CONTENTS

PETERSON'S

COMPUTER SCIENCE & ELECTRICAL ENGINEERING PROGRAMS

A COMPLETE RESOURCE OF GRADUATE EDUCATIONAL AND CAREER OPPORTUNITIES

Peterson's
Princeton, New Jersey

About Peterson's

Peterson's is the country's largest educational information/communications company, providing the academic, consumer, and professional communities with books, software, and online services in support of lifelong education access and career choice. Well-known references include Peterson's annual guides to private schools, summer programs, colleges and universities, graduate and professional programs, financial aid, international study, adult learning, and career guidance. Peterson's Web site at petersons.com is the only comprehensive—and most heavily traveled—education resource on the Internet. The site carries all of Peterson's fully searchable major databases and includes financial aid sources, test-prep help, job postings, direct inquiry and application features, and specially created Virtual Campuses for every accredited academic institution and summer program in the U.S. and Canada that offers in-depth narratives, announcements, and multimedia features.

Visit Peterson's Education Center on the Internet (World Wide Web) at www.petersons.com

Editorial inquiries concerning this book should be addressed to the editor at Peterson's, 202 Carnegie Center, P.O. Box 2123, Princeton, New Jersey 08543-2123 (609-243-9111).

ISSN 1089-3350
ISBN 1-56079-874-2

Executive Editor: Robert Crepeau
Senior Editor: Art Stickney
Production Editor: Karen Rae
Interior Design: Cynthia Boone
Composition: Linda Williams
Director of Research for Higher Education: Kimberly J. Hoeritz
Programming: Barbara A. Dedecker

Printed in the United States of America

10 9 8 7 6 5 4 3 2 1

FOREWORD

Over the past two decades, men and women working in computer science and electrical engineering careers have literally changed the world. They've made it possible to communicate with anyone, anywhere. They've brought the power of imagination to life in homes, research institutions, and businesses around the world. And they're not about to stop now.

You are embarking on a wondrous journey as you further your knowledge of technology and its applications. Now more than ever it is time for you to begin seeing yourself in a new light. Your career begins today. As a graduate student of computer science or electrical engineering, you have the opportunity to follow your own path in the twenty-first century. However, while you will have a breadth of information and knowledge from which to draw, the power to use it lies with you alone.

Being a part of the world of technology doesn't mean that you can escape the world at large, however. Technology today is an incredible blend of theory, passion, and application. Learn your fundamentals, then dive headlong into using those skills to feed the stirrings of your soul. If it is music you love, find out how you can add to the resonance of the note or to the clarity of the recording. Consider the artists of Pixar, the company at the heart of the movie *Toy Story*. With a team of animators, artists, and technologists, Pixar made the impossible possible. But that is one mission of technology.

I welcome you to an exciting and fulfilling career. And I urge you to seize ownership of your future. As you work to select a graduate program, conduct your interviews and assessments with an eye toward your own growth and fulfillment. It's not a question of who will accept you into their program, it's a question of whose program you want to buy into. Talk to the faculty members. Find out about the work the department is doing and what opportunities exist for academic and corporate research.

Remember, too, that technological knowledge is not enough in today's marketplace. Learn to present yourself and your ideas. Accept the challenge of teamwork, and you will find its rewards. The graduate student chapters of societies such as the Computer Society and the Association of Computing Machinery will allow you to gain entry and introduction into your field.

Above all, engineer yourself. There is no greater technology than what lies inside you. Graduate school is simply another tool to help you apply that energy to your life.

Gwen Bell
Founding President, The Computer Museum

HOW TO USE THIS BOOK

eterson's *Computer Science & Electrical Engineering Programs* provides prospective students with comprehensive information on graduate computer science and electrical engineering education in the United States and Canada. For those seeking to enter these professions or to further their careers, *Peterson's Computer Science & Electrical Engineering Programs* includes just the help they need to make important college and career decisions.

The following overview describes the various components of the book, as well as criteria used to select institutions and computer science and electrical engineering programs for the guide. Additional explanatory material will help users to interpret details presented within the guide.

RESEARCH PROCEDURES

Peterson's Computer Science & Electrical Engineering Programs covers accredited institutions in the United States, U.S. territories, and Canada that grant master's, doctorate, and combined graduate degrees. To be included in this guide, an institution must have full accreditation or candidate-for-accreditation status granted by an institutional or specialized accrediting body recognized by the U.S. Department of Education or the Council on Higher Education Accreditation (formerly the Council on Postsecondary Accreditation). A Canadian institution must be chartered and authorized to grant degrees by the provincial government, affiliated with a chartered institution, or accredited by a recognized accrediting body. Areas of study in computer science and electrical engineering are defined as artificial intelligence/robotics, computer engineering, computer science, electrical engineering, information science, and software engineering.

The data contained in the school profiles were collected through a survey conducted by Peterson's in the spring of 1997. Letters and questionnaires were sent to U.S. and Canadian colleges and universities with graduate programs in computer science and electrical engineering. Data included in this edition, with minor exceptions, have been submitted by officials (usually the deans of the departments of computer science and electrical engineering or the directors of institutional research) at the schools themselves. In addition, the great majority of schools that submitted information were contacted directly by Peterson's research staff to verify unusual figures or facts, to resolve discrepancies, or to obtain additional information.

All usable information received in time for publication has been included. The omission of a particular item from a profile signifies that data were not available or usable. In the cases where no data were submitted regarding an eligible computer science or electrical engineering program, the name, location, and some general information regarding the program appear in the profile section to indicate the existence of the program. Because of the extensive system of checks performed on the data collected by Peterson's, we have every reason to believe that the information presented in this guide is accurate. Nonetheless, some errors and omissions are possible in a data collection and processing endeavor of this scope, and facts and figures, such as tuition and fees, do change. Therefore, students should check with a specific college or university at the time of application to verify all pertinent information.

ORGANIZATION OF THE GUIDE

The table of contents will give you a quick idea of this guide's contents, but, in a nutshell, *Peterson's Computer Science & Electrical Engineering Programs* is divided into four main sections:

The Career Advisory section includes useful articles, employment charts, and a financial aid list to help guide graduate education choices and career opportunities in the computer science and electrical engineering fields. The Profiles of Graduate Computer Science and Electrical Engineering Programs section contains detailed information about U.S. and Canadian institutions. This section is organized geographically; U.S. schools are listed alphabetically by state, followed by Canadian schools listed alphabetically by province. The Full Descriptions of Computer Science and Electrical Engineering Programs section is an open forum for computer science and electrical engineering programs to communicate, on a voluntary basis, their particular message to prospective students. The absence of any college or university from this section does not constitute an editorial decision on the part of Peterson's. Those who have chosen to write these descriptions are responsible for the accuracy of the content. Statements regarding a school's objectives and accomplishments are a reflection of its own beliefs and are not the opinions of the editors. The School Index and Program Index section at the back of the book refers to profiles and descriptions by institution name and by type of program offered.

The profiles contain detailed information about the colleges and universities offering computer science and electrical engineering programs. While the profiles have been designed to be as self-explanatory as possible, the following outline of the profile discusses the items that each section covers. Any item that does not apply to a particular college or university, or for which no information was supplied, is omitted from the profile.

SAMPLE PROFILE

HAMILTON SQUARE UNIVERSITY
Hamilton Square, NJ 08690-3930

OVERVIEW
Hamilton Square University is an independent coed university.

ENROLLMENT
7,318 graduate, professional, and undergraduate students; 1,663 full-time matriculated graduate/professional students (450 women), 752 part-time matriculated graduate/professional students (222 women).

GRADUATE FACULTY
531 full-time (87 women), 417 part-time (158 women); includes 29 minority (5 African-Americans, 19 Asian-Americans, 5 Hispanics).

EXPENSES
Tuition $19,400 per year full-time, $269 per unit part-time. Fees $100 per year.

HOUSING
On-campus housing not available.

STUDENT SERVICES
Low-cost medical care, low-cost health insurance, free psychological counseling, career counseling, day-care facilities, emergency short-term loans, campus safety program, campus employment opportunities, counseling/support services for international students.

FACILITIES
Library: Hunt Library plus 2 additional on-campus libraries; total holdings of 873,540 volumes, 809,527 microforms, 3,561 current periodical subscriptions. A total of 220 personal computers in all libraries. Access provided to on-line information retrieval services. *Special:* In arts and humanities: Communications Design Center, Center for the Study of Writing, Center for the Materials of the Artist and Conservator, Center for Building Performance and Diagnostics. In science and engineering: Software Engineering Institute, Center for Machine Translation, Engineering Design Research Center, Robotics Institute, Soybean Institute, SRC/CMU Research Center for Computer-Aided Design, Center for Molecular Genetics. In social sciences: Center for the Study of Public Policy, Center for the Management of Technology.

COMPUTER ENGINEERING

Steele Institute of Technology, Department of Electrical and Computer Engineering

Programs Offers programs in biomedical engineering (MS, PhD), electrical and computer engineering (MS, PhD). Part-time programs available.

Faculty 33 full-time (0 women), 18 part-time (1 woman).

Faculty Research Computer-aided design, solid-state devices, VLSI, optical data processing, robotics and controls.

Students 207 full-time (25 women), 23 part-time (1 woman); includes 47 minority (4 African-Americans, 38 Asian-Americans, 5 Hispanics), 76 international.

Degrees Awarded In 1996, 32 master's, 38 doctorates awarded.

Entrance Requirements GRE General Test, TOEFL.

Degree Requirements For master's, foreign language not required; for doctorate, computer language, dissertation, qualifying exam required, foreign language not required.

Financial Aid Fellowships, research assistantships, teaching assistantships, institutionally sponsored loans available. *Financial aid application deadline: 1/15.*

Applying *Deadline:* 1/15 (11/1 for spring admission). *Fee:* $35.

Contact *Marla Givens*
Graduate Coordinator
609-987-7800

See in-depth description on page 435.

Institutional Details

Heading with the school's name and location, plus institutional control, total graduate student enrollment, total graduate faculty members, expenses, housing, student services, and library, computer, and special facilities.

Program Details

School or department name, graduate programs offered, number of faculty members and key faculty research, number of students, degrees awarded and postgraduate work, entrance requirements, degree requirements, financial aid availability, applying, and admissions contact.

DESIGNING THE 21ST CENTURY: COMPUTER SCIENCE AND ELECTRICAL ENGINEERING GRADUATE STUDENTS TAKE ON THE FUTURE

BY TOM FERRELL

"Science cannot live by science alone. Research needs education, just as education thrives when it is conducted in an atmosphere of inquiry and discovery."

—Neal Lane
Director, National Science Foundation

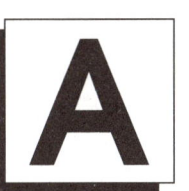

As students of computer science and electrical engineering, you are taking part in the grandest experiment of all: the future. In some ways, yours is the same as all the generations of technical visionaries before you. Technology, after all, has always driven civilization. But no generation has ever had the tools you have at your disposal. Today, more than half the population of the United States uses a computer at home or at work. A hand-held computer can now accomplish more than yesterday's mainframes. Technology has never played a greater role in society. It has changed the way we communicate on a personal level, thanks to innovations such as Internet, e-mail, and the World Wide Web. In turn, technology has changed the way we think. By becoming integrated with virtually every aspect of our personal and professional environments, it has changed the way we live.

You have already made a commitment to learning and to using the power of technology to create and improve. Now you're ready to take another step. There is more to postgraduate education than an enhanced standing in the job market, though certainly that will come. As a member of an advanced degree program in computer science or electrical engineering, you take your place as an architect of the next century. The research you take part in as a graduate student in these fields will help chart the course of learning, discovery, implementation, and adoption, not only in the academic world but in the worlds of commerce and industry as well.

In other words, you will be playing a large role in creating your own career opportunities and the technological landscape in which you pursue them. That's a lot of power you hold in your hands.

Few fields provide the quality of work, the earnings potential, and the satisfaction of high technology. And in terms of industry resilience, you would be hard pressed to find another field as durable. High tech survived the defense industry cutbacks and continues to thrive as new applications appear with blinding speed.

"You can't count the way technology is being applied right now," says Dudley Kay, an executive editor with the Institute of Electrical and Electronics Engineers (IEEE). "I mean, Hertz has just announced that they'll be putting satellite navigational systems in all of their rental cars. This is the stuff that used to be science fiction."

In computer science and electrical engineering, anything you can imagine you can also make real. Graduate programs offer you the tools to do it. The selection you're about to make—where to go to graduate school—is a major factor in the development of your career. The projects you work on, the relationships you make—these are the ingredients that will launch you toward an as-yet unknown destination.

Congratulations on your decision to follow one of the most dynamic professional paths in history. Here's to going further.

KEEPING UP WITH THE FIELD

The opportunities for skilled technological professionals are limitless. On this, academic officials, industry analysts, and research organizations all agree. Keep in mind, however, that high-technology occupations can be difficult to classify. Even well-crafted analysis has failed to predict some of the hottest career markets in the high-tech arena. The personal computer industry grew from a curiosity to one of the largest forces in the global economy in less than a decade. More recently, the Internet has provided fertile ground for commercial success by exploding from a small group of online devotees to a standard communications channel serving more than 60 million people.

Internet access and related services—design of networking and other communications hardware, application programming, and database management—constitute an industry that literally did not exist in 1990. Today, Internet-related businesses generate hundreds of millions of dollars and produce new fields, markets, and success stories almost daily.

This constant change is what makes high tech both exciting and challenging. It also underscores the need for learning more than existing technologies. In order to stay competitive, you have to learn to research, and you have to learn to learn.

"Just look at what wasn't possible ten years ago," says Dr. Stu Zweben, chair of the computer and information science department at Ohio State University. "You come to a graduate program to learn the foundations. It's important that the program offers the latest technology. But what you want people to learn is how to change, how to extend and integrate those existing technologies."

John Michalenko, associate director of the career center at Carnegie Mellon University, agrees. "The most important thing is to stay current. There's no decline in any of the computing areas. It's all headed up, and it's constantly growing. If you stay abreast of your field, your prospects are outstanding."

The U.S. Bureau of Labor Statistics (BLS) supports this view of the high-technology industry's future. To simplify tracking, the organization has created several career classifications. All promise continued growth and opportunity.

Computer Scientists and Systems Analysts

Computer scientists and systems analysts constitute one of the most sought-after professional groups in industry. Government and academic institutions also provide an excellent employment market. With the proliferation of computing and networking throughout society, prospects are expected to remain high through at least the year 2005. And because employers are requiring higher levels of technical expertise to help maximize their investments in highly technical equipment and systems, holders of advanced degrees enjoy a strong career advantage over those with undergraduate degrees. The BLS estimates that computer science positions accounted for more than 828,000 jobs in 1994, with very high growth forecast for the next ten years.

Income is high as well, with median annual salaries of about $44,000. Again, advanced degree holders enjoy much stronger earnings power than their baccalaureate counterparts, with salaries often topping $65,000.

Advancement paths lead to standards boards, management, and entrepreneurial consulting ventures. A growing number of companies are now turning to outside consultants, called systems integrators, to handle basic systems analysis and implementation. These consulting firms present another entry-level employment opportunity for students familiar with a variety of hardware, operating systems, and networking topologies.

Computer Programmers

Computer programmers held more than 537,000 jobs in 1994, according to the BLS. In the corporate world, programmers often work with systems analysts, writing software that allows the computer systems to achieve the goals of management. Programming can be an excellent vehicle for later movement to systems analyst or other management positions.

With advanced, graphically based languages such as C++ at their disposal, programmers are capable of dazzling achievements without much of the torturous coding their predecessors had to endure. These advances lead many industry experts to pick programming as the brightest spot of all in the computing industry.

"The market for programmers is absolutely incredible," says Matt McConnell, president of Compatible Systems Corporation, a network hardware manufacturer in Boulder, Colorado. "Software drives so many products today, from networking products all the way down to general-use products like cars and even home appliances. I don't see the demand for programmers slowing any in the coming years, either."

In addition, new server-based programming languages such as Java will open doors for software authors in the coming years. Skilled programmers with degrees and relevant experience will have little trouble finding suitable employment. Though job growth is not expected to match the rate of other computing professions, there will always be a place for a good programmer.

Median pay for full-time programmers is about $38,500 per year. The more technical and systems-oriented programmers can earn considerably higher. Application programmers, however, can sometimes negotiate royalties—a percentage of gross or net profits—on their work, enhancing earnings opportunities.

Electronics Engineers

Electronics engineers make up the largest force of the broad engineering category, with a total of about 349,000 jobs in 1994. While these engineers felt the sting from the aerospace cutbacks of the late 1980s, the job outlook is good.

The electrical engineering disciplines almost always benefit from the rapid pace of change in technology. Automation of factory and office processes creates demand for new systems development.

"Most chip vendors are shifting people over from desktop PC development," notes Loring Wirbel of *Electronic Engineering Times* magazine. "Some areas of the field have been gutted, but for the most part we're defining 'slow' growth as low double-digits. Wireless development is huge, so RF (radio frequency) is a good area to pursue. And keep an eye on vertical markets such as health care or transportation. There are so many good opportunities."

WOMEN AND COMPUTING

Women planning to enter the world of computing often feel that they must break into a man's world. But that is changing. Computer science and electrical engineering are growing, changing, exciting fields with significant opportunities for talented and motivated women. In fact, nearly one third of all computer systems analysts and computer scientists are women, according to the Bureau of Labor Statistics. However, old traditions die hard, and the world of high technology can still come off as a male-dominated and sometimes oppressive industry.

As computers become more integrated into businesses and households throughout the world, university programs are trying to woo more women into the field, and successful women are beginning to show up in high-profile places. How far can women go? Take a look at Martha Sloan, the first woman president of the Institute of Electrical and Electronics Engineers, or Arati Prabhakar, head of the National Institute of Standards and Technology.

So what's a woman to do to succeed in a master's program and beyond?

- Determine whether a program is "woman-friendly" or not. When Laura Downey, a computer scientist with the federal government, was checking into graduate schools, she wanted to identify programs with positive, encouraging environments for women. "You hear so many negative things out there...I just wanted to dwell on the positive," says Downey. "The first thing I would do is check out how many female staff members are part of the department. Then I would see if they've implemented any programs that are designed to encourage women in computer science." Downey's own research has resulted in the WCARLIST, a compilation of colleges and universities that have formal and/or informal programs for encouraging and retaining women in computer science, and, while she notes that the list is only one tool that women can use to assess what school they might want to attend, it at

least offers them a starting point. You can send e-mail to Downey for a copy of the list at wcarlist@acm.org. You can also find excellent resources devoted to women in computing, including information on the video "Minerva's Machine: Women in Computing," a PBS special.

- Look to other women in the field. Everyone agrees that finding a female role model or mentor in the field is one of the best things a young woman can do, whether it's actually connecting with another woman through a formal mentoring program or simply following the successes of high-profile women in the field. Once enrolled in a program, make it a point to try to get a woman as an academic adviser and seek out the classes taught by women. "There are definitely programs out there to help with mentoring," says Elisabeth Freeman, a graduate researcher at Yale and codeveloper of The Ada Project (TAP), a network resource for women in computing (http://www.cs.yale.edu/homes/tap/cs-women-projs.html). She cites the Computing Research Association Distributed Mentor Project, a program that brings undergraduates and professors together for a summer of research.

- Check out the online newsgroups and resources for women. Increasingly available Internet access has made it easier to connect with other women, regardless of their home base. And women in the field are recognizing the power that comes from sharing their experiences and knowledge online. Motivated to help make resources available to women, Freeman and fellow graduate researcher Susanne Hupfer developed TAP. In addition, there are numerous online communities specifically for women (such as Systers, founded by Anita Borg, a researcher at Digital Equipment Corporation). As with most newsgroups and networks, one connection often leads to another. Spend some time in the relevant computing bulletin boards and newsgroups and seek out the contacts that can help you in your planned studies.

Many of those opportunities have more to do with information signaling than with the more traditional movement of electricity. The availability of new information processing technology has allowed for new automation applications that simply were not possible just a few years ago.

"Traditional electrical engineering is giving way to information technology," says the IEEE's Kay. "Internet, wireless, satellite. That's the industry right now, and that's where the research money is going. MEMs (MicroElectronic Mechanism) technology is in high demand. These devices

gather information and effect an action. You've simply got to think about what you can do with information."

THE TECHNICAL PROFESSIONAL

One of the changes wrought by the impact of technology on society is that technical professionals today play a much larger role in industry than their predecessors. In the past, the technical people were often disparagingly thought of as "nerds." Today, as Scott Adams, creator of the popular Dilbert comic strip observes, "nerds are the sex symbols of the '90s."

This much is certain: today's computer professional must be more general and well rounded than those of the past. Companies no longer sweep their technical personnel into the back offices. More and more, they're looking for cross-discipline skills.

Graduate programs offer some inherent cross-discipline advantages. For one, industry is working more closely with universities, funding more research and placing graduate students in competitive, real-world situations. "Departments used to train graduate students for careers in academia," says Zweben of Ohio State. "That's no longer the case."

Now more than ever, students must take an active role in designing a comprehensive educational program that will prepare them for the competitive and unpredictable world that lies beyond the university gates.

Jack Wilson is president of Career Sciences, a career consulting firm. He believes that the heads-up student today is always looking for that something extra that will separate him or her during the job search process.

"The mistake students make," Wilson says, "is that they think technical skill is the only thing they need to get a good job. That may be true in some cases. But it's just not true universally anymore."

Companies use technical people on product teams, in customer support positions, for sales training and education, and as product promoters. All good businesses are looking to stretch their hiring dollar.

"There seems to be increased interest in students understanding business principles," says Zweben. "We as a university have to respond. A lot of the cross-discipline curriculum has to come at the undergraduate level. In a graduate program, you want to become more specialized, more career oriented. At every level, however, teamwork and communication skills are vital."

Wilson goes so far as to encourage computer science and electrical engineering students to take humanities and literature classes to improve their critical thinking, writing, and listening skills.

The quest for multidisciplinary curricula is creating some confusion, even in university programs themselves. Today's business school graduates are stronger in technological areas and are competing with technical students for high-paying, fast-track positions. With the line between business and computing constantly getting more blurry, staying current on both technology and business trends should enhance your value in a workplace in which employees can expect to change jobs seven times during a career.

"What we're going through right now is a change that is second only to the Industrial Revolution," says Jack Wilson. "The notion of going to school for four years, graduating, and getting a lifetime job with one company is going to be very, very rare."

The loss of long-term job stability is one argument for the hybrid curriculum, but not everyone agrees. "Business schooling simply isn't necessary," says Gwen Bell of The Computer Museum. "If you perform in the technical capac-ity in which you were hired, you'll get the opportunity to receive the business training you need.

"Focus on mastering the fundamentals of your technology while developing good presentation skills. The likelihood of having a master's degree in a technology field and rising in the business is just as great as it is for M.B.A. graduates."

INDUSTRY AND THE UNIVERSITY

The name of the game for most graduate programs is research. Today's technology graduate students are reaping the benefits of closer relations between universities and business. As a result, research projects are more likely to allow students to develop excellent corporate contacts and opportunities. While federal research and development support to corporate R&D firms has dropped dramatically, reliance on university programs for required research is rising.

"If you can get the chance to be a research assistant, do it," says Bell. "Careers—even some teaching careers—start in industry, and it is industry that is driving research today. Work you do in research becomes a career opportunity. Research assistants get their names on papers, and they get invitations to conferences. They become recognized people in the field."

Of the three major R&D performing sectors—the federal government, private industry, and universities—only universities have registered an increase in research grants. While most research done on college campuses is funded by the federal government, industry is playing a larger role, providing $1.5 billion in 1995 to research institutions.

Industry works with graduate programs in a number of ways, often licensing research findings and paying royalties to the institution. Graduate students become vital parts of this research, important both to the institution and to industry. And technology firms continue to gobble up students from research-oriented universities.

Perhaps the most famous story is that of Marc Andreessen, who worked as a student researcher in the National Center for Supercomputing Applications (NCSA) at the University of Illinois. Fascinated by the Internet and enamored with the possibilities of the then text-based World Wide Web, he set out to create a graphical user interface (GUI) for displaying Web documents. He called his program Mosaic and made it available on the Internet for free. More than one million people downloaded Mosaic and made it an Internet standard. Then Andreessen got a phone call from the CEO of Silicon Graphics and became a partner in a new software venture—Netscape Communications.

"Colleges today offer so many more business opportunities than they did ten or fifteen years ago," says Compatible Systems' McConnell. "We hire interns throughout the year and assign them to some excellent projects. We're always looking for real-world experience. And real-world experience combined with a solid academic background is a powerful force. We'll always try to support university students who want to gain valuable work experience, and we look for those same kinds of people when we're hiring."

MAKING THE RIGHT CHOICE

The decisions you are ready to make are important ones. Your inspiration and your work are going to carry America into the twenty-first century, a century that will be defined by its technology and the way you put it to use.

At the graduate level, you cannot afford to make a choice based solely on program reputation. The importance of fitting a university's program to your career outlook is crucial.

Here are some comments designed to help you make the right choice:

- Know What You Want. Graduate work is specialization. Narrow your focus and look inside the program. No school is strong in every phase of a technology program.

- Consult With Faculty. These are the men and women you will rely on for guidance through a very important stage in your career. Call them up and talk to them about your specific interests and concerns. As a graduate student, you will be part of the university's academic team. Find out what projects the faculty has worked on. Do they match your interests and goals?

- Use Technology. The World Wide Web has put a wealth of information on your desktop. Let your fingers do the walking on your computer's keyboard to help you find out what you need to know before making a selection.

It's your move now. You've chosen a great field of study, ripe with chances to create an exciting and dynamic career.

Now it's time to make it your own.

Tom Ferrell is technical marketing manager for Compatible Systems Corporation in Boulder, Colorado. He is also a business and technology writer with more than ten years' experience covering the networking and telecommunications industries.

SELECTING AND APPLYING TO COMPUTER SCIENCE AND ELECTRICAL ENGINEERING SCHOOLS

The decision to attend graduate school and the choice of an institution and degree program require serious consideration. The time, money, and energy you will expend doing graduate work are significant, and you will want to analyze your options carefully. Before you begin filing applications, you should evaluate your interests and goals, know what programs are available, and be clear about your reasons for pursuing a particular degree.

DEGREES

Traditionally, graduate education has involved acquiring and communicating knowledge gained through original research in a particular academic field. The highest earned academic degree, which requires the pursuit of original research, is the Doctor of Philosophy (Ph.D.). In contrast, professional training stresses the practical application of knowledge and skills; this is true, for example, in the fields of computer science and electrical engineering. Master's degrees are offered in most fields and may also be academic or professional in orientation. In many fields, the master's degree may be the only professional degree needed for employment.

Some people decide to earn a master's degree at one institution and then select a different university or a somewhat different program of study for doctoral work. This can be a way of acquiring a broad background: you can choose a master's program with one emphasis or orientation and a doctoral program with another. The total period of graduate study may be somewhat lengthened by proceeding this way, but probably not by much.

In recent years, the distinctions between traditional academic programs and professional programs have become blurred. The course of graduate education has changed direction in the last thirty years, and many programs have redefined their shape and focus. There are centers and institutes for research, many graduate programs are now interdepartmental and interdisciplinary, off-campus graduate programs have multiplied, and part-time graduate programs have increased. Colleges and universities have also established dual-degree programs, in many cases in order to enable students to combine academic and professional studies. As a result of such changes, you now have considerable freedom in determining the program best suited to your current needs as well as your long-term goals.

CHOOSING A SPECIALIZATION AND RESEARCHING PROGRAMS

There are several sources of information you should make use of in choosing a specialization and a program. A good way to begin is to consult this guide for programs of interest to you. Each program listing provides information on degrees, research facilities, the faculty, financial aid resources, tuition and other costs, application requirements, and so on.

Talk with your college adviser and professors about your areas of interest and ask for their advice about the best programs to research. Besides being very well informed themselves, these faculty members may have colleagues at institutions you are investigating, and they can give you inside information about individual programs and the kind of background they seek in candidates for admission.

The valuable perspective of educators should not be overlooked. If the faculty members you know through your courses are not involved in your field of interest, do not hesitate to contact other appropriate professors at your institution or neighboring institutions to ask for advice on programs that might suit your goals. In addition, talk to graduate students studying in your field of interest; their advice can be valuable also.

Your decision about a field of study may be determined by your research interests or, if you choose to enter a professional school, by the appeal of a particular career. In either case, as you attempt to limit the number of institutions you will apply to, you will want to familiarize yourself with publications describing current research in your discipline. Find related professional journals and note who is publishing in the areas of specialization that interest you, as well as where they are teaching. Take note of the institutions represented on the publications' editorial boards (they are usually listed on the inside cover); such representation usually reflects strength in the discipline.

Being aware of who the top people are and where they are will pay off in a number of ways. A graduate department's reputation rests heavily on the reputation of its faculty, and in some disciplines it is more important to study under someone of note than it is to study at a college or university with a prestigious name. In addition, in certain fields graduate funds are often tied to a particular research project and, as a result, to the faculty member directing that project. Finally, most Ph.D. candidates (and nonprofessional master's degree candidates) must pick an adviser and one or more other faculty members who form a committee that directs and approves their work. Many times this choice must be made during the first semester, so it is important to learn as much as you can about faculty members before you begin your studies. As you research the faculties of various departments, keep in mind the following questions: What is their academic training? What are their research activities? What kind of concern do they have for teaching and student development?

There are other important factors to consider in judging the educational quality of a program. First, what kind of students enroll in the program? What are their academic abilities, achievements, skills, geographic representation, and level of professional success upon completion of the program? Second, what are the program's resources? What kind of financial support does it have? How complete is the library? What laboratory equipment and computer facilities are available? And third, what does the program have to offer in terms of both curriculum and services? What are its purposes, its course offerings, and its job placement and student advisement services? What is the student-faculty ratio, and what kind of interaction is there between students and professors? What internships, assistantships, and other experiential education opportunities are available?

When evaluating a particular institution's reputation in a given field, you may also want to look at published graduate program ratings. There is no single rating that is universally accepted, so you would be well advised to read several and not place too much importance on any one. Most consist of what are known as "peer ratings;" that is, they are the results of polls of respected scholars who are asked to rate graduate departments in their field of expertise. Many academicians feel that these ratings are too heavily based upon traditional concepts of what constitutes quality—such as the publications of the faculty—and that they perpetuate the notion of a research-oriented department as the only model of excellence in graduate education. Depending on whether your own goals are research-oriented, you may want to attribute more or less importance to this type of rating.

If possible, visit the institutions that interest you and talk with faculty members and currently enrolled students. Be sure, however, to write or call the admissions office a week in advance to give the person in charge a chance to set up appointments for you with faculty members and students.

THE APPLICATION PROCESS

Timetable

It is important to start gathering information early to be able to complete your applications on time. Most people should start the process a full year and a half before their anticipated date of matriculation. There are, however, some exceptions to this rule. The time frame will be different if you are applying for national scholarships or if your undergraduate institution has an evaluation committee through which you are applying. In such a situation, you may have to begin the process two years before your date of matriculation in order to take your graduate admission test and arrange for letters of recommendation early enough to meet deadlines.

Application deadlines may range from August (a year prior to matriculation) for early decision programs to late spring or summer (when beginning graduate school in the fall) for a few programs with rolling admissions. Most deadlines for entry in the fall are between January and March. You should in all cases plan to meet formal deadlines; beyond this, you should be aware of the fact that many schools with rolling admissions encourage and act upon early applications. Applying early to a school with rolling admissions is usually advantageous, as it shows your enthusiasm for the program and gives admissions committees more time to evaluate the subjective components of your application, rather than just the "numbers." Applicants are not rejected early unless they are clearly below an institution's standards.

The timetable that appears below represents the ideal for most applicants.

Six months prior to applying

- Research areas of interest, institutions, and programs.
- Talk to advisers about application requirements.
- Register and prepare for appropriate graduate admission tests.
- Investigate national scholarships.
- If appropriate, obtain letters of recommendation.

Three months prior to applying

- Take required graduate admission tests.
- Write for application materials.
- Write your application essay.
- Check on application deadlines and rolling admissions policies.

Fall, a year before matriculating

- Obtain letters of recommendation.
- Take graduate admission tests if you haven't already.
- Send in completed applications.

Winter, before matriculating in the fall

- Complete the Free Application for Federal Student Aid (FAFSA) and Financial Aid PROFILE, if required.

Spring, before matriculating in the fall

- Check with all institutions before their deadlines to make sure your file is complete.
- Visit institutions that accept you.
- Send a deposit to your institution of choice.
- Notify other colleges and universities that accepted you of your decision so that they can admit students on their waiting list.
- Send thank-you notes to people who wrote your recommendation letters, informing them of your success.

You may not be able to adhere to this timetable if your application deadlines are very early or if you decide to attend graduate school at the last minute. In any case, keep in mind the various application requirements and be sure to meet all deadlines. If deadlines are impossible to meet, call the institution to see if a late application will be considered.

Obtaining Application Forms and Information

To obtain the materials you need, send a neatly typed or handwritten postcard requesting an application, a bulletin, and financial aid information to the address provided in this Guide. However, you may want to request an application by writing a formal letter directly to the department chair in which you briefly describe your training, experience, and specialized research interests. If you want to write to a particular faculty member about your background and interests in order to explore the possibility of an assistantship, you should also feel free to do so. However, do not ask a faculty member for an application, as this may cause a significant delay in your receipt of the forms.

Meeting Application Requirements

Requirements vary from one field to another and from one institution to another. Read each program's requirements carefully; the importance of this cannot be overemphasized.

Graduate Admission Tests

Colleges and universities usually require a specific graduate admission test, and departments sometimes have their own requirements as well. Scores are used in evaluating the likelihood of your success in a particular program (based upon the success rate of past students with similar scores). Most programs will not accept scores more than three to five years old. The various tests are described a little later in this book.

Transcripts

Admissions committees require official transcripts of your grades to evaluate your academic preparation for graduate study. Grade point averages are important but are not examined in isolation; the rigor of the courses you have taken, your course load, and the reputation of the undergraduate institution you have attended are also scrutinized. To have your college transcript sent to graduate institutions, contact your college registrar.

Letters of Recommendation

Choosing people to write recommendations can be difficult, and most graduate schools require two or three letters. While recommendations from faculty members are essential for academically oriented programs, professional programs may seriously consider nonacademic recommendations from professionals in the field. Indeed, often these nonacademic recommendations are as respected as those from faculty members.

To begin the process of choosing references, identify likely candidates from among those you know through your classes, extracurricular activities, and jobs. A good reference will meet several of the following criteria: he or she has a high opinion of you, knows you well in more than one area of your life, is familiar with the institutions to which you are applying as well as the kind of study you are pursuing, has taught or worked with a large number of students and can make a favorable comparison of you with your peers, is known by the admissions committee and is regarded as someone whose judgment should be given weight, and has good written communication skills. No one person is likely to satisfy all these criteria, so choose those people who come closest to the ideal.

Once you have decided whom to ask for letters, you may wonder how to approach them. Ask them if they think they know you well enough to write a meaningful letter. Be aware that the later in the semester you ask, the more likely they are to hesitate because of time constraints; ask early in the fall semester of your senior year. Once those you ask to write letters agree in a suitably enthusiastic manner, make an appointment to talk with them. Go to the appointment with recommendation forms in hand, being sure to include addressed, stamped envelopes for their convenience. In addition, give them other supporting materials that will assist them in writing a good, detailed letter on your behalf. Such documents as transcripts, a résumé, a copy of your application essay, and a copy of a research paper can help them write a thorough recommendation.

On the recommendation form, you will be asked to indicate whether you wish to waive or retain the right to see the recommendation. Before you decide, discuss the confidentiality of the letter with each writer. Many faculty members will not write a letter unless it is confidential. This does not necessarily mean that they will write a negative letter but, rather, that they believe it will carry more weight as part of your application if it is confidential. Waiving the right to see a letter does, in fact, usually increase its validity.

If you will not be applying to graduate school as a senior but you plan to pursue further education in the future, open a credentials file if your college or university offers this service. Letters of recommendation can be kept on file for you until you begin the application process. If you are returning to school after working for several years and did not establish a credentials file, it may be difficult to obtain letters of recommendation from professors at your undergraduate institution. In this case, contact the graduate schools you are applying to and ask what their policies are regarding your situation. They may waive the requirement of recommendation letters, allow you to substitute letters from employment supervisors, or suggest you enroll in relevant courses at a nearby institution and obtain letters from professors upon completion of the course work. Program policies vary considerably, so it is best to check with each school.

Application Essays

Writing an essay, or personal statement, is often the most difficult part of the application process. Requirements vary widely in this regard. Some programs request only one or two paragraphs about why you want to pursue graduate study, while others require five or six separate essays in which you are expected to write at length about your motivation for graduate study, your strengths and weaknesses, your greatest achievements, and solutions to hypothetical problems.

An essay or personal statement for an application should be essentially a statement of your ideas and goals. Usually it includes a certain amount of personal history, but, unless an institution specifically requests autobiographical information, you do not have to supply any. Even when the requirement is a "personal statement," the possibilities are almost unlimited. There is no set formula to follow, and, if you do write an autobiographical piece, it does not have to be arranged chronologically. Your aim should be a clear, succinct statement showing that you have a definite sense of what you want to do and enthusiasm for the field of study you have chosen. Your essay should reflect your writing abilities; more important, it should reveal the clarity, the focus, and the depth of your thinking.

Before writing anything, stop and consider what your reader might be looking for; the general directions or other parts of the application may give you an indication of this. Admissions committees may be trying to evaluate a number of things from your statement, including the following things about you:

- Motivation and commitment to a field of study
- Expectations with regard to the program and career opportunities
- Writing ability
- Major areas of interest
- Research or work experience
- Educational background
- Immediate and long-term goals
- Reasons for deciding to pursue graduate education in a particular field and at a particular institution
- Maturity
- Personal uniqueness—what you would add to the diversity of the entering class

There are two main approaches to organizing an essay. You can outline the points you want to cover and then expand on them, or you can put your ideas down on paper as they come to you, going over them, eliminating certain sentences, and moving others around until you achieve a logical sequence. Making an outline will probably lead to a well-organized essay, whereas writing spontaneously may yield a more inspired piece of writing. Use the approach you feel most comfortable with. Whichever approach you use, you will want someone to critique your essay. Your adviser and those who write your letters of recommendation may be very helpful to you in this regard. If they are in the field you plan to pursue, they will be able to tell you what things to stress and what things to keep brief. Do not be surprised, however, if you get differing opinions on the content of your essay. In the end, only you can decide on the best way of presenting yourself.

If there is information in your application that might reflect badly on you, such as poor grades or a low admission test score, it is better not to deal with it in your essay unless you are asked to. Keep your essay positive. You will need to explain anything that could be construed as negative in your application, however, as failure to do so may eliminate you from consideration. You can do this on a separate sheet entitled "Addendum," which you attach to the application, or in a cover letter that you enclose. In either form, your explanation should be short and to the point, avoiding long, tedious excuses. In addition to supplying your own explanation, you may find it appropriate to ask one or more of your recommenders to address the issue in their recommendation letter. Ask them to do this only if they are already familiar with your problem and could talk about it from a positive perspective.

In every case, essays should be word processed or typed. It is usually acceptable to attach pages to your application if the space provided is insufficient. Neatness, spelling, and grammar are important.

Interviews

Some graduate programs will require you to appear for an interview. Interviewers will be interested in the way you think and approach problems and will probably concentrate on questions that enable them to assess your thinking skills, rather than questions that call upon your grasp of technical knowledge. Some interviewers will ask controversial questions or give you hypothetical situations and ask how you would handle them. Bear in mind that the interviewer is more interested in how you think than in what you think. As in your essay, you may be asked to address such topics as your motivation for graduate study, personal philosophy, career goals, related research and work experience, and areas of interest.

You should prepare for a graduate school interview as you would for a job interview. Think about the questions you are likely to be asked and practice verbalizing your answers. Think too about what you want interviewers to know about you so that you can present this information when the opportunity is given. Dress as you would for an employment interview.

Mailing Completed Applications

Graduate schools have established a wide variety of procedures for filing applications, so read each institution's instructions carefully. Some may request that you send all application materials in one package (including letters of recommendation). Others may have a two-step application process. This system requires the applicant to file a preliminary application; if this is reviewed favorably, he or she submits a second set of documents and a second application fee. Pay close attention to each school's instructions.

Graduate schools generally require an application fee. Sometimes this fee may be waived if you meet certain financial criteria. Check with your undergraduate financial aid office and the graduate schools to which you are applying to see if you qualify.

Admission Decisions

At most institutions, once the graduate school office has received all of your application materials, your file is sent directly to the academic department. A faculty committee (or the department chairperson) then makes a recommendation to the chief graduate school officer (usually a graduate dean or vice president), who is responsible for the final admission decision. Professional schools at most institutions act independently of the graduate school office; applications

INTERNATIONAL STUDENTS

If you are an international student, you will follow the same application procedures as other graduate school applicants. However, you will have to meet additional requirements.

Since your success as a graduate student will depend on your ability to understand, write, read, and speak English, if English is not your native language, you will be required to take the Test of English as a Foreign Language (TOEFL) or a similar test. Some schools will waive the language test requirement, however, if you have a degree from a college or university in a country where the native language is English or if you have studied two or more years in an undergraduate or graduate program in a country where the native language is English. As for all other tests, score requirements vary, but some schools admit students with lower scores on the condition that they enroll in an intensive English program before or during their graduate study. You should ask each school or department about its policies.

In addition to scores on your English test, or proof of competence in English, your formal application must be accompanied by a certified English translation of your academic transcripts. You may also be required to submit records of immunization and certain health certificates as well as documented evidence of financial support at the time of application. However, since you may apply for financial assistance from graduate schools as well as other sources, some institutions require evidence of financial support only as the last step in your formal admittance and may grant you conditional acceptance first.

Once you have been formally admitted into a graduate program and have submitted evidence of your source or sources of financial support, the school will send you Form I-20 or Form IAP-66, Certificate of Eligibility for Non-Immigrant Status. You must present this document, along with a passport from your own government, and evidence of financial support (some schools will require evidence of support for the entire course of study, while others require evidence of support only for the first year of study if there is also documentation to show reasonable expectation of continued support) to a U.S. embassy or consulate to obtain an international student visa (F-1 with the Form I-20 or J-1 with the Form IAP-66).

Your own government may have other requirements you must meet to study in the United States. Be sure to investigate those requirements as well.

Once all the paperwork has been completed and approved, you are ready to make your travel arrangements. If your port of entry into the United States will be New York's Kennedy Airport, you can arrange, for a fee, to be met and assisted by a representative of the YMCA Arrivals Program. This person will help you through customs and assist you in making travel connections. He or she can also help you find temporary overnight accommodations, if needed. To inquire about fees for this service, contact the Arrivals Program by phone (212-727-8800 Ext. 130), fax (212-727-8814), or e-mail (ips@ymca.nyc.org). If you decide to take advantage of this assistance, you must provide the Arrivals Program with the following information: your name, age, sex, date and time of arrival, airline and flight number, college or university you will be attending, sponsoring agency (if any), and connecting flight information. Include a photo to help identify you, and note if you need overnight accommodations in New York. This information should be sent well in advance to YMCA Arrivals Program, 71 West 23rd Street, Suite 1904, New York, New York 10010.

When you arrive on your American college campus, you will want to contact the international student adviser. This person's job is to help international students in their academic and social adjustment. The adviser often coordinates special orientation programs for new students, which may consist of lectures on American culture, intensive language instruction, campus tours, academic placement examinations, and visits to places of cultural interest in the community. This adviser will also help you with travel and employment questions as well as financial concerns and will keep copies of your visa documents on file, which is required by U.S. immigration law.

A number of nonprofit educational organizations are available throughout the world to assist international students in planning graduate study in the United States. To learn how to get in touch with these organizations to obtain detailed information, contact the U.S. embassy in your country.

are submitted to them directly, and they make their own admission decisions.

Usually a student's grade point average, letters of recommendation, and graduate admission test scores are the primary factors considered by admissions committees. The appropriate-ness of the undergraduate degree, an interview, and evidence of creative talent may also be taken into account. Normally the student's total record is examined closely, and the weight assigned to specific factors fluctuates from program to program. Few, if any, institutions base their decisions purely on numbers, that is, admission test scores and grade point average. A study by the Graduate Record Examinations Board found that grades and recommendations by known faculty members were considered to be somewhat more important than GRE General Test scores and that GRE Subject Test scores were rated as relatively unimportant (Oltman and Hartnett, 1984). This indicates that some graduate admission test scores may be of less importance than is commonly believed, but this will of course differ from program to program.

Some of the common reasons applicants are rejected for admission to graduate schools are inappropriate undergraduate curriculum, poor grades or lack of academic prerequisites, low admission test scores, weak or ineffective recommendation letters, poor interviews, and lack of extracurricular activities, volunteer experience, or research activities. To give yourself the best chances of being admitted where you apply, try to make a realistic assessment of an institution's admission standards and your own qualifications. Remember, too, that missing deadlines and filing an incomplete application can also be a cause for rejection; be sure that your transcripts and recommendation letters are received on time.

RETURNING STUDENTS

Many graduate programs not only accept the older, returning student but actually prefer these "seasoned" candidates. Some programs value mature applicants with work experience, for they have found that these students often show a higher level of motivation and commitment and work harder than 21-year-olds. Many programs also seek the diversity older students bring to the student body, as differences in perspective and experience make for interesting—and often intense—class discussions. Nonprofessional programs also view older students favorably if their academic and experiential preparation is recent enough and sufficient for the proposed fields of study.

Many institutions have programs designed to make the transition to academic life easier for the returning student. Such programs include low-cost child-care centers, emotional support programs for both the returning student and his or her spouse, and review courses of various kinds.

Other than making the necessary changes in their life-style, older students report that the most difficult aspect of returning to school is recovering, or developing, appropriate study habits. Initially, older students often feel at a disadvantage compared to students fresh out of an undergraduate program who are accustomed to preparing research papers and taking tests. This feeling can be overcome by taking advantage of noncredit courses in study skills and time management and review courses in math and writing, as well as by taking a tour of the library and becoming thoroughly familiar with it. By the end of the graduate program, most returning students feel that their life experience gave them an edge, because they could use concrete experiences to help them understand academic theory.

If you choose to go back to school, you are not alone. A significant number of adults are currently enrolled in some kind of educational program in order to make their lives or careers more rewarding.

PART-TIME STUDENTS

As graduate education has changed over the past thirty years, the number of part-time graduate programs has increased. Traditionally, graduate programs were completed by full-time students. Graduate schools instituted residence requirements, demanding that students take a full course load for a certain number of consecutive semesters. It was felt that total immersion in the field of study and extensive interaction with the faculty were necessary to achieve mastery of an academic area.

In most academic Ph.D. programs, this is still the only approach. However, many other programs now admit part-time students or allow a portion of the requirements to be completed on a part-time basis. Professional schools are more likely to allow part-time study because many students work full-time in the field and pursue their degree in order to enhance their career credentials. Other applicants choose part-time study because of financial considerations. By continuing to work full-time while attending school, they take fewer economic risks.

Part-time programs vary considerably in quality and admissions standards. When evaluating a part-time program, use the same criteria you would use in judging the reputation of any graduate program. Some schools use more adjunct faculty members with weaker academic training for their night and weekend courses, and this could lower the quality of the program; however, adjunct lecturers often have excellent experiential knowledge. Admissions standards may be lower for a part-time program than for an equivalent full-time program at the same school, but, again, your fellow students in the part-time program may be practicing in the field and may have much to add to class discussions. Another concern is placement opportunities upon completion of the program. Some schools may not offer placement services to part-time students, and many employers do not value part-time training as highly as a full-time education. However, if a part-time program is the best option for you, do not hesitate to enroll after carefully researching available programs.

Jane E. Levy
Senior Associate Director
University Career Center
Cornell University
and
Elinor R. Workman
Director of Career Services
Graduate School of Business
University of Chicago

TESTS REQUIRED OF APPLICANTS

any graduate schools require that applicants submit scores on one or more standardized tests, often the Graduate Record Examinations (GRE) or the Miller Analogies Test (MAT). Professional schools usually require that applicants take a specific admission test. Virtually all graduate and professional schools ask students whose native language is not English to take the Test of English as a Foreign Language (TOEFL), and some also ask for TOEFL's Test of Written English (TWE) or the Test of Spoken English (TSE).

Brief descriptions of these tests and the addresses to write to for additional information are given below.

Graduate Record Examinations

The GRE General Test and Subject Tests are designed to assess academic knowledge and skills relevant to graduate study. The General Test measures verbal, quantitative, and analytical reasoning abilities, and the Subject Tests measure achievement in particular fields of study. The GRE tests are administered worldwide by Educational Testing Service (ETS) of Princeton, New Jersey, under policies established by the Graduate Record Examinations Board, an independent board affiliated with the Association of Graduate Schools and the Council of Graduate Schools.

The General Test is offered both as a computer-based test (CBT) and a paper-based test. Subject Tests are offered only as paper-based tests. Subject Tests are available in sixteen areas: biochemistry, cell and molecular biology; biology; chemistry; computer science; economics; education; engineering; geology; history; literature in English; mathematics; music; physics; political science; psychology; and sociology.

The CBT General Test is offered year-round at more than 300 test centers around the world. The CBT offers easier scheduling, immediate viewing of scores, and faster score reporting. Call 800-GRE-CALL to schedule an appointment, or refer to the 1997–98 *GRE Information and Registration Bulletin* for a list of test centers. The 1997–98 *GRE Bulletin* contains registration and program services information for both computer-based and paper-based testing.

The 1997–98 GRE paper-based test dates are November 1, December 13, and April 4. The General Test is offered at the November and April test dates only. Subject Tests are offered on all three test dates; however, the economics, geology, history, music, revised education, revised political science, and sociology tests will not be offered on the November test date. Additionally, the revised education and revised political science tests will be discontinued after April 1998.

Fees for the CBT General Test, the paper-based General Test, and the Subject Tests are $96 if testing in the United States, U.S. Territories, or Puerto Rico. In all other locations, fees are $120 for the General Test and $96 for a Subject Test. Fees are subject to change.

Nonstandard testing accommodations are available for test takers with disabilities through both the CBT and paper-based testing programs. Refer to the *GRE Bulletin* for more information.

Students who, for religious reasons, cannot take tests on Saturdays may request a Monday administration immediately following a regular Saturday test date.

To receive GRE registration material, write to GRE, P.O. Box 6000, Princeton, New Jersey 08541-6000, call 609-771-7670, or visit the GRE Web site at http://www.gre. org.

Peterson's offers *GRE Success*, a complete guide to the GRE. Visit your local bookstore or contact Peterson's at 800-225-0261.

Miller Analogies Test

The MAT is published and administered by The Psychological Corporation, a division of Harcourt Brace & Company. The MAT is a high-level mental ability test that requires the solution of 100 problems stated in the form of analogies. The MAT is accepted by more than 2,300 graduate school programs as part of their admission process. The test items use different types of analogies to sample general information and a variety of fields, such as fine arts, literature, mathematics, natural science, and social science. Examinees are allowed 50 minutes to complete the test.

The MAT is offered at more than 600 test centers in the United States and Canada. For examinee convenience, the test is given on an as-needed basis at most test centers. Fees are also determined by each test center.

Additional information about the MAT, including preparatory materials and test center locations, is available from The Psychological Corporation, 555 Academic Court, San Antonio, Texas 78204. Telephone: 210-299-1061 or 800-622-3231 (7 a.m. to 7 p.m., Monday through Friday, Central time).

Test of English as a Foreign Language

The purpose of TOEFL is to evaluate the English proficiency of people whose native language is not English. Given in a single session of about 3 hours, the test consists of three sections: listening comprehension, structure and written expression, and reading comprehension. The test is given at more than 1,275 centers in 180 countries and areas and is administered by Educational Testing Service (ETS) under the general direction of a policy council established by the College Board and the Graduate Record Examinations Board.

The 1997–98 test dates are December 12, January 10, February 7, March 13, April 18, May 9, and June 5. Examinees who take the test during the December February, and May administrations are required to write a short essay. This essay, the Test of Written English (TWE), is a 30-minute test of the ability to compose in English. Examinees receive a TWE score separate from their TOEFL score. The fee for the TOEFL is $55. There is no additional charge for the TWE essay. This fee is for testing in the United States. Overseas bulletins contain information on local fees and registration procedures. Registration material is available from TOEFL, P.O. Box 6151, Princeton, New Jersey 08541-6151, U.S.A. Telephone: 609-771-7100. E-mail: toefl@ets.org. World Wide Web: http://www.toefl.org.

Peterson's offers *TOEFL Success*, a complete guide to the TOEFL. Visit your local bookstore or contact Peterson's at 800-225-0261.

Test of Spoken English

The major purpose of the TSE is to evaluate the spoken English proficiency of people whose native language is not English. The test, which takes about 30 minutes, requires examinees to demonstrate their ability to speak English by answering a variety of questions presented in printed and recorded form. All the answers to test questions are recorded on tape; no writing is required. TSE is given at selected TOEFL test centers worldwide. The test is administered by Educational Testing Service (ETS) under the general direction of a policy council established by the College Board and the Graduate Record Examinations Board.

The 1997–98 test dates are December 12, January 10, February 7, March 13, April 18, May 9, and June 5. The registration fee is $100, which must be paid in U.S. dollars.

Registration material is found in the *Bulletin of Information for TOEFL and TSE* available from TOEFL, P.O. Box 6151, Princeton, New Jersey 08541-6151, U.S.A. Telephone: 609-771-7100.

CAREER ADVISORY • CAREER ADVISORY • CAREER ADVISORY

ACCREDITATION AND ACCREDITING AGENCIES

olleges and universities in the United States, and their individual academic and professional programs, are accredited by non-governmental agencies concerned with monitoring the quality of education in this country. Agencies with both regional and national jurisdictions grant accreditation to institutions as a whole, while specialized bodies acting on a nationwide basis—often national professional associations—grant accreditation to departments and programs in specific fields.

Institutional and specialized accrediting agencies share the same basic concerns: the purpose an academic unit—whether university or program—has set for itself and how well it fulfills that purpose, the adequacy of its financial and other resources, the quality of its academic offerings, and the level of services it provides. Agencies that grant institutional accreditation take a broader view, of course, and examine universitywide or college-wide services that a specialized agency may not concern itself with.

Both types of agencies follow the same general procedures when considering an application for accreditation. The academic unit prepares a self-evaluation, focusing on the concerns mentioned above and usually including an assessment of both its strengths and weaknesses; a team of representatives of the accrediting body reviews this evaluation, visits the campus, and makes its own report; and finally, the accrediting body makes a decision on the application. Often, even when accreditation is granted, the agency makes a recommendation regarding how the institution or program can improve. All institutions and programs are also reviewed every few years to determine whether they continue to meet established standards; if they do not, they may lose their accreditation.

Accrediting agencies themselves are reviewed and evaluated periodically by the U.S. Department of Education and the Council for Higher Education Accreditation (CHEA). Agencies recognized adhere to certain standards and practices, and their authority in matters of accreditation is widely accepted in the educational community.

This does not mean, however, that accreditation is a simple matter, either for schools wishing to become accredited or for students deciding where to apply. Indeed, in certain fields the very meaning and methods of accreditation are the subject of a good deal of debate. For their part, those applying to graduate school should be aware of the safeguards provided by regional accreditation, especially in terms of degree acceptance and institutional longevity. Beyond this, applicants should understand the role that specialized accreditation plays in their field, as this varies considerably from one discipline to another. In certain professional fields, it is necessary to have graduated from a program that is accredited in order to be eligible for a license to practice, and in some fields the federal government also makes this a hiring requirement. In other disciplines, however, accreditation is not as essential, and there can be excellent programs that are not accredited. In fact, some programs choose not to seek accreditation, although most do.

Institutions and programs that present themselves for accreditation are sometimes granted the status of candidate for accreditation, or what is known as "preaccreditation." This may happen, for example, when an academic unit is too new to have met all the requirements for accreditation. Such status signifies initial recognition and indicates that the school or program in question is working to fulfill all requirements; it does not, however, guarantee that accreditation will be granted.

Readers are advised to contact agencies directly for answers to their questions about accreditation. The names and addresses of all agencies recognized by the U.S. Department of Education and the Council for Higher Education Accreditation are listed below.

Institutional Accrediting Agencies– Regional

Middle States Association of Colleges and Schools

Accredits institutions in Delaware, District of Columbia, Maryland, New Jersey, New York, Pennsylvania, Puerto Rico, and the Virgin Islands.

> Jean Avnet Morse, Executive Director
> Commission on Higher Education
> 3624 Market Street
> Philadelphia, Pennsylvania 19104-2680
> Telephone: 215-662-5606

New England Association of Schools and Colleges

Accredits institutions in Connecticut, Maine, Massachusetts, New Hampshire, Rhode Island, and Vermont.

> Dr. Charles M. Cook, Director
> Commission on Institutions of Higher Education
> 209 Burlington Road
> Bedford, Massachusetts 01730-1433
> Telephone: 617-271-0022

North Central Association of Colleges and Schools

Accredits institutions in Arizona, Arkansas, Colorado, Illinois, Indiana, Iowa, Kansas, Michigan, Minnesota, Missouri, Nebraska, New Mexico, North Dakota, Ohio, Oklahoma, South Dakota, West Virginia, Wisconsin, and Wyoming.

> Steve Crow, Executive Director
> Commission on Institutions of Higher Education
> 30 North LaSalle, Suite 2400
> Chicago, Illinois 60602-2504
> Telephone: 312-263-0456

Northwest Association of Schools and Colleges

Accredits institutions in Alaska, Idaho, Montana, Nevada, Oregon, Utah, and Washington.

> Sandra Elman, Executive Director
> Commission on Colleges
> 11130 Northeast 33rd Place, Suite 120
> Bellevue, Washington 98004
> Telephone: 206-827-2005

Southern Association of Colleges and Schools

Accredits institutions in Alabama, Florida, Georgia, Kentucky, Louisiana, Mississippi, North Carolina, South Carolina, Tennessee, Texas, and Virginia.

> James T. Rogers, Executive Director
> Commission on Colleges
> 1866 Southern Lane
> Decatur, Georgia 30033-4097
> Telephone: 404-679-4501 Ext. 512

Western Association of Schools and Colleges

Accredits institutions in California, Guam, and Hawaii.

> Ralph Wolff, Executive Director
> Accrediting Commission for Senior Colleges and
>   Universities
> Mills College
> P.O. Box 9990
> Oakland, California 94613-0990
> Telephone: 510-632-5000

Institutional Accrediting Agencies–Other

Accrediting Council for Independent Colleges and Schools

> Stephen D. Parker, Executive Director
> 750 First Street, NE, Suite 980
> Washington, D.C. 20002-4241
> Telephone: 202-336-6780

Distance Education and Training Council

> Michael P. Lambert, Executive Director
> Accrediting Commission
> 1601 Eighteenth Street, NW
> Washington, D.C. 20009-2529
> Telephone: 202-234-5100
> Fax: 202-332-1386

Specialized Accrediting Agencies
ENGINEERING

> George D. Peterson, Executive Director
> Accreditation Board for Engineering and
>   Technology, Inc.
> 111 Market Place, Suite 1050
> Baltimore, Maryland 21202
> Telephone: 410-347-7710
> Fax: 410-625-2238

QUICK REFERENCE TO PROGRAMS OFFERED

	Artificial Intelligence/ Robotics	Computer Engineering	Computer Science/ Systems Science	Electrical Engineering	Information Science/Medical Informatics	Software Engineering
UNITED STATES						
▶ **Alabama**						
Alabama Agricultural and Mechanical University			•			
Auburn University		•	•	•		
Tuskegee University				•		
The University of Alabama (Tuscaloosa)			•	•		
The University of Alabama at Birmingham		•	•	•	•	
The University of Alabama in Huntsville		•	•	•		
University of South Alabama			•	•	•	
▶ **Alaska**						
University of Alaska Fairbanks			•	•		
▶ **Arizona**						
Arizona State University			•	•		
Arizona State University East		•		•	•	
University of Arizona		•	•	•		
University of Phoenix			•		•	
▶ **Arkansas**						
Arkansas State University			•			
University of Arkansas (Fayetteville)		•	•	•		
University of Arkansas at Little Rock			•		•	
▶ **California**						
Azusa Pacific University			•			•
California Institute of Technology			•	•		
California Polytechnic State University, San Luis Obispo		•	•	•		
California State Polytechnic University, Pomona			•	•		
California State University, Chico			•	•		
California State University, Fresno			•	•		
California State University, Fullerton			•	•	•	
California State University, Hayward			•			
California State University, Long Beach		•	•	•		
California State University, Los Angeles				•		
California State University, Northridge		•	•	•		
California State University, Sacramento			•	•		•
California State University, San Bernardino			•			
Claremont Graduate University					•	
Coleman College					•	
Loyola Marymount University			•	•		
Mills College			•			
National University						•
Naval Postgraduate School		•	•	•		
San Diego State University			•	•		
San Francisco State University			•			
San Jose State University	•	•	•	•		•
Santa Clara University		•	•	•		•
Stanford University			•	•	•	
University of California, Berkeley			•	•		
University of California, Davis		•	•	•		
University of California, Irvine		•	•	•	•	
University of California, Los Angeles			•	•		

	Artificial Intelligence/ Robotics	Computer Engineering	Computer Science/ Systems Science	Electrical Engineering	Information Science/Medical Informatics	Software Engineering
University of California, Riverside			•			
University of California, San Diego	•	•	•	•		
University of California, Santa Barbara		•	•	•		
University of California, Santa Cruz		•	•			
University of San Francisco			•			
University of Southern California	•	•	•	•		•
▶ Colorado						
Colorado School of Mines			•			
Colorado State University			•	•		
Colorado Technical University		•	•	•		
National Technological University		•	•	•		•
University of Colorado at Boulder		•	•	•		
University of Colorado at Colorado Springs		•	•	•		
University of Colorado at Denver			•	•		
University of Denver			•	•		
▶ Connecticut						
Fairfield University					•	
Rensselaer at Hartford			•	•	•	
Sacred Heart University			•		•	
University of Bridgeport		•	•	•		
University of Connecticut (Storrs)			•			•
University of New Haven				•		•
Western Connecticut State University			•			
Yale University			•	•		
▶ Delaware						
University of Delaware			•	•	•	
▶ District of Columbia						
American University			•		•	
The Catholic University of America	•			•		
The George Washington University			•	•		
Howard University	•		•	•		
Southeastern University			•			
▶ Florida						
Embry-Riddle Aeronautical University (FL)						•
Florida Agricultural and Mechanical University				•		
Florida Atlantic University		•	•	•		
Florida Institute of Technology		•	•	•	•	
Florida International University		•	•	•		
Florida State University			•	•		
Nova Southeastern University			•		•	
University of Central Florida		•	•	•		
University of Florida		•	•	•	•	
University of Miami			•	•		
University of North Florida			•		•	
University of South Florida		•	•	•		
University of West Florida			•			
▶ Georgia						
Clark Atlanta University			•		•	
Columbus State University			•			
Emory University			•			
Georgia Institute of Technology		•	•	•		
Georgia Southwestern State University			•			
Medical College of Georgia					•	
Mercer University (Macon)			•	•	•	•
Mercer University, Cecil B. Day Campus				•		
Southern Polytechnic State University			•			
University of Georgia	•					
▶ Hawaii						
University of Hawaii at Manoa			•	•	•	
▶ Idaho						
University of Idaho		•	•	•		

	Artificial Intelligence/ Robotics	Computer Engineering	Computer Science/ Systems Science	Electrical Engineering	Information Science/Medical Informatics	Software Engineering
▶ Illinois						
Bradley University			•	•	•	
DePaul University			•		•	•
Governors State University			•			
Illinois Institute of Technology		•	•	•		
Illinois State University			•			
Knowledge Systems Institute			•		•	
Loyola University Chicago			•			
North Central College			•			
Northeastern Illinois University			•			
Northern Illinois University			•	•		
Northwestern University		•	•	•	•	
Roosevelt University			•		•	
Southern Illinois University at Carbondale			•	•	•	
Southern Illinois University at Edwardsville			•	•		
University of Chicago			•			
University of Illinois at Chicago		•	•	•		
University of Illinois at Springfield			•			
University of Illinois at Urbana–Champaign		•	•	•		
Western Illinois University			•			
▶ Indiana						
Ball State University			•		•	
Indiana State University		•				
Indiana University Bloomington			•			
Indiana University–Purdue University Fort Wayne			•			
Indiana University–Purdue University Indianapolis			•	•		
Purdue University (West Lafayette)		•	•	•		
Rose-Hulman Institute of Technology		•		•		
University of Notre Dame		•	•	•		
▶ Iowa						
Iowa State University of Science and Technology		•	•	•		
Maharishi University of Management			•			
Marycrest International University			•			
The University of Iowa		•	•	•		
University of Northern Iowa			•			
▶ Kansas						
Kansas State University		•	•	•	•	•
University of Kansas			•	•		
Wichita State University				•		
▶ Kentucky						
University of Kentucky			•	•		
University of Louisville		•	•	•		
Western Kentucky University			•			
▶ Louisiana						
Louisiana State University and Agricultural and Mechanical College		•	•	•		
Louisiana Tech University			•	•		
Loyola University New Orleans			•			
McNeese State University			•	•		
Southern University and Agricultural and Mechanical College			•			
Tulane University			•	•		
University of New Orleans			•	•		
University of Southwestern Louisiana		•	•			
▶ Maine						
University of Maine (Orono)		•	•	•		
University of Southern Maine			•			
▶ Maryland						
Bowie State University			•			
Capitol College					•	
Hood College			•		•	
Johns Hopkins University		•	•	•		
Towson University			•			

	Artificial Intelligence/ Robotics	Computer Engineering	Computer Science/ Systems Science	Electrical Engineering	Information Science/Medical Informatics	Software Engineering
University of Maryland, Baltimore County		•	•	•	•	
University of Maryland, College Park			•	•		•
University of Maryland Eastern Shore			•			
University of Maryland University College						•
▶ **Massachusetts**						
Boston University		•	•	•		
Brandeis University			•			
Bridgewater State College			•			
Fitchburg State College			•			
Harvard University			•			
Massachusetts Institute of Technology			•	•		
Northeastern University		•	•	•	•	
Suffolk University			•			
Tufts University			•	•		
University of Massachusetts Amherst		•	•	•		
University of Massachusetts Boston			•			
University of Massachusetts Dartmouth			•	•		
University of Massachusetts Lowell		•	•	•		
Western New England College				•		
Worcester Polytechnic Institute		•	•	•		
▶ **Michigan**						
Central Michigan University			•			•
GMI Engineering & Management Institute		•		•		
Grand Valley State University					•	•
Michigan State University			•	•		
Michigan Technological University			•	•		
Oakland University		•	•	•		
University of Detroit Mercy			•	•		
University of Michigan (Ann Arbor)		•	•	•		
University of Michigan–Dearborn		•	•	•	•	
Wayne State University		•	•	•		•
Western Michigan University		•	•	•		
▶ **Minnesota**						
College of St. Scholastica					•	
Mankato State University			•	•		
St. Cloud State University			•			
University of Minnesota, Duluth			•			
University of Minnesota, Twin Cities Campus	•		•	•	•	
University of St. Thomas (MN)						•
▶ **Mississippi**						
Alcorn State University			•		•	
Jackson State University			•			
Mississippi College			•			
Mississippi State University		•	•	•		
University of Southern Mississippi			•			
▶ **Missouri**						
Northwest Missouri State University			•			
University of Missouri–Columbia		•	•	•		
University of Missouri–Kansas City			•			•
University of Missouri–Rolla			•	•		
Washington University			•	•		
Webster University			•			
▶ **Montana**						
Montana State University–Bozeman		•	•	•		
The University of Montana–Missoula			•			
▶ **Nebraska**						
Creighton University			•			
University of Nebraska at Omaha			•			
University of Nebraska–Lincoln		•	•	•		
▶ **Nevada**						
University of Nevada, Las Vegas		•	•	•		
University of Nevada, Reno			•	•		

	Artificial Intelligence/ Robotics	Computer Engineering	Computer Science/ Systems Science	Electrical Engineering	Information Science/Medical Informatics	Software Engineering
▶ New Hampshire						
Dartmouth College		•	•	•		
New Hampshire College	•					
Rivier College			•		•	
University of New Hampshire (Durham)			•	•		
▶ New Jersey						
Fairleigh Dickinson University, Florham-Madison Campus			•			
Fairleigh Dickinson University, Teaneck–Hackensack		•	•	•		
Monmouth University			•			•
Montclair State University			•			
New Jersey Institute of Technology		•	•	•	•	
Princeton University		•	•	•	•	
Rutgers, The State University of New Jersey, New Brunswick		•	•	•		
Stevens Institute of Technology		•	•	•	•	
University of Medicine and Dentistry of New Jersey					•	
▶ New Mexico						
New Mexico Institute of Mining and Technology			•			
New Mexico State University		•	•	•		
University of New Mexico		•	•	•		
▶ New York						
Alfred University				•		
Brooklyn College of the City University of New York			•		•	
City College of the City University of New York			•	•		
Clarkson University		•	•	•		
College of Staten Island of the City University of New York			•			
Columbia University			•	•	•	
Cornell University	•	•	•	•		
Fordham University			•			
Graduate School and University Center of the City University of New York			•	•		
Hofstra University			•			
Hunter College of the City University of New York			•			
Iona College (New Rochelle)			•			
Lehman College of the City University of New York			•			
Long Island University, Brooklyn Campus			•			
Long Island University, C.W. Post Campus					•	
Manhattan College		•		•		
Marist College			•		•	
New York Institute of Technology			•	•		
New York University			•			
Pace University			•		•	
Polytechnic University, Brooklyn Campus			•	•	•	
Polytechnic University, Farmingdale Campus			•	•	•	
Polytechnic University, Westchester Graduate Center			•	•	•	
Queens College of the City University of New York			•			
Rensselaer Polytechnic Institute		•	•	•		
Rochester Institute of Technology		•	•	•	•	•
St. John's University (NY)			•			
State University of New York at Binghamton			•	•		
State University of New York at Buffalo		•	•	•		
State University of New York at New Paltz			•			
State University of New York at Stony Brook			•	•	•	•
State University of New York Institute of Technology at Utica/Rome			•		•	
Syracuse University		•	•	•	•	
Union College (NY)			•	•		
University at Albany, State University of New York			•		•	
University of Rochester			•	•		
▶ North Carolina						
Appalachian State University			•			
Duke University		•	•	•	•	

	Artificial Intelligence/ Robotics	Computer Engineering	Computer Science/ Systems Science	Electrical Engineering	Information Science/Medical Informatics	Software Engineering
East Carolina University			•			
North Carolina Agricultural and Technical State University			•	•		
North Carolina State University		•	•	•		
The University of North Carolina at Chapel Hill			•			
University of North Carolina at Charlotte			•	•		
Wake Forest University			•			
Western Carolina University			•			
▶ North Dakota						
North Dakota State University			•	•		
University of North Dakota			•	•		
▶ Ohio						
Air Force Institute of Technology		•	•	•		
Bowling Green State University			•			
Case Western Reserve University		•	•	•		
Cleveland State University		•				
Kent State University			•			
Miami University			•			
The Ohio State University			•	•	•	
Ohio University	•			•		
The University of Akron			•	•		
University of Cincinnati		•	•	•		
University of Dayton			•	•		
University of Toledo			•	•		
Wright State University		•	•	•		
Youngstown State University				•		
▶ Oklahoma						
Oklahoma City University			•			
Oklahoma State University		•	•	•		
University of Central Oklahoma			•			
University of Oklahoma			•	•		
University of Tulsa			•	•		
▶ Oregon						
Oregon Graduate Institute of Science and Technology		•	•	•		
Oregon Health Sciences University					•	
Oregon Institute of Technology		•				
Oregon State University		•	•	•		
Portland State University		•	•	•		
Southern Oregon University			•			
University of Oregon			•		•	
University of Portland				•		
▶ Pennsylvania						
Allentown College of St. Francis de Sales					•	
Bucknell University				•		
Carnegie Mellon University	•	•	•	•	•	•
Drexel University		•	•	•	•	•
East Stroudsburg University of Pennsylvania			•			
Gannon University				•		•
Kutztown University of Pennsylvania			•		•	
La Salle University			•			
Lehigh University		•	•	•		
Pennsylvania State University Great Valley Graduate Center				•	•	
Pennsylvania State University Harrisburg Campus of the Capital College				•		
Pennsylvania State University University Park Campus		•	•	•		
Saint Joseph's University			•			
Shippensburg University of Pennsylvania			•		•	
Temple University (Philadelphia)		•	•	•	•	
University of Pennsylvania			•	•	•	
University of Pittsburgh			•	•	•	
University of Scranton						•
Villanova University		•	•	•		
West Chester University of Pennsylvania			•			

Pennsylvania (continued)	Artificial Intelligence/ Robotics	Computer Engineering	Computer Science/ Systems Science	Electrical Engineering	Information Science/Medical Informatics	Software Engineering
Widener University		•		•		•
Wilkes University				•		
▶ **Rhode Island**						
Brown University			•	•		
Salve Regina University			•			
University of Rhode Island		•	•	•		
▶ **South Carolina**						
Clemson University		•	•	•		
Medical University of South Carolina					•	
University of South Carolina (Columbia)		•	•	•		
▶ **South Dakota**						
South Dakota School of Mines and Technology			•	•		
South Dakota State University			•	•		
University of South Dakota			•			
▶ **Tennessee**						
East Tennessee State University			•		•	
Middle Tennessee State University			•			
Tennessee Technological University				•		
The University of Memphis		•	•	•		
University of Tennessee at Chattanooga			•			
University of Tennessee, Knoxville			•	•	•	
University of Tennessee Space Institute			•	•		
Vanderbilt University		•	•	•		
▶ **Texas**						
Angelo State University			•			
Baylor University			•			
Lamar University			•	•		
Midwestern State University			•			
Rice University		•	•	•		
St. Mary's University of San Antonio		•	•	•	•	
Sam Houston State University			•			
Southern Methodist University		•	•	•		•
Southwest Texas State University			•			
Stephen F. Austin State University			•			
Texas A&M University (College Station)			•	•		
Texas A&M University–Commerce			•			
Texas A&M University–Corpus Christi			•			
Texas A&M University–Kingsville			•	•		
Texas Christian University						•
Texas Tech University			•	•		
University of Houston		•	•			
University of Houston–Clear Lake		•	•		•	•
University of North Texas			•		•	
The University of Texas at Arlington		•	•			•
The University of Texas at Austin		•	•	•		
The University of Texas at Dallas			•	•		
The University of Texas at El Paso		•	•	•		
The University of Texas at San Antonio			•			
The University of Texas at Tyler			•			
The University of Texas–Pan American			•			
▶ **Utah**						
Brigham Young University			•	•		
University of Utah			•	•	•	
Utah State University			•	•		
▶ **Vermont**						
University of Vermont			•	•		
▶ **Virginia**						
Christopher Newport University			•			
College of William and Mary			•			
George Mason University			•	•	•	•
Hampton University			•			
Hollins College			•			

	Artificial Intelligence/ Robotics	Computer Engineering	Computer Science/ Systems Science	Electrical Engineering	Information Science/Medical Informatics	Software Engineering
James Madison University			•			
Marymount University			•			
Old Dominion University		•	•	•		
University of Virginia			•	•	•	
Virginia Commonwealth University			•			
Virginia Polytechnic Institute and State University			•	•	•	
▶ **Washington**						
Eastern Washington University			•			
Gonzaga University				•		
Seattle University						•
University of Washington			•	•		
Washington State University			•	•		
Western Washington University			•			
▶ **West Virginia**						
West Virginia Graduate College					•	
West Virginia University		•	•	•		
▶ **Wisconsin**						
Concordia University Wisconsin			•			
Marquette University		•		•		
Milwaukee School of Engineering					•	
University of Wisconsin–Madison			•	•		
University of Wisconsin–Milwaukee			•			
▶ **Wyoming**						
University of Wyoming			•	•		
US TERRITORIES						
▶ **Puerto Rico**						
University of Puerto Rico, Mayagüez Campus		•		•		
CANADA						
▶ **Alberta**						
University of Alberta		•	•	•		
The University of Calgary		•	•	•		
▶ **British Columbia**						
Simon Fraser University			•			
University of British Columbia			•	•		
University of Victoria			•	•		
▶ **Manitoba**						
University of Manitoba		•	•	•		
▶ **New Brunswick**						
University of New Brunswick (Fredericton)			•			
▶ **Newfoundland**						
Memorial University of Newfoundland			•	•		
▶ **Nova Scotia**						
Acadia University			•			
Dalhousie University			•			
Technical University of Nova Scotia			•	•		
▶ **Ontario**						
Carleton University			•	•	•	
Lakehead University			•			
McMaster University			•	•		
Queen's University at Kingston			•	•	•	•
Trent University			•			
University of Guelph			•			
University of Ottawa			•	•		
University of Toronto		•	•	•		•
University of Waterloo		•	•	•		
The University of Western Ontario			•			
University of Windsor			•	•		
York University			•			
▶ **Quebec**						
Concordia University (Canada)		•	•	•		•
École Polytechnique de Montréal		•	•	•		
McGill University			•	•		

Quebec (continued)	Artificial Intelligence/ Robotics	Computer Engineering	Computer Science/ Systems Science	Electrical Engineering	Information Science/Medical Informatics	Software Engineering
Université de Montréal			•			
Université de Sherbrooke		•		•		
Université du Québec à Trois-Rivières			•	•		
Université Laval			•	•		
▶ Saskatchewan						
University of Regina		•	•			
University of Saskatchewan				•		

PAYING FOR SCHOOL—FINANCING YOUR GRADUATE EDUCATION

Support for graduate study can take many forms, depending upon the field of study and program you pursue. For example, some 60 percent of doctoral students receive support in the form of either grants/fellowships or assistantships, whereas most students in master's programs rely on loans to pay for their graduate study. In addition, doctoral candidates are more likely to receive grants/fellowships and assistantships than master's degree students, and students in the sciences are more likely to receive aid than those in the arts and humanities.

For those of you who applied for financial aid as an undergraduate, there are some differences for graduate students you'll notice right away. For one, aid to undergraduates is based primarily on need (although the number of colleges that now offer undergraduate merit-based aid is increasing), but graduate aid is often based on academic merit. Second, as a graduate student, you are automatically declared "independent" for federal financial aid purposes, meaning your parents' income and asset information is not required in assessing your need for federal aid. Third, at some graduate schools, the awarding of aid may be administered by the academic departments or the graduate school itself, not the financial aid office. That means that at some schools, you may be involved with as many as three offices: a central financial aid office, the graduate school, *and* your academic department.

BE PREPARED

Being prepared for graduate school means you have to put together a financial plan. So, before you enter graduate school, you should have answers to these questions:

- What should I be doing now to prepare for the cost of my graduate education?
- What can I do to minimize my costs once I arrive on campus?
- What financial aid programs are available at each of the schools to which I am applying?
- What financial aid programs are available outside the university, at the federal, state, or private level?
- What financing options do I have if I cannot pay the full cost from my own resources and those of my family?
- What should I know about the loans I am being offered?

- What impact will these loans have on me when I complete my program?

You'll find your answers in three guiding principles: think ahead, live within your means, and keep your head above water.

THINK AHEAD

The first step to putting together your financial plan comes from thinking about the future: the loss of your income while you're attending school, your projected income after you graduate, the annual rate of inflation, additional expenses you will incur as a student and after you graduate, and any loss of income you may experience later on from unintentional periods of unemployment, pregnancy, or disability. The cornerstone of thinking ahead is following a step-by-step process.

1. *Set your goals.* Decide what and where you want to study, whether you will attend full- or part-time, whether you'll work while attending, and what an appropriate level of debt would be. Consider whether you would attend full-time if you had enough financial aid or whether keeping your full-time job is an important priority in your life. Keep in mind that some employers have tuition reimbursement plans for full-time employees.
2. *Take inventory.* Collect your financial information and add up your assets—bank accounts, stocks, bonds, real estate, business and personal property. Then subtract your liabilities—money owed on your assets, including credit card debt and car loans—to yield your net worth.
3. *Calculate your need.* Compare your net worth with the costs at the schools you are considering to get a rough estimate of how much of your assets you can use for your schooling.
4. *Create an action plan.* Determine how much you'll earn while in school, how much you think you will receive in grants and scholarships, and how much you plan to borrow. Don't forget to consider inflation and possible life changes that could affect your overall financial plan.
5. *Review your plan regularly.* Measure the progress of your plan every year and make adjustments for such things as increases in salary or other changes in your goals or circumstances.

LIVE WITHIN YOUR MEANS

The second step in being prepared is knowing how much you spend now so you can determine how much you'll spend when you're in school. Use the standard cost of attendance budget published by your school as a guide, but don't be surprised if your estimated budget is higher than the one the school provides, especially if you've been out of school for a while. Once you've figured out your budget, see if you can pare down your current costs and financial obligations so the lean years of graduate school don't come as too large a shock.

KEEP YOUR HEAD ABOVE WATER

Finally, the third step is managing the debt you'll accrue as a graduate student. Debt is manageable only when considered in terms of five things:

1. Your future income
2. The amount of time it takes to repay the loan
3. The interest rate you are being charged
4. Your personal lifestyle and expenses after graduation
5. Unexpected circumstances that change your income or your ability to repay what you owe

To make sure your educational debt is manageable, you should borrow an amount that requires payments of between 8 and 15 percent of your starting salary.

The approximate monthly installments for repaying borrowed principal at 5, 8–10, 12, and 14 percent are indicated below.

Estimated Loan Repayment Schedule
Monthly Payments for Every $1000 Borrowed

Rate	5 years	10 years	15 years	20 years	25 years
5%	$18.87	$10.61	$ 7.91	$ 6.60	$ 5.85
8%	20.28	12.13	9.56	8.36	7.72
9%	20.76	12.67	10.14	9.00	8.39
10%	21.74	13.77	10.75	9.65	9.09
12%	22.24	14.35	12.00	11.01	10.53
14%	23.27	15.53	13.32	12.44	12.04

You can use this table to estimate your monthly payments on a loan for any of the five repayment periods (5, 10, 15, 20, and 25 years). The amounts listed are the monthly payments for a $1000 loan for each of the interest rates. To estimate your monthly payment, choose the closest interest rate and multiply the amount of the payment listed by the total amount of your loan and then divide by 1,000. For example, for a total loan of $15,000 at 9 percent to be paid back over ten years, multiply $12.67 times 15,000 (190,050) divided by 1,000. This yields $190.05 per month.

If you're wondering just how much of a loan payment you can afford monthly without running into payment problems, consult the chart below.

HOW MUCH CAN YOU AFFORD TO REPAY?

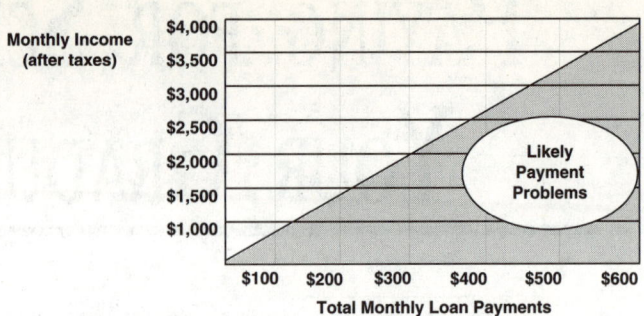

This graph shows the monthly cash-flow outlook based on your total monthly loan payments in comparison with your monthly income earned after taxes. Ideally, to eliminate likely payment problems, your monthly loan payment should be less than 15 percent of your monthly income.

Of course, the best way to manage your debt is to borrow less. While cutting your personal budget may be one option, there are a few others you may want to consider:

- *Ask Your Family for Help:* Although the federal government considers you "independent," your parents and family may still be willing and able to help pay for your graduate education. If your family is not open to just giving you money, they may be open to making a low-interest (or deferred-interest) loan. Family loans usually have more attractive interest rates and repayment terms than commercial loans. They may also have tax consequences, so you may want to check with a tax adviser.
- *Push to Graduate Early:* It's possible to reduce your total indebtedness by completing your program ahead of schedule. You can either take more courses per semester or during the summer. Keep in mind, though, that these options reduce the time you have available to work.
- *Work More, Attend Less:* Another alternative is to enroll part-time, leaving more time to work. Remember, though, to qualify for aid, you must be enrolled at least half time, which is usually considered six credits per term. If you're enrolled less than half time, you'll have to start repaying your loans once the grace period has expired.

ROLL YOUR LOANS INTO ONE

There's a good chance that as a graduate student you will have two or more loans included in your aid package, plus any money you borrowed as an undergraduate. That means when you start repaying, you could be making loan payments to several different lenders. Not only can the recordkeeping be a nightmare, but with each loan having a minimum payment, your total monthly payments may be more than you can handle. If you owe more than $7500 in federal loans, you can combine your loans into one consolidated loan at either a flat 9 percent interest rate or a weighted average of the rates on the loans consolidated. Your repayment can also be extended to up to thirty years, depending on the total amount you borrow, which will make your monthly payments lower (of course, you'll also be paying more total interest). With a consolidated loan, some lenders offer graduated or income-sensitive repayment options. Consult with your lender or the U.S. Department of Education about the types of consolidation provisions offered.

CREDIT: DON'T LET YOUR PAST HAUNT YOU

Many schools will check your credit history before they process any private educational loans for you. To make sure your credit rating is accurate, you may want to request a copy of your credit report before you start graduate school. You can get a copy of your report by sending a signed, written request to one of the four national credit reporting agencies at the addresses listed below. Include your full name, social security number, current address, any previous addresses for the past five years, date of birth, and daytime phone number. Call the agency before you request your report so you know whether there is a fee for this report. Note that you are entitled to a free copy of your credit report if you have been denied credit within the last sixty days. In addition, TRW currently provides complimentary credit reports once every twelve months.

Credit criteria used to review and approve student loans can include the following:

- Absence of negative credit
- No bankruptcies, foreclosures, repossessions, charge-offs, or open judgments
- No prior educational loan defaults, unless paid in full or making satisfactory repayments
- Absence of excessive past due accounts; that is, no 30-, 60-, or 90-day delinquencies on consumer loans or revolving charge accounts within the past two years

CREDIT REPORTING AGENCIES

Equifax Information Service Center
P.O. Box 740241
Atlanta, GA 30374-0241
800-685-1111

Experian National Consumer Assistance Center
P.O. Box 949
Allen, TX 75013-0949
888-397-3742

Trans Union Corporation
P.O. Box 390
Springfield, PA 19064-0390
610-690-4909

TYPES OF AID AVAILABLE

There are three types of aid: money given to you (grants, scholarships, and fellowships), money you earn through work, and loans.

Grants, Scholarships, and Fellowships

Most grants, scholarships, and fellowships are outright awards that require no service in return. Often they provide the cost of tuition and fees plus a stipend to cover living expenses. Some are based exclusively on financial need, some exclusively on academic merit, and some on a combination of need and merit. As a rule, grants are awarded to those with financial need, although they may require the recipient to have expertise in a certain field. Fellowships and scholarships often connote selectivity based on ability—financial need is usually not a factor.

Federal Support

Several federal agencies fund fellowship and trainee programs for graduate and professional students. The amounts and types of assistance offered vary considerably by field of study. The following are programs available for those studying engineering or applied sciences:

National Science Foundation. Graduate Research Program Fellowships include tuition and fees plus a $14,000 stipend and a $1000 total allowance for three years of graduate study in engineering, mathematics, the natural sciences, the social sciences, and the history and philosophy of science. The application deadline is in early November. For more information, write to the National Science Foundation at Oak Ridge Associated Universities, P.O. Box 3010, Oak Ridge, TN 37831-3010, or call 423-241-4300.

National Institutes of Health (NIH). NIH sponsors many different fellowship opportunities. For example, it offers training grants administered through schools' research departments. Training grants provide tuition plus a twelve-month stipend of $10,008. For more information, call 301-435-0714.

Graduate Assistantships in Areas of National Need. This program was designed to offer fellowships to outstanding doctoral candidates of superior ability. It is designed to offer financial assistance to students enrolled in specific programs for which there is both a national need and lack of qualified personnel. The definition of national need is determined by the Secretary of Education. Current areas include chemistry, engineering, mathematics, physics, and area studies. Funds are awarded to schools who then select their recipients, based on academic merit. Awardees must also demonstrate financial need. Awards include tuition plus a living expense stipend of up to $14,000. Awards are not to exceed four years. Contact the graduate dean's office or academic department to see whether the school participates in this program.

Veterans' Benefits. Veterans may use their educational benefits for training at the graduate and professional levels. Contact your regional office of the Veterans Administration for more details.

State Support

Many states offer grants for graduate study, with California, Michigan, New York, North Carolina, Texas, and Virginia offering the largest programs. States grant approximately $64 million per year to graduate students. Due to fiscal constraints, however, some states have had to reduce or eliminate their financial aid programs for graduate study. To qualify for a particular state's aid you must be a resident of that state.

Residency is established in most states after you have lived there for at least twelve consecutive months prior to enrolling in school. Many states provide funds for in-state students only; that is, funds are not transferable out of state. Contact your state scholarship office to determine what aid it offers.

Institutional Aid

Educational institutions using their own funds provide between $2 billion and $3 billion in graduate assistance in the form of fellowships, tuition waivers, and assistantships. Consult each school's catalog for information about aid programs.

Corporate Aid

Some corporations provide graduate student support as part of the employee benefits package. Most employees who receive aid study at the master's level or take courses without enrolling in a particular degree program.

Aid from Foundations

Most foundations provide support in areas of interest to them. The Foundation Center of New York City publishes several reference books on foundation support for graduate study. For more information, call 212-620-4230 or access their Web site at http://fdncenter.org.

Financial Aid for Minorities and Women

Patricia Roberts Harris Fellowships. This federal award provides support for minorities and women. Awards are made to schools, and the schools decide who receives these funds. Grants provide tuition and a stipend of $14,000 for up to four years. Consult the graduate school for more information.

Bureau of Indian Affairs. The Bureau of Indian Affairs (BIA) offers aid to students who are at least one quarter American Indian or native Alaskan and from a federally recognized tribe. Contact your tribal education officer, BIA area office, or call the Bureau of Indian Affairs at 202-208-3710.

The Ford Foundation Doctoral Fellowship for Minorities. Provides three-year doctoral fellowships and one-year dissertation fellowships. Predoctoral fellowships include an annual stipend of $11,500 to the fellow and an annual institutional grant of $6000 to the fellowship institution in lieu of tuition and fees. Dissertation fellows receive a stipend of $18,000 for a twelve-month period. Applications are due in early November. For more information, contact the Fellowship Office, National Research Council at 202-334-2872.

National Consortium for Graduate Degrees in Engineering and Science (GEM). GEM was founded in 1976 to help minority men and women pursue graduate study in engineering by helping them obtain practical experience through summer internships at consortium work-sites and finance graduate study toward a master's or Ph.D. degree. GEM administers the following programs:

Engineering Fellowship Program. Each fellow receives a GEM-sponsored summer internship and a portable fellowship tenable at one of seventy-seven GEM universities. The fellowship consists of tuition, fees, and a $6000 stipend per academic year.

Ph.D. Fellowship Program. The Ph.D. Science Fellowship and the Engineering Fellowship programs provide opportunities for minority students to obtain a Ph.D. in the natural sciences or in engineering through a program of paid summer research internships and financial support. Open to U.S. citizens who belong to one of the ethnic groups underrepresented in the natural sciences and engineering, GEM fellowships are awarded for a twelve-month period. Fellowships are tenable at universities participating in the GEM science or engineering Ph.D. programs. Awards include tuition, fees, and a $12,000 stipend. After the first year of study fellows are supported completely by their respective universities and support may include teaching or research assistantships. Forty fellowships are awarded annually in each program. The application deadline is December. Contact GEM, Box 537, Notre Dame, IN 46556, or call 219-631-7771.

National Physical Sciences Consortium. Graduate fellowships are available in astronomy, chemistry, computer science, geology, materials science, mathematics, and physics for women and Black, Hispanic, and Native American students. These fellowships are available only at member universities. Awards may vary by year in school; the application deadline is November 1. Fellows receive tuition plus a stipend between $10,000 and $15,000. Contact National Physical Sciences Consortium, Department 3NPS, c/o New Mexico State University, P.O. Box 30001, Las Cruces, New Mexico 88033-8001, or call 505-646-6037.

In addition, below are some books available that describe financial aid opportunities for women and minorities.

The Directory of Financial Aids for Women by Gail Ann Schlachter (Reference Service Press, 1997) lists sources of support and identifies foundations and other organizations interested in helping women secure funding for graduate study.

The Association for Women in Science publishes *Grants-at-a-Glance,* a booklet highlighting fellowships for women in science. It can be ordered by calling 202-326-8940.

Books such as the *Financial Aid for Minorities* (Garrett Park, MD: Garrett Park Press, 1994) describe financial aid opportunities for minority students.

Reference Service Press also publishes four directories specifically for minority students: *Financial Aid for African Americans, Financial Aid for Asian Americans, Financial Aid for Hispanic Americans,* and *Financial Aid for Native Americans.*

In addition, if you register with the *Minority Graduate Student Locator Service,* sponsored by the Educational Testing Service, you will be contacted by schools interested in increasing their minority student enrollment. Such schools may have funds designated for minority students.

Disabled students are eligible to receive aid from a number of organizations. *Financial Aid for the Disabled and Their Families, 1996–98* by Gail Ann Schlachter and David R. Weber (Reference Service Press) lists aid opportunities for disabled students. The Vocational Rehabilitation Services in your home state can also provide information.

Researching Grants and Fellowships

The books listed below are good sources of information on grant and fellowship support for graduate education and should be consulted before you resort to borrowing. Keep in mind that grant support varies dramatically from field to field.

Annual Register of Grant Support: A Directory of Funding Sources, Wilmette, Illinois: National Register Publishing Co. This is a comprehensive guide to grants and awards from government agencies, foundations, and business and professional organizations.

Corporate Foundation Profiles, 8th ed. New York: Foundation Center, 1994. This is an in-depth, analytical profile of 250 of the largest company-sponsored foundations in the United States. Brief descriptions of all 700 company-sponsored foundations are also included. There is an index of subjects, types of support, and geographical locations.

The Foundation Directory, 16th ed. Edited by Stan Olsen. New York: Foundation Center, 1994. This directory, with a supplement, gives detailed information on U.S. foundations with brief descriptions of the purpose and activities of each.

The Grants Register 1995–97, 14th ed. Edited by Lisa Williams. New York: St. Martin's, 1995. This lists grant agencies alphabetically and gives information on awards available to graduate students, young professionals, and scholars for study and research.

Peterson's Grants for Graduate and Postdoctoral Study, 4th ed. Princeton: Peterson's, 1994. This book includes information on 1,400 grants, scholarships, awards, fellowships, and prizes. Originally compiled by the Office of Research Affairs at the Graduate School of the University of Massachusetts at Amherst, this guide is updated periodically by Peterson's.

Graduate schools sometimes publish listings of support sources in their catalogs, and some provide separate publications, such as the *Graduate Guide to Grants,* compiled by the Harvard Graduate School of Arts and Sciences. For more information, call 617-495-1814.

World Wide Web: A New Source of Funding Information

If you have not explored the financial resources on the World Wide Web (the Web, for short), your research is not complete. Now available on the Web is a wealth of information ranging from loan and entrance applications to minority grants and scholarships.

Web Mailing Lists

There is a mailing list or newsgroup, called GRANTS-L, for announcements of grants and fellowships of interest to graduate students. To subscribe, send mail to listproc@listproc.gsu.edu with "subscribe GRANTS-L YOUR NAME" in the body of the message.

University-Specific Information on the Web

Universities are now in the process of creating Web financial aid directories. Florida, Virginia Tech, Massachusetts, Emory, and Georgetown are just a few. Applications of admission can now be downloaded from the Web to start the graduate process. After that, detailed information can be obtained on financial aid processes, forms, and deadlines. University-specific grant and scholarship information can also be found, and more may be learned about financing by using the Web than by an actual visit. Questions can often be answered online.

Scholarships on the Web

Dictionary-sized books listing scholarships will be obsolete in the future. When searching for scholarship opportunities, one can search the Web. First, many benefactors and other scholarship donors are creating pages on the Web listing pertinent information with regard to their specific scholarship. You can reach this information through a variety of methods. For example, you can find a directory listing minority scholarships, quickly look at the information on-line, decide if it applies to you, and then move on. New scholarship pages are being added to the Web daily.

The Web also lists many services that will look for scholarships for you. *FastWeb* is one of these services. Some of these services cost money and advertise more scholarships per dollar than any other service. While some of these might be helpful, surfing the Web and using the traditional library resources on available scholarships (now often listed on the Web as stated above) are often just as productive and free. Some services such as FastWeb, which is an acronym for Financial aid search through the Web, may be free through your university. Check with your financial aid office to see if these services are available to you.

Bank and Loan Information on the Web

Banks and loan servicing centers are creating pages on the Web, making it easier to access loan information. Having the information on screen in front of you instantaneously is more convenient than being put on hold on the phone. Any loan information such as interest rate variations, descriptions of loans, loan consolidation programs, and repayment charts can all be found on the Web.

Work Programs

Certain types of support, such as teaching, research, and administrative assistantships, require recipients to provide service to the university in exchange for a salary or stipend; sometimes tuition is also provided or waived.

Teaching Assistantships

Because science and engineering classes are taught at the undergraduate level, you stand a good chance of securing a teaching assistantship. These positions usually involve conducting small classes, delivering lectures, correcting class work, grading papers, counseling students, and supervising laboratory groups. Usually about 20 hours of work is required each week.

Teaching assistantships provide excellent educational experience as well as financial support. Teaching Assistants generally receive a salary (now considered taxable income). Sometimes tuition is provided or waived as well. In addition, at some schools, TAs can be declared state residents, qualifying them for the in-state tuition rates. Appointments are based on academic qualifications and are subject to the availability of funds within a department. If you are interested in a teaching assistantship, contact the academic department.

Ordinarily you are not considered for such positions until you have been admitted to the graduate school.

Research Assistantships

Research assistantships usually require that you assist in the research activities of a faculty member. Appointments are ordinarily made for the academic year. They are rarely offered to first-year students. Contact the academic department, describing your particular research interests. As is the case with teaching assistantships, research assistantships provide excellent academic training as well as practical experience and financial support.

Administrative Assistantships

These positions usually require 10 to 20 hours of work each week in an administrative office of the university. For example, those seeking a graduate degree in education may work in the admissions, financial aid, student affairs, or placement office of the school they are attending. Some administrative assistantships provide a tuition waiver, others a salary. Details concerning these positions can be found in the school catalog or by contacting the academic department directly.

Federal Work Study (FWS)

This federally funded program provides eligible students with employment opportunities, usually in public and private nonprofit organizations. Federal funds pay up to 75 percent of the wages, with the remainder paid by the employing agency. FWS is available to graduate students who demonstrate financial need. Not all schools have these funds, and some only award undergraduates. Each school sets its application deadline and work-study earnings limits. Wages vary and are related to the type of work done.

Additional Employment Opportunities

Many schools provide on-campus employment opportunities that do not require demonstrated financial need. The student employment office on most campuses assists students in securing jobs both on and off the campus.

Loans

Most needy graduate students, except those pursuing Ph.D.'s in certain fields, borrow to finance their graduate programs. There are two sources of student loans—the federal government and private loan programs. You should read and understand the terms of these loan programs before submitting your loan application.

Federal Loans

Federal Stafford Loans. The Federal Stafford Loan Program offers government-sponsored, low-interest loans to students through a private lender such as a bank, credit union, or savings and loan association.

There are two components of the Federal Stafford Loan program. Under the *subsidized* component of the program, the federal government pays the interest accruing on the loan while you are enrolled in graduate school on at least a half-time basis. Under the *unsubsidized* component of the program, you pay the interest on the loan from the day proceeds are issued. Eligibility for the federal subsidy is based on demonstrated financial need as determined by the financial aid office from the information you provide on the Free

Application for Federal Student Aid (FAFSA). A cosigner is not required, since the loan is not based on creditworthiness.

Although Unsubsidized Federal Stafford Loans may not be as desirable as Subsidized Federal Stafford Loans from the consumer's perspective, they are a useful source of support for those who may not qualify for the subsidized loans or who need additional financial assistance.

Eligible borrowers may borrow up to $8500 per year through the Subsidized Stafford Loan Program, up to a maximum of $65,000, including undergraduate borrowing. In addition to loans through the Subsidized Stafford Loan Program, graduate students may borrow up to an additional $10,000 per year through the *unsubsidized* component of the Federal Stafford Loan Program. You may borrow up to the cost of the school in which you are enrolled or will attend, minus estimated financial assistance from other federal, state, and private sources, with a maximum of $138,500, including undergraduate borrowing. Graduate students who borrow the maximum allowable amounts each year can receive a total of $18,500: $8500 through the *subsidized* program and an additional $10,000 through the *unsubsidized* program.

The interest rate for the Federal Stafford Loans varies annually and is set every July. The rate during in-school, grace, and deferment periods is based on the 91-Day U.S. Treasury Bill rate plus 2.5 percent, capped at 8.25 percent. The rate in repayment is based on the 91-Day U.S. Treasury Bill rate plus 3.1 percent, capped at 8.25 percent.

Two fees are deducted from the loan proceeds upon disbursement: a guarantee fee of up to 1 percent, which is deposited in an insurance pool to ensure repayment to the lender if the borrower defaults, and a federally mandated 3 percent origination fee, which is used to offset the administrative cost of the Federal Stafford Loan Program.

Under the *subsidized* Federal Stafford Loan program, repayment begins six months after your last enrollment on at least a half-time basis. Under the *unsubsidized* program, repayment of interest begins within thirty days from disbursement of the loan proceeds, and repayment of the principal begins six months after your last enrollment on at least a half-time basis. Some lenders may require that some payments be made even while you are in school, although most lenders will allow you to defer payments and will add the accrued interest to the loan balance. Under both components of the program, repayment may extend over a maximum of ten years with no prepayment penalty.

Federal Direct Loans. Some schools participate in the Department of Education's Direct Lending Program instead of offering Federal Stafford Loans. The two programs are essentially the same except that with Direct Loans, schools themselves originate the loans with funds provided from the federal government. Terms and interest rates are virtually the same except that there are a few more repayment options with Federal Direct Loans.

Federal Perkins Loans. The Federal Perkins Loan is a long-term loan available to students demonstrating financial need and is administered directly by the school. Not all schools have these funds, and some may award them to undergraduates only. Eligibility is determined from the information you provide on the FAFSA. The school will notify you of your eligibility.

Eligible graduate students may borrow up to $5000 per year, up to a maximum of $30,000, including undergraduate borrowing (even if your previous Perkins Loans have been repaid). The interest rate for Federal Perkins Loans is 5 percent, and no interest accrues while you remain in school at least half-time. There are no guarantee, loan, or disbursement fees. Repayment begins nine months after your last enrollment on at least a half-time basis and may extend over a maximum of ten years with no prepayment penalty.

Deferring Your Federal Loan Repayments. If you borrowed under the Federal Stafford Loan Program or the Federal Perkins Loan program for previous undergraduate or graduate study, some of your repayments may be deferred (i.e., suspended) when you return to graduate school, depending on when you borrowed and under which program. There are other deferment options available if you are temporarily unable to repay your loan. Information about these deferments is provided at your entrance and exit interviews. If you believe you are eligible for a deferment of your loan repayments, you must contact your lender to complete a deferment form. The deferment must be filed prior to the time your repayment is due, and it must be refiled when it expires if you remain eligible for deferment at that time.

Supplemental Loans

Many lending institutions offer supplemental loan programs and other financing plans to students seeking assistance in meeting their expected contribution toward educational expenses.

If you are considering borrowing through a supplemental loan program, you should carefully consider the terms of the program and be sure to "read the fine print." Check with the program sponsor for the most current terms that will be applicable to the amounts you intend to borrow for graduate study. Most supplemental loan programs for graduate study offer unsubsidized, credit-based loans. In general, a credit-ready borrower is one who has a satisfactory credit history or no credit history at all. A creditworthy borrower generally must pass a credit test to be eligible to borrow or act as a cosigner for the loan funds.

Many supplemental loan programs have a minimum annual loan limit and a maximum annual loan limit. Some offer amounts equal to the cost of attendance minus any other aid you will receive for graduate study. If you are planning to borrow for several years of graduate study, consider whether there is a cumulative or aggregate limit on the amount you may borrow. Often this cumulative or aggregate limit will include any amounts you borrowed and have not repaid for undergraduate or previous graduate study.

The combination of the annual interest rate, loan fees, and the repayment terms you choose will determine how much the amount is that you will repay over time. Compare these features in combination before you decide which loan program to use. Some loans offer interest rates that are adjusted monthly, some quarterly, some annually. Some offer interest rates that are lower during the in-school, grace, and deferment periods, and then increase when you begin repayment. Most programs include a loan "origination" fee, which is usually deducted from the principal amount you receive when the loan is disbursed, and must be repaid along with the interest and other principal when you graduate, withdraw from school, or drop below half-time study. Sometimes the loan fees are reduced if you borrow with a qualified cosigner. Some programs allow you to defer interest and/or principal payments while you are enrolled in graduate school. Many programs allow you to capitalize your interest payments; the interest due on your loan is added to the outstanding balance of your loan, so you don't have to repay immediately, but this increases the amount you owe. Other programs allow you to pay the interest as you go, which will reduce the amount you later have to repay.

For more information about supplemental loan programs or to obtain applications, access the sponsor's site on the World Wide Web or visit your school's financial aid office.

INTERNATIONAL EDUCATION AND STUDY ABROAD

A variety of funding sources are offered for study abroad and for foreign nationals studying in the United States. The Institute of International Education in New York assists students in locating such aid. It publishes *Funding for U.S. Study—A Guide for International Students and Professionals* and *Financial Resources for International Study,* a guide to organizations offering awards for overseas study. The Council on International Educational Exchange in New York publishes the *Student Travel Catalogue,* which lists fellowship sources and explains the council's services both for United States students traveling abroad and for foreign students coming to the United States.

The U.S. Department of Education administers programs that support fellowships related to international education. Foreign Language and Area Studies Fellowships and Fulbright-Hays Doctoral Dissertation Awards were established to promote knowledge and understanding of other countries and cultures. They offer support to graduate students interested in foreign languages and international relations. Discuss these and other foreign study opportunities with the financial aid officer or someone in the graduate school dean's office at the school you will attend.

HOW TO APPLY

All applicants for federal aid must complete the Free Application for Federal Student Aid (FAFSA). This application must be completed *after* January 1 preceding enrollment in the fall. On this form you report your income and asset information for the preceding calendar year and specify which schools will receive the data. Two to four weeks later you'll receive an acknowledgment on which you can make any corrections. The schools you've designated will also receive the information and may begin asking you to send them documents, usually your U.S. income tax return, verifying what you reported.

In addition to the FAFSA, some graduate schools want additional information and will ask you to complete the CSS Financial Aid PROFILE. Schools requiring this form are listed in the PROFILE registration form available in college financial aid offices. Other schools use their own supplemental application. Check with your financial aid office to confirm which forms they require.

If you have already filed your federal income tax for the year, it will be much easier for you to complete these forms. If not, use estimates, but be certain to notify the financial aid office if your estimated figures differ from the actual ones once you have calculated them.

APPLICATION DEADLINES

Application deadlines vary. Some schools require you to apply for aid when applying for admission; others require that you be admitted before applying for aid. Aid application instructions and deadlines should be clearly stated in each school's application material. The FAFSA must be filed after January 1 of the year you are applying for aid but the Financial Aid PROFILE should be completed earlier, in October or November.

DETERMINING FINANCIAL NEED

Eligibility for need-based financial aid is based on your income during the calendar year prior to the academic year in which you apply for aid. Prior-year income is used because it is a good predictor of current-year income and is verifiable. If you have a significant reduction in income or assets after your aid application is completed, consult a financial aid counselor. If, for example, you are returning to school after working, you should let the financial aid counselor know your projected income for the year you will be in school. Aid counselors may use their "professional judgment" to revise your financial need, based on the actual income you will earn while you are in graduate school.

Need is determined by examining the difference between the cost of attendance at a given institution and the financial resources you bring to the table. Eligibility for aid is calculated by subtracting your resources from the total cost of attendance budget. These standard student budgets are generally on the low side of the norm. So if your expenses are higher because of medical bills, higher research travel, or more costly books, for example, a financial aid counselor can make an adjustment. Of course, you'll have to document any unusual expenses. Also, keep in mind that with limited grant and scholarship aid, a higher budget will probably mean either more loan or more working hours for you.

TAX ISSUES

Since the passage of the Tax Reform Act of 1986, grants, scholarships, and fellowships may be considered taxable income. That portion of the grant used for payment of tuition and course-required fees, books, supplies, and equipment is excludable from taxable income. Grant support for living expenses is taxable. A good rule of thumb for determining the tax liability for grants and scholarships is to view anything that exceeds the actual cost of tuition, required fees, books, supplies related to courses, and required equipment as taxable.

- If you are employed by an educational institution or other organization that gives tuition reimbursement, you must pay tax on the value that exceeds $5250.
- If your tuition is waived in exchange for working at the institution, the tuition waiver is taxable. This includes waivers that come with teaching or research assistantships.
- Other student support, such as stipends and wages paid to research assistants and teaching assistants, is also taxable income. Student loans, however, are not taxable.
- If you are an international student you may or may not owe taxes depending upon the agreement the U.S. has negotiated with your home country. The United States has tax treaties with more than forty countries. You are responsible for making sure that the school you attend follows the terms of the tax treaty. If your country does not have a tax treaty with the U.S., you may have as much as 30 percent withheld from your paycheck.

A FINAL NOTE

While amounts and eligibility criteria vary from field to field as well as from year to year, with thorough research you can uncover many opportunities for graduate financial assistance. If you are interested in graduate study, discuss your plans with faculty members and advisers. Explore all options. Plan ahead, complete forms on time, and be tenacious in your search for support. No matter what your financial situation, if you are academically qualified and knowledgeable about the different sources of aid, you should be able to attend the graduate school of your choice.

Patricia McWade
Dean of Student Financial Services
Georgetown University

SOURCES OF FINANCIAL AID FOR COMPUTER SCIENCE AND ELECTRICAL ENGINEERING STUDENTS

or many families or individuals, financial aid from private sources is an excellent way to help defray higher education expenses. Private aid is particularly attractive for students who have been disqualified for need-based aid by family financial sources. The following presents private and other non-need sources of financial aid specifically for graduate computer science and electrical engineering students.

American Association of University Women Educational Foundation

Award Name: AAUW Educational Foundation Selected Professions Fellowships

Program Description: One-time award for minority women pursuing graduate degrees in architecture, math, computer science, or engineering. Must be U.S. citizens or permanent residents and have minimum 3.0 GPA. Write for deadline information. Application fee: $25.

Application Contact: American Association of University
Women Educational Foundation
111 16th Street, NW
Washington, DC 20036-4873

American Society for Engineering Education

Award Names: Navy-ASEE Summer Faculty Research Program, ONR-ASEE Postdoctoral Fellowship

Program Description: Research Program is a one-time award for postdoctoral work in a scientific/technical area of interest and relevance to the Navy. Must be a U.S. citizen and hold a teaching or research position at a U.S. college/university. Fellowship is a renewable postdoctoral award for highly trained scientists and engineers to pursue scientific research/technical development of interest and relevance to the Navy. Submit research proposal.

Application Contact: American Society for Engineering
Education
Program Manager
1818 N Street, NW, Suite 600
Washington, DC 20036-2479

American Society for Information Science

Award Names: ASIS Doctoral Dissertation Award, ISI Doctoral Dissertation Scholarship, Outstanding Information Science Teacher Award, Pratt-Severn Student Research Award, SIG/STI BIOSIS Student Award, SIG/STI Chemical Abstracts Service Student Award, ASIS Award of Merit, ASIS Best Information Science Book Award, ASIS Research Award, ASIS Student Paper Award, Cretsos Leadership Award, Watson Davis Award

Program Description: One dozen one-time awards available at various levels of study in information science. Most awards are based on achievement in a research area. Some awards require applicants to be nominated.

Application Contact: American Society for Information
Science
Awards Coordinator
8720 Georgia Avenue, Suite 501
Silver Spring, MD 20910

American Society of Heating, Refrigeration, and Air-Conditioning Engineers, Inc.

Award Name: Alwin B. Newton Scholarship Fund

Program Description: Renewable award of $2000 for studies relating to heating, refrigeration, and air-conditioning. Must be enrolled in an ABET-accredited program. Minimum 3.0 GPA required.

Application Contact: American Society of Heating,
Refrigeration, and Air-Conditioning
Engineers, Inc.
1791 Tullie Circle, NE
Atlanta, GA 30329-1683

American-Scandinavian Foundation

Award Name: ASF Training Program in Scandinavia

Program Description: One-time internship for American students ages 21–30 to live and work in Scandinavia for two to six months. Must have three years' undergraduate study completed in engineering, computer science, chemistry, or agriculture. Stipend is living expenses. Application fee: $20.

Application Contact: American-Scandinavian Foundation
725 Park Avenue
New York, NY 10021

Argonne National Laboratory

Award Name: ANL Student Summer Research Fellowships

Program Description: Summer student fellowships for juniors, seniors, and graduate students. Must conduct nonthesis work on nuclear reactors. Must be a U.S. citizen or permanent resident. Minimum 3.0 GPA required.

Application Contact: Argonne National Laboratory
Division of Educational Programs
Idaho National Engineering Laboratory
Idaho Falls, ID 83209

ARRL Foundation, Inc.

Award Names: Nemal Electronics Scholarship, ARRL Mississippi Scholarship, ARRL Ph.D. Scholarship, Charles N. Fisher Memorial Scholarship, Edmond A. Metzger Scholarship Fund, F. Charles Ruling "N6FR" Memorial Scholarship, Fred R. McDaniel Memorial Scholarship, Irving W. Cook "WA7CGS" Scholarship, L. Phil Wicker Scholarship, Paul and Helen L. Grauer Scholarship, Perry F. Hadlock Memorial Scholarship

Program Description: Eleven awards available to students pursuing a degree in electronics, electrical engineering, communications, or a related field or who are licensed amateur radio operators. Some awards have state residency requirements.

Application Contact: ARRL Foundation, Inc.
Scholarship Director
225 Main Street
Newington, CT 06111

Business and Professional Women's Foundation

Award Names: Avon Products Foundation Scholarship for Women in Business, BPW Foundation Career Advancement Scholarship, BPW Loan Fund for Women in Engineering Studies

Program Description: Scholarships are one-time awards for women at least 25 years old who are studying a business-related subject such as management, business administration, sales, computer science, education, engineering, science, paralegal studies, or a professional degree. The one-time loan is available to female college juniors, seniors, and graduate students who are studying engineering at an ABET-accredited school. Applications available from October 1 to April 1.

Application Contact: Business and Professional Women's Foundation
Scholarship and Loan Officer
2012 Massachusetts Avenue, NW
Washington, DC 20036

Center for Campus Organizing

Award Name: Computer Specialist Internship

Program Description: Year-long internship at national office in Massachusetts to work on upgrading CCO internal networks and presence on the World Wide Web and install and train staff on new software. Submit resume. Duration, start time, and hours are flexible.

Application Contact: Center for Campus Organizing
Internship Coordinator

Box 748
Cambridge, MA 02142

Charles Babbage Institute

Award Name: Adelle and Erwin Tomash Fellowship

Program Description: One-time award for graduate students addressing a topic in the history of computer and information processing. Submit research proposal and biographical information. Priority given to students who have completed all requirements for doctoral degree except the dissertation.

Application Contact: Charles Babbage Institute
Director
103 Walter Library, University of Minnesota
117 Pleasant Street, SE
Minneapolis, MN 55455

Connecticut Building Congress Scholarship Fund

Award Name: Connecticut Building Congress Scholarships

Program Description: Renewable award for Connecticut residents pursuing postsecondary studies in a construction-related field. Must be a U.S. citizen and attend a two- or four-year institution.

Application Contact: Connecticut Building Congress
Scholarship Fund
Scholarship Director
2600 Dixwell Avenue
Hamden, CT 65141

Council of Energy Resource Tribes

Award Name: CERT Scholarship Program

Program Description: Renewable scholarship for alumni of Tribal Resource Institute in Business, Engineering, and Science (TRIBES) or Tribal Internship program only. Must present tribal affiliation certification. Deadlines are July 15 and January 30.

Application Contact: Council of Energy Resource Tribes
CERT Scholarship Program
1999 Broadway, Suite 2600
Denver, CO 80202-5726

Council on Library Resources

Award Name: Council on Library Resources Fellows Program

Program Description: One-time award of $4000 for a graduate student showing great promise of technical innovation and leadership in computer or data management. Applications available in January.

Application Contact: Council on Library Resources
Fellowship Director
1400 16th Street, NW, Suite 715
Washington, DC 20036-2217

Educational Testing Service

Award Names: ETS Postdoctoral Fellowship Program, ETS Summer Program in Research for Graduate Students, NAEP Visiting Scholar Program

Program Description: Fellowship Program is a one-time award of $35,000 for an individual with doctorate in

relevant discipline. Summer Program provides internships for graduate students with 40 or more credits in a doctoral program of education, business, social science, or computer science. Visiting Scholar Program is an internship to conduct research addressing issues that affect the National Assessment of Educational Progress. Candidate should hold a Ph.D. in education, business, social studies, or computer science. Must submit resume, detailed description of research experiment, and research proposal.
Application Contact: Educational Testing Service
Rosedale Road
Mail Stop 16T
Princeton, NJ 05411

Electrochemical Society, Inc.
Award Names: Department of Energy Summer Fellowship; Electrochemical Society, Inc. Summer Fellowship Award Program; Electrochemical Society Energy Research Fellowship; F.M. Becket Memorial Award
Program Description: One-time awards for graduate students in electrochemical or solid-state science. Must be enrolled in a U.S. or Canadian institution and must continue studies post-fellowship. Submit statement of educational and research objectives. Cannot have other summer fellowships. Becket Memorial Award is for study overseas in a laboratory of a recognized research institution selected from a list of host institutions in the field of electrochemical science and technology concerned with specialty material and processing.
Application Contact: Electrochemical Society, Inc.
10 South Main Street
Pennington, NJ 08534-2896

Electronic Industries Foundation Scholarship Fund
Award Name: Electronic Industries Foundation Scholarship
Program Description: One-time award for disabled students pursuing or about to pursue undergraduate or graduate studies in fields directly related to the electronics industry. Must be a U.S. citizen or permanent resident and demonstrate financial need. Must provide proof of acceptance to an accredited four-year college or university.
Application Contact: Electronic Industries Foundation
Scholarship Fund
2500 Wilson Boulevard, Suite 210
Arlington, VA 22201-3834

Fannie and John Hertz Foundation
Award Name: Fannie and John Hertz Foundation Fellowship
Program Description: Award for graduate students of outstanding potential in the applied physical sciences. Stipend is $20,000, with up to $12,000 in expenses at specified schools. Must have minimum 3.75 GPA in last two undergraduate years. Renewable up to five years.
Application Contact: Fannie and John Hertz Foundation
Box 5032
Livermore, CA 94551-5032

Foundation for Science and Disability
Award Name: Foundation for Science and Disability–Student Grant
Program Description: One-time award available to graduate students who have some physical disability. Awards are given for an assistive device or as financial support for scientific research. Seniors may apply.
Application Contact: Foundation for Science and Disability
Grants Committee Chair
115 South Brainard Avenue
La Grange, IL 60525-2114

Henry Luce Foundation, Inc.
Award Name: Clare Boothe Luce Program/Women in Science
Program Description: One-time awards available through thirteen participating institutions for women interested in a career in science or engineering. Must be college junior, senior, or graduate student. Henry Luce Foundation accepts no individual applications.
Application Contact: Henry Luce Foundation, Inc.
Program Director
111 West 50th Street, Suite 3710
New York, NY 10020

International Union for Vacuum Science, Technique and Applications
Award Name: Welch Foundation Scholarship
Program Description: One-time award of $12,500 available to a promising scholar who wishes to contribute to the study of vacuum science techniques or their application in any field. Must hold at least a bachelor's degree and plan to spend a year in a research lab in another country. Must submit curriculum vitae, two recommendations, and a research proposal.
Application Contact: International Union for Vacuum
Science, Technique and Applications
Welch Foundation Scholarship
Box 3511, Station C
Ottawa, ON K1Y 4H7

National Academy of Sciences—National Research Council—Office for Central Europe and Eurasia
Award Name: Collaboration in Basic Science and Engineering Grants
Program Description: Several one-time short- and long-term grants available to American specialists who hold a Ph.D. in a field funded by NSF. Applicant must be a U.S. citizen; government employees are not eligible. Time period ranges from two weeks to six months. Application deadlines: April 7 for short-term, July for long-term grants.
Application Contact: National Academy of Sciences—
National Research Council—Office for
Central Europe and Eurasia
Program Assistant
2101 Constitution Avenue, NW
Washington, DC 20418

National Association of Water Companies
Award Names: David L. Owens Scholarship, J. J. Barr
Scholarship, NAWC Utilities, Inc. Scholarship
Program Description: One-time awards of varying amounts
for graduating seniors or graduate students pursuing studies
leading to a career in the investor-owned public water
supply business. Must be a U.S. citizen.
Application Contact: National Association of Water
           Companies
           Scholarship Committee
           1725 K Street, NW, Suite 1212
           Washington, DC 20006

National Federation of the Blind
Award Name: NFB Computer Science Scholarship
Program Description: One-time award for legally blind
students studying computer science. Must submit
recommendation from state officer of National Federation
of the Blind. Based on financial need, minimum 3.5 GPA,
scholarship, and community service.
Application Contact: National Federation of the Blind
           NFB Computer Science Scholarship
           Chairperson
           814 4th Avenue, Suite 200
           Grinnell, IA 50112

National Science Foundation
Award Name: NSF Minority Graduate Research
Fellowships
Program Description: Renewable fellowships for minority
graduate students pursuing research-based master's or
doctoral degrees in science, mathematics, or engineering.
Include transcript, test scores, essay, and reference with
application.
Application Contact: National Science Foundation
           Program Director
           4201 Wilson Boulevard, Room 907N
           Arlington, VA 22230

National Security Industrial Association
Award Name: Rocky Mountain Chapter Scholarship
Program Description: Up to 5 one-time awards of varying
amounts available to students interested in the aerospace
industry. Limited to the Colorado Springs local area.
Application Contact: National Security Industrial Association
           Rocky Mountain Chapter Scholarship
           Scholarship Committee
           P.O. Box 15200
           Colorado Springs, CO 80935

Naval Research Laboratory
Award Name: NRL Postdoctoral Fellowships
Program Description: Forty one-time internships with
$36,000–$43,000 stipend for scientists/engineers from
academia/industry to pursue research in areas of relevance
to the Navy. Submit research proposal with application.
Deadlines are January 1, April 1, July 1, and October 1.
Application Contact: Naval Research Laboratory
           NRL Postdoctoral Fellowships
           Fellowship Coordinator

           1818 N Street, NW, Suite 600
           Washington, DC 20036

North Carolina State Education Assistance Authority
Award Name: North Carolina Student Loan Program for
Health, Science and Math
Program Description: Renewable award for North Carolina
residents studying health-related fields or science or math
education. Based on merit, need, and promise of service as
a health professional or educator in an underserved area of
North Carolina.
Application Contact: North Carolina State Education
           Assistance Authority
           North Carolina Student Loan Program
           for Health, Science and Math
           P.O. Box 20549
           Raleigh, NC 27619

Society of Women Engineers
Award Names: General Motors Foundation Graduate
Scholarship, GTE Foundation Scholarships, Microsoft
Corporation Graduate Scholarships
Program Description: One-time awards for women
sophomores, juniors, seniors, or graduate students with
career interests in engineering technology, computer
science, computer engineering, or electrical, mechanical,
chemical, industrial, automotive, or manufacturing
engineering. Minimum 3.5 GPA. Send self-addressed
stamped envelope for application.
Application Contact: Society of Women Engineers
           Scholarships
           120 Wall Street, 11th Floor
           New York, NY 10005-3902

U.S. Department of Defense
Award Name: NDSEG Fellowship Program
Program Description: Three-year fellowship for U.S. citizens
at or near the beginning of doctoral study in science or
engineering. Award amount is full tuition and fees (not
including room and board) plus a stipend. Award is
renewable.
Application Contact: U.S. Department of Defense
           NDSEG Fellowship Program
           P.O. Box 13444
           200 Park Drive, Suite 211
           Research Triangle Park, NC
           27709-3444

U.S. Department of Energy
Award Name: Hollaender Postdoctoral Fellowships
Program Description: Renewable award for recent Ph.D.
recipients to conduct research in life, biomedical, or
environmental sciences. Must be U.S. citizen. Submit
proposal, application, transcript, autobiography, and
references by January 15.
Application Contact: U.S. Department of Energy
           Program Specialist
           P.O. Box 117
           Oak Ridge, TN 37831

Vertical Flight Foundation
Award Name: Vertical Flight Foundation Scholarship
Program Description: One-time award available for
undergraduate and graduate study in aerospace, electrical,
or mechanical engineering. Applicants must have an
interest in vertical flight technology.
Application Contact: Vertical Flight Foundation
     217 North Washington Street
     Alexandria, VA 22314

Woods Hole Oceanographic Institution
Award Name: WHOI Summer Student Fellowship
Program Description: Awarded to upper-class undergraduates
and beginning graduate students studying in any science or
engineering field with an interest in ocean sciences,
oceanographic engineering, mathematics, or marine policy.
Must submit research plan and career goals.
Application Contact: Woods Hole Oceanographic Institution
     Associate Dean
     Clark 223, Education Office MS 31
     Woods Hole, MA 02543

ABBREVIATIONS USED IN THIS GUIDE

The following list includes abbreviations of degree names used in the profiles in this book.

AC	Advanced Certificate
App Sc	Applied Scientist
CAS	Certificate of Advanced Studies
CSE	Computer Systems Engineer
DA	Doctor of Arts
DCS	Doctor of Computer Science
DE	Doctor of Engineering
D Eng	Doctor of Engineering
DESS	Diplôme Études Supérieures Spécialisées
D Sc	Doctor of Science
Ed D	Doctor of Education
EE	Electrical Engineer
Eng	Engineer
Engr	Engineer
Eng Sc D	Doctor of Engineering Science
MA	Master of Arts
MA Ed	Master of Arts in Education
MAIS	Master of Arts in Interdisciplinary Studies
MAMS	Master of Applied Mathematical Sciences
MA Sc	Master of Applied Science
MBA	Master of Business Administration
MCIS	Master of Computer and Information Science
M Co E	Master of Computer Engineering
M Cp E	Master of Computer Engineering
MCS	Master of Computer Science
MC Sc	Master of Computer Science
ME	Master of Engineering
MECE	Master of Electrical and Computer Engineering
M Ed	Master of Education
MEE	Master of Electrical Engineering
M Elec E	Master of Electrical Engineering
M Eng	Master of Engineering
M Engr	Master of Engineering
MES	Master of Engineering Science
MHCI	Master of Human-Computer Interaction
MIS	Master of Information Systems
M Math	Master of Mathematics
MME	Master of Mechanical Engineering
M Phil	Master of Philosophy
MS	Master of Science
MSA	Master of Science Administration

MSAI	Master of Science in Artificial Intelligence
MSBME	Master of Science in Biomedical Engineering
M Sc	Master of Science
M Sc A	Master of Science (Applied)
M Sc CS	Master of Science in Computer Science
MSCE	Master of Science in Computer Engineering
M Sc Eng	Master of Science in Engineering
MSCIS	Master of Science in Computer and Information Systems
	Master of Science in Computer Information Science
MS Cp E	Master of Science in Computer Engineering
MSCS	Master of Science in Computer Science
MSCSE	Master of Science in Computer and Systems Engineering
	Master of Science in Computer Science and Engineering
MSDD	Master of Software Design and Development
MSE	Master of Science in Engineering
MSE	Master of Software Engineering
MSECE	Master of Science in Electrical and Computer Engineering
MSEE	Master of Science in Electrical Engineering
	Master of Science in Electronic Engineering
MSEM	Master of Science in Engineering Management
MS Eng	Master of Science in Engineering
MS Engr	Master of Science in Engineering
MS Engr Sci	Master of Science in Engineering Science
MSES	Master of Science in Engineering Science
MSHCI	Master of Science in Human-Computer Interaction
MSIS	Master of Science in Information Systems
MSMCS	Master of Science in Management and Computer Science
MSMIS	Master of Science in Management Information Systems
MST	Master of Science in Teaching
MSWE	Master of Software Engineering
M Sw En	Master of Software Engineering
M Tech	Master of Technology
PhD	Doctor of Philosophy
Sc D	Doctor of Science
Sc M	Master of Science
SM	Master of Science

Profiles of Graduate Computer Science and Electrical Engineering Programs

UNITED STATES

ALABAMA

ALABAMA AGRICULTURAL AND MECHANICAL UNIVERSITY
Normal, AL 35762-1357

OVERVIEW
Alabama Agricultural and Mechanical University is a public coed university.

ENROLLMENT
5,263 graduate, professional, and undergraduate students; 373 full-time matriculated graduate/professional students (243 women), 1,038 part-time matriculated graduate/professional students (693 women).

GRADUATE FACULTY
139 full-time (39 women), 14 part-time (2 women); includes 97 minority (60 African-Americans, 35 Asian-Americans, 2 Hispanics).

EXPENSES
Tuition $117 per credit hour for state residents; $234 per credit hour for nonresidents. Fees $20 per year.

HOUSING
Rooms and/or apartments available to single students at an average cost of $2400 per year ($4008 including board); on-campus housing not available to married students. Housing application deadline: 5/1. Graduate housing contact: Mr. William Thigpen, 205-851-5797.

STUDENT SERVICES
Low-cost health insurance, career counseling, day-care facilities, campus employment opportunities, international student services.

FACILITIES
Library: J. F. Drake Memorial Learning Resources Center; total holdings of 263,026 volumes, 605,516 microforms, 1,729 current periodical subscriptions. A total of 35 personal computers in all libraries. Access provided to on-line information retrieval services. *Computer:* Campuswide network is available with full Internet access. Total number of PCs/terminals supplied for student use: 155. Computer services are offered at no charge. *Special:* In science and engineering: Agriculture Research Center, Biological Research Center, Remote Sensor Center, agricultural extension service, Optics Center. In social sciences: Teacher Education Service Center.

COMPUTER SCIENCE

School of Arts and Sciences, Department of Mathematics and Computer Science
Programs Offers program in computer science (MS). Evening/weekend programs available.
Faculty 10 full-time (0 women), 5 part-time (0 women).
Faculty Research Computer-assisted instruction, database management, software engineering, operating systems, neural networks.

Students 24 full-time (12 women), 26 part-time (8 women); includes 13 minority (all African-Americans), 37 international. Average age 26.
Degrees Awarded In 1996, 37 degrees awarded.
Entrance Requirements GRE General Test (minimum score 500 on each section), TOEFL (minimum score 500).
Degree Requirements Computer language, comprehensive exam required, thesis optional, foreign language not required.
Financial Aid Fellowships, research assistantships, teaching assistantships, and career-related internships or fieldwork available. *Financial aid application deadline: 4/1.*
Applying *Deadline: 5/1. Fee:* $15 ($20 for international students).
Contact *Surendar Pulusani*
Coordinator
205-851-5570

AUBURN UNIVERSITY
Auburn University, AL 36849-0001

OVERVIEW
Auburn University is a public coed university.

ENROLLMENT
21,778 graduate, professional, and undergraduate students; 1,864 full-time matriculated graduate/professional students (864 women), 1,518 part-time matriculated graduate/professional students (622 women).

GRADUATE FACULTY
1,171 full-time (235 women); includes 110 minority (30 African-Americans, 64 Asian-Americans, 11 Hispanics, 5 Native Americans).

EXPENSES
Tuition $2565 per year full-time, $71 per credit hour part-time for state residents; $7695 per year full-time, $213 per credit hour part-time for nonresidents. Fees $145 per quarter part-time for state residents; $435 per quarter part-time for nonresidents.

HOUSING
Rooms and/or apartments available to single students at an average cost of $1794 per year ($4727 including board); available to married students (359 units) at an average cost of $3054 per year. Housing application deadline: 9/1. Graduate housing contact: Student Housing Office, 334-844-4580.

STUDENT SERVICES
Disabled student services, low-cost health insurance, career counseling, campus safety program, campus employment opportunities, international student services.

FACILITIES
Library: Ralph B. Draughon Library plus 2 additional on-campus libraries; total holdings of 2,303,326 volumes, 2,248,480 microforms, 19,410 current periodical subscriptions. A total of 18 personal computers in all libraries. Access provided to on-line information retrieval services. *Computer:* Campuswide network is available

with full Internet access. Total number of PCs/terminals supplied for student use: 300. *Special:* In arts and humanities: Center for the Arts and Humanities, Center for Aging Studies. In science and engineering: Space Power Institute, International Center for Aquaculture, Scott-Ritchey Small Animal Research Facility, National Center for Asphalt Technology, Center for Advanced Technology. In social sciences: Truman Pierce Institute for the Advancement of Teacher Education, Economic Development Institution.

COMPUTER ENGINEERING

College of Engineering, Department of Computer Science and Engineering
Programs   Awards MCSE, MS, PhD. Part-time programs available.
Faculty   11 full-time (3 women).
Faculty Research   Parallelizable, scalable software translations; graphical representations of algorithms, structures, and processes; graph drawing. *Total annual research expenditures:* $400,000.
Students   45 full-time (16 women), 34 part-time (6 women); includes 15 minority (12 African-Americans, 2 Asian-Americans, 1 Hispanic), 31 international.
Degrees Awarded   In 1996, 26 master's, 2 doctorates awarded.
Entrance Requirements   For master's, GRE General Test, GRE Subject Test; for doctorate, GRE General Test (minimum score 400 on each section), GRE Subject Test.
Degree Requirements   For master's, thesis (MS) required, foreign language not required; for doctorate, dissertation required, foreign language not required.
Financial Aid   Research assistantships, teaching assistantships, Federal Work-Study available. Aid available to part-time students. *Financial aid application deadline:* 3/15.
Applying   61 applicants, 49% accepted. *Deadline:* 9/1 (rolling processing; 3/1 for spring admission). *Fee:* $25 ($50 for international students).
Contact   *Dr. John F. Pritchett*
Dean of the Graduate School
334-844-4700

COMPUTER SCIENCE

College of Engineering, Department of Computer Science and Engineering
Programs   Awards MCSE, MS, PhD. Part-time programs available.
Faculty   11 full-time (3 women).
Faculty Research   Parallelizable, scalable software translations; graphical representations of algorithms, structures, and processes; graph drawing. *Total annual research expenditures:* $400,000.
Students   45 full-time (16 women), 34 part-time (6 women); includes 15 minority (12 African-Americans, 2 Asian-Americans, 1 Hispanic), 31 international.
Degrees Awarded   In 1996, 26 master's, 2 doctorates awarded.
Entrance Requirements   For master's, GRE General Test, GRE Subject Test; for doctorate, GRE General Test (minimum score 400 on each section), GRE Subject Test.
Degree Requirements   For master's, thesis (MS) required, foreign language not required; for doctorate, dissertation required, foreign language not required.
Financial Aid   Research assistantships, teaching assistantships, Federal Work-Study available. Aid available to part-time students. *Financial aid application deadline:* 3/15.
Applying   61 applicants, 49% accepted. *Deadline:* 9/1 (rolling processing; 3/1 for spring admission). *Fee:* $25 ($50 for international students).

Contact   *Dr. John F. Pritchett*
Dean of the Graduate School
334-844-4700

ELECTRICAL ENGINEERING

College of Engineering, Department of Electrical Engineering
Programs   Awards MEE, MS, PhD. Part-time programs available.
Faculty   28 full-time (1 woman).
Faculty Research   Power systems, energy conversion, electronics, electromagnetics, digital systems.
Students   33 full-time (5 women), 52 part-time (4 women); includes 5 minority (2 African-Americans, 3 Asian-Americans), 30 international.
Degrees Awarded   In 1996, 19 master's, 3 doctorates awarded.
Entrance Requirements   For master's, GRE General Test, GRE Subject Test; for doctorate, GRE General Test (minimum score 400 on each section), GRE Subject Test.
Degree Requirements   For master's, thesis (MS), comprehensive exam required, foreign language not required; for doctorate, dissertation.
Financial Aid   Fellowships, research assistantships, teaching assistantships, Federal Work-Study available. Aid available to part-time students. *Financial aid application deadline:* 3/15.
Applying   75 applicants, 52% accepted. *Deadline:* 9/1 (rolling processing; 3/1 for spring admission). *Fee:* $25 ($50 for international students).
Contact   *Dr. John F. Pritchett*
Dean of the Graduate School
334-844-4700

TUSKEGEE UNIVERSITY
Tuskegee, AL 36088

OVERVIEW
Tuskegee University is an independent coed comprehensive institution.

ENROLLMENT
3,175 graduate, professional, and undergraduate students; 303 full-time matriculated graduate/professional students (174 women), 84 part-time matriculated graduate/professional students (44 women).

GRADUATE FACULTY
112 full-time (17 women), 11 part-time (5 women); includes 101 minority (67 African-Americans, 32 Asian-Americans, 2 Hispanics).

TUITION
$8662 per year full-time, $1948 per semester (minimum) part-time.

HOUSING
Rooms and/or apartments available to single students at an average cost of $3750 (including board); available to married students (48 units). Housing application deadline: 5/1. Graduate housing contact: Mary Wheeler, 334-727-8915.

STUDENT SERVICES
Low-cost health insurance, career counseling, free psychological counseling, day-care facilities, campus safety program, international student services.

FACILITIES

Library: Hollis Burke Frissell Library plus 3 additional on-campus libraries; total holdings of 293,656 volumes, 110,201 microforms, 1,020 current periodical subscriptions. *Special:* In science and engineering: Carver Research Foundation, agricultural experiment station, materials research laboratory.

ELECTRICAL ENGINEERING

College of Engineering, Architecture and Physical Sciences, Department of Electrical Engineering
Programs Awards MSEE.
Faculty 8 full-time (0 women).
Faculty Research Photovoltaic insulation, automatic guidance and control, wind energy.
Students 9 full-time (1 woman), 5 part-time (2 women); includes 14 minority (12 African-Americans, 2 Asian-Americans). Average age 24.
Degrees Awarded In 1996, 6 degrees awarded.
Entrance Requirements GRE General Test, GRE Subject Test.
Degree Requirements Computer language, thesis or alternative required, foreign language not required.
Financial Aid Fellowships available. *Financial aid application deadline:* 4/15.
Applying *Deadline:* 7/15 (rolling processing). *Fee:* $25 ($35 for international students).
Contact Dr. Numam Dogen
    Acting Head
    334-727-8298

THE UNIVERSITY OF ALABAMA
Tuscaloosa, AL 35487

OVERVIEW

The University of Alabama is a public coed university.

ENROLLMENT

17,810 graduate, professional, and undergraduate students; 2,587 full-time matriculated graduate/professional students (1,238 women), 1,534 part-time matriculated graduate/professional students (953 women).

GRADUATE FACULTY

800 full-time (370 women), 195 part-time (75 women); includes 97 minority (53 African-Americans, 36 Asian-Americans, 5 Hispanics, 3 Native Americans).

TUITION

$2594 per year full-time, $568 per year (minimum) part-time for state residents; $6808 per year full-time, $1174 per year (minimum) part-time for nonresidents.

HOUSING

Rooms and/or apartments available to single students (2,000 units) at an average cost of $2000 per year; available to married students (458 units) at an average cost of $3480 per year. Housing application deadline: 6/1. Graduate housing contact: Ms. Coress Brondon, 205-348-8086.

STUDENT SERVICES

Low-cost health insurance, career counseling, free psychological counseling, day-care facilities, campus safety program, campus employment opportunities, international student services.

FACILITIES

Library: Amelia Gayle Gorgas Library plus 8 additional on-campus libraries; total holdings of 2,057,586 volumes, 3,224,111 microforms, 14,426 current periodical subscriptions. Access provided to on-line information retrieval services. *Computer:* Campuswide network is available with full Internet access. Total number of PCs/terminals supplied for student use: 1,250. Computer service fees are included with tuition and fees. *Special:* In arts and humanities: Synclavier Synthesizer Laboratory, Center for Southern History and Culture, Critical Language Center, Strode House/Program for Renaissance Studies. In science and engineering: Freshwater Biology Center, School of Mines and Energy Development, computer design laboratory, robotics laboratory, artificial intelligence laboratory, biomass laboratory, herbarium, ichthyological collection. In social sciences: Center for Business and Economic Research, Institute for Social Science Research, Archaeological Research Center at Moundville, Brewer Porch Children's Center.

COMPUTER SCIENCE

College of Engineering, Department of Computer Science
Programs Awards MSCS, PhD.
Faculty 10 full-time (3 women).
Faculty Research Software engineering, artificial intelligence, database management, algorithms, human-computer interaction. *Total annual research expenditures:* $650,000.
Students 25 full-time (4 women), 12 part-time (4 women); includes 2 minority (both African-Americans), 22 international. Average age 27.
Degrees Awarded In 1996, 9 master's, 1 doctorate awarded.
Entrance Requirements For master's, GRE General Test (minimum combined score of 1600 on three sections), minimum GPA of 3.0 in last 60 hours; for doctorate, GRE General Test (minimum combined score of 1800 on three sections), minimum GPA of 3.0.
Degree Requirements For master's, thesis or alternative required, foreign language not required; for doctorate, dissertation required, foreign language not required.
Financial Aid In 1996–97, 22 students received aid, including 2 fellowships, 4 research assistantships averaging $889 per month and totaling $16,000, 16 teaching assistantships (3 to first-year students) averaging $889 per month and totaling $68,000; Federal Work-Study also available.
Applying 96 applicants, 24% accepted. *Deadline:* 7/6 (rolling processing). *Fee:* $25.
Contact Dr. Hui-Chuan Chen
    205-348-6363

See in-depth description on page 579.

ELECTRICAL ENGINEERING

College of Engineering, Department of Electrical Engineering
Programs Awards MSEE, PhD.
Faculty 17 full-time (2 women).
Faculty Research Computer engineering, microelectronics, power systems, electromagnetics, control systems.
Students 19 full-time (1 woman), 22 part-time (3 women); includes 2 minority (1 African-American, 1 Asian-American), 18 international. Average age 28.
Degrees Awarded In 1996, 6 master's, 3 doctorates awarded.

Entrance Requirements GRE General Test (minimum combined score of 1500 on three sections), minimum GPA of 3.0 in last 60 hours.

Degree Requirements For master's, thesis or alternative required, foreign language not required; for doctorate, 1 foreign language (computer language can substitute), dissertation.

Financial Aid In 1996–97, 28 students received aid, including 7 research assistantships (2 to first-year students), 21 teaching assistantships (8 to first-year students); fellowships, Federal Work-Study also available.

Applying 76 applicants, 36% accepted. *Deadline:* 7/6 (rolling processing). *Fee:* $25.

Contact *Dr. Russell L. Pimmel*
Head
205-348-6351

THE UNIVERSITY OF ALABAMA AT BIRMINGHAM
Birmingham, AL 35294

OVERVIEW
The University of Alabama at Birmingham is a public coed university.

ENROLLMENT
15,274 graduate, professional, and undergraduate students; 3,154 full-time matriculated graduate/professional students (1,614 women), 1,428 part-time matriculated graduate/professional students (959 women).

EXPENSES
Tuition $96 per credit hour for state residents; $192 per credit hour for nonresidents. Fees $647 per year (minimum) full-time, $344 per year (minimum) part-time.

HOUSING
Rooms and/or apartments available to single students at an average cost of $5175 (including board); available to married students. Graduate housing contact: Coordinator of Student Housing, 205-934-2092.

STUDENT SERVICES
Low-cost health insurance, career counseling, daycare facilities, campus safety program, campus employment opportunities, international student services, teacher training.

FACILITIES
Library: Mervyn Sterne Library plus 1 additional on-campus library; total holdings of 1,567,770 volumes, 1,171,772 microforms, 5,144 current periodical subscriptions. A total of 210 personal computers in all libraries. Access provided to on-line information retrieval services. *Computer:* Campuswide network is available. Total number of PCs/terminals supplied for student use: 400. Computer service fees are applied as a separate charge. *Special:* In science and engineering: Institute of Dental Research, Cardiovascular Research and Training Center, Comprehensive Cancer Center, Diabetes Research and Training Center, Arthritis Center, Cystic Fibrosis Research

Center. In social sciences: Center for Urban Affairs, Small Business Development Center.

COMPUTER ENGINEERING

Graduate School, School of Engineering, Department of Electrical and Computer Engineering

Programs Awards MSEE. Evening/weekend programs available.

Students 10 full-time (5 women), 18 part-time (3 women); includes 5 minority (4 African-Americans, 1 Asian-American), 6 international.

Degrees Awarded In 1996, 10 degrees awarded.

Entrance Requirements GRE General Test, BSEE.

Degree Requirements Thesis or alternative required, foreign language not required.

Applying *Deadline:* rolling. *Fee:* $30 ($55 for international students).

Contact *Dr. Gregg Vaughan*
Interim Chair
205-934-8440

COMPUTER SCIENCE

Graduate School, School of Natural Sciences and Mathematics, Department of Computer and Information Sciences

Programs Awards MS, PhD.

Faculty Research Theory and software systems, intelligent systems, systems architecture.

Students 30 full-time (9 women), 20 part-time (5 women); includes 11 minority (5 African-Americans, 5 Asian-Americans, 1 Hispanic), 21 international.

Degrees Awarded In 1996, 13 master's, 3 doctorates awarded.

Entrance Requirements For master's, GRE General Test (minimum combined score of 1100); for doctorate, GRE Subject Test.

Degree Requirements For doctorate, dissertation.

Financial Aid In 1996–97, 23 students received aid, including 4 fellowships, 1 research assistantship, 8 teaching assistantships; Federal Work-Study and career-related internships or fieldwork also available. *Financial aid application deadline:* 3/15.

Applying 87 applicants, 75% accepted. *Deadline:* rolling. *Fee:* $30 ($55 for international students).

Contact *Dr. Warren T. Jones*
Chairman
205-934-2213

See in-depth description on page **581.**

ELECTRICAL ENGINEERING

Graduate School, School of Engineering, Department of Electrical and Computer Engineering

Programs Awards MSEE. Evening/weekend programs available.

Students 10 full-time (5 women), 18 part-time (3 women); includes 5 minority (4 African-Americans, 1 Asian-American), 6 international.

Degrees Awarded In 1996, 10 degrees awarded.

Entrance Requirements GRE General Test, BSEE.

Degree Requirements Thesis or alternative required, foreign language not required.

Applying *Deadline:* rolling. *Fee:* $30 ($55 for international students).

Contact *Dr. Gregg Vaughan*
Interim Chair
205-934-8440

INFORMATION SCIENCE

Graduate School, School of Natural Sciences and Mathematics, Department of Computer and Information Sciences

Programs Awards MS, PhD.

Faculty Research Theory and software systems, intelligent systems, systems architecture.

Students 30 full-time (9 women), 20 part-time (5 women); includes 11 minority (5 African-Americans, 5 Asian-Americans, 1 Hispanic), 21 international.

Degrees Awarded In 1996, 13 master's, 3 doctorates awarded.

Entrance Requirements For master's, GRE General Test (minimum combined score of 1100); for doctorate, GRE Subject Test.

Degree Requirements For doctorate, dissertation.

Financial Aid In 1996–97, 23 students received aid, including 4 fellowships, 1 research assistantship, 8 teaching assistantships; Federal Work-Study and career-related internships or fieldwork also available. *Financial aid application deadline: 3/15.*

Applying 87 applicants, 75% accepted. *Deadline:* rolling. *Fee:* $30 ($55 for international students).

Contact *Dr. Warren T. Jones*
Chairman
205-934-2213

See in-depth description on page **581.**

MEDICAL INFORMATICS

Graduate School, School of Health Related Professions, Program in Health Informatics

Programs Awards MS.

Faculty Research Healthcare/medical informatics, natural language processing, application of expert systems, graphical user interface design.

Students 21 full-time (14 women), 14 part-time (5 women); includes 6 minority (5 African-Americans, 1 Asian-American), 2 international.

Degrees Awarded In 1996, 11 degrees awarded.

Entrance Requirements GRE General Test (minimum combined score of 1500), GMAT (minimum score 480), MAT (minimum score 50).

Degree Requirements Computer language, thesis or alternative.

Financial Aid Federal Work-Study and career-related internships or fieldwork available.

Applying 20 applicants, 95% accepted. *Fee:* $30 ($55 for international students).

Contact *Dr. Merida Johns*
Director
205-934-3509
Fax: 205-975-6608

THE UNIVERSITY OF ALABAMA IN HUNTSVILLE
Huntsville, AL 35899

OVERVIEW

The University of Alabama in Huntsville is a public coed university.

ENROLLMENT

4,982 graduate, professional, and undergraduate students; 400 full-time matriculated graduate/professional students (164 women), 701 part-time matriculated graduate/professional students (279 women).

GRADUATE FACULTY

221 full-time (45 women), 17 part-time (5 women), 227.6 FTE; includes 33 minority (3 African-Americans, 25 Asian-Americans, 4 Hispanics, 1 Native American).

TUITION

$3550 per year full-time, $521 per semester (minimum) part-time for state residents; $7260 per year full-time, $1059 per semester (minimum) part-time for nonresidents.

HOUSING

Rooms and/or apartments available to single students (48 units) at an average cost of $4100 per year ($5100 including board); available to married students (60 units) at an average cost of $5040 per year. Housing application deadline: 6/15. Graduate housing contact: John Maxon, 205-890-6108.

STUDENT SERVICES

Multicultural affairs office, low-cost health insurance, career counseling, free psychological counseling, campus safety program, campus employment opportunities, international student services.

FACILITIES

Library: Main library; total holdings of 418,219 volumes, 627,376 microforms, 2,766 current periodical subscriptions. A total of 78 personal computers in all libraries. Access provided to on-line information retrieval services. *Computer:* Campuswide network is available with full Internet access. Total number of PCs/terminals supplied for student use: 300. Computer service fees are included with tuition and fees. *Special:* In arts and humanities: Humanities Center, Center for International Research and Education. In science and engineering: Johnson Environmental and Energy Center, Center for Microgravity and Materials Research, Center for Space Plasma and Aeronomic Research, Center for Robotics, Consortium for Space Life Sciences, Center of Applied Optics, earth systems sciences laboratory.

COMPUTER ENGINEERING

College of Engineering, Department of Electrical and Computer Engineering

Programs Offers programs in computer engineering (PhD), electrical and computer engineering (MSE), electrical engineering (PhD), optical science and engineering (PhD). Part-time and evening/weekend programs available.

Faculty 26 full-time (1 woman), 1 part-time (0 women), 26.25 FTE.

Faculty Research Optical signal processing, electromagnetics, photonics, nonlinear waves, computer architecture. *Total annual research expenditures:* $641,916.

Students 56 full-time (10 women), 81 part-time (11 women); includes 31 minority (4 African-Americans, 25 Asian-Americans, 2 Hispanics), 25 international. Average age 31.

Degrees Awarded In 1996, 46 master's, 8 doctorates awarded.

Entrance Requirements For master's, GRE General Test (minimum combined score of 1500 on three sections), appropriate bachelor's degree, minimum GPA of 3.0; for doctorate, GRE General Test (minimum combined score of 1500 on three sections), minimum GPA of 3.0.

Degree Requirements For master's, computer language, oral and written exams required, thesis optional, foreign language not required; for doctorate, computer language, dissertation, oral and written exams required, foreign language not required.

Financial Aid In 1996–97, 34 students received aid, including 18 research assistantships averaging $1,000 per month and totaling $162,000, 16 teaching assistantships averaging $1,000 per month and totaling $144,000; fellowships, grants, scholarships, full and partial tuition waivers, Federal Work-Study, institutionally sponsored loans, and career-related internships or fieldwork also available. Aid available to part-time students. *Financial aid application deadline:* 4/1; applicants required to submit FAFSA.

Applying 97 applicants, 61% accepted. *Deadline:* 7/24 (priority date; rolling processing; 11/15 for spring admission). *Fee:* $20.

Contact Dr. Stephen T. Kowel
Chair
205-890-6316
Fax: 205-890-6803
E-mail: kowel@ebs330.uah.edu

See in-depth description on page 583.

COMPUTER SCIENCE

College of Science, Department of Computer Science

Programs Awards MS, PhD. Part-time and evening/weekend programs available.

Faculty 15 full-time (2 women), 1 part-time (0 women), 15.5 FTE.

Faculty Research Numerical analysis, programming languages, software systems, artificial intelligence, visualization systems. *Total annual research expenditures:* $873,479.

Students 27 full-time (9 women), 67 part-time (18 women); includes 11 minority (2 African-Americans, 7 Asian-Americans, 2 Hispanics), 22 international. Average age 33.

Degrees Awarded In 1996, 36 master's, 2 doctorates awarded.

Entrance Requirements GRE General Test (minimum combined score of 1500 on three sections), GRE Subject Test, minimum GPA of 3.0.

Degree Requirements For master's, computer language, oral and written exams required, thesis optional, foreign language not required; for doctorate, computer language, dissertation, oral and written exams required, foreign language not required.

Financial Aid In 1996–97, 13 students received aid, including 2 research assistantships averaging $900 per month and totaling $16,200, 11 teaching assistantships averaging $850 per month and totaling $34,150; fellowships, grants, full and partial tuition waivers, Federal Work-Study, institutionally sponsored loans, and career-related internships or fieldwork also available. Aid available to part-time students. *Financial aid application deadline:* 4/1; applicants required to submit FAFSA.

Applying 48 applicants, 79% accepted. *Deadline:* 7/24 (priority date; rolling processing; 11/15 for spring admission). *Fee:* $20.

Contact Dr. Carl Davis
Chair
205-890-6088
Fax: 205-890-6239
E-mail: cdavis@cs.uah.edu

ELECTRICAL ENGINEERING

College of Engineering, Department of Electrical and Computer Engineering

Programs Offers programs in computer engineering (PhD), electrical and computer engineering (MSE), electrical engineering (PhD), optical science and engineering (PhD). Part-time and evening/weekend programs available.

Faculty 26 full-time (1 woman), 1 part-time (0 women), 26.25 FTE.

Faculty Research Optical signal processing, electromagnetics, photonics, nonlinear waves, computer architecture. *Total annual research expenditures:* $641,916.

Students 56 full-time (10 women), 81 part-time (11 women); includes 31 minority (4 African-Americans, 25 Asian-Americans, 2 Hispanics), 25 international. Average age 31.

Degrees Awarded In 1996, 46 master's, 8 doctorates awarded.

Entrance Requirements For master's, GRE General Test (minimum combined score of 1500 on three sections), appropriate

bachelor's degree, minimum GPA of 3.0; for doctorate, GRE General Test (minimum combined score of 1500 on three sections), minimum GPA of 3.0.

Degree Requirements For master's, computer language, oral and written exams required, thesis optional, foreign language not required; for doctorate, computer language, dissertation, oral and written exams required, foreign language not required.

Financial Aid In 1996–97, 34 students received aid, including 18 research assistantships averaging $1,000 per month and totaling $162,000, 16 teaching assistantships averaging $1,000 per month and totaling $144,000; fellowships, grants, scholarships, full and partial tuition waivers, Federal Work-Study, institutionally sponsored loans, and career-related internships or fieldwork also available. Aid available to part-time students. *Financial aid application deadline:* 4/1; applicants required to submit FAFSA.

Applying 97 applicants, 61% accepted. *Deadline:* 7/24 (priority date; rolling processing; 11/15 for spring admission). *Fee:* $20.

Contact Dr. Stephen T. Kowel
Chair
205-890-6316
Fax: 205-890-6803
E-mail: kowel@ebs330.uah.edu

See in-depth description on page 583.

UNIVERSITY OF SOUTH ALABAMA
Mobile, AL 36688-0002

OVERVIEW
University of South Alabama is a public coed university.

ENROLLMENT
11,832 graduate, professional, and undergraduate students; 1,103 full-time matriculated graduate/professional students (599 women), 929 part-time matriculated graduate/professional students (676 women).

GRADUATE FACULTY
450 full-time (107 women), 27 part-time (9 women); includes 51 minority (13 African-Americans, 25 Asian-Americans, 9 Hispanics, 4 Native Americans).

EXPENSES
Tuition $71 per quarter hour for state residents; $142 per quarter hour for nonresidents. Fees $198 per year.

HOUSING
Rooms and/or apartments available to single students at an average cost of $1485 per year ($3465 including board); available to married students (600 units) at an average cost of $2230 per year. Housing application deadline: 6/1. Graduate housing contact: Tom Martin, 334-460-6195.

STUDENT SERVICES
Low-cost health insurance, career counseling, free psychological counseling, campus employment opportunities, international student services.

FACILITIES
Library: Main library plus 2 additional on-campus libraries; total holdings of 463,784 volumes, 861,050 microforms, 3,735 current periodical subscriptions. Access provided to on-line information retrieval services. *Special:* In arts and humanities: Mobile Townhouse Gallery, university photographic archives, communications library laboratory.

In science and engineering: Big Creek Lake Biological Station, Cancer Research Center, Coastal Research and Development Center, laboratory of molecular biology, Primate Center, Dauphin Island Sea Laboratory. In social sciences: Archaeology laboratory.

COMPUTER SCIENCE

Division of Computer and Information Sciences
Programs   Offers programs in computer science (MS), information science (MS). Part-time and evening/weekend programs available.
Faculty   10 full-time (1 woman).
Faculty Research   Numerical analysis, artificial intelligence, simulation, medical applications, software engineering.
Students   71 full-time (19 women), 36 part-time (13 women); includes 8 minority (4 African-Americans, 3 Asian-Americans, 1 Hispanic), 62 international.
Degrees Awarded   In 1996, 19 degrees awarded.
Entrance Requirements   GRE General Test (minimum combined score of 1000), minimum GPA of 2.5.
Degree Requirements   Computer language, project required, thesis optional, foreign language not required.
Financial Aid   In 1996–97, 4 research assistantships were awarded; institutionally sponsored loans and career-related internships or fieldwork also available. Aid available to part-time students. *Financial aid application deadline: 4/1.*
Applying   177 applicants, 44% accepted. *Deadline:* 9/1 (priority date; rolling processing). *Fee:* $25.
Contact   *Dr. David Feinstein*
Chairman
334-460-6390

ELECTRICAL ENGINEERING

College of Engineering, Department of Computer and Electrical Engineering
Programs   Awards MSEE. Part-time programs available.
Faculty   9 full-time (0 women).
Students   6 full-time (0 women), 19 part-time (4 women); includes 21 international.
Degrees Awarded   In 1996, 9 degrees awarded.
Entrance Requirements   GRE General Test (minimum combined score of 1000), BS in engineering, minimum GPA of 3.0.
Degree Requirements   Project or thesis required, foreign language not required.
Financial Aid   In 1996–97, 1 research assistantship was awarded; institutionally sponsored loans and career-related internships or fieldwork also available. Aid available to part-time students.
Applying   110 applicants, 34% accepted. *Deadline:* 9/1 (priority date; rolling processing). *Fee:* $25.
Contact   *Dr. Martin Parker*
Chairperson
334-460-6117

INFORMATION SCIENCE

Division of Computer and Information Sciences
Programs   Offers programs in computer science (MS), information science (MS). Part-time and evening/weekend programs available.
Faculty   10 full-time (1 woman).
Faculty Research   Numerical analysis, artificial intelligence, simulation, medical applications, software engineering.
Students   71 full-time (19 women), 36 part-time (13 women); includes 8 minority (4 African-Americans, 3 Asian-Americans, 1 Hispanic), 62 international.

Degrees Awarded   In 1996, 19 degrees awarded.
Entrance Requirements   GRE General Test (minimum combined score of 1000), minimum GPA of 2.5.
Degree Requirements   Computer language, project required, thesis optional, foreign language not required.
Financial Aid   In 1996–97, 4 research assistantships were awarded; institutionally sponsored loans and career-related internships or fieldwork also available. Aid available to part-time students. *Financial aid application deadline: 4/1.*
Applying   177 applicants, 44% accepted. *Deadline:* 9/1 (priority date; rolling processing). *Fee:* $25.
Contact   *Dr. David Feinstein*
Chairman
334-460-6390

ALASKA

UNIVERSITY OF ALASKA FAIRBANKS
Fairbanks, AK 99775-7480

OVERVIEW
University of Alaska Fairbanks is a public coed university.

ENROLLMENT
8,360 graduate, professional, and undergraduate students; 522 full-time matriculated graduate/professional students (217 women), 322 part-time matriculated graduate/professional students (150 women).

GRADUATE FACULTY
291 full-time (55 women), 59 part-time (27 women).

EXPENSES
Tuition $2844 per year full-time, $158 per credit part-time for state residents; $5544 per year full-time, $308 per credit part-time for nonresidents. Fees $340 per year full-time, $95 per semester (minimum) part-time.

HOUSING
Rooms and/or apartments available to single students at an average cost of $3095 (including board); available to married students at an average cost of $3780 per year. Housing application deadline: 3/15. Graduate housing contact: Director of Housing, 907-474-7247.

STUDENT SERVICES
Low-cost health insurance, career counseling, free psychological counseling, day-care facilities, campus safety program, campus employment opportunities, international student services.

FACILITIES
Library: Rasmuson Library plus 1 additional on-campus library; total holdings of 750,000 volumes, 882,765 microforms, 6,700 current periodical subscriptions. Access provided to on-line information retrieval services. *Computer:* Campuswide network is available with full Internet access. Computer service fees are included with tuition and fees. *Special:* In arts and humanities: Alaska Native Language Center. In science and engineering: Geophysical Institute, Institute of Marine Science, Institute of Arctic Biology, Institute of Northern Engineering, mineral industry research laboratory, engineering experiment station, Institute of Water Resources, Arctic Environmental Information and Data

Center, agricultural and forestry experiment station. In social sciences: Center for Cross-Cultural Studies, Sea Grant Program.

COMPUTER SCIENCE

Graduate School, College of Liberal Arts, Department of Mathematical Sciences
Programs   Offerings include computer science (MS).
Department Faculty   23 full-time (3 women), 1 part-time (0 women).
Applying   *Deadline:* 8/1 (priority date). *Fee:* $35.
Contact   *Dr. Clifton Lando*
Head
907-474-7332

ELECTRICAL ENGINEERING

Graduate School, School of Engineering, Department of Electrical Engineering
Programs   Awards MEE, MS.
Faculty   7 full-time (0 women), 2 part-time (1 woman).
Faculty Research   Geomagnetically-induced currents in power lines, telecommunications.
Students   5 full-time (1 woman), 3 part-time (0 women); includes 3 international. Average age 30.
Degrees Awarded   In 1996, 4 degrees awarded.
Entrance Requirements   GRE General Test, TOEFL (minimum score 550).
Degree Requirements   Thesis or alternative, comprehensive exam required, foreign language not required.
Financial Aid   In 1996–97, 5 research assistantships totaling $33,000, 7 teaching assistantships totaling $14,100 were awarded; career-related internships or fieldwork also available.
Applying   5 applicants, 0% accepted. *Deadline:* 8/1 (rolling processing). *Fee:* $35.
Contact   *Dr. John D. Aspnes*
Head
907-474-7137

ARIZONA

ARIZONA STATE UNIVERSITY
Tempe, AZ 85287-2203

OVERVIEW
Arizona State University is a public coed university.

ENROLLMENT
42,189 graduate, professional, and undergraduate students; 4,985 full-time matriculated graduate/professional students (2,378 women), 2,946 part-time matriculated graduate/professional students (1,543 women).

GRADUATE FACULTY
1,627 full-time (485 women), 134 part-time (69 women); includes 354 minority (45 African-Americans, 152 Asian-Americans, 135 Hispanics, 22 Native Americans).

EXPENSES
Tuition $2059 per year full-time, $105 per hour part-time for state residents; $8711 per year full-time, $360 per hour part-time for nonresidents. Fees $71 per year full-time, $36 per year part-time.

HOUSING
Rooms and/or apartments available to single students (540 units) at an average cost of $3460 per year ($4850 including board); on-campus housing not available to married students. Graduate housing contact: Residential Life Office, 602-965-3515.

STUDENT SERVICES
Disabled student services, multicultural affairs office, low-cost health insurance, career counseling, free psychological counseling, exercise/wellness program, day-care facilities, campus safety program, campus employment opportunities, international student services, writing training, grant writing training, teacher training.

FACILITIES
Library: Charles Trumbull Hayden Library plus 6 additional on-campus libraries; total holdings of 3 million volumes, 6.3 million microforms, 35,000 current periodical subscriptions. A total of 200 personal computers in all libraries. Access provided to on-line information retrieval services. *Computer:* Campuswide network is available with full Internet access. Computer services are offered at no charge. *Special:* In arts and humanities: Center for Medieval and Renaissance Studies, Center for the Study of the Arts, Hispanic Research Center. In science and engineering: Center for Meteorite Studies, Center for Solid State Science, Cancer Research Institute, Center for Research in Engineering and Applied Sciences, Center for Environmental Studies. In social sciences: Center for Asian Studies, Center for Latin American Studies, Exercise and Sport Research Institute, Center for Bilingual/Bicultural Education, Center for Business Research, Center for Indian Education.

COMPUTER SCIENCE

College of Engineering and Applied Sciences, Department of Computer Science and Engineering
Programs   Offers program in computer science (MCS, MS, PhD).
Faculty   31 full-time (5 women), 5 part-time (0 women).
Students   174 full-time (30 women), 127 part-time (24 women); includes 20 minority (5 African-Americans, 13 Asian-Americans, 1 Hispanic, 1 Native American), 174 international. Average age 28.
Degrees Awarded   In 1996, 88 master's, 10 doctorates awarded.
Entrance Requirements   GRE General Test (recommended).
Degree Requirements   For master's, thesis or alternative; for doctorate, dissertation.
Financial Aid   In 1996–97, 2 fellowships were awarded.
Applying   333 applicants, 64% accepted. *Fee:* $35.
Contact   *Dr. Timothy Lindquist*
Assistant Chair
602-965-3190

See in-depth description on page **373.**

ELECTRICAL ENGINEERING

College of Engineering and Applied Sciences, Department of Electrical Engineering
Programs   Awards MS, MSE, PhD.
Faculty   41 full-time (4 women), 2 part-time (0 women).
Faculty Research   Solid-state electronics, computer applications, power systems, communications.

Students 234 full-time (25 women), 179 part-time (37 women); includes 58 minority (5 African-Americans, 30 Asian-Americans, 22 Hispanics, 1 Native American), 198 international. Average age 29.

Degrees Awarded In 1996, 129 master's, 16 doctorates awarded.

Entrance Requirements GRE General Test (recommended), TOEFL (minimum score 550).

Degree Requirements For master's, thesis or alternative; for doctorate, dissertation.

Financial Aid In 1996–97, 5 fellowships were awarded; research assistantships, teaching assistantships also available.

Applying 565 applicants, 52% accepted. *Fee:* $35.

Contact *Dr. Joseph C. Palais*
Director of Graduate Studies
602-965-3590
Fax: 602-965-3837
E-mail: eeinfo@enpop1.eas.asu.edu

See in-depth description on page 375.

ARIZONA STATE UNIVERSITY EAST
Mesa, AZ 85206-0903

OVERVIEW
Arizona State University East is a public coed university.

ENROLLMENT
1,000 graduate, professional, and undergraduate students; 67 full-time, 237 part-time matriculated graduate/professional students.

TUITION
$2130 per year for state residents; $8780 per year for nonresidents.

HOUSING
Rooms and/or apartments available to single and married students.

COMPUTER ENGINEERING

College of Technology and Applied Sciences, Department of Electronics and Computer Engineering Technology
Programs Awards MT.
Contact *Director of Academic Services*
602-727-1028
E-mail: asueast@asu.edu

ELECTRICAL ENGINEERING

College of Technology and Applied Sciences, Department of Electronics and Computer Engineering Technology
Programs Awards MT.
Contact *Director of Academic Services*
602-727-1028
E-mail: asueast@asu.edu

INFORMATION SCIENCE

College of Technology and Applied Sciences, Department of Information and Management Technology
Programs Awards MT.
Contact *Director of Academic Services*
602-727-1028
E-mail: asueast@asu.edu

UNIVERSITY OF ARIZONA
Tucson, AZ 85721

OVERVIEW
University of Arizona is a public coed university.

ENROLLMENT
33,504 graduate, professional, and undergraduate students; 5,327 full-time matriculated graduate/professional students (2,482 women), 2,884 part-time matriculated graduate/professional students (1,610 women).

GRADUATE FACULTY
1,415 full-time (351 women), 86 part-time (23 women), 1,466 FTE; includes 167 minority (22 African-Americans, 73 Asian-Americans, 59 Hispanics, 13 Native Americans).

EXPENSES
Tuition $0 for state residents; $6652 per year full-time, $765 per semester (minimum) part-time for nonresidents. Fees $2058 per year full-time, $333 per semester (minimum) part-time.

HOUSING
Rooms and/or apartments available to single students (2,100 units) at an average cost of $2430 per year ($4410 including board); available to married students (318 units) at an average cost of $4756 per year ($6736 including board). Graduate housing contact: Residence Life Office, 520-621-6500.

STUDENT SERVICES
Disabled student services, low-cost health insurance, career counseling, free psychological counseling, campus employment opportunities, international student services.

FACILITIES
Library: Main library plus 3 additional on-campus libraries; total holdings of 4,113,794 volumes, 4,814,585 microforms, 26,967 current periodical subscriptions. A total of 20 personal computers in all libraries. Access provided to on-line information retrieval services. *Computer:* Campuswide network is available with full Internet access. Computer services are offered at no charge. *Special:* In arts and humanities: Language Research Center. In science and engineering: Office of Arid Lands Studies, Laboratory of Tree Ring Research, Optical Sciences Center, Steward Observatory, lunar and planetary laboratory. In social sciences: Bureau of Applied Research in Anthropology, Division of Medieval/Reformation Studies, Southwest Institute for Research on Women, Southwest Studies Center.

COMPUTER ENGINEERING

College of Engineering and Mines, Department of Electrical and Computer Engineering
Programs Awards MS, PhD. Part-time programs available.
Faculty Research Communication systems, control systems, signal processing, computer-aided logic.
Entrance Requirements For master's, GRE General Test, TOEFL (minimum score 575); for doctorate, GRE General Test, TOEFL (minimum score 600).
Degree Requirements For master's, thesis required (for some programs), foreign language not required; for doctorate, dissertation required, foreign language not required.

Applying *Deadline:* 6/15 (rolling processing). *Fee:* $35.

See in-depth description on page 589.

COMPUTER SCIENCE

College of Science, Department of Computer Science
Programs Awards MS, PhD. Part-time programs available.
Faculty 13 full-time (1 woman).
Faculty Research Operating systems, theory of computation, programming languages, databases, algorithms, networks, web searching. *Total annual research expenditures:* $2 million.
Students 68 full-time (7 women), 2 part-time (1 woman); includes 5 minority (all Asian-Americans), 37 international. Average age 27.
Degrees Awarded In 1996, 10 master's awarded (90% found work related to degree, 10% continued full-time study); 5 doctorates awarded (20% entered university research/teaching, 80% found other work related to degree). Terminal master's awarded for partial completion of doctoral program.
Entrance Requirements For master's, GRE General Test, TOEFL, minimum GPA of 3.2; for doctorate, GRE General Test, GRE Subject Test, TOEFL, minimum undergraduate GPA of 3.5.
Degree Requirements For master's, computer language required, thesis optional, foreign language not required; for doctorate, computer language, dissertation required, foreign language not required.
Financial Aid In 1996–97, 54 students received aid, including 2 fellowships (1 to a first-year student), 24 research assistantships, 11 teaching assistantships (4 to first-year students), 23 scholarships (11 to first-year students); full tuition waivers, institutionally sponsored loans, and career-related internships or fieldwork also available. *Financial aid application deadline:* 2/1.
Applying 255 applicants, 36% accepted. *Deadline:* 2/1 (rolling processing; 8/1 for spring admission). *Fee:* $35.
Contact *Wendy Swartz*
Graduate Coordinator
520-621-4049
Fax: 520-621-4246
E-mail: wjs@cs.arizona.edu

See in-depth description on page 587.

ELECTRICAL ENGINEERING

College of Engineering and Mines, Department of Electrical and Computer Engineering
Programs Awards MS, PhD. Part-time programs available.
Faculty Research Communication systems, control systems, signal processing, computer-aided logic.
Entrance Requirements For master's, GRE General Test, TOEFL (minimum score 575); for doctorate, GRE General Test, TOEFL (minimum score 600).
Degree Requirements For master's, thesis required (for some programs), foreign language not required; for doctorate, dissertation required, foreign language not required.
Applying *Deadline:* 6/15 (rolling processing). *Fee:* $35.

See in-depth description on page 589.

UNIVERSITY OF PHOENIX
Phoenix, AZ 85072-2069

OVERVIEW
University of Phoenix is a proprietary coed comprehensive institution.

ENROLLMENT
34,720 graduate, professional, and undergraduate students; 11,079 full-time matriculated graduate/professional students (5,650 women), 0 part-time matriculated graduate/professional students.

GRADUATE FACULTY
25 full-time (11 women), 2,070 part-time (787 women), 370 FTE.

TUITION
$223 per credit hour.

HOUSING
On-campus housing not available.

STUDENT SERVICES
Campus safety program.

FACILITIES
Library: Learning Resource Services Center plus 4 additional on-campus libraries; total holdings of 14,000 volumes, 494,000 microforms, 3,388 current periodical subscriptions. A total of 20 personal computers in all libraries. Access provided to on-line information retrieval services. *Computer:* Total number of PCs/terminals supplied for student use: 120. *Special:* In social sciences: Phoenix Institute.

COMPUTER SCIENCE

Graduate Programs, Computer Science and Information Technology Program
Programs Awards MSCIS. Programs offered at campuses in Colorado, New Mexico, Northern California, Tucson, Utah, and Online. Evening/weekend programs available.
Students 356 full-time (69 women), includes 83 minority (23 African-Americans, 18 Asian-Americans, 37 Hispanics, 5 Native Americans). Average age 35.
Degrees Awarded In 1996, 64 degrees awarded.
Entrance Requirements TOEFL (minimum score 580), minimum GPA of 2.5, 3 years of work experience, comprehensive cognitive assessment (COCA).
Degree Requirements Thesis or alternative.
Applying *Deadline:* rolling. *Fee:* $50.
Contact *Campus Information Center*
602-966-9577

INFORMATION SCIENCE

Graduate Programs, Computer Science and Information Technology Program
Programs Awards MSCIS. Programs offered at campuses in Colorado, New Mexico, Northern California, Tucson, Utah, and Online. Evening/weekend programs available.
Students 356 full-time (69 women), includes 83 minority (23 African-Americans, 18 Asian-Americans, 37 Hispanics, 5 Native Americans). Average age 35.
Degrees Awarded In 1996, 64 degrees awarded.
Entrance Requirements TOEFL (minimum score 580), minimum GPA of 2.5, 3 years of work experience, comprehensive cognitive assessment (COCA).
Degree Requirements Thesis or alternative.
Applying *Deadline:* rolling. *Fee:* $50.
Contact *Campus Information Center*
602-966-9577

ARKANSAS

ARKANSAS STATE UNIVERSITY
State University, AR 72467

OVERVIEW
Arkansas State University is a public coed comprehensive institution.

ENROLLMENT
9,828 graduate, professional, and undergraduate students; 249 full-time matriculated graduate/professional students (121 women), 670 part-time matriculated graduate/ professional students (443 women).

GRADUATE FACULTY
245 full-time (52 women), 16 part-time (13 women); includes 4 minority (3 African-Americans, 1 Asian-American).

EXPENSES
Tuition $2784 per year full-time, $116 per credit hour part-time for state residents; $6576 per year full-time, $274 per credit hour part-time for nonresidents. Fees $30 per year.

HOUSING
Rooms and/or apartments available to single students at an average cost of $3030 (including board); available to married students (190 units) at an average cost of $2000 per year. Graduate housing contact: Director of Housing, 501-972-2042.

STUDENT SERVICES
Disabled student services, low-cost health insurance, career counseling, free psychological counseling, campus safety program, campus employment opportunities, international student services.

FACILITIES
Library: Dean B. Ellis Library; total holdings of 520,305 volumes, 564,670 microforms, 2,481 current periodical subscriptions. A total of 84 personal computers in all libraries. Access provided to on-line information retrieval services. *Computer:* Campuswide network is available with full Internet access. Total number of PCs/terminals supplied for student use: 421. Computer services are offered at no charge. *Special:* In arts and humanities: Center for Radio and Television. In science and engineering: Electron Microscopy Center, high-temperature chemistry area, telecommunications facility.

COMPUTER SCIENCE

College of Arts and Sciences, Department of Computer Science and Mathematics
Programs Offers programs in computer science (MS), mathematics (MS, MSE). Part-time programs available.
Faculty 13 full-time (1 woman), 1 part-time (0 women).
Students 20 full-time (6 women), 15 part-time (6 women); includes 18 minority (1 African-American, 16 Asian-Americans, 1 Hispanic), 17 international. Average age 28.
Degrees Awarded In 1996, 14 degrees awarded.
Entrance Requirements GRE General Test or MAT, appropriate bachelor's degree.
Degree Requirements Thesis or alternative, comprehensive exam.

Financial Aid Teaching assistantships available. Aid available to part-time students. *Financial aid application deadline:* 6/1; applicants required to submit FAFSA.
Applying *Deadline:* 7/1 (priority date; rolling processing; 11/15 for spring admission). *Fee:* $15 ($25 for international students).
Contact Dr. Roger Abernathy
Chairman
501-972-3090
Fax: 501-972-3950
E-mail: raber@caddo.astate.edu

UNIVERSITY OF ARKANSAS
Fayetteville, AR 72701-1201

OVERVIEW
University of Arkansas is a public coed university.

ENROLLMENT
14,692 graduate, professional, and undergraduate students; 992 full-time matriculated graduate/professional students (429 women), 1,363 part-time matriculated graduate/professional students (662 women).

GRADUATE FACULTY
808 full-time, 76 part-time, 838.7 FTE; includes 63 minority (20 African-Americans, 29 Asian-Americans, 6 Hispanics, 8 Native Americans).

EXPENSES
Tuition $3506 per year full-time, $147 per credit hour part-time for state residents; $7984 per year full-time, $334 per credit hour part-time for nonresidents. Fees $124 per year full-time, $76 per semester (minimum) part-time.

HOUSING
Rooms and/or apartments available to single students (86 units) at an average cost of $2540 per year ($4190 including board); available to married students (329 units) at an average cost of $2800 per year. Housing application deadline: 4/15. Graduate housing contact: Residence Life and Dining Services, 501-575-3951.

STUDENT SERVICES
Low-cost health insurance, career counseling, free psychological counseling, campus safety program, campus employment opportunities, international student services.

FACILITIES
Library: Mullins Library plus 5 additional on-campus libraries; total holdings of 1,452,137 volumes, 820,675 microforms, 16,298 current periodical subscriptions. A total of 150 personal computers in all libraries. Access provided to on-line information retrieval services. *Computer:* Campuswide network is available with full Internet access. Total number of PCs/terminals supplied for student use: 800. Computer services are offered at no charge. *Special:* In arts and humanities: Center for Arkansas and Regional Studies. In science and engineering: Center for Advanced Spatial Technologies, Mack Blackwell Transportation Center, Arkansas Water Resources Research Center, Biomass Research Center, Center of Excellence for Poultry Science, agricultural experiment station. In social sciences: Bureau

of Business and Economic Research, Fulbright Institute of International Relations.

COMPUTER ENGINEERING

College of Engineering, Department of Computer Systems Engineering
Programs Awards MSCSE.
Faculty 7 full-time (0 women).
Students 17 full-time (3 women), 10 part-time (0 women); includes 2 minority (1 African-American, 1 Asian-American), 16 international.
Degrees Awarded In 1996, 6 degrees awarded.
Degree Requirements Computer language required, thesis optional, foreign language not required.
Financial Aid Teaching assistantships, Federal Work-Study, and career-related internships or fieldwork available. Aid available to part-time students. *Financial aid application deadline:* 4/1; applicants required to submit FAFSA.
Applying 19 applicants, 68% accepted. *Fee:* $25 ($35 for international students).
Contact Dr. Ron Skeith
          Chair
          501-575-6036

COMPUTER SCIENCE

J. William Fulbright College of Arts and Sciences, Department of Computer Science
Programs Awards MS.
Faculty 5 full-time (0 women).
Students 16 full-time (5 women), includes 1 minority (Asian-American), 7 international.
Degrees Awarded In 1996, 8 degrees awarded.
Degree Requirements Computer language required, foreign language and thesis not required.
Financial Aid Teaching assistantships, Federal Work-Study, and career-related internships or fieldwork available. Aid available to part-time students. *Financial aid application deadline:* 4/1; applicants required to submit FAFSA.
Applying 29 applicants, 28% accepted. *Fee:* $25 ($35 for international students).
Contact Dr. Dennis Brewer
          Chairman
          501-575-6427

ELECTRICAL ENGINEERING

College of Engineering, Department of Electrical Engineering
Programs Awards MSEE.
Faculty 17 full-time (0 women).
Students 60 full-time (9 women), 9 part-time (1 woman); includes 7 minority (3 African-Americans, 2 Asian-Americans, 2 Hispanics), 37 international.
Degrees Awarded In 1996, 29 degrees awarded.
Degree Requirements Thesis optional, foreign language not required.
Financial Aid Fellowships, research assistantships, teaching assistantships, Federal Work-Study, and career-related internships or fieldwork available. Aid available to part-time students. *Financial aid application deadline:* 4/1; applicants required to submit FAFSA.
Applying 70 applicants, 66% accepted. *Fee:* $25 ($35 for international students).
Contact J. S. Charlton
          Graduate Coordinator
          501-575-3005

UNIVERSITY OF ARKANSAS AT LITTLE ROCK
Little Rock, AR 72204–1099

OVERVIEW
University of Arkansas at Little Rock is a public coed university.

ENROLLMENT
10,720 graduate, professional, and undergraduate students; 702 full-time matriculated graduate/professional students (404 women), 1,012 part-time matriculated graduate/professional students (642 women).

TUITION
$2547 per year full-time, $142 per credit hour part-time for state residents; $5211 per year full-time, $290 per credit hour part-time for nonresidents.

HOUSING
Rooms and/or apartments available to single students (320 units) at an average cost of $2435 per year; on-campus housing not available to married students. Graduate housing contact: Debra Gentry, 501-569-3392.

STUDENT SERVICES
Low-cost health insurance, career counseling, free psychological counseling, campus safety program, campus employment opportunities.

FACILITIES
Library: Ottenheimer Library plus 1 additional on-campus library; total holdings of 394,780 volumes, 691,612 microforms, 2,626 current periodical subscriptions. A total of 100 personal computers in all libraries. Access provided to on-line information retrieval services. *Computer:* Campuswide network is available with full Internet access. Total number of PCs/terminals supplied for student use: 750. Computer service fees are included with tuition and fees. *Special:* In arts and humanities: Fine Arts Galleries I, II, and III; Community School of the Arts. In science and engineering: Planetarium and observatory, Summer Chemistry Institute. In social sciences: Mid-South Center on Alcohol and Other Drug Abuse Problems, Arkansas Institute of Government, Arkansas Institute for Economic Advancement, Center for Research on Teaching and Writing, Speech-Language and Hearing Clinic, Criminal Justice Institute, Center for Arkansas Studies, Arkansas International Center.

COMPUTER SCIENCE

College of Sciences and Engineering Technology, Department of Computer and Information Science
Programs Awards MS. Part-time and evening/weekend programs available.
Students 3 full-time (1 woman), 3 part-time (1 woman); includes 4 minority (all Asian-Americans). Average age 33.
Degrees Awarded In 1996, 3 degrees awarded.
Entrance Requirements GRE General Test, minimum GPA of 3.0, bachelor's degree in computer science, mathematics, or appropriate alternative.
Degree Requirements Computer language required, thesis optional, foreign language not required.

Financial Aid   Research assistantships, teaching assistantships, graduate assistantships, Federal Work-Study, institutionally sponsored loans available. Aid available to part-time students.

Applying   *Deadline:* 8/1 (priority date).

Contact   *Dr. Rama Reddy*
Coordinator
501-569-8130

INFORMATION SCIENCE

College of Sciences and Engineering Technology, Department of Computer and Information Science

Programs   Awards MS. Part-time and evening/weekend programs available.

Students   3 full-time (1 woman), 3 part-time (1 woman); includes 4 minority (all Asian-Americans). Average age 33.

Degrees Awarded   In 1996, 3 degrees awarded.

Entrance Requirements   GRE General Test, minimum GPA of 3.0, bachelor's degree in computer science, mathematics, or appropriate alternative.

Degree Requirements   Computer language required, thesis optional, foreign language not required.

Financial Aid   Research assistantships, teaching assistantships, graduate assistantships, Federal Work-Study, institutionally sponsored loans available. Aid available to part-time students.

Applying   *Deadline:* 8/1 (priority date).

Contact   *Dr. Rama Reddy*
Coordinator
501-569-8130

CALIFORNIA

AZUSA PACIFIC UNIVERSITY
Azusa, CA 91702-7000

OVERVIEW
Azusa Pacific University is an independent-religious coed comprehensive institution.

ENROLLMENT
4,840 graduate, professional, and undergraduate students; 473 full-time matriculated graduate/professional students (257 women), 1,892 part-time matriculated graduate/professional students (1,124 women).

GRADUATE FACULTY
97 full-time, 99 part-time.

TUITION
$335 per unit.

HOUSING
Rooms and/or apartments available to single students at an average cost of $3120 (including board); on-campus housing not available to married students.

STUDENT SERVICES
Low-cost health insurance, career counseling, free psychological counseling.

FACILITIES
Library: Marshburn Memorial Library plus 1 additional on-campus library; total holdings of 140,000 volumes, 565,000 microforms, 1,400 current periodical subscriptions. A total of 4 personal computers in all libraries. Access provided to on-line information retrieval services.

Computer: Campuswide network is available with full Internet access. Computer services are offered at no charge.

COMPUTER SCIENCE

College of Liberal Arts and Sciences, Department of Computer Science

Programs   Offers programs in applied computer science and technology (MS), including client/server technology, computer information systems, end user support, inter-emphasis, software engineering, technical programming, telecommunications; client/server technology (Certificate); computer information systems (Certificate); computer science (Certificate); end-user training and support (Certificate); software engineering (MSE, Certificate); technical programming (Certificate); telecommunications (Certificate). Part-time and evening/weekend programs available.

Faculty   9 full-time (1 woman), 10 part-time (2 women).

Faculty Research   Applied artificial intelligence, programming languages, engineering, database system.

Students   83 full-time (22 women), 140 part-time (32 women).

Degrees Awarded   In 1996, 36 master's awarded.

Entrance Requirements   For master's, minimum GPA of 3.0, proficiency in one programming language, college-level algebra, and applied calculus.

Degree Requirements   For master's, computer language, thesis or alternative, project required, foreign language not required.

Financial Aid   Teaching assistantships and career-related internships or fieldwork available.

Applying   *Deadline:* 9/1 (priority date; rolling processing). *Fee:* $45 ($65 for international students).

Contact   *Dr. Samuel E. Sambasivam*
Acting Chairman
818-815-5476
Fax: 818-815-5323

See in-depth description on page 377.

SOFTWARE ENGINEERING

College of Liberal Arts and Sciences, Department of Computer Science

Programs   Offerings include applied computer science and technology (MS), with options in client/server technology, computer information systems, end user support, inter-emphasis, software engineering, technical programming, telecommunications; software engineering (MSE, Certificate).

Department Faculty   9 full-time (1 woman), 10 part-time (2 women).

Entrance Requirements   For master's, minimum GPA of 3.0, proficiency in one programming language, college-level algebra, and applied calculus.

Degree Requirements   For master's, computer language, thesis or alternative, project required, foreign language not required.

Applying   *Deadline:* 9/1 (priority date; rolling processing). *Fee:* $45 ($65 for international students).

Contact   *Dr. Samuel E. Sambasivam*
Acting Chairman
818-815-5476
Fax: 818-815-5323

See in-depth description on page 377.

CALIFORNIA INSTITUTE OF TECHNOLOGY
Pasadena, CA 91125-0001

OVERVIEW
California Institute of Technology is an independent coed university.

ENROLLMENT
1,046 full-time matriculated graduate/professional students (238 women), 0 part-time matriculated graduate/professional students.

GRADUATE FACULTY
552 full-time (76 women), 60 part-time (21 women).

EXPENSES
Tuition $18,600 per year. Fees $16 per year.

HOUSING
Rooms and/or apartments available to single students (560 units) at an average cost of $4800 per year ($6900 including board); available to married students (30 units) at an average cost of $8760 per year. Housing application deadline: 5/1. Graduate housing contact: Linda Chappell, 818-395-6178.

STUDENT SERVICES
Low-cost health insurance, career counseling, free psychological counseling, day-care facilities, campus safety program, campus employment opportunities, international student services.

FACILITIES
Library: Caltech Library Systems plus 4 additional on-campus libraries; total holdings of 550,325 volumes, 542,270 microforms, 2,740 current periodical subscriptions. A total of 75 personal computers in all libraries. Access provided to on-line information retrieval services. *Computer:* Campuswide network is available with full Internet access. Total number of PCs/terminals supplied for student use: 200. Computer service fees are included with tuition and fees. *Special:* In science and engineering: Jet propulsion laboratory, Hale Observatories, seismological laboratory, Kerckhoff Marine Laboratory, Big Bear Solar Observatory, Palomar Observatory, Owens Valley Radio Observatory, aeronautics laboratory, environmental quality laboratory, Kellog Radiation Laboratory, submillimeter observatory, W. M. Keck Observatory.

COMPUTER SCIENCE

Division of Engineering and Applied Science, Option in Computer Science
Programs Awards MS, PhD.
Faculty 5 full-time (0 women).
Faculty Research VLSI systems, concurrent computation, high-level programming languages, signal and image processing, graphics.
Students 23 full-time (4 women), includes 8 international.
Degrees Awarded In 1996, 5 master's, 1 doctorate awarded.
Degree Requirements Thesis/dissertation required, foreign language not required.
Applying 239 applicants, 2% accepted. *Deadline:* 1/15. *Fee:* $0.
Contact Dr. Alain J. Martin
Executive Officer
818-395-6549

See in-depth description on page 383.

ELECTRICAL ENGINEERING

Division of Engineering and Applied Science, Option in Electrical Engineering
Programs Awards MS, PhD, Engr.
Faculty 16 full-time (2 women).
Faculty Research Solid-state electronics, power electronics, communications, controls, submillimeter-wave integrated circuits.
Students 102 full-time (18 women), includes 2 minority, 67 international.
Degrees Awarded In 1996, 19 master's, 19 doctorates, 1 Engr awarded.
Degree Requirements For doctorate, dissertation required, foreign language not required.
Applying 669 applicants, 3% accepted. *Deadline:* 1/15. *Fee:* $0.
Contact Dr. P. P. Vaidyanathan
Representative
818-395-4681

CALIFORNIA POLYTECHNIC STATE UNIVERSITY, SAN LUIS OBISPO
San Luis Obispo, CA 93407

OVERVIEW
California Polytechnic State University, San Luis Obispo is a public coed comprehensive institution.

ENROLLMENT
17,000 graduate, professional, and undergraduate students; 649 full-time matriculated graduate/professional students (347 women), 340 part-time matriculated graduate/professional students (198 women).

EXPENSES
Tuition $0 for state residents; $164 per unit for nonresidents. Fees $2244 per year full-time, $1578 per year part-time.

HOUSING
Rooms and/or apartments available to single students at an average cost of $2753 per year ($4810 including board); on-campus housing not available to married students. Housing application deadline: 6/15. Graduate housing contact: Housing Office, 805-756-1225.

STUDENT SERVICES
Disabled student services, multicultural affairs office, low-cost health insurance, career counseling, free psychological counseling, exercise/wellness program, day-care facilities, campus safety program, campus employment opportunities, international student services, writing training, grant writing training, teacher training.

FACILITIES
Library: Robert F. Kennedy Library; total holdings of 631,151 volumes, 3,267,581 microforms, 3,500 current periodical subscriptions. A total of 16 personal computers in all libraries. Access provided to on-line information retrieval services. *Computer:* Campuswide network is available with full Internet access. Total number of PCs/terminals supplied for student use: 1,600. Computer services are offered at no charge. *Special:* In science and engineering: Dairy Products Technology Center, Computer Integrated Manufacturing Center, Engineering Research and Development Center. In social sciences:

Institute for Practical Politics, Center for Business and Economic Research.

COMPUTER ENGINEERING

College of Engineering, Department of Computer Engineering
Programs Awards MS. Part-time programs available.
Faculty Research Microprocessors, computer systems.
Students 2 full-time (1 woman), 1 (woman) part-time.
Entrance Requirements GRE General Test, GRE Subject Test, minimum GPA of 3.0 during previous 2 years.
Degree Requirements Thesis or alternative required, foreign language not required.
Financial Aid Career-related internships or fieldwork available. *Financial aid application deadline:* 4/15.
Applying *Deadline:* 5/31 (priority date; rolling processing; 12/31 for spring admission). *Fee:* $55.
Contact Dr. James Harris
Coordinator
805-756-1229
Fax: 805-756-1458
E-mail: jharris@ohm.calpoly.edu

COMPUTER SCIENCE

College of Engineering, Department of Computer Science
Programs Awards MSCS. Part-time programs available.
Faculty Research Computer systems, software, graphics, hardware design, expert systems, software engineering and computer networks.
Students 20 full-time (2 women), 17 part-time (4 women); includes 11 minority (1 African-American, 10 Asian-Americans). Average age 26.
Degrees Awarded In 1996, 18 degrees awarded.
Entrance Requirements GRE General Test (minimum combined score of 1650 on three sections required, 400 on verbal), minimum GPA of 3.0 during previous 2 years.
Degree Requirements Thesis required, foreign language not required.
Financial Aid In 1996–97, 20 teaching assistantships (4 to first-year students) totaling $60,000 were awarded; Federal Work-Study, institutionally sponsored loans, and career-related internships or fieldwork also available. *Financial aid application deadline:* 4/15.
Applying 43 applicants, 49% accepted. *Deadline:* 5/31 (priority date; rolling processing; 2/28 for spring admission). *Fee:* $55.
Contact Dr. Pat Wheatley
Coordinator
805-756-6168
Fax: 805-756-2956
E-mail: pwheatle@calpoly.edu

ELECTRICAL ENGINEERING

College of Engineering, Department of Electrical Engineering
Programs Awards MS. Part-time programs available.
Faculty Research Communications, systems analysis, control systems, electronic devices, microprocessors.
Students 13 full-time (1 woman), 5 part-time (0 women); includes 7 minority (all Asian-Americans). Average age 27.
Degrees Awarded In 1996, 13 degrees awarded (88% found work related to degree, 12% continued full-time study).
Entrance Requirements GRE General Test, GRE Subject Test, minimum GPA of 2.5 during previous 2 years.
Degree Requirements Thesis or alternative required, foreign language not required.
Financial Aid In 1996–97, 6 fellowships, 7 research assistantships, 8 teaching assistantships were awarded; career-related internships or fieldwork also available. *Financial aid application deadline:* 4/15.

Applying 26 applicants, 42% accepted. *Deadline:* 5/31 (priority date; rolling processing; 12/31 for spring admission). *Fee:* $55.
Contact Dr. Jerome Breitenbach
Coordinator
805-756-5710
Fax: 805-756-1458
E-mail: jbreiten@ohm.calpoly.edu

CALIFORNIA STATE POLYTECHNIC UNIVERSITY, POMONA
Pomona, CA 91768-2557

OVERVIEW
California State Polytechnic University, Pomona is a public coed comprehensive institution.

ENROLLMENT
16,803 graduate, professional, and undergraduate students; 193 full-time matriculated graduate/professional students (96 women), 866 part-time matriculated graduate/professional students (391 women).

EXPENSES
Tuition $0 for state residents; $164 per unit for nonresidents. Fees $1923 per year full-time, $1257 per year part-time.

HOUSING
Rooms and/or apartments available to single students (1,184 units); on-campus housing not available to married students. Housing application deadline: 5/1. Graduate housing contact: Leticia Vasquez, 909-869-3308.

STUDENT SERVICES
Disabled student services, low-cost health insurance, career counseling, free psychological counseling, day-care facilities, campus safety program, campus employment opportunities, international student services.

FACILITIES
Library: University Library; total holdings of 621,184 volumes, 2,106,948 microforms, 2,855 current periodical subscriptions. A total of 105 personal computers in all libraries. Access provided to on-line information retrieval services. *Computer:* Campuswide network is available with full Internet access. Total number of PCs/terminals supplied for student use: 2,061. *Special:* In arts and humanities: Center for Community Affairs. In science and engineering: Equine Research Center, Institute for Cellular and Molecular Biology, Center for Science and Mathematics Education. In social sciences: Business Education Center, Center for Regenerative Studies, Social Data Center.

COMPUTER SCIENCE

College of Science, Program in Computer Science
Programs Awards MS. Part-time and evening/weekend programs available.
Students 2 full-time (1 woman), 33 part-time (11 women); includes 20 minority (17 Asian-Americans, 3 Hispanics), 9 international.
Degrees Awarded In 1996, 5 degrees awarded.
Entrance Requirements GRE General Test.
Degree Requirements Thesis.

Financial Aid   4 students received aid; Federal Work-Study, institutionally sponsored loans, and career-related internships or fieldwork available. Aid available to part-time students. *Financial aid application deadline:* 3/2; applicants required to submit FAFSA.
Applying   36 applicants, 44% accepted. *Deadline:* rolling. *Fee:* $55.
Contact   Dr. Norton Riley
Coordinator
909-869-3444
E-mail: hnriley@csupomona.edu

ELECTRICAL ENGINEERING

College of Engineering
Programs   Offerings include electrical engineering (MSEE).
College Faculty   36 full-time (3 women), 6 part-time (1 woman).
Applying   *Deadline:* rolling. *Fee:* $55.
Contact   Dr. Elhami T. Ibrahim
Director, Engineering Graduate Studies
909-869-2476
Fax: 909-869-4370
E-mail: etibrahim@csupomona.edu

CALIFORNIA STATE UNIVERSITY, CHICO
Chico, CA 95929-0722

OVERVIEW
California State University, Chico is a public coed comprehensive institution.

EXPENSES
Tuition $0 for state residents; $246 per unit for nonresidents. Fees $2070 per year full-time, $1405 per year part-time.

HOUSING
Rooms and/or apartments available to single students; on-campus housing not available to married students. Graduate housing contact: Sherri Jacobs, 916-898-6328.

FACILITIES
Library: Meriam Library plus 2 additional on-campus libraries. *Special:* In arts and humanities: Performing Arts Center, Laxson Auditorium, university gallery. In science and engineering: Eagle Lake Biological Field Station, scanning and transmission electron microscope facilities, vertebrate museum, university farm. In social sciences: Survey Research Center, Instructional Media Center, television laboratory, anthropology museum, political processes simulation laboratory.

COMPUTER SCIENCE

College of Engineering, Computer Science, and Technology, Department of Computer Science
Programs   Awards MS.
Entrance Requirements   GRE General Test.
Degree Requirements   Thesis or alternative required, foreign language not required.
Applying   *Deadline:* 4/1 (rolling processing). *Fee:* $55.

ELECTRICAL ENGINEERING

College of Engineering, Computer Science, and Technology, Department of Electrical Engineering
Programs   Awards MS.
Entrance Requirements   GRE General Test.
Degree Requirements   Thesis or alternative required, foreign language not required.
Applying   *Deadline:* 4/1 (rolling processing). *Fee:* $55.

CALIFORNIA STATE UNIVERSITY, FRESNO
Fresno, CA 93740

OVERVIEW
California State University, Fresno is a public coed comprehensive institution.

ENROLLMENT
17,460 graduate, professional, and undergraduate students; 950 full-time matriculated graduate/professional students (589 women), 824 part-time matriculated graduate/professional students (479 women).

GRADUATE FACULTY
404 full-time (112 women), 36 part-time (16 women); includes 118 minority (15 African-Americans, 53 Asian-Americans, 48 Hispanics, 2 Native Americans).

EXPENSES
Tuition $0 for state residents; $246 per unit for nonresidents. Fees $1806 per year full-time, $1140 per year part-time.

HOUSING
Rooms and/or apartments available to single students (1,000 units) at an average cost of $5339 (including board); on-campus housing not available to married students. Graduate housing contact: Karen Johnson, 209-278-2345.

STUDENT SERVICES
Low-cost health insurance, career counseling, free psychological counseling, day-care facilities, campus safety program, campus employment opportunities, international student services.

FACILITIES
Library: Henry Madden Library; total holdings of 896,544 volumes, 1,186,772 microforms, 2,616 current periodical subscriptions. A total of 63 personal computers in all libraries. *Computer:* Campuswide network is available. Total number of PCs/terminals supplied for student use: 1,500. Computer services are offered at no charge. *Special:* In arts and humanities: Interdisciplinary Center for Human Services, Instructional Technology Resource Center. In science and engineering: Center for Irrigation Technology, agricultural research farm, Viticulture Ecology Research Center, Center for Agricultural Business, California Construction Institute, Computer Integrated Manufacturing Center, engineering research laboratory. In social sciences: Center for Business Research and Service; computer laboratory; language, hearing,

and speech clinical research facility; social research laboratory; human performance laboratory.

COMPUTER SCIENCE

Division of Graduate Studies, School of Engineering, Department of Computer Science

Programs Awards MS. Part-time programs available.

Faculty 6 full-time (2 women).

Faculty Research Software design, parallel processing, computer engineering.

Students 19 full-time (8 women), 16 part-time (4 women); includes 8 minority (6 Asian-Americans, 2 Hispanics), 19 international. Average age 31.

Degrees Awarded In 1996, 8 degrees awarded.

Entrance Requirements GRE General Test, TOEFL (minimum score 550), minimum GPA of 3.0.

Degree Requirements Thesis or alternative required, foreign language not required.

Financial Aid 4 students received aid; fellowships, research assistantships, teaching assistantships, scholarships, Federal Work-Study, and career-related internships or fieldwork available. *Financial aid application deadline:* 3/1; applicants required to submit FAFSA.

Applying 33 applicants, 73% accepted. *Deadline:* 8/1 (priority date; rolling processing; 12/1 for spring admission). *Fee:* $55.

Contact *Henderson Yeung*
Coordinator
209-278-4373
Fax: 209-278-4197
E-mail: henderson_yeung@csufresno.edu

ELECTRICAL ENGINEERING

Division of Graduate Studies, School of Engineering

Programs Offerings include electrical engineering (MS). MS (electrical engineering, mechanical engineering) offered jointly with Edwards Air Force Base.

School Faculty 17 full-time (2 women).

Entrance Requirements GRE General Test, TOEFL (minimum score 550).

Degree Requirements Thesis or alternative required, foreign language not required.

Applying *Deadline:* 8/1 (priority date; rolling processing; 12/1 for spring admission). *Fee:* $55.

Contact *Karl Longley*
Graduate Program Coordinator
209-278-2889
Fax: 209-278-7071

CALIFORNIA STATE UNIVERSITY, FULLERTON
Fullerton, CA 92834-9480

OVERVIEW

California State University, Fullerton is a public coed comprehensive institution.

ENROLLMENT

24,040 graduate, professional, and undergraduate students; 303 full-time matriculated graduate/professional students (185 women), 2,386 part-time matriculated graduate/professional students (1,341 women).

GRADUATE FACULTY

543 full-time (156 women), 578 part-time (296 women), 719.1 FTE.

EXPENSES

Tuition $0 for state residents; $246 per unit for nonresidents. Fees $1947 per year full-time, $1281 per year part-time.

HOUSING

Rooms and/or apartments available to single students at an average cost of $3476 per year; on-campus housing not available to married students.

STUDENT SERVICES

Disabled student services, multicultural affairs office, low-cost health insurance, career counseling, free psychological counseling, exercise/wellness program, day-care facilities, campus safety program, campus employment opportunities, international student services, writing training.

FACILITIES

Library: Total holdings of 717,389 volumes, 970,429 microforms, 2,603 current periodical subscriptions. Access provided to on-line information retrieval services. *Special:* In arts and humanities: Institute for Research in Reading and Related Disciplines, Sport and Movement Institute, speech and hearing clinic, phonetic research laboratory. In science and engineering: Tucker Wildlife Sanctuary, Institute for Molecular Biology and Nutrition, California State University Desert Studies, Institute for Geophysics. In social sciences: Center for Economic Education, Center for Governmental Studies, Center for International Business, Institute for Early Childhood Education, anthropology museum.

COMPUTER SCIENCE

School of Engineering and Computer Science, Department of Computer Science

Programs Offers programs in applications administrative information systems (MS), applications mathematical methods (MS), computer science (MS), information processing systems (MS). Part-time programs available.

Faculty 13 full-time (5 women), 26 part-time (5 women), 21.5 FTE.

Faculty Research Software engineering, development of computer networks.

Students 4 full-time (2 women), 118 part-time (38 women); includes 54 minority (2 African-Americans, 46 Asian-Americans, 6 Hispanics), 24 international. Average age 32.

Degrees Awarded In 1996, 26 degrees awarded.

Entrance Requirements GRE General Test (minimum combined score of 1100), minimum undergraduate GPA of 2.5.

Degree Requirements Computer language, comprehensive exam, project or thesis required, foreign language not required.

Financial Aid State grants, Federal Work-Study, institutionally sponsored loans, and career-related internships or fieldwork available. Aid available to part-time students. *Financial aid application deadline:* 3/1.

Applying 93 applicants, 60% accepted. *Fee:* $55.

Contact *Dr. Martin Maskarinec*
Adviser
714-773-3700

ELECTRICAL ENGINEERING

School of Engineering and Computer Science, Department of Electrical Engineering

Programs Awards MS. Part-time programs available.

Faculty 13 full-time (2 women), 1 part-time (0 women), 13.6 FTE.
Students 15 full-time (2 women), 57 part-time (5 women); includes 29 minority (2 African-Americans, 23 Asian-Americans, 4 Hispanics), 17 international. Average age 31.
Degrees Awarded In 1996, 38 degrees awarded.
Entrance Requirements GRE General Test, GRE Subject Test, minimum GPA of 2.5 (undergraduate), 3.0 (graduate).
Degree Requirements Computer language, comprehensive exam, project or thesis required, foreign language not required.
Financial Aid State grants, Federal Work-Study, institutionally sponsored loans, and career-related internships or fieldwork available. Aid available to part-time students. *Financial aid application deadline:* 3/1.
Applying 58 applicants, 59% accepted. *Fee:* $55.
Contact Dr. Karim Hamidian
  Acting Chair
  714-773-3013

INFORMATION SCIENCE

School of Engineering and Computer Science, Department of Computer Science
Programs Offerings include applications administrative information systems (MS), information processing systems (MS).
Department Faculty 13 full-time (5 women), 26 part-time (5 women), 21.5 FTE.
Entrance Requirements GRE General Test (minimum combined score of 1100), minimum undergraduate GPA of 2.5.
Degree Requirements Computer language, comprehensive exam, project or thesis required, foreign language not required.
Applying *Fee:* $55.
Contact Dr. Martin Maskarinec
  Adviser
  714-773-3700

CALIFORNIA STATE UNIVERSITY, HAYWARD
Hayward, CA 94542-3000

OVERVIEW
California State University, Hayward is a public coed comprehensive institution.

ENROLLMENT
12,650 graduate, professional, and undergraduate students; 728 full-time matriculated graduate/professional students (508 women), 1,299 part-time matriculated graduate/professional students (774 women).

GRADUATE FACULTY
368 full-time (117 women); includes 165 minority (40 African-Americans, 85 Asian-Americans, 36 Hispanics, 4 Native Americans).

EXPENSES
Tuition $0 for state residents; $164 per unit for nonresidents. Fees $1815 per year full-time, $1149 per year part-time.

HOUSING
Rooms and/or apartments available to single students (404 units) at an average cost of $3200 per year; on-campus housing not available to married students.

Housing application deadline: 3/1. Graduate housing contact: Regina Metayer, 510-885-3601.

STUDENT SERVICES
Disabled student services, low-cost health insurance, career counseling, free psychological counseling, day-care facilities, campus safety program, campus employment opportunities.

FACILITIES
Library: University Library; total holdings of 740,894 volumes, 649,873 microforms, 2,390 current periodical subscriptions. A total of 49 personal computers in all libraries. Access provided to on-line information retrieval services. *Computer:* Campuswide network is available with full Internet access. Total number of PCs/terminals supplied for student use: 400. Computer service fees are included with tuition and fees. *Special:* In arts and humanities: Gallery West, art gallery, computer art laboratory, electronic music studio. In science and engineering: Moss Landing Marine Laboratories, geology field camp, ecology field station, wetlands field station. In social sciences: Clarence Smith Museum of Anthropology, cartographic laboratory.

COMPUTER SCIENCE

School of Science, Department of Mathematics and Computer Science, Computer Science Program
Programs Awards MS.
Faculty 17 full-time (2 women).
Students 48 full-time (34 women), 65 part-time (29 women); includes 50 minority (48 Asian-Americans, 2 Hispanics), 33 international.
Degrees Awarded In 1996, 32 degrees awarded.
Entrance Requirements Minimum GPA of 3.0 in field, 2.75 overall.
Degree Requirements Computer language, comprehensive exam or thesis required, foreign language not required.
Financial Aid Federal Work-Study, institutionally sponsored loans, and career-related internships or fieldwork available. Aid available to part-time students. *Financial aid application deadline:* 3/1.
Applying 52 applicants, 46% accepted. *Deadline:* 4/19 (priority date; rolling processing; 1/5 for spring admission). *Fee:* $55.
Contact Dr. Maria De Anda-Ramos
  Executive Director, Admissions and Outreach
  510-885-2624

CALIFORNIA STATE UNIVERSITY, LONG BEACH
Long Beach, CA 90840-0119

OVERVIEW
California State University, Long Beach is a public coed comprehensive institution.

ENROLLMENT
26,403 graduate, professional, and undergraduate students; 1,205 full-time matriculated graduate/professional students (749 women), 2,310 part-time matriculated graduate/professional students (1,183 women).

GRADUATE FACULTY

836 full-time (283 women), 709 part-time (329 women), 1,023 FTE; includes 281 minority (53 African-Americans, 138 Asian-Americans, 80 Hispanics, 10 Native Americans).

EXPENSES

Tuition $0 for state residents; $246 per unit for nonresidents. Fees $1846 per year full-time, $1180 per year part-time.

HOUSING

Rooms and/or apartments available to single students (1,844 units) at an average cost of $5300 (including board); on-campus housing not available to married students. Housing application deadline: 6/1. Graduate housing contact: Gary Little, 310-985-4187.

STUDENT SERVICES

Low-cost health insurance, career counseling, free psychological counseling, day-care facilities, campus safety program, campus employment opportunities, international student services.

FACILITIES

Library: Total holdings of 1,076,111 volumes, 1,546,918 microforms, 5,877 current periodical subscriptions. A total of 350 personal computers in all libraries. Access provided to on-line information retrieval services. *Computer:* Campuswide network is available with full Internet access. Total number of PCs/terminals supplied for student use: 1,100. Computer service fees are included with tuition and fees. *Special:* In arts and humanities: Art museum, Institute for the Preservation of Jazz. In science and engineering: R/V *Yellowfin* (ocean studies research vessel).

COMPUTER ENGINEERING

College of Engineering, Department of Computer Engineering and Computer Science
Programs   Offers programs in computer engineering (MS), computer science (MS). Part-time programs available.
Faculty   17 full-time (3 women), 8 part-time (0 women).
Faculty Research   Artificial intelligence, software engineering, computer simulation and modeling, user-interface design, networking.
Students   61 full-time (19 women), 121 part-time (35 women); includes 72 minority (3 African-Americans, 65 Asian-Americans, 4 Hispanics), 40 international. Average age 32.
Degrees Awarded   In 1996, 38 degrees awarded.
Entrance Requirements   TOEFL (minimum score 550).
Degree Requirements   Computer language, thesis or alternative required, foreign language not required.
Financial Aid   In 1996–97, 5 teaching assistantships (3 to first-year students) were awarded; assistantships also available. *Financial aid application deadline: 3/2.*
Applying   178 applicants, 51% accepted. *Deadline: 8/1. Fee: $55.*
Contact   *Dr. Wayne Dick*
Graduate Adviser
562-985-1551
Fax: 562-985-7561
E-mail: wed@csulb.edu

COMPUTER SCIENCE

College of Engineering, Department of Computer Engineering and Computer Science
Programs   Offers programs in computer engineering (MS), computer science (MS). Part-time programs available.
Faculty   17 full-time (3 women), 8 part-time (0 women).

Faculty Research   Artificial intelligence, software engineering, computer simulation and modeling, user-interface design, networking.
Students   61 full-time (19 women), 121 part-time (35 women); includes 72 minority (3 African-Americans, 65 Asian-Americans, 4 Hispanics), 40 international. Average age 32.
Degrees Awarded   In 1996, 38 degrees awarded.
Entrance Requirements   TOEFL (minimum score 550).
Degree Requirements   Computer language, thesis or alternative required, foreign language not required.
Financial Aid   In 1996–97, 5 teaching assistantships (3 to first-year students) were awarded; assistantships also available. *Financial aid application deadline: 3/2.*
Applying   178 applicants, 51% accepted. *Deadline: 8/1. Fee: $55.*
Contact   *Dr. Wayne Dick*
Graduate Adviser
562-985-1551
Fax: 562-985-7561
E-mail: wed@csulb.edu

ELECTRICAL ENGINEERING

College of Engineering, Department of Electrical Engineering
Programs   Awards MSE, MSEE. Part-time programs available.
Faculty   24 full-time (0 women), 6 part-time (0 women).
Faculty Research   Health care systems, IC, VLSI, communications, CAD/CAM.
Students   24 full-time (3 women), 76 part-time (10 women); includes 40 minority (1 African-American, 31 Asian-Americans, 8 Hispanics), 30 international. Average age 32.
Degrees Awarded   In 1996, 28 degrees awarded.
Entrance Requirements   TOEFL (minimum score 550).
Degree Requirements   Comprehensive exam or thesis required, foreign language not required.
Financial Aid   In 1996–97, 2 teaching assistantships, 2 assistantships were awarded; career-related internships or fieldwork also available. *Financial aid application deadline: 3/2.*
Applying   97 applicants, 51% accepted. *Deadline: 8/1. Fee: $55.*
Contact   *Dr. Michael Singh-Chelian*
Graduate Adviser
562-985-1516
Fax: 562-985-5327
E-mail: mchelian@engr.csulb.edu

CALIFORNIA STATE UNIVERSITY, LOS ANGELES
Los Angeles, CA 90032-8530

OVERVIEW

California State University, Los Angeles is a public coed comprehensive institution.

ENROLLMENT

18,849 graduate, professional, and undergraduate students; 893 full-time matriculated graduate/professional students (556 women), 2,116 part-time matriculated graduate/professional students (1,267 women).

GRADUATE FACULTY

504 full-time, 605 part-time; includes 291 minority (53 African-Americans, 134 Asian-Americans, 102 Hispanics, 2 Native Americans).

EXPENSES
Tuition $0 for state residents; $164 per unit for nonresidents. Fees $1763 per year full-time, $1097 per year part-time.

HOUSING
Rooms and/or apartments available to single students (192 units) at an average cost of $2915 per year; on-campus housing not available to married students. Graduate housing contact: Denzil Suite, 213-343-4800.

STUDENT SERVICES
Career counseling, free psychological counseling, day-care facilities, campus employment opportunities, international student services.

FACILITIES
Library: John F. Kennedy Memorial Library; total holdings of 1,147,573 volumes, 909,989 microforms, 1,971 current periodical subscriptions. A total of 121 personal computers in all libraries. Access provided to on-line information retrieval services. *Computer:* Campuswide network is available with full Internet access. Total number of PCs/terminals supplied for student use: 1,200. Computer services are offered at no charge. *Special:* In science and engineering: Desert Studies Center (Mojave Desert). In social sciences: Center for the Study of Business in Society, Chinese Studies Center, Center for Korean-American and Korean Studies, Center for the Study of Armament and Disarmament.

ELECTRICAL ENGINEERING

School of Engineering and Technology, Department of Electrical and Computer Engineering

Programs Offers program in electrical engineering (MS). Part-time and evening/weekend programs available.

Faculty 11 full-time, 7 part-time.

Students 12 full-time (0 women), 52 part-time (3 women); includes 38 minority (2 African-Americans, 31 Asian-Americans, 5 Hispanics), 7 international.

Degrees Awarded In 1996, 29 degrees awarded.

Entrance Requirements GRE General Test, GRE Subject Test, TOEFL (minimum score 550).

Degree Requirements Computer language, comprehensive exam or thesis required, foreign language not required.

Financial Aid 18 students received aid; Federal Work-Study available. Aid available to part-time students. *Financial aid application deadline:* 3/1.

Applying *Deadline:* 6/30 (rolling processing; 2/1 for spring admission). *Fee:* $55.

Contact *Dr. Helen Boussalis*
Chair
213-343-4470

CALIFORNIA STATE UNIVERSITY, NORTHRIDGE
Northridge, CA 91330

OVERVIEW
California State University, Northridge is a public coed comprehensive institution.

ENROLLMENT
27,189 graduate, professional, and undergraduate students; 501 full-time matriculated graduate/professional students (366 women), 2,370 part-time matriculated graduate/professional students (1,409 women).

GRADUATE FACULTY
817 full-time, 672 part-time.

EXPENSES
Tuition $0 for state residents; $246 per unit for nonresidents. Fees $1970 per year full-time, $1304 per year part-time.

HOUSING
Rooms and/or apartments available to single students (1,400 units) at an average cost of $5840 per year; on-campus housing not available to married students. Graduate housing contact: Housing Office, 818-677-2160.

STUDENT SERVICES
Low-cost health insurance, career counseling, free psychological counseling, day-care facilities, campus safety program, campus employment opportunities, international student services.

FACILITIES
Library: Oviatt Library plus 1 additional on-campus library; total holdings of 990,938 volumes, 7,566 current periodical subscriptions. Access provided to on-line information retrieval services. *Special:* In arts and humanities: Urban Archives Center. In science and engineering: Cancer Research Center, solar observatory, Desert Studies Consortium, Ocean Studies Institute. In social sciences: San Fernando Teaching Center, Northridge Center for Public Archaeology, child guidance clinic, geography map library.

COMPUTER ENGINEERING

College of Engineering and Computer Science, Department of Electrical and Computer Engineering

Programs Offers programs in biomedical engineering (MS), communications/radar engineering (MS), control engineering (MS), digital/computer engineering (MS), electronics engineering (MS), microwave/antenna engineering (MS). Part-time and evening/weekend programs available.

Faculty 21 full-time.

Faculty Research Reflector antenna study, radome study.

Students 8 full-time (0 women), 148 part-time (17 women); includes 57 minority (2 African-Americans, 45 Asian-Americans, 10 Hispanics), 14 international. Average age 32.

Entrance Requirements GRE General Test, TOEFL, minimum GPA of 2.5.

Degree Requirements Thesis or alternative required, foreign language not required.

Financial Aid *Application deadline:* 3/1.

Applying 110 applicants, 75% accepted. *Deadline:* 11/30. *Fee:* $55.

Contact *Nagi El Naga*
Graduate Coordinator
818-677-2180

COMPUTER SCIENCE

College of Engineering and Computer Science, Department of Computer Science

Programs Awards MS. Part-time and evening/weekend programs available.

Faculty 17 full-time, 20 part-time.

Faculty Research Radar data processing.

Students 2 full-time (0 women), 94 part-time (20 women); includes 33 minority (1 African-American, 26 Asian-Americans, 6 Hispanics), 17 international. Average age 32.

Entrance Requirements GRE General Test, TOEFL, minimum GPA of 2.5.

Degree Requirements Computer language, thesis required, foreign language not required.

Financial Aid *Application deadline: 3/1.*

Applying 63 applicants, 60% accepted. *Deadline: 11/30. Fee: $55.*

Contact *Dr. Diane Schwartz*
Chair
818-677-3398

ELECTRICAL ENGINEERING

College of Engineering and Computer Science, Department of Electrical and Computer Engineering

Programs Offers programs in biomedical engineering (MS), communications/radar engineering (MS), control engineering (MS), digital/computer engineering (MS), electronics engineering (MS), microwave/antenna engineering (MS). Part-time and evening/weekend programs available.

Faculty 21 full-time.

Faculty Research Reflector antenna study, radome study.

Students 8 full-time (0 women), 148 part-time (17 women); includes 57 minority (2 African-Americans, 45 Asian-Americans, 10 Hispanics), 14 international. Average age 32.

Entrance Requirements GRE General Test, TOEFL, minimum GPA of 2.5.

Degree Requirements Thesis or alternative required, foreign language not required.

Financial Aid *Application deadline: 3/1.*

Applying 110 applicants, 75% accepted. *Deadline: 11/30. Fee: $55.*

Contact *Nagi El Naga*
Graduate Coordinator
818-677-2180

CALIFORNIA STATE UNIVERSITY, SACRAMENTO

Sacramento, CA 95819-6048

OVERVIEW

California State University, Sacramento is a public coed comprehensive institution.

ENROLLMENT

17,835 graduate, professional, and undergraduate students; 2,199 full-time matriculated graduate/professional students (1,461 women), 2,508 part-time matriculated graduate/professional students (1,559 women).

GRADUATE FACULTY

1,314; includes 88 minority (22 African-Americans, 27 Asian-Americans, 32 Hispanics, 7 Native Americans).

EXPENSES

Tuition $0 for state residents; $246 per unit for nonresidents. Fees $1982 per year full-time, $1316 per year part-time.

HOUSING

Rooms and/or apartments available to single students (400 units) at an average cost of $4583 (including board); on-campus housing not available to married students. Housing application deadline: 4/1.

STUDENT SERVICES

Low-cost health insurance, career counseling, free psychological counseling, day-care facilities.

FACILITIES

Library: Main library; total holdings of 846,011 volumes, 40,214 microforms, 4,332 current periodical subscriptions. Access provided to on-line information retrieval services. *Special:* In science and engineering: Moss Landing Marine Laboratories.

COMPUTER SCIENCE

School of Engineering and Computer Science, Department of Computer Science

Programs Offers programs in computer systems (MS), software engineering (MS). Part-time and evening/weekend programs available.

Faculty 23 full-time (6 women).

Students 38 full-time (10 women), 73 part-time (20 women); includes 26 minority (2 African-Americans, 24 Asian-Americans).

Degrees Awarded In 1996, 24 degrees awarded.

Entrance Requirements TOEFL (minimum score 550).

Degree Requirements Computer language, thesis or alternative, writing proficiency exam required, foreign language not required.

Financial Aid Research assistantships, teaching assistantships, Federal Work-Study, and career-related internships or fieldwork available. Aid available to part-time students. *Financial aid application deadline: 3/1.*

Applying *Deadline: 4/15 (11/1 for spring admission). Fee: $55.*

Contact *Dr. Fred Blackwell*
Coordinator
916-278-6834

ELECTRICAL ENGINEERING

School of Engineering and Computer Science, Department of Electrical and Electronic Engineering

Programs Offers programs in biomedical engineering (MS), electrical engineering (MS). Part-time and evening/weekend programs available.

Faculty 18 (2 women).

Students 32 full-time (6 women), 72 part-time (14 women); includes 53 minority (8 African-Americans, 34 Asian-Americans, 11 Hispanics).

Degrees Awarded In 1996, 18 degrees awarded.

Entrance Requirements TOEFL (minimum score 550).

Degree Requirements Writing proficiency exam required, foreign language not required.

Financial Aid Research assistantships, teaching assistantships, Federal Work-Study, and career-related internships or fieldwork available. Aid available to part-time students. *Financial aid application deadline: 3/1.*

Applying *Deadline: 4/15 (11/1 for spring admission). Fee: $55.*

Contact *Dr. C. Desmond*
Graduate Coordinator
916-278-6873

SOFTWARE ENGINEERING

School of Engineering and Computer Science, Department of Computer Science

Programs Offerings include software engineering (MS).

Department Faculty 23 full-time (6 women).

Entrance Requirements   TOEFL (minimum score 550).
Degree Requirements   Computer language, thesis or alternative, writing proficiency exam required, foreign language not required.
Applying   *Deadline:* 4/15 (11/1 for spring admission). *Fee:* $55.
Contact   *Dr. Fred Blackwell*
              Coordinator
              916-278-6834

CALIFORNIA STATE UNIVERSITY, SAN BERNARDINO
San Bernardino, CA 92407-2397

OVERVIEW
California State University, San Bernardino is a public coed comprehensive institution.

ENROLLMENT
11,957 graduate, professional, and undergraduate students; 905 full-time matriculated graduate/professional students (564 women), 674 part-time matriculated graduate/professional students (426 women).

EXPENSES
Tuition $0 for state residents; $164 per unit for nonresidents. Fees $1896 per year full-time, $1230 per year part-time.

HOUSING
Rooms and/or apartments available to single students (400 units) at an average cost of $4950 (including board); on-campus housing not available to married students. Housing application deadline: 8/1.

STUDENT SERVICES
Career counseling, free psychological counseling, day-care facilities, campus safety program, campus employment opportunities, international student services.

FACILITIES
Library: Pfau Library; total holdings of 550,000 volumes, 585,000 microforms, 1,650 current periodical subscriptions. A total of 12 personal computers in all libraries. Access provided to on-line information retrieval services. *Special:* In arts and humanities: Art museum. In science and engineering: Desert Research Center. In social sciences: Institute for Social and Public Policy Research.

COMPUTER SCIENCE

School of Natural Sciences, Department of Computer Science
Programs   Awards MS.
Students   20 full-time (4 women), 14 part-time (3 women); includes 11 minority (2 African-Americans, 8 Asian-Americans, 1 Hispanic), 14 international. Average age 31.
Applying   39 applicants, 85% accepted. *Fee:* $55.
Contact   *Dr. Arturo Concepcion*
              Graduate Coordinator
              909-880-5330

CLAREMONT GRADUATE UNIVERSITY
Claremont, CA 91711-6163

OVERVIEW
Claremont Graduate University is an independent coed graduate-only institution.

ENROLLMENT
511 full-time matriculated graduate/professional students (233 women), 1,510 part-time matriculated graduate/professional students (744 women).

GRADUATE FACULTY
82 full-time (23 women), 100 part-time (30 women); includes 6 minority (1 African-American, 2 Asian-Americans, 3 Hispanics).

EXPENSES
Tuition $19,500 per year full-time, $880 per unit part-time. Fees $130 per year.

HOUSING
Rooms and/or apartments available to single students (60 units) at an average cost of $2835 per year; available to married students (29 units) at an average cost of $5782 per year. Graduate housing contact: Dana McLellan, 909-621-8036.

STUDENT SERVICES
Multicultural affairs office, low-cost health insurance, career counseling, free psychological counseling, campus safety program, campus employment opportunities, international student services, writing training, teacher training.

FACILITIES
Library: Honnold Library plus 3 additional on-campus libraries; total holdings of 2 million volumes, 1.3 million microforms, 4,319 current periodical subscriptions. A total of 30 personal computers in all libraries. Access provided to on-line information retrieval services. *Computer:* Campuswide network is available with full Internet access. Total number of PCs/terminals supplied for student use: 90. Computer service fees are included with tuition and fees. *Special:* In arts and humanities: Institute for Antiquity and Christianity. In social sciences: Institute for Economic Policy Studies, Claremont Graduate University Research Institute.

INFORMATION SCIENCE

Department of Information Sciences
Programs   Awards MIS, MSMIS, PhD, MBA/PhD. Programs in information systems (MIS), management of information systems (MSMIS, PhD). Part-time programs available.
Faculty   5 full-time (1 woman), 4 part-time (0 women).
Faculty Research   GDSS, man-machine interaction, organizational aspects of computing, implementation of information systems, information systems practice.
Students   17 full-time (10 women), 84 part-time (20 women); includes 29 minority (6 African-Americans, 19 Asian-Americans, 4 Hispanics), 20 international. Average age 38.
Degrees Awarded   In 1996, 21 master's, 6 doctorates awarded. Terminal master's awarded for partial completion of doctoral program.
Entrance Requirements   For master's, GMAT, GRE General Test.
Degree Requirements   For doctorate, dissertation.

Financial Aid Fellowships, research assistantships, teaching assistant-ships, Federal Work-Study, institutionally sponsored loans available. Aid available to part-time students. *Financial aid application deadline:* 2/15; applicants required to submit FAFSA.
Applying 61 applicants, 61% accepted. *Deadline:* 2/15 (priority date; rolling processing). *Fee:* $40.
Contact *Nancy Back*
Program Coordinator
909-621-8209
Fax: 909-621-8390
E-mail: infosci@cgs.edu

See in-depth description on page 397.

COLEMAN COLLEGE
La Mesa, CA 91942-1532

OVERVIEW
Coleman College is an independent coed comprehensive institution.

ENROLLMENT
1,100 graduate, professional, and undergraduate students; 15 matriculated graduate/professional students.

GRADUATE FACULTY
1 full-time (0 women), 15 part-time (1 woman); includes 0 minority.

EXPENSES
Tuition $155 per unit. Fees $100 (one-time charge).

HOUSING
On-campus housing not available.

STUDENT SERVICES
Campus employment opportunities, international student services.

FACILITIES
Library: Total holdings of 21,000 volumes. Access provided to on-line information retrieval services.

INFORMATION SCIENCE

Graduate Program in Information Systems
Programs Awards MS. Evening/weekend programs available.
Faculty 9 part-time (1 woman).
Students 15; includes 1 international.
Degree Requirements Computer language required, thesis optional, foreign language not required.
Applying 50% of applicants accepted. *Deadline:* rolling. *Fee:* $100.
Contact *William Fall*
Registrar
619-465-3990
Fax: 619-463-0162

LOYOLA MARYMOUNT UNIVERSITY
Los Angeles, CA 90045-8350

OVERVIEW
Loyola Marymount University is an independent-religious coed comprehensive institution.

ENROLLMENT
6,687 graduate, professional, and undergraduate students; 1,706 full-time, 820 part-time matriculated graduate/professional students.

GRADUATE FACULTY
132 full-time (38 women), 163 part-time (71 women); includes 31 minority (10 African-Americans, 13 Asian-Americans, 8 Hispanics).

EXPENSES
Tuition $475 per unit. Fees $56 per year full-time, $28 per year part-time.

HOUSING
Rooms and/or apartments available to single students (20 units) at an average cost of $4952 per year; on-campus housing not available to married students. Housing application deadline: 5/1. Graduate housing contact: Carole Kropp, 310-338-2963.

STUDENT SERVICES
Disabled student services, multicultural affairs office, low-cost health insurance, career counseling, free psychological counseling, campus safety program, campus employment opportunities, international student services, writing training, teacher training.

FACILITIES
Library: Charles Von der Ahe Library; total holdings of 487,232 volumes, 1,176,395 microforms, 9,505 current periodical subscriptions. A total of 30 personal computers in all libraries. Access provided to on-line information retrieval services. *Computer:* Campuswide network is available with full Internet access. Total number of PCs/terminals supplied for student use: 200. Computer service fees are included with tuition and fees.

COMPUTER SCIENCE

College of Science and Engineering, Department of Electrical Engineering and Computer Science, Program in Computer Science
Programs Awards MS. Part-time and evening/weekend programs available.
Faculty 2 part-time (1 woman).
Students 12 full-time (3 women), 7 part-time (4 women); includes 10 minority (2 African-Americans, 6 Asian-Americans, 2 Hispanics), 1 international.
Degrees Awarded In 1996, 8 degrees awarded.
Entrance Requirements TOEFL (minimum score 550).
Degree Requirements Computer language, research seminar required, foreign language and thesis not required.
Financial Aid 1 student received aid; grants available. Aid available to part-time students. *Financial aid application deadline:* 3/2; applicants required to submit FAFSA.
Applying 6 applicants, 67% accepted. *Fee:* $35.
Contact *Dr. Paul A. Rude*
Graduate Director
310-338-2774

ELECTRICAL ENGINEERING

College of Science and Engineering, Department of Electrical Engineering and Computer Science, Program in Electrical Engineering
Programs Awards MSE. Part-time and evening/weekend programs available.
Faculty 7 full-time (0 women), 2 part-time (0 women).
Students 2 full-time (0 women), 4 part-time (0 women); includes 4 minority (3 Asian-Americans, 1 Native American), 1 international.

Degrees Awarded   In 1996, 4 degrees awarded.
Entrance Requirements   TOEFL (minimum score 550).
Degree Requirements   Computer language, research seminar required, foreign language and thesis not required.
Financial Aid   2 students received aid; scholarships available. Aid available to part-time students. *Financial aid application deadline:* 3/2; applicants required to submit FAFSA.
Applying   12 applicants, 67% accepted. *Fee:* $35.
Contact   Dr. Paul A. Rude
Graduate Director
310-338-2774

MILLS COLLEGE
Oakland, CA 94613-1000

OVERVIEW
Mills College is an independent coed comprehensive institution.

ENROLLMENT
1,182 graduate, professional, and undergraduate students; 281 full-time matriculated graduate/professional students (244 women), 35 part-time matriculated graduate/professional students (31 women).

GRADUATE FACULTY
44 full-time (28 women), 42 part-time (32 women), 55 FTE; includes 12 minority (3 African-Americans, 7 Asian-Americans, 2 Hispanics).

EXPENSES
Tuition $9910 per year full-time, $2510 per year part-time. Fees $438 per year.

HOUSING
Rooms and/or apartments available to single students (50 units) at an average cost of $3400 per year ($6800 including board); available to married students (11 units) at an average cost of $5000 per year. Housing application deadline: 3/1. Graduate housing contact: Dean of Students Office, 510-430-2130.

STUDENT SERVICES
Disabled student services, low-cost health insurance, career counseling, free psychological counseling, exercise/wellness program, day-care facilities, campus safety program, campus employment opportunities, international student services, teacher training.

FACILITIES
Library: F. W. Olin Library; total holdings of 215,760 volumes, 8,000 microforms, 738 current periodical subscriptions. A total of 20 personal computers in all libraries. Access provided to on-line information retrieval services. *Computer:* Campuswide network is available with full Internet access. Total number of PCs/terminals supplied for student use: 100. Computer services are offered at no charge. *Special:* In arts and humanities: Center for Contemporary Music, Mills College Art Galleries, Scholars' Multimedia Workroom, Heller Rare Book Collection, music instrument collection. In science and engineering: Academic Computing Center. In social sciences: Children's school.

COMPUTER SCIENCE

New Horizons Program in Mathematics and Computer Science
Programs   Offers computer science (Certificate). Part-time programs available.

Faculty   6 full-time (3 women), 3 part-time (2 women), 6.5 FTE.
Faculty Research   Dynamical systems, human interface, parallel computation, compiling techniques, fault tolerance, operating systems.
Students   5 full-time (4 women), includes 1 minority (African-American), 1 international.
Degrees Awarded   In 1996, 1 degree awarded.
Entrance Requirements   TOEFL (minimum score 600).
Degree Requirements   Computer language required, thesis not required.
Financial Aid   Fellowships, teaching assistantships, residence awards, institutionally sponsored loans, and career-related internships or fieldwork available. Aid available to part-time students. *Financial aid application deadline:* 2/1; applicants required to submit FAFSA.
Applying   4 applicants, 75% accepted. *Deadline:* 2/1 (priority date; rolling processing; 11/1 for spring admission). *Fee:* $50.
Contact   Margaret Stephan
Assistant Director
510-430-3309
Fax: 510-430-3314

COMPUTER SCIENCE

Program in Interdisciplinary Computer Science
Programs   Awards MA. Part-time programs available.
Faculty   6 full-time (3 women), 3 part-time (2 women), 6.5 FTE.
Faculty Research   Dynamical systems, linear programming, theory of computer viruses, interface design, intelligent tutoring systems.
Students   8 full-time (all women), includes 1 minority (Asian-American), 2 international.
Degrees Awarded   In 1996, 2 degrees awarded (100% found work related to degree).
Entrance Requirements   TOEFL (minimum score 600).
Degree Requirements   Computer language, thesis.
Financial Aid   In 1996–97, 4 fellowships (2 to first-year students) totaling $9,000, 7 teaching assistantships (3 to first-year students) totaling $37,000, 1 residence award (to a first-year student) totaling $3,000 were awarded; institutionally sponsored loans and career-related internships or fieldwork also available. Aid available to part-time students. *Financial aid application deadline:* 2/1; applicants required to submit CSS PROFILE or FAFSA.
Applying   7 applicants, 86% accepted. *Deadline:* 2/1 (priority date; rolling processing; 11/1 for spring admission). *Fee:* $50.
Contact   Margaret Stephan
Assistant Director
510-430-3309
Fax: 510-430-3314

NATIONAL UNIVERSITY
La Jolla, CA 92037-1011

OVERVIEW
National University is an independent coed comprehensive institution.

TUITION
$7425 per year full-time, $825 per course part-time.

HOUSING
On-campus housing not available.

FACILITIES
Library: Main library plus 1 additional on-campus library.

SOFTWARE ENGINEERING

School of Management and Technology, Department of Technology Studies
Programs Offerings include software engineering (MS).
Applying *Deadline:* rolling. *Fee:* $60 ($100 for international students).

NAVAL POSTGRADUATE SCHOOL
Monterey, CA 93943

OVERVIEW
Naval Postgraduate School is a public coed graduate-only institution.

ENROLLMENT
1,505 full-time, 0 part-time matriculated graduate/professional students.

GRADUATE FACULTY
334 full-time, 33 part-time.

TUITION
$9500 per year.

HOUSING
Rooms and/or apartments available to single students; available to married students (1,491 units). Graduate housing contact: Housing Office, 408-656-2321.

STUDENT SERVICES
Career counseling, day-care facilities.

FACILITIES
Library: Dudley Knox Library; total holdings of 500,000 volumes, 520,000 microforms, 1,700 current periodical subscriptions. Access provided to on-line information retrieval services. *Computer:* Campuswide network is available with full Internet access. Total number of PCs/terminals supplied for student use: 1,700. Computer services are offered at no charge. *Special:* In science and engineering: Laboratories in aeronautics and astronautics; command, control, and communications; computer, electrical, and mechanical engineering; computer science; meteorology; oceanography; and physics.

COMPUTER ENGINEERING

Department of Electrical and Computer Engineering
Programs Awards MS, PhD, Eng. One or more programs accredited by ABET. Program only open to commissioned officers of the United States and friendly nations and selected United States federal civilian employees.
Students 117 full-time, includes 36 international.
Degrees Awarded In 1996, 45 master's, 2 doctorates, 1 Eng awarded.
Degree Requirements For master's and Eng, computer language, thesis required, foreign language not required; for doctorate, 1 foreign language, computer language, dissertation.

Contact *Theodore H. Calhoon*
Director of Admissions
408-656-3093
Fax: 408-656-2891

COMPUTER SCIENCE

Department of Computer Science
Programs Awards MS, PhD. Program only open to commissioned officers of the United States and friendly nations and selected United States federal civilian employees. Part-time programs available.
Students 92 full-time, includes 19 international.
Degrees Awarded In 1996, 46 master's, 2 doctorates awarded. Terminal master's awarded for partial completion of doctoral program.
Degree Requirements For master's, computer language, thesis required, foreign language not required; for doctorate, 1 foreign language, computer language, dissertation.
Contact *Theodore H. Calhoon*
Director of Admissions
408-656-3093
Fax: 408-656-2891

ELECTRICAL ENGINEERING

Department of Electrical and Computer Engineering
Programs Awards MS, PhD, Eng. One or more programs accredited by ABET. Program only open to commissioned officers of the United States and friendly nations and selected United States federal civilian employees.
Students 117 full-time, includes 36 international.
Degrees Awarded In 1996, 45 master's, 2 doctorates, 1 Eng awarded.
Degree Requirements For master's and Eng, computer language, thesis required, foreign language not required; for doctorate, 1 foreign language, computer language, dissertation.
Contact *Theodore H. Calhoon*
Director of Admissions
408-656-3093
Fax: 408-656-2891

SAN DIEGO STATE UNIVERSITY
San Diego, CA 92182

OVERVIEW
San Diego State University is a public coed university.

ENROLLMENT
27,430 graduate, professional, and undergraduate students; 5,617 matriculated graduate/professional students (3,300 women).

GRADUATE FACULTY
952 full-time, 460 part-time; includes 129 minority (24 African-Americans, 50 Asian-Americans, 52 Hispanics, 3 Native Americans).

EXPENSES
Tuition $0 for state residents; $246 per unit for nonresidents. Fees $1932 per year full-time, $1266 per year part-time.

HOUSING
Rooms and/or apartments available to single students (3,018 units) at an average cost of $3736 per year ($5172 including board); on-campus housing not available to

married students. Graduate housing contact: Housing and Resident Life Office, 619-594-5742.

STUDENT SERVICES
Low-cost health insurance, career counseling, free psychological counseling, day-care facilities, campus safety program, campus employment opportunities, international student services.

FACILITIES
Library: Malcolm A. Love Library plus 1 additional on-campus library; total holdings of 1,095,581 volumes, 3,554,052 microforms, 5,979 current periodical subscriptions. A total of 45 personal computers in all libraries. Access provided to on-line information retrieval services. *Special:* In arts and humanities: Lupinski Institute for Judaic Studies, Institute for International Security and Conflict Resolution. In science and engineering: Mt. Laguna Observatory, biological field stations, Center for Energy Studies, Molecular Biology Institute, Center for Research In Mathematics and Science Education. In social sciences: Social science research laboratory, University Center on Aging, California Border Area Research Center, International Center for Communications.

COMPUTER SCIENCE

College of Sciences, Department of Mathematical Sciences, Program in Computer Science

Programs Awards MS.
Students 93 (22 women); includes 25 minority (20 Asian-Americans, 5 Hispanics), 9 international. Average age 28.
Degrees Awarded In 1996, 18 degrees awarded.
Entrance Requirements GRE General Test (minimum combined score of 950), TOEFL (minimum score 550).
Degree Requirements Computer language, comprehensive exam or thesis required, foreign language not required.
Applying *Deadline:* 6/1 (priority date; rolling processing; 12/1 for spring admission). *Fee:* $55.
Contact Carl Eckberg
　　　　　　Graduate Coordinator
　　　　　　619-594-6834
　　　　　　Fax: 619-594-6746
　　　　　　E-mail: eckberg@saturn.sdsu.edu

ELECTRICAL ENGINEERING

College of Engineering, Department of Electrical and Computer Engineering

Programs Offers program in electrical engineering (MS). Evening/weekend programs available.
Faculty 18 (1 woman).
Faculty Research Ultra-high speed integral circuits and systems, naval command control and ocean surveillance, signal processing and analysis. *Total annual research expenditures:* $525,000.
Students 128 (14 women); includes 28 minority (1 African-American, 21 Asian-Americans, 6 Hispanics), 9 international. Average age 29.
Degrees Awarded In 1996, 34 degrees awarded.
Entrance Requirements GRE General Test (minimum combined score of 950), TOEFL (minimum score 550).
Financial Aid Career-related internships or fieldwork available.
Applying *Deadline:* 6/1 (priority date; rolling processing; 12/1 for spring admission). *Fee:* $55.

Contact M. Lin
　　　　　　Graduate Coordinator
　　　　　　619-594-2493
　　　　　　Fax: 619-594-6005
　　　　　　E-mail: maolin@sdsu.edu

SAN FRANCISCO STATE UNIVERSITY
San Francisco, CA 94132-1722

OVERVIEW
San Francisco State University is a public coed comprehensive institution.

ENROLLMENT
25,716 graduate, professional, and undergraduate students; 5,918 matriculated graduate/professional students.

GRADUATE FACULTY
795 full-time (285 women).

EXPENSES
Tuition $0 for state residents; $246 per unit for nonresidents. Fees $1982 per year full-time, $1316 per year part-time.

HOUSING
Rooms and/or apartments available to single students at an average cost of $4000 per year ($5000 including board); on-campus housing not available to married students. Graduate housing contact: Housing Director, 415-338-1067.

STUDENT SERVICES
Low-cost health insurance, career counseling, free psychological counseling, day-care facilities, campus safety program, campus employment opportunities.

FACILITIES
Library: J. Paul Leonard Library; total holdings of 900,000 volumes, 2 million microforms, 4,300 current periodical subscriptions. A total of 200 personal computers in all libraries. Access provided to on-line information retrieval services. *Computer:* Campuswide network is available with full Internet access. Computer services are offered at no charge. *Special:* In arts and humanities: Frank V. de Bellis Italian Collection, Sutro Egyptian Collection. In science and engineering: J. Paul Leonard Sierra Nevada Science Field Campus, Romberg Tiburon Center for Environmental Studies. In social sciences: Treganza Anthropology Museum, Labor Library and Archives.

COMPUTER SCIENCE

College of Science, Department of Computer Science

Programs Awards MS. Part-time programs available.
Faculty 9 full-time (1 woman), 4 part-time (0 women).
Faculty Research Parallel computing, real time systems, database systems, neural networks, computer graphics.
Students 59 (12 women); includes 25 minority (23 Asian-Americans, 1 Hispanic, 1 Native American). Average age 26.
Degrees Awarded In 1996, 16 degrees awarded.
Entrance Requirements GRE, minimum GPA of 2.5 in last 60 units.
Degree Requirements Thesis or alternative.

Financial Aid In 1996–97, 2 research assistantships, 4 teaching assistantships (1 to a first-year student), 4 graduate assistantships (2 to first-year students) were awarded. *Financial aid application deadline:* 3/1.
Applying *Deadline:* 11/30 (priority date; rolling processing). *Fee:* $55.
Contact *Dr. Gerald Eisman*
Chair
415-338-1008
Fax: 415-338-6136
E-mail: eisman@cs.sfsu.edu

SAN JOSE STATE UNIVERSITY
San Jose, CA 95192-0001

OVERVIEW
San Jose State University is a public coed comprehensive institution.

ENROLLMENT
26,543 graduate, professional, and undergraduate students; 2,075 full-time matriculated graduate/professional students (1,391 women), 2,806 part-time matriculated graduate/professional students (1,582 women).

GRADUATE FACULTY
933 full-time (216 women), 488 part-time (152 women); includes 314 minority (43 African-Americans, 157 Asian-Americans, 88 Hispanics, 26 Native Americans).

EXPENSES
Tuition $0 for state residents; $246 per unit for nonresidents. Fees $2017 per year full-time, $1351 per year part-time.

HOUSING
Rooms and/or apartments available to single students (900 units) at an average cost of $5919 (including board); on-campus housing not available to married students. Graduate housing contact: Housing Office, 408-924-6160.

STUDENT SERVICES
Low-cost health insurance, career counseling, free psychological counseling, day-care facilities, campus safety program, campus employment opportunities.

FACILITIES
Library: Clark Library plus 1 additional on-campus library; total holdings of 700,000 volumes, 650,000 microforms, 11,000 current periodical subscriptions. Access provided to on-line information retrieval services. *Computer:* Campuswide network is available with full Internet access. Computer services are offered at no charge. *Special:* In science and engineering: Nuclear science facility.

ARTIFICIAL INTELLIGENCE/ROBOTICS

College of Engineering, Department of Computer Engineering
Programs Offerings include computer science (MS), with options in computer engineering, computer software, computerized robots and computer applications, microprocessors and microcomputers.
Department Faculty 5 full-time (0 women), 12 part-time (1 woman).

Entrance Requirements GRE General Test (minimum combined score of 1500 on three sections), BS in computer science or 24 credits in related area.
Degree Requirements Computer language, thesis, comprehensive exam required, foreign language not required.
Applying *Deadline:* 6/1 (rolling processing). *Fee:* $59.
Contact *Dr. Haluk Ozemek*
Chair
408-924-4100

COMPUTER ENGINEERING

College of Engineering, Department of Computer Engineering
Programs Offers program in computer science (MS), including computer engineering, computer software, computerized robots and computer applications, microprocessors and microcomputers.
Faculty 5 full-time (0 women), 12 part-time (1 woman).
Faculty Research Robotics, database management systems, computer networks.
Students 36 full-time (19 women), 57 part-time (13 women); includes 81 minority (1 African-American, 78 Asian-Americans, 2 Hispanics), 10 international. Average age 29.
Degrees Awarded In 1996, 16 degrees awarded.
Entrance Requirements GRE General Test (minimum combined score of 1500 on three sections), BS in computer science or 24 credits in related area.
Degree Requirements Computer language, thesis, comprehensive exam required, foreign language not required.
Financial Aid Teaching assistantships, Federal Work-Study, institutionally sponsored loans, and career-related internships or fieldwork available. Aid available to part-time students. *Financial aid application deadline:* 5/1.
Applying 111 applicants, 52% accepted. *Deadline:* 6/1 (rolling processing). *Fee:* $59.
Contact *Dr. Haluk Ozemek*
Chair
408-924-4100

COMPUTER SCIENCE

College of Engineering, Department of Computer Engineering
Programs Offerings include computer science (MS), with options in computer engineering, computer software, computerized robots and computer applications, microprocessors and microcomputers.
Department Faculty 5 full-time (0 women), 12 part-time (1 woman).
Entrance Requirements GRE General Test (minimum combined score of 1500 on three sections), BS in computer science or 24 credits in related area.
Degree Requirements Computer language, thesis, comprehensive exam required, foreign language not required.
Applying *Deadline:* 6/1 (rolling processing). *Fee:* $59.
Contact *Dr. Haluk Ozemek*
Chair
408-924-4100

COMPUTER SCIENCE

College of Science, Department of Mathematics and Computer Science
Programs Offers programs in computer science (MS), mathematics (MA, MS). Part-time and evening/weekend programs available.
Faculty 51 full-time (5 women), 3 part-time (0 women).
Faculty Research Artificial intelligence, algorithms, numerical analysis, software database, number theory.
Students 33 full-time (16 women), 74 part-time (34 women); includes 64 minority (4 African-Americans, 58 Asian-Americans, 2 Hispanics), 27 international. Average age 31.

Degrees Awarded In 1996, 17 degrees awarded.
Entrance Requirements GRE Subject Test.
Degree Requirements Thesis (for some programs), comprehensive exam required, foreign language not required.
Financial Aid In 1996–97, 20 teaching assistantships (10 to first-year students) were awarded; Federal Work-Study and career-related internships or fieldwork also available. Aid available to part-time students.
Applying 196 applicants, 41% accepted. *Deadline:* 6/1 (rolling processing). *Fee:* $59.
Contact *Dr. John Mitchem*
Graduate Adviser
408-924-5135

ELECTRICAL ENGINEERING

College of Engineering, Department of Electrical Engineering
Programs Awards MS.
Faculty 15 full-time (2 women), 27 part-time (4 women).
Students 74 full-time (22 women), 197 part-time (30 women); includes 203 minority (6 African-Americans, 193 Asian-Americans, 4 Hispanics), 38 international. Average age 30.
Degrees Awarded In 1996, 68 degrees awarded.
Entrance Requirements GRE General Test (minimum combined score of 1500 on three sections), minimum GPA of 3.0.
Degree Requirements Thesis.
Applying 188 applicants, 60% accepted. *Deadline:* 6/1 (rolling processing). *Fee:* $59.
Contact *Dr. Rangaiya Rao*
Graduate Coordinator
408-924-3914

SOFTWARE ENGINEERING

College of Engineering, Department of Computer Engineering
Programs Offerings include computer science (MS), with options in computer engineering, computer software, computerized robots and computer applications, microprocessors and microcomputers.
Department Faculty 5 full-time (0 women), 12 part-time (1 woman).
Entrance Requirements GRE General Test (minimum combined score of 1500 on three sections), BS in computer science or 24 credits in related area.
Degree Requirements Computer language, thesis, comprehensive exam required, foreign language not required.
Applying *Deadline:* 6/1 (rolling processing). *Fee:* $59.
Contact *Dr. Haluk Ozemek*
Chair
408-924-4100

SANTA CLARA UNIVERSITY
Santa Clara, CA 95053-0001

OVERVIEW
Santa Clara University is an independent-religious coed comprehensive institution.

ENROLLMENT
7,863 graduate, professional, and undergraduate students; 1,357 full-time matriculated graduate/professional students (696 women), 1,969 part-time matriculated graduate/professional students (782 women).

GRADUATE FACULTY
137 full-time (35 women), 115 part-time (31 women); includes 61 minority (7 African-Americans, 44 Asian-Americans, 9 Hispanics, 1 Native American).

TUITION
$6912 per year full-time, $432 per unit part-time.

HOUSING
On-campus housing not available.

STUDENT SERVICES
Career counseling, free psychological counseling, day-care facilities, campus employment opportunities, international student services.

FACILITIES
Library: Orradre Library plus 1 additional on-campus library; total holdings of 735,064 volumes, 1,241,034 microforms, 9,529 current periodical subscriptions. A total of 67 personal computers in all libraries. Access provided to on-line information retrieval services. *Computer:* Campuswide network is available with full Internet access. Total number of PCs/terminals supplied for student use: 350. Computer service fees are included with tuition and fees. *Special:* In science and engineering: Institute on Information Storage Technology, microwave laboratory, microelectronics laboratory, semiconductor teaching and research laboratory.

COMPUTER ENGINEERING

School of Engineering, Department of Computer Science and Engineering
Programs Offers programs in computer science and engineering (MSCSE, PhD), high performance computing (Certificate), software engineering (Certificate). Part-time and evening/weekend programs available.
Students 138 full-time (76 women), 238 part-time (78 women); includes 272 minority (3 African-Americans, 263 Asian-Americans, 5 Hispanics, 1 Native American). Average age 34.
Degrees Awarded In 1996, 100 master's, 1 doctorate awarded.
Entrance Requirements For master's, GRE General Test, TOEFL (minimum score 550), minimum GPA of 2.75; for doctorate, GRE General Test, GRE Subject Test, TOEFL (minimum score 550), master's degree or equivalent; for Certificate, master's degree, published paper.
Degree Requirements For master's, computer language, thesis or alternative required, foreign language not required; for doctorate and Certificate, computer language, thesis/dissertation required, foreign language not required.
Financial Aid Research assistantships, teaching assistantships, Federal Work-Study available. Aid available to part-time students. *Financial aid application deadline:* 2/1.
Applying 190 applicants, 63% accepted. *Deadline:* 6/1 (rolling processing; 1/1 for spring admission). *Fee:* $35.
Contact *Tina Samms*
Assistant Director of Graduate Admissions
408-554-4313
Fax: 408-551-1857

COMPUTER SCIENCE

School of Engineering, Department of Computer Science and Engineering
Programs Offers programs in computer science and engineering (MSCSE, PhD), high performance computing (Certificate), software engineering (Certificate). Part-time and evening/weekend programs available.

Students 138 full-time (76 women), 238 part-time (78 women); includes 272 minority (3 African-Americans, 263 Asian-Americans, 5 Hispanics, 1 Native American). Average age 34.

Degrees Awarded In 1996, 100 master's, 1 doctorate awarded.

Entrance Requirements For master's, GRE General Test, TOEFL (minimum score 550), minimum GPA of 2.75; for doctorate, GRE General Test, GRE Subject Test, TOEFL (minimum score 550), master's degree or equivalent; for Certificate, master's degree, published paper.

Degree Requirements For master's, computer language, thesis or alternative required, foreign language not required; for doctorate and Certificate, computer language, thesis/dissertation required, foreign language not required.

Financial Aid Research assistantships, teaching assistantships, Federal Work-Study available. Aid available to part-time students. *Financial aid application deadline:* 2/1.

Applying 190 applicants, 63% accepted. *Deadline:* 6/1 (rolling processing; 1/1 for spring admission). *Fee:* $35.

Contact *Tina Samms*
Assistant Director of Graduate Admissions
408-554-4313
Fax: 408-551-1857

ELECTRICAL ENGINEERING

School of Engineering, Department of Electrical Engineering

Programs Offers programs in ASIC design and test (Certificate), data storage technologies (Certificate), electrical engineering (MSEE, PhD, Engineer). Part-time and evening/weekend programs available.

Students 43 full-time (8 women), 197 part-time (28 women); includes 132 minority (1 African-American, 125 Asian-Americans, 6 Hispanics), 56 international. Average age 35.

Degrees Awarded In 1996, 53 master's awarded.

Entrance Requirements For master's, GRE General Test, TOEFL (minimum score 550), minimum GPA of 2.75; for doctorate, GRE General Test, GRE Subject Test, TOEFL (minimum score 550), master's degree or equivalent; for other advanced degree, master's degree, published paper.

Degree Requirements For master's, computer language, thesis or alternative required, foreign language not required; for doctorate and other advanced degree, computer language, thesis/dissertation required, foreign language not required.

Financial Aid Research assistantships, teaching assistantships, Federal Work-Study available. Aid available to part-time students. *Financial aid application deadline:* 2/1.

Applying 129 applicants, 71% accepted. *Deadline:* 6/1 (rolling processing; 1/1 for spring admission). *Fee:* $35.

Contact *Tina Samms*
Assistant Director of Graduate Admissions
408-554-4313
Fax: 408-551-1857

SOFTWARE ENGINEERING

School of Engineering, Department of Computer Science and Engineering

Programs Offerings include software engineering (Certificate).

Entrance Requirements Master's degree, published paper.

Degree Requirements Computer language, thesis required, foreign language not required.

Applying *Deadline:* 6/1 (rolling processing; 1/1 for spring admission). *Fee:* $35.

Contact *Tina Samms*
Assistant Director of Graduate Admissions
408-554-4313
Fax: 408-551-1857

STANFORD UNIVERSITY
Stanford, CA 94305-9991

OVERVIEW
Stanford University is an independent coed university.

ENROLLMENT
14,044 graduate, professional, and undergraduate students; 6,061 full-time matriculated graduate/professional students (1,935 women), 1,409 part-time matriculated graduate/professional students (484 women).

GRADUATE FACULTY
1,459 full-time (259 women); includes 198 minority (39 African-Americans, 122 Asian-Americans, 35 Hispanics, 2 Native Americans).

EXPENSES
Tuition $21,300 per year. Fees $156 per year.

HOUSING
Rooms and/or apartments available to single students (2,152 units) and married students (747 units). Housing application deadline: 5/13. Graduate housing information: 650-725-2810.

STUDENT SERVICES
Low-cost health insurance, career counseling, free psychological counseling, day-care facilities, campus safety program, campus employment opportunities, international student services.

FACILITIES
Library: Cecil H. Green Library plus 16 additional on-campus libraries; total holdings of 6.5 million volumes, 4.5 million microforms, 43,800 current periodical subscriptions. A total of 600 personal computers in all libraries. Access provided to on-line information retrieval services. *Computer:* Campuswide network is available with full Internet access. *Special:* In arts and humanities: Humanities Center. In science and engineering: Stanford Linear Accelerator, Hopkins Marine Station, Stanford Electronics Laboratories, Hansen Experimental Ginzton Laboratory, physics laboratory, Center for Materials Research. In social sciences: Hoover Institute on War, Revolution, and Peace; Center for Research in International Studies; Institute for Research on Women and Gender; Center for Chicano Research; Center for Study of Language and Information; Center for Economic Policy Research; Center for Behavioral Sciences.

COMPUTER SCIENCE

School of Engineering, Department of Computer Science

Programs Awards MS, PhD.

Faculty 33 full-time (4 women).

Students 329 full-time (50 women), 83 part-time (15 women); includes 81 minority (9 African-Americans, 64 Asian-Americans, 5 Hispanics, 3 Native Americans), 159 international. Average age 26.

Degrees Awarded In 1996, 136 master's, 22 doctorates awarded. Terminal master's awarded for partial completion of doctoral program.

Entrance Requirements For master's, GRE General Test, TOEFL; for doctorate, GRE General Test, GRE Subject Test, TOEFL.

Degree Requirements For master's, computer language required, foreign language and thesis not required; for doctorate, computer language, dissertation required, foreign language not required.
Financial Aid Fellowships, research assistantships, teaching assistantships, Federal Work-Study, institutionally sponsored loans available. *Financial aid application deadline: 1/1.*
Applying 652 applicants, 25% accepted. *Deadline: 1/1. Fee: $65 ($75 for international students).*
Contact *Graduate Administrator*
650-723-1519

See in-depth description on page 547.

COMPUTER SCIENCE

School of Engineering, Program in Scientific Computing and Computational Mathematics
Programs Awards MS, PhD.
Students 35 full-time (7 women), 3 part-time (0 women); includes 6 minority (5 Asian-Americans, 1 Hispanic), 19 international. Average age 27.
Degrees Awarded In 1996, 10 master's, 3 doctorates awarded. Terminal master's awarded for partial completion of doctoral program.
Entrance Requirements For master's, GRE General Test, TOEFL; for doctorate, GRE General Test, GRE Subject Test, TOEFL.
Degree Requirements For doctorate, dissertation.
Financial Aid Fellowships, research assistantships, institutionally sponsored loans available. *Financial aid application deadline: 2/15.*
Applying 54 applicants, 24% accepted. *Deadline: 2/15. Fee: $65 ($75 for international students).*
Contact *Admissions Coordinator*
650-723-0572

See in-depth description on page 553.

ELECTRICAL ENGINEERING

School of Engineering, Department of Electrical Engineering
Programs Awards MS, PhD, Eng.
Faculty 50 full-time (2 women).
Students 616 full-time (86 women), 139 part-time (11 women); includes 163 minority (17 African-Americans, 122 Asian-Americans, 21 Hispanics, 3 Native Americans), 329 international. Average age 26.
Degrees Awarded In 1996, 205 master's, 68 doctorates awarded. Terminal master's awarded for partial completion of doctoral program.
Entrance Requirements GRE General Test, TOEFL.
Degree Requirements For doctorate, dissertation required, foreign language not required; for Eng, thesis.
Financial Aid Fellowships, research assistantships, teaching assistantships, Federal Work-Study, institutionally sponsored loans available. *Financial aid application deadline: 1/1.*
Applying 1,039 applicants, 39% accepted. *Deadline: 1/7. Fee: $65 ($75 for international students).*
Contact *Director of Graduate Admissions*
650-723-4115

See in-depth description on page 549.

MEDICAL INFORMATICS

School of Medicine, Graduate Programs in Medicine, Medical Information Sciences Program
Programs Offers medical computer science (MS, PhD), medical decision science (MS, PhD).

Students 19 full-time (8 women), 9 part-time (3 women); includes 10 minority (2 African-Americans, 6 Asian-Americans, 2 Hispanics), 7 international. Average age 30.
Degrees Awarded In 1996, 2 doctorates awarded. Terminal master's awarded for partial completion of doctoral program.
Entrance Requirements For master's, GRE or MCAT; for doctorate, GRE or MCAT, TOEFL.
Degree Requirements Computer language, thesis/dissertation.
Financial Aid Research assistantships available. *Financial aid application deadline: 1/1.*
Applying 42 applicants, 10% accepted. *Deadline: 1/1. Fee: $65 ($75 for international students).*
Contact *Darlene Vian*
Administrator
650-725-3388
Fax: 650-725-7944
E-mail: vian@smi.stanford.edu

See in-depth description on page 551.

UNIVERSITY OF CALIFORNIA, BERKELEY
Berkeley, CA 94720-1500

OVERVIEW
University of California, Berkeley is a public coed university.

ENROLLMENT
30,372 graduate, professional, and undergraduate students; 8,439 matriculated graduate/professional students (3,661 women).

GRADUATE FACULTY
1,654; includes 189 minority (38 African-Americans, 100 Asian-Americans, 46 Hispanics, 5 Native Americans).

EXPENSES
Tuition $0 for state residents; $8984 per year for nonresidents. Fees $4395 per year.

HOUSING
Rooms and/or apartments available to single and married students. Graduate housing information: 510-642-3642.

STUDENT SERVICES
Disabled student services, multicultural affairs office, low-cost health insurance, career counseling, free psychological counseling, exercise/wellness program, day-care facilities, campus safety program, campus employment opportunities, international student services, grant writing training.

FACILITIES
Library: Doe Library plus 55 additional on-campus libraries; total holdings of 7 million volumes, 3 million microforms, 100,000 current periodical subscriptions. Access provided to on-line information retrieval services. *Computer:* Campuswide network is available with full Internet access. Computer service fees are included with tuition and fees. *Special:* In science and engineering: Lawrence Berkeley Laboratory, Earthquake Engineering Research Center, Institute of Transportation Studies, agricultural experiment station, botanical garden, space sciences laboratory, laboratory of chemical biodynamics, cancer

research laboratory. In social sciences: Center for Research in Management.

COMPUTER SCIENCE

College of Engineering, Department of Electrical Engineering and Computer Sciences, Computer Science Division

Programs Awards MS, PhD.

Degrees Awarded In 1996, 33 master's, 16 doctorates awarded.

Entrance Requirements GRE General Test, GRE Subject Test, TOEFL, minimum GPA of 3.0.

Degree Requirements For master's, comprehensive exam or thesis; for doctorate, dissertation, qualifying exam required, foreign language not required.

Financial Aid Fellowships, research assistantships, teaching assistantships, scholarships available.

Applying *Deadline:* 1/5. *Fee:* $40.

Contact *Patrick Hernan*
Graduate Assistant for Admission
510-642-3068
Fax: 510-642-2845
E-mail: hernan@eecs.berkeley.edu

ELECTRICAL ENGINEERING

College of Engineering, Department of Electrical Engineering and Computer Sciences

Programs Offers programs in computer science (MS, PhD), electrical engineering (M Eng, MS, D Eng, PhD).

Students 468 full-time (76 women), includes 127 minority (17 African-Americans, 99 Asian-Americans, 10 Hispanics, 1 Native American), 131 international.

Degrees Awarded In 1996, 47 master's, 52 doctorates awarded.

Entrance Requirements GRE General Test, GRE Subject Test, TOEFL, minimum GPA of 3.0.

Degree Requirements For master's, comprehensive exam or thesis (MS); for doctorate, dissertation, qualifying exam required, foreign language not required.

Financial Aid Fellowships, research assistantships, teaching assistantships, scholarships available.

Applying 1,435 applicants, 16% accepted. *Deadline:* 1/5. *Fee:* $40.

Contact *Mary Byrnes*
Graduate Assistant for Admission
510-642-3694
Fax: 510-642-2845
E-mail: mkbyrnes@eecs.berkeley.edu

UNIVERSITY OF CALIFORNIA, DAVIS
Davis, CA 95616

OVERVIEW

University of California, Davis is a public coed university.

ENROLLMENT

23,931 graduate, professional, and undergraduate students; 5,112 matriculated graduate/professional students (2,331 women).

GRADUATE FACULTY

1,331 full-time, 267 part-time, 1,486 FTE; includes 178 minority (21 African-Americans, 109 Asian-Americans, 42 Hispanics, 6 Native Americans).

EXPENSES

Tuition $0 for state residents; $8984 per year for nonresidents. Fees $4498 per year.

HOUSING

Rooms and/or apartments available to single students (178 units) at an average cost of $6690 (including board); available to married students (476 units) at an average cost of $5800 per year. Housing application deadline: 4/1. Graduate housing contact: Student Housing Office, 916-752-2033.

STUDENT SERVICES

Disabled student services, multicultural affairs office, low-cost health insurance, career counseling, free psychological counseling, exercise/wellness program, day-care facilities, campus safety program, campus employment opportunities, international student services, writing training, grant writing training, teacher training.

FACILITIES

Library: Peter J. Shields Library plus 5 additional on-campus libraries; total holdings of 2.802 million volumes, 3.58 million microforms, 46,855 current periodical subscriptions. Access provided to on-line information retrieval services. *Computer:* Campuswide network is available with full Internet access. Total number of PCs/terminals supplied for student use: 300. Computer services are offered at no charge. *Special:* In arts and humanities: Carl N. Gorman Museum (Native American artists), Humanities Institute, Richard Nelson Gallery, Walker Design Gallery, Main Theatre and Wyatt Pavilion Theatre. In science and engineering: Primate Research Center; Bodega Marine Laboratory; Natural Reserve System; Arboretum; Institute for Transpotation Studies; Facilities for Advanced Instrumentation, Nuclear Magnetic Resonance, X-Ray Crystallography; Theoretical Dynamics Institute; John Muir Institute; Germplasm Repository; Laboratories for Food Intake, Health Sciences Research, Human Performance, Radio Astronomy, Veterinary Genetics; Tucker Herbarium; Institute of Toxicology and Environmental Health; Mann Laboratory; Sustainable Agriculture Experimental Farm; Centers for Geotechnical Modeling, Image Processing and Integrated Computing Research; Crocker Nuclear Laboratory; Geology Museum; Institute for Particle Accelerator Research. In social sciences: Center for Consumer Research; Institute of Governmental Affairs; Center for Comparative Research in History, Society and Culture; Institute on Global Conflict and Cooperation; Public Service Research Program; Child and Family Study Center; Washington Center.

COMPUTER ENGINEERING

College of Engineering, Program in Electrical and Computer Engineering

Programs Awards MS, PhD.

Faculty 33 full-time (2 women), 2 part-time (0 women).

Students 102 full-time (21 women), 8 part-time (0 women); includes 25 minority (2 African-Americans, 20 Asian-Americans, 3 Hispanics), 31 international.

Degrees Awarded In 1996, 30 master's, 8 doctorates awarded. Terminal master's awarded for partial completion of doctoral program.

Entrance Requirements For master's, GRE General Test, minimum GPA of 3.2; for doctorate, minimum graduate GPA of 3.5.

Degree Requirements For master's, thesis optional, foreign language not required; for doctorate, dissertation, preliminary and qualifying exams, thesis defense required, foreign language not required.

Financial Aid Fellowships, research assistantships, teaching assistantships, Federal Work-Study available. *Financial aid application deadline:* 3/1; applicants required to submit FAFSA.

Applying 346 applicants, 29% accepted. *Deadline:* 2/15. *Fee:* $40.

Contact *Anita Morales*
Graduate Staff Assistant
916-752-8251
E-mail: gradinfo@ucdavis.edu

COMPUTER SCIENCE

Program in Computer Science
Programs Awards MS, PhD.
Faculty 35 full-time (0 women), 8 part-time (1 woman).
Faculty Research Intrusion detection, malicious code detection, next generation light wave computer networks, biological algorithms, parallel processing.
Students 50 full-time (6 women), 1 part-time (0 women); includes 10 international.
Degrees Awarded In 1996, 15 master's, 8 doctorates awarded.
Entrance Requirements GRE General Test, GRE Subject Test, minimum GPA of 3.0.
Degree Requirements For master's, thesis optional, foreign language not required; for doctorate, dissertation required, foreign language not required.
Financial Aid Fellowships, research assistantships, teaching assistantships, readerships available.
Applying *Deadline:* 1/15 (priority date; rolling processing). *Fee:* $40.
Contact *Graduate Adviser*
916-752-7004
Fax: 916-752-4767
E-mail: gradinfo@cs.ucdavis.edu

See in-depth description on page 593.

ELECTRICAL ENGINEERING

College of Engineering, Program in Electrical and Computer Engineering
Programs Awards MS, PhD.
Faculty 33 full-time (2 women), 2 part-time (0 women).
Students 102 full-time (21 women), 8 part-time (0 women); includes 25 minority (2 African-Americans, 20 Asian-Americans, 3 Hispanics), 31 international.
Degrees Awarded In 1996, 30 master's, 8 doctorates awarded. Terminal master's awarded for partial completion of doctoral program.
Entrance Requirements For master's, GRE General Test, minimum GPA of 3.2; for doctorate, minimum graduate GPA of 3.5.
Degree Requirements For master's, thesis optional, foreign language not required; for doctorate, dissertation, preliminary and qualifying exams, thesis defense required, foreign language not required.
Financial Aid Fellowships, research assistantships, teaching assistantships, Federal Work-Study available. *Financial aid application deadline:* 3/1; applicants required to submit FAFSA.
Applying 346 applicants, 29% accepted. *Deadline:* 2/15. *Fee:* $40.
Contact *Anita Morales*
Graduate Staff Assistant
916-752-8251
E-mail: gradinfo@ucdavis.edu

UNIVERSITY OF CALIFORNIA, IRVINE
Irvine, CA 92697

OVERVIEW
University of California, Irvine is a public coed university.

ENROLLMENT
17,221 graduate, professional, and undergraduate students; 2,797 full-time matriculated graduate/professional students (1,107 women), 71 part-time matriculated graduate/professional students (24 women).

GRADUATE FACULTY
1,438 (421 women); includes 335 minority (33 African-Americans, 227 Asian-Americans, 72 Hispanics, 3 Native Americans).

EXPENSES
Tuition $0 for state residents; $8984 per year full-time, $1497 per quarter part-time for nonresidents. Fees $4845 per year full-time, $1101 per quarter part-time.

HOUSING
Rooms and/or apartments available to single students (263 units) and married students (862 units). Graduate housing contact: Housing Office, 714-824-6811.

STUDENT SERVICES
Disabled student services, multicultural affairs office, low-cost health insurance, career counseling, free psychological counseling, exercise/wellness program, day-care facilities, campus safety program, campus employment opportunities, international student services, writing training, grant writing training, teacher training.

FACILITIES
Library: Main library plus 2 additional on-campus libraries; total holdings of 1.5 million volumes, 2,143,825 microforms, 17,500 current periodical subscriptions. A total of 178 personal computers in all libraries. Access provided to on-line information retrieval services. *Computer:* Campuswide network is available with full Internet access. Total number of PCs/terminals supplied for student use: 100. Computer service fees are included with tuition and fees. *Special:* In arts and humanities: *Thesaurus Linguae Graecae* Project, Humanities Research Institute, Critical Theory Institute. In science and engineering: Developmental Biology Center, Institute of Transportation Studies, Institute for Surface and Interface Science, Cancer Research Institute, Institute for Brain Aging and Dementia. In social sciences: Mathematical Behavioral Sciences Research Institute, Center for Research on Information Technology and Organizations.

COMPUTER ENGINEERING

School of Engineering, Department of Electrical and Computer Engineering
Programs Awards MS, PhD. Part-time programs available.
Faculty 19 full-time (1 woman), 1 part-time (0 women).
Faculty Research Optical and solid-state devices, systems and signal processing.
Students 99 full-time (14 women), 28 part-time (9 women); includes 46 minority (1 African-American, 45 Asian-Americans), 47 international.
Degrees Awarded In 1996, 38 master's, 11 doctorates awarded. Terminal master's awarded for partial completion of doctoral program.

Entrance Requirements For master's, GRE General Test, minimum GPA of 3.0; for doctorate, GRE General Test.
Degree Requirements For doctorate, dissertation required, foreign language not required.
Financial Aid Fellowships, research assistantships, teaching assistantships, full and partial tuition waivers, institutionally sponsored loans available. *Financial aid application deadline:* 3/2; applicants required to submit FAFSA.
Applying 197 applicants, 36% accepted. *Deadline:* 1/15 (priority date; rolling processing). *Fee:* $40.
Contact *Linda Le*
Graduate Admissions Coordinator
714-824-5489
Fax: 714-824-4152
E-mail: ttle@uci.edu

See in-depth description on page **595.**

COMPUTER SCIENCE

Department of Information and Computer Science
Programs Awards PhD.
Faculty 27 full-time (3 women).
Faculty Research Artificial intelligence, computer system design, software, biomedical computing, theory, computing policy and society.
Students 111 full-time (26 women), 1 part-time (0 women); includes 24 minority (20 Asian-Americans, 3 Hispanics, 1 Native American), 31 international. Average age 32.
Degrees Awarded In 1996, 8 master's, 14 doctorates awarded. Terminal master's awarded for partial completion of doctoral program.
Entrance Requirements For doctorate, GRE General Test, GRE Subject Test.
Degree Requirements For doctorate, dissertation required, foreign language not required.
Financial Aid Fellowships, research assistantships, teaching assistantships, full and partial tuition waivers, institutionally sponsored loans available. *Financial aid application deadline:* 3/2; applicants required to submit FAFSA.
Applying 205 applicants, 25% accepted. *Deadline:* 1/15 (priority date; rolling processing). *Fee:* $40.
Contact *Theresa Klonecky*
714-824-2277

See in-depth description on page **597.**

ELECTRICAL ENGINEERING

School of Engineering, Department of Electrical and Computer Engineering
Programs Awards MS, PhD. Part-time programs available.
Faculty 19 full-time (1 woman), 1 part-time (0 women).
Faculty Research Optical and solid-state devices, systems and signal processing.
Students 99 full-time (14 women), 28 part-time (9 women); includes 46 minority (1 African-American, 45 Asian-Americans), 47 international.
Degrees Awarded In 1996, 38 master's, 11 doctorates awarded. Terminal master's awarded for partial completion of doctoral program.
Entrance Requirements For master's, GRE General Test, minimum GPA of 3.0; for doctorate, GRE General Test.
Degree Requirements For doctorate, dissertation required, foreign language not required.
Financial Aid Fellowships, research assistantships, teaching assistantships, full and partial tuition waivers, institutionally sponsored loans available. *Financial aid application deadline:* 3/2; applicants required to submit FAFSA.

Applying 197 applicants, 36% accepted. *Deadline:* 1/15 (priority date; rolling processing). *Fee:* $40.
Contact *Linda Le*
Graduate Admissions Coordinator
714-824-5489
Fax: 714-824-4152
E-mail: ttle@uci.edu

See in-depth description on page **595.**

INFORMATION SCIENCE

Department of Information and Computer Science
Programs Awards PhD.
Faculty 27 full-time (3 women).
Faculty Research Artificial intelligence, computer system design, software, biomedical computing, theory, computing policy and society.
Students 111 full-time (26 women), 1 part-time (0 women); includes 24 minority (20 Asian-Americans, 3 Hispanics, 1 Native American), 31 international. Average age 32.
Degrees Awarded In 1996, 8 master's, 14 doctorates awarded. Terminal master's awarded for partial completion of doctoral program.
Entrance Requirements For doctorate, GRE General Test, GRE Subject Test.
Degree Requirements For doctorate, dissertation required, foreign language not required.
Financial Aid Fellowships, research assistantships, teaching assistantships, full and partial tuition waivers, institutionally sponsored loans available. *Financial aid application deadline:* 3/2; applicants required to submit FAFSA.
Applying 205 applicants, 25% accepted. *Deadline:* 1/15 (priority date; rolling processing). *Fee:* $40.
Contact *Theresa Klonecky*
714-824-2277

See in-depth description on page **597.**

UNIVERSITY OF CALIFORNIA, LOS ANGELES
Los Angeles, CA 90095

OVERVIEW
University of California, Los Angeles is a public coed university.

ENROLLMENT
32,625 graduate, professional, and undergraduate students; 9,717 matriculated graduate/professional students (4,613 women).

GRADUATE FACULTY
1,906 (385 women); includes 286 minority (50 African-Americans, 162 Asian-Americans, 70 Hispanics, 4 Native Americans).

EXPENSES
Tuition $0 for state residents; $8982 per year for nonresidents. Fees $4496 per year.

HOUSING
Rooms and/or apartments available to single students (334 units) at an average cost of $5602 (including board); available to married students (977 units). Housing application deadline: 5/15. Graduate housing contact: Maria Marshall, 310-825-4271.

STUDENT SERVICES

Disabled student services, multicultural affairs office, low-cost health insurance, career counseling, free psychological counseling, day-care facilities, campus safety program, campus employment opportunities, international student services.

FACILITIES

Library: University Research Library plus 13 additional on-campus libraries; total holdings of 6,247,320 volumes, 6,377,470 microforms, 94,156 current periodical subscriptions. *Computer:* Campuswide network is available with full Internet access. Computer service fees are included with tuition and fees. *Special:* In science and engineering: Institute of Geophysics and Planetary Physics, Molecular Biology Institute, Brain Research Institute, biomedical and environmental sciences laboratory, Crump Institute of Medical Engineering, Dental Research Institute, Mental Retardation Research Center.

COMPUTER SCIENCE

School of Engineering and Applied Science, Department of Computer Science

Programs   Awards MS, PhD, Engr, MBA/MS.

Faculty   22 full-time (2 women), 12 part-time (0 women).

Students   231 full-time (20 women), includes 78 minority (5 African-Americans, 69 Asian-Americans, 3 Hispanics, 1 Native American), 74 international.

Degrees Awarded   In 1996, 39 master's, 16 doctorates, 1 Engr awarded.

Entrance Requirements   For master's, GRE General Test, GRE Subject Test, minimum GPA of 3.0; for doctorate, GRE General Test, GRE Subject Test, minimum GPA of 3.25.

Degree Requirements   For master's, comprehensive exam or thesis required, foreign language not required; for doctorate, dissertation, qualifying exams required, foreign language not required.

Financial Aid   Fellowships, research assistantships, teaching assistantships, full and partial tuition waivers, Federal Work-Study, institutionally sponsored loans available. *Financial aid application deadline:* 1/15; applicants required to submit FAFSA.

Applying   407 applicants, 45% accepted. *Deadline:* 1/15 (8/15 for spring admission). *Fee:* $40.

Contact   *Verra Morgan*
Student Affairs Officer
310-825-6830
Fax: 310-UCLA-CSD
E-mail: verra@es.ucla.edu

ELECTRICAL ENGINEERING

School of Engineering and Applied Science, Department of Electrical Engineering

Programs   Offers programs in electrical engineering (MS, PhD, Engr), operations research (MS, PhD).

Faculty   40 full-time (2 women), 18 part-time (0 women).

Students   301 full-time (32 women), includes 122 minority (3 African-Americans, 107 Asian-Americans, 11 Hispanics, 1 Native American), 95 international.

Degrees Awarded   In 1996, 49 master's, 37 doctorates, 4 Engrs awarded.

Entrance Requirements   For master's, GRE General Test, minimum GPA of 3.0; for doctorate, GRE General Test, minimum GPA of 3.25.

Degree Requirements   For master's, comprehensive exam or thesis required, foreign language not required; for doctorate, dissertation, qualifying exams required, foreign language not required.

Financial Aid   Fellowships, research assistantships, teaching assistantships, full and partial tuition waivers, Federal Work-Study, institutionally sponsored loans, and career-related internships or fieldwork available. *Financial aid application deadline:* 1/15; applicants required to submit FAFSA.

Applying   754 applicants, 35% accepted. *Deadline:* 1/15. *Fee:* $40.

Contact   *Maida Bassili*
Student Affairs Officer
310-825-9383
E-mail: mbassili@ea.ucla.edu

See in-depth description on page **599.**

UNIVERSITY OF CALIFORNIA, RIVERSIDE
Riverside, CA 92521-0102

OVERVIEW

University of California, Riverside is a public coed university.

ENROLLMENT

9,056 graduate, professional, and undergraduate students; 1,198 full-time matriculated graduate/professional students (541 women), 35 part-time matriculated graduate/professional students (11 women).

GRADUATE FACULTY

456 full-time (115 women); includes 97 minority (11 African-Americans, 58 Asian-Americans, 26 Hispanics, 2 Native Americans).

EXPENSES

Tuition $0 for state residents; $8988 per year for nonresidents. Fees $4872 per year.

HOUSING

Rooms and/or apartments available to single students at an average cost of $5750 (including board); available to married students (268 units) at an average cost of $4800 per year. Housing application deadline: 6/1. Graduate housing contact: Pat Newman, 909-787-5723.

STUDENT SERVICES

Low-cost health insurance, career counseling, free psychological counseling, day-care facilities, international student services.

FACILITIES

Library: Tomas Rivera Library plus 4 additional on-campus libraries; total holdings of 1,717,626 volumes, 1,481,372 microforms, 13,296 current periodical subscriptions. Access provided to on-line information retrieval services. *Computer:* Campuswide network is available with full Internet access. Computer services are offered at no charge. *Special:* In arts and humanities: California Museum of Photography, Center for Ideas and Society, J. Lloyd Eaton Collection of Science Fiction. In science and engineering: 8 natural reserves, biotechnology instrumentation facility, Institute of Geophysics and Planetary Physics, computer graphics and visual imaging laboratory, radiocarbon dating laboratory, Statewide Air Pollution Research Center, U.C. Mexus. In social sciences: Archaeological research laboratory, Center for Bibliographic Studies, Center for Social and Behavioral Science Research, laboratory for historical research.

COMPUTER SCIENCE

Graduate Division, College of Engineering, Department of Computer Science

Programs Awards MS, PhD. Part-time programs available.
Faculty 8 full-time (0 women).
Faculty Research Compiler construction, operating systems, theory of computation, computer architecture, computer networks, design automation.
Students 43 full-time (7 women), includes 4 minority (all Asian-Americans), 22 international. Average age 27.
Degrees Awarded In 1996, 10 master's awarded.
Entrance Requirements GRE General Test (minimum combined score of 1100), TOEFL (minimum score 550).
Degree Requirements For master's, comprehensive exams required, foreign language and thesis not required; for doctorate, dissertation, qualifying exams required, foreign language not required.
Financial Aid Fellowships, research assistantships, teaching assistantships, full and partial tuition waivers, Federal Work-Study, institutionally sponsored loans, and career-related internships or fieldwork available. *Financial aid application deadline:* 2/1; applicants required to submit FAFSA.
Applying 142 applicants, 38% accepted. *Deadline:* 5/1 (rolling processing; 12/1 for spring admission). *Fee:* $40.
Contact *Graduate Student Affairs*
909-787-5639
Fax: 909-787-4643
E-mail: gradadmissions@cs.ucr.edu

See in-depth description on page 601.

See in-depth description on page 601.

UNIVERSITY OF CALIFORNIA, SAN DIEGO
La Jolla, CA 92093-5003

OVERVIEW
University of California, San Diego is a public coed university.

ENROLLMENT
18,119 graduate, professional, and undergraduate students; 2,960 matriculated graduate/professional students (1,137 women).

GRADUATE FACULTY
1,800.

EXPENSES
Tuition $0 for state residents; $8984 per year full-time, $4492 per year part-time for nonresidents. Fees $4851 per year full-time, $3308 per year part-time.

HOUSING
Rooms and/or apartments available to single and married students. Graduate housing contact: Jana Black, 619-534-2952.

STUDENT SERVICES
Low-cost health insurance, career counseling, free psychological counseling, day-care facilities, campus safety program, campus employment opportunities, international student services.

FACILITIES
Library: Geisel Library plus 11 additional on-campus libraries; total holdings of 2.37 million volumes, 2.5 million microforms, 23,906 current periodical subscriptions. A total of 450 personal computers in all libraries. Access provided to on-line information retrieval services. *Computer:* Campuswide network is available with full Internet access. *Special:* In arts and humanities: Center for Music Experiments, Center for Research in Language. In science and engineering: California Space Institute, Institute for Geophysics and Planetary Physics, Institute of Marine Resources, Institute for Cognitive Sciences, Institute for Pure and Applied Physical Sciences, Cancer Center, Center for Astrophysics and Space Sciences, Center for Developmental Biology, Energy Center, San Diego Super Computer Center, Center for Magnetic Recording Research. In social sciences: Center for Human Information Processing, Center for Iberian and Latin American Studies, Center for United States–Mexican Studies.

ARTIFICIAL INTELLIGENCE/ROBOTICS

Department of Electrical and Computer Engineering
Programs Offerings include intelligent systems, robotics and control (MS, PhD).
Department Faculty 35.
Entrance Requirements GRE General Test.
Applying *Fee:* $40.
Contact *Graduate Coordinator*
619-534-6606

See in-depth description on page 605.

See in-depth description on page 605.

COMPUTER ENGINEERING

Department of Computer Science and Engineering
Programs Offers programs in computer engineering (MS, PhD), computer science (MS, PhD).
Faculty 18.
Faculty Research Analysis of algorithms, combinatorial algorithms, discrete optimization.
Students 116 (21 women); includes 26 international.
Degrees Awarded In 1996, 23 master's, 6 doctorates awarded.
Entrance Requirements GRE General Test.
Degree Requirements For doctorate, variable foreign language requirement, dissertation.
Applying 329 applicants, 32% accepted. *Deadline:* 1/15. *Fee:* $40.
Contact *Graduate Coordinator*
619-534-6005

See in-depth description on page 603.

See in-depth description on page 603.

COMPUTER ENGINEERING

Department of Electrical and Computer Engineering
Programs Offers programs in applied ocean science (MS, PhD); applied physics (MS, PhD); communication theory and systems (MS, PhD); computer engineering (MS, PhD); electrical engineering (MS, PhD); electronic circuits and systems (MS, PhD); intelligent systems, robotics and control (MS, PhD); photonics (MS, PhD); signal and image processing (MS, PhD).
Faculty 35.
Students 174 (13 women); includes 37 international.
Degrees Awarded In 1996, 33 master's, 21 doctorates awarded.
Entrance Requirements GRE General Test.
Applying 329 applicants, 34% accepted. *Fee:* $40.

Contact *Graduate Coordinator*
619-534-6606

See in-depth description on page 605.

COMPUTER ENGINEERING

Interdisciplinary Program in Cognitive Science
Programs Offerings include cognitive science/computer science and engineering (PhD). Offered in cooperation with the Departments of Anthropology, Communication, Computer Science and Engineering, Linguistics, Neurosciences, Philosophy, Psychology, and Sociology; admissions through affiliated departments.
Program Faculty 56 full-time (10 women).
Entrance Requirements GRE General Test.
Degree Requirements Dissertation.
Applying *Deadline:* rolling. *Fee:* $40.
Contact *Gris Arellano-Ramirez*
Graduate Coordinator
619-534-7141
Fax: 619-534-1128
E-mail: gradinfo@cogsci.ucsd.edu

COMPUTER SCIENCE

Department of Computer Science and Engineering
Programs Offers programs in computer engineering (MS, PhD), computer science (MS, PhD).
Faculty 18.
Faculty Research Analysis of algorithms, combinatorial algorithms, discrete optimization.
Students 116 (21 women); includes 26 international.
Degrees Awarded In 1996, 23 master's, 6 doctorates awarded.
Entrance Requirements GRE General Test.
Degree Requirements For doctorate, variable foreign language requirement, dissertation.
Applying 329 applicants, 32% accepted. *Deadline:* 1/15. *Fee:* $40.
Contact *Graduate Coordinator*
619-534-6005

See in-depth description on page 603.

COMPUTER SCIENCE

Interdisciplinary Program in Cognitive Science
Programs Offerings include cognitive science/computer science and engineering (PhD). Offered in cooperation with the Departments of Anthropology, Communication, Computer Science and Engineering, Linguistics, Neurosciences, Philosophy, Psychology, and Sociology; admissions through affiliated departments.
Program Faculty 56 full-time (10 women).
Entrance Requirements GRE General Test.
Degree Requirements Dissertation.
Applying *Deadline:* rolling. *Fee:* $40.
Contact *Gris Arellano-Ramirez*
Graduate Coordinator
619-534-7141
Fax: 619-534-1128
E-mail: gradinfo@cogsci.ucsd.edu

ELECTRICAL ENGINEERING

Department of Electrical and Computer Engineering
Programs Offers programs in applied ocean science (MS, PhD); applied physics (MS, PhD); communication theory and systems (MS, PhD); computer engineering (MS, PhD); electrical engineering (MS, PhD); electronic circuits and systems (MS, PhD); intelligent systems, robotics and control (MS, PhD); photonics (MS, PhD); signal and image processing (MS, PhD).

Faculty 35.
Students 174 (13 women); includes 37 international.
Degrees Awarded In 1996, 33 master's, 21 doctorates awarded.
Entrance Requirements GRE General Test.
Applying 329 applicants, 34% accepted. *Fee:* $40.
Contact *Graduate Coordinator*
619-534-6606

See in-depth description on page 605.

UNIVERSITY OF CALIFORNIA, SANTA BARBARA
Santa Barbara, CA 93106

OVERVIEW
University of California, Santa Barbara is a public coed university.

ENROLLMENT
18,531 graduate, professional, and undergraduate students; 2,250 full-time matriculated graduate/professional students (938 women), 0 part-time matriculated graduate/professional students.

GRADUATE FACULTY
684 full-time, 165 part-time.

EXPENSES
Tuition $0 for state residents; $8985 per year for nonresidents. Fees $4886 per year.

HOUSING
Rooms and/or apartments available to single students (383 units) and married students (592 units) at an average cost of $6960 per year. Graduate housing contact: Housing and Residential Services Office, 805-893-2760.

STUDENT SERVICES
Low-cost health insurance, career counseling, free psychological counseling, day-care facilities, campus safety program, campus employment opportunities, international student services.

FACILITIES
Library: Davidson Library; total holdings of 2.2 million volumes, 24,325 current periodical subscriptions. Access provided to on-line information retrieval services. *Computer:* Campuswide network is available with full Internet access. Computer services are offered at no charge. *Special:* In arts and humanities: Interdisciplinary Humanities Center. In science and engineering: Alegbra Institute, Institute for Polymers and Organic Solids, Marine Science Institute, Quantum Institute, Institute for Crystal Studies, Neuroscience Research Institute, seawater laboratories. In social sciences: Community Organization Research Institute, Center for Chicano Studies, Center for Black Studies.

COMPUTER ENGINEERING

College of Engineering, Department of Electrical and Computer Engineering
Programs Awards MS, PhD.
Faculty Research Solid-state device theory, physics of solid-state materials, computer architecture.

Students 194 full-time (33 women), includes 22 minority (1 African-American, 17 Asian-Americans, 3 Hispanics, 1 Native American), 101 international.

Degrees Awarded In 1996, 58 master's, 27 doctorates awarded.

Entrance Requirements GRE General Test, TOEFL (minimum score 560).

Degree Requirements For master's, thesis or alternative required, foreign language not required; for doctorate, dissertation required, foreign language not required.

Financial Aid Fellowships, research assistantships, teaching assistantships, full and partial tuition waivers, Federal Work-Study, institutionally sponsored loans, and career-related internships or fieldwork available. *Financial aid application deadline:* 1/15; applicants required to submit FAFSA.

Applying 338 applicants, 58% accepted. *Deadline:* 1/15. *Fee:* $40.

Contact *Linda James*
Graduate Secretary
805-893-3114
E-mail: james@ece.ucsb.edu

See in-depth description on page **609.**

COMPUTER SCIENCE

College of Engineering, Department of Computer Science

Programs Awards MS, PhD.

Students 98 full-time (16 women), includes 12 minority (11 Asian-Americans, 1 Hispanic), 57 international.

Degrees Awarded In 1996, 16 master's, 2 doctorates awarded.

Entrance Requirements GRE, TOEFL (minimum score 600).

Degree Requirements For master's, thesis or alternative required, foreign language not required; for doctorate, dissertation required, foreign language not required.

Financial Aid Fellowships, research assistantships, teaching assistantships, full and partial tuition waivers, Federal Work-Study, institutionally sponsored loans, and career-related internships or fieldwork available. *Financial aid application deadline:* 1/15; applicants required to submit FAFSA.

Applying 335 applicants, 63% accepted. *Deadline:* 5/1. *Fee:* $40.

Contact *Louise Sciutto*
Graduate Secretary
805-893-4323
E-mail: gradadvisor@cs.ucsb.edu

See in-depth description on page **607.**

ELECTRICAL ENGINEERING

College of Engineering, Department of Electrical and Computer Engineering

Programs Awards MS, PhD.

Faculty Research Solid-state device theory, physics of solid-state materials, computer architecture.

Students 194 full-time (33 women), includes 22 minority (1 African-American, 17 Asian-Americans, 3 Hispanics, 1 Native American), 101 international.

Degrees Awarded In 1996, 58 master's, 27 doctorates awarded.

Entrance Requirements GRE General Test, TOEFL (minimum score 560).

Degree Requirements For master's, thesis or alternative required, foreign language not required; for doctorate, dissertation required, foreign language not required.

Financial Aid Fellowships, research assistantships, teaching assistantships, full and partial tuition waivers, Federal Work-Study, institutionally sponsored loans, and career-related internships or fieldwork available. *Financial aid application deadline:* 1/15; applicants required to submit FAFSA.

Applying 338 applicants, 58% accepted. *Deadline:* 1/15. *Fee:* $40.

Contact *Linda James*
Graduate Secretary
805-893-3114
E-mail: james@ece.ucsb.edu

See in-depth description on page **609.**

UNIVERSITY OF CALIFORNIA, SANTA CRUZ
Santa Cruz, CA 95064

OVERVIEW
University of California, Santa Cruz is a public coed university.

ENROLLMENT
10,117 graduate, professional, and undergraduate students; 1,056 full-time matriculated graduate/professional students (518 women), 0 part-time matriculated graduate/professional students.

GRADUATE FACULTY
499 full-time.

EXPENSES
Tuition $0 for state residents; $8982 per year for nonresidents. Fees $4950 per year.

HOUSING
Rooms and/or apartments available to single students (80 units) at an average cost of $7398 (including board); available to married students (199 units).

STUDENT SERVICES
Low-cost health insurance, career counseling, free psychological counseling, day-care facilities, campus employment opportunities, international student services.

FACILITIES
Library: McHenry Library plus 2 additional on-campus libraries; total holdings of 1,007,969 volumes, 610,740 microforms, 9,106 current periodical subscriptions. Access provided to on-line information retrieval services. *Special:* In arts and humanities: Syntax Research Center, Baskin Art Center, feminist studies research group, bilingual studies research group. In science and engineering: Center for Non-Linear Science, Tectonics Institute, Lick Observatory, Long Marine Laboratory, Santa Cruz Institute for Particle Physics, Landels-Hill Big Creek Reserve, arboretum. In social sciences: Third World Teaching Resource Center, Stevenson Nuclear Policy Group, Social Policy Research Group, Lesbian and Gay Center for Cultural Studies.

COMPUTER ENGINEERING

Division of Natural Sciences, Program in Computer Engineering

Programs Awards MS, PhD.

Faculty 8 full-time.

Faculty Research Computer-aided design of digital systems.

Students 70 full-time (9 women), includes 15 minority (12 Asian-Americans, 3 Hispanics), 22 international.

Degrees Awarded In 1996, 19 master's, 8 doctorates awarded. Terminal master's awarded for partial completion of doctoral program.

Entrance Requirements GRE General Test, GRE Subject Test.

Degree Requirements For doctorate, 1 foreign language, dissertation, comprehensive and oral exams.

Financial Aid Fellowships, research assistantships, teaching assistantships, Federal Work-Study, institutionally sponsored loans, and career-related internships or fieldwork available. *Financial aid application deadline: 2/1.*

Applying 60 applicants, 73% accepted. *Deadline: 2/1. Fee: $40.*

Contact *Graduate Admissions*
408-459-2301

See in-depth description on page 611.

COMPUTER SCIENCE

Division of Natural Sciences, Department of Computer Science
Programs Awards MS, PhD.
Faculty 12 full-time.
Faculty Research Algorithm analysis, artificial intelligence, computer graphics, information and communication theory, problem-solving techniques.
Students 61 full-time (14 women), includes 13 minority (3 African-Americans, 6 Asian-Americans, 3 Hispanics, 1 Native American), 11 international.
Degrees Awarded In 1996, 11 master's, 2 doctorates awarded.
Entrance Requirements GRE General Test, GRE Subject Test.
Degree Requirements For master's, thesis; for doctorate, 1 foreign language, dissertation, qualifying exam.
Financial Aid Fellowships, research assistantships, teaching assistantships, Federal Work-Study, institutionally sponsored loans available. *Financial aid application deadline: 2/1.*
Applying 104 applicants, 38% accepted. *Deadline: 2/1. Fee: $40.*
Contact *Graduate Admissions*
408-459-2301

See in-depth description on page 613.

UNIVERSITY OF SAN FRANCISCO
San Francisco, CA 94117-1080

OVERVIEW
University of San Francisco is an independent-religious coed university.

ENROLLMENT
7,510 graduate, professional, and undergraduate students; 2,235 full-time matriculated graduate/professional students (1,307 women), 745 part-time matriculated graduate/professional students (422 women).

GRADUATE FACULTY
165 full-time (52 women), 313 part-time (114 women); includes 67 minority (24 African-Americans, 24 Asian-Americans, 19 Hispanics).

TUITION
$627 per unit (minimum).

HOUSING
Rooms and/or apartments available to single students at an average cost of $4396 per year ($6868 including board); on-campus housing not available to married students. Graduate housing contact: Gary Maslowski, 415-422-6824.

STUDENT SERVICES
Low-cost health insurance, career counseling, free psychological counseling, campus employment opportunities, international student services.

FACILITIES
Library: Gleeson Library plus 2 additional on-campus libraries; total holdings of 757,000 volumes, 788,000 microforms, 2,711 current periodical subscriptions. A total of 60 personal computers in all libraries. Access provided to on-line information retrieval services. *Computer:* Campuswide network is available with full Internet access. Total number of PCs/terminals supplied for student use: 300. *Special:* In science and engineering: Institute for Chemical Biology, radiation laboratory.

COMPUTER SCIENCE

College of Arts and Sciences, Department of Computer Science
Programs Awards MS. Part-time programs available.
Faculty 4 full-time (0 women), 2 part-time (0 women).
Faculty Research Software engineering, computer graphics, computer networks.
Students 20 full-time (6 women), 5 part-time (3 women); includes 3 minority (all Asian-Americans), 21 international. Average age 27.
Degrees Awarded In 1996, 4 degrees awarded.
Entrance Requirements GRE General Test, GRE Subject Test, TOEFL, BS in computer science or related field.
Degree Requirements Computer language required, thesis optional, foreign language not required.
Financial Aid 11 students received aid; fellowships, teaching assistantships, Federal Work-Study, and career-related internships or fieldwork available. *Financial aid application deadline: 3/2.*
Applying 61 applicants, 75% accepted. *Deadline: 7/1 (priority date; rolling processing; 12/1 for spring admission). Fee: $40 ($50 for international students).*
Contact *Dr. Benjamin Wells*
Graduate Adviser
415-422-6530
E-mail: wells@usfca.edu

UNIVERSITY OF SOUTHERN CALIFORNIA
Los Angeles, CA 90089

OVERVIEW
University of Southern California is an independent coed university.

ENROLLMENT
28,081 graduate, professional, and undergraduate students; 10,217 full-time matriculated graduate/professional students (4,746 women), 4,490 part-time matriculated graduate/professional students (1,826 women).

GRADUATE FACULTY
2,331 full-time (644 women); includes 430 minority (57 African-Americans, 302 Asian-Americans, 71 Hispanics).

TUITION
$16,224 per year full-time, $676 per unit part-time.

HOUSING
Rooms and/or apartments available to single students (700 units) at an average cost of $3600 per year; available to married students (80 units) at an average cost of $8900 per year. Graduate housing contact: Housing Department, 800-872-4632.

STUDENT SERVICES

Disabled student services, low-cost health insurance, career counseling, free psychological counseling, exercise/wellness program, day-care facilities, campus safety program, campus employment opportunities, international student services.

FACILITIES

Library: Doheny Memorial Library plus 19 additional on-campus libraries; total holdings of 3.1 million volumes, 3.9 million microforms, 38,000 current periodical subscriptions. A total of 334 personal computers in all libraries. Access provided to on-line information retrieval services. *Computer:* Campuswide network is available with full Internet access. Total number of PCs/terminals supplied for student use: 7,200. Computer services are offered at no charge. *Special:* In arts and humanities: East Asian Studies Center, Max Kade Institute. In science and engineering: Institute for Genetic Medicine, USC/Norris Comprehensive Cancer Center, Institute for Toxicology, Center for Craniofacial Molecular Biology, Center for Laser Studies, Center for the Management of Engineering Research and Technology, Center for Neural Engineering, Institute for Robotics and Intelligent Systems, Signal and Image Processing Institute, Center for Applied Mathematical Sciences, Center for Earth Sciences, Center for Space Sciences, Loker Hydrocarbon Research Institute, Southern California Earthquake Center, Atherosclerosis Research Institute, Center for Software Engineering. In social sciences: Center for Feminist Research, Social Science Research Institute, Center for Multiethnic and Transnational Studies.

ARTIFICIAL INTELLIGENCE/ROBOTICS

Graduate School, School of Engineering, Department of Computer Science, Program in Robotics and Automation
Programs Awards MS.
Students 2 full-time (0 women), 2 part-time (0 women); includes 1 minority (Asian-American). Average age 29.
Degrees Awarded In 1996, 1 degree awarded.
Entrance Requirements GRE General Test.
Financial Aid In 1996–97, 1 research assistantship, 1 scholarship were awarded; fellowships, teaching assistantships, Federal Work-Study, institutionally sponsored loans also available. Aid available to part-time students. *Financial aid application deadline:* 2/15; applicants required to submit FAFSA.
Applying 15 applicants, 67% accepted. *Deadline:* 6/1 (priority date; rolling processing; 10/1 for spring admission). *Fee:* $55.
Contact *Dr. Ellis Horowitz*
Chairman
213-740-4494

COMPUTER ENGINEERING

Graduate School, School of Engineering, Department of Electrical Engineering, Program in Computer Engineering
Programs Awards MS, PhD.
Students 85 full-time (13 women), 86 part-time (6 women); includes 27 minority (1 African-American, 24 Asian-Americans, 2 Hispanics), 126 international. Average age 29.
Degrees Awarded In 1996, 62 master's, 9 doctorates awarded.
Entrance Requirements GRE General Test.
Degree Requirements For master's, thesis optional; for doctorate, dissertation.
Financial Aid In 1996–97, 12 fellowships, 52 research assistantships, 20 teaching assistantships, 11 scholarships were awarded;

Federal Work-Study, institutionally sponsored loans also available. Aid available to part-time students. *Financial aid application deadline:* 2/15; applicants required to submit FAFSA.
Applying 141 applicants, 76% accepted. *Deadline:* 6/1 (priority date; 9/1 for spring admission). *Fee:* $55.
Contact *Dr. Victor Prasanna*
Director

See in-depth description on page **713.**

COMPUTER ENGINEERING

Departments of Electrical Engineering and Computer Science, Program in Computer Networks
Programs Awards MS.
Students 10 full-time (1 woman), 10 part-time (0 women); includes 4 minority (3 Asian-Americans, 1 Hispanic), 12 international. Average age 29.
Degrees Awarded In 1996, 7 degrees awarded.
Entrance Requirements GRE General Test.
Degree Requirements Thesis optional.
Financial Aid In 1996–97, 1 research assistantship was awarded; fellowships, teaching assistantships, Federal Work-Study, institutionally sponsored loans also available. Aid available to part-time students. *Financial aid application deadline:* 2/15; applicants required to submit FAFSA.
Applying 42 applicants, 67% accepted. *Deadline:* 6/1 (priority date; 10/1 for spring admission). *Fee:* $55.
Contact *John Sylvester*
Director

See in-depth description on page **713.**

COMPUTER SCIENCE

Graduate School, School of Engineering, Department of Computer Science, Program in Computer Science
Programs Awards MS, PhD.
Students 177 full-time (34 women), 112 part-time (17 women); includes 42 minority (1 African-American, 38 Asian-Americans, 3 Hispanics), 200 international. Average age 29.
Degrees Awarded In 1996, 97 master's, 22 doctorates awarded.
Entrance Requirements GRE General Test.
Degree Requirements For doctorate, dissertation.
Financial Aid In 1996–97, 12 fellowships, 124 research assistantships, 30 teaching assistantships, 7 scholarships were awarded; Federal Work-Study, institutionally sponsored loans also available. Aid available to part-time students. *Financial aid application deadline:* 2/15; applicants required to submit FAFSA.
Applying 611 applicants, 62% accepted. *Deadline:* 6/1 (priority date; rolling processing; 10/1 for spring admission). *Fee:* $55.
Contact *Dr. Ellis Horowitz*
Chairman
213-740-4494

See in-depth description on page **711.**

ELECTRICAL ENGINEERING

Graduate School, School of Engineering, Department of Electrical Engineering, Program in Electrical Engineering
Programs Awards MS, PhD, Engr.
Students 298 full-time (23 women), 396 part-time (52 women); includes 140 minority (13 African-Americans, 107 Asian-Americans, 19 Hispanics, 1 Native American), 397 international. Average age 31.
Degrees Awarded In 1996, 227 master's, 50 doctorates awarded.
Entrance Requirements GRE General Test.
Degree Requirements For master's, thesis optional; for doctorate, dissertation.

Financial Aid In 1996–97, 37 fellowships, 170 research assistantships, 52 teaching assistantships, 6 scholarships were awarded; Federal Work-Study, institutionally sponsored loans also available. Aid available to part-time students. *Financial aid application deadline:* 2/15; applicants required to submit FAFSA.

Applying 1,069 applicants, 67% accepted. *Deadline:* 2/1 (priority date; 9/1 for spring admission). *Fee:* $55.

Contact *Robert Shultz*
Chair
213-740-4446

See in-depth description on page **713.**

SOFTWARE ENGINEERING

Graduate School, School of Engineering, Department of Computer Science, Program in Software Engineering
Programs Awards MS.
Students 8 full-time (2 women), 18 part-time (5 women); includes 9 minority (1 African-American, 8 Asian-Americans), 12 international. Average age 29.
Degrees Awarded In 1996, 8 degrees awarded.
Entrance Requirements GRE General Test.
Financial Aid In 1996–97, 2 research assistantships, 1 scholarship were awarded; fellowships, teaching assistantships, Federal Work-Study, institutionally sponsored loans also available. Aid available to part-time students. *Financial aid application deadline:* 2/15; applicants required to submit FAFSA.
Applying 58 applicants, 69% accepted. *Deadline:* 6/1 (priority date; rolling processing; 10/1 for spring admission). *Fee:* $55.
Contact *Dr. Ellis Horowitz*
Chairman
213-740-4494

COLORADO

COLORADO SCHOOL OF MINES
Golden, CO 80401-1887

OVERVIEW
Colorado School of Mines is a public coed university.

ENROLLMENT
2,943 graduate, professional, and undergraduate students; 538 full-time matriculated graduate/professional students (110 women), 241 part-time matriculated graduate/professional students (39 women).

GRADUATE FACULTY
83 full-time (10 women), 18 part-time (1 woman), 88.96 FTE; includes 6 minority (4 Asian-Americans, 2 Hispanics).

EXPENSES
Tuition $4468 per year full-time, $149 per semester hour part-time for state residents; $13,968 per year full-time, $466 per semester hour part-time for nonresidents. Fees $553 per year.

HOUSING
Rooms and/or apartments available to single students (450 units) at an average cost of $4600 (including board); available to married students (72 units) at an average cost of $4500 (including board). Graduate housing contact: Bob Francisco, 303-273-3353.

STUDENT SERVICES
Low-cost health insurance, career counseling, free psychological counseling, exercise/wellness program, campus safety program, campus employment opportunities, international student services.

FACILITIES
Library: Arthur Lakes Library; total holdings of 145,000 volumes, 400,000 microforms, 2,000 current periodical subscriptions. A total of 23 personal computers in all libraries. Access provided to on-line information retrieval services. *Computer:* Campuswide network is available with full Internet access. Total number of PCs/terminals supplied for student use: 80. Computer service fees are included with tuition and fees. *Special:* In science and engineering: Colorado Advanced Materials Institute, Center for Risk Assessment.

COMPUTER SCIENCE

Department of Mathematical and Computer Sciences
Programs Awards MS, PhD. Part-time programs available.
Faculty 3 full-time (0 women).
Faculty Research Operations research, applied statistics, numerical computation, artificial intelligence, linear optimization.
Students 33 full-time (8 women), 26 part-time (4 women); includes 8 minority (2 African-Americans, 5 Asian-Americans, 1 Hispanic), 19 international.
Degrees Awarded In 1996, 23 master's, 4 doctorates awarded.
Entrance Requirements GRE General Test (combined average 1680 on three sections), minimum GPA of 3.0.
Degree Requirements For master's, thesis required, foreign language not required; for doctorate, dissertation, written comprehensive exams required, foreign language not required.
Financial Aid In 1996–97, 4 fellowships averaging $900 per month and totaling $14,994, 12 research assistantships averaging $900 per month, 14 teaching assistantships averaging $900 per month and totaling $162,566, 4 graduate assistantships averaging $900 per month were awarded. Financial aid applicants required to submit FAFSA.
Applying 34 applicants, 88% accepted. *Deadline:* rolling. *Fee:* $40.
Contact *Dr. Graeme Fairweather*
Head
303-273-3860

COLORADO STATE UNIVERSITY
Fort Collins, CO 80523-0015

OVERVIEW
Colorado State University is a public coed university.

ENROLLMENT
21,970 graduate, professional, and undergraduate students; 2,478 full-time matriculated graduate/professional students (1,306 women), 1,273 part-time matriculated graduate/professional students (572 women).

GRADUATE FACULTY
1,004 full-time (219 women); includes 91 minority (8 African-Americans, 51 Asian-Americans, 21 Hispanics, 11 Native Americans).

EXPENSES

Tuition $2600 per year full-time, $108 per credit hour part-time for state residents; $9890 per year full-time, $412 per credit hour part-time for nonresidents. Fees $675 per year full-time, $30 per semester (minimum) part-time.

HOUSING

Rooms and/or apartments available to single students (302 units) at an average cost of $3510 per year; available to married students (718 units) at an average cost of $4950 per year. Graduate housing contact: Housing and Food Services Office, 303-491-4743.

STUDENT SERVICES

Disabled student services, multicultural affairs office, low-cost health insurance, career counseling, free psychological counseling, exercise/wellness program, day-care facilities, campus safety program, campus employment opportunities, international student services.

FACILITIES

Library: Morgan Library; total holdings of 1,656,039 volumes, 2,327,921 microforms, 21,081 current periodical subscriptions. A total of 266 personal computers in all libraries. Access provided to on-line information retrieval services. *Computer:* Campuswide network is available with full Internet access. Total number of PCs/terminals supplied for student use: 8,000. Computer services are offered at no charge. *Special:* In arts and humanities: Center for Biomedical Research in Music, Center for Research on Writing and Communication Technologies, Cooperative Leadership in Networking Colorado, Gustafson Gallery, Hatton Gallery, Human Dimensions in Natural Resources Unit, Laboratory for Human Identification. In science and engineering: Agricultural Research Development and Education Center; animal reproduction and biotechnology laboratory; arthropod-borne and infectious disease laboratory; Center for Ecological Management of Military Lands; Center for Environmental Toxicology and Technology; Center for Geosciences; Center for Science, Mathematics and Technology Education; Colorado Bioprocessing Center; Cooperative Institute for Research in the Atmosphere; Engineering Research Center; Manufacturing Excellence Center; Mid-America Manufacturing Technology Center; natural resources ecology laboratory; Optoelectronic Computing Systems Center; Veterinary Teaching Hospital. In social sciences: Assistive Technology Resource Center, Center for Applied Studies in American Ethnicity, Center for Community Participation, Early Childhood Laboratories, Human Services Training and Research Consortium, Professional Development Schools, Research and Development Schools, Research and Development Center for the Advancement of Student Learning, Tri-Ethnic Center for Prevention Research.

COMPUTER SCIENCE

College of Natural Sciences, Department of Computer Science
Programs Awards MS, PhD.
Faculty 15 full-time (2 women).
Faculty Research Architecture, artificial intelligence, parallel and distributed computing, software engineering. *Total annual research expenditures:* $1.1 million.

Students 32 full-time (5 women), 12 part-time (4 women); includes 2 minority (1 African-American, 1 Asian-American), 15 international. Average age 31.
Degrees Awarded In 1996, 14 master's, 4 doctorates awarded. Terminal master's awarded for partial completion of doctoral program.
Entrance Requirements GRE General Test, GRE Subject Test, TOEFL (minimum score 580), minimum GPA of 3.2.
Degree Requirements For master's, thesis or alternative required, foreign language not required; for doctorate, dissertation, qualifying, preliminary, and final exams required, foreign language not required.
Financial Aid In 1996–97, 1 fellowship, 15 research assistantships averaging $1,200 per month and totaling $162,000, 22 teaching assistantships averaging $1,200 per month and totaling $237,600 were awarded; Federal Work-Study and career-related internships or fieldwork also available.
Applying 172 applicants, 54% accepted. *Deadline:* 3/1 (priority date; rolling processing). *Fee:* $30.
Contact Graduate Coordinator
970-491-5792
Fax: 970-491-6639
E-mail: gradinfo@cs.colostate.edu

See in-depth description on page **403.**

ELECTRICAL ENGINEERING

College of Engineering, Department of Electrical Engineering
Programs Awards MS, PhD.
Faculty 19 full-time (2 women).
Faculty Research Optoelectronics and microelectronics, radar remote sensing and nuclear device testing, controls, computer engineering. *Total annual research expenditures:* $2.8 million.
Students 32 full-time (7 women), 27 part-time (3 women); includes 2 minority (1 African-American, 1 Hispanic), 28 international. Average age 29.
Degrees Awarded In 1996, 20 master's, 14 doctorates awarded.
Entrance Requirements For master's, GRE General Test (minimum combined score of 1100), TOEFL, minimum GPA of 3.0; for doctorate, GRE General Test (minimum combined score of 1100), TOEFL, minimum GPA of 3.5.
Degree Requirements For master's, thesis (for some programs), final exam required, foreign language not required; for doctorate, dissertation, qualifying, preliminary, and final exams required, foreign language not required.
Financial Aid In 1996–97, 1 fellowship, 25 research assistantships, 7 teaching assistantships, 2 traineeships were awarded; Federal Work-Study, institutionally sponsored loans, and career-related internships or fieldwork also available.
Applying 189 applicants, 45% accepted. *Deadline:* 3/1 (priority date; rolling processing). *Fee:* $30.
Contact Audrey M. Mohr
Graduate Coordinator
970-491-6600
Fax: 970-491-2498
E-mail: amohr@engr.colostate.edu

COLORADO TECHNICAL UNIVERSITY
Colorado Springs, CO 80907-3896

OVERVIEW

Colorado Technical University is a proprietary coed comprehensive institution.

ENROLLMENT

1,822 graduate, professional, and undergraduate students; 468 full-time matriculated graduate/professional students (94 women), 0 part-time matriculated graduate/professional students.

GRADUATE FACULTY

21 full-time (4 women), 14 part-time (2 women), 29 FTE; includes 4 minority (2 African-Americans, 1 Asian-American, 1 Hispanic).

EXPENSES

Tuition $225 per quarter hour. Fees $50 per quarter.

HOUSING

On-campus housing not available.

STUDENT SERVICES

Low-cost health insurance, career counseling, exercise/wellness program, campus safety program, campus employment opportunities, international student services.

FACILITIES

Library: Resource Center; total holdings of 14,620 volumes, 1,650 microforms, 365 current periodical subscriptions. A total of 14 personal computers in all libraries. Access provided to on-line information retrieval services. *Computer:* Campuswide network is available with full Internet access. Total number of PCs/terminals supplied for student use: 8. Computer services are offered at no charge.

COMPUTER ENGINEERING

Graduate Studies, Program in Computer Engineering
Programs Awards MSCE. Part-time and evening/weekend programs available.
Faculty 7 full-time (1 woman).
Students 4 full-time (0 women). Average age 32.
Entrance Requirements Minimum undergraduate GPA of 3.0.
Degree Requirements Computer language, thesis or alternative required, foreign language not required.
Financial Aid Institutionally sponsored loans and career-related internships or fieldwork available. Financial aid applicants required to submit FAFSA.
Applying 2 applicants, 100% accepted. *Deadline:* 10/4 (rolling processing; 4/5 for spring admission). *Fee:* $100.
Contact *Judy Galante*
   Graduate Admissions
   719-590-6720
   Fax: 719-598-3740

COMPUTER SCIENCE

Graduate Studies, Program in Computer Science
Programs Awards MSCS, DCS. Part-time and evening/weekend programs available.
Faculty 10 full-time (2 women), 7 part-time (1 woman), 14 FTE.
Faculty Research Software engineering, systems engineering.
Students 216 full-time (56 women), includes 28 minority (11 African-Americans, 10 Asian-Americans, 7 Hispanics), 3 international. Average age 36.
Degrees Awarded In 1996, 89 master's awarded (100% found work related to degree).
Entrance Requirements For master's, minimum undergraduate GPA of 3.0; for doctorate, minimum graduate GPA of 3.0, 5 years of related work experience.

Degree Requirements For master's, computer language, thesis or alternative required, foreign language not required; for doctorate, computer language, dissertation required, foreign language not required.
Financial Aid Institutionally sponsored loans and career-related internships or fieldwork available. Financial aid applicants required to submit FAFSA.
Applying 69 applicants, 90% accepted. *Deadline:* 10/4 (rolling processing; 4/5 for spring admission). *Fee:* $100.
Contact *Judy Galante*
   Graduate Admissions
   719-590-6720
   Fax: 719-598-3740

ELECTRICAL ENGINEERING

Graduate Studies, Program in Electrical Engineering
Programs Awards MSEE. Part-time and evening/weekend programs available.
Faculty 5 full-time (1 woman), 4 part-time (0 women), 7 FTE.
Faculty Research Electronic systems design, communication systems design.
Students 36 full-time (4 women), includes 3 minority (1 African-American, 1 Asian-American, 1 Hispanic). Average age 36.
Degrees Awarded In 1996, 11 degrees awarded (100% found work related to degree).
Entrance Requirements Minimum undergraduate GPA of 3.0.
Degree Requirements Thesis or alternative required, foreign language not required.
Financial Aid Career-related internships or fieldwork available. Financial aid applicants required to submit FAFSA.
Applying 12 applicants, 92% accepted. *Deadline:* 10/4 (rolling processing; 4/5 for spring admission). *Fee:* $100.
Contact *Judy Galante*
   Graduate Admissions
   719-590-6720
   Fax: 719-598-3740

NATIONAL TECHNOLOGICAL UNIVERSITY
Fort Collins, CO 80526-1842

OVERVIEW

National Technological University is an independent coed graduate-only institution.

ENROLLMENT

1,866 graduate, professional, and undergraduate students; 0 full-time matriculated graduate/professional students, 1,456 part-time matriculated graduate/professional students (217 women).

GRADUATE FACULTY

0 full-time, 600 part-time (20 women).

TUITION

$585 per credit.

HOUSING

On-campus housing not available.

STUDENT SERVICES

Career counseling.

COMPUTER ENGINEERING

Graduate Programs in Engineering
Programs Offerings include computer engineering (M Eng).
Faculty 600 part-time (20 women).

Applying *Deadline:* rolling. *Fee:* $50.
Contact *Lionel V. Baldwin*
President
970-495-6400
Fax: 970-484-0668
E-mail: baldwin@mail.ntu.edu

COMPUTER SCIENCE

Graduate Programs in Engineering
Programs Offerings include computer science (M Eng).
Faculty 600 part-time (20 women).
Applying *Deadline:* rolling. *Fee:* $50.
Contact *Lionel V. Baldwin*
President
970-495-6400
Fax: 970-484-0668
E-mail: baldwin@mail.ntu.edu

ELECTRICAL ENGINEERING

Graduate Programs in Engineering
Programs Offerings include electrical engineering (M Eng).
Faculty 600 part-time (20 women).
Applying *Deadline:* rolling. *Fee:* $50.
Contact *Lionel V. Baldwin*
President
970-495-6400
Fax: 970-484-0668
E-mail: baldwin@mail.ntu.edu

SOFTWARE ENGINEERING

Graduate Programs in Engineering
Programs Offerings include software engineering (M Eng).
Faculty 600 part-time (20 women).
Applying *Deadline:* rolling. *Fee:* $50.
Contact *Lionel V. Baldwin*
President
970-495-6400
Fax: 970-484-0668
E-mail: baldwin@mail.ntu.edu

UNIVERSITY OF COLORADO AT BOULDER
Boulder, CO 80309

OVERVIEW
University of Colorado at Boulder is a public coed university.

ENROLLMENT
24,622 graduate, professional, and undergraduate students; 4,189 full-time matriculated graduate/professional students (1,753 women), 549 part-time matriculated graduate/professional students (242 women).

GRADUATE FACULTY
1,150 full-time (272 women); includes 130 minority (19 African-Americans, 62 Asian-Americans, 42 Hispanics, 7 Native Americans).

EXPENSES
Tuition $3130 per year full-time, $525 per semester (minimum) part-time for state residents; $14,184 per year full-time, $2364 per semester (minimum) part-time for nonresidents. Fees $653 per year full-time, $114 per semester (minimum) part-time.

HOUSING
Rooms and/or apartments available to single students (6,000 units) at an average cost of $2514 per year ($4370 including board); available to married students (1,000 units) at an average cost of $5100 per year. Graduate housing contact: Assistant Director of Housing, 303-492-6871.

STUDENT SERVICES
Low-cost health insurance, career counseling, free psychological counseling, day-care facilities, campus safety program, campus employment opportunities, international student services.

FACILITIES
Library: Norlin Library plus 6 additional on-campus libraries; total holdings of 2,575,290 volumes, 5,319,494 microforms, 28,444 current periodical subscriptions. A total of 500 personal computers in all libraries. Access provided to on-line information retrieval services. *Computer:* Campuswide network is available with full Internet access. Computer service fees are included with tuition and fees. *Special:* In arts and humanities: Center for Computer Research in the Humanities. In science and engineering: Institute of Behavioral Genetics, Institute of Arctic and Alpine Research, laboratory of atmospheric and space physics, Joint Institute for Laboratory Astrophysics, Cooperative Institute for Research and Environmental Sciences, Center for Applied Mathematics, Joint Institute for Laboratory Physics, Center for Space and Geosciences Policy. In social sciences: Institute of Behavioral Science, Institute for Cognitive Science, Center for Study of Ethnicity and Race in America.

COMPUTER ENGINEERING

College of Engineering and Applied Science, Department of Electrical and Computer Engineering
Programs Offers program in electrical engineering (ME, MS, PhD), including computer engineering.
Faculty 43 full-time (5 women).
Faculty Research *Total annual research expenditures:* $8.6 million.
Students 202 full-time (27 women), 35 part-time (9 women); includes 24 minority (2 African-Americans, 17 Asian-Americans, 4 Hispanics, 1 Native American), 66 international. Average age 30.
Degrees Awarded In 1996, 58 master's, 34 doctorates awarded.
Entrance Requirements For master's, GRE General Test, minimum undergraduate GPA of 3.0; for doctorate, GRE General Test, minimum undergraduate GPA of 3.5.
Degree Requirements For master's, thesis or alternative, comprehensive exam; for doctorate, 1 foreign language, dissertation, departmental qualifying exam.
Financial Aid Fellowships, research assistantships, teaching assistantships, full tuition waivers available. *Financial aid application deadline:* 1/15.
Applying 230 applicants, 59% accepted. *Deadline:* 3/1 (priority date; rolling processing). *Fee:* $40 ($60 for international students).

Contact *Pamela Wheeler*
Graduate Secretary
303-492-1190
Fax: 303-492-2758

See in-depth description on page 621.

COMPUTER SCIENCE

College of Engineering and Applied Science, Department of Computer Science
Programs Awards ME, MS, PhD.
Faculty 19 full-time (2 women).
Faculty Research Parallel and numerical computation, human computer interaction, neural networks, software systems, theory. *Total annual research expenditures:* $6.6 million.
Students 122 full-time (26 women), 34 part-time (11 women); includes 24 minority (6 African-Americans, 13 Asian-Americans, 4 Hispanics, 1 Native American), 41 international. Average age 31.
Degrees Awarded In 1996, 59 master's, 12 doctorates awarded.
Entrance Requirements For master's, minimum undergraduate GPA of 3.0.
Degree Requirements For master's, thesis or alternative, comprehensive exam; for doctorate, 1 foreign language, dissertation.
Financial Aid Fellowships, research assistantships, teaching assistantships, full tuition waivers available. *Financial aid application deadline:* 3/1.
Applying 195 applicants, 54% accepted. *Deadline:* 3/1 (priority date; rolling processing). *Fee:* $40 ($60 for international students).
Contact *Vicki Emken*
Graduate Secretary
303-492-6361
Fax: 303-492-2844
E-mail: vicki.emken@colorado.edu

ELECTRICAL ENGINEERING

College of Engineering and Applied Science, Department of Electrical and Computer Engineering
Programs Offers program in electrical engineering (ME, MS, PhD), including computer engineering.
Faculty 43 full-time (5 women).
Faculty Research *Total annual research expenditures:* $8.6 million.
Students 202 full-time (27 women), 35 part-time (9 women); includes 24 minority (2 African-Americans, 17 Asian-Americans, 4 Hispanics, 1 Native American), 66 international. Average age 30.
Degrees Awarded In 1996, 58 master's, 34 doctorates awarded.
Entrance Requirements For master's, GRE General Test, minimum undergraduate GPA of 3.0; for doctorate, GRE General Test, minimum undergraduate GPA of 3.5.
Degree Requirements For master's, thesis or alternative, comprehensive exam; for doctorate, 1 foreign language, dissertation, departmental qualifying exam.
Financial Aid Fellowships, research assistantships, teaching assistantships, full tuition waivers available. *Financial aid application deadline:* 1/15.
Applying 230 applicants, 59% accepted. *Deadline:* 3/1 (priority date; rolling processing). *Fee:* $40 ($60 for international students).
Contact *Pamela Wheeler*
Graduate Secretary
303-492-1190
Fax: 303-492-2758

See in-depth description on page 621.

UNIVERSITY OF COLORADO AT COLORADO SPRINGS
Colorado Springs, CO 80933-7150

OVERVIEW
University of Colorado at Colorado Springs is a public coed comprehensive institution.

ENROLLMENT
5,840 graduate, professional, and undergraduate students; 608 full-time matriculated graduate/professional students (298 women), 421 part-time matriculated graduate/professional students (216 women).

GRADUATE FACULTY
146; includes 22 minority (12 African-Americans, 2 Asian-Americans, 8 Hispanics).

EXPENSES
Tuition $2670 per year full-time, $114 per credit hour part-time for state residents; $9824 per year full-time, $402 per credit hour part-time for nonresidents. Fees $192 per year (minimum) full-time, $71 per year (minimum) part-time.

HOUSING
Rooms and/or apartments available to single students (600 units); on-campus housing not available to married students. Graduate housing contact: Housing Village Office, 719-262-4042.

STUDENT SERVICES
Multicultural affairs office, low-cost health insurance, career counseling, free psychological counseling, day-care facilities, campus employment opportunities.

FACILITIES
Library: Kraemer Family Library; total holdings of 328,009 volumes, 516,108 microforms, 2,374 current periodical subscriptions. A total of 26 personal computers in all libraries. Access provided to on-line information retrieval services. *Computer:* Campuswide network is available with full Internet access. Total number of PCs/terminals supplied for student use: 250. Computer service fees are included with tuition and fees. *Special:* In science and engineering: Anechoic chamber, microprocessor clean room.

COMPUTER ENGINEERING

College of Engineering and Applied Science, Department of Electrical and Computer Engineering
Programs Awards MS, PhD. Part-time and evening/weekend programs available.
Faculty 10 full-time (0 women), 2 part-time (0 women).
Faculty Research Signal processing, neural networks, integrated ferroelectric devices, applied electromagnetics, circuit design.
Students 38 full-time (3 women), 29 part-time (4 women); includes 6 minority (1 African-American, 5 Asian-Americans), 14 international. Average age 29.
Degrees Awarded In 1996, 20 master's awarded (100% found work related to degree); 6 doctorates awarded (100% found work related to degree).
Entrance Requirements For master's, GRE General Test (minimum combined score of 1200), TOEFL (minimum score 550), minimum GPA of 3.0; for doctorate, GRE General Test

(minimum combined score of 1200), TOEFL (minimum score 550), minimum GPA of 3.3.

Degree Requirements For master's, thesis required (for some programs), foreign language not required; for doctorate, dissertation, comprehensive exams required, foreign language not required.

Financial Aid Fellowships, research assistantships, teaching assistantships, Federal Work-Study, and career-related internships or fieldwork available. *Financial aid application deadline: 5/1.*

Applying 27 applicants, 93% accepted. *Fee:* $40 ($50 for international students).

Contact *Susan Bennis*
Academic Adviser
719-262-3351
Fax: 719-262-3589
E-mail: sbennis@mail.uccs.edu

COMPUTER SCIENCE

College of Engineering and Applied Science, Department of Computer Science

Programs Awards MS. Part-time programs available.

Faculty 12 full-time (1 woman), 1 (woman) part-time.

Faculty Research Analytical intelligence, software engineering, networks, database systems, graphics. *Total annual research expenditures:* $45,000.

Students 35 full-time (12 women), 37 part-time (7 women); includes 9 minority (1 African-American, 6 Asian-Americans, 1 Hispanic, 1 Native American), 10 international. Average age 29.

Degrees Awarded In 1996, 22 degrees awarded (100% found work related to degree).

Entrance Requirements GRE General Test (minimum combined score of 1200), TOEFL (minimum score 550), minimum GPA of 3.0.

Degree Requirements Oral final exam required, thesis optional, foreign language not required.

Financial Aid Teaching assistantships available. *Financial aid application deadline: 5/1.*

Applying 26 applicants, 81% accepted. *Deadline:* 7/1 (priority date; rolling processing; 12/1 for spring admission). *Fee:* $40 ($50 for international students).

Contact *Marijke Augusteijn*
Academic Adviser
719-262-3325
Fax: 719-262-3369

ELECTRICAL ENGINEERING

College of Engineering and Applied Science, Department of Electrical and Computer Engineering

Programs Awards MS, PhD. Part-time and evening/weekend programs available.

Faculty 10 full-time (0 women), 2 part-time (0 women).

Faculty Research Signal processing, neural networks, integrated ferroelectric devices, applied electromagnetics, circuit design.

Students 38 full-time (3 women), 29 part-time (4 women); includes 6 minority (1 African-American, 5 Asian-Americans), 14 international. Average age 29.

Degrees Awarded In 1996, 20 master's awarded (100% found work related to degree); 6 doctorates awarded (100% found work related to degree).

Entrance Requirements For master's, GRE General Test (minimum combined score of 1200), TOEFL (minimum score 550), minimum GPA of 3.0; for doctorate, GRE General Test (minimum combined score of 1200), TOEFL (minimum score 550), minimum GPA of 3.3.

Degree Requirements For master's, thesis required (for some programs), foreign language not required; for doctorate, dissertation, comprehensive exams required, foreign language not required.

Financial Aid Fellowships, research assistantships, teaching assistantships, Federal Work-Study, and career-related internships or fieldwork available. *Financial aid application deadline: 5/1.*

Applying 27 applicants, 93% accepted. *Fee:* $40 ($50 for international students).

Contact *Susan Bennis*
Academic Adviser
719-262-3351
Fax: 719-262-3589
E-mail: sbennis@mail.uccs.edu

UNIVERSITY OF COLORADO AT DENVER
Denver, CO 80217-3364

OVERVIEW

University of Colorado at Denver is a public coed university.

ENROLLMENT

10,855 graduate, professional, and undergraduate students; 1,415 full-time matriculated graduate/professional students (752 women), 3,549 part-time matriculated graduate/professional students (1,952 women).

GRADUATE FACULTY

389 (142 women); includes 58 minority (4 African-Americans, 28 Asian-Americans, 24 Hispanics, 2 Native Americans).

TUITION

$3216 per year full-time, $308 per semester hour part-time for state residents; $11,836 per year full-time, $824 per semester hour part-time for nonresidents.

HOUSING

On-campus housing not available.

STUDENT SERVICES

Low-cost health insurance, career counseling, free psychological counseling, day-care facilities, campus safety program, campus employment opportunities, international student services.

FACILITIES

Library: Auraria Library; total holdings of 544,194 volumes, 848,365 microforms, 3,233 current periodical subscriptions. A total of 75 personal computers in all libraries. Access provided to on-line information retrieval services. *Computer:* Campuswide network is available with full Internet access. Total number of PCs/terminals supplied for student use: 480. Computer service fees are included with tuition and fees. *Special:* In arts and humanities: Laboratory for Audio Engineering Faculty. In science and engineering: Expansive Soil Research Center, Land and Water Information Systems Group, Telemedia Center, Transportation Research Center, bioengineering laboratory. In social sciences: National Leadership Institute on Aging, Center for Applied Psychology, 4th World Center for the Study of Indigenous Law and

Politics, Center for Research on Economic and Social Policy.

COMPUTER SCIENCE

College of Engineering and Applied Science, Department of Computer Science
Programs Awards MS. Part-time and evening/weekend programs available.
Faculty 9 full-time (1 woman).
Students 19 full-time (5 women), 66 part-time (13 women); includes 17 minority (1 African-American, 15 Asian-Americans, 1 Hispanic), 10 international. Average age 31.
Degrees Awarded In 1996, 19 degrees awarded.
Entrance Requirements GRE.
Degree Requirements Thesis or alternative.
Financial Aid Research assistantships, teaching assistantships, Federal Work-Study, and career-related internships or fieldwork available. *Financial aid application deadline:* 3/1; applicants required to submit FAFSA.
Applying 45 applicants, 78% accepted. *Deadline:* 2/1 (rolling processing; 10/1 for spring admission). *Fee:* $50 ($60 for international students).
Contact *Mary Stephens*
Program Assistant
303-556-4314
Fax: 303-556-8369

ELECTRICAL ENGINEERING

College of Engineering and Applied Science, Department of Electrical Engineering
Programs Awards MS. Part-time and evening/weekend programs available.
Faculty 12 full-time (1 woman).
Students 9 full-time (2 women), 44 part-time (3 women); includes 10 minority (3 African-Americans, 6 Asian-Americans, 1 Hispanic), 5 international. Average age 31.
Degrees Awarded In 1996, 19 degrees awarded.
Entrance Requirements GRE.
Degree Requirements Thesis or alternative.
Financial Aid Research assistantships, teaching assistantships, Federal Work-Study, and career-related internships or fieldwork available. *Financial aid application deadline:* 3/1; applicants required to submit FAFSA.
Applying 24 applicants, 75% accepted. *Deadline:* 3/15 (rolling processing; 9/15 for spring admission). *Fee:* $50 ($60 for international students).
Contact *Christy Mourning*
Program Assistant
303-556-2872
Fax: 303-556-2383
E-mail: cmournin@carbon.cudenver.edu

UNIVERSITY OF DENVER
Denver, CO 80208

OVERVIEW
University of Denver is an independent coed university.

ENROLLMENT
8,724 graduate, professional, and undergraduate students; 3,334 matriculated graduate/professional students.

GRADUATE FACULTY
402 full-time (125 women), 18 part-time (8 women); includes 44 minority (10 African-Americans, 15 Asian-Americans, 16 Hispanics, 3 Native Americans).

EXPENSES
Tuition $17,532 per year full-time, $487 per credit hour part-time. Fees $255 per year full-time.

HOUSING
Rooms and/or apartments available to single students (216 units) at an average cost of $5743 (including board); available to married students (54 units). Graduate housing contact: Mary Duarte, 303-871-2246.

STUDENT SERVICES
Disabled student services, multicultural affairs office, low-cost health insurance, career counseling, free psychological counseling, exercise/wellness program, campus safety program, campus employment opportunities, international student services.

FACILITIES
Library: Penrose Library plus 2 additional on-campus libraries; total holdings of 1,896,796 volumes, 934,060 microforms, 5,540 current periodical subscriptions. A total of 120 personal computers in all libraries. Access provided to on-line information retrieval services. *Computer:* Campuswide network is available with full Internet access. *Special:* In arts and humanities: Humanities Institute. In science and engineering: Mt. Evans High Altitude Laboratory, Denver Research Institute, geographic information systems laboratory, Mt. Evans Astronomical Observatory, Chamberlin Observatory. In social sciences: Child Study Center, Center for Marital Studies, Center for Public Policy and Contemporary Issues, Center for Study of Self and Others, Center for Infant Development, Infant and Childhood Research Center.

COMPUTER SCIENCE

Graduate Studies, Faculty of Natural Sciences, Mathematics and Engineering, Department of Mathematics and Computer Science
Programs Offers programs in applied mathematics (MA, MS), computer science (MS), mathematics and computer science (PhD). Part-time programs available.
Faculty 16 full-time (3 women).
Faculty Research *Total annual research expenditures:* $28,000.
Students 51 (18 women); includes 2 minority (both Asian-Americans), 24 international.
Degrees Awarded In 1996, 19 master's awarded. Terminal master's awarded for partial completion of doctoral program.
Entrance Requirements GRE General Test, TOEFL (minimum score 550).
Degree Requirements For master's, foreign language, computer language, or laboratory experience required, thesis not required; for doctorate, 1 foreign language (computer language can substitute), dissertation, oral and written exams.
Financial Aid In 1996–97, 4 fellowships totaling $12,000, 2 research assistantships averaging $911 per month and totaling $16,398, 15 teaching assistantships averaging $911 per month and totaling $123,001, 1 scholarship totaling $6,975 were awarded; Federal Work-Study, institutionally sponsored loans, and career-related internships or fieldwork also available. Aid available to part-time students. *Financial aid application deadline:* 3/1; applicants required to submit FAFSA.
Applying 63 applicants, 98% accepted. *Deadline:* rolling. *Fee:* $40.

Contact *Rick Ball*
Graduate Adviser
303-871-2453

ELECTRICAL ENGINEERING

Graduate Studies, Faculty of Natural Sciences, Mathematics and Engineering, Department of Engineering
Programs Offerings include electrical engineering (MS). MSMGEN offered jointly with Daniels College of Business.
Department Faculty 13 full-time (2 women).
Applying *Deadline:* rolling. *Fee:* $40.
Contact *Louise Carlson*
Assistant to Chair
303-871-2107

CONNECTICUT

FAIRFIELD UNIVERSITY
Fairfield, CT 06430-5195

OVERVIEW
Fairfield University is an independent-religious coed comprehensive institution.

ENROLLMENT
5,111 graduate, professional, and undergraduate students; 158 full-time matriculated graduate/professional students (121 women), 722 part-time matriculated graduate/professional students (514 women).

GRADUATE FACULTY
55 full-time (23 women), 34 part-time (17 women), 66 FTE; includes 6 minority (1 African-American, 4 Asian-Americans, 1 Hispanic).

EXPENSES
Tuition $335 per credit hour (minimum). Fees $20 per semester.

HOUSING
Rooms and/or apartments available to single students (6 units) at an average cost of $6800 (including board); on-campus housing not available to married students. Housing application deadline: 6/15. Graduate housing contact: Fran Koerting, 203-254-4215.

STUDENT SERVICES
Disabled student services, multicultural affairs office, low-cost health insurance, career counseling, free psychological counseling, campus safety program, campus employment opportunities, international student services, teacher training.

FACILITIES
Library: Nyselius Library; total holdings of 326,000 volumes, 468,000 microforms, 1,850 current periodical subscriptions. A total of 20 personal computers in all libraries. Access provided to on-line information retrieval services. *Computer:* Campuswide network is available with full Internet access. Total number of PCs/terminals supplied for student use: 140. Computer service fees are included with tuition and fees.

INFORMATION SCIENCE

School of Business
Programs Offerings include information technology (MBA, CAS).
School Faculty 35 full-time (11 women), 2 part-time (1 woman).
Applying *Deadline:* 8/1 (priority date; rolling processing; 12/1 for spring admission). *Fee:* $40.
Contact *Dr. Cynthia S. Chegwidden*
Director of Graduate Programs
203-254-4070 Ext.
Fax: 203-254-4105
E-mail: cchegwidden@fairl.fairfield.edu

RENSSELAER AT HARTFORD
Hartford, CT 06120-2991

OVERVIEW
Rensselaer at Hartford is an independent coed graduate-only institution.

ENROLLMENT
1,903 graduate, professional, and undergraduate students; 82 full-time matriculated graduate/professional students (27 women), 1,333 part-time matriculated graduate/professional students (407 women).

GRADUATE FACULTY
26 full-time (3 women), 87 part-time (10 women).

TUITION
$490 per credit hour.

HOUSING
On-campus housing not available.

STUDENT SERVICES
Career counseling.

FACILITIES
Library: Main library; total holdings of 30,000 volumes, 43,141 microforms, 535 current periodical subscriptions. A total of 12 personal computers in all libraries. Access provided to on-line information retrieval services. *Computer:* Campuswide network is available with full Internet access. Total number of PCs/terminals supplied for student use: 125. Computer services are offered at no charge. *Special:* In science and engineering: Software systems laboratory, computer engineering laboratory, human-computer interaction laboratory, computer graphics laboratory, computer vision laboratory.

COMPUTER SCIENCE

Lolly School of Management and Technology, Program in Computer and Information Science
Programs Awards MS. Offered through Rensselaer Polytechnic Institute. Part-time and evening/weekend programs available.
Faculty 5 full-time (1 woman), 11 part-time (2 women).
Students 9 full-time (3 women), 162 part-time (26 women); includes 19 minority (1 African-American, 17 Asian-Americans, 1 Hispanic), 15 international. Average age 31.
Degrees Awarded In 1996, 51 degrees awarded.
Entrance Requirements TOEFL (minimum score 570).

Degree Requirements Computer language, seminar required, thesis optional, foreign language not required.

Financial Aid Research assistantships, student assistantships, full and partial tuition waivers available. Aid available to part-time students. Financial aid applicants required to submit FAFSA.

Applying 84 applicants, 90% accepted. *Deadline:* 8/6 (priority date; rolling processing). *Fee:* $25.

Contact *Rebecca Danchak*
Admissions Office
860-548-2420
Fax: 860-548-7823
E-mail: beckyd@hgc.edu

ELECTRICAL ENGINEERING

School of Engineering, Program in Electrical Engineering
Programs Awards MS. Offered through Rensselaer Polytechnic Institute. Part-time and evening/weekend programs available.
Faculty 2 full-time (0 women), 4 part-time (0 women).
Students 45 part-time (1 woman); includes 8 minority (2 African-Americans, 6 Asian-Americans). Average age 31.
Degrees Awarded In 1996, 30 degrees awarded.
Entrance Requirements TOEFL (minimum score 570).
Degree Requirements Seminar required, thesis optional, foreign language not required.
Financial Aid Research assistantships, student assistantships, full and partial tuition waivers available. Aid available to part-time students. Financial aid applicants required to submit FAFSA.
Applying 17 applicants, 100% accepted. *Deadline:* 8/6 (priority date; rolling processing). *Fee:* $25.
Contact *Rebecca Danchek*
Admissions Office
860-548-2420
Fax: 860-548-7823

INFORMATION SCIENCE

Lolly School of Management and Technology, Program in Computer and Information Science
Programs Awards MS. Offered through Rensselaer Polytechnic Institute. Part-time and evening/weekend programs available.
Faculty 5 full-time (1 woman), 11 part-time (2 women).
Students 9 full-time (3 women), 162 part-time (26 women); includes 19 minority (1 African-American, 17 Asian-Americans, 1 Hispanic), 15 international. Average age 31.
Degrees Awarded In 1996, 51 degrees awarded.
Entrance Requirements TOEFL (minimum score 570).
Degree Requirements Computer language, seminar required, thesis optional, foreign language not required.
Financial Aid Research assistantships, student assistantships, full and partial tuition waivers available. Aid available to part-time students. Financial aid applicants required to submit FAFSA.
Applying 84 applicants, 90% accepted. *Deadline:* 8/6 (priority date; rolling processing). *Fee:* $25.
Contact *Rebecca Danchek*
Admissions Office
860-548-2420
Fax: 860-548-7823
E-mail: beckyd@hgc.edu

SACRED HEART UNIVERSITY
Fairfield, CT 06432-1000

OVERVIEW
Sacred Heart University is an independent-religious coed comprehensive institution.

ENROLLMENT
5,545 graduate, professional, and undergraduate students; 226 full-time matriculated graduate/professional students (166 women), 1,215 part-time matriculated graduate/professional students (768 women).

GRADUATE FACULTY
129 full-time, 241 part-time.

EXPENSES
Tuition $350 per credit. Fees $71 per semester.

HOUSING
Rooms and/or apartments available to single students at an average cost of $4490 per year; on-campus housing not available to married students. Graduate housing contact: Daniel Connelly, 203-371-2511.

STUDENT SERVICES
Low-cost health insurance, career counseling, free psychological counseling, campus safety program, campus employment opportunities, international student services.

FACILITIES
Library: Ryan-Matura Library plus 1 additional on-campus library; total holdings of 163,500 volumes, 81,045 microforms, 2,041 current periodical subscriptions. A total of 25 personal computers in all libraries. Access provided to on-line information retrieval services. *Computer:* Campuswide network is available with full Internet access. *Special:* In arts and humanities: Center for Ethnic Studies. In social sciences: Center for Policy Issues.

COMPUTER SCIENCE

Faculty of Computer and Information Science
Programs Awards MS.
Students 42 part-time (7 women); includes 12 minority (2 African-Americans, 5 Asian-Americans, 3 Hispanics, 2 Native Americans), 1 international.
Degree Requirements Thesis optional.
Applying *Deadline:* rolling. *Fee:* $40 ($100 for international students).
Contact *Mike Kennedy*
Graduate Admissions Counselor
203-371-7880
Fax: 203-365-4732
E-mail: gradstudies@sacredheart.edu

INFORMATION SCIENCE

Faculty of Computer and Information Science
Programs Awards MS.
Students 42 part-time (7 women); includes 12 minority (2 African-Americans, 5 Asian-Americans, 3 Hispanics, 2 Native Americans), 1 international.
Degree Requirements Thesis optional.
Applying *Deadline:* rolling. *Fee:* $40 ($100 for international students).
Contact *Mike Kennedy*
Graduate Admissions Counselor
203-371-7880
Fax: 203-365-4732
E-mail: gradstudies@sacredheart.edu

UNIVERSITY OF BRIDGEPORT
Bridgeport, CT 06601

OVERVIEW
University of Bridgeport is an independent coed comprehensive institution.

ENROLLMENT
2,147 graduate, professional, and undergraduate students; 542 full-time matriculated graduate/professional students (250 women), 604 part-time matriculated graduate/ professional students (338 women).

GRADUATE FACULTY
83 full-time (15 women), 185 part-time (102 women), 145 FTE; includes 28 minority (11 African-Americans, 13 Asian-Americans, 3 Hispanics, 1 Native American).

EXPENSES
Tuition $13,000 per year full-time, $320 per credit part-time. Fees $590 per year.

HOUSING
Rooms and/or apartments available to single students (500 units) at an average cost of $3700 per year ($6810 including board); on-campus housing not available to married students. Graduate housing contact: David Ostreicher, 203-576-4295.

STUDENT SERVICES
Low-cost health insurance, career counseling, free psychological counseling, campus safety program, campus employment opportunities, international student services.

FACILITIES
Library: Magnus Wahlstom Library plus 1 additional on-campus library; total holdings of 273,489 volumes, 1,011,758 microforms, 1,630 current periodical subscriptions. A total of 200 personal computers in all libraries. Access provided to on-line information retrieval services. *Computer:* Campuswide network is available with full Internet access. Total number of PCs/terminals supplied for student use: 200. Computer services are offered at no charge. *Special:* In arts and humanities: Bernhard Center for Arts and Humanities, Carlson Art Gallery. In science and engineering: Connecticut Technology Institute. In social sciences: Center for Venture Management and Entrepreneurial Studies, New England Center for Regional and International Studies.

COMPUTER ENGINEERING

College of Graduate and Undergraduate Studies, School of Science, Engineering, and Technology, Department of Computer Science and Engineering
Programs   Offers programs in computer engineering (MS), computer science (MS).
Faculty   7 full-time (0 women), 1 (woman) part-time.
Students   50 full-time (8 women), 40 part-time (4 women); includes 8 minority (all Asian-Americans), 82 international.
Degrees Awarded   In 1996, 11 degrees awarded.
Entrance Requirements   TOEFL.
Degree Requirements   Thesis optional, foreign language not required.
Financial Aid   4 students received aid; research assistantships, teaching assistantships, partial tuition waivers, Federal Work-Study, institutionally sponsored loans, and career-related internships or fieldwork available. Aid available to part-time students. *Financial aid application deadline:* 6/1; applicants required to submit FAFSA.
Applying   181 applicants, 86% accepted. *Deadline:* rolling. *Fee:* $35 ($50 for international students).
Contact   Dr. Stephen Grodzinsky
Chairman
203-576-4145

See in-depth description on page **591.**

COMPUTER SCIENCE

College of Graduate and Undergraduate Studies, School of Science, Engineering, and Technology, Department of Computer Science and Engineering
Programs   Offers programs in computer engineering (MS), computer science (MS).
Faculty   7 full-time (0 women), 1 (woman) part-time.
Students   50 full-time (8 women), 40 part-time (4 women); includes 8 minority (all Asian-Americans), 82 international.
Degrees Awarded   In 1996, 11 degrees awarded.
Entrance Requirements   TOEFL.
Degree Requirements   Thesis optional, foreign language not required.
Financial Aid   4 students received aid; research assistantships, teaching assistantships, partial tuition waivers, Federal Work-Study, institutionally sponsored loans, and career-related internships or fieldwork available. Aid available to part-time students. *Financial aid application deadline:* 6/1; applicants required to submit FAFSA.
Applying   181 applicants, 86% accepted. *Deadline:* rolling. *Fee:* $35 ($50 for international students).
Contact   Dr. Stephen Grodzinsky
Chairman
203-576-4145

See in-depth description on page **591.**

ELECTRICAL ENGINEERING

College of Graduate and Undergraduate Studies, School of Science, Engineering, and Technology, Department of Electrical Engineering
Programs   Awards MS.
Faculty   3 full-time (0 women), 1 part-time (0 women).
Students   7 full-time (0 women), 2 part-time (1 woman); includes 1 minority (Asian-American), 6 international.
Degrees Awarded   In 1996, 2 degrees awarded.
Entrance Requirements   TOEFL.
Degree Requirements   Thesis optional, foreign language not required.
Financial Aid   Research assistantships, teaching assistantships, partial tuition waivers, Federal Work-Study, institutionally sponsored loans, and career-related internships or fieldwork available. Aid available to part-time students. *Financial aid application deadline:* 6/1; applicants required to submit FAFSA.
Applying   103 applicants, 86% accepted. *Deadline:* rolling. *Fee:* $35 ($50 for international students).
Contact   Dr. Wenelin Janeff
Chairman
203-576-4296

UNIVERSITY OF CONNECTICUT
Storrs, CT 06269

OVERVIEW
University of Connecticut is a public coed university.

ENROLLMENT

22,316 graduate, professional, and undergraduate students; 3,992 full-time matriculated graduate/professional students (1,865 women), 2,475 part-time matriculated graduate/professional students (1,277 women).

GRADUATE FACULTY

1,103; includes 128 minority (29 African-Americans, 74 Asian-Americans, 23 Hispanics, 2 Native Americans).

EXPENSES

Tuition $5118 per year full-time, $284 per credit part-time for state residents; $13,298 per year full-time, $739 per credit part-time for nonresidents. Fees $878 per year full-time, $352 per year part-time.

HOUSING

Rooms and/or apartments available to single students (440 units) at an average cost of $3080 per year ($5766 including board); on-campus housing not available to married students. Housing application deadline: 4/1. Graduate housing contact: Jacqueline Seide, 860-486-3430.

STUDENT SERVICES

Disabled student services, multicultural affairs office, low-cost health insurance, career counseling, free psychological counseling, day-care facilities, campus safety program, campus employment opportunities, international student services.

FACILITIES

Library: Homer D. Babbidge Library plus 3 additional on-campus libraries; total holdings of 2,079,395 volumes, 2,976,273 microforms, 8,253 current periodical subscriptions. A total of 440 personal computers in all libraries. Access provided to on-line information retrieval services. *Computer:* Campuswide network is available with full Internet access. Total number of PCs/terminals supplied for student use: 10,004. Computer services are offered at no charge. *Special:* In science and engineering: Advanced Technology Center for Precision Manufacturing, Institute of Materials Science, Electrical Insulation Research Center, Polymer Compatibilization Research Consortium, Marine Sciences Institute, Marine Sciences and Technology Center, Environmental Research Institute, Connecticut Environmental Entrepreneurial Center, Photonics Research Center. In social sciences: Institute of Social Inquiry, Connecticut Center for Economic Analysis.

COMPUTER SCIENCE

School of Engineering, Field of Computer Science and Engineering
Programs Offers programs in artificial intelligence (MS, PhD), computer architecture (MS, PhD), computer science (MS, PhD), operating systems (MS, PhD), robotics (MS, PhD), software engineering (MS, PhD).
Faculty 21.
Students 47 full-time (11 women), 16 part-time (1 woman); includes 3 minority (1 Asian-American, 1 Hispanic, 1 Native American), 36 international. Average age 30.
Degrees Awarded In 1996, 11 master's, 2 doctorates awarded. Terminal master's awarded for partial completion of doctoral program.
Entrance Requirements GRE General Test.
Degree Requirements For master's, thesis or alternative; for doctorate, dissertation.

Financial Aid In 1996–97, 2 fellowships totaling $7,000, 15 research assistantships (2 to first-year students) totaling $189,842, 23 teaching assistantships (7 to first-year students) totaling $193,422 were awarded. *Financial aid application deadline:* 2/15.
Applying 59 applicants, 42% accepted. *Deadline:* 6/1 (priority date; rolling processing; 11/1 for spring admission). *Fee:* $40 ($45 for international students).
Contact *Bernard W. Lovell*
Chairperson
860-486-2772

ELECTRICAL ENGINEERING

School of Engineering, Field of Electrical and Systems Engineering
Programs Offers programs in biological engineering (MS), control and communication systems (MS, PhD), electromagnetics and physical electronics (MS, PhD).
Faculty 25.
Students 75 full-time (9 women), 30 part-time (3 women); includes 8 minority (2 African-Americans, 4 Asian-Americans, 2 Hispanics), 61 international. Average age 30.
Degrees Awarded In 1996, 19 master's, 14 doctorates awarded. Terminal master's awarded for partial completion of doctoral program.
Entrance Requirements GRE General Test, TOEFL.
Degree Requirements For master's, thesis or alternative; for doctorate, dissertation.
Financial Aid In 1996–97, 8 fellowships totaling $25,735, 53 research assistantships (14 to first-year students) totaling $602,755, 12 teaching assistantships (3 to first-year students) totaling $65,567 were awarded. *Financial aid application deadline:* 2/15.
Applying 199 applicants, 21% accepted. *Deadline:* 6/1 (priority date; rolling processing; 11/1 for spring admission). *Fee:* $40 ($45 for international students).
Contact *Rajeev Bansal*
Chairperson
860-486-4816

See in-depth description on page 623.

SOFTWARE ENGINEERING

School of Engineering, Field of Computer Science and Engineering
Programs Offerings include software engineering (MS, PhD). Terminal master's awarded for partial completion of doctoral program.
Faculty 21.
Entrance Requirements GRE General Test.
Degree Requirements For master's, thesis or alternative; for doctorate, dissertation.
Applying *Deadline:* 6/1 (priority date; rolling processing; 11/1 for spring admission). *Fee:* $40 ($45 for international students).
Contact *Bernard W. Lovell*
Chairperson
860-486-2772

UNIVERSITY OF NEW HAVEN
West Haven, CT 06516-1916

OVERVIEW

University of New Haven is an independent coed comprehensive institution.

ENROLLMENT
4,753 graduate, professional, and undergraduate students; 536 full-time matriculated graduate/professional students (286 women), 1,586 part-time matriculated graduate/professional students (714 women).

GRADUATE FACULTY
150 full-time, 100 part-time.

EXPENSES
Tuition $1080 per course. Fees $13 per trimester.

HOUSING
Rooms and/or apartments available to single students (17 units) at an average cost of $4725 per year; on-campus housing not available to married students. Graduate housing contact: Rebecca Johnson, 203-932-7076.

STUDENT SERVICES
Disabled student services, multicultural affairs office, low-cost health insurance, career counseling, free psychological counseling, campus safety program, campus employment opportunities, international student services, writing training.

FACILITIES
Library: Marvin K. Peterson Library. Access provided to on-line information retrieval services.

ELECTRICAL ENGINEERING

School of Engineering and Applied Science, Program in Electrical Engineering
Programs Awards MSEE. Part-time and evening/weekend programs available.
Students 8 full-time (1 woman), 25 part-time (2 women); includes 3 minority (1 African-American, 1 Asian-American, 1 Hispanic), 11 international.
Entrance Requirements Bachelor's degree in electrical engineering.
Degree Requirements Thesis or alternative required, foreign language not required.
Financial Aid Federal Work-Study available. Aid available to part-time students. *Financial aid application deadline:* 5/1; applicants required to submit FAFSA.
Applying 22 applicants, 86% accepted. *Deadline:* rolling. *Fee:* $50.
Contact Dr. Bouzid Aliane
Coordinator
203-932-7160

SOFTWARE ENGINEERING

School of Engineering and Applied Science, Program in Computer and Information Science
Programs Offerings include applications software (MS), systems software (MS).
Degree Requirements Thesis or alternative required, foreign language not required.
Applying *Deadline:* rolling. *Fee:* $50.
Contact Dr. Roger Frey
Coordinator
203-932-7065

WESTERN CONNECTICUT STATE UNIVERSITY
Danbury, CT 06810-6885

OVERVIEW
Western Connecticut State University is a public coed comprehensive institution.

ENROLLMENT
5,208 graduate, professional, and undergraduate students; 17 full-time matriculated graduate/professional students (11 women), 557 part-time matriculated graduate/professional students (419 women).

GRADUATE FACULTY
42 full-time (14 women), 9 part-time (2 women).

EXPENSES
Tuition $4127 per year (minimum) full-time, $178 per credit hour part-time for state residents; $9581 per year (minimum) full-time, $178 per credit hour part-time for nonresidents. Fees $25 per year part-time.

HOUSING
Rooms and/or apartments available to single students (900 units) and married students (150 units) at an average cost of $2478 per year ($4496 including board). Housing application deadline: 6/13. Graduate housing contact: J. Wallace, 203-837-8543.

STUDENT SERVICES
Low-cost health insurance, career counseling, free psychological counseling, day-care facilities, campus employment opportunities.

FACILITIES
Library: Ruth A. Haas Library plus 1 additional on-campus library; total holdings of 157,428 volumes, 206,461 microforms, 1,614 current periodical subscriptions. Access provided to on-line information retrieval services. *Computer:* Campuswide network is available with full Internet access. Computer service fees are applied as a separate charge. *Special:* In arts and humanities: Charles Ives Center for the Arts. In science and engineering: Center for Galactic Astronomy, Laboratory Information Management System.

COMPUTER SCIENCE

School of Arts and Sciences, Department of Mathematics and Computer Science
Programs Offers programs in mathematics and computer science (MA), theoretical mathematics (MA). Part-time and evening/weekend programs available.
Students 1 full-time, 11 part-time.
Entrance Requirements Minimum GPA of 2.5.
Degree Requirements Thesis, comprehensive exam required, foreign language not required.
Financial Aid Fellowships, Federal Work-Study, and career-related internships or fieldwork available. Aid available to part-time students. *Financial aid application deadline:* 5/1.
Applying *Deadline:* 8/1 (priority date; rolling processing). *Fee:* $40.
Contact Dr. Josephine Hamer
Chair
203-837-9347

YALE UNIVERSITY
New Haven, CT 06520

OVERVIEW
Yale University is an independent coed university.

ENROLLMENT
11,085 graduate, professional, and undergraduate students; 5,438 full-time, 208 part-time matriculated graduate/professional students.

GRADUATE FACULTY
2,986.

TUITION
$20,300 per year.

HOUSING
Rooms and/or apartments available to single students (825 units) and married students (280 units). Housing application deadline: 6/1. Graduate housing contact: Housing Department, 203-432-9756.

STUDENT SERVICES
Disabled student services, career counseling, free psychological counseling, campus employment opportunities.

FACILITIES
Library: Sterling Memorial Library plus 40 additional on-campus libraries; total holdings of 10.8 million volumes, 5.2 million microforms, 57,377 current periodical subscriptions. Access provided to on-line information retrieval services. *Computer:* Campuswide network is available with full Internet access. Total number of PCs/terminals supplied for student use: 250. Computer service fees are applied as a separate charge. *Special:* In arts and humanities: Peabody Museum of Natural History, Institute of Sacred Music, Yale Center for British Art, university art gallery, Whitney Humanities Center. In science and engineering: J. W. Gibbs Research Laboratories, Boyer Center for Molecular Medicine, Bass Center for Molecular and Structural Biology, Chemical Instrumentation Center, Arthur W. Wright Nuclear Structure Laboratory, Osborn Memorial Laboratories. In social sciences: Center for International and Area Studies, Child Study Center, video archive of Holocaust survivor testimonies.

COMPUTER SCIENCE

Graduate School of Arts and Sciences, Department of Computer Science
Programs Awards PhD.
Faculty 16 full-time (1 woman).
Students 43 (9 women); includes 1 minority (Asian–American), 24 international.
Degrees Awarded In 1996, 11 master's, 9 doctorates awarded. Terminal master's awarded for partial completion of doctoral program.
Entrance Requirements For doctorate, GRE General Test, GRE Subject Test.
Degree Requirements For doctorate, dissertation required, foreign language not required.
Financial Aid Fellowships, research assistantships, teaching assistantships, Federal Work-Study, institutionally sponsored loans available. Aid available to part-time students.
Applying 198 applicants, 15% accepted. *Deadline: 1/2. Fee: $65.*

Contact *Admissions Information*
203-432-2770

See in-depth description on page 771.

ELECTRICAL ENGINEERING

Graduate School of Arts and Sciences, Council of Engineering and Applied Science, Program of Electrical Engineering
Programs Awards MS, PhD.
Faculty 14 full-time (0 women), 1 part-time (0 women).
Students 39 (9 women); includes 31 international.
Degrees Awarded In 1996, 10 master's, 6 doctorates awarded. Terminal master's awarded for partial completion of doctoral program.
Entrance Requirements GRE General Test, TOEFL.
Degree Requirements For doctorate, dissertation, exam required, foreign language not required.
Financial Aid Federal Work-Study, institutionally sponsored loans available. Aid available to part-time students.
Applying 99 applicants, 14% accepted. *Deadline: 1/2. Fee: $65.*
Contact *Admissions Information*
203-432-2770

DELAWARE

UNIVERSITY OF DELAWARE
Newark, DE 19716

OVERVIEW
University of Delaware is a public coed university.

ENROLLMENT
21,722 graduate, professional, and undergraduate students; 1,686 full-time matriculated graduate/professional students (732 women), 1,661 part-time matriculated graduate/professional students (860 women).

GRADUATE FACULTY
964.

EXPENSES
Tuition $4120 per year full-time, $229 per credit hour part-time for state residents; $11,750 per year full-time, $653 per credit hour part-time for nonresidents. Fees $100 per year.

HOUSING
Rooms and/or apartments available to single students at an average cost of $6120 per year; available to married students (21 units) at an average cost of $6360 per year. Graduate housing contact: David Butler, 302-831-6573.

STUDENT SERVICES
Low-cost health insurance, career counseling, free psychological counseling, campus employment opportunities, international student services.

FACILITIES
Library: Hugh M. Morris Library plus 4 additional on-campus libraries; total holdings of 2.1 million volumes, 2.6 million microforms, 24,000 current periodical subscriptions. Access provided to on-line information retrieval services. *Computer:* Campuswide network is available with full

Internet access. *Special:* In science and engineering: Institute for Energy Conversion, Center for the Study of Catalysts, Center for the Study of Composite Materials, Institute of Applied Mathematics, marine studies laboratory.

COMPUTER SCIENCE

College of Arts and Science, Department of Computer and Information Sciences
Programs Awards MS, PhD. Part-time programs available.
Faculty 21 full-time (3 women), 1 part-time (0 women).
Faculty Research Computer networks and distributed systems, natural language processing and artificial intelligence, parallel computing, scientific computation, theory.
Students 64 full-time (18 women), 13 part-time (3 women); includes 3 minority (all Asian-Americans), 42 international. Average age 24.
Degrees Awarded In 1996, 30 master's, 4 doctorates awarded. Terminal master's awarded for partial completion of doctoral program.
Entrance Requirements GRE General Test (minimum combined score of 1750 on three sections), TOEFL (average 550).
Degree Requirements For master's, thesis optional, foreign language not required; for doctorate, dissertation required, foreign language not required.
Financial Aid In 1996–97, 46 students received aid, including 10 fellowships, 18 research assistantships (3 to first-year students), 17 teaching assistantships (9 to first-year students), 1 laboratory assistantship; full tuition waivers also available. *Financial aid application deadline:* 3/1.
Applying *Deadline:* 7/1 (rolling processing; 12/1 for spring admission). *Fee:* $40.
Contact Dr. K. Vijayashanker
   Coordinator of Graduate Studies
   302-831-2713
   Fax: 302-831-8458
   E-mail: gradprgm@cis.udel.edu
   See in-depth description on page 625.

ELECTRICAL ENGINEERING

College of Engineering, Department of Electrical Engineering
Programs Awards MEE, PhD. Part-time programs available.
Faculty 17 full-time (0 women), 4 part-time (0 women), 17.9 FTE.
Faculty Research Signal and image processing, communications, devices and materials, optoelectronics, computer engineering. *Total annual research expenditures:* $68,000.
Students 48 full-time (7 women), 33 part-time (5 women); includes 5 minority (2 African-Americans, 3 Asian-Americans), 35 international. Average age 25.
Degrees Awarded In 1996, 11 master's awarded; 6 doctorates awarded (100% found work related to degree). Terminal master's awarded for partial completion of doctoral program.
Entrance Requirements GRE General Test.
Degree Requirements For master's, thesis optional, foreign language not required; for doctorate, dissertation required, foreign language not required.
Financial Aid In 1996–97, 36 students received aid, including 3 fellowships (2 to first-year students) averaging $1,200 per month and totaling $31,500, 12 research assistantships (1 to a first-year student) totaling $129,500, 12 teaching assistantships (3 to first-year students) totaling $119,600, 3 tuition assistantships (1 to a first-year student) totaling $26,825; Federal Work-Study, institutionally sponsored loans also available. *Financial aid application deadline:* 3/1.

Applying 767 applicants, 46% accepted. *Deadline:* 7/1 (rolling processing; 12/1 for spring admission). *Fee:* $40.
Contact Dr. Robert G. Hunsperger
   Chair, Graduate Committee
   302-831-8031
   Fax: 302-831-4316
   E-mail: hunsperg@ee.udel.edu

INFORMATION SCIENCE

College of Arts and Science, Department of Computer and Information Sciences
Programs Awards MS, PhD. Part-time programs available.
Faculty 21 full-time (3 women), 1 part-time (0 women).
Faculty Research Computer networks and distributed systems, natural language processing and artificial intelligence, parallel computing, scientific computation, theory.
Students 64 full-time (18 women), 13 part-time (3 women); includes 3 minority (all Asian-Americans), 42 international. Average age 24.
Degrees Awarded In 1996, 30 master's, 4 doctorates awarded. Terminal master's awarded for partial completion of doctoral program.
Entrance Requirements GRE General Test (minimum combined score of 1750 on three sections), TOEFL (average 550).
Degree Requirements For master's, thesis optional, foreign language not required; for doctorate, dissertation required, foreign language not required.
Financial Aid In 1996–97, 46 students received aid, including 10 fellowships, 18 research assistantships (3 to first-year students), 17 teaching assistantships (9 to first-year students), 1 laboratory assistantship; full tuition waivers also available. *Financial aid application deadline:* 3/1.
Applying *Deadline:* 7/1 (rolling processing; 12/1 for spring admission). *Fee:* $40.
Contact Dr. K. Vijayashanker
   Coordinator of Graduate Studies
   302-831-2713
   Fax: 302-831-8458
   E-mail: gradprgm@cis.udel.edu
   See in-depth description on page 625.

DISTRICT OF COLUMBIA

AMERICAN UNIVERSITY
Washington, DC 20016-8001

OVERVIEW
American University is an independent-religious coed university.

ENROLLMENT
9,954 graduate, professional, and undergraduate students; 2,458 full-time matriculated graduate/professional students (1,465 women), 2,454 part-time matriculated graduate/professional students (1,321 women).

GRADUATE FACULTY
403 full-time (138 women), 206 part-time (72 women); includes 80 minority (32 African-Americans, 32 Asian-Americans, 12 Hispanics, 4 Native Americans).

EXPENSES

Tuition $655 per credit hour. Fees $230 per year full-time, $120 per year part-time.

HOUSING

On-campus housing not available.

STUDENT SERVICES

Disabled student services, multicultural affairs office, low-cost health insurance, career counseling, free psychological counseling, day-care facilities, campus safety program, campus employment opportunities, international student services, teacher training.

FACILITIES

Library: University Library plus 1 additional on-campus library; total holdings of 866,964 volumes, 1,884,538 microforms, 11,554 current periodical subscriptions. A total of 53 personal computers in all libraries. Access provided to on-line information retrieval services. *Computer:* Campuswide network is available with full Internet access. Computer services are offered at no charge. *Special:* In science and engineering: Advanced technology computing laboratory. In social sciences: National Center for Health/Fitness, social science research computing laboratory.

COMPUTER SCIENCE

College of Arts and Sciences, Department of Computer Science and Information Systems, Program in Computer Science
Programs   Awards MS. Part-time and evening/weekend programs available.
Faculty   13 full-time (4 women), 2 part-time (0 women).
Students   16 full-time (4 women), 22 part-time (9 women); includes 9 minority (3 African-Americans, 4 Asian-Americans, 1 Hispanic, 1 Native American), 18 international.
Degrees Awarded   In 1996, 23 degrees awarded.
Degree Requirements   Computer language, thesis or alternative, comprehensive exam.
Financial Aid   Fellowships, assistantships, Federal Work-Study, institutionally sponsored loans, and career-related internships or fieldwork available. *Financial aid application deadline:* 2/1.
Applying   67 applicants, 85% accepted. *Deadline:* 2/1 (10/1 for spring admission). *Fee:* $50.
Contact   *Dr. Michael Gray*
Chair
202-885-1470

See in-depth description on page **371.**

COMPUTER SCIENCE

College of Arts and Sciences, Department of Mathematics and Statistics, Program in Statistical Computing
Programs   Awards MS. Part-time and evening/weekend programs available.
Faculty   22 full-time (8 women).
Faculty Research   Data analysis; random processes; environmental, meteorological, and biological applications.
Students   1 (woman) full-time, 2 part-time (1 woman); includes 1 international.
Degrees Awarded   In 1996, 1 degree awarded.
Entrance Requirements   BA in mathematics.
Degree Requirements   1 foreign language required (computer language can substitute), thesis optional.
Financial Aid   Fellowships, teaching assistantships, Federal Work-Study, institutionally sponsored loans, and career-related internships

or fieldwork available. Aid available to part-time students. *Financial aid application deadline:* 2/1.
Applying   3 applicants, 67% accepted. *Deadline:* 2/1 (10/1 for spring admission). *Fee:* $50.
Contact   *Dr. Robert Jeinigan*
Chair
202-885-3120
Fax: 202-885-3155

INFORMATION SCIENCE

College of Arts and Sciences, Department of Computer Science and Information Systems, Program in Information Systems
Programs   Awards MS, Certificate. Part-time and evening/weekend programs available.
Faculty   13 full-time (4 women), 5 part-time (0 women).
Students   27 full-time (11 women), 122 part-time (47 women); includes 44 minority (27 African-Americans, 7 Asian-Americans, 9 Hispanics, 1 Native American), 23 international.
Degrees Awarded   In 1996, 71 master's awarded.
Degree Requirements   For master's, computer language, thesis or alternative, comprehensive exam required, foreign language not required.
Financial Aid   Fellowships, teaching assistantships, assistantships, Federal Work-Study, institutionally sponsored loans, and career-related internships or fieldwork available. *Financial aid application deadline:* 2/1.
Applying   101 applicants, 61% accepted. *Deadline:* 2/1 (10/1 for spring admission). *Fee:* $50.
Contact   *Dr. Michael Gray*
Chair
202-885-1470

See in-depth description on page **371.**

THE CATHOLIC UNIVERSITY OF AMERICA
Washington, DC 20064

OVERVIEW

The Catholic University of America is an independent-religious coed university.

ENROLLMENT

5,974 graduate, professional, and undergraduate students; 1,663 full-time matriculated graduate/professional students (833 women), 1,931 part-time matriculated graduate/professional students (1,024 women).

GRADUATE FACULTY

370 full-time (118 women), 291 part-time (104 women), 467 FTE; includes 66 minority (25 African-Americans, 29 Asian-Americans, 12 Hispanics).

EXPENSES

Tuition $16,500 per year full-time, $636 per credit hour part-time. Fees $610 per year full-time, $280 per year part-time.

HOUSING

Rooms and/or apartments available to single students (129 units) at an average cost of $3978 per year ($7036 including board); on-campus housing not available to married students. Housing application deadline: 6/1. Graduate housing contact: Office of Housing and Residential Services, 202-319-5615.

STUDENT SERVICES

Disabled student services, multicultural affairs office, low-cost health insurance, career counseling, free psychological counseling, exercise/wellness program, day-care facilities, campus safety program, campus employment opportunities, international student services, writing training.

FACILITIES

Library: Mullen Library plus 7 additional on-campus libraries; total holdings of 1,388,428 volumes, 128,694 microforms, 10,684 current periodical subscriptions. A total of 95 personal computers in all libraries. Access provided to on-line information retrieval services. *Computer:* Campuswide network is available with full Internet access. Total number of PCs/terminals supplied for student use: 300. Computer service fees are included with tuition and fees. *Special:* In arts and humanities: Latin American Center for Graduate Studies in Music. In science and engineering: Vitreous state laboratory, Center for Advanced Training in Cell and Molecular Biology. In social sciences: Center for the Study of Youth Development, Life Cycle Institute.

ARTIFICIAL INTELLIGENCE/ROBOTICS

School of Engineering, Department of Mechanical Engineering, Program in Design and Robotics

Programs Awards MME, D Engr, PhD. Part-time and evening/weekend programs available.

Faculty Research Active constrained damping, smart traversing beams. *Total annual research expenditures:* $86,000.

Entrance Requirements For master's, minimum GPA of 3.0; for doctorate, minimum GPA of 3.5.

Degree Requirements For master's, comprehensive exam required, thesis optional, foreign language not required; for doctorate, dissertation, comprehensive and oral exams required, foreign language not required.

Financial Aid Research assistantships, teaching assistantships, full and partial tuition waivers, Federal Work-Study, institutionally sponsored loans, and career-related internships or fieldwork available. Aid available to part-time students. *Financial aid application deadline:* 2/1.

Applying *Deadline:* 8/1 (priority date; rolling processing; 12/1 for spring admission). *Fee:* $50.

Contact Dr. Amr Baz
Director
202-319-5170

ELECTRICAL ENGINEERING

School of Engineering, Department of Electrical Engineering

Programs Awards MEE, MS Engr, D Engr, PhD. Part-time and evening/weekend programs available.

Faculty 7 full-time (0 women), 4 part-time (0 women), 8 FTE.

Faculty Research Signal and image processing, computer communications, robotics, intelligent controls, bioelectromagnetics, properties of materials. *Total annual research expenditures:* $320,000.

Students 11 full-time (0 women), 18 part-time (3 women); includes 10 minority (4 African-Americans, 2 Asian-Americans, 4 Hispanics), 13 international. Average age 34.

Degrees Awarded In 1996, 12 master's, 1 doctorate awarded.

Entrance Requirements For master's, TOEFL (minimum score 550), minimum GPA of 3.0; for doctorate, TOEFL (minimum score 550), minimum GPA of 3.4.

Degree Requirements For master's, thesis optional, foreign language not required; for doctorate, dissertation, comprehensive and oral exams required, foreign language not required.

Financial Aid Research assistantships, graduate assistantships, full and partial tuition waivers, Federal Work-Study, institutionally sponsored loans, and career-related internships or fieldwork available. Aid available to part-time students. *Financial aid application deadline:* 2/1.

Applying 41 applicants, 66% accepted. *Deadline:* 8/1 (priority date; rolling processing; 12/1 for spring admission). *Fee:* $50.

Contact Dr. Robert Meister
Chair
202-319-5193

THE GEORGE WASHINGTON UNIVERSITY
Washington, DC 20052

OVERVIEW

The George Washington University is an independent coed university.

ENROLLMENT

18,986 graduate, professional, and undergraduate students; 5,121 full-time matriculated graduate/professional students (2,475 women), 5,251 part-time matriculated graduate/professional students (2,467 women).

GRADUATE FACULTY

1,403 full-time (450 women), 2,962 part-time (900 women); includes 585 minority (172 African-Americans, 298 Asian-Americans, 103 Hispanics, 12 Native Americans).

EXPENSES

Tuition $655 per semester hour. Fees $33 per semester hour.

HOUSING

On-campus housing not available.

STUDENT SERVICES

Disabled student services, multicultural affairs office, low-cost health insurance, career counseling, free psychological counseling, exercise/wellness program, campus safety program, campus employment opportunities, international student services, writing training, teacher training.

FACILITIES

Library: Melvin Gelman Library plus 2 additional on-campus libraries; total holdings of 1,730,733 volumes, 2,016,655 microforms, 14,129 current periodical subscriptions. A total of 6 personal computers in all libraries. Access provided to on-line information retrieval services. *Computer:* Campuswide network is available with full Internet access. Total number of PCs/terminals supplied for student use: 550. Computer service fees are included with tuition and fees. *Special:* In science and engineering: Institute for the Study of Fatigue Fracture and Structural Reliability, Institute for Management Science and Engineering, Joint Institute for Advancement of Flight Sciences, Institute for Information Science and Technology, Institute for Artificial Intelligence, Institute for Reliability and Risk Analysis, International Water Resources Institute, Institute for Technology and Strategic Research,

Institute for Medical Imaging and Image Analysis. In social sciences: Sigur Center for East Asian Studies; Space Policy Institute; Center for International Science and Technology Policy; Labor Management Institute for Health Policy Research; Center for Washington Area Studies; Center for History in the Media; Institute for European, Russian, and Eurasian Studies.

COMPUTER SCIENCE

School of Engineering and Applied Science, Department of Electrical Engineering and Computer Science, Program in Computer Science
Programs Awards MS, D Sc, App Sc, Engr. Part-time and evening/weekend programs available.
Faculty 18 full-time (2 women), 11 part-time (1 woman), 21 FTE.
Faculty Research Computer graphics, multimedia, VLSI, parallel processing.
Students 103 full-time (27 women), 272 part-time (52 women); includes 73 minority (23 African-Americans, 40 Asian-Americans, 8 Hispanics, 2 Native Americans), 139 international. Average age 32.
Entrance Requirements For master's, TOEFL (minimum score 550; average 580) or George Washington University English as a Foreign Language Test, appropriate bachelor's degree, minimum GPA of 3.0; for doctorate, TOEFL (minimum score 550; average 580) or George Washington University English as a Foreign Language Test, appropriate bachelor's or master's degree, minimum GPA of 3.4 (undergraduate), 3.0 (graduate); for other advanced degree, TOEFL (minimum score 550; average 580) or George Washington University English as a Foreign Language Test, appropriate master's degree, minimum GPA of 3.4.
Degree Requirements For master's, thesis optional, foreign language not required; for doctorate, dissertation defense, qualifying exam required, foreign language not required.
Financial Aid Fellowships, research assistantships, teaching assistantships, institutionally sponsored loans, and career-related internships or fieldwork available. *Financial aid application deadline:* 3/1; applicants required to submit FAFSA.
Applying 308 applicants, 90% accepted. *Deadline:* 4/1 (rolling processing; 10/1 for spring admission). *Fee:* $50.
Contact *Carole Landau*
Student Services
202-994-1803
E-mail: clandau@seas.gwu.edu

See in-depth description on page **439.**

ELECTRICAL ENGINEERING

School of Engineering and Applied Science, Department of Electrical Engineering and Computer Science, Program in Electrical Engineering
Programs Awards MS, D Sc, App Sc, Engr. Part-time and evening/weekend programs available.
Faculty 21 full-time (2 women), 29 part-time (1 woman), 34 FTE.
Faculty Research Communications, magnetics, medical engineering, robotics, electrophysics.
Students 126 full-time (28 women), 261 part-time (36 women); includes 73 minority (20 African-Americans, 48 Asian-Americans, 5 Hispanics), 117 international. Average age 32.
Entrance Requirements For master's, TOEFL (minimum score 550; average 580) or George Washington University English as a Foreign Language Test, appropriate bachelor's degree, minimum GPA of 3.0; for doctorate, TOEFL (minimum score 550; average 580) or George Washington University English as a Foreign Language Test, appropriate bachelor's or master's degree, minimum GPA of 3.4 (undergraduate), 3.0 (graduate).

Degree Requirements For master's, thesis optional, foreign language not required; for doctorate, dissertation defense, qualifying exam required, foreign language not required.
Financial Aid Fellowships, research assistantships, teaching assistantships available. *Financial aid application deadline:* 3/1; applicants required to submit FAFSA.
Applying 264 applicants, 84% accepted. *Deadline:* 4/1 (rolling processing; 10/1 for spring admission). *Fee:* $45.
Contact *Carole Landau*
Student Services
202-994-1803
E-mail: clandau@seas.gwu.edu

See in-depth description on page **439.**

HOWARD UNIVERSITY
Washington, DC 20059-0002

OVERVIEW
Howard University is an independent coed university.

ENROLLMENT
10,248 graduate, professional, and undergraduate students; 2,836 full-time matriculated graduate/professional students (1,611 women), 727 part-time matriculated graduate/professional students (400 women).

GRADUATE FACULTY
335; includes 228 minority.

TUITION
$9900 per year full-time, $330 per credit hour part-time.

HOUSING
Rooms and/or apartments available to single students at an average cost of $1500 per year ($3300 including board); available to married students at an average cost of $3800 per year ($5600 including board). Housing application deadline: 4/1. Graduate housing contact: Dean William Keene, 202-806-6131.

STUDENT SERVICES
Disabled student services, multicultural affairs office, low-cost health insurance, career counseling, free psychological counseling, campus safety program, campus employment opportunities, international student services, writing training, teacher training.

FACILITIES
Library: Founders Library plus 10 additional on-campus libraries; total holdings of 2.2 million volumes, 3.7 million microforms, 14,000 current periodical subscriptions. A total of 606 personal computers in all libraries. Access provided to on-line information retrieval services. *Computer:* Campuswide network is available with full Internet access. Total number of PCs/terminals supplied for student use: 606. Computer services are offered at no charge. *Special:* In arts and humanities: African-American Resource Center. In science and engineering: Center for the Study of Terrestrial and Extraterrestrial Atomospheres, Computational Science and Engineering Research Center, Cancer Research Center, Center for Sickle Cell Disease. In social sciences: Center for Disability and Socioeconomic Policy Studies, W. Montague Cobb Human Skeletal Collections.

ARTIFICIAL INTELLIGENCE/ROBOTICS

School of Engineering, Department of Mechanical Engineering, Field of CAD/CAM and Robotics
Programs Awards M Eng, PhD. Offered through the Graduate School of Arts and Sciences.
Entrance Requirements For master's, GRE General Test, TOEFL, bachelor's degree in mechanical engineering or related field, minimum GPA of 3.0; for doctorate, GRE General Test, TOEFL, minimum GPA of 3.0.
Degree Requirements For master's, computer language, comprehensive exam required, thesis optional, foreign language not required; for doctorate, 1 foreign language, computer language, dissertation, comprehensive exam.
Financial Aid *Application deadline: 4/1.*
Applying *Deadline:* 4/1 (11/1 for spring admission). *Fee:* $45.
Contact Dr. Lewis Thigpen
    Acting Chairman
    202-806-6600

COMPUTER SCIENCE

School of Engineering, Department of Systems and Computer Science
Programs Awards MSCS, MU Sys E. Offered through the Graduate School of Arts and Sciences. Part-time programs available.
Faculty Research Analysis of blending algorithms, software metrics and their limitations.
Entrance Requirements GRE General Test, TOEFL, minimum GPA of 3.0.
Degree Requirements Computer language, comprehensive exam required, thesis optional, foreign language not required.
Financial Aid Fellowships, research assistantships, teaching assistantships, grants, institutionally sponsored loans, and career-related internships or fieldwork available. *Financial aid application deadline: 4/1.*
Applying *Deadline:* 4/1 (11/1 for spring admission). *Fee:* $45.
Contact Dr. Ronald Leach
    Acting Chair
    202-806-6595

ELECTRICAL ENGINEERING

School of Engineering, Department of Electrical Engineering
Programs Awards M Eng, PhD. Offered through the Graduate School of Arts and Sciences. Part-time programs available.
Faculty Research Solid state electronics, antennas and microwaves, communications and signal processing, controls and powersystems, applied electromagnetics.
Entrance Requirements For master's, GRE General Test, TOEFL, bachelor's degree in electrical engineering, minimum GPA of 3.0; for doctorate, GRE General Test, TOEFL, minimum GPA of 3.0.
Degree Requirements For master's, computer language, comprehensive exam required, thesis optional, foreign language not required; for doctorate, 1 foreign language, computer language, dissertation, qualifying exam.
Financial Aid Fellowships, research assistantships, teaching assistantships, grants, institutionally sponsored loans, and career-related internships or fieldwork available. *Financial aid application deadline: 4/1.*
Applying *Deadline:* 4/1 (11/1 for spring admission). *Fee:* $45.
Contact Dr. James A. Momoh
    Chairman
    202-806-6585

See in-depth description on page 445.

SYSTEMS SCIENCE

School of Engineering, Department of Systems and Computer Science
Programs Awards MSCS, MU Sys E. Offered through the Graduate School of Arts and Sciences. Part-time programs available.

Faculty Research Analysis of blending algorithms, software metrics and their limitations.
Entrance Requirements GRE General Test, TOEFL, minimum GPA of 3.0.
Degree Requirements Computer language, comprehensive exam required, thesis optional, foreign language not required.
Financial Aid Fellowships, research assistantships, teaching assistantships, grants, institutionally sponsored loans, and career-related internships or fieldwork available. *Financial aid application deadline: 4/1.*
Applying *Deadline:* 4/1 (11/1 for spring admission). *Fee:* $45.
Contact Dr. Ronald Leach
    Acting Chair
    202-806-6595

SOUTHEASTERN UNIVERSITY
Washington, DC 20024-2788

OVERVIEW
Southeastern University is an independent coed comprehensive institution.

ENROLLMENT
1,120 graduate, professional, and undergraduate students; 113 full-time matriculated graduate/professional students (50 women), 115 part-time matriculated graduate/professional students (51 women).

GRADUATE FACULTY
12 full-time (2 women), 60 part-time (5 women), 22 FTE.

EXPENSES
Tuition $228 per credit hour. Fees $100 per quarter (minimum).

HOUSING
On-campus housing not available.

STUDENT SERVICES
Career counseling, campus employment opportunities, international student services.

FACILITIES
Library: Total holdings of 38,000 volumes, 1,300 current periodical subscriptions. Access provided to on-line information retrieval services.

COMPUTER SCIENCE

Program in Computer Science
Programs Awards MS. Part-time and evening/weekend programs available.
Students 14 full-time (9 women), 13 part-time (3 women); includes 1 African-American, 25 Asian-Americans.
Degrees Awarded In 1996, 17 degrees awarded.
Entrance Requirements GRE General Test, TOEFL.
Applying *Deadline:* rolling. *Fee:* $45.
Contact Jack Flinter
    Director of Admissions
    202-265-5343
    Fax: 202-488-8093

FLORIDA

EMBRY-RIDDLE AERONAUTICAL UNIVERSITY
Daytona Beach, FL 32114-3900

OVERVIEW
Embry-Riddle Aeronautical University is an independent coed comprehensive institution.

ENROLLMENT
4,135 graduate, professional, and undergraduate students; 119 full-time matriculated graduate/professional students (23 women), 86 part-time matriculated graduate/professional students (31 women).

GRADUATE FACULTY
37 full-time (2 women), 7 part-time (1 woman); includes 5 minority (all Asian-Americans).

EXPENSES
Tuition $400 per credit hour. Fees $130 per year.

HOUSING
Rooms and/or apartments available to single students at an average cost of $2700 per year ($5226 including board); available to married students at an average cost of $5000 per year. Graduate housing contact: Sonja Taylor, 904-226-6555.

STUDENT SERVICES
Low-cost health insurance, career counseling, free psychological counseling, campus safety program, campus employment opportunities, international student services.

FACILITIES
Library: Jack R. Hunt Memorial Library; total holdings of 79,657 volumes, 251,457 microforms, 1,931 current periodical subscriptions. A total of 45 personal computers in all libraries. Access provided to on-line information retrieval services. *Computer:* Campuswide network is available with full Internet access. Total number of PCs/terminals supplied for student use: 425. Computer services are offered at no charge. *Special:* In science and engineering: Air traffic flow control laboratory, total airspace and airport modeler, differential GPS applications laboratory, aviation human factors laboratory, space physics laboratory.

SOFTWARE ENGINEERING

Department of Computer Science and Software Engineering
Programs Offers program in software engineering (MSE). Part-time and evening/weekend programs available.
Faculty 8 full-time (1 woman), 1 (woman) part-time.
Faculty Research Beta testing for support of flight data processing, real-time systems software. *Total annual research expenditures:* $186,000.
Students 21 full-time (1 woman), 20 part-time (6 women); includes 13 minority (6 African-Americans, 4 Asian-Americans, 3 Hispanics), 16 international. Average age 27.
Degrees Awarded In 1996, 4 degrees awarded.
Entrance Requirements TOEFL (minimum score 550), minimum GPA of 3.0 senior year, 2.5 overall; previous course work in computer science.

Degree Requirements Computer language, thesis or alternative required, foreign language not required.
Financial Aid In 1996–97, 11 research assistantships averaging $950 per month, 7 teaching assistantships averaging $950 per month, 18 assistantships averaging $950 per month were awarded; fellowships, Federal Work-Study, and career-related internships or fieldwork also available. *Financial aid application deadline:* 4/15.
Applying 23 applicants, 78% accepted. *Deadline:* rolling. *Fee:* $30 ($50 for international students).
Contact *Ginny Tait*
Graduate Admissions Specialist
904-226-6115
Fax: 904-226-6299

See in-depth description on page 427.

FLORIDA AGRICULTURAL AND MECHANICAL UNIVERSITY
Tallahassee, FL 32307

OVERVIEW
Florida Agricultural and Mechanical University is a public coed university.

ENROLLMENT
10,693 graduate, professional, and undergraduate students; 1,381 matriculated graduate/professional students (889 women).

GRADUATE FACULTY
714 full-time (309 women), 111 part-time (49 women); includes 667 minority (601 African-Americans, 53 Asian-Americans, 13 Hispanics).

EXPENSES
Tuition $138 per credit hour for state residents; $436 per credit hour for nonresidents. Fees $96 per year.

HOUSING
Rooms and/or apartments available to single students (20 units) and married students (69 units) at an average cost of $1976 per year ($3854 including board). Housing application deadline: 7/1. Graduate housing contact: Housing Office, 904-599-3681.

STUDENT SERVICES
Disabled student services, low-cost health insurance, career counseling, free psychological counseling, daycare facilities.

FACILITIES
Library: Coleman Library plus 8 additional on-campus libraries; total holdings of 529,151 volumes, 102,166 microforms, 5,501 current periodical subscriptions. Access provided to on-line information retrieval services. *Computer:* Campuswide network is available with full Internet access. Total number of PCs/terminals supplied for student use: 100. Computer services are offered at no charge. *Special:* In science and engineering: Mulrennan Research Center.

ELECTRICAL ENGINEERING

Division of Graduate Studies, Research, and Continuing Education, FAMU-FSU College of Engineering, Department of Electrical Engineering
Programs Awards MS, PhD.
Students 6 (3 women); includes 6 minority (all African-Americans).

Degrees Awarded In 1996, 1 master's awarded.
Entrance Requirements For master's, GRE General Test (minimum combined score of 1000), minimum GPA of 3.0.
Applying *Deadline:* 7/1. *Fee:* $20.
Contact *Dr. C. J. Chen*
Dean
904-487-6100
Fax: 904-487-6486

FLORIDA ATLANTIC UNIVERSITY
Boca Raton, FL 33431-0991

OVERVIEW
Florida Atlantic University is a public coed university.

ENROLLMENT
18,362 graduate, professional, and undergraduate students; 878 full-time matriculated graduate/professional students (490 women), 1,760 part-time matriculated graduate/professional students (1,078 women).

GRADUATE FACULTY
706 full-time (269 women), 6 part-time (5 women); includes 135 minority (38 African-Americans, 63 Asian-Americans, 31 Hispanics, 3 Native Americans).

EXPENSES
Tuition $2380 per year full-time, $132 per credit hour part-time for state residents; $7877 per year full-time, $438 per credit hour part-time for nonresidents. Fees $5 per year (minimum).

HOUSING
Rooms and/or apartments available to single students (1,582 units) at an average cost of $1790 per year ($4160 including board); available to married students (521 units) at an average cost of $1790 per year ($5090 including board). Housing application deadline: 5/14. Graduate housing contact: Housing Office, 561-367-2880.

STUDENT SERVICES
Disabled student services, multicultural affairs office, low-cost health insurance, career counseling, free psychological counseling, exercise/wellness program, day-care facilities, campus safety program, campus employment opportunities, international student services, teacher training.

FACILITIES
Library: S. E. Wimberly Library; total holdings of 662,269 volumes, 1,281,435 microforms, 4,171 current periodical subscriptions. A total of 118 personal computers in all libraries. Access provided to on-line information retrieval services. *Computer:* Campuswide network is available with full Internet access. Total number of PCs/terminals supplied for student use: 180. Computer services are offered at no charge. *Special:* In arts and humanities: Griswold University Theatre, Ritter Art Gallery, Schmidt Center Gallery, Schmidt Institute for Comparative Studies. In science and engineering: Communications Technology Center, non-native fish research laboratory, ocean engineering corrosion research laboratory, Robotics Center, Center for Complex Systems. In social sciences: Joint Center for Environmental and Urban Problems,

South Atlantic Regional Resources Center, Florida Center for Environmental Studies.

COMPUTER ENGINEERING

College of Engineering, Department of Computer Science and Engineering, Program in Computer Engineering
Programs Awards MS, PhD. Part-time and evening/weekend programs available.
Faculty 11 full-time (1 woman).
Faculty Research VLSI and neural networks, data communications, fault-tolerance, data security, parallel systems.
Students 28 full-time (7 women), 35 part-time (5 women); includes 17 minority (3 African-Americans, 14 Asian-Americans), 26 international.
Degrees Awarded In 1996, 40 master's, 3 doctorates awarded. Terminal master's awarded for partial completion of doctoral program.
Entrance Requirements For master's, GRE General Test (minimum combined score of 1000), TOEFL (minimum score 550), minimum GPA of 3.0; for doctorate, TOEFL (minimum score 550), GRE General Test (minimum combined score of 1100) and minimum GPA of 3.0 or GRE General Test (minimum combined score of 1000) and minimum GPA of 3.5.
Degree Requirements For master's, thesis required (for some programs), foreign language not required; for doctorate, dissertation, qualifying exam required, foreign language not required.
Financial Aid In 1996–97, 39 students received aid, including 1 fellowship, 13 research assistantships, 7 teaching assistantships, 11 graduate assistantships; Federal Work-Study and career-related internships or fieldwork also available. Aid available to part-time students. *Financial aid application deadline:* 4/1; applicants required to submit FAFSA.
Applying *Deadline:* 4/10 (priority date; rolling processing; 10/1 for spring admission). *Fee:* $20.
Contact *Patricia Capozziello*
Graduate Admissions Coordinator
561-367-2694
Fax: 561-367-2659

COMPUTER SCIENCE

College of Engineering, Department of Computer Science and Engineering, Program in Computer Science
Programs Awards MS, PhD. Part-time and evening/weekend programs available.
Faculty 11 full-time (1 woman).
Faculty Research Software engineering, artificial intelligence, performance evaluation, queuing theory.
Students 36 full-time (10 women), 46 part-time (13 women); includes 24 minority (1 African-American, 17 Asian-Americans, 6 Hispanics), 39 international.
Degrees Awarded In 1996, 28 master's, 4 doctorates awarded.
Entrance Requirements For master's, GRE General Test (minimum combined score of 1000), TOEFL (minimum score 550), minimum GPA of 3.0 in last 60 hours of undergraduate work; for doctorate, TOEFL (minimum score 550), GRE General Test (minimum combined score of 1100) and minimum GPA of 3.0 or GRE General Test (minimum combined score of 1000) and minimum GPA of 3.5.
Degree Requirements For master's, computer language, thesis (for some programs) required, foreign language not required; for doctorate, computer language, dissertation, qualifying exam required, foreign language not required.
Financial Aid Fellowships, research assistantships, teaching assistantships, graduate assistantships, Federal Work-Study, and career-related internships or fieldwork available. Aid available to part-time

students. *Financial aid application deadline:* 4/1; applicants required to submit FAFSA.

Applying   *Deadline:* 4/10 (priority date; rolling processing; 10/1 for spring admission). *Fee:* $20.

Contact   *Patricia Capozziello*
Graduate Admissions Coordinator
561-367-2694
Fax: 561-367-2659

ELECTRICAL ENGINEERING

College of Engineering, Department of Electrical Engineering

Programs   Awards MS, PhD. Part-time and evening/weekend programs available.

Faculty   16 full-time (3 women), 2 part-time (0 women).

Faculty Research   Robotics, digital signal processing, electromagnetics, imaging systems, controls. *Total annual research expenditures:* $658,000.

Students   21 full-time (3 women), 40 part-time (7 women); includes 12 minority (4 African-Americans, 3 Asian-Americans, 5 Hispanics), 16 international.

Degrees Awarded   In 1996, 20 master's, 4 doctorates awarded. Terminal master's awarded for partial completion of doctoral program.

Entrance Requirements   GRE General Test (minimum combined score of 1000), TOEFL (minimum score 550), minimum GPA of 3.0.

Degree Requirements   For master's, thesis required (for some programs), foreign language not required; for doctorate, dissertation, qualifying exam required, foreign language not required.

Financial Aid   In 1996–97, 47 students received aid, including 2 fellowships totaling $19,658, 21 research assistantships totaling $92,109, 26 teaching assistantships totaling $121,810, 4 graduate assistantships totaling $4,045; Federal Work-Study and career-related internships or fieldwork also available. Aid available to part-time students. *Financial aid application deadline:* 4/1; applicants required to submit FAFSA.

Applying   *Deadline:* 4/10 (priority date; rolling processing; 10/1 for spring admission). *Fee:* $20.

Contact   *Patricia Capozziello*
Graduate Admissions Coordinator
561-367-2694
Fax: 561-367-2659

FLORIDA INSTITUTE OF TECHNOLOGY
Melbourne, FL 32901-6975

OVERVIEW
Florida Institute of Technology is an independent coed university.

ENROLLMENT
4,185 graduate, professional, and undergraduate students; 394 full-time matriculated graduate/professional students (162 women), 1,906 part-time matriculated graduate/professional students (723 women).

GRADUATE FACULTY
191 full-time (29 women), 244 part-time (43 women); includes 17 minority (1 African-American, 13 Asian-Americans, 3 Hispanics).

TUITION
$517 per credit hour.

HOUSING
Rooms and/or apartments available to single students (507 units) at an average cost of $1970 per year ($4640 including board); available to married students (16 units) at an average cost of $6456 per year ($8928 including board). Graduate housing contact: Philip Cortese, 407-768-8000 Ext. 8080.

STUDENT SERVICES
Disabled student services, low-cost health insurance, career counseling, free psychological counseling, campus employment opportunities, international student services.

FACILITIES
Library: Evans Library; total holdings of 323,068 volumes, 203,465 microforms, 1,524 current periodical subscriptions. A total of 55 personal computers in all libraries. Access provided to on-line information retrieval services. *Computer:* Campuswide network is available with full Internet access. Total number of PCs/terminals supplied for student use: 400. Computer services are offered at no charge. *Special:* In science and engineering: Vero Beach Marine Science Research Center, Center for Electronics Manufacturability, Claude Pepper Institute for Aging and Therapeutic Research, Southern Association for Research in Astronomy. In social sciences: East Central Florida Memory Disorder Clinic.

COMPUTER ENGINEERING

College of Engineering, Division of Electrical and Computer Science and Engineering, Program in Computer Engineering

Programs   Awards MS, PhD. Part-time and evening/weekend programs available.

Faculty   6 full-time (0 women), 2 part-time (0 women).

Faculty Research   Neural networks, parallel processing, reliability testing, image processing. *Total annual research expenditures:* $113,554.

Students   12 full-time (2 women), 22 part-time (2 women); includes 2 minority (both Hispanics), 22 international. Average age 30.

Degrees Awarded   In 1996, 10 master's, 1 doctorate awarded.

Entrance Requirements   For master's, minimum GPA of 3.0; for doctorate, minimum GPA of 3.2.

Degree Requirements   For master's, thesis optional, foreign language not required; for doctorate, dissertation, comprehensive exam required, foreign language not required.

Financial Aid   In 1996–97, 1 teaching assistantship averaging $903 per month and totaling $3,610, 1 tuition remission averaging $777 per month and totaling $3,108 were awarded; research assistantships also available. *Financial aid application deadline:* 3/1; applicants required to submit FAFSA.

Applying   64 applicants, 63% accepted. *Deadline:* rolling. *Fee:* $50.

Contact   *Carolyn P. Farrior*
Associate Dean of Graduate Admissions
407-768-8000 Ext. 7118
Fax: 407-723-9468
E-mail: cfarrior@fit.edu

See in-depth description on page 431.

COMPUTER SCIENCE

College of Engineering, Division of Electrical and Computer Science and Engineering, Department of Computer Science, Program in Computer Science

Programs   Awards MS, PhD. Part-time and evening/weekend programs available.

Students 14 full-time (8 women), 90 part-time (18 women); includes 11 minority (6 African-Americans, 1 Asian-American, 2 Hispanics, 2 Native Americans), 22 international. Average age 33.

Degrees Awarded In 1996, 23 master's, 3 doctorates awarded.

Entrance Requirements For master's, minimum GPA of 3.0; for doctorate, GRE General Test, GRE Subject Test (computer science), minimum GPA of 3.2.

Degree Requirements For master's, computer language required, foreign language not required; for doctorate, computer language, dissertation, comprehensive exam required, foreign language not required.

Financial Aid In 1996–97, 4 research assistantships (1 to a first-year student) averaging $1,033 per month and totaling $16,530, 10 teaching assistantships (1 to a first-year student) averaging $946 per month and totaling $37,830, 15 tuition remissions (2 to first-year students) averaging $932 per month and totaling $55,944 were awarded. *Financial aid application deadline:* 3/1; applicants required to submit FAFSA.

Applying 110 applicants, 66% accepted. *Deadline:* rolling. *Fee:* $50.

Contact *Carolyn P. Farrior*
Associate Dean of Graduate Admissions
407-768-8000 Ext. 7118
Fax: 407-723-9468

See in-depth description on page 429.

ELECTRICAL ENGINEERING

College of Engineering, Division of Electrical and Computer Science and Engineering, Program in Electrical Engineering

Programs Awards MS, PhD.

Faculty 7 full-time (0 women), 1 part-time (0 women).

Faculty Research Electrooptics, electromagnetics, microelectronics, signals and controls, neural network applications. *Total annual research expenditures:* $1.08 million.

Students 13 full-time (1 woman), 104 part-time (9 women); includes 20 minority (4 African-Americans, 6 Asian-Americans, 10 Hispanics), 32 international. Average age 31.

Degrees Awarded In 1996, 33 master's, 9 doctorates awarded.

Entrance Requirements For master's, minimum GPA of 3.0; for doctorate, minimum GPA of 3.2.

Degree Requirements For master's, thesis optional, foreign language not required; for doctorate, dissertation, comprehensive exam.

Financial Aid In 1996–97, 11 research assistantships averaging $850 per month and totaling $37,391, 10 teaching assistantships (2 to first-year students) averaging $874 per month and totaling $34,960, 17 tuition remissions (2 to first-year students) averaging $788 per month and totaling $53,613 were awarded. *Financial aid application deadline:* 3/1; applicants required to submit FAFSA.

Applying 132 applicants, 74% accepted. *Deadline:* rolling. *Fee:* $50.

Contact *Carolyn P. Farrior*
Associate Dean of Graduate Admissions
407-768-8000 Ext. 7118
Fax: 407-723-9468
E-mail: cfarrior@fit.edu

See in-depth description on page 431.

INFORMATION SCIENCE

College of Engineering, Division of Electrical and Computer Science and Engineering, Department of Computer Science, Program in Computer Information Systems

Programs Awards MS. Part-time and evening/weekend programs available.

Faculty Research Artificial intelligence, software engineering, parallel processing, computer graphics.

Students 34 full-time (8 women), 81 part-time (25 women); includes 14 minority (7 African-Americans, 1 Asian-American, 6 Hispanics), 35 international. Average age 32.

Degrees Awarded In 1996, 34 degrees awarded.

Entrance Requirements Minimum GPA of 3.0.

Degree Requirements Computer language, comprehensive exam required, foreign language and thesis not required.

Financial Aid Research assistantships, teaching assistantships, tuition remissions available. *Financial aid application deadline:* 3/1; applicants required to submit FAFSA.

Applying 53 applicants, 72% accepted. *Deadline:* rolling. *Fee:* $50.

Contact *Carolyn P. Farrior*
Associate Dean of Graduate Admissions
407-768-8000 Ext. 7118
Fax: 407-723-9468
E-mail: cfarrior@fit.edu

See in-depth description on page 429.

FLORIDA INTERNATIONAL UNIVERSITY
Miami, FL 33199

OVERVIEW
Florida International University is a public coed university.

ENROLLMENT
29,720 graduate, professional, and undergraduate students; 1,717 full-time matriculated graduate/professional students (999 women), 2,641 part-time matriculated graduate/professional students (1,627 women).

GRADUATE FACULTY
746 full-time (252 women), 53 part-time (25 women), 779 FTE; includes 222 minority (64 African-Americans, 53 Asian-Americans, 104 Hispanics, 1 Native American).

EXPENSES
Tuition $130 per credit hour for state residents; $435 per credit hour for nonresidents. Fees $46 per semester.

HOUSING
Rooms and/or apartments available to single students (1,246 units) at an average cost of $3480 per year; available to married students (36 units) at an average cost of $4365 per year. Graduate housing contact: James Wassenaar, 305-348-4190.

STUDENT SERVICES
Disabled student services, low-cost health insurance, career counseling, free psychological counseling, day-care facilities, campus safety program, campus employment opportunities, international student services.

FACILITIES
Library: University Park Campus Library; total holdings of 1,112,111 volumes, 3,029,225 microforms, 11,930 current periodical subscriptions. A total of 600 personal computers in all libraries. Access provided to on-line information retrieval services. *Computer:* Campuswide network is available with full Internet access. Total number of PCs/terminals supplied for student use: 1,500. Computer services are offered at no charge. *Special:* In arts and humanities: Art museum. In science and engineering: Drinking Water Research Center, Biomedical Research

and Innovation Center, robotics/automated manufacturing laboratory. In social sciences: Latin American and Caribbean Center, Southeast Florida Center on Aging, Multilingual/Multicultural Center, Institute for Public Policy Opinion Research, Institute for Public Policy and Citizenship, Center for the Administration of Justice, infancy laboratory.

COMPUTER ENGINEERING

College of Engineering and Design, School of Engineering, Department of Electrical Engineering, Program in Computer Engineering
Programs Awards MS. Part-time and evening/weekend programs available.
Faculty 3 full-time (0 women), 2 part-time (0 women), 3.5 FTE.
Students 2 full-time (1 woman), 12 part-time (2 women); includes 8 minority (2 Asian-Americans, 6 Hispanics), 5 international. Average age 30.
Degrees Awarded In 1996, 5 degrees awarded.
Applying 13 applicants, 31% accepted. *Deadline:* 4/1 (priority date; rolling processing; 10/1 for spring admission). *Fee:* $20.
Contact Dr. James Story
Chairperson
305-348-2807
Fax: 305-348-3707

COMPUTER SCIENCE

College of Arts and Sciences, School of Computer Science
Programs Awards MS, PhD. Part-time and evening/weekend programs available.
Faculty 24 full-time (4 women), 1 part-time (0 women), 24.5 FTE.
Faculty Research Computer graphics, database management systems, simulation.
Students 42 full-time (9 women), 34 part-time (8 women); includes 24 minority (5 African-Americans, 5 Asian-Americans, 14 Hispanics). Average age 28.
Degrees Awarded In 1996, 9 master's, 2 doctorates awarded.
Entrance Requirements For master's, GRE General Test (minimum combined score of 1650 on three sections), TOEFL; for doctorate, GRE General Test (minimum combined score of 1650 on three sections).
Degree Requirements For master's, computer language required, thesis optional, foreign language not required; for doctorate, computer language, dissertation.
Financial Aid *Application deadline:* 4/1.
Applying 163 applicants, 43% accepted. *Deadline:* 4/1 (priority date; rolling processing; 10/1 for spring admission). *Fee:* $20.
Contact Dr. Michael Evangelist
Director
305-348-2744
Fax: 305-348-3549
E-mail: wme@cs.fiu.edu
See in-depth description on page **433.**

ELECTRICAL ENGINEERING

College of Engineering and Design, School of Engineering, Department of Electrical Engineering, Program in Electrical Engineering
Programs Awards MS, PhD. Part-time and evening/weekend programs available.
Faculty 14 full-time (1 woman).
Students 23 full-time (2 women), 39 part-time (6 women); includes 26 minority (4 African-Americans, 4 Asian-Americans, 18 Hispanics), 20 international. Average age 31.
Degrees Awarded In 1996, 9 master's, 2 doctorates awarded.

Applying 55 applicants, 47% accepted. *Deadline:* 4/1 (priority date; rolling processing; 10/1 for spring admission). *Fee:* $20.
Contact Dr. James Story
Chairperson
305-348-2807
Fax: 305-348-3707

FLORIDA STATE UNIVERSITY
Tallahassee, FL 32306

OVERVIEW
Florida State University is a public coed university.

ENROLLMENT
30,264 graduate, professional, and undergraduate students; 3,746 full-time matriculated graduate/professional students (1,940 women), 2,182 part-time matriculated graduate/professional students (1,277 women).

GRADUATE FACULTY
873 full-time (250 women), 36 part-time (7 women); includes 81 minority (27 African-Americans, 33 Asian-Americans, 21 Hispanics).

TUITION
$131 per credit hour for state residents; $436 per credit hour for nonresidents.

HOUSING
Rooms and/or apartments available to single students at an average cost of $3180 per year; available to married students at an average cost of $5136 per year. Graduate housing contact: Housing Office, 904-644-2860.

STUDENT SERVICES
Disabled student services, multicultural affairs office, low-cost health insurance, career counseling, free psychological counseling, exercise/wellness program, day-care facilities, campus safety program, campus employment opportunities, international student services.

FACILITIES
Library: Robert Manning Strozier Library plus 6 additional on-campus libraries; total holdings of 2,116,510 volumes, 4,545,276 microforms, 18,296 current periodical subscriptions. Access provided to on-line information retrieval services. *Special:* In arts and humanities: Center for Music Research. In science and engineering: Super Computer Research Institute, Institute of Molecular Biophysics, super tandam Van de Graaff accelerator laboratory, National High Magnetic Field Laboratory. In social sciences: Institute for Social Research.

COMPUTER SCIENCE

College of Arts and Sciences, Department of Computer Science
Programs Awards MA, MS, PhD. Part-time programs available.
Faculty 14 full-time (2 women).
Faculty Research Expert systems, fuzzy logic programming languages, compiler design, artificial intelligence, neural networks, computer vision. *Total annual research expenditures:* $812,000.
Students 76 full-time (22 women), 24 part-time (4 women); includes 15 minority (13 African-Americans, 1 Asian-American, 1 Hispanic), 39 international. Average age 24.

Degrees Awarded   In 1996, 17 master's awarded (12% entered university research/teaching, 53% found other work related to degree, 35% continued full-time study); 2 doctorates awarded (100% entered university research/teaching).

Entrance Requirements   For master's, GRE General Test (minimum score 650 on quantitative section, 1100 combined), minimum undergraduate GPA of 3.0; for doctorate, GRE General Test (minimum score 650 on quantitative section, 1100 combined), minimum GPA of 3.0.

Degree Requirements   For master's, computer language, thesis or alternative required, foreign language not required; for doctorate, computer language, dissertation required, foreign language not required.

Financial Aid   In 1996–97, 42 students received aid, including 8 fellowships (3 to first-year students) averaging $1,000 per month, 8 research assistantships averaging $1,000 per month, 29 teaching assistantships (10 to first-year students) averaging $1,000 per month; Federal Work-Study, institutionally sponsored loans, and career-related internships or fieldwork also available. *Financial aid application deadline: 3/3.*

Applying   200 applicants, 20% accepted. *Deadline:* 3/3 (rolling processing; 7/1 for spring admission). *Fee:* $20.

Contact   R. C. Lacher
Chairman
904-644-2296
Fax: 904-644-0058

See in-depth description on page **435.**

ELECTRICAL ENGINEERING

FAMU/FSU College of Engineering, Department of Electrical Engineering

Programs   Awards MS, PhD. Part-time programs available.

Faculty   17 full-time (2 women), 2 part-time (0 women), 17.25 FTE.

Faculty Research   Electromagnetics, digital signal processing, computer systems, image processing, laser optics. *Total annual research expenditures:* $692,800.

Students   44 full-time (11 women), 10 part-time (2 women); includes 17 minority (8 African-Americans, 6 Asian-Americans, 3 Hispanics), 9 international. Average age 26.

Degrees Awarded   In 1996, 20 master's, 1 doctorate awarded.

Entrance Requirements   For master's, GRE General Test (minimum combined score of 1000), TOEFL (minimum score 550), minimum GPA of 3.0, BS in electrical engineering; for doctorate, GRE General Test (minimum combined score of 1100), TOEFL (minimum score 550), minimum GPA of 3.5 (graduate), MS in electrical engineering.

Degree Requirements   For master's, thesis optional, foreign language not required; for doctorate, dissertation required, foreign language not required.

Financial Aid   In 1996–97, 1 fellowship, 8 research assistantships (3 to first-year students) averaging $900 per month and totaling $54,000, 11 teaching assistantships (5 to first-year students) averaging $900 per month and totaling $99,000 were awarded; institutionally sponsored loans and career-related internships or fieldwork also available. *Financial aid application deadline:* 6/15.

Applying   500 applicants, 14% accepted. *Deadline:* 7/15 (rolling processing; 11/23 for spring admission). *Fee:* $20.

Contact   *Graduate Studies Assistant*
904-487-6454
Fax: 904-487-6479

NOVA SOUTHEASTERN UNIVERSITY
Fort Lauderdale, FL 33314–7721

OVERVIEW
Nova Southeastern University is an independent coed university.

ENROLLMENT
15,739 graduate, professional, and undergraduate students; 4,590 full-time matriculated graduate/professional students (2,561 women), 6,749 part-time matriculated graduate/professional students (4,129 women).

GRADUATE FACULTY
376 full-time (155 women), 750 part-time; includes 61 minority (22 African-Americans, 17 Asian-Americans, 22 Hispanics).

TUITION
$230 per credit hour (minimum).

HOUSING
Rooms and/or apartments available to single students (545 units) and married students (60 units) at an average cost of $3180 per year ($5380 including board). Graduate housing contact: Residential Life Office, 954-262-7052.

STUDENT SERVICES
Low-cost health insurance, career counseling, exercise/wellness program, campus safety program, campus employment opportunities, international student services.

FACILITIES
Library: Einstein Library plus 3 additional on-campus libraries; total holdings of 313,420 volumes, 1,157,300 microforms, 8,073 current periodical subscriptions. A total of 88 personal computers in all libraries. Access provided to on-line information retrieval services. *Computer:* Campuswide network is available with full Internet access. Computer services are offered at no charge. *Special:* In science and engineering: Institute for Marine and Coastal Studies. In social sciences: Center for Youth Policy, Family Center for Child Development, Institute for Social Services to Families.

COMPUTER SCIENCE

School of Computer and Information Sciences

Programs   Offers programs in computer information systems (MS, PhD), computer science (MS, PhD), computer technology in education (MS), computing technology in education (Ed D, PhD), information sciences (PhD), management information systems (MS, PhD). Part-time and evening/weekend programs available.

Faculty   29.

Faculty Research   Artificial intelligence, database management, human-computer interaction, distance education, computer education.

Students   650 full-time (214 women), 81 part-time (27 women); includes 114 minority (41 African-Americans, 22 Asian-Americans, 29 Hispanics, 22 Native Americans), 35 international. Average age 41.

Degrees Awarded   In 1996, 77 master's, 23 doctorates awarded. Terminal master's awarded for partial completion of doctoral program.

Entrance Requirements   For master's, GRE or portfolio; for doctorate, GRE, master's degree, or portfolio.

Degree Requirements For master's, computer language required, thesis optional; for doctorate, computer language, dissertation required, foreign language not required.

Financial Aid In 1996–97, 3 teaching assistantships averaging $1,200 per month were awarded; Federal Work-Study also available. Aid available to part-time students. *Financial aid application deadline:* 5/1.

Applying 121 applicants, 99% accepted. *Deadline:* 6/1 (priority date; rolling processing; 1/1 for spring admission). *Fee:* $50.

Contact *Liz Gawelek*
Program Representative
800-986-2247 Ext. 2000
Fax: 954-262-3915
E-mail: scisinfo@scis.nova.edu

See in-depth description on page 499.

INFORMATION SCIENCE

School of Computer and Information Sciences
Programs Offers programs in computer information systems (MS, PhD), computer science (MS, PhD), computer technology in education (MS), computing technology in education (Ed D, PhD), information sciences (PhD), management information systems (MS, PhD). Part-time and evening/weekend programs available.

Faculty 29.

Faculty Research Artificial intelligence, database management, human-computer interaction, distance education, computer education.

Students 650 full-time (214 women), 81 part-time (27 women); includes 114 minority (41 African-Americans, 22 Asian-Americans, 29 Hispanics, 22 Native Americans), 35 international. Average age 41.

Degrees Awarded In 1996, 77 master's, 23 doctorates awarded. Terminal master's awarded for partial completion of doctoral program.

Entrance Requirements For master's, GRE or portfolio; for doctorate, GRE, master's degree, or portfolio.

Degree Requirements For master's, computer language required, thesis optional; for doctorate, computer language, dissertation required, foreign language not required.

Financial Aid In 1996–97, 3 teaching assistantships averaging $1,200 per month were awarded; Federal Work-Study also available. Aid available to part-time students. *Financial aid application deadline:* 5/1.

Applying 121 applicants, 99% accepted. *Deadline:* 6/1 (priority date; rolling processing; 1/1 for spring admission). *Fee:* $50.

Contact *Liz Gawelek*
Program Representative
800-986-2247 Ext. 2000
Fax: 954-262-3915
E-mail: scisinfo@scis.nova.edu

See in-depth description on page 499.

UNIVERSITY OF CENTRAL FLORIDA
Orlando, FL 32816

OVERVIEW
University of Central Florida is a public coed university.

ENROLLMENT
27,411 graduate, professional, and undergraduate students; 2,652 full-time matriculated graduate/professional students (1,392 women), 1,498 part-time matriculated graduate/professional students (755 women).

GRADUATE FACULTY
650; includes 97 minority (25 African-Americans, 47 Asian-Americans, 24 Hispanics, 1 Native American).

EXPENSES
Tuition $3096 per year full-time, $129 per credit hour part-time for state residents; $10,440 per year full-time, $435 per credit hour part-time for nonresidents. Fees $114 per year.

HOUSING
Rooms and/or apartments available to single students (899 units) at an average cost of $2260 per year ($4305 including board); on-campus housing not available to married students. Housing application deadline: 3/1.

STUDENT SERVICES
Low-cost health insurance, career counseling, free psychological counseling, day-care facilities, campus employment opportunities.

FACILITIES
Library: Total holdings of 864,415 volumes, 1,191,233 microforms, 4,981 current periodical subscriptions. Access provided to on-line information retrieval services. *Computer:* Campuswide network is available with full Internet access. *Special:* In science and engineering: Florida Solar Energy Center, Institute for Simulation and Training, Center for Electro Optics and Lasers. In social sciences: Management Institute, Small Business Institute, Educational Research Institute, Institute for Statistics, Institute for Social Behavioral Sciences, Center for Economic Education, Caracol Field Station.

COMPUTER ENGINEERING

College of Engineering, Department of Electrical and Computer Engineering
Programs Offers programs in computer engineering (MSE, PhD), electrical engineering (MSE, PhD), optical science and engineering (MS, PhD). Part-time and evening/weekend programs available.

Faculty 26.

Faculty Research Communication theory, solid-state devices, electromagnetics, electrooptics, digital signal processing.

Students 152 full-time (20 women), 121 part-time (16 women); includes 43 minority (7 African-Americans, 19 Asian-Americans, 17 Hispanics), 86 international.

Degrees Awarded In 1996, 60 master's, 13 doctorates awarded.

Entrance Requirements GRE General Test (minimum combined score of 1000).

Degree Requirements For master's, thesis required, foreign language not required; for doctorate, dissertation, departmental qualifying exam required, foreign language not required.

Financial Aid Research assistantships, teaching assistantships, Federal Work-Study, institutionally sponsored loans, and career-related internships or fieldwork available. *Financial aid application deadline:* 2/15.

Applying 163 applicants, 82% accepted. *Deadline:* 7/15 (priority date; rolling processing; 12/15 for spring admission). *Fee:* $20.

Contact *Dr. J. Liou*
Coordinator
407-823-5339
E-mail: liou@pegasus.cc.ucf.edu

See in-depth description on page 617.

COMPUTER SCIENCE

College of Arts and Sciences, Program in Computer Science
Programs Awards MS, PhD. Part-time and evening/weekend programs available.

Faculty 19.

Faculty Research Parallel processing, databases, algorithms, virtual reality.

Students 67 full-time (19 women), 71 part-time (12 women); includes 23 minority (9 African-Americans, 11 Asian-Americans, 3 Hispanics), 40 international.

Degrees Awarded In 1996, 13 master's, 2 doctorates awarded.

Entrance Requirements For master's, GRE General Test, GRE Subject Test, minimum GPA of 3.0 in last 60 hours; for doctorate, GRE Subject Test, minimum GPA of 3.0 in last 60 hours or master's qualifying exam.

Degree Requirements For master's, computer language, thesis or alternative required, foreign language not required; for doctorate, computer language, dissertation, departmental candidacy exam required, foreign language not required.

Financial Aid Research assistantships, teaching assistantships, Federal Work-Study, institutionally sponsored loans, and career-related internships or fieldwork available. Aid available to part-time students.

Applying 66 applicants, 41% accepted. *Deadline:* 7/15 (rolling processing; 12/15 for spring admission). *Fee:* $20.

Contact Dr. Ronald Dutton
Coordinator
407-823-2920
Fax: 407-823-5419
E-mail: dutton@cs.ucf.edu

See in-depth description on page **615.**

ELECTRICAL ENGINEERING

College of Engineering, Department of Electrical and Computer Engineering

Programs Offers programs in computer engineering (MSE, PhD), electrical engineering (MSE, PhD), optical science and engineering (MS, PhD). Part-time and evening/weekend programs available.

Faculty 26.

Faculty Research Communication theory, solid-state devices, electromagnetics, electrooptics, digital signal processing.

Students 152 full-time (20 women), 121 part-time (16 women); includes 43 minority (7 African-Americans, 19 Asian-Americans, 17 Hispanics), 86 international.

Degrees Awarded In 1996, 60 master's, 13 doctorates awarded.

Entrance Requirements GRE General Test (minimum combined score of 1000).

Degree Requirements For master's, thesis required, foreign language not required; for doctorate, dissertation, departmental qualifying exam required, foreign language not required.

Financial Aid Research assistantships, teaching assistantships, Federal Work-Study, institutionally sponsored loans, and career-related internships or fieldwork available. *Financial aid application deadline:* 2/15.

Applying 163 applicants, 82% accepted. *Deadline:* 7/15 (priority date; rolling processing; 12/15 for spring admission). *Fee:* $20.

Contact Dr. J. Liou
Coordinator
407-823-5339
E-mail: liou@pegasus.cc.ucf.edu

See in-depth description on page **617.**

UNIVERSITY OF FLORIDA
Gainesville, FL 32611-8140

OVERVIEW

University of Florida is a public coed university.

ENROLLMENT

39,137 graduate, professional, and undergraduate students; 6,877 full-time, 2,081 part-time matriculated graduate/professional students.

GRADUATE FACULTY

2,500.

TUITION

$129 per credit hour for state residents; $434 per credit hour for nonresidents.

HOUSING

Rooms and/or apartments available to single students (104 units) at an average cost of $2472 per year; available to married students (980 units) at an average cost of $2884 per year. Graduate housing contact: Director of Housing, 352-392-2161.

STUDENT SERVICES

Disabled student services, multicultural affairs office, low-cost health insurance, career counseling, free psychological counseling, exercise/wellness program, day-care facilities, campus safety program, campus employment opportunities, international student services, writing training, grant writing training, teacher training.

FACILITIES

Library: University Library plus 8 additional on-campus libraries; total holdings of 3 million volumes, 4.2 million microforms. Access provided to on-line information retrieval services. *Computer:* Campuswide network is available with full Internet access. *Special:* In arts and humanities: Florida Museum of Natural History, Samuel P. Harn Museum of Art, Harn Center for the Performing Arts, Grinter Galleries, University Art Gallery. In science and engineering: Center for Intelligent Machines and Robotics, Center for Biomass Energy Studies, General Clinical Research Center, space astronomy laboratory, NSF Engineering Center for Particle Science and Technology, Whitney Marine Laboratory, Interdisciplinary Center for Biotechnology Research. In social sciences: Center for Latin American Studies, Bureau of Economics and Business Research, Center for International Studies.

COMPUTER ENGINEERING

College of Engineering, Department of Electrical and Computer Engineering

Programs Awards ME, MS, PhD, Engr. Part-time programs available.

Faculty 41 full-time (2 women), 5 part-time (0 women).

Faculty Research Communications, computer engineering, electronics, digital signal processing, photonics. *Total annual research expenditures:* $3.6 million.

Students 162 full-time (13 women), 122 part-time (11 women); includes 46 minority (5 African-Americans, 17 Asian-Americans, 21 Hispanics, 3 Native Americans), 121 international.

Degrees Awarded In 1996, 64 master's, 17 doctorates, 2 Engrs awarded. Terminal master's awarded for partial completion of doctoral program.

Entrance Requirements For master's, GRE General Test (minimum score 350 on verbal section, 1000 combined), TOEFL (minimum score 550), minimum GPA of 3.0; for doctorate, GRE General Test (minimum score 350 on verbal section, 1200 combined on three sections), TOEFL (minimum score 550), minimum GPA of 3.5; for Engr, GRE General Test.

Degree Requirements For master's, thesis optional, foreign language not required; for doctorate and Engr, thesis/dissertation required, foreign language not required.

Financial Aid In 1996–97, 161 students received aid, including 20 fellowships averaging $990 per month, 89 research assistantships averaging $789 per month, 34 teaching assistantships averaging $600 per month, 18 graduate assistantships averaging $480 per month. *Financial aid application deadline: 4/15.*

Applying 304 applicants, 79% accepted. *Deadline: 6/7* (priority date; rolling processing). *Fee:* $20.

Contact Dr. Gijs Bosman
Graduate Coordinator
352-392-6607
Fax: 352-392-8671
E-mail: gbosm@admin.ee.ufl.edu

See in-depth description on page **633.**

COMPUTER SCIENCE

College of Engineering, Department of Computer and Information Science and Engineering

Programs Offers programs in computer organization (MS, PhD, Engr), information systems (MS, PhD, Engr), manufacturing systems engineering (Certificate), software systems (MS, PhD, Engr).

Faculty 33.

Faculty Research Artifical intelligence, expert systems, network security, distributed computing systems, parallel processing system.

Students 94 full-time (18 women), 58 part-time (8 women); includes 17 minority (3 African-Americans, 8 Asian-Americans, 5 Hispanics, 1 Native American), 93 international.

Degrees Awarded In 1996, 34 master's, 10 doctorates awarded.

Entrance Requirements For master's and doctorate, GRE General Test (minimum combined score of 1100), minimum GPA of 3.0; for other advanced degree, GRE General Test.

Degree Requirements For master's, computer language, thesis (for some programs) required, foreign language not required; for doctorate, computer language, dissertation required, foreign language not required.

Financial Aid In 1996–97, 88 students received aid, including 8 fellowships averaging $916 per month, 60 research assistantships averaging $803 per month, 8 teaching assistantships averaging $951 per month, 12 graduate assistantships averaging $679 per month. *Financial aid application deadline: 6/1.*

Applying 511 applicants, 29% accepted. *Deadline: 6/7* (priority date; rolling processing; 11/1 for spring admission). *Fee:* $20.

Contact Dr. Doug Dankel
Graduate Coordinator
352-392-1387
Fax: 352-392-1220
E-mail: ddd@cise.ufl.edu

See in-depth description on page **631.**

ELECTRICAL ENGINEERING

College of Engineering, Department of Electrical and Computer Engineering

Programs Awards ME, MS, PhD, Engr. Part-time programs available.

Faculty 41 full-time (2 women), 5 part-time (0 women).

Faculty Research Communications, computer engineering, electronics, digital signal processing, photonics. *Total annual research expenditures:* $3.6 million.

Students 162 full-time (13 women), 122 part-time (11 women); includes 46 minority (5 African-Americans, 17 Asian-Americans, 21 Hispanics, 3 Native Americans), 121 international.

Degrees Awarded In 1996, 64 master's, 17 doctorates, 2 Engrs awarded. Terminal master's awarded for partial completion of doctoral program.

Entrance Requirements For master's, GRE General Test (minimum score 350 on verbal section, 1000 combined), TOEFL (minimum score 550), minimum GPA of 3.0; for doctorate, GRE General Test (minimum score 350 on verbal section, 1200 combined on three sections), TOEFL (minimum score 550), minimum GPA of 3.5; for Engr, GRE General Test.

Degree Requirements For master's, thesis optional, foreign language not required; for doctorate and Engr, thesis/dissertation required, foreign language not required.

Financial Aid In 1996–97, 161 students received aid, including 20 fellowships averaging $990 per month, 89 research assistantships averaging $789 per month, 34 teaching assistantships averaging $600 per month, 18 graduate assistantships averaging $480 per month. *Financial aid application deadline: 4/15.*

Applying 304 applicants, 79% accepted. *Deadline: 6/7* (priority date; rolling processing). *Fee:* $20.

Contact Dr. Gijs Bosman
Graduate Coordinator
352-392-6607
Fax: 352-392-8671
E-mail: gbosm@admin.ee.ufl.edu

See in-depth description on page **633.**

INFORMATION SCIENCE

College of Engineering, Department of Computer and Information Science and Engineering

Programs Offers programs in computer organization (MS, PhD, Engr), information systems (MS, PhD, Engr), manufacturing systems engineering (Certificate), software systems (MS, PhD, Engr).

Faculty 33.

Faculty Research Artifical intelligence, expert systems, network security, distributed computing systems, parallel processing system.

Students 94 full-time (18 women), 58 part-time (8 women); includes 17 minority (3 African-Americans, 8 Asian-Americans, 5 Hispanics, 1 Native American), 93 international.

Degrees Awarded In 1996, 34 master's, 10 doctorates awarded.

Entrance Requirements For master's and doctorate, GRE General Test (minimum combined score of 1100), minimum GPA of 3.0; for other advanced degree, GRE General Test.

Degree Requirements For master's, computer language, thesis (for some programs) required, foreign language not required; for doctorate, computer language, dissertation required, foreign language not required.

Financial Aid In 1996–97, 88 students received aid, including 8 fellowships averaging $916 per month, 60 research assistantships averaging $803 per month, 8 teaching assistantships averaging $951 per month, 12 graduate assistantships averaging $679 per month. *Financial aid application deadline: 6/1.*

Applying 511 applicants, 29% accepted. *Deadline: 6/7* (priority date; rolling processing; 11/1 for spring admission). *Fee:* $20.

Contact Dr. Doug Dankel
Graduate Coordinator
352-392-1387
Fax: 352-392-1220
E-mail: ddd@cise.ufl.edu

See in-depth description on page **631.**

UNIVERSITY OF MIAMI
Coral Gables, FL 33124

OVERVIEW
University of Miami is an independent coed university.

ENROLLMENT
13,677 graduate, professional, and undergraduate students; 4,715 matriculated graduate/professional students.

GRADUATE FACULTY
2,365; includes 225 minority (32 African-Americans, 55 Asian-Americans, 135 Hispanics, 3 Native Americans).

EXPENSES
Tuition $779 per credit hour. Fees $124 per year.

HOUSING
Rooms and/or apartments available to single students at an average cost of $4140 per year ($7298 including board); on-campus housing not available to married students. Graduate housing contact: Department of Residence Halls, 305-284-4505.

STUDENT SERVICES
Low-cost health insurance, career counseling, free psychological counseling, day-care facilities, campus safety program, international student services.

FACILITIES
Library: Otto G. Richter Library plus 6 additional on-campus libraries; total holdings of 2.08 million volumes, 3.13 million microforms, 19,601 current periodical subscriptions. Access provided to on-line information retrieval services. *Special:* In arts and humanities: Lowe Art Museum. In science and engineering: Bascom Palmer Eye Institute, Comprehensive Cancer Center for Florida. In social sciences: Mailman Center for Child Development.

COMPUTER SCIENCE

College of Arts and Sciences, Department of Mathematics and Computer Science
Programs   Offers programs in computer science (MA, MS), mathematics (MA, MS, DA, PhD). Part-time and evening/weekend programs available.
Faculty   27 (2 women).
Students   31 full-time (7 women), 19 part-time (4 women); includes 14 minority (1 African-American, 3 Asian-Americans, 10 Hispanics), 12 international. Average age 30.
Degrees Awarded   In 1996, 7 master's awarded (100% found work related to degree); 3 doctorates awarded (100% entered university research/teaching). Terminal master's awarded for partial completion of doctoral program.
Entrance Requirements   GRE General Test (minimum combined score of 1000), TOEFL (minimum score 550), minimum GPA of 3.0.
Degree Requirements   For master's, comprehensive exam or project required, foreign language and thesis not required; for doctorate, 1 foreign language, dissertation, qualifying exams.
Financial Aid   In 1996–97, 30 students received aid, including 1 fellowship, 25 teaching assistantships (8 to first-year students); institutionally sponsored loans and career-related internships or fieldwork also available. Aid available to part-time students. *Financial aid application deadline: 3/1.*
Applying   74 applicants, 82% accepted. *Deadline:* 7/1 (rolling processing). *Fee:* $35.

Contact   *Dr. Marvin Mielke*
Graduate Adviser
305-284-2348

ELECTRICAL ENGINEERING

College of Engineering, Department of Electrical and Computer Engineering
Programs   Offers program in electrical engineering (MSECE, PhD). Part-time programs available.
Faculty   15 (0 women).
Faculty Research   Computer network, computer vision and image processing, database systems, digital signal processing, machine intelligence. *Total annual research expenditures:* $203,792.
Students   39 full-time (9 women), 30 part-time (5 women); includes 35 minority (2 African-Americans, 16 Asian-Americans, 17 Hispanics), 34 international. Average age 23.
Degrees Awarded   In 1996, 10 master's, 5 doctorates awarded.
Entrance Requirements   For master's, GRE General Test (minimum combined score of 1000), TOEFL (minimum score 550), minimum GPA of 3.0; for doctorate, GRE General Test (minimum combined score of 1100), TOEFL (minimum score 550), minimum GPA of 3.5.
Degree Requirements   For master's, thesis optional, foreign language not required; for doctorate, dissertation, comprehensive exam required, foreign language not required.
Financial Aid   In 1996–97, 39 students received aid, including 2 fellowships, 8 research assistantships (3 to first-year students), 13 teaching assistantships (4 to first-year students), 16 graduate assistantships; Federal Work-Study, institutionally sponsored loans, and career-related internships or fieldwork also available. Aid available to part-time students.
Applying   135 applicants, 37% accepted. *Deadline:* 4/1 (priority date; 11/1 for spring admission). *Fee:* $35.
Contact   *Dr. Claude Lindquist*
Graduate Adviser
305-284-3291

UNIVERSITY OF NORTH FLORIDA
Jacksonville, FL 32224-2645

OVERVIEW
University of North Florida is a public coed comprehensive institution.

ENROLLMENT
10,000 graduate, professional, and undergraduate students; 356 full-time matriculated graduate/professional students (236 women), 1,092 part-time matriculated graduate/professional students (690 women).

GRADUATE FACULTY
191 full-time (64 women), 13 part-time (5 women); includes 32 minority (15 African-Americans, 12 Asian-Americans, 5 Hispanics).

TUITION
$3168 per year full-time, $132 per credit hour part-time for state residents; $10,488 per year full-time, $437 per credit hour part-time for nonresidents.

HOUSING
Rooms and/or apartments available to single students (1,120 units) at an average cost of $4900 (including board); available to married students at an average

cost of $9800 (including board). Housing application deadline: 7/1. Graduate housing contact: Brahan Woodham, 904-646-2636.

STUDENT SERVICES

Disabled student services, multicultural affairs office, low-cost health insurance, career counseling, free psychological counseling, exercise/wellness program, day-care facilities, campus safety program, campus employment opportunities, international student services, writing training, teacher training.

FACILITIES

Library: Thomas G. Carpenter Library; total holdings of 485,033 volumes, 714,579 microforms. Access provided to on-line information retrieval services. *Computer:* Campuswide network is available with full Internet access. Total number of PCs/terminals supplied for student use: 200. Computer service fees are included with tuition and fees. *Special:* In arts and humanities: Council for the Humanities. In science and engineering: Center for Membrane Physics, Center for Alcohol and Drug Abuse. In social sciences: Florida Institute of Education, Small Business Development Center, Center for Local Government Administration.

COMPUTER SCIENCE

College of Computer Sciences and Engineering
Programs Offers program in computer and information sciences (MA). Part-time programs available.
Faculty 14 full-time (3 women).
Faculty Research Parallel processing, software engineering, artificial intelligence, human factors, human–machine interfacing.
Students 9 full-time (5 women), 42 part-time (12 women); includes 10 minority (all Asian-Americans), 1 international. Average age 36.
Degrees Awarded In 1996, 8 degrees awarded.
Entrance Requirements GRE General Test (minimum combined score of 1000).
Degree Requirements Thesis required, foreign language not required.
Financial Aid Research assistantships, teaching assistantships, partial tuition waivers available.
Applying 23 applicants, 35% accepted. *Deadline:* rolling. *Fee:* $20.
Contact Dr. Charles Winton
  Interim Dean
  904-646-2985

COMPUTER SCIENCE

College of Arts and Sciences, Department of Mathematics and Statistics
Programs Offerings include computer science (MS).
Department Faculty 15 full-time (5 women).
Entrance Requirements GRE General Test, GRE Subject Test, TOEFL, minimum GPA of 3.0.
Degree Requirements Comprehensive exam required, thesis optional, foreign language not required.
Applying *Deadline:* rolling. *Fee:* $20.
Contact Dr. Adel Boules
  Graduate Director
  904-646-2653

INFORMATION SCIENCE

College of Computer Sciences and Engineering
Programs Offers program in computer and information sciences (MA). Part-time programs available.

Faculty 14 full-time (3 women).
Faculty Research Parallel processing, software engineering, artificial intelligence, human factors, human–machine interfacing.
Students 9 full-time (5 women), 42 part-time (12 women); includes 10 minority (all Asian-Americans), 1 international. Average age 36.
Degrees Awarded In 1996, 8 degrees awarded.
Entrance Requirements GRE General Test (minimum combined score of 1000).
Degree Requirements Thesis required, foreign language not required.
Financial Aid Research assistantships, teaching assistantships, partial tuition waivers available.
Applying 23 applicants, 35% accepted. *Deadline:* rolling. *Fee:* $20.
Contact Dr. Charles Winton
  Interim Dean
  904-646-2985

UNIVERSITY OF SOUTH FLORIDA
Tampa, FL 33620-9951

OVERVIEW

University of South Florida is a public coed university.

ENROLLMENT

30,938 graduate, professional, and undergraduate students; 2,791 full-time, 3,829 part-time matriculated graduate/professional students.

GRADUATE FACULTY

1,654.

TUITION

$134 per credit hour for state residents; $440 per credit hour for nonresidents.

HOUSING

Rooms and/or apartments available to single students; on-campus housing not available to married students. Graduate housing contact: Joan E. Tallis, 813-974-2764.

STUDENT SERVICES

Disabled student services, career counseling, free psychological counseling, day-care facilities, campus safety program, campus employment opportunities, international student services.

FACILITIES

Library: Main library plus 6 additional on-campus libraries; total holdings of 1.5 million volumes, 4 million microforms, 10,000 current periodical subscriptions. Access provided to on-line information retrieval services. *Computer:* Campuswide network is available with full Internet access. *Special:* In science and engineering: Florida Institute of Oceanography, Center for Engineering Development and Research, Long Term Care Gerontology Center, Center for Nearshore Marine Science, Center for Microelectronics Research. In social sciences: Juvenile Justice Training Academy.

COMPUTER ENGINEERING

College of Engineering, Department of Computer Science and Engineering, Program of Computer Engineering
Programs Awards M Cp E, MS Cp E. Part-time programs available.

Entrance Requirements GRE General Test (minimum combined score of 1150), minimum GPA of 3.0 during previous 2 years.
Degree Requirements Thesis required, foreign language not required.
Applying *Deadline:* 6/1 (rolling processing; 10/23 for spring admission). *Fee:* $20.
Contact Dr. Lawrence Hall
   Graduate Program Director
   813-974-3033
   Fax: 813-974-5456

See in-depth description on page **715.**

COMPUTER SCIENCE

College of Engineering, Department of Computer Science and Engineering, Program of Computer Science
Programs Awards MCS, MSCS. Part-time programs available.
Entrance Requirements GRE General Test (minimum combined score of 1150), minimum GPA of 3.0 during previous 2 years.
Degree Requirements Computer language, thesis (for some programs) required, foreign language not required.
Applying *Deadline:* 6/1 (rolling processing; 10/23 for spring admission). *Fee:* $20.
Contact Head
   813-974-4195

See in-depth description on page **715.**

ELECTRICAL ENGINEERING

College of Engineering, Department of Electrical Engineering
Programs Awards ME, MEE, MSE, MSEE, PhD. Part-time programs available.
Faculty 23 full-time (0 women).
Faculty Research Controls, including system parameter identification; computer-aided design and modeling; microwave and hybrid circuits.
Students 69 full-time (11 women), 77 part-time (10 women); includes 22 minority (6 African-Americans, 11 Asian-Americans, 5 Hispanics), 54 international. Average age 31.
Degrees Awarded In 1996, 46 master's, 12 doctorates awarded. Terminal master's awarded for partial completion of doctoral program.
Entrance Requirements For master's, GRE General Test (minimum combined score of 1000), minimum GPA of 3.0 during previous 2 years; for doctorate, GRE General Test (minimum combined score of 1000).
Degree Requirements For master's, thesis or alternative required, foreign language not required; for doctorate, dissertation, 2 tools of research as specified by dissertation required, foreign language not required.
Financial Aid In 1996–97, 66 students received aid, including 1 fellowship averaging $778 per month and totaling $7,000, 45 research assistantships averaging $778 per month, 20 teaching assistantships averaging $778 per month and totaling $140,000; partial tuition waivers, Federal Work-Study, institutionally sponsored loans, and career-related internships or fieldwork also available. Aid available to part-time students. Financial aid applicants required to submit FAFSA.
Applying *Deadline:* 6/1 (rolling processing; 10/23 for spring admission). *Fee:* $20.
Contact Dr. Kenneth A. Buckle
   Graduate Program Coordinator
   813-974-2369
   Fax: 813-974-5250
   E-mail: buckle@eng.usf.edu

See in-depth description on page **717.**

UNIVERSITY OF WEST FLORIDA
Pensacola, FL 32514-5750

OVERVIEW
University of West Florida is a public coed comprehensive institution.

ENROLLMENT
6,987 graduate, professional, and undergraduate students; 398 full-time matriculated graduate/professional students (240 women), 905 part-time matriculated graduate/professional students (508 women).

GRADUATE FACULTY
155 full-time (50 women), 90 part-time (29 women), 194.4 FTE; includes 19 minority (9 African-Americans, 7 Asian-Americans, 1 Hispanic, 2 Native Americans).

TUITION
$116 per credit hour (minimum) for state residents; $387 per credit hour (minimum) for nonresidents.

HOUSING
Rooms and/or apartments available to single students (500 units) at an average cost of $2053 per year; available to married students (16 units) at an average cost of $3248 per year. Graduate housing contact: Frank Kelly, 904-474-2463.

STUDENT SERVICES
Low-cost health insurance, career counseling, free psychological counseling, day-care facilities, campus safety program, campus employment opportunities, international student services.

FACILITIES
Library: Pace Library; total holdings of 570,769 volumes, 1,061,599 microforms, 3,333 current periodical subscriptions. A total of 87 personal computers in all libraries. Access provided to on-line information retrieval services. *Computer:* Campuswide network is available with full Internet access. Computer services are offered at no charge. *Special:* In science and engineering: Center for Environmental Diagnostics and Bioremediation, Institute for Human and Machine Cognition. In social sciences: Educational Research and Development Center, Small Business Development Center.

COMPUTER SCIENCE

College of Science and Technology, Department of Computer Science
Programs Offers programs in computer science (MS), systems and control engineering (MS). Part-time and evening/weekend programs available.
Students 24 full-time (3 women), 95 part-time (18 women); includes 18 minority (4 African-Americans, 7 Asian-Americans, 6 Hispanics, 1 Native American), 8 international. Average age 34.
Degrees Awarded In 1996, 42 degrees awarded.
Entrance Requirements GRE General Test (minimum combined score of 1000).
Degree Requirements Computer language, thesis or alternative required, foreign language not required.
Financial Aid Fellowships, research assistantships available.
Applying 49 applicants, 94% accepted. *Deadline:* 7/29. *Fee:* $20.
Contact Dr. Ed Rodgers
   Chairperson
   904-474-2542

GEORGIA

CLARK ATLANTA UNIVERSITY
Atlanta, GA 30314

OVERVIEW
Clark Atlanta University is an independent-religious coed university.

ENROLLMENT
5,798 graduate, professional, and undergraduate students; 751 full-time matriculated graduate/professional students (536 women), 656 part-time matriculated graduate/professional students (421 women).

EXPENSES
Tuition $4584 per year full-time, $382 per credit hour part-time. Fees $100 per year.

HOUSING
Rooms and/or apartments available to single students; on-campus housing not available to married students. Housing application deadline: 6/1. Graduate housing contact: Jerryl Briggs, 404-880-8072.

STUDENT SERVICES
Low-cost health insurance, career counseling, free psychological counseling.

FACILITIES
Library: Robert W. Woodruff Library; total holdings of 535,815 volumes, 756,448 microforms, 2,271 current periodical subscriptions. Access provided to on-line information retrieval services. *Special:* In arts and humanities: Center on Aging, Center for African and African-American Studies, Institute for Humanistic Studies. In science and engineering: Polymer Research Center. In social sciences: Government and Public Policy Institute, Institute for Applied Social Research, Institute for Criminal Justice, Institute for International Affairs, Rural Poverty Institute, Institute for Defense Analysis, Institute for Organization and Management, Cuban Mental Health Residential Facility.

COMPUTER SCIENCE

School of Arts and Sciences, Department of Computer and Information Science
Programs Awards MS.
Students 27 full-time (13 women), 22 part-time (5 women); includes 40 minority (35 African-Americans, 5 Asian-Americans), 9 international.
Degrees Awarded In 1996, 26 degrees awarded.
Entrance Requirements GRE General Test, minimum GPA of 2.5.
Degree Requirements 1 foreign language (computer language can substitute), thesis.
Financial Aid Fellowships, research assistantships available. *Financial aid application deadline: 4/30.*
Applying 28 applicants, 50% accepted. *Deadline:* 4/1 (rolling processing; 11/1 for spring admission). *Fee:* $40.
Contact *Yvette McKinney*
Assistant Director of Graduate Programs
404-880-8709

COMPUTER SCIENCE

School of Arts and Sciences, Department of Mathematical Sciences
Programs Offerings include computer science (MS).

Entrance Requirements GRE General Test, minimum GPA of 2.5.
Degree Requirements 1 foreign language (computer language can substitute), thesis.
Applying *Deadline:* 4/1 (rolling processing; 11/1 for spring admission). *Fee:* $40.
Contact *Yvette McKinney*
Assistant Director of Graduate Programs
404-880-8709

INFORMATION SCIENCE

School of Arts and Sciences, Department of Computer and Information Science
Programs Awards MS.
Students 27 full-time (13 women), 22 part-time (5 women); includes 40 minority (35 African-Americans, 5 Asian-Americans), 9 international.
Degrees Awarded In 1996, 26 degrees awarded.
Entrance Requirements GRE General Test, minimum GPA of 2.5.
Degree Requirements 1 foreign language (computer language can substitute), thesis.
Financial Aid Fellowships, research assistantships available. *Financial aid application deadline: 4/30.*
Applying 28 applicants, 50% accepted. *Deadline:* 4/1 (rolling processing; 11/1 for spring admission). *Fee:* $40.
Contact *Yvette McKinney*
Assistant Director of Graduate Programs
404-880-8709

COLUMBUS STATE UNIVERSITY
Columbus, GA 31907-5645

OVERVIEW
Columbus State University is a public coed comprehensive institution.

ENROLLMENT
5,536 graduate, professional, and undergraduate students; 356 full-time matriculated graduate/professional students (220 women), 414 part-time matriculated graduate/professional students (261 women).

GRADUATE FACULTY
108 full-time (43 women), 27 part-time (11 women), 117 FTE; includes 11 minority (3 African-Americans, 3 Asian-Americans, 5 Hispanics).

TUITION
$2112 per year full-time, $90 per quarter hour part-time for state residents; $7032 per year full-time, $228 per quarter hour part-time for nonresidents.

HOUSING
Rooms and/or apartments available to single students (300 units) at an average cost of $3458 (including board); on-campus housing not available to married students. Housing application deadline: 7/1. Graduate housing contact: Larry Kees, 706-568-2273.

STUDENT SERVICES
Disabled student services, multicultural affairs office, career counseling, free psychological counseling, exercise/wellness program, day-care facilities, campus

safety program, campus employment opportunities, international student services, teacher training.

FACILITIES

Library: Schwob Memorial Library; total holdings of 250,429 volumes, 823,752 microforms, 1,426 current periodical subscriptions. A total of 60 personal computers in all libraries. Access provided to on-line information retrieval services. *Computer:* Campuswide network is available with full Internet access. Total number of PCs/terminals supplied for student use: 300. Computer services are offered at no charge. *Special:* In arts and humanities: Columbus Child Care Resource and Referral Center. In science and engineering: Space Science (Challenger) Center, Oxbow Meadows Environmental Learning Center, Columbus Regional Mathematics Collaborative.

COMPUTER SCIENCE

School of Science
Programs Offerings include applied computer science (MS).
School Faculty 16.
Entrance Requirements GRE General Test (minimum combined score of 800) (environmental science).
Degree Requirements Thesis (environmental science) required, foreign language not required.
Applying *Deadline:* 9/4 (priority date; rolling processing; 3/12 for spring admission). *Fee:* $20.
Contact Katie Thornton
Graduate Admissions
706-568-2279
Fax: 706-568-2462

EMORY UNIVERSITY
Atlanta, GA 30322-1100

OVERVIEW

Emory University is an independent-religious coed university.

ENROLLMENT

11,270 graduate, professional, and undergraduate students; 3,889 full-time matriculated graduate/professional students (2,008 women), 1,354 part-time matriculated graduate/professional students (762 women).

GRADUATE FACULTY

1,494 full-time, 157 part-time; includes 273 minority.

TUITION

$21,070 per year full-time, $940 per semester hour part-time.

HOUSING

Rooms and/or apartments available to single students (3,110 units) at an average cost of $3702 per year; available to married students (276 units) at an average cost of $6442 per year. Graduate housing contact: Residential Services, 404-727-7631.

STUDENT SERVICES

Low-cost health insurance, career counseling, free psychological counseling.

FACILITIES

Library: Robert W. Woodruff Library plus 6 additional on-campus libraries; total holdings of 2,311,985 volumes, 3,178,980 microforms, 24,687 current periodical subscriptions. Access provided to on-line information retrieval services. *Computer:* Campuswide network is available with full Internet access. Computer service fees are included with tuition and fees. *Special:* In arts and humanities: Institute of the Liberal Arts. In science and engineering: Yerkes Regional Primate Research Center, R/V *Baker-Lester* (50-foot diesel), School of Medicine Teaching Hospital, Winship Cancer Center, scanning electron microscope facility. In social sciences: Center for Research in Social Change, Carter Center.

COMPUTER SCIENCE

Graduate School of Arts and Sciences, Department of Mathematics and Computer Science
Programs Offers programs in mathematics (MA, MS, PhD), mathematics/computer science (MS).
Faculty 22 full-time (4 women), 4 part-time (0 women), 26 FTE.
Faculty Research *Total annual research expenditures:* $1.1 million.
Students 37 full-time (17 women), 6 part-time (3 women); includes 3 minority (1 African-American, 1 Asian-American, 1 Hispanic), 18 international.
Degrees Awarded In 1996, 5 master's, 5 doctorates awarded. Terminal master's awarded for partial completion of doctoral program.
Entrance Requirements For master's, GRE General Test (combined average 1600 on three sections); for doctorate, GRE General Test (combined average 1800 on three sections).
Degree Requirements For master's, thesis; for doctorate, 1 foreign language, dissertation, comprehensive exams.
Financial Aid In 1996–97, 33 fellowships (6 to first-year students) averaging $1,185 per month and totaling $398,400, 27 tuition scholarships (6 to first-year students) totaling $474,480 were awarded; teaching assistantships also available.
Applying 79 applicants, 25% accepted. *Deadline:* 1/20. *Fee:* $45.
Contact Ron Gould
Director of Graduate Studies
404-727-7580
Fax: 404-727-5611
E-mail: dgs@mathcs.emory.edu

GEORGIA INSTITUTE OF TECHNOLOGY
Atlanta, GA 30332-0001

OVERVIEW

Georgia Institute of Technology is a public coed university.

ENROLLMENT

12,985 graduate, professional, and undergraduate students; 2,712 full-time matriculated graduate/professional students (644 women), 800 part-time matriculated graduate/professional students (168 women).

GRADUATE FACULTY

679 full-time (95 women), 7 part-time (1 woman); includes 127 minority (17 African-Americans, 101 Asian-Americans, 9 Hispanics).

EXPENSES

Tuition $2472 per year full-time, $91 per credit hour part-time for state residents; $9888 per year full-time, $297 per credit hour part-time for nonresidents. Fees $660 per year full-time, $46 per quarter (minimum) part-time.

HOUSING

Rooms and/or apartments available to single students (669 units) at an average cost of $3492 per year ($6550 including board); available to married students (300 units) at an average cost of $5040 per year ($7740 including board). Housing application deadline: 5/1. Graduate housing information: 404-894-2470.

STUDENT SERVICES

Low-cost health insurance, career counseling, free psychological counseling, exercise/wellness program, campus safety program, campus employment opportunities, international student services, writing training.

FACILITIES

Library: Price Gilbert Memorial Library; total holdings of 3 million volumes, 3,721,197 microforms, 12,713 current periodical subscriptions. A total of 149 personal computers in all libraries. Access provided to on-line information retrieval services. *Computer:* Campuswide network is available with full Internet access. Computer service fees are included with tuition and fees. *Special:* In science and engineering: Georgia Tech Research Institute, Computer Integrated Manufacturing Systems Research Center, Microelectronic Research Center, Bioengineering Center. In social sciences: Technology, Policy, and Assessment Center; Center for International Strategy, Technology, and Policy.

COMPUTER ENGINEERING

College of Engineering, School of Electrical and Computer Engineering
Programs Awards MS, MSEE, PhD. Part-time programs available.
Faculty 86 full-time (7 women), 20 part-time (1 woman).
Faculty Research Telecommunications, computer systems, microelectronics, optical engineering, digital signal processing. *Total annual research expenditures:* $8.773 million.
Students 493 full-time (64 women), 221 part-time (27 women); includes 155 minority (43 African-Americans, 87 Asian-Americans, 24 Hispanics, 1 Native American), 238 international. Average age 23.
Degrees Awarded In 1996, 216 master's, 52 doctorates awarded. Terminal master's awarded for partial completion of doctoral program.
Entrance Requirements For master's, GRE General Test (minimum score 500 on verbal section, 700 on quantitative and analytical), TOEFL (minimum score 550), minimum GPA of 3.0; for doctorate, GRE General Test (minimum score 500 on verbal section, 700 on quantitative and analytical), TOEFL (minimum score 550), minimum GPA of 3.5.
Degree Requirements For master's, thesis optional, foreign language not required; for doctorate, dissertation required, foreign language not required.
Financial Aid In 1996–97, 428 students received aid, including 41 fellowships, 319 research assistantships, 68 teaching assistantships; partial tuition waivers, Federal Work-Study, institutionally sponsored loans, and career-related internships or fieldwork also available.
Applying 583 applicants, 56% accepted. *Deadline:* 7/1 (priority date; rolling processing; 2/1 for spring admission). *Fee:* $50.

Contact *Dr. D. C. Ray*
Vice Chair
404-894-2904
Fax: 404-894-4641

COMPUTER SCIENCE

College of Computing
Programs Offers programs in computer science (MS, MSCS, PhD), human computer interaction (MSHCI). Part-time programs available.
Faculty 44 full-time (5 women), 3 part-time (1 woman), 46 FTE.
Faculty Research Computer systems, graphics, intelligent systems and artificial intelligence, networks and telecommunications, software engineering. *Total annual research expenditures:* $4.1 million.
Students 150 full-time (25 women), 41 part-time (8 women); includes 24 minority (13 African-Americans, 7 Asian-Americans, 3 Hispanics, 1 Native American), 62 international.
Degrees Awarded In 1996, 50 master's, 26 doctorates awarded. Terminal master's awarded for partial completion of doctoral program.
Entrance Requirements For master's, GRE General Test, TOEFL (minimum score 600), GRE Subject Test, minimum GPA of 3.0; for doctorate, GRE General Test, GRE Subject Test, TOEFL (minimum score 600), minimum GPA of 3.3.
Degree Requirements For master's, thesis optional, foreign language not required; for doctorate, dissertation, comprehensive exam required, foreign language not required.
Financial Aid In 1996–97, 132 students received aid, including 4 fellowships, 77 research assistantships, 49 teaching assistantships, 2 traineeships; partial tuition waivers, Federal Work-Study, institutionally sponsored loans, and career-related internships or fieldwork also available. *Financial aid application deadline:* 1/3.
Applying 278 applicants, 35% accepted. *Deadline:* 1/3 (rolling processing). *Fee:* $50.
Contact *Dr. Kurt Eiselt*
Director, Student Services
404-894-6170
Fax: 404-894-9846

See in-depth description on page **441.**

COMPUTER SCIENCE

Ivan Allen College of Management, Policy and International Affairs, Multidisciplinary Program in Human Computer Interaction
Programs Awards MSHCI. Offered jointly through the College of Computing, the Program in Information Design and Technology, and the School of Psychology; program new for fall 1997.
Entrance Requirements TOEFL.
Applying *Fee:* $50.
Contact *Dr. Albert Badre*
Director
404-894-0075
Fax: 404-894-0673
E-mail: badre@cc.gatech.edu

ELECTRICAL ENGINEERING

College of Engineering, School of Electrical and Computer Engineering
Programs Awards MS, MSEE, PhD. Part-time programs available.
Faculty 86 full-time (7 women), 20 part-time (1 woman).
Faculty Research Telecommunications, computer systems, microelectronics, optical engineering, digital signal processing. *Total annual research expenditures:* $8.773 million.
Students 493 full-time (64 women), 221 part-time (27 women); includes 155 minority (43 African-Americans, 87 Asian-Americans, 24 Hispanics, 1 Native American), 238 international. Average age 23.

Degrees Awarded In 1996, 216 master's, 52 doctorates awarded. Terminal master's awarded for partial completion of doctoral program.

Entrance Requirements For master's, GRE General Test (minimum score 500 on verbal section, 700 on quantitative and analytical), TOEFL (minimum score 550), minimum GPA of 3.0; for doctorate, GRE General Test (minimum score 500 on verbal section, 700 on quantitative and analytical), TOEFL (minimum score 550), minimum GPA of 3.5.

Degree Requirements For master's, thesis optional, foreign language not required; for doctorate, dissertation required, foreign language not required.

Financial Aid In 1996–97, 428 students received aid, including 41 fellowships, 319 research assistantships, 68 teaching assistantships; partial tuition waivers, Federal Work-Study, institutionally sponsored loans, and career-related internships or fieldwork also available.

Applying 583 applicants, 56% accepted. *Deadline:* 7/1 (priority date; rolling processing; 2/1 for spring admission). *Fee:* $50.

Contact Dr. D. C. Ray
Vice Chair
404-894-2904
Fax: 404-894-4641

GEORGIA SOUTHWESTERN STATE UNIVERSITY
Americus, GA 31709-4693

OVERVIEW
Georgia Southwestern State University is a public coed comprehensive institution.

ENROLLMENT
2,500 graduate, professional, and undergraduate students; 147 full-time matriculated graduate/professional students (110 women), 309 part-time matriculated graduate/professional students (245 women).

GRADUATE FACULTY
40 full-time (8 women), 3 part-time (all women); includes 11 minority (3 African-Americans, 6 Asian-Americans, 1 Hispanic, 1 Native American).

EXPENSES
Tuition $1851 per year full-time, $52 per quarter hour part-time for state residents; $6771 per year full-time, $190 per quarter hour part-time for nonresidents. Fees $155 per quarter.

HOUSING
Rooms and/or apartments available to single students at an average cost of $3033 (including board); on-campus housing not available to married students. Housing application deadline: 9/1. Graduate housing contact: Office of Student Life, 912-928-1387.

STUDENT SERVICES
Career counseling, campus safety program, campus employment opportunities, international student services.

FACILITIES
Library: James Earl Carter Library; total holdings of 167,558 volumes, 436,355 microforms, 857 current periodical subscriptions. *Computer:* Campuswide network is

available with full Internet access. Computer service fees are applied as a separate charge.

COMPUTER SCIENCE

School of Computer and Applied Sciences
Programs Awards MS.
Faculty 5 full-time (0 women).
Students 10 full-time (2 women), 6 part-time (3 women); includes 9 minority (2 African-Americans, 7 Asian-Americans), 7 international.
Entrance Requirements GRE General Test (minimum combined score of 900), minimum GPA of 2.5.
Financial Aid *Application deadline:* 9/1.
Applying *Deadline:* 9/1 (rolling processing; 3/15 for spring admission). *Fee:* $10.
Contact Chris Laney
Graduate Admissions Specialist
912-931-2027
Fax: 912-931-2059

MEDICAL COLLEGE OF GEORGIA
Augusta, GA 30912-1003

OVERVIEW
Medical College of Georgia is a public coed university.

ENROLLMENT
2,061 graduate, professional, and undergraduate students; 1,093 full-time matriculated graduate/professional students (389 women), 123 part-time matriculated graduate/professional students (83 women).

GRADUATE FACULTY
677 full-time (199 women), 98 part-time (40 women); includes 69 minority (27 African-Americans, 28 Asian-Americans, 14 Hispanics).

TUITION
$2757 per year full-time, $69 per credit hour part-time for state residents; $9318 per year full-time, $252 per credit hour part-time for nonresidents.

HOUSING
Rooms and/or apartments available to single students (266 units) at an average cost of $1950 per year; available to married students (64 units) at an average cost of $4892 per year. Graduate housing contact: Thomas J. Fitts, 706-721-3471.

STUDENT SERVICES
Low-cost health insurance, career counseling, free psychological counseling, day-care facilities, campus safety program, campus employment opportunities, international student services.

FACILITIES
Library: Robert B. Greenblatt Library; total holdings of 170,856 volumes, 6,008 microforms, 1,287 current periodical subscriptions. A total of 115 personal computers in all libraries. Access provided to on-line information retrieval services. *Computer:* Campuswide network is available with full Internet access. Total number of PCs/terminals supplied for student use: 75. Computer services are offered at no charge. *Special:* In science and engineering: Animal Behavior Center, Institute of Molecular

Medicine and Genetics, Sickle Cell Center, Transgenic Mouse Facility, Flow Cytometry Center.

MEDICAL INFORMATICS

Program in Allied Health Sciences
Programs Offerings include health information management (MHE).
Program Faculty 5 full-time (3 women), 2 part-time (both women).
Applying *Deadline:* 6/30 (priority date; rolling processing). *Fee:* $0.
Contact Dr. Gary C. Bond
Associate Dean
706-721-3278
Fax: 706-721-6829
E-mail: gbond@mail.mcg.edu

MERCER UNIVERSITY
Macon, GA 31207-0003

OVERVIEW
Mercer University is an independent-religious coed comprehensive institution.

ENROLLMENT
6,942 graduate, professional, and undergraduate students; 2,768 matriculated graduate/professional students.

GRADUATE FACULTY
395 full-time, 118 part-time.

TUITION
$160 per credit hour.

HOUSING
Rooms and/or apartments available to single students (175 units) and married students. Graduate housing contact: Mr. Tim Coley, 912-752-2478.

STUDENT SERVICES
Low-cost health insurance, career counseling, free psychological counseling, campus safety program, campus employment opportunities, international student services.

FACILITIES
Library: Stetson Memorial Library plus 2 additional on-campus libraries; total holdings of 404,808 volumes, 241,010 microforms, 3,346 current periodical subscriptions. A total of 35 personal computers in all libraries. Access provided to on-line information retrieval services. *Special:* In science and engineering: Mercer Engineering Research Center.

COMPUTER SCIENCE

School of Engineering
Programs Offerings include computer and information systems (MS).
School Faculty 23 full-time (1 woman), 6 part-time (0 women).
Applying *Deadline:* 8/9. *Fee:* $35 ($50 for international students).
Contact Kathy Olivier
Coordinator, Special Programs
912-752-2196

ELECTRICAL ENGINEERING

School of Engineering
Programs Offerings include electrical engineering (MSE).
School Faculty 23 full-time (1 woman), 6 part-time (0 women).
Applying *Deadline:* 8/9. *Fee:* $35 ($50 for international students).
Contact Kathy Olivier
Coordinator, Special Programs
912-752-2196

INFORMATION SCIENCE

School of Engineering
Programs Offerings include computer and information systems (MS).
School Faculty 23 full-time (1 woman), 6 part-time (0 women).
Applying *Deadline:* 8/9. *Fee:* $35 ($50 for international students).
Contact Kathy Olivier
Coordinator, Special Programs
912-752-2196

SOFTWARE ENGINEERING

School of Engineering
Programs Offerings include software engineering (MSE).
School Faculty 23 full-time (1 woman), 6 part-time (0 women).
Applying *Deadline:* 8/9. *Fee:* $35 ($50 for international students).
Contact Kathy Olivier
Coordinator, Special Programs
912-752-2196

MERCER UNIVERSITY, CECIL B. DAY CAMPUS
Atlanta, GA 30341-4155

OVERVIEW
Mercer University, Cecil B. Day Campus is an independent-religious coed upper-level institution.

ENROLLMENT
1,819 graduate, professional, and undergraduate students; 1,596 matriculated graduate/professional students.

GRADUATE FACULTY
63 full-time, 29 part-time.

TUITION
$200 per semester hour.

HOUSING
On-campus housing not available.

STUDENT SERVICES
Low-cost health insurance, career counseling, campus employment opportunities.

FACILITIES
Library: Monroe F. Swilley Jr. Library plus 1 additional on-campus library; total holdings of 81,668 volumes, 351,241 microforms, 742 current periodical subscriptions. A total of 8 personal computers in all libraries. Access provided to on-line information retrieval services.

ELECTRICAL ENGINEERING

Graduate Engineering Programs
Programs Offerings include electrical engineering (MSE).
Faculty 4 full-time, 1 part-time.

Applying *Deadline:* (8/9 for spring admission). *Fee:* $35 ($50 for international students).
Contact Dr. David Leonard
Director of Admissions
770-986-3203

SOUTHERN POLYTECHNIC STATE UNIVERSITY
Marietta, GA 30060-2896

OVERVIEW
Southern Polytechnic State University is a public coed comprehensive institution.

ENROLLMENT
3,923 graduate, professional, and undergraduate students; 217 full-time matriculated graduate/professional students (85 women), 357 part-time matriculated graduate/professional students (132 women).

GRADUATE FACULTY
31 full-time (8 women), 10 part-time (2 women), 35.5 FTE; includes 5 minority (3 African-Americans, 1 Asian-American, 1 Hispanic).

TUITION
$1878 per year full-time, $366 per quarter (minimum) part-time for state residents; $5448 per year full-time, $1056 per quarter (minimum) part-time for nonresidents.

HOUSING
Rooms and/or apartments available to single students (470 units) at an average cost of $1725 per year ($3930 including board); on-campus housing not available to married students. Housing application deadline: 8/1. Graduate housing contact: Ed Klein, 770-528-7335.

STUDENT SERVICES
Disabled student services, low-cost health insurance, career counseling, free psychological counseling, campus safety program, campus employment opportunities, international student services.

FACILITIES
Library: Main library; total holdings of 105,000 volumes, 42,900 microforms, 1,500 current periodical subscriptions. A total of 20 personal computers in all libraries. Access provided to on-line information retrieval services. *Computer:* Campuswide network is available with full Internet access. Total number of PCs/terminals supplied for student use: 200. Computer services are offered at no charge.

COMPUTER SCIENCE

Program in Computer Science
Programs Awards MS. Part-time and evening/weekend programs available.
Faculty 11 full-time (4 women), 3 part-time (0 women), 12 FTE.
Students 100 full-time (37 women), 130 part-time (40 women); includes 68 minority (18 African-Americans, 43 Asian-Americans, 7 Hispanics), 59 international. Average age 33.
Degrees Awarded In 1996, 72 degrees awarded (100% found work related to degree).
Entrance Requirements GRE General Test.

Degree Requirements Thesis optional, foreign language not required.
Financial Aid In 1996–97, 101 students received aid, including 15 teaching assistantships (5 to first-year students) averaging $300 per month and totaling $45,000; Federal Work-Study and career-related internships or fieldwork also available. Aid available to part-time students. *Financial aid application deadline:* 3/15; applicants required to submit FAFSA.
Applying 51 applicants, 98% accepted. *Deadline:* 8/1 (priority date; rolling processing; 2/1 for spring admission). *Fee:* $0.
Contact Dr. Michael G. Murphy
Head, Computer Science Department
770-528-7406

UNIVERSITY OF GEORGIA
Athens, GA 30602

OVERVIEW
University of Georgia is a public coed university.

ENROLLMENT
29,404 graduate, professional, and undergraduate students; 3,940 full-time, 1,492 part-time matriculated graduate/professional students.

GRADUATE FACULTY
1,407 full-time (310 women); includes 147 minority.

TUITION
$3069 per year full-time, $544 per quarter (minimum) part-time for state residents; $9630 per year full-time, $1459 per quarter (minimum) part-time for nonresidents.

HOUSING
Rooms and/or apartments available to single students; available to married students (579 units). Graduate housing contact: Housing Office, 706-542-1421.

STUDENT SERVICES
Career counseling, free psychological counseling.

FACILITIES
Library: Ilah Dunlap Little Memorial Library; total holdings of 3.3 million volumes, 5.4 million microforms, 48,190 current periodical subscriptions. A total of 252 personal computers in all libraries. Access provided to on-line information retrieval services.

ARTIFICIAL INTELLIGENCE/ROBOTICS

College of Arts and Sciences, Department of Computer Science, Program in Artificial Intelligence
Programs Awards MSAI.
Students 23 full-time, 5 part-time (2 women); includes 13 international.
Entrance Requirements GRE General Test.
Degree Requirements Thesis required, foreign language not required.
Financial Aid Assistantships available.
Applying 28 applicants, 57% accepted. *Fee:* $30.
Contact Dr. Walter D. Potter
Graduate Coordinator
706-542-0361
E-mail: potter@uga.cc.uga.edu

COMPUTER SCIENCE

College of Arts and Sciences, Department of Computer Science
Programs Offers programs in applied mathematical science (MAMS), artificial intelligence (MSAI), computer science (MSCS, PhD).
Faculty 15 full-time (0 women).
Students 51 full-time (17 women), 14 part-time (4 women); includes 2 minority (both African-Americans), 19 international.
Degrees Awarded In 1996, 12 master's awarded.
Entrance Requirements GRE General Test.
Degree Requirements For doctorate, dissertation.
Financial Aid Fellowships, research assistantships, teaching assistantships, assistantships available.
Applying 151 applicants, 30% accepted. *Fee:* $30.
Contact *Dr. Walter D. Potter*
Graduate Coordinator, Artificial Intelligence
706-542-0361
E-mail: potter@uga.cc.uga.edu

HAWAII

UNIVERSITY OF HAWAII AT MANOA
Honolulu, HI 96822

OVERVIEW
University of Hawaii at Manoa is a public coed university.

ENROLLMENT
17,005 graduate, professional, and undergraduate students; 2,321 full-time matriculated graduate/professional students (1,304 women), 2,468 part-time matriculated graduate/professional students (1,345 women).

GRADUATE FACULTY
1,705 (342 women).

EXPENSES
Tuition $3909 per year full-time, $209 per credit hour part-time for state residents; $9967 per year full-time, $521 per credit hour part-time for nonresidents. Fees $100 per year.

HOUSING
Rooms and/or apartments available to single students (1,363 units) at an average cost of $2863 per year ($4528 including board); available to married students at an average cost of $5257 per year ($8587 including board). Housing application deadline: 5/1. Graduate housing contact: Laurie Furutani, 808-956-8177.

STUDENT SERVICES
Low-cost health insurance, career counseling, free psychological counseling, day-care facilities, campus safety program, campus employment opportunities, international student services.

FACILITIES
Library: Hamilton Library plus 1 additional on-campus library; total holdings of 2,888,498 volumes, 5,657,508 microforms, 17,753 current periodical subscriptions. A total of 105 personal computers in all libraries. Access provided to on-line information retrieval services. *Computer:* Campuswide network is available with full Internet access. Total number of PCs/terminals supplied for student use: 500. Computer services are offered at no charge. *Special:* In science and engineering: Institute for Astronomy, Hawaii Institute of Geophysics, Pacific Biomedical Research Center, Hawaii Institute of Marine Biology. In social sciences: Social Science Research Institute.

COMPUTER SCIENCE

College of Arts and Sciences, College of Natural Sciences, Department of Information and Computer Sciences
Programs Offers programs in computer science (MS, PhD), information science (MS, PhD). PhD (computer science) new for fall 1997.
Faculty 14 full-time (1 woman).
Faculty Research Software engineering, telecommunications, artificial intelligence, multimedia.
Students 31 full-time (8 women), 5 part-time (3 women); includes 11 minority (9 Asian-Americans, 2 Hispanics), 17 international.
Degrees Awarded In 1996, 15 master's awarded.
Entrance Requirements For master's, GRE General Test.
Financial Aid In 1996–97, 23 students received aid, including 3 research assistantships (1 to a first-year student), 5 teaching assistantships (1 to a first-year student); full tuition waivers also available.
Applying *Deadline:* 10/15 (8/10 for spring admission).
Contact *Dr. Will Gersch*
Graduate Field Chairperson
808-956-8249
E-mail: gersch@hawaii.edu

ELECTRICAL ENGINEERING

College of Engineering, Department of Electrical Engineering
Programs Awards MS, PhD.
Faculty 24 full-time (2 women), 2 part-time (0 women).
Faculty Research Computers and artificial intelligence, communication and networking, control theory, physical electronics, VLSI design, micromillimeter waves. *Total annual research expenditures:* $2 million.
Students 64 full-time (15 women), 15 part-time (5 women); includes 69 international.
Degrees Awarded In 1996, 24 master's, 5 doctorates awarded.
Entrance Requirements For master's, TOEFL (minimum score 540; average 607); for doctorate, GRE General Test, GRE Subject Test, TOEFL (minimum score 540; average 607).
Degree Requirements For master's, thesis required, foreign language not required; for doctorate, 1 foreign language, dissertation, exams.
Financial Aid In 1996–97, 54 research assistantships (7 to first-year students) averaging $1,153 per month, 17 teaching assistantships (4 to first-year students) averaging $985 per month were awarded; full and partial tuition waivers also available.
Applying 282 applicants, 72% accepted. *Deadline:* 3/1 (priority date; rolling processing; 8/1 for spring admission). *Fee:* $0.
Contact *Dr. N.T. Gaarder*
Graduate Field Chairperson
808-956-7443
Fax: 808-956-3427
E-mail: gaarder@spectra.eng.hawaii.edu

INFORMATION SCIENCE

College of Arts and Sciences, College of Natural Sciences, Department of Information and Computer Sciences
Programs Offers programs in computer science (MS, PhD), information science (MS, PhD). PhD (computer science) new for fall 1997.

Faculty 14 full-time (1 woman).

Faculty Research Software engineering, telecommunications, artificial intelligence, multimedia.

Students 31 full-time (8 women), 5 part-time (3 women); includes 11 minority (9 Asian-Americans, 2 Hispanics), 17 international.

Degrees Awarded In 1996, 15 master's awarded.

Entrance Requirements For master's, GRE General Test.

Financial Aid In 1996–97, 23 students received aid, including 3 research assistantships (1 to a first-year student), 5 teaching assistantships (1 to a first-year student); full tuition waivers also available.

Applying *Deadline:* 10/15 (8/10 for spring admission).

Contact Dr. Will Gersch
Graduate Field Chairperson
808-956-8249
E-mail: gersch@hawaii.edu

IDAHO

UNIVERSITY OF IDAHO
Moscow, ID 83844–4140

OVERVIEW
University of Idaho is a public coed university.

ENROLLMENT
11,133 graduate, professional, and undergraduate students; 1,082 full-time matriculated graduate/professional students (424 women), 1,180 part-time matriculated graduate/professional students (518 women).

GRADUATE FACULTY
548 full-time (112 women), 51 part-time (25 women), 574.7 FTE; includes 43 minority (3 African-Americans, 29 Asian-Americans, 6 Hispanics, 5 Native Americans).

EXPENSES
Tuition $0 for state residents; $5900 per year full-time, $95 per credit part-time for nonresidents. Fees $2482 per year full-time, $122 per credit part-time.

HOUSING
Rooms and/or apartments available to single students (85 units) at an average cost of $3150 (including board); available to married students (276 units) at an average cost of $3680 (including board). Graduate housing contact: Roger Oettli, 208-885-6571.

STUDENT SERVICES
Disabled student services, multicultural affairs office, low-cost health insurance, career counseling, free psychological counseling, exercise/wellness program, day-care facilities, campus safety program, campus employment opportunities, international student services, writing training, grant writing training.

FACILITIES
Library: Main library plus 1 additional on-campus library; total holdings of 996,095 volumes, 129,787 microforms, 13,077 current periodical subscriptions. A total of 229 personal computers in all libraries. Access provided to on-line information retrieval services. *Computer:* Campuswide network is available with full Internet access. Total number of PCs/terminals supplied for student use: 800. Computer service fees are included with tuition and fees. *Special:* In arts and humanities: Institute for Pacific Northwest Studies. In science and engineering: Taylor Ranch Wilderness Research Area; agricultural experiment station; forest, wildlife, and range experiment station. In social sciences: Bowers Anthropology Laboratory, Bureau of Public Affairs Research.

COMPUTER ENGINEERING

College of Graduate Studies, College of Engineering, Department of Electrical Engineering, Program in Computer Engineering

Programs Awards M Engr, MS.

Students 1 full-time (0 women), 7 part-time (0 women); includes 2 international.

Degrees Awarded In 1996, 2 degrees awarded.

Entrance Requirements Minimum GPA of 2.8.

Degree Requirements Computer language, thesis required, foreign language not required.

Financial Aid Federal Work-Study available. *Financial aid application deadline:* 2/15.

Applying *Deadline:* 8/1 (12/15 for spring admission). *Fee:* $35 ($45 for international students).

Contact Dr. David Egolf
Chairman
208-885-6554

COMPUTER SCIENCE

College of Graduate Studies, College of Engineering, Department of Computer Science

Programs Awards MS, PhD.

Faculty 14 full-time (2 women).

Faculty Research Artificial intelligence, theory of computation, software engineering.

Students 13 full-time (2 women), 42 part-time (10 women); includes 3 minority (2 African-Americans, 1 Hispanic), 14 international.

Degrees Awarded In 1996, 11 master's, 1 doctorate awarded.

Entrance Requirements For master's, GRE General Test, TOEFL (minimum score 550), minimum GPA of 3.0; for doctorate, minimum undergraduate GPA of 2.8, 3.0 graduate.

Degree Requirements For master's, thesis required, foreign language not required; for doctorate, dissertation.

Financial Aid In 1996–97, 6 research assistantships (3 to first-year students) averaging $1,016 per month and totaling $54,878, 2 teaching assistantships (1 to a first-year student) averaging $1,051 per month and totaling $18,924 were awarded; career-related internships or fieldwork also available. *Financial aid application deadline:* 2/15.

Applying *Deadline:* 8/1 (12/15 for spring admission). *Fee:* $35 ($45 for international students).

Contact Dr. John Dickinson
Chair
208-885-6589

ELECTRICAL ENGINEERING

College of Graduate Studies, College of Engineering, Department of Electrical Engineering

Programs Offers programs in computer engineering (M Engr, MS), electrical engineering (M Engr, MS, PhD).

Faculty 17 full-time (0 women), 4 part-time (1 woman), 18.98 FTE.

Faculty Research Digital systems, energy systems.

Students 15 full-time (0 women), 58 part-time (2 women); includes 6 minority (5 Asian-Americans, 1 Hispanic), 16 international.

Degrees Awarded In 1996, 23 master's, 4 doctorates awarded.

Entrance Requirements For master's, minimum GPA of 2.8; for doctorate, minimum undergraduate GPA of 2.8, 3.0 graduate.
Degree Requirements For master's, computer language, thesis required, foreign language not required; for doctorate, computer language, dissertation.
Financial Aid In 1996–97, 4 research assistantships (1 to a first-year student) averaging $765 per month and totaling $27,547, 6 teaching assistantships (5 to first-year students) averaging $645 per month and totaling $34,832 were awarded; fellowships, Federal Work-Study, and career-related internships or fieldwork also available. *Financial aid application deadline:* 2/15.
Applying *Deadline:* 8/1 (12/15 for spring admission). *Fee:* $35 ($45 for international students).
Contact *Dr. David Egolf*
Chairman
208-885-6554

ILLINOIS

BRADLEY UNIVERSITY
Peoria, IL 61625-0002

OVERVIEW
Bradley University is an independent coed comprehensive institution.

ENROLLMENT
5,900 graduate, professional, and undergraduate students; 167 full-time, 592 part-time matriculated graduate/professional students.

GRADUATE FACULTY
251.

TUITION
$12,610 per year full-time, $342 per credit hour (minimum) part-time.

HOUSING
On-campus housing not available.

STUDENT SERVICES
Multicultural affairs office, low-cost health insurance, career counseling, free psychological counseling, day-care facilities, campus safety program, campus employment opportunities, international student services, teacher training.

FACILITIES
Library: Cullom-Davis Library; total holdings of 636,000 volumes, 775,895 microforms, 1,841 current periodical subscriptions. Access provided to on-line information retrieval services. *Computer:* Campuswide network is available with full Internet access. *Special:* In science and engineering: Technology Commercialization Center.

COMPUTER SCIENCE

College of Liberal Arts and Sciences, Department of Computer Science
Programs Offers programs in computer information systems (MS), computer science (MS). Part-time and evening/weekend programs available.
Faculty 8 (0 women).
Students 33 full-time, 64 part-time.
Degrees Awarded In 1996, 22 degrees awarded.

Entrance Requirements TOEFL (minimum score 500).
Degree Requirements Thesis or alternative, comprehensive exam required, foreign language not required.
Financial Aid In 1996–97, 22 research assistantships (1 to a first-year student), 50 scholarships (30 to first-year students) were awarded; teaching assistantships also available. *Financial aid application deadline:* 3/1.
Applying 131 applicants, 85% accepted. *Deadline:* 7/1 (priority date; rolling processing; 11/1 for spring admission). *Fee:* $35.
Contact *Dr. Jiang-Bo Liu*
Graduate Adviser
309-677-2386

ELECTRICAL ENGINEERING

College of Engineering and Technology, Department of Electrical Engineering
Programs Awards MSEE. Part-time and evening/weekend programs available.
Faculty 13 (0 women).
Students 7 full-time, 18 part-time.
Degrees Awarded In 1996, 8 degrees awarded.
Entrance Requirements GRE, TOEFL (minimum score 525), minimum GPA of 3.0.
Degree Requirements Comprehensive exam required, foreign language and thesis not required.
Financial Aid In 1996–97, 10 research assistantships (4 to first-year students), 8 scholarships (all to first-year students) were awarded; teaching assistantships also available. *Financial aid application deadline:* 3/1.
Applying 124 applicants, 60% accepted. *Deadline:* 7/1 (priority date; rolling processing; 11/1 for spring admission). *Fee:* $35.
Contact *Dr. Winfred Anakwa*
Graduate Adviser
309-677-2933

INFORMATION SCIENCE

College of Liberal Arts and Sciences, Department of Computer Science
Programs Offers programs in computer information systems (MS), computer science (MS). Part-time and evening/weekend programs available.
Faculty 8 (0 women).
Students 33 full-time, 64 part-time.
Degrees Awarded In 1996, 22 degrees awarded.
Entrance Requirements TOEFL (minimum score 500).
Degree Requirements Thesis or alternative, comprehensive exam required, foreign language not required.
Financial Aid In 1996–97, 22 research assistantships (1 to a first-year student), 50 scholarships (30 to first-year students) were awarded; teaching assistantships also available. *Financial aid application deadline:* 3/1.
Applying 131 applicants, 85% accepted. *Deadline:* 7/1 (priority date; rolling processing; 11/1 for spring admission). *Fee:* $35.
Contact *Dr. Jiang-Bo Liu*
Graduate Adviser
309-677-2386

DEPAUL UNIVERSITY
Chicago, IL 60604-2287

OVERVIEW
DePaul University is an independent-religious coed university.

ENROLLMENT

17,294 graduate, professional, and undergraduate students; 3,383 full-time matriculated graduate/professional students (1,677 women), 3,473 part-time matriculated graduate/professional students (1,632 women).

GRADUATE FACULTY

491 full-time (180 women), 817 part-time (315 women); includes 155 minority (72 African-Americans, 48 Asian-Americans, 33 Hispanics, 2 Native Americans).

EXPENSES

Tuition $306 per credit hour. Fees $30 per year.

HOUSING

On-campus housing not available.

STUDENT SERVICES

Disabled student services, multicultural affairs office, low-cost health insurance, career counseling, free psychological counseling, campus safety program, campus employment opportunities, international student services.

FACILITIES

Library: John T. Richardson Library plus 6 additional on-campus libraries; total holdings of 727,682 volumes, 306,733 microforms, 11,779 current periodical subscriptions. A total of 275 personal computers in all libraries. Access provided to on-line information retrieval services. *Computer:* Campuswide network is available with full Internet access. Total number of PCs/terminals supplied for student use: 530. Computer services are offered at no charge. *Special:* In arts and humanities: DePaul Performance Center, Blackstone Theatre. In science and engineering: Institute for Applied Artificial Intelligence. In social sciences: Center for Church/State Studies, Chicago Area Studies Center, Hispanic Research Center, Center for the Study of Values, Social Science Skills Center, International Human Rights Law Institute, Health Law Institute.

COMPUTER SCIENCE

School of Computer Science, Telecommunications, and Information Systems, Program in Computer Science

Programs   Awards MS, PhD. Part-time and evening/weekend programs available.

Students   161 full-time (47 women), 265 part-time (63 women); includes 160 minority (30 African-Americans, 108 Asian-Americans, 22 Hispanics), 32 international. Average age 32.

Degrees Awarded   In 1996, 88 master's, 1 doctorate awarded.

Entrance Requirements   For master's, passing grade on the department's Graduate Assessment Examination; for doctorate, GRE, master's degree in computer science.

Degree Requirements   For master's, computer language, comprehensive exam required, foreign language and thesis not required; for doctorate, computer language, dissertation, comprehensive exam required, foreign language not required.

Financial Aid   Fellowships, research assistantships, teaching assistantships, assistantships, partial tuition waivers, Federal Work-Study available. Aid available to part-time students. *Financial aid application deadline:* 3/20.

Applying   244 applicants, 73% accepted. *Deadline:* 8/15 (priority date; rolling processing). *Fee:* $25.

Contact   *Anne B. Morley*
Director of Student Services
312-362-8714
Fax: 312-362-6116

See in-depth description on page **417.**

COMPUTER SCIENCE

School of Computer Science, Telecommunications, and Information Systems, Program in Human Computer Interaction

Programs   Awards MS.

Students   5.

Entrance Requirements   Passing grade on the department's Graduate Assessment Examination.

Degree Requirements   Computer language, comprehensive exam required, foreign language not required.

Applying   6 applicants, 100% accepted. *Deadline:* 8/15 (rolling processing). *Fee:* $25.

Contact   *Anne B. Morley*
Director of Student Services
312-362-8714
Fax: 312-362-6116

See in-depth description on page **417.**

INFORMATION SCIENCE

School of Computer Science, Telecommunications, and Information Systems, Program in Information Systems

Programs   Awards MS. Part-time and evening/weekend programs available.

Students   90 full-time (43 women), 95 part-time (34 women); includes 77 minority (14 African-Americans, 41 Asian-Americans, 22 Hispanics), 7 international. Average age 30.

Degrees Awarded   In 1996, 39 degrees awarded.

Entrance Requirements   Passing grade on the department's Graduate Assessment Examination.

Degree Requirements   Computer language, comprehensive exam required, foreign language and thesis not required.

Financial Aid   Research assistantships, teaching assistantships, assistantships, partial tuition waivers, Federal Work-Study available. *Financial aid application deadline:* 4/1.

Applying   79 applicants, 91% accepted. *Deadline:* 8/15 (priority date; rolling processing). *Fee:* $25.

Contact   *Anne B. Morley*
Director of Student Services
312-362-8714
Fax: 312-362-6116

See in-depth description on page **417.**

SOFTWARE ENGINEERING

School of Computer Science, Telecommunications, and Information Systems, Program in Software Engineering

Programs   Awards MS. Part-time and evening/weekend programs available.

Faculty Research   Formal methods, object oriented technolgy, measurement human computer interaction, architecture.

Students   19 full-time (3 women), 44 part-time (9 women); includes 17 minority (1 African-American, 13 Asian-Americans, 3 Hispanics), 3 international. Average age 32.

Entrance Requirements   Passing grade on the department's Graduate Assessment Examination.

Degree Requirements   Computer language, thesis, comprehensive exam required, foreign language not required.

Financial Aid   Fellowships, partial tuition waivers, Federal Work-Study available. *Financial aid application deadline:* 4/1.

Applying   23 applicants, 96% accepted. *Deadline:* 8/15 (priority date; rolling processing). *Fee:* $25.

Contact   *Anne B. Morley*
Director of Student Services
312-362-8714
Fax: 312-362-6116

See in-depth description on page **417.**

GOVERNORS STATE UNIVERSITY
University Park, IL 60466

OVERVIEW
Governors State University is a public coed upper-level institution.

ENROLLMENT
6,200 graduate, professional, and undergraduate students; 117 full-time matriculated graduate/professional students (83 women), 1,822 part-time matriculated graduate/professional students (1,271 women).

GRADUATE FACULTY
150 full-time (54 women), 160 part-time (74 women); includes 65 minority (31 African-Americans, 23 Asian-Americans, 9 Hispanics, 2 Native Americans).

EXPENSES
Tuition $1104 per trimester full-time, $92 per credit hour part-time for state residents; $3312 per trimester full-time, $276 per credit hour part-time for nonresidents. Fees $85 per trimester.

HOUSING
On-campus housing not available.

STUDENT SERVICES
Disabled student services, low-cost health insurance, career counseling, free psychological counseling, exercise/wellness program, day-care facilities, campus safety program, campus employment opportunities, international student services.

FACILITIES
Library: University Library; total holdings of 241,000 volumes, 715,000 microforms, 2,510 current periodical subscriptions. Access provided to on-line information retrieval services. *Computer:* Campuswide network is available with full Internet access. Total number of PCs/terminals supplied for student use: 162. Computer service fees are included with tuition and fees. *Special:* In arts and humanities: Nathan Manilow Monumental Sculpture Park, Infinity Gallery (photography), art gallery. In social sciences: Public Policy Institute, Small Business Development Center Cooperative.

COMPUTER SCIENCE

College of Arts and Sciences, Division of Science, Program in Computer Science
Programs   Awards MS. Part-time and evening/weekend programs available.
Faculty   8 full-time (1 woman), 8 part-time (1 woman).
Degrees Awarded   In 1996, 5 degrees awarded.
Entrance Requirements   Minimum GPA of 2.75.
Degree Requirements   Computer language, thesis or alternative required, foreign language not required.
Financial Aid   Research assistantships, scholarships, Federal Work-Study, institutionally sponsored loans, and career-related internships or fieldwork available. Aid available to part-time students. *Financial aid application deadline: 5/1.*
Applying   *Deadline:* 7/15 (priority date; rolling processing; 11/10 for spring admission). *Fee:* $0.
Contact   Dr. Edwin Cehelnik
        Chairperson
        708-534-4520

ILLINOIS INSTITUTE OF TECHNOLOGY
Chicago, IL 60616-3793

OVERVIEW
Illinois Institute of Technology is an independent coed university.

ENROLLMENT
6,287 graduate, professional, and undergraduate students; 1,515 full-time matriculated graduate/professional students (581 women), 2,775 part-time matriculated graduate/professional students (868 women).

GRADUATE FACULTY
275 full-time (51 women), 248 part-time (38 women), 369 FTE; includes 58 minority (12 African-Americans, 45 Asian-Americans, 1 Hispanic).

EXPENSES
Tuition $17,250 per year full-time, $575 per credit hour part-time. Fees $60 per year full-time, $1.50 per credit hour part-time.

HOUSING
Rooms and/or apartments available to single students (800 units) at an average cost of $5550 (including board); available to married students (400 units) at an average cost of $6500 per year. Housing application deadline: 7/15. Graduate housing contact: Housing Director, 312-567-5075.

STUDENT SERVICES
Multicultural affairs office, low-cost health insurance, career counseling, free psychological counseling, campus safety program, campus employment opportunities, international student services.

FACILITIES
Library: Paul V. Galvin Library; total holdings of 522,000 volumes, 556,330 microforms, 800 current periodical subscriptions. Access provided to on-line information retrieval services. *Computer:* Campuswide network is available with full Internet access. Total number of PCs/terminals supplied for student use: 250. Computer services are offered at no charge. *Special:* In arts and humanities: Center for the Study of Ethics in the Professions. In science and engineering: Pritzker Institute of Medical Engineering, Fluid Dynamics Research Center, Center for Law and Computers, Center for Excellence in Polymer Science and Engineering, Center for Synchrotron Radiation Research and Instrumentation, Fuel Cell and Battery Technology Research Hub Program, Grainger Power Engineering Laboratory, Instrumental Factory for Gears. In social sciences: National Center for Food Safety and Technology; Center for Research on Industrial Strategy and Policy; Center for Research in Financial Markets and Trading; Center for Innovative Learning and Education; Center for Consultation, Psychological Services, and Research; Center for Research on the Impact of Information Systems.

COMPUTER ENGINEERING

Armour College of Engineering and Sciences, Department of Electrical and Computer Engineering
Programs   Offers programs in computer systems engineering (MS), electrical and computer engineering (MECE), electrical engineer-

ing (MS, PhD), manufacturing engineering (MME, MS). Part-time and evening/weekend programs available.

Faculty 23 full-time (1 woman), 9 part-time (0 women).

Faculty Research Computer system design, photonics, biomedical engineering, power systems analysis, communications theory. *Total annual research expenditures: $750,000.*

Students 54 full-time (5 women), 292 part-time (34 women); includes 96 minority (11 African-Americans, 73 Asian-Americans, 12 Hispanics), 78 international.

Degrees Awarded In 1996, 73 master's, 7 doctorates awarded. Terminal master's awarded for partial completion of doctoral program.

Entrance Requirements For master's, GRE Subject Test, TOEFL (minimum score 550); for doctorate, GRE, TOEFL (minimum score 550).

Degree Requirements For master's, thesis (for some programs), comprehensive exam required, foreign language not required; for doctorate, dissertation, comprehensive exam required, foreign language not required.

Financial Aid In 1996–97, 9 research assistantships, 20 teaching assistantships, 4 graduate assistantships, tuition scholarships were awarded; fellowships, Federal Work-Study, institutionally sponsored loans also available. *Financial aid application deadline: 3/1.*

Applying 626 applicants, 60% accepted. *Deadline:* 7/1 (rolling processing; 12/1 for spring admission). *Fee:* $30.

Contact *Graduate College*
312-567-3024
Fax: 312-567-7517
E-mail: grad@minna.cas.iit.edu

See in-depth description on page 449.

COMPUTER SCIENCE

Armour College of Engineering and Sciences, Department of Computer Science and Applied Mathematics

Programs Awards MS, PhD. Part-time and evening/weekend programs available.

Faculty 27 full-time (7 women), 27 part-time (4 women).

Faculty Research Networking, computer graphics, database, parallel computing, software engineering. *Total annual research expenditures: $250,000.*

Students 53 full-time (7 women), 594 part-time (147 women); includes 214 minority (59 African-Americans, 142 Asian-Americans, 13 Hispanics), 150 international.

Degrees Awarded In 1996, 116 master's, 27 doctorates awarded. Terminal master's awarded for partial completion of doctoral program.

Entrance Requirements GRE, TOEFL (minimum score 550).

Degree Requirements For master's, computer language, thesis (for some programs), comprehensive exam required, foreign language not required; for doctorate, computer language, dissertation, comprehensive exam required, foreign language not required.

Financial Aid In 1996–97, 4 fellowships, 3 research assistantships, 20 teaching assistantships were awarded; graduate assistantships, tuition scholarships, Federal Work-Study, institutionally sponsored loans also available. *Financial aid application deadline: 3/1.*

Applying 588 applicants, 84% accepted. *Deadline:* 7/1 (rolling processing; 11/1 for spring admission). *Fee:* $30.

Contact *Graduate College*
312-567-3024
Fax: 312-567-7517
E-mail: grad@minna.cas.iit.edu

See in-depth description on page 447.

ELECTRICAL ENGINEERING

Armour College of Engineering and Sciences, Department of Electrical and Computer Engineering

Programs Offers programs in computer systems engineering (MS), electrical and computer engineering (MECE), electrical engineering (MS, PhD), manufacturing engineering (MME, MS). Part-time and evening/weekend programs available.

Faculty 23 full-time (1 woman), 9 part-time (0 women).

Faculty Research Computer system design, photonics, biomedical engineering, power systems analysis, communications theory. *Total annual research expenditures: $750,000.*

Students 54 full-time (5 women), 292 part-time (34 women); includes 96 minority (11 African-Americans, 73 Asian-Americans, 12 Hispanics), 78 international.

Degrees Awarded In 1996, 73 master's, 7 doctorates awarded. Terminal master's awarded for partial completion of doctoral program.

Entrance Requirements For master's, GRE Subject Test, TOEFL (minimum score 550); for doctorate, GRE, TOEFL (minimum score 550).

Degree Requirements For master's, thesis (for some programs), comprehensive exam required, foreign language not required; for doctorate, dissertation, comprehensive exam required, foreign language not required.

Financial Aid In 1996–97, 9 research assistantships, 20 teaching assistantships, 4 graduate assistantships, tuition scholarships were awarded; fellowships, Federal Work-Study, institutionally sponsored loans also available. *Financial aid application deadline: 3/1.*

Applying 626 applicants, 60% accepted. *Deadline:* 7/1 (rolling processing; 12/1 for spring admission). *Fee:* $30.

Contact *Graduate College*
312-567-3024
Fax: 312-567-7517
E-mail: grad@minna.cas.iit.edu

See in-depth description on page 449.

ILLINOIS STATE UNIVERSITY
Normal, IL 61790-2200

OVERVIEW

Illinois State University is a public coed university.

ENROLLMENT

19,722 graduate, professional, and undergraduate students; 1,045 full-time matriculated graduate/professional students (579 women), 1,242 part-time matriculated graduate/professional students (744 women).

GRADUATE FACULTY

493 full-time (134 women), 16 part-time (4 women), 498.9 FTE; includes 49 minority (10 African-Americans, 28 Asian-Americans, 10 Hispanics, 1 Native American).

EXPENSES

Tuition $2386 per year full-time, $99 per hour part-time for state residents; $7157 per year full-time, $298 per hour part-time for nonresidents. Fees $1017 per year full-time, $42 per hour part-time.

HOUSING

Rooms and/or apartments available to single students at an average cost of $3077 per year ($3840 including board); available to married students (292 units) at an average cost of $2394 per year. Graduate housing contact: Pat O'Connell, 309-438-5967.

STUDENT SERVICES

Low-cost health insurance, career counseling, free psychological counseling, day-care facilities, campus safety program, campus employment opportunities, international student services.

FACILITIES

Library: Milner Library; total holdings of 1,301,788 volumes, 1,882,332 microforms, 8,987 current periodical subscriptions. A total of 150 personal computers in all libraries. Access provided to on-line information retrieval services. *Computer:* Campuswide network is available with full Internet access. Computer service fees are included with tuition and fees.

COMPUTER SCIENCE

College of Applied Science and Technology, Department of Applied Computer Science

Programs   Awards MS.

Faculty   17 full-time (4 women), 1 part-time (0 women), 17.5 FTE.

Faculty Research   *Total annual research expenditures:* $268,386.

Students   44 full-time (15 women), 42 part-time (13 women); includes 9 minority (3 African-Americans, 6 Asian-Americans), 28 international.

Degrees Awarded   In 1996, 15 degrees awarded.

Entrance Requirements   GRE General Test (minimum score 400 on verbal section, 1000 combined), minimum GPA of 3.0 in last 60 hours; proficiency in COBOL, Fortran, Pascal, or P12.

Degree Requirements   Computer language, thesis (for some programs).

Financial Aid   In 1996–97, 1 research assistantship, 8 teaching assistantships averaging $612 per month, 13 assistantships were awarded; fellowships, full tuition waivers also available. *Financial aid application deadline: 4/1.*

Applying   56 applicants, 73% accepted. *Deadline:* rolling. *Fee:* $0.

Contact   Dr. Robert Zant
            Chairperson
            309-438-8338

KNOWLEDGE SYSTEMS INSTITUTE
Skokie, IL 60076

OVERVIEW

Knowledge Systems Institute is an independent coed graduate-only institution.

ENROLLMENT

58 full-time matriculated graduate/professional students (19 women), 42 part-time matriculated graduate/professional students (13 women).

GRADUATE FACULTY

4 full-time (0 women), 23 part-time (3 women), 10 FTE.

TUITION

$6240 per course full-time, $780 per course part-time for state residents; $6240 per year full-time, $780 per course part-time for nonresidents.

HOUSING

Rooms and/or apartments available to single students at an average cost of $3600 per year; available to married students at an average cost of $4320 per year. Graduate housing information: 847-679-3135.

STUDENT SERVICES

Low-cost health insurance, campus employment opportunities, international student services.

FACILITIES

Library: Main library; total holdings of 1,400 volumes, 60 current periodical subscriptions. A total of 3 personal computers in all libraries. Access provided to on-line information retrieval services. *Computer:* Campuswide network is available with full Internet access. Total number of PCs/terminals supplied for student use: 45. Computer service fees are included with tuition and fees.

COMPUTER SCIENCE

Program in Computer and Information Sciences

Programs   Offers programs in art and design (MS), education (MS), management information systems (MS).

Faculty   4 full-time (0 women), 23 part-time (3 women), 10 FTE.

Students   58 full-time (19 women), 42 part-time (13 women).

Applying   *Fee:* $40.

Contact   *Judy Pan*
            Executive Director
            847-679-3135
            Fax: 847-679-3166
            E-mail: judy@ksi.edu

INFORMATION SCIENCE

Program in Computer and Information Sciences

Programs   Offers programs in art and design (MS), education (MS), management information systems (MS).

Faculty   4 full-time (0 women), 23 part-time (3 women), 10 FTE.

Students   58 full-time (19 women), 42 part-time (13 women).

Applying   *Fee:* $40.

Contact   *Judy Pan*
            Executive Director
            847-679-3135
            Fax: 847-679-3166
            E-mail: judy@ksi.edu

LOYOLA UNIVERSITY CHICAGO
Chicago, IL 60611-2196

OVERVIEW

Loyola University Chicago is an independent-religious coed university.

ENROLLMENT

13,759 graduate, professional, and undergraduate students; 2,415 full-time matriculated graduate/professional students (1,445 women), 3,675 part-time matriculated graduate/professional students (2,356 women).

GRADUATE FACULTY

1,382; includes 47 minority (18 African-Americans, 15 Asian-Americans, 14 Hispanics).

TUITION
$441 per semester hour.

HOUSING
Rooms and/or apartments available to single students (22 units) at an average cost of $6380 (including board); on-campus housing not available to married students. Graduate housing contact: Sarah Griesse, 773-508-3300.

STUDENT SERVICES
Low-cost health insurance, career counseling, free psychological counseling, day-care facilities, campus safety program, campus employment opportunities, international student services.

FACILITIES
Library: Elizabeth M. Cudahy Memorial Library plus 4 additional on-campus libraries; total holdings of 1,349,058 volumes, 1,208,416 microforms, 11,545 current periodical subscriptions. A total of 245 personal computers in all libraries. Access provided to on-line information retrieval services. *Special:* In arts and humanities: Rome Center for the Liberal Arts, Center for Ethics across the University, Newberry Library Center for Renaissance Studies. In science and engineering: Parmly Hearing Institute, Neuroscience Institute, Oncology Institute. In social sciences: Center for Children and Families.

COMPUTER SCIENCE

Graduate School, Department of Mathematical and Computer Sciences
Programs Offers programs in computer science (MS), mathematical sciences (MS). Part-time and evening/weekend programs available.
Faculty 29 full-time (4 women), 18 part-time (7 women), 38 FTE.
Faculty Research Parallel computing, programming language, analysis of algorithms, logic. *Total annual research expenditures:* $1.3 million.
Students 82 full-time (42 women), 56 part-time (24 women); includes 38 minority (2 African-Americans, 36 Asian-Americans), 70 international. Average age 27.
Degrees Awarded In 1996, 47 degrees awarded.
Entrance Requirements GRE or TOEFL (minimum score 550), minimum B average.
Degree Requirements Oral and written comprehensive exams required, foreign language not required.
Financial Aid In 1996–97, 18 students received aid, including 9 research assistantships (4 to first-year students) averaging $850 per month, 9 teaching assistantships (4 to first-year students) averaging $850 per month; Federal Work-Study, institutionally sponsored loans, and career-related internships or fieldwork also available. *Financial aid application deadline:* 2/1; applicants required to submit FAFSA.
Applying 190 applicants, 84% accepted. *Deadline:* 8/1 (rolling processing; 12/1 for spring admission). *Fee:* $35.
Contact *Dr. Chandra Selharan*
Graduate Director
773-508-3572
E-mail: chandra@math.luc.edu

See in-depth description on page 467.

NORTH CENTRAL COLLEGE
Naperville, IL 60566-7063

OVERVIEW
North Central College is an independent-religious coed comprehensive institution.

ENROLLMENT
2,446 graduate, professional, and undergraduate students; 435 matriculated graduate/professional students.

GRADUATE FACULTY
40 full-time, 22 part-time; includes 4 minority (1 African-American, 3 Asian-Americans).

TUITION
$1366 per course.

HOUSING
On-campus housing not available.

STUDENT SERVICES
Career counseling, free psychological counseling, campus safety program, campus employment opportunities, international student services.

FACILITIES
Library: Oesterle Library; total holdings of 121,000 volumes, 425 microforms, 730 current periodical subscriptions. A total of 12 personal computers in all libraries. Access provided to on-line information retrieval services. *Computer:* Campuswide network is available with full Internet access. Total number of PCs/terminals supplied for student use: 40. Computer service fees are included with tuition and fees.

COMPUTER SCIENCE

Graduate Programs, Department of Computer Science
Programs Awards MS. Part-time and evening/weekend programs available.
Faculty 7 full-time (1 woman), 11 part-time (1 woman).
Faculty Research Experimental broadband network.
Students 90. Average age 28.
Degrees Awarded In 1996, 18 degrees awarded.
Entrance Requirements GMAT or GRE General Test, minimum GPA of 2.75.
Degree Requirements Computer language, project required, thesis not required.
Financial Aid Available to part-time students.
Applying *Deadline:* 8/15 (rolling processing). *Fee:* $25.
Contact *Dr. Steven Renk*
Coordinator
630-637-5170
Fax: 630-637-5844

NORTHEASTERN ILLINOIS UNIVERSITY
Chicago, IL 60625-4699

OVERVIEW
Northeastern Illinois University is a public coed comprehensive institution.

ENROLLMENT

10,306 graduate, professional, and undergraduate students; 205 full-time matriculated graduate/ professional students (119 women), 1,350 part-time matriculated graduate/professional students (938 women).

GRADUATE FACULTY

242 full-time (92 women), 118 part-time (50 women); includes 104 minority (38 African-Americans, 39 Asian-Americans, 25 Hispanics, 2 Native Americans).

EXPENSES

Tuition $1074 per year full-time, $90 per credit hour part-time for state residents; $3222 per year full-time, $269 per credit hour part-time for nonresidents. Fees $156 per year full-time, $13 per credit hour part-time.

HOUSING

On-campus housing not available.

STUDENT SERVICES

Low-cost health insurance, career counseling, free psychological counseling, day-care facilities, campus safety program, campus employment opportunities, international student services.

FACILITIES

Library: Ronald Williams University Library; total holdings of 667,035 volumes, 209,677 microforms, 3,816 current periodical subscriptions. A total of 112 personal computers in all libraries. Access provided to on-line information retrieval services. *Computer:* Campuswide network is available with full Internet access. Total number of PCs/terminals supplied for student use: 280. Computer service fees are included with tuition and fees. *Special:* In arts and humanities: Art gallery, Little Theater on Campus. In science and engineering: Mazon Creek Paleontological Collection, Center for Exercise Science and Cardiovascular Research. In social sciences: Center for Inner Cities Studies, Chicago Teachers' Center, computer cartography/geographic information systems laboratory.

COMPUTER SCIENCE

College of Arts and Sciences, Department of Computer Science, Program in Computer Science

Programs Awards MS. Part-time and evening/weekend programs available.

Faculty 12 full-time (3 women), 5 part-time (2 women).

Faculty Research Telecommunications, database inference problems, decision making under uncertainty, belief networks, analysis of algorithms.

Students 10 full-time (1 woman), 48 part-time (12 women); includes 24 minority (21 Asian-Americans, 3 Hispanics), 7 international. Average age 35.

Degrees Awarded In 1996, 30 degrees awarded.

Entrance Requirements Minimum GPA of 2.75, proficiency in 2 higher level computer languages, one course in discrete mathematics.

Degree Requirements Computer language, comprehensive exam, research project, or thesis required, thesis optional, foreign language not required.

Financial Aid In 1996–97, 25 students received aid, including 6 research assistantships averaging $450 per month; full and partial tuition waivers, Federal Work-Study, institutionally sponsored loans, and career-related internships or fieldwork also available. Aid available to part-time students. Financial aid applicants required to submit FAFSA.

Applying 50 applicants, 32% accepted. *Deadline:* 3/18 (priority date; rolling processing; 9/30 for spring admission). *Fee:* $0.

Contact Dr. Mohan K. Sood
Dean of Graduate College
773-583-4050 Ext. 6143
Fax: 773-794-6670

NORTHERN ILLINOIS UNIVERSITY
De Kalb, IL 60115-2854

OVERVIEW

Northern Illinois University is a public coed university.

ENROLLMENT

21,609 graduate, professional, and undergraduate students; 1,831 full-time matriculated graduate/ professional students (953 women), 2,989 part-time matriculated graduate/professional students (1,701 women).

GRADUATE FACULTY

1,034 full-time (324 women), 49 part-time (14 women); includes 86 minority (14 African-Americans, 55 Asian-Americans, 14 Hispanics, 3 Native Americans).

TUITION

$3704 per year full-time, $143 per credit hour part-time for state residents; $8792 per year full-time, $355 per credit hour part-time for nonresidents.

HOUSING

Rooms and/or apartments available to single students at an average cost of $3972 (including board); available to married students (80 units) at an average cost of $2835 per year. Graduate housing contact: Student Housing Services Office, 815-753-1525.

STUDENT SERVICES

Low-cost health insurance, career counseling, free psychological counseling, day-care facilities, campus safety program, campus employment opportunities, international student services.

FACILITIES

Library: Founders Library plus 3 additional on-campus libraries; total holdings of 1,446,931 volumes, 2,747,779 microforms, 11,882 current periodical subscriptions. Access provided to on-line information retrieval services. *Computer:* Campuswide network is available with full Internet access. *Special:* In arts and humanities: Center for Southeast Asian Studies, Regional History Center, Burma Studies Center. In science and engineering: Plant Molecular Biology Center, Microelectronics Research and Development Laboratories. In social sciences: Social Science Research Institute, Center for Governmental Studies, Center for Black Studies, Women's Studies Program, Gerontology Program, Center for Latino and Latin American Studies.

COMPUTER SCIENCE

College of Liberal Arts and Sciences, Department of Computer Science

Programs Awards MS. Part-time and evening/weekend programs available.

Faculty 11 full-time (1 woman).

Faculty Research Databases, theorem proving.

Students 73 full-time (30 women), 43 part-time (17 women); includes 19 minority (all Asian-Americans), 57 international. Average age 28.
Degrees Awarded In 1996, 44 degrees awarded.
Entrance Requirements GRE General Test, TOEFL (minimum score 550), minimum GPA of 2.75.
Degree Requirements Computer language, comprehensive exam required, foreign language and thesis not required.
Financial Aid In 1996–97, 11 research assistantships, 19 teaching assistantships, 2 staff assistantships were awarded; fellowships, full tuition waivers, Federal Work-Study, and career-related internships or fieldwork also available. Aid available to part-time students.
Applying 124 applicants, 54% accepted. *Deadline:* 6/1 (rolling processing; 11/1 for spring admission). *Fee:* $30.
Contact *Dr. Rodney Angotti*
 Chair
 815-753-0378

ELECTRICAL ENGINEERING

College of Engineering and Engineering Technology, Department of Electrical Engineering
Programs Awards MS. Part-time programs available.
Faculty 11 full-time (0 women).
Students 24 full-time (5 women), 32 part-time (3 women); includes 5 minority (1 African-American, 4 Asian-Americans), 35 international. Average age 29.
Degrees Awarded In 1996, 13 degrees awarded.
Entrance Requirements GRE General Test, TOEFL (minimum score 550), minimum GPA of 2.75.
Degree Requirements Comprehensive exam required, thesis optional, foreign language not required.
Financial Aid In 1996–97, 18 research assistantships, 1 teaching assistantship were awarded; fellowships, staff assistantships, full tuition waivers, Federal Work-Study also available. Aid available to part-time students.
Applying 159 applicants, 55% accepted. *Deadline:* 6/1 (rolling processing; 11/1 for spring admission). *Fee:* $30.
Contact *Dr. Vincent McGinn*
 Chair
 815-753-9962

NORTHWESTERN UNIVERSITY
Evanston, IL 60208

OVERVIEW
Northwestern University is an independent coed university.

ENROLLMENT
17,880 graduate, professional, and undergraduate students; 6,103 full-time matriculated graduate/professional students (2,656 women), 1,806 part-time matriculated graduate/professional students (693 women).

GRADUATE FACULTY
1,955 full-time (505 women), 170 part-time (48 women), 2,012 FTE; includes 256 minority (45 African-Americans, 175 Asian-Americans, 35 Hispanics, 1 Native American).

TUITION
$19,152 per year full-time, $2128 per course part-time.

HOUSING
Rooms and/or apartments available to single students (438 units) at an average cost of $4455 per year; available to married students (201 units) at an average cost of $7515 per year. Housing application deadline: 9/1. Graduate housing contact: Housing Office, 847-491-5127.

STUDENT SERVICES
Low-cost health insurance, career counseling, free psychological counseling, campus safety program, campus employment opportunities, international student services.

FACILITIES
Library: University Library plus 6 additional on-campus libraries; total holdings of 3,840,439 volumes, 3,284,677 microforms, 39,033 current periodical subscriptions. A total of 523 personal computers in all libraries. Access provided to on-line information retrieval services. *Computer:* Campuswide network is available with full Internet access. Total number of PCs/terminals supplied for student use: 500. Computer service fees are included with tuition and fees. *Special:* In arts and humanities: African Humanities Institute, Block Gallery, Center for the Humanities, Mitchell Media Center. In science and engineering: Center for Catalysis and Surface Science, Center for Circadian Biology and Medicine, Center for Experimental Animal Resources, Center for Reproductive Science, Center for Quantum Devices, Information Technology, Institute for the Learning Sciences, Institute for Neuroscience, Materials Research Center, Science and Technology Center for Superconductivity. In social sciences: Buehler Center on Aging, Center for Mathematical Studies in Economics and Management Science, Institute for Health Services Research and Policy Studies, Institute for Policy Research, Program of African Studies, Searle Center for Teaching Excellence, The Transportation Center.

COMPUTER ENGINEERING

Robert R. McCormick School of Engineering and Applied Science, Department of Electrical and Computer Engineering
Programs Offers programs in electrical and computer engineering (MS, PhD), information technology (MIT). MS and PhD admissions and degrees offered through The Graduate School. Part-time programs available.
Faculty 34 full-time (5 women).
Faculty Research Optics, devices, communication and signal processing, computer engineering. *Total annual research expenditures:* $3.262 million.
Students 121 full-time (28 women), 14 part-time (0 women); includes 16 minority (7 African-Americans, 8 Asian-Americans, 1 Hispanic), 61 international.
Degrees Awarded In 1996, 19 master's, 11 doctorates awarded. Terminal master's awarded for partial completion of doctoral program.
Entrance Requirements GRE General Test.
Degree Requirements For master's, thesis or project required, foreign language not required; for doctorate, dissertation required, foreign language not required.
Financial Aid In 1996–97, 70 students received aid, including 20 fellowships (all to first-year students) averaging $1,256 per month, 35 research assistantships (3 to first-year students) averaging $1,592 per month, 19 teaching assistantships averaging $1,296 per month; tuition scholarships, Federal Work-Study, institutionally sponsored loans, and career-related internships or fieldwork also available. *Financial aid application deadline:* 1/15; applicants required to submit FAFSA.

Applying 449 applicants, 18% accepted. *Deadline:* 8/30 (rolling processing). *Fee:* $50 ($55 for international students).
Contact *Lawrence Henschen*
Admission Officer
847-491-3338
Fax: 847-491-4455
E-mail: henschen@ece.nwu.edu

See in-depth description on page 497.

COMPUTER SCIENCE

Robert R. McCormick School of Engineering and Applied Science, Department of Computer Science
Programs Awards PhD. Admissions and degrees offered through The Graduate School.
Faculty 7 full-time (0 women), 3 part-time (0 women).
Faculty Research Artificial intelligence, multimedia networked databases, human-computer interaction, complex interactive systems, robotics. *Total annual research expenditures:* $500,000.
Students 39 full-time (5 women), 2 part-time (0 women); includes 4 minority (2 African-Americans, 1 Asian-American, 1 Hispanic), 6 international.
Degrees Awarded In 1996, 9 degrees awarded.
Entrance Requirements GRE General Test (minimum combined score of 1500 on three sections; average 2000).
Degree Requirements Dissertation.
Financial Aid In 1996–97, 23 students received aid, including 4 fellowships averaging $1,256 per month, research assistantships averaging $1,592 per month, 9 tuition scholarships averaging $1,296 per month; teaching assistantships, Federal Work-Study, institutionally sponsored loans also available. *Financial aid application deadline:* 1/15; applicants required to submit FAFSA.
Applying 244 applicants, 7% accepted. *Deadline:* 8/30. *Fee:* $50 ($55 for international students).
Contact *Christopher Riesbeck*
Admission Officer
847-491-7279
E-mail: criesbeck@nwu.edu

See in-depth description on page 495.

ELECTRICAL ENGINEERING

Robert R. McCormick School of Engineering and Applied Science, Department of Electrical and Computer Engineering
Programs Offers programs in electrical and computer engineering (MS, PhD), information technology (MIT). MS and PhD admissions and degrees offered through The Graduate School. Part-time programs available.
Faculty 34 full-time (5 women).
Faculty Research Optics, devices, communication and signal processing, computer engineering. *Total annual research expenditures:* $3.262 million.
Students 121 full-time (28 women), 14 part-time (0 women); includes 16 minority (7 African-Americans, 8 Asian-Americans, 1 Hispanic), 61 international.
Degrees Awarded In 1996, 19 master's, 11 doctorates awarded. Terminal master's awarded for partial completion of doctoral program.
Entrance Requirements GRE General Test.
Degree Requirements For master's, thesis or project required, foreign language not required; for doctorate, dissertation required, foreign language not required.
Financial Aid In 1996–97, 70 students received aid, including 20 fellowships (all to first-year students) averaging $1,256 per month, 35 research assistantships (3 to first-year students) averaging $1,592 per month, 19 teaching assistantships averaging $1,296 per month; tuition scholarships, Federal Work-Study, institutionally sponsored

loans, and career-related internships or fieldwork also available. *Financial aid application deadline:* 1/15; applicants required to submit FAFSA.
Applying 449 applicants, 18% accepted. *Deadline:* 8/30 (rolling processing). *Fee:* $50 ($55 for international students).
Contact *Lawrence Henschen*
Admission Officer
847-491-3338
Fax: 847-491-4455
E-mail: henschen@ece.nwu.edu

See in-depth description on page 497.

INFORMATION SCIENCE

Robert R. McCormick School of Engineering and Applied Science, Department of Electrical and Computer Engineering, Program in Information Technology
Programs Awards MIT.
Students 29 full-time (6 women), includes 2 minority (1 African-American, 1 Asian-American), 4 international.
Entrance Requirements GRE General Test.
Applying *Deadline:* 8/30. *Fee:* $50 ($55 for international students).
Contact *Srikanta Kumar*
Director

ROOSEVELT UNIVERSITY
Chicago, IL 60605-1394

OVERVIEW
Roosevelt University is an independent coed comprehensive institution.

EXPENSES
Tuition $7614 per year full-time, $423 per credit hour part-time. Fees $150 per year.

HOUSING
Rooms and/or apartments available to single students; on-campus housing not available to married students. Graduate housing contact: Contact Office, 312-341-2004.

FACILITIES
Library: Murray-Green Library plus 1 additional on-campus library.

COMPUTER SCIENCE

College of Arts and Sciences, Faculty of Mathematical Sciences, Program in Computing and Information Science
Programs Awards MS. Part-time and evening/weekend programs available.
Applying *Deadline:* 6/1 (priority date; rolling processing). *Fee:* $25 ($35 for international students).

INFORMATION SCIENCE

College of Arts and Sciences, Faculty of Mathematical Sciences, Program in Computing and Information Science
Programs Awards MS. Part-time and evening/weekend programs available.

Applying *Deadline:* 6/1 (priority date; rolling processing). *Fee:* $25 ($35 for international students).

SOUTHERN ILLINOIS UNIVERSITY AT CARBONDALE
Carbondale, IL 62901-6806

OVERVIEW
Southern Illinois University at Carbondale is a public coed university.

ENROLLMENT
21,863 graduate, professional, and undergraduate students; 2,863 full-time matriculated graduate/professional students (1,359 women), 624 part-time matriculated graduate/professional students (357 women).

GRADUATE FACULTY
1,079 full-time (236 women), 115 part-time (49 women); includes 84 minority (15 African-Americans, 62 Asian-Americans, 6 Hispanics, 1 Native American).

EXPENSES
Tuition $2550 per year full-time, $85 per semester hour part-time for state residents; $8100 per year full-time, $270 per semester hour part-time for nonresidents. Fees $798 per year (minimum) full-time, $244 per semester (minimum) part-time.

HOUSING
Rooms and/or apartments available to single students at an average cost of $3416 (including board); available to married students (560 units) at an average cost of $3138 per year. Graduate housing contact: Housing Office, 618-453-2301.

STUDENT SERVICES
Low-cost health insurance, career counseling, free psychological counseling, day-care facilities, campus safety program, campus employment opportunities, international student services.

FACILITIES
Library: Morris Library; total holdings of 2 million volumes, 2.4 million microforms, 15,000 current periodical subscriptions. Access provided to on-line information retrieval services. *Computer:* Campuswide network is available with full Internet access. Computer services are offered at no charge. *Special:* In arts and humanities: Center for Dewey Studies. In science and engineering: Coal Extraction and Utilization Center, Materials Technology Center, cooperative fisheries laboratory, cooperative wildlife laboratory. In social sciences: Center for Archaeological Investigations.

COMPUTER SCIENCE

College of Science, Department of Computer Science
Programs Offers programs in architecture information systems (MS), computer systems (MS), software theory (MS).
Faculty 14 full-time (0 women).
Faculty Research Analysis of algorithms, data structures, database systems, artificial intelligence, computer architecture.

Students 40 full-time (15 women), 1 part-time (0 women); includes 2 minority (both Asian-Americans), 30 international.
Degrees Awarded In 1996, 27 degrees awarded.
Entrance Requirements TOEFL (minimum score 550), previous undergraduate course work in computer science, minimum GPA of 2.7.
Degree Requirements Computer language, thesis required, foreign language not required.
Financial Aid In 1996–97, 3 research assistantships, 30 teaching assistantships were awarded; fellowships, full tuition waivers, Federal Work-Study, institutionally sponsored loans also available. Aid available to part-time students. *Financial aid application deadline:* 3/1.
Applying 67 applicants, 39% accepted. *Deadline:* rolling. *Fee:* $20.
Contact Dr. Kenneth Danhof
Chairperson
618-536-2327

ELECTRICAL ENGINEERING

College of Engineering, Department of Electrical Engineering
Programs Awards MS.
Faculty 21 full-time (1 woman).
Faculty Research Circuits and power systems, communications and signal processing, controls and systems, electromagnetics and optics, electronics instrumentation and bioengineering. *Total annual research expenditures:* $254,257.
Students 34 full-time (6 women), 4 part-time (0 women); includes 3 minority (2 African-Americans, 1 Asian-American), 24 international.
Degrees Awarded In 1996, 22 degrees awarded.
Entrance Requirements TOEFL (minimum score 550), minimum GPA of 2.7.
Degree Requirements Thesis, comprehensive exam required, foreign language not required.
Financial Aid In 1996–97, 6 research assistantships, 29 teaching assistantships were awarded; fellowships, full tuition waivers, Federal Work-Study, institutionally sponsored loans also available. Aid available to part-time students. *Financial aid application deadline:* 1/15.
Applying 53 applicants, 40% accepted. *Deadline:* rolling. *Fee:* $20.
Contact Dr. Glafkos D. Galanos
Chair
618-536-2364

See in-depth description on page 541.

ELECTRICAL ENGINEERING

College of Engineering, Program in Engineering Sciences
Programs Offerings include electrical systems (PhD).
Program Faculty 57 full-time (1 woman).
Entrance Requirements GRE General Test, TOEFL (minimum score 600), minimum GPA of 3.5.
Degree Requirements Dissertation.
Applying *Fee:* $20.
Contact Dr. James Evers
Associate Dean
618-453-4321
Fax: 618-453-4235
E-mail: evers@sysa.c_engri.siu.edu

INFORMATION SCIENCE

College of Science, Department of Computer Science
Programs Offerings include architecture information systems (MS).
Department Faculty 14 full-time (0 women).
Entrance Requirements TOEFL (minimum score 550), previous undergraduate course work in computer science, minimum GPA of 2.7.

Degree Requirements Computer language, thesis required, foreign language not required.
Applying *Deadline:* rolling. *Fee:* $20.
Contact *Dr. Kenneth Danhof*
Chairperson
618-536-2327

SOUTHERN ILLINOIS UNIVERSITY AT EDWARDSVILLE
Edwardsville, IL 62026-0001

OVERVIEW
Southern Illinois University at Edwardsville is a public coed comprehensive institution.

ENROLLMENT
11,151 graduate, professional, and undergraduate students; 1,198 full-time matriculated graduate/professional students (624 women), 970 part-time matriculated graduate/professional students (634 women).

GRADUATE FACULTY
453 full-time, 200 part-time; includes 42 minority (14 African-Americans, 26 Asian-Americans, 2 Hispanics).

EXPENSES
Tuition $1623 per year full-time, $90 per credit hour part-time for state residents; $4868 per year full-time, $270 per credit hour part-time for nonresidents. Fees $446 per year full-time, $417 per year part-time.

HOUSING
Rooms and/or apartments available to single students (396 units) at an average cost of $2127 per year; available to married students (96 units) at an average cost of $5400 per year. Graduate housing contact: Michael Schultz, 618-692-3931.

STUDENT SERVICES
Low-cost health insurance, career counseling, free psychological counseling, day-care facilities, campus safety program, campus employment opportunities, international student services.

FACILITIES
Library: Lovejoy Library; total holdings of 797,000 volumes, 1.091 million microforms, 6,980 current periodical subscriptions. A total of 450 personal computers in all libraries. Access provided to on-line information retrieval services. *Special:* In arts and humanities: Black Literature Collection, Drum Voices Revue, Louis Sullivan Ornamental Collection, Katherine Dunham Center for the Performing Arts. In science and engineering: Speech, Language, and Hearing Center; Illinois Transportation Research Center; planning design laboratory; scanning and transmission electron microscope. In social sciences: Regional Research and Development Services, East St. Louis Center.

COMPUTER SCIENCE

School of Engineering, Department of Computer Information Systems
Programs Awards MS.

Students 35 full-time (7 women), 14 part-time (3 women); includes 3 minority (all Asian-Americans), 24 international.
Degrees Awarded In 1996, 1 degree awarded.
Degree Requirements Thesis or alternative, final exam.
Financial Aid In 1996–97, 3 research assistantships, 4 teaching assistantships, 8 assistantships were awarded; fellowships also available.
Applying 47 applicants, 34% accepted. *Deadline:* 7/19. *Fee:* $20.
Contact *Robert Klepper*
Director
618-692-2386

ELECTRICAL ENGINEERING

School of Engineering, Program in Electrical Engineering
Programs Awards MS. Part-time programs available.
Students 39 full-time (5 women), 24 part-time (6 women); includes 11 minority (4 African-Americans, 7 Asian-Americans), 28 international.
Degrees Awarded In 1996, 25 degrees awarded.
Degree Requirements Thesis or research paper, final exam required, foreign language not required.
Financial Aid In 1996–97, 1 fellowship, 5 research assistantships, 25 assistantships were awarded; teaching assistantships, Federal Work-Study, institutionally sponsored loans also available. Aid available to part-time students.
Applying 90 applicants, 61% accepted. *Deadline:* 7/19. *Fee:* $20.
Contact *Dr. Raghu Bollini*
Chair
618-692-2500

UNIVERSITY OF CHICAGO
Chicago, IL 60637-1513

OVERVIEW
University of Chicago is an independent coed university.

ENROLLMENT
12,293 graduate, professional, and undergraduate students; 6,538 full-time matriculated graduate/professional students (2,548 women), 2,124 part-time matriculated graduate/professional students (796 women).

GRADUATE FACULTY
1,937 full-time (457 women), 335 part-time (123 women); includes 397 minority (52 African-Americans, 315 Asian-Americans, 29 Hispanics, 1 Native American).

EXPENSES
Tuition $22,491 per year full-time, $3103 per course part-time. Fees $366 per year.

HOUSING
Rooms and/or apartments available to single students (1,822 units) at an average cost of $4500 per year ($6750 including board); available to married students (1,200 units) at an average cost of $5850 per year ($9000 including board). Graduate housing contact: Jo Reizner, 773-753-2200.

STUDENT SERVICES
Low-cost health insurance, career counseling, free psychological counseling, exercise/wellness program, campus safety program, campus employment opportunities, international student services, writing training.

FACILITIES

Library: Joseph Regenstein Library plus 8 additional on-campus libraries; total holdings of 5,982,101 volumes, 2,308,586 microforms, 40,711 current periodical subscriptions. A total of 597 personal computers in all libraries. Access provided to on-line information retrieval services. *Computer:* Campuswide network is available with full Internet access. Computer services are offered at no charge. *Special:* In arts and humanities: Oriental Institute, Midway Studios, Court Theater, Smart Museum of Art, Chicago Humanities Institute. In science and engineering: Franklin McLean Memorial Research Institute, Ben My Laboratory for Cancer Research, Enrico Fermi Institute, James Franck Institute. In social sciences: National Opinion Research Center, Morris Fishbein Center for Study of the History of Medicine, Center for Urban Studies, Population Research Center.

COMPUTER SCIENCE

Division of the Physical Sciences, Department of Computer Science
Programs Awards SM, PhD.
Faculty 12 full-time (0 women), 2 part-time (1 woman).
Faculty Research Theory of computing, artificial intelligence, programming languages, robotics, computational geometry.
Students 34 full-time (5 women), includes 2 minority (1 African-American, 1 Asian-American), 10 international. Average age 23.
Degrees Awarded In 1996, 3 master's awarded (100% continued full-time study); 3 doctorates awarded (100% entered university research/teaching). Terminal master's awarded for partial completion of doctoral program.
Entrance Requirements For doctorate, GRE Subject Test.
Degree Requirements For master's, computer language, thesis or alternative required, foreign language not required; for doctorate, 1 foreign language, computer language, dissertation.
Financial Aid In 1996–97, 34 students received aid, including 4 fellowships (2 to first-year students), 13 research assistantships (3 to first-year students), 17 teaching assistantships (3 to first-year students). *Financial aid application deadline: 1/5.*
Applying 175 applicants, 11% accepted. *Deadline:* 1/5 (priority date; rolling processing). *Fee:* $50 ($55 for international students).
Contact *Margaret Jaffey*
Secretary to the Chairman
773-702-6011
Fax: 773-702-8487
E-mail: admissions@cs.uchicago.edu

UNIVERSITY OF ILLINOIS AT CHICAGO
Chicago, IL 60607-7128

OVERVIEW

University of Illinois at Chicago is a public coed university.

ENROLLMENT

24,589 graduate, professional, and undergraduate students; 4,922 full-time, 3,525 part-time matriculated graduate/professional students.

GRADUATE FACULTY

1,319 full-time (326 women), 94 part-time (15 women).

TUITION

$4942 per year full-time, $1215 per semester (minimum) part-time for state residents; $11,384 per year full-time, $2289 per semester (minimum) part-time for nonresidents.

HOUSING

Rooms and/or apartments available to single students at an average cost of $4400 per year ($5300 including board); on-campus housing not available to married students. Graduate housing contact: C. William Schnackel, 312-413-5418.

STUDENT SERVICES

Low-cost health insurance, career counseling, free psychological counseling, day-care facilities, campus employment opportunities, international student services.

FACILITIES

Library: University Library plus 4 additional on-campus libraries; total holdings of 1.6 million volumes. Access provided to on-line information retrieval services. *Computer:* Campuswide network is available with full Internet access. Computer service fees are included with tuition and fees. *Special:* In arts and humanities: Institute for the Humanities. In science and engineering: Engineering Research Facility, Molecular Sciences Building, Center for Pharmaceutical Biotechnology, Energy Resources Center, Research Resources Center, Microphysics Laboratory, Urban Transportation Center. In social sciences: Office of Social Science Research, Center for Research on Women and Gender, John Nuveen Center for International Affairs, Midwest Latino Health Research Training and Policy Center.

COMPUTER ENGINEERING

College of Engineering, Department of Electrical Engineering and Computer Science, Program in Computer Science and Engineering
Programs Awards MS, PhD. Evening/weekend programs available.
Entrance Requirements For master's, TOEFL (minimum score 550), minimum GPA of 3.75 on a 5.0 scale, BS in related field; for doctorate, GRE General Test, TOEFL (minimum score 550), minimum GPA of 3.75 on a 5.0 scale, MS in related field.
Degree Requirements For master's, computer language, thesis or alternative required, foreign language not required; for doctorate, computer language, dissertation, departmental qualifying exam required, foreign language not required.
Financial Aid Fellowships, research assistantships, teaching assistantships available.
Applying *Deadline:* 6/7 (11/1 for spring admission).
Contact *Gyan Agarwal*
Director of Graduate Studies
312-996-2290
Fax: 312-413-2290

See in-depth description on page 639.

COMPUTER SCIENCE

College of Engineering, Department of Electrical Engineering and Computer Science, Program in Computer Science and Engineering
Programs Awards MS, PhD. Evening/weekend programs available.
Entrance Requirements For master's, TOEFL (minimum score 550), minimum GPA of 3.75 on a 5.0 scale, BS in related field; for doctorate, GRE General Test, TOEFL (minimum score 550), minimum GPA of 3.75 on a 5.0 scale, MS in related field.
Degree Requirements For master's, computer language, thesis or alternative required, foreign language not required; for doctorate, computer language, dissertation, departmental qualifying exam required, foreign language not required.
Financial Aid Fellowships, research assistantships, teaching assistantships available.
Applying *Deadline:* 6/7 (11/1 for spring admission).

Contact *Gyan Agarwal*
Director of Graduate Studies
312-996-2290
Fax: 312-413-2290

See in-depth description on page 639.

COMPUTER SCIENCE

College of Liberal Arts and Sciences, Department of Mathematics, Statistics, and Computer Science, Program in Computer Science
Programs Awards MS, DA, PhD.
Entrance Requirements GRE General Test, TOEFL (minimum score 550), minimum GPA of 3.75 on a 5.0 scale.
Degree Requirements For master's, comprehensive exam required, foreign language and thesis not required; for doctorate, 1 foreign language, dissertation.
Applying *Deadline:* 7/3 (11/8 for spring admission). *Fee:* $30 ($40 for international students).
Contact *David Radford*
Director of Graduate Studies
312-996-3041

ELECTRICAL ENGINEERING

College of Engineering, Department of Electrical Engineering and Computer Science, Program in Electrical Engineering
Programs Awards MS, PhD. Evening/weekend programs available.
Entrance Requirements For master's, TOEFL (minimum score 550), minimum GPA of 3.75 on a 5.0 scale, BS in related field; for doctorate, GRE General Test, TOEFL (minimum score 550), minimum GPA of 3.75 on a 5.0 scale, MS in related field.
Degree Requirements For master's, computer language, thesis or alternative required, foreign language not required; for doctorate, computer language, dissertation, departmental qualifying exam required, foreign language not required.
Financial Aid Fellowships, research assistantships, teaching assistantships available.
Applying *Deadline:* 6/7 (11/1 for spring admission).
Contact *Gyan Agarwal*
Director of Graduate Studies
312-996-2290
Fax: 312-413-2290

See in-depth description on page 641.

UNIVERSITY OF ILLINOIS AT SPRINGFIELD
Springfield, IL 62794-9243

OVERVIEW
University of Illinois at Springfield is a public coed upper-level institution.

ENROLLMENT
4,611 graduate, professional, and undergraduate students; 389 full-time matriculated graduate/professional students (223 women), 1,296 part-time matriculated graduate/professional students (746 women).

GRADUATE FACULTY
106 full-time (27 women), 44 part-time (24 women), 116.4 FTE; includes 19 minority (10 African-Americans, 7 Asian-Americans, 2 Hispanics).

EXPENSES
Tuition $93 per credit hour for state residents; $280 per credit hour for nonresidents. Fees $400 per year full-time, $30 per semester (minimum) part-time.

HOUSING
Rooms and/or apartments available to single students (374 units) at an average cost of $1980 per year; available to married students (26 units) at an average cost of $3060 per year. Housing application deadline: 7/15.

STUDENT SERVICES
Low-cost health insurance, career counseling, free psychological counseling, exercise/wellness program, day-care facilities, campus safety program, campus employment opportunities, international student services.

FACILITIES
Library: Norris L. Brookens Library; total holdings of 508,673 volumes, 1,590,773 microforms, 2,500 current periodical subscriptions. A total of 54 personal computers in all libraries. Access provided to on-line information retrieval services. *Computer:* Campuswide network is available with full Internet access. *Special:* In arts and humanities: Visual arts gallery, studio theater. In science and engineering: Observatory, physics laboratory, biology laboratory, L. S. McClung anaerobic bacteria and bacteriophage collections. In social sciences: Center for Legal Studies, Illinois Legislative Studies Center, Institute for Public Affairs, public radio station, television office.

COMPUTER SCIENCE

School of Liberal Arts and Sciences, Program in Mathematical Sciences
Programs Offerings include computer science (MA).
Program Faculty 6 full-time (0 women), 2 part-time (0 women), 6.5 FTE.
Entrance Requirements Proficiency in calculus and programming, BA in computer science or mathematics.
Degree Requirements Thesis or alternative required, foreign language not required.
Applying *Fee:* $0.
Contact *Chung-Hsien Sung*
Convener
217-786-7330

UNIVERSITY OF ILLINOIS AT URBANA–CHAMPAIGN
Champaign, IL 61820-5711

OVERVIEW
University of Illinois at Urbana–Champaign is a public coed university.

ENROLLMENT
36,164 graduate, professional, and undergraduate students; 9,426 matriculated graduate/professional students (4,008 women).

GRADUATE FACULTY
1,991 full-time (376 women), 111 part-time (34 women).

EXPENSES
Tuition $3770 per year full-time, $629 per semester (minimum) part-time for state residents; $10,444 per year

full-time, $1741 per semester (minimum) part-time for nonresidents. Fees $1064 per year full-time, $220 per semester (minimum) part-time.

HOUSING

Rooms and/or apartments available to single students (979 units) at an average cost of $2500 per year ($5300 including board); available to married students (750 units) at an average cost of $4548 per year. Graduate housing contact: Housing Information Office, 217-333-1420.

STUDENT SERVICES

Disabled student services, multicultural affairs office, low-cost health insurance, career counseling, free psychological counseling, exercise/wellness program, campus safety program, campus employment opportunities, international student services, teacher training.

FACILITIES

Library: University Library plus 37 additional on-campus libraries; total holdings of 8 million volumes. Access provided to on-line information retrieval services. *Computer:* Campuswide network is available with full Internet access. Computer service fees are included with tuition and fees. *Special:* In arts and humanities: Krannert Art Museum, World Heritage Museum, language learning laboratory. In science and engineering: Center for Supercomputing Applications, Beckman Institute for Advanced Science and Technology, Biotechnology Center. In social sciences: Centers for Asian, African, East European, and Latin American Studies; social science quantitative laboratory.

COMPUTER ENGINEERING

College of Engineering, Department of Electrical and Computer Engineering
Programs Offers programs in computer engineering (MS, PhD), electrical engineering (MS, PhD).
Faculty 89 full-time (3 women).
Students 445 full-time (41 women), includes 80 minority (6 African-Americans, 67 Asian-Americans, 7 Hispanics), 149 international.
Degrees Awarded In 1996, 99 master's, 41 doctorates awarded.
Entrance Requirements For master's, minimum GPA of 4.0 on a 5.0 scale.
Degree Requirements Thesis/dissertation required, foreign language not required.
Financial Aid In 1996–97, 29 fellowships, 274 research assistantships, 101 teaching assistantships were awarded; full and partial tuition waivers also available. *Financial aid application deadline: 1/15.*
Applying 802 applicants, 32% accepted. *Deadline:* 1/15 (rolling processing). *Fee:* $40 ($50 for international students).
Contact *Sung Mo Kang*
Head
217-333-2301

See in-depth description on page 643.

COMPUTER SCIENCE

College of Engineering, Department of Computer Science
Programs Awards MCS, MS, MST, PhD.
Faculty 45 full-time (4 women).
Students 372 full-time (62 women), includes 49 minority (2 African-Americans, 44 Asian-Americans, 3 Hispanics), 178 international.
Degrees Awarded In 1996, 104 master's, 37 doctorates awarded.
Entrance Requirements GRE General Test.

Degree Requirements Thesis/dissertation required, foreign language not required.
Financial Aid In 1996–97, 14 fellowships, 254 research assistantships, 53 teaching assistantships were awarded; full and partial tuition waivers also available. *Financial aid application deadline: 1/15.*
Applying 749 applicants, 10% accepted. *Deadline:* 1/15 (rolling processing). *Fee:* $4 ($50 for international students).
Contact *Daniel A. Reed*
Head
217-333-3373

ELECTRICAL ENGINEERING

College of Engineering, Department of Electrical and Computer Engineering
Programs Offers programs in computer engineering (MS, PhD), electrical engineering (MS, PhD).
Faculty 89 full-time (3 women).
Students 445 full-time (41 women), includes 80 minority (6 African-Americans, 67 Asian-Americans, 7 Hispanics), 149 international.
Degrees Awarded In 1996, 99 master's, 41 doctorates awarded.
Entrance Requirements For master's, minimum GPA of 4.0 on a 5.0 scale.
Degree Requirements Thesis/dissertation required, foreign language not required.
Financial Aid In 1996–97, 29 fellowships, 274 research assistantships, 101 teaching assistantships were awarded; full and partial tuition waivers also available. *Financial aid application deadline: 1/15.*
Applying 802 applicants, 32% accepted. *Deadline:* 1/15 (rolling processing). *Fee:* $40 ($50 for international students).
Contact *Sung Mo Kang*
Head
217-333-2301

See in-depth description on page 643.

WESTERN ILLINOIS UNIVERSITY
Macomb, IL 61455-1390

OVERVIEW

Western Illinois University is a public coed comprehensive institution.

ENROLLMENT

12,184 graduate, professional, and undergraduate students; 701 full-time matriculated graduate/professional students (338 women), 1,088 part-time matriculated graduate/professional students (762 women).

GRADUATE FACULTY

438 full-time (113 women); includes 36 minority (8 African-Americans, 24 Asian-Americans, 3 Hispanics, 1 Native American).

EXPENSES

Tuition $2232 per year full-time, $93 per semester hour part-time for state residents; $6696 per year full-time, $279 per semester hour part-time for nonresidents. Fees $918 per year full-time, $32 per semester hour part-time.

HOUSING

Rooms and/or apartments available to single students at an average cost of $3083 per year ($4643 including board); available to married students (336 units) at an average cost of $3660 per year. Graduate housing contact: Dr. Robert Caruso, 309-298-3320.

STUDENT SERVICES

Disabled student services, multicultural affairs office, low-cost health insurance, career counseling, free psychological counseling, exercise/wellness program, campus safety program, campus employment opportunities, international student services, writing training.

FACILITIES

Library: University Library plus 3 additional on-campus libraries; total holdings of 1 million volumes, 446,700 microforms, 3,309 current periodical subscriptions. A total of 183 personal computers in all libraries. Access provided to on-line information retrieval services. *Computer:* Campuswide network is available with full Internet access. Total number of PCs/terminals supplied for student use: 509. Computer service fees are included with tuition and fees. *Special:* In arts and humanities: Art gallery. In science and engineering: Kibbe Life Science Station, Institute for Environmental Management, geology museum, Horn Field Campus. In social sciences: Center for Business and Economic Research, Illinois Institute for Rural Affairs, Public Policy Research Institute, Social Policy Research Center.

COMPUTER SCIENCE

College of Business and Technology, Department of Computer Science
Programs Awards MS. Part-time programs available.
Faculty 12 full-time (2 women).
Faculty Research Space-based life support, public Internet services.
Students 26 full-time (9 women), 17 part-time (7 women); includes 4 minority (1 African-American, 3 Asian-Americans), 21 international. Average age 31.
Degrees Awarded In 1996, 21 degrees awarded.
Entrance Requirements Proficiency in PASCAL.
Degree Requirements Thesis or alternative required, foreign language not required.
Financial Aid In 1996–97, 14 students received aid, including 11 research assistantships averaging $570 per month, 3 teaching assistantships averaging $745 per month. Financial aid applicants required to submit FAFSA.
Applying 47 applicants, 55% accepted. *Deadline:* rolling. *Fee:* $0 ($25 for international students).
Contact *Barbara Baily*
Director of Graduate Studies
309-298-1806
Fax: 309-298-2245

INDIANA

BALL STATE UNIVERSITY
Muncie, IN 47306-1099

OVERVIEW

Ball State University is a public coed university.

ENROLLMENT

19,500 graduate, professional, and undergraduate students; 789 full-time, 1,243 part-time matriculated graduate/professional students.

GRADUATE FACULTY

652.

EXPENSES

Tuition $3316 per year full-time, $498 per semester (minimum) part-time for state residents; $8872 per year full-time, $1163 per semester (minimum) part-time for nonresidents. Fees $6 per credit hour.

HOUSING

Rooms and/or apartments available to single students (119 units) at an average cost of $4634 (including board); available to married students (581 units) at an average cost of $4314 per year. Graduate housing contact: Dr. John E. Collins, 765-285-8011.

STUDENT SERVICES

Low-cost health insurance, career counseling, free psychological counseling, day-care facilities, campus safety program, campus employment opportunities.

FACILITIES

Library: Bracken Library plus 2 additional on-campus libraries; total holdings of 1,047,697 volumes, 695,219 microforms, 4,131 current periodical subscriptions. A total of 150 personal computers in all libraries. Access provided to on-line information retrieval services. *Special:* In arts and humanities: Reading laboratory. In science and engineering: Burris Laboratory School, human performance laboratory. In social sciences: Social Research and Service Center, school psychology clinic.

COMPUTER SCIENCE

College of Sciences and Humanities, Department of Computer Science
Programs Awards MA, MS.
Faculty 10.
Faculty Research Numerical methods, programmer productivity, graphics.
Students 30 full-time (5 women), 43 part-time (8 women); includes 1 minority (Asian-American), 37 international.
Degrees Awarded In 1996, 30 degrees awarded.
Financial Aid Teaching assistantships available.
Applying *Fee:* $15.
Contact *Dr. Clinton Fuelling*
Chairman
765-285-8641

INFORMATION SCIENCE

College of Communication, Information, and Media, Center for Information and Communication Sciences
Programs Awards MS.
Faculty 8.
Students 72 full-time (16 women), 51 part-time (16 women); includes 9 minority (6 African-Americans, 2 Asian-Americans, 1 Hispanic), 6 international.
Degrees Awarded In 1996, 84 degrees awarded.
Financial Aid Teaching assistantships available.
Applying *Fee:* $15.
Contact *Dr. Rayford Steele*
Director
765-285-1889

INDIANA STATE UNIVERSITY
Terre Haute, IN 47809-1401

OVERVIEW
Indiana State University is a public coed university.

ENROLLMENT
10,934 graduate, professional, and undergraduate students; 615 full-time matriculated graduate/professional students (315 women), 570 part-time matriculated graduate/professional students (318 women).

GRADUATE FACULTY
420 full-time (142 women), 14 part-time (8 women); includes 34 minority (9 African-Americans, 19 Asian-Americans, 5 Hispanics, 1 Native American).

TUITION
$138 per credit hour for state residents; $312 per credit hour for nonresidents.

HOUSING
Rooms and/or apartments available to single students at an average cost of $3332 (including board); available to married students (382 units) at an average cost of $4044 per year. Graduate housing contact: Ginny Jones, 812-237-7697.

STUDENT SERVICES
Low-cost health insurance, career counseling, free psychological counseling, day-care facilities, campus employment opportunities, international student services.

FACILITIES
Library: Cunningham Memorial Library plus 3 additional on-campus libraries; total holdings of 1,070,350 volumes, 712,734 microforms, 5,867 current periodical subscriptions. A total of 120 personal computers in all libraries. Access provided to on-line information retrieval services. *Special:* In arts and humanities: Turman Art Gallery, foreign languages multimedia laboratory, New Theater, Dreiser Theater. In science and engineering: Remote sensing/geographic information systems laboratory, physics computation and research laboratory, Interdisciplinary Biotech Center, Technology Services Center, radiation laboratory. In social sciences: Special Education Center, Center for Urban-Regional Studies, Center for Governmental Studies, interactive multimedia laboratory, clinical psychology clinic, School Psychology Center, Audiology and Speech Pathology Center, Hearing Disorders Center.

COMPUTER ENGINEERING

School of Technology, Department of Electronics and Computer Technology
Programs Awards MA, MS.
Faculty 3 full-time (0 women).
Students 14 full-time (2 women), 7 part-time (0 women); includes 3 minority (all African-Americans), 9 international. Average age 25.
Degrees Awarded In 1996, 10 degrees awarded.
Entrance Requirements TOEFL (minimum score 550), bachelor's degree in industrial technology or related field, minimum undergraduate GPA of 2.5.
Degree Requirements Thesis required, foreign language not required.

Financial Aid In 1996–97, 3 research assistantships (2 to first-year students), 3 teaching assistantships (all to first-year students) were awarded; fellowships, Federal Work-Study, institutionally sponsored loans also available. *Financial aid application deadline:* 3/1.
Applying 48 applicants, 77% accepted. *Deadline:* rolling. *Fee:* $20.
Contact *Dr. Robert English*
Chairperson
812-237-3456

INDIANA UNIVERSITY BLOOMINGTON
Bloomington, IN 47405

OVERVIEW
Indiana University Bloomington is a public coed university.

ENROLLMENT
34,700 graduate, professional, and undergraduate students; 4,914 full-time matriculated graduate/professional students (2,335 women), 2,998 part-time matriculated graduate/professional students (1,572 women).

GRADUATE FACULTY
1,468; includes 118 minority (44 African-Americans, 57 Asian-Americans, 16 Hispanics, 1 Native American).

EXPENSES
Tuition $160 per credit hour for state residents; $448 per credit hour for nonresidents. Fees $343 per year.

HOUSING
Rooms and/or apartments available to single students (1,295 units) and married students (1,296 units). Graduate housing contact: Halls of Residence Office, 812-855-5603.

STUDENT SERVICES
Disabled student services, multicultural affairs office, low-cost health insurance, career counseling, free psychological counseling, exercise/wellness program, day-care facilities, campus safety program, campus employment opportunities, international student services.

FACILITIES
Library: Main library plus 19 additional on-campus libraries; total holdings of 5,789,924 volumes, 3,743,511 microforms, 41,064 current periodical subscriptions. Access provided to on-line information retrieval services. *Computer:* Campuswide network is available with full Internet access. Computer service fees are applied as a separate charge. *Special:* In arts and humanities: Research Center for Language and Semiotic Studies, East Asian Studies Center, Center for Excellence in Education. In science and engineering: G. A. Black Archaeology Laboratory; Kinsey Institute for Research in Sex, Gender, and Reproduction; cyclotron facility. In social sciences: Institute of Social Research, Institute for Advanced Study, Population Institute for Research and Training, Mathers Museum of World Culture.

COMPUTER SCIENCE

College of Arts and Sciences, Department of Computer Science
Programs Awards MS, PhD. PhD offered through the University Graduate School.
Faculty 18 full-time (0 women).

Faculty Research Hardware/VLSI, parallel programming, graphics/visualization, programming language, cognitive science/artificial intelligence.

Students 134 full-time (28 women), includes 7 minority (1 African-American, 4 Asian-Americans, 2 Hispanics), 70 international. Average age 26.

Degrees Awarded In 1996, 47 master's, 11 doctorates awarded. Terminal master's awarded for partial completion of doctoral program.

Entrance Requirements GRE General Test, TOEFL.

Degree Requirements For master's, computer language required, thesis optional, foreign language not required; for doctorate, computer language, dissertation, oral and written exams.

Financial Aid Fellowships, research assistantships, teaching assistantships, graduate traineeships, Federal Work-Study available. *Financial aid application deadline: 2/1.*

Applying 264 applicants, 32% accepted. *Deadline:* 1/15 (priority date; 9/1 for spring admission). *Fee:* $35.

Contact Pam Larson
Graduate Secretary
812-855-6487
Fax: 812-855-4829
E-mail: gradvise@cs.indiana.edu

See in-depth description on page 451.

INDIANA UNIVERSITY–PURDUE UNIVERSITY FORT WAYNE
Fort Wayne, IN 46805-1499

OVERVIEW
Indiana University–Purdue University Fort Wayne is a public coed comprehensive institution.

ENROLLMENT
10,749 graduate, professional, and undergraduate students; 52 full-time matriculated graduate/professional students (27 women), 808 part-time matriculated graduate/professional students (451 women).

GRADUATE FACULTY
120 full-time (32 women), 30 part-time (13 women), 130 FTE; includes 38 minority (7 African-Americans, 24 Asian-Americans, 5 Hispanics, 2 Native Americans).

EXPENSES
Tuition $1512 per year full-time, $126 per credit hour part-time for state residents; $3336 per year full-time, $278 per credit hour part-time for nonresidents. Fees $9.50 per credit hour.

HOUSING
On-campus housing not available.

STUDENT SERVICES
Disabled student services, multicultural affairs office, low-cost health insurance, career counseling, free psychological counseling, exercise/wellness program, day-care facilities, campus safety program, campus employment opportunities, international student services, writing training, teacher training.

FACILITIES
Library: Walter E. Helmke Library; total holdings of 409,102 volumes, 481,537 microforms, 2,576 current periodical subscriptions. A total of 25 personal computers in all libraries. Access provided to on-line information retrieval

services. *Computer:* Campuswide network is available with full Internet access. Total number of PCs/terminals supplied for student use: 200. Computer service fees are included with tuition and fees. *Special:* In science and engineering: Crooked Lake Biological Station, Preventive Dentistry Research Institute, life sciences research facilities.

COMPUTER SCIENCE

School of Engineering, Technology, and Computer Science, Department of Computer Science

Programs Offers program in applied computer science (MS). Part-time and evening/weekend programs available.

Faculty 8 full-time (0 women).

Students 1 (woman) full-time, 24 part-time (1 woman); includes 2 minority (both Asian-Americans).

Entrance Requirements GRE, TOEFL.

Degree Requirements Computer language required, foreign language and thesis not required.

Financial Aid Career-related internships or fieldwork available. *Financial aid application deadline: 3/1.*

Applying 30 applicants, 83% accepted. *Deadline:* 2/15 (priority date; 9/1 for spring admission). *Fee:* $30.

Contact James L. Silver
Chair
219-481-6803

INDIANA UNIVERSITY–PURDUE UNIVERSITY INDIANAPOLIS
Indianapolis, IN 46202-2896

OVERVIEW
Indiana University–Purdue University Indianapolis is a public coed university.

ENROLLMENT
27,011 graduate, professional, and undergraduate students; 2,871 full-time matriculated graduate/professional students (1,329 women), 2,013 part-time matriculated graduate/professional students (1,184 women).

GRADUATE FACULTY
739 full-time (181 women), 56 part-time (20 women); includes 110 minority (20 African-Americans, 80 Asian-Americans, 9 Hispanics, 1 Native American).

EXPENSES
Tuition $2592 per year full-time, $144 per credit hour part-time for state residents; $7488 per year full-time, $416 per credit hour part-time for nonresidents. Fees $97 per year (minimum) full-time, $39 per year (minimum) part-time.

HOUSING
Rooms and/or apartments available to single students (350 units) at an average cost of $3500 per year; available to married students (113 units) at an average cost of $4900 per year. Graduate housing contact: Housing Office, 317-274-7200.

STUDENT SERVICES
Disabled student services, multicultural affairs office, low-cost health insurance, career counseling, free psychologi-

cal counseling, day-care facilities, campus safety program, campus employment opportunities, international student services.

FACILITIES

Library: University Library plus 4 additional on-campus libraries; total holdings of 1,091,127 volumes, 2,230,724 microforms, 14,172 current periodical subscriptions. A total of 200 personal computers in all libraries. Access provided to on-line information retrieval services. *Computer:* Campuswide network is available with full Internet access. Total number of PCs/terminals supplied for student use: 500. Computer service fees are included with tuition and fees. *Special:* In arts and humanities: Center for Religion and American Culture, Center on Philanthropy. In science and engineering: Krannert Institute of Cardiology, Institute of Psychiatric Research, CAD/CAM Center, Diabetes Research and Training Center, Bowen Center for Health Care Research. In social sciences: Osgood Laboratory for Cross Cultural Research, Center for Urban Policy and the Environment, Center for Law and Health.

COMPUTER SCIENCE

School of Science, Department of Computer and Information Science
Programs Offers program in computer science (MS). Part-time and evening/weekend programs available.
Faculty 7 full-time (0 women), 2 part-time (0 women).
Faculty Research Artificial intelligence, scientific computing, computational geometry, parallel computing, database systems. *Total annual research expenditures:* $200,000.
Students 14 full-time (4 women), 11 part-time (1 woman); includes 7 minority (all Asian-Americans), 7 international. Average age 30.
Degrees Awarded In 1996, 3 degrees awarded (100% found work related to degree).
Entrance Requirements GRE, BS or equivalent in computer science.
Degree Requirements Computer language required, thesis optional, foreign language not required.
Financial Aid In 1996–97, 5 students received aid, including 2 research assistantships (1 to a first-year student) averaging $800 per month and totaling $8,000, 2 teaching assistantships (both to first-year students) averaging $800 per month and totaling $8,000; fellowships, full and partial tuition waivers, institutionally sponsored loans, and career-related internships or fieldwork also available. Aid available to part-time students. *Financial aid application deadline:* 3/1; applicants required to submit FAFSA.
Applying 2 applicants, 100% accepted. *Deadline:* 3/1 (priority date; rolling processing; 9/1 for spring admission). *Fee:* $25 ($50 for international students).
Contact *Carla L. Boyd*
Research Curriculum and Administrative Coordinator
317-274-9727
Fax: 317-274-9742
E-mail: staff@cs.iupui.edu

ELECTRICAL ENGINEERING

School of Engineering and Technology, Department of Electrical Engineering
Programs Offers programs in biomedical engineering (MSBME), electrical engineering (MSEE).
Faculty 13 full-time (2 women).
Faculty Research Control and automation, signal processing, robotics, medical imaging, neural networks. *Total annual research expenditures:* $172,654.

Students 20 full-time (1 woman), 23 part-time (1 woman); includes 4 minority (2 African-Americans, 2 Asian-Americans), 10 international. Average age 27.
Degrees Awarded In 1996, 11 degrees awarded.
Entrance Requirements GRE, TOEFL, minimum B average.
Degree Requirements Thesis optional, foreign language not required.
Financial Aid Fellowships, research assistantships, full and partial tuition waivers, Federal Work-Study available. *Financial aid application deadline:* 3/1.
Applying 34 applicants, 29% accepted. *Deadline:* 7/1. *Fee:* $25 ($50 for international students).
Contact *Vickie Lawrence*
Graduate Program Secretary
317-274-9740
Fax: 317-274-4567
E-mail: grad@engr.iupui.edu

PURDUE UNIVERSITY
West Lafayette, IN 47907-1968

OVERVIEW
Purdue University is a public coed university.

ENROLLMENT
34,117 graduate, professional, and undergraduate students; 4,464 full-time matriculated graduate/professional students (1,647 women), 1,552 part-time matriculated graduate/professional students (607 women).

GRADUATE FACULTY
1,837; includes 349 minority (30 African-Americans, 274 Asian-Americans, 40 Hispanics, 5 Native Americans).

TUITION
$3336 per year full-time, $120 per credit hour part-time for state residents; $11,168 per year full-time, $369 per credit hour part-time for nonresidents.

HOUSING
Rooms and/or apartments available to single students (1,050 units) at an average cost of $4200 per year; available to married students (1,244 units) at an average cost of $4776 per year. Graduate housing information: 765-494-7045.

STUDENT SERVICES
Disabled student services, multicultural affairs office, low-cost health insurance, career counseling, free psychological counseling, exercise/wellness program, campus safety program, campus employment opportunities, international student services, writing training, grant writing training, teacher training.

FACILITIES
Library: Main library plus 15 additional on-campus libraries; total holdings of 2,201,543 volumes, 2,259,260 microforms, 20,542 current periodical subscriptions. A total of 300 personal computers in all libraries. Access provided to on-line information retrieval services. *Computer:* Campuswide network is available with full Internet access. Computer services are offered at no charge. *Special:* In arts and humanities: Centers for Asian Studies, Classical Studies, Comparative Literature, Film Studies, Medieval Studies, Philosophy and Literature,

and Science and Culture. In science and engineering: Animal Scis Research Ctr, Automotive Transportation Ctr, Ctr for AIDS Research, Ctr for Applied Math, Ctr for Information & Numerical Data Analysis & Synthesis, Ctr for Paralysis Research, Ctr for Plant Environmental Stress Physiology, Ctr for Statistical Decision Scis, Ctr for Technology Transfer & Pollution Prevention Projects, Engineering Research Ctr for Intelligent Manufacturing Systems, Indian Pine Natural Resources Field Station, Ctr for New Crops & Plant Products, Mining & Minerals Resource Research Ctr, Lucille P. Markey Ctr for Structural Biology, Natural Resources Research Inst, NSF Ctr for Advanced Cement-Based Materials, Optoelectronic Ctr, Crop Diagnostics Training & Research Ctr, Vision Research Ctr, Software Engineering Ctr, Thermal Scis & Propulsion Ctr, Water Resources Re. In social sciences: Center for Applied Ethology and Human/Animal Interaction, Center for Leadership Studies, Center for Rural Development, Gifted Education Resource Center, Marriage and Family Therapy Center, Policy Center for Life Long Learning, Retail Institute, School Mathematics and Science Center, Social Research Institute.

COMPUTER ENGINEERING

Schools of Engineering, School of Electrical and Computer Engineering
Programs Offers programs in biomedical engineering (MS Bm E, PhD), computer engineering (MS, MSE, PhD), electrical engineering (MS, MSE, MSEE, PhD). MS Bm E and PhD (biomedical engineering) new for fall 1997 and offered jointly with the Schools of Chemical Engineering and Mechanical Engineering. Part-time programs available.
Faculty 60 full-time (5 women), 12 part-time (0 women).
Faculty Research Biomedical communications and signal processing; solid-state materials and devices; fields and optics; control, power, and circuit systems. *Total annual research expenditures:* $9.5 million.
Students 447 full-time (70 women), 16 part-time (3 women); includes 65 minority (11 African-Americans, 47 Asian-Americans, 7 Hispanics), 294 international. Average age 25.
Degrees Awarded In 1996, 116 master's, 38 doctorates awarded. Terminal master's awarded for partial completion of doctoral program.
Entrance Requirements GRE General Test (combined average 2070 on three sections), TOEFL (minimum score 575; average 635).
Degree Requirements For master's, thesis optional, foreign language not required; for doctorate, dissertation required, foreign language not required.
Financial Aid In 1996–97, 262 students received aid, including 22 fellowships (8 to first-year students) averaging $900 per month, 166 research assistantships (31 to first-year students) averaging $1,250 per month, 75 teaching assistantships (17 to first-year students) averaging $1,110 per month. Aid available to part-time students. Financial aid applicants required to submit FAFSA.
Applying 834 applicants, 54% accepted. *Deadline:* 1/15 (priority date; rolling processing; 9/1 for spring admission). *Fee:* $30.
Contact Dr. A. M. Weiner
Director of Admissions
765-494-3392
Fax: 765-494-3393
E-mail: ecegrad@ecn.purdue.edu

See in-depth description on page 529.

COMPUTER SCIENCE

School of Science, Department of Computer Sciences
Programs Awards MS, PhD. Part-time programs available.
Faculty 29 full-time (1 woman), 8 part-time (1 woman).
Faculty Research Computer systems, geometric modeling, information security, scientific computing, software systems, theory and algorithms. *Total annual research expenditures:* $3.87 million.
Students 107 full-time (18 women), 11 part-time (3 women); includes 8 minority (2 African-Americans, 6 Asian-Americans), 91 international. Average age 27.
Degrees Awarded In 1996, 41 master's awarded; 13 doctorates awarded (38% entered university research/teaching, 62% found other work related to degree). Terminal master's awarded for partial completion of doctoral program.
Entrance Requirements GRE General Test, TOEFL (minimum score 577), TWE, minimum GPA of 3.5.
Degree Requirements For master's, thesis optional, foreign language not required; for doctorate, dissertation required, foreign language not required.
Financial Aid In 1996–97, 108 students received aid, including 8 fellowships (3 to first-year students) averaging $1,329 per month, 53 research assistantships (9 to first-year students) averaging $1,164 per month and totaling $480,700, 35 teaching assistantships (8 to first-year students) averaging $1,034 per month and totaling $339,200, 1 facilities assistantship averaging $1,025 per month and totaling $10,250. Aid available to part-time students. *Financial aid application deadline:* 12/15; applicants required to submit FAFSA.
Applying 508 applicants, 31% accepted. *Deadline:* 12/15. *Fee:* $30.
Contact Dr. W. J. Gorman
Assistant to the Head
765-494-6004
Fax: 765-494-0739
E-mail: grad_info@cs.purdue.edu

See in-depth description on page 527.

COMPUTER SCIENCE

School of Science, Department of Statistics
Programs Offerings include statistics and computer science (MS).
Department Faculty 25.
Entrance Requirements TOEFL (minimum score 550).
Applying *Fee:* $30.
Contact Angie Murphy
Graduate Secretary
765-494-5794
Fax: 765-494-0558
E-mail: graduate@stat.purdue.edu

ELECTRICAL ENGINEERING

Schools of Engineering, School of Electrical and Computer Engineering
Programs Offers programs in biomedical engineering (MS Bm E, PhD), computer engineering (MS, MSE, PhD), electrical engineering (MS, MSE, MSEE, PhD). MS Bm E and PhD (biomedical engineering) new for fall 1997 and offered jointly with the Schools of Chemical Engineering and Mechanical Engineering. Part-time programs available.
Faculty 60 full-time (5 women), 12 part-time (0 women).
Faculty Research Biomedical communications and signal processing; solid-state materials and devices; fields and optics; control, power, and circuit systems. *Total annual research expenditures:* $9.5 million.
Students 447 full-time (70 women), 16 part-time (3 women); includes 65 minority (11 African-Americans, 47 Asian-Americans, 7 Hispanics), 294 international. Average age 25.

Degrees Awarded In 1996, 116 master's, 38 doctorates awarded. Terminal master's awarded for partial completion of doctoral program.

Entrance Requirements GRE General Test (combined average 2070 on three sections), TOEFL (minimum score 575; average 635).

Degree Requirements For master's, thesis optional, foreign language not required; for doctorate, dissertation required, foreign language not required.

Financial Aid In 1996–97, 262 students received aid, including 22 fellowships (8 to first-year students) averaging $900 per month, 166 research assistantships (31 to first-year students) averaging $1,250 per month, 75 teaching assistantships (17 to first-year students) averaging $1,110 per month. Aid available to part-time students. Financial aid applicants required to submit FAFSA.

Applying 834 applicants, 54% accepted. *Deadline:* 1/15 (priority date; rolling processing; 9/1 for spring admission). *Fee:* $30.

Contact Dr. A. M. Weiner
Director of Admissions
765-494-3392
Fax: 765-494-3393
E-mail: ecegrad@ecn.purdue.edu

See in-depth description on page 529.

ROSE-HULMAN INSTITUTE OF TECHNOLOGY
Terre Haute, IN 47803-3920

OVERVIEW
Rose-Hulman Institute of Technology is an independent primarily male comprehensive institution.

ENROLLMENT
1,420 graduate, professional, and undergraduate students; 93 full-time matriculated graduate/professional students (19 women), 42 part-time matriculated graduate/professional students (6 women).

GRADUATE FACULTY
72 full-time (7 women); includes 0 minority.

TUITION
$16,863 per year full-time, $471 per quarter hour part-time.

HOUSING
Rooms and/or apartments available to single students at an average cost of $2556 per year ($4956 including board); on-campus housing not available to married students. Housing application deadline: 4/1. Graduate housing contact: Peter Gustafson, 812-877-8257.

STUDENT SERVICES
Low-cost health insurance, career counseling, international student services.

FACILITIES
Library: John A. Logan Library; total holdings of 70,000 volumes. Access provided to on-line information retrieval services. *Computer:* Campuswide network is available with full Internet access. Total number of PCs/terminals supplied for student use: 200. Computer services are offered at no charge. *Special:* In science and engineering:

Rotz Mechanical Engineering Laboratory, Center for Applied Optics, Center for Technology Assessment.

COMPUTER ENGINEERING

Department of Electrical and Computer Engineering
Programs Awards MS. Part-time programs available.
Faculty 19 full-time (1 woman).
Faculty Research Network synthesis, digital electronics, control systems, image processing, electromagnetics. *Total annual research expenditures: $777,147.*
Students 35 full-time (9 women), includes 27 international. Average age 23.
Degrees Awarded In 1996, 13 degrees awarded.
Entrance Requirements GRE, TOEFL (minimum score 580), minimum GPA of 3.0.
Degree Requirements Thesis required, foreign language not required.
Financial Aid In 1996–97, 19 students received aid, including 6 fellowships (4 to first-year students) averaging $665 per month and totaling $36,000, 13 tuition grants (6 to first-year students) totaling $130,100; research assistantships, teaching assistantships, full and partial tuition waivers, institutionally sponsored loans also available. *Financial aid application deadline: 2/1.*
Applying 36 applicants, 81% accepted. *Deadline:* 4/1 (priority date; rolling processing). *Fee:* $0.
Contact Dr. Buck F. Brown
Dean for Research and Graduate Studies
812-877-8403
Fax: 812-877-8102
E-mail: buck.brown@rose-hulman.edu

ELECTRICAL ENGINEERING

Department of Electrical and Computer Engineering
Programs Awards MS. Part-time programs available.
Faculty 19 full-time (1 woman).
Faculty Research Network synthesis, digital electronics, control systems, image processing, electromagnetics. *Total annual research expenditures: $777,147.*
Students 35 full-time (9 women), includes 27 international. Average age 23.
Degrees Awarded In 1996, 13 degrees awarded.
Entrance Requirements GRE, TOEFL (minimum score 580), minimum GPA of 3.0.
Degree Requirements Thesis required, foreign language not required.
Financial Aid In 1996–97, 19 students received aid, including 6 fellowships (4 to first-year students) averaging $665 per month and totaling $36,000, 13 tuition grants (6 to first-year students) totaling $130,100; research assistantships, teaching assistantships, full and partial tuition waivers, institutionally sponsored loans also available. *Financial aid application deadline: 2/1.*
Applying 36 applicants, 81% accepted. *Deadline:* 4/1 (priority date; rolling processing). *Fee:* $0.
Contact Dr. Buck F. Brown
Dean for Research and Graduate Studies
812-877-8403
Fax: 812-877-8102
E-mail: buck.brown@rose-hulman.edu

UNIVERSITY OF NOTRE DAME
Notre Dame, IN 46556

OVERVIEW
University of Notre Dame is an independent-religious coed university.

ENROLLMENT
10,281 graduate, professional, and undergraduate students; 2,423 matriculated graduate/professional students.

GRADUATE FACULTY
670 (113 women); includes 94 minority (12 African-Americans, 54 Asian-Americans, 28 Hispanics).

EXPENSES
Tuition $19,680 per year full-time, $1093 per credit hour part-time. Fees $45 per year.

HOUSING
Rooms and/or apartments available to single students (524 units) at an average cost of $2050 per year; available to married students (131 units) at an average cost of $3912 per year. Housing application deadline: 5/1. Graduate housing contact: Kevin Cannon, 219-631-5878.

STUDENT SERVICES
Low-cost health insurance, career counseling, free psychological counseling, day-care facilities, campus safety program, campus employment opportunities, international student services.

FACILITIES
Library: Theodore M. Hesburgh Library plus 8 additional on-campus libraries; total holdings of 2,458,987 volumes, 2,661,435 microforms, 23,131 current periodical subscriptions. A total of 315 personal computers in all libraries. Access provided to on-line information retrieval services. *Computer:* Campuswide network is available with full Internet access. Total number of PCs/terminals supplied for student use: 600. Computer services are offered at no charge. *Special:* In arts and humanities: Ambrosiana Library Microfilm; photograph and drawings collection; Charles and Margaret Hall Cushwa Center for the Study of American Catholicism; Reilly Center for Science, Technology and Values; Snite Museum of Art; Medieval Institute. In science and engineering: Center for Applied Mathematics, Center for Bioengineering and Pollutions Control, radiation laboratory, vector biology laboratory. In social sciences: Center for the Study of Contemporary Society, Helen Kellogg Institute for International Studies, Joan B. Kroc Institute for International Peace Studies, Laboratory for Social Research.

COMPUTER ENGINEERING

College of Engineering, Department of Computer Science and Engineering
Programs Awards MS, PhD. Part-time programs available.
Faculty 13 full-time (1 woman), 2 part-time (0 women).
Faculty Research VLSI design, VLSI architectures, parallel and distributed computing, artificial intelligence. *Total annual research expenditures:* $300,000.

Students 40 full-time (10 women), 4 part-time (1 woman); includes 3 minority (1 African-American, 2 Asian-Americans), 27 international. Average age 25.
Degrees Awarded In 1996, 5 master's, 3 doctorates awarded. Terminal master's awarded for partial completion of doctoral program.
Entrance Requirements GRE General Test (minimum combined score of 2000 on three sections), TOEFL (minimum score 620).
Degree Requirements Computer language, thesis/dissertation required, foreign language not required.
Financial Aid In 1996–97, 40 students received aid, including 9 fellowships (2 to first-year students) averaging $1,184 per month, 10 research assistantships averaging $1,183 per month, 13 teaching assistantships (1 to a first-year student) averaging $1,010 per month. *Financial aid application deadline:* 2/1.
Applying 94 applicants, 18% accepted. *Deadline:* 2/1 (priority date; rolling processing; 10/15 for spring admission). *Fee:* $40.
Contact Dr. Terrence J. Akai
Director of Graduate Admissions
219-631-7706
Fax: 219-631-4183

See in-depth description on page 691.

COMPUTER SCIENCE

College of Engineering, Department of Computer Science and Engineering
Programs Awards MS, PhD. Part-time programs available.
Faculty 13 full-time (1 woman), 2 part-time (0 women).
Faculty Research VLSI design, VLSI architectures, parallel and distributed computing, artificial intelligence. *Total annual research expenditures:* $300,000.
Students 40 full-time (10 women), 4 part-time (1 woman); includes 3 minority (1 African-American, 2 Asian-Americans), 27 international. Average age 25.
Degrees Awarded In 1996, 5 master's, 3 doctorates awarded. Terminal master's awarded for partial completion of doctoral program.
Entrance Requirements GRE General Test (minimum combined score of 2000 on three sections), TOEFL (minimum score 620).
Degree Requirements Computer language, thesis/dissertation required, foreign language not required.
Financial Aid In 1996–97, 40 students received aid, including 9 fellowships (2 to first-year students) averaging $1,184 per month, 10 research assistantships averaging $1,183 per month, 13 teaching assistantships (1 to a first-year student) averaging $1,010 per month. *Financial aid application deadline:* 2/1.
Applying 94 applicants, 18% accepted. *Deadline:* 2/1 (priority date; rolling processing; 10/15 for spring admission). *Fee:* $40.
Contact Dr. Terrence J. Akai
Director of Graduate Admissions
219-631-7706
Fax: 219-631-4183

See in-depth description on page 691.

ELECTRICAL ENGINEERING

College of Engineering, Department of Electrical Engineering
Programs Awards MS, PhD. Part-time programs available.
Faculty 22 full-time (0 women), 5 part-time (0 women).
Faculty Research Electronic properties of materials and devices, signal and imaging processing, communication theory, control theory and applications, optoelectronics.
Students 53 full-time (10 women), 12 part-time (0 women); includes 3 minority (all Hispanics), 48 international. Average age 26.

Degrees Awarded In 1996, 8 master's, 9 doctorates awarded. Terminal master's awarded for partial completion of doctoral program.

Entrance Requirements GRE General Test, TOEFL (minimum score 600).

Degree Requirements Thesis/dissertation required, foreign language not required.

Financial Aid In 1996–97, 6 fellowships (2 to first-year students) averaging $1,282 per month, 18 research assistantships (3 to first-year students) averaging $1,268 per month, 21 teaching assistantships (15 to first-year students) averaging $1,266 per month were awarded; scholarships, full and partial tuition waivers also available. *Financial aid application deadline:* 2/1.

Applying 160 applicants, 29% accepted. *Deadline:* 2/1 (priority date; rolling processing; 10/1 for spring admission). *Fee:* $40.

Contact *Dr. Terrence J. Akai*
Director of Graduate Admissions
219-631-7706
Fax: 219-631-4183

See in-depth description on page 693.

IOWA

IOWA STATE UNIVERSITY OF SCIENCE AND TECHNOLOGY
Ames, IA 50011

OVERVIEW

Iowa State University of Science and Technology is a public coed university.

ENROLLMENT

24,899 graduate, professional, and undergraduate students; 2,725 full-time matriculated graduate/professional students (1,092 women), 1,549 part-time matriculated graduate/professional students (689 women).

GRADUATE FACULTY

1,817 full-time, 160 part-time; includes 143 minority.

EXPENSES

Tuition $3048 per year full-time, $170 per credit part-time for state residents; $8974 per year full-time, $499 per credit part-time for nonresidents. Fees $200 per year for state residents; $200 per year full-time for nonresidents.

HOUSING

Rooms and/or apartments available to single students (134 units) and married students (822 units) at an average cost of $4596 per year. Graduate housing contact: Department of Residence Life, 515-294-2900.

STUDENT SERVICES

Disabled student services, low-cost health insurance, career counseling, free psychological counseling, exercise/wellness program, day-care facilities, campus safety program, campus employment opportunities, international student services, teacher training.

FACILITIES

Library: University Library plus 5 additional on-campus libraries; total holdings of 2,104,204 volumes, 2,888,345 microforms, 21,775 current periodical subscriptions. A total of 149 personal computers in all libraries. Access provided to on-line information retrieval services. *Computer:* Campuswide network is available with full Internet access. Computer service fees are included with tuition and fees. *Special:* In science and engineering: Ames Center for Animal Health; Biotechnology Instrumentation Center; Centers for Advanced Technology Development, Agricultural and Rural Development, Transportation Research and Education; Computation Center; Iowa Center for Emerging Manufacturing Technology; Iowa Energy Center; Leopold Center for Sustainable Agriculture; Microanalytical Instrumentation Center; Microelectronics Research Center; Seed Science Center; statistical laboratory; Utilization Center for Agricultural Products. In social sciences: Social and Behavioral Research Center for Rural Health.

COMPUTER ENGINEERING

College of Engineering, Department of Electrical and Computer Engineering

Programs Offers programs in computer engineering (MS, PhD); electrical engineering (M Eng, MS, PhD), including computer engineering (M Eng).

Faculty 44 full-time, 2 part-time.

Students 172 full-time (35 women), 48 part-time (6 women); includes 8 minority (4 African-Americans, 2 Asian-Americans, 2 Hispanics), 167 international.

Degrees Awarded In 1996, 58 master's, 15 doctorates awarded.

Entrance Requirements TOEFL, GRE General Test.

Degree Requirements For master's, thesis or alternative required, foreign language not required; for doctorate, dissertation required, foreign language not required.

Financial Aid In 1996–97, 138 research assistantships (33 to first-year students), 31 teaching assistantships (3 to first-year students), 2 scholarships (1 to a first-year student) were awarded; fellowships also available.

Applying 637 applicants, 22% accepted. *Deadline:* 1/15 (priority date; 9/15 for spring admission). *Fee:* $20 ($30 for international students).

Contact *William Lord*
515-294-2667
E-mail: ecegrad@iastate.edu

COMPUTER SCIENCE

College of Liberal Arts and Sciences, Department of Computer Science

Programs Awards MS, PhD.

Faculty 19 full-time, 1 part-time.

Students 37 full-time (9 women), 29 part-time (7 women); includes 2 minority (1 African-American, 1 Asian-American), 38 international.

Degrees Awarded In 1996, 24 master's, 2 doctorates awarded.

Entrance Requirements GRE General Test, TOEFL.

Degree Requirements For master's, thesis or alternative; for doctorate, 1 foreign language, dissertation.

Financial Aid In 1996–97, 32 research assistantships (3 to first-year students), 30 teaching assistantships (8 to first-year students), 13 scholarships (10 to first-year students) were awarded; fellowships also available.

Applying 254 applicants, 15% accepted. *Fee:* $20 ($30 for international students).

Contact *Dr. Arthur E. Oldehoeft*
Chair
515-294-4377
E-mail: grad_adm@cs.iastate.edu

See in-depth description on page 453.

ELECTRICAL ENGINEERING

College of Engineering, Department of Electrical and Computer Engineering

Programs   Offers programs in computer engineering (MS, PhD); electrical engineering (M Eng, MS, PhD), including computer engineering (M Eng).

Faculty   44 full-time, 2 part-time.

Students   172 full-time (35 women), 48 part-time (6 women); includes 8 minority (4 African-Americans, 2 Asian-Americans, 2 Hispanics), 167 international.

Degrees Awarded   In 1996, 58 master's, 15 doctorates awarded.

Entrance Requirements   TOEFL, GRE General Test.

Degree Requirements   For master's, thesis or alternative required, foreign language not required; for doctorate, dissertation required, foreign language not required.

Financial Aid   In 1996–97, 138 research assistantships (33 to first-year students), 31 teaching assistantships (3 to first-year students), 2 scholarships (1 to a first-year student) were awarded; fellowships also available.

Applying   637 applicants, 22% accepted. *Deadline:* 1/15 (priority date; 9/15 for spring admission). *Fee:* $20 ($30 for international students).

Contact   *William Lord*
515-294-2667
E-mail: ecegrad@iastate.edu

molecular biology laboratory. In social sciences: Statistical software for social science research.

COMPUTER SCIENCE

Program in Computer Science

Programs   Awards MS.

Faculty   15 (1 woman).

Faculty Research   Parallel processing, computer systems in architecture.

Students   11 full-time (1 woman), 3 part-time (0 women); includes 8 international. Average age 27.

Degrees Awarded   In 1996, 5 degrees awarded.

Entrance Requirements   GRE General Test, TOEFL (minimum score 550), minimum GPA of 3.0.

Degree Requirements   Computer language, thesis or alternative required, foreign language not required.

Financial Aid   In 1996–97, 5 fellowships (4 to first-year students) were awarded; full and partial tuition waivers, Federal Work-Study also available. *Financial aid application deadline:* 4/30.

Applying   *Deadline:* 4/15 (priority date; rolling processing). *Fee:* $40.

Contact   *Harry Bright*
Director of Admissions
515-472-1166

MAHARISHI UNIVERSITY OF MANAGEMENT
Fairfield, IA 52557

OVERVIEW
Maharishi University of Management is an independent coed university.

ENROLLMENT
796 graduate, professional, and undergraduate students; 201 full-time matriculated graduate/professional students (96 women), 57 part-time matriculated graduate/professional students (28 women).

GRADUATE FACULTY
73 (12 women); includes 3 minority (all African-Americans).

HOUSING
Rooms and/or apartments available to single students (350 units) and married students (50 units) at an average cost of $1864 per year ($3560 including board). Housing application deadline: 8/1. Graduate housing contact: Housing Office, 515-472-1126.

STUDENT SERVICES
Career counseling, day-care facilities, campus employment opportunities, international student services.

FACILITIES
Library: Main library plus 1 additional on-campus library; total holdings of 142,800 volumes, 49,240 microforms, 1,650 current periodical subscriptions. A total of 8 personal computers in all libraries. Access provided to on-line information retrieval services. *Special:* In science and engineering: Cellular and biochemical laboratory, physiological and neurophysiological laboratory, EEG and brain topographical mapping laboratory,

---

MARYCREST INTERNATIONAL UNIVERSITY
Davenport, IA 52804–4096

OVERVIEW
Marycrest International University is an independent coed comprehensive institution.

ENROLLMENT
905 graduate, professional, and undergraduate students; 10 full-time matriculated graduate/professional students (2 women), 365 part-time matriculated graduate/professional students (314 women).

GRADUATE FACULTY
6 full-time (4 women), 4 part-time (0 women), 7.3 FTE; includes 0 minority.

EXPENSES
Tuition $393 per credit hour. Fees $12 per credit hour.

HOUSING
Rooms and/or apartments available to single students (25 units); on-campus housing not available to married students. Housing application deadline: 7/15. Graduate housing information: 319-326-9225.

STUDENT SERVICES
Career counseling, day-care facilities.

FACILITIES
Library: Cone Library; total holdings of 110,582 volumes, 26,028 microforms, 522 current periodical subscriptions. A total of 10 personal computers in all libraries. Access provided to on-line information retrieval services. *Computer:* Campuswide network is available with full Internet access. Total number of PCs/terminals supplied

for student use: 85. Computer service fees are included with tuition and fees.

COMPUTER SCIENCE

Department of Computer Science
Programs   Awards MS. Part-time and evening/weekend programs available.
Faculty   2 full-time (0 women), 1 part-time (0 women), 2.5 FTE.
Faculty Research   Distributed database, network management, distributed fault tolerance, object-oriented systems.
Students   10 full-time (3 women), 11 part-time (3 women); includes 1 minority (Asian-American), 8 international. Average age 30.
Degrees Awarded   In 1996, 9 degrees awarded (100% found work related to degree).
Entrance Requirements   Minimum undergraduate GPA of 2.8.
Degree Requirements   Computer language, comprehensive exams required, foreign language and thesis not required.
Financial Aid   In 1996–97, 10 students received aid, including 10 research assistantships (5 to first-year students); Federal Work-Study also available. *Financial aid application deadline: 3/1.*
Applying   20 applicants, 75% accepted. *Deadline:* rolling. *Fee:* $25.
Contact   *Mark McGinn*
Chairman
319-326-9252
Fax: 319-326-9250
E-mail: mcginn@mcrest.edu

THE UNIVERSITY OF IOWA
Iowa City, IA 52242

OVERVIEW
The University of Iowa is a public coed university.

ENROLLMENT
27,921 graduate, professional, and undergraduate students; 5,717 full-time matriculated graduate/professional students (2,644 women), 2,889 part-time matriculated graduate/professional students (1,508 women).

GRADUATE FACULTY
1,686 full-time, 61 part-time; includes 192 minority (34 African-Americans, 123 Asian-Americans, 31 Hispanics, 4 Native Americans).

EXPENSES
Tuition $3048 per year full-time, $170 per semester hour part-time for state residents; $9820 per year full-time, $170 per semester hour part-time for nonresidents. Fees $194 per year full-time, $170 per year part-time.

HOUSING
Rooms and/or apartments available to single students (5,540 units) at an average cost of $2557 per year ($4351 including board); available to married students (749 units) at an average cost of $3420 per year. Graduate housing information: 319-335-3009.

STUDENT SERVICES
Disabled student services, low-cost health insurance, career counseling, free psychological counseling, campus employment opportunities, international student services, teacher training.

FACILITIES
Library: Main library plus 11 additional on-campus libraries; total holdings of 3,751,596 volumes, 5,819,830 microforms, 38,370 current periodical subscriptions. Access provided to on-line information retrieval services. *Computer:* Campuswide network is available with full Internet access. Total number of PCs/terminals supplied for student use: 885. Computer service fees are included with tuition and fees. *Special:* In arts and humanities: Museum of Art, Museum of Natural History, Lakeside Laboratories. In science and engineering: High Field Nuclear Magnetic Resonance Facility, Fermentor Facility, Computer-Assisted Image AnalysisFacility, High Resolution Mass Spectrometry Facility, Institute of Hydraulic Research, Electron Microscopy Research Facility, Optical Science and Technology Center. In social sciences: Social Science Institute, Public Policy Center.

COMPUTER ENGINEERING

College of Engineering, Department of Electrical and Computer Engineering
Programs   Awards MS, PhD.
Faculty   17 full-time, 1 part-time.
Faculty Research   Computer systems and applications, biomedical image processing, robotics, acousto-optics.
Students   43 full-time (2 women), 37 part-time (5 women); includes 3 minority (all Asian-Americans), 37 international.
Degrees Awarded   In 1996, 17 master's, 4 doctorates awarded.
Entrance Requirements   GRE, TOEFL.
Degree Requirements   For master's, thesis optional, foreign language not required; for doctorate, dissertation, comprehensive exam required, foreign language not required.
Financial Aid   In 1996–97, 1 fellowship (to a first-year student), 25 research assistantships (8 to first-year students), 25 teaching assistantships (16 to first-year students) were awarded. Financial aid applicants required to submit FAFSA.
Applying   195 applicants, 46% accepted. *Deadline:* rolling. *Fee:* $20 ($30 for international students).
Contact   *Dr. Sudhakar M. Reddy*
Chair
319-335-5196

COMPUTER SCIENCE

College of Liberal Arts, Department of Computer Science
Programs   Awards MS, PhD.
Faculty   20 full-time.
Students   39 full-time (5 women), 64 part-time (18 women); includes 7 minority (1 African-American, 4 Asian-Americans, 2 Hispanics), 60 international.
Degrees Awarded   In 1996, 48 master's, 1 doctorate awarded.
Entrance Requirements   GRE General Test, GRE Subject Test.
Degree Requirements   For master's, thesis optional, foreign language not required; for doctorate, dissertation, comprehensive exam required, foreign language not required.
Financial Aid   In 1996–97, 3 fellowships (1 to a first-year student), 27 research assistantships (9 to first-year students), 39 teaching assistantships (16 to first-year students) were awarded. Financial aid applicants required to submit FAFSA.
Applying   307 applicants, 35% accepted. *Deadline:* rolling. *Fee:* $20 ($30 for international students).
Contact   *Steven C. Bruell*
Chair
319-335-0713

See in-depth description on page **645.**

ELECTRICAL ENGINEERING

College of Engineering, Department of Electrical and Computer Engineering
Programs Awards MS, PhD.
Faculty 17 full-time, 1 part-time.
Faculty Research Computer systems and applications, biomedical image processing, robotics, acousto-optics.
Students 43 full-time (2 women), 37 part-time (5 women); includes 3 minority (all Asian-Americans), 37 international.
Degrees Awarded In 1996, 17 master's, 4 doctorates awarded.
Entrance Requirements GRE, TOEFL.
Degree Requirements For master's, thesis optional, foreign language not required; for doctorate, dissertation, comprehensive exam required, foreign language not required.
Financial Aid In 1996–97, 1 fellowship (to a first-year student), 25 research assistantships (8 to first-year students), 25 teaching assistantships (16 to first-year students) were awarded. Financial aid applicants required to submit FAFSA.
Applying 195 applicants, 46% accepted. *Deadline:* rolling. *Fee:* $20 ($30 for international students).
Contact *Dr. Sudhakar M. Reddy*
 Chair
 319-335-5196

Access provided to on-line information retrieval services. *Computer:* Campuswide network is available with full Internet access. Computer service fees are included with tuition and fees. *Special:* In science and engineering: Iowa Teachers Conservation Camp, Iowa Lakeside Laboratory, Institute for Environmental Education.

COMPUTER SCIENCE

College of Natural Sciences, Department of Computer Science
Programs Offers programs in computer science (MS), computer science education (MA). MA being phased out; applicants no longer accepted.
Students 5 full-time (2 women), 5 part-time (4 women); includes 3 international. Average age 33.
Degrees Awarded In 1996, 2 degrees awarded.
Degree Requirements Thesis or alternative required, foreign language not required.
Financial Aid *Application deadline: 3/1.*
Applying 8 applicants, 38% accepted. *Deadline:* 8/1 (priority date; rolling processing). *Fee:* $20 ($30 for international students).
Contact *Dr. John McCormick*
 Head
 319-273-2618

UNIVERSITY OF NORTHERN IOWA
Cedar Falls, IA 50614

OVERVIEW
University of Northern Iowa is a public coed comprehensive institution.

ENROLLMENT
12,957 graduate, professional, and undergraduate students; 458 full-time matriculated graduate/professional students (276 women), 595 part-time matriculated graduate/professional students (387 women).

GRADUATE FACULTY
411 full-time (107 women); includes 88 minority (27 African-Americans, 39 Asian-Americans, 18 Hispanics, 4 Native Americans).

EXPENSES
Tuition $3046 per year full-time, $340 per semester (minimum) part-time for state residents; $7512 per year full-time, $340 per semester (minimum) part-time for nonresidents. Fees $186 per year full-time.

HOUSING
Rooms and/or apartments available to single students at an average cost of $3452 (including board); available to married students (365 units) at an average cost of $2742 per year. Graduate housing contact: Department of Residence, 319-273-2333.

STUDENT SERVICES
Disabled student services, multicultural affairs office, low-cost health insurance, career counseling, free psychological counseling, exercise/wellness program, day-care facilities, campus employment opportunities, international student services, grant writing training.

FACILITIES
Library: Rod Library; total holdings of 785,000 volumes, 690,512 microforms, 3,033 current periodical subscriptions.

KANSAS

KANSAS STATE UNIVERSITY
Manhattan, KS 66506

OVERVIEW
Kansas State University is a public coed university.

ENROLLMENT
20,476 graduate, professional, and undergraduate students; 3,390 matriculated graduate/professional students (1,731 women).

GRADUATE FACULTY
1,109.

TUITION
$162 per credit hour for state residents; $321 per credit hour for nonresidents.

HOUSING
Rooms and/or apartments available to single students at an average cost of $3990 (including board); available to married students (475 units) at an average cost of $2833 per year. Graduate housing contact: Housing Office, 913-532-6453.

STUDENT SERVICES
Low-cost health insurance, career counseling, free psychological counseling, day-care facilities, campus safety program, campus employment opportunities, international student services.

FACILITIES
Library: Farrell Library plus 4 additional on-campus libraries; total holdings of 1,304,443 volumes, 3,813,071 microforms, 8,900 current periodical subscriptions. A total of 200 personal computers in all libraries. Access provided to on-line information retrieval services. *Computer:* Campuswide network is available with full Internet

access. Total number of PCs/terminals supplied for student use: 500. Computer service fees are included with tuition and fees. *Special:* In arts and humanities: McCain Auditorium, Nichols Theater. In science and engineering: Konza Prairie Research Natural Area, Wheat Genetics Resource Center, J. R. MacDonald Particle Accelerator Laboratory, Institute for Environmental Research, Food and Feed Grain Institute, Sensory Analysis Center. In social sciences: Institute for Social and Behavioral Research, Center for Aging, early childhood laboratory.

COMPUTER ENGINEERING

College of Engineering, Department of Electrical and Computer Engineering

Programs Offers programs in bioengineering (MS, PhD), communications (MS, PhD), computer engineering (MS, PhD), control systems (MS, PhD), electric energy systems (MS, PhD), instrumentation (MS, PhD), signal processing (MS, PhD).

Faculty 20 full-time (3 women).

Faculty Research Digital signal processing, communications systems. *Total annual research expenditures:* $643,944.

Students 27 (3 women); includes 7 minority (3 African-Americans, 4 Asian-Americans).

Degrees Awarded In 1996, 20 master's awarded (95% found work related to degree, 5% continued full-time study); 1 doctorate awarded (100% found work related to degree).

Entrance Requirements GRE General Test (minimum score 400 on verbal section, 600 on quantitative).

Degree Requirements For master's, thesis optional; for doctorate, dissertation.

Financial Aid In 1996–97, 21 research assistantships (2 to first-year students) averaging $950 per month, 4 teaching assistantships averaging $1,000 per month were awarded; career-related internships or fieldwork also available.

Applying 285 applicants, 12% accepted. *Deadline:* 3/1 (rolling processing; 9/1 for spring admission).

Contact *Dr. David Soldan*
Head
913-532-5600
E-mail: grad@eece.ksu.edu

COMPUTER SCIENCE

College of Engineering, Department of Computing and Information Sciences

Programs Offers programs in computer science (MS, PhD), software engineering (MSE).

Faculty 13 full-time (0 women), 1 (woman) part-time, 13.1 FTE.

Faculty Research Programming language semantics, distributed systems, real-time systems and algorithms, database management systems.

Students 67 (18 women); includes 5 minority (2 African-Americans, 1 Asian-American, 2 Hispanics), 50 international. Average age 28.

Degrees Awarded In 1996, 40 master's, 3 doctorates awarded.

Entrance Requirements GRE, TOEFL.

Degree Requirements For master's, computer language required, thesis optional, foreign language not required; for doctorate, computer language, dissertation required, foreign language not required.

Financial Aid In 1996–97, 1 fellowship averaging $1,111 per month, 6 research assistantships (1 to a first-year student) averaging $1,350 per month, 30 teaching assistantships (7 to first-year students) averaging $1,050 per month were awarded; institutionally sponsored

loans and career-related internships or fieldwork also available. *Financial aid application deadline:* 2/15.

Applying 274 applicants, 36% accepted. *Deadline:* 4/1 (priority date; rolling processing; 11/1 for spring admission). *Fee:* $0 ($25 for international students).

Contact *Rod Howell*
Graduate Coordinator
913-532-6350
Fax: 913-532-7353
E-mail: howell@cis.ksu.edu

See in-depth description on page **459.**

ELECTRICAL ENGINEERING

College of Engineering, Department of Electrical and Computer Engineering

Programs Offers programs in bioengineering (MS, PhD), communications (MS, PhD), computer engineering (MS, PhD), control systems (MS, PhD), electric energy systems (MS, PhD), instrumentation (MS, PhD), signal processing (MS, PhD).

Faculty 20 full-time (3 women).

Faculty Research Digital signal processing, communications systems. *Total annual research expenditures:* $643,944.

Students 27 (3 women); includes 7 minority (3 African-Americans, 4 Asian-Americans).

Degrees Awarded In 1996, 20 master's awarded (95% found work related to degree, 5% continued full-time study); 1 doctorate awarded (100% found work related to degree).

Entrance Requirements GRE General Test (minimum score 400 on verbal section, 600 on quantitative).

Degree Requirements For master's, thesis optional; for doctorate, dissertation.

Financial Aid In 1996–97, 21 research assistantships (2 to first-year students) averaging $950 per month, 4 teaching assistantships averaging $1,000 per month were awarded; career-related internships or fieldwork also available.

Applying 285 applicants, 12% accepted. *Deadline:* 3/1 (rolling processing; 9/1 for spring admission).

Contact *Dr. David Soldan*
Head
913-532-5600
E-mail: grad@eece.ksu.edu

INFORMATION SCIENCE

College of Engineering, Department of Computing and Information Sciences

Programs Offers programs in computer science (MS, PhD), software engineering (MSE).

Faculty 13 full-time (0 women), 1 (woman) part-time, 13.1 FTE.

Faculty Research Programming language semantics, distributed systems, real-time systems and algorithms, database management systems.

Students 67 (18 women); includes 5 minority (2 African-Americans, 1 Asian-American, 2 Hispanics), 50 international. Average age 28.

Degrees Awarded In 1996, 40 master's, 3 doctorates awarded.

Entrance Requirements GRE, TOEFL.

Degree Requirements For master's, computer language required, thesis optional, foreign language not required; for doctorate, computer language, dissertation required, foreign language not required.

Financial Aid In 1996–97, 1 fellowship averaging $1,111 per month, 6 research assistantships (1 to a first-year student) averaging $1,350 per month, 30 teaching assistantships (7 to first-year students) averaging $1,050 per month were awarded; institutionally sponsored loans and career-related internships or fieldwork also available. *Financial aid application deadline:* 2/15.

Applying 274 applicants, 36% accepted. *Deadline:* 4/1 (priority date; rolling processing; 11/1 for spring admission). *Fee:* $0 ($25 for international students).

Contact *Rod Howell*
Graduate Coordinator
913-532-6350
Fax: 913-532-7353
E-mail: howell@cis.ksu.edu

See in-depth description on page **459.**

SOFTWARE ENGINEERING

College of Engineering, Department of Computing and Information Sciences, Program in Software Engineering
Programs Awards MSE.
Students 22 (10 women).
Entrance Requirements GRE, TOEFL.
Degree Requirements Computer language required, thesis optional, foreign language not required.
Financial Aid *Application deadline:* 2/15.
Applying *Deadline:* 4/1 (priority date; rolling processing; 11/1 for spring admission). *Fee:* $0 ($25 for international students).
Contact *Dr. David Gustafson*
Graduate Chairperson
913-532-6350

See in-depth description on page **459.**

UNIVERSITY OF KANSAS
Lawrence, KS 66045

OVERVIEW
University of Kansas is a public coed university.

ENROLLMENT
27,407 graduate, professional, and undergraduate students; 3,861 full-time matriculated graduate/professional students (2,053 women), 4,003 part-time matriculated graduate/professional students (2,270 women).

GRADUATE FACULTY
1,888; includes 158 minority (34 African-Americans, 98 Asian-Americans, 20 Hispanics, 6 Native Americans).

EXPENSES
Tuition $2347 per year full-time, $98 per credit hour part-time for state residents; $7712 per year full-time, $321 per credit hour part-time for nonresidents. Fees $420 per year full-time, $30 per credit hour part-time.

HOUSING
Rooms and/or apartments available to single students (1,900 units) at an average cost of $3736 (including board); available to married students (300 units) at an average cost of $2600 per year. Housing application deadline: 2/15. Graduate housing contact: Kennith L. Stoner, 785-864-4560.

STUDENT SERVICES
Disabled student services, multicultural affairs office, low-cost health insurance, career counseling, free psychological counseling, day-care facilities, campus safety program, campus employment opportunities, international student services.

FACILITIES
Library: Watson Library plus 12 additional on-campus libraries; total holdings of 3,450,463 volumes, 2,983,680 microforms, 32,341 current periodical subscriptions. A total of 250 personal computers in all libraries. Access provided to on-line information retrieval services. *Computer:* Campuswide network is available with full Internet access. Total number of PCs/terminals supplied for student use: 670. Computer service fees are applied as a separate charge. *Special:* In arts and humanities: Spencer Museum of Art, Hall Center for the Humanities, Spencer Research Library, Lied Performing Arts Center. In science and engineering: Cancer Center, Higuchi Bioscience Center, Museum of Natural History, remote sensing laboratory, Center for Environmental Health, Mental Retardation Research Center. In social sciences: Center for Aging, Museum of Anthropology, Schiefelbusch Institute for Life Span Studies.

COMPUTER SCIENCE

School of Engineering, Department of Electrical Engineering and Computer Science, Program in Computer Science
Programs Awards MS, PhD.
Degrees Awarded Terminal master's awarded for partial completion of doctoral program.
Entrance Requirements GRE, TOEFL (minimum score 600), minimum GPA of 3.0.
Degree Requirements For master's, exam required, thesis optional, foreign language not required; for doctorate, 1 foreign language (computer language can substitute), dissertation, comprehensive and qualifying exams.
Financial Aid Fellowships, research assistantships, teaching assistantships, and career-related internships or fieldwork available.
Applying *Deadline:* 4/15 (priority date; rolling processing; 10/15 for spring admission). *Fee:* $30.
Contact *Victor Wallace*
Graduate Director
785-864-4487
Fax: 785-864-3226
E-mail: grad.admissions@eecs.ukans.edu

See in-depth description on page **647.**

ELECTRICAL ENGINEERING

School of Engineering, Department of Electrical Engineering and Computer Science, Program in Electrical Engineering
Programs Awards MS, DE, PhD.
Degrees Awarded Terminal master's awarded for partial completion of doctoral program.
Entrance Requirements GRE, TOEFL (minimum score 600), minimum GPA of 3.0.
Degree Requirements For master's, exam required, thesis optional, foreign language not required; for doctorate, 1 foreign language (computer language can substitute), dissertation, comprehensive and qualifying exams.
Financial Aid Fellowships, research assistantships, teaching assistantships, and career-related internships or fieldwork available.
Applying *Deadline:* 4/15 (priority date; rolling processing; 10/15 for spring admission). *Fee:* $30.
Contact *Victor Wallace*
Graduate Director
785-864-4487
Fax: 785-864-3226
E-mail: grad.admissions@eecs.ukans.edu

See in-depth description on page **647.**

WICHITA STATE UNIVERSITY
Wichita, KS 67260

OVERVIEW
Wichita State University is a public coed university.

ENROLLMENT
14,049 graduate, professional, and undergraduate students; 925 full-time matriculated graduate/professional students (527 women), 2,059 part-time matriculated graduate/professional students (1,173 women).

GRADUATE FACULTY
455 full-time (141 women), 198 part-time; includes 40 minority (11 African-Americans, 18 Asian-Americans, 11 Hispanics).

EXPENSES
Tuition $2698 per year full-time, $113 per credit hour part-time for state residents; $7964 per year full-time, $332 per credit hour part-time for nonresidents. Fees $15 (one-time charge).

HOUSING
Rooms and/or apartments available to single students (400 units) at an average cost of $5603 (including board); available to married students (300 units) at an average cost of $3400 per year. Housing application deadline: 7/1. Graduate housing contact: Randy Alexander, 316-978-3693.

STUDENT SERVICES
Low-cost health insurance, career counseling, free psychological counseling, day-care facilities, campus safety program, campus employment opportunities, international student services, teacher training.

FACILITIES
Library: Ablah Library plus 2 additional on-campus libraries; total holdings of 938,817 volumes, 907,837 microforms, 6,319 current periodical subscriptions. A total of 70 personal computers in all libraries. Access provided to on-line information retrieval services. *Computer:* Campuswide network is available with full Internet access. Total number of PCs/terminals supplied for student use: 100. Computer service fees are included with tuition and fees. *Special:* In science and engineering: Subsonic and supersonic wind tunnels, crash dynamics laboratory, biology core laboratories, Institute for Rehabilitation Research and Service. In social sciences: Center for Urban Studies, social science research laboratory, L. Holmes Museum of Anthropology.

ELECTRICAL ENGINEERING

College of Engineering, Department of Electrical Engineering
Programs Awards MS, PhD. Part-time and evening/weekend programs available.
Faculty 16 full-time (0 women).
Faculty Research Rehabilitation engineering, control systems, power systems, digital systems, communications/signal processing.
Students 82 full-time (8 women), 42 part-time (8 women); includes 9 minority (all Asian-Americans), 90 international. Average age 28.
Degrees Awarded In 1996, 38 master's, 4 doctorates awarded.
Entrance Requirements For master's, TOEFL (minimum score 550); for doctorate, GRE, TOEFL (minimum score 550).

Degree Requirements For master's, computer language, thesis or alternative, oral exam required, foreign language not required; for doctorate, 1 foreign language (computer language can substitute), dissertation, comprehensive exam.
Financial Aid Fellowships, research assistantships, teaching assistantships, assistantships, Federal Work-Study, institutionally sponsored loans available. *Financial aid application deadline:* 4/1; applicants required to submit FAFSA.
Applying 278 applicants, 29% accepted. *Deadline:* 7/1 (priority date; rolling processing; 1/1 for spring admission). *Fee:* $0 ($40 for international students).
Contact *Dr. E. Sawan*
Graduate Coordinator
316-978-3415
Fax: 316-978-3307
E-mail: ed@ee.twsu.edu

KENTUCKY

UNIVERSITY OF KENTUCKY
Lexington, KY 40506-0032

OVERVIEW
University of Kentucky is a public coed university.

ENROLLMENT
24,061 graduate, professional, and undergraduate students; 3,893 full-time matriculated graduate/professional students (1,905 women), 2,647 part-time matriculated graduate/professional students (1,535 women).

GRADUATE FACULTY
2,204 full-time (557 women), 301 part-time (76 women); includes 242 minority (98 African-Americans, 130 Asian-Americans, 12 Hispanics, 2 Native Americans).

TUITION
$2916 per year full-time, $150 per credit hour part-time for state residents; $8076 per year full-time, $436 per credit hour part-time for nonresidents.

HOUSING
Rooms and/or apartments available to single students at an average cost of $4560 per year; available to married students at an average cost of $4728 per year. Graduate housing information: 606-257-3721.

STUDENT SERVICES
Low-cost health insurance, career counseling, free psychological counseling, exercise/wellness program, day-care facilities, campus employment opportunities, international student services.

FACILITIES
Library: King Library plus 14 additional on-campus libraries; total holdings of 2,556,807 volumes, 5,239,342 microforms, 26,637 current periodical subscriptions. A total of 1,000 personal computers in all libraries. Access provided to on-line information retrieval services. *Computer:* Campuswide network is available with full Internet access. *Special:* In arts and humanities: Gaines Center for the Humanities, Black Box Theater, Center for the Arts, Reynolds Studio Art Facilities, recording computer, metal casting foundry, synthesizing facilities. In science

and engineering: Institute for Mining/Minerals Research, Water Resources Institute, Wenner Gren Bioengineering Laboratory, Van de Graaff accelerator, magnetic resonance imaging facility, neutron activation analysis system, pilot scale liquefaction units, Sanders-Brown Center on Aging, Lucille Parker Markey Cancer Center, Maxwell H. Gluck Equine Research Center. In social sciences: Appalachian Center, Center for Business and Economic Research, Kentucky Transportation Research Center, Multidisciplinary Center on Gerontology, Survey Research Center, anthropology research facility and museum.

COMPUTER SCIENCE

Graduate School Programs from the College of Engineering, Program in Computer Science

Programs Awards MS, PhD.
Faculty 19 full-time (1 woman), 1 part-time (0 women).
Faculty Research Artificial intelligence and databases, communication networks and operating systems, graphics and vision, numerical analysis, theory. *Total annual research expenditures:* $174,500.
Students 44 full-time (7 women), 28 part-time (5 women); includes 5 minority (all Asian-Americans), 32 international.
Degrees Awarded In 1996, 21 master's, 3 doctorates awarded.
Entrance Requirements For master's, GRE General Test, minimum undergraduate GPA of 2.5; for doctorate, GRE General Test, minimum graduate GPA of 3.0.
Degree Requirements For master's, comprehensive exam required, thesis optional, foreign language not required; for doctorate, 1 foreign language, dissertation, comprehensive exam.
Financial Aid In 1996–97, 5 fellowships, 12 research assistantships, 25 teaching assistantships were awarded; Federal Work-Study, institutionally sponsored loans also available. Aid available to part-time students.
Applying 157 applicants, 44% accepted. *Deadline:* 7/19 (rolling processing). *Fee:* $30 ($35 for international students).
Contact Dr. Constance L. Wood
Associate Dean
606-257-4613
Fax: 606-323-1928

See in-depth description on page 649.

ELECTRICAL ENGINEERING

Graduate School Programs from the College of Engineering, Program in Electrical Engineering

Programs Awards MSEE, PhD.
Faculty 24 full-time (3 women).
Faculty Research Signal processing, systems, and control; electromagnetic field theory; power electronics and machines; computer engineering and very large scale integration; materials and devices. *Total annual research expenditures:* $1.516 million.
Students 52 full-time (7 women), 41 part-time (11 women); includes 2 minority (both Asian-Americans), 48 international.
Degrees Awarded In 1996, 20 master's, 1 doctorate awarded.
Entrance Requirements For master's, GRE General Test (minimum combined score of 1100 on three sections), minimum undergraduate GPA of 3.0; for doctorate, GRE General Test (minimum combined score of 1200 on three sections), minimum graduate GPA of 3.0.
Degree Requirements For master's, comprehensive exam required, thesis optional, foreign language not required; for doctorate, 1 foreign language, dissertation, comprehensive exam.
Financial Aid In 1996–97, 5 fellowships, 28 research assistantships, 15 teaching assistantships were awarded; Federal Work-

Study, institutionally sponsored loans also available. Aid available to part-time students. *Financial aid application deadline:* 3/1.
Applying 166 applicants, 60% accepted. *Deadline:* 7/19 (rolling processing). *Fee:* $30 ($35 for international students).
Contact Dr. Constance L. Wood
Associate Dean
606-257-4613
Fax: 606-323-1928

UNIVERSITY OF LOUISVILLE
Louisville, KY 40292-0001

OVERVIEW
University of Louisville is a public coed university.

ENROLLMENT
21,020 graduate, professional, and undergraduate students; 3,102 full-time matriculated graduate/professional students (1,593 women), 1,975 part-time matriculated graduate/professional students (1,143 women).

GRADUATE FACULTY
1,077 full-time (278 women), 463 part-time (214 women), 1,216 FTE; includes 265 minority (82 African-Americans, 130 Asian-Americans, 39 Hispanics, 14 Native Americans).

TUITION
$2870 per year for state residents; $8150 per year for nonresidents.

HOUSING
Rooms and/or apartments available to single students (1,809 units) at an average cost of $3300 per year ($4480 including board); available to married students (124 units) at an average cost of $4500 per year ($5680 including board). Graduate housing contact: Frank Mianzo, 502-852-6636.

STUDENT SERVICES
Disabled student services, multicultural affairs office, low-cost health insurance, career counseling, free psychological counseling, exercise/wellness program, day-care facilities, campus safety program, campus employment opportunities, international student services, grant writing training.

FACILITIES
Library: Ekstrom Library plus 4 additional on-campus libraries; total holdings of 1,359,140 volumes, 13,139 current periodical subscriptions. Access provided to on-line information retrieval services. *Computer:* Campuswide network is available with full Internet access. Total number of PCs/terminals supplied for student use: 1,000. Computer service fees are included with tuition and fees. *Special:* In arts and humanities: Photographic archives, Center for the Humanities, Kentucky Institute for the Environment and Sustainable Development. In science and engineering: Applied Microcirculation Center, Cancer Center, Vogt Automated Engineering Laboratory, rapid prototyping facilities. In social sciences:

McConnell Center for Leadership Studies, Urban Studies Institute.

COMPUTER ENGINEERING

Speed Scientific School, Department of Engineering Mathematics and Computer Science
Programs   Offerings include computer science and engineering (PhD).
Department Faculty   18 full-time (2 women), 1 part-time (0 women).
Entrance Requirements   GRE General Test.
Degree Requirements   Dissertation required, foreign language not required.
Applying   *Deadline:* rolling. *Fee:* $25.
Contact   *Dr. Khaled A. Kamel*
　　　　　Chair
　　　　　502-852-6304

COMPUTER SCIENCE

Speed Scientific School, Department of Engineering Mathematics and Computer Science
Programs   Offers programs in computer science (M Eng, MS), computer science and engineering (PhD). One or more programs accredited by ABET.
Faculty   18 full-time (2 women), 1 part-time (0 women).
Students   4 full-time (0 women), 35 part-time (6 women); includes 4 minority (3 Asian-Americans, 1 Hispanic).
Degrees Awarded   In 1996, 14 master's, 4 doctorates awarded.
Entrance Requirements   GRE General Test.
Degree Requirements   Thesis/dissertation required, foreign language not required.
Applying   *Deadline:* rolling. *Fee:* $25.
Contact   *Dr. Khaled A. Kamel*
　　　　　Chair
　　　　　502-852-6304

ELECTRICAL ENGINEERING

Speed Scientific School, Department of Electrical Engineering
Programs   Awards M Eng, MS. One or more programs accredited by ABET.
Faculty   15 full-time (0 women), 1 part-time (0 women).
Students   30 full-time (8 women), 99 part-time (12 women); includes 24 minority (5 African-Americans, 14 Asian-Americans, 4 Hispanics, 1 Native American), 17 international.
Degrees Awarded   In 1996, 5 degrees awarded.
Entrance Requirements   GRE General Test.
Degree Requirements   Thesis required, foreign language not required.
Applying   *Deadline:* rolling. *Fee:* $25.
Contact   *Darrel L. Chenoweth*
　　　　　Chair
　　　　　502-852-6289

WESTERN KENTUCKY UNIVERSITY
Bowling Green, KY 42101-3576

OVERVIEW
Western Kentucky University is a public coed comprehensive institution.

ENROLLMENT
14,613 graduate, professional, and undergraduate students; 443 full-time matriculated graduate/professional students (291 women), 1,239 part-time matriculated graduate/professional students (923 women).

GRADUATE FACULTY
362 full-time (93 women), 15 part-time (10 women), 368 FTE; includes 20 minority (10 African-Americans, 8 Asian-Americans, 1 Hispanic, 1 Native American).

TUITION
$2268 per year full-time, $126 per credit hour part-time for state residents; $6228 per year full-time, $346 per credit hour part-time for nonresidents.

HOUSING
Rooms and/or apartments available to single students at an average cost of $1600 per year; available to married students (14 units) at an average cost of $3600 per year. Housing application deadline: 4/1. Graduate housing contact: Housing Office, 502-745-4359.

STUDENT SERVICES
Low-cost health insurance, career counseling, free psychological counseling, day-care facilities, campus employment opportunities, international student services.

FACILITIES
Library: Helm-Cravens Library plus 2 additional on-campus libraries; total holdings of 555,016 volumes, 2,444,513 microforms, 4,603 current periodical subscriptions. A total of 50 personal computers in all libraries. Access provided to on-line information retrieval services. *Computer:* Campuswide network is available with full Internet access. Total number of PCs/terminals supplied for student use: 750. Computer service fees are included with tuition and fees. *Special:* In arts and humanities: Kentucky Museum/Library. In science and engineering: Center for Cave and Karst Studies, materials science laboratory. In social sciences: Social research laboratory.

COMPUTER SCIENCE

Ogden College of Science, Technology, and Health, Department of Computer Science
Programs   Awards MS. Part-time programs available.
Faculty   8 full-time (3 women).
Faculty Research   Artificial intelligence.
Students   14 full-time (6 women), 14 part-time (5 women); includes 4 minority (3 Asian-Americans, 1 Native American), 14 international. Average age 29.
Degrees Awarded   In 1996, 9 degrees awarded.
Entrance Requirements   GRE General Test (minimum combined score of 1150 on three sections; average 1685), minimum GPA of 2.5.
Financial Aid   In 1996–97, 9 service awards (3 to first-year students) averaging $338 per month and totaling $21,300 were awarded; research assistantships, Federal Work-Study, institutionally sponsored loans also available. Aid available to part-time students. *Financial aid application deadline:* 4/1; applicants required to submit FAFSA.
Applying   24 applicants, 96% accepted. *Deadline:* 8/1 (priority date; rolling processing; 12/1 for spring admission). *Fee:* $20.
Contact   *Dr. Arthur Shindhelm*
　　　　　Head
　　　　　502-745-4642

LOUISIANA

LOUISIANA STATE UNIVERSITY AND AGRICULTURAL AND MECHANICAL COLLEGE
Baton Rouge, LA 70803-3103

OVERVIEW
Louisiana State University and Agricultural and Mechanical College is a public coed university.

ENROLLMENT
26,851 graduate, professional, and undergraduate students; 3,380 full-time matriculated graduate/professional students (1,556 women), 1,536 part-time matriculated graduate/professional students (806 women).

GRADUATE FACULTY
1,268 full-time (222 women), 38 part-time (12 women); includes 126 minority (19 African-Americans, 88 Asian-Americans, 16 Hispanics, 3 Native Americans).

TUITION
$2672 per year full-time, $285 per semester (minimum) part-time for state residents; $5972 per year full-time, $435 per semester (minimum) part-time for nonresidents.

HOUSING
Rooms and/or apartments available to single students (4,495 units) at an average cost of $1920 per year ($3570 including board); available to married students (579 units) at an average cost of $2230 per year ($3880 including board). Graduate housing contact: Department of Residential Housing, 504-388-8663.

STUDENT SERVICES
Low-cost health insurance, career counseling, free psychological counseling, campus safety program, campus employment opportunities, international student services.

FACILITIES
Library: Troy H. Middleton Library plus 4 additional on-campus libraries; total holdings of 2,950,079 volumes, 4,995,722 microforms, 18,570 current periodical subscriptions. Access provided to on-line information retrieval services. *Computer:* Campuswide network is available with full Internet access. Computer services are offered at no charge. *Special:* In arts and humanities: Center for French and Francophone Studies, Eric Voegelin Institute, CADGIS research laboratory. In science and engineering: Museum of Natural Science, Museum of Geoscience, mycological herbarium, Center for Advanced Microstructures and Devices, Pennington Biomedical Institute. In social sciences: United States Civil War Center, Public Administration Institute.

COMPUTER ENGINEERING

College of Engineering, Department of Electrical and Computer Engineering
Programs Awards MSEE, PhD.
Faculty 24 full-time (2 women).
Faculty Research Electronics, power engineering, systems and signal processing, communications.

Students 91 full-time (13 women), 19 part-time (1 woman); includes 9 minority (3 African-Americans, 5 Asian-Americans, 1 Hispanic), 89 international. Average age 26.
Degrees Awarded In 1996, 21 master's, 6 doctorates awarded. Terminal master's awarded for partial completion of doctoral program.
Entrance Requirements For master's, GRE General Test, minimum GPA of 3.0; for doctorate, GRE General Test, minimum GPA of 3.5.
Degree Requirements For master's, thesis optional, foreign language not required; for doctorate, dissertation required, foreign language not required.
Financial Aid In 1996–97, 58 students received aid, including 6 fellowships (2 to first-year students), 19 research assistantships (4 to first-year students), 16 teaching assistantships (2 to first-year students), 15 service assistantships (8 to first-year students); institutionally sponsored loans also available. *Financial aid application deadline:* 2/28.
Applying 356 applicants, 40% accepted. *Deadline:* 1/25 (priority date; rolling processing). *Fee:* $25.
Contact Dr. Jorge L. Aravena
          Graduate Adviser
          504-388-5478

See in-depth description on page 465.

COMPUTER SCIENCE

College of Basic Sciences, Department of Computer Science, Program in Computer Science
Programs Awards MSSS, PhD.
Entrance Requirements For master's, GRE General Test (minimum combined score of 1000), minimum GPA of 3.0; for doctorate, GRE General Test (minimum combined score of 1200), minimum GPA of 3.0.
Degree Requirements Computer language, thesis/dissertation required, foreign language not required.
Applying *Deadline:* rolling. *Fee:* $25.
Contact Dr. Doris Carver
          Graduate Program Coordinator
          504-388-1495
          Fax: 504-388-1465

ELECTRICAL ENGINEERING

College of Engineering, Department of Electrical and Computer Engineering
Programs Awards MSEE, PhD.
Faculty 24 full-time (2 women).
Faculty Research Electronics, power engineering, systems and signal processing, communications.
Students 91 full-time (13 women), 19 part-time (1 woman); includes 9 minority (3 African-Americans, 5 Asian-Americans, 1 Hispanic), 89 international. Average age 26.
Degrees Awarded In 1996, 21 master's, 6 doctorates awarded. Terminal master's awarded for partial completion of doctoral program.
Entrance Requirements For master's, GRE General Test, minimum GPA of 3.0; for doctorate, GRE General Test, minimum GPA of 3.5.
Degree Requirements For master's, thesis optional, foreign language not required; for doctorate, dissertation required, foreign language not required.
Financial Aid In 1996–97, 58 students received aid, including 6 fellowships (2 to first-year students), 19 research assistantships (4 to first-year students), 16 teaching assistantships (2 to first-year students), 15 service assistantships (8 to first-year students); institutionally sponsored loans also available. *Financial aid application deadline:* 2/28.

Applying 356 applicants, 40% accepted. *Deadline:* 1/25 (priority date; rolling processing). *Fee:* $25.
Contact Dr. Jorge L. Aravena
Graduate Adviser
504-388-5478

See in-depth description on page 465.

SYSTEMS SCIENCE

College of Basic Sciences, Department of Computer Science, Program in Systems Science
Programs Awards MSSS.
Faculty 1 full-time (0 women).
Faculty Research Robotics, artificial intelligence, algorithms, database software engineering, high-performance computing. *Total annual research expenditures:* $391,000.
Students 45 full-time (7 women), 12 part-time (3 women); includes 6 minority (all Asian-Americans), 51 international. Average age 23.
Degrees Awarded In 1996, 21 degrees awarded.
Entrance Requirements GRE General Test (minimum combined score of 1200), minimum GPA of 3.0.
Degree Requirements Computer language, thesis required, foreign language not required.
Financial Aid 21 students received aid; fellowships, research assistantships, teaching assistantships available. *Financial aid application deadline:* 2/1.
Applying 67 applicants, 57% accepted. *Deadline:* 5/15 (priority date; rolling processing; 10/15 for spring admission). *Fee:* $25.
Contact Dr. Doris Carver
Graduate Program Coordinator
504-388-1495
Fax: 504-388-1465

LOUISIANA TECH UNIVERSITY
Ruston, LA 71272

OVERVIEW
Louisiana Tech University is a public coed university.

ENROLLMENT
9,313 graduate, professional, and undergraduate students; 717 full-time matriculated graduate/professional students (349 women), 307 part-time matriculated graduate/professional students (195 women).

GRADUATE FACULTY
253 full-time (66 women); includes 15 minority (1 African-American, 13 Asian-Americans, 1 Hispanic).

TUITION
$2367 per year full-time, $222 per quarter (minimum) part-time for state residents; $4362 per year full-time, $222 per quarter (minimum) part-time for nonresidents.

HOUSING
Rooms and/or apartments available to single students at an average cost of $2385 (including board); available to married students (42 units) at an average cost of $1935 per year. Housing application deadline: 7/15. Graduate housing contact: Dickie Crawford, 318-257-4917.

STUDENT SERVICES
Low-cost health insurance, career counseling, campus employment opportunities, international student services.

FACILITIES
Library: Prescott Memorial Library; total holdings of 365,636 volumes, 485,347 microforms, 2,611 current periodical subscriptions. A total of 39 personal computers in all libraries. Access provided to on-line information retrieval services. *Special:* In science and engineering: Biomedical Engineering Center, Water Resources Center, Center for Robotics and Automated Manufacturing, Personal Licensed Vehicles Center for Development. In social sciences: Small Business Institute, Rehabilitation Engineering Research Development and Training Center.

COMPUTER SCIENCE

College of Engineering and Science, Department of Computer Science
Programs Awards MS. Part-time programs available.
Faculty 6 full-time (0 women).
Faculty Research Computer systems organization, artificial intelligence, expert systems, graphics, program language. *Total annual research expenditures:* $308,259.
Students 19 full-time (2 women), 4 part-time (all women); includes 2 minority (1 African-American, 1 Asian-American), 14 international. Average age 27.
Degrees Awarded In 1996, 2 degrees awarded.
Entrance Requirements GRE General Test (minimum combined score of 1070), TOEFL (minimum score 550), minimum GPA of 3.0 in last 60 hours.
Degree Requirements Computer language, thesis or alternative required, foreign language not required.
Financial Aid In 1996–97, 14 students received aid, including 6 research assistantships (1 to a first-year student) totaling $52,400, 8 assistantships (1 to a first-year student) totaling $42,000; Federal Work-Study also available. *Financial aid application deadline:* 4/1.
Applying *Deadline:* 8/1 (rolling processing; 2/1 for spring admission). *Fee:* $20 ($30 for international students).
Contact Dr. Barry L. Kurtz
Academic Director
318-257-2436
Fax: 318-257-2562
E-mail: kurtz@engr.latech.edu

ELECTRICAL ENGINEERING

College of Engineering and Science, Department of Electrical Engineering
Programs Awards MS, D Eng. Part-time programs available.
Faculty 11 full-time (0 women).
Faculty Research Communications, computers and microprocessors, electrical and power systems, pattern recognition, robotics. *Total annual research expenditures:* $234,532.
Students 27 full-time (4 women), 1 (woman) part-time; includes 24 international. Average age 27.
Degrees Awarded In 1996, 13 master's awarded. Terminal master's awarded for partial completion of doctoral program.
Entrance Requirements For master's, GRE General Test (minimum combined score of 1070), TOEFL (minimum score 550), minimum GPA of 3.0 in last 60 hours; for doctorate, TOEFL (minimum score 550), minimum graduate GPA of 3.25 (with MS) or GRE General Test (minimum combined score of 1270 required without MS).
Degree Requirements Thesis/dissertation required, foreign language not required.
Financial Aid In 1996–97, 17 students received aid, including 6 research assistantships totaling $41,200, 4 teaching assistantships averaging $1,000 per month and totaling $27,000, 7 assistantships (1 to a first-year student) totaling $53,000; fellowships, Federal Work-Study also available. *Financial aid application deadline:* 4/1.

Applying   *Deadline:* 8/1 (rolling processing; 2/1 for spring admission). *Fee:* $20 ($30 for international students).
Contact   *Dr. Richard Gibbs Jr.*
Academic Director
318-257-4358
Fax: 318-257-2562
E-mail: gibbs@latech.edu

LOYOLA UNIVERSITY NEW ORLEANS
New Orleans, LA 70118-6195

OVERVIEW
Loyola University New Orleans is an independent-religious coed comprehensive institution.

ENROLLMENT
4,993 graduate, professional, and undergraduate students; 492 full-time matriculated graduate/professional students (250 women), 1,126 part-time matriculated graduate/professional students (638 women).

GRADUATE FACULTY
270 full-time (96 women), 165 part-time (67 women); includes 50 minority (23 African-Americans, 12 Asian-Americans, 15 Hispanics).

EXPENSES
Tuition $494 per credit hour. Fees $326 per year full-time, $169 per year part-time.

HOUSING
Rooms and/or apartments available to single students (1,070 units) at an average cost of $3260 per year ($5830 including board); on-campus housing not available to married students. Housing application deadline: 8/1. Graduate housing contact: Mr. Robert Reed, 504-865-3735.

STUDENT SERVICES
Disabled student services, low-cost health insurance, career counseling, free psychological counseling, day-care facilities, campus safety program, international student services.

FACILITIES
Library: University Library plus 3 additional on-campus libraries; total holdings of 460,784 volumes, 777,934 microforms, 4,472 current periodical subscriptions. Access provided to on-line information retrieval services. *Special:* In social sciences: Institute of Human Relations, Institute of Politics.

COMPUTER SCIENCE

College of Arts and Sciences, Department of Mathematics and Computer Science
Programs   Awards MS. Part-time and evening/weekend programs available.
Faculty   12 full-time (3 women), 7 part-time (4 women).
Students   11 part-time (7 women); includes 2 minority (both African-Americans). Average age 45.
Degrees Awarded   In 1996, 38 degrees awarded.
Entrance Requirements   Documentation of previous work, courses currently being taught, minimum GPA of 3.0 in last 30 hours.

Financial Aid   Partial tuition waivers, institutionally sponsored loans, and career-related internships or fieldwork available. Aid available to part-time students. *Financial aid application deadline:* 5/1; applicants required to submit FAFSA.
Applying   2 applicants, 100% accepted. *Deadline:* 8/1 (rolling processing; 12/1 for spring admission). *Fee:* $20.
Contact   *Dr. Antonio Lopez Jr.*
Adviser
504-865-2657
Fax: 504-865-2051

McNEESE STATE UNIVERSITY
Lake Charles, LA 70609-2495

OVERVIEW
McNeese State University is a public coed comprehensive institution.

TUITION
$2002 per year for state residents; $6442 per year for nonresidents.

HOUSING
Rooms and/or apartments available to single and married students. Graduate housing contact: Director of Student Housing, 318-475-5706.

FACILITIES
Library: Lether E. Frazar Memorial Library.

COMPUTER SCIENCE

College of Science, Department of Mathematics, Computer Science, and Statistics
Programs   Offers programs in computer science (MS), mathematics (MS), statistics (MS). Evening/weekend programs available.
Entrance Requirements   GRE General Test.
Degree Requirements   Computer language, thesis or alternative, written exam required, foreign language not required.
Applying   *Deadline:* 7/15 (priority date; rolling processing). *Fee:* $10 ($25 for international students).

ELECTRICAL ENGINEERING

College of Engineering and Technology
Programs   Offerings include electrical engineering (M Eng).
Degree Requirements   Computer language, thesis or alternative required, foreign language not required.
Applying   *Deadline:* 7/15 (priority date; rolling processing). *Fee:* $10 ($25 for international students).

SOUTHERN UNIVERSITY AND AGRICULTURAL AND MECHANICAL COLLEGE
Baton Rouge, LA 70813

OVERVIEW
Southern University and Agricultural and Mechanical College is a public coed comprehensive institution.

TUITION

$2086 per year full-time, $252 per semester (minimum) part-time for state residents; $4992 per year full-time, $1705 per semester (minimum) part-time for nonresidents.

HOUSING

Rooms and/or apartments available to single students; on-campus housing not available to married students. Graduate housing contact: Yvonne Hughes, 504-771-3590.

FACILITIES

Library: J. B. Cade Library. *Special:* In science and engineering: Health Research Center, Environmental and Energy Institute, Center for Sickle Cell Disease Research. In social sciences: Center for Social Research.

COMPUTER SCIENCE

College of Sciences, Department of Computer Science

Programs Offers programs in information systems (MS), micro/minicomputer architecture (MS), operating systems (MS).

Faculty Research Price and policy software development, expert systems, software for advanced AC plasma display technology, computer-assisted instruction.

Entrance Requirements GMAT or GRE General Test, TOEFL, minimum GPA of 2.7, bachelor's degree in computer science or related field.

Degree Requirements Computer language, project or thesis.

Applying *Deadline:* 6/1 (priority date; rolling processing; 11/1 for spring admission). *Fee:* $5.

TULANE UNIVERSITY
New Orleans, LA 70118-5669

OVERVIEW

Tulane University is an independent coed university.

ENROLLMENT

11,246 graduate, professional, and undergraduate students; 4,385 full-time matriculated graduate/professional students (2,042 women), 459 part-time matriculated graduate/professional students (204 women).

GRADUATE FACULTY

1,063 full-time, 397 part-time; includes 241 minority.

EXPENSES

Tuition $20,930 per year full-time, $1163 per hour part-time. Fees $1136 per year.

HOUSING

Rooms and/or apartments available to single students (100 units) at an average cost of $4500 per year; available to married students (175 units) at an average cost of $4815 per year. Housing application deadline: 3/24. Graduate housing contact: Director of Housing, 504-865-5724.

STUDENT SERVICES

Low-cost health insurance, career counseling, free psychological counseling, day-care facilities, campus safety program, international student services.

FACILITIES

Library: Howard Tilton Library plus 6 additional on-campus libraries; total holdings of 20,029,777 volumes, 2,405,379 microforms, 14,846 current periodical subscriptions. Access provided to on-line information retrieval services. *Computer:* Campuswide network is available with full Internet access. Total number of PCs/terminals supplied for student use: 400. Computer services are offered at no charge. *Special:* In arts and humanities: Southeastern Architectural Archives, William Ransom Hogan Jazz Archives, Amistad Research Center, Newcomb College Center for Research on Women. In science and engineering: Museum of Natural History, Mease Natural History Library, Institute for Health Services Research, Hayward Genetics Center, Tulane Regional Primate Research Center, Endocrine Poly-Peptide and Cancer Institute, Tulane/Xavier Center for Bioenvironmental Research, Center for Cardiovascular Health, Tulane Cancer Center, General Clinical Research Center, Center for International Health and Development, Tulane/LSU Adult and Pediatric AIDS Clinical Trial Units, U.S./China Institute. In social sciences: Elizabeth Wisner Social Welfare Research Center for Families and Children; Institute for Research and Training on HIV Counseling; Middle American Research Institute; Murphy Institute of Political Economy; Tulane Center on Aging Research, Education and Services; Roger Thayer Center for Latin American Studies.

COMPUTER SCIENCE

School of Engineering, Department of Computer Science

Programs Awards MS, MSCS, PhD, Sc D. MS and PhD offered through the Graduate School. Part-time programs available.

Faculty Research Software engineering, robotics, artificial intelligence, fuzzy sets, programming languages, neural nets.

Students 38 full-time (7 women), 3 part-time (1 woman); includes 5 minority (2 African-Americans, 2 Asian-Americans, 1 Hispanic), 18 international.

Degrees Awarded In 1996, 5 master's, 2 doctorates awarded. Terminal master's awarded for partial completion of doctoral program.

Entrance Requirements GRE General Test, TOEFL, minimum B average in undergraduate course work.

Degree Requirements For master's, thesis or alternative required, foreign language not required; for doctorate, computer language, dissertation required, foreign language not required.

Financial Aid In 1996–97, 3 fellowships (all to first-year students) totaling $65,000 were awarded; research assistantships, teaching assistantships, full and partial tuition waivers, institutionally sponsored loans, and career-related internships or fieldwork also available. *Financial aid application deadline:* 2/1.

Applying 74 applicants, 45% accepted. *Deadline:* 7/1 (priority date; rolling processing; 11/1 for spring admission). *Fee:* $35.

Contact Dr. E. Michaelides
Associate Dean
504-865-5764

ELECTRICAL ENGINEERING

School of Engineering, Department of Electrical Engineering

Programs Awards MS, MSE, PhD, Sc D. MS and PhD offered through the Graduate School. Part-time programs available.

Faculty Research Control systems, digital signal processing, image processing, power systems.

Students 32 full-time (6 women), includes 3 minority (2 African-Americans, 1 Hispanic), 16 international.

Degrees Awarded In 1996, 8 master's, 1 doctorate awarded. Terminal master's awarded for partial completion of doctoral program.

Entrance Requirements For master's, GRE General Test (combined average 1361), TOEFL, minimum B average in undergraduate course work; for doctorate, GRE General Test, TOEFL, minimum B average in undergraduate course work.

Degree Requirements Thesis/dissertation.

Financial Aid Research assistantships, teaching assistantships, full and partial tuition waivers, Federal Work-Study, institutionally sponsored loans available. *Financial aid application deadline: 2/1.*

Applying 113 applicants, 19% accepted. *Deadline: 7/1. Fee:* $35.

Contact *Dr. E. Michaelides*
Associate Dean
504-865-5764

UNIVERSITY OF NEW ORLEANS
New Orleans, LA 70148

OVERVIEW
University of New Orleans is a public coed university.

ENROLLMENT
15,665 graduate, professional, and undergraduate students; 1,290 full-time matriculated graduate/professional students (649 women), 2,686 part-time matriculated graduate/professional students (1,684 women).

GRADUATE FACULTY
440.

EXPENSES
Tuition $2362 per year full-time, $373 per semester (minimum) part-time for state residents; $5154 per year full-time, $903 per semester (minimum) part-time for nonresidents. Fees $120 per year full-time, $15 per semester (minimum) part-time.

HOUSING
Rooms and/or apartments available to single students (610 units) at an average cost of $1030 per year; available to married students (120 units) at an average cost of $4200 per year. Graduate housing contact: Margaret Vinti, 504-280-6585.

STUDENT SERVICES
Low-cost health insurance, career counseling, free psychological counseling, day-care facilities, campus safety program, campus employment opportunities, international student services.

FACILITIES
Library: Earl K. Long Library. A total of 12 personal computers in all libraries. Access provided to on-line information retrieval services. *Special:* In arts and humanities: Electronic imaging laboratory. In science and engineering: Center for Energy Resources Management, Gulf Coast Region Maritime Technology Center, Urban Waste Management and Research Center, geophysical research laboratory, Center for the Industrial Application of Electric Power and Instrumentation, Energy and Environmental Materials Research Institute, New Orleans Advanced Computation Laboratory. In social sciences: Small Business Development Center, Division of Business and Economic Research, Environmental

Social Science Research Institute, Division of Urban Research and Policy Studies.

COMPUTER SCIENCE

College of Sciences, Department of Computer Science

Programs Awards MS.

Students 26 full-time (6 women), 33 part-time (7 women); includes 13 minority (1 African-American, 9 Asian-Americans, 3 Hispanics), 26 international. Average age 32.

Degrees Awarded In 1996, 14 degrees awarded.

Entrance Requirements GRE General Test.

Applying *Deadline: 7/1 (priority date; rolling processing). Fee:* $20.

Contact *Dr. Shengru Tu*
Graduate Coordinator
504-280-7108
Fax: 504-280-7228
E-mail: stcs@uno.edu

ELECTRICAL ENGINEERING

College of Engineering, Concentration in Electrical Engineering

Programs Awards MS Engr Sci.

Faculty 10 full-time (0 women), 2 part-time (0 women).

Faculty Research Optics, ellipsometry, power systems, power-harmonics, optimal controls.

Students 34 full-time (4 women), 14 part-time (2 women); includes 6 minority (3 Asian-Americans, 2 Hispanics, 1 Native American), 29 international. Average age 28.

Entrance Requirements GRE General Test (minimum combined score of 1200), minimum GPA of 3.0.

Degree Requirements Thesis optional, foreign language not required.

Financial Aid Research assistantships, teaching assistantships available.

Applying *Deadline: 7/1 (priority date; rolling processing). Fee:* $20.

Contact *Dr. Russell Trahan*
Graduate Coordinator
504-280-6176
Fax: 504-286-3950
E-mail: retee@uno.edu

UNIVERSITY OF SOUTHWESTERN LOUISIANA
Lafayette, LA 70503

OVERVIEW
University of Southwestern Louisiana is a public coed university.

ENROLLMENT
16,742 graduate, professional, and undergraduate students; 642 full-time matriculated graduate/professional students (273 women), 580 part-time matriculated graduate/professional students (357 women).

GRADUATE FACULTY
336 full-time (97 women).

TUITION
$1884 per year full-time, $281 per semester (minimum) part-time for state residents; $6540 per year (minimum) full-time, $281 per semester (minimum) part-time for nonresidents.

HOUSING
Rooms and/or apartments available to single students (165 units) at an average cost of $2196 (including board); available to married students (165 units) at an average cost of $2940 per year. Graduate housing contact: John Wales, 318-482-6471.

STUDENT SERVICES
Disabled student services, low-cost health insurance, career counseling, free psychological counseling, day-care facilities, campus safety program, campus employment opportunities, international student services.

FACILITIES
Library: Dupre Library; total holdings of 687,142 volumes, 1,714,506 microforms, 6,188 current periodical subscriptions. A total of 30 personal computers in all libraries. Access provided to on-line information retrieval services. *Computer:* Campuswide network is available with full Internet access. Computer service fees are included with tuition and fees. *Special:* In arts and humanities: Center for Louisiana Studies, University Art Museum. In science and engineering: Louisiana Productivity Center, Acadiana Research Laboratory, New Iberia Research Center, Center for Advanced Computer Studies. In social sciences: Educational Technology Review Center, Center for Socioeconomic Education.

COMPUTER ENGINEERING

College of Engineering, Center for Advanced Computer Studies
Programs   Offers programs in computer engineering (MS, PhD), computer science (MS, PhD). Part-time programs available.
Faculty   32 full-time (5 women).
Students   160 full-time (29 women), 34 part-time (6 women); includes 10 minority (3 African-Americans, 5 Asian-Americans, 2 Hispanics), 139 international.
Degrees Awarded   In 1996, 46 master's, 11 doctorates awarded. Terminal master's awarded for partial completion of doctoral program.
Entrance Requirements   For master's, GRE General Test, TOEFL, minimum GPA of 2.75; for doctorate, GRE General Test, TOEFL, minimum GPA of 3.0.
Degree Requirements   For master's, computer language, thesis or alternative required, foreign language not required; for doctorate, computer language, dissertation, final oral exam required, foreign language not required.
Financial Aid   In 1996–97, 105 students received aid, including 12 fellowships (3 to first-year students) averaging $1,154 per month, 47 research assistantships (15 to first-year students) averaging $360 per month and totaling $169,635, 45 teaching assistantships (11 to first-year students) averaging $360 per month and totaling $162,415; full tuition waivers, Federal Work-Study also available. *Financial aid application deadline:* 3/1.
Applying   518 applicants, 57% accepted. *Deadline:* 8/15. *Fee:* $5 ($15 for international students).
Contact   *Dr. Harold Szu*
Director
318-482-6284

See in-depth description on page **719.**

COMPUTER SCIENCE

College of Engineering, Center for Advanced Computer Studies
Programs   Offers programs in computer engineering (MS, PhD), computer science (MS, PhD). Part-time programs available.
Faculty   32 full-time (5 women).
Students   160 full-time (29 women), 34 part-time (6 women); includes 10 minority (3 African-Americans, 5 Asian-Americans, 2 Hispanics), 139 international.
Degrees Awarded   In 1996, 46 master's, 11 doctorates awarded. Terminal master's awarded for partial completion of doctoral program.
Entrance Requirements   For master's, GRE General Test, TOEFL, minimum GPA of 2.75; for doctorate, GRE General Test, TOEFL, minimum GPA of 3.0.
Degree Requirements   For master's, computer language, thesis or alternative required, foreign language not required; for doctorate, computer language, dissertation, final oral exam required, foreign language not required.
Financial Aid   In 1996–97, 105 students received aid, including 12 fellowships (3 to first-year students) averaging $1,154 per month, 47 research assistantships (15 to first-year students) averaging $360 per month and totaling $169,635, 45 teaching assistantships (11 to first-year students) averaging $360 per month and totaling $162,415; full tuition waivers, Federal Work-Study also available. *Financial aid application deadline:* 3/1.
Applying   518 applicants, 57% accepted. *Deadline:* 8/15. *Fee:* $5 ($15 for international students).
Contact   *Dr. Harold Szu*
Director
318-482-6284

See in-depth description on page **719.**

COMPUTER SCIENCE

College of Sciences, Department of Computer Science
Programs   Awards MS.
Entrance Requirements   GRE General Test, minimum GPA of 2.75.
Applying   *Deadline:* 8/15. *Fee:* $5 ($15 for international students).
Contact   *Dr. Duane D. Blumberg*
Interim Dean
318-482-6986

MAINE

UNIVERSITY OF MAINE
Orono, ME 04469

OVERVIEW
University of Maine is a public coed university.

ENROLLMENT
10,000 graduate, professional, and undergraduate students; 927 full-time matriculated graduate/professional students (500 women), 659 part-time matriculated graduate/professional students (451 women).

GRADUATE FACULTY
600.

EXPENSES

Tuition $188 per credit hour for state residents; $531 per credit hour for nonresidents. Fees $336 per year full-time, $89 per year (minimum) part-time.

HOUSING

Rooms and/or apartments available to single students (124 units) at an average cost of $4537 (including board); available to married students (40 units). Housing application deadline: 8/1. Graduate housing information: 207-581-4584.

STUDENT SERVICES

Disabled student services, multicultural affairs office, low-cost health insurance, career counseling, free psychological counseling, campus safety program, campus employment opportunities, international student services, teacher training.

FACILITIES

Library: Fogler Library plus 1 additional on-campus library; total holdings of 815,000 volumes, 1.25 million microforms, 5,300 current periodical subscriptions. Access provided to on-line information retrieval services. *Computer:* Campuswide network is available with full Internet access. Computer service fees are included with tuition and fees. *Special:* In arts and humanities: Canadian-American Center, National Poetry Foundation, Northeast Archives of Folklore and Oral History. In science and engineering: Migratory Fish Research Institute, Pulp and Paper Foundation, surface science technology laboratory, Ira C. Darling Center. In social sciences: Psychology Services Center, Conley Speech and Hearing Center.

COMPUTER ENGINEERING

College of Engineering, Department of Electrical and Computer Engineering
Programs Offers programs in computer engineering (MS), electrical engineering (MS). Part-time programs available.
Faculty 14 full-time.
Students 30 full-time, 8 part-time; includes 1 international. Average age 25.
Degrees Awarded In 1996, 6 degrees awarded.
Entrance Requirements GRE General Test, TOEFL (minimum score 550).
Degree Requirements Thesis required (for some programs), foreign language not required.
Financial Aid In 1996–97, 6 research assistantships, 8 teaching assistantships were awarded; full tuition waivers, Federal Work-Study, institutionally sponsored loans also available. *Financial aid application deadline: 3/1.*
Applying 45 applicants, 71% accepted. *Deadline:* 2/1 (priority date; rolling processing; 10/15 for spring admission). *Fee:* $50.
Contact *Scott Delcourt*
Director of Graduate Admissions
207-581-3218
Fax: 207-581-3232
E-mail: delcourt@maine.maine.edu

COMPUTER SCIENCE

College of Liberal Arts and Sciences, Department of Computer Science
Programs Awards MS. Part-time programs available.
Faculty 5 full-time (0 women), 1 part-time (0 women).
Faculty Research Theory, software engineering, graphics, applications, artificial intelligence.

Students 12 full-time (3 women), 3 part-time (1 woman); includes 2 international.
Entrance Requirements GRE General Test, GRE Subject Test, TOEFL (minimum score 550).
Degree Requirements Thesis optional.
Financial Aid In 1996–97, 1 research assistantship, 7 teaching assistantships (3 to first-year students) were awarded; full tuition waivers, Federal Work-Study, institutionally sponsored loans, and career-related internships or fieldwork also available. *Financial aid application deadline: 3/1.*
Applying *Deadline:* 2/1 (priority date; rolling processing; 10/15 for spring admission). *Fee:* $50.
Contact *Scott Delcourt*
Director of Graduate Admissions
207-581-3218
Fax: 207-581-3232

ELECTRICAL ENGINEERING

College of Engineering, Department of Electrical and Computer Engineering
Programs Offers programs in computer engineering (MS), electrical engineering (MS). Part-time programs available.
Faculty 14 full-time.
Students 30 full-time, 8 part-time; includes 1 international. Average age 25.
Degrees Awarded In 1996, 6 degrees awarded.
Entrance Requirements GRE General Test, TOEFL (minimum score 550).
Degree Requirements Thesis required (for some programs), foreign language not required.
Financial Aid In 1996–97, 6 research assistantships, 8 teaching assistantships were awarded; full tuition waivers, Federal Work-Study, institutionally sponsored loans also available. *Financial aid application deadline: 3/1.*
Applying 45 applicants, 71% accepted. *Deadline:* 2/1 (priority date; rolling processing; 10/15 for spring admission). *Fee:* $50.
Contact *Scott Delcourt*
Director of Graduate Admissions
207-581-3218
Fax: 207-581-3232
E-mail: delcourt@maine.maine.edu

UNIVERSITY OF SOUTHERN MAINE
Portland, ME 04104-9300

OVERVIEW

University of Southern Maine is a public coed comprehensive institution.

ENROLLMENT

9,966 graduate, professional, and undergraduate students; 831 full-time matriculated graduate/professional students (493 women), 588 part-time matriculated graduate/professional students (366 women).

GRADUATE FACULTY

122.

EXPENSES

Tuition $173 per credit hour for state residents; $477 per credit hour for nonresidents. Fees $136 per year (minimum) full-time, $43 per semester (minimum) part-time.

HOUSING

Rooms and/or apartments available to single students at an average cost of $3134 per year ($4554 including board); on-campus housing not available to married students. Graduate housing contact: Joe Austin, 207-780-5158.

STUDENT SERVICES

Low-cost health insurance, career counseling, free psychological counseling, day-care facilities, international student services.

FACILITIES

Library: Main library plus 2 additional on-campus libraries; total holdings of 554,474 volumes, 1,151,835 microforms, 7,132 current periodical subscriptions. A total of 33 personal computers in all libraries. Access provided to on-line information retrieval services. *Computer:* Campuswide network is available with full Internet access. Computer service fees are included with tuition and fees.

COMPUTER SCIENCE

School of Applied Science, Department of Computer Science
Programs   Awards MS. Part-time programs available.
Faculty   6 full-time (0 women).
Faculty Research   Computer networks, database systems, software engineering, theory of computability, human factors. *Total annual research expenditures:* $27,173.
Students   10 full-time (3 women), 5 part-time (0 women); includes 2 international. Average age 30.
Degrees Awarded   In 1996, 1 degree awarded (100% found work related to degree).
Entrance Requirements   GRE Subject Test, minimum GPA of 3.0.
Degree Requirements   Computer language, thesis required, foreign language not required.
Financial Aid   In 1996–97, 4 students received aid, including 4 teaching assistantships (3 to first-year students) averaging $778 per month and totaling $28,008; research assistantships, Federal Work-Study also available. Aid available to part-time students. *Financial aid application deadline:* 4/1; applicants required to submit FAFSA.
Applying   9 applicants, 67% accepted. *Deadline:* 3/1 (priority date; 10/1 for spring admission). *Fee:* $25.
Contact   *Mary Sloan*
Assistant Director of Graduate Studies and Research
207-780-4386
Fax: 207-780-4969
E-mail: msloan@usm.maine.edu

MARYLAND

BOWIE STATE UNIVERSITY
Bowie, MD 20715

OVERVIEW

Bowie State University is a public coed comprehensive institution.

ENROLLMENT

5,067 graduate, professional, and undergraduate students; 1,817 matriculated graduate/professional students.

GRADUATE FACULTY

31 full-time (20 women), 43 part-time (21 women).

EXPENSES

Tuition $158 per credit hour for state residents; $268 per credit hour for nonresidents. Fees $169 per year.

HOUSING

Rooms and/or apartments available to single students (1,000 units) at an average cost of $2764 per year ($4455 including board); on-campus housing not available to married students. Graduate housing contact: Housing Department, 301-464-7135.

STUDENT SERVICES

Low-cost health insurance, career counseling, free psychological counseling, day-care facilities, campus safety program, campus employment opportunities, international student services.

FACILITIES

Library: Thurgood Marshall Library; total holdings of 208,680 volumes, 632,317 microforms, 1,364 current periodical subscriptions. Access provided to on-line information retrieval services. *Special:* In science and engineering: Center for Research in Distributed Computing.

COMPUTER SCIENCE

Program in Computer Science
Programs   Awards MS. Part-time and evening/weekend programs available.
Faculty   10 full-time (3 women).
Faculty Research   Holographics, launch vehicle ground truth ephemeras.
Students   95.
Degree Requirements   Research paper, written comprehensive exam required, thesis optional.
Financial Aid   Institutionally sponsored loans and career-related internships or fieldwork available. *Financial aid application deadline:* 4/1.
Applying   *Fee:* $30.
Contact   *Dr. Nagi Wakim*
Chairperson
301-464-7241
Fax: 301-464-7827

CAPITOL COLLEGE
Laurel, MD 20708-9759

OVERVIEW

Capitol College is an independent coed comprehensive institution.

ENROLLMENT

800 graduate, professional, and undergraduate students; 6 full-time matriculated graduate/professional students (3 women), 145 part-time matriculated graduate/professional students (39 women).

GRADUATE FACULTY

1 full-time (0 women), 24 part-time (4 women); includes 2 minority (1 African-American, 1 Hispanic).

TUITION
$355 per credit.

HOUSING
On-campus housing not available.

STUDENT SERVICES
Career counseling.

FACILITIES
Library: Puente Library; total holdings of 10,000 volumes, 75 current periodical subscriptions. Access provided to on-line information retrieval services. *Computer:* Campuswide network is available with partial Internet access (e-mail only). Total number of PCs/terminals supplied for student use: 45. Computer services are offered at no charge.

INFORMATION SCIENCE

Graduate School
Programs   Offerings include information and telecommunications systems management (MS).
School Faculty   1 full-time (0 women), 24 part-time (4 women).
Applying   *Deadline:* 7/1 (priority date; rolling processing). *Fee:* $25 ($100 for international students).
Contact   *Sandy Perriello*
Coordinator of Graduate Administration
703-998-5503
Fax: 703-379-8239

HOOD COLLEGE
Frederick, MD 21701-8575

OVERVIEW
Hood College is an independent-religious coed comprehensive institution.

ENROLLMENT
1,870 graduate, professional, and undergraduate students; 50 full-time matriculated graduate/professional students (35 women), 786 part-time matriculated graduate/professional students (544 women).

GRADUATE FACULTY
26.

TUITION
$270 per credit.

HOUSING
On-campus housing not available.

STUDENT SERVICES
Campus safety program, international student services.

FACILITIES
Library: Beneficial-Hodson Library; total holdings of 176,754 volumes, 600,621 microforms, 1,366 current periodical subscriptions. Access provided to on-line information retrieval services.

COMPUTER SCIENCE

Programs in Computer and Information Sciences
Programs   Awards MS.

Students   18 full-time (8 women), 124 part-time (56 women); includes 32 minority (6 African-Americans, 25 Asian-Americans, 1 Hispanic), 11 international. Average age 33.
Degrees Awarded   In 1996, 22 degrees awarded.
Entrance Requirements   Minimum GPA of 2.5.
Financial Aid   Fellowships, partial tuition waivers, institutionally sponsored loans, and career-related internships or fieldwork available. Aid available to part-time students. Financial aid applicants required to submit FAFSA.
Applying   *Deadline:* rolling. *Fee:* $30.
Contact   *Dr. Paul Gowen*
Chairperson
301-696-3731
Fax: 301-696-3597
E-mail: gowen@nimue.hood.edu

INFORMATION SCIENCE

Programs in Computer and Information Sciences
Programs   Awards MS.
Students   18 full-time (8 women), 124 part-time (56 women); includes 32 minority (6 African-Americans, 25 Asian-Americans, 1 Hispanic), 11 international. Average age 33.
Degrees Awarded   In 1996, 22 degrees awarded.
Entrance Requirements   Minimum GPA of 2.5.
Financial Aid   Fellowships, partial tuition waivers, institutionally sponsored loans, and career-related internships or fieldwork available. Aid available to part-time students. Financial aid applicants required to submit FAFSA.
Applying   *Deadline:* rolling. *Fee:* $30.
Contact   *Dr. Paul Gowen*
Chairperson
301-696-3731
Fax: 301-696-3597
E-mail: gowen@nimue.hood.edu

JOHNS HOPKINS UNIVERSITY
Baltimore, MD 21218-2699

OVERVIEW
Johns Hopkins University is an independent coed university.

ENROLLMENT
13,829 graduate, professional, and undergraduate students; 3,814 full-time matriculated graduate/professional students (1,872 women), 5,441 part-time matriculated graduate/professional students (2,763 women).

GRADUATE FACULTY
2,209 full-time (715 women), 2,359 part-time (827 women), 2,995 FTE; includes 380 minority (72 African-Americans, 257 Asian-Americans, 50 Hispanics, 1 Native American).

EXPENSES
Tuition $21,700 per year full-time, $725 per credit part-time. Fees $500 per year.

HOUSING
Rooms and/or apartments available to single students (176 units) at an average cost of $5000 per year; available to married students (75 units) at an average cost of $6600 per year. Housing application deadline: 6/1. Graduate housing contact: Carol Mohr, 410-516-7960.

STUDENT SERVICES

Disabled student services, multicultural affairs office, low-cost health insurance, career counseling, free psychological counseling, exercise/wellness program, campus safety program, campus employment opportunities, international student services, writing training, teacher training.

FACILITIES

Library: Eisenhower Library plus 3 additional on-campus libraries; total holdings of 2,337,797 volumes, 3,495,289 microforms, 13,958 current periodical subscriptions. A total of 248 personal computers in all libraries. Access provided to on-line information retrieval services. *Computer:* Campuswide network is available with full Internet access. Total number of PCs/terminals supplied for student use: 250. Computer service fees are included with tuition and fees. *Special:* In arts and humanities: Villa Spelman (Florence, Italy). In science and engineering: McCollum-Pratt Institute, Center for Astrophysical Sciences, applied physics laboratory. In social sciences: Center for Social Organization of Schools, Nanjing Center (People's Republic of China), Bologna Center (Italy).

COMPUTER ENGINEERING

G. W. C. Whiting School of Engineering, Department of Electrical and Computer Engineering
Programs Awards MSE, PhD. Part-time and evening/weekend programs available.
Faculty 15 full-time (0 women), 9 part-time (0 women).
Faculty Research Communications systems, quantum electronics and optics, signal and image processing, VLSI, microwaves. *Total annual research expenditures:* $3.267 million.
Students 56 full-time (7 women), 13 part-time (1 woman); includes 2 minority (1 African-American, 1 Asian-American), 29 international. Average age 25.
Degrees Awarded In 1996, 11 master's awarded (100% found work related to degree); 5 doctorates awarded. Terminal master's awarded for partial completion of doctoral program.
Entrance Requirements For doctorate, GRE General Test, TOEFL.
Degree Requirements For doctorate, dissertation required, foreign language not required.
Financial Aid In 1996–97, 49 students received aid, including 6 fellowships averaging $1,395 per month and totaling $75,300, 27 research assistantships averaging $1,386 per month and totaling $336,798, 11 teaching assistantships averaging $1,386 per month and totaling $137,214, 5 grants averaging $1,386 per month and totaling $62,370; partial tuition waivers, Federal Work-Study, institutionally sponsored loans also available. *Financial aid application deadline:* 2/1.
Applying 2,362 applicants, 2% accepted. *Deadline:* 1/1. *Fee:* $50.
Contact Gail M. O'Connor
Academic Coordinator II
410-516-4808
Fax: 410-516-5566
E-mail: gradadm@ece.jhu.edu

See in-depth description on page **457.**

COMPUTER SCIENCE

G. W. C. Whiting School of Engineering, Department of Computer Science
Programs Awards MSE, PhD.
Faculty 15 full-time (2 women), 12 part-time (0 women).

Faculty Research Artificial intelligence, networking parallel algorithms, programming languages, fault-tolerant computing, geometric computing. *Total annual research expenditures:* $1.109 million.
Students 55 full-time (9 women), 8 part-time (0 women); includes 4 minority (all Asian-Americans), 32 international. Average age 27.
Degrees Awarded In 1996, 14 master's, 6 doctorates awarded. Terminal master's awarded for partial completion of doctoral program.
Entrance Requirements For master's, GRE General Test; for doctorate, GRE General Test (average 654 verbal, 793 quantitative, 767 analytical), TOEFL.
Degree Requirements For master's, thesis optional; for doctorate, 1 foreign language, dissertation.
Financial Aid In 1996–97, 34 students received aid, including 1 fellowship (to a first-year student) averaging $1,386 per month and totaling $12,105, 17 research assistantships (2 to first-year students) averaging $1,386 per month and totaling $205,785, 9 teaching assistantships (4 to first-year students) averaging $1,386 per month and totaling $108,945, 24 grants averaging $1,386 per month and totaling $290,520; full and partial tuition waivers, Federal Work-Study, institutionally sponsored loans also available. *Financial aid application deadline:* 2/1.
Applying 215 applicants, 9% accepted. *Deadline:* 2/1. *Fee:* $50.
Contact Linda Rorke
Admissions Secretary
410-516-8775
Fax: 410-516-6134

See in-depth description on page **455.**

ELECTRICAL ENGINEERING

G. W. C. Whiting School of Engineering, Department of Electrical and Computer Engineering
Programs Awards MSE, PhD. Part-time and evening/weekend programs available.
Faculty 15 full-time (0 women), 9 part-time (0 women).
Faculty Research Communications systems, quantum electronics and optics, signal and image processing, VLSI, microwaves. *Total annual research expenditures:* $3.267 million.
Students 56 full-time (7 women), 13 part-time (1 woman); includes 2 minority (1 African-American, 1 Asian-American), 29 international. Average age 25.
Degrees Awarded In 1996, 11 master's awarded (100% found work related to degree); 5 doctorates awarded. Terminal master's awarded for partial completion of doctoral program.
Entrance Requirements For doctorate, GRE General Test, TOEFL.
Degree Requirements For doctorate, dissertation required, foreign language not required.
Financial Aid In 1996–97, 49 students received aid, including 6 fellowships averaging $1,395 per month and totaling $75,300, 27 research assistantships averaging $1,386 per month and totaling $336,798, 11 teaching assistantships averaging $1,386 per month and totaling $137,214, 5 grants averaging $1,386 per month and totaling $62,370; partial tuition waivers, Federal Work-Study, institutionally sponsored loans also available. *Financial aid application deadline:* 2/1.
Applying 2,362 applicants, 2% accepted. *Deadline:* 1/1. *Fee:* $50.
Contact Gail M. O'Connor
Academic Coordinator II
410-516-4808
Fax: 410-516-5566
E-mail: gradadm@ece.jhu.edu

See in-depth description on page **457.**

TOWSON UNIVERSITY
Towson, MD 21252-0001

OVERVIEW
Towson University is a public coed comprehensive institution.

ENROLLMENT
15,105 graduate, professional, and undergraduate students; 452 full-time matriculated graduate/professional students (333 women), 1,245 part-time matriculated graduate/professional students (966 women).

GRADUATE FACULTY
136 full-time (54 women), 19 part-time (12 women).

EXPENSES
Tuition $3132 per year full-time, $174 per credit hour part-time for state residents; $6120 per year full-time, $340 per credit hour part-time for nonresidents. Fees $648 per year full-time, $36 per credit hour part-time.

HOUSING
Rooms and/or apartments available to single students at an average cost of $2749 per year ($4280 including board); on-campus housing not available to married students. Graduate housing contact: Residence Department, 410-830-2516.

STUDENT SERVICES
Multicultural affairs office, low-cost health insurance, career counseling, free psychological counseling, exercise/wellness program, day-care facilities, campus employment opportunities, international student services, writing training, teacher training.

FACILITIES
Library: Albert S. Cook Library; total holdings of 536,976 volumes, 400,045 microforms, 1,995 current periodical subscriptions. A total of 18 personal computers in all libraries. Access provided to on-line information retrieval services. *Computer:* Campuswide network is available with full Internet access. *Special:* In arts and humanities: Center for the Teaching and Study of Writing. In science and engineering: Applied mathematics laboratory, Center for Mathematics and Sciences Education. In social sciences: Institute for Teaching and Research on Women, Center for Suburban and Regional Studies, Speech-Language-Hearing Clinic.

COMPUTER SCIENCE

Program in Computer Science
Programs Awards MS. Part-time and evening/weekend programs available.
Faculty 4 full-time (0 women).
Faculty Research Deductive databases, neural nets, software engineering, data communications and networks.
Students 55 full-time (27 women), 87 part-time (38 women); includes 28 minority (5 African-Americans, 18 Asian-Americans, 2 Hispanics, 3 Native Americans), 57 international.
Degrees Awarded In 1996, 3 degrees awarded.
Degree Requirements Exam required, thesis optional.
Financial Aid In 1996–97, 11 students received aid, including 11 assistantships; Federal Work-Study also available. Aid available to part-time students. *Financial aid application deadline:* 4/1; applicants required to submit FAFSA.

Applying *Deadline:* 3/1 (rolling processing; 10/1 for spring admission). *Fee:* $40.
Contact *Angela DeVito*
Assistant Director of Graduate Admissions
410-830-2501
Fax: 410-830-3434

UNIVERSITY OF MARYLAND, BALTIMORE COUNTY
Baltimore, MD 21250-5398

OVERVIEW
University of Maryland, Baltimore County is a public coed university.

EXPENSES
Tuition $253 per credit hour for state residents; $455 per credit hour for nonresidents. Fees $384 per year full-time, $32 per credit hour part-time.

HOUSING
Rooms and/or apartments available to single students; on-campus housing not available to married students. Graduate housing contact: Nancy Young, 410-455-2591.

FACILITIES
Library: Albin O. Kuhn Library. *Special:* In science and engineering: Bioimaging Center, Molecular Graphics Center, Center for Fluorescence Spectroscopy, Structural Biochemistry Center. In social sciences: Center for Educational Research and Development, Institute for Policy Analysis and Research, Bradley Center for Employment and Training.

COMPUTER ENGINEERING

Graduate School, College of Engineering, Department of Mechanical Engineering, Concentration in Computer-Integrated Manufacturing and Design
Programs Awards MS, PhD.
Entrance Requirements For master's, GRE General Test, minimum GPA of 3.0; for doctorate, GRE General Test, GRE Subject Test, TOEFL, minimum GPA of 3.5.
Applying *Deadline:* 7/1. *Fee:* $40.

COMPUTER SCIENCE

Graduate School, College of Engineering, Department of Computer Science and Electrical Engineering, Program in Computer Science
Programs Awards MS, PhD.
Entrance Requirements GRE General Test, GRE Subject Test, minimum GPA of 3.2.
Applying *Deadline:* 7/1. *Fee:* $40.

See in-depth description on page 651.

ELECTRICAL ENGINEERING

Graduate School, College of Engineering, Department of Computer Science and Electrical Engineering, Program in Electrical Engineering
Programs Awards MS, PhD.
Entrance Requirements GRE General Test.
Applying *Deadline:* 7/1. *Fee:* $40.

See in-depth description on page 651.

INFORMATION SCIENCE

Graduate School, Department of Information Systems
Programs Offers program in operations analysis (MS, PhD).
Entrance Requirements GRE General Test, minimum GPA of 3.0.
Applying *Deadline:* 7/1. *Fee:* $40.

See in-depth description on page 653.

UNIVERSITY OF MARYLAND, COLLEGE PARK
College Park, MD 20742

OVERVIEW
University of Maryland, College Park is a public coed university.

ENROLLMENT
31,471 graduate, professional, and undergraduate students; 4,202 full-time matriculated graduate/ professional students (1,902 women), 3,511 part-time matriculated graduate/professional students (1,762 women).

GRADUATE FACULTY
2,239 (498 women); includes 449 minority (163 African-Americans, 236 Asian-Americans, 46 Hispanics, 4 Native Americans).

EXPENSES
Tuition $272 per credit hour for state residents; $400 per credit hour for nonresidents. Fees $487 per year full-time, $293 per year part-time.

HOUSING
Rooms and/or apartments available to single students (476 units) at an average cost of $5880 per year; available to married students (476 units) at an average cost of $7296 per year. Housing application deadline: 6/15. Graduate housing contact: Sharon Tims, 301-422-0147.

STUDENT SERVICES
Disabled student services, low-cost health insurance, career counseling, free psychological counseling, daycare facilities, campus safety program, campus employment opportunities, international student services.

FACILITIES
Library: T. R. McKeldin Library plus 7 additional on-campus libraries; total holdings of 2,539,110 volumes, 5,072,411 microforms, 26,259 current periodical subscriptions. Access provided to on-line information retrieval services. *Computer:* Campuswide network is available with full Internet access. Total number of PCs/terminals supplied for student use: 3,470. Computer services are offered at no charge. *Special:* In arts and humanities: Center for Language, Center for Renaissance and Baroque Studies. In science and engineering: Center for Estuarine and Environmental Sciences, Transportation Studies Center, Institute for Physical Science and Technology, Neutral Buoyancy Research Center, Automation Research Center, Laboratory Plasma Center. In social sciences: Institute for Philosophy and Public Policy, Institute of Criminal Justice and Criminology, Survey Research Center, Center on Aging.

COMPUTER SCIENCE

College of Computer, Mathematical and Physical Sciences, Department of Computer Science
Programs Awards MS, PhD.
Faculty 51 (2 women).
Faculty Research Artificial intelligence, computer applications, information processing.
Students 136 full-time (17 women), 88 part-time (17 women); includes 28 minority (7 African-Americans, 16 Asian-Americans, 5 Hispanics), 123 international.
Degrees Awarded In 1996, 38 master's, 15 doctorates awarded.
Entrance Requirements For master's, GRE General Test, GRE Subject Test, minimum GPA of 3.0; for doctorate, GRE General Test, GRE Subject Test.
Degree Requirements For master's, thesis or alternative required, foreign language not required; for doctorate, variable foreign language requirement, dissertation.
Financial Aid In 1996–97, 7 fellowships, 79 research assistantships, 59 teaching assistantships were awarded; career-related internships or fieldwork also available.
Applying 545 applicants, 21% accepted. *Deadline:* rolling. *Fee:* $50 ($70 for international students).
Contact *John Mollish*
Director, Graduate Admissions and Records
301-405-4191

ELECTRICAL ENGINEERING

A. James Clark School of Engineering, Department of Electrical Engineering
Programs Offers programs in electrical engineering (M Eng, MS, PhD), telecommunications (MS). M Eng offered in conjunction with Professional Program in Engineering.
Faculty 83 (2 women).
Faculty Research Communication and control, electrophysics, solid-state electronics.
Students 196 full-time (24 women), 132 part-time (22 women); includes 41 minority (7 African-Americans, 32 Asian-Americans, 2 Hispanics), 194 international.
Degrees Awarded In 1996, 51 master's, 26 doctorates awarded.
Entrance Requirements For master's, minimum GPA of 3.0.
Degree Requirements For master's, thesis or alternative required, foreign language not required; for doctorate, variable foreign language requirement, dissertation.
Financial Aid In 1996–97, 23 fellowships, 84 research assistantships, 28 teaching assistantships were awarded; career-related internships or fieldwork also available.
Applying 952 applicants, 18% accepted. *Deadline:* rolling. *Fee:* $50 ($70 for international students).
Contact *John Mollish*
Director, Graduate Admissions and Records
301-405-4198
Fax: 301-314-9305

See in-depth description on page 655.

ELECTRICAL ENGINEERING

A. James Clark School of Engineering, Professional Program in Engineering
Programs Offerings include electrical engineering (M Eng).
Applying *Fee:* $50 ($70 for international students).

Contact *John Mollish*
Director, Graduate Admissions and Records
301-405-4198
Fax: 301-314-9305

SOFTWARE ENGINEERING

College of Computer, Mathematical and Physical Sciences, Software Engineering Program

Programs   Awards MSWE. Offered jointly with University of Maryland University College. Part-time programs available.

Students   28 part-time (7 women); includes 10 minority (2 African-Americans, 5 Asian-Americans, 2 Hispanics, 1 Native American), 1 international.

Entrance Requirements   Minimum GPA of 3.0, previous experience in software design.

Degree Requirements   Computer language.

Financial Aid   Federal Work-Study available. Aid available to part-time students. Financial aid applicants required to submit FAFSA.

Applying   21 applicants, 48% accepted. *Deadline:* rolling. *Fee:* $50 ($70 for international students).

Contact *DeAnn Buss*
Admissions Representative, University College
301-985-7155

UNIVERSITY OF MARYLAND EASTERN SHORE
Princess Anne, MD 21853-1299

OVERVIEW

University of Maryland Eastern Shore is a public coed university.

ENROLLMENT

3,166 graduate, professional, and undergraduate students; 147 full-time matriculated graduate/professional students (90 women), 114 part-time matriculated graduate/professional students (70 women).

GRADUATE FACULTY

60 full-time (13 women), 6 part-time (3 women); includes 24 minority (21 African-Americans, 3 Asian-Americans).

EXPENSES

Tuition $143 per credit hour for state residents; $253 per credit hour for nonresidents. Fees $50 per year.

HOUSING

Rooms and/or apartments available to single students at an average cost of $2330 per year ($4130 including board); on-campus housing not available to married students. Housing application deadline: 6/15. Graduate housing contact: Residence Life Office, 410-651-6141.

STUDENT SERVICES

Disabled student services, career counseling, free psychological counseling, exercise/wellness program, day-care facilities, campus safety program, campus employment opportunities, international student services, grant writing training, teacher training.

FACILITIES

Library: Frederick Douglass Library; total holdings of 170,000 volumes, 1,603 current periodical subscriptions. Access provided to on-line information retrieval services.

Computer: Campuswide network is available with full Internet access. Computer service fees are included with tuition and fees. *Special:* In science and engineering: Soybean Research Institute, Small Farm Institute, air pollution laboratory, crab research laboratory, water pollution laboratory.

COMPUTER SCIENCE

Department of Mathematics and Computer Sciences

Programs   Offers program in applied computer science (MS).

Faculty   7 full-time (1 woman).

Faculty Research   Parallel processing.

Students   20 full-time (6 women), 29 part-time (7 women); includes 11 minority (8 African-Americans, 2 Asian-Americans, 1 Hispanic), 25 international. Average age 31.

Degrees Awarded   In 1996, 17 degrees awarded (100% found work related to degree).

Entrance Requirements   TOEFL (minimum score 550), minimum GPA of 3.0.

Degree Requirements   Computer language, thesis or alternative, research project required, foreign language not required.

Financial Aid   In 1996–97, 23 students received aid, including 5 research assistantships, 3 teaching assistantships, 15 grants; fellowships, Federal Work-Study also available. Aid available to part-time students. *Financial aid application deadline: 3/1.*

Applying   53 applicants, 75% accepted. *Deadline:* 4/15 (priority date; rolling processing; 10/15 for spring admission). *Fee:* $30.

Contact *Dr. James Nelson Jr.*
Coordinator
410-651-6420
Fax: 410-651-6259
E-mail: jnelson@mcs.umes.umd.edu

UNIVERSITY OF MARYLAND UNIVERSITY COLLEGE
College Park, MD 20742-1600

OVERVIEW

University of Maryland University College is a public coed comprehensive institution.

ENROLLMENT

13,618 graduate, professional, and undergraduate students; 126 full-time matriculated graduate/professional students (54 women), 3,175 part-time matriculated graduate/professional students (1,555 women).

GRADUATE FACULTY

0 full-time, 124 part-time (12 women), 41 FTE; includes 19 minority (8 African-Americans, 8 Asian-Americans, 1 Hispanic, 2 Native Americans).

TUITION

$6552 per year full-time, $273 per semester hour part-time for state residents; $8472 per year full-time, $353 per semester hour part-time for nonresidents.

HOUSING

On-campus housing not available.

STUDENT SERVICES

Campus employment opportunities.

FACILITIES

Library: Access provided to on-line information retrieval services. *Computer:* Campuswide network is available with full Internet access. Total number of PCs/terminals supplied for student use: 375.

SOFTWARE ENGINEERING

Graduate School of Management and Technology, Program in Software Engineering

Programs   Awards MS. Offered evenings and weekends only; offered jointly with University of Maryland, College Park. Part-time and evening/weekend programs available.

Financial Aid   Federal Work-Study available. Aid available to part-time students. *Financial aid application deadline:* 5/1; applicants required to submit FAFSA.

Applying   *Deadline:* rolling. *Fee:* $50.

Contact   *Director of Graduate Admissions*
301-985-7155
Fax: 301-985-7175
E-mail: gradschool@europa.umuc.edu

MASSACHUSETTS

BOSTON UNIVERSITY
Boston, MA 02215

OVERVIEW

Boston University is an independent coed university.

ENROLLMENT

30,035 graduate, professional, and undergraduate students; 7,676 full-time matriculated graduate/professional students (3,982 women), 3,331 part-time matriculated graduate/professional students (1,675 women).

EXPENSES

Tuition $21,970 per year full-time, $687 per credit part-time. Fees $208 per year full-time, $40 per semester part-time.

HOUSING

Rooms and/or apartments available to single students (140 units) and married students. Graduate housing contact: Office of Housing, 617-353-3511.

STUDENT SERVICES

Low-cost health insurance, career counseling, free psychological counseling, day-care facilities, campus safety program, campus employment opportunities, international student services.

FACILITIES

Library: Mugar Memorial Library plus 16 additional on-campus libraries; total holdings of 2,051,555 volumes, 3,564,394 microforms, 28,949 current periodical subscriptions. Access provided to on-line information retrieval services. *Computer:* Campuswide network is available with full Internet access. *Special:* In arts and humanities: Center for Archaeological Studies. In science and engineering: Center for Adaptive Systems, Center for Polymer Studies, Center for Remote Sensing, Center for Space Physics, Science and Mathematics Education Center, Neuromuscular Research Center, marine laboratories, Cardiovascular Institute, Biomolecular Engineering Research Center, Center for Advanced Biotechnology. In social sciences: Institute for the Study of Economic Culture; Center for Health and Advanced Policy Studies; Institute for the Study of Small States; Institute for the Study of Conflict, Ideology, and Policy; African Studies Center; Health Policy Institute.

COMPUTER ENGINEERING

College of Engineering, Department of Electrical and Computer Engineering

Programs   Offers programs in computer engineering (MS, PhD); electrical engineering (MS, PhD); systems engineering (MS, PhD), including software engineering (MS). Part-time programs available.

Faculty   35 full-time (4 women), 6 part-time (0 women), 36.2 FTE.

Faculty Research   Optoelectronic devices and materials, speech and signal processing, multimedia communications, high performance computing, electromagnetics, software systems. *Total annual research expenditures:* $2.85 million.

Students   109 full-time (18 women), 37 part-time (5 women); includes 6 minority (1 African-American, 4 Asian-Americans, 1 Hispanic), 62 international. Average age 29.

Degrees Awarded   In 1996, 68 master's, 4 doctorates awarded. Terminal master's awarded for partial completion of doctoral program.

Entrance Requirements   GRE General Test, TOEFL.

Degree Requirements   For doctorate, dissertation required, foreign language not required.

Financial Aid   In 1996–97, 84 students received aid, including 11 fellowships (1 to a first-year student) averaging $1,190 per month, 58 research assistantships (13 to first-year students) averaging $1,268 per month, 18 teaching assistantships (7 to first-year students) averaging $1,312 per month, 10 scholarships (2 to first-year students); Federal Work-Study, institutionally sponsored loans, and career-related internships or fieldwork also available. *Financial aid application deadline:* 1/15; applicants required to submit FAFSA.

Applying   505 applicants, 21% accepted. *Deadline:* 4/1 (rolling processing; 10/15 for spring admission). *Fee:* $50.

Contact   *Dr. Bahaa Saleh*
Chairman
617-353-7176
Fax: 617-353-6440

See in-depth description on page 379.

COMPUTER SCIENCE

Graduate School of Arts and Sciences, Department of Computer Science

Programs   Awards MA, PhD. Part-time programs available.

Faculty   11 full-time (1 woman), 2 part-time (0 women).

Faculty Research   Networking, real time systems, computational complexity, database systems, mathematical logic, algorithmic information theory.

Students   50 full-time (11 women), 13 part-time (3 women); includes 2 minority (both Asian-Americans), 33 international. Average age 29.

Degrees Awarded   In 1996, 18 master's, 6 doctorates awarded.

Entrance Requirements   GRE General Test, TOEFL (minimum score 550).

Degree Requirements   For master's, 1 foreign language, project required, thesis optional; for doctorate, 1 foreign language, dissertation, oral and written qualifying exams.

Financial Aid   In 1996–97, 24 students received aid, including 9 fellowships (1 to a first-year student), 8 research assistantships, 4 scholarships; teaching assistantships, Federal Work-Study also available. Aid available to part-time students. *Financial aid application deadline:* 1/15; applicants required to submit FAFSA.

Applying 170 applicants, 56% accepted. *Deadline:* 6/1 (priority date; rolling processing; 10/15 for spring admission). *Fee:* $50.

Contact *Marina Chen*
Chairman
617-353-3840
Fax: 617-353-6457
E-mail: mcchen@bu.edu

COMPUTER SCIENCE

Metropolitan College, Program in Computer Science

Programs Offers computer information systems (MS), computer science (MS). Part-time and evening/weekend programs available.

Faculty 8 full-time (2 women), 64 part-time.

Faculty Research Software engineering, information systems architecture, process control, operating systems, parallel processing, object-oriented methods.

Students 14 full-time (2 women), 174 part-time (36 women); includes 37 minority (3 African-Americans, 33 Asian-Americans, 1 Hispanic), 24 international. Average age 33.

Degrees Awarded In 1996, 150 degrees awarded.

Degree Requirements Computer language required, foreign language and thesis not required.

Financial Aid In 1996–97, 2 research assistantships totaling $15,200 were awarded; full and partial tuition waivers, Federal Work-Study, and career-related internships or fieldwork also available. Aid available to part-time students.

Applying *Deadline:* rolling. *Fee:* $50.

Contact *Linda Goldberg*
Administrative Secretary
617-353-2566
Fax: 617-353-2367
E-mail: linda@bumeta.bu.edu

ELECTRICAL ENGINEERING

College of Engineering, Department of Electrical and Computer Engineering

Programs Offers programs in computer engineering (MS, PhD); electrical engineering (MS, PhD); systems engineering (MS, PhD), including software engineering (MS). Part-time programs available.

Faculty 35 full-time (4 women), 6 part-time (0 women), 36.2 FTE.

Faculty Research Optoelectronic devices and materials, speech and signal processing, multimedia communications, high performance computing, electromagnetics, software systems. *Total annual research expenditures:* $2.85 million.

Students 109 full-time (18 women), 37 part-time (5 women); includes 6 minority (1 African-American, 4 Asian-Americans, 1 Hispanic), 62 international. Average age 29.

Degrees Awarded In 1996, 68 master's, 4 doctorates awarded. Terminal master's awarded for partial completion of doctoral program.

Entrance Requirements GRE General Test, TOEFL.

Degree Requirements For doctorate, dissertation required, foreign language not required.

Financial Aid In 1996–97, 84 students received aid, including 11 fellowships (1 to a first-year student) averaging $1,190 per month, 58 research assistantships (13 to first-year students) averaging $1,268 per month, 18 teaching assistantships (7 to first-year students) averaging $1,312 per month, 10 scholarships (2 to first-year students); Federal Work-Study, institutionally sponsored loans, and career-related internships or fieldwork also available. *Financial aid application deadline:* 1/15; applicants required to submit FAFSA.

Applying 505 applicants, 21% accepted. *Deadline:* 4/1 (rolling processing; 10/15 for spring admission). *Fee:* $50.

Contact *Dr. Bahaa Saleh*
Chairman
617-353-7176
Fax: 617-353-6440

See in-depth description on page 379.

BRANDEIS UNIVERSITY
Waltham, MA 02254-9110

OVERVIEW
Brandeis University is an independent coed university.

ENROLLMENT
4,008 graduate, professional, and undergraduate students; 984 full-time matriculated graduate/professional students (468 women), 325 part-time matriculated graduate/professional students (237 women).

GRADUATE FACULTY
364 full-time (109 women), 150 part-time (71 women); includes 43 minority (10 African-Americans, 20 Asian-Americans, 13 Hispanics).

EXPENSES
Tuition $22,360 per year full-time, $2795 per course part-time. Fees $45 per year.

HOUSING
Rooms and/or apartments available to single students (85 units) at an average cost of $3685 per year; on-campus housing not available to married students. Housing application deadline: 6/15. Graduate housing contact: Andy Simmons, 617-736-3550.

STUDENT SERVICES
Low-cost health insurance, career counseling, free psychological counseling, day-care facilities, campus safety program, campus employment opportunities, international student services.

FACILITIES
Library: Goldfarbl Farber Libraries plus 3 additional on-campus libraries; total holdings of 1 million volumes, 835,000 microforms, 4,027 current periodical subscriptions. A total of 100 personal computers in all libraries. Access provided to on-line information retrieval services. *Computer:* Campuswide network is available with full Internet access. Total number of PCs/terminals supplied for student use: 125. Computer services are offered at no charge. *Special:* In arts and humanities: Humanities Center, Rose Museum of Art, Spingold Theatre Arts Center. In science and engineering: Volen National Center for Complex Systems, Rosenstiel Basic Medical Sciences Research Center. In social sciences: Center for Mental Retardation, Brandeis Institute for Health Policy, Policy Center on Aging, Family and Children's Policy Center.

COMPUTER SCIENCE

Graduate School of Arts and Sciences, Michtom School of Computer Science

Programs Awards MA, PhD.

Faculty 12 full-time (1 woman), 1 part-time.

Faculty Research Artificial intelligence, programming languages, parallel computing, computer linguistics, data compression.
Students 27 full-time (5 women), 2 part-time (1 woman); includes 2 minority (both Asian-Americans), 15 international.
Degrees Awarded In 1996, 11 master's, 5 doctorates awarded. Terminal master's awarded for partial completion of doctoral program.
Entrance Requirements GRE.
Degree Requirements For doctorate, dissertation, general exam.
Financial Aid 29 students received aid; fellowships, research assistantships, teaching assistantships, scholarships, full and partial tuition waivers, institutionally sponsored loans available. Aid available to part-time students. *Financial aid application deadline:* 4/15; applicants required to submit FAFSA.
Applying 85 applicants, 25% accepted. *Deadline:* 3/1. *Fee:* $60.
Contact *Myrna Fox*
 Department Administrator
 617-736-2701

BRIDGEWATER STATE COLLEGE
Bridgewater, MA 02325-0001

OVERVIEW
Bridgewater State College is a public coed comprehensive institution.

ENROLLMENT
8,569 graduate, professional, and undergraduate students; 1,339 matriculated graduate/professional students.

GRADUATE FACULTY
140 full-time.

TUITION
$3312 per year full-time, $138 per credit part-time.

HOUSING
On-campus housing not available.

STUDENT SERVICES
Low-cost health insurance, career counseling, day-care facilities.

FACILITIES
Library: Maxwell Library.

COMPUTER SCIENCE

School of Arts and Sciences, Department of Mathematics and Computer Science
Programs Offerings include computer science (MS).
Applying *Deadline:* 4/1 (10/1 for spring admission). *Fee:* $25.
Contact *Graduate School*
 508-697-1300

FITCHBURG STATE COLLEGE
Fitchburg, MA 01420-2697

OVERVIEW
Fitchburg State College is a public coed comprehensive institution.

ENROLLMENT
6,513 graduate, professional, and undergraduate students; 40 full-time, 865 part-time matriculated graduate/professional students.

GRADUATE FACULTY
0 full-time, 162 part-time (54 women); includes 9 minority (5 African-Americans, 3 Asian-Americans, 1 Native American).

EXPENSES
Tuition $140 per credit. Fees $139 per semester full-time, $76 per semester (minimum) part-time.

HOUSING
Rooms and/or apartments available to single students at an average cost of $2340 per year ($4110 including board); on-campus housing not available to married students. Graduate housing contact: Residence Life Office, 508-665-3219.

STUDENT SERVICES
Low-cost health insurance, career counseling, day-care facilities, campus safety program, international student services.

FACILITIES
Library: Hammond Library; total holdings of 206,884 volumes, 1,776 current periodical subscriptions. A total of 10 personal computers in all libraries. Access provided to on-line information retrieval services. *Computer:* Campuswide network is available with partial Internet access (e-mail only). Total number of PCs/terminals supplied for student use: 500. Computer services are offered at no charge.

COMPUTER SCIENCE

Program in Computer Science
Programs Awards MS. Part-time and evening/weekend programs available.
Entrance Requirements GRE General Test or MAT (minimum score 47), appropriate bachelor's degree, interview.
Degree Requirements Computer language, thesis required, foreign language not required.
Financial Aid Graduate assistantships, Federal Work-Study available. Aid available to part-time students. *Financial aid application deadline:* 3/30; applicants required to submit FAFSA.
Applying *Deadline:* rolling. *Fee:* $10.
Contact *James DuPont*
 Director of Admissions
 508-665-3144
 Fax: 508-665-4540

HARVARD UNIVERSITY
Cambridge, MA 02138

OVERVIEW
Harvard University is an independent coed university.

ENROLLMENT
18,649 graduate, professional, and undergraduate students; 10,639 full-time matriculated graduate/professional students (4,684 women), 921 part-time matriculated graduate/professional students (545 women).

GRADUATE FACULTY
2,134 (526 women).

EXPENSES
Tuition $20,600 per year. Fees $666 per year.

HOUSING
Rooms and/or apartments available to single and married students. Housing application deadline: 5/1.

STUDENT SERVICES
Low-cost health insurance, career counseling, free psychological counseling, day-care facilities, campus safety program, campus employment opportunities, international student services.

FACILITIES
Library: Widener Library plus 90 additional on-campus libraries; total holdings of 13,369,855 volumes, 7,953,568 microforms. Access provided to on-line information retrieval services. *Computer:* Campuswide network is available with full Internet access. Computer services are offered at no charge. *Special:* In arts and humanities: Carpenter Center for the Visual Arts, Fogg Art Museum, Arthur M. Sackler Museum, Busch-Reisinger Museum, Peabody Museum of Archaeology and Ethnology, Semitic Museum. In science and engineering: Museum of Comparative Zoology, mineralogical and geological Museum, botanical museum.

COMPUTER SCIENCE

Graduate School of Arts and Sciences, Division of Engineering and Applied Sciences
Programs Offerings include computer science (ME, SM, PhD), computing technology (PhD). Terminal master's awarded for partial completion of doctoral program.
Entrance Requirements For master's, GRE General Test, GRE Subject Test, TOEFL (minimum score 550).
Applying *Deadline:* 12/15. *Fee:* $60.
Contact *Office of Admissions and Financial Aid*
        617-495-5315

COMPUTER SCIENCE

Graduate School of Arts and Sciences, Division of Engineering and Applied Sciences, Center for Research in Computing Technology
Programs Awards PhD.
Entrance Requirements GRE General Test, GRE Subject Test, TOEFL (minimum score 550).
Degree Requirements Dissertation required, foreign language not required.
Financial Aid Federal Work-Study, institutionally sponsored loans, and career-related internships or fieldwork available. *Financial aid application deadline:* 12/30.
Applying *Deadline:* 12/15. *Fee:* $60.
Contact *Office of Admissions and Financial Aid*
        617-495-5315

See in-depth description on page 443.

MASSACHUSETTS INSTITUTE OF TECHNOLOGY
Cambridge, MA 02139-4307

OVERVIEW
Massachusetts Institute of Technology is an independent coed university.

ENROLLMENT
9,791 graduate, professional, and undergraduate students; 5,357 full-time matriculated graduate/professional students (1,309 women), 21 part-time matriculated graduate/professional students (4 women).

GRADUATE FACULTY
879 full-time (120 women), 17 part-time (4 women); includes 117 minority (20 African-Americans, 79 Asian-Americans, 18 Hispanics).

TUITION
$23,100 per year.

HOUSING
Rooms and/or apartments available to single students (1,060 units) at an average cost of $4898 per year; available to married students (407 units) at an average cost of $9351 per year. Housing application deadline: 4/30. Graduate housing contact: Betsey Walsh, 617-253-5148.

STUDENT SERVICES
Low-cost health insurance, career counseling, free psychological counseling, day-care facilities, campus safety program, campus employment opportunities, international student services.

FACILITIES
Library: Charles Hayden Memorial Library plus 22 additional on-campus libraries; total holdings of 2,448,647 volumes, 2,163,900 microforms, 21,764 current periodical subscriptions. A total of 400 personal computers in all libraries. Access provided to on-line information retrieval services. *Computer:* Campuswide network is available with full Internet access. Total number of PCs/terminals supplied for student use: 700. Computer services are offered at no charge. *Special:* In arts and humanities: Weisner Arts and Media Technology Building. In science and engineering: Bates Laboratory, Center for Cancer Research, Center for Space Research, Francis Bitter National Magnet Laboratory, microsystems technology laboratory, spectroscopy laboratory. In social sciences: Organizational Learning Center.

COMPUTER SCIENCE

School of Engineering, Department of Electrical Engineering and Computer Science, Program in Computer Science
Programs Awards M Eng, SM, PhD, Sc D, EE.
Faculty 42 full-time (3 women), 2 part-time (0 women).
Faculty Research Artificial intelligence, programming and systems, algorithms and theory.
Students 237 full-time (46 women), includes 46 minority (5 African-Americans, 37 Asian-Americans, 4 Hispanics), 64 international. Average age 26.
Degrees Awarded In 1996, 69 master's, 24 doctorates, 1 EE awarded.
Degree Requirements For master's and EE, thesis; for doctorate, dissertation, comprehensive exams.
Financial Aid In 1996–97, 2 fellowships averaging $1,295 per month, 131 research assistantships (29 to first-year students) averaging $1,430 per month, 25 teaching assistantships (4 to first-year students) averaging $1,470 per month were awarded; Federal Work-Study, institutionally sponsored loans, and career-related internships or fieldwork also available.
Applying 726 applicants, 9% accepted. *Deadline:* 1/15 (11/1 for spring admission). *Fee:* $50.

Contact *Peggy Carney*
Administrator
617-253-4603

ELECTRICAL ENGINEERING

School of Engineering, Department of Electrical Engineering and Computer Science

Programs Offers programs in computer science (M Eng, SM, PhD, Sc D, EE), electrical engineering (EE), electrical engineering and computer science (M Eng, SM, PhD, Sc D).

Faculty 119 full-time (7 women), 4 part-time (0 women).

Faculty Research Systems, communication, control, and signal processing; electronics, computers, and systems; energy and electromagnetic systems; materials and devices; bioelectrical engineering.

Students 792 full-time (130 women), includes 199 minority (21 African-Americans, 165 Asian-Americans, 13 Hispanics), 188 international. Average age 26.

Degrees Awarded In 1996, 291 master's, 70 doctorates, 8 EEs awarded.

Degree Requirements For master's and EE, thesis; for doctorate, dissertation, comprehensive exams.

Financial Aid In 1996–97, 7 fellowships (5 to first-year students) averaging $1,295 per month, 430 research assistantships (61 to first-year students) averaging $1,430 per month, 109 teaching assistantships (28 to first-year students) averaging $1,470 per month were awarded; Federal Work-Study, institutionally sponsored loans, and career-related internships or fieldwork also available.

Applying 1,741 applicants, 15% accepted. *Deadline:* 1/15 (11/1 for spring admission). *Fee:* $50.

Contact *Peggy Carney*
Administrator
617-253-4603

NORTHEASTERN UNIVERSITY
Boston, MA 02115-5096

OVERVIEW

Northeastern University is an independent coed university.

ENROLLMENT

24,579 graduate, professional, and undergraduate students; 2,748 full-time matriculated graduate/professional students (1,463 women), 2,051 part-time matriculated graduate/professional students (965 women).

GRADUATE FACULTY

745 full-time (246 women).

EXPENSES

Tuition $415 per credit hour. Fees $165 per year full-time, $40 per year part-time.

HOUSING

Rooms and/or apartments available to single students; on-campus housing not available to married students. Graduate housing contact: Sheryl Bunnell, 800-240-7666.

STUDENT SERVICES

Disabled student services, multicultural affairs office, low-cost health insurance, career counseling, free psychological counseling, exercise/wellness program, day-care facilities, campus safety program, campus employment opportunities, international student services.

FACILITIES

Library: Snell Library plus 5 additional on-campus libraries; total holdings of 829,140 volumes, 1,947,538 microforms, 8,878 current periodical subscriptions. Access provided to on-line information retrieval services. *Computer:* Campuswide network is available with full Internet access. Total number of PCs/terminals supplied for student use: 950. Computer services are offered at no charge. *Special:* In arts and humanities: Institute on Writing and Teaching. In science and engineering: Barnett Institute of Chemical Analysis and Materials Science, Center for Biotechnology Engineering, Center for Digital Signal Processing, Marine Science Center. In social sciences: Center for Labor Market Studies, Center of European Economic Studies, Center for Criminal Justice Policy Research, Center for the Study of Sport in Society.

COMPUTER ENGINEERING

Graduate School of Engineering, Computer Systems Engineering Program

Programs Awards MS. Part-time programs available.

Faculty Research Engineering software design, CAD/CAM, robotics.

Students 26 full-time (7 women), 37 part-time (7 women); includes 5 minority (4 Asian-Americans, 1 Hispanic), 14 international. Average age 25.

Degrees Awarded In 1996, 25 degrees awarded.

Entrance Requirements GRE General Test.

Degree Requirements Computer language required, thesis optional, foreign language not required.

Financial Aid In 1996–97, 9 students received aid, including 1 fellowship averaging $1,150 per month, 1 research assistantship averaging $1,150 per month, 3 teaching assistantships averaging $1,150 per month, 4 tuition assistantships (all to first-year students); Federal Work-Study and career-related internships or fieldwork also available. Aid available to part-time students. *Financial aid application deadline:* 2/15; applicants required to submit FAFSA.

Applying 57 applicants, 91% accepted. *Deadline:* 4/15 (rolling processing). *Fee:* $50.

Contact *Stephen L. Gibson*
Associate Director
617-373-2711
Fax: 617-373-2501

COMPUTER ENGINEERING

Graduate School of Engineering, Department of Electrical and Computer Engineering

Programs Awards MS, PhD, Engr. Part-time programs available.

Faculty 40 full-time (4 women).

Faculty Research Digital communications, digital signal processing, electromagnetics, control systems, microelectronics. *Total annual research expenditures:* $6.7 million.

Students 143 full-time (32 women), 196 part-time (19 women); includes 7 minority (5 Asian-Americans, 2 Hispanics), 106 international. Average age 25.

Degrees Awarded In 1996, 79 master's, 12 doctorates awarded. Terminal master's awarded for partial completion of doctoral program.

Entrance Requirements GRE General Test.

Degree Requirements For master's, thesis optional, foreign language not required; for doctorate, dissertation, departmental qualifying exam required, foreign language not required; for Engr, thesis required, foreign language not required.

Financial Aid In 1996–97, 120 students received aid, including 7 fellowships (6 to first-year students) averaging $1,150 per month,

80 research assistantships (13 to first-year students) averaging $1,150 per month, 26 teaching assistantships (9 to first-year students) averaging $1,150 per month, 7 tuition assistantships (3 to first-year students); Federal Work-Study and career-related internships or fieldwork also available. *Financial aid application deadline:* 2/15; applicants required to submit FAFSA.

Applying 526 applicants, 40% accepted. *Deadline:* 4/15 (rolling processing). *Fee:* $50.

Contact *Stephen L. Gibson*
Associate Director
617-373-2711
Fax: 617-373-2501

See in-depth description on page 493.

COMPUTER SCIENCE

College of Computer Science
Programs Awards MS, PhD. Part-time and evening/weekend programs available.
Faculty 18 full-time (5 women), 3 part-time (0 women).
Faculty Research Database theory, parallel computing, programming languages and software development, artifical intelligence, network and cryptography. *Total annual research expenditures:* $1.2 million.
Students 97 full-time (34 women), 65 part-time (12 women); includes 2 minority (1 African-American, 1 Hispanic), 85 international. Average age 26.
Degrees Awarded In 1996, 51 master's, 4 doctorates awarded. Terminal master's awarded for partial completion of doctoral program.
Entrance Requirements GRE General Test, TOEFL.
Degree Requirements For master's, computer language required, thesis optional; for doctorate, computer language, dissertation.
Financial Aid In 1996–97, 32 students received aid, including 1 fellowship (to a first-year student) averaging $1,333 per month and totaling $16,000, 5 research assistantships (all to first-year students), 8 teaching assistantships (all to first-year students), 4 industrial research assistantships; Federal Work-Study, institutionally sponsored loans, and career-related internships or fieldwork also available. *Financial aid application deadline:* 2/15.
Applying 358 applicants, 55% accepted. *Deadline:* 8/15 (rolling processing; 2/15 for spring admission). *Fee:* $50.
Contact *Dr. Agnes Chan*
Associate Dean and Director of Graduate Program
617-373-2462
Fax: 617-373-5121

See in-depth description on page 491.

ELECTRICAL ENGINEERING

Graduate School of Engineering, Department of Electrical and Computer Engineering
Programs Awards MS, PhD, Engr. Part-time programs available.
Faculty 40 full-time (4 women).
Faculty Research Digital communications, digital signal processing, electromagnetics, control systems, microelectronics. *Total annual research expenditures:* $6.7 million.
Students 143 full-time (32 women), 196 part-time (19 women); includes 7 minority (5 Asian-Americans, 2 Hispanics), 106 international. Average age 25.
Degrees Awarded In 1996, 79 master's, 12 doctorates awarded. Terminal master's awarded for partial completion of doctoral program.
Entrance Requirements GRE General Test.
Degree Requirements For master's, thesis optional, foreign language not required; for doctorate, dissertation, departmental

qualifying exam required, foreign language not required; for Engr, thesis required, foreign language not required.
Financial Aid In 1996–97, 120 students received aid, including 7 fellowships (6 to first-year students) averaging $1,150 per month, 80 research assistantships (13 to first-year students) averaging $1,150 per month, 26 teaching assistantships (9 to first-year students) averaging $1,150 per month, 7 tuition assistantships (3 to first-year students); Federal Work-Study and career-related internships or fieldwork also available. *Financial aid application deadline:* 2/15; applicants required to submit FAFSA.
Applying 526 applicants, 40% accepted. *Deadline:* 4/15 (rolling processing). *Fee:* $50.
Contact *Stephen L. Gibson*
Associate Director
617-373-2711
Fax: 617-373-2501

See in-depth description on page 493.

INFORMATION SCIENCE

Graduate School of Engineering, Information Systems Program
Programs Awards MS. Part-time programs available.
Faculty Research Simulation analysis.
Students 114 full-time (63 women), 62 part-time (30 women); includes 1 minority (Asian-American), 56 international. Average age 26.
Degrees Awarded In 1996, 40 degrees awarded.
Entrance Requirements GRE General Test.
Degree Requirements Computer language required, thesis optional, foreign language not required.
Financial Aid In 1996–97, 27 students received aid, including 1 fellowship averaging $1,150 per month, 2 research assistantships averaging $1,150 per month, 8 teaching assistantships (3 to first-year students) averaging $1,150 per month, 16 tuition assistantships (9 to first-year students). Financial aid applicants required to submit FAFSA.
Applying 91 applicants, 97% accepted. *Deadline:* 4/15 (rolling processing). *Fee:* $50.
Contact *Stephen L. Gibson*
Associate Director
617-373-2711
Fax: 617-373-2501

SUFFOLK UNIVERSITY
Boston, MA 02108-2770

OVERVIEW
Suffolk University is an independent coed comprehensive institution.

ENROLLMENT
6,401 graduate, professional, and undergraduate students; 1,269 full-time matriculated graduate/professional students (666 women), 2,062 part-time matriculated graduate/professional students (937 women).

GRADUATE FACULTY
175 full-time, 239 part-time; includes 31 minority (14 African-Americans, 11 Asian-Americans, 6 Hispanics).

EXPENSES
Tuition $13,644 per year full-time, $1932 per course part-time. Fees $20 per year full-time, $10 per year part-time.

HOUSING

Rooms and/or apartments available to single students (30 units) at an average cost of $8350 (including board); on-campus housing not available to married students. Graduate housing contact: Dean of Students, 617-573-8239.

STUDENT SERVICES

Disabled student services, multicultural affairs office, low-cost health insurance, career counseling, free psychological counseling, exercise/wellness program, campus safety program, campus employment opportunities, international student services, writing training.

FACILITIES

Library: Sawyer Library plus 2 additional on-campus libraries; total holdings of 281,000 volumes, 558,000 microforms, 6,965 current periodical subscriptions. Access provided to on-line information retrieval services. *Computer:* Campuswide network is available with full Internet access. Total number of PCs/terminals supplied for student use: 250. Computer service fees are included with tuition and fees. *Special:* In arts and humanities: C. Walsh Theatre. In science and engineering: Robert S. Friedman Marine Biology Field Station. In social sciences: Beacon Hill Institute.

COMPUTER SCIENCE

College of Liberal Arts and Sciences, Department of Mathematics and Computer Science
Programs Offers program in computer science (MS). Part-time and evening/weekend programs available.
Faculty 5 full-time (0 women).
Degree Requirements Computer language required, thesis optional, foreign language not required.
Financial Aid In 1996–97, 1 student received aid, including 1 fellowship (to a first-year student) totaling $12,593; Federal Work-Study, institutionally sponsored loans, and career-related internships or fieldwork also available. *Financial aid application deadline:* 4/1; applicants required to submit FAFSA.
Applying 21 applicants, 52% accepted. *Deadline:* 6/15 (priority date; rolling processing; 11/15 for spring admission). *Fee:* $50.
Contact *Marsha Ginn*
Director of Graduate Admissions
617-573-8302
Fax: 617-523-0116
E-mail: grad.admission@admin.suffolk.edu

TUFTS UNIVERSITY
Medford, MA 02155

OVERVIEW

Tufts University is an independent coed university.

ENROLLMENT

8,500 graduate, professional, and undergraduate students; 3,134 full-time, 492 part-time matriculated graduate/professional students.

GRADUATE FACULTY

561 full-time, 523 part-time.

EXPENSES

Tuition $22,867 per year. Fees $1200 per year.

HOUSING

Rooms and/or apartments available to single students (60 units) at an average cost of $4323 per year ($7643 including board); on-campus housing not available to married students. Graduate housing contact: Campus Housing Office, 612-627-3248.

STUDENT SERVICES

Disabled student services, low-cost health insurance, career counseling, free psychological counseling, daycare facilities, campus safety program, campus employment opportunities, international student services, writing training, teacher training.

FACILITIES

Library: Tisch Library plus 1 additional on-campus library; total holdings of 739,778 volumes, 1,098,592 microforms, 3,465 current periodical subscriptions. Access provided to on-line information retrieval services. *Computer:* Campuswide network is available. *Special:* In science and engineering: Center for Environmental Management, Electro-Optics Technology Center, Science and Technology Center. In social sciences: Center for Applied Child Development, Lincoln Filene Center for Science and Math Teaching.

COMPUTER SCIENCE

Graduate School of Arts and Sciences, College of Engineering, Department of Electrical Engineering and Computer Science
Programs Offers programs in computer science (MS, PhD), electrical engineering (MS, PhD). Part-time programs available.
Faculty 21 full-time, 9 part-time.
Students 86 (15 women); includes 4 minority (all Asian-Americans), 30 international.
Degrees Awarded In 1996, 22 master's, 6 doctorates awarded. Terminal master's awarded for partial completion of doctoral program.
Entrance Requirements GRE General Test, TOEFL (minimum score 550).
Degree Requirements For master's, thesis or alternative required, foreign language not required; for doctorate, dissertation required, foreign language not required.
Financial Aid Research assistantships, teaching assistantships, scholarships, partial tuition waivers, Federal Work-Study available. *Financial aid application deadline:* 2/15; applicants required to submit FAFSA.
Applying 127 applicants, 64% accepted. *Deadline:* 3/15 (rolling processing; 10/15 for spring admission). *Fee:* $50.
Contact *Robert Gonsalves*
Chair
617-627-3217

ELECTRICAL ENGINEERING

Professional and Continuing Studies, Microwave and Wireless Engineering Program
Programs Awards Certificate. Part-time and evening/weekend programs available.
Students 5 part-time (0 women). Average age 28.
Financial Aid Available to part-time students. *Financial aid application deadline:* 5/1; applicants required to submit FAFSA.
Applying 2 applicants, 100% accepted. *Deadline:* 8/15 (priority date; rolling processing; 12/12 for spring admission). *Fee:* $40.
Contact *Liz Regan*
Program Administrator
617-627-3562
Fax: 617-627-3017

ELECTRICAL ENGINEERING

Graduate School of Arts and Sciences, College of Engineering, Department of Electrical Engineering and Computer Science
Programs Offers programs in computer science (MS, PhD), electrical engineering (MS, PhD). Part-time programs available.
Faculty 21 full-time, 9 part-time.
Students 86 (15 women); includes 4 minority (all Asian-Americans), 30 international.
Degrees Awarded In 1996, 22 master's, 6 doctorates awarded. Terminal master's awarded for partial completion of doctoral program.
Entrance Requirements GRE General Test, TOEFL (minimum score 550).
Degree Requirements For master's, thesis or alternative required, foreign language not required; for doctorate, dissertation required, foreign language not required.
Financial Aid Research assistantships, teaching assistantships, scholarships, partial tuition waivers, Federal Work-Study available. *Financial aid application deadline:* 2/15; applicants required to submit FAFSA.
Applying 127 applicants, 64% accepted. *Deadline:* 3/15 (rolling processing; 10/15 for spring admission). *Fee:* $50.
Contact *Robert Gonsalves*
Chair
617-627-3217

UNIVERSITY OF MASSACHUSETTS AMHERST
Amherst, MA 01003-0001

OVERVIEW
University of Massachusetts Amherst is a public coed university.

ENROLLMENT
24,296 graduate, professional, and undergraduate students; 2,337 full-time matriculated graduate/professional students (1,272 women), 2,357 part-time matriculated graduate/professional students (1,186 women).

GRADUATE FACULTY
1,118 full-time (261 women), 7 part-time (3 women); includes 182 minority (60 African-Americans, 65 Asian-Americans, 50 Hispanics, 7 Native Americans).

TUITION
$3941 per year full-time, $110 per credit part-time for state residents; $8705 per year full-time, $373 per credit part-time for nonresidents.

HOUSING
Rooms and/or apartments available to single students (190 units) at an average cost of $2416 per year ($4228 including board); available to married students (345 units) at an average cost of $5712 per year ($7524 including board). Housing application deadline: 8/1. Graduate housing contact: Gerald Quarles, 413-545-2100.

STUDENT SERVICES
Low-cost health insurance, career counseling, free psychological counseling, day-care facilities, campus safety program.

FACILITIES
Library: University Library plus 4 additional on-campus libraries; total holdings of 5 million volumes, 2.8 million microforms, 15,500 current periodical subscriptions. Access provided to on-line information retrieval services. *Computer:* Campuswide network is available with full Internet access. Computer service fees are applied as a separate charge. *Special:* In science and engineering: Environmental Institute, Polymer Research Institute, Remote Sensing Center, marine station, suburban experiment station.

COMPUTER ENGINEERING

College of Engineering, Department of Electrical and Computer Engineering
Programs Awards MS, PhD. Part-time and evening/weekend programs available.
Faculty 32 full-time (1 woman).
Students 76 full-time (12 women), 60 part-time (6 women); includes 5 minority (all Asian-Americans), 93 international. Average age 28.
Degrees Awarded In 1996, 25 master's, 22 doctorates awarded. Terminal master's awarded for partial completion of doctoral program.
Entrance Requirements GRE General Test.
Degree Requirements For doctorate, dissertation required, foreign language not required.
Financial Aid In 1996–97, 4 fellowships, 68 research assistantships, 31 teaching assistantships were awarded; Federal Work-Study also available. Aid available to part-time students. *Financial aid application deadline:* 2/15.
Applying 418 applicants, 42% accepted. *Deadline:* 2/15 (priority date; rolling processing; 10/1 for spring admission). *Fee:* $40.
Contact *Dr. Donald E. Scott*
Chair, Admissions Committee
413-545-0937
Fax: 413-545-4611
E-mail: scott@ecs.umass.edu

COMPUTER SCIENCE

College of Natural Sciences and Mathematics, Department of Computer Science
Programs Awards MS, PhD. Part-time programs available.
Faculty 33 full-time (3 women).
Faculty Research Artificial intelligence, systems, theory, robotics.
Students 49 full-time (13 women), 86 part-time (13 women); includes 5 minority (4 Asian-Americans, 1 Hispanic), 74 international. Average age 29.
Degrees Awarded In 1996, 25 master's, 11 doctorates awarded. Terminal master's awarded for partial completion of doctoral program.
Entrance Requirements GRE General Test.
Degree Requirements For doctorate, dissertation required, foreign language not required.
Financial Aid In 1996–97, 4 fellowships, 129 research assistantships, 40 teaching assistantships were awarded; Federal Work-Study also available. Aid available to part-time students. *Financial aid application deadline:* 1/15.
Applying 489 applicants, 14% accepted. *Deadline:* 1/15 (priority date; rolling processing). *Fee:* $40.
Contact *Chair, Admissions Committee*
413-545-3640

See in-depth description on page 657.

ELECTRICAL ENGINEERING

College of Engineering, Department of Electrical and Computer Engineering

Programs Awards MS, PhD. Part-time and evening/weekend programs available.

Faculty 32 full-time (1 woman).

Students 76 full-time (12 women), 60 part-time (6 women); includes 5 minority (all Asian-Americans), 93 international. Average age 28.

Degrees Awarded In 1996, 25 master's, 22 doctorates awarded. Terminal master's awarded for partial completion of doctoral program.

Entrance Requirements GRE General Test.

Degree Requirements For doctorate, dissertation required, foreign language not required.

Financial Aid In 1996–97, 4 fellowships, 68 research assistantships, 31 teaching assistantships were awarded; Federal Work-Study also available. Aid available to part-time students. *Financial aid application deadline:* 2/15.

Applying 418 applicants, 42% accepted. *Deadline:* 2/15 (priority date; rolling processing; 10/1 for spring admission). *Fee:* $40.

Contact *Dr. Donald E. Scott*
Chair, Admissions Committee
413-545-0937
Fax: 413-545-4611
E-mail: scott@ecs.umass.edu

UNIVERSITY OF MASSACHUSETTS BOSTON
Boston, MA 02125-3393

OVERVIEW
University of Massachusetts Boston is a public coed university.

ENROLLMENT
10,236 graduate, professional, and undergraduate students; 667 full-time matriculated graduate/professional students (442 women), 1,748 part-time matriculated graduate/professional students (1,097 women).

GRADUATE FACULTY
449 full-time (169 women); includes 84 minority (33 African-Americans, 36 Asian-Americans, 14 Hispanics, 1 Native American).

EXPENSES
Tuition $2640 per year full-time, $110 per credit part-time for state residents; $8842 per year full-time, $369 per credit part-time for nonresidents. Fees $547 per year (minimum) full-time, $261 per semester (minimum) part-time.

HOUSING
On-campus housing not available.

STUDENT SERVICES
Disabled student services, multicultural affairs office, low-cost health insurance, career counseling, free psychological counseling, exercise/wellness program, day-care facilities, campus safety program, campus employment opportunities, international student services, teacher training.

FACILITIES
Library: Joseph P. Healey Library; total holdings of 572,397 volumes, 743,479 microforms, 3,120 current periodical subscriptions. Access provided to on-line information retrieval services. *Computer:* Campuswide network is available with full Internet access. Total number of PCs/terminals supplied for student use: 440. Computer service fees are included with tuition and fees. *Special:* In science and engineering: Center for Advancement of Teaching in the Sciences. In social sciences: McCormack Institute of Public Affairs, Center for Survey Research, Joiner Center for the Study of War and Social Consequences, Urban Harbors Institute, Gerontology Institute, Trotter Institute for the Study of Black Culture, Gaston Institute for Latino Affairs, Institute for Learning and Teaching, Field Center for Teaching and Learning, Asian American Institute.

COMPUTER SCIENCE

College of Arts and Sciences, Faculty of Sciences, Program in Computer Science

Programs Awards MS, PhD.

Students 36 full-time (13 women), 59 part-time (15 women).

Degrees Awarded In 1996, 26 master's awarded.

Entrance Requirements GRE General Test, minimum GPA of 2.75.

Degree Requirements For master's, comprehensive exams required, thesis optional, foreign language not required; for doctorate, dissertation, comprehensive exams required, foreign language not required.

Financial Aid Research assistantships, teaching assistantships, administrative assistantships available. *Financial aid application deadline:* 3/1; applicants required to submit FAFSA.

Applying 113 applicants, 46% accepted. *Deadline:* 3/1 (priority date; 11/1 for spring admission). *Fee:* $20 ($35 for international students).

Contact *Lisa Lavely*
Director of Graduate Admissions and Records
617-287-6400
Fax: 617-287-6236

UNIVERSITY OF MASSACHUSETTS DARTMOUTH
North Dartmouth, MA 02747-2300

OVERVIEW
University of Massachusetts Dartmouth is a public coed comprehensive institution.

ENROLLMENT
5,436 graduate, professional, and undergraduate students; 172 full-time matriculated graduate/professional students (81 women), 287 part-time matriculated graduate/professional students (178 women).

GRADUATE FACULTY
199 (57 women); includes 41 minority (9 African-Americans, 28 Asian-Americans, 3 Hispanics, 1 Native American).

EXPENSES
Tuition $3106 per year full-time, $86 per credit part-time for state residents; $10,788 per year full-time, $300 per

credit part-time for nonresidents. Fees $5002 per year full-time, $143 per credit part-time for state residents; $6830 per year full-time, $194 per credit part-time for nonresidents.

HOUSING

Rooms and/or apartments available to single students at an average cost of $3134 per year ($5074 including board); on-campus housing not available to married students. Graduate housing contact: Housing Office, 508-999-8140.

STUDENT SERVICES

Low-cost health insurance, career counseling, free psychological counseling, day-care facilities, campus safety program, campus employment opportunities, international student services.

FACILITIES

Library: Library Communications Center; total holdings of 430,194 volumes, 269,454 microforms, 3,118 current periodical subscriptions. A total of 50 personal computers in all libraries. Access provided to on-line information retrieval services. *Computer:* Campuswide network is available with full Internet access. Computer services are offered at no charge. *Special:* In science and engineering: Center for Marine Sciences and Technology, marine science laboratory, Northeast Regional Aquaculture Center.

COMPUTER SCIENCE

Graduate School, College of Engineering, Program in Computer Science
Programs   Awards MS. Part-time programs available.
Faculty   7 (1 woman).
Faculty Research   Learning software design, computer architecture, parallel architecture.
Students   7 full-time (3 women), 8 part-time (1 woman); includes 3 minority (all Asian-Americans), 6 international.
Degrees Awarded   In 1996, 12 degrees awarded.
Entrance Requirements   GRE General Test, GRE Subject Test, TOEFL.
Degree Requirements   Thesis or alternative required, foreign language not required.
Financial Aid   In 1996–97, 7 teaching assistantships totaling $14,000 were awarded; research assistantships, graduate assistantships, Federal Work-Study also available. Aid available to part-time students. *Financial aid application deadline:* 3/15; applicants required to submit FAFSA.
Applying   14 applicants, 86% accepted. *Deadline:* 4/20 (priority date; rolling processing; 11/15 for spring admission). *Fee:* $40.
Contact   *Carol A. Novo*
Graduate Admissions Office
508-999-8604
Fax: 508-999-8375
E-mail: graduate@umassd.edu

ELECTRICAL ENGINEERING

Graduate School, College of Engineering, Department of Electrical and Computer Engineering
Programs   Offers program in electrical engineering (MS, PhD). Part-time programs available.
Faculty   19 (1 woman).
Faculty Research   Signal processing, systems analysis, underwater acoustics.
Students   25 full-time (5 women), 27 part-time (5 women); includes 19 international.

Degrees Awarded   In 1996, 28 master's awarded.
Entrance Requirements   For master's, GRE General Test, TOEFL.
Degree Requirements   For master's, thesis or alternative required, foreign language not required.
Financial Aid   In 1996–97, 14 research assistantships totaling $62,038, 15 teaching assistantships totaling $61,226 were awarded; graduate assistantships, Federal Work-Study also available. Aid available to part-time students. *Financial aid application deadline:* 3/15; applicants required to submit FAFSA.
Applying   123 applicants, 88% accepted. *Deadline:* 4/20 (priority date; rolling processing; 11/15 for spring admission). *Fee:* $40.
Contact   *Carol A. Novo*
Graduate Admissions Office
508-999-8604
Fax: 508-999-8375
E-mail: graduate@umassd.edu

See in-depth description on page **659.**

UNIVERSITY OF MASSACHUSETTS LOWELL
Lowell, MA 01854–2881

OVERVIEW

University of Massachusetts Lowell is a public coed university.

ENROLLMENT

12,350 graduate, professional, and undergraduate students; 747 full-time matriculated graduate/professional students (308 women), 2,006 part-time matriculated graduate/professional students (802 women).

GRADUATE FACULTY

406 full-time (105 women), 94 part-time (34 women).

EXPENSES

Tuition $4868 per year full-time, $618 per semester (minimum) part-time for state residents; $10,068 per year full-time, $1268 per semester (minimum) part-time for nonresidents. Fees $640 per year full-time, $85 per semester part-time.

HOUSING

Rooms and/or apartments available to single students (73 units) at an average cost of $3480 per year; available to married students (48 units) at an average cost of $4800 per year. Housing application deadline: 4/1.

STUDENT SERVICES

Disabled student services, multicultural affairs office, low-cost health insurance, career counseling, free psychological counseling, day-care facilities, campus safety program, campus employment opportunities, international student services, grant writing training.

FACILITIES

Library: Lydon Library plus 1 additional on-campus library; total holdings of 433,000 volumes, 611,799 microforms, 3,500 current periodical subscriptions. Access provided to on-line information retrieval services. *Computer:* Campuswide network is available with full Internet access. Computer service fees are included with tuition and fees. *Special:* In arts and humanities: Center for

Field Services and Studies, Tsongas Industrial History Center. In science and engineering: Advanced Biomaterials Center; Advanced Electronics Technology Center; Center for Advanced Computation and Telecommunications; Center for Advanced Materials; Center for Atmospheric Research; Center for Electromagnetic Materials and Optical Systems; Center for Environmentally Appropriate Materials; Center for Environmental Engineering and Science Technologies; Center for Recording Arts, Technology, and Industry; Computer Aided Engineering and Design Center; distributed multimedia systems laboratory; Institute for Plastics Innovation; Kerr Ergonomics Institute; Massachusetts Bioprocess Development Center; NSF Centre for Biodegradable Polymer Research; radiation laboratory; submillimeter technology laboratory; Toxics Use Reduction Institute. In social sciences: Center for Industrial Competitiveness; Center for Productivity Enhancement; Center for Telecommunications Applications in Management; Center for Family, Work, and Community; Institute for Visualization and Perception Research; Manufacturing Laboratory; Small Business Incubator, Center for Health Promotion.

COMPUTER ENGINEERING

James B. Francis College of Engineering, Department of Electrical Engineering, Program in Computer Engineering

Programs Awards MS Eng, D Eng.
Students 7 full-time (2 women), 30 part-time (6 women); includes 7 minority (all Asian-Americans), 12 international.
Degrees Awarded In 1996, 27 master's awarded.
Entrance Requirements GRE General Test.
Degree Requirements For master's, thesis optional, foreign language not required; for doctorate, 2 foreign languages, computer language, dissertation.
Financial Aid Career-related internships or fieldwork available. *Financial aid application deadline: 4/1.*
Applying *Deadline:* 4/1 (priority date; rolling processing; 10/1 for spring admission). *Fee:* $20 ($35 for international students).
Contact *Dr. Ross Holmstrom*
Coordinator
508-934-3307

COMPUTER SCIENCE

College of Arts and Sciences, Department of Computer Science
Programs Awards MS, Sc D. Part-time programs available.
Faculty 18 full-time (0 women), 4 part-time (0 women).
Faculty Research Networks, multimedia systems, human-computer interaction, graphics and visualization databases.
Students 60 full-time (14 women), 212 part-time (58 women); includes 44 minority (4 African-Americans, 33 Asian-Americans, 6 Hispanics, 1 Native American), 93 international.
Degrees Awarded In 1996, 48 master's, 4 doctorates awarded.
Entrance Requirements GRE General Test.
Degree Requirements For master's, thesis optional, foreign language not required; for doctorate, computer language, dissertation.
Financial Aid In 1996–97, 2 research assistantships, 12 teaching assistantships were awarded; fellowships, Federal Work-Study, and career-related internships or fieldwork also available. *Financial aid application deadline: 4/1.*
Applying 122 applicants, 71% accepted. *Deadline:* 4/1 (priority date; rolling processing; 10/1 for spring admission). *Fee:* $20 ($35 for international students).
Contact *Charles Steele*
Coordinator
508-934-3615

ELECTRICAL ENGINEERING

James B. Francis College of Engineering, Department of Electrical Engineering, Program in Electrical Engineering
Programs Awards MS Eng, D Eng. Part-time and evening/weekend programs available.
Degrees Awarded Terminal master's awarded for partial completion of doctoral program.
Entrance Requirements GRE General Test.
Degree Requirements For master's, thesis required, foreign language not required; for doctorate, 2 foreign languages, computer language, dissertation.
Financial Aid Federal Work-Study, institutionally sponsored loans, and career-related internships or fieldwork available. Aid available to part-time students. *Financial aid application deadline: 4/1.*
Applying *Deadline:* 4/1 (priority date; rolling processing; 10/1 for spring admission). *Fee:* $20 ($35 for international students).
Contact *Dr. Ross Holmstrom*
Coordinator
508-934-3307

WESTERN NEW ENGLAND COLLEGE
Springfield, MA 01119-2654

OVERVIEW
Western New England College is an independent coed comprehensive institution.

ENROLLMENT
4,283 graduate, professional, and undergraduate students; 420 full-time matriculated graduate/professional students (204 women), 1,106 part-time matriculated graduate/professional students (452 women).

GRADUATE FACULTY
64 full-time (10 women), 58 part-time (12 women); includes 6 minority (2 African-Americans, 3 Asian-Americans, 1 Native American).

EXPENSES
Tuition $317 per credit hour. Fees $32 per semester (minimum).

HOUSING
On-campus housing not available.

STUDENT SERVICES
Disabled student services, low-cost health insurance, career counseling, free psychological counseling, exercise/wellness program, campus safety program, writing training.

FACILITIES
Library: D'Amour Library plus 1 additional on-campus library; total holdings of 277,619 volumes, 1,081,689 microforms, 4,274 current periodical subscriptions. A total of 94 personal computers in all libraries. Access provided to on-line information retrieval services. *Computer:* Campuswide network is available with full Internet access. Total number of PCs/terminals supplied for student use: 150. Computer services are offered at no charge.

ELECTRICAL ENGINEERING

School of Engineering, Department of Electrical Engineering
Programs Awards MSEE. Part-time and evening/weekend programs available.

Faculty 7 full-time (0 women).

Faculty Research Superconductors, microwave cooking, computer voice output, digital filters, computer engineering.

Students 11 part-time (1 woman). Average age 29.

Degrees Awarded In 1996, 5 degrees awarded.

Entrance Requirements Bachelor's degree in engineering or related field.

Degree Requirements Computer language, comprehensive exam required, thesis optional, foreign language not required.

Financial Aid Teaching assistantships available. Aid available to part-time students. *Financial aid application deadline:* 4/1; applicants required to submit FAFSA.

Applying *Deadline:* rolling. *Fee:* $30.

Contact *Rod Pease*
Director of Student Administrative Services
413-796-2080

WORCESTER POLYTECHNIC INSTITUTE
Worcester, MA 01609-2280

OVERVIEW
Worcester Polytechnic Institute is an independent coed university.

ENROLLMENT
3,765 graduate, professional, and undergraduate students; 401 full-time matriculated graduate/professional students (85 women), 330 part-time matriculated graduate/professional students (67 women).

GRADUATE FACULTY
177 full-time (24 women), 40 part-time (4 women); includes 22 minority (16 Asian-Americans, 6 Hispanics).

TUITION
$612 per credit hour.

HOUSING
On-campus housing not available. Graduate housing contact: Philip Clay, 508-831-5308.

STUDENT SERVICES
Low-cost health insurance, career counseling, free psychological counseling, campus employment opportunities, international student services.

FACILITIES
Library: Gordon Library; total holdings of 345,000 volumes, 77,103 microforms, 1,200 current periodical subscriptions. A total of 55 personal computers in all libraries. Access provided to on-line information retrieval services. *Computer:* Campuswide network is available with full Internet access. Computer services are offered at no charge. *Special:* In science and engineering: Manufacturing Engineering Applications Center, aluminum casting research laboratory, ultrasound research laboratory, Center for Holographic Studies, Applied Bioengineering Center, Powder Metallurgy Center.

COMPUTER ENGINEERING

Department of Electrical and Computer Engineering

Programs Offers programs in electrical and computer engineering (MS, PhD), power systems engineering (MS, PhD). Part-time and evening/weekend programs available.

Faculty 16 full-time (1 woman), 9 part-time (0 women), 17.5 FTE.

Faculty Research Solid-state electronics, power systems, processing, image processing, computer engineering, ultrasonics.

Students 53 full-time (4 women), 39 part-time (4 women); includes 10 minority (2 African-Americans, 7 Asian-Americans, 1 Hispanic), 30 international.

Degrees Awarded In 1996, 37 master's, 2 doctorates awarded. Terminal master's awarded for partial completion of doctoral program.

Entrance Requirements GRE (required for non-native speakers of English), TOEFL (minimum score 550; average 610).

Degree Requirements For master's, thesis optional, foreign language not required; for doctorate, dissertation required, foreign language not required.

Financial Aid In 1996–97, 48 students received aid, including 8 fellowships (2 to first-year students) averaging $1,167 per month and totaling $84,024, 19 research assistantships (8 to first-year students) averaging $1,080 per month and totaling $184,680, 16 teaching assistantships (6 to first-year students) averaging $1,060 per month and totaling $152,640; institutionally sponsored loans and career-related internships or fieldwork also available. *Financial aid application deadline:* 2/15.

Applying 132 applicants, 55% accepted. *Deadline:* 2/15 (priority date; rolling processing; 10/15 for spring admission). *Fee:* $50.

Contact *Dr. Fred Loobt*
Graduate Coordinator
508-831-5231
Fax: 508-831-5491
E-mail: fjloobt@ece.wpi.edu

COMPUTER SCIENCE

Department of Computer Science

Programs Awards MS, PhD. Part-time and evening/weekend programs available.

Faculty 13 full-time (2 women), 7 part-time (2 women), 15 FTE.

Faculty Research Artificial intelligence, language, networks, operating systems, databases.

Students 42 full-time (6 women), 47 part-time (3 women); includes 12 minority (1 African-American, 11 Asian-Americans), 23 international.

Degrees Awarded In 1996, 38 master's, 1 doctorate awarded. Terminal master's awarded for partial completion of doctoral program.

Entrance Requirements GRE General Test (combined average 1815 on three sections, TOEFL (minimum score 550; average 602).

Degree Requirements For master's, computer language required, thesis optional, foreign language not required; for doctorate, computer language, dissertation required, foreign language not required.

Financial Aid In 1996–97, 15 students received aid, including 3 research assistantships averaging $1,166 per month and totaling $31,482, 12 teaching assistantships (3 to first-year students) averaging $1,060 per month and totaling $114,480; fellowships, institutionally sponsored loans, and career-related internships or fieldwork also available. *Financial aid application deadline:* 2/15.

Applying 316 applicants, 60% accepted. *Deadline:* 2/15 (priority date; rolling processing; 10/15 for spring admission). *Fee:* $50.

Contact *Dr. R. E. Kinicki*
Head
508-831-5670
Fax: 508-831-5776
E-mail: rek@cs.wpi.edu

See in-depth description on page 765.

ELECTRICAL ENGINEERING

Department of Electrical and Computer Engineering
Programs Offers programs in electrical and computer engineering (MS, PhD), power systems engineering (MS, PhD). Part-time and evening/weekend programs available.
Faculty 16 full-time (1 woman), 9 part-time (0 women), 17.5 FTE.
Faculty Research Solid-state electronics, power systems, processing, image processing, computer engineering, ultrasonics.
Students 53 full-time (4 women), 39 part-time (4 women); includes 10 minority (2 African-Americans, 7 Asian-Americans, 1 Hispanic), 30 international.
Degrees Awarded In 1996, 37 master's, 2 doctorates awarded. Terminal master's awarded for partial completion of doctoral program.
Entrance Requirements GRE (required for non-native speakers of English), TOEFL (minimum score 550; average 610).
Degree Requirements For master's, thesis optional, foreign language not required; for doctorate, dissertation required, foreign language not required.
Financial Aid In 1996–97, 48 students received aid, including 8 fellowships (2 to first-year students) averaging $1,167 per month and totaling $84,024, 19 research assistantships (8 to first-year students) averaging $1,080 per month and totaling $184,680, 16 teaching assistantships (6 to first-year students) averaging $1,060 per month and totaling $152,640; institutionally sponsored loans and career-related internships or fieldwork also available. *Financial aid application deadline: 2/15.*
Applying 132 applicants, 55% accepted. *Deadline:* 2/15 (priority date; rolling processing; 10/15 for spring admission). *Fee:* $50.
Contact *Dr. Fred Loobt*
Graduate Coordinator
508-831-5231
Fax: 508-831-5491
E-mail: fjloobt@ece.wpi.edu

MICHIGAN

CENTRAL MICHIGAN UNIVERSITY
Mount Pleasant, MI 48859

OVERVIEW
Central Michigan University is a public coed university.

ENROLLMENT
16,597 graduate, professional, and undergraduate students; 11,223 matriculated graduate/professional students.

GRADUATE FACULTY
2,040.

EXPENSES
Tuition $131 per credit for state residents; $261 per credit for nonresidents. Fees $235 per year full-time, $90 per year part-time.

HOUSING
Rooms and/or apartments available to single students (108 units) at an average cost of $2500 per year ($4300 including board); available to married students (428 units) at an average cost of $4000 per year. Graduate housing contact: Joan Schmidt, 517-774-3284.

STUDENT SERVICES
Low-cost health insurance, career counseling, free psychological counseling, campus safety program, campus employment opportunities, international student services.

FACILITIES
Library: Park Library; total holdings of 900,000 volumes, 1,182,320 microforms, 5,000 current periodical subscriptions. A total of 135 personal computers in all libraries. Access provided to on-line information retrieval services. *Computer:* Campuswide network is available with full Internet access. Computer service fees are included with tuition and fees. *Special:* In arts and humanities: Clarke Historical Library, English Language Institute. In science and engineering: Beaver Island, Nethercut Woods, Center for Computer Vision and Robotics, Center for Cultural and Natural History, Dow Science Building. In social sciences: Michigan Geographic Alliance, Center for Applied Research and Rural Studies, Psychology Training andConsulting Center.

COMPUTER SCIENCE

College of Arts and Sciences, Department of Computer Science
Programs Awards MS.
Faculty 15 full-time (1 woman).
Faculty Research Compiler construction, artificial intelligence, database theory, software engineering, operating systems.
Students 28 full-time (5 women), 13 part-time (6 women); includes 5 minority (all Asian-Americans), 29 international. Average age 28.
Degrees Awarded In 1996, 11 degrees awarded.
Entrance Requirements TOEFL (minimum score 550), minimum GPA of 2.5 in last 2 undergraduate years.
Degree Requirements Computer language, thesis or alternative required, foreign language not required.
Financial Aid In 1996–97, 12 teaching assistantships were awarded; fellowships, Federal Work-Study, and career-related internships or fieldwork also available. *Financial aid application deadline: 3/7.*
Applying *Deadline:* 3/15 (priority date; rolling processing). *Fee:* $30.
Contact *Dr. Gongzhu Hu*
Chairperson
517-774-3774
Fax: 517-774-6652
E-mail: hu@cps201.cps.cmich.edu

SOFTWARE ENGINEERING

College of Extended Learning, Program in Administration
Programs Offerings include software engineering administration (MSA, Certificate).
Entrance Requirements For master's, minimum GPA of 2.5 in major.
Applying *Fee:* $50.
Contact *Marketing Office*
800-950-1144
Fax: 517-774-2461

GMI ENGINEERING & MANAGEMENT INSTITUTE
Flint, MI 48504-4898

OVERVIEW
GMI Engineering & Management Institute is an independent coed comprehensive institution.

ENROLLMENT
3,027 graduate, professional, and undergraduate students; 5 full-time matriculated graduate/professional students (4 women), 790 part-time matriculated graduate/professional students (147 women).

GRADUATE FACULTY
34 full-time (2 women), 2 part-time (0 women); includes 9 minority (1 African-American, 8 Asian-Americans).

EXPENSES
Tuition $379 per credit. Fees $15 per credit.

HOUSING
Rooms and/or apartments available to single students (600 units); on-campus housing not available to married students. Graduate housing contact: D. Stewart, 810-762-9503.

STUDENT SERVICES
Low-cost health insurance, free psychological counseling, campus employment opportunities.

FACILITIES
Library: Main library; total holdings of 54,000 volumes, 15,000 microforms, 815 current periodical subscriptions. Access provided to on-line information retrieval services. *Special:* In arts and humanities: Humanities Art Gallery. In science and engineering: Optics and lasers laboratory, analytical chemistry laboratory, manufacturing laboratory. In social sciences: Industrial history archive.

COMPUTER ENGINEERING

Electrical and Computer Engineering Department
Programs Offers program in controls and signal processing (MS Eng).
Entrance Requirements GRE General Test.
Financial Aid Fellowships, research assistantships, teaching assistantships, partial tuition waivers, Federal Work-Study, institutionally sponsored loans available. Aid available to part-time students.
Applying *Deadline:* 7/15 (rolling processing). *Fee:* $0.
Contact *David Leffen*
Head
810-762-7900

ELECTRICAL ENGINEERING

Electrical and Computer Engineering Department
Programs Offers program in controls and signal processing (MS Eng).
Entrance Requirements GRE General Test.
Financial Aid Fellowships, research assistantships, teaching assistantships, partial tuition waivers, Federal Work-Study, institutionally sponsored loans available. Aid available to part-time students.
Applying *Deadline:* 7/15 (rolling processing). *Fee:* $0.
Contact *David Leffen*
Head
810-762-7900

GRAND VALLEY STATE UNIVERSITY
Allendale, MI 49401-9403

OVERVIEW
Grand Valley State University is a public coed comprehensive institution.

ENROLLMENT
14,662 graduate, professional, and undergraduate students; 454 full-time matriculated graduate/professional students (347 women), 1,286 part-time matriculated graduate/professional students (852 women).

GRADUATE FACULTY
100 full-time (40 women), 131 part-time (51 women).

TUITION
$162 per credit hour for state residents; $330 per credit hour for nonresidents.

HOUSING
Rooms and/or apartments available to single students at an average cost of $4380 (including board); on-campus housing not available to married students. Housing application deadline: 2/1. Graduate housing contact: Andrew Beachnau, 616-895-3531.

STUDENT SERVICES
Disabled student services, multicultural affairs office, low-cost health insurance, career counseling, free psychological counseling, exercise/wellness program, day-care facilities, campus safety program, campus employment opportunities, international student services, teacher training.

FACILITIES
Library: Zumberge Library; total holdings of 352,411 volumes, 66,338 microforms, 2,774 current periodical subscriptions. A total of 79 personal computers in all libraries. Access provided to on-line information retrieval services. *Computer:* Campuswide network is available with full Internet access. Total number of PCs/terminals supplied for student use: 637. Computer service fees are included with tuition and fees. *Special:* In science and engineering: Manitou Computer Center, R/V *Angus.*

INFORMATION SCIENCE

Science and Mathematics Division, Department of Computer Science and Information Systems
Programs Offers programs in information systems (MS), software engineering (MS). Part-time and evening/weekend programs available.
Faculty 7 full-time (0 women), 1 part-time (0 women).
Faculty Research Object technology, distributed computing, information systems management.
Students 6 full-time (4 women), 29 part-time (8 women); includes 12 minority (1 African-American, 11 Asian-Americans), 7 international. Average age 34.
Degrees Awarded In 1996, 8 degrees awarded.

Entrance Requirements GMAT or GRE General Test.
Degree Requirements Computer language, thesis or alternative required, foreign language not required.
Applying *Deadline: 2/1. Fee: $20.*
Contact *Bruce J. Klein*
Associate Professor
616-895-2048
Fax: 616-895-3506
E-mail: kleinb@gvsu.edu

SOFTWARE ENGINEERING

Science and Mathematics Division, Department of Computer Science and Information Systems
Programs Offers programs in information systems (MS), software engineering (MS). Part-time and evening/weekend programs available.
Faculty 7 full-time (0 women), 1 part-time (0 women).
Faculty Research Object technology, distributed computing, information systems management.
Students 6 full-time (4 women), 29 part-time (8 women); includes 12 minority (1 African-American, 11 Asian-Americans), 7 international. Average age 34.
Degrees Awarded In 1996, 8 degrees awarded.
Entrance Requirements GMAT or GRE General Test.
Degree Requirements Computer language, thesis or alternative required, foreign language not required.
Applying *Deadline: 2/1. Fee: $20.*
Contact *Bruce J. Klein*
Associate Professor
616-895-2048
Fax: 616-895-3506
E-mail: kleinb@gvsu.edu

MICHIGAN STATE UNIVERSITY
East Lansing, MI 48824-1020

OVERVIEW
Michigan State University is a public coed university.

ENROLLMENT
41,545 graduate, professional, and undergraduate students; 5,509 full-time matriculated graduate/professional students (2,791 women), 3,718 part-time matriculated graduate/professional students (2,136 women).

GRADUATE FACULTY
2,022 (476 women); includes 253 minority (91 African-Americans, 122 Asian-Americans, 33 Hispanics, 7 Native Americans).

EXPENSES
Tuition $3888 per year full-time, $216 per credit hour (minimum) part-time for state residents; $7366 per year full-time, $437 per credit hour (minimum) part-time for nonresidents. Fees $566 per year full-time, $468 per year part-time.

HOUSING
Rooms and/or apartments available to single students (872 units) at an average cost of $3942 (including board); available to married students (2,284 units). Graduate housing contact: Charles Gagliano, 517-355-7457.

STUDENT SERVICES
Low-cost health insurance, career counseling, free psychological counseling, day-care facilities, campus safety program, campus employment opportunities, international student services.

FACILITIES
Library: Main library plus 15 additional on-campus libraries; total holdings of 4,047,477 volumes, 4,993,512 microforms, 27,917 current periodical subscriptions. Access provided to on-line information retrieval services. *Computer:* Campuswide network is available with full Internet access. Computer service fees are included with tuition and fees. *Special:* In arts and humanities: Kresge Art Center and Museum, university museum, voice library. In science and engineering: Center for Remote Sensing, MSU/DOE Plant Research Laboratory, Pesticide Research Center, W. K. Kellogg Biological Station, Water Research Center, cyclotron. In social sciences: Center for Urban Affairs; Institute for Research on Teaching; preschool laboratory; Institute for Children, Youth, and Families; Institute for Public Policy and Social Research; psychological laboratory.

COMPUTER SCIENCE

College of Engineering, Department of Computer Science
Programs Awards MS, PhD.
Faculty 22 (2 women).
Students 153 (30 women); includes 14 minority (7 African-Americans, 6 Asian-Americans, 1 Native American), 85 international.
Degrees Awarded In 1996, 35 master's, 11 doctorates awarded.
Entrance Requirements GRE General Test, GRE Subject Test, TOEFL.
Degree Requirements For master's, written exam or substantial design project required, foreign language and thesis not required; for doctorate, dissertation, comprehensive and qualifying exams.
Financial Aid In 1996–97, 6 fellowships, 46 research assistantships, 70 teaching assistantships were awarded.
Applying *Deadline: rolling. Fee: $30 ($40 for international students).*
Contact *Dr. George C. Stockman*
Graduate Coordinator
517-353-1679

See in-depth description on page **471.**

ELECTRICAL ENGINEERING

College of Engineering, Department of Electrical Engineering
Programs Awards MS, PhD.
Faculty 26 (1 woman).
Students 133 (20 women); includes 24 minority (8 African-Americans, 11 Asian-Americans, 5 Hispanics), 81 international.
Degrees Awarded In 1996, 23 master's, 8 doctorates awarded.
Entrance Requirements GRE General Test (minimum combined score of 1800 on three sections), TOEFL (minimum score 580).
Degree Requirements For master's, exit exam required, thesis optional, foreign language not required; for doctorate, dissertation, comprehensive and qualifying exams required, foreign language not required.
Financial Aid In 1996–97, 15 fellowships, 45 research assistantships, 20 teaching assistantships were awarded.
Applying *Deadline: rolling. Fee: $30 ($40 for international students).*
Contact *Dr. Jes Asmussen Jr.*
Chairperson
517-355-4620

See in-depth description on page **473.**

MICHIGAN TECHNOLOGICAL UNIVERSITY
Houghton, MI 49931-1295

OVERVIEW
Michigan Technological University is a public coed university.

ENROLLMENT
6,195 graduate, professional, and undergraduate students; 628 full-time matriculated graduate/professional students (206 women), 26 part-time matriculated graduate/professional students (9 women).

GRADUATE FACULTY
321 full-time (52 women), 12 part-time (3 women), 328.3 FTE; includes 55 minority (5 African-Americans, 45 Asian-Americans, 4 Hispanics, 1 Native American).

EXPENSES
Tuition $3276 per year full-time, $182 per credit hour part-time for state residents; $7506 per year full-time, $417 per credit hour part-time for nonresidents. Fees $126 per year.

HOUSING
Rooms and/or apartments available to single students at an average cost of $1904 per year ($4284 including board); available to married students (350 units) at an average cost of $3912 per year. Housing application deadline: 7/15. Graduate housing contact: Housing Office, 906-487-2682.

STUDENT SERVICES
Disabled student services, low-cost health insurance, career counseling, free psychological counseling, exercise/wellness program, campus safety program, campus employment opportunities, international student services, writing training, grant writing training, teacher training.

FACILITIES
Library: J. Robert Van Pelt Library; total holdings of 803,041 volumes, 463,889 microforms, 10,154 current periodical subscriptions. A total of 53 personal computers in all libraries. Access provided to on-line information retrieval services. *Computer:* Campuswide network is available with full Internet access. Total number of PCs/terminals supplied for student use: 1,025. Computer service fees are included with tuition and fees. *Special:* In science and engineering: A. E. Seaman Mineralogical Museum, Institute of Materials Processing, Ford Forestry Center, Keweenaw Research Center, Center for Clean Manufacturing and Treatment Technologies, Center for Lake Superior Ecosystems Research, Institute of Wood Research.

COMPUTER SCIENCE

College of Sciences and Arts, Department of Computer Science
Programs Offers programs in computer science (MS), engineering-computational science (PhD). Part-time programs available.
Faculty 9 full-time (1 woman).
Faculty Research Software engineering, parallel algorithms, graphics and computational biology, geometric modeling/graphics, instruction level parallelism.

Students 23 full-time (5 women), 2 part-time (0 women); includes 14 international. Average age 27.
Degrees Awarded In 1996, 10 master's awarded.
Entrance Requirements For master's, GRE General Test (minimum combined score of 1780 on three sections; average 1998), TOEFL (minimum score 600; average 631); for doctorate, GRE General Test (combined average 2145 on three sections), TOEFL (minimum score 575; average 588).
Degree Requirements For master's, computer language required, foreign language not required; for doctorate, computer language, dissertation required, foreign language not required.
Financial Aid In 1996–97, 24 students received aid, including 1 fellowship (to a first-year student) averaging $1,007 per month and totaling $9,060, 9 research assistantships (2 to first-year students) averaging $809 per month and totaling $65,553, 13 teaching assistantships (5 to first-year students) averaging $920 per month and totaling $107,724, 1 exceptional student award (to a first-year student); Federal Work-Study also available. Aid available to part-time students. *Financial aid application deadline: 3/15.*
Applying 71 applicants, 65% accepted. *Deadline:* 3/15 (priority date; rolling processing). *Fee:* $30 ($35 for international students).
Contact Dr. Steve Carr
Assistant Professor
906-487-2950
Fax: 906-487-2283
E-mail: carr@mtu.edu

See in-depth description on page **475.**

ELECTRICAL ENGINEERING

College of Engineering, Department of Electrical Engineering
Programs Offers programs in electrical engineering (MS, PhD), sensing and signal processing (PhD). Part-time programs available.
Faculty 24 full-time (3 women).
Faculty Research Signal and image processing, power systems, intelligent systems, electrophysics. *Total annual research expenditures:* $624,686.
Students 45 full-time (14 women), 3 part-time (0 women); includes 31 international. Average age 26.
Degrees Awarded In 1996, 19 master's, 1 doctorate awarded.
Entrance Requirements For master's, GRE General Test (combined average 1960 on three sections), TOEFL (minimum score 600; average 605), BSEE or equivalent; for doctorate, GRE General Test (combined average 2020 on three sections), TOEFL (minimum score 600; average 634).
Degree Requirements For master's, thesis or alternative required, foreign language not required; for doctorate, dissertation required, foreign language not required.
Financial Aid In 1996–97, 40 students received aid, including 6 fellowships (1 to a first-year student) averaging $989 per month and totaling $53,400, 11 research assistantships averaging $1,015 per month and totaling $100,467, 18 teaching assistantships (6 to first-year students) averaging $821 per month and totaling $132,990; Federal Work-Study and career-related internships or fieldwork also available. Aid available to part-time students. *Financial aid application deadline: 3/1.*
Applying 125 applicants, 57% accepted. *Deadline:* 3/15 (priority date; rolling processing). *Fee:* $30 ($35 for international students).
Contact *Graduate Coordinator*
906-487-2550
Fax: 906-487-2949

OAKLAND UNIVERSITY
Rochester, MI 48309-4401

OVERVIEW
Oakland University is a public coed university.

ENROLLMENT
13,956 graduate, professional, and undergraduate students; 594 full-time matriculated graduate/professional students (360 women), 2,066 part-time matriculated graduate/professional students (1,337 women).

GRADUATE FACULTY
269 full-time, 49 part-time; includes 71 minority (20 African-Americans, 43 Asian-Americans, 7 Hispanics, 1 Native American).

EXPENSES
Tuition $3744 per year full-time, $208 per credit hour part-time for state residents; $8298 per year full-time, $461 per credit hour part-time for nonresidents. Fees $262 per year (minimum).

HOUSING
Rooms and/or apartments available to single students at an average cost of $4400 (including board); available to married students (48 units) at an average cost of $4560 per year. Housing application deadline: 9/1. Graduate housing contact: Eleanor Reynolds, 248-370-3570.

STUDENT SERVICES
Low-cost health insurance, career counseling, day-care facilities, campus safety program, campus employment opportunities, international student services.

FACILITIES
Library: Kresge Library plus 1 additional on-campus library; total holdings of 622,621 volumes, 1,070,184 microforms, 2,078 current periodical subscriptions. A total of 350 personal computers in all libraries. Access provided to on-line information retrieval services. *Special:* In science and engineering: Kettering Magnetics Laboratory, Eye Research Institute, clinical research laboratory, robotics laboratory, Biochemistry and Biotechnology Institute.

COMPUTER ENGINEERING

School of Engineering and Computer Science, Program in Computer Science and Engineering

Programs Awards MS. Part-time and evening/weekend programs available.
Faculty 13 full-time, 1 part-time.
Students 45 full-time (18 women), 95 part-time (22 women); includes 16 minority (3 African-Americans, 11 Asian-Americans, 2 Hispanics), 44 international. Average age 30.
Degrees Awarded In 1996, 37 degrees awarded.
Entrance Requirements Minimum GPA of 3.0 for unconditional admission.
Financial Aid Full tuition waivers, Federal Work-Study, institutionally sponsored loans available. *Financial aid application deadline:* 3/1; applicants required to submit FAFSA.
Applying 113 applicants, 87% accepted. *Deadline:* 7/15 (3/15 for spring admission). *Fee:* $30.

Contact Dr. S. Ganesan
Chair
248-370-2200

COMPUTER ENGINEERING

School of Engineering and Computer Science, Program in Electrical and Computer Engineering

Programs Awards MS. Part-time and evening/weekend programs available.
Faculty 6 full-time, 1 part-time.
Students 26 full-time (5 women), 48 part-time (8 women); includes 7 minority (4 African-Americans, 2 Asian-Americans, 1 Hispanic), 15 international. Average age 29.
Degrees Awarded In 1996, 16 degrees awarded.
Entrance Requirements Minimum GPA of 3.0 for unconditional admission.
Financial Aid Full tuition waivers, Federal Work-Study, institutionally sponsored loans available. *Financial aid application deadline:* 3/1; applicants required to submit FAFSA.
Applying 38 applicants, 74% accepted. *Deadline:* 7/15 (3/15 for spring admission). *Fee:* $30.
Contact Dr. Naim A. Kheir
Chair
248-370-2245

COMPUTER SCIENCE

School of Engineering and Computer Science, Program in Computer Science and Engineering

Programs Awards MS. Part-time and evening/weekend programs available.
Faculty 13 full-time, 1 part-time.
Students 45 full-time (18 women), 95 part-time (22 women); includes 16 minority (3 African-Americans, 11 Asian-Americans, 2 Hispanics), 44 international. Average age 30.
Degrees Awarded In 1996, 37 degrees awarded.
Entrance Requirements Minimum GPA of 3.0 for unconditional admission.
Financial Aid Full tuition waivers, Federal Work-Study, institutionally sponsored loans available. *Financial aid application deadline:* 3/1; applicants required to submit FAFSA.
Applying 113 applicants, 87% accepted. *Deadline:* 7/15 (3/15 for spring admission). *Fee:* $30.
Contact Dr. S. Ganesan
Chair
248-370-2200

ELECTRICAL ENGINEERING

School of Engineering and Computer Science, Program in Electrical and Computer Engineering

Programs Awards MS. Part-time and evening/weekend programs available.
Faculty 6 full-time, 1 part-time.
Students 26 full-time (5 women), 48 part-time (8 women); includes 7 minority (4 African-Americans, 2 Asian-Americans, 1 Hispanic), 15 international. Average age 29.
Degrees Awarded In 1996, 16 degrees awarded.
Entrance Requirements Minimum GPA of 3.0 for unconditional admission.
Financial Aid Full tuition waivers, Federal Work-Study, institutionally sponsored loans available. *Financial aid application deadline:* 3/1; applicants required to submit FAFSA.
Applying 38 applicants, 74% accepted. *Deadline:* 7/15 (3/15 for spring admission). *Fee:* $30.

Contact *Dr. Naim A. Kheir*
Chair
248-370-2245

UNIVERSITY OF DETROIT MERCY
Detroit, MI 48219-0900

OVERVIEW
University of Detroit Mercy is an independent-religious coed university.

EXPENSES
Tuition $468 per credit hour. Fees $230 per year full-time, $75 per semester part-time.

HOUSING
Rooms and/or apartments available to single and married students.

FACILITIES
Library: Main library. *Special:* In arts and humanities: Folklore archives. In science and engineering: Manufacturing Institute, magnetic resonance laboratory, automotive electronics laboratory, Polymer Institute, Center for Excellence in Environmental Engineering and Science. In social sciences: Center for the Study of Development and Aging, Institute for Business and Community Services, Kellstadt Consumer Research Center, child psychodiagnostic clinic, psychology clinic.

COMPUTER SCIENCE

College of Engineering and Science, Department of Mathematics and Computer Science, Program in Computer Science
Programs Awards MSCS. Evening/weekend programs available.
Entrance Requirements Minimum GPA of 3.0.
Degree Requirements Computer language required, foreign language not required.
Applying *Deadline:* 8/1 (priority date; rolling processing). *Fee:* $25 ($35 for international students).

See in-depth description on page 629.

ELECTRICAL ENGINEERING

College of Engineering and Science, Department of Electrical Engineering
Programs Awards ME, DE. Evening/weekend programs available.
Faculty Research Electromagnetics, computer architecture, systems.
Degree Requirements For master's, computer language required, foreign language not required; for doctorate, dissertation.
Applying *Deadline:* 8/1 (priority date; rolling processing). *Fee:* $25 ($35 for international students).

See in-depth description on page 627.

UNIVERSITY OF MICHIGAN
Ann Arbor, MI 48109

OVERVIEW
University of Michigan is a public coed university.

ENROLLMENT
36,450 graduate, professional, and undergraduate students; 14,975 matriculated graduate/professional students (6,285 women).

GRADUATE FACULTY
2,678 (589 women); includes 398 minority (131 African-Americans, 206 Asian-Americans, 53 Hispanics, 8 Native Americans).

EXPENSES
Tuition $9822 per year full-time, $2717 per semester part-time for state residents; $19,930 per year full-time, $5522 per semester part-time for nonresidents. Fees $184 per year full-time, $46 per year part-time.

HOUSING
Rooms and/or apartments available to single students (750 units) and married students (1,650 units). Graduate housing contact: Housing Information Office, 313-763-3164.

STUDENT SERVICES
Disabled student services, multicultural affairs office, low-cost health insurance, career counseling, free psychological counseling, exercise/wellness program, campus safety program, campus employment opportunities, international student services, writing training, grant writing training, teacher training.

FACILITIES
Library: Hatcher Graduate Library plus 35 additional on-campus libraries. Access provided to on-line information retrieval services. *Computer:* Campuswide network is available with full Internet access. *Special:* In arts and humanities: Eva Jessye Afro-American Music Collection, Kelsey Museum of Archaeology, art museum, William Clements Library, Gerald Ford Library, Bentley Historical Library. In science and engineering: Biological station, Institute for Science and Technology, Phoenix Memorial Laboratory, Kresge Hearing and Research Institute, Matthaei Botanical Gardens. In social sciences: Institute for Social Research, Mental Health Research Institute, Institute for Public Policy Studies, Population Studies Center, Institute of Gerontology, Transportation Research Institute.

COMPUTER ENGINEERING

College of Engineering, Department of Electrical Engineering and Computer Science, Program in Computer Science and Engineering
Programs Awards MS, MSE, PhD.
Faculty 32 full-time (2 women), 1 part-time (0 women).
Faculty Research Computer architecture, programming languages, software engineering, artificial intelligence, VLSI. *Total annual research expenditures:* $7.322 million.
Students 213 full-time (27 women), includes 35 minority (9 African-Americans, 25 Asian-Americans, 1 Hispanic), 85 international.
Degrees Awarded In 1996, 50 master's, 25 doctorates awarded. Terminal master's awarded for partial completion of doctoral program.
Entrance Requirements For master's, GRE General Test (minimum combined score of 1900 on three sections; average 2062); for doctorate, GRE General Test (minimum combined score of 1900 on three sections; average 2062), master's degree.
Degree Requirements For doctorate, dissertation, oral defense of dissertation, preliminary exams.
Financial Aid In 1996–97, 150 students received aid, including 28 fellowships (4 to first-year students) averaging $1,280 per month,

89 research assistantships (8 to first-year students) averaging $1,280 per month, 33 teaching assistantships (7 to first-year students) averaging $1,280 per month. *Financial aid application deadline:* 1/15.
Applying 572 applicants, 41% accepted. *Deadline:* 1/15 (rolling processing). *Fee:* $55.
Contact *Toby Teorey*
Division Associate Chair
313-647-1807

See in-depth description on page **661.**

COMPUTER SCIENCE

College of Engineering, Department of Electrical Engineering and Computer Science, Program in Computer Science and Engineering
Programs Awards MS, MSE, PhD.
Faculty 32 full-time (2 women), 1 part-time (0 women).
Faculty Research Computer architecture, programming languages, software engineering, artificial intelligence, VLSI. *Total annual research expenditures:* $7.322 million.
Students 213 full-time (27 women), includes 35 minority (9 African-Americans, 25 Asian-Americans, 1 Hispanic), 85 international.
Degrees Awarded In 1996, 50 master's, 25 doctorates awarded. Terminal master's awarded for partial completion of doctoral program.
Entrance Requirements For master's, GRE General Test (minimum combined score of 1900 on three sections; average 2062); for doctorate, GRE General Test (minimum combined score of 1900 on three sections; average 2062), master's degree.
Degree Requirements For doctorate, dissertation, oral defense of dissertation, preliminary exams.
Financial Aid In 1996–97, 150 students received aid, including 28 fellowships (4 to first-year students) averaging $1,280 per month, 89 research assistantships (8 to first-year students) averaging $1,280 per month, 33 teaching assistantships (7 to first-year students) averaging $1,280 per month. *Financial aid application deadline:* 1/15.
Applying 572 applicants, 41% accepted. *Deadline:* 1/15 (rolling processing). *Fee:* $55.
Contact *Toby Teorey*
Division Associate Chair
313-647-1807

See in-depth description on page **661.**

ELECTRICAL ENGINEERING

College of Engineering, Department of Electrical Engineering and Computer Science, Program in Electrical Engineering
Programs Awards MS, MSE, PhD, EE.
Faculty 33 full-time (3 women).
Faculty Research Circuits, optics, VLSI, electromagnetics, solid-state. *Total annual research expenditures:* $18.6 million.
Students 254 full-time (28 women), includes 25 minority (9 African-Americans, 12 Asian-Americans, 3 Hispanics, 1 Native American), 150 international.
Degrees Awarded In 1996, 62 master's, 32 doctorates awarded. Terminal master's awarded for partial completion of doctoral program.
Entrance Requirements For master's, GRE General Test (minimum combined score of 1900 on three sections; average 1934); for doctorate, GRE General Test (minimum combined score of 1900 on three sections; average 1934), master's degree; for EE, GRE.
Degree Requirements For doctorate, dissertation, oral defense of dissertation, preliminary exams.
Financial Aid In 1996–97, 200 students received aid, including 49 fellowships (5 to first-year students) averaging $1,280 per month, 130 research assistantships (11 to first-year students) averaging $1,280

per month, 21 teaching assistantships (8 to first-year students) averaging $1,280 per month. *Financial aid application deadline:* 1/15.
Applying 359 applicants, 62% accepted. *Deadline:* 1/15 (rolling processing). *Fee:* $55.
Contact *T. B. A. Senior*
Division Associate Chair
313-764-2390

See in-depth description on page **661.**

UNIVERSITY OF MICHIGAN–DEARBORN
Dearborn, MI 48128-1491

OVERVIEW
University of Michigan–Dearborn is a public coed comprehensive institution.

ENROLLMENT
8,324 graduate, professional, and undergraduate students; 43 full-time matriculated graduate/professional students (17 women), 1,537 part-time matriculated graduate/professional students (591 women).

GRADUATE FACULTY
79; includes 27 minority (4 African-Americans, 22 Asian-Americans, 1 Hispanic).

EXPENSES
Tuition $4320 per year full-time, $240 per credit hour part-time for state residents; $12,492 per year full-time, $694 per credit hour part-time for nonresidents. Fees $160 per year (minimum) for state residents; $160 per year full-time, $160 per year (minimum) part-time for nonresidents.

HOUSING
On-campus housing not available.

STUDENT SERVICES
Disabled student services, low-cost health insurance, career counseling, free psychological counseling, exercise/wellness program, day-care facilities, campus safety program, campus employment opportunities, international student services, writing training, teacher training.

FACILITIES
Library: Mardigian Library; total holdings of 306,000 volumes, 1,150 current periodical subscriptions. Access provided to on-line information retrieval services. *Computer:* Campuswide network is available with full Internet access. Total number of PCs/terminals supplied for student use: 1,100. Computer service fees are applied as a separate charge. *Special:* In arts and humanities: Armenian Research Center, Henry Ford Estate Natural Area. In science and engineering: CAD/CAM/CAE and robotics laboratory, machine vision laboratory, chemistry manufacturing systems engineering laboratory.

COMPUTER ENGINEERING

School of Engineering, Department of Electrical Engineering
Programs Offerings include computer engineering (MSE).
Department Faculty 11 full-time (1 woman), 10 part-time (1 woman).

Entrance Requirements Bachelor's degree in electrical and computer engineering or equivalent, minimum GPA of 3.0.

Degree Requirements Computer language required, thesis optional, foreign language not required.

Applying *Deadline:* 8/1 (rolling processing). *Fee:* $55.

Contact *Karen Claiborne*
Administrative Assistant I
313-593-5420
Fax: 313-593-9967
E-mail: karen@umdsun2.umd.umich.edu

COMPUTER SCIENCE

School of Engineering, Department of Computer and Information Science

Programs Awards MS. Part-time and evening/weekend programs available.

Faculty 9 full-time (0 women), 2 part-time (0 women).

Faculty Research Object-oriented computing, geometric modelling (rapid prototyping), computer controlled systems.

Students 5 full-time (2 women), 86 part-time (17 women); includes 20 minority (5 African-Americans, 14 Asian-Americans, 1 Hispanic), 7 international. Average age 29.

Degrees Awarded In 1996, 9 degrees awarded.

Entrance Requirements Bachelor's degree in applied mathematics, computer science, engineering, or physical science; minimum GPA of 3.0.

Degree Requirements Computer language required, thesis optional, foreign language not required.

Financial Aid In 1996–97, 1 research assistantship (to a first-year student) was awarded.

Applying 54 applicants, 80% accepted. *Deadline:* 6/15 (rolling processing). *Fee:* $55.

Contact *Mary Tamsen*
Graduate Secretary
313-436-9145
Fax: 313-593-9967
E-mail: mtamsen@umdsun2.umd.umich.edu

ELECTRICAL ENGINEERING

School of Engineering, Department of Electrical Engineering

Programs Offers programs in computer engineering (MSE), electrical engineering (MSE). Part-time programs available.

Faculty 11 full-time (1 woman), 10 part-time (1 woman).

Faculty Research Process control, fuzzy systems design, machine vision image processing and pattern recognition.

Students 5 full-time (1 woman), 87 part-time (15 women); includes 19 minority (5 African-Americans, 11 Asian-Americans, 3 Hispanics), 2 international. Average age 29.

Degrees Awarded In 1996, 44 degrees awarded.

Entrance Requirements Bachelor's degree in electrical and computer engineering or equivalent, minimum GPA of 3.0.

Degree Requirements Computer language required, thesis optional, foreign language not required.

Financial Aid In 1996–97, 5 research assistantships averaging $800 per month and totaling $48,000, 2 teaching assistantships averaging $800 per month and totaling $19,200 were awarded; fellowships, Federal Work-Study also available.

Applying 34 applicants, 100% accepted. *Deadline:* 8/1 (rolling processing). *Fee:* $55.

Contact *Karen Claiborne*
Administrative Assistant I
313-593-5420
Fax: 313-593-9967
E-mail: karen@umdsun2.umd.umich.edu

INFORMATION SCIENCE

School of Engineering, Department of Computer and Information Science

Programs Awards MS. Part-time and evening/weekend programs available.

Faculty 9 full-time (0 women), 2 part-time (0 women).

Faculty Research Object-oriented computing, geometric modelling (rapid prototyping), computer controlled systems.

Students 5 full-time (2 women), 86 part-time (17 women); includes 20 minority (5 African-Americans, 14 Asian-Americans, 1 Hispanic), 7 international. Average age 29.

Degrees Awarded In 1996, 9 degrees awarded.

Entrance Requirements Bachelor's degree in applied mathematics, computer science, engineering, or physical science; minimum GPA of 3.0.

Degree Requirements Computer language required, thesis optional, foreign language not required.

Financial Aid In 1996–97, 1 research assistantship (to a first-year student) was awarded.

Applying 54 applicants, 80% accepted. *Deadline:* 6/15 (rolling processing). *Fee:* $55.

Contact *Mary Tamsen*
Graduate Secretary
313-436-9145
Fax: 313-593-9967
E-mail: mtamsen@umdsun2.umd.umich.edu

WAYNE STATE UNIVERSITY
Detroit, MI 48202

OVERVIEW

Wayne State University is a public coed university.

ENROLLMENT

31,185 graduate, professional, and undergraduate students; 4,898 full-time matriculated graduate/professional students (2,454 women), 6,404 part-time matriculated graduate/professional students (3,504 women).

GRADUATE FACULTY

1,872.

EXPENSES

Tuition $159 per credit hour for state residents; $341 per credit hour for nonresidents. Fees $138 per year.

HOUSING

Rooms and/or apartments available to single students (750 units) and married students (300 units). Graduate housing contact: Housing Office, 313-577-2116.

STUDENT SERVICES

Low-cost health insurance, career counseling, free psychological counseling, day-care facilities, international student services.

FACILITIES

Library: Purdy/Kresge Library plus 5 additional on-campus libraries; total holdings of 2.96 million volumes, 3.4 million microforms, 24,691 current periodical subscriptions. Access provided to on-line information retrieval services. *Computer:* Campuswide network is available with full Internet access. Computer services are offered at no charge. *Special:* In arts and humanities: Humanities Center, Center for Arts and Public Policy, Legal Studies Center, African-American Film Institute. In science and engineering: Addiction Research Institute, Institute of Gerontology, Institute of Chemical Toxicology, Bioengineering Center, Center for Molecular Medicine and Genetics. In social sciences: Reuther Archives of Labor and Urban Affairs, Merrill-Palmer Institute for Human and Family Development, Center for Urban Studies, Center for Chicago-Boricua Studies.

COMPUTER ENGINEERING

College of Engineering, Interdisciplinary Program in Electronics and Computer Control Systems
Programs Awards MS.
Students 26 full-time (5 women), 76 part-time (11 women).
Degrees Awarded In 1996, 65 degrees awarded.
Degree Requirements Thesis optional, foreign language not required.
Applying 38 applicants, 50% accepted. *Deadline:* 7/1 (priority date; rolling processing; 3/15 for spring admission). *Fee:* $20 ($30 for international students).
Contact *Dr. Donald Silversmith*
Associate Dean
313-577-3861

COMPUTER ENGINEERING

College of Engineering, Department of Electrical and Computer Engineering, Program in Computer Engineering
Programs Awards MS, PhD.
Faculty 11 full-time (0 women), 8 part-time (1 woman).
Faculty Research Neural networks, parallel processing, pattern recognition, VLSI, computer architecture.
Students 74 full-time (20 women), 43 part-time (13 women).
Degrees Awarded In 1996, 73 master's, 3 doctorates awarded.
Degree Requirements For master's, thesis optional, foreign language not required; for doctorate, dissertation required, foreign language not required.
Financial Aid *Application deadline:* 3/16.
Applying 110 applicants, 51% accepted. *Deadline:* 7/1 (priority date; rolling processing; 3/15 for spring admission). *Fee:* $20 ($30 for international students).
Contact *Dr. Pepe Siy*
Graduate Committee Chair
313-577-3841
Fax: 313-577-1101

See in-depth description on page **763.**

COMPUTER SCIENCE

College of Science, Department of Computer Science
Programs Offers programs in computer science (MA, MS, PhD), electronics and computer control systems (MS).
Faculty 21.
Faculty Research Neural computation, artificial intelligence, software engineering, distributed systems, databases. *Total annual research expenditures:* $391,330.
Students 62 full-time (25 women), 138 part-time (56 women).
Degrees Awarded In 1996, 94 master's, 7 doctorates awarded.
Entrance Requirements For master's, TOEFL (minimum score 550), GRE General Test (minimum combined score of 1700 on three sections); for doctorate, TOEFL (minimum score 550), GRE General Test (minimum combined score of 1800 on three sections).
Degree Requirements For master's, computer language, thesis (for some programs) required, foreign language not required; for doctorate, computer language, dissertation required, foreign language not required.

Financial Aid In 1996–97, 1 fellowship averaging $950 per month, 25 teaching assistantships averaging $1,150 per month were awarded; research assistantships, Federal Work-Study, and career-related internships or fieldwork also available.
Applying 371 applicants, 28% accepted. *Deadline:* 7/1. *Fee:* $20 ($30 for international students).
Contact *Dr. Robert Reynolds*
Associate Professor
313-577-2477
Fax: 313-577-6868
E-mail: reynolds@cs.wayne.edu

See in-depth description on page **761.**

ELECTRICAL ENGINEERING

College of Engineering, Interdisciplinary Program in Electronics and Computer Control Systems
Programs Awards MS.
Students 26 full-time (5 women), 76 part-time (11 women).
Degrees Awarded In 1996, 65 degrees awarded.
Degree Requirements Thesis optional, foreign language not required.
Applying 38 applicants, 50% accepted. *Deadline:* 7/1 (priority date; rolling processing; 3/15 for spring admission). *Fee:* $20 ($30 for international students).
Contact *Dr. Donald Silversmith*
Associate Dean
313-577-3861

ELECTRICAL ENGINEERING

College of Engineering, Department of Electrical and Computer Engineering, Program in Electrical Engineering
Programs Awards MS, PhD.
Faculty 25 full-time (2 women), 8 part-time (0 women).
Faculty Research Biomedical systems, control systems, solid state materials, optical materials, hybrid vehicle.
Students 85 full-time (6 women), 70 part-time (11 women).
Degrees Awarded In 1996, 29 master's, 8 doctorates awarded.
Degree Requirements For master's, thesis optional, foreign language not required; for doctorate, dissertation required, foreign language not required.
Financial Aid *Application deadline:* 3/16.
Applying 357 applicants, 52% accepted. *Deadline:* 7/1 (priority date; rolling processing; 3/15 for spring admission). *Fee:* $20 ($30 for international students).
Contact *Dr. Pepe Siy*
Graduate Committee Chair
313-577-3841
Fax: 313-577-1101

See in-depth description on page **763.**

SOFTWARE ENGINEERING

College of Science, Department of Computer Science
Programs Offerings include electronics and computer control systems (MS).
Department Faculty 21.
Applying *Deadline:* 7/1. *Fee:* $20 ($30 for international students).
Contact *Dr. Robert Reynolds*
Associate Professor
313-577-2477
Fax: 313-577-6868
E-mail: reynolds@cs.wayne.edu

See in-depth description on page **761.**

WESTERN MICHIGAN UNIVERSITY
Kalamazoo, MI 49008

OVERVIEW
Western Michigan University is a public coed university.

ENROLLMENT
25,699 graduate, professional, and undergraduate students; 1,160 full-time matriculated graduate/professional students (677 women), 4,736 part-time matriculated graduate/professional students (2,847 women).

GRADUATE FACULTY
817 full-time (251 women), 414 part-time (235 women), 1,129 FTE; includes 136 minority (52 African-Americans, 61 Asian-Americans, 20 Hispanics, 3 Native Americans).

EXPENSES
Tuition $142 per credit hour for state residents; $345 per credit hour for nonresidents. Fees $578 per year.

HOUSING
Rooms and/or apartments available to single students at an average cost of $1747 per year ($4257 including board); available to married students (585 units) at an average cost of $3424 per year. Graduate housing contact: University Apartments Office, 800-882-9819.

STUDENT SERVICES
Low-cost health insurance, career counseling, free psychological counseling, day-care facilities, campus safety program, campus employment opportunities, international student services.

FACILITIES
Library: Waldo Library plus 3 additional on-campus libraries; total holdings of 3,440,181 volumes, 1,503,237 microforms, 6,619 current periodical subscriptions. A total of 288 personal computers in all libraries. Access provided to on-line information retrieval services. *Computer:* Campuswide network is available with full Internet access. Total number of PCs/terminals supplied for student use: 2,000. Computer service fees are included with tuition and fees. *Special:* In arts and humanities: Cistercian Studies Library, Dalton Center, regional history collection, Medieval Institute, music therapy clinic. In science and engineering: Institute for Water Sciences, geographic information systems, Paper Pilot Plant, Printing and Research Center, particle accelerator laboratory. In social sciences: Evaluation Center, Kercher Center for Social Research, Community Information System, Service Quality Institute.

COMPUTER ENGINEERING

College of Engineering and Applied Sciences, Department of Electrical Engineering and Computer Engineering
Programs Offers programs in computer engineering (MSE), electrical engineering (MSE). Part-time programs available.
Faculty Research Fiber optics, computer architecture, bioelectromagnetics, acoustics.
Students 3 full-time (0 women), 53 part-time (16 women); includes 2 minority (1 African-American, 1 Asian-American), 22 international.
Degrees Awarded In 1996, 7 degrees awarded.
Entrance Requirements Minimum GPA of 3.0.
Degree Requirements Thesis optional.

Financial Aid Fellowships, research assistantships, teaching assistantships, Federal Work-Study, and career-related internships or fieldwork available. *Financial aid application deadline:* 2/15; applicants required to submit FAFSA.
Applying 77 applicants, 56% accepted. *Deadline:* 2/15 (priority date; rolling processing). *Fee:* $25.
Contact *Paula J. Boodt*
Coordinator, Graduate Admissions and Recruitment
616-387-2000

COMPUTER SCIENCE

College of Arts and Sciences, Department of Computer Science
Programs Awards MS, PhD.
Students 33 full-time (12 women), 52 part-time (10 women); includes 4 minority (1 African-American, 3 Asian-Americans), 64 international.
Degrees Awarded In 1996, 27 master's awarded.
Entrance Requirements GRE General Test.
Degree Requirements For master's, oral exams required, thesis not required; for doctorate, dissertation.
Financial Aid Fellowships, research assistantships, teaching assistantships, institutionally sponsored loans, and career-related internships or fieldwork available. *Financial aid application deadline:* 2/15; applicants required to submit FAFSA.
Applying 144 applicants, 38% accepted. *Deadline:* 2/15 (priority date; rolling processing). *Fee:* $25.
Contact *Paula J. Boodt*
Coordinator, Graduate Admissions and Recruitment
616-387-2000

COMPUTER SCIENCE

College of Arts and Sciences, Department of Mathematics and Statistics
Programs Offerings include graph theory and computer science (PhD).
Entrance Requirements GRE General Test.
Degree Requirements 1 foreign language, dissertation.
Applying *Deadline:* 2/15 (priority date; rolling processing). *Fee:* $25.
Contact *Paula J. Boodt*
Coordinator, Graduate Admissions and Recruitment
616-387-2000

ELECTRICAL ENGINEERING

College of Engineering and Applied Sciences, Department of Electrical Engineering and Computer Engineering
Programs Offers programs in computer engineering (MSE), electrical engineering (MSE). Part-time programs available.
Faculty Research Fiber optics, computer architecture, bioelectromagnetics, acoustics.
Students 3 full-time (0 women), 53 part-time (16 women); includes 2 minority (1 African-American, 1 Asian-American), 22 international.
Degrees Awarded In 1996, 7 degrees awarded.
Entrance Requirements Minimum GPA of 3.0.
Degree Requirements Thesis optional.
Financial Aid Fellowships, research assistantships, teaching assistantships, Federal Work-Study, and career-related internships or fieldwork available. *Financial aid application deadline:* 2/15; applicants required to submit FAFSA.
Applying 77 applicants, 56% accepted. *Deadline:* 2/15 (priority date; rolling processing). *Fee:* $25.
Contact *Paula J. Boodt*
Coordinator, Graduate Admissions and Recruitment
616-387-2000

MINNESOTA

COLLEGE OF ST. SCHOLASTICA
Duluth, MN 55811-4199

OVERVIEW
College of St. Scholastica is an independent-religious coed comprehensive institution.

ENROLLMENT
2,089 graduate, professional, and undergraduate students; 212 full-time matriculated graduate/professional students (147 women), 415 part-time matriculated graduate/professional students (315 women).

GRADUATE FACULTY
28 full-time, 18 part-time.

TUITION
$2480 per year full-time, $310 per credit part-time.

HOUSING
Rooms and/or apartments available to single students at an average cost of $2163 per year ($4164 including board); on-campus housing not available to married students. Graduate housing contact: Linda Olcott, 218-723-6483.

STUDENT SERVICES
Disabled student services, career counseling, free psychological counseling, day-care facilities, campus safety program, campus employment opportunities, international student services.

FACILITIES
Library: Total holdings of 99,518 volumes, 1,147 microforms, 800 current periodical subscriptions. A total of 27 personal computers in all libraries. Access provided to on-line information retrieval services. *Computer:* Campuswide network is available with full Internet access. Total number of PCs/terminals supplied for student use: 110. Computer service fees are included with tuition and fees.

MEDICAL INFORMATICS

Program in Health Information Management
Programs   Awards MA. Part-time programs available.
Faculty   1 (woman) full-time, 3 part-time (all women).
Financial Aid   Available to part-time students. Financial aid applicants required to submit FAFSA.
Applying   *Fee:* $50.
Contact   Shirley Eichenwald
Admissions Office
218-723-6448
Fax: 218-733-2239
E-mail: seichenw@css.edu

MANKATO STATE UNIVERSITY
Mankato, MN 56002-8400

OVERVIEW
Mankato State University is a public coed comprehensive institution.

ENROLLMENT
11,366 graduate, professional, and undergraduate students; 1,018 full-time matriculated graduate/professional students (613 women), 824 part-time matriculated graduate/professional students (568 women).

GRADUATE FACULTY
394 full-time (131 women), 24 part-time (11 women); includes 18 minority.

TUITION
$92 per credit (minimum) for state residents; $137 per credit for nonresidents.

HOUSING
Rooms and/or apartments available to single students at an average cost of $2228 per year ($3313 including board); on-campus housing not available to married students. Housing application deadline: 4/1. Graduate housing contact: Residential Life Office, 507-389-1011.

STUDENT SERVICES
Disabled student services, multicultural affairs office, low-cost health insurance, career counseling, free psychological counseling, day-care facilities, campus safety program, campus employment opportunities, international student services.

FACILITIES
Library: Memorial Library; total holdings of 825,000 volumes, 225,000 microforms, 3,500 current periodical subscriptions. A total of 90 personal computers in all libraries. Access provided to on-line information retrieval services. *Computer:* Campuswide network is available with full Internet access. *Special:* In arts and humanities: Performing Arts Center, Conkling Art Gallery. In science and engineering: Biotechnology Research Center, Trafton Science Center, microelectronics clean room laboratory, Andreas and Standeford Astronomy Observatories, Water Resource Center. In social sciences: Urban Studies Institute, weather laboratory.

COMPUTER SCIENCE

College of Science, Engineering and Technology, Department of Computer Science
Programs   Awards MS.
Faculty   13 full-time (2 women).
Students   11 full-time (1 woman), 2 part-time (0 women); includes 7 international. Average age 29.
Degrees Awarded   In 1996, 3 degrees awarded.
Entrance Requirements   GRE General Test (minimum combined score of 1500 on three sections), minimum GPA of 3.0 during previous 2 years.
Degree Requirements   Thesis or alternative, comprehensive exam.
Financial Aid   Teaching assistantships available. *Financial aid application deadline:* 3/15; applicants required to submit FAFSA.
Applying   26 applicants, 50% accepted. *Deadline:* 8/6 (priority date; rolling processing; 2/10 for spring admission). *Fee:* $20.
Contact   Joni Roberts
Admissions Coordinator
507-389-2321
Fax: 501-389-5974

COMPUTER SCIENCE

College of Science, Engineering and Technology, Department of Mathematics and Statistics, Program in Computers
Programs   Offers mathematics: computer science (MS).

Students 11 full-time (0 women), 2 part-time (0 women); includes 7 international. Average age 30.

Degrees Awarded In 1996, 3 degrees awarded.

Entrance Requirements GRE General Test, GRE Subject Test, minimum GPA of 3.0 during previous 2 years.

Degree Requirements 1 foreign language, computer language, thesis or alternative, comprehensive exam.

Financial Aid Fellowships, research assistantships, teaching assistantships, Federal Work-Study, institutionally sponsored loans available. Aid available to part-time students. *Financial aid application deadline:* 3/15; applicants required to submit FAFSA.

Applying 26 applicants, 50% accepted. *Deadline:* 8/6 (priority date; rolling processing; 2/10 for spring admission). *Fee:* $20.

Contact *Joni Roberts*
Admissions Coordinator
507-389-2321
Fax: 501-389-5974

ELECTRICAL ENGINEERING

College of Science, Engineering and Technology, Program in Electrical Engineering and Electronic Engineering Technology

Programs Awards MSE. Program new for fall 1997.

Faculty 9 full-time (0 women).

Entrance Requirements GRE General Test, minimum GPA of 3.0 during previous 2 years.

Degree Requirements Thesis, comprehensive exam.

Financial Aid *Application deadline:* 3/15.

Applying *Deadline:* 8/6 (priority date; rolling processing; 2/10 for spring admission). *Fee:* $20.

Contact *Joni Roberts*
Admissions Coordinator
507-389-2321
Fax: 501-389-5974

STUDENT SERVICES

Low-cost health insurance, career counseling, day-care facilities, campus safety program, campus employment opportunities, international student services.

FACILITIES

Library: Centennial Hall Learning Resource Center; total holdings of 2.025 million volumes, 1,850,030 microforms, 2,000 current periodical subscriptions. A total of 50 personal computers in all libraries. Access provided to on-line information retrieval services. *Computer:* Campuswide network is available with full Internet access. Computer service fees are included with tuition and fees.

COMPUTER SCIENCE

College of Science and Technology, Department of Computer Science

Programs Awards MS.

Faculty 13 full-time (2 women), 1 (woman) part-time.

Students 2 full-time (0 women), 1 (woman) part-time.

Degrees Awarded In 1996, 1 degree awarded.

Entrance Requirements GRE General Test, minimum GPA of 2.75.

Degree Requirements Thesis or alternative required, foreign language not required.

Financial Aid In 1996–97, 3 graduate assistantships were awarded. *Financial aid application deadline:* 3/1.

Applying *Fee:* $20 ($100 for international students).

Contact *Dr. James Howatt*
Chairperson
320-255-4966

ST. CLOUD STATE UNIVERSITY
St. Cloud, MN 56301-4498

OVERVIEW

St. Cloud State University is a public coed comprehensive institution.

ENROLLMENT

13,994 graduate, professional, and undergraduate students; 332 full-time matriculated graduate/professional students (202 women), 352 part-time matriculated graduate/professional students (238 women).

GRADUATE FACULTY

466 full-time (154 women), 92 part-time (35 women); includes 51 minority (16 African-Americans, 25 Asian-Americans, 6 Hispanics, 4 Native Americans).

TUITION

$93 per credit for state residents; $130 per credit for nonresidents.

HOUSING

Rooms and/or apartments available to single students at an average cost of $1215 per year ($2620 including board); on-campus housing not available to married students. Graduate housing contact: Michael Hayman, 320-255-2166.

UNIVERSITY OF MINNESOTA, DULUTH
Duluth, MN 55812-2496

OVERVIEW

University of Minnesota, Duluth is a public coed comprehensive institution.

ENROLLMENT

7,348 graduate, professional, and undergraduate students; 403 full-time matriculated graduate/professional students (240 women), 173 part-time matriculated graduate/professional students (95 women).

GRADUATE FACULTY

194 full-time (42 women), 53 part-time (16 women); includes 17 minority (1 African-American, 10 Asian-Americans, 6 Native Americans).

EXPENSES

Tuition $4980 per year full-time, $290 per credit part-time for state residents; $9780 per year full-time, $520 per credit part-time for nonresidents. Fees $507 per year.

HOUSING

Rooms and/or apartments available to single students at an average cost of $1810 per year ($4105 including board); on-campus housing not available to married students. Housing application deadline: 3/1. Graduate housing information: 218-726-8178.

STUDENT SERVICES

Low-cost health insurance, career counseling, day-care facilities, campus employment opportunities, international student services.

FACILITIES

Library: Main library plus 3 additional on-campus libraries; total holdings of 412,600 volumes, 375,200 microforms, 3,018 current periodical subscriptions. A total of 193 personal computers in all libraries. Access provided to on-line information retrieval services. *Computer:* Campuswide network is available with full Internet access. Total number of PCs/terminals supplied for student use: 380. Computer service fees are included with tuition and fees. *Special:* In arts and humanities: Tweed Musuem of Art, Marshall Performing Arts Center. In science and engineering: Natural Resources Research Institute, Sea Grant Program, cartography laboratory, clinical biochemistry and toxicology laboratory, remote sensing laboratory, Large Lakes Observatory. In social sciences: Small Business Development Center, Alworth Institute for International Studies.

COMPUTER SCIENCE

Graduate School, College of Science and Engineering, Department of Computer Science

Programs Awards MS. Part-time programs available.
Faculty 8 full-time (1 woman).
Faculty Research Software engineering, information retrieval, user-system interfaces, neural networks, artificial intelligence. *Total annual research expenditures:* $64,008.
Students 17 full-time (3 women), 2 part-time (0 women); includes 15 international. Average age 27.
Degrees Awarded In 1996, 6 degrees awarded (100% found work related to degree).
Entrance Requirements GRE General Test (minimum combined score of 1790 on three sections; average 2010), TOEFL (minimum score 600; average 620), minimum GPA of 3.0.
Degree Requirements Computer language, thesis (for some programs) required, foreign language not required.
Financial Aid In 1996–97, 13 students received aid, including 1 fellowship averaging $487 per month and totaling $3,000, 3 research assistantships (2 to first-year students) averaging $919 per month and totaling $27,040, 9 teaching assistantships (5 to first-year students) averaging $919 per month and totaling $81,121; partial tuition waivers, institutionally sponsored loans also available. *Financial aid application deadline:* 3/15.
Applying 52 applicants, 75% accepted. *Deadline:* 7/15 (rolling processing; 1/15 for spring admission). *Fee:* $40 ($50 for international students).
Contact Dr. Carolyn J. Crouch
Director of Graduate Studies
218-726-7607
E-mail: cs@d.umn.edu

UNIVERSITY OF MINNESOTA, TWIN CITIES CAMPUS
Minneapolis, MN 55455-0213

OVERVIEW

University of Minnesota, Twin Cities Campus is a public coed university.

ENROLLMENT

37,018 graduate, professional, and undergraduate students; 11,793 matriculated graduate/professional students.

GRADUATE FACULTY

3,200.

EXPENSES

Tuition $4980 per year full-time, $750 per quarter (minimum) part-time for state residents; $9780 per year full-time, $1440 per quarter (minimum) part-time for nonresidents. Fees $474 per year.

HOUSING

Rooms and/or apartments available to single students at an average cost of $4500 (including board); available to married students at an average cost of $5150 per year. Graduate housing contact: Mary Ann Ryan, 612-624-1499.

STUDENT SERVICES

Disabled student services, multicultural affairs office, low-cost health insurance, career counseling, free psychological counseling, exercise/wellness program, day-care facilities, campus safety program, campus employment opportunities, international student services, writing training, grant writing training, teacher training.

FACILITIES

Library: O. Meredith Wilson Library plus 17 additional on-campus libraries; total holdings of 5.376 million volumes, 5.243 million microforms, 48,000 current periodical subscriptions. Access provided to on-line information retrieval services. *Special:* In arts and humanities: Weisman Art Museum, Center for European Studies, Center for Medieval Studies, Immigration History Research Center. In science and engineering: Center for Interfacial Engineering, Institute for Mathematics and Applications, Minnesota Landscape Arboretum, Lake Itasca Forestry and Biological Station. In social sciences: Center for Philosophy of Science, Center for Feminist Studies, Center for Youth Development.

COMPUTER ENGINEERING

Institute of Technology, Department of Electrical and Computer Engineering

Programs Awards MEE, MSEE, PhD. Part-time programs available.
Faculty 46 full-time (2 women), 1 part-time (0 women).
Faculty Research Signal processing, microelectronics, computers, controls, power electronics. *Total annual research expenditures:* $7 million.
Students 184 full-time (21 women), 74 part-time (9 women); includes 17 minority (all Asian-Americans), 125 international.
Degrees Awarded In 1996, 78 master's, 23 doctorates awarded.
Entrance Requirements TOEFL (minimum score 550).
Degree Requirements For master's, thesis or alternative required, foreign language not required; for doctorate, dissertation required, foreign language not required.
Financial Aid In 1996–97, 7 fellowships, 103 research assistantships, 38 teaching assistantships were awarded; partial tuition waivers also available. *Financial aid application deadline:* 12/15.
Applying 516 applicants, 22% accepted. *Deadline:* 7/1 (rolling processing). *Fee:* $40 ($50 for international students).

Contact *Richard Kain*
Director of Graduate Studies
612-625-3564
Fax: 612-625-4583

See in-depth description on page 667.

COMPUTER ENGINEERING

Institute of Technology, Program in Computer Engineering
Programs Awards M Comp E, MS.
Entrance Requirements TOEFL (minimum score 550).
Degree Requirements Thesis or alternative required, foreign language not required.
Financial Aid Fellowships, research assistantships, teaching assistantships available. *Financial aid application deadline:* 12/15.
Applying *Deadline:* 7/1 (rolling processing). *Fee:* $40 ($50 for international students).
Contact *Director of Graduate Studies*
612-625-3300
Fax: 612-625-4583
E-mail: gradinfo@compeng.umn.edu

See in-depth description on page 663.

COMPUTER SCIENCE

Scientific Computation Program
Programs Awards MS, PhD.
Faculty Research Parallel computations, quantum mechanical dynamics, computational materials science, computational fluid dynamics.
Applying *Deadline:* 1/15 (priority date; rolling processing). *Fee:* $40 ($50 for international students).

COMPUTER SCIENCE

Institute of Technology, Department of Computer Science
Programs Offers program in computer and information sciences (MCIS, MS, PhD). Part-time programs available.
Faculty 31 full-time (3 women), 3 part-time (0 women).
Faculty Research Software systems, numerical analysis, theory, artificial intelligence, computer engineering. *Total annual research expenditures:* $3.5 million.
Students 86 full-time (15 women), 165 part-time (27 women); includes 15 minority (1 African-American, 12 Asian-Americans, 1 Hispanic, 1 Native American), 111 international.
Degrees Awarded In 1996, 55 master's awarded; 21 doctorates awarded (33% entered university research/teaching, 67% found other work related to degree). Terminal master's awarded for partial completion of doctoral program.
Entrance Requirements GRE General Test.
Degree Requirements For doctorate, dissertation.
Financial Aid In 1996–97, 109 students received aid, including 7 fellowships (5 to first-year students) averaging $1,300 per month, 64 research assistantships (11 to first-year students) averaging $1,150 per month, 46 teaching assistantships (14 to first-year students) averaging $1,150 per month; full and partial tuition waivers, Federal Work-Study, institutionally sponsored loans, and career-related internships or fieldwork also available. *Financial aid application deadline:* 1/2.
Applying 418 applicants, 56% accepted. *Deadline:* 5/31 (rolling processing). *Fee:* $40 ($50 for international students).
Contact *Jaideep Srivastava*
Director of Graduate Studies
612-625-4002
Fax: 612-625-0572
E-mail: dgs@cs.umn.edu

See in-depth description on page 665.

ELECTRICAL ENGINEERING

Institute of Technology, Department of Electrical and Computer Engineering
Programs Awards MEE, MSEE, PhD. Part-time programs available.
Faculty 46 full-time (2 women), 1 part-time (0 women).
Faculty Research Signal processing, microelectronics, computers, controls, power electronics. *Total annual research expenditures:* $7 million.
Students 184 full-time (21 women), 74 part-time (9 women); includes 17 minority (all Asian-Americans), 125 international.
Degrees Awarded In 1996, 78 master's, 23 doctorates awarded.
Entrance Requirements TOEFL (minimum score 550).
Degree Requirements For master's, thesis or alternative required, foreign language not required; for doctorate, dissertation required, foreign language not required.
Financial Aid In 1996–97, 7 fellowships, 103 research assistantships, 38 teaching assistantships were awarded; partial tuition waivers also available. *Financial aid application deadline:* 12/15.
Applying 516 applicants, 22% accepted. *Deadline:* 7/1 (rolling processing). *Fee:* $40 ($50 for international students).
Contact *Richard Kain*
Director of Graduate Studies
612-625-3564
Fax: 612-625-4583

See in-depth description on page 667.

INFORMATION SCIENCE

Institute of Technology, Department of Computer Science
Programs Offers program in computer and information sciences (MCIS, MS, PhD). Part-time programs available.
Faculty 31 full-time (3 women), 3 part-time (0 women).
Faculty Research Software systems, numerical analysis, theory, artificial intelligence, computer engineering. *Total annual research expenditures:* $3.5 million.
Students 86 full-time (15 women), 165 part-time (27 women); includes 15 minority (1 African-American, 12 Asian-Americans, 1 Hispanic, 1 Native American), 111 international.
Degrees Awarded In 1996, 55 master's awarded; 21 doctorates awarded (33% entered university research/teaching, 67% found other work related to degree). Terminal master's awarded for partial completion of doctoral program.
Entrance Requirements GRE General Test.
Degree Requirements For doctorate, dissertation.
Financial Aid In 1996–97, 109 students received aid, including 7 fellowships (5 to first-year students) averaging $1,300 per month, 64 research assistantships (11 to first-year students) averaging $1,150 per month, 46 teaching assistantships (14 to first-year students) averaging $1,150 per month; full and partial tuition waivers, Federal Work-Study, institutionally sponsored loans, and career-related internships or fieldwork also available. *Financial aid application deadline:* 1/2.
Applying 418 applicants, 56% accepted. *Deadline:* 5/31 (rolling processing). *Fee:* $40 ($50 for international students).
Contact *Jaideep Srivastava*
Director of Graduate Studies
612-625-4002
Fax: 612-625-0572
E-mail: dgs@cs.umn.edu

See in-depth description on page 665.

MEDICAL INFORMATICS

Program in Health Informatics
Programs Awards MS, PhD. Part-time programs available.
Faculty 15 full-time (5 women), 7 part-time (0 women).

Faculty Research Medical decision making, physiological control systems, population studies, clinical information systems, telemedicine.
Students 22 full-time (10 women), 14 part-time (7 women); includes 2 minority (1 Asian-American, 1 Hispanic), 10 international. Average age 37.
Degrees Awarded In 1996, 10 master's awarded (10% entered university research/teaching, 50% found other work related to degree, 40% continued full-time study); 1 doctorate awarded (100% found work related to degree).
Entrance Requirements For master's, GRE General Test, previous course work in calculus, linear algebra, life sciences, programming, and biology; for doctorate, GRE General Test, previous course work in life sciences, programming, and differential equations.
Degree Requirements For master's, thesis or alternative, project paper; for doctorate, dissertation.
Financial Aid In 1996–97, 22 students received aid, including 1 fellowship (to a first-year student), 9 research assistantships (2 to first-year students), 1 teaching assistantship, 11 grants, traineeships (2 to first-year students); full and partial tuition waivers, Federal Work-Study also available. *Financial aid application deadline: 1/15.*
Applying 32 applicants, 47% accepted. *Deadline:* 6/30 (rolling processing). *Fee:* $40 ($50 for international students).
Contact *Dr. Stanley Finkelstein*
Director
612-625-8440

UNIVERSITY OF ST. THOMAS
St. Paul, MN 55105-1096

OVERVIEW
University of St. Thomas is an independent-religious coed university.

HOUSING
On-campus housing not available.

FACILITIES
Library: O'Shaughnessy Frey Library plus 2 additional on-campus libraries.

SOFTWARE ENGINEERING

Graduate School of Applied Science and Engineering, Program in Software
Programs Awards MS, MSDD, Certificate. Part-time and evening/weekend programs available.
Faculty Research Distributed databases, fault tolerant computing, expert systems, object-oriented software.
Entrance Requirements For master's, TOEFL.
Degree Requirements For master's, computer language, thesis or alternative required, foreign language not required.
Applying *Deadline:* 8/15 (priority date; rolling processing; 1/15 for spring admission). *Fee:* $30.

MISSISSIPPI

ALCORN STATE UNIVERSITY
Lorman, MS 39096-9402

OVERVIEW
Alcorn State University is a public coed comprehensive institution.

TUITION
$2208 per year full-time, $335 per semester (minimum) part-time for state residents; $3460 per year full-time, $543 per semester (minimum) part-time for nonresidents.

HOUSING
Rooms and/or apartments available to single students; on-campus housing not available to married students. Graduate housing contact: Mr. Laplose Jackson, 601-877-6478.

FACILITIES
Library: J. D. Boyd Library.

COMPUTER SCIENCE

School of Arts and Sciences, Department of Mathematical Sciences
Programs Offers program in computer and information sciences (MS).
Applying *Deadline:* 7/1 (priority date; rolling processing; 12/1 for spring admission). *Fee:* $10.

INFORMATION SCIENCE

School of Arts and Sciences, Department of Mathematical Sciences
Programs Offers program in computer and information sciences (MS).
Applying *Deadline:* 7/1 (priority date; rolling processing; 12/1 for spring admission). *Fee:* $10.

JACKSON STATE UNIVERSITY
Jackson, MS 39217

OVERVIEW
Jackson State University is a public coed university.

TUITION
$2380 per year full-time, $132 per semester hour part-time for state residents; $4974 per year full-time, $276 per semester hour part-time for nonresidents.

HOUSING
Rooms and/or apartments available to single students; on-campus housing not available to married students. Graduate housing contact: Edward Curtis, 601-968-2326.

FACILITIES
Library: H. T. Sampson Library plus 1 additional on-campus library. *Special:* In arts and humanities: Margaret W. Alexander Research Center. In science and engineering: Electronics laboratory, environmental analysis laboratory, observatory, Academic Research and Computing Center, Urban Research Center.

COMPUTER SCIENCE

School of Science and Technology, Department of Computer Science
Programs Awards MS. Part-time and evening/weekend programs available.
Entrance Requirements GRE General Test.
Degree Requirements Computer language, thesis.

Applying *Deadline:* 3/1 (priority date; rolling processing; 10/1 for spring admission). *Fee:* $20.

MISSISSIPPI COLLEGE
Clinton, MS 39058

OVERVIEW
Mississippi College is an independent-religious coed comprehensive institution.

HOUSING
Rooms and/or apartments available to single students; on-campus housing not available to married students. Graduate housing contact: Dean of Students, 601-925-3248.

FACILITIES
Library: Leland Speed Library.

COMPUTER SCIENCE

College of Arts and Sciences, Department of Mathematics and Computer Science
Programs Offers programs in computer science (MS), mathematics (MS).
Entrance Requirements Minimum GPA of 2.5.
Degree Requirements Comprehensive exam.
Applying *Fee:* $25 ($75 for international students).

MISSISSIPPI STATE UNIVERSITY
Mississippi State, MS 39762

OVERVIEW
Mississippi State University is a public coed university.

ENROLLMENT
14,064 graduate, professional, and undergraduate students; 1,329 full-time matriculated graduate/professional students (560 women), 573 part-time matriculated graduate/professional students (271 women).

GRADUATE FACULTY
700 full-time, 98 part-time; includes 92 minority.

TUITION
$2731 per year full-time, $152 per credit hour part-time for state residents; $5551 per year full-time, $308 per credit hour part-time for nonresidents.

HOUSING
Rooms and/or apartments available to single students at an average cost of $1500 per year ($4100 including board); available to married students (268 units) at an average cost of $1575 per year. Housing application deadline: 8/1. Graduate housing contact: University Village Office, 601-325-2133.

STUDENT SERVICES
Disabled student services, multicultural affairs office, low-cost health insurance, career counseling, free psychological counseling, exercise/wellness program, day-care facilities, campus safety program, campus employment opportunities, international student services.

FACILITIES
Library: Mitchell Memorial Library plus 2 additional on-campus libraries; total holdings of 873,003 volumes, 2,107,709 microforms, 7,527 current periodical subscriptions. A total of 44 personal computers in all libraries. Access provided to on-line information retrieval services. *Computer:* Campuswide network is available with full Internet access. Total number of PCs/terminals supplied for student use: 3,000. Computer services are offered at no charge. *Special:* In arts and humanities: Center for Small Town Research and Design, Institute for the Humanities, Cobb Institute of Archaeology. In science and engineering: Center for Robotics, Automation, and Artificial Intelligence; Electron Microscope Center; Mississippi Energy Research Center; Mississippi State Chemical Laboratory; MSU/NSTL Research Center; Mississippi Technology Transfer Office; Radiological Safety Office; Water Resources Research Institute; Biological and Physical Science Research Institute; University/Industry Chemical Research Center; MHD Energy Center. In social sciences: Center for International Security and Strategic Studies, Social Science Research Center, Mississippi Alcohol Safety Education Program, Cobb Institute of Archaeology, John C. Stennis Institute of Government.

COMPUTER ENGINEERING

College of Engineering, Department of Electrical and Computer Engineering
Programs Offers programs in computer engineering (MS, PhD), electrical engineering (MS, PhD). Part-time and evening/weekend programs available.
Faculty 25 full-time.
Faculty Research Digital computing, power, controls, communication systems, microelectronics.
Students 60 full-time (15 women), 19 part-time (2 women); includes 7 minority (5 African-Americans, 2 Asian-Americans), 47 international. Average age 25.
Degrees Awarded In 1996, 38 master's, 4 doctorates awarded.
Entrance Requirements For master's, GRE General Test, TOEFL.
Degree Requirements For master's, comprehensive oral or written exam required, foreign language not required; for doctorate, computer language, dissertation, comprehensive oral or written exam required, foreign language not required.
Financial Aid In 1996–97, 2 fellowships, 21 research assistantships (18 to first-year students), 21 teaching assistantships (5 to first-year students) were awarded. *Financial aid application deadline:* 4/1.
Applying 132 applicants, 38% accepted. *Deadline:* 7/1 (priority date; rolling processing; 11/1 for spring admission). *Fee:* $0 ($25 for international students).
Contact *Dr. Franklin M. Ingels*
  Graduate Coordinator
  601-325-3912

See in-depth description on page 477.

COMPUTER SCIENCE

College of Engineering, Department of Computer Science
Programs Awards MCS, MS, PhD. Part-time programs available.
Faculty 16 full-time (5 women), 1 part-time (0 women).

Faculty Research Artificial intelligence, software engineering, computer architecture, visualization, parallel computing. *Total annual research expenditures:* $401,139.

Students 40 full-time (6 women), 11 part-time (4 women); includes 1 minority (African-American), 27 international. Average age 26.

Degrees Awarded In 1996, 17 master's, 1 doctorate awarded.

Entrance Requirements For master's, GRE General Test, TOEFL; for doctorate, TOEFL.

Degree Requirements For master's, comprehensive oral or written exam required, thesis optional, foreign language not required; for doctorate, 1 foreign language, dissertation, comprehensive oral or written exam.

Financial Aid In 1996–97, 36 students received aid, including 18 research assistantships (5 to first-year students) averaging $868 per month and totaling $140,600, 15 teaching assistantships (5 to first-year students) averaging $737 per month and totaling $99,624; fellowships, service assistantships, Federal Work-Study, and career-related internships or fieldwork also available. Aid available to part-time students. *Financial aid application deadline:* 4/1.

Applying 75 applicants, 71% accepted. *Deadline:* 4/1 (priority date; rolling processing; 11/15 for spring admission). *Fee:* $0 ($25 for international students).

Contact Dr. Susan M. Bridges
Graduate Coordinator
601-325-2756

See in-depth description on page **477.**

ELECTRICAL ENGINEERING

College of Engineering, Department of Electrical and Computer Engineering

Programs Offers programs in computer engineering (MS, PhD), electrical engineering (MS, PhD). Part-time and evening/weekend programs available.

Faculty 25 full-time.

Faculty Research Digital computing, power, controls, communication systems, microelectronics.

Students 60 full-time (15 women), 19 part-time (2 women); includes 7 minority (5 African-Americans, 2 Asian-Americans), 47 international. Average age 25.

Degrees Awarded In 1996, 38 master's, 4 doctorates awarded.

Entrance Requirements For master's, GRE General Test, TOEFL.

Degree Requirements For master's, comprehensive oral or written exam required, foreign language not required; for doctorate, computer language, dissertation, comprehensive oral or written exam required, foreign language not required.

Financial Aid In 1996–97, 2 fellowships, 21 research assistantships (18 to first-year students), 21 teaching assistantships (5 to first-year students) were awarded. *Financial aid application deadline:* 4/1.

Applying 132 applicants, 38% accepted. *Deadline:* 7/1 (priority date; rolling processing; 11/1 for spring admission). *Fee:* $0 ($25 for international students).

Contact Dr. Franklin M. Ingels
Graduate Coordinator
601-325-3912

See in-depth description on page **477.**

UNIVERSITY OF SOUTHERN MISSISSIPPI
Hattiesburg, MS 39406-5167

OVERVIEW

University of Southern Mississippi is a public coed university.

ENROLLMENT

13,657 graduate, professional, and undergraduate students; 1,236 full-time matriculated graduate/professional students (686 women), 934 part-time matriculated graduate/professional students (635 women).

GRADUATE FACULTY

462 full-time (141 women), 66 part-time (16 women); includes 31 minority (11 African-Americans, 15 Asian-Americans, 4 Hispanics, 1 Native American).

TUITION

$2590 per year full-time, $136 per credit hour part-time for state residents; $5410 per year full-time, $136 per credit hour part-time for nonresidents.

HOUSING

Rooms and/or apartments available to single students at an average cost of $2505 (including board); available to married students (296 units) at an average cost of $873 per year. Graduate housing contact: Resident Life Office, 601-266-4783.

STUDENT SERVICES

Disabled student services, career counseling, free psychological counseling, campus employment opportunities, international student services.

FACILITIES

Library: Cook Memorial Library plus 2 additional on-campus libraries; total holdings of 791,450 volumes, 2,275,141 microforms, 5,212 current periodical subscriptions. A total of 125 personal computers in all libraries. Access provided to on-line information retrieval services. *Special:* In science and engineering: Gulf Coast Research Laboratory, Automation and Robotics Application Center.

COMPUTER SCIENCE

College of Science and Technology, School of Mathematical Sciences, Department of Computer Science

Programs Awards MS.

Faculty 14 full-time (1 woman), 1 part-time (0 women).

Faculty Research Satellite telecommunications, advanced life-support systems, artificial intelligence.

Students 18 full-time (4 women), 11 part-time (8 women); includes 14 minority (1 African-American, 13 Asian-Americans), 14 international. Average age 32.

Degrees Awarded In 1996, 14 master's awarded.

Entrance Requirements For master's, GRE General Test (minimum combined score of 1000), TOEFL (minimum score 580), minimum GPA of 2.75.

Degree Requirements For master's, thesis or alternative, oral/written comprehensive exam required, foreign language not required.

Financial Aid Research assistantships, teaching assistantships, Federal Work-Study, institutionally sponsored loans available. *Financial aid application deadline:* 3/15.

Applying 43 applicants, 60% accepted. *Deadline:* 8/9 (priority date; rolling processing). *Fee:* $0 ($25 for international students).

Contact Dr. Frank Nagurney
Chair
601-266-4949

COMPUTER SCIENCE

College of Science and Technology, School of Mathematical Sciences, Program in Scientific Computing

Programs Awards PhD. Part-time programs available.

Faculty 6 part-time (0 women).

Students 13 full-time (3 women), 9 part-time (1 woman); includes 10 minority (2 African-Americans, 8 Asian-Americans), 8 international. Average age 33.

Degrees Awarded In 1996, 2 doctorates awarded. Terminal master's awarded for partial completion of doctoral program.

Entrance Requirements For doctorate, GRE General Test (minimum combined score of 1000), minimum GPA of 3.5.

Degree Requirements For doctorate, 2 foreign languages (computer language can substitute for one), dissertation, written comprehensive exam.

Financial Aid Teaching assistantships, Federal Work-Study, institutionally sponsored loans available. *Financial aid application deadline:* 3/15.

Applying 20 applicants, 95% accepted. *Deadline:* 8/9 (priority date; rolling processing). *Fee:* $0 ($25 for international students).

Contact *Dr. Grayson Rayborn*
Director
601-266-4739

MISSOURI

NORTHWEST MISSOURI STATE UNIVERSITY
Maryville, MO 64468-6001

OVERVIEW
Northwest Missouri State University is a public coed comprehensive institution.

ENROLLMENT
6,001 graduate, professional, and undergraduate students; 340 full-time matriculated graduate/professional students (245 women), 167 part-time matriculated graduate/professional students (113 women).

GRADUATE FACULTY
174 full-time (44 women).

EXPENSES
Tuition $105 per semester hour for state residents; $187 per semester hour for nonresidents. Fees $3 per semester hour.

HOUSING
Rooms and/or apartments available to single students at an average cost of $3690 (including board); on-campus housing not available to married students. Graduate housing contact: Wayne Viner, 816-562-1214.

STUDENT SERVICES
Low-cost health insurance, career counseling, free psychological counseling, campus safety program, campus employment opportunities, international student services.

FACILITIES
Library: B. D. Owens Library plus 1 additional on-campus library; total holdings of 352,792 volumes, 784,022 microforms, 1,462 current periodical subscriptions. A total of 80 personal computers in all libraries. Access provided to on-line information retrieval services. *Computer:* Campuswide network is available with full Internet access. Total number of PCs/terminals supplied for student use: 3,000. Computer service fees are applied as a separate charge. *Special:* In science and

engineering: Alternative Crops Center, Poultry Compost Research Center, Biomass Applied Research Center, Institute for Quality Productivity.

COMPUTER SCIENCE

College of Professional and Applied Studies, Department of Computer Science and Information Systems

Programs Offers program in school computer studies (MS). Part-time programs available.

Faculty 9 full-time (3 women).

Students 1 full-time (0 women), 1 (woman) part-time; includes 1 international.

Entrance Requirements GRE General Test (minimum combined score of 700), TOEFL (minimum score 550), minimum GPA of 3.0.

Degree Requirements Comprehensive exam required, foreign language and thesis not required.

Financial Aid In 1996–97, 1 research assistantship averaging $555 per month, 1 teaching assistantship averaging $555 per month were awarded. *Financial aid application deadline:* 3/1.

Applying 0 applicants. *Deadline:* rolling. *Fee:* $0 ($50 for international students).

Contact *Dr. Frances Shipley*
Dean of Graduate School
816-562-1145

UNIVERSITY OF MISSOURI–COLUMBIA
Columbia, MO 65211

OVERVIEW
University of Missouri–Columbia is a public coed university.

ENROLLMENT
22,483 graduate, professional, and undergraduate students; 3,117 full-time matriculated graduate/professional students (1,507 women), 2,201 part-time matriculated graduate/professional students (1,162 women).

GRADUATE FACULTY
1,911; includes 208 minority (50 African-Americans, 122 Asian-Americans, 30 Hispanics, 6 Native Americans).

TUITION
$3114 per year full-time, $173 per credit hour part-time for state residents; $8820 per year full-time, $490 per credit hour part-time for nonresidents.

HOUSING
Rooms and/or apartments available to single students (215 units) at an average cost of $4100 (including board); available to married students (322 units) at an average cost of $3700 per year. Graduate housing contact: Residential Life Office, 573-882-7275.

STUDENT SERVICES
Disabled student services, multicultural affairs office, career counseling, free psychological counseling, exercise/wellness program, day-care facilities, campus safety program, campus employment opportunities, international student services, writing training, grant writing training, teacher training.

FACILITIES

Library: Ellis Library plus 9 additional on-campus libraries; total holdings of 2.5 million volumes, 4.8 million microforms. Access provided to on-line information retrieval services. *Computer:* Campuswide network is available with full Internet access. Computer service fees are included with tuition and fees. *Special:* In arts and humanities: Museum of Art and Archaeology. In science and engineering: Dalton Research Reactor, Cardiovascular Research Center, Clinical Coordinating Center of the National Continuous Ambilatory Peritoneal Dialysis Registry, low-level radiation laboratory, research farms for agriculture and veterinary medicine. In social sciences: Center for Study of Aging, Business and Public Administration Research Center, Center for Advanced Social Research.

COMPUTER ENGINEERING

College of Engineering, Department of Computer Engineering and Computer Science

Programs Awards MS. Part-time programs available.
Faculty 8 full-time (0 women), 1 (woman) part-time.
Students 28 full-time (6 women), 23 part-time (5 women); includes 6 minority (1 African-American, 2 Asian-Americans, 3 Hispanics), 28 international.
Degrees Awarded In 1996, 15 degrees awarded.
Entrance Requirements GRE General Test, minimum GPA of 3.0.
Applying *Deadline:* 7/1 (priority date; rolling processing). *Fee:* $25 ($50 for international students).
Contact *Dr. Gordon Soringer*
Director of Graduate Studies
573-882-7422

See in-depth description on page 669.

COMPUTER SCIENCE

College of Engineering, Department of Computer Engineering and Computer Science

Programs Awards MS. Part-time programs available.
Faculty 8 full-time (0 women), 1 (woman) part-time.
Students 28 full-time (6 women), 23 part-time (5 women); includes 6 minority (1 African-American, 2 Asian-Americans, 3 Hispanics), 28 international.
Degrees Awarded In 1996, 15 degrees awarded.
Entrance Requirements GRE General Test, minimum GPA of 3.0.
Applying *Deadline:* 7/1 (priority date; rolling processing). *Fee:* $25 ($50 for international students).
Contact *Dr. Gordon Soringer*
Director of Graduate Studies
573-882-7422

See in-depth description on page 669.

ELECTRICAL ENGINEERING

College of Engineering, Department of Electrical Engineering
Programs Awards MS, PhD.
Faculty 30 full-time (1 woman).
Students 33 full-time (4 women), 56 part-time (6 women); includes 7 minority (3 African-Americans, 4 Asian-Americans), 74 international.
Degrees Awarded In 1996, 30 master's, 14 doctorates awarded.

Entrance Requirements For master's, GRE General Test, TOEFL, minimum GPA of 3.0; for doctorate, GRE General Test, GRE Subject Test, TOEFL, minimum GPA of 3.0.
Degree Requirements For master's, thesis or alternative required, foreign language not required; for doctorate, dissertation required, foreign language not required.
Applying *Deadline:* 7/1 (priority date; rolling processing). *Fee:* $25 ($50 for international students).
Contact *Dr. Kenneth Unklesbay*
Chair
573-882-2781
Fax: 573-882-0397
E-mail: unk@ece.missouri.edu

See in-depth description on page 671.

UNIVERSITY OF MISSOURI–KANSAS CITY
Kansas City, MO 64110-2499

OVERVIEW
University of Missouri–Kansas City is a public coed university.

ENROLLMENT
10,298 graduate, professional, and undergraduate students; 2,046 full-time matriculated graduate/professional students (972 women), 2,582 part-time matriculated graduate/professional students (1,639 women).

GRADUATE FACULTY
521 full-time (149 women), 240 part-time (101 women), 615.6 FTE; includes 31 minority (5 African-Americans, 21 Asian-Americans, 5 Hispanics).

EXPENSES
Tuition $176 per credit hour for state residents; $493 per credit hour for nonresidents. Fees $60 per year.

HOUSING
Rooms and/or apartments available to single students (325 units) at an average cost of $4000 (including board); on-campus housing not available to married students. Graduate housing contact: Residence Housing Office, 816-235-2800.

STUDENT SERVICES
Disabled student services, multicultural affairs office, career counseling, free psychological counseling, exercise/wellness program, day-care facilities, campus safety program, campus employment opportunities, international student services, writing training.

FACILITIES
Library: Miller Nichols Library plus 3 additional on-campus libraries; total holdings of 981,149 volumes, 1,841,946 microforms, 8,787 current periodical subscriptions. Access provided to on-line information retrieval services. *Computer:* Campuswide network is available with full Internet access. Total number of PCs/terminals supplied for student use: 440. Computer service fees are included with tuition and fees. *Special:* In arts and humanities: Institute for Studies in American Music, electronic music laboratory. In science and engineering: Laboratory Animal Center, Center for Underground Space Studies,

Drug Information Center, biopharmacokinetics laboratory, hormone research laboratory. In social sciences: Center for the Study of Metropolitan Problems in Education, Center for Labor Studies, Institute for Human Development.

COMPUTER SCIENCE

Program in Computer Science Telecommunications

Programs Offers computer networking (MS, PhD), software engineering (MS), telecommunications networking (MS, PhD). PhD offered through the School of Graduate Studies. Part-time programs available.

Faculty 15 full-time (1 woman).

Faculty Research Multimedia networking, distributed systems/databases, data/network security.

Students 46 full-time (7 women), 54 part-time (19 women); includes 11 minority (1 African-American, 9 Asian-Americans, 1 Hispanic), 63 international. Average age 29.

Degrees Awarded In 1996, 21 master's awarded.

Entrance Requirements For master's, GRE General Test (score in 75th percentile or higher on quantitative section required, 50th percentile or higher on verbal), minimum GPA of 3.0; for doctorate, GRE General Test (score in 85th percentile or higher on quantitative section required, 50th percentile or higher on verbal), minimum GPA of 3.5.

Degree Requirements For master's, computer language required, foreign language not required; for doctorate, computer language, dissertation required, foreign language not required.

Financial Aid In 1996–97, 15 research assistantships, 15 teaching assistantships were awarded; partial tuition waivers, Federal Work-Study, institutionally sponsored loans, and career-related internships or fieldwork also available. Aid available to part-time students. *Financial aid application deadline:* 3/1.

Applying 107 applicants, 62% accepted. *Deadline:* 3/1 (priority date; rolling processing; 10/1 for spring admission). *Fee:* $25.

Contact Dr. Richard Hetherington
Director
816-235-1193
Fax: 816-235-5159
E-mail: info@cstp.umkc.edu

See in-depth description on page **673.**

SOFTWARE ENGINEERING

Program in Computer Science Telecommunications

Programs Offerings include software engineering (MS).

Program Faculty 15 full-time (1 woman).

Entrance Requirements GRE General Test (score in 75th percentile or higher on quantitative section required, 50th percentile or higher on verbal), minimum GPA of 3.0.

Degree Requirements Computer language required, foreign language not required.

Applying *Deadline:* 3/1 (priority date; rolling processing; 10/1 for spring admission). *Fee:* $25.

Contact Dr. Richard Hetherington
Director
816-235-1193
Fax: 816-235-5159
E-mail: info@cstp.umkc.edu

See in-depth description on page **673.**

UNIVERSITY OF MISSOURI–ROLLA
Rolla, MO 65409

OVERVIEW
University of Missouri–Rolla is a public coed university.

EXPENSES
Tuition $3790 per year full-time, $158 per credit hour part-time for state residents; $11,398 per year full-time, $475 per credit hour part-time for nonresidents. Fees $579 per year (minimum) full-time, $115 per year (minimum) part-time.

HOUSING
Rooms and/or apartments available to single and married students. Graduate housing contact: James Murphy, 573-341-4218.

FACILITIES
Library: Curtis Laws Wilson Library. *Special:* In science and engineering: Graduate Center for Materials Research, Graduate Center for Cloud Physics Research, Rock Mechanics and Explosives Research Center, Institute for River Studies, Intelligent Systems Center.

COMPUTER SCIENCE

College of Arts and Sciences, Department of Computer Science

Programs Awards MS, PhD. Part-time programs available.

Faculty 14 full-time (0 women).

Faculty Research Intelligent systems, software engineering, distributed systems, database systems, computer systems.

Students 60 full-time (12 women), 57 part-time (12 women); includes 5 minority (1 African-American, 4 Asian-Americans), 54 international. Average age 30.

Degrees Awarded In 1996, 36 master's, 4 doctorates awarded. Terminal master's awarded for partial completion of doctoral program.

Entrance Requirements For master's, GRE General Test (minimum combined score of 1200); for doctorate, GRE Subject Test.

Degree Requirements For doctorate, dissertation, departmental qualifying exam required, foreign language not required.

Financial Aid In 1996–97, 18 students received aid, including 8 fellowships (2 to first-year students) totaling $34,600, 8 research assistantships (1 to a first-year student) averaging $1,387 per month and totaling $98,350, 9 teaching assistantships (2 to first-year students) averaging $1,387 per month and totaling $110,644; institutionally sponsored loans also available.

Applying 122 applicants, 83% accepted. *Deadline:* 7/1 (rolling processing). *Fee:* $20.

Contact Dr. George Zobrist
Chairman
573-341-4491
Fax: 573-341-4501
E-mail: zobrist@umr.edu

ELECTRICAL ENGINEERING

School of Engineering, Department of Electrical Engineering

Programs Awards MS, DE, PhD. Part-time and evening/weekend programs available.

Faculty 29 full-time (2 women).

Faculty Research Digital, signal, and image processing; power systems and machines; communications; waves and devices; computer engineering. *Total annual research expenditures:* $760,890.

Students 80 full-time (5 women), 22 part-time (1 woman); includes 10 minority (3 African-Americans, 5 Asian-Americans, 1 Hispanic, 1 Native American), 51 international. Average age 28.

Degrees Awarded In 1996, 25 master's, 2 doctorates awarded. Terminal master's awarded for partial completion of doctoral program.

Entrance Requirements GRE, TOEFL.

Degree Requirements For master's, thesis or alternative required, foreign language not required; for doctorate, dissertation, departmental qualifying exam.

Financial Aid In 1996–97, 54 students received aid, including 27 fellowships (6 to first-year students) totaling $69,946, 33 research assistantships (5 to first-year students) averaging $1,354 per month and totaling $402,138, 21 teaching assistantships (3 to first-year students) averaging $1,511 per month and totaling $285,579; partial tuition waivers, institutionally sponsored loans, and career-related internships or fieldwork also available. Aid available to part-time students. *Financial aid application deadline: 3/1.*

Applying 299 applicants, 41% accepted. *Deadline:* 6/1 (rolling processing; 11/1 for spring admission). *Fee:* $20.

Contact *Paul D. Stigall*
Assistant Chairman
573-341-4533
Fax: 573-341-4532
E-mail: stigall@ee.umr.edu

WASHINGTON UNIVERSITY
St. Louis, MO 63130-4899

OVERVIEW
Washington University is an independent coed university.

ENROLLMENT
11,636 graduate, professional, and undergraduate students; 3,424 full-time matriculated graduate/professional students (1,726 women), 1,643 part-time matriculated graduate/professional students (679 women).

GRADUATE FACULTY
1,862 full-time, 1,509 part-time.

TUITION
$21,000 per year full-time, $875 per credit hour part-time.

HOUSING
On-campus housing not available.

STUDENT SERVICES
Low-cost health insurance, career counseling, free psychological counseling, campus safety program, campus employment opportunities, international student services.

FACILITIES
Library: John M. Olin Library plus 13 additional on-campus libraries; total holdings of 3 million volumes, 2.7 million microforms, 18,988 current periodical subscriptions. Access provided to on-line information retrieval services. *Special:* In arts and humanities: International Writers Center, Center for the History of Freedom, Joint Center for East Asian Studies, Center for Study of Islamic Societies and Civilizations. In science and engineering: Center for Air Pollution Impact and Trend Analysis, McDonnell Center for Space Sciences, biomedical computer laboratory, computer systems laboratory, materials research laboratory. In social sciences: Center for Mental Health Research, Center in Political Economy, Central Institute for the Deaf, Center for the Study of American Business.

COMPUTER SCIENCE

School of Engineering and Applied Science, Sever Institute of Technology, Department of Computer Science

Programs Awards MS, D Sc. Part-time programs available.

Faculty 18 full-time (2 women), 6 part-time (0 women).

Faculty Research Multimedia networking, distributed systems, artificial intelligence, computational science, multimedia-user interfaces.

Students 52 full-time (7 women), 23 part-time (3 women); includes 3 minority (1 African-American, 2 Asian-Americans), 42 international.

Degrees Awarded In 1996, 17 master's, 3 doctorates awarded. Terminal master's awarded for partial completion of doctoral program.

Entrance Requirements GRE General Test, GRE Subject Test, TOEFL (minimum score 575), TWE (minimum score 4.5).

Degree Requirements For master's, thesis optional, foreign language not required; for doctorate, dissertation, departmental qualifying exam required, foreign language not required.

Financial Aid In 1996–97, 38 research assistantships (14 to first-year students) averaging $1,260 per month, 3 teaching assistantships (1 to a first-year student) averaging $1,260 per month and totaling $30,064 were awarded; fellowships, Federal Work-Study, and career-related internships or fieldwork also available. *Financial aid application deadline: 1/15.*

Applying 204 applicants, 20% accepted. *Deadline:* 5/1 (priority date; 9/15 for spring admission). *Fee:* $20.

Contact *Jean Grothe*
Graduate Admissions Coordinator
314-935-6160
Fax: 314-935-7302
E-mail: admissions@cs.wustl.edu

See in-depth description on page **757.**

ELECTRICAL ENGINEERING

School of Engineering and Applied Science, Sever Institute of Technology, Department of Electrical Engineering

Programs Awards MSEE, D Sc. Part-time programs available.

Faculty 19 full-time (1 woman), 12 part-time (0 women), 22 FTE.

Faculty Research Applied physics, signal and image processing, computer engineering, telecommunications, biomedical engineering. *Total annual research expenditures:* $1.6 million.

Students 88 full-time (13 women), 36 part-time (4 women); includes 9 minority (2 African-Americans, 7 Asian-Americans), 69 international. Average age 25.

Degrees Awarded In 1996, 36 master's, 7 doctorates awarded. Terminal master's awarded for partial completion of doctoral program.

Entrance Requirements For master's, minimum GPA of 3.0 during previous two years.

Degree Requirements For master's, thesis optional, foreign language not required; for doctorate, variable foreign language requirement, dissertation, departmental qualifying exam.

Financial Aid In 1996–97, 41 students received aid, including 7 fellowships (3 to first-year students) averaging $1,150 per month, 30 research assistantships (9 to first-year students) averaging $1,150 per month; Federal Work-Study, institutionally sponsored loans also available. *Financial aid application deadline: 2/1.*

Applying 391 applicants, 33% accepted. *Deadline:* 8/18 (priority date; rolling processing; 1/10 for spring admission). *Fee:* $20.
Contact Dr. Barry Spielman
Chairman
314-935-6170
Fax: 314-935-7500
E-mail: bes@ee.wustl.edu

See in–depth description on page 759.

SYSTEMS SCIENCE

School of Engineering and Applied Science, Sever Institute of Technology, Department of Systems Science and Mathematics
Programs Offers programs in systems science and mathematics (MS, D Sc); systems science, mathematics, and economics (D Sc). Part-time programs available. Terminal master's awarded for partial completion of doctoral program.
Degree Requirements For master's, thesis optional, foreign language not required; for doctorate, variable foreign language requirement, dissertation, departmental qualifying exam.
Applying *Fee:* $20.

WEBSTER UNIVERSITY
St. Louis, MO 63119-3194

OVERVIEW
Webster University is an independent coed comprehensive institution.

ENROLLMENT
12,319 graduate, professional, and undergraduate students; 5,272 full-time, 3,965 part-time matriculated graduate/professional students.

GRADUATE FACULTY
86 full-time (40 women), 1,477 part-time; includes 8 minority (2 African-Americans, 4 Asian-Americans, 2 Hispanics).

TUITION
$332 per credit hour.

HOUSING
Rooms and/or apartments available to single students at an average cost of $4614 (including board); on-campus housing not available to married students. Housing application deadline: 7/1. Graduate housing contact: Kris McPeak, 314-968-7030.

STUDENT SERVICES
Career counseling, free psychological counseling, campus safety program, campus employment opportunities, international student services.

FACILITIES
Library: Eden-Webster Library; total holdings of 249,500 volumes, 108,994 microforms, 1,260 current periodical subscriptions. A total of 65 personal computers in all libraries. Access provided to on-line information retrieval services. *Computer:* Campuswide network is available with full Internet access. Total number of PCs/terminals supplied for student use: 175. Computer services are offered at no charge. *Special:* In arts and humanities: Center for International Education, Loretto Hilton Media Center.

COMPUTER SCIENCE

School of Business and Technology, Department of Mathematics and Computer Science
Programs Offers programs in computer distributed systems (Certificate), computer science (MS).
Faculty 3 full-time (1 woman).
Students 29 full-time, 44 part-time.
Financial Aid 31 students received aid; Federal Work-Study available. Aid available to part-time students. *Financial aid application deadline:* 4/1; applicants required to submit FAFSA.
Applying *Deadline:* 8/1 (priority date; rolling processing; 1/1 for spring admission). *Fee:* $25.
Contact Beth Russel
Director of Graduate Admissions
314-968-7089
Fax: 314-968-7115

MONTANA
MONTANA STATE UNIVERSITY–BOZEMAN
Bozeman, MT 59717

OVERVIEW
Montana State University–Bozeman is a public coed university.

ENROLLMENT
11,611 graduate, professional, and undergraduate students; 472 full-time matriculated graduate/professional students (184 women), 452 part-time matriculated graduate/professional students (213 women).

GRADUATE FACULTY
422 full-time (90 women), 8 part-time (2 women); includes 13 minority (8 Asian-Americans, 5 Native Americans).

EXPENSES
Tuition $1508 per year full-time, $84 per credit part-time for state residents; $4732 per year full-time, $263 per credit part-time for nonresidents. Fees $621 per year full-time, $34 per semester (minimum) part-time for state residents; $675 per year full-time, $37 per semester (minimum) part-time for nonresidents.

HOUSING
Rooms and/or apartments available to single students (106 units) at an average cost of $4025 (including board); available to married students (598 units) at an average cost of $4025 per year. Graduate housing contact: Residence Life Office, 406-994-2661.

STUDENT SERVICES
Disabled student services, multicultural affairs office, career counseling, free psychological counseling, exercise/wellness program, day-care facilities, campus employment opportunities, international student services, writing training, teacher training.

FACILITIES
Library: Renne Library plus 1 additional on-campus library; total holdings of 578,909 volumes, 1,388,931

microforms, 3,854 current periodical subscriptions. A total of 96 personal computers in all libraries. Access provided to on-line information retrieval services. *Computer:* Campuswide network is available with full Internet access. Total number of PCs/terminals supplied for student use: 769. Computer service fees are applied as a separate charge. *Special:* In arts and humanities: Wheeler Center. In science and engineering: Engineering Research Center, Agricultural Biosciences, Plant Growth Center, Optical Technology Center (OpTec), Chemical Instrumentation Laboratory, Center for Computational Biology, Water Resources Center. In social sciences: Local Government Center, Northern Plains and Rockies Center for the Study of Western Hemisphere Trade.

COMPUTER ENGINEERING

College of Engineering, Department of Electrical and Computer Engineering
Programs Offers programs in electrical engineering (MS); engineering (PhD), including electrical and computer engineering. Part-time programs available.
Faculty 14 full-time (0 women), 1 part-time (0 women).
Faculty Research Electromagnetic fields interacting with biological systems, communications, power/power systems, feedback and control on large scale systems, biomedical engineering. *Total annual research expenditures:* $342,904.
Students 7 full-time (3 women), 9 part-time (0 women). Average age 34.
Degrees Awarded In 1996, 9 master's awarded.
Entrance Requirements GRE General Test (minimum combined score of 1700 on three sections), TOEFL (minimum score 600).
Degree Requirements For master's, thesis or alternative required, foreign language not required; for doctorate, dissertation required, foreign language not required.
Financial Aid Research assistantships, teaching assistantships available. *Financial aid application deadline:* 3/1.
Applying *Deadline:* 6/1 (priority date; rolling processing; 11/1 for spring admission). *Fee:* $50.
Contact Dr. Bruce McLeod
Acting Head
406-994-2505
Fax: 406-994-5958
E-mail: eedept@ee.montana.edu

See in-depth description on page 479.

COMPUTER SCIENCE

College of Engineering, Department of Computer Science
Programs Offers programs in computer science (MS), engineering (PhD). Part-time programs available.
Faculty 5 full-time (0 women).
Faculty Research Graphics, artificial intelligence, networks, algorithms, computer science education. *Total annual research expenditures:* $104,150.
Students 19 full-time (4 women), 18 part-time (5 women); includes 14 international. Average age 29.
Degrees Awarded In 1996, 13 master's awarded.
Entrance Requirements For master's, GRE General Test (minimum combined score of 1200), TOEFL (minimum score 580), minimum GPA of 3.0; for doctorate, GRE General Test (minimum combined score of 1200), TOEFL (minimum score 580).
Degree Requirements For master's, thesis or alternative required, foreign language not required; for doctorate, dissertation required, foreign language not required.

Financial Aid In 1996–97, 4 research assistantships (1 to a first-year student) averaging $764 per month and totaling $27,504, 16 teaching assistantships (8 to first-year students) averaging $764 per month and totaling $110,016 were awarded. *Financial aid application deadline:* 3/1.
Applying *Deadline:* 6/1 (priority date; rolling processing; 11/1 for spring admission). *Fee:* $50.
Contact Dr. J. Denbigh Starkey
Head
406-994-4780
E-mail: gradappl@cs.montana.edu

ELECTRICAL ENGINEERING

College of Engineering, Department of Electrical and Computer Engineering
Programs Offers programs in electrical engineering (MS); engineering (PhD), including electrical and computer engineering. Part-time programs available.
Faculty 14 full-time (0 women), 1 part-time (0 women).
Faculty Research Electromagnetic fields interacting with biological systems, communications, power/power systems, feedback and control on large scale systems, biomedical engineering. *Total annual research expenditures:* $342,904.
Students 7 full-time (3 women), 9 part-time (0 women). Average age 34.
Degrees Awarded In 1996, 9 master's awarded.
Entrance Requirements GRE General Test (minimum combined score of 1700 on three sections), TOEFL (minimum score 600).
Degree Requirements For master's, thesis or alternative required, foreign language not required; for doctorate, dissertation required, foreign language not required.
Financial Aid Research assistantships, teaching assistantships available. *Financial aid application deadline:* 3/1.
Applying *Deadline:* 6/1 (priority date; rolling processing; 11/1 for spring admission). *Fee:* $50.
Contact Dr. Bruce McLeod
Acting Head
406-994-2505
Fax: 406-994-5958
E-mail: eedept@ee.montana.edu

See in-depth description on page 479.

THE UNIVERSITY OF MONTANA–MISSOULA
Missoula, MT 59812-0002

OVERVIEW
The University of Montana–Missoula is a public coed university.

ENROLLMENT
11,565 graduate, professional, and undergraduate students; 1,049 full-time matriculated graduate/professional students (441 women), 153 part-time matriculated graduate/professional students (74 women).

GRADUATE FACULTY
450 full-time (117 women), 31 part-time (3 women); includes 36 minority (9 African-Americans, 9 Asian-Americans, 8 Hispanics, 10 Native Americans).

TUITION

$3046 per year full-time, $142 per credit part-time for state residents; $8048 per year full-time, $350 per credit part-time for nonresidents.

HOUSING

Rooms and/or apartments available to single students at an average cost of $2208 per year ($4000 including board); available to married students (566 units) at an average cost of $3300 per year. Graduate housing information: 406-549-0134.

STUDENT SERVICES

Disabled student services, multicultural affairs office, low-cost health insurance, career counseling, free psychological counseling, exercise/wellness program, day-care facilities, campus safety program, campus employment opportunities, international student services.

FACILITIES

Library: Maureen and Mike Mansfield Library plus 2 additional on-campus libraries; total holdings of 678,852 volumes, 1,934,727 microforms, 4,803 current periodical subscriptions. *Computer:* Campuswide network is available with full Internet access. Computer service fees are included with tuition and fees. *Special:* In arts and humanities: Performing Arts and Radio/Television Center. In science and engineering: Lubrecht Experimental Forest, Montana Conservation Experiment Station, Freshwater Research Institute, Stella Duncan Memorial Institute for Respiratory Disease Research, forest sciences laboratory, wood chemistry laboratory, animal behavior laboratory, biological station.

COMPUTER SCIENCE

College of Arts and Sciences, Department of Computer Science
Programs Awards MS. Part-time programs available.
Faculty 5 full-time (0 women), 1 part-time (0 women).
Faculty Research Parallel and distributed systems, neural networks, genetic algorithms, machine learning, data visualization, artificial intelligence.
Students 29 (2 women); includes 14 international. Average age 33.
Degrees Awarded In 1996, 2 degrees awarded.
Entrance Requirements GRE General Test, TOEFL, bachelor's degree in technical field.
Degree Requirements Computer language, project or thesis required, foreign language not required.
Financial Aid In 1996–97, 4 research assistantships, 6 teaching assistantships were awarded; Federal Work-Study also available. *Financial aid application deadline:* 3/1.
Applying 12 applicants, 92% accepted. *Deadline:* 3/15 (priority date; rolling processing; 10/15 for spring admission). *Fee:* $30.
Contact *Kathy Lockridge*
Graduate Secretary
406-243-2883

NEBRASKA

CREIGHTON UNIVERSITY
Omaha, NE 68178-0001

OVERVIEW

Creighton University is an independent-religious coed university.

ENROLLMENT

6,241 graduate, professional, and undergraduate students; 1,927 full-time matriculated graduate/professional students (799 women), 412 part-time matriculated graduate/professional students (225 women).

GRADUATE FACULTY

251 (42 women).

EXPENSES

Tuition $382 per credit hour. Fees $510 per year full-time, $26 per semester part-time.

HOUSING

Rooms and/or apartments available to single students at an average cost of $2612 per year ($4726 including board); available to married students at an average cost of $4200 per year.

STUDENT SERVICES

Disabled student services, multicultural affairs office, low-cost health insurance, career counseling, free psychological counseling, exercise/wellness program, day-care facilities, campus safety program, campus employment opportunities, international student services.

FACILITIES

Library: Alumni Memorial Library; total holdings of 644,634 volumes, 123,176 microforms. *Computer:* Campuswide network is available with full Internet access. Computer service fees are included with tuition and fees. *Special:* In science and engineering: Dr. C. C. and Mabel L. Criss Health Sciences Center Medical Research Wing, Dr. Harry and Maude Boyne School of Dental Science Dental Clinic, Bioinformation Center, Allergic Disease Center.

COMPUTER SCIENCE

College of Arts and Sciences, Department of Mathematics, Statistics, and Computer Science, Program in Computer Sciences
Programs Awards MCS.
Degrees Awarded In 1996, 6 degrees awarded.
Entrance Requirements GRE General Test, TOEFL (minimum score 550).
Applying 20 applicants, 80% accepted. *Deadline:* 3/15 (rolling processing). *Fee:* $30.
Contact *Dr. Barbara J. Braden*
Dean, Graduate School
402-280-2870
Fax: 402-280-5762

UNIVERSITY OF NEBRASKA AT OMAHA
Omaha, NE 68182

OVERVIEW

University of Nebraska at Omaha is a public coed university.

ENROLLMENT

15,000 graduate, professional, and undergraduate students; 568 full-time matriculated graduate/

professional students (358 women), 1,718 part-time matriculated graduate/professional students (1,098 women).

GRADUATE FACULTY

308 full-time (65 women), 9 part-time (1 woman); includes 29 minority (7 African-Americans, 16 Asian-Americans, 5 Hispanics, 1 Native American).

EXPENSES

Tuition $1602 per year full-time, $89 per credit hour part-time for state residents; $3870 per year full-time, $215 per credit hour part-time for nonresidents. Fees $200 per year full-time, $90 per semester part-time.

HOUSING

On-campus housing not available.

STUDENT SERVICES

Disabled student services, multicultural affairs office, low-cost health insurance, career counseling, free psychological counseling, exercise/wellness program, day-care facilities, campus safety program, campus employment opportunities, international student services, writing training, grant writing training, teacher training.

FACILITIES

Library: University Library; total holdings of 736,918 volumes, 1,753,914 microforms, 4,085 current periodical subscriptions. Access provided to on-line information retrieval services. *Computer:* Campuswide network is available with partial Internet access (e-mail only). Total number of PCs/terminals supplied for student use: 450. Computer service fees are included with tuition and fees. *Special:* In arts and humanities: Center for Afghanistan Studies, Center for Faculty Development, Center for International Telecommunications Management. In social sciences: Center for Urban Education, Small Business Development Center, Center for Public Affairs Research.

COMPUTER SCIENCE

College of Arts and Sciences, Department of Computer Science
Programs Awards MA, MS. Part-time programs available.
Faculty 8 full-time (1 woman), 1 part-time (0 women).
Students 15 full-time (5 women), 71 part-time (9 women); includes 4 minority (2 Asian-Americans, 2 Hispanics), 20 international. Average age 34.
Degrees Awarded In 1996, 15 degrees awarded.
Entrance Requirements GRE General Test, minimum GPA of 3.0, previous course work in computer science.
Degree Requirements Thesis (for some programs), comprehensive exams required, foreign language not required.
Financial Aid 9 students received aid; research assistantships, teaching assistantships, full tuition waivers, institutionally sponsored loans available. Aid available to part-time students. *Financial aid application deadline:* 3/1; applicants required to submit FAFSA.
Applying 62 applicants, 66% accepted. *Deadline:* 7/1 (priority date; rolling processing; 12/1 for spring admission). *Fee:* $25.
Contact *Prof. Stanley Wileman*
Chairperson
402-554-2834

OVERVIEW

University of Nebraska–Lincoln is a public coed university.

ENROLLMENT

23,887 graduate, professional, and undergraduate students; 2,297 full-time matriculated graduate/professional students (1,014 women), 1,523 part-time matriculated graduate/professional students (788 women).

GRADUATE FACULTY

913 full-time (159 women), 20 part-time (2 women), 924 FTE; includes 77 minority (5 African-Americans, 54 Asian-Americans, 15 Hispanics, 3 Native Americans).

EXPENSES

Tuition $104 per credit hour for state residents; $256 per credit hour for nonresidents. Fees $414 per year full-time, $100 per semester part-time.

HOUSING

Rooms and/or apartments available to single students (444 units) at an average cost of $3570 (including board); available to married students (153 units) at an average cost of $3640 (including board). Graduate housing contact: Douglas Zatechka, 402-472-3561.

STUDENT SERVICES

Disabled student services, multicultural affairs office, low-cost health insurance, career counseling, free psychological counseling, exercise/wellness program, day-care facilities, campus safety program, campus employment opportunities, international student services, grant writing training.

FACILITIES

Library: Love Memorial Library plus 11 additional on-campus libraries; total holdings of 2,384,200 volumes, 4,062,246 microforms. Access provided to on-line information retrieval services. *Computer:* Campuswide network is available with full Internet access. Computer service fees are included with tuition and fees. *Special:* In arts and humanities: Sheldon Art Gallery, Lied Center for Performing Arts. In science and engineering: Barkley Memorial Center, Midwest Center for Mass Spectrometry, Walter Scott Research Laboratories, atomic physics laboratory, G. W. Beadle Center for Genetics and Biomaterials Research. In social sciences: Nebraska State Museum of Natural History, Bureau of Sociological Research, Government Research Institute.

COMPUTER ENGINEERING

College of Arts and Sciences, Department of Computer Science and Engineering
Programs Awards MS, PhD.
Faculty 19 full-time (1 woman).
Faculty Research Scheduling theory and digital image processing, artificial intelligence, coding theory, VLSI design, theoretical computer science. *Total annual research expenditures:* $363,340.
Students 59 full-time (12 women), 29 part-time (8 women); includes 11 minority (all Asian-Americans), 46 international. Average age 31.
Degrees Awarded In 1996, 23 master's, 4 doctorates awarded.

Entrance Requirements GRE General Test, GRE Subject Test, TOEFL (minimum score 550).

Degree Requirements For master's, thesis optional, foreign language not required; for doctorate, dissertation, comprehensive exams.

Financial Aid In 1996–97, 4 fellowships totaling $38,000, 11 research assistantships totaling $100,750, 22 teaching assistantships totaling $166,400 were awarded; Federal Work-Study also available. Aid available to part-time students. *Financial aid application deadline:* 2/15.

Applying 124 applicants, 57% accepted. *Deadline:* 3/1 (10/1 for spring admission). *Fee:* $25.

Contact Dr. Stephen Reichenbach
Interim Chair
402-472-3200

See in-depth description on page 675.

COMPUTER SCIENCE

College of Arts and Sciences, Department of Computer Science and Engineering

Programs Awards MS, PhD.

Faculty 19 full-time (1 woman).

Faculty Research Scheduling theory and digital image processing, artificial intelligence, coding theory, VLSI design, theoretical computer science. *Total annual research expenditures:* $363,340.

Students 59 full-time (12 women), 29 part-time (8 women); includes 11 minority (all Asian-Americans), 46 international. Average age 31.

Degrees Awarded In 1996, 23 master's, 4 doctorates awarded.

Entrance Requirements GRE General Test, GRE Subject Test, TOEFL (minimum score 550).

Degree Requirements For master's, thesis optional, foreign language not required; for doctorate, dissertation, comprehensive exams.

Financial Aid In 1996–97, 4 fellowships totaling $38,000, 11 research assistantships totaling $100,750, 22 teaching assistantships totaling $166,400 were awarded; Federal Work-Study also available. Aid available to part-time students. *Financial aid application deadline:* 2/15.

Applying 124 applicants, 57% accepted. *Deadline:* 3/1 (10/1 for spring admission). *Fee:* $25.

Contact Dr. Stephen Reichenbach
Interim Chair
402-472-3200

See in-depth description on page 675.

ELECTRICAL ENGINEERING

College of Engineering and Technology, Department of Electrical Engineering

Programs Offers programs in electrical engineering (MS), engineering (PhD).

Faculty 23 full-time (1 woman).

Faculty Research Communication and signal processing systems, electromagnetics, gaseous electronics and plasmas, power/control/digital systems, remote sensing. *Total annual research expenditures:* $808,642.

Students 48 full-time (16 women), 6 part-time (1 woman); includes 20 international. Average age 27.

Degrees Awarded In 1996, 24 master's awarded.

Entrance Requirements GRE General Test, TOEFL (minimum score 550).

Degree Requirements For master's, thesis optional, foreign language not required; for doctorate, dissertation, comprehensive exams.

Financial Aid In 1996–97, 15 fellowships totaling $41,800, 23 research assistantships totaling $164,265, 14 teaching assistantships totaling $112,500 were awarded; Federal Work-Study also available. Aid available to part-time students. *Financial aid application deadline:* 2/15.

Applying 129 applicants, 37% accepted. *Deadline:* 4/15 (priority date; rolling processing; 10/15 for spring admission). *Fee:* $25.

Contact Dr. Rodney Soukup
Chair
402-472-3771

See in-depth description on page 677.

NEVADA

UNIVERSITY OF NEVADA, LAS VEGAS
Las Vegas, NV 89154-9900

OVERVIEW
University of Nevada, Las Vegas is a public coed university.

ENROLLMENT
19,683 graduate, professional, and undergraduate students; 731 full-time matriculated graduate/professional students (404 women), 1,349 part-time matriculated graduate/professional students (817 women).

GRADUATE FACULTY
515 full-time (117 women), 25 part-time (6 women); includes 66 minority (9 African-Americans, 39 Asian-Americans, 14 Hispanics, 4 Native Americans).

EXPENSES
Tuition $90 per credit for state residents; $90 per credit full-time, $132 per credit part-time for nonresidents. Fees $5435 per year full-time for nonresidents.

HOUSING
Rooms and/or apartments available to single students (1,079 units) at an average cost of $2691 (including board); on-campus housing not available to married students. Graduate housing contact: Karen Strong, 702-895-3489.

STUDENT SERVICES
Disabled student services, multicultural affairs office, low-cost health insurance, career counseling, free psychological counseling, day-care facilities, campus safety program, campus employment opportunities, international student services.

FACILITIES
Library: James R. Dickinson Library; total holdings of 781,734 volumes, 1,527,522 microforms, 7,500 current periodical subscriptions. Access provided to on-line information retrieval services. *Computer:* Campuswide network is available with full Internet access. Computer services are offered at no charge. *Special:* In arts and humanities: Educational Equity Resource Center; Center for In-service, Training, and Educational Research; Arnold Shaw Popular Music Research Center; Center for Advanced Research; Center for Public Data Research; Center for the Study of Public Policy; Center for Survey Research. In science and engineering: Harry Reid Center,

Supercomputing Center for Energy and the Environment, Center for Energy Research, Information Science Research Institute, Transportation Research Center, ventilation and acoustic systems technology laboratory, biomechanics laboratory, exercise physiology laboratory, motor behavior laboratory, muscle metabolism laboratory, Sports Injury Research Center, Center for Volcanic and Tectonic Studies, Desert Biology Research Center, Limnological Research Center, National Park Service Cooperative Park Studies Unit. In social sciences: Nevada Small Business Development Center, International Gaming Institute, Barbara Schick Center for Economic Education, Southwestern Social Science Research Center.

COMPUTER ENGINEERING

Howard R. Hughes College of Engineering, Department of Electrical and Computer Engineering
Programs Awards MSE, PhD.
Faculty 12 full-time (1 woman).
Students 13 full-time (3 women), 13 part-time (2 women); includes 7 minority (2 African-Americans, 5 Asian-Americans), 10 international.
Degrees Awarded In 1996, 8 master's awarded.
Entrance Requirements For master's, TOEFL (minimum score 550), bachelor's degree in electrical engineering or related field, GRE General Test or minimum GPA of 3.0; for doctorate, minimum GPA of 3.5.
Degree Requirements For master's, comprehensive exam required, thesis optional, foreign language not required; for doctorate, dissertation.
Financial Aid In 1996–97, 3 research assistantships, 7 teaching assistantships were awarded; full tuition waivers also available. *Financial aid application deadline: 3/1.*
Applying 47 applicants, 30% accepted. *Deadline:* 6/15 (priority date; rolling processing; 11/15 for spring admission). *Fee:* $40 ($95 for international students).
Contact *Admissions and Information*
    702-895-4183

COMPUTER SCIENCE

Howard R. Hughes College of Engineering, Department of Computer Science
Programs Awards MS, PhD. Part-time programs available.
Faculty 10 full-time (0 women).
Students 20 full-time (4 women), 14 part-time (2 women); includes 5 minority (all Asian-Americans), 10 international.
Degrees Awarded In 1996, 14 master's, 1 doctorate awarded.
Entrance Requirements For master's, GRE General Test, GRE Subject Test, minimum GPA of 3.0; for doctorate, minimum GPA of 3.5.
Degree Requirements For master's, comprehensive exam required, thesis optional, foreign language not required; for doctorate, dissertation.
Financial Aid In 1996–97, 12 teaching assistantships were awarded; research assistantships also available. *Financial aid application deadline: 3/1.*
Applying 35 applicants, 63% accepted. *Deadline:* 6/15 (priority date; rolling processing; 11/15 for spring admission). *Fee:* $40 ($95 for international students).
Contact *Graduate College Admissions Evaluator*
    702-895-3320

See in–depth description on page 679.

ELECTRICAL ENGINEERING

Howard R. Hughes College of Engineering, Department of Electrical and Computer Engineering
Programs Awards MSE, PhD.
Faculty 12 full-time (1 woman).
Students 13 full-time (3 women), 13 part-time (2 women); includes 7 minority (2 African-Americans, 5 Asian-Americans), 10 international.
Degrees Awarded In 1996, 8 master's awarded.
Entrance Requirements For master's, TOEFL (minimum score 550), bachelor's degree in electrical engineering or related field, GRE General Test or minimum GPA of 3.0; for doctorate, minimum GPA of 3.5.
Degree Requirements For master's, comprehensive exam required, thesis optional, foreign language not required; for doctorate, dissertation.
Financial Aid In 1996–97, 3 research assistantships, 7 teaching assistantships were awarded; full tuition waivers also available. *Financial aid application deadline: 3/1.*
Applying 47 applicants, 30% accepted. *Deadline:* 6/15 (priority date; rolling processing; 11/15 for spring admission). *Fee:* $40 ($95 for international students).
Contact *Admissions and Information*
    702-895-4183

UNIVERSITY OF NEVADA, RENO
Reno, NV 89557

OVERVIEW
University of Nevada, Reno is a public coed university.

ENROLLMENT
12,000 graduate, professional, and undergraduate students; 2,203 matriculated graduate/professional students.

GRADUATE FACULTY
556; includes 61 minority (10 African-Americans, 36 Asian-Americans, 10 Hispanics, 5 Native Americans).

EXPENSES
Tuition $0 for state residents; $5435 per year full-time, $166 per credit part-time for nonresidents. Fees $90 per credit.

HOUSING
Rooms and/or apartments available to single students (1,116 units) at an average cost of $2972 per year ($4997 including board); available to married students (40 units) at an average cost of $3240 per year. Graduate housing contact: Housing Services Office, 702-784-6107.

STUDENT SERVICES
Low-cost health insurance, career counseling, free psychological counseling, exercise/wellness program, day-care facilities, campus safety program, campus employment opportunities, international student services, writing training.

FACILITIES
Library: Getchell Library plus 7 additional on-campus libraries; total holdings of 880,000 volumes, 2,720,024 microforms, 9,800 current periodical subscriptions. A total of 115 personal computers in all libraries. Access provided to on-line information retrieval services. *Computer:* Campuswide network is available with full Internet

access. Computer services are offered at no charge. *Special:* In arts and humanities: Center for Advanced Study, University of Nevada Press, Center for Environmental Arts and Humanities. In science and engineering: Engineering Research and Development Center, Mackay Mineral Resources Research Institute, Nevada Mining Analytical Laboratory, Senator Alan Bible Center for Applied Research, agricultural research station, seismological laboratory, Desert Research Institute (Atmospheric Sciences Center, Biological Sciences Center, Energy and Environmental Engineering Center, Quaternary Sciences Center, Water Resources Center). In social sciences: Bureau of Business and Economic Research, Center for Justice Studies, Center for Applied Research, Survey Research Center.

COMPUTER SCIENCE

Mackay School of Mines, Program in Computer Science
Programs Awards MS.
Faculty 4 (0 women).
Students 13 full-time (4 women), 27 part-time (10 women); includes 11 minority (all Asian-Americans), 18 international.
Entrance Requirements GRE, TOEFL (minimum score 500), minimum GPA of 2.75.
Degree Requirements Thesis optional, foreign language not required.
Financial Aid Research assistantships, teaching assistantships available. *Financial aid application deadline:* 3/1.
Applying 56 applicants, 38% accepted. *Deadline:* 3/1 (priority date; rolling processing). *Fee:* $40.
Contact Dr. Carl Looney
　　　　　Director of Graduate Studies
　　　　　702-784-6974

ELECTRICAL ENGINEERING

College of Engineering, Department of Electrical Engineering
Programs Awards MS, PhD.
Faculty 9 full-time (1 woman), 1 part-time (0 women).
Students 5 full-time (0 women), 33 part-time (3 women); includes 1 minority (Hispanic), 17 international.
Degrees Awarded In 1996, 10 master's, 1 doctorate awarded.
Entrance Requirements For master's, GRE General Test, TOEFL (minimum score 500), minimum GPA of 2.75; for doctorate, GRE General Test, TOEFL (minimum score 500), minimum GPA of 3.0.
Degree Requirements For master's, thesis optional, foreign language not required; for doctorate, 1 foreign language, dissertation.
Financial Aid Research assistantships, teaching assistantships, full tuition waivers, Federal Work-Study, institutionally sponsored loans available. *Financial aid application deadline:* 3/1.
Applying 67 applicants, 12% accepted. *Deadline:* 3/1 (priority date; rolling processing). *Fee:* $40.
Contact Dr. M. Sami Fadali
　　　　　Director of Graduate Studies
　　　　　702-784-6927

NEW HAMPSHIRE

DARTMOUTH COLLEGE
Hanover, NH 03755

OVERVIEW
Dartmouth College is an independent coed university.

ENROLLMENT
5,249 graduate, professional, and undergraduate students; 1,249 full-time matriculated graduate/professional students (467 women), 86 part-time matriculated graduate/professional students (54 women).

GRADUATE FACULTY
306 full-time, 716 part-time; includes 12 minority (5 African-Americans, 5 Asian-Americans, 2 Hispanics).

TUITION
$30,528 per year.

HOUSING
Rooms and/or apartments available to single students (35 units) at an average cost of $4300 per year ($7000 including board); available to married students (130 units) at an average cost of $6000 per year ($9000 including board). Graduate housing contact: Office of Rental Housing, 603-646-2170.

STUDENT SERVICES
Disabled student services, low-cost health insurance, career counseling, free psychological counseling, campus safety program, international student services, writing training, teacher training.

FACILITIES
Library: Baker Library plus 8 additional on-campus libraries; total holdings of 2,057,421 volumes, 2,378,886 microforms, 20,764 current periodical subscriptions. A total of 150 personal computers in all libraries. Access provided to on-line information retrieval services. *Computer:* Campuswide network is available with full Internet access. Computer service fees are included with tuition and fees. *Special:* In science and engineering: McGraw Hill Observatory (Tucson, Arizona), Dartmouth-Hitchcock Medical Center.

COMPUTER ENGINEERING

Thayer School of Engineering, Program in Computer Engineering
Programs Awards MS, PhD.
Faculty Research Multimedia systems and networks, distributed agents, parallel and distributed computing simulation and performance analysis, VLSI design and testing. *Total annual research expenditures:* $300,000.
Entrance Requirements GRE General Test.
Degree Requirements For master's, thesis; for doctorate, dissertation, candidacy oral exam.
Financial Aid Fellowships, research assistantships, teaching assistantships, full and partial tuition waivers, Federal Work-Study, institutionally sponsored loans, and career-related internships or fieldwork available. *Financial aid application deadline:* 1/15.
Applying *Deadline:* 1/15 (priority date). *Fee:* $20 ($40 for international students).
Contact Candace S. Potter
　　　　　Admissions Coordinator
　　　　　603-646-3844
　　　　　Fax: 603-646-3856
　　　　　E-mail: candace.potter@dartmouth.edu

COMPUTER SCIENCE

School of Arts and Sciences, Department of Computer Science
Programs Awards PhD.
Faculty 14 full-time (2 women), 1 part-time (0 women).
Students 26 full-time (3 women), 1 part-time (0 women); includes 1 minority (Asian-American), 8 international.

Degrees Awarded In 1996, 8 master's awarded (25% found work related to degree, 75% continued full-time study); 3 doctorates awarded (67% entered university research/teaching, 33% found other work related to degree). Terminal master's awarded for partial completion of doctoral program.

Entrance Requirements For doctorate, GRE General Test, GRE Subject Test.

Degree Requirements For doctorate, dissertation required, foreign language not required.

Financial Aid In 1996–97, 27 students received aid, including 11 fellowships (6 to first-year students) averaging $1,150 per month and totaling $151,800, 8 research assistantships averaging $1,150 per month and totaling $110,400; full and partial tuition waivers, institutionally sponsored loans, and career-related internships or fieldwork also available. Aid available to part-time students. *Financial aid application deadline:* 2/1.

Applying 143 applicants, 17% accepted. *Deadline:* 2/1 (priority date). *Fee:* $30.

Contact *Phyllis Bellmore*
Administrative Assistant
603-646-2206

See in-depth description on page **415.**

ELECTRICAL ENGINEERING

Thayer School of Engineering, Program in Electrical Engineering
Programs Awards MS, PhD.

Faculty Research Electronics and microengineering, image and signal processing, optics, lasers and optoelectronics, electromagnetic fields, waves and antennas, aerospace environment and plasma science. *Total annual research expenditures:* $1.1 million.

Entrance Requirements GRE General Test.

Degree Requirements For master's, thesis; for doctorate, dissertation, candidacy oral exam.

Financial Aid Full and partial tuition waivers, Federal Work-Study, institutionally sponsored loans, and career-related internships or fieldwork available. *Financial aid application deadline:* 1/15.

Applying *Deadline:* 1/15 (priority date). *Fee:* $20 ($40 for international students).

Contact *Candace S. Potter*
Admissions Coordinator
603-646-3844
Fax: 603-646-3856

NEW HAMPSHIRE COLLEGE
Manchester, NH 03106-1045

OVERVIEW
New Hampshire College is an independent coed comprehensive institution.

ENROLLMENT
6,500 graduate, professional, and undergraduate students; 330 full-time matriculated graduate/professional students (120 women), 1,532 part-time matriculated graduate/professional students (644 women).

GRADUATE FACULTY
23 full-time (4 women), 116 part-time (25 women), 77 FTE.

EXPENSES
Tuition $16,080 per year full-time, $891 per course part-time. Fees $450 per year full-time, $80 per year part-time.

HOUSING
Rooms and/or apartments available to single students (32 units) at an average cost of $5500 per year ($6840 including board); on-campus housing not available to married students. Graduate housing contact: Robert Schiavoni, 603-668-2211.

STUDENT SERVICES
Low-cost health insurance, career counseling, free psychological counseling, campus safety program, campus employment opportunities, international student services.

FACILITIES
Library: H. A. B. Shapiro Memorial Library; total holdings of 77,000 volumes, 5,561 microforms, 821 current periodical subscriptions. A total of 35 personal computers in all libraries. Access provided to on-line information retrieval services. *Computer:* Campuswide network is available with full Internet access. Total number of PCs/terminals supplied for student use: 190.

ARTIFICIAL INTELLIGENCE/ROBOTICS

Graduate School of Business, Program in Business Administration
Programs Offerings include artificial intelligence (Certificate).

Program Faculty 7 full-time (1 woman), 66 part-time (11 women), 47 FTE.

Applying *Deadline:* rolling. *Fee:* $0.

Contact *Dr. Jacqueline F. Mara*
Dean
603-644-3102
Fax: 603-644-3150

RIVIER COLLEGE
Nashua, NH 03060-5086

OVERVIEW
Rivier College is an independent-religious coed comprehensive institution.

HOUSING
On-campus housing not available.

FACILITIES
Library: Regina Library.

COMPUTER SCIENCE

Department of Computer Science and Mathematics
Programs Offers programs in computer science (MS), information science (MS), mathematics (MS). Part-time and evening/weekend programs available.

Entrance Requirements GRE Subject Test.

Applying *Deadline:* rolling. *Fee:* $25.

INFORMATION SCIENCE

Department of Computer Science and Mathematics
Programs Offerings include information science (MS).

Applying *Deadline:* rolling. *Fee:* $25.

UNIVERSITY OF NEW HAMPSHIRE
Durham, NH 03824

OVERVIEW
University of New Hampshire is a public coed university.

ENROLLMENT
12,701 graduate, professional, and undergraduate students; 967 full-time matriculated graduate/professional students (512 women), 1,134 part-time matriculated graduate/professional students (675 women).

GRADUATE FACULTY
577 full-time.

EXPENSES
Tuition $4900 per year full-time, $272 per credit hour part-time for state residents; $13,760 per year full-time, $561 per credit hour part-time for nonresidents. Fees $789 per year full-time, $212 per semester part-time.

HOUSING
Rooms and/or apartments available to single students (180 units) at an average cost of $2876 per year ($4676 including board); available to married students (153 units). Housing application deadline: 7/15. Graduate housing information: 603-862-2120.

STUDENT SERVICES
Low-cost health insurance, career counseling, free psychological counseling, day-care facilities, campus safety program, campus employment opportunities, international student services.

FACILITIES
Library: Dimond Library plus 4 additional on-campus libraries; total holdings of 1,034,946 volumes, 6,500 current periodical subscriptions. Access provided to on-line information retrieval services. *Computer:* Campuswide network is available with full Internet access. *Special:* In arts and humanities: Center for the Humanities, writing process laboratory. In science and engineering: Institute for the Study of Earth, Oceans, and Space; Water Resource Research Center; agricultural experiment station. In social sciences: Family research laboratory, Institute for Policy and Social Science Research, Institute on Disability.

COMPUTER SCIENCE

College of Engineering and Physical Sciences, Department of Computer Science
Programs Awards MS, PhD. Part-time and evening/weekend programs available.
Faculty 12 full-time.
Faculty Research Programming languages, compiler design, parallel algorithms, computer graphics, artificial intelligence.
Students 23 full-time (5 women), 31 part-time (7 women); includes 3 minority (1 African-American, 2 Asian-Americans), 19 international. Average age 31.
Degrees Awarded In 1996, 9 master's awarded.
Entrance Requirements GRE General Test, GRE Subject Test.
Degree Requirements For master's, computer language, thesis or alternative required, foreign language not required; for doctorate, computer language, dissertation required, foreign language not required.

Financial Aid In 1996–97, 6 research assistantships, 14 teaching assistantships (6 to first-year students), 2 scholarships were awarded; fellowships, full and partial tuition waivers, Federal Work-Study, and career-related internships or fieldwork also available. Aid available to part-time students. *Financial aid application deadline: 2/15.*
Applying 32 applicants, 72% accepted. *Deadline:* 4/1 (priority date; rolling processing). *Fee:* $50.
Contact Pilar de la Torre
Graduate Coordinator
603-862-2682

See in-depth description on page 681.

ELECTRICAL ENGINEERING

College of Engineering and Physical Sciences, Programs in Engineering
Programs Offerings include electrical and computer engineering (MS), with option in electrical engineering; engineering (PhD), with options in chemical engineering, civil engineering, electrical engineering, mechanical engineering, systems design engineering.
Faculty 63 full-time.
Degree Requirements For doctorate, dissertation.
Applying *Deadline:* 4/1 (priority date; rolling processing). *Fee:* $50.
Contact Dr. Roy B. Torbert
Dean
603-862-1781

ELECTRICAL ENGINEERING

College of Engineering and Physical Sciences, Programs in Engineering, Department of Electrical and Computer Engineering
Programs Offers program in electrical engineering (MS).
Faculty 19 full-time.
Faculty Research Biomedical engineering, communications systems and information theory, digital systems, illumination engineering.
Students 9 full-time (0 women), 32 part-time (3 women); includes 5 minority (4 Asian-Americans, 1 Hispanic), 3 international. Average age 34.
Degrees Awarded In 1996, 13 degrees awarded.
Degree Requirements Thesis or alternative required, foreign language not required.
Financial Aid In 1996–97, 10 research assistantships (4 to first-year students), 7 teaching assistantships (3 to first-year students) were awarded; scholarships, full and partial tuition waivers, Federal Work-Study also available. Aid available to part-time students. *Financial aid application deadline: 2/15.*
Applying 25 applicants, 80% accepted. *Deadline:* 4/1 (priority date; rolling processing). *Fee:* $50.
Contact Dr. Michael J. Carter
Graduate Coordinator
603-862-4328

See in-depth description on page 683.

NEW JERSEY

FAIRLEIGH DICKINSON UNIVERSITY, FLORHAM-MADISON CAMPUS
Madison, NJ 07940-1099

OVERVIEW
Fairleigh Dickinson University, Florham-Madison Campus is an independent coed comprehensive institution.

ENROLLMENT

3,307 graduate, professional, and undergraduate students; 190 full-time matriculated graduate/professional students (102 women), 1,199 part-time matriculated graduate/ professional students (605 women).

GRADUATE FACULTY

62 full-time (7 women), 84 part-time (12 women); includes 8 minority (1 African-American, 5 Asian-Americans, 2 Hispanics).

EXPENSES

Tuition $496 per credit. Fees $302 per year full-time, $69 per semester part-time.

HOUSING

Rooms and/or apartments available to single students (16 units) at an average cost of $3144 per year ($5550 including board); on-campus housing not available to married students. Housing application deadline: 6/15. Graduate housing contact: Robert Brown, 201-593-8586.

STUDENT SERVICES

Low-cost health insurance, career counseling, free psychological counseling, campus safety program, campus employment opportunities, international student services.

FACILITIES

Library: Friendship Library; total holdings of 182,302 volumes, 115,770 microforms, 923 current periodical subscriptions. A total of 22 personal computers in all libraries. Access provided to on-line information retrieval services. *Special:* In arts and humanities: Wroxton College (Wroxton, England).

COMPUTER SCIENCE

Maxwell Becton College of Arts and Sciences, Department of Mathematics, Computer Science and Physics

Programs Offers programs in computer science (MS), mathematics (MS).

Faculty 5 full-time (0 women), 1 part-time (0 women).

Students 0.

Entrance Requirements GRE General Test.

Degree Requirements Computer language required, foreign language and thesis not required.

Financial Aid Fellowships, research assistantships, teaching assistantships available.

Applying 13 applicants, 100% accepted. *Deadline:* rolling. *Fee:* $35.

Contact Dr. Richard Wagner
Acting Chairperson
201-593-8691

FAIRLEIGH DICKINSON UNIVERSITY, TEANECK–HACKENSACK
Teaneck, NJ 07666-1914

OVERVIEW

Fairleigh Dickinson University, Teaneck–Hackensack is an independent coed comprehensive institution.

ENROLLMENT

4,014 graduate, professional, and undergraduate students; 575 full-time matriculated graduate/professional students (273 women), 1,419 part-time matriculated graduate/ professional students (762 women).

GRADUATE FACULTY

107 full-time (27 women), 67 part-time (33 women); includes 12 minority (1 African-American, 7 Asian-Americans, 4 Hispanics).

EXPENSES

Tuition $496 per credit. Fees $302 per year full-time, $69 per semester part-time.

HOUSING

Rooms and/or apartments available to single students (64 units) at an average cost of $3144 per year ($5550 including board); on-campus housing not available to married students. Housing application deadline: 6/15. Graduate housing contact: Douglas Samuels, 201-692-2250.

STUDENT SERVICES

Low-cost health insurance, career counseling, free psychological counseling, campus safety program, campus employment opportunities, international student services.

FACILITIES

Library: Weiner Library plus 1 additional on-campus library; total holdings of 274,188 volumes, 190,181 microforms, 1,613 current periodical subscriptions. A total of 17 personal computers in all libraries. Access provided to on-line information retrieval services. *Special:* In arts and humanities: Wroxton College (Wroxton, England). In science and engineering: Health Research Center, Electrooptics Research Center.

COMPUTER ENGINEERING

University College: Arts, Sciences, and Professional Studies, Department of Systems Science

Programs Offerings include computer engineering (MS).

Department Faculty 5 full-time (0 women), 4 part-time (2 women).

Entrance Requirements GRE General Test.

Degree Requirements Thesis required, foreign language not required.

Applying *Fee:* $35.

Contact Dr. Dario A. Cortes
Dean
201-692-2132

COMPUTER SCIENCE

University College: Arts, Sciences, and Professional Studies, Department of Mathematics and Computer Science, Program in Computer Science

Programs Awards MS.

Faculty 15 full-time (2 women), 7 part-time (2 women).

Students 50 full-time (15 women), 116 part-time (28 women); includes 29 minority (7 African-Americans, 15 Asian-Americans, 6 Hispanics, 1 Native American), 62 international. Average age 32.

Degrees Awarded In 1996, 50 degrees awarded.

Entrance Requirements GRE General Test.

Degree Requirements Computer language required, thesis optional, foreign language not required.

Applying *Deadline:* rolling. *Fee:* $35.

Contact *Dr. Gilbert Steiner*
Chairperson
201-692-2260

ELECTRICAL ENGINEERING

University College: Arts, Sciences, and Professional Studies, Department of Electrical Engineering
Programs Awards MSEE.
Faculty 7 full-time (1 woman), 2 part-time (0 women).
Students 38 full-time (3 women), 22 part-time (2 women); includes 11 minority (3 African-Americans, 6 Asian-Americans, 2 Hispanics), 39 international. Average age 28.
Degrees Awarded In 1996, 28 degrees awarded.
Entrance Requirements GRE General Test.
Degree Requirements Thesis optional, foreign language not required.
Financial Aid Fellowships available.
Applying *Deadline:* rolling. *Fee:* $35.
Contact *Dr. Howard Silver*
Chairperson
201-692-2830

SYSTEMS SCIENCE

University College: Arts, Sciences, and Professional Studies, Department of Systems Science
Programs Offers programs in computer engineering (MS), pollution studies (MS).
Faculty 5 full-time (0 women), 4 part-time (2 women).
Students 2 full-time (1 woman), 9 part-time (4 women); includes 1 international. Average age 33.
Degrees Awarded In 1996, 3 degrees awarded.
Entrance Requirements GRE General Test.
Degree Requirements Thesis required, foreign language not required.
Applying *Fee:* $35.
Contact *Dr. Dario A. Cortes*
Dean
201-692-2132

MONMOUTH UNIVERSITY
West Long Branch, NJ 07764-1898

OVERVIEW
Monmouth University is an independent coed comprehensive institution.

ENROLLMENT
4,915 graduate, professional, and undergraduate students; 236 full-time matriculated graduate/professional students (151 women), 892 part-time matriculated graduate/professional students (497 women).

GRADUATE FACULTY
53 full-time (15 women), 30 part-time (8 women); includes 11 minority (2 African-Americans, 8 Asian-Americans, 1 Hispanic).

EXPENSES
Tuition $439 per credit. Fees $548 per year full-time, $137 per semester part-time.

HOUSING
On-campus housing not available.

STUDENT SERVICES
Career counseling, free psychological counseling, campus employment opportunities, international student services.

FACILITIES
Library: Guggenheim Memorial Library; total holdings of 248,416 volumes, 323,970 microforms, 1,306 current periodical subscriptions. A total of 7 personal computers in all libraries. Access provided to on-line information retrieval services. *Computer:* Campuswide network is available with full Internet access. Total number of PCs/terminals supplied for student use: 375. Computer service fees are included with tuition and fees. *Special:* In arts and humanities: Center for the Study of Public Issues. In science and engineering: Center for Technology Development and Transfer.

COMPUTER SCIENCE

Department of Computer Science
Programs Awards MS.
Faculty 6 full-time (1 woman), 2 part-time (0 women).
Faculty Research Databases, natural language processing, protocols, performance analysis, communications networks (systems), telecommunications.
Students 18 full-time (8 women), 50 part-time (15 women); includes 14 minority (1 African-American, 12 Asian-Americans, 1 Hispanic), 27 international. Average age 31.
Degrees Awarded In 1996, 29 degrees awarded.
Entrance Requirements Minimum GPA of 3.0 in major, 2.5 overall.
Degree Requirements Computer language, thesis required, foreign language not required.
Financial Aid In 1996–97, 23 students received aid, including 2 assistantships; full tuition waivers, Federal Work-Study also available. Aid available to part-time students. *Financial aid application deadline:* 3/1; applicants required to submit FAFSA.
Applying 97 applicants, 84% accepted. *Deadline:* 8/15 (priority date; rolling processing; 12/1 for spring admission). *Fee:* $35.
Contact *Office of Graduate Admissions*
732-571-3452
Fax: 732-571-5123

SOFTWARE ENGINEERING

Department of Software Engineering
Programs Awards MS. Part-time and evening/weekend programs available.
Faculty 4 full-time (0 women), 4 part-time (0 women).
Faculty Research Formal protocol modeling with abstract data types and finite state machines, network computing, object orientation, distributed object base, artificial intelligence, real-time systems.
Students 35 full-time (6 women), 104 part-time (35 women); includes 15 minority (6 African-Americans, 6 Asian-Americans, 3 Hispanics), 10 international. Average age 35.
Degrees Awarded In 1996, 62 degrees awarded.
Entrance Requirements Bachelor's degree in computer science, engineering, mathematics, or physics; minimum GPA of 3.0; 1 year of software development experience.
Degree Requirements Computer language required, thesis optional, foreign language not required.
Financial Aid In 1996–97, 11 students received aid, including 5 assistantships; full and partial tuition waivers, Federal Work-Study, and career-related internships or fieldwork also available. Aid available to part-time students. *Financial aid application deadline:* 3/1; applicants required to submit FAFSA.

Applying 65 applicants, 95% accepted. *Deadline:* 8/1 (priority date; rolling processing; 12/1 for spring admission). *Fee:* $35.
Contact *Office of Graduate Admissions*
732-571-3452
Fax: 732-571-5123

Financial Aid Available to part-time students. *Financial aid application deadline:* 3/1; applicants required to submit FAFSA.
Applying *Deadline:* 4/1 (rolling processing; 11/1 for spring admission). *Fee:* $40.
Contact *Dr. Helen Roberts*
Adviser
201-655-7262

MONTCLAIR STATE UNIVERSITY
Upper Montclair, NJ 07043-1624

OVERVIEW
Montclair State University is a public coed comprehensive institution.

ENROLLMENT
13,034 graduate, professional, and undergraduate students; 517 full-time matriculated graduate/professional students (338 women), 1,771 part-time matriculated graduate/professional students (1,218 women).

GRADUATE FACULTY
444 full-time (171 women); includes 82 minority (30 African-Americans, 28 Asian-Americans, 23 Hispanics, 1 Native American).

EXPENSES
Tuition $186 per credit for state residents; $236 per credit for nonresidents. Fees $18.05 per credit.

HOUSING
Rooms and/or apartments available to single students at an average cost of $3826 per year ($5658 including board); on-campus housing not available to married students. Graduate housing contact: Residence Life, 201-655-5188.

STUDENT SERVICES
Disabled student services, low-cost health insurance, career counseling, free psychological counseling, exercise/wellness program, day-care facilities, campus safety program, international student services, teacher training.

FACILITIES
Library: Sprague Library; total holdings of 418,547 volumes, 1,134,242 microforms, 3,793 current periodical subscriptions. Access provided to on-line information retrieval services. *Computer:* Campuswide network is available with full Internet access. Total number of PCs/terminals supplied for student use: 450. Computer service fees are included with tuition and fees. *Special:* In social sciences: Psycho-Educational Center, School of Conservation, International Trade Counseling Center.

COMPUTER SCIENCE

College of Science and Mathematics, Department of Mathematics and Computer Science, Programs in Mathematics, Concentration in Computer Science
Programs Awards MS.
Faculty 39 full-time.
Entrance Requirements GRE General Test, minimum GPA of 2.67.
Degree Requirements Written comprehensive exam required, foreign language and thesis not required.

NEW JERSEY INSTITUTE OF TECHNOLOGY
Newark, NJ 07102-1982

OVERVIEW
New Jersey Institute of Technology is a public coed university.

ENROLLMENT
7,837 graduate, professional, and undergraduate students; 964 full-time matriculated graduate/professional students (257 women), 1,119 part-time matriculated graduate/professional students (293 women).

GRADUATE FACULTY
348 full-time (41 women), 182 part-time (27 women), 394 FTE; includes 107 minority (15 African-Americans, 84 Asian-Americans, 8 Hispanics).

TUITION
$6660 per year (minimum) full-time, $346 per credit part-time for state residents; $9478 per year (minimum) full-time, $479 per credit part-time for nonresidents.

HOUSING
Rooms and/or apartments available to single students (870 units) at an average cost of $3840 per year ($5500 including board); on-campus housing not available to married students. Housing application deadline: 3/31. Graduate housing contact: Ralph Choonoo, 973-596-3041.

STUDENT SERVICES
Low-cost health insurance, career counseling, free psychological counseling, campus safety program, campus employment opportunities, international student services.

FACILITIES
Library: Van Houten Library plus 1 additional on-campus library; total holdings of 208,000 volumes, 3,715 microforms, 1,120 current periodical subscriptions. A total of 25 personal computers in all libraries. Access provided to on-line information retrieval services. *Computer:* Campuswide network is available with full Internet access. Computer service fees are included with tuition and fees. *Special:* In science and engineering: Hazardous Substance Management Research Center, Center for Biomedical Engineering, Center for Manufacturing Systems, Center for Transportation Studies and Research.

COMPUTER ENGINEERING

Department of Electrical and Computer Engineering
Programs Offers programs in computer engineering (MS); electrical engineering (MS, PhD, Engineer), including biomedical systems (MS, PhD), communication and signal processing (MS, PhD),

computer systems (MS, PhD), control systems (MS, PhD), microwave and lightwave engineering (MS, PhD), solid-state materials and devices (MS, PhD). Part-time and evening/weekend programs available.

Faculty 40 full-time (1 woman), 13 part-time (2 women), 43 FTE.

Faculty Research Communications systems design, digital signal processing. *Total annual research expenditures:* $1.8 million.

Students 129 full-time (21 women), 55 part-time (4 women); includes 29 minority (5 African-Americans, 18 Asian-Americans, 5 Hispanics), 110 international. Average age 33.

Degrees Awarded In 1996, 51 master's, 9 doctorates awarded. Terminal master's awarded for partial completion of doctoral program.

Entrance Requirements For master's, GRE General Test (minimum score 450 on verbal section, 600 on quantitative, 550 on analytical); for doctorate, GRE General Test (minimum score 450 on verbal section, 600 on quantitative, 550 on analytical), minimum graduate GPA of 3.5.

Degree Requirements For master's, thesis required (for some programs), foreign language not required; for doctorate, dissertation, residency required, foreign language not required.

Financial Aid Fellowships, research assistantships, teaching assistantships, assistantships, Federal Work-Study, institutionally sponsored loans, and career-related internships or fieldwork available. *Financial aid application deadline:* 3/15.

Applying 445 applicants, 66% accepted. *Deadline:* 6/5 (priority date; rolling processing; 11/5 for spring admission). *Fee:* $35.

Contact *Kathy Kelly*
Director of Admissions
973-596-3300
Fax: 973-596-3461
E-mail: admissions@admin.njit.edu

See in-depth description on page **483.**

COMPUTER SCIENCE

Department of Computer and Information Science

Programs Offers programs in bioinformatics (MS, PhD), computer and information science (PhD), computer science (MS), information systems (MS). MS and PhD (bioinformatics) offered jointly with the University of Medicine and Dentistry of New Jersey. Part-time and evening/weekend programs available.

Faculty 36 full-time (4 women), 14 part-time (2 women), 40 FTE.

Faculty Research Computer systems, communications and networking, artificial intelligence, database engineering, systems analysis. *Total annual research expenditures:* $2 million.

Students 321 full-time (104 women), 322 part-time (85 women); includes 135 minority (16 African-Americans, 103 Asian-Americans, 15 Hispanics, 1 Native American), 250 international. Average age 30.

Degrees Awarded In 1996, 189 master's, 8 doctorates awarded. Terminal master's awarded for partial completion of doctoral program.

Entrance Requirements For master's, GRE General Test (minimum score 450 on verbal section, 600 on quantitative, 550 on analytical); for doctorate, GRE General Test (minimum score 450 on verbal section, 600 on quantitative, 550 on analytical), minimum graduate GPA of 3.5.

Degree Requirements For master's, computer language, thesis required, foreign language not required; for doctorate, computer language, dissertation, residency required, foreign language not required.

Financial Aid Fellowships, research assistantships, teaching assistantships, assistantships, Federal Work-Study, institutionally sponsored loans, and career-related internships or fieldwork available. *Financial aid application deadline:* 3/15.

Applying 733 applicants, 61% accepted. *Deadline:* 6/5 (priority date; rolling processing; 11/5 for spring admission). *Fee:* $35.

Contact *Kathy Kelly*
Director of Admissions
973-596-3300
Fax: 973-596-3461
E-mail: admissions@admin.njit.edu

See in-depth description on page **481.**

ELECTRICAL ENGINEERING

Department of Electrical and Computer Engineering

Programs Offers programs in computer engineering (MS); electrical engineering (MS, PhD, Engineer), including biomedical systems (MS, PhD), communication and signal processing (MS, PhD), computer systems (MS, PhD), control systems (MS, PhD), microwave and lightwave engineering (MS, PhD), solid-state materials and devices (MS, PhD). Part-time and evening/weekend programs available.

Faculty 40 full-time (1 woman), 13 part-time (2 women), 43 FTE.

Faculty Research Communications systems design, digital signal processing. *Total annual research expenditures:* $1.8 million.

Students 129 full-time (21 women), 55 part-time (4 women); includes 29 minority (5 African-Americans, 18 Asian-Americans, 5 Hispanics), 110 international. Average age 33.

Degrees Awarded In 1996, 51 master's, 9 doctorates awarded. Terminal master's awarded for partial completion of doctoral program.

Entrance Requirements For master's, GRE General Test (minimum score 450 on verbal section, 600 on quantitative, 550 on analytical); for doctorate, GRE General Test (minimum score 450 on verbal section, 600 on quantitative, 550 on analytical), minimum graduate GPA of 3.5.

Degree Requirements For master's, thesis required (for some programs), foreign language not required; for doctorate, dissertation, residency required, foreign language not required.

Financial Aid Fellowships, research assistantships, teaching assistantships, assistantships, Federal Work-Study, institutionally sponsored loans, and career-related internships or fieldwork available. *Financial aid application deadline:* 3/15.

Applying 445 applicants, 66% accepted. *Deadline:* 6/5 (priority date; rolling processing; 11/5 for spring admission). *Fee:* $35.

Contact *Kathy Kelly*
Director of Admissions
973-596-3300
Fax: 973-596-3461
E-mail: admissions@admin.njit.edu

See in-depth description on page **483.**

INFORMATION SCIENCE

Department of Computer and Information Science

Programs Offers programs in bioinformatics (MS, PhD), computer and information science (PhD), computer science (MS), information systems (MS). MS and PhD (bioinformatics) offered jointly with the University of Medicine and Dentistry of New Jersey. Part-time and evening/weekend programs available.

Faculty 36 full-time (4 women), 14 part-time (2 women), 40 FTE.

Faculty Research Computer systems, communications and networking, artificial intelligence, database engineering, systems analysis. *Total annual research expenditures:* $2 million.

Students 321 full-time (104 women), 322 part-time (85 women); includes 135 minority (16 African-Americans, 103 Asian-Americans, 15 Hispanics, 1 Native American), 250 international. Average age 30.

Degrees Awarded In 1996, 189 master's, 8 doctorates awarded. Terminal master's awarded for partial completion of doctoral program.

Entrance Requirements For master's, GRE General Test (minimum score 450 on verbal section, 600 on quantitative, 550 on analytical); for doctorate, GRE General Test (minimum score 450 on verbal section, 600 on quantitative, 550 on analytical), minimum graduate GPA of 3.5.

Degree Requirements For master's, computer language, thesis required, foreign language not required; for doctorate, computer language, dissertation, residency required, foreign language not required.

Financial Aid Fellowships, research assistantships, teaching assistantships, assistantships, Federal Work-Study, institutionally sponsored loans, and career-related internships or fieldwork available. *Financial aid application deadline: 3/15.*

Applying 733 applicants, 61% accepted. *Deadline:* 6/5 (priority date; rolling processing; 11/5 for spring admission). *Fee:* $35.

Contact *Kathy Kelly*
Director of Admissions
973-596-3300
Fax: 973-596-3461
E-mail: admissions@admin.njit.edu

See in-depth description on page **481.**

MEDICAL INFORMATICS

Department of Computer and Information Science

Programs Offerings include bioinformatics (MS, PhD). MS and PhD (bioinformatics) offered jointly with the University of Medicine and Dentistry of New Jersey. Terminal master's awarded for partial completion of doctoral program.

Department Faculty 36 full-time (4 women), 14 part-time (2 women), 40 FTE.

Entrance Requirements For master's, GRE General Test (minimum score 450 on verbal section, 600 on quantitative, 550 on analytical); for doctorate, GRE General Test (minimum score 450 on verbal section, 600 on quantitative, 550 on analytical), minimum graduate GPA of 3.5.

Degree Requirements For master's, computer language, thesis required, foreign language not required; for doctorate, computer language, dissertation, residency required, foreign language not required.

Applying *Deadline:* 6/5 (priority date; rolling processing; 11/5 for spring admission). *Fee:* $35.

Contact *Kathy Kelly*
Director of Admissions
973-596-3300
Fax: 973-596-3461
E-mail: admissions@admin.njit.edu

See in-depth description on page **481.**

PRINCETON UNIVERSITY
Princeton, NJ 08544-1019

OVERVIEW

Princeton University is an independent coed university.

ENROLLMENT

6,400 graduate, professional, and undergraduate students; 1,719 full-time matriculated graduate/professional students (616 women), 0 part-time matriculated graduate/professional students.

GRADUATE FACULTY

718 full-time (168 women); includes 95 minority (14 African-Americans, 69 Asian-Americans, 12 Hispanics).

TUITION

$23,500 per year.

HOUSING

Rooms and/or apartments available to single students (884 units) at an average cost of $3688 per year ($6774 including board); available to married students (310 units) at an average cost of $6618 per year. Housing application deadline: 4/15. Graduate housing contact: Patricia McArdle, 609-258-3720.

STUDENT SERVICES

Low-cost health insurance, career counseling, free psychological counseling, day-care facilities, campus employment opportunities, international student services, teacher training.

FACILITIES

Library: Firestone Library plus 18 additional on-campus libraries; total holdings of 5 million volumes, 1.5 million microforms, 45,000 current periodical subscriptions. Access provided to on-line information retrieval services. *Computer:* Campuswide network is available with full Internet access. Computer services are offered at no charge. *Special:* In arts and humanities: Index of Christian Art, art museum. In science and engineering: Center for Energy and Environmental Studies, geophysical fluid dynamics laboratory, plasma physics laboratory. In social sciences: Office of Population Research.

COMPUTER ENGINEERING

School of Engineering and Applied Science, Department of Electrical Engineering

Programs Offerings include computer engineering (MSE, PhD).

Department Faculty 25 full-time (2 women).

Entrance Requirements GRE General Test.

Degree Requirements For master's, thesis optional; for doctorate, dissertation.

Applying *Deadline:* 1/8. *Fee:* $55 ($60 for international students).

Contact *Director of Graduate Admissions*
609-258-3034

See in-depth description on page **525.**

COMPUTER SCIENCE

School of Engineering and Applied Science, Department of Computer Science

Programs Awards MSE, PhD.

Faculty 18 full-time (2 women).

Faculty Research Algorithms, complexity, systems, VLSI.

Students 46 full-time (7 women), includes 2 minority (both Asian-Americans), 24 international.

Degrees Awarded In 1996, 6 doctorates awarded (33% entered university research/teaching, 67% found other work related to degree).

Entrance Requirements GRE General Test, GRE Subject Test.

Degree Requirements For master's, computer language required, thesis not required; for doctorate, computer language, dissertation.

Financial Aid Fellowships, research assistantships, teaching assistantships, Federal Work-Study, institutionally sponsored loans available. *Financial aid application deadline: 1/5.*

Applying 188 applicants, 23% accepted. *Deadline:* 1/5. *Fee:* $55 ($60 for international students).

Contact *Director of Graduate Admissions*
609-258-3034

See in-depth description on page 523.

ELECTRICAL ENGINEERING

School of Engineering and Applied Science, Department of Electrical Engineering

Programs Offers programs in computer engineering (MSE, PhD), electronic materials and devices (MSE, PhD), information sciences and systems (MSE, PhD), optoelectronics (MSE, PhD).
Faculty 25 full-time (2 women).
Students 105 full-time (13 women), 2 part-time (0 women); includes 63 minority (62 Asian-Americans, 1 Hispanic).
Degrees Awarded In 1996, 15 doctorates awarded.
Entrance Requirements GRE General Test.
Degree Requirements For master's, thesis optional; for doctorate, dissertation.
Financial Aid Fellowships, research assistantships, teaching assistantships, Federal Work-Study, institutionally sponsored loans available. *Financial aid application deadline: 1/8.*
Applying 519 applicants, 13% accepted. *Deadline: 1/8. Fee: $55 ($60 for international students).*
Contact *Director of Graduate Admissions*
609-258-3034

See in-depth description on page 525.

INFORMATION SCIENCE

School of Engineering and Applied Science, Department of Electrical Engineering

Programs Offerings include information sciences and systems (MSE, PhD).
Department Faculty 25 full-time (2 women).
Entrance Requirements GRE General Test.
Degree Requirements For master's, thesis optional; for doctorate, dissertation.
Applying *Deadline: 1/8. Fee: $55 ($60 for international students).*
Contact *Director of Graduate Admissions*
609-258-3034

See in-depth description on page 525.

RUTGERS, THE STATE UNIVERSITY OF NEW JERSEY, NEW BRUNSWICK
New Brunswick, NJ 08903

OVERVIEW
Rutgers, The State University of New Jersey, New Brunswick is a public coed university.

ENROLLMENT
47,812 graduate, professional, and undergraduate students; 4,538 full-time matriculated graduate/professional students (2,308 women), 8,215 part-time matriculated graduate/professional students (4,637 women).

EXPENSES
Tuition $6066 per year full-time, $250 per credit part-time for state residents; $8894 per year full-time, $369 per credit part-time for nonresidents. Fees $634 per year full-time, $84 per semester (minimum) part-time.

HOUSING
Rooms and/or apartments available to single students (705 units) at an average cost of $4084 per year; available to married students (368 units) at an average cost of $7440 per year. Graduate housing contact: Michael Imperiale, 732-932-1002.

STUDENT SERVICES
Low-cost health insurance, career counseling, free psychological counseling, day-care facilities, campus employment opportunities, international student services.

FACILITIES
Library: Alexander Library plus 18 additional on-campus libraries; total holdings of 5,418,327 volumes, 3,662,034 microforms, 24,891 current periodical subscriptions. Access provided to on-line information retrieval services. *Computer:* Campuswide network is available with full Internet access. Computer service fees are included with tuition and fees.

COMPUTER ENGINEERING

Department of Electrical and Computer Engineering

Programs Offers programs in communications and solid-state electronics (MS, PhD), computer engineering (MS, PhD), control systems (MS, PhD), digital signal processing (MS, PhD). Part-time programs available.
Faculty 28 full-time (2 women).
Faculty Research Communication and information processing, wireless information networks, micro-vacuum devices, machine vision, VLSI design. *Total annual research expenditures: $5.31 million.*
Students 59 full-time (6 women), 128 part-time (8 women); includes 80 minority (3 African-Americans, 75 Asian-Americans, 2 Hispanics).
Degrees Awarded In 1996, 32 master's awarded (80% found work related to degree, 20% continued full-time study); 12 doctorates awarded. Terminal master's awarded for partial completion of doctoral program.
Entrance Requirements GRE General Test.
Degree Requirements For master's, thesis optional, foreign language not required; for doctorate, dissertation required, foreign language not required.
Financial Aid In 1996–97, 86 students received aid, including 2 fellowships, 54 research assistantships (14 to first-year students), 30 teaching assistantships (10 to first-year students); full tuition waivers, Federal Work-Study also available. *Financial aid application deadline: 2/1.*
Applying 400 applicants, 26% accepted. *Deadline: 2/1 (priority date; rolling processing; 11/1 for spring admission). Fee: $40.*
Contact *Dr. David G. Daut*
Director
732-445-2578
Fax: 732-445-2820

See in-depth description on page 539.

COMPUTER SCIENCE

Department of Computer Science

Programs Awards MS, PhD. Part-time programs available.
Faculty 38 full-time (4 women), 4 part-time (0 women).
Faculty Research Artificial intelligence software and hardware systems, numerical computing, algorithms and complexity theory, programming languages and program transformation.
Students 92 full-time (12 women), 95 part-time (21 women); includes 5 minority (1 African-American, 4 Hispanics), 114 international.

Degrees Awarded In 1996, 44 master's, 14 doctorates awarded. Terminal master's awarded for partial completion of doctoral program.

Entrance Requirements GRE General Test, GRE Subject Test, bachelor's degree in computer science.

Degree Requirements For doctorate, dissertation required, foreign language not required.

Financial Aid In 1996–97, 79 students received aid, including 4 fellowships (all to first-year students), 28 research assistantships (5 to first-year students), 59 teaching assistantships (18 to first-year students); Federal Work-Study also available. *Financial aid application deadline:* 3/1.

Applying 307 applicants, 35% accepted. *Deadline:* 4/1 (rolling processing; 11/1 for spring admission). *Fee:* $40.

Contact Valentine Rolfe
Secretary
732-445-3547
Fax: 732-445-0537
E-mail: rolfe@cs.rutgers.edu

See in–depth description on page 537.

ELECTRICAL ENGINEERING

Department of Electrical and Computer Engineering

Programs Offers programs in communications and solid-state electronics (MS, PhD), computer engineering (MS, PhD), control systems (MS, PhD), digital signal processing (MS, PhD). Part-time programs available.

Faculty 28 full-time (2 women).

Faculty Research Communication and information processing, wireless information networks, micro-vacuum devices, machine vision, VLSI design. *Total annual research expenditures:* $5.31 million.

Students 59 full-time (6 women), 128 part-time (8 women); includes 80 minority (3 African-Americans, 75 Asian-Americans, 2 Hispanics).

Degrees Awarded In 1996, 32 master's awarded (80% found work related to degree, 20% continued full-time study); 12 doctorates awarded. Terminal master's awarded for partial completion of doctoral program.

Entrance Requirements GRE General Test.

Degree Requirements For master's, thesis optional, foreign language not required; for doctorate, dissertation required, foreign language not required.

Financial Aid In 1996–97, 86 students received aid, including 2 fellowships, 54 research assistantships (14 to first-year students), 30 teaching assistantships (10 to first-year students); full tuition waivers, Federal Work-Study also available. *Financial aid application deadline:* 2/1.

Applying 400 applicants, 26% accepted. *Deadline:* 2/1 (priority date; rolling processing; 11/1 for spring admission). *Fee:* $40.

Contact Dr. David G. Daut
Director
732-445-2578
Fax: 732-445-2820

See in–depth description on page 539.

STEVENS INSTITUTE OF TECHNOLOGY
Hoboken, NJ 07030

OVERVIEW

Stevens Institute of Technology is an independent coed university.

ENROLLMENT

2,800 graduate, professional, and undergraduate students; 353 full-time matriculated graduate/professional students (70 women), 1,073 part-time matriculated graduate/professional students (297 women).

GRADUATE FACULTY

102 full-time (7 women), 72 part-time (6 women), 126 FTE.

EXPENSES

Tuition $13,000 per year full-time, $650 per credit part-time. Fees $150 per year.

HOUSING

Rooms and/or apartments available to single students (40 units) at an average cost of $3364 per year ($6724 including board); available to married students (90 units) at an average cost of $7365 per year ($8565 including board). Graduate housing contact: Douglas James, 201-216-5128.

STUDENT SERVICES

Low-cost health insurance, career counseling, free psychological counseling, exercise/wellness program, day-care facilities, campus safety program, campus employment opportunities, international student services.

FACILITIES

Library: Samuel C. Williams Library; total holdings of 107,843 volumes, 10,461 microforms, 2,622 current periodical subscriptions. A total of 11 personal computers in all libraries. Access provided to on-line information retrieval services. *Computer:* Campuswide network is available with full Internet access. Total number of PCs/terminals supplied for student use: 200. Computer services are offered at no charge. *Special:* In arts and humanities: Humanities Resource Center. In science and engineering: Design Manufacturing Institute, Nichol's Environmental Laboratory, Surface Materials Center, telecommunications laboratory, Highly Filled Materials Institute, Davidson Oceanographic Laboratory. In social sciences: Schacht Management Laboratory, Laboratory of Psychological Studies.

COMPUTER ENGINEERING

Charles V. Schaefer Jr. School of Engineering, Department of Electrical and Computer Engineering, Program in Computer Engineering

Programs Offers computer and communications security (Certificate), computer and information engineering (M Eng, PhD, Engr), computer architecture and digital system design (M Eng, PhD, Engr), digital systems and VLSI design (Certificate), image and signal processing (M Eng, PhD, Engr), information networks (Certificate), robotics and automation (M Eng, PhD, Engr), software engineering (M Eng, PhD, Engr). Part-time and evening/weekend programs available.

Degrees Awarded Terminal master's awarded for partial completion of doctoral program.

Entrance Requirements For master's and doctorate, GRE, TOEFL; for other advanced degree, GRE.

Degree Requirements For master's and other advanced degree, computer language required, foreign language not required; for doctorate, computer language, dissertation.

Financial Aid Fellowships, research assistantships, teaching assistantships, Federal Work-Study, institutionally sponsored loans available.

Applying 48 applicants, 83% accepted. *Deadline:* rolling. *Fee:* $40.

Contact *Lawrence Russ*
Acting Director
201-216-5623
Fax: 201-216-8246

COMPUTER SCIENCE

School of Applied Sciences and Liberal Arts, Department of Computer Science

Programs Offers programs in advanced programming: theory, design and verification (Certificate); artificial intelligence and robotics (MS, PhD); computer and information systems (MS, PhD); computer architecture and digital system design (MS, PhD); database systems (Certificate); elements of computer science (Certificate); information systems (MS, Certificate); network and graph theory (Certificate); software design (MS, PhD); software engineering (Certificate); theoretical computer science (MS, PhD, Certificate); wireless communications (Certificate). MS and Certificate offered in cooperation with the Program in Information Systems. Part-time and evening/weekend programs available.
Faculty 7 full-time (1 woman), 14 part-time (0 women), 14 FTE.
Faculty Research Semantics, reliability theory.
Students 315 (77 women); includes 162 minority (8 African-Americans, 139 Asian-Americans, 15 Hispanics), 86 international.
Degrees Awarded In 1996, 106 master's, 6 doctorates awarded. Terminal master's awarded for partial completion of doctoral program.
Entrance Requirements For master's and doctorate, GRE, TOEFL.
Degree Requirements For master's, computer language required, thesis optional, foreign language not required; for doctorate, variable foreign language requirement, computer language, dissertation; for Certificate, computer language required, foreign language not required.
Financial Aid Fellowships, Federal Work-Study available. *Financial aid application deadline: 4/15.*
Applying 295 applicants, 87% accepted. *Fee:* $40.
Contact *Stephen L. Bloom*
Director
201-216-5439
Fax: 201-216-8246
E-mail: bloom@cs.stevens-tech.edu

ELECTRICAL ENGINEERING

Charles V. Schaefer Jr. School of Engineering, Department of Electrical and Computer Engineering, Program in Electrical Engineering

Programs Offers computer architecture and digital system design (M Eng, PhD, Engr), robotics/control/instrumentation (M Eng, PhD, Engr), signal and image processing (M Eng, PhD, Engr), telecommunications engineering (M Eng, PhD, Engr), telecommunications management (MS, PhD, Certificate). MS, PhD, and Certificate offered in cooperation with the Program in Telecommunications Management.
Entrance Requirements For master's and doctorate, GRE, TOEFL; for other advanced degree, GRE.
Degree Requirements For master's, computer language required, thesis optional, foreign language not required; for doctorate, variable foreign language requirement, computer language, dissertation; for other advanced degree, computer language required, foreign language not required.
Applying 167 applicants, 69% accepted. *Deadline:* rolling. *Fee:* $40.
Contact *Lawrence Russ*
Acting Director
201-216-5623
Fax: 201-216-8246

INFORMATION SCIENCE

Wesley J. Howe School of Technology Management, Program in Information Systems

Programs Awards MS, Certificate. Offered in cooperation with the Department of Computer Science.
Entrance Requirements For master's, GMAT, GRE, TOEFL.
Degree Requirements For master's, computer language required, thesis optional, foreign language not required; for Certificate, computer language required, foreign language not required.
Applying 16 applicants, 63% accepted. *Fee:* $40.
Contact *J. Luftman*
Head
201-216-8255

UNIVERSITY OF MEDICINE AND DENTISTRY OF NEW JERSEY
Newark, NJ 07107-3001

OVERVIEW
University of Medicine and Dentistry of New Jersey is a public coed graduate-only institution.

ENROLLMENT
4,476 graduate, professional, and undergraduate students; 3,056 full-time matriculated graduate/professional students (1,390 women), 621 part-time matriculated graduate/professional students (422 women).

GRADUATE FACULTY
1,694 full-time (562 women), 321 part-time (130 women), 1,829 FTE; includes 415 minority (101 African-Americans, 257 Asian-Americans, 57 Hispanics).

EXPENSES
Tuition $4949 per year full-time, $205 per credit part-time for state residents; $7169 per year full-time, $292 per credit part-time for nonresidents. Fees $240 per year.

HOUSING
On-campus housing not available.

STUDENT SERVICES
Low-cost health insurance, career counseling, free psychological counseling, day-care facilities, campus safety program, campus employment opportunities, international student services.

FACILITIES
Library: George F. Smith Library plus 3 additional on-campus libraries; total holdings of 204,267 volumes, 22,219 microforms, 2,981 current periodical subscriptions. A total of 100 personal computers in all libraries. Access provided to on-line information retrieval services. *Computer:* Campuswide network is available with full Internet access. Computer services are offered at no charge. *Special:* In science and engineering: Center for Advanced Biotechnology and Medicine, Environmental and Occupational Health Science Institute, New Jersey Cancer Institute, Eye Institute.

MEDICAL INFORMATICS

School of Health Related Professions

Programs Offerings include biomedical informatics (MS), health care informatics (Certificate). MS (biomedical informatics) offered jointly with New Jersey Institute of Technology; MA and MS (health science, physician assistant) offered jointly with Seton Hall University; MPT offered jointly with Rutgers, The State University of New Jersey, Camden.

School Faculty 44 full-time (36 women), 15 part-time (10 women), 51.55 FTE.

Entrance Requirements For Certificate, RN license (nurse midwifery).

Applying *Deadline:* rolling. *Fee:* $35.

Contact *Dr. Laura Nelson*
Associate Dean of Academic and Student Services
973-982-5453
Fax: 973-982-7028
E-mail: shrp.adm@umdnj.edu

NEW MEXICO

New Mexico Institute of Mining and Technology
Socorro, NM 87801

OVERVIEW
New Mexico Institute of Mining and Technology is a public primarily male university.

ENROLLMENT
1,201 graduate, professional, and undergraduate students; 231 full-time matriculated graduate/professional students (67 women), 2 part-time matriculated graduate/professional students (both women).

GRADUATE FACULTY
77 full-time, 2 part-time; includes 8 minority (1 African-American, 4 Asian-Americans, 1 Hispanic, 2 Native Americans).

EXPENSES
Tuition $2048 per year full-time, $85 per hour part-time for state residents; $8440 per year full-time, $352 per hour part-time for nonresidents. Fees $860 per year.

HOUSING
Rooms and/or apartments available to single students (11 units) at an average cost of $1966 per year; available to married students (36 units) at an average cost of $4536 per year. Graduate housing contact: Barbara Romero, 505-835-5900.

STUDENT SERVICES
Low-cost health insurance, career counseling, free psychological counseling, day-care facilities, campus employment opportunities, international student services.

FACILITIES
Library: Martin Speare Memorial Library plus 3 additional on-campus libraries; total holdings of 137,000 volumes, 130,000 microforms, 910 current periodical subscriptions. A total of 8 personal computers in all libraries. Access provided to on-line information retrieval services. *Special:* In science and engineering: New Mexico Bureau of Mines and Mineral Resources, Petroleum Recovery Research Center, Center for Explosives Technology

Research, Geophysical Research Center, Langmuir Laboratory for Atmospheric Research.

COMPUTER SCIENCE

Department of Computer Science
Programs Awards MS, PhD.
Faculty 6 full-time (0 women).
Students 24 full-time (7 women), 1 (woman) part-time; includes 18 international. Average age 25.
Degrees Awarded In 1996, 6 master's awarded.
Entrance Requirements For master's, GRE General Test, TOEFL (minimum score 540); for doctorate, GRE General Test, GRE Subject Test, TOEFL (minimum score 540).
Degree Requirements For master's, computer language required, thesis optional, foreign language not required; for doctorate, 1 foreign language, computer language, dissertation.
Financial Aid In 1996–97, 17 students received aid, including 9 research assistantships (3 to first-year students) averaging $800 per month and totaling $34,932, 8 teaching assistantships (4 to first-year students) averaging $800 per month and totaling $26,444; fellowships, Federal Work-Study, institutionally sponsored loans also available. *Financial aid application deadline:* 3/1; applicants required to submit CSS PROFILE or FAFSA.
Applying 90 applicants, 67% accepted. *Deadline:* 3/1 (priority date; rolling processing; 6/1 for spring admission). *Fee:* $16.
Contact *Dr. J. A. Smoake*
Dean of Graduate Studies
505-835-5513
Fax: 505-835-5476
E-mail: graduate@nmt.edu

New Mexico State University
Las Cruces, NM 88003-8001

OVERVIEW
New Mexico State University is a public coed university.

ENROLLMENT
14,748 graduate, professional, and undergraduate students; 1,428 full-time matriculated graduate/professional students (667 women), 1,017 part-time matriculated graduate/professional students (576 women).

GRADUATE FACULTY
571 full-time (145 women), 40 part-time (10 women); includes 86 minority (33 Asian-Americans, 51 Hispanics, 2 Native Americans).

TUITION
$2352 per year full-time, $98 per credit hour part-time for state residents; $7344 per year full-time, $306 per credit hour part-time for nonresidents.

HOUSING
Rooms and/or apartments available to single students at an average cost of $1730 per year; available to married students (490 units). Housing application deadline: 7/1. Graduate housing contact: Robert Smiggen, 505-646-3203.

STUDENT SERVICES
Low-cost health insurance, career counseling, free psychological counseling, campus employment opportunities, international student services.

FACILITIES

Library: New Library; total holdings of 953,352 volumes, 956,989 microforms, 7,328 current periodical subscriptions. A total of 61 personal computers in all libraries. Access provided to on-line information retrieval services. *Computer:* Campuswide network is available with full Internet access. Computer service fees are included with tuition and fees. *Special:* In arts and humanities: Arts and Sciences Research Center, Center for Business Research and Services, Center for Latin American Studies, computing research laboratory, Educational Research Center. In science and engineering: Astrophysical Research Consortium, Engineering Research Center, New Mexico Water Resources Institute. In social sciences: Border Research Institute, Center for International Programs, Institute for Gerontological Research and Education.

COMPUTER ENGINEERING

College of Engineering, Department of Electrical and Computer Engineering
Programs   Awards MSEE, PhD. Part-time programs available.
Faculty   25 full-time (1 woman), 4 part-time (0 women).
Faculty Research   Software engineering, high performance computing, telemetering and space telecommunications, computational electromagnetics.
Students   52 full-time (4 women), 30 part-time (1 woman); includes 15 minority (1 Asian-American, 13 Hispanics, 1 Native American), 24 international. Average age 30.
Degrees Awarded   In 1996, 54 master's awarded.
Entrance Requirements   For doctorate, departmental qualifying exam, minimum GPA of 3.0.
Degree Requirements   For master's, thesis (for some programs); for doctorate, 2 foreign languages (computer language can substitute for one), dissertation.
Financial Aid   Fellowships, research assistantships, teaching assistantships, Federal Work-Study, and career-related internships or fieldwork available. Aid available to part-time students. *Financial aid application deadline: 3/1.*
Applying   69 applicants, 88% accepted. *Deadline:* 7/1 (priority date; rolling processing; 11/1 for spring admission). *Fee:* $15 ($35 for international students).
Contact   *Dr. Jay B. Jordan*
Head
505-646-3115
Fax: 505-646-1435
E-mail: jjordan@nmsu.edu

COMPUTER SCIENCE

College of Arts and Sciences, Department of Computer Science
Programs   Awards MS, PhD. PhD offered jointly with the University of New Mexico. Part-time programs available.
Faculty   19 full-time (2 women), 1 part-time (0 women).
Faculty Research   Programming languages, artificial intelligence, databases, operating systems, computer networks.
Students   45 full-time (7 women), 18 part-time (3 women); includes 5 minority (1 Asian-American, 4 Hispanics), 37 international. Average age 31.
Degrees Awarded   In 1996, 11 master's, 2 doctorates awarded.
Entrance Requirements   GRE General Test.
Degree Requirements   For master's, computer language, thesis or alternative required, foreign language not required; for doctorate, 1 foreign language, computer language, dissertation.

Financial Aid   Research assistantships, teaching assistantships, Federal Work-Study, and career-related internships or fieldwork available. Aid available to part-time students. *Financial aid application deadline: 3/1.*
Applying   83 applicants, 60% accepted. *Deadline:* 7/1 (priority date; rolling processing; 11/1 for spring admission). *Fee:* $15 ($35 for international students).
Contact   *Dr. Arthur Karshmer*
Head
505-646-3723
Fax: 505-646-1002
E-mail: arthur@nmsu.edu

ELECTRICAL ENGINEERING

College of Engineering, Department of Electrical and Computer Engineering
Programs   Awards MSEE, PhD. Part-time programs available.
Faculty   25 full-time (1 woman), 4 part-time (0 women).
Faculty Research   Software engineering, high performance computing, telemetering and space telecommunications, computational electromagnetics.
Students   52 full-time (4 women), 30 part-time (1 woman); includes 15 minority (1 Asian-American, 13 Hispanics, 1 Native American), 24 international. Average age 30.
Degrees Awarded   In 1996, 54 master's awarded.
Entrance Requirements   For doctorate, departmental qualifying exam, minimum GPA of 3.0.
Degree Requirements   For master's, thesis (for some programs); for doctorate, 2 foreign languages (computer language can substitute for one), dissertation.
Financial Aid   Fellowships, research assistantships, teaching assistantships, Federal Work-Study, and career-related internships or fieldwork available. Aid available to part-time students. *Financial aid application deadline: 3/1.*
Applying   69 applicants, 88% accepted. *Deadline:* 7/1 (priority date; rolling processing; 11/1 for spring admission). *Fee:* $15 ($35 for international students).
Contact   *Dr. Jay B. Jordan*
Head
505-646-3115
Fax: 505-646-1435
E-mail: jjordan@nmsu.edu

UNIVERSITY OF NEW MEXICO
Albuquerque, NM 87131-2039

OVERVIEW
University of New Mexico is a public coed university.

ENROLLMENT
23,617 graduate, professional, and undergraduate students; 2,742 full-time, 2,248 part-time matriculated graduate/professional students.

GRADUATE FACULTY
1,375 full-time (451 women), 367 part-time (179 women), 1,512 FTE; includes 202 minority (13 African-Americans, 66 Asian-Americans, 109 Hispanics, 14 Native Americans).

TUITION
$2349 per year full-time, $99 per credit hour part-time for state residents; $8386 per year full-time, $99 per credit hour (minimum) part-time for nonresidents.

HOUSING

Rooms and/or apartments available to single students (2,300 units) at an average cost of $300 per year ($4500 including board); available to married students (200 units) at an average cost of $5000 per year. Housing application deadline: 5/1. Graduate housing contact: Robert A. Schulte, 505-277-4707.

STUDENT SERVICES

Low-cost health insurance, career counseling, free psychological counseling, exercise/wellness program, day-care facilities, campus safety program, campus employment opportunities, international student services.

FACILITIES

Library: Zimmerman Library plus 9 additional on-campus libraries; total holdings of 1.6 million volumes, 5 million microforms. Access provided to on-line information retrieval services. *Computer:* Campuswide network is available with full Internet access. Total number of PCs/terminals supplied for student use: 10,000. Computer service fees are included with tuition and fees. *Special:* In arts and humanities: Tamarind Institute, Latin American Institute. In science and engineering: New Mexico Engineering Research Institute, Technology Application Center, Institute for Modern Optics, Institute of Meteoritics, Office of Contract Archaeology, Bureau of Engineering Research, Museum of Southwestern Biology. In social sciences: Maxwell Museum of Anthropology.

COMPUTER ENGINEERING

School of Engineering, Department of Electrical and Computer Engineering
Programs Offers programs in computer engineering (MS, PhD), manufacturing engineering (ME, MS), microelectronics (MS, PhD), network and control systems (MS, PhD), optoelectronics (MS, PhD), pulsed power and plasma science (MS, PhD), signal processing and communications (MS, PhD). Part-time and evening/weekend programs available.
Faculty 38 full-time (2 women), 9 part-time (1 woman), 42.4 FTE.
Faculty Research Pulsed power, microelectronics, optoelectronics, signal processing.
Students 44 full-time (7 women), 52 part-time (6 women); includes 8 minority (7 Hispanics, 1 Native American), 27 international. Average age 30.
Degrees Awarded In 1996, 48 master's awarded.
Entrance Requirements GRE General Test, minimum GPA of 3.0.
Degree Requirements For master's, thesis or alternative required, foreign language not required; for doctorate, dissertation required, foreign language not required.
Financial Aid In 1996–97, 67 students received aid, including 4 fellowships, 50 research assistantships (19 to first-year students) averaging $1,100 per month and totaling $464,432, 13 teaching assistantships (5 to first-year students) averaging $980 per month and totaling $132,825; Federal Work-Study and career-related internships or fieldwork also available. *Financial aid application deadline:* 5/31.
Applying 53 applicants, 51% accepted. *Deadline:* 6/1. *Fee:* $25.
Contact *Ronald DeVries*
Coordinator of Graduate Studies
505-277-6562
Fax: 505-277-1439
E-mail: devries@houdini.eece.unm.edu

See in-depth description on page 685.

COMPUTER SCIENCE

School of Engineering, Department of Computer Science
Programs Awards MS, PhD.
Faculty 16 full-time (2 women), 4 part-time (1 woman), 17.42 FTE.
Faculty Research Programming methodology, operating systems, artificial intelligence, computer graphics and visualization, deductive databases. *Total annual research expenditures:* $1.539 million.
Students 34 full-time (5 women), 50 part-time (11 women); includes 6 minority (3 Asian-Americans, 3 Hispanics), 20 international. Average age 33.
Degrees Awarded In 1996, 17 master's, 2 doctorates awarded.
Entrance Requirements Minimum GPA of 3.0.
Degree Requirements For master's, thesis required, foreign language not required; for doctorate, dissertation.
Financial Aid In 1996–97, 52 students received aid, including 1 fellowship totaling $2,000, 32 research assistantships (8 to first-year students) averaging $1,500 per month and totaling $368,800, 19 teaching assistantships (11 to first-year students) averaging $922 per month; Federal Work-Study and career-related internships or fieldwork also available. *Financial aid application deadline:* 4/15.
Applying 62 applicants, 47% accepted. *Deadline:* 6/30. *Fee:* $25.
Contact *Dr. James Hollan*
Chair
505-277-3112
Fax: 505-277-6927
E-mail: hollan@cs.unm.edu

ELECTRICAL ENGINEERING

School of Engineering, Department of Electrical and Computer Engineering
Programs Offers programs in computer engineering (MS, PhD), manufacturing engineering (ME, MS), microelectronics (MS, PhD), network and control systems (MS, PhD), optoelectronics (MS, PhD), pulsed power and plasma science (MS, PhD), signal processing and communications (MS, PhD). Part-time and evening/weekend programs available.
Faculty 38 full-time (2 women), 9 part-time (1 woman), 42.4 FTE.
Faculty Research Pulsed power, microelectronics, optoelectronics, signal processing.
Students 44 full-time (7 women), 52 part-time (6 women); includes 8 minority (7 Hispanics, 1 Native American), 27 international. Average age 30.
Degrees Awarded In 1996, 48 master's awarded.
Entrance Requirements GRE General Test, minimum GPA of 3.0.
Degree Requirements For master's, thesis or alternative required, foreign language not required; for doctorate, dissertation required, foreign language not required.
Financial Aid In 1996–97, 67 students received aid, including 4 fellowships, 50 research assistantships (19 to first-year students) averaging $1,100 per month and totaling $464,432, 13 teaching assistantships (5 to first-year students) averaging $980 per month and totaling $132,825; Federal Work-Study and career-related internships or fieldwork also available. *Financial aid application deadline:* 5/31.
Applying 53 applicants, 51% accepted. *Deadline:* 6/1. *Fee:* $25.
Contact *Ronald DeVries*
Coordinator of Graduate Studies
505-277-6562
Fax: 505-277-1439
E-mail: devries@houdini.eece.unm.edu

See in-depth description on page 685.

NEW YORK

ALFRED UNIVERSITY
Alfred, NY 14802-1205

OVERVIEW
Alfred University is an independent coed university.

ENROLLMENT
2,397 graduate, professional, and undergraduate students; 187 full-time matriculated graduate/professional students (93 women), 199 part-time matriculated graduate/ professional students (120 women).

GRADUATE FACULTY
103 (22 women); includes 4 minority (1 African-American, 3 Asian-Americans).

EXPENSES
Tuition $19,414 per year full-time, $370 per credit hour (minimum) part-time. Fees $502 per year.

HOUSING
Rooms and/or apartments available to single students at an average cost of $3488 per year ($6394 including board); on-campus housing not available to married students. Housing application deadline: 7/1. Graduate housing contact: Tomas Gonzalez, 607-871-2186.

STUDENT SERVICES
Multicultural affairs office, low-cost health insurance, career counseling, free psychological counseling, campus safety program, campus employment opportunities, international student services, writing training.

FACILITIES
Library: Herrick Library plus 1 additional on-campus library; total holdings of 410,000 volumes, 70,000 microforms, 1,900 current periodical subscriptions. Access provided to on-line information retrieval services. *Computer:* Campuswide network is available with full Internet access. Computer services are offered at no charge. *Special:* In science and engineering: Center for Advanced Ceramic Technology, Center for Glass Research.

ELECTRICAL ENGINEERING

Graduate School, Program in Electrical Engineering
Programs Awards MS. Part-time programs available.
Faculty 5 full-time (0 women).
Students 2 full-time (0 women), 2 part-time (1 woman).
Degrees Awarded In 1996, 2 degrees awarded.
Entrance Requirements TOEFL.
Degree Requirements Thesis required, foreign language not required.
Financial Aid Research assistantships, partial tuition waivers available. Aid available to part-time students. Financial aid applicants required to submit FAFSA.
Applying 12 applicants, 92% accepted. *Deadline:* rolling. *Fee:* $50.
Contact *Kathleen M. Torrey*
Associate Director of Admissions
607-871-2141
Fax: 607-871-2198
E-mail: hudak@bigvax.alfred.edu

BROOKLYN COLLEGE OF THE CITY UNIVERSITY OF NEW YORK
Brooklyn, NY 11210-2889

OVERVIEW
Brooklyn College of the City University of New York is a public coed comprehensive institution.

EXPENSES
Tuition $4350 per year full-time, $185 per credit part-time for state residents; $7600 per year full-time, $320 per credit part-time for nonresidents. Fees $120 per year.

HOUSING
On-campus housing not available.

FACILITIES
Library: Harry D. Gideonse Library. *Special:* In arts and humanities: Humanities Institute, Institute for Studies in American Music, electronic music studio. In science and engineering: Applied Science Institute, Archaeological Research Institute, Center for Nuclear Theory. In social sciences: Center for Italian American Studies, Infant Study Center, Africana Research Institute, Center for Health Promotion, Center for Responsive Psychology, Center for Human Relations Training, Center for Latino Studies, Center for Child and Adult Development.

COMPUTER SCIENCE

Department of Computer and Information Science
Programs Awards MA, MS, PhD. Part-time and evening/ weekend programs available.
Faculty Research Theoretical computer science, operating systems, modeling and computer applications, algorithms, artificial intelligence.
Entrance Requirements For master's, TOEFL, previous course work in computer science.
Degree Requirements For master's, computer language, comprehensive exam or thesis required, foreign language not required.
Applying *Deadline:* 3/1. *Fee:* $35.

COMPUTER SCIENCE

Department of Health and Nutrition Science, Program in Community Health
Programs Offerings include computer science and health science (MS).
Applying *Deadline:* 3/1 (11/1 for spring admission). *Fee:* $35.

INFORMATION SCIENCE

Department of Computer and Information Science
Programs Awards MA, MS, PhD. Part-time and evening/ weekend programs available.
Faculty Research Theoretical computer science, operating systems, modeling and computer applications, algorithms, artificial intelligence.
Entrance Requirements For master's, TOEFL, previous course work in computer science.
Degree Requirements For master's, computer language, comprehensive exam or thesis required, foreign language not required.
Applying *Deadline:* 3/1. *Fee:* $35.

CITY COLLEGE OF THE CITY UNIVERSITY OF NEW YORK
New York, NY 10031-6977

OVERVIEW
City College of the City University of New York is a public coed university.

ENROLLMENT
12,506 graduate, professional, and undergraduate students; 265 full-time matriculated graduate/professional students (134 women), 1,961 part-time matriculated graduate/professional students (1,133 women).

EXPENSES
Tuition $4350 per year full-time, $185 per credit part-time for state residents; $7600 per year full-time, $320 per credit part-time for nonresidents. Fees $41 per year.

HOUSING
On-campus housing not available.

STUDENT SERVICES
Career counseling, free psychological counseling, day-care facilities.

FACILITIES
Library: Cohen Library plus 3 additional on-campus libraries; total holdings of 1.2 million volumes, 644 microforms, 2,000 current periodical subscriptions. Access provided to on-line information retrieval services. *Computer:* Campuswide network is available with full Internet access. Total number of PCs/terminals supplied for student use: 3,000. Computer services are offered at no charge. *Special:* In arts and humanities: Leonard Davis Center for the Performing Arts, Rifkind Center for the Humanities, Latin American Writers Institute. In science and engineering: Institute for Marine and Atmospheric Sciences, Clean Fuels Institute, Institute for Applied Chemical Physics, Northeast Resource Center for Science and Engineering, picosecond laser and spectroscopy laboratory. In social sciences: Rosenberg/Humphrey Program in Public Affairs, Greenberg Center for Legal Education and Urban Policy.

COMPUTER SCIENCE

Graduate School, School of Engineering, Department of Computer Sciences
Programs Awards MS, PhD. PhD offered through the Graduate School and University Center of the City University of New York.
Faculty Research Complexities of algebraic research, human issues in computer science, scientific computing, supercompilers, parallel algorithms.
Students 51 full-time (13 women), 144 part-time (47 women).
Degrees Awarded In 1996, 112 master's awarded.
Entrance Requirements For master's, TOEFL (minimum score 500); for doctorate, GRE General Test, TOEFL.
Degree Requirements For master's, computer language required, thesis optional, foreign language not required; for doctorate, 1 foreign language, dissertation, comprehensive exams.
Financial Aid Fellowships, teaching assistantships, partial tuition waivers, Federal Work-Study available. Aid available to part-time students. *Financial aid application deadline: 6/1.*

Applying 121 applicants, 96% accepted. *Deadline:* rolling. *Fee:* $40.
Contact *Graduate Admissions Office*
212-650-6977

ELECTRICAL ENGINEERING

Graduate School, School of Engineering, Department of Electrical Engineering
Programs Awards ME, MS, PhD. PhD offered through the Graduate School and University Center of the City University of New York. Part-time programs available.
Faculty Research Optical electronics, microwaves, communication, signal processing, control systems.
Students 9 full-time (1 woman), 36 part-time (0 women).
Degrees Awarded In 1996, 61 master's awarded.
Entrance Requirements For master's, TOEFL (minimum score 500); for doctorate, GRE General Test, TOEFL.
Degree Requirements For master's, computer language required, thesis optional, foreign language not required; for doctorate, 1 foreign language (computer language can substitute), dissertation, comprehensive exams.
Financial Aid Fellowships, research assistantships, full and partial tuition waivers, Federal Work-Study available. Aid available to part-time students. *Financial aid application deadline: 5/1.*
Applying 44 applicants, 95% accepted. *Deadline:* rolling. *Fee:* $40.
Contact *Graduate Admissions Office*
212-650-6977

CLARKSON UNIVERSITY
Potsdam, NY 13699

OVERVIEW
Clarkson University is an independent coed university.

ENROLLMENT
2,670 graduate, professional, and undergraduate students; 300 full-time matriculated graduate/professional students (71 women), 14 part-time matriculated graduate/professional students (6 women).

GRADUATE FACULTY
145 full-time (21 women), 15 part-time (9 women), 151 FTE; includes 16 minority (1 African-American, 15 Asian-Americans).

EXPENSES
Tuition $18,250 per year. Fees $373 per year.

HOUSING
On-campus housing not available.

STUDENT SERVICES
Low-cost health insurance, career counseling, free psychological counseling, campus safety program, campus employment opportunities, international student services.

FACILITIES
Library: Andrew S. Schuler Educational Resources Center; total holdings of 229,242 volumes, 272,114 microforms, 2,561 current periodical subscriptions. A total of 118 personal computers in all libraries. Access provided to on-line information retrieval services. *Computer:* Campuswide network is available with full Internet access. Total number of PCs/terminals supplied for student use: 199. Computer services are offered at no

charge. *Special:* In science and engineering: Center for Advanced Material Processing.

COMPUTER ENGINEERING

School of Engineering, Department of Electrical and Computer Engineering

Programs Offers programs in computer engineering (ME, MS), electrical and computer engineering (PhD), electrical engineering (ME, MS). Part-time programs available.

Faculty 12 full-time (1 woman).

Faculty Research Robotics, electrical machines, electrical circuits, dielectric liquids, controls. *Total annual research expenditures:* $389,000.

Students 38 full-time (6 women), 1 (woman) part-time; includes 2 minority (1 African-American, 1 Asian-American), 28 international. Average age 26.

Degrees Awarded In 1996, 13 master's, 1 doctorate awarded.

Degree Requirements For master's, thesis required, foreign language not required; for doctorate, dissertation, departmental qualifying exam required, foreign language not required.

Financial Aid In 1996–97, 2 fellowships, 6 research assistantships, 6 teaching assistantships were awarded.

Applying 233 applicants, 63% accepted. *Deadline:* rolling. *Fee:* $25.

Contact *Dr. Susan E. Conry*
Interim Chair
315-268-6511
Fax: 315-268-7600
E-mail: conry@sun.soe.clarkson.edu

COMPUTER SCIENCE

School of Science, Department of Mathematics and Computer Science

Programs Offers programs in computer science (MS), mathematics (MS, PhD).

Faculty 13 full-time (2 women), 2 part-time (0 women), 14 FTE.

Faculty Research Automated deduction, solitons, cryptography, computational theory, neutral network. *Total annual research expenditures:* $348,000.

Students 11 full-time (3 women), 2 part-time (1 woman); includes 4 international. Average age 29.

Degrees Awarded In 1996, 1 master's, 1 doctorate awarded. Terminal master's awarded for partial completion of doctoral program.

Degree Requirements For doctorate, dissertation, departmental qualifying exam required, foreign language not required.

Financial Aid In 1996–97, 7 teaching assistantships were awarded; fellowships, research assistantships also available.

Applying 80 applicants, 35% accepted. *Deadline:* rolling. *Fee:* $25.

Contact *Dr. David L. Powers*
Chair
315-268-2369
Fax: 315-268-6670
E-mail: dpowers@craft.cam0.edu

ELECTRICAL ENGINEERING

School of Engineering, Department of Electrical and Computer Engineering

Programs Offers programs in computer engineering (ME, MS), electrical and computer engineering (PhD), electrical engineering (ME, MS). Part-time programs available.

Faculty 12 full-time (1 woman).

Faculty Research Robotics, electrical machines, electrical circuits, dielectric liquids, controls. *Total annual research expenditures:* $389,000.

Students 38 full-time (6 women), 1 (woman) part-time; includes 2 minority (1 African-American, 1 Asian-American), 28 international. Average age 26.

Degrees Awarded In 1996, 13 master's, 1 doctorate awarded.

Degree Requirements For master's, thesis required, foreign language not required; for doctorate, dissertation, departmental qualifying exam required, foreign language not required.

Financial Aid In 1996–97, 2 fellowships, 6 research assistantships, 6 teaching assistantships were awarded.

Applying 233 applicants, 63% accepted. *Deadline:* rolling. *Fee:* $25.

Contact *Dr. Susan E. Conry*
Interim Chair
315-268-6511
Fax: 315-268-7600
E-mail: conry@sun.soe.clarkson.edu

COLLEGE OF STATEN ISLAND OF THE CITY UNIVERSITY OF NEW YORK
Staten Island, NY 10314-6600

OVERVIEW

College of Staten Island of the City University of New York is a public coed comprehensive institution.

ENROLLMENT

12,203 graduate, professional, and undergraduate students; 55 full-time matriculated graduate/professional students (37 women), 1,025 part-time matriculated graduate/professional students (810 women).

GRADUATE FACULTY

55 full-time, 51 part-time.

EXPENSES

Tuition $4350 per year full-time, $185 per credit part-time for state residents; $7600 per year full-time, $320 per credit part-time for nonresidents. Fees $116 per year full-time, $64 per year part-time.

HOUSING

On-campus housing not available.

STUDENT SERVICES

Disabled student services, low-cost health insurance, career counseling, free psychological counseling, day-care facilities, campus employment opportunities, international student services.

FACILITIES

Library: Main library; total holdings of 197,872 volumes, 688,812 microforms, 1,343 current periodical subscriptions. A total of 60 personal computers in all libraries. Access provided to on-line information retrieval services. *Computer:* Campuswide network is available with full Internet access. Total number of PCs/terminals supplied for student use: 1,000. Computer services are offered at no charge. *Special:* In science and engineering: Air pollution research facility, mechanical research laboratory, computer science research laboratory, polymer chemistry research laboratory.

COMPUTER SCIENCE

Program in Computer Science

Programs Awards MS, PhD. PhD offered jointly with the Graduate School and University Center of the City University of New York. Part-time and evening/weekend programs available.

Faculty 7 full-time (2 women).

Faculty Research Knowledge engineering, image processing, performance evaluation, database networks, neural computing.

Students 7 full-time (4 women), 49 part-time (9 women); includes 12 minority (1 African-American, 10 Asian-Americans, 1 Native American), 21 international. Average age 30.

Degrees Awarded In 1996, 12 master's awarded.

Entrance Requirements For master's, previous undergraduate course work in computer science.

Degree Requirements For master's, thesis optional; for doctorate, dissertation.

Financial Aid In 1996–97, 6 teaching assistantships were awarded; research assistantships also available.

Applying 32 applicants, 38% accepted. *Deadline:* 6/1 (priority date; rolling processing; 12/1 for spring admission). *Fee:* $40.

Contact *Earl Teasley*
Director of Admissions
718-982-2010
Fax: 718-982-2500

COLUMBIA UNIVERSITY
New York, NY 10027

OVERVIEW
Columbia University is an independent coed university.

ENROLLMENT
19,975 graduate, professional, and undergraduate students; 10,401 full-time matriculated graduate/professional students (4,931 women), 2,078 part-time matriculated graduate/professional students (1,211 women).

GRADUATE FACULTY
2,557 full-time (777 women), 763 part-time (219 women), 2,811 FTE; includes 722 minority (279 African-Americans, 325 Asian-Americans, 117 Hispanics, 1 Native American).

TUITION
$22,400 per year full-time, $12,140 per year part-time.

HOUSING
Rooms and/or apartments available to single students at an average cost of $4988 per year ($7938 including board); available to married students at an average cost of $6700 per year. Graduate housing information: 212-854-9300.

STUDENT SERVICES
Low-cost health insurance, career counseling, free psychological counseling, campus safety program, campus employment opportunities, international student services.

FACILITIES
Library: Butler Library plus 23 additional on-campus libraries; total holdings of 6,792,274 volumes, 4,460,914 microforms, 65,275 current periodical subscriptions. Access provided to on-line information retrieval services. *Computer:* Campuswide network is available with full Internet access. Computer service fees are included with tuition and fees. *Special:* In arts and humanities: Heyman Center, Miller Theater, Temple Hoyne Buell Center for the Study of American Architecture, Ctr for Preservation Research, Research Ctr for Arts and Culture, Society of Fellows in the Humanities, Electronic Music Center, Center for U.S.-China Arts Exchange. In science and engineering: Lamont Doherty Earth Observatory; Nevis Laboratories; radiation laboratory; Center for Biomedical Engineering; Center for Earth Engineering; Image Technology for New Media Center; Center for Infrastructure Studies; Langmuir Center for Colloids and Interfaces; N. Y. State Center of Advanced Technology; Center for Telecommunications Research; Carleton Materials Laboratory; laboratories for microelectronics and plasma physics; Center for Chemical Research; Alzheimer's Disease Research Center; Irving Comprehensive Cancer Center; Centers for Molecular Recognition, Radiological Research, and Reproductive Sciences; Center for Neurobiology and Behavior; Institute of Cancer Research; Biosphere 2. In social sciences: Center for the Social Sciences, AIDS Prevention Research Center, New York City Social Indicators Survey Center, Center for the Study of Social Policy and Practice in the Workplace, Center for the Study of Social Work Practice, Institute on Aging and Adult Human Development, Italian Academy for Advanced Studies in America, Center for Israel and Jewish Studies, Center for Iranian Studies, Donald Keene Center of Japanese Culture, Institute for Research in African American Studies.

COMPUTER SCIENCE

School of Engineering and Applied Science, Department of Computer Science

Programs Awards MS, PhD, CSE. PhD offered through the Graduate School of Arts and Sciences. Part-time programs available.

Faculty 24 full-time (3 women), 7 part-time (1 woman).

Faculty Research Algorithms and complexity, robotics, software systems, parallel processing, artificial intelligence. *Total annual research expenditures:* $4.719 million.

Students 94 full-time (15 women), 73 part-time (19 women); includes 29 minority (28 Asian-Americans, 1 Hispanic), 69 international.

Degrees Awarded In 1996, 48 master's, 8 doctorates, 2 CSEs awarded. Terminal master's awarded for partial completion of doctoral program.

Entrance Requirements GRE General Test, GRE Subject Test, TOEFL.

Degree Requirements For master's, computer language required, thesis optional, foreign language not required; for doctorate, computer language, dissertation, 4 qualifying exams required, foreign language not required; for CSE, computer language required, foreign language not required.

Financial Aid In 1996–97, 82 students received aid, including 2 fellowships averaging $1,420 per month, 70 research assistantships (7 to first-year students) averaging $1,420 per month, 10 teaching assistantships (2 to first-year students) averaging $1,420 per month; outside fellowships, Federal Work-Study also available. *Financial aid application deadline:* 1/5; applicants required to submit FAFSA.

Applying 407 applicants, 27% accepted. *Deadline:* 1/5 (10/1 for spring admission). *Fee:* $45.

Contact *Graduate Program Office*
212-939-7000
Fax: 212-666-0140
E-mail: gradinfo@cs.columbia.edu

See in-depth description on page **405.**

ELECTRICAL ENGINEERING

School of Engineering and Applied Science, Department of Electrical Engineering

Programs Offers programs in electrical engineering (MS, Eng Sc D, PhD, EE), new media technology (MS), solid state science and engineering (MS, Eng Sc D, PhD), telecommunications (MS). PhD offered through the Graduate School of Arts and Sciences. Part-time programs available.

Faculty   19 full-time (0 women), 7 part-time (0 women).

Faculty Research   Plasma and electromagnetics, microelectronics, signal and communications processing, VLSI and circuits, optoelectronics. *Total annual research expenditures:* $6.5 million.

Students   119 full-time (12 women), 84 part-time (10 women); includes 32 minority (2 African-Americans, 30 Asian-Americans), 113 international.

Degrees Awarded   In 1996, 64 master's, 15 doctorates awarded. Terminal master's awarded for partial completion of doctoral program.

Entrance Requirements   For master's and doctorate, GRE General Test, TOEFL.

Degree Requirements   For doctorate, dissertation, qualifying exam required, foreign language not required.

Financial Aid   In 1996–97, 51 research assistantships totaling $1.495 million, 12 teaching assistantships totaling $292,000 were awarded; readers, preceptors, Federal Work-Study also available. *Financial aid application deadline:* 1/5; applicants required to submit FAFSA.

Applying   576 applicants, 25% accepted. *Deadline:* 1/5 (10/1 for spring admission). *Fee:* $45.

Contact   *Marlene Mansfield*
Student Coordinator
212-854-3104
Fax: 212-932-9421
E-mail: mansfld@ee.columbia.edu

See in-depth description on page **407.**

MEDICAL INFORMATICS

College of Physicians and Surgeons and Graduate School of Arts and Sciences, Graduate School of Arts and Sciences at the College of Physicians and Surgeons, Department of Medical Informatics

Programs   Awards MA, M Phil, PhD, MD/PhD.

Students   9 full-time (4 women), includes 6 international.

Degrees Awarded   In 1996, 1 doctorate awarded.

Entrance Requirements   For master's, GRE General Test, TOEFL (minimum score 550).

Degree Requirements   For doctorate, dissertation.

Financial Aid   In 1996–97, 6 research assistantships (5 to first-year students) were awarded. Aid available to part-time students. *Financial aid application deadline:* 1/5.

Applying   28 applicants, 18% accepted. *Deadline:* 1/2. *Fee:* $65.

Contact   *Dr. Richard E. Abbott*
Assistant Dean for Graduate Affairs
212-305-8058
Fax: 212-305-1031

See in-depth description on page **409.**

CORNELL UNIVERSITY
Ithaca, NY 14853-0001

OVERVIEW

Cornell University is an independent coed university.

ENROLLMENT

18,849 graduate, professional, and undergraduate students; 5,337 full-time matriculated graduate/professional students (2,168 women), 0 part-time matriculated graduate/professional students.

GRADUATE FACULTY

1,466 full-time (281 women), 60 part-time (13 women); includes 152 minority (38 African-Americans, 82 Asian-Americans, 27 Hispanics, 5 Native Americans).

EXPENSES

Tuition $21,840 per year. Fees $36 per year.

HOUSING

Rooms and/or apartments available to single students (507 units) at an average cost of $5100 per year; available to married students (478 units) at an average cost of $7800 per year. Graduate housing contact: Missy Riker, 607-255-5368.

STUDENT SERVICES

Disabled student services, low-cost health insurance, career counseling, free psychological counseling, exercise/wellness program, campus safety program, campus employment opportunities, international student services.

FACILITIES

Library: Olin Library plus 17 additional on-campus libraries; total holdings of 5,952,217 volumes, 6,980,459 microforms, 61,673 current periodical subscriptions. A total of 500 personal computers in all libraries. Access provided to on-line information retrieval services. *Computer:* Campuswide network is available with full Internet access. Total number of PCs/terminals supplied for student use: 700. Computer services are offered at no charge. *Special:* In arts and humanities: Johnson Museum of Art, Einaudi Center for International Studies, Performing Arts Center. In science and engineering: Baker Institute for Animal Health; Boyce Thompson Institute for Plant Research; Cornell Plantations Botanical Gardens; Centers for Advanced Technology in Biotechnology, the Environment, Radiophysics and Space Research; Statistics, Theory and Simulation in Science and Engineering, High-Energy Synchrotron Studies, and Manufacturing Enterprise; Institute for Comparative and Environmental Toxicology; Institute for the Study of Continents; Mathematical Sciences Institute; National Astronomy and Ionosphere Center (Arecibo, Puerto Rico); National Nanofabrication Facility; New York State Agricultural Experiment Stations; Newman Laboratory of Nuclear Studies; Northeast Regional Climate Center; Ward Laboratory of Nuclear Engineering; atomic and solid state physics, ornithology, and plasma studies la. In social sciences: Africana Studies and Research Center; Bronfenbrenner Life Course Center; Community and Rural Development Institute; Cornell Institute for Social and Economic Research; Cornell International Institute for Food, Agriculture and Development; Family Life Development Center.

ARTIFICIAL INTELLIGENCE/ROBOTICS

Graduate Fields of Engineering, Field of Computer Science

Programs   Offerings include artificial intelligence (M Eng, PhD), robotics (M Eng, PhD). Terminal master's awarded for partial completion of doctoral program.

Faculty   34 full-time.

Entrance Requirements   GRE General Test, GRE Subject Test, TOEFL.

Degree Requirements   For doctorate, dissertation.

Applying   *Deadline:* 1/10 (priority date). *Fee:* $65.

Contact *Graduate Field Assistant*
            607-255-8593
            Fax: 607-255-4428
            E-mail: phd@cs.cornell.edu

See in-depth description on page **411.**

COMPUTER ENGINEERING

Graduate Fields of Engineering, Field of Electrical Engineering
Programs Offerings include computer engineering (M Eng, PhD).
Faculty 44 full-time.
Entrance Requirements GRE General Test, TOEFL.
Degree Requirements For doctorate, dissertation required, foreign language not required.
Applying *Deadline:* 1/10 (priority date). *Fee:* $65.
Contact *Graduate Field Assistant*
            607-255-4304
            E-mail: ee_msphd@cornell.edu

See in-depth description on page **413.**

COMPUTER SCIENCE

Graduate Fields of Engineering, Field of Computer Science
Programs Offers programs in algorithms (M Eng, PhD), applied logic and automated reasoning (M Eng, PhD), artificial intelligence (M Eng, PhD), computer graphics (M Eng, PhD), computer science (M Eng, PhD), computer vision (M Eng, PhD), concurrency and distributed computing (M Eng, PhD), information organization and retrieval (M Eng, PhD), operating systems (M Eng, PhD), parallel computing (M Eng, PhD), programming environments (M Eng, PhD), programming languages and methodology (M Eng, PhD), robotics (M Eng, PhD), scientific computing (M Eng, PhD), theory of computation (M Eng, PhD).
Faculty 34 full-time.
Faculty Research Numerical analysis, distributed systems, multimedia.
Students 133 full-time (27 women), includes 16 minority (1 African-American, 12 Asian-Americans, 3 Hispanics), 73 international.
Degrees Awarded In 1996, 65 master's, 11 doctorates awarded. Terminal master's awarded for partial completion of doctoral program.
Entrance Requirements GRE General Test, GRE Subject Test, TOEFL.
Degree Requirements For doctorate, dissertation.
Financial Aid In 1996–97, 71 students received aid, including 8 fellowships (5 to first-year students), 42 research assistantships, 21 teaching assistantships (12 to first-year students); full and partial tuition waivers, institutionally sponsored loans also available. Financial aid applicants required to submit FAFSA.
Applying 680 applicants, 24% accepted. *Deadline:* 1/10 (priority date). *Fee:* $65.
Contact *Graduate Field Assistant*
            607-255-8593
            Fax: 607-255-4428
            E-mail: phd@cs.cornell.edu

See in-depth description on page **411.**

ELECTRICAL ENGINEERING

Graduate Fields of Engineering, Field of Electrical Engineering
Programs Offers programs in computer engineering (M Eng, PhD), electrical engineering (M Eng, PhD), electrical systems (M Eng, PhD), electrophysics (M Eng, PhD).
Faculty 44 full-time.
Faculty Research Communications, information theory, signal processing and power and control; plasma science and technology;

space and upper-atmospheric science; remote sensing; solid state electronics and optoelectronics.
Students 207 full-time (29 women), includes 50 minority (6 African-Americans, 31 Asian-Americans, 13 Hispanics), 83 international.
Degrees Awarded In 1996, 128 master's, 20 doctorates awarded.
Entrance Requirements GRE General Test, TOEFL.
Degree Requirements For doctorate, dissertation required, foreign language not required.
Financial Aid In 1996–97, 90 students received aid, including 11 fellowships (4 to first-year students), 51 research assistantships (4 to first-year students), 28 teaching assistantships (7 to first-year students); full and partial tuition waivers, institutionally sponsored loans also available. Financial aid applicants required to submit FAFSA.
Applying 815 applicants, 37% accepted. *Deadline:* 1/10 (priority date). *Fee:* $65.
Contact *Graduate Field Assistant*
            607-255-4304
            E-mail: ee_msphd@cornell.edu

See in-depth description on page **413.**

FORDHAM UNIVERSITY
New York, NY 10458

OVERVIEW
Fordham University is an independent-religious coed university.

ENROLLMENT
13,158 graduate, professional, and undergraduate students; 6,612 matriculated graduate/professional students (3,713 women).

GRADUATE FACULTY
370 full-time (116 women), 470 part-time (237 women); includes 69 minority (26 African-Americans, 19 Asian-Americans, 24 Hispanics).

EXPENSES
Tuition $525 per credit. Fees $64 per year.

HOUSING
Rooms and/or apartments available to single students (300 units); on-campus housing not available to married students. Housing application deadline: 4/15. Graduate housing contact: Iris Remon, 718-817-3080.

STUDENT SERVICES
Disabled student services, low-cost health insurance, career counseling, free psychological counseling, campus safety program, campus employment opportunities, international student services, writing training, teacher training.

FACILITIES
Library: Main library; total holdings of 1,233,575 volumes, 1,420,920 microforms, 5,505 current periodical subscriptions. A total of 30 personal computers in all libraries. Access provided to on-line information retrieval services. *Computer:* Campuswide network is available with full Internet access. Total number of PCs/terminals supplied for student use: 400. *Special:* In arts and humanities: Regional Education Technology Center. In science and engineering: Calder Conservation and Ecology Center. In social sciences: Center for Family and Children's

Services, Third Age Center, Hispanic Research Center, Institute for Social Research.

COMPUTER SCIENCE

Graduate School of Arts and Sciences, Department of Computer Science and Information Systems
Programs Offers program in computer science (MS).
Students 6 full-time (5 women), 14 part-time (5 women); includes 1 minority (African-American), 4 international.
Entrance Requirements GRE General Test.
Degree Requirements Computer language, comprehensive exam required, thesis not required.
Financial Aid In 1996–97, 3 students received aid, including 3 teaching assistantships; research assistantships, full and partial tuition waivers, institutionally sponsored loans, and career-related internships or fieldwork also available. *Financial aid application deadline:* 2/1.
Applying 15 applicants, 67% accepted. *Deadline:* 5/1 (priority date; rolling processing; 12/1 for spring admission). *Fee:* $50.
Contact *Dr. Craig Pilant*
Director of Admissions
718-817-4416

See in-depth description on page 437.

GRADUATE SCHOOL AND UNIVERSITY CENTER OF THE CITY UNIVERSITY OF NEW YORK
New York, NY 10036-8099

OVERVIEW
Graduate School and University Center of the City University of New York is a public coed graduate-only institution.

ENROLLMENT
3,879 graduate, professional, and undergraduate students; 3,464 full-time matriculated graduate/professional students (1,817 women), 343 part-time matriculated graduate/professional students (192 women).

GRADUATE FACULTY
1,471 full-time (318 women); includes 5 minority (3 African-Americans, 2 Hispanics).

TUITION
$4350 per year full-time, $245 per credit part-time for state residents; $7600 per year full-time, $425 per credit part-time for nonresidents.

HOUSING
Rooms and/or apartments available to single students (114 units) at an average cost of $6300 per year; available to married students (10 units) at an average cost of $10,800 per year. Housing application deadline: 5/1. Graduate housing contact: Roberta Zalkin, 212-642-2803.

STUDENT SERVICES
Low-cost health insurance, career counseling, free psychological counseling.

FACILITIES
Library: Mina Rees Library; total holdings of 204,000 volumes, 409,000 microforms, 1,680 current periodical subscriptions. Access provided to on-line information retrieval services. *Special:* In arts and humanities: Répertoire Internationale de Littérature Musale. In science and engineering: Center for Research in Speech and Hearing Sciences. In social sciences: Center for Social Research, Center for Urban and Policy Studies, Center for Advanced Study in Education, Center for Jewish Studies, Center for the Study of Women and Sex Roles, Center for Research in Cognition and Affect.

COMPUTER SCIENCE

Program in Computer Science
Programs Awards PhD. Offered jointly with the College of Staten Island of the City University of New York.
Faculty 56 full-time (12 women).
Students 95 full-time (26 women), 3 part-time (1 woman); includes 23 minority (9 African-Americans, 12 Asian-Americans, 2 Hispanics), 16 international. Average age 36.
Degrees Awarded In 1996, 4 degrees awarded.
Entrance Requirements GRE General Test.
Degree Requirements 1 foreign language (computer language can substitute), dissertation.
Financial Aid In 1996–97, 36 students received aid, including 26 fellowships (2 to first-year students), 3 teaching assistantships (1 to a first-year student); research assistantships also available. *Financial aid application deadline:* 2/1; applicants required to submit FAFSA.
Applying 76 applicants, 30% accepted. *Deadline:* 4/15. *Fee:* $40.
Contact *Dr. Stanley Habib*
Executive Officer
212-642-2201

ELECTRICAL ENGINEERING

Program in Engineering
Programs Offerings include electrical engineering (PhD). Terminal master's awarded for partial completion of doctoral program.
Program Faculty 68 full-time (1 woman).
Entrance Requirements GRE General Test.
Degree Requirements Dissertation.
Applying *Deadline:* 4/15. *Fee:* $40.
Contact *Dr. Gerard G. Lowen*
Executive Officer
212-650-8030

HOFSTRA UNIVERSITY
Hempstead, NY 11550-1090

OVERVIEW
Hofstra University is an independent coed university.

ENROLLMENT
12,279 graduate, professional, and undergraduate students; 1,364 full-time matriculated graduate/professional students (687 women), 2,147 part-time matriculated graduate/professional students (1,416 women).

GRADUATE FACULTY
177 full-time (63 women), 132 part-time (60 women); includes 27 minority (9 African-Americans, 13 Asian-Americans, 5 Hispanics).

EXPENSES
Tuition $6188 per year full-time, $442 per credit part-time. Fees $662 per year full-time, $222 per semester (minimum) part-time.

HOUSING
Rooms and/or apartments available to single students (3,375 units) at an average cost of $4060 per year ($6450 including board); on-campus housing not available to married students. Graduate housing contact: Office of Residential Life, 516-463-6930.

STUDENT SERVICES
Disabled student services, low-cost health insurance, career counseling, free psychological counseling, exercise/wellness program, day-care facilities, campus safety program, campus employment opportunities, international student services, teacher training.

FACILITIES
Library: Axinn Library plus 1 additional on-campus library; total holdings of 1.35 million volumes, 1.152 million microforms, 5,483 current periodical subscriptions. A total of 70 personal computers in all libraries. Access provided to on-line information retrieval services. *Computer:* Campuswide network is available with full Internet access. Total number of PCs/terminals supplied for student use: 250. Computer services are offered at no charge. *Special:* In arts and humanities: Hofstra Museum. In science and engineering: Arboretum, marine laboratory in Jamaica, bird sanctuary. In social sciences: Psychological Evaluation and Research Center.

COMPUTER SCIENCE

College of Liberal Arts and Sciences, Division of Natural Sciences, Mathematics, Engineering, and Computer Science, Department of Computer Science

Programs Awards MA, MS. Part-time and evening/weekend programs available.

Faculty 8 full-time (2 women), 4 part-time (0 women).

Faculty Research Graphics, medical imaging, modeling graphics, artificial intelligence.

Students 42 part-time (5 women); includes 2 minority (1 African-American, 1 Native American), 4 international. Average age 33.

Degrees Awarded In 1996, 11 degrees awarded.

Entrance Requirements GRE General Test (minimum combined score of 1650 on three sections), minimum GPA of 3.0.

Degree Requirements Computer language, thesis, projects (MA) required, foreign language not required.

Financial Aid 8 students received aid; fellowships, institutionally sponsored loans available. Aid available to part-time students. Financial aid applicants required to submit FAFSA.

Applying 28 applicants, 43% accepted. *Deadline:* rolling. *Fee:* $40 ($75 for international students).

Contact *Mary Beth Carey*
Dean of Admissions
516-463-6700
Fax: 516-560-7660

OVERVIEW
Hunter College of the City University of New York is a public coed comprehensive institution.

ENROLLMENT
18,772 graduate, professional, and undergraduate students; 680 full-time matriculated graduate/professional students (502 women), 2,629 part-time matriculated graduate/professional students (2,070 women).

GRADUATE FACULTY
548 full-time (270 women), 458 part-time (272 women).

EXPENSES
Tuition $4350 per year full-time, $185 per credit part-time for state residents; $7600 per year full-time, $320 per credit part-time for nonresidents. Fees $26 per year.

HOUSING
Rooms and/or apartments available to single students (500 units); on-campus housing not available to married students. Graduate housing contact: Pamela Burthwright, 212-481-4311.

STUDENT SERVICES
Disabled student services, career counseling, free psychological counseling, day-care facilities, campus safety program, campus employment opportunities, international student services.

FACILITIES
Library: Jacqueline Grennan Wexler Library plus 2 additional on-campus libraries; total holdings of 742,041 volumes, 1,071,213 microforms, 2,275 current periodical subscriptions. A total of 80 personal computers in all libraries. Access provided to on-line information retrieval services. *Computer:* Campuswide network is available with full Internet access. Total number of PCs/terminals supplied for student use: 600. *Special:* In arts and humanities: Center for Puerto Rican Studies. In science and engineering: Center for Communication Disorders, Institute for Biomolecular Structure and Function, Center for Occupational and Environmental Health. In social sciences: Urban Research Center; Center for AIDS, Drugs, and Community Health; Brookdale Center on Aging.

COMPUTER SCIENCE

Division of Sciences and Mathematics, Department of Computer Science

Programs Awards MA, PhD. PhD jointly offered with the Graduate School and University Center of the City University of New York; MA admissions temporarily suspended. Part-time and evening/weekend programs available.

Faculty 10 full-time (3 women).

Faculty Research Artificial intelligence, software engineering, graph theory, combinatorics.

Students 0.

Degrees Awarded Terminal master's awarded for partial completion of doctoral program.

Degree Requirements For doctorate, 1 foreign language, computer language, dissertation.

Financial Aid Fellowships available.

Applying *Fee:* $40.
Contact *Dr. Howard Rubin*
             Chair
             212-772-5213

IONA COLLEGE
New Rochelle, NY 10801-1890

OVERVIEW
Iona College is an independent coed comprehensive institution.

ENROLLMENT
5,136 graduate, professional, and undergraduate students; 56 full-time matriculated graduate/professional students (35 women), 840 part-time matriculated graduate/professional students (485 women).

GRADUATE FACULTY
70 full-time (17 women), 55 part-time (12 women); includes 41 minority (14 African-Americans, 12 Asian-Americans, 15 Hispanics).

EXPENSES
Tuition $435 per credit. Fees $45 per semester.

HOUSING
On-campus housing not available.

STUDENT SERVICES
Career counseling, free psychological counseling, campus employment opportunities, international student services.

FACILITIES
Library: Ryan Library; total holdings of 243,888 volumes, 409,737 microforms. A total of 1,079 personal computers in all libraries. Access provided to on-line information retrieval services. *Computer:* Campuswide network is available with full Internet access. Computer service fees are included with tuition and fees. *Special:* In arts and humanities: Library Technology Center. In science and engineering: Machine Intelligence Institute.

COMPUTER SCIENCE

School of Arts and Science, Program in Computer Science
Programs Awards MS. Part-time and evening/weekend programs available.
Faculty 7 full-time (2 women).
Faculty Research Telecommunications, computer graphics, expert systems, database design, compiler design.
Students 71 part-time (27 women); includes 5 minority (1 African-American, 4 Asian-Americans), 1 international. Average age 29.
Degrees Awarded In 1996, 17 degrees awarded.
Entrance Requirements Minimum GPA of 3.0.
Degree Requirements Thesis or alternative.
Financial Aid In 1996–97, 2 graduate assistantships were awarded; partial tuition waivers also available. Aid available to part-time students.
Applying *Deadline:* rolling. *Fee:* $25.
Contact *Arlene Melillo*
             Director of Graduate Recruitment
             914-633-2328
             Fax: 914-633-2023

LEHMAN COLLEGE OF THE CITY UNIVERSITY OF NEW YORK
Bronx, NY 10468-1589

OVERVIEW
Lehman College of the City University of New York is a public coed comprehensive institution.

ENROLLMENT
10,352 graduate, professional, and undergraduate students; 78 full-time matriculated graduate/professional students (50 women), 1,371 part-time matriculated graduate/professional students (1,027 women).

GRADUATE FACULTY
285 full-time (108 women), 351 part-time (197 women).

EXPENSES
Tuition $4350 per year full-time, $185 per credit part-time for state residents; $7600 per year full-time, $320 per credit part-time for nonresidents. Fees $115 per year full-time, $68 per year part-time.

HOUSING
On-campus housing not available.

STUDENT SERVICES
Low-cost health insurance, career counseling, day-care facilities.

FACILITIES
Library: Main library; total holdings of 529,143 volumes, 460,000 microforms, 1,460 current periodical subscriptions. Access provided to on-line information retrieval services. *Computer:* Campuswide network is available. Total number of PCs/terminals supplied for student use: 400. Computer service fees are included with tuition and fees. *Special:* In arts and humanities: Institute for Literacy Studies, Speech and Hearing Center, Center for School/College Collaboratives, Latino Urban Policy Institute, The Bronx Institute.

COMPUTER SCIENCE

Division of Natural and Social Sciences, Department of Mathematics and Computer Science, Program in Computer Science
Programs Awards MS.
Students 13 full-time (1 woman), 20 part-time (7 women).
Degree Requirements 1 foreign language, computer language, thesis or alternative.
Financial Aid Full and partial tuition waivers, Federal Work-Study available. Aid available to part-time students. *Financial aid application deadline:* 5/15; applicants required to submit FAFSA.
Applying *Deadline:* 4/1 (rolling processing; 11/1 for spring admission). *Fee:* $40.
Contact *Charles Berger*
             Adviser
             718-960-8868
             Fax: 718-960-8969

LONG ISLAND UNIVERSITY, BROOKLYN CAMPUS
Brooklyn, NY 11201-8423

OVERVIEW
Long Island University, Brooklyn Campus is an independent coed comprehensive institution.

ENROLLMENT
8,264 graduate, professional, and undergraduate students; 712 full-time matriculated graduate/professional students (460 women), 1,233 part-time matriculated graduate/professional students (839 women).

EXPENSES
Tuition $457 per credit. Fees $520 per year (minimum) full-time, $60 per semester (minimum) part-time.

HOUSING
Rooms and/or apartments available to single students at an average cost of $4230 per year ($6000 including board); available to married students at an average cost of $4970 per year ($7500 including board). Housing application deadline: 9/1. Graduate housing contact: Tom Iseley, 718-488-1046.

STUDENT SERVICES
Disabled student services, career counseling, free psychological counseling, day-care facilities, international student services.

FACILITIES
Library: Salena Library Learning Center; total holdings of 230,000 volumes. Access provided to on-line information retrieval services. *Computer:* Campuswide network is available with full Internet access. Total number of PCs/terminals supplied for student use: 400. Computer service fees are included with tuition and fees.

COMPUTER SCIENCE

School of Business and Public Administration, Department of Computer Science
Programs Awards MS.
Faculty 5 full-time (0 women).
Students 24 full-time, 25 part-time; includes 32 minority (12 African-Americans, 19 Asian-Americans, 1 Hispanic).
Degrees Awarded In 1996, 21 degrees awarded.
Entrance Requirements GMAT or GRE.
Financial Aid 13 students received aid; assistantships available.
Applying 51 applicants, 59% accepted. *Deadline:* rolling. *Fee:* $30.
Contact Bernard W. Sullivan
    Associate Director of Admissions
    718-488-1011

LONG ISLAND UNIVERSITY, C.W. POST CAMPUS
Brookville, NY 11548-1300

OVERVIEW
Long Island University, C.W. Post Campus is an independent coed comprehensive institution.

ENROLLMENT
8,060 graduate, professional, and undergraduate students; 906 full-time matriculated graduate/professional students (579 women), 2,955 part-time matriculated graduate/professional students (2,049 women).

GRADUATE FACULTY
215 full-time (70 women), 170 part-time (50 women); includes 40 minority (10 African-Americans, 21 Asian-Americans, 9 Hispanics).

EXPENSES
Tuition $457 per credit. Fees $520 per year (minimum) full-time, $60 per semester (minimum) part-time.

HOUSING
Rooms and/or apartments available to single students (1,500 units) at an average cost of $3650 per year ($5650 including board); on-campus housing not available to married students. Housing application deadline: 6/1. Graduate housing contact: John Farkas, 516-299-2326.

STUDENT SERVICES
Low-cost health insurance, career counseling, free psychological counseling, day-care facilities, campus employment opportunities, international student services.

FACILITIES
Library: B. Davis Schwartz Memorial Library; total holdings of 1,057,934 volumes, 932,072 microforms, 9,784 current periodical subscriptions. A total of 15 personal computers in all libraries. Access provided to on-line information retrieval services. *Computer:* Campuswide network is available with full Internet access. Total number of PCs/terminals supplied for student use: 400. Computer services are offered at no charge. *Special:* In arts and humanities: Hillwood Art Museum, Tilles Center for Performing Arts. In social sciences: Accounting and Tax Research Library, Center for Business Research, Center for Aging.

INFORMATION SCIENCE

College of Liberal Arts and Sciences, Department of Computer Sciences
Programs Offerings include information systems (MS).
Department Faculty 7 full-time (2 women), 1 part-time (0 women).
Entrance Requirements Bachelor's degree in science, mathematics, or engineering.
Degree Requirements Computer language, thesis or alternative, comprehensive exam required, foreign language not required.
Applying *Deadline:* rolling. *Fee:* $30.
Contact John Keane
    Graduate Adviser
    516-299-2923

MANHATTAN COLLEGE
Riverdale, NY 10471

OVERVIEW
Manhattan College is an independent-religious coed comprehensive institution.

ENROLLMENT
3,121 graduate, professional, and undergraduate students; 69 full-time matriculated graduate/professional students

(28 women), 457 part-time matriculated graduate/professional students (180 women).

GRADUATE FACULTY
63 full-time (12 women), 28 part-time (12 women).

EXPENSES
Tuition $370 per credit. Fees $100 per year.

HOUSING
Rooms and/or apartments available to single students at an average cost of $3500 per year; on-campus housing not available to married students.

STUDENT SERVICES
Low-cost health insurance, career counseling, free psychological counseling.

FACILITIES
Library: Cardinal Hayes Library plus 1 additional on-campus library; total holdings of 244,680 volumes, 347,290 microforms, 2,540 current periodical subscriptions. A total of 6 personal computers in all libraries. Access provided to on-line information retrieval services. *Special:* In arts and humanities: Peace Studies Institute, Center for Professional Ethics. In science and engineering: Plant morphogenesis laboratory, nuclear reactor laboratory, advanced separation laboratory, manufacturing engineering laboratory, Northeast Regional Community Environmental Center. In social sciences: School of Business Research Institute.

COMPUTER ENGINEERING

Leo School of Engineering, Program in Electrical Engineering, Program in Computer Engineering
Programs   Awards MS. Part-time and evening/weekend programs available.
Faculty   10 full-time (1 woman), 1 part-time (0 women).
Students   1 full-time (0 women), 18 part-time (1 woman); includes 7 minority (2 Asian-Americans, 5 Hispanics), 1 international. Average age 28.
Degrees Awarded   In 1996, 18 degrees awarded.
Entrance Requirements   GRE, TOEFL, minimum GPA of 3.0.
Degree Requirements   Computer language, thesis or alternative.
Financial Aid   In 1996–97, 5 laboratory assistantships (all to first-year students) were awarded; Federal Work-Study also available. *Financial aid application deadline: 2/1.*
Applying   5 applicants, 100% accepted. *Deadline:* 8/10 (priority date; rolling processing; 1/7 for spring admission). *Fee:* $50.
Contact   *William Bisset*
Dean of Admissions/Financial Aid
718-920-0200
Fax: 718-548-1008

ELECTRICAL ENGINEERING

Leo School of Engineering, Program in Electrical Engineering
Programs   Offers computer engineering (MS), electrical engineering (MS). Part-time and evening/weekend programs available.
Faculty   10 full-time (1 woman), 1 part-time (0 women).
Faculty Research   Computer modeling of magnetic resonance imaging.
Students   6 full-time (1 woman), 18 part-time (3 women); includes 10 minority (4 Asian-Americans, 6 Hispanics), 1 international. Average age 27.
Degrees Awarded   In 1996, 10 degrees awarded.
Entrance Requirements   GRE, TOEFL, minimum GPA of 3.0.
Degree Requirements   Computer language, thesis or alternative.

Financial Aid   In 1996–97, 9 laboratory assistantships, scholarships (8 to first-year students) were awarded; Federal Work-Study also available. *Financial aid application deadline: 2/1.*
Applying   26 applicants, 88% accepted. *Deadline:* 8/10 (priority date; rolling processing; 1/7 for spring admission). *Fee:* $50.
Contact   *William Bisset*
Dean of Admissions/Financial Aid
718-920-0200
Fax: 718-548-1008

MARIST COLLEGE
Poughkeepsie, NY 12601-1387

OVERVIEW
Marist College is an independent coed comprehensive institution.

ENROLLMENT
4,465 graduate, professional, and undergraduate students; 86 full-time matriculated graduate/professional students (51 women), 370 part-time matriculated graduate/professional students (150 women).

GRADUATE FACULTY
47 full-time (11 women), 24 part-time (4 women).

EXPENSES
Tuition $399 per credit hour. Fees $50 per year.

HOUSING
On-campus housing not available.

STUDENT SERVICES
Low-cost health insurance, career counseling, free psychological counseling, campus employment opportunities.

FACILITIES
Library: Main library; total holdings of 156,638 volumes, 182,983 microforms, 1,822 current periodical subscriptions. Access provided to on-line information retrieval services. *Computer:* Campuswide network is available with full Internet access. Total number of PCs/terminals supplied for student use: 258. Computer services are offered at no charge. *Special:* In social sciences: Marist Institute for Public Opinion.

COMPUTER SCIENCE

Division of Sciences
Programs   Offers program in computer science (MS), including information systems, software development. Part-time and evening/weekend programs available.
Faculty   9 full-time (4 women), 3 part-time (0 women).
Students   22 full-time (2 women), 86 part-time (25 women). Average age 33.
Degrees Awarded   In 1996, 37 degrees awarded.
Degree Requirements   Thesis optional, foreign language not required.
Financial Aid   Partial tuition waivers, Federal Work-Study available. Aid available to part-time students. *Financial aid application deadline:* 8/15; applicants required to submit FAFSA.
Applying   123 applicants, 78% accepted. *Deadline:* 8/1 (priority date; rolling processing; 12/15 for spring admission). *Fee:* $30.

Contact   *Carol A. Vari*
Acting Director of Graduate Admissions
914-575-3530
Fax: 914-575-3640

INFORMATION SCIENCE

Division of Sciences
Programs   Offerings include computer science (MS), with options in information systems, software development.
Division Faculty   9 full-time (4 women), 3 part-time (0 women).
Degree Requirements   Thesis optional, foreign language not required.
Applying   *Deadline:* 8/1 (priority date; rolling processing; 12/15 for spring admission). *Fee:* $30.
Contact   *Carol A. Vari*
Acting Director of Graduate Admissions
914-575-3530
Fax: 914-575-3640

NEW YORK INSTITUTE OF TECHNOLOGY
Old Westbury, NY 11568-8000

OVERVIEW
New York Institute of Technology is an independent coed comprehensive institution.

ENROLLMENT
9,396 graduate, professional, and undergraduate students; 1,629 full-time matriculated graduate/professional students (694 women), 2,132 part-time matriculated graduate/professional students (1,103 women).

GRADUATE FACULTY
116 full-time (22 women), 247 part-time (65 women); includes 25 minority (5 African-Americans, 15 Asian-Americans, 4 Hispanics, 1 Native American).

TUITION
$390 per credit.

HOUSING
Rooms and/or apartments available to single students at an average cost of $3260 per year ($6060 including board); available to married students. Graduate housing contact: Office of Residential Life, 516-348-3340.

STUDENT SERVICES
Low-cost health insurance, career counseling, free psychological counseling, campus employment opportunities, international student services.

FACILITIES
Library: Wisser Library plus 2 additional on-campus libraries; total holdings of 202,271 volumes, 598,428 microforms, 3,989 current periodical subscriptions. A total of 71 personal computers in all libraries. Access provided to on-line information retrieval services. *Computer:* Campuswide network is available with full Internet access. Total number of PCs/terminals supplied for student use: 300. Computer service fees are applied as a separate charge. *Special:* In science and engineering: Electromagnetics laboratory, Science and Technology Research Center, Video Center, Management Information Systems Center.

COMPUTER SCIENCE

School of Engineering and Technology, Program in Computer Science
Programs   Awards MS. Part-time and evening/weekend programs available.
Faculty   12 full-time (0 women), 7 part-time (0 women).
Faculty Research   Computer graphics, artificial intelligence, databases, computer laboratory work, multimedia.
Students   151 full-time (38 women), 160 part-time (35 women); includes 95 minority (18 African-Americans, 65 Asian-Americans, 12 Hispanics), 156 international. Average age 30.
Degrees Awarded   In 1996, 145 degrees awarded.
Entrance Requirements   GRE General Test, TOEFL, minimum QPA of 2.85, BS in computer science or related field.
Degree Requirements   Computer language, project required, foreign language and thesis not required.
Financial Aid   Fellowships, research assistantships, teaching assistantships, full and partial tuition waivers, institutionally sponsored loans available. Aid available to part-time students.
Applying   191 applicants, 85% accepted. *Deadline:* 8/1 (rolling processing). *Fee:* $50.
Contact   *Glenn Berman*
Director of Graduate Admissions
516-686-7519
Fax: 516-626-0419

ELECTRICAL ENGINEERING

School of Engineering and Technology, Program in Electrical Engineering
Programs   Awards MS. Part-time and evening/weekend programs available.
Faculty   6 full-time (0 women), 1 part-time (0 women).
Faculty Research   Computer networks, control theory, lightwaves and optics, robotics, signal processing.
Students   15 full-time (3 women), 32 part-time (1 woman); includes 17 minority (8 African-Americans, 6 Asian-Americans, 3 Hispanics), 14 international.
Degrees Awarded   In 1996, 21 degrees awarded.
Entrance Requirements   GRE General Test, TOEFL, BS in electrical engineering or related field, minimum QPA of 2.85.
Financial Aid   Fellowships, research assistantships, full and partial tuition waivers, institutionally sponsored loans available. Aid available to part-time students.
Applying   37 applicants, 86% accepted. *Deadline:* 8/1 (rolling processing). *Fee:* $50.
Contact   *Glenn Berman*
Director of Graduate Admissions
516-686-7519
Fax: 516-626-0419

NEW YORK UNIVERSITY
New York, NY 10012-1019

OVERVIEW
New York University is an independent coed university.

ENROLLMENT
36,305 graduate, professional, and undergraduate students; 9,742 full-time matriculated graduate/

professional students (5,175 women), 9,503 part-time matriculated graduate/professional students (5,564 women).

GRADUATE FACULTY
2,146 full-time (666 women), 3,087 part-time (1,341 women).

EXPENSES
Tuition $675 per credit. Fees $1038 per year full-time, $224 per semester (minimum) part-time.

HOUSING
Rooms and/or apartments available to single students at an average cost of $5858 per year; on-campus housing not available to married students. Graduate housing contact: Housing Office, 212-998-4600.

STUDENT SERVICES
Disabled student services, multicultural affairs office, low-cost health insurance, career counseling, free psychological counseling, campus safety program, campus employment opportunities, international student services.

FACILITIES
Library: Elmer H. Bobst Library plus 6 additional on-campus libraries; total holdings of 3,653,477 volumes, 3,236,036 microforms, 28,689 current periodical subscriptions. A total of 300 personal computers in all libraries. Access provided to on-line information retrieval services. *Computer:* Campuswide network is available with full Internet access. Computer service fees are included with tuition and fees. *Special:* In arts and humanities: Grey Art Gallery and Study Center, Institute of Fine Arts, Institute of French Studies, Hagop Kevorkian Center for Near Eastern Studies, Institute of Film Studies, American Language Institute, Alexander S. Onassis Center for Hellenic Studies. In science and engineering: Institute of Environmental Medicine, Courant Institute of Mathematical Sciences, Center for Neural Science, Sackler Institute of Graduate Biomedical Sciences, Institute for Dental Research. In social sciences: Institute for Economic Analysis, C. V. Starr Center for Applied Economics, Real Estate Institute, Center for Japan-U.S. Business and Economic Studies, Vincent C. Ross Institute of Accounting Research, Salomon Brothers Center for the Study of Financial Institutions, Center for Graphic Communications Management and Technology, Metropolitan Center for Educational Research Development.

COMPUTER SCIENCE

Graduate School of Arts and Science, Courant Institute of Mathematical Sciences, Department of Computer Science
Programs Awards MS, PhD. Part-time and evening/weekend programs available.
Faculty 35 full-time (1 woman).
Faculty Research Distributed and parallel computing, multimedia and graphics, algorithmics and theory of computation, programming languages, artificial intelligence.
Students 104 full-time (16 women), 312 part-time (71 women); includes 49 minority (5 African-Americans, 35 Asian-Americans, 9 Hispanics), 184 international. Average age 28.
Degrees Awarded In 1996, 69 master's, 24 doctorates awarded.
Entrance Requirements GRE General Test, GRE Subject Test, TOEFL.
Degree Requirements For master's, computer language, thesis or alternative required, foreign language not required; for doctor-

ate, 1 foreign language, computer language, dissertation, oral and written exams.
Financial Aid Fellowships, research assistantships, teaching assistantships, full and partial tuition waivers, Federal Work-Study available. *Financial aid application deadline:* 1/4; applicants required to submit FAFSA.
Applying 360 applicants, 61% accepted. *Deadline:* 1/4 (priority date; 11/1 for spring admission). *Fee:* $60.
Contact *Ernest Davis*
Director of Graduate Studies
212-998-3011
E-mail: admissions@cs.nyu.edu

See in-depth description on page 485.

PACE UNIVERSITY
New York, NY 10038

OVERVIEW
Pace University is an independent coed university.

ENROLLMENT
13,577 graduate, professional, and undergraduate students; 1,294 full-time matriculated graduate/professional students (727 women), 3,052 part-time matriculated graduate/professional students (1,485 women).

GRADUATE FACULTY
273 full-time, 281 part-time, 367 FTE.

EXPENSES
Tuition $495 per credit. Fees $350 per year full-time, $52 per semester (minimum) part-time.

HOUSING
Rooms and/or apartments available to single students at an average cost of $4300 per year; on-campus housing not available to married students.

STUDENT SERVICES
Low-cost health insurance, career counseling, free psychological counseling, campus employment opportunities, international student services.

FACILITIES
Library: Main library plus 3 additional on-campus libraries; total holdings of 1 million volumes, 655,000 microforms, 2,500 current periodical subscriptions. Access provided to on-line information retrieval services. *Computer:* Campuswide network is available with full Internet access. Computer services are offered at no charge. *Special:* In science and engineering: Center for Applied Research, Haskins Laboratories, Center for Nursing Research and Clinical Practice. In social sciences: Center for International Business Studies.

COMPUTER SCIENCE

School of Computer Science and Information Systems
Programs Offers programs in computer communications and networks (Certificate), computer science (MS), information systems (MS), object-oriented programming (Certificate), telecommunications (MS, Certificate). Part-time and evening/weekend programs available.
Faculty 36 full-time, 44 part-time, 51 FTE.

Students 64 full-time (35 women), 495 part-time (176 women); includes 102 minority (36 African-Americans, 47 Asian-Americans, 19 Hispanics), 53 international. Average age 32.

Degrees Awarded In 1996, 145 master's, 2 Certificates awarded.

Entrance Requirements For master's, GRE General Test.

Degree Requirements For master's, computer language required, foreign language and thesis not required.

Financial Aid Research assistantships and career-related internships or fieldwork available. Aid available to part-time students. Financial aid applicants required to submit FAFSA.

Applying 293 applicants, 83% accepted. *Deadline:* 7/31 (priority date; rolling processing; 11/30 for spring admission). *Fee:* $60.

Contact *Lois Rich*
Associate Director
914-422-4283
Fax: 914-422-4287
E-mail: gradwp@ny2.pace.edu

See in-depth description on page 515.

INFORMATION SCIENCE

School of Computer Science and Information Systems

Programs Offerings include information systems (MS).

School Faculty 36 full-time, 44 part-time, 51 FTE.

Entrance Requirements GRE General Test.

Degree Requirements Computer language required, foreign language and thesis not required.

Applying *Deadline:* 7/31 (priority date; rolling processing; 11/30 for spring admission). *Fee:* $60.

Contact *Lois Rich*
Associate Director
914-422-4283
Fax: 914-422-4287
E-mail: gradwp@ny2.pace.edu

See in-depth description on page 515.

```
POLYTECHNIC UNIVERSITY, BROOKLYN
CAMPUS
Brooklyn, NY 11201-2990
```

OVERVIEW

Polytechnic University, Brooklyn Campus is an independent coed university.

ENROLLMENT

2,219 graduate, professional, and undergraduate students; 207 full-time matriculated graduate/professional students (43 women), 813 part-time matriculated graduate/professional students (139 women).

GRADUATE FACULTY

158 full-time (19 women), 145 part-time (28 women).

EXPENSES

Tuition $18,690 per year full-time, $645 per credit part-time. Fees $460 per year full-time, $85 per semester part-time.

HOUSING

Rooms and/or apartments available to single students at an average cost of $4700 (including board); on-campus housing not available to married students. Graduate housing contact: Jeanne Swanson, 718-260-3137.

STUDENT SERVICES

Career counseling, campus safety program, campus employment opportunities, international student services.

FACILITIES

Library: Bern Dibner Library of Science and Technology; total holdings of 192,738 volumes, 375 microforms, 1,762 current periodical subscriptions. A total of 160 personal computers in all libraries. Access provided to on-line information retrieval services. *Computer:* Campuswide network is available with full Internet access. Total number of PCs/terminals supplied for student use: 350. Computer services are offered at no charge. *Special:* In arts and humanities: Philosophy and Technology Studies Center. In science and engineering: Weber Research Institute, Polymer Research Institute, Transportation Training and Research Center, Center for Digital Systems, Institute of Imaging Sciences, Center for Applied Large-Scale Computing, Center for Advanced Technology in Telecommunications.

COMPUTER SCIENCE

Division of Engineering, Department of Computer Science and Information

Programs Offers programs in computer science (MS, PhD), distributed information systems engineering (MS). Part-time and evening/weekend programs available.

Faculty 20.

Students 23 full-time (7 women), 208 part-time (43 women).

Degrees Awarded In 1996, 36 master's, 3 doctorates awarded.

Entrance Requirements For master's, BA or BS in computer science, math, science or engineering; working knowledge of a high-level program; for doctorate, GRE General Test, GRE Subject Test, qualifying exam, BA or BS in science, engineering, or management, MS or 1 year of graduate work.

Degree Requirements For master's, computer language required, thesis not required; for doctorate, computer language, dissertation.

Financial Aid Research assistantships, teaching assistantships, institutionally sponsored loans available. Aid available to part-time students. Financial aid applicants required to submit FAFSA.

Applying *Deadline:* rolling. *Fee:* $45.

Contact *Ellen Hartigan*
Vice President for Student Affairs and Dean of Admissions
718-260-3200
Fax: 718-260-3446

See in-depth description on page 519.

ELECTRICAL ENGINEERING

Division of Engineering, Department of Electrical Engineering

Programs Offers programs in electrical engineering (MS, PhD), electrophysics (MS), system engineering (MS), telecommunications networks (MS). Part-time and evening/weekend programs available.

Faculty 36.

Faculty Research Microelectronic devices and systems, computer engineering and computer science, telecommunications, speech and imaging processing, microwave engineering.

Students 70 full-time (8 women), 197 part-time (15 women).

Degrees Awarded In 1996, 95 master's, 12 doctorates awarded.

Entrance Requirements For master's, BS in electrical engineering; for doctorate, qualifying exam, MS in electrical engineering.

Degree Requirements For master's, thesis optional; for doctorate, dissertation.

Financial Aid Fellowships, research assistantships, teaching assistantships, institutionally sponsored loans available. Aid available to part-time students. Financial aid applicants required to submit FAFSA.

Applying *Deadline:* rolling. *Fee:* $45.
Contact *Ellen Hartigan*
Vice President for Student Affairs and Dean of Admissions
718-260-3200
Fax: 718-260-3446

See in-depth description on page 521.

INFORMATION SCIENCE

Division of Engineering, Department of Computer Science and Information
Programs Offers programs in computer science (MS, PhD), distributed information systems engineering (MS). Part-time and evening/weekend programs available.
Faculty 20.
Students 23 full-time (7 women), 208 part-time (43 women).
Degrees Awarded In 1996, 36 master's, 3 doctorates awarded.
Entrance Requirements For master's, BA or BS in computer science, math, science or engineering; working knowledge of a high-level program; for doctorate, GRE General Test, GRE Subject Test, qualifying exam, BA or BS in science, engineering, or management, MS or 1 year of graduate work.
Degree Requirements For master's, computer language required, thesis not required; for doctorate, computer language, dissertation.
Financial Aid Research assistantships, teaching assistantships, institutionally sponsored loans available. Aid available to part-time students. Financial aid applicants required to submit FAFSA.
Applying *Deadline:* rolling. *Fee:* $45.
Contact *Ellen Hartigan*
Vice President for Student Affairs and Dean of Admissions
718-260-3200
Fax: 718-260-3446

See in-depth description on page 519.

POLYTECHNIC UNIVERSITY, FARMINGDALE CAMPUS
Farmingdale, NY 11735-3995

OVERVIEW
Polytechnic University, Farmingdale Campus is an independent coed university.

ENROLLMENT
697 graduate, professional, and undergraduate students; 11 full-time matriculated graduate/professional students (2 women), 297 part-time matriculated graduate/professional students (48 women).

GRADUATE FACULTY
156 full-time (19 women), 145 part-time (28 women).

EXPENSES
Tuition $18,690 per year full-time, $645 per credit part-time. Fees $460 per year full-time, $85 per semester part-time.

HOUSING
Rooms and/or apartments available to single students at an average cost of $4700 (including board); on-campus housing not available to married students. Graduate housing contact: Chris Caramore, 516-755-4325.

STUDENT SERVICES
Career counseling, campus employment opportunities, international student services.

FACILITIES
Library: Long Island Center Library plus 1 additional on-campus library; total holdings of 192,738 volumes, 375 microforms, 1,762 current periodical subscriptions. A total of 160 personal computers in all libraries. Access provided to on-line information retrieval services. *Computer:* Campuswide network is available with full Internet access. Total number of PCs/terminals supplied for student use: 75. Computer services are offered at no charge. *Special:* In science and engineering: Weber Research Institute, Polymer Research Institute, Transportation Training and Research Center, Center for Digital Systems, Institute of Imaging Sciences, Center for Advanced Technology in Telecommunications, Friar Research Institute. In social sciences: Center for Philosophy and Technology Studies, Materials Research Group, Center for Applied Large-Scale Computing (calculus).

COMPUTER SCIENCE

Division of Engineering, Department of Computer and Information Science
Programs Offers program in computer science (MS), including distributed information systems engineering. Part-time and evening/weekend programs available.
Faculty 56.
Faculty Research Ultra-wideband electromagnetics, high resolution space-time signal, medical image compression, microwave-plasma interaction. *Total annual research expenditures:* $4.7 million.
Students 70 part-time (10 women).
Degrees Awarded In 1996, 29 degrees awarded.
Degree Requirements Computer language.
Financial Aid Institutionally sponsored loans available. Aid available to part-time students. Financial aid applicants required to submit FAFSA.
Applying *Deadline:* rolling. *Fee:* $45.
Contact *Ellen Hartigan*
Vice President for Student Affairs and Dean of Admissions
718-260-3200
Fax: 718-260-3446

ELECTRICAL ENGINEERING

Division of Engineering, Department of Electrical Engineering
Programs Offers programs in electrical engineering (MS), electrophysics (MS), systems engineering (MS). Part-time and evening/weekend programs available.
Students 10 full-time (1 woman), 98 part-time (10 women).
Degree Requirements Computer language.
Financial Aid Institutionally sponsored loans available. Aid available to part-time students. Financial aid applicants required to submit FAFSA.
Applying *Deadline:* rolling. *Fee:* $45.
Contact *Ellen Hartigan*
Vice President for Student Affairs and Dean of Admissions
718-260-3200
Fax: 718-260-3446

INFORMATION SCIENCE

Division of Engineering, Department of Computer and Information Science
Programs Offers program in computer science (MS), including distributed information systems engineering. Part-time and evening/weekend programs available.
Faculty 56.

Faculty Research Ultra-wideband electromagnetics, high resolution space-time signal, medical image compression, microwave-plasma interaction. *Total annual research expenditures: $4.7 million.*
Students 70 part-time (10 women).
Degrees Awarded In 1996, 29 degrees awarded.
Degree Requirements Computer language.
Financial Aid Institutionally sponsored loans available. Aid available to part-time students. Financial aid applicants required to submit FAFSA.
Applying *Deadline:* rolling. *Fee:* $45.
Contact *Ellen Hartigan*
Vice President for Student Affairs and Dean of Admissions
718-260-3200
Fax: 718-260-3446

POLYTECHNIC UNIVERSITY, WESTCHESTER GRADUATE CENTER
Hawthorne, NY 10532-1507

OVERVIEW
Polytechnic University, Westchester Graduate Center is an independent coed graduate-only institution.

ENROLLMENT
9 full-time matriculated graduate/professional students (1 woman), 418 part-time matriculated graduate/professional students (69 women).

GRADUATE FACULTY
158 full-time (19 women), 145 part-time (28 women).

EXPENSES
Tuition $18,690 per year full-time, $645 per credit part-time. Fees $460 per year full-time, $85 per semester part-time.

HOUSING
On-campus housing not available.

STUDENT SERVICES
Low-cost health insurance, career counseling, campus employment opportunities, international student services.

FACILITIES
Library: Richard Laster Library plus 2 additional on-campus libraries; total holdings of 192,738 volumes, 375 microforms, 1,762 current periodical subscriptions. A total of 160 personal computers in all libraries. Access provided to on-line information retrieval services. *Special:* In science and engineering: Weber Research Institute, Polymer Research Institute, Center for Advanced Technology in Telecommunication, materials research group, Philosophy and Technology Studies Center.

COMPUTER SCIENCE

Department of Computer and Information Science
Programs Offers programs in computer science (MS), distributed information systems engineering (MS). Part-time and evening/weekend programs available.
Faculty Research Ultra-wideband electromagnetics, high resolution space-time signal, medical image compression, microwave-plasma interaction.
Students 3 full-time (0 women), 148 part-time (23 women).
Degree Requirements Computer language.

Financial Aid Institutionally sponsored loans available. Aid available to part-time students. Financial aid applicants required to submit FAFSA.
Applying *Deadline:* rolling. *Fee:* $45.
Contact *Ellen Hartigan*
Vice President for Student Services and Dean of Admissions
718-260-3200
Fax: 718-260-3446

ELECTRICAL ENGINEERING

Department of Electrical Engineering
Programs Offers programs in electrical engineering (MS), electrophysics (MS), systems engineering (MS), telecommunications networks (MS). Part-time and evening/weekend programs available.
Students 2 full-time (0 women), 46 part-time (6 women).
Degree Requirements Computer language.
Financial Aid Institutionally sponsored loans available. Aid available to part-time students. Financial aid applicants required to submit FAFSA.
Applying *Deadline:* rolling. *Fee:* $45.
Contact *Ellen Hartigan*
Vice President for Student Services and Dean of Admissions
718-260-3200
Fax: 718-260-3446

INFORMATION SCIENCE

Department of Computer and Information Science
Programs Offers programs in computer science (MS), distributed information systems engineering (MS). Part-time and evening/weekend programs available.
Faculty Research Ultra-wideband electromagnetics, high resolution space-time signal, medical image compression, microwave-plasma interaction.
Students 3 full-time (0 women), 148 part-time (23 women).
Degree Requirements Computer language.
Financial Aid Institutionally sponsored loans available. Aid available to part-time students. Financial aid applicants required to submit FAFSA.
Applying *Deadline:* rolling. *Fee:* $45.
Contact *Ellen Hartigan*
Vice President for Student Services and Dean of Admissions
718-260-3200
Fax: 718-260-3446

QUEENS COLLEGE OF THE CITY UNIVERSITY OF NEW YORK
Flushing, NY 11367-1597

OVERVIEW
Queens College of the City University of New York is a public coed comprehensive institution.

ENROLLMENT
15,557 graduate, professional, and undergraduate students; 300 full-time matriculated graduate/professional students (225 women), 2,747 part-time matriculated graduate/professional students (1,978 women).

GRADUATE FACULTY
518 full-time (164 women), 513 part-time (247 women); includes 185 minority (65 African-Americans, 66 Asian-Americans, 51 Hispanics, 3 Native Americans).

EXPENSES
Tuition $4350 per year full-time, $185 per credit part-time for state residents; $7600 per year full-time, $320 per credit part-time for nonresidents. Fees $114 per year.

HOUSING
On-campus housing not available.

STUDENT SERVICES
Disabled student services, multicultural affairs office, low-cost health insurance, career counseling, free psychological counseling, day-care facilities, campus employment opportunities, international student services, writing training, teacher training.

FACILITIES
Library: Benjamin Rosenthal Library plus 1 additional on-campus library; total holdings of 698,051 volumes, 736,100 microforms, 2,582 current periodical subscriptions. A total of 17 personal computers in all libraries. Access provided to on-line information retrieval services. *Computer:* Campuswide network is available with full Internet access. Total number of PCs/terminals supplied for student use: 345. Computer services are offered at no charge. *Special:* In arts and humanities: Center for Byzantine and Modern Greek Studies, electronic music studio. In science and engineering: Computer Center, Gertz Speech and Hearing Center, applied physiology performance laboratory, solid-state magnetics laboratory. In social sciences: Center for the Improvement of Education, social science computer research laboratory.

COMPUTER SCIENCE

Mathematics and Natural Sciences Division, Department of Computer Science

Programs Awards MA. Part-time and evening/weekend programs available.

Faculty Research Fifth-generation computing, hardware/software development, analysis of algorithms and theoretical computer science.

Students 6 full-time (3 women), 138 part-time (53 women); includes 48 minority (1 African-American, 46 Asian-Americans, 1 Hispanic), 61 international.

Degrees Awarded In 1996, 48 degrees awarded.

Entrance Requirements GRE, TOEFL (minimum score 550), minimum GPA of 3.0.

Degree Requirements Computer language, comprehensive exam required, thesis optional, foreign language not required.

Financial Aid Graduate assistantships, adjunct lectureships, partial tuition waivers, Federal Work-Study, institutionally sponsored loans, and career-related internships or fieldwork available. Aid available to part-time students. *Financial aid application deadline:* 4/1; applicants required to submit FAFSA.

Applying 146 applicants, 78% accepted. *Deadline:* 4/1 (rolling processing; 11/1 for spring admission). *Fee:* $40.

Contact Dr. K. Yukawa
Graduate Adviser
718-997-3500

RENSSELAER POLYTECHNIC INSTITUTE
Troy, NY 12180-3590

OVERVIEW
Rensselaer Polytechnic Institute is an independent coed university.

ENROLLMENT
6,101 graduate, professional, and undergraduate students; 1,602 full-time matriculated graduate/professional students (383 women), 350 part-time matriculated graduate/professional students (80 women).

GRADUATE FACULTY
345 full-time (45 women), 135 part-time (12 women); includes 6 minority.

EXPENSES
Tuition $600 per credit hour. Fees $710 per year.

HOUSING
Rooms and/or apartments available to single students (250 units) at an average cost of $3400 per year ($7000 including board); available to married students (265 units) at an average cost of $5400 per year ($9200 including board). Housing application deadline: 6/1. Graduate housing contact: Peter Snyder, 518-276-6284.

STUDENT SERVICES
Disabled student services, multicultural affairs office, low-cost health insurance, career counseling, free psychological counseling, campus safety program, campus employment opportunities, international student services, writing training, teacher training.

FACILITIES
Library: Richard G. Folsom Library plus 1 additional on-campus library; total holdings of 454,145 volumes, 3,496 current periodical subscriptions. A total of 75 personal computers in all libraries. Access provided to on-line information retrieval services. *Computer:* Campuswide network is available with full Internet access. Total number of PCs/terminals supplied for student use: 800. Computer service fees are included with tuition and fees. *Special:* In arts and humanities: EAR Studios, communications research laboratory. In science and engineering: Center for Integrated Electronics and Electronics Manufacturing; Center for Polymer Synthesis; Darrin Fresh Water Institute; Center for Multiphase Research; Scientific Computation Research Center; Center for Advanced Technology in Automation, Robotics and Manufacturing. In social sciences: Center for Science and Technology Policy, Center for Services Sector Research, Center for Entrepreneurship of New Technological Ventures.

COMPUTER ENGINEERING

School of Engineering, Department of Electrical, Computer, and Systems Engineering, Program in Computer and Systems Engineering

Programs Awards M Eng, MS, D Eng, PhD, M Eng/MBA. Part-time programs available.

Faculty 35 full-time (1 woman), 4 part-time (0 women).

Faculty Research Multimedia via ATM, mobile robotics, thermophotovoltaic devices, microelectronic interconnections, agile manufacturing. *Total annual research expenditures:* $2.4 million.

Students 46 full-time (11 women), 9 part-time (2 women); includes 9 minority (2 African-Americans, 7 Asian-Americans), 17 international.
Degrees Awarded In 1996, 18 master's, 11 doctorates awarded.
Entrance Requirements GRE, TOEFL (minimum score 550).
Degree Requirements For master's, thesis required (for some programs), foreign language not required; for doctorate, dissertation required, foreign language not required.
Financial Aid Fellowships, research assistantships, teaching assistantships, institutionally sponsored loans, and career-related internships or fieldwork available. *Financial aid application deadline:* 2/1.
Applying 97 applicants, 48% accepted. *Deadline:* 2/1 (rolling processing; 11/1 for spring admission). *Fee:* $35.
Contact *Barbara Konchanin*
        Manager of Graduate Admissions and Financial Aid
        518-276-2719
        Fax: 518-276-2433

                    See in–depth description on page 533.

COMPUTER SCIENCE

School of Science, Department of Computer Science
Programs Awards MS, PhD. Part-time programs available.
Faculty 14 full-time (1 woman).
Faculty Research Parallel programming, computer vision, genetic algorithms, engineering databases. *Total annual research expenditures:* $1 million.
Students 85 full-time (21 women), 18 part-time (6 women); includes 14 minority (4 African-Americans, 7 Asian-Americans, 3 Hispanics), 30 international.
Degrees Awarded In 1996, 49 master's, 7 doctorates awarded.
Entrance Requirements GRE General Test, TOEFL (minimum score 550).
Degree Requirements For master's, thesis or alternative; for doctorate, dissertation required, foreign language not required.
Financial Aid In 1996–97, 50 students received aid, including 20 research assistantships, 28 teaching assistantships (7 to first-year students); fellowships, institutionally sponsored loans, and career-related internships or fieldwork also available. *Financial aid application deadline:* 2/1.
Applying 240 applicants, 36% accepted. *Deadline:* 2/1 (priority date; rolling processing; 11/1 for spring admission). *Fee:* $35.
Contact *Dr. Robert Ingalls*
        Coordinator of Graduate Admissions
        518-276-2819

                    See in–depth description on page 531.

ELECTRICAL ENGINEERING

School of Engineering, Department of Electrical, Computer, and Systems Engineering, Program in Electrical Engineering
Programs Awards M Eng, MS, D Eng, PhD, M Eng/MBA. Part-time programs available.
Faculty 35 full-time (1 woman), 4 part-time (0 women).
Faculty Research Multimedia via ATM, thermophotovoltaic devices, microelectronic interconnections, agile manufacturing, mobile robotics. *Total annual research expenditures:* $2.4 million.
Students 114 full-time (9 women), 22 part-time (0 women); includes 18 minority (4 African-Americans, 10 Asian-Americans, 4 Hispanics), 60 international.
Degrees Awarded In 1996, 40 master's, 12 doctorates awarded.
Entrance Requirements GRE, TOEFL (minimum score 550).
Degree Requirements For master's, thesis required (for some programs), foreign language not required; for doctorate, dissertation required, foreign language not required.

Financial Aid Fellowships, research assistantships, teaching assistantships, institutionally sponsored loans, and career-related internships or fieldwork available. *Financial aid application deadline:* 2/1.
Applying 477 applicants, 28% accepted. *Deadline:* 2/1 (rolling processing; 11/1 for spring admission). *Fee:* $35.
Contact *Barbara Konchanin*
        Manager of Graduate Admissions and Financial Aid
        518-276-2719
        Fax: 518-276-2433

                    See in–depth description on page 533.

ROCHESTER INSTITUTE OF TECHNOLOGY
Rochester, NY 14623-5604

OVERVIEW
Rochester Institute of Technology is an independent coed comprehensive institution.

ENROLLMENT
12,933 graduate, professional, and undergraduate students; 695 full-time matriculated graduate/professional students (294 women), 1,105 part-time matriculated graduate/professional students (421 women).

TUITION
$18,054 per year full-time, $507 per hour part-time.

HOUSING
Rooms and/or apartments available to single and married students at an average cost of $3486 per year ($6417 including board). Housing application deadline: 4/30. Graduate housing contact: Mary Webster, 716-475-6914.

STUDENT SERVICES
Low-cost health insurance, career counseling, free psychological counseling, day-care facilities, campus safety program, campus employment opportunities, international student services.

FACILITIES
Library: Wallace Memorial Library; total holdings of 351,294 volumes, 402,355 microforms, 4,034 current periodical subscriptions. Access provided to on-line information retrieval services. *Computer:* Campuswide network is available. *Special:* In science and engineering: National Technical Institute for the Deaf, Rochester Institute of Technology Research Corporation.

COMPUTER ENGINEERING

College of Engineering, Department of Computer Engineering
Programs Awards ME.
Students 3 full-time (0 women), 12 part-time (1 woman); includes 1 minority (Hispanic), 1 international.
Degrees Awarded In 1996, 8 degrees awarded.
Entrance Requirements TOEFL, minimum GPA of 3.0.
Applying 31 applicants, 55% accepted. *Deadline:* 3/1 (priority date; rolling processing). *Fee:* $40.
Contact *Dr. Richard Reeves*
        Associate Dean
        716-475-7048

COMPUTER SCIENCE

College of Applied Science and Technology, Department of Computer Science and Information Technology, Program in Applied Computer Studies
Programs Awards AC.
Students 4 part-time (0 women).
Degrees Awarded In 1996, 2 degrees awarded.
Entrance Requirements GRE, TOEFL (minimum score 550), minimum GPA of 3.0.
Financial Aid Assistantships available.
Applying 4 applicants, 100% accepted. *Deadline:* 3/1 (priority date; rolling processing). *Fee:* $40.
Contact *Dr. Guy Johnson*
  Chair
  716-475-2161

COMPUTER SCIENCE

College of Applied Science and Technology, Department of Computer Science and Information Technology, Program in Computer Science
Programs Awards MS.
Students 37 full-time (12 women), 114 part-time (31 women); includes 16 minority (1 African-American, 15 Asian-Americans), 55 international.
Degrees Awarded In 1996, 27 degrees awarded.
Entrance Requirements GRE General Test, TOEFL, minimum GPA of 3.0.
Degree Requirements Computer language, thesis.
Financial Aid Research assistantships, teaching assistantships, scholarships available.
Applying 117 applicants, 74% accepted. *Deadline:* 3/1 (priority date; rolling processing). *Fee:* $40.
Contact *Dr. Peter Anderson*
  Chairperson
  716-475-2979

ELECTRICAL ENGINEERING

College of Engineering, Department of Electrical Engineering
Programs Awards MSEE.
Faculty Research Integrated optics, control systems, digital signal processing, robotic vision.
Students 7 full-time (1 woman), 64 part-time (4 women); includes 12 minority (3 African-Americans, 3 Asian-Americans, 5 Hispanics, 1 Native American), 10 international.
Degrees Awarded In 1996, 27 degrees awarded.
Entrance Requirements TOEFL, minimum GPA of 3.0.
Degree Requirements Thesis optional, foreign language not required.
Financial Aid Research assistantships available.
Applying 77 applicants, 64% accepted. *Deadline:* 3/1 (priority date; rolling processing). *Fee:* $40.
Contact *Dr. Richard Reeves*
  Associate Dean
  716-475-7048

ELECTRICAL ENGINEERING

College of Engineering, Department of Microelectronic Engineering
Programs Awards ME.
Faculty Research Semiconductor device fabrication, lithography, materials, gallium arsenide.
Students 12 full-time (2 women), 5 part-time (0 women); includes 2 minority (both Asian-Americans), 4 international.
Degrees Awarded In 1996, 16 degrees awarded.
Entrance Requirements TOEFL, minimum GPA of 3.0.

Financial Aid Fellowships, research assistantships, teaching assistantships, Federal Work-Study, institutionally sponsored loans, and career-related internships or fieldwork available. Aid available to part-time students.
Applying 29 applicants, 86% accepted. *Deadline:* 3/1 (priority date; rolling processing). *Fee:* $40.
Contact *Dr. Richard Reeves*
  Associate Dean
  716-475-7048

INFORMATION SCIENCE

College of Applied Science and Technology, Department of Computer Science and Information Technology, Program in Information Technology
Programs Awards MS.
Students 24 full-time (5 women), 47 part-time (10 women); includes 7 minority (3 African-Americans, 1 Asian-American, 3 Hispanics), 9 international.
Entrance Requirements Minimum GPA of 3.0.
Applying 55 applicants, 82% accepted. *Deadline:* 3/1 (priority date; rolling processing). *Fee:* $40.
Contact *Dr. Evelyn Rozanski*
  Graduate Program Coordinator
  716-475-2114

SOFTWARE ENGINEERING

College of Applied Science and Technology, Department of Computer Science and Information Technology, Program in Interactive Media Design
Programs Awards AC.
Students 6 part-time (2 women).
Degrees Awarded In 1996, 8 degrees awarded.
Entrance Requirements GRE, TOEFL (minimum score 550), minimum GPA of 3.0.
Financial Aid Assistantships available.
Applying 7 applicants, 86% accepted. *Deadline:* 3/1 (priority date; rolling processing). *Fee:* $40.
Contact *Dr. Evelyn Rozanski*
  Graduate Program Coordinator
  716-475-2114

SOFTWARE ENGINEERING

College of Applied Science and Technology, Department of Computer Science and Information Technology, Program in Software Development and Management
Programs Awards MS.
Students 11 full-time (5 women), 68 part-time (25 women); includes 9 minority (6 African-Americans, 3 Asian-Americans), 5 international.
Degrees Awarded In 1996, 38 degrees awarded.
Entrance Requirements GRE General Test, TOEFL, minimum GPA of 3.0.
Degree Requirements Computer language, thesis.
Financial Aid Scholarships, assistantships available.
Applying 46 applicants, 80% accepted. *Deadline:* 3/1 (priority date; rolling processing). *Fee:* $40.
Contact *Dr. Guy Johnson*
  Chair
  716-475-2161

SOFTWARE ENGINEERING

College of Applied Science and Technology, Department of Computer Science and Information Technology, Program in Telecommunications Software Technology
Programs Awards MS.

Students 12 part-time (2 women); includes 1 minority (Asian-American).
Entrance Requirements Minimum GPA of 3.0.
Degree Requirements Computer language, thesis.
Financial Aid Assistantships available.
Applying 0 applicants. *Deadline:* 3/1 (priority date; rolling processing). *Fee:* $35.
Contact Dr. Evelyn Rozanski
Graduate Program Coordinator
716-475-2114

ST. JOHN'S UNIVERSITY
Jamaica, NY 11439

OVERVIEW
St. John's University is an independent-religious coed university.

ENROLLMENT
18,787 graduate, professional, and undergraduate students; 1,644 full-time matriculated graduate/professional students (858 women), 2,602 part-time matriculated graduate/professional students (1,441 women).

GRADUATE FACULTY
468 full-time (138 women), 146 part-time (53 women).

EXPENSES
Tuition $500 per credit (minimum). Fees $150 per year.

HOUSING
On-campus housing not available.

STUDENT SERVICES
Low-cost health insurance, career counseling, free psychological counseling, campus employment opportunities, international student services.

FACILITIES
Library: St. Augustine Hall plus 2 additional on-campus libraries; total holdings of 1,233,148 volumes, 2,555,273 microforms, 15,169 current periodical subscriptions. A total of 154 personal computers in all libraries. Access provided to on-line information retrieval services. *Computer:* Campuswide network is available with full Internet access. Total number of PCs/terminals supplied for student use: 675. Computer service fees are included with tuition and fees. *Special:* In arts and humanities: Center for Asian Studies, Hugh Carey Collection. In science and engineering: Speech and hearing clinic. In social sciences: Television Center, Instructional Media Center, Center for Psychological Services, Center for Clinical Studies, reading clinic.

COMPUTER SCIENCE

Graduate School of Arts and Sciences, Department of Mathematics and Computer Science
Programs Offers programs in algebra (MA), analysis (MA), applied mathematics (MA), computer science (MA), geometry-topology (MA), logic and foundations (MA), probability and statistics (MA). Part-time and evening/weekend programs available.
Faculty 20 full-time (3 women).

Students 5 full-time (3 women), 4 part-time (2 women); includes 5 minority (2 African-Americans, 2 Asian-Americans, 1 Hispanic), 3 international. Average age 27.
Entrance Requirements Minimum GPA of 3.0.
Degree Requirements Thesis optional.
Financial Aid In 1996–97, 3 research assistantships (1 to a first-year student) averaging $660 per month were awarded; Federal Work-Study also available. Aid available to part-time students. *Financial aid application deadline:* 4/1.
Applying *Deadline:* rolling. *Fee:* $40.
Contact Jeanne Umland
Associate Vice President for Admissions
718-990-6114

STATE UNIVERSITY OF NEW YORK AT BINGHAMTON
Binghamton, NY 13902-6000

OVERVIEW
State University of New York at Binghamton is a public coed university.

ENROLLMENT
11,960 graduate, professional, and undergraduate students; 1,394 full-time matriculated graduate/professional students (631 women), 868 part-time matriculated graduate/professional students (465 women).

GRADUATE FACULTY
466 full-time (123 women), 218 part-time (102 women), 494.2 FTE; includes 94 minority (20 African-Americans, 50 Asian-Americans, 22 Hispanics, 2 Native Americans).

EXPENSES
Tuition $5100 per year full-time, $213 per credit hour part-time for state residents; $8416 per year full-time, $351 per credit hour part-time for nonresidents. Fees $491 per year full-time, $42 per semester (minimum) part-time.

HOUSING
Rooms and/or apartments available to single students (320 units) at an average cost of $3710 per year ($5754 including board); available to married students (28 units) at an average cost of $5990 per year ($7824 including board). Graduate housing contact: Graduate Student Organization, 607-777-2904.

STUDENT SERVICES
Low-cost health insurance, career counseling, free psychological counseling.

FACILITIES
Library: Glenn G. Bartle Library plus 5 additional on-campus libraries; total holdings of 1.545 million volumes, 1.471 million microforms, 8,800 current periodical subscriptions. Access provided to on-line information retrieval services. *Computer:* Campuswide network is available with full Internet access. *Special:* In arts and humanities: Center for Medieval and Early Renaissance Studies, Center for Research in Translation. In science and engineering: Center for Developmental Psychobiology, Integrated Electronics Engineering Center, Center for Cognitive and Psycholinguistic Sciences, Center for Computing Technologies, Center for Intelligent Systems. In social sciences:

Institute of Global Cultural Studies, Center for Leadership Studies, Fernand Braudel Center for the Study of Economics.

COMPUTER SCIENCE

School of Arts and Sciences, Department of Mathematical Sciences
Programs   Offerings include computer science (MA, PhD). Terminal master's awarded for partial completion of doctoral program.
Entrance Requirements   GRE General Test, GRE Subject Test, TOEFL.
Degree Requirements   For master's, thesis or alternative; for doctorate, 2 foreign languages, dissertation.
Applying   *Deadline:* 4/15 (priority date; rolling processing; 11/1 for spring admission). *Fee:* $50.
Contact   *Dr. David Hanson*
Chairperson
607-777-2147

COMPUTER SCIENCE

Thomas J. Watson School of Engineering and Applied Science, Program in Computer Science
Programs   Awards MS, PhD.
Students   58 full-time (11 women), 47 part-time (10 women); includes 11 minority (1 African-American, 8 Asian-Americans, 1 Hispanic, 1 Native American), 39 international. Average age 31.
Degrees Awarded   In 1996, 33 master's, 3 doctorates awarded.
Entrance Requirements   GRE General Test, GRE Subject Test, TOEFL (minimum score 550).
Degree Requirements   For master's, thesis or alternative required, foreign language not required; for doctorate, dissertation required, foreign language not required.
Financial Aid   In 1996–97, 37 students received aid, including 2 fellowships averaging $760 per month and totaling $15,200, 12 research assistantships (3 to first-year students) averaging $773 per month and totaling $92,713, 18 teaching assistantships (4 to first-year students) averaging $743 per month and totaling $133,654, 5 graduate assistantships (4 to first-year students) averaging $729 per month and totaling $36,455. *Financial aid application deadline:* 2/15.
Applying   77 applicants, 62% accepted. *Deadline:* 4/15 (priority date; rolling processing; 11/1 for spring admission). *Fee:* $50.
Contact   *Dr. Sudhir Aggarwal*
Chair
607-777-4802

See in-depth description on page **555.**

ELECTRICAL ENGINEERING

Thomas J. Watson School of Engineering and Applied Science, Program in Electrical Engineering
Programs   Awards MS, PhD. Part-time and evening/weekend programs available.
Students   40 full-time (2 women), 45 part-time (10 women); includes 19 minority (7 African-Americans, 10 Asian-Americans, 2 Hispanics), 23 international. Average age 31.
Degrees Awarded   In 1996, 39 master's, 11 doctorates awarded.
Entrance Requirements   GRE General Test, GRE Subject Test, TOEFL (minimum score 550).
Degree Requirements   For master's, thesis or alternative required, foreign language not required; for doctorate, dissertation required, foreign language not required.
Financial Aid   In 1996–97, 21 students received aid, including 9 research assistantships averaging $1,067 per month and totaling $96,027, 11 teaching assistantships averaging $785 per month and totaling $86,400, 1 graduate assistantship (to a first-year student)

averaging $800 per month and totaling $8,000; fellowships, Federal Work-Study, institutionally sponsored loans, and career-related internships or fieldwork also available. Aid available to part-time students. *Financial aid application deadline:* 2/15.
Applying   63 applicants, 71% accepted. *Deadline:* 4/15 (priority date; rolling processing; 11/1 for spring admission). *Fee:* $50.
Contact   *Dr. George Sackman*
Chairperson
607-777-4856

See in-depth description on page **557.**

SYSTEMS SCIENCE

Thomas J. Watson School of Engineering and Applied Science, Program in Systems Science
Programs   Awards MS, MSAT, PhD. Part-time and evening/weekend programs available.
Faculty Research   Problem restructuring, protein modeling.
Students   19 full-time (3 women), 30 part-time (8 women); includes 5 minority (2 African-Americans, 2 Asian-Americans, 1 Hispanic), 11 international. Average age 35.
Degrees Awarded   In 1996, 4 master's, 1 doctorate awarded. Terminal master's awarded for partial completion of doctoral program.
Entrance Requirements   GRE General Test, GRE Subject Test, TOEFL (minimum score 550).
Degree Requirements   For master's, thesis or alternative required, foreign language not required; for doctorate, dissertation required, foreign language not required.
Financial Aid   In 1996–97, 16 students received aid, including 10 research assistantships (1 to a first-year student) averaging $903 per month and totaling $90,335, 2 teaching assistantships averaging $680 per month and totaling $13,600, 4 graduate assistantships (2 to first-year students) averaging $912 per month and totaling $36,464; fellowships, Federal Work-Study, institutionally sponsored loans, and career-related internships or fieldwork also available. Aid available to part-time students. *Financial aid application deadline:* 2/15.
Applying   18 applicants, 83% accepted. *Deadline:* 4/15 (priority date; rolling processing; 11/1 for spring admission). *Fee:* $50.
Contact   *Dr. Robert Emerson*
Chair
607-777-6509

STATE UNIVERSITY OF NEW YORK AT BUFFALO
Buffalo, NY 14260

OVERVIEW
State University of New York at Buffalo is a public coed university.

ENROLLMENT
23,577 graduate, professional, and undergraduate students; 5,308 full-time matriculated graduate/professional students (2,467 women), 2,253 part-time matriculated graduate/professional students (1,237 women).

GRADUATE FACULTY
1,860 full-time (461 women), 385 part-time (135 women); includes 348 minority (110 African-Americans, 188 Asian-Americans, 41 Hispanics, 9 Native Americans).

TUITION

$5792 per year full-time, $272 per credit hour part-time for state residents; $9108 per year full-time, $410 per credit hour part-time for nonresidents.

HOUSING

Rooms and/or apartments available to single students (5,400 units) at an average cost of $3224 per year ($4374 including board); on-campus housing not available to married students. Housing application deadline: 5/1. Graduate housing contact: University Residence Halls, 716-645-2171.

STUDENT SERVICES

Low-cost health insurance, career counseling, free psychological counseling, day-care facilities, campus safety program, campus employment opportunities, international student services.

FACILITIES

Library: Lockwood Library plus 8 additional on-campus libraries; total holdings of 2,991,288 volumes, 4,740,453 microforms, 21,085 current periodical subscriptions. A total of 300 personal computers in all libraries. Access provided to on-line information retrieval services. *Computer:* Campuswide network is available with full Internet access. Total number of PCs/terminals supplied for student use: 1,800. Computer service fees are applied as a separate charge. *Special:* In arts and humanities: Center for Comparative and Global Studies in Education, Center for Studies in American Culture, Center for the Study of Psychoanalysis and Recognition. In science and engineering: Center for Advanced Molecular Biology and Immunology, Center for Advanced Photonic and Electronic Materials, Center of Excellence in Document Analysis and Recognition, Center for Hazardous Waste Management, Center for Structural Biology, Industry-University Center for Biosurfaces, Periodontal Disease Research Center, Research Center in Oral Biology. In social sciences: Center for Cognitive Science, Center for Hearing and Deafness, Canada-United States Trade Center, National Center for Geographic Information and Analysis.

COMPUTER ENGINEERING

Graduate School, School of Engineering and Applied Sciences, Department of Electrical and Computer Engineering

Programs Offers programs in applied physics (MS, PhD), electrical and computer engineering (M Eng, MS, PhD). Part-time programs available.

Faculty 27 full-time (1 woman), 11 part-time (2 women).

Faculty Research High power electronics and plasmas, electronic materials signal and image processing, photonics and communications, computers and VLSI. *Total annual research expenditures:* $1.66 million.

Students 105 full-time (18 women), 71 part-time (6 women); includes 19 minority (3 African-Americans, 16 Asian-Americans), 108 international. Average age 24.

Degrees Awarded In 1996, 64 master's, 20 doctorates awarded. Terminal master's awarded for partial completion of doctoral program.

Entrance Requirements GRE General Test, TOEFL (minimum score 550).

Degree Requirements For master's, exam, project required, foreign language not required; for doctorate, dissertation required, foreign language not required.

Financial Aid In 1996–97, 65 students received aid, including 4 fellowships (1 to a first-year student), 28 research assistantships (10 to first-year students), 28 teaching assistantships (13 to first-year students), 5 graduate assistantships (2 to first-year students); full and partial tuition waivers, Federal Work-Study, institutionally sponsored loans, and career-related internships or fieldwork also available. *Financial aid application deadline:* 2/1.

Applying 499 applicants, 45% accepted. *Deadline:* 2/1 (priority date; rolling processing; 9/28 for spring admission). *Fee:* $35.

Contact Dr. Donald Givone
Director of Graduate Admissions
716-645-2422 Ext. 2129
Fax: 716-645-3656
E-mail: elekosik@ubvms.cc.buffalo.edu

See in-depth description on page **561.**

COMPUTER SCIENCE

Graduate School, Faculty of Natural Sciences and Mathematics, Department of Computer Science

Programs Awards MS, PhD.

Faculty 16 full-time (6 women), 4 part-time (1 woman).

Faculty Research Artificial intelligence, computer vision, theoretical computer science, parallel architecture, operating systems. *Total annual research expenditures:* $3.026 million.

Students 68 full-time (13 women), 10 part-time (5 women); includes 2 minority (1 Asian-American, 1 Hispanic), 60 international. Average age 25.

Degrees Awarded In 1996, 26 master's, 8 doctorates awarded. Terminal master's awarded for partial completion of doctoral program.

Entrance Requirements GRE General Test, GRE Subject Test (computer science), TOEFL (minimum score 550).

Degree Requirements For master's, computer language, thesis or alternative required, foreign language not required; for doctorate, computer language, dissertation, comprehensive qualifying exam required, foreign language not required.

Financial Aid In 1996–97, 3 fellowships (1 to a first-year student) totaling $11,970, 15 research assistantships (3 to first-year students), 41 teaching assistantships (20 to first-year students) totaling $9,970, 3 graduate assistantships (2 to first-year students) totaling $9,970 were awarded; Federal Work-Study, institutionally sponsored loans also available. *Financial aid application deadline:* 12/31.

Applying 327 applicants, 65% accepted. *Deadline:* 12/31. *Fee:* $35.

Contact Dr. Jin-Yi Cai
Director of Graduate Studies
716-645-3180
Fax: 716-645-3464
E-mail: cai.cs.buffalo.edu

See in-depth description on page **559.**

ELECTRICAL ENGINEERING

Graduate School, School of Engineering and Applied Sciences, Department of Electrical and Computer Engineering

Programs Offers programs in applied physics (MS, PhD), electrical and computer engineering (M Eng, MS, PhD). Part-time programs available.

Faculty 27 full-time (1 woman), 11 part-time (2 women).

Faculty Research High power electronics and plasmas, electronic materials signal and image processing, photonics and communications, computers and VLSI. *Total annual research expenditures:* $1.66 million.

Students 105 full-time (18 women), 71 part-time (6 women); includes 19 minority (3 African-Americans, 16 Asian-Americans), 108 international. Average age 24.

Degrees Awarded In 1996, 64 master's, 20 doctorates awarded. Terminal master's awarded for partial completion of doctoral program.

Entrance Requirements GRE General Test, TOEFL (minimum score 550).

Degree Requirements For master's, exam, project required, foreign language not required; for doctorate, dissertation required, foreign language not required.

Financial Aid In 1996–97, 65 students received aid, including 4 fellowships (1 to a first-year student), 28 research assistantships (10 to first-year students), 28 teaching assistantships (13 to first-year students), 5 graduate assistantships (2 to first-year students); full and partial tuition waivers, Federal Work-Study, institutionally sponsored loans, and career-related internships or fieldwork also available. *Financial aid application deadline:* 2/1.

Applying 499 applicants, 45% accepted. *Deadline:* 2/1 (priority date; rolling processing; 9/28 for spring admission). *Fee:* $35.

Contact Dr. Donald Givone
Director of Graduate Admissions
716-645-2422 Ext. 2129
Fax: 716-645-3656
E-mail: elekosik@ubvms.cc.buffalo.edu

See in-depth description on page **561.**

STATE UNIVERSITY OF NEW YORK AT NEW PALTZ
New Paltz, NY 12561-2499

OVERVIEW
State University of New York at New Paltz is a public coed comprehensive institution.

ENROLLMENT
7,539 graduate, professional, and undergraduate students; 292 full-time matriculated graduate/professional students (195 women), 783 part-time matriculated graduate/professional students (589 women).

GRADUATE FACULTY
268 full-time (101 women), 292 part-time (162 women); includes 59 minority (16 African-Americans, 19 Asian-Americans, 20 Hispanics, 4 Native Americans).

EXPENSES
Tuition $5100 per year full-time, $213 per credit hour part-time for state residents; $8416 per year full-time, $351 per credit hour part-time for nonresidents. Fees $425 per year full-time, $14.60 per credit hour (minimum) part-time.

HOUSING
Rooms and/or apartments available to single students at an average cost of $2920 per year ($4980 including board); on-campus housing not available to married students. Graduate housing contact: Jeff Hurrin, 914-257-4444.

STUDENT SERVICES
Low-cost health insurance, career counseling, free psychological counseling, day-care facilities, campus safety program, campus employment opportunities.

FACILITIES
Library: Sojourner Truth Library; total holdings of 420,000 volumes, 1 million microforms, 1,300 current periodical subscriptions. Access provided to on-line information retrieval services. *Computer:* Campuswide network is available with full Internet access. Total number of PCs/terminals supplied for student use: 400. Computer services are offered at no charge. *Special:* In science and engineering: Class 1000 Clean Room, Institute for Science and Technology, electron microscopy laboratory.

COMPUTER SCIENCE

Faculty of Liberal Arts and Sciences, Department of Mathematics and Computer Science, Program in Computer Science

Programs Awards MS.

Students 16 full-time (7 women), 27 part-time (14 women); includes 14 minority (all Asian-Americans), 24 international.

Degrees Awarded In 1996, 19 degrees awarded.

Entrance Requirements GRE General Test, minimum GPA of 3.0, proficiency in program assembly.

Degree Requirements Computer language, thesis (for some programs), comprehensive exam required, foreign language not required.

Financial Aid Teaching assistantships, full tuition waivers available.

Applying *Deadline:* 3/15 (priority date; rolling processing). *Fee:* $50.

Contact Kequin Li
Graduate Adviser
914-257-3535

STATE UNIVERSITY OF NEW YORK AT STONY BROOK
Stony Brook, NY 11794

OVERVIEW
State University of New York at Stony Brook is a public coed university.

ENROLLMENT
17,316 graduate, professional, and undergraduate students; 3,232 full-time matriculated graduate/professional students (1,554 women), 1,747 part-time matriculated graduate/professional students (1,174 women).

GRADUATE FACULTY
1,220 full-time (317 women), 390 part-time (159 women); includes 194 minority (48 African-Americans, 110 Asian-Americans, 32 Hispanics, 4 Native Americans).

EXPENSES
Tuition $5100 per year full-time, $213 per credit hour part-time for state residents; $8416 per year full-time, $351 per credit hour part-time for nonresidents. Fees $140 per year full-time, $112 per year part-time.

HOUSING
Rooms and/or apartments available to single students at an average cost of $3494 per year ($5594 including board); available to married students. Graduate housing contact: Al DeVries, 516-632-6750.

STUDENT SERVICES
Disabled student services, multicultural affairs office, low-cost health insurance, career counseling, free psychological counseling, exercise/wellness program, day-care facilities, campus safety program, campus employ-

ment opportunities, international student services, writing training, grant writing training, teacher training.

FACILITIES

Library: F. Melville Memorial Library plus 7 additional on-campus libraries; total holdings of 1,777,489 volumes, 2,484,798 microforms, 11,139 current periodical subscriptions. Access provided to on-line information retrieval services. *Computer:* Campuswide network is available with full Internet access. Total number of PCs/terminals supplied for student use: 1,500. Computer service fees are included with tuition and fees. *Special:* In arts and humanities: Institute for American Studies, Humanities Institute. In science and engineering: Marine Sciences Research Center, Institute for Theoretical Physics, Institute for Mathematical Science, Institute for Mineral Physics, Institute for Terrestrial and Planetary Atmosphere. In social sciences: Institute for Conservation of Tropical Environments, Center for Regional Policy Studies.

COMPUTER SCIENCE

College of Engineering and Applied Sciences, Department of Computer Science
Programs Offers programs in computer science (MS, PhD), information systems management (Certificate).
Faculty 25.
Faculty Research Artificial intelligence, computer architecture, database management systems, VLSI, operating systems. *Total annual research expenditures:* $1.7 million.
Students 110 full-time (29 women), 34 part-time (11 women); includes 20 minority (2 African-Americans, 18 Asian-Americans), 97 international.
Degrees Awarded In 1996, 42 master's, 6 doctorates, 10 Certificates awarded.
Entrance Requirements For master's and doctorate, GRE General Test, TOEFL.
Degree Requirements For master's, computer language, thesis or alternative required, foreign language not required; for doctorate, computer language, dissertation, comprehensive exams required, foreign language not required.
Financial Aid In 1996–97, 6 fellowships, 19 research assistantships, 34 teaching assistantships were awarded.
Applying 224 applicants, 72% accepted. *Deadline:* 1/15. *Fee:* $50.
Contact *Dr. David Smith*
Director
516-632-8471

See in-depth description on page 563.

ELECTRICAL ENGINEERING

College of Engineering and Applied Sciences, Department of Electrical Engineering
Programs Offers programs in biomedical engineering (Certificate), electrical engineering (MS, PhD). Evening/weekend programs available.
Faculty 29.
Faculty Research System science, solid-state electronics, computer engineering. *Total annual research expenditures:* $773,655.
Students 75 full-time (7 women), 27 part-time (6 women); includes 16 minority (2 African-Americans, 11 Asian-Americans, 3 Hispanics), 66 international.
Degrees Awarded In 1996, 36 master's, 6 doctorates awarded.
Entrance Requirements For master's and doctorate, GRE General Test, TOEFL.

Degree Requirements For master's, thesis or alternative required, foreign language not required; for doctorate, dissertation, comprehensive exams required, foreign language not required.
Financial Aid In 1996–97, 1 fellowship, 15 research assistantships, 24 teaching assistantships were awarded.
Applying 350 applicants, 69% accepted. *Deadline:* 1/15. *Fee:* $50.
Contact *Dr. Chi-Tsong Chen*
Director
516-632-8400

See in-depth description on page 565.

INFORMATION SCIENCE

College of Engineering and Applied Sciences, Department of Computer Science
Programs Offerings include information systems management (Certificate).
Department Faculty 25.
Applying *Deadline:* 1/15. *Fee:* $50.
Contact *Dr. David Smith*
Director
516-632-8471

See in-depth description on page 563.

SOFTWARE ENGINEERING

School of Professional Development and Continuing Studies
Programs Offerings include software engineering (Certificate).
School Faculty 102.
Applying *Deadline:* 1/15. *Fee:* $50.
Contact *Sandra Romansky*
Director of Admissions and Advisement
516-632-7050
Fax: 516-632-9046
E-mail: sandra.romansky@sunysb.edu

STATE UNIVERSITY OF NEW YORK INSTITUTE OF TECHNOLOGY AT UTICA/ROME
Utica, NY 13504-3050

OVERVIEW
State University of New York Institute of Technology at Utica/Rome is a public coed upper-level institution.

ENROLLMENT
2,559 graduate, professional, and undergraduate students; 81 full-time matriculated graduate/professional students (36 women), 214 part-time matriculated graduate/professional students (117 women).

GRADUATE FACULTY
30 full-time (12 women); includes 6 minority (2 Asian-Americans, 4 Hispanics).

EXPENSES
Tuition $5100 per year full-time, $213 per credit hour part-time for state residents; $8416 per year full-time, $351 per credit hour part-time for nonresidents. Fees $278 per year full-time, $16.60 per credit hour part-time.

HOUSING
Rooms and/or apartments available to single students (35 units) at an average cost of $3780 per year ($5880

including board); on-campus housing not available to married students. Graduate housing contact: John Borner, 315-792-7810.

STUDENT SERVICES

Disabled student services, low-cost health insurance, career counseling, exercise/wellness program, campus safety program, campus employment opportunities, international student services.

FACILITIES

Library: Main library; total holdings of 159,092 volumes, 161,041 microforms, 981 current periodical subscriptions. A total of 17 personal computers in all libraries. Access provided to on-line information retrieval services. *Computer:* Campuswide network is available with full Internet access. Total number of PCs/terminals supplied for student use: 325. Computer service fees are included with tuition and fees. *Special:* In science and engineering: Natural and physical science laboratory.

COMPUTER SCIENCE

School of Information Systems and Engineering Technology, Program in Computer and Information Science
Programs Awards MS. Part-time and evening/weekend programs available.
Faculty 12 full-time (3 women).
Faculty Research Client/server computing, flexible computing, distributed systems, computers in education, database theory. *Total annual research expenditures:* $124,761.
Students 14 full-time (1 woman), 42 part-time (10 women); includes 7 minority (3 African-Americans, 2 Asian-Americans, 1 Hispanic, 1 Native American), 4 international. Average age 35.
Degrees Awarded In 1996, 14 degrees awarded.
Entrance Requirements GRE General Test, TOEFL (minimum score 550), minimum GPA of 3.0.
Degree Requirements Computer language, comprehensive exam required, thesis optional, foreign language not required.
Financial Aid In 1996–97, 13 students received aid, including 2 graduate assistantships; Federal Work-Study and career-related internships or fieldwork also available. Aid available to part-time students. Financial aid applicants required to submit FAFSA.
Applying 25 applicants, 80% accepted. *Deadline:* 6/15 (priority date; rolling processing). *Fee:* $50.
Contact *Marybeth Lyons*
Interim Director of Admissions
315-792-7500
Fax: 315-792-7837

INFORMATION SCIENCE

School of Information Systems and Engineering Technology, Program in Computer and Information Science
Programs Awards MS. Part-time and evening/weekend programs available.
Faculty 12 full-time (3 women).
Faculty Research Client/server computing, flexible computing, distributed systems, computers in education, database theory. *Total annual research expenditures:* $124,761.
Students 14 full-time (1 woman), 42 part-time (10 women); includes 7 minority (3 African-Americans, 2 Asian-Americans, 1 Hispanic, 1 Native American), 4 international. Average age 35.
Degrees Awarded In 1996, 14 degrees awarded.
Entrance Requirements GRE General Test, TOEFL (minimum score 550), minimum GPA of 3.0.
Degree Requirements Computer language, comprehensive exam required, thesis optional, foreign language not required.

Financial Aid In 1996–97, 13 students received aid, including 2 graduate assistantships; Federal Work-Study and career-related internships or fieldwork also available. Aid available to part-time students. Financial aid applicants required to submit FAFSA.
Applying 25 applicants, 80% accepted. *Deadline:* 6/15 (priority date; rolling processing). *Fee:* $50.
Contact *Marybeth Lyons*
Interim Director of Admissions
315-792-7500
Fax: 315-792-7837

SYRACUSE UNIVERSITY
Syracuse, NY 13244-0003

OVERVIEW

Syracuse University is an independent coed university.

ENROLLMENT

3,024 full-time matriculated graduate/professional students (1,460 women), 2,931 part-time matriculated graduate/professional students (1,343 women).

GRADUATE FACULTY

949 full-time (207 women), 139 part-time (67 women).

TUITION

$12,696 per year full-time, $529 per credit hour part-time.

HOUSING

Rooms and/or apartments available to single students (160 units) at an average cost of $4680 per year ($6591 including board); available to married students (400 units) at an average cost of $8544 (including board). Housing application deadline: 6/1.

STUDENT SERVICES

Low-cost health insurance, career counseling, free psychological counseling, day-care facilities, campus safety program, campus employment opportunities, international student services.

FACILITIES

Library: Ernest Stevenson Bird Library plus 6 additional on-campus libraries; total holdings of 2.01 million volumes, 2.069 million microforms. Access provided to on-line information retrieval services. *Computer:* Campuswide network is available with full Internet access. Computer service fees are included with tuition and fees. *Special:* In arts and humanities: Dorthea Ilgen Shaffer Art Building, Regent Theater Complex. In science and engineering: Institute for Sensory Research, Heroy Geological Laboratory, S. I. Newhouse Telecommunications Studios, Center for Advanced Technology in Computer Applications and Software Engineering, Northeastern Parallel Architectures Center, biological research library. In social sciences: Global Affairs Institute, International Exploratorium, Metropolitan Studies Program.

COMPUTER ENGINEERING

L. C. Smith College of Engineering and Computer Science, Department of Electrical and Computer Engineering, Program in Computer Engineering
Programs Awards MS, PhD, CE.
Faculty 36 full-time, 8 part-time.

Faculty Research Hardware, software, computer applications.

Students 76 full-time (12 women), 82 part-time (19 women); includes 10 minority (3 African-Americans, 6 Asian-Americans, 1 Native American), 99 international.

Degrees Awarded In 1996, 43 master's, 7 doctorates awarded.

Entrance Requirements For master's and doctorate, GRE General Test.

Degree Requirements For doctorate, computer language, dissertation required, foreign language not required.

Financial Aid Fellowships, research assistantships, teaching assistantships, partial tuition waivers, Federal Work-Study available. *Financial aid application deadline: 3/1.*

Applying 165 applicants, 73% accepted. *Deadline: rolling. Fee:* $40.

Contact *James Fawcett*
Graduate Program Director
315-443-4370

COMPUTER SCIENCE

L. C. Smith College of Engineering and Computer Science, School of Computer and Information Science, Program in Computer Science

Programs Offers computer and information science (PhD), computer science (MS).

Students 28 full-time (6 women), 45 part-time (8 women); includes 2 minority (1 African-American, 1 Asian-American), 51 international.

Degrees Awarded In 1996, 25 master's awarded.

Entrance Requirements For master's, GRE General Test.

Degree Requirements For master's, thesis required, foreign language not required.

Financial Aid Fellowships, research assistantships, teaching assistantships, partial tuition waivers, Federal Work-Study available. *Financial aid application deadline: 3/1.*

Applying 305 applicants, 85% accepted. *Deadline: rolling. Fee:* $40.

Contact *Carlos Hartmann*
Head
315-443-2369

ELECTRICAL ENGINEERING

L. C. Smith College of Engineering and Computer Science, Department of Electrical and Computer Engineering, Program in Electrical Engineering

Programs Awards MS, PhD, EE.

Faculty Research Electromagnetics, electronic devices, systems.

Students 53 full-time (4 women), 63 part-time (8 women); includes 6 minority (3 African-Americans, 3 Asian-Americans), 66 international.

Degrees Awarded In 1996, 29 master's, 10 doctorates awarded.

Entrance Requirements For master's and doctorate, GRE General Test.

Degree Requirements For doctorate, computer language, dissertation required, foreign language not required.

Financial Aid Fellowships, research assistantships, teaching assistantships, Federal Work-Study available. *Financial aid application deadline: 3/1.*

Applying 299 applicants, 77% accepted. *Deadline: rolling. Fee:* $40.

Contact *James Fawcett*
Contact
315-443-2655

INFORMATION SCIENCE

L. C. Smith College of Engineering and Computer Science, School of Computer and Information Science, Program in Systems and Information Science

Programs Awards MS, PhD.

Students 67 full-time (14 women), 20 part-time (6 women); includes 2 minority (both Asian-Americans), 76 international.

Degrees Awarded In 1996, 5 doctorates awarded.

Entrance Requirements GRE General Test.

Financial Aid Fellowships, research assistantships, teaching assistantships, partial tuition waivers, Federal Work-Study available. *Financial aid application deadline: 3/1.*

Applying 93 applicants, 78% accepted. *Deadline: rolling. Fee:* $40.

Contact *Carlos Hartmann*
Head
315-443-2369

UNION COLLEGE
Schenectady, NY 12308-2311

OVERVIEW
Union College is an independent coed comprehensive institution.

ENROLLMENT
2,333 graduate, professional, and undergraduate students; 123 full-time matriculated graduate/professional students (58 women), 124 part-time matriculated graduate/professional students (31 women).

GRADUATE FACULTY
9 full-time, 18 part-time.

TUITION
$1370 per course.

HOUSING
On-campus housing not available.

STUDENT SERVICES
Low-cost health insurance, career counseling, free psychological counseling, campus safety program.

FACILITIES
Library: Schaffer Library; total holdings of 507,665 volumes, 665,886 microforms, 1,972 current periodical subscriptions. A total of 38 personal computers in all libraries. Access provided to on-line information retrieval services. *Computer:* Campuswide network is available with full Internet access. Total number of PCs/terminals supplied for student use: 250. Computer services are offered at no charge.

COMPUTER SCIENCE

Graduate and Continuing Studies, Division of Engineering and Applied Science, Department of Electrical Engineering and Computer Science, Program in Computer Science

Programs Awards MS.

Faculty Research Microprocessor applications.

Students 5 full-time (3 women), 18 part-time (2 women); includes 3 minority (all Asian-Americans), 1 international.

Degrees Awarded In 1996, 8 degrees awarded.

Entrance Requirements Minimum GPA of 3.0.

Degree Requirements Computer language, comprehensive exam, project, or thesis required, foreign language not required.
Applying 5 applicants, 100% accepted. *Deadline:* rolling. *Fee:* $35.
Contact *Dr. George H. Williams*
Chair
518-388-6273

ELECTRICAL ENGINEERING

Graduate and Continuing Studies, Division of Engineering and Applied Science, Department of Electrical Engineering and Computer Science, Program in Electrical Engineering
Programs Awards MS.
Students 4 full-time (0 women), 3 part-time (0 women).
Degrees Awarded In 1996, 16 degrees awarded.
Entrance Requirements Minimum GPA of 3.0.
Degree Requirements Computer language, comprehensive and departmental qualifying exams required, foreign language and thesis not required.
Applying 2 applicants, 50% accepted. *Deadline:* rolling. *Fee:* $35.
Contact *Dr. Michael Rudko*
Chair
518-388-6316

UNIVERSITY AT ALBANY, STATE UNIVERSITY OF NEW YORK
Albany, NY 12222-0001

OVERVIEW
University at Albany, State University of New York is a public coed university.

ENROLLMENT
15,773 graduate, professional, and undergraduate students; 2,473 full-time matriculated graduate/professional students (1,381 women), 1,737 part-time matriculated graduate/professional students (1,044 women).

GRADUATE FACULTY
618 full-time, 277 part-time; includes 86 minority (21 African-Americans, 37 Asian-Americans, 26 Hispanics, 2 Native Americans).

EXPENSES
Tuition $5100 per year full-time, $213 per credit hour part-time for state residents; $8416 per year full-time, $351 per credit hour part-time for nonresidents. Fees $555 per year full-time, $20.85 per credit hour part-time.

HOUSING
Rooms and/or apartments available to single students (250 units) at an average cost of $3488 per year ($5241 including board); available to married students at an average cost of $6976 per year ($10,482 including board). Housing application deadline: 9/1. Graduate housing information: 518-442-5875.

STUDENT SERVICES
Disabled student services, multicultural affairs office, low-cost health insurance, career counseling, free psychological counseling, day-care facilities, campus safety program, campus employment opportunities, international student services, writing training, grant writing training, teacher training.

FACILITIES
Library: University Library plus 1 additional on-campus library; total holdings of 1,842,937 volumes, 2,814,892 microforms, 7,000 current periodical subscriptions. Access provided to on-line information retrieval services. *Special:* In arts and humanities: New York State Writers' Institute. In science and engineering: Atmospheric Sciences Research Center, Center for Molecular Genetics, Joint Laboratories for Advanced Materials. In social sciences: Center for Social and Demograph Analysis, Center for Stress and Anxiety Disorders, Child Research and Study Center, Hindelang Criminal Justice Center.

COMPUTER SCIENCE

College of Arts and Sciences, Department of Computer Science
Programs Awards MS, PhD.
Faculty 13 full-time (2 women), 1 part-time (0 women).
Faculty Research Algorithm design and analysis, artificial intelligence, computational logic, databases, numerical analysis.
Students 40 full-time (11 women), 25 part-time (6 women); includes 3 minority (all Asian-Americans), 40 international. Average age 25.
Degrees Awarded In 1996, 23 master's, 1 doctorate awarded.
Entrance Requirements GRE General Test, TOEFL.
Degree Requirements For master's, comprehensive exam, project or thesis required, foreign language not required; for doctorate, dissertation, area and comprehensive exams required, foreign language not required.
Financial Aid Fellowships, research assistantships, teaching assistantships, Federal Work-Study, and career-related internships or fieldwork available.
Applying 109 applicants, 47% accepted. *Fee:* $50.
Contact *Neil V. Murray*
518-442-3393

See in-depth description on page 575.

INFORMATION SCIENCE

Nelson A. Rockefeller College of Public Affairs and Policy, Information Science Program
Programs Awards MS, PhD.
Students 13 full-time (4 women), 23 part-time (11 women); includes 7 minority (4 African-Americans, 1 Asian-American, 2 Hispanics).
Entrance Requirements For doctorate, GRE General Test.
Degree Requirements For doctorate, dissertation.
Applying 32 applicants, 34% accepted. *Fee:* $50.
Contact *Dr. Thomas J. Galvin*
Director
518-442-3306

See in-depth description on page 577.

UNIVERSITY OF ROCHESTER
Rochester, NY 14627-0001

OVERVIEW
University of Rochester is an independent coed university.

ENROLLMENT
8,761 graduate, professional, and undergraduate students; 2,164 full-time matriculated graduate/professional students

(844 women), 1,186 part-time matriculated graduate/professional students (682 women).

GRADUATE FACULTY

1,604; includes 166 minority.

EXPENSES

Tuition $20,540 per year full-time, $642 per credit hour part-time. Fees $320 per year.

HOUSING

Rooms and/or apartments available to single and married students. Graduate housing contact: Office of Residential Life, 716-275-1081.

STUDENT SERVICES

Low-cost health insurance, career counseling, free psychological counseling, campus safety program, campus employment opportunities, international student services.

FACILITIES

Library: University Library plus 7 additional on-campus libraries; total holdings of 2,882,023 volumes, 3,649,451 microforms, 11,460 current periodical subscriptions. A total of 141 personal computers in all libraries. Access provided to on-line information retrieval services. *Computer:* Campuswide network is available with full Internet access. Total number of PCs/terminals supplied for student use: 300. Computer service fees are included with tuition and fees. *Special:* In arts and humanities: Memorial Art Gallery, Summer Theatre. In science and engineering: Center for Advanced Technology, C. E. K. Mees Observatory, laboratory for laser energetics, nuclear structure research laboratory with 24-MeV tandem Van de Graaff accelerator. In social sciences: Rochester Center for Economic Research, Center for Research and Government Policy and Business, Frederick Douglass Institute for African-American Studies, Susan B. Anthony Center for Women's Studies, Center for Manufacturing and Operations Management.

COMPUTER SCIENCE

The College, Arts and Sciences, Department of Computer Science
Programs   Awards MS, PhD.
Faculty   11 full-time.
Students   42 full-time (7 women), 1 part-time (0 women); includes 2 minority (1 Asian-American, 1 Native American), 24 international.
Degrees Awarded   In 1996, 7 master's, 5 doctorates awarded. Terminal master's awarded for partial completion of doctoral program.
Entrance Requirements   For master's, GRE General Test; for doctorate, GRE General Test, TOEFL.
Degree Requirements   For doctorate, dissertation, qualifying exam required, foreign language not required.
Financial Aid   Fellowships, research assistantships, teaching assistantships, full and partial tuition waivers available. *Financial aid application deadline:* 2/1.
Applying   281 applicants, 9% accepted. *Deadline:* 2/1 (priority date). *Fee:* $25.
Contact   *Peggy Franz*
 Graduate Program Secretary
 716-275-5478

See in-depth description on page 705.

ELECTRICAL ENGINEERING

The College, School of Engineering and Applied Sciences, Department of Electrical Engineering
Programs   Awards MS, PhD. Part-time programs available.
Faculty   15 full-time.
Students   68 full-time (8 women), 9 part-time (1 woman); includes 19 minority (4 African-Americans, 14 Asian-Americans, 1 Native American), 26 international.
Degrees Awarded   In 1996, 8 master's, 14 doctorates awarded. Terminal master's awarded for partial completion of doctoral program.
Entrance Requirements   GRE, TOEFL.
Degree Requirements   For doctorate, dissertation, preliminary and oral exams required, foreign language not required.
Financial Aid   Fellowships, research assistantships, teaching assistantships, full and partial tuition waivers available. *Financial aid application deadline:* 2/1.
Applying   357 applicants, 6% accepted. *Deadline:* 2/1 (priority date). *Fee:* $25.
Contact   *Ruth Williams*
 Graduate Program Secretary
 716-275-7417

See in-depth description on page 707.

NORTH CAROLINA

APPALACHIAN STATE UNIVERSITY
Boone, NC 28608

OVERVIEW

Appalachian State University is a public coed comprehensive institution.

ENROLLMENT

11,641 graduate, professional, and undergraduate students; 662 full-time matriculated graduate/professional students (396 women), 369 part-time matriculated graduate/professional students (235 women).

GRADUATE FACULTY

415 full-time (95 women), 21 part-time (11 women); includes 12 minority (7 African-Americans, 3 Asian-Americans, 2 Hispanics).

TUITION

$1760 per year full-time, $344 per semester (minimum) part-time for state residents; $8914 per year full-time, $2133 per semester (minimum) part-time for nonresidents.

HOUSING

Rooms and/or apartments available to single and married students at an average cost of $3000 per year. Graduate housing information: 704-262-2160.

STUDENT SERVICES

Low-cost health insurance, career counseling, free psychological counseling, day-care facilities, campus safety program, campus employment opportunities, international student services.

FACILITIES

Library: Carol Grotnes Belk Library plus 2 additional on-campus libraries. A total of 30 personal computers in all libraries. Access provided to on-line information retrieval services. *Computer:* Campuswide network is available with full Internet access. Total number of PCs/terminals supplied for student use: 600. Computer service fees are included with tuition and fees. *Special:* In science and engineering: Dark Sky Observatory, speech and hearing clinic. In social sciences: Center for Appalachian Studies, Center for Management Development, Early Childhood Learning Center, Western Carolina Research Center, reading curriculum laboratory.

COMPUTER SCIENCE

College of Arts and Sciences, Department of Mathematics, Program in Computer Science

Programs   Awards MS. Program new for fall 1997.
Entrance Requirements   GRE General Test (minimum combined score of 1000).
Degree Requirements   1 foreign language (computer language can substitute), comprehensive exam.
Financial Aid   *Application deadline: 7/31.*
Applying   *Deadline:* 7/31 (priority date). *Fee:* $35.
Contact   Dr. James Wilkes
              Adviser
              704-262-3050
              Fax: 704-265-8617
              E-mail: wilkesjt@appstate.edu

DUKE UNIVERSITY
Durham, NC 27708-0586

OVERVIEW
Duke University is an independent-religious coed university.

ENROLLMENT
12,346 graduate, professional, and undergraduate students; 5,286 full-time matriculated graduate/professional students (2,096 women), 276 part-time matriculated graduate/professional students (190 women).

GRADUATE FACULTY
3,466; includes 76 minority (25 African-Americans, 40 Asian-Americans, 11 Hispanics).

EXPENSES
Tuition $15,840 per year full-time, $660 per unit part-time. Fees $2674 per year.

HOUSING
Rooms and/or apartments available to single students (112 units) at an average cost of $3698 per year; available to married students. Graduate housing contact: Housing Administration Office, 919-684-4304.

STUDENT SERVICES
Low-cost health insurance, career counseling, free psychological counseling, campus safety program, campus employment opportunities, international student services.

FACILITIES
Library: William R. Perkins Library plus 12 additional on-campus libraries; total holdings of 4,534,208 volumes, 3,314,158 microforms, 33,205 current periodical subscriptions. A total of 425 personal computers in all libraries. Access provided to on-line information retrieval

services. *Computer:* Campuswide network is available with full Internet access. *Special:* In arts and humanities: Museum of Art, Mary Lou Williams Center for Black Culture. In science and engineering: Center for Resource and Environmental Policy Research, Duke Comprehensive Cancer Center, F. G. Hall Laboratory for Environmental Research (includes hypohyperbaric chamber), Paul M. Gross Chemical Laboratory, marine laboratory, phytotron, Primate Center. In social sciences: Center for Demographic Studies, Center for the Study of Aging and Human Development, psychology laboratories.

COMPUTER ENGINEERING

Graduate School, School of Engineering, Department of Electrical and Computer Engineering

Programs   Awards MS, PhD.
Faculty   20 full-time, 21 part-time.
Students   76 full-time (14 women), includes 3 minority (1 African-American, 2 Asian-Americans), 44 international.
Degrees Awarded   In 1996, 18 master's, 8 doctorates awarded. Terminal master's awarded for partial completion of doctoral program.
Entrance Requirements   GRE General Test.
Degree Requirements   For doctorate, dissertation required, foreign language not required.
Financial Aid   In 1996–97, 59 students received aid, including fellowships totaling $555,036, research assistantships totaling $612,551; Federal Work-Study also available. *Financial aid application deadline:* 12/31.
Applying   162 applicants, 27% accepted. *Deadline:* 12/31 (11/1 for spring admission). *Fee:* $75.
Contact   Dr. Loren W. Nolte
              Director of Graduate Studies
              919-660-5251

COMPUTER SCIENCE

Graduate School, Department of Computer Science

Programs   Awards MS, PhD.
Faculty   25 full-time, 9 part-time.
Students   61 full-time (13 women), includes 4 minority (1 African-American, 2 Asian-Americans, 1 Hispanic), 41 international.
Degrees Awarded   In 1996, 14 master's, 6 doctorates awarded. Terminal master's awarded for partial completion of doctoral program.
Entrance Requirements   For master's, GRE General Test; for doctorate, GRE General Test, GRE Subject Test (recommended).
Degree Requirements   For doctorate, dissertation.
Financial Aid   In 1996–97, 22 students received aid, including fellowships totaling $520,988, research assistantships totaling $265,679, teaching assistantships totaling $116,268; Federal Work-Study also available. *Financial aid application deadline:* 12/31.
Applying   207 applicants, 22% accepted. *Deadline:* 12/31. *Fee:* $75.
Contact   Robert Wagner
              Director of Graduate Studies
              919-660-6538

See in-depth description on page 425.

ELECTRICAL ENGINEERING

Graduate School, School of Engineering, Department of Electrical and Computer Engineering

Programs   Awards MS, PhD.
Faculty   20 full-time, 21 part-time.

Students 76 full-time (14 women), includes 3 minority (1 African-American, 2 Asian-Americans), 44 international.

Degrees Awarded In 1996, 18 master's, 8 doctorates awarded. Terminal master's awarded for partial completion of doctoral program.

Entrance Requirements GRE General Test.

Degree Requirements For doctorate, dissertation required, foreign language not required.

Financial Aid In 1996–97, 59 students received aid, including fellowships totaling $555,036, research assistantships totaling $612,551; Federal Work-Study also available. *Financial aid application deadline:* 12/31.

Applying 162 applicants, 27% accepted. *Deadline:* 12/31 (11/1 for spring admission). *Fee:* $75.

Contact Dr. Loren W. Nolte
Director of Graduate Studies
919-660-5251

MEDICAL INFORMATICS

School of Nursing

Programs Offerings include nursing informatics (MSN, Certificate).

School Faculty 14 full-time (all women), 3 part-time (all women), 15.75 FTE.

Entrance Requirements For master's, GRE General Test or MAT, BSN, minimum GPA of 3.0, previous course work in statistics, RN license, 1 year of nursing experience.

Degree Requirements For master's, computer language required, thesis optional, foreign language not required.

Applying *Deadline:* 4/1 (priority date; rolling processing; 11/1 for spring admission). *Fee:* $50.

Contact Judy Carter
Admissions Officer
919-684-4248
Fax: 919-681-8899
E-mail: carte26@mc.duke.edu

EAST CAROLINA UNIVERSITY
Greenville, NC 27858-4353

OVERVIEW
East Carolina University is a public coed university.

ENROLLMENT
16,805 graduate, professional, and undergraduate students; 1,383 full-time matriculated graduate/professional students (834 women), 1,109 part-time matriculated graduate/professional students (719 women).

GRADUATE FACULTY
526 full-time (131 women), 4 part-time (0 women); includes 29 minority (11 African-Americans, 17 Asian-Americans, 1 Hispanic).

TUITION
$1806 per year full-time, $452 per semester (minimum) part-time for state residents; $8960 per year full-time, $2240 per semester (minimum) part-time for nonresidents.

HOUSING
Rooms and/or apartments available to single students at an average cost of $1660 per year ($3480 including board); on-campus housing not available to married students. Housing application deadline: 5/1. Graduate housing contact: Margie Bradley, 919-328-4928.

STUDENT SERVICES
Disabled student services, multicultural affairs office, low-cost health insurance, career counseling, free psychological counseling, exercise/wellness program, campus safety program, campus employment opportunities, international student services, writing training, grant writing training, teacher training.

FACILITIES
Library: Joyner Library plus 1 additional on-campus library; total holdings of 1.2 million volumes, 1.6 million microforms, 7,702 current periodical subscriptions. A total of 184 personal computers in all libraries. Access provided to on-line information retrieval services. *Computer:* Campuswide network is available with full Internet access. Total number of PCs/terminals supplied for student use: 2,000. Computer service fees are included with tuition and fees. *Special:* In arts and humanities: Mental Health Training Institute, East Carolina Development Institute, Center on Aging. In science and engineering: Institute for Coastal and Marine Resources. In social sciences: Reading laboratory, speech and hearing clinic.

COMPUTER SCIENCE

College of Arts and Sciences, Department of Mathematics, Program in Computer Science

Programs Awards MS.

Students 3 part-time (0 women); includes 1 minority (African-American). Average age 27.

Entrance Requirements GRE General Test, TOEFL.

Degree Requirements Comprehensive exams required, thesis optional, foreign language not required.

Financial Aid Research assistantships, teaching assistantships available. *Financial aid application deadline:* 6/1.

Applying 9 applicants, 44% accepted. *Deadline:* 6/1 (priority date; rolling processing; 10/15 for spring admission). *Fee:* $40.

Contact Dr. Karl Abrahamson
Director of Graduate Studies
919-328-6461
Fax: 919-328-6414
E-mail: maabraha@ecuvm.cis.ecu.edu

NORTH CAROLINA AGRICULTURAL AND TECHNICAL STATE UNIVERSITY
Greensboro, NC 27411

OVERVIEW
North Carolina Agricultural and Technical State University is a public coed university.

ENROLLMENT
7,533 graduate, professional, and undergraduate students; 384 full-time matriculated graduate/professional students (206 women), 609 part-time matriculated graduate/professional students (402 women).

TUITION
$1596 per year full-time, $261 per semester (minimum) part-time for state residents; $8750 per year full-time, $2049 per semester (minimum) part-time for nonresidents.

HOUSING

Rooms and/or apartments available to single students at an average cost of $1790 per year ($3120 including board); on-campus housing not available to married students. Housing application deadline: 5/8. Graduate housing contact: Dr. Charles Williams, 910-334-7920.

STUDENT SERVICES

Career counseling, free psychological counseling, day-care facilities, campus employment opportunities, international student services.

FACILITIES

Library: F. D. Bluford Library; total holdings of 416,021 volumes, 905,087 microforms, 250 current periodical subscriptions. Access provided to on-line information retrieval services. *Computer:* Campuswide network is available with full Internet access. Computer services are offered at no charge. *Special:* In science and engineering: Transportation Institute, solid-state engineering laboratory, agriculture farm laboratory, Waste Management Institute.

COMPUTER SCIENCE

Graduate School, College of Engineering, Department of Computer Science
Programs Awards MSCS.
Faculty 9 full-time (1 woman), 1 part-time (0 women), 9.25 FTE.
Faculty Research Object-oriented analysis, artificial intelligence, distributed computing, societal implications of computing, testing. *Total annual research expenditures:* $800,000.
Students 53 full-time (20 women), 34 part-time (16 women); includes 73 minority (50 African-Americans, 22 Asian-Americans, 1 Hispanic). Average age 25.
Degrees Awarded In 1996, 18 degrees awarded.
Degree Requirements Thesis (for some programs), comprehensive exam required, foreign language not required.
Financial Aid In 1996–97, 24 students received aid, including 16 research assistantships (6 to first-year students) averaging $1,050 per month and totaling $16,800, 4 teaching assistantships (2 to first-year students) averaging $1,050 per month and totaling $4,200; fellowships and career-related internships or fieldwork also available. *Financial aid application deadline:* 3/30.
Applying 51 applicants, 47% accepted. *Deadline:* 7/1 (priority date; rolling processing; 1/9 for spring admission). *Fee:* $25.
Contact Dr. David Bellin
　　　　　Graduate Coordinator
　　　　　910-334-7245
　　　　　Fax: 910-334-7244
　　　　　E-mail: dbellin@ncat.edu

ELECTRICAL ENGINEERING

Graduate School, College of Engineering, Department of Electrical Engineering
Programs Awards MSEE, PhD. Part-time programs available.
Faculty 21 full-time (2 women).
Faculty Research Semiconductor compounds, VLSI design, image processing, optical systems and devices, fault-tolerant computing. *Total annual research expenditures:* $1.082 million.
Students 37 full-time (9 women), 27 part-time (6 women); includes 45 minority (37 African-Americans, 7 Asian-Americans, 1 Hispanic), 15 international. Average age 24.
Degrees Awarded In 1996, 14 master's awarded.
Entrance Requirements For master's, GRE General Test, GRE Subject Test (recommended).

Degree Requirements For master's, project, thesis defense required, foreign language not required.
Financial Aid In 1996–97, 59 students received aid, including 10 fellowships, 15 research assistantships, 17 teaching assistantships. *Financial aid application deadline:* 3/30.
Applying 64 applicants, 63% accepted. *Deadline:* 7/1 (rolling processing; 1/9 for spring admission). *Fee:* $25.
Contact Dr. Chung Yu
　　　　　Graduate Coordinator
　　　　　910-334-7760
　　　　　Fax: 910-334-7716
　　　　　E-mail: yu@genesis.ncat.edu

NORTH CAROLINA STATE UNIVERSITY
Raleigh, NC 27695

OVERVIEW

North Carolina State University is a public coed university.

ENROLLMENT

27,169 graduate, professional, and undergraduate students; 3,481 full-time matriculated graduate/professional students (1,354 women), 1,655 part-time matriculated graduate/professional students (742 women).

GRADUATE FACULTY

1,329 full-time (176 women), 634 part-time (49 women); includes 195 minority (18 African-Americans, 107 Asian-Americans, 24 Hispanics, 46 Native Americans).

TUITION

$2206 per year full-time, $484 per semester (minimum) part-time for state residents; $10,738 per year full-time, $2617 per semester (minimum) part-time for nonresidents.

HOUSING

Rooms and/or apartments available to single students at an average cost of $3360 per year; available to married students (295 units) at an average cost of $4790 per year. Graduate housing contact: Jim Pappenhagen, 919-515-2440.

STUDENT SERVICES

Low-cost health insurance, career counseling, free psychological counseling, day-care facilities, campus safety program, campus employment opportunities, international student services.

FACILITIES

Library: D. H. Hill Library plus 5 additional on-campus libraries; total holdings of 2,540,328 volumes, 4,427,896 microforms, 21,586 current periodical subscriptions. A total of 274 personal computers in all libraries. Access provided to on-line information retrieval services. *Computer:* Campuswide network is available. Total number of PCs/terminals supplied for student use: 2,500. Computer service fees are included with tuition and fees. *Special:* In science and engineering: Sea Grant College Program, Electron Microscope Center, Nuclear Reactor Program, Precision Engineering Center, Materials Research Center, Center for Communications and Signal Processing, Center for Electric Power Research, Center for Sound and Vibration, Integrated Manufacturing Systems Engineering Institute, reproductive physiology research laboratory, phytotron, biological field laboratory, pesticide residue research laboratory, Mars Mission Research Center. In social sciences: Counseling Laboratory, Diagnostic Technology Clinic, Psychoeducational Clinic and Laboratories.

COMPUTER ENGINEERING

College of Engineering, Department of Electrical and Computer Engineering
Programs   Awards MS, PhD. Part-time programs available.
Faculty   4 full-time (0 women).
Faculty Research   Microwave devices, communications, signal processing, solid-state power systems, VLSI. *Total annual research expenditures:* $9.159 million.
Students   279 full-time (45 women), 83 part-time (7 women); includes 64 minority (29 African-Americans, 30 Asian-Americans, 4 Hispanics, 1 Native American), 123 international. Average age 28.
Degrees Awarded   In 1996, 82 master's, 32 doctorates awarded. Terminal master's awarded for partial completion of doctoral program.
Entrance Requirements   For master's, GRE, TOEFL (minimum score 575), minimum GPA of 3.2 in electrical engineering course work; for doctorate, GRE, TOEFL (minimum score 625), minimum GPA of 3.5 in electrical engineering course work.
Degree Requirements   For master's, thesis optional, foreign language not required; for doctorate, dissertation required, foreign language not required.
Financial Aid   In 1996–97, 35 fellowships (3 to first-year students) averaging $1,371 per month and totaling $215,916, 124 research assistantships (22 to first-year students) averaging $1,168 per month and totaling $631,486, 57 teaching assistantships (26 to first-year students) totaling $255,203 were awarded; career-related internships or fieldwork also available. *Financial aid application deadline:* 3/1.
Applying   367 applicants, 37% accepted. *Deadline:* 6/25 (rolling processing; 11/25 for spring admission). *Fee:* $45.
Contact   Connie Reno
Administrative Assistant
919-515-5085
Fax: 919-515-5523
E-mail: reno@eos.ncsu.edu

See in-depth description on page 489.

COMPUTER SCIENCE

College of Engineering, Department of Computer Science
Programs   Awards MC Sc, MS, PhD. Part-time programs available.
Faculty   27 full-time (2 women), 13 part-time (2 women).
Faculty Research   Software systems, networking and performance analysis, theory and algorithms, architecture, multimedia systems. *Total annual research expenditures:* $1.53 million.
Students   77 full-time (14 women), 35 part-time (5 women); includes 11 minority (3 African-Americans, 6 Asian-Americans, 2 Hispanics), 33 international. Average age 29.
Degrees Awarded   In 1996, 36 master's, 7 doctorates awarded.
Entrance Requirements   For master's, GRE General Test, GRE Subject Test, TOEFL, minimum GPA of 3.0; for doctorate, GRE General Test, GRE Subject Test, TOEFL, minimum GPA of 3.5.
Degree Requirements   For master's, computer language, thesis (for some programs) required, foreign language not required; for doctorate, computer language, dissertation required, foreign language not required.
Financial Aid   In 1996–97, 6 fellowships (3 to first-year students) averaging $1,349 per month and totaling $36,427, 23 research assistantships (4 to first-year students) averaging $1,218 per month and totaling $126,036, 37 teaching assistantships (15 to first-year

students) totaling $310,315 were awarded; institutionally sponsored loans and career-related internships or fieldwork also available. *Financial aid application deadline:* 2/1.
Applying   196 applicants, 32% accepted. *Deadline:* 4/1 (priority date; 10/1 for spring admission). *Fee:* $45.
Contact   Dr. Rex A. Dwyer
Director of Graduate Programs
919-515-7028
Fax: 919-515-7896
E-mail: dgp@csc.ncsu.edu

See in-depth description on page 487.

COMPUTER SCIENCE

College of Management, Program in Management
Programs   Offerings include computer science (MS).
Program Faculty   37 full-time (4 women), 3 part-time (0 women).
Entrance Requirements   GRE or GMAT, TOEFL (minimum score 550), minimum undergraduate GPA of 3.0.
Degree Requirements   Computer language required, foreign language and thesis not required.
Applying   *Deadline:* 6/25 (rolling processing; 11/25 for spring admission). *Fee:* $45.
Contact   Carol Smith
Graduate Secretary
919-515-5584
Fax: 919-515-5564
E-mail: carol_smith@ncsu.edu

ELECTRICAL ENGINEERING

College of Engineering, Department of Electrical and Computer Engineering
Programs   Awards MS, PhD. Part-time programs available.
Faculty   4 full-time (0 women).
Faculty Research   Microwave devices, communications, signal processing, solid-state power systems, VLSI. *Total annual research expenditures:* $9.159 million.
Students   279 full-time (45 women), 83 part-time (7 women); includes 64 minority (29 African-Americans, 30 Asian-Americans, 4 Hispanics, 1 Native American), 123 international. Average age 28.
Degrees Awarded   In 1996, 82 master's, 32 doctorates awarded. Terminal master's awarded for partial completion of doctoral program.
Entrance Requirements   For master's, GRE, TOEFL (minimum score 575), minimum GPA of 3.2 in electrical engineering course work; for doctorate, GRE, TOEFL (minimum score 625), minimum GPA of 3.5 in electrical engineering course work.
Degree Requirements   For master's, thesis optional, foreign language not required; for doctorate, dissertation required, foreign language not required.
Financial Aid   In 1996–97, 35 fellowships (3 to first-year students) averaging $1,371 per month and totaling $215,916, 124 research assistantships (22 to first-year students) averaging $1,168 per month and totaling $631,486, 57 teaching assistantships (26 to first-year students) totaling $255,203 were awarded; career-related internships or fieldwork also available. *Financial aid application deadline:* 3/1.
Applying   367 applicants, 37% accepted. *Deadline:* 6/25 (rolling processing; 11/25 for spring admission). *Fee:* $45.

Contact *Connie Reno*
Administrative Assistant
919-515-5085
Fax: 919-515-5523
E-mail: reno@eos.ncsu.edu

See in-depth description on page 489.

See in-depth description on page 489.

THE UNIVERSITY OF NORTH CAROLINA AT CHAPEL HILL
Chapel Hill, NC 27599

OVERVIEW
The University of North Carolina at Chapel Hill is a public coed university.

ENROLLMENT
22,626 graduate, professional, and undergraduate students; 6,679 full-time, 611 part-time matriculated graduate/professional students.

GRADUATE FACULTY
2,337 (707 women); includes 250 minority (91 African-Americans, 115 Asian-Americans, 39 Hispanics, 5 Native Americans).

EXPENSES
Tuition $1428 per year full-time, $357 per semester (minimum) part-time for state residents; $10,414 per year full-time, $2604 per semester (minimum) part-time for nonresidents. Fees $782 per year full-time, $332 per semester (minimum) part-time.

HOUSING
Rooms and/or apartments available to single students (630 units) and married students (306 units).

STUDENT SERVICES
Disabled student services, low-cost health insurance, career counseling, free psychological counseling, day-care facilities, writing training, teacher training.

FACILITIES
Library: Davis Library plus 3 additional on-campus libraries; total holdings of 4,674,502 volumes, 4,044,679 microforms, 45,571 current periodical subscriptions. *Computer:* Campuswide network is available with full Internet access. *Special:* In science and engineering: Cancer Research Center, Biological Sciences Research Center, Dental Research Center, Clinical Research Unit, Health Services Research Center. In social sciences: Institute for Research in Social Sciences, Carolina Population Center, Center for Urban and Regional Studies, Center for Alcohol Studies.

COMPUTER SCIENCE

College of Arts and Sciences, Department of Computer Science
Programs Awards MS, PhD.
Faculty 37 full-time.
Students 119 full-time, includes 49 minority (3 African-Americans, 41 Asian-Americans, 5 Hispanics), 54 international.
Degrees Awarded In 1996, 32 master's, 10 doctorates awarded.
Entrance Requirements GRE General Test, minimum GPA of 3.0.

Degree Requirements For master's, comprehensive exam required, foreign language not required; for doctorate, dissertation, comprehensive exam required, foreign language not required.
Financial Aid In 1996–97, 61 research assistantships, 13 teaching assistantships were awarded; fellowships also available. *Financial aid application deadline: 3/1.*
Applying 343 applicants, 25% accepted. *Deadline:* 1/31 (priority date; rolling processing). *Fee:* $55.
Contact *Dr. Stephen F. Weiss Jr.*
Chairman
919-962-1888

See in-depth description on page 687.

See in-depth description on page 687.

UNIVERSITY OF NORTH CAROLINA AT CHARLOTTE
Charlotte, NC 28223-0001

OVERVIEW
University of North Carolina at Charlotte is a public coed university.

ENROLLMENT
15,795 graduate, professional, and undergraduate students; 627 full-time matriculated graduate/professional students (323 women), 1,437 part-time matriculated graduate/professional students (812 women).

GRADUATE FACULTY
439 full-time (114 women), 19 part-time (11 women), 445 FTE; includes 55 minority (15 African-Americans, 34 Asian-Americans, 4 Hispanics, 2 Native Americans).

TUITION
$1718 per year full-time, $326 per semester (minimum) part-time for state residents; $8872 per year full-time, $2114 per semester (minimum) part-time for nonresidents.

HOUSING
Rooms and/or apartments available to single students (3,646 units) at an average cost of $2104 per year ($3724 including board); on-campus housing not available to married students. Housing application deadline: 6/1. Graduate housing contact: Residence Life Office, 704-547-2585.

STUDENT SERVICES
Disabled student services, career counseling, free psychological counseling, campus safety program, campus employment opportunities, international student services.

FACILITIES
Library: J. Murrey Atkins Library; total holdings of 622,559 volumes, 1,266,280 microforms, 4,900 current periodical subscriptions. Access provided to on-line information retrieval services. *Computer:* Campuswide network is available with full Internet access. Total number of PCs/terminals supplied for student use: 650. Computer service fees are included with tuition and fees. *Special:* In science and engineering: Cameron Applied Research

Center. In social sciences: Small Business and Technology Development Center, Urban Institute.

COMPUTER SCIENCE

The William States Lee College of Engineering, Department of Computer Science
Programs Awards MS.
Faculty 12 full-time (1 woman).
Faculty Research Computer programming, data retrieval and processing, robotics.
Students 41 full-time (5 women), 93 part-time (26 women); includes 14 minority (3 African-Americans, 10 Asian-Americans, 1 Hispanic), 70 international. Average age 28.
Degrees Awarded In 1996, 39 degrees awarded.
Entrance Requirements GRE General Test, minimum GPA of 3.0 during previous 2 years, 2.8 overall.
Financial Aid In 1996–97, 22 research assistantships averaging $1,629 per month and totaling $286,844, 14 teaching assistantships (2 to first-year students) averaging $830 per month and totaling $93,000 were awarded. *Financial aid application deadline: 4/1.*
Applying 121 applicants, 90% accepted. *Deadline: 7/1. Fee: $35.*
Contact *Diane Locklin*
Director of Graduate Admissions
704-547-3366
Fax: 704-547-3279

ELECTRICAL ENGINEERING

The William States Lee College of Engineering, Department of Electrical Engineering
Programs Awards MSEE, PhD. Part-time and evening/weekend programs available.
Faculty 19 full-time (1 woman).
Faculty Research Power systems, dynamics and control of flexibility, power load management, microelectronics.
Students 19 full-time (2 women), 35 part-time (6 women); includes 5 minority (all Asian-Americans), 19 international. Average age 28.
Degrees Awarded In 1996, 28 master's awarded.
Entrance Requirements For master's, GRE General Test, minimum GPA of 3.0 in undergraduate major, 2.5 overall.
Financial Aid In 1996–97, 1 fellowship, 16 research assistantships averaging $1,237 per month and totaling $158,336, 16 teaching assistantships averaging $810 per month and totaling $103,700 were awarded; Federal Work-Study also available. *Financial aid application deadline: 4/1.*
Applying 112 applicants, 75% accepted. *Deadline: 7/1. Fee: $35.*
Contact *Diane Locklin*
Director of Graduate Admissions
704-547-3366
Fax: 704-547-3279

WAKE FOREST UNIVERSITY
Winston-Salem, NC 27109

OVERVIEW
Wake Forest University is an independent coed university.

ENROLLMENT
5,748 graduate, professional, and undergraduate students; 1,191 full-time matriculated graduate/professional students (465 women), 346 part-time matriculated graduate/professional students (138 women).

GRADUATE FACULTY
1,448.

TUITION
$16,300 per year full-time, $500 per hour part-time.

HOUSING
On-campus housing not available.

STUDENT SERVICES
Low-cost health insurance, career counseling, free psychological counseling.

FACILITIES
Library: Z. Smith Reynolds Library plus 3 additional on-campus libraries; total holdings of 1,299,805 volumes, 1,602,327 microforms, 17,585 current periodical subscriptions. A total of 100 personal computers in all libraries.

COMPUTER SCIENCE

Department of Computer Science
Programs Awards MS. Part-time programs available.
Faculty 4 full-time (0 women).
Students 10 full-time (2 women), 4 part-time (0 women); includes 1 minority (Hispanic), 1 international. Average age 27.
Degrees Awarded In 1996, 5 degrees awarded.
Entrance Requirements GRE General Test, GRE Subject Test.
Degree Requirements 1 foreign language required (computer language can substitute), thesis optional.
Financial Aid In 1996–97, 11 students received aid, including 3 fellowships (all to first-year students) averaging $400 per month and totaling $12,000, 7 teaching assistantships (2 to first-year students) averaging $800 per month and totaling $56,000, 1 scholarship (to a first-year student) totaling $14,750. Aid available to part-time students. *Financial aid application deadline: 2/15; applicants required to submit FAFSA.*
Applying 24 applicants, 38% accepted. *Deadline: 2/15. Fee: $25.*
Contact *Dr. Stan Thomas*
Director
910-758-5354
E-mail: sjt@wfu.edu

WESTERN CAROLINA UNIVERSITY
Cullowhee, NC 28723

OVERVIEW
Western Carolina University is a public coed comprehensive institution.

ENROLLMENT
6,511 graduate, professional, and undergraduate students; 332 full-time matriculated graduate/professional students (197 women), 505 part-time matriculated graduate/professional students (356 women).

GRADUATE FACULTY
275 (81 women); includes 6 minority (3 African-Americans, 3 Asian-Americans).

TUITION
$1729 per year full-time, $140 per credit hour (minimum) part-time for state residents; $8857 per year full-time, $1030 per credit hour (minimum) part-time for nonresidents.

HOUSING

Rooms and/or apartments available to single students at an average cost of $1350 per year ($2674 including board); available to married students (48 units) at an average cost of $3750 (including board). Graduate housing contact: Randy Rice, 704-227-7303.

STUDENT SERVICES

Low-cost health insurance, career counseling, free psychological counseling, exercise/wellness program, campus employment opportunities, international student services.

FACILITIES

Library: Hunter Library; total holdings of 496,970 volumes, 1,263,098 microforms, 2,788 current periodical subscriptions. A total of 34 personal computers in all libraries. Access provided to on-line information retrieval services. *Computer:* Campuswide network is available with full Internet access. Total number of PCs/terminals supplied for student use: 400. Computer service fees are included with tuition and fees. *Special:* In arts and humanities: Mountain Heritage Center. In science and engineering: Highlands Biological Station, Mountain Aquaculture Research Center. In social sciences: Mountain Resources Center.

COMPUTER SCIENCE

College of Arts and Sciences, Department of Mathematics and Computer Science

Programs   Awards MA Ed, MS. Part-time and evening/weekend programs available.

Faculty   18 (3 women).

Students   6 full-time (1 woman), 2 part-time (1 woman); includes 1 international.

Degrees Awarded   In 1996, 12 degrees awarded.

Entrance Requirements   GRE General Test.

Degree Requirements   Comprehensive exam required, thesis optional, foreign language not required.

Financial Aid   In 1996–97, 5 students received aid, including 5 research assistantships (1 to a first-year student) totaling $22,000; fellowships, teaching assistantships, Federal Work-Study, institutionally sponsored loans also available. *Financial aid application deadline:* 3/15.

Applying   9 applicants, 56% accepted. *Deadline:* rolling. *Fee:* $25.

Contact   *Kathleen Owen*
Assistant to the Dean
704-227-7398
Fax: 704-227-7480

NORTH DAKOTA

NORTH DAKOTA STATE UNIVERSITY
Fargo, ND 58105

OVERVIEW

North Dakota State University is a public coed university.

ENROLLMENT

9,598 graduate, professional, and undergraduate students; 556 full-time matriculated graduate/professional students (233 women), 359 part-time matriculated graduate/professional students (151 women).

GRADUATE FACULTY

400 full-time (58 women), 15 part-time (6 women); includes 42 minority (37 Asian-Americans, 4 Hispanics, 1 Native American).

TUITION

$2448 per year full-time, $102 per credit part-time for state residents; $6528 per year full-time, $272 per credit part-time for nonresidents.

HOUSING

Rooms and/or apartments available to single students at an average cost of $1108 per year ($2968 including board); available to married students (305 units) at an average cost of $2910 per year. Graduate housing contact: Mr. Prakash Mathew, 701-231-7557.

STUDENT SERVICES

Low-cost health insurance, career counseling, free psychological counseling, day-care facilities, international student services.

FACILITIES

Library: Main library plus 3 additional on-campus libraries; total holdings of 504,113 volumes, 272,697 microforms, 4,210 current periodical subscriptions. A total of 100 personal computers in all libraries. Access provided to on-line information retrieval services. *Computer:* Campuswide network is available with full Internet access. Total number of PCs/terminals supplied for student use: 350. Computer services are offered at no charge.

COMPUTER SCIENCE

College of Science and Mathematics, Department of Computer Science

Programs   Offers programs in computer science (MS, PhD), operations research (MS). Part-time programs available.

Faculty   12 full-time (0 women), 2 part-time (1 woman).

Faculty Research   Operating systems, artificial intelligence, database systems, software engineering, algorithm analysis.

Students   46 full-time (11 women), 35 part-time (9 women); includes 59 minority (7 African-Americans, 52 Asian-Americans). Average age 25.

Degrees Awarded   In 1996, 19 master's, 3 doctorates awarded.

Entrance Requirements   For master's, TOEFL (minimum score 600), minimum GPA of 3.0, BS in computer science or related field; for doctorate, TOEFL (minimum score 600), minimum GPA of 3.25, MS in computer science or related field.

Degree Requirements   For master's, computer language, comprehensive exam required, thesis optional, foreign language not required; for doctorate, computer language, dissertation, qualifying exam required, foreign language not required.

Financial Aid   Research assistantships, teaching assistantships, Federal Work-Study, institutionally sponsored loans, and career-related internships or fieldwork available. *Financial aid application deadline:* 4/15.

Applying   197 applicants, 36% accepted. *Deadline:* 8/1 (rolling processing; 10/1 for spring admission). *Fee:* $25.

Contact   *Dr. Kendall Nygard*
Chair
701-231-8562
Fax: 701-231-8255
E-mail: nygard@plains.nodak.edu

ELECTRICAL ENGINEERING

College of Engineering and Architecture, Department of Electrical Engineering

Programs   Awards MS.

Faculty   16 full-time (1 woman), 2 part-time (0 women).

Faculty Research Computers, power and control systems, microwaves, communications and signal processing, bioengineering.
Students 22 full-time (4 women), 10 part-time (0 women). Average age 28.
Degrees Awarded In 1996, 12 degrees awarded (100% found work related to degree).
Entrance Requirements TOEFL (minimum score 525).
Degree Requirements Computer language, thesis or alternative required, foreign language not required.
Financial Aid Research assistantships, teaching assistantships, full tuition waivers, Federal Work-Study, institutionally sponsored loans, and career-related internships or fieldwork available. *Financial aid application deadline: 4/15.*
Applying 52 applicants, 71% accepted. *Deadline:* 6/1 (priority date; rolling processing). *Fee:* $25.
Contact *Dr. Orlando Baiocchi*
Chair
701-231-7608
Fax: 701-231-8677

UNIVERSITY OF NORTH DAKOTA
Grand Forks, ND 58202

OVERVIEW
University of North Dakota is a public coed university.

ENROLLMENT
11,512 graduate, professional, and undergraduate students; 1,094 full-time matriculated graduate/professional students (548 women), 1,075 part-time matriculated graduate/professional students (640 women).

GRADUATE FACULTY
416 full-time (116 women).

EXPENSES
Tuition $2446 per year full-time, $102 per credit hour part-time for state residents; $6532 per year full-time, $272 per credit hour part-time for nonresidents. Fees $440 per year full-time, $41 per credit hour part-time.

HOUSING
Rooms and/or apartments available to single students at an average cost of $2750 (including board); available to married students (560 units) at an average cost of $3300 per year. Graduate housing contact: Darold Dewald, 701-777-4251.

STUDENT SERVICES
Low-cost health insurance, career counseling, free psychological counseling, day-care facilities, campus employment opportunities, international student services.

FACILITIES
Library: Chester Fritz Library plus 5 additional on-campus libraries; total holdings of 2.3 million volumes, 8,200 current periodical subscriptions. A total of 1,500 personal computers in all libraries. Access provided to on-line information retrieval services. *Computer:* Campuswide network is available with full Internet access. Computer services are offered at no charge. *Special:* In science and engineering: Ireland Cancer Research Laboratory, Energy and Environmental Research Center, biological field stations.

COMPUTER SCIENCE

Center for Aerospace Studies, Department of Computer Science
Programs Awards MS. Part-time programs available.
Faculty 7 full-time (1 woman).
Faculty Research Operating systems, simulation, parallel computation, hypermedia, graph theory.
Students 9 full-time (3 women), 6 part-time (1 woman).
Degrees Awarded In 1996, 3 degrees awarded.
Entrance Requirements GRE General Test, TOEFL (minimum score 550), minimum GPA of 3.0.
Degree Requirements Comprehensive exam required, thesis optional, foreign language not required.
Financial Aid In 1996–97, 11 students received aid, including 2 research assistantships totaling $14,000, 9 teaching assistantships totaling $59,500; fellowships, full and partial tuition waivers, Federal Work-Study, institutionally sponsored loans also available. *Financial aid application deadline: 3/15.*
Applying 15 applicants, 80% accepted. *Deadline:* 3/15 (priority date; rolling processing). *Fee:* $20.
Contact *Dr. Tom O'Neil*
Director
701-777-4107
E-mail: oneil@cs.und.edu

ELECTRICAL ENGINEERING

School of Engineering and Mines, Department of Electrical Engineering
Programs Awards M Engr, MS. Part-time programs available.
Faculty 6 full-time (0 women).
Faculty Research Controls and robotics, signal processing, energy conversion, microwaves, computer engineering.
Students 6 full-time (1 woman), 1 part-time (0 women).
Degrees Awarded In 1996, 2 degrees awarded.
Entrance Requirements GRE General Test, TOEFL (minimum score 550), minimum GPA of 3.0.
Degree Requirements Thesis or alternative.
Financial Aid In 1996–97, 6 students received aid, including 2 research assistantships totaling $7,295, 4 teaching assistantships totaling $14,640; fellowships, full and partial tuition waivers, Federal Work-Study, institutionally sponsored loans also available. *Financial aid application deadline: 3/15.*
Applying 8 applicants, 100% accepted. *Deadline:* 3/15 (priority date; rolling processing). *Fee:* $20.
Contact *Dr. Nagy Bengiamin*
Chairperson
701-777-4331
E-mail: bengiami@plains.nodak.edu

OHIO

AIR FORCE INSTITUTE OF TECHNOLOGY
Wright-Patterson AFB, OH 45433-7765

OVERVIEW
Air Force Institute of Technology is a public coed graduate-only institution.

ENROLLMENT
522 full-time matriculated graduate/professional students (34 women), 0 part-time matriculated graduate/professional students.

GRADUATE FACULTY
255 full-time (6 women).

TUITION
$0.

HOUSING
Rooms and/or apartments available to married students; on-campus housing not available to single students.

STUDENT SERVICES
Low-cost health insurance, career counseling, free psychological counseling, exercise/wellness program, day-care facilities, campus safety program, international student services.

FACILITIES
Library: Main library; total holdings of 88,500 volumes, 801,877 microforms, 1,250 current periodical subscriptions. Access provided to on-line information retrieval services. *Computer:* Campuswide network is available with full Internet access.

COMPUTER ENGINEERING

School of Engineering, Department of Electrical and Computer Engineering, Program in Computer Science and Engineering
Programs   Awards MS, PhD. One or more programs accredited by ABET.
Faculty   46 full-time (0 women).
Students   66 full-time (2 women), includes 4 minority (1 African-American, 2 Asian-Americans, 1 Hispanic), 4 international. Average age 29.
Degrees Awarded   In 1996, 37 master's awarded (100% found work related to degree); 5 doctorates awarded.
Entrance Requirements   For master's, GRE General Test (minimum combined score of 1100), minimum GPA of 3.0; must be military officer, DOD civilian, or government employee; for doctorate, GRE General Test (minimum combined score of 1200), minimum GPA of 3.5; must be military officer, DOD civilian, or government employee.
Degree Requirements   For master's, computer language, thesis required, foreign language not required.
Applying   100% of applicants accepted.
Contact   *Dr. Thomas Hartrum*
Head
937-255-4281

COMPUTER SCIENCE

School of Engineering, Department of Electrical and Computer Engineering, Program in Computer Science and Engineering
Programs   Awards MS, PhD. One or more programs accredited by ABET.
Faculty   46 full-time (0 women).
Students   66 full-time (2 women), includes 4 minority (1 African-American, 2 Asian-Americans, 1 Hispanic), 4 international. Average age 29.
Degrees Awarded   In 1996, 37 master's awarded (100% found work related to degree); 5 doctorates awarded.
Entrance Requirements   For master's, GRE General Test (minimum combined score of 1100), minimum GPA of 3.0; must be military officer, DOD civilian, or government employee; for doctorate, GRE General Test (minimum combined score of 1200), minimum GPA of 3.5; must be military officer, DOD civilian, or government employee.
Degree Requirements   For master's, computer language, thesis required, foreign language not required.
Applying   100% of applicants accepted.

Contact   *Dr. Thomas Hartrum*
Head
937-255-4281

ELECTRICAL ENGINEERING

School of Engineering, Department of Electrical and Computer Engineering, Program in Electrical Engineering
Programs   Awards MS, PhD. Part-time programs available.
Faculty   46 full-time (0 women).
Students   77 full-time (2 women), includes 4 minority (1 African-American, 3 Asian-Americans), 7 international. Average age 29.
Degrees Awarded   In 1996, 23 master's awarded (100% found work related to degree); 13 doctorates awarded.
Entrance Requirements   For master's, GRE General Test (minimum combined score of 1100), minimum GPA of 3.0; must be military officer, DOD civilian, or government employee; for doctorate, GRE General Test (minimum combined score of 1200), minimum GPA of 3.5; must be military officer, DOD civilian, or government employee.
Degree Requirements   For master's, computer language, thesis required, foreign language not required; for doctorate, dissertation required, foreign language not required.
Applying   100% of applicants accepted.
Contact   *Lt. Col. David M. Norman*
Head
937-255-9270

BOWLING GREEN STATE UNIVERSITY
Bowling Green, OH 43403

OVERVIEW
Bowling Green State University is a public coed university.

ENROLLMENT
18,868 graduate, professional, and undergraduate students; 1,503 full-time matriculated graduate/professional students (814 women), 894 part-time matriculated graduate/professional students (498 women).

GRADUATE FACULTY
543 full-time (155 women), 185 part-time (45 women).

TUITION
$5762 per year full-time, $270 per credit hour part-time for state residents; $10,776 per year full-time, $509 per credit hour part-time for nonresidents.

HOUSING
Rooms and/or apartments available to single students (26 units) at an average cost of $5482 (including board); on-campus housing not available to married students. Graduate housing contact: Student Housing and Residential Programs, 419-372-2011.

STUDENT SERVICES
Disabled student services, multicultural affairs office, low-cost health insurance, career counseling, free psychological counseling, exercise/wellness program, day-care facilities, campus safety program, campus employment opportunities, international student services.

FACILITIES
Library: William T. Jerome Library plus 6 additional on-campus libraries; total holdings of 1.9 million volumes, 2 million microforms, 5,000 current periodical subscriptions.

A total of 200 personal computers in all libraries. Access provided to on-line information retrieval services. *Computer:* Campuswide network is available with full Internet access. Total number of PCs/terminals supplied for student use: 700. Computer service fees are included with tuition and fees. *Special:* In arts and humanities: Center for Archival Collections, Mid-American Center for Contemporary Music, Philosophy Documentation Center. In science and engineering: Center for Microscopy and Microanalysis, Center for Photochemical Sciences, Institute for Great Lakes Research, Mid-American *Drosophila* Stock Center, Statistical Consulting Center. In social sciences: Institute for Psychological Research and Application Management Center, Philosophy Documentation Center, Population and Society Research Center, Reading Center, Social Philosophy and Policy Center.

COMPUTER SCIENCE

College of Arts and Sciences, Department of Computer Science
Programs Awards MS. Part-time and evening/weekend programs available.
Faculty 12 full-time (4 women), 1 part-time (0 women).
Faculty Research Artificial intelligence, real time and concurrent programming languages, behavioral aspects of computing, network protocols.
Students 41 full-time (11 women), 18 part-time (5 women); includes 1 minority (Asian-American), 37 international.
Degrees Awarded In 1996, 32 degrees awarded.
Entrance Requirements GRE General Test, TOEFL (minimum score 550).
Degree Requirements Thesis or alternative required, foreign language not required.
Financial Aid In 1996–97, 30 assistantships were awarded; full and partial tuition waivers and career-related internships or fieldwork also available. *Financial aid application deadline:* 2/15.
Applying 79 applicants, 48% accepted. *Fee:* $30.
Contact Dr. Mohammad Dadfar
Graduate Coordinator
419-372-2977

CASE WESTERN RESERVE UNIVERSITY
Cleveland, OH 44106

OVERVIEW
Case Western Reserve University is an independent coed university.

ENROLLMENT
9,970 graduate, professional, and undergraduate students; 3,543 full-time matriculated graduate/professional students (1,682 women), 2,748 part-time matriculated graduate/professional students (1,304 women).

GRADUATE FACULTY
1,879 (531 women); includes 230 minority (54 African-Americans, 143 Asian-Americans, 30 Hispanics, 3 Native Americans).

TUITION
$17,800 per year full-time, $742 per credit hour part-time.

HOUSING
Rooms and/or apartments available to single students (85 units) at an average cost of $3890 per year ($6100 including board); on-campus housing not available to married students. Housing application deadline: 5/1. Graduate housing contact: James Salerno, 216-368-3780.

STUDENT SERVICES
Disabled student services, low-cost health insurance, career counseling, free psychological counseling, campus safety program, campus employment opportunities, international student services, writing training, grant writing training, teacher training.

FACILITIES
Library: Kelvin Smith Library plus 3 additional on-campus libraries; total holdings of 1,938,840 volumes, 2,226,822 microforms, 13,599 current periodical subscriptions. A total of 90 personal computers in all libraries. Access provided to on-line information retrieval services. *Computer:* Campuswide network is available with full Internet access. Total number of PCs/terminals supplied for student use: 200. Computer services are offered at no charge. *Special:* In arts and humanities: Center for Regional and Comparative History. In science and engineering: Center for Applied Polymer Research; Center for Adhesives, Sealants, and Coatings; Center for Electrochemical Sciences; Genetics Center; Electronics Design Center; Center for Neurosciences; Center for Automations and Intelligent Systems Research. In social sciences: Mandel Center for Nonprofit Organization, Health Systems Management Center, Center for Aging and Health, Criminal Justice Center, Mental Development Center.

COMPUTER ENGINEERING

The Case School of Engineering, Department of Computer Engineering and Science
Programs Offers programs in computer engineering (MS, PhD), computing and information science (MS, PhD). Part-time programs available.
Faculty 11 full-time (3 women), 4 part-time (0 women).
Faculty Research Artificial intelligence, distributed computing and simulation, database design, computer architecture, parallel processing. *Total annual research expenditures:* $720,000.
Students 80 full-time (20 women), 31 part-time (6 women); includes 45 minority (2 African-Americans, 43 Asian-Americans), 65 international. Average age 24.
Degrees Awarded In 1996, 25 master's awarded (88% found work related to degree, 12% continued full-time study); 3 doctorates awarded (33% entered university research/teaching, 67% found other work related to degree). Terminal master's awarded for partial completion of doctoral program.
Entrance Requirements GRE General Test (minimum combined score of 1700 on three sections; 2100 for financial aid), TOEFL (minimum score 550).
Degree Requirements For master's, thesis optional, foreign language not required; for doctorate, dissertation required, foreign language not required.
Financial Aid In 1996–97, 38 students received aid, including 25 research assistantships, 13 teaching assistantships (5 to first-year students); institutionally sponsored loans and career-related internships or fieldwork also available. *Financial aid application deadline:* 2/15.

Applying 307 applicants, 85% accepted. *Deadline:* 2/15 (11/15 for spring admission). *Fee:* $25.
Contact *Kate Coleman*
Executive/Graduate Secretary
216-368-2802
Fax: 216-368-2801
E-mail: coleman@alpha.ces.cwru.edu

COMPUTER ENGINEERING

The Case School of Engineering, Practice-Oriented Master's Degree Program in Engineering
Programs Offerings include computer engineering (MS).
Entrance Requirements TOEFL (minimum score 550).
Applying *Deadline:* 8/15 (priority date; rolling processing; 12/15 for spring admission). *Fee:* $25.
Contact *Dr. Marcus Buchner*
Director
216-368-8760
Fax: 216-368-0327
E-mail: epom@po.cwru.edu

COMPUTER SCIENCE

The Case School of Engineering, Department of Computer Engineering and Science
Programs Offers programs in computer engineering (MS, PhD), computing and information science (MS, PhD). Part-time programs available.
Faculty 11 full-time (3 women), 4 part-time (0 women).
Faculty Research Artificial intelligence, distributed computing and simulation, database design, computer architecture, parallel processing. *Total annual research expenditures:* $720,000.
Students 80 full-time (20 women), 31 part-time (6 women); includes 45 minority (2 African-Americans, 43 Asian-Americans), 65 international. Average age 24.
Degrees Awarded In 1996, 25 master's awarded (88% found work related to degree, 12% continued full-time study); 3 doctorates awarded (33% entered university research/teaching, 67% found other work related to degree). Terminal master's awarded for partial completion of doctoral program.
Entrance Requirements GRE General Test (minimum combined score of 1700 on three sections; 2100 for financial aid), TOEFL (minimum score 550).
Degree Requirements For master's, thesis optional, foreign language not required; for doctorate, dissertation required, foreign language not required.
Financial Aid In 1996–97, 38 students received aid, including 25 research assistantships, 13 teaching assistantships (5 to first-year students); institutionally sponsored loans and career-related internships or fieldwork also available. *Financial aid application deadline:* 2/15.
Applying 307 applicants, 85% accepted. *Deadline:* 2/15 (11/15 for spring admission). *Fee:* $25.
Contact *Kate Coleman*
Executive/Graduate Secretary
216-368-2802
Fax: 216-368-2801
E-mail: coleman@alpha.ces.cwru.edu

ELECTRICAL ENGINEERING

The Case School of Engineering, Department of Electrical Engineering and Applied Physics
Programs Offerings include electrical engineering (MS, PhD).
Department Faculty 12 full-time (0 women), 1 part-time (0 women).

Entrance Requirements For master's, GRE General Test (minimum combined score of 2000 on three sections), TOEFL (minimum score 550); for doctorate, TOEFL (minimum score 550).
Degree Requirements For master's, thesis or alternative required, foreign language not required; for doctorate, dissertation, qualifying exam required, foreign language not required.
Applying *Deadline:* 4/1 (priority date; 11/1 for spring admission). *Fee:* $25.
Contact *Elizabethanne Fuller*
Admissions Secretary
216-368-4080
Fax: 216-368-2668
E-mail: emf4@po.cwru.edu

ELECTRICAL ENGINEERING

The Case School of Engineering, Practice-Oriented Master's Degree Program in Engineering
Programs Offerings include electrical engineering (MS).
Entrance Requirements TOEFL (minimum score 550).
Applying *Deadline:* 8/15 (priority date; rolling processing; 12/15 for spring admission). *Fee:* $25.
Contact *Dr. Marcus Buchner*
Director
216-368-8760
Fax: 216-368-0327
E-mail: epom@po.cwru.edu

CLEVELAND STATE UNIVERSITY
Cleveland, OH 44115

OVERVIEW
Cleveland State University is a public coed university.

ENROLLMENT
15,522 graduate, professional, and undergraduate students; 1,473 full-time matriculated graduate/professional students (712 women), 3,313 part-time matriculated graduate/professional students (1,843 women).

GRADUATE FACULTY
465 full-time (122 women), 238 part-time (171 women).

EXPENSES
Tuition $3266 per year full-time, $126 per credit hour part-time for state residents; $6531 per year full-time, $251 per credit hour part-time for nonresidents. Fees $1.50 per credit hour.

HOUSING
Rooms and/or apartments available to single students at an average cost of $4419 (including board); available to married students at an average cost of $5700 per year ($8838 including board). Graduate housing contact: Judith La Riccia-Grant, 216-687-5196.

STUDENT SERVICES
Low-cost health insurance, career counseling, free psychological counseling, day-care facilities, campus safety program, campus employment opportunities, international student services.

FACILITIES
Library: Main library plus 1 additional on-campus library; total holdings of 907,661 volumes, 642,683 microforms,

5,957 current periodical subscriptions. A total of 177 personal computers in all libraries. Access provided to on-line information retrieval services. *Computer:* Campuswide network is available with full Internet access. Computer service fees are included with tuition and fees. *Special:* In arts and humanities: Center for Teaching Excellence. In science and engineering: Advanced Manufacturing Center. In social sciences: Urban Center.

COMPUTER ENGINEERING

Fenn College of Engineering, Department of Electrical and Computer Engineering

Programs   Awards MS, D Eng. Part-time programs available.

Faculty   11 full-time (1 woman), 1 part-time (0 women).

Faculty Research   Computer networks, knowledge-based control systems, artificial intelligence, electromagnetic interference, semiconducting materials for solar cell digital communications.

Students   18 full-time (3 women), 51 part-time (4 women); includes 9 minority (1 African-American, 7 Asian-Americans, 1 Hispanic), 16 international. Average age 31.

Degrees Awarded   In 1996, 19 master's, 4 doctorates awarded.

Entrance Requirements   For master's, GRE General Test, GRE Subject Test, TOEFL (minimum score 550), minimum GPA of 3.0; for doctorate, GRE General Test, GRE Subject Test, TOEFL, minimum GPA of 3.5.

Degree Requirements   For master's, exam or thesis required, foreign language not required; for doctorate, dissertation, candidacy and qualifying exams required, foreign language not required.

Financial Aid   In 1996–97, 1 research assistantship, 3 teaching assistantships were awarded; career-related internships or fieldwork also available.

Applying   229 applicants, 49% accepted. *Deadline:* 9/1 (priority date; rolling processing). *Fee:* $0.

Contact   *Dr. James H. Burghart*
Chairperson
216-687-2586
Fax: 216-687-9280
E-mail: burghart@csvax.csuohio.edu

ELECTRICAL ENGINEERING

Fenn College of Engineering, Department of Electrical and Computer Engineering

Programs   Awards MS, D Eng. Part-time programs available.

Faculty   11 full-time (1 woman), 1 part-time (0 women).

Faculty Research   Computer networks, knowledge-based control systems, artificial intelligence, electromagnetic interference, semiconducting materials for solar cell digital communications.

Students   18 full-time (3 women), 51 part-time (4 women); includes 9 minority (1 African-American, 7 Asian-Americans, 1 Hispanic), 16 international. Average age 31.

Degrees Awarded   In 1996, 19 master's, 4 doctorates awarded.

Entrance Requirements   For master's, GRE General Test, GRE Subject Test, TOEFL (minimum score 550), minimum GPA of 3.0; for doctorate, GRE General Test, GRE Subject Test, TOEFL, minimum GPA of 3.5.

Degree Requirements   For master's, exam or thesis required, foreign language not required; for doctorate, dissertation, candidacy and qualifying exams required, foreign language not required.

Financial Aid   In 1996–97, 1 research assistantship, 3 teaching assistantships were awarded; career-related internships or fieldwork also available.

Applying   229 applicants, 49% accepted. *Deadline:* 9/1 (priority date; rolling processing). *Fee:* $0.

Contact   *Dr. James H. Burghart*
Chairperson
216-687-2586
Fax: 216-687-9280
E-mail: burghart@csvax.csuohio.edu

KENT STATE UNIVERSITY
Kent, OH 44242-0001

OVERVIEW
Kent State University is a public coed university.

ENROLLMENT
20,600 graduate, professional, and undergraduate students; 2,054 full-time matriculated graduate/professional students (1,205 women), 2,588 part-time matriculated graduate/professional students (1,721 women).

GRADUATE FACULTY
765.

TUITION
$4752 per year full-time, $216 per credit hour part-time for state residents; $9213 per year full-time, $419 per credit hour part-time for nonresidents.

HOUSING
Rooms and/or apartments available to single students (250 units) at an average cost of $2556 per year; available to married students (240 units) at an average cost of $4836 per year. Graduate housing contact: Douglas Berger, 330-672-7000.

STUDENT SERVICES
Low-cost health insurance, career counseling, free psychological counseling, day-care facilities, campus employment opportunities, international student services.

FACILITIES
Library: Main library plus 4 additional on-campus libraries; total holdings of 1.8 million volumes, 1 million microforms, 8,000 current periodical subscriptions. *Special:* In arts and humanities: Kent/Blossom Arts Festivals, Institute for Bibliography, Editing Center for the Study of World Musics. In science and engineering: Liquid Crystal Institute, Center for Aquatic Ecology, Center for Nuclear Physics. In social sciences: Center for NATO Studies.

COMPUTER SCIENCE

College of Arts and Sciences, Department of Mathematics and Computer Science

Programs   Offers programs in applied mathematics (MA, MS, PhD), computer science (MA, MS, PhD), pure mathematics (MA, MS, PhD).

Faculty   41 full-time.

Students   66 full-time (13 women), 56 part-time (14 women); includes 2 minority (1 African-American, 1 Asian-American), 51 international.

Degrees Awarded   In 1996, 13 master's, 2 doctorates awarded.

Entrance Requirements   For master's, GRE, minimum GPA of 2.75; for doctorate, GRE, minimum GPA of 3.0.

Degree Requirements   For master's, thesis optional, foreign language not required; for doctorate, 1 foreign language, dissertation.

Contact   *Dr. James H. Burghart*
Chairperson
216-687-2586
Fax: 216-687-9280
E-mail: burghart@csvax.csuohio.edu

Financial Aid Fellowships, research assistantships, teaching assistantships, full tuition waivers, Federal Work-Study, institutionally sponsored loans available. *Financial aid application deadline:* 2/1.
Applying 132 applicants, 77% accepted. *Deadline:* 7/12 (rolling processing; 11/29 for spring admission). *Fee:* $30.
Contact Dr. Austin C. Melton
　　　　　Chairman
　　　　　330-672-2430
　　　　　Fax: 330-672-7824

MIAMI UNIVERSITY
Oxford, OH 45056

OVERVIEW
Miami University is a public coed university.

ENROLLMENT
19,743 graduate, professional, and undergraduate students; 1,013 full-time matriculated graduate/professional students (546 women), 293 part-time matriculated graduate/professional students (171 women).

GRADUATE FACULTY
798; includes 41 minority.

EXPENSES
Tuition $5604 per year full-time, $242 per credit hour part-time for state residents; $11,704 per year full-time, $496 per credit hour part-time for nonresidents. Fees $15 per semester (minimum).

HOUSING
Rooms and/or apartments available to single students (22 units) at an average cost of $2400 per year ($5200 including board); available to married students (108 units) at an average cost of $3600 per year ($5200 including board). Housing application deadline: 3/1. Graduate housing contact: Student Housing Services Office, 513-529-5000.

STUDENT SERVICES
Disabled student services, multicultural affairs office, low-cost health insurance, career counseling, free psychological counseling, exercise/wellness program, day-care facilities, campus safety program, campus employment opportunities, international student services, writing training.

FACILITIES
Library: King Library plus 4 additional on-campus libraries; total holdings of 1.4 million volumes, 2 million microforms, 6,500 current periodical subscriptions. Access provided to on-line information retrieval services. *Computer:* Campuswide network is available with full Internet access. Computer service fees are included with tuition and fees. *Special:* In science and engineering: Bachelor Wildlife Reserve, Willard Sherman Turrell Herbarium, Institute of Environmental Sciences, Scripps Gerontology Center.

COMPUTER SCIENCE

School of Applied Science, Program in Systems Analysis
Programs Awards MS.
Faculty 12.

Students 22 full-time (8 women), 6 part-time (2 women); includes 3 minority (1 African-American, 2 Asian-Americans), 10 international.
Degrees Awarded In 1996, 9 degrees awarded.
Entrance Requirements GRE, minimum undergraduate GPA of 3.0 during previous 2 years or 2.75 overall.
Degree Requirements Computer language, thesis, final exam required, foreign language not required.
Financial Aid In 1996–97, 3 research assistantships, 5 teaching assistantships were awarded; full tuition waivers, Federal Work-Study also available. *Financial aid application deadline:* 3/1.
Applying 37 applicants, 84% accepted. *Deadline:* 3/1 (priority date; rolling processing). *Fee:* $35.
Contact Dr. Douglas Troy
　　　　　Director of Graduate Studies
　　　　　513-529-5928

THE OHIO STATE UNIVERSITY
Columbus, OH 43210

OVERVIEW
The Ohio State University is a public coed university.

ENROLLMENT
54,726 graduate, professional, and undergraduate students; 13,478 matriculated graduate/professional students.

GRADUATE FACULTY
2,979.

TUITION
$5214 per year full-time, $527 per quarter (minimum) part-time for state residents; $13,500 per year full-time, $1356 per quarter (minimum) part-time for nonresidents.

HOUSING
Rooms and/or apartments available to single students (890 units) at an average cost of $2810 per year ($4865 including board); available to married students (383 units) at an average cost of $3900 per year. Graduate housing contact: Office of Housing, 614-292-8266.

STUDENT SERVICES
Disabled student services, multicultural affairs office, low-cost health insurance, career counseling, free psychological counseling, day-care facilities, campus safety program, campus employment opportunities, international student services, writing training, teacher training.

FACILITIES
Library: William Oxley Thompson Library plus 14 additional on-campus libraries; total holdings of 4,977,610 volumes, 4,196,464 microforms, 33,280 current periodical subscriptions. A total of 410 personal computers in all libraries. Access provided to on-line information retrieval services. *Computer:* Campuswide network is available with full Internet access. Total number of PCs/terminals supplied for student use: 3,000. Computer services are offered at no charge. *Special:* In arts and humanities: Center for Medieval and Renaissance Studies, Center for Epigraphical Studies, Wexner Center for Visual Arts. In science and engineering: Byrd Polar Research Center, Biotechnology Center, Center for Welding Research, Center for Net Shape Manufacturing, Center for Materials Research, Center for Mapping. In social sciences: Mershon Center for Public Policy, Center for Human

Resources Research, Center for Education and Training for Employment, Center for Labor Research.

COMPUTER SCIENCE

College of Engineering, Department of Computer and Information Science
Programs Awards MS, PhD.
Faculty 34.
Students 129 full-time (19 women), 50 part-time (4 women); includes 18 minority (6 African-Americans, 10 Asian-Americans, 2 Hispanics), 87 international.
Degrees Awarded In 1996, 40 master's, 9 doctorates awarded.
Entrance Requirements GRE General Test.
Degree Requirements For master's, computer language required, thesis optional, foreign language not required; for doctorate, computer language, dissertation required, foreign language not required.
Financial Aid Fellowships, research assistantships, teaching assistantships, administrative assistantships, Federal Work-Study, institutionally sponsored loans, and career-related internships or fieldwork available. Aid available to part-time students.
Applying 306 applicants, 28% accepted. *Deadline:* 8/15 (rolling processing). *Fee:* $30 ($40 for international students).
Contact *Stuart H. Zweben*
  Chairman
  614-292-5813
  Fax: 614-292-2911

See in-depth description on page **501.**

ELECTRICAL ENGINEERING

College of Engineering, Department of Electrical Engineering
Programs Awards MS, PhD.
Faculty 41.
Students 195 full-time (19 women), 23 part-time (4 women); includes 14 minority (1 African-American, 12 Asian-Americans, 1 Hispanic), 130 international.
Degrees Awarded In 1996, 61 master's, 24 doctorates awarded.
Entrance Requirements GRE General Test, GRE Subject Test, or minimum GPA of 3.0.
Degree Requirements For master's, computer language required, thesis optional, foreign language not required; for doctorate, computer language, dissertation required, foreign language not required.
Financial Aid Fellowships, research assistantships, teaching assistantships, Federal Work-Study, institutionally sponsored loans, and career-related internships or fieldwork available. Aid available to part-time students.
Applying 696 applicants, 24% accepted. *Deadline:* 8/15 (rolling processing). *Fee:* $30 ($40 for international students).
Contact *Yuan F. Zheng*
  Chair
  614-292-2572
  Fax: 614-292-7596

INFORMATION SCIENCE

College of Engineering, Department of Computer and Information Science
Programs Awards MS, PhD.
Faculty 34.
Students 129 full-time (19 women), 50 part-time (4 women); includes 18 minority (6 African-Americans, 10 Asian-Americans, 2 Hispanics), 87 international.
Degrees Awarded In 1996, 40 master's, 9 doctorates awarded.
Entrance Requirements GRE General Test.

Degree Requirements For master's, computer language required, thesis optional, foreign language not required; for doctorate, computer language, dissertation required, foreign language not required.
Financial Aid Fellowships, research assistantships, teaching assistantships, administrative assistantships, Federal Work-Study, institutionally sponsored loans, and career-related internships or fieldwork available. Aid available to part-time students.
Applying 306 applicants, 28% accepted. *Deadline:* 8/15 (rolling processing). *Fee:* $30 ($40 for international students).
Contact *Stuart H. Zweben*
  Chairman
  614-292-5813
  Fax: 614-292-2911

See in-depth description on page **501.**

OHIO UNIVERSITY
Athens, OH 45701-2979

OVERVIEW
Ohio University is a public coed university.

ENROLLMENT
27,386 graduate, professional, and undergraduate students; 2,507 full-time matriculated graduate/professional students (1,128 women), 808 part-time matriculated graduate/professional students (482 women).

GRADUATE FACULTY
817 full-time (241 women), 304 part-time (119 women), 969 FTE; includes 131 minority (49 African-Americans, 62 Asian-Americans, 16 Hispanics, 4 Native Americans).

TUITION
$5124 per year full-time, $204 per quarter hour part-time for state residents; $9843 per year full-time, $399 per quarter hour part-time for nonresidents.

HOUSING
Rooms and/or apartments available to single students (1,200 units) at an average cost of $2094 per year ($4260 including board); available to married students (239 units) at an average cost of $5556 per year. Housing application deadline: 7/1. Graduate housing contact: Dale Tampke, 614-593-4088.

STUDENT SERVICES
Low-cost health insurance, career counseling, free psychological counseling, day-care facilities, campus safety program, campus employment opportunities, international student services.

FACILITIES
Library: Alden Library plus 1 additional on-campus library; total holdings of 178,600 volumes, 235,200 microforms, 12,120 current periodical subscriptions. A total of 89 personal computers in all libraries. Access provided to on-line information retrieval services. *Computer:* Campuswide network is available with full Internet access. Total number of PCs/terminals supplied for student use: 2,396. *Special:* In arts and humanities: Kennedy Museum of American Art. In science and engineering: Edwards Accelerator Laboratory, Irvine Hall,

Avionics Engineering Center, Edison Biotechnology Center. In social sciences: Anderson Psychology Laboratory.

ARTIFICIAL INTELLIGENCE/ROBOTICS

Graduate Studies, College of Engineering and Technology, Department of Integrated Engineering
Programs Offerings include intelligent systems (PhD).
Entrance Requirements GRE General Test, MS in engineering or related field.
Degree Requirements Computer language, dissertation required, foreign language not required.
Applying *Deadline:* 3/15 (rolling processing). *Fee:* $30.
Contact Dr. Jerre L. Mitchell
Director
614-593-1482
E-mail: mitchellj@ouvaxa.cats.ohiou.edu

ELECTRICAL ENGINEERING

Graduate Studies, College of Engineering and Technology, School of Electrical Engineering and Computer Science
Programs Offers program in electrical engineering (MS, PhD).
Faculty 20 full-time (1 woman), 2 part-time (0 women).
Faculty Research Communication, control, circuits, industrial, electromagnetics.
Students 86 full-time (12 women), 22 part-time (0 women); includes 4 minority (1 African-American, 2 Asian-Americans, 1 Native American), 59 international.
Degrees Awarded In 1996, 18 master's, 6 doctorates awarded.
Entrance Requirements For master's, GRE, BSEE, minimum GPA of 3.0; for doctorate, GRE, MSEE, minimum GPA of 3.0.
Degree Requirements For master's, thesis required, foreign language not required; for doctorate, dissertation, comprehensive and qualifying exams.
Financial Aid In 1996–97, 10 fellowships (8 to first-year students), 6 research assistantships (2 to first-year students), 4 teaching assistantships (1 to a first-year student) were awarded; Federal Work-Study, institutionally sponsored loans also available.
Applying 241 applicants, 65% accepted. *Fee:* $30.
Contact Dr. Douglas A. Lawrence
Graduate Chair
614-593-1922

See in-depth description on page 503.

THE UNIVERSITY OF AKRON
Akron, OH 44325-0001

OVERVIEW
The University of Akron is a public coed university.

ENROLLMENT
24,252 graduate, professional, and undergraduate students; 2,281 full-time, 1,934 part-time matriculated graduate/professional students.

GRADUATE FACULTY
498 full-time, 255 part-time.

TUITION
$171 per credit hour for state residents; $314 per credit hour for nonresidents.

HOUSING
Rooms and/or apartments available to single students (29 units) at an average cost of $5300 (including board); on-campus housing not available to married students. Graduate housing contact: Lisa K. Wray, 330-972-7800.

STUDENT SERVICES
Career counseling, free psychological counseling, day-care facilities, campus safety program, campus employment opportunities, international student services.

FACILITIES
Library: Bierce Library plus 2 additional on-campus libraries; total holdings of 1,198,600 volumes, 1,771,830 microforms, 9,392 current periodical subscriptions. A total of 120 personal computers in all libraries. Access provided to on-line information retrieval services. *Computer:* Campuswide network is available with full Internet access. Computer services are offered at no charge. *Special:* In arts and humanities: E. J. Thomas Performing Arts Hall, University of Akron Press, instructional television center, WAUP-FM radio workshops. In science and engineering: Institute of Polymer Science, Polymer Engineering Institute, Institute for Biomedical Engineering, Oak Hill Center for Environmental Studies, Polymer Processing Centers. In social sciences: Archives of the History of American Psychology, Center for Urban Studies, Political Science Survey Research Center, Bliss Institute for Applied Politics.

COMPUTER SCIENCE

Buchtel College of Arts and Sciences, Department of Mathematical Sciences, Program in Computer Science
Programs Awards MS.
Entrance Requirements Minimum GPA of 2.75.
Degree Requirements Thesis optional, foreign language not required.
Financial Aid *Application deadline:* 3/1.
Applying *Deadline:* 3/1 (rolling processing). *Fee:* $25 ($50 for international students).
Contact Dr. Wolfgang Pelz
Coordinator
330-972-8019
E-mail: wolfgangpelz@uakron.edu

ELECTRICAL ENGINEERING

College of Engineering, Department of Electrical Engineering
Programs Awards MSEE, PhD. Evening/weekend programs available.
Faculty Research Signal processing, digital control systems, computer interfacing, nondestructive testing.
Degrees Awarded In 1996, 17 master's awarded.
Entrance Requirements For master's, TOEFL (minimum score 550), minimum GPA of 2.75; for doctorate, GRE, TOEFL (minimum score 550).
Degree Requirements For master's, thesis or alternative required, foreign language not required; for doctorate, variable foreign language requirement, dissertation, candidacy exam, qualifying exam.
Financial Aid In 1996–97, 24 students received aid, including 20 teaching assistantships; fellowships, research assistantships, full tuition waivers, and career-related internships or fieldwork also available. *Financial aid application deadline:* 3/1.
Applying *Deadline:* 3/1 (rolling processing). *Fee:* $25 ($50 for international students).

Contact Dr. Max S. Willis
Associate Dean for Research and Graduate Studies
330-972-6580

UNIVERSITY OF CINCINNATI
Cincinnati, OH 45221

OVERVIEW
University of Cincinnati is a public coed university.

ENROLLMENT
34,951 graduate, professional, and undergraduate students; 4,398 full-time matriculated graduate/professional students (2,202 women), 3,068 part-time matriculated graduate/professional students (1,769 women).

GRADUATE FACULTY
771.

TUITION
$7260 per year full-time, $181 per credit hour part-time for state residents; $13,844 per year full-time, $346 per credit hour part-time for nonresidents.

HOUSING
Rooms and/or apartments available to single students (308 units) and married students (308 units) at an average cost of $5382 per year. Housing application deadline: 7/1. Graduate housing contact: Deborah Cohan, 513-556-6461.

STUDENT SERVICES
Disabled student services, low-cost health insurance, career counseling, free psychological counseling, day-care facilities, campus safety program, campus employment opportunities, international student services, teacher training.

FACILITIES
Library: Walter C. Langsam Library plus 16 additional on-campus libraries; total holdings of 2,113,966 volumes, 3,009,059 microforms, 19,431 current periodical subscriptions. A total of 338 personal computers in all libraries. Access provided to on-line information retrieval services. *Computer:* Campuswide network is available with full Internet access. *Special:* In arts and humanities: Lessing Society, Center for Cultural Resources. In science and engineering: Biomedical Chemistry Research Center, Center for Computational Fluid Dynamics, Center for Hazardous Waste Research, Environmental Health Center, Center for Geographic Information Systems and Spatial Analysis. In social sciences: Center for Economic Education, Center for Neighborhood and Community Studies, Institute of Policy Research, Center for Urban and Regional Analysis, Goering Center for Family/Private Business.

COMPUTER ENGINEERING

College of Engineering, Department of Electrical and Computer Engineering and Computer Science, Program in Computer Engineering
Programs Awards MS, PhD.
Faculty Research Digital signal processing, large-scale systems, picture processing.

Degrees Awarded Terminal master's awarded for partial completion of doctoral program.
Entrance Requirements For master's, GRE General Test, TOEFL (minimum score 550), BS in electrical engineering or related field; for doctorate, GRE General Test, TOEFL (minimum score 550).
Degree Requirements Thesis/dissertation required, foreign language not required.
Financial Aid Fellowships, graduate assistantships, full tuition waivers available. *Financial aid application deadline: 2/1.*
Applying *Deadline:* 2/1 (priority date). *Fee:* $40.
Contact Atam P. Dhawan
Graduate Program Director
513-556-4713
Fax: 513-556-7326
E-mail: adhawan@ece.uc.edu
See in-depth description on page 619.

COMPUTER SCIENCE

College of Engineering, Department of Electrical and Computer Engineering and Computer Science, Program in Computer Science
Programs Awards MS.
Entrance Requirements GRE General Test, TOEFL (minimum score 520), BS in electrical engineering or related field.
Degree Requirements Thesis or alternative required, foreign language not required.
Financial Aid Fellowships, graduate assistantships, full tuition waivers available. *Financial aid application deadline: 2/1.*
Applying *Deadline:* 2/1 (priority date). *Fee:* $40.
Contact Atam P. Dhawan
Graduate Program Director
513-556-4713
Fax: 513-556-7326
E-mail: adhawan@ece.uc.edu
See in-depth description on page 619.

COMPUTER SCIENCE

College of Engineering, Department of Electrical and Computer Engineering and Computer Science, Program in Computing Sciences
Programs Awards MS, PhD.
Degrees Awarded Terminal master's awarded for partial completion of doctoral program.
Entrance Requirements For master's, GRE General Test, TOEFL, BS in electrical engineering or related field; for doctorate, GRE General Test, TOEFL.
Degree Requirements Thesis/dissertation required, foreign language not required.
Financial Aid Fellowships, graduate assistantships, full tuition waivers available. *Financial aid application deadline: 2/1.*
Applying *Deadline:* 2/1 (priority date). *Fee:* $40.
Contact Atam P. Dhawan
Graduate Program Director
513-556-4713
Fax: 513-556-7326
E-mail: adhawan@ece.uc.edu
See in-depth description on page 619.

ELECTRICAL ENGINEERING

College of Engineering, Department of Electrical and Computer Engineering and Computer Science, Program in Electrical Engineering
Programs Awards MS, PhD.
Faculty Research Integrated circuits and optical devices, charge-coupled devices, photosensitive devices.
Degrees Awarded In 1996, 19 master's, 9 doctorates awarded.

Entrance Requirements For master's, GRE General Test, TOEFL (minimum score 525), BS in electrical engineering or related field; for doctorate, GRE General Test, TOEFL.
Degree Requirements Thesis/dissertation required, foreign language not required.
Financial Aid Fellowships, graduate assistantships, full tuition waivers available. Aid available to part-time students. *Financial aid application deadline: 2/1.*
Applying 93 applicants, 74% accepted. *Deadline:* 2/1 (priority date). *Fee:* $40.
Contact *Atam P. Dhawan*
Graduate Program Director
513-556-4713
Fax: 513-556-7326
E-mail: adhawan@ece.uc.edu

See in-depth description on page 619.

UNIVERSITY OF DAYTON
Dayton, OH 45469–1611

OVERVIEW
University of Dayton is an independent-religious coed university.

ENROLLMENT
10,315 graduate, professional, and undergraduate students; 1,771 full-time matriculated graduate/professional students (768 women), 1,766 part-time matriculated graduate/professional students (1,096 women).

GRADUATE FACULTY
339 (67 women); includes 37 minority (13 African-Americans, 18 Asian-Americans, 6 Hispanics).

EXPENSES
Tuition $4728 per year full-time, $394 per semester hour part-time. Fees $50 per year.

HOUSING
On-campus housing not available.

STUDENT SERVICES
Low-cost health insurance, career counseling, free psychological counseling, day-care facilities, campus safety program, campus employment opportunities.

FACILITIES
Library: Roesch Library plus 1 additional on-campus library; total holdings of 1,304,438 volumes, 719,487 microforms, 3,106 current periodical subscriptions. A total of 84 personal computers in all libraries. Access provided to on-line information retrieval services. *Computer:* Campuswide network is available with full Internet access. Total number of PCs/terminals supplied for student use: 480. Computer service fees are included with tuition and fees. *Special:* In arts and humanities: Center for the Study of Family Development. In science and engineering: CAD/CAM/CIM Center, surface analysis laboratory, impact physics laboratory, structural analysis laboratory, signal processing laboratory, information systems laboratory, stereolithography laboratory. In

social sciences: Center for Advanced Manufacturing, Center for Business and Economic Research.

COMPUTER SCIENCE

College of Arts and Sciences, Department of Computer Science
Programs Awards MCS. Part-time and evening/weekend programs available.
Faculty 9 full-time, 8 part-time, 10.5 FTE.
Faculty Research Software engineering, networking, databases. *Total annual research expenditures:* $30,000.
Students 22 full-time (5 women), 19 part-time (7 women).
Degrees Awarded In 1996, 25 degrees awarded (100% found work related to degree).
Entrance Requirements GRE General Test, 4 undergraduate courses in computer science, minimum undergraduate GPA of 3.0.
Degree Requirements Computer language, project required, foreign language and thesis not required.
Financial Aid In 1996–97, 5 students received aid, including 4 teaching assistantships (2 to first-year students).
Applying *Deadline:* 8/1 (rolling processing). *Fee:* $30.
Contact *Dr. Barbara Smith*
Chair
937-229-3831
Fax: 937-229-4000
E-mail: smithb@cps.udayton.edu

ELECTRICAL ENGINEERING

School of Engineering, Department of Electrical Engineering
Programs Awards MSEE, DE, PhD. Part-time and evening/weekend programs available.
Faculty 16 full-time (1 woman), 4 part-time (0 women).
Faculty Research Analog and signal processing, electromagnetics, electro-optics, digital computer architectures.
Students 29 full-time (4 women), 41 part-time (3 women); includes 11 minority (4 African-Americans, 5 Asian-Americans, 2 Hispanics), 7 international. Average age 24.
Degrees Awarded In 1996, 32 master's, 4 doctorates awarded.
Entrance Requirements For master's, TOEFL.
Degree Requirements For master's, thesis optional, foreign language not required; for doctorate, variable foreign language requirement, dissertation, departmental qualifying exam.
Financial Aid In 1996–97, 9 students received aid, including 2 fellowships averaging $1,000 per month, 6 research assistantships averaging $1,000 per month, 1 teaching assistantship averaging $900 per month; institutionally sponsored loans also available. *Financial aid application deadline: 5/1.*
Applying *Deadline:* 8/1 (rolling processing). *Fee:* $30.
Contact *Dr. Donald L. Moon*
Associate Dean
937-229-2241
Fax: 937-229-2471

UNIVERSITY OF TOLEDO
Toledo, OH 43606–3398

OVERVIEW
University of Toledo is a public coed university.

ENROLLMENT
21,692 graduate, professional, and undergraduate students; 1,656 full-time matriculated graduate/

professional students (673 women), 1,849 part-time matriculated graduate/professional students (1,044 women).

GRADUATE FACULTY
499 full-time (95 women), 53 part-time (3 women); includes 85 minority (31 African-Americans, 46 Asian-Americans, 7 Hispanics, 1 Native American).

TUITION
$5770 per year full-time, $233 per hour part-time for state residents; $11,362 per year full-time, $466 per hour part-time for nonresidents.

HOUSING
On-campus housing not available.

STUDENT SERVICES
Disabled student services, multicultural affairs office, low-cost health insurance, career counseling, free psychological counseling, exercise/wellness program, day-care facilities, campus safety program, campus employment opportunities, international student services, writing training, grant writing training, teacher training.

FACILITIES
Library: William S. Carlson Library; total holdings of 1,649,681 volumes, 1,561,283 microforms, 4,636 current periodical subscriptions. A total of 36 personal computers in all libraries. Access provided to on-line information retrieval services. *Computer:* Campuswide network is available with full Internet access. Total number of PCs/terminals supplied for student use: 300. Computer services are offered at no charge. *Special:* In arts and humanities: Humanities Institute. In science and engineering: Eitel Institute for Silicate Research, Polymer Institute, Ritter Astrophysical Research Center, Thin Films Institute, Crystallography Center. In social sciences: Urban Affairs Center, Center for International Studies and Programs.

COMPUTER SCIENCE

College of Engineering, Department of Electrical Engineering and Computer Science

Programs Offers programs in computer science (MSES), electrical engineering (MSEE), engineering sciences (PhD). Part-time programs available.

Faculty 22 full-time (3 women), 1 part-time (0 women), 22.3 FTE.

Faculty Research Power electronics, digital television, satellite communications, computer networks, fault-tolerant computing, weather and intelligent transportation. *Total annual research expenditures:* $311,410.

Students 177 full-time (36 women), 19 part-time (6 women); includes 155 international. Average age 25.

Degrees Awarded In 1996, 31 master's, 5 doctorates awarded.

Entrance Requirements For master's, GRE General Test (minimum combined score of 1700 on three sections), TOEFL (minimum score 550), minimum GPA of 2.7; for doctorate, GRE General Test (minimum combined score of 1700 on three sections), TOEFL (minimum score 550).

Degree Requirements For master's, thesis or alternative required, foreign language not required; for doctorate, dissertation required, foreign language not required.

Financial Aid In 1996–97, 103 students received aid, including 2 fellowships (1 to a first-year student) averaging $1,778 per month and totaling $32,004, 6 research assistantships (3 to first-year students) averaging $1,000 per month and totaling $54,000, 23 teaching assistantships (9 to first-year students) averaging $1,000 per month and totaling $207,000, 72 tuition scholarships; full tuition waivers, Federal Work-Study also available. Aid available to part-time students. *Financial aid application deadline:* 4/1.

Applying 375 applicants, 81% accepted. *Deadline:* 5/31 (priority date; rolling processing). *Fee:* $30.

Contact *Sylvia Pinkerman*
Academic Program Coordinator
419-530-8144
Fax: 419-530-8146
E-mail: spinkerm@eng.utoledo.edu

ELECTRICAL ENGINEERING

College of Engineering, Department of Electrical Engineering and Computer Science

Programs Offers programs in computer science (MSES), electrical engineering (MSEE), engineering sciences (PhD). Part-time programs available.

Faculty 22 full-time (3 women), 1 part-time (0 women), 22.3 FTE.

Faculty Research Power electronics, digital television, satellite communications, computer networks, fault-tolerant computing, weather and intelligent transportation. *Total annual research expenditures:* $311,410.

Students 177 full-time (36 women), 19 part-time (6 women); includes 155 international. Average age 25.

Degrees Awarded In 1996, 31 master's, 5 doctorates awarded.

Entrance Requirements For master's, GRE General Test (minimum combined score of 1700 on three sections), TOEFL (minimum score 550), minimum GPA of 2.7; for doctorate, GRE General Test (minimum combined score of 1700 on three sections), TOEFL (minimum score 550).

Degree Requirements For master's, thesis or alternative required, foreign language not required; for doctorate, dissertation required, foreign language not required.

Financial Aid In 1996–97, 103 students received aid, including 2 fellowships (1 to a first-year student) averaging $1,778 per month and totaling $32,004, 6 research assistantships (3 to first-year students) averaging $1,000 per month and totaling $54,000, 23 teaching assistantships (9 to first-year students) averaging $1,000 per month and totaling $207,000, 72 tuition scholarships; full tuition waivers, Federal Work-Study also available. Aid available to part-time students. *Financial aid application deadline:* 4/1.

Applying 375 applicants, 81% accepted. *Deadline:* 5/31 (priority date; rolling processing). *Fee:* $30.

Contact *Sylvia Pinkerman*
Academic Program Coordinator
419-530-8144
Fax: 419-530-8146
E-mail: spinkerm@eng.utoledo.edu

WRIGHT STATE UNIVERSITY
Dayton, OH 45435

OVERVIEW
Wright State University is a public coed university.

ENROLLMENT
15,697 graduate, professional, and undergraduate students; 1,476 full-time matriculated graduate/professional students (756 women), 1,714 part-time matriculated graduate/professional students (1,106 women).

GRADUATE FACULTY

689 full-time (212 women), 323 part-time (143 women); includes 135 minority (50 African-Americans, 70 Asian-Americans, 14 Hispanics, 1 Native American).

TUITION

$4689 per year full-time, $148 per credit hour part-time for state residents; $8397 per year full-time, $263 per credit hour part-time for nonresidents.

HOUSING

Rooms and/or apartments available to single students (1,906 units) at an average cost of $4800 per year ($6450 including board); available to married students (133 units) at an average cost of $5472 per year. Graduate housing contact: Office of Residence Services, 937-775-4172.

STUDENT SERVICES

Low-cost health insurance, career counseling, free psychological counseling, day-care facilities, campus safety program, campus employment opportunities, international student services.

FACILITIES

Library: Paul Laurence Dunbar Library plus 1 additional on-campus library; total holdings of 676,299 volumes, 1,231,091 microforms, 5,312 current periodical subscriptions. A total of 152 personal computers in all libraries. Access provided to on-line information retrieval services. *Computer:* Campuswide network is available with full Internet access. Total number of PCs/terminals supplied for student use: 500. Computer service fees are included with tuition and fees. *Special:* In arts and humanities: Center for Healthy Communities, Bolinga Cultural Resources Center, Center for Arts for Disabled and Handicapped Persons, Public Education Regional Studies Center, art galleries. In science and engineering: Groundwater Management Center, Region II Cancer Resource Center, biomedical imaging laboratory (Center for Health Education, Miami Valley Hospital), Cox Research Institute, Center for Artificial Intelligence Applications. In social sciences: Center for Urban and Public Affairs, Center for Labor-Management Cooperation, Center for Professional Services in Education, Institute for Environmental Quality.

COMPUTER ENGINEERING

College of Engineering and Computer Science, Department of Computer Science and Engineering, Computer Engineering Program

Programs Awards MSCE, PhD.

Faculty 7 full-time (0 women).

Faculty Research Networking and digital communications, parallel and concurrent computing, robotics and control, computer vision, optical computing.

Students 26 full-time (7 women), 12 part-time (1 woman); includes 2 minority (both Asian-Americans), 19 international.

Degrees Awarded In 1996, 13 master's, 1 doctorate awarded.

Entrance Requirements For master's, GRE General Test, TOEFL (minimum score 550), minimum GPA of 3.0 in major, 2.7 overall; for doctorate, GRE General Test, TOEFL (minimum score 550), minimum GPA of 3.3.

Degree Requirements For master's, thesis required, foreign language not required; for doctorate, dissertation, candidacy and general exams.

Financial Aid In 1996–97, 3 fellowships (all to first-year students) were awarded; research assistantships, teaching assistantships also

available. Aid available to part-time students. *Financial aid application deadline:* 3/31; applicants required to submit FAFSA.

Applying 79 applicants, 37% accepted. *Fee:* $50.

Contact *Dr. Oscar N. Garcia*
Chair
937-775-5134
Fax: 937-775-5133

See in-depth description on page 767.

COMPUTER SCIENCE

College of Engineering and Computer Science, Department of Computer Science and Engineering, Computer Science Program

Programs Awards MS, PhD.

Faculty 7 full-time (0 women).

Faculty Research Artificial intelligence, human–computer interaction, graphics, software engineering, logic and symbolic programming.

Students 62 full-time (16 women), 27 part-time (5 women); includes 10 minority (1 African-American, 7 Asian-Americans, 2 Hispanics), 42 international.

Degrees Awarded In 1996, 31 master's awarded.

Entrance Requirements For master's, GRE General Test, TOEFL (minimum score 550), minimum GPA of 3.0 in major, 2.7 overall; for doctorate, GRE General Test, TOEFL (minimum score 550), minimum GPA of 3.3.

Degree Requirements For master's, thesis required, foreign language not required; for doctorate, dissertation, candidacy and general exams.

Financial Aid In 1996–97, 4 fellowships (all to first-year students), 10 research assistantships, 10 teaching assistantships, 1 graduate assistantship were awarded. Aid available to part-time students. *Financial aid application deadline:* 3/31; applicants required to submit FAFSA.

Applying 191 applicants, 40% accepted. *Fee:* $50.

Contact *Dr. Oscar N. Garcia*
Chair
937-775-5134
Fax: 937-775-5133

See in-depth description on page 769.

ELECTRICAL ENGINEERING

College of Engineering and Computer Science, Programs in Engineering, Program in Electrical Engineering

Programs Awards MSE. Part-time and evening/weekend programs available.

Faculty 15 full-time (0 women), 3 part-time (0 women).

Faculty Research Robotics, circuit design, power electronics, image processing, communication systems.

Students 62 full-time (4 women), 74 part-time (5 women); includes 11 minority (1 African-American, 5 Asian-Americans, 3 Hispanics, 2 Native Americans), 53 international. Average age 27.

Degrees Awarded In 1996, 44 degrees awarded.

Entrance Requirements TOEFL (minimum score 550).

Degree Requirements Thesis or course option alternative required, foreign language not required.

Financial Aid In 1996–97, 5 fellowships (all to first-year students), 7 research assistantships, 9 teaching assistantships were awarded; graduate assistantships also available. Aid available to part-time students. *Financial aid application deadline:* 3/1; applicants required to submit FAFSA.

Applying 192 applicants, 66% accepted. *Deadline:* rolling. *Fee:* $50.

Contact *Dr. Larry Smith*
Graduate Adviser
937-775-5037
Fax: 937-775-5009

YOUNGSTOWN STATE UNIVERSITY
Youngstown, OH 44555-0002

OVERVIEW
Youngstown State University is a public coed comprehensive institution.

ENROLLMENT
12,801 graduate, professional, and undergraduate students; 294 full-time matriculated graduate/professional students (149 women), 953 part-time matriculated graduate/professional students (651 women).

GRADUATE FACULTY
274 full-time (76 women), 64 part-time (25 women); includes 26 minority (6 African-Americans, 16 Asian-Americans, 4 Hispanics).

EXPENSES
Tuition $86 per credit hour for state residents; $182 per credit hour for nonresidents. Fees $19 per credit.

HOUSING
Rooms and/or apartments available to single students (913 units) at an average cost of $4350 (including board); on-campus housing not available to married students. Housing application deadline: 9/1. Graduate housing contact: Jack Fahey, 330-742-3547.

STUDENT SERVICES
Disabled student services, multicultural affairs office, low-cost health insurance, career counseling, free psychological counseling, campus safety program, campus employment opportunities, international student services.

FACILITIES
Library: Maag Library; total holdings of 675,912 volumes, 1,346,263 microforms, 3,363 current periodical subscriptions. A total of 33 personal computers in all libraries. Access provided to on-line information retrieval services. *Special:* In arts and humanities: Center for Historic Preservation, McDonough Museum of Art, Ethics Center, Professional Communication Design and Production Center. In science and engineering: Fluid-flow laboratory, chemical engineering chamber, molecular/cellular laboratory, x-ray laboratory. In social sciences: Animal laboratory, child development laboratory, counseling laboratory, testing and experimental laboratory, Public Service Institute.

ELECTRICAL ENGINEERING

William Rayen College of Engineering, Department of Electrical Engineering
Programs Awards MSE. Part-time and evening/weekend programs available.
Faculty 5 full-time (0 women).
Faculty Research Computer-aided design, power systems, electromagnetic energy conversion, sensors, control systems.

Students 5 full-time (2 women), 3 part-time (0 women); includes 1 minority (Asian-American), 2 international.
Degrees Awarded In 1996, 7 degrees awarded.
Entrance Requirements TOEFL (minimum score 550), minimum GPA of 2.75 in field.
Degree Requirements Computer language required, thesis optional, foreign language not required.
Financial Aid In 1996–97, 2 students received aid, including 2 research assistantships averaging $833 per month and totaling $21,300; teaching assistantships, scholarships, Federal Work-Study, institutionally sponsored loans also available. Aid available to part-time students. *Financial aid application deadline: 3/1.*
Applying 6 applicants, 33% accepted. *Deadline:* 8/15 (priority date; rolling processing; 2/15 for spring admission). *Fee:* $30 ($75 for international students).
Contact *Dr. Peter J. Kasvinsky*
Dean of Graduate Studies
330-742-3091
Fax: 330-742-1580
E-mail: amgrad03@ysub.ysu.edu

OKLAHOMA

OKLAHOMA CITY UNIVERSITY
Oklahoma City, OK 73106-1402

OVERVIEW
Oklahoma City University is an independent-religious coed comprehensive institution.

ENROLLMENT
4,696 graduate, professional, and undergraduate students; 1,414 full-time matriculated graduate/professional students (532 women), 722 part-time matriculated graduate/professional students (254 women).

GRADUATE FACULTY
168 full-time (64 women), 215 part-time; includes 23 minority (2 African-Americans, 12 Asian-Americans, 2 Hispanics, 7 Native Americans).

EXPENSES
Tuition $300 per hour. Fees $100 per year full-time, $90 per year part-time.

HOUSING
Rooms and/or apartments available to single students (1,079 units) at an average cost of $1900 per year ($4180 including board); available to married students (58 units) at an average cost of $5022 per year. Graduate housing contact: Charlene Kitch, 405-521-5177.

STUDENT SERVICES
Disabled student services, low-cost health insurance, career counseling, free psychological counseling, campus safety program, campus employment opportunities, international student services, teacher training.

FACILITIES
Library: Dulaney-Browne Library plus 1 additional on-campus library; total holdings of 310,749 volumes, 648,989 microforms, 4,644 current periodical subscriptions. A total of 56 personal computers in all libraries. Access provided to on-line information retrieval services. *Computer:* Campuswide network is available with full

Internet access. Total number of PCs/terminals supplied for student use: 180. Computer service fees are applied as a separate charge. *Special:* In arts and humanities: Norick Art Center's Hulsey Gallery.

COMPUTER SCIENCE

Petree College of Arts and Sciences, Division of Mathematics and Science, Program in Computer Science

Programs Awards MS. Part-time and evening/weekend programs available.

Faculty 6 full-time (1 woman).

Students 104 full-time (15 women), 32 part-time (4 women); includes 4 minority (all Asian-Americans), 108 international.

Degrees Awarded In 1996, 109 degrees awarded.

Entrance Requirements Minimum GPA of 3.0.

Degree Requirements Computer language required, thesis optional, foreign language not required.

Financial Aid Fellowships, partial tuition waivers, Federal Work-Study, institutionally sponsored loans, and career-related internships or fieldwork available. Aid available to part-time students. *Financial aid application deadline:* 8/1; applicants required to submit FAFSA.

Applying *Deadline:* 8/25 (priority date; rolling processing; 1/15 for spring admission). *Fee:* $35 ($55 for international students).

Contact Laura L. Rahhal
Director of Graduate Admissions
800-633-7242 Ext. 2
Fax: 405-521-5356

OKLAHOMA STATE UNIVERSITY
Stillwater, OK 74078

OVERVIEW
Oklahoma State University is a public coed university.

ENROLLMENT
19,125 graduate, professional, and undergraduate students; 1,748 full-time matriculated graduate/professional students (730 women), 2,569 part-time matriculated graduate/professional students (1,205 women).

GRADUATE FACULTY
812 full-time (155 women), 9 part-time (1 woman), 814.2 FTE.

EXPENSES
Tuition $80 per credit hour for state residents; $254 per credit hour for nonresidents. Fees $14.56 per credit hour (minimum).

HOUSING
Rooms and/or apartments available to single students (40 units) at an average cost of $1880 per year ($3816 including board); available to married students (771 units) at an average cost of $3860 per year. Graduate housing contact: Bob Huss, 405-744-9164.

STUDENT SERVICES
Low-cost health insurance, career counseling, free psychological counseling, campus safety program, campus employment opportunities, international student services.

FACILITIES
Library: Edmond Low Library; total holdings of 1.8 million volumes, 2.1 million microforms, 15,000 current periodical subscriptions. Access provided to on-line information retrieval services. *Special:* In arts and humanities: Center for Global Studies. In science and engineering: Remote Sensing Center, University Center for Water Research, Institute for Energy Analysis, Laser Center, agricultural experiment station. In social sciences: Center for Local Government and Technology, Center for International Trade and Development.

COMPUTER ENGINEERING

College of Engineering, Architecture and Technology, School of Electrical and Computer Engineering

Programs Awards M Elec E, MS, PhD.

Faculty 15 full-time (0 women), 1 part-time (0 women), 15.25 FTE.

Students 82 full-time (8 women), 63 part-time (5 women); includes 14 minority (1 African-American, 13 Asian-Americans), 78 international. Average age 29.

Degrees Awarded In 1996, 62 master's, 3 doctorates awarded.

Entrance Requirements TOEFL (minimum score 575).

Degree Requirements For master's, thesis or alternative required, foreign language not required; for doctorate, dissertation required, foreign language not required.

Financial Aid In 1996–97, 42 students received aid, including 18 research assistantships (2 to first-year students) averaging $1,125 per month and totaling $182,296, 24 teaching assistantships (8 to first-year students) averaging $795 per month and totaling $171,798; partial tuition waivers, Federal Work-Study, and career-related internships or fieldwork also available. Aid available to part-time students. *Financial aid application deadline:* 3/1.

Applying *Deadline:* 7/1 (priority date). *Fee:* $25.

Contact Dr. Rainikani Patel
Head
405-744-5151

COMPUTER SCIENCE

College of Arts and Sciences, Department of Computer Science

Programs Offers programs in computer education (Ed D), computer science (MS, PhD).

Faculty 9 full-time (2 women).

Students 53 full-time (11 women), 82 part-time (20 women); includes 19 minority (4 African-Americans, 15 Asian-Americans), 84 international. Average age 31.

Degrees Awarded In 1996, 31 master's, 1 doctorate awarded.

Entrance Requirements For master's, GRE General Test (minimum score 700 on quantitative section), TOEFL (minimum score 550); for doctorate, GRE General Test (minimum score 700 on quantitative section), GRE Subject Test (score in 50th percentile or higher), TOEFL (minimum score 550).

Degree Requirements Thesis/dissertation.

Financial Aid In 1996–97, 26 students received aid, including 8 research assistantships (1 to a first-year student) averaging $1,120 per month and totaling $80,660, 18 teaching assistantships (1 to a first-year student) averaging $936 per month and totaling $151,551; partial tuition waivers, Federal Work-Study, and career-related internships or fieldwork also available. Aid available to part-time students. *Financial aid application deadline:* 3/1.

Applying *Deadline:* 7/1 (priority date). *Fee:* $25.

Contact Dr. Blaine Mayfield
Head
405-744-5668
Fax: 405-774-9097

See in-depth description on page 505.

ELECTRICAL ENGINEERING

College of Engineering, Architecture and Technology, School of Electrical and Computer Engineering
Programs Awards M Elec E, MS, PhD.
Faculty 15 full-time (0 women), 1 part-time (0 women), 15.25 FTE.
Students 82 full-time (8 women), 63 part-time (5 women); includes 14 minority (1 African-American, 13 Asian-Americans), 78 international. Average age 29.
Degrees Awarded In 1996, 62 master's, 3 doctorates awarded.
Entrance Requirements TOEFL (minimum score 575).
Degree Requirements For master's, thesis or alternative required, foreign language not required; for doctorate, dissertation required, foreign language not required.
Financial Aid In 1996–97, 42 students received aid, including 18 research assistantships (2 to first-year students) averaging $1,125 per month and totaling $182,296, 24 teaching assistantships (8 to first-year students) averaging $795 per month and totaling $171,798; partial tuition waivers, Federal Work-Study, and career-related internships or fieldwork also available. Aid available to part-time students. *Financial aid application deadline:* 3/1.
Applying *Deadline:* 7/1 (priority date). *Fee:* $25.
Contact *Dr. Rainikani Patel*
Head
405-744-5151

UNIVERSITY OF CENTRAL OKLAHOMA
Edmond, OK 73034-5209

OVERVIEW
University of Central Oklahoma is a public coed comprehensive institution.

ENROLLMENT
14,481 graduate, professional, and undergraduate students; 324 full-time matriculated graduate/professional students (148 women), 1,589 part-time matriculated graduate/professional students (1,026 women).

GRADUATE FACULTY
297 full-time (124 women), 60 part-time (23 women); includes 19 minority (6 African-Americans, 8 Asian-Americans, 5 Native Americans).

TUITION
$75 per credit hour for state residents; $176 per credit hour for nonresidents.

HOUSING
Rooms and/or apartments available to single students at an average cost of $2915 (including board); available to married students (158 units) at an average cost of $3600 per year. Housing application deadline: 7/1. Graduate housing contact: Housing Office, 405-341-2980 Ext. 3344.

STUDENT SERVICES
Disabled student services, multicultural affairs office, low-cost health insurance, career counseling, free psychological counseling, day-care facilities, campus employment opportunities, international student services.

FACILITIES
Library: Max Chambers Library; total holdings of 750,000 volumes, 520,000 microforms, 3,185 current periodical subscriptions. Access provided to on-line information retrieval services. *Special:* In social sciences: Center for Urban Economics and Business Analysis.

COMPUTER SCIENCE

College of Mathematics and Science, Department of Mathematics
Programs Offerings include applied mathematical sciences (MS), with options in computer science, mathematics, mathematics/computer science teaching, statistics.
Department Faculty 11 full-time (1 woman).
Degree Requirements Computer language, thesis required, foreign language not required.
Applying *Deadline:* 8/18 (priority date; rolling processing). *Fee:* $15.
Contact *Dr. David Bridge*
Chairperson
405-341-2980 Ext. 5253

UNIVERSITY OF OKLAHOMA
Norman, OK 73019-0390

OVERVIEW
University of Oklahoma is a public coed university.

ENROLLMENT
19,432 graduate, professional, and undergraduate students; 2,001 full-time matriculated graduate/professional students (918 women), 2,181 part-time matriculated graduate/professional students (1,091 women).

GRADUATE FACULTY
812 full-time (175 women), 180 part-time (78 women); includes 122 minority (22 African-Americans, 56 Asian-Americans, 28 Hispanics, 16 Native Americans).

EXPENSES
Tuition $1440 per year full-time, $80 per credit hour part-time for state residents; $4320 per year full-time, $240 per credit hour part-time for nonresidents. Fees $498 per year full-time, $129 per semester (minimum) part-time.

HOUSING
Rooms and/or apartments available to single students (3,852 units) at an average cost of $3800 (including board); available to married students (921 units) at an average cost of $3900 (including board). Graduate housing information: 405-325-2511.

STUDENT SERVICES
Low-cost health insurance, career counseling, free psychological counseling, day-care facilities, campus safety program, campus employment opportunities, international student services.

FACILITIES
Library: Bizzell Memorial Library plus 8 additional on-campus libraries; total holdings of 2,430,404 volumes, 3,394,894 microforms, 17,400 current periodical subscriptions. A total of 55 personal computers in all libraries. Access provided to on-line information retrieval services. *Computer:* Campuswide network is available with full Internet access. Total number of PCs/terminals supplied for student use: 800. *Special:* In arts and

humanities: Oklahoma Museum of Natural History. In science and engineering: Fears Structural Laboratory, biological station (Lake Texoma), Rock Mechanics Laboratory, Fracturing Fluids Characterization Center.

COMPUTER SCIENCE

College of Engineering, School of Computer Science
Programs Awards MS, PhD. Part-time programs available.
Faculty 6 full-time (2 women).
Faculty Research Artificial intelligence, database, parallel processing and distributed computation, computer architecture. *Total annual research expenditures: $250,000.*
Students 35 full-time (6 women), 31 part-time (9 women); includes 4 minority (1 African-American, 3 Asian-Americans), 46 international. Average age 30.
Degrees Awarded In 1996, 19 master's, 4 doctorates awarded.
Entrance Requirements GRE General Test (minimum combined score of 1150), TOEFL (minimum score 550).
Degree Requirements For master's, qualifying exam, oral exams required, thesis optional, foreign language not required; for doctorate, dissertation, qualifying exam, general exam required, foreign language not required.
Financial Aid In 1996–97, 6 research assistantships, 7 teaching assistantships were awarded; fellowships, partial tuition waivers also available. *Financial aid application deadline: 4/15.*
Applying 221 applicants, 36% accepted. *Deadline:* 4/1 (priority date; rolling processing; 9/1 for spring admission). *Fee:* $25.
Contact Dr. Changwook Kim
   Graduate Adviser
   405-325-4042

ELECTRICAL ENGINEERING

College of Engineering, School of Electrical Engineering
Programs Awards MS, PhD.
Faculty 18 full-time (1 woman), 2 part-time (1 woman).
Faculty Research Communications, biomedical engineering, digital systems, solid-state, power systems control. *Total annual research expenditures: $1 million.*
Students 23 full-time (3 women), 63 part-time (8 women); includes 12 minority (2 African-Americans, 7 Asian-Americans, 2 Hispanics, 1 Native American), 36 international. Average age 28.
Degrees Awarded In 1996, 31 master's, 2 doctorates awarded.
Entrance Requirements GRE General Test (minimum combined score of 1150), TOEFL (minimum score 550).
Degree Requirements For master's, thesis, oral exam required, foreign language not required; for doctorate, dissertation, qualifying exam, general exam, oral exam required, foreign language not required.
Financial Aid In 1996–97, 26 research assistantships, 12 teaching assistantships were awarded; fellowships, partial tuition waivers, Federal Work-Study, institutionally sponsored loans also available. *Financial aid application deadline: 4/15.*
Applying 251 applicants, 39% accepted. *Deadline:* 4/1 (priority date; rolling processing; 9/1 for spring admission). *Fee:* $25.
Contact Dr. William Kuriger
   Graduate Adviser
   405-325-4721

UNIVERSITY OF TULSA
Tulsa, OK 74104-3189

OVERVIEW
University of Tulsa is an independent-religious coed university.

ENROLLMENT
4,236 graduate, professional, and undergraduate students; 862 full-time matriculated graduate/professional students (348 women), 429 part-time matriculated graduate/professional students (202 women).

GRADUATE FACULTY
238 full-time (58 women), 27 part-time (6 women), 245.3 FTE; includes 30 minority (4 African-Americans, 12 Asian-Americans, 5 Hispanics, 9 Native Americans).

EXPENSES
Tuition $480 per credit hour. Fees $2 per credit hour.

HOUSING
Rooms and/or apartments available to single students (325 units) at an average cost of $3700 per year ($5900 including board); available to married students (325 units) at an average cost of $4800 per year ($8100 including board). Graduate housing contact: Gordon Wilson, 918-631-5248.

STUDENT SERVICES
Disabled student services, multicultural affairs office, low-cost health insurance, career counseling, free psychological counseling, exercise/wellness program, day-care facilities, campus safety program, campus employment opportunities, international student services, teacher training.

FACILITIES
Library: McFarlin Library plus 1 additional on-campus library; total holdings of 794,821 volumes, 1,938,417 microforms, 7,504 current periodical subscriptions. A total of 87 personal computers in all libraries. Access provided to on-line information retrieval services. *Computer:* Campuswide network is available with full Internet access. Computer services are offered at no charge. *Special:* In arts and humanities: Alexander Hogue Art Gallery, Chapman Theatre, Tyrell Hall Auditorium. In science and engineering: Born Technical Library Abstracting Service; oil and gas research facilities; biology facilities for electron microscopy, cell sorting analysis, and DNA sequencing. In social sciences: Anthropological research sites, speech science laboratory, venture capital exchange.

COMPUTER SCIENCE

Colleges of Business Administration and Engineering and Applied Sciences, Department of Engineering and Technology Management
Programs Offerings include computer science (METM).
Entrance Requirements GRE General Test (minimum score 430 on verbal section, 600 on quantitative), TOEFL (minimum score 575).
Applying *Deadline:* rolling. *Fee:* $30.
Contact Dr. Richard C. Burgess
   Assistant Dean/Director of Graduate Business Studies
   918-631-2242
   Fax: 918-631-2142

COMPUTER SCIENCE

College of Engineering and Applied Sciences, Department of Mathematical and Computer Sciences, Program in Computer Science
Programs Awards MS, PhD. Part-time programs available.
Students 22 full-time (7 women), 1 (woman) part-time; includes 4 minority (3 Asian-Americans, 1 Native American), 11 international. Average age 32.

Degrees Awarded In 1996, 6 master's, 2 doctorates awarded.

Entrance Requirements GRE General Test, TOEFL (minimum score 550).

Degree Requirements For master's, computer language required, thesis optional, foreign language not required; for doctorate, computer language, dissertation, comprehensive exams required, foreign language not required.

Financial Aid In 1996–97, 19 students received aid, including 13 research assistantships (3 to first-year students) averaging $903 per month and totaling $170,937, 6 teaching assistantships (1 to a first-year student) averaging $939 per month and totaling $94,860; fellowships, tuition scholarships, partial tuition waivers, Federal Work-Study also available. Aid available to part-time students. *Financial aid application deadline:* 2/1; applicants required to submit FAFSA.

Applying 34 applicants, 88% accepted. *Deadline:* rolling. *Fee:* $30.

Contact *Dr. Roger L. Wainwright*
Adviser
918-631-3143
Fax: 918-631-3077

ELECTRICAL ENGINEERING

Colleges of Business Administration and Engineering and Applied Sciences, Department of Engineering and Technology Management

Programs Offerings include electrical engineering (METM).

Entrance Requirements GRE General Test (minimum score 430 on verbal section, 600 on quantitative), TOEFL (minimum score 575).

Applying *Deadline:* rolling. *Fee:* $30.

Contact *Dr. Richard C. Burgess*
Assistant Dean/Director of Graduate Business Studies
918-631-2242
Fax: 918-631-2142

ELECTRICAL ENGINEERING

College of Engineering and Applied Sciences, Department of Electrical Engineering

Programs Awards ME, MSE. Part-time programs available.

Faculty 9 full-time (0 women).

Faculty Research Simulation, linear and digital electronics, VLSI microprocessors, radar scattering, computer-aided design.

Students 15 full-time (2 women), 1 part-time (0 women); includes 13 international. Average age 24.

Degrees Awarded In 1996, 6 degrees awarded.

Entrance Requirements GRE General Test (minimum score 650 on quantitative section), TOEFL (minimum score 550).

Degree Requirements Computer language, thesis (MSE), design report (ME) required, foreign language not required.

Financial Aid In 1996–97, 14 students received aid, including 5 research assistantships (3 to first-year students) averaging $670 per month and totaling $55,560, 8 teaching assistantships (1 to a first-year student) averaging $823 per month and totaling $84,640, 1 tuition scholarship totaling $2,880; fellowships, partial tuition waivers, Federal Work-Study also available. Aid available to part-time students. *Financial aid application deadline:* 2/1; applicants required to submit FAFSA.

Applying 26 applicants, 92% accepted. *Deadline:* rolling. *Fee:* $30.

Contact *Dr. Heng-Ming Tai*
Adviser
918-631-3271
Fax: 918-631-3344

OREGON

OREGON GRADUATE INSTITUTE OF SCIENCE AND TECHNOLOGY
Portland, OR 97291-1000

OVERVIEW
Oregon Graduate Institute of Science and Technology is an independent coed graduate-only institution.

ENROLLMENT
206 full-time matriculated graduate/professional students (44 women), 159 part-time matriculated graduate/professional students (36 women).

GRADUATE FACULTY
63 full-time (6 women), 92 part-time (10 women); includes 19 minority (2 African-Americans, 16 Asian-Americans, 1 Hispanic).

TUITION
$16,200 per year full-time, $405 per credit part-time.

HOUSING
On-campus housing not available.

STUDENT SERVICES
Campus safety program, campus employment opportunities, international student services.

FACILITIES
Library: Samuel L. Diack Memorial Library; total holdings of 31,000 volumes, 13,000 microforms, 535 current periodical subscriptions. A total of 8 personal computers in all libraries. Access provided to on-line information retrieval services. *Computer:* Campuswide network is available with full Internet access. Computer services are offered at no charge. *Special:* In science and engineering: Large experimental aquifer program, electroslag welding and surfacing laboratory, computer speech recognition laboratory.

COMPUTER ENGINEERING

Department of Computer Science and Engineering

Programs Offers programs in computer engineering (MS, PhD), computer science (MS, PhD). MS (computer science) offered in conjunction with Lewis & Clark College, Pacific University, Reed College, and Willamette University. Part-time programs available.

Faculty 16 full-time (2 women), 31 part-time (6 women).

Faculty Research Computer systems architecture, intelligent and interactive systems, programming models and systems, theory of computation.

Students 57 full-time (11 women), 43 part-time (11 women); includes 3 minority (1 African-American, 2 Asian-Americans), 25 international. Average age 31.

Degrees Awarded In 1996, 22 master's awarded (90% found work related to degree, 10% continued full-time study); 7 doctorates awarded (40% entered university research/teaching, 60% found other work related to degree). Terminal master's awarded for partial completion of doctoral program.

Entrance Requirements GRE General Test, TOEFL (minimum score 550).

Degree Requirements For master's, computer language required, thesis optional, foreign language not required; for doctorate, computer language, comprehensive exam, oral defense of dissertation required, foreign language not required.

Financial Aid In 1996–97, 41 students received aid, including 38 research assistantships (6 to first-year students) averaging $960 per month and totaling $437,000, 3 teaching assistantships; fellowships, Federal Work-Study also available. *Financial aid application deadline:* 3/1.
Applying 208 applicants, 24% accepted. *Deadline:* 3/1 (priority date; rolling processing). *Fee:* $50.
Contact *Frances M. Hewitt*
Enrollment Manager
800-685-2423
Fax: 503-690-1285

See in-depth description on page **509.**

COMPUTER SCIENCE

Department of Computer Science and Engineering
Programs Offers programs in computer engineering (MS, PhD), computer science (MS, PhD). MS (computer science) offered in conjunction with Lewis & Clark College, Pacific University, Reed College, and Willamette University. Part-time programs available.
Faculty 16 full-time (2 women), 31 part-time (6 women).
Faculty Research Computer systems architecture, intelligent and interactive systems, programming models and systems, theory of computation.
Students 57 full-time (11 women), 43 part-time (11 women); includes 3 minority (1 African-American, 2 Asian-Americans), 25 international. Average age 31.
Degrees Awarded In 1996, 22 master's awarded (90% found work related to degree, 10% continued full-time study); 7 doctorates awarded (40% entered university research/teaching, 60% found other work related to degree). Terminal master's awarded for partial completion of doctoral program.
Entrance Requirements GRE General Test, TOEFL (minimum score 550).
Degree Requirements For master's, computer language required, thesis optional, foreign language not required; for doctorate, computer language, comprehensive exam, oral defense of dissertation required, foreign language not required.
Financial Aid In 1996–97, 41 students received aid, including 38 research assistantships (6 to first-year students) averaging $960 per month and totaling $437,000, 3 teaching assistantships; fellowships, Federal Work-Study also available. *Financial aid application deadline:* 3/1.
Applying 208 applicants, 24% accepted. *Deadline:* 3/1 (priority date; rolling processing). *Fee:* $50.
Contact *Frances M. Hewitt*
Enrollment Manager
800-685-2423
Fax: 503-690-1285

See in-depth description on page **509.**

ELECTRICAL ENGINEERING

Department of Electrical Engineering
Programs Awards MS, PhD. Part-time programs available.
Faculty 13 full-time (0 women), 34 part-time (1 woman).
Faculty Research Semiconductor materials, microwave circuits, atmospheric optics, surface physics, electron and ion optics.
Students 46 full-time (5 women), 32 part-time (4 women); includes 5 minority (4 Asian-Americans, 1 Hispanic), 29 international. Average age 29.
Degrees Awarded In 1996, 17 master's awarded (82% found work related to degree, 18% continued full-time study); 6 doctorates awarded. Terminal master's awarded for partial completion of doctoral program.

Entrance Requirements For master's, TOEFL (minimum score 550); for doctorate, GRE General Test, GRE Subject Test, TOEFL (minimum score 550).
Degree Requirements For master's, thesis optional, foreign language not required; for doctorate, comprehensive exam, oral defense of dissertation required, foreign language not required.
Financial Aid In 1996–97, 20 students received aid, including 20 research assistantships (5 to first-year students) averaging $960 per month and totaling $220,000; fellowships, Federal Work-Study also available. *Financial aid application deadline:* 3/1.
Applying 285 applicants, 28% accepted. *Deadline:* 3/1 (priority date; rolling processing). *Fee:* $50.
Contact *Frances M. Hewitt*
Enrollment Manager
800-685-2423
Fax: 503-690-1285

See in-depth description on page **511.**

OREGON HEALTH SCIENCES UNIVERSITY
Portland, OR 97201-3098

OVERVIEW
Oregon Health Sciences University is a public coed upper-level institution.

ENROLLMENT
1,757 graduate, professional, and undergraduate students; 1,002 full-time matriculated graduate/professional students (477 women), 146 part-time matriculated graduate/professional students (132 women).

GRADUATE FACULTY
769 (244 women); includes 61 minority (7 African-Americans, 46 Asian-Americans, 7 Hispanics, 1 Native American).

HOUSING
Rooms and/or apartments available to single students (87 units) at an average cost of $2352 per year; on-campus housing not available to married students. Graduate housing contact: Kay Kendall, 503-494-7747.

STUDENT SERVICES
Low-cost health insurance, career counseling, free psychological counseling, campus safety program, campus employment opportunities.

FACILITIES
Library: Main library plus 3 additional on-campus libraries; total holdings of 205,023 volumes, 0 microforms, 1,257 current periodical subscriptions. A total of 32 personal computers in all libraries. Access provided to on-line information retrieval services.

MEDICAL INFORMATICS

School of Medicine, Graduate Programs in Medicine, Medical Informatics Program
Programs Awards MS. Part-time programs available.
Faculty 7 full-time (1 woman), 6 part-time (2 women), 8 FTE.
Faculty Research Information retrieval, outcomes research, telemedicine, consumer health informatics, information needs assessment. *Total annual research expenditures:* $3 million.

Students 10 full-time (4 women), includes 1 minority (Asian-American). Average age 27.

Entrance Requirements GRE General Test (combined average 1600 on three sections), MCAT (average 8).

Degree Requirements Computer language, thesis required, foreign language not required.

Financial Aid Research assistantships available.

Applying 20 applicants, 50% accepted. *Deadline:* 3/1 (priority date; rolling processing). *Fee:* $40.

Contact Dr. William Hersh
Associate Professor
503-494-4563
Fax: 503-494-4551
E-mail: hersh@ohsu.edu

OREGON INSTITUTE OF TECHNOLOGY
Klamath Falls, OR 97601-8801

OVERVIEW
Oregon Institute of Technology is a public coed comprehensive institution.

ENROLLMENT
2,339 graduate, professional, and undergraduate students.

GRADUATE FACULTY
3 full-time (1 woman).

HOUSING
Rooms and/or apartments available to single students at an average cost of $3910 (including board); on-campus housing not available to married students. Graduate housing contact: George Abendschein, 541-885-1080.

STUDENT SERVICES
Career counseling, campus employment opportunities, international student services.

FACILITIES
Library: Main library; total holdings of 120,000 volumes, 94,888 microforms, 1,270 current periodical subscriptions. A total of 41 personal computers in all libraries. Access provided to on-line information retrieval services. *Computer:* Campuswide network is available with full Internet access. Total number of PCs/terminals supplied for student use: 1,000. Computer services are offered at no charge. *Special:* In science and engineering: Geo-Heat Center.

COMPUTER ENGINEERING

Program in Computer Engineering Technology

Programs Offers program in engineering technology (MS). Part-time programs available.

Faculty 3 full-time (1 woman).

Entrance Requirements GRE General Test (minimum combined score of 1500 on three sections), TOEFL (minimum score 600).

Degree Requirements 1 foreign language, computer language, project required, thesis not required.

Financial Aid Federal Work-Study available. Aid available to part-time students. *Financial aid application deadline:* 3/1; applicants required to submit FAFSA.

Applying *Deadline:* 5/1. *Fee:* $50.

Contact Barbara Kratochvit
Director of Admissions
541-885-1152
Fax: 541-885-1115
E-mail: oit@oit.edu

OREGON STATE UNIVERSITY
Corvallis, OR 97331

OVERVIEW
Oregon State University is a public coed university.

TUITION
$6009 per year full-time, $785 per quarter (minimum) part-time for state residents; $10,227 per year full-time, $1250 per quarter (minimum) part-time for nonresidents.

HOUSING
Rooms and/or apartments available to single and married students. Graduate housing contact: Thomas Scheuermann, 541-737-4771.

FACILITIES
Library: William Jasper Kerr Library. *Special:* In arts and humanities: Center for the Humanities, university archives. In science and engineering: Marine Science Center, International Plant Protection Center, Radiation Center, forest research laboratory, agricultural experiment station. In social sciences: Western Rural Development Center.

COMPUTER ENGINEERING

Graduate School, College of Engineering, Department of Electrical and Computer Engineering

Programs Awards MAIS, MS, PhD. Part-time programs available.

Faculty Research Analog and mixed mode IC's; materials, devices, and electroluminescence; microwave and optoelectrics; control systems and signal processing; novel electrical machines.

Entrance Requirements TOEFL (minimum score 575), minimum GPA of 3.0 in last 90 hours.

Degree Requirements For master's, minimum GPA of 3.0 required, foreign language not required; for doctorate, dissertation, departmental qualifying exam, overall minimum GPA of 3.0 required, foreign language not required.

Applying *Deadline:* 3/1 (rolling processing). *Fee:* $50.

COMPUTER SCIENCE

Graduate School, College of Engineering, Department of Computer Science

Programs Awards MA, MAIS, MS, PhD. Part-time programs available. Terminal master's awarded for partial completion of doctoral program.

Faculty Research Artificial intelligence, software systems, theory and algorithms, parallel computing.

Entrance Requirements GRE General Test, TOEFL (minimum score 550), minimum GPA of 3.0 in last 90 hours.

Degree Requirements For master's, thesis or alternative, minimum GPA of 3.0 required, foreign language not required; for doctorate, dissertation, minimum GPA of 3.0 required, foreign language not required.

Applying *Deadline:* 3/1 (rolling processing). *Fee:* $50.

See in-depth description on page 513.

ELECTRICAL ENGINEERING

Graduate School, College of Engineering, Department of Electrical and Computer Engineering
Programs Awards MAIS, MS, PhD. Part-time programs available.
Faculty Research Analog and mixed mode IC's; materials, devices, and electroluminescence; microwave and optoelectrics; control systems and signal processing; novel electrical machines.
Entrance Requirements TOEFL (minimum score 575), minimum GPA of 3.0 in last 90 hours.
Degree Requirements For master's, minimum GPA of 3.0 required, foreign language not required; for doctorate, dissertation, departmental qualifying exam, overall minimum GPA of 3.0 required, foreign language not required.
Applying *Deadline:* 3/1 (rolling processing). *Fee:* $50.

PORTLAND STATE UNIVERSITY
Portland, OR 97207-0751

OVERVIEW

Portland State University is a public coed university.

ENROLLMENT

11,733 graduate, professional, and undergraduate students; 1,550 full-time matriculated graduate/professional students (918 women), 1,378 part-time matriculated graduate/professional students (756 women).

GRADUATE FACULTY

515 full-time (176 women), 228 part-time (107 women), 547.7 FTE; includes 112 minority (32 African-Americans, 51 Asian-Americans, 23 Hispanics, 6 Native Americans).

TUITION

$5868 per year full-time, $663 per quarter (minimum) part-time for state residents; $10,086 per year full-time, $663 per quarter (minimum) part-time for nonresidents.

HOUSING

Rooms and/or apartments available to single students at an average cost of $4128 per year; available to married students at an average cost of $4872 per year. Graduate housing contact: College Housing Northwest, 503-725-4333.

STUDENT SERVICES

Disabled student services, multicultural affairs office, low-cost health insurance, career counseling, free psychological counseling, day-care facilities, campus safety program, campus employment opportunities, international student services, teacher training.

FACILITIES

Library: Branford Millar Library; total holdings of 1,030,666 volumes, 2,220,138 microforms, 10,734 current periodical subscriptions. A total of 130 personal computers in all libraries. Access provided to on-line information retrieval services. *Computer:* Campuswide network is available with full Internet access. Total number of PCs/terminals supplied for student use: 357. Computer service fees are included with tuition and fees. *Special:* In arts and humanities: Art computer laboratory, statistical consulting laboratory, writing laboratory, Mid-East Studies Center, Autzen Gallery, Gallery 299, visual instruction laboratory, autoCAD laboratory. In science and engineering: Civil, electrical, and mechanical engineering laboratories; geology museum; speech and hearing clinic; hazardous waste disposal laboratory. In social sciences: Center for Sociological Research, Center for Urban Studies, Regional Research Institute for Human Services, Institute on Aging, Center for Population Research and Census, Mental Health Policy Research Center, Regional Research Institute for Human Services.

COMPUTER ENGINEERING

School of Engineering and Applied Science, Department of Electrical Engineering
Programs Offers program in electrical and computer engineering (MS, PhD). Part-time and evening/weekend programs available.
Faculty 13 full-time (1 woman), 2 part-time (0 women), 14 FTE.
Faculty Research Optics and laser systems, design automation, VLSI design, computer systems, power electronics. *Total annual research expenditures:* $400,000.
Students 39 full-time (4 women), 62 part-time (14 women); includes 7 minority (5 Asian-Americans, 2 Hispanics), 65 international. Average age 31.
Degrees Awarded In 1996, 16 master's, 1 doctorate awarded.
Entrance Requirements For master's, TOEFL (minimum score 550), minimum GPA of 3.0 in upper-division course work or 2.75 overall; for doctorate, GRE General Test, GRE Subject Test, minimum GPA of 3.0 in upper-division course work.
Degree Requirements For master's, variable foreign language requirement, computer language, thesis or alternative, oral exam; for doctorate, 1 foreign language, computer language, dissertation, oral and written exams.
Financial Aid In 1996–97, 10 research assistantships (5 to first-year students), 11 teaching assistantships (7 to first-year students) were awarded; Federal Work-Study, institutionally sponsored loans, and career-related internships or fieldwork also available. Aid available to part-time students. *Financial aid application deadline:* 3/1; applicants required to submit FAFSA.
Applying 95 applicants, 52% accepted. *Deadline:* 3/1 (priority date; rolling processing; 11/1 for spring admission). *Fee:* $50.
Contact *Dr. Y. C. Jenq*
503-725-3806
Fax: 503-725-3807
E-mail: jenq@ee.pdx.edu

COMPUTER SCIENCE

School of Engineering and Applied Science, Department of Computer Science
Programs Awards MS. Part-time programs available.
Faculty 12 full-time (2 women), 6 part-time (1 woman), 13 FTE.
Faculty Research Formal methods, database systems, parallel programming environments, computer security, software tools. *Total annual research expenditures:* $300,000.
Students 19 full-time (8 women), 25 part-time (7 women); includes 7 minority (5 Asian-Americans, 1 Hispanic, 1 Native American), 19 international. Average age 31.
Degrees Awarded In 1996, 13 degrees awarded.
Entrance Requirements GRE General Test, TOEFL (minimum score 550), minimum GPA of 3.0 in upper-division course work or 2.75 overall.
Degree Requirements Thesis optional, foreign language not required.
Financial Aid In 1996–97, 6 research assistantships (3 to first-year students), 9 teaching assistantships (6 to first-year students) were awarded; Federal Work-Study and career-related internships or fieldwork also available. Aid available to part-time students. *Financial aid application deadline:* 3/1; applicants required to submit FAFSA.

Applying 78 applicants, 37% accepted. *Deadline:* 3/15 (priority date; rolling processing). *Fee:* $50.
Contact *Graduate Office*
503-725-4036
Fax: 503-725-3211

ELECTRICAL ENGINEERING

School of Engineering and Applied Science, Department of Electrical Engineering
Programs Offers program in electrical and computer engineering (MS, PhD). Part-time and evening/weekend programs available.
Faculty 13 full-time (1 woman), 2 part-time (0 women), 14 FTE.
Faculty Research Optics and laser systems, design automation, VLSI design, computer systems, power electronics. *Total annual research expenditures:* $400,000.
Students 39 full-time (4 women), 62 part-time (14 women); includes 7 minority (5 Asian-Americans, 2 Hispanics), 65 international. Average age 31.
Degrees Awarded In 1996, 16 master's, 1 doctorate awarded.
Entrance Requirements For master's, TOEFL (minimum score 550), minimum GPA of 3.0 in upper-division course work or 2.75 overall; for doctorate, GRE General Test, GRE Subject Test, minimum GPA of 3.0 in upper-division course work.
Degree Requirements For master's, variable foreign language requirement, computer language, thesis or alternative, oral exam; for doctorate, 1 foreign language, computer language, dissertation, oral and written exams.
Financial Aid In 1996–97, 10 research assistantships (5 to first-year students), 11 teaching assistantships (7 to first-year students) were awarded; Federal Work-Study, institutionally sponsored loans, and career-related internships or fieldwork also available. Aid available to part-time students. *Financial aid application deadline:* 3/1; applicants required to submit FAFSA.
Applying 95 applicants, 52% accepted. *Deadline:* 3/1 (priority date; rolling processing; 11/1 for spring admission). *Fee:* $50.
Contact *Dr. Y. C. Jenq*
503-725-3806
Fax: 503-725-3807
E-mail: jenq@ee.pdx.edu

SYSTEMS SCIENCE

Systems Science Program
Programs Offers systems science/anthropology (PhD), systems science/business administration (PhD), systems science/civil engineering (PhD), systems science/economics (PhD), systems science/engineering management (PhD), systems science/general (PhD), systems science/mathematical sciences (PhD), systems science/mechanical engineering (PhD), systems science/psychology (PhD), systems science/sociology (PhD).
Faculty 3 full-time (0 women), 2 part-time (0 women), 4 FTE.
Faculty Research Systems theory and methodology, AI neural networks, information theory, nonlinear dynamics/chaos, modeling and simulation. *Total annual research expenditures:* $140,000.
Students 48 full-time (21 women), 24 part-time (4 women); includes 5 minority (1 African-American, 3 Asian-Americans, 1 Hispanic), 12 international. Average age 38.
Degrees Awarded In 1996, 7 degrees awarded.
Entrance Requirements GMAT (score in 75th percentile or higher), GRE General Test (score in 75th percentile or higher), TOEFL (minimum score 575), minimum undergraduate GPA of 3.0.
Degree Requirements Variable foreign language requirement, computer language, dissertation.
Financial Aid In 1996–97, 7 research assistantships (1 to a first-year student) were awarded; teaching assistantships, Federal Work-Study, institutionally sponsored loans, and career-related internships or fieldwork also available. Aid available to part-time students. *Financial aid application deadline:* 3/1; applicants required to submit FAFSA.
Applying 105 applicants, 15% accepted. *Deadline:* 2/1 (11/1 for spring admission). *Fee:* $50.
Contact *Dawn Kuenle*
503-725-4960
E-mail: dawn@sysc.pdx.edu

SOUTHERN OREGON UNIVERSITY
Ashland, OR 97520

OVERVIEW
Southern Oregon University is a public coed comprehensive institution.

ENROLLMENT
4,726 graduate, professional, and undergraduate students; 155 full-time matriculated graduate/professional students (111 women), 110 part-time matriculated graduate/professional students (73 women).

GRADUATE FACULTY
119 full-time (35 women).

TUITION
$5061 per year full-time, $564 per quarter (minimum) part-time for state residents; $8985 per year full-time, $564 per quarter (minimum) part-time for nonresidents.

HOUSING
Rooms and/or apartments available to single students at an average cost of $3780 per year; available to married students (130 units). Graduate housing contact: Mr. Wayne Schumacher, 541-488-4401.

STUDENT SERVICES
Low-cost health insurance, career counseling, free psychological counseling, day-care facilities, international student services.

FACILITIES
Library: Main library; total holdings of 275,000 volumes, 750,000 microforms, 2,150 current periodical subscriptions. Access provided to on-line information retrieval services. *Computer:* Campuswide network is available. Total number of PCs/terminals supplied for student use: 300. Computer service fees are included with tuition and fees. *Special:* In arts and humanities: Theatre Arts Center, music recital hall. In science and engineering: Natural History Museum. In social sciences: Small Business Institute, Southern Oregon Regional Services Institute.

COMPUTER SCIENCE

School of Sciences
Programs Offerings include mathematics/computer science (MA, MS).
Entrance Requirements GRE General Test, minimum GPA of 3.0.
Degree Requirements Comprehensive exam (MA) required, thesis optional.
Applying *Deadline:* rolling. *Fee:* $50.

Contact *Dr. Joseph Graf*
Dean
541-552-6474

UNIVERSITY OF OREGON
Eugene, OR 97403

OVERVIEW
University of Oregon is a public coed university.

ENROLLMENT
17,269 graduate, professional, and undergraduate students; 2,684 full-time matriculated graduate/professional students (1,296 women), 527 part-time matriculated graduate/professional students (281 women).

GRADUATE FACULTY
747 full-time (272 women), 445 part-time (223 women); includes 112 minority (11 African-Americans, 64 Asian-Americans, 31 Hispanics, 6 Native Americans).

TUITION
$6150 per year full-time, $1238 per semester (minimum) part-time for state residents; $10,449 per year full-time, $1947 per semester (minimum) part-time for nonresidents.

HOUSING
Rooms and/or apartments available to single students (3,125 units) at an average cost of $4646 (including board); available to married students (820 units) at an average cost of $4500 per year. Graduate housing contact: Michael Eyster, 541-346-4277.

STUDENT SERVICES
Disabled student services, multicultural affairs office, low-cost health insurance, career counseling, free psychological counseling, day-care facilities, campus safety program, campus employment opportunities, international student services, writing training, grant writing training, teacher training.

FACILITIES
Library: Knight Library plus 5 additional on-campus libraries; total holdings of 2,082,684 volumes, 1,888,835 microforms, 17,259 current periodical subscriptions. A total of 200 personal computers in all libraries. Access provided to on-line information retrieval services. *Computer:* Campuswide network is available with full Internet access. Total number of PCs/terminals supplied for student use: 1,000. Computer service fees are included with tuition and fees. *Special:* In arts and humanities: Humanities Center. In science and engineering: Institute of Chemical Physics, Oregon Institute of Marine Biology, Institute of Molecular Biology, Institute of Neuroscience. In social sciences: Center for Study of Women in Society, Institute on Violence and Destructive Behavior.

COMPUTER SCIENCE

Graduate School, College of Arts and Sciences, Department of Computer and Information Science
Programs Awards MA, MS, PhD. Part-time programs available.
Faculty 15 full-time (5 women), 9 part-time (2 women).

Faculty Research Artificial intelligence, graphics, natural-language processing, expert systems, operating systems.
Students 59 full-time (11 women), 5 part-time (1 woman); includes 5 minority (all Asian-Americans), 29 international.
Degrees Awarded In 1996, 22 master's awarded (100% found work related to degree); 2 doctorates awarded (100% entered university research/teaching). Terminal master's awarded for partial completion of doctoral program.
Entrance Requirements GRE General Test, TOEFL, TSE (for teaching assistants).
Degree Requirements For master's, computer language required, foreign language and thesis not required; for doctorate, computer language, dissertation required, foreign language not required.
Financial Aid In 1996–97, 47 students received aid, including 17 research assistantships (11 to first-year students) averaging $905 per month and totaling $138,439, 22 teaching assistantships (3 to first-year students) averaging $847 per month and totaling $167,668; fellowships, Federal Work-Study, institutionally sponsored loans also available. *Financial aid application deadline: 2/1.*
Applying 105 applicants, 47% accepted. *Deadline:* 2/1 (priority date). *Fee:* $50.
Contact *Betty Lockwood*
Graduate Secretary
541-346-4408
Fax: 541-346-5373

See in-depth description on page 695.

INFORMATION SCIENCE

Graduate School, College of Arts and Sciences, Department of Computer and Information Science
Programs Awards MA, MS, PhD. Part-time programs available.
Faculty 15 full-time (5 women), 9 part-time (2 women).
Faculty Research Artificial intelligence, graphics, natural-language processing, expert systems, operating systems.
Students 59 full-time (11 women), 5 part-time (1 woman); includes 5 minority (all Asian-Americans), 29 international.
Degrees Awarded In 1996, 22 master's awarded (100% found work related to degree); 2 doctorates awarded (100% entered university research/teaching). Terminal master's awarded for partial completion of doctoral program.
Entrance Requirements GRE General Test, TOEFL, TSE (for teaching assistants).
Degree Requirements For master's, computer language required, foreign language and thesis not required; for doctorate, computer language, dissertation required, foreign language not required.
Financial Aid In 1996–97, 47 students received aid, including 17 research assistantships (11 to first-year students) averaging $905 per month and totaling $138,439, 22 teaching assistantships (3 to first-year students) averaging $847 per month and totaling $167,668; fellowships, Federal Work-Study, institutionally sponsored loans also available. *Financial aid application deadline: 2/1.*
Applying 105 applicants, 47% accepted. *Deadline:* 2/1 (priority date). *Fee:* $50.
Contact *Betty Lockwood*
Graduate Secretary
541-346-4408
Fax: 541-346-5373

See in-depth description on page 695.

UNIVERSITY OF PORTLAND
Portland, OR 97203-5798

OVERVIEW
University of Portland is an independent-religious coed comprehensive institution.

ENROLLMENT
2,819 graduate, professional, and undergraduate students; 112 full-time matriculated graduate/professional students (61 women), 449 part-time matriculated graduate/professional students (253 women).

GRADUATE FACULTY
72 full-time (16 women), 26 part-time (6 women).

TUITION
$490 per semester hour.

HOUSING
Rooms and/or apartments available to single students (20 units); on-campus housing not available to married students. Housing application deadline: 8/1. Graduate housing contact: Student Housing Office, 503-283-7205.

STUDENT SERVICES
Low-cost health insurance, career counseling, free psychological counseling, campus safety program, campus employment opportunities, international student services.

FACILITIES
Library: Wilson W. Clark Library; total holdings of 310,000 volumes, 2,100 microforms, 9 current periodical subscriptions. Access provided to on-line information retrieval services. *Computer:* Campuswide network is available with full Internet access. Total number of PCs/terminals supplied for student use: 150. Computer service fees are included with tuition and fees. *Special:* In science and engineering: Materials testing laboratory, noise and vibrations laboratories.

ELECTRICAL ENGINEERING

Multnomah School of Engineering
Programs   Offerings include electrical engineering (MSEE).
Applying   *Deadline:* 8/1. *Fee:* $30.
Contact   Dr. Khalid Khan
Graduate Program Director
503-283-7276

PENNSYLVANIA

ALLENTOWN COLLEGE OF ST. FRANCIS DE SALES
Center Valley, PA 18034-9568

OVERVIEW
Allentown College of St. Francis de Sales is an independent-religious coed comprehensive institution.

ENROLLMENT
2,204 graduate, professional, and undergraduate students; 0 full-time matriculated graduate/professional students, 488 part-time matriculated graduate/professional students (301 women).

GRADUATE FACULTY
28 full-time (10 women), 46 part-time (7 women); includes 8 minority (3 African-Americans, 4 Asian-Americans, 1 Hispanic).

TUITION
$395 per credit.

HOUSING
On-campus housing not available.

STUDENT SERVICES
Career counseling.

FACILITIES
Library: Trexler Library; total holdings of 126,000 volumes, 353,979 microforms, 910 current periodical subscriptions. A total of 180 personal computers in all libraries. Access provided to on-line information retrieval services. *Computer:* Campuswide network is available with full Internet access. Total number of PCs/terminals supplied for student use: 180. Computer service fees are included with tuition and fees. *Special:* In arts and humanities: Labunda Center for the Performing Arts.

INFORMATION SCIENCE

Graduate Division, Program in Information Systems
Programs   Awards MSIS. Part-time and evening/weekend programs available.
Faculty   1 full-time (0 women), 8 part-time (1 woman).
Faculty Research   Digital communication, numerical analysis, database design.
Students   98 part-time (30 women); includes 5 minority (1 African-American, 4 Asian-Americans). Average age 31.
Degrees Awarded   In 1996, 8 degrees awarded.
Degree Requirements   Computer language, comprehensive exam required, thesis optional, foreign language not required.
Applying   17 applicants, 100% accepted. *Deadline:* 8/30 (priority date; rolling processing). *Fee:* $35.
Contact   Dr. Julius G. Bede
Director
610-282-1100 Ext. 1280
E-mail: bede@accnov.allencol.edu

BUCKNELL UNIVERSITY
Lewisburg, PA 17837

OVERVIEW
Bucknell University is an independent coed comprehensive institution.

ENROLLMENT
3,661 graduate, professional, and undergraduate students; 93 full-time matriculated graduate/professional students (54 women), 35 part-time matriculated graduate/professional students (17 women).

GRADUATE FACULTY

231 full-time (68 women), 11 part-time (4 women); includes 29 minority (10 African-Americans, 13 Asian-Americans, 5 Hispanics, 1 Native American).

TUITION

$2410 per course.

HOUSING

On-campus housing not available.

STUDENT SERVICES

Multicultural affairs office, low-cost health insurance, career counseling, free psychological counseling, campus employment opportunities, international student services.

FACILITIES

Library: Bertrand Library; total holdings of 610,760 volumes, 690,998 microforms, 4,784 current periodical subscriptions. A total of 35 personal computers in all libraries. Access provided to on-line information retrieval services. *Computer:* Campuswide network is available with full Internet access. Computer service fees are included with tuition and fees. *Special:* In social sciences: Animal behavior laboratory (primate facility).

ELECTRICAL ENGINEERING

College of Engineering, Department of Electrical Engineering
Programs Awards MS, MSEE.
Faculty 7 full-time.
Students 6 full-time (0 women),
Entrance Requirements GRE General Test (minimum combined score of 1000), GRE Subject Test, TOEFL (minimum score 550), minimum GPA of 2.8.
Degree Requirements Thesis required, foreign language not required.
Financial Aid Assistantships available. *Financial aid application deadline:* 3/1.
Applying *Deadline:* 6/1 (priority date; rolling processing; 12/1 for spring admission). *Fee:* $25.
Contact Dr. Maurice Aburdene
Head
717-524-1234

CARNEGIE MELLON UNIVERSITY
Pittsburgh, PA 15213-3891

OVERVIEW

Carnegie Mellon University is an independent coed university.

ENROLLMENT

7,758 graduate, professional, and undergraduate students; 2,086 full-time matriculated graduate/professional students (564 women), 723 part-time matriculated graduate/professional students (268 women).

GRADUATE FACULTY

648 full-time (121 women), 371 part-time (114 women); includes 74 minority (6 African-Americans, 56 Asian-Americans, 12 Hispanics).

EXPENSES

Tuition $20,275 per year full-time, $282 per unit part-time. Fees $100 per year.

HOUSING

On-campus housing not available.

STUDENT SERVICES

Disabled student services, multicultural affairs office, low-cost health insurance, career counseling, free psychological counseling, day-care facilities, campus safety program, campus employment opportunities, international student services.

FACILITIES

Library: Hunt Library plus 2 additional on-campus libraries; total holdings of 889,252 volumes, 839,392 microforms, 3,854 current periodical subscriptions. A total of 220 personal computers in all libraries. Access provided to on-line information retrieval services. *Computer:* Campuswide network is available with full Internet access. Computer service fees are included with tuition and fees. *Special:* In arts and humanities: Studio for Creative Inquiry, Center for Cultural Analysis, Center for the Study of Writing and Literacy, Center for History and Policy, Pittsburgh Center for Social History. In science and engineering: Engineering Design Research Center, Language Technology Institute, Human-Computer Interaction Institute, Carnegie Mellon Research Institute, Robotics Institute. In social sciences: Center for Economic Development, Center for African American Urban Studies and the Economy, Center for Computations in Methodology and Logic, Center for the Advancement of Applied Ethics, Center for the Neural Basis of Cognition.

ARTIFICIAL INTELLIGENCE/ROBOTICS

School of Computer Science and Graduate School of Industrial Administration and Carnegie Institute of Technology, Robotics Doctoral Program
Programs Awards PhD.
Faculty 23 full-time (1 woman), 15 part-time (0 women).
Faculty Research Perception, cognition, manipulation, robot systems, manufacturing. *Total annual research expenditures:* $14 million.
Students 66 full-time (11 women), 2 part-time (0 women); includes 1 minority (Hispanic), 35 international.
Degrees Awarded In 1996, 12 degrees awarded.
Entrance Requirements GRE General Test, GRE Subject Test, TOEFL.
Degree Requirements Dissertation required, foreign language not required.
Financial Aid Full support grants available.
Applying *Deadline:* 2/1. *Fee:* $50.
Contact Marcella Zaragoza
Coordinator
412-268-3733
E-mail: robotics.admissions@cmu.edu

See in-depth description on page 393.

COMPUTER ENGINEERING

Carnegie Institute of Technology, Department of Electrical and Computer Engineering
Programs Offers programs in biomedical engineering (MS, PhD), electrical and computer engineering (MS, PhD). Part-time programs available.
Faculty 38 full-time (0 women), 12 part-time (0 women).
Faculty Research Computer-aided design, solid-state devices, VLSI, optical data processing, robotics and controls.

Students 214 full-time (28 women), 20 part-time (0 women); includes 18 minority (4 African-Americans, 14 Asian-Americans), 126 international.
Degrees Awarded In 1996, 61 master's, 36 doctorates awarded.
Entrance Requirements GRE General Test, TOEFL.
Degree Requirements For doctorate, computer language, dissertation, qualifying exam required, foreign language not required.
Financial Aid Fellowships, research assistantships, teaching assistantships, institutionally sponsored loans available. *Financial aid application deadline: 1/15.*
Applying *Deadline: 1/15 (10/15 for spring admission). Fee: $45.*
Contact Lynn E. Philibin
　　　　　Graduate Coordinator
　　　　　412-268-3291

See in-depth description on page 387.

COMPUTER SCIENCE

School of Computer Science, Department of Computer Science
Programs Offers programs in algorithms, combinatorics, and optimization (PhD); computer science (PhD); pure and applied logic (PhD). PhD (pure and applied logic) offered jointly with the Departments of Mathematical Sciences and Philosophy; PhD (algorithms, combinatorics, and optimization) offered jointly with the Department of Mathematical Sciences and the Graduate School of Industrial Administration.
Faculty 63 full-time (6 women), 23 part-time (1 woman).
Faculty Research Software systems, theory of computations, artificial intelligence, computer systems, programming languages.
Students 131 full-time (19 women), 13 part-time (2 women); includes 3 minority (2 African-Americans, 1 Hispanic), 63 international.
Degrees Awarded In 1996, 12 master's, 21 doctorates awarded. Terminal master's awarded for partial completion of doctoral program.
Entrance Requirements For doctorate, GRE General Test, GRE Subject Test, TOEFL, BS in computer science or equivalent.
Degree Requirements For doctorate, dissertation required, foreign language not required.
Financial Aid In 1996–97, research assistantships averaging $1,284 per month, teaching assistantships averaging $1,284 per month were awarded; fellowships, outside fellowships also available.
Applying *Deadline: 1/1. Fee: $65.*
Contact Martha Clarke
　　　　　Admissions Coordinator
　　　　　412-268-3863
　　　　　Fax: 412-681-5739
　　　　　E-mail: grad_admin@cs.cmu.edu

See in-depth description on page 385.

COMPUTER SCIENCE

School of Computer Science, Department of Human-Computer Interaction
Programs Awards MHCI.
Faculty 4 full-time (0 women), 2 part-time (both women).
Students 7 full-time (1 woman), 5 part-time (1 woman); includes 5 international.
Entrance Requirements GRE General Test, GRE Subject Test.
Applying *Deadline: 2/1. Fee: $50.*
Contact Admissions Coordinator
　　　　　412-268-6493
　　　　　E-mail: hcii-masters@cs.cmu.edu

See in-depth description on page 389.

ELECTRICAL ENGINEERING

Carnegie Institute of Technology, Department of Electrical and Computer Engineering
Programs Offers programs in biomedical engineering (MS, PhD), electrical and computer engineering (MS, PhD). Part-time programs available.
Faculty 38 full-time (0 women), 12 part-time (0 women).
Faculty Research Computer-aided design, solid-state devices, VLSI, optical data processing, robotics and controls.
Students 214 full-time (28 women), 20 part-time (0 women); includes 18 minority (4 African-Americans, 14 Asian-Americans), 126 international.
Degrees Awarded In 1996, 61 master's, 36 doctorates awarded.
Entrance Requirements GRE General Test, TOEFL.
Degree Requirements For doctorate, computer language, dissertation, qualifying exam required, foreign language not required.
Financial Aid Fellowships, research assistantships, teaching assistantships, institutionally sponsored loans available. *Financial aid application deadline: 1/15.*
Applying *Deadline: 1/15 (10/15 for spring admission). Fee: $45.*
Contact Lynn E. Philibin
　　　　　Graduate Coordinator
　　　　　412-268-3291

See in-depth description on page 387.

INFORMATION SCIENCE

Information Networking Institute
Programs Awards MS.
Faculty 32 full-time (5 women).
Students 29 full-time (4 women), 2 part-time (1 woman); includes 12 minority (1 African-American, 10 Asian-Americans, 1 Native American), 17 international. Average age 25.
Degrees Awarded In 1996, 30 degrees awarded.
Entrance Requirements GRE General Test, previous course work in computer science, computer engineering, or electrical engineering.
Financial Aid In 1996–97, scholarships averaging $1,000 per month were awarded; full tuition waivers, Federal Work-Study also available. *Financial aid application deadline: 2/1.*
Applying *Deadline: 2/1 (priority date; rolling processing). Fee: $30.*
Contact Susan Jones
　　　　　Graduate Program Coordinator
　　　　　412-268-5721

See in-depth description on page 391.

INFORMATION SCIENCE

Graduate School of Industrial Administration, Program in Information Science
Programs Awards PhD.
Faculty 6 full-time (0 women).
Entrance Requirements GRE General Test.
Degree Requirements Dissertation required, foreign language not required.
Financial Aid Fellowships available. *Financial aid application deadline: 5/1.*
Applying *Deadline: 2/1. Fee: $50.*
Contact Jackie Cavendish
　　　　　Administrative Assistant
　　　　　412-268-2301

SOFTWARE ENGINEERING

Graduate School of Industrial Administration
Programs Offerings include business management and software engineering (MBMSE).

School Faculty 64 full-time (8 women), 33 part-time (5 women).
Applying *Deadline:* rolling. *Fee:* $50.
Contact *Director of Admissions*
  412-268-2272

SOFTWARE ENGINEERING

School of Computer Science, Software Engineering Program
Programs Awards MSE.
Faculty 23 full-time (4 women), 14 part-time (2 women).
Degrees Awarded In 1996, 11 degrees awarded (100% found work related to degree).
Entrance Requirements GRE General Test, GRE Subject Test (computer science), 2 years of experience in large-scale software development project.
Financial Aid Teaching assistantships available.
Applying *Deadline:* 3/1. *Fee:* $50.
Contact *Program Coordinator*
  412-268-7713
  Fax: 412-681-5739
  E-mail: mse-info@cs.cmu.edu

See in-depth description on page **395.**

DREXEL UNIVERSITY
Philadelphia, PA 19104–2875

OVERVIEW
Drexel University is an independent coed university.

ENROLLMENT
9,590 graduate, professional, and undergraduate students; 861 full-time matriculated graduate/professional students (354 women), 1,914 part-time matriculated graduate/professional students (746 women).

GRADUATE FACULTY
367 full-time, 402 part-time, 520 FTE; includes 102 minority (20 African-Americans, 68 Asian-Americans, 14 Hispanics).

EXPENSES
Tuition $477 per credit. Fees $117 per trimester full-time, $63 per trimester part-time.

HOUSING
Rooms and/or apartments available to single students at an average cost of $4660 per year; on-campus housing not available to married students. Graduate housing contact: Jacquelyn Ford-Edwards, 215-590-8708.

STUDENT SERVICES
Low-cost health insurance, career counseling, campus safety program, campus employment opportunities, international student services.

FACILITIES
Library: W. W. Hagerty Library; total holdings of 494,626 volumes, 748,887 microforms, 2,016 current periodical subscriptions. A total of 65 personal computers in all libraries. Access provided to on-line information retrieval services. *Computer:* Campuswide network is available with full Internet access. Computer services are offered at no charge. *Special:* In arts and humanities: Art museum, historic costume collection. In science and engineering: Image Processing Center, bioelectrode research laboratory, biophysics laser laboratory,

Geosynthetic Research Institute. In social sciences: Physiological psychology laboratory, experimental psychology and learning laboratory.

COMPUTER ENGINEERING

College of Engineering, Department of Electrical and Computer Engineering
Programs Offers programs in electrical and computer engineering (PhD), electrical engineering (MSEE), telecommunications engineering (MSEE). Part-time and evening/weekend programs available.
Faculty 29 full-time, 9 part-time, 33.33 FTE.
Faculty Research Power systems planning and control, semiconductors, photovoltaics, electronic systems, image processing.
Students 61 full-time (13 women), 142 part-time (14 women); includes 27 minority (7 African-Americans, 17 Asian-Americans, 3 Hispanics), 67 international. Average age 30.
Degrees Awarded In 1996, 49 master's, 5 doctorates awarded. Terminal master's awarded for partial completion of doctoral program.
Entrance Requirements For master's, TOEFL (minimum score 570), minimum GPA of 3.0, BS in electrical engineering or physics; for doctorate, TOEFL (minimum score 570), minimum GPA of 3.5, MS in electrical engineering.
Degree Requirements For master's, thesis required (for some programs), foreign language not required; for doctorate, dissertation required, foreign language not required.
Financial Aid In 1996–97, 28 research assistantships (6 to first-year students), 26 teaching assistantships (7 to first-year students), 43 graduate assistantships (6 to first-year students) were awarded; fellowships and career-related internships or fieldwork also available. *Financial aid application deadline:* 2/1.
Applying 473 applicants, 64% accepted. *Deadline:* 8/21 (rolling processing). *Fee:* $35.
Contact *Dr. Mohana Shankar*
  Graduate Adviser
  215-895-6632

See in-depth description on page **421.**

COMPUTER SCIENCE

College of Arts and Sciences, Department of Mathematics and Computer Science, Program in Computer Science
Programs Awards MS.
Students 23 full-time (8 women), 46 part-time (7 women); includes 7 minority (6 Asian-Americans, 1 Native American), 19 international. Average age 29.
Degrees Awarded In 1996, 29 degrees awarded.
Entrance Requirements GRE, TOEFL (minimum score 570), TSE (for teaching assistants).
Financial Aid In 1996–97, 3 research assistantships (1 to a first-year student), 15 teaching assistantships (6 to first-year students), 1 graduate assistantship were awarded. *Financial aid application deadline:* 2/1.
Applying *Deadline:* 8/21 (rolling processing). *Fee:* $35.
Contact *Dr. Ron Perline*
  Graduate Adviser
  215-895-6673
  Fax: 215-895-5939

See in-depth description on page **419.**

ELECTRICAL ENGINEERING

College of Engineering, Department of Electrical and Computer Engineering
Programs Offers programs in electrical and computer engineering (PhD), electrical engineering (MSEE), telecommunications

engineering (MSEE). Part-time and evening/weekend programs available.

Faculty   29 full-time, 9 part-time, 33.33 FTE.

Faculty Research   Power systems planning and control, semiconductors, photovoltaics, electronic systems, image processing.

Students   61 full-time (13 women), 142 part-time (14 women); includes 27 minority (7 African-Americans, 17 Asian-Americans, 3 Hispanics), 67 international. Average age 30.

Degrees Awarded   In 1996, 49 master's, 5 doctorates awarded. Terminal master's awarded for partial completion of doctoral program.

Entrance Requirements   For master's, TOEFL (minimum score 570), minimum GPA of 3.0, BS in electrical engineering or physics; for doctorate, TOEFL (minimum score 570), minimum GPA of 3.5, MS in electrical engineering.

Degree Requirements   For master's, thesis required (for some programs), foreign language not required; for doctorate, dissertation required, foreign language not required.

Financial Aid   In 1996–97, 28 research assistantships (6 to first-year students), 26 teaching assistantships (7 to first-year students), 43 graduate assistantships (6 to first-year students) were awarded; fellowships and career-related internships or fieldwork also available. *Financial aid application deadline: 2/1.*

Applying   473 applicants, 64% accepted. *Deadline:* 8/21 (rolling processing). *Fee:* $35.

Contact   Dr. Mohana Shankar
Graduate Adviser
215-895-6632

See in-depth description on page **421.**

INFORMATION SCIENCE

College of Information Science and Technology

Programs   Offers programs in information studies (PhD, CAS), information systems (MSIS), library and information science (MS). Part-time and evening/weekend programs available.

Faculty   11 full-time, 18 part-time, 19.42 FTE.

Faculty Research   Bibliometric analysis, information management, scientific communication, expert systems, man-machine interfaces in information transfer.

Students   95 full-time (55 women), 442 part-time (241 women); includes 68 minority (35 African-Americans, 27 Asian-Americans, 4 Hispanics, 2 Native Americans), 28 international. Average age 35.

Degrees Awarded   In 1996, 124 master's awarded.

Entrance Requirements   For master's, GRE General Test, TOEFL (minimum score 600); for doctorate, GRE General Test, TOEFL (minimum score 600), master's degree.

Degree Requirements   For doctorate, dissertation required, foreign language not required.

Financial Aid   In 1996–97, 7 research assistantships (2 to first-year students), 39 teaching assistantships (8 to first-year students), 39 graduate assistantships (6 to first-year students) were awarded; fellowships, partial tuition waivers, Federal Work-Study, institutionally sponsored loans, and career-related internships or fieldwork also available. Aid available to part-time students. *Financial aid application deadline: 2/1.*

Applying   233 applicants, 79% accepted. *Deadline:* 8/21 (rolling processing). *Fee:* $35.

Contact   Anne B. Tanner
Associate Dean
215-895-2474

See in-depth description on page **423.**

SOFTWARE ENGINEERING

College of Arts and Sciences, Department of Mathematics and Computer Science

Programs   Offerings include software engineering (MS).

Department Faculty   29 full-time, 10 part-time, 33.7 FTE.

Entrance Requirements   GRE, TOEFL (minimum score 570), TSE (for teaching assistants).

Applying   *Deadline: 8/21 (rolling processing). Fee: $35.*

Contact   Dr. Robert Boyer
Graduate Adviser
215-895-1854

EAST STROUDSBURG UNIVERSITY OF PENNSYLVANIA
East Stroudsburg, PA 18301-2999

OVERVIEW
East Stroudsburg University of Pennsylvania is a public coed comprehensive institution.

ENROLLMENT
5,552 graduate, professional, and undergraduate students; 248 full-time matriculated graduate/professional students (149 women), 493 part-time matriculated graduate/professional students (348 women).

GRADUATE FACULTY
94 full-time (33 women), 1 part-time (0 women), 94.75 FTE; includes 4 minority (3 Asian-Americans, 1 Native American).

EXPENSES
Tuition $3468 per year full-time, $193 per credit part-time for state residents; $6236 per year full-time, $346 per credit part-time for nonresidents. Fees $698 per year full-time, $39 per credit part-time.

HOUSING
Rooms and/or apartments available to single students at an average cost of $3626 (including board); on-campus housing not available to married students. Graduate housing contact: Joseph Catanzaro, 717-422-3460.

STUDENT SERVICES
Disabled student services, low-cost health insurance, career counseling, free psychological counseling, exercise/wellness program, day-care facilities, campus safety program, campus employment opportunities, international student services.

FACILITIES
Library: Kemp Library; total holdings of 423,652 volumes, 1,219,134 microforms, 2,087 current periodical subscriptions. A total of 20 personal computers in all libraries. Access provided to on-line information retrieval services. *Computer:* Campuswide network is available with full Internet access. Total number of PCs/terminals supplied for student use: 250. Computer service fees are included with tuition and fees. *Special:* In science and engineering: Human performance laboratory, biology research laboratory.

COMPUTER SCIENCE

School of Arts and Sciences, Department of Computer Science

Programs   Awards MS. Part-time and evening/weekend programs available.

Faculty 6 full-time (1 woman).

Students 5 full-time (1 woman), 10 part-time (1 woman); includes 1 international. Average age 35.

Degrees Awarded In 1996, 4 degrees awarded.

Entrance Requirements Bachelor's degree in computer science or related field.

Degree Requirements Computer language, thesis or alternative, comprehensive exam.

Financial Aid Research assistantships, Federal Work-Study, institutionally sponsored loans, and career-related internships or fieldwork available. *Financial aid application deadline:* 3/1; applicants required to submit FAFSA.

Applying *Deadline:* 7/31 (priority date; rolling processing; 11/30 for spring admission). *Fee:* $15.

Contact *Dr. Richard Prince*
Graduate Coordinator
717-422-3772
Fax: 717-422-3777
E-mail: rprince@esu.edu

GANNON UNIVERSITY
Erie, PA 16541

OVERVIEW
Gannon University is an independent-religious coed comprehensive institution.

ENROLLMENT
3,327 graduate, professional, and undergraduate students; 108 full-time matriculated graduate/professional students (66 women), 373 part-time matriculated graduate/professional students (216 women).

GRADUATE FACULTY
47 full-time (17 women), 20 part-time (5 women), 53 FTE; includes 5 minority (all Asian-Americans).

EXPENSES
Tuition $405 per credit. Fees $200 per year full-time, $8 per credit part-time.

HOUSING
On-campus housing not available.

STUDENT SERVICES
Low-cost health insurance, career counseling, free psychological counseling, campus safety program, campus employment opportunities, international student services.

FACILITIES
Library: Nash Library; total holdings of 296,253 volumes, 415,978 microforms, 1,195 current periodical subscriptions. A total of 45 personal computers in all libraries. Access provided to on-line information retrieval services. *Computer:* Campuswide network is available with full Internet access. Total number of PCs/terminals supplied for student use: 375. Computer service fees are included with tuition and fees. *Special:* In arts and humanities: Schuster Theatre, Schuster Art Gallery. In science and engineering: Zurn Science Center, Computer Center, Bahama Field Station.

ELECTRICAL ENGINEERING

School of Graduate Studies, College of Sciences, Engineering, and Health Sciences, School of Sciences and Engineering, Program in Engineering

Programs Offerings include electrical engineering (MS).

Entrance Requirements GRE Subject Test, minimum QPA of 2.5, bachelor's degree in engineering.

Degree Requirements Thesis or alternative, comprehensive exam.

Applying *Deadline:* rolling. *Fee:* $25.

Contact *Beth Nemenz*
Director of Admissions
814-871-7240
Fax: 814-871-5803

SOFTWARE ENGINEERING

School of Graduate Studies, College of Sciences, Engineering, and Health Sciences, School of Sciences and Engineering, Program in Engineering

Programs Offerings include embedded software engineering (MS).

Entrance Requirements GRE Subject Test, minimum QPA of 2.5, bachelor's degree in engineering.

Degree Requirements Thesis or alternative, comprehensive exam.

Applying *Deadline:* rolling. *Fee:* $25.

Contact *Beth Nemenz*
Director of Admissions
814-871-7240
Fax: 814-871-5803

KUTZTOWN UNIVERSITY OF PENNSYLVANIA
Kutztown, PA 19530

OVERVIEW
Kutztown University of Pennsylvania is a public coed comprehensive institution.

ENROLLMENT
7,843 graduate, professional, and undergraduate students; 127 full-time matriculated graduate/professional students (86 women), 791 part-time matriculated graduate/professional students (611 women).

GRADUATE FACULTY
54 full-time (15 women); includes 7 minority (4 African-Americans, 1 Asian-American, 2 Hispanics).

TUITION
$5247 per year full-time, $224 per credit hour part-time for state residents; $8933 per year full-time, $392 per credit hour part-time for nonresidents.

HOUSING
On-campus housing not available.

STUDENT SERVICES
Low-cost health insurance, career counseling, free psychological counseling, day-care facilities, campus employment opportunities, international student services.

FACILITIES
Library: Rohrbach Library; total holdings of 414,564 volumes, 1,201,101 microforms, 1,926 current periodical subscriptions. A total of 50 personal computers in all libraries. Access provided to on-line information retrieval services. *Computer:* Campuswide network is available with full Internet access. Computer services are offered

at no charge. *Special:* In science and engineering: Seismic observatory. In social sciences: Speech clinic.

COMPUTER SCIENCE

Graduate School, College of Liberal Arts and Sciences, Program in Computer and Information Science
Programs Awards MS.
Faculty 10 full-time (3 women).
Faculty Research Artificial intelligence, expert systems, neural networks.
Students 5 full-time (2 women), 8 part-time (2 women); includes 3 minority (all Asian-Americans), 5 international. Average age 33.
Degrees Awarded In 1996, 5 degrees awarded.
Entrance Requirements GRE General Test, TOEFL, TSE.
Degree Requirements Computer language, comprehensive exam or thesis required, foreign language not required.
Financial Aid Graduate assistantships, partial tuition waivers, Federal Work-Study, and career-related internships or fieldwork available. *Financial aid application deadline:* 3/15; applicants required to submit FAFSA.
Applying *Deadline:* 3/1 (8/1 for spring admission). *Fee:* $25.
Contact *Dr. Cherry C. Mauk*
Chairperson
610-683-4410

INFORMATION SCIENCE

Graduate School, College of Liberal Arts and Sciences, Program in Computer and Information Science
Programs Awards MS.
Faculty 10 full-time (3 women).
Faculty Research Artificial intelligence, expert systems, neural networks.
Students 5 full-time (2 women), 8 part-time (2 women); includes 3 minority (all Asian-Americans), 5 international. Average age 33.
Degrees Awarded In 1996, 5 degrees awarded.
Entrance Requirements GRE General Test, TOEFL, TSE.
Degree Requirements Computer language, comprehensive exam or thesis required, foreign language not required.
Financial Aid Graduate assistantships, partial tuition waivers, Federal Work-Study, and career-related internships or fieldwork available. *Financial aid application deadline:* 3/15; applicants required to submit FAFSA.
Applying *Deadline:* 3/1 (8/1 for spring admission). *Fee:* $25.
Contact *Dr. Cherry C. Mauk*
Chairperson
610-683-4410

LA SALLE UNIVERSITY
Philadelphia, PA 19141-1199

OVERVIEW
La Salle University is an independent-religious coed comprehensive institution.

ENROLLMENT
5,130 graduate, professional, and undergraduate students; 1,320 matriculated graduate/professional students (720 women).

GRADUATE FACULTY
76 full-time, 38 part-time; includes 11 minority (3 African-Americans, 5 Asian-Americans, 3 Hispanics).

TUITION
$365 per credit.

HOUSING
Rooms and/or apartments available to single students at an average cost of $3500 per year ($5800 including board); on-campus housing not available to married students. Housing application deadline: 7/1. Graduate housing contact: Ron Diment, 215-951-1550.

STUDENT SERVICES
Career counseling, free psychological counseling, day-care facilities, campus employment opportunities.

FACILITIES
Library: Connelly Library; total holdings of 340,000 volumes, 50,000 microforms, 1,650 current periodical subscriptions. A total of 50 personal computers in all libraries. Access provided to on-line information retrieval services. *Computer:* Campuswide network is available with full Internet access. Total number of PCs/terminals supplied for student use: 200. Computer service fees are included with tuition and fees. *Special:* In arts and humanities: Art museum, Japanese Tea House.

COMPUTER SCIENCE

School of Arts and Sciences, Program in Computer Information Science
Programs Awards MA. Part-time and evening/weekend programs available.
Faculty 8 full-time (3 women).
Faculty Research Human-computer interaction, networks, technology trends, databases, groupware.
Students 58 part-time (10 women); includes 4 minority (3 African-Americans, 1 Asian-American), 1 international. Average age 35.
Entrance Requirements GRE, MAT, 18 undergraduate credits in computer science, professional experience.
Degree Requirements Computer language required, foreign language not required.
Financial Aid In 1996–97, 8 grants were awarded; institutionally sponsored loans also available. Aid available to part-time students.
Applying *Deadline:* 7/15 (priority date; rolling processing; 11/1 for spring admission). *Fee:* $30.
Contact *Dr. Margaret McManus*
Director
215-951-1222
Fax: 215-951-1805
E-mail: macis@lasalle.edu

LEHIGH UNIVERSITY
Bethlehem, PA 18015-3094

OVERVIEW
Lehigh University is an independent coed university.

ENROLLMENT
6,233 graduate, professional, and undergraduate students; 753 full-time matriculated graduate/professional students (260 women), 981 part-time matriculated graduate/professional students (450 women).

GRADUATE FACULTY
399 full-time (83 women), 89 part-time (42 women); includes 50 minority (12 African-Americans, 29 Asian-Americans, 7 Hispanics, 2 Native Americans).

EXPENSES

Tuition $800 per credit. Fees $12 per semester full-time, $6 per semester part-time.

HOUSING

Rooms and/or apartments available to single students at an average cost of $4500 per year; available to married students at an average cost of $5700 per year. Graduate housing contact: Office of Residential Services, 610-758-3500.

STUDENT SERVICES

Low-cost health insurance, career counseling, free psychological counseling, day-care facilities, campus safety program, campus employment opportunities, international student services.

FACILITIES

Library: Fairchild-Martindale Library and Computing Center plus 2 additional on-campus libraries; total holdings of 1,077,299 volumes, 1,610,454 microforms, 9,700 current periodical subscriptions. A total of 63 personal computers in all libraries. Access provided to on-line information retrieval services. *Computer:* Campuswide network is available with full Internet access. Total number of PCs/terminals supplied for student use: 500. Computer services are offered at no charge. *Special:* In arts and humanities: Center for International Studies, Lawrence Henry Gieson Institute for Eighteenth-Century Studies. In science and engineering: Fairchild Solid State Laboratory, Fritz Structural Engineering Laboratory, Materials Research Center, electron microscopy laboratory, surface chemistry and coatings laboratory. In social sciences: Center for Social Research, Iacocca Institute.

COMPUTER ENGINEERING

College of Engineering and Applied Science, Department of Electrical Engineering and Computer Science, Program in Computer Engineering
Programs Awards MS. Part-time programs available.
Entrance Requirements GRE General Test, TOEFL (minimum score 550), minimum GPA of 3.0.
Degree Requirements Oral presentation of thesis.
Financial Aid Fellowships, research assistantships, teaching assistantships available. *Financial aid application deadline:* 1/15.
Applying *Deadline:* 4/1 (rolling processing; 11/1 for spring admission). *Fee:* $40.
Contact *Naomi Gulden*
Graduate Coordinator
610-758-3079
Fax: 610-758-6279

See in-depth descriptions on pages 463 and 461.

COMPUTER SCIENCE

College of Engineering and Applied Science, Department of Electrical Engineering and Computer Science, Program in Computer Science
Programs Awards MS, PhD. Part-time programs available.
Entrance Requirements For master's, GRE General Test, TOEFL (minimum score 550), minimum GPA of 3.0; for doctorate, GRE General Test, TOEFL (minimum score 550), MS, minimum GPA of 3.25.
Degree Requirements For master's, oral presentation of thesis; for doctorate, dissertation, qualifying, general, and oral exams.
Financial Aid Fellowships, research assistantships, teaching assistantships available. *Financial aid application deadline:* 1/15.
Applying *Deadline:* 4/1 (rolling processing; 11/1 for spring admission). *Fee:* $40.

Contact *Naomi Gulden*
Graduate Coordinator
610-758-3079
Fax: 610-758-6279

See in-depth description on page 461.

ELECTRICAL ENGINEERING

College of Engineering and Applied Science, Department of Electrical Engineering and Computer Science, Program in Electrical Engineering
Programs Awards M Eng, MS, PhD. Part-time programs available.
Entrance Requirements For master's, GRE General Test, TOEFL (minimum score 550), minimum GPA of 3.0; for doctorate, GRE General Test, TOEFL (minimum score 550), MS, minimum GPA of 3.25.
Degree Requirements For master's, oral presentation of thesis; for doctorate, dissertation, qualifying, general, and oral exams.
Financial Aid Fellowships, research assistantships, teaching assistantships available. *Financial aid application deadline:* 1/15.
Applying *Deadline:* 4/1 (rolling processing; 11/1 for spring admission). *Fee:* $40.
Contact *Naomi Gulden*
Graduate Coordinator
610-758-3079
Fax: 610-758-6279

See in-depth description on page 463.

PENNSYLVANIA STATE UNIVERSITY GREAT VALLEY GRADUATE CENTER
Malvern, PA 19355-1488

OVERVIEW

Pennsylvania State University Great Valley Graduate Center is a public coed graduate-only institution.

ENROLLMENT

1,179 graduate, professional, and undergraduate students; 85 full-time matriculated graduate/professional students (40 women), 1,092 part-time matriculated graduate/professional students (478 women).

GRADUATE FACULTY

27 full-time (11 women), 72 part-time (14 women); includes 9 minority (2 African-Americans, 7 Asian-Americans).

EXPENSES

Tuition $5940 per year full-time, $330 per credit hour part-time for state residents; $10,620 per year full-time, $590 per credit hour part-time for nonresidents. Fees $150 per year full-time, $26 per semester (minimum) part-time.

HOUSING

On-campus housing not available.

STUDENT SERVICES

Low-cost health insurance, career counseling, international student services.

FACILITIES

Library: Total holdings of 23,126 volumes, 10,640 microforms, 242 current periodical subscriptions. Access provided to on-line information retrieval services.

ELECTRICAL ENGINEERING

Graduate Studies and Continuing Education, College of Engineering, Program in Electrical Engineering
Programs Awards M Eng.
Faculty 3.
Students 25 part-time (1 woman). Average age 34.
Entrance Requirements GRE.
Applying *Fee:* $40.
Contact Dr. David Russell
　　　　　　Adviser
　　　　　　610-648-3277

INFORMATION SCIENCE

Graduate Studies and Continuing Education, College of Engineering, Program in Information Science
Programs Awards MS, M Eng/MS.
Faculty 10.
Students 11 full-time (1 woman), 180 part-time (54 women). Average age 34.
Applying *Fee:* $40.
Contact Dr. David Russell
　　　　　　Adviser
　　　　　　610-648-3277

PENNSYLVANIA STATE UNIVERSITY HARRISBURG CAMPUS OF THE CAPITAL COLLEGE
Middletown, PA 17057-4898

OVERVIEW
Pennsylvania State University Harrisburg Campus of the Capital College is a public coed comprehensive institution.

ENROLLMENT
2,923 graduate, professional, and undergraduate students; 111 full-time matriculated graduate/professional students (60 women), 981 part-time matriculated graduate/professional students (577 women).

GRADUATE FACULTY
139 full-time (36 women), 95 part-time (41 women); includes 21 minority (6 African-Americans, 13 Asian-Americans, 2 Hispanics).

EXPENSES
Tuition $6302 per year full-time, $266 per credit hour part-time for state residents; $12,516 per year full-time, $523 per credit hour part-time for nonresidents. Fees $200 per year full-time, $35 per semester (minimum) part-time.

HOUSING
Rooms and/or apartments available to single students at an average cost of $2580 per year ($4350 including board); available to married students at an average cost of $4815 per year.

STUDENT SERVICES
Low-cost health insurance, career counseling, free psychological counseling, international student services.

FACILITIES
Library: Richard H. Heindel Library; total holdings of 241,514 volumes, 1,095,202 microforms, 1,567 current periodical subscriptions. Access provided to on-line information retrieval services.

ELECTRICAL ENGINEERING

Division of Science, Engineering and Technology, Program in Electrical Engineering
Programs Awards M Eng.
Students 13 part-time (0 women).
Applying *Fee:* $40.
Contact Dr. Jerry Sharp
　　　　　　Chair
　　　　　　717-948-6114

PENNSYLVANIA STATE UNIVERSITY UNIVERSITY PARK CAMPUS
University Park, PA 16802-1503

OVERVIEW
Pennsylvania State University University Park Campus is a public coed university.

ENROLLMENT
37,881 graduate, professional, and undergraduate students; 4,288 full-time matriculated graduate/professional students (1,712 women), 1,781 part-time matriculated graduate/professional students (809 women).

GRADUATE FACULTY
2,584 full-time (663 women), 426 part-time (215 women); includes 374 minority (70 African-Americans, 250 Asian-Americans, 52 Hispanics, 2 Native Americans).

EXPENSES
Tuition $6302 per year full-time, $266 per credit hour part-time for state residents; $12,980 per year full-time, $541 per credit hour part-time for nonresidents. Fees $50 per year (minimum).

HOUSING
Rooms and/or apartments available to single students at an average cost of $2150 per year ($4420 including board); available to married students at an average cost of $4365 per year.

STUDENT SERVICES
Low-cost health insurance, career counseling, free psychological counseling, international student services.

FACILITIES
Library: Pattee Library plus 7 additional on-campus libraries; total holdings of 2,680,414 volumes, 2,143,699 microforms, 24,628 current periodical subscriptions. Access provided to on-line information retrieval services. *Special:* In arts and humanities: Institute of Arts and Humanistic Studies. In science and engineering: Biotechnology Institute, Center for Air Environment Studies, Land and Water Resources Research Institute, applied research laboratory, laboratory for human performance, materials research laboratory.

COMPUTER ENGINEERING

College of Engineering, Department of Computer Science and Engineering
Programs Awards M Eng, MS, PhD.
Faculty 26.
Students 65 full-time (19 women), 34 part-time (4 women).
Degrees Awarded In 1996, 33 master's, 13 doctorates awarded.
Entrance Requirements GRE General Test.
Degree Requirements For doctorate, dissertation.
Applying *Fee:* $40.
Contact *Dr. Joseph M. Lambert*
　　　　　Head
　　　　　814-865-9505

COMPUTER SCIENCE

College of Engineering, Department of Computer Science and Engineering
Programs Awards M Eng, MS, PhD.
Faculty 26.
Students 65 full-time (19 women), 34 part-time (4 women).
Degrees Awarded In 1996, 33 master's, 13 doctorates awarded.
Entrance Requirements GRE General Test.
Degree Requirements For doctorate, dissertation.
Applying *Fee:* $40.
Contact *Dr. Joseph M. Lambert*
　　　　　Head
　　　　　814-865-9505

ELECTRICAL ENGINEERING

College of Engineering, Department of Electrical Engineering
Programs Awards MS, PhD.
Faculty 71.
Students 168 full-time (19 women), 64 part-time (7 women).
Degrees Awarded In 1996, 45 master's, 19 doctorates awarded.
Entrance Requirements GRE General Test.
Degree Requirements For doctorate, dissertation required, foreign language not required.
Applying *Fee:* $40.
Contact *Dr. James W. Robinson*
　　　　　Chair
　　　　　814-863-7295

See in-depth description on page 517.

See in-depth description on page 517.

SAINT JOSEPH'S UNIVERSITY
Philadelphia, PA 19131-1395

OVERVIEW
Saint Joseph's University is an independent-religious coed comprehensive institution.

ENROLLMENT
6,963 graduate, professional, and undergraduate students; 307 full-time matriculated graduate/professional students (150 women), 2,579 part-time matriculated graduate/professional students (1,422 women).

GRADUATE FACULTY
66 full-time (23 women), 76 part-time (28 women); includes 4 minority (1 African-American, 3 Asian-Americans).

TUITION
$440 per credit hour.

HOUSING
On-campus housing not available.

STUDENT SERVICES
Low-cost health insurance, career counseling, free psychological counseling, campus employment opportunities.

FACILITIES
Library: Francis A. Drexel Library plus 1 additional on-campus library; total holdings of 355,000 volumes, 727,000 microforms, 2,029 current periodical subscriptions. Access provided to on-line information retrieval services. *Computer:* Campuswide network is available with full Internet access. Total number of PCs/terminals supplied for student use: 143. Computer services are offered at no charge.

COMPUTER SCIENCE

Program in Computer Science
Programs Awards MS. Part-time and evening/weekend programs available.
Students 98 (37 women).
Degrees Awarded In 1996, 21 degrees awarded.
Entrance Requirements GRE General Test, TOEFL.
Degree Requirements Computer language.
Applying *Deadline:* 7/15. *Fee:* $30.
Contact *Dr. Gary Laison*
　　　　　Director
　　　　　610-660-1571

SHIPPENSBURG UNIVERSITY OF PENNSYLVANIA
Shippensburg, PA 17257-2299

OVERVIEW
Shippensburg University of Pennsylvania is a public coed comprehensive institution.

ENROLLMENT
6,683 graduate, professional, and undergraduate students; 225 full-time matriculated graduate/professional students (126 women), 651 part-time matriculated graduate/professional students (360 women).

GRADUATE FACULTY
155 full-time (48 women), 1 part-time (0 women); includes 7 minority (5 African-Americans, 2 Asian-Americans).

EXPENSES
Tuition $3468 per year full-time, $193 per credit hour part-time for state residents; $6236 per year full-time, $346 per credit hour part-time for nonresidents. Fees $676 per year full-time, $195 per semester (minimum) part-time.

HOUSING
On-campus housing not available.

STUDENT SERVICES

Low-cost health insurance, career counseling, free psychological counseling, day-care facilities, campus safety program, campus employment opportunities, international student services.

FACILITIES

Library: Ezra Lehman Memorial Library plus 1 additional on-campus library; total holdings of 441,732 volumes, 1,621,054 microforms, 1,782 current periodical subscriptions. A total of 60 personal computers in all libraries. Access provided to on-line information retrieval services. *Computer:* Campuswide network is available. Total number of PCs/terminals supplied for student use: 300. Computer services are offered at no charge.

COMPUTER SCIENCE

College of Arts and Sciences, Department of Mathematics and Computer Science
Programs Offers programs in computer education (M Ed), computer science (MS), information systems (MS), mathematics (M Ed, MS).
Faculty 20 full-time (1 woman).
Students 15 full-time (3 women), 83 part-time (20 women); includes 9 minority (4 African-Americans, 2 Asian-Americans, 1 Hispanic, 2 Native Americans), 9 international. Average age 34.
Degrees Awarded In 1996, 28 degrees awarded.
Entrance Requirements GRE General Test or minimum GPA of 2.5.
Financial Aid In 1996–97, 13 graduate assistantships were awarded. *Financial aid application deadline:* 3/1.
Applying *Deadline:* rolling. *Fee:* $25.
Contact *Dr. Fred Nordai*
      Chairperson
      717-532-1431

INFORMATION SCIENCE

College of Arts and Sciences, Department of Mathematics and Computer Science
Programs Offerings include information systems (MS).
Department Faculty 20 full-time (1 woman).
Applying *Deadline:* rolling. *Fee:* $25.
Contact *Dr. Fred Nordai*
      Chairperson
      717-532-1431

TEMPLE UNIVERSITY
Philadelphia, PA 19122-6096

OVERVIEW

Temple University is a public coed university.

ENROLLMENT

25,468 graduate, professional, and undergraduate students; 8,957 matriculated graduate/professional students (4,651 women).

GRADUATE FACULTY

878 (269 women); includes 150 minority (62 African-Americans, 64 Asian-Americans, 23 Hispanics, 1 Native American).

EXPENSES

Tuition $308 per semester hour for state residents; $429 per semester hour for nonresidents. Fees $280 per year full-time, $107 per semester (minimum) part-time.

HOUSING

Rooms and/or apartments available to single students (186 units) at an average cost of $4998 per year; available to married students (186 units) at an average cost of $6684 per year. Housing application deadline: 6/1. Graduate housing contact: Helen Ball, 215-204-7223.

STUDENT SERVICES

Disabled student services, multicultural affairs office, low-cost health insurance, career counseling, free psychological counseling, exercise/wellness program, day-care facilities, campus safety program, campus employment opportunities, international student services, writing training.

FACILITIES

Library: Paley Library plus 12 additional on-campus libraries; total holdings of 2,361,209 volumes, 2,504,569 microforms, 14,413 current periodical subscriptions. A total of 400 personal computers in all libraries. Access provided to on-line information retrieval services. *Computer:* Campuswide network is available with full Internet access. Computer service fees are applied as a separate charge. *Special:* In arts and humanities: Center for Research in Human Development, Center for Environmental Research. In science and engineering: Fels Institute for Molecular Biology and Genetics, Thrombosis Research Center. In social sciences: Center for Public Policy, Center for Black Culture and History, Social Policy and Community Development Center.

COMPUTER ENGINEERING

College of Engineering, Program in Electrical and Computer Engineering
Programs Awards MSE. Part-time programs available.
Faculty 10 full-time (0 women).
Faculty Research Neural networks, adaptive control, robotics, multiprocessor systems, vacuum microelectronics. *Total annual research expenditures:* $425,000.
Students 9; includes 7 minority (1 African-American, 6 Asian-Americans), 1 international. Average age 25.
Degrees Awarded In 1996, 1 degree awarded.
Entrance Requirements GRE General Test (minimum combined score of 1500), TOEFL (minimum score 575).
Degree Requirements Thesis required, foreign language not required.
Financial Aid Fellowships, research assistantships, teaching assistantships, Federal Work-Study, institutionally sponsored loans available. *Financial aid application deadline:* 2/15.
Applying 75 applicants, 4% accepted. *Deadline:* 7/1 (rolling processing; 1/15 for spring admission). *Fee:* $30.
Contact *Dr. Richard Klafter*
      Director
      215-204-4523
      Fax: 215-204-5960
      E-mail: rklafter@thunder.ocis.temple.edu

COMPUTER SCIENCE

College of Arts and Sciences, Department of Computer and Information Sciences
Programs Awards MS, PhD. Part-time programs available.
Faculty 16 full-time (1 woman).

Faculty Research Artificial intelligence, information systems, software engineering, network-distributed systems.

Students 63 (22 women); includes 41 minority (40 Asian-Americans, 1 Hispanic). Average age 29.

Degrees Awarded In 1996, 37 master's, 8 doctorates awarded.

Entrance Requirements GRE General Test, TOEFL, minimum GPA of 2.8.

Degree Requirements For master's, computer language required, foreign language and thesis not required; for doctorate, computer language, dissertation required, foreign language not required.

Financial Aid In 1996–97, 25 students received aid, including 17 teaching assistantships totaling $9,750, 8 laboratory assistantships totaling $7,600; fellowships, research assistantships also available. *Financial aid application deadline:* 2/1.

Applying 218 applicants, 70% accepted. *Deadline:* 2/1 (rolling processing; 9/30 for spring admission). *Fee:* $30.

Contact *Dr. Robert Aiken*
  Graduate Chair
  215-204-8450

ELECTRICAL ENGINEERING

College of Engineering, Program in Electrical and Computer Engineering

Programs Awards MSE. Part-time programs available.

Faculty 10 full-time (0 women).

Faculty Research Neural networks, adaptive control, robotics, multiprocessor systems, vacuum microelectronics. *Total annual research expenditures:* $425,000.

Students 9; includes 7 minority (1 African-American, 6 Asian-Americans), 1 international. Average age 25.

Degrees Awarded In 1996, 1 degree awarded.

Entrance Requirements GRE General Test (minimum combined score of 1500), TOEFL (minimum score 575).

Degree Requirements Thesis required, foreign language not required.

Financial Aid Fellowships, research assistantships, teaching assistantships, Federal Work-Study, institutionally sponsored loans available. *Financial aid application deadline:* 2/15.

Applying 75 applicants, 4% accepted. *Deadline:* 7/1 (rolling processing; 1/15 for spring admission). *Fee:* $30.

Contact *Dr. Richard Klafter*
  Director
  215-204-4523
  Fax: 215-204-5960
  E-mail: rklafter@thunder.ocis.temple.edu

INFORMATION SCIENCE

College of Arts and Sciences, Department of Computer and Information Sciences

Programs Awards MS, PhD. Part-time programs available.

Faculty 16 full-time (1 woman).

Faculty Research Artificial intelligence, information systems, software engineering, network-distributed systems.

Students 63 (22 women); includes 41 minority (40 Asian-Americans, 1 Hispanic). Average age 29.

Degrees Awarded In 1996, 37 master's, 8 doctorates awarded.

Entrance Requirements GRE General Test, TOEFL, minimum GPA of 2.8.

Degree Requirements For master's, computer language required, foreign language and thesis not required; for doctorate, computer language, dissertation required, foreign language not required.

Financial Aid In 1996–97, 25 students received aid, including 17 teaching assistantships totaling $9,750, 8 laboratory assistantships totaling $7,600; fellowships, research assistantships also available. *Financial aid application deadline:* 2/1.

Applying 218 applicants, 70% accepted. *Deadline:* 2/1 (rolling processing; 9/30 for spring admission). *Fee:* $30.

Contact *Dr. Robert Aiken*
  Graduate Chair
  215-204-8450

UNIVERSITY OF PENNSYLVANIA
Philadelphia, PA 19104

OVERVIEW
University of Pennsylvania is an independent coed university.

ENROLLMENT
21,869 graduate, professional, and undergraduate students; 8,493 full-time matriculated graduate/professional students (3,992 women), 1,868 part-time matriculated graduate/professional students (1,097 women).

GRADUATE FACULTY
2,035 full-time (459 women); includes 170 minority (51 African-Americans, 87 Asian-Americans, 31 Hispanics, 1 Native American).

EXPENSES
Tuition $21,738 per year full-time, $2752 per course part-time. Fees $1420 per year full-time, $163 per course part-time.

HOUSING
Rooms and/or apartments available to single students (1,050 units) at an average cost of $7260 per year ($10,760 including board); available to married students (100 units) at an average cost of $10,080 per year ($17,076 including board). Graduate housing contact: Shelli Mueller, 215-898-8271.

STUDENT SERVICES
Low-cost health insurance, career counseling, free psychological counseling, campus safety program, international student services.

FACILITIES
Library: Van Pelt Library plus 14 additional on-campus libraries; total holdings of 4.2 million volumes, 1.5 million microforms, 33,000 current periodical subscriptions. Access provided to on-line information retrieval services. *Computer:* Campuswide network is available with full Internet access. Computer services are offered at no charge. *Special:* In arts and humanities: Institute for Contemporary Art, university museum, Morris Arboretum. In science and engineering: Cancer Center, Laboratory for Research on the Structure of Matter, Mahoney Institute for Neurological Sciences, Institute for Environmental Medicine. In social sciences: Lauder Institute, Population Studies Center, Leonard Davis Institute of Health Economics, Center for the Study of Aging, Real Estate Center, Early American Studies Center.

COMPUTER SCIENCE

School of Engineering and Applied Science, Department of Computer and Information Science

Programs Awards MSE, PhD, MSE/MBA. Part-time programs available.

Faculty   22 full-time (4 women), 7 part-time (3 women).

Faculty Research   Robotics, graphics, theory, ai, networks and distributed systems, databases, computational biology, natural language processing. *Total annual research expenditures:* $22 million.

Students   151 full-time (25 women), 56 part-time (11 women); includes 21 minority (5 African-Americans, 15 Asian-Americans, 1 Hispanic), 90 international. Average age 26.

Degrees Awarded   In 1996, 67 master's awarded (2% entered university research/teaching, 85% found other work related to degree, 13% continued full-time study); 18 doctorates awarded (67% entered university research/teaching, 33% found other work related to degree). Terminal master's awarded for partial completion of doctoral program.

Entrance Requirements   GRE General Test, TOEFL (minimum score 600).

Degree Requirements   For master's, computer language required, thesis optional, foreign language not required; for doctorate, computer language, dissertation required, foreign language not required.

Financial Aid   In 1996–97, 99 students received aid, including 17 fellowships (13 to first-year students) averaging $1,333 per month, 82 research assistantships; teaching assistantships, institutionally sponsored loans also available. *Financial aid application deadline:* 1/2.

Applying   352 applicants, 34% accepted. *Deadline:* 1/15 (priority date; rolling processing). *Fee:* $65.

Contact   *Mike Felker*
   Graduate Coordinator
   215-898-8560
   Fax: 215-898-0587
   E-mail: cis-grad-admin@central.cis.upenn.edu

See in-depth description on page **697.**

ELECTRICAL ENGINEERING

School of Engineering and Applied Science, Department of Electrical Engineering

Programs   Awards MSE, PhD. Part-time programs available.

Faculty   15 full-time (1 woman), 3 part-time (0 women).

Faculty Research   Electro-optics, microwave and millimeter-wave optics, solid-state and chemical electronics, electromagnetic propagation, inverse scattering.

Students   41 full-time (4 women), 22 part-time (3 women); includes 12 minority (3 African-Americans, 7 Asian-Americans, 2 Hispanics), 33 international. Average age 25.

Degrees Awarded   In 1996, 29 master's, 4 doctorates awarded. Terminal master's awarded for partial completion of doctoral program.

Entrance Requirements   TOEFL (minimum score 600).

Degree Requirements   For master's, thesis optional, foreign language not required; for doctorate, dissertation required, foreign language not required.

Financial Aid   In 1996–97, 18 students received aid, including 3 fellowships (all to first-year students), 15 research assistantships, 2 teaching assistantships; institutionally sponsored loans also available. *Financial aid application deadline:* 1/2.

Applying   177 applicants, 36% accepted. *Deadline:* 1/15 (priority date; rolling processing; 11/1 for spring admission). *Fee:* $65.

Contact   *Dr. Nader Engheta*
   Graduate Group Chair
   215-898-9241
   Fax: 215-573-2068
   E-mail: engheta@pender.ee.upenn.edu

See in-depth description on page **699.**

INFORMATION SCIENCE

School of Engineering and Applied Science, Department of Computer and Information Science

Programs   Awards MSE, PhD, MSE/MBA. Part-time programs available.

Faculty   22 full-time (4 women), 7 part-time (3 women).

Faculty Research   Robotics, graphics, theory, ai, networks and distributed systems, databases, computational biology, natural language processing. *Total annual research expenditures:* $22 million.

Students   151 full-time (25 women), 56 part-time (11 women); includes 21 minority (5 African-Americans, 15 Asian-Americans, 1 Hispanic), 90 international. Average age 26.

Degrees Awarded   In 1996, 67 master's awarded (2% entered university research/teaching, 85% found other work related to degree, 13% continued full-time study); 18 doctorates awarded (67% entered university research/teaching, 33% found other work related to degree). Terminal master's awarded for partial completion of doctoral program.

Entrance Requirements   GRE General Test, TOEFL (minimum score 600).

Degree Requirements   For master's, computer language required, thesis optional, foreign language not required; for doctorate, computer language, dissertation required, foreign language not required.

Financial Aid   In 1996–97, 99 students received aid, including 17 fellowships (13 to first-year students) averaging $1,333 per month, 82 research assistantships; teaching assistantships, institutionally sponsored loans also available. *Financial aid application deadline:* 1/2.

Applying   352 applicants, 34% accepted. *Deadline:* 1/15 (priority date; rolling processing). *Fee:* $65.

Contact   *Mike Felker*
   Graduate Coordinator
   215-898-8560
   Fax: 215-898-0587
   E-mail: cis-grad-admin@central.cis.upenn.edu

See in-depth description on page **697.**

UNIVERSITY OF PITTSBURGH
Pittsburgh, PA 15260

OVERVIEW

University of Pittsburgh is a public coed university.

ENROLLMENT

25,479 graduate, professional, and undergraduate students; 5,943 full-time matriculated graduate/professional students (2,797 women), 3,487 part-time matriculated graduate/professional students (1,903 women).

GRADUATE FACULTY

2,882 full-time (870 women), 583 part-time (269 women); includes 495 minority (133 African-Americans, 311 Asian-Americans, 49 Hispanics, 2 Native Americans).

EXPENSES

Tuition $7710 per year full-time, $317 per credit part-time for state residents; $15,874 per year full-time, $654 per credit part-time for nonresidents. Fees $444 per year full-time, $102 per year part-time.

HOUSING

Rooms and/or apartments available to single students; available to married students (533 units). Graduate housing contact: Office of Property Management, 412-624-4317.

STUDENT SERVICES
Disabled student services, low-cost health insurance, career counseling, free psychological counseling, exercise/wellness program, day-care facilities, campus safety program, campus employment opportunities, international student services.

FACILITIES
Library: Hillman Library plus 26 additional on-campus libraries; total holdings of 3,391,033 volumes, 3,602,572 microforms, 23,052 current periodical subscriptions. Access provided to on-line information retrieval services. *Computer:* Campuswide network is available with full Internet access. Total number of PCs/terminals supplied for student use: 620. Computer service fees are included with tuition and fees. *Special:* In arts and humanities: Stephen Foster Memorial, Frick Fine Arts Building. In science and engineering: Applied Research Center, Michael L. Benedum Hall of Engineering, Bituminous Coal Research National Laboratory, Mid-Atlantic Technology Applications Center, Cancer Institute. In social sciences: Learning Research and Development Center, Center for Social and Urban Research, Center for International Studies.

COMPUTER SCIENCE

Faculty of Arts and Sciences, Department of Computer Science
Programs Awards MS, PhD. Part-time programs available.
Faculty 22 full-time (3 women), 8 part-time (1 woman).
Faculty Research Algorithms and theory, artificial intelligence, parallel and distributed systems, software systems and interfaces. *Total annual research expenditures:* $1.144 million.
Students 55 full-time (11 women), 33 part-time (5 women); includes 8 minority (3 African-Americans, 4 Asian-Americans, 1 Hispanic), 39 international.
Degrees Awarded In 1996, 21 master's, 3 doctorates awarded. Terminal master's awarded for partial completion of doctoral program.
Entrance Requirements GRE General Test, TOEFL.
Degree Requirements For master's, computer language, thesis or alternative required, foreign language not required; for doctorate, computer language, dissertation, comprehensive and preliminary exams required, foreign language not required.
Financial Aid In 1996–97, 4 fellowships (1 to a first-year student) averaging $1,406 per month, 23 research assistantships (2 to first-year students) averaging $1,040 per month, 36 teaching assistantships (15 to first-year students) averaging $1,249 per month were awarded; partial tuition waivers, Federal Work-Study, institutionally sponsored loans, and career-related internships or fieldwork also available. *Financial aid application deadline:* 2/1.
Applying 209 applicants, 25% accepted. *Deadline:* 3/1 (rolling processing; 10/1 for spring admission). *Fee:* $30 ($40 for international students).
Contact Loretta Shabatura
Graduate Secretary
412-624-8495
Fax: 412-624-8854

ELECTRICAL ENGINEERING

School of Engineering, Department of Electrical Engineering
Programs Awards MSEE, PhD. Part-time and evening/weekend programs available.
Faculty 20 full-time (2 women), 1 part-time (0 women).

Faculty Research Computer engineering, image processing/computer vision, signal processing/communications, power engineering. *Total annual research expenditures:* $601,997.
Students 72 full-time (11 women), 54 part-time (3 women); includes 13 minority (4 African-Americans, 8 Asian-Americans, 1 Hispanic), 66 international.
Degrees Awarded In 1996, 32 master's, 11 doctorates awarded. Terminal master's awarded for partial completion of doctoral program.
Entrance Requirements For master's, GRE General Test, TOEFL (minimum score 550), minimum QPA of 3.0; for doctorate, GRE General Test, TOEFL (minimum score 550), minimum QPA of 3.3.
Degree Requirements For master's, computer language, comprehensive and oral exams required, thesis optional, foreign language not required; for doctorate, computer language, dissertation, comprehensive, final oral, and preliminary exams required, foreign language not required.
Financial Aid In 1996–97, 42 students received aid, including 3 fellowships averaging $1,428 per month, 17 research assistantships (2 to first-year students) averaging $1,249 per month, 14 teaching assistantships (2 to first-year students) averaging $1,274 per month; Federal Work-Study, institutionally sponsored loans also available. *Financial aid application deadline:* 2/15.
Applying 362 applicants, 77% accepted. *Deadline:* 8/1 (rolling processing; 12/1 for spring admission). *Fee:* $30 ($40 for international students).
Contact Luis F. Chaparro
Graduate Program Coordinator
412-624-9665
Fax: 412-624-8003
E-mail: chaparro@ee.pitt.edu

See in-depth description on page **701.**

INFORMATION SCIENCE

Faculty of Arts and Sciences, Program in Intelligent Systems
Programs Awards MS, PhD.
Faculty Research Medical artificial intelligence, expert systems, computer-assisted instruction, natural language processing, knowledge.
Students 21 full-time (7 women), 2 part-time (0 women); includes 1 minority (Hispanic), 12 international.
Degrees Awarded In 1996, 4 master's, 2 doctorates awarded. Terminal master's awarded for partial completion of doctoral program.
Entrance Requirements For master's, GRE General Test, TOEFL (average 640); for doctorate, GRE General Test, TOEFL.
Degree Requirements For master's, computer language required, foreign language and thesis not required; for doctorate, computer language, dissertation required, foreign language not required.
Financial Aid In 1996–97, 4 assistantships, scholarships (3 to first-year students) totaling $36,800 were awarded; Federal Work-Study, institutionally sponsored loans also available. *Financial aid application deadline:* 2/1.
Applying 38 applicants, 29% accepted. *Deadline:* 2/1 (priority date; rolling processing). *Fee:* $30 ($40 for international students).
Contact Stefni Agin
Secretary
412-624-5755
Fax: 412-624-6089
E-mail: stefni@pogo.isp.pitt.edu

INFORMATION SCIENCE

School of Information Sciences, Department of Information Science and Telecommunications, Program in Information Science
Programs Awards MSIS, PhD, Certificate, MSIS/MPA, MSIS/MPIA, MSIS/MURP. Part-time and evening/weekend programs available.
Faculty 13 full-time (1 woman), 2 part-time (0 women).
Faculty Research Visualization, information storage and retrieval, systems analysis and design, telecommunications and networking, cognitive science. *Total annual research expenditures:* $156,348.
Students 94 full-time (31 women), 122 part-time (54 women); includes 14 minority (3 African-Americans, 9 Asian-Americans, 2 Hispanics), 51 international.
Degrees Awarded In 1996, 53 master's, 2 doctorates awarded.
Entrance Requirements For master's, GRE General Test (combined average 1625 on three sections), minimum QPA 0f 3.0; previous course work in cognitive science, mathematics, and statistics; for doctorate, GRE General Test (combined average 1810 on three sections), master's degree; minimum QPA of 3.0; previous course work in cognitive science, mathematics, and statistics.
Degree Requirements For master's and doctorate, computer language, thesis/dissertation required, foreign language not required.
Financial Aid In 1996–97, 3 fellowships averaging $1,167 per month, 16 research assistantships (2 to first-year students) averaging $1,217 per month and totaling $169,360, 5 teaching assistantships averaging $1,300 per month and totaling $62,700, 17 assistantships (5 to first-year students) averaging $780 per month were awarded; full and partial tuition waivers, Federal Work-Study, institutionally sponsored loans, and career-related internships or fieldwork also available. *Financial aid application deadline:* 1/15; applicants required to submit FAFSA.
Applying 133 applicants, 76% accepted. *Deadline:* 7/1 (priority date; rolling processing; 11/1 for spring admission). *Fee:* $30 ($40 for international students).
Contact *Ninette Kay*
Admissions Coordinator
412-624-5146
Fax: 412-624-5231
E-mail: nk@sis.pitt.edu

See in-depth description on page **703.**

MEDICAL INFORMATICS

School of Health and Rehabilitation Sciences, Interdisciplinary Program in Health and Rehabilitation Sciences
Programs Offerings include health information systems (MS).
Entrance Requirements GRE General Test, TOEFL.
Degree Requirements Comprehensive exam required, foreign language and thesis not required.
Applying *Deadline:* 6/1 (rolling processing). *Fee:* $30 ($40 for international students).
Contact *Shameem Gangjee*
Director of Admissions
412-647-1252
Fax: 412-647-1255
E-mail: shameem@shrs.upmc.edu

UNIVERSITY OF SCRANTON
Scranton, PA 18510-4622

OVERVIEW

University of Scranton is an independent-religious coed comprehensive institution.

ENROLLMENT

4,931 graduate, professional, and undergraduate students; 165 full-time matriculated graduate/professional students (97 women), 493 part-time matriculated graduate/professional students (293 women).

GRADUATE FACULTY

137 full-time (46 women), 41 part-time (17 women).

EXPENSES

Tuition $439 per credit. Fees $25 per semester.

HOUSING

On-campus housing not available.

STUDENT SERVICES

Career counseling, free psychological counseling, campus employment opportunities, international student services.

FACILITIES

Library: Harry and Jeanette Weinberg Memorial Library; total holdings of 356,713 volumes, 324,620 microforms, 2,124 current periodical subscriptions. A total of 80 personal computers in all libraries. Access provided to on-line information retrieval services. *Computer:* Campuswide network is available with full Internet access. Total number of PCs/terminals supplied for student use: 300. Computer service fees are included with tuition and fees. *Special:* In arts and humanities: Center for Eastern Christian Studies, Ethics Center. In science and engineering: CAD/CAM Center, Joseph M. McDade Center for Technology and Applied Research, Institute for Molecular Biology. In social sciences: Center for Economic Education, Small Business Development Center.

SOFTWARE ENGINEERING

Program in Software Engineering
Programs Awards MS. Part-time and evening/weekend programs available.
Faculty 8 full-time (0 women).
Faculty Research Database, parallel and distributed systems, computer network, real-time systems.
Students 11 full-time (7 women), 18 part-time (9 women); includes 3 minority (2 Asian-Americans, 1 Hispanic), 7 international. Average age 30.
Degrees Awarded In 1996, 6 degrees awarded.
Entrance Requirements GMAT or GRE, TOEFL (minimum score 550), minimum GPA of 3.0.
Degree Requirements Computer language, thesis required, foreign language not required.
Financial Aid In 1996–97, 7 students received aid, including 1 teaching assistantship averaging $633 per month and totaling $5,700, 6 teaching fellowships (1 to a first-year student) averaging $844 per month and totaling $53,199; Federal Work-Study and career-related internships or fieldwork also available. Aid available to part-time students. *Financial aid application deadline:* 3/1.
Applying 15 applicants, 93% accepted. *Deadline:* 3/1 (priority date). *Fee:* $35.
Contact *Dr. Yaodong Bi*
Director
717-941-6108
Fax: 717-941-4250
E-mail: bi@cs.uofs.edu

VILLANOVA UNIVERSITY
Villanova, PA 19085-1699

OVERVIEW
Villanova University is an independent-religious coed comprehensive institution.

ENROLLMENT
10,141 graduate, professional, and undergraduate students; 1,105 full-time matriculated graduate/professional students (518 women), 1,841 part-time matriculated graduate/professional students (814 women).

EXPENSES
Tuition $385 per credit. Fees $60 per year.

HOUSING
On-campus housing not available.

STUDENT SERVICES
Multicultural affairs office, low-cost health insurance, career counseling, free psychological counseling, international student services.

FACILITIES
Library: Falvey Memorial Library plus 2 additional on-campus libraries. Access provided to on-line information retrieval services. *Computer:* Campuswide network is available with full Internet access.

COMPUTER ENGINEERING

College of Engineering, Department of Electrical and Computer Engineering, Program in Computer Engineering
Programs Awards MSCE. Part-time and evening/weekend programs available.
Faculty 3 full-time (0 women), 4 part-time (0 women).
Faculty Research Expert systems, computer vision, neural networks, image processing, computer architectures.
Students 7 full-time (2 women), 25 part-time (2 women); includes 1 minority (African-American), 7 international. Average age 27.
Degrees Awarded In 1996, 20 degrees awarded (100% found work related to degree).
Entrance Requirements GRE General Test (for applicants with degrees from foreign universities), BEE, minimum GPA of 3.0.
Degree Requirements Thesis optional, foreign language not required.
Financial Aid In 1996–97, 10 students received aid, including 1 research assistantship, 6 teaching assistantships (3 to first-year students), 4 tuition scholarships (all to first-year students). *Financial aid application deadline: 3/15.*
Applying 44 applicants, 55% accepted. *Deadline:* 8/1 (priority date; rolling processing; 12/1 for spring admission). *Fee:* $40.
Contact Dr. S. S. Rao
　　　　　Chairman
　　　　　610-519-4971
　　　　　Fax: 610-519-4436

See in-depth description on page 751.

COMPUTER SCIENCE

Graduate School of Liberal Arts and Sciences, Department of Computing Sciences
Programs Awards MS. Part-time and evening/weekend programs available.

Students 45 full-time (17 women), 111 part-time (27 women); includes 60 minority (5 African-Americans, 54 Asian-Americans, 1 Hispanic), 59 international. Average age 31.
Degrees Awarded In 1996, 71 degrees awarded.
Entrance Requirements Minimum GPA of 3.0.
Degree Requirements Computer language, independent study project required, thesis optional, foreign language not required.
Financial Aid Research assistantships, scholarships, Federal Work-Study available. *Financial aid application deadline: 4/1.*
Applying 112 applicants, 78% accepted. *Deadline:* 8/1 (priority date; 12/1 for spring admission). *Fee:* $25.
Contact Dr. Don Goelman
　　　　　Director
　　　　　610-519-7310

ELECTRICAL ENGINEERING

College of Engineering, Department of Electrical and Computer Engineering, Program in Electrical Engineering
Programs Awards MSEE. Part-time and evening/weekend programs available.
Students 21 full-time (5 women), 21 part-time (2 women); includes 1 minority (Hispanic), 28 international.
Degrees Awarded In 1996, 18 degrees awarded (100% found work related to degree).
Entrance Requirements GRE General Test (for applicants with degrees from foreign universities), BEE, minimum GPA of 3.0.
Degree Requirements Thesis optional, foreign language not required.
Financial Aid Research assistantships, teaching assistantships, tuition scholarships, Federal Work-Study available. *Financial aid application deadline: 3/15.*
Applying 106 applicants, 77% accepted. *Deadline:* 8/1 (priority date; rolling processing; 12/1 for spring admission). *Fee:* $40.
Contact Dr. S. S. Rao
　　　　　Chairman
　　　　　610-519-4971
　　　　　Fax: 610-519-4436

See in-depth description on page 751.

WEST CHESTER UNIVERSITY OF PENNSYLVANIA
West Chester, PA 19383

OVERVIEW
West Chester University of Pennsylvania is a public coed comprehensive institution.

ENROLLMENT
15,168 graduate, professional, and undergraduate students; 357 full-time matriculated graduate/professional students (226 women), 1,556 part-time matriculated graduate/professional students (1,091 women).

EXPENSES
Tuition $3368 per year full-time, $187 per credit part-time for state residents; $6054 per year full-time, $336 per credit part-time for nonresidents. Fees $546 per year full-time, $31 per credit part-time.

HOUSING
Rooms and/or apartments available to single students (38 units) at an average cost of $4500 (including board);

on-campus housing not available to married students. Graduate housing contact: Pete Galloway, 610-436-3307.

STUDENT SERVICES
Low-cost health insurance, career counseling, free psychological counseling, day-care facilities, campus safety program, campus employment opportunities, international student services.

FACILITIES
Library: Francis Harvey Green Library plus 1 additional on-campus library; total holdings of 510,349 volumes, 1,033,227 microforms, 3,026 current periodical subscriptions. A total of 72 personal computers in all libraries. Access provided to on-line information retrieval services. *Computer:* Campuswide network is available with full Internet access. *Special:* In arts and humanities: IGA Art Gallery, Center for Music Technology. In science and engineering: Schmucker Science Center, Darlington Herbarium, Robert B. Gordon Natural Area for Environmental Studies, speech and hearing clinic. In social sciences: Psychology laboratory.

COMPUTER SCIENCE

College of Arts and Sciences, Department of Computer Science
Programs   Awards MS.
Entrance Requirements   GRE General Test, interview.
Degree Requirements   Comprehensive exam required, foreign language and thesis not required.
Financial Aid   Research assistantships available. Aid available to part-time students. *Financial aid application deadline:* 2/15.
Applying   *Deadline:* 4/15 (priority date; 10/15 for spring admission). *Fee:* $25.
Contact   Dr. Elaine Milito
Graduate Coordinator
610-436-2590

WIDENER UNIVERSITY
Chester, PA 19013-5792

OVERVIEW
Widener University is an independent coed comprehensive institution.

ENROLLMENT
8,517 graduate, professional, and undergraduate students; 1,880 full-time, 2,525 part-time matriculated graduate/professional students.

GRADUATE FACULTY
242 full-time, 338 part-time.

TUITION
$445 per credit.

HOUSING
Rooms and/or apartments available to single students (46 units) at an average cost of $4170 per year; available to married students (46 units) at an average cost of $6690 per year. Housing application deadline: 5/30. Graduate housing contact: Simone Calvin, 610-499-4390.

STUDENT SERVICES
Career counseling, free psychological counseling, day-care facilities, campus employment opportunities, international student services.

FACILITIES
Library: Wolfgram Library plus 1 additional on-campus library; total holdings of 728,600 volumes. Access provided to on-line information retrieval services. *Special:* In arts and humanities: Art museum, Child Development Center, Curriculum Material Center, curriculum laboratory. In science and engineering: Prime-Medusa Computer-Aided Design Laboratory, Center for Computer-Assisted Instruction, Engineering Research Center. In social sciences: Business Research Center, social science research laboratory.

COMPUTER ENGINEERING

School of Engineering, Program in Computer, Software, and Telecommunication Engineering
Programs   Awards ME, ME/MBA. Part-time and evening/weekend programs available.
Students   18 full-time (2 women), 29 part-time (6 women); includes 5 minority (2 African-Americans, 2 Asian-Americans, 1 Hispanic), 21 international.
Degrees Awarded   In 1996, 11 degrees awarded.
Entrance Requirements   GMAT (ME/MBA).
Degree Requirements   Thesis optional, foreign language not required.
Financial Aid   Graduate assistantships available. *Financial aid application deadline:* 3/15.
Applying   41 applicants, 88% accepted. *Deadline:* 8/1 (priority date; rolling processing; 12/1 for spring admission). *Fee:* $25.
Contact   Dr. D. H. T. Chen
Assistant Dean for Graduate Programs
610-499-4049

ELECTRICAL ENGINEERING

School of Engineering, Program in Electrical Engineering
Programs   Awards ME, ME/MBA. Part-time and evening/weekend programs available.
Students   4 full-time (0 women), 5 part-time (0 women); includes 2 minority (1 African-American, 1 Asian-American), 3 international.
Degrees Awarded   In 1996, 5 degrees awarded.
Entrance Requirements   GMAT (ME/MBA).
Degree Requirements   Thesis optional, foreign language not required.
Financial Aid   Graduate assistantships available. *Financial aid application deadline:* 3/15.
Applying   5 applicants, 80% accepted. *Deadline:* 8/1 (priority date; rolling processing; 12/1 for spring admission). *Fee:* $25.
Contact   Dr. D. H. T. Chen
Assistant Dean for Graduate Programs
610-499-4049

SOFTWARE ENGINEERING

School of Engineering, Program in Computer, Software, and Telecommunication Engineering
Programs   Awards ME, ME/MBA. Part-time and evening/weekend programs available.
Students   18 full-time (2 women), 29 part-time (6 women); includes 5 minority (2 African-Americans, 2 Asian-Americans, 1 Hispanic), 21 international.
Degrees Awarded   In 1996, 11 degrees awarded.

Entrance Requirements GMAT (ME/MBA).
Degree Requirements Thesis optional, foreign language not required.
Financial Aid Graduate assistantships available. *Financial aid application deadline: 3/15.*
Applying 41 applicants, 88% accepted. *Deadline:* 8/1 (priority date; rolling processing; 12/1 for spring admission). *Fee:* $25.
Contact *Dr. D. H. T. Chen*
Assistant Dean for Graduate Programs
610-499-4049

WILKES UNIVERSITY
Wilkes-Barre, PA 18766-0002

OVERVIEW
Wilkes University is an independent coed comprehensive institution.

ENROLLMENT
2,473 graduate, professional, and undergraduate students; 96 full-time matriculated graduate/professional students (60 women), 185 part-time matriculated graduate/ professional students (86 women).

GRADUATE FACULTY
56 full-time, 11 part-time; includes 5 minority (all Asian-Americans).

EXPENSES
Tuition $12,072 per year full-time, $503 per credit hour part-time. Fees $240 per year full-time, $10 per credit hour (minimum) part-time.

HOUSING
On-campus housing not available.

STUDENT SERVICES
Low-cost health insurance, career counseling.

FACILITIES
Library: E. S. Farley Library plus 1 additional on-campus library; total holdings of 209,000 volumes, 623,000 microforms, 1,154 current periodical subscriptions. A total of 45 personal computers in all libraries. Access provided to on-line information retrieval services.

ELECTRICAL ENGINEERING

School of Science and Engineering
Programs Offers program in electrical engineering (MSEE).
Faculty 7 full-time.
Students 5 full-time (0 women), 10 part-time (1 woman); includes 6 minority (all Asian-Americans).
Entrance Requirements GRE General Test.
Financial Aid *Application deadline: 2/28;* applicants required to submit FAFSA.
Applying *Deadline:* rolling. *Fee:* $30.
Contact *Dr. Umid Nejib*
Dean
717-831-4800

RHODE ISLAND

BROWN UNIVERSITY
Providence, RI 02912

OVERVIEW
Brown University is an independent coed university.

EXPENSES
Tuition $22,592 per year. Fees $426 per year.

HOUSING
Rooms and/or apartments available to single students; on-campus housing not available to married students. Graduate housing contact: William Silvia, 401-863-2253.

FACILITIES
Library: John D. Rockefeller Library plus 3 additional on-campus libraries. *Special:* In science and engineering: Biomedical Center, Computer Center, Geological Sciences/Chemistry Research Building, materials research laboratory. In social sciences: Haffenreffer Museum of Anthropology, Population Studies and Training Center.

COMPUTER SCIENCE

Department of Computer Science
Programs Awards Sc M, PhD.
Entrance Requirements GRE General Test, GRE Subject Test.
Degree Requirements For master's, thesis or alternative required, foreign language not required; for doctorate, 1 foreign language, dissertation, comprehensive exam.
Applying *Deadline:* 1/1.

See in-depth description on page 381.

ELECTRICAL ENGINEERING

Division of Engineering, Program in Electrical Sciences
Programs Awards Sc M, PhD.
Degree Requirements For doctorate, dissertation, preliminary exam required, foreign language not required.
Applying *Deadline:* 1/2.

SALVE REGINA UNIVERSITY
Newport, RI 02840-4192

OVERVIEW
Salve Regina University is an independent-religious coed comprehensive institution.

ENROLLMENT
2,036 graduate, professional, and undergraduate students; 58 full-time matriculated graduate/professional students (39 women), 515 part-time matriculated graduate/ professional students (260 women).

GRADUATE FACULTY
14 full-time (5 women), 41 part-time (16 women), 26.25 FTE; includes 1 minority (Asian-American).

EXPENSES
Tuition $275 per credit hour. Fees $70 per year.

HOUSING
On-campus housing not available.

STUDENT SERVICES
Career counseling, free psychological counseling.

FACILITIES
Library: McKillop Library; total holdings of 107,280 volumes, 20,600 microforms, 891 current periodical subscriptions. A total of 21 personal computers in all libraries. Access provided to on-line information retrieval services. *Computer:* Campuswide network is available with full Internet access. Total number of PCs/terminals supplied for student use: 110. Computer service fees are applied as a separate charge.

SYSTEMS SCIENCE

Program in Information Systems Science
Programs Awards MS. Part-time and evening/weekend programs available.
Faculty 1 full-time (0 women), 2 part-time (0 women), 1.75 FTE.
Students 5 full-time (2 women), 27 part-time (9 women); includes 3 minority (1 African-American, 2 Asian-Americans), 1 international. Average age 31.
Degrees Awarded In 1996, 7 degrees awarded.
Entrance Requirements GMAT, GRE General Test, or MAT.
Financial Aid Federal Work-Study and career-related internships or fieldwork available. Aid available to part-time students. *Financial aid application deadline: 3/1.*
Applying 9 applicants, 78% accepted. *Deadline:* rolling. *Fee:* $35.
Contact *Laura E. McPhie*
Dean of Enrollment Services
401-847-6650 Ext. 2908
Fax: 401-848-2823

UNIVERSITY OF RHODE ISLAND
Kingston, RI 02881

OVERVIEW
University of Rhode Island is a public coed university.

ENROLLMENT
13,261 graduate, professional, and undergraduate students; 2,021 full-time matriculated graduate/professional students (1,104 women), 1,104 part-time matriculated graduate/professional students (604 women).

GRADUATE FACULTY
813 (241 women); includes 75 minority (13 African-Americans, 50 Asian-Americans, 10 Hispanics, 2 Native Americans).

EXPENSES
Tuition $3362 per year for state residents; $9380 per year for nonresidents. Fees $1210 per year.

HOUSING
Rooms and/or apartments available to married students (142 units) at an average cost of $4500 per year; on-campus housing not available to single students. Housing application deadline: 8/1. Graduate housing contact: Residential Life Office, 401-874-2935.

STUDENT SERVICES
Low-cost health insurance, career counseling, campus safety program, campus employment opportunities, international student services.

FACILITIES
Library: Main library plus 2 additional on-campus libraries; total holdings of 935,800 volumes, 1,112,117 microforms, 7,150 current periodical subscriptions. Access provided to on-line information retrieval services. *Special:* In arts and humanities: Labor Research Center. In science and engineering: Biotechnology Center, Center for Ocean Management Studies, Center for Energy Studies, International Center for Marine Resource Development, Robotics Research Center, R/V *Edson Shock*, R/V *Endeavor*, R/V *Laurie Lee*, agricultural experiment station, information science laboratory, Coastal Research Center. In social sciences: Research Center in Business and Economics, Bureau of Government Research, Institute of Human Science and Services, Child Development Center, Marriage and Family Center.

COMPUTER ENGINEERING

College of Engineering, Department of Electrical and Computer Engineering
Programs Awards MS, PhD. Part-time programs available.
Faculty 22 full-time, 2 part-time.
Faculty Research Digital signal processing, computer engineering, VLSI, fiber optics and materials, communication and control systems, biomedical engineering.
Students 75 full-time (10 women), 45 part-time (5 women); includes 49 international.
Degrees Awarded In 1996, 18 master's, 6 doctorates awarded.
Entrance Requirements GRE General Test, TOEFL.
Degree Requirements For master's, thesis or alternative; for doctorate, dissertation, comprehensive exam.
Financial Aid 33 students received aid.
Applying 225 applicants, 67% accepted. *Deadline:* 4/15 (rolling processing). *Fee:* $25.
Contact *Director of Graduate Studies*
401-874-2506

COMPUTER SCIENCE

College of Arts and Sciences, Department of Computer Science and Statistics
Programs Awards MS, PhD.
Faculty 19 (1 woman).
Students 30 full-time (7 women), 31 part-time (10 women); includes 1 minority (Asian-American), 9 international.
Degrees Awarded In 1996, 17 master's awarded.
Entrance Requirements For master's, GRE Subject Test.
Degree Requirements For master's, thesis optional; for doctorate, 1 foreign language, dissertation.
Financial Aid Assistantships available.
Applying *Deadline:* 4/15 (priority date; rolling processing). *Fee:* $35.
Contact *Dr. Edward Lamagna*
Chair
401-874-2701

ELECTRICAL ENGINEERING

College of Engineering, Department of Electrical and Computer Engineering
Programs Awards MS, PhD. Part-time programs available.
Faculty 22 full-time, 2 part-time.

Faculty Research Digital signal processing, computer engineering, VLSI, fiber optics and materials, communication and control systems, biomedical engineering.
Students 75 full-time (10 women), 45 part-time (5 women); includes 49 international.
Degrees Awarded In 1996, 18 master's, 6 doctorates awarded.
Entrance Requirements GRE General Test, TOEFL.
Degree Requirements For master's, thesis or alternative; for doctorate, dissertation, comprehensive exam.
Financial Aid 33 students received aid.
Applying 225 applicants, 67% accepted. *Deadline:* 4/15 (rolling processing). *Fee:* $25.
Contact *Director of Graduate Studies*
401-874-2506

SOUTH CAROLINA

CLEMSON UNIVERSITY
Clemson, SC 29634

OVERVIEW
Clemson University is a public coed university.

ENROLLMENT
15,097 graduate, professional, and undergraduate students; 1,855 full-time matriculated graduate/professional students (710 women), 2,017 part-time matriculated graduate/professional students (1,239 women).

GRADUATE FACULTY
794 full-time (130 women), 61 part-time (25 women), 819.2 FTE; includes 72 minority (24 African-Americans, 45 Asian-Americans, 3 Hispanics).

EXPENSES
Tuition $3062 per year full-time, $126 per credit hour part-time for state residents; $6144 per year full-time, $252 per credit hour part-time for nonresidents. Fees $190 per year.

HOUSING
Rooms and/or apartments available to single students (160 units) at an average cost of $3780 per year ($5678 including board); available to married students (110 units) at an average cost of $3780 per year. Housing application deadline: 1/30. Graduate housing contact: Verna Howell, 864-656-2295.

STUDENT SERVICES
Disabled student services, low-cost health insurance, career counseling, free psychological counseling, exercise/wellness program, campus safety program, international student services.

FACILITIES
Library: Robert Muldrow Cooper Library plus 4 additional on-campus libraries; total holdings of 1,533,971 volumes, 1,052,414 microforms, 11,574 current periodical subscriptions. A total of 100 personal computers in all libraries. Access provided to on-line information retrieval services. *Computer:* Campuswide network is available with full Internet access. Total number of PCs/terminals supplied for student use: 1,700. Computer service fees are included with tuition and fees. *Special:* In arts and

humanities: Brooks Center for the Performing Arts, Daniel Center, Lee Hall Art Gallery, Pearce Center for Professional Communications. In science and engineering: Apparel Research Center, Archibold Center for Tropical Studies, Center for Advanced Manufacturing, Center for Engineering Ceramic Manufacturing, Emerging Technology Center, Energy Research and Development Center. In social sciences: Center for Excellence in Mathematics and Science Education; National Dropout Prevention Center; Nursing Center; Recreation, Travel and Tourism Institute; Small Business Development Center; Spiro Center for Entrepreneurial Leadership; Thurmond Institute.

COMPUTER ENGINEERING

College of Engineering and Science, Department of Electrical and Computer Engineering, Program in Computer Engineering
Programs Awards MS, PhD.
Faculty Research Interface applications, software development, multisystem communications, artificial intelligence, robotics.
Students 28 full-time (3 women), 6 part-time (0 women); includes 3 minority (2 African-Americans, 1 Hispanic), 16 international.
Degrees Awarded In 1996, 13 master's awarded.
Entrance Requirements GRE General Test, TOEFL.
Degree Requirements For master's, thesis or alternative required, foreign language not required; for doctorate, dissertation, departmental qualifying exam required, foreign language not required.
Financial Aid Fellowships, research assistantships, teaching assistantships, and career-related internships or fieldwork available.
Applying 75 applicants, 40% accepted. *Deadline:* 6/1. *Fee:* $35.
Contact *Dr. David Lubkeman*
Graduate Coordinator
864-656-5932
Fax: 864-656-5910

See in-depth description on page **401.**

COMPUTER SCIENCE

College of Engineering and Science, Department of Computer Science
Programs Awards MS, PhD.
Faculty Research Parallel computation, performance modeling, operating systems, software engineering, design and analysis of algorithms. *Total annual research expenditures:* $537,017.
Students 91 full-time (16 women), 16 part-time (3 women); includes 3 minority (2 African-Americans, 1 Hispanic), 50 international.
Degrees Awarded In 1996, 23 master's, 4 doctorates awarded. Terminal master's awarded for partial completion of doctoral program.
Entrance Requirements GRE General Test, TOEFL.
Degree Requirements For master's, thesis optional, foreign language not required; for doctorate, dissertation required, foreign language not required.
Financial Aid Fellowships, research assistantships, teaching assistantships, institutionally sponsored loans available. *Financial aid application deadline:* 3/1.
Applying 201 applicants, 67% accepted. *Deadline:* 5/1 (rolling processing; 10/1 for spring admission). *Fee:* $35.
Contact *Dr. James Westall*
Graduate Coordinator
864-656-3444
Fax: 864-656-0145
E-mail: westall@clemson.edu

See in-depth description on page **399.**

ELECTRICAL ENGINEERING

College of Engineering and Science, Department of Electrical and Computer Engineering, Program in Electrical Engineering
Programs Awards M Engr, MS, PhD.
Faculty Research Microelectronics, robotics, signal processing/communications, power systems, control.
Students 90 full-time (13 women), 22 part-time (3 women); includes 7 minority (6 African-Americans, 1 Asian-American), 61 international.
Degrees Awarded In 1996, 42 master's, 10 doctorates awarded.
Entrance Requirements For master's, GRE General Test (MS), TOEFL; for doctorate, GRE General Test, TOEFL.
Degree Requirements For master's, thesis or alternative required, foreign language not required; for doctorate, dissertation, departmental qualifying exam required, foreign language not required.
Financial Aid Fellowships, research assistantships, teaching assistantships, and career-related internships or fieldwork available.
Applying 261 applicants, 35% accepted. *Deadline: 6/1. Fee: $35.*
Contact Dr. David Lubkeman
Graduate Coordinator
864-656-5932
Fax: 864-656-5910

See in-depth description on page 401.

MEDICAL UNIVERSITY OF SOUTH CAROLINA
Charleston, SC 29425-0002

OVERVIEW
Medical University of South Carolina is a public coed upper-level institution.

ENROLLMENT
2,265 graduate, professional, and undergraduate students; 1,207 full-time, 213 part-time matriculated graduate/professional students.

GRADUATE FACULTY
725.

EXPENSES
Tuition $3100 per year (minimum) full-time, $150 per semester hour (minimum) part-time for state residents; $4000 per semester hour (minimum) full-time, $200 per semester hour (minimum) part-time for nonresidents. Fees $290 per year (minimum).

HOUSING
On-campus housing not available.

STUDENT SERVICES
Low-cost health insurance, free psychological counseling, campus safety program, campus employment opportunities, international student services.

FACILITIES
Library: Health Affairs Library plus 1 additional on-campus library; total holdings of 212,502 volumes, 3,087 microforms, 2,480 current periodical subscriptions. A total of 50 personal computers in all libraries. Access provided to on-line information retrieval services. *Computer:* Campuswide network is available with full Internet access. Computer service fees are included with tuition

and fees. *Special:* In arts and humanities: Waring Historical Library, McCauley Dental Museum.

MEDICAL INFORMATICS

College of Health Professions, Department of Health Administration and Policy, Program in Health Information Administration
Programs Awards MHS, MHA/MHS.
Faculty 10 full-time (4 women), 2 part-time (1 woman).
Degrees Awarded In 1996, 2 degrees awarded (100% found work related to degree).
Entrance Requirements GRE General Test (minimum combined score of 1500 on three sections), GMAT (minimum score 500), TOEFL (minimum score 500), interview, minimum GPA of 3.0.
Financial Aid Fellowships, research assistantships available. *Financial aid application deadline: 3/1.*
Applying *Fee: $55.*
Contact Kelly Long
Student Services Coordinator
803-792-2118
Fax: 803-792-3327

UNIVERSITY OF SOUTH CAROLINA
Columbia, SC 29208

OVERVIEW
University of South Carolina is a public coed university.

ENROLLMENT
25,489 graduate, professional, and undergraduate students; 4,671 full-time matriculated graduate/professional students (2,465 women), 4,208 part-time matriculated graduate/professional students (3,142 women).

GRADUATE FACULTY
1,407 (421 women); includes 91 minority (55 African-Americans, 26 Asian-Americans, 10 Hispanics).

TUITION
$3724 per year full-time, $185 per credit hour part-time for state residents; $7634 per year full-time, $380 per credit hour part-time for nonresidents.

HOUSING
Rooms and/or apartments available to single students (319 units) at an average cost of $4700 per year; available to married students (334 units) at an average cost of $3860 per year. Graduate housing contact: Allen Shealy, 803-777-4571.

STUDENT SERVICES
Low-cost health insurance, career counseling, free psychological counseling, day-care facilities, campus employment opportunities, international student services.

FACILITIES
Library: Thomas Cooper Library plus 6 additional on-campus libraries; total holdings of 2,714,060 volumes, 4,186,737 microforms, 17,940 current periodical subscriptions. A total of 289 personal computers in all libraries. Access provided to on-line information retrieval services. *Computer:* Campuswide network is available with full Internet access. Computer service fees are included with tuition and fees. *Special:* In arts and humanities: Center for the Study of Suicide and Life

Threatening Behavior, McKissick Museum, National Center for the Study of the Freshman Year Experience. In science and engineering: Belle W. Baruch Institute for Marine Biology and Coastal Research, Center for Economic Education, Center for Fracture Mechanics and Nondestructive Evaluation, Center for Industrial Research, Center for Industry Policy and Strategy, Center for Machine Intelligence, Center for Science Education, Earth Sciences and Resources Institute, Electron Microscopy Center, International Center for Public Health Research, Nuclear Magnetic Resonance Facility. In social sciences: Center for Developmental Disabilities, Counseling and Human Development Centers, Institute for Families in Society.

COMPUTER ENGINEERING

Graduate School, College of Engineering, Department of Electrical and Computer Engineering, Program in Computer Engineering
Programs Awards ME, MS, PhD.
Students 24 full-time (3 women), 7 part-time (3 women); includes 3 minority (1 African-American, 2 Asian-Americans), 20 international.
Degrees Awarded In 1996, 28 master's awarded.
Entrance Requirements GRE General Test (minimum combined score of 1100), TOEFL (minimum score 550).
Degree Requirements For master's, thesis or alternative required, foreign language not required; for doctorate, dissertation required, foreign language not required.
Financial Aid Career-related internships or fieldwork available.
Applying *Deadline:* 3/1 (priority date; rolling processing; 11/1 for spring admission). *Fee:* $35.
Contact *Leck Mason*
  Graduate Administration
  803-777-7522

COMPUTER SCIENCE

Graduate School, College of Science and Mathematics, Department of Computer Science
Programs Awards MS, PhD.
Faculty 12 full-time (1 woman).
Faculty Research Computer vision, pattern recognition, artificial intelligence, database management.
Students 71 full-time (10 women), 49 part-time (15 women); includes 8 minority (5 African-Americans, 3 Asian-Americans), 68 international.
Degrees Awarded In 1996, 23 master's awarded.
Entrance Requirements GRE General Test.
Degree Requirements Thesis/dissertation required, foreign language not required.
Financial Aid In 1996–97, 2 fellowships (1 to a first-year student), 6 research assistantships (2 to first-year students), 32 teaching assistantships (9 to first-year students) were awarded; Federal Work–Study also available. *Financial aid application deadline:* 3/1.
Applying 157 applicants, 58% accepted. *Deadline:* 3/1 (priority date; rolling processing). *Fee:* $35.
Contact *Dr. Robert Cannon*
  Chair
  803-777-2880

See in-depth description on page **709.**

ELECTRICAL ENGINEERING

Graduate School, College of Engineering, Department of Electrical and Computer Engineering, Program in Electrical Engineering
Programs Awards ME, MS, PhD.

Students 29 full-time (5 women), 8 part-time (1 woman); includes 3 minority (1 African-American, 2 Asian-Americans), 25 international.
Degrees Awarded In 1996, 16 master's, 2 doctorates awarded.
Entrance Requirements GRE General Test (minimum combined score of 1100), TOEFL (minimum score 550).
Degree Requirements For master's, thesis or alternative required, foreign language not required; for doctorate, dissertation required, foreign language not required.
Financial Aid Fellowships and career-related internships or fieldwork available.
Applying *Deadline:* 3/1 (priority date; rolling processing; 11/1 for spring admission). *Fee:* $35.
Contact *Leck Mason*
  Graduate Administration
  803-777-7522

SOUTH DAKOTA

SOUTH DAKOTA SCHOOL OF MINES AND TECHNOLOGY
Rapid City, SD 57701-3995

OVERVIEW
South Dakota School of Mines and Technology is a public coed university.

ENROLLMENT
2,356 graduate, professional, and undergraduate students; 144 full-time matriculated graduate/professional students (30 women), 88 part-time matriculated graduate/professional students (14 women).

GRADUATE FACULTY
71 full-time (3 women), 20 part-time (0 women); includes 10 minority (9 Asian-Americans, 1 Hispanic).

EXPENSES
Tuition $82 per credit hour for state residents; $242 per credit hour for nonresidents. Fees $51 per credit hour (minimum).

HOUSING
Rooms and/or apartments available to single students at an average cost of $1650 per year ($3200 including board); on-campus housing not available to married students. Graduate housing contact: Arthur Alleger, 605-394-2348.

STUDENT SERVICES
Low-cost health insurance, career counseling, free psychological counseling, international student services.

FACILITIES
Library: Devereaux Library; total holdings of 98,690 volumes, 209,000 microforms, 919 current periodical subscriptions. A total of 15 personal computers in all libraries. Access provided to on-line information retrieval services. *Computer:* Campuswide network is available with full Internet access. Computer service fees are included with tuition and fees. *Special:* In science and engineering: Institute of Atmospheric Sciences, Museum of Geology, engineering and mining experiment station.

COMPUTER SCIENCE

Department of Mathematics and Computer Science
Programs Offers program in computer science (MS). Part-time programs available.

Faculty 6 full-time (1 woman).

Faculty Research Database systems, remote sensing, numerical modeling, artificial intelligence, neural networks.

Students 15 full-time (5 women), 7 part-time (0 women); includes 1 minority (Hispanic), 13 international. Average age 30.

Degrees Awarded In 1996, 5 degrees awarded.

Entrance Requirements TOEFL (minimum score 520), TWE.

Financial Aid In 1996–97, 2 research assistantships, 7 teaching assistantships were awarded; fellowships, Federal Work-Study, institutionally sponsored loans also available. Aid available to part-time students. *Financial aid application deadline: 5/15.*

Applying *Deadline:* 6/15 (priority date; 10/15 for spring admission). *Fee:* $15.

Contact *Lori Jensen*
Admissions Counselor
800-554-8162

ELECTRICAL ENGINEERING

Department of Electrical Engineering

Programs Awards MS. Part-time programs available.

Faculty 11 full-time (0 women), 1 part-time (0 women).

Faculty Research Semiconductors, systems, digital systems, computers, superconductivity. *Total annual research expenditures:* $49,294.

Students 14 full-time (1 woman), 7 part-time (0 women); includes 4 international. Average age 27.

Degrees Awarded In 1996, 6 degrees awarded.

Entrance Requirements GRE (for applicants from schools without ABET accreditation), TOEFL (minimum score 520), TWE.

Degree Requirements Thesis required, foreign language not required.

Financial Aid In 1996–97, 15 students received aid, including 15 teaching assistantships; fellowships, research assistantships, Federal Work-Study, institutionally sponsored loans also available. Aid available to part-time students. *Financial aid application deadline: 5/15.*

Applying *Deadline:* 6/15 (priority date; 10/15 for spring admission). *Fee:* $15.

Contact *Lori Jensen*
Admissions Counselor
800-554-8162

SOUTH DAKOTA STATE UNIVERSITY
Brookings, SD 57007

OVERVIEW

South Dakota State University is a public coed university.

ENROLLMENT

8,350 graduate, professional, and undergraduate students; 385 full-time matriculated graduate/professional students (198 women), 505 part-time matriculated graduate/professional students (273 women).

GRADUATE FACULTY

296 full-time (57 women); includes 27 minority (3 African-Americans, 20 Asian-Americans, 1 Hispanic, 3 Native Americans).

EXPENSES

Tuition $1476 per year full-time, $82 per credit hour part-time for state residents; $2016 per year (minimum) full-time, $112 per credit hour (minimum) part-time for nonresidents. Fees $37 per credit hour (minimum).

HOUSING

Rooms and/or apartments available to single students at an average cost of $1498 per year ($2664 including board); available to married students (88 units) at an average cost of $2268 per year. Graduate housing contact: Janet Peterson, 605-688-5148.

STUDENT SERVICES

Low-cost health insurance, career counseling, free psychological counseling, day-care facilities, campus employment opportunities.

FACILITIES

Library: Briggs Library; total holdings of 530,000 volumes, 770,000 microforms, 3,497 current periodical subscriptions. A total of 69 personal computers in all libraries. Access provided to on-line information retrieval services. *Computer:* Campuswide network is available with full Internet access. Total number of PCs/terminals supplied for student use: 300. Computer service fees are included with tuition and fees. *Special:* In arts and humanities: South Dakota Art Museum. In science and engineering: Northern Great Plains Water Resources Research Center, Northern Plains Biological Field Station, Oak Lake Engineering and Environmental Research Center, Water Resources Institute. In social sciences: Census Data Center.

COMPUTER SCIENCE

College of Engineering, Department of Computer Science

Programs Offers program in engineering (MS), including computer science.

Faculty 4 full-time (0 women).

Students 17 full-time (5 women), 14 part-time (5 women); includes 24 international.

Entrance Requirements TOEFL (minimum score 520).

Degree Requirements Thesis, oral exam required, foreign language not required.

Financial Aid In 1996–97, 2 research assistantships (1 to a first-year student), 5 teaching assistantships (2 to first-year students), 3 administrative assistantships (1 to a first-year student) were awarded.

Applying *Deadline:* rolling. *Fee:* $15.

Contact *Dr. Gerald Bergum*
Head
605-688-5719

ELECTRICAL ENGINEERING

College of Engineering, Department of Electrical Engineering

Programs Awards MS.

Faculty 9 full-time (1 woman).

Faculty Research Image processing, electromagnetics communications, power systems, electrical materials and sensors. *Total annual research expenditures:* $139,000.

Students 10 full-time (0 women), 8 part-time (0 women); includes 13 international.

Entrance Requirements TOEFL (minimum score 550).

Degree Requirements Thesis, oral exam required, foreign language not required.

Financial Aid In 1996–97, 9 research assistantships (5 to first-year students), 3 teaching assistantships (1 to a first-year student) were awarded.

Applying *Deadline:* rolling. *Fee:* $15.

Contact *Dr. Bob Finch*
Graduate Coordinator
605-688-4526

UNIVERSITY OF SOUTH DAKOTA
Vermillion, SD 57069-2390

OVERVIEW
University of South Dakota is a public coed university.

ENROLLMENT
7,750 graduate, professional, and undergraduate students; 1,726 matriculated graduate/professional students.

GRADUATE FACULTY
369 full-time, 309 part-time; includes 18 minority (1 African-American, 11 Asian-Americans, 2 Hispanics, 4 Native Americans).

EXPENSES
Tuition $1476 per year full-time, $82 per credit hour part-time for state residents; $4356 per year full-time, $242 per credit hour part-time for nonresidents. Fees $723 per year full-time, $40 per credit hour (minimum) part-time.

HOUSING
Rooms and/or apartments available to single students (100 units) at an average cost of $1624 per year; available to married students (80 units) at an average cost of $1718 per year. Graduate housing contact: Irma Burback, 605-677-5663.

STUDENT SERVICES
Career counseling, free psychological counseling, day-care facilities, international student services.

FACILITIES
Library: I. D. Weeks Library plus 2 additional on-campus libraries; total holdings of 667,110 volumes, 645,989 microforms, 8,147 current periodical subscriptions. A total of 138 personal computers in all libraries. Access provided to on-line information retrieval services. *Computer:* Campuswide network is available with full Internet access. *Special:* In arts and humanities: Shrine to Music Museum, Historical Preservation Center, Institute of American Indian Studies, Oral History Center. In science and engineering: South Dakota Geological Society, W. H. Over Museum, natural sciences field station. In social sciences: Governmental Research Bureau, Business Research Bureau.

COMPUTER SCIENCE

College of Arts and Sciences, Department of Computer Science
Programs Awards MA.
Faculty 5 full-time (0 women), 1 part-time (0 women).
Students 11 full-time (3 women), 3 part-time (1 woman); includes 4 international.
Degrees Awarded In 1996, 6 degrees awarded.
Entrance Requirements GRE General Test.
Degree Requirements Computer language, thesis required, foreign language not required.
Financial Aid Teaching assistantships available. Aid available to part-time students.
Applying 25 applicants, 32% accepted. *Fee:* $15.
Contact *Dr. Rich McBride*
Graduate Adviser
605-677-5388

TENNESSEE

EAST TENNESSEE STATE UNIVERSITY
Johnson City, TN 37614-0734

OVERVIEW
East Tennessee State University is a public coed university.

ENROLLMENT
10,706 graduate, professional, and undergraduate students; 893 full-time matriculated graduate/professional students (501 women), 762 part-time matriculated graduate/professional students (443 women).

GRADUATE FACULTY
290 full-time (76 women), 50 part-time (28 women); includes 14 minority (1 African-American, 13 Asian-Americans).

TUITION
$2722 per year full-time, $141 per credit hour part-time for state residents; $7318 per year full-time, $342 per credit hour part-time for nonresidents.

HOUSING
Rooms and/or apartments available to single students (36 units) at an average cost of $2200 per year ($3400 including board); available to married students (80 units) at an average cost of $2450 per year. Housing application deadline: 7/1. Graduate housing contact: Harry Steele, 423-439-4446.

STUDENT SERVICES
Disabled student services, multicultural affairs office, low-cost health insurance, career counseling, free psychological counseling, day-care facilities, campus safety program, campus employment opportunities, international student services, grant writing training, teacher training.

FACILITIES
Library: Sherrod Library plus 2 additional on-campus libraries; total holdings of 594,080 volumes, 1,506,980 microforms, 4,201 current periodical subscriptions. A total of 107 personal computers in all libraries. Access provided to on-line information retrieval services. *Computer:* Campuswide network is available with full Internet access. Total number of PCs/terminals supplied for student use: 400. *Special:* In arts and humanities: Center for Appalachian Studies. In science and engineering: Bays Mountain Field Station, Eastman Center for Nutrition. In social sciences: Early Childhood Center, Institute for Public Service Evaluation and Research.

COMPUTER SCIENCE

College of Applied Science and Technology, Department of Computer and Information Sciences
Programs Offers programs in computer science (MS), information sciences (MS). Part-time and evening/weekend programs available.
Faculty 12 full-time (3 women).
Faculty Research Operating systems, database design, artificial intelligence, simulation, parallel algorithms.
Students 27 full-time (5 women), 26 part-time (10 women); includes 3 minority (2 African-Americans, 1 Hispanic), 15 international. Average age 30.
Degrees Awarded In 1996, 12 degrees awarded.

Entrance Requirements GRE General Test (minimum combined score of 1050), TOEFL (minimum score 550), minimum GPA of 2.5.

Degree Requirements Computer language, thesis, written comprehensive exam required, foreign language not required.

Financial Aid In 1996–97, 4 research assistantships (2 to first-year students), 4 teaching assistantships (2 to first-year students), 3 grants were awarded. Aid available to part-time students. *Financial aid application deadline:* 7/1; applicants required to submit FAFSA.

Applying *Deadline:* 7/15 (priority date; rolling processing; 11/15 for spring admission). *Fee:* $5.

Contact Dr. James Pleasant
Graduate Coordinator
423-439-6962
Fax: 423-439-7119

INFORMATION SCIENCE

College of Applied Science and Technology, Department of Computer and Information Sciences

Programs Offers programs in computer science (MS), information sciences (MS). Part-time and evening/weekend programs available.

Faculty 12 full-time (3 women).

Faculty Research Operating systems, database design, artificial intelligence, simulation, parallel algorithms.

Students 27 full-time (5 women), 26 part-time (10 women); includes 3 minority (2 African-Americans, 1 Hispanic), 15 international. Average age 30.

Degrees Awarded In 1996, 12 degrees awarded.

Entrance Requirements GRE General Test (minimum combined score of 1050), TOEFL (minimum score 550), minimum GPA of 2.5.

Degree Requirements Computer language, thesis, written comprehensive exam required, foreign language not required.

Financial Aid In 1996–97, 4 research assistantships (2 to first-year students), 4 teaching assistantships (2 to first-year students), 3 grants were awarded. Aid available to part-time students. *Financial aid application deadline:* 7/1; applicants required to submit FAFSA.

Applying *Deadline:* 7/15 (priority date; rolling processing; 11/15 for spring admission). *Fee:* $5.

Contact Dr. James Pleasant
Graduate Coordinator
423-439-6962
Fax: 423-439-7119

MIDDLE TENNESSEE STATE UNIVERSITY
Murfreesboro, TN 37132

OVERVIEW
Middle Tennessee State University is a public coed university.

ENROLLMENT
17,924 graduate, professional, and undergraduate students; 553 full-time matriculated graduate/professional students (312 women), 1,267 part-time matriculated graduate/professional students (767 women).

GRADUATE FACULTY
353 full-time (111 women), 20 part-time (8 women).

EXPENSES
Tuition $2438 per year full-time, $123 per semester hour part-time for state residents; $7034 per year full-time, $324 per semester hour part-time for nonresidents. Fees $310 per year full-time, $9 per semester (minimum) part-time.

HOUSING
Rooms and/or apartments available to single students at an average cost of $2054 per year ($3369 including board); available to married students (192 units) at an average cost of $4272 per year. Graduate housing contact: Vicki Justice-Lowe, 615-898-2971.

STUDENT SERVICES
Disabled student services, multicultural affairs office, low-cost health insurance, career counseling, free psychological counseling, campus safety program, campus employment opportunities, international student services.

FACILITIES
Library: Todd Library; total holdings of 616,671 volumes, 162,065 microforms, 3,485 current periodical subscriptions. A total of 35 personal computers in all libraries. Access provided to on-line information retrieval services. *Computer:* Campuswide network is available with full Internet access. Total number of PCs/terminals supplied for student use: 200. Computer service fees are included with tuition and fees. *Special:* In arts and humanities: Governor's School for the Arts.

COMPUTER SCIENCE

College of Basic and Applied Sciences, Department of Computer Science

Programs Awards MS.

Faculty 9 full-time (4 women).

Students 31 full-time (13 women), 18 part-time (3 women); includes 22 minority (4 African-Americans, 14 Asian-Americans, 4 Hispanics), 17 international. Average age 30.

Degrees Awarded In 1996, 12 degrees awarded.

Entrance Requirements GRE or MAT.

Degree Requirements 1 foreign language, comprehensive exams required, thesis not required.

Financial Aid Teaching assistantships, institutionally sponsored loans available. Aid available to part-time students. *Financial aid application deadline:* 5/1; applicants required to submit FAFSA.

Applying 45 applicants, 33% accepted. *Deadline:* 8/1 (priority date). *Fee:* $5.

Contact Dr. Thomas J. Cheatham
Chair
615-898-2397
Fax: 615-898-5567
E-mail: cheatham@mtsu.edu

TENNESSEE TECHNOLOGICAL UNIVERSITY
Cookeville, TN 38505

OVERVIEW
Tennessee Technological University is a public coed university.

ENROLLMENT
8,163 graduate, professional, and undergraduate students; 393 full-time matriculated graduate/professional students (154 women), 551 part-time matriculated graduate/professional students (378 women).

GRADUATE FACULTY
341 full-time (62 women); includes 13 minority (all African-Americans).

TUITION
$2638 per year full-time, $132 per semester hour part-time for state residents; $4596 per year full-time, $333 per semester hour part-time for nonresidents.

HOUSING
Rooms and/or apartments available to single students at an average cost of $1550 per year; available to married students (300 units) at an average cost of $2400 per year. Housing application deadline: 6/1. Graduate housing contact: Edwin Boucher, 615-372-3414.

STUDENT SERVICES
Low-cost health insurance, career counseling, free psychological counseling, day-care facilities, campus safety program, campus employment opportunities, international student services.

FACILITIES
Library: University Library; total holdings of 1 million volumes. A total of 50 personal computers in all libraries. Access provided to on-line information retrieval services. *Special:* In science and engineering: Upper Cumberland Biological Research Center.

ELECTRICAL ENGINEERING

College of Engineering, Department of Electrical Engineering
Programs Awards MS, PhD. Part-time programs available.
Faculty 19 full-time (0 women).
Faculty Research Control, digital, and power systems.
Students 32 full-time (7 women), 5 part-time (0 women); includes 1 minority (African-American), 24 international. Average age 27.
Degrees Awarded In 1996, 15 master's awarded.
Entrance Requirements For master's, GRE General Test, TOEFL (minimum score 525); for doctorate, GRE Subject Test, TOEFL (minimum score 525), minimum GPA of 3.5.
Degree Requirements For master's, thesis required, foreign language not required; for doctorate, 1 foreign language (computer language can substitute), dissertation.
Financial Aid In 1996–97, 33 students received aid, including 16 research assistantships (3 to first-year students), 17 teaching assistantships (10 to first-year students); career-related internships or fieldwork also available. *Financial aid application deadline:* 4/1.
Applying 119 applicants, 39% accepted. *Deadline:* 3/1 (priority date; 8/1 for spring admission). *Fee:* $5 ($30 for international students).
Contact Dr. Rebecca F. Quattlebaum
　　　　　Dean of the Graduate School
　　　　　615-372-3233
　　　　　Fax: 615-372-3497

THE UNIVERSITY OF MEMPHIS
Memphis, TN 38152

OVERVIEW
The University of Memphis is a public coed university.

ENROLLMENT
19,271 graduate, professional, and undergraduate students; 2,315 full-time matriculated graduate/professional students (1,155 women), 2,662 part-time matriculated graduate/professional students (1,599 women).

TUITION
$2934 per year full-time, $151 per credit hour part-time for state residents; $7530 per year full-time, $352 per credit hour part-time for nonresidents.

HOUSING
Rooms and/or apartments available to single students (2,502 units) at an average cost of $3600 per year; available to married students (150 units) at an average cost of $5184 per year. Graduate housing contact: Daniel Armitage, 901-678-2295.

STUDENT SERVICES
Disabled student services, low-cost health insurance, career counseling, free psychological counseling, day-care facilities, campus safety program, campus employment opportunities, international student services.

FACILITIES
Library: Ned R. McWherter Library plus 5 additional on-campus libraries; total holdings of 1,020,842 volumes, 2,950,512 microforms, 8,500 current periodical subscriptions. A total of 200 personal computers in all libraries. Access provided to on-line information retrieval services. *Computer:* Campuswide network is available with full Internet access. Total number of PCs/terminals supplied for student use: 319. Computer service fees are included with tuition and fees. *Special:* In arts and humanities: Center for Egyptian Art and Archaeology, Marcus W. Orr Center for the Humanities, Center for Research on Women. In science and engineering: Integrated Microscopy Center, Center for Earthquake Research and Information, Ecological Research Center, Feinstone Institute of Molecular Biology, Wellness Institute, Universities Prevention Center. In social sciences: Center for Applied Psychological Research, Center for Innovative Services for the Communicatively Impaired, Center for Teacher Education.

COMPUTER ENGINEERING

Herff College of Engineering, Department of Electrical Engineering
Programs Offerings include engineering computer systems (MS).
Department Faculty 11 full-time (0 women), 3 part-time (0 women).
Entrance Requirements GRE General Test (minimum combined score of 1000) or MAT, minimum undergraduate GPA of 2.5.
Degree Requirements Thesis or alternative, written comprehensive exam.
Applying *Deadline:* 8/1 (12/1 for spring admission). *Fee:* $5 ($25 for international students).
Contact Dr. Steven T. Griffin
　　　　　Coordinator of Graduate Studies
　　　　　901-678-3250

COMPUTER SCIENCE

College of Arts and Sciences, Department of Mathematical Sciences
Programs Offerings include computer science (PhD), computer sciences (MS).

Department Faculty 21 full-time (2 women), 7 part-time (1 woman).

Entrance Requirements For master's, GRE General Test (minimum combined score of 800), MAT (minimum score 30), TOEFL (minimum score 550), minimum GPA of 2.5; for doctorate, GRE General Test (minimum combined score of 1000).

Degree Requirements For master's, comprehensive exams required, thesis not required; for doctorate, 1 foreign language, dissertation.

Applying *Deadline:* 8/1 (rolling processing; 12/1 for spring admission). *Fee:* $5 ($30 for international students).

Contact *Dr. Anna Kaminska*
Coordinator of Graduate Studies
901-678-2482

ELECTRICAL ENGINEERING

Herff College of Engineering, Department of Electrical Engineering

Programs Offers programs in automatic control systems (MS), communications and propagation systems (MS), electrical engineering (PhD), electro-optical systems (MS), engineering computer systems (MS).

Faculty 11 full-time (0 women), 3 part-time (0 women).

Faculty Research Ventricular arrhythmias, cerebral palsy, automatic computer troubleshooting, noninvasive monitoring of gastric motor functions.

Students 17 full-time (5 women), 12 part-time (1 woman); includes 2 minority (both Asian-Americans), 15 international.

Degrees Awarded In 1996, 19 master's awarded.

Entrance Requirements For master's, GRE General Test (minimum combined score of 1000) or MAT, minimum undergraduate GPA of 2.5.

Degree Requirements For master's, thesis or alternative, written comprehensive exam.

Financial Aid In 1996–97, 13 research assistantships totaling $12,450, 8 teaching assistantships totaling $28,900 were awarded; career-related internships or fieldwork also available.

Applying 112 applicants, 31% accepted. *Deadline:* 8/1 (12/1 for spring admission). *Fee:* $5 ($25 for international students).

Contact *Dr. Steven T. Griffin*
Coordinator of Graduate Studies
901-678-3250

UNIVERSITY OF TENNESSEE AT CHATTANOOGA
Chattanooga, TN 37403-2598

OVERVIEW
University of Tennessee at Chattanooga is a public coed comprehensive institution.

ENROLLMENT
8,296 graduate, professional, and undergraduate students; 329 full-time matriculated graduate/professional students (193 women), 839 part-time matriculated graduate/professional students (445 women).

GRADUATE FACULTY
106 full-time (39 women), 16 part-time (7 women); includes 30 minority (16 African-Americans, 10 Asian-Americans, 4 Hispanics).

TUITION
$2790 per year full-time, $151 per credit hour part-time for state residents; $7386 per year full-time, $351 per credit hour part-time for nonresidents.

HOUSING
Rooms and/or apartments available to single students (421 units) at an average cost of $1600 per year; on-campus housing not available to married students. Graduate housing contact: Richard MacDougall, 423-755-4246.

STUDENT SERVICES
Career counseling, free psychological counseling, day-care facilities, campus employment opportunities, international student services.

FACILITIES
Library: T. Carter and Margaret Rawlings Lupton Library; total holdings of 449,148 volumes, 1,181,670 microforms, 3,025 current periodical subscriptions. Access provided to on-line information retrieval services. *Computer:* Total number of PCs/terminals supplied for student use: 300. *Special:* In arts and humanities: Cadek Conservatory of Music. In science and engineering: Odor Research Center. In social sciences: Center for Economic Education, Center for Environmental/Energy Education, Institute of Archaeology.

COMPUTER SCIENCE

School of Engineering, Department of Computer Science

Programs Awards MS. Part-time and evening/weekend programs available.

Faculty 4 full-time (1 woman).

Students 18 full-time (4 women), 10 part-time (2 women); includes 2 minority (both Asian-Americans), 13 international.

Degrees Awarded In 1996, 2 degrees awarded.

Entrance Requirements GRE General Test.

Degree Requirements Computer language, thesis required, foreign language not required.

Financial Aid Fellowships, research assistantships, Federal Work-Study, institutionally sponsored loans available. Aid available to part-time students. *Financial aid application deadline:* 4/1.

Applying *Deadline:* rolling. *Fee:* $25.

Contact *Dr. Deborah Arfken*
Assistant Provost for Graduate Studies
423-755-4667
Fax: 423-755-4478

UNIVERSITY OF TENNESSEE, KNOXVILLE
Knoxville, TN 37996

OVERVIEW
University of Tennessee, Knoxville is a public coed university.

ENROLLMENT
25,924 graduate, professional, and undergraduate students; 3,900 full-time matriculated graduate/professional students (2,081 women), 2,293 part-time matriculated graduate/professional students (1,170 women).

GRADUATE FACULTY

1,254 full-time (356 women), 205 part-time (108 women); includes 142 minority (48 African-Americans, 68 Asian-Americans, 22 Hispanics, 4 Native Americans).

TUITION

$3142 per year full-time, $171 per credit hour part-time for state residents; $7824 per year full-time, $429 per credit hour part-time for nonresidents.

HOUSING

Rooms and/or apartments available to single students (1,500 units) at an average cost of $2355 per year; available to married students (800 units) at an average cost of $3546 per year. Housing application deadline: 2/1. Graduate housing contact: Director of University Housing, 423-974-3411.

STUDENT SERVICES

Disabled student services, multicultural affairs office, low-cost health insurance, career counseling, free psychological counseling, day-care facilities, campus safety program, campus employment opportunities, international student services, teacher training.

FACILITIES

Library: John C. Hodges Library plus 4 additional on-campus libraries; total holdings of 2 million volumes, 3 million microforms, 10,000 current periodical subscriptions. Access provided to on-line information retrieval services. *Computer:* Campuswide network is available with full Internet access. Computer service fees are applied as a separate charge. *Special:* In arts and humanities: Stokely Institute for Liberal Arts, McClung Museum. In science and engineering: Energy, Environment, and Resources Center; Transportation Center; Science Alliance; Measurement and Control Engineering Center. In social sciences: Center for Business and Economic Research, Management Development Center, Forensic Anthropology Center, Social Science Research Institute.

COMPUTER SCIENCE

College of Arts and Sciences, Department of Computer Science
Programs Awards MS, PhD. Part-time programs available.
Faculty 16 full-time (0 women).
Students 39 full-time (15 women), 76 part-time (19 women); includes 6 minority (4 African-Americans, 1 Asian-American, 1 Hispanic), 15 international.
Degrees Awarded In 1996, 21 master's, 6 doctorates awarded.
Entrance Requirements GRE General Test, TOEFL (minimum score 550), minimum GPA of 2.7.
Degree Requirements For master's, computer language, thesis or alternative required, foreign language not required; for doctorate, computer language, dissertation required, foreign language not required.
Financial Aid In 1996–97, 1 fellowship, 23 research assistantships, 35 teaching assistantships, 2 graduate assistantships were awarded; Federal Work-Study, institutionally sponsored loans also available. *Financial aid application deadline: 2/1.*
Applying 178 applicants, 24% accepted. *Deadline:* 2/1 (priority date; rolling processing). *Fee:* $15.
Contact *Dr. David Straight*
Graduate Representative
E-mail: straight@cs.utk.edu

See in-depth description on page 721.

ELECTRICAL ENGINEERING

College of Engineering, Department of Electrical Engineering
Programs Awards MS, PhD. Part-time programs available.
Faculty 26 full-time (0 women), 4 part-time (0 women).
Students 31 full-time (7 women), 57 part-time (3 women); includes 12 minority (4 African-Americans, 6 Asian-Americans, 2 Native Americans), 16 international. Average age 33.
Degrees Awarded In 1996, 26 master's, 6 doctorates awarded.
Entrance Requirements For master's, TOEFL (minimum score 580), minimum GPA of 2.7; for doctorate, GRE General Test, TOEFL (minimum score 580), minimum GPA of 2.7.
Degree Requirements Thesis/dissertation required, foreign language not required.
Financial Aid In 1996–97, 38 research assistantships, 7 graduate assistantships were awarded; fellowships, teaching assistantships, Federal Work-Study, institutionally sponsored loans, and career-related internships or fieldwork also available. *Financial aid application deadline: 2/1.*
Applying 102 applicants, 50% accepted. *Deadline:* 2/1 (priority date; rolling processing). *Fee:* $15.
Contact *Dr. Jack Lawler*
Graduate Representative
423-974-5462
E-mail: jsl@utk.edu

INFORMATION SCIENCE

College of Communications
Programs Offerings include information sciences (PhD).
College Faculty 25 full-time (8 women).
Entrance Requirements GRE General Test, TOEFL (minimum score 550), minimum GPA of 2.7.
Degree Requirements Dissertation required, foreign language not required.
Applying *Deadline:* 2/1 (priority date; rolling processing). *Fee:* $15.
Contact *Dr. Herbert Howard*
Program Head
423-974-6651
Fax: 423-974-3896
E-mail: hhowarda@utk.edu

UNIVERSITY OF TENNESSEE SPACE INSTITUTE
Tullahoma, TN 37388-8897

OVERVIEW

University of Tennessee Space Institute is a public coed graduate-only institution.

ENROLLMENT

73 full-time matriculated graduate/professional students (13 women), 194 part-time matriculated graduate/professional students (25 women).

GRADUATE FACULTY

40 full-time (1 woman), 8 part-time (0 women); includes 11 minority (1 African-American, 10 Asian-Americans).

TUITION

$2662 per year full-time, $150 per semester hour part-time for state residents; $7344 per year full-time, $408 per semester hour part-time for nonresidents.

HOUSING

Rooms and/or apartments available to single students (40 units) at an average cost of $1440 per year; on-campus housing not available to married students. Graduate housing contact: Dr. Edwin M. Gleason, 615-393-7432.

STUDENT SERVICES

Low-cost health insurance, career counseling, campus employment opportunities, international student services.

FACILITIES

Library: Main library plus 1 additional on-campus library; total holdings of 19,692 volumes, 194,200 microforms, 161 current periodical subscriptions. A total of 2 personal computers in all libraries. Access provided to on-line information retrieval services. *Computer:* Campuswide network is available with full Internet access. Computer services are offered at no charge. *Special:* In science and engineering: Center for Laser Application; Flight Test and Performance Center; water tunnel, subsonic, and transonic wind tunnels in the Gas Dynamic Facilities; Magnetohydrodynamic Coal Field Flow Facilities.

COMPUTER SCIENCE

Program in Computer Science
Programs Awards MS.
Faculty 2 full-time (0 women), 1 part-time (0 women).
Students 3 full-time (2 women), 6 part-time (3 women); includes 1 minority (African-American).
Degrees Awarded In 1996, 3 degrees awarded.
Entrance Requirements GRE General Test.
Degree Requirements Thesis required (for some programs), foreign language not required.
Financial Aid Research assistantships, Federal Work-Study available. Financial aid applicants required to submit FAFSA.
Applying *Deadline:* rolling. *Fee:* $15.
Contact *Dr. Edwin M. Gleason*
Assistant Dean for Admissions and Student Affairs
615-393-7432
Fax: 615-393-7346
E-mail: egleason@utsi.edu

ELECTRICAL ENGINEERING

Program in Electrical Engineering
Programs Awards MS, PhD.
Faculty 4 full-time (0 women), 1 part-time (0 women).
Students 1 (woman) full-time, 7 part-time (0 women); includes 1 minority (African-American).
Degrees Awarded In 1996, 2 master's awarded.
Degree Requirements For master's, thesis required (for some programs), foreign language not required; for doctorate, 1 foreign language, dissertation.
Financial Aid Research assistantships, full and partial tuition waivers, Federal Work-Study, and career-related internships or fieldwork available. Financial aid applicants required to submit FAFSA.
Applying *Deadline:* rolling. *Fee:* $15.
Contact *Dr. Edwin M. Gleason*
Assistant Dean for Admissions and Student Affairs
615-393-7432
Fax: 615-393-7346
E-mail: egleason@utsi.edu

VANDERBILT UNIVERSITY
Nashville, TN 37240-1001

OVERVIEW

Vanderbilt University is an independent coed university.

ENROLLMENT

10,253 graduate, professional, and undergraduate students; 3,894 full-time matriculated graduate/professional students (1,788 women), 482 part-time matriculated graduate/professional students (282 women).

GRADUATE FACULTY

1,875 full-time (536 women), 1,274 part-time (431 women); includes 228 minority (45 African-Americans, 151 Asian-Americans, 31 Hispanics, 1 Native American).

EXPENSES

Tuition $15,678 per year full-time, $871 per credit hour part-time. Fees $226 per year (minimum).

HOUSING

Rooms and/or apartments available to single students (115 units) at an average cost of $7380 per year; available to married students (51 units) at an average cost of $7740 per year. Housing application deadline: 5/1. Graduate housing contact: Housing Office, 615-322-2591.

STUDENT SERVICES

Disabled student services, multicultural affairs office, low-cost health insurance, career counseling, free psychological counseling, exercise/wellness program, day-care facilities, campus safety program, campus employment opportunities, international student services, writing training, teacher training.

FACILITIES

Library: Central Library plus 8 additional on-campus libraries; total holdings of 2.4 million volumes, 2.7 million microforms, 17,009 current periodical subscriptions. Access provided to on-line information retrieval services. *Computer:* Campuswide network is available with full Internet access. Computer services are offered at no charge. *Special:* In arts and humanities: Center for Baudelaire Studies, Fine Arts Gallery, Robert Penn Warren Center for the Humanities. In science and engineering: Stevenson Center for the Natural Sciences, Arthur J. Dyer Observatory, A. B. Learned Laboratories, Free-electron Laser Center. In social sciences: John F. Kennedy Center for Research on Education and Human Development, Vanderbilt Institute for Public Policy Studies, television news archive.

COMPUTER ENGINEERING

School of Engineering, Department of Electrical and Computer Engineering, Program in Electrical and Computer Engineering
Programs Awards M Eng, MS, PhD. MS and PhD offered through the Graduate School.
Faculty 17 full-time (1 woman).
Faculty Research Robotics microelectronics, signal and image processing. *Total annual research expenditures:* $2.7 million.
Students 87 full-time (10 women), includes 2 minority (both African-Americans), 42 international. Average age 26.
Degrees Awarded In 1996, 9 master's, 3 doctorates awarded.

Entrance Requirements For master's, GRE General Test (minimum combined score of 1200), GRE Subject Test, TOEFL (minimum score 550); for doctorate, GRE General Test (minimum combined score of 1200), GRE Subject Test, TOEFL (minimum score 575).

Degree Requirements Thesis/dissertation required, foreign language not required.

Financial Aid In 1996–97, 3 fellowships, 19 research assistantships (5 to first-year students), 21 teaching assistantships (7 to first-year students) were awarded; institutionally sponsored loans also available. *Financial aid application deadline:* 1/15.

Applying 80 applicants, 38% accepted. *Deadline:* 1/15 (priority date; 11/1 for spring admission). *Fee:* $40.

Contact *F. Wells*
          Director of Graduate Studies
          615-322-2771

COMPUTER SCIENCE

School of Engineering, Department of Computer Science

Programs Awards M Eng, MS, PhD. MS and PhD offered through the Graduate School. Part-time programs available.

Faculty 9 full-time (1 woman), 1 (woman) part-time.

Faculty Research Artificial intelligence, performance evaluation, databases, software engineering, computational science, image processing, graph algorithms, learning theory. *Total annual research expenditures:* $605,400.

Students 47 full-time (13 women), 6 part-time (3 women); includes 4 minority (2 African-Americans, 1 Asian-American, 1 Hispanic), 30 international. Average age 26.

Degrees Awarded In 1996, 6 master's awarded (100% found work related to degree); 2 doctorates awarded (100% entered university research/teaching).

Entrance Requirements For master's, GRE General Test (minimum combined score of 1700 on three sections), TOEFL (minimum score 600); for doctorate, GRE General Test (minimum combined score of 1800 on three sections), TOEFL (minimum score 600).

Degree Requirements For master's, thesis required (for some programs), foreign language not required; for doctorate, dissertation required, foreign language not required.

Financial Aid In 1996–97, 33 students received aid, including 4 fellowships (2 to first-year students), 4 research assistantships (2 to first-year students) averaging $1,100 per month, 15 teaching assistantships (3 to first-year students) averaging $1,050 per month; full and partial tuition waivers, institutionally sponsored loans also available. *Financial aid application deadline:* 1/15.

Applying 84 applicants, 42% accepted. *Deadline:* 1/15. *Fee:* $40.

Contact *Douglas Fisher*
          Director of Graduate Studies
          615-322-2976
          Fax: 615-343-8006
          E-mail: csdgs@vuse.vanderbilt.edu

ELECTRICAL ENGINEERING

School of Engineering, Department of Electrical and Computer Engineering, Program in Electrical and Computer Engineering

Programs Awards M Eng, MS, PhD. MS and PhD offered through the Graduate School.

Faculty 17 full-time (1 woman).

Faculty Research Robotics microelectronics, signal and image processing. *Total annual research expenditures:* $2.7 million.

Students 87 full-time (10 women), includes 2 minority (both African-Americans), 42 international. Average age 26.

Degrees Awarded In 1996, 9 master's, 3 doctorates awarded.

Entrance Requirements For master's, GRE General Test (minimum combined score of 1200), GRE Subject Test, TOEFL (minimum score 550); for doctorate, GRE General Test (minimum combined score of 1200), GRE Subject Test, TOEFL (minimum score 575).

Degree Requirements Thesis/dissertation required, foreign language not required.

Financial Aid In 1996–97, 3 fellowships, 19 research assistantships (5 to first-year students), 21 teaching assistantships (7 to first-year students) were awarded; institutionally sponsored loans also available. *Financial aid application deadline:* 1/15.

Applying 80 applicants, 38% accepted. *Deadline:* 1/15 (priority date; 11/1 for spring admission). *Fee:* $40.

Contact *F. Wells*
          Director of Graduate Studies
          615-322-2771

TEXAS

ANGELO STATE UNIVERSITY
San Angelo, TX 76909

OVERVIEW
Angelo State University is a public coed comprehensive institution.

ENROLLMENT
62,796 graduate, professional, and undergraduate students; 131 full-time matriculated graduate/professional students (73 women), 268 part-time matriculated graduate/professional students (170 women).

GRADUATE FACULTY
112 full-time (26 women), 8 part-time (2 women).

EXPENSES
Tuition $816 per year full-time, $34 per semester hour part-time for state residents; $5904 per year full-time, $246 per semester hour part-time for nonresidents. Fees $840 per year full-time, $150 per semester (minimum) part-time.

HOUSING
Rooms and/or apartments available to single students at an average cost of $2100 per year ($3968 including board); available to married students at an average cost of $2532 per year. Housing application deadline: 7/15. Graduate housing contact: Gary Poole, 915-942-2035.

STUDENT SERVICES
Low-cost health insurance, career counseling, campus safety program, campus employment opportunities.

FACILITIES
Library: Porter Henderson Library; total holdings of 262,673 volumes, 625,016 microforms, 2,029 current periodical subscriptions. A total of 40 personal computers in all libraries. Access provided to on-line information retrieval services. *Computer:* Campuswide network is available with full Internet access. Total number of PCs/terminals supplied for student use: 300. Computer service fees are included with tuition and fees.

COMPUTER SCIENCE

College of Professional Studies, Department of Computer Science
Programs Awards MBA. Part-time and evening/weekend programs available.
Faculty 4 full-time (1 woman).
Students 1 part-time (0 women). Average age 27.
Degrees Awarded In 1996, 1 degree awarded.
Entrance Requirements GRE General Test, minimum GPA of 2.5.
Degree Requirements Computer language, comprehensive exam required, thesis optional, foreign language not required.
Financial Aid In 1996–97, 1 fellowship was awarded; partial tuition waivers, Federal Work-Study also available. Aid available to part-time students. *Financial aid application deadline: 8/1.*
Applying 0 applicants. *Deadline:* 8/7 (priority date; rolling processing; 1/2 for spring admission). *Fee:* $0 ($50 for international students).
Contact *Dr. Fred Homeyer*
Head
915-942-2101

BAYLOR UNIVERSITY
Waco, TX 76798

OVERVIEW
Baylor University is an independent-religious coed university.

ENROLLMENT
12,391 graduate, professional, and undergraduate students; 1,149 full-time matriculated graduate/professional students (431 women), 710 part-time matriculated graduate/professional students (367 women).

GRADUATE FACULTY
350; includes 28 minority (9 African-Americans, 4 Asian-Americans, 10 Hispanics, 5 Native Americans).

EXPENSES
Tuition $6912 per year full-time, $288 per semester hour part-time. Fees $788 per year full-time, $27 per semester hour part-time.

HOUSING
Rooms and/or apartments available to single students (47 units) at an average cost of $4254 (including board); available to married students (47 units). Graduate housing contact: Residence Life Department, 817-755-3642.

STUDENT SERVICES
Low-cost health insurance, career counseling, free psychological counseling.

FACILITIES
Library: Moody Memorial Library plus 5 additional on-campus libraries; total holdings of 1,555,014 volumes, 1,090,804 microforms, 9,424 current periodical subscriptions. A total of 67 personal computers in all libraries. Access provided to on-line information retrieval services. *Computer:* Campuswide network is available with full Internet access. Total number of PCs/terminals supplied for student use: 634. Computer service fees are included with tuition and fees. *Special:* In science and engineering: Glasscock Energy Center, Van de Graaff accelerator laboratory, Institute for Famine Research and Alterna-

tive Agriculture, Institute of Environmental Studies, Strecker Museum, vector genetics mosquito laboratory.

COMPUTER SCIENCE

School of Engineering and Computer Science
Programs Offers program in computer science (MS). Part-time programs available.
Faculty Research Database systems, advanced architecture, operations research.
Students 5 full-time (0 women), 13 part-time (3 women); includes 2 minority (1 African-American, 1 Hispanic), 9 international.
Degrees Awarded In 1996, 6 degrees awarded.
Entrance Requirements GRE General Test (minimum combined score of 1050), minimum GPA of 3.0.
Degree Requirements Computer language required, thesis optional, foreign language not required.
Financial Aid Teaching assistantships available. *Financial aid application deadline: 3/15.*
Applying *Deadline:* 8/1 (rolling processing). *Fee:* $25.
Contact *Dr. Greg Speegle*
Director of Graduate Studies
817-755-3871

LAMAR UNIVERSITY
Beaumont, TX 77710

OVERVIEW
Lamar University is a public coed university.

ENROLLMENT
8,417 graduate, professional, and undergraduate students; 314 full-time matriculated graduate/professional students (143 women), 262 part-time matriculated graduate/professional students (138 women).

GRADUATE FACULTY
110 full-time (18 women), 40 part-time (11 women); includes 24 minority (3 African-Americans, 17 Asian-Americans, 3 Hispanics, 1 Native American).

TUITION
$1532 per year full-time, $259 per year (minimum) part-time for state residents; $6668 per year full-time, $877 per year (minimum) part-time for nonresidents.

HOUSING
Rooms and/or apartments available to single students at an average cost of $2264 per year ($3824 including board); on-campus housing not available to married students. Housing application deadline: 9/1. Graduate housing contact: Kent Kelso, 409-880-8111.

STUDENT SERVICES
Disabled student services, low-cost health insurance, career counseling, free psychological counseling, exercise/wellness program, day-care facilities, campus employment opportunities, international student services.

FACILITIES
Library: Mary and John Gray Library; total holdings of 645,673 volumes, 1,095,985 microforms, 2,834 current periodical subscriptions. A total of 109 personal computers in all libraries. Access provided to on-line information retrieval services. *Computer:* Campuswide network is available with full Internet access. Total number of

PCs/terminals supplied for student use: 751. Computer service fees are included with tuition and fees. *Special:* In arts and humanities: Gladys City Oil Boomtown Museum, Dishman Art Gallery. In science and engineering: Gulf Coast Hazardous Substance Research Center, Environmental Chromatography Institute, Space Exploration Center, environmental chemistry laboratory. In social sciences: Center for Public Policy Studies.

COMPUTER SCIENCE

College of Engineering, Department of Computer Science
Programs Awards MS.
Faculty 7 full-time (1 woman).
Faculty Research Artificial intelligence, complexity, databases, networks, distributed systems.
Students 44 full-time (9 women), 26 part-time (9 women); includes 2 minority (both Asian-Americans), 48 international.
Degrees Awarded In 1996, 13 degrees awarded.
Entrance Requirements GRE General Test (minimum combined score of 1050), TOEFL (minimum score 500), minimum GPA of 3.0 or 3.3 in last 60 hours of undergraduate course work.
Degree Requirements Computer language, comprehensive exams and project or thesis required, foreign language not required.
Financial Aid In 1996–97, 29 students received aid, including 4 research assistantships averaging $300 per month, 6 teaching assistantships (2 to first-year students) averaging $300 per month; partial tuition waivers, institutionally sponsored loans also available. *Financial aid application deadline:* 4/1.
Applying 50 applicants, 90% accepted. *Deadline:* rolling. *Fee:* $0.
Contact *Sandy Drane*
Graduate Admissions Office
800-443-5638
E-mail: dranes1@lub002.lamar.edu

ELECTRICAL ENGINEERING

College of Engineering, Department of Electrical Engineering
Programs Awards ME, MES, DE.
Faculty 4 full-time (0 women), 2 part-time (1 woman), 5.6 FTE.
Students 15 full-time (3 women), 3 part-time (1 woman); includes 14 international.
Entrance Requirements For master's, GRE General Test (minimum combined score of 950), TOEFL (minimum score 500); for doctorate, GRE General Test, TOEFL (minimum score 530).
Degree Requirements For master's, thesis required (for some programs), foreign language not required; for doctorate, computer language, dissertation required, foreign language not required.
Financial Aid In 1996–97, 2 fellowships, 1 research assistantship, 3 teaching assistantships were awarded. *Financial aid application deadline:* 4/1.
Applying 250 applicants, 40% accepted. *Deadline:* rolling. *Fee:* $0.
Contact *Dr. Bernard Maxum*
Chair
409-880-8746

Midwestern State University
Wichita Falls, TX 76308-2096

OVERVIEW

Midwestern State University is a public coed comprehensive institution.

ENROLLMENT

5,643 graduate, professional, and undergraduate students; 137 full-time matriculated graduate/professional students (66 women), 411 part-time matriculated graduate/professional students (208 women).

GRADUATE FACULTY

75 full-time, 1 part-time; includes 4 minority (1 African-American, 1 Asian-American, 2 Hispanics).

EXPENSES

Tuition $1062 per year full-time, $42 per hour part-time for state residents; $4273 per year full-time, $256 per hour part-time for nonresidents. Fees $90 per year (minimum) full-time, $9 per semester (minimum) part-time.

HOUSING

Rooms and/or apartments available to single students at an average cost of $1770 per year ($3266 including board); available to married students at an average cost of $2610 per year ($3500 including board). Graduate housing contact: Housing Office, 817-689-4217.

STUDENT SERVICES

Low-cost health insurance, career counseling, free psychological counseling, campus employment opportunities.

FACILITIES

Library: Moffett Library; total holdings of 622,410 volumes. A total of 25 personal computers in all libraries. Access provided to on-line information retrieval services. *Computer:* Campuswide network is available with full Internet access. Total number of PCs/terminals supplied for student use: 250. Computer service fees are included with tuition and fees. *Special:* In science and engineering: Bolin Science Hall.

COMPUTER SCIENCE

Division of Mathematical Sciences, Computer Science Program
Programs Awards MS. Part-time and evening/weekend programs available.
Faculty 3 full-time (1 woman).
Students 30 full-time (2 women), 18 part-time (2 women). Average age 35.
Degrees Awarded In 1996, 14 degrees awarded (100% found work related to degree).
Entrance Requirements GRE General Test, TOEFL (minimum score 550).
Degree Requirements Computer language, thesis or alternative required, foreign language not required.
Financial Aid In 1996–97, 19 research assistantships, 2 assistantships were awarded; teaching assistantships, partial tuition waivers, Federal Work-Study, institutionally sponsored loans also available. Aid available to part-time students.
Applying 40 applicants, 95% accepted. *Deadline:* 8/7 (12/15 for spring admission). *Fee:* $0 ($50 for international students).
Contact *Dr. Stewart Carpenter*
Graduate Adviser
817-689-4279

RICE UNIVERSITY
Houston, TX 77005

OVERVIEW
Rice University is an independent coed university.

ENROLLMENT
4,257 graduate, professional, and undergraduate students; 1,404 full-time matriculated graduate/professional students (462 women), 74 part-time matriculated graduate/professional students (29 women).

GRADUATE FACULTY
434 full-time, 150 part-time.

TUITION
$14,300 per year full-time, $795 per credit hour part-time.

HOUSING
Rooms and/or apartments available to single students (150 units) at an average cost of $3600 per year; available to married students (50 units) at an average cost of $4800 per year. Housing application deadline: 7/15. Graduate housing contact: Marion Hicks, 713-522-1096.

STUDENT SERVICES
Low-cost health insurance, career counseling, free psychological counseling, campus employment opportunities, international student services.

FACILITIES
Library: Fondren Library plus 5 additional on-campus libraries; total holdings of 1,534,750 volumes, 1.95 million microforms, 14,108 current periodical subscriptions. Access provided to on-line information retrieval services. *Special:* In science and engineering: NMR spectroscopy laboratory, sedimentology laboratory, electron microprobe and scanning electron microscope, biomedical engineering laboratory.

COMPUTER ENGINEERING

George R. Brown School of Engineering, Department of Electrical and Computer Engineering
Programs Offers programs in bioengineering (MS, PhD); circuits, controls, and communication systems (MS, PhD); computer science and engineering (MS, PhD); electrical engineering (MEE); lasers, microwaves, and solid-state electronics (MS, PhD). Part-time programs available.
Faculty Research Physical electronics.
Entrance Requirements GRE General Test, GRE Subject Test, TOEFL (minimum score 550), minimum GPA of 3.0.
Degree Requirements For master's, thesis required (for some programs), foreign language not required; for doctorate, dissertation required, foreign language not required.
Applying *Deadline:* 2/1 (priority date; rolling processing; 11/1 for spring admission). *Fee:* $25.

COMPUTER SCIENCE

George R. Brown School of Engineering, Department of Computer Science
Programs Awards MCS, MS, PhD. Part-time programs available. Terminal master's awarded for partial completion of doctoral program.
Faculty Research Operating systems, distributed systems, programming languages, algorithms, automatic program testing.

Entrance Requirements GRE General Test, GRE Subject Test, TOEFL (minimum score 550), minimum GPA of 3.0.
Degree Requirements For master's, thesis required (for some programs), foreign language not required; for doctorate, dissertation required, foreign language not required.
Applying *Deadline:* 2/1 (priority date; rolling processing; 11/1 for spring admission). *Fee:* $25.

See in-depth description on page **535.**

ELECTRICAL ENGINEERING

George R. Brown School of Engineering, Department of Electrical and Computer Engineering
Programs Offers programs in bioengineering (MS, PhD); circuits, controls, and communication systems (MS, PhD); computer science and engineering (MS, PhD); electrical engineering (MEE); lasers, microwaves, and solid-state electronics (MS, PhD). Part-time programs available.
Faculty Research Physical electronics.
Entrance Requirements GRE General Test, GRE Subject Test, TOEFL (minimum score 550), minimum GPA of 3.0.
Degree Requirements For master's, thesis required (for some programs), foreign language not required; for doctorate, dissertation required, foreign language not required.
Applying *Deadline:* 2/1 (priority date; rolling processing; 11/1 for spring admission). *Fee:* $25.

ST. MARY'S UNIVERSITY OF SAN ANTONIO
San Antonio, TX 78228-8507

OVERVIEW
St. Mary's University of San Antonio is an independent-religious coed comprehensive institution.

ENROLLMENT
4,000 graduate, professional, and undergraduate students; 1,556 matriculated graduate/professional students (741 women).

GRADUATE FACULTY
58 full-time, 100 part-time.

EXPENSES
Tuition $365 per credit hour. Fees $212 per year.

HOUSING
Rooms and/or apartments available to single students (93 units) at an average cost of $2500 per year ($4500 including board); on-campus housing not available to married students. Graduate housing contact: Lisa McDougle, 210-436-3534.

STUDENT SERVICES
Low-cost health insurance, career counseling, free psychological counseling.

FACILITIES
Library: Main library plus 1 additional on-campus library; total holdings of 525,000 volumes, 17,000 microforms, 1,400 current periodical subscriptions. A total of 66 personal computers in all libraries. Access provided to on-line information retrieval services. *Computer:* Campuswide network is available with full Internet access. Total number of PCs/terminals supplied for

student use: 125. Computer service fees are included with tuition and fees.

COMPUTER ENGINEERING

Department of Engineering, Program in Electrical/Computer Engineering
Programs   Awards MS.
Faculty
Faculty Research   Robotics, artificial intelligence, manufacturing engineering.
Students   23 (4 women). Average age 25.
Degrees Awarded   In 1996, 4 degrees awarded.
Entrance Requirements   GRE General Test, BS in science or engineering.
Degree Requirements   Computer language, thesis required, foreign language not required.
Financial Aid   Teaching assistantships, Federal Work-Study available.
Applying   *Deadline:* 8/1. *Fee:* $15.
Contact   *Dr. Abe Yazdani*
   Adviser
   210-436-3305

COMPUTER SCIENCE

Program in Computer Information Systems
Programs   Awards MS.
Faculty   6 full-time (0 women), 3 part-time (1 woman).
Faculty Research   Artificial intelligence, database/knowledge base, software engineering, expert systems.
Students   83 (22 women). Average age 30.
Degrees Awarded   In 1996, 14 degrees awarded (100% found work related to degree).
Entrance Requirements   GMAT or GRE General Test.
Degree Requirements   Computer language, comprehensive exams required, thesis optional, foreign language not required.
Financial Aid   Research assistantships, institutionally sponsored loans, and career-related internships or fieldwork available.
Applying   *Deadline:* 8/1. *Fee:* $15.
Contact   *Dr. Douglas Hall*
   Adviser
   210-436-3317

ELECTRICAL ENGINEERING

Department of Engineering, Program in Electrical/Computer Engineering
Programs   Awards MS.
Faculty
Faculty Research   Robotics, artificial intelligence, manufacturing engineering.
Students   23 (4 women). Average age 25.
Degrees Awarded   In 1996, 4 degrees awarded.
Entrance Requirements   GRE General Test, BS in science or engineering.
Degree Requirements   Computer language, thesis required, foreign language not required.
Financial Aid   Teaching assistantships, Federal Work-Study available.
Applying   *Deadline:* 8/1. *Fee:* $15.
Contact   *Dr. Abe Yazdani*
   Adviser
   210-436-3305

INFORMATION SCIENCE

Program in Computer Information Systems
Programs   Awards MS.
Faculty   6 full-time (0 women), 3 part-time (1 woman).

Faculty Research   Artificial intelligence, database/knowledge base, software engineering, expert systems.
Students   83 (22 women). Average age 30.
Degrees Awarded   In 1996, 14 degrees awarded (100% found work related to degree).
Entrance Requirements   GMAT or GRE General Test.
Degree Requirements   Computer language, comprehensive exams required, thesis optional, foreign language not required.
Financial Aid   Research assistantships, institutionally sponsored loans, and career-related internships or fieldwork available.
Applying   *Deadline:* 8/1. *Fee:* $15.
Contact   *Dr. Douglas Hall*
   Adviser
   210-436-3317

SAM HOUSTON STATE UNIVERSITY
Huntsville, TX 77341

OVERVIEW
Sam Houston State University is a public coed comprehensive institution.

ENROLLMENT
12,564 graduate, professional, and undergraduate students; 214 full-time matriculated graduate/professional students (115 women), 835 part-time matriculated graduate/professional students (584 women).

TUITION
$1314 per year (minimum) full-time, $273 per semester (minimum) part-time for state residents; $5166 per year (minimum) full-time, $897 per semester (minimum) part-time for nonresidents.

HOUSING
Rooms and/or apartments available to single students at an average cost of $1580 per year ($3160 including board); available to married students (102 units) at an average cost of $3000 (including board). Graduate housing contact: Department of Housing, 409-294-1812.

STUDENT SERVICES
Disabled student services, career counseling, free psychological counseling, day-care facilities, campus employment opportunities, international student services.

FACILITIES
Library: Newton Gresham Library; total holdings of 795,910 volumes, 576,788 microforms, 3,363 current periodical subscriptions. Access provided to on-line information retrieval services. *Computer:* Campuswide network is available with full Internet access. Computer service fees are included with tuition and fees. *Special:* In arts and humanities: Sam Houston Memorial Museum. In science and engineering: Texas Regional Institute for Environmental Studies.

COMPUTER SCIENCE

College of Arts and Sciences, Division of Mathematical and Information Sciences, Program in Computing Science
Programs   Awards M Ed, MS. Part-time programs available.
Faculty Research   Language design, networks, database, operating systems, multimedia.

Students 3 full-time (1 woman), 32 part-time (12 women); includes 3 minority (2 Asian-Americans, 1 Hispanic), 22 international.
Degrees Awarded In 1996, 8 degrees awarded.
Entrance Requirements GRE General Test (minimum combined score of 1000), TOEFL (minimum score 550).
Financial Aid In 1996–97, 5 teaching assistantships were awarded.
Applying *Deadline:* rolling. *Fee:* $15.
Contact *Dr. David Burris*
Graduate Adviser
409-294-1568
Fax: 409-294-1882
E-mail: csc_dsb@shsu.edu

SOUTHERN METHODIST UNIVERSITY
Dallas, TX 75275

OVERVIEW
Southern Methodist University is an independent-religious coed university.

ENROLLMENT
9,464 graduate, professional, and undergraduate students; 1,781 full-time matriculated graduate/professional students (735 women), 1,982 part-time matriculated graduate/professional students (645 women).

GRADUATE FACULTY
455 full-time (114 women), 289 part-time (100 women); includes 70 minority (10 African-Americans, 40 Asian-Americans, 20 Hispanics).

EXPENSES
Tuition $11,196 per year full-time, $622 per credit part-time. Fees $1440 per year full-time, $80 per credit part-time.

HOUSING
Rooms and/or apartments available to single students (208 units) at an average cost of $3412 per year; available to married students (76 units) at an average cost of $3725 per year. Housing application deadline: 5/31. Graduate housing contact: Office of Housing, 214-768-2407.

STUDENT SERVICES
Low-cost health insurance, career counseling, free psychological counseling, day-care facilities, campus safety program, campus employment opportunities, international student services.

FACILITIES
Library: Central University Library plus 9 additional on-campus libraries; total holdings of 3,012,359 volumes, 704,168 microforms, 6,417 current periodical subscriptions. Access provided to on-line information retrieval services. *Computer:* Campuswide network is available with full Internet access. Total number of PCs/terminals supplied for student use: 339. Computer services are offered at no charge. *Special:* In arts and humanities: Meadows Museum. In science and engineering: Dallas Seismological Observatory, Fort Burgwin Research Center, Shuler Museum of Paleontology, electron microscope labora-

tory, pollen analysis laboratory. In social sciences: N. L. Heroy Science Hall.

COMPUTER ENGINEERING

School of Engineering and Applied Science, Department of Computer Science and Engineering
Programs Offers programs in computer engineering (MS Cp E, PhD), computer science (MS, PhD), engineering management (MSEM, DE), operations research (MS, PhD), software engineering (MS). Part-time programs available.
Faculty 12 full-time (1 woman), 4 part-time (0 women).
Faculty Research Data and knowledge-based systems, artificial intelligence, parallel processing, scientific computing.
Students 35 full-time (11 women), 307 part-time (51 women); includes 66 minority (15 African-Americans, 37 Asian-Americans, 14 Hispanics), 34 international.
Degrees Awarded In 1996, 62 master's, 6 doctorates awarded.
Entrance Requirements For master's, GRE General Test (minimum score 650 on quantitative section), TOEFL (minimum score 550), minimum GPA of 3.0 in last 2 years.
Degree Requirements For master's, comprehensive exam or thesis required, foreign language not required; for doctorate, dissertation, oral and written qualifying exams.
Financial Aid Fellowships, research assistantships, teaching assistantships available. Financial aid applicants required to submit FAFSA.
Applying *Deadline:* 8/1 (priority date; rolling processing; 12/15 for spring admission). *Fee:* $25.
Contact *Dr. James B. Dunham*
Assistant Dean
214-768-3484

See in-depth description on page 543.

COMPUTER SCIENCE

School of Engineering and Applied Science, Department of Computer Science and Engineering
Programs Offers programs in computer engineering (MS Cp E, PhD), computer science (MS, PhD), engineering management (MSEM, DE), operations research (MS, PhD), software engineering (MS). Part-time programs available.
Faculty 12 full-time (1 woman), 4 part-time (0 women).
Faculty Research Data and knowledge-based systems, artificial intelligence, parallel processing, scientific computing.
Students 35 full-time (11 women), 307 part-time (51 women); includes 66 minority (15 African-Americans, 37 Asian-Americans, 14 Hispanics), 34 international.
Degrees Awarded In 1996, 62 master's, 6 doctorates awarded.
Entrance Requirements For master's, GRE General Test (minimum score 650 on quantitative section), TOEFL (minimum score 550), minimum GPA of 3.0 in last 2 years.
Degree Requirements For master's, comprehensive exam or thesis required, foreign language not required; for doctorate, dissertation, oral and written qualifying exams.
Financial Aid Fellowships, research assistantships, teaching assistantships available. Financial aid applicants required to submit FAFSA.
Applying *Deadline:* 8/1 (priority date; rolling processing; 12/15 for spring admission). *Fee:* $25.
Contact *Dr. James B. Dunham*
Assistant Dean
214-768-3484

See in-depth description on page 543.

ELECTRICAL ENGINEERING

School of Engineering and Applied Science, Department of Electrical Engineering
Programs   Awards MS, MSEE, PhD.
Faculty   14 full-time (1 woman), 6 part-time (1 woman).
Faculty Research   Communications, solid-state digital signal processing, solid-state circuits and devices, telecommunications.
Students   22 full-time (3 women), 411 part-time (62 women); includes 104 minority (14 African-Americans, 64 Asian-Americans, 24 Hispanics, 2 Native Americans), 26 international.
Degrees Awarded   In 1996, 50 master's, 17 doctorates awarded.
Entrance Requirements   For master's, GRE General Test (minimum score 650 on quantitative section), TOEFL (minimum score 550), minimum GPA of 3.0 in last 2 years; for doctorate, minimum GPA of 3.0.
Degree Requirements   For master's, thesis optional, foreign language not required; for doctorate, dissertation, oral and written qualifying exams.
Financial Aid   Fellowships, research assistantships, teaching assistantships, full tuition waivers, institutionally sponsored loans available. Financial aid applicants required to submit FAFSA.
Applying   *Deadline:* 8/1 (priority date; rolling processing; 12/15 for spring admission). *Fee:* $25.
Contact   *Dr. James B. Dunham*
Interim Chair
214-768-3113

See in-depth description on page **545.**

SOFTWARE ENGINEERING

School of Engineering and Applied Science, Department of Computer Science and Engineering
Programs   Offerings include software engineering (MS).
Department Faculty   12 full-time (1 woman), 4 part-time (0 women).
Applying   *Deadline:* 8/1 (priority date; rolling processing; 12/15 for spring admission). *Fee:* $25.
Contact   *Dr. James B. Dunham*
Assistant Dean
214-768-3484

See in-depth description on page **543.**

SOUTHWEST TEXAS STATE UNIVERSITY
San Marcos, TX 78666

OVERVIEW
Southwest Texas State University is a public coed comprehensive institution.

ENROLLMENT
20,776 graduate, professional, and undergraduate students; 736 full-time matriculated graduate/professional students (462 women), 1,605 part-time matriculated graduate/professional students (932 women).

GRADUATE FACULTY
277 full-time (91 women), 23 part-time (8 women); includes 32 minority (4 African-Americans, 10 Asian-Americans, 17 Hispanics, 1 Native American).

TUITION
$1780 per year full-time, $416 per course part-time for state residents; $5632 per year full-time, $1040 per course part-time for nonresidents.

HOUSING
Rooms and/or apartments available to single students (50 units) at an average cost of $3787 (including board); available to married students (194 units) at an average cost of $2272 per year. Housing application deadline: 7/1. Graduate housing contact: Residence Life Office, 512-245-2382.

STUDENT SERVICES
Disabled student services, multicultural affairs office, low-cost health insurance, career counseling, free psychological counseling, campus safety program, campus employment opportunities, international student services, teacher training.

FACILITIES
Library: Alkek Library; total holdings of 2,946,607 volumes, 1,591,317 microforms, 5,339 current periodical subscriptions. A total of 50 personal computers in all libraries. Access provided to on-line information retrieval services. *Computer:* Campuswide network is available with full Internet access. Total number of PCs/terminals supplied for student use: 600. Computer service fees are included with tuition and fees. *Special:* In arts and humanities: Southwestern Writers Collection, Center for Studies of the Southwest, writing laboratory, modern language laboratory. In science and engineering: Edwards Aquifer Research and Data Center; Traffic Safety Center; speech, hearing, and language clinic; university farm. In social sciences: Institute of Corridor Studies, Center for International Studies, Center for Multicultural and Gender Studies.

COMPUTER SCIENCE

School of Science, Department of Computer Science
Programs   Awards MA, MS. Part-time programs available.
Faculty   9 full-time (1 woman).
Faculty Research   Software engineering, artificial intelligence, multimedia, distributed/parallel computing, database systems, operating systems.
Students   62 full-time (31 women), 54 part-time (13 women); includes 10 minority (9 Asian-Americans, 1 Native American), 59 international. Average age 33.
Degrees Awarded   In 1996, 37 degrees awarded.
Entrance Requirements   GRE General Test (minimum combined score of 1000), TOEFL (minimum score 550), minimum GPA of 2.75 in last 60 hours.
Degree Requirements   Computer language, thesis (for some programs), comprehensive exam required, foreign language not required.
Financial Aid   In 1996–97, 15 teaching assistantships were awarded; Federal Work-Study, institutionally sponsored loans, and career-related internships or fieldwork also available. Aid available to part-time students. *Financial aid application deadline:* 4/1; applicants required to submit FAFSA.
Applying   *Deadline:* 7/15 (priority date; rolling processing; 11/15 for spring admission). *Fee:* $25 ($50 for international students).
Contact   *Dr. Tom McCabe*
Graduate Adviser
512-245-3409
Fax: 512-245-8750
E-mail: tm03@swt.edu

STEPHEN F. AUSTIN STATE UNIVERSITY
Nacogdoches, TX 75962

OVERVIEW
Stephen F. Austin State University is a public coed comprehensive institution.

ENROLLMENT
11,687 graduate, professional, and undergraduate students; 562 full-time matriculated graduate/professional students (317 women), 937 part-time matriculated graduate/professional students (592 women).

GRADUATE FACULTY
214 full-time, 75 part-time; includes 6 minority.

EXPENSES
Tuition $816 per year full-time, $120 per semester (minimum) part-time for state residents; $5952 per year full-time, $248 per semester (minimum) part-time for nonresidents. Fees $890 per year full-time, $119 per semester (minimum) part-time.

HOUSING
Rooms and/or apartments available to single students at an average cost of $4300 (including board); available to married students (351 units) at an average cost of $4185 (including board). Housing application deadline: 6/1. Graduate housing contact: Jammie Fain, 409-468-2601.

STUDENT SERVICES
Disabled student services, multicultural affairs office, low-cost health insurance, career counseling, free psychological counseling, day-care facilities, campus employment opportunities, international student services.

FACILITIES
Library: Ralph W. Steen Library; total holdings of 601,441 volumes, 1,144,620 microforms, 3,200 current periodical subscriptions. Access provided to on-line information retrieval services. *Computer:* Campuswide network is available with full Internet access. Computer service fees are included with tuition and fees. *Special:* In arts and humanities: Center for East Texas Studies. In science and engineering: Center for Applied Studies in Forestry, forestry field station, observatory.

COMPUTER SCIENCE

College of Business, Department of Computer Science
Programs   Awards MS. Part-time programs available.
Faculty   6 full-time (1 woman), 1 part-time (0 women).
Students   6 full-time (1 woman), 7 part-time (4 women); includes 2 minority (1 African-American, 1 Asian-American), 3 international.
Degrees Awarded   In 1996, 4 degrees awarded.
Entrance Requirements   GRE General Test (minimum combined score of 1000).
Degree Requirements   Computer language, comprehensive exam required, foreign language and thesis not required.
Financial Aid   In 1996–97, research assistantships totaling $6,200, teaching assistantships totaling $37,800 were awarded; Federal Work-Study also available. *Financial aid application deadline:* 3/1.
Applying   5 applicants, 80% accepted. *Deadline:* 8/1 (priority date; rolling processing; 12/15 for spring admission). *Fee:* $0 ($25 for international students).

Contact   *Dr. Craig A. Wood*
Chair
409-468-2508

TEXAS A&M UNIVERSITY
College Station, TX 77843-1244

OVERVIEW
Texas A&M University is a public coed university.

ENROLLMENT
41,790 graduate, professional, and undergraduate students; 8,408 matriculated graduate/professional students (3,225 women).

GRADUATE FACULTY
2,054 full-time (343 women), 482 part-time (143 women), 2,220 FTE; includes 309 minority (32 African-Americans, 175 Asian-Americans, 97 Hispanics, 5 Native Americans).

EXPENSES
Tuition $72 per semester hour for state residents; $285 per semester hour for nonresidents. Fees $1318 per year full-time, $480 per semester (minimum) part-time.

HOUSING
Rooms and/or apartments available to single students (405 units) at an average cost of $2832 per year ($2832 including board); available to married students (650 units) at an average cost of $3480 per year ($3480 including board). Graduate housing contact: Director of Student Housing, 409-845-1741.

STUDENT SERVICES
Disabled student services, multicultural affairs office, low-cost health insurance, career counseling, free psychological counseling, exercise/wellness program, campus safety program, campus employment opportunities, international student services, writing training, grant writing training, teacher training.

FACILITIES
Library: Sterling C. Evans Library plus 3 additional on-campus libraries; total holdings of 2,168,963 volumes, 4,323,592 microforms, 17,322 current periodical subscriptions. A total of 400 personal computers in all libraries. Access provided to on-line information retrieval services. *Computer:* Campuswide network is available with full Internet access. Total number of PCs/terminals supplied for student use: 3,000. Computer service fees are included with tuition and fees. *Special:* In arts and humanities: World Shakespeare Bibliography; Runyon Art Collection; Benz Gallery of Floral Design; Santa Chiara Study Center in Castiglione d'Fiorentino, Italy. In science and engineering: Institute for Biosciences and Technology, Institute for Scientific Computation, Cyclotron Institute, Texas Transportation Institute, Nuclear Science Center. In social sciences: Institute for Nautical Archaeology; Public Policy Research Institute; Center for International Business Studies; Race and Ethnic Studies Institute; Presidential Studies Center; Center for Biotechnology, Policy, and Ethics.

COMPUTER SCIENCE

College of Engineering, Department of Computer Science
Programs   Awards MCS, MS, PhD.

Faculty 32 full-time (3 women), 4 part-time (0 women), 34.1 FTE.

Faculty Research Software development, numerical applications and controls, data structures.

Students 174 full-time (42 women), 87 part-time (18 women); includes 25 minority (4 African-Americans, 14 Asian-Americans, 7 Hispanics), 111 international. Average age 28.

Degrees Awarded In 1996, 68 master's, 17 doctorates awarded.

Entrance Requirements GRE General Test, TOEFL.

Degree Requirements For master's, computer language, thesis (MS) required, foreign language not required; for doctorate, computer language, dissertation required, foreign language not required.

Financial Aid Fellowships, research assistantships, teaching assistantships available.

Applying 457 applicants, 49% accepted. *Deadline:* 5/1 (priority date). *Fee:* $35 ($75 for international students).

Contact *Fabrizio Lombardi*
Graduate Adviser
409-845-5534

See in-depth description on page **567.**

ELECTRICAL ENGINEERING

College of Engineering, Department of Electrical Engineering

Programs Awards M Eng, MS, PhD.

Faculty 49 full-time (3 women), 8 part-time (3 women), 52.6 FTE.

Faculty Research Solid-state, electric power systems, and communications engineering.

Students 324 full-time (52 women), 68 part-time (10 women); includes 56 minority (10 African-Americans, 34 Asian-Americans, 12 Hispanics), 181 international. Average age 28.

Degrees Awarded In 1996, 49 master's, 29 doctorates awarded.

Entrance Requirements GRE General Test, TOEFL.

Degree Requirements For master's, thesis (MS) required, foreign language not required; for doctorate, dissertation required, foreign language not required.

Financial Aid Fellowships, research assistantships, teaching assistantships, and career-related internships or fieldwork available.

Applying 391 applicants, 76% accepted. *Fee:* $35 ($75 for international students).

Contact *Norman Griswold*
Graduate Adviser
409-845-7441

See in-depth description on page **569.**

TEXAS A&M UNIVERSITY–COMMERCE
Commerce, TX 75429-3011

OVERVIEW

Texas A&M University–Commerce is a public coed university.

ENROLLMENT

7,457 graduate, professional, and undergraduate students; 442 full-time matriculated graduate/professional students (235 women), 1,225 part-time matriculated graduate/professional students (781 women).

GRADUATE FACULTY

166 full-time (36 women), 36 part-time (6 women), 205 FTE; includes 23 minority (10 African-Americans, 6 Asian-Americans, 7 Hispanics).

TUITION

$2283 per year full-time, $341 per semester (minimum) part-time for state residents; $7633 per year full-time, $965 per semester (minimum) part-time for nonresidents.

HOUSING

Rooms and/or apartments available to single students at an average cost of $2631 per year ($4740 including board); available to married students (250 units) at an average cost of $3240 per year. Graduate housing contact: Jimmie Sadler, 903-886-5797.

STUDENT SERVICES

Disabled student services, low-cost health insurance, career counseling, free psychological counseling, exercise/wellness program, day-care facilities, campus employment opportunities, international student services, writing training, grant writing training, teacher training.

FACILITIES

Library: James G. Gee Library; total holdings of 1,117,245 volumes, 479,797 microforms, 1,882 current periodical subscriptions. A total of 144 personal computers in all libraries. Access provided to on-line information retrieval services. *Computer:* Campuswide network is available with full Internet access. Total number of PCs/terminals supplied for student use: 500. Computer service fees are included with tuition and fees.

COMPUTER SCIENCE

College of Arts and Sciences, Department of Computer Science

Programs Awards MS.

Faculty 3 full-time (0 women).

Students 58 full-time (16 women), 30 part-time (3 women); includes 11 minority (4 African-Americans, 7 Asian-Americans), 58 international.

Entrance Requirements GMAT or GRE General Test.

Degree Requirements Thesis (for some programs), comprehensive exam.

Financial Aid Research assistantships, teaching assistantships, Federal Work-Study, institutionally sponsored loans available.

Applying *Deadline:* rolling. *Fee:* $0 ($25 for international students).

Contact *Pam Hammonds*
Graduate Admissions Adviser
903-886-5167
Fax: 903-886-5165

TEXAS A&M UNIVERSITY–CORPUS CHRISTI
Corpus Christi, TX 78412-5503

OVERVIEW

Texas A&M University–Corpus Christi is a public coed comprehensive institution.

ENROLLMENT

5,671 graduate, professional, and undergraduate students; 310 full-time matriculated graduate/professional students

(192 women), 1,131 part-time matriculated graduate/professional students (728 women).

GRADUATE FACULTY

198 full-time (69 women), 182 part-time (86 women), 269 FTE; includes 62 minority (5 African-Americans, 10 Asian-Americans, 45 Hispanics, 2 Native Americans).

TUITION

$1954 per year full-time, $219 per credit hour part-time for state residents; $5366 per year full-time, $347 per credit hour part-time for nonresidents.

HOUSING

Rooms and/or apartments available to single students (650 units) at an average cost of $2280 per year; on-campus housing not available to married students. Graduate housing contact: Mark Center, 512-994-5963.

STUDENT SERVICES

Low-cost health insurance, career counseling, free psychological counseling, campus safety program, campus employment opportunities, international student services.

FACILITIES

Library: Mary and Jeff Bell Library; total holdings of 321,134 volumes, 505,817 microforms, 1,582 current periodical subscriptions. A total of 20 personal computers in all libraries. Access provided to on-line information retrieval services. *Computer:* Campuswide network is available with full Internet access. Total number of PCs/terminals supplied for student use: 500. Computer service fees are applied as a separate charge. *Special:* In arts and humanities: Weil Gallery. In science and engineering: Conrad Blucher Institute, Center for Coastal Studies, Environmental Research Consortium.

COMPUTER SCIENCE

College of Science and Technology, Program in Computing and Mathematical Sciences

Programs Offers computer science (MS), mathematics (MS). Part-time and evening/weekend programs available.

Students 16 full-time (4 women), 49 part-time (16 women); includes 18 minority (4 Asian-Americans, 14 Hispanics), 3 international. Average age 36.

Degrees Awarded In 1996, 7 degrees awarded.

Entrance Requirements GRE General Test.

Degree Requirements Computer language, thesis required, foreign language not required.

Financial Aid Federal Work-Study, institutionally sponsored loans, and career-related internships or fieldwork available. Aid available to part-time students. *Financial aid application deadline:* 3/15; applicants required to submit FAFSA.

Applying 23 applicants, 100% accepted. *Deadline:* 7/15 (priority date; rolling processing; 11/15 for spring admission). *Fee:* $10 ($30 for international students).

Contact *Mary Margaret Dechant*
Director of Admissions
512-994-2624
Fax: 512-994-5887

See in-depth description on page 571.

TEXAS A&M UNIVERSITY–KINGSVILLE
Kingsville, TX 78363

OVERVIEW

Texas A&M University–Kingsville is a public coed university.

ENROLLMENT

6,113 graduate, professional, and undergraduate students; 291 full-time, 800 part-time matriculated graduate/professional students.

GRADUATE FACULTY

157 (33 women).

EXPENSES

Tuition $816 per year full-time, $120 per semester (minimum) part-time for state residents; $5952 per year full-time, $744 per semester (minimum) part-time for nonresidents. Fees $958 per year full-time, $161 per semester (minimum) part-time.

HOUSING

Rooms and/or apartments available to single students at an average cost of $3484 (including board); available to married students (40 units) at an average cost of $2640 per year. Housing application deadline: 8/1. Graduate housing contact: Antonia Alvarez, 512-593-3419.

STUDENT SERVICES

Low-cost health insurance, career counseling, free psychological counseling, day-care facilities, campus safety program, campus employment opportunities, international student services.

FACILITIES

Library: James C. Jernigan Library; total holdings of 494,195 volumes, 270,911 microforms, 2,313 current periodical subscriptions. A total of 100 personal computers in all libraries. Access provided to on-line information retrieval services. *Computer:* Campuswide network is available with full Internet access. Total number of PCs/terminals supplied for student use: 350. Computer service fees are included with tuition and fees. *Special:* In arts and humanities: J. E. Conner Museum, Frank C. Smith Fine Arts Group. In science and engineering: Caesar Kleberg Wildlife Research Institute, Citrus Center in Weslaco, Center for Semi-Arid Forest Resources, Welhausen Water Resource Center.

COMPUTER SCIENCE

College of Engineering, Department of Electrical Engineering and Computer Science, Program in Computer Science

Programs Awards MS.

Faculty 3 full-time, 1 part-time.

Faculty Research Operating systems, programming languages, database systems, computer architecture, artificial intelligence.

Students 26; includes 2 minority (1 Asian-American, 1 Hispanic), 22 international. Average age 33.

Degrees Awarded In 1996, 6 degrees awarded.

Entrance Requirements GRE General Test (minimum combined score of 1000), TOEFL (minimum score 525), minimum GPA of 3.0.

Degree Requirements Computer language, thesis or alternative, comprehensive exam required, foreign language not required.

Financial Aid Research assistantships available. *Financial aid application deadline:* 5/15.

Applying *Deadline:* 6/1 (rolling processing; 11/15 for spring admission). *Fee:* $15 ($25 for international students).

Contact *H. D. Gorakhpurwalla*
Graduate Coordinator
512-593-2004

ELECTRICAL ENGINEERING

College of Engineering, Department of Electrical Engineering and Computer Science, Program in Electrical Engineering

Programs Awards ME, MS.

Students 42; includes 15 minority (all Hispanics), 22 international.

Degrees Awarded In 1996, 10 degrees awarded.

Entrance Requirements GRE General Test (minimum combined score of 1000), TOEFL (minimum score 525), minimum GPA of 3.0.

Degree Requirements Computer language, thesis or alternative, comprehensive exam required, foreign language not required.

Financial Aid *Application deadline:* 5/15.

Applying *Deadline:* 6/1 (rolling processing; 11/15 for spring admission). *Fee:* $15 ($25 for international students).

Contact *H. D. Gorakhpurwalla*
Graduate Coordinator
512-593-2004

TEXAS CHRISTIAN UNIVERSITY
Fort Worth, TX 76129-0002

OVERVIEW

Texas Christian University is an independent-religious coed university.

ENROLLMENT

6,961 graduate, professional, and undergraduate students; 530 full-time matriculated graduate/professional students (238 women), 621 part-time matriculated graduate/professional students (314 women).

GRADUATE FACULTY

209 full-time; includes 22 minority (6 African-Americans, 8 Asian-Americans, 8 Hispanics).

EXPENSES

Tuition $7920 per year full-time, $330 per semester hour part-time. Fees $1190 per year full-time, $35 per semester hour part-time.

HOUSING

On-campus housing not available.

STUDENT SERVICES

Disabled student services, low-cost health insurance, career counseling, free psychological counseling, campus safety program, campus employment opportunities, international student services.

FACILITIES

Library: Mary Couts Burnett Library; total holdings of 1,183,312 volumes, 492,215 microforms, 4,470 current periodical subscriptions. Access provided to on-line information retrieval services. *Computer:* Campuswide network is available with full Internet access. Total number of PCs/terminals supplied for student use: 1,288. Computer services are offered at no charge. *Special:* In science and engineering: Center for Remote Sensing, Experimental Mesocosm Facility, Lake Worth Fish Hatchery, NMR facility, X-ray diffraction facility, Mathemat-

ics and Science Education Institute. In social sciences: Institute of Behavioral Research.

SOFTWARE ENGINEERING

Add Ran College of Arts and Sciences, Department of Computer Science

Programs Offers program in software engineering (MSE).

Students 17 (2 women); includes 2 minority (1 Asian-American, 1 Hispanic).

Degrees Awarded In 1996, 3 degrees awarded.

Entrance Requirements GRE General Test (minimum combined score of 1000), TOEFL (minimum score 550).

Financial Aid *Application deadline:* 3/1.

Applying 8 applicants, 75% accepted. *Deadline:* 3/1 (rolling processing; 12/1 for spring admission). *Fee:* $0 ($60 for international students).

Contact *Dr. James Comer*
Chairperson
817-921-7166

TEXAS TECH UNIVERSITY
Lubbock, TX 79409

OVERVIEW

Texas Tech University is a public coed university.

ENROLLMENT

24,717 graduate, professional, and undergraduate students; 2,793 full-time matriculated graduate/professional students (1,122 women), 1,504 part-time matriculated graduate/professional students (845 women).

GRADUATE FACULTY

678 full-time (158 women), 32 part-time (8 women), 694 FTE; includes 76 minority (7 African-Americans, 45 Asian-Americans, 24 Hispanics).

EXPENSES

Tuition $56 per credit hour for state residents; $268 per credit hour for nonresidents. Fees $1454 per year full-time, $412 per semester (minimum) part-time.

HOUSING

Rooms and/or apartments available to single students at an average cost of $4200 (including board); on-campus housing not available to married students. Housing application deadline: 6/1. Graduate housing contact: James Burkhalter, 806-742-2661.

STUDENT SERVICES

Disabled student services, multicultural affairs office, low-cost health insurance, career counseling, free psychological counseling, campus safety program, campus employment opportunities, international student services, writing training.

FACILITIES

Library: Main library plus 4 additional on-campus libraries; total holdings of 1,987,162 volumes, 1,874,171 microforms, 20,949 current periodical subscriptions. A total of 342 personal computers in all libraries. Access provided to on-line information retrieval services. *Computer:* Campuswide network is available with full Internet access. Total number of PCs/terminals supplied for student use: 293. Computer services are offered at no charge. *Special:* In arts and humanities: Texas Wine Marketing Research Center, Center for the Study of the Vietnam Conflict, Turkish Oral Archives. In science and engineering: International Textile Research Center, Plant Stress and Water Conservation Institute. In social sciences: Ranching Heritage Center, Lubbock Lake Landmark (architectural dig site and state park), International Cultural Center.

COMPUTER SCIENCE

Graduate School, College of Engineering, Department of Computer Science

Programs   Awards MS, PhD. Part-time programs available.
Faculty   9 full-time (0 women).
Faculty Research   Generic controller software development, neural networks/speech recognition, neural-type network for solving 2-point boundary value. *Total annual research expenditures:* $309,057.
Students   56 full-time (12 women), 26 part-time (2 women); includes 1 minority (Hispanic), 64 international. Average age 29.
Degrees Awarded   In 1996, 25 master's, 1 doctorate awarded.
Entrance Requirements   For master's, GRE General Test (minimum combined score of 1000; average 1228), minimum GPA of 3.0; for doctorate, GRE General Test (minimum combined score of 1000), minimum GPA of 3.0.
Degree Requirements   Computer language, thesis/dissertation required, foreign language not required.
Financial Aid   In 1996–97, 46 students received aid, including 10 research assistantships (3 to first-year students) averaging $965 per month, 5 teaching assistantships averaging $893 per month; fellowships, Federal Work-Study, institutionally sponsored loans also available. Aid available to part-time students. *Financial aid application deadline:* 5/15; applicants required to submit FAFSA.
Applying   84 applicants, 62% accepted. *Deadline:* 4/15 (priority date; rolling processing; 11/1 for spring admission). *Fee:* $25 ($50 for international students).
Contact   *Dr. William J. B. Oldham*
Director
806-742-3527

ELECTRICAL ENGINEERING

Graduate School, College of Engineering, Department of Electrical Engineering

Programs   Awards MSEE, PhD. Part-time programs available.
Faculty   18 full-time (2 women), 1 part-time (0 women), 18.61 FTE.
Faculty Research   High-voltage space power, accuracy enhancement in optical computing, computer vision in image processing. *Total annual research expenditures:* $2.213 million.
Students   50 full-time (5 women), 13 part-time (2 women); includes 3 minority (1 African-American, 2 Hispanics), 41 international. Average age 28.
Degrees Awarded   In 1996, 21 master's, 5 doctorates awarded.
Entrance Requirements   For master's, GRE General Test (minimum combined score of 1000; average 1227), minimum GPA of 3.0; for doctorate, GRE General Test (minimum combined score of 1000), minimum GPA of 3.0.
Degree Requirements   Computer language, thesis/dissertation required, foreign language not required.
Financial Aid   In 1996–97, 37 research assistantships (7 to first-year students) averaging $981 per month, 1 teaching assistantship averaging $1,300 per month were awarded; fellowships, Federal Work-Study, institutionally sponsored loans also available. Aid available to part-time students. *Financial aid application deadline:* 5/15; applicants required to submit FAFSA.

Applying   139 applicants, 50% accepted. *Deadline:* 4/15 (priority date; rolling processing; 11/1 for spring admission). *Fee:* $25 ($50 for international students).
Contact   *Dr. Jon G. Bredeson*
Chair
806-742-3533

See in-depth description on page 573.

UNIVERSITY OF HOUSTON
Houston, TX 77204-2163

OVERVIEW
University of Houston is a public coed university.

ENROLLMENT
30,774 graduate, professional, and undergraduate students; 3,925 full-time matriculated graduate/professional students (1,918 women), 3,039 part-time matriculated graduate/professional students (1,605 women).

GRADUATE FACULTY
747 full-time (185 women), 295 part-time (97 women), 837.7 FTE; includes 143 minority (30 African-Americans, 80 Asian-Americans, 32 Hispanics, 1 Native American).

EXPENSES
Tuition $1344 per year full-time, $56 per credit hour part-time for state residents; $5952 per year full-time, $248 per credit hour part-time for nonresidents. Fees $1177 per year full-time, $117 per semester (minimum) part-time.

HOUSING
Rooms and/or apartments available to single students (2,600 units) at an average cost of $2500 per year ($4435 including board); available to married students (200 units) at an average cost of $5400 per year ($6900 including board). Housing application deadline: 6/1. Graduate housing contact: Sandy Coltharp, 800-247-7184.

STUDENT SERVICES
Disabled student services, low-cost health insurance, career counseling, free psychological counseling, exercise/wellness program, day-care facilities, campus safety program, campus employment opportunities, international student services.

FACILITIES
Library: M. D. Anderson Library plus 5 additional on-campus libraries; total holdings of 1,899,229 volumes, 3,733,365 microforms, 15,133 current periodical subscriptions. A total of 300 personal computers in all libraries. Access provided to on-line information retrieval services. *Computer:* Campuswide network is available with full Internet access. Total number of PCs/terminals supplied for student use: 850. Computer service fees are included with tuition and fees. *Special:* In arts and humanities: Blaffer Gallery, Center for Study of African-American Culture, Institute for Public History, Center for Asian Studies. In science and engineering: Texas Center for Superconductivity, Space Vacuum Expitaxy Center, Institute for Molecular Design, Composites Engineering Applications Center. In social sciences: Center for

Immigration Studies, Center for Public Policy, Energy Institute, Institute for Enterprise Excellence.

COMPUTER ENGINEERING

Cullen College of Engineering, Program in Computer and Systems Engineering

Programs Awards MSCSE, PhD. Part-time and evening/weekend programs available.

Faculty Research Parallel processing, parallel algorithms and architectures, neural networks.

Students 10 full-time (4 women), 13 part-time (3 women); includes 2 minority (both Asian-Americans), 9 international. Average age 28.

Degrees Awarded In 1996, 6 master's awarded. Terminal master's awarded for partial completion of doctoral program.

Entrance Requirements GRE General Test, TOEFL.

Degree Requirements For master's, thesis required (for some programs), foreign language not required; for doctorate, dissertation, departmental qualifying exams required, foreign language not required.

Financial Aid Fellowships, research assistantships, teaching assistantships, partial tuition waivers, Federal Work-Study available. *Financial aid application deadline: 7/1.*

Applying 81 applicants, 16% accepted. *Deadline:* 7/3 (priority date; rolling processing; 12/4 for spring admission). *Fee:* $25 ($75 for international students).

Contact Mylyssa McDonald
Graduate Analyst
713-743-4403
Fax: 713-743-4444
E-mail: mmm05866@jetson.uh.edu

See in-depth description on page **637.**

COMPUTER SCIENCE

College of Technology

Programs Offerings include microcomputer systems (MT).

College Faculty 23 full-time (7 women), 3 part-time (0 women), 24 FTE.

Applying *Deadline:* 7/1 (11/1 for spring admission). *Fee:* $35 ($75 for international students).

Contact Curtis D. Johnson
Associate Dean
713-743-4025
Fax: 713-743-4032
E-mail: cjohnsn@uh.edu

COMPUTER SCIENCE

College of Natural Sciences and Mathematics, Department of Computer Science

Programs Awards MS, PhD. Part-time programs available.

Faculty 18 full-time (0 women), 6 part-time (0 women).

Faculty Research Parallel and distributed systems, software engineering, numerical analysis, databases.

Students 159 full-time (42 women), 111 part-time (36 women); includes 45 minority (2 African-Americans, 39 Asian-Americans, 4 Hispanics), 173 international. Average age 30.

Degrees Awarded In 1996, 38 master's, 1 doctorate awarded. Terminal master's awarded for partial completion of doctoral program.

Entrance Requirements GRE General Test, TOEFL (minimum score 550).

Degree Requirements Computer language, thesis/dissertation.

Financial Aid In 1996–97, research assistantships averaging $850 per month, teaching assistantships averaging $850 per month were awarded; Federal Work-Study, institutionally sponsored loans also available. Aid available to part-time students. *Financial aid application deadline: 3/1;* applicants required to submit FAFSA.

Applying 282 applicants, 55% accepted. *Deadline:* 7/3 (priority date; rolling processing; 12/4 for spring admission). *Fee:* $0 ($75 for international students).

Contact Amanda Vaughan
Graduate Academic Advising Assistant
713-743-3364
Fax: 713-743-3335
E-mail: vaughan@cs.uh.edu

See in-depth description on page **635.**

ELECTRICAL ENGINEERING

Cullen College of Engineering, Department of Electrical and Computer Engineering

Programs Awards MEE, MSEE, PhD. Part-time and evening/weekend programs available.

Faculty 29 full-time (3 women), 4 part-time (0 women).

Faculty Research Applied electromagnetics and microelectronics, signal and image processing, biomedical engineering, geophysical applications, control engineering. *Total annual research expenditures:* $1.998 million.

Students 121 full-time (25 women), 65 part-time (9 women); includes 20 minority (3 African-Americans, 14 Asian-Americans, 3 Hispanics), 108 international. Average age 30.

Degrees Awarded In 1996, 57 master's, 11 doctorates awarded. Terminal master's awarded for partial completion of doctoral program.

Entrance Requirements GRE General Test, TOEFL.

Degree Requirements For master's, thesis required (for some programs), foreign language not required; for doctorate, dissertation, departmental qualifying exam required, foreign language not required.

Financial Aid Research assistantships, teaching assistantships, partial tuition waivers, Federal Work-Study, institutionally sponsored loans, and career-related internships or fieldwork available. *Financial aid application deadline: 7/1.*

Applying 180 applicants, 18% accepted. *Deadline:* 7/3 (priority date; rolling processing; 12/4 for spring admission). *Fee:* $25 ($75 for international students).

Contact Mylyssa McDonald
Graduate Analyst
713-743-4403
Fax: 713-743-4444
E-mail: mmm05866@jetson.uh.edu

See in-depth description on page **637.**

UNIVERSITY OF HOUSTON–CLEAR LAKE
Houston, TX 77058-1098

OVERVIEW

University of Houston–Clear Lake is a public coed upper-level institution.

ENROLLMENT

7,136 graduate, professional, and undergraduate students; 943 full-time matriculated graduate/professional students (531 women), 2,672 part-time matriculated graduate/professional students (1,544 women).

GRADUATE FACULTY
78.

TUITION
$201 per credit hour for state residents; $327 per credit hour for nonresidents.

HOUSING
On-campus housing not available.

STUDENT SERVICES
Low-cost health insurance, career counseling, free psychological counseling, campus safety program, campus employment opportunities, international student services.

FACILITIES
Library: Neumann Library; total holdings of 339,254 volumes, 2,455 current periodical subscriptions. A total of 20 personal computers in all libraries. Access provided to on-line information retrieval services. *Special:* In science and engineering: Gas chromatograph, mass spectrometer, scanning electron microscope, Autoteknicon SMA 6-60 autoanalyzer.

COMPUTER ENGINEERING

School of Natural and Applied Sciences, Program in Computer Engineering
Programs Awards MS.
Faculty 5 full-time (1 woman), 1 part-time (0 women).
Students 19 full-time (7 women), 37 part-time (5 women); includes 17 minority (1 African-American, 14 Asian-Americans, 2 Hispanics), 14 international. Average age 32.
Degrees Awarded In 1996, 7 degrees awarded.
Entrance Requirements GRE General Test.
Financial Aid Research assistantships, teaching assistantships available. *Financial aid application deadline: 5/1.*
Applying *Fee:* $30 ($60 for international students).
Contact *Dr. Robert Ferebee*
Interim Associate Dean
281-283-3700
Fax: 281-283-3707

COMPUTER SCIENCE

School of Natural and Applied Sciences, Program in Computer Science
Programs Awards MS.
Faculty 10 full-time (2 women), 1 part-time (0 women).
Students 82 full-time (17 women), 163 part-time (37 women); includes 73 minority (58 Asian-Americans, 15 Hispanics), 65 international. Average age 32.
Degrees Awarded In 1996, 40 degrees awarded.
Entrance Requirements GRE General Test.
Financial Aid Research assistantships, teaching assistantships available. *Financial aid application deadline: 5/1.*
Applying *Fee:* $30 ($60 for international students).
Contact *Dr. Robert Ferebee*
Interim Associate Dean
281-283-3700
Fax: 281-283-3707

INFORMATION SCIENCE

School of Natural and Applied Sciences, Program in Computer Information Systems
Programs Awards MA.
Faculty 7 full-time (1 woman).

Students 41 full-time (14 women), 92 part-time (40 women); includes 36 minority (6 African-Americans, 20 Asian-Americans, 10 Hispanics), 3 international. Average age 32.
Degrees Awarded In 1996, 9 degrees awarded.
Entrance Requirements GRE General Test.
Financial Aid Research assistantships, teaching assistantships available. *Financial aid application deadline: 5/1.*
Applying *Fee:* $30 ($60 for international students).
Contact *Dr. Robert Ferebee*
Interim Associate Dean
281-283-3700
Fax: 281-283-3707

SOFTWARE ENGINEERING

School of Natural and Applied Sciences, Program in Software Engineering
Programs Awards MS.
Faculty 5 full-time (0 women), 2 part-time (0 women).
Students 4 full-time (1 woman), 20 part-time (7 women); includes 3 minority (1 Asian-American, 2 Hispanics), 6 international.
Entrance Requirements GRE General Test.
Financial Aid *Application deadline: 5/1.*
Applying *Fee:* $30 ($60 for international students).
Contact *Dr. Robert Ferebee*
Interim Associate Dean
281-283-3700
Fax: 281-283-3707

UNIVERSITY OF NORTH TEXAS
Denton, TX 76203-6737

OVERVIEW
University of North Texas is a public coed university.

ENROLLMENT
24,957 graduate, professional, and undergraduate students; 1,998 full-time matriculated graduate/professional students (1,037 women), 3,032 part-time matriculated graduate/professional students (1,906 women).

GRADUATE FACULTY
694; includes 76 minority (25 African-Americans, 22 Asian-Americans, 25 Hispanics, 4 Native Americans).

EXPENSES
Tuition $1512 per year full-time, $696 per year part-time for state residents; $4896 per year full-time, $3260 per year part-time for nonresidents. Fees $736 per year full-time, $538 per year part-time.

HOUSING
Rooms and/or apartments available to single students (4,000 units) at an average cost of $1877 per year ($3777 including board); available to married students (50 units). Graduate housing contact: Dr. Betsy McGuire, 940-565-2605.

STUDENT SERVICES
Disabled student services, multicultural affairs office, low-cost health insurance, career counseling, free psychological counseling, exercise/wellness program, day-care facilities, campus safety program, campus employment opportunities, international student services.

FACILITIES

Library: A. M. Willis Library plus 5 additional on-campus libraries; total holdings of 1,292,539 volumes, 2,902,046 microforms, 10,302 current periodical subscriptions. A total of 300 personal computers in all libraries. Access provided to on-line information retrieval services. *Computer:* Campuswide network is available with full Internet access. Computer service fees are applied as a separate charge. *Special:* In arts and humanities: North Texas Institute for Educators on the Visual Arts, University Center for Texas Studies. In science and engineering: Center for Network Neuroscience, Center for Organometallic Research and Education, Center for Remote Sensing and Land-Use Analysis, Industry/University Cooperative Research Center for Nanostructural Materials, Institute of Applied Sciences, University Center for Materials Characterization. In social sciences: Center for Economic Education, Center for Environmental Economic Studies and Research, Center for Inter-American Studies and Research, Labor and Industrial Relations Institute, Center for Studies in Aging, Center for Behavior Analysis, Center for Public Service, Institute for Anthropology, Institute of Criminal Justice, Institute for Emergency Administration and Planning, Center for Rehabilitation Studies, Institute of Applied Economics, Institute for Studies in Addiction.

COMPUTER SCIENCE

College of Arts and Sciences, Department of Computer Sciences
Programs Awards MA, MS, PhD.
Faculty 20 full-time (1 woman).
Faculty Research Parallel algorithms, artificial intelligence, operating systems, software engineering, databases.
Students 87 full-time (19 women), 45 part-time (6 women); includes 8 minority (2 African-Americans, 6 Asian-Americans), 92 international.
Degrees Awarded In 1996, 43 master's, 10 doctorates awarded. Terminal master's awarded for partial completion of doctoral program.
Entrance Requirements For master's, GRE General Test (minimum combined score of 1050), minimum undergraduate GPA of 3.0; for doctorate, GRE General Test (minimum combined score of 1150), minimum GPA of 3.5.
Degree Requirements For master's, thesis (for some programs), comprehensive exam required, foreign language not required; for doctorate, dissertation, comprehensive exam required, foreign language not required.
Financial Aid Fellowships, research assistantships, teaching assistantships, Federal Work-Study, institutionally sponsored loans, and career-related internships or fieldwork available. *Financial aid application deadline:* 4/1.
Applying Deadline: 7/15. *Fee:* $25 ($50 for international students).
Contact C. Q. Yang
Graduate Coordinator
940-565-2767

See in-depth description on page 689.

INFORMATION SCIENCE

Interdisciplinary Studies
Programs Offerings include information science (PhD).
Degree Requirements 1 foreign language (computer language can substitute), dissertation.
Applying Deadline: 7/15. *Fee:* $25 ($50 for international students).

Contact *Dr. Sandra L. Terrell*
Associate Dean
940-565-2383
Fax: 940-565-2141

THE UNIVERSITY OF TEXAS AT ARLINGTON
Arlington, TX 76019-0407

OVERVIEW

The University of Texas at Arlington is a public coed university.

ENROLLMENT

21,000 graduate, professional, and undergraduate students; 1,707 full-time matriculated graduate/professional students (755 women), 2,121 part-time matriculated graduate/professional students (1,017 women).

GRADUATE FACULTY

467 full-time (112 women), 29 part-time (8 women).

TUITION

$2901 per year full-time, $421 per semester (minimum) part-time for state residents; $8279 per year full-time, $1093 per semester (minimum) part-time for nonresidents.

HOUSING

Rooms and/or apartments available to single students at an average cost of $2500 per year; available to married students at an average cost of $4500 per year. Graduate housing contact: Wyl Parker, 817-273-2791.

STUDENT SERVICES

Disabled student services, multicultural affairs office, career counseling, free psychological counseling, exercise/wellness program, day-care facilities, campus safety program, campus employment opportunities, international student services.

FACILITIES

Library: Central Library plus 2 additional on-campus libraries; total holdings of 1.5 million volumes, 1.25 million microforms, 5,800 current periodical subscriptions. Access provided to on-line information retrieval services. *Computer:* Campuswide network is available with full Internet access. *Special:* In arts and humanities: Center for Research in Contemporary Art, Center for Rhetorical and Critical Theory. In science and engineering: Center for Positron Studies, Energy Systems Research Center, Automation and Robotics Research Institute, electronic materials and devices engineering laboratory. In social sciences: Community Services Development Center, Center for Social Research, Center for Greater Southwestern Studies and History of Cartography.

COMPUTER ENGINEERING

College of Engineering, Department of Computer Science and Engineering
Programs Awards MCS, M Engr, MS, M Sw En, PhD.
Faculty 19 full-time (3 women).

Students 172 full-time (37 women), 122 part-time (23 women); includes 34 minority (3 African-Americans, 28 Asian-Americans, 3 Hispanics), 175 international.
Degrees Awarded In 1996, 138 master's, 2 doctorates awarded.
Entrance Requirements For master's, GRE General Test (minimum combined score of 1100), TOEFL (minimum score 560); for doctorate, GRE General Test (minimum combined score of 1250), TOEFL (minimum score 560).
Degree Requirements For master's, computer language, thesis (for some programs) required, foreign language not required; for doctorate, computer language, dissertation required, foreign language not required.
Financial Aid Research assistantships, teaching assistantships, partial tuition waivers, and career-related internships or fieldwork available.
Applying 389 applicants, 31% accepted. *Deadline:* rolling. *Fee:* $25 ($50 for international students).
Contact Dr. Bob Weems
Graduate Adviser
817-272-3785

See in-depth description on page **723.**

COMPUTER SCIENCE

College of Engineering, Department of Computer Science and Engineering
Programs Awards MCS, M Engr, MS, M Sw En, PhD.
Faculty 19 full-time (3 women).
Students 172 full-time (37 women), 122 part-time (23 women); includes 34 minority (3 African-Americans, 28 Asian-Americans, 3 Hispanics), 175 international.
Degrees Awarded In 1996, 138 master's, 2 doctorates awarded.
Entrance Requirements For master's, GRE General Test (minimum combined score of 1100), TOEFL (minimum score 560); for doctorate, GRE General Test (minimum combined score of 1250), TOEFL (minimum score 560).
Degree Requirements For master's, computer language, thesis (for some programs) required, foreign language not required; for doctorate, computer language, dissertation required, foreign language not required.
Financial Aid Research assistantships, teaching assistantships, partial tuition waivers, and career-related internships or fieldwork available.
Applying 389 applicants, 31% accepted. *Deadline:* rolling. *Fee:* $25 ($50 for international students).
Contact Dr. Bob Weems
Graduate Adviser
817-272-3785

See in-depth description on page **723.**

ELECTRICAL ENGINEERING

College of Engineering, Department of Electrical Engineering
Programs Awards M Engr, MS, PhD.
Faculty 22 full-time (1 woman), 1 part-time (0 women).
Students 132 full-time (6 women), 139 part-time (18 women); includes 45 minority (7 African-Americans, 33 Asian-Americans, 4 Hispanics, 1 Native American), 124 international.
Degrees Awarded In 1996, 80 master's, 14 doctorates awarded.
Entrance Requirements GRE General Test, TOEFL.
Degree Requirements For master's, thesis required (for some programs), foreign language not required; for doctorate, dissertation required, foreign language not required.
Financial Aid Fellowships, research assistantships, teaching assistantships available.
Applying 375 applicants, 41% accepted. *Deadline:* rolling. *Fee:* $25 ($50 for international students).

Contact Ronald Carter
Graduate Adviser
817-272-2671

See in-depth description on page **725.**

SOFTWARE ENGINEERING

College of Engineering, Department of Computer Science and Engineering
Programs Awards MCS, M Engr, MS, M Sw En, PhD.
Faculty 19 full-time (3 women).
Students 172 full-time (37 women), 122 part-time (23 women); includes 34 minority (3 African-Americans, 28 Asian-Americans, 3 Hispanics), 175 international.
Degrees Awarded In 1996, 138 master's, 2 doctorates awarded.
Entrance Requirements For master's, GRE General Test (minimum combined score of 1100), TOEFL (minimum score 560); for doctorate, GRE General Test (minimum combined score of 1250), TOEFL (minimum score 560).
Degree Requirements For master's, computer language, thesis (for some programs) required, foreign language not required; for doctorate, computer language, dissertation required, foreign language not required.
Financial Aid Research assistantships, teaching assistantships, partial tuition waivers, and career-related internships or fieldwork available.
Applying 389 applicants, 31% accepted. *Deadline:* rolling. *Fee:* $25 ($50 for international students).
Contact Dr. Bob Weems
Graduate Adviser
817-272-3785

See in-depth description on page **723.**

THE UNIVERSITY OF TEXAS AT AUSTIN
Austin, TX 78712

OVERVIEW
The University of Texas at Austin is a public coed university.

ENROLLMENT
48,008 graduate, professional, and undergraduate students; 12,219 matriculated graduate/professional students (5,538 women).

GRADUATE FACULTY
1,774 (417 women); includes 238 minority (50 African-Americans, 100 Asian-Americans, 80 Hispanics, 8 Native Americans).

EXPENSES
Tuition $2448 per year full-time, $102 per credit part-time for state residents; $7584 per year full-time, $316 per year part-time for nonresidents. Fees $750 per year full-time, $36 per semester (minimum) part-time.

HOUSING
Rooms and/or apartments available to single students (4,933 units) and married students (790 units).

STUDENT SERVICES
Disabled student services, low-cost health insurance, career counseling, free psychological counseling, exercise/wellness program, day-care facilities, campus safety program, campus employment opportunities, international student services, writing training, grant writing training, teacher training.

FACILITIES

Library: Perry-Castaneda Library plus 18 additional on-campus libraries; total holdings of 7,329,663 volumes, 5,295,504 microforms, 51,562 current periodical subscriptions. Access provided to on-line information retrieval services. *Computer:* Campuswide network is available. Computer service fees are included with tuition and fees.

COMPUTER ENGINEERING

Graduate School, College of Engineering, Department of Electrical and Computer Engineering

Programs Offers program in electrical engineering (MSE, PhD).
Students 350 full-time (47 women), 164 part-time (17 women); includes 80 minority (8 African-Americans, 55 Asian-Americans, 17 Hispanics), 256 international.
Degrees Awarded In 1996, 114 master's, 56 doctorates awarded.
Entrance Requirements For master's, GRE General Test (minimum combined score of 1100; average 1350), minimum GPA of 3.3 in upper-division course work; for doctorate, GRE General Test (combined average 1350).
Financial Aid Fellowships, research assistantships, teaching assistantships available. *Financial aid application deadline:* 1/2.
Applying 911 applicants, 37% accepted. *Deadline:* 1/2 (rolling processing). *Fee:* $50 ($75 for international students).
Contact Dr. G. Jack Lipovski
Graduate Adviser
512-471-8511

See in-depth description on page 729.

COMPUTER SCIENCE

Graduate School, College of Natural Sciences, Department of Computer Sciences

Programs Awards MA, MSCS, PhD.
Students 225 (44 women); includes 31 minority (2 African-Americans, 19 Asian-Americans, 10 Hispanics), 113 international.
Degrees Awarded In 1996, 53 master's, 17 doctorates awarded.
Entrance Requirements GRE General Test, GRE Subject Test.
Degree Requirements For master's, thesis optional; for doctorate, dissertation, qualifying exam.
Financial Aid Fellowships, research assistantships, teaching assistantships, institutionally sponsored loans available. *Financial aid application deadline:* 1/2.
Applying 247 applicants, 54% accepted. *Deadline:* 1/2. *Fee:* $50 ($75 for international students).
Contact Dr. Bruce Porter
Graduate Adviser
512-471-9502

See in-depth description on page 727.

ELECTRICAL ENGINEERING

Graduate School, College of Engineering, Department of Electrical and Computer Engineering

Programs Offers program in electrical engineering (MSE, PhD).
Students 350 full-time (47 women), 164 part-time (17 women); includes 80 minority (8 African-Americans, 55 Asian-Americans, 17 Hispanics), 256 international.
Degrees Awarded In 1996, 114 master's, 56 doctorates awarded.
Entrance Requirements For master's, GRE General Test (minimum combined score of 1100; average 1350), minimum GPA of 3.3 in upper-division course work; for doctorate, GRE General Test (combined average 1350).

Financial Aid Fellowships, research assistantships, teaching assistantships available. *Financial aid application deadline:* 1/2.
Applying 911 applicants, 37% accepted. *Deadline:* 1/2 (rolling processing). *Fee:* $50 ($75 for international students).
Contact Dr. G. Jack Lipovski
Graduate Adviser
512-471-8511

See in-depth description on page 729.

THE UNIVERSITY OF TEXAS AT DALLAS
Richardson, TX 75083-0688

OVERVIEW
The University of Texas at Dallas is a public coed university.

ENROLLMENT
9,378 graduate, professional, and undergraduate students; 1,219 full-time matriculated graduate/professional students (589 women), 1,538 part-time matriculated graduate/professional students (681 women).

GRADUATE FACULTY
288 full-time (64 women), 138 part-time (61 women); includes 52 minority (9 African-Americans, 31 Asian-Americans, 11 Hispanics, 1 Native American).

TUITION
$3808 per year full-time, $482 per semester (minimum) part-time for state residents; $10,228 per year full-time, $1124 per semester (minimum) part-time for nonresidents.

HOUSING
Rooms and/or apartments available to single students (800 units) and married students (800 units) at an average cost of $5255 (including board). Graduate housing contact: Kim Winkler, 972-883-6391.

STUDENT SERVICES
Low-cost health insurance, career counseling, free psychological counseling, day-care facilities, campus safety program, campus employment opportunities.

FACILITIES
Library: Eugene McDermott Library; total holdings of 594,913 volumes, 1,603,235 microforms, 3,811 current periodical subscriptions. A total of 19 personal computers in all libraries. Access provided to on-line information retrieval services. *Computer:* Campuswide network is available with full Internet access. Computer service fees are applied as a separate charge. *Special:* In arts and humanities: Translation Center. In science and engineering: Callier Center for Communication Disorders, Center for Applied Optics, Center for Lithospheric Studies, Center for Quantum Electronics, Center for Space Sciences, Institute for Environmental Sciences, Center for Engineering Mathematics, Center for Genetic Technology, Communications and Learning Center. In social sciences: Center for China/U.S. Management Studies, Center for Research in Teaching and Learning, Bruton Center for Development Studies, Morris Hite Center for

Product Development and Marketing Science, Center for International Accounting Development.

COMPUTER SCIENCE

Erik Jonsson School of Engineering and Computer Science, Program in Computer Science

Programs Awards MS, PhD. Part-time and evening/weekend programs available.

Faculty 19 full-time (3 women), 8 part-time (1 woman).

Faculty Research Telecommunication networks, parallel processing, analysis of algorithms, artificial intelligence, software engineering.

Students 236 full-time (97 women), 195 part-time (54 women); includes 101 minority (7 African-Americans, 92 Asian-Americans, 2 Hispanics), 221 international. Average age 30.

Degrees Awarded In 1996, 103 master's, 2 doctorates awarded.

Entrance Requirements For master's, GRE General Test (minimum combined score of 1100), TOEFL (minimum score 550), minimum GPA of 3.0 in undergraduate course work, 3.3 in quantitative course work; for doctorate, GRE General Test (minimum combined score of 1100 required with master's degree, 1300 with bachelor's degree), TOEFL (minimum score 550), minimum GPA of 3.5.

Degree Requirements For master's, minimum GPA of 3.0 required, thesis optional, foreign language not required; for doctorate, dissertation, minimum grade of B in core courses required, foreign language not required.

Financial Aid 43 students received aid; fellowships, research assistantships, teaching assistantships, Federal Work-Study, and career-related internships or fieldwork available. Aid available to part-time students. *Financial aid application deadline:* 11/1.

Applying 289 applicants, 73% accepted. *Deadline:* 7/15 (rolling processing; 11/15 for spring admission). *Fee:* $25 ($75 for international students).

Contact Deborah Chen
Graduate Secretary
972-883-2185
Fax: 972-883-2344

*See in-depth description on page **731**.*

ELECTRICAL ENGINEERING

Erik Jonsson School of Engineering and Computer Science, Programs in Electrical Engineering

Programs Offerings in electrical engineering (MSEE, PhD), microelectronics (MSEE), telecommunications (MSEE). Part-time and evening/weekend programs available.

Faculty 15 full-time (0 women).

Faculty Research Communications and signal processing, solid-state devices and circuits, digital systems, optical devices, materials and systems, lasers and photonics.

Students 61 full-time (15 women), 114 part-time (22 women); includes 39 minority (3 African-Americans, 29 Asian-Americans, 7 Hispanics), 65 international. Average age 29.

Degrees Awarded In 1996, 39 master's, 6 doctorates awarded.

Entrance Requirements For master's, GRE General Test (minimum score 500 on verbal section, 700 on quantitative, 600 on analytical), TOEFL (minimum score 550), minimum GPA of 3.0 in related bachelor's degree; for doctorate, GRE General Test (minimum score 500 on verbal section, 700 on quantitative, 600 on analytical), TOEFL (minimum score 550), minimum GPA of 3.5.

Degree Requirements For master's, thesis (for some programs), minimum GPA of 3.0, thesis or major design project required, foreign language not required; for doctorate, dissertation, minimum GPA of 3.5 required, foreign language not required.

Financial Aid 36 students received aid; fellowships, research assistantships, teaching assistantships, Federal Work-Study available. Aid available to part-time students. *Financial aid application deadline:* 11/1.

Applying 134 applicants, 86% accepted. *Deadline:* 7/15 (rolling processing; 11/15 for spring admission). *Fee:* $25 ($75 for international students).

Contact Secretary
972-883-2648
Fax: 972-883-2710

*See in-depth description on page **733**.*

THE UNIVERSITY OF TEXAS AT EL PASO
El Paso, TX 79968-0001

OVERVIEW
The University of Texas at El Paso is a public coed university.

ENROLLMENT
15,386 graduate, professional, and undergraduate students; 607 full-time matriculated graduate/professional students (280 women), 1,000 part-time matriculated graduate/professional students (567 women).

GRADUATE FACULTY
418 full-time (104 women), 374 part-time (186 women); includes 203 minority (12 African-Americans, 20 Asian-Americans, 168 Hispanics, 3 Native Americans).

TUITION
$1585 per year full-time, $259 per credit hour part-time for state residents; $6079 per year full-time, $368 per credit hour part-time for nonresidents.

HOUSING
Rooms and/or apartments available to single students (700 units) at an average cost of $1800 per year; available to married students (60 units). Graduate housing contact: Carlos Garcia, 915-747-5352.

STUDENT SERVICES
Disabled student services, low-cost health insurance, career counseling, free psychological counseling, exercise/wellness program, day-care facilities, campus employment opportunities, international student services, grant writing training, teacher training.

FACILITIES
Library: Main library; total holdings of 840,773 volumes, 1,601,630 microforms, 2,541 current periodical subscriptions. A total of 130 personal computers in all libraries. Access provided to on-line information retrieval services. *Computer:* Campuswide network is available with full Internet access. Computer service fees are included with tuition and fees. *Special:* In arts and humanities: El Paso Centennial Museum, Oral History Institute. In science and engineering: NSF Materials Science Center, El Paso Solar Pond Research Station, Institute for Manufacturing and Materials Management, Center for Environmental Resource Management, Material Research Institute. In social sciences: Inter-American and Border Studies

Center; Center for Entrepreneurial Development, Advancement Research and Support.

COMPUTER ENGINEERING

College of Engineering, Department of Electrical and Computer Engineering

Programs Offers programs in computer engineering (MS, PhD), electrical engineering (MS, PhD). MS offered jointly with the University of Texas of the Permian Basin. Part-time and evening/weekend programs available.

Faculty 17 full-time (1 woman), 8 part-time (0 women).

Faculty Research Signal and image processing, computer architecture, fiber optics, computational electromagnetics, electronic displays and thin films. *Total annual research expenditures:* $436,501.

Students 50 full-time (8 women), 29 part-time (3 women); includes 27 minority (2 Asian-Americans, 25 Hispanics), 38 international. Average age 29.

Degrees Awarded In 1996, 16 master's awarded.

Entrance Requirements For master's, GRE General Test, TOEFL (minimum score 550), minimum GPA of 3.0; for doctorate, GRE General Test, TOEFL, qualifying exam, minimum graduate GPA of 3.0.

Degree Requirements For master's, thesis optional; for doctorate, dissertation.

Financial Aid In 1996–97, 60 students received aid, including research assistantships averaging $1,000 per month, teaching assistantships averaging $1,000 per month; fellowships, partial tuition waivers, Federal Work-Study, institutionally sponsored loans also available. *Financial aid application deadline:* 2/15.

Applying 58 applicants, 48% accepted. *Deadline:* 7/1 (priority date; rolling processing; 11/1 for spring admission). *Fee:* $15 ($65 for international students).

Contact Susan Jordan
Director, Graduate Student Services
915-747-5491
Fax: 915-747-5788
E-mail: sjordan@utep.edu

COMPUTER SCIENCE

College of Engineering, Department of Computer Science

Programs Awards MS. Part-time and evening/weekend programs available.

Faculty 7 full-time (1 woman), 3 part-time (0 women).

Faculty Research *Total annual research expenditures:* $395,129.

Students 16 full-time (2 women), 15 part-time (5 women); includes 7 minority (all Hispanics), 17 international. Average age 27.

Degrees Awarded In 1996, 10 degrees awarded.

Entrance Requirements GRE General Test, TOEFL (minimum score 550), minimum GPA of 3.0.

Degree Requirements Thesis optional, foreign language not required.

Financial Aid Research assistantships, teaching assistantships, partial tuition waivers, Federal Work-Study, institutionally sponsored loans available. *Financial aid application deadline:* 2/15; applicants required to submit FAFSA.

Applying 45 applicants, 49% accepted. *Deadline:* 7/1 (priority date; rolling processing; 11/1 for spring admission). *Fee:* $15 ($65 for international students).

Contact Susan Jordan
Director, Graduate Student Services
915-747-5491
Fax: 915-747-5788
E-mail: sjordan@utep.edu

ELECTRICAL ENGINEERING

College of Engineering, Department of Electrical and Computer Engineering

Programs Offers programs in computer engineering (MS, PhD), electrical engineering (MS, PhD). MS offered jointly with the University of Texas of the Permian Basin. Part-time and evening/weekend programs available.

Faculty 17 full-time (1 woman), 8 part-time (0 women).

Faculty Research Signal and image processing, computer architecture, fiber optics, computational electromagnetics, electronic displays and thin films. *Total annual research expenditures:* $436,501.

Students 50 full-time (8 women), 29 part-time (3 women); includes 27 minority (2 Asian-Americans, 25 Hispanics), 38 international. Average age 29.

Degrees Awarded In 1996, 16 master's awarded.

Entrance Requirements For master's, GRE General Test, TOEFL (minimum score 550), minimum GPA of 3.0; for doctorate, GRE General Test, TOEFL, qualifying exam, minimum graduate GPA of 3.0.

Degree Requirements For master's, thesis optional; for doctorate, dissertation.

Financial Aid In 1996–97, 60 students received aid, including research assistantships averaging $1,000 per month, teaching assistantships averaging $1,000 per month; fellowships, partial tuition waivers, Federal Work-Study, institutionally sponsored loans also available. *Financial aid application deadline:* 2/15.

Applying 58 applicants, 48% accepted. *Deadline:* 7/1 (priority date; rolling processing; 11/1 for spring admission). *Fee:* $15 ($65 for international students).

Contact Susan Jordan
Director, Graduate Student Services
915-747-5491
Fax: 915-747-5788
E-mail: sjordan@utep.edu

THE UNIVERSITY OF TEXAS AT SAN ANTONIO
San Antonio, TX 78249-0617

OVERVIEW
The University of Texas at San Antonio is a public coed comprehensive institution.

ENROLLMENT
17,547 graduate, professional, and undergraduate students; 607 full-time matriculated graduate/professional students (305 women), 2,024 part-time matriculated graduate/professional students (1,206 women).

GRADUATE FACULTY
376 full-time (108 women), 475 part-time (228 women); includes 190 minority (13 African-Americans, 62 Asian-Americans, 107 Hispanics, 8 Native Americans).

TUITION
$2926 per year full-time, $421 per semester (minimum) part-time for state residents; $8062 per year full-time, $1063 per semester (minimum) part-time for nonresidents.

HOUSING
Rooms and/or apartments available to single students (1,060 units) and married students (940 units) at an aver-

age cost of $2833 per year ($4880 including board). Graduate housing contact: Peg Layton, 210-354-7676.

STUDENT SERVICES

Disabled student services, multicultural affairs office, low-cost health insurance, career counseling, free psychological counseling, campus employment opportunities, international student services.

FACILITIES

Library: John Peace Library; total holdings of 490,394 volumes, 2,385,025 microforms, 2,297 current periodical subscriptions. Access provided to on-line information retrieval services. *Computer:* Campuswide network is available. Computer service fees are included with tuition and fees. *Special:* In arts and humanities: Institute for the Arts and Humanities, Research Center for the Visual Arts, Institute for Music Research. In science and engineering: Center for Water Research, Institute for Research in Sciences and Engineering. In social sciences: Institute for Research in Social and Behavioral Sciences, Center for Archaeological Research, Center for Learning and Development Research in Education, Center for the Study of Women and Gender, Hispanic Research Center, Institute for Studies in Business, Center for Professional Excellence.

COMPUTER SCIENCE

College of Sciences and Engineering, Division of Computer Science
Programs Awards MS, PhD.
Faculty 13 full-time (1 woman), 12 part-time (0 women).
Students 14 full-time (4 women), 36 part-time (10 women). Average age 34.
Degrees Awarded In 1996, 12 master's awarded.
Entrance Requirements For master's, GRE General Test; for doctorate, GRE General Test (minimum combined score of 1000), TOEFL (minimum score 550), minimum GPA of 3.0.
Degree Requirements For doctorate, dissertation, comprehensive exam.
Applying 70 applicants, 27% accepted. *Deadline:* 7/1 (rolling processing). *Fee:* $20.
Contact Dr. Robert Hiromoto
Interim Director
210-458-4453

ELECTRICAL ENGINEERING

College of Sciences and Engineering, Division of Engineering
Programs Offerings include electrical engineering (MS).
Division Faculty 25 full-time (4 women), 21 part-time (1 woman).
Entrance Requirements GRE General Test.
Degree Requirements Thesis optional, foreign language not required.
Applying *Deadline:* 7/1 (rolling processing; 12/1 for spring admission). *Fee:* $20.
Contact Dr. Lex Akers
Director
210-458-4490

THE UNIVERSITY OF TEXAS AT TYLER
Tyler, TX 75799-0001

OVERVIEW

The University of Texas at Tyler is a public coed upper-level institution.

ENROLLMENT

3,790 graduate, professional, and undergraduate students; 286 full-time matriculated graduate/professional students (159 women), 1,193 part-time matriculated graduate/professional students (796 women).

GRADUATE FACULTY

115 full-time (43 women), 33 part-time (14 women); includes 4 minority (2 Asian-Americans, 2 Hispanics).

TUITION

$2048 per year full-time, $331 per semester (minimum) part-time for state residents; $7184 per year full-time, $955 per semester (minimum) part-time for nonresidents.

HOUSING

On-campus housing not available.

STUDENT SERVICES

Career counseling, free psychological counseling.

FACILITIES

Library: Robert R. Muntz Library; total holdings of 193,519 volumes, 523,816 microforms, 1,282 current periodical subscriptions. A total of 107 personal computers in all libraries. Access provided to on-line information retrieval services. *Special:* In science and engineering: Zuckerman Electron Microscope Laboratory, University of Texas High Speed Computational Center. In social sciences: Center for Policy Studies, Child and Family Abuse Clearinghouse.

COMPUTER SCIENCE

School of Sciences and Mathematics, Department of Mathematics, Program in Computer Science
Programs Offers computer science (MS), interdisciplinary studies (MA, MS).
Faculty 6 full-time (2 women).
Faculty Research Artificial neural systems, artificial intelligence, image processing, computer graphics, protein identification using the computer.
Degrees Awarded In 1996, 39 degrees awarded.
Entrance Requirements GRE General Test (minimum combined score of 1000), previous course work in data structures and computer organization.
Degree Requirements Computer language, comprehensive exam required, thesis optional, foreign language not required.
Financial Aid *Application deadline:* 7/1.
Applying *Fee:* $0.
Contact Martha D. Wheat
Director of Admissions and Student Records
903-566-7201
Fax: 903-566-7068

THE UNIVERSITY OF TEXAS–PAN AMERICAN
Edinburg, TX 78539-2999

OVERVIEW

The University of Texas–Pan American is a public coed comprehensive institution.

TUITION

$2085 per year full-time, $231 per semester (minimum) part-time for state residents; $6187 per year full-time, $856 per semester (minimum) part-time for nonresidents.

HOUSING

Rooms and/or apartments available to single students; on-campus housing not available to married students. Graduate housing contact: Housing Office, 210-381-3439.

FACILITIES

Library: Main library. *Special:* In arts and humanities: Speech and hearing clinic. In science and engineering: Coastal marine biology laboratory. In social sciences: Rio Grande Valley Archives.

COMPUTER SCIENCE

College of Science and Engineering, Department of Computer Science
Programs Awards MS.
Entrance Requirements GRE General Test, TOEFL, minimum GPA of 3.0 in last 60 hours.
Degree Requirements Final written exam, project.
Financial Aid Research assistantships, teaching assistantships available. Financial aid applicants required to submit FAFSA.
Applying *Fee:* $0.
Contact *Graduate Coordinator*
956-381-2320
Fax: 956-384-5099
E-mail: graduate-studies@cs.panam.edu
See in-depth description on page 735.

UTAH

BRIGHAM YOUNG UNIVERSITY
Provo, UT 84602-1001

OVERVIEW

Brigham Young University is an independent-religious coed university.

ENROLLMENT

31,419 graduate, professional, and undergraduate students; 2,070 full-time matriculated graduate/professional students (687 women), 1,476 part-time matriculated graduate/professional students (580 women).

GRADUATE FACULTY

1,176 (152 women).

TUITION

$3100 per year full-time, $172 per credit hour part-time for state residents; $4650 per year full-time, $258 per credit hour part-time for nonresidents.

HOUSING

Rooms and/or apartments available to single students at an average cost of $1715 per year ($3425 including board); available to married students (1,324 units) at an average cost of $2760 per year. Graduate housing contact: Harold Redd, 801-378-2853.

STUDENT SERVICES

Disabled student services, multicultural affairs office, low-cost health insurance, career counseling, free psychological counseling, exercise/wellness program, campus safety program, campus employment opportunities, international student services, writing training, teacher training.

FACILITIES

Library: Harold B. Lee Library plus 2 additional on-campus libraries; total holdings of 2,411,754 volumes, 2,311,821 microforms, 16,487 current periodical subscriptions. A total of 250 personal computers in all libraries. Access provided to on-line information retrieval services. *Computer:* Campuswide network is available with full Internet access. Total number of PCs/terminals supplied for student use: 1,800. Computer service fees are applied as a separate charge. *Special:* In arts and humanities: Center for Computer Based Education, art museum, Humanities Research Center, Harris Fine Arts Center. In science and engineering: Monte L. Bean Life Science Museum, environmental analysis laboratory, Benson Agricultural Institute, Advanced Combustion Engineering Research Center, animal science farm. In social sciences: Family and Demographic Research Institute, Women's Research Institute, Redd Institute of Western Studies, Kennedy Center for International Studies.

COMPUTER SCIENCE

College of Physical and Mathematical Sciences, Department of Computer Science
Programs Awards MS, PhD.
Faculty 20 full-time (0 women).
Faculty Research Software development, graphics, image processing, neural networks and machine learning.
Students 20 full-time (2 women), 84 part-time (10 women); includes 31 minority (29 Asian-Americans, 2 Hispanics), 29 international. Average age 26.
Degrees Awarded In 1996, 18 master's, 2 doctorates awarded. Terminal master's awarded for partial completion of doctoral program.
Entrance Requirements For master's, GRE General Test, minimum GPA of 3.0 in last 60 hours; for doctorate, GRE General Test, GRE Subject Test.
Degree Requirements For master's, thesis; for doctorate, dissertation required, foreign language not required.
Financial Aid Research assistantships, teaching assistantships available.
Applying 50 applicants, 62% accepted. *Deadline:* 2/15 (9/15 for spring admission). *Fee:* $30.
Contact *Scott Woodfield*
Graduate Coordinator
801-378-2915
Fax: 801-378-7775
E-mail: gradinfo@cs.byu.edu

ELECTRICAL ENGINEERING

College of Engineering and Technology, Department of Electrical and Computer Engineering
Programs Offers programs in electrical engineering (MS), engineering (PhD). Part-time programs available.
Faculty 21 full-time (0 women), 1 part-time (0 women).
Faculty Research Digital signal processing, VLSI design tool development, fiber optics communication, upper atmospheric research, solid-state devices.

Students 60 full-time (4 women), 2 part-time (0 women); includes 8 minority (4 Asian-Americans, 4 Hispanics), 12 international. Average age 23.

Degrees Awarded In 1996, 20 master's awarded (90% found work related to degree, 10% continued full-time study); 4 doctorates awarded (25% entered university research/teaching, 75% found other work related to degree).

Entrance Requirements For master's, GRE General Test, TOEFL (minimum score 550), minimum GPA of 3.0 in last 60 hours; for doctorate, minimum GPA of 3.4 in last 60 hours.

Degree Requirements For doctorate, 2 foreign languages (computer language can substitute for one), dissertation.

Financial Aid In 1996–97, 54 students received aid, including 6 fellowships, 14 research assistantships (7 to first-year students), 27 teaching assistantships (11 to first-year students), 7 scholarships. *Financial aid application deadline: 2/15.*

Applying 37 applicants, 84% accepted. *Deadline:* 2/15 (rolling processing). *Fee:* $30.

Contact Dr. Michael Rice
Graduate Coordinator
801-378-4469
Fax: 801-378-6586

UNIVERSITY OF UTAH
Salt Lake City, UT 84112

OVERVIEW
University of Utah is a public coed university.

ENROLLMENT
26,359 graduate, professional, and undergraduate students; 3,974 full-time matriculated graduate/professional students (1,554 women), 977 part-time matriculated graduate/professional students (486 women).

GRADUATE FACULTY
1,454 full-time (329 women); includes 128 minority (10 African-Americans, 84 Asian-Americans, 29 Hispanics, 5 Native Americans).

TUITION
$2790 per year full-time, $359 per quarter (minimum) part-time for state residents; $8709 per year full-time, $1037 per quarter (minimum) part-time for nonresidents.

HOUSING
Rooms and/or apartments available to single students (1,238 units) at an average cost of $2125 per year; available to married students (1,094 units) at an average cost of $5688 per year. Graduate housing contact: Norman Chambers, 801-581-8667.

STUDENT SERVICES
Low-cost health insurance, career counseling, day-care facilities, campus safety program, campus employment opportunities, international student services.

FACILITIES
Library: Marriott Library plus 2 additional on-campus libraries; total holdings of 3,394,737 volumes, 3,366,654 microforms, 26,393 current periodical subscriptions. A total of 136 personal computers in all libraries. Access provided to on-line information retrieval services. *Computer:* Campuswide network is available with full Internet access. Total number of PCs/terminals supplied

for student use: 1,000. Computer service fees are included with tuition and fees. *Special:* In arts and humanities: Middle East Center, Pioneer Theatre Company, Utah Museum of Fine Arts, Utah Museum of Natural History. In science and engineering: Huntsman Cancer Institute, Institute for Biomedical Engineering, Intermountain Burn Center, Center for Human Toxicology, cosmic ray observatory for ultra high-energy processes. In social sciences: Hinckley Institute of Politics, Bennion Center.

COMPUTER SCIENCE

College of Engineering, Department of Computer Science
Programs Awards ME, M Phil, MS, PhD.
Faculty 18 full-time (2 women), 11 part-time (0 women).
Faculty Research Computer-aided graphic design, VLSI, information retrieval, portable AI systems, functional programming.
Students 77 full-time (10 women), 6 part-time (0 women); includes 1 minority (Asian-American), 26 international. Average age 29.
Degrees Awarded In 1996, 11 master's, 7 doctorates awarded.
Entrance Requirements GRE General Test, GRE Subject Test, TOEFL (minimum score 500), minimum GPA of 3.0.
Degree Requirements For master's, thesis (for some programs), thesis (MS) required, foreign language not required; for doctorate, dissertation required, foreign language not required.
Financial Aid In 1996–97, 25 teaching assistantships were awarded; fellowships, research assistantships also available.
Applying *Deadline:* 7/1. *Fee:* $30 ($50 for international students).
Contact Gary Linstrom
Director of Graduate Admissions
801-581-5586

See in-depth description on page **737.**

ELECTRICAL ENGINEERING

College of Engineering, Department of Electrical Engineering
Programs Awards ME, M Phil, MS, PhD, EE. Part-time programs available.
Faculty 17 full-time (1 woman), 11 part-time (1 woman).
Faculty Research Semiconductors, VLSI design, control systems, electromagnetics and applied optics, communication theory and digital signal processing.
Students 70 full-time (8 women), 16 part-time (3 women); includes 1 minority (Hispanic), 40 international. Average age 29.
Degrees Awarded In 1996, 16 master's, 5 doctorates awarded. Terminal master's awarded for partial completion of doctoral program.
Entrance Requirements For master's and doctorate, GRE, TOEFL (minimum score 560), minimum GPA of 3.0.
Degree Requirements For master's, thesis (for some programs), comprehensive exam (MS) required, foreign language not required; for doctorate, dissertation, comprehensive exam required, foreign language not required.
Financial Aid In 1996–97, 14 teaching assistantships were awarded; fellowships, research assistantships, Federal Work-Study, institutionally sponsored loans also available. *Financial aid application deadline:* 2/1.
Applying *Deadline:* 2/1. *Fee:* $30 ($50 for international students).
Contact Bob Benner
Director, Graduate Studies
801-581-6684

MEDICAL INFORMATICS

School of Medicine and Graduate School, Graduate Programs in Medicine, Department of Medical Informatics
Programs Awards MS, PhD. Part-time programs available.
Faculty 17 full-time (3 women), 11 part-time (4 women).

Faculty Research Health information systems, expert systems, genetic epidemiology, medical imaging. *Total annual research expenditures:* $5.6 million.

Students 33 full-time (9 women), 5 part-time (1 woman); includes 2 minority (1 Asian-American, 1 Hispanic), 10 international. Average age 30.

Degrees Awarded In 1996, 6 master's, 4 doctorates awarded.

Entrance Requirements For master's, GRE General Test, TOEFL (minimum score 600), minimum GPA of 3.3; for doctorate, GRE, TOEFL (minimum score 600), minimum GPA of 3.3.

Degree Requirements Computer language, thesis/dissertation required, foreign language not required.

Financial Aid In 1996–97, 27 students received aid, including 1 fellowship averaging $1,300 per month, 26 research assistantships (10 to first-year students) averaging $1,300 per month; career-related internships or fieldwork also available. *Financial aid application deadline:* 3/1.

Applying 40 applicants, 45% accepted. *Deadline:* 3/1 (priority date; rolling processing). *Fee:* $40 ($60 for international students).

Contact *Dinny Abaunza*
Graduate Student Adviser
801-581-3121
Fax: 801-581-4297
E-mail: dabaunza@medinfo.med.utah.edu

UTAH STATE UNIVERSITY
Logan, UT 84322

OVERVIEW

Utah State University is a public coed university.

ENROLLMENT

20,808 graduate, professional, and undergraduate students; 1,663 full-time, 646 part-time matriculated graduate/professional students.

EXPENSES

Tuition $1008 per year full-time, $609 per year part-time for state residents; $3540 per year full-time, $2136 per year part-time for nonresidents. Fees $189 per year full-time, $147 per year part-time.

HOUSING

Rooms and/or apartments available to single students (2,599 units) at an average cost of $1590 per year ($3500 including board); available to married students (676 units) at an average cost of $5000 per year. Graduate housing contact: Housing Office, 801-797-3113.

STUDENT SERVICES

Disabled student services, multicultural affairs office, low-cost health insurance, career counseling, free psychological counseling, campus safety program, campus employment opportunities, international student services, writing training.

FACILITIES

Library: Merrill Library and Learning Resource Center plus 5 additional on-campus libraries; total holdings of 1,217,218 volumes, 2,031,556 microforms, 14,035 current periodical subscriptions. Access provided to on-line information retrieval services. *Computer:* Campuswide network is available with full Internet access. Total number of PCs/terminals supplied for student use: 709. Computer service fees are included with tuition and fees. *Special:* In arts and humanities: Jensen Living Histori-

cal Farm, Mountain West Center for Regional Studies, Fife Folklore Archive, university special collections and archives. In science and engineering: Space Dynamics Laboratory, Agriculture Experiment Station, Atmospheric and Space Sciences, Utah Water Research Laboratory, Center for Space Engineering, Center for Biocatalysis, Huntsman EnvironmentalResearch Center. In social sciences: Center for Persons with Disabilities, Edith Bowen Laboratory School, Sky Hi Institute.

COMPUTER SCIENCE

College of Science, Department of Computer Science

Programs Awards MS. Part-time and evening/weekend programs available.

Faculty 12 full-time (1 woman).

Faculty Research Artificial intelligence, software engineering, parallelism. *Total annual research expenditures:* $225,000.

Students 36 full-time, 51 part-time; includes 5 minority (all Asian-Americans), 57 international. Average age 26.

Degrees Awarded In 1996, 24 degrees awarded.

Entrance Requirements GRE General Test (score in 40th percentile or higher), GRE Subject Test, TOEFL (minimum score 550), minimum GPA of 3.0.

Degree Requirements Computer language, thesis (for some programs), research project required, foreign language not required.

Financial Aid In 1996–97, 23 students received aid, including 2 fellowships (both to first-year students) averaging $1,555 per month and totaling $25,000, 7 research assistantships (2 to first-year students) averaging $1,125 per month and totaling $45,000, 8 teaching assistantships (4 to first-year students) averaging $860 per month and totaling $46,500; partial tuition waivers, Federal Work-Study, institutionally sponsored loans, and career-related internships or fieldwork also available. Aid available to part-time students. *Financial aid application deadline:* 3/15.

Applying 75 applicants, 71% accepted. *Deadline:* 7/15 (priority date; rolling processing; 1/15 for spring admission). *Fee:* $30 ($35 for international students).

Contact *Greg Jones*
Graduate Adviser
801-797-3267
Fax: 801-797-3265
E-mail: jones@greg.cs.usu.edu

ELECTRICAL ENGINEERING

College of Engineering, Department of Electrical and Computer Engineering

Programs Offers program in electrical engineering (ME, MES, MS, PhD, EE). Part-time programs available.

Faculty 18 full-time (1 woman), 1 (woman) part-time.

Faculty Research Parallel processing, networking, control systems, digital signal processing, communications, real-time systems.

Students 35 full-time, 27 part-time; includes 25 international. Average age 26.

Degrees Awarded In 1996, 30 master's, 3 doctorates awarded.

Entrance Requirements For master's and doctorate, GRE General Test (score in 40th percentile or higher), TOEFL (minimum score 560), minimum GPA of 3.0.

Degree Requirements For master's, thesis required (for some programs), foreign language not required; for doctorate, dissertation required, foreign language not required.

Financial Aid In 1996–97, 35 students received aid, including 2 fellowships (both to first-year students) averaging $1,250 per month and totaling $20,000, 29 research assistantships (11 to first-year students) averaging $750 per month and totaling $195,750, 6 teaching assistantships (4 to first-year students) averaging $400 per month and totaling $19,200; Federal Work-Study, institutionally sponsored loans also available.

Applying 146 applicants, 26% accepted. *Deadline:* 1/1 (priority date). *Fee:* $30 ($35 for international students).

Contact Robert W. Gunderson
Graduate Adviser
801-797-2924

VERMONT

UNIVERSITY OF VERMONT
Burlington, VT 05405-0160

OVERVIEW
University of Vermont is a public coed university.

ENROLLMENT
9,341 graduate, professional, and undergraduate students; 1,550 matriculated graduate/professional students.

GRADUATE FACULTY
702 full-time, 604 part-time.

EXPENSES
Tuition $293 per credit for state residents; $733 per credit for nonresidents. Fees $414 per year full-time, $80 per year part-time.

HOUSING
Rooms and/or apartments available to single students (235 units) at an average cost of $4600 per year; available to married students (130 units). Graduate housing contact: Ethan Allen Housing, 802-656-0661.

STUDENT SERVICES
Low-cost health insurance, career counseling, free psychological counseling.

FACILITIES
Library: Bailey-Howe Library plus 2 additional on-campus libraries; total holdings of 1,185,252 volumes, 851,895 microforms, 8,000 current periodical subscriptions. A total of 38 personal computers in all libraries. Access provided to on-line information retrieval services. *Special:* In science and engineering: Bruker 250-MHz Nuclear Magnetic Resonance Facility, Vermont Regional Cancer Center, flow cytometry facility.

COMPUTER SCIENCE

College of Engineering and Mathematics, Department of Computer Science and Electrical Engineering, Program in Computer Science

Programs Awards MS.

Students 15; includes 2 international.

Degrees Awarded In 1996, 5 degrees awarded.

Entrance Requirements GRE General Test, TOEFL (minimum score 550).

Degree Requirements Thesis or alternative required, foreign language not required.

Financial Aid Research assistantships, teaching assistantships available. *Financial aid application deadline:* 3/1.

Applying 14 applicants, 71% accepted. *Deadline:* 4/1 (priority date; rolling processing). *Fee:* $25.

Contact Dr. S. Hegner
Coordinator
802-656-3330

ELECTRICAL ENGINEERING

College of Engineering and Mathematics, Department of Computer Science and Electrical Engineering, Program in Electrical Engineering

Programs Awards MS, PhD.

Students 38; includes 3 minority (1 Asian-American, 1 Hispanic, 1 Native American), 8 international.

Degrees Awarded In 1996, 11 master's, 2 doctorates awarded.

Entrance Requirements GRE General Test, TOEFL (minimum score 550).

Degree Requirements For master's, thesis or alternative required, foreign language not required; for doctorate, 1 foreign language, dissertation.

Financial Aid Fellowships, research assistantships, teaching assistantships available. *Financial aid application deadline:* 3/1.

Applying 75 applicants, 71% accepted. *Deadline:* 4/1 (priority date; rolling processing). *Fee:* $25.

Contact Dr. R. Snapp
Coordinator
802-656-3330

VIRGINIA

CHRISTOPHER NEWPORT UNIVERSITY
Newport News, VA 23606-2998

OVERVIEW
Christopher Newport University is a public coed comprehensive institution.

ENROLLMENT
4,490 graduate, professional, and undergraduate students; 18 full-time matriculated graduate/professional students (9 women), 57 part-time matriculated graduate/professional students (33 women).

GRADUATE FACULTY
51 full-time (17 women), 2 part-time (0 women); includes 7 minority (1 African-American, 5 Asian-Americans, 1 Hispanic).

EXPENSES
Tuition $143 per credit hour for state residents; $338 per credit hour for nonresidents. Fees $20 per semester.

HOUSING
Rooms and/or apartments available to single students at an average cost of $4650 (including board); on-campus housing not available to married students. Graduate housing contact: University Housing, 757-594-7756.

STUDENT SERVICES
Disabled student services, multicultural affairs office, low-cost health insurance, career counseling, exercise/wellness program, day-care facilities, campus safety program, campus employment opportunities, international student services, writing training.

FACILITIES
Library: Captain John Smith Library; total holdings of 164,028 volumes, 171,652 microforms, 1,513 current periodical subscriptions. A total of 83 personal comput-

ers in all libraries. Access provided to on-line information retrieval services. *Computer:* Campuswide network is available with full Internet access. Total number of PCs/terminals supplied for student use: 250. Computer services are offered at no charge. *Special:* In arts and humanities: Institute for Critical Thinking, Cary McMurran Music Library. In science and engineering: S. Hunter Creech computer, superconductivity, electro-optics, microbiology, and methane measurements laboratories. In social sciences: Information science laboratory.

COMPUTER SCIENCE

Graduate Studies, Department of Physics and Computer Science
Programs   Offers program in applied physics and computer science (MS). Part-time and evening/weekend programs available.
Faculty   13 full-time (1 woman), 1 part-time (0 women).
Faculty Research   Experimental nuclear physics, semiconductor nanophysics, laser and optical fiber sensors, superconductivity applications, VLSI systems design.
Students   4 full-time (0 women), 11 part-time (2 women); includes 4 minority (3 Asian-Americans, 1 Hispanic). Average age 35.
Degrees Awarded   In 1996, 5 degrees awarded (100% found work related to degree).
Entrance Requirements   GRE, minimum GPA of 3.0.
Degree Requirements   Computer language, thesis required, foreign language not required.
Financial Aid   In 1996–97, 1 student received aid, including 1 research assistantship (to a first-year student) totaling $5,000; Federal Work-Study and career-related internships or fieldwork also available. Aid available to part-time students. *Financial aid application deadline:* 4/1; applicants required to submit FAFSA.
Applying   *Deadline:* 8/1 (priority date; rolling processing; 12/15 for spring admission). *Fee:* $40.
Contact   Graduate Admissions
                    800-333-4268
                    Fax: 757-594-7333
                    E-mail: admit@cnu.edu

COLLEGE OF WILLIAM AND MARY
Williamsburg, VA 23187-8795

OVERVIEW
College of William and Mary is a public coed university.

ENROLLMENT
7,373 graduate, professional, and undergraduate students; 1,384 full-time matriculated graduate/professional students (641 women), 500 part-time matriculated graduate/professional students (282 women).

GRADUATE FACULTY
575 full-time (157 women), 121 part-time (44 women); includes 61 minority (25 African-Americans, 30 Asian-Americans, 5 Hispanics, 1 Native American).

TUITION
$5116 per year full-time, $165 per credit part-time for state residents; $15,404 per year full-time, $480 per credit part-time for nonresidents.

HOUSING
Rooms and/or apartments available to single students (239 units) at an average cost of $2940 per year ($4920 including board); available to married students (10 units)

at an average cost of $5460 per year. Graduate housing contact: Residence Life Office, 757-221-4314.

STUDENT SERVICES
Disabled student services, multicultural affairs office, low-cost health insurance, career counseling, free psychological counseling, exercise/wellness program, day-care facilities, campus safety program, campus employment opportunities, international student services, grant writing training, teacher training.

FACILITIES
Library: Swem Library plus 8 additional on-campus libraries; total holdings of 1,312,615 volumes, 1,950,732 microforms, 10,747 current periodical subscriptions. A total of 50 personal computers in all libraries. Access provided to on-line information retrieval services. *Computer:* Campuswide network is available with full Internet access. Total number of PCs/terminals supplied for student use: 280. Computer services are offered at no charge. *Special:* In arts and humanities: Muscarelle Museum of Art. In science and engineering: Virginia Institute of Marine Science, endocrinology and population ecology laboratory, William Small Physical Laboratory. In social sciences: William and Mary Archaeological Conservation Center, Institute of Early American History and Culture, Institute for the Bill of Rights.

COMPUTER SCIENCE

Faculty of Arts and Sciences, Department of Computer Science
Programs   Awards MS, PhD. Part-time programs available.
Faculty   16 full-time (4 women).
Faculty Research   Simulation, stochastic modeling, parallel systems, networks, image processing. *Total annual research expenditures:* $450,798.
Students   38 full-time (12 women), 27 part-time (6 women); includes 6 minority (3 African-Americans, 2 Asian-Americans, 1 Hispanic), 12 international. Average age 30.
Degrees Awarded   In 1996, 9 master's awarded (22% entered university research/teaching, 56% found other work related to degree, 22% continued full-time study). Terminal master's awarded for partial completion of doctoral program.
Entrance Requirements   For master's, GRE General Test, minimum GPA of 2.5; for doctorate, GRE General Test (minimum combined score of 1700 on three sections; average 2010), minimum GPA of 3.0.
Degree Requirements   For master's, computer language, research project required, thesis optional; for doctorate, computer language, dissertation, oral exam.
Financial Aid   In 1996–97, 28 students received aid, including 6 research assistantships (1 to a first-year student) averaging $1,300 per month, 20 teaching assistantships (8 to first-year students) averaging $1,167 per month; fellowships also available. *Financial aid application deadline:* 3/1.
Applying   189 applicants, 25% accepted. *Deadline:* 3/1 (rolling processing; 11/1 for spring admission). *Fee:* $30.
Contact   *Vanessa Godwin*
                    Administrative Director
                    757-221-3453
                    E-mail: gradinfo@cs.wm.edu

GEORGE MASON UNIVERSITY
Fairfax, VA 22030-4444

OVERVIEW
George Mason University is a public coed university.

ENROLLMENT
24,368 graduate, professional, and undergraduate students; 2,094 full-time matriculated graduate/professional students (1,180 women), 5,665 part-time matriculated graduate/professional students (2,950 women).

GRADUATE FACULTY
765 full-time (262 women), 543 part-time (261 women), 941 FTE; includes 161 minority (44 African-Americans, 78 Asian-Americans, 38 Hispanics, 1 Native American).

EXPENSES
Tuition $4296 per year full-time, $179 per credit hour part-time for state residents; $12,240 per year full-time, $510 per credit hour part-time for nonresidents. Fees $75 (one-time charge).

HOUSING
Rooms and/or apartments available to single students (3,006 units) at an average cost of $3200 per year ($5020 including board); available to married students at an average cost of $6000 per year. Housing application deadline: 6/1. Graduate housing information: 703-993-2720.

STUDENT SERVICES
Disabled student services, multicultural affairs office, low-cost health insurance, career counseling, free psychological counseling, exercise/wellness program, day-care facilities, campus safety program, campus employment opportunities, international student services, writing training.

FACILITIES
Library: Fenwick Library plus 1 additional on-campus library; total holdings of 710,013 volumes, 2,023,751 microforms, 10,979 current periodical subscriptions. Access provided to on-line information retrieval services. *Computer:* Campuswide network is available with full Internet access. Total number of PCs/terminals supplied for student use: 425. *Special:* In arts and humanities: Federal Theatre Archives; Institute of the Arts; Center for Government, Society and the Arts. In science and engineering: Shared Research Instrumentation Facility; Instructional Development Office; Center for New Engineer; High Performance Computing Facility; Institute for Computational Sciences and Informatics; Center for Command, Control, Communications and Intelligence. In social sciences: Institute of Public Policy, Center for Cognitive and Behavioral Studies, Northern Virginia Survey Research Laboratory, Center for Human Disabilities, Institute for Conflict Analysis and Resolution.

COMPUTER SCIENCE

School of Information Technology and Engineering, Department of Computer Science
Programs Awards MS. Offered jointly with Old Dominion University, the University of Virginia, Virginia Commonwealth University, and Virginia Polytechnic Institute and State University. Part-time and evening/weekend programs available.
Faculty 21 full-time (4 women), 9 part-time (0 women), 26 FTE.
Faculty Research Artificial intelligence, image processing/graphics, parallel/distributed systems, software engineering systems. *Total annual research expenditures:* $1.8 million.
Students 54 full-time (21 women), 286 part-time (75 women); includes 89 minority (9 African-Americans, 74 Asian-Americans, 4 Hispanics, 2 Native Americans), 97 international. Average age 30.
Degrees Awarded In 1996, 74 degrees awarded.
Entrance Requirements GRE General Test, TOEFL (minimum score 575), minimum GPA of 3.0 in last 60 hours.
Degree Requirements Thesis optional, foreign language not required.
Financial Aid Fellowships, research assistantships, teaching assistantships, Federal Work-Study, and career-related internships or fieldwork available. Aid available to part-time students. *Financial aid application deadline:* 3/1; applicants required to submit FAFSA.
Applying 273 applicants, 83% accepted. *Deadline:* 5/1 (11/1 for spring admission). *Fee:* $30.
Contact *Graduate Coordinator*
703-993-1530
Fax: 703-993-3729
E-mail: csinfo@cs.gmu.edu

ELECTRICAL ENGINEERING

School of Information Technology and Engineering, Department of Electrical and Computer Engineering
Programs Offers program in electrical engineering (MS). Offered jointly with Old Dominion University, the University of Virginia, Virginia Commonwealth University, and Virginia Polytechnic Institute and State University. Part-time and evening/weekend programs available.
Faculty 23 full-time (1 woman), 3 part-time (0 women), 24 FTE.
Faculty Research Communication networks, signal processing, system failure diagnosis, multiprocessors, material processing using microwave energy.
Students 29 full-time (5 women), 167 part-time (25 women); includes 57 minority (11 African-Americans, 41 Asian-Americans, 5 Hispanics), 30 international. Average age 30.
Degrees Awarded In 1996, 44 degrees awarded.
Entrance Requirements GMAT or GRE General Test, TOEFL (minimum score 575), bachelor's degree in electrical engineering or related field, minimum GPA of 3.0 in last 60 hours.
Degree Requirements Computer language required, thesis optional, foreign language not required.
Financial Aid Fellowships, research assistantships, teaching assistantships, Federal Work-Study, and career-related internships or fieldwork available. Aid available to part-time students. *Financial aid application deadline:* 3/1; applicants required to submit FAFSA.
Applying 163 applicants, 93% accepted. *Deadline:* 5/1 (11/1 for spring admission). *Fee:* $30.
Contact *Dr. Gerald Cook*
Chairman
703-993-1569
Fax: 703-993-1601
E-mail: ece@bass.gmu.edu

INFORMATION SCIENCE

School of Information Technology and Engineering, Department of Information and Software Systems Engineering
Programs Offers programs in information systems (MS), software systems engineering (MS). Offered jointly with Old Dominion University, the University of Virginia, Virginia Commonwealth

University, and Virginia Polytechnic Institute and State University. Part-time and evening/weekend programs available.

Faculty 13 full-time (0 women), 9 part-time (0 women), 15 FTE.

Faculty Research Security, database management, real time systems, software quality. *Total annual research expenditures:* $380,638.

Students 76 full-time (35 women), 522 part-time (157 women); includes 155 minority (33 African-Americans, 102 Asian-Americans, 18 Hispanics, 2 Native Americans), 69 international. Average age 32.

Degrees Awarded In 1996, 151 degrees awarded.

Entrance Requirements GMAT or GRE General Test, TOEFL (minimum score 575), minimum GPA of 3.0 in last 60 hours.

Degree Requirements Computer language required, thesis optional, foreign language not required.

Financial Aid Fellowships, research assistantships, teaching assistantships available. Aid available to part-time students. *Financial aid application deadline:* 3/1; applicants required to submit FAFSA.

Applying 353 applicants, 78% accepted. *Deadline:* 5/1 (11/1 for spring admission). *Fee:* $30.

Contact *Sandy Mayo*
Student Adviser
703-993-1640
Fax: 703-993-1638

INFORMATION SCIENCE

School of Information Technology and Engineering, Interdisciplinary Program in Information Technology

Programs Awards PhD. Part-time and evening/weekend programs available.

Faculty 1 (woman) full-time.

Students 47 full-time (9 women), 262 part-time (53 women); includes 66 minority (17 African-Americans, 43 Asian-Americans, 5 Hispanics, 1 Native American), 82 international. Average age 38.

Degrees Awarded In 1996, 19 degrees awarded.

Entrance Requirements GRE General Test, TOEFL (minimum score 575), minimum graduate GPA of 3.5.

Degree Requirements Dissertation, comprehensive oral and written exams required, foreign language not required.

Financial Aid Fellowships, research assistantships, teaching assistantships, Federal Work-Study, institutionally sponsored loans available. Aid available to part-time students. *Financial aid application deadline:* 3/1; applicants required to submit FAFSA.

Applying 150 applicants, 79% accepted. *Deadline:* 5/1 (11/1 for spring admission). *Fee:* $30.

Contact *Student Services*
703-993-1499
Fax: 703-993-1497
E-mail: sitegrad@gmu.edu

SOFTWARE ENGINEERING

School of Information Technology and Engineering, Department of Information and Software Systems Engineering

Programs Offers programs in information systems (MS), software systems engineering (MS). Offered jointly with Old Dominion University, the University of Virginia, Virginia Commonwealth University, and Virginia Polytechnic Institute and State University. Part-time and evening/weekend programs available.

Faculty 13 full-time (0 women), 9 part-time (0 women), 15 FTE.

Faculty Research Security, database management, real time systems, software quality. *Total annual research expenditures:* $380,638.

Students 76 full-time (35 women), 522 part-time (157 women); includes 155 minority (33 African-Americans, 102 Asian-Americans, 18 Hispanics, 2 Native Americans), 69 international. Average age 32.

Degrees Awarded In 1996, 151 degrees awarded.

Entrance Requirements GMAT or GRE General Test, TOEFL (minimum score 575), minimum GPA of 3.0 in last 60 hours.

Degree Requirements Computer language required, thesis optional, foreign language not required.

Financial Aid Fellowships, research assistantships, teaching assistantships available. Aid available to part-time students. *Financial aid application deadline:* 3/1; applicants required to submit FAFSA.

Applying 353 applicants, 78% accepted. *Deadline:* 5/1 (11/1 for spring admission). *Fee:* $30.

Contact *Sandy Mayo*
Student Adviser
703-993-1640
Fax: 703-993-1638

HAMPTON UNIVERSITY
Hampton, VA 23668

OVERVIEW

Hampton University is an independent coed comprehensive institution.

ENROLLMENT

5,078 graduate, professional, and undergraduate students; 186 full-time matriculated graduate/professional students (136 women), 164 part-time matriculated graduate/professional students (122 women).

GRADUATE FACULTY

90 full-time (54 women), 11 part-time (8 women), 95 FTE.

EXPENSES

Tuition $8608 per year full-time, $210 per credit part-time. Fees $70 per year.

HOUSING

Rooms and/or apartments available to single and married students at an average cost of $3518 (including board). Housing application deadline: 6/1. Graduate housing contact: Office of Auxiliary Services, 757-727-5210.

STUDENT SERVICES

Low-cost health insurance, career counseling, free psychological counseling, campus employment opportunities, international student services.

FACILITIES

Library: William R. and Norma B. Harvey Library plus 4 additional on-campus libraries; total holdings of 400,000 volumes, 350,000 microforms, 1,500 current periodical subscriptions. A total of 75 personal computers in all libraries. Access provided to on-line information retrieval services. *Special:* In science and engineering: Marine Science Center, Turner Observatory, Graduate Physics Research Center.

COMPUTER SCIENCE

Department of Computer Science

Programs Awards MS. Part-time and evening/weekend programs available.

Faculty 8 full-time (3 women).

Faculty Research Software testing, neural networks, parallel processing, computer graphics, natural language processing.

Students 6 full-time (4 women), 15 part-time (8 women); includes 19 minority (15 African-Americans, 4 Asian-Americans), 1 international.

Degrees Awarded In 1996, 3 degrees awarded.
Entrance Requirements GRE General Test (minimum score 450 on verbal section).
Degree Requirements Computer language, thesis or alternative required, foreign language not required.
Financial Aid Research assistantships, scholarships, Federal Work-Study, and career-related internships or fieldwork available. Aid available to part-time students. *Financial aid application deadline:* 5/1; applicants required to submit FAFSA.
Applying *Deadline:* 6/1 (priority date; rolling processing; 11/1 for spring admission). *Fee:* $25.
Contact *Erika Henderson*
Director, Graduate Programs
757-727-5454
Fax: 757-727-5084

HOLLINS COLLEGE
Roanoke, VA 24020-1688

OVERVIEW
Hollins College is an independent primarily female comprehensive institution.

ENROLLMENT
1,094 graduate, professional, and undergraduate students; 71 full-time matriculated graduate/professional students (62 women), 153 part-time matriculated graduate/professional students (121 women).

GRADUATE FACULTY
41 full-time (20 women), 7 part-time (4 women); includes 1 minority (African-American).

TUITION
$15,070 per year.

HOUSING
On-campus housing not available.

STUDENT SERVICES
Low-cost health insurance, career counseling, campus employment opportunities, writing training.

FACILITIES
Library: Fishburn Library plus 1 additional on-campus library; total holdings of 212,140 volumes, 211,240 microforms, 1,242 current periodical subscriptions. A total of 24 personal computers in all libraries. Access provided to on-line information retrieval services. *Computer:* Campuswide network is available with full Internet access. Total number of PCs/terminals supplied for student use: 100. Computer services are offered at no charge. *Special:* In science and engineering: Research Institute for Speech Pathology, Research and Rehabilitation Institute for Head Trauma.

COMPUTER SCIENCE

Program in Liberal Studies
Programs Offerings include computer science (MALS, CAS).
Program Faculty 16 full-time (6 women), 4 part-time (2 women).
Entrance Requirements For master's, TOEFL (minimum score 550), interview.
Degree Requirements For master's, thesis required, foreign language not required.

Applying *Deadline:* 9/1 (priority date; rolling processing; 2/3 for spring admission). *Fee:* $25.
Contact *Cathy S. Koon*
Administrative Assistant
540-362-6575
Fax: 540-362-6288
E-mail: cakoon@hollins.edu

JAMES MADISON UNIVERSITY
Harrisonburg, VA 22807

OVERVIEW
James Madison University is a public coed comprehensive institution.

ENROLLMENT
12,963 graduate, professional, and undergraduate students; 416 full-time matriculated graduate/professional students (276 women), 343 part-time matriculated graduate/professional students (222 women).

GRADUATE FACULTY
160 full-time (60 women), 29 part-time (6 women); includes 13 minority (6 African-Americans, 3 Asian-Americans, 2 Hispanics, 2 Native Americans).

TUITION
$2376 per year full-time, $132 per credit hour part-time for state residents; $6930 per year full-time, $385 per credit hour part-time for nonresidents.

HOUSING
On-campus housing not available.

STUDENT SERVICES
Disabled student services, multicultural affairs office, career counseling, free psychological counseling, campus safety program, campus employment opportunities, international student services, teacher training.

FACILITIES
Library: Carrier Library plus 1 additional on-campus library; total holdings of 445,066 volumes, 1,018,915 microforms, 2,414 current periodical subscriptions. A total of 150 personal computers in all libraries. Access provided to on-line information retrieval services. *Computer:* Campuswide network is available with full Internet access. Total number of PCs/terminals supplied for student use: 500. Computer services are offered at no charge. *Special:* In science and engineering: Speech and Hearing Center. In social sciences: Human Development Center, Center for Economics Education, Center for Entrepreneurship.

COMPUTER SCIENCE

College of Integrated Science and Technology, Department of Computer Science
Programs Awards MS.
Faculty 6 full-time (0 women).
Students 29 full-time (11 women), 12 part-time (1 woman); includes 4 minority (3 Asian-Americans, 1 Native American), 10 international. Average age 30.
Degrees Awarded In 1996, 7 degrees awarded.
Entrance Requirements GRE General Test.

Degree Requirements Thesis or alternative required, foreign language not required.

Financial Aid In 1996–97, 5 teaching assistantships totaling $33,250, 17 assistantships totaling $96,050 were awarded; fellowships, Federal Work-Study also available. *Financial aid application deadline:* 2/15; applicants required to submit FAFSA.

Applying *Deadline:* 7/1 (priority date; rolling processing). *Fee:* $50.

Contact *Dr. Charles W. Reynolds*
Program Coordinator
540-568-2770

Financial Aid Career-related internships or fieldwork available. Aid available to part-time students. Financial aid applicants required to submit FAFSA.

Applying 12 applicants, 67% accepted. *Deadline:* 8/15 (priority date; rolling processing; 12/15 for spring admission). *Fee:* $35.

Contact *Dr. Vanessa Job*
Chairperson
703-284-1670
Fax: 703-284-3859
E-mail: vanessa.job@marymount.edu

MARYMOUNT UNIVERSITY
Arlington, VA 22207-4299

OVERVIEW

Marymount University is an independent-religious coed comprehensive institution.

ENROLLMENT

3,579 graduate, professional, and undergraduate students; 107 full-time matriculated graduate/professional students (91 women), 1,273 part-time matriculated graduate/professional students (833 women).

GRADUATE FACULTY

60 full-time (29 women), 80 part-time (34 women), 87 FTE.

TUITION

$445 per credit hour.

HOUSING

Rooms and/or apartments available to single students at an average cost of $5810 (including board); on-campus housing not available to married students. Graduate housing contact: Carlton Sauls, 703-284-1608.

STUDENT SERVICES

Low-cost health insurance, career counseling, campus safety program, campus employment opportunities, international student services.

FACILITIES

Library: Reinsch Library plus 1 additional on-campus library; total holdings of 166,927 volumes, 251,442 microforms, 1,072 current periodical subscriptions. A total of 8 personal computers in all libraries. Access provided to on-line information retrieval services. *Computer:* Campuswide network is available with full Internet access. Total number of PCs/terminals supplied for student use: 205. Computer service fees are included with tuition and fees. *Special:* In science and engineering: Cell biology laboratory.

COMPUTER SCIENCE

School of Arts and Sciences, Program in Computer Science
Programs Awards MS.
Students 19 part-time (2 women); includes 6 minority (all Asian-Americans), 3 international. Average age 33.
Degrees Awarded In 1996, 6 degrees awarded.
Entrance Requirements GRE, interview.
Degree Requirements Thesis optional, foreign language not required.

OLD DOMINION UNIVERSITY
Norfolk, VA 23529

OVERVIEW

Old Dominion University is a public coed university.

ENROLLMENT

14,688 graduate, professional, and undergraduate students; 1,556 full-time matriculated graduate/professional students (836 women), 2,156 part-time matriculated graduate/professional students (1,204 women).

GRADUATE FACULTY

546 full-time (166 women), 25 part-time (12 women), 552.4 FTE; includes 145 minority (76 African-Americans, 57 Asian-Americans, 8 Hispanics, 4 Native Americans).

EXPENSES

Tuition $176 per credit hour for state residents; $464 per credit hour for nonresidents. Fees $140 per year full-time, $32 per semester part-time.

HOUSING

Rooms and/or apartments available to single students at an average cost of $3508 per year; on-campus housing not available to married students. Housing application deadline: 5/1. Graduate housing contact: Ramonsa White, 757-683-4283.

STUDENT SERVICES

Disabled student services, multicultural affairs office, low-cost health insurance, career counseling, free psychological counseling, campus safety program, campus employment opportunities, international student services, grant writing training, teacher training.

FACILITIES

Library: University Library; total holdings of 754,614 volumes, 1,185,185 microforms, 5,363 current periodical subscriptions. A total of 78 personal computers in all libraries. Access provided to on-line information retrieval services. *Computer:* Campuswide network is available with full Internet access. Total number of PCs/terminals supplied for student use: 400. Computer services are offered at no charge. *Special:* In arts and humanities: Institute for the Study of Minority Issues, Institute of Asian Studies, Institute of the Humanities. In science and engineering: Technology Applications Center, applied marine research laboratory, Center for Coastal Physical Oceanography, Center for Biotechnology. In social sciences: Center for Economic Education, Center for Research in International Studies, Entrepreneurial Center.

COMPUTER ENGINEERING

College of Engineering and Technology, Department of Electrical and Computer Engineering

Programs Awards ME, MS, PhD. Part-time programs available.
Faculty 16 full-time (1 woman).
Faculty Research Computers, signal processing, controls pulsed power, semiconductor devices and opto-electronics. *Total annual research expenditures:* $689,929.
Students 46 full-time (10 women), 23 part-time (5 women); includes 5 minority (1 African-American, 3 Asian-Americans, 1 Hispanic), 37 international. Average age 29.
Degrees Awarded In 1996, 19 master's, 1 doctorate awarded.
Entrance Requirements For master's, GRE, TOEFL (minimum score 550), minimum GPA of 3.0; for doctorate, GRE, TOEFL (minimum score 550), minimum GPA of 3.25.
Degree Requirements For master's, computer language, thesis (for some programs), comprehensive exam required, foreign language not required; for doctorate, computer language, dissertation, candidacy exam required, foreign language not required.
Financial Aid In 1996–97, 38 students received aid, including 17 research assistantships (2 to first-year students) totaling $134,169, 3 teaching assistantships (1 to a first-year student) totaling $18,500, 16 grants (3 to first-year students) totaling $110,346; fellowships, institutionally sponsored loans, and career-related internships or fieldwork also available. Aid available to part-time students. Financial aid applicants required to submit FAFSA.
Applying *Deadline:* 7/1 (rolling processing; 11/1 for spring admission). *Fee:* $30.
Contact Dr. Vishnu Lakdawala
  Graduate Program Director
  757-683-3741
  Fax: 757-683-3220
  E-mail: vkl100f@eefs01.ee.odu.edu

COMPUTER SCIENCE

College of Sciences, Department of Computer Science

Programs Awards MS, PhD. Part-time programs available.
Faculty 17 full-time (0 women).
Faculty Research Software engineering, artificial intelligence, foundations, high-performance computing, networking. *Total annual research expenditures:* $1.129 million.
Students 44 full-time (9 women), 66 part-time (23 women); includes 8 minority (2 African-Americans, 2 Asian-Americans, 3 Hispanics, 1 Native American), 48 international. Average age 31.
Degrees Awarded In 1996, 25 master's, 3 doctorates awarded. Terminal master's awarded for partial completion of doctoral program.
Entrance Requirements For master's, GRE General Test, GRE Subject Test, TOEFL (minimum score 550), minimum GPA of 3.0 in major, 2.5 overall; for doctorate, GRE General Test (minimum combined score of 1000), GRE Subject Test (minimum score 600), TOEFL.
Degree Requirements For master's, computer language, comprehensive diagnostic exam required, thesis optional, foreign language not required; for doctorate, computer language, dissertation, comprehensive exam required, foreign language not required.
Financial Aid In 1996–97, 52 students received aid, including 25 research assistantships (6 to first-year students) totaling $210,745, 4 teaching assistantships totaling $29,800, 20 tuition grants (6 to first-year students) totaling $92,462; fellowships and career-related internships or fieldwork also available. *Financial aid application deadline:* 4/1; applicants required to submit FAFSA.

Applying *Deadline:* 7/1 (rolling processing). *Fee:* $30.
Contact Dr. Hussein Abdel-Wahab
  Graduate Program Director
  757-683-3915
  E-mail: wahab@ccs.odu.edu

See in-depth description on page 507.

ELECTRICAL ENGINEERING

College of Engineering and Technology, Department of Electrical and Computer Engineering

Programs Awards ME, MS, PhD. Part-time programs available.
Faculty 16 full-time (1 woman).
Faculty Research Computers, signal processing, controls pulsed power, semiconductor devices and opto-electronics. *Total annual research expenditures:* $689,929.
Students 46 full-time (10 women), 23 part-time (5 women); includes 5 minority (1 African-American, 3 Asian-Americans, 1 Hispanic), 37 international. Average age 29.
Degrees Awarded In 1996, 19 master's, 1 doctorate awarded.
Entrance Requirements For master's, GRE, TOEFL (minimum score 550), minimum GPA of 3.0; for doctorate, GRE, TOEFL (minimum score 550), minimum GPA of 3.25.
Degree Requirements For master's, computer language, thesis (for some programs), comprehensive exam required, foreign language not required; for doctorate, computer language, dissertation, candidacy exam required, foreign language not required.
Financial Aid In 1996–97, 38 students received aid, including 17 research assistantships (2 to first-year students) totaling $134,169, 3 teaching assistantships (1 to a first-year student) totaling $18,500, 16 grants (3 to first-year students) totaling $110,346; fellowships, institutionally sponsored loans, and career-related internships or fieldwork also available. Aid available to part-time students. Financial aid applicants required to submit FAFSA.
Applying *Deadline:* 7/1 (rolling processing; 11/1 for spring admission). *Fee:* $30.
Contact Dr. Vishnu Lakdawala
  Graduate Program Director
  757-683-3741
  Fax: 757-683-3220
  E-mail: vkl100f@eefs01.ee.odu.edu

UNIVERSITY OF VIRGINIA
Charlottesville, VA 22903

OVERVIEW
University of Virginia is a public coed university.

ENROLLMENT
17,746 graduate, professional, and undergraduate students; 5,438 full-time matriculated graduate/professional students (2,360 women), 290 part-time matriculated graduate/professional students (168 women).

GRADUATE FACULTY
1,804 full-time (435 women), 224 part-time (90 women), 1,895 FTE; includes 198 minority (64 African-Americans, 105 Asian-Americans, 29 Hispanics).

TUITION
$4790 per year full-time, $918 per semester (minimum) part-time for state residents; $15,034 per year full-time, $2612 per semester (minimum) part-time for nonresidents.

HOUSING

Rooms and/or apartments available to single students (350 units) at an average cost of $3420 per year ($5770 including board); available to married students (323 units). Housing application deadline: 2/20. Graduate housing contact: Wanda Weaver, 804-924-6873.

STUDENT SERVICES

Disabled student services, multicultural affairs office, low-cost health insurance, career counseling, free psychological counseling, exercise/wellness program, day-care facilities, campus safety program, campus employment opportunities, international student services, writing training, grant writing training, teacher training.

FACILITIES

Library: Alderman Library plus 11 additional on-campus libraries; total holdings of 4,276,435 volumes, 4,569,358 microforms, 40,905 current periodical subscriptions. A total of 325 personal computers in all libraries. Access provided to on-line information retrieval services. *Computer:* Campuswide network is available with full Internet access. Total number of PCs/terminals supplied for student use: 1,745. Computer service fees are included with tuition and fees. *Special:* In science and engineering: Fan Mountain Observatory, Mountain Lake Biological Station, reactor facility. In social sciences: White Burkett Miller Center of Public Affairs, Center for Oceans Law and Policy, Center for Public Service.

COMPUTER SCIENCE

School of Engineering and Applied Science, Department of Computer Science
Programs Awards MCS, MS, PhD.
Faculty 21 full-time (2 women).
Faculty Research Systems programming, operating systems, analysis of programs and computation theory, programming languages, software engineering.
Students 60 full-time (8 women), 8 part-time (1 woman); includes 8 minority (4 African-Americans, 3 Asian-Americans, 1 Hispanic), 9 international. Average age 26.
Degrees Awarded In 1996, 15 master's, 6 doctorates awarded.
Entrance Requirements GRE General Test.
Degree Requirements For master's, thesis required (for some programs), foreign language not required; for doctorate, dissertation, comprehensive exam required, foreign language not required.
Financial Aid Fellowships available.
Applying 105 applicants, 37% accepted. *Deadline:* 8/1 (12/1 for spring admission). *Fee:* $40.
Contact *J. Milton Adams*
Assistant Dean
804-924-3897

See in-depth description on page **739.**

ELECTRICAL ENGINEERING

School of Engineering and Applied Science, Department of Electrical Engineering
Programs Awards ME, MS, PhD.
Faculty 20 full-time (3 women), 3 part-time (1 woman), 21 FTE.
Students 99 full-time (13 women), 3 part-time (1 woman); includes 13 minority (5 African-Americans, 7 Asian-Americans, 1 Hispanic), 41 international. Average age 26.
Degrees Awarded In 1996, 31 master's, 17 doctorates awarded.
Entrance Requirements GRE General Test.

Degree Requirements For master's, thesis (MS) required, foreign language not required; for doctorate, dissertation, comprehensive exam required, foreign language not required.
Financial Aid Fellowships available.
Applying 183 applicants, 46% accepted. *Deadline:* 8/1 (12/1 for spring admission). *Fee:* $40.
Contact *J. Milton Adams*
Assistant Dean
804-924-3897

See in-depth description on page **741.**

MEDICAL INFORMATICS

Graduate School of Arts and Sciences, Program in Health Evaluation Sciences
Programs Offerings include health care informatics (MS).
Contact *Program Coordinator*
804-924-8646
Fax: 804-924-8437
E-mail: ms-hes@virginia.edu

VIRGINIA COMMONWEALTH UNIVERSITY
Richmond, VA 23284-9005

OVERVIEW

Virginia Commonwealth University is a public coed university.

ENROLLMENT

21,349 graduate, professional, and undergraduate students; 3,541 full-time matriculated graduate/professional students (2,128 women), 1,899 part-time matriculated graduate/professional students (1,277 women).

GRADUATE FACULTY

817.

TUITION

$4782 per year full-time, $248 per credit part-time for state residents; $12,265 per year full-time, $663 per credit part-time for nonresidents.

HOUSING

Rooms and/or apartments available to single students at an average cost of $2500 per year ($4000 including board); on-campus housing not available to married students. Graduate housing contact: Bernard A. Mann, 804-828-7666.

STUDENT SERVICES

Multicultural affairs office, low-cost health insurance, career counseling, free psychological counseling, exercise/wellness program, campus safety program, campus employment opportunities, international student services, grant writing training, teacher training.

FACILITIES

Library: Cabell/Tompkins-McCaw Libraries; total holdings of 1.2 million volumes, 2.5 million microforms, 10,200 current periodical subscriptions. A total of 78 personal computers in all libraries. Access provided to on-line information retrieval services. *Computer:* Campuswide network is available with full Internet access. *Special:* In arts and humanities: Anderson Art Gallery, School of the Arts Library and Slide Collection, conservation laboratory. In science and engineering: Burn Trauma Clinic, Institute of Biotechnology, Institute of Statistics, Massey Cancer Center, Sickle Cell Anemia Clinic, nuclear magnetic resonance facility, pharmacokinetics laboratory. In social sciences: Business Management Center, Virginia Center for Public/Private Initiatives, Virginia Center on Aging, survey research laboratory.

COMPUTER SCIENCE

College of Humanities and Sciences, Department of Mathematical Sciences, Program in Computer Science
Programs   Awards MS.
Faculty   8.
Students   13 full-time (5 women), 18 part-time (2 women); includes 4 minority (all Asian-Americans), 8 international. Average age 32.
Degrees Awarded   In 1996, 8 degrees awarded.
Entrance Requirements   GRE General Test, GRE Subject Test.
Applying   23 applicants, 57% accepted. *Deadline:* 7/1 (11/15 for spring admission). *Fee:* $25.
Contact   Dr. James A. Wood
  Director of Graduate Studies
  804-828-1301
  Fax: 804-828-8785
  E-mail: jwoods@atlas.vcu.edu

VIRGINIA POLYTECHNIC INSTITUTE AND STATE UNIVERSITY
Blacksburg, VA 24061-0202

OVERVIEW
Virginia Polytechnic Institute and State University is a public coed university.

ENROLLMENT
26,659 graduate, professional, and undergraduate students; 3,668 full-time matriculated graduate/professional students (1,441 women), 2,463 part-time matriculated graduate/professional students (1,067 women).

TUITION
$4769 per year full-time, $757 per semester (minimum) part-time for state residents; $7199 per year full-time, $1162 per semester (minimum) part-time for nonresidents.

HOUSING
Rooms and/or apartments available to single students at an average cost of $1024 per year; on-campus housing not available to married students. Housing application deadline: 5/16. Graduate housing contact: Edward Spencer, 540-231-6204.

STUDENT SERVICES
Career counseling, free psychological counseling, campus employment opportunities, international student services.

FACILITIES
Library: Carol M. Newman Library plus 3 additional on-campus libraries; total holdings of 1.545 million volumes, 3.927 million microforms, 17,200 current periodical subscriptions. Access provided to on-line information retrieval services. *Special:* In science and engineering:

Center for the Study of Composite Materials, Center for Coal and Energy Research, anaerobe laboratory, spatial analysis laboratory.

COMPUTER SCIENCE

College of Arts and Sciences, Department of Computer Science
Programs   Offers programs in computer science (MS, PhD), information systems (MIS). Part-time programs available.
Faculty   22 full-time (2 women).
Faculty Research   Software engineering, operating systems, simulation, artificial intelligence.
Students   73 full-time (15 women), 53 part-time (14 women); includes 18 minority (7 African-Americans, 9 Asian-Americans, 2 Hispanics), 45 international. Average age 24.
Degrees Awarded   In 1996, 55 master's, 5 doctorates awarded.
Entrance Requirements   GRE General Test (minimum combined score of 1200), TOEFL.
Degree Requirements   For master's, computer language, thesis (for some programs); for doctorate, computer language.
Financial Aid   In 1996–97, 21 research assistantships (6 to first-year students), 25 teaching assistantships (3 to first-year students), 15 assistantships (8 to first-year students) were awarded; fellowships, Federal Work-Study also available. *Financial aid application deadline:* 4/1.
Applying   348 applicants, 35% accepted. *Deadline:* 12/1 (priority date; rolling processing). *Fee:* $25.
Contact   Dr. Verna Schuetz
  Assistant Head
  540-231-6931

See in-depth description on page **753.**

ELECTRICAL ENGINEERING

College of Engineering, Department of Electrical Engineering
Programs   Awards MS, PhD.
Students   283 full-time (39 women), 150 part-time (14 women); includes 46 minority (8 African-Americans, 33 Asian-Americans, 5 Hispanics), 203 international.
Degrees Awarded   In 1996, 91 master's, 16 doctorates awarded.
Entrance Requirements   GRE General Test, GRE Subject Test, TOEFL (minimum score 600).
Degree Requirements   For doctorate, 1 foreign language, dissertation.
Financial Aid   In 1996–97, 56 research assistantships, 47 teaching assistantships, 21 graduate assistantships were awarded; fellowships and career-related internships or fieldwork also available. *Financial aid application deadline:* 4/1.
Applying   605 applicants, 60% accepted. *Deadline:* 12/1 (priority date; rolling processing). *Fee:* $25.
Contact   Dr. Ira Jacobs
  Interim Head
  540-231-6646

See in-depth description on page **755.**

INFORMATION SCIENCE

College of Arts and Sciences, Department of Computer Science, Program in Information Systems
Programs   Awards MIS. Part-time programs available.
Faculty   22 full-time (2 women).
Faculty Research   Software engineering, operating systems, simulation, artificial intelligence.
Students   3 full-time (2 women), 41 part-time (14 women); includes 8 minority (2 African-Americans, 3 Asian-Americans, 2 Hispanics, 1 Native American), 1 international. Average age 24.
Degrees Awarded   In 1996, 16 degrees awarded.

Entrance Requirements GRE General Test (minimum combined score of 1200), TOEFL.
Degree Requirements Computer language.
Financial Aid Fellowships, research assistantships, teaching assistantships, Federal Work-Study available. *Financial aid application deadline:* 4/1.
Applying 31 applicants, 23% accepted. *Deadline:* 12/1 (priority date; rolling processing). *Fee:* $25.
Contact *Dr. Verna Schuetz*
　　　　　 Assistant Head
　　　　　 540-231-6931

See in-depth description on page 753.

WASHINGTON

EASTERN WASHINGTON UNIVERSITY
Cheney, WA 99004-2431

OVERVIEW
Eastern Washington University is a public coed comprehensive institution.

ENROLLMENT
8,078 graduate, professional, and undergraduate students; 439 full-time matriculated graduate/professional students (263 women), 349 part-time matriculated graduate/professional students (227 women).

GRADUATE FACULTY
288 (70 women); includes 45 minority (3 African-Americans, 24 Asian-Americans, 12 Hispanics, 6 Native Americans).

TUITION
$4041 per year full-time, $135 per credit part-time for state residents; $12,291 per year full-time, $410 per credit part-time for nonresidents.

HOUSING
On-campus housing not available.

STUDENT SERVICES
Low-cost health insurance, career counseling, free psychological counseling, campus safety program, campus employment opportunities, international student services.

FACILITIES
Library: John F. Kennedy Library plus 3 additional on-campus libraries; total holdings of 441,562 volumes, 1,121,239 microforms, 5,231 current periodical subscriptions. Access provided to on-line information retrieval services. *Computer:* Campuswide network is available with full Internet access. *Special:* In science and engineering: Turnbull Laboratory for Ecological Research, primate center. In social sciences: Robert Reid Laboratory School.

COMPUTER SCIENCE

College of Science, Mathematics and Technology, Department of Computer Science
Programs Awards M Ed, MS. Part-time programs available.
Faculty 10 full-time (2 women).
Students 5 full-time (1 woman), 12 part-time (2 women).
Degrees Awarded In 1996, 4 degrees awarded.

Entrance Requirements Minimum GPA of 3.0.
Degree Requirements Thesis or alternative, comprehensive oral exam.
Financial Aid In 1996–97, 1 research assistantship, 7 teaching assistantships were awarded; Federal Work-Study, institutionally sponsored loans also available. *Financial aid application deadline:* 2/1.
Applying 18 applicants, 78% accepted. *Deadline:* 4/1 (priority date; rolling processing; 1/15 for spring admission). *Fee:* $35.
Contact *Dr. Steve Simmons*
　　　　　 Adviser
　　　　　 509-359-6064

GONZAGA UNIVERSITY
Spokane, WA 99258

OVERVIEW
Gonzaga University is an independent-religious coed comprehensive institution.

ENROLLMENT
4,613 graduate, professional, and undergraduate students; 1,748 full-time matriculated graduate/professional students (891 women), 0 part-time matriculated graduate/professional students.

GRADUATE FACULTY
154 full-time (34 women), 45 part-time (15 women); includes 30 minority (8 African-Americans, 11 Asian-Americans, 3 Hispanics, 8 Native Americans).

TUITION
$5925 per year (minimum) full-time, $395 per credit hour (minimum) part-time.

HOUSING
Rooms and/or apartments available to single students at an average cost of $3400 per year; available to married students at an average cost of $6600 per year. Graduate housing contact: Housing/Residence Life, 509-328-4220.

STUDENT SERVICES
Disabled student services, multicultural affairs office, low-cost health insurance, career counseling, free psychological counseling, campus employment opportunities, writing training, grant writing training.

FACILITIES
Library: Foley Center plus 2 additional on-campus libraries; total holdings of 550,000 volumes, 290,000 microforms, 4,200 current periodical subscriptions. A total of 120 personal computers in all libraries. Access provided to on-line information retrieval services. *Computer:* Campuswide network is available with full Internet access. Computer service fees are applied as a separate charge.

ELECTRICAL ENGINEERING

Graduate School, School of Engineering, Program in Electrical Engineering
Programs Awards MSEE.
Faculty 9 full-time (1 woman).
Students 12 full-time (3 women), includes 10 international. Average age 30.
Degrees Awarded In 1996, 1 degree awarded.

Entrance Requirements GRE General Test, TOEFL (minimum score 550), minimum GPA of 3.0 during previous 2 years.

Degree Requirements Project required, foreign language and thesis not required.

Financial Aid Available to part-time students. *Financial aid application deadline: 3/1.*

Applying 23 applicants, 39% accepted. *Deadline: 7/20 (priority date; rolling processing; 11/1 for spring admission). Fee: $40.*

Contact *Dr. Grigore Braileanu*
Chairman
509-328-4220 Ext. 3536

SEATTLE UNIVERSITY
Seattle, WA 98122

OVERVIEW
Seattle University is an independent-religious coed comprehensive institution.

ENROLLMENT
5,990 graduate, professional, and undergraduate students; 1,080 full-time matriculated graduate/professional students (598 women), 1,613 part-time matriculated graduate/professional students (882 women).

GRADUATE FACULTY
153; includes 13 minority (5 African-Americans, 5 Asian-Americans, 2 Hispanics, 1 Native American).

EXPENSES
Tuition $329 per credit hour (minimum). Fees $70 per year.

HOUSING
Rooms and/or apartments available to single students (40 units) at an average cost of $4620 per year ($6465 including board); on-campus housing not available to married students. Graduate housing contact: Housing Office, 206-296-6274.

STUDENT SERVICES
Disabled student services, low-cost health insurance, career counseling, free psychological counseling, day-care facilities, campus safety program, campus employment opportunities, international student services.

FACILITIES
Library: A. A. Lemieux Library; total holdings of 209,543 volumes, 396,663 microforms, 2,694 current periodical subscriptions. A total of 26 personal computers in all libraries. Access provided to on-line information retrieval services. *Computer:* Campuswide network is available with full Internet access. Computer services are offered at no charge.

SOFTWARE ENGINEERING

School of Science and Engineering, Program in Software Engineering
Programs Awards MSE. Part-time and evening/weekend programs available.
Faculty 7 full-time (2 women).
Students 3 full-time (0 women), 86 part-time (22 women); includes 19 minority (7 African-Americans, 10 Asian-Americans, 1 Hispanic, 1 Native American), 4 international. Average age 34.
Degrees Awarded In 1996, 36 degrees awarded.

Entrance Requirements GRE General Test, 2 years of related work experience.

Degree Requirements Thesis or alternative required, foreign language not required.

Financial Aid Assistantships, Federal Work-Study, and career-related internships or fieldwork available. Aid available to part-time students. *Financial aid application deadline: 2/1;* applicants required to submit FAFSA.

Applying 22 applicants, 68% accepted. *Deadline: 4/1 (priority date). Fee: $55.*

Contact *Dr. David Umphress*
Director
206-296-5510

UNIVERSITY OF WASHINGTON
Seattle, WA 98195

OVERVIEW
University of Washington is a public coed university.

ENROLLMENT
35,954 graduate, professional, and undergraduate students; 7,570 full-time matriculated graduate/professional students (3,685 women), 1,738 part-time matriculated graduate/professional students (963 women).

GRADUATE FACULTY
2,720.

TUITION
$5232 per year full-time, $748 per quarter (minimum) part-time for state residents; $12,966 per year full-time, $1854 per quarter (minimum) part-time for nonresidents.

HOUSING
Rooms and/or apartments available to single students (4,300 units) at an average cost of $3377 per year ($4671 including board); available to married students (443 units) at an average cost of $4634 per year. Housing application deadline: 5/1. Graduate housing contact: Student Services Office, 206-543-4059.

STUDENT SERVICES
Disabled student services, multicultural affairs office, low-cost health insurance, career counseling, day-care facilities, campus safety program, campus employment opportunities, international student services, teacher training.

FACILITIES
Library: Suzzallo Library plus 18 additional on-campus libraries; total holdings of 5,601,263 volumes, 6,432,950 microforms, 56,295 current periodical subscriptions. A total of 550 personal computers in all libraries. Access provided to on-line information retrieval services. *Computer:* Campuswide network is available with full Internet access. Total number of PCs/terminals supplied for student use: 3,000. Computer service fees are included with tuition and fees. *Special:* In arts and humanities: Center for the Humanities, Henry Art Gallery, Burke Memorial Washington State Museum. In science and engineering: Fisheries Research Institute, applied physics laboratory, Friday Harbor Laboratories, Quaternary Research Center, Center for Urban Horticulture, Regional Primate Research Center, Institute

for Nuclear Theory. In social sciences: Center for Law and Justice, Institute for Ethnic Studies in the United States, Northwest Center for Research on Women, Institute on Aging, Center on Human Development and Disability.

COMPUTER SCIENCE

College of Engineering, Department of Computer Science and Engineering

Programs Offers program in computer science (MS, PhD).

Faculty 30 full-time (3 women).

Students 114 full-time (16 women), 17 part-time (1 woman); includes 19 minority (5 African-Americans, 12 Asian-Americans, 2 Hispanics), 38 international.

Degrees Awarded In 1996, 20 master's awarded (10% found work related to degree, 90% continued full-time study); 16 doctorates awarded (44% entered university research/teaching, 56% found other work related to degree).

Entrance Requirements GRE General Test, TOEFL (minimum score 550), minimum GPA of 3.0.

Degree Requirements For master's, thesis or alternative required, foreign language not required; for doctorate, dissertation, comprehensive exam, depth exam required, foreign language not required.

Financial Aid In 1996–97, 15 fellowships (1 to a first-year student), 50 research assistantships (5 to first-year students), 35 teaching assistantships (15 to first-year students) were awarded. *Financial aid application deadline: 2/1.*

Applying 588 applicants, 16% accepted. *Deadline: 1/10. Fee: $45.*

Contact *Graduate Admissions*
   206-543-1695
   E-mail: grad_admissions@cs.u.washington.edu
See in-depth description on page 743.

ELECTRICAL ENGINEERING

College of Engineering, Department of Electrical Engineering

Programs Awards MSEE, PhD.

Faculty Research Controls and robotics, communications and signal processing, electromagnetics, optics and acoustics, electronic devices and photonics.

Entrance Requirements For master's, GRE General Test, TOEFL (minimum score 580), minimum GPA of 3.0; for doctorate, GRE General Test, TOEFL (minimum score 580), MS, minimum GPA of 3.0.

Degree Requirements For master's, thesis optional, foreign language not required; for doctorate, dissertation required, foreign language not required.

Applying *Deadline: 2/1. Fee: $45.*

See in-depth description on page 745.

WASHINGTON STATE UNIVERSITY
Pullman, WA 99164–1610

OVERVIEW
Washington State University is a public coed university.

ENROLLMENT
17,379 graduate, professional, and undergraduate students; 1,846 full-time matriculated graduate/professional students (856 women), 1,192 part-time matriculated graduate/professional students (595 women).

GRADUATE FACULTY
770 full-time (100 women), 50 part-time (25 women); includes 113 minority (13 African-Americans, 65 Asian-Americans, 31 Hispanics, 4 Native Americans).

TUITION
$5132 per year full-time, $257 per credit hour part-time for state residents; $12,866 per year full-time, $643 per credit hour part-time for nonresidents.

HOUSING
Rooms and/or apartments available to single students (320 units) at an average cost of $3500 per year ($5500 including board); available to married students at an average cost of $3900 per year ($5500 including board). Graduate housing contact: Housing Services Office, 509-335-4577.

STUDENT SERVICES
Disabled student services, multicultural affairs office, low-cost health insurance, career counseling, free psychological counseling, exercise/wellness program, day-care facilities, campus safety program, campus employment opportunities, international student services, writing training, grant writing training, teacher training.

FACILITIES
Library: Holland Library plus 4 additional on-campus libraries; total holdings of 185,000 volumes, 310,000 microforms, 24,250 current periodical subscriptions. A total of 92 personal computers in all libraries. Access provided to on-line information retrieval services. *Computer:* Campuswide network is available with full Internet access. Computer service fees are applied as a separate charge. *Special:* In arts and humanities: Humanities Research Center. In science and engineering: Environmental Research Center, laboratory for atmospheric research, Bioanalytic Center, Electron Microscopy Center, Center for Visualization Analysis and Design in Molecular Science. In social sciences: Small Business Research Center, Social and Economic Research Center.

COMPUTER SCIENCE

College of Engineering and Architecture, School of Electrical Engineering and Computer Science, Program in Computer Science

Programs Awards MS, PhD.

Faculty 10 full-time (0 women).

Students 39 full-time (8 women), 6 part-time (4 women); includes 2 minority (both Asian-Americans), 34 international.

Degrees Awarded In 1996, 14 master's awarded.

Entrance Requirements GRE General Test, GRE Subject Test, minimum GPA of 3.0.

Degree Requirements Thesis/dissertation, oral exam required, foreign language not required.

Financial Aid In 1996–97, 9 research assistantships, 20 teaching assistantships were awarded; teaching associateships, partial tuition waivers, Federal Work-Study, institutionally sponsored loans, and career-related internships or fieldwork also available. *Financial aid application deadline: 4/1;* applicants required to submit FAFSA.

Applying *Deadline: 3/1 (priority date; rolling processing). Fee: $35.*

Contact *Dr. C. Raghavendra*
   Graduate Coordinator
   509-335-8246
   Fax: 509-335-3818

ELECTRICAL ENGINEERING

College of Engineering and Architecture, School of Electrical Engineering and Computer Science, Program in Electrical Engineering
Programs   Awards MS, PhD.
Students   61 full-time (7 women), 12 part-time (0 women); includes 3 minority (1 African-American, 2 Asian-Americans), 31 international.
Degrees Awarded   In 1996, 29 master's, 6 doctorates awarded.
Entrance Requirements   GRE General Test, minimum GPA of 3.0.
Degree Requirements   Thesis/dissertation, oral exam required, foreign language not required.
Financial Aid   In 1996–97, 25 research assistantships, 24 teaching assistantships were awarded; partial tuition waivers, Federal Work-Study, institutionally sponsored loans, and career-related internships or fieldwork also available. *Financial aid application deadline:* 4/1; applicants required to submit FAFSA.
Applying   *Deadline:* 3/1 (priority date; rolling processing). *Fee:* $35.
Contact   *Dr. Robert Olsen*
Graduate Coordinator
509-335-4950
Fax: 509-335-3818

WESTERN WASHINGTON UNIVERSITY
Bellingham, WA 98225-5996

OVERVIEW
Western Washington University is a public coed comprehensive institution.

ENROLLMENT
10,708 graduate, professional, and undergraduate students; 588 full-time matriculated graduate/professional students (338 women), 245 part-time matriculated graduate/professional students (155 women).

GRADUATE FACULTY
303 (79 women).

EXPENSES
Tuition $4041 per year full-time, $135 per credit part-time for state residents; $12,291 per year full-time, $410 per credit part-time for nonresidents. Fees $240 per year.

HOUSING
Rooms and/or apartments available to single students at an average cost of $4400 (including board); available to married students at an average cost of $3321 per year. Housing application deadline: 5/1. Graduate housing contact: Kay Rich, 360-650-2971.

STUDENT SERVICES
Disabled student services, multicultural affairs office, low-cost health insurance, career counseling, free psychological counseling, exercise/wellness program, day-care facilities, campus safety program, campus employment opportunities, international student services.

FACILITIES
Library: Mabel Zoe Wilson Library plus 1 additional on-campus library; total holdings of 600,000 volumes, 1.906 million microforms, 4,804 current periodical subscriptions. A total of 150 personal computers in all libraries. Access provided to on-line information retrieval services. *Computer:* Campuswide network is available with full Internet access. Total number of PCs/terminals supplied for student use: 1,000. Computer service fees are included with tuition and fees. *Special:* In science and engineering: Sundquist Marine Laboratory.

COMPUTER SCIENCE

College of Arts and Sciences, Department of Computer Science
Programs   Awards MS. Part-time programs available.
Faculty   9 (0 women).
Students   12 full-time (1 woman), 5 part-time (0 women).
Degrees Awarded   In 1996, 4 degrees awarded.
Entrance Requirements   GRE General Test, TOEFL (minimum score 565), minimum GPA of 3.0 in last 60 semester hours or last 90 quarter hours.
Degree Requirements   Computer language, project required, thesis optional, foreign language not required.
Financial Aid   Teaching assistantships, partial tuition waivers, Federal Work-Study, institutionally sponsored loans available. Aid available to part-time students. *Financial aid application deadline:* 3/31.
Applying   13 applicants, 62% accepted. *Deadline:* 6/1 (rolling processing; 2/1 for spring admission). *Fee:* $35.
Contact   *Dr. Gary Eerkes*
Graduate Program Adviser
360-650-3807

WEST VIRGINIA

WEST VIRGINIA GRADUATE COLLEGE
South Charleston, WV 25303-1600

OVERVIEW
West Virginia Graduate College is a public coed graduate-only institution.

ENROLLMENT
152 full-time matriculated graduate/professional students (95 women), 1,482 part-time matriculated graduate/professional students (1,014 women).

GRADUATE FACULTY
51 full-time (13 women), 92 part-time (42 women), 70.41 FTE; includes 2 minority (both African-Americans).

TUITION
$1738 per year full-time, $97 per credit hour part-time for state residents; $6264 per year full-time, $348 per credit hour part-time for nonresidents.

HOUSING
On-campus housing not available.

STUDENT SERVICES
Career counseling.

FACILITIES
Library: Drain-Jordan Library; total holdings of 45,752 volumes, 509,972 microforms, 457 current periodical subscriptions. A total of 6 personal computers in all libraries. Access provided to on-line information retrieval services. *Computer:* Campuswide network is available with full Internet access. Total number of PCs/terminals

supplied for student use: 20. Computer services are offered at no charge.

INFORMATION SCIENCE

School of Engineering and Science, Program in Information Systems

Programs Awards MS. Part-time and evening/weekend programs available.

Faculty 1 full-time (0 women), 2 part-time (1 woman), 1.4 FTE.

Students 5 full-time (2 women), 34 part-time (16 women); includes 5 minority (all Asian-Americans). Average age 35.

Degrees Awarded In 1996, 7 degrees awarded.

Entrance Requirements GRE General Test, minimum undergraduate GPA of 2.5.

Degree Requirements Computer language, final project, oral exam.

Financial Aid Full tuition waivers available. Aid available to part-time students. *Financial aid application deadline:* 8/1; applicants required to submit FAFSA.

Applying *Deadline:* 8/1 (priority date; rolling processing). *Fee:* $0.

Contact Dr. Thomas Hankins
  Adviser
  304-746-2044
  Fax: 304-746-2503

WEST VIRGINIA UNIVERSITY
Morgantown, WV 26506-6201

OVERVIEW
West Virginia University is a public coed university.

ENROLLMENT
1,743 graduate, professional, and undergraduate students; 3,046 full-time matriculated graduate/professional students (1,421 women), 2,149 part-time matriculated graduate/professional students (1,369 women).

GRADUATE FACULTY
1,380 full-time (388 women), 212 part-time (115 women), 1,465 FTE; includes 166 minority (32 African-Americans, 102 Asian-Americans, 27 Hispanics, 5 Native Americans).

EXPENSES
Tuition $2490 per year full-time, $107 per credit hour part-time for state residents; $7606 per year full-time, $391 per credit hour part-time for nonresidents. Fees $608 per year full-time, $34 per credit hour part-time.

HOUSING
Rooms and/or apartments available to single students (154 units) at an average cost of $3175 per year ($4500 including board); available to married students (120 units) at an average cost of $3475 per year. Graduate housing contact: Housing and Residence Life Office, 304-293-5840.

STUDENT SERVICES
Disabled student services, low-cost health insurance, career counseling, free psychological counseling, campus safety program, campus employment opportunities, international student services, writing training.

FACILITIES
Library: Charles C. Wise, Jr. Library plus 9 additional on-campus libraries; total holdings of 1,530,955 volumes, 2,518,386 microforms, 11,666 current periodical subscriptions. A total of 120 personal computers in all libraries. Access provided to on-line information retrieval services. *Computer:* Campuswide network is available with full Internet access. Total number of PCs/terminals supplied for student use: 1,500. Computer services are offered at no charge. *Special:* In arts and humanities: Institute for the History of Technology and Industrial Archaeology, World Music Center. In science and engineering: National Research Center for Coal and Energy, Constructed Facilities Center, Concurrent Engineering Research Center, Alternate Transportation Fuels Center. In social sciences: Women's Studies Center, Regional Research Institute, Bureau of Business Research, Geographic Information Systems Laboratory.

COMPUTER ENGINEERING

College of Engineering and Mineral Resources, Department of Electrical and Computer Engineering, Program in Computer Engineering

Programs Offers engineering (PhD).

Faculty Research Software engineering, microprocessor applications, microelectronic systems, fault tolerance, advanced computer architectures and networks, neural networks.

Degrees Awarded Terminal master's awarded for partial completion of doctoral program.

Entrance Requirements For doctorate, GRE General Test (score in 80th percentile or higher), TOEFL (minimum score 550), minimum GPA of 3.0.

Degree Requirements For doctorate, computer language, dissertation, comprehensive exam required, foreign language not required.

Financial Aid Fellowships, research assistantships, teaching assistantships, full and partial tuition waivers, Federal Work-Study, institutionally sponsored loans available. *Financial aid application deadline:* 2/1; applicants required to submit FAFSA.

Applying 20 applicants, 65% accepted. *Deadline:* 7/1 (priority date; rolling processing). *Fee:* $45.

Contact Dr. Wils Cooley
  Graduate Coordinator
  304-293-6371

COMPUTER SCIENCE

Eberly College of Arts and Sciences, Department of Statistics and Computer Science, Program in Computer Science

Programs Awards MS, PhD.

Faculty Research Artificial intelligence, knowledge-based simulation, data communications, mathematical computations, software engineering.

Students 67 full-time (13 women), 16 part-time (3 women); includes 2 minority (both Asian-Americans), 33 international. Average age 26.

Degrees Awarded In 1996, 27 master's awarded.

Entrance Requirements For master's, GRE General Test (score in 50th percentile or higher), TOEFL (minimum score 550), minimum GPA of 3.0; for doctorate, GRE General Test (score in 50th percentile or higher), GRE Subject Test, TOEFL (minimum score 550).

Degree Requirements For master's, computer language, thesis required, foreign language not required; for doctorate, 1 foreign language, computer language, dissertation, comprehensive exam.

Financial Aid In 1996–97, 8 research assistantships (4 to first-year students) averaging $900 per month and totaling $64,800, 15 teaching assistantships (6 to first-year students) averaging $885 per month were awarded; full and partial tuition waivers, Federal Work-Study, institutionally sponsored loans also available. *Financial aid application deadline:* 2/1; applicants required to submit FAFSA.

Applying 155 applicants, 46% accepted. *Deadline:* 3/15 (priority date; rolling processing). *Fee:* $45.

Contact Dr. John Atkins
Professor
304-293-3607 Ext. 3514
Fax: 304-293-7226

ELECTRICAL ENGINEERING

College of Engineering and Mineral Resources, Department of Electrical and Computer Engineering, Program in Electrical Engineering

Programs Offers electrical engineering (MSEE), engineering (MSE, PhD).

Faculty Research Power and control systems, communications and signal processing, electromechanical systems, microelectronics and photonics. *Total annual research expenditures:* $1.211 million.

Students 25 full-time (4 women), 11 part-time (0 women); includes 1 minority (Asian-American), 21 international. Average age 24.

Degrees Awarded In 1996, 21 master's, 1 doctorate awarded. Terminal master's awarded for partial completion of doctoral program.

Entrance Requirements GRE General Test (score in 80th percentile or higher), TOEFL (minimum score 550), minimum GPA of 3.0.

Degree Requirements For master's, computer language, thesis or alternative required, foreign language not required; for doctorate, computer language, dissertation, comprehensive exam required, foreign language not required.

Financial Aid Fellowships, research assistantships, teaching assistantships, full and partial tuition waivers, Federal Work-Study, institutionally sponsored loans available. *Financial aid application deadline:* 2/1; applicants required to submit FAFSA.

Applying 154 applicants, 64% accepted. *Deadline:* 7/1 (priority date; rolling processing). *Fee:* $45.

Contact Dr. Wils Cooley
Graduate Coordinator
304-293-6375

WISCONSIN

OVERVIEW

Concordia University Wisconsin is an independent-religious coed comprehensive institution.

ENROLLMENT

4,000 graduate, professional, and undergraduate students; 69 full-time matriculated graduate/professional students (40 women), 624 part-time matriculated graduate/professional students.

GRADUATE FACULTY

13 full-time (5 women), 10 part-time (5 women); includes 2 minority (1 African-American, 1 Hispanic).

TUITION

$250 per credit.

HOUSING

On-campus housing not available.

STUDENT SERVICES

Low-cost health insurance, career counseling, free psychological counseling, campus safety program, international student services, writing training.

FACILITIES

Library: Rincker Library; total holdings of 90,000 volumes, 128,000 microforms, 750 current periodical subscriptions. Access provided to on-line information retrieval services. *Computer:* Campuswide network is available with full Internet access. Total number of PCs/terminals supplied for student use: 150. Computer services are offered at no charge.

COMPUTER SCIENCE

Division of Graduate Studies, Master's Program in Guided Independent Study, Program in Computer Science

Programs Awards MS. Part-time and evening/weekend programs available.

Contact Gary Locklair
Director
414-243-4217
E-mail: locklair@luther.cuw.edu

OVERVIEW

Marquette University is an independent-religious coed university.

ENROLLMENT

10,527 graduate, professional, and undergraduate students; 854 full-time matriculated graduate/professional students (373 women), 1,304 part-time matriculated graduate/professional students (607 women).

GRADUATE FACULTY

519 full-time, 290 part-time.

TUITION

$475 per credit.

HOUSING

Rooms and/or apartments available to single students (118 units) and married students (114 units) at an average cost of $4000 per year ($6000 including board). Graduate housing contact: Residence Life Office, 414-288-7678.

STUDENT SERVICES

Disabled student services, multicultural affairs office, low-cost health insurance, career counseling, free psychological counseling, exercise/wellness program, day-care facilities, campus safety program, campus employment opportunities, international student services, writing training, grant writing training, teacher training.

FACILITIES

Library: Memorial Library plus 2 additional on-campus libraries; total holdings of 700,000 volumes, 268,607 microforms, 9,400 current periodical subscriptions. A total of 69 personal computers in all libraries. Access provided to on-line information retrieval services. *Computer:*

Campuswide network is available with full Internet access. Computer service fees are included with tuition and fees.

COMPUTER ENGINEERING

College of Engineering, Department of Electrical and Computer Engineering
Programs Awards MS, PhD. Part-time and evening/weekend programs available.
Faculty 14 full-time (2 women), 2 part-time (0 women).
Faculty Research Electric machines, drives, and controls; applied solid-state electronics; computers and signal processing; microwaves and antennas; electronic and ultrasonic sensors. *Total annual research expenditures:* $1 million.
Students 39 full-time (4 women), 66 part-time (9 women); includes 8 minority (2 African-Americans, 2 Asian-Americans, 4 Hispanics), 37 international. Average age 28.
Degrees Awarded In 1996, 18 master's awarded (100% found work related to degree); 5 doctorates awarded (100% found work related to degree). Terminal master's awarded for partial completion of doctoral program.
Entrance Requirements For master's, TOEFL (minimum score 575), GRE General Test or minimum GPA of 3.0; for doctorate, GRE General Test (minimum score 700 on quantitative section), TOEFL (minimum score 575).
Degree Requirements For master's, thesis optional, foreign language not required; for doctorate, computer language, dissertation defense, qualifying exam required, foreign language not required.
Financial Aid In 1996–97, 40 students received aid, including 10 fellowships averaging $962 per month, 13 research assistantships (2 to first-year students) averaging $962 per month, 10 teaching assistantships (4 to first-year students) averaging $962 per month, 7 scholarship (1 to a first-year student); Federal Work-Study, institutionally sponsored loans also available. *Financial aid application deadline:* 2/15.
Applying 111 applicants, 45% accepted. *Deadline:* 7/15 (priority date; rolling processing; 11/15 for spring admission). *Fee:* $40.
Contact Dr. Thomas K. Ishii
  Director of Graduate Studies
  414-288-6998
  Fax: 414-288-5579
  E-mail: ishiit@vms.csd.mu.edu

ELECTRICAL ENGINEERING

College of Engineering, Department of Electrical and Computer Engineering
Programs Awards MS, PhD. Part-time and evening/weekend programs available.
Faculty 14 full-time (2 women), 2 part-time (0 women).
Faculty Research Electric machines, drives, and controls; applied solid-state electronics; computers and signal processing; microwaves and antennas; electronic and ultrasonic sensors. *Total annual research expenditures:* $1 million.
Students 39 full-time (4 women), 66 part-time (9 women); includes 8 minority (2 African-Americans, 2 Asian-Americans, 4 Hispanics), 37 international. Average age 28.
Degrees Awarded In 1996, 18 master's awarded (100% found work related to degree); 5 doctorates awarded (100% found work related to degree). Terminal master's awarded for partial completion of doctoral program.
Entrance Requirements For master's, TOEFL (minimum score 575), GRE General Test or minimum GPA of 3.0; for doctorate, GRE General Test (minimum score 700 on quantitative section), TOEFL (minimum score 575).

Degree Requirements For master's, thesis optional, foreign language not required; for doctorate, computer language, dissertation defense, qualifying exam required, foreign language not required.
Financial Aid In 1996–97, 40 students received aid, including 10 fellowships averaging $962 per month, 13 research assistantships (2 to first-year students) averaging $962 per month, 10 teaching assistantships (4 to first-year students) averaging $962 per month, 7 scholarship (1 to a first-year student); Federal Work-Study, institutionally sponsored loans also available. *Financial aid application deadline:* 2/15.
Applying 111 applicants, 45% accepted. *Deadline:* 7/15 (priority date; rolling processing; 11/15 for spring admission). *Fee:* $40.
Contact Dr. Thomas K. Ishii
  Director of Graduate Studies
  414-288-6998
  Fax: 414-288-5579
  E-mail: ishiit@vms.csd.mu.edu

MILWAUKEE SCHOOL OF ENGINEERING
Milwaukee, WI 53202-3109

OVERVIEW
Milwaukee School of Engineering is an independent coed comprehensive institution.

ENROLLMENT
2,957 graduate, professional, and undergraduate students; 62 full-time matriculated graduate/professional students (13 women), 358 part-time matriculated graduate/professional students (47 women).

GRADUATE FACULTY
1 full-time (0 women), 38 part-time (5 women), 13.09 FTE; includes 0 minority.

HOUSING
Rooms and/or apartments available to single students at an average cost of $2430 per year ($3630 including board); on-campus housing not available to married students. Graduate housing contact: Bill Gorman, 414-277-7400.

STUDENT SERVICES
Disabled student services, multicultural affairs office, low-cost health insurance, career counseling, free psychological counseling, exercise/wellness program, campus safety program, campus employment opportunities, international student services, writing training.

FACILITIES
Library: Walter Schroeder Memorial Library; total holdings of 59,000 volumes, 60,000 microforms, 623 current periodical subscriptions. A total of 25 personal computers in all libraries. Access provided to on-line information retrieval services. *Computer:* Campuswide network is available with full Internet access. Total number of PCs/terminals supplied for student use: 550. Computer services are offered at no charge. *Special:* In science and engineering: Applied Technology Center; Rapid Prototyping Center; Fluid Power Institute; High Impact

Materials and Structures, Photonics and Applied Optics Center.

Tenure Center Library, Arthur H. Robinson Map Library, Social Science Reference Library, Social Science Research Institute.

MEDICAL INFORMATICS

Department of Electrical Engineering and Computer Science, Program in Medical Informatics
Programs   Awards MS.
Contact   *Cheryl Donnelly*
Director of Graduate Enrollment
800-321-6763
Fax: 414-277-7475
E-mail: donnelly@admin.msoe.edu

COMPUTER SCIENCE

College of Letters and Science, Department of Computer Sciences
Programs   Awards MS, PhD.
Entrance Requirements   GRE General Test, GRE Subject Test.
Degree Requirements   For doctorate, dissertation.
Financial Aid   Fellowships, research assistantships, teaching assistantships available.
Applying   *Fee:* $38.
Contact   *Marvin H. Solomon*
Chair
608-262-7967

See in-depth description on page **747.**

ELECTRICAL ENGINEERING

College of Engineering, Department of Electrical and Computer Engineering
Programs   Offers program in electrical engineering (MS, PhD). Part-time programs available.
Faculty   42 full-time (4 women), 2 part-time (0 women).
Faculty Research   Microelectronics, computer architecture, power electronics and systems, communications, signal processing. *Total annual research expenditures:* $9.7 million.
Students   231 full-time (26 women), 39 part-time (4 women); includes 12 minority (5 African-Americans, 2 Asian-Americans, 5 Hispanics), 150 international.
Degrees Awarded   In 1996, 55 master's, 23 doctorates awarded. Terminal master's awarded for partial completion of doctoral program.
Entrance Requirements   GRE General Test, TOEFL (minimum score 580).
Degree Requirements   For master's, thesis or alternative required, foreign language not required; for doctorate, dissertation required, foreign language not required.
Financial Aid   In 1996–97, 190 students received aid, including 21 fellowships (7 to first-year students) totaling $202,124, 114 research assistantships (13 to first-year students) averaging $1,396 per month and totaling $1.43 million, 55 teaching assistantships (17 to first-year students) averaging $1,003 per month and totaling $450,422; Federal Work-Study, institutionally sponsored loans, and career-related internships or fieldwork also available. Aid available to part-time students. *Financial aid application deadline:* 12/1.
Applying   400 applicants, 78% accepted. *Deadline:* 6/1 (rolling processing; 11/1 for spring admission). *Fee:* $38.
Contact   *Graduate Secretary*
608-262-2745
Fax: 608-262-1267
E-mail: gradapp@ece.wisc.edu

UNIVERSITY OF WISCONSIN–MADISON
Madison, WI 53706-1380

OVERVIEW
University of Wisconsin–Madison is a public coed university.

TUITION
$4692 per year full-time, $881 per semester (minimum) part-time for state residents; $14,395 per year full-time, $2670 per semester (minimum) part-time for nonresidents.

HOUSING
Rooms and/or apartments available to single and married students. Graduate housing contact: Assignment Office, 608-262-2522.

FACILITIES
Library: Memorial Library plus 44 additional on-campus libraries. *Special:* In arts and humanities: Elvehjem Art Museum, Institute for Research in the Humanities, Kohler Art Library, Mills Music Library, Newberry Library Center for Renaissance Studies, Vilas Communication Hall Theatres and Studios, Women's Studies Research Center. In science and engineering: Agricultural experiment station, arboretum, Biotechnology Center, Biotron, Center for Quality and Productivity Improvement, Center for X-Ray Lithography, Enzyme Institute, Food Research Institute, integrated microscopy facility, Materials Science Research Center, W. S. Middleton Health Sciences, physical sciences laboratory, Space Science and Engineering Center, Synchrotron Radiation Center, university experimental farms, Waisman Center on Mental Retardation and Human Development, Weston Library, Wisconsin Center for Applied Microelectronics, Wisconsin Clinical Cancer Center, Wisconsin Regional Primate Center, Steenbock Memorial Library. In social sciences: Center for Demography and Ecology, Cooperative Children's Book Center, data and program library services, demography library, Education Research and Development Center, geography library, Industrial Relations Research Institute, Information Studies Library, Institute for Environmental Studies, Institute for Research on Poverty, Institute on Aging, Instructional Materials Center, journalism reading room, Robert M. LaFollotte Institute of Public Affairs, Land Tenure Center, Land

---

UNIVERSITY OF WISCONSIN–MILWAUKEE
Milwaukee, WI 53201-0413

OVERVIEW
University of Wisconsin–Milwaukee is a public coed university.

ENROLLMENT

21,877 graduate, professional, and undergraduate students; 1,601 full-time matriculated graduate/professional students (909 women), 2,598 part-time matriculated graduate/professional students (1,521 women).

GRADUATE FACULTY

773 full-time (239 women).

TUITION

$4771 per year full-time, $980 per semester (minimum) part-time for state residents; $14,433 per year full-time, $2790 per semester (minimum) part-time for nonresidents.

HOUSING

Rooms and/or apartments available to single students (1,950 units) at an average cost of $3350 (including board); available to married students (16 units). Graduate housing contact: Director of Housing, 419-229-4065.

STUDENT SERVICES

Low-cost health insurance, career counseling, free psychological counseling, day-care facilities, campus safety program, campus employment opportunities, international student services.

FACILITIES

Library: Golda Meir Library; total holdings of 1.8 million volumes, 1.2 million microforms. A total of 100 personal computers in all libraries. Access provided to on-line information retrieval services. *Computer:* Campuswide network is available with full Internet access. Total number of PCs/terminals supplied for student use: 320. Computer services are offered at no charge. *Special:* In arts and humanities: Center for Twentieth-Century Studies. In science and engineering: Center for Great Lakes Study, surface studies laboratory, Advanced Analysis Facility. In social sciences: Urban Research Center.

COMPUTER SCIENCE

College of Engineering and Applied Science, Department of Electrical Engineering and Computer Science

Programs Offers program in computer science (MS, PhD). Part-time programs available.

Faculty 22 full-time (2 women).

Students 10 full-time (4 women), 50 part-time (8 women); includes 7 minority (5 Asian-Americans, 2 Hispanics), 17 international.

Degrees Awarded In 1996, 11 master's awarded.

Entrance Requirements For master's, minimum GPA of 2.75; for doctorate, minimum GPA of 3.5.

Degree Requirements For master's, thesis or alternative required, foreign language not required; for doctorate, dissertation, internship required, foreign language not required.

Financial Aid In 1996–97, 9 teaching assistantships were awarded; fellowships, research assistantships, project assistantships, and career-related internships or fieldwork also available. Aid available to part-time students. *Financial aid application deadline:* 4/15.

Applying 84 applicants, 50% accepted. *Deadline:* 1/1 (priority date; rolling processing; 9/1 for spring admission). *Fee:* $38 ($68 for international students).

Contact *K. Vairavan*
Co-Chair
414-229-4677

WYOMING

UNIVERSITY OF WYOMING
Laramie, WY 82071

OVERVIEW

University of Wyoming is a public coed university.

ENROLLMENT

11,251 graduate, professional, and undergraduate students; 1,023 full-time matriculated graduate/professional students (444 women), 708 part-time matriculated graduate/professional students (374 women).

GRADUATE FACULTY

582 (117 women).

EXPENSES

Tuition $2430 per year full-time, $135 per credit hour part-time for state residents; $7520 per year full-time, $418 per credit hour part-time for nonresidents. Fees $382 per year full-time, $7.25 per credit hour part-time.

HOUSING

Rooms and/or apartments available to single students at an average cost of $1512 per year ($3520 including board); available to married students (456 units) at an average cost of $4800 per year. Housing application deadline: 5/25. Graduate housing contact: Nicky Veneigas, 307-766-3179.

STUDENT SERVICES

Disabled student services, multicultural affairs office, low-cost health insurance, career counseling, free psychological counseling, day-care facilities, campus employment opportunities, international student services.

FACILITIES

Library: Coe Library plus 5 additional on-campus libraries; total holdings of 1,151,109 volumes, 2,765,643 microforms, 11,818 current periodical subscriptions. A total of 65 personal computers in all libraries. Access provided to on-line information retrieval services. *Computer:* Campuswide network is available with full Internet access. Total number of PCs/terminals supplied for student use: 372. Computer service fees are included with tuition and fees. *Special:* In arts and humanities: American Heritage Center, Survey Research Center, art museum. In science and engineering: Anthropology museum, Enhanced Oil Recovery Institute, Composite Materials Research Group, environmental simulation laboratory, Graphics and Image Processing Center, Information Technology, geological museum, mycological herbarium, Survey Research Center, UN-National Park Service Research Center, Red Buttes Environmental Biology Facility, Rocky Mountain Herbarium, U.S. Geological Survey, USDA-arthropod-borne animal diseases research laboratory, vertebrate museum, Williams Botany Conservatory, Wyoming Cooperative Research Unit, Wyoming State Veterinary Laboratory, Wyoming Water Research Center, Mineral Research and Reclamation Center, Elk Mountain Atmospheric Science Observatory, Atmospheric Science Flight Facility.

COMPUTER SCIENCE

College of Arts and Sciences, Department of Computer Science

Programs Offers programs in computer science (MS, PhD), mathematics–computer science (PhD). Part-time programs available.

Faculty 10 full-time (0 women), 1 (woman) part-time.

Faculty Research Fault-tolerant computing, distributed systems, knowledge representation, case-based reasoning, automated reasoning, parallel database access, parallel compilers. *Total annual research expenditures:* $169,701.

Students 17 full-time (1 woman), 11 part-time (5 women); includes 7 international.

Degrees Awarded In 1996, 19 master's, 3 doctorates awarded. Terminal master's awarded for partial completion of doctoral program.

Entrance Requirements For master's, GRE General Test (minimum combined score of 900), minimum GPA of 3.0; for doctorate, GRE General Test (minimum combined score of 1000), minimum GPA of 3.0.

Degree Requirements For master's, thesis; for doctorate, 1 foreign language, dissertation.

Financial Aid 20 students received aid; research assistantships, teaching assistantships, partial tuition waivers, Federal Work–Study, and career-related internships or fieldwork available. *Financial aid application deadline:* 3/1.

Applying 25 applicants, 48% accepted. *Deadline:* 3/1 (rolling processing; 10/1 for spring admission). *Fee:* $40.

Contact *Graduate Coordinator*
307-766-5190
Fax: 307-766-4036
E-mail: cosc@uwyo.edu

See in-depth description on page 749.

ELECTRICAL ENGINEERING

College of Engineering, Department of Electrical Engineering

Programs Offers program in electrical engineering (MS, PhD). Part-time programs available.

Faculty 12 (0 women).

Faculty Research Robotics and controls, signal and speech processing, power electronics, power systems, fuzzy and neural systems, instrumentation.

Students 20 full-time (3 women), 12 part-time (1 woman); includes 1 minority (Native American), 12 international.

Degrees Awarded In 1996, 18 master's awarded (100% found work related to degree); 1 doctorate awarded.

Entrance Requirements For master's, GRE General Test (minimum combined score of 1375), TOEFL (minimum score 550), minimum GPA of 3.0; for doctorate, GRE General Test (minimum combined score of 1475), TOEFL (minimum score 550), minimum GPA of 3.0.

Degree Requirements For master's, thesis; for doctorate, dissertation required, foreign language not required.

Financial Aid In 1996–97, 5 research assistantships (2 to first-year students), 18 teaching assistantships (5 to first-year students) were awarded. *Financial aid application deadline:* 3/1.

Applying 9 applicants, 78% accepted. *Deadline:* 6/1 (priority date; rolling processing). *Fee:* $40.

Contact *John E. McInroy*
Graduate Program Coordinator
307-766-6137

US TERRITORY

PUERTO RICO

UNIVERSITY OF PUERTO RICO, MAYAGÜEZ CAMPUS
Mayagüez, PR 00681-5000

OVERVIEW
University of Puerto Rico, Mayagüez Campus is a public coed university.

ENROLLMENT
12,594 graduate, professional, and undergraduate students; 658 full-time matriculated graduate/professional students (295 women), 141 part-time matriculated graduate/professional students (70 women).

GRADUATE FACULTY
382 (75 women).

EXPENSES
Tuition $75 per credit for commonwealth residents; $219 per credit for nonresidents. Fees $302 per year for commonwealth residents; $418 per year for nonresidents.

HOUSING
Rooms and/or apartments available to married students (44 units); on-campus housing not available to single students. Graduate housing contact: Gladys Hernández, 787-832-4040 Ext. 2078.

STUDENT SERVICES
Low-cost health insurance, career counseling, free psychological counseling, international student services.

FACILITIES
Library: Main library plus 1 additional on-campus library; total holdings of 875,138 volumes, 585,542 microforms, 3,062 current periodical subscriptions. A total of 57 personal computers in all libraries. Access provided to on-line information retrieval services. *Computer:* Campuswide network is available with full Internet access. Total number of PCs/terminals supplied for student use: 1,000. Computer services are offered at no charge. *Special:* In science and engineering: Center for Energy and Environment Research, Engineering Research Center, Magueyes Island Marine Station, Agricultural Experiment Station.

COMPUTER ENGINEERING

College of Engineering, Department of Electrical Engineering
Programs Offerings include computer engineering (M Co E, MS).
Department Faculty 27 (0 women).
Applying *Deadline:* 2/28 (rolling processing; 9/15 for spring admission). *Fee:* $15.
Contact *Dr. Samuel R. Irizarry*
Chairperson
787-832-4040 Ext. 3821

ELECTRICAL ENGINEERING

College of Engineering, Department of Electrical Engineering
Programs Offers programs in computer engineering (M Co E, MS), electrical engineering (MEE, MS). Part-time programs available.
Faculty 27 (0 women).
Faculty Research Microcomputer interfacing, control systems, power systems, electronics.
Students 63 full-time (15 women), 5 part-time (0 women); includes 57 minority (all Hispanics), 11 international.
Degrees Awarded In 1996, 11 degrees awarded.
Entrance Requirements Minimum GPA of 2.5, proficiency in English and Spanish.
Degree Requirements Thesis, comprehensive exam required, foreign language not required.
Financial Aid In 1996–97, 47 students received aid, including 2 fellowships averaging $200 per month, 27 research assistantships (7 to first-year students) averaging $664 per month, 18 teaching assistantships (8 to first-year students) averaging $700 per month; Federal Work-Study, institutionally sponsored loans also available.
Applying 44 applicants, 64% accepted. *Deadline:* 2/28 (rolling processing; 9/15 for spring admission). *Fee:* $15.
Contact *Dr. Samuel R. Irizarry*
Chairperson
787-832-4040 Ext. 3821

CANADA

ALBERTA

UNIVERSITY OF ALBERTA
Edmonton, AB T6G 2E1, Canada

OVERVIEW
University of Alberta is a public coed university.

ENROLLMENT
29,924 graduate, professional, and undergraduate students; 4,641 full-time matriculated graduate/professional students (2,134 women), 1,353 part-time matriculated graduate/professional students (773 women).

EXPENSES
Tuition $358 per course for Canadian residents; $716 per course for nonresidents. Fees $481 per year full-time, $185 per year part-time.

HOUSING
Rooms and/or apartments available to single students (1,310 units) at an average cost of $3012 per year ($5718 including board); available to married students (550 units) at an average cost of $6000 per year. Graduate housing contact: Housing and Food Services Office, 403-492-4281.

STUDENT SERVICES
Disabled student services, career counseling, free psychological counseling, exercise/wellness program, day-care facilities, campus employment opportunities, international student services, writing training, teacher training.

FACILITIES
Library: Cameron Library plus 8 additional on-campus libraries; total holdings of 4,968,292 volumes, 3,625,992 microforms, 26,424 current periodical subscriptions. A total of 125 personal computers in all libraries. Access provided to on-line information retrieval services. *Computer:* Campuswide network is available with full Internet access. Total number of PCs/terminals supplied for student use: 900. Computer service fees are included with tuition and fees. *Special:* In arts and humanities: Convocation Hall, Timms Centre for the Arts. In science and engineering: University farm, vascular plant herbarium, clothing and textiles collection, George Lake field site. In social sciences: Population Research Laboratory.

COMPUTER ENGINEERING

Faculty of Graduate Studies and Research, Department of Electrical and Computing Engineering
Programs Offers programs in computational optics (PhD), computer engineering (M Eng, M Sc, PhD), control systems (M Eng, M Sc, PhD), engineering management (M Eng), laser physics (M Sc, PhD), plasma physics (M Sc, PhD), power engineering (M Eng, M Sc, PhD), telecommunications (M Eng, M Sc, PhD).
Faculty 31 full-time (1 woman), 12 part-time (0 women), 35 FTE.

Faculty Research Controls, lasers and plasmas, microelectronics. *Total annual research expenditures:* $3 million.
Students 78 full-time (4 women), 25 part-time (2 women); includes 19 international. Average age 26.
Degrees Awarded Terminal master's awarded for partial completion of doctoral program.
Entrance Requirements TOEFL (minimum score 580; average 610).
Degree Requirements Thesis/dissertation required, foreign language not required.
Financial Aid 75 students received aid; fellowships, research assistantships, teaching assistantships available.
Applying 180 applicants, 19% accepted. *Deadline:* 4/30 (priority date; rolling processing). *Fee:* $0.
Contact Department Office
403-492-0161
Fax: 403-492-1811
E-mail: eegrad@ee.ualberta.ca

COMPUTER SCIENCE

Faculty of Graduate Studies and Research, Department of Computing Science
Programs Awards M Sc, PhD. Part-time programs available.
Faculty 27 full-time (5 women), 6 part-time (0 women), 27.5 FTE.
Faculty Research Artificial intelligence, multimedia, distributed computing, theory, software engineering.
Students 80 full-time (14 women), 16 part-time (2 women); includes 32 international.
Degrees Awarded In 1996, 22 master's awarded (77% found work related to degree, 23% continued full-time study); 4 doctorates awarded (100% found work related to degree). Terminal master's awarded for partial completion of doctoral program.
Degree Requirements Thesis/dissertation, oral exam, seminar.
Financial Aid In 1996–97, 5 fellowships averaging $1,100 per month, 8 research assistantships (1 to a first-year student) averaging $1,250 per month, 61 teaching assistantships (19 to first-year students) averaging $1,250 per month were awarded; career-related internships or fieldwork also available. Aid available to part-time students. *Financial aid application deadline:* 3/1.
Applying 160 applicants, 55% accepted. *Deadline:* 3/1 (priority date; rolling processing). *Fee:* $60.
Contact Edith Drummond
Department of Computing Science
403-492-4194
Fax: 403-492-1071
E-mail: gradinfo@cs.ualberta.ca

See in-depth description on page 585.

ELECTRICAL ENGINEERING

Faculty of Graduate Studies and Research, Department of Electrical and Computing Engineering
Programs Offers programs in computational optics (PhD), computer engineering (M Eng, M Sc, PhD), control systems (M Eng, M Sc, PhD), engineering management (M Eng), laser physics (M Sc, PhD), plasma physics (M Sc, PhD), power engineering (M Eng, M Sc, PhD), telecommunications (M Eng, M Sc, PhD).
Faculty 31 full-time (1 woman), 12 part-time (0 women), 35 FTE.

Faculty Research   Controls, lasers and plasmas, microelectronics. *Total annual research expenditures:* $3 million.

Students   78 full-time (4 women), 25 part-time (2 women); includes 19 international. Average age 26.

Degrees Awarded   Terminal master's awarded for partial completion of doctoral program.

Entrance Requirements   TOEFL (minimum score 580; average 610).

Degree Requirements   Thesis/dissertation required, foreign language not required.

Financial Aid   75 students received aid; fellowships, research assistantships, teaching assistantships available.

Applying   180 applicants, 19% accepted. *Deadline:* 4/30 (priority date; rolling processing). *Fee:* $0.

Contact   *Department Office*
403-492-0161
Fax: 403-492-1811
E-mail: eegrad@ee.ualberta.ca

THE UNIVERSITY OF CALGARY
Calgary, AB T2N 1N4, Canada

OVERVIEW
The University of Calgary is a public coed university.

EXPENSES
Tuition $3354 per year full-time, $838 per course part-time for Canadian residents; $6708 per year full-time, $1676 per year part-time for nonresidents. Fees $146 per year.

HOUSING
Rooms and/or apartments available to single and married students. Graduate housing contact: Manager of Student Housing Office, 403-220-3210.

FACILITIES
Library: MacKimmie Library plus 5 additional on-campus libraries. *Special:* In arts and humanities: Calgary Institute for the Humanities, International Center. In science and engineering: Kananaskis Centre for Environmental Research, Institute for Space Research, Artic Institute of North America. In social sciences: Institute for Transportation Studies, Research Centre for Canadian Ethnic Studies, Centre for Gifted Education.

COMPUTER ENGINEERING

Faculty of Engineering, Department of Electrical and Computer Engineering

Programs   Awards M Eng, M Sc, PhD. Part-time programs available.

Faculty   22 full-time (0 women), 1 part-time (0 women).

Faculty Research   Control, electronics, power systems, signal and image processing, telecommunications, software engineering. *Total annual research expenditures:* $1.8 million.

Students   65 full-time (7 women), 29 part-time (2 women); includes 32 international.

Degrees Awarded   In 1996, 16 master's, 3 doctorates awarded.

Entrance Requirements   TOEFL (minimum score 550), minimum GPA of 3.0.

Degree Requirements   For master's, thesis (M Sc) required, foreign language not required; for doctorate, dissertation, candidacy exam required, foreign language not required.

Financial Aid   59 students received aid; fellowships, research assistantships, teaching assistantships available. *Financial aid application deadline:* 5/30.

Applying   160 applicants, 31% accepted. *Deadline:* 5/31 (priority date; rolling processing). *Fee:* $60.

Contact   *R. A. Stein*
Associate Head
403-220-6175
Fax: 403-282-6855
E-mail: grad_studies@enel.ucalgary.ca

COMPUTER SCIENCE

Faculty of Science, Department of Computer Science

Programs   Awards M Sc, PhD.

Faculty Research   Artificial intelligence, computer graphics, human computer interaction, numerical computation, programming languages.

Entrance Requirements   TOEFL (minimum score 600), GRE General Test (requested for overseas applicants).

Degree Requirements   For master's, thesis required, foreign language not required; for doctorate, dissertation, candidacy exam required, foreign language not required.

Applying   *Deadline:* 4/15 (rolling processing; 8/15 for spring admission). *Fee:* $60.

ELECTRICAL ENGINEERING

Faculty of Engineering, Department of Electrical and Computer Engineering

Programs   Awards M Eng, M Sc, PhD. Part-time programs available.

Faculty   22 full-time (0 women), 1 part-time (0 women).

Faculty Research   Control, electronics, power systems, signal and image processing, telecommunications, software engineering. *Total annual research expenditures:* $1.8 million.

Students   65 full-time (7 women), 29 part-time (2 women); includes 32 international.

Degrees Awarded   In 1996, 16 master's, 3 doctorates awarded.

Entrance Requirements   TOEFL (minimum score 550), minimum GPA of 3.0.

Degree Requirements   For master's, thesis (M Sc) required, foreign language not required; for doctorate, dissertation, candidacy exam required, foreign language not required.

Financial Aid   59 students received aid; fellowships, research assistantships, teaching assistantships available. *Financial aid application deadline:* 5/30.

Applying   160 applicants, 31% accepted. *Deadline:* 5/31 (priority date; rolling processing). *Fee:* $60.

Contact   *R. A. Stein*
Associate Head
403-220-6175
Fax: 403-282-6855
E-mail: grad_studies@enel.ucalgary.ca

BRITISH COLUMBIA

SIMON FRASER UNIVERSITY
Burnaby, BC V5A 1S6, Canada

OVERVIEW
Simon Fraser University is a public coed university.

ENROLLMENT

19,000 graduate, professional, and undergraduate students; 2,048 full-time matriculated graduate/professional students (953 women), 402 part-time matriculated graduate/professional students (240 women).

GRADUATE FACULTY

626 full-time (145 women), 5 part-time (2 women).

EXPENSES

Tuition $2304 per year full-time, $443 per trimester part-time. Fees $309 per year full-time, $75 per trimester part-time.

HOUSING

Rooms and/or apartments available to single students (940 units) at an average cost of $3375 per year; available to married students (209 units) at an average cost of $5952 per year. Housing application deadline: 1/2. Graduate housing contact: Housing Office, 604-291-4201.

STUDENT SERVICES

Disabled student services, low-cost health insurance, career counseling, free psychological counseling, exercise/wellness program, day-care facilities, campus safety program, campus employment opportunities, international student services, writing training, grant writing training, teacher training.

FACILITIES

Library: W. A. C. Bennett Library plus 1 additional on-campus library; total holdings of 1,231,669 volumes, 943,523 microforms, 9,663 current periodical subscriptions. A total of 285 personal computers in all libraries. Access provided to on-line information retrieval services. *Computer:* Campuswide network is available with full Internet access. Total number of PCs/terminals supplied for student use: 140. Computer service fees are included with tuition and fees. *Special:* In arts and humanities: Historical Records Institute. In science and engineering: Gerontology Research Center, laboratory for computer and communications research, Energy Research Institute, Chemical Ecology Research Group, surface science laboratory, Center for Systems Science. In social sciences: Institute for Studies in Criminal Justice Policy, Psychology and Law Institute, archaeological museum collection.

COMPUTER SCIENCE

Faculty of Applied Science, School of Computing Science
Programs Awards M Sc, PhD.
Faculty 34 full-time (4 women), 1 part-time (0 women).
Faculty Research Artificial intelligence, computer graphics, computer hardware, computer systems, database systems.
Students 83 full-time (23 women), 8 part-time (1 woman). Average age 30.
Degrees Awarded In 1996, 4 master's, 3 doctorates awarded.
Entrance Requirements For master's, GRE General Test, GRE Subject Test (minimum score 570), TOEFL, TWE or International English Language Test (minimum score 7.5), minimum GPA of 3.0; for doctorate, GRE General Test, GRE Subject Test (minimum score 570), TOEFL, TWE or International English Language Test (minimum score 7.5), minimum GPA of 3.5.
Degree Requirements For master's, thesis; for doctorate, dissertation, qualifying exams.
Financial Aid In 1996–97, 28 fellowships were awarded; research assistantships, teaching assistantships also available.

Applying *Deadline:* 3/31 (7/31 for spring admission). *Fee:* $45.
Contact *Graduate Secretary*
604-291-4842
E-mail: gradpgm@cs.sfu.ca

UNIVERSITY OF BRITISH COLUMBIA
Vancouver, BC V6T 1Z2, Canada

OVERVIEW

University of British Columbia is a public coed university.

ENROLLMENT

31,500 graduate, professional, and undergraduate students; 6,178 matriculated graduate/professional students (3,050 women).

GRADUATE FACULTY

2,280.

EXPENSES

Tuition $2315 per year full-time, $1331 per year part-time for Canadian residents; $7200 per year full-time, $4140 per year part-time for nonresidents. Fees $256 per year full-time, $149 per year part-time.

HOUSING

Rooms and/or apartments available to single students (4,354 units) at an average cost of $4069 per year ($6100 including board); available to married students (762 units) at an average cost of $8196 per year. Housing application deadline: 3/1. Graduate housing contact: Housing Office, 604-822-2811/4411.

STUDENT SERVICES

Disabled student services, low-cost health insurance, career counseling, free psychological counseling, day-care facilities, campus safety program, campus employment opportunities, international student services, teacher training.

FACILITIES

Library: Main library plus 11 additional on-campus libraries; total holdings of 3.5 million volumes, 4.3 million microforms, 21,400 current periodical subscriptions. Access provided to on-line information retrieval services. *Computer:* Campuswide network is available with full Internet access. *Special:* In arts and humanities: Norman MacKenzie Centre for Fine Arts, fine arts gallery, Frederic Wood Theatre, Dorothy Somerset Studio. In science and engineering: Tri-University Meson Facility, Bamfield Marine Station, B. C. Cancer Research Centre, Pulp and Paper Research Institute of Canada, Centre for Integrated Computer Systems Research, Fisheries Centre, Westwater Research Centre, Media and Graphics Interdisciplinary Centre, biotechnology laboratory, Institute of Health Promotion Research, Centre for Advanced Technology in Microelectronics, Ocean Studies Council, botanical gardens, M. Y. Williams Geological Museum, zoological museum, herbarium. In social sciences: Museum of Anthropology, Institute of Asian Research, First Nations House of Learning, Centre for Human Settlements, Centre for Research in Women's Studies and Gender Relations, Sustainable Development Research Institute, Centre for Applied Ethics, Institute of International Relations, Centre for Transportation Studies.

COMPUTER SCIENCE

Faculty of Science, Department of Computer Science
Programs   Awards M Sc, PhD. Part-time programs available.
Faculty   28 full-time (1 woman).
Faculty Research   Artificial intelligence, databases, robotics, graphics, systems. *Total annual research expenditures:* $1 million.
Students   99 full-time (24 women), 3 part-time (1 woman); includes 21 international. Average age 25.
Degrees Awarded   In 1996, 15 master's awarded; 14 doctorates awarded (100% entered university research/teaching).
Entrance Requirements   GRE, TOEFL (minimum score 600).
Degree Requirements   For master's, computer language required, foreign language and thesis not required; for doctorate, computer language, dissertation required, foreign language not required.
Financial Aid   Fellowships, research assistantships, teaching assistantships, and career-related internships or fieldwork available.
Applying   *Deadline:* 3/31 (rolling processing). *Fee:* $60.
Contact   Joyce Poon
　　　　　Graduate Program Administrator
　　　　　604-822-3061
　　　　　Fax: 604-822-5485
　　　　　E-mail: grad_info@cs.ubc.ca

ELECTRICAL ENGINEERING

Faculty of Applied Science, Department of Electrical Engineering
Programs   Awards MA Sc, M Eng, PhD.
Faculty   34 full-time (1 woman), 9 part-time (0 women).
Faculty Research   Applied electromagnetics, biomedical engineering, communications and signal processing, computer and software engineering, power engineering, robotics, solid-state, systems and control.
Students   155 full-time (28 women), 21 part-time (4 women); includes 50 international. Average age 26.
Degrees Awarded   In 1996, 31 master's, 8 doctorates awarded.
Entrance Requirements   TOEFL (minimum score 600).
Degree Requirements   For master's, thesis required (for some programs), foreign language not required; for doctorate, dissertation required, foreign language not required.
Financial Aid   In 1996–97, 30 fellowships (10 to first-year students) averaging $1,250 per month, 84 research assistantships (33 to first-year students) averaging $1,100 per month, 119 teaching assistantships (22 to first-year students) averaging $310 per month were awarded; career-related internships or fieldwork also available.
Applying   275 applicants, 41% accepted. *Deadline:* 3/15 (priority date; rolling processing). *Fee:* $60.
Contact   D. Metcalf
　　　　　Graduate Admissions
　　　　　604-822-3368

UNIVERSITY OF VICTORIA
Victoria, BC V8W 2Y2, Canada

OVERVIEW
University of Victoria is a public coed university.

ENROLLMENT
17,000 graduate, professional, and undergraduate students; 2,062 full-time, 312 part-time matriculated graduate/professional students.

GRADUATE FACULTY
567 full-time (170 women), 161 part-time (44 women).

HOUSING
Rooms and/or apartments available to single students (120 units) at an average cost of $2960 per year ($4968 including board); available to married students (181 units) at an average cost of $8652 per year. Housing application deadline: 2/1. Graduate housing contact: Housing Services Office, 250-721-8395.

STUDENT SERVICES
Low-cost health insurance, career counseling, free psychological counseling, day-care facilities, campus safety program, campus employment opportunities, international student services.

FACILITIES
Library: McPherson Library plus 4 additional on-campus libraries; total holdings of 1,677,614 volumes, 1,804,934 microforms, 12,000 current periodical subscriptions. A total of 85 personal computers in all libraries. Access provided to on-line information retrieval services. *Computer:* Campuswide network is available with full Internet access. Total number of PCs/terminals supplied for student use: 400. Computer service fees are applied as a separate charge. *Special:* In arts and humanities: Language Centre, Phoenix Theatre, Maltwood Museum. In science and engineering: Strickland Biological Research Vessel, NSERC Toxicology Research Unit, nuclear magnetic resonance spectrometer, physics observatory. In social sciences: Automated Cartography (GIS) Laboratories, Centre for Asia-Pacific Initiatives, Centre for Earth and Ocean Research, human interaction laboratory.

COMPUTER SCIENCE

Faculty of Engineering, Department of Computer Science
Programs   Awards MA, M Sc, PhD. Part-time programs available.
Faculty   21 full-time (3 women), 8 part-time (0 women).
Faculty Research   Functional and logic programming, numerical analysis, parallel and distributed computing, software systems, theoretical computer science, VLSI design and testing. *Total annual research expenditures:* $1.091 million.
Students   70 full-time (15 women), 6 part-time (0 women); includes 27 international. Average age 30.
Degrees Awarded   In 1996, 7 master's, 4 doctorates awarded.
Entrance Requirements   For master's, TOEFL (minimum score 550), BS in computer science (recommended); for doctorate, TOEFL (minimum score 575), MS in computer science (recommended).
Degree Requirements   Thesis/dissertation.
Financial Aid   In 1996–97, 50 students received aid, including 4 fellowships (2 to first-year students) averaging $1,200 per month, 35 research assistantships (20 to first-year students) averaging $730 per month and totaling $283,000, 35 teaching assistantships (16 to first-year students) averaging $440 per month and totaling $185,000, 4 awards (2 to first-year students) averaging $200 per month and totaling $8,000; institutionally sponsored loans and career-related internships or fieldwork also available. *Financial aid application deadline:* 2/15.
Applying   178 applicants, 15% accepted. *Deadline:* 5/1 (priority date; rolling processing; 10/1 for spring admission). *Fee:* $45.
Contact   Dr. B. Ehle
　　　　　Graduate Adviser
　　　　　250-721-8941
　　　　　Fax: 250-721-7292
　　　　　E-mail: behle@csr.uvic.ca

ELECTRICAL ENGINEERING

Faculty of Engineering, Department of Electrical Engineering
Programs Awards MA Sc, M Eng, PhD. Part-time programs available.
Faculty 20 full-time (1 woman), 8 part-time (0 women), 24.5 FTE.
Faculty Research Communications and computers; electromagnetics, microwaves, and optics; electronics; power; systems, signal processing, and control.
Students 74 full-time (8 women), 1 part-time (0 women); includes 35 international. Average age 30.
Degrees Awarded In 1996, 6 master's, 20 doctorates awarded.
Entrance Requirements For master's, TOEFL (minimum score 575), bachelor's degree in engineering; for doctorate, TOEFL (minimum score 575), master's degree.
Degree Requirements Thesis/dissertation required, foreign language not required.
Financial Aid Fellowships, research assistantships, teaching assistantships, awards, institutionally sponsored loans, and career-related internships or fieldwork available. *Financial aid application deadline:* 2/15.
Applying 214 applicants, 9% accepted. *Deadline:* 3/15 (priority date; rolling processing; 9/15 for spring admission). *Fee:* $45.
Contact *Dr. Kin Li*
Graduate Adviser
250-721-8683
Fax: 250-721-6052
E-mail: kinli@ece.uvic.ca

MANITOBA

UNIVERSITY OF MANITOBA
Winnipeg, MB R3T 2N2, Canada

OVERVIEW
University of Manitoba is a public coed university.

ENROLLMENT
21,833 graduate, professional, and undergraduate students; 2,063 full-time, 828 part-time matriculated graduate/professional students.

HOUSING
Rooms and/or apartments available to single students (1,140 units) at an average cost of $4141 (including board); available to married students. Graduate housing contact: Garth Wannan, 204-474-9981.

STUDENT SERVICES
Low-cost health insurance, career counseling, free psychological counseling, day-care facilities, campus safety program, campus employment opportunities, international student services.

FACILITIES
Library: Elizabeth Dafoe Library plus 12 additional on-campus libraries; total holdings of 1.55 million volumes, 1.057 million microforms, 12,800 current periodical subscriptions. Access provided to on-line information retrieval services. *Special:* In science and engineering: Fetherstonhaugh High Voltage Laboratory, Taiga Biological Station, Glenlea Experimental Station, Accelerator

Centre, Delta Waterfowl Research Station, Delta Marsh Field Station, university field station.

COMPUTER ENGINEERING

Faculty of Engineering, Department of Electrical and Computer Engineering
Programs Awards M Eng, M Sc, PhD.
Degree Requirements Thesis/dissertation.

COMPUTER SCIENCE

Faculty of Science, Department of Computer Science
Programs Awards M Sc, PhD.
Degree Requirements For master's, thesis or alternative; for doctorate, dissertation.

ELECTRICAL ENGINEERING

Faculty of Engineering, Department of Electrical and Computer Engineering
Programs Awards M Eng, M Sc, PhD.
Degree Requirements Thesis/dissertation.

NEW BRUNSWICK

UNIVERSITY OF NEW BRUNSWICK
Fredericton, NB E3B 5A3, Canada

OVERVIEW
University of New Brunswick is a public coed university.

HOUSING
Rooms and/or apartments available to single and married students.

FACILITIES
Library: Harriet Irving Library plus 3 additional on-campus libraries. *Special:* In arts and humanities: Center for Conflict Studies. In science and engineering: Institute of Biomedical Engineering, Fire Science Center. In social sciences: Center for Family Violence.

COMPUTER SCIENCE

Faculty of Engineering, School of Computer Science
Programs Awards M Sc CS, PhD. Part-time programs available.
Entrance Requirements For master's, TOEFL, TWE, minimum GPA of 3.0; for doctorate, TOEFL, TWE.
Degree Requirements For master's, thesis required, foreign language not required; for doctorate, dissertation, qualifying exam required, foreign language not required.
Applying *Deadline:* 3/1 (priority date; rolling processing). *Fee:* $25.

NEWFOUNDLAND

MEMORIAL UNIVERSITY OF NEWFOUNDLAND
St. John's, NF A1C 5S7, Canada

OVERVIEW
Memorial University of Newfoundland is a public coed university.

ENROLLMENT
16,122 graduate, professional, and undergraduate students; 1,183 full-time matriculated graduate/professional students (564 women), 580 part-time matriculated graduate/professional students (323 women).

EXPENSES
Tuition $1806 per year (minimum). Fees $60 per year for Canadian residents; $415 per year for nonresidents.

HOUSING
Rooms and/or apartments available to single students (40 units) at an average cost of $3000 per year ($6500 including board); available to married students (15 units) at an average cost of $6700 per year. Graduate housing contact: Dr. K. B. Johnston, 709-737-7590.

STUDENT SERVICES
Disabled student services, low-cost health insurance, career counseling, free psychological counseling, daycare facilities, campus safety program, campus employment opportunities, international student services, writing training, teacher training.

FACILITIES
Library: Queen Elizabeth II Library plus 3 additional on-campus libraries; total holdings of 1,256,107 volumes, 1,803,430 microforms, 10,450 current periodical subscriptions. Access provided to on-line information retrieval services. *Computer:* Campuswide network is available with full Internet access. Total number of PCs/terminals supplied for student use: 900. Computer services are offered at no charge. *Special:* In arts and humanities: Institute Frecker, maritime history archive, folklore and language archive. In science and engineering: Ocean Sciences Centre, Ocean Engineering Research Centre, botanical garden, cartography laboratory, Marine Institute. In social sciences: Institute for Social And Economic Research, Labrador Institute of Northern Studies.

COMPUTER SCIENCE

School of Graduate Studies, Department of Computer Science
Programs   Offers program in very large scale integrated design (M Sc).
Faculty   16.
Students   15 full-time (6 women), 4 part-time (2 women); includes 11 international.
Degrees Awarded   In 1996, 2 degrees awarded.
Degree Requirements   Thesis.
Financial Aid   Fellowships, research assistantships, teaching assistantships available.
Applying   77 applicants, 8% accepted. *Fee:* $30.

Contact   *Dr. John Shieh*
Graduate Officer
709-737-8627
E-mail: shunen@cs.mun.ca

ELECTRICAL ENGINEERING

School of Graduate Studies, Faculty of Engineering and Applied Science
Programs   Offerings include electrical engineering (M Eng, PhD).
Faculty   51 full-time (1 woman), 6 part-time (0 women).
Degree Requirements   For master's, thesis optional; for doctorate, dissertation, comprehensive exam.
Applying   *Fee:* $30.
Contact   *Dr. J. J. Sharp*
Associate Dean
709-737-8901
Fax: 709-737-4042
E-mail: jsharp@engr.mun.ca

NOVA SCOTIA

ACADIA UNIVERSITY
Wolfville, NS B0P 1X0, Canada

OVERVIEW
Acadia University is a public coed comprehensive institution.

ENROLLMENT
4,205 graduate, professional, and undergraduate students; 173 full-time matriculated graduate/professional students (74 women), 130 part-time matriculated graduate/professional students (78 women).

EXPENSES
Tuition $3955 per year for Canadian residents; $5935 per year for nonresidents. Fees $144 per year for Canadian residents; $1844 per year for nonresidents.

HOUSING
Rooms and/or apartments available to single students at an average cost of $3008 per year ($4898 including board); available to married students (6 units). Housing application deadline: 6/30. Graduate housing contact: Student Accomodations Supervisor, 902-542-2201 Ext. 1418.

STUDENT SERVICES
Disabled student services, low-cost health insurance, career counseling, free psychological counseling, exercise/wellness program, campus safety program, campus employment opportunities, international student services.

FACILITIES
Library: Vaughan Memorial Library; total holdings of 703,309 volumes, 266,000 microforms, 3,450 current periodical subscriptions. A total of 66 personal computers in all libraries. Access provided to on-line information retrieval services. *Computer:* Campuswide network is available with full Internet access. Total number of PCs/terminals supplied for student use: 25. Computer service fees are included with tuition and fees. *Special:* In arts and humanities: Planters Collection, Atlantic Baptist Archives. In science and engineering: Estuarine

Center, vascular plant herbarium, mycology collection, Acadia Center for Wildlife and Conservation Biology. In social sciences: Infant and Family Research Center.

COMPUTER SCIENCE

Faculty of Pure and Applied Science, School of Computer Science
Programs Awards M Sc.
Faculty 11 full-time (1 woman).
Faculty Research Visual and object-oriented programming, concurrency, artificial intelligence, hypertext and multimedia, algorithm analysis.
Students 8 full-time (2 women), includes 6 international. Average age 22.
Degrees Awarded In 1996, 2 degrees awarded.
Entrance Requirements Honors degree in computer science.
Degree Requirements Thesis required, foreign language not required.
Financial Aid Fellowships and career-related internships or fieldwork available. *Financial aid application deadline: 2/1.*
Applying *Deadline: 2/1. Fee: $25.*
Contact *Rosie Hare*
Secretary
902-585-1585
Fax: 902-585-1067
E-mail: cs@acadiau.ca

DALHOUSIE UNIVERSITY
Halifax, NS B3H 3J5, Canada

OVERVIEW
Dalhousie University is a public coed university.

ENROLLMENT
10,910 graduate, professional, and undergraduate students; 2,301 matriculated graduate/professional students.

GRADUATE FACULTY
1,401.

EXPENSES
Tuition $3855 per year (minimum) full-time, $1285 per year (minimum) part-time for Canadian residents; $6555 per year (minimum) full-time, $3985 per year (minimum) part-time for nonresidents. Fees $229 per year full-time, $107 per year part-time.

HOUSING
Rooms and/or apartments available to single students at an average cost of $4750 (including board); available to married students. Housing application deadline: 7/15. Graduate housing contact: Terry Gallivan, 902-494-3365.

STUDENT SERVICES
Career counseling, free psychological counseling, daycare facilities, campus safety program, campus employment opportunities, international student services.

FACILITIES
Library: Killam Library plus 3 additional on-campus libraries; total holdings of 1,385,446 volumes, 285,338 microforms, 9,421 current periodical subscriptions. Access provided to on-line information retrieval services. *Special:* In arts and humanities: J. J. Stewart Canadiana Collection, J.

M. Stewart Kipling Collection, Bacon Collection, university archives. In science and engineering: Atlantic Institute of Biotechnology, Centre for Marine Biology, Trace Analysis Research Centre, Atlantic Region Magnetic Resonance Centre, Neuroscience Institute. In social sciences: Atlantic Institute of Criminology, Centre of Foreign Policy Studies, Centre for International Business Studies, Lester Pearson Institute for International Development, Oceans Institute of Canada.

COMPUTER SCIENCE

College of Arts and Science, Faculty of Science, Department of Mathematics, Statistics, and Computing Science, Program in Computing Science
Programs Awards M Sc.
Entrance Requirements TOEFL (minimum score 580).
Degree Requirements Thesis required, foreign language not required.
Applying *Deadline: 6/1 (rolling processing). Fee: $55.*
Contact *Dr. W. R. S. Sutherland*
Graduate Coordinator
902-494-8851

TECHNICAL UNIVERSITY OF NOVA SCOTIA
Halifax, NS B3J 2X4, Canada

OVERVIEW
Technical University of Nova Scotia is a public coed upper-level institution.

ENROLLMENT
1,401 graduate, professional, and undergraduate students; 424 full-time matriculated graduate/professional students (111 women), 33 part-time matriculated graduate/professional students (6 women).

GRADUATE FACULTY
91.

HOUSING
Rooms and/or apartments available to single students (146 units) at an average cost of $4890 (including board); available to married students (8 units) at an average cost of $6000 per year. Graduate housing contact: Suzanne Kolmer, 902-420-7505.

STUDENT SERVICES
Low-cost health insurance, career counseling, campus safety program, international student services.

FACILITIES
Library: Main library; total holdings of 100,000 volumes, 82,000 microforms, 900 current periodical subscriptions. Access provided to on-line information retrieval services. *Computer:* Campuswide network is available with full Internet access. *Special:* In science and engineering: Centre for Energy Studies, fisheries research and technology laboratory, Centre for Water Resource Studies, Applied Microelectronics Institute.

COMPUTER SCIENCE

School of Computer Science
Programs Awards MC Sc, PhD.

Students   38 full-time (8 women), 10 part-time (3 women); includes 3 international. Average age 30.
Degrees Awarded   In 1996, 9 master's, 1 doctorate awarded.
Entrance Requirements   TOEFL (minimum score 575).
Applying   66 applicants, 44% accepted. *Deadline:* rolling.
Contact   *Dr. J. Barzilai*
Director
902-420-7718

ELECTRICAL ENGINEERING

Faculty of Engineering, Department of Electrical Engineering
Programs   Awards MA Sc, M Eng, PhD.
Faculty   9 full-time (0 women), 4 part-time (0 women).
Students   45 full-time (7 women), 6 part-time (0 women); includes 18 international. Average age 29.
Degrees Awarded   In 1996, 8 master's, 3 doctorates awarded.
Entrance Requirements   TOEFL (minimum score 550).
Degree Requirements   Thesis/dissertation required, foreign language not required.
Applying   92 applicants, 48% accepted. *Deadline:* rolling.
Contact   *Dr. W. Robertson*
Head
902-420-7721

ONTARIO

CARLETON UNIVERSITY
Ottawa, ON K1S 5B6, Canada

OVERVIEW
Carleton University is a public coed university.

ENROLLMENT
21,768 graduate, professional, and undergraduate students; 1,662 full-time matriculated graduate/professional students (768 women), 787 part-time matriculated graduate/professional students (392 women).

GRADUATE FACULTY
640 full-time (167 women).

EXPENSES
Tuition $4908 per year full-time, $785 per credit part-time for Canadian residents; $9324 per year full-time, $3043 per credit part-time for nonresidents. Fees $383 per year full-time.

HOUSING
Rooms and/or apartments available to single students (93 units) at an average cost of $5625 (including board); on-campus housing not available to married students. Housing application deadline: 5/31. Graduate housing contact: K. Haarbosch, 613-520-5612.

STUDENT SERVICES
Low-cost health insurance, career counseling, free psychological counseling, day-care facilities, campus safety program, campus employment opportunities, international student services.

FACILITIES
Library: Maxwell MacOdrum Library; total holdings of 1,620,912 volumes, 1,128,216 microforms, 10,520 current periodical subscriptions. A total of 307 personal comput-

ers in all libraries. Access provided to on-line information retrieval services. *Computer:* Campuswide network is available with partial Internet access (e-mail only). Total number of PCs/terminals supplied for student use: 1,000. Computer services are offered at no charge. *Special:* In arts and humanities: Art laboratory. In science and engineering: Gas turbine research laboratory, scanning analytical microscope facility. In social sciences: Life Sciences Research Centre.

COMPUTER SCIENCE

Faculty of Science, Ottawa-Carleton Institute for Computer Science
Programs   Awards MCS, PhD. Offered jointly with the University of Ottawa. Part-time programs available.
Faculty   17 full-time.
Faculty Research   Programming systems, theory of computing, computer applications, computer systems.
Students   58 full-time (15 women), 17 part-time (4 women).
Degrees Awarded   In 1996, 10 master's, 1 doctorate awarded.
Entrance Requirements   For master's, TOEFL (minimum score 550), honors degree; for doctorate, TOEFL (minimum score 550).
Degree Requirements   For master's, project required, thesis optional; for doctorate, dissertation, comprehensive exam.
Financial Aid   *Application deadline:* 3/1.
Applying   *Deadline:* 2/1 (priority date; rolling processing). *Fee:* $35.
Contact   *B. J. Oommen*
Director
613-520-2600 Ext. 4358
Fax: 613-520-4334
E-mail: scs@carleton.ca

ELECTRICAL ENGINEERING

Faculty of Engineering, Ottawa-Carleton Institute for Electrical Engineering, Department of Electronics
Programs   Awards MA Sc, M Eng, M Sc, PhD. MA Sc and M Sc offered jointly with the University of Ottawa.
Faculty   12 full-time (0 women).
Students   51 full-time (7 women), 26 part-time (2 women).
Entrance Requirements   For master's, TOEFL (minimum score 550), honors degree; for doctorate, TOEFL (minimum score 550), MA Sc or M Eng.
Degree Requirements   For master's, thesis optional; for doctorate, dissertation, comprehensive exam.
Financial Aid   *Application deadline:* 3/1.
Applying   *Deadline:* 3/1 (priority date; rolling processing). *Fee:* $35.
Contact   *R. G. Harrison*
Supervisor of Graduate Studies
613-520-5776
Fax: 613-520-5708
E-mail: rgh@doe.carleton.ca

ELECTRICAL ENGINEERING

Faculty of Engineering, Ottawa-Carleton Institute for Electrical Engineering, Department of Systems and Computer Engineering, Program in Electrical Engineering
Programs   Awards MA Sc, M Eng, PhD. MA Sc offered jointly with the University of Ottawa.
Students   51 full-time (7 women), 26 part-time (2 women).
Entrance Requirements   For master's, TOEFL (minimum score 550), honors degree; for doctorate, TOEFL (minimum score 550), MA Sc or M Eng.

Degree Requirements For master's, thesis optional; for doctorate, dissertation, comprehensive exam.
Financial Aid *Application deadline: 3/1.*
Applying *Deadline: 3/1 (rolling processing). Fee: $35.*
Contact *John W. Chinneck*
Supervisor of Graduate Studies
613-520-5733
Fax: 613-520-5727

INFORMATION SCIENCE

Faculty of Science, Information and Systems Science Committee
Programs Awards M Sc. Offered jointly with the Department of Systems and Computer Engineering, the Ottawa-Carleton Institute for Computer Science, and the Ottawa-Carleton Institute of Mathematics and Statistics.
Faculty 17 full-time.
Faculty Research Software engineering, real-time and microprocessor programming, computer communications.
Students 35 full-time (16 women), 27 part-time (11 women).
Degrees Awarded In 1996, 5 degrees awarded.
Entrance Requirements TOEFL (minimum score 550), honors degree.
Degree Requirements Computer language required, thesis optional.
Financial Aid *Application deadline: 3/1.*
Applying *Deadline: 3/1 (priority date; rolling processing). Fee: $35.*
Contact *M. J. Moore*
Coordinator
613-520-2600 Ext. 2160
Fax: 613-520-5733

INFORMATION SCIENCE

Faculty of Engineering, Ottawa-Carleton Institute for Electrical Engineering, Department of Systems and Computer Engineering
Programs Offerings include information and systems science (M Sc).
Department Faculty 21 full-time (1 woman).
Applying *Deadline: 3/1 (rolling processing). Fee: $35.*
Contact *John W. Chinneck*
Supervisor of Graduate Studies
613-520-5733
Fax: 613-520-5727
E-mail: chinneck@sce.carleton.ca

SYSTEMS SCIENCE

Faculty of Science, Information and Systems Science Committee
Programs Awards M Sc. Offered jointly with the Department of Systems and Computer Engineering, the Ottawa-Carleton Institute for Computer Science, and the Ottawa-Carleton Institute of Mathematics and Statistics.
Faculty 17 full-time.
Faculty Research Software engineering, real-time and microprocessor programming, computer communications.
Students 35 full-time (16 women), 27 part-time (11 women).
Degrees Awarded In 1996, 5 degrees awarded.
Entrance Requirements TOEFL (minimum score 550), honors degree.
Degree Requirements Computer language required, thesis optional.
Financial Aid *Application deadline: 3/1.*
Applying *Deadline: 3/1 (priority date; rolling processing). Fee: $35.*

Contact *M. J. Moore*
Coordinator
613-520-2600 Ext. 2160
Fax: 613-520-5733

LAKEHEAD UNIVERSITY
Thunder Bay, ON P7B 5E1, Canada

OVERVIEW
Lakehead University is a public coed comprehensive institution.

EXPENSES
Tuition $4420 per year full-time, $1768 per course part-time for Canadian residents; $7500 per year full-time, $3000 per course part-time for nonresidents. Fees $338 per year.

HOUSING
Rooms and/or apartments available to single students; on-campus housing not available to married students. Graduate housing contact: Mr. David Hare, 807-343-8097.

FACILITIES
Library: Chancellor Norman M. Paterson Library plus 1 additional on-campus library. *Special:* In arts and humanities: Centre for Archaeological Resource Prediction, Native Philosophy Project, International Indigenous Knowledge Centre. In science and engineering: Centre for the Application of Resources Information Systems, Pulp and Paper Centre of Excellence. In social sciences: Northern Human Health Resource Research Unit, Northern Educational Centre for Aging and Health, Nordic Sports Research Centre.

COMPUTER SCIENCE

Faculty of Arts and Science, School of Mathematical Sciences
Programs Offerings include computer science (MA, M Sc).
Degree Requirements Thesis or alternative required, foreign language not required.
Applying *Deadline: 2/1 (priority date; rolling processing). Fee: $0.*

McMASTER UNIVERSITY
Hamilton, ON L8S 4M2, Canada

OVERVIEW
McMaster University is a public coed university.

ENROLLMENT
17,890 graduate, professional, and undergraduate students; 3,057 matriculated graduate/professional students.

GRADUATE FACULTY
826 full-time, 33 part-time.

EXPENSES
Tuition $4422 per year full-time, $1590 per year part-time for Canadian residents; $12,000 per year full-time, $6165 per year part-time for nonresidents. Fees $231 per year full-time, $162 per year part-time.

HOUSING

Rooms and/or apartments available to single students at an average cost of $5900 (including board); on-campus housing not available to married students.

STUDENT SERVICES

Career counseling, free psychological counseling, day-care facilities, campus safety program, campus employment opportunities, international student services.

FACILITIES

Library: Mills Memorial Library plus 4 additional on-campus libraries; total holdings of 1.5 million volumes, 990,000 microforms, 14,400 current periodical subscriptions. Access provided to on-line information retrieval services. *Computer:* Campuswide network is available with full Internet access. *Special:* In science and engineering: Institute for Energy Studies, Institute for Materials Research, Van de Graaff accelerator, communications research laboratory, nuclear reactor.

COMPUTER SCIENCE

Faculty of Science, Department of Computer Science and Systems
Programs Awards M Sc. Part-time programs available.
Faculty 10 full-time (0 women).
Faculty Research Software engineering; theory of non-sequential systems; parallel and distributed computing; artificial intelligence; complexity, design, and analysis of algorithms; combinatorial computing, especially applications to molecular biology. *Total annual research expenditures:* $420,000.
Students 12 full-time (2 women), 2 part-time (0 women).
Degrees Awarded In 1996, 1 degree awarded.
Degree Requirements Thesis required, foreign language not required.
Financial Aid In 1996–97, 12 students received aid, including 6 teaching assistantships (4 to first-year students); research assistantships also available.
Applying 75 applicants, 100% accepted. *Deadline:* 1/15 (rolling processing). *Fee:* $50.
Contact Dr. W. F. Smyth
   Chair
   905-525-9140 Ext. 23437
   Fax: 905-546-9995
   E-mail: dcss@maccs.dcss.mcmaster.ca

ELECTRICAL ENGINEERING

Faculty of Engineering, Department of Electrical and Computer Engineering
Programs Offers program in electrical engineering (M Eng, PhD).
Faculty 20 full-time, 4 part-time.
Students 76 full-time (11 women), 51 part-time (4 women); includes 27 international.
Degrees Awarded In 1996, 25 master's, 6 doctorates awarded.
Degree Requirements For master's, thesis required, foreign language not required; for doctorate, dissertation, comprehensive exam required, foreign language not required.
Financial Aid Fellowships, research assistantships, teaching assistantships available.
Applying *Deadline:* 3/1 (priority date; rolling processing). *Fee:* $50.
Contact Dr. D. R. Conn
   Chair
   905-525-9140 Ext. 24826

QUEEN'S UNIVERSITY AT KINGSTON
Kingston, ON K7L 3N6, Canada

OVERVIEW

Queen's University at Kingston is a public coed university.

ENROLLMENT

15,940 graduate, professional, and undergraduate students; 3,185 matriculated graduate/professional students.

GRADUATE FACULTY

1,695.

TUITION

$5339 per year (minimum) full-time, $827 per year (minimum) part-time for Canadian residents; $10,472 per year (minimum) full-time, $1683 per year (minimum) part-time for nonresidents.

HOUSING

Rooms and/or apartments available to single students at an average cost of $5600 (including board); available to married students. Graduate housing contact: Apartment and Housing Office, 613-545-2501.

STUDENT SERVICES

Career counseling, free psychological counseling, day-care facilities, campus safety program, international student services.

FACILITIES

Library: Stauffer Library plus 18 additional on-campus libraries. Access provided to on-line information retrieval services. *Computer:* Campuswide network is available with full Internet access. *Special:* In arts and humanities: Agnes Etherington Gallery, Disraeli Project, John Deutsch Institute. In science and engineering: Canadian Microelectronics Corporation, Ontario Centre for Materials Research. In social sciences: Centre for Resource Studies, Studies in National and International Development, Institute of Intergovernmental Relations, Social Progress Evaluation Unit.

COMPUTER SCIENCE

Faculty of Arts and Sciences, Department of Computing and Information Science
Programs Offers programs in computer science (M Sc, PhD), information systems (M Sc, PhD), software engineering (M Sc, PhD). Part-time programs available.
Students 59 full-time (11 women), 21 part-time (2 women); includes 6 international.
Degrees Awarded In 1996, 11 master's, 2 doctorates awarded.
Entrance Requirements TOEFL (minimum score 600).
Degree Requirements For master's, thesis optional, foreign language not required; for doctorate, dissertation, comprehensive exam.
Financial Aid Fellowships, research assistantships, teaching assistantships, institutionally sponsored loans available. *Financial aid application deadline:* 3/1.
Applying *Deadline:* 2/28 (priority date). *Fee:* $60.
Contact Dr. D. Rappaport
   Graduate Coordinator
   613-545-6055

ELECTRICAL ENGINEERING

Faculty of Applied Science, Department of Electrical Engineering
Programs Awards M Sc, M Sc Eng, PhD. Part-time programs available.
Faculty Research Communications and signal processing systems.
Students 88 full-time (12 women), 23 part-time (2 women); includes 23 international.
Degrees Awarded In 1996, 20 master's, 7 doctorates awarded.
Entrance Requirements TOEFL (minimum score 550).
Degree Requirements For master's, thesis optional, foreign language not required; for doctorate, dissertation, comprehensive exam required, foreign language not required.
Financial Aid Fellowships, research assistantships, teaching assistantships, institutionally sponsored loans available. *Financial aid application deadline:* 3/1.
Applying *Deadline:* 2/28 (priority date). *Fee:* $60.
Contact *Dr. S. E. Tavares*
Graduate Coordinator
613-545-2945

INFORMATION SCIENCE

Faculty of Arts and Sciences, Department of Computing and Information Science
Programs Offers programs in computer science (M Sc, PhD), information systems (M Sc, PhD), software engineering (M Sc, PhD). Part-time programs available.
Students 59 full-time (11 women), 21 part-time (2 women); includes 6 international.
Degrees Awarded In 1996, 11 master's, 2 doctorates awarded.
Entrance Requirements TOEFL (minimum score 600).
Degree Requirements For master's, thesis optional, foreign language not required; for doctorate, dissertation, comprehensive exam.
Financial Aid Fellowships, research assistantships, teaching assistantships, institutionally sponsored loans available. *Financial aid application deadline:* 3/1.
Applying *Deadline:* 2/28 (priority date). *Fee:* $60.
Contact *Dr. D. Rappaport*
Graduate Coordinator
613-545-6055

SOFTWARE ENGINEERING

Faculty of Arts and Sciences, Department of Computing and Information Science, Program in Software Engineering
Programs Awards M Sc, PhD.
Entrance Requirements TOEFL (minimum score 600).
Degree Requirements For master's, thesis optional, foreign language not required; for doctorate, dissertation, comprehensive exam.
Applying *Deadline:* 2/28 (priority date). *Fee:* $60.
Contact *Dr. D. Rappaport*
Graduate Coordinator
613-545-6055

TRENT UNIVERSITY
Peterborough, ON K9J 7B8, Canada

OVERVIEW
Trent University is a public coed comprehensive institution.

HOUSING
Rooms and/or apartments available to single students; on-campus housing not available to married students.

FACILITIES
Library: Thomas J. Bata Library. *Special:* In arts and humanities: Frost Centre for Canadian Heritage and Development Studies. In science and engineering: Archaeology Centre, Environmental and Resource Centre, climatological field station.

COMPUTER SCIENCE

Program in Applications of Modelling in the Natural and Social Sciences, Department of Computer Studies
Programs Awards M Sc.
Degree Requirements Computer language, thesis required, foreign language not required.
Applying *Deadline:* 2/15 (priority date; rolling processing). *Fee:* $35.

UNIVERSITY OF GUELPH
Guelph, ON N1G 2W1, Canada

OVERVIEW
University of Guelph is a public coed university.

ENROLLMENT
13,834 graduate, professional, and undergraduate students; 1,502 full-time matriculated graduate/professional students (726 women), 201 part-time matriculated graduate/professional students (74 women).

GRADUATE FACULTY
650 full-time.

EXPENSES
Tuition $4725 per year full-time, $3165 per year part-time for Canadian residents; $6999 per year for nonresidents. Fees $400 per year.

HOUSING
Rooms and/or apartments available to single students (56 units) at an average cost of $4386 per year; available to married students (340 units). Housing application deadline: 6/1. Graduate housing contact: Merike Poirier, 519-824-4120 Ext. 2551.

STUDENT SERVICES
Low-cost health insurance, career counseling, free psychological counseling, day-care facilities, campus safety program, campus employment opportunities, international student services.

FACILITIES
Library: McLaughlin Library plus 1 additional on-campus library; total holdings of 2.06 million volumes, 1.38 million microforms, 12,400 current periodical subscriptions. A total of 200 personal computers in all libraries. Access provided to on-line information retrieval services. *Computer:* Campuswide network is available with full Internet access. Computer services are offered at no charge. *Special:* In arts and humanities: Scottish Collection (manuscripts, print material, and artifacts), George Bernard Shaw Collection, archives for major Ontario theatre performance troupes. In science and engineering:

Equine Research Centre, Stewardship Information Bureau, Toxicology Centre, Guelph Transgenic Plant Research Complex, magnetic resonance imaging facility, Animal Embryo Biotechnology Laboratory, aqualab for marine and fresh water species and systems, Institute of Ichthyology. In social sciences: Gerontology Research Centre, Guelph Centre for Occupational Research Inc., Institute for Environmental Policy.

COMPUTER SCIENCE

College of Physical and Engineering Science, Department of Computing and Information Science

Programs Offers programs in applied computer science (M Sc), computer science (M Sc). Part-time programs available.

Faculty 20 full-time (4 women).

Faculty Research Interactive systems, distributed systems, information management, knowledge-based systems, VLSI-(A). *Total annual research expenditures:* $476,000.

Students 35 full-time (9 women), 11 part-time (0 women); includes 2 international.

Degrees Awarded In 1996, 6 degrees awarded (80% found work related to degree, 20% continued full-time study).

Entrance Requirements Minimum B- average during last 2 years.

Degree Requirements Thesis.

Financial Aid In 1996–97, 10 students received aid, including research assistantships averaging $400 per month, teaching assistantships averaging $900 per month; fellowships also available.

Applying 82 applicants, 18% accepted. *Deadline:* 4/1 (priority date; rolling processing). *Fee:* $35.

Contact *S. MacKenzie*
Graduate Coordinator
519-824-4120 Ext. 8268
Fax: 519-837-0323
E-mail: gradinfo@snowhite.cis.uoguelph.ca

UNIVERSITY OF OTTAWA
Ottawa, ON K1N 6N5, Canada

OVERVIEW

University of Ottawa is a public coed university.

ENROLLMENT

23,755 graduate, professional, and undergraduate students; 2,133 full-time matriculated graduate/professional students (1,023 women), 1,347 part-time matriculated graduate/professional students (713 women).

GRADUATE FACULTY

884 full-time, 367 part-time.

EXPENSES

Tuition $4266 per year (minimum) full-time, $550 per course part-time for Canadian residents; $8700 per year (minimum) full-time, $798 per course part-time for nonresidents. Fees $227 per year full-time, $112 per year part-time.

HOUSING

Rooms and/or apartments available to single students (1,938 units) at an average cost of $2458 per year; available to married students (60 units) at an average cost of $9480 per year. Housing application deadline: 7/31. Graduate housing information: 613-562-5885.

STUDENT SERVICES

Disabled student services, multicultural affairs office, low-cost health insurance, career counseling, free psychological counseling, day-care facilities, campus safety program, campus employment opportunities, international student services, writing training, teacher training.

FACILITIES

Library: Morisset Library plus 7 additional on-campus libraries; total holdings of 1,383,649 volumes, 1,175,700 microforms, 11,200 current periodical subscriptions. A total of 65 personal computers in all libraries. Access provided to on-line information retrieval services. *Computer:* Campuswide network is available with full Internet access. Total number of PCs/terminals supplied for student use: 500. Computer service fees are included with tuition and fees. *Special:* In arts and humanities: Human Rights Research and Education Centre, Institute for Research on Environment and the Economy. In science and engineering: Electrochemical Science and Technology Centre, International Water Engineering Centre, Neuroscience Research Institute, Telecommunications Research Institute. In social sciences: Accounting Research Centre, Institute of Mental Health Research.

COMPUTER SCIENCE

Faculty of Science, Ottawa-Carleton Institute for Computer Science

Programs Awards MCS, PhD. Offered jointly with Carleton University.

Faculty 19 full-time, 7 part-time.

Faculty Research Algorithms and complexity, artificial intelligence, simulation software engineering.

Students 38 full-time (7 women), 33 part-time (7 women); includes 13 international. Average age 30.

Degrees Awarded In 1996, 21 master's, 1 doctorate awarded.

Entrance Requirements For master's, honors degree or equivalent, minimum B average; for doctorate, minimum B+ average.

Degree Requirements For master's, computer language, thesis or alternative required, foreign language not required; for doctorate, computer language, dissertation, computer exam required, foreign language not required.

Financial Aid Fellowships, research assistantships, teaching assistantships available. *Financial aid application deadline:* 2/15.

Applying *Deadline:* 3/1 (priority date; rolling processing). *Fee:* $15.

Contact *Ginette Trottier*
Academic Assistant
613-562-5800 Ext. 6701
Fax: 613-562-5187

ELECTRICAL ENGINEERING

Faculty of Engineering, Ottawa-Carleton Institute for Electrical Engineering

Programs Awards MA Sc, M Eng, PhD. Offered jointly with Carleton University.

Faculty 19 full-time, 5 part-time.

Students 58 full-time (6 women), 76 part-time (8 women); includes 19 international. Average age 31.

Degrees Awarded In 1996, 18 master's, 7 doctorates awarded.

Entrance Requirements For master's, honors degree or equivalent, minimum B average; for doctorate, minimum A- average.

Degree Requirements For master's, thesis or alternative required, foreign language not required; for doctorate, dissertation required, foreign language not required.
Financial Aid Fellowships, research assistantships, teaching assistantships available.
Applying *Deadline:* 3/1 (priority date). *Fee:* $15.
Contact *Lucette Lepage*
Academic Assistant
613-562-5800 Ext. 6212
Fax: 613-562-5175

SYSTEMS SCIENCE

Systems Science Program
Programs Awards M Sc. Part-time programs available.
Faculty 15 full-time (1 woman), 3 part-time (0 women).
Faculty Research Deterministic and probabilistic modelling, optimization, computer science, information systems.
Students 27 full-time (10 women), 13 part-time (3 women); includes 7 international. Average age 31.
Degrees Awarded In 1996, 7 degrees awarded.
Entrance Requirements Honors degree or equivalent, minimum B average.
Degree Requirements Computer language required, thesis optional, foreign language not required.
Financial Aid Fellowships, research assistantships, teaching assistantships available.
Applying *Deadline:* 2/1 (priority date; rolling processing). *Fee:* $15.
Contact *Diane Sarrazin*
Administrator
613-562-5884
Fax: 613-562-5164

UNIVERSITY OF TORONTO
Toronto, ON M5S 1A1, Canada

OVERVIEW
University of Toronto is a public coed university.

ENROLLMENT
55,000 graduate, professional, and undergraduate students; 8,723 full-time matriculated graduate/professional students (4,213 women), 2,372 part-time matriculated graduate/professional students (1,474 women).

GRADUATE FACULTY
7,417.

TUITION
$4283 per year (minimum) full-time, $1282 per year (minimum) part-time for Canadian residents; $8653 per year (minimum) full-time, $2992 per year (minimum) part-time for nonresidents.

HOUSING
Rooms and/or apartments available to single students (300 units) at an average cost of $4000 per year ($6000 including board); available to married students (710 units) at an average cost of $6000 per year ($8000 including board). Graduate housing contact: Housing Services Office, 416-978-8045.

STUDENT SERVICES
Career counseling, free psychological counseling, day-care facilities, campus safety program, campus employment opportunities, international student services.

FACILITIES
Library: John P. Roberts Library plus 50 additional on-campus libraries; total holdings of 8 million volumes, 3 million microforms, 35,000 current periodical subscriptions. Access provided to on-line information retrieval services. *Computer:* Campuswide network is available with full Internet access. Computer services are offered at no charge. *Special:* In arts and humanities: Centre for Medieval Studies, Centre for Computing in the Humanities and Social Sciences, Institute for History and Philosophy of Science and Technology, Centre for South Asian Studies. In science and engineering: David Dunlap Observatory, Institute for Aerospace Studies, Banting and Best Department of Medical Research. In social sciences: Centre for International Studies, Centre for Industrial Relations, Institute for Policy Analysis, Centre for Urban and Community Studies.

COMPUTER ENGINEERING

School of Graduate Studies, Physical Sciences Division, Faculty of Applied Science and Engineering, Department of Electrical and Computer Engineering
Programs Offers programs in biomedical engineering (MA Sc, M Eng, PhD), communications (MA Sc, M Eng, PhD), computer engineering and systems (MA Sc, M Eng, PhD), electromagnetics (MA Sc, M Eng, PhD), electronics (MA Sc, M Eng, PhD), photonics (MA Sc, M Eng, PhD), power devices and systems (MA Sc, M Eng, PhD), systems control (MA Sc, M Eng, PhD). Part-time programs available.
Faculty 54.
Students 253 full-time (23 women), 56 part-time (6 women); includes 36 international.
Degrees Awarded In 1996, 72 master's, 26 doctorates awarded.
Degree Requirements For master's, thesis required (for some programs), foreign language not required; for doctorate, dissertation required, foreign language not required.
Financial Aid *Application deadline:* 2/1.
Applying 485 applicants, 46% accepted. *Deadline:* 4/15. *Fee:* $60.
Contact *Secretary*
416-978-3122
Fax: 416-978-7423
E-mail: cherian@ecf.utoronto.ca

COMPUTER SCIENCE

School of Graduate Studies, Physical Sciences Division, Department of Computer Science
Programs Awards M Sc, PhD. Part-time programs available.
Faculty 45.
Students 126 full-time (20 women), 22 part-time (6 women); includes 25 international.
Degrees Awarded In 1996, 31 master's, 19 doctorates awarded.
Degree Requirements Thesis/dissertation.
Financial Aid *Application deadline:* 2/1.
Applying 336 applicants, 27% accepted. *Deadline:* 4/15. *Fee:* $50.
Contact *Secretary*
416-978-8762
Fax: 416-978-1931
E-mail: grad-inq@cdf.utoronto.ca

ELECTRICAL ENGINEERING

School of Graduate Studies, Physical Sciences Division, Faculty of Applied Science and Engineering, Department of Electrical and Computer Engineering

Programs Offers programs in biomedical engineering (MA Sc, M Eng, PhD), communications (MA Sc, M Eng, PhD), computer engineering and systems (MA Sc, M Eng, PhD), electromagnetics (MA Sc, M Eng, PhD), electronics (MA Sc, M Eng, PhD), photonics (MA Sc, M Eng, PhD), power devices and systems (MA Sc, M Eng, PhD), systems control (MA Sc, M Eng, PhD). Part-time programs available.

Faculty 54.

Students 253 full-time (23 women), 56 part-time (6 women); includes 36 international.

Degrees Awarded In 1996, 72 master's, 26 doctorates awarded.

Degree Requirements For master's, thesis required (for some programs), foreign language not required; for doctorate, dissertation required, foreign language not required.

Financial Aid *Application deadline: 2/1.*

Applying 485 applicants, 46% accepted. *Deadline:* 4/15. *Fee:* $60.

Contact *Secretary*
416-978-3122
Fax: 416-978-7423
E-mail: cherian@ecf.utoronto.ca

SOFTWARE ENGINEERING

School of Graduate Studies, Physical Sciences Division, Collaborative Program in Software Engineering

Programs Awards M Eng, M Sc.

Degree Requirements Thesis (for some programs).

Financial Aid *Application deadline: 2/1.*

Applying *Deadline:* 4/15. *Fee:* $60.

Contact *N. K. Wagle*
Director
416-978-4294

UNIVERSITY OF WATERLOO
Waterloo, ON N2L 3G1, Canada

OVERVIEW
University of Waterloo is a public coed university.

ENROLLMENT
21,903 graduate, professional, and undergraduate students; 1,487 full-time matriculated graduate/professional students (546 women), 258 part-time matriculated graduate/professional students (84 women).

GRADUATE FACULTY
691 full-time (128 women), 259 part-time (48 women).

HOUSING
Rooms and/or apartments available to single students (72 units) at an average cost of $3942 per year; available to married students (600 units) at an average cost of $6108 per year. Graduate housing information: 519-888-4567.

STUDENT SERVICES
Disabled student services, low-cost health insurance, career counseling, free psychological counseling, exercise/wellness program, day-care facilities, campus safety program, campus employment opportunities, international student services.

FACILITIES
Library: Dana Porter Library plus 2 additional on-campus libraries; total holdings of 1.77 million volumes, 1.39 million microforms, 14,148 current periodical subscriptions. A total of 200 personal computers in all libraries. Access provided to on-line information retrieval services. *Computer:* Campuswide network is available with full Internet access. Total number of PCs/terminals supplied for student use: 4,000. Computer services are offered at no charge. *Special:* In arts and humanities: Centre for Accounting Research and Education, Centre for Advanced Studies in Finance, Centre for Cultural Management, Institute for Insurance and Pension Research. In science and engineering: Institute for Computer Research, Institute for Groundwater Research, Institute for Polymer Research, Institute for Innovation Research, Institute for Risk Research, Centre for Materials Technology, Centre for Biotechnology Research, Centre for Contact Lens Research, Centre for Wetlands Research. In social sciences: Institute for Improvement in Quality and Productivity; Centre for Heritage Resources; Centre for Applied Health Research; Centre for Society, Technology, and Values.

COMPUTER ENGINEERING

Faculty of Engineering, Department of Electrical and Computer Engineering

Programs Awards MA Sc, PhD. Part-time programs available.

Faculty 40 full-time (3 women), 10 part-time (1 woman).

Faculty Research Communications, computers, systems and control, silicon devices, power engineering, antennas, microwaves, wave-optics, high-voltage, VLSI.

Students 115 full-time (13 women), 17 part-time (2 women); includes 33 international.

Degrees Awarded In 1996, 36 master's, 23 doctorates awarded.

Entrance Requirements For master's, TOEFL (minimum score 550), honors degree, minimum B+ average; for doctorate, TOEFL (minimum score 550), master's degree.

Degree Requirements For master's, project or thesis; for doctorate, dissertation, comprehensive exam.

Financial Aid Fellowships, research assistantships, teaching assistantships available.

Applying *Deadline:* 2/1 (10/1 for spring admission). *Fee:* $50.

Contact *Dr. A. Vannelli*
Graduate Officer
519-888-4567 Ext. 3330
E-mail: vannelli@cheetah.vlsi.uwaterloo.ca

COMPUTER SCIENCE

Faculty of Mathematics, Department of Computer Science

Programs Awards M Math, PhD. Part-time programs available.

Faculty 41 full-time (6 women), 13 part-time (3 women).

Faculty Research Computer graphics, data structures, artificial intelligence, symbolic computation, theory of computing. *Total annual research expenditures:* $2.245 million.

Students 106 full-time (25 women), 25 part-time (4 women); includes 11 international.

Degrees Awarded In 1996, 51 master's, 16 doctorates awarded.

Entrance Requirements For master's, TOEFL (minimum score 580), honors degree in field, minimum B+ average; for doctorate, TOEFL (minimum score 580), master's degree.

Degree Requirements For master's, computer language, essay or thesis required, foreign language not required; for doctorate, computer language, dissertation required, foreign language not required.

Financial Aid   108 students received aid; research assistantships, teaching assistantships, scholarships available.

Applying   151 applicants, 54% accepted. *Deadline:* 2/28 (priority date; rolling processing; 1/31 for spring admission). *Fee:* $50.

Contact   Dr. E. P. F. Chan
Graduate Officer
519-888-4567 Ext. 4439
E-mail: csgrad@jeeves.uwaterloo.ca

ELECTRICAL ENGINEERING

Faculty of Engineering, Department of Electrical and Computer Engineering

Programs   Awards MA Sc, PhD. Part-time programs available.

Faculty   40 full-time (3 women), 10 part-time (1 woman).

Faculty Research   Communications, computers, systems and control, silicon devices, power engineering, antennas, microwaves, wave-optics, high-voltage, VLSI.

Students   115 full-time (13 women), 17 part-time (2 women); includes 33 international.

Degrees Awarded   In 1996, 36 master's, 23 doctorates awarded.

Entrance Requirements   For master's, TOEFL (minimum score 550), honors degree, minimum B+ average; for doctorate, TOEFL (minimum score 550), master's degree.

Degree Requirements   For master's, project or thesis; for doctorate, dissertation, comprehensive exam.

Financial Aid   Fellowships, research assistantships, teaching assistantships available.

Applying   *Deadline:* 2/1 (10/1 for spring admission). *Fee:* $50.

Contact   Dr. A. Vannelli
Graduate Officer
519-888-4567 Ext. 3330
E-mail: vannelli@cheetah.vlsi.uwaterloo.ca

THE UNIVERSITY OF WESTERN ONTARIO
London, ON N6A 5B8, Canada

OVERVIEW
The University of Western Ontario is a public coed university.

HOUSING
Rooms and/or apartments available to single and married students.

FACILITIES
Library: D. B. Weldon Library plus 7 additional on-campus libraries.

COMPUTER SCIENCE

Physical Sciences Division, Department of Computer Science

Programs   Awards M Sc, PhD.

Faculty Research   Artificial intelligence and logic programming, graphics and image processing, software and systems, theory of computing.

Entrance Requirements   For master's, TOEFL (minimum score 580), M Sc in computer science or comparable academic qualifications.

Degree Requirements   For master's, thesis or project required, foreign language not required; for doctorate, dissertation required, foreign language not required.

Applying   *Deadline:* rolling.

UNIVERSITY OF WINDSOR
Windsor, ON N9B 3P4, Canada

OVERVIEW
University of Windsor is a public coed university.

ENROLLMENT
13,726 graduate, professional, and undergraduate students; 656 full-time matriculated graduate/professional students (264 women), 208 part-time matriculated graduate/professional students (115 women).

GRADUATE FACULTY
287 full-time (57 women), 46 part-time (10 women).

EXPENSES
Tuition $4242 per year full-time, $2121 per year part-time for Canadian residents; $8250 per year for nonresidents. Fees $400 per year full-time, $180 per year part-time for Canadian residents; $400 per year for nonresidents.

HOUSING
Rooms and/or apartments available to single students at an average cost of $3231 per year ($4881 including board); available to married students at an average cost of $6012 per year. Graduate housing contact: Margaret Bickerstaff, 519-253-4232 Ext. 3279.

STUDENT SERVICES
Disabled student services, low-cost health insurance, career counseling, free psychological counseling, daycare facilities, campus safety program, campus employment opportunities, international student services, writing training, teacher training.

FACILITIES
Library: Leddy Library plus 3 additional on-campus libraries; total holdings of 2.188 million volumes, 776,000 microforms, 8,000 current periodical subscriptions. A total of 85 personal computers in all libraries. Access provided to on-line information retrieval services. *Computer:* Campuswide network is available with full Internet access. Total number of PCs/terminals supplied for student use: 132. Computer service fees are included with tuition and fees. *Special:* In arts and humanities: Humanities Research Group. In science and engineering: Great Lakes Institute, Fluid Dynamics Research Institute, VSLI Group.

COMPUTER SCIENCE

Faculty of Science, School of Computer Science

Programs   Awards M Sc. Part-time programs available.

Faculty   9 full-time (3 women).

Faculty Research   Database management, information retrieval systems, programming languages, computer graphics, artificial intelligence.

Students   36 full-time (10 women), 2 part-time (both women); includes 3 international.

Degrees Awarded   In 1996, 7 degrees awarded.

Entrance Requirements   GRE, TOEFL (minimum score 550), minimum B average.

Degree Requirements   Thesis optional.

Financial Aid In 1996–97, teaching assistantships averaging $1,067 per month and totaling $123,987 were awarded. *Financial aid application deadline:* 2/15.

Applying *Deadline:* 7/1 (priority date; rolling processing). *Fee:* $50.

Contact *Liaison and Applicant Services*
519-253-4232 Ext. 7014
Fax: 519-971-3653

ELECTRICAL ENGINEERING

Faculty of Engineering, Department of Electrical Engineering
Programs Awards MA Sc, PhD. Part-time programs available.
Faculty 9 full-time (0 women), 2 part-time (0 women).
Faculty Research Systems, signals, power.
Students 28 full-time (4 women), 8 part-time (0 women); includes 8 international.
Degrees Awarded In 1996, 4 master's, 1 doctorate awarded.
Entrance Requirements For master's, TOEFL (minimum score 550), minimum B average; for doctorate, TOEFL, master's degree.
Degree Requirements Thesis/dissertation required, foreign language not required.
Financial Aid In 1996–97, 3 fellowships averaging $713 per month and totaling $8,557, teaching assistantships averaging $1,067 per month and totaling $153,147 were awarded; research assistantships also available. *Financial aid application deadline:* 2/15.
Applying *Deadline:* 7/1 (priority date; rolling processing). *Fee:* $50.
Contact *Liaison and Applicant Services*
519-253-4232 Ext. 7014
Fax: 519-971-3653

YORK UNIVERSITY
North York, ON M3J 1P3, Canada

OVERVIEW
York University is a public coed university.

HOUSING
Rooms and/or apartments available to single and married students. Graduate housing information: 416-736-5152.

FACILITIES
Library: Scott Library plus 4 additional on-campus libraries. *Special:* In arts and humanities: Robart's Centre for Canadian Studies. In science and engineering: Centre for Research in Earth and Space Science, Institute for Space and Terrestrial Science, Centre for Study of Computers in Education. In social sciences: Institute for Social Research, Centre for Research on Latin America and the Caribbean, Centre for Feminist Research, Centre for Refugee Studies, Centre for International and Strategic Studies.

COMPUTER SCIENCE

Faculty of Science, Program in Computer Science
Programs Awards M Sc.
Degree Requirements Thesis required, foreign language not required.
Applying *Deadline:* 3/1. *Fee:* $60.

QUEBEC

CONCORDIA UNIVERSITY
Montréal, PQ H3G 1M8, Canada

OVERVIEW
Concordia University is a public coed university.

ENROLLMENT
22,324 graduate, professional, and undergraduate students; 2,349 full-time matriculated graduate/professional students (1,094 women), 875 part-time matriculated graduate/professional students (451 women).

EXPENSES
Tuition $55 per credit (minimum) for Canadian residents; $248 per credit (minimum) for nonresidents. Fees $282 per year full-time, $66 per year (minimum) part-time.

HOUSING
Rooms and/or apartments available to single students (144 units) at an average cost of $2215 per year; on-campus housing not available to married students. Graduate housing contact: Mimi Littman, 514-848-4755.

STUDENT SERVICES
Disabled student services, career counseling, free psychological counseling, day-care facilities, campus safety program, campus employment opportunities, international student services.

FACILITIES
Library: Webster Library plus 2 additional on-campus libraries; total holdings of 1,590,999 volumes, 923,790 microforms, 9,055 current periodical subscriptions. A total of 180 personal computers in all libraries. Access provided to on-line information retrieval services. *Computer:* Campuswide network is available with full Internet access. Total number of PCs/terminals supplied for student use: 1,000. Computer services are offered at no charge. *Special:* In arts and humanities: Conservatory of Cinematographic Art, Centre for Research in Human Development, Concordia Centre for Broadcasting Studies. In science and engineering: Concordia Computer-Aided Vehicle Engineering, Centre for Industrial Control, Centre for Pattern Recognition and Machine Intelligence, Centre for Composites. In social sciences: Centre for Studies in Behavioral Neurobiology, Centre for Human Relations and Community Studies, Concordia Transportation Management Centre.

COMPUTER ENGINEERING

Faculty of Engineering and Computer Science, Department of Electrical and Computer Engineering
Programs Awards MA Sc, M Eng, PhD.
Faculty Research Computer communications and protocols, circuits and systems, graph theory, VLSI systems, microelectronics.
Students 142 full-time (18 women), 15 part-time (0 women); includes 47 international.
Degrees Awarded In 1996, 28 master's, 8 doctorates awarded.
Degree Requirements For master's, computer language required, thesis optional, foreign language not required; for doctorate, computer language, dissertation, comprehensive exam required, foreign language not required.
Applying *Deadline:* 6/1 (10/1 for spring admission). *Fee:* $30.

Contact *Dr. O. Schwelb*
Director
514-848-3103
Fax: 514-848-2802

COMPUTER SCIENCE

Faculty of Engineering and Computer Science, Department of Computer Science

Programs Offers programs in computer science (MCS, PhD, Diploma), software engineering (MCS).

Faculty Research Computer systems and applications, mathematics of computation, pattern recognition, artificial intelligence and robotics.

Students 238 full-time (69 women), 85 part-time (21 women); includes 20 international.

Degrees Awarded In 1996, 15 master's, 4 doctorates, 29 Diplomas awarded.

Degree Requirements For master's, 1 foreign language, computer language required, thesis optional; for doctorate, 1 foreign language, computer language, dissertation, comprehensive exam.

Applying *Deadline:* 6/1 (10/1 for spring admission). *Fee:* $30.

Contact *Dr. H. F. Li*
Director
514-848-3043
Fax: 514-848-2830

ELECTRICAL ENGINEERING

Faculty of Engineering and Computer Science, Department of Electrical and Computer Engineering

Programs Awards MA Sc, M Eng, PhD.

Faculty Research Computer communications and protocols, circuits and systems, graph theory, VLSI systems, microelectronics.

Students 142 full-time (18 women), 15 part-time (0 women); includes 47 international.

Degrees Awarded In 1996, 28 master's, 8 doctorates awarded.

Degree Requirements For master's, computer language required, thesis optional, foreign language not required; for doctorate, computer language, dissertation, comprehensive exam required, foreign language not required.

Applying *Deadline:* 6/1 (10/1 for spring admission). *Fee:* $30.

Contact *Dr. O. Schwelb*
Director
514-848-3103
Fax: 514-848-2802

SOFTWARE ENGINEERING

Faculty of Engineering and Computer Science, Department of Computer Science

Programs Offerings include software engineering (MCS).

Degree Requirements 1 foreign language, computer language required, thesis optional.

Applying *Deadline:* 6/1 (10/1 for spring admission). *Fee:* $30.

Contact *Dr. H. F. Li*
Director
514-848-3043
Fax: 514-848-2830

ÉCOLE POLYTECHNIQUE DE MONTRÉAL
Montréal, PQ H3C 3A7, Canada

OVERVIEW
École Polytechnique de Montréal is a public coed graduate-only institution.

HOUSING
Rooms and/or apartments available to single students; on-campus housing not available to married students. Graduate housing contact: Student Services Office, 514-340-4843.

FACILITIES
Special: In science and engineering: Slowpoke Nuclear Reactor; solid-state physics, CAD/CAM, refractories, biomedical modeling, microscopic characterization, and polymer processing facilities.

COMPUTER ENGINEERING

Department of Electrical and Computer Engineering

Programs Awards M Eng, M Sc A, PhD, DESS. Programs in automation (M Eng, M Sc A, PhD), computer science (M Eng, M Sc A, PhD), electrotechnology (M Eng, M Sc A, PhD), microelectronics (M Eng, M Sc A, PhD), microwave technology (M Eng, M Sc A, PhD). Part-time and evening/weekend programs available.

Faculty Research Microwaves, telecommunications, software engineering.

Entrance Requirements For master's, minimum GPA of 2.75; for doctorate, minimum GPA of 3.0.

Degree Requirements For master's and doctorate, 1 foreign language, computer language, thesis/dissertation.

Applying *Deadline:* 3/1 (priority date; rolling processing; 2/1 for spring admission). *Fee:* $15.

COMPUTER SCIENCE

Department of Electrical and Computer Engineering

Programs Offerings include computer science (M Eng, M Sc A, PhD).

Degree Requirements 1 foreign language, computer language, thesis/dissertation.

Applying *Deadline:* 3/1 (priority date; rolling processing; 2/1 for spring admission). *Fee:* $15.

ELECTRICAL ENGINEERING

Department of Electrical and Computer Engineering

Programs Awards M Eng, M Sc A, PhD, DESS. Programs in automation (M Eng, M Sc A, PhD), computer science (M Eng, M Sc A, PhD), electrotechnology (M Eng, M Sc A, PhD), microelectronics (M Eng, M Sc A, PhD), microwave technology (M Eng, M Sc A, PhD). Part-time and evening/weekend programs available.

Faculty Research Microwaves, telecommunications, software engineering.

Entrance Requirements For master's, minimum GPA of 2.75; for doctorate, minimum GPA of 3.0.

Degree Requirements For master's and doctorate, 1 foreign language, computer language, thesis/dissertation.

Applying *Deadline:* 3/1 (priority date; rolling processing; 2/1 for spring admission). *Fee:* $15.

McGILL UNIVERSITY
Montréal, PQ H3A 2T5, Canada

OVERVIEW
McGill University is a public coed university.

ENROLLMENT
31,592 graduate, professional, and undergraduate students; 7,126 matriculated graduate/professional students.

EXPENSES
Tuition $1668 per year for Canadian residents; $8268 per year for nonresidents. Fees $828 per year for Canadian residents; $1216 per year for nonresidents.

HOUSING
Rooms and/or apartments available to single students; on-campus housing not available to married students. Graduate housing information: 514-398-6363.

STUDENT SERVICES
Disabled student services, low-cost health insurance, career counseling, free psychological counseling, day-care facilities, campus employment opportunities, international student services.

FACILITIES
Library: Human and Social Sciences Library plus 18 additional on-campus libraries; total holdings of 2,509,999 volumes, 1,039,889 microforms, 17,516 current periodical subscriptions. A total of 79 personal computers in all libraries. Access provided to on-line information retrieval services. *Special:* In arts and humanities: Institute of Islamic Studies. In science and engineering: Aids Centre, Centre for Studies on Aging, Artificial Cells and Organs Research Centre, Cancer Centre, Centre for Research in Neuroscience, Centre for Plant Molecular Biology, Institute of Parasitology, Research Centre for Intelligent Machines, Centre for Climate and Global Change, Centre for the Physics of Materials. In social sciences: Centre of Air and Space Law; Cognitive Science Centre; Centre for Developing Area Studies; Economics Centre; Centre for Applied Family Studies; Centre for Research on Instruction; Centre for Medicine, Ethics, and Law; Centre for Society, Technology, and Development; Quebec Research Centre of Private and Comparative Law.

COMPUTER SCIENCE

Faculty of Graduate Studies and Research, School of Computer Science
Programs Awards M Sc, PhD.
Faculty 17 full-time (2 women).
Faculty Research Computational geometry and robotics, parallel computer systems (ACAPS), software engineering, database systems and speech recognition. *Total annual research expenditures:* $1.6 million.
Students 93 full-time (21 women), includes 29 international.
Degrees Awarded In 1996, 27 master's awarded; 3 doctorates awarded (100% found work related to degree). Terminal master's awarded for partial completion of doctoral program.
Entrance Requirements TOEFL (minimum score 580).

Degree Requirements For master's, project or thesis; for doctorate, dissertation, comprehensive exam.
Financial Aid Fellowships, research assistantships, teaching assistantships, full and partial tuition waivers available. *Financial aid application deadline:* 2/1.
Applying 288 applicants, 26% accepted. *Deadline:* 4/1 (rolling processing). *Fee:* $60.
Contact *Franca Cianci*
Graduate Secretary
514-398-3744

ELECTRICAL ENGINEERING

Faculty of Graduate Studies and Research, Faculty of Engineering, Department of Electrical Engineering
Programs Awards M Eng, PhD.
Faculty 28 full-time (1 woman).
Students 189 full-time (25 women), 40 part-time (8 women); includes 43 international.
Degrees Awarded In 1996, 36 master's, 22 doctorates awarded.
Entrance Requirements TOEFL (minimum score 600).
Degree Requirements For master's, thesis optional; for doctorate, dissertation, qualifying exam.
Financial Aid In 1996–97, 112 teaching assistantships (12 to first-year students) averaging $525 per month were awarded.
Applying 200 applicants, 31% accepted. *Deadline:* 2/1 (rolling processing). *Fee:* $60.
Contact *J. Webb*
Associate Chair, Graduate Program
514-398-7126
Fax: 514-398-4470

See in-depth description on page 469.

UNIVERSITÉ DE MONTRÉAL
Montréal, PQ H3C 3J7, Canada

OVERVIEW
Université de Montréal is an independent coed university.

ENROLLMENT
33,532 graduate, professional, and undergraduate students; 7,899 full-time matriculated graduate/professional students (3,935 women), 2,723 part-time matriculated graduate/professional students (1,526 women).

GRADUATE FACULTY
2,600.

TUITION
$975 per trimester for Canadian residents; $3875 per trimester for nonresidents.

HOUSING
Rooms and/or apartments available to single students (1,130 units) at an average cost of $1900 per year; on-campus housing not available to married students. Housing application deadline: 3/1. Graduate housing information: 514-343-6531.

STUDENT SERVICES
Disabled student services, low-cost health insurance, career counseling, free psychological counseling, day-care facilities, campus safety program, international student services.

FACILITIES

Library: Total holdings of 2,439,628 volumes, 1,438,865 microforms, 15,006 current periodical subscriptions. A total of 230 personal computers in all libraries. Access provided to on-line information retrieval services. *Computer:* Campuswide network is available with full Internet access. Computer services are offered at no charge. *Special:* In arts and humanities: Public Law Research Center, orchestra. In science and engineering: Mont Megantic Observatory, nuclear physics laboratory, veterinarian hospital, Plant Biology Research Institute, Biology Station St. Hypolythe. In social sciences: Center for Research and Development Economics, Center for Research in Transportation.

COMPUTER SCIENCE

Faculty of Arts and Sciences, Department of Computer Science and Operations Research

Programs Offers program in computer systems (M Sc, PhD). Part-time programs available.

Faculty 40 full-time (5 women), 1 part-time (0 women).

Faculty Research Optimization statistics, programming languages, telecommunications, theoretical computer science, artificial intelligence.

Students 143 full-time (27 women), 9 part-time (2 women).

Degrees Awarded In 1996, 28 master's, 15 doctorates awarded. Terminal master's awarded for partial completion of doctoral program.

Entrance Requirements For master's, B Sc in related field; for doctorate, MA or M Sc in related field.

Degree Requirements For master's, 1 foreign language, computer language, thesis; for doctorate, 1 foreign language, computer language, dissertation, general exam.

Financial Aid Available to part-time students. *Financial aid application deadline:* 10/31.

Applying 87 applicants, 34% accepted. *Deadline:* 2/1 (priority date). *Fee:* $30.

Contact *Patrice Marcotte*
Graduate Studies Assistant
514-343-6111 Ext. 5941

UNIVERSITÉ DE SHERBROOKE
Sherbrooke, PQ J1K 2R1, Canada

OVERVIEW

Université de Sherbrooke is an independent coed university.

HOUSING

Rooms and/or apartments available to single students; on-campus housing not available to married students. Graduate housing contact: Pierre Gelinas, 819-821-7663.

FACILITIES

Library: Bibliothèque générale plus 4 additional on-campus libraries. *Special:* In arts and humanities: Institut de Recherche et d'Enseignement Cooperatif, Centre d'Études sur la Renaissance. In science and engineering: Centre de Recherche sur les Mécanismes de Sécrétion, Centre de Recherche sur la Physique de l'État Solide, Centre de Recherche sur les Communications, Centre d'Applications et de Recherches en Télédétection.

COMPUTER ENGINEERING

Faculty of Applied Sciences, Department of Electrical Engineering and Computer Engineering

Programs Awards M Sc A, PhD.

Faculty Research Minielectronics, biomedical engineering, digital signal prolonging and telecommunications, software engineering and artificial intelligence.

Degree Requirements Thesis/dissertation.

Applying *Deadline:* 6/1 (priority date; rolling processing). *Fee:* $15.

ELECTRICAL ENGINEERING

Faculty of Applied Sciences, Department of Electrical Engineering and Computer Engineering

Programs Awards M Sc A, PhD.

Faculty Research Minielectronics, biomedical engineering, digital signal prolonging and telecommunications, software engineering and artificial intelligence.

Degree Requirements Thesis/dissertation.

Applying *Deadline:* 6/1 (priority date; rolling processing). *Fee:* $15.

UNIVERSITÉ DU QUÉBEC À TROIS-RIVIÈRES
Trois-Rivières, PQ G9A 5H7, Canada

OVERVIEW

Université du Québec à Trois-Rivières is a public coed university.

ENROLLMENT

10,869 graduate, professional, and undergraduate students; 789 full-time matriculated graduate/professional students (385 women), 416 part-time matriculated graduate/professional students (137 women).

GRADUATE FACULTY

1,200 full-time (720 women).

HOUSING

Rooms and/or apartments available to single students (812 units) at an average cost of $2500 per year; on-campus housing not available to married students. Graduate housing contact: Sylvain Desforset, 819-378-0385.

STUDENT SERVICES

Career counseling, free psychological counseling, day-care facilities, campus safety program, campus employment opportunities, international student services.

FACILITIES

Library: Total holdings of 959,591 volumes, 512,690 microforms, 3,047 current periodical subscriptions. Access provided to on-line information retrieval services. *Computer:* Campuswide network is available with full Internet access. *Special:* In arts and humanities: Groupe de recherche en philosophie analytique. In science and engineering: Centre de Recherche en P&(ates et Papiers, Centre de Recherche en Photobiophysique, groupe de recherche en biotechnologie des membranes, groupe de recherche en diélectrique, groupe de recherche sur les insectes piquers, laboratoire départmental de recherche sur les communatés aquatiques, groupe de recherche en électronique industrielle. In social sciences: Centre de Recherche en Études Québécoises, groupe de recherche en économie et gestion des petites et moyennes organisations et de leur environnent, groupe de recherche en développement de l'enfant, laboratoire départemental de recherche sur les pratiques du temps libre, laboratoire départemental de recherche en gérontologie.

COMPUTER SCIENCE

Program in Mathematics and Computer Science
Programs Awards M Sc.
Students 30.
Applying *Deadline: 2/1. Fee: $30.*
Contact *Suzanne Camirand*
Admissions Officer
819-376-5045 Ext. 2591
Fax: 819-376-5210

ELECTRICAL ENGINEERING

Program in Electrical Engineering
Programs Awards PhD.
Students 10 full-time (2 women), includes 2 international.
Entrance Requirements Appropriate master's degree, proficiency in French.
Degree Requirements Dissertation.
Financial Aid Fellowships, research assistantships, teaching assistantships available.
Applying 2 applicants, 100% accepted. *Deadline: 2/1. Fee: $30.*
Contact *Suzanne Camirand*
Admissions Officer
819-376-5045 Ext. 2591
Fax: 819-376-5210

ELECTRICAL ENGINEERING

Program in Industrial Engineering
Programs Offerings include electrical engineering (PhD).
Applying *Deadline: 2/1. Fee: $30.*
Contact *Suzanne Camirand*
Admissions Officer
819-376-5045 Ext. 2591
Fax: 819-376-5210

UNIVERSITÉ LAVAL
Sainte-Foy, PQ G1K 7P4, Canada

OVERVIEW
Université Laval is an independent coed university.

ENROLLMENT
31,545 graduate, professional, and undergraduate students; 4,858 full-time matriculated graduate/professional students (2,422 women), 2,446 part-time matriculated graduate/professional students (1,386 women).

EXPENSES
Tuition $1334 per year (minimum) full-time, $56 per credit (minimum) part-time for Canadian residents; $5976 per year (minimum) full-time, $249 per credit (minimum) part-time for nonresidents. Fees $138 per year full-time, $5.75 per credit part-time.

HOUSING
Rooms and/or apartments available to single students (2,291 units) at an average cost of $1440 per year; on-campus housing not available to married students. Housing application deadline: 2/15. Graduate housing contact: Fernand Lehoux, 418-656-2921.

STUDENT SERVICES
Career counseling, free psychological counseling, daycare facilities, campus safety program, campus employment opportunities, international student services.

FACILITIES
Library: Main library plus 1 additional on-campus library; total holdings of 2,217,793 volumes, 1,206,230 microforms, 14,369 current periodical subscriptions. A total of 147 personal computers in all libraries. Access provided to on-line information retrieval services. *Computer:* Campuswide network is available with full Internet access. Total number of PCs/terminals supplied for student use: 1,600. Computer services are offered at no charge. *Special:* In arts and humanities: Centre d'Études sur la Langue, les Arts et les Traditions Populaires des Francophones en Amérique du Nord, Centre de Recherche en Littérature Québécoise, Centre International de Recherche ena Ménagement Linguistique. In science and engineering: Centre d'Études Nordiques, Centre de Recherche sur les Propriétés des Interfaces et la Catalyse, Centre de Recherches en Aménagement et Développement, Centre de Recherche en Biologie Forestiére, Centre de Recherche en Sciences et Ingénierie des Macromolécules, groupe interuniversitaire de recherches océanographiques du Québec, Centre de Recherche en Sciences et Technologie du Lait, Centre de Recherche en Géomatique, Centre de Recherche en Horticulture, Centre d'Optique, Photonique et Laser, Centre de Recherche en Cancérologie. In social sciences: Centre Québécois de Relations Internationales,Centre de Recherche sur le Sahel, groupe de recherche en économie de l'énergie et des ressources naturelles.

COMPUTER SCIENCE

Faculty of Sciences and Engineering, Department of Computer Science
Programs Awards M Sc, PhD.
Faculty Research Software and information systems design, networking, management-oriented computer science and office automation.
Students 61 full-time (13 women), 23 part-time (3 women).
Degrees Awarded In 1996, 28 master's awarded.
Applying 90 applicants, 64% accepted. *Deadline: 3/1. Fee: $30.*
Contact *Pierre Marchand*
Director
418-656-2131 Ext. 7409
Fax: 418-656-2324
E-mail: pierre.marchand@ift.ulaval.ca

ELECTRICAL ENGINEERING

Faculty of Sciences and Engineering, Department of Electrical and Computer Engineering
Programs Awards M Sc, PhD.
Faculty Research Telecommunication, frequency standards, biomedical engineering and electronic instrumentation.

Students 93 full-time (9 women), 24 part-time (3 women).
Degrees Awarded In 1996, 23 master's, 6 doctorates awarded.
Applying 84 applicants, 43% accepted. *Deadline:* 3/1. *Fee:* $30.
Contact *Denis Angers*
Director
418-656-2131 Ext. 3556
Fax: 418-656-3159
E-mail: denis.angers@gel.ulaval.ca

SASKATCHEWAN

UNIVERSITY OF REGINA
Regina, SK S4S 0A2, Canada

OVERVIEW
University of Regina is a public coed university.

ENROLLMENT
11,715 graduate, professional, and undergraduate students; 249 full-time, 668 part-time matriculated graduate/professional students.

GRADUATE FACULTY
418 full-time (121 women), 32 part-time.

HOUSING
Rooms and/or apartments available to single students (12 units) at an average cost of $3058 per year; on-campus housing not available to married students. Graduate housing contact: College West Residence, 306-585-4001.

STUDENT SERVICES
Low-cost health insurance, career counseling, free psychological counseling, exercise/wellness program, day-care facilities, campus safety program, campus employment opportunities, international student services.

FACILITIES
Library: Main library plus 5 additional on-campus libraries; total holdings of 808,854 volumes, 1,158,374 microforms, 3,017 current periodical subscriptions. A total of 120 personal computers in all libraries. Access provided to on-line information retrieval services. *Computer:* Campuswide network is available with full Internet access. Computer services are offered at no charge. *Special:* In arts and humanities: Centre for Franco-Canadian and Canadian Studies, Language Institute, Summer Centre for International Languages. In science and engineering: Canadian Institute for Broadband and Information Network Technologies, Centre for Advanced Systems, Centre for Geographic Information Systems, energy research unit, Genbiotek, Water Research Institute. In social sciences: Asia-Pacific Management Institute, Canadian Plains Research Center, Social Administrative Research Unit, Seniors Education Center, Dr. Paul Schwann Applied Health Center and Research.

COMPUTER ENGINEERING

Faculty of Graduate Studies and Research, Faculty of Engineering, Program in Electronic Systems Engineering
Programs Awards MA Sc, PhD. M Eng new for fall 1997.

Faculty Research Signal image processing, fibre optic network, analog/digital VLS1, expert system communication network.
Students 4 full-time, 12 part-time.
Degrees Awarded In 1996, 4 master's awarded.
Entrance Requirements For master's, TOEFL (minimum score 550); for doctorate, TOEFL (minimum score 550), master's degree.
Degree Requirements Thesis/dissertation.
Financial Aid In 1996–97, 7 students received aid, including fellowships averaging $1,131 per month, 1 research assistantship averaging $1,000 per month, 2 teaching assistantships averaging $880 per month, 4 scholarships averaging $750 per month; career-related internships or fieldwork also available.
Applying 26 applicants, 35% accepted. *Deadline:* rolling. *Fee:* $0.
Contact *Dr. R. Mason*
Coordinator
306-585-4470
Fax: 306-585-4855
E-mail: ralph.mason@uregina.ca

COMPUTER SCIENCE

Faculty of Graduate Studies and Research, Faculty of Science, Department of Computer Science
Programs Awards M Sc, PhD.
Faculty 15 full-time (1 woman), 4 part-time (0 women).
Faculty Research Expert systems, image processing, artificial intelligence, parallel computing data and knowledge bases. *Total annual research expenditures:* $387,000.
Students 25 full-time, 41 part-time.
Degrees Awarded In 1996, 7 master's awarded.
Entrance Requirements For master's, TOEFL (minimum score 550); for doctorate, M Sc in computer science.
Degree Requirements Computer language, thesis/dissertation required, foreign language not required.
Financial Aid In 1996–97, 24 students received aid, including fellowships averaging $1,131 per month, 4 research assistantships averaging $1,000 per month, 7 teaching assistantships averaging $880 per month, 13 scholarships averaging $750 per month; career-related internships or fieldwork also available.
Applying 89 applicants, 28% accepted. *Deadline:* rolling. *Fee:* $0.
Contact *Dr. L. Saxton*
Head
306-585-4632
Fax: 306-585-4745
E-mail: saxton@cs.uregina.ca

UNIVERSITY OF SASKATCHEWAN
Saskatoon, SK S7N 5A2, Canada

OVERVIEW
University of Saskatchewan is a public coed university.

HOUSING
Rooms and/or apartments available to single and married students.

FACILITIES
Library: Main library plus 7 additional on-campus libraries. *Special:* In science and engineering: National Research Council, National Hydrology Research Institute, Plant Biotechnology Institute, Institute of Space and

Atmospheric Studies, Crop Development Centre, Institute of Pedology, Veterinary Infectious Disease Organization, 100 MEV linear accelerator laboratory. In social sciences: Institute of Child Guidance and Development, Regional Psychiatric Centre, Wanuskewin Archaeological and Cultural Native Canadian Centre, Saskatchewan Native Law Centre.

ELECTRICAL ENGINEERING

College of Engineering, Department of Electrical Engineering

Programs   Awards M Eng, M Sc, PhD.

Entrance Requirements   GRE, TOEFL.

Degree Requirements   Thesis/dissertation required, foreign language not required.

Applying   *Deadline:* 7/1 (priority date; rolling processing). *Fee:* $0.

In-Depth Descriptions of Computer Science and Electrical Engineering Programs

AMERICAN UNIVERSITY
W A S H I N G T O N , DC

DEPARTMENT OF COMPUTER SCIENCE AND INFORMATION SYSTEMS

PROGRAMS OF STUDY

The Department of Computer Science and Information Systems offers programs leading to the M.S. degree in computer science or the M.S. degree in information systems, both in a broad array of formats. Both programs balance the practical and theoretical aspects of computer science and information systems. The 30-credit-hour M.S. in computer science provides a thorough background in computer science and its applications. The 36-credit-hour M.S. in information systems is a professionally oriented program covering all aspects of the analysis, design, development, and maintenance of computerized information systems. Formats include traditional day and evening classes as well as cohort-based weekend classes that meet in twelve sequenced courses, each course running for six weekend sessions. The Master of Science in statistical computing program, offered jointly with the Department of Mathematics and Statistics, emphasizes computer-oriented data analysis, including the design of algorithms, data structures, and numerical and graphical procedures for statistical applications. The department also offers professional advancement courses through its graduate certificate programs in information systems, information resources management, and systems and project management. Graduate degree programs are designed to prepare students for professional careers or for further doctoral study. Department emphasis is on software, with concentrations in intelligent systems, database management, and software development.

RESEARCH FACILITIES

The campus is fully networked with Windows-based, UNIX-based, and Macintosh workstations, and all are accessible through EagleNet, the University's campuswide fiber-optic network. Network-based software for personal computers and workstations is provided on EagleNet, which also serves as the University's gateway to the Internet. The department supports five specialized laboratories, including an intelligent systems laboratory, an Oracle development laboratory, and a multimedia laboratory. Labs are used for instruction and research and are maintained by department personnel to ensure smooth operation. Graduate students have ample opportunities to develop a variety of experience and skills. The Bender Library and Learning Resources Center houses more than 600,000 volumes and 3,000 periodicals as well as extensive microform collections and a nonprint media center. In addition, more than fourteen indexes in compact disk format are searchable using library microcomputers. Students have unlimited book check-out privileges and access to on-line bibliographical search services. As a member of the Washington Research Library Consortium, AU graduate students have borrowing privileges at six college and university libraries in the Washington, D.C., area. Dozens of other private and governmental collections, including the Library of Congress, are easily accessible.

FINANCIAL AID

Fellowships, scholarships, and graduate assistantships are available to full-time students. There are special awards for members of minority groups and international students. Part-time work is also available, as are loans and deferred-payment programs. Duties of graduate fellows and assistants usually include helping students in the department's computer center and assisting faculty members in their research.

COST OF STUDY

Graduate tuition for 1997–98 is $655 per semester hour.

LIVING AND HOUSING COSTS

Although many graduate students live off campus, the University provides graduate dormitory rooms and apartments. The Off-Campus Housing Office maintains a referral file of rooms and apartments. Housing costs in Washington, D.C., are comparable to those in most other major metropolitan areas.

STUDENT GROUP

The department has approximately 200 graduate students, with a number of these in part-time status. The University's favorable student-faculty ratio of 14:1 allows ample opportunity for one-on-one interaction among faculty members and fellow students.

STUDENT OUTCOMES

Graduates from the master's programs have begun their own start-up ventures or are employed in networking, databases, and system development and administration with government organizations such as the Census Bureau, the Department of Defense, Fannie Mae, and with private companies such as Oracle Corporation, America Online, Discovery Corporation, and Hughes Network Systems.

LOCATION

The University is located on an 84-acre site in a residential area of northwest Washington. The national capital area offers students access to a variety of educational, governmental, and cultural resources that enrich the student's degree program with opportunities for practical applications of theoretical studies. In recent years, students have completed internships at organizations such as IBM, AT&T, MCI, the American Council on Education, the Internal Revenue Service, the Department of Treasury, the General Accounting Office, and the National Security Agency.

THE UNIVERSITY

American University was founded as a Methodist institution, chartered by Congress in 1893, and intended originally for graduate study only. As a member of the Consortium of Universities of the Washington Area, AU offers its degree candidates the option of taking courses at other consortium universities for residence credit.

APPLYING

Applications for admission should be submitted prior to February 1 if the student is also applying for financial aid. Deadlines vary for different fields of study, but early application is always encouraged. The application fee is $50.

CORRESPONDENCE AND INFORMATION

To contact faculty members and for specific program information:

Department of Computer Science and Information
 Systems
College of Arts and Sciences
American University
4400 Massachusetts Avenue, NW
Washington, D.C. 20016-8116
Telephone: 202-885-1470
E-mail: csis@american.edu
WWW: http://www.american.edu/academic.depts/cas/

For an application and University catalog:

Graduate Admissions Office
American University
4400 Massachusetts Avenue, NW
Washington, D.C. 20016-8001
Telephone: 202-885-3120
E-mail: afa@american.edu

AMERICAN UNIVERSITY
THE FACULTY AND THEIR RESEARCH

Judith Barlow, Assistant Professor; Ph.D., Colorado. Databases, decision support systems, simulation.

Shirley Becker, Associate Professor; Ph.D., Maryland. Computer-assisted software engineering, expert systems, database and information systems.

Thomas J. Bergin, Professor; Ph.D., American. History of computing, information resources management, ethical issues in computing.

Frank W. Connolly, Professor; Ph.D., American. Legal and ethical issues of technology, educational computing, intellectual property.

Richard Gibson, Assistant Professor; Ph.D., Maryland. Global information technology and software process improvement.

Michael A. Gray, Associate Professor and Chairperson; Ph.D., Penn State. Artificial intelligence (AI), distributed AI, intelligent systems architecture.

Reza Khorramshahgol, Associate Professor; Ph.D., George Washington. Data communications, quantitative methods, software engineering.

Anita J. La Salle, Associate Professor; Ph.D., Stevens. Software engineering, expert systems, communications, multimedia design and development.

Jack Ligon, Assistant Professor; Ph.D., Maryland. Information resources management and business process re-engineering.

Gene McGuire, Assistant Professor; Ph.D., George Mason. Organizational and behavior aspects of information systems, software quality, hypermedia computing, expert systems, educational computing.

Larry Medsker, Professor; Ph.D., Indiana. Hybrid intelligent systems, expert systems, fuzzy logic, neural networks, database systems.

Mehdi Owrang, Associate Professor; Ph.D., Oklahoma. Database systems, expert systems, knowledge discovery in databases.

Angela Wu, Professor; Ph.D., Maryland. Computer vision systems and computational geometry.

ARIZONA STATE UNIVERSITY

COLLEGE OF ENGINEERING AND APPLIED SCIENCES
DEPARTMENT OF COMPUTER SCIENCE AND ENGINEERING

PROGRAMS OF STUDY

The Department of Computer Science and Engineering at Arizona State University offers three graduate degree programs: the M.C.S., M.S., and Ph.D. The M.C.S. is primarily a course work master's program. The M.S. combines course work and research at the master's level, and the Ph.D. is a research-intensive program. Highly qualified and research-motivated candidates are encouraged to apply for the Ph.D. program. Professionally inclined applicants are encouraged to apply for the M.C.S. program. Those wishing to follow a well-rounded education and research path choose the M.S. program.

RESEARCH FACILITIES

The department maintains various instructional laboratories with UNIX workstations (Sun, Silicon Graphics, DEC, etc.), Pentium PCs, and Macintosh computers. These laboratories support special applications required for computer science and engineering courses not available elsewhere on the ASU campus. The department has three laboratories with equipment and software specifically designed for instructions at the microprocessor level. They support Motorola and Intel processors and VLSI design.

The department has various research laboratories ranging from personal computers to UNIX and graphics workstations to parallel computers such as the IBM RISC workstation cluster and the Silicon Graphics Power Challenge Supercomputer located at ASU Information Technology in the Computing Commons.

All computers in the department are networked, with some research laboratories using high-speed ATM switches, Myrinet, mobile ATM, and 100 mbps LAN Hubs. The College of Engineering and Applied Sciences provides various servers to support client/server applications and development in the department. All computers in the department are connected through networking to ASU Information Technology. IT maintains the general-purpose computer laboratories throughout the campus.

FINANCIAL AID

Approximately 90 graduate teaching or research assistantships are available, including sponsored research support. Students should write to the Graduate Office for further information. Positions are highly competitive, and only exceptional new students are offered financial aid upon admission to the Ph.D. program. Arrangements are made for numerous graduate students who are supported around the campus.

COST OF STUDY

In 1996–97, registration and tuition for 12 hours or more were $970 per semester for Arizona residents; nonresidents paid $4154 per semester (prorated for fewer than 12 hours).

LIVING AND HOUSING COSTS

Limited on-campus housing is available for unmarried students. In 1997–98, room and board range from $2200 to $3830 per academic year. Twelve different meal plans are available (per week or per semester).

STUDENT GROUP

There are more than 42,000 students at Arizona State, including more than 10,500 graduate students. More than 1,766 of the 5,188 students in the College of Engineering and Applied Sciences are enrolled in graduate programs. There are 409 doctoral students enrolled in the College. More than 300 of the 900 students in the Department of Computer Science and Engineering are enrolled in the graduate programs. There are about 65 students enrolled in the Ph.D. program within the department.

STUDENT OUTCOMES

Excellent opportunities exist for graduates of the program, either in the local high-technology industry or in the major software/hardware organizations. The department fosters contacts with industry during graduate studies through colloquia, assistantships, and contacts with part-time graduate students who are full-time employees.

LOCATION

Arizona is well known for its scenic attractions, which range from desert to mountain woodlands, lakes, and streams. The urban community immediately surrounding Arizona State University thrives on high-technology industries that have large research and development staffs involved with computers, airborne electronics, semiconductors, turbines, energy production and conservation, food processing, and health services. Approximately 11,000 scientists and engineers are employed in the immediate vicinity of the University.

THE COLLEGE

The rapid growth of the College began in 1956 with the authorization of the B.S.E. degree. The faculty now numbers about 230. Enrollment in the graduate program in engineering is the largest among engineering colleges in the Rocky Mountain region. The College has several research centers targeted toward specific research areas.

APPLYING

Application forms may be obtained by writing to the Admissions Office of the Graduate College or by accessing the Web site http://www.asu.edu/forms/adm.html. At the beginning of the semester prior to the student's enrollment (by August 15 for spring semester enrollment or by January 15 for fall semester enrollment), the Graduate College should have received the application for admission and two copies of transcripts of all undergraduate and graduate work. If the applicant is an international student, then a TOEFL score is required before evaluation can begin. It is required that scores on the General Test of the Graduate Record Examinations also be submitted. Regular admission requires a grade point average of at least 3.0 (on a scale of 4.0) in the last two years of course work leading to the bachelor's degree.

Graduate admission to the M.C.S., M.S., and Ph.D. programs in the Department of Computer Science and Engineering is based on a competitive evaluation of the applicant's background. The evaluation includes scholastic background, experience, and performance on the GRE and TOEFL (for international applicants). The equivalent of a bachelor's degree in computer science in previous academic experience is expected. However, highly accomplished candidates from related disciplines are also considered. In addition, applicants to the Ph.D. program are expected to provide three letters of recommendation, a statement of purpose, and GRE General and Subject Test scores.

The department looks for demonstrable academic capabilities in the prior degree program. Most of the admitted applicants have GRE scores above 50 percent in verbal, 90 percent in quantitative, and 70 percent in analytical. Admitted applicants to the M.S. and M.C.S. programs typically have a grade point average of 3.25 out of 4.0. Admissible applicants to the Ph.D. program normally have a grade point average of 3.5 out of 4.0. In addition, nearly all successful international applicants score the Graduate College standard of 550 or higher on the TOEFL.

CORRESPONDENCE AND INFORMATION

Graduate Office
Department of Computer Science and Engineering
Arizona State University, Box 875406
Tempe, Arizona 85287-5406

Telephone: 602-965-3190
Fax: 602-965-2751
E-mail: cse.graduate.office@asu.edu
World Wide Web: http://www.eas.asu.edu/~csedept

ARIZONA STATE UNIVERSITY
THE FACULTY AND THEIR RESEARCH

Stephen S. Yau, Professor and Chair; Ph.D., Illinois at Urbana-Champaign, 1961. Software engineering, parallel processing and distributed computing systems, fault-tolerant computing systems.

Edward A. Ashcroft, Professor; Ph.D., Imperial College (London), 1970. Program verification, declarative language, intensional programming, high-level parallel programming language, language Lucid.

Rida A. Bazzi, Assistant Professor; Ph.D., Georgia Tech, 1994. Distributed computing, software engineering for distributed systems, fault-tolerance algorithms, computer vision.

Sourav Bhattacharya, Associate Professor; Ph.D., Minnesota, 1993. Networked and parallel computing, dependable communication, ATM networks.

Vernon Blackledge, Professor; Ph.D., Arizona State, 1969. Microprocessor systems.

K. Selcuk Candan, Assistant Professor; Ph.D., Maryland, 1997. Distributed multimedia authoring systems, video servers for video-on-demand systems, content-based video indexing, query/retrieval of multimedia data, security, query processing.

James S. Collofello, Professor; Ph.D., Northwestern, 1978. Software engineering, project management.

Partha Dasgupta, Associate Professor; Ph.D., SUNY at Stony Brook, 1984. Distributed operating systems, system software.

Suzanne W. Dietrich, Associate Professor; Ph.D., SUNY at Stony Brook, 1987. Databases, knowledge management, object management, active features.

Leonard Faltz, Associate Professor; Ph.D., Berkeley, 1977. Formal linguistics, computational linguistics.

Gerald E. Farin, Professor; Ph.D., Braunschweig (Germany), 1979. Computer-aided geometric design, NURBS.

Nicholas V. Findler, Emeritus Professor; Ph.D., Budapest Technical, 1956. Artificial intelligence, heuristic programming, expert systems, pattern recognition, information retrieval.

Sumit Ghosh, Associate Professor; Ph.D., Stanford, 1984. Networking and distributed algorithms.

Forouzan Golshani, Professor; Ph.D., Warwick (England), 1982. Multimedia information system, digital video processing, advanced databases, intelligent systems.

Chun-Nan Hsu, Assistant Professor; Ph.D., USC, 1996. Artificial intelligence, machine learning, knowledge discovery in databases, inductive logic programming, self-organizing/evolving databases.

Ben M. Huey, Associate Professor and Associate Chair for Undergraduate Program; Ph.D., Arizona, 1975. Language-based models for architecture, silicon compilation, design verification, automatic test generation.

Subbarao Kambhampati, Associate Professor; Ph.D., Maryland, 1989. Artificial intelligence, automated planning, machine learning.

William E. Lewis, Professor and Vice Provost for Information Technology; Ph.D., Northwestern, 1966. Analytical modeling, information systems.

Timothy E. Lindquist, Associate Professor; Ph.D., Iowa State, 1979. Programming language, software engineering, human-computer interaction, software engineering environments.

Donald S. Miller, Associate Professor; Ph.D., USC, 1972. Address space operating systems, distributed and multiprocessor operating systems, computer architecture, local area networks.

Gregory M. Nielson, Professor; Ph.D. Utah, 1970. Interactive design of curves and surfaces, multivariate data fitting, computer-aided geometric design, computer graphics, visualization of scientific computing.

Pearse O'Grady, Associate Professor; Ph.D., Arizona, 1969. Parallel processing, computer architecture, continuous system simulation.

Sethuraman Panchanathan, Associate Professor; Ph.D., Ottawa, 1989. Multimedia computing and communications, multimedia hardware architectures, VLSI architectures for real-time video processing, indexing/storage/browsing/retrieval of images and video.

David C. Pheanis, Associate Professor; Ph.D., Arizona State, 1974. Software/hardware interface in embedded microprocessor system, real-time system.

Alyn P. Rockwood, Associate Professor; Ph.D., Cambridge, 1988. Mechanical CAD, computer graphics.

Arunabha Sen, Associate Professor; Ph.D., South Carolina, 1987. Parallel computing, computer interconnection networks, combinatorial optimization.

Joseph E. Urban, Professor and Associate Chair for Research and Graduate Programs; Ph.D., Southwestern Louisiana, 1977. CASE, computer languages, data engineering, distributed computing, executable specification languages, software prototyping.

Susan D. Urban, Associate Professor; Ph.D., Southwestern Louisiana, 1987. Active database systems, heterogeneous database systems, object-oriented database systems.

Michael G. Wagner, Assistant Professor; Ph.D., Technical University of Vienna, 1994. Computer-aided geometric design, geometric modeling and processing, computer animation, theoretical kinematics, robotics and robot dynamics.

Marvin C. Woodfill, Professor; Ph.D., Iowa State, 1964. Digital logic, microcomputers.

RESEARCH CONCENTRATIONS

Artificial Intelligence
Internationally recognized in distributed planning systems, incremental planning, and applications. Funded by the NSF and the U.S. Coast Guard.

Computer-Aided Geometric Design/Graphics
Internationally recognized. The new IEEE *Transactions on Visualization and Computer Graphics* and the *CAGD Journal* edited at ASU. Funding from NSF, DOE, and NASA. Recent work in biomedical application (with University of Arizona Medical Center, Good Samaritan) is funded by the Flinn Foundation. A new project on multiresolution flow visualization is being funded by NASA/Ames.

Database/Multimedia Systems
There is a strong foundation in advanced database research and multimedia information systems. Current research is targeted toward commercial and manufacturing applications. Funded by NSF and industrial sources. Emerging national leadership.

Distributed Computing and Networking
Internationally recognized group working on distributed systems and networking, including distributed algorithms, fault-tolerant applications, software development, protocols, and security. Government and industrial support.

Microprocessors
Extensive research collaboration with industries such as AT&T, En. Gen. Inc., Enhanced Software Inc., Inter-Tel, Motorola, Municipal Services & Software, and Unizone, Inc.

Software Engineering
This internationally recognized group spans software life cycle and covers central as well as distributed and parallel systems. It has strong DoD and industrial support.

ARIZONA STATE UNIVERSITY

DEPARTMENT OF ELECTRICAL ENGINEERING

PROGRAMS OF STUDY

The department offers graduate programs leading to the Master of Science in Engineering, the Master of Science, and the Doctor of Philosophy degrees. Graduate courses and programs are offered in solid-state electronics, power engineering, electromagnetics, control systems, communications, signal processing, and coherent optics.

The Master of Science in Engineering degree (M.S.E.) is a professional degree. General requirements include 30 semester hours of graduate-level course work and a final examination.

The Master of Science degree (M.S.) is a research degree, culminating in a thesis. Course work includes 12 semester hours in the major and two 6-hour minors. Typically, two years of study are required to complete the degree. Only those who are granted graduate assistantships or who are outstanding students showing research potential are admitted to the M.S. program.

The Doctor of Philosophy degree (Ph.D.) is awarded based upon evidence of excellence in research leading to a scholarly dissertation that contributes to scientific knowledge. A total of 84 semester hours of graduate study beyond the bachelor's degree is required. A minimum of 30 semester hours of course work must be completed in residence at ASU. Twenty-four semester hours of research and dissertation complete the 84-hour program. A departmental qualifying examination is taken near the beginning of the program, and an individualized comprehensive examination is administered after all course work is completed.

RESEARCH FACILITIES

Centers of research excellence have been established in several areas. Those closely affiliated with electrical engineering are the Center for Solid State Electronics Research, the Center for System Science and Engineering, the Telecommunications Research Center, the Center for Advanced Control of Energy and Power Systems, and the Center for Innovation in Engineering Education.

The department maintains an active program of research and development supported by funds from federal agencies, private foundations, private corporations, and the University. Opportunities for research are offered to students whose goals are research, development, design, manufacturing, systems, engineering management, teaching, or other professional activities in electrical engineering. Significant research activities exist in solid-state electronics (nanoelectronics, optoelectronics, materials processing and science, neural VLSI networks, low-power electronics, and semiconductor theory), power engineering (power systems, power quality, system control, transmission and distribution, power electronics, high-voltage engineering, computer applications, and solar energy), electromagnetics (antennas, propagation, scattering, microwaves, radio frequency, and radar), coherent optics (lasers, integrated optics, and fiber optics), control systems (linear, nonlinear, real-time, adaptive, and robust control systems) and communications (digital communications, signal processing, wireless, and coding).

FINANCIAL AID

Teaching and research assistantships are available on a competitive basis. Annual stipends range from $8573 to $12,324. Teaching assistants usually supervise undergraduate teaching labs, while research assistants perform research applicable to their theses and dissertations. Out-of-state tuition is waived for all graduate assistants. Graduate Tuition Scholarships (GTS), which cover out-of-state tuition, and Graduate Academic Scholarships (GAS), which cover in-state registration fees, are also available on a competitive basis. An Industrial Fellows program provides part-time work experience in local industry.

Application forms for GTS, GAS, and assistantships should be submitted to the Department of Electrical Engineering. Loans and college work-study support are available through the Student Financial Assistance Office and require filing the FAFSA. The University Graduate Scholars (UGS) award provides research assistantships with a stipend of more than $18,000 and payment of all tuition and fees. Information about loans, work-study, and employment is available through Student Financial Assistance (telephone: 602-965-3355).

COST OF STUDY

The registration fee for full-time Arizona residents was $1940 per academic year in 1996–97. Out-of-state tuition was $8308.

LIVING AND HOUSING COSTS

The cost of room and board in University residences ranged from $2300 to $3830 for the 1996–97 school year. Abundant housing is also available near the campus at prices that vary widely.

STUDENT GROUP

There are approximately 413 graduate students in the department. About 150 of these are Ph.D. students. The remainder are master's degree candidates. The department televises many of its graduate courses to major local companies. The students attending the televised classes are included as regularly enrolled graduate students. The department also participates in the National Technological University (NTU) system of nationally televised classes.

LOCATION

The University's main campus is located in Tempe, Arizona, a city of 165,000 in the Phoenix metropolitan area. Strong academic programs and faculty are complemented by the attractions of year-round sunshine, cultural diversity on campus and in the community, and the resources of one of the nation's fastest-growing cities.

THE UNIVERSITY

Arizona State University (ASU) is the nation's fifth-largest university. Of ASU's 42,000 students, 10,500 are pursuing graduate study. ASU's main campus comprises nearly 700 acres and offers outstanding physical facilities to support the University's educational and research programs. Included within the more than 125 buildings are twelve colleges and schools, a University-wide computer system, seven libraries (including an $8-million building dedicated solely to the Noble Science and Engineering Library), and more than two dozen specialized centers of research. ASU's commitment to permanently establish itself as a major research institution is demonstrated by the construction and acquisition of research facilities and resources as well as the addition of new research faculty and staff.

APPLYING

All students must apply for admission through the Graduate College. For application forms, students should contact Graduate Admissions, Arizona State University, Tempe, Arizona 85287-1003 or call 602-965-6113. An applicant whose undergraduate degree is not from a program accredited by the Accreditation Board of Engineering and Technology (ABET) must submit scores from the Graduate Record Examinations (GRE) General Test. Students whose first language is not English must achieve a minimum score of 550 on the TOEFL.

CORRESPONDENCE AND INFORMATION

Director of Graduate Studies
Department of Electrical Engineering
Arizona State University
Tempe, Arizona 85287-5706

Telephone: 602-965-3590
Fax: 602-965-3837
E-mail: eeinfo@enpop1.eas.asu.edu
World Wide Web: http://www.eas.asu.edu:7001/

ARIZONA STATE UNIVERSITY

THE FACULTY AND THEIR RESEARCH

Control Systems

Peter E. Crouch, Dean, College of Engineering and Applied Sciences; Ph.D., Harvard. Nonlinear control systems, applied mathematics, semiconductor manufacturing, power systems.

Walter T. Higgins Jr., Professor; Ph.D., Arizona. Digital control systems.

Armando A. Rodriguez, Associate Professor; Ph.D., MIT. Robust and nonlinear distributed control theory.

Jennie Si, Associate Professor; Ph.D., Notre Dame. Control theory, learning systems.

Konstantinos S. Tsakalis, Associate Professor; Ph.D., USC. Adaptive and nonlinear control systems, semiconductor manufacturing.

Electromagnetics, Antennas, Microwaves, Radar, Coherent Optics

James T. Aberle, Associate Professor; Ph.D., Massachusetts. Computational electromagnetics, conformal antennas, electromagnetic scattering, radar cross section, numerical techniques.

Constantine A. Balanis, Professor, Regents' Professor of Engineering, and Director, Telecommunications Research Center; Ph.D., Ohio State. Antennas, propagation, scattering, computational electromagnetics, transients in MMICs.

Samir M. El-Ghazaly, Associate Professor; Ph.D., Texas at Austin. Microwave active and passive devices, electromagnetics, semiconductor device simulation, numerical techniques.

El-Badawy A. El-Sharawy, Associate Professor; Ph.D., Massachusetts. Printed microwave circuits, anisotropic devices, numerical techniques, composite material antennas.

Joseph C. Palais, Professor and Director, Graduate Studies in Electrical Engineering; Ph.D., Michigan. Fiber optics, optical communications, fiber sensors, holography, lasers.

George W. Pan, Professor; Ph.D., Kansas. Packaging and interconnections, MCMS/MMICS, rough surface scattering, computational EM.

Power Engineering

Ravi S. Gorur, Professor; Ph.D., Windsor. High-voltage engineering, insulating materials and systems for electric power, smart materials, pulse power.

Gerald T. Heydt, Professor; Ph.D., Purdue. Electric power quality, power systems.

Keith E. Holbert, Associate Professor; Ph.D., Tennessee, Knoxville. Power plant modeling, dynamics and diagnostics, signal validation, noise analysis, instrument calibration reduction.

George G. Karady, Professor and SRP Professor of Engineering; Ph.D., Budapest University for Technical Sciences. Power electronics, high-voltage engineering, variable speed drives, thyristor control, power supplies, electric insulation, neural networks for power, pollution flashover.

Daniel J. Tylavsky, Associate Professor; Ph.D., Penn State. Power systems analysis, computational methods, large electrical systems.

Signal Processing and Communication Systems

Chaitali Chakrabarti, Associate Professor; Ph.D., Maryland. VLSI architectures for digital signal processing.

Douglas Cochran, Associate Professor; Ph.D., Harvard. Mathematical signal analysis, signal detection, wavelet analysis, sonar.

Lina J. Karam, Assistant Professor; Ph.D., Georgia Tech. Multidimensional digital signal processing, image and video processing and coding.

Darryl R. Morrell, Associate Professor; Ph.D., Brigham Young. Estimation and detection, stochastic filtering, statistical signal processing, epistemology, target tracking, data compression, image compression.

John S. Sadowsky, Associate Professor; Ph.D., Wisconsin. Digital communications, statistical communications and information theory.

Andreas S. Spanias, Associate Professor; Ph.D., West Virginia. Digital signal processing, adaptive filters, speech processing and coding, active noise control.

Solid-State Electronics

Lex A. Akers, Professor; Ph.D., Texas Tech. Neural networks, VLSI design, small geometry MOSFETs.

David R. Allee, Assistant Professor; Ph.D., Stanford. Nanometer scale fabrication, nanolithography, low-power analog circuit design.

Thomas A. DeMassa, Professor; Ph.D., Michigan. Semiconductor electronic devices, modeling.

David K. Ferry, Regents' Professor of Engineering; Ph.D., Texas at Austin. Nanoelectronics, lithography, and quantum structured devices.

Stephen Goodnick, Department Chair and Professor; Ph.D., Colorado State. Semiconductor transport, quantum and nanostructure device technology, and high frequency devices.

Edwin W. Greeneich, Associate Professor; Ph.D., Berkeley. Semiconductor device modeling, analog integrated circuits, BiCMOS devices and circuits.

Robert O. Grondin, Associate Professor; Ph.D., Michigan. Small high-speed devices, physics of electrical engineering.

Michael N. Kozicki, Professor; Ph.D., Edinburgh. Semiconductor processing, manufacturing, nanoelectronics, rapid thermal processing, lithographic materials, vapor etching.

Ronald J. Roedel, Professor; Ph.D., UCLA. Semiconductor materials and devices.

Dieter K. Schroder, Professor; Ph.D., Illinois at Urbana-Champaign. Semiconductor devices, characterization, low-power electronics, defects.

C. C. Shen, Associate Professor; Ph.D., Stanford. Photovoltaic devices.

Jun Shen, Associate Professor; Ph.D., Notre Dame. Solid-state device physics.

Brian J. Skromme, Associate Professor; Ph.D., Illinois at Urbana–Champaign. Compound semiconductor materials and devices.

Yong-Hang Zhang, Associate Professor; Ph.D., Max-Planck Institute. Semiconductor materials and devices.

AZUSA PACIFIC UNIVERSITY

DEPARTMENT OF COMPUTER SCIENCE
GRADUATE PROGRAMS

PROGRAMS OF STUDY

The Department offers the Master of Software Engineering (M.S.E.) and the Master of Science (M.S.) in applied computer science and technology. The department also offers three undergraduate programs. The Master of Science in applied computer science and technology is a practical and applied degree with seven program emphases. A minimum of 40 semester units is required to complete the Master of Science program with a capstone option. Without the capstone, 46 units are needed. Each emphasis requires core course work totaling 24 units, plus 16 units in the emphasis (including a capstone project) or 22 units in the emphasis without a capstone project. These emphases are client/server, computer information systems, end-user support, inter-emphasis, software engineering, technical programming, and telecommunications.

The department also offers graduate certificate programs in several emphasis areas. Each certificate comprises 18 units of graduate course work that may also be applied to the appropriate master's degree. Graduate certificate programs include client/server, which provides for a career in networked client/server database applications; computer information systems, which provides a foundation for a career in computer information systems; end-user training and support, which provides knowledge and skills needed for a career in end-user support; software engineering, which addresses current software engineering knowledge, research, and practice; technical programming, which focuses on skills and knowledge for employment as a technical programmer; and telecommunications, which teaches practical and theoretical networking and telecommunications.

The Master of Software Engineering (M.S.E.) degree is designed for those engaged in the development and maintenance of large-scale software products. The M.S.E. program addresses the three key components of software development: people, process, and technology. The M.S.E. program requires 30 units but has higher prerequisites than the 46-unit M.S. program.

Graduate computer science programs at Azusa Pacific University are offered in a nine-week half-semester format with five terms per year. Because the graduate program is geared toward working professionals, classes usually meet one evening per week from 5:30 p.m. to 9:45 p.m., with some classes scheduled on Saturdays. Six units per term is considered a full load, but students may take more or less than that.

RESEARCH FACILITIES

The computer science department operates six computer science laboratories (including the telecommunications lab, the multimedia lab, the advanced technologies lab, the computer engineering lab, two PC labs and one Macintosh lab) and also shares access through the University's T1 line as well as access to a variety of software available on the various department servers. Most workstations are Pentium class machines running multiple operating systems, including Windows 95, OS/2, DOS, and UNIX. The University library system include extensive book collections, numerous electronic search facilities, and other research support resources.

FINANCIAL AID

Students at the University are eligible for financial aid in the form of employment, California Graduate Fellowships, and Federal Stafford, Federal Perkins, and CLAS loans. For more information, students should contact the Office of Student Financial Services.

COST OF STUDY

Tuition for the M.S. and the M.A. programs is $370 per unit in 1997–98 and $500 per unit for most M.S.E. courses.

LIVING AND HOUSING COSTS

There is no on-campus housing offered for graduate students attending Azusa Pacific University, but private housing is widely available in the area at various prices.

STUDENT GROUP

Approximately 2,100 graduate students are enrolled in the various master's and doctoral programs at the University in fall 1997. Approximately fifty percent are women. More than 200 students are enrolled in graduate computer science programs.

STUDENT OUTCOMES

More than 200 graduate students are enrolled in computer science department graduate programs. The student population is divided between full-time students and working professionals. Working professional frequently obtain promotions during the course of their studies, generally avoiding company downsizing and layoffs. Most students find excellent employment in their professions soon after graduation. Graduates are working in every aspect of computer science and technology, with positions as network administrators, software engineers, technical programmers, software developers, consultants, client/server specialists, and in many other areas.

LOCATION

Azusa Pacific University is located 30 miles east of downtown Los Angeles. The area offers students a wide variety of cultural, recreational, intellectual, and athletic opportunities. The climate is moderate.

THE UNIVERSITY

Azusa Pacific University, founded in 1899, is coeducational, independent, nondenominational Christian university. APU remains committed to the goal of fostering each student's personal, spiritual, physical, and academic growth.

APPLYING

Applicants for master's programs must hold a bachelor's degree from an accredited university or college with a minimum GPA of 3.0. Applicants must file a university and department application, pay a nonrefundable application fee of $45, and have all materials sent to the Graduate Admissions Office. The University operates under a policy of continuous admission. Students should call or write for an information packet with applications.

CORRESPONDENCE AND INFORMATION

Graduate Admissions Office
Azusa Pacific University
901 East Alosta
P.O. Box 7000
Azusa, California 91702-7000
Telephone: 800-TALK-APU (toll-free)

Dr. Samuel E. Sambasivam, Chairman
Department of Computer Science
Azusa Pacific University
901 East Alosta
P.O. Box 7000
Azusa, California 91702-7000
Telephone 626-815-5310
E-mail: cs@apu.edu
World Wide Web: http://www.apu.edu/~cs

AZUSA PACIFIC UNIVERSITY
THE FACULTY AND THEIR RESEARCH

Gerald Boerner, M.A. (experimental psychology). Professor Boerner has more than twenty years of significant experience in various aspects of computing. He has taught for APU since 1986. He is widely recognized for his expertise in end-user support, including applications software on many computer platforms. His experience includes educational evaluation, research and testing, data processing, telecommunications and networking, printing, desktop publishing, customized training programs, and extensive university teaching. Professor Boerner coordinates the end-user support emphasis and telecommunications.

Thomas Plew, Ph.D. (instructional systems technology); B.R.E. religious education. He has more than ten years of teaching experience. He possesses diverse experience, skills, and qualifications, including several management positions, a senior pastorate, curriculum and course development; evaluation, selection, and implementation of computer systems; and instructional development and delivery of a variety of courses in programming, software engineering, systems analysis and design, software applications, artificial intelligence, and computer theory courses. His professional involvement includes the development and management of the first computer access training center for the blind and visually impaired in the United States. Professor Plew has numerous significant presentations and publications to his credit. He is a member of the Association of Computing Machinery, the American Educational Research Association, the National Society for Performance and Instruction, and the Sigma Zeta Honor Society. Professor Plew coordinates the computer information systems emphasis.

Samuel E. Sambasivam, Chairman, Department of Computer Science; Ph.D. (mathematics), M.S. (computer science). Professor Sambasivam has done extensive research, publications, and presentations in both computer science and mathematics. He has taught computer science courses for ten years at three universities in the U.S. He also has taught mathematics courses for fourteen years at five universities, both in the U.S. and in India. Professor Sambasivam was the director of a regional Association for Computing Machinery (ACM) Programming Contest for six years. He has developed and introduced several new courses for computer science majors for eight years. Professor Sambasivam teaches database management systems, information structures and algorithm design, microcomputer programming with C++, discrete structures, client/server applications development, advanced database applications, applied artificial intelligence, and other courses. Professor Sambasivam is a voting member of the ACM for the Kappa Mu Epsilon and the Upsilon Pi Epsilon. He is named in Marquis's *Who's Who in the World, Who's Who in America,* and *Who's Who in the Midwest.* Professor Sambasivam coordinates the client/server technology emphasis for the Department of Computer Science.

Wendel Scarbrough, M.A. (educational administration). Professor Scarbrough has extensive course work in mathematics and computing from six other universities including the Universities of Texas, New Mexico, and Oklahoma. Professor Scarbrough has more than forty years of varied teaching and computing experience, including analysis, design, and implementation of computer systems; software engineering; scientific programming; information systems management; and computer consulting. He has more than twenty years of instructional design, including development, implementation, and teaching of several major programs with more than fifty different computer courses. He has also taught a wide variety of mathematics courses. After joining the faculty of Azusa Pacific University in 1983, Professor Scarbrough developed the undergraduate computer science program in 1984, the Master of Educational Computing in 1985, and the Master of Science in applied computer science and technology in 1987. He has received numerous awards and fellowships, including several National Science Fellowships, the Walter Anderson Fellowship, the Chase Sawtell Inspirational Teacher Award (1991), and the Uncommon Faculty Citizen Award (1996). Professor Scarbrough is a member of the ACM (Association of Computer Machinists) and the IEEE (Institute of Electrical and Electronics Engineers) Computer Society.

Carol Stoker, Ph.D. in education. Among Professor Stoker's many contributions to Azusa Pacific University, she developed numerous courses and was the leader in the redesign of the undergraduate computer science curriculum in 1990. She taught a variety of computer science courses and other courses. Professor Stoker is a member of the faculty senate of Azusa Pacific University, the American Educational Researchers Association, the American Psychological Association, and the Computer Using Educators' Association. Professor Stoker helps coordinate the undergraduate computer science program.

Peter A. Yoon, Ph.D. (computer science). Professor Yoon has done extensive research, publications, and presentations in the mathematics and computer fields. His experience includes the development of an algorithm for the generation of synthetic range-Doppler map for accurate image analysis using the radial basis functions multidimensional interpolation approach. Professor Yoon taught mathematics at Purdue University for three years. His publications includes "Modifying the singular value decomposition on the connection machine" (*International Journal of High Speed Computing*). He worked for IBM Corporation for three years as a systems programmer. He also sponsors a Christian Fellowship for International Students.

BOSTON UNIVERSITY

COLLEGE OF ENGINEERING
DEPARTMENT OF ELECTRICAL AND COMPUTER ENGINEERING

PROGRAMS OF STUDY

Ph.D. and M.S. programs prepare students for the application of state-of-the-art analysis and design methods to research and development problems in electrical and computer engineering. Primary research areas in the department include photonics, signal processing and recognition, electronic materials and devices, high-performance computing applications, ionospheric physics, computer hardware testing and fault-tolerant design, communication networks, multimedia, microprocessor development, and software engineering. Both post-bachelor's and post-master's Ph.D. tracks are available, leading to degrees in electrical, computer, and systems engineering. Ph.D. study requires 32 credits (eight courses) beyond the M.S. requirements. Ph.D. study also requires at least two consecutive semesters of residence, passing qualifying exams, and the dissertation. M.S. degrees are offered in electrical and computer systems engineering. The M.S. programs require a minimum of 36 credits (nine courses), including the completion of a thesis or project, and can be completed by a full-time student in one calendar year.

RESEARCH FACILITIES

Facilities include the following research laboratories: applied electromagnetics; complex systems dynamics; design and testing of computer and communications systems; embedded systems; functorial electromagnetics; high-performance computing; integrated circuit fabrication; knowledge-based signal processing; magnetic and optical devices; microprocessor research; liquid crystal display; molecular beam epitaxy; multidimensional signal processing; multimedia communications; near-field optical microscopy/spectroscopy; picosecond spectroscopy; quantum optics; radio communications and plasma research; semiconductor device research; sensors, actuators, and micromechanics; signal processing and interpretation; space sciences; speech research; VLSI process modeling and characterization; and VLSI research. These laboratories are complemented by a superb computational/networking environment with equipment ranging from personal computers to multimedia workstations to a 38-processor SGI Power Challenge Array scalable parallel supercomputer. Many ECE students also conduct their research in interdisciplinary centers such as those in photonics, computational science, space physics, and adaptive systems. In 1997, the department's facilities will expand into a new building of a quarter million square feet.

FINANCIAL AID

A full range of financial aid is available, including Presidential University Graduate Fellowships, Dean's Scholarships, GAANN Fellowships in Photonics, graduate teaching fellowships, research assistantships, and various scholarships. In 1997–98, teaching fellowships provide stipends of $10,500 per academic year and require approximately 20 hours a week of instructional duties. Recipients receive a tuition waiver for 16 credits. Research assistantship stipends are comparable to or higher than those of teaching fellowships and are also supplemented by tuition waivers. University and Dean's scholarships range up to $33,500 (including stipend and tuition) per year; the department encourages GEM scholars to apply. Federally funded work-study applications may be obtained from the Graduate Programs Office. Federal Stafford Student Loan applicants must submit a Free Application for Federal Student Aid (FAFSA) to the College Scholarship Office.

COST OF STUDY

In 1997–98, tuition and fees for full-time study are $21,970. For part-time students, the cost is $687 per credit hour.

LIVING AND HOUSING COSTS

Privately owned apartments or rooms are readily available. Living expenses for a single student are estimated at $12,535 for the 1997–98 nine-month academic year.

STUDENT GROUP

The department has 64 students in the M.S. programs and 67 students pursuing the Ph.D. In 1996–97, 19 ECE students were supported as graduate teaching fellows; another 47 were supported as research assistants.

STUDENT OUTCOMES

Most graduates of the M.S. programs enter industry. With a growing base of funded research, increasing numbers are pursuing Ph.D. research at Boston University.

LOCATION

Boston offers a sophisticated environment with world-renowned academic and scientific resources. The area's seminar and colloquium programs allow students to participate at the cutting edge of research. Access to nearby concentrations of high-technology industry provides another vital element.

THE UNIVERSITY AND THE DEPARTMENT

Boston University, incorporated in 1869, is an independent, coeducational, nonsectarian university, fully open to women and to all minority groups. Its 23,672 full-time students and 3,009 faculty members make it one of the largest independent universities in the world. The department is the largest in the College of Engineering and has experienced remarkable growth over the last decade. The faculty of the department has sought to build a stronger research program while maintaining its traditional commitment to the educational experience of its students. Interaction with local industry has created a focus on state-of-the-art educational and research issues. The other departments in the College are Biomedical Engineering, Manufacturing Engineering, and Aerospace and Mechanical Engineering.

APPLYING

Applicants to the M.S., post-bachelor's Ph.D., and post-master's Ph.D. programs should show a high degree of scholarship in an undergraduate program in engineering or science at an accredited college or university. Outstanding post-bachelor's candidates can be admitted directly to Ph.D. studies. Students desiring financial aid should apply by January 15 for fall admission and October 1 for spring. Applications for admission without financial aid can be submitted until April 1 and October 15, respectively. Required credentials include official transcripts, specific letters of recommendation, and GRE General Test scores. There are more requirements for international applicants, including the TOEFL.

CORRESPONDENCE AND INFORMATION

For program information:
ECE Department-Graduate Programs
Boston University
44 Cummington Street
Boston, Massachusetts 02215

Telephone: 617-353-1048
Fax: 617-353-6440
E-mail: ecegrad@enga.bu.edu
World Wide Web: http://www-eng.bu.edu/ECE

For application forms:
Graduate Programs
Boston University
110 Cummington Street
Boston, Massachusetts 02215

Telephone: 617-353-9760
Fax: 617-353-0259
E-mail: eng-grad@bu.edu

BOSTON UNIVERSITY
THE FACULTY AND THEIR RESEARCH

Dimiter Avresky, Assistant Professor; Ph.D., Russian Academy of Sciences. Software implemented fault tolerance in parallel and distributed systems, verification, testing and validation of software protocols, performance analysis of networks, parallel programming.

Paul Blasche, Associate Professor; Ph.D., Ohio. Electro-optical sensor systems and components and their applications, including sensor systems for target acquisition and tracking, navigation and guidance, and remote sensing.

John Brackett, Professor; Ph.D., Purdue. Software requirements definition and software architecture; software testing, especially of large object-oriented software systems.

Richard Brower, Professor; Ph.D., Berkeley. Quantum field theory, strings, molecular dynamics.

David Castañon, Associate Professor; Ph.D., MIT. Stochastic control, estimation, optimization, image processing, parallel and distributed computing.

Krish Chakrabarty, Assistant Professor; Ph.D., Michigan. Design automation, synthesis, verification, and testing of VLSI systems, computer architecture, and fault-tolerant computing.

Scott Dunham, Associate Professor; Ph.D., Stanford. Modeling and simulation of VLSI fabrication processes, point defect interaction in semiconductors, kinetics of extended defect evolution.

Solomon Eisenberg, Associate Professor; Ph.D., MIT. Electrokinetic and other electromagnetic interactions in connective tissues and membranes.

Carol Espy-Wilson, Assistant Professor; Ph.D., MIT. Speech recognition, speech processing, acoustic phonetics, and digital signal processing.

Azza Fahim, Research Assistant Professor; Ph.D., Cairo. Electric machines, computations in electromagnetics.

Leopold Felsen, Professor; D.E.E., Polytechnic of Brooklyn. Wave propagation and diffraction in various disciplines, high-frequency asymptotics, wave-oriented data processing and imaging.

Roscoe Giles, Associate Professor; Ph.D., Stanford. Advanced computer architectures, distributed and parallel computing.

Bennett Goldberg, Associate Professor and Associate Professor of Physics; Ph.D., Brown. Optical processes in semiconductors and devices, near-field scanning optical microscopy and spectroscopy, low-temperature magneto-optics and transport of quantum confined electron systems.

Mark Horenstein, Associate Professor; Ph.D., MIT. Applied electromagnetics and electrostatics, instrumentation and measurement, microelectronics.

Allyn Hubbard, Associate Professor; Ph.D., Wisconsin. VLSI circuit design: digital, analog, subthreshold analog, biCMOS, and CMOS; special-purpose integrated circuits: neural-net, image processing, sonar signal processing DNA and large-molecule analysis, neural tissue interface; auditory research: theory and models of mammalian auditory signal processing, electronic ears.

Floyd Humphrey, Research Professor; Ph.D., Caltech. Magnetic materials, magnetic digital storage.

W. Clem Karl, Assistant Professor; Ph.D., MIT. Multidimensional and multiscale statistical signal and image processing, geometric estimation, medical signal and image processing.

Mark Karpovsky, Professor; Ph.D., Leningrad Electrotechnical Institute. Testing and diagnosis of computer hardware, fault-tolerant computing, error correcting codes.

Thomas Kincaid, Professor; Ph.D., MIT. Signal and image processing, neurodynamics, nondestructive testing.

Robert Kotiuga, Associate Professor; Ph.D., McGill. Mathematical and computational methods in electromagnetics.

Min-Chang Lee, Associate Professor; Ph.D., California, San Diego. Radio communications, applied plasma physics and ionospheric radio physics.

Lev Levitin, Distinguished Professor; Ph.D., Moscow. Information theory, VLSI diagnostics and fault detection.

Thomas D. C. Little, Assistant Professor; Ph.D., Syracuse. Multimedia computing, computer networking, software engineering.

Michael Mendillo, Professor and Professor of Astronomy; Ph.D., Boston University. Instrumentation for low-light imaging of astronomical targets, digital image processing, optical tomography, Monte Carlo simulations of extended atmospheres of Jupiter and the Moon.

Theodore Moustakas, Professor; Ph.D., Columbia. III-V nitrides, semiconductor properties and devices (visible-UV emitters, detectors, and high-temperature transistors).

Syed Hamid Nawab, Associate Professor; Ph.D., MIT. Digital signal processing and signal processing for real-time, low-power, and communications applications.

Truong Q. Nguyen, Assistant Professor; Ph.D., Caltech. Digital signal processing; image processing; signal compression and analysis; wavelets, filter banks, and applications.

William Oliver, Associate Professor; Ph.D., Illinois. Upper-atmosphere/ionosphere physics, radar experimentation and data analysis, global atmosphere modeling and simulation.

Mari Ostendorf, Associate Professor; Ph.D., Stanford. Statistical modeling for signal interpretation, enhancement, and data compression, particularly speech processing.

David Perreault, Professor; Ph.D., Purdue. Nonlinear networks, computer-aided design, microprocessors, distributed-signal networks.

Tatyana Roziner, Associate Professor; Ph.D., Moscow Scientific Research Institute. Digital design, testing and diagnostics of computer hardware, fault-tolerant computing.

Michael Ruane, Associate Professor; Ph.D., MIT. Magneto-optical materials and devices, optical systems, communications.

Bahaa Saleh, Professor and Department Chairman; Ph.D., MIT. Nonlinear and quantum optics, optical communication, liquid crystal displays, image processing.

Fred Schubert, Professor; Doktor Ingenieur, Stuttgart (Germany). Technology and physics of lasers and light-emitting diodes, concepts for novel semiconductor devices.

Alexander Sergienko, Assistant Professor; Ph.D., Moscow. Femtosecond quantum optics, fundamental interactions of quantum light with matter, presize optical measurement and quantum metrology, quantum communications and quantum cryptography.

Thomas Skinner, Associate Professor; Ph.D., Boston University. Microprocessors, computer networks, operating systems, distributed systems, object-oriented programming.

Johannes Smits, Associate Professor; Ph.D., Twente University of Technology (Netherlands). Micromechanics, microsensors and actuators, device fabrication.

Malvin Teich, Professor; Ph.D., Cornell. Quantum optics, photonics, lightwave systems, fractal point processes in physical and biological systems, information transmission in biological sensory systems.

Tommaso Toffoli, Research Professor; Ph.D., Michigan. Programmable matter: design and use of fine-grained mesh computers; information mechanics; fundamental connections between physics and computation; quantum computation; information theory of fine-grained processes.

M. Selim Unlü, Assistant Professor; Ph.D., Illinois at Urbana-Champaign. Design, processing, characterization, and simulation of optoelectronic devices, resonant cavity enhanced photonic devices, near-field optical microscopy and spectroscopy.

Richard Vidale, Professor; Ph.D., Wisconsin. Modeling and simulation, software engineering, real-time systems.

Moe Wasserman, Associate Professor; Ph.D., Michigan. Semiconductor processing, electronic circuits.

BROWN UNIVERSITY

DEPARTMENT OF COMPUTER SCIENCE

PROGRAMS OF STUDY

The Department of Computer Science at Brown University offers a full range of programs of research and education at the graduate level, leading to the Sc.M. and Ph.D. degrees. The department emphasizes a combination of theory and practice in computer science; students develop considerable practical and analytical skills as well as an appreciation for the importance of theory. The informal atmosphere of the department together with its facilities and programs, which are typical of a much larger department, provide an attractive setting for graduate education.

RESEARCH FACILITIES

Brown has remarkably good and easily accessible computer facilities. The department manages a large network of more than 190 Sun SPARCstation-10 Model 41 workstations for research and instruction. Other systems owned by the department include a number of DECstations, Hewlett-Packard 9000s, a variety of systems from SGI, several IBM RS/6000s, and a number of Macintoshes and PCs. All workstations are connected to a department-wide Ethernet and to the Internet. Faculty and students have developed a large number of tools for the effective use of graphics workstations, some of which are used in instruction. Other computing resources available on campus include IBM PCs, Macs, and an IBM 3090, the University's central facility.

FINANCIAL AID

Fellowships and scholarships are available for qualified full-time graduate students. In addition, a number of research assistants and teaching assistants are appointed annually. Summer support can usually be provided for students working on research projects.

COST OF STUDY

Tuition and fees for full-time students are $22,592 for the 1997–98 academic year. Teaching assistants and research assistants are charged three quarters of this amount and are reimbursed for tuition charges.

LIVING AND HOUSING COSTS

The cost of living in Providence is below the national average. Housing for graduate students is available in the Graduate Center for $4240 for the 1997–98 academic year.

STUDENT GROUP

Brown University has about 5,500 undergraduate and 1,450 graduate students, including those in the medical program. The Department of Computer Science has about 100 full-time graduate students, of whom about 50 receive financial support from the University.

LOCATION

Brown University is located in a pleasant residential area of Providence, a medium-sized city 1 hour from Boston and 3 hours from New York. Seminars, colloquia, and other events are presented by the University and the nearby Rhode Island School of Design. Many cultural resources, including concert halls, theaters, museums, and art galleries, are available. The possibilities for recreational activity are numerous. Excellent indoor and outdoor University-owned sports facilities, Rhode Island's many beaches, and New England ski areas are available.

THE UNIVERSITY

Brown University is the seventh-oldest institution of higher learning in America. Founded as Rhode Island College in Warren, Rhode Island, in 1764, it moved to its present location on College Hill, overlooking the capital city of Providence, in 1770. In 1804, it took its present name of Brown University in recognition of a gift. Pembroke College, the women's college associated with Brown, was merged with the University in 1971. Today, the University consists of the undergraduate college, the Graduate School, and the Program in Medicine.

APPLYING

The deadline for receipt of applications, including GRE scores and letters of recommendation, is January 1 for the fall term. Applications are considered after this date, but the late applicant may be at a disadvantage in the awarding of financial support.

Applicants are urged to express clearly their area or areas of academic and research interest; applicants who do not provide such information are difficult to evaluate for admission.

CORRESPONDENCE AND INFORMATION

For information:

Graduate Representative
Department of Computer Science
Brown University
Box 1910
Providence, Rhode Island 02912

Telephone: 401-863-7600
E-mail: gradinfo@cs.brown.edu.
Further information is available via anonymous ftp in
wilma.cs.brown.edu:pub/info.

For applications:

Graduate School Admissions Office
Brown University
Box 1867
Providence, Rhode Island 02912

BROWN UNIVERSITY
THE FACULTY AND THEIR RESEARCH

Eugene Charniak, Professor and Chairman; Ph.D., MIT, 1972. Artificial intelligence, natural-language processing.

Thomas L. Dean, Professor; Ph.D., Yale, 1986. Artificial intelligence, deductive retrieval systems, logic programming, planning, robot problem solving.

Thomas W. Doeppner Jr., Associate Professor (Research); Ph.D., Princeton, 1977. Operating systems, concurrent and distributed programming.

Maurice Herlihy, Associate Professor; Ph.D., MIT, 1984. Concurrent and distributed systems.

John F. Hughes, Assistant Professor; Ph.D., Berkeley, 1982. Computer graphics, low-dimensional topology.

Leslie Kaelbling, Associate Professor; Ph.D., Stanford, 1990. Artificial intelligence.

Philip N. Klein, Associate Professor; Ph.D., MIT, 1988. Algorithms, parallel processing, combinatorial optimization, graph theory.

Robert H. B. Netzer, Assistant Professor; Ph.D., Wisconsin–Madison, 1991. Parallel and distributed program debugging, languages and compilers for distributed computing.

Franco P. Preparata, An Wang Professor; Dr.Ing., Rome, 1959. Design and analysis of algorithms, computational geometry, parallel computation.

Steven P. Reiss, Professor; Ph.D., Yale, 1977. Theory of programming, graphical programming, programming languages and systems, semantics, compilers, database management systems, computational geometry.

John E. Savage, Professor; Ph.D., MIT, 1965. Analysis of parallel and serial algorithms, complexity theory, VLSI systems and theory.

Roberto Tamassia, Associate Professor; Ph.D., Illinois, 1988. Computational geometry, analysis of algorithms, representation of graphical objects.

Andries van Dam, Professor; Ph.D., Pennsylvania, 1966. Computer graphics, multimedia document preparation systems, workstations in research and education.

Pascal Van Hentenryck, Associate Professor; Ph.D., Namur (Belgium), 1987. Constraint logic programming.

Peter Wegner, Professor; Ph.D., London, 1968. Programming languages, software engineering.

Stanley B. Zdonik Jr., Professor; Ph.D., MIT, 1983. Database management systems, software engineering, object-oriented systems.

CALIFORNIA INSTITUTE OF TECHNOLOGY

PROGRAM IN COMPUTER SCIENCE

PROGRAM OF STUDY

Graduate study leading to M.S. and Ph.D. degrees in computer science is oriented principally toward doctoral research. The first two years are typically devoted to course work and master's thesis research as preliminaries to the candidacy examination and Ph.D. thesis research. The program requires a minimum of three academic years of residence.

Students have unusual opportunities for research in the following areas: VLSI systems; concurrent (parallel) computation; computer graphics; theory of computation; computational complexity and information theory; programming languages; semantics; programming methods and correctness; the human-machine interface, including natural language; computer vision; and computer-aided design. Research projects frequently involve work in several of these areas, as well as connections with fields such as mathematics, physics, biology, linguistics, and electrical engineering.

RESEARCH FACILITIES

The Department of Computer Science and its research groups operate extensive computing facilities that are interconnected by a department network, which includes connections to the national research networks. All faculty members, graduate students, research staff, support staff, and the librarian have terminals, personal computers, or workstations for access to these computing facilities.

In addition to eighty conventional computers and workstations, most of which are UNIX systems, the research groups maintain facilities that are important to particular research areas. The department computers include twenty-five Intel Pentiums, fifteen HP 715 and seven HP 735 workstations, fifteen Indy workstations, and twenty-five SPARCstations. The Intel Touchstone Delta System and an IBM SP2 are also on the department network for system and application experiments. The computer graphics laboratory is the Caltech site of the NSF STC for Computer Graphics and Scientific Visualization and is associated with Caltech's Biological Imaging Center and computational biology projects in the Beckman Institute. The lab is well-equipped with high-performance workstations and has specialized equipment for fast rendering of models and generating computer animation sequences. Software used in courses and research activities includes compilers and/or interpreters for thirty programming languages, extensive VLSI computer-aided design and analysis tools, TeX typesetting software, and libraries of advanced computer graphics routines. The digital systems and VLSI laboratories are equipped with complete facilities for constructing experimental systems and for testing and probing integrated circuits. Students also have access to facilities provided by the NSF center for research in parallel computing.

The computer science library subscribes to eighty journals in the computer science field and maintains collections of technical reports from the department and computer science departments at other universities, as well as text and reference books.

FINANCIAL AID

Most computer science graduate students receive financial aid from one or more of the following sources: research assistantships, teaching assistantships, and fellowships. In 1996–97, full-time research and teaching assistantships for the academic year paid stipends ranging from $15,000 to $18,000 and also covered tuition expenses. Students are also encouraged to apply for outside fellowships, which can be supplemented by the department.

Summer research appointments on campus are available, or students may choose to accept summer positions in industry.

COST OF STUDY

Tuition, health plan coverage, and other graduate student fees for the academic year 1997–98 are approximately $18,600. A typical figure for books and supplies is $900 a year.

LIVING AND HOUSING COSTS

Single-student dormitory-style accommodations in the on-campus Graduate Houses cost $339.30 a month for a private room; single-student apartment-style accommodations (four bedrooms, two bathrooms) in the Catalina Complex I cost $396 a month per student, plus utilities. Married- and single-student apartment-style accommodations (two bedrooms, one bathroom) in Catalina Complex II and III cost $865.80 a month per family or $432 a month per single student, plus utilities. Single apartments (one bedroom, one bath, one double bed) in Complex III cost $727 per month, plus utilities.

STUDENT GROUP

Currently enrolled at Caltech are 900 undergraduate students, including 237 women, and 1,092 graduate students, including 235 women. There are 32 students currently enrolled in the graduate program in computer science.

LOCATION

Pasadena, a city of approximately 125,000, is located about 10 miles northeast of Los Angeles. The Institute, although located in the center of a residential district, is within a few blocks of shopping facilities. Pasadena and the Metropolitan Los Angeles area provide abundant cultural and recreational opportunities.

THE INSTITUTE

Caltech is an independent, privately supported institution. With its off-campus facilities (such as the Jet Propulsion Laboratory), it constitutes one of the world's major research centers. Because of the Institute's relatively small size (1,061 faculty members and 1,992 students), close interaction exists between students and research staff members.

Caltech scientists have achieved wide recognition for their distinguished achievements. Twenty-two Nobel Prizes have been awarded to Caltech alumni and faculty, and 23 alumni and faculty members have received the National Medal of Science for outstanding contributions to the development of science and engineering. Of all the educational institutions in the country, Caltech has both the highest percentage of faculty members elected to the National Academy of Sciences and the highest percentage of engineering faculty members elected to the National Academy of Engineering.

APPLYING

Applications for September admission should be received by January 15. GRE General Test scores are required. Admission to graduate study in computer science is highly competitive; only about 6 new students are admitted each year. The department seeks applicants with exceptional promise for scientific research.

Application materials may be obtained from the Office of the Dean of Graduate Studies. Inquiries for further information should be sent to the computer science department. Caltech is an Affirmative Action institution and encourages women and members of minority groups to apply.

CORRESPONDENCE AND INFORMATION

Dean of Graduate Studies, 02-31
California Institute of Technology
Pasadena, California 91125
Telephone: 818-395-6346
Fax: 818-577-9246

CALIFORNIA INSTITUTE OF TECHNOLOGY

THE FACULTY AND THEIR RESEARCH

Yaser S. Abu-Mostafa, Professor of Electrical Engineering and Computer Science; Ph.D., Caltech, 1983. Learning theory, neural networks, information theory, computational complexity, pattern recognition.

James R. Arvo, Associate Professor; Ph.D., Yale, 1995. Computational methods and mathematical foundations of physically and perceptually based image synthesis, interactive computer graphics for exploration and instruction.

Alan H. Barr, Associate Professor; Ph.D., Rensselaer, 1983. Three-dimensional mathematical and computational modeling techniques, image synthesis and computer graphics, biomechanics and simulation of natural phenomena.

K. Mani Chandy, Professor; Ph.D., MIT, 1969. Concurrent computation: formal methods, performance modeling, software engineering.

Alain J. Martin, Professor; Engineer in Applied Mathematics, Grenoble Polytechnic (France), 1969. Asynchronous VLSI design, concurrent and distributed computations, highly parallel computers, computer architecture, verification.

Carver A. Mead, Gordon and Betty Moore Professor; Ph.D., Caltech, 1960. VLSI design, ultraconcurrent systems, physics of computation, real-time vision and hearing.

Peter Schroder, Assistant Professor; Ph.D., Princeton, 1994. Illumination computations, wavelets, massively parallel graphics, scientific visualization, scientific computation.

Frederick Burtis Thompson, Professor Emeritus of Applied Science and Philosophy; Ph.D., Berkeley, 1951. Philosophy of information, computational linguistics, user interface, dynamics of information.

The following faculty members and professionals at Caltech actively contribute to the computer science research and curriculum:

Jehoshua Bruck, Associate Professor of Computation and Neural Systems and Electrical Engineering; Ph.D., Stanford, 1989. Parallel and distributed computing, computation theory and neural systems, fault-tolerant computing and error-correcting codes.

Joel N. Franklin, Professor of Applied Mathematics; Ph.D., Stanford, 1953. Mathematical programming, numerical analysis, computer algorithms.

John J. Hopfield, Roscoe Gilkey Dickinson Professor of Chemistry and Biology; Ph.D., Cornell, 1958. Collective computation and collective circuits.

Alexander S. Kechris, Professor of Mathematics; Ph.D., UCLA, 1972. Mathematical logic, computability theory.

Herbert B. Keller, Professor of Applied Mathematics; Ph.D., NYU (Courant), 1954. Numerical analysis, bifurcation theory, large-scale scientific computing.

Carl Kesselman, Visiting Associate; Ph.D., UCLA, 1991. Parallel programming languages and environments, high-performance computing, computational biology.

Richard F. Lyon, Visiting Associate; M.S., Stanford, 1975. Speech recognition and computational models of hearing, VLSI systems, architectural methodologies.

Robert J. McEliece, Professor of Electrical Engineering; Ph.D., Caltech, 1967. Information theory, error-correcting codes, applied mathematics.

Daniel I. Meiron, Professor of Applied Mathematics; Sc.D., MIT, 1981. Computational physics, large-scale scientific computing.

Paul C. Messina, Assistant Vice President for Scientific Computing and Director of CACR; Ph.D., Cincinnati, 1972. Director of Caltech Concurrent Supercomputing Facilities, Executive Director of Concurrent Supercomputing Consortium, Project Leader for CASA gigabit network testbed.

Philip G. Saffman, Professor of Applied Mathematics; Ph.D., Cambridge, 1956. Computational fluid mechanics.

Bozena Henisz Thompson, Senior Research Associate in Linguistics; Ph.D., Georgetown, 1965. Experimental psycholinguistics, theoretical linguistics, computational linguistics, user interface.

W. Hugh Woodin, Professor of Mathematics; Ph.D., Berkeley, 1984. Mathematical logic, computational complexity.

CARNEGIE MELLON UNIVERSITY

SCHOOL OF COMPUTER SCIENCE
DOCTORAL PROGRAM IN COMPUTER SCIENCE

PROGRAM OF STUDY

The Department of Computer Science offers the degree of Doctor of Philosophy. Requirements for the Ph.D. are successful completion of eight core course requirements and submission of a thesis describing original, independent research. An initial acculturation program (the "Immigration Course") involves students in all the activities of the Department. Participation in one or more of the ongoing research projects is a key factor in a student's education. Visitors come to Carnegie Mellon in a steady stream from universities and laboratories throughout the world for various lengths of time, joining the faculty members and students in an active colloquium program.

RESEARCH FACILITIES

The School of Computer Science (SCS) has a research facility that provides both a large number and a wide variety of computers for faculty and graduate student use—more than 2200 machines. Personal computing employs various UNIX machines—primarily from Sun, DEC, HP, IBM, and SGI—along with numerous Macintosh and PC systems. Nearly every person in the School has the individual use of a workstation. Many of the UNIX workstations run Mach, a 4.3BSD variant developed at Carnegie Mellon for distributed parallel processing. All UNIX workstations have transparent access to the Andrew File System, a large, shared filespace, and to one another through Network File System and/or Remote File System protocols. Total disk space within SCS currently exceeds one terabyte. Beyond these resources, the University maintains various independent facilities for general computation.

Carnegie Mellon's campus network is a fully-interconnected, multimedia, multiprotocol infrastructure spanning more than 100 segments. Segments are attached to an "inverted" backbone, thus enabling mutual access among all campus systems, including the PSC's supercomputers. Numerous communication media, such as fiber optics and shielded and unshielded twisted-pair, support Ethernet, Token Ring, LocalTalk, ATM, and HIPPI. Network protocols include IP/TCP, AppleTalk, and IPX. In a joint venture with Bell Atlantic, SCS also developed a Wide-Area Network telecommuting infrastructure based on Data-over-Voice technology. This system provides low-cost, synchronous, 64Kb/s links to student, staff, and faculty homes.

FINANCIAL AID

Most students in the department are supported by graduate research fellowships during the academic year. In 1997–98, each student receives full tuition plus a stipend of $1400 per month for the academic year. Dependency allowances are available; students who receive external fellowships may be given supplementary stipends.

Summer support is normally available for many students, particularly those working on the dissertation. However, since the University believes that it is also good for students to gain experience in industry for one or two summers during their careers at Carnegie Mellon, faculty and staff members are able to provide valuable help in finding suitable summer employment.

COST OF STUDY

Tuition and fees for full-time graduate students in 1997–98 are $20,275 for the academic year. This figure is subject to change.

LIVING AND HOUSING COSTS

The University does not provide housing for graduate students, but accommodations are available in the community at a variety of costs.

STUDENT GROUP

Carnegie Mellon has a total enrollment of approximately 7,500 students. About 150 full-time students are enrolled in the Doctoral Program in Computer Science, which makes the student-faculty member ratio about 2:1. Admission to the program is highly competitive; about 25 students are admitted each year.

STUDENT OUTCOMES

Carnegie Mellon's Computer Science doctoral program aims to produce well-educated researchers and future leaders in computer science. Approximately 25 students graduate each year, with slightly more than half accepting positions in industrial research laboratories such as DEC, IBM, Intel, Lucent Labs, and Xerox; those preferring academic careers accept both tenure- and research-track positions at many of the top universities in the country, including the University of California at Berkeley, Cornell University, the University of Pennsylvania, and Stanford University.

LOCATION

Carnegie Mellon is located in Oakland, the cultural center of Pittsburgh, on a 90-acre campus adjacent to Schenley Park, the largest city park. The campus is close to the many cultural and sports activities of the city and is only 4 miles from the downtown business district. Pittsburgh is the headquarters for many of the nation's biggest corporations. There is a large concentration of research laboratories in the area.

THE UNIVERSITY

Founded in 1900 by Andrew Carnegie, the Carnegie Institute of Technology joined with Mellon Institute (now the Carnegie Mellon Research Institute) in 1967 to become Carnegie Mellon University. With this merger, one of the leading research and education institutions in the country was established.

APPLYING

The application, Graduate Record Examinations scores, and letters of reference must be received by January 1. Notification of acceptance and financial aid awards is made by March 15. Minimum preparation normally includes an undergraduate program in mathematics, physics, electrical engineering, or computer science and some experience in computer programming. Excellence and promise may balance a lack of formal preparation. No applications are considered unless accompanied by the GRE scores (the General Test and Subject Test in mathematics, computer science, physics, or engineering).

CORRESPONDENCE AND INFORMATION

Admissions Committee
Department of Computer Science
Carnegie Mellon University
5000 Forbes Avenue
Pittsburgh, Pennsylvania 15213

Telephone: 412-268-3863
E-mail: grad-adm@cs.cmu.edu
World Wide Web: http://www.cs.cmu.edu

CARNEGIE MELLON UNIVERSITY
THE FACULTY AND THEIR RESEARCH

J. Anderson, Professor. Cognitive psychology, artificial intelligence, human computer interaction.

D. Baraff, Assistant Professor. Computer graphics, dynamic simulation, animation.

H. Berliner, Principal Research Scientist. AI, representation of knowledge for large domains, tree searching, structures that could support learning, usually in a game-playing or puzzle environment.

G. Blelloch, Associate Professor. Compilers, parallel architectures, parallel languages, parallel algorithms.

A. Blum, Associate Professor. Machine-learning theory, on-line algorithms, approximation algorithms.

S. Brookes, Associate Professor. Mathematical theory of computation, theory and semantics of programming languages.

B. Bruegge, Senior Systems Scientist. Programming environments, distributed debugging, high-speed networking, software engineering.

R. Bryant, Professor. Formal verification of digital systems, data structures and algorithms for representing and reasoning about discrete functions.

J. Carbonell, Professor. Artificial intelligence, natural-language processing, machine learning, machine translation.

E. Clarke, FORE Professor. Hardware and software verification, automatic theorem proving, symbolic computation, parallel algorithms, programming.

S. Cochran, Systems Scientist. Image understanding, aerial photo interpretation, stereo vision.

A. Corbett, Research Scientist. Application of AI in education, use of cognitive models in computer-based learning environments.

R. Dannenberg, Senior Research Scientist. Computer languages, computer music, human-computer interaction.

M. Erdmann, Associate Professor. Robotics, motion planning, probabilistic/sensing strategies, mechanics of manipulation, cooperating robots.

S. Fahlman, Principal Research Scientist. AI, artificial neural networks, software development environments (Gwydion/Dylan), image processing, natural language processing.

A. Fisher, Principal Systems Scientist and Associate Dean. VLSI architecture, parallel computing.

M. Furst, Professor. Algorithm design, computational complexity, learning theory.

D. Garlan, Associate Professor. Software engineering, software architecture, formal methods, programming environments.

G. Gibson, Associate Professor. Computer systems, computer architecture, performance evaluation, disk arrays, networks.

T. Gross, Associate Professor. Computer systems, parallel computing, compilers, debugging, software construction.

R. Harper, Associate Professor. Type theory, logic and semantics, programming language design and implementation.

A. Hauptmann, Systems Scientist. Integrating speech recognition, language processing and information retrieval research.

P. Heckbert, Assistant Professor. Computer graphics and image processing.

S. Issar, Systems Scientist. Very large vocabulary real-time continuous speech recognition, modeling dialogue.

B. John, Assistant Professor. Human-computer interaction, engineering models of human performance.

D. Johnson, Assistant Professor. Wireless/mobile networking, fault tolerance, network protocols, operating systems, distributed systems.

T. Kanade, Professor. Computer vision, mobile robots, medical robotics, sensors, virtualized reality.

R. Kannan, Professor. Geometric and mathematical algorithms, optimization.

K. Koedinger, Research Scientist. Cognitive science, intelligent tutor agents, HCI, diagrammatic reasoning, interactive representations.

R. Kraut, Professor. HCI, social impact of technology, interpersonal communication, psychology of work.

J. Lafferty, Research Scientist. Probability and information theory, natural-language processing, stochastic modeling.

P. Lee, Associate Professor. Compilers for advanced programming languages, semantics-based analysis and optimization, functional programming, formal semantics.

T. Lee, Assistant Professor. Medical engineering, computational neuroscience, computer vision.

J. Fain Lehman, Research Scientist. Natural-language understanding, generation, and acquisition; machine learning; cognitive modeling.

C. Love, Senior Systems Scientist. Parallel computing and high-speed, multicomputer networks.

B. Maggs, Associate Professor. Networks for parallel and distributed computer systems.

M. Mason, Professor. Automatic planning of robot manipulator tasks, mechanics of manipulation, artificial intelligence.

R. Maxion, Senior Systems Scientist. Human and machine diagnosis of complex systems, discovery of structure, fault tolerance.

C. McGlone, Systems Scientist. Photogrammetry and image understanding.

D. McKeown, Principal Research Scientist. Image understanding, remote sensing, cartography, spatial databases.

G. Miller, Professor. Parallel computation; sparse matrix, graph and number-theoretic algorithms.

P. Miller, Principal Lecturer and Introductory Programming Director. Programming environments, computer science education.

T. Mitchell, Professor. AI-machine learning/applications to datamining, information agents, robotics, process optimization.

A. Moore, Assistant Professor. Reinforcement learning, machine learning, AI in manufacturing, scheduling, Markov decision processes.

J. Morris, Professor and Department Head. Distributed personal computer systems, functional programming, user interfaces.

T. Mowry, Associate Professor. Computer systems, computer architecture, compiler algorithms for prefetching in uniprocessors and shared-memory multiprocessors.

D. Nagle, Assistant Professor. Computer architecture, embedded systems, I/O.

D. O'Hallaron, Research Scientist. Architectures, compilers, and applications for parallel computer systems.

D. Olsen, Director, HCI Institute. Human-computer interaction, user interface architectures, computer-based education.

R. Pausch, Associate Professor. HCI, user interfaces, interactive computer graphics, virtual reality.

M. Perlin, Senior Research Scientist. Computational molecular genetics, genome mapping, user interfaces, artificial intelligence methods.

F. Pfenning, Senior Research Scientist. Logic and computation, type theory, logic programming, functional programming, automated deduction.

D. Plaut, Assistant Professor. Computational modeling of normal and impaired cognitive processes in vision, attention, and language.

D. Pomerleau, Research Scientist. Computer vision, robotics, development of neural network learning techniques to achieve flexibility.

R. Rajkumar, Systems Scientist. Speech recognition and search algorithms, computer architecture, parallel processing.

M. Ravishankar, Systems Scientist. Speech decoding algorithms, acoustic modeling, speech applications, interface design.

R. Reddy, University Professor and Dean. AI, speech recognition and understanding, integrated manufacturing systems.

J. Reynolds, Professor. Design of computer programming languages, mathematical semantics, programming methodology.

R. Rosenfeld, Research Scientist. Human language technologies, statistical language modeling, speech recognition, stochastic modeling.

S. Roth, Senior Research Scientist. Information visualization and exploration, user interface design.

S. Rudich, Associate Professor. Complexity theory, cryptography, combinatorics, probability.

A. Rudnicky, Senior Systems Scientist. Speech recognition, spoken language interaction, interface design.

R. Rutenbar, Professor. VLSI design automation, synthesis techniques to transform specifications into circuits, geometric layout algorithms.

M. Satyanarayanan, Professor. Mobile computing, distributed file systems, measurement and evaluation, security.

W. Scherlis, Senior Research Scientist. Software engineering, program manipulation and analysis, information structuring for collaborative work.

D. Scott, Hillman Professor. Foundations of logic and mathematics, semantics of natural and computer languages.

M. Shaw, Perlis Professor and Associate Dean. Software architecture, software engineering, programming systems and methodologies.

D. Siewiorek, Buhl Professor. Computer architecture, fault-tolerance, design automation, parallel processing, mobile computing, rapid prototyping.

R. Simmons, Senior Research Scientist. AI, autonomous mobile robots, task-level control architectures, planning, reasoning under uncertainty.

H. Simon, University Professor. Computer simulation of cognitive processes, artificial intelligence, management science.

D. Sleator, Professor. Data structures, graph algorithms, on-line algorithms, parsing natural languages.

P. Steenkiste, Senior Research Scientist. High-performance networking, parallel and distributed computing.

J. Subhlok, Systems Scientist. Compilers and programming tools for parallel and network computers.

S. Thrun, Research Scientist. Artificial intelligence, machine learning, neural networks and their applications to robotics and intelligent control.

J. Tomayko, Principal Lecturer. Reliability of embedded real-time systems, software development management, history of computing.

D. Touretzky, Senior Research Scientist. Computational neuroscience, knowledge representation in connectionist nets.

D. Tygar, Associate Professor. Computer security, applied randomized algorithms, distributed computation.

R. Valdes-Perez, Senior Research Scientist. AI-computational science, interactive discovery tools for biology, chemistry, physics, and other sciences.

M. Veloso, Associate Professor. AI, integration of planning and learning, analogical/case-based reasoning, machine vision and learning.

W. Ward, Research Scientist. Artificial intelligence, speech understanding, stochastic modeling.

J. Wing, Professor. Formal methods, security, concurrent and distributed systems, programming languages, programming methodology.

A. Witkin, Professor. Computer graphics and animation, simulation, computational vision.

Y. Yang, Senior Research Scientist. Natural language analysis systems, machine translation, text retrieval and categorization.

H. Zhang, Assistant Professor. Computer networking and telecommunication systems, multimedia systems, distributed systems.

CARNEGIE MELLON UNIVERSITY

DEPARTMENT OF ELECTRICAL AND COMPUTER ENGINEERING

Carnegie Mellon

PROGRAMS OF STUDY

The department offers several graduate degree programs. Students who have earned a B.S. degree may apply to the M.S. degree program, which has two options: the course option and the project option. Students who have earned an M.S. degree may apply to the Ph.D. program. (The Direct Ph.D. Program is for highly qualified students who are interested in pursuing a Ph.D. immediately after completing a B.S. degree.)

Students in the project option are required to submit a project report. The completion time for an M.S. degree is usually one year to eighteen months. Fulfillment of the Ph.D. requirements takes three to four years beyond the M.S. degree and requires passing a qualifying examination, completing an internship in university teaching, writing a thesis that describes the results of independent research, and passing an oral defense of the research. All full-time Ph.D. students and project option master's students engage in research under faculty guidance. Currently, the department has 50 faculty members; all are actively engaged in research in addition to their regular teaching responsibilities. While several faculty members hold joint appointments with other departments, many of the faculty also have close ties with various interdisciplinary research centers in the University, such as the Information Networking Institute, the Robotics Institute, and the Engineering Design Research Center. The department is home for several internationally recognized research centers: an NSF Engineering Research Center in Data Storage Systems and the SRC-CMU Research Center for Computer-Aided Design. Major areas of research include neural networks; artificial intelligence; biomedical engineering; communications/information engineering; computer engineering; electronic design; computer-aided manufacturing of VLSI circuits; control systems engineering; electrical engineering and public policy; electronic design automation; high-speed computing and communication networks; electromagnetics/electrophysics; electronics; fault-tolerant computing and real-time computing; data storage technology and systems, including magnetic and optical recording; high-performance parallel and application-specific architectures; magnetooptical devices; optical data processing; signal processing; solid-state electronics; speech and image processing; video compression; robotics; and VLSI.

RESEARCH FACILITIES

The department has extensive computational facilities that include over 250 advanced workstations supporting research and education. Research projects also make frequent use of supercomputers, available to the department through the Pittsburgh Supercomputing Center. The facilities also include numerous laser printers and color-printing and slide-making capabilities. These systems are all connected to the CMU campuswide computer network via an Ethernet local area network. A fully equipped 4000-square-foot, class 100 clean room supports research in semiconductor and magnetic and optical device research and can be used to produce state-of-the-art solid-state and recording devices. In addition to the clean room, the department has a molecular-beam epitaxy system and extensive facilities for measuring the electrical and optical properties of semiconducting and superconducting materials, structures, and devices. Computer-controlled systems for performing photoluminescence spectroscopy, deep-level transient spectroscopy, device parameter analysis, capacitance voltage measurements, and other functions are all available.

Data Storage Systems laboratories contain several test stands for evaluating both rigid and flexible magnetic and optical recording media and heads, a high-resolution magnetooptic photometer, and several polarized-light microscopes equipped with drive electronics for testing magnetooptic recording media. Facilities also include a vibrating sample magnetometer, an inductive hysteresis loop tracer, a torque magnetometer, a SQUID magnetometer, an alternating gradient magnetometer, an atomic magnetic force microscope, a 35-GHz ferromagnetic resonance spectrometer, and a spin polarized electron microscope for magnetic domain observation.

The optical and digital processing labs contain large vibration-isolated tables, lasers, associated optical components, and extensive optical and electrical detection and measurement facilities. Optical systems include image processing, pattern recognition, feature generation, and optical neural networks.

FINANCIAL AID

Graduate research and teaching assistantships are available to U.S. and international students and include a typical stipend of about $1325–$1425 per month plus tuition. In the award of financial aid, consideration is given to the student's undergraduate and graduate academic records, GRE scores, and letters of reference indicating outstanding academic potential.

COST OF STUDY

Tuition for graduate students enrolled in the Department of Electrical and Computer Engineering is $20,275 for the academic year 1997–98. Books and supplies cost about $1400 per year.

LIVING AND HOUSING COSTS

Graduate accommodations are not provided, although there are various board plans available in nearby rooms or apartments. Approximate living expenses, including room and board, insurance, transportation, and miscellaneous expenses, average $14,525 per academic year, exclusive of tuition.

STUDENT GROUP

The campus enrollment averages 7,318 students; 2,611 are graduate students. The University has 881 full-time faculty members. Within the Department of Electrical and Computer Engineering, there are 212 full-time graduate students, with 98 in the master's program and 114 in the Ph.D. program.

LOCATION

The Greater Pittsburgh metropolitan area has more than 2 million residents. The Carnegie Mellon campus encompasses approximately 100 acres and adjoins a 500-acre city park and quiet residential communities with abundant student housing.

THE UNIVERSITY

The University is composed of the Carnegie Institute of Technology (the Engineering School), Mellon College of Science, the College of Fine Arts, the Graduate School of Industrial Administration, the Heinz School, the College of Humanities and Social Sciences, and the School of Computer Sciences.

APPLYING

All applicants are required to take the GRE (General Test) at least six weeks prior to the application deadline. All students whose native language is other than English are required to take the Test of English as a Foreign Language (TOEFL). Applications for the fall semester must be received by January 15. Official transcripts, three letters of recommendation, and GRE scores must be provided. Application materials may be obtained by writing to the department.

CORRESPONDENCE AND INFORMATION

Graduate Admissions
Department of Electrical and Computer Engineering
Carnegie Mellon University
Pittsburgh, Pennsylvania 15213

Telephone: 412-268-3200
World Wide Web: http://www.ece.cmu.edu

CARNEGIE MELLON UNIVERSITY

THE FACULTY AND THEIR RESEARCH

J. A. Bain, Research Engineer; Ph.D., Stanford, 1993. Thin film magnetic device design, fabrication, and testing; tape recording.

R. P. Bianchini Jr., Associate Professor; Ph.D., Carnegie Mellon, 1989. Distributed fault-tolerant computing, and computer networks.

S. Blanton, Assistant Professor; Ph.D., Michigan, 1995. Design and test of VLSI circuits, fault-tolerant computing, computer architecture.

R. E. Bryant , Professor of Computer Science; Ph.D., MIT, 1981. Digital system simulation and verification.

L. R. Carley, Professor; Ph.D., MIT, 1984. CAD and design of analog signal processing circuits.

D. P. Casasent, George Westinghouse Professor; Ph.D., Illinois at Urbana–Champaign, 1969. Pattern recognition, neural nets, and optical data processing.

Z. J. Cendes, Adjunct Professor; Ph.D., McGill, 1973. Computer-aided design of high-speed digital interconnects, microwave and antenna field simulation, modeling of magnetic and semiconductor devices, numerical methods.

S. H. Charap, Emeritus Professor; Ph.D., Rutgers, 1959. Magnetic phenomena and devices, theory and modeling, magnetic recording.

E. Clarke, FORE Systems Professor of Computer Science; Ph.D., Cornell, 1976. Hardware and software verification, automatic theorem proving, symbolic computation.

S. W. Director, Adjunct Professor of Electrical and Computer Engineering; Ph.D., Berkeley, 1968. Computer-aided VLSI design, CAD frameworks, statistical design.

G. K. Fedder, Assistant Professor; Ph.D., Berkeley, 1994. Microelectromechanical systems (MEMS), MEMS CAD, micro-robotics.

R. M. Feenstra, Professor of Physics; Ph.D., Caltech, 1982. Molecular beam epitaxy, scanning tunneling microscopy.

A. Fisher, Principal Systems Scientist and Associate Dean of Computer Science; Ph.D., Carnegie Mellon, 1984. Network architecture, parallel computing.

K. Gabriel, Professor of Electrical and Computer Engineering and Robotics; Sc.D., MIT, 1983. Microelectromechanical systems.

G. Ganger, Assistant Professor; Ph.D., Michigan, 1995. Computer engineering.

G. A. Gibson, Associate Professor of Computer Science; Ph.D., Berkeley, 1991. Computer architecture, operating systems, file systems, disk arrays.

S. C. Goldstein, Assistant Professor of Computer Science; Ph.D., Berkeley, 1997. Parallel systems, reconfigurable computing.

D. W. Greve, Professor; Ph.D., Lehigh, 1979. Epitaxy of germanium silicon alloys and applications, semiconductor technology, wide gap semiconductors.

J. B. Hampshire II, Research Engineer; Ph.D., Carnegie Mellon, 1993. Learning theory, pattern recognition, neural networks.

J. F. Hoburg, Professor; Ph.D., MIT, 1975. Electromagnetics, electromechanics, magnetic shielding.

D. B. Johnson, Assistant Professor of Computer Science; Ph.D., Rice, 1990. Network protocols, distributed systems, operating systems, mobile computing, fault tolerance.

R. E. Jones, Jr., Principal Research Engineer; Ph.D., Berkeley, 1957. Magnetic recording head technology.

A. G. Jordan, Keithley University Professor of Electrical and Computer Engineering and Robotics; Ph.D., Carnegie Tech, 1959. Advanced video systems, robotics.

T. Kanade, Director of the Robotics Institute and U. A. and Helen Whitaker Professor of Computer Science, Robotics, and Electrical and Computer Engineering; Ph.D., Kyoto, 1973. Autonomous systems, medical robotics, computer vision.

P. K. Khosla, Professor of Electrical and Computer Engineering and Robotics and Director, Institute for Complex Engineered Systems; Ph.D., Carnegie Mellon, 1986. Mechatronics, agent-based design and control, S/W engineering for real-time systems, collaborating robot systems, gesture-based programming.

H. S. Kim, Associate Professor; Ph.D., Toronto, 1990. Computer networks, advanced switch architectures, high-speed networks.

P. J. Koopman, Assistant Professor; Ph.D., Carnegie Mellon, 1989. Robust distributed embedded systems, computer architecture, methodical system design.

B. H. Krogh, Professor; Ph.D., Illinois at Urbana–Champaign, 1982. Discrete and continuous control systems.

M. H. Kryder, Stephen J. Jatras University Professor and Director, Data Storage Systems Center; Ph.D., Caltech, 1970. Magnetic and optical recording.

B. V. K. Vijaya Kumar, Professor; Ph.D., Carnegie Mellon, 1980. Optical pattern recognition, neural networks, signal processing for storage.

D. N. Lambeth, Professor and Associate Director, Data Storage Systems Center; Ph.D., MIT, 1973. Magnetism, recording systems, media, precision instrumentation, transducers and sensors.

W. Maly, U. A. and Helen Whitaker Professor; Ph.D., Polish Academy of Sciences, 1975. Computer-aided design and manufacturing of VLSICs.

W. C. Messner, Assistant Professor of Mechanical Engineering; Ph.D., Berkeley, 1992. Control theory, control for data storage systems, robot control.

A. G. Milnes, Emeritus Professor; D.Sc., Bristol, 1956. Semiconductor phenomena and devices.

M. G. Morgan, Lord Professor of Electrical and Computer Engineering and of Engineering and Public Policy and Department Head of Engineering and Public Policy; Ph.D., California, San Diego, 1969. Technology and public policy including risk analysis.

J. M. F. Moura, Professor; D.Sc., MIT, 1975. Communications, statistical signal/image video processing, multiresolution transforms.

T. Mukherjee, Research Engineer, Electrical and Computer Engineering and Assistant Director, Center for Electronic Design Automation; Ph.D., Carnegie Mellon, 1995. CAD for MEMS, analog circuit synthesis.

D. Nagle, Assistant Professor; Ph.D., Michigan, 1994. Computer architecture, operating systems, storage technologies.

C. P. Neuman, Professor and Undergraduate Advisor; Ph.D., Harvard, 1968. Control engineering and robotics.

J. M. Peha, Assistant Professor; Ph.D., Stanford, 1991. Telecommunications, computer networks, wireless networks, telecom policy.

L. T. Pileggi, Associate Professor; Ph.D., Carnegie Mellon, 1989. Circuit-level analysis and design automation for electronic systems.

R. Rajkumar, Senior Research Engineer and Senior Systems Scientist; Ph.D., Carnegie Mellon, 1989. Multimedia and real-time systems.

R. A. Rohrer, Adjunct Professor; Ph.D., Berkeley, 1963. Electronic circuits, systems design automation.

R. A. Rutenbar, Professor, Center for Electronic Design Automation; Ph.D., Michigan, 1984. VLSI CAD, algorithms.

T. E. Schlesinger, Professor, Associate Department Head, and Director, Center for Electronic Design Automation; Ph.D., Caltech, 1985. III–V semiconductors, optoelectronics, nuclear detectors.

H. H. Schmit, Research Engineer; Ph.D., Carnegie Mellon, 1995. Behavioral synthesis, reconfigurable custom computing.

J. P. Shen, Professor; Ph.D., USC, 1981. Modern superscaler processor design, instruction-level parallelism and code scheduling.

D. P. Siewiorek, Buhl Professor of Electrical and Computer Engineering and Computer Science and Associate Director, Institute for Complex Engineered Systems; Ph.D., Stanford, 1972. Computer architecture, reliability, CAD, mobile computing.

M. A. Sirbu, Professor of Engineering and Public Policy and Industrial Administration; Sc.D., MIT, 1973. Telecommunications policy and economics.

D. D. Stancil, Professor and Associate Dean of CIT; Ph.D., MIT, 1981. Wireless communication, integrated optics, optical data storage.

R. M. Stern Jr., Professor; Ph.D., MIT, 1976. Automatic speech recognition, auditory perception, signal processing.

A. J. Strojwas, Professor; Ph.D., Carnegie Mellon, 1982. Statistically based CAD/CAM of VLSI circuits.

J. K. Strosnider, Associate Professor; Ph.D., Carnegie Mellon, 1988. Performance engineering real-time/multimedia systems, design automation of large scale distributed systems.

S. N. Talukdar, Professor; Ph.D., Purdue, 1970. Machine cooperation, CAD, distributed problem solving, power systems, organization design.

A. A. Thiele, Senior Research Engineer and Distinguished Scholar; Ph.D., MIT, 1965. Micromagnetics, topology, and statistics of domain wall motion.

D. E. Thomas Jr., Professor and Associate Director, Center for Electronics Design Automation; Ph.D., Carnegie Mellon, 1977. Computer-aided design of mixed hardware and software systems.

R. M. Unetich, Adjunct Professor; B.S.E.E., Carnegie Mellon, 1968. Wireless communication systems.

R. M. White, University Professor and Head of the Department of Electrical and Computer Engineering; Ph.D., Stanford, 1964. Magnetic device phenomena, technology policy.

H. Zhang, Assistant Professor of Computer Science; Ph.D., Berkeley, 1993. Computer networks, real-time communication, multimedia networking.

J. G. Zhu, Associate Professor; Ph.D., California, San Diego, 1989. Micromagnetics, magnetoelectronic devices, magnetic recording.

CARNEGIE MELLON UNIVERSITY

HUMAN-COMPUTER INTERACTION INSTITUTE
MASTER OF HUMAN-COMPUTER INTERACTION

PROGRAM OF STUDY

The computer industry is spending an increasing proportion of its development funds in human-computer interaction (HCI), but has a shortage of personnel with the breadth of training or experience to effectively work on the multidisciplinary teams that produce software with a significant HCI component. With instructors from the School of Computer Science, the Graduate School of Industrial Administration, the School of Humanities and Social Sciences, the College of Fine Arts, the Engineering Design Research Center, the Robotics Institute, and the Software Engineering Institute, the Human Computer Interaction Institute at Carnegie Mellon is one of the few institutes in the country with the breadth of expertise to offer such a program.

The program prepares students to participate in the design and implementation of software systems that can be used easily, effectively, and enjoyably. Students are expected to have a strong undergraduate degree or comparable work experience in either computer science, a behavioral science (psychology, sociology, anthropology, or organizational behavior), or visual or information design. All students are expected to have had at least one prerequisite course in statistics, design, and elementary programming.

During the first two semesters of the twelve-month program, students complete courses to give them a broad background in computer science, human behavior, evaluation and assessment, and design. The curriculum consists of four core courses and six courses in one of three specialty areas: design, implementation, or analysis and evaluation. In the summer, students participate in the extensive team-oriented Human-Computer Interaction Project, in which they apply their classroom knowledge and develop skills by working on a multidisciplinary team.

RESEARCH FACILITIES

The joint computing facility of the HCI program and the School of Computer Science has a large number and a wide variety of computers available to faculty members and graduate students, ranging from Macintosh and Intel-based personal computers to large multiprocessors from DEC (8800) and Encore (Multimax-16). All personal computers provide transparent access to the Adrew File System.

The User Studies Labs are University-wide facilities for research on human-computer interaction. The three laboratory facilities have space for studying single individuals and groups applications. Equipment includes facilities for recording of video and analysis of video data.

FINANCIAL AID

There are a small number of teaching assistantships. In addition, students may be assisted in finding employment to complement the program. University-wide work-study opportunities are available to graduate students. Students may apply for Stafford loans.

COST OF STUDY

Tuition for full-time graduate students accepted in 1997–98 is $10,138 per semester. This figure is subject to change.

LIVING AND HOUSING COSTS

Graduate students are responsible for their own housing needs. There is no on-campus graduate housing; however, housing is available in the area within a range of costs. The Office of International Education suggests living costs of $9100 for single students and $12,100 for married students.

STUDENT GROUP

The first group of students accepted into the program in August 1995 was 3 men. The first group of 12 accepted for the academic year 1996–97 includes 4 women. Of the 12, 8 are from the United States. The current class of 18 students includes 5 women.

LOCATION

Carnegie Mellon University is located 5 miles east of Pittsburgh in Oakland, the cultural center of Pittsburgh. The University is adjacent to Schenley Park, the city's largest park, and is close to many cultural and sports activities.

THE UNIVERSITY

Founded in 1900 by Andrew Carnegie, the Carnegie Institute of Technology joined with Mellon Institute (now the Carnegie Mellon Research Institute) in 1967 to become Carnegie Mellon University. With this merger, one of the leading research and education institutions in the country was established. Approximately 4,500 undergraduate and 2,500 graduate students are enrolled at Carnegie Mellon.

APPLYING

The application, Graduate Record Examinations scores, a statement of purpose, an up-to-date résumé, letters of reference, and the application fee must be received by February 1. A strong undergraduate degree or comparable work in computer science, a behavioral science (psychology, sociology, anthropology, or organizational behavior), or visual or information design is required, as is at least one course in statistics, design, and elementary programming.

CORRESPONDENCE AND INFORMATION

Admissions Coordinator
Human-Computer Interaction Program
School of Computer Science
Carnegie Mellon University
Pittsburgh, Pennsylvania 15213
Telephone: 412-268-6493
E-mail: hcii-masters@cs.cmu.edu
World Wide Web: http://www.cs.cmu.edu/~hcii

CARNEGIE MELLON UNIVERSITY

THE FACULTY

Members of the faculty are drawn from the membership of the Human-Computer Interaction Institute (HCII) of Carnegie Mellon.

Human-Computer Interaction Institute Faculty and Members

Dan Olsen, Professor of Computer Science and Director of the HCII. Human-computer interfaces, artificial intelligence, programming environments, computer graphics, DEC computers.

John Anderson, Professor of Psychology and Computer Science. Cognitive psychology, artificial intelligence, human-computer interaction.

Daniel Boyarski, Professor of Design. How words, pictures, sound, and motion may be combined for effective communication.

Albert T. Corbett, Research Computer Scientist, HCII. Development and evaluation of computer-based learning environments.

Bonnie E. John, Assistant Professor of Computer Science and Psychology. Usability evaluation methods, engineering models of human performance.

Sara Kiesler, Professor of Social and Decision Sciences. Social and behavioral aspects of computers and computer-based communication technologies.

Roberta L. Klatzky, Professor and Head of Department, Psychology. Perceptual/motor interactions and their implications for interface design.

Kenneth R. Koedinger, Research Computer Scientist, HCII. Cognitive modeling of problem solving, intelligent tutoring systems.

Robert Kraut, Professor of Social Psychology and Human-Computer Interaction, Computer Science, Social and Decision Sciences, and Graduate School of Industrial Administration. Use of emerging computer and telecommunication technologies for communication by groups and individuals.

F. Javier Lerch, Associate Professor, Graduate School of Industrial Administration. Working memory, problem representation.

James H. Morris, Professor and Head of Department, Computer Science. Distributed personal computer systems, software engineering, functional programming, user interfaces.

Brad A. Myers, Senior Research Computer Scientist, Computer Science Department. User interface design, user interface software, demonstrational interfaces, programming environments.

Christine M. Neuwirth, Associate Professor of English and Computer Science. Computer-supported cooperative work, collaborative writing.

Randy Pausch, Associate Professor of Human-Computer Interaction, Computer Science and Design, HCII. Virtual reality, interactive 3D graphics, theme park and entertainment technologies, design of consumer market devices.

Steven Roth, Senior Research Scientist, Robotics Institute. Presentation of information, visualization.

Jane Siegel, Senior Systems Scientist, HCII. Usability evaluation methods and measures, behavioral aspects of computer-supported cooperative work systems.

Alex Waibel, Senior Research Scientist, Computer Science, Center for Machine Translation, Robotics, and Computational Linguistics. Speech understanding and translation, multimodal interfaces, neural networks, machine learning.

Joseph M. Ballay, Professor of Design. Design for human-computer interaction, nonverbal communication.

David Baraff, Assistant Professor of Robotics. Computer graphics, dynamic simulation, animation.

Len Bass, Senior Member, Technical Staff, Software Engineering Institute. Evaluating user interface tools, user interfaces for hands-free operation.

Malcolm Bauer, Research Associate, School of Computer Science. Characterizing the learning and problem-solving abilities of people at work.

Richard Buchanan, Professor and Head of Department, Design. Rhetorical theory and its application in graphic and communications design, industrial design, strategic planning, design management.

Kathleen M. Carley, Associate Professor of Sociology and Information Systems. Joint cognitive, technological, and structural basis for social and organizational behavior in dynamic settings.

Michael Christel, Member, Technical Staff, Software Engineering Institute. Multimedia interfaces, digital video computer systems.

Stephen E. Cross, Director, Software Engineering Institute. Broad adoption of innovative software development methods, transition of advanced technology, application of intelligent systems to strategic decision making, models of technology transition.

Roger B. Dannenberg, Senior Research Computer Scientist, School of Computer Science. Computer languages, computer music.

Maxine Eskenazi, Visiting Research Scholar, Robotics Institute. Phonetics, automatic speech processing, assessment of speech recognition systems.

Scott E. Fahlman, Principal Research Scientist, School of Computer Science. Artificial intelligence, artificial neural networks, software development environments, biomedical image processing.

Nick V. Flor, Assistant Professor, Graduate School of Industrial Administration. Distributed cognition frameworks, distributed collaboration tools.

Jolene Galegher, Associate Professor of English. Communication in small, collaborative workgroups, collaborative writing.

David Garlan, Assistant Professor of Computer Science. Software engineering, software architecture, formal methods, programming environments.

William E. Hefley, Lecturer of Social and Decision Sciences. Intelligent human-computer interaction, training systems.

Suguru Ishizaki, Assistant Professor of Communication Design. Kinetic typography, facilitation of dynamic design solutions.

Takeo Kanade, Professor of Computer Science and Robotics and Director of the Robotics Institute. Computer vision and sensors, development of self-mobile space manipulators.

David Kaufer, Professor and Head of Department, English. Computer interfaces for supporting individual writing and collaborative writing.

Stephan Kerpedjiev, Project Scientist, Robotics Institute. Information visualization, task-centered visualization, multimedia generation, text and graphics coordination.

Jill Fain Lehman, Research Computer Scientist, Computer Science Department. Natural language understanding, language acquisition, machine learning, cognitive modeling.

Richard L. Martin, Senior Systems Scientist, Robotics Institute. Systems engineering and development of software-intensive systems, evolutionary development models.

Roy Maxion, Systems Scientist, Computer Science Department. Human and machine diagnosis of complex systems, discovery of structure in high-dimensional knowledge bases, distributed systems.

John F. McClusky, Assistant Professor of Industrial Design. User-centered product design, the flow and utilization of computer data throughout the product design and development process.

Philip Miller, Principal Lecturer and Director of Introductory Programming, School of Computer Science. Computer support for education.

Tom M. Mitchell, Professor of Computer Science and Robotics. Artificial intelligence, machine learning, robotics, interfaces that learn.

Jack Mostow, Senior Research Scientist, Robotics Institute, HCII, and Language Technologies Institute, and Director of Project LISTEN. Applying speech recognition and artificial intelligence to literacy.

Dean A. Pomerleau, Research Scientist, Robotics Institute and Computer Science Department. Computer vision, robotics, development of neural network learning techniques to achieve flexibility.

Raj Reddy, Professor and Dean, School of Computer Science. Artificial intelligence, speech recognition and understanding, integrated manufacturing systems.

Lynne M. Reder, Professor of Psychology. Human memory, cognitive skill learning, transfer of training.

Alexander I. Rudnicky, Senior Research Scientist, School of Computer Science. Speech recognition, spoken language interaction, interface design.

Richard Scheines, Senior Research Scientist, Department of Philosophy. Intelligent computer tutors, Web-based courseware on statistical and casual reasoning.

William L. Scherlis, Senior Research Computer Scientist, Computer Science Department. Software engineering, work on the technological foundations for effective long-term collaboration in distributed groups.

Mary Shaw, Professor and Associate Dean for Professional Programs, School of Computer Science. Software architecture, software engineering, programming systems and methodologies.

Mel Siegel, Senior Research Scientist, School of Computer Science, and Director of the Measurement and Control Lab, Robotics Institute. Measurement, diagnosis, and control; perception system invention and modeling; stereoscopic computer and TV systems.

Dan Siewiorek, Professor of Electrical and Computer Engineering and Computer Science, and Director of the Engineering Design Research Center. Computer architecture, design automation, fault-tolerant computing, reliability modeling.

Herbert A. Simon, Richard King Mellon University Professor of Computer Science and Psychology. Computer simulation of cognitive processes, artificial intelligence, management science.

Scott M. Stevens, Senior Member, Technical Staff, Software Engineering Institute. Multimedia, digital video.

Susan G. Straus, Assistant Professor, Graduate School of Industrial Administration. Work groups and technology, how communication media affect performance.

Katia P. Sycara, Senior Research Scientist, Robotics Institute. Case-based and analogical reasoning and learning, group problem solving, negotiation, intelligent agents.

Andrew P. Witkin, Professor of Computer Science. Computer graphics and animation, simulation, computational vision.

PROGRAM OF STUDY

The M.S. in information networking is an alternative to the conventional one-year computer science or electrical engineering graduate programs in that it integrates both and adds some features of a two-year M.B.A. program. The program is unique because it brings together subjects not traditionally offered in one program and provides students with a solid foundation in each.

The information networking degree has been designed as a fourteen-month program with three major elements: technology, business applications, and an intensive design project. The first two elements constitute a ten-month program of study, equivalent to 2½ semesters. In each semester, students carry five courses with associated lab work. The final four months are devoted to a thesis or a design project on which students and faculty collaborate in order to design an information network that meets the needs of a real business.

The technology courses cover the fields of computer science and electrical engineering, for example, packet switching, computer operating systems, distributed systems design, software engineering, and broadband networks. In addition, students have the opportunity to pursue in greater depth those areas with which they are already familiar or in which they have a special interest.

In the business applications section, specially designed courses show how businesses use and process information, how to analyze information flows in the firm and identify opportunities to use information networking, how telecommunications and information regulation both constrain and create opportunities, and the use of information networking as an element of competitive strategy. This group of courses also provides an introduction to fundamental principles of management and economics.

For the final element of the program, students may choose either an interdisciplinary thesis or an intensive design project that is equivalent in rigor to a thesis in current graduate programs at Carnegie Mellon and other leading universities. The group project offers students the opportunity to apply their new knowledge of information networking technology and applications derived from formal course work to solving typical information networking problems. Projects are based on real-world situations, and have frequently contributed to the Institute's research programs.

RESEARCH FACILITIES

The Information Networking Institute has a computer cluster exclusively for use by its students. The cluster contains more than two dozen UNIX workstations from HP, Sun, and DEC, as well as numerous IBM-compatible and Apple computers. Cluster equipment also includes a variety of portable computers and wireless access devices. The Institute has a continuous program of refreshing software and machines. In addition, the University has exceptional computer and library facilities, including extensive on-line access to citation and full-text databases. The campus is served by broadband wireless access to the major distributed networked system known as Andrew. Research facilities are available through the School of Computer Science and the Department of Electrical and Computer Engineering.

FINANCIAL AID

The Information Networking Institute provides financial aid for approximately 20 percent of its graduate students. Aid can be in the form of research assistantships. Support includes a competitive stipend and reduction in tuition. There are a small number of full scholarships for exceptional applicants (who must be U.S. citizens).

COST OF STUDY

The Institute has successfully kept its tuition unchanged for the last three years. Tuition is $37,700 for the fourteen-month program during the 1997–98 academic year. Additional fees may be required for students wishing to extend the program to two years.

LIVING AND HOUSING COSTS

All graduate students attending Carnegie Mellon University live off campus in nearby areas. The estimated living expense for 1997–98, including room and board, insurance, transportation, and miscellaneous expenses, is $13,000.

STUDENT GROUP

The graduate enrollment at Carnegie Mellon University totals more than 2,600 students, who come from colleges and universities throughout the United States and from many countries. In 1996, the Information Networking Institute had 33 students.

STUDENT OUTCOMES

Although heavily represented in the traditional telecommunications companies, Information Networking Institute alumni currently work in more than fifty corporations worldwide.

LOCATION

Carnegie Mellon is located in Oakland, the cultural center of Pittsburgh, on a 90-acre campus adjacent to Schenley Park, the city's largest park. The campus is conveniently located near access to many cultural and sports events and is only four miles from the downtown business district. Pittsburgh is the headquarters for many of the nation's largest corporations and is also home to numerous research laboratories. Many recreational facilities, including ski areas and state parks, are located nearby.

THE UNIVERSITY

Founded by Andrew Carnegie, the Carnegie Institute of Technology joined the Mellon Institute (now the Carnegie Mellon Research Institute) in 1967 to become Carnegie Mellon University. With this merger, one of the leading research institutions in the country was established. The Information Networking Institute is a joint endeavor of the College of Engineering, the School of Computer Science, and the Graduate School of Industrial Administration.

APPLYING

The application, Graduate Record Examinations General Test scores, and letters of reference must be received by February 1. Early application is encouraged. Notification of acceptance and financial aid awards is made by April 15. Minimum preparation normally includes an undergraduate program in electrical engineering, computer engineering, or computer science.

CORRESPONDENCE AND INFORMATION

Admissions Coordinator
Information Networking Institute
Carnegie Mellon University
Pittsburgh, Pennsylvania 15213-3890

Telephone: 412-268-7195
Fax: 412-268-7196
E-mail: ini-admissions+@andrew.cmu.edu
World Wide Web: http://www.ini.cmu.edu

CARNEGIE MELLON UNIVERSITY
THE FACULTY AND THEIR RESEARCH

Ilker Baybars, Deputy Dean and Director, Master's Program, and Professor of Operations Management and Manufacturing; Ph.D., Carnegie Mellon. Production/operations management, assembly line balancing, operations research, heuristic algorithms, design of telecommunications networks.

Linda Argote, David M. and Barbara A. Kirr Professor of Industrial Administration; Ph.D., Michigan. Organizational learning, productivity, technology transfer, organizational structure, group decision making and performance.

Alex Hills, Distinguished Service Professor, Engineering and Public Policy; Ph.D., Carnegie Mellon. Telecommunications in rural and remote areas, telecommunications policy, radio-based communications technology.

Hyong Kim, Associate Professor of Electrical and Computer Engineering; Ph.D., Toronto. Computer networks, high-speed multimedia networks, advanced switching system, BISDN.

Charles H. Kriebel, Professor of Industrial Administration (Graduate School of Industrial Administration); Ph.D., MIT. Computers and information systems, information economics, management science, operations management, robotics, applied economics, productivity, manufacturing control systems, information resources management.

B. V. K. Vijaya Kumar, Professor of Electrical and Computer Engineering; Ph.D., Carnegie Mellon. Information theory, statistical signal processing, pattern recognition, optical data processing, magnetic recording.

F. Javier Lerch, Associate Professor of Information Systems (Graduate School of Industrial Administration); Ph.D., Michigan. Human-computer interaction, including detection and correction of human errors in computer-based managerial tasks, design and evaluation of user interfaces for computer decision support and office automation, trust in machine advice, and cognitive modeling of organizations.

José Moura, Professor of Electrical and Computer Engineering; Sc.D., MIT. Statistical communications, signal processing, and stochastic control, with applications to modulation systems, guidance tracking, high-resolution spectral estimation, parameter identification, and statistical image processing.

Tridas Mukhopadhyay, Associate Professor of Industrial Administration (Graduate School of Industrial Administration); Ph.D., Michigan. Business value of information technology, electronic data interchange, software cost estimation, cost analysis.

Jon M. Peha, Assistant Professor of Electrical and Computer Engineering and of Engineering and Public Policy; Ph.D., Stanford. Computer and telecommunications networks (e.g., congestion control for (B)ISDN, reliability, wireless networks, telecommunications policy).

Mahadev Satyanarayanan, Professor of Computer Science; Ph.D., Carnegie Mellon. Distributed systems, particularly Coda, a distributed file system that is resilient to server and network failures.

Daniel Siewiorek, Buhl Professor of Electrical and Computer Engineering and Computer Science; Ph.D. Stanford. Modular design of reliable computing structures, with emphasis on design automation and multiprocessors.

Marvin Sirbu, Professor of Engineering and Public Policy, Industrial Administration, and Electrical and Computer Engineering; Sc.D., MIT. Telecommunications technology, policy, and management; communication and computer standards; integrated voice, data, and video in the home and implications for regulatory policy.

Sandra Slaughter, Assistant Professor of Information Systems; Ph.D., Minnesota. Productivity and quality in software development and maintenance, software project management, information systems employment strategies.

Richard Stern, Professor of Computer Science and of Electrical and Computer Engineering; Ph.D., MIT. Automatic speech recognition, particularly statistical classification of features and adaptation to new speakers; auditory perception, including the application of optical detection and estimation theory.

Jay Strosnider, Associate Professor of Electrical and Computer Engineering; Ph.D., Carnegie Mellon. High-reliability, high-performance, real-time computing systems whose performance properties can be validated without extensive testing.

Donald Thomas, Professor of Electrical and Computer Engineering; Ph.D., Carnegie Mellon. Computer-aided design for integrated circuits and systems, including design and synthesis of such systems from an abstract description.

Michael Trick, Associate Professor of Operations Research; Ph.D., Georgia Tech. Combinatorial optimization and network optimization.

Doug Tygar, Associate Professor of Computer Science; Ph.D., Harvard. Secure operating systems; algorithms and protocols that allow exploitation of special hardware to achieve strong levels of security; copy production, electronic software distribution, and secure electronic currency.

INFORMATION NETWORKING INSTITUTE MAJOR RESEARCH INITIATIVES

The Institute has taken a leadership role in several areas of research. They include:

The Wireless Research Initiative: This includes systems research, innovative computer platforms for mobile use, compression research, and human factors of mobile usage. In addition, the Institute was the prime initiator and implementer of Wireless Andrew, a 1.5 Mb-per-second wireless access network covering most of the campus buildings. The Institute has also been a leader in developing mobile applications for emergency response, health care, and vehicle maintenance systems. Additional information is available at the World Wide Web site (http://www.ini.cmu.edu/WIRELESS/Wireless.html).

NetBill: This project is an Internet billing system developed at the Information Networking Institute that supports electronic commerce. NetBill functions as an intermediary between a merchant and consumer who wish to conduct business. It provides the mechanisms for consumer-merchant pairs to securely transfer goods and perform financial transactions. More information is available at the World Wide Web site (http://www.ini.cmu.edu/netbill).

CARNEGIE MELLON UNIVERSITY

ROBOTICS DOCTORAL PROGRAM

PROGRAM OF STUDY

The Robotics Doctoral Program is a unique program that brings together areas of robotics research that would otherwise be spread across different departments or even separate universities, preparing students to take a leading role in the research and development of future generations of integrated robotic technologies and systems. Requirements for the Ph.D. include course work in the key areas of perception, cognition, and manipulation; completion of a specialized qualifier and a research qualifier; and the submission of a thesis describing original, independent research.

Students are expected to split their time evenly between course work and research during the first two years of the program, after which they concentrate entirely on research. Students are involved in every aspect of research, from initial problem formulation to the final publication of results. Research is conducted in the laboratories of the Robotics Institute under the supervision of faculty advisers and in collaboration with student colleagues. Advisers are chosen in the first semester after students spend several weeks assimilating into the environment of the Robotics Institute. The expected duration of the program is four to six years.

RESEARCH FACILITIES

Students in the Robotics Doctoral Program work in the Robotics Institute's various research laboratories at the University, including the following laboratories: Advanced Manipulators, Calibrated Imaging, Intelligent Modeling, Intelligent Sensors, Learning Hand-Eye Robot, Manipulation, Manufacturing Logistics, Manufacturing Systems Architecture, Medical Robotics, Mobile Robot, Field Robotics, Intelligent Measurement and Control, Production Planning, Rapid Manufacturing, Shape Deposition, Concurrent Engineering, Production Control, Task-Oriented Vision, and High Definition Systems.

The Institute's research laboratories hold and maintain a multitude of unique and general research equipment. In the area of mobile robots, Carnegie Mellon is known for the Navlab vehicles, Ambler, Dante, Terregator, Neptune, and Uranus. Robotic manipulators include the Troikabot system, Pumas, Adepts, a Direct-Drive Arm, a Reconfigurable Modular Manipulator System, Robot World, IMB-RS, and others. Institute laboratories house more than a dozen vision systems, a stereolithographer, Silicon Graphics Reality Engines, a shape deposition facility, and special sensors such as fast range finders (ERIM), ground penetrating radar, and olfactory and photometric sensors. Computer-controlled moving platforms, high-precision calibration equipment, and solid modeling systems are also used in the robotic research conducted in the laboratories. In addition, the Robotics Institute's own electronic labs, machine shops, and fabrication facilities support all of these activities.

The joint computing facility of the Robotics Institute and the School of Computer Science (SCS) has more than 2,200 machines of a wide variety available for faculty members and graduate students. All new students in the robotics program are assigned personal workstations such as Sun SPARCs or Power Macintoshes.

FINANCIAL AID

All students in the robotics program are supported by graduate fellowships during the academic year. This support is provided on the basis of the student's participation in one or more of the ongoing robotics research projects. This participation is an integral part of the student's education. In 1997–98, each student receives full tuition and fees plus a stipend of $1900 per month for the nine-month academic year. Additional allowances for dependents are available. Students holding outside fellowships may be given supplementary stipends. In the summer, students may accept research support from the University or seek employment in industry.

COST OF STUDY

Tuition and fees for 1997–98 are $20,375, which is generally paid through fellowships.

LIVING AND HOUSING COSTS

The University does not provide housing for graduate students. Accommodations in the community are available at a variety of costs.

STUDENT GROUP

Carnegie Mellon has a total enrollment of approximately 7,500 students, of whom about 2,700 are graduate students. Within the robotics program there are 40 faculty members and approximately 60 students.

STUDENT OUTCOMES

The goal of the Robotics Doctoral Program is to prepare students to conduct independent research and become the future leaders formulating the ideas and building the systems that determine the basic understanding of robots and purposeful behavior in general. Graduates of the program are in positions at top universities, research groups, and government research laboratories all over the world.

LOCATION

Carnegie Mellon is located in Oakland, the cultural center of Pittsburgh. The 90-acre campus is adjacent to Schenley Park, the largest city park. The campus is close to the many cultural and sports activities of the city and is only 4 miles from the downtown business district. Pittsburgh is the headquarters for many of the nation's biggest corporations. There is a large concentration of research laboratories in the area.

THE UNIVERSITY AND THE PROGRAM

Founded in 1900 by Andrew Carnegie, the Carnegie Institute of Technology joined with the Mellon Institute (now the Carnegie Mellon Research Institute) in 1967 to become Carnegie Mellon University. Through this merger one of the nation's leading research and education institutions was established.

The Robotics Doctoral Program is a joint effort of the College of Engineering, the School of Computer Science, and the Graduate School of Industrial Administration. It is administered by the Robotics Institute, which is part of the School of Computer Science.

APPLYING

Application materials are available by writing to the address below. The application, official transcripts, Graduate Record Examination General Test scores, and three letters of recommendation must be received by January 1. The TOEFL is required for students whose native language is not English. While formal admission requirements are flexible, minimum preparation normally includes an undergraduate program in science or engineering and some experience in computer programming. Excellence and promise may balance a lack of formal preparation.

CORRESPONDENCE AND INFORMATION

Robotics Doctoral Program
Carnegie Mellon University
5000 Forbes Avenue
Pittsburgh, Pennsylvania 15213-3890

Telephone: 412-268-3733
E-mail: robotics.admissions@ri.cmu.edu
World Wide Web: http://www.ri.cmu.edu

CARNEGIE MELLON UNIVERSITY
THE FACULTY AND THEIR RESEARCH

O. Amidi, Systems Scientist, Robotics. Aerial robotics, vision-based robot navigation and control, high-speed industrial inspection.

D. Baraff, Assistant Professor, Robotics. Dynamic simulation with collision, contact, and constraints; computer graphics and animation; modeling friction; interactive simulation for manufacturing and design.

J. Bares, Research Scientist, Robotics. Full-cycle conception to testing of intelligent machines for hazardous environments, construction, and heavy industry applications.

D. A. Bourne, Senior Systems Scientist, Robotics. Real-time expert systems, languages for flexible manufacturing, manufacturing process, and computer vision.

V. M. Brajovic, Research Scientist, Robotics. VLSI vision sensors (computational sensors), computer vision, perception for robot guidance and navigation, perception for human-machine interaction.

H. Choset, Assistant Professor, Mechanical Engineering and Robotics. Sensor-based exploration, motion planning, coverage, highly articulated robots, mobile robots, sensors, inspection, computational geometry (Voronoi diagrams).

S. Cross, Senior Research Scientist, Robotics and Software Engineering Institute (SEI), and Director, SEI. Artificial intelligence, large multimedia information systems, knowledge banks for medicine, articulate agents, associate systems.

M. Erdmann, Associate Professor, Computer Science and Robotics. Automatic synthesis of robotic programs, planning with uncertainty, mechanics of assembly, randomized manipulation strategies, information requirements of robot tasks, cooperating robots, nonprehensile manipulation.

G. K. Fedder, Assistant Professor, Electrical and Computer Engineering and Robotics. Microelectromechanical systems (MEMS), microrobotics, MEMS computer-aided design.

K. J. Gabriel, Professor, Electrical and Computer Engineering and Robotics. Microelectromechanical systems (MEMS), human-machine interfaces, biomimetic systems.

S. K. Gupta, Research Scientist, Robotics. Rapid product realization, simulation of manufacturing processes, electromechanical assembly design and planning, computer-aided process planning, mass customization, and design for manufacturing.

M. Hebert, Senior Research Scientist, Robotics. Range data analysis for an autonomous land vehicle, 3-D perception for manipulation in unstructured environments, perception for an autonomous underwater vehicle.

P. Heckbert, Assistant Professor, Computer Science. Computer graphics, image processing.

R. Hollis, Senior Research Scientist, Robotics. Mechatronic design, micro electromechanical systems, real-time control of dynamic systems, multi-degree-of-freedom magnetic actuators, robotic systems that demonstrate "human-like" skills, scaled teleoperation, intelligent mobile robots.

T. Jochem, Systems Scientist, Robotics. Automated vehicle control systems, multisensor integration, tactical action execution for mobile robots, active vision.

A. Jordan, University Professor of Electrical and Computer Engineering. High-definition systems, digital television, studies of computer industries.

T. Kanade, U. A. and Helen Whitaker Professor of Computer Science and Robotics and Director, Robotics Institute. Computer vision, robotic sensors, manipulators, navigational vision systems, medical robotics.

P. K. Khosla, Professor, Electrical and Computer Engineering and Robotics. Sensory-based manipulator control, modular robots, automatic assembly, mobile manipulator systems, human systems interface, real-time software composition.

E. Krotkov, Senior Research Scientist, Robotics. Machine perception (vision, audition, haptics), mobile robotics (especially for planetary exploration).

R. Martin, Senior Systems Scientist, Robotics. Systems engineering and development of software-intensive systems using evolutionary development processes, methods, and tools.

M. T. Mason, Professor of Computer Science and Robotics and Chair, Robotics Doctoral Program. Manipulation, particularly automatic planning of robot manipulator programs, and the mechanics of manipulation.

T. M. Mitchell, Professor, Computer Science and Robotics. Artificial intelligence, machine learning and their applications to robotics, process optimization, information agents, data mining.

A. Moore, Assistant Professor, Computer Science and Robotics. Machine learning, especially as applied to robotics, control, and manufacturing processes; reinforcement learning; heuristic search; probabilistic reasoning; mobile robotics.

H. P. Moravec, Principal Research Scientist, Robotics. Mobile robots, computer vision, three-dimensional modeling, robot manipulators, and space applications.

J. Mostow, Senior Research Scientist, Robotics. Artificial intelligence, machine learning, using automated speech recognition to help children learn to read by getting computers to listen to them read aloud.

D. Navin-Chandra, Research Scientist, Robotics. Theories and methodologies of design, knowledge-aided design, automation, case-based memories, green engineering, concurrent engineering, and computational creativity.

I. R. Nourbakhsh, Assistant Professor, Robotics. Robot architecture, robot communication and cooperation, Automated Highway System, real-world robot campus navigation, nonprehensile manipulation, real-world robot learning from primitives.

S. Penny, Assistant Professor, Art and Robotics. Robotic art, simulation, electronic media.

D. Pomerleau, Research Scientist, Computer Science and Robotics. Connectionism, vision, and mobile robots.

R. Reddy, Herbert A. Simon University Professor and Dean, School of Computer Science. Spoken language systems, multimedia/human computer interaction, learning from example.

S. F. Roth, Senior Research Scientist, Robotics. Information visualization and exploration, HCI, application of artificial intelligence to visualization design and multimedia explanation generation.

N. Sadeh, Research Scientist, Robotics. Constraint-directed reasoning, heuristic search, distributed problem solving, multiagent architectures, probabilistic reasoning, learning mechanisms, planning, scheduling, diagnostics, computer-integrated manufacturing, knowledge-based decision support systems for management and engineering problems.

H. Schempf, Systems Scientist, Robotics. Development of mobile robots for hazardous-waste inspection and remediation and long-reach manipulators for space and infrastructure inspection, research in design and controls of high-fidelity controllable actuation systems.

M. W. Siegel, Senior Research Scientist, Robotics. State-of-the-art sensors and sensor technology, mobile robots for making difficult measurements in difficult environments, 3-D-stereoscopic optics, computer graphics, video and display systems.

R. Simmons, Senior Research Scientist, Computer Science and Robotics. Planning and control for mobile robots, robot architectures, self-reliant robots, learning robots, probabilistic reasoning, autonomous spacecraft.

S. Singh, Systems Scientist, Robotics. Forceful robot-world interaction, motion planning, machine learning, automated earthmoving, land mine detection.

S. F. Smith, Senior Research Scientist, Robotics. Artificial intelligence, constraint-based planning and scheduling, distributed problem solving, machine learning, genetic algorithms, knowledge-based production management.

A. X. Stentz, Senior Research Scientist, Robotics. Robotic excavation, mining, and farming; mobile robots; artificial intelligence; robot architectures; computer vision.

K. P. Sycara, Research Scientist, Robotics. Artificial intelligence, constraint-directed planning and scheduling, case-based reasoning, distributed problem solving, coordination of multiple autonomous agents, enterprise integration, decision support for manufacturing problems, AI applications in design and production management.

S. N. Talukdar, Professor, Electrical and Computer Engineering. Design, manufacturing, distributed systems.

R. H. Thibadeau, Senior Research Scientist, Robotics. Design and construction of automated optical inspection devices, research in computer models of intelligent visual and verbal perception, rule-system languages, and models of computation.

C. Thorpe, Principal Research Scientist, Robotics. Vision, navigation, and systems for mobile robots; the Automated Highway System.

L. E. Weiss, Senior Research Scientist, Robotics. Rapid prototyping, micromechanisms, human tissue engineering.

W. L. Whittaker, Principal Research Scientist, Robotics. Robots for unstructured environments, sensing and image understanding, modeling and planning, navigation and manipulation, control computing and integration of competent robot systems.

A. Witkin, Professor, Computer Science and Robotics. Animation, vision, physically based modeling.

Y. Xu, Senior Research Scientist, Robotics. Space robotics, human control modeling and interface, mechatronics design and control.

CARNEGIE MELLON UNIVERSITY

MASTER OF SOFTWARE ENGINEERING

PROGRAM OF STUDY

Software engineering is that form of computer science that applies the principles of computer science, mathematics, engineering, and management to achieve cost-effective solutions to software problems. Carnegie Mellon University, in response to industry's growing demand for skilled software professionals, offers a one-year master's degree program in software engineering aimed at practitioners from industry. The Master of Software Engineering (M.S.E.) program is sponsored jointly by the University's School of Computer Science (SCS) and the Software Engineering Institute (SEI).

A set of core courses develops skills in the fundamentals of software engineering, with an emphasis on design, analysis, and management of large-scale software systems. A rich collection of elective courses, selected not only from the offerings of the School of Computer Science but also from other schools within the University, allows students to develop deeper technical expertise in one of several specialties, such as real-time systems, human-computer interaction, business, or the economic and organizational environment of software systems.

The capstone of the program is the software development studio component that runs throughout the entire program. The studio provides an opportunity for students to apply the knowledge and skills gained in other courses. Students work in teams to analyze a problem, plan a software development project, and find a solution. Recent studio projects include the movement software for a robot that services the Space Shuttle tiles, a robot for lunar exploration studies, and a tool for integrating architectural information.

RESEARCH FACILITIES

The School of Computer Science research facility has both a large number and a wide variety of computers available for faculty and graduate student use. Personal computing facilities include DEC-Alpha (64 bit architecture running OSF/1 or DEC UNIX), Sun (running SUNOS or Solaris), HP, SGI, and DEC Stations (running Ultrix). The M.S.E. computing environment has personal computers running Windows and LINUX, Sun's running SUNOS, and several Macintoshes. All personal computers in SCS have transparent access to the Andrew File System. The Carnegie Mellon Internet is a fully interconnected, multimedia, multiprotocol infrastructure spanning over 100 segments. These segments are attached to an inverted backbone, enabling access between all systems on the campus. Various media such as fiber optics, shielded and unshielded twisted pair support Fast Ethernet, Ethernet, ATM, HIPPI, Token Ring, and LocalTalk Network protocols utilized are IP/TCP, AppleTalk, and IPX. Carnegie Mellon is connected to the Internet with a T3 (45Mbit/sec) link and will participate in the VBNS.

FINANCIAL AID

Students in the M.S.E. program are generally supported by their companies. There are a small number of teaching assistantships. Students may be able to find employment to complement the program. University-wide work-study opportunities are available to graduate students. Students may apply for Stafford loans.

COST OF STUDY

Tuition for the full-time graduate students accepted for the 1997–98 academic year is $10,138 per semester. This figure is subject to change.

LIVING AND HOUSING COSTS

Graduate students are responsible for their own housing needs. Housing is available in the area within a range of costs.

STUDENT GROUP

The number of students admitted to the M.S.E. program is dependent on the number of qualified applicants. The present class has 22 students from the United States and seven other countries, all with at least two years' industrial experience. Previous classes have averaged 15 students, with an average of seven years of work experience.

STUDENT OUTCOMES

The program's graduates do exceptionally well in obtaining important professional positions after graduation. Some graduates have received starting salaries as high as $70,000 (salaries in some areas of the country are higher than others.) Graduates advance rapidly in their careers, and many have achieved influential management and policy positions within a few years after graduating.

LOCATION

Located 5 miles east of the city in Oakland, the cultural center of Pittsburgh, the University is adjacent to Schenley Park, the city's largest, and close to many cultural and sports activities.

THE UNIVERSITY

Founded in 1900 by Andrew Carnegie, the Carnegie Institute of Technology joined with Mellon Institute (now the Carnegie Mellon Research Institute) in 1967 to become Carnegie Mellon University. With this merger, one of the leading research and education institutions in the country was established.

APPLYING

The application, Graduate Record Examinations scores (General Test and Subject Test in computer science), statement of purpose, up-to-date résumé, letters of reference, and application fee must be received by January 31. Minimum preparation normally includes at least two years' experience working in a sizable software development project; foundation in discrete mathematics and programming-in-the-small; competence in using an imperative block-structured language; an undergraduate degree in computer science, engineering, mathematics, or physics (this requirement is flexible); and practical knowledge of programming methods, computer organization, data structures, compiling techniques, comparative programming languages, operating systems, and database systems.

CORRESPONDENCE AND INFORMATION

Admissions Coordinator
Master of Software Engineering Program
School of Computer Science
Carnegie Mellon University
Pittsburgh, Pennsylvania 15213
Telephone: 412-268-6493
E-mail: mse-info@cs.cmu.edu

CARNEGIE MELLON UNIVERSITY
THE FACULTY AND THEIR RESEARCH

Members of the M.S.E. faculty are drawn from the SEI staff as well as the School of Computer Science. In addition, members of SEI technical projects often act as advisers to student teams in the M.S.E. studio course.

David Garlan, Assistant Professor, School of Computer Science; Ph.D., Carnegie Mellon. Formal methods in software engineering, programming environments, domain-specific software architectures.

Daniel Jackson, Assistant Professor, School of Computer Science; Ph.D., MIT. Software engineering, requirements analysis, design methods, automatic specification checking, reverse engineering.

Nancy R. Mead, Senior Member of the Technical Staff, Software Engineering Institute; Ph.D., Polytechnic of New York. Development of professional infrastructure for software engineers, software requirements engineering, software architectures, software metrics, and real-time systems.

Mary M. Shaw, Alan J. Perlis Professor of Computer Science and Associate Dean for Professional Programs, School of Computer Science; Ph.D., Carnegie Mellon. Programming systems and software engineering, particularly software architecture, programming languages, specifications, and abstraction techniques.

James E. Tomayko, Acting Director of the M.S.E. Program and Coordinator of the M.S.E. Program's Software Development Studio; D.A., Carnegie Mellon. Fault tolerance of distributed embedded systems, history of software development practices and techniques.

Associated Faculty in the School of Computer Science
Bernd O. Bruegge. Debugging and programming environments.

Roger B. Dannenberg. Various aspects of computer music.

Allan L. Fisher. Theory, design, and implementation of efficient, high-performance computing systems.

Merrick L. Furst. Establishing connections between computer science and mathematics, with the goal of developing new computational tools and methods.

Bonnie E. John. Creating engineering models of human performance to be used in the design of human-computer interaction.

James H. Morris. Developing distributed computer systems and their use for human communication.

Brad A. Myers. Human-computer interaction, especially ways to make interfaces easier to use, more functional, and easier to implement.

Raj Reddy. Spoken language systems, multimedia collaboration technologies, learning by reading, 90 percent self-reproducing factories, learning from observation.

M. Satyanarayanan. Data sharing in distributed systems, distributed file systems.

William Scherlis. Program manipulation, information structures, HomeNet research, information infrastructure.

Doug Tygar. Computer security, concentrating on providing mechanisms for secure remote execution.

Jeannette M. Wing. Programming languages and distributed systems, with a specific emphasis on the application of formal methods to reason about complex software systems.

Associated Technical Staff in the Software Engineering Institute
Mario R. Barbacci. Software architecture description languages.

Richard E. Barbour. Software process improvement, capability maturity model–based appraisals, Internal Process Improvement (IPI), Software Capability Evaluation (SCE).

Joe Batman. Real-time systems.

Alan Brown. Computer-aided software engineering environments.

Mary Beth Chrissis. Software process.

Stephen E. Cross, Director, Software Engineering Institute. Broad adoption of innovative software development methods, transition of advanced technology, application of intelligent systems to strategic decision-making models of technology transition.

David Gluch. Dependable system upgrade and reliable real-time systems.

Clifford H. Huff. Software visualization, information, respositories, Web technologies.

Watts Humphrey, Fellow, Software Engineering Institute. Software process research.

Mark Klein. Rate monotonic analysis for real-time systems.

Tom Longstaff. Computer and information security, research on survivable systems.

Linda Northrop. Object-oriented development, system design, databases, minicomputers in business environments, micrographics.

Mark Paulk. Software process.

Linda Hutz Pesante. Communication of technical information to multiple audiences, particularly international audiences.

Ragunathan Rajkumar. Real-time networking and multimedia.

James Rozum. Software measurement methods and software process improvement methods and evaluation techniques.

Lui Sha. Fault-tolerant software for control system management of software- and system-related project risks.

CLAREMONT GRADUATE UNIVERSITY

PROGRAM IN INFORMATION SCIENCE

PROGRAMS OF STUDY
The Claremont Graduate University (CGU) offers three academic programs in information science: the Master of Information Systems (M.I.S.), the Master of Science in the management of information systems (M.S.M.I.S.), and the Ph.D. in the management of information systems.

The 32-unit Master of Information Systems degree program is designed for professionals in information systems and information systems users who want to improve both their professional and management skills and do not plan to continue beyond the master's level. Courses focus on information science issues. The fifty-six-unit Master of Science in the management of information systems degree program is designed for professionals who want a master's degree that leads to management or senior staff positions in information systems organizations or for students who plan to continue on to a doctoral program.

The Ph.D. program in the management of information systems is designed to prepare graduates to make advanced contributions in either university or applied organizational settings. Specially designed courses allow students in each program to be exposed to the areas emphasized in all three programs.

The comprehensive combination of the technical, organizational, and systems elements in the curricula trains future managers to interact effectively with the technical specialists within their organization and trains technical specialists to be more sensitive to the management aspects of information systems. It is this integrated, two-culture approach that distinguishes the CGU vision of information science from a more modest data processing emphasis or from the highly theoretical training of traditional computer science programs. The programs in information sciences are affiliated with the Peter F. Drucker Graduate Management Center. Students take management courses as part of their studies.

As part of its staffing concept in applied fields, the Graduate University appoints adjunct faculty members from industry to teach courses in specialized areas. Because of the University's location in the Los Angeles basin, a large pool of qualified professionals with relevant experience and superior teaching skills is readily available.

RESEARCH FACILITIES
Among the facilities available for research is the Decision Laboratory. Its purpose is to support the study of organizational decision making by senior executives in a technologically enhanced environment, and it provides the appearance and comfort appropriate for executive conferences. The Academic Computing Building houses the Graduate University's computers and the Program in Information Science and has several distinctive features: a wide-band local area network, personal computer laboratories, and a decision support system laboratory. The library system, which includes the central Honnold Library, has extensive holdings of more than 1.9 million volumes, 6,000 periodicals and other serials, and a large collection of materials in microtext format.

FINANCIAL AID
Numerous financial aid packages are available through the information science program and the Graduate University's Financial Aid Office. Institutional fellowships are awarded by the program faculty. Federal and state loans and grants are also available. Information about need-based aid is available from the Financial Aid Office (telephone: 909-621-8337).

COST OF STUDY
For 1997–98, full-time tuition at CGU is $9750 per semester. Part-time tuition is $880 per unit of credit.

LIVING AND HOUSING COSTS
CGU residences accommodate single students, couples, and couples with children at rents ranging from $300 to $700 per month. Most students make their own residential arrangements, living off campus in Claremont or in one of the surrounding communities. Further information may be obtained from the Housing Office, 1263 North Dartmouth Street, Claremont, California 91711 (telephone: 909-607-2609).

STUDENT GROUP
The approximately 115 students enrolled in the Program in Information Science are a diverse and stimulating group. Students come from across the country and represent a broad range of undergraduate disciplines (humanities—6 percent, economics/social sciences—15 percent, business—26 percent, science/computer sciences/engineering—48 percent, other—5 percent). A small group of international students offers a critical perspective on information systems. Thirty-five percent of the students are between 25 and 35 years of age, and practical insights are provided by the many students who have several years of full-time work experience.

LOCATION
The Claremont Graduate University is located in Claremont, a residential community of 36,000, located 35 miles east of Los Angeles. Situated in the foothills of the San Gabriel Mountains, Claremont is ideally located for those who enjoy skiing, hiking, swimming, and camping. Mt. Baldy is a half hour away, with deserts and Pacific Ocean beaches within an hour's drive to the east and west. The climate is sunny most of the year.

THE UNIVERSITY
Founded in 1925, the Claremont Graduate University is affiliated with a group of five undergraduate colleges (Pomona, Scripps, Claremont McKenna, Harvey Mudd, and Pitzer), which together form the Claremont Colleges. The small-college atmosphere at CGU offers students close relationships with faculty members and ample opportunity for individual development. The Graduate University cooperates with other colleges in Claremont to provide facilities and services characteristic of a much larger university. CGU awards master's and doctoral degrees in traditional academic and professional programs with an interdisciplinary emphasis. Enrollment is approximately 2,000, and the regular CGU faculty of 74 appointees is supplemented by more than 200 faculty members from the undergraduate colleges in Claremont and other affiliated institutions.

APPLYING
Students are admitted on a rolling basis to the fall, spring, and summer semesters. Application forms are available from the program office. A complete application includes official graduate and undergraduate transcripts, GRE or GMAT scores, three letters of recommendation, a résumé, and a personal statement. The TOEFL is required of applicants whose native language is not English and who do not hold a degree from a U.S. college or university. Applications for institutional fellowships must be completed by February 15 to receive priority consideration.

CORRESPONDENCE AND INFORMATION
For more information, application materials, or a campus visit, students should contact:

Nancy M. Back, Program Coordinator
Program in Information Science
Academic Computing Building
Claremont Graduate University
130 East Ninth Street
Claremont, California 91711-6190
Telephone: 909-621-8209
Fax: 909-621-8564
E-mail: infosci@cgs.edu
World Wide Web: http://www.cgs.edu

CLAREMONT GRADUATE UNIVERSITY
THE FACULTY AND THEIR RESEARCH

Paul Gray, Ph.D., Stanford. Professor Gray, professor of information science, was the founding chair of the Claremont Graduate University's Program in Information Science. He specializes in decision support systems and is the originator of the Graduate University's Decision Laboratory. He worked for eighteen years in research and development organizations, including nine years at SRI. Before coming to Claremont in 1983, he was a faculty member at Stanford University, the Georgia Institute of Technology, the University of Southern California, and Southern Methodist University. He has held numerous offices in national professional societies. He was president of the Institute of Management Sciences for 1992–93 and was formerly president-elect, vice president, and secretary of the Institute. He is on the editorial board of several journals. He is the author of twelve books and more than seventy-five journal articles.

M. Lynne Markus, Ph.D., Case Western Reserve. Professor Markus, professor of information science, joined Claremont in 1992 after teaching at the University of California, Los Angeles, and the Massachusetts Institute of Technology. Her current research interests include "reengineering" the organization through the use of information technology, the information systems professional as "change agent," and the management of information technology from the perspective of the general manager. Among her publications is the book *Systems in Organizations: Bugs and Features*.

Magid Igbaria, Ph.D., Tel Aviv (Israel). Professor Igbaria, professor of information science, joined Claremont in 1995. Before he joined the faculty, he taught at the University of Hawaii and at Drexel University. He has published numerous articles in journals such as the *Communications of ACM, MIS Quarterly Journal in MIS, Omega,* and *Information and Management*. His current research interests focus on IS personnel, computer technology acceptance, management of IS, the virtual workplace, impact of technology on individuals, organizations and society, cross-cultural differences in IS, and international IS.

Lorne Olfman, Ph.D., Indiana. Professor Olfman, associate professor of information science, joined the faculty in 1987. His teaching specialties are system analysis design and planning, end-user computing, and research methodology. He is actively involved in research projects on the design and adoption of group work technologies, end-user training, and the impact of information systems on organizational memory. He served as chair of the 1996 conference of the Association for Computing Machinery Computer Personnel Research and Management Information Systems. He has been an economist and a systems analyst in transportation and telecommunications organizations, and had previously worked as a programmer.

The Program in Information Science benefits enormously from a unique arrangement between CGU and Israel's Tel Aviv University, widely recognized for the strength of its IS program. Each year, a Tel Aviv University faculty member serves as a visiting professor at CGU; the following Tel Aviv University professors have taught at CGU:

Niv Ahituv is a professor of information systems at Tel Aviv University and former dean of its faculty of management.

Cad Ariav, professor on the faculty of management at Tel Aviv University, specializes in database management and decision support systems.

Israel Borovits is a professor of computers and information systems on the faculty of management at Tel Aviv University, where he served for a number of years as the chair of its CIS program.

Phillip Ein-Dor is a professor on the faculty of management at Tel Aviv University and has served as chairperson for the Program in Information Science.

Seev Neumann was highly influential in the establishment of the Ph.D. program at the Claremont Graduate University's Program in Information Science and has served as chair of the program.

Eli Segev is a professor on the faculty of management at Tel Aviv University.

Israel Spiegler is chair of the Computers and Information Systems Department of the faculty of management at Tel Aviv University.

CLEMSON UNIVERSITY

COLLEGE OF ENGINEERING AND SCIENCE
DEPARTMENT OF COMPUTER SCIENCE

PROGRAMS OF STUDY

The Department of Computer Science offers programs leading to both Master of Science and Doctor of Philosophy degrees in computer science.

Requirements for a Ph.D. degree include passing a written qualification examination on core computer science subjects, a comprehensive examination in the student's specialization, and an oral defense of the dissertation. The areas of possible research span computer science. Interdisciplinary work is possible.

Programs leading to the M.S. degree are tailored to the student's interest, while ensuring a strong base in core subjects. Typical requirements include ten courses and a scholarly paper plus a written examination.

RESEARCH FACILITIES

The Department of Computer Science uses a wide variety of computer systems and networks. It operates an Intel Hypercube, a Sun LAN with four servers, a Data General Aviion systems performance lab with two dual processor servers and a RAID (disk array) system, and a Silicon Graphics LAN that includes an Onyx Reality Engine. There are over eighty workstations and terminals. Both UNIX System V and BSD UNIX environments are supported.

FINANCIAL AID

Financial support for graduate students is available through limited research assistantships associated with grants and contracts, teaching assistantships, and graduate fellowships. Students with assistantships are normally expected to work an average of 20 hours each week while taking three courses per semester (two courses for Ph.D. students). Both twelve-month and nine-month assistantships are available. Alternative employment opportunities for qualified applicants are sometimes available.

COST OF STUDY

In-state tuition for 1996–97 was $1461 per semester for graduate students without assistantships and $460 per semester for graduate students with assistantships. Out-of-state tuition was $2922 per semester for graduate students without assistantships and $460 per semester for graduate students with assistantships.

LIVING AND HOUSING COSTS

In 1996–97, double-occupancy rooms in the dormitories ranged in cost from $755 to $1190 per semester. All are air conditioned, and most include the cost of a room telephone. University apartments ranged in cost from $1050 per semester to $1150 per semester for duplex units; the cost of utilities varied. Many privately owned apartments are available; costs vary considerably.

STUDENT GROUP

Clemson University's on-campus enrollment of more than 17,000 students includes approximately 4,000 graduate students. The Department of Computer Science enrolls about 110 full-time graduate students.

STUDENT OUTCOMES

Many M.S. graduates find employment in the computer industry, with salaries typically starting around $40,000. Recent graduates have taken positions with AT&T, Bell Northern Research, Data General, IBM, Intel, Microsoft, Sun Microsystems, and Transarc.

LOCATION

Clemson, South Carolina, is a small college town that enjoys the beauty and water sports of Lakes Hartwell (61,350 acres), Keowee (18,500 acres), and Jocassee (7,500 acres); the scenery of the South Carolina, Georgia, and North Carolina mountains (40-minute drive); and the challenge of many wild and scenic rivers such as the nearby Chattooga. Opportunities to participate in and enjoy plays, concerts, lectures, films, and sports events are provided by many University and community groups. While shopping in Clemson is limited to specialty stores and shopping centers, Seneca, Greenville, and Anderson are only a few minutes away and offer more extensive shopping and entertainment.

THE UNIVERSITY

Clemson University is a fully accredited, state-supported, coeducational, land-grant university founded in 1889. The main campus is situated on a 1,400-acre site, part of which was once the John C. Calhoun plantation. The campus is surrounded by 21,000 acres of agricultural research land and bordered by Lake Hartwell. Clemson offers sixty-eight undergraduate and ninety-five graduate curricula.

APPLYING

Applications for admission are considered at any time of the year. Applications for financial assistance, however, should be submitted before March 1 for full consideration.

CORRESPONDENCE AND INFORMATION

Student Services Specialist
Department of Computer Science
Clemson University
Box 341906
Clemson, South Carolina 29634-1906
Telephone: 864-656-5853

CLEMSON UNIVERSITY

THE FACULTY AND THEIR RESEARCH

Robert M. Geist III, Professor; Ph.D., Notre Dame. Systems modeling, performance evaluation, reliability modeling, graphics.

Harold C. Grossman, Associate Professor; Ph.D., Michigan State. Programming language theory, design, and implementation; software development methodology.

Eleanor O'M. Hare, Assistant Professor; Ph.D., Clemson. Graph algorithms, graph representation.

Sandra M. Hedetniemi, Professor; Ph.D., Virginia. Data structures, analysis of algorithms.

Stephen T. Hedetniemi, Professor and Head; Ph.D., Michigan. Design and analysis of algorithms, parallel algorithms, computational complexity and combinatorial optimization.

David P. Jacobs, Associate Professor; Ph.D., Missouri. Algorithms, algebraic computation.

A. Wayne Madison, Associate Professor; Ph.D., Virginia. Operating systems, performance measurement and evaluation.

Brian A. Malloy, Assistant Professor; Ph.D., Pittsburgh. Languages, compilers, parallel processing, software maintenance and testing, simulation modeling.

John D. McGregor, Associate Professor; Ph.D., Vanderbilt. Software engineering, graphical systems, object-oriented development.

Edward W. Page III, Professor; Ph.D., Duke. Neural computation, computer architecture, telecommunications.

Roy P. Pargas, Associate Professor; Ph.D., North Carolina. Parallel computation, genetic algorithms.

John C. Peck, Professor; Ph.D., Southwestern Louisiana. Operating systems, database systems, real-time manufacturing systems.

Mark K. Smotherman, Associate Professor; Ph.D., North Carolina. Computer architecture, superscalar processors, reliability.

D. E. Stevenson, Associate Professor; Ph.D., Clemson. Computational science, numerical analysis, computation theory.

Albert J. Turner, Professor; Ph.D., Maryland. Software engineering, computer science education.

James M. Westall, Professor; Ph.D., North Carolina. Systems software, performance measurement and evaluation, character recognition, neural networks.

CLEMSON UNIVERSITY

DEPARTMENT OF ELECTRICAL AND COMPUTER ENGINEERING

PROGRAMS OF STUDY

The department offers programs leading to M.S. and Ph.D. degrees in electrical engineering and in computer engineering. The M.S. programs have three options: thesis, report, and all course work. The first two options require 24 semester hours of course work and 6 hours of research credit. The all–course work option requires 33 hours of course work. The report option is reserved for special programs. Each M.S. student must satisfy a minor area requirement outside the department as part of the 24-hour or 33-hour requirements described above, and each M.S. program must include a core of courses in a specialty area. Computer engineering students must satisfy the computer engineering core and can select from such specialty areas as computer communications, computer systems architecture, communications/digital signal processing, and controls/robotics. Electrical engineering students may select from computational electromagnetics, communications/digital signal processing, computer communications, controls/robotics, electronics, and power systems. An exit examination is required for the all–course work option. The Ph.D. degree requires 24 hours of course work past the M.S. degree. The student is also required to pass qualifying and comprehensive examinations and complete a dissertation that must produce an original contribution to the field. Because of the requirement to do original work, no fixed time limit for the degree can be specified, although three years past the M.S. is considered typical. The typical student completes the M.S. degree before beginning the Ph.D., although direct entry into the Ph.D. program from the B.S. degree is an option for qualified students.

RESEARCH FACILITIES

The ECE department's laboratories are primarily located in the Fluor Daniel Engineering Innovation Building, which was dedicated in 1995 and constructed to house research facilities. Research in the areas of communications and digital signal processing is supported by the Holcombe Laboratory for Advanced Communications, the ITT Laboratory for Spread Spectrum Communications, the Barnes Communications Laboratory, the Image Acquisition and Analysis Laboratory, the Radar Systems Laboratory, and the Speech Analysis Laboratory. Facilities for computer systems architecture research include the Software Standards and Technology Laboratory, the Parallel Architecture Research Laboratory, and the Instruction-Level Parallelism Laboratory. The controls and robotics area maintains a Mechatronics Laboratory and shares the Robotics and Machine Automation Laboratory (RAMAL). Electromagnetics research is supported by the Computational Electromagnetics Laboratory, which includes a ground plane, HP Vector Network Analyzers, a microwave/millimeter wave instrumentation receiver system, a Cascade probe station, and fabrication equipment. Work within the electronics area is supported by the Rapid Photothermal Processing Laboratory, an Oxide Reliability Laboratory, the Reliability and Failure Analysis Laboratory, and the MOCVD Laboratory. Electric power area activities are supported by the Power System Protection Laboratory, the Duke Power Quality Laboratory, and the Union Camp Power Electronics/Variable Frequency Drive Laboratory. The ECE department also houses a 2,000-square-foot Microstructures Laboratory, which contains a 900-square-foot cleanroom with class 100 areas. This laboratory is equipped for silicon micromachining, mask-making metal deposition, wet etching, photolithography, and packaging of semiconductor integrated circuits. The ECE department also hosts the Center for Semiconductor Device Reliability Research and the Clemson University Electric Power Research Association (CUEPRA) and is associated with the Center for Advanced Manufacturing.

FINANCIAL AID

In 1996–97, the nine-month rates for teaching assistantships were $9000 for Ph.D. students and $7500 for M.S. students. Recommended nine-month rates for externally funded research assistantships were $12,000 and $10,000 for Ph.D. and M.S. students, respectively. These rates are for half-time appointments. A number of fellowships ranging from $3000 to $5000 are awarded on a competitive basis.

COST OF STUDY

Tuition and fees for graduate students in 1997–98 are $120 per credit hour for in-state students. However, the rate for graduate assistants is $460 per semester, independent of the number of hours taken. Out-of-state tuition is $2922 per semester for 12 or more credits or $240 per credit hour for fewer than 12 credits.

LIVING AND HOUSING COSTS

Rents for University dormitory rooms and apartments range from about $630 to $930 per semester. Cafeteria service is available on campus for all meals. Married student housing is available in apartments whose cost ranges from about $290 to $365 a month. Graduate assistants and graduate fellows are given priority in assignment to married student housing if applications are received sufficiently early.

STUDENT GROUP

Currently, about two thirds of the students in the department hold assistantships. Approximately half of the assistantships are for teaching-related duties, and half are for externally funded research. Approximately half of the graduate assistants are U.S. natives. About 10 percent of the students in the department are women. Representation from minority groups is low among the U.S. native component, but the department is actively trying to recruit qualified students who are members of minority groups.

LOCATION

Clemson is a small college town located in the scenic northwest corner of South Carolina. It is situated in the foothills of the Blue Ridge Mountains, on the 1,000-mile shoreline of Lake Hartwell. Clemson is 3 hours from Great Smoky Mountain National Park, 5 hours from Atlantic beaches, and 2 hours from Atlanta. Nearby cities of moderate size include Anderson and Greenville, home of the Greenville-Spartanburg airport.

THE UNIVERSITY AND THE DEPARTMENT

Clemson is a fully accredited, state-supported, coeducational land-grant institution founded in 1889. It is built on the former plantation of John C. Calhoun, U.S. Vice President and statesman of the mid-1800s. The beautiful campus comprises 1,400 acres and represents an investment of approximately $200 million in academic buildings, student housing, and service facilities. Total enrollment is approximately 17,000, which includes about 4,000 graduate students. The Department of Electrical and Computer Engineering has an enrollment of about 500, including 140 graduate students. Two thirds of these graduate students are electrical engineering majors, and one third are computer engineering majors. Approximately 45 students in the department are Ph.D. candidates. In addition, a number of M.S. candidates plan to continue in Ph.D. programs.

APPLYING

Applications for admission and financial assistance are considered at any time of the year. However, opportunities for financial support are much better for students whose applications are received well in advance of the desired entry date. Transcripts of undergraduate work and scores on the General Test of the Graduate Record Examinations are required. Undergraduate corequisite course requirements are specified for applicants not having a B.S. degree in the intended graduate degree area.

CORRESPONDENCE AND INFORMATION

Graduate Program Coordinator
Department of Electrical and Computer Engineering
Clemson University, Riggs Hall
Clemson, South Carolina 29634-0915
Telephone: 864-656-5902

CLEMSON UNIVERSITY
THE FACULTY AND THEIR RESEARCH

Carl W. Baum, Assistant Professor; Ph.D., Illinois at Urbana-Champaign. Digital communications, wireless communications, spread-spectrum communications, detection theory, signal acquisition.

Ernest G. Baxa, Associate Professor; Ph.D., Duke. Radar signal processing, spectral analysis.

Michael A. Bridgwood, Associate Professor; Ph.D., Portsmouth (England). VLSI reliability, electromagnetic compatibility.

Chalmers M. Butler, Professor; Ph.D., Wisconsin. Applied electromagnetic theory, mathematical and numerical methods, aperture penetration, communication antennas.

E. Randolph Collins Jr., Associate Professor; Ph.D., Georgia Tech. Power electronics, electric machines, adjustable speed motor drives, industrial applications, compatibility of power systems and industrial automation equipment.

Darren M. Dawson, Professor; Ph.D., Georgia Tech. Nonlinear control techniques for mechatronic systems such as electric machinery, robotic manipulator systems, overhead cranes, and magnetic bearings; boundary control of distributed parameter systems such as textile machines, flexible beams/robots/rotors, and cable structures.

Thomas L. Drake, Professor; Ph.D., Michigan State. Real-time applications of minicomputer and microcomputer systems, computer organization and architecture, design of digital computer systems, Ada programming language, electrical geophysical prospecting techniques.

David J. Dumin, Professor; Ph.D., Stanford. Solid-state devices and materials, ultra-small MOS devices, VLSI reliability.

Manoj Franklin, Assistant Professor; Ph.D., Wisconsin–Madison. Computer architecture, parallel processing, fault-tolerant computing, digital testing.

Adly A. Girgis, Professor; Ph.D., Iowa State. Power systems transients and protection; Kalman filtering; signal processing and microprocessor applications in power system instrumentation, control, and protection; application of artificial intelligence in power systems.

John N. Gowdy, Professor and Department Chair; Ph.D., Missouri–Columbia. Speech recognition and synthesis, neural networks, digital signal processing, microcomputer systems.

Joseph L. Hammond, Professor; Ph.D., Georgia Tech. Computer communication networks, local area networks, performance modeling.

James W. Harrison, Professor; Ph.D., North Carolina State. VLSI reliability, electromigration, IC processing, GaAs devices.

James E. Harriss, Research Associate; Ph.D., Georgia Tech. VLSI reliability, integrated circuit manufacturing, silicon materials, applied statistics (SPC,DOE).

John J. Komo, Professor; Ph.D., Missouri–Rolla. Error control coding, spreading sequences, spread-spectrum communications.

James F. Leathrum, Professor; Ph.D., Princeton. Computer engineering, software engineering, programming systems, Ada applications and environments, control theory and practice.

Walter B. Ligon III, Assistant Professor; Ph.D., Georgia Tech. Computer architecture, parallel processing, computer vision, compilers, VLSI design.

David L. Lubkeman, Associate Professor; Ph.D., Purdue. Electric power distribution system modeling and analysis and operations, distribution automation, distribution power quality, industrial power systems.

Johnson Y. S. Luh, Professor; Ph.D., Minnesota. Intelligent robotic systems, industrial automation, machine vision, learning control, differential games.

Elham B. Makram, Professor; Ph.D., Iowa State. Computer modeling of machinery and power systems, power system analysis, power system harmonics and measurements, power system planning.

Anthony Q. Martin, Assistant Professor; Ph.D., Clemson. Computer simulation of power systems, high impedance faults and power quality.

Dan McAuliff, Lecturer, B.S.E.E., Southern Methodist (plus thirty-two years in industry). Lectures all classes for nonelectrical engineering majors and is responsible for the College of Engineering and Science Effective Technical Communications Program.

Daniel L. Noneaker, Assistant Professor; Ph.D., Illinois at Urbana-Champaign. Digital communications, wireless communications, spread-spectrum communications, error-control coding for fading channels, cellular telephoning, data communications.

L. Wilson Pearson, Professor; Ph.D., Illinois. Millimeter wave systems, circuit design employing monolithic microwave integrated circuits (MMICs), asymptotic methods in electromagnetics, the finite-element method applied to electromagnetics; currently leads a multi-university team of workers (University of Colorado, University of Central Florida, University of Leeds [England], University of Michigan, and North Carolina State University) in a Multidisciplinary University Research Initiative (MURI) on spatial power combining at millimeter wavelengths.

Kelvin F. Poole, Professor; Ph.D., Manchester (England). Integrated circuit design, VLSI reliability, computer-aided design, materials, vacuum.

Michael B. Pursley, Professor; Ph.D., USC. Digital communications and information theory, wireless communications, spread-spectrum communications, communication over fading channels, applications of error-control coding, protocols for packet radio networks, adaptive methods for time-varying communication channels, and mobile communication systems and networks.

Robert J. Schalkoff, Professor; Ph.D., Virginia. Electronic systems, solid-state electronics, integrated circuits manufacturing, solar cells, electronic and optical materials.

Rajendra Singh, Professor; Ph.D., McMaster (Canada). Electronic systems, solid-state electronics, IC processing.

Robert W. Snelsire, Professor; Ph.D., Carnegie Mellon. Radar systems, finite fields.

John D. Spragins, Professor; Ph.D., Stanford. Computer communications, local area networks, network reliability, performance modeling, communications protocols.

Ian D. Walker, Associate Professor, Ph.D., Texas at Austin. Robotics and control—multiple manipulator mechanisms, robotic hands and grasping, fault tolerance, redundant manipulators, contact modeling and dynamics, application of robotics to space and remote systems.

Xiao-Bang Xu, Associate Professor; Ph.D., Mississippi. Integral equation methods, numerical analysis, and electromagnetic theory; development and application of hybrid numerical methods for the solution of scattering problems, for the analysis of extremely low frequency fields, and for the treatment of nonlinear problems.

COLORADO STATE UNIVERSITY

COMPUTER SCIENCE DEPARTMENT

PROGRAMS OF STUDY

The Computer Science Department at Colorado State University seeks outstanding students for study leading to the M.S. and Ph.D. degrees. The M.S. program provides maximum flexibility so participants may prepare for professional employment or advanced graduate study. The Ph.D. program is meant for well-qualified individuals who desire to prepare for careers in academic or industrial research. While students may work in many areas, active research programs in algorithms, applicative languages, architecture, artificial intelligence, distributed systems, fault tolerance, genetic algorithms, graphics, languages and compilers, neural networks, operating systems, parallel processing, performance evaluation, and software engineering provide special opportunities for thesis research topics and assistantship support.

The department retains an applied orientation, with industrial adjunct faculty supplying insight into practical issues and industrial approaches. Weekly seminars with speakers from many academic and industrial organizations provide students with a broad introduction to many research areas.

The M.S. curriculum requires at least 39 credits. M.S. students pass an oral final examination on their thesis or project work. Highly successful M.S. students may transfer to the Ph.D. program with no loss of efficiency. The Ph.D. curriculum requires at least 72 credits in total, comprising both course work and research. Required examinations are a written qualifying examination, an oral preliminary examination, and a final examination in defense of the dissertation.

RESEARCH FACILITIES

The department maintains several laboratories: architecture studies—an HP9000/S400 and five 715/33 workstations; artificial intelligence/neural nets—five IBM RS6000/320H workstations and five X terminals; graphics—an HP9000/433VRX system and twelve 715/50 workstations; networks and distributed computing—an AT&T server and eighteen workstations; software engineering—fifteen 9000/700 series workstations. Numerous HP, Sun, and DEC workstations and servers provide additional computing. The department houses a CNAPS 128-processor SIMD machine and a Motorola MONSOON dataflow system for parallel processing research. All the preceding run UNIX and are fully networked. Researchers have access to other multiprocessor systems at remote locations. In addition, the department has a variety of X terminals, workstations, and microcomputers for instructional and research purposes. Laser printers are available.

The University maintains several IBM RS6000 servers running AIX and a Visualization Laboratory. The campus network connects many sites and provides access to Internet.

FINANCIAL AID

The University has grants, loans, and work-study opportunities available to graduate students. The department offers teaching and research assistantships that require duties of 20 hours per week. Assistantships pay a competitive stipend and tuition; supported students pay only fees.

COST OF STUDY

In 1997–98, full-time graduate tuition is $1300 per semester for Colorado residents and $4945 for nonresidents. Fees are $337.56 per semester.

LIVING AND HOUSING COSTS

On-campus apartments for single students rent for $300 to $475 per month. Family housing ranges from $460 to $680 per month (utilities included). Off-campus, rent for a two-bedroom apartment averages $588 per month (plus utilities).

STUDENT GROUP

The University enrolled about 22,000 regular, on-campus students in 1996–97, including 3,512 graduate students. Thirty percent of approximately 65 computer science graduate students are noncitizens. More than 50 percent receive financial aid from the department, and more than 20 percent work in the computer industry while pursuing graduate work.

LOCATION

Fort Collins is a community of 100,000 located along the foothills of the Rocky Mountains, 60 miles north of Denver. The climate is moderate—15 inches of precipitation and 290 days of sunshine annually. Cultural offerings include a museum, library, symphony, chorale, and community center, all with many activities and performances. The spectrum of cultural and outdoor activities, the climate, and the mountain setting contribute to making Fort Collins an attractive community.

THE UNIVERSITY

Colorado State was designated Colorado's land-grant college in 1879; it was named Colorado State University in 1957. Today the University has 8 colleges, 56 departments, and more than 100 academic programs. The central 666-acre campus includes nearly 100 academic buildings, research facilities, dormitories, married students' housing, and the Veterinary Teaching Hospital. Other campuses support instruction and research in agriculture, engineering, natural resources, and biological sciences.

APPLYING

Applications are considered throughout the year. Applicants who desire financial assistance should apply six months prior to their first semester. Applicants should have an undergraduate GPA of at least 3.2 on a 4.0 scale. All applicants must take both the GRE General Test and the Subject Test in computer science. International applicants must also take the TOEFL; a score of at least 580 is strictly required. A nonrefundable application fee of $30 is required from all applicants.

CORRESPONDENCE AND INFORMATION

Graduate Programs Coordinator
Department of Computer Science
Colorado State University
Fort Collins, Colorado 80523

Telephone: 970-491-5792
Fax: 970-491-2466
E-mail: csgradinfo@cs.colostate.edu

COLORADO STATE UNIVERSITY
THE FACULTY AND THEIR RESEARCH

Charles W. Anderson, Associate Professor; Ph.D., Massachusetts. Neural networks, machine learning, artificial intelligence, pattern classification, adaptive control, graphics.

J. Ross Beveridge, Assistant Professor; Ph.D., Massachusetts. Computer vision, robot navigation, model matching.

James Bieman, Associate Professor; Ph.D., Southwestern Louisiana. Software engineering, executable specifications, software analysis and testing, programming languages.

A. P. Wim Böhm, Professor; Ph.D., Utrecht (Netherlands). Parallel and dataflow architectures, software, and languages.

Bruce Draper, Assistant Professor; Ph.D., Massachusetts. Computer vision, machine learning, image understanding.

Dale H. Grit, Associate Professor; Ph.D., Minnesota. Parallel functional languages and architectures, operating systems.

Sandeep Gupta, Assistant Professor; Ph.D., Ohio State. Parallel and distributed systems, scientific computing, compilers.

Adele Howe, Assistant Professor; Ph.D., Massachusetts. Artificial intelligence, planning, agent architectures, failure recovery.

Robert Kelman, Professor Emeritus; Ph.D., Berkeley. Computational methods, mathematical software.

Yashwant Malaiya, Professor; Ph.D., Utah State. Fault-tolerant computing, architecture, VLSI design, hardware and software reliability evaluation.

Walid Najjar, Associate Professor; Ph.D., USC. Parallel processing, dataflow architectures, performance and reliability evaluation, parallel simulation.

Rodney Oldehoeft, Professor; Ph.D., Purdue. Parallel processing software and systems, functional programming, operating systems.

Stephen Seidman, Professor and Chair; Ph.D., Michigan. Parallel computation, formal methods in software engineering.

Pradip Srimani, Professor; Ph.D., Calcutta. Parallel and distributed computing, operating systems, graph theory applications.

Anneliese von Mayrhauser, Professor; Ph.D., Duke. Software engineering, maintenance, metrics, testing, reliability, performance evaluation.

Darrell Whitley, Professor; Ph.D., Southern Illinois. Artificial intelligence, machine learning, genetic algorithms, neural networks.

Affiliate Faculty

Anura Jayasumana, Ph.D., Michigan State. Computer networks, VLSI.

Julian Kately, Ph.D., Michigan State. Computer systems evaluation, computer center management.

Selected Research Areas

Artificial Intelligence: Learning algorithms for neural networks, neural networks for control and signal processing, genetic algorithms and applications to scheduling problems.

Software Engineering: Evaluation of testing criteria, executable specifications, foundations of software measurement, automatic analysis from algebraic specifications, static evaluation of sequencing constraints, software maintenance toolkit, software reliability simulation.

Parallel and Distributed Computing: Applicative language features, dataflow parallelisms versus locality, SISAL language and implementations, representation of parallel programs, distributed algorithms.

Graphics and Computer Vision: Detail enhancement in volume images, ray tracing of fractal terrain, image understanding.

Architecture and Networks: Reliability management through self-testing; reliability, performability, and scalability of large-scale distributed systems; network reliability and topology.

COLUMBIA UNIVERSITY

DEPARTMENT OF COMPUTER SCIENCE

PROGRAMS OF STUDY

The doctoral program of the Department of Computer Science is geared toward the exceptional student. The faculty believes that the best way to learn how to do research is by doing it. Starting in their first year, students do joint research with the faculty. They also prepare themselves for the Ph.D. qualifying examination, which tests breadth in computer science. The primary educational goal is to prepare students for research and teaching careers either in universities or in industry.

The department enjoys a low doctoral student–faculty ratio (about 4:1). Ph.D. students are viewed as colleagues by the faculty.

Current research areas include algorithmic analysis, artificial intelligence, collaborative work, computational complexity, computer-aided design of digital systems, databases, distributed computing, graphics, logic synthesis, network management, parallel processing, software development environments, vision, robotics, user interfaces, and virtual environments.

The department also offers the Master of Science degree in computer science. This program can be completed within one academic year of full-time classwork. However, completing the optional thesis generally stretches the program to two years. The M.S. degree can also be earned through part-time study.

RESEARCH FACILITIES

The department has well-equipped lab areas for research in robotics, computer vision, networking, distributed and mobile computing, user interfaces, computer graphics, and collaborative work. The computer facilities include a shared infrastructure of Sun file servers (both multiprocessors and single processors), a student research lab of workstations and various X terminals, a department-wide Ethernet (with numerous subnets), high-speed dial-up lines, FDDI rings connecting the file servers and HP cluster, and an ATM testbed connected to NYNET, plus a research project infrastructure and numerous Sun, HP, DEC, IBM, and SGI workstations, including an Onyx 2 server and an HP Distributed Parallel Cluster. Research labs contain Unimate Puma 500 and IBM robotic arms; a UTAH-MIT dextrous hand; an Aspex PIPE (an eight-stage parallel pipelined low-level image processor); a DataCube image processor; an Adept-1 robot; a real-time defocus range sensor; SGI, Sun, and HP 3-D–shaded graphics workstations with true 3-D input (via a VPL DataGlove hand-tracking system and ascension and Logitech trackers); a StereoGraphics stereo display system; see-through head-mounted displays; a high-resolution color scanner; an HP 6300 optical jukebox and a 600 GB exabyte tape jukebox; experimental packet-radio-based workstations; additional network gateways; and a departmental network that is gatewayed to a campuswide backbone network as well as to Internet (through Nysernet) and Usenet. The research facility is supported by a full-time staff of professional systems programmers and engineers, aided by many part-time student technicians.

FINANCIAL AID

Most doctoral students receive graduate research assistantships. The stipend for 1997–98 is $1420 per month for the academic year. In addition, graduate research assistants receive full tuition exemption.

COST OF STUDY

Tuition and fees total approximately $21,320 for the 1997–98 academic year.

LIVING AND HOUSING COSTS

In 1997–98, dormitory rooms are available for approximately $4445–$4495 for the academic year. Apartments in University-owned buildings cost $700 per month and up. Rooms are also available at International House; these cost from $450 to $600 per month.

STUDENT GROUP

There are 57 Ph.D. students in the department. A large proportion of Columbia University's student body is at the graduate level: of approximately 18,800 students, 10,500 are in the graduate or professional schools.

LOCATION

New York City is the intellectual, artistic, cultural, gastronomic, corporate, financial, and media center of the United States, and perhaps of the world. The city is renowned for its theaters, museums, libraries, restaurants, opera, and music. Inexpensive student tickets for cultural and sporting events are frequently available, and the museums are open to students at very modest cost or are free. The ethnic variety of the city adds to its appeal.

The city is bordered by uncongested areas of great beauty that provide varied types of recreation, such as hiking, camping, skiing, and ocean and lake swimming. There are superb beaches on Long Island and in New Jersey, while to the north lie the Catskill, Green, Berkshire, and Adirondack mountains. Close at hand is the beautiful Hudson River valley.

THE UNIVERSITY

Columbia University was established as King's College in 1754. Today it consists of sixteen schools and faculties and is one of the leading universities in the world. The University draws students from many countries. The high caliber of the students and faculty makes it an intellectually stimulating place to be. Columbia University is located on Morningside Heights, close to Lincoln Center for the Performing Arts, Greenwich Village, Central Park, and midtown Manhattan. Columbia athletic teams compete in the Ivy League.

APPLYING

For maximum consideration for admission to the doctoral program, students should submit the following before January 1: official applications for the fall term, transcripts, two recommendation letters, and a $45 application fee. The General and Subject tests of the Graduate Record Examinations are required for all computer science graduate students and should be taken by October for doctoral admission or December for master's admission. The deadlines for applications to the master's program are March 15 for fall admission and October 1 for spring admission.

CORRESPONDENCE AND INFORMATION

For information about the programs:
Admissions Committee
Department of Computer Science
450 Computer Science Building
Columbia University
New York, New York 10027
Telephone: 212-939-7000
E-mail: gradinfo@cs.columbia.edu
World Wide Web: http://www.cs.columbia.edu

For applications:
Office of Engineering Admissions
530 S. W. Mudd Building
Columbia University
New York, New York 10027
Telephone: 212-854-6438

COLUMBIA UNIVERSITY

THE FACULTY AND THEIR RESEARCH

Alfred V. Aho, Professor and Chairman. Evolvable information systems and networks, software production, algorithms for information retrieval.

Peter K. Allen, Associate Professor. Sensor-based robotics, computer vision, 3-D modeling.

Mukesh Dalal, Assistant Professor. Artificial intelligence, knowledge representation and reasoning, logic, databases, user interfaces, information systems.

Steven K. Feiner, Associate Professor. Computer graphics, knowledge-based picture generation, user interfaces, animation, virtual worlds, augmented reality, visual languages, hypermedia.

Zvi Galil, Morris A. and Alma Schapiro Professor of Engineering and Julian Clarence Levi Professor of Computer Science. Analysis of algorithms, computational complexity, cryptography, parallel processing, theory of computation.

Leana Golubchik, Assistant Professor. Multimedia information systems, high-performance I/O, computer systems modeling and performance evaluation.

Jonathan L. Gross, Professor of Computer Science, Mathematics, and Mathematical Statistics. Combinatorial and probabilistic models, parallel architectural models, topological graph theory and low-dimensional algebraic topology.

Gail E. Kaiser, Associate Professor. Software development environments, software process, object-oriented databases, collaborative work, workflow applications, cooperative transactions.

John R. Kender, Associate Professor. Computer vision, robotic navigation, artificial intelligence.

Kathleen R. McKeown, Associate Professor. Artificial intelligence, natural-language processing, language generation, multimedia explanation, user interfaces, user modeling.

Shree K. Nayar, Professor. Computer vision, physical models, vision sensors, realistic rendering, robotics.

Steven M. Nowick, Associate Professor. Computer-aided digital design, asynchronous circuits, logic synthesis, high-power and high-performance systems, formal hardware verification.

Kenneth A. Ross, Assistant Professor. Databases, query optimization, declarative languages for database systems, logic programming.

Henning Schulzrinne, Associate Professor. Internet real-time and multimedia services and protocols, modeling and analysis of computer-communication networks, operating systems, network security.

Salvatore J. Stolfo, Associate Professor. Artificial intelligence, parallel processing, knowledge discovery in databases.

Joseph F. Traub, Edwin Howard Armstrong Professor and Professor of Mathematics. Computational complexity, information-based complexity, financial computations, limits to scientific knowledge.

Athanasios M. Tsantilas, Lecturer. Parallel computing, randomized algorithms, computational complexity.

Stephen H. Unger, Professor of Computer Science and Electrical Engineering. Logic circuits theory, digital systems, self-timed systems, parallel processing, technology-society interface, engineering ethics.

Henryk Woźniakowski, Professor. Computational complexity, information-based complexity, algorithmic analysis, numerical mathematics.

Yechiam Yemini, Professor. Algorithms and protocols for computer networks, network management, high-speed networks, organization of distributed systems, modeling and analysis of computer-communication networks.

Associated Faculty

Theodore R. Bashkow, Professor Emeritus. Computer architecture, data communications.

Matthew Blaze, Adjunct Lecturer. Cryptography and cryptographic protocols, computer security, file systems, large-scale systems, networks.

Judith Klavans, Research Scientist and Adjunct Associate Professor. Text databases, natural language processing, digital library, computing and the humanities, artificial intelligence, computational lexicons, electronic dictionaries.

Jaron Lanier, Visiting Scholar. Visualization of extremely complex systems, "slow machine"—an exotic hypothetical computation device, programming language design and virtual reality systems.

Paul Michelman, Research Scientist. Robotics and biomedical engineering.

Ron Mraz, Adjunct Lecturer. Computer architecture, real-time systems, operating systems, parallel systems.

Soumitra Sengupta, Assistant Professor, Department of Medical Informatics. Distributed systems, deductive and object-oriented databases, concurrency control, medical informatics, application system development.

Arthur G. Werschulz, Visiting Scholar. Information-based complexity theory, optimal solution of integral and differential equations, numerical analysis.

George Wolberg, Adjunct Lecturer. Image processing, computer graphics, computer vision, and image warping, reconstruction, and enhancement.

COLUMBIA UNIVERSITY

DEPARTMENT OF ELECTRICAL ENGINEERING

PROGRAMS OF STUDY

The Department of Electrical Engineering offers programs of study leading to the degrees of Master of Science (M.S.), Electrical Engineer (E.E.), Doctor of Engineering Science (Eng.Sc.D.), and Doctor of Philosophy (Ph.D.). Registration as a nondegree candidate (special student) is also permitted.

There are no prescribed course requirements for these degrees. Students, in consultation with their faculty advisers, design their own programs focusing on particular fields. Among them are semiconductor physics materials and devices; telecommunication systems and computer networks; high-speed analog, RF analog, and mixed analog/digital integrated circuits and systems; image and video processing; electromagnetic theory and applications; plasma physics; quantum electronics; sensory perception; and medical electronics.

Graduate studies are closely associated with research. Faculty members are engaged in theoretical and experimental research in various areas of their disciplines (see reverse of this page).

Access also exists to a number of interdisciplinary programs such as Computer Engineering, Solid-State Science and Engineering, and Bioengineering. In addition, substantial research interactions occur with the Departments of Applied Physics, Computer Science, and Industrial Engineering and Operations Research and with the College of Physicians and Surgeons.

The requirements for the Ph.D. and Eng.Sc.D. degrees are identical. Both require a dissertation based on the candidate's original research, conducted under the supervision of a faculty member. The work may be theoretical or experimental or both. The E.E. degree program does not require a thesis. It provides specialization beyond the M.S. degree in a field chosen by the student and is particularly suited to those who wish to advance their professional development after a period of industrial employment.

RESEARCH FACILITIES

Every phase of current research activities is fully supported and carried out in one of more than a dozen well-equipped research laboratories run by the department.

Specifically, laboratory research is conducted in the following laboratories: Multimedia Networking Laboratory; Ultrafast Opto-Electronics Laboratory; Photonics Laboratory; Microelectronics Device Fabrication Laboratory; Molecular Beam Epitaxy Laboratory; Laser Processing and Surface Analysis Laboratory; VLSI Design Laboratory; Image and Advanced Television Laboratory; Lightwave Communications Laboratory; Mixed Analog-Digital VLSI Laboratory; Plasma Physics Laboratory (in conjunction with the Department of Applied Physics); and Fowler Memorial Laboratory for Auditory Research (in conjunction with the Department of Otolaryngology at Columbia College of Physicians and Surgeons).

FINANCIAL AID

Teaching assistantships and graduate research assistantships are available. Stipends range from $1222 to $1317 per month plus tuition exemption.

COST OF STUDY

The annual tuition for 1997–98 is estimated at $22,500, plus fees.

LIVING AND HOUSING COSTS

The University provides limited housing for graduate men and women who are registered either for an approved program of full-time academic study or for doctoral dissertation research. University residence halls include traditional dormitory facilities as well as suites and apartments for single and married students; furnishings and utilities may be included. An estimated minimum of $16,500 should be allowed for board, room, and personal expenses for the academic year.

University Real Estate properties include apartments owned and managed by the University in the immediate vicinity of the Morningside Heights campus. These are leased yearly, as they become available, to single and married students at rates that reflect the size and location of each apartment as well as whether furnishings or utilities are included.

Requests for additional information and application forms should be directed to the Assignments Office, 111 Wallach Hall, Columbia University, New York, New York 10027.

STUDENT GROUP

In 1996–97, enrollment in the Department of Electrical Engineering totaled 320 students and included 69 undergraduates (juniors and seniors), 153 master's degree candidates, 83 doctoral candidates with master's degrees, and 15 professional and part-time special students. The student population has a diverse and international character.

LOCATION

The proximity of many local industries provides strong student-industry contact and excellent job opportunities. Cooperative research projects are available in neighboring industrial laboratories, which are engaged in research and development in computers, telecommunications, electronics, defense, and health care. Adjunct faculty from industry provide courses in areas of current professional interest. Frequent colloquia are given on current research by distinguished speakers from industry and neighboring universities.

THE UNIVERSITY

Since its founding in 1754, Columbia University has attracted students interested in the issues of their times. Opened as King's College under charter of King George II to "prevent the growth of republican principles which prevail already too much in the colonies," it instead educated founders of a new and powerful nation: Alexander Hamilton, John Jay, Robert Livingston, and Gouverneur Morris. Since then such notable figures as Michael Pupin, Edwin Armstrong, and Jacob Millman have served as professors of electrical engineering at Columbia.

APPLYING

Application forms should be requested from the Office of Engineering Admissions, 530 Seeley W. Mudd. Applications should be filed by January 1 for admission the following September. Notification of admission decisions are mailed beginning March 1.

CORRESPONDENCE AND INFORMATION

Student Coordinator
Department of Electrical Engineering
Columbia University
500 West 120th Street, Room 1312
New York, New York 10027-6699
Telephone: 212-854-3104

COLUMBIA UNIVERSITY
THE FACULTY AND THEIR RESEARCH

Dimitris Anastassiou, Professor; Ph.D., Berkeley, 1979. Digital image/video communications and processing with emphasis on multimedia applications. (Telephone: 212-854-3113; e-mail: anastas@ee.columbia.edu)

Andrew Campbell, Assistant Professor; Ph.D., Lancaster (England), 1996. Open interfaces for signaling, control, and management of broadband networks; ATM-based networks; multimedia communications. (Telephone: 212-854-3109; e-mail: campbell@ee.columbia.edu)

Shih-Fu Chang, Assistant Professor; Ph.D., Berkeley, 1993. Visual signal processing and communications, multimedia systems and communications, visual information systems. (E-mail: sfchang@ee.columbia.edu)

Paul Diament, Professor; Ph.D., Columbia, 1963. Free electron lasers, fiber optics, waveguiding in VLSI chips, electromagnetics. (Telephone: 212-854-3111; e-mail: diament@ee.columbia.edu)

Alexandros Eleftheriadis, Assistant Professor; Ph.D., Columbia, 1995. Image and video signal processing and compression; video communication systems; operating system and network support for digital video; information and rate distortion theories. (Telephone: 212-854-8670; e-mail: eleft@ee.columbia.edu)

Tony Heinz, Professor; Ph.D., Berkeley, 1982. Ultrafast optoelectronics and spectroscopy; nonlinear optics; surface dynamics; optical diagnostics of surface processes. (Telephone: 212-854-6564; e-mail: t.f.heinz@columbia.edu)

John Khoury, Associate Professor; Eng.Sc.D., Columbia, 1988. Design and analysis of mixed analog-digital integrated circuits and systems with application to telecommunications, wireless systems, and related fields. (Telephone: 212-854-6414; e-mail: khoury@elab.columbia.edu)

Aurel A. Lazar, Professor; Ph.D., Princeton, 1980. Multimedia networking: control, management, and telemedia; the mathematics of networks and intelligent systems. (e-mail: aurel@ctr.columbia.edu)

Q. Y. Ma, Assistant Professor; Ph.D., Columbia, 1990. Superconductor electronics, biomedical sensors, magnetic sensors. (Telephone: 212-854-5080; e-mail: qyma@ee.columbia.edu).

Richard M. Osgood Jr., Higgins Professor; Ph.D., MIT, 1973. Integrated optical devices and design, semiconductor surface physics, laser sources. (Telephone: 212-854-4462; e-mail: osgood@columbia.edu)

Amiya K. Sen, Professor; Ph.D., Columbia, 1963. Plasma instabilities and their feedback control, plasma turbulence and anomalous transport.

Kenneth Shepard, Assistant Professor; Ph.D., Stanford, 1992. Interconnect analysis and design for submicron devices and integrated circuits, passive and active components, VLSI tools and technology of advanced microprocessors.

Thomas E. Stern, Dicker Professor; Sc.D., MIT, 1956. Integrated digital communication networks, lightwave networks, analysis of queueing systems. (Telephone: 212-854-3119; e-mail: tom@ee.columbia.edu)

Yannis P. Tsividis, Professor; Ph.D., Berkeley, 1976. Microelectronic circuit design, circuit theory, solid-state device modeling.

Wen I. Wang, Professor; Ph.D., Cornell, 1981. Heterostructure devices and physics, material properties, molecular-beam epitaxy. (E-mail: wen@ee.columbia.edu)

Edward S. Yang, Professor; Ph.D., Yale, 1965. GaAs heterojunction bipolar transistors, SiGe MOS devices, high-speed circuits. (E-mail: esyang@ee.columbia.edu)

Charles A. Zukowski, Associate Professor; Ph.D., MIT, 1985. Design and analysis of digital VLSI circuits, circuit simulation, communication circuits.

COLUMBIA UNIVERSITY

GRADUATE SCHOOL OF ARTS AND SCIENCES
COLLEGE OF PHYSICIANS AND SURGEONS
DEPARTMENT OF MEDICAL INFORMATICS
TRAINING PROGRAMS IN MEDICAL INFORMATICS

PROGRAMS OF STUDY

Medical informatics studies the organization of medical information, the effective management of information using computer technology, and the impact of such technology on medical research, education, and patient care. Columbia University offers two programs in medical informatics: an advanced degree program leading to the M.A., M.Phil., or Ph.D. degree and a postdoctoral training program.

The degree program focuses on the theory and application of information science in the domain of medicine. The program trains students for academic careers as researchers and teachers as well as for professional positions in health-care information processing. The curriculum incorporates course work from computer science, public health, and biostatistics, with core courses and projects in medical informatics serving to integrate approaches and illustrate practical applications. The predoctoral program requires three years of full-time study to complete the M.Phil. and typically two additional years to conduct research and write the dissertation. The M.A. degree can be completed in two years of part-time study.

The postdoctoral training program trains medical informatics scientists for careers as productive researchers and teachers. The fellowship is funded by the National Library of Medicine, an agency of the National Institutes of Health, and is open to United States citizens or permanent residents with an M.D. or Ph.D. degree. Support for each fellow will be for three years in most cases. The program is individualized to address the needs and directions of each fellow. Fellows will be expected to develop, conduct, and report on an original research project.

RESEARCH FACILITIES

Computing resources for medical informatics research at Columbia include the Integrated Academic Information Management System (IAIMS), a sophisticated, heterogeneous distributed information system for patient care, administration, research, and scholarship. This environment provides an unparalleled living laboratory for informatics projects. The Health Sciences Library provides access to medical informatics journals, on-line materials, and a microcomputer classroom. Additional computer laboratories and modern classroom facilities are available in a newly renovated Student Learning Center located in Presbyterian Hospital.

FINANCIAL AID

All students accepted into the predoctoral program are awarded support that fully provides for the tuition and the medical insurance fees required by the University. Students also receive a stipend toward living expenses that commences with registration and normally continues throughout graduate study. This stipend is $17,556 for the 1997–98 academic year. International students as well as U.S. citizens are eligible for these fellowships. The postdoctoral training program includes a stipend and tuition support for course work.

COST OF STUDY

Fees for the 1997–98 year for the part-time master's program are tuition, $5727 per semester; required Student Health Service, $840; and Blue Cross insurance, $515.

LIVING AND HOUSING COSTS

Housing is available on the Health Sciences Campus and on the Morningside Heights Campus of Columbia University. Accommodations include University residence halls, which consist of furnished 2- or 4-person suites, and institutional Real Estate Apartments, which include studios and one-, two-, and three-bedroom apartments. Membership at the Athletic Club is free to students. The club contains a swimming pool, squash courts, a gymnasium, a sauna, and exercise equipment and is accessible to the handicapped.

STUDENT GROUP

There are currently 7 part-time master's students, 10 predoctoral students, and 8 postdoctoral fellows. Eight are women, and 10 are international students. Approximately one third will seek academic positions, while the others intend to pursue professional careers in health-care information processing.

LOCATION

The Department of Medical Informatics at the College of Physicians and Surgeons of Columbia University is located on the Health Sciences Campus at 165th Street and Fort Washington Avenue in upper Manhattan. The complex includes the Columbia-Presbyterian Medical Center and its subdivisions and the New York Psychiatric Institute. New York's world-renowned cultural activities are easily accessible by public transportation, as are sporting events and other recreational opportunities.

THE UNIVERSITY

Columbia University, a privately supported institution, is one of the world's leading educational, scholarly, and research centers. Founded by charter as King's College in 1754, it is one of the oldest universities in the country. Medical informatics programs enjoy close collaborative relationships with the Columbia University Health Sciences Library, basic and clinical science departments on the Health Sciences Campus, and the computer science department at the Morningside Campus.

APPLYING

The basic requirement for admission as an M.A. student in the medical informatics degree program is a bachelor's degree. Applicants should indicate clearly on the application whether they are applying for the part-time M.A. degree program or the full-time Ph.D. program.

The postdoctoral training program is open to U.S. citizens or permanent residents with an M.D. or Ph.D. degree. Applicants should send a letter of purpose, transcripts (from college and from medical or graduate school), a curriculum vitae, and three letters of reference.

CORRESPONDENCE AND INFORMATION

For Advanced Degree Program:
Office of Graduate Affairs, Room 406
College of Physicians and Surgeons
Columbia University
701 West 168th Street
New York, New York 10032
Telephone: 212-305-8058
Fax: 212-305-1031
E-mail: midegree@cucis.cpmc.columbia.edu
World Wide Web: http://www.cpmc.columbia.edu

For Postdoctoral Training Program:
James J. Cimino, M.D.
Atchley Pavilion 1310
161 Fort Washington Avenue
New York, New York 10032
Telephone: 212-305-8127
Fax: 212-305-3302
E-mail: ciminoj@cucis.cis.columbia.edu

COLUMBIA UNIVERSITY

THE FACULTY AND THEIR RESEARCH

Paul D. Clayton, Chair, Ph.D. Generation and sharing of medical knowledge, linking literature sources to computer-generated suggestions.

Barry A. Allen, Ph.D. Advanced user interfaces, genome informatics.

Randolph C. Barrows Jr., M.D. Outpatient applications, practice guidelines, prevention, computer-based medical records.

James J. Cimino, M.D. Medical concept representation and the exploitation of that representation to provide clinical decision support.

Bruce H. Forman, M.D. Methods and standards for data interchange in health-care informatics.

Carol Friedman, Ph.D. Natural language processing.

George M. Hripcsak, M.D. Automated decision support, data acquisition and access, mobile computing.

Nilesh L. Jain, D.Sc. Evaluation, clinical practice guidelines, clinical decision support.

Robert A. Jenders, M.D. Expert systems, electronic medical records, medical vocabulary.

Stephen B. Johnson, Ph.D. Natural language processing, knowledge representation, database design.

Pat Molholt, M.L.S. Knowledge structuring and management.

Soumitra Sengupta, Ph.D. Networking, security, systems architecture.

Justin B. Starrem, M.D., Ph.D. User interface design, radiologic information systems, community health information systems.

John L. Zimmerman, D.D.S. Dental informatics, informatics training, WWW, information technologies in education, electronic oral health records.

CORNELL UNIVERSITY
DEPARTMENT OF COMPUTER SCIENCE

PROGRAM OF STUDY

The Department of Computer Science is oriented primarily toward doctoral study. The emphasis is on research, and most graduates of the program are employed in research positions. The department offers strong programs of study in the theory of computation, the design and analysis of algorithms, programming languages and methodology, numerical analysis, concurrency and distributed systems, artificial intelligence, information retrieval and text processing, networking, multimedia, databases, and computer graphics.

The dominant characteristic of the department, and its principal advantage for a graduate student, is the unusual opportunity for close interaction between faculty and students. All faculty members are actively engaged in research, their teaching load is relatively light, and the student-faculty ratio is quite favorable. One indication of the degree of interaction is the large number of papers coauthored by faculty and students.

A typical Ph.D. program requires about five years of study. The first two years are largely devoted to course work and the search for a thesis topic. A comprehensive examination is taken in the first or second year.

RESEARCH FACILITIES

The department's research computing facility consists of more than 300 high-performance engineering workstations from Sun, HP, and Intel, together with color X-window terminals, back-end file servers, and back-end compute servers. Specialized machines include a 32-node Intel iPSC/860 and an 8-node IBM SP2. Departmental machines are on a local network with gateways to University-wide, national, and international networks. There are special departmental laboratories for research in robotics, vision, and distributed computing. Other Cornell computing facilities include a number of IBM mainframes, computer graphics research and instructional facilities, and two instructional workstation laboratories—one with twenty-five HP 700 series machines and the other with forty Sun Microsystems workstations. There are also a large number of personal computers for instructional use. Cornell is the site of a National Science Foundation–funded supercomputer center, the Cornell Theory Center, located in the building adjacent to the Department of Computer Science. The Center consists of a 516-node IBM SP2 and many other facilities.

The Cornell University library, one of the largest in the country, maintains an excellent collection in computer science.

FINANCIAL AID

All Ph.D. students receive financial aid in the form of a fellowship, research assistantship, or teaching assistantship. For 1997–98, fellowship stipends range from $12,000 to $18,000 for nine months, and assistantship stipends are $12,500. Financial aid includes tuition in addition to the amounts cited.

COST OF STUDY

For 1997–98, tuition for the two-semester academic year is approximately $21,400.

LIVING AND HOUSING COSTS

For 1997–98, graduate dormitory accommodations cost about $7000 per academic year. University-operated married student apartments rent for about $800 per month. In addition, a considerable range of privately owned accommodations can be found within commuting distance.

STUDENT GROUP

There are 150 resident graduate students (90 Ph.D. and 60 M.Eng.) in the department; all are full-time. Each year, about 15 to 20 new Ph.D. students are enrolled.

STUDENT OUTCOMES

The department's graduates are a good source of information about the Cornell program—they hold computer science positions at Arizona, Berkeley, Brown, Carnegie Mellon, Colorado, Colorado State, CUNY, Dartmouth, Florida State, Harvard, Illinois, Johns Hopkins, Kansas, Maryland, Massachusetts, Minnesota, Montreal, North Carolina, Ohio, Penn State, Pennsylvania, Princeton, Purdue, Queens, Rhode Island, Rice, Stanford, SUNY at Albany, SUNY at Stony Brook, Toronto, Washington, and Wisconsin. Many graduates have gone into research positions in industry (Hewlett-Packard, IBM, ITT, Bell Labs, Control Data, Ford Aerospace, Mitre, Softech, Microsoft, and Xerox) and government, and several have formed their own companies.

LOCATION

Ithaca, New York, is a small town in the heart of the Finger Lakes region. It offers the cultural activities of a large university and the pleasures of a rural environment. Facilities for skiing, sailing, camping, hiking, soaring, and other sports are close at hand.

THE UNIVERSITY AND THE DEPARTMENT

Cornell is a prominent research university, one of the largest producers of Ph.D.'s in the country, and it stands out as a major contributor of women scholars. Computer Science interacts most closely with Cornell's distinguished Departments of Mathematics, Operations Research, Mechanical Engineering, Linguistics, Electrical Engineering, and Architecture, as well as the interdisciplinary Center for Applied Mathematics.

The computer science department, which was organized in 1965, is one of the oldest departments of its kind in the country. It has a full-time faculty of 27, associated faculty members from other departments, and numerous visitors each year.

APPLYING

To be admitted to the Graduate School, an applicant must have a B.A. or equivalent degree. In addition, applicants are expected to have had significant programming experience, a solid background in mathematics (at least calculus and linear algebra and preferably other subjects such as logic, statistics, or analysis), and, depending on the specialization chosen, an appropriate background that would permit immediate enrollment in graduate-level courses in that specialization.

CORRESPONDENCE AND INFORMATION

Graduate Field Office
Department of Computer Science
4126 Upson Hall
Cornell University
Ithaca, New York 14853-7501

CORNELL UNIVERSITY
THE FACULTY AND THEIR RESEARCH

Kenneth P. Birman, Professor; Ph.D., Berkeley, 1981. Distributed systems, signal processing.
Geoffrey Brown, Assistant Professor; Ph.D., Texas at Austin, 1987. VLSI.
Claire Cardie, Assistant Professor; Ph.D., Massachusetts, 1994. Natural language processing, machine learning, artificial intelligence.
Tom Coleman, Professor; Ph.D., Waterloo, 1979. Numerical analysis, sparse optimization, algorithms.
Robert L. Constable, Professor; Ph.D, Wisconsin, 1968. Computational complexity, formal semantics, applied logic, automated reasoning.
Bruce Donald, Associate Professor; Ph.D., MIT, 1987. Robotics, computational geometry, artificial intelligence.
Michael Godfrey, Assistant Professor; Ph.D., Toronto, 1996. Software engineering.
Donald P. Greenberg, Jacob Gould Schurman Professor of Computer Graphics; Ph.D., Cornell, 1968. Realistic image synthesis, modeling, scientific visualization, computer-aided design, image processing.
David Gries, Professor; Ph.D., Munich, 1966. Programming methodology, programming languages, compiler construction.
Joseph Halpern, Professor; Ph.D., Harvard, 1981. Logics, artificial intelligence, distributed computing.
Juris Hartmanis, Walter R. Read Professor of Engineering; Ph.D., Caltech, 1955. Theory of computation.
Shelia S. Hemami, Assistant Professor; Ph.D., Stanford, 1995. Image processing, networks.
Daniel P. Huttenlocher, Associate Professor; Ph.D., MIT, 1988. Computer vision.
S. Keshav, Associate Professor; Ph.D., Berkeley, 1991. Networking, multimedia.
Dexter Kozen, Professor; Ph.D., Cornell, 1977. Theory of computation.
Gregory Morrisett, Assistant Professor; Ph.D., Carnegie Mellon, 1996. Programming languages, compilers.
Anil Nerode, Professor; Ph.D., Chicago, 1956. Logic, applied mathematics.
Keshav Pingali, Associate Professor; Ph.D., MIT, 1986. Data flow machines, functional and logic programming.
Ronitt Rubinfeld, Assistant Professor; Ph.D., Berkeley, 1990. Theory of computation, randomized algorithms, computational complexity.
Fred B. Schneider, Professor; Ph.D., SUNY at Stony Brook, 1978. Concurrent programming, fault tolerance, distributed systems.
Praveen Seshadri, Assistant Professor; Ph.D., Wisconsin, 1996. Database systems.
David Shmoys, Associate Professor; Ph.D., Berkeley, 1984. Scheduling, computational complexity.
Brian Smith, Assistant Professor; Ph.D., Berkeley, 1994. Multimedia systems.
Éva Tardos, Associate Professor; Ph.D., Eötvös, 1981. Combinatorics, complexity theory.
Ray (Tim) Teitelbaum, Associate Professor; Ph.D., Carnegie-Mellon, 1975. Programming languages and systems.
Sam Toueg, Professor; Ph.D., Princeton, 1979. Distributed computing, fault tolerance.
Lloyd N. Trefethen, Professor; Ph.D., Stanford, 1982. Numerical analysis and scientific computing.
Charles Van Loan, Professor; Ph.D., Michigan, 1973. Matrix computations.
Stephen Vavasis, Associate Professor; Ph.D., Stanford, 1989. Numerical analysis, optimization.
Thorsten von Eicken, Assistant Professor; Ph.D., Berkeley, 1993. Parallel and distributed systems.
Ramin Zabih, Assistant Professor; Ph.D., Stanford, 1993. Multimedia, computer vision.

RESEARCH AREAS

Algorithms. Work in this traditionally strong area continues but with a more applied flavor. Some of the problems under investigation in the robotics area fall under the heading of analysis of algorithms. In addition, several faculty members are studying various combinatorial algorithms that are used to solve sparse matrix problems arising in numerical analysis.

Artificial Intelligence. Faculty interests include automated theorem proving, machine learning, robotics, and machine vision.

Computer Vision. Includes object recognition, shape comparison, structure from motion, motion tracking, and robot localization.

Computing Theory. This area is concerned with fundamental mathematical problems of computer science. Specific topics include computational complexity, analysis of algorithms, formal languages and automata, semantics, and program verification. Computational complexity has always been a major research interest at Cornell, and current work is concerned with the intrinsic difficulty of computing problems and the relationships among various measures of computational and structural complexity, such as run time, space, and program size. Recently, there has been extensive work on the classification of problems and algorithms.

Concurrency and Distributed Computing. Several researchers are investigating theoretical issues in concurrent programming, with particular attention focused on decentralized control (i.e., distributed systems) and on fault tolerance. In addition, the ISIS/HORUS project has developed a tool kit for actually building this sort of software and has distributed it to more than 500 cities worldwide.

Information Organization and Retrieval. Current theoretical work is in the areas of file organization and information-retrieval algorithms, using concepts from mathematics, computer science, and linguistics. The material under study includes automatic indexing techniques; automatic classification; interactive search and retrieval methods; retrieval evaluation; automatic thesaurus construction techniques; and dynamic file management, including collection, growth, and retirement.

Numerical Analysis. Research is conducted in the field of matrix computations, sparse optimization, and differential equations. Topics include parallel-matrix algorithms, generalized and inverse eigenvalue problems, matrix problems in statistics, control engineering, signal processing, graph methods for handling matrix sparsity, and grid generation.

Programming Environments. The Synthesizer Generator, a system for creating interactive, language-based environments from formal specifications, continues to be a focal point of much research. It is being used to create interactive environments for theorem proving as well as for programming and has been licensed to over 290 sites worldwide.

Programming Languages and Methodology. Proofs of program correctness and their influence on program development are being studied for concurrent as well as sequential programs. A related project is PRL (Program Refinement Logic), which permits interactive development and verification of programs specified in a top-down fashion, using constructive mathematical proofs. There are significant efforts in developing semantic theories of concurrency and of types, as well as in extracting parallelism from sequential programs for various parallel machines.

CORNELL UNIVERSITY

COLLEGE OF ENGINEERING
SCHOOL OF ELECTRICAL ENGINEERING

PROGRAMS OF STUDY

The Graduate Field of Electrical Engineering at Cornell University offers study leading to the M.S. and Ph.D. degrees and to the professional Master of Engineering (Electrical) degree. A wide range of interests are covered. The major areas of concentration are communications, information theory, signal processing, and power and control systems; computer engineering; plasma physics, space plasma physics, and electromagnetics; solid-state electronics; and optoelectronics. There are two avenues by which a student may proceed: the one-year Master of Engineering (Electrical) degree program, which places major emphasis on design capability at a high level of professional competence, and the Master of Science/Doctor of Philosophy (M.S./Ph.D.) degree program, which requires several years of study and is oriented toward research. Students who want to limit their study to the master's degree should consider the M.Eng. (Electrical) program. The M.Eng. (Electrical) program requires 30 credits of advanced technical work, including a design project. Degree requirements for the M.S./Ph.D. degrees are kept at a minimum to give the student maximum flexibility in choosing a program of study. Independent thesis research is an important part of the M.S. and Ph.D. programs. Candidates for the Ph.D. degree must pass an EE qualifying examination before the beginning of their second term; a comprehensive admission-to-candidacy examination, required for formal admission to doctoral candidacy, may be taken after a student has earned 2 units of residence credit (a unit is given for each term of full-time graduate study successfully completed) but must be taken before the student begins the seventh unit of residence. Final examinations are given after completion of the M.S. and the Ph.D. dissertations. They cover subject matter related to the topics of the dissertations.

RESEARCH FACILITIES

The College of Engineering has a substantial campus with well-equipped buildings. The classrooms, offices, undergraduate laboratories, and many of the graduate research laboratories of the School of Electrical Engineering are housed in Phillips Hall and in the adjacent Rhodes Hall. Among the graduate research laboratories are those devoted to communications, computer engineering, control systems, digital signal processing, high-energy particle beams, integrated circuits, ionospheric physics and radio-wave propagation, lasers and optoelectronics, microwave and semiconductor devices, and semiconductor material preparation and characterization. Electrical Engineering faculty members and graduate students use the facilities of the following centers, laboratories, and programs: the Center for Applied Mathematics, the Electronic Packaging Program, the Joint Services Electronics Program, the Kettering Energy Systems Laboratory, the Laboratory of Plasma Studies, the Materials Science Center, the Microscience and Technology Program, the Optoelectronics Technology Center, and the Center for Theory and Simulation in Science and Engineering. In addition, the facilities of the National Nanofabrication Facility (adjacent to Phillips Hall), the National Astronomy and Ionosphere Center (Arecibo, Puerto Rico), and the Jicamarca Radio Observatory (Peru) are available. All research areas are served by a variety of computing resources. These include networked multi-MIP workstations, PCs, and the Cornell National Supercomputing Facility, which is located in Rhodes Hall.

FINANCIAL AID

Teaching assistantships, graduate research assistantships, and fellowships are available. Nearly all M.S./Ph.D. students in electrical engineering are enrolled full-time and receive full financial support. Students are strongly encouraged to apply for National Science Foundation and Department of Defense Fellowships. Application information is available at the 230 Phillips Hall address listed below.

COST OF STUDY

Tuition for a full-time program of study is $21,840 for the 1997–98 academic year.

LIVING AND HOUSING COSTS

Living costs vary according to the family situation of the student, the particular housing accommodations secured, and other factors. A rough estimate for a single student, exclusive of tuition but including room and board, books, and medical insurance, is $11,600 for the academic year.

STUDENT GROUP

The University has 13,500 undergraduate and 5,300 graduate and professional students. The Graduate Field of Electrical Engineering currently has 225 full-time students. Approximately 20 new M.S./Ph.D. and 90 M.Eng. (Electrical) students enter the Graduate Field of Electrical Engineering each fall. The EE School also has 22 postdoctoral associates and visiting scientists.

LOCATION

Ithaca, a city of 45,000 on Cayuga Lake, is the home of both Ithaca College and Cornell and is one of the country's great educational communities, offering cultural advantages that rival those of many large cities. State parks and recreational facilities, including those for camping, boating, skiing, and hiking, are located nearby.

THE UNIVERSITY

Cornell University was founded in 1865. Studies in electrical engineering began in 1883. Today, the faculty of the Graduate Field of Electrical Engineering consists of 40 distinguished members.

APPLYING

Applicants should have a baccalaureate degree from an accredited institution, or its equivalent, in an area of study that adequately prepares them for advanced study in electrical engineering. They must have maintained a minimum undergraduate grade point average of 3.5 (A = 4.0). A minimum TOEFL score of 600 is required of international students who are not studying in the United States. Scores on the GRE General Test are required of all M.S./Ph.D. and M.Eng. (Electrical) applicants (scores on a Subject Test are optional). Applications are considered for the fall term only. Applicants are encouraged to download application materials at any time. Students may request application materials via the World Wide Web at http://www.gradschool.cornell.edu for the M.S./Ph.D. program or http://www.ee.cornell.edu/meng.html for the M.Eng. (Electrical) program. Printed applications are not mailed out until after August 1 for consideration for the fall term of the following year. Application deadlines are January 15 for fellowship consideration and February 15 for other applicants.

CORRESPONDENCE AND INFORMATION

For M.S./Ph.D. degree information:

Director of Graduate Studies
School of Electrical Engineering
230 Phillips Hall
Cornell University
Ithaca, New York 14853-5401

Telephone: 607-255-4304
Fax: 607-254-4565
E-mail: ee_msphd@cornell.edu
World Wide Web: http://www.ee.cornell.edu

For M.Eng. (Electrical) degree information:

Master of Electrical Engineering Program
School of Electrical Engineering
222 Phillips Hall
Cornell University
Ithaca, New York 14853-5401

Telephone: 607-255-8414
Fax: 607-254-4565
E-mail: meng@ee.cornell.edu
World Wide Web: http://www.ee.cornell.edu

CORNELL UNIVERSITY
THE FACULTY AND THEIR RESEARCH

J. M. Ballantyne, Professor; Ph.D., MIT. Optoelectronic materials and devices, integrated optoelectronics, device nanofabrication, optical interconnects.

T. Berger, Professor; Ph.D., Harvard. Information theory, signal processing, communication theory, data and video compression.

A. W. Bojanczyk, Associate Professor; Ph.D., Warsaw. Parallel algorithms and architectures for engineering and scientific computing.

G. Brown, Associate Professor; Ph.D., Texas. Hardware specification and verification, distributed systems, computer engineering.

H. D. Chiang, Associate Professor; Ph.D., Berkeley. Nonlinear circuits and systems, power systems, artificial neural networks, control systems, optimization theory.

R. C. Compton, Associate Professor; Ph.D., Caltech. Millimeter/microwave solid-state devices and integrated circuits.

D. F. Delchamps, Associate Professor; Ph.D., Harvard. Dynamical systems, control theory, mixed digital/analog systems, hybrid systems, cognitive science.

L. F. Eastman, Professor; Ph.D., Cornell. Microwave, millimeter-wave, optical, and high-speed solid-state devices; compound semiconductor growth by molecular-beam epitaxy; submicron fabrication technology.

D. T. Farley, Professor; Ph.D., Cornell. Ionospheric physics, space-plasma physics, radar techniques.

T. L. Fine, Professor; Ph.D., Harvard. Neural networks, stochastic modeling, estimation.

Z. J. Haas, Associate Professor; Ph.D., Stanford. Wireless networks, wireless communication, ad-hoc networks, mobile systems, computer networks, data communication, high-speed protocols, optical networks.

D. A. Hammer, Professor; Ph.D., Cornell. Plasma physics, controlled fusion, intense ion beams, plasma radiation sources.

C. Heegard, Associate Professor; Ph.D., Stanford. Information theory, coding theory, digital communications, VLSI systems.

S. S. Hemami, Assistant Professor; Ph.D., Stanford. Image and video coding and transmission, signal processing, joint coding and network design.

C. R. Johnson Jr., Professor; Ph.D., Stanford. Adaptive digital signal processing in communication systems, blind equalization, recursive system identification for control, active noise control.

E. C. Kan, Assistant Professor; Ph.D., Illinois at Urbana-Champaign. Microelectronics device and process modeling, technology CAD software development and integration, scientific computing.

M. C. Kelley, Professor; Ph.D., Berkeley. Space plasma physics, atmospheric science, radar and lidar, rocket and satellite instrumentation.

P. M. Kintner, Professor; Ph.D., Minnesota. Global Positioning System, space plasma physics, spacecraft systems.

J. P. Krusius, Professor; Ph.D., Helsinki University of Technology. Silicon nanoelectronics, nanofabrication, device physics, electronic system packaging.

R. L. Liboff, Professor; Ph.D., NYU. Transport in metals and semiconductors, superlattice analysis, mesoscopic metal elements, localization, percolation and hopping phenomena, nonlinearity, classical and quantum chaos.

Y. H. Lo, Associate Professor; Ph.D., Berkeley. Optoelectronic materials and devices, semiconductor lasers, microelectronics, MicroElectroMechanical Systems (MEMS).

N. C. MacDonald, Professor; Ph.D., Berkeley. Nanostructure science; MEMS: microinstruments, micro-optics, and scanned-probe instruments in silicon; MEMS-based silicon processes.

P. R. McIsaac, Professor; Ph.D., Michigan. Electromagnetic theory, microwave circuits and devices.

B. A. Minch, Assistant Professor; Ph.D., Caltech. Analog IC design, low-power analog and digital circuits and systems, analog information processing systems, information theory.

J. A. Nation, Professor; Ph.D., Imperial College (London). Plasma physics, applied electrodynamics, high-energy electron and ion beams, accelerator physics, high-power microwave generation.

T. W. Parks, Professor; Ph.D., Cornell. Digital signal processing, signal analysis, array processing for sonar and seismic signals, pattern classification.

C. R. Pollock, Professor; Ph.D., Rice. Solid-state and tunable lasers, fiber optics, ultrashort pulse generation.

C. Pottle, Professor; Ph.D., Illinois. Computer-aided design, power system simulation, parallel computer processing.

A. P. Reeves, Associate Professor; Ph.D., Kent (England). Parallel processing, computer vision, image processing.

C. E. Seyler, Professor; Ph.D., Iowa. Theoretical and computational plasma physics, space plasmas, controlled fusion, relativistic electron beams.

Y. Y. Shacham, Assistant Professor; Ph.D., Technion (Israel). VLSI circuits and technology, nanofabrication, microlithography, process integration.

J. R. Shealy, Associate Professor; Ph.D., Cornell. Vapor-phase epitaxial growth of III-V compounds, optoelectronic devices and integration.

R. N. Sudan, Professor; Ph.D., Imperial College (London). Plasma physics, thermonuclear fusion, space and solar physics, high-power electron- and ion-beam physics, intense laser-plasma interaction.

C. L. Tang, Professor; Ph.D., Harvard. Lasers, quantum electronics, semiconductor materials and devices, ultrafast optical processes, nonlinear optics and devices.

R. J. Thomas, Professor; Ph.D., Wayne State. Control and analysis of linear and nonlinear systems, with applications to power systems.

J. S. Thorp, Professor and Director; Ph.D., Cornell. Applications of optimization and control theory to power systems.

N. C. Tien, Assistant Professor; Ph.D., California, San Diego. Silicon MEMS, design and fabrication of microactuators, microsensors, micromechanical structures, and systems.

H. C. Torng, Professor; Ph.D., Cornell. Computer engineering, telecommunications, superscalar processors.

V. V. Veeravalli, Assistant Professor; Ph.D. Illinois. Mobile and wireless communications, detection and estimation theory, information theory.

S. B. Wicker, Associate Professor; Ph.D., USC. Wireless information networks, digital communication systems, error control coding, cryptography.

RESEARCH AREAS

Communications, Information Theory, Signal Processing, and Power and Control. Pattern classification, neural networks, and signal processing; energy conversion and power systems; networks, coding, data compression, and information theory; adaptive and nonlinear dynamical systems; image and video processing and compression.

Computer Engineering. CAD for reconfigurable systems; image processing and computer vision; parallel and distributed processing; software technology and applications; VLSI design; wireless and high speed information networks.

Plasma Science and Technology, Space and Upper-Atmospheric Science, and Remote Sensing. Pulsed power, fusion, electron and ion beams, radiation sources, and plasma fabrication; space plasma physics, solar-terrestrial weather, plasma theory and simulation; remote sensing of the geospace environment: satellites, sounding rockets, radar, Global Positioning System, lidar.

Solid-State Electronics and Optoelectronics. Electronic and optoelectronic materials; microfabrication and nanofabrication technology; electronic devices, circuits, and system integration; optoelectronic, optical, and laser devices; millimeter-wave devices and systems; sensors, micromechanics, and nanoelectromechanics.

DARTMOUTH COLLEGE

DEPARTMENT OF COMPUTER SCIENCE

PROGRAMS OF STUDY

The Department of Computer Science offers a program leading to the Ph.D. degree in computer science. The department is in the process of establishing a terminal M.S. program. The Ph.D. program faculty includes all members of the Department of Computer Science and adjunct members from the Department of Mathematics and the Thayer School of Engineering.

Active research areas include algorithms, combinatorial optimization, computational geometry, discrete-event simulation, distributed systems, graphics, information retrieval, multimedia, operating systems, parallel computing, performance modeling, robotics, and signal processing.

The requirements for the Ph.D. degree include the following: six core courses and four advanced topics courses; passing five written qualifying exams (algorithms, architecture, operating systems, programming languages, and one of theory, artificial intelligence, or numerical analysis) by the end of the second year; participation in teaching; an oral thesis proposal; six terms in residence at Dartmouth; and acceptance and public defense of a thesis. Most students who complete the Ph.D. program do so in four to five years.

The Department of Computer Science is housed in the Sudikoff Laboratory for Computer Science, a modern building with offices for all faculty and graduate students. Each office has Ethernet and Appletalk connections. A weekly colloquium series and a weekly graduate student seminar series add to a lively environment for the exchange of ideas.

RESEARCH FACILITIES

Graduate students have access to many computer laboratories in Sudikoff Laboratory with networks of DEC, Silicon Graphics, Sun, and Macintosh computers. All graduate student offices have computing facilities.

Other research facilities in the Department of Computer Science include a DEC 2100 high-end server with multiple processors, very large memory, and several disk drives; the FLEET laboratory for file system experimentation, consisting of a cluster of workstations each with multiple disk drives and connected by a high-speed local network; a robotics laboratory with two RWI B12 autonomous mobile robots with on-board vision and communication, workstations to control the robots, and hardware benches; the Dartmouth Experimental Visualization Laboratory, which conducts research in multimedia technology.

FINANCIAL AID

All graduate students accepted into the Department of Computer Science are granted a tuition scholarship. Most students are supported either by Dartmouth Fellowships or by faculty member grants; the stipend is $1193 per month for nine months in 1997–98. Summer support is often available for students working with faculty members.

COST OF STUDY

Tuition for 1997–98 is $22,896 for nine months, but all full-time graduate students receive full tuition scholarships. A health plan fee of approximately $1050 for a single student is required unless the student can verify equivalent coverage from another plan. Stipends are subject to federal income tax.

LIVING AND HOUSING COSTS

A single graduate student should expect to spend up to $5500 per year on rent and utilities, $4000 per year on food, and $4000 per year on transportation and personal items. Many Dartmouth graduate students are able to spend much less. College housing is available for single and married students on a priority basis. Rents in Hanover are relatively high for New Hampshire, but rents are considerably lower in many nearby towns.

STUDENT GROUP

The Department of Computer Science currently has 28 graduate students, 26 of whom are full-time. Approximately one third are international students. Almost all the full-time students have fellowship or grant support.

STUDENT OUTCOMES

Graduates have gone into both academia (e.g., tenure-track positions at Wellesley, Puget Sound, Hartford, Vermont, and Southern Illinois; a postdoctoral position at Carnegie Mellon; and a position at the University of Minnesota Supercomputing Center) and industry (e.g., BBN, Transarc, Thinking Machines, and IBM Almaden Research Center).

LOCATION

Hanover lies along the eastern bank of the Connecticut River, between the Green Mountains of Vermont and the White Mountains of New Hampshire. It is a small town of about 9,200 residents. Hanover has tried hard to preserve traditional New England small town qualities. Outdoor activities—especially hiking, skiing, canoeing, and bicycling—are popular. Hanover also offers a modest but active cultural life. The Hopkins Center at Dartmouth is a magnet for the arts in New Hampshire and Vermont; it sponsors concerts by visiting and local musicians, film series, art shows, and theater. Dartmouth provides a full assortment of athletic facilities.

Because Hanover is near the junction of Interstates 89 and 91, students can drive to Boston in 2½ hours, Montréal in 3½ hours, and New York in 5 hours. The airport in Lebanon, New Hampshire, is about 10 minutes from campus and is served by USAir Express and Business Express with direct flights to Boston, New York, and Philadelphia.

THE COLLEGE AND THE DEPARTMENT

Founded in 1769, Dartmouth College combines the advantages of a liberal arts college and a research university. The approximately 4,300 undergraduates benefit from a faculty renowned for its teaching excellence, and the approximately 300 graduate students in the arts and sciences and 800 graduate students in the engineering, business, and medical schools enjoy close working relationships with faculty members actively involved in research.

Dartmouth has a long tradition of leadership in computing, pioneering time-sharing availability to all students and the BASIC programming language in the 1960s. The undergraduate major in computer science was created in 1979, the Ph.D. program in computer science started in 1986, and the Department of Computer Science was formed in 1994.

APPLYING

Applicants should send to the address below a completed application form; $20 application fee (fee may be waived based on need); three letters of recommendation; college transcripts; GRE scores, including an advanced test score in computer science, mathematics, or engineering (originals only); and TOEFL scores (originals only, but not required for native speakers of English). Applications must be completed by February 1. Admissions will be announced by March 15. Applicants have until April 15 to accept or decline.

CORRESPONDENCE AND INFORMATION

Ph.D. Program
Department of Computer Science
Dartmouth College
6211 Sudikoff Laboratory
Hanover, New Hampshire 03755-3510

Telephone: 603-646-2206
E-mail: phd@cs.dartmouth.edu
World Wide Web: http://www.cs.dartmouth.edu/

DARTMOUTH COLLEGE
THE FACULTY AND THEIR RESEARCH

Javed A. Aslam, Visiting Assistant Professor; Ph.D., MIT, 1994. Machine learning, design and analysis of algorithms, computational biology, computational geometry.

Carl Beckmann, Assistant Professor (Adjunct, Thayer); Ph.D., Illinois at Urbana-Champaign, 1993. Computer architecture, performance analysis, networked multimedia systems, parallelizing and optimizing compilers.

Thomas H. Cormen, Assistant Professor; Ph.D., MIT, 1992. Parallel computing, languages, and disk systems; analysis of algorithms; VLSI.

George Cybenko, Dorothy and Walter Gramm Professor of Engineering Sciences (Adjunct, Thayer); Ph.D., Princeton, 1978. Signal processing, networked information systems, parallel computing.

John Danskin, Assistant Professor; Ph.D., Princeton, 1994. Network protocol compression, lossy image transmission, hardware and software systems for supporting graphics and multimedia applications.

Geoffrey Davis, Assistant Professor (Adjunct, Mathematics); Ph.D., NYU (Courant), 1994. Image and signal processing.

Robert L. (Scot) Drysdale III, Professor and Chair; Ph.D., Stanford, 1979. Algorithms, computational geometry, Voronoi diagrams, triangulations.

Dennis M. Healy Jr., Associate Professor; Ph.D., California, San Diego, 1986. Nonabelian harmonic analysis, architectures for distributed statistical pattern recognition.

Prasad Jayanti, Assistant Professor; Ph.D., Cornell, 1993. Asynchronous concurrent systems, synchronization, fault tolerance.

David Kotz, Associate Professor; Ph.D., Duke, 1991. Operating systems, concurrent data structures, parallel architectures and systems.

Donald L. Kreider, Professor; Ph.D., MIT, 1959. Numerical analysis, recursive function theory, logic.

Fillia S. Makedon, Associate Professor; Ph.D., Northwestern, 1982. Multimedia systems and analysis, information retrieval of multimedia data, electronic publishing, multimedia data access.

David M. Nicol, Associate Professor; Ph.D., Virginia, 1985. Performance modeling, analysis, optimization, and tools, parallel processing; discrete-event simulation; reliability modeling and tools.

Daniel Rockmore, Assistant Professor (Adjunct, Mathematics); Ph.D., Harvard, 1989. Algorithms related to representation theory of finite groups with applications in statistics.

Daniela Rus, Assistant Professor; Ph.D., Cornell, 1992. Multimedia information capture and access, electronic libraries, applications of geometric algorithms, robotics.

Clifford Stein, Assistant Professor; Ph.D., MIT, 1992. Design and analysis of algorithms, combinatorial optimization, network algorithms, parallel algorithms, scheduling, computational biology.

Linda Wilson, Assistant Professor (Adjunct, Thayer); Ph.D., Texas at Austin, 1994. Parallel and distributed computing, parallel discrete-event simulation, computer performance analysis, computer architecture.

Neal Young, Assistant Professor; Ph.D., Princeton, 1991. Design and analysis of approximation algorithms for combinatorial optimization, network design, and on-line problems.

Sudikoff Laboratory for Computer Science.

Dartmouth Hall.

Baker Library.

DEPAUL UNIVERSITY

SCHOOL OF COMPUTER SCIENCE, TELECOMMUNICATIONS AND INFORMATION SYSTEMS

PROGRAMS OF STUDY

The School of Computer Science, Telecommunications and Information Systems (CTI) offers programs leading to the M.S. degree in computer science, human-computer interaction, information systems, management information systems, software engineering, and telecommunication systems and to the Ph.D. degree in computer science. Separate master's degree concentrations allow specialization in the areas of artificial intelligence, computer science, computer science telecommunications, data analysis, database, data communications, information systems, quality management, software engineering, standard telecommunications systems, and visual computing.

All master's programs are organized into three phases: Prerequisite, Core Knowledge, and Advanced. Most degree candidates are admitted conditionally into the Prerequisite Phase and become fully admitted to the graduate program by achieving a passing grade on the department's Graduate Assessment Examination, or by proving equivalent competence in undergraduate course work or work experience. In order to obtain the M.S. degree, students must complete three to six Core Knowledge Phase courses and eight to ten Advanced Phase courses. A comprehensive examination covering material from Core Knowledge Phase courses is required to enter the Advanced Phase.

The M.S. curriculum is flexible and appropriate for students seeking professional development through academic study. Each student, in consultation with a faculty adviser, plans a phase-by-phase program suited to the student's interests and goals. The Ph.D. program prepares computer scientists for positions in industry or academia. A Ph.D. candidate must complete fifteen courses beyond the master's degree, pass a doctoral candidacy examination, pass an oral examination on the dissertation area, present a dissertation proposal, and prepare and successfully defend the dissertation.

RESEARCH FACILITIES

DePaul's Information Services (IS) division houses a large network of computers and allows students access to a rich computing environment. The configuration includes several Sun SPARCcenters for student use. In addition, students have access to IBM PC laboratories and Macintosh laboratories at the Loop and Lincoln Park campuses. There are numerous dial-up phone numbers available for off-campus work. DePaul's suburban campuses, in the Naperville, O'Hare, and South areas, also offer excellent student laboratory facilities. Permanent student Internet access accounts are available along with dial-in SLIP connections.

The School itself operates specialized laboratories for artificial intelligence, computer vision and graphics, software engineering, telecommunications, local area networks, and computer telephony. One laboratory allows students to explore specialized software. The laboratories include both PCs and UNIX workstations. The School also operates an IBM ES 9000/9221.

FINANCIAL AID

The School provides a number of full and partial graduate assistantships that carry stipends and tuition waivers. Application should be made directly to the School. Students should apply for autumn, from February 2 to May 1; for winter, from September 1 to November 1; and for spring, from November 2 to February 1.

The University's Financial Aid Office assists interested students in applying to the Federal Perkins Loan and Federal Stafford Student Loan programs. Students are encouraged to apply before May 1 to receive maximum consideration.

COST OF STUDY

Graduate tuition for the 1997–98 academic year is $359 per quarter hour. Full-time graduate study generally consists of 8 to 12 hours per quarter.

LIVING AND HOUSING COSTS

There is no on-campus housing for graduate students, but the Housing Office has listings of apartments and residential hotels near the Lincoln Park campus. Apartments in the Chicago area are available at various rents.

STUDENT GROUP

CTI has approximately 1,000 students in the graduate program; nearly half attend full-time. This sizable enrollment allows the School to offer a wide variety of courses each quarter. Many students are already employed in a computer or computer-related profession and enroll in the program for career enhancement.

STUDENT OUTCOMES

Graduates of CTI have experienced a high degree of success in locating employment. Many graduates have reported starting salaries that exceed national averages. The Career Development Center assists students with job searches through career development seminars, job fairs, networking programs, interviewing skills workshops, and on-campus recruiting.

LOCATION

The city of Chicago offers DePaul students a wide range of cultural and recreational opportunities. The Loop campus is minutes from the Art Institute; Orchestra Hall; museums of art, natural history, and science; and the LaSalle Street business district. The 25-acre Lincoln Park campus is less than 1 mile from Lake Michigan beaches, the lakefront bicycle and running paths, the zoo, and other public recreational facilities. The stores, theaters, musical groups, and other attractions of the Lincoln Park community reflect the broad interests of people who live and work there. The Naperville, O'Hare, and South campuses serve students in the outlying suburbs.

THE UNIVERSITY

DePaul University was founded in 1898 by the Vincentian Fathers and is now one of the largest Catholic universities in the world. Urban in style, the University today still strives to maintain the heritage of St. Vincent DePaul.

Numerous student organizations offer considerable opportunities for participation in both community and University activities. There are music performance groups, theater groups, student publications, sports, and honor and service societies. Athletic facilities include two gymnasiums, a swimming pool, racquetball courts, and extensive physical education equipment.

APPLYING

Master's degree students may begin their course work in any academic quarter; Ph.D. degree students are admitted to the fall quarter only. Application materials for the graduate programs in computer science, information systems, software engineering, telecommunication systems, or management information systems may be obtained by sending a request to the address given below. The application fee is $25.

The CTI Web site offers information and resources for current and prospective students. Students can order admission applications, view the class schedule, and visit faculty member and student home pages.

CORRESPONDENCE AND INFORMATION

School of Computer Science, Telecommunications and Information Systems
Graduate Programs
DePaul University
243 South Wabash
Chicago, Illinois 60604
World Wide Web: http://www.cs.depaul.edu

DEPAUL UNIVERSITY
THE FACULTY AND THEIR RESEARCH

L. Edward Allemand, Professor Emeritus; Ph.D., Louvain (Belgium), 1970. Information systems, human-computer interaction.

Gary Andrus, Associate Professor; Ph.D., Wayne State, 1977. Formal language theory, compiler design.

Karen Bernstein, Assistant Professor; Ph.D., SUNY at Stony Brook, 1996. Programming environments, programming languages, software engineering and concurrent systems.

Michael Borella, Assistant Professor; Ph.D., California, Davis, 1995. Computer networks, security, performance evaluation.

Gregory Brewster, Assistant Professor; Ph.D., Wisconsin–Madison, 1994. Telecommunication systems, data communications, computer networks, performance analysis of communication systems.

Susy Chan, Associate Professor; Ph.D., Syracuse, 1979. IT management, planning, and strategies; systems analysis and design; electronic commerce.

I-Ping Chu, Associate Professor; Ph.D., SUNY at Stony Brook, 1981. Data communication, computer networks, combinatorial algorithms, database, distributed database.

Anthony Wai Man Chung, Assistant Professor; Ph.D., Maryland, 1992. Communication networks, distributed systems, automated tools for software development, operating systems, programming languages.

Kamal Dahbur, Instructor; M.S., DePaul, 1993. Artificial intelligence, information systems.

Br. Michael Driscoll, Instructor; M.S., DePaul, 1985. Database.

Clark Elliott, Assistant Professor; Ph.D., Northwestern, 1992. Artificial intelligence.

Helmut Epp, Associate Professor and Dean; Ph.D., Northwestern, 1966. Expert systems, artificial intelligence, computer security, hardware description languages.

Robert Fisher, Associate Professor; Ph.D., Harvard, 1975. Graphics, operating systems.

Gerald Gordon, Associate Professor; Ph.D., Berkeley, 1968. Computer vision.

Henry Harr, Associate Professor; Ph.D., IIT, 1988. Parallel processing, operating systems.

Xiaoping Jia, Assistant Professor; Ph.D., Northwestern, 1989. Software engineering, formal methods, object-oriented software development.

Richard Johnsonbaugh, Professor; Ph.D., Oregon, 1969. Combinatorial algorithms, pattern recognition.

Steve Jost, Associate Professor; Ph.D., Northwestern, 1985. Statistics, pattern recognition, image processing.

Martin Kalin, Professor; Ph.D., Northwestern, 1969. Artificial intelligence, databases, industrial scheduling.

George Knafl, Professor; Ph.D., Northwestern, 1978. Statistical computing, software quality and reliability.

Warren Krueger, Professor; Ph.D., Wisconsin, 1966. Computer vision, image processing.

Glenn Lancaster, Associate Professor; Ph.D., California, Irvine, 1972. Compiler design.

Chengwen Liu, Assistant Professor; Ph.D., Illinois, 1991. Database management systems, information retrieval, data compression.

Steve Lytinen, Associate Professor; Ph.D., Yale, 1984. Artificial intelligence, natural language processing.

David Miller, Associate Professor and Associate Dean; Ph.D., Chicago, 1981. Artificial intelligence, computation theory.

Thomas Muscarello, Assistant Professor; Ph.D., Illinois, 1993. Artificial intelligence, hospital/medical informatics, information systems.

John Rogers, Assistant Professor; Ph.D., Chicago, 1995. Computational complexity, mathematical logic.

LoriLee Sadler, Visiting Assistant Professor; Ph.D. candidate, Indiana. High-speed data networking, human-computer interaction, human cognition.

Andrew Sears, Assistant Professor; Ph.D., Maryland, 1993. Human-computer interaction, data visualization, computer graphics.

Amber Settle, Instructor; M.S., Chicago, 1994. Distributed algorithms.

Rosalee Wolfe, Associate Professor; Ph.D., Indiana, 1987. Computer graphics, human-computer interaction.

DREXEL UNIVERSITY

COLLEGE OF ARTS AND SCIENCES
PROGRAM IN COMPUTER SCIENCE

PROGRAMS OF STUDY

Drexel University prepares students through its comprehensive graduate programs in mathematics and computer science leading to the Master of Science (M.S.) and Doctor of Philosophy (Ph.D.) degrees.

In the M.S. program in computer science, areas of emphasis include artificial intelligence, computer graphics, compiler design, software engineering, parallel and distributed computing, computer algebra systems, and scientific computation. The program is intended to prepare students for employment as computing professionals in business, industry, or government. Studies are offered on a full- or part-time basis; full-time students normally complete the program within two years. A minimum of 45 quarter credits is required. The Ph.D. program emphasizes computer algebra systems and parallel and distributed computing. Details on this program can be obtained from the Department of Mathematics and Computer Science.

Students with strong backgrounds in both mathematics and computer science are encouraged to pursue the dual M.S. in mathematics and computer science. Typically, this requires an additional one-half year of study beyond the time required for an M.S. degree in one field. The degrees are awarded simultaneously upon completion of the program.

RESEARCH FACILITIES

A department-wide local area network, MCSNET, is the cornerstone for the computing facilities in the Department of Mathematics and Computer Science. MCSNET directly supports the administrative, instructional, and research activities of the department and provides access to centralized resources operated by Drexel's Office of Computing Services; resources operated by other Drexel departments, making possible joint instructional and research efforts; remote resources via the Internet (PREPnet and NSFnet); and Drexel's Hagerty Library, which has more than 480,000 volumes, including approximately 120,000 in the science and technology section. Currently, MCSNET includes a variety of Sun servers and/or multiprocessors–a Sun Ultra Enterprise 3000, a Sun Ultra Enterprise 150, a Sun SPARC 10-514, a Sun SPARCserver 390MP, and two Ultra 2170s.

The department's Instructional Computing Facility has been extensively remodeled and consists of Sun Ultras, Sun SPARCstations, and Apple Macintoshes. Research computing includes a variety of other Sun Workstations and X-terminals. A broad selection of software is supported on the UNIX and Apple Macintosh systems. Languages include C, C++, FORTRAN, Modula-2, LISP, Pascal, APL, PCL, and PROLOG. Additional software includes C-Linda, GKS, Mathematica, MATLAB, MAPLE, NAG FORTRAN Library and Graphical Supplement, PHIGS, PVM, Perl, Eli, SAC-2C, Macaulay, A#, Axiom, SR, and X-Windows.

Drexel's Office of Computing Services supports computing facilities for general use on campus, including an IBM 9121, Model 320, and a four-processor Sun SPARCserver 670 MP. These are accessible via the campuswide Ethernet, modem, terminals attached to a central dataswitch, and clusters of microcomputers equipped with Ethernet connections and terminal emulation software. An open-access cluster of Macintoshes and printers is available to faculty and students. A file server system is in place for students to download Drexel-developed and public domain software and templates required for course work.

FINANCIAL AID

A significant number of teaching and research assistantships are available. A teaching assistant position includes a teaching stipend and a tuition stipend. For 1996–97, teaching stipends averaged $10,000 per academic year. The tuition stipend includes tuition remission of up to 27 credits for the academic year.

COST OF STUDY

Tuition varies with the program of study. For 1997–98, tuition for computer science students is $546 per credit hour. The general University fee is $117 per term for full-time students and $63 per term for part-time students.

LIVING AND HOUSING COSTS

Accommodations for single students are available in University residence halls. Ample housing is also available in the neighborhood bordering campus. For the nine-month academic year, transportation and living expenses for a single student are estimated at $11,450.

STUDENT GROUP

The University has a total enrollment of 9,590 students, including 2,785 at the graduate level. Approximately 70 graduate students are enrolled in the computer science program. Evening course offerings are sufficient to offer a robust degree program for part-time evening students.

The Philadelphia/Delaware Valley area is part of a technological corridor with a wealth of companies that hire Drexel graduates as full-time computing professionals. In most cases, students get jobs involving some aspect of software development. The graduate student body is a diverse mixture of part-time students with full-time jobs in the computing industry, students with backgrounds other than computing science, students from other countries spanning the globe, and full-time students with interests in advanced graduate study. Job opportunities exist not only in the Delaware Valley but all over the country and the world.

LOCATION

As a part of the University City area of west Philadelphia, Drexel is conveniently located within minutes of downtown Philadelphia, a great cultural, educational, and industrial center. From campus, New York City and Washington, D.C., are easily reached by train, bus, or car. Amtrak's 30th Street Station, a hub for national and local transportation, is located within three blocks of the University.

THE UNIVERSITY

Founded in 1891, Drexel University is a private institution offering undergraduate and graduate programs in arts and sciences, business and administration, design arts, engineering, and information studies. The University operates on an academic calendar of four terms per year.

APPLYING

Graduate students may apply with the intention of enrolling in any of Drexel's four terms (these begin in January, March, June, and September; application deadlines vary accordingly). Transcripts and letters of recommendation are required. The GRE General Test (aptitude portion) is recommended for the program in computer science. For assistantship consideration, students must submit their application by February 1.

CORRESPONDENCE AND INFORMATION

For further information and an application form, students should contact:

Office of Graduate Admissions, Box P
Drexel University
Philadelphia, Pennsylvania 19104

Telephone: 215-895-6700
E-mail: admissions-grad@post.drexel.edu

DREXEL UNIVERSITY
THE FACULTY AND THEIR RESEARCH

Loren N. Argabright, Professor; Ph.D., Washington (Seattle). Functional analysis, wavelets, abstract harmonic analysis and the theory of group representations.

Robert P. Boyer, Professor; Ph.D., Pennsylvania. Functional analysis, C* algebras and the theory of group representations.

Robert C. Busby, Professor; Ph.D., Pennsylvania. Functional analysis, C* algebras and group representations, computer science.

Robin R. Carr, Assistant Professor; Ph.D., Toronto. Mathematical physics, symbolic algebra.

Bruce W. Char, Professor; Ph.D., Berkeley. Symbolic mathematical computation, algorithms and systems for computer algebra, automatic scientific programming, parallel and distributed computation.

William M. Y. Goh, Associate Professor; Ph.D., Ohio State. Number theory, approximation theory and special functions, combinatorial enumeration, asymptotic analysis.

Herman Gollwitzer, Associate Professor; Ph.D., Minnesota. Applied mathematics, differential equations, data analysis, user interface design, visualization and scientific computing.

William J. Gordon, Professor; Ph.D., Brown. Numerical analysis, multivariate interpolation and approximation, numerical solution of partial differential equations, computer graphics.

Stephen J. Hartley, Assistant Professor; Ph.D., Virginia. Languages, operating systems for distributed and parallel computing, genetic algorithms, combinatorial optimization.

Nira Herrmann, Associate Professor; Ph.D., Stanford. Mathematical and applied statistics, early decision problems, expert systems in statistics, computer science, computer science education, multivariate analysis, biostatistics.

Jeremy R. Johnson, Associate Professor; Ph.D., Ohio State. Computer algebra, parallel computation, algebraic algorithms, scientific computing.

Bernard Kolman, Professor; Ph.D., Pennsylvania. Lie algebras; theory, applications, and computational techniques; operations research.

Yagati N. Lakshman, Assistant Professor; Ph.D., RPI. Computational algebra, design and analysis of algorithms, symbolic computation systems.

Spiros Mancoridis, Assistant Professor; Ph.D., Toronto. Software engineering.

Charles J. Mode, Professor; Ph.D., California, Davis. Probability and statistics, biostatistics, epidemiology, mathematical demography, data analysis, computer-intensive methods.

Ronald K. Perline, Associate Professor; Ph.D., Berkeley. Applied mathematics, numerical analysis, symbolic computation, differential geometry, mathematical physics.

Marci A. Perlstadt, Associate Professor; Ph.D., Berkeley. Applied mathematics, special functions, numerical analysis of function reconstruction, signal processing, combinatorics.

Jeffrey L. Popyack, Associate Professor and Associate Department Head; Ph.D., Virginia. Operations research, stochastic optimization, computational methods for Markov decision processes, artificial intelligence, computer science education.

Chris Rorres, Professor; Ph.D., NYU (Courant). Applied mathematics, scattering theory, mathematical modeling in biological sciences, dynamical systems.

Eric Schmutz, Associate Professor; Ph.D., Pennsylvania. Discrete mathematics and combinatorial probability, number theory, probabilistic methods in combinatorics, graph theory and computer science.

Justin Smith, Professor; Ph.D., NYU (Courant). Computer science; parallel algorithms, artificial intelligence, and computer vision.

Robert P. Weaver, Assistant Professor; Ph.D., Colorado at Boulder. Languages for parallel numerical computation, programming languages and compilers, human-computer interaction.

Jet Wimp, Professor; Ph.D., Edinburgh. Applied mathematics; special functions, approximation theory, numerical techniques, and asymptotic analysis.

Stanley Zietz, Associate Professor; Ph.D., Berkeley. Population dynamics, applied mathematics, mathematical biology, biophysics, image analysis.

DREXEL UNIVERSITY

ELECTRICAL AND COMPUTER ENGINEERING

PROGRAM OF STUDY

Graduate study in the department leads to a Master of Science in Electrical and Computer Engineering (M.S.E.E.), a Master of Science in Telecommunications Engineering (M.S.E.E./Telecommunications Engineering), and a Doctor of Philosophy (Ph.D.) in electrical and computer engineering.

The degree offerings for electrical and computer engineering are focused on four general areas: electrophysics, systems, power systems, and computers and digital circuits. The field of electrophysics includes electronic devices, electromagnetics, acoustics, lightwaves, and microwaves. The study of systems includes controls, communications, telecommunications, signal processing, and robotics. The study of power systems can include resources planning and allocation and system security and stability. The study of computers and digital circuits can entail parallel processing, digital circuits, fault-tolerant design, networks, and imaging.

The curriculum for the Master of Science in Electrical and Computer Engineering encompasses 45 approved quarter credits (approximately 15 courses). The curriculum is structured on predesigned sequences of foundation courses that provide a background for advanced studies. The Ph.D. degree in electrical and computer engineering requires 90 quarter credits beyond the B.S. and a dissertation. At least one year of full-time study on campus is required. In addition to the basic University guidelines, a written preliminary examination is also required by the department. All Ph.D. candidates must participate in teaching, research, and the department's seminar program. Prospective Ph.D. students are welcome to contact the department to discuss their research interests.

The Master of Science in Electrical Engineering/Telecommunications Engineering degree program provides a specialization in telecommunications engineering. The program responds to the tremendous and growing demand for engineers with telecommunications expertise. This demand is being generated by the spread of such technologies as computer networks, e-mail systems, mobile phone systems, and interactive cable television. The degree requires 45 or 48 approved course credits. The requirements include a 27-credit core, 12 to 15 credits of electives, and 3 to 6 credits for thesis work or a full-time professional internship through Drexel's Career-Integrated Education (CIE) option.

RESEARCH FACILITIES

The following are the major facilities in use in the department: Computer-Based Interactive Systems Laboratory (CBIS); Electrophysics Laboratories: Microwave Laboratory, Solar Cell Experimental Station, Thick-Film Hybrid Circuit Lab, and Thin-Film Lab; VLSI Design Center; Image Processing Center (IPC); Laboratory of Applied Machine Intelligence and Robotics (LAMIR); Lightwave Engineering Laboratory; Emory Long Computer Center; Power Systems Laboratories; Signal Processing Laboratory (SPL); Systems Laboratory; and laboratories related to biomedical engineering: Bioelectrode Research Laboratory (BERL), Cardiovascular Dynamics Laboratory, Telemetry, Sensor and Instrumentation Laboratory, and Ultrasound Laboratories. Telecommunications and Wireless Systems labs are being developed.

FINANCIAL AID

Teaching, research, and graduate assistantships are available and are awarded on a full-time or half-time basis. Full-time appointments carry an average monthly stipend of $1250 and 9 credits of tuition per term. The Dean's Fellowship for full-time study provides 40 percent of a student's tuition for the first term when another form of assistantship is not available. This fellowship is renewable after the first term depending on the student's academic performance.

COST OF STUDY

Tuition is $546 per credit hour in the 1997–98 academic year for both the M.S. and Ph.D. The University fee is $117 per term for full-time students and $63 per term for part-time graduate students.

LIVING AND HOUSING COSTS

University-approved residences cost $1300 to $1600 per term for room and board. Housing of all types is available around the Drexel community for single and married students. Job opportunities are available for the spouses of married students.

STUDENT GROUP

Drexel has 9,590 students from forty-two states and 102 countries. Of these, 1,925 are part-time graduate students and 860 are full-time graduate students. There are 145 part-time and 60 full-time graduate students within the graduate curriculum of the department.

LOCATION

Drexel is located in Philadelphia, a city of 2 million people and a center of science and industry. The campus is easily reached by bus, subway, railroad, and car. It is only a few minutes walk from the heart of Philadelphia, close to its many centers of education, entertainment, culture, and industry. It is a convenient train or car ride to New York City; Washington, D.C.; the Atlantic City boardwalk; and the Pocono Mountain resort and ski area. Philadelphia International Airport is only 15 minutes away by car or high-speed rail link.

THE UNIVERSITY

Drexel was founded in 1891. Its students are enrolled in five academic units: engineering, arts and sciences, business administration, the Nesbitt College of Design Arts, and information science and technology. Drexel has one of the largest private undergraduate engineering colleges in the country, and it is one of the top twenty private universities in the granting of master's degrees.

APPLYING

Graduate students may apply with the intention of enrolling in any of Drexel's four academic terms (fall, winter, spring, summer). Completed applications for admission and supporting transcripts and references should be on file six weeks prior to the start of classes each term. Requests for financial aid should accompany applications for admission. Applications for financial aid must be received by February 1 for consideration for the next fall term. Inquiries may be directed to any member of the graduate faculty listed on the back of this page doing research in the student's area of interest.

CORRESPONDENCE AND INFORMATION

Graduate Advisor
Department of Electrical and Computer Engineering
Drexel University
3141 Chestnut Street
Philadelphia, Pennsylvania 19104
World Wide Web: http://coe.drexel.edu/ECE/ece_home.html

DREXEL UNIVERSITY
THE FACULTY

The following lists current full-time faculty members and their areas of research interests. Prospective students are welcome to contact individual faculty members.

Izhak Bar-Kana, Research Professor; Ph.D., Rensselaer. Systems and control, guidance, adoptive control. (E-mail: barkana@duvm.ocs.drexel.edu)

Richard B. Beard, Professor Emeritus; Ph.D., Pennsylvania. Electrophysics and biomedical: bioelectrochemistry and acoustic properties of materials, biocompatibility studies. (E-mail: beardrb@post.drexel.edu)

Nihat M. Bilgutay, Professor and Department Head; Ph.D., Purdue. Systems and biomedical: communication theory, ultrasonic imaging, nondestructive testing, and signal processing. (E-mail: bilgutay@ece.drexel.edu)

Fernand Cohen, Associate Professor; Ph.D., Brown. Computer vision, image processing, texture. (E-mail: fernand_cohen@cbis.ece.drexel.edu)

Richard L. Coren, Professor; Ph.D., Polytechnic of Brooklyn. Electromagnetic fields, antennas, shielding, RFI. (E-mail: corenr@duvm.ocs.drexel.edu)

Afshin Daryoush, Associate Professor; Ph.D., Drexel. Electrophysics: electromagnetic fields, antennas, telecommunications, microwave and millimeter-wave solid state devices and circuits, heterostructures, electrooptics, optoelectronics, fiber optics, integrated optics, electromagnetic sensors. (E-mail: daryoush@ece.drexel.edu)

Bruce A. Eisenstein, Arthur A. Rowland Professor; Ph.D., Pennsylvania. Systems and biomedical: digital signal processing, pattern recognition, communication theory. (E-mail: eisenstein@ece.drexel.edu)

Robert Fischl, Professor Emeritus and Director of Electrical Power Research; Ph.D., Michigan. Power: systems, networks, controls, computer-aided design, power systems, solar energy. (E-mail: fischl@cbis.ece.drexel.edu)

William Freedman, Associate Professor; Ph.D., Drexel. Biomedical systems, rehabilitation, neural systems, computer engineering. (E-mail: freedman@ece.drexel.edu)

Eli Fromm, Roy A. Brothers University Professor and Vice President for Educational Research and Development; Ph.D., Thomas Jefferson. Bioengineering: biotelemetry, sensors, bioinstrumentation, communications, professional society activities. (E-mail: fromme@duvm.ocs.drexel.edu)

Edwin L. Gerber, Professor; Ph.D., Pennsylvania. Electrophysics: physical electronics, electronic devices, computerized instrumentation. (E-mail: gerbere@duvm.ocs.drexel.edu)

Allon Guez, Associate Professor; Ph.D., Florida. Linear systems, nonlinear systems, robotics, optimal control. (E-mail: guez@cbis.ece.drexel.edu)

Peter R. Herczfeld, Lester A. Kraus Professor; Ph.D., Minnesota. Microwaves and millimeter waves, lightwave engineering, fiber optics, solar energy, solid-state electronics. (E-mail: herczfeld@ece.drexel.edu)

Leonid Hrebien, Associate Professor and Associate Dean; Ph.D., Drexel. Systems and biomedical: cardiovascular system characterization; tissue excitability measurement; acceleration effects on cardiovascular and cerebrovascular functions. (E-mail: hrebienl@duvm.ocs.drexel.edu)

Dov Jaron, Professor; Ph.D., Pennsylvania. Development, physiologic evaluation, and clinical implementation of mechanical devices to assist the failing heart, control and optimization of circulatory devices, computer application to patient monitoring, properties of bioelectrodes, instrumentation. (E-mail: dov.jaron@coe.drexel.edu)

Paul R. Kalata, Associate Professor; Ph.D., IIT. Systems: estimation, identification and control theory, adaptive control and filtering, computer control systems.

Moshe Kam, Professor; Ph.D., Drexel. Systems: information theory, control theory; artificial intelligence: neural networks, distributed parallel processing. (E-mail: kam@lorelei.ece.drexel.edu)

Stanislav B. Kesler, Associate Professor; Ph.D., McMaster. Systems: communication, satellite communications, signal processing, spectral analysis, array signal processing. (E-mail: keslerb@post.drexel.edu)

Peter A. Lewin, Professor; Ph.D., Technical University of Denmark. Ultrasonic characterization of materials, propagation of ultrasonic waves in inhomogeneous media, electroacoustic transducers, biological effects of ultrasound, physical acoustics, underwater acoustics. (E-mail: lewin@ece.drexel.edu)

Alexander M. Meystel, Professor and Director of Laboratory of Applied Machine Intelligence and Robotics; Ph.D., ENIMS (Moscow). Intelligent control, machine intelligence, autonomous systems, robotics. (E-mail: meysteam@duvm.ocs.drexel.edu)

Bahram Nabet, Associate Professor; Ph.D., Washington (Seattle). Electrophysics: compound semiconductor devices and circuits; fabrication and modeling; neural networks; vision. (E-mail: nabetb@duvm.ocs.drexel.edu)

Prawat Nagvajara, Associate Professor; Ph.D., Boston University. Design and testing of computer hardware; fault-tolerant computing; error-correcting code. (E-mail: prawat_nagvajara@cbis.ece.drexel.edu)

Vernon L. Newhouse, Professor Emeritus; Ph.D., Leeds (England). Biomedical and electrophysics: ultrasonic flow measurement, imaging and texture analysis in medicine, ultrasonic nondestructive testing and robot sensing, clinical engineering. (E-mail: newhouse@ece.drexel.edu)

Dagmar Niebur, Visiting Assistant Professor; Ph.D., Swiss Federal Institute of Technology (Lausanne). Intelligent information processing techniques for power system monitoring and control. (E-mail: niebur@ece.drexel.edu)

Chikaodinaka O. D. Nwankpa, Associate Professor; Ph.D., IIT. Power: power systems planning and operation; systems: modeling and control of nonlinear systems; stochastic systems theory. (E-mail: chika_nwankpa@cbis.ece.drexel.edu)

Banu Onaral, Professor and Interim Director, School of Biomedical Engineering, Science, and Health Systems; Ph.D. Pennsylvania. Biomedical: bioelectrodes, biological signal processing, measurement of very low frequency phenomena, microcomputer applications, automated measurements, fractals, sealing. (E-mail: onaral@cbis.ece.drexel.edu)

Athina P. Petropulu, Assistant Professor; Ph.D., Northeastern. Telecommunications, wavelets, blind deconvolution. (E-mail: althina@cbis.ece.drexel.edu)

Kambiz Pourrezaei, Associate Professor; Ph.D., Rensselaer. Electrophysics: focused ion beams, lithography, plasma engineering. (E-mail: pourrezk@duvm.ocs.drexel.edu)

Robert G. Quinn, Francis C. Powell Professor; Ph.D., Catholic University. Optoelectronics and plasmas: optical fibers, devices and systems, cosmic and geophysical plasma phenomena. (E-mail: quinnrg@duvm.ocs.drexel.edu)

John Reid, Professor Emeritus; Ph.D., Pennsylvania. Biomedical: ultrasonics and ultrasound, medical instrumentation, echocardiography. (E-mail: reid@coe.drexel.edu)

Allen Rothwarf, Ernest O. Lange Professor; Ph.D., Pennsylvania. Electrophysics: solid-state physics, photovoltaics, pn junctions, integrated circuit modeling. (E-mail: rothwarf@ece.drexel.edu)

Kevin J. Scoles, Associate Professor and Assistant Department Head for Undergraduate Studies; Ph.D., Dartmouth. Electrophysics: device fabrication, photovoltaics, solid-state physics, digital circuit design, computer-aided design. (E-mail: scoles@ece.drexel.edu)

P. Mohana Shankar, Professor and Assistant Department Head for Graduate Affairs and Graduate Adviser; Ph.D., Indian Institute of Technology (Delhi). Telecommunications, mobile systems, fiber optics, speckle, biomedical ultrasonics. (E-mail: shankar@ece.drexel.edu)

Ernest L. Stagliano Jr., Lecturer; M.S.E.E., Drexel. Power, protective relaying, systems, circuits.

Hun H. Sun, Professor Emeritus; Ph.D., Cornell. Systems and biomedical: control systems, network analysis and synthesis.

Lazar Trachtenberg, Professor; Sc.D., Technion (Israel). Design and testing of hardware (multilevel gage arrays), fault tolerant computing, design of reliable suboptimal digital filters. (E-mail: lazar_trachtenberg@coe.drexel.edu)

Oleh J. Tretiak, Robert C. Disque Professor and Director of Image Processing Center; Sc.D., MIT. Computers and image processing: microcomputer image processing workstation, computer tomography, pattern recognition, computer systems. (E-mail: tretiak@ece.drexel.edu)

DREXEL UNIVERSITY

COLLEGE OF INFORMATION SCIENCE AND TECHNOLOGY

PROGRAMS OF STUDY

Drexel University's College of Information Science and Technology prepares practitioners and researchers for the information systems professions. The College's systems-related graduate degrees are Master of Science in Information Systems (M.S.I.S.) and Ph.D. The Certificate of Advanced Study (C.A.S.) program enrolls professionals who already hold a master's degree in information systems or a related field.

The M.S.I.S. normally requires 60 credits and may be completed on a full- or part-time basis. The Drexel University calendar includes four terms per calendar year; most information science and technology courses carry 4 credits. The program includes required core courses, distribution courses, and free electives as well as a strong focus on the design, implementation, and evaluation of software-intensive information systems. Subjects taught include systems analysis, implementation, and evaluation; database design and management; user interfaces; knowledge-based systems; abstracting and indexing; cognition and information retrieval; data communications; language processing; information systems policy and administration; and information services management. Workshops and other special offerings allow students to pursue studies in various programming languages and research or professionally oriented topics. M.S.I.S. applicants are asked to demonstrate competencies in basic statistics, the use of basic software packages (word processors, spreadsheets, and database management systems), and basic computer programming in either Pascal, C, COBOL, Ada, or FORTRAN. Students lacking one or more of these competencies may enroll in foundation courses that do not count toward the degree. The Ph.D. program comprises an approved plan of study, candidacy examinations, and a dissertation. One year of full-time residency is required; otherwise, doctoral students may pursue studies on either a full- or a part-time basis. The doctoral program offers two tracks of study, computer information systems and information and library science; one track must be chosen for program planning and examinations. The Ph.D. normally requires 60 credits beyond the master's, or 90 credits beyond the bachelor's if no applicable master's is held. The C.A.S. requires 32 credits and offers specialization beyond the master's. This program is regarded as continuing professional education.

RESEARCH FACILITIES

The College's Computing Resource Center supports students and faculty with such features as microcomputer hardware and software, access to the University's mainframes, a networked computer training room, on-line and CD-ROM information resources, a collection of reference books and 50 periodicals, and audio and video equipment. The College is also home to the Alfred P. Sloan Center for Asynchronous Learning and Training, which conducts research and development for Internet-based distance learning.

The University's library holds extensive collections of materials for all major fields in library and information science, computer science, systems engineering, and information systems. Students also have access to libraries on the adjacent University of Pennsylvania campus as well as to other libraries and information centers in the Philadelphia area.

FINANCIAL AID

A number of library, graduate, research, and teaching assistantships are awarded each year to incoming students, as are partial tuition scholarships. Assistants receive tuition remission and stipends in return for fulfilling specific work requirements in the College or the University's library. Teaching assistantships are available only for Ph.D. or advanced master's students. Enrolled students may also borrow limited funds through a College-administered loan program. Information on federal and state loan programs is available from Drexel's Graduate Financial Aid Office (Room 241, Randell Hall). No financial aid is available for international students.

COST OF STUDY

In 1997–98, tuition is $422 per credit. Each term, students are also charged a general University fee, based on full-time ($117) or part-time ($63) status. The cost of books and materials averages $100 per term for a full-time student.

LIVING AND HOUSING COSTS

Accommodations for single students are available in University residence halls. Ample housing is also available in the neighborhood bordering campus. For the nine-month academic year, transportation and living expenses for a single student are estimated at $11,450.

STUDENT GROUP

The students represent diverse academic and professional backgrounds and hold varied career expectations. In addition to the M.S.I.S and Ph.D. degrees, graduate students can pursue the M.S., Library and Information Science, and undergraduates can pursue the B.S. in Information Systems. About 75 percent of the 530 graduate students come from the mid-Atlantic region, with other regions and countries also represented.

The College of Information Science and Technology maintains its own placement office with a full-time director. The director helps students find preprofessional positions and internships and assists graduates in locating professional employment. The placement rate for graduates is high. Recent master's graduates have accepted systems positions in corporate, government, and academic settings.

The business, industry, and government resources of Philadelphia also provide ample opportunities for students to pursue preprofessional employment, internships, and permanent employment.

LOCATION

The campus is located in the University City section of Philadelphia. As one of the nation's oldest and largest cities, Philadelphia is rich in cultural, historical, and academic institutions and is home to an extraordinary variety of general and special libraries.

THE UNIVERSITY

Drexel is a private institution with an enrollment of 10,000 graduate and undergraduate students. In addition to the information science and technology curricula, degree programs are offered in the arts and sciences, business and administration, design arts, and engineering. These varied programs feature a strong professional orientation.

With College approval, graduate students may include courses from other Drexel departments in their program of study; related curricula include computer science, management and other business specializations, neuropsychology, and technical and science communication.

APPLYING

Graduate students may apply for admission in any term. Those seeking assistantships and scholarships should apply by February 1 for admission in the following September. An application and fee, transcripts, letters of recommendation, and a personal statement are required. Scores for the GRE General Test are required for some master's and all Ph.D. applicants; scores for the GRE are required for all applicants seeking assistantships.

CORRESPONDENCE AND INFORMATION

Anne B. Tanner, Associate Dean
College of Information Science and Technology-P
Drexel University
Philadelphia, Pennsylvania 19104
Telephone: 215-895-2474
World Wide Web: http://www.cis.drexel.edu

DREXEL UNIVERSITY
THE FACULTY AND THEIR RESEARCH

Thomas Childers, Alice B. Kroeger Professor; Ph.D., Rutgers. Management and evaluation of information organizations and services, foundations of information work, the quality of information services, effectiveness of information organizations.

M. Carl Drott, Associate Professor; Ph.D., Michigan. Computer programming for information processing, search strategy techniques for information retrieval and dissemination, use of systems analysis techniques for dealing with problems in large organizations such as libraries.

Lee Scott Ehrhart, Assistant Professor; Ph.D., George Mason. Information and software systems engineering; cognitive and behavioral sciences; management and organizational theory; multidisciplinary approaches to system life-cycle engineering activities, including requirements identification and modeling, design, and evaluation; human-computer interaction; planning and decision making; multimedia information systems.

Belver Griffith, Research Professor and Professor Emeritus; Ph.D., Connecticut. Research methods; design, planning, and evaluation of information services and products; functions of information in technical and scientific work; communications.

John Hall, Associate Professor; Ph.D., Florida State. Academic library service, library administration, organization of materials, technical processes, social aspects of information systems, academic library management information systems and their relation to management decision making, academic library services and use, collective bargaining, cooperation among libraries, application of simulation and gaming techniques to library education.

Lewis Hassell, Visiting Professor; Ph.D., Drexel. Systems analysis techniques, database management systems, computer-supported cooperative work (CSCW), use of computers to support collaboration, applications of linguistics to CSCW, object-oriented analysis and design.

Gregory W. Hislop, Assistant Professor; Ph.D., Drexel. Software development and modification, software evaluation and reuse, and organizing and staffing information systems groups; systems management, software product development, and technology support for large organizations.

Maxwell Hughes, Research Professor of Management and Information Science and Technology; Ph.D., Cambridge. Management of information systems, generally in large organizations, specifically in the health care industry.

Richard H. Lytle, Isaac L. Auerbach Professor and Dean of the College; Ph.D., Maryland. Information management in large, complex organizations; information resource management, with special emphasis on techniques and methodologies to connect organization strategic direction to implementation of automated information systems; records management; archives management.

Jacqueline C. Mancall, Professor; Ph.D., Drexel. Collection development, management, delivery of information services to children and adolescents, instructional role of the information specialist, design of library collections and services for user groups based on their communication behavior, application of survey methodology and statistical analysis to collection planning and management.

Katherine W. McCain, Professor; Ph.D., Drexel. Resources in science and technology, serial literature, abstracting and indexing, bibliometric studies of scholarly literatures, information transfer in the biomedical sciences.

Il-Yeol Song, Associate Professor; Ph.D., LSU. Database management systems and systems analysis and design, database modeling and design, object-oriented analysis and design, object-oriented database systems, client-server systems, data warehousing, digital libraries.

Howard D. White, Professor; Ph.D., Berkeley. Issues surrounding information work with well-defined clienteles concentrating on services that involve resources of the social sciences, improvement of statistics for use by library management, foundations of information work, expert systems in reference service, library collection evaluation, co-citation mapping of subject specialties, and American attitudes toward censorship.

Associate Professor John Hall chats with prospective students during the College's annual Open House.

Students at work in the College's Computing Resource Center.

DUKE UNIVERSITY

DEPARTMENT OF COMPUTER SCIENCE

PROGRAM OF STUDY

The Department of Computer Science has many exciting research efforts in the areas of systems and architecture, algorithms and complexity, scientific computing, and artificial intelligence. Scalable parallel computing is a unifying theme in much of the department's research. The department offers instruction leading to the M.S. and Ph.D. degrees and cooperates with the School of Medicine in offering an M.D./Ph.D. program. There are strong ties and collaborations with researchers in chemistry, engineering, mathematics, physics, and medicine through faculty members who have joint appointments in these areas. Students must take 60 units of credit for the Ph.D. degree, which takes about five years to earn. The Ph.D. program emphasizes early research experience in the first two years. The M.S. degree program is designed to allow completion in twelve months and provides practical training with a strong theoretical base. The department especially encourages M.S. candidates in the areas of operating systems, parallel computation, scientific computing, and VLSI design.

RESEARCH FACILITIES

The Department of Computer Science maintains state-of-the-art computing facilities to satisfy a variety of research and teaching needs. An SGI Powerchallenge L 4-processor machine with 2 gb RAM provides both a powerful computing environment and a systems research platform, and an SGI Octane dual-processor R10000 machine provides a powerful environment for graphics research. Workstations are installed in all faculty and graduate student offices and consist primarily of Sun Workstations but also include twenty-five Dell Pentium Pro 200 MHz Intel-based machines. Other facilities include six AlphaStation 600 266 MHz machines and eight AlphaStation 500 266 MHz machines used primarily for research on high-speed networking and next-generation collaborative computing, a 4-node SGI 4D/44OVGX with video generation capabilities, six Sun Ultra 140 workstations, four Sun SPARCstation 20 compute servers with 2 each 90-MHz HyperSPARC processors, two Alpha AXP compute servers with 128 MB RAM each, two SPARCstation 4 Model 110 login servers, two Sun SPARCstation 2 file servers with Weitek processor upgrades, one Sun SPARCstation 10 file server with 4 Ross Technology 90-MHz SuperSPARC processors, one Sun SPARCstation 20 file server with 2 50-MHz HyperSPARC processors, and three AlphaStation 400 4/233 NFS servers. Computers and workstations are connected via 10- and 100-megabit Ethernet through the department to a campus fiber-optic network that provides high-speed data paths to other University resources and to the Internet. Duke students and faculty members have ready access to a 4-processor CRAY Y-MP and a 48-cell KSR-1 at the nearby North Carolina Supercomputing Center.

FINANCIAL AID

Most full-time Ph.D. students receive support throughout their affiliation with the department. Full-time Ph.D. students are supported by fellowships, teaching assistantships, or research assistantships during their first two years. By the third year, students are expected to work with an adviser as a research assistant. Financial support provides tuition, most fees, and a stipend of $12,000 for the academic year. Additional support for the summer can be provided by research assistantships or instructorships. Financial support is typically not available for M.S. candidates.

COST OF STUDY

For 1997–98, tuition, registration, and fees are about $18,470 for a nine-month year of full-time study toward the M.S. or Ph.D. degree.

LIVING AND HOUSING COSTS

The cost of living in Durham for a single student is estimated at $10,500 per academic year. Comfortable and affordable student housing is either on or close to campus.

STUDENT GROUP

All full-time students are provided with office space within the Department of Computer Science. In the last few years, about half of the graduate students have been from other countries, and 30 percent have been women. The department is quite successful in placing graduates in strong positions in industry, consulting, and academics.

LOCATION

Duke is located on a beautiful 1,635-acre campus in Durham, North Carolina, a city of approximately 137,000 inhabitants. Durham sits at the apex of North Carolina's famous Research Triangle, which includes the nearby University of North Carolina at Chapel Hill and North Carolina State University in Raleigh. The adjacent Research Triangle Park, situated in 6,750 acres of rolling woodland, is home to many sophisticated research and manufacturing facilities. Duke is centrally located for a variety of cultural activities, and the mild climate makes the area a sports paradise. There are also outstanding recreational opportunities in the Outer Banks (eastern coast of the state) and in the Blue Ridge mountain range (western part of the state).

THE UNIVERSITY

Duke University was founded by James Buchanan Duke in 1924 and is now recognized as one of the top educational and research schools in the country. The University currently enrolls more than 9,000 students annually.

APPLYING

Applicants should have a strong background in mathematics, preferably three semesters of calculus and one semester of linear algebra. They should also have some knowledge of data structures, assembly language, and a higher-level computer programming language, especially C++. Most students accepted into the Ph.D. program have a grade point average of 3.5 or higher (on a 4.0 scale) and GRE scores in the 90th percentile or above. The GRE Subject Test in computer science is recommended but not required. Once the GRE testing program has changed in 1997, applicants should take the package of General Test measures containing the Mathematical Reasoning test. International students must score well in the TOEFL test. Excellent references and transcripts, prior research experience, and a good essay explaining the applicant's research interests and plan of study play important roles in the admissions process.

CORRESPONDENCE AND INFORMATION

Further information about the Department of Computer Science can be obtained by telephoning the Assistant to the Director of Graduate Studies at 919-660-6538, by sending e-mail to dgs@cs.duke.edu., or by connecting to the department's World Wide Web home page http://www.cs.duke.edu. Applications and application information can be obtained from Duke's Graduate School at the address below or by completing a Web request at http://www.cs.duke.edu/cgi-bin/education/infoplease.

Graduate School Admissions Office
127 Allen Building
Duke University
Durham, North Carolina 27706

Telephone: 919-684-3913
E-mail: grad-admissions@acpub.duke.edu
World Wide Web: http://www.gradschool.duke.edu/admissions

DUKE UNIVERSITY
THE FACULTY AND THEIR RESEARCH

Full-Time Faculty

Pankaj K. Agarwal, Associate Professor; Ph.D., NYU (Courant), 1989. Analysis of algorithms, computational and combinatorial geometry, robotics, data structures. (E-mail: pankaj@cs.duke.edu; telephone: 919-660-6540)

Lars Arge, Assistant Research Professor; Ph.D., Aarhus (Denmark), 1996. Design and analysis of algorithms and data structures, I/O efficient computation, computational geometry. (E-mail: large@cs.duke.edu; telephone: 919-660-6557)

Owen L. Astrachan, Associate Professor of the Practice and Director of Undergraduate Studies; Ph.D., Duke, 1992. Automated theorem proving, parallel and distributed computing, computer science education. (E-mail: ola@cs.duke.edu; telephone: 919-660-6522)

Alan W. Biermann, Professor; Ph.D., Berkeley, 1968. Artificial intelligence, automatic program synthesis, learning and inference theory, natural language processing. (E-mail: awb@cs.duke.edu; telephone: 919-660-6539)

Jeffrey S. Chase, Assistant Professor; Ph.D., Washington (Seattle), 1995. Operating systems, distributed systems, storage systems, parallel programming. (E-mail: chase@cs.duke.edu; telephone: 919-660-6559)

Robert Duvall, Lecturer; M.S., Brown, 1997. Computer science education. (E-mail: rcd@cs.duke.edu; telephone: 919-660-6567)

Carla S. Ellis, Associate Professor; Ph.D., Washington (Seattle), 1979. Operating systems, parallel systems, distributed data structures. (E-mail: carla@cs.duke.edu; telephone: 919-660-6523)

Gershon Kedem, Associate Professor of Computer Science and of Electrical and Computer Engineering; Ph.D., Wisconsin–Madison, 1978. Parallel architecture and VLSI design algorithms. (E-mail: kedem@cs.duke.edu; telephone: 919-660-6555)

Alvin R. Lebeck, Assistant Professor of Computer Science and of Electrical and Computer Engineering; Ph.D., Wisconsin–Madison, 1995. Computer architecture, memory systems, parallel and distributed systems, performance analysis. (E-mail: alvy@cs.duke.edu; telephone: 919-660-6551)

Michael L. Littman, Assistant Professor; Ph.D., Brown, 1996. Artificial intelligence, machine learning, planning under uncertainty, statistical natural language processing, algorithms and complexity, user interfaces. (E-mail: mlittman@cs.duke.edu; telephone: 919-660-6537)

Donald W. Loveland, Professor; Ph.D., NYU, 1964. Automated theorem proving, logic programming, test and treatment problem, knowledge evaluation. (E-mail: dwl@cs.duke.edu; telephone: 919-660-6542)

Dietolf Ramm, Associate Professor of the Practice and Associate Chair; Ph.D., Duke, 1969. Communications, applications of personal computers to education. (E-mail: dr@cs.duke.edu; telephone: 919-660-6532)

John H. Reif, Professor; Ph.D., Harvard, 1977. Theoretical computer science, efficient algorithms, parallel computation, robotics. (E-mail: reif@cs.duke.edu; telephone: 919-660-6568)

Susan H. Rodger, Assistant Professor of the Practice; Ph.D., Purdue, 1989. Interactive and visual tools for theoretical computer science, computer science education, algorithm animation, analysis of algorithms, parallel algorithms, data structures, computational geometry. (E-mail: rodger@cs.duke.edu; telephone: 919-660-6595)

Donald J. Rose, Professor; Ph.D., Harvard, 1970. Numerical solution of PDEs, numerical algebra, numerical methods for semiconductor device and circuit simulation. (E-mail: djr@cs.duke.edu; telephone: 919-660-6544)

C. Franklin Starmer Jr., Professor of Computer Science and of Experimental Medicine; Ph.D., North Carolina at Chapel Hill, 1968. Cellular communication, biological modeling, medical research databases. (E-mail: cfs@cs.duke.edu; telephone: 919-660-6524)

Xiaobai Sun, Assistant Professor; Ph.D., Maryland College Park, 1991. Successive band reduction and banded approaches to eigenvalue problems, block householder transformations, numerical libraries for high-performance architectures, numerical methods for the solutions of Markov chains. (E-mail: xiaobai@cs.duke.edu; telephone: 919-660-6518)

Jeffrey S. Vitter, Gilbert, Louis, and Edward Lehrman Professor and Chair; Ph.D., Stanford, 1980. Design and analysis of algorithms, large-scale computation (including I/O efficiency, parallel computation, incremental algorithms), computational geometry, data compression, machine learning, order statistics. (E-mail: jsv@cs.duke.edu; telephone: 919-660-6548)

Robert A. Wagner, Associate Professor and Director of Graduate Studies; Ph.D., Carnegie Mellon, 1969. Experimental VLSI architectures, applications of dynamic programming to algorithm design and systems design, design of optimal software and hardware systems, time-cost tradeoffs in abstract parallel computer models. (E-mail: raw@cs.duke.edu; telephone: 919-660-6536)

Adjunct, Associate, and Emeritus Faculty

Robert P. Behringer, James B. Duke Professor of Physics, of Mechanical Engineering and Material Science, and of Computer Science; Ph.D., Duke. Experiment and computation in nonlinear dynamics, Rayleigh-Bénard convection, flow in porous media, dynamics of granular materials, low-temperature physics.

John A. Board Jr., Associate Professor of Electrical and Computer Engineering and of Computer Science; D.Phil., Oxford. Application of high-performance computing technology to large scientific and industrial computing problems.

Franc Brglez, Adjunct Associate Professor; Ph.D., Colorado at Boulder. CAD for VLSI circuits, theory, and applications.

William W. Coughran, Head, Scientific Computing Research, AT&T Bell, and Adjunct Professor of Computer Science; Ph.D., Stanford. Differential equations, distributed computing, and scientific programming environments.

Thomas M. Gallie, Professor Emeritus; Ph.D., Rice. Complex variable theory, numerical analysis, compiler design, computer graphics, real-time computing, computing services for education and cardiology.

Erol Gelenbe, Nello L. Teer Professor of Electrical and Computer Engineering and of Computer Science and Chair, Department of Electrical and Computer Engineering; Ph.D., Polytechnic; D.Sc., Pierre et Marie Curie (Paris). Distributed and parallel computing, networks, neural computation, image understanding and compression.

Henry S. Greenside, Associate Professor of Physics and of Computer Science; Ph.D., Princeton, 1981. Nonlinear dynamics, computational fluid dynamics, vector and parallel scientific computing.

Peter N. Marinos, Professor of Electrical and Computer Engineering and of Computer Science; Ph.D., North Carolina State. Design of digital systems, fault diagnosis, applied automata theory.

Tassos Markas, Research Engineer at Research Triangle Institute and Adjunct Assistant Professor; Ph.D, Duke, 1993. Multimedia, data compression, ASIC and system design. (E-mail: am@cs.duke.edu; telephone: 919-462-6541)

Thomas Narten, Research staff member at IBM-RTP and Adjunct Assistant Professor; Ph.D., Purdue, 1988. Operating systems, networking and software systems. (E-mail: narten@cs.duke.edu; telephone: 919-660-6500)

Richard G. Palmer, Professor of Physics, of Psychology-Experimental, and of Computer Science; Ph.D., Cambridge. Theory and modeling of complex systems including glasses, neural networks, genetic algorithms, and economic markets.

Merrell L. Patrick, Professor Emeritus; Ph.D., Carnegie Mellon (at National Science Foundation). Research administration, computer and information science and engineering.

Michael Prisant, Assistant Professor of Chemistry and of Computer Science; Ph.D., Stanford. Experimental and computational chemical physics, massively parallel algorithms for molecular dynamics, computer visualization and animation.

Kishor S. Trivedi, Professor of Electrical and Computer Engineering and of Computer Science; Ph.D., Illinois. Computer architecture, performance evaluation, systems modeling and fault-tolerant computing.

Senol Utku, Professor of Civil and Environmental Engineering and of Computer Science; Ph.D., MIT. Finite element methods and parallel processing.

Turner Whitted, Research Professor of Computer Science at the University of North Carolina at Chapel Hill and Adjunct Professor of Computer Science; Ph.D., North Carolina State. Computer graphics, computer geometry, parallel algorithms for graphics, graphics architecture.

EMBRY-RIDDLE AERONAUTICAL UNIVERSITY

OFFICE OF GRADUATE STUDIES
DEPARTMENT OF COMPUTER SCIENCE AND SOFTWARE ENGINEERING

PROGRAM OF STUDY

Embry-Riddle Aeronautical University offers the Master of Software Engineering (M.S.E.) degree program through the Department of Computer Science. The M.S.E. degree is designed to give recent college graduates, or college graduates who have had several years of professional life, an opportunity to enhance their careers and work on the cutting edge of modern software development. Students learn technical tools and techniques in combination with skills in communication, group interaction, management, and planning. The program provides graduates with in-depth understanding and ability in the areas of software process engineering, software project planning and management, software analysis and design, communications, and teamwork. In addition, the M.S.E. curriculum takes full notice of the Software Engineering Institute's Capability Maturity Model (CMM) by incorporating the key practices throughout the course work.

The curriculum is structured into three groups of courses: core (15 credits), specified electives (6 or 9 credits), and recommended electives (9 credits). In addition, each student is required to complete a graduate project (3 credits). Courses such as modeling and simulation, knowledge-based systems, and concurrent and distributed systems are available as specified electives. The electives allow a student to customize the program toward one or more software architectures. The curriculum addresses the issue of target software architecture as opposed to a generic architecture. The approach of applying software engineering tools and techniques to different software architectures (real-time, AI, and simulation) is one of the distinguishing features of the curriculum.

RESEARCH FACILITIES

The Software Engineering Education & Research Laboratory (SEER-LAB) supports the Master of Software Engineering program. The SEER-LAB provides framework services that allow integration of procedures, methods, and tools in the form of a process-oriented software engineering environment that accommodates the educational and research requirements of the M.S.E. program and operates on a UNIX-based hardware platform consisting of three Sun servers and a network of more than fifty Sun Workstations. The lab supports a wide range of software development tools and provides a variety of CASE tools for full life-cycle support. Both front-end tools for analysis, design, project and configuration management activities and back-end tools in support of integration, testing, regression analysis, documentation, and maintenance phases of a software development life cycle are supplied. Numerous programming languages such as Ada, C, C++, LISP, and FORTRAN are available. In addition, the SEER-LAB is connected, via a local area network (LAN), to the Airway Science Simulation Laboratory (ASSL), housing a network of Silicon Graphics IRIS Workstations, Apollo/DOMAIN workstations, and personal computers. Flight simulators (e.g., FRASCA and a Boeing 707) and a Kavouras weather station, located in the ASSL, provide a realistic environment for real-time software development applications.

FINANCIAL AID

Embry-Riddle makes every effort, within the limitations of the financial resources available, to ensure that no qualified student is denied the opportunity to obtain an education because of inadequate funds. However, the primary responsibility for financing an education must be assumed by the student. A number of graduate assistantships, providing a stipend and a tuition waiver, are available on a competitive basis each year. Opportunities for graduate research and teaching assistantships are excellent, since most University functions employ M.S.E. students to assist them with their information technology needs. Other financial aid programs include Federal Stafford Student Loans, the Embry-Riddle Student Employment Program, Embry-Riddle short-term loans, and scholarship and fellowship programs. All graduate programs are approved for Veterans Administration education benefits.

COST OF STUDY

In 1997–98, tuition costs are $415 per semester hour. International students pay an additional fee of $50 per semester. Books and supplies cost approximately $270 per semester.

LIVING AND HOUSING COSTS

Some on-campus housing is available to graduate students. The cost for a standard double-occupancy room is $1350 per semester; a privacy or efficiency apartment is $1550 per semester. Off-campus housing is reasonably priced. Single students who are sharing rental and utility expenses with someone can expect off-campus room and board yearly expenses of $3800. Married students can expect higher average yearly expenses.

STUDENT GROUP

The graduate programs currently enroll approximately 235 graduate students on the Daytona Beach campus. The College of Career Education enrolls about 3,000 students in graduate degree programs off campus, at more than 100 locations throughout the United States and Western Europe. Of the graduate students on the Daytona campus, 25 percent are from other countries, 19 percent are women, and 11 percent, not including the international students, are members of minority groups. Approximately 14 percent of the campus-based graduate students are employed full-time, many holding professional positions in the aviation industry.

STUDENT OUTCOMES

Employment opportunities are excellent for graduates of the M.S.E. degree program. In an era of information technology, software engineers are in high demand. Recent M.S.E. graduates were recruited by companies such as Motorola, Andersen Consulting, Lockheed Martin, and McDonnell–Douglas.

LOCATION

The campus is 10 minutes from Daytona Beach. Within an hour's drive are Disney World and EPCOT, the Kennedy Space Center, Sea World, and the city of St. Augustine.

THE UNIVERSITY

Within the field of aviation, Embry-Riddle Aeronautical University has built a reputation for the high quality of instruction in its programs since its founding in 1926. The University comprises the main campus at Daytona Beach; a western campus in Prescott, Arizona; and the College of Career Education.

APPLYING

Applications for admission should be submitted to the Graduate Admissions Department. The minimum desired undergraduate cumulative GPA is 2.5 out of a possible 4.0, with a 3.0 in the senior year. Applications from U.S. citizens and permanent residents should be received at least thirty days prior to the first day of the term in which they plan to enroll. International students should submit all of their documents at least ninety days prior to the first day of the term in which they plan to enroll.

CORRESPONDENCE AND INFORMATION

Graduate Admissions
Embry-Riddle Aeronautical University
600 South Clyde Morris Boulevard
Daytona Beach, Florida 32114-3900

Telephone: 904-226-6115
         800-388-ERAU (toll-free nationwide)
Fax: 904-226-6299
E-mail: taitg@cts.db.erau.edu
World Wide Web: http://erau.db.erau.edu/curriculum/mseprog.html

EMBRY-RIDDLE AERONAUTICAL UNIVERSITY
THE FACULTY AND THEIR AREAS OF SPECIALIZATION

The following professors are members of the graduate faculty at the Daytona Beach Campus.

Thomas Hilburn, Professor, Computer Science; Ph.D., Louisiana Tech. Software engineering, fuzzy clustering, Ada programming.

Iraj Hirmanpour, Professor and Chair, Computer Science; Ed.D., Florida Atlantic. Software engineering, information modeling.

Soheil Khajenoori, Professor, Computer Science; Ph.D., Central Florida. Software development methodologies, CASE, software metrics and software process engineering.

Andrew Kornecki, Professor, Computer Science; Ph.D., University of Mining and Metallurgy, Krakow (Poland). Computer simulation, object-oriented programming, real-time systems, microprocessor applications, AI, applications, air traffic control automation.

Rodney O. Rogers, Associate Professor, Computer Science; Ph.D., Central Florida. Computer graphics, design and analysis of algorithms, parallel computation, theory of computation, programming languages.

Massood Towhidnejad, Associate Professor, Computer Science; Ph.D., Central Florida. AI, intelligent CBT systems, multimedia, computer networking and architecture.

FLORIDA INSTITUTE OF TECHNOLOGY

COLLEGE OF ENGINEERING
COMPUTER SCIENCE PROGRAM

PROGRAMS OF STUDY

The Computer Science Program offers programs of graduate study leading to the degrees of Master of Science in Computer Information Systems, Master of Science in Computer Science, and Doctor of Philosophy. Major areas of study include software engineering, artificial intelligence/expert systems, computer graphics, programming languages, and database systems.

The master's degree in computer information systems is geared for students who may not have an undergraduate degree in computer science but who wish to obtain advanced training in this field. The course work required for this degree provides a broad background in the major areas of computer science. All students must pass a final program examination during their last semester.

The master's degree in computer science offers the student the opportunity to pursue advanced studies in various areas of computer science. The program is designed for students with baccalaureate degrees in computer science and provides a solid preparation for those who may pursue a doctorate. All students must complete and defend a thesis.

The doctoral program is designed to provide research in the disciplines of computer science. The program requires understanding the fundamentals of computer science, mastery of a specialized subject, and the creativity to produce a dissertation based on original research.

RESEARCH FACILITIES

The Computer Science Program occupies approximately 5,450 square feet of laboratory and office space. Computer laboratories support research programs in graphics design and implementation, software engineering, systems development, and artificial intelligence. Computer resources include X-terminals and Sun workstations as well as PC and Apple Macintosh networks.

FINANCIAL AID

Graduate teaching and research assistantships are available to qualified students. For 1997–98, stipends range from $7220 to $12,480 for twelve months. All assistantships include tuition remission. Computer-based information on scholarships, loan funds, and other student assistance may be obtained from the Financial Aid Office. A limited number of assistantships providing tuition remission only or stipend only are also available.

COST OF STUDY

In 1997–98, tuition is $533 per semester credit hour for all graduate students. As noted above, however, tuition is remitted for some graduate assistants.

LIVING AND HOUSING COSTS

Room and board on campus cost approximately $2200 per semester in 1997–98. On-campus housing (dormitories and apartments) is available for full-time single and married graduate students, but priority for dormitory rooms is given to undergraduate students. Many apartment complexes and rental houses are available near the campus.

STUDENT GROUP

The program currently has an enrollment of 215 graduate students from colleges throughout the United States. Approximately 17 percent of the graduate students are women.

STUDENT OUTCOMES

Graduates of the College of Engineering have found employment with such firms as IBM, Texas Instruments, NASA, Harris Corp., AT&T, General Electric, Keane Inc., Matrox, Northrop Grumman, Lockheed Martin, McDonnell Douglas, DBA Systems, Rockwell International, Advanced Micro Devices, USF&G, United Technologies, Honeywell, Computer Sciences Raytheon, ITT Aerospace, U.S. Patent Office, CIA, KPMG Audit, Los Alamos National Laboratory, Hewlett-Packard, Intel, Naval Air Systems Command, Naval Undersea Warfare Center, Macintosh Software Development, and Computer Task Group.

LOCATION

Florida Tech's main campus is located in Melbourne, a residential community on Florida's Space Coast. Melbourne is the key city in south Brevard County, which also encompasses nine other smaller communities on the mainland and beachside. The Kennedy Space Center and Disney World are within a 90-minute drive of the Institute. The area's economy is a well-balanced mix of electronics, aviation, light manufacturing, opticals, communications, agriculture, and tourism.

THE INSTITUTE AND THE PROGRAM

Florida Tech was founded in 1958 and has developed rapidly into a university that provides both undergraduate and graduate education in the sciences and engineering for selected students from throughout the United States and many countries. Current enrollment on the Melbourne campus is about 4,000. In addition to computer science, Florida Tech offers graduate programs in aerospace engineering, airport development management, applied mathematics, aquaculture, aviation science, biotechnology, business administration, cell and molecular biology, chemical engineering, chemistry, civil engineering, computer information systems, computer education, ecology, electrical engineering, environmental engineering, environmental management, environmental resource management, environmental science, industrial/organizational psychology, managerial communication, marine biology, mathematics education, mechanical engineering, ocean engineering, oceanography, operations research, physics, science education, space sciences, systems engineering, and technical and professional communication.

APPLYING

Further information and application forms for admission may be obtained from the Graduate Admissions Office. Students are encouraged to take the GRE General Test and Subject Test in computer science and submit scores for program consideration. Separate application for financial aid must be made on forms available from the Graduate School and must be submitted to the department by March 1.

CORRESPONDENCE AND INFORMATION

Graduate Admissions Office
Florida Institute of Technology
150 West University Boulevard
Melbourne, Florida 32901-6975
Telephone: 407-768-8000 Ext. 8027
Fax: 407-723-9468
World Wide Web: http://www.fit.edu

Dr. W. D. Shoaff, Chair
Computer Science Program
Florida Institute of Technology
150 West University Boulevard
Melbourne, Florida 32901-6975
Telephone: 407-768-8000 Ext. 8062
E-mail: wds@cs.fit.edu

FLORIDA INSTITUTE OF TECHNOLOGY
THE FACULTY AND THEIR RESEARCH

Frederick B. Buoni, Professor and Associate Dean; Ph.D., Ohio State, 1971. Decision analysis, artificial intelligence, systems simulations modeling, reliability and risk assessment, operations research applications, engineering quality control, engineering reliability. Introducing "quality" into an undergraduate computer science curriculum. *Fifty-Fourth Annual Meeting of the Florida Academy of Sciences.* Melbourne, Florida, March 23, 1990 (with Hadjilogiou and Newman). Comparison of performance for fuzzy expert system shell implementations in Pascal and in ADA. *Proceedings of AIDA-89, Fifth Annual Conference on Artificial Intelligence and Ada.* George Mason University, November 16–17, 1989 (with Schneider and Cornett).

David W. Clay, Assistant Professor; M.S., Florida Tech, 1984. Advanced data structures, object-oriented design, concurrency in operating systems, parallel processing systems, computer science education. Internet: Features and resources—an unexplored infoscape. *Proceedings of the Third National Conference on College Teaching and Learning.* Jacksonville, Florida, 1992. *Information Structures—Implementing Imagination.* St. Paul, Minn.: West Publishing, 1985.

Charles B. Engle Jr., Associate Professor; Ph.D., Polytechnic, 1991. Software engineering, real-time systems, software project management, Ada/Ada 9X, rate monotonic scheduling theory, computer education. An undergraduate curriculum in software engineering. *Proceedings of the Fourth Annual Conference on Software Engineering Education, SEI.* April 1990 (with Mills and Newman).

Lina Khatib, Assistant Professor; Ph.D., Florida Tech, 1994. Artificial intelligence, temporal reasoning, constraint satisfaction, analysis of algorithms. *Path Consistency in a Network of Non-Convex Intervals,* IJCAI, 1993.

Robert A. Morris, Associate Professor; Ph.D., Indiana, 1984. Temporal reasoning theory and applications, distributed artificial intelligence, model-based diagnostic reasoning, knowledge representation. An interval-based temporal relational calculus for events with gaps. *J. Exp. Theoret. Artific. Intell.* 3:87–107, 1991 (with Al-Khatib). Distributed intelligent monitoring and control for space applications. *Proceedings of the Fourth International Conference on Industrial/Engineering Applications of Artificial Intelligence and Expert Systems (AEI/AIE-91).* Kauai, Hawaii, June 2–5, 1991 (with Gonzalez and Raval).

J. Richard Newman, Professor and Associate Dean; Ph.D., Southwestern Louisiana, 1976. Software engineering, information systems management, CASE tools for clean room software engineering, legal issues, program specification tools. An undergraduate curriculum in software engineering. *Proceedings of the Fourth Annual Conference on Software Engineering Education, SEI.* April 1990 (with Mills and Engle). Performance issues for an expert system written in Ada. *Fifty-Fourth Annual Meeting of the Florida Academy of Sciences.* Melbourne, Florida, March 23, 1990 (with Buoni and Baggs).

William D. Shoaff, Associate Professor; Ph.D., Southern Illinois, 1981. Mathematical programming, parallel algorithms, parallel processing, supercomputers, computer modeling in genetics, computer graphics. The recognition of imperfect strings generated by fuzzy context sensitive grammars. *Int. J. Fuzzy Sets Syst.* 62:21–29, 1994 (with Inui, Fausett, and Schneider). Supercomputer simulation of chromosomes. In *Proceedings of the First International Conference on Electrophoresis, Supercomputing and the Human Genome,* eds. H. A. Lim and C. R. Cantor. Teaneck, N.J.: Supercomputer Computations Research Institute and Florida State University, 1990 (with Newman, Nuttall, and Hozier). A parallel algorithm for the singular value decomposition of rectangular matrices. In *Parallel Processing for Scientific Computing,* ed. Garry Rodrique. SIAM, 1989.

Ryan Stansifer, Associate Professor; Ph.D., Cornell, 1985. Programming languages, compilers, information systems, internationalization. *The Study of Programming Languages,* Prentice Hall, 1994; *M. L. Primer,* Prentice Hall, 1992; *The Foundation of Program Verification,* Wiley, 1987.

Dan E. Tamir, Professor; Ph.D., Florida State, 1989. Image processing, pattern recognition, computer architecture, parallel processing, digital signal processing, artificial intelligence, data communication. A pattern recognition interpretation of implications. *Inf. Sci.* 54, 1992. An axiomatic approach to fuzzy set theory. *Info. Sciences* 52:75–83, 1990.

James Whittaker, Assistant Professor; Ph.D., Tennessee, 1992. Statistical testing of software, software reliability engineering, software metrics, clean room software engineering. *Clean Room Systems Engineering Practices,* IDEA Publishing, 1996.

FLORIDA INSTITUTE OF TECHNOLOGY

COLLEGE OF ENGINEERING
PROGRAMS IN ELECTRICAL AND COMPUTER ENGINEERING

PROGRAMS OF STUDY

Florida Institute of Technology offers programs of study leading to the Master of Science and Doctor of Philosophy degrees in electrical engineering and computer engineering. These programs are designed to provide opportunities for students' development of professional engineering competence and scholarly achievement.

RESEARCH FACILITIES

There are more than 12,000 square feet of well-equipped laboratory facilities available for use by students, faculty, and researchers. Networked computing facilities include more than twenty-five Sun SPARCstations and sixty Macintosh and PC-compatible microcomputers, as well as a VAX and a Harris superminicomputer. Computing resources are networked via Ethernet and allow supercomputer and worldwide computer access via Internet. Research facilities support basic and applied research in electronics, communications, microwave systems, microelectronics, photonics, controls and robotics, and neural networks, as well as VLSI and computer system design. The Centers for Electronics Manufacturability and Enhancement of Quality in Engineering Education provide challenging opportunities for students. Agencies of the federal and state governments, as well as major corporations support research efforts in these and other technical areas.

FINANCIAL AID

Graduate teaching and research assistantships are available to qualified students. For 1997–98, typical stipends range upward from $9600 for twelve months for approximately half-time duties. Some assistantships include tuition.

COST OF STUDY

For 1997–98, tuition is $533 per semester credit hour for all students. As noted above, tuition is waived for some graduate assistants.

LIVING AND HOUSING COSTS

Room and board on campus cost approximately $2200 per semester in 1997–98. On-campus housing (dormitories and apartments) is available for full-time single and married graduate students, but priority for dormitory rooms is given to undergraduate students. Many apartment complexes and rental houses are available near the campus.

STUDENT OUTCOMES

Graduates of the programs in electrical and computer engineering are employed by such companies as IBM, Texas Instruments, NASA, Harris Corporation, AT&T, General Electric, Keane Inc., Matrox, Northrup Grumman, Lockheed Martin, McDonnell Douglas, DBA Systems, Rockwell International, Advanced Micro Devices, USF&G, United Technologies, Honeywell, Computer Sciences Raytheon, ITT Aerospace, U.S. Patent Office, CIA, KPMG Audit, Los Alamos National Lab, Hewlett-Packard, Intel, Naval Air Systems Command, Naval Undersea Warfare Center, Macintosh Software Development, and Computer Task Group.

LOCATION

The campus is located in Melbourne, on Florida's east coast. It is an area 3 miles from Atlantic Ocean beaches, with a year-round subtropical climate. The area's economy is supported by a well-balanced mix of industries in electronics, aviation, light manufacturing, optics, communications, agriculture, and tourism. Many companies support activities at the Kennedy Space Center.

THE INSTITUTE

Florida Institute of Technology, founded in 1958, has developed into a distinctive independent university that provides undergraduate and graduate education in engineering and sciences for students from throughout the United States and many other countries. Florida Tech is supported by local industry and is the recipient of many research grants and contracts.

APPLYING

Applicants for graduate study in electrical engineering should have an undergraduate degree in electrical engineering, while those applying for graduate study in computer engineering should have an undergraduate degree in computer engineering. An applicant whose degree is in another field of engineering or in the applied sciences will be reviewed; however, undergraduate course work in the field of study may be required prior to starting the Master of Science program.

Forms and instructions for applying for admission and assistantships are sent upon request. Doctoral applicants are asked to submit three letters of recommendation from academic references and a statement of purpose giving their reason for graduate study. Although the GRE is not required, it is considered for students with marginal undergraduate academic performance. International students applying for assistantships must have a TOEFL score greater than 600 and a TSE score of 45. International students without English proficiency and with a TOEFL score of less than 550 may need to enroll in language courses before beginning their graduate studies. Separate application for an assistantship should be made on forms available from the Graduate School.

CORRESPONDENCE AND INFORMATION

Graduate Admissions Office
Florida Institute of Technology
150 West University Boulevard
Melbourne, Florida 32901-6988
Telephone: 407-768-8000 Ext. 8027
          800-944-4348 (toll-free)
Fax: 407-723-9468
World Wide Web: http://www.fit.edu

Dr. Charles Beach
Electrical and Computer Engineering Programs
Florida Institute of Technology
150 West University Boulevard
Melbourne, Florida 32901-6988
Telephone: 407-768-8000 Ext. 8060
Fax: 407-984-8461
E-mail: cbeach@fit.edu

FLORIDA INSTITUTE OF TECHNOLOGY
THE FACULTY AND THEIR RESEARCH

Electrical Engineering

C. D. Beach, Associate Professor. Nonlinear systems, non-Gaussian noise, radio communications, signal processing.

B. G. Grossman, Professor and Electrical Engineering Program Chair. Optic fiber-optic sensors; optical computing and signal processing; optical neural networks; optical communication systems; electrooptic, acoustooptic, and nonlinear optical devices/systems; optical artificial neural networks; smart structures.

F. Ham, Professor. Linear and nonlinear control systems, robust control, optimal tracking systems, biosensor research, neural networks, robotics.

W. M. Nunn Jr., Professor. Electromagnetic theory, electromagnetic scattering, antennas, radar systems, microwave, electron physics.

T. J. Sanders, Harris Professor and Division Director, Electrical and Computer Science and Engineering. Microelectronics design for manufacturability, advanced IC process development, optoelectronics, radiation hardening, microelectronics packaging.

N. Tepedelenlioglu, Associate Professor. Neural networks, adaptive filtering, digital signal processing.

M. Thursby, Associate Professor. Artificial neural networks, smart antenna systems, nondestructive testing, automated RF measurements.

Computer Engineering

H. K. Brown, Associate Professor. Microelectronic devices and processes, ASIC design for supercomputers, neural networks, VLSI design and testing, computer architectures and networks.

R. H. Cofer, Associate Professor. VLSI design, image processing, high-performance computational structures, perception and biosensor research, neural networks and parallel processing.

R. G. Deshmukh, Associate Professor. High-performance computer architectures, neural networks and parallel processing, microprocessor applications, digital systems.

J. Hadjilogiou, Professor, Computer Engineering Program Chair, and Director of the Center for Enhancement of Quality in Engineering Education. Automata theory, computer organization and architecture, fault diagnosis and reliable system design, statistical process control, design for manufacturability, integration of quality issues into the curriculum.

S. Kozaitis, Associate Professor. Pattern recognition, optical signal processing, fiber-optic sensing.

M. M. Shahsavari, Assistant Professor. Computer-aided design, VLSI circuits, high-performance computer architectures, computer networks and communications, microprocessor applications.

FLORIDA INTERNATIONAL UNIVERSITY

SCHOOL OF COMPUTER SCIENCE

PROGRAMS OF STUDY

The School offers programs leading to Master of Science (M.S.) and Doctor of Philosophy (Ph.D.) degrees in computer science.

The master's degree in computer science is a terminal professional degree; the degree program offers the student course work in the most current concepts and theory of computer science. The program consists of 30 semester hours of course work, including a thesis. The intent of this degree program is to prepare students to assume professional leadership positions in industry, government, and education.

The doctoral program in computer science consists initially of nine required graduate courses, followed by a qualifying examination. The student then participates in a number of advanced seminars that culminate in the Ph.D. candidacy examination. Upon being admitted to candidacy, the student prepares and presents a thesis for review by a committee, after which the degree may be awarded.

RESEARCH FACILITIES

The library has more than 8,000 volumes in the mathematical and computer sciences and receives more than 125 periodicals.

The School's research is performed on an integrated ATM/Ethernet network of Sun and SGI enterprise servers, workstations, and personal computers. Researchers typically collaborate on distributed databases, parallel processing, and software engineering interest with NASA, DOD, and other government and commercial settings.

FINANCIAL AID

There are several Presidential Doctoral Fellowships available for exceptional students, carrying an initial stipend of $24,750 per year (plus tuition and fee waiver) and eventually rising to $29,354. Regular research assistantships are also awarded to excellent students. These carry an initial stipend of $15,350 (plus tuition and fees), eventually rising to $18,400.

COST OF STUDY

In 1996–97, tuition for in-state graduate students was $114.99 per semester hour for regular course work and $114.99 per hour for dissertation or thesis credit. In addition, there was a $46 assessment each semester for the use of the campus health center. Tuition for out-of-state graduate students was $385.73 per semester hour for regular course work and $385.73 per hour for dissertation or thesis credit. (These figures are subject to change without notice in 1997–98.)

LIVING AND HOUSING COSTS

Recently built, privately owned off-campus apartments were available for approximately $1000–$2000 per semester in 1996–97. (These figures are subject to change without notice in 1997–98.)

STUDENT GROUP

There are 22,000 students on campus, with more than 106 graduate students in computer science. Graduate students come from many areas of the United States and from a number of other countries.

LOCATION

Florida International University is located at the gateway to the Everglades in suburban Dade County, 10 miles from downtown Miami. There are ample recreational activities available, and the mild weather allows these activities to be enjoyed the year round.

THE UNIVERSITY

Florida International University, a public institution, is a member of the State University System of Florida. It comprises a College of Arts and Sciences, a College of Engineering and Design, and Schools of Computer Science, Business Administration, Hospitality Management, Public Administration, Education, Health Sciences, and Nursing.

APPLYING

Graduate study may begin in any semester, but assistantships are usually awarded for the fall semester. Applicants must submit up-to-date transcripts and current Graduate Record Examinations scores to the graduate program director as early as possible. The GRE General Test is required of all applicants, and the minimum acceptable score is a combined total score (verbal, quantitative, and analytical) of 1650; the scores must have been earned within the last five years. The department requires a grade average of at least B in all upper-division undergraduate classwork and a background in mathematics that includes calculus and statistics.

CORRESPONDENCE AND INFORMATION

Graduate Program Coordinator
School of Computer Science
Florida International University
Miami, Florida 33199-2788

Telephone: 305-348-1038
World Wide Web: http://www.cs.fiu.edu.

FLORIDA INTERNATIONAL UNIVERSITY
THE FACULTY AND THEIR RESEARCH

Walid Akache, Instructor; M.S., Miami, 1984. Computer science.

Paul C. Attie, Assistant Professor; Ph.D., Texas, 1995. Temporal logic, distributed computing, verification of programs.

David Barton, Professor; Ph.D., Cambridge, 1966. Distributed systems and data communications.

Rida Bazzi, Assistant Professor; Ph.D., Georgia Tech, 1994. Theory of distributed computing.

Toby S. Berk, Professor; Ph.D., Purdue, 1972. Computer graphics and operating systems.

Chungmin Chen, Assistant Professor; Ph.D., Maryland, 1994. Databases.

Yi Deng, Assistant Professor; Ph.D., Pittsburgh, 1992. Software engineering and knowledge engineering, distributed systems, multimedia systems.

Timothy Downey, Instructor; M.S., SUNY at Albany, 1986. Computer science.

Raimund Ege, Associate Professor; Ph.D., Oregon Graduate Center, 1987. Object-oriented programming.

Michael Evangelist, Professor and Director of the School; Ph.D., Northwestern, 1978. Distributed computing and software engineering.

Mbola Fanomezantsoa, Instructor; M.S., SUNY Institute of Technology, 1994. Computer science.

Dawn J. Holmes, Instructor; Ph.D., Florida State, 1991. Artificial intelligence, intelligent tutoring systems.

Bill Kraynek, Associate Professor and Associate Director; Ph.D., Carnegie Mellon, 1968. Programming languages and computer science education.

Masoud Milani, Associate Professor; Ph.D., Central Florida, 1986. Programming language environments.

Jainendra Navlakha, Professor and Graduate Program Director; Ph.D., Case Western Reserve, 1977. Analysis of algorithms, program verification, software metrics.

Cyril U. Orji, Assistant Professor; Ph.D., Illinois at Chicago, 1991. I/O systems, operating systems, database systems, and file systems.

Ana Pasztor, Professor; D.R.N., Darmstadt, 1979. Cognitive sciences, program verification.

Alexander Pelin, Associate Professor; Ph.D., Pennsylvania, 1977. Automated reasoning.

Norman Pestaina, Instructor; M.S., Penn State, 1979. Computer science.

Nagarajan Prabhakaran, Associate Professor; Ph.D., Queensland (Australia), 1985. Database systems, graphics.

Naphtali Rishe, Professor; Ph.D., Tel-Aviv, 1984. Database management and systems.

Orlando Sauleda, Instructor; M.S., Florida International, 1977. Computer science.

Rakesh Sinha, Assistant Professor; Ph.D., Washington (Seattle), 1995. Theory of computation, parallel algorithms.

Wei Sun, Associate Professor; Ph.D., Illinois at Chicago, 1990. Database systems and knowledge-based systems.

Mark A. Weiss, Associate Professor; Ph.D., Princeton, 1987. Data structures and algorithm analysis.

FLORIDA STATE UNIVERSITY

COLLEGE OF ARTS AND SCIENCES
DEPARTMENT OF COMPUTER SCIENCE

PROGRAMS OF STUDY

The department offers programs leading to the M.S. and Ph.D. degrees.

The department offers three majors at the master's level: computer science, software engineering, and computer system administration. Each major offers both thesis and project tracks. The project tracks in any of these majors, while no less rigorous and demanding than thesis tracks, are considered professional degree tracks. A student considering continuing into the Ph.D. program is encouraged to follow a thesis track.

In addition to the master's with a major in computer science, the department offers majors designed for the computer professional: software engineering and computer system administration.

Each of the master's tracks requires 27 hours of course work and 6 additional hours for the completion of a suitable project or thesis. Most students complete the requirements for a master's in two years.

The Doctor of Philosophy is regarded as a research degree and is awarded on the basis of accomplishment in a recognized specialty in computer science. Such accomplishment should include scholarly mastery of the field, significant contributions to new knowledge in the field, and written and oral communication skills appropriate to the field.

The Ph.D. requires an additional 12 hours of course work beyond the master's degree and a minimum of 24 hours of acceptable dissertation.

RESEARCH FACILITIES

Computer science students have access to a large variety of computer systems. Course work and research are supported by a network of Sun Microsystems UNIX-based workstations, Windows NT and Windows 95 PCs, and Linux-based PCs. The department also maintains several computer labs that support undergraduate and graduate courses. These labs contain 486 and Pentium-based machines, all with color capability. Specialized equipment available for research and instruction includes a variety of high-speed black-and-white laser printers, a color printer, a Silicon Graphics O2 multimedia workstation, and a multimedia PC complete with a flatbed scanner.

Network connectivity is available to machines and systems via a 100 Mbit/second FDDI connection to the FSU campus backbone. Routing and bridging provide fast Ethernet capability to a number of servers and workstations throughout the department. Fiber-optic cables connect interbuilding department offices and labs. Internet connectivity is via the FSU campus connection.

FINANCIAL AID

Teaching assistantships, requiring 20 hours per week for instruction and related duties, are available. The stipend ranges between $12,000 and $14,000 per calendar year. Research assistantship appointments are comparable to those awarded for teaching assistantships; duties involve working on the research program of an individual faculty member, with whom an interested applicant should correspond directly. Fellowship stipends total up to $11,000 per year. Students on assistantships and fellowships are eligible to receive remission of their tuition fees.

COST OF STUDY

The 1997–98 registration fees for Florida residents are $118.29 per graduate credit hour. Fees for out-of-state students are $389.03 per graduate credit hour.

A reasonable estimate of the cost of attending Florida State University is approximately $10,347 for the academic year for in-state graduate students living in University residences and participating in a campus meal plan.

LIVING AND HOUSING COSTS

University facilities on the main campus include an apartment facility, Rodgers Hall, with ninety-four 1-bedroom, double-occupancy apartments reserved for single graduate students. Monthly charges are $273 per student.

Graduate students, either single or with dependents, are also eligible for housing in Alumni Village, an apartment complex 1½ miles from campus. Alumni Village offers 790 one-, two-, and three-bedroom furnished apartments. Residents have access to a preschool, laundry facilities, and recreational facilities. Monthly charges range from $254 to $442 and do not include utilities.

For more information concerning on- and off-campus housing, interested students should contact the University Housing Office.

STUDENT GROUP

Florida State University is a public coeducational institution with an enrollment of approximately 30,000, including more than 5,500 graduate students. Approximately 100 graduate students are pursuing studies in computer science. More than one third of graduate students in computer science are women.

STUDENT OUTCOMES

Recent graduates from the department have accepted positions in research and development, software engineering, systems administration, and higher education.

LOCATION

The University is located in Tallahassee, the capital of Florida, which has a population of approximately 175,000. The rolling hills of north Florida, with their cover of pine and live oak, provide a pleasant variety of landscapes. The nearby Gulf of Mexico (35 miles away) tempers the climate and offers diverse recreational opportunities. Tallahassee is one of the oldest cities in Florida and has many points of historic interest. Music and the arts are well supported by the community. A number of state and community parks in and around the city have trails for hiking and spring-fed rivers and streams for snorkeling and canoeing.

THE UNIVERSITY

The main campus of the University encompasses 346 highly populated acres. Valued at more than $170 million, the physical plant ranges in architectural style from gothic to ultramodern. Founded in 1857, the University places special emphasis on graduate programs.

APPLYING

Applications for admission should be sent to the Office of Admissions. Applications for departmental financial aid, with all supporting documents, should be submitted to the Department of Computer Science. The deadline for applying for the fall semester is July 15 for U.S. students and March 1 for international applicants.

CORRESPONDENCE AND INFORMATION

Applications and information may be obtained by contacting:
Graduate Admissions
Department of Computer Science 4019
203 James J. Love Building
Florida State University
Tallahassee, Florida 32306-4019

Telephone: 904-644-2296
Fax: 904-644-0058
E-mail: info@cs.fsu.edu
World Wide Web: http://www.cs.fsu.edu

FLORIDA STATE UNIVERSITY
THE FACULTY AND THEIR RESEARCH

Theodore P. Baker, Professor; Ph.D., Cornell, 1974. Real-time systems; theory of parsing, translation, and compiling; Ada run-time environments; tools and high-level languages for real-time software interfaces.

Jeff Bauer, Instructor and System Administrator; M.S., South Florida, 1988. Parallel processing, distributed computations, system administration.

Kyle Gallivan, Associate Professor; Ph.D., Illinois at Urbana-Champaign, 1983. Parallel numerical algorithms, architectures for scientific computation, computational electromagnetics, signal processing.

Lois Wright Hawkes, Professor; Ph.D., London, 1977. Fault tolerance, coding theory, intelligent tutoring systems.

Susan I. Hruska, Associate Professor; Ph.D., Alabama at Birmingham, 1988. Neural networks, hybrid AI systems, machine learning, statistics.

Charles Kacmar, Associate Professor; Ph.D., Texas A&M, 1990. Hypertext/hypermedia, human-computer interaction, object-oriented systems, software engineering, software development tools.

Ladislav Kohout, Professor; Ph.D., Essex (England), 1978. Knowledge engineering, fuzzy sets and systems, artificial intelligence, knowledge-based systems, fuzzy relational architectures, medical computing.

Christopher Lacher, Professor and Chair; Ph.D., Georgia, 1966. Neural computation, hybrid systems, machine learning, artificial life.

Stephen P. Leach, Associate Chair; Ph.D., Florida State, 1990. Knowledge-based systems, software engineering, artificial intelligence.

Hilbert Levitz, Professor; Ph.D., Penn State, 1965. Automated reasoning, logic, recursive functions.

Ernest L. McDuffie, Assistant Professor; Ph.D., Florida Tech, 1995. Expert systems, fuzzy logic, temporal reasoning, scheduling.

Gregory Riccardi, Professor; Ph.D., SUNY at Buffalo, 1980. Supercomputer applications, parallel processing, software engineering.

Daniel Schwartz, Associate Professor; Ph.D., Portland State, 1981. Models of human reasoning, logic programming, expert systems, programming languages.

David Whalley, Associate Professor; Ph.D., Virginia, 1990. Computer architecture, compiler theory, performance evaluation.

FORDHAM UNIVERSITY

GRADUATE SCHOOL OF ARTS AND SCIENCES
DEPARTMENT OF COMPUTER SCIENCE AND INFORMATION SYSTEMS

PROGRAM OF STUDY

The Department of Computer Science offers a program of study leading to an M.S. degree in computer science. The degree is designed to prepare students for technical and/or supervisory careers in computer science, information technology, and telecommunications and/or as a preparation for study at the doctoral level. Course offerings are at the Lincoln Center campus. Area concentrations are available in database systems and applications, artificial intelligence, data communications and networks, and computation and algorithms.

The main criterion for admission to the computer science program is the clear indication that the student has the ability and motivation to pursue graduate study successfully, evidenced by undergraduate work in computer science or a related field, letters of recommendation, and a reasonable score on the Graduate Record Examinations (GRE) General Test. (Requests to take the GRE during the first semester are considered by the admissions committee.) Students who lack an undergraduate degree in computer science may be asked to take selected undergraduate courses or preparatory graduate courses before matriculation in the graduate program.

RESEARCH FACILITIES

The University's computing facilities at the Rose Hill campus include six Digital Alpha systems, one VAX, two MicroVAX systems, and a lab containing fifty network computers; there are two VAX systems and one Alpha system at the Lincoln Center campus. Both campuses have various LANs, and the campuses are connected with a T-3 connection that carries both voice and data. The University is connected to the Internet via a T-1 connection and has easy access to other research institutions and high-technology companies around the world. Both campuses also maintain several microcomputer laboratories with more than 100 stations at each campus.

In addition to the University computing facilities, the Department of Computer Science and Information Systems has a configuration of two local-area research networks with three RISC/6000 nodes running AIX/UNIX, a node running UNIXWARE, and a number of X-stations and Sun Workstations.

FINANCIAL AID

Financial support in the form of assistantships and teaching fellowships is available for full-time graduate students. Tuition remission scholarships are usually held jointly with these awards. In 1996–97, stipends ranged from $8000 to $14,000. Opportunities for support in the form of research assistantships are also available.

COST OF STUDY

For 1997–98, tuition is $525 per credit. The student activities fee is $40 per year. The annual cost for books and supplies is approximately $800.

LIVING AND HOUSING COSTS

On-campus housing is available for unmarried students at approximately $5000 per twelve-month lease (1997–98). Most students live in off-campus housing near the University or elsewhere in the New York City area. Rents vary widely.

STUDENT GROUP

The total enrollment of Fordham University is approximately 12,000 students. The Graduate School of Arts and Sciences has an enrollment of approximately 1,100 students. Students enrolled in the Department of Computer Science represent diverse ethnic, cultural, and religious backgrounds. Most graduates of the program are engaged in teaching, research, or both.

STUDENT OUTCOMES

Opportunities to gain teaching experience are available through many adjunct positions offered at New York–area colleges. Graduates of Fordham teach at various major colleges and universities, both in the United States as well as overseas. Many are recognized authors and specialists in their particular fields of expertise.

LOCATION

The program is based at the Lincoln Center campus of the University, located at West 60th Street and Columbus Avenue in Manhattan. Opportunities for cultural and social enrichment in New York are virtually unlimited. The Lincoln Center for the Performing Arts, the Museum of Natural History, and the Metropolitan Museum of Art are among just a few of the many cultural attractions within walking distance of the campus.

THE UNIVERSITY AND THE DEPARTMENT

Fordham University, founded in 1841, consists of ten colleges and schools. The Graduate School of Arts and Sciences offers a wide range of master's and doctoral degree programs and participates in the New York City Doctoral Consortium.

APPLYING

Applicants must hold a bachelor's degree in the computer sciences or its equivalent, have a minimum undergraduate GPA of 3.0 (on a 4.0 scale), submit GRE scores, and arrange for official transcripts and at least two letters of recommendation to be sent to the University. TOEFL scores are required for most international students. Early application is encouraged. The deadlines are May 1 (fall term) and December 1 (spring term). Applications for financial aid must be received by January 15. The application fee is $50.

CORRESPONDENCE AND INFORMATION

For applications and further information, students should contact:

Assistant Dean
Office of Graduate Admissions
Graduate School of Arts and Sciences
Fordham University
Bronx, New York 10458
Telephone: 718-817-4416
E-mail: fuga@murray.fordham.edu
World Wide Web: http://www.fordham.edu

Specific questions can be addressed to:

Chairperson
Department of Computer Science
Fordham University, LL813
113 West 60th Street
New York, New York 10023
Telephone: 212-636-7925 or
                    718-817-4480
World Wide Web: http://www.cis.fordham.edu/

FORDHAM UNIVERSITY

THE FACULTY AND THEIR RESEARCH

Members of the faculty of the Department of Computer Science are engaged in various research activities on a variety of topics and projects. They have collaborated with colleagues from all over the world and have received funding and support from many government and private agencies. Recent examples of funding include research in computer-automated reasoning with RUE resolution, supported by the National Science Foundation; database and distributed database, supported by the Texaco Corporation; advanced technology systems for the design of communications networks, supported by the Defense Information Systems Agency; and reducing the intractability of differential and integral equations, supported by the National Science Foundation. Members of the department are actively involved as reviewers, referees, and consultants for professional and technical journals and publications, government agencies, and industry and business institutions.

T. Michael Houlihan, Associate Professor and Department Chair; Ph.D., Polytechnic. Object-oriented programming and object-oriented databases for large systems, specifically databases used in the development and verification of digital circuits.

D. Frank Hsu, Professor and Director or Graduate Studies; Ph.D., Michigan. Interconnection networks for massively parallel computer systems, communication networks and VLSI designs, parallel algorithms and architectures, telecommunication network design and optimization, graph theory and combinatorial problems.

David T. K. Chen, Associate Professor; Ph.D., Erlangen-Nuremberg (Germany). Database systems, object-oriented design, software engineering (software reliability, quality, and security).

Vincent J. Digricoli, Associate Professor; Ph.D., NYU (Courant). Artificial intelligence and programming languages: automated reasoning, logic programming and PROLOG, compiler design.

Valery Frants, Associate Professor; Ph.D., Academy of Science/VINITI (Moscow). Information science theory, information retrieval system design, software engineering, computer algorithms and artificial intelligence.

Robert K. Moniot, Associate Professor; Ph.D., Berkeley. Scale-space and equation-error minimization approaches to problems in image reconstruction and solution of partial differential equations.

Tadeusz Strzemecki, Assistant Professor; Ph.D., Stevens. Design and analysis of algorithms, computational complexity, complexity of algorithms, theory of computation.

Arthur G. Werschulz, Professor; Ph.D., Carnegie Mellon. Information-based computational complexity, numerical mathematics, special interest in the computational complexity of differential and integral equations.

THE GEORGE WASHINGTON UNIVERSITY

SCHOOL OF ENGINEERING AND APPLIED SCIENCE
DEPARTMENT OF ELECTRICAL ENGINEERING AND COMPUTER SCIENCE

PROGRAMS OF STUDY

The department offers the M.S., Engineer (Engr.), and Applied Scientist (App.Sc.) professional degrees and the D.Sc. in three fields of study: computer science, electrical engineering, and telecommunication and computers (M.S. only). Computer science concentrations include algorithms and theory, artificial intelligence and computer vision, computer and communications security, computer engineering and architecture, computer graphics and multimedia systems, parallel and distributed computing, and software engineering and systems. Electrical engineering concentrations include communications; electrical power and engineering management; electrophysics and fiber optics; energy conversion, power, and transmission; biomedical engineering; control systems and signal processing; and microelectronics and VLSI systems. The interdisciplinary field of telecommunication and computers combines study in the areas of computer science, electrical engineering, and engineering management. M.S. programs require a minimum of 24 semester hours of graduate-level courses and 6 semester hours of thesis or a minimum of 30 semester hours for the nonthesis option. Engr. and App.Sc. professional degree programs emphasize applied subject material. At least two years of professional experience beyond a master's degree are required for admission to these programs, which require at least 30 semester hours of approved post-master's courses. The D.Sc. program normally consists of one major and two minor areas of concentration, totaling a minimum of 30 course semester hours beyond the master's level or a minimum of 54 credit hours of approved graduate work for students whose highest earned degree is a baccalaureate, and 24 dissertation research semester hours. Each doctoral student is assigned an adviser whose research specialty is in the student's major area of study; together they determine the major and minor areas of study.

RESEARCH FACILITIES

The electronics and communications labs have been expanded and reequipped, while the microwave and laser lab continues to add new equipment. The medical engineering lab's own 8-, 16-, and 32-bit microcomputers are capable of conducting and analyzing evoked-potential experiments. A controls lab offers opportunity for research in real-time computer control and in CAD and simulation control systems. The electrical power lab has both large and small machinery and power transmission equipment. The School's dedicated Academic Computing Facility provides UNIX-based HP and Sun workstations and file servers and a Sun Microsystems SPARCserver 1000 multiprocessor system supporting terminal server and remote access. High-level graphics computing is supported with color workstations and printers, laser printers, and a large-scale plotter. These systems are fully integrated by Ethernet and through the School's UNIX system organization and are equipped with a wide range of software. Remote access to systems at the School of Engineering and Applied Science (SEAS) is provided by the Computing Facility's dial-up 2400/9600 baud modems and the University's AT&T ISN serial switching system, which provides campuswide asynchronous communications and dial-up support. Also, SEAS Macintosh and PC labs provide microcomputer-based computing support, utilizing LAN technology with laser printers, plotters, and input scanners. SEAS's networks of computers are connected to the University's high-speed FDDI backbone, linking the School to University computer resources, as well as Internet/SURAnet for access to national supercomputer centers, universities, and worldwide research facilities. The University's dedicated academic computer resources include an IBM 4381 mainframe VM/CMS, PC and Macintosh classroom labs, and a UNIX Sequent computer. University libraries contain 1.7 million volumes. Their computer system provides on-line access to the shared catalog of all seven member libraries of the Washington Research Library Consortium, as well as to periodical and newspaper index databases. Gelman Library provides additional databases on CD-ROM, including several specific to engineering, and offers research consultation services. Students have ready access to the Library of Congress.

FINANCIAL AID

Teaching assistantships provide remission of tuition for 9 hours per semester and a salary ranging from $1200 to $3500 for each course taught per semester in 1997–98. Research assistants receive a salary of $8000–$16,000 for the calendar year. School Graduate Fellow, Dean's Fellow, and Department Fellow awards range from $7500 to $15,000 for eligible full-time students. Full-time students who are U.S. citizens or permanent residents may be eligible for Graduate Engineering Honors Fellowships.

COST OF STUDY

For the 1997–98 academic year, tuition is charged at the rate of $655 per semester hour, payable on a course-by-course basis.

LIVING AND HOUSING COSTS

Apartments for students enrolled in the School of Engineering and Applied Science are available in the surrounding area at a wide range of costs. These costs start at about $600 a month.

STUDENT GROUP

At SEAS, about 1,400 students are working on master's degrees, 31 on professional degrees, and 406 on the doctorate. The department has about 565 M.S. students, 20 professional degree students, and 200 D.Sc. students.

LOCATION

The Washington area has the second-largest concentration of research and development activity in the nation. Library facilities are unsurpassed in scope. The campus is in the Foggy Bottom historic district of Washington, D.C.

THE UNIVERSITY AND THE SCHOOL

The School, organized in 1884, offers limited course work in engineering, engineering administration, operations research, physical science, mathematics, economics, and statistics during summer sessions.

APPLYING

Admission to the M.S. program requires an appropriate bachelor's degree from a recognized institution and evidence of a capacity for productive work in the field. Admission to professional degree programs requires an appropriate master's degree from a recognized institution and evidence of capacity for productive work in the field. Applicants for doctoral study must have adequate preparation for advanced study, including a bachelor's or a master's degree or the equivalent and a capacity for creative scholarship. March 1 and October 1 are the respective priority deadlines for applications for the fall and spring; applications are accepted on a space-available basis thereafter.

CORRESPONDENCE AND INFORMATION

Professor Mona E. Zaghloul, Chair
Department of Electrical Engineering
    and Computer Science
School of Engineering and Applied Science
The George Washington University
Washington, D.C. 20052
Telephone: 202-994-6083
Fax: 202-994-0227
E-mail: eecs@seas.gwu.edu

Dean Gideon Frieder
School of Engineering and Applied Science
The George Washington University
Washington, D.C. 20052
Telephone: 202-994-3096
            800-537-7327(toll-free)
Fax: 202-994-4522

THE GEORGE WASHINGTON UNIVERSITY
THE FACULTY AND THEIR RESEARCH

Nikitas A. Alexandridis, Professor; Ph.D., UCLA, 1971. Microprocessors, parallel computer architectures, multiprocessor systems, adaptable computer architectures, multilevel vision systems.

Simon Y. Berkovich, Professor; Ph.D., Institute of Precise Mechanics and Computer Technology (Moscow), 1964. Information systems, data structures, associative memories and processors, computer organization.

Peter Bock, Professor; M.S., Purdue, 1964. Computer systems, artificial intelligence, robotics, simulation, programming languages, microprocessor systems.

Giorgio V. Borgiotti, Professor; D.E.E., Rome, 1957. Electrophysics, acoustic radiation and scattering, structural acoustics, signal processing, modal analysis of vibration, radar systems.

Robert L. Carroll Jr., Professor; Ph.D., Connecticut, 1973. Control systems, adaptive and learning systems, multidimensional systems, robotic systems, multitarget tracking.

Hyeong-Ah Choi, Associate Professor; Ph.D., Northwestern, 1986. Graph theory, design and analysis of algorithms, computational complexity.

Milos Doroslovacki, Assistant Professor; Ph.D., Cincinnati, 1994. Communications theory, mobile communications, coding theory.

Edward Della Torre, Professor; D.Eng.Sc., Columbia, 1964. Numerical device modeling, magnetic recording and bubble memory, magnetic phenomena.

Sajjad H. Durrani, Research Professor; Sc.D., New Mexico, 1962. Space communications: new services, systems planning, policy issues, research and development, and research planning and management.

Burton I. Edelson, Research Professor; Ph.D., Yale, 1960. Space science and technology, satellite communications systems.

Marvin F. Eisenberg, Professor; Ph.D., Florida, 1961. Medical engineering, thermography, evoked response, ultrasonics.

Kie-Bum Eom, Associate Professor; Ph.D., Purdue, 1986. Computer vision, pattern recognition, image modeling.

Michael B. Feldman, Professor; Ph.D., Pennsylvania, 1973. Computer science, programming languages, data structures, software engineering, concurrency and parallelism.

Gideon Frieder, A. James Clark Professor of Computer Science and Dean of the School; D.Sc., Technion (Israel), 1967. Computer architecture, operating systems, assembly languages and machine organization.

Arthur D. Friedman, Professor; Ph.D., Columbia, 1965. Computer architecture and organization, switching theory and logic design, microprocessors, diagnosis and fault-tolerant design of digital circuits.

James K. Hahn, Assistant Professor; Ph.D., Ohio State, 1989. Computer graphics, computer animation, display algorithms.

Robert J. Harrington, Professor of Engineering and Applied Science and Chairman of the Department; Ph.D., Liverpool, 1965. Simulation and control of electrical machinery and power systems, transient stability, transmission line switching transients, power system planning and operation.

Hermann J. Helgert, Professor; Ph.D., SUNY at Buffalo, 1966. Communications and information theory, coding theory, data communications, computer networks.

Rachelle S. Heller, Associate Professor; Ph.D., Maryland, 1986. Computer literacy, computers in education, programming languages.

Robert B. Heller, Professor Emeritus; Ph.D., Saint Louis, 1951. Information processing, computer-to-computer communication networks, satellite communications, electromagnetic radiation.

Lance J. Hoffman, Professor; Ph.D., Stanford, 1970. Computer science, security and privacy, viruses, social implications.

Walter K. Kahn, Professor; D.E.E., Polytechnic of Brooklyn, 1960. Antennas, microwave components, fiber optics, electrophysics.

Can E. Korman, Assistant Professor; Ph.D., Maryland, 1990. Numerical modeling of semiconductor devices, VLSI, magnetics, signal processing.

Nicholas Kyriakopoulos, Professor; D.Sc., George Washington, 1968. Computer-aided network design, systems theory, control theory, digital filtering.

Roger H. Lang, Professor; Ph.D., Polytechnic of Brooklyn, 1968. Wave propagation in random media, remote sensing, and adaptive arrays.

Ting N. Lee, Professor; Ph.D., Wisconsin, 1972. Networks, linear systems.

Murray H. Loew, Professor; Ph.D., Purdue, 1972. Pattern recognition, medical engineering, image processing.

C. Dianne Martin, Associate Professor; Ed.D., George Washington, 1987. Computer literacy, computers in education, computers and society, computer ethics.

W. Douglas Maurer, Professor; Ph.D., Berkeley, 1965. Computer science, correctness of programs, analysis of algorithms, semantics of programming languages.

Arnold C. Meltzer, Professor; D.Sc., George Washington, 1967. Computer architecture, design of computer systems, database systems, multiprocessor systems, information storage and retrieval.

Forest K. Musgrave, Assistant Professor; Ph.D., Yale, 1993. Computer graphics, modeling of natural phenomena.

Bhagirath Narahari, Assistant Professor; Ph.D., Pennsylvania, 1987. Parallel processing, algorithms and interconnection networks, reconfigurable parallel computer architectures, special-purpose computing.

Martha Pardavi-Horvath, Professor; Ph.D., Hungarian Academy of Sciences, 1985. Magnetic phenomena, magnetic recording processes and materials, magnetooptic devices and materials.

Raymond L. Pickholtz, Professor; Ph.D., Polytechnic of Brooklyn, 1966. Data communications, computer communication networks, communications theory, secure communications.

Shmuel Rotenstreich, Associate Professor; Ph.D., California, San Diego, 1983. Software engineering, operation systems.

Debabrata Saha, Associate Professor; Ph.D., Michigan, 1986. Communication theory, modulation and coding techniques.

John L. Sibert, Associate Professor; Ph.D., Michigan, 1974. Computer graphics, human-computer interaction.

Branimir R. Vojcic, Assistant Professor; Ph.D., Belgrade, 1989. Communications theory, spread spectrum, mobile and fading communications.

Wasyl Wasylkiwskyj, Professor; Ph.D., Polytechnic of Brooklyn, 1968. Electromagnetic waves, propagation, signal processing, remote sensing.

Abdou Youssef, Assistant Professor; Ph.D., Princeton, 1988. Interconnection networks, parallel computer architecture, parallel algorithms, algorithms and data structures, theory of computing.

Mona E. Zaghloul, Professor; Ph.D., Waterloo, 1975. Computer-aided analysis and design of integrated circuits; analog and digital VLSI modeling, design, and testing.

GEORGIA INSTITUTE OF TECHNOLOGY
A Unit of the University System of Georgia

COLLEGE OF COMPUTING

PROGRAMS OF STUDY

The College of Computing currently offers programs of study leading to the degrees of Doctor of Philosophy and Master of Science in computer science. The College also offers an interdisciplinary program leading to the degree of Doctor of Philosophy in algorithms, combinatorics, and optimization. In addition, the College awards an interdisciplinary Ph.D. certificate in cognitive science. The principal requirements for the Ph.D. are successful completion of certain comprehensive examinations and submission of a dissertation that describes original independent research. The degree of Doctor of Philosophy is awarded in recognition of high achievement in research and is intended for people who intend to pursue research careers. A student may earn the M.S. degree by completing one of the following: 50 quarter hours of approved course work, 38 to 41 hours of approved course work and a master's project, or 33 hours of approved course work and a thesis. The master's degree is intended for people who have a variety of career objectives, including technical and managerial positions in industry and government. A wide variety of graduate courses and research seminars are offered, and several active colloquium series featuring outside speakers are held.

RESEARCH FACILITIES

The College maintains a variety of computer systems for general support of academic and research activities. These include thirty-six Sun systems used as file and compute servers, eight of which are quad-processor machines; a Sun/Epoch file server with a read-write optical library unit; more than 350 workstation class machines from Sun, Digital, Hewlett-Packard, Silicon Graphics, IBM, Apple, and Intel; and over 150 X-terminals. A number of specialized facilities augment the College's general-purpose computing capabilities. The Graphics, Visualization, and Usability (GVU) Center houses a variety of graphics and multimedia equipment, including high-performance systems from Silicon Graphics, Hewlett-Packard, Sun, Digital, Apple, and Intel, as well as extensive video and audio facilities for recording and editing. A Scientific Visualization Laboratory with additional equipment from Digital and Silicon Graphics is jointly operated by the GVU Center and the Institute's Office of Information Technology (OIT). The High-Performance and Parallel Computation Experimentation Laboratory (HPPCEL), another joint operation between the College and OIT, serves as a focus for interdisciplinary research involving high-performance computer systems. Shared facilities include two Silicon Graphics Power Challenge XL systems, with twenty-two R10000 and twelve R8000 superscalar RISC processors, respectively; an 8-node IBM SP-2; a Cray Y/MP-EL dual-processor supercomputer; a cluster of sixteen Silicon Graphics R4400 processors utilizing an ATM interconnect; a cluster of sixteen Sun UltraSPARC processors and five UltraSPARC dual processors utilizing Myrinet (eight systems), Dolphin (four systems), and ATM interconnects (all systems); a Sun Media Center 1000E video server; and a laboratory of Silicon Graphics, Sun, and IBM workstations. A 32-node Intel iPSC/860 and a 1,024-node MASPAR MP-2 SIMD multiprocessor are jointly operated with the School of Electrical Engineering. HPPCEL facilities are linked by a dedicated high-performance network utilizing ATM and FDDI. Other specialized laboratories support research in databases, robotics, open systems, software engineering, computer networking and communications systems, and artificial intelligence. All of the College's facilities are connected via local area networks, which, in turn, are linked to a campuswide network, providing access to systems throughout the Georgia Tech community. Both the College and campus networks enjoy an excellent high-performance ATM and FDDI backbone. As a regional backbone site, Georgia Tech also employs a means of high-speed communication worldwide through a direct connection to the Internet at forty-five megabits per second. Additional computing facilities are provided to the Georgia Tech campus by OIT, including eight public-access clusters of Apple, IBM, Dell, and Sun workstations; a Sun SPARCcenter 2000 with twelve superscalar RISC processors; various mainframes; and public-access interactive terminals.

FINANCIAL AID

Most doctoral students and some master's students are supported throughout the year by assistantships. Research assistants participate in the College's ongoing research projects. The range of teaching assistants' duties includes grading, instructional laboratory support, and some teaching. The full-time base pay for assistants averaged $36,000 per fiscal year in 1996–97. Assistantships are usually awarded on a ⅜ time basis at a corresponding fraction of the full-time base pay, plus the cost of reduced tuition and fees. Some tuition waivers are available. A limited number of fellowships are available, as is an industry-college cooperative program. In addition, Georgia Tech President's Fellowships at $5000 per calendar year are available as supplements to normal assistantships or fellowship awards given to chosen students.

COST OF STUDY

In 1997–98, total fees are $930 per quarter for residents of the state of Georgia and $3121 per quarter for nonresidents. Resident and nonresident students with at least ⅓ time research or teaching assistantships pay reduced total fees of $215 per quarter.

LIVING AND HOUSING COSTS

The Housing Office supervises 6,267 single spaces and 300 married student apartments. In 1997–98, room rent costs $803–$1118 per quarter; board costs $349 to $686 per quarter. Total expenses for a single student living on campus, excluding tuition and fees, are estimated to be $2000–$2660 per quarter.

STUDENT GROUP

The Georgia Institute of Technology has a total enrollment of about 13,000 students, of whom approximately 3,600 are graduate students. The College's graduate enrollment exceeds 200.

STUDENT OUTCOMES

Recent Ph.D. graduates have taken faculty positions at Washington (St. Louis), Penn State, and University of Virginia and research positions at Xerox PARC, Sun Microsystems, Silicon Graphics, and Hewlett-Packard.

LOCATION

Situated close to the center of Atlanta on a 330-acre campus, Georgia Tech is near the many cultural and sports activities of the city. Atlanta, the site of the 1996 Olympic Games, is the headquarters of many large corporations and is the financial hub of the rapidly growing southeastern United States.

THE INSTITUTE

The Georgia Institute of Technology was founded in 1885. It offers graduate and undergraduate degrees in computing, the sciences, engineering, architecture, management, the social sciences, and the humanities. As the site of the Olympic Village for the 1996 Olympic Games, the Georgia Tech campus was improved by a significant building program that included a coliseum, a natatorium, and dormitories.

APPLYING

Students with a variety of backgrounds are encouraged to apply, provided they have strong computer science and mathematics preparation. All applicants must submit GRE scores on the General Test and one of the Subject Tests, preferably in computer science. The M.S. program requires that the Subject Test be in computer science. All international students from countries where English is not the native language must submit their TOEFL results. For Ph.D. applicants, completed applications for fall quarter should be received by January 3; for M.S. applicants, by May 1.

CORRESPONDENCE AND INFORMATION

College of Computing
Georgia Institute of Technology
Atlanta, Georgia 30332-0280

Telephone: 404-894-3152
World Wide Web: http://www.cc.gatech.edu

GEORGIA INSTITUTE OF TECHNOLOGY

THE FACULTY AND THEIR RESEARCH

G. Abowd, Assistant Professor; D.Phil., Oxford. Software engineering, formal methods, human-computer interaction, software architecture, requirements engineering.

M. Ahamad, Associate Professor; Ph.D., SUNY at Stony Brook. Distributed operating systems, distributed algorithms, software fault tolerance, networks.

A. Amir, Associate Professor; Ph.D., Bar-Ilan (Israel). Structural complexity, analysis of algorithms, pattern matching, computational molecular biology.

M. H. Ammar, Associate Professor; Ph.D., Waterloo. Computer networks, communication protocols, performance evaluation, distributed database systems, distributed computing systems.

R. C. Arkin, Professor; Ph.D., Massachusetts. Artificial intelligence, computer vision and mobile robotics.

C. Atkeson, Associate Professor; Ph.D., MIT. Intelligent systems and robotics.

A. N. Badre, Professor; Ph.D., Michigan. Human factors in computer systems, software engineering.

K. L. Calvert, Assistant Professor; Ph.D., Texas at Austin. Computer networks and protocols, formal methods, distributed computing.

A. Chervenak, Assistant Professor; Ph.D., Berkeley. Computer systems, computer architecture, performance modeling and evaluation.

R. Das, Assistant Professor; Ph.D., William and Mary. High-performance computing systems, programming languages.

C. Eastman, Professor; M.S., Berkeley. Computer-based design environments, geometric modeling, integrated databases.

K. P. Eiselt, Assistant Dean; Ph.D., California, Irvine. Artificial intelligence, cognitive science, natural-language understanding, models of human sentence processing, computational psycholinguistics.

P. H. Enslow Jr., Professor; Ph.D., Stanford. Computer networks, telecommunication systems, data communications, distributed processing, operating systems, computer systems.

I. Essa, Assistant Professor; Ph.D., MIT. Computational perception, computer vision, computer graphics, perception and cognition.

N. F. Ezquerra, Associate Professor; Ph.D., Florida State. Medical informatics, artificial intelligence, computer vision.

P. A. Freeman, Professor and Dean; Ph.D., Carnegie Mellon. Software engineering, design processes, science and technology policy.

R. M. Fujimoto, Professor; Ph.D., Berkeley. Computer architecture, parallel processing, simulation.

J. J. Goda Jr., Assistant Professor; M.S., Georgia Tech. Computer programming, programming languages.

A. K. Goel, Associate Professor; Ph.D., Ohio State. Artificial intelligence, planning and design, problem solving, qualitative modeling and model-based reasoning, case-based reasoning and learning.

J. K. Greenlee, Instructor; M.S., Georgia Tech. Computer architecture.

M. Guzdial, Assistant Professor; Ph.D., Michigan. Human-computer interactions, design support environments, interactive technologies for learning.

L. F. Hodges, Associate Professor; Ph.D., North Carolina State. Computer graphics, scientific visualization, 3-D display technology, virtual environments.

J. Hodgins, Associate Professor; Ph.D., Carnegie Mellon. Computer graphics and artificial intelligence, with emphasis on robotics.

S. Hudson, Associate Professor; Ph.D., Colorado. Interactive computer graphics, database management systems, computer applications to molecular biology.

H. Karloff, Associate Professor; Ph.D., Berkeley. Theoretical computer science, randomized and parallel algorithms.

J. L. Kolodner, Professor; Ph.D., Yale. Artificial intelligence, cognitive science, learning and problem solving, case-based reasoning.

R. J. LeBlanc Jr., Professor and Associate Dean; Ph.D., Wisconsin–Madison. Programming languages and environments, compilers, distributed processing, software engineering.

J. Limb, Professor; Ph.D., Western Australia. High-speed networks, multimedia telecommunications, interactive video systems, video coding, video teleconferencing.

L. Mark, Associate Professor; Ph.D., Aarhus (Denmark). Database system architecture, data models, database design, Metadata management, data dictionary systems, information exchange.

W. M. McCracken, Principal Research Scientist; M.S., Georgia Tech. Design cognition, learning theory, software engineering.

M. Moore, Research Scientist II; M.S., Georgia Tech. User interface reengineering, software engineering education.

S. B. Navathe, Professor; Ph.D., Michigan. Database modeling, database design, manufacturing systems, CAD/CAM and office systems, information systems analysis and design, distributed and heterogeneous databases.

N. Nersessian, Professor; Ph.D., Case Western Reserve. Philosophy and history of science, conceptual change, creativity, learning.

E. R. Omiecinski, Associate Professor; Ph.D., Northwestern. Database systems, file management, parallel algorithms.

C. Potts, Associate Professor; Ph.D., Sheffield (England). Software requirements analysis and design methods with related interodes in hypertext software, documentation and computer support for design decision making.

A. Ram, Associate Professor; Ph.D., Yale. Artificial intelligence, story understanding, memory, learning.

U. Ramachandran, Associate Professor; Ph.D., Wisconsin–Madison. Computer architecture and VLSI, distributed operating systems, networking.

D. Randall, Assistant Professor; Ph.D., Berkeley. Algorithms, computational complexity, discrete mathematics.

W. Ribarsky, Senior Research Scientist; Ph.D., Cincinnati. Visualization and virtual environments.

J. Rossignac, Professor and Director of Graphics, Visualization and Usability; Ph.D., Rochester. 3-D modeling, compression, graphics acceleration, user interface technologies and system architecture.

J. S. Rugaber, Senior Research Scientist; Ph.D., Yale. Software engineering, program understanding.

L. Schulman, Assistant Professor; Ph.D., MIT. Theory of computation and discrete mathematics.

K. Schwan, Professor; Ph.D., Carnegie Mellon. Operating and programming systems for parallel and distributed computers, real-time systems.

R. Shackelford, Assistant Professor; Ph.D., Georgia Tech. Computing education, teaching information systems, modeling of human experiential structures, history of technology and consciousness.

J. T. Stasko, Associate Professor; Ph.D., Brown. Software and information visualization, human-computer interaction, programming environments.

C. Tovey, Professor; Ph.D., Stanford. Industrial and systems engineering.

G. Turk, Assistant Professor; Ph.D., North Carolina at Chapel Hill. Computer graphics, scientific visualization, geometric modeling, image processing.

V. Vazirani, Professor; Ph.D., Berkeley. Design and analysis of algorithms, complexity theory.

H. Venkateswaran, Associate Professor; Ph.D., Washington (Seattle). Theoretical computer science, computational complexity, parallel computation, algorithms.

E. W. Zegura, Assistant Professor; Ph.D., Washington (St. Louis). Advanced communication systems, analysis of switching networks, parallel and distributed algorithms.

HARVARD UNIVERSITY

CENTER FOR RESEARCH IN COMPUTING TECHNOLOGY

PROGRAM OF STUDY

Teaching and research in computer science at Harvard are organized within the Center for Research in Computing Technology. The Center was formed in 1971 to provide a focal point for research in computer science at Harvard and to bridge relationships between computer science and other departments, disciplines, and faculties in working with computing and communications technology. The Center is closely tied to the Division of Engineering and Applied Sciences in order to encourage this interaction with related disciplines.

Members of the Center teach and coordinate courses in computer science, train graduate students, and conduct computer science research. In addition, they provide the faculty and students in other parts of the University with expertise in computer science.

Faculty members bring particular strength to the program in the areas of computer systems, computer and communications networks, programming languages, parallel computing, theory of computation, artificial intelligence, computational linguistics, robotics, computer vision, and related areas of electrical engineering. In addition, other faculty members bring breadth to the computer science program through their interests in applied mathematics, biology, and the interaction of science and public policy. Several of the professors hold joint appointments with other departments.

Graduate students interested in computer science are normally admitted to study for the Ph.D. degree under the Division of Engineering and Applied Sciences. The program of study is quite flexible and stresses an interdisciplinary approach to graduate study.

The Massachusetts Institute of Technology and certain other institutions have agreements with Harvard covering course credits, thesis research, and the use of facilities.

RESEARCH FACILITIES

The Center for Research in Computing Technology is housed in the Aiken Computation Laboratory. The Center maintains a computer science research facility that includes a network of Sun Workstations and computation and file servers, a Silicon Graphics workstation for graphics research and instruction, and a Connection Machine and other parallel computers. Next door, laboratories in Pierce Hall house other computing facilities, including a MasPar parallel computer, an extensive laboratory for research in computer vision and robotics, and a CAD/CAM facility for use by students.

In the nearby Science Center are networks of DECstations and VAX's running both UNIX (Ultrix) and VMS operating systems and large networks of Macintosh and PC-compatible computers. All of these computer systems are interconnected by a campuswide high-speed network that is connected to the Internet.

FINANCIAL AID

Financial support is available from a number of possible sources, which include employment in teaching or research, fellowships, scholarships, and loans.

COST OF STUDY

In 1997–98, tuition for the two-term academic year is $20,600, health insurance is $554, and University health service is $666. After the second year of study, tuition charges drop substantially.

LIVING AND HOUSING COSTS

Graduate dormitory accommodations are available to single students. Rents are approximately $3060–$4950 for the 1997–98 academic year. Meals are available at the graduate commons. University-operated apartments for married students, from efficiency to three-bedroom units, are available. The cost varies according to accommodations sought. A wide range of private housing can be found within commuting distance.

STUDENT GROUP

In 1996–97, there were 63 graduate students in computer science; as of March 1997, no Ph.D. degrees had been awarded.

LOCATION

Cambridge, Massachusetts, the home of Harvard University, is just across the Charles River from Boston. Harvard, therefore, is not only near the resources of Boston but also within an easy drive of the New England shoreline and countryside. The Cambridge area is justly famous as a cultural, scientific, and intellectual center.

THE UNIVERSITY

Harvard is the oldest college in the United States. It draws students from all corners of the world and from every part of the United States.

APPLYING

Students with a bachelor's degree may apply to the Division of Engineering and Applied Sciences, stating the nature of their interest. Admission and financial aid applications must be received in the Graduate School Admissions Office before 5 p.m. on December 30.

CORRESPONDENCE AND INFORMATION

Information about the Center:

Director
Center for Research in Computing Technology
Harvard University
Cambridge, Massachusetts 02138
Telephone: 617-495-3989
World Wide Web: http://www.deas.harvard.edu

Application forms for admission and financial aid:

Admissions Office
Graduate School of Arts and Sciences
Byerly Hall
Harvard University
8 Garden Street
Cambridge, Massachusetts 02138
Telephone: 617-495-5315

HARVARD UNIVERSITY
THE FACULTY AND THEIR RESEARCH

Donald G. M. Anderson, Gordon McKay Professor of Applied Mathematics. Methodological problems in numerical mathematics and scientific computing with applications to physical sciences and engineering.

William H. Bossert, David B. Arnold Jr. Professor of Science. Models of the transmission of malaria, environmental policy: species diversity of the White Mountain National Forest, management of marine fisheries, rapid evolution in ecosystems.

Michael S. Brandstein, Assistant Professor of Electrical Engineering on the Gordon McKay Endowment. Speech and audio signal processing.

Roger W. Brockett, An Wang Professor of Electrical Engineering and Computer Science. Motion control, intelligent control, pulsed analog computing, tactile sensing, learning approach to estimation theory.

Thomas E. Cheatham Jr., Gordon McKay Professor of Computer Science and Director of the Center for Research in Computing Technology. BSP programming languages, extensible programming languages, program development and maintenance environments, program transformations, activity coordination, quantum computers, abstract interpreters.

J. Bradley Chen, Assistant Professor of Computer Science on the Gordon McKay Endowment. Operating systems, computer architecture, computer systems performance evaluation, executable editing.

Ugo O. Gagliardi, Gordon McKay Professor of the Practice of Computer Engineering. Data persistency and sharing in OOP software development environments (object-oriented databases), software systems architecture and object-oriented software engineering (object-oriented design and analysis), methods for deriving performance models from architectural descriptions: nested queuing networks.

Steven J. Gortler, Assistant Professor of Computer Science on the Gordon McKay Endowment. Computer graphics, including image-based rendering, photo-realistic rendering, and geometric modeling; application of hierarchical and wavelet techniques to problems in computer graphics.

Barbara J. Grosz, Gordon McKay Professor of Computer Science. Computational theories of discourse and discourse processing, intonation and discourse structure, collaborative planning, coordination of natural language and graphics for human-computer communication, natural-language processing systems.

R. Victor Jones, Robert L. Wallace Professor of Applied Physics. Photonics hardware design languages (PHDL): computer-aided methods for treating design problems in optics and optoelectronics, optical and optoelectronic computing; photoneural model, optical and optoelectronic computing: dataflow model.

H. T. Kung, Gordon McKay Professor of Electrical Engineering and Computer Science. Design and experiment of gigabit networks, congestion control in ATM networks, wireless networking.

Harry Lewis, Gordon McKay Professor of Computer Science and Dean of Harvard College. Formal specification and verification.

David Mumford, Higgins Professor of Mathematics. Intelligent systems.

Anthony G. Oettinger, Gordon McKay Professor of Applied Mathematics and Professor of Information Resources Policy. Program on information resources policy; intelligence, command, and control in business and government.

Michael O. Rabin, Thomas J. Watson Sr. Professor of Computer Science. Asynchronous parallel computing, fault tolerance and randomization.

Margo I. Seltzer, Assistant Professor of Computer Science on the Gordon McKay Endowment. Software systems, database support for audio and video data, application-oriented operating systems.

Stuart M. Shieber, Gordon McKay Professor of Computer Science. Computational linguistics, natural-language processing, automated graphic design, combinatorial optimization.

Michael D. Smith, Assistant Professor of Electrical Engineering and Computer Science on the Gordon McKay Endowment. High-performance computer architectures, optimizing compilers.

Leslie G. Valiant, Gordon McKay Professor of Computer Science and Applied Mathematics. Computational complexity, parallel computation, machine learning, neural computation.

Woodward Yang, Associate Professor of Electrical Engineering on the Gordon McKay Endowment. CCD/CMOS sensors and signal processors, high-performance digital VLSI systems, neuromorphic pulse computing, analysis of sigma-delta modulators.

Lecturer
Henry H. Leitner, Senior Lecturer on Computer Science.

HOWARD UNIVERSITY

DEPARTMENT OF ELECTRICAL ENGINEERING

PROGRAMS OF STUDY

The Department of Electrical Engineering offers programs leading to the Master of Engineering and Doctor of Philosophy degrees in electrical engineering. At the master's level, major areas of study and research are solid-state electronics, control engineering, power systems, antennas, microwaves, communications, and signal processing. The Master of Engineering program offers the thesis or nonthesis option. The thesis option requires 24 credit hours of courses and a 6-credit-hour thesis. The nonthesis option requires 33 credit hours of course work and a comprehensive exam. Some specialization areas also require an engineering project. In the Ph.D. program, major areas of study and research are solid-state electronics, control engineering, power systems, communications, signal processing, and applied electromagnetics. The Ph.D. program requires 72 credit hours beyond the bachelor's degree, four semesters of residence and full-time study (two of the four semesters must be consecutive), passing grades on preliminary and qualifying exams, and evidence of submittal of a manuscript based on the student's dissertation research to a refereed journal or professional conference.

RESEARCH FACILITIES

The Materials Science Research Center of Excellence (MSRCE) has an interdisciplinary research team dedicated to the resolution of problems associated with the growth, characterization, and fabrication of novel electronic and electrooptic materials and devices for high-power, high-frequency, and high-temperature applications. State-of-the-art laboratories for growth and epitaxy, fabrication, characterization, and testing and an ultrafast laser facility are housed in the MSRCE.

The Computations Science and Engineering Research Center (ComSERC), funded by the Army High Performance Computing Research Center, includes faculty and other researchers from engineering, physics, and mathematics who are involved in research related to supercomputers located at Howard University, the University of Minnesota, and Army research laboratories.

The Center for Energy Systems and Controls (CESC) is dedicated to research and development of efficient tools for analysis and design of power system operations and planning. System theories and emerging technologies such as artificial intelligence (expert system), artificial neural network, and fuzzy logic are investigated to improve analysis of decision making for power system design and studies. Investigators of the center apply modern control theories to solve large-scale engineering problems.

In addition to the laboratories housed within the centers, students have access to other departmental laboratories, including the Communications and Signal Processing Laboratory, which is equipped for simulation of communications and signal processing systems and functions, detection and estimation algorithms, adaptive filters and arrays, emulation and applications studies of digital signal processing chips, and time-domain and frequency-domain measurements and analysis of real-time signals. The Microwave Laboratory provides fixed and swept-frequency systems for a wide range of millimeter-wave, microwave, waveguide, and coaxial component studies and designs.

Students also have access to excellent computing resources at Howard, including the School of Engineering's centralized facility, the Computer Learning and Design Center. This center provides a full spectrum of computer resources for research, such as computer-aided designs, programming and engineering problem solving, and document publishing. The center's major systems include HP and DEC VAX microcomputers, various peripherals, and remote-access capability. Ten Sun workstations and an Alliant minisupercomputer are available for advanced research.

FINANCIAL AID

Financial aid is available to qualified students on a competitive basis through graduate, teaching, and research assistantships. In 1997–98, graduate and teaching assistantships provide stipends ranging from $5000 to $8000, plus tuition waivers. Some research assistantships offer support of up to $18,000. Recipients are required to work up to 20 hours per week.

COST OF STUDY

Tuition and fees for full-time graduate study are $4950 per year in 1997–98.

LIVING AND HOUSING COSTS

Most graduate students live off campus. Howard Plaza Towers, a high-rise complex, has some accommodations for students. Those who desire assistance in locating housing in the Washington metropolitan area should write to the Supervisor of Off-Campus Housing, Howard University.

STUDENT GROUP

Approximately 60 students, including students from various regions of the United States and several other countries, are enrolled in the electrical engineering graduate programs.

LOCATION

Howard University is located in Washington, D.C., a city that offers opportunities for study and research.

THE UNIVERSITY

Founded in 1867, Howard University is a privately governed institution. It has eighteen schools and colleges, and its main campus occupies almost 90 acres. Howard is a member of the National Consortium for Graduate Degrees for Minorities in Engineering and the Consortium of Universities of the Washington Metropolitan Area, which includes Georgetown, George Washington, American, and Gallaudet universities; the University of the District of Columbia; The Catholic University of America; and Mount Vernon and Trinity colleges.

APPLYING

Regular admission to the master's program is considered for individuals who hold a bachelor's degree in electrical engineering from an accredited institution and whose undergraduate grade point average is at least 3.0 (out of 4.0). In special circumstances, individuals having a lower grade point average or those with degrees in other disciplines or branches of engineering may be provisionally admitted. Admission to the doctoral program may be sought by persons holding a degree in electrical engineering from a nationally or regionally accredited institution. These persons must have maintained a minimum grade point average of 3.0. Candidates with equivalent qualifications earned at foreign institutions will be considered.

Additional information and application forms are obtainable on request. Applicants should provide credentials before April 1 for August admission and before November 1 for January admission. All applicants to the Graduate School of Arts and Sciences are required to submit scores on the General Test of the Graduate Record Examinations as part of their application. Applicants requiring financial assistance should provide all supporting materials as soon as possible before the above deadlines. International students whose native language is not English must report scores from the TOEFL.

CORRESPONDENCE AND INFORMATION

Chairman
Graduate Studies Committee
Department of Electrical Engineering
Howard University
Washington, D.C. 20059

HOWARD UNIVERSITY

THE GRADUATE FACULTY AND THEIR RESEARCH

Professors

Tepper L. Gill, Ph.D., Wayne State. Mathematical physics, quantum field theory, magnetism.

Gary L. Harris, Ph.D., Cornell. Electrophysics, device fabrication, characterization in materials and devices.

James A. Momoh, Chairman, Electrical Engineering Department; Ph.D., Howard. Systems engineering, power systems and controls, expert systems, neural networks.

Steven L. Richardson, Ph.D., Ohio State. Condensed matter, theoretical physics, electronic structure theory of semiconductor crystals, surfaces and computational physics.

Michael G. Spencer, Ph.D., Cornell. Electrophysics, device fabrication, microwave devices and materials characterization.

Yen-chu Wang, Ph.D., NYU. Antennas, microwaves, applied superconductivity.

Associate Professors

Ajit K. Choudhury, Ph.D., UCLA. Controls and communications.

Mohammed Chouikha, Ph.D., Colorado. Estimation theory and detection, image and signal processing.

S. Noor Mohammad, Ph.D., Calcutta. Semiconductor materials and devices.

Ahmed Rubaai, Ph.D., Cleveland State. Power systems and controls.

Raj C. Yalamanchili, Chairman, Graduate Studies Committee; Ph.D., Georgetown. Microwave amplifiers and antennas.

Assistant Professors

Peter Bofah, Ph.D., Howard. Power devices and systems and controls.

Jamshid Goshtasbi, Ph.D., SUNY at Binghamton. Computer architecture, digital design.

Adjunct Professors

Leonard Rockett, Ph.D., Columbia. Solid-state electronics, device and materials characterization, integrated circuit design and fabrication.

Woodford Zachary, Ph.D., Maryland. Theoretical physics.

ILLINOIS INSTITUTE OF TECHNOLOGY

DEPARTMENT OF COMPUTER SCIENCE AND APPLIED MATHEMATICS

PROGRAMS OF STUDY

Graduate programs lead to the Master of Science (M.S.) and Doctor of Philosophy (Ph.D.) degrees in computer science and the Master of Science in Teaching (M.S.T.) for teachers/trainers of computer science. The graduate programs provide both a practical preparation for those seeking careers in the computer industry and a solid foundation for those aiming at careers in research and education. The programs offer the necessary background in the core areas and exposure to cutting-edge computer technologies that have high impact in the academic and industrial worlds. Courses are offered on IIT's Main Campus in Chicago, at the Daniel F. and Ada L. Rice Campus in suburban Wheaton, and via IITV, the University's interactive television network, at twenty-six public and corporate sites in the greater Chicago area.

The M.S. degree program prepares the research-oriented student for candidacy into the Ph.D. program. Faculty members supervise Ph.D. research in computer algorithms, computer networks and data communication, compilers and operating systems, distributed systems, graphics and image processing, intelligent tutoring/information systems, natural language processing, neural networks, performance analysis and evaluation, programming languages, relational and object-oriented information systems, robotics, software engineering, and software verification and testing. The M.S. degree program also includes several program options designed for working professionals. Popular among these are concentrated programs in software engineering, computer networking and telecommunications, intelligent information systems, and distributed system software.

The M.S.T. program is designed for experienced certified teachers and corporate trainers to strengthen their knowledge of computer science and the effective utilization of educational technologies in computer instruction.

The field of applied mathematics explores those branches of mathematics that form the foundation of science and engineering, including probability and statistics, numerical analysis, and mathematical modeling. Collectively, these branches define the emerging field of computational science and engineering, in which techniques drawn from mathematics and computer science are used to solve problems in many disciplines.

RESEARCH FACILITIES

Research computing facilities include Sun SPARC and Silicon Graphics UNIX workstations; Challenge, Encore, and NCUBE multiprocessor systems; and Windows-based PCs.

FINANCIAL AID

Financial assistance is available for new and continuing students through fellowships, teaching assistantships, and research assistantships that include both varying stipends and full or partial tuition and through scholarships that provide all or some portion of tuition. Loans for eligible students may be arranged through the Financial Aid Office. Primary consideration for financial aid is given to applications received before March 1.

COST OF STUDY

For 1997–98, tuition is $575 per credit hour. Students must register for a minimum of 2 credit hours. International students are required to register for a minimum of 9 credit hours or the equivalent per semester.

LIVING AND HOUSING COSTS

Housing is available for graduate students in IIT residence halls; the 1997–98 cost of room and board ranges from $4760 to $6485. Unfurnished IIT apartments are available for graduate students at costs ranging from $430 to $880 per month, including utilities. Early application for apartments is recommended. Several off-campus apartment complexes are located within a mile of the Main Campus.

STUDENT GROUP

IIT's total enrollment in 1996–97 was approximately 6,300; of this number, 671 were enrolled as full-time graduate students and 2,391 as part-time graduate students. Total undergraduate enrollment was 1,959. The remainder were enrolled in the Chicago-Kent College of Law. Computer Science is the largest department on the Main Campus; 641 students were enrolled in computer science graduate programs in 1996–97.

LOCATION

IIT's Main Campus is located near the heart of Chicago, just 3 miles south of the Loop and central to the greater Chicago area's thriving technological community of business, industry, and research institutions. Internationally known for its architecture, museums, symphony, and theater; its beautiful lakefront on the western shore of Lake Michigan; and the unusually rich variety of its ethnic communities, Chicago offers a vast array of recreational and cultural opportunities. Among its immediate neighbors are Comiskey Park (home of the Chicago White Sox), two major medical centers, and the McCormick Place Exposition Center. The Downtown Campus is in the Loop near the city's financial trading, banking, and legal centers. The Rice Campus is in suburban Wheaton, convenient to the Interstate 88 research and technology corridor west of the city. The Moffett Campus is in southwest suburban Summit-Argo.

THE INSTITUTE

Illinois Institute of Technology was formed in 1940 by the merger of Armour Institute of Technology (founded in 1890) and Lewis Institute (founded in 1896). IIT offers programs of study in engineering and the sciences, architecture, design, public administration, technical communications and information design, psychology, business, and law. IIT is a member of the prestigious Association of Independent Technological Universities (AITU).

The Main Campus, designed by Ludwig Mies van der Rohe and regarded internationally as a landmark of twentieth-century architecture, occupies fifty buildings on a 120-acre site and includes research institutes, libraries, laboratories, residence halls, a sports center, and other facilities.

APPLYING

Applicants must submit an application form, official transcripts (or certified copies) of all college-level work, letters of recommendation, and required GRE and TOEFL scores. Application forms and additional information may be found at the Graduate College's Web site (http://www.iit.edu/colleges/grad). Applications should be received no later than June 1 for fall matriculation and November 1 for spring matriculation.

CORRESPONDENCE AND INFORMATION

Department of Computer Science and Applied Mathematics
Illinois Institute of Technology
10 West 31st Street
Chicago, Illinois 60616-3793

Telephone: 312-567-5150
Fax: 312-567-5067
E-mail: info@csam.iit.edu
World Wide Web: http://www.csam.iit.edu/

ILLINOIS INSTITUTE OF TECHNOLOGY

THE FACULTY AND THEIR RESEARCH

Charles Bauer, Associate Professor; M.Ed., Loyola. Computer science education, computers in education and educational technology.

Sam Biardo, Instructor; M.S., IIT. Software engineering, performance evaluation and database systems.

Ilene Burnstein, Associate Professor; Ph.D., IIT. Software engineering, knowledge-based testing and debugging tools, test management.

Graham Campbell, Professor; Ph.D., Penn State. Computer networking, wideband communication protocols, protocol verification, and computer performance analysis.

C. Robert Carlson, Professor and Chairman; Ph.D., Iowa. Relational databases, database design tools and methodologies, information modeling techniques and tools, software design patterns and information architecture.

Morris Chang, Assistant Professor; Ph.D., North Carolina State. Computer architecture, object-oriented co-design.

Thomas Christopher, Associate Professor; Ph.D., IIT. Message driven computing, distributed and parallel computing, programming languages and compilers.

Phillips Dickens, Assistant Professor; Ph.D., Virginia. Parallel and distributed computation, parallel simulation, network-based distributed computation, thread-based computation.

Trilla Elrad, Associate Professor; Ph.D., Technion (Israel). Concurrent programming, formal verification, embedded real-time systems and ADA standards.

Martha Evens, Professor; Ph.D., Northwestern. Natural language processing, expert systems and intelligent tutoring/information systems.

Peter Greene, Associate Professor; Ph.D., Chicago. Neural networks, feeling-based reasoning, artificial intelligence and robotics.

Cynthia Hood, Assistant Professor; Ph.D., Rensselaer. Network management, statistical signal processing, learning processing.

Bogden Korel, Associate Professor; Ph.D., Oakland. Software engineering, program testing and operating systems.

James Roberge, Associate Professor; Ph.D., Northwestern. Computer graphics, medical imaging, image processing, educational technology, pedagogy.

ILLINOIS INSTITUTE OF TECHNOLOGY

ARMOUR COLLEGE OF ENGINEERING
DEPARTMENT OF ELECTRICAL AND COMPUTER ENGINEERING

PROGRAMS OF STUDY

The Department of Electrical and Computer Engineering offers a full spectrum of graduate degree programs at the master's and doctoral levels, both full-time and part-time. The Master of Electrical and Computer Engineering (M.E.C.E.) is a one-year course of study that prepares students for professional practice in electrical and computer engineering. The Master of Science in Electrical Engineering (M.S.E.E.) is a two- to three-semester program combining breadth across several areas of study within electrical engineering and specialization within one area, with an option to pursue thesis research under the guidance of a faculty adviser. Areas of study include communication and signal processing; networks, electronics, and electromagnetics; power and control systems; and computer engineering. The Master of Science in Computer Systems Engineering (M.S.C.S.E.) is similar to the M.S.E.E., but the M.S.C.S.E. emphasizes computer engineering with areas of study that include computer hardware design, computer networking and communications, and system and application software. The Doctor of Philosophy (Ph.D.) degree is awarded to recognize a high level of mastery in electrical engineering and requires a research dissertation representing an original contribution to knowledge in the field. The Ph.D. program is appropriate for those students with M.S. degrees who are interested in pursuing an academic or industrial research career. To be admitted to candidacy, the student must pass an oral qualifying examination and an oral comprehensive examination, both conducted by an appointed committee. Research, conducted in consultation with a faculty adviser, culminates in an oral defense of the dissertation. The program length is typically three to four years beyond the M.S. degree.

RESEARCH FACILITIES

The department operates research laboratories for work in CAD for VLSI, communications, computer networking, image processing and medical imaging, microwave electronics, optical fiber components, power systems, signal processing, and ultrasonic diagnostics. The department also collaborates with and utilizes the research resources of the IIT Research Institute and the Pritzker Institute of Medical Engineering.

The department operates a Sun Workstation network and several minicomputers and personal computer networks for student use. University computer resources include an SGI Challenge L system, an SGI workstation cluster, DEC VAX's, and more than 350 personal computers.

FINANCIAL AID

Financial support in the forms of fellowships, teaching assistantships, research assistantships, and scholarships are awarded on a competitive basis. Support varies from tuition only to tuition plus stipend for nine to twelve months. Approximately 80 percent of full-time students receive some form of financial aid. Primary consideration for graduate financial aid is given to applications received before March 1.

COST OF STUDY

Graduate tuition for 1997–98 is $575 per credit hour. Full-time study is a minimum of 9 hours per semester. International students must register for a minimum of 12 credits or the equivalent per semester.

LIVING AND HOUSING COSTS

Housing is available for graduate students in IIT residence halls. In 1997–98 the cost of room and board ranges from $4760 to $6485. Unfurnished IIT apartments are available at costs ranging from $430 to $880 per month, including utilities. Early application for apartments is recommended. Several off-campus apartment complexes are located within a mile of the Institute.

STUDENT GROUP

IIT's total enrollment in 1996–97 was approximately 6,300. Graduate enrollment in electrical and computer engineering numbers about 50 full-time and 300 part-time students, including the enrollment of IIT-Rice campus in the western suburbs of Chicago and IIT/V, the Institute's interactive television network. Five continents are represented in the student group, making for a diverse and stimulating atmosphere.

STUDENT OUTCOMES

Graduates of the master's programs are typically employed by the engineering industry, at corporations both large and small, or at one of a wide range of technology companies located in the greater Chicago area. Graduates of the doctoral program most frequently enter research positions in industry at locations throughout the United States. Several recent doctoral graduates are pursuing academic careers at major universities.

LOCATION

IIT is located near the heart of Chicago, just 3 miles south of the Loop, and is central to the greater Chicago area's thriving technological community of business, industry, and research institutions. Internationally known for its architecture, museums, symphony, and theater as well as its beautiful lakefront on the western shore of Lake Michigan and the unusually rich variety of its ethnic communities, Chicago offers a vast array of recreational and cultural opportunities. The main campus, designed by Ludwig Mies van der Rohe and regarded internationally as a landmark of twentieth-century architecture, occupies fifty buildings on a 120-acre site and includes research institutes, libraries, laboratories, residence halls, a sports center, and other facilities. Among its immediate neighbors are Comiskey Park, home of the Chicago White Sox; two major medical centers; and the McCormick Place Exposition Center. The downtown campus is in the Loop near the city's financial trading, banking, and legal centers. The Rice campus is in suburban Wheaton, convenient to the Interstate 88 research and technology corridor west of the city. The Moffett campus is in southwest suburban Bedford Park.

THE INSTITUTE

Illinois Institute of Technology was formed in 1940 by the merger of Armour Institute of Technology (founded in 1890) and Lewis Institute (founded 1896). ITT offers programs of study in engineering and the sciences, architecture, design, psychology, business, and law. ITT is a member of the prestigious Association of Independent Technological Universities (AITU).

APPLYING

Applications and supporting documents, including transcripts, GRE General Test scores, and three letters of recommendation, should be received by June 1 for fall, November 1 for spring, or May 1 for summer matriculation. Applicants whose native language is not English must also submit TOEFL scores.

Applications for financial aid, which is usually awarded for the academic year beginning in the fall term, should be received by March 1.

CORRESPONDENCE AND INFORMATION

Department of Electrical and Computer Engineering
Illinois Institute of Technology
Chicago, Illinois 60616-3793

Telephone: 312-567-3400
Fax: 312-567-8976
E-mail: gradinfo@ece.iit.edu
World Wide Web: http://www.ece.iit.edu/

ILLINOIS INSTITUTE OF TECHNOLOGY
THE FACULTY AND THEIR RESEARCH

Robert C. Arzbaecher, Professor and Director of the Pritzker Institute of Medical Engineering; Ph.D., Illinois. Biomedical engineering, signal processing and control.

Guillermo E. Atkin, Associate Professor; Ph.D., Waterloo. Modulation and coding for bandwidth efficient communication, digital mobile and wireless communication, spread-spectrum and optical communication systems.

Wai-Yip Geoffrey Chan, Motorola Assistant Professor; Ph.D., California, Santa Barbara. Signal compression, audiovisual communication, vector quantization.

Alexander J. Flueck, Assistant Professor; Ph.D., Cornell. Power systems, computational methods, control systems.

Nikolas Galatsanos, Associate Professor; Ph.D., Wisconsin. Image processing, image restoration, image coding, multidimensional signal processing.

Sanjay Gupta, Assistant Professor; Ph.D., Pennsylvania. Computer networks and communications, packet radio networks, performance modeling.

Robert J. Jaeger, Professor; Ph.D., Illinois. Neural control and biomechanics of human movement, biomedical engineering.

Joseph L. LoCicero, Professor; Ph.D., CUNY. Communication and digital signal processing, speech and image processing, wireless communications, photonic switching, pure phase gratings, automatic speech recognition, ultra-wideband communications.

Jeffrey P. Mills, Visiting Assistant Professor; Ph.D., IIT. Electromagnetic compatibility.

John A. Nestor, Associate Professor and Associate Chairman, Computer Engineering Program; Ph.D., Carnegie Mellon. Computer-aided design, VLSI design.

David B. Patterson, Assistant Professor; Ph.D., Stanford. Optical fiber components and devices, integrated optics.

V. C. Ramesh, Assistant Professor; Ph.D., Carnegie Mellon. Intelligent systems, power electronics, computational engineering.

Gerald F. Saletta, Associate Professor and Associate Dean of Undergraduate Studies; Ph.D., IIT. Electronics, digital systems.

Jafar Saniie, Professor; Ph.D., Purdue. Digital signal and image processing, ultrasonic imaging, pattern recognition, detection and estimation, diffraction tomography, nondestructive testing.

Mohammad Shahidehpour, Professor and Graduate Dean; Ph.D., Missouri. Large-scale power systems, nonlinear stochastic systems, optimization theory.

Henry Stark, Bodine Distinguished Professor and Chairman; Ph.D., Columbia. Image reconstruction, medical imaging, pattern recognition, signal processing and sampling theory, stochastic phenomena.

Andres Takach, Assistant Professor; Ph.D., Princeton. VLSI circuits, design automation, hardware/software codesign.

Philip Troyk, Associate Professor; Ph.D., Illinois. Polymers for electronics, neural implants, solid-state power systems.

Donald R. Ucci, Associate Professor and Associate Chairman; Ph.D., CUNY Graduate Center. Adaptive systems, signal processing, communications, computer systems, stochastic processes.

Erwin W. Weber, Associate Professor and Director of IIT-Rice Campus; Ph.D., IIT. Electromagnetic compatibility, network theory.

Miles Wernick, Assistant Professor; Ph.D., Rochester. Optics, medical imaging, image processing.

Geoffrey A. Williamson, Associate Professor and Graduate Program Director; Ph.D., Cornell. Adaptive control and signal processing, parameter estimation and system identification, control systems, robust control theory.

Thomas T. Y. Wong, Professor; Ph.D., Northwestern. Microwave communications systems, nonlinear device measurement, semiconductor device theory, microwave electronics and instrumentation.

Yongyi Yang, Visiting Assistant Professor; Ph.D., IIT. Image recovery, signal compression, computer vision, applied mathematical and statistical methods.

Research Areas

Active research programs are conducted in the general areas of communication systems and signal processing; power and control systems; electromagnetics, networks, and electronics; digital and computer systems; and bioengineering. Specific topics include adaptive control and signal processing; automated diagnosis; automatic speech recognition; biomedical engineering; bionics (including prosthesis and drug infusion); CAD for VLSI; coding theory; computer communications and networking; computer performance evaluation; design automation; diffraction tomography; digital and data communication; digital filters; distributed processing and parallel computing; electrical machine analysis and optimization; electron devices; fault-tolerant computing; fiber and integrated optics; high-definition video; human motor control; image processing; intelligent systems; microwave electronics; millimeter-wave communications systems; neural network; nondestructive testing; nonlinear device characterization; optimum communication system design; pattern recognition; photonic switching; power electronics; power system stability, operation, and control; sampling and signal recovery; signal analysis techniques; speech processing; spread spectrum techniques; and transient electromagnetics.

INDIANA UNIVERSITY BLOOMINGTON

DEPARTMENT OF COMPUTER SCIENCE

PROGRAMS OF STUDY
The department offers a broad spectrum of graduate programs. The master's and doctoral programs lead to the degrees of Master of Science and Doctor of Philosophy. A professional master's program is designed to lead to both the Bachelor of Science and Master of Science degrees in five years of study.

The Ph.D. program prepares students to attain cutting-edge expertise in one research area, combined with a solid command of computer science in general. The requirements include written qualifying examinations, an oral area exam, a thesis proposal, and a thesis defense.

The department's strong master's program opened in 1973 and has awarded more than 900 degrees to date. Requirements include 30 credit hours of course work, of which 20 must be in computer science; a balanced course distribution; and evidence of creativity (options include a master's thesis and a programming project).

All incoming graduate students who are not native English speakers must take an English proficiency test.

RESEARCH FACILITIES
In 1991, the department moved back into Lindley Hall after a $3.5-million department-specified renovation. Lindley Hall is designed to serve as a modern facility for research and education in computer science well into the next century. The department's computing environment, based upon UNIX, Ethernet and high-speed ATM networking, NFS, and X, is fully connected to the Internet. Sun, SGI, and BSDI Intel-based UNIX workstations along with DOS/Windows and Macintosh personal computers provide desktop computing for faculty, staff, and students. Silicon Graphics workstations provide powerful graphics capabilities along with Sun and Macintosh systems with special graphics enhancements. There are more than 200 computing systems in the department with access to more than 100 GB of on-line and near-line disk storage. The department is on the standard national and international research networks. A 10-processor SGI Power Challenge with a total capacity of 3 GFLOPS and 2 GB of main memory provides support for various research groups in the department. There is also an SGI Origin 2000 on campus for parallel computing research support. For input and output, there are more than thirty laser printers, two color printers, a large format plotter, multiple scanners, video frame-grabbers, and CD-ROM players and recorders. There is a digital hardware lab with logic design and PC-board fabrication facilities. The computing facilities are complemented by a research, instructional, and administrative support staff.

FINANCIAL AID
Most Ph.D. and some M.S. students receive financial aid in the form of research (twenty-five) or teaching (sixty) assistantships. For teaching awards, all students who are not native speakers of English must pass an English proficiency exam designed for teachers. The best Ph.D. students receive full or partial fellowships (six). Most awards include a stipend of at least $11,000 for ten months plus tuition support for all fees except an unremittable portion of $21 per credit hour. About twenty summer teaching assistantships are available in addition to research assistantships. Many computer-related jobs are also available throughout the University and the Bloomington area.

COST OF STUDY
Tuition and fees were $140 per credit hour for in-state students and $408 per credit hour for out-of-state students for the 1996–97 academic year. Mandatory fees and student health fees total about $400 per year.

LIVING AND HOUSING COSTS
The cost of a single room and board in the graduate dorm is about $4700 for the academic year. Average University family housing costs range from $400 to $730 per month, including utilities. There are a large number of apartment complexes, condominiums, and houses for rent, as well as studios, efficiencies, and single rooms with shared kitchen and bathroom privileges. The standard lease is twelve months and begins in August.

STUDENT GROUP
Indiana University has about 26,200 undergraduates and 7,600 graduate students. The Department of Computer Science has about 140 graduate and 190 undergraduate students.

LOCATION
The 1,800-acre main campus of Indiana University is located in Bloomington, a city of 60,000 (excluding students), 45 miles southwest of Indianapolis in the rolling hills of southern Indiana. Bloomington combines small-town charm with a wide variety of cultural activities, including Indiana University's School of Music (ranked in the top five music schools in the country), the theater and drama department, and the School of Fine Arts. With the Hoosier National Forest, three state parks, and Lake Monroe all less than an hour away, there are ample opportunities for outdoor recreation.

THE UNIVERSITY AND THE DEPARTMENT
Founded in 1820, Indiana University is a liberal arts school with professional programs in medicine, law, nursing, and optometry. The computer science department has grown from an interdisciplinary program in 1967 to a robust research and teaching department. Faculty, staff, and students relish the department's collegiality and interdisciplinary nature. With the Cognitive Science Program, the Indiana University Logic Group, and the Center for Innovative Computer Applications, there is strong interaction with the linguistics, philosophy, mathematics, and psychology departments. Students should contact the department at the address below to receive the most recent computer science annual report and to arrange to visit the department.

APPLYING
All applicants must have an accredited baccalaureate degree or its equivalent. A strong computer science background is not required, but maturity in mathematics and writing is expected. Three letters of recommendation, official transcripts from all previously attended institutions, current GRE scores, TOEFL scores (for international students), and a 300–500-word statement of purpose must accompany the official graduate school application. Admission decisions are based on a careful review of these documents. Decisions are not made until all application materials have arrived. The application priority date for the fall semester is January 15 for admission with aid and April 1 for admission only.

CORRESPONDENCE AND INFORMATION
Admissions Secretary
Department of Computer Science
Lindley Hall 215
Indiana University
Bloomington, Indiana 47405
E-mail: admissions@cs.indiana.edu
World Wide Web: http://www.cs.indiana.edu

INDIANA UNIVERSITY BLOOMINGTON
THE FACULTY AND THEIR RESEARCH

K. Jon Barwise (1990), University Professor of Philosophy, Mathematics, and Logic Philosophy and Adjunct Professor of Computer Science; Ph.D. (mathematics), Stanford, 1967. Logic, information-theoretic approaches to semantics, heterogeneous inference. (E-mail: barwise@cs.indiana.edu)

Randall Bramley (1992), Associate Professor of Computer Science; Ph.D., (computer science), Illinois at Urbana-Champaign, 1989. Scientific computation, parallel numerical algorithms, computational optimization, numerical linear algebra. (E-mail: bramley@cs.indiana.edu)

J. Michael Dunn (1987), Professor of Computer Science, Oscar R. Ewing Professor of Philosophy, and Associate Dean, College of Arts and Sciences; Ph.D. (philosophy), Pittsburgh, 1966. Algebraic logic, proof theory, nonstandard logics (especially relevance logic), relations between logic and computer science. (E-mail: dunn@cs.indiana.edu)

R. Kent Dybvig (1985), Associate Professor of Computer Science; Ph.D. (computer science), North Carolina at Chapel Hill, 1987. Programming language design and implementation, parallel architectures and languages, compiler design, code optimization. (E-mail: dyb@cs.indiana.edu)

Daniel P. Friedman (1973), Professor of Computer Science; Ph.D. (computer science), Texas at Austin, 1973. Programming languages. (E-mail: dfried@cs.indiana.edu)

Dennis Gannon (1985), Professor of Computer Science; Ph.D. (mathematics), California, Davis, 1974; Ph.D. (computer science), Illinois, 1980. Parallel computation, programming systems, graphics and tool design, computer architecture. (E-mail: gannon@cs.indiana.edu)

Michael E. Gasser (1988), Associate Professor of Computer Science; Ph.D. (applied linguistics), UCLA, 1988. Natural language processing, language acquisition, machine translation, speech acts, and the lexicon; knowledge representation; connectionist models of cognition. (E-mail: gasser@cs.indiana.edu)

Andrew J. Hanson (1989), Professor of Computer Science; Ph.D. (physics), MIT, 1971. Artificial intelligence, machine vision, computer graphics, shape modeling for vision and graphics, interactive human interfaces, scientific visualization of mathematical physics. (E-mail: hanson@cs.indiana.edu)

Christopher T. Haynes (1982), Associate Professor of Computer Science; Ph.D. (computer science), Iowa, 1982. Programming languages. (E-mail: chaynes@cs.indiana.edu)

Douglas R. Hofstadter (1988), University Professor of Cognitive Science and Computer Science; Adjunct Professor of Psychology, Philosophy, History and Philosophy of Science, and Comparative Literature; and Director, Center for Research on Concepts and Cognition; Ph.D. (physics), Oregon, 1975. Artificial intelligence, philosophy of mind, cognitive science. (E-mail: dughof@cs.indiana.edu)

Steven D. Johnson (1982), Associate Professor of Computer Science and Chair; Ph.D. (computer science), Indiana, 1983. Formal design methods, program verification and synthesis, hardware verification and synthesis, functional programming, parallel computation. (E-mail: sjohnson@cs.indiana.edu)

David Leake (1990), Associate Professor of Computer Science; Ph.D. (computer science), Yale, 1990. Artificial intelligence and cognitive science, especially case-based reasoning, explanation-based learning, natural language processing, story understanding, and memory. (E-mail: leake@cs.indiana.edu)

Daniel Leivant (1991), Professor of Computer Science and Adjunct Professor of Philosophy; Ph.D. (mathematics), Amsterdam, 1975. Theory of computing, theory of programming languages, mathematical logic and foundations of mathematics. (E-mail: leivant@cs.indiana.edu)

Annie E. Liu (1997), Assistant Professor of Computer Science; Ph.D. (computer science), Cornell, 1996. Programming languages, compilers, and software systems. (E-mail: liu@cs.indiana.edu)

Jonathan W. Mills (1988), Associate Professor of Computer Science; Ph.D. (computer science), Arizona State, 1988. Computer architecture, analog VLSI circuits, robotics, computational sensors, neural networks, continuous-valued logic. (E-mail: jwmills@cs.indiana.edu)

Lawrence S. Moss (1990), Associate Professor of Mathematics and Adjunct Assistant Professor of Computer Science; Ph.D. (mathematics), UCLA, 1984. Logic, theory and semantics of computation, interaction of logic, linguistics, and computer science. (E-mail: moss@cs.indiana.edu)

Benjamin C. Pierce (1997), Assistant Professor of Computer Science; Ph.D. (computer science), Carnegie Mellon, 1991. Programming languages design and implementation, object-oriented programming, static type systems, subtyping, concurrency, process calculi, and distributed programming. (E-mail: pierce@cs.indiana.edu)

Robert F. Port (1986), Professor of Computer Science and Linguistics; Ph.D. (linguistics), Connecticut, 1976. Artificial intelligence, speech recognition, cognitive science, natural language processing. (E-mail: port@cs.indiana.edu)

Franklin Prosser (1969), Professor of Computer Science; Ph.D. (physical chemistry), Penn State, 1961. Digital hardware, computer science education. (E-mail: fpp@cs.indiana.edu)

Paul W. Purdom (1971), Professor of Computer Science; Ph.D. (physics), Caltech, 1966. Analysis of algorithms, rewriting systems, compilers, game playing. (E-mail: pwp@cs.indiana.edu)

Gregory J. E. Rawlins (1987), Associate Professor of Computer Science; Ph.D. (computer science), Waterloo, 1987. Combinatorial algorithms, computational geometry, shape editors and computer animation, models of machine learning. (E-mail: rawlins@cs.indiana.edu)

Edward L. Robertson (1978), Professor of Computer Science; Ph.D. (computer science), Wisconsin, 1970. Database systems, theory of computation, computational complexity, software engineering. (E-mail: edrbtsn@cs.indiana.edu)

Brian Cantwell Smith (1997), Professor of Computer Science and Cognitive Science; Ph.D. (computer science), MIT, 1982. Conceptual foundations of computing, use of computational metaphors in other fields, computational reflection, meta-level architectures, programming languages, knowledge representation. (E-mail: bcsmith@cs.indiana.edu)

George Springer (1986), Emeritus Professor of Computer Science and Mathematics; Ph.D. (mathematics), Harvard, 1949. Programming languages, numerical analysis, complex analysis. (E-mail: springer@cs.indiana.edu)

Scott D. Stoller (1997), Assistant Professor of Computer Science; Ph.D. (computer science), Cornell, 1997. Techniques and supporting tools for design, optimization, and validation of distributed systems. (E-mail: stoller@cs.indiana.edu)

Dirk Van Gucht (1985), Associate Professor of Computer Science; Ph.D. (computer science), Vanderbilt, 1985. Database theory and systems, machine learning. (E-mail: vgucht@cs.indiana.edu)

David E. Winkel (1983), Emeritus Professor of Computer Science; Ph.D. (chemistry), Iowa State, 1957. Digital design, applicative architectures. (E-mail: winkel@cs.indiana.edu)

David S. Wise (1972), Professor of Computer Science; Ph.D. (computer science), Wisconsin, 1971. Applicative programming, multiprocessing architectures and algorithms. (E-mail: dswise@cs.indiana.edu)

IOWA STATE UNIVERSITY

DEPARTMENT OF COMPUTER SCIENCE

PROGRAMS OF STUDY

The Department of Computer Science at Iowa State University offers programs of study leading to either the M.S. or the Ph.D. degree, with areas of concentration in AI databases, programming languages, complexity theory, algorithms, computer architecture, software engineering, operating systems, distributed and parallel computing, and VLSI systems.

For the M.S. degree, students must complete 31 credits and either a master's thesis or a formal paper. Ph.D. candidates must complete 72 credits, fulfill the proficiency requirement in three areas, pass a preliminary exam, and complete and defend a dissertation.

RESEARCH FACILITIES

Faculty and graduate student research is supported by local area networks with workstations, personal computers, and X-terminals. Access is available to machines throughout campus and to the Internet. Parallel processing is provided by the University Scalable Computing Laboratory.

Computer science graduate students are involved in research projects within the department and in numerous research centers and laboratories across the campus.

The University library collections total more than 5.6 million items, including more than 2 million books and bound serials and 2.7 million microforms. The library receives more than 21,000 journals and other serial publications.

FINANCIAL AID

Many qualified graduate students in computer science receive financial support in the form of teaching or research assistantships. Assistantship stipends start at $1235 per month in 1997–98. Graduate students on research or teaching assistantships of quarter time or more and not on restricted admission or academic probation are considered Iowa residents. They receive a Graduate College tuition scholarship, which covers a portion of the tuition and fee assessment. The tuition scholarship for 1997–98 is $762 per semester for students on at least half-time appointment and $381 per semester for students on at least quarter-time but less than half-time appointment. Appointments are normally made on a half-time basis, committing the student to 20 hours of work per week. Ordinarily, the student is eligible for reappointment if academic progress and the performance of duties of the previous appointment have been satisfactory. The Graduate College permits a student holding a half-time graduate assistantship to register for no more than 12 semester credits.

Applicants who have outstanding undergraduate records are eligible for nomination for a Premium for Academic Excellence (PACE) Award. The amount of the PACE Award is equal to one half of the resident tuition. A nomination for the PACE Award is initiated by the department and must be awarded prior to enrollment.

COST OF STUDY

Fall 1997 fees for full-time study are $1524 per semester for Iowa residents and $4487 per semester for nonresidents. Fees and tuition are subject to change without notice.

LIVING AND HOUSING COSTS

The University provides graduate housing facilities for approximately 336 students and 920 families. There is also apartment space for 131 single graduate students. Private rooms and apartments are available in Ames and other nearby communities.

Buchanan (air-conditioned) is the graduate residence hall. In 1997–98, the proposed Buchanan rates are $2068 for double occupancy and $2704 for single occupancy. A full meal plan costs $1768.

STUDENT GROUP

In spring 1997, there were 68 M.S. students and 14 Ph.D. students in the department.

STUDENT OUTCOMES

Graduates of the program are heavily recruited by major computer companies, energy corporations, software producers, and application developers. The types of employment include both research and development positions and range from internal system design to application development. During the course of their studies, some students accept summer internships with corporations. Many Ph.D. graduates have elected to assume research and teaching positions in academic institutions.

LOCATION

Ames, a city with a population of 50,000, is located near the geographical center of Iowa and is 35 miles north of the state capital, Des Moines. Ames is 300 miles west of Chicago, 200 miles south of Minneapolis–St. Paul, and 200 miles north of Kansas City. Students new to the area are generally pleased with the range of available cultural, social, and recreational activities.

THE UNIVERSITY

Iowa State University was founded in 1858 as one of the first land-grant institutions in the United States. The campus occupies more than 1,000 acres of land on the west side of Ames. Currently, nearly 25,000 students are enrolled in the University and of those, 4,500 are graduate students. The computer science department is part of the College of Liberal Arts and Sciences.

APPLYING

Fall semester admission is preferred, but applications for spring semester admission are considered. Applications for fall semester admission with financial aid should be received by March 1. The department requires submission of GRE General Test scores and recommends submission of scores on the GRE Subject Test in computer science. International students are required to submit TOEFL results. Applicants are expected to have been in the upper quartile of their undergraduate class and must normally have a strong background in computer science. Provisional admission is sometimes granted to promising students whose prior training is outside the discipline.

CORRESPONDENCE AND INFORMATION

Inquiries about the graduate program or requests for information can be made by regular mail, telephone, or fax. Students can also send e-mail to "grad__adm" or to "almanac"; the former generates a package of information that is returned by e-mail and a secretary will request the Graduate Admissions Office to send the necessary application forms. Information about the graduate program (without application forms) may be electronically obtained by sending e-mail directly to "almanac" as described below or by accessing either the departmental Internet Gopher (gopher.cs.iastate.edu) or World Wide Web (www.cs.iastate.edu) servers.

Traditional correspondence:

Graduate Admissions
Department of Computer Science
Iowa State University
Ames, Iowa 50011-1040

Telephone: 515-294-8361
Fax: 515-294-0258
E-mail: grad__adm@cs.iastate.edu

Almanac Mail Server:

Send e-mail to:

almanac@cs.iastate.edu
with the following lines in the message
send gi pamphlet
send gi faculty__interests
send gi evaluation
send gi catalog

IOWA STATE UNIVERSITY
THE FACULTY AND THEIR RESEARCH

Albert L. Baker, Associate Professor; Ph.D., Ohio State. Software engineering, specification languages and CASE tools, natural language text analysis.

J. Peter Boysen, Adjunct Assistant Professor; Ph.D., Iowa State. Computer-assisted instruction, programming languages, object-oriented software development.

Harrington C. Brearley, Professor Emeritus; Ph.D., Illinois at Urbana-Champaign. Computer architecture, switching theory, fault detection.

Soma Chaudhuri, Assistant Professor; Ph.D., Washington (Seattle). Theory of distributed computing, parallel computation and complexity, theory of computation.

Carolina Cruz-Neira, Adjunct Assistant Professor; Ph.D., Illinois at Chicago. Virtual reality, scientific visualization, real-time computer graphics, integrated high-performance computing and communications systems.

David Fernandez-Baca, Associate Professor; Ph.D., California, Davis. Design and analysis of algorithms, combinatorial optimization.

Shashi K. Gadia, Associate Professor; Ph.D., Illinois at Urbana-Champaign. Temporal databases, databases, geographical information systems.

Dale D. Grosvenor, Associate Professor; Ph.D., Iowa State. Mathematical programming, operating systems.

John Gustafson, Adjunct Associate Professor; Ph.D., Iowa State. Massively parallel computing, architecture application fit, analysis of algorithms, performance models, computational physics and chemistry.

Don E. Heller, Adjunct Associate Professor; Ph.D., Carnegie Mellon. Programming and debugging support tools for distributed memory systems, performance evaluation and analysis, parallel algorithms.

Vasant Honavar, Associate Professor; Ph.D., Wisconsin. Artificial intelligence; neural networks; artificial life; cognitive science; computational neuroscience; neural, parallel, and distributed algorithms for AI; machine learning; machine perception; evolutionary computation; intelligent multimedia information systems; computer networks.

Suresh C. Kothari, Professor; Ph.D., Purdue. Computer architecture, parallel and distributed computing, performance analysis, neural networks, computational science.

Gary T. Leavens, Associate Professor; Ph.D., MIT. Programming language design and semantics, programming methodology, specification, verification, distributed systems, object-oriented programming.

Jack H. Lutz, Professor; Ph.D., Caltech. Computational complexity, algorithmic information, randomness and pseudorandomness.

Robyn R. Lutz, Affiliate Assistant Professor; Ph.D., Kansas. High-integrity systems, software safety, real-time embedded software, spacecraft.

Leslie L. Miller, Professor; Ph.D., SMU. Database design, file organization and parallel searching.

Arthur E. Oldehoeft, Professor and Chairman; Ph.D., Purdue. Operating systems, parallel processing, distributed processing, computer security.

Wayne Ostendorf, Associate Professor; B.S., Iowa State. Applied systems technology, computer-based information systems, data center management, large databases, interactive systems.

G. M. Prabhu, Associate Professor; Ph.D., Washington State. Parallel processing, computer architecture and information technology.

Giora Slutzki, Professor; Ph.D., Tel-Aviv. Algorithms, computational complexity, formal languages, automata theory, relational database theory.

Robert M. Stewart, Professor Emeritus; Ph.D., Iowa State. Computer architecture.

George O. Strawn, Associate Professor; Ph.D., Iowa State. Expert systems, optimizing compilers, programming language translation theory, data structures.

Rex Thomas, Adjunct Professor; Ph.D., Iowa State. Instructional use of computers, teaching of programming.

Akhilesh Tyagi, Assistant Professor; Ph.D., Washington (Seattle). VLSI: complexity theory, design, and architectures; computer architecture; parallel computers.

Johnny S. K. Wong, Associate Professor; Ph.D., Sydney. Computer networks, operating systems, performance evaluation of communication protocols, distributed computing, object-oriented database, multimedia and hypermedia systems.

JOHNS HOPKINS UNIVERSITY

G. W. C. WHITING SCHOOL OF ENGINEERING
DEPARTMENT OF COMPUTER SCIENCE

PROGRAM OF STUDY

Graduate study is oriented toward the Ph.D. degree. Faculty research interests are concentrated in the following areas: algorithms, distributed and fault-tolerant computing and networks, biomedical applications of computer science, object-oriented programming languages and methodologies, robotics and computer vision, geometric computing and computer graphics, concurrent and parallel computer systems, machine learning, computational biology, and natural language processing. The department encourages students to become involved in research-oriented studies guided by a faculty research adviser shortly after enrolling in the program. Ph.D. students must qualify for the Ph.D. by satisfactorily completing both course and project requirements by the end of the second academic year of graduate study. A mutually agreeable selection of a faculty research adviser is then made. The student and research adviser together plan the remainder of the graduate program. Ph.D. students must also pass a Graduate Board oral examination, prepare and defend a preliminary research proposal, and present a department seminar. Once the thesis is completed, there is a dissertation defense open to the public.

The department also offers both full-time and part-time Master of Science in Engineering programs, which require successful completion of a minimum of 8 one-semester courses at an acceptable level, plus satisfactory completion of either a master's thesis/project or 2 additional one-semester courses.

RESEARCH FACILITIES

The department maintains extensive facilities for research and teaching in the New Engineering Building on the Homewood Campus of Johns Hopkins. Department laboratories include a Center for Geometric Computing, a Center for Networks and Distributed Systems, a Computed Integrated Surgery Lab, a Computer Vision Lab, a Machine Learning and Computational Biology Lab, and a Natural Language Processing Lab. The department's general computing facilities include numerous Sun and SGI workstations, Macs and PCs, X-terminals, scanners, and laser printers.

FINANCIAL AID

Financial assistance is available through tuition scholarships, teaching assistantships, research assistantships, and fellowships, including the Abel Wolman Graduate Fellowship, as well as fellowships from the Center for Geometric Computing, the Networks and Distributed Systems Center, and the Center for Language and Speech Processing. Financial assistance should be requested when applying for admission. The standard assistantship stipend is $12,850. Normally, financial aid is not available for students working toward only an M.S. degree.

COST OF STUDY

Tuition for 1997–98 is $21,700.

LIVING AND HOUSING COSTS

University-owned apartments are available for single and married students. Private off-campus housing in Baltimore is available in a wide range of prices.

STUDENT GROUP

The department currently has approximately 60 full-time graduate students.

LOCATION

The campus is in a residential neighborhood of both single-family homes and apartments, located 4 miles from downtown Baltimore. There are churches, restaurants, drugstores, grocery stores, and other shops nearby. The 140-acre tree-lined Homewood campus offers a wide variety of areas for gatherings and recreation. Generally, graduate students find that their academic and social lives tend to center on their departments. The three most widely used buildings are the Milton S. Eisenhower Library; the Newton H. White, Jr. Athletic Center; and the Hopkins Union (Levering Hall), which is the University student center.

THE UNIVERSITY

Privately endowed, the Johns Hopkins University was founded in 1876 as the first American educational institution committed to the university idea: giving students and faculty the freedom of choice and opportunity necessary for learning and creativity. It remains committed to this idea today. Johns Hopkins is a small coeducational university. To preserve close intellectual association, the University community and the student-faculty ratio are intentionally small. Approximately 3,400 undergraduates, 1,400 graduates, and 140 postdoctoral students are currently enrolled. There are more than 350 faculty members.

APPLYING

Admissions materials should be requested between June 1 and December 1; completed applications must be received by February 1. Students may also apply by electronic mail by sending to the address below. Acceptance letters are sent by mid-March. Students should take the Graduate Record Examinations (both the General Test and a Subject Test in computer science, mathematics, or engineering) no later than December and should specify the Department of Computer Science when having scores sent. Students without a degree from an American college or university must also take the Test of English as a Foreign Language (TOEFL) and have the score sent to the Department of Computer Science.

Qualified individuals are encouraged to visit the campus to discuss their plans for graduate study with the faculty. Midyear entrance into the graduate program is difficult and not recommended.

CORRESPONDENCE AND INFORMATION

Chair, Graduate Admissions
Department of Computer Science
Johns Hopkins University
3400 North Charles Street
Baltimore, Maryland 21218-2694
Telephone: 410-516-8775
Fax: 410-516-6134
E-mail: admissions@cs.jhu.edu
World Wide Web: http://www.cs.jhu.edu/

JOHNS HOPKINS UNIVERSITY
THE FACULTY AND THEIR RESEARCH

Yair Amir, Assistant Professor; Ph.D., Hebrew (Jerusalem), 1995. Distributed systems, communication protocol, conferencing replication.

Baruch Awerbuch, Professor; D.Sc., Technion (Israel), 1984. Algorithmic theory of communications, on-line and distributed computing.

Eric Brill, Assistant Professor; Ph.D., Pennsylvania, 1993. Natural language and speech processing, machine learning and artificial intelligence.

Michael T. Goodrich, Professor; Ph.D., Purdue, 1987. Design and analysis of algorithms, parallel algorithms, computational geometry, computer graphics.

S. Rao Kosaraju, Edward J. Schaefer Professor; Ph.D., Pennsylvania, 1969. Design of algorithms, parallel computation, pattern matching computation geometry, computational biology.

Subodh Kumar, Assistant Professor; Ph.D., North Carolina, 1996. Interactive 3D computer graphics, virtual environments, computational geometry.

F. Thomson Leighton, Professor MIT, Adjunct Professor; Ph.D., MIT, 1981. Algorithms, parallel computation, cryptography.

Gerald M. Masson, Professor and Chair; Ph.D., Northwestern, 1971. Computer and communication networking, fault-tolerant computing, interconnection structures.

Steven L. Salzberg, Associate Professor; Ph.D., Harvard, 1989. Artificial intelligence, machine learning, computational biology.

Scott F. Smith, Associate Professor; Ph.D., Cornell, 1988. Programming languages, semantics.

Russell Taylor, Professor; Ph.D., Stanford, 1976. Medical robotics and computer-assisted surgery.

Lawrence B. Wolff, Associate Professor; Ph.D., Columbia, 1990. Computer vision.

David Yarowsky, Assistant Professor; Ph.D., Pennsylvania, 1995. Speech and natural language processing, machine translation, information retrieval and machine learning.

Research Faculty

Arthur L. Delcher, Research Scientist; Ph.D., Johns Hopkins, 1989. Artificial intelligence, parallel algorithms, parallel programming.

Gregory Sullivan, Research Scholar; Ph.D., Yale, 1986. Design of algorithms and fault-tolerant computing.

Joint and Visiting Appointments

Andreas Andreou, Associate Professor (joint appointment with Electrical and Computer Engineering); Ph.D., Johns Hopkins, 1986. Electron devices, analog VLSI, sensor micropower electronics.

Yossi Azar, Visiting Research Scholar; Ph.D., Tel Aviv, 1989. On-line algorithms.

Amnon Barak, Visiting Professor; Ph.D., Illinois at Urbana-Champaign, 1971. Distributed operating systems.

Michael R. Brent, Assistant Professor (joint appointment with Cognitive Science); Ph.D., MIT, 1991. Computational linguistics and algorithms for learning natural languages.

Eugene Charniak, Professor; Ph.D., MIT, 1972. Statistical language processing.

Greg Chirikjian, Assistant Professor (joint appointment with Mechanical Engineering); Ph.D., Caltech, 1992. Design, kinematics, dynamics, and control of mechanisms, robotics, and controls.

Lenore Cowen, Assistant Professor (joint appointment with Mathematical Sciences); Ph.D., MIT, 1993. Combinatorics graph theory routing and scheduling, probabilistic method.

Simon Kasif, Visiting Associate Professor; Ph.D., Maryland, 1985. Artificial intelligence, logic programming, parallel computation.

Frederick Jelinek, Professor (joint appointment with Electrical and Computer Engineering) and Director of Center for Speech Processing; Ph.D., MIT, 1962. Speech recognition, statistical methods of natural language processing, information theory.

Stanley Letovsky, Assistant Professor (joint appointment with Neuroradiology); Ph.D., Yale, 1988. Computational biology, machine learning.

Edward R. Scheinerman, Professor (joint appointment with Mathematical Sciences); Ph.D., Princeton, 1984. Graph theory, partially ordered sets and random graphs.

Jack Snoeyink, Visiting Associate Professor; Ph.D., Stanford, 1990. Computational geometry, GIS, CAD, robotics.

Raimond L. Winslow, Associate Professor (joint appointment with Biomedical Engineering); Ph.D., Johns Hopkins, 1985. Modeling of biological systems, large-scale computation, visualization and nonlinear dynamical systems theory.

Yaacov Yesha, Visiting Professor; Ph.D., 1979. Weizmann (Israel). Algorithmic theory of communications and distributed computing.

Yelena Yesha, Visiting Research Scholar; Ph.D., Ohio State, 1989. Electronic commerce and databases.

Amy E. Zwarico, Visiting Assistant Professor; Ph.D., Pennsylvania, 1988. Programming languages, distributed and real-time processing.

Undergraduate Lecturers

Lewis L. Beach, M.S., West Virginia, 1989. General computer science.

Mark E. Giuliano, Ph.D., Maryland, 1990. Parallel languages, artificial intelligence, logic programming.

Joanne Houlahan, Ph.D., Johns Hopkins, 1996. Fault-tolerant computing.

Harold Lehmann, Ph.D., Stanford, 1992. Medical informatics, Bayesian reasoning, statistical software.

Robert Massof, Ph.D., Indiana, 1975. Ophthalmology, virtual reality and vision.

Fernando Pineda, Ph.D., Maryland, 1986. Neural computation, machine learning.

John Sadowsky, Ph.D., Maryland, 1980. Sensory engineering, virtual reality, applied number theory, signal and image processing.

Paul B. Schneck, Ph.D., NYU (Courant), 1979. Supercomputing and parallel processing.

Dwight Wilson, Ph.D., Johns Hopkins, 1996. Fault-tolerant computing.

THE JOHNS HOPKINS UNIVERSITY

DEPARTMENT OF ELECTRICAL AND COMPUTER ENGINEERING

PROGRAMS OF STUDY

Graduate study is oriented toward the Ph.D., with emphasis on applicable research and scholarship rather than on engineering practice. Research interests of the faculty are concentrated in communications, computer engineering, solid-state electronics, information processing, nonlinear and quantum optics and electronics, systems and control theory, and language and speech processing.

The program encourages students to become involved in research-oriented studies as early as possible. A departmental examination must be passed before the beginning of the fourth semester of graduate study. Then a member of the faculty is selected as the research sponsor, and the student and sponsor plan together the remainder of the graduate program. The program requirements include passing a Graduate Board oral examination given by a panel of 5 faculty members, preparing a brief research proposal, and presenting a departmental seminar. Finally, there is a dissertation defense open to the public.

The department also offers both full-time and part-time M.S. programs. Such programs require at least eight 1-semester courses at the graduate level, plus satisfactory completion of either a master's essay, a special project, or two additional 1-semester courses.

RESEARCH FACILITIES

The department occupies Barton Hall and portions of Latrobe Hall, both of which contain extensive laboratory and computing facilities. Major research laboratories include the Image Analysis and Communications, Parallel Processing, Solid State Electronics, Quantum Electronics, Optical Communications, Sensory Aids, and Nonlinear Optics laboratories.

Computing facilities include a departmental time-sharing system running UNIX, a CAD laboratory for electronics and VLSI, and numerous workstations, in addition to the Homewood Computing Facility's DEC VAX 6000-410 running VMS, SGI Server running UNIX, and an IBM 3081.

FINANCIAL AID

Financial assistance is available through tuition scholarships, teaching assistantships, and research assistantships. The nominal assistantship salary in 1997–98 is $12,850 for nine months. Limited financial aid is available for terminal M.S. students. The department accepts candidates with a bachelor's degree directly into the Ph.D. programs and offers full financial aid support to outstanding applicants.

COST OF STUDY

Annual tuition for 1997–98 is $21,700.

LIVING AND HOUSING COSTS

University-owned apartments are available for single and married students. Private off-campus housing in Baltimore is readily available in a wide range of prices.

STUDENT GROUP

The department has about 75 graduate students, of whom about 50 are working toward the Ph.D. degree, and about 150 undergraduates. In Arts and Sciences and Engineering, there are 3,336 undergraduates, 1,323 graduate students, and 356 faculty members.

LOCATION

The University is located in Homewood, a residential area located only a short distance north of downtown Baltimore. The 140-acre campus is wooded and quiet, providing an appropriate atmosphere for study and research. The Johns Hopkins medical institutions are separately located in east Baltimore. The Johns Hopkins Applied Physics Laboratory is located 20 miles south of Baltimore.

THE UNIVERSITY

Founded in 1876, Johns Hopkins was the first university to offer graduate education as it is known today in America. From the start, the University was dedicated to the idea of "creative scholarship." Its faculty members were scholars as well as teachers. Students were to engage not merely in the absorption of knowledge dispensed by their elders but also in the creation of knowledge through their own research. Thus, although small in size, Johns Hopkins has had a profound influence on American higher education.

APPLYING

Qualified individuals are encouraged to visit the campus to discuss their plans for graduate study with the faculty. The deadline for applying for admission is January 1. Notification of awards is made by March 15. Submission of scores on the Graduate Record Examinations is required. Midyear entrance into the graduate programs is difficult and not recommended. Applications, forms, and instructions are available on the World Wide Web to download, complete, and submit. The address is http://www.ece.jhu.edu/, sub-heading "GRADUATE ADMISSIONS." Due to increased mailing costs, international applicants who do not have access to the Internet must complete a preliminary application.

CORRESPONDENCE AND INFORMATION

Graduate Admissions Committee
Department of Electrical and Computer Engineering
The Johns Hopkins University
Baltimore, Maryland 21218
Telephone: 410-516-4808
Fax: 410-516-5566
E-mail: gradadm@mail.ece.jhu.edu

THE JOHNS HOPKINS UNIVERSITY

THE FACULTY AND THEIR RESEARCH

A. G. Andreou, Associate Professor; Ph.D., Johns Hopkins, 1986. Electron devices, analog VLSI, sensors and micropower electronics, physics of computation.

G. Cauwenberghs, Assistant Professor; Ph.D., Caltech, 1994. Analog and digital VLSI systems, distributed parallel processing, analog neural computation.

F. M. Davidson, Professor and Chair; Ph.D., Rochester, 1969. Quantum optics, optical coherence, optical communications.

J. I. Goutsias, Associate Professor; Ph.D., USC, 1986. Signal processing, image processing, and analysis.

B. Hughes, Research Professor; Ph.D., Maryland, 1985. Information theory, communication theory, signal processing.

P. A. Iglesias, Assistant Professor; Ph.D., Cambridge, 1991. Linear control, H-infinity control, adaptive control.

F. Jelinek, Professor and Director, Center for Language and Speech Processing; Ph.D., MIT, 1962. Speech recognition, statistical methods of natural language processing, information theory.

R. I. Joseph, Professor; Ph.D., Harvard, 1962. Electromagnetic theory, nonlinear wave propagation, solitons.

A. E. Kaplan, Professor; Ph.D., USSR Academy of Sciences, 1967. Quantum electronics, nonlinear optics, optical bistability.

J. B. Khurgin, Professor; Ph.D., Polytechnic, 1986. Quantum electronics, nonlinear optics.

G. G. L. Meyer, Professor; Ph.D., Berkeley, 1970. Parallel computing, computational methods, fault-tolerant computing.

T. O. Poehler, Research Professor; Ph.D., Johns Hopkins, 1961. Quantum electronics, solid-state physics.

J. L. Prince, Associate Professor; Ph.D., MIT, 1988. Multidimensional signal processing, medical imaging, computational geometry.

W. J. Rugh, Professor; Ph.D., Northwestern, 1969. Linear and nonlinear systems theory, control theory.

H. L. Weinert, Professor; Ph.D., Stanford, 1972. Statistical signal and image processing.

C. R. Westgate, Professor and Associate Dean for Academic Affairs, Whiting School of Engineering; Ph.D., Princeton, 1966. Solid-state electronics, design and circuit modeling, microwaves, high-speed circuits.

Associated Faculty: Joint Appointments and Part-Time Members

William R. Brody, Professor and President of the University. Medical imaging, magnetic resonance imaging.

William J. Byrne, Lecturer; Ph.D., Maryland, 1993. Speech recognition, information theory and statistics.

R. E. Glaser, Lecturer (part-time); Ph.D., Johns Hopkins, 1981. Advanced digital logic systems.

W. C. Gore, Professor (part-time); Dr.Engr., Johns Hopkins, 1952. Information theory, error-correcting codes, communication systems.

Douglas M. Green, Research Professor and Associate Dean for Research, Whiting School of Engineering; Ph.D., Texas at Austin, 1977. Microcirculation trauma, highly parallel architectures, computer design for microelectronics, fault-tolerant wafer-scale processors.

Elliot McVeigh, Associate Professor, Biomedical Engineering; Ph.D., Toronto, 1988. Magnetic resonance imaging.

Michael Stern, Assistant Professor, Cardiology, School of Medicine; Ph.D., MIT, 1968; M.D., Pennsylvania, 1972. Application of coherent optics to cardiology.

Larry Wolff, Associate Professor, Computer Science; Ph.D., Columbia, 1991. Computer vision, computational sensors for vision/robotics, computer graphics.

KANSAS STATE UNIVERSITY

DEPARTMENT OF COMPUTING AND INFORMATION SCIENCES

PROGRAMS OF STUDY

The Department of Computing and Information Sciences at Kansas State University offers graduate programs leading to the Master of Software Engineering, Master of Science, and Doctor of Philosophy degrees.

The program of study for the M.S.E. program consists of 33 credits. Each student specializes in an application area and does a project related to that application area. Each student produces and presents a software portfolio that contains a collection of documents related to the software development activity.

The M.S. degree requires a minimum of 30 credit hours of graduate-level course work. The degree program can take one of three forms: a nonthesis-report option requiring 33 hours, a report option requiring 30 hours, and a thesis option requiring 30 hours. An oral presentation is required for each option, and further original research is required for the thesis option.

The Ph.D. degree requirements include 90 semester hours of graduate-level credit. General requirements include passing a preliminary examination, writing a research proposal about the dissertation research, and writing and successfully defending the dissertation in an open forum.

Kansas State University maintains research programs in programming languages, distributed and real-time systems, software engineering, and database systems.

RESEARCH FACILITIES

The Department of Computing and Information Sciences maintains a large network of servers, workstations, and graphics display terminals for graduate study and faculty research. Servers include symmetrical multiprocessors manufactured by Sun and Solbourne. Access to these servers is available in offices and laboratories equipped with more than 120 workstations, including Sun SPARCstations, X window system terminals, PCs, and Macintoshes. Direct access to the Internet permits communication with computer science researchers worldwide. Programming languages include Ada, C, C++, Concurrent C, Java, FORTRAN-77, Common LISP, LISP, Miranda, ML, OBJ3, Parlog, Pascal, PROLOG, and Scheme. Many other software packages are available, including CASE tools, relational database management systems, simulation, expert systems, interface builders, and document publishing. Additional campuswide computer facilities are provided by central Computing and Network Services. These facilities include an IBM 3090 mainframe, Sun servers, Sun Workstations, and several labs throughout campus with PCs and Apple Macintoshes.

Farrell Library subscribes to the standard computer science publications and is able to obtain nearly any title through a nationwide interlibrary loan system.

FINANCIAL AID

Graduate teaching assistantships carry stipends for the academic year and are normally offered on a half-time basis. Resident staff tuition is available for teaching assistants, with a substantial additional fee reduction based on the time of the appointment. A few graduate research assistantships are available and are in effect for the full year. University fellowships are available to qualified U.S. citizens and permanent residents who are interested in pursuing doctoral degrees.

COST OF STUDY

For 1997–98, basic fees for all students are $65.50, plus $17 per credit hour up to 12 hours. In addition, graduate tuition for state residents is $97.80 per credit hour; nonresident graduate tuition is $321.35 per credit hour. Tuition is waived for graduate teaching assistants.

LIVING AND HOUSING COSTS

The cost of a dormitory room and board for single students is $2225 per semester in 1997–98, with the contract taken on a yearly basis. There is a $25 application fee for housing. Married student housing on campus ranges in cost from $235 to $312 per month plus electricity. Off-campus one-bedroom apartments rent for $250 per month and up. Overall living costs are among the lowest in the nation.

STUDENT GROUP

The total enrollment at Kansas State University in 1996–97 was 20,325; of this figure, 3,390 were graduate students. Forty-eight percent of the graduate students were women. Students are drawn from every state in the Union and from seventy-one countries. The graduate enrollment in computer science was about 60 students; 36 of these students received some form of financial support.

LOCATION

Manhattan, Kansas, a pleasant, tree-shaded city of 38,000 in the northern Flint Hills, is the trade and cultural center of a five-county area. The area enjoys a stable economy based on agriculture and ranching, trade, light industry, education, and government installations. Manhattan offers most of the advantages of a big city, yet it retains the wholesome flavor and attractions of small-town living. Tuttle Creek Lake, with 165 miles of shoreline and nearly 16,000 surface acres, offers some of the finest recreational areas in Kansas. Manhattan is located about 100 miles west of Kansas City via Interstate 70.

THE UNIVERSITY

Kansas State University was founded in 1863 as a land-grant institution under the Morrill Act. The University was first located on the grounds of the old Bluemont Central College, which was chartered in 1858, but in 1875 most of the work of the University was moved to its present site. The 315-acre campus is in northern Manhattan, convenient to both business and residential sections. Most of the buildings on campus are constructed of native limestone.

APPLYING

Applications for admission are considered throughout the year but should be completed as early as possible. Application for financial aid should be made by February 15 for the following academic year. Applicants are required to take the GRE General Test; international students must take the TOEFL, and they must score at least 50 out of 60 on the TSE to be considered for financial assistance.

CORRESPONDENCE AND INFORMATION

Dr. Virgil E. Wallentine, Head
Department of Computing and Information Sciences
Nichols Hall
Kansas State University
Manhattan, Kansas 66506-2302

Telephone: 913-532-6350
Fax: 913-532-7353
E-mail: virg@cis.ksu.edu
    gradinfo@cis.ksu.edu
World Wide Web: http://www.cis.ksu.edu/

KANSAS STATE UNIVERSITY
THE FACULTY AND THEIR RESEARCH

Professors

Virgil E. Wallentine, Head of the Department; Ph.D., Iowa State. Operating systems, computer networks, parallel simulation, concurrent programming systems, knowledge engineering.

David A. Gustafson, Ph.D., Wisconsin–Madison. Software engineering, AI techniques in software development, software measures, expert systems, software testing.

William J. Hankley, Ph.D., Ohio State. Formal specification of software systems, verification of specifications, software engineering, graphical user interfaces, World Wide Web technologies.

David A. Schmidt, Ph.D., Kansas State. Programming language semantics, abstract interpretation.

Elizabeth A. Unger, Ph.D., Kansas. Data and knowledge based systems, security, integrity of data, office automation systems.

Maarten van Swaay, Emeritus; Ph.D., Leiden (Netherlands). Laboratory instrumentation, social and ethical issues in computing.

Associate Professors

Myron A. Calhoun (Emeritus), Ph.D., Arizona State. Digital systems design, computer applications.

Rodney Howell, Ph.D., Texas at Austin. Distributed and real-time systems, design and analysis of algorithms, Petri nets, computational complexity.

Masaaki Mizuno, Ph.D., Iowa State. Distributed systems, operating systems.

Allen Stoughton, Ph.D., Edinburgh (Scotland). Programming language semantics, intuitionistic logic.

Maria Zamfir-Bleyberg, Ph.D., UCLA. Database and knowledge-base systems, data mining, semantics of programming language.

Assistant Professors

Matthew Dwyer, Ph.D., Massachusetts Amherst. Analysis of concurrent systems, software validation and verification, parallel software architectures.

Michael R. A. Huth, Ph.D., Tulane. Quantitative performance analysis, model checking, computation and logic, programming language semantics, computers and society.

Michael A. Miller, M.S., Iowa State. Operating systems, microcomputer applications.

Mitchell L. Neilsen, Ph.D., Kansas State. Operating systems, computer networks, distributed systems.

Gurdip Singh, Ph.D., SUNY at Stony Brook. Concurrent and distributed systems, network management protocols, modular verification, specification languages, database concurrency control.

REPRESENTATIVE PUBLICATIONS

Dwyer, M. B., and L. A. Clarke. Data flow analysis for verifying properties of concurrent programs. *Proc. 2nd SIGSOFT Symposium on Foundations of Software Engineering. Software Eng. Notes* 19(5):62–75, 1994.

Dwyer, M., and L. A. Clarke. A flexible architecture for building data flow analyzers. *Proc. 18th Intl. Conf. Software Eng.,* March 1996.

Gustafson, D. A., J. T. Tan, and P. Weaver. Software metric specifications. In *Software Measurement,* ed. A. Melton. International Thomson Publishing, 1995.

Gustafson, D. A. Kansas State's "Slick Willie" robot software. *AI Magazine* 18(1): 33–6, Spring 1997.

Hankley, W., and P. Tsai. A verification helper for task specifications. *Proc. 1993 ACM/SIGAPP Symp. Appl. Comput.,* pp. 193–202, February 1993.

Paryavi, M., and **W. Hankley.** OOSPEC: An executable object-oriented specification language. *Proc. 1995 ACM Comp. Sci. Conf.,* 1995.

Cherkosova, L., **R. Howell,** and L. Rosier. Bounded self-stabilizing petri nets. *Acta Informatica* 32:189–207, 1995.

Howell, R., and M. Venkatrao. On nonpreemptive scheduling of recurring tasks using inserted idle times. *Information and Computation* 117:50–62, 1995.

Huth, M., and M. Kwiatkowska. Quantitative analysis and model checking. *IEEE Symposium Logic Comput. Sci. 1997,* to appear, June 1997.

Huth, M., and M. Kwiatkowska. Finite but unbounded delay in synchronous CCS. Advances in theory and formal methods of computing. *Proc. Third Imperial College Workshop,* April 1996. Imperial College Press, 312–23, 1996.

Mizuno, M., and H. Kakugawa. A timestamp based transformation of self-stabilizing programs for distributed computing environments. *10th International Workshop on Distributed Algorithms (WDAG '96).* Springer Verlag LNCS 1151:304–21, 1966.

Mizuno, M., M. Rayal, and J. Zhou. Sequential consistency in distributed systems. Theory and practice in distributed computing. Springer Verlag LNCS 938:224–41, 1995.

Neilsen, M. Properties of nondominated k-coteries. *J. Syst. Software,* in press.

Neilsen, M. A dynamic probe strategy for quorum systems. *Proc. 17th Int. Conference Distributed Syst.,* May 1997, in press.

Schmidt, D. Abstract interpretation of small-step semantics. *5th LOMAPS Workshop on Analysis and Verification of Multiple-Agent Languages, Stockholm. Springer Lect. Notes Computer Sci.,* June 1996.

Schmidt, D. Programming language semantics. In *CRC Handbook of Computer Science,* ed. A. Tucker. Boca Raton, Florida: CRC Press, 1996.

Singh, G., and Z. Mao. Structured design of distributed protocols. *Proc. IEEE Int. Conference Distributed Comput. Syst.,* Hong Kong, 1996.

Singh, G. Leader election in compete networks. *SIAM J. Computing* 26(3), 1997.

Stoughton, A. Porgi: A proof-or-refutation generator for intuitionistic propositional logic. *CADE-13 Workshop Proof Search Type-Theor. Lang.* Rutgers University 109–16, 1996.

Stoughton, A. Fully abstract models of programming languages. *Research Notes in Theoretical Computer Science.* New York: Pitman/Wiley, 1988.

McNulty, S. K., and **E. A. Unger.** Database systems: inferential security. *J. Official Statistics,* 1993.

Slack, J. M. and **E. A. Unger.** Integrity in object-oriented database systems. *Comp. Sec. J.,* 1994.

van Swaay, M. The value and protection of privacy. *Computer Networks and ISDN Systems* 26(4):149, 1995.

van Swaay, M. Magic or mischief: The illusions of cyberspace as a "technological fix". *National Computer Ethics Conference,* Washington, D.C., pp. 27–8, April 1995.

Wallentine, V., et al. Multiprocessing. *Advan. Comp.,* ed. Marshall C. Yovits, vol. 33. Academic Press, 1994.

Wallentine, V., and J. Butler. A performance study of the RPE mechanism for PDES. *Proceedings of the 1994 International Workshop on Modeling, Analysis and Simulation of Computer and Telecommunications Systems,* eds. Madisetti, Gelenbe, and Walrand. IEEE Computer Society Press, January 1994.

Zamfir-Bleyberg, M. Modeling concurrency with AND/OR algebraic theories. *Proc. of the 2nd Internat. Conf. on Algebraic Methodology and Software Technology,* Iowa City, May 1991.

Zamfir-Bleyberg, M. A categorical view of databases. *Libertas Mathematica J.,* vol. 12, 1992.

LEHIGH UNIVERSITY

COMPUTER SCIENCE AND COMPUTER ENGINEERING

PROGRAMS OF STUDY

The department offers programs of study leading to the M.S. and Ph.D. degrees in computer science and to the M.S. degree in computer engineering. The computer science and computer engineering programs span the spectrum from VLSI design and image processing to natural-language processing, artificial intelligence, and theories of computing. The M.S. degree requires 30 credit hours of work, which may include a 3-credit-hour thesis for the computer science degree program and a 6-credit-hour thesis for the computer engineering degree program. The M.S. in computer science has 9 credit hours of specific course requirements. An oral presentation of the thesis or project is required. The Ph.D. degree requires completing 42 credit hours of work (including the dissertation) beyond the master's degree (48 credit hours if the master's degree is not from Lehigh), passing a departmental qualifying examination within one year after completion of the master's degree and passing a general examination in the area of specialization, fulfilling the University's residence requirements, and writing and defending a dissertation. Competence in a foreign language is not required. Major areas of emphasis in computer science and computer engineering include expert systems, artificial intelligence, data-based systems, natural-language interfacing, software engineering, computer vision, large-scale software, distributed operation systems, programming languages, computational linguistics, parallel processing and program semantics, VLSI design, integrated circuit testing, ultrahigh-performance semiconductor circuits, image processing, signal processing algorithms, pattern recognition, error-control coding, computer network architectures and protocols, logic design and verification, design automation, computer architecture, computer arithmetic, hierarchical robot control systems, and robot programming languages.

RESEARCH FACILITIES

The department's research laboratories include the computer architectures laboratory, design and computing systems laboratory, electron device physics laboratory, microelectronics fabrication laboratory, microwave measurements laboratory, microwave monolithic circuits laboratory, multimedia laboratory, parallel processing laboratory, optical computing and communications laboratory, and VLSI measurements laboratory. The department facilities include Sun SPARCstations, a 64-node transputer, a variety of personal computers, and a complete CMOS integrated-circuit processing laboratory. Facilities available for graduate research include the University Computer Center's IBM RS6000 workstations in public sites. Collaborative research is ongoing with the facilities of the Sherman Fairchild Laboratory of Solid State Studies, the Energy Research Center, the Materials Research Center, and the Engineering Research Center for Advanced Technology for Large Structural Systems.

FINANCIAL AID

Approximately 50 of the department's graduate students receive financial aid in the form of fellowships and scholarships from Lehigh University and departmental research and teaching assistantships. Beginning teaching assistants in 1997–98 receive $10,710 and a 20 hours' tuition award for the academic year and are obligated for 20 hours per week of teaching service.

COST OF STUDY

Tuition for the 1997–98 academic year is $800 per credit hour.

LIVING AND HOUSING COSTS

The University's Saucon Valley apartments for married and single students provide one- to three-bedroom garden-style efficiency apartments in a rural setting near the athletic complex, with rates from $375 to $510 per month in 1997–98. For further information, students should contact the Office of Residence Operations, Rathbone Hall 63, Lehigh University. Many graduate students live in rooms or apartments in the neighboring community. Living costs are below the national average.

STUDENT GROUP

Lehigh has more than 4,000 undergraduates and 2,000 graduate students. The Department of Electrical Engineering and Computer Science has 160 graduate students; 59 are full-time and 84 are Ph.D. students.

LOCATION

Lehigh University, located on the north slope of South Mountain, overlooks the Lehigh Valley and its cities of Allentown, Bethlehem, and Easton. The Lehigh Saucon Valleys provide a choice of urban or rural living with ready access to the Poconos, the Appalachian Trail, the Delaware and Lehigh River systems, and the Pennsylvania Dutch region. The Jersey shore is a 2- to 3-hour drive east, and buses run frequently to Atlantic City. Downtown Philadelphia and New York can be reached in 1 and 2 hours, respectively, by car or bus. Lehigh is readily accessible by air and by bus or car on Interstate 78.

THE UNIVERSITY

Lehigh is a private, coeducational university, founded in 1865 by Asa Pacer to "provide students with a scientific education tempered by humanistic study." This innovative concept of offering contiguous technical and nontechnical courses of study continues to provide Lehigh's unusual and successful flavor today. Approximately 35 percent of the students are enrolled in the College of Engineering and Applied Sciences. Research is conducted in all major departments and in the thirteen interdepartmental and interdisciplinary research centers and institutes.

APPLYING

Application forms for admission and financial aid may be obtained from the department. The admission decision is based on the applicant's transcripts, letters of recommendation, research, and professional goals. GRE scores are required of all applicants. Scores on the Test of English as a Foreign Language (TOEFL) and the Test of Spoken English (TSE) are required of all applicants whose native language is not English. Applicants who wish to be considered for financial aid must apply by January 15.

CORRESPONDENCE AND INFORMATION

Graduate Coordinator
Department of Electrical Engineering and Computer Science
Packard Laboratory
Lehigh University
19 Memorial Drive, West
Bethlehem, Pennsylvania 18015-3084

Telephone: 610-758-4072
Fax: 610-758-6279
E-mail: gradinfo@eecs.lehigh.edu
World Wide Web: http://www.eecs.lehigh.edu

LEHIGH UNIVERSITY
THE FACULTY AND THEIR RESEARCH

Richard Beigel, Associate Professor; Ph.D. (computer science), Stanford, 1988. User interfaces, parallel fault diagnosis, complexity theory.

Glenn D. Blank, Associate Professor; Ph.D. (cognitive science), Wisconsin, 1984. Computational linguistics, artificial intelligence, cognitive science.

Rick S. Blum, Assistant Professor; Ph.D. (electrical engineering), Pennsylvania, 1991. Signal processing, communications.

Terrance Boult, Associate Professor; Ph.D. (computer science), Columbia, 1986. Computer vision, software systems.

Dragana Brzakovic, Associate Professor; Ph.D. (electrical engineering), Florida, 1984. Image processing, pattern recognition.

Demetrios Christodoulides, Associate Professor; Ph.D. (electrical engineering), Johns Hopkins, 1986. Light-wave technology, nonlinear optics, solitons.

D. Richard Decker, Professor; Ph.D. (electrical engineering), Lehigh, 1970. Microwave integrated circuit design, packaging design.

Douglas R. Frey, Associate Professor; Ph.D. (electrical engineering), Lehigh, 1977. Nonlinear circuit analysis.

Bruce D. Fritchman, Professor; Ph.D. (electrical engineering), Lehigh, 1967. Image processing.

Samuel L. Gulden, Professor; M.A. (mathematics), Princeton, 1950. Distributed operating systems, program verification.

Miltiadis Hatalis, Professor; Ph.D. (electrical engineering), Carnegie Mellon, 1987. Microelectronic device structures and fabrication processes for active matrix displays.

Frank H. Hielscher, Professor; Ph.D. (electrical engineering), Illinois, 1966. VLSI design and testing.

Donald J. Hillman, Professor; Ph.D. (mathematics, logic), Cambridge, 1961. Database systems, expert systems.

Carl S. Holzinger, Professor; Ph.D. (electrical engineering), Lehigh, 1963. Microprocessor system design.

James C. M. Hwang, Professor; Ph.D. (material science), Cornell, 1976. Compound semiconductor materials and devices.

Edwin J. Kay, Associate Professor; Ph.D. (mathematics), 1968, Ph.D. (psychology), 1971, Lehigh. Computer applications in psychology, cognitive science.

Weiping Li, Associate Professor; Ph.D. (electrical engineering), Stanford, 1987. Signal processing and computer algorithms, processor architecture, ASIC design.

Alastair D. McAulay, Chandler-Weaver Professor and Chair; Ph.D. (electrical engineering), Carnegie-Mellon, 1974. Optical information processing, communications.

Roger Nagel, Harvey E. Wagner Professor of Manufacturing Systems Engineering; Ph.D. (computer science), Maryland, 1976. Robotics, computer-aided manufacturing.

Karl H. Norian, Associate Professor; Ph.D. (electrical materials), London, 1977. Electronic materials, electrical properties of thin films and biomembranes.

Peggy A. Ota, Vice Provost for Academic Administration; Ph.D. (computer and information sciences), Pennsylvania, 1972. Software testing, pattern recognition.

Eunice E. Santos, Assistant Professor; Ph.D. (computer science), Berkeley, 1995. Parallel and distributed computing, algorithm design and implementation.

Michael Schulte, Assistant Professor; Ph.D. (electrical engineering), Texas, 1992. Computer architecture, computer arithmetic, VLSI design.

Kenneth K. Tzeng, Professor; Ph.D. (electrical engineering), Illinois, 1969. Coding theory computer networks.

Meghanad D. Wagh, Associate Professor; Ph.D. (electrical engineering), Indian Institute of Technology (Bombay), 1977. Computer architecture, signal processing algorithms.

Richard S. Wallace, Assistant Professor; Ph.D. (computer science), Carnegie-Mellon, 1986. Robotics, computer vision, network programming.

Marvin H. White, Sherman Fairchild Professor; Ph.D. (electrical engineering), Ohio State, 1969. Submicron device physics, solid-state device modeling, VLSI design.

LEHIGH UNIVERSITY

DEPARTMENT OF ELECTRICAL ENGINEERING AND COMPUTER ENGINEERING

PROGRAMS OF STUDY

The department offers programs of study leading to the M.S., M.E., and Ph.D. degrees in electrical engineering and to the M.S. degree in computer engineering. The departmental programs span the spectrum from the mathematical and physical end of electrical engineering through computer engineering. The Master of Science degree in electrical engineering or computer engineering requires 30 credit hours of work, which may include a 6-credit-hour thesis. Alternatively, the Master of Engineering degree requires 30 credit hours of work, which includes design-oriented courses and an engineering project. An oral presentation of the thesis or project is required. The Ph.D. degree requires the completion of 42 credit hours of work (including the dissertation) beyond the master's degree (48 credit hours if the master's is not from Lehigh), passing a departmental qualifying examination within one year after completion of the master's, passing a general examination in the area of specialization, the fulfillment of the University's residence requirement, and the writing and defense of a dissertation. Competence in a foreign language is not required. Major areas of emphasis in electrical engineering and computer engineering include VLSI design, semiconductor device physics, monolithic microwave circuit design and characterization, fiber optics and optical computing, CMOS/VLSI chip technology, digital signal processing, image processing, special audio chips, signal processing algorithms for HDTV, pattern recognition, error-control coding, nonlinear optics and electromagnetics, logic design and verification, computer architectures, microrobotics and anthropomorphic robots, and computer vision. Major areas of emphasis in computer engineering include computer architectures, operating systems, software engineering, VLSI design and design automation, parallel and distributed computing, digital signal processing algorithms and architectures, communication systems, network architectures, and optical communications.

RESEARCH FACILITIES

The department's research laboratories include the computer architectures laboratory, design and computing systems laboratory, electron device physics laboratory, microelectronics fabrication laboratory, microwave measurements laboratory, microwave monolithic circuits laboratory, multimedia laboratory, parallel processing laboratory, optical computing and communications laboratory, and VLSI measurements laboratory. The departmental facilities include Sun SPARCstations, a 64-node transputer, a variety of personal computers, and a complete CMOS integrated-circuit processing laboratory. Facilities available for graduate research include the University Computer Center's IBM RS 6000 Workstations in public sites. Collaborative research is ongoing with the facilities of the Sherman Fairchild Laboratory of Solid State Studies, the Energy Research Center, the Materials Research Center, and the Engineering Research Center for Advanced Technology for Large Structural Systems.

FINANCIAL AID

Approximately 50 of the department's graduate students are receiving financial aid in the form of fellowships and scholarships from Lehigh University and in the form of departmental research and teaching assistantships. Beginning teaching assistants in 1997–98 receive $10,710 and a 20 hours' tuition award for the academic year and are obligated for 20 hours per week of teaching service.

COST OF STUDY

Tuition for the 1997–98 academic year is $800 per credit hour.

LIVING AND HOUSING COSTS

The University's Saucon Valley apartments for married and graduate students provide one- to three-bedroom garden-style efficiency apartments in a rural setting near the athletic complex, with rates that range from $375 to $510 per month in 1997–98. For further information, students should contact the Office of Residence Operations, Rathbone Hall 63, Lehigh University. Many graduate students live in rooms or apartments in the neighboring community. Living costs are below the national average.

STUDENT GROUP

Lehigh has more than 4,000 undergraduates and 2,000 graduate students. The EECS department has 160 graduate students; 59 are full-time and 84 are Ph.D. students.

LOCATION

Lehigh University, located on the north slope of South Mountain, overlooks the Lehigh Valley, with its cities of Allentown, Bethlehem, and Easton. The Lehigh and Saucon Valleys provide a choice of urban or rural living with ready access to the Poconos, the Appalachian Trail, the Delaware and Lehigh river systems, and the Pennsylvania Dutch region. The Jersey shore is a 2- to 3-hour drive east, and buses run frequently to Atlantic City. Downtown Philadelphia and New York can be reached in 1 and 2 hours, respectively, by car or bus. Lehigh is readily accessible by air, by bus, or by car on Interstate 78.

THE UNIVERSITY

Lehigh is a private, coeducational university, founded in 1865 by Asa Packer to "provide students with a scientific education tempered by humanistic study." This innovative concept of offering contiguous technical and nontechnical courses of study continues to provide Lehigh's unusual and successful flavor today. Approximately 35 percent of the students are enrolled in the College of Engineering and Applied Sciences. Research is conducted in all major departments and in the thirteen interdepartmental and interdisciplinary research centers and institutes.

APPLYING

Application forms for admission and financial aid may be obtained from the department. The admission decision is based on the applicant's transcripts, letters of recommendation, and research and professional goals. GRE scores are required from all applicants. Scores on the Test of English as a Foreign Language (TOEFL), as well as the Test of Spoken English (TSE), are required of all applicants whose native language is not English. Applicants who wish to be considered for financial aid must apply by January 15.

CORRESPONDENCE AND INFORMATION

Graduate Coordinator
Department of Electrical Engineering and Computer Science
Packard Laboratory
Lehigh University
19 Memorial Drive, West
Bethlehem, Pennsylvania 18015-3084

Telephone: 610-758-4072
Fax: 610-758-6279
E-mail: gradinfo@eecs.lehigh.edu
World Wide Web: http://www.eecs.lehigh.edu

LEHIGH UNIVERSITY
THE FACULTY AND THEIR RESEARCH

Richard Beigel, Associate Professor; Ph.D. (computer science), Stanford, 1988. User interfaces, parallel fault diagnosis, complexity theory.

Glenn D. Blank, Associate Professor; Ph.D. (cognitive science), Wisconsin, 1984. Computational linguistics, artificial intelligence, cognitive science.

Rick S. Blum, Assistant Professor; Ph.D. (electrical engineering), Pennsylvania, 1991. Signal processing, communications.

Terrance Boult, Associate Professor; Ph.D. (computer science), Columbia, 1986. Computer vision, software systems.

Dragana Brzakovic, Associate Professor; Ph.D. (electrical engineering), Florida, 1984. Image processing, pattern recognition.

Demetrios Christodoulides, Associate Professor; Ph.D. (electrical engineering), Johns Hopkins, 1986. Light-wave technology, nonlinear optics, solitons.

D. Richard Decker, Professor; Ph.D. (electrical engineering), Lehigh, 1970. Microwave integrated circuit design, packaging design.

Douglas R. Frey, Associate Professor; Ph.D. (electrical engineering), Lehigh, 1977. Nonlinear circuit analysis.

Bruce D. Fritchman, Professor; Ph.D. (electrical engineering), Lehigh, 1967. Image processing.

Samuel L. Gulden, Professor; M.A. (mathematics), Princeton, 1950. Distributed operating systems, program verification.

Miltiadis Hatalis, Professor; Ph.D. (electrical engineering), Carnegie Mellon, 1987. Microelectronic device structures and fabrication processes, active matrix displays.

Frank H. Hielscher, Professor; Ph.D. (electrical engineering), Illinois, 1966. VLSI design and testing.

Donald J. Hillman, Professor; Ph.D. (mathematics, logic), Cambridge, 1961. Database systems, expert systems.

Carl S. Holzinger, Professor; Ph.D. (electrical engineering), Lehigh, 1963. Microprocessor system design.

James C. M. Hwang, Professor; Ph.D. (material science), Cornell, 1976. Compound semiconductor materials and devices.

Edwin J. Kay, Associate Professor; Ph.D. (mathematics), 1968, Ph.D. (psychology), 1971, Lehigh. Computer applications in psychology, cognitive science.

Weiping Li, Associate Professor; Ph.D. (electrical engineering), Stanford, 1987. Signal processing and computer algorithms, processor architecture, ASIC design.

Alastair D. McAulay, Chandler-Weaver Professor and Chair; Ph.D. (electrical engineering), Carnegie Mellon, 1974. Optical information processing, communications.

Roger Nagel, Professor; Ph.D. (computer science), Maryland, 1976. Robotics, computer-aided manufacturing.

Karl H. Norian, Associate Professor; Ph.D. (electrical materials), London, 1977. Electronic materials, electrical properties of thin films and biomembranes.

Peggy A. Ota, Vice Provost for Academic Administration; Ph.D. (computer and information sciences), Pennsylvania, 1972. Software testing, pattern recognition.

Eunice E. Santos, Assistant Professor; Ph.D. (computer science), Berkeley, 1995. Parallel and distributed computing, algorithm design and implementation.

Michael Schulte, Assistant Professor; Ph.D. (electrical engineering), Texas at Austin, 1992. Computer architecture, computer arithmetic, VLSI design.

Kenneth K. Tzeng, Professor; Ph.D. (electrical engineering), Illinois, 1969. Coding theory, computer networks.

Meghanad D. Wagh, Associate Professor; Ph.D. (electrical engineering), Indian Institute of Technology (Bombay), 1977. Computer architecture, signal processing algorithms.

Richard S. Wallace, Assistant Professor; Ph.D. (computer science), Carnegie-Mellon, 1986. Robotics, computer vision, network programming.

Marvin H. White, Sherman Fairchild Professor; Ph.D. (electrical engineering), Ohio State, 1969. Submicron device physics, solid-state device modeling, VLSI design.

LOUISIANA STATE UNIVERSITY

DEPARTMENT OF ELECTRICAL AND COMPUTER ENGINEERING

PROGRAMS OF STUDY

The department is the focus for research and graduate education in electrical and computer engineering in the state of Louisiana. It offers programs of study leading to the M.S. and Ph.D. degrees. Areas of study are computers (including computer architectures, parallel and distributed processing, and fault-tolerant computing), electronics (including device-oriented electronics and solid-state materials), communication systems (including digital communication, data compression, and digital signal processing), control systems (including robust, adaptive, and time-varying control), and electric power (including power systems and power electronics). Students seeking the M.S. degree may select either a thesis (24 semester hours of course work plus 6 semester hours of thesis credit) or a nonthesis (36 semester hours of course work) option. The Ph.D. degree requires a dissertation and a minimum of 18 semester hours of course work beyond the requirements for the M.S. Students are encouraged to enter the Ph.D. program directly after receiving the B.S., in which case requirements are a dissertation and 48 semester hours of approved course work.

RESEARCH FACILITIES

The department possesses modern research facilities, including laboratories for materials science, VLSI, computer engineering, control systems, and power systems and electrical machines. The departmental computing facilities include a network of workstations, minicomputers, and personal computers supporting a variety of operating systems and applications. A University-wide System Network Computing Center offers supercomputer and mainframe power. The department's Solid State Laboratory is the only one of its kind in Louisiana to carry out interdisciplinary research in the areas of semiconductor material growth, characterization, device fabrication, and measurements. The laboratory has a 200-square-foot class 100 clean room for photolithography. The department's faculty is involved in the Center for Advanced Microstructures and Devices (CAMD), established by the University for carrying out research in X-ray lithography for submicron devices. The VLSI systems design laboratory houses graphics terminals, state-of-the-art Sun Workstations, and Berkeley CAD VLSI tools. The laboratory is used for instructional and research purposes, both for the designing of smart silicon VLSI chips and for VLSI device modeling. Designs can be sent via electronic mail to Silicon Foundry (MOSIS) for chip fabrication. The Systems Laboratory supports research in automatic control, communications, and signal processing. The laboratory houses several high-powered Sun Workstations and personal computers, a television camera and signal acquisition hardware and software, process simulators, and advanced system simulation software. The Power Electronics Laboratory offers the student hands-on experience with several power electronic devices, many of them rated at more than 6 kilowatts. Also available are facilities for experimenting with new power electronic circuit designs capable of handling large amounts of power. The department has access to the Remote Sensing and Image Processing Laboratory, the Nuclear Science Center, and other University facilities. The Division of Engineering Research provides additional support for research activities. The University library has holdings of about 2.1 million volumes and receives more than 23,800 periodical titles.

FINANCIAL AID

The department attempts to provide financial support to all qualified Ph.D. students and to outstanding M.S. students. Graduate assistantships in 1996–97 carried stipends ranging upward from $9200 for approximately half-time duties performed during the academic year. Assistantships for the fiscal year carried proportionately higher stipends. Graduate assistants are considered Louisiana residents for the purpose of fee assessments. Research performed under an assistantship normally provides the basis for the thesis. Fellowships, some of which cover fees, are also available; they require no duties of the recipient and included the $15,000-per-year LSU Graduate Fellowships and $17,000-per-year Board of Regents' Fellowships. Summer employment can be found in private industry.

COST OF STUDY

Tuition and fees in 1996–97 for full-time graduate students who are residents of Louisiana totaled $1336 per semester; nonresidents paid $2986 per semester. Diploma and thesis-binding fees were $40 and $20, respectively, for the master's degree and $60 and $45 for the doctorate.

LIVING AND HOUSING COSTS

The cost of dormitory rooms for single students in 1996–97 ranged from $715 to $1350 per semester. Unfurnished married student apartments were available for $245 to $320 per month. Off-campus apartments are plentiful; they rented for $250 to $550 per month.

STUDENT GROUP

Enrollment on the Baton Rouge campus is 25,317 (50 percent are women); graduate and professional enrollments total 5,131. Enrollment in the department for the fall of 1996 was 110 full-time graduate students, including 33 Ph.D. candidates. Students come to the University from every state in the Union and more than sixty other countries.

LOCATION

Baton Rouge, the state capital, is a growing industrial metropolis of 350,000. It is centered on the oil and petrochemical industries and is a deepwater port on the Mississippi River. The semitropical climate makes outdoor activities, such as golf and tennis, popular throughout the year, and the area is widely known for its fishing, boating, and hunting. Social life in Baton Rouge, relaxed and informal, is enhanced by a symphony orchestra, a little theater, and a Civic Center Complex. New Orleans, renowned for its southern hospitality, historic sites, antebellum charm, and recreational facilities, is located just 70 miles to the southeast.

THE UNIVERSITY

Louisiana State, founded in 1860, is on the southern edge of Baton Rouge, ½ mile east of the Mississippi River. The principal buildings, grouped on a landscaped 300-acre tract, exhibit a blend of contemporary design and the older Italian style, with its tile roofs and colonnaded passageways. Growth and improvements in buildings, facilities, and staff have been steady, and the University is now a modern multicampus facility well equipped to meet the educational, social, and cultural needs of its students. More than 26,000 graduate degrees have been awarded. The University is the largest and most comprehensive in Louisiana.

APPLYING

Applications for admission are considered throughout the year but should be submitted as early as possible. If financial assistance is desired, applications should be completed by March 1 for the fall and November 1 for the spring semesters. An application fee of $25 is required. Applicants are required to submit scores on the GRE General Test, and international students must pass the TOEFL with a minimum score of 550.

CORRESPONDENCE AND INFORMATION

For formal applications:

Office of the Registrar
Louisiana State University
Baton Rouge, Louisiana 70803-2804
Telephone: 504-388-1686

For further information and financial assistance:

Graduate Coordinator
Department of Electrical and Computer Engineering
Louisiana State University
Baton Rouge, Louisiana 70803-5901
Telephone: 504-388-5241
E-mail: ecegrad@ee.lsu.edu
World Wide Web: http://www.ee.lsu.edu/

LOUISIANA STATE UNIVERSITY
THE FACULTY AND THEIR RESEARCH

Pratul K. Ajmera, Professor; Ph.D., North Carolina State, 1975. Semiconductor materials and devices.

Jorge L. Aravena, Associate Professor; Ph.D., Michigan, 1980. System theory, computer-based control systems, signal processing.

Jack C. Cho, Associate Professor; Ph.D., Iowa State, 1967. Magnetic devices, magnetic bubble memory.

Leszeck Czarnecki, Associate Professor; Ph.D., 1969, D.Sc., 1984, Silesia Technical (Poland). Power electronics, nonsinusoidal systems, network analysis and synthesis.

Fred I. Denny, Associate Professor; Ph.D., Mississippi State, 1973. Electrical power systems, energy efficiency, control centers, distributed resources.

Ahmed A. El-Amawy, Professor; Ph.D., Iowa State, 1983. Microprocessors, computer architecture, VLSI processor arrays.

Martin Feldman, Professor; Ph.D., Cornell, 1962. Applied optics, integrated circuit lithography, metrology.

Guoxiang Gu, Associate Professor; Ph.D., Minnesota, 1988. Digital signal processing, controls.

Charles H. Harlow, Professor; Ph.D., Texas at Austin, 1967. Digital systems, image analysis, software engineering.

Manjunath Hegde, Associate Professor; Ph.D., Michigan, 1987. Communication and information theory, controls.

Kiki Ikossi-Anastasiou, Associate Professor; Ph.D., Cincinnati, 1986. Semiconductor heterostructure material and devices, molecular-beam epitaxy, measurement techniques for device characterization.

Subhash C. Kak, Professor; Ph.D., Indian Institute of Technology (Delhi), 1970. Information structures, parallel processing, data security, artificial intelligence.

Ralph A. Kinney, Professor; Ph.D., Florida, 1967. Field theory, fiber optics, computer applications.

David M. Koppelman, Assistant Professor; Ph.D., RPI, 1988. Advanced computer architectures, parallel processing, neural networks.

Gil S. Lee, Associate Professor; Ph.D., North Carolina State, 1987. Solid-state materials and devices, molecular-beam epitaxy quantum well structures, optoelectronics.

Alan H. Marshak, Professor and Chairman; Ph.D., Arizona, 1969. Semiconductor device physics, device analysis, transport theory, heterostructures.

Morteza Naraghi-Pour, Associate Professor; Ph.D., Michigan, 1986. Communication theory, image processing, signal processing.

Suresh Rai, Associate Professor; Ph.D., Kurukshetra (India), 1980. Computer networking, parallel processing, microprocessors, reliability.

Jagannathan Ramanujam, Associate Professor; Ph.D., Ohio State, 1990. Operating systems and programs for parallel machines, computer architecture.

Alexander Skavantzos, Associate Professor; Ph.D., Florida, 1987. Computer architecture, digital signal processing, parallel processing.

Ashok Srivastava, Associate Professor; Ph.D., Indian Institute of Technology (Delhi), 1975. Semiconductor device modeling, IC design and fabrication.

Jerry Trahan, Associate Professor; Ph.D., Illinois at Urbana-Champaign, 1988. Theory of computation, parallel processing, computational complexity, algorithm design and analysis.

Ramachandran Vaidyanathan, Associate Professor; Ph.D., Syracuse, 1990. Parallel computation, problem decomposition, parallel algorithms, interconnection networks, algorithm complexity.

Charles H. Voss, Professor; Ph.D., North Carolina State, 1963. Electronics and electrical systems.

Kemin Zhou, Associate Professor; Ph.D., Minnesota, 1988. Control and system theory, computer-aided system design, signal processing, industrial applications of advanced control theory.

Jianchao Zhu, Assistant Professor; Ph.D., Alabama in Huntsville, 1989. Control and system theory, communications, artificial intelligence, digital signal processing.

Publications and Research Grants

The graduate faculty of the department publishes an average of thirty-five refereed journal papers and forty-one conference presentations per year; graduate student collaborators often appear as coauthors. A complete list of publications of the last three years is available from the departmental graduate office.

Several faculty members hold associate editorships in prestigious scientific journals, and all faculty members are frequent reviewers for *IEEE Transactions* and other journals. Members of the faculty have also organized special sessions or given invited presentations at various events.

Faculty research is supported by grants from federal, state, and industrial sources, including LEQSF; NSF; U.S. Air Force; U.S. Army; U.S. Navy; Fingerhut Corporation; EPRI; LSU Utilities Power Research Consortium; Optek Technology, Inc.; Southern University and A&M, Meretel, Formosa Plastic Corporation; and Washington University. During the last three years, sponsored research contracts exceeded $5.2 million. Recent research grants include "Parallelizing Programs for Distributed Memory Multiprocessors," "Fault-Tolerant Neural Networks: Design Theories and Applications," "Dynamic Clustering," "High Efficiency Monolithic Tandem Solar Cells," "Parallel Computing with Reconfigurable Buses," "High Speed Heterojunction Bipolar Transistors," "Modeling and Control of Uncertain Systems with Applications," "Theory and Design of Branch-and-Combine Clock Networks," "Loop Transformations and Scheduling Techniques for Distributed Memory Processors," "Robust Stability and Stabilization of Systems with Real Parameter Uncertainty," "Neural Network Approach Towards Logic Testing and Design-for-Testability," "Alignment System for Anorad X-Ray Exposure Tool," "Development of High Speed Complementary Heterojunction Bipolar Transistors," "Modeling and Control of Uncertain Systems with Applications to Air Force Problems," "Employing Instruction History in the Management of Shared Memory Coherent Caches," "Languages, Compilers, and Runtime Systems for Parallel Architectures," "Robust Adaptive Control & Its Application to Missile Autopilots," "Algorithmic Scalability in Reconfigurable Bus-Based Models," "New Information Technology for Financial Data Processing," "Evaluation and Development of Methods and Equipment for Power Quality Improvement," "Multi-Channel Switching in Optical Fiber Networks," "Control of HSPS and SVC for Enhancing Power System Stability," "Fabrication of INSB Magnetoresistor," "High Performance Control Systems Design," "Learning and Generalization Using Neural Network with Applications to On-Line F-16 Reference Model," "A Coherent-Cache Computer for Research and Education," "Investigation of Capacity, Microwave Coexistence and Security in Wireless Network," "Power System Stability Study," and "Robust System Identification and Control Design."

LOYOLA UNIVERSITY CHICAGO

DEPARTMENT OF MATHEMATICAL AND COMPUTER SCIENCES
COMPUTER SCIENCE PROGRAM

PROGRAMS OF STUDY

The M.S. program at Loyola University Chicago offers a rigorous course of study to introduce students to new modes of inquiry and to deepen their awareness and understanding of recent progress in computer science. This program appeals to the computer science professional seeking an advanced degree, to professionals in other disciplines contemplating a career change, and to students who wish to prepare for entering a Ph.D. program in computer science.

The program consists of nine graduate courses: five are core courses in algorithms, architecture, operating systems, software engineering, and object-oriented programming; four are elective courses. Students may choose electives in various areas, including artificial intelligence, database design, programming languages, computer networks, parallel processing, and computer graphics. These course offerings parallel faculty research interests. A student may choose, as an elective course, individual study and research or a programming project directed by a faculty member.

A well-prepared student may finish the program in 1 to 1½ years. A student attending part-time may require a minimum of two years to complete the degree.

RESEARCH FACILITIES

The department has approximately thirty Sun Workstations and a similar number of Pentium PCs. These are all networked with the University computer system and the Internet and have access to Loyola's larger machines, which include an IBM 3081D mainframe and an IBM RS/6000. Dial-up and SLIP access is also available. The department runs its own Gopher and World Wide Web servers offering information about the department, courses offered, and faculty research. A variety of programming languages is available, including Ada, C, C++, Haskell, Java, LISP, ML, Pascal, Perl, PROLOG, S+, Scheme, and Tcl/Tk. Installed UNIX software includes FrameMaker, Gopher, IslandWrite, Mathematica, Mosaic, Netscape, SoftWindows, Tex/LaTex, XEmacs, Xess (a spreadsheet), and others.

Loyola's Sullivan Science Library contains an excellent collection of books in computer science, mathematics, and statistics and receives most major national and international journals in these areas.

FINANCIAL AID

The department offers teaching assistantships that pay full tuition and a stipend of $10,600 for nine months. Also available are research assistantships within the department and the data center.

COST OF STUDY

Tuition in 1997–98 for a 3-hour graduate course is $1323, and there is a University services and programs fee of $40 ($55 for students taking 6 or more hours). Tuition is waived for students holding graduate assistantships.

LIVING AND HOUSING COSTS

There are two campus residence halls that are exclusively for graduate students. Rooms and apartments are available in the campus neighborhood as well as throughout the Chicago area at widely varying costs.

STUDENT GROUP

There are about 155 graduate students in the department, with 120 studying full-time. It is an international group, with students coming from the United States, Canada, Europe, and Asia. Approximately 50 students graduate each year, and the majority of these take positions in software companies, research institutes, high schools, and colleges. Other graduates continue their studies toward a Ph.D. degree.

LOCATION

The department is located at the Lake Shore Campus of the University, which is on the north side of Chicago on the shore of Lake Michigan. The University has an active theater program and a museum of medieval art and sponsors many cultural events. The Chicago area has a large concentration of universities and colleges, and there are many world-renowned museums such as the Art Institute, the Museum of Science and Industry, and the Field Museum of Natural History. Chicago also has an outstanding array of musical organizations, including the Chicago Symphony Orchestra and the Lyric Opera.

THE UNIVERSITY AND THE DEPARTMENT

Loyola University Chicago was founded by the Society of Jesus in 1870 and is committed to the Jesuit tradition of education. Loyola is a Carnegie Doctoral I institution and enrolls 13,800 students. The University offers bachelor's degrees in forty-two fields, master's degrees in forty, and doctoral degrees in thirty-two. In fall 1996, there were 5,700 students enrolled in graduate and professional programs at the University. The department offers undergraduate and graduate degrees in computer science, mathematics, and statistics.

APPLYING

Applicants must take the GRE General Test and have the equivalent of a four-year undergraduate degree with a major in computer science or a related area. The Graduate School requires a minimum undergraduate GPA of 3.0 for admission, and international applicants must submit a TOEFL score of at least 550. Three letters of recommendation are required. Applicants who wish to be considered for an assistantship must submit applications by February 1 for the following academic year. Students may apply to be admitted for fall, spring, or summer sessions. Loyola University is an equal opportunity educator and employer.

CORRESPONDENCE AND INFORMATION

Graduate Program Director
Department of Mathematical and Computer Sciences
Loyola University Chicago
6525 North Sheridan Road
Chicago, Illinois 60626
Telephone: 773-508-3322
E-mail: info@math.luc.edu
World Wide Web: http://www.math.luc.edu/

LOYOLA UNIVERSITY CHICAGO
THE FACULTY AND THEIR RESEARCH

Emmanuel Nicholas Barron, Professor; Ph.D., Northwestern.
Martin Buntinas, Professor; Ph.D., IIT.
Christopher Colby, Assistant Professor; Ph.D., Carnegie Mellon.
John Del Greco, Associate Professor; Ph.D., Purdue.
Peter Lars Dordal, Associate Professor; Ph.D., Harvard.
Stephen Doty, Professor; Ph.D., Notre Dame.
Gerald Funk, Associate Professor; Ph.D., Michigan State.
Ronald Greenberg, Associate Professor; Ph.D., MIT.
Andrew N. Harrington, Associate Professor; Ph.D., Stanford.
Christine Haught, Associate Professor; Ph.D., Cornell.
William Cary Huffman, Professor; Ph.D., Caltech.
Anne Peters Hupert, Associate Professor; Ph.D., Chicago.
Radha Jagadeesan, Associate Professor; Ph.D., Cornell.
Robert Jensen, Professor; Ph.D., Northwestern.
Konstantin Läufer, Assistant Professor; Ph.D., NYU.
Wenxiong Liu, Assistant Professor; Ph.D., Minnesota.
Satya Lokam, Assistant Professor; Ph.D., Chicago.
Richard J. Lucas, Professor; Ph.D., Illinois at Chicago.
Richard J. Maher, Associate Professor; Ph.D., Northwestern.
Joseph H. Mayne, Associate Professor; Ph.D., IIT.
Anne Leggett McDonald, Associate Professor; Ph.D., Yale.
Gerard McDonald, Associate Professor; Ph.D., SUNY at Stony Brook.
Alan Saleski, Associate Professor; Ph.D., Berkeley.
Chandra Sekharan, Associate Professor; Ph.D., Clemson.
J. Richard VandeVelde, S.J., Associate Professor; Ph.D., Chicago.

Faculty research interests include programming languages, algorithms, software engineering, parallel processing, architecture, database design, artificial intelligence, graphics, system performance evaluation, combinatorics, graph theory, logic and automata, and algebraic coding theory.

McGILL UNIVERSITY

DEPARTMENT OF ELECTRICAL ENGINEERING

PROGRAMS OF STUDY

The Department of Electrical Engineering offers programs of graduate study leading to the degrees of Master of Engineering and Doctor of Philosophy. The areas of concentration include biomedical engineering, communication systems, computational analysis and design for electromagnetics, computer engineering, computer vision, control systems, engineering software, microwaves, optical waveguides, photonic systems, power electronics, power systems, robotics, solid-state devices, and VLSI systems.

The M.Eng. program requires the equivalent of one calendar year of full-time study but is normally completed in 1½ years. The degree may be obtained by the completion of six graduate courses and an externally examined thesis or nine graduate courses and an internally examined project.

The Ph.D. program requires the equivalent of two years of full-time study beyond the master's degree. While there are no formal course requirements for the degree, which is awarded upon completion of a satisfactory thesis, students usually select courses applicable to their research interests.

RESEARCH FACILITIES

The Department of Electrical Engineering has extensive facilities for all its main research areas. Laboratories for research into robotics, control, and vision are available in the associated Center for Intelligent Machines. The telecommunications laboratories have been recently reequipped and are centred on work in signal compression and wireless communication. These laboratories form part of the Canadian Institute for Telecommunications Research (CITR)—a federally funded network of Centres of Excellence. Digital and analogue design test laboratories form part of the Microelectronics and Computer Systems Laboratory. There are extensive research laboratories for antenna and microwave work as well as a fully equipped facility for optical fiber and integrated optics research. There is a fully equipped laboratory for photonic systems research, which includes continuous wave and femtosecond Ti:Sapphire lasers, diode lasers, extensive optics and optomechanics, and sophisticated electronic and imaging equipment. Solid-state facilities include measurement equipment for optical and electronic properties of materials and vacuum deposition and RF sputtering systems. The Computational Analysis and Design Laboratory provides tools for numerical analysis, visualization, interface design, and knowledge-based system development, as does the power systems facility. There is a well-equipped laboratory for power electronics and machines research. The department has extensive computer facilities available. Almost all the research machines are networked, providing access to a vast array of different hardware. In addition, there are links to the Centre de Recherche Informatique de Montreal (CRIM) and the University Computing Centre.

FINANCIAL AID

The department awards a number of graduate assistantships that carry an annual stipend of approximately Can$15,000 to qualified full-time graduate students. These are normally tenable for a maximum period of eighteen months for students registered for the M.Eng. degree and for thirty-six months for Ph.D. candidates. Graduate assistants and holders of other scholarships or fellowships may, with the approval of their supervisors, also undertake a teaching assistantship for an additional remuneration of between Can$400 and Can$3000 per year. Ample job opportunities exist for spouses because of McGill's proximity to Montreal's business section.

COST OF STUDY

In 1997–98, tuition for international students is Can$4453 per term for the M.Eng. program and Can$4048 per term for the Ph.D. program, which reduces to Can$1589 per term after the minimum residence period. For Canadian citizens and landed immigrants who are Quebec residents, the tuition fee is Can$1248 per term, which reduces to Can$1239 per term after the minimum residence period. For Canadian citizens and permanent residents who are not Quebec residents, tuition fees are Can$1848 per term for the M.Eng. program and Can$1248 per term for the Ph.D. program, which reduces to Can$1239 per term after the minimum residence period. Required health insurance is Can$578 per year for a single student (Can$2537 per year for family coverage). Books and supplies cost approximately Can$550 per year. These fees are set by the Quebec government and are subject to change.

LIVING AND HOUSING COSTS

The average living expenses for a student are Can$800 per month for a single student and Can$1100 per month for a married student. A large variety of apartments in subdivided older houses and apartment blocks are available within walking distance of the University. Monthly rents range upward from Can$300 for a one-room apartment and Can$400 for a two-room apartment.

STUDENT GROUP

The department has approximately 235 graduate students, almost all full-time, who come from all provinces of Canada and countries around the world to form a diverse and participative academic and social group. Most eventually take up careers in consulting engineering, university teaching, government professions, and industry, especially in high-technology sectors.

LOCATION

The University is situated on a beautiful campus in the heart of Montreal. The city is attractive and cosmopolitan, with a population of 2.5 million, the majority of whom speak French and the remainder English. Cultural activities abound: the main museums and concert halls are all within a few blocks of the University. An excellent and inexpensive public transport system of buses and subway trains allows for easy travelling in and around the city. Outdoor activities—skiing, sailing, cycling, and walking—are easily accessible.

THE UNIVERSITY

McGill University was founded in 1821. It is a nondenominational institution and operates in the English language. Other than engineering, its faculties are agriculture, arts, dentistry, education, graduate studies and research, law, management, medicine, religious studies, and science. Of 15,000 full-time students, about 3,000 are studying for advanced degrees. The Faculty of Engineering is one of Canada's oldest. It also has Departments of Chemical Engineering, Civil Engineering and Applied Mechanics, and Mining and Metallurgical Engineering and Schools of Architecture, Computer Science, and Urban Planning.

APPLYING

Applications can be obtained from the department. Completed applications, including official transcripts, reference letters, and Test of English as a Foreign Language (TOEFL) scores, Graduate Record Examinations (GRE) scores, and Advanced Engineering Test scores, must be received in the departmental office by February 1 for September admission.

Scores on the GRE General Test and Advanced Engineering Test are required of all applicants from colleges and universities outside Canada. A minimum total GRE score of 1800 is required. International applicants must give evidence of adequate proficiency in the English language by achieving a score of at least 600 on the Test of English as a Foreign Language (TOEFL). Admission and financial aid decisions are based on the student's transcripts, general academic background, letters of recommendation, and specific research goals. Applications are considered for admission for the fall session only.

CORRESPONDENCE AND INFORMATION

For further information:

Graduate Program Admissions
Department of Electrical Engineering
Room 603, McConnell Engineering Building
3480 University Street
McGill University
Montreal, Quebec H3A 2A7
Canada

Telephone: 514-398-7344
Fax: 514-398-4470
E-mail: grad@ee.lan.mcgill.ca

MCGILL UNIVERSITY
THE FACULTY AND THEIR RESEARCH

P. R. Bélanger, Ph.D., MIT. Control systems, industrial process control, parameter identification, robotics.

M. L. Blostein, Ph.D., Illinois. Digital signal processing, telecommunication networks and systems.

P. E. Caines, Ph.D., London; PE. Systems and control theory: stochastic systems, adaptive control, logic, hybrid and hierarchical systems.

J. J. Clark, Ph.D., British Columbia. Computer vision, analogue VLSI sensors, robotics.

F. Ferrie, Ph.D., McGill. Computer vision, robotics, image processing.

K. Fraser, M.Eng., McGill. Electronics.

F. D. Galiana, Ph.D., MIT. Power systems planning, operation and control, expert systems.

V. Hayward, Ph.D., Paris XI. Artificial intelligence, robotics and programming languages for robotics, applied control.

P. Kabal, Ph.D., Toronto. Digital signal/speech processing, adaptive filters/systems, data communications.

A. Kirk, Ph.D., London. Photonics, free-space digital optical systems, optically interconnected smart pixel arrays.

K. Khordoc, Ph.D., McGill. Formal specification and verification, timing verification, real-time systems.

H. Leib, Ph.D., Toronto. Digital communication, telecommunication systems, signal processing, statistical communication and information theory.

M. D. Levine, Ph.D., London. Computer vision, robotics, image processing.

D. A. Lowther, Ph.D., CNAA (U.K.). Numerical methods in electromagnetics, interactive graphics and visualization of electromagnetic fields, intelligent design systems for electromagnetic devices.

A. S. Malowany, Ph.D., McGill. Real-time, computer systems, robotics, virtual reality systems.

S. McFee, Ph.D., McGill. Computer modelling; simulation and visualization of electromagnetic fields in microwave, optical, and power-frequency devices.

H. Michalska, Ph.D., London. Control theory, nonlinear systems, stabilization, optimal control.

S. D. Morgera, Ph.D., Brown. Information theory, wireless/wireline networks, pattern recognition, digital signal and image processing, fast algorithms, optical enhanced computing, quantum computing.

B. T. Ooi, Ph.D., McGill. Power electronics, flexible AC transmission systems (FACTS), power quality conditioner, matrix converters.

D. V. Plant, Ph.D., Brown. Photonic/optoelectronic devices and systems, optomechanics, smart pixels, optical interconnects.

G. W. Roberts, Ph.D., Toronto. Analogue IC design and test, filter theory, synthesis and design.

N. C. Rumin, Ph.D., McGill. Circuit simulation and timing analysis, device modelling of VLSI systems.

I. S. Shih, Ph.D., McGill. Semiconducting properties and devices; properties of selenium, tellurium, and related semiconductors.

T. Szymanski, Ph.D., Toronto. Telecommunications, parallel computing, ATM switching, optical networks, optical switching.

J. Webb, Ph.D., Cambridge. Computer modelling, simulation and visualization of electromagnetic fields in microwave, optical, and power-frequency devices.

G. L. Yip, Ph.D., Toronto. Electromagnetic wave theory, fibers and integrated optics, guided-wave photonic devices, optical communication systems.

G. D. Zames, Sc.D., MIT. Control theory, multivariable feedback, H-∞ optimization, multivariable systems, adaptive systems, nonlinear feedback.

Associate Faculty

J. H. T. Bates, Ph.D., Canterbury (New Zealand). Biomedical engineering, mathematical modelling and instrumentation in respiratory physiology.

E. Cerny, Ph.D., McGill. Computer-aided design and verification (formal and by simulation) of microelectronic systems.

E. Dubois, Ph.D., Toronto. Image coding and processing, multidimensional signal processing.

G. L. Dudek, Ph.D., Toronto. Computational vision, artificial intelligence, robotic navigation, operating systems.

L.-G. Durand, Ph.D., Ecole Polytechnique/Montreal. Biomedical engineering.

A. Evans, Ph.D., Leeds (England). Brain imaging research using PET (positron emission tomography) and MRI (magnetic resonance imaging), 3-D image processing, cognitive neuroimaging, imaging physics.

M. J. Ferguson, Ph.D., Stanford. Telecommunication software, design, specification, formal methods.

W. R. J. Funnell, Ph.D., McGill. Biomedical engineering, hearing mechanics, finite-element method, medical informatics.

H. L. Galiana, Ph.D., McGill. Oculomotor and gaze control, signal processing, clinical and robotic applications.

G. Gao, Ph.D., MIT. Computer architecture, high-performance computer systems, parallel language compilers.

B. J. Gevay, M.Eng., McGill. Power system analysis, generation of electricity from renewable energy sources, energy conservation methods, environmental analysis, power system economics.

J. Gotman, Ph.D., McGill. Neurophysiology, biomedical engineering, analysis of electroencephalograms.

C. K. Jen, Ph.D., McGill. Ultrasonic sensors for on-line process control, ultrasonic nondestructive testing of materials and composites, fiber-optic smart materials.

G. Joos, Ph.D., McGill. Power electronics, flexible AC transmission systems (FACTS).

M. Kaplan, Ph.D., Cornell. Analysis and control of telecommunication networks.

R. E. Kearney, Ph.D., McGill. Biomedical engineering, human motor control, nonlinear identification.

J. Konrad, Ph.D., McGill. Image and video coding/processing, stereoscopic video, multidimensional signal processing.

M. A. Marin, Ph.D., UCLA. Computer systems, logic design, expert systems for maintenance and design, parallel computing.

D. McGillis, B.Eng., McGill. Power system planning and expert systems.

D. O'Shaughnessy, Ph.D., MIT. Digital speech coding, speech synthesis by rule, automatic speech recognition.

T. M. Peters, Ph.D., Canterbury (New Zealand). Biomedical engineering, medical imaging, neurosurgical instrumentation.

M. R. Solyemani, Ph.D., Concordia. Information theory, digital signal processing, satellite communications.

K. L. Watkin, Ph.D., Washington (Seattle). Biomedical engineering, medical imaging, ultrasound.

L. A. Wegrowicz, Ph.D., Leningrad; D.Sc., IFTR (Warsaw). Applied electrodynamics, antenna and propagation engineering.

MICHIGAN STATE UNIVERSITY

DEPARTMENT OF COMPUTER SCIENCE

PROGRAMS OF STUDY

The Department of Computer Science offers graduate study leading to the Master of Science and Doctor of Philosophy degrees. Advanced study is available in the areas of computer architecture, high-performance computing, design automation, distributed systems, computer networks, artificial intelligence, knowledge-based systems, database systems, parallel systems and algorithms, pattern recognition, image processing, computer vision, software engineering, and theory of computing. Interdisciplinary work with other departments is encouraged. There are three options for the M.S. program: thesis, project, and course work and qualifying examination. Ph.D. students must pass a written four-part qualifying exam within the first two years. A comprehensive examination with both written and oral parts is administered by the guidance committee prior to the dissertation work.

RESEARCH FACILITIES

The department operates a number of different laboratories with a variety of modern computing equipment. These include research laboratories for Intelligent Systems, High-Speed Networks and Performance (HSNP), High-Performance Computing, Software Engineering, and Pattern Recognition and Image Processing (PRIP). In addition, other laboratories support instruction in computer architecture, operating systems and networks, and software engineering and are at most times open for all uses by students. The department maintains more than 250 workstations and several subnets.

All computer science graduate students have a permanent account and electronic mail address. Students can keep in contact with colleagues, research groups, databases, and agencies throughout the world.

FINANCIAL AID

The department supports a total of about 100 graduate teaching and research assistants. Stipends range from about $1200 to $1400 per month for half-time appointments. A health plan is included with all assistantships. Assistants qualify for in-state tuition rates and receive tuition grants for 6 credits of study per term. Additional fellowship opportunities are available. Many students avail themselves of the opportunity to work as teaching or research assistants for other campus units.

COST OF STUDY

In 1996–97, graduate tuition was $203.50 per semester credit for Michigan residents and $411.75 per semester credit for nonresidents. In addition, per-semester fees included a $269 registration fee for students enrolling for more than 4 credits ($228 for students enrolling for 4 or fewer credits), a $218 engineering program fee for students enrolling for more than 4 credits ($120 for students enrolling for 4 or fewer credits), a $3 FM radio tax, a $9 student information technology fee, a $4.25 student newspaper tax (for students enrolling for 10 or more credits), and a $4.50 Council of Graduate Students tax.

LIVING AND HOUSING COSTS

Owen Graduate Residence Hall offers comfortable living in an atmosphere conducive to advanced study and the exchange of ideas. The 1996–97 rates were $1820 per single room occupancy per semester and $1558 per double room occupancy per semester, including residence hall tax. Furnished University apartments are available for married students. The 1996–97 family monthly rates were $370 for a one-bedroom apartment and $410 for a two-bedroom.

STUDENT GROUP

Currently, there are 100 M.S. and 62 Ph.D. students. Seventy students are supported as teaching assistants, 37 are supported as research assistants by the department, and approximately 20 are supported by other departments. Thirty-five M.S. and 11 Ph.D. students graduated in 1996.

LOCATION

Located near the center of lower Michigan, the East Lansing campus is famous for its beauty. The campus consists of 5,263 acres crossed by the Red Cedar River. There are more than 400 buildings and 8,000 trees. The metropolitan area has a population of about 400,000. Nearby Lansing is the capital of Michigan. There are cultural events to suit nearly every taste. The Wharton Center for the Performing Arts and the Breslin Student Events Center bring world-famous entertainment to campus. The cost of living is moderate and the secondary schools excellent. The area has many of the amenities of a large city without the congestion or pollution.

THE DEPARTMENT

The Department of Computer Science was formed in 1968 and continues to expand its graduate and research programs. Michigan State has been a pioneer in computing, providing computer courses for more than thirty years. The faculty members have varied research interests covering the areas mentioned under Program of Study. Related courses are offered in the Departments of Mathematics, Statistics, Electrical Engineering, Business, Psychology, and Linguistics and in the School of Communication.

APPLYING

In addition to other University and College of Engineering requirements, applicants must provide scores from the GRE General Test and from a Subject Test in computer science or in a closely related area. Applicants for the M.S. program must score in at least the 50th percentile on the Subject Test of the GRE. Ph.D. applicants must score in at least the 85th percentile on the GRE Subject Test in computer science; a related field may be accepted for students with exceptional records. Ph.D. applicants are encouraged to contact faculty members in their area of research interest. International students must submit a minimum score of 600 on the TOEFL.

CORRESPONDENCE AND INFORMATION

Graduate Director
Department of Computer Science
Michigan State University
East Lansing, Michigan 48824-1027
Telephone: 517-353-1679
Fax: 517-432-1061
E-mail: graddir@cps.msu.edu

MICHIGAN STATE UNIVERSITY
THE FACULTY AND THEIR RESEARCH

Betty H. C. Cheng, Assistant Professor; Ph.D., Illinois. Software tools, synthesis of procedural and data abstractions from formal specifications.

Moon Jung Chung, Associate Professor; Ph.D., Northwestern. Theoretical computer science, algorithms, design automation.

Laura K. Dillon, Associate Professor; Ph.D., Massachusetts at Amherst. Specification and analysis of real-time systems, temporal test oracles, formal methods.

Richard Enbody, Associate Professor; Ph.D., Minnesota. Design automation for digital systems, CAD, parallel algorithms, computer architecture.

Abdol H. Esfahanian, Associate Professor; Ph.D., Northwestern. Applied graph theory, fault-tolerant computing, analysis of algorithms.

John B. Eulenberg, Associate Professor; Ph.D., California, San Diego. Computational linguistics, communication enhancement systems.

John J. Forsyth, Associate Professor; Ph.D., Michigan State. Database theory.

Lewis H. Greenberg, Professor; Ph.D., Michigan State. Operating systems, programming languages, networks.

Herman D. Hughes, Professor; Ph.D., Southwestern Louisiana. Performance measurement and evaluation, programming languages, simulation.

Anil K. Jain, Professor; Ph.D., Ohio State. Pattern recognition, image processing, artificial intelligence.

Hans E. Lee, Associate Professor; Ph.D., Stanford. Artificial intelligence, man/machine interface.

Sridhar Mahadevan, Assistant Professor; Ph.D., Rutgers. Artificial intelligence, autonomous agents, machine learning, robotics.

Philip K. McKinley, Assistant Professor; Ph.D., Illinois. Computer networks, distributed systems, parallel processing, fault-tolerant systems.

Matthew W. Mutka, Assistant Professor; Ph.D., Wisconsin. Resource management in distributed and parallel systems, operating systems, modeling and simulation.

Lionel M. Ni, Professor; Ph.D., Purdue. Parallel and distributed processing, networks, operating systems, computer architecture.

Sakti Pramanik, Professor; Ph.D., Yale. Database systems, distributed database systems, parallel processing, optical computing, parallel architectures.

William F. Punch, Assistant Professor; Ph.D., Ohio State. Artificial intelligence, expert systems, diagnostic reasoning, genetic algorithms.

Richard J. Reid, Professor; Ph.D., Michigan State. Communication enhancement systems, computer system design.

Jon Sticklen, Associate Professor; Ph.D., Ohio State. Artificial intelligence, expert systems, knowledge engineering.

R. E. Kurt Stirewalt, Assistant Professor; Ph.D., Georgia Tech. Formal methods, user interfaces, software engineering.

George C. Stockman, Professor; Ph.D., Maryland. Computer vision, artificial intelligence.

Eric K. Torng, Assistant Professor; Ph.D., Stanford. On-line algorithms, scheduling, computational complexity, computational biology.

Bernhard L. Weinberg, Associate Professor; Ph.D., Wisconsin. Operating systems, compiler theory, alternate energy sources.

Donald J. Weinshank, Professor; Ph.D., Wisconsin. Computer simulations for science education, textual analysis via computer.

John J. Weng, Assistant Professor; Ph.D., Illinois. Computer vision, parallel architectures for real-time vision systems, neural networks, robotics.

Anthony S. Wojcik, Professor and Chairperson; Ph.D., Illinois. Design automation for digital systems, computer architecture, software engineering, automated reasoning.

MICHIGAN STATE UNIVERSITY

COLLEGE OF ENGINEERING
DEPARTMENT OF ELECTRICAL ENGINEERING

PROGRAMS OF STUDY

The department offers graduate programs leading to the Master of Science and Doctor of Philosophy degrees. The student's graduate program is designed in consultation with a faculty adviser of his or her choice. There are excellent opportunities for advanced theoretical and experimental study in the areas of communication sciences, computer engineering, controls, electronic devices and circuits, electrophysics, power, and robotics.

The master's degree requires 30 semester credits and is normally completed in twelve to eighteen months. The student may choose either the nonthesis or the thesis option (6 to 8 thesis credits). The Ph.D. candidate must pass a qualifying examination and a comprehensive examination. Normally, 42 credits of course work beyond the bachelor's degree and a minimum of 24 research credits are taken in a typical Ph.D. program, which requires approximately three to four years to complete. The Ph.D. program prepares the student for a career in advanced research and/or teaching.

RESEARCH FACILITIES

The electrical engineering department occupies approximately 7,200 square feet of research space in the 66,000-square-foot Engineering Research Facility. There are excellent laboratories and facilities for experimental research in backscattering, plasma science, microfabrication, robotics, antennas, computer design, and CAD/CAM. Computer facilities available to the department include Sun-4/390 SPARCservers, many Sun and HP workstations, and a large number of IBM-compatible personal computers. In addition, the department has the use of an NCUBE computer and parallel computers at industrial sites. The College of Engineering computer facilities, administered through the A. H. Case Center for Computer-Aided Engineering and Manufacturing, include numerous 386/486 microcomputers in open labs and numerous Sun and HP workstations featuring high-resolution color graphics. Many commercial-grade design, finite-element, graphics, simulation, and support software packages are available. Students have access to various University mainframe computers. College-wide and University-wide Ethernet and FDDI fiber-optic networking is well established. Access to supercomputers is provided through connections to all major academic and research networks.

The College's engineering library contains 58,000 volumes and 630 journal subscriptions. The University library system has more than 3 million volumes and more than 21,000 journal subscriptions.

FINANCIAL AID

Research and teaching assistantships and fellowships are available to qualified students. In 1996–97, annual half-time assistantship stipends were $15,191 for first-year M.S. students and $18,184 for senior M.S. students and Ph.D. students. Up to 6 credits of tuition per semester are waived for students with assistantships, and nonresident graduate assistants pay the resident tuition rate on all additional credits. Fellowships range from $100 per semester to $16,152 per calendar year.

COST OF STUDY

In 1997–98, graduate tuition is $216 per semester credit for Michigan residents and $437 per semester credit for nonresidents. In addition, per semester fees include a $283 registration fee for students enrolling for more than 4 credits ($234 for students enrolling for 4 or fewer credits), a $232 engineering program fee for students enrolling for more than 4 credits ($128 for students enrolling for 4 or fewer credits), a $3 FM radio tax, a $9 student information technology fee, a $4.25 student newspaper tax (for students enrolling for 10 or more credits), and a $4.50 Council of Graduate Students tax.

LIVING AND HOUSING COSTS

Owen Graduate Residence Hall offers comfortable living in an atmosphere conducive to advanced study and the exchange of ideas. The 1996–97 rates were $1114 per double-room occupancy per semester, including residence hall tax. Furnished University apartments are available for married students. The 1996–97 family monthly rates were $370 for a one-bedroom apartment and $410 for a two-bedroom apartment.

STUDENT GROUP

For the 1996 fall term, 41,545 students were enrolled on Michigan State University's East Lansing campus; 31,637 were undergraduates, 6,616 were graduate students, and 1,395 were professional students. Students come from every state in the Union and about 107 other countries. Enrollment in the College of Engineering in the 1996 fall semester was 4,112, of whom 3,457 were undergraduate students and 670 were graduate students.

LOCATION

Michigan State University is located in the south-central part of the state in East Lansing, which is approximately 80 miles northwest of Detroit and about 210 miles northeast of Chicago. East Lansing is a city of about 30,000 people in a metropolitan area of more than 270,000. Lansing, the capital of Michigan, is located just 4 miles to the west. Many summer and winter recreational activities are located within driving distance of East Lansing.

THE UNIVERSITY

Michigan State University, founded in 1855, was the prototype institution for the nation's land-grant colleges. The enrollment of 42,000 makes MSU one of the largest single-campus universities in the nation. Such a large campus provides the engineering student with wide exposure to and interdisciplinary opportunities with the natural sciences, medicine, and business. Engineering is one of the most popular and demanding majors on campus. The number of graduate students and faculty members and the amount of research expenditures have grown considerably in the past ten years.

APPLYING

Application forms and instructions for submitting transcripts, letters of recommendation, and related material may be obtained from the department. Study may begin in September, January, or May; applications are accepted at any time but should be received at least two months prior to the expected starting date. Most fellowship and assistantship opportunities arise in the fall semester; applications for the fall semester should be submitted by February 1 if financial aid is desired. The GRE General Test is required for international students and recommended for domestic students, and the TOEFL is required for international students. A minimum TOEFL score of 580 is necessary for consideration.

CORRESPONDENCE AND INFORMATION

Professor Michael Shanblatt, Graduate Program Coordinator
Department of Electrical Engineering
2120 Engineering Building
Michigan State University
East Lansing, Michigan 48824-1226
Telephone: 517-355-5066
         517-353-6773
E-mail: eegradoff@egr.msu.edu

MICHIGAN STATE UNIVERSITY
THE FACULTY AND THEIR RESEARCH

Dean M. Aslam, Associate Professor; Ph.D., Rhenish-Westphalian Technical (Aachen), 1983. Diamond film microsensors, Si cold cathodes, MOS technology. (Telephone: 353-6329; e-mail: aslam@egr.msu.edu)

Jes Asmussen Jr., Professor and Chairperson; Ph.D., Wisconsin, 1967. Plasmas, microwave processing of materials, ion and electrothermal thrusters. (Telephone: 355-4620; e-mail: asmussen@egr.msu.edu)

Virginia Ayres, Associate Professor; Ph.D., Purdue, 1985. Electronic and thermal properties of diamond material, electron beam sources and devices, plasmas. (Telephone: 355-5066; e-mail: ayres@egr.msu.edu)

Theodore A. Bickart, Professor and Dean of Engineering; Ph.D., Johns Hopkins, 1960. Dynamical systems, network theory, digital systems, mathematical software. (Telephone: 355-5113; e-mail: bickart@egr.msu.edu)

Kun-Mu Chen, Professor; Ph.D., Harvard, 1960. Electromagnetic fields, antennas, radar detection, medical applications. (Telephone: 355-6502; e-mail: chen@egr.mus.edu)

John R. Deller Jr., Professor; Ph.D., Michigan, 1979. Speech processing, system identification, neural network models in speech, biomedical signal processing. (Telephone: 353-8840; e-mail: deller@egr.msu.edu)

P. David Fisher, Professor; Ph.D., Johns Hopkins, 1967. Digital circuit design, instrumentation. (Telephone: 355-5241, e-mail: fisher@egr.msu.edu)

Ronald J. Fredericks, Adjunct Professor; Ph.D., Michigan, 1970. Half-time Associate Professor, Grand Valley State University; private consulting engineer. Electronic devices, optoelectronic sensors and systems. (Telephone: 616-791-9134)

Erik D. Goodman, Professor; Ph.D., Michigan, 1972. Computer-aided design and manufacturing (CAD/CAM), interactive computer graphics, genetic algorithms. (Telephone: 353-9695; e-mail: goodman@egr.msu.edu)

Timothy Grotjohn, Associate Professor; Ph.D., Purdue, 1986. Semiconductor physics and devices, integrated-circuits modeling, plasmas modeling and diagnostics. (Telephone: 353-8906; e-mail: grotjohn@egr.msu.edu)

Hassan Khalil, Professor; Ph.D., Illinois, 1978. Nonlinear control, singular perturbation methods, robust control. (Telephone: 355-6689; e-mail: khalil@egr.msu.edu)

James D. Mosko, Adjunct Professor; Ph.D., Purdue, 1968. Senior Scientist and Director of Diometrics Evaluation Laboratory, CTA Incorporated, Rockville, Maryland. Speech science and speech processing, intelligent signal processing, biometrics. (Telephone: 301-816-1399; e-mail: jmosko@smtplink.cta.com)

Majid Nayeri, Assistant Professor; Ph.D., Illinois, 1988. Parameter estimation, system identification, adaptive signal processing, multirate signal processing (Telephone: 353-1857; e-mail: majid@egr.msu.edu)

Robert D. Nowak, Assistant Professor; Ph.D., Wisconsin, 1995. Signal and image processing, nonlinear and statistical signal processing, applications in medicine and communications. (Telephone: 355-5235; e-mail: nowak@egr.msu.edu)

Dennis P. Nyquist, Professor; Ph.D., Michigan State, 1966. Electromagnetic theory, radiation, scattering, layered media, integrated circuits, guided-wave optics. (Telephone: 355-1771; e-mail: nyquist@egr.msu.edu)

Percy A. Pierre, Professor; Ph.D., Johns Hopkins, 1967. Communications theory, stochastic processes, signal detection and estimation. (Telephone: 432-5148; e-mail: pierre@egr.msu.edu)

Donnie K. Reinhard, Professor; Ph.D., MIT, 1973. Electronic materials and devices, plasma-assisted etching and deposition. (Telephone: 355-5214; e-mail: reinhard@egr.msu.edu)

James A. Resh, Associate Professor; Ph.D., Illinois, 1963. Nonlinear systems, computer-aided circuit analysis and design, microcomputers. (Telephone: 355-7649; e-mail: resh@egr.msu.edu)

Edward J. Rothwell, Associate Professor; Ph.D., Michigan State, 1985. Transient electromagnetic scattering, antennas, radar target identification, electromagnetic theory. (Telephone: 355-5231; e-mail: rothwell@egr.msu.edu)

Diane Thiede Rover, Associate Professor; Ph.D., Iowa State, 1989. Computer engineering, advanced architecture computers, performance measurement and visualization. (Telephone: 353-7735; e-mail: rover@egr.msu.edu)

Fathi M. A. Salam, Professor; Ph.D., Berkeley, 1983. Nonlinear systems and circuits, analog VLSI and neural networks, adaptive and robust control. (Telephone: 355-7695; e-mail: salam@egr.msu.edu)

Robert A. Schlueter, Professor; Ph.D., Polytechnic of Brooklyn, 1972. Stability; planning, operation, and control; and nonlinear and adaptive control applied to power systems. (Telephone: 355-5244; e-mail: schluete@egr.msu.edu)

Michael A. Shanblatt, Professor; Ph.D., Pittsburgh, 1980. Computer engineering, VLSI architectures for enhanced control, neural networks, VLSI design methodologies. (Telephone: 353-7249; e-mail: mas@egr.msu.edu)

John R. Short, Adjunct Professor; Ph.D., Michigan State, 1971. Director for Submarine Combat Systems, Naval Undersea Warfare Center Division, Newport. Underwater acoustics and signal processing, decision and estimation theory, advanced submarine combat system design. (Telephone: 401-841-3924; e-mail: shortjr@npt.nuwc.navy.mil)

Marvin Siegel, Professor; Ph.D., Harvard, 1970. Electromagnetic theory, communication theory, biomedical signal processing. (Telephone: 355-7688; e-mail: siegel@egr.msu.edu)

Elias G. Strangas, Associate Professor; Ph.D., Pittsburgh, 1980. Electrical machinery, finite-element methods for electromagnetic fields, electrical drives, power electronics. (Telephone: 353-3517; e-mail: strangas@egr.msu.edu)

Alexander Y. Tetelbaum, Adjunct Professor; Ph.D., Kiev Polytechnical Institute, 1975. Zycad Company. Design automation of VLSI systems, system design methodologies, graph theory, artificial intelligence, computer architecture.

R. Lal Tummala, Professor; Ph.D., Michigan State, 1970. Robotics, digital control, and manufacturing systems. (Telephone: 355-7453; e-mail: tummala@egr.msu.edu)

Mervin C. Vincent, Adjunct Professor; Ph.D., Michigan State, 1967. Technical Fellow, Electromagnetics Technology, Boeing Defense and Space Group. Electromagnetic fields, antennas, and radar detection. (Telephone: 206-662-0459)

Chin-Long Wey, Professor; Ph.D., Texas Tech, 1983. Fault-tolerant design of microelectronics structures, VLSI design and testing, logic synthesis for testability, and analog/digital circuits faults diagnosis. (Telephone: 353-0665; e-mail: wey@egr.msu.edu)

Gregory M. Wierzba, Associate Professor; Ph.D., Wisconsin, 1978. Analog electronics, macromodeling, computer-aided design, active filters. (Telephone: 355-5225; e-mail: wierzba@egr.msu.edu)

Ning Xi, Assistant Professor; D.Sc., Washington (St. Louis), 1993. Manufacturing, automation and robotics, nonlinear control, intelligent planning and distributed computing. (Telephone: 355-5066)

H. Roland Zapp, Associate Professor and Associate Chairperson; Ph.D., Stanford, 1969. Signal processing, data acquisition, communication, ultrasonic imaging, alternative energy systems. (Telephone: 355-5230; e-mail: zapp@egr.msu.edu)

MICHIGAN TECHNOLOGICAL UNIVERSITY

DEPARTMENT OF COMPUTER SCIENCE

PROGRAM OF STUDY

The Department of Computer Science offers a Master of Science in computer science and, through the College of Engineering, the department offers an interdisciplinary Ph.D. in computational science and engineering.

The M.S. program requires the completion of 45 quarter credits. Breadth is achieved through course work in operating systems, software engineering, design and analysis of algorithms, and theory of computation, programming languages, and computer architecture. Students are expected to do additional course work in computer science and/or related areas as well as select an area in which they will achieve greater depth. This depth is generally achieved through the preparation of a thesis, though students can also fulfill this requirement with a project or additional course work. Students with a half-time assistantship usually take two years to complete the M.S. program.

The computational science and engineering Ph.D. program is open to students who have completed an M.S. degree in the sciences or engineering. It is an interdisciplinary program that allows students either to focus on how to solve large-scale, computationally intensive problems in the sciences and engineering or to pursue traditional computer science research programs at the doctoral level. The program also supports research activities that produce environments and methods for solving computationally intensive problems in the sciences and engineering. Students must complete a minimum of 24 credits of course work, pass a comprehensive examination, and successfully defend a dissertation. After completing the first two of these requirements, students spend the majority of their efforts contributing to a research project with a faculty member or research group. Students with a half-time assistantship are expected to take approximately four years to complete the Ph.D. program.

RESEARCH FACILITIES

Departmental research equipment available to faculty members and graduate students includes high-end Sun Workstations as well as special-purpose DEC Alpha machines and SCIs. Department faculty members and graduate students also have access to research computing facilities in the Center for Experimental Computation, which supports various UNIX machines and other special-purpose hardware. Access to supercomputer centers off campus is also available.

FINANCIAL AID

A number of graduate teaching assistantships are available within the department. The 1996–97 stipends were $2600 for M.S. students and $3020 for Ph.D. students, plus tuition for each of the three quarters of the academic year. Graduate research assistantships are available on a limited basis.

COST OF STUDY

For 1996–97, tuition costs were $110 per credit hour for Michigan residents and $253 per credit hour for all other students.

LIVING AND HOUSING COSTS

Apartments and dormitory rooms for students are available in University-owned buildings; room and board costs start at $4284 (double occupancy) for the 1996–97 academic year. Housing for married students is $326 per month for a one-bedroom apartment and $397 for a two-bedroom apartment. Utilities are included, and the apartments are partially furnished. Reasonably priced off-campus housing is located nearby.

STUDENT GROUP

Approximately 25 students are currently enrolled in the M.S. program. Most of these students are supported by graduate teaching assistantships, graduate research assistantships, or other forms of University-funded support. The CS&E Ph.D. program started in 1994 and currently has 4 students enrolled. Michigan Technological University has more than 6,000 students enrolled in its undergraduate and graduate programs. The department has approximately 270 undergraduate majors and 30 graduate students.

STUDENT OUTCOMES

Graduates of the program have found employment in the commercial sector and in government laboratories. Some have gone on to earn Ph.D. degrees at other institutions, and several have started their own companies. Commercial sector employers include AT&T, EDS, Ford, General Dynamics, GE Aerospace, HP, Honeywell, IBM, Motorola, Sprint, Sun Microsystems, TI, and Xerox. Government laboratory employers include Goddard Spaceflight Center, NASA Ames Research Center, and Los Alamos National Laboratory. Graduates completed their doctorates at such institutions as Clemson, Georgia Tech, Michigan State, and Rice Universities.

LOCATION

Michigan Technological University is located in Houghton, Michigan, a town of 7,000 on the Keweenaw Peninsula, on the northwestern side of the Upper Peninsula of Michigan. In the lee of Lake Superior, summers are mild and winters are temperate, with an average of 250 inches of snow. Autumn and spring are cool and colorful. The remoteness imposed by geography is mitigated by the beauty of the countryside, which is unspoiled and free of pollution. There are abundant opportunities for outdoor recreational activities, such as hiking, fishing, boating, and cross-country and Alpine skiing.

THE UNIVERSITY

Michigan Technological University has an excellent reputation in engineering and science education. By national standards, the University has superior laboratories and equipment and excels in several spheres of science and technology. Michigan Tech was founded in 1885 as a school of mining and metallurgical engineering, and, although it maintains leadership in these areas, it has expanded its curriculum to encompass all areas of science and technology.

There are approximately twenty buildings on the main campus. They house laboratories, classrooms, lecture halls, gymnasiums, the student union, and the library. The University also operates an indoor ice arena, an eighteen-hole golf course, 8 kilometers of Nordic ski trails, its own ski hill with a chair lift, and an indoor tennis center. A major athletic-recreational complex contains a ½-mile indoor track, two pools, handball courts, volleyball courts, basketball courts, dance rooms, and a rifle range. A variety of cultural attractions, many of which are presented at the new fine arts and cultural center, are sponsored by the University.

APPLYING

Application forms and instructions for submitting the appropriate materials can be obtained from the department and the department's Web site. Applicants for the M.S. program should have a B.S. degree in computer science. Students with a background in another area are considered for admission if there is evidence in their backgrounds to indicate likelihood of success in the M.S. program. Evaluations are based on GRE scores, previous academic performance, experience in computer science, and letters of recommendation. Students may also submit papers or projects in the area of computer science for consideration by the admission committee.

Applicants for the CS&E Ph.D. program should have an M.S. degree in some field of science, engineering, or mathematics. Applicants backgrounds are matched with on-going interdisciplinary research projects across the University.

GRE General Test scores are required for all applicants whose degrees are not from a U.S. institution. Although not required, the GRE Subject Test in computer science is also strongly recommended for M.S. applicants. TOEFL scores are required for all applicants whose native language is not English.

Applications for the fall term received by February 15 are generally evaluated by March 30. Most financial aid decisions are also made at this time. Applications received later, as well as applications for other terms, are evaluated on an individual basis.

CORRESPONDENCE AND INFORMATION

Graduate Admissions Committee
Department of Computer Science
Michigan Technological University
Houghton, Michigan 49931-1295

Telephone: 906-487-2209
Fax: 906-487-2283
E-mail: csdept@mtu.edu
World Wide Web: http://cs.mtu.edu

MICHIGAN TECHNOLOGICAL UNIVERSITY
THE FACULTY AND THEIR RESEARCH

S. Carr, Assistant Professor; Ph.D. (computer science), Rice, 1993. Compiler optimization.

X. Huang, Associate Professor; Ph.D. (computer science), Penn State, 1990. Sequence comparison algorithms, parallel applications in computational biology.

J. Lowther, Associate Professor; Ph.D. (computer science), Iowa, 1975. Artificial intelligence, computer graphics.

J. Mayo, Assistant Professor; Ph.D. (computer science), William and Mary, 1997. Distributed systems, clock synchronization, and operating systems.

L. Ott, Chair and Associate Professor; Ph.D. (computer science), Purdue, 1978. Software metrics.

D. Poplawski, Associate Professor; Ph.D. (computer science), Purdue, 1978. Parallel computer architectures, parallel processing, performance evaluation.

S. Seidel, Associate Professor; Ph.D. (computer science), Iowa, 1979. Interprocessor communication algorithms, massively parallel computers, interconnection networks.

C. Shene, Assistant Professor; Ph.D. (computer science), Johns Hopkins, 1992. Geometric/solid modeling, computer-aided design, computer graphics, computational geometry.

P. Sweany, Assistant Professor; Ph.D. (computer science), Colorado State, 1992. Compiler optimization and parallel architectures.

RESEARCH AREAS

Artificial Intelligence. Work in artificial intelligence has emphasized issues in knowledge representation. The acquisition, use, verification, inference, and/or revision of knowledge is crucial in the operation of problem solvers. To study these issues in knowledge representation, various representation techniques and representation languages are used to develop specific problem solvers.

Computer Architecture. Current work is focused on two areas of instruction level parallelism: highly efficient speculative execution and reduction in average memory access times. Efficient speculative execution requires fetching and executing instructions before it is known whether the instructions are supposed to execute. Current research looks at finding ways to quickly fetch a large amount of instructions in the presence of conditional branch instructions. Reduction in average memory access time involves new cache structures and burst transfers of large blocks of memory to cache.

Compiler Optimization. Current work is in developing techniques to generate excellent code for instruction-level parallel (ILP) architecture such as VLIW and superscalar computers. Efficient code generation for ILP architecture requires careful ordering of the operations to be performed during execution. This ordering, called instruction scheduling, is the driving force behind ILP code generation. Within that larger context, on-going projects include developing and testing novel techniques to perform register assignment for ILP architectures, improving existing loop scheduling ("software piplining") methods, and making effective use of an ILP architecture's memory hierarchy, including cache.

Computational Biology. Current work is focused on the development of algorithms and software for finding similarity correlations among DNA and protein sequences. A similarity correlation between two sequences is represented by an alignment of the sequences in a way that maximizes the pairs of identical symbols of the sequences. Dynamic programming is used to compute an optimal alignment of two sequences. This research contributes to the Human Genome Project, whose ultimate goal is to obtain the complete human DNA sequence of about three billion nucleotides.

Computational Science. Research in this area is interdisciplinary in nature, combining current computing practices and applied mathematics with applications from the sciences and engineering. Work in this area is determined on the basis of the combined expertise of the students and faculty members and often involves faculty members from other departments of the University.

Communication Algorithms. Interprocessor communication is often an expensive part of applications designed for massively parallel distributed memory computers. Recent work has centered on the development of a communication model for the Intel Paragon mesh. Algorithms have been studied for frequently encountered communication problems, such as the broadcast, scatter/gather, and complete exchange problems. Modeling of message passing protocols is also being developed in order to study the behavior of those protocols and to discover ways in which the latency of message passing can be reduced.

Geometric Modeling. Geometric modeling is the technique for describing the shape of an object and to simulate dynamic processes. It is a primary ingredient in computer-aided design and computer-aided manufacturing (CAD/CAM), computer graphics, computer art, animation, simulation, computer vision, visualization, and robotics. Recent research has been aimed at investigating the possible use of lower degree algebraic surfaces in geometric modeling. This includes robust algorithms for detecting and calculating the intersection of two geometric models, simple geometric representations for lower degree (i.e., three or four) algebraic surfaces, and surface approximation, interpolation, and reconstruction. Another important focus is in developing techniques for visualizing and interrogating surfaces with animation.

Distributed Systems. Recent work includes the development of methods for the efficient evaluation of the global state of distributed computations based on the use of roughly synchronized clocks. Changes in technology for both hardware and software clock synchronization are providing ever tighter clock skews at lower costs. Research in this area will consider the design of new distributed applications based on an assumption of the availability of a global time base.

Software Measurement. A significant difficulty in improving the software development process and the quality of software produced is in identifying when actual improvements have occurred. One technique for identifying such improvements is through measurement. Recent research has focused on measuring the functional cohesion of software developed using an imperative paradigm and exploring the existence of relationships between functional cohesion and other software quality and software process attributes in that paradigm. Research is also underway to formulate methodologies to quantitatively evaluate other paradigms such as the object-oriented paradigm

MISSISSIPPI STATE UNIVERSITY

COLLEGE OF ENGINEERING
PROGRAMS IN COMPUTER SCIENCE, COMPUTER ENGINEERING, AND COMPUTATIONAL ENGINEERING

PROGRAMS OF STUDY

The College of Engineering offers graduate programs of study and research leading to the M.S. and Ph.D. degrees in three computing fields: computer science, computer engineering, and computational engineering. The computer science (CS) and computer engineering (CPE) graduate programs are administered by the Department of Computer Science and the Department of Electrical and Computer Engineering, respectively. The computational engineering (CME) graduate program is interdisciplinary and includes faculty members from most engineering disciplines, computer science, and mathematics.

Areas of research and study supported by the three fields are artificial intelligence (CS), graphics and visualization (CS, CPE, CME), software engineering (CS), digital integrated circuit design (CPE), high-performance computing (CS, CPE, CME), signal and information processing (CPE), embedded microprocessor systems (CPE), communications (CPE, CS), domain-specific computational technologies (CME), computational mathematics (CME), and parallel and distributed computing (CS, CPE, CME). The computational engineering program requires students to complete a program of study with adequate work in a specific computational engineering application area, high-performance computing, and computational mathematics.

All three M.S. programs require 30 to 35 credit hours and offer both thesis and nonthesis options. The Ph.D. programs consist of course work, examinations, a dissertation that reports original scholarly research, and an oral presentation and defense of the dissertation.

RESEARCH FACILITIES

Research facilities are housed in the Simrall Electrical Engineering Building, a modern 95,000-square-foot facility; the Butler Computer Science Building, a newly renovated 35,000-square-foot facility; and the Engineering Research Center for Computational Field Simulation, a 44,000-square-foot building designed for cross-disciplinary research. Both Simrall and Butler house faculty offices, modern classrooms, research laboratories, and workstation laboratories for graduate students. The Engineering Research Center Building has an electronic classroom, a state-of-the-art workstation laboratory/classroom, and a general-purpose workstation laboratory supplementing the extensive desktop infrastructure. Computer equipment includes three Silicon Graphics Onyx RealityEngine2 servers, two Silicon Graphics Power Challenge XL servers, one Power Challenge L computer server, four SUN4/690 servers, a dedicated Archive/FTP/WWW server, a 32-node Intel parallel processor, a 32-processor SuperMSPARC (designed and constructed at the ERC), 139 Sun SPARCstation class workstations, seventy-nine Silicon Graphics workstations, two virtual reality pushbooms, and assorted other personal computers, printers, and peripherals.

FINANCIAL AID

Research and teaching assistantships are available for highly qualified applicants. Stipends for assistantships vary. The College of Engineering offers Barrier and Honda Graduate Fellowships for both M.S. and Ph.D. students. MSU is a member of the National Consortium for Graduate Degrees for Minorities in Engineering and Science (GEM), which supports students from minority groups in advanced study in engineering. Approximately 90 percent of graduate students are on assistantship or fellowship.

COST OF STUDY

In 1996–97, tuition and fees were $1315.50 per semester for Mississippi residents and $2725.50 per semester for nonresidents. Assistantships and fellowships include a waiver of both resident and nonresident tuition.

LIVING AND HOUSING COSTS

Critz Hall is an on-campus dormitory for graduate students that costs $250 to $300 per month, which includes all utilities, including cable television. Each unit contains a refrigerator-freezer-microwave combination. Housing for married students is available in Aiken Village, where the cost of unfurnished one- and two-bedroom apartments is $200 to $225, including all utilities except electricity. Off-campus apartments rent for $300 to $600 per month.

STUDENT GROUP

Approximately 100 graduate students are enrolled on campus in the three programs. Because of the nature of the programs and the location of the University, almost all of the students are full-time. More than one third are enrolled in the doctoral programs. Additional students are enrolled in programs at the U.S. Corps of Engineers Waterways Experiment Station and at the Stennis Space Flight Center.

STUDENT OUTCOMES

Students who are awarded graduate degrees in computing fields at Mississippi State University work for a wide variety of high-tech companies, including Microsoft, Intel, Federal Express, Intergraph, Texas Instruments, and many others. Graduates are also placed in a variety of government positions and at universities involved in both teaching and research.

LOCATION

Mississippi State University is located in a rural area of east Mississippi and adjoins the small town of Starkville (population 18,500). Mississippi State is within easy driving distance of Jackson, Mississippi (120 miles); Birmingham, Alabama (140 miles); Memphis, Tennessee (179 miles); and New Orleans, Louisiana (307 miles). Air service is available through the Golden Triangle Regional Airport, located 16 miles east of the campus.

THE UNIVERSITY AND THE COLLEGE

Mississippi State was established as a land-grant college in 1880 and has grown to be the largest university in the state of Mississippi. It is the only institution in the state listed among the nation's top 100 research institutions by the National Science Foundation and designated as a Doctoral I university by the Southern Regional Educational Board. The College of Engineering consists of ten operating departments and units. Since the first freshman class enrolled in engineering in 1892, more than 15,000 engineers have gone on to become respected leaders in many diverse fields across the state, nation, and world.

APPLYING

Applications for graduate study for the 1998–99 academic year are accepted at any time. Preference for awarding assistantships is given to applications received by February 1 for summer or fall semester admission or October 1 for spring semester admission. All applicants are required to submit scores for the general test of the GRE, and the TOEFL is required of international students whose native language is not English.

CORRESPONDENCE AND INFORMATION

Computer Science Graduate Program
Graduate Studies Committee
Box 9637
Mississippi State, Mississippi 39762
Telephone: 601-325-2756
Fax: 601-325-8997
E-mail:
   grad-coord@cs.msstate.edu
WWW: http://www.cs.msstate.edu/

Computer Engineering Graduate Program
Electrical and Computer Engineering
Box 9571
Mississippi State, Mississippi 39762
Telephone: 601-325-3667
Fax: 601-325-2298
E-mail: harden@ece.msstate.edu
WWW: http://www.ece.msstate.edu/

Computational Engineering Graduate Program
Coordinator of Graduate Studies
NSF Engineering Research Center
Box 9627
Mississippi State, Mississippi 39762
Telephone: 601-325-8278
Fax: 601-325-7692
E-mail: grad-coord@erc.msstate.edu
WWW: http://www.erc.msstate.edu/

MISSISSIPPI STATE UNIVERSITY

THE FACULTY AND THEIR RESEARCH

Artificial Intelligence, Information and Signal Processing
G. Boggess, Assistant Professor; Ph.D., Illinois. Cognitive science, neural networks, genetic algorithms, computational linguistics.
L. Boggess, Professor; Ph.D., Illinois. Artificial intelligence, natural language processing, speech recognition.
S. Bridges, Associate Professor; Ph.D., Alabama in Huntsville. Expert systems, knowledge discovery in databases.
D. Dearholt, Professor; Ph.D., Washington (Seattle). Human-computer interaction, associative graphs.
J. Hodges, Professor; Ph.D., Southwestern Louisiana. Knowledge representation, knowledge discovery in databases, expert systems, document understanding.
R. King, Professor; Ph.D., Wales. Neural networks, knowledge-based expert systems.
J. Picone, Associate Professor; Ph.D., IIT. Signal processing, speech processing.

Graphics and Visualization
D. Banks, Assistant Professor; Ph.D., North Carolina. Graphics, flow visualization, mathematical visualization.
R. Machiraju, Assistant Professor; Ph.D., Ohio State. Graphics, visualization, image analysis.
R. Moorhead, Associate Professor; Ph.D., North Carolina State. Scientific visualization, digital image processing.

High Performance, Distributed, and Parallel Computing
I. Banicescu, Assistant Professor; Ph.D., Polytechnic. Parallel algorithms, scientific computing.
J. Harden, Professor; Ph.D., Texas A&M. Performance monitoring, memory-hierarchy design, real-time embedded systems.
S. Howard, Assistant Professor; Ph.D., North Carolina State. Algorithms, parallel computing, signal processing.
R. Little, Associate Professor; Ph.D., Louisiana Tech. Data compression, instruction set architecture.
D. Reese, Associate Professor; Ph.D., Texas A&M. Distributed computing, computer architecture, object-oriented programming.
S. Russ, Assistant Professor; Ph.D., Georgia Tech. Distributed computing, resource allocation, computer architecture.
A. Skjellum, Associate Professor; Ph.D., Caltech. Parallel algorithms, parallel and distributed software, scientific computing.

Software Engineering
B. Carter, Professor; Ph.D., Arkansas. Software engineering, software metrics.
T. Philip, Professor; Ph.D., Mississippi State. Software engineering, real-time systems, software design and testing.

Domain Specific Computational Applications
J. Beggs, Assistant Professor; Ph.D., Penn State. Computational electromagnetics, solution algorithms, time-domain electromagnetics.
R. Briley, Professor; Ph.D., Texas. Computational fluid dynamics, parallel computing.
P. Cinnella, Associate Professor; Ph.D., Virginia Tech. Computational fluid dynamics, hypersonic flow.
B. Gatlin, Associate Professor; Ph.D., Mississippi State. Computational biofluid mechanics, computational particle dynamics.
D. Huddleston, Associate Professor; Ph.D., Tennessee. Computational fluid dynamics, computational methods in water resources.
M. Janus, Associate Professor; Ph.D., Mississippi State. Computational fluids, algorithms, unsteady flows, dynamic grids.
D. Whitfield, Distinguished Professor; Ph.D., Tennessee. Computational fluid dynamics.

Grid Technology and Computational Mathematics
M. Li, Assistant Professor; Ph.D., Alberta. Differential equations, mathematical biology.
D. Marcum, Professor; Ph.D., Purdue. Fluid mechanics, computational fluid dynamics, unstructured grid generation, numerical methods.
B. Soni, Professor; Ph.D., Texas. Computational fluid dynamics, numerical grid generation, computer-aided geometry design.
J. Thompson, Distinguished Professor; Ph.D., Georgia Tech. Grid generation computational fluid dynamics, high-performance computing.
J. Zhu, Associate Professor; Ph.D., SUNY at Stony Brook. Numerical analysis, parallel computing, mathematical modeling.

Microelectronics
B. Blalock, Assistant Professor; Ph.D., Georgia Tech. Circuit design, CMOS design, monolithic sensors.
D. Linder, Assistant Professor; Ph.D., Mississippi State. Computer architecture, CAD tools.
R. Reese, Associate Professor; Ph.D., Texas A&M. CAD for integrated circuits, digital systems.
D. Trotter, Professor; Ph.D., Texas. Microelectronics design, VLSI.

Research Centers

The National Science Foundation Engineering Research Center (ERC) at Mississippi State University has as its mission the enhancement of global competitiveness of United States industry by reducing the time and cost necessary for complex field simulations for engineering analysis and design. The ERC for CFS is an interdisciplinary research center within the College of Engineering, with faculty members and students from most engineering programs, computer science, mathematics, and physics. The Center conducts coordinated cross-disciplinary research (approximately $7 million per year), with industrial affiliate interactions (twenty-eight government laboratories and agencies and sixteen industrial companies).

The Diagnostic Instrumentation and Analysis Laboratory (DIAL) is an interdisciplinary research department in the College of Engineering. DIAL is supported primarily through funding from the Office of Technology Development within the Office of Environmental Management in the U.S. Department of Energy (DOE). DIAL's mission is to improve effectiveness and competitiveness by employing modern diagnostic techniques to monitor, control, and optimize processes, thereby improving process understanding while minimizing environmental impact. Measurements are made in extremely hot, highly corrosive atmospheres in which conventional measurement devices are ineffective.

The Institute for Signal and Information Processing (ISIP) is a multidisciplinary program to develop next generation information-processing techniques. Research at ISIP is centered on intelligent information processing. ISIP draws upon a wide range of research experience in areas such as signal processing, communications, natural language, database query, intelligent systems, and discrete controls. Its vision is to develop systems capable of intelligent interactions with users by the integration of multiple interface technologies, including speech, natural language, database query, and imaging.

The High Performance Computing Laboratory (HPC Lab) is located in the Engineering Research Center and the Butler Computer Science Building. Addressing high-performance system software, including parallel and distributed middleware for scientific and real-time settings, the HPC Lab research includes leading standards-based efforts involving the Message-Passing Interface, IETF PacketWay, and high-speed networking protocol software. A well-equipped laboratory includes ATM and Myrinet networking, connecting modern multiprocessor PC's and UltraSPARC systems, and several small-scale parallel machines. Research is supported by DARPA, NSF, DOE, and industry.

The Microsystems Prototyping Laboratory (MPL) is located at the Engineering Research Center and represents a growing presence in the government, industrial, and academic research communities. By aligning its capabilities with existing and projected Department of Defense projects relating to a variety of microsystem topics, the MPL provides a state-of-the-art research environment in the following areas: VLSI design and test; microsystem specification, design, and test; VHDL (VHSIC hardware description language) modeling, simulation, and test; and military microcircuit obsolescence.

The Computational Fluid Dynamics Laboratory (CFD Lab), located at the Engineering Research Center (ERC), has the objective of advancing the state of the art in the computational solution of real-world problems involving complex geometry and complex physics. Strengths of the ERC are brought to bear on computational problems dealing with complex flows, which include results from various grid generation projects; research in parallel and vector computational methods; and data visualization. Experiences with these state-of-the-art computational challenges shape the details of a research program involved in numerical solution algorithms, with emphasis on three-dimensional time-dependent compressible and incompressible viscous flows. The CFD Lab produces a family of codes known as UNCLE (Unsteady Computation of Field Equations).

MONTANA STATE UNIVERSITY–BOZEMAN

DEPARTMENT OF ELECTRICAL AND COMPUTER ENGINEERING

PROGRAMS OF STUDY

The Department of Electrical and Computer Engineering (ECE) offers programs of study leading to a Master of Science in Electrical Engineering (M.S.E.E.) and the Ph.D. in engineering, with an option in electrical and computer engineering (E&CpE). Graduate courses and research programs are offered in communications, computers, control systems, electronics, electromagnetics, filters, image processing, optics, and power systems.

Both thesis and nonthesis M.S. options are available: the nonthesis option requires a minimum of 30 credit hours of acceptable course work, including a minimum of 3 credits of research experience, and the thesis option requires the completion of at least 20 credits of acceptable course work and an M.S. thesis. Master's candidates take an oral comprehensive examination near the completion of their graduate program. Research experience is required of all master's students and is satisfied in one of three ways: an approved M.S. thesis; satisfactory participation in an acceptable research project approved by the student's committee; or approved industrial experience.

The Ph.D. degree in engineering (E&CpE option) is one of four Ph.D. options offered by the College of Engineering. All Ph.D. candidates must satisfy a set of core requirements, including a 3-credit course in Research and Experimental Methods in Engineering. The E&CpE option forms a natural area of collaboration between the electrical and computer engineering department and the computer science department, which is also within the College of Engineering. Examinations required for the Ph.D. degree are the Ph.D. qualifying examination, given during the first year of the student's doctoral program; the Ph.D. comprehensive examination, to be taken within two years of qualifying for the Ph.D. program; and the Ph.D. thesis defense.

RESEARCH FACILITIES

The principal offices and laboratories of the ECE department are in Cobleigh Hall (fifth and sixth floors); the offices and laboratories of the computer science department are in the adjoining Engineering and Physical Sciences Building, a new building opened in 1997 that is equipped with modern telecommunications equipment in addition to a variety of networked computers. Much of the recent equipment acquisitions in the E&CpE department have been the result of the generosity of many of the companies that hire its graduates.

FINANCIAL AID

Financial aid is available in the form of teaching assistantships, research assistantships, and student loans. Inquiries should be directed to the Graduate Program Coordinator at the address below. In 1997–1998, teaching assistantships provide substantial tuition waivers and pay approximately $7200 for nine months on a half-time basis. Research assistantships range from $7200 to $9000 (depending on graduate level and funding source) on a half-time basis for nine months, plus possible tuition reduction, with additional remuneration for summer activities.

COST OF STUDY

Tuition and fees for 1997–98 are approximately $1320 for 9 credit hours for Montana residents and $3000 for 9 credit hours for nonresidents. All graduate students enrolled for 7 credit hours or more are eligible for health insurance, the cost of which is included in student fees.

LIVING AND HOUSING COSTS

Housing costs in residence halls (with meals) are about $4000 for the nine-month academic year. Married student housing rentals vary from $220 to $430 per month. For more information, students can visit the Montana University System Web site (www.montana.edu) and link to Services for Students, MSU-Bozeman Catalog, Expenses, and Estimated Expenses.

STUDENT GROUP

The E&CpE department has approximately 300 students, of whom 20 are full-time M.S.E.E. students. About 8 students are working toward the Ph.D. in E&CpE. The low graduate student-to-staff ratio results in close working relationships between students and faculty.

LOCATION

MSU–Bozeman is in the Gallatin Valley, 90 miles from Yellowstone Park. Outdoor activities include mountain hiking, skiing, fishing, golf, and hunting. The neighboring area has a population of approximately 50,000. Local theater and university plays provide entertainment, and several small high-technology companies are located in Bozeman. More information on Bozeman and the region can be obtained on the Web (montana.avicom.net/bozemanmt/).

THE UNIVERSITY

The Bozeman campus of the University has about 12,000 students and is the land-grant University for the state of Montana. Since 1990, 13 students have been selected as All USA-Academic by *USA Today*, placing MSU among the top schools in the nation with multiple academic all-American selections.

APPLYING

Prospective students can apply at any time, but those requesting financial assistance for the fall semester should apply by March 1. Application forms can be obtained by writing to the address below or by e-mail via monicah@ee.montana.edu.

CORRESPONDENCE AND INFORMATION

Graduate Program Coordinator
Department of Electrical and Computer Engineering
Montana State University
Bozeman, Montana 59717
Telephone: 406-994-2502
Fax: 406-994-5958
E-mail: bruce_m@ee.montana.edu

MONTANA STATE UNIVERSITY—BOZEMAN

THE FACULTY AND THEIR RESEARCH

Electrical and Computer Engineering Department Faculty

Fredrick M. Cady, Associate Professor; Ph.D. (electrical engineering), Canterbury (New Zealand). Microcomputers, image processing, electrooptic systems. (e-mail: fcady@ee.montana.edu)

Victor Gerez, Professor; Ph.D. (engineering), Berkeley. Power systems, energy conversion, alternate energy systems. (e-mail: victorg@ee.montana.edu)

John P. Hanton, Professor; Ph.D. (electrical engineering), Minnesota. Solid-state materials, semiconductor devices, engineering teaching. (e-mail: johnh@ee.montana.edu)

William J. Jameson Jr., Associate Professor; Ph.D. (applied mathematics), Iowa State. Telecommunications, networking, numerical analysis. (e-mail: billj@ee.montana.edu)

Roy M. Johnson, Professor; Ph.D. (electrical engineering), Naval Postgraduate School. Digital computers, electromagnetic theory, magnetohydrodynamics, electrical power conversion. (e-mail: royj@ee.montana.edu)

Murari L. Kejariwal, Associate Professor; Ph.D. (electrical engineering), Houston. Electronics, biomedical instrumentation. (e-mail: murarik@ee.montana.edu)

Harley A. Leach, Lecturer; B.S. (electrical engineering), Montana State. Digital engineering. (e-mail: harley@ee.montana.edu)

Daniel N. March, Professor; Ph.D. (electrical engineering), Montana State. Communications systems, radio frequency interference. (e-mail: dan@ee.montana.edu)

Bruce R. McLeod, Professor; Ph.D. (electrical engineering), Colorado. Electromagnetic theory, microwaves, em fields and biological effects. (e-mail: mcleod@ee.montana.edu)

Hobart F. McWilliams, Associate Professor; M.S. (electrical engineering), SMU. Digital and analog electronics, reliability engineering. (e-mail: hobart@ee.montana.edu)

John F. Myers, Associate Professor; M.S. (electrical engineering), Purdue. Control systems, circuits. (e-mail: jackm@ee.montana.edu)

M. Hashem Nehrir, Professor; Ph.D. (electrical engineering), Oregon State. Electric power systems, electric machines. (e-mail: hashemn@ee.montana.edu)

Donald A. Pierre, Professor; Ph.D. (electrical engineering), Wisconsin. Control systems, power system dynamics, optimization techniques. (e-mail: donp@ee.montana.edu)

James R. Smith, Associate Professor; Ph.D. (electrical engineering), Montana State. Control systems, power system dynamics and stability. (e-mail: jims@ee.montana.edu)

Baldev Thapar, Professor; Ph.D. (electrical engineering), IIT. Power system analysis, protection, and grounding. (e-mail: baldevt@ee.montana.edu)

Giri Venkataramanan, Assistant Professor; Ph.D. (electrical engineering), Wisconsin. Power and energy conversion, industrial applications. (e-mail: giriv@ee.montana.edu)

Computer Science Department Faculty

Ray S. Babcock, Assistant Professor; M.S. (electrical engineering), Montana State. Image processing, computer graphics, user interfaces. (e-mail: babcock@cs.montana.edu)

Robert J. Cimikowski, Associate Professor; Ph.D. (computer science), New Mexico State. Graph theory, analysis of algorithms. (e-mail: cimo@cs.montana.edu)

Gary J. Harkin, Associate Professor; Ph.D. (computer science), Washington State. Image processing, pattern recognition, parallel systems, artificial intelligence, computer architecture. (e-mail: harkin@cs.montana.edu)

John T. Paxton, Associate Professor; Ph.D. (computer science), Michigan. Artificial intelligence, computer science education. (e-mail: paxton@cs.montana.edu)

Rockford J. Ross, Professor; Ph.D. (computer science), Washington State. Formal language theory, theory of computation, program animation systems, computer science education. (e-mail: ross@cs.montana.edu)

J. Denbigh Starkey, Professor; Ph.D. (computer science), Pennsylvania. Computer graphics, scientific visualization, user interfaces. (e-mail: starkey@cs.montana.edu)

Year-Back Yoo, Associate Professor; Ph.D. (computer science), Washington State. Analysis of algorithms, parallel processing, operations research. (e-mail: yoo@cs.montana.edu)

NEW JERSEY INSTITUTE OF TECHNOLOGY

DEPARTMENT OF COMPUTER AND INFORMATION SCIENCE

PROGRAMS OF STUDY

Doctoral and Master of Science programs are offered. The Ph.D. programs in computer science and information systems are individually designed in consultation with the department's doctoral directors. Each program includes 24 credits of advanced courses beyond the master's degree in an area of specialization, a doctoral seminar, and 30 credits of doctoral dissertation and research. A qualifying examination that tests general academic preparation and proficiency in computer science or information systems must be passed before progressing to the 24 credits of advanced courses.

Doctoral research areas include artificial intelligence, algorithms, collaborative systems, computer and information systems management, computer systems, computer vision and pattern recognition, communications, distributed processing and parallel computation, graphics and image processing, data and knowledge engineering, networking, real-time computing, simulation and modeling, software engineering, systems analysis, systems integration, and theory of computing.

The M.S. in computer science requires a minimum of 31 credits, including three core courses, a project or thesis, and courses in an area of specialization. The M.S. in information systems requires a minimum of 36 credits, including six core courses, a project or thesis, and courses in areas of specialization. Areas of specialization are artificial intelligence, collaborative systems, computer algorithms and theory of computing, computer and information systems management, computer systems, computer vision, data communications and networks, database engineering, design support systems, expert systems, graphics and image processing, human-computer interaction, knowledge-based systems, numerical computation, parallel and distributed processing, process engineering, real-time systems, simulation and modeling, software engineering, systems analysis, and systems integration. Applicants to the master's program in computer science or information systems should have backgrounds in mathematics and computer science or information systems.

For the convenience of students throughout New Jersey, NJIT offers courses to complete the master's degree in computer science at selected corporate headquarters and on the campuses of Ramapo College in Mahwah, Drew University in Madison, and at the NJIT/BCC Technology and Engineering Center.

RESEARCH FACILITIES

The Institute of Integrated Systems Research is the research arm of the Department of Computer and Information Science. It concentrates on improving productivity in the service and manufacturing industries by integrating existing and new hardware and software into single systems. The Institute also supports interdisciplinary research in microelectronics, computer engineering, and other disciplines.

Other research laboratories are dedicated to advanced computer architecture and parallel processing, artificial intelligence, collaborative systems, computer communications and networking, computer vision research on image processing, data and knowledge engineering, integrated systems and document preparation, real-time computing, and software engineering. In addition to the university's extensive, networked computing resources, the Department of Computer and Information Science maintains its NCUBE, Sun file servers, MASPAR, and Symbolic Machines. NJIT is a member of the Newark Remote Access Center (NRAC). NRAC promotes supercomputer education, research, training, and applications at its three member universities: NJIT, Stevens Institute of Technology, and the University of Medicine and Dentistry of New Jersey. NJIT is also a member of the Partnership for Academic Consulting and Training in Supercomputing at the Pittsburgh Supercomputing Center (PSC), thereby providing access to a CRAY Y-MP/832.

FINANCIAL AID

Support is available to full-time students in the form of teaching, graduate, and research assistantships. Support for summer research is also available. Tuition remission is often included in assistantships. Securing financial support is highly competitive, so early application is strongly recommended.

COST OF STUDY

Tuition for part-time students in 1996–97 was $326 per credit for residents of New Jersey and $451 for nonresidents. Full-time tuition (12 to 19 credits) was $3170 per semester for residents and $4579 for nonresidents. The tuition costs cited do not include student fees.

LIVING AND HOUSING COSTS

A limited amount of on-campus housing, the cost of which averages $4050 annually, is available for graduate students. A fourth residence hall is scheduled for completion in September 1997. Average room and board total $5800 per academic year. The Office of Residence Life assists in finding off-campus housing in Newark and surrounding communities.

STUDENT GROUP

Of the 7,837 students enrolled at NJIT, 2,830 are either full- or part-time graduate students.

LOCATION

NJIT's 45-acre campus is located in the University Heights section of New Jersey's largest city, Newark. Its location offers many activities. It is home to the New Jersey Performing Arts Center, the New Jersey Symphony, and the Newark Museum. Branch Brook Park is minutes from the campus, New York City is 10 miles away, and blocks away are campuses of Rutgers University, the University of Medicine and Dentistry of New Jersey, Seton Hall Law School, and Essex County College. Many programs operate collaboratively with these institutions. Public transportation is available, and the New Jersey shore is close by.

THE UNIVERSITY

New Jersey Institute of Technology is the state's public technological research university. Founded in 1881, NJIT has maintained close ties with industry by preparing generations of students to assume leadership roles in an increasingly technological society. The university's first and largest school is Newark College of Engineering, which was established in 1919 to reflect the institution's evolution into a four-year college. When the School of Architecture was established in 1973, a name change to New Jersey Institute of Technology reflected a broadened mission. The College of Science and Liberal Arts, founded in 1982; the School of Management, founded in 1988; and the Albert Dorman Honors College, founded in 1993, round out the university's educational offerings.

APPLYING

Applicants should contact the Office of University Admissions for admission instructions and forms. Completed applications must be received before June 5 for fall admission and November 5 for spring admission. Students can also apply on-line via the World Wide Web. February 1 is the deadline for applying for financial support for the following fall. GRE scores are required for admission to all doctoral programs and most master's degree programs, for all students seeking financial support, and for those whose last prior degree was from outside the U.S. Transcripts, letters of recommendation, and a $35 nonrefundable application fee are also required. The application fee is $50 for applications submitted from outside the U.S. International students must provide TOEFL scores as well as equivalent academic credentials from their countries of origin.

CORRESPONDENCE AND INFORMATION

Office of University Admissions
New Jersey Institute of Technology
University Heights
Newark, New Jersey 07102-1982
Telephone: 973-596-3300
Fax: 973-596-3461
World Wide Web: http://www.njit.edu

NEW JERSEY INSTITUTE OF TECHNOLOGY

THE FACULTY

Chairperson
Peter Ng, Ph.D.

Associate Chairpersons
D. C. Hung, Ph.D.
James McHugh, Ph.D.
Julian Scher, Ph.D.

Distinguished Professors
Starr Roxanne Hiltz, Ph.D., Columbia.
Murray Turoff, Ph.D., Brandeis.
Raymond T. Yeh, Ph.D., Illinois.

Professors
James A. M. McHugh, Ph.D., NYU (Courant).
Peter A. Ng, Chairman; Ph.D., Texas at Austin.
Yehoshua Perl, Ph.D., Weizmann (Israel).
Boris Verkhovsky, Ph.D., Latvian SSR Academy of Sciences
   (Latvia).

Associate Professors
Michael A. Baltrush, Ph.D., Connecticut.
Tom Featheringham, Ph.D., Pittsburgh.
James Geller, Ph.D., SUNY at Buffalo.
Dao-Chuan Hung, Ph.D., Purdue.
David Nassimi, Ph.D., Minnesota.
John W. Ryon III, Ph.D., Stevens.
Edward Sarian, Ph.D., Stevens.
Julian M. Scher, Ph.D., NYU.
Frank Y. Shih, Ph.D., Purdue.
Alexander Stoyenko, Ph.D., Toronto.

Assistant Professors
Michael P. Bieber, Ph.D., Pennsylvania.
James Calvin, Ph.D., Stanford.
Mary M. Eshaghian, Ph.D., USC.
Michael Hinchey, Ph.D., Cambridge.
Dennis Karvelas, Ph.D., Toronto.
Dina Kravets, Ph.D., MIT.
Franz Kurfess, Ph.D., Munich.
Qianhong Liu, Ph.D., NJIT.
Marvin Nakayama, Ph.D., Stanford.
Ajaz Rana, Ph.D., Rutgers.
Suresh Rao, Ph.D., Syracuse.
Wilhelm Rossak, Ph.D., Vienna Technical.
Richard Scherl, Ph.D., Illinois.
Ami Silberman, Ph.D., Illinois.
Andrew Sohn, Ph.D., USC.
Neeraj Suri, Ph.D., Massachusetts.
Murat Tanik, Ph.D., Texas A&M.
David Wang, Ph.D., Carnegie Mellon.
Jason T. L. Wang, Ph.D., NYU (Courant).
Bulent Yener, Ph.D., Columbia.

Special Lecturers
Fadi Pierre Deek, Ph.D., NJIT.
Leon Jololian, Ph.D. candidate.

RESEARCH AREAS

Artificial Intelligence and Knowledge-Based Systems: Database management, knowledge-based management, object-oriented databases, multimedia databases, semantic models, knowledge representation formalisms and methods, expert systems, machine learning, natural-language processing, automatic programming, case-based reasoning, fuzzy set theory and artificial intelligence. Geller, Kurfess, Liu, Ng, Perl, Scherl, Shih, J. Wang.

Computer Vision, Graphics, and Image Processing: Pattern recognition, computer graphics, parallel architecture, neural network, geometric modeling, robotics, expert systems, intelligent systems manipulation and control, advanced image processing, partial shape recognition, autonomous navigation systems. Hung, Shih, D. Wang.

Real-Time Computing and Distributed and Parallel Processing: Advanced computer architecture, operating systems and multiprogramming, parallel and distributed computing, computer systems modeling, evaluation and performance measurement, real-time systems, programming languages and methodology, interconnection networks, microprocessors. Baltrush, Eshaghian, Hinchey, Kravets, Kurfess, McHugh, Nassimi, Perl, Silberman, Sohn, Stoyenko, Welch.

Data Communication and Networking: Computer communication networks; network management, protocols, and standards; local area networks; integrated services digital networks; data compression; performance analysis and evaluation. Eshaghian, Karvelas, Perl, Sohn, Verkhovsky, Yener.

Software Development and Systems Integration: Software engineering, rapid prototyping, computer-aided software engineering, software requirements engineering, user interface design, virtual classroom systems, intelligent text processing systems, systems integration. Geller, Hiltz, Hinchey, Ng, Rana, Rossak, Scherl, Turoff, J. Wang, Welch, Yeh.

Information Systems: Computer-mediated communications, management information systems, human-computer interface, decision support systems, evaluation of systems, collaborative systems, hypertext systems, simulation and modeling, management and social impacts of computing, information retrieval. Bieber, Featheringham, Hiltz, Liu, Rana, Rao, Rossak, Scher, Turoff, J. Wang, Yeh.

Theory of Computing: Theory of computation, design and analysis of algorithms, algorithmic graph theory, complexity theory, formal languages and automata, nonnumerical algorithms and problems, numerical computation, parallel computational complexity, computational geometry. Hinchey, Kravets, McHugh, Nassimi, Perl, Sarian, Stoyenko, Verkhovsky.

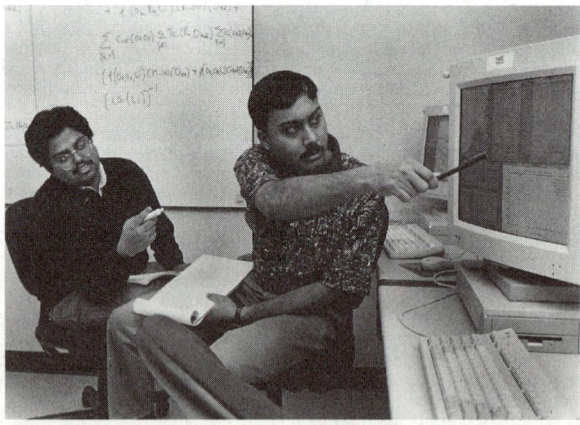

Laboratory instruction on real-time computing.

NEW JERSEY INSTITUTE OF TECHNOLOGY

DEPARTMENT OF ELECTRICAL AND COMPUTER ENGINEERING

PROGRAMS OF STUDY

The Department of Electrical and Computer Engineering offers the Doctor of Philosophy, the Master of Science in electrical engineering and in computer engineering, and the Degree of Engineer. Students may choose from a wide variety of areas of specialization. General areas in electrical engineering include biomedical systems, communication and signal processing, computer systems, control systems, energy conversion and power, microwave and light-wave engineering, and solid-state materials and devices. Specialty areas in computer engineering include microprocessor-based systems, parallel computing systems, computer networking, VLSI system design and test, and machine vision systems.

Starting in fall 1997 (pending approval), the department will offer two new interdisciplinary programs: the Master of Science in Telecommunications, which seeks to provide students with tools and skills for understanding and creating advanced telecommunications networks, hardware, and systems; and the Master of Science in Power Engineering, which seeks to provide engineers working in the electric power industry and those who seek to enter it with advanced education relevant to their chosen occupation.

The requirements listed are for individuals with appropriate undergraduate backgrounds. Those lacking preparation must make up deficiencies with additional courses not counted toward a degree. Doctoral candidates must pass qualifying examinations and complete at least 24 credits of advanced course work and 36 credits of dissertation research. Candidates for the M.S. must complete at least 30 credits. Students receiving financial support include a thesis within their program of study. Other students can select from the following three program options: I) complete 24 course credits plus a 6-credit thesis; II) complete 27 course credits plus a 3-credit project; III) complete 30 course credits. Candidates for the Degree of Engineer must pass a qualifying exam, complete at least 24 course credits beyond the master's degree, and complete a design project. Complete requirements for each degree are found in the latest graduate catalog, which is available through the Office of University Admissions.

In one of the few graduate cooperative education programs in the United States, master's candidates at NJIT may benefit from a study/employment combination with both academic and financial advantages. Employment is within the student's field of study and may be concurrent or may alternate with academic work.

In fall 1994, the Division of Continuing Professional Education designed and implemented a 12-credit Graduate Certificate Program, which offers certificates in subjects that are in demand by business and industry. Each certificate functions as a stand-alone credential or as a springboard to a corresponding NJIT master's degree.

RESEARCH FACILITIES

Research facilities include the Microelectronics Research Center with a class 10 cleanroom, the New Jersey Center for Multimedia Research, the Center for Microwave and Lightwave Engineering, the Center for Communications and Signal Processing, Drexler Thin Film Laboratory, the Electronic Imaging Center, and the Molecular Beam Epitaxy/III-V Device Processing Laboratory. These facilities provide students with firsthand knowledge of applications for industries such as consumer electronics (VCRs and high-definition television), air traffic controls, weather prediction, automobile controls and remote sensing, and microwave communications systems.

Major corporations, the New Jersey Commission on Science and Technology, and the U.S. Environmental Protection Agency are among the many industry and government resources that contribute both financial support and working partnerships for these research efforts. Extensive computing facilities support both academic study and research. NJIT has centralized its computing services through a number of powerful systems. Minicomputers and microcomputers are located throughout the campus in academic departments and in computer laboratories. A fiber-optic spine connects nearly 2,000 campus locations and beyond. NJIT is a member of the Partnership for Academic Consulting and Training in Supercomputing at the Pittsburgh Supercomputing Center (PSC), which provides access to a CRAY Y-MP/832.

FINANCIAL AID

Support is available to full-time students in the form of teaching, graduate, and research assistantships. Support for summer research is also available. Tuition remission is often included in assistantships. Securing financial support is highly competitive, so early application is strongly recommended.

COST OF STUDY

Tuition for part-time students in 1996–97 was $326 per credit for residents of New Jersey and $451 for nonresidents. Full-time tuition (12 to 19 credits) was $3170 per semester for residents and $4579 for nonresidents. The tuition costs cited do not include student fees.

LIVING AND HOUSING COSTS

A limited amount of on-campus housing, the cost of which averages $4050 annually, is available for graduate students. Average room and board total $5800 per academic year. A fourth residence hall is scheduled for completion in September 1997. The Office of Residence Life assists in finding off-campus housing in Newark and surrounding communities.

STUDENT GROUP

Of the 7,837 students enrolled at NJIT, 2,830 are full- or part-time graduate students.

LOCATION

NJIT's 45-acre campus is located in the University Heights section of New Jersey's largest city, Newark. Its location offers many activities. It is home to the New Jersey Performing Arts Center, the New Jersey Symphony, and the Newark Museum. Branch Brook Park is minutes from the campus, New York City is 10 miles away, and blocks away are campuses of Rutgers University, the University of Medicine and Dentistry of New Jersey, Seton Hall Law School, and Essex County College. Many programs operate collaboratively with these institutions. Public transportation is available, and the New Jersey shore is close by.

THE UNIVERSITY

New Jersey Institute of Technology is the state's public technological research university. Founded in 1881, NJIT has maintained close ties with industry by preparing generations of students to assume leadership roles in an increasingly technological society. The university's first and largest school is Newark College of Engineering, which was established in 1919 to reflect the institution's evolution into a four-year college. When the School of Architecture was established in 1973, a name change to New Jersey Institute of Technology reflected a broadened mission. The College of Science and Liberal Arts, founded in 1982; the School of Management, founded in 1988; and the Albert Dorman Honors College, founded in 1993; round out the university's comprehensive educational offerings.

APPLYING

Applicants should contact the Office of University Admissions for admission instructions and form. Completed applications must be received before June 5 for fall admission and November 5 for spring admission. Students can also apply on-line via the Internet World Wide Web. February 1 is the deadline for applying for financial support for the following fall. GRE scores are required for admission to all doctoral programs and most master's degree programs, for all students seeking financial support, and for those whose last prior degree was from outside the United States. Transcripts, letters of recommendation, and a $35 nonrefundable application fee are required. The application fee is $50 for applications submitted from outside the United States. International students must provide TOEFL scores as well as equivalent academic credentials from their countries of origin. GMAT scores are required for management programs.

CORRESPONDENCE AND INFORMATION

Office of University Admissions
New Jersey Institute of Technology
University Heights
Newark, New Jersey 07102-1982

Telephone: 973-596-3300
Fax: 973-596-3461
World Wide Web: http://www.njit.edu

Administrative Coordinator
Department of Electrical and
    Computer Engineering
New Jersey Institute of Technology
University Heights
Newark, New Jersey 07102-1982

Telephone: 973-596-3513
Fax: 973-596-5680

NEW JERSEY INSTITUTE OF TECHNOLOGY

THE FACULTY

Chairperson
Richard A. Haddad, Ph.D., Polytechnic.

Associate Chairpersons
Nirwan Ansari, Ph.D., Purdue.
Kenneth Sohn, Sc.D., Stevens.

Computer Engineering Program
Jacob Savir, Program Director; Ph.D., Stanford.

Distinguished Professors.
Yeheskel Bar-Ness, Ph.D., Brown.
Bernard Friedland, Ph.D., Columbia.

Professors
William Carr, Ph.D., Carnegie Mellon.
Edwin Cohen, Ph.D., Polytechnic.
Roy Cornely, Ph.D., Rutgers.
Haim Grebel, Ph.D., Weizmann (Israel).
Richard Haddad, Ph.D., Polytechnic.
Jacob Klapper, Eng.Sc.D., NYU.
Marshall Kuo, Ph.D., Michigan.
Andrew Meyer, Ph.D., Northwestern.
Stanley Reisman, Ph.D., Polytechnic.
Sol Rosenstark, Ph.D., NYU.
Jacob Savir, Ph.D., Stanford.
Kenneth Sohn, Sc.D., Stevens.
Joseph Strano, Ph.D., Rutgers.
Gary Thomas, Provost; Ph.D., Berkeley.
Gerald Whitman, Ph.D., Polytechnic.

Associate Professors
Ali Akansu, Ph.D., Polytechnic.
Nirwan Ansari, Ph.D., Purdue.
Timothy Chang, Ph.D., Toronto.

Wayne Clements, M.S., Pennsylvania.
Peter Engler, Ph.D., SUNY at Buffalo.
Joseph Frank, Ph.D., Polytechnic.
Alex Haimovich, Ph.D., Pennsylvania.
Edwin Hou, Ph.D., Purdue.
Walid Hubbi, Ph.D., Queens.
C. N. Manikopoulos, Ph.D., Princeton.
Durga Misra, Ph.D., Waterloo.
Edip Niver, Ph.D., Middle East Technical (Turkey).
Yung-Qing Shi, Ph.D., Pittsburgh.
Marek Sosnowski, Ph.D., Warsaw.
William Troop, Ph.D., Stevens.
Mengchu Zhou, Ph.D., Rensselaer.
Sotirios Ziavras, Ph.D., George Washington.

Assistant Professors
Hongya Ge, Ph.D., Rhode Island.
Zoran Siveski, Ph.D., CUNY.
Shi-Chang Wu, Ph.D., UCLA.

Research Professor
Robert Marcus, Ph.D., Michigan.

JOINT APPOINTMENTS

Associate Professors
Frank Shi, Ph.D., Computer and Information Science.
Alexander Stoyenko, Ph.D., Computer and Information Science.

Assistant Professors
Mary Eshagian, Ph.D., Computer and Information Science.
Dennis Karvelas, Ph.D., Computer and Information Science.
Eliza Michalopoulou, Ph.D., Mathematics.

RESEARCH AREAS

Biomedical Systems: Medical instrumentation, biomedical signal processing, medical imaging, computer simulation of physiological systems, biomedical informatics. Particular areas include heart rate variability studies, signal processing of bioelectrical signals, gait analysis, and studies of the effects of stress and relaxation techniques on the nervous system. Carpinelli, Chang, Clements, Engler, Grebel, Klapper, Meyer, Reisman, Shi, Strano.

Communication and Signal Processing: Mobile and personal wireless communications, coherent communications and phase-locked loops application, spread spectrum systems and satellite communication, co-channel demodulation, surface acoustic wave applications, optical communication systems synchronization, equalization source coding for data compression, error control coding, detection and estimation, adaptive signal processing and arrays. Fast algorithms for signal separation, multidimensional signal processing, subband filter banks and wavelet transforms for feature extraction and compression; time-frequency localization; interference and cross-polarization canceler; interference canceler in radar, digital, and image processing; pattern recognition; ATM networking. Akansu, Ansari, Bar-Ness, Frank, Ge, Haddad, Haimovich, Klapper, Shi, Siveski.

Computer Systems: Advanced computer architecture, computer communications networks, multiprocessor and multicomputer systems, parallel and distributed processing, microprocessor applications, computer systems modeling and performance evaluation, discrete event systems, VLSI design and microengineering, image processing and machine vision systems, microcontroller systems, intelligent instrumentation, medical instrumentation, process scheduling, flexible manufacturing systems, robotics, neural networks, computer-aided instruction; testing, fault-tolerant computing, computer-aided design. Ansari, Carpinelli, Carr, Clements, Hou, Manikopoulos, Reisman, Rosenstark, Savir, Zhou, Ziavras.

Computer Engineering Research: Communication networks; multiprocessor system architecture; parallel and distributed processing; scheduling; neural networks and genetic algorithms; infrared imaging; discrete event system models and tools, robotics, VLSI design, and microengineering; computer-aided instruction; testing, fault-tolerant computing, computer-aided design. Carpinelli, Hou, Manikopoulos, Rosenstark, Savir, Zhou, Ziavras.

Control Systems: Application of system concepts to biomedical engineering problems; modeling and control of flexible robot arms; stochastic and robust optimal control; adaptive digital control; machine vision in robotics; system identification; computer implementation of modern control algorithms; algebraic system theory; nonlinear system dynamics, including study of bifurcation and chaotic motion; aerospace navigation guidance and control; precision motion control; human factors in control system design. Bar-Ness, Chang, Clements, Friedland, Kuo, Meyer, Shi, Strano.

Energy Systems: Computer applications to solve energy system problems, power electronics, alternative energy sources, reliability of insulation systems for electrical machines. Cohen, Hubbi.

Microwave and Lightwave Engineering: Microstrip and dielectric antennas, wave propagation indoors, in vegetation, in inhomogeneous media; scattering from periodic and rough surfaces; RF/microwave device modeling and measurements, CAD of microwave components and systems; numerical methods; artificial dielectrics; optical interconnects; laser processing in semiconductor surfaces. Grebel, Niver, Thomas, Whitman, Wu.

Solid-State Materials, Devices, and Circuits: Processing and micromachining of solid-state materials for electronic and optical devices, solid-state sensor technology of visible and infrared imaging for industrial and medical applications, micromechanical devices with integrated microelectronic circuits for "smart sensors" (e.g., accelerometers, humidity and tactile sensors), application specific integrated circuit ASIC design utilizing CMOS technology, fabrication and testing of germanium-silicon devices, development of novel thin-film and surface modification technologies, novel composite thin films and materials for nonlinear optical devices and optically controlled waveguides. Carr, Cornely, Grebel, Marcus, Misra, Sohn, Sosnowski.

NEW YORK UNIVERSITY

COURANT INSTITUTE OF MATHEMATICAL SCIENCES
DEPARTMENT OF COMPUTER SCIENCE

PROGRAMS OF STUDY

The Department of Computer Science offers courses leading to the M.S. and Ph.D. degrees. The program offers instruction in the principles, design, and application of computer systems. The M.S. degree is obtained through course work plus a comprehensive examination. A thesis option is also available. An accelerated M.S. program is available to highly qualified students and can be completed in a year of full-time study. Students who obtain an M.S. degree are qualified to do significant development work in the computer industry and in important application areas. The Ph.D. degree program entails more extensive requirements, namely, three comprehensive exams, an oral exam, a thesis proposal, and a doctoral dissertation. An essential aspect of the doctoral program is active participation in the department's varied research programs. Those who receive a doctoral degree are in a position to hold faculty appointments and do research and development work at the forefront of this rapidly changing and expanding field.

Established in 1969 as a part of the Courant Institute of Mathematical Sciences, the department has experienced substantial growth in its faculty, student body, research staff, and funding. There is major support for research in compilers, computer vision, distributed computing, multimedia, natural-language processing, and scientific computing. Research areas also include algorithmics, computational biology, databases, design of computer systems, high-level programming languages, mathematical programming, numerical analysis, parallel distributed systems, real-time systems, symbolic computation, and theory of computation. Courses are offered regularly in all of these areas.

RESEARCH FACILITIES

The department provides a general-purpose, state-of-the-art computing environment. All supported Ph.D. students receive an individual computer. All graduate students have access to public laboratories in Warren Weaver Hall, which contains about forty Suns and Xterminals. In addition, there are specialized laboratories for compiler optimization and instruction level scheduling, computer graphics and multimedia, computer vision, and parallel and distributed computing.

Warren Weaver Hall is the original home of the Courant Institute of Mathematical Sciences, which is shared by the mathematics and computer science departments, as well as the Institute's outstanding mathematical sciences library. In recent years, the department's growth has led to an expansion of its facilities. A nearby campus building now houses the language, multimedia, distributed computing, and parallel computing laboratories plus additional faculty offices.

FINANCIAL AID

Fellowships and assistantships are awarded exclusively to students who study full-time for the Ph.D. degree. They cover tuition and, in 1996–97, provided a stipend of $16,300 for the nine-month academic year. Additional summer support may be available. Students who perform well have their awards renewed for a period of four to five years. Low-interest loans (available to students who qualify on the basis of need) are another source of support for graduate study in the department.

COST OF STUDY

In 1997–98, tuition and fees are calculated at $675 per point. A full-time program normally consists of four 3-point courses per term (24 points for the year). A limited deferred-tuition plan is in effect.

LIVING AND HOUSING COSTS

University housing for graduate students is limited. It consists mainly of shared studio apartments in buildings adjacent to Warren Weaver Hall and shared suites in residence halls within walking distance of the University. University housing rents in 1997–98 range from approximately $6250 to $8650 for the nine-month academic year.

STUDENT GROUP

The department has a substantial number of both full- and part-time students. Most of the part-time students are computer professionals employed by a wide range of corporations in the metropolitan area, including IBM and AT&T Bell Laboratories, as well as many banking and finance corporations. The student body numbers approximately 380.

LOCATION

New York University is located at Washington Square in Greenwich Village in a residential neighborhood consisting of apartments, art galleries, theaters, restaurants, and shops.

THE UNIVERSITY AND THE INSTITUTE

New York University, founded in 1831, enrolls 46,000 students and is the largest private university in the country. Its various schools offer a wide range of undergraduate, graduate, and professional degrees. Among its units of international stature is the Courant Institute of Mathematical Sciences. The Institute combines research of mathematics and computer science with advanced training at the graduate and postdoctoral levels. Its activities are supported by the University, government, industry, private foundations, and individuals.

APPLYING

The requirements for admission are discussed in detail in the admission and computer science sections of the Graduate School of Arts and Science bulletin and in the department's booklet *The Graduate Program in Computer Science*. Much information, including the department's booklet, is accessible on the Internet using the World Wide Web. Admission is granted to applicants who are judged to have the greatest potential for success in the graduate program. Students seeking admission are required to file applications before April 15 for the summer and fall terms and before November 1 for the spring term. Scores on the GRE General and Subject Tests are required of all Ph.D. applicants. Applicants for the master's degree programs need only submit GRE General Test scores. An applicant whose native language is not English must submit a TOEFL score; scores of less than 590 are generally not acceptable. Students who make application for financial aid when they apply for admission are considered for all awards available to graduate students of computer science at New York University, including departmental fellowships and assistantships. The major review of applications for financial aid occurs in early February each year; all such applications must be received by January 4. The application deadline for general admission is April 15.

CORRESPONDENCE AND INFORMATION

For program and financial aid information:
Computer Science Department
Courant Institute of Mathematical Sciences
New York University
251 Mercer Street
New York, New York 10012-1185
Telephone: 212-998-3063
E-mail: admissions@cs.nyu.edu
World Wide Web: http://cs.nyu.edu

For applications and a bulletin:
Office of Admissions and Financial Aid
Graduate School of Arts and Science
New York University
P.O. Box 907, Cooper Station
New York, New York 10276-0907
Telephone: 212-998-8050
E-mail: gsas.admissions@nyu.edu
World Wide Web: http://nyu.edu/gsas/degree/admission

NEW YORK UNIVERSITY
THE FACULTY AND THEIR RESEARCH

Professors

Marsha J. Berger. Computational fluid dynamics, adaptive methods for partial differential equations, parallel computing. berger@cs.nyu.edu

Richard J. Cole. Algorithmics, parallel algorithms, amortized complexity, pattern matching. cole@cs.nyu.edu

Martin D. Davis (Emeritus). Mathematical logic, theory of computation, diophantine decision problems, history of logic. davism@cs.nyu.edu

Robert B. K. Dewar. Programming languages, compilers, operating systems, microprocessor architectures. dewar@cs.nyu.edu

Allan Gottlieb. Parallel computing/supercomputing, computer architecture, operating systems, experimental systems. gottlieb@cs.nyu.edu

Ralph Grishman. Computational linguistics (natural language processing). grishman@cs.nyu.edu

Malcolm C. Harrison. Programming language design. harrison@cs.nyu.edu

Zvi M. Kedem. Metacomputing, reliable distributed computing, parallel computing. kedem@cs.nyu.edu

Bhubaneswar Mishra. Mathematical and theoretical computer science, computational biology, computational finance and robotics. mishra@cs.nyu.edu

Michael L. Overton. Numerical optimization, numerical linear algebra, mathematical programming, linear and semidefinite programming. overton@cs.nyu.edu

Robert Paige. Program transformations, compilers and programming languages, software environments, algorithms. paige@cs.nyu.edu

Edmond Schonberg. Programming languages, compiler construction, software engineering, software prototyping. schonberg@cs.nyu.edu

Jacob T. Schwartz. Design of algorithms and systems for computational logic, interactive multimedia systems and their applications to education. schwartz@cs.nyu.edu

Dennis E. Shasha. Transaction processing, combinatorial pattern recognition, real-time algorithms, parallel computing systems, document tailoring. shasha@cs.nyu.edu

Joel H. Spencer. Discrete mathematics, theoretical computer science, probabilistic methods, random graphs. spencer@cs.nyu.edu

Olof B. Widlund. Numerical analysis, parallel computing, partial differential equations, continuum mechanics. widlund@cs.nyu.edu

Chee K. Yap. Computational geometry, computer algebra, visualization, robotics, complexity theory. yap@cs.nyu.edu

Research Professors

Naomi Sager. Natural language processing, science information structures, medical informatics, speech recognition. sager@cs.nyu.edu

Micha Sharir. Robotics, computational geometry, analysis of algorithms, combinatorial geometry. sharir@cs.nyu.edu

Associate Professors

Ravi Boppana. Theoretical computer science, computational complexity, probabilistic methods, analysis of algorithms. boppana@cs.nyu.edu

Ernest Davis. Knowledge representation, commonsense reasoning, physical and spatial reasoning. davise@cs.nyu.edu

Benjamin F. Goldberg. Program analysis and optimization, programming language design and implementation, functional programming languages, languages for parallel computation. goldberg@cs.nyu.edu

Robert A. Hummel. Computer vision, evidential reasoning, automatic target recognition, medical image processing. hummel@cs.nyu.edu

Krishna Palem. Compilers and optimization, programming tools for embedded and configurable computing, parallel computing, string and pattern matching. palem@cs.nyu.edu

Kenneth Perlin. Computer graphics, computer/human interfaces, multimedia, simulation. perlin@cs.nyu.edu

Alan R. Siegel. Probabilistic computation, parallel computation, graphics design systems. siegel@cs.nyu.edu

Research Associate Professors

Anne Greenbaum. Numeric linear algebra and partial differential equations, parallel computing. greenbau@cs.nyu.edu

Stephane Mallat. Computer vision, signal processing, harmonic analysis. mallat@cs.nyu.edu

Assistant Professor

Thomas Anantharaman. Large-scale software development, statistical techniques for genomics, computer chess. tsa@cs.nyu.edu

Associated Faculty

Richard Pollack, Professor of Mathematics and Computer Science. Discrete geometry, computational geometry and algorithmic real algebraic geometry. pollack@cims.nyu.edu

Tamar Schlick, Associate Professor of Chemistry, Mathematics and Computer Science. Mathematical biology, numerical analysis, computational chemistry.

David Schwartz, Associate Professor of Chemistry and Computer Science. Genomics, DNA, physical chemistry, microscopy.

MAJOR RESEARCH AREAS

Algorithmics and computational complexity: probabilistic methods, computational geometry, string and pattern matching, computer vision and biology, on-line algorithms and real-time computation, parallel and distributed computation, computer algebra.

Artificial intelligence and natural language processing: natural language processing, neural networks, reasoning with uncertainty, commonsense reasoning, learning, database modeling.

Image processing and computer vision: analysis and synthesis of digital images, human-machine interfaces, object recognition and image data representation.

Multimedia: computer graphics, human/computer interface, authoring tools, digital audio and video, high-level visual languages, multiuser simulation worlds, new input and output technologies.

Numerical analysis: computations in specific application domains, scientific computing, optimization and control.

Parallel and distributed systems: reliable distributed computing, parallel computer architectures, systems software, databases.

Programming languages and compilers: programming language design and implementation, program development methodology (including automatic derivation of programs from high-level specifications), languages for parallel computation, instruction level scheduling.

NORTH CAROLINA STATE UNIVERSITY

DEPARTMENT OF COMPUTER SCIENCE

PROGRAMS OF STUDY

The department confers the Ph.D., the M.S., and the M.C.S. Each Ph.D. candidate completes written qualifying examinations in three broad areas, individualized in-depth written and oral preliminary examinations, and a public defense of a dissertation describing substantial original independent scholarly work. Ph.D. students typically complete 72 semester hours of postbaccalaureate course work. The M.S. requires 30 hours of graduate work, including thesis research. The thesis requirement may be waived for students who gain admission to the Ph.D. program by passing the Ph.D. Qualifying Exams. The Master of Computer Science (M.C.S.) is a terminal professional degree granted upon successful completion of 30 hours of course work. The department also contributes to graduate distance learning programs of the College of Engineering and the National Technological University.

RESEARCH FACILITIES

The Department crossed a watershed in early 1997 as it began to occupy built-to-suit space in the Engineering Graduate Research Center on the University's new 1,000-acre Centennial Campus. By 1999, the EGRC will be connected to the Historical Campus by an underground maglev monorail system.

Basic computing services are provided by the College of Engineering's Eos system, a modern networked computing environment with more than 1,000 public UNIX-based workstations, predominantly Sun Sparc 4s and 5s. Personal desktop workstations are typical for graduate students engaged in research, and other computer science students have exclusive access to dozens of workstations in departmental laboratories. The Multimedia Laboratory includes facilities for video capture and editing, color printers, video disk recorders, stereo viewing systems, voice synthesizers, and an experimental 25 M-bit ATM network. Students can also gain access to the state-funded NC Supercomputing Center. The state-wide NC-REN network was the subject of the November 1994 issue of *IEEE Network*.

Graduate students enjoy the use of excellent library facilities both on campus and through cooperative arrangements with other Triangle institutions. NCSU libraries' array of full-text and image databases is among the largest offered at any university and is available 24 hours a day through its networked information system. In fact, the Association of Research Libraries recently recognized NCSU Libraries as one of six "Research Libraries of the Future" for its rapid assimilation of computing and networking technologies.

FINANCIAL AID

Around 60 students are supported as graduate assistants. Traditional teaching and research assistantships are complemented by the Industrial Assistantship program, which allows selected students to combine theoretical training with real-world experience at local sites of major software developers.

In fall 1997, the value of a new Assistant's Award will exceed $21,200, including full tuition support, year-round health insurance coverage, and a nine-month salary of $10,000. Several outstanding applicants will receive supplemental Dean's Fellowships.

COST OF STUDY

In 1997–98, graduate assistants receive full tuition support and pay fees estimated at $350 per semester. Other full-time graduate students pay tuition and fees estimated at $1100 (North Carolina residents) or $5350 (non-residents) per semester.

LIVING AND HOUSING COSTS

Residence hall rooms for unmarried students cost $995–$1420 per semester in 1997–98; University efficiency apartments cost $1360 per semester for double occupancy and $2635 for single occupancy. University housing for married students is extremely limited. Many graduate students live off campus. Estimated living costs for 1997–98 are $1015 per month for a single student. Raleigh's cost-of-living index is 2.6 percent below the national average.

STUDENT GROUP

In spring 1997, 142 graduate students enrolled, including 20 women, 3 African Americans, 2 Hispanics, and 36 international students from six countries. Thirty-three were classified as doctoral students.

STUDENT OUTCOMES

Graduates at all levels are highly respected and well paid locally and elsewhere. Many M.S. and M.C.S. graduates begin or continue careers performing and supervising advanced software development in and around the Research Triangle Park. Most recent Ph.D. graduates assumed positions of technical leadership in well-known, large companies. Despite a competitive academic market, 2 assumed tenure-track faculty positions and 2 others declined such offers; 2 more pursued postdoctoral research.

LOCATION

Raleigh, North Carolina's capital city, is home to the North Carolina Symphony Orchestra and the North Carolina Museums of Art, History, and Natural History. The Research Triangle Park is home to major installations of the computer, telecommunications, and pharmaceutical industries; federal agencies such as the Army Research Office and the Environmental Protection Agency; and nonprofit organizations such as the National Humanities Center, Sigma Xi, MCNC, and the North Carolina Biotechnology Center. Atlantic Coast Conference basketball teams at the vertices of the Research Triangle—NCSU's Wolfpack, Duke's Blue Devils, and UNC–Chapel Hill's Tar Heels—make it a hotbed of athletic as well as intellectual endeavor. Beyond the Triangle, the Old North State's natural beauty extends from the Great Smoky Mountains National Park and Blue Ridge Parkway in the west to the Cape Hatteras National Seashore "down east." The many graduates who choose to accept permanent employment here apparently concur with *Money* magazine's September 1994 report that the Triangle is "America's Best Place to Live."

THE UNIVERSITY AND THE DEPARTMENT

The University's 110-year Land Grant tradition is exemplified by its strong Colleges of Agriculture, Engineering, Forestry, Textiles, and Veterinary Medicine. In spring 1997, 19,456 undergraduate and 5,681 graduate students enrolled.

The department is among both the oldest and the youngest in the nation. Although its first undergraduate degrees were awarded in 1967, Ph.D.'s were not conferred until 1990. Nine of 31 members of the graduate faculty have arrived within the past five years, making it among the nation's fastest growing.

In 1995–96, ninety-one bachelor's, thirty-eight master's, and seven doctor's degrees were conferred. The graduate student body grows steadily, while undergraduate programs have become somewhat smaller and distinctly more selective.

APPLYING

The Department actively seeks a diverse pool of qualified applicants. All applicants must have an accredited baccalaureate degree with a B average, including undergraduate course work in calculus, statistics, computer programming, computer organization, and data structures. Scores for the General and Computer Science Subject Tests of the Graduate Record Examinations and three letters of recommendation are required. Most international applicants must submit TOEFL scores. Fall and spring admission deadlines are: for all international applicants, February 1 and August 15; for aid (U.S. residents), February 1 and September 1; and for admission only (U.S. residents), April 1 and November 1.

CORRESPONDENCE AND INFORMATION

Requests for application information should include the prospective applicant's undergraduate institution, major, and degree date; GRE scores are appreciated if available. Students should direct inquiries to:
Computer Science Graduate Admissions
North Carolina State University
Box 8207
Raleigh, North Carolina 27695-8207

Telephone: 919-515-2654
E-mail: gradprogram@csc.ncsu.edu
World Wide Web: http://www.csc.ncsu.edu/graduate

NORTH CAROLINA STATE UNIVERSITY
THE FACULTY AND THEIR RESEARCH

Dennis R. Bahler, Associate Professor; Ph.D., Virginia, 1987. Artificial intelligence, including constraint processing, machine learning, approximate reasoning, and hybrid neural-symbolic computing; application of artificial intelligence to concurrent engineering and molecular biology.

Donald L. Bitzer, Distinguished University Research Professor; Ph.D., Illinois, 1960. Convolutional codes; high-speed, error-free channels for satellite and land communications; computer-based instruction for discrete mathematics in computer science.

Wushow Chou, Professor; Ph.D., Berkeley, 1968. Optimization and performance evaluation of communications networks and computer and communications systems, focusing on applying heuristic algorithms and approximation models to real systems.

Kenneth Clark, Adjunct Associate Professor; Ph.D., North Carolina State, 1986. Numerical analysis, numerical solution of constrained ordinary and partial differential equations, numerical methods for parallel architectures, algorithmic techniques, applications of large-scale computing in economics.

W. Rance Cleaveland II, Associate Professor; Ph.D., Cornell, 1987. Automated and interactive tools for reasoning about computer systems, specification and verification of concurrent and distributed systems, formal methods in system design and analysis, semantics of programming languages and logics, applications of logic in computer science.

Edward W. Davis, Associate Professor and Director of Undergraduate Programs; Ph.D., Illinois, 1972. Computer architecture with emphasis on the design and application of highly parallel computers.

Rex A. Dwyer, Associate Professor and Director of Graduate Programs; Ph.D., Carnegie-Mellon, 1988. Algorithms and data structures, computational geometry, geometric probability, algorithms for problems in human and evolutionary genetics.

Robert J. Fornaro, Professor; Ph.D., Penn State, 1969. Real-time operating systems and architectures, applications of real-time systems in manufacturing, control and multimedia systems.

Robert E. Funderlic, Professor; Ph.D., Tennessee, 1970. Scientific and high-performance computing, including the design and implementation of algorithms for parallel computers; design and analysis of numerical methods, especially in linear algebra.

Edward F. Gehringer, Associate Professor (with Electrical and Computer Engineering); Ph.D., Purdue, 1979. Object-oriented software systems—memory management, performance studies, persistent storage, very large address spaces, distributed object systems; computer architecture—performance of memory hierarchies, caches; algorithm/architecture interaction.

Thomas L. Honeycutt, Associate Professor; Ph.D., North Carolina State, 1969. Management information systems, computer modeling and simulation, computer literacy.

S. Purushothaman Iyer, Associate Professor; Ph.D., Utah, 1986. Formal methods and programming languages, compile-time analysis of programs, reasoning about designs for concurrent systems.

Vicki E. Jones, Assistant Professor; Ph.D., Illinois, 1996. Data, information, and knowledge management; security and performance evaluation for object-oriented, parallel, and distributed systems.

Garrison Q. Kenney, Adjunct Assistant Professor; Ph.D., North Carolina State, 1993. Software engineering, software reliability estimation, networking technologies.

James C. Lester, Assistant Professor; Ph.D., Texas at Austin, 1994. Artificial intelligence, intelligent multimedia technologies, knowledge-based learning environments, computational linguistics, computational biology.

David F. McAllister, Professor; Ph.D., North Carolina at Chapel Hill, 1972. Computer graphics, software reliability modeling, numerical analysis.

Harry G. Perros, Professor; Ph.D., Dublin, 1975. Performance analysis of ATM networks, congestion control, design and performance evaluation of optical networks, performance evaluation of software systems, analysis of queueing networks.

Douglas S. Reeves, Associate Professor (with Electrical and Computer Engineering); Ph.D., Penn State, 1987. Distributed multimedia, real-time communication and high-speed networks, parallel signal processing architectures.

Woodrow E. Robbins, Professor; Ph.D., Syracuse, 1971. Computer graphics, true three-dimensional graphic imaging techniques, the role of color, parallel graphics algorithms.

Robert D. Rodman, Associate Professor; Ph.D., UCLA, 1973. Voice processing, including automatic speaker and language recognition; applied voice input/out systems; use of computers for elder care; computational linguistics.

Jonathan Rossie, Assistant Professor; Ph.D., Indiana, 1996. Implementation and foundations of object-oriented programming languages.

George N. Rouskas, Assistant Professor; Ph.D., Georgia Tech, 1994. Lightwave high-speed networks, distributed systems, multicasting, and their performance evaluation.

Robert St. Amant, Assistant Professor; Ph.D., Massachusetts, 1996. Human-computer interaction, artificial intelligence, intelligent user interfaces, statistical expert systems.

Carla D. Savage, Professor; Ph.D., Illinois, 1977. Combinatorial algorithms, generating combinatorial structures, Gray codes, discrete mathematics, graph theory.

Mona Singh, Adjunct Assistant Professor; Ph.D. Texas, 1994. Natural language processing, dialogue systems, user interfaces.

Munindar Singh, Assistant Professor; Ph.D., Texas, 1993. Databases: semantic and transactional issues in databases; information management and access in open environments; intelligent agents; multiagent systems; formal methods for databases.

Matthias F. M. Stallmann, Associate Professor; Ph.D., Colorado, 1982. Algorithm design and analysis for both serial and parallel models of computation, combinatorial optimization, graph and matroid algorithms, graph algorithm animation.

William J. Stewart, Professor; Ph.D., Queen's (Belfast), 1974. Performance evaluation, approximate and numerical solution of general queueing-network models, numerical linear algebra, operating systems and parallel architectures and algorithms.

Kuo-Chung Tai, Professor; Ph.D., Cornell, 1977. Software testing; concurrent programming languages; specification, verification, testing, and debugging of concurrent programs and communication protocols.

Alan L. Tharp, Alumni Distinguished Professor and Department Head; Ph.D., Northwestern, 1969. File and data structures, human-computer interfaces, database management systems.

Karen J. Ulberg, Adjunct Assistant Professor; Ph.D., North Carolina State, 1994. Extending the relational database model to handle constraints, databases for software engineering.

Mladen A. Vouk, Associate Professor; Ph.D., King's (London), 1976. Software engineering, software testing and reliability, software process and risk management, development of large-scale numerical and scientific systems, computer-based education, multimedia, error-coding in high-speed networks.

Shyhtsun Felix Wu, Assistant Professor; Ph.D., Columbia, 1995. Network security, network control and management, mobile networking, real-time systems, software engineering.

Atef Zaghloul, Adjunct Assistant Professor; Ph.D., North Carolina State, 1993. Network performance modeling.

Associate Faculty Members

Dharma P. Agrawal, Professor of Electrical and Computer Engineering; D.Sc., Lausanne Federal Polytechnic (Switzerland), 1975. Parallel processing, parallelism detection and scheduling, reliability, large network design and routing protocols.

John W. Baugh Jr., Associate Professor of Civil Engineering; Ph.D., Carnegie Mellon, 1989. Computer-aided engineering, parallel and distributed computing, formal specification and verification of software systems, mathematical modeling and optimization.

Erich Kaltofen, Professor of Mathematics; Ph.D., Rensselaer, 1982. Computational algebra and number theory, design and analysis of sequential and parallel algorithms, symbolic manipulation systems and languages.

Carl D. Meyer, Professor of Mathematics; Ph.D., Colorado State, 1968. Numerical analysis, applied linear algebra, discrete Markov chains.

Wesley E. Snyder, Professor of Electrical and Computer Engineering; Ph.D., Illinois, 1975. Computer-based image analysis: robot vision, satellite-based target tracking, and medical imaging; better reconstruction of CT and PET images.

Ioannis Viniotis, Associate Professor of Electrical and Computer Engineering; Ph.D., Maryland, 1988. High-speed networks, queueing systems, stochastic control, multimedia applications.

NORTH CAROLINA STATE UNIVERSITY

DEPARTMENT OF ELECTRICAL AND COMPUTER ENGINEERING

PROGRAMS OF STUDY

The Department of Electrical and Computer Engineering offers programs leading to the Master of Science (M.S.), Master of Engineering (M.E.), and Doctor of Philosophy (Ph.D.) degrees in either computer engineering or electrical engineering. The M.S. degree may be earned under either the thesis or nonthesis option. Either option of the M.S. degree may be designed to provide the background for professional practice or prepare for Ph.D. study. The M.S. program requires 30 hours of course work, 9 of which must be from a designated area of specialization. If the thesis option is selected, up to 6 credit hours of research may be selected. Students seldom need more than two years to meet these requirements. Normally, a student pursuing a Ph.D. takes approximately 72 semester hours of course credits beyond the B.S. degree. Students must pass a qualifying examination (within three semesters of admission into the Ph.D. program), an in-depth examination set by the student's advisory committee, and preliminary and final oral examinations. The Ph.D. degree typically requires four to five years. The department offers the opportunity for study in a large variety of specialties and cross-disciplines. These specialties include digital, analog circuits, and microwave communications and signal processing, biomedical engineering, computer communications, digital systems, electromagnetics, power and control systems, power electronics, solid state, system software, and VLSI design. The department has highly qualified faculty members in all of the above areas. The department cooperates closely with computer science, materials engineering, and operations research. M.S. students following the nonthesis option may choose to either sharply focus their studies on a particular area or study in several of the above areas. M.S. students following the thesis option, as well as Ph.D. students, generally tailor their studies to match their research interests.

RESEARCH FACILITIES

The department has numerous laboratories that support both education and research. These laboratories provide access to special-purpose hardware and software that are not available through other departmental and college computing resources. The department is organized into several research units whose disciplinary areas coincide with faculty research interests. The Solid State Electronics Laboratory emphasizes the study of devices, material processes, and manufacturing equipment for very advanced devices and circuits in both silicon and compound semiconductor technologies. The National Science Foundation's Center for Advanced Electronic Materials Processing (AEMP) has established collaborative research programs with other NCSU departments, North Carolina universities, and institutions to develop new generations of semiconductor manufacturing processes that will enable efficient manufacture of VLSI chips with submicron features. The Power Semiconductor Research Center (PSRC) is supported by an industrial consortium and focuses on advanced smart and integrated devices and circuits for power systems. The Center for Advanced Computing and Communication (CACC) addresses a range of challenges arising in the design of complex, very high performance telecommunications and signal processing systems. The Electronics Research Laboratory focuses on modeling, simulation, and validation of antennas, signal propagation, and micro- and millimeter-wave devices and systems. Research in the Center for Robotics and Intelligent Machines explores a wide range of technological and theoretical issues arising in the design and prototyping of machines that operate with minimal intervention. The Electric Power Research Center (EPRC), operated jointly with the Department of Nuclear Engineering, conducts studies in a range of areas that include distribution systems, load modeling, intelligent fault detection systems, and power quality.

FINANCIAL AID

The department offers a number of graduate teaching, research, and industrial assistantships each year to qualified applicants. The current stipend ranges from $2000 to $14,000 for nine months. A typical academic year assistantship requires 20 hours of work per week and carries a stipend of $8000–$14,000. The College of Engineering offers fellowships of $6000 and $3000. Full-time students holding teaching or research assistantships are eligible to receive tuition remission and health insurance.

COST OF STUDY

The 1996–97 tuition and fees for full-time students were $1,103 per semester for state residents and $5369 for nonresidents.

LIVING AND HOUSING COSTS

On-campus dormitory facilities are provided for unmarried graduate students. In 1996–97, the rent in these dormitories started at $995 per semester. There are a limited number of University-owned apartments for married students; rent for those started at $345 per month.

STUDENT GROUP

Enrollment in the graduate program is more than 380 students, with approximately two thirds of the students in the M.S. programs and the other one third studying for the Ph.D. degree.

STUDENT OUTCOMES

All graduates of the department have found opportunities across the spectrum of industry, government, and education. The industrial employment ranges from self-employed consultants to positions at organizations such as AT&T, Motorola, and Texas Instruments. In government, employment has been gained at institutions such as the Army Research Office, and in education, graduates have obtained positions at various universities.

LOCATION

Raleigh is a relatively small and uncrowded city with a population of about 250,000. The city defines one point of the Research Triangle. The area offers a wide range of cultural activities. The climate is moderate, with four distinct seasons.

THE UNIVERSITY

North Carolina State University is a major research university in the land-grant tradition. The University was founded in 1887, to provide education and encourage economic development in agriculture and engineering. Fall 1996 enrollment exceeded 27,000 students, including 18,500 full-time undergraduate, 5,000 graduate, and 3,400 lifelong education students.

APPLYING

Applicants must have a bachelor's degree from an accredited institution. Ideally this degree should be in electrical engineering or computer engineering. All applicants must have taken the GRE General Test within the past two years. The TOEFL is required for international students whose native language is not English. All application materials for the fall semester must be received by June 25 for U.S. students and by May 1 for international students. For the spring semester, application materials must be received by November 25 and September 15, respectively.

CORRESPONDENCE AND INFORMATION

Dr. A. Reisman, Professor
Director of Graduate Programs
Department of Electrical and Computer Engineering, Box 7911
North Carolina State University
Raleigh, North Carolina 27695-7911

Telephone: 919-515-5091
Fax: 919-515-5601
E-mail: reisman@eos.ncsu.edu
World Wide Web: http://www.ece.ncsu.edu/

NORTH CAROLINA STATE UNIVERSITY
THE FACULTY AND THEIR RESEARCH

D. P. Agrawal, D.Sc., Swiss Federal Institute of Technology. Computer engineering.
S. T. Alexander, Ph.D., North Carolina State. Signal processing.
W. E. Alexander, Ph.D., New Mexico. Signal processing.
W. D. Allen, Ph.D., North Carolina State. Computer engineering.
B. J. Baliga, Ph.D., Rensselaer. Semiconductor devices.
M. E. Baran, Ph.D., Berkeley. Power systems.
S. M. Bedair, Ph.D., Berkeley. Semiconductor materials and devices.
G. Bilbro, Ph.D., Illinois. Communications and signal processing.
D. Bitzer, Ph.D., Illinois. Computer science.
S. Blanchard, Ph.D., Duke. Biomedical engineering.
J. J. Brickley, Ph.D., Virginia. Biomedical devices and systems.
M.-Y. Chow, Ph.D., Cornell. Power systems.
T. M. Conte, Ph.D., Illinois. Computer engineering.
E. Davis, Ph.D., Illinois. Computer architecture.
A. Duel-Hallen, Ph.D., Cornell. Communications.
A. E. Eichenberger, Ph.D., Michigan. Computer engineering.
P. D. Franzon, Ph.D., Adelaide (Australia). Microelectronic systems.
E. D. Gehringer, Ph.D., Purdue. Computer systems, architecture.
T. H. Glisson, Ph.D., SMU. Solid-state device modeling.
C. S. Gloster, Ph.D., North Carolina State. Digital systems.
J. J. Grainger, Ph.D., Wisconsin. Power systems.
E. Grant, Ph.D., Sheffield (Scotland). Robotics.
R. S. Gyurcsik, Ph.D., Berkeley. Computer-aided manufacturing.
J. R. Hauser, Ph.D., Duke. Semiconductor materials and devices.
W. Jasper, Ph.D., Stanford. Real-time control.
J. F. Kauffnam, Ph.D., North Carolina State. Antennas and electromagnetics.
A. W. Kelley, Ph.D., Duke. Power systems.
K. W. Kim, Ph.D., Illinois. Semiconductor devices.
R. M. Kolbas, Ph.D., Illinois. Semiconductor devices.
R. T. Kuehn, Ph.D., North Carolina State. Semiconductor devices.
M. A. Littlejohn, Ph.D., North Carolina State. Semiconductor devices.
W. Liu, Ph.D., Michigan. Microelectronic systems.
G. Lucovsky, Ph.D., Temple. Solid-state physics.
R. C. Luo, Ph.D., Technische Universität Berlin. Artificial intelligence.
N. A. Masnari, Ph.D., Michigan. Semiconductor materials and devices.
N. F. J. Matthews, Ph.D., Princeton. Electromagnetics.
D. McAllister, Ph.D., North Carolina at Chapel Hill. Computer graphics.
J. W. Mink, Ph.D., Wisconsin. Microwave devices and systems.
T. Mitchell, Ph.D., North Carolina State. Communications.
H. T. Nagle, Ph.D., Auburn; M.D., Miami (Florida). Medical electronics.
J. Narayan, Ph.D., Berkeley. Solid-state science.
A. A. Nilsson, Ph.D., Lunds Universitet (Sweden). Communications.
J. B. O'Neal, Ph.D., Florida. Communications.
C. M. Osburn, Ph.D., Purdue. Semiconductor devices.
H. A. Ozturk, Ph.D., North Carolina State. Communications/signal processing.
M. C. Ozturk, Ph.D., North Carolina State. Semiconductor devices.
H. Perros, Ph.D., Trinity (Dublin). Queuing theory.
S. A. Rajala, Ph.D., Rice. Communications and signal processing.
D. S. Reeves, Ph.D., Penn State. Computer systems.
A. Reisman, Ph.D., Polytechnic of Brooklyn. Semiconductor materials and devices.
W. Robbins, Ph.D., Syracuse. Computer graphics.
W. E. Snyder, Ph.D., Illinois. Signal and image processing.
M. Stallmann, Ph.D., Colorado. Network algorithms.
M. B. Steer, Ph.D., Queensland (Australia). Analog and microwave systems.
K. Tai, Ph.D., Cornell. Software systems.
C. Townsend, M.S., Kansas. Circuits.
J. K. Townsend, Ph.D., Kansas. Communications.
H. J. Trussell, Ph.D., New Mexico. Image and signal processing.
I. Viniotis, Ph.D., Maryland. Communications.
M. Vouk, Ph.D., King's College (London). Software testing.
M. K. White, Ph.D., Berkeley. Signal processing.
J. J. Wortman, Ph.D., Duke. Solid-state materials and devices.

NORTHEASTERN UNIVERSITY

COLLEGE OF COMPUTER SCIENCE

PROGRAMS OF STUDY

The College of Computer Science offers programs leading to the M.S. and Ph.D. degrees. The M.S. program is designed for those who are seeking to prepare themselves for organizations that design, develop, market, or utilize computing systems. Forty-eight quarter hours of study are required. Seven areas of concentration are offered: artificial intelligence, communications and networks, databases, graphics and imaging, operating systems, programming languages and compilers, and theory. Admission normally requires a B.S. in computer science. College graduates with equivalent industrial or technical experience may also apply.

The goal of the Ph.D. program is to equip its graduates to conduct state-of-the-art research in computer science, either in academia or in industry. The curriculum aims to fulfill this goal by providing the student with a broad background in the fundamentals of computer science, advanced courses in the dissertation area, and an intensive research experience, culminating in the writing of a dissertation.

The Graduate School of the College of Computer Science offers courses the year round; with careful planning, full-time students may be able to complete the M.S. program in one year. Part-time students usually elect one or two courses per academic quarter and can complete the M.S. degree in two or three years. Most of the graduate courses are offered in the late afternoon and early evening, which enables many students to pursue their graduate degrees while continuing with their daytime employment.

RESEARCH FACILITIES

Equipment in the College of Computer Science is constantly upgraded to keep pace with advances in the computer industry. This equipment currently includes a network of over 80 UNIX workstations, including SUN, DEC, and SPARC. The main server is an Auspex with 10 gigabytes of storage. Additional research equipment includes a network of alphas for high-performance computing, Symbolics LISP machines, an 8K-processor CM-29 from Thinking Machines, and more than 100 microcomputers, including Macintoshes and PCs from a variety of manufacturers.

The Computing Resource Center (CRC) of the Division of Academic Computing provides student access to computing resources. A high-speed data network links users and facilities on the central campus and on three satellite campuses. The campus network is also connected via the global Internet to computing resources around the world. At the University, students have access to Digital VAX systems, labs of microcomputers, a computer mail-and-conferencing system, and an array of specialized computing equipment.

The University Libraries system contains more than 650,000 volumes, 1.5 million microforms, 250,000 documents, 7,000 serial subscriptions, and 15,000 audiotape, videotape, and software titles. A recently constructed, large central library contains technologically sophisticated library services, including an on-line catalog and circulation system, an information gateway, and a seventeen-station network of CD-ROM optical disk databases. Graduate students also have access to other major research collections in the area through the Boston Library Consortium.

FINANCIAL AID

Northeastern University awards need-based financial aid to graduate students through the Federal Perkins Loan, Federal Work-Study, and Federal Stafford Student Loan programs. The University offers a limited number of fellowships and Martin Luther King Jr. Scholarships to students from minority groups. The Graduate School of the College of Computer Science also provides financial assistance through teaching, research, and administrative assistantship awards that include tuition remission and a stipend, typically ranging from $11,000 to $12,500. These assistantships require a maximum of 20 hours of work per week. Also available are a limited number of tuition assistantships, which provide partial or full tuition remission and require a maximum of 10 hours of work per week.

COST OF STUDY

Tuition for 1996–97 was $425 per quarter hour of credit. Where applicable, special tuition charges are made for theses, dissertations, teaching, practicums, and fieldwork. Other charges include the Student Center fee and the health and accident insurance fee required of all full-time students.

LIVING AND HOUSING COSTS

On-campus living expenses are estimated at $900 per month, with on-campus housing available on a limited basis to newly accepted students. Off-campus living expenses are estimated at $1000 per month. A public transportation system services the Greater Boston area, and there are convenient subway and bus services.

STUDENT GROUP

Approximately 30,600 students are enrolled at Northeastern University, representing a wide variety of academic, professional, geographic, and cultural backgrounds. The Graduate School of the College of Computer Science has 170 students, 67 percent of whom attended on a full-time basis.

LOCATION

Boston, the capital city of Massachusetts, offers students extraordinary academic, cultural, and recreational opportunities. In addition to the abundant resources available within Northeastern, there are those of the other educational and cultural institutions of Greater Boston. Boston is a mixture of Colonial tradition and modern America, and it is home to people of every intellectual, political, economic, racial, ethnic, and religious background. It is a place where the past is appreciated, the present enjoyed, and the future anticipated.

THE UNIVERSITY AND THE COLLEGE

Founded in 1898, Northeastern is a privately endowed nonsectarian institution of higher learning and is among the largest private universities in the country. Today, Northeastern has nine undergraduate schools and colleges, ten graduate and professional schools, two undergraduate divisions offering part-time study, a number of continuing and special education programs and institutes, several suburban campuses, and a large research division. The College of Computer Science is a fully accredited, degree-granting academic unit in the United States, now offering the M.S. and Ph.D. in computer science, dedicated to computer science under the cooperative education program. Northeastern's proximity to leading computer companies aids it in promoting exchanges of ideas and improved research and teaching.

APPLYING

An applicant must submit an application form, a nonrefundable application fee, complete official transcripts indicating the award of a bachelor's degree from a recognized institution, a typed 250- to 300-word personal statement, an official copy of scores on the GRE General Test, and three letters of recommendation. Applicants whose native language is not English must submit official TOEFL scores. Acceptance into the College of Computer Science is granted to an applicant upon recommendation of the College's Graduate Committee after a review of the completed application. Applicants may begin their study in any quarter.

CORRESPONDENCE AND INFORMATION

Director of Graduate Studies
College of Computer Science
169 Cullinane Hall
Northeastern University
360 Huntington Avenue
Boston, Massachusetts 02115

Telephone: 617-373-2462
Fax: 617-373-5121
E-mail: csgradinfo@ccs.neu.edu

NORTHEASTERN UNIVERSITY
THE FACULTY AND THEIR RESEARCH

Larry A. Finkelstein, Dean of the College; Ph.D., Birmingham (England). Symbolic problems in algebra, application of group theory to searching, fast algorithms for signal processing, term rewriting systems.

Professors

Agnes H. Chan, Ph.D., Ohio State. Coding and cryptography.

Gene D. Cooperman, Ph.D., Brown. Computer algebra, term rewriting systems, scientific and engineering simulations, aspects of artificial intelligence.

Harriet J. Fell, Ph.D., MIT. Interactive graphics systems, raster graphics algorithms, digital typography, cryptography.

R. Mark Goresky, Ph.D., Brown (Joint with Mathematics). Computational geometry, coding theory, computer experiments and explorations in pure mathematics.

Karl J. Lieberherr, Ph.D., Swiss Federal Institute of Technology. Tools for object-oriented programming, knowledge-based tools for design automation for VLSI, analysis of algorithms.

Richard A. Rasala, Ph.D., Harvard. Image generation, text processing, graphics algorithms.

Betty J. Salzberg, Ph.D., Michigan. Database implementation issues: query optimization, concurrency, recovery and storage options.

Raoul N. Smith, Ph.D., Brown. Intelligent interfaces, knowledge representation, natural-language processing.

Mitchell Wand, Ph.D., MIT. Semantics of programming languages, program verification and construction, algebra and logic.

Patrick S. P. Wang, Ph.D., Oregon State. Artificial intelligence, pattern recognition, programming languages, automata.

Associate Professors

Kenneth P. Baclawski, Ph.D., Harvard. Distributed and object-oriented database systems, high-performance concurrency control methods, data semantics and view integration.

John Casey, B.A., Boston College. Exploring the possibilities of cooperation among numbers of computers on common tasks.

William Clinger, Ph.D., MIT. Semantics and implementation of programming languages.

Robert P. Futrelle, Ph.D., MIT. Artificial intelligence and the construction of expert "scientists' assistants," foundations of social and personal knowledge and cognition relevant to such systems, cellular sensory-motor biophysics.

Carole D. Hafner, Ph.D., Michigan. Natural-language processing, computer representations of real-world knowledge.

Viera K. Proulx, Ph.D., Columbia. Parallel processing, distributed computer systems and architectures.

Ronald J. Williams, Ph.D., California, San Diego. Connectionist networks, cognition, machine learning.

Bryant York, Ph.D., Massachusetts at Amherst. Parallel programming, computer algebra, computing and the handicapped.

Assistant Professors

Jill Crisman, Ph.D., Carnegie Mellon (Joint with ECE). Intelligent robotic systems and active computer vision.

Ibrahim Matta, Ph.D., Maryland. Computer network, numerical analysis.

Boaz Patt-Shamir, Ph.D., MIT. Distributed computing, network protocol, packet-routing algorithms, complexity theory.

Adjunct Professors

John Makhoul, Ph.D., MIT. Image processing.

Eytan Modiano, Ph.D., Maryland. Communication network.

Homer Pieu, Ph.D., Northeastern. Computer vision, image processing

NORTHEASTERN UNIVERSITY

DEPARTMENT OF ELECTRICAL AND COMPUTER ENGINEERING

PROGRAMS OF STUDY

The department offers graduate programs on either a full-time or part-time basis leading to the Master of Science, Electrical Engineer, and Doctor of Philosophy degrees in six areas of concentration: communications and signal processing; computer engineering; control systems and signal processing; electromagnetics, plasma, and optics; electronic circuits and semiconductor devices; and power systems. Techniques from these disciplines are applied to a variety of research problems, including speech and image processing, integrated circuits and VLSI, computer architecture and software development, digital communications, adaptive filtering, electromagnetic scattering, antennas, radar systems, telemetry, and robotics.

The M.S. degree requires 44 quarter hours (equivalent to eleven 4-quarter-hour courses, each of which is one quarter or twelve weeks in duration), which may include at the student's option an 8-quarter-hour master's thesis. The Electrical Engineer degree requires 70 quarter hours of work beyond the B.S. degree, including a thesis of 6 to 10 quarter hours. There is a residence requirement of two academic quarters of full-time study in the same academic year. The Ph.D. degree requires 70 quarter hours of work beyond the B.S. degree, a dissertation representing an original contribution to knowledge in the field, and a technical writing requirement. Students must pass a Ph.D. qualifying examination, consisting of both a written and an oral part, and a comprehensive examination in the major field, and they must present a successful oral defense of the dissertation. The Ph.D. residence requirement is one academic year.

RESEARCH FACILITIES

The department and its two research centers maintain modern laboratory and computer facilities for graduate research. The Center for Electromagnetics Research enables students interested in electromagnetics, optics, microwaves, and plasmas to pursue graduate theses in industry- and government-sponsored research at the University. The Center for Communications and Digital Signal Processing offers students a variety of opportunities for research in digital signal processing, communications, control systems, and robotics. The department has a VLSI/CAD computer facility that includes over seventy DEC and Sun workstations. The Center for Communications and Digital Signal Processing maintains a computing research laboratory for student research. There are also research groups and laboratories in electron devices and computer engineering.

FINANCIAL AID

Northeastern University awards need-based financial aid to graduate students through the Federal Perkins Loan, Federal Work-Study, and Federal Stafford Student Loan programs and offers a limited number of minority fellowships and Martin Luther King Jr. Scholarships. The graduate schools offer financial assistance through teaching, research, and administrative assistantship awards that include tuition remission and a stipend of approximately $11,500 (departmentally specific). These assistantships require a maximum of 20 hours of work per week. There are also a limited number of tuition assistantships that provide partial or full tuition remission and require a maximum of 10 hours of work per week.

COST OF STUDY

The tuition rate for 1997–98 is $440 per quarter hour of credit. There are special tuition charges for theses and dissertations, where applicable. The Student Center fee and health and accident insurance fee required for all full-time students is approximately $950 per academic year.

LIVING AND HOUSING COSTS

On-campus living expenses are estimated at $1000 per month, with on-campus housing available on a limited basis to newly accepted students. Off-campus living expenses are estimated at $950 per month. A public transportation system serves the Greater Boston area, and there are subway and bus services nearby.

STUDENT GROUP

In fall 1996, the department had 143 full-time graduate students and 119 part-time graduate students.

STUDENT OUTCOMES

The majority of graduates find employment in various high-technology industries across the United States. Several Ph.D. graduates are employed by academic institutions in teaching and research.

LOCATION

Northeastern University is located in the heart of Boston, a city that has played a pioneering role in American education. Within a 25-mile radius of the campus there are over fifty degree-granting institutions. Within walking distance of the campus there are numerous renowned cultural centers, such as the Museum of Fine Arts, Isabella Stewart Gardner Museum, Symphony Hall, Horticultural Hall, and Boston Public Library. Theater in Boston includes everything from pre-Broadway to experimental and college productions. The Boston area is also the site of all home games of the Red Sox, Celtics, Bruins, and New England Patriots.

THE UNIVERSITY AND THE DEPARTMENT

Northeastern University is among the nation's largest private universities, with an international reputation as a leader in cooperative education. The cooperative plan of education, initiated by the College of Engineering in 1909 and subsequently adopted by the other colleges of the University, enables students to alternate periods of work and study. The cooperative education plan is available to selected graduate students. Today, Northeastern has eight undergraduate colleges, eight graduate and professional schools, several suburban campuses, and an extensive research division. The Department of Electrical and Computer Engineering offers its full-time day graduate programs at the University's Boston campus and its part-time evening programs at both the Boston campus and the suburban Burlington campus.

APPLYING

All applicants to the M.S. degree program must have a B.S. degree in electrical engineering with an acceptable quality of work from an ABET-accredited undergraduate program. Applicants with a B.S. degree in other engineering or related scientific fields and an appropriate background and preparation may also pursue this program. Applicants to the Electrical Engineer and Ph.D. degree programs should have either a B.S.E.E. or M.S.E.E. with a high quality of work. International students holding undergraduate degrees from recognized engineering institutions outside the United States must submit GRE and TOEFL scores. All applicants must submit a completed application form, including official transcripts and a nonrefundable $50 processing fee. The application deadline for fall admission to the full-time program is April 15. To be considered for an assistantship, the application must be submitted by February 15.

CORRESPONDENCE AND INFORMATION

Cynthia Bates, Coordinator
Office of Graduate Student Affairs
Department of Electrical and Computer Engineering
Northeastern University
360 Huntington Avenue
Boston, Massachusetts 02115

NORTHEASTERN UNIVERSITY
THE FACULTY AND THEIR RESEARCH

D. Brady, Associate Professor; Ph.D., Princeton. Digital communications, multiuser communications.

D. Brooks, Associate Professor; Ph.D., Northeastern. Digital signal processing.

S. Buus, Professor; Ph.D., Northeastern. Speech processing, psychoacoustics.

C. Chan, Professor; Ph.D., Iowa. Plasmas, electromagnetics.

J. Crisman, Associate Professor; Ph.D., Carnegie Mellon. Robotics, robot vision.

A. Devaney, Professor; Ph.D., Rochester. Tomography, electromagnetic wave propagation, inverse scattering, signal processing.

J. Feldman, Professor; Ph.D., Carnegie Mellon. Physical electronics, computers.

A. Grabel, Professor; Sc.D., NYU. Circuit theory, electronics.

J. Hanania, Professor; Ph.D., Leeds. Power systems.

J. Hopwood, Assistant Professor; Ph.D., Michigan State. Plasma processing, IC fabrication.

V. Ingle, Associate Professor; Ph.D., RPI. Signal processing, image processing.

D. Kaeli, Assistant Professor; Ph.D., Rutgers. Computer architecture, software engineering.

M. Kokar, Associate Professor; Ph.D., Technical University of Wroclaw. Artificial intelligence, operating systems.

M. Leeser, Associate Professor; Ph.D., Cambridge. CAD, VLSI design, rapid system prototyping.

B. Lehman, Assistant Professor; Ph.D., Georgia Tech. Control systems, power systems.

H. Lev-Ari, Associate Professor; Ph.D., Stanford. Digital signal processing, adaptive filtering.

E. Manolakos, Associate Professor; Ph.D., USC. Computer architecture, VLSI design, pattern recognition.

N. McGruer, Associate Professor; Ph.D., Michigan State. Solid-state devices, IC fabrication.

L. McIlrath, Assistant Professor; Ph.D., MIT. Analog electronics, VLSI.

S. McKnight, Associate Professor; Ph.D., Maryland. Solid-state devices, electromagnetics.

D. McLaughlin, Associate Professor; Ph.D., Massachusetts. Radar systems, remote sensing.

W. Meleis, Assistant Professor; Ph.D., Michigan. Computer engineering, computer architecture, performance optimization.

E. Miller, Assistant Professor; Ph.D., MIT. Signal and image processing, inverse problems, wavelet and multiscale methods, statistical methods.

S. Mulukutla, Professor; Ph.D., Colorado. Power systems, electrical machinery, electromagnetic theory and its applications to electrical machines.

S. Prasad, Professor; Ph.D., Harvard. Microwave solid-state devices and circuits, high-frequency device modeling.

J. Proakis, Professor; Ph.D., Harvard. Digital communications, adaptive filtering, estimation, digital signal processing.

R. Raghavan, Associate Professor; Ph.D., Massachusetts. Microwaves, remote sensing, electromagnetics.

C. Rappaport, Associate Professor; Sc.D., MIT. Electromagnetics, microwaves.

M. Salehi, Associate Professor; Ph.D., Stanford. Information theory, coding.

S. Sandler, Professor; Ph.D., Harvard. Electromagnetics, antennas, pattern recognition, robotics.

M. Schetzen, Professor; Sc.D., MIT. Systems theory, control systems, theory of nonlinear systems.

P. Serafim, Professor; Sc.D., MIT. Electromagnetics, remote sensing.

B. Shafai, Associate Professor; Ph.D., George Washington. Control systems, digital signal processing.

M. Silevitch, Professor; Ph.D., Northeastern. Computer engineering, plasma theory, applications of plasma theory to auroral phenomena.

A. Stankovic, Assistant Professor; Sc.D., MIT. Power electronics, control systems.

I. Stavrakakis, Associate Professor; Ph.D., Virginia. Communications, networks.

G. Tadmor, Associate Professor; Ph.D., Weizmann (Israel). Control systems.

M. Vai, Associate Professor; Ph.D., Michigan State. VLSI design, computer engineering.

C. Vittoria, Professor; Ph.D., Yale. Electromagnetics, magnetic materials, microwave circuits.

P. Zavracky, Associate Professor; Ph.D., Tufts. Microsensor devices and device fabrication.

Research Areas

Nonlinear systems theory.
Control systems.
Large-scale systems.
Distributed parameter systems.
Machine vision and robotics.
Autonomous intelligent machines.
Speech processing.
Psychoacoustics.
Biomedical signal processing.
Signal and systems analysis.
Plasma theory.
Electromagnetics.
Antennas.
Microwave devices.
High-vacuum phenomena.
Semiconductor devices.
Integrated circuits.
VLSI fabrication, design, and testing.
Active networks.
Gallium arsenide circuits.

Optical electronics and communications.
Holography.
Digital image processing.
Upper-atmosphere phenomena.
Space telemetry and instrumentation.
Radio frequency phenomena and systems.
Computer systems.
Graph theory.
Computer architecture.
Power systems.
Electrical machines.
Digital communications.
Communication networks.
Random-access communications.
Coding theory.
Digital signal processing.
Numerical methods.
Circuit theory.
Stochastic systems.
Information theory.

NORTHWESTERN UNIVERSITY

MCCORMICK SCHOOL OF ENGINEERING AND APPLIED SCIENCE
DEPARTMENT OF COMPUTER SCIENCE

PROGRAM OF STUDY

The department offers a comprehensive program of course work and research leading to the degree of Doctor of Philosophy. A Master of Science degree may be obtained upon completion of a two-year program of courses; however, students are normally admitted only if they intend to complete the Ph.D. program and exhibit the ability to successfully do so. A candidate for the Ph.D. degree is required to complete nine quarters of full-time registration (normally three years, but credits may be transferred from other graduate institutions), pass the departmental qualifying examination, prepare a thesis that presents the results of original research, and pass an oral examination based on the thesis.

Most course work is accomplished in the first two years. Involvement in research typically commences as early as the second quarter. At the close of their second year, students take their Ph.D. qualifying examinations. After admission to candidacy, students work primarily on research.

RESEARCH FACILITIES

The department maintains an extensive network of more than 150 high-end personal computers and workstations, with eighteen assorted servers. The internal network is an FDDI Ring with switched 10T hubs linked to Northwestern's backbone network by ATM fiber. The entire infrastructure is maintained by a professional support staff. Specific services include a 24-gigabyte real-time video server, an Oracle server, and a code manager server. Multimedia production is supported by a complete graphics and video production facility with ten dedicated high-end Macintosh computers. The Autonomous Mobile Robot Laboratory has two high-performance robot systems. The robots are equipped with real-time color vision, simple object grippers, radio modems, and high-end speech synthesizers. The lab also has workstations, video equipment, hardware assembly, and test equipment.

FINANCIAL AID

All applicants for admission are automatically considered for financial aid. Students receiving teaching assistantships are given a nine-month stipend ($11,304 in 1997–98) plus full tuition. Teaching assistants spend 7 to 8 contact hours per week in laboratory teaching or other equivalent duties and approximately another 3 to 4 hours per week in preparation. Fellowships are also available; fellows may receive up to $20,000 over twelve months, with no teaching duties. Students normally receive financial support during the summer.

COST OF STUDY

Tuition in 1997–98 is $19,152 for the three-quarter academic year. (Full tuition remission is offered with teaching assistantships, as noted above.) Books and supplies vary in cost, but a typical figure is $450 per year.

LIVING AND HOUSING COSTS

In 1996, rental rates in the Evanston area ranged from $600 to $900 per month for a one-bedroom apartment and $800 to $1300 per month for a three-bedroom apartment, depending upon location and amenities. Single rooms in shared houses ranged from $300 to $600 per month. Campus dining facilities are available.

STUDENT GROUP

There are currently 40 graduate students in computer science and most receive full financial support. The undergraduate enrollment in the University is 7,300 with approximately equal numbers of men and women. The graduate enrollment on the Evanston campus of Northwestern is 4,000.

STUDENT OUTCOMES

Recent graduates have accepted tenure-track positions at Columbia University and University of Michigan. They have also accepted industrial and business positions in companies such as Xerox and Learning Sciences Corporation as well as becoming independent consultants.

LOCATION

The Evanston campus of Northwestern University stretches for a mile along the western shore of Lake Michigan. Evanston is the first suburb north of Chicago and is one of the most pleasant residential towns of the area. It has an excellent shopping district within walking distance of the campus and four lakefront parks with sandy beaches and picnic areas. Chicago, with its wide variety of shopping facilities, cultural activities, and entertainment, is easily reached by the elevated railroad running close to the campus. A wide variety of activities in the form of sports events, plays, concerts, and public lectures are an integral part of life at Northwestern University.

THE UNIVERSITY

Northwestern's geographical location enables the student to profit from the cultural advantages of a large city, the recreational opportunities of the local environment, and the quieter pace of town life when on campus. There is housing within a 20-minute walk of the campus.

APPLYING

Except in special cases, students are admitted only in September. Completed applications for the forthcoming year should be received by February 1. The General Test of the Graduate Record Examinations is required and students are encouraged to take a Subject Test. These tests should be taken early enough so that test scores are available by February 1. TOEFL scores are required of candidates from non-English-speaking countries. Completed applications and Graduate Record Examinations scores must be submitted by February 1 to be considered for financial support.

CORRESPONDENCE AND INFORMATION

Graduate Admission Coordinator
Computer Science Department
Northwestern University
1890 Maple Avenue
Evanston, Illinois 60201
Telephone: 847-467-7114
E-mail: compsci@cs.nwu.edu

NORTHWESTERN UNIVERSITY
THE FACULTY AND THEIR RESEARCH

Bradley Adelberg, Assistant Professor; Ph.D., Stanford, 1997. Databases, real-time systems, computer architecture.

Lawrence A. Birnbaum, Associate Professor; Ph.D., Yale, 1986. Semantic information processing, educational software design, natural-language processing, memory and learning, interface design/HCI, computer vision.

Eric A. Domeshek, Assistant Professor; Ph.D., Yale, 1992. Case-based design, social representation and simulations, information repositories, applications to computer-based learning environments.

Daniel Edelson, Assistant Professor; Ph.D., Northwestern, 1993. Computer-based learning environments, case-based teaching, computer-supported collaborative learning (CSCL), scientific visualization tools for open-ended inquiry.

Kenneth Forbus, Professor; Ph.D., MIT, 1984. Qualitative physics, analogical reasoning and learning, cognitive simulation.

Louis M. Gomez, Associate Professor; Ph.D., Berkeley, 1979. Design of collaborative learning environments, computer-supported collaborative work, human-computer interaction.

Ian Horswill, Assistant Professor; Ph.D., MIT, 1993. Autonomous agents, robotics, and computer vision; cognitive architecture and situated agency and biological modeling.

Christopher K. Riesbeck, Associate Professor; Ph.D., Stanford, 1974. Natural-language understanding, case-based reasoning, intelligent tutoring systems, intelligent interfaces for knowledge acquisition and teaching, authoring tools for "thick" interfaces.

Roger C. Schank, John Evans Professor and Director of the Institute for the Learning Sciences; Ph.D., Texas, 1969. Artificial intelligence, cognitive science, natural-language processing, learning, models of human reasoning and human memory, computers and education.

RESEARCH FACULTY

Ray Bareiss, Research Associate Professor; Ph.D., Texas, 1988. Computer-based learning environments, corporate memory and computer-based performance support, case-based reasoning, multimedia computing.

Alex Kass, Research Associate Professor; Ph.D., Yale, 1990. Simulation-based training and case presentation, theory-rich authoring tools for learning environments, case-based reasoning, story understanding, hypothesis formation, machine learning, computational creativity.

RESEARCH ACTIVITIES

Northwestern's Department of Computer Science currently emphasizes research in the following five areas:

Artificial intelligence.
Models of memory and reasoning, knowledge of representation, natural-language understanding, planning and problem solving, mobile robots with perceptual systems.

Human computer interaction.
Interface design, task modeling, intelligent interfaces, authoring tools.

Distributed interactive systems.
Client-server and Web-based applications, learning environments for education and training.

Software engineering.
Analysis, design, implementation, evaluation, and maintenance of large applications.

Theoretical computer science.
Algorithm design and the analysis of their worst- and average-case behavior.

MAJOR RESEARCH EFFORTS

Computer-based education and training.
Design of intelligent learning-by-doing environments, construction and evaluation of education and training systems, development of theory-rich authoring tools to speed high-quality system construction.

Intelligent task support.
Generation and use of task models, multimedia corporate memory, semantically appropriate interfaces.

Cognitive simulation of analogical processing.
Structure-mapping engine, MAC/FAC models similarity-based retrieval, MARS models analogical problem solving, problem of solving and reasoning technology.

Qualitative physics.
Qualitative process theory, compositional modeling, qualitative spatial reasoning, self-explanatory simulation, articulate virtual laboratories for science and engineering education.

Autonomous robots.
Development of autonomous robots that seamlessly integrate sensory-motor activities such as navigation and object manipulation with cognitive activities such as following a set of instructions, techniques for real-time visual obstacle avoidance and navigation, object tracking and real-time parallel reasoning systems that interface cleanly with active vision systems.

NORTHWESTERN UNIVERSITY

ROBERT R. MCCORMICK SCHOOL OF ENGINEERING
AND APPLIED SCIENCE OF THE TECHNOLOGICAL INSTITUTE
DEPARTMENT OF ELECTRICAL AND COMPUTER ENGINEERING

PROGRAMS OF STUDY

The Department of Electrical and Computer Engineering offers a broad range of programs in electrical and computer engineering, or a combination of both, leading to the degrees of Master of Science and Doctor of Philosophy. The M.S. requires a minimum of one academic year of full-time study, and the Ph.D. requires a minimum of three years beyond the B.S. degree. Fields of study include biomedical electronics, communication systems and networks, computational electromagnetics, computer architecture, control systems and robotics, detection and estimation, digital circuits, digital signal and image processing, electronic devices and materials, lasers, neural networks, nonlinear and quantum optics, numerical analysis, numerical optimization, optical communications, optical materials, quantum electronics, distributed and parallel computing, VLSI and CAD, and embedded systems.

RESEARCH FACILITIES

The department has well-equipped laboratories for electronic circuits, digital circuits, solid-state electronics, thin-film device development, biomedical electronics, microwave techniques, real-time control systems, guided-wave and nonlinear optics, fiber optics, biological control systems, digital systems design, digital signal processing, neural information processing, image and speech processing, MOCVD, MOMBE reactors for optoelectronic materials and devices fabrication, numerical analysis, computer architecture, distributed computing systems, robotics, VLSI/CAD, communication networks, and microprocessor systems design. The department also uses the facilities of the Center for Quantum Devices, Materials Research Center, Manufacturing Engineering Center, and Advanced Cement Based Materials Center.

The department's ECE Computing Laboratory has a number of interconnected UNIX computers, including several NFS file servers and a public access lab containing client workstations and X terminals. The departmental ethernet LAN interconnects all faculty and graduate student offices and lab spaces. The department offers the standard panoply of Internet services, including USENET news, anonymous FTP, WWW, and gopher, and is directly connected to the campus high-speed backbone. In addition, it offers an extensive software library for teaching and research. A dedicated modem-pool, which supports standard dial-up access, SLIP, and PPP, provides users with remote access to the LAN.

The Robert R. McCormick School of Engineering and Applied Science (MEAS) is located in the Technological Institute. Connected to the Technological Institute is the Science and Engineering Library. The University's main library is also close to the Technological Institute.

FINANCIAL AID

Many types of financial support, awarded on a competitive basis, are available for graduate students at Northwestern. Full institutional stipends range from $11,304 to $13,300 plus tuition for nine months. Veterans' benefits may be received simultaneously with other aid. University awards include the Walter P. Murphy fellowships, teaching assistantships, and research assistantships. Other fellowships provided by various government agencies and industry pay for tuition and offer stipends to cover living expenses. Stipends usually increase after the first year of study.

COST OF STUDY

Tuition for 1997–98 is $6384 per quarter, except for students who have been admitted to candidacy for the Ph.D., for whom tuition is $2012 per quarter.

LIVING AND HOUSING COSTS

Northwestern operates two apartment buildings in Evanston for single and married graduate students. Additional accommodations at reasonable costs are available in Evanston and nearby communities for students who choose to rent rooms, apartments, or houses from private owners.

STUDENT GROUP

The schools on the Evanston campus annually enroll 7,604 full-time undergraduates and 4,148 full-time graduate students. The University's total annual enrollment of about 17,880 students includes 2,262 full-time students on the Chicago campus and all men and women registered in the summer session, evening divisions, and part-time programs on both campuses. MEAS has a current graduate enrollment of 932 students, of whom 154 are in the Department of Electrical and Computer Engineering.

LOCATION

In addition to enjoying the extensive cultural activities and sports offered at the University, graduate students make good use of the cultural advantages of the Chicago area. The location provides a good combination of urban amenities and the pleasant environment of a suburban residential community.

THE UNIVERSITY AND THE SCHOOL

Northwestern University, founded in 1851, is a coeducational institution and the only privately supported university in the Big Ten. Northwestern has two campuses on the shore of Lake Michigan, one in suburban Evanston and the other near the downtown center of Chicago. There are 2,072 full-time faculty members at Northwestern; 89 percent of them hold doctorates or the equivalent.

The McCormick School of Engineering and Applied Science is located on the Evanston campus. Within MEAS are the Departments of Biomedical Engineering, Chemical Engineering, Civil Engineering, Electrical and Computer Engineering, Computer Science, Engineering Sciences and Applied Mathematics, Industrial Engineering and Management Sciences, Materials Science and Engineering, and Mechanical Engineering. Currently, several million dollars is being spent for graduate education and research.

Interdisciplinary research opportunities are available at various centers, including the Center for Quantum Devices, the Center for Information and Telecommunication Technology, the Manufacturing Engineering Center, the Materials Research Center, and the Institute for the Learning Sciences.

APPLYING

Graduate students are admitted primarily for the fall quarter. Completed applications for admission and for financial aid should be received by January 15.

CORRESPONDENCE AND INFORMATION

Graduate Director
Department of Electrical and Computer Engineering
Technological Institute
Northwestern University
Evanston, Illinois 60208-3118

Telephone: 847-491-7092
E-mail: grad@ece.nwu.edu
World Wide Web: http://www.ece.nwu.edu

NORTHWESTERN UNIVERSITY
THE FACULTY AND THEIR RESEARCH

A. H. Haddad, Henry and Isabelle Dever Professor and Chairman of the Department; Ph.D., Princeton. Stochastic systems, modeling, estimation, detection, nonlinear filtering, singular perturbation, applications to communications and control.

Prithviraj Banerjee, Walter P. Murphy Professor; Ph.D., Illinois at Urbana-Champaign. Parallel compilers and software, parallel architectures, parallel algorithms for VLSI CAD.

Alvin Bayliss, Professor; Ph.D., NYU. Numerical analysis, large-scale scientific computing, computational fluid dynamics.

Morris E. Brodwin, Emeritus Professor; Ph.D., Johns Hopkins. Electromagnetic characterization and thermal processing of materials.

Arthur R. Butz, Associate Professor; Ph.D., Minnesota. Digital signal processing.

Robert P. H. Chang, Professor; Ph.D., Princeton. Thin films for electronic and optoelectronic device applications.

Alok N. Choudhary, Associate Professor; Ph.D., Illinois at Urbana-Champaign. High-performance computing and communication, input-output, compiler and runtime systems for HPCC, multimedia systems and databases.

Randy A. Freeman, Assistant Professor; Ph.D., California, Santa Barbara. Robust nonlinear control, optimal control.

Scott A. Hauck, Assistant Professor; Ph.D., Washington, Seattle. Multi-FPGA systems, FPGA architectures and CAD tools, rapid-prototyping, asynchronous circuit and VLSI design, parallel processing and parallel programming languages.

Lisa Hellerstein, Assistant Professor; Ph.D., Berkeley. Computational learning theory, complexity theory, algorithms.

Lawrence J. Henschen, Professor; Ph.D., Illinois at Urbana-Champaign. AI, theorem proving, deductive databases.

Seng-Tiong Ho, Associate Professor; Ph.D., MIT. Quantum optics, nonlinear optics, ultrafast optical devices, microcavity lasers.

Michael L. Honig, Ameritech Professor; Ph.D., Berkeley. Digital communications, wireless communications, networks, signal processing.

Carl R. Kannewurf, Professor; Ph.D., Northwestern. Electronic materials: electrical and optical phenomena in semiconductors and metals, high-T_c superconductors, low dimensional materials and devices.

Aggelos K. Katsaggelos, Professor; Ph.D., Georgia Tech. Multidimensional digital signal processing, processing of moving images, video coding, computational vision, parallel implementation of signal processing algorithms.

Andrew E. Kertesz, Professor and Chairman of the Department of Biomedical Engineering; Ph.D., Northwestern. Binocular information processing and oculomotor control by the human visual system, medical instrumentation.

Gilbert K. Krulee, Professor; Ph.D., MIT. Natural language systems, two-level grammars, intelligent support systems.

Prem Kumar, Professor; Ph.D., SUNY at Buffalo. Nonlinear and quantum optics, picosecond and subpicosecond phenomena, laser and atomic physics, optical communications and networks.

Srikanta P. Kumar, Associate Professor; Ph.D., Yale. Communication and computer networks, wireless and personal communication systems, stochastic modeling, performance analysis, distributed systems and protocols, queuing, adaptive control.

Chung-Chieh Lee, Professor; Ph.D., Princeton. Digital communications, communication network performance modeling and analysis, distributed multisensor detection and estimation.

Der-Tsai Lee, Professor; Ph.D., Illinois at Urbana-Champaign. Design and analysis of algorithms, data structures, VLSI systems, computational geometry, computational complexity, algorithm visualization.

Wei-Chung Lin, Associate Professor; Ph.D., Purdue. Computer vision, pattern recognition, neural networks, computer graphics.

Michel E. Marhic, Professor; Ph.D., UCLA. Optical networks, optical coding, nonlinear optics of fibers, optical storage.

Gordon J. Murphy, Emeritus Professor; Ph.D., Minnesota. Integrated computer-control systems, automated manufacturing systems, digital signal processing, microprocessor-based systems.

Nathan Newman, Associate Professor; Ph.D., Stanford. Fabrication of novel solid-state materials and devices, characterization and modeling of surface, interface and bulk phenomena in solids.

Jorge Nocedal, Professor; Ph.D., Rice. Numerical analysis, nonlinear optimization, applied linear algebra, numerical software.

Martin A. Plonus, Professor; Ph.D., Michigan. Electromagnetic theory, particularly propagation and scattering of electromagnetic waves and optical communication through the turbulent atmosphere, consumer electronics.

Mort Rahimi, Professor and Vice President of the University; Ph.D., Iowa. Artificial languages, computer networks, IT management.

Manijeh Razeghi, Walter P. Murphy Professor and Director of the Center for Quantum Devices; Ph.D., Paris. Solid-state science and technology; semiconductors: materials growth, physics, optical, electrical and structural characterization; opto-electronic device modeling and fabrication.

Alan V. Sahakian, Associate Professor; Ph.D., Wisconsin-Madison. Instrumentation, signal processing for medical applications.

Majid Sarrafzadeh, Professor; Ph.D., Illinois at Urbana-Champaign. VLSI design, computer-aided design, high-performance architectural design, design and analysis of algorithms, computational complexity, low power systems.

Peter I. Scheuermann, Associate Professor; Ph.D., SUNY at Stony Brook. Physical database design, pictorial databases, parallel I/O systems, parallel algorithms for data-intensive applications, distributed database systems.

Eric J. Schwabe, Assistant Professor; Ph.D., MIT. Parallel algorithms and architectures, network emulations, graph theory.

Allen Taflove, Professor; Ph.D., Northwestern. Applied electromagnetic field theory and applications, computational electromagnetics, scattering and diffraction, supercomputing, Maxwell's equations–based computational nonlinear optics, electromagnetic waves in nonlinear dispersive media, femtosecond optical switches.

Valerie E. Taylor, Assistant Professor; Ph.D., Berkeley. Computer architecture, parallel processing, hardware development and analysis for scientific computations, and special-purpose processors.

James E. Van Ness, Emeritus Professor; Ph.D., Northwestern. Use of the digital computer to study large dynamic systems, numerical analysis, control systems, power systems.

Bruce W. Wessels, Professor; Ph.D., MIT. Compound semiconductors, materials preparation, defect studies by deep-level transient spectroscopy, MOCVD processing of ceramic superconductors.

Chi-Haur Wu, Associate Professor; Ph.D., Purdue. Robotics, CAD/CAM, industrial control, neural network, surgical robots.

Horace P. Yuen, Professor; D.Sc., MIT. Optical communication, theoretical quantum optics, measurement theory.

NOVA SOUTHEASTERN UNIVERSITY

THE SCHOOL OF COMPUTER AND INFORMATION SCIENCES

PROGRAMS OF STUDY

The School has become a major force in educational innovation, distinguished by its ability to offer both traditional and nontraditional choices in educational programs and formats that enable professionals to pursue advanced degrees without career interruption. M.S. degrees are available in several areas, including computer information systems, computer science, computing technology in education, and management information systems. The School offers the Ph.D. in computer information systems, computer science, information systems, and information science and the Ph.D. or Ed.D. in computing technology in education. Professionals may earn the M.S. degree in eighteen months. M.S. programs in computer science, computer information systems, and management information systems can be taken in the evening on the Main Campus. M.S. programs in computer science, computer information systems, management information systems, and computing technology in education can be taken on-line following an on-campus weekend orientation. Terms start in September, January, April, and July. Depending on the program, doctoral students may take one of two formats: cluster or institute. Cluster students attend four cluster meetings per year, held quarterly over an extended weekend (Friday, Saturday, and half of Sunday) at the University. Cluster terms start in March and September. Cluster weekends take place in March, June, September, and December. Institute students attend weeklong institutes in January and July at the University. Clusters and institutes bring together students and faculty members for participation in courses, workshops, training, and dissertation counseling. Between meetings, students complete assignments, research papers and projects, and participate in on-line activities that facilitate frequent interaction among faculty members, classmates, and colleagues. The on-line component may involve NSU's real-time electronic classroom, computer conferences, submission of assignments, electronic mail, the electronic library, and use of the Internet. The Ph.D.'s in computer science and computer information systems are offered in cluster format and require 68 credits, including eight 3-credit courses, six 4-credit projects, and the dissertation. They may be completed in four years. Doctoral programs in information systems, information science, and computing technology in education are offered in cluster and institute formats and require 64 credits, including eight 3-credit courses, four 4-credit projects, and the dissertation. They may be completed in three years.

RESEARCH FACILITIES

Computing facilities include ten Sun servers, nine of which are SPARCserver 1000E's and one of which is a SPARCserver 20 running Solaris; a DEC 5910 running Ultrix; and a DEC VAX 6610 and DEC VAX 4500 running VMS. The Sun servers are connected to two Sun storage arrays that provide a total of 30 gigabytes of mirrored critical data using RAID 0+1. The two VAX machines are connected to a DEC storage works box with 24 gigabytes of disk space. There are also fourteen Sun workstations used by faculty members and staff. Students have access to four Sun workstations, 320 IBM personal computers, and fifty Apple Macintoshes in fourteen microcomputer laboratories. The PCs are connected to six servers with an application storage area of 16 gigabytes. The network includes a T-1 Internet connection, capacity for more than 200 dial-up connections via a local modem pool and a national switched public data network, five WAN connections to satellite campus locations in the area, FDDI connections between all major buildings, and support for 5,700 connections at all the campus locations.

FINANCIAL AID

The Office of Student Financial Aid administers the University's financial aid programs of grants, loans, scholarships, and student employment and provides professional financial advisers to help students plan for the most efficient use of their financial resources for education. To qualify for financial aid, a student must be admitted into a University program, must be a U.S. citizen or a U.S. immigrant, and must plan on registering for a minimum of 6 credit hours per term. A prospective student who requires financial assistance should apply for financial aid while a candidate for admission. For financial aid information or application forms, students should call 800-522-3243.

COST OF STUDY

For the 1997–98 academic year, tuition is $350 per credit for master's students; for doctoral students, semiannual tuition is $3925.

LIVING AND HOUSING COSTS

There are many furnished apartments available for lease on an annual basis to graduate students and married students without children. These apartments are located in several buildings on the Main Campus. Application for housing for the fall term should be submitted prior to May 31. For additional information, students should call the Office of Student Housing at 800-541-6682 Ext. 5654.

STUDENT GROUP

The School of Computer and Information Sciences has more than 600 graduate students from across the U.S. and other countries and has been awarding graduate degrees since 1984.

LOCATION

The School is located on NSU's East Campus in Fort Lauderdale, Florida. In addition to the Main Campus and East Campus, NSU has facilities in downtown Fort Lauderdale, Coral Springs, and Port Everglades.

THE UNIVERSITY

NSU is the forty-seventh-largest independent academic institution in the U.S. and the largest in Florida. It has a 250-acre campus in Fort Lauderdale, with more than 10,000 students on campus and 4,000 students in programs elsewhere in Florida, in twenty-four other states, and in several other countries. In addition to The School of Computer and Information Sciences, the University has an undergraduate college and graduate schools of law, medicine, clinical psychology, education, business, oceanography, pharmacy, and social and systemic studies. It is also the home of the Miami Dolphins' training facility. NSU has enjoyed full accreditation by the Commission on Colleges of the Southern Association of Colleges and Schools since 1971.

APPLYING

Applications, including transcripts and recommendations, should be submitted at least three months before the anticipated starting term. Students who wish to matriculate in a shorter amount of time must contact the SCIS admissions office by telephone to begin the process. Copies of transcripts are acceptable for unofficial early review. Students applying late may be granted provisional acceptance pending completion of the application process. Master's terms start in September, January, April, and July. Doctoral cluster terms start in September and March. Doctoral institute terms start in January and July.

CORRESPONDENCE AND INFORMATION

The School of Computer and Information Sciences
Nova Southeastern University
3100 Southwest 9th Avenue
Fort Lauderdale, Florida 33315
Telephone: 954-262-2000
        800-986-2247 Ext. 2000 (toll-free)
E-mail: scisinfo@scis.nova.edu
World Wide Web: http://www.scis.nova.edu

NOVA SOUTHEASTERN UNIVERSITY
THE FACULTY AND THEIR RESEARCH AREAS

Gertrude W. Abramson, Professor; Ed.D., Columbia. Computer education, hypermedia/multimedia, authoring systems, courseware design, distance learning.

Wilker S. Bruce, Assistant Professor; Ph.D., Nova Southeastern. Artificial intelligence, genetic algorithms, operating systems.

Maxine S. Cohen, Assistant Professor; Ph.D., SUNY. Human-computer interaction, usability engineering, database systems, computer science education.

Laurie P. Dringus, Assistant Professor; Ph.D., Nova Southeastern. Human-computer interaction, group support systems, learning theory, distance education.

George K. Fornshell, Associate Professor; Ph.D., Nova Southeastern. Instructional systems development, multimedia, authoring systems, human factors, distance education.

Rollins Guild, Assistant Professor; Ph.D., Nova Southeastern. Mathematical modeling, computer graphics, programming languages, artificial intelligence.

Michael J. Laszlo, Associate Professor; Ph.D., Princeton. Computer graphics, data structures and algorithms, software engineering, programming.

Jacques Levin, Professor; Ph.D., Grenoble (France). Database management, modeling, distance education, decision support systems, numerical analysis.

Edward Lieblein, Professor and Dean; Ph.D., Pennsylvania. Software engineering, object-oriented design, programming languages, automata theory.

Marlyn Kemper Littman, Professor; Ph.D., Nova Southeastern. Computer networks, broadband communications, multimedia, telecommunications, emerging technologies.

Frank Mitropoulos, Instructor; M.S., Nova Southeastern. Programming languages, data structures, software engineering, object-oriented design, on-line systems for distance learning.

Sumitra Mukherjee, Assistant Professor; Ph.D., Carnegie Mellon. Database security, decision support systems, artificial intelligence applications.

Raul Salazar, Assistant Professor; Ph.D., Nova Southeastern. Multimedia, computer networks, programming languages, computer systems, computer graphics.

John Scigliano, Professor; Ed.D., Florida. On-line information systems, information systems management, distance education.

Junping Sun, Associate Professor; Ph.D., Wayne State. Database management systems, object-oriented database systems, artificial neural networks.

Raisa Szabo, Instructor; M.S., Budapest Technical Institute. Computer architecture, artificial intelligence, neural networks, robotics, operations research.

Steven R. Terrell, Associate Professor; Ed.D., Florida International. Research methodology and statistics, learning theory, distance education, computer-managed instruction.

Adjunct Faculty

Alfred Adler, Ph.D., Michigan. Computer-aided design, numerical control, operating systems, algorithms.

Muchuan M. Chen, Ph.D., Pennsylvania. Signal processing algorithms, computer architecture, database design.

Richard D. Manning, Sc.D., Nova Southeastern. Strategic planning of management information systems, decision support systems, telecommunications.

Michael R. Mocciola, Ed.D., Columbia. Multimedia applications, distance education, mathematics education.

Michael Moody, Ph.D., Nova Southeastern. Decision support systems, computer networks, database systems, artificial intelligence, systems usability assessment.

Angela Trujillo, Ph.D., Nova Southeastern. Data communications, telecommunications.

Steven Zink, Ph.D., Nova Southeastern. Information science, information systems, digital libraries, information policy.

The Mailman Hollywood building houses the computer link to students through out the world.

Students attending class in NSU's state-of-the-art computer facilities.

NSU is located on a 315-acre campus in Ft. Lauderdale, Florida.

THE OHIO STATE UNIVERSITY

DEPARTMENT OF COMPUTER AND INFORMATION SCIENCE

PROGRAMS OF STUDY

The department offers graduate programs leading to the M.S. and Ph.D. degrees. It also offers joint M.S. degree programs with the Departments of Mathematics and Biomedical Engineering and with the Center for Mapping. Research areas include artificial intelligence, combinatorial algorithms, computational geometry, concurrent programming, database systems, data translation, graphics, image analysis, multimedia, networking, neural networks, object-oriented applications, parallel and distributed computing, parallel computer architecture, performance evaluation, reusable software, robotics, scientific computing, software engineering, theoretical computer science, and visualization.

Requirements for the Ph.D. degree include course work and a preliminary examination based on initial and proposed thesis research. The M.S. degree, whether completed with a thesis option or a comprehensive examination option, usually takes two years.

RESEARCH FACILITIES

Computing facilities used for instruction and research include workstations and PCs (347 HP workstations, 230 Sun workstations, various Macintoshes and PCs); file servers (thirty-eight HP, thirty-one Sun, eight NT); peripherals (twenty-six HP 4si/mx laser printers, four Apple LaserWriters, eight Sony 1271 projection units); ATM, Fast Ethernet, and Myrinet interconnections; supercomputer access through the Ohio Supercomputer Center; Cray T90 (four processors); Cray T3E (128 processors); Convex Exemplar (sixteen processors); SGI PowerChallenge (sixteen processors); and IBM SP-2 (eight processors).

FINANCIAL AID

Financial aid is available to students in the form of teaching assistantships, research assistantships, and fellowships. These all provide tuition and fee waivers and a significant stipend. Special fellowships for members of minority groups are also available.

COST OF STUDY

In-state tuition for 1997–98 is $1767 per quarter, and out-of-state tuition is $4397 per quarter.

LIVING AND HOUSING COSTS

In addition to dormitories, University-operated one- and two-bedroom apartments are available for married students; the cost is $365–$465 per month. There is also a substantial amount of off-campus housing in the immediate area with similar costs.

STUDENT GROUP

The department has about 180 graduate students, with about 50 new students entering each year. About sixteen Ph.D. degrees and forty-five M.S. degrees are awarded each year.

STUDENT OUTCOMES

Of the Ph.D. graduates, approximately 70 percent take jobs in industry and 30 percent in academia.

LOCATION

The Ohio State University is located about 3 miles north of downtown Columbus, the capital of Ohio. The city has a metro population of about 1.4 million and is one of the fastest-growing urban areas in the United States. Columbus is a global center for high technology (especially in information services), home to an active arts community, and serves as the corporate and divisional headquarters for a number of major corporations.

THE UNIVERSITY AND THE DEPARTMENT

The University was founded as a land-grant institution in 1870. It has one of the most comprehensive academic programs of any university in the world, many of which are ranked among the top twenty-five in the country. *U.S. News & World Report* recently ranked the Ohio State University fifteenth among public universities in the United States for overall academic reputation.

The Department of Computer and Information Science, formed in 1968, has a tenure-track faculty of 33 members, all of whom hold a Ph.D., as well as several auxiliary and part-time faculty members. All regular faculty members lead active research programs, and a high-quality graduate student population contributes to the intellectual vitality of the department. In 1996, a survey published in *Communications of the ACM* ranked the department fourteenth among academic computer science departments in the number of research publications appearing in prestigious IEEE and ACM transactions.

APPLYING

For autumn quarter admission, all application materials must be received by August 15 (or by July 1 for those applying from abroad). All assistantship and fellowship applications must be received in the Admissions Office by January 15. Applicants must take the GRE General Test, and it is strongly recommended that they submit scores from the GRE Subject Test in Computer Science or another Subject Test (such as Engineering, Mathematics, or Physics). The TOEFL is required and the TSE highly recommended for applicants whose native language is not English. If an applicant's undergraduate course work is not in computer science, significant related course work is expected.

CORRESPONDENCE AND INFORMATION

Graduate Admissions Secretary
Department of Computer and Information Science
2015 Neil Avenue
The Ohio State University
Columbus, Ohio 43210-1277
Telephone: 614-292-7084
Fax: 614-292-2911
E-mail: oncill@cis.ohio-state.edu
World Wide Web: http://www.cis.ohio-state.edu/
   ~grad-adm/

Office of Admissions
The Ohio State University
3rd Floor, Lincoln Tower
1800 Cannon Drive
Columbus, Ohio 43210-1277
Telephone: 614-292-3980
World Wide Web: http://www.afa.adm.ohio-state.edu/

THE OHIO STATE UNIVERSITY
THE FACULTY AND THEIR RESEARCH

Anish Arora, Assistant Professor; Ph.D., Texas at Austin, 1992. Fault-tolerance, distributed systems, concurrency semantics. (E-mail: anish@cis.ohio-state.edu)

Wayne Carlson, Associate Professor; Ph.D., Ohio State, 1982. Computer graphics and animation. (E-mail: waynec@cis.ohio-state.edu)

B. Chandrasekaran, Professor; Ph.D., Pennsylvania, 1967. Intelligence–problem solving, understanding, explanation. (E-mail: chandra@cis.ohio-state.edu)

Roger Crawfis, Assistant Professor; Ph.D., California, Davis, 1995. Computer graphics and scientific visualization. (E-mail: crawfis@cis.ohio-state.edu)

Wu-Chi Feng, Assistant Professor; Ph.D., Michigan, 1996. Multimedia networking and computing. (E-mail: wuchi@cis.ohio-state.edu)

Kikuo Fujimura, Assistant Professor; Ph.D., Maryland, 1989. Computer graphics, image analysis, robotics. (E-mail: fujimura@cis.ohio-state.edu)

Eitan M. Gurari, Associate Professor; Ph.D., Minnesota, 1978. Literate programming, graphic languages. (E-mail: gurari@cis.ohio-state.edu)

Mary Jean Harrold, Assistant Professor; Ph.D., Pittsburgh, 1988. Program analysis–based software engineering, Aristotle Analysis System. (E-mail: harrold@cis.ohio-state.edu)

Chua-Huang Huang, Associate Professor; Ph.D., Texas, 1987. Parallelizing compiler, parallel programming methodology. (E-mail: chh@cis.ohio-state.edu)

Raj Jain, Professor; Ph.D., Harvard, 1978. Computer networking architectures. (E-mail: jain@cis.ohio-state.edu)

Douglas S. Kerr, Associate Professor; Ph.D., Purdue, 1967. Database systems, performance measurement. (E-mail: doug@cis.ohio-state.edu)

Ten-Hwang Lai, Associate Professor; Ph.D., Minnesota, 1982. Parallel and distributed computing. (E-mail: lai@cis.ohio-state.edu)

Richard Lewis, Assistant Professor; Ph.D., Carnegie Mellon, 1993. Cognitive modeling, computational psycholinguistics, architectures for intelligence. (E-mail: rick@cis.ohio-state.edu)

Ming-Tsan Liu, Professor; Ph.D., Pennsylvania, 1964. Distributed computing, computer networking. (E-mail: liu@cis.ohio-state.edu)

Timothy J. Long, Associate Professor; Ph.D., Purdue, 1978. Theoretical computer science, complexity theory. (E-mail: long@cis.ohio-state.edu)

Sandra A. Mamrak, Professor; Ph.D., Illinois, 1975. Data translation, object-oriented applications. (E-mail: mamrak@cis.ohio-state.edu)

Renee Miller, Assistant Professor; Ph.D., Wisconsin, 1994. Heterogeneous databases and semantic interoperability. (E-mail: rjmiller@cis.ohio-state.edu)

Ramon E. Moore, Professor; Ph.D., Stanford, 1963. Reliable scientific computing. (E-mail: moore-r@cis.ohio-state.edu)

Mervin E. Muller, Professor; Ph.D., UCLA, 1954. Distributed computing, performance analysis. (E-mail; muller-m@cis.ohio-state.edu)

William F. Ogden, Associate Professor; Ph.D., Stanford, 1969. Software engineering. (E-mail: ogden@cis.ohio-state.edu)

Thomas Page, Assistant Professor; Ph.D., UCLA, 1989. Distributed systems and performance analysis. (E-mail: page@cis.ohio-state.edu)

Dhabaleswar K. Panda, Assistant Professor; Ph.D., USC, 1991. Parallel computer architectures, interprocessor communication. (E-mail: panda@cis.ohio-state.edu)

Richard Parent, Associate Professor; Ph.D., Ohio State, 1977. Computer graphics and animation. (E-mail: parent@cis.ohio-state.edu)

Ponnuswamy Sadayappan, Associate Professor; Ph.D., SUNY at Stony Brook, 1983. Parallel algorithms and computation. (E-mail: saday@cis.ohio-state.edu)

Mukesh Singhal, Associate Professor; Ph.D., Maryland, 1986. Distributed systems, performance evaluation, operating systems. (E-mail: singhal@cis.ohio-state.edu)

Jack Smith, Associate Professor, Ph.D., West Virginia. Medical artificial intelligence systems (E-mail: smith@cis.ohio-state.edu)

Neelamegam Soundarajan, Associate Professor; Ph.D., Bombay, 1978. Semantics of distributed, concurrent programs. (E-mail: neelam@cis.ohio-state.edu)

Kenneth J. Supowit, Associate Professor; Ph.D., Illinois, 1981. Combinatorial algorithms. (E-mail; supowit@cis.ohio-state.edu)

DeLiang Wang, Assistant Professor; Ph.D., USC, 1991. Neural networks and cognitive modeling. (E-mail: dwang@cis.ohio-state.edu)

Bruce W. Weide, Associate Professor; Ph.D., Carnegie-Mellon, 1978. Reusable software. (E-mail: weide@cis.ohio-state.edu)

Rephael Wenger, Assistant Professor; Ph.D., McGill, 1988. Computational geometry. (E-mail: wenger@cis.ohio-state.edu)

Roni Yagel, Assistant Professor; Ph.D., SUNY at Stony Brook, 1991. Computer graphics, volume rendering, scientific visualization. (E-mail: yagel@cis.ohio-state.edu)

Feng Zhao, Assistant Professor; Ph.D., MIT, 1992. Expert reasoning, intelligent scientific/engineering computation. (E-mail: fz@cis.ohio-state.edu)

Stuart H. Zweben, Professor and Chairman; Ph.D., Purdue, 1974. Software engineering. (E-mail: zweben@cis.ohio-state.edu)

OHIO UNIVERSITY

FRITZ J. & DOLORES H. RUSS COLLEGE OF ENGINEERING AND TECHNOLOGY
SCHOOL OF ELECTRICAL ENGINEERING AND COMPUTER SCIENCE

PROGRAMS OF STUDY

Programs leading to the M.S. and Ph.D. degrees in electrical engineering are available. Major areas of study include avionics, computers, applied and theoretical computer science, communications, controls, information theory, solid-state electronics, energy conversion, power electronics, power systems, electromagnetics, signal processing, manufacturing, VLSI design, computer vision, electronic circuits, and optoelectronics. Successful applicants for the Ph.D. degree program are expected to hold an M.S. degree in electrical engineering, computer science, or a related field of engineering or the physical sciences. Typically, Ph.D. students complete two academic years of formal course work in a major area, a minor area, and either mathematics or physics, followed by a written comprehensive examination and an oral examination that includes the presentation of a dissertation research proposal. The remainder of the Ph.D. degree program consists of dissertation research, preparation of the dissertation, and the dissertation defense. The average duration of the program is four years. Ohio University regulations require that candidates for the Ph.D. degree be in residence for a minimum of three academic quarters. Recipients of the Ph.D. degree are prepared for research careers in the private, public, and academic sectors. Successful applicants for the M.S. degree are expected to hold a B.S degree in electrical engineering, computer science, or a related field of engineering or the physical sciences. The typical M.S. degree program consists of one year of formal course work followed by thesis research, preparation of the thesis, and a combined oral examination and thesis defense. The average duration of the M.S. program is two years. Recipients of the M.S. degree are prepared to enter the engineering profession at an advanced level or to pursue more advanced graduate work.

RESEARCH FACILITIES

The School of Electrical Engineering and Computer Science occupies the entire third floor of the five-story, 159,000-square-foot C. Paul and Beth K. Stocker Engineering and Technology Center and the fourth floor of Morton Hall. The Avionics Engineering Center, an administrative unit of the School, occupies a large portion of the second floor of Stocker Center. State-of-the-art laboratories are maintained to support research activities in avionics, computer networking, communications, computer vision, optoelectronics, controls, VLSI design, manufacturing, and large-scale software integration. Computing facilities include more than 35 UNIX workstations, access to the Ohio University mainframes and the Ohio Supercomputer, and numerous late-model personal computers. Licenses for recent releases of all major software tools in areas of current research activity are maintained. Historically, the School has been highly successful in maintaining its computer hardware and software capabilities at a state-of-the-art level. Roughly half of the $15-million Stocker Endowment is dedicated to the School and currently generates $500,000 annually in support of its research activities.

FINANCIAL AID

All financial aid is awarded competitively based on standardized test scores and academic performance. In some cases, supplemental aid is available for highly qualified U.S. citizens. Financial aid consists of tuition scholarships, graduate assistantships, teaching assistantships, research assistantships, International Student Graduate Study Initiation Grants, International Student Stocker Initiation Grants, Stocker Research Associateships, and Stocker Fellowships. Stocker Research Associateships and Stocker Fellowships are open to U.S. citizens only. Stipends range from $5925 per academic year for graduate assistantships to $15,000 per academic year for Stocker Fellowships. All financial aid includes, at a minimum, a tuition scholarship. Financial aid for international students is contingent on placement by the Ohio Program of Intensive English (OPIE) in full-time academic study; the cost for remedying English-language deficiencies are borne by the student. International students are strongly encouraged to sit for the Test of Written English (TWE) before applying for admission. For more information regarding financial aid, including current stipends and the number of awards made annually, interested students should visit the School's World Wide Web site (http://www.ent.ohiou.edu/eecs/).

COST OF STUDY

In 1996–97, tuition and fees (9–18 credit hours) were $1542 per quarter for in-state students and $2955 per quarter for out-of-state students. Tuition and fees are subject to change without notice. The most current information on tuition and fees may be obtained at the Web site (http://www.cats.ohiou.edu/ohiou/about/factsandfigures.html).

LIVING AND HOUSING COSTS

The 1996–97 quarterly dormitory rates were $902 for a standard single room and $733 for a standard double room. Board costs ranged from $515 per quarter for the one-meal-a-day plan to $758 for the three-meal-a-day plan. University-owned apartments are also available. A one-bedroom unfurnished unit was $463 per month (furnished, $526); a two-bedroom unfurnished unit was $546 per month (furnished, $610). All apartments have a stove and refrigerator; utilities are included in the costs. Students interested in these apartments should apply by January. Many private apartments are also available close by. For more information and the latest rates, interested students should visit the Web site (http://www.cats.ohiou.edu/~auxserv/houscost.htm#Costs).

STUDENT GROUP

Total enrollment at Ohio University is 27,939. Enrollment at the Athens campus is 19,143 and includes students from more than ninety countries. The Russ College of Engineering and Technology enrolls more than 1,700 students, including approximately 260 graduate students. The graduate enrollment in the School of Electrical Engineering and Computer Science is 108, including about 35 Ph.D. students. Approximately 40 percent of the graduate students enrolled in the School are U.S. citizens. The School currently supports roughly 50 students on various forms of financial aid.

LOCATION

Ohio University is located in the small city of Athens in scenic southeast Ohio. Athens is 75 miles southeast of Columbus, the state capital and a major metropolitan area. Cincinnati, Cleveland, and Pittsburgh are all roughly a 4-hour car ride away. The Athens area is rural, with beautiful rolling hills and woodlands and numerous state parks offering camping, hiking, and fishing. The Ohio River is only 30 miles from Athens and offers boating and waterskiing opportunities. Several professional bicycle races are held in the area on an annual basis, as is a major woodcraft festival.

THE UNIVERSITY AND THE SCHOOL

Ohio University was chartered by the state of Ohio in 1804 and was the first university in the Northwest Territory. Today, the main campus in Athens consists of 1,700 acres and 197 buildings. Ohio University was recently designated a Research University II by the Carnegie Foundation for the Advancement of Teaching. Only 125 schools—3.4 percent—of the 3,600 schools assessed by the Carnegie Foundation are classified as research universities. Others in the Research II classification include Auburn University, Clemson University, Kansas State University, the University of Notre Dame, the University of Oklahoma, and Washington State University. According to the Carnegie Foundation definition, a Research University II "offers a full range of baccalaureate programs, is committed to graduate education through the doctorate, and gives high priority to research."

APPLYING

Applications are reviewed for admissions continuously. However, in order to be fully considered for financial aid, application files must be completed by the end of March. GRE scores are required for all international applicants and for applicants graduating from programs in the U.S. that are not ABET accredited. Although there is no minimum GRE score required for admission, most successful applicants score in the top 25th percentile on the quantitative and analytical portions. The Test of English as a Foreign Language (TOEFL) is required for nonnative speakers of English. Most successful applicants score 550 or above on the TOEFL. Nonnative speakers of English who are interested in financial aid are also strongly encouraged to take the TWE. Applications must be submitted to the Office of Graduate Student Services, Ohio University, Athens, Ohio 45701. For more information, applicants may visit the Web site (http://www.ohiou.edu/about/admit/index.html).

CORRESPONDENCE AND INFORMATION

Graduate Chair
School of Electrical Engineering and Computer Science
Ohio University
Athens, Ohio 45701-2979

Telphone: 614-593-1568
Fax: 614-593-0007
E-mail: schaefer@homer.ece.ohiou.edu
World Wide Web: http://www.ent.ohiou.edu/eecs/

OHIO UNIVERSITY

THE FACULTY AND THEIR RESEARCH

Michael S. Braasch, Assistant Professor; Ph.D., Ohio. Electronic navigation systems, navigation system simulation, GPS receiver design, GPS multipath analysis and mitigation.

Liming Cai, Assistant Professor; Ph.D., Texas A&M. Algorithms design and analysis, compiler systems, programming languages, theory of computation.

Mehmet Celenk, Associate Professor; Ph.D., Stevens. Digital image processing, computer and robot vision, multiprocessor systems and distributed computing, multimedia communications systems, parallel processing, computer architecture and digital design, pattern recognition.

David Chelberg, Associate Professor; Ph.D., Stanford. Computer vision, object recognition, medical image processing, artificial intelligence, scientific visualization, computer graphics.

Hollis C. Chen, Professor; Ph.D., Syracuse. Electromagnetic wave propagation and radiation in isotropic and anisotropic environment in moving media, plasmas, and ferrites; fiber optics; computer applications to electromagnetic problems; applied mathematics.

Robert A. Curtis, Associate Professor; Ph.D., NYU. Digital and analog electronic systems, semiconductor physics, microprocessors, charge-coupled devices.

Jeffrey C. Dill, Associate Professor; Ph.D., USC. Spread spectrum communications, error correcting/detecting codes, personal communications/multiple access, wavelet applications to communications.

Joseph E. Essman, Professor Emeritus (part-time); Ph.D., Purdue. Communication system—digital and analog, modulation and detection, adaptive systems, digital signal processing, image processing and data compression, adaptive arrays.

Voula Georgopoulos, Assistant Professor; Ph.D., Tufts. Time-frequency analysis, optical communications and optical signal processing, application of neural networks to signal processing, perception systems modeling.

Jeffrey J. Giesey, Associate Professor; Ph.D., Michigan. Ultrasonic imaging, image processing, biomedical applications.

John D. Gillam, Professor; Ph.D., Michigan State. Algorithms, graphics.

Herman W. Hill, Professor; Ph.D., West Virginia. Power electronics, electromechanical energy conversion.

Larry Irwin, Assistant Professor; M.S., Ohio. Programming languages, software engineering.

R. Dennis Irwin, Professor; Ph.D., Mississippi State. Reliable numerical algorithms for computer-aided analysis and design, sampled-data and digital robust control design, model identification, control system design for flexible structures.

Robert Judd, Cooper Industries Professor; Ph.D., Oakland. Control of manufacturing systems, discrete event systems, simulation, controls.

David W. Juedes, Assistant Professor; Ph.D., Iowa State. Complexity theory, automatic differentiation, information theory.

Harold Klock, Professor Emeritus (part-time); Ph.D., Northwestern. Digital systems design, computer-aided design of digital systems, digital computer architecture and design, microcomputer design and programming, particularly 16-bit and 32-bit systems.

Douglas A. Lawrence, Associate Professor; Ph.D., Johns Hopkins. Linear and nonlinear system theory, analytical aspects of gain scheduling, flight control systems.

Robert W. Lilley, Professor (part-time); Ph.D., Ohio. Airborne data collection systems, GPS instrument approach criteria, wake vortex avoidance, Loran-C navigation system.

Henryk J. Lozykowski, Professor; Ph.D., Copernicus (Poland). Fundamental optical properties of semiconductors, luminescence and optical absorption, exciton and impurity recombination, rare earth of heterostructures, semiconductors, lasers, integrated optics, fundamental properties of layered and alloyed semiconductors relevant to lasers, detectors, and other optoelectronic devices.

Brian Manhire, Professor; Ph.D., Ohio State. Electric power engineering, power system planning.

Richard H. McFarland, Russ Professor Emeritus (part-time); Ph.D., Ohio State. Avionics, aircraft navigation systems, radar antennas.

Jerrel R. Mitchell, Russ Professor; Ph.D., Mississippi State. Control system computer-aided analysis and design, frequency response system identification, analysis and design of sampled-data control systems, multivariable frequency response methods for control systems, parameter estimation techniques, optimal control theory, analysis and design of control systems for large space structures.

M. Ebrahim Mokari, Professor; Ph.D., Illinois. VLSI circuit simulations, computer-aided circuit design, microwave integrated circuits, analog and digital filters, device modeling and sensitivity analysis.

Joseph H. Nurre, Assistant Professor; Ph.D., Cincinnati. 3-D data processing, computer graphics, manufacturing and automation, computer-aided design for mechanical systems.

Shawn Ostermann, Assistant Professor; Ph.D., Purdue. Computer Internetworking and network protocols, data communications, operating systems.

Roger D. Radcliff, Professor; Ph.D., West Virginia. Antenna theory and design, computer solution of electromagnetic problems, electromagnetics and wave propagation.

Janusz A. Starzyk, Professor; Ph.D., Warsaw Technical. VLSI and VHDL design, design and applications of neural networks, analog and digital testing, CAD methods for large analog systems.

John A. Tague, Associate Professor; Ph.D., Penn State. Underwater signal processing, spectrum estimation, characterization of stochastic processes.

Frank van Graas, Associate Professor; Ph.D., Ohio. Electronic navigation systems, satellite positioning, differential GPS, inertial navigation.

Constantinos Vassiliadis, Associate Professor; Ph.D., Mississippi State. Artificial intelligence, expert systems, inference engines and knowledge bases, knowledge acquisition, representation and programming, knowledge engineering, neural intelligence, learning algorithms, Internet intelligent agents.

OKLAHOMA STATE UNIVERSITY

COMPUTER SCIENCE DEPARTMENT

PROGRAMS OF STUDY

The Computer Science Department of Oklahoma State University offers graduate programs leading to the Master of Science, Doctor of Philosophy, and Doctor of Education degrees.

The M.S. degree requires 30 hours of course work, including a thesis. For all M.S. students, the department requires courses in programming languages, operating systems, advanced data structures, and computer architecture. Graduates of the M.S. program are well prepared to serve as industry leaders in software development or to move into a doctoral program.

The Ph.D. program requires at least 30 semester hours of course work beyond the master's degree and an additional 30 semester hours of research. The presentation and defense of a dissertation describing original research are required. Ph.D. graduates have a sound background for original research in educational and industrial environments.

The Ed.D. program requires at least 30 hours of course work beyond the master's degree and an additional component consisting of 30 hours of research and advanced course work. The presentation and defense of an expository dissertation are required. Graduates of the Ed.D. program are prepared to teach in colleges and universities.

The Computer Science Department is also a participant in the cross-disciplinary Master's of Science in Telecommunications Management (M.S.T.M.) degree, representing the College of Arts and Sciences. This program combines the expertise of the Computer Science Department with that of the College of Engineering, Architecture and Technology and the College of Business Administration. Students in this program may choose computer science as their home department.

RESEARCH FACILITIES

Graduate students have access to departmental and University computers as well as a dedicated research computer running the UNIX operating system. There is an on-campus network linking research, departmental, and University computers. OSU is an active participant in national networks and the ONENET regional network.

The Edmond Low Library subscribes to numerous publications in the computing area and can obtain additional publications through the interlibrary loan system.

FINANCIAL AID

Graduate assistantships require one-quarter-time or one-half-time teaching or research duties and carry a stipend for an academic year. Several such assistantships are available each year. Most Ph.D. students who apply for a teaching assistantship receive one. Students on assistantships pay Oklahoma resident tuition. A limited number of fellowships are available for Ph.D.-level study. Some students may qualify for jobs as computer programmers in any of several departments on campus.

COST OF STUDY

In 1996–97, state resident tuition and fees totaled approximately $850 per semester; nonresident tuition and fees were approximately $2300 per semester. Costs are subject to change.

LIVING AND HOUSING COSTS

In 1996–97, the cost of dormitory room and board for single students ranged from $1700 to $2000 per academic year. Married student housing ranged upward from $294 to $500 per month. Off-campus, one-bedroom apartments rented for approximately $400 or higher per month, including utilities.

STUDENT GROUP

In 1996–97, student enrollment on the Stillwater campus was approximately 19,000, of whom about 7,000 were pursuing graduate degrees. Graduate enrollment in the Computer Science Department was 150 full-time students.

The majority of graduate students in the department earned their undergraduate degrees in the sciences, but students with undergraduate degrees in other areas have completed a graduate program successfully. The majority of graduate students are studying for the M.S. and spend 1½–2 years on campus. Ed.D. and Ph.D. students usually require 3 to 4 years beyond the master's degree. Most graduate students in the department are active in the local chapter of the Association for Computing Machinery.

STUDENT OUTCOMES

Graduates of the M.S. program have been extremely successful in finding software development and research positions all over the world. Most of these positions are in the fields of scientific computing, business applications, and telecommunications.

The majority of recent doctoral graduates have taken university positions. Many others have accepted industrial research positions.

LOCATION

Stillwater is a small, attractive university city of about 38,000, located on the prairie in north-central Oklahoma. The city is 65 miles west of Tulsa and 65 miles north of Oklahoma City. There are numerous cultural activities to be found in the Stillwater community and many more within a 2-hour drive of Stillwater.

THE UNIVERSITY

Oklahoma State University was founded in 1890 as Oklahoma Agricultural and Mechanical College. The name was changed to reflect its university status in 1957. Proud of its land-grant heritage, the University takes seriously the commitment to promote liberal and practical education on the campus, throughout the state of Oklahoma, and in those areas of the nation and world where its special talents can be put to use.

The OSU campus is one of exceptional beauty, with modified Georgian architecture in all buildings. University property includes the main campus of 415 acres at Stillwater and lands and farms totaling 5,300 acres. In addition, the University holds title to the Lake Carl Blackwell area, which contains 19,364 acres and a lake covering 3,380 acres that provides recreational and experimental facilities as well as the University's water supply.

APPLYING

Applications for admission are considered throughout the year, but they should be submitted early enough to allow six weeks for processing prior to initial enrollment. Application for financial aid should be made by March 1 for the following academic year. All applicants are urged to take the GRE General Test, and Ph.D. students are required to submit scores on the Subject Test in computer science. International students whose native language is not English must take the TOEFL, and international students seeking financial aid must take the TSE.

CORRESPONDENCE AND INFORMATION

John P. Chandler, Ph.D.
Director of Graduate Programs
Computer Science Department
Math Sciences Building 219
Oklahoma State University
Stillwater, Oklahoma 74078-1053

Telephone: 405-744-5668
E-mail: grad_info@cs.okstate.edu
World Wide Web: http://www.cs.okstate.edu/

OKLAHOMA STATE UNIVERSITY
THE FACULTY AND THEIR RESEARCH

John P. Chandler, Professor; Ph.D., Indiana. Numerical methods, data structures, statistical computation.

Judy Edgmand, Adjunct Assistant Professor; Ed.D., Oklahoma State. Statistical computing, social issues of computing.

K. M. George, Professor; Ph.D., SUNY at Stony Brook. Mathematical foundations, programming language theory.

John Hatcliff, Assistant Professor; Ph.D., Kansas State. Programming languages, program specialization and verification, logic and type theory.

G. E. Hedrick, Regents' Service Professor; Ph.D., Iowa State. Programming languages, compiler implementation, scientific applications.

Kathleen Kaplan, Assistant Professor; D.Sc., George Washington. Pattern recognition, string matching, computational biology.

Jacques LaFrance, Adjunct Associate Professor; Ph.D., Illinois. Artificial intelligence, programming languages.

Huizhu Lu, Associate Professor; Ph.D., Oklahoma. Computer architecture, automata theory, database theory.

Blayne Mayfield, Associate Professor and Department Head; Ph.D., Missouri–Rolla. Artificial intelligence, data structures.

Mansur H. Samadzadeh, Associate Professor; Ph.D., Southwestern Louisiana. Software engineering, systems measurement.

Nick Street, Assistant Professor; Ph.D., Wisconsin. Machine learning, medical applications, optimization.

Emeritus Faculty
Donald D. Fisher, Regents' Service Professor; Ph.D., Stanford. Computer organization, data and information, numerical analysis.

Donald W. Grace, Professor; Ph.D., Stanford. Optimization, combinatorics, numerical analysis.

Supporting Faculty
Herman G. Burchard (mathematics), Ph.D., Purdue. Numerical analysis.

Louis G. Johnson (computer engineering), Ph.D., MIT. Computer architecture, software engineering.

Marilyn G. Kletke (management), Ph.D., Oklahoma State. Management information systems, business applications.

J. Scott Turner (management), Ph.D., SMU. Optimization.

OLD DOMINION UNIVERSITY

DEPARTMENT OF COMPUTER SCIENCE

PROGRAMS OF STUDY

The Department of Computer Science offers graduate programs leading to the Ph.D. and Master of Science degrees with a concentration in networking, software engineering, high-performance scientific computing, artificial intelligence, or foundations. The department offers two additional master's degree options. The computer engineering option, offered jointly with the Department of Electrical and Computer Engineering, is designed for the student with a strong interest in hardware and software who has an undergraduate degree in computer science, electrical engineering, or computer engineering. The computer information sciences option, offered jointly with the Department of Management Information Systems, is appropriate for the student with both software management and technical interests who has an undergraduate degree in computer science or management information systems.

The master's degree programs generally have two tracks—thesis and nonthesis. The thesis option requires a minimum of 31 credit hours, including 24 hours of course work, 6 hours of thesis work, and 1 hour of colloquium attendance. The nonthesis option requires a minimum of 34 credit hours, including 30 hours of course work, 3 hours of project work, and 1 hour of colloquium attendance. In addition to the above requirements, an M.S. candidate must pass a comprehensive examination at the master's level.

The doctoral program requires the candidate to pass a comprehensive examination during the first year. The Ph.D. degree program requires a minimum of 27 credit hours of course work beyond the master's degree, the passing of a candidacy exam, 24 credit hours of dissertation work, and the successful defense of the dissertation. A candidate is required to spend at least two semesters engaged in full-time graduate study.

RESEARCH FACILITIES

The department has several instructional and research laboratories. The problem-solving Instructional Laboratory and the Advanced Projects Instructional Laboratory have more than thirty-two color Sun SPARCstations. The Interactive Remote Instruction (IRI) lab has more than fifteen SPARCstations for use by research assistants and faculty members.

All faculty members have workstations or PCs running NT in their offices. Each funded student has a UNIX workstation. The department has more than 150 UNIX workstations and PCs running NT on local area networks connected to the Internet. In addition, the University currently has more than 3,000 microcomputers and more than fifty PC networks for teaching and research as well as for student use.

FINANCIAL AID

Doctoral students may receive financial aid in the form of a University fellowship, a research assistantship, or a teaching assistantship. For 1996–97, fully supported Ph.D. students received from $10,000 to $16,000. In addition, all supported Ph.D. students received a full tuition waiver. Financial support is also available for master's students.

COST OF STUDY

For 1996–97, the tuition per credit hour per semester was $174 for Virginia residents and $453 for nonresidents. In addition, there was a mandatory health service fee of $38 per semester, except in summer.

LIVING AND HOUSING COSTS

A limited number of University-owned apartments and dormitories are available, ranging in cost from $1751 to $2433 per semester.

STUDENT GROUP

The department has 45 full-time and 50 part-time graduate students, coming from a variety of backgrounds and geographic areas. Approximately one third are women, and 30 are Ph.D. students at various stages.

LOCATION

Old Dominion University is located in Norfolk, Virginia. Situated at the mouth of the Chesapeake Bay, Norfolk is ideal for fishing, sailing, and other water activities. In addition, historic Williamsburg, Jamestown, Yorktown, and scenic Virginia Beach are nearby, and Shenandoah National Park is just a few hours' drive away. The NASA Langley Research Center, the Continuous Electron Beam Acceleration Facility (CEBAF) at Thomas Jefferson Laboratories, U.S. Navy bases, and Newport News Shipbuilding are nearby.

THE UNIVERSITY AND THE DEPARTMENT

The University had its formal beginning in 1930 as a branch of the College of William and Mary and became autonomous in 1962. It is a state-supported university and currently enrolls about 17,000 students in the Colleges of Arts and Letters, Business and Public Administration, Health Sciences, and Sciences; the School of Engineering; the Darden School of Education; and the doctoral program in urban services.

The Department of Computer Science was founded in 1979 and is in the College of Sciences. It is a vigorous department striving for national and international recognition in research and education.

APPLYING

Prospective students should contact the Office of Admissions for application forms for admission and financial assistance. The deadlines for application are June 15 for the fall term, November 1 for the spring term, and April 1 for the summer session. The deadline for financial aid applications for fall term enrollment is April 1. For international students, a TOEFL score of at least 550 is required. Preference is given to applicants who score above 600. High scores on the General Test of the GRE are also required.

CORRESPONDENCE AND INFORMATION

Graduate Program Director
Department of Computer Science
Old Dominion University
Norfolk, Virginia 23529-0162

Telephone: 757-683-3915
Fax: 757-683-4900
E-mail: office@cs.odu.edu
World Wide Web: http://www.cs.odu.edu/ODUCS.html

OLD DOMINION UNIVERSITY
THE FACULTY AND THEIR RESEARCH

Hussein M. Abdel-Wahab, Professor; Ph.D., Waterloo, 1976. Multimedia communications and collaboration, computer networks, systems programming, operating systems. (wahab@cs.odu.edu)

Chester E. Grosch, Professor; Ph.D., Stevens, 1967. Parallel processing, high-performance computing. (grosch@cs.odu.edu)

David E. Keyes, Associate Professor; Ph.D., Harvard, 1984. Scientific computing parallel algorithms for differential and integral equations, modeling cluster computing performance. (keyes@cs.odu.edu)

Irwin B. Levinstein, Assistant Professor; Ph.D., Chicago, 1973. Theory of computation, database systems, expert systems. (ibl@cs.odu.edu)

Kurt J. Maly, Kaufman Professor and Chair; Ph.D., NYU, 1973. Software engineering, computer networks. (maly@cs.odu.edu)

Ravi Mukkamala, Associate Professor; Ph.D., Iowa, 1987. Distributed systems, distributed databases, operating systems. (mukka@cs.odu.edu)

Stephan Olariu, Associate Professor; Ph.D., McGill, 1986. Parallel algorithms and architectures, image processing, computational geometry. (olariu@cs.odu.edu)

C. Michael Overstreet, Associate Professor; Ph.D., Virginia Tech, 1982. Code analysis techniques, simulation, computer networks. (cmo@cs.odu.edu)

Alex Pothen, Associate Professor; Ph.D., Cornell, 1984. Parallel algorithms, scientific computing, numerical linear algebra, algorithmic graph theory. (pothen@cs.odu.edu)

G. Hill Price, Lecturer; M.S., Old Dominion, 1984. (price@cs.odu.edu)

Dennis E. Ray, Lecturer; M.S., Naval Postgraduate School, 1971. Robotics. (ray@cs.odu.edu)

James L. Schwing, Professor; Ph.D., Utah, 1976. Computer graphics, numerical analysis, parallel algorithms. (schwing@cs.odu.edu)

Stewart N. T. Shen, Professor; Ph.D., Northwestern, 1972. Databases, artificial intelligence, expert systems, distributed hypermedia. (shen@cs.odu.edu)

Shunichi Toida, Professor; Ph.D., Illinois at Urbana–Champaign, 1969. VLSI testing, stochastic algorithms, design for test of logic circuit. (toida@cs.odu.edu)

J. Christian Wild Jr., Associate Professor; Ph.D., Rutgers, 1977. Artificial intelligence, software engineering. (wild@cs.odu.edu)

Larry W. Wilson, Associate Professor; Ph.D., Texas at Austin, 1971. Software reliability, parallel algorithms. (wilson@cs.odu.edu)

Steven Zeil, Associate Professor; Ph.D., Ohio State, 1981. Software testing, software development environments. (zeil@cs.odu.edu)

M. Zubair, Associate Professor; Ph.D., Indian Institute of Technology, 1986. Parallel processing, computer architecture, high-performance computing. (zubair@cs.odu.edu)

Selected Research Projects

User interface for integrated computer-aided design systems.
Knowledge-oriented hypermedia methodology.
Computer productivity initiative.
Extending schedulability analysis in distributed real-time systems.
Automatic code transformation.
Modeling of distributed database systems.
Knowledge-based refinement during testing.
Robotic receptionist.
X share.
Intelligent forces/what-if simulation system for advanced research and development.
Real-time dynamic reasoning for process control.
Automation of cargo transfer information management and display.
A decomposition-based investigation of large classes of graphs.
Hybrid intelligent systems.
Perturbation testing.
Geometric modeling for computer-aided design.
Group collaboration research.
Concurrency control in collaborative environments.
Group broadcasting in heterogeneous distributed systems.
Building a generalized distributed system model.
Fault diagnosis.
Neural networks and theorem proving.
Software reliability in flight control.
Parallel/concurrent Euler equation solvers.
Information technology: A tool to cut health-care costs.
CoReview: An interactive information exchange and retrieval tool.
Decision-based systems development.
Interactive remote instruction technology (IRIT).
Solution-adaptive grid partitioning and variable ordering for PDEs.
Spectral algorithms for envelope reduction.
Large-scale least squares problems.
Spectral algorithms for graph and mesh partitioning.
Orderings for parallel sparse matrix factorization.
Highly parallel triangular solution.
VLSI-optimal algorithms for reconfigurable architectures.
Linear structure of graphs.
Fractal-based image processing.
Parallel algorithms for convection-diffusion-reaction systems.
Full-potential, Euler, and Navier-Stokes aerodynamics.
Geophysical flows.
Modeling communication costs in distributed environments.
A parallel and distributed environment for scientific applications.
Networked Computer Science Technical Report Library (NCSTRL).
Intelligent medical information system.
Reliability modeling of directed testing.

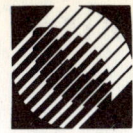

OREGON GRADUATE INSTITUTE OF SCIENCE & TECHNOLOGY

DEPARTMENT OF COMPUTER SCIENCE AND ENGINEERING

PROGRAMS OF STUDY

Close cooperation among faculty and students is a vital element of the Oregon Graduate Institute (OGI) academic experience. Because faculty members have no undergraduate teaching responsibilities, they can devote careful attention to the graduate students working with them on research projects. Faculty and students enjoy the facilities, administrative support, and academic intensity characteristic of a major research university.

The department currently has 30 faculty members—24 full-time and 6 part-time. Local computer science professionals also serve as adjunct faculty to teach courses in their area of technical specialty. The curriculum covers a broad spectrum of the computer science and engineering field. The department offers M.S. and Ph.D. degrees.

Departmental research strengths include programming techniques and computer architectures for parallel computing, functional and logic programming languages, support for scientific computing, databases, distributed systems, human-computer communication, operating systems, object-oriented systems, and neural networks and their application to computer speech recognition.

As part of its educational program the department runs open reading groups on a variety of topics. Participants include OGI faculty and students, faculty and students from other educational institutions in Oregon, and professionals from local industry.

The department's goal is to give its students the knowledge and intellectual discipline they need to become innovators and leaders within their professional communities. In addition to training students how to use today's technologies, the department gives them the skills necessary to develop tomorrow's technologies.

RESEARCH FACILITIES

The CSE computing environment is a state-of-the-art heterogeneous environment composed of Sun, DEC, HP, NeXT, and Apple computers. A combination of high-performance, multiprocessor servers and more than 100 X-terminals allows the department to remain flexible in meeting the needs of research and education. The CSE department network is connected to NorthWestNet and has interfaces to NERO (an ATM network for research and education in Oregon). The Computing Facilities staff of 4 provides support for this diverse and demanding environment through the careful use of vendor, third-party, public domain, and custom solutions.

FINANCIAL AID

Tuition scholarships and research assistantships are available on a competitive basis. The Institute provides guidance for students who wish to secure external fellowships or student loans.

COST OF STUDY

Tuition for 1997–98 is $4050 per academic quarter or $405 per credit hour.

LIVING AND HOUSING COSTS

In general, the cost of living in Portland is less than in most major metropolitan areas on the West Coast. All graduate students live off campus, and most share rent with other students. Monthly rent for off-campus apartments ranges from $550 to $850.

STUDENT GROUP

The department currently has approximately 100 matriculated graduate students. Of the matriculated students, 30 percent are women and about 40 percent are international. In addition, more than 200 students, primarily engineers and scientists from nearby high-technology firms, take advantage of the department's continuing education opportunities.

LOCATION

OGI's location in the beautiful Pacific Northwest provides a very enjoyable setting for study. OGI is 12 miles west of Portland and just 60 miles from the famous Oregon Coast or from excellent downhill and cross-country skiing on Mount Hood. World-class windsurfing in the scenic Columbia Gorge is also an easy drive from the campus. Olympic National Park is within a day's drive. Mount Rainier National Park, Crater Lake National Park, the Oregon Dunes National Recreation Area, the rugged desert country of eastern Oregon, North Cascades National Park, and the breathtaking redwood forests of northern California are at driving distances ranging from a few hours to one day.

THE INSTITUTE

The Oregon Graduate Institute is a private, graduate-only technical university dedicated to contemporary scientific research and education. Founded in 1963, OGI combines the vigorous research emphasis and instrumentation of a large university with the personal interaction and collaboration characteristics of a small research institution.

Approximately 350 graduate students from all regions of the United States and sixteen countries pursue M.S. and Ph.D. degrees. In addition to computer science and engineering, degree programs are offered in environmental science and engineering; electrical engineering; materials science and engineering; chemistry, biochemistry, and molecular biology; and management in science and technology.

APPLYING

Applications are accepted at any time, but those requesting financial assistance should be submitted by March 1. Required admissions materials include three letters of recommendation, transcripts, and GRE General Test scores. The OGI institutional code for the GRE is 4592. TOEFL results are required of those applicants whose native language is not English. The TOEFL requirement may be waived if the student received a prior degree in the United States.

CORRESPONDENCE AND INFORMATION

Director of Admissions
Office of Admissions
Oregon Graduate Institute
P.O. Box 91000
Portland, Oregon 97291-1000
Telephone: 503-690-1027
        800-685-2423 (toll-free)
E-mail: admissions@admin.ogi.edu
      csedept@cse.ogi.edu
World Wide Web: http://www.ogi.edu/
      http://www.cse.ogi.edu/

OREGON GRADUATE INSTITUTE OF SCIENCE & TECHNOLOGY

THE FACULTY AND THEIR RESEARCH

Full-Time Faculty

Andrew Black, Professor and Department Head; D.Phil., Oxford. Programming languages, distributed systems, wide area networking (particularly World Wide Web), object-oriented languages and systems, and types for objects.

Etienne Barnard, Associate Professor; Ph.D., Carnegie Mellon, 1989. Theory and practice of pattern-recognition systems, generalization, neural networks, speech recognition, image recognition, control systems.

Philip R. Cohen, Professor; Ph.D., Toronto, 1978. Multimodal interfaces, human-computer interaction, intelligent agents, dialogue, natural language processing, collaboration theory and technology, speech act theory, delegation technology, knowledge-based simulation, applications to mobile computing, information management, manufacturing.

Ronald A. Cole, Professor and Director, Center for Spoken Language Understanding; Ph.D., California, Riverside, 1971. Spoken language systems, integrating expert knowledge of human perception and communication into systems that recognize spoken language, speaker- and vocabulary-independent recognition of telephone speech in different languages, multilanguage speech data collection and transcription, automatic language identification.

Crispin Cowan, Research Assistant Professor; Ph.D., Western Ontario, 1995. Operating systems, distributed and parallel systems, computer architecture, programming languages, optimism.

Lois M. L. Delcambre, Associate Professor, Director of The Data-Intensive Systems Center, Pacific Northwest Laboratories Affiliate Staff Scientist, and Department Chair for Education; Ph.D., Southwestern Louisiana, 1982. Database systems, data models, object-oriented databases, scientific databases, design databases, expert database systems.

Mark Fanty, Research Associate Professor; Ph.D., Rochester, 1988. Speech recognition.

Hynek Hermansky, Associate Professor; Dr.Eng., Tokyo, 1983. Communication between human and machine; computer simulation of human perception; speech recognition, coding, and enhancement.

James Hook, Associate Professor; Ph.D., Cornell, 1988. Type theory, programming language semantics, theorem proving and program verification, software specification.

Richard B. Kieburtz, Professor and Director of Pacific Software Research Center; Ph.D., Washington (Seattle), 1961. Functional programming, software specification, deriving programs from specifications, computer architecture, semantics of programming languages.

John Launchbury, Assistant Professor; Ph.D., Glasgow, 1990. Functional programming languages, semantics-based program analysis, program transformation and partial evaluation.

Todd K. Leen, Associate Professor; Ph.D., Wisconsin, 1982. Learning algorithms, stochastic and deterministic learning dynamics, feature selection and data compression, application of computer algebra systems to design and dynamical analysis, visualization, applications to signal processing and speech recognition.

David Maier, Professor; Ph.D., Princeton, 1978. Database systems, object-oriented databases, query optimization, scientific data management, data display, algorithms and complexity, object-oriented languages.

Dylan McNamee, Visiting Assistant Professor; Ph.D., Washington (Seattle), 1996. High-performance and maintainable operating systems, application/operating systems interaction, distributed and parallel systems support, middleware support for application-development.

John Moody, Professor; Ph.D., Princeton, 1984. Design and analysis of learning algorithms; statistical learning theory, including generalization and model selection; optimization methods, both deterministic and stochastic; applications to signal processing, control, time series prediction, and finance.

David G. Novick, Associate Professor; Ph.D., Oregon, 1988; J.D., Harvard, 1977. Interactive systems, spoken-language understanding, human-computer interaction, natural language processing, knowledge engineering.

Sharon L. Oviatt, Associate Professor; Ph.D., Toronto, 1979. Human language technology and multimodal systems, modality effects in communication models, telecommunications, interactive systems, human-computer interaction, empirically based design and evaluation of human-computer interfaces, cognitive science, research methodology.

Misha Pavel, Associate Professor; Ph.D., NYU, 1980. Multimedia information communication comprising anthropomorphic signal processing; adaptive systems, including pattern recognition, decision making, and visual, image, and speech processing.

Calton Pu, Professor; Ph.D., Washington (Seattle), 1986. Transaction processing, database systems, scientific data management, object-oriented databases, operating systems, distributed and parallel operating systems.

Tim Sheard, Assistant Professor; Ph.D., Massachusetts at Amherst, 1985. Functional programming, software specification, automatic theorem proving, linguistic reflection, partial evaluation, database safety.

David Steere, Assistant Professor; Ph.D., Carnegie Mellon, 1997. Operating systems, mobile computing, distributed information systems.

Jonathan Walpole, Associate Professor; Ph.D., Lancaster (England), 1988. Operating systems, operating system support for multimedia computing, operating system support for scientific computing in loosely coupled distributed systems.

Eric Wan, Assistant Professor; Ph.D., Stanford, 1994. Learning algorithms and architectures for neural networks and adaptive signal processing; applications to time series prediction, adaptive control, active noise cancellation, and telecommunications.

Yonghong Yan, Assistant Research Professor; Ph.D., Oregon Tech, 1995. Speech recognition, spoken language system, signal processing, language identification and language modeling.

Part-Time Faculty

Francoise Bellegarde, Associate Research Faculty; Ph.D., Nancy I (France), 1985. Formal methods for software engineering, formal specifications, software verification, program derivation from formal specifications and prototyping, automatic demonstration and theorem proving, functional programming term rewriting systems, program derivation, program transformation.

Charles Consel, Assistant Professor; Ph.D., Paris VI (Curie), 1989. Program transformation by partial evaluation, program analysis, compilation compiler generation, programming environments, programming language semantics, prototyping.

Gil Neiger, Associate Research Professor; Ph.D., Cornell, 1988. Research scientist at Intel's MicroComputer Research Labs. Principles of distributed computing.

Daniel W. Hammerstrom, Associate Professor; Ph.D., Illinois, 1977. Massively parallel VLSI architectures for connectionist, neural network emulation and pattern recognition; VLSI design.

Michael Wolfe, Associate Professor; Ph.D., Illinois, 1982. Senior Software Engineer, The Portland Group, Inc. Compiler optimizations for high-performance and parallel computer systems.

Eleanor Wynn, Associate Professor; Ph.D., Berkeley, 1979. Owner, Interactive Intelligence, Inc. Software development paradigms and processes.

The OGI campus and Science Park share a beautiful natural setting.

The Cooley Science Center.

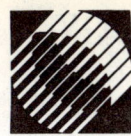

OREGON GRADUATE INSTITUTE OF SCIENCE & TECHNOLOGY

DEPARTMENT OF ELECTRICAL ENGINEERING

PROGRAMS OF STUDY

The Department of Electrical Engineering offers programs of study leading to the M.S. and Ph.D. degrees in electrical engineering. Both thesis and nonthesis M.S. options are available, the former requiring 36 credit hours of classes and 12 credit hours of research and the latter requiring 44 course credits and 4 credits of research. An intensive M.S. program (minimum 48 credits for nonthesis) is also available. The Ph.D. requires that both a written and an oral qualifying examination covering core course areas be passed before admission to Ph.D. candidacy. M.S. (thesis) and Ph.D. candidates must submit satisfactory theses and defend them in oral examinations. There is a two-year minimum residency requirement for the Ph.D. Full-time students are expected to complete their degree requirements within five years for the Ph.D. and three years for the M.S.

Research specialty areas include digital signal processing, with emphasis on human-like speech and image processing; adaptive neural net systems; advanced display technology; field emission; display technology; semiconductor materials, devices, and processing; biomedical engineering; and VLSI design and processing. The emphasis is on scientific and engineering investigations that have well-defined goals and real utility, pursued in an atmosphere resembling that of a working research and development laboratory. The relatively small size of the department, with a student-faculty ratio of about 4:1, and the overall educational philosophy guarantee that each student receives close individual supervision from his or her research adviser.

RESEARCH FACILITIES

The department utilizes a Sun Microsystems network with X-Windows terminals. In addition, the department maintains a student computer lab with terminals stationed throughout the department. Semiconductor device, circuit, and applications facilities include MOCVD growth characterization laboratories (III-V, II-VI, and β-SiC), device and IC processing laboratories, and materials and device characterization laboratories. The department also houses laser characterization equipment and two picosecond streak cameras. Laser application laboratories are available for the study of atmospheric optics and laser interactions with matter. High-resolution (submicrometer) focused ion beam facilities include a combination SEM-focused ion beam system used for optoelectronics device modification and a system for investigating ion beam–induced chemistry. Equipment supporting display technology research includes an atomic layer epitaxy reactor for growth of multilayered electroluminescent flat panel displays and a sputtering system with 3-inch RF and DC guns.

FINANCIAL AID

Financial aid for entering students is awarded on a competitive basis to students with financial need and outstanding promise. Full-time Ph.D. students may be supported on research fellowships, which include full tuition scholarships. Full-time M.S. students may receive partial tuition scholarships. The Institute provides guidance for students who wish to secure external fellowships or student loans. Good opportunities exist for student spouse employment in local industry.

COST OF STUDY

Tuition for 1997–98 is $4050 per academic quarter or $405 per credit hour.

LIVING AND HOUSING COSTS

In general, the cost of living in Portland is less than in most major metropolitan areas on the West Coast. All graduate students live off campus, and most share rent with other students. Monthly rent for off-campus apartments ranges from $550 to $850.

STUDENT GROUP

As of January 1997, the department had 27 full-time students. Of these, 52 percent were Ph.D. students. Since 1992, the department has graduated 102 students—78 percent M.S. and 22 percent Ph.D.

LOCATION

OGI is located in a rapidly developing rural area 12 miles west of downtown Portland, a city that provides diverse cultural activities, including art, music, entertainment, and sports. The Oregon coast is about 60 miles to the west, and the Cascade Mountains are 50 miles to the east. Oregon has a large number of state parks, as well as national forest land and wilderness areas. These natural areas provide outstanding opportunities for skiing, hiking, fishing, and other outdoor activities.

THE INSTITUTE AND THE DEPARTMENT

The goal of the department is to provide education of the highest quality in electrical engineering through first-class research in areas of scientific importance. This philosophy ensures that graduates are actively recruited by internationally recognized industries and universities.

APPLYING

Applications are accepted at any time, but those requesting financial assistance should be submitted by March 1. Required admissions materials include three letters of recommendation, transcripts, and GRE scores for Ph.D. applicants. The OGI institutional code for the GRE is 4592. TOEFL results are also required of those whose native language is not English. The TOEFL requirement may be waived if the student received a prior degree in the United States.

CORRESPONDENCE AND INFORMATION

Director of Admissions
Office of Admissions
Oregon Graduate Institute
P.O. Box 91000
Portland, Oregon 97291-1000
Telephone: 503-690-1027
         800-685-2423 (toll-free)
E-mail: admissions@admin.ogi.edu
World Wide Web: http://www.ogi.edu/

OREGON GRADUATE INSTITUTE OF SCIENCE & TECHNOLOGY

THE FACULTY AND THEIR RESEARCH

*Etienne Barnard, Assistant Professor; Ph.D. (electrical and computer engineering), Carnegie Mellon, 1989. Theoretical pattern recognition; applications of pattern recognition, including speech and image recognition; neural networks; language identification.

Anthony E. Bell, Associate Professor; Ph.D. (physical chemistry), London, 1962. Development of liquid-metal field ion sources; field ionization, surface physics, and chemistry; field emission microscopy; energy distribution measurements; selected area processing for microcircuit fabrication, using focused electron beams.

C. Neil Berglund, Professor; Ph.D. (electrical engineering), Stanford, 1964. Optical and electron beam lithography, mask and reticle technology, metrology in semiconductor processing, management of technology, display technology.

*Ronald A. Cole, Professor and Director, Center for Spoken Language Understanding; Ph.D. (psychology), California, Riverside, 1971. Spoken language systems, integrating expert knowledge of human perception and communication into systems that recognize spoken language; speaker- and vocabulary-independent recognition of telephone speech in different languages, multilanguage speech data collection and transcription, automatic language identification.

Reinhart Engelmann, Professor; Dr.rer.nat. (nuclear physics), Munich, 1961. Optoelectronic semiconductor devices: quantum well lasers, modulators, and detectors; optical waveguide devices for integrated optics; modeling and design.

V. S. Rao Gudimetla, Assistant Professor; Ph.D. (applied physics), Oregon Graduate Center, 1982. Microwave circuits, device simulation, laser speckle, applied mathematics.

*Hynek Hermansky, Associate Professor; Dr.Eng. (electrical engineering), Tokyo, 1983. Communication between human and machine; human perception and its computer simulation; speech production and perception; automatic recognition of speech, speech coding, synthesis, and enhancement; identification and extraction of linguistic information in realistic communication environments.

J. Fred Holmes, Professor and Department Head; Ph.D. (electrical engineering), Washington (Seattle), 1968. Speckle propagation through turbulence, remote sensing of wind and turbulence, electrooptic systems for industrial process control applications, instrumentation signal processing.

Steven Jacques, Associate Professor; Ph.D. (biophysics and medical physics), Berkeley, 1984. Laser effects on biological systems using light-activated drugs, thermal processes, or photoacoustic shock waves; modeling of photon migration using Monte Carlo or Feynman path integrals.

*Todd K. Leen, Associate Professor; Ph.D. (physics), Wisconsin, 1982. Neural learning algorithms, architecture and theory, dynamics, noise, model complexity and pruning, applications to speech processing.

Michael Macon, Assistant Professor; Ph.D. (electrical engineering), Georgia Tech, 1996. Speech synthesis, speech and audio coding, speech enhancement, music synthesis, human auditory perception and modeling, digital signal processing.

*John E. Moody, Associate Professor; Ph.D. (physics), Princeton, 1984. Design and analysis of learning algorithms; statistical learning theory, including generalization and model selection; optimization methods (both deterministic and stochastic) and applications to signal processing, time series, macroeconomics, and finance.

James D. Parsons, Associate Professor; Ph.D. (engineering), UCLA, 1981. Relationships of semiconductor properties, solid-state device performance, and MOCVD growth; new semiconductors and device processing technologies; new solid-state device and monolithic IC design concepts in β-SiC, III-V, and II-VI semiconductors.

*Misha Pavel, Research Associate Professor; Ph.D. (experimental psychology), NYU, 1980. Representation of uncertainty, decision making, and choice behavior; pattern recognition and categorization in humans and machines; information retrieval and decision support systems; image processing and sensor fusion.

Scott A. Prahl, Assistant Professor; Ph.D. (biomedical engineering), Texas at Austin, 1988. Interaction of light with tissue, pulsed photothermal radiometry, laser angioplasty, optical properties of biological materials, noninvasive medical diagnostics.

Raj Solanki, Associate Professor; Ph.D. (physics), Colorado State, 1982. Gas lasers, laser spectroscopy, gas plasmas, photon- and electron-beam-induced materials processing.

Pieter Vermeulen, Associate Professor; Ph.D. (electrical and computer engineering), Carnegie Mellon, 1989. Speech processing/recognition, pattern recognition, neural networks and computer architecture.

*Eric A. Wan, Assistant Professor; Ph.D. (electrical engineering), Stanford, 1993. Neural networks and adaptive signal processing, time series prediction, adaptive control, active noise cancellation, telecommunications.

The OGI campus and Science Park share a beautiful natural setting.

The Cooley Science Center.

---

*Joint appointment with Department of Computer Science and Engineering

OREGON STATE UNIVERSITY

COLLEGE OF ENGINEERING
DEPARTMENT OF COMPUTER SCIENCE

PROGRAMS OF STUDY

Graduate degree programs leading to the M.A., M.A.I.S., M.S., and Ph.D. degrees in computer science are offered in the following areas of concentration: parallel computing, artificial intelligence, programming languages, theory of computation, software engineering, information-based systems, numerical analysis (with the Department of Mathematics), and computer architecture (with the Department of Electrical and Computer Engineering).

OSU operates on the quarter system. There are three quarters in the academic year. The master's degree programs require 45 hours of graduate-level courses, a final oral examination, and a thesis or research paper. The doctoral program requires approximately 120 graduate credit hours, demonstration of both breadth and depth of knowledge, and completion of significant independent research.

RESEARCH FACILITIES

The department has an exceptional computing environment. Parallel computing facilities include a 17-node Meiko CS-2 multicomputer, an 8-node Sun Enterprise 4000, a cluster of Sun multiprocessors, and a 128-node Adaptive Systems CNAPS neural net builder. Open laboratories on campus contain dozens of state-of-the-art workstations and X terminals, a multimedia laboratory with dozens of PowerPC Macintosh computers, and hundreds of IBM PC-compatible computers. The department also maintains dozens of Hewlett-Packard, IBM, and Sun workstations and Macintosh computers distributed to faculty, research assistants, and teaching assistants.

The Valley Library contains more than 1 million volumes and subscribes to most computer science journals.

FINANCIAL AID

Financial support is available for qualified graduate students in the form of teaching and research assistantships. New graduate students with teaching assistantships receive a package paying $11,000 over the academic year. Stipends for half-time research assistants usually range between $12,000 and $16,000 for a twelve-month appointment.

COST OF STUDY

Estimated resident tuition and fees for 1997–98 total $2000 for 9 to 16 term hours; nonresidents pay tuition and fees of $3406 per term. These figures are reduced to $269 per term for students with assistantships. (Figures are subject to change without notice.)

LIVING AND HOUSING COSTS

For 1997–98, the rate for double occupancy in University dormitories and election of a full meal plan is $4963 for the academic year. A few University apartments are available for married students and rent for $310–$350 per month. Off-campus one-bedroom apartments rent for approximately $450–$550 per month, excluding electricity.

STUDENT GROUP

The total enrollment for 1996–97 was 13,784, including 2,765 graduate students. About 43 percent of the graduate students were women. There were 92 on-campus computer science graduate majors in 1996–97.

LOCATION

Corvallis, a city of 46,000, is located in the Willamette Valley. Portland is 80 miles to the north, the Oregon coast is 50 miles to the west, and the Cascade mountain range is 60 miles to the east. Skiing, camping, hiking, and climbing opportunities are all within easy driving distance. The climate is mild (ranging from the low 30s in the winter to 85 in the summer).

The University and the community offer concerts, plays, movies, and art exhibits.

THE UNIVERSITY AND THE DEPARTMENT

Oregon State University is a land-grant and sea-grant university and dates back to 1868. Graduate work and research are carried out in many disciplines, including science, engineering, agriculture, and oceanography. The campus is a visual delight, beautifully landscaped with trees, flowering shrubs, and flowing lawns—all of which contribute to a relaxed atmosphere.

The Department of Computer Science was formed in 1972 and now has 13 graduate faculty members. The department maintains close ties with neighboring institutions and high-technology industry.

APPLYING

A $50 fee is required of all applicants. Application for graduate admission should be made to the Office of Admissions, Oregon State University. Applications for financial assistance should be submitted to the department by March 1 for the following academic year. All graduate applicants are required to submit scores on the General Test (quantitative and verbal sections) of the GRE. International students must pass the TOEFL to be considered for University admission. Oregon State University supports equal educational opportunity without regard to sex, race, handicap, national origin, marital status, or religion.

CORRESPONDENCE AND INFORMATION

For additional information:
Graduate Advisor
Department of Computer Science
Dearborn Hall 303
Oregon State University
Corvallis, Oregon 97331
Telephone: 541-737-3273
Fax: 541-737-3014
World Wide Web: http://www.cs.orst.edu

For application forms:
Director of Admissions
Oregon State University
Corvallis, Oregon 97331
Telephone: 541-737-4411

OREGON STATE UNIVERSITY
THE FACULTY AND THEIR RESEARCH

Bella Bose, Professor; Ph.D., SMU, 1980. Error-control codes, VLSI testing, parallel processing.

William S. Bregar, Adjunct Associate Professor (at Hewlett-Packard, Vancouver, Washington); Ph.D., Wisconsin–Madison, 1974. Artificial intelligence—problem solving, intelligent-computer-assisted instruction, representation of knowledge.

Timothy A. Budd, Associate Professor; Ph.D., Yale, 1980. Programming languages, programming environments, program testing.

Margaret M. Burnett, Associate Professor; Ph.D., Kansas, 1991. Visual programming languages; alternative programming paradigms, especially object-oriented and functional.

Curtis R. Cook, Professor; Ph.D., Iowa, 1970. Software quality, software complexity measures, program comprehension.

Paul Cull, Professor; Ph.D., Chicago, 1970. Analysis of algorithms, mathematical biology.

Bruce D. D'Ambrosio, Associate Professor; Ph.D., Berkeley, 1986. Artificial intelligence, management of uncertainty, real-time problem solving, qualitative reasoning.

Thomas G. Dietterich, Professor; Ph.D., Stanford, 1984. Machine learning.

Toshimi Minoura, Associate Professor; Ph.D., Stanford, 1980. Actionbase system for manufacturing control.

Cherri M. Pancake, Professor; Ph.D., Auburn, 1986. Software support for parallel computing, graphical user interface design, parallel languages.

Michael J. Quinn, Professor and Interim Department Head; Ph.D., Washington State, 1983. Parallel algorithms, parallel programming languages and environments.

Gregg Rothermel, Assistant Professor; Ph.D., Clemson, 1996. Software engineering.

Walter G. Rudd, Professor; Ph.D., Rice, 1969. Computer architecture, parallel computing, computational science.

Prasad Tadepalli, Associate Professor, Ph.D., Rutgers, 1989. Artificial intelligence, machine learning, problem solving, computer-integrated manufacturing.

PACE UNIVERSITY

SCHOOL OF COMPUTER SCIENCE AND INFORMATION SYSTEMS

PROGRAMS OF STUDY

Graduate degrees offered by the School of Computer Science and Information Systems at both the White Plains and New York City campuses are the Master of Science (M.S.) in computer science, the Master of Science (M.S.) in information systems, and the Master of Science (M.S.) in telecommunications. The M.S. program in computer science emphasizes a hands-on approach to software systems engineering. The 36-credit curriculum balances theory and practice in software design and development, culminating in the implementation of a large software system. The program usually requires three semesters of full-time study or five semesters of part-time study.

The M.S. in information systems provides the technological-organizational balance necessary for effectively dealing with information systems in all organizations. The program integrates information systems technology, information systems concepts and processes, and organizational functions and management into a unified information systems approach, making the relationship between information systems technology and managerial effectiveness more apparent. The 36-credit curriculum can generally be completed in three semesters of full-time study or five semesters of part-time study.

The M.S. in telecommunications is designed to integrate the technology, management, and policy disciplines underlying telecommunications with up-to-date coverage of the issues and trends. Case studies and the use of computer-based tools and simulations integrate the concepts and disciplines learned in the program by providing a context for complex problem analysis in the planning and management of telecommunications networks. The 36-credit curriculum can generally be completed in three semesters of full-time study or five semesters of part-time study.

Certificate programs are available in computer communications and networks, telecommunications, object-oriented programming, and computing science for teachers.

RESEARCH FACILITIES

Extensive library facilities are available at the University. Holdings of about 1 million volumes and 7,500 cataloged periodicals. Database searching facilities are also available. Students using the University-wide computing network employ the latest in state-of-the-art hardware and software. Currently, there are 80 mainframe terminals (3170/3270), 200 IBM microcomputers (ValuePoint 486 and PS/2), and 35 Macintosh microcomputers available to students, faculty, and staff in the computer labs and classrooms of the New York and Westchester campuses. An IBM RISC 6000 running AIX is connected to the Pace network.

FINANCIAL AID

A number of graduate scholarships and assistantships are available. Grants are made on the basis of outstanding academic performance as indicated by the applicant's previous college record, test scores, and demonstrated financial need. Research assistantships are available for full- and part-time students and are awarded on the basis of previous academic achievement. Graduate assistants received stipends of up to $5100 for 1996–97 and 24 credits in tuition remission. Half assistantships are also available. For further information, students should contact the Financial Aid Office, Pace University, 78 North Broadway, White Plains, New York 10603, 914-422-4050, or Pace Plaza, New York, New York 10038, 212-346-1300.

COST OF STUDY

Tuition for graduate courses is $520 per credit in 1997–98; the registration and library fees vary according to the number of credits taken.

LIVING AND HOUSING COSTS

Dormitory rooms for graduate students at Pace University cost $4300 for the 1997–98 academic year. A variety of housing is available in the area.

STUDENT GROUP

Current enrollment in the computer science and information systems graduate programs is about 600 students. One third are professionals in the field, one third are recent graduates, and the other third are preparing for a career change. Most students attend classes part-time in the evening.

LOCATION

The Civic Center campus and Midtown branch are located in Manhattan, the cultural and financial center of the Eastern Seaboard. The nearby city of White Plains is a major retail center and home to national and international corporate headquarters. It is surrounded by towns and villages that have resident artisans, local musical and theatrical groups, and rural museums. New York City is easily accessible from White Plains by bus, train, or car.

THE UNIVERSITY AND THE SCHOOL

Founded in 1906, Pace University is a private, nonsectarian, coeducational institution. It has three campuses—one in Manhattan and two in Westchester County. In 1948 Pace Institute became Pace College; in 1973 the New York Board of Regents approved a charter change to designate Pace a university. The School of Computer Science and Information Systems was established in 1983.

APPLYING

Admission to the M.S. in computer science, M.S. in information systems, and M.S. in telecommunications programs requires satisfactory completion of a baccalaureate degree at an accredited institution. Applicants are expected to have a GPA of at least 3.0 and evidence of a successful performance on the GRE General Test. In addition to the application, official GRE test scores, two letters of reference, an essay, and official college transcripts must be submitted. International students must also submit official TOEFL score reports and professional translations of their university transcripts. Official copies of transcripts in the original language must also be submitted. For admission information, students should write to Graduate Admission, Graduate Center, Pace University, 1 Martine Avenue, White Plains, New York 10606 (telephone: 914-422-4283; fax: 914-422-4287; e-mail: gradwp@ny2.pace.edu) or Graduate Admission, Pace University, Pace Plaza, New York, New York 10038 (telephone: 212-346-1531; fax: 212-346-1585; e-mail: gradnyc@ny2.pace.edu). Applications should be received by July 31 for the fall semester, by November 30 for the spring semester, and by May 1 for the summer semester. Although applications for admission are accepted throughout the year, those received after the deadline for a particular semester may not be acted upon in time for attendance that semester.

CORRESPONDENCE AND INFORMATION

Computer Science and Information
  Systems Programs
Pace University
1 Martine Avenue
White Plains, New York 10606

Telephone: 914-422-4191
E-mail: kleinb@pace.edu

Computer Science and Information
  Systems Programs
Pace University
Pace Plaza
New York, New York 10038

Telephone: 212-346-1687
E-mail: norzs@pace.edu

PACE UNIVERSITY

THE FACULTY

Hamid Ahmadi, Adjunct Associate Professor; Ph.D., Columbia, 1988.
Mehdi Badii, Associate Professor; Ph.D., Loughborough (England), 1987.
Joseph Bergin, Professor; Ph.D., Michigan State, 1989.
Howard Blum, Professor; Ph.D., Polytechnic of Brooklyn, 1973.
Don M. M. Booker, Associate Professor; D.B.A., Nova, 1985.
Thomas Brier, Adjunct Professor; M.B.A., Iona, 1977.
Frederick B. Bunt, Professor Emeritus-in-Residence; Ed.D., Columbia, 1966.
Alexander L. Cheng, Adjunct Lecturer; Ph.D., Polytechnic of New York, 1992.
Mary F. Courtney, Associate Professor; Ed.D., Columbia, 1991.
John S. Craparo, Adjunct Associate Professor; Sc.D., Nova, 1990.
Paul M. Dantzig, Adjunct Lecturer; M.S., Stanford, 1975.
Edgar G. DuCasse, Professor; Ph.D., Illinois at Urbana-Champaign, 1973.
Leonard Fagen, Adjunct Instructor; M.S., CCNY, 1961.
Daniel J. Farkas, Assistant Professor; M.A., NYU, 1977.
Dietrich Fischer, Professor; Ph.D., NYU, 1976.
Ronald I. Frank, Adjunct Lecturer; M.S., NYU, 1964.
Yair Fussman, Adjunct Assistant Professor; M.S., Polytechnic of New York, 1991.
Michael L. Gargano, Professor; Ph.D., CUNY Graduate Center, 1980.
Myron H. Goldberg, Professor; M.S., Arizona, 1960.
Walter Goralski, Adjunct Assistant Professor; M.S., Pace, 1983.
Fred Grossman, Professor; Ph.D., NYU, 1973.
Frances Gustavson, Professor; Ph.D., Polytechnic of Brooklyn, 1971.
Murray J. Haims, Adjunct Professor; Ph.D., NYU, 1978.
Constance Knapp, Associate Professor; Ph.D., CUNY Graduate Center, 1995.
Babette Kronstadt, Instructor; Ed.S., Michigan, 1989.
Frank Lo Sacco, Professor; Ph.D., Columbia, 1960.
Joseph Malerba, Associate Professor; Ph.D., Yale, 1977.
Francis T. Marchese, Professor; Ph.D., Cincinnati, 1983.
Miroslav Martinovic, Adjunct Lecturer; Ph.D., Belgrade, 1983.
Susan M. Merritt, Professor; Ph.D., NYU, 1982.
John C. Molluzzo, Professor; Ph.D., Yeshiva, 1972.
Narayan Murthy, Professor; Ph.D., Rhode Island, 1981.
Richard M. Nemes, Associate Professor; Ph.D., CUNY Graduate Center, 1983.
Farrell Patrick, Professor; Ph.D., American, 1966.
Said Reda, Adjunct Lecturer; M.S., Pace, 1987.
Michael F. Riggio, Adjunct Instructor; M.S., Polytechnic of New York, 1994.
Sylvia Russakoff, Adjunct Instructor; M.B.A., Pace, 1991.
David A. Sachs, Professor; Ed.D., Columbia, 1978.
Marian V. Sackson, Professor; Ph.D., CUNY Graduate Center, 1989.
Allen Stix, Associate Professor; Ph.D., Pittsburgh, 1973.
James Swingle, Adjunct Lecturer; M.S., NYU, 1984.
Sylvester Tuohy, Professor; Ph.D., Stevens, 1978.
Stuart Varden, Professor; Ed.D., Columbia, 1974.
William von Heyn, Adjunct Instructor; M.S., Polytechnic of New York, 1991.
Melvyn Weisel, Associate Professor; Ed.D., Columbia, 1977.
Robert Williams, Assistant Professor; Ph.D., Massachusetts, 1991.
Gerald Wohl, Professor; M.B.A., CCNY, 1961.
Carol E. Wolf, Professor; Ph.D., Cornell, 1964.
Charles T. Zahn, Professor; M.A., Wisconsin–Madison, 1983.

PENNSTATE

THE PENNSYLVANIA STATE UNIVERSITY

COLLEGE OF ENGINEERING
DEPARTMENT OF ELECTRICAL ENGINEERING

PROGRAMS OF STUDY

The Department of Electrical Engineering offers M.S. degrees (either thesis or paper option) that lead to positions with government and industry as well as to Ph.D. degrees where graduates find research and teaching positions. Each student requests the appointment of a committee that oversees and approves the student's research. With the exception of the M.S. paper option, the degrees are strongly research-oriented. Master's degree students need 32 or 34 credits requiring typically seventeen to twenty-four months if they have assistantships, and doctoral degree students require 50 credits beyond the baccalaureate plus research work requiring typically three or four years beyond the master's degree. Doctoral degree students take written and oral candidacy exams within the first year and an oral comprehensive exam when course work is completed.

The department provides research opportunities in antennas; wave propagation; radar remote sensing; microwaves; computational electromagnetics; in situ ionospheric research; laser remote sensing; radiometry; multidimensional signal processing; signal compression; medical imaging; computer vision; neural nets; artificial intelligence; condition-based maintenance; data communications; optical communications; communication systems; data fusion; nonlinear, robust, intelligent, and adaptive controls; power systems; amorphous semiconductors; ferroelectrics; photonic devices; microelectronic and micromechanical devices; silicon processing; quantum well devices; fiber optics; nonlinear optics; and optical information processing.

RESEARCH FACILITIES

The Electronic Materials and Processing Research Laboratory has clean-room facilities providing III-V MBE deposition, ion implantation, dry etching, photolithography, E-beam evaporation, PECVD, and supporting facilities. The optics laboratories have high-power CW and pulsed picosecond lasers and programmable spatial light modulators. The Communications and Space Sciences Laboratory uses facilities at the Arecibo Observatory and Poker Flats, Alaska; four locally developed lidar systems; masers; sounding rockets; and radars. Other electromagnetic equipment includes an anechoic chamber, a microwave network analyzer, antennas, and electromagnetic simulation tools. The power systems and controls laboratories contain a Bailey Network 90 control system and power electronic systems. Signal and image processing laboratories contain numerous dedicated workstations and massively parallel computers that support a variety of research projects. Other Penn State resources include IBM mainframe and parallel processing facilities, extensive materials processing equipment associated with the Materials Research Institute, and the facilities of the Applied Research Laboratory.

FINANCIAL AID

The department provides fellowships, research assistantships, and teaching assistantships. Assistantships require nominally 20 hours per week and stipulate that students take between 8 and 11 credits each semester. These awards provide stipends worth from $5000 to $7500 per semester, and in addition tuition is paid.

COST OF STUDY

Full-time tuition and fees were $3334 per semester in spring 1997 for Pennsylvania residents and $6553 per semester for nonresidents who scheduled 12 or more credits. Thesis fees were $17 for the master's degree and $70 for the doctorate.

LIVING AND HOUSING COSTS

University housing and privately owned housing are available to graduate students. Examples of University housing costs for spring 1997 included double-occupancy rooms at $985 and up per semester. With board, the price ranged from $1985 to $2235. Four-bedroom apartments with common areas were available at $1315 and up per student per semester. Apartments were available at $305 and up per month.

STUDENT GROUP

Approximately 6,800 graduate students are enrolled at the University Park campus, with 1,400 in the College of Engineering and 230 in electrical engineering. About 10 percent are women, one half are non–U.S. citizens, and one half receive financial aid.

STUDENT OUTCOMES

Recent M.S. graduates have found positions with large corporations, small entrepreneurial companies, government labs and agencies, U.S. military branches, and consulting firms. Recent Ph.D. graduates have taken faculty positions at large and small universities, research positions with large corporations, and research positions in government laboratories and start-up companies. Some noncitizens have found positions in the United States, and some have returned to positions with their sponsors or to industrial and teaching positions in their home countries.

LOCATION

Penn State's main campus, University Park, is located in the borough of State College in the center of the state. The town and its surrounding area, with a population of about 71,000, are located in low, rolling mountain country and offer a variety of recreational activities. The community and the University present a wide array of cultural and athletic events.

THE UNIVERSITY AND THE COLLEGE

Penn State is a land-grant university founded in 1855, with graduate work beginning in 1862. Today, the Graduate School has more than 2,000 faculty members and grants degrees in more than 140 majors. With 268 faculty members, the College of Engineering last year registered 1,370 graduate students and had research expenditures of $44 million.

APPLYING

Qualified candidates may apply to begin study in August or January, though August is preferred. Accordingly, application materials should be on file by late fall in order for the student to be considered for all forms of financial aid and to establish contacts with professors who share the same fields of interest. The applicant should have a B.S. degree in electrical engineering, although a closely related degree is also considered—the student may be expected to complete extra course work. Applicants are invited to submit a personal statement of career goals in addition to the required transcripts, scores on the General Test of the Graduate Record Examinations, and two letters of recommendation.

CORRESPONDENCE AND INFORMATION

To obtain additional information, students should contact:

Electrical Engineering Graduate Program Office
121 Electrical Engineering East
The Pennsylvania State University
University Park, Pennsylvania 16802

Telephone: 814-863-7295
Fax: 814-865-7065
E-mail: grad_info_ee@engr.psu.edu
World Wide Web: http://www.ee.psu.edu/

THE PENNSYLVANIA STATE UNIVERSITY
THE FACULTY AND THEIR RESEARCH

S. Ashok, Professor; Ph.D., RPI, 1978. Metal-semiconductor interfaces, ion implantation, radiation effects, photovoltaics.

Osama O. Awadelkarim, Associate Professor; Ph.D., Reading (England), 1982. Electronic materials and devices, MEMS, nanofabrication.

Kultegin Aydin, Associate Professor; Ph.D., Middle East Technical (Ankara), 1979. Radar, atmospheric remote sensing.

Amar S. Bhalla, Professor; Ph.D., Penn State, 1971. Smart materials, optoelectronics, microwave materials and devices.

Nirmal K. Bose, HRB Systems Professor; Ph.D., Syracuse, 1967. Multidimensional signal processing, robust processors.

James K. Breakall, Professor; Ph.D., Case Western Reserve, 1983. Electromagnetics, antennas, remote sensing.

Larry C. Burton, Professor and Head; Ph.D., Penn State, 1970. Electronic materials and devices, photovoltaics, electronic ceramics.

Octavia I. Camps, Assistant Professor; Ph.D., Washington, 1992. Computer vision, pattern recognition, graphics, and AI.

Lynn A. Carpenter, Associate Professor; Ph.D., Illinois, 1971. Ionospheric electric fields, propagation, microwaves, electrical safety.

Lee D. Coraor, Associate Professor; Ph.D., Iowa, 1978. Computer architecture, real-time microprocessor systems, digital systems.

Charles L. Croskey, Professor; Ph.D., Penn State, 1976. Microwave remote sensing, middle atmosphere, instrumentation.

L. Eric Cross, Evan Pugh Professor; Ph.D., Leeds, 1952. Ferroelectrics, ferroelastics, electrooptic and acoustooptic crystals, piezoelectrics.

Derald O. Cummings, Associate Professor; Ph.D., Penn State, 1982. RF/microwave and light-wave communications and devices.

Chita R. Das, Associate Professor; Ph.D., Southwestern Louisiana, 1986. Distributed processing, fault tolerance, local area nets.

John F. Doherty, Associate Professor; Ph.D., Rutgers, 1990. Communications technology and signal processing.

Joseph P. Dougherty, Associate Professor; Ph.D., Penn State, 1972. Electronic packaging, piezoelectrics, dielectric devices.

John E. Dzielski, Assistant Professor; Ph.D., MIT, 1988. Underwater vehicle control and identification, signal processing.

Tse-yun Feng, Binder Professor; Ph.D., Michigan, 1967. Computer design and engineering, computers and systems, supercomputers.

Anthony J. Ferraro, Professor; Ph.D., Penn State, 1959. Electromagnetics, antenna engineering, chemical models of the lower ionosphere.

Steven J. Fonash, Professor; Ph.D., Pennsylvania, 1968. Thin films, microelectronic and photovoltaic devices, ion implantation.

David B. Geselowitz, Professor; Ph.D., Pennsylvania, 1958. Cardiac electrophysiology, electrocardiography, magnetocardiography.

Gennady Gildenblat, Professor; Ph.D., RPI, 1984. Semiconductor device physics, microelectronics, wide-gap semiconductors.

Claire Gu, Assistant Professor; Ph.D., Caltech, 1989. Optical computing, optical interconnections, memories, and neural networks.

David L. Hall, Professor; Ph.D., Penn State, 1976. Signal processing, condition-based maintenance.

William E. Higgins, Associate Professor; Ph.D., Illinois, 1984. Computer vision, scientific visualization, medical imaging.

Thomas W. Hilands, Research Associate; Ph.D., Penn State, 1992. Signal processing, detection/estimation theory, arrays.

Paul T. Hulina, Associate Professor; Ph.D., Penn State, 1969. Microprocessor-based systems, memory systems, real-time systems.

Ali R. Hurson, Associate Professor; Ph.D., Central Florida, 1980. Concurrent and parallel systems, text-retrieval machines, data-driven architecture.

Thomas N. Jackson, Professor; Ph.D., Michigan, 1980. Exploratory electron devices including high-speed III-V's, ultrasmall devices, and quantum devices; microfabrication.

Timothy J. Kane, Assistant Professor; Ph.D., Illinois, 1992. Optical remote sensing, laser radar, atmospheric dynamics.

Rangachar Kasturi, Professor; Ph.D., Texas Tech, 1982. Computer vision, pattern recognition, image analysis, artificial intelligence.

Mohsen Kavehrad, Weiss Professor; Ph.D., Polytechnic, 1977. Information and communication technology.

Iam-Choon Khoo, Professor; Ph.D., Rochester, 1976. Quantum electronics, nonlinear optics, lasers and novel materials.

Karl S. Kunz, Professor; Ph.D., New Mexico State, 1971. Numerical modeling of electromagnetic coupling and shielding, antennas, radars, plasma physics, computer-aided instruction.

Stewart K. Kurtz, Murata Professor of Materials Research; Ph.D., Ohio State, 1960. Nonlinear electrooptic materials, semiconductor reliability, ferroelectrics, microstructural simulation of polycrystalline electronic materials.

David L. Landis, Professor; Ph.D., Penn State, 1982. Microelectronics, electronic design.

Kwang Y. Lee, Professor; Ph.D., Michigan State, 1971. Optimal and robust control, power systems, distributed systems, robotics, neural networks.

Raymond J. Luebbers, Professor; Ph.D., Ohio State, 1975. Computational electromagnetics, geometrical theory of diffraction, method of moments, finite difference time domain.

John D. Mathews, Professor; Ph.D., Case Western Reserve, 1972. Radar remote sensing, ionospheric physical and chemical processes, electrical-failure analysis.

Jeffrey S. Mayer, Assistant Professor; Ph.D., Purdue, 1991. Power system dynamics, electric machines, electromechanical systems.

Theresa Stellwag Mayer, Assistant Professor; Ph.D., Purdue, 1993. III-V compound semiconductor device physics.

John J. Metzner, Professor; Eng.Sc.D., NYU, 1958. Data communications, error correction, information theory.

David J. Miller, Assistant Professor; Ph.D., California, Santa Barbara, 1995. Data compression, pattern recognition.

David L. Miller, Professor; Ph.D., Illinois, 1973. III-V compound semiconductor materials, devices, and processing; MBE.

John D. Mitchell, Professor; Ph.D., Penn State, 1973. Electronics, instrumentation, atmospheric electrodynamics.

Simin Pakzad, Associate Professor; Ph.D., Oklahoma, 1986. Interconnection networks, fault tolerance, databases.

Jay S. Patel, Professor; Ph.D., SUNY at Stony Brook, 1982. Liquid crystals and related devices.

C. Russell Philbrick, Professor; Ph.D., North Carolina State, 1966. Atmospheric and ionospheric dynamics and composition, laser remote sensing (lidar).

Shashi Phoha, Professor; Ph.D., Michigan, 1976. Command/control systems, knowledge-based systems, information fusion.

Ashok Ray, Professor; Ph.D., Northeastern, 1976. Control systems, computer networks, mechatronics.

James W. Robinson, Professor; Ph.D., Michigan, 1965. Plasma and ion-beam systems for semiconductor device processing.

Christopher S. Ruf, Associate Professor; Ph.D., Massachusetts, 1987. Atmospheric propagation, microwave interferometer imaging.

David W. Russell, Associate Professor; Ph.D., CNAA, Manchester, 1971. Artificial intelligence, ill-defined processes, cognition.

Jerzy Ruzyllo, Professor; Ph.D., Warsaw Technical, 1977. Integrated circuit and device processing, semiconductor materials and surfaces.

Jeffrey L. Schiano, Assistant Professor; Ph.D., Illinois, 1991. Controls, quantum control, microelectromechanical systems.

Raymond A. Schulz, Assistant Professor; M.S., Syracuse, 1962. Linear integrated circuits, device models, data acquisition.

Leon H. Sibul, Professor; Ph.D., Penn State, 1968. Adaptive signal processing, optimum arrays, stochastic systems.

Frank W. Symons Jr., Senior Research Associate; Ph.D., Penn State, 1975. Adaptive filters, nonlinear control, complex systems.

Mario Sznaier, Assistant Professor; Ph.D., Washington (Seattle), 1989. Robust and optimal control, robotics, power systems.

Richard L. Tutwiler, Research Associate; Ph.D., Penn State, 1992. Pattern recognition, machine vision, ultrasonic imaging.

Kenji Uchino, Professor; Ph.D., Tokyo Institute of Technology, 1981. Ferroelectric materials and piezoelectric ceramics.

Robert E. Van Dyck, Assistant Professor; Ph.D., North Carolina State, 1991. Video compression, broadband communication.

Vasundara V. Varadan, Professor; Ph.D., Illinois, 1974. Tailored composites, electromagnetic/acoustic coatings, chiral composites.

Vijay K. Varadan, Professor; Ph.D., Northwestern, 1974. Electronic ceramics, conducting polymers, chiral composites, sonar, radar.

Douglas H. Werner, Research Associate; Ph.D., Penn State, 1989. Electromagnetics, antennas, propagation, fractals.

Christopher R. Wronski, Leonhard Professor; Ph.D., Imperial College (London), 1963. Hydrogenated amorphous silicon and diamond, thin-film optoelectronic and heterojunction devices, photovoltaics.

Shizhuo Yin, Assistant Professor; Ph.D., Penn State, 1993. Optical signal processing, photorefractive materials.

Randy K. Young, Research Associate; Ph.D., Penn State, 1991. Signal processing; wideband, wavelet, multisensor processing.

Francis T. S. Yu, Evan Pugh Professor; Ph.D., Michigan, 1964. Electrooptics, optical information processing, holography, information theory, neural networks.

Qiming Zhang, Associate Professor; Ph.D., Penn State, 1986. Piezoelectric actuators, sensors, transducers.

COMPUTER SCIENCE AND INFORMATION DEPARTMENT

PROGRAMS OF STUDY

Polytechnic's Computer Science and Information Department offers programs of study leading to the M.S. and Ph.D. degrees. The M.S. program is intended to develop competence in a broad range of fundamental areas, including data structures and algorithms, programming languages, compilers, architecture, operating systems, and artificial intelligence. Graduates are prepared for challenging careers in software and hardware development in such industries as telecommunications, financial services, and computer manufacturing. Degree requirements include completion of 36 credits, including six required courses, two 2-semester course sequences, and additional electives. The M.S. program is offered on all three of Polytechnic's campuses in the New York metropolitan area (Brooklyn, Long Island, and Westchester). Evening classes are an option. A sequence of preparatory courses is available for students whose undergraduate background is not in computer science.

The Ph.D. program is intended to develop competence in a broad range of areas and expertise in one or more specific areas, as well as critical thinking ability and the ability to conduct independent research. Graduates are prepared for state-of-the-art industrial research and for academic research and teaching careers. The main requirement of the Ph.D. program is completion of a thesis embodying significant original research. Preliminary conditions include the completion of the M.S. requirements, the passing of written qualifying exams, and the writing of a survey paper. The relatively small size of the program affords students the opportunity for close collaboration with faculty members working in such research areas as combinatorial optimization, computational biology, computational geometry, databases, image processing and understanding, pattern matching, parallel and distributed architectures and systems, parallel algorithms, network design and management, randomized algorithms, and software engineering, reliability, and testing. The Ph.D. program is centered at Polytechnic's main campus in Brooklyn.

RESEARCH FACILITIES

Polytechnic's research facilities include a network of workstations (Sun SPARC, IBM RS-6000, HP 9000/425), a Convex C120 superminicomputer, several Sun SPARC-10s serving a network of X-terminals, a Silicon Graphics Indigo, a Tandem fault-tolerant computer, a DataCube Image Processing system, and other special purpose equipment for image analysis.

FINANCIAL AID

A limited number of teaching and research assistantships are available to exceptionally qualified Ph.D. students. In 1996–97, these awards covered full tuition and carried a stipend of $1145 per month for junior graduate students (before passing the qualifying exam) and of $1330 per month for advanced students. These awards are renewed annually for up to five years, provided the student is making satisfactory progress. The National Science Foundation awards several graduate research traineeships for Ph.D. students studying at Polytechnic University who are U.S. citizens or permanent residents. Other forms of financial support include grants and loans from state and national programs.

COST OF STUDY

In 1997–98, tuition is $18,670 for full-time study and $645 per credit for part-time study.

LIVING AND HOUSING COSTS

A limited number of dormitory rooms are available at Pratt Institute and Long Island University (near Polytechnic's Brooklyn campus) and at Polytechnic's Farmingdale, Long Island, campus. Shared dormitory rooms cost about $1300 per semester. Privately owned apartments are available near campus.

STUDENT GROUP

Polytechnic's computer science program draws students from across the United States and around the world. The M.S. program has about 300 students and the Ph.D. program about 50 students. Approximately 20 percent of the students are women. Most of the M.S. students and some of the Ph.D. students pursue their degrees on a part-time basis.

LOCATION

Polytechnic is located on three campuses in the New York City metropolitan area. The main campus is in downtown Brooklyn, adjacent to Brooklyn Heights, one of New York's more desirable residential communities. The department is located in a University building that is part of the 16-acre Metrotech Center for academic, research, and commercial activities. As a result of the University's favorable location, faculty members and students enjoy close interactions with major companies in the financial, telecommunications, and computer industries. Two suburban campuses are located in Farmingdale, Long Island, and in Hawthorne, Westchester County. New York City's many and diverse cultural attractions are easily accessible from all three campuses.

THE UNIVERSITY AND THE DEPARTMENT

Founded in 1854 as the Polytechnic Institute of Brooklyn ("Brooklyn Poly"), Polytechnic University is one of the major technological universities in the Greater New York area. Programs of full-time and part-time study are offered during the day and evening at all three campuses. The evening graduate program of Polytechnic allows students unusual latitude in adjusting their programs to the dictates of employment. The Computer Science and Information Department enjoys close relationships with the Departments of Electrical Engineering and Mathematics and with Polytechnic's Center for Advanced Technology in Telecommunications and Center for Applied Large Scale Computing.

APPLYING

Applications to the M.S. program will be processed until shortly before the beginning of the semester, but earlier application is strongly encouraged. Deadlines for Ph.D. program and fellowship applications are September 15 for the spring semester and February 15 for the fall semester. The GRE General Test is required for Ph.D. applicants. TOEFL scores are required for students whose native language is not English. The application fee is $45.

CORRESPONDENCE AND INFORMATION

For application material and general information:
Office of Graduate Admissions
Polytechnic University
Six Metrotech Center
Brooklyn, New York 11210
Telephone: 718-260-3200
 800-POLYTECH (toll-free)

For specific questions about the Computer Science Program:
Dr. Joseph L. Cina, Academic Administrator
Computer Science and Information Department
Polytechnic University
Six Metrotech Center
Brooklyn, New York 11210
Telephone: 718-260-3210
E-mail: jcina@duke.poly.edu

POLYTECHNIC UNIVERSITY
THE FACULTY AND THEIR RESEARCH

Boris Aronov, Associate Professor; Ph.D., NYU (Courant), 1989. Algorithms, computational and combinatorial geometry.

Alex Delis, Assistant Professor; Ph.D., Maryland College Park, 1993. Database management systems, analysis of systems, and software engineering.

David R. Doucette, Industry Professor; Ph.D., Polytechnic of Brooklyn, 1974. Systems integration, software engineering, operating systems.

Robert J. Flynn, Industry Professor; Ph.D., Polytechnic of Brooklyn, 1966. Computer architecture, operating systems.

Phyllis G. Frankl, Associate Professor; Ph.D., NYU (Courant), 1987. Software testing and analysis.

Ivan T. Frisch, Professor and Provost; Ph.D., Columbia, 1962. Information systems, computer network and network control.

Linda Ann Grieco, Coordinator of Advising; Ph.D., Rutgers, 1976. Programming and computer software.

Haldun Hadimioglu, Industry Assistant Professor; Ph.D., Polytechnic, 1991. Heterogeneous computing, including architectures and operating systems; performance analysis.

Donald J. Hockney, Professor and Vice President of Strategic Initiatives; Ph.D., Cornell, 1966. Logic, network design and applications, database theory and design.

Aaron Kershenbaum, Industry Professor; Ph.D., Polytechnic of New York, 1976. Algorithms, telecommunication network design.

Gad Landau, Associate Professor; Ph.D., Tel-Aviv, 1987. Algorithms, string matching, computational biology, pattern recognition, communication networks.

Burton Lieberman, Professor and Head of the Computer Science and Information Department; Ph.D., NYU (Courant), 1967. Statistical analysis.

Jeanette Schmidt, Associate Professor; Ph.D., Weizmann (Israel), 1986. Data structures, randomized algorithms, probabilistic analysis, string matching, computational biology.

Martin L. Shooman, Professor; D.E.E., Polytechnic of Brooklyn, 1961. Software engineering, system reliability and safety.

Stuart Steele, Industry Professor; Ph.D., Penn State, 1965. Software engineering.

Vassilis J. Tsotras, Assistant Professor; Ph.D., Columbia, 1990. Database systems, access methods, parallel databases and computer networks.

Richard Van Slyke, Professor; Ph.D., Berkeley, 1965. Combinatorial optimization, information network design, algorithms.

Joel Wein, Assistant Professor; Ph.D., MIT, 1991. Parallel and distributed computing, combinatorial optimization, scheduling theory, algorithms, network optimization.

Edward K. Wong, Associate Professor; Ph.D., Purdue, 1986. Computer vision, image analysis, pattern recognition.

The Computer Science and Information Department is located in the Dibner Building, part of the Metrotech academic/industrial complex in downtown Brooklyn.

POLYTECHNIC UNIVERSITY

DEPARTMENT OF ELECTRICAL ENGINEERING

PROGRAMS OF STUDY

The Department of Electrical Engineering offers M.S. and Ph.D. degrees in electrical engineering and M.S. degrees in systems engineering, telecommunication networks, and electrophysics. Large enrollments allow courses to be offered in a wide variety of areas, including telecommunication networks, wireless networks, communication theory, multimedia, systems, controls and robotics, image and signal processing, optoelectronics and fiber optics, electromagnetics and microwaves, plasmas, electronics, VLSI design, power systems, and material science. In addition to electrical engineering courses, students may also use courses in computer science, mathematics, physics, and other engineering disciplines toward the M.S. and Ph.D. degrees. A recent Gourman Report of M.S. programs in the United States ranks Polytechnic's electrical engineering program thirteenth in the nation. The electrophysics program is intended for students with a bachelor's degree in electrical engineering, physics, or related disciplines who are interested in studying the physical properties of devices and materials. The systems engineering program allows students with bachelor's degrees in mathematics, computer science, or other engineering disciplines to study the system and networking aspects of electrical sciences. The telecommunications program admits students with bachelor's degrees in computer science, computer engineering, or electrical engineering.

The M.S. degree requires 36 units of course work, which is equivalent to twelve standard semester-long courses meeting 2½ hours per week. Students may elect to do a 9-unit master's thesis, and up to 9 units may be transferred from other universities. For the telecommunications M.S. degree, students must complete a 6-unit project. In order to receive the degree, a student must maintain an average grade of at least a B. Students seeking the Ph.D. must take a minimum of 30 course units and 24 dissertation units past the M.S. In addition, they must pass a written and oral qualifying examination prior to taking dissertation credits and make a successful oral defense of the dissertation.

RESEARCH FACILITIES

Research activities related to the M.S. and Ph.D. programs are primarily organized through the Center for Advanced Technology in Telecommunications (CATT) and the Weber Research Institute (WRI). The CATT research programs encompass telecommunication networks, distributed systems, wireless networks, SONET and ATM networks, and image processing and compression. The WRI activities deal with ultrawideband short-pulse electromagnetics and signal processing, underwater propagation, microwave-integrated circuits, optoelectronics, plasmas, power systems, high-power sources, and acoustic devices. In addition, there are research programs in controls and robotics and in communication theory. These research activities are supported by $2.9 million in grants and contracts from industry and from federal and state agencies. Research facilities are divided between the primary campus in Brooklyn and the Long Island campus in Farmingdale. The Brooklyn campus has research laboratories devoted to image processing, signal processing, VLSI design, high-speed switching, optoelectronics, control and robotics, short-pulse electromagnetic scattering, and power systems. On the Long Island campus, there are laboratories for studying plasmas, microwave-integrated circuits, high-power sources, wireless communication systems, materials, and acoustic devices.

FINANCIAL AID

Financial aid includes half-tuition remission, research and teaching fellowships, graduate assistantships, and graduate traineeships. Stipends ranged from $1180 to $1365 per month for 1996–97.

COST OF STUDY

In 1996–97, tuition for full-time study was $8945 per semester; for part-time study, the cost was $615 per unit.

LIVING AND HOUSING COSTS

In Brooklyn, there are dormitory facilities for single students. In addition, private rooming accommodations are available for all students. For students enrolled at the 25-acre Long Island campus in Farmingdale, accommodations are available in the residence hall. Private rooms for men, women, and families can be rented nearby. Basic living expenses for a single student are approximately $2000 per month.

STUDENT GROUP

The student body consists of men and women who hold baccalaureate and graduate degrees from over 350 institutions worldwide. The graduate students represent about fifty other countries. In 1996, 101 M.S. degrees and 21 Ph.D. degrees were awarded by the department.

LOCATION

The main campus of Polytechnic is in the recently developed MetroTech Center in downtown Brooklyn, which is one of the five boroughs making up New York City. New York is a center for science, technology, medicine, the arts, and theater. With its mix of people and cultures from all over the world, it is perhaps the most exciting city in the world. The Long Island campus is located 40 miles east in Farmingdale, a major center of the aerospace and electronics industry. Some graduate courses are also offered at the Westchester campus in Hawthorne. The main campus is accessible by public transportation, and all campuses are easily reached by car.

THE UNIVERSITY

The University was formed in 1973 by the merger of the Polytechnic Institute of Brooklyn and the NYU School of Engineering and Science. It has the nation's third-largest graduate engineering enrollment. Graduate programs are offered at the main campus in Brooklyn, the Long Island campus in Farmingdale, and the Westchester Center in White Plains. The evening sessions allow unusual latitude in adapting programs to the requirements of employment. The faculty has 147 full-time professors and a large adjunct staff. The University conducted more than $9.9 million of funded research in 1996. In 1983, New York designated Polytechnic the state's Center for Advanced Technology in Telecommunications.

APPLYING

For admission to the M.S. programs, the applicant must have a bachelor's degree from an accredited university with a grade point average indicative of success in graduate study. For the electrical engineering program, a B.S. in electrical engineering is required. Admission to the electrophysics program requires a B.S. in electrical engineering, physics, or a related discipline. Admission to the system engineering program requires a bachelor's degree in engineering, mathematics, or computer science. Admission to the telecommunications program requires a bachelor's degree in computer science, computer engineering, or electrical engineering. Students lacking some background may qualify for admission by taking specified deficiency courses. Students may be admitted directly into the Ph.D. programs with a bachelor's degree or with a master's degree. Those entering with a bachelor's will ordinarily satisfy the requirements for the M.S. on the way to the Ph.D. Students receiving a master's in systems engineering or electrophysics may go on for a Ph.D. in electrical engineering.

Applicants should submit credentials as early as possible. Deadlines are July 1 for September registration, November 1 for January registration, and May 1 for the summer session, although late admission is possible. The financial aid deadline is April 1.

CORRESPONDENCE AND INFORMATION

Graduate Committee
Department of Electrical Engineering
Polytechnic University
6 Metrotech Center
Brooklyn, New York 11201
Telephone: 718-260-3056

POLYTECHNIC UNIVERSITY
THE FACULTY AND THEIR RESEARCH

S. Bergstein, Industry Professor; Ph.D. (electrical engineering), Polytechnic of New York. Optical communications, fiber optics.

H. Bertoni, Professor; Ph.D. (electrical engineering), Polytechnic of Brooklyn. Acoustics, electromagnetics.

D. Bolle, Professor; Ph.D. (electrical engineering), Purdue. Guided wave propagation, nonreciprocal devices.

R. Boorstyn, Professor; Ph.D. (electrical engineering), Polytechnic of Brooklyn. Computer communication networks, telecommunications.

M. Boukli, Instructor; Ph.D. (electrical engineering), Polytechnic of Brooklyn. Communication systems, fiber optics.

F. Cassara, Professor; Ph.D. (electrical engineering), Polytechnic of Brooklyn. Communication electronics.

E. Cassedy Jr., Professor; D.Eng. (electrical engineering), Johns Hopkins. Plasma studies, power, energy policies.

J. Chao, Associate Professor; Ph.D. (electrical engineering), Ohio. High-speed networks, ATM and photonic switch design, VLSI.

D. Czarkowski, Assistant Professor; Ph.D., Florida. Power electronics, power quality.

N. Das, Assistant Professor; Ph.D. (electrical engineering), Massachusetts. Electromagnetics, antennas.

G. Griffel, Associate Professor; Ph.D. (electrical engineering), Tel-Aviv (Israel). Optoelectronics, semiconductor lasers.

D. Hunt, Professor; B.S.E.E., Pennsylvania. Networks, systems.

F. Khorrami, Associate Professor; Ph.D. (electrical engineering), Ohio State. Control systems and robotics.

M. Kouar, Instructor; Ph.D. (electrical engineering), Polytechnic of Brooklyn. Electronic circuits, telecommunication systems.

S.-P. Kuo, Professor; Ph.D. (electrophysics), Polytechnic of New York. Magnetohydrodynamics, plasmas.

I.-T. Lu, Associate Professor; Ph.D. (electrical engineering), Polytechnic of New York. Acoustics, wireless communications.

Z. Pan, Assistant Professor; Ph.D. (electrical engineering), Illinois at Urbana–Champaign. Control systems.

S. Panwar, Associate Professor; Ph.D. (electrical engineering), Massachusetts. Communication networks.

S. Pillai, Professor; Ph.D. (systems engineering), Pennsylvania. Signal processing and communications.

L. Shaw, Professor; Ph.D. (electrical engineering), Stanford. Signal processing, reliability.

J. Snyder, Senior Industry Professor; M.S.E.E., Polytechnic of New York. Microprocessors, data acquisition, signal processing.

T. Tamir, University Professor; Ph.D. (electrophysics), Polytechnic of Brooklyn. Electromagnetics, electrooptics.

N. Uzun, Assistant Industry Professor; Ph.D. (electrical engineering), Polytechnic of Brooklyn. VLSI, high-speed networking, signal processing.

P. Voltz, Associate Professor; Ph.D. (electrical engineering), Polytechnic. Communications, signal processing.

Y. Wang, Associate Professor; Ph.D. (electrical engineering), California, Santa Barbara. Medical imaging, computer vision, image and video signal processing.

D. Youla, University Professor; M.S.E.E., NYU. Networks, control systems.

Z. Zabar, Professor and Department Head; Sc.D. (electrical engineering), Technion (Israel). Power electronics, electrical drives, power systems.

PRINCETON UNIVERSITY

DEPARTMENT OF COMPUTER SCIENCE

PROGRAMS OF STUDY

The Department of Computer Science offers programs of study leading to the Master of Science in Engineering (M.S.E.) and Doctor of Philosophy (Ph.D.) degrees. The requirements for the M.S.E. can normally be completed in one academic year of full-time graduate study. Requirements for the Ph.D. degree are to (1) complete at least one academic year of full-time residence as a degree candidate; (2) present a research seminar and sustain the Ph.D. general examination; (3) submit a doctoral dissertation and have it accepted by the faculty; and (4) satisfactorily sustain a final public oral examination, which includes a presentation and a defense of the dissertation.

Dissertation topics are selected through an informal matching of students' interests and faculty expertise. Graduate courses, seminars, and informal work groups have a major influence on this process. External speakers in a regular seminar series also play a role, and student interactions are important as well.

RESEARCH FACILITIES

The Department of Computer Science is located in a recently constructed four-story building. The department has a number of computer systems to support instruction and research in architecture, graphics, networking, and systems, including a High End and DEC mainframes, and a variety of personal workstations and special equipment. These machines are networked and connected via a broadband cable to various University and national networks.

Princeton's libraries include the Mathematics Library and the Engineering Library, both of which are nearby and are well-stocked with primary reference materials in computer science.

FINANCIAL AID

Financial assistance, equivalent to tuition plus $13,000 to $15,360 for the 1997–98 academic year, is normally available to all doctoral students in the form of fellowships or assistantships in instruction or research. The assistantships are so arranged as to be an integral part of the student's training and to permit a full program of study. Additional compensation in the summer is available. No financial aid is provided to M.S.E. students.

COST OF STUDY

Tuition is $23,500 for the 1997–98 academic year; this includes use of University facilities and comprehensive health and accident insurance coverage.

LIVING AND HOUSING COSTS

The Graduate College provides rooms for about 500 single students at costs of $2117 to $3688 for the 1997–98 academic year. Some rooms are available in the Princeton area for about $600 a month, and students may take meals at the Graduate College for the board rate, which varies from $2407 to $3086. University housing at $440 to $1202 a month plus utilities is available for 400 married students. Jobs are available at the University or nearby for graduate students' spouses.

STUDENT GROUP

Of the 6,250 students at Princeton University, approximately 1,700 are graduate students. The Department of Computer Science has 60 graduate students and 90 undergraduates. The student population represents many universities and countries.

LOCATION

The University is located in the historic town of Princeton, about 50 miles from both New York City and Philadelphia. There are a variety of athletic and cultural activities in the area. The University has many athletic facilities for such sports as golf, tennis, sailing, swimming, and squash, plus two large gymnasiums. The Pocono Mountains, about 85 miles away, offer skiing and camping. The beaches of the Jersey shore are an hour's drive away. In addition, McCarter Theatre and Richardson Auditorium present an outstanding variety of concerts and plays.

THE UNIVERSITY AND THE DEPARTMENT

Founded in 1746 by charter of King George II, Princeton is the country's fourth-oldest university. The University annually enrolls about 6,250 students (4,550 undergraduate students and 1,700 graduate students). The faculty, numbering about 800, engages in teaching at both the undergraduate and graduate levels and in a diversity of research and scholarly activities.

Research in computer science at Princeton has a distinguished history that dates back to von Neumann and Turing. The primary center of research activity has shifted from mathematics in the forties and fifties to electrical engineering in the sixties and seventies to an independent Department of Computer Science since 1985. The department has intellectual ties throughout the University, ranging from mathematics to mechanical engineering to molecular biology to music.

APPLYING

Completed applications for admission received before January 7 receive first consideration; fellowship and assistantship appointments are made from these applications. Applicants are notified of the results around March 15. Applicants should include the results of the Graduate Record Examinations, including scores on the General Test and a Subject Test, as part of their application for admission. Students who are in doubt as to which Subject Test to take usually should register for the one covering their field of undergraduate concentration. The TOEFL is required if English was not the primary language of undergraduate instruction.

CORRESPONDENCE AND INFORMATION

Director of Graduate Studies
Department of Computer Science
35 Olden Street
Princeton University
Princeton, New Jersey 08544
Telephone: 609-258-5387
E-mail: gradinfo@cs.princeton.edu
World Wide Web: http://www.cs.princeton.edu

PRINCETON UNIVERSITY
THE FACULTY AND THEIR RESEARCH

Andrew Appel, Ph.D., Carnegie Mellon. Programming languages.
Sanjeev Arora, Ph.D., Berkeley. Complexity theory.
Bernard Chazelle, Ph.D., Yale. Computational geometry, data structures.
Douglas Clark, Ph.D., Carnegie Mellon. Architecture.
Perry Cook, Ph.D., Stanford. Computer music, human/computer interface.
David Dobkin, Ph.D., Harvard. Graphics, analysis of algorithms, geometry.
Edward Felten, Ph.D., Washington (Seattle). Computer security, distributed computing.
Adam Finkelstein, Ph.D., Washington (Seattle). Computer graphics.
Hisashi Kobayashi, Ph.D., Princeton. Performance analysis.
Andrea LaPaugh, Ph.D., MIT. Combinatorial algorithms, VLSI design.
Kai Li, Ph.D., Yale. Operating systems, architecture.
Richard Lipton, Ph.D., Carnegie Mellon. Architecture, complexity, DNA computing.
Robert Sedgewick, Ph.D., Stanford. Analysis of algorithms, algorithm visualization.
J. P. Singh, Ph.D., Stanford. Scientific applications of high-performance computers.
Kenneth Steiglitz, Ph.D., NYU. Highly parallel computation, combinatorial optimization, computer music.
Robert Tarjan, Ph.D., Stanford. Data structures, graph algorithms, complexity.
Andrew Yao, Ph.D., Illinois. Computational complexity, analysis of algorithms.

Areas of Graduate Study and Research

Architecture for high-performance systems; complexity; computational geometry; data structures and combinatorial algorithms; distributed computer systems; graphics systems and algorithms; language recognition; parallel computation; programming languages and environments; VLSI design, simulation, and testing.

PRINCETON UNIVERSITY

SCHOOL OF ENGINEERING AND APPLIED SCIENCE
DEPARTMENT OF ELECTRICAL ENGINEERING

PROGRAMS OF STUDY

The Department of Electrical Engineering offers programs of study leading to the Ph.D. and M.S.E. degrees. The requirements for the M.S.E. can normally be completed in one academic year of full-time graduate study. (There are a few students, supported by local industry, who proceed on a half-time basis for two years in the Industrial M.S.E. Program.) Requirements for the Ph.D. degree are completing at least one academic year of full-time residence as a degree candidate, presenting a research seminar and passing the Ph.D. general examination, submitting a doctoral dissertation and having it accepted by the faculty, and satisfactorily sustaining a final public oral examination, which includes a presentation and a defense of the dissertation.

RESEARCH FACILITIES

The Department of Electrical Engineering, located in the Engineering Quadrangle, has facilities for experimental research in multiuser communication systems, VLSI array processors, computer-aided design and testing of digital systems, and digital signal processing. The image processing lab is equipped with a network of Sony NEWS 3710 and Sun SPARC color workstations, a Sony HDM-2830 high-definition color monitor, a DVS-ISP 1024 image sequence storage and simulation system, and a Sony LVR/LVS 5000 laser videodisc recording system. Pulse-compressed mode-locked lasers, custom-built fiber-optic linear filters, optical bistable devices, and integrated-optic photonic switches are used for light-wave communications research. In the area of electronic materials and devices, research instrumentation includes molecular-beam epitaxy (MBE), electron diffraction and spectroscopy equipment, scanning tunneling microscopy, superconducting magnets (including a 16T magnet with dilution refrigerator), various cw and pulsed (picosecond and femtosecond) lasers, and other equipment for electrical, optical, and magnetic measurements and for materials synthesis and processing. One laboratory is dedicated to the deposition and characterization of amorphous semiconductors, and a clean-room laboratory is available for the general processing, fabrication, and measurement of semiconductor structures and devices. Facilities include diffusion furnaces; electron-beam and thermal evaporators; and plasma etching and deposition, optical lithography, direct-write electron-beam patterning, and automated electrical measurement equipment.

In addition to the mainframe at the Computer Center, the department's own computing facilities consist of a network of Sun and Sony workstations, HP 9000 series 200 and 550 workstations, and a complement of Macintosh PCs. The department also has an NSF-funded center for experimental computing research, which operates an SGI Challenge multiprocessor, a system of SGI Indigo workstations, and a Viewgraphics HDTV frame buffer. Free access to these computers is provided to graduate students for their research. Undergraduate microcomputer laboratories for systems and signal processing with IBM PC/ATs and an IBM PS/2S and for microcomputer development with an HP 64000 system are also available for graduate student use. The research groups also have access to the Interactive Computer Graphics Laboratory (ICGL) and the Center for Information Technology (CIT) microcomputer clusters in the EQUAD located near the campus.

The Engineering Library is fully equipped with texts and reference material in all of the major areas of engineering, including both domestic and international periodicals and files of project research reports. The Fine Hall Library contains a large amount of reference material, including texts, periodicals, and reports in mathematics, physics, and statistics.

FINANCIAL AID

Financial assistance, equivalent to tuition plus $13,000 for the 1997–98 academic year, is normally available to all doctoral students in the form of fellowships or as assistantships in instruction or research. The assistantships are arranged as part of the student's training and permit a full program of study. Additional compensation is available in the summer.

COST OF STUDY

The tuition, $23,500 for the 1997–98 academic year, includes use of University facilities and comprehensive health and accident insurance coverage.

LIVING AND HOUSING COSTS

The Graduate College provides rooms for about 500 single students at $2390 to $3850 per academic year. Some rooms are available in the Princeton area for about $505 a month, and students may take meals at the Graduate College for the board rate. University housing is available for about 300 married students at approximately $430 to $800 a month plus utilities. Jobs for graduate students' spouses are available at the University or nearby.

STUDENT GROUP

Of the 6,438 students at Princeton University, 1,913 are graduate students from many universities and countries. The Department of Electrical Engineering has 119 graduate students and 103 undergraduates.

LOCATION

The University is located in the historic town of Princeton, 50 miles from both New York City and Philadelphia. The area offers sports, cultural, and entertainment activities, including an outstanding variety of concerts and plays at McCarter Theatre. The University has many facilities for such sports as golf, tennis, sailing, swimming, and squash, plus two large gymnasiums. The Pocono Mountains, 85 miles away, offer skiing and camping. The Jersey shore beaches are an hour's drive away.

THE UNIVERSITY AND THE SCHOOL

Princeton's first engineering program was offered in 1873 in civil engineering. In 1922, the School of Engineering was formed by the Departments of Electrical Engineering, Civil Engineering, and Mechanical Engineering. The widening scope of today's engineering and the University's responsibilities for developing new areas of applied science, particularly those spreading across or falling outside traditional fields, led Princeton in 1962 to rename its engineering school the School of Engineering and Applied Science. There are currently five departments in the School: Chemical Engineering, Civil Engineering and Operations Research, Computer Science, Electrical Engineering, and Mechanical and Aerospace Engineering.

APPLYING

Completed applications for admission received before January 3 receive first consideration; fellowship and assistantship appointments are made from these applications. Applicants are notified of the results around March 15 and should include results of the Graduate Record Examinations (GRE) General Test as part of their application for admission. Students may also request an application electronically.

CORRESPONDENCE AND INFORMATION

Director of Graduate Studies
Department of Electrical Engineering
Princeton University
Princeton, New Jersey 08544

Telephone: 609-258-3335
World Wide Web: http://www.ee.princeton.edu/maildgs.html

PRINCETON UNIVERSITY
THE FACULTY AND THEIR RESEARCH

Keren Bergman, Ph.D., MIT. Fiber optic systems and devices, nonlinear quantum noise, high bit-rate lasers.

Ravindra Bhatt, Ph.D., Illinois. Condensed-matter theory.

Stephen Y. Chou, Ph.D., MIT. Nanotechnology, nanoelectronics, nano-optoelectronics, nanomagnetics.

Bradley W. Dickinson, Ph.D., Stanford. Systems theory, signal processing.

Stephen R. Forrest, Ph.D., Michigan. Optoelectronics and organic semiconductors.

Niraj Jha, Ph.D., Illinois. Digital system testing, fault-tolerant computing, computer-aided design of integrated circuits, parallel processing.

Antoine Kahn, Ph.D., Princeton. Semiconductor surfaces and interfaces.

Hisashi Kobayashi, Ph.D., Princeton. Communication networks, digital communication, system performance analysis, queueing theory.

Sanjeev R. Kulkarni, Ph.D., MIT. Signal processing, image processing, machine vision, machine learning.

Sun-Yuan Kung, Ph.D., Stanford. VLSI signal processing, array processors, digital signal processing, modern spectrum analysis, neural computing.

Bede Liu, Ph.D., Polytechnic of Brooklyn. Image/video/signal processing.

Stephen A. Lyon, Ph.D., Caltech. Device physics and laser spectroscopy.

Sharad Malik, Ph.D., Berkeley. Design methodology and design tools for electronic systems.

Margaret R. Martonosi, Ph.D., Stanford. Computer analysis and performance monitoring, parallel architectures and software.

Michael Orchard, Ph.D., Princeton. Image processing and video coding.

H. Vincent Poor, Ph.D., Princeton. Statistical signal processing, digital communications, multiuser communication systems.

Paul Prucnal, Ph.D., Columbia. Photonic switching, optical networks, VLSI optical interconnects and optical signal processing.

Peter Ramadge, Ph.D., Toronto. System theory, control theory.

Stuart C. Schwartz, Ph.D., Michigan. Signal and image processing, communication theory.

Mordechai Segev, Ph.D., Technion (Israel). Nonlinear optics.

Mansour Shayegan, Ph.D., MIT. Physics and technology of low-dimensional semiconductor structures.

James C. Sturm, Ph.D., Stanford. Physics and technology of semiconductors, fabrication processes.

Daniel C. Tsui, Ph.D., Chicago. Physics of thin films and interfaces.

Sergio Verdu, Ph.D., Illinois. Communication and information theory.

Sigurd Wagner, Ph.D., Vienna. Device materials and thin-film electronics, including solar cells.

Wayne H. Wolf, Ph.D., Stanford. VLSI-CAD, layout design and compaction.

Andrew Wolfe, Ph.D., Carnegie Mellon. Computer architecture and implementation, parallel processor architecture, advanced compilation methods.

RESEARCH AREAS

Computer Engineering

This program aims to prepare students for teaching and research in computer architecture, fault-tolerant systems, digital system testing, parallel processing, neural computing, logic and high-level synthesis, embedded system design, and related areas. Courses offered by the Department of Electrical Engineering include VLSI design, switching and sequential systems, digital system testing, computer architecture, neural computing, VLSI array processors, and computer-aided design of integrated circuits. In addition, students elect appropriate courses offered by the Departments of Computer Science and Mathematics. Ongoing research focuses on digital system testing, synthesis for testability, fault-tolerant computing, systolic and wavefront architectures, parallel processing, optical computing, computer architecture, special-purpose supercomputers, neural networks, and computer-aided design of digital systems.

Research in computer engineering has a strong theoretical component and often involves experimental work in design, testing, and simulation. Departmental facilities are available to support the research, and students gain substantial experience with hardware and software as part of an academic program in this area.

Electronic Materials and Devices

This program is directed toward preparing the student for research, advanced development, or teaching in the areas of solid-state electronics, physical electronics, electronic materials, or the physical aspects of electrotechnology in general. The student takes courses in the Department of Physics on appropriate topics, such as electromagnetic theory and quantum mechanics. Courses in solid-state and semiconductor physics, transport theory, semiconductor surface phenomena, solid-state devices, optical properties of solids, electronic materials, and heterojunction structures are given within the Department of Electrical Engineering.

The research in the program combines the theoretical and experimental aspects of unsolved challenges in the field. The laboratories of the department provide extensive facilities for experimental research, and each student is provided with properly equipped space and apparatus for his or her own work. Current student research includes work on surfaces and interfaces of semiconductors; molecular-beam epitaxy growth of compound semiconductors and organic solids; deposition and application of amorphous semiconductors; optoelectronic devices for VLSI interconnects; optical processes in semiconductors, including subpicosecond phenomena; and transport along interfaces, especially two-dimensional magnetotransport.

Information Sciences and Systems

This program is broadly formulated to prepare the student for research and teaching in the general area of systems, with emphasis on stochastic systems, communication theory, systems theory, and signal and image processing. Current research activities include work in estimation and detection, stochastic processes, optimization of stochastic systems, adaptive and learning systems, artificial neural networks, control theory, nonlinear filtering, computer communication, data communication, digital signal processing, image processing, discrete event systems, information theory, multiuser communication systems, optical channels, and fiber-optic networks and photonic switching.

The research program is oriented mainly toward theoretical work and toward extensive use of computers for signal processing and for system simulation and optimization. Facilities are available to conduct a wide range of experimental research, particularly in the areas of digital and optical signal processing, random processes, and light-wave communication.

Optical and Optoelectronic Engineering

This program prepares students for research, advanced development, and teaching in the areas of optical communications, optoelectronic devices, and optical system design, with applications to fiber optic networks, telecommunications systems, and multiprocessor interconnections. In addition to the core curriculum, the program of study can include selected courses in the Electronic Materials and Devices Group and the Information Sciences and Systems Group, as well as courses in the Physics, Chemistry, and Mechanical and Aerospace Engineering departments.

The research program is both experimental and theoretical, and the projects can range from areas such as photonic switching, broadband optical networks, and optical computing to smart pixels. The laboratory facilities for optical communications systems are equipped with Argon, YAG, YLF, Titanium Sapphire, and Color-Center short-pulse laser systems, as well as a variety of semiconductor lasers, optical hardware, and systems test equipment. The facilities for sample growth are equipped with inorganic and organic MBE growth systems, a vapor deposition system, and an LPE growth system. The sample preparation and characterization facilities include reactive ion etching, an electron beam etching chamber, RHEED, STM, and a picosecond dye laser. For device processing, packaging, and microelectronics, the facilities include a mask aligner, a wire bonder, and a probe station.

526

PURDUE UNIVERSITY, WEST LAFAYETTE

DEPARTMENT OF COMPUTER SCIENCES

PROGRAM OF STUDY

The Department of Computer Sciences offers challenging programs leading to the Master of Science and Doctor of Philosophy degrees. The areas of the department include the analysis of algorithms and the theory of computation; artificial intelligence and heuristic problem solving; distributed systems; geometric modeling, computer graphics, and scientific visualization; information security; scientific computing; and software systems.

The requirements for the Ph.D. include a qualifying process involving four examinations, seven specified courses (21 semester hours), a master's thesis or some other demonstration of research potential, seven elective courses, a preliminary examination, and a thesis, the novel results of which merit publication in a refereed journal. For students starting after a bachelor's degree, the qualifying process takes three or four semesters. Courses taken as part of a master's program in computer science at another university can often be counted toward the Ph.D. course requirements.

For the M.S., students must complete at least ten courses (30 semester hours) or eight courses and a thesis. The department offers a terminal M.S. degree (33 semester hours) jointly with the Department of Statistics and master's and doctoral specializations in computational science and engineering.

RESEARCH FACILITIES

The department, committed to experimental as well as theoretical research, has established more than a dozen laboratories. The department has state-of-the-art UNIX and Windows NT systems and direct access to research computing facilities in the Purdue University Computing Center (PUCC). Departmental facilities include two 4-processor Sun SPARC server 1000s (one with a 30-gigabyte storage array), two Sun 4/470 multiprocessors, a 64-node nCube 2 hypercube multiprocessor, and about 350 Sun, Intel, and Silcon Graphics workstations. These machines are connected by sixteen Ethernet networks, an ATM network, and several gateways to each other and to the campus network, which include a 10-megabit-per-second link to the Internet. Additional facilities include another 30 gigabytes of disk storage, thirty-five laser printers, and a fully equipped video production facility.

The PUCC facilities include an IBM SP2, a 161-node Intel Paragon supercomputer, a 16-node Intel iPSC/860 hypercube, an IBM 3090, and two SPARC server 1000s.

FINANCIAL AID

Prospective doctoral students may apply for a first-year fellowship, which may be extended for an additional year. United States citizens and permanent residents who are members of certain ethnic minority groups, including African American, American Indian, Native Alaskan (Eskimo or Aleut), Native Pacific Islander (Polynesian or Micronesian), and Hispanic, may be eligible for special master's and doctoral fellowships.

The usual form of support is the graduate assistantship. Duties may include teaching classes or recitation sections, grading papers, assisting students with their programs, or working on a research project. A few summer assistantships are usually available. Teaching assistantships require high proficiency in spoken English. The normal stipend for graduate assistants in 1997–98 is in the range of $1100 to $1300 per month for ten months.

COST OF STUDY

In 1997–98, all graduate assistants and fellows paid fees of $294 per semester. Tuition and fees were $1668 per semester for Indiana residents and $5584 per semester for others. Summer rates are half of those for other semesters.

LIVING AND HOUSING COSTS

In 1997–98, single accommodations in the Graduate Houses cost $11.65 to $15.55 per day. University-operated apartments for married students cost $397.50 to $487.50 per month. The rent for most two-bedroom unfurnished apartments in West Lafayette and Lafayette ranges from $450 to $650 per month.

STUDENT GROUP

In the Department of Computer Sciences, there are about 570 undergraduate students and 120 graduate students, of whom almost all are full-time. Nearly 50 percent of the graduate students have listed the Ph.D. as a degree objective. About 20 percent of the graduate students have successfully completed the doctoral qualifying process. Approximately 80 percent have assistantships or fellowships. About 20 percent are women, and about 75 percent are international students.

LOCATION

West Lafayette is a university community across the Wabash River from Lafayette, 65 miles northwest of Indianapolis, the state capital, and 126 miles southeast of Chicago. The population of the two cities exceeds 70,000, not including Purdue's student population. Cultural and athletic events are available throughout the academic year. Convenient transportation is provided by air (Purdue University Airport), bus, and rail (Amtrak) carriers. U.S. 52 passes through both cities, and Interstate 65 is nearby.

THE UNIVERSITY

Purdue is a public land-grant university with principal emphases in engineering, science, and agriculture. The first regular classes began in September 1874, and the first degree was awarded in June 1875. The West Lafayette Campus has almost 2,100 full-time faculty members who teach and engage in scholarly activities and research within more than 145 principal buildings located on 650 acres. Instructional work is organized in the Schools of Agriculture, Consumer and Family Sciences, Education, Engineering, Health Sciences, Liberal Arts, Management, Nursing, Pharmacy and Pharmacal Sciences, Science, Technology, and Veterinary Medicine.

There are about 35,000 undergraduate students and 6,000 graduate students at the West Lafayette Campus.

APPLYING

Applications and all supporting documents should be submitted by December 15 for the following fall semester, which begins about the third week of August. Supporting documents must include an official report of GRE General Test scores. Students whose native language is not English normally must submit TOEFL and TWE scores. If these students apply for teaching assistantships, it is recommended that they take the TSE.

Applicants should have completed or be close to completing a bachelor's or equivalent degree with a major or the near equivalent of a major in computer science and have general and major GPAs of at least 3.5 on a 4.0 scale.

CORRESPONDENCE AND INFORMATION

Graduate Admissions
Department of Computer Sciences
1398 Computer Science Building
Purdue University
West Lafayette, Indiana 47907-1398

Telephone: 765-494-6004
Fax: 765-494-0739
E-mail: grad-info@cs.purdue.edu
World Wide Web: http://www.cs.purdue.edu

PURDUE UNIVERSITY, WEST LAFAYETTE

THE FACULTY AND THEIR RESEARCH

S. S. Abhyankar, Marshall Distinguished Professor; Ph.D. (mathematics), Harvard, 1955. Algebraic geometry, commutative algebra, local algebra, theory of functions of several complex variables, circuit theory, combinatorics, computer-aided design, robotics.

D. C. Anderson, Professor; Ph.D. (mechanical engineering), Purdue, 1974. Computer-aided design, computer graphics, mechanical engineering design.

A. Apostolico, Professor; Dr.Eng. (electronics engineering), Naples, 1973. Algorithmic analysis and design, parallel computation, computational molecular biology.

M. J. Atallah, Professor; Ph.D. (computer science), Johns Hopkins, 1982. Algorithms in computer security, geometry, and parallel computation.

C. Bajaj, Professor; Ph.D. (computer science), Cornell, 1984. Computational science, geometric modeling, computational geometry, computer graphics, data visualization, computational robotics.

B. Bhargava, Professor; Ph.D. (electrical engineering), Purdue, 1974. Transaction processing in distributed systems, video conferencing, multimedia and communication software, experiments in distributed systems and networks.

D. E. Comer, Professor; Ph.D. (computer science), Penn State, 1976. Design of computer operating systems and network protocols.

H. E. Dunsmore, Associate Professor; Ph.D. (computer science), Maryland, 1978. The Internet, the World Wide Web, Web browsers, Web site design and implementation, object-oriented design and programming, object-oriented implementation using C++, software engineering, information systems.

W. R. Dyksen, Associate Professor and Associate Head, Department of Computer Sciences; Ph.D. (applied mathematics), Purdue, 1982. Numerical analysis, user interface design.

A. K. Elmagarmid, Professor; Ph.D. (computer and information science), Ohio State, 1985. Consistency aspects of distributed databases; heterogeneous, federated, and multidatabases; transaction management for advanced database applications.

G. N. Frederickson, Professor; Ph.D. (computer science), Maryland, 1977. Analysis of algorithms, data structures, graph and network algorithms.

W. Gautschi, Professor; Ph.D. (mathematics), Basel (Switzerland), 1953. Numerical analysis.

A. Y. Grama, Assistant Professor; Ph.D. (computer science), Minnesota, 1996. Parallel algorithms, architectures, and applications; scientific computation.

C. Guerra, Associate Professor; Dr.Sc.Math. (mathematics), Naples, 1972. Computer vision, image processing.

S. E. Hambrusch, Professor; Ph.D. (computer science), Penn State, 1982. Parallel and distributed computation, analysis of algorithms.

C. M. Hoffmann, Professor; Ph.D. (computer science), Wisconsin–Madison, 1974. Geometric and solid modeling.

A. L. Hosking, Assistant Professor; Ph.D. (computer science), Massachusetts, 1994. Programming language design and implementation; compilation, interpretation, and optimization; run-time systems; object-oriented database systems; database and persistent programming languages and systems; empirical performance evaluation of prototype systems.

E. N. Houstis, Professor; Ph.D. (mathematics), Purdue, 1974. Numerical analysis; parallel, neural, and mobile computing; performance evaluation and modeling; expert systems for scientific computing; problem-solving environments.

Z. Li, Associate Professor; Ph.D. (computer science), Illinois at Urbana-Champaign, 1989. Optimizing compilers for advanced processors and computer systems, interface between compilers and operating systems, static analysis of large programs, performance evaluation of concurrent systems, object-oriented compiler design.

B. J. Lucier, Professor; Ph.D. (applied mathematics), Chicago, 1981. Wavelets, image processing, numerical analysis.

R. E. Lynch, Professor; Ph.D. (applied mathematics), Harvard, 1963. Differential equations, linear algebra, software for solving elliptic partial differential equations, computational biology.

D. C. Marinescu, Professor; Ph.D. (EECS), Polytechnic Institute (Bucharest), 1975. Real-time systems, computer networks, performance evaluation of computer and communication systems, parallel and distributed systems, scientific computing.

A. P. Mathur, Professor; Ph.D. (computer science), BITS, 1977. Software testing and reliability.

J. Palsberg, Associate Professor; Ph.D. (computer science), Aarhus (Denmark), 1992. Programming languages.

K. Park, Assistant Professor; Ph.D. (computer science), Boston University, 1996. QoS in high-speed networks; design/control of distributed operating systems; cellular automata and fault-tolerant distributed computing.

J. Peters, Associate Professor; Ph.D. (computer science), Wisconsin–Madison, 1990. Representation and analysis of geometry on the computer.

V. J. Rego, Professor; Ph.D. (computer science), Michigan State, 1985. Software systems for parallel and distributed computing, threads systems, network protocols, distributed systems, distributed simulation, probabilistic performance and software engineering.

J. R. Rice, W. Brooks Fortune Distinguished Professor; Ph.D. (mathematics), Caltech, 1959. Analysis of numerical methods and problem solving environments for scientific computing.

E. P. Sacks, Associate Professor; Ph.D. (computer science), MIT, 1988. Scientific and engineering problem solving, geometric reasoning, artificial intelligence.

A. H. Sameh, Professor and Head, Department of Computer Sciences; Ph.D. (civil engineering), Illinois at Urbana-Champaign, 1968. Parallel algorithms in numerical linear algebra.

E. H. Spafford, Professor; Ph.D. (information and computer science), Georgia Tech, 1986. Security, software engineering and computing systems.

J. M. Steele, Associate Professor and Director, Purdue University Computing Center; M.S. (electrical engineering), Purdue, 1965. Computer data communications, computer circuits and systems.

W. Szpankowski, Professor; Ph.D. (electrical engineering and computer science), Gdansk Technical, 1980. Performance evaluation, analysis and design of algorithms, computational pattern matching, data compression, computational combinatorics, queueing theory.

S. S. Wagstaff Jr., Professor; Ph.D. (mathematics), Cornell, 1970. Cryptography, parallel computation, analysis of algorithms.

D. K. Y. Yau, Assistant Professor; Ph.D. (computer science) Texas at Austin, 1997. Networking with quality of service guarantees, operating systems, distributed multimedia.

PURDUE UNIVERSITY

SCHOOL OF ELECTRICAL AND COMPUTER ENGINEERING

PROGRAMS OF STUDY

The School of Electrical and Computer Engineering offers M.S.E.E., M.S.B.M.E., M.S.E., M.S., and Ph.D. degrees with specialization in automatic control, biomedical engineering, communications and signal processing, computer engineering, energy sources and systems, fields and optics, solid-state devices and materials, and VLSI and circuit design. Interdisciplinary programs are also offered.

Master's students whose undergraduate degree is in electrical engineering are eligible for an M.S.E.E. degree. Typically, master's students whose bachelor's degree is in an engineering discipline outside electrical engineering complete the M.S.E. degree. Master's students whose undergraduate degree is in science or mathematics usually complete the M.S. degree. The master's program has both nonthesis and thesis options. The nonthesis option requires 30 hours of course work; the thesis option requires 18 hours of course work plus a master's thesis. Master's students typically take three semesters to complete their degree.

The Ph.D. program requires 21 hours of course work beyond the master's degree or 42 hours beyond the bachelor's degree. In the Ph.D. program, the student establishes a major area and two minor areas of study. Students must pass a qualifying exam covering graduate course work, written and oral preliminary exams, and a dissertation defense. There is no foreign language requirement. The typical length of the Ph.D. program is four to five years beyond the master's degree.

RESEARCH FACILITIES

Laboratory facilities in the School of Electrical and Computer Engineering include the Advanced Digital Systems/Embedded Microcontroller Design Laboratory, the Applied Ultrasonics Laboratory, the Articulated Motion Laboratory, the Basil S. Turner Laboratory for Electroceramics, the Biomedical Acoustics Laboratory, the Communications Research Laboratory, the Computer Vision and Image Processing Laboratory, the Digital Signal Processing Laboratory, the Distributed Multimedia Systems Laboratory, the Electronic Imaging Systems Laboratory (EISL), the Energy System Simulation Laboratory, the Engineering Research Center for Collaborative Manufacturing, the III-V Molecular Beam Epitaxy Laboratory, the Magnetics Laboratory, the Materials Research Science and Engineering Center for Technology-Enabling Heterostructure Materials, the Microprocessor Systems and Interfacing Laboratory, the Microwave Laboratory, the Modern Optics Research Laboratory, the Multispectral Image Processing Laboratory (MIP Lab), the Optical Information Processing Laboratory, the Optoelectronics Research Center, the Parallel Processing Facilities, the Purdue Electric Power Center (PEPC), the Purdue Multimedia Testbed, the Purdue–Notre Dame NSF Materials Research Group, the Robot Vision Lab, the Sensor-Based Robot Control Laboratory, the Silicon Epitaxial Laboratory, the Solid-State Device and Materials Laboratory, the Ultrafast Optics and Fiber Communications Laboratory, the Video and Image Systems Engineering (VISE) Laboratory, the VLSI Design Laboratory, and the Wide Bandgap Photonics Molecular Beam Epitaxy Facility.

Extensive computing facilities for research are provided by the Engineering Computer Network (ECN). Computer systems within the School of Electrical and Computer Engineering that are networked on the ECN include 2 Sun 2000 series, 11 Sun Ultra-1c series, 9 Sun Ultra-2 series, 5 Sun Sparc 1000 series, 12 Sun Sparc 20 series, 7 Sun Sparc 10 series, 334 Sun IPC or Sparc 5 workstations, 57 Hewlett-Packard 9000/700 Series workstations, 30 Hewlett-Packard C110 Series workstations, 1 Hewlett-Packard J-Class server, 1 Hewlett-Packard K-Class server, 6 Tatung workstations, 4 SGI workstations, and 10 Macintosh personal computers, available to all graduate students, and 30 Intel/NT workstations, available only to teaching assistants.

FINANCIAL AID

Various fellowships are awarded by Purdue University, by state and federal agencies, and by industrial sponsors. Departmental teaching and research assistantships are awarded on a competitive merit basis. Stipends range from approximately $920 to $1400 per month in 1997–98. The stipends also carry exemptions from University fees and tuition, except for $268 per semester.

COST OF STUDY

In 1997–98, Indiana residents pay approximately $1684 per semester for tuition and fees, and nonresidents pay approximately $5584 per semester. Books and supplies average $300 per semester.

LIVING AND HOUSING COSTS

In 1997–98, University-supervised graduate residences cost an average of $3000 over a ten-month period (these figures are subject to change). The University operates 1,244 married-student apartments renting for an average of $4200 over a ten-month period. A variety of privately owned housing facilities are available for rent in the surrounding community. A helpful publication entitled *Housing and Financial Guide for Off-Campus Students* is available from the Office of the Dean of Students. Purdue estimates that the total cost of attending graduate school is approximately $25,585 per year for a non-Indiana resident.

STUDENT GROUP

There are approximately 250 master's students and 250 Ph.D. students in the School of Electrical and Computer Engineering. Students represent all parts of the United States and many other countries. The electrical and computer engineering undergraduate program has approximately 850 students.

LOCATION

The West Lafayette campus of Purdue University is located on 1,565 acres in north-central Indiana. The cities of Lafayette and West Lafayette, which are separated by the Wabash River, have a combined population of approximately 70,000. West Lafayette and the surrounding areas offer a variety of cultural activities as well as historic landmarks and recreational attractions. The Purdue airport was the first university-owned airport in the United States. The campus is located 60 miles from Indianapolis, with a population of approximately 1.25 million in the metropolitan area, and 130 miles from Chicago.

THE UNIVERSITY

Purdue University was established as a land-grant institution in 1869. The main campus at West Lafayette has 31,999 students, of whom 5,846 are enrolled in graduate programs. Engineering students number 5,457, of whom 1,859 are graduate students. Purdue has graduated more female engineers than any other engineering school in the United States and has the founding chapter of the National Society of Black Engineers.

APPLYING

Applicants may apply for fall, spring, or summer admission (August, January, or June, respectively). Applications and supporting material should be submitted at least four months prior to the beginning of the semester for which admission is sought. For consideration for fellowships or assistantships, applications should be submitted by December 1 (for fall admission) or by September 15 (for spring or summer admission). The General Test of the Graduate Record Examinations (GRE) is required for all applicants. The Test of English as a Foreign Language (TOEFL) is required for all applicants whose native language is not English, regardless of prior education in the United States. For admission, a minimum TOEFL score of 575 is required.

CORRESPONDENCE AND INFORMATION

Electrical and Computer Engineering Graduate Office
Purdue University
1285 Electrical Engineering Building
West Lafayette, Indiana 47907-1285

Telephone: 765-494-3392
Fax: 765-494-3393
E-mail: ecegrad@ecn.purdue.edu

PURDUE UNIVERSITY
THE FACULTY AND THEIR RESEARCH

Seth Abraham, Assistant Professor. Parallel processing, computer architecture, interconnection networks, parallelizing techniques for software.

Jan P. Allebach, Professor. Electronic imaging systems, image capture and rendering, color image processing, image quality, multispectral imaging.

Philip F. Bagwell, Associate Professor. Quantum mechanical electron transport, electron transport in small devices, physics of semiconductors and metals, superconductivity and superconducting devices.

V. Ragu Balakrishnan, Assistant Professor. Numerical methods and optimization for systems and control, control theory, control system analysis and design, signal processing.

Mark R. Bell, Associate Professor. Information theory, communication theory and systems, radar systems and signal processing, signal theory.

Arden Bement, Basil S. Turner Distinguished Professor of Engineering. Electroceramics, high-temperature superconducting thin films and hybrid structures, smart materials and functional gradient interfaces.

Charles A. Bouman, Associate Professor. Image processing, statistical modeling, pattern recognition, image database search, inverse problems.

Carla E. Brodley, Assistant Professor. Artificial intelligence, machine learning, computer vision, pattern recognition.

Jessica C. P. Chang, Assistant Professor. Structural properties of semiconductor heterointerfaces, compound semiconductor materials, transmission electron microscopy, X-ray diffraction.

Chin-Lin Chen, Professor. Integrated optics, fiber optics.

Edwin K. P. Chong, Assistant Professor. Discrete event systems, queuing systems in communication/computer networks, wireless systems.

James A. Cooper Jr., Professor. Semiconductor device physics, wide band gap semiconductor devices (SiC and AlGaN), electron transport in semiconductors, MOS interface characterization.

Edward J. Coyle, Professor. Computer networks: performance analysis of ATM networks, architecture and performance of all-optical networks, queuing theory and stochastic processes, characterization of video traffic on networks; nonlinear signal and image processing.

Supriyo Datta, Professor. Electronic transport in small devices, nanoelectronics, superconductivity.

Ray A. DeCarlo, Associate Professor. Large-scale systems, geometric multivariable control, decentralized pole placement and eigenvalue placement, decentralized variable structure control, fault analysis and diagnosis, system and parameter identification.

Edward J. Delp, Professor. Image and video compression, multimedia systems, image processing, parallel processing, computer vision, medical imaging, communication and information theory.

Henry G. Dietz, Associate Professor. Optimizing and parallelizing compilers, computer architecture, linguistics, digital imaging, real-time systems.

Peter C. Doerschuk, Associate Professor. Statistical signal processing, multidimensional signal processing, inverse problems, X-ray crystallography.

Rudolf Eigenmann, Assistant Professor. Parallel computing, compilers, computational engineering, performance evaluation, parallel architectures.

Daniel S. Elliott, Professor. Nonlinear optics, multiphoton processes, photoionization, competition between optical processes.

Okan K. Ersoy, Associate Professor. Digital signal and image processing, neural networks, information processing based on fields and optics, probability and statistics, Fourier-related transforms and convolution techniques, parallel processing, applied mathematics.

José A. B. Fortes, Professor. Parallel and distributed computing, computer architecture, network computing.

Fritz J. Friedlaender, Professor. Magnetics.

W. Kent Fuchs, Professor and Head. Dependable high-performance computing, diagnosis, test and failure analysis of integrated circuits.

Keinosuke Fukunaga, Professor. Information processing systems, pattern recognition, pattern processing, learning computer control systems.

Eric S. Furgason, Professor. Applied ultrasonics, acoustic emissions, nondestructive evaluation of materials, acoustic propagation and scattering.

Leslie A. Geddes, Showalter Distinguished Professor Emeritus of Bioengineering. Biomedical engineering (experimental physiology and cardiology).

Saul B. Gelfand, Associate Professor. Digital communications, statistical signal processing, optimization and pattern recognition.

Arif Ghafoor, Associate Professor. Multimedia systems, databases, distributed computing systems, broadband multimedia networking.

Jeffery L. Gray, Associate Professor. Computer modeling of semiconductor devices, semiconductor physics, solar cells.

Robert L. Gunshor, Thomas Duncan Distinguished Professor of Microelectronics. Molecular beam epitaxy, optical devices.

Mary P. Harper, Associate Professor. Artificial intelligence, natural language processing, speech understanding, algorithms.

Leah H. Jamieson, Professor. Speech analysis and recognition, parallel processing, parallel algorithms, parallel speech processing, parallel image processing, algorithm complexity theory.

Avinash C. Kak, Professor. Artificial intelligence, robotics, computer vision.

Rangasami L. Kashyap, Professor. Pattern recognition, image processing, system identification, time series, database management systems.

Antti J. Koivo, Professor. Robotics, computer control, biomedical systems.

Kevin T. Kornegay, Assistant Professor. VLSI design, intelligent power electronics, high-temperature electronics, VLSI for high-performance communications, CAD for VLSI.

Paul C. Krause, Professor. Electromechanical energy conversion, electric drive systems, analysis and control of electric energy systems..

James V. Krogmeier, Assistant Professor. Multidimensional signal processing, digital communications, equalization, adaptive filtering.

David A. Landgrebe, Professor. Signal representation, pattern recognition applications, image data processing, remote sensing systems.

C. S. George Lee, Professor. Neural fuzzy systems, robotics, assembly systems, sensor-based robotic systems.

James S. Lehnert, Associate Professor. Communication theory, information theory, spread spectrum signaling, packet radio systems, fading communication channels, channel equalization techniques, signal design and coding.

John C. Lindenlaub, Professor. Computer engineering, microprocessor systems, educational technology.

Mark S. Lundstrom, Professor. Semiconductor device physics, transport in ultrasmall devices, modeling and simulation.

Anthony A. Maciejewski, Associate Professor. Failure-tolerant and redundant robotic systems, image synthesis and computer graphic simulation.

Michael R. Melloch, Professor. Semiconductor physics, molecular beam epitaxy, heterostructures, superlattices, ultrasmall devices.

David G. Meyer, Associate Professor. Information technology, distance education, effectiveness of student learning in nontraditional environments.

Frederic J. Mowle, Professor. Data structures, software engineering, software testing, software metrics, testing tools, software management.

Gerold W. Neudeck, Professor. Semiconductor devices, silicon fabrication processes, advanced MOSFET and BJT devices, epitaxial lateral overgrowth, SOI devices, Si-Ge growth and advanced devices.

John A. Nyenhuis, Professor. Magnetic materials, magnetic sensors, magnetic bubbles, magnetic stimulation, electromagnetic calculations.

Lawrence L. Ogborn, Associate Professor. Electronic circuits, device applications and limitations, instrumentation, power electronics, circuit theory.

Chee-Mun Ong, Professor. Interactions between converters, electric machines, and power systems; methods of operation and control of electric power systems.

Robert F. Pierret, Professor and Assistant Head for Education. Measurement of parameters characterizing solid-state materials and devices, metal-oxide/insulator-semiconductor (MOS or MIS) devices, semiconductor device physics.

Kaushik Roy, Assistant Professor. Low-power VLSI for portable computing and wireless communications, accurate power estimation techniques, low voltage design, VLSI signal processing, reconfigurable computing, field programmable gate arrays, VLSI testing and verification.

Vwani Roychowdhury, Associate Professor. Parallel algorithms and architectures, computational models for nanoelectronics, neural networks.

Richard J. Schwartz, Professor and Dean of the Schools of Engineering. Semiconductor devices, direct energy conversion, solar cells.

Ness B. Shroff, Assistant Professor. High-speed communication networks (B-ISDN and ATM), mobile communications, multimedia applications, network management, traffic management, performance modeling, congestion control, queuing theory, load balancing and routing, optimization.

H. J. Siegel, Professor. Parallel processing, parallel architectures, parallel algorithms, heterogeneous computing, interconnection networks.

LeRoy F. Silva, Ball Brothers Professor of Engineering and Director of the Business and Industrial Development Center.

Philip H. Swain, Professor and Director of Continuing Engineering Education. Pattern recognition, image processing, remote sensing, distance learning, adult education.

Oleg Wasynczuk, Professor. Power systems, power system modeling and control, solid-state power conversion.

Kevin J. Webb, Associate Professor. Numerical electromagnetics, quantum electronic devices, microwave and optical measurements.

Andrew M. Weiner, Professor. Femtosecond optics, ultrafast photonics, ultrafast nonlinear optics, femtosecond pulse shaping, high-speed fiber communications, time-resolved spectroscopy in semiconductors, ultrafast laser control of quantum processes, imaging in scattering media.

George R. Wodicka, Associate Professor. Biomedical acoustics, biomedical signal processing, medical instrumentation, active noise reduction.

Jerry M. Woodall, Charles William Harrison Distinguished Professor of Microelectronics. Exploratory compound semiconductor materials and devices.

Stanislaw H. Zak, Associate Professor. Nonlinear systems, chaos, neural networks, fuzzy logic, genetic algorithms, dynamic system control.

Michael D. Zoltowski, Associate Professor. Space-time adaptive processing, mobile and wireless communications, adaptive antennas for GPS, spread spectrum (CDMA) communications, narrowband (TDMA) digital communications.

RENSSELAER POLYTECHNIC INSTITUTE

DEPARTMENT OF COMPUTER SCIENCE

PROGRAMS OF STUDY

The Department of Computer Science offers the degrees of Master of Science and Doctor of Philosophy. The computer science program emphasizes the study of parallel computing, computer systems, programming systems and languages, human-computer interfaces, numerical analysis, databases, computer vision, algorithm analysis, theory, and the application of computer technology and science to other areas.

The master's degree program requires the equivalent of a full year's work beyond the baccalaureate. Courses are required in each of four basic areas: software systems, hardware systems, theory of computation, and applications. Other courses are chosen according to the individual student's interests. The M.S. candidate participates in computer science seminars and colloquia and completes a project under the guidance of a faculty adviser.

The doctoral degree is obtained by passing a preliminary written examination that covers core areas of computer science, achieving candidacy by means of an oral examination that covers a proposed research area and topic, and presenting a research thesis. Doctoral research possibilities include parallel computing, numerical analysis, programming languages, programming semantics, CAD, computer graphics, database systems, mathematical computation, computational complexity, automata theory, medical imaging, and computer vision. Occasionally a student arranges research in a related area of mathematics or engineering.

RESEARCH FACILITIES

The department's laboratory has a network of more than fifty Sun and Silicon Graphics workstations as well as a number of computers with specialized architectures, including a Maspar SIMD computer with more than 2,000 processors, two MIMD multiprocessor computers from Sequent, and a Stardent graphics supercomputer. The department also has a computer vision laboratory with a 384 processor AIS 5000 for image processing, motorized cameras, and a structured light range sensor.

In addition, students have access to the Rensselaer Computer System, a network of more than 600 Sun and IBM UNIX workstations for instruction and research. Some students also use the IBM SP-2 supercomputer and numerous specialized computers in the Scientific Computation Research Center. All computers have network connections to local and worldwide networks.

FINANCIAL AID

Rensselaer Scholar Fellowships, competitive across the University, provide stipends of $15,000 together with full remission of tuition and fees. Graduate assistantships, involving teaching, research, or a combination of these, provide stipends ranging up to $10,200 plus tuition for up to 18 credits for the academic year. Full- or partial-tuition scholarships, low-interest loans, and part-time work are also available.

COST OF STUDY

Tuition for 1997–98 is $600 per credit hour. Other fees amount to approximately $500 per semester. Books and supplies cost about $1500 per year.

LIVING AND HOUSING COSTS

The cost of rooms for single students in residence halls or apartments ranges from $3000 to $4800 for the 1997–98 academic year. Family student housing, with a monthly rent of $592 to $720, is available. Local telephone service is included in all residences and apartments.

STUDENT GROUP

There are about 3,900 undergraduates and 1,875 graduate students representing all fifty states and more than eighty countries at Rensselaer.

STUDENT OUTCOMES

Eight-five percent of Rensselaer's 1996 graduating students were hired after graduation with starting salaries that averaged $47,000 for master's degree recipients and $55,000–$75,000 for doctoral degree recipients.

LOCATION

Rensselaer is situated on a scenic 260-acre hillside campus in Troy, New York, across the Hudson River from the state capital of Albany. Troy's central Northeast location provides students with a supportive, active, medium-sized community in which to live; an easy commute to Boston, New York, and Montreal; and some of the country's finest outdoor recreation sites, including Lake George, Lake Placid, and the Adirondack, Catskill, Berkshire, and Green Mountains. The Capital Region has one of the largest concentrations of academic institutions in the United States. Sixty thousand students attend fourteen area colleges and benefit from shared activities and courses.

THE UNIVERSITY

Founded in 1824 and the first American college to award degrees in engineering and science, Rensselaer Polytechnic Institute today is accredited by the Middle States Association of Colleges and Schools and is a private, nonsectarian, coeducational university. Rensselaer has five schools—Architecture, Engineering, Management, Science, and Humanities and Social Sciences—that offer a total of ninety-four graduate degrees in forty-four fields.

APPLYING

Students with varied backgrounds are encouraged to apply. Minimum requirements include a knowledge of several higher-level programming languages, assembly language programming, and data structures. In addition, an applicant should have taken at least two years of college-level mathematics, including calculus, discrete mathematics, and linear algebra. GRE General Test scores are required.

Admissions applications and all supporting credentials should be submitted well in advance of the preferred semester of entry to allow sufficient time for departmental review and processing. The application fee is $35. Since the first departmental awards are made in February for the next full academic year, applicants requesting financial aid are encouraged to submit all required credentials by February 1 to ensure consideration.

CORRESPONDENCE AND INFORMATION

For written information about graduate study:

Graduate Admissions
Department of Computer Science
Rensselaer Polytechnic Institute
110 8th Street
Troy, New York 12180-3590

Telephone: 518-276-8326
World Wide Web: http://www.cs.rpi.edu

For application and admissions information:

Director of Graduate Academic and Enrollment
    Services, Graduate Center
Rensselaer Polytechnic Institute
110 8th Street
Troy, New York 12180-3590

Telephone: 518-276-6789
E-mail: grad-services@rpi.edu
World Wide Web: http://www.rpi.edu

RENSSELAER POLYTECHNIC INSTITUTE
THE FACULTY AND THEIR RESEARCH

Sibel Adali, Assistant Professor; Ph.D., Maryland, 1996. Heterogeneous distributed information systems, database interoperability.

Joseph E. Flaherty, Amos Eaton Professor; Ph.D., Polytechnic of Brooklyn, 1969. Numerical analysis, scientific computation, and parallel computation.

W. Randolph Franklin, Associate Professor; Ph.D., Harvard, 1978. Computer graphics, computational geometry, parallel computation, geographic information systems.

Lester A. Gerhardt, Professor; Ph.D., SUNY at Buffalo, 1969. Adaptive learning systems, pictorial data processing, information theory.

Ephraim P. Glinert, Associate Professor; Ph.D., Washington (Seattle), 1985. Visual and multimodal human-computer interfaces, multiparadigm programming languages and systems, computer-based assistive technology for the disabled, CASE tools for very large scale systems.

Mark Goldberg, Professor; Ph.D., Mathematical Institute of the Academy of Science, Novosibirsk, 1968. Algorithm design, combinatorial optimization, graph theory.

Martin Hardwick, Professor; Ph.D., Bristol (England), 1982. Database systems for concurrent engineering, computer graphics and VLSI.

Robert P. Ingalls, Executive Officer; Ph.D., Connecticut, 1972. Systems programming.

David Isaacson, Professor; Ph.D., NYU, 1976. Numerical analysis, medical imaging.

Mukkai S. Krishnamoorthy, Associate Professor; Ph.D., Indian Institute of Technology (Kanpur), 1976. Graph and algebraic algorithms, algorithm animation, language translators.

Franklin T. Luk, Professor and Chairman; Ph.D., Stanford, 1978. Numerical linear algebra, parallel computation, signal processing.

Paul A. McGloin, Professor Emeritus; Ph.D., Rensselaer, 1968. Data processing, graph theory.

Harry W. McLaughlin, Professor; Ph.D., Maryland, 1966. Applied geometry.

Robert McNaughton, Professor Emeritus; Ph.D., Harvard, 1951. Automata theory, formal languages, combinatorics on words.

Joseph Mundy, Adjunct Professor; Ph.D., Rensselaer, 1969. Artificial intelligence.

David R. Musser, Professor; Ph.D., Wisconsin, 1971. Generic software libraries, software verification, automated theorem proving.

Edwin H. Rogers, Professor; Ph.D., Carnegie Mellon, 1962. Parallel systems, CAD, software engineering.

Richard Shuey, Adjunct Professor; Ph.D., Berkeley, 1950. Distributed computer architecture, communications, data engineering.

Michael Skolnick, Associate Professor; Ph.D., Michigan, 1984. Computer vision, image processing, learning algorithms.

David L. Spooner, Professor; Ph.D., Penn State, 1981. Database management, engineering and object-oriented database systems, database security.

Charles Stewart, Assistant Professor; Ph.D., Wisconsin, 1988. Computer vision, robotics, parallel computation.

Boleslaw Szymanski, Professor; Ph.D., National Academy of Science (Warsaw), 1976. Parallel computation, large-scale scientific computations, programming languages, operating systems.

Research Areas

The department has an international reputation for the quality of its research. The philosophy of the department is to develop a critical mass of researchers in selected research areas rather than trying to cover all aspects of computer science. The most important of these areas include the following:

Parallel Computation. Students and faculty are involved in all phases of parallel computation, from algorithm design to the design of new languages to support parallelism to the design of highly parallel hardware. To support these efforts, the department has a number of parallel (multiprocessor) computers.

Computational Science. Students and faculty are working on the application of computational methods to the solution of problems in other sciences such as physics, chemistry, biology, and astronomy. Specific research includes adaptive methods for solving partial differential equations, the development of finite element software, and the development of fast and stable matrix algorithms for scientific and engineering computations.

Computer Vision. This research involves parallel cellular array transformations to obtain measurements of biomedical, scientific, and industrial images; algorithms for inferring three-dimensional depth information from stereo images; geometric reasoning algorithms for interpreting visual information; and visual learning algorithms employing neural networks and genetic algorithms. The department has a well-equipped computer vision laboratory.

Engineering Database Development. This research includes databases for CAD and other engineering applications. This research uses object-oriented data abstraction methods to develop databases for graphical and other nontextual information. This research group has a large grant in concurrent engineering.

Fundamentals of Computing. Several faculty members develop algorithms for performing operations on graphs and sets. Faculty and students are involved in developing two large software systems in this area: SetPlayer for manipulation of sets and GraphPack for performing operations on graphs. In addition, Rensselaer is well known for its research in symbolic computation and computer algebra.

In addition, there are a number of other smaller research areas that do not fit easily into one of the five major areas. These include program verification, the development of graphical programming environments, and automated design tools.

RENSSELAER POLYTECHNIC INSTITUTE

DEPARTMENT OF ELECTRICAL, COMPUTER, AND SYSTEMS ENGINEERING

PROGRAMS OF STUDY

The department offers the M.Eng., M.S., D.E., and Ph.D. degrees in two curricula, electrical engineering and computer and systems engineering, which cover a wide range of disciplines and are sufficiently flexible to accommodate individual interests. The M.S. degree is for those interested in research careers and who may also want to pursue a Ph.D. The M.S. requires 30 credits, including a 6-credit thesis, and generally takes three academic semesters to complete. The M.Eng. degree is designed for students interested in becoming practicing professional engineers and also requires 30 credits, but no thesis, and can be completed in two academic semesters. The department jointly offers a 72-credit dual M.B.A./M.Eng. degree program with the Lally School of Management and Technology; this program can be completed in two calendar years.

RESEARCH FACILITIES

Much of the research in the department is conducted in the extensive facilities associated with Rensselaer's multidisciplinary research centers, including the Center for Integrated Electronics and Electronics Manufacturing; the New York State Center for Advanced Technology in Automation, Robotics and Manufacturing; the Center for Image Processing Research; the Scientific Computation Research Center; and the International Center for Multimedia Education. In addition, department facilities include the Speech Processing Laboratory, the Document Analysis and Geometric Modeling Laboratory, the Networking Laboratory, the Neural Net Computing Laboratory, the Advanced Imaging Systems Laboratory, the Solid State Microwave Laboratory, the Electronic Materials Laboratory, the Device Fabrication and Testing Laboratory, the Device Characterization Laboratory, and the Plasma Dynamics Laboratory. Research is also supported by Computing and Information Services, which operates and supports a sophisticated campuswide computing, information, and networking environment that includes campus site licenses for software, laptop hookups, desktop devices, advanced workstations, a visualization laboratory for scientific computation, a numerically intensive computing cluster, a 36-node SP2 parallel computer, and the Rensselaer Libraries, where modern library systems allow on-line access to collections, databases, and Internet resources.

FINANCIAL AID

Financial aid is available in the form of fellowships, research or teaching assistantships, and scholarships. The stipend for graduate assistantships ranges from approximately $9700 to $10,400 for the 1997–98 academic year. In addition, full tuition is granted. Additional compensation for study in the summer months is usually available. Outstanding students may qualify for either industrial, Graduate School, or Rensselaer Scholar fellowships. These awards provide stipends of up to $15,000 and a full tuition and fees scholarship for the nine-month academic year. Low-interest, deferred-repayment graduate loans are also available to U.S. citizens with demonstrated need.

COST OF STUDY

Tuition for 1997–98 is $600 per credit hour. Other fees amount to approximately $500 per semester. Books and supplies cost about $1500 per year.

LIVING AND HOUSING COSTS

The cost of rooms for single students in residence halls or apartments ranges from $3000 to $4800 for the 1997–98 academic year. Family student housing, with a monthly rent of $592 to $720, is available. Local telephone service is included in all residence halls and apartments.

STUDENT GROUP

There are about 3,900 undergraduates and 1,875 graduate students representing all fifty states and more than eighty countries at Rensselaer.

STUDENT OUTCOMES

Eighty-five percent of Rensselaer's 1996 graduate students were hired after graduation, with starting salaries that averaged $47,000 for master's degree recipients and $55,000–$75,000 for doctoral degree recipients.

LOCATION

Rensselaer is situated on a scenic 260-acre hillside campus in Troy, New York, across the Hudson River from the state capital of Albany. Troy's central Northeast location provides students with a supportive, active, medium-sized community in which to live and an easy commute to Boston, New York, and Montreal and some of the country's finest outdoor recreation, including Lake George, Lake Placid, and the Adirondack, Catskill, Berkshire, and Green Mountains. The Capital Region has one of the largest concentrations of academic institutions in the United States. Sixty thousand students attend fourteen area colleges and benefit from shared activities and courses.

THE UNIVERSITY

Founded in 1824 and the first American college to award degrees in engineering and science, Rensselaer Polytechnic Institute today is accredited by the Middle States Association of Colleges and Schools and is a private, nonsectarian, coeducational university. Rensselaer has five schools—Architecture, Engineering, Management, Science, and Humanities and Social Sciences. The School of Engineering is ranked among the top twenty engineering schools nationally by the *U.S. News & World Report* survey and is ranked in the top ten by practicing engineers.

APPLYING

Admissions applications and all supporting credentials should be submitted well in advance of the preferred semester of entry to allow sufficient time for departmental review and processing. Scores on the General Test of the Graduate Record Examinations are required of all applicants. The application fee is $35. Due to the high level of competition for awards, the department requires that both U.S. and international applicants requesting financial aid submit all credentials by February 1 for fall and by October 1 for spring.

CORRESPONDENCE AND INFORMATION

For written information about graduate study:

Manager of Graduate Admissions
and Financial Aid
Department of Electrical, Computer,
and Systems Engineering
Rensselaer Polytechnic Institute
110 8th Street
Troy, New York 12180-3590
Telephone: 518-276-6313
E-mail: grad-info@ecse.rpi.edu
World Wide Web: http://www.ecse.rpi.edu

For applications and admissions information:

Director of Graduate Academic and Enrollment
Services, Graduate Center
Rensselaer Polytechnic Institute
110 8th Street
Troy, New York 12180-3590
Telephone: 518-276-6789
E-mail: grad-services@rpi.edu
World Wide Web: http://www.rpi.edu

RENSSELAER POLYTECHNIC INSTITUTE

THE FACULTY AND THEIR RESEARCH

John B. Anderson, Professor; Ph.D., Cornell. Communications and coding theory.

Ishwara B. Bhat, Associate Professor; Ph.D., Rensselaer. Solid state, electronic materials.

A. Bruce Carlson, Professor and Curriculum Chair; Ph.D., Stanford. Communications systems, educational methods, social context of engineering.

Joseph H. Chow, Professor; Ph.D., Illinois. Large-scale modeling, multivariable control systems.

T. Paul Chow, Associate Professor; Ph.D., Rensselaer. Semiconductor device physics and processing technology, integrated circuits.

Kenneth A. Connor, Professor; Ph.D., Polytechnic of New York. Electromagnetic theory, wave propagation, plasmas for fusion research.

Thomas P. Crowley, Associate Professor; Ph.D., Princeton. Fusion and space plasmas, wave propagation, microwaves.

Alan A. Desrochers, Professor; Ph.D., Purdue. Nonlinear systems, robotics, control of automated manufacturing systems.

Frank DiCesare, Professor; Ph.D., Carnegie Mellon. Design theory and software tools for intelligent control of discrete event dynamic systems, computer-integrated manufacturing systems.

W. Randolph Franklin, Associate Professor; Ph.D., Harvard. Computational geometry, graphics and CAD, cartography, parallel algorithms, large databases, expert system verification.

Lester A. Gerhardt, Professor and Associate Dean of Engineering; Ph.D., SUNY at Buffalo. Communication systems, digital voice and image processing, adaptive systems and pattern recognition, computer-integrated manufacturing.

Ronald J. Gutmann, Professor; Ph.D., Rensselaer. Semiconductor devices, microwave monolithic integrated circuits, microwave nondestructive testing techniques, interconnect technology.

Timothy J. Holmes, Associate Professor of Biomedical Engineering and Affiliated Faculty of Electrical, Computer, and Systems Engineering; Ph.D., Washington (St. Louis). Internal imaging, signal processing and systems.

William C. Jennings, Professor and Department Chair for Electrical, Computer, and Systems Engineering; Ph.D., Rensselaer. Plasmas, gas lasers, microwaves.

Chuanyi Ji, Assistant Professor; Ph.D., Caltech. Neural networks, communications and information processing, pattern recognition.

Howard Kaufman, Professor; Ph.D., Rensselaer. Adaptive systems theory and applications, image restoration, optimization, estimation and identification.

Robert B. Kelley, Professor; Ph.D., UCLA. Robotic systems, machine intelligence, machine vision, expert systems.

Yannick L. LeCoz, Associate Professor; Ph.D., MIT. Solid-state devices.

Edward W. Maby, Associate Professor; Sc.D., MIT. Solid-state electronics, semiconductor-device simulation, circuit implementation of parallel algorithms.

John F. McDonald, Professor; Ph.D., Yale. Communication theory, coding and switching theory, computer architecture, digital signal processing.

James W. Modestino, Institute Professor and Director of the Center for Imaging Processing Research; Ph.D., Princeton. Information theory and coding, communications and signal processing, image processing and computer vision.

George Nagy, Professor; Ph.D., Cornell. Pattern recognition, computer vision, computational geometry, solid modeling, knowledge-based systems, digitizing camera performance.

William A. Pearlman, Professor; Ph.D., Stanford. Information theory and source coding, rate-distortion theory, image and optical data restoration, image coding, communication theory.

Kenneth Rose, Professor; Ph.D., Illinois. Semiconductor and superconductor materials and processing, VLSI design and testing.

Badrinath Roysam, Associate Professor; Ph.D., Washington (St. Louis). Massively parallel computation, joint symbolic/stochastic inference, hierarchical imaging and image processing.

Arthur C. Sanderson, Professor; Ph.D., Carnegie Mellon. Robotics, knowledge-based systems, computer vision.

Gary J. Saulnier, Associate Professor; Ph.D., Rensselaer. Circuits and electronics, communication systems, digital signal processing.

Michael Savic, Professor; Eng.Sc.D., Belgrade. Digital processing of speech and other signals, hardware and software implementation of fast signal processors, analog and digital electronics.

Paul M. Schoch, Associate Professor; Ph.D., Rensselaer. Plasma diagnostics, power electronics.

Michael S. Shur, Professor and Patricia W. and C. Sheldon Roberts Professor of Solid State Electronics; Ph.D., Ioffe (Russia). Semiconductor materials and devices, integrated circuit simulation, characterization and design.

Michael M. Skolnick, Associate Professor of Computer Science and Affiliated Faculty of Electrical, Computer, and Systems Engineering; Ph.D., Michigan. Image processing, computer vision, learning algorithms.

Harry E. Stephanou, Associate Professor and Director, Center for Advanced Technology in Automation and Robotics; Ph.D., Purdue. Robotics and automation, pattern recognition, neural networks.

James M. Tien, Professor and Chair of Decision Sciences and Engineering Systems and Affiliated Faculty of Electrical, Computer, and Systems Engineering; Ph.D., MIT. Information and decision systems methodology and applications.

David A. Torrey, Associate Professor of Electric Power Engineering and Affiliated Faculty of Electrical, Computer, and Systems Engineering; Ph.D., MIT. Power electronics, electric machine drives, and motion control.

Kenneth S. Vastola, Associate Professor; Ph.D., Illinois. Computer-communication networks, statistical signal processing and communications.

John T. Wen, Associate Professor; Ph.D., Rensselaer. Robot control, control of flexible structures, adaptive control.

John W. Woods, Professor; Ph.D., MIT. Digital signal processing; image processing, estimation theory.

Michael J. Wozny, Professor; Ph.D., Arizona. Computer graphics, computer-aided design, digital simulation, rapid prototyping systems.

RICE UNIVERSITY
DEPARTMENT OF COMPUTER SCIENCE

PROGRAMS OF STUDY

Rice University offers graduate study programs leading to Master of Computer Science, Master of Science, and Doctor of Philosophy degrees. The M.C.S. is a professional degree that usually takes one to two years to complete. It prepares students for careers as practitioners rather than researchers and does not require a thesis or oral examination. The M.S. program requires a thesis in addition to course work. M.S. recipients usually go on to pursue a Ph.D. The Ph.D. is a research degree that prepares its recipients for careers in independent research, teaching, and advanced development. Four to six years are normally needed to earn a Ph.D. The first year of the program provides the student with a sound basis for independent research. Doctoral students must take comprehensive and qualifying examinations during their first three years. The comprehensive exam covers eight areas: algorithms, architecture, automata, compilers, graphics, logic, operating systems, and programming languages, five of which must be passed during a student's first academic year in the program. The qualifying exam covers one area of computer science, presumably that in which the student wishes to pursue thesis research. Students typically take it after their second year. Ph.D. students are encouraged to become involved in research as quickly as possible after entering the program. While researching with a faculty member, the student finds a problem of interest and develops it into a thesis proposal. Eventually, the student presents the proposal in a departmental colloquium, solves the problem raised by the proposal, and writes a dissertation on the work. Teaching is an integral part of graduate education at Rice. Ph.D. students are required to work as teaching assistants for four semesters. The amount of work varies by course, but is not expected to exceed 10 hours a week averaged over a semester.

RESEARCH FACILITIES

Department research is supported by a shared computing research facility available to all Ph.D. students. The resources are in public laboratories on a local area network of heterogeneous machines running variations of UNIX operating systems and various networking software. Ph.D. student offices are equipped with at least one X-terminal. Students working on projects with the Computer and Information Technology Institute at Rice have access to an 8-way cluster of 4-way high-performance multiprocessors. Rice is the lead institution in the Center for Research on Parallel Computation, a consortium that uses the parallel computing laboratories at seven participating institutions for physically distributed, shared computing resources. The LAN at Rice consists of a 10Mb Ethernet. The campus has a fiber-optic backbone network to connect department networks, and Rice is the hub of SesquiNet, the southwest regional network of NSFNET. The DOE ESNET and the NASA Science Internet provide additional connections to the international research network. The Fondren Library's collection of 1.7 million volumes, 2.2 million microforms, and 14,000 periodical and serial titles is also an excellent resource for students.

FINANCIAL AID

In their first academic year, Ph.D. students in the department normally receive financial support in the form of Rice University fellowships, which carry a stipend of between $1444 and $1667 per month, plus tuition. In subsequent years, most students receive financial support, including stipend and tuition, through research assistantships supported by various grants. M.S. students are eligible for research assistantships. M.C.S. students are not eligible for financial aid.

COST OF STUDY

The tuition for full-time graduate study in 1997–98 is $14,300 per year, but is waived for most Ph.D. graduate students. Health insurance and other miscellaneous fees are about $230 annually. The cost of books varies by course, and the 1996–97 thesis fee was $93.

LIVING AND HOUSING COSTS

The cost of living in Houston is low compared to other large cities in the U.S. One-bedroom apartments or shared larger apartments can cost $350–$500 in middle-class neighborhoods. The Graduate House, located adjacent to the campus, offers private or shared rooms, group kitchens, a commons room, and free transportation to academic buildings. Rooms are reserved as space is available and cost $300–400 per month.

STUDENT GROUP

The number of Ph.D. students in computer science at Rice is about 40, and 15 students are in the M.C.S. program. Most Ph.D. students are full-time with full fellowships or research assistantships. Acceptance into the programs is based on scholastic record as reflected by the courses chosen and quality of performance, evaluation of former teachers and advisers, GRE scores, and TOEFL scores (if applicable). M.S. and Ph.D. students are also evaluated on their to ability to conduct independent research. M.C.S. students are evaluated by their ability to take advanced courses.

STUDENT OUTCOMES

Students who have completed the Ph.D. program in computer science at Rice can be found in the nation's premier universities and corporate research labs. Graduates are teaching or have taught at the California Institute of Technology, Stanford University, Carnegie Mellon University, University of Maryland–College Park, University of Victoria, and Rutgers University, among others. They are working or have worked as researchers for IBM, Tera Computers, Lucent Technologies, Motorola, Daimler Benz, and Hewlett-Packard.

LOCATION

Rice University is located 3 miles from downtown Houston, Texas, the nation's fourth-largest city. Houston's diverse population is reflected in the city's restaurants and cultural events. The city has a symphony, ballet, opera, and theater, as well as professional football, basketball, baseball, and hockey teams. Houston's seaport, the nation's third largest, is linked to the Gulf of Mexico by a 50-mile channel.

THE UNIVERSITY

Rice University is a private, coeducational nondenominational university founded in 1891 from the estate of William Marsh Rice. It has faculties of liberal arts, science, and engineering and about 2,500 undergraduate and 1,300 graduate students. Rice has a 9:1 student-faculty ratio and is regarded as a top teaching and research university. Students work closely with faculty members and have many opportunities for participation in research activities. The graduate program in computer science is ranked in the top twenty among American universities.

APPLYING

Typical GRE scores for admitted applicants are in the 90–99th percentile for the quantitative, analytical, and Subject Tests. Completed applications should be sent directly to the computer science department and must be received by February 1.

CORRESPONDENCE AND INFORMATION

Chairman
Department of Computer Science
Rice University
6100 Main, MS-132
Houston, Texas 77005-1892

Telephone: 713-527-4834
Fax: 713-285-5930
E-mail: cs@rice.edu
World Wide Web: http://www.cs.rice.edu/

RICE UNIVERSITY
THE FACULTY AND THEIR RESEARCH

Robert S. Cartwright Jr., Professor; Ph.D., Stanford, 1977. Programming languages and methodology, with an emphasis on type inference to verify program invariants and eliminate run-time checks, a technique dubbed "soft typing;" codirector with M. Felleisen of the Rice Education Infrastructure Project, the goal of which is to create a new core computer science curriculum that integrates the algebraic model, embodied in advanced languages such as Scheme and ML, and the physical model, embodied in languages such as C and C++.

Keith D. Cooper, Associate Professor; Ph.D., Rice, 1983. Code optimization for modern microprocessors, interprocedural analysis and optimization, code generation issues such as register allocation and scheduling, rethinking classical optimizations, practical and effective techniques for interprocedural optimizations, classical optimization, compiler management of latency, issues that arise in the design and use of deep memory hierarchies.

Alan L. Cox, Associate Professor; Ph.D., Rochester, 1992. Parallel computing, operating systems for distributed and multiprocessor systems, computer architecture; member of the Rice team that developed TreadMarks, a state-of-the-art distributed shared-memory system that enables parallel programs written using the shared-memory paradigm to run efficiently on networks of workstations; recipient of the National Science Foundation Young Investigator Award (1994).

Hristo Djidjev, Lecturer; Ph.D., Sofia (Bulgaria), 1984. Graph theory and graph algorithms, graph drawing, computational geometry, parallel algorithms, finding separators of graphs, graph planarization, convex drawing of planar graphs, like distance problems, algorithms of combinatorial problems; developer of the most efficient known algorithm that embeds a graph on a surface of minimum genus.

Peter Druschel, Assistant Professor; Ph.D., Arizona, 1994. Operating systems, networks, computer architecture, providing operating system support for high-speed networking; recipient of an NSF CAREER grant for early career development as an educator and researcher (1995).

Matthias Felleisen, Professor; Ph.D., Indiana, 1987. High-level programming languages, including semantics, implementation, analysis tools, pragmatics, and teaching; developer of syntax-based methods for describing the behavior of almost all Scheme programs, which are used to study implementation strategies of advanced programming languages; codirector with R. Cartwright of the Rice Education Infrastructure Project.

Ron Goldman, Professor; Ph.D., Johns Hopkins, 1973. Mathematical representation, manipulation, and analysis of shape using computers; algorithms for polynomial and piece-wise polynomial curves and surfaces; parametrically and implicitly represented geometry; computer-aided geometric design, solid modeling, computer graphics, and splines.

G. Anthony Gorry, Professor; Ph.D., MIT, 1967. Impact of information technology on organizations and society, application of artificial intelligence in medicine and the development of decision support systems; director of Rice's Center for Technology in Teaching and Learning, which is developing computing and telecommunications for sharing knowledge in schools, universities, the workplace, and the home; member of the Institute of Medicine of the National Academy of Sciences; Fellow of the American College of Medical Informatics.

Lydia E. Kavraki, Assistant Professor; Ph.D, Stanford, 1995. Physical algorithms with applications to robotics (path planning, assembly sequencing, mechanical part orientation), medicine (noninvasive radiosurgery), and computational chemistry (computer-aided pharmaceutical drug design); recipient of the NSF CAREER Award for early career development as researcher and educator (1996).

Ken Kennedy, Noah Harding Professor of Mathematics; Ph.D., NYU, 1971. Parallel computing in science and engineering, scientific programming environments, optimization of compiled code, computer architecture, performance analysis, graph algorithms, extending the techniques of program analysis and parallelization to provide language support for highly parallel supercomputers and advanced programming environments for scientific and engineering professionals; director of the Center for Research on Parallel Computation, a consortium that uses the parallel computing laboratories at seven participating institutions for physically distributed, shared computing resources; recipient of the IEEE Computer Society W. Wallace McDowell Award (1995); Fellow of the ACM, IEEE, and the American Association for the Advancement of Science; member of the National Academy of Engineering; cochair, President's Advisory Committee on High-Performance Computing and Communications, Information Technology, and the Next Generation Internet (1997).

John Mellor-Crummey, Faculty Fellow; Ph.D., Rochester, 1989. Topics in large-scale parallel computation, including architectures, operating systems, programming environments, and algorithms; compiler and programming environment support for data-parallel languages.

Devika Subramanian, Associate Professor; Ph.D., Stanford, 1989. Artificial intelligence aimed at the design and analysis of adaptive, discrete, limited-resource agents that perform tasks in dynamic environments; recipient of the George Forsythe Memorial Award for Excellence in Teaching, Stanford University (1986), and the Outstanding Educator Award, Merrill Presidential Scholar Program, Cornell University (1991, 1993).

Linda M. Torczon, Faculty Fellow; Ph.D., Rice, 1985. Code generation, interprocedural data-flow analysis and optimization, programming environments; one of the key implementors of an optimizing compiler for FORTRAN and one of the principal investigators on the Massively Scalar Compiler Project at Rice; principal architect of the framework for whole program analysis in the ParaScope programming environment; executive director of the Center for Research on Parallel Computation.

Moshe Y. Vardi, Noah Harding Professor of Computer Science and Chair, Department of Computer Science; Ph.D., Hebrew (Jerusalem), 1981. Applications of logic to computer science, specifically to databases, finite-model theory, knowledge theory, and program specification and verification; connection between finite-model theory and areas of computer science such as complexity theory and database theory; developer of a theory of knowledge-based agents that will have applications to the design and analysis of multiagent systems, such as distributed computer systems or teams of cooperating robots; recipient of the IBM Research Outstanding Innovation Award (1987, 1989, 1992).

Joe Warren, Associate Professor; Ph.D., Cornell, 1986. Application of computers to geometric problems centered around the general problem of representing geometric shapes, geometric modeling (the construction and manipulation of data structures for representing geometric objects), computational geometry (using algorithms to solve geometric problems), algorithms for solving and manipulating systems of polynomial equations.

Willy E. Zwaenepoel, Noah Harding Professor of Computer Science and Professor of Electrical and Computer Engineering; Ph.D., Stanford, 1984. Distributed parallel systems, fault tolerance, operating systems, the extent to which a network of workstations can be used to construct a loosely coupled multicomputer; director of Rice's NSF Research Infrastructure Award, which provides funds to build a state-of-the-art cluster of shared-memory multiprocessors; director of Computer Information Technology Institute.

RUTGERS, THE STATE UNIVERSITY OF NEW JERSEY, NEW BRUNSWICK

GRADUATE SCHOOL
DEPARTMENT OF COMPUTER SCIENCE

PROGRAM OF STUDY

The Department of Computer Science at Rutgers University, New Brunswick, offers a comprehensive program of study in most areas of computer science leading to either an M.S. or a Ph.D. degree. The department's program includes these areas: algorithms, artificial intelligence (with applications to design, genetics, law, medicine), combinatorics, complexity theory, computational geometry, databases, data structures, distributed systems, expert systems, logical foundations of knowledge-based systems, machine learning, mathematical programming, numerical analysis, optical computing, optimization, parallel computation, programming languages, and software engineering.

For the M.S. degree, a student must complete 24 credits of course work and a master's thesis or 30 credits and an expository essay and pass a comprehensive examination. A candidate for the Ph.D. degree must complete 48 credits of course work and pass a written and oral qualifying examination. A student who enters with a master's degree may apply to transfer up to 24 credits toward the 48 required. The candidate must also complete a research project and successfully defend a dissertation written about the project. Normally, a one-year residence in the department is required.

RESEARCH FACILITIES

Computing facilities for the department are run by the staff of the Laboratory for Computer Science Research (LCSR), which is a member of NSFNET and has access to other nets. The principal facility consists of a network of about 100 Sun Workstations and file servers. There are also dedicated special-purpose facilities and high-performance graphics terminals. IBM mainframe–type computing is available through the Rutgers University Computing Services (RUCS), and supercomputing is accessible. NCUBE and Butterfly computers are also available for experimental and smaller-scale parallel computing by special arrangement with the state-sponsored Center for Aids to Industrial Productivity (CAIP). Instructional computing is supported by the RUCS. Computing for introductory courses is provided by networks of Apple Macintosh computers; other undergraduate courses are served by Sun Workstations. Graduate instruction is, except for some special-purpose computing, provided through the network of Suns.

The excellent Mathematical Sciences Library, which includes the computer science collection, is housed in the same building as the department.

FINANCIAL AID

A large number of full-time graduate students receive financial support, which includes University fellowships, teaching assistantships, and graduate assistantships. In 1996–97 stipends ranged from $10,000 to $12,000. Tuition is remitted for all assistants. Summer support is available for graduate assistants on some research projects.

COST OF STUDY

Full-time graduate tuition during the 1996–97 academic year was $5734 per year (24 credits) for residents of New Jersey and $8406 for nonresidents, and there was a student fee of $764. For part-time students, resident tuition was $236.25 per credit, nonresident tuition was $348.75, and the student fee was about $500 per year. (These fees are likely to rise.) Books cost approximately $800 per semester.

LIVING AND HOUSING COSTS

Graduate student apartments cost about $4526 per year. Graduate dormitory rooms cost from $3692 to $3842 with various possible meal plans. Married student housing is available at a cost of $526 per month for a one-bedroom apartment and $688 per month for a two-bedroom apartment. (These fees are likely to rise.)

STUDENT GROUP

In fall 1996, there were 91 full-time and 92 part-time graduate students in the department. Between January 1990 and January 1997, fifty-nine Ph.D.'s were awarded.

LOCATION

New Brunswick is located on a main railroad line, 33 miles from New York City and 60 miles from Philadelphia. Mountains and shore areas are close by and are easily reached by car. There is an active program of concerts, art exhibits, lectures, and recreational activities at the University, and the unsurpassed cultural advantages of New York and Philadelphia are within easy reach.

THE UNIVERSITY

Rutgers was founded before the American Revolution; it was the eighth college to be established in this country. In the nineteenth century the state of New Jersey began to provide support for certain programs, and in 1945 Rutgers as a whole became the state university. Currently, about 49,000 students are enrolled in the three principal divisions of the University—at New Brunswick, Newark, and Camden. In New Brunswick there are four resident undergraduate colleges: Rutgers, Douglass, Livingston, and Cook. These colleges are spread over four areas in and around New Brunswick. The computer science department is part of the Faculty of Arts and Sciences, and it is located in the Hill Center for Mathematical Sciences on the Busch campus. An outstanding gymnasium is a block away. This suburban area is also the home of the chemistry, mathematics, geology, psychology, and physics departments; the Engineering School; the College of Pharmacy; Robert Wood Johnson School of Medicine of the University of Medicine and Dentistry of New Jersey; and the New Jersey Mental Health Center.

APPLYING

Applications for September admission with financial aid must be received by March 1. Applications for September that do not request financial aid are accepted until April 1; for January admission, until November 1. The application fee is $40. The applicant's academic record should exhibit at least a B+ average and must show distinction in computer science, mathematics, and related fields. Results of the Graduate Record Examinations (General Test and Subject Test in computer science) are required in addition to letters of recommendation and all transcripts. International applicants are required to submit TOEFL results. Applicants whose undergraduate degree is not in computer science must have completed with distinction the equivalent of an undergraduate core curriculum in the discipline or demonstrated proficiency through a high score on the GRE Subject Test in computer science.

CORRESPONDENCE AND INFORMATION

For information on the program:
Department of Computer Science, PG
Hill Center for Mathematical Sciences
Rutgers, The State University of New Jersey
New Brunswick, New Jersey 08903

For applications:
Graduate Admissions Office, PG
Rutgers, The State University of New Jersey
New Brunswick, New Jersey 08903

RUTGERS, THE STATE UNIVERSITY OF NEW JERSEY
THE FACULTY AND THEIR RESEARCH

Eric Allender, Associate Professor; Ph.D., Georgia Tech. Complexity theory, parallel and probabilistic computation.

Saul Amarel, Turing Professor of Computer Science; D.Eng.Sc., Columbia. Artificial intelligence: representation, theory formation, computational design.

B. R. Badrinath, Associate Professor; Ph.D., Massachusetts. Distributed systems and databases, mobile wireless computing.

Alexander T. Borgida, Professor; Ph.D., Toronto. Artificial intelligence in the design of information systems.

Vaclav Chvátal, Professor; Ph.D., Waterloo. Algorithms, combinatorics, graph theory, operations research.

Sven Dickinson, Assistant Professor; Ph.D., Maryland. Computer vision, object modeling, artificial intelligence.

Thomas Ellman, Assistant Professor; Ph.D., Columbia. Artificial intelligence, machine learning, knowledge compilation, qualitative physics.

Martin Farach, Assistant Professor; M.D., Johns Hopkins; Ph.D., Maryland. Computational biology, design and analysis of algorithms.

Michael L. Fredman, Professor; Ph.D., Stanford. Algorithms, data structures, computational complexity.

Andrew Gelsey, Assistant Professor; Ph.D., Yale. Artificial intelligence, reasoning about physical systems, application of AI to engineering problems.

Apostolos Gerasoulis, Professor; Ph.D., SUNY at Stony Brook. Parallel processing, algorithms, numerical analysis.

Michael D. Grigoriadis, Professor; Ph.D., Wisconsin–Madison. Algorithms for network optimization.

Charles L. Hedrick, Director of the Laboratory for Computer Science Research Computing Facility; Ph.D., Carnegie Mellon. Network technology and distributed computing environments.

Haym Hirsh, Associate Professor; Ph.D., Stanford. Machine learning and artificial intelligence.

Tomasz Imielinski, Professor; Ph.D., Polish Academy of Sciences. Logical foundations of databases, mobile wireless computing.

Bahman Kalantari, Associate Professor; Ph.D., Minnesota. Mathematical programming, global and discrete optimization.

Kenneth R. Kaplan, Associate Professor and Chairman; Ph.D., Polytechnic of Brooklyn. Algorithms, queuing theory, modeling, discrete simulation.

Leonid Khachiyan, Professor; Ph.D., D.Sc., USSR Academy of Sciences. Mathematical programming, computational complexity, discrete optimization.

Ulrich Kremer, Assistant Professor; Ph.D., Rice. Computation techniques and interactive programming environments for distributed-memory and shared-memory multiprocessor.

Casimir Kulikowski, Professor and Director of the Laboratory for Computer Science Research; Ph.D., Hawaii. Artificial intelligence, pattern recognition, imaging, biomedical applications.

Saul Levy, Associate Professor; Ph.D., Yeshiva. Massively parallel architectures, algorithms, environments.

L. Thorne McCarty, Professor of Computer Science and Law; J.D., Harvard. Artificial intelligence, legal reasoning, logic programming.

Naftaly Minsky, Professor; Ph.D., Hebrew (Jerusalem). Software engineering, programming languages, distributed systems.

Miles Murdocca, Assistant Professor; Ph.D., Rutgers. Optical computing, adaptive architectures, parallel processing.

Michiel Noordewier, Assistant Professor; Ph.D., Wisconsin–Madison. Artificial intelligence (including machine learning) in the context of genetics and biochemistry, molecular biology.

Marvin C. Paull, Professor; B.S., Clarkson. Design and analysis of algorithms—principles and practice.

Gerard Richter, Professor; Ph.D., Harvard. Numerical solution of differential and integral equations.

Barbara Ryder, Professor; Ph.D., Rutgers. Programming languages, software engineering, parallel computation.

Donald Smith, Assistant Professor; Ph.D., Rutgers. Massively parallel architectures, VLSI, artificial intelligence.

Diane L. Souvaine, Associate Professor; Ph.D., Princeton. Development and analysis of geometric and graph-theoretic algorithms, the applications of these algorithms to practical problems, parallel algorithms.

Chitoor V. Srinivasan, Associate Professor; Dr.Eng.Sc., Columbia. Knowledge-based systems, concurrent computation.

William Steiger, Professor; Ph.D., Australian National. Computational geometry, parallel computation, probabilistic algorithms.

Louis Steinberg, Associate Professor; Ph.D., Stanford. Artificial intelligence, computer-aided design with applications to the design of thermodynamic, aerodynamic, and hydrodynamic structures.

Suzanne Stevenson, Assistant Professor; Ph.D., Maryland. Computational linguistics, cognitive modeling.

Endre Szemerédi, State of New Jersey Professor of Computer Science; Ph.D., Moscow. Number theory, extremal graph theory, parallel algorithms, theoretical computer science.

Robert Vichnevetsky, Professor; Ph.D., Brussels. Numerical analysis, computer methods for partial differential equations, optimization theory, modeling and simulation systems, environmental systems, computational fluid dynamics.

Sholom M. Weiss, Research Professor; Ph.D., Rutgers. Expert systems, artificial intelligence.

Ann Yasuhara, Associate Professor; Ph.D., Illinois. Recursive function theory, logic, theoretical computer science.

Affiliated Faculty

Stanley Dunn, Associate Professor of Biomedical Engineering; Ph.D., Maryland. Computer vision, image understanding, pattern recognition, software engineering for vision, signal-processing applications.

Herbert Freeman, Professor of Computer Engineering; Dr.Eng.Sc., Columbia. Computer graphics, pattern recognition, image processing, computer vision.

Peter L. Hammer, Professor and Director of the Center for Operations Research; Ph.D., Bucharest. Boolean methods in operations research and related areas, theory of graphs and networks.

Jeffry Kahn, Professor of Mathematics; Ph.D., Ohio State. Combinatorics.

János Komlós, Professor of Mathematics; Ph.D., Eotvos Lorand (Budapest). Combinatorics, probability, theoretical computer science.

Evangelina Micheli-Tzanakou, Professor of Biomedical Engineering; Ph.D., Syracuse. Pattern recognition, computer vision, brain information processing, neural networks.

Michael Saks, Professor of Mathematics; Ph.D., MIT. Combinatorics, complexity theory, distributed computing, on-line algorithms.

Charles Schmidt, Professor of Psychology; Ph.D., Iowa. Human and machine planning and plan recognition, human and machine problem-solving and learning, human-computer interaction.

Eduardo D. Sontag, Professor of Mathematics; Ph.D., Florida. Nonlinear control, neural nets, learning theory.

RUTGERS, THE STATE UNIVERSITY OF NEW JERSEY, NEW BRUNSWICK

DEPARTMENT OF ELECTRICAL AND COMPUTER ENGINEERING

PROGRAM OF STUDY

The graduate program in electrical and computer engineering, which leads to the M.S. and Ph.D. degrees, has facilities for education and research in computer engineering, integrated systems encompassing control systems, digital signal processing, and communications and solid-state electronics. Computer engineering involves the architecture and design of computing machines, information processing, and software engineering. Control systems is concerned with the design, analysis, simulation, and mathematical modeling of systems to ensure that an automatic process, such as that of a robot or spacecraft, meets and maintains certain criteria. Digital signal processing deals with discrete-time information processing, digital filter design, spectral analysis, and special-purpose signal processors. Electrical communications systems analysis and design is concentrated in the areas of source and channel encoding, analog and digital modulation methods, information theory, and telecommunication networks. Solid-state electronics encompasses the areas of microwave switching devices, semiconductor lasers, electrooptical modulation, solar cells, integrated circuits, and characterization of semiconductor materials and devices.

Master of Science degree candidates may elect either a thesis or nonthesis option. The thesis option consists of 24 credits of course work, 6 credits of research in a specialized area, and a final thesis presentation. In the nonthesis option, a candidate must complete 30 credits of course work, pass a written comprehensive examination, and submit a satisfactory tutorial paper in a course. Requirements for the M.S. degree may be satisfied for all options in a part-time evening program designed specifically for students employed in industry and other students whose obligations preclude full-time study.

Admission into the Ph.D. program requires an M.S. in electrical and/or computer engineering. Applicants having an M.S. in a closely related discipline may be admitted into the program provided their preparation has no significant deficiencies. A student is considered to be a Ph.D. candidate after satisfactory completion of the qualifying exam and presentation of the dissertation topic. A Ph.D. candidate, in conjunction with an adviser, is required to select a dissertation committee, submit a plan of study, and orally present a dissertation proposal. Minimum requirements for the Ph.D. degree include 48 credits beyond the baccalaureate in courses approved by the dissertation adviser and 24 credits of dissertation research beyond the M.S. degree. A public defense serves as the final Ph.D. dissertation exam. There is no foreign language requirement.

RESEARCH FACILITIES

There are three centers within the department: the Center for Digital Signal Processing, the Wireless Information Networks Laboratory (WINLAB), and the Microelectronics Research Laboratory (MERL), a semiconductor device processing clean room. Additional research is conducted with various Rutgers research centers established by the New Jersey Commission of Science and Technology, particularly the Center for Computer Aids for Industrial Productivity (CAIP) and the Fiber Optic Materials Research Program (FOMRP). In addition to the extensive facilities available at these centers, the department maintains the Digital Communications and Image Transmission Laboratory, Digital Signal Processing Laboratory, Digital Signal Processing Systems Laboratory, Digital Signal Processing Research and Graduate Instruction Laboratory, Local Area Network Laboratory, Machine Vision Laboratory, Robotics and Sensorics Laboratory, VLSI CAD Laboratory, Laboratory for Engineering Information Systems, and solid-state experimental facilities for crystal growth and preparation, electrical characterization, design and fabrication, optical measurements, structure and composition analysis, and thin-film deposition measurements. For detailed information on these and other facilities available to graduate students, contact the Graduate Director at the address given below.

FINANCIAL AID

Assistantships and fellowships are available, each with a typical stipend of about $11,500 plus tuition for the academic year 1997–98. In the award of financial aid, consideration is given to the student's undergraduate academic record, performance on the GRE, and letters of reference indicating outstanding ability.

COST OF STUDY

Tuition is $5700 for state residents and $8400 for out-of-state residents for the academic year 1997–98. Fees, books, and supplies are about $1600 per year.

LIVING AND HOUSING COSTS

Graduate housing is available. Graduate students in the Department of Electrical and Computer Engineering may also reside in nearby rooms or apartments. Various board plans are available.

STUDENT GROUP

The department has about 230 graduate students.

LOCATION

New Brunswick (population 42,000), is in central New Jersey off Exit 9 of the New Jersey Turnpike and along the New York–Philadelphia railroad line. It is about 33 miles from New York City; frequent express bus service is available from a station near the College Avenue campus to terminals in central Manhattan. Princeton is 16 miles south, Philadelphia about 60 miles south, and Washington, D.C., within 200 miles.

THE UNIVERSITY

Rutgers, The State University of New Jersey, with more than 47,000 students on three campuses in Camden, Newark, and New Brunswick, is one of the major state university systems in the nation. The University comprises twenty-five degree-granting divisions: thirteen undergraduate colleges, eleven graduate schools, and one school offering both undergraduate and graduate degrees. Four are located in Camden, seven in Newark, and fourteen in New Brunswick. Rutgers has a unique history as a Colonial college, a land-grant institution, and a state university. Chartered in 1766 as Queen's College, the eighth institution of higher learning to be founded in the colonies before the Revolution, the school opened its doors in New Brunswick in 1771 with one instructor, one sophomore, and a handful of freshmen. In 1825, the name of the college was changed to Rutgers to honor a former trustee and revolutionary war veteran, Colonel Henry Rutgers.

APPLYING

Admission materials are available from the Office of Graduate and Professional Admissions, Van Nest Hall, Rutgers, The State University of New Jersey, New Brunswick, NJ 08903 (908-932-7711). A complete application consists of the application form, letters of recommendation, the application fee, official transcripts of previous academic work, a personal statement or essay, and scores on the GRE General Test. Detailed procedures and instructions accompany the application forms.

CORRESPONDENCE AND INFORMATION

Graduate Director
Department of Electrical and Computer Engineering
Rutgers University GPECE
P.O. Box 909
Piscataway, New Jersey 08855-0909
Telephone: 908-445-2578

RUTGERS, THE STATE UNIVERSITY OF NEW JERSEY

THE FACULTY AND THEIR RESEARCH

Grigore Burdea, Associate Professor of Electrical and Computer Engineering; Ph.D., NYU. Robotic systems, computer engineering.

Michael L. Bushnell, Associate Professor of Electrical and Computer Engineering; Ph.D., Carnegie Mellon. Computer engineering: computer-aided design of VLSI integrated circuits, silicon compilers, artificial intelligence techniques.

Michael F. Caggiano, Assistant Professor of Electrical and Computer Engineering; Ph.D., UCLA. High-performance and microwave IC device packaging.

Todd Cook, Assistant Professor of Electrical and Computer Engineering; Ph.D., North Carolina State. Computer architectures, embedded systems design, custom computing machines, high-level synthesis, retargetable compilers.

Sekhar Darbha, Assistant Professor of Electrical and Computer Engineering; Ph.D., North Carolina State. Parallel computing, task scheduling for multiprocessor systems, load balancing, process migration.

David G. Daut, Professor of Electrical and Computer Engineering; Ph.D., RPI. Communications and information processing: digital communication system design and analysis, image coding and transmission.

James Flanagan, Board of Governors' Professor of Electrical and Computer Engineering and Director of the Center for Computer Aids for Industrial Productivity; Eng.Sc.D., MIT. Digital communications; speech processing; coding, recognition, and synthesis; acoustic systems; robotics; artificial intelligence; human/computer interfaces.

Herbert Freeman, Professor of Electrical and Computer Engineering; Eng.Sc.D., Columbia. Computer engineering: digital computer systems, computer architecture, image processing and graphics.

Zoran R. Gajic, Associate Professor of Electrical and Computer Engineering; Ph.D., Michigan State. Systems and controls: singular perturbation methods in control system analysis, linear stochastic estimation.

David J. Goodman, Professor of Electrical and Computer Engineering and Director of the Wireless Information Networks Laboratory; Ph.D., Imperial College, London. Communication systems, wireless access radio and systems.

Jack M. Holtzman, Research Professor of Electrical and Computer Engineering; Ph.D., Polytechnic. Telecommunications, wireless communications, performance analysis.

Joseph Hui, Professor of Electrical and Computer Engineering; Ph.D., MIT. Communications networks: integrated broadband networks, switching and traffic theory, information and coding theory, parallel processing and adaptive computing.

Bogoljub Lalevic, Professor of Electrical and Computer Engineering; Ph.D., Temple. Solid-state electronics: gaseous and chemical semiconducting device sensors, high-power and microwave switching devices.

Morton H. Lewin, Professor of Electrical and Computer Engineering; Ph.D., Princeton. Computer engineering: digital logic and microprocessor system design, UNIX operating system.

Yicheng Lu, Associate Professor of Electrical and Computer Engineering; Ph.D., Colorado. Semiconductor materials (GaAs and Si), metal-semiconductor contacts, device physics and fabrication.

Richard Mammone, Professor of Electrical and Computer Engineering; Ph.D., CUNY Graduate Center. Digital signal processing: image restoration, speech recognition, medical imaging.

Narayan B. Mandayam, Assistant Professor of Electrical and Computer Engineering; Ph.D., Rice. Communication theory, spread spectrum, wireless systems, multi-access protocols.

Thomas G. Marshall, Professor of Electrical and Computer Engineering and Director of the Center for Digital Signal Processing; Ph.D., Chalmers (Sweden). Digital signal processing: algorithms and specialized signal processing computers.

Sigrid R. McAfee, Associate Professor of Electrical and Computer Engineering; Ph.D., Polytechnic of New York. Solid-state electronics: deep levels in semiconductors, molecular beam epitaxy and MO-CVD gallium arsenide, AlGaAs and GaAs on silicon.

Peter Meer, Associate Professor of Electrical and Computer Engineering; D.Sc., Technion (Israel). Computer vision, pattern recognition, applied robust estimation, probabilistic algorithms for machine-vision problems.

Sophocles J. Orfanidis, Associate Professor of Electrical and Computer Engineering; Ph.D., Yale. Digital signal processing: signal estimation and modeling methods, adaptive signal processing and spectrum estimation.

Paul Panayotatos, Associate Professor of Electrical and Computer Engineering; Eng.Sc.D., Columbia. Organic semiconductor solar cells, optical interconnects, microelectromechanical devices.

Narindra N. Puri, Professor of Electrical and Computer Engineering; Ph.D., Pennsylvania. Systems and controls: optimal adaptive control systems.

Christopher Rose, Associate Professor of Electrical Engineering; Ph.D., MIT. Complex systems (neural networks, communication networks), neurophysiology, communication network topologies, novel applications of superconducting materials.

Peddapullaiah Sannuti, Professor of Electrical and Computer Engineering; Ph.D., Illinois. Communication and control systems: singular perturbation analysis of Kalman filter with weak measurement noise.

Deborah Silver, Associate Professor of Electrical and Computer Engineering; Ph.D., Princeton. Computer graphics, computational geometry, numerical analysis.

Joseph Wilder, Research Professor of Electrical and Computer Engineering; Ph.D., Pennsylvania. Image processing, pattern recognition, machine vision.

Roy Yates, Associate Professor of Electrical and Computer Engineering; Ph.D., MIT. Routing and flow control for integrated broadband networks, reversible queuing systems, wireless cellular communication systems.

Jian Zhao, Associate Professor of Electrical and Computer Engineering; Ph.D., Carnegie Mellon. Heterojunctions and their optoelectronic device applications, computer modeling of III-V devices, deep traps in semiconductors, electromigration.

SOUTHERN ILLINOIS UNIVERSITY
AT CARBONDALE

DEPARTMENT OF ELECTRICAL ENGINEERING

PROGRAMS OF STUDY

Graduate programs are offered leading to the Doctor of Philosophy (Ph.D.) in engineering science with a concentration in electrical systems and to the Master of Science (M.S.) in electrical engineering.

To earn the Ph.D., a minimum of 32 semester hours of course work and 24 semester hours of dissertation research is required. The course work must be completed in two areas: the area of concentration and the program core. A student must complete a minimum of 15 semester hours of course work relevant to an area of concentration and 17 hours of courses in the program core, which is required of all students. A dissertation must be completed in the student's area of research interest, with the approval of the dissertation committee. Written candidacy exams covering all course work taken are required, and an oral defense of the dissertation must be accomplished.

Students who choose the M.S. thesis option must complete a minimum of 30 semester hours of acceptable graduate credit, including 18 semester hours within the major department. Each candidate must also pass a comprehensive examination covering all graduate work, including the thesis. Students who choose the M.S. nonthesis option must complete a minimum of 36 semester hours of acceptable graduate credit, including at least 21 semester hours within the major department. Of these 21 semester hours, 3 should be in a course that can be devoted to the preparation of a research paper. In addition, each candidate is required to successfully complete a research paper and a written comprehensive examination.

RESEARCH FACILITIES

The air-conditioned laboratory facilities are furnished with modern equipment and are located in the newly constructed wing of the College of Engineering building complex near the 26-acre campus lake. Laboratories are available for research in the areas of biomedical engineering, circuits and systems, electrochemical engineering, electronics, electric machines, information processing, lasers, power systems and power electronics, microelectronics, microprocessors and digital systems, microwaves, optics, control and robotics, signal processing and pattern recognition, and intelligent and expert systems.

FINANCIAL AID

Graduate teaching and/or research assistantships that include a stipend of approximately $8400 for the 1997–98 academic year and a tuition waiver are available in the department. A few fellowships, with stipends ranging from $9900 to $16,500 per calendar year and a tuition waiver, are also available on a competitive basis.

COST OF STUDY

The tuition and fee charge for students enrolled in the 1996–97 academic year was $3522 for Illinois residents and $8125 for nonresidents.

LIVING AND HOUSING COSTS

During the 1996–97 academic year, the cost for on-campus room and board was $3472. There are 571 furnished and unfurnished apartments available for married students; rents ranged from $325 to $377 a month, including utilities.

STUDENT GROUP

In 1996–97, there were 21,863 students at the University. The electrical engineering department had 42 students working toward the master's degree and 17 students working toward the Ph.D.

STUDENT OUTCOMES

Approximately 20 percent of the graduates of the M.S. degree program continue their studies to obtain a Ph.D. degree. All graduates are in high demand by industry and receive attractive job offers well before finishing their thesis. Graduates are employed by high-technology industries in high-skill positions, such as design and development engineers, in areas closely related to their specific field of specialization. Some recent employers hiring Southern Illinois University at Carbondale electrical engineering graduate students include AT&T Bell Labs, Ericsson, Motorola, McDonnell Douglas, Caterpillar, Toyota, IBM, INTEL, Microsoft, and Texas Instruments.

LOCATION

The city of Carbondale is approximately 100 miles southeast of St. Louis, Missouri, in Jackson County, the western border of which is the Mississippi River. Immediately south of Carbondale is some of the most rugged and picturesque terrain in Illinois. The region immediately surrounding Carbondale is noted for its large peach and apple orchards. Within 10 miles of the campus are two state parks and four lakes, and much of the area is part of the Shawnee National Forest.

THE UNIVERSITY

Southern Illinois University is in its second 100 years of providing high-quality education. Graduate studies were first offered in 1943, and the first doctoral degree was granted in 1959.

APPLYING

Students interested in graduate studies in electrical engineering should seek admission to the Graduate School and acceptance into a degree program offered by the electrical engineering department. The applicant must have a bachelor's degree with a major in engineering, mathematics, physical science, or life science and demonstrate competence in mathematics. A student whose undergraduate training is deficient may be required to take course work without graduate credit. To be admitted to the Ph.D. program, students must have a master's degree, or the equivalent, in engineering.

CORRESPONDENCE AND INFORMATION

For information about the M.S. program in electrical engineering:

Chairman, Department of Electrical Engineering
Southern Illinois University at Carbondale
Carbondale, Illinois 62901-6603

Telephone: 618-536-2364
Fax: 618-453-7972
E-mail: eedept@siu.edu
World Wide Web: http://www.siu.edu/gradschl/gc96ee.htm
http://howard.engr.siu.edu/elec/siu_ee.html

For information about the Ph.D. program:

Associate Dean, College of Engineering
Southern Illinois University at Carbondale
Carbondale, Illinois 62901-6603

SOUTHERN ILLINOIS UNIVERSITY AT CARBONDALE

THE FACULTY AND THEIR RESEARCH

Nazeih M. Botros, Associate Professor; Ph.D., Oklahoma, 1985. Digital hardware design, digital signal processing, digital instrumentation, neural networks, robot sensing, bioengineering.

David P. Brown, Professor; Ph.D., Michigan State, 1964. Active network theory, circuit and system theory, graph theory, matrix theory, large-scale networks and systems, signal processing.

Morteza Daneshdoost, Associate Professor; Ph.D., Drexel, 1984. Electric power systems, linear systems and circuits, control systems, optimization techniques, expert systems, computer graphics, MMI.

Shirshak Dhali, Professor; Ph.D., Texas Tech, 1984. Plasma processing, gaseous electronics, lasers and laser applications.

Ralph Etienne-Cummings, Assistant Professor; Ph.D., Pennsylvania, 1994. Analog and digital VLSI systems for machine perception, biological and artificial computational sensors, visual motion detection and navigation in hardware, image processing and computer vision.

Vernold K. Feiste, Associate Professor; Ph.D., Missouri–Columbia, 1966. Electric power systems, electrical machines, electric power distribution, distribution automation.

Glafkos Galanos, Professor; Ph.D., Manchester (England), 1970. Power systems, HVDC transmission, power electronic systems.

Charles A. Goben, Professor; Ph.D., Iowa State, 1965. Physical electronics; surface and interface properties; nuclear and space radiation effects; integrated optics; fiber optics; optical, infrared, and microwave surface wave properties.

Lalit Gupta, Associate Professor; Ph.D., SMU, 1986. Computer vision, pattern recognition, digital signal processing, neural networks.

Frances J. Harackiewicz, Associate Professor; Ph.D., Massachusetts Amherst, 1990. Electromagnetics, antenna theory and design, microwaves, microstrip phased arrays and anisotropic materials.

Constantine Hatziadoniu, Associate Professor; Ph.D., West Virginia, 1987. Power systems modeling, simulation, and control; high-voltage DC transmission; power electronics; power systems transient.

Chia-Lun John Hu, Professor; Ph.D., Colorado at Boulder, 1966. Microwaves and applied optics (Fourier optics, holograph, electrooptics), nonlinear and parametric wave systems (phase conjugation), neural networks.

Dimitrios Kagaris, Assistant Professor; Ph.D., Dartmouth, 1994. VLSI design automation, digital circuit testing, communication networks.

Mahmoud A. Manzoul, Associate Professor; Ph.D., West Virginia, 1985. Computer architecture, special-purpose computers, parallel and array processing, multiple-valued logic.

Farzad Pourboghrat, Associate Professor; Ph.D., Iowa, 1984. Systems control, robust and adaptive control, robotics, motion planning and self-organization, neural networks and learning systems.

Charles A. Rawlings, Professor; Ph.D., Southern Illinois at Carbondale, 1974. Biomedical engineering, clinical engineering, instrumentation, electronics.

Mohammad Sayeh, Associate Professor; Ph.D., Oklahoma State, 1985. Neural networks, optical computing, image processing, stochastic modeling, quantum electronics.

R. Viswanathan, Professor; Ph.D., SMU, 1983. Detection and estimation theory, spread spectrum communication and communication theory.

SOUTHERN METHODIST UNIVERSITY

DEPARTMENT OF COMPUTER SCIENCE AND ENGINEERING

PROGRAMS OF STUDY

The department offers the following degrees: Master of Science in Computer Engineering, Master of Science (with majors in computer science, operations research, and software engineering), Master of Science in Engineering Management, Ph.D. (with majors in computer engineering, computer science, and operations research), and D.Eng. (with a major in engineering management). SMU's CSE department emphasizes the following major areas of interest: algorithms engineering, artificial intelligence, computer architecture, computer networks, data and knowledge engineering, mathematical programming, natural-language processing, parallel and distributed processing, and software engineering and systems.

RESEARCH FACILITIES

Students in the Department of Computer Science and Engineering have access to a wide range of facilities and equipment. The department's computing environment has evolved into an Ethernet-based network of minicomputers and workstations. It now includes workstations from Sun Microsystems and Digital Equipment Corporation, including four fast (250–300 megahertz) Alpha Server 2100s. These are networked with a Sequent Symmetry S81 configured with twenty CPUs.

FINANCIAL AID

The Graduate Admissions Committee awards a limited number of merit-based research and teaching assistantships to incoming students, which pay up to $1600 per month and cover tuition. Separate tuition assistantships are also available.

COST OF STUDY

Tuition and fees for graduate study in 1997–98 are $600 per semester hour.

LIVING AND HOUSING COSTS

Dormitory housing charges each semester are approximately $1800 per person for double occupancy. Board, including tax, costs $1427 per semester. Furnished efficiency and one- and two-bedroom apartments are available on campus, some with paid utilities, at costs ranging from $1900 to $2000 per semester. The Dallas area offers inexpensive housing options within driving distance of the campus, with apartments starting at $300 per month.

STUDENT GROUP

The department has about 85 doctoral students and 350 master's degree students. Approximately 10 to 15 doctorates and 40 to 50 master's degrees are awarded each year.

STUDENT OUTCOMES

Recent graduates have obtained appointments at the University of Oklahoma, the University of Arkansas, and the College of the Ozarks, as well as industrial research positions at Texas Instruments, Sabre Decision Technologies (American Airlines), DSC Communications, MCI, Sun Microsystems, Bell (AT&T), Cyrix, Alcatel, and Science Applications International Corporation.

LOCATION

Dallas is the center of an attractive metropolitan area of 2 million people. It has fine parks, lakes, museums, theaters, orchestras, libraries, and places of worship. Clean and progressive, the city continues to grow as a center of business and light industry. The manufacturing, microelectronics, and telecommunications industries provide many opportunities for employment.

THE UNIVERSITY AND THE SCHOOL

Southern Methodist University is a private, nonprofit, coeducational institution located in suburban University Park, an incorporated residential district of Dallas, Texas. The School of Engineering and Applied Science (SEAS) traces its roots to 1925, when the Technical Club of Dallas, a professional organization of practicing engineers, petitioned SMU to fulfill the need for an engineering school in the Southwest.

APPLYING

Students may apply for admission at any time. However, initial review for admission in a given semester depends upon receipt by the Graduate Division of all requisite application materials no later than August 1 for fall admission, December 15 for spring admission, or May 15 for summer admission. All international students must use the following dates: July 1 for fall admission, November 15 for spring admission, and April 15 for summer admission. GRE General Test scores are required.

CORRESPONDENCE AND INFORMATION

Graduate Admissions
School of Engineering and Applied Science
Southern Methodist University
Dallas, Texas 75275-0335
Telephone: 214-768-3900
World Wide Web: http://www.seas.smu.edu/

SOUTHERN METHODIST UNIVERSITY
THE FACULTY AND THEIR RESEARCH

The following is a partial list of faculty members affiliated with the Department of Computer Science and Engineering.

Professors

Dan I. Moldovan, Chairman; Ph.D., Columbia, 1978. Computer architecture, parallel and distributed processing, artificial intelligence, natural-language processing.

Jeffery L. Kennington, Ph.D., Georgia Tech, 1973; PE. Network optimization, mathematical programming, telecommunications networks.

David W. Matula, Ph.D., Berkeley, 1966. Computer arithmetic, network and graph algorithms, algorithm engineering.

Associate Professors

Richard S. Barr, Ph.D., Texas at Austin, 1978. Network optimization, data mining, system modeling.

Weidong Chen, Ph.D., SUNY at Stony Brook, 1990. Databases, mobile computing, computer networking and communication.

Margaret H. Dunham, Ph.D., SMU, 1984. Database recovery, data mining, mobile computing, temporal databases.

Richard V. Helgason, Ph.D., SMU, 1980. Network optimization, mathematical programming, computational geometry.

Sukumaran Nair, Ph.D., Illinois at Urbana–Champaign, 1990. Fault-tolerant computing, computer networks, VLSI systems.

Assistant Professors

Rebecca Bruce, Ph.D., New Mexico State, 1995. Natural-language processing, machine learning, expert system development.

Eric Lin, Ph.D., USC, 1994. Distributed operating systems, telecommunications software, mobile computing.

Jeff Tian, Ph.D., Maryland, 1992. Software testing techniques and tools, measurement and analysis of software products and processes, software reliability and safety, software engineering.

Lecturers

Frank Coyle, Ph.D., SMU, 1992. Software engineering.

Mary Alys Lillard, M.S., SMU, 1983. Computer education, telecommunications.

SOUTHERN METHODIST UNIVERSITY

DEPARTMENT OF ELECTRICAL ENGINEERING

PROGRAMS OF STUDY

The department offers M.S. and Ph.D. degrees. The SMU electrical engineering department emphasizes the following major areas of interest: biomedical engineering (biomedical devices and instrumentation and biomedical signal capture, processing, and modeling); communications and information theory (detection and estimation theory, digital communications, spread spectrum, cellular communications, coding, encryption, radar/sonar, optical communications, and information theory); control systems and robotics (linear and nonlinear systems, robotics, and computer and robot vision); digital signal processing (digital filter design, system identification, spectral estimation, adaptive filters, and neural networks); image processing and computer vision (digital image processing, computer vision, and pattern recognition); lasers, optoelectronics, electromagnetic theory, and microwave electronics (classical optics, fiber optics, laser recording, integrated optics, dielectric waveguides, antennas, transmission lines, laser diodes, signal processors, and superconductive microwave and optoelectronic devices); solid-state circuits, computer-aided circuit design, and VLSI design (electronic circuits, computer-aided design, VLSI design, neural network implementation, parallel array architectures, and memory interfaces); electronic materials and solid-state devices (fabrication and characterization of devices and materials, device physics, microelectromechanical systems, noise in solid-state devices, infrared detectors, AlGaAs and GaAs devices and materials, thin films, superconductivity, superconductive devices and electronics, hybrid superconductor-semiconductor devices, ultrafast electronics, and applications of the scanning tunneling microscope); and telecommunications (telecommunication components and systems, data communications, digital telephony, and digital switching).

RESEARCH FACILITIES

The Biomedical Engineering Laboratory is equipped for the study of problems in biomedical engineering. The Cryoelectronics Laboratory includes Dewars, refrigerators, temperature controllers and sensors, computer workstations, and fiber-optic instrumentation to support low-temperature device characterization and superconductivity research. The Digital Signal Processing Laboratory is equipped with PC-based DSP workstations. The Image Processing and Analysis Laboratory incorporates two Recognition Concepts TRAPIX 5500 series real-time color image processing systems. The Microwave Electronics Laboratory has high-frequency oscilloscopes, synthesizers, power meters, generators, analyzers, and computer stations for design and analysis of microwave circuits. The Optical and Millimeter Wave Electronics Laboratory consists of lasers, optical equipment, millimeter-wave active and passive components, and system controllers. Major apparatus in the Robotics Laboratory are used for design and development of robot arm, robot hand, and vision systems. The Solid-State Device Characterization Laboratory is used for the computerized I-V, C-V, and noise characterization of devices. The lab contains a shielded room and various programmable and nonprogrammable instruments. The Solid-State Fabrication Laboratory consists of a class-10,000 clean room with class-100 laminar-flow work areas. It has photolithography, deposition, etching, and optical inspection equipment for the fabrication of solid-state devices.

FINANCIAL AID

The Graduate Admissions Committee awards a limited number of merit-based research and teaching assistantships to incoming students, paying up to $1600 per month and covering tuition. Separate tuition assistantships are also available.

COST OF STUDY

Tuition and fees for graduate study in 1997–98 are $600 per semester hour.

LIVING AND HOUSING COSTS

Dormitory housing charges each semester are approximately $1800 per person for double occupancy. Board on campus, including tax, costs $1427 per semester. Furnished efficiency and one- and two-bedroom apartments are available on campus, with utilities paid in some, at costs ranging from $1900 to $2000 per semester. The Dallas area offers inexpensive housing options within driving distance of the campus, with apartments starting from $300 per month.

STUDENT GROUP

The department has about 50 doctoral students and 90 master's students. There are also postdoctoral research fellows. Approximately ten to twenty doctoral and twenty to thirty master's degrees are awarded each year. In addition, the department has about 300 students in the telecommunications program.

STUDENT OUTCOMES

Recent graduates have obtained appointments at prestigious universities and industrial research positions at firms such as Texas Instruments.

LOCATION

Dallas is the center of an attractive metropolitan area of 2 million people. It has fine parks, lakes, museums, theaters, orchestras, libraries, and places of worship. Clean and progressive, the city continues to grow as a center of business and light industry. The manufacturing, microelectronics, and telecommunications industries provide many opportunities for employment.

THE UNIVERSITY AND THE SCHOOL

Southern Methodist University is a private, nonprofit coeducational institution located in suburban University Park, an incorporated residential district surrounded by Dallas, Texas. The School of Engineering and Applied Science (SEAS) traces its roots to 1925, when the Technical Club of Dallas, a professional organization of practicing engineers, petitioned SMU to fulfill the need for an engineering school in the Southwest.

APPLYING

Students may apply for admission at any time. However, initial review for admission in a given semester is dependent upon receipt by the Graduate Division of all requisite application materials no later than August 1 for fall admission, December 15 for spring admission, and May 15 for summer admission. International students should use the following dates: July 1 for fall admission, November 15 for spring admission, and April 15 for summer admission. GRE General Test scores are required.

CORRESPONDENCE AND INFORMATION

Graduate Admissions
School of Engineering and Applied Science
Southern Methodist University
Dallas, Texas 75275-0335
Telephone: 214-768-3900
World Wide Web: http://www.seas.smu.edu/

SOUTHERN METHODIST UNIVERSITY
THE FACULTY AND THEIR RESEARCH

The following is a partial list of faculty members affiliated with the Department of Electrical Engineering:

Kenneth L. Ashley, Professor; Ph.D., Carnegie Mellon; PE. Semiconductor optoelectronic devices, gallium arsenide circuits.

Donald P. Butler, Associate Professor; Ph.D., Rochester. Infrared detectors, microelectromechanics, optoelectronic and microwave devices, superconductive devices.

Jerome K. Butler, University Distinguished Professor; Ph.D., Kansas; PE. Integrated optical communications, solid-state injection lasers, surface-emitting lasers.

Zeynep Çelik-Butler, Associate Professor; Ph.D., Rochester. Infrared detectors, microelectromechanics, noise modeling of solid-state devices, high-T_c superconductors.

Carlos E. Davila, Associate Professor; Ph.D., Texas at Austin. Adaptive signal processing, spectral estimation, system identification.

James G. Dunham, Associate Professor; Ph.D., Stanford; PE. Data compression, cryptography, information and telecommunications theory.

Gary Evans, Professor; Ph.D., Caltech; PE. Design, fabrication, and analysis of surface-emitting lasers.

Robert R. Fossum, Professor; Ph.D., Oregon State. Communications.

Jerry D. Gibson, Professor and Chairman; Ph.D., SMU. Data, speech, image, and video compression; multimedia over networks; wireless communications; information theory.

W. Milton Gosney, Cecil and Ida Green Professor; Ph.D., Berkeley; PE. VLSI circuits and biomedical applications, scanning tunneling microscopy.

Someshwar C. Gupta, Cecil H. Green Professor; Ph.D., Berkeley; PE. Cellular, navigational, and personal communications.

Alireza Khotanzad, Associate Professor; Ph.D., Purdue; PE. Computer vision and pattern recognition, applications of neural networks.

Choon S. Lee, Associate Professor; Ph.D., Illinois at Urbana-Champaign. Electromagnetic scattering, reflector and microstrip antennas, millimeter-wave applications.

Behrouz Peikari, Professor; Ph.D., Berkeley; PE. Nonlinear circuits, filter design, image processing, robotics.

Mandyam D. Srinath, Professor; Ph.D., Illinois at Urbana-Champaign; PE. Adaptive filters, shape classification, neural networks.

André G. Vacroux, Professor; Ph.D., Purdue; PE. Microcomputer networks, switched networks, ISDN, biomedical systems.

Emeritus Professors

Kenneth W. Heizer, Ph.D., Illinois at Urbana-Champaign; PE.

Lorn L. Howard, Ph.D., Michigan State; PE. Neutral electronics and circuits.

John A. Savage, M.S.E.E., Texas at Austin; PE.

STANFORD UNIVERSITY

COMPUTER SCIENCE DEPARTMENT

PROGRAMS OF STUDY

Founded in 1965, the Computer Science Department is a center for research and education at the graduate level. Strong research groups exist in the areas of analysis of algorithms and theory of computation, artificial intelligence, scientific computing, robotics, and systems. Basic research in computer science is the main goal of these groups, but there is also a strong emphasis on interdisciplinary work and on applications. Fields in which interdisciplinary work has been undertaken include chemistry, genetics, linguistics, physics, engineering, and medicine. Close ties are maintained with researchers in the Departments of Electrical Engineering, Mathematics, Statistics, Operations Research, and others with similar interests. In addition, both faculty and students commonly work with investigators at nearby research or industrial institutions. The main educational goal is to prepare students for research and teaching careers, either in universities or in industry.

Students admitted to the Ph.D. program usually combine course work and participation in a research group during their first year and devote themselves entirely to research thereafter. Students must pass comprehensive examinations that test the breadth of their computer science knowledge and a qualifying examination in their specialty area.

The department also offers the Master of Science in Computer Science (M.S.C.S.). The M.S.C.S. program chiefly involves course work and usually takes from four to six quarters to complete.

RESEARCH FACILITIES

In addition to equipment provided by the University, the department provides a wide variety of machines used by students and researchers, such as Xenon, a Sun-4/670 with 4 CPUs, the primary student machine; Radon, an HP 9000-755 compute server for student use; various medium to large UNIX machines; and hundreds of workstations and X terminals from Sun Microsystems, Digital Equipment Corporation, Hewlett-Packard, Silicon Graphics, NeXT, IBM, and NCD.

FINANCIAL AID

All incoming Ph.D. students are supported by a departmental assistantship or by a fellowship. Assistantship holders receive a stipend plus a 9-unit tuition credit each quarter. If there is an insufficient number of Ph.D. students to staff teaching and research assistantships, then such positions are offered to qualified students in the M.S.C.S. program.

COST OF STUDY

For 1997–98, tuition charges for all students not holding assistantships are approximately $7500 per quarter or $22,500 per academic year.

LIVING AND HOUSING COSTS

On-campus housing for single students costs approximately $2800 for the 1997–98 academic year. Housing for married students is available and averages about $600 per month. Off-campus housing tends to be more expensive. The cost of living in the area is relatively high.

STUDENT GROUP

The department has approximately 160 doctoral students and 350 master's students; they come from all parts of the nation and the world. Approximately 30 Ph.D. degrees and 150 master's degrees are awarded each year. Career choices are divided about evenly between academic and industrial positions.

LOCATION

Stanford University is located on a spacious campus on the San Francisco peninsula, 30 miles south of the city of San Francisco. A wide variety of natural attractions are located within a short drive, including the Pacific Ocean and the Sierra Nevada. The climate is mild the year round. The San Francisco Bay Area is a major and diverse cultural center and is also the site of many industrial corporations and research centers in computer and other technologies.

THE UNIVERSITY

Stanford is a private, nonsectarian, coeducational university with an international reputation as an outstanding educational institution. It operates on the quarter system with a shortened summer session. Enrollment is approximately 14,000, including 7,000 graduate students. Among the approximately 1,300 faculty members are 10 Nobel laureates and many others who have achieved wide academic distinction. The University provides superb academic and athletic facilities.

APPLYING

Applications and all supporting documentation for admission to the Ph.D. and the M.S.C.S. programs must be received before December 1. Exceptions are made for applicants to the M.S.C.S. program who are either Honors Co-op applicants or already students at Stanford. Information on these deadlines is available from the department. Absolutely no exceptions will be made for the Ph.D. program. Application forms and information packets may be obtained from the Office of Graduate Admissions or, for non-U.S. citizens, the Office of Foreign Graduate Admissions. Financial aid information for Ph.D. students will be made available upon the students' acceptance.

CORRESPONDENCE AND INFORMATION

Admissions Central
Computer Science Department
Gates 1B, Room 196
Stanford University
Stanford, California 94305-9015
World Wide Web: http://www.stanford.edu

STANFORD UNIVERSITY
THE FACULTY AND THEIR RESEARCH

The following is a partial list of faculty members affiliated with the Department of Computer Science.

Charles Bigelow, Associate Professor of Art and Computer Science; B.A., Reed, 1967. Digital typographic design.

Thomas O. Binford, Professor of Research in Computer Science; Ph.D., Wisconsin, 1965. Computer vision, robotics, artificial intelligence, computer-aided design, manufacturing.

David R. Cheriton, Associate Professor; Ph.D., Waterloo, 1978. Computer operating system design, distributed systems, computer communications, multiprocessor architectures, parallel computation.

William J. Dally, Professor; Ph.D., Caltech, 1986. Computer architecture and the implementation of multiprocessors.

George B. Dantzig, Professor Emeritus of Operations Research and Computer Science; Ph.D., Berkeley, 1946. Modeling and optimization of large-scale energy systems, combinatorial mathematics, mathematical programming.

David L. Dill, Assistant Professor; Ph.D., Carnegie Mellon, 1987. Concurrency, hardware verification, asynchronous circuits, compilers, LISP.

Edward A. Feigenbaum, Professor; Ph.D., Carnegie Tech, 1960. Knowledge engineering, expert systems, artificial intelligence, large-scale knowledge-based systems.

Richard E. Fikes, Professor of Research and Co-Scientific Director of the HPP in the Knowledge Systems Laboratory; Ph.D., Carnegie Mellon, 1968. Knowledge-based systems technology, declarative knowledge representation.

Robert W. Floyd, Professor; B.A., 1953, B.S., 1958, Chicago. Design and analysis of algorithms.

Hector Garcia-Molina, Professor; Ph.D., Stanford, 1979. Database systems, distributed computing.

Michael R. Genesereth, Associate Professor; Ph.D., Harvard, 1978. Artificial intelligence, logic, automated reasoning, and agent architecture with applications in engineering and robotics.

Gene H. Golub, Professor; Ph.D., Illinois, 1959. Numerical analysis, scientific computing, mathematical programming, statistical computing.

Leonidas J. Guibas, Professor; Ph.D., Stanford, 1976. Computational geometry, computer graphics, VLSI algorithms and design aids, analysis of algorithms and data structures, complexity theory, programming techniques, personal computing.

Anoop Gupta, Assistant Professor; Ph.D., Carnegie Mellon, 1985. Highly parallel computer architectures, programming languages and operating systems for such machines, parallel applications studies.

Pat Hanrahan, Professor; Ph.D., Wisconsin, 1986. Computer graphics, rendering algorithms and high-performance graphics systems.

John Hennessy, Willard and Inez Bell Professor of Electrical Engineering and Computer Science; Ph.D., SUNY at Stony Brook, 1977. Computer architecture and optimizing compilers, especially the interaction between compiler technology and architecture; multiprocessors; parallel computing.

John G. Herriot, Professor Emeritus; Ph.D., Brown, 1941. Numerical analysis.

Oussama Khatib, Associate Professor; Ph.D., Toulouse (France), 1980. Robotics, control architectures, strategies, sensing, design.

Donald E. Knuth, Professor of the Art of Computer Programming; Ph.D., Caltech, 1963. Analysis of algorithms, programming languages, mathematical typography, combinatorial mathematics, history of computer science.

Daphne Koller, Assistant Professor of Computer Science; Ph.D., Stanford, 1993. AI: creating systems that reason and act under uncertainty.

Monica S. Lam, Assistant Professor; Ph.D., Carnegie Mellon, 1987. Parallel computer systems, programming languages, optimizing compilers, computer architectures.

Jean-Claude Latombe, Associate Professor; Thèse d'état, Grenoble (France), 1977. Robotics, artificial intelligence, geometrical reasoning, planning.

Marc Levoy, Assistant Professor of Computer Science and Electrical Engineering; Ph.D., North Carolina at Chapel Hill, 1989. Computer graphics, scientific visualization, interactive techniques.

Zohar Manna, Professor; Ph.D., Carnegie Mellon, 1968. Mathematical theory of computation, logic of programs, automated deduction, logic programming, concurrent programming, artificial intelligence.

John McCarthy, Charles Piggot Professor of Computer Science; Ph.D., Princeton, 1951. Artificial intelligence, computing with symbolic expressions, time sharing, formalizing common sense, nonmonotonic logic.

Edward J. McCluskey, Professor of Electrical Engineering and Computer Science; Sc.D., MIT, 1956. Fault-tolerant computing, computer reliability, diagnosis, and testing; organization of computer systems; switching theory and logic design.

Nick McKeown, Assistant Professor of Computer Science; Ph.D., Berkeley, 1995. Architectures for high-speed switched, scheduling algorithms, multicast support, traffic management.

William F. Miller, Professor of Computer Science and Public and Private Management, Graduate School of Business; Ph.D., Purdue, 1956. Computer systems design, software systems, strategic planning and management, economic technological development.

John C. Mitchell, Associate Professor; Ph.D., MIT, 1984. Programming language theory, functional programming, object-oriented programming, applications of classical and nonclassical logic to computational problems.

Rajeev Motwani, Assistant Professor; Ph.D., Berkeley, 1988. Design and analysis of algorithms, data structures, complexity theory.

Nils J. Nilsson, Professor; Ph.D., Stanford, 1958. Artificial intelligence, knowledge representation, reasoning systems.

Joseph Oliger, Professor; Ph.D., Uppsala (Sweden), 1973. Numerical analysis, numerical methods for partial differential equations, applications in meteorology, oceanography, and geophysics.

Serge A. Plotkin, Assistant Professor; Ph.D., MIT, 1988. Parallel and distributed computation, analysis of algorithms, combinatorial optimization.

Vaughan Pratt, Professor; Ph.D., Stanford, 1972. Process specification languages, models of concurrency, applications of algebraic geometry and category theory, digital typography.

Eric Roberts, Associate Professor and Assistant Chair for Educational Affairs; Ph.D., Harvard, 1980. Computer science education, social implications of computing, programming languages, programming environments.

Mendel Rosenblum, Assistant Professor of Computer Science; Ph.D., Berkeley, 1992. Operating systems, computer architecture.

Arthur L. Samuel, Professor Emeritus of Research in Computer Science; S.M., MIT, 1926. Artificial intelligence.

Yoav Shoham, Assistant Professor; Ph.D., Yale, 1987. Artificial intelligence, spatiotemporal reasoning, formalizing common sense.

Andrew M. Stuart, Assistant Professor of Computer Science and Mechanical Engineering; D.Phil., Oxford, 1986. Dynamical systems.

Jeffrey D. Ullman, Professor; Ph.D., Princeton, 1966. Database systems, logic programming, parallel computation.

Gio Wiederhold, Professor of Research in Medicine and Computer Science; Ph.D., California, San Francisco, 1976. Databases, knowledge bases, information systems, parallel problem solving.

Terry Winograd, Professor; Ph.D., MIT, 1970. Artificial intelligence, human-computer interaction, work-centered system design.

STANFORD UNIVERSITY

DEPARTMENT OF ELECTRICAL ENGINEERING

PROGRAMS OF STUDY

The department awards three advanced degrees: the Master of Science, the Engineer, and the Doctor of Philosophy. The M.S. degree normally requires one year of course work beyond a bachelor's degree and the Engineer degree, an additional year after that. The Ph.D. degree is intended for students who wish to pursue a career in teaching and advanced academic or industrial research. It requires at least nine quarters of equivalent full-time residence, successful completion of the departmental qualifying exams, the preparation of a major dissertation on the results of independent research in the student's chosen field, and a University Oral Examination on the dissertation research. Research at Stanford is not an end in itself but a means of training graduate students. The typical faculty member supervises 6 or 7 Ph.D. research students. Department activities are organized around six research laboratories: the Computer Systems Laboratory (jointly with the Department of Computer Science), the Ginzton Laboratory (jointly with the Department of Applied Physics), the Information Systems Laboratory, the Integrated Circuits Laboratory, the Solid State Laboratory, and the Space, Telecommunications and Radioscience (STAR) Laboratory. In addition to the laboratories, there are interdisciplinary centers that bring together faculty members from different laboratories and departments. The Center for Integrated Systems brings together researchers in solid-state physics, materials science, and computer science who cooperate to develop VLSI technology. The Center for Telecommunications coordinates research of faculty members from several departments on networks and systems for telecommunication.

RESEARCH FACILITIES

The department occupies a cluster of three buildings on one side of the main University quadrangle. Research laboratories, classrooms, and faculty offices are all in proximity to one another. A fourth building, housing the Center for Integrated Systems with its 10,000-square-foot class 100 VLSI laboratory, is located a short distance away. The Engineering Library, with more than 1,700 active serial titles, 45,000 monographs, and thousands of technical reports, is part of a network of libraries serving the Stanford community. Seven other science libraries, as well as the two general reference libraries, contain additional scientific and technological materials. The department has extensive computing equipment to support all aspects of research and course work, including UNIX-based DEC, Sun, and HP workstations; graphics workstations; multiprocessors; and personal computers. The Stanford University Network (SUNet) connects more than 24,000 host computers, microcomputers, and advanced workstations, plus several thousand computer terminals on campus and provides access to off-campus computers, including national supercomputer centers. Individual laboratories often have special purpose equipment devoted to particular projects.

FINANCIAL AID

The Graduate Admission Committee awards a limited number of merit-based fellowships, research assistantships, and half-time teaching assistantships to incoming students. As financial aid is limited, it is strongly recommended that applicants apply for external aid (e.g., NSF, DOD). Tuition waivers are not available. Students are expected to make their own contacts for research assistantship support for post-master's work leading to the Ph.D. Students employed by local industry or research laboratories may attend Stanford on a part-time basis through the Honors Cooperative Program.

COST OF STUDY

Full tuition for 1997–98 is $22,740 for three quarters ($7580 per quarter). Books and supplies cost approximately $335 per quarter.

LIVING AND HOUSING COSTS

Stanford is able to house approximately 45 percent of its graduate students on campus, and most students who request on-campus housing are able to be assigned to one of the residences. On-campus accommodations for the 1997–98 nine-month academic year are priced as follows (all figures are approximate): dormitories, $4683; single student furnished housing, $9770; and double occupancy furnished housing, $4885 for two bedrooms. Furnished student housing for families costs approximately $815 per month for one bedroom, $934 per month for two bedrooms, $1128 per month for three bedrooms, and $1341 per month for four bedrooms. Living costs and medical insurance for a single on-campus student are estimated at $9600 for nine months. Off-campus living costs, including local transportation, are estimated at $12,900 for nine months.

STUDENT GROUP

The University has approximately 7,300 graduate and 6,600 undergraduate students. The EE department has 423 doctoral and 431 master's students and an additional 120 students enrolled part-time through the Honors Cooperative Program. These students of remarkable ability and achievements, from all parts of the nation and the world, form a professional and cultural resource of almost limitless scope.

LOCATION

Stanford University's spacious campus is located on the San Francisco peninsula, 35 miles southeast of the city of San Francisco. The climate is mild the year round. The San Francisco Bay Area is a major and diverse cultural center and is also the site of many industrial corporations and research centers related to computers and other technologies.

THE UNIVERSITY AND THE DEPARTMENT

Stanford is a private, nonsectarian, coeducational university with an international reputation as an outstanding educational institution. The atmosphere is an unusual blend of a pleasant uncrowded environment, a spirited and dynamic student body and faculty, and high standards of academic achievement. The EE faculty is one of the most distinguished in the world, including 19 members of the National Academy of Engineering, 6 members of the National Academy of Sciences, 39 Fellows of the IEEE, and recipients of numerous awards for research and education.

APPLYING

Applications for full-time study are considered for the autumn quarter only. The application deadline is January 5. Application deadlines for the Honors Cooperative Program are: autumn quarter, August 1; winter quarter, November 1; spring quarter, February 1; and summer quarter, May 1. Application forms and information packets may be obtained by writing to the Graduate Admissions Support Section of the Registrar's Office, Old Union Room 137, Stanford, California 94305-3052 or by calling 650-723-4291.

CORRESPONDENCE AND INFORMATION

Chairman of Admissions
Department of Electrical Engineering
Stanford University
Stanford, California 94305-9505
Telephone: 650-723-4115

STANFORD UNIVERSITY
THE FACULTY AND THEIR RESEARCH

Computer Systems Laboratory. Programming language theory, program verification, integrated circuit design, special computer architectures.

Hector Garcia-Molina, Professor (jointly with Computer Science) and Director; Ph.D., Stanford, 1979.
Mark A. Horowitz, Professor and Director; Ph.D., Stanford, 1984.
Mary G. Baker, Assistant Professor (jointly with Computer Science); Ph.D., Berkeley, 1993.
William J. Dally, Professor (jointly with Computer Science); Ph.D., Caltech, 1986.
Giovanni De Micheli, Professor; Ph.D., Berkeley, 1983.
Michael J. Flynn, Professor; Ph.D., Purdue, 1961.
Anoop Gupta, Associate Professor (jointly with Computer Science); Ph.D., Carnegie Mellon, 1985.
Patrick M. Hanrahan, Professor (jointly with Computer Science); Ph.D., Wisconsin, 1985.
John L. Hennessy, Willard and Inez Kerr Bell Professor of Engineering (jointly with Computer Science) and Dean of the School of Engineering; Ph.D., SUNY at Stony Brook, 1977.
Marc S. Levoy, Associate Professor (jointly with Computer Science); Ph.D., North Carolina at Chapel Hill, 1989.
David Luckham, Professor (Research); Ph.D., MIT, 1963.
Edward J. McCluskey, Professor (jointly with Computer Science); Sc.D., MIT, 1956.
Nicholas W. McKeown, Assistant Professor (jointly with Computer Science); Ph.D., Berkeley, 1995.
Teresa H. Y. Meng, Associate Professor; Ph.D., Berkeley, 1988.
Oyekunle A. Olukotun, Assistant Professor; Ph.D., Michigan, 1991.
Fouad A. Tobagi, Professor; Ph.D., UCLA, 1974.
Jennifer Widom, Associate Professor (jointly with Computer Science); Ph.D., Cornell, 1987.

Ginzton Laboratory. Superconductivity; superconducting materials and devices; lasers; fiber optics; ultrafast electrooptics; acoustooptic imaging; materials measurements using acoustic, photoacoustic, and optical techniques.

Butrus Khuri-Yakub, Professor (Research) and Associate Director; Ph.D., Stanford, 1975.
Stephen E. Harris, Barbara and Kenneth Oshman Professor of Engineering (jointly with Applied Physics); Ph.D., Stanford, 1963.
David A. B. Miller, W. M. Keck Foundation Professor of Electrical Engineering; Ph.D., Heriot-Watt (Edinburgh), 1979.
Calvin F. Quate, Leland T. Edwards Professor of Engineering (Research); Ph.D., Stanford, 1950.
Anthony E. Siegman, Burton J. and Ann M. McMurty Professor of Electrical Engineering; Ph.D., Stanford, 1957.
Yoshihisa Yamamoto, Professor (jointly with Applied Physics); Ph.D., Tokyo, 1978.

Information Systems Laboratory. Information and communication theory; signal processing; medical imaging; multivariable systems; optical information processing; storage systems; pattern recognition; fast algorithms; image and speech processing and coding; data compression and quantization; adaptive filtering; linear, nonlinear, and digital control; modeling complexity in VLSI systems.

Stephen P. Boyd, Professor and Director; Ph.D., Berkeley, 1985.
John M. Cioffi, Associate Professor; Ph.D., Stanford. 1984.
Thomas M. Cover, Kwoh-Ting Li Professor (jointly with Statistics); Ph.D., Stanford, 1964.
Abbas El Gamal, Associate Professor; Ph.D., Stanford, 1978.
John T. Gill III, Associate Professor; Ph.D., Berkeley, 1972.
Joseph W. Goodman, William Ayer Professor of Electrical Engineering and Senior Associate Dean; Ph.D., Stanford, 1963.
Robert M. Gray, Professor and Vice Chair; Ph.D., USC, 1969.
Lambertus Hesselink, Professor (jointly with Aeronautics and Astronautics); Ph.D., Caltech, 1977.
Thomas Kailath, Hitachi America Professor of Engineering; Sc.D., MIT, 1961.
Dwight G. Nishimura, Associate Professor; Ph.D., Stanford, 1984.
Arogyaswami Paulraj, Professor (Research); Ph.D., Indian Institute of Technology, 1973.
Bernard Widrow, Professor; Sc.D., MIT, 1956.

Integrated Circuits Laboratory. Materials research, including oxidation, diffusion, ion implantation, epitaxy, rapid thermal processing, deposition, and etching; integrated devices research in both silicon and GaAs; integrated circuits and integrated systems; fabrication processes.

Bruce A. Wooley, Professor and Director; Ph.D., Berkeley, 1970.
Robert W. Dutton, Professor; Ph.D., Berkeley, 1970.
Gregory Kovacs, Assistant Professor; Ph.D., Stanford, 1990.
Thomas H. Lee, Assistant Professor; Ph.D., MIT, 1990.
James D. Plummer, John M. Fluke Professor of Electrical Engineering and Chair; Ph.D., Stanford, 1971.
Krishna C. Saraswat, Professor; Ph.D., Stanford, 1974.
Simon S. Wong, Professor; Ph.D., Berkeley, 1983.

Solid State Laboratory. Physics and technology of solid-state materials, devices, and processes, especially nanotechnology.

James S. Harris, James and Ellenor Chesebrough Professor of Engineering and Director; Ph.D., Stanford, 1969.
James F. Gibbons, Frederick Emmons Terman Professor of Engineering; Ph.D., Stanford, 1956.
C. Robert Helms, Professor (Research); Ph.D., Stanford, 1973.
Ingolf Lindau, Professor (Research); Ph.D., Chalmers (Sweden), 1971.
R. Fabian Pease, Professor; Ph.D., Cambridge, 1964.
Piero A. Pianetta, Professor (Research) (jointly with SSRL); Ph.D., Stanford, 1977.
Shan Wang, Assistant Professor (jointly with Materials Science); Ph.D., Carnegie Mellon, 1993.

Space, Telecommunications and Radioscience Laboratory (STARLab). Electromagnetic waves to probe remote environments and develop communications systems. The Center for Telecommunications research includes space, mobile radio, and optical fiber communications systems.

G. Leonard Tyler, Professor and Director; Ph.D., Stanford, 1967.
Donald C. Cox, Harald Trap Friis Professor; Ph.D., Stanford, 1968.
Antony C. Fraser-Smith, Professor (Research) (jointly with School of Earth Sciences); Ph.D., New Zealand, 1966.
Umran S. Inan, Professor; Ph.D., Stanford, 1977.
Leonid G. Kazovsky, Professor; Ph.D., Leningrad, 1972.
Bruce Lusignan, Associate Professor; Ph.D., Stanford, 1963.
Howard A. Zebker, Associate Professor (jointly with Geophysics); Ph.D., Stanford, 1984.

STANFORD UNIVERSITY

MEDICAL INFORMATION SCIENCES PROGRAM

PROGRAM OF STUDY

The Medical Information Sciences (MIS) Program is an interdepartmental program offering instruction and research opportunities leading to an M.S. or a Ph.D. in medical information sciences (medical informatics). The program is administered by the School of Medicine, but its curriculum and degree requirements are coordinated with the Office of Graduate Studies of the University. The program is designed to train researchers and educators in the field of medical informatics. Emphasis is placed on providing innovations of relevance to clinical medicine or biomedical research. Although Stanford researchers have expertise in a cross section of MIS activities, the University is recognized in particular for its studies of clinical decision making and of the interface between developing technology and the decision sciences. These topics are accordingly emphasized in the program's curriculum. Required courses come from five major topic areas: medical informatics, computer science, decision theory and statistics, biomedicine, and health policy and social issues.

RESEARCH FACILITIES

Five large computing servers and allied student computing clusters are located around campus and are available to all students in the University for instruction, unsponsored research, e-mail, and World Wide Web services. In addition, a number of systems are available to students of computer science, to which MIS trainees may have access for relevant work. Many MIS trainees use the CAMIS computer resources, which are supported by the National Library of Medicine of the NIH. These resources include two large servers and a variety of UNIX, Macintosh, and PC client workstations for instruction and research. Essentially all computing and information resources at Stanford are linked together by a high-speed Internet communications network. Students can consult Stanford's World Wide Web page (http://www-smi.stanford.edu) for more information.

FINANCIAL AID

A limited amount of funding is available to provide research stipend support for students in the program. Most students become associated with projects that provide them with support soon after their arrival at Stanford.

COST OF STUDY

Tuition in 1997–98 is $7100 per quarter. This figure is expected to increase annually.

LIVING AND HOUSING COSTS

Housing is available for both on-campus and off-campus living. On-campus housing for graduate students is limited. The cost of living in the area is relatively high.

STUDENT GROUP

Stanford University has a faculty of about 1,300 members and a total student enrollment of more than 13,000, of whom nearly half are graduate students. The MIS Program, now in its fourteenth year, has 27 graduate students.

STUDENT OUTCOMES

There is a high demand for individuals with formal training in medical informatics. Among the program's 48 graduates, 20 are in academic positions, 19 work in industry, 1 works for a hospital, 2 work for the federal government, 4 are in clinical practice, and 2 are completing residency training.

LOCATION

Stanford is located next to Palo Alto, a community of 60,000, about 35 miles south of San Francisco.

THE UNIVERSITY

Stanford (founded in 1885) is a private, nonsectarian, coeducational university with an international reputation as an outstanding educational and research institution. It operates on the quarter system with a shortened summer session. Among the almost 1,350 faculty members are 9 Nobel laureates and many others who have achieved wide academic distinction. The Medical Information Sciences Program is administered from the offices and laboratory of the Section on Medical Informatics, located in the Stanford Medical Center complex. The University is committed to the principles of affirmative action in the admission of students and in the employment of faculty and staff, and does not use any racial, religious, ethnic, geographic, or sex-related quotas.

APPLYING

Applications for the master's and Ph.D. programs are normally considered for admission in the autumn quarter only and must be submitted with supporting documents no later than the preceding January 1. Applicants must report either GRE or MCAT scores.

CORRESPONDENCE AND INFORMATION

Darlene Vian, Program Administrator
Stanford Medical Center, MSOB X-215
Stanford University
Stanford, California 94305-5479
Telephone: 415-725-3388
Fax: 415-725-7944
E-mail: vian@smi.stanford.edu

For application forms:
Office of Graduate Admissions
Old Union 141
Stanford University
Stanford, California 94305-3005

STANFORD UNIVERSITY
THE FACULTY AND THEIR RESEARCH

Edward H. Shortliffe, M.D., Ph.D., Program Director; Department of Medicine (General Internal Medicine) and, by courtesy, Computer Science. Computer-based medical consultation systems, with emphasis on integrating decision analytic and artificial intelligence techniques.

Lawrence M. Fagan, M.D., Ph.D., Program Co-Director; Department of Medicine (Medical Informatics). Techniques for relating qualitative and quantitative physiological models, design of speech and graphic interfaces for expert systems.

Mark A. Musen, M.D., Ph.D., Director of Admissions; Department of Medicine (General Internal Medicine) and, by courtesy, Computer Science. Computer-based tools for describing the knowledge of how to conduct clinical trials, knowledge-based systems for clinical-trial design and administration.

Russ B. Altman, M.D., Ph.D., Department of Medicine. Application of computing technologies to basic molecular biological problems, particularly the analysis of protein structure and function.

Thomas O. Binford, Ph.D., Department of Computer Science. Sensing, machine perception and computer vision, robotics, geometric modeling, reasoning with geometry, evidential reasoning.

Terrence Blaschke, M.D., Department of Medicine (Clinical Pharmacology). Automated monitoring of therapeutic decisions, pharmacokinetic modeling of drug distribution.

Byron W. Brown Jr., Ph.D., Departments of Statistics and Health Research and Policy. Methodologies for the design and analysis of experiments in all phases of medical research, using mathematical work and computer simulation.

Douglas Brutlag, Ph.D., Department of Biochemistry. Knowledge representation and reasoning, pattern recognition and sequence classification in biological-sequence databases.

Robert W. Carlson, M.D., Department of Medicine (Oncology). Computer-based physician consultation systems for treating patients with cancer and AIDS.

Stanley N. Cohen, M.D., Departments of Genetics and Medicine. Molecular genetics and use of computers for monitoring drug use to assist in therapeutic decisions.

Parvati Dev, Ph.D., SUMMIT. Computers in medical education, hypermedia, 3-D medical imaging, simulation of clinical encounters, virtual reality, cognitive modeling of students.

Alain C. Enthoven, Ph.D., Graduate School of Business. Use of decision analysis techniques in reforming the financing and delivery of health care in the United States.

Edward A. Feigenbaum, Ph.D., Department of Computer Science. Mechanization of scientific reasoning, formalization of scientific knowledge, design of computers for artificial intelligence applications.

James F. Fries, M.D., Department of Medicine (Immunology). National chronic-disease computer databank systems, formal approaches to clinical decision making.

Victor R. Fuchs, Ph.D., Department of Economics. Socioeconomic determinants of health, functioning of health-care markets, relation between health and postindustrial society.

David M. Gaba, M.D., Department of Anesthesia. Human error in anesthesia-related accidents, intelligent decision support for decision making in anesthesia.

Alan M. Garber, M.D., Ph.D., Department of Medicine (General Internal Medicine) and, by courtesy, Economics. Health policy and health economics, particularly methods to forecast the utilization of and expenditures for long-term care of the elderly.

Michael R. Genesereth, Ph.D., Department of Computer Science. Study of logic, with special attention to knowledge representation, automated reasoning, and architecture of agents that operate in the physical world.

Gary H. Glover, Ph.D., Department of Radiology. MR imaging and spectroscopy, particularly chemical-shift resolved tissue characterization.

Mark A. Hlatky, M.D., Departments of Health Research and Policy and Medicine. Costs and outcomes of cardiovascular care, technology assessment, physician decision making, clinical epidemiology.

Samuel Holtzman, Ph.D., Department of Engineering–Economic Systems. Computer-based decision aids for industry and medicine, economics and ethics of medical decision making, modeling of medical preferences.

Ronald A. Howard, Ph.D., Department of Engineering–Economic Systems. Development of systematic, logical procedures for decision making in uncertain, complex, and dynamic settings.

Emmet J. Lamb, M.D., Department of Obstetrics and Gynecology. Clinical infertility, reproductive endocrinology, clinical decision analysis.

Leslie Lenert, M.D., Department of Medicine. Use of mathematical modeling for clinical decision making and quality assurance, with an emphasis on drug therapies.

Marc Levoy, Ph.D., Departments of Computer Science and Electrical Engineering. Computer graphics for scientific data visualization.

Albert Macovski, Ph.D., Department of Electrical Engineering. Systems approach to the imaging of the internal structures of the body.

Sandy A. Napel, Ph.D., Department of Radiology. Visualization of flow from magnetic resonance images; segmentation of tumors from 3-D medical imaging data; multidimensional, multimodality image correlation and display.

Richard A. Olshen, Ph.D., Department of Health Research and Policy. Statistics and mathematics as applied to problems in medicine.

Douglas K. Owens, M.D., Department of Medicine. Technology assessment and the application of decision theory to clinical and health policy problems.

Norbert J. Pelc, Sc.D., Department of Diagnostic Radiology and Nuclear Medicine. Medical imaging modalities, medical imaging, magnetic resonance.

Thomas C. Rindfleisch, Department of Medicine (Medical Informatics), Director, Lane Medical Library. Symbolic systems, integrated workstations for biomedicine, information retrieval from optical databases.

Ross D. Schachter, Ph.D., Department of Engineering–Economic Systems and of Operations Research. Modeling of uncertain processes over time, decision making under uncertainty.

Yuval Shahar, M.D., Ph.D., Department of Medicine. Planning, temporal reasoning, knowledge representation, problem-solving methods, medical decision analysis.

Lee S. Shulman, Ph.D., Graduate School of Education. Clinical judgment and problem solving in medicine and teaching, assessment of professional and clinical expertise in teaching and medicine.

Richard E. Snow, Ph.D., Graduate School of Education. The nature of intelligence, information-processing theories of cognition, evaluation of medical education.

Howard H. Sussman, M.D., Department of Pathology. Laboratory information systems, networking for data sharing.

Amos N. Tversky, Ph.D., Department of Psychology. Heuristics, biases in judgments, decisions under uncertainty.

Gio Wiederhold, Ph.D., Departments of Computer Science, Medicine, and Electrical Engineering. Effective information systems, acquisition of real-time data.

Terry Winograd, Ph.D., Department of Computer Science. Development of conceptual models and interactive structures.

STANFORD UNIVERSITY

SCIENTIFIC COMPUTING AND COMPUTATIONAL MATHEMATICS PROGRAM

PROGRAMS OF STUDY

The SCCM Program was founded in 1988 to provide interdisciplinary graduate training and to foster research in areas of the applied sciences and engineering that require interactions among modeling, mathematical and numerical analysis, and scientific computing. The primary educational goal is to prepare students for research or teaching positions within universities or in industry. Both M.S. and Ph.D. degrees are offered.

Successful research in scientific computing involves formulation of a mathematical model of a phenomenon; mathematical analysis of the model; reduction to a finite dimensional form appropriate for numerical simulation, together with attendant numerical analysis; and computer implementation, including exploitation of appropriate computer architecture. The SCCM program provides training that recognizes the broad interrelation of these four areas but that is also sufficiently focused to provide intellectual rigor and challenge. Mathematical and numerical analysis form the core of the course work offered in the SCCM Program; however, it is important to recognize that such analysis can and should be significantly influenced by an understanding of the application areas of interest on the one hand and developments in computer science and scientific computing on the other. Hence a thorough study of an application area, together with fundamental knowledge of computer science, is also required. A training of the kind outlined is not available through traditional departments; the SCCM program provides unification and coherence to doctoral training involving many disciplines. This is reflected in the truly interdisciplinary nature of the group of faculty members involved in the program.

For Ph.D. students, the majority of the first year is spent taking core courses in mathematical and numerical analysis that form the basis of a written comprehensive exam, usually taken twelve months after arrival. During the first eighteen months, students also typically associate themselves with a research group; thereafter, the majority of time is spent in research, leading to a thesis defense and thesis in this area. Additional course work, augmenting the core material, giving a firm foundation in an application area, and covering important issues in computer science, is also required.

Studying for the M.S. degree primarily involves course work of the same type taken for the Ph.D. degree and usually takes between four and six quarters to complete.

RESEARCH FACILITIES

A variety of computer systems are available to all students in the University. In addition, the SCCM group has a cluster of computers: DECs, SPARCstations, and SGI workstations. Parallel computers are also available through specific research groups. All computers are linked by a University-wide Ethernet system.

FINANCIAL AID

Incoming Ph.D. students are generally supported by a departmental assistantship or by a fellowship. Assistantship holders receive a stipend plus a 9-unit tuition credit each quarter. Master's students are not guaranteed aid. If additional research assistantships become available, they are offered to M.S. students.

COST OF STUDY

For 1997–98, tuition charges for all students not holding assistantships are $7580 per quarter.

LIVING AND HOUSING COSTS

Housing is available both on campus and off campus. On-campus housing is available for married graduate students. The cost of living in the area is relatively high.

STUDENT GROUP

Stanford University has a total student enrollment of 14,000, of whom over half are graduate students. The SCCM Program averages between 30 and 40 graduate students a year.

LOCATION

Stanford has a spacious campus located on the San Francisco peninsula. The San Francisco Bay area is a major and diverse cultural center and is also the site of many industrial corporations and research centers.

THE UNIVERSITY

Stanford is a private, nonsectarian, coeducational university with an international reputation as an outstanding educational and research institution. It operates on the quarter system with a shortened summer session. There are over 1,300 faculty members, many of whom have achieved wide academic distinction.

APPLYING

Applications and all supporting documentation for admission to the Ph.D. program must be received before February 15. Applications for the M.S. program are accepted until August 1, though it is beneficial to apply before March 1 to be eligible for the initial on-campus housing pool. Applicants must submit GRE scores; Ph.D. applicants must also take a GRE Subject Test in math, CS, engineering, or physics.

CORRESPONDENCE AND INFORMATION

Admissions
SCCM Program
Gates 2B, MC 9025, Room 291
Stanford University
Stanford, California 94305-9025

Telephone: 415-723-0572
Fax: 415-723-2411
E-mail: admissions@sccm.stanford.edu

STANFORD UNIVERSITY
THE FACULTY AND THEIR RESEARCH

Program Director
Gene H. Golub.

Associate Program Director
Andrew Stuart.

Core Faculty
Robert Dutton, Ph.D., Department of Electrical Engineering. Computational electronics for the design and manufacturing of integrated circuits.
Gene H. Golub, Ph.D., Department of Computer Science. Design and analysis of algorithms arising in linear algebra, matrix methods in signal processing, large sparse systems of equations.
George M. Homsy, Ph.D., Department of Chemical Engineering. Transport and stability of flows in physical systems, fluid/particle systems, instability and transition in non-Newtonian fluids.
Joseph Keller, Ph.D., Department of Mathematics. Applied mathematics, wave propagation, asymptotic analysis, electromagnetic theory, optics and acoustics.
Walter Murray, Ph.D., Department of Operations Research. Linear and nonlinear programming, sparse matrix methods, linear algebra, theoretical and practical optimization problems.
Joseph Oliger, Ph.D., Department of Computer Science. Numerical analysis, numerical methods for partial differential equations, computer simulation or analysis of physical processes.
George Papanicolaou, Ph.D., Department of Mathematics. Stochastic equations and random media, seismic signal processing and wavelets, singularities in nonlinear waves.
Andrew Stuart, Ph.D., Department of Computer Science and Mechanical Engineering. Numerical analysis of evolution equations, dynamical systems, applied and computational mathematics.

Associate Faculty
Khalid Aziz, Ph.D., Department of Petroleum Engineering. Multiphase flow of oil/gas mixtures and steam in pipes and wells, multiphase flow in porous media, reservoir simulation.
Joel Ferziger, Ph.D., Department of Mechanical Engineering. Computational fluid dynamics, simulation of turbulent flows, flow phenomena, numerical methods for solving the equations of fluid mechanics.
Thomas J. Hughes, Ph.D., Department of Mechanical Engineering. Computational methods to problems in solid and fluid mechanics, including finite element methods for nonlinear plate and shell response.
Thomas Kailath, Ph.D., Department of Electrical Engineering. Signal processing algorithms for various applications, emphasizing speed, numerical robustness, and ease of design and implementation in current technology.
Tai-Ping Liu, Ph.D., Department of Mathematics. Hyperbolic equations and conservation laws.

STATE UNIVERSITY OF NEW YORK AT BINGHAMTON

DEPARTMENT OF COMPUTER SCIENCE

PROGRAMS OF STUDY

The computer science department in the Thomas J. Watson School of Engineering and Applied Science offers graduate degrees leading to the M.S. and Ph.D. degrees in computer science. The department offers a wide variety of courses. Recent and current faculty research areas include computer architecture, computer networks, database systems, distributed systems, information retrieval, fault testing and diagnosis, operating systems, parallel processing, real-time systems, software specification and verification, and VLSI systems.

Doctoral students are required to have a minimum of 24 credit hours in residence. Students have to pass two qualifying exams: a general comprehensive exam and a specialization exam covering the intended area of research. The general comprehensive exam covers the following five areas: algorithms, architecture, operating systems, programming languages, and one of the following: AI, compilers, database, automata theory, or networks. The doctoral candidate is also required to present and defend a prospectus that describes the intended research topic. Finally, the Ph.D. dissertation has to be successfully defended.

To fulfill the requirements for the M.S. degree, students must (1) complete one course in each of the three core areas of architecture and operating systems, programming languages and compilers, and theoretical computer science; (2) complete seven additional courses and pass a comprehensive examination or complete five additional courses and write and defend a thesis; and (3) maintain a B average in all course work.

RESEARCH FACILITIES

In addition to the facilities available through the University Computing Center and the Watson School of Engineering, the department operates several research laboratories. These laboratories are equipped with workstations, high-end PCs, multimedia equipment, and multiprocessor systems. The department is also currently developing an experimental high-bandwidth testbed for addressing research issues in a network of tightly coupled workstations.

The department has research collaborations with local industry such as IBM, Loral, Lockheed Martin, Hughes Training, and Universal. The department also has strong ties with Watson School research centers such as the Center for Computing Technologies and the Integrated Electronics Engineering Center.

FINANCIAL AID

The department awards approximately twenty teaching assistantships and a number of research assistantships each year. Requests for assistantships can be indicted on the Graduate Admissions application form; no separate form is required.

COST OF STUDY

For full-time matriculated graduate students, tuition in 1996–97 cost $2779 per semester for state residents and $4437 per semester for nonresidents.

LIVING AND HOUSING COSTS

A recently completed apartment complex, the Graduate Community, has 3- and 4-person apartments, with living room, dining area, kitchen, and bath. Based on a 1996–97 academic-year lease, the semester rate for a single bedroom was $1975, and for a double bedroom, $1710 per person and $2995 per couple. The cost of meal plans per semester is as follows: basic, $767; standard, $927; and ultra, $1027. Assistance in locating off-campus housing is provided by the listing services of Off-Campus College.

STUDENT GROUP

Of the 11,978 students enrolled at Binghamton University, 2,697 are graduate students. In the Watson School, there are 566 undergraduates and 384 graduate students. Many obtain jobs in local high-technology enterprises during their enrollment at the School and after graduation.

LOCATION

The University's 606-acre campus is in a suburban setting just west of Binghamton. More than 300,000 people live within commuting distance of the campus. Cultural offerings in the community include the museum and programs of the Roberson Center for the Arts and Sciences as well as performances by the Binghamton Symphony, Tri-Cities Opera, Civic Theater, and other groups. The University's Art Gallery has a permanent collection representing all periods and also displays works from special loan exhibitions. The annual concert series of the Anderson Center brings a wide variety of performing artists to campus. The Department of Theater stages more than twenty-five productions each year.

THE UNIVERSITY AND THE SCHOOL

The State University of New York at Binghamton is one of four university centers in the State University of New York System. The faculty numbers about 700. Graduate programs were initiated in 1961 with the establishment of Master of Arts programs in English and mathematics.

The Watson School was created in 1983 by combining the established graduate programs in computer science and systems science from the School of Advanced Technology with new programs in electrical and mechanical engineering.

APPLYING

Applicants should have a baccalaureate degree in computer science or a closely related field and must submit official transcripts, GRE scores, two letters of recommendation (three for Ph.D. applicants), and a statement of personal academic goals. For international students, TOEFL results and a statement of financial means are also required. Application forms are available from the Office of Graduate Admissions. To ensure consideration for assistantships, admission credentials should be received by February 15.

CORRESPONDENCE AND INFORMATION

Associate Dean for Academic Affairs
Computer Science Admissions
Thomas J. Watson School
State University of New York at Binghamton
P.O. Box 6000
Binghamton, New York 13902-6000
World Wide Web: http://www.cs.binghamton.edu

STATE UNIVERSITY OF NEW YORK AT BINGHAMTON

THE FACULTY AND THEIR RESEARCH

Sudhir Aggarwal, Professor and Department Chair; Ph.D., Michigan, 1975. Distributed systems, protocols, simulation, networks, real-time systems.

Joseph V. Cornacchio, Professor; Ph.D., Syracuse, 1962. Distributed computer systems with emphasis on design, distributed operating systems.

Michal Cutler, Associate Professor; Ph.D., Weizmann (Israel), 1979. Design automation, information retrieval, expert systems.

Richard Eckert, Associate Professor; Ph.D., Kansas, 1971. Computer graphics, human-computer interaction, computer architecture, microprocessor-based systems, computer science education.

Dennis Foreman, Lecturer; M.S., SUNY at Binghamton, 1974. Design and development of operating systems and computers.

Kanad Ghose, Associate Professor; Ph.D., Iowa State, 1988. Parallel processing, computer architecture, VLSI architectures, distributed systems, operating systems.

Vipul Gupta, Assistant Professor; Ph.D., Rutgers, 1994. Parallel and distributed processing, architecture, networks.

Margaret E. Iwobi, Lecturer; M.S., SUNY at Binghamton, 1975. Software engineering principles, software development environments.

Walker Land, Lecturer; M.S., George Washington, 1964. Neural networks, evolutionary computing, object-oriented design, systematic design and applications.

Leslie Lander, Associate Professor; Ph.D., Liverpool, 1973. Formal aspects of software engineering, programming languages and paradigms.

Weiyi Meng, Assistant Professor; Ph.D., Illinois at Chicago, 1992. Internet-based information retrieval, heterogeneous database systems, query optimization and translation.

Walter G. Piotrowski, Associate Professor; Ph.D., SUNY at Binghamton, 1990. Operating systems, distributed systems and networks.

Stephen Y. H. Su, Professor; Ph.D., Wisconsin–Madison, 1967. Fault-tolerant computing, design automation, computer architecture.

William L. Ziegler, Associate Professor; M.S., Syracuse, 1982. Programming languages and paradigms, computer architecture, university-industry collaboration.

STATE UNIVERSITY OF NEW YORK AT BINGHAMTON

DEPARTMENT OF ELECTRICAL ENGINEERING

PROGRAMS OF STUDY

The Department of Electrical Engineering in the Thomas J. Watson School of Engineering and Applied Science offers the B.S., M.S., and Ph.D. degrees. Course work for both the M.S. and Ph.D. is available through EngiNet, the Watson School system for distance learning.

The M.S.E.E. requires the student to complete either of two optional courses of study. The thesis option requires seven lecture courses plus a thesis and a seminar course. The project option requires nine lecture courses plus a project and a seminar focused on research literature. In both options, the lecture courses selected must meet breadth and depth requirements. M.S.E.E. students specialize in one of the research areas listed below. The normal period for completion of a master's degree is 1½ years of full-time study.

Requirements for the Ph.D. degree are based on individual learning contracts and normally take three years beyond the master's degree. There is a broad preliminary examination and a comprehensive examination followed by the satisfactory defense of a dissertation. Residence requirement is 24 credit hours.

RESEARCH FACILITIES

The Watson School has excellent access to advanced computing facilities. An IBM 9121 linked to a network of Sun workstations and advanced PCs, as well as to the University computer networks and mainframes.

Since the Watson School was first established in 1983, it has developed an international reputation in the multidisciplinary research speciality of electronics packaging. This research is housed in the Watson School's Integrated Electronics Engineering Center (IEEC). The IEEC is also a designated National Science Foundation state/industry/university cooperative research center and in 1993, it became a New York State Center for Advanced Technology (CAT). The IEEC also administers equipment that supports both local industry and University research.

The Science and Engineering Library is part of the University library system, which has a total collection of more than 2 million items. On-line access to other SUNY collections exists through the campus computer network. Resources are supplemented by membership in academic library consortia, notably the Research Libraries Group, Inc.

FINANCIAL AID

Many students hold fellowships, traineeships, or assistantships (graduate, research, or teaching). Most awards include a full or partial waiver of tuition and medical benefits. Other sources of financial aid include the New York State Tuition Assistance Program, the Federal Stafford Student Loan Program, the graduate and professional school College Work-Study Program, and campus jobs.

COST OF STUDY

For full-time matriculated graduate students, tuition in 1996–97 was $2779 per semester for state residents and $4437 per semester for nonresidents.

LIVING AND HOUSING COSTS

The campus graduate community housing has 3- and 4-person apartments, with living room, dining area, kitchen, and bath. Based on a 1996–97 academic-year lease, the semester rate for a single bedroom was $1975, and for a double bedroom, $1710 per person and $2995 per family apartment. The cost of meal plans per semester was as follows: basic, $767; standard, $927; and ultra, $1027. Assistance in locating cheaper off-campus housing is provided by the listing services of the Off-Campus College.

STUDENT GROUP

Of the 11,978 students enrolled at Binghamton University, 3,000 are graduate students. In the Watson School, there are 566 undergraduates and 384 graduate students.

The Department of Electrical Engineering enrolled its first freshmen in 1995, having offered only upper-division undergraduate programs previously. Current approximate enrollments of 40 juniors, 40 seniors, 30 full-time and 35 part-time master's students, and 22 Ph.D. students permit the individual faculty attention for which the Department is known.

LOCATION

The University's 606-acre campus is in a suburban setting just west of Binghamton, which is itself conveniently situated among the major cities of the Northeast: 200 miles from New York, Philadelphia, and Buffalo and 300 miles from Toronto, Boston, Montreal, Pittsburgh, and Washington, D.C. More than 300,000 people live within commuting distance of the campus. Cultural offerings in the community include the museum and programs of the Roberson Center for the Arts and Sciences, as well as performances by the Binghamton Symphony Tri-Cities Opera, Cider Mill Theater, and other groups.

THE UNIVERSITY AND THE SCHOOL

The State University of New York at Binghamton is one of the four university centers in the 64-campus State University of New York system. The faculty numbers about 700. Graduate programs were initiated in 1961 with the establishment of Master of Arts programs in English and mathematics.

The University's Art Gallery has a permanent collection representing all periods and also displays works from special loan exhibitions. The Anderson Center's annual concert series brings a wide variety of performing artists to campus. The Department of Theater stages more than twenty-five productions each year.

The Watson School was created in 1983 by combining the established graduate programs in computer science and systems science from the School of Advanced Technology with new graduate programs in electrical and mechanical engineering. The first electrical engineering juniors were admitted in 1984.

APPLYING

Holders of a bachelor's degree in electrical engineering or related discipline from any recognized college or university are eligible to apply. Application forms are available from the Office of Graduate Admissions. Applicants should submit GRE General Test scores. (Graduates of ABET–accredited engineering programs may apply for waiver of this requirement.) International applicants must submit TOEFL scores and provide proof of their ability to meet academic expenses. All credentials should be on file at least one month prior to anticipated enrollment. To ensure consideration for assistantship and fellowship awards, admission credentials should be received by February 15.

CORRESPONDENCE AND INFORMATION

Graduate Adviser, Department of Electrical Engineering
Thomas J. Watson School of Engineering and Applied Science
Binghamton University, State University of New York
Binghamton, New York 13902-6000
Telephone: 607-777-4856
Fax: 607-777-4464

STATE UNIVERSITY OF NEW YORK AT BINGHAMTON

THE FACULTY

Craig Bergman, Lecturer; M.S., Illinois at Urbana–Champaign, 1975. Digital design, microprocessors, human factors. (cbergman@binghamton.edu)

William Blose, Lecturer; M.S., SUNY at Binghamton, 1979. Semiconductor device modeling, semiconductor processing, VLSI chip design. (blose@binghamton.edu)

Nikolaos Bourbakis, Associate Professor; Ph.D, Patras (Greece), 1983. Applied AI robotics, knowledge-based VLSI design, computer vision, text and image processing, multiprocessor system architectures, neural nets, automated software environment. (bourbaki@binghamton.edu)

Monish Chatterjee, Associate Professor; Ph.D, Iowa, 1985. Nonlinear wave phenomena, nonlinear modeling, quantum electronics, acoustooptics, fiber-optics and optical communications. (mrchat@binghamton.edu)

James Constable, Professor; Ph.D, Ohio State, 1969; PE. Instrumentation, cryogenics, electrical noise, contact resistance, electronics packaging. (constab@binghamton.edu)

Jose Delgado-Frias, Associate Professor; Ph.D, Texas A&M, 1986. Computer engineering, VLSI/WSI design, parallel computer architectures, interconnection networks, novel computing paradigms. (jdf@parallel.ee.binghamton.edu)

Jiayuan Fang, Associate Professor; Ph.D, Berkeley, 1989. Computational electromagnetics, electronic packaging and interconnects, microwaves. (fangj@binghamton.edu)

Linda Head, Assistant Professor; Ph.D, South Florida, 1990. Thin-film reliability, noise theory, surface mount technology. (lhead@binghamton.edu)

Douglas Hopkins, Assistant Professor; Ph.D., Virginia Tech, 1989. Power electronics, high-density power packaging. (hopkins@bingsuns.cc.binghamton.edu)

James Morris, Professor; Ph.D, Saskatchewan, 1971; PE. Thick and thin films, semiconductor devices, electronics, engine sensors and control, electronics packaging, materials, engineering education. (jmorris@binghamton.edu)

Dhananjay Phatak, Assistant Professor; Ph.D, Massachusetts Amherst, 1994. Computer architectures, computer arithmetic, neural networks and applications. (phatak@ee.binghamton.edu)

George Sackman, Professor; Ph.D, Stanford, 1964; PE. Signal processing, acoustic space-time array processing, digital audio, microwave electronics, engineering education. (sackman@bingtjw.cc.binghamton.edu)

Richard Schwartz, Emeritus Professor; Ph.D, Pennsylvania, 1959; PE. Microwave theory, antennas and propagation, acoustics, signal processing, engineering education. (schwartz@bingtjw.cc.binghamton.edu)

Victor Skormin, Professor; Ph.D, Moscow, 1975. Control engineering, operations research, computer simulation. (skormin@binghamton.edu)

Charles Taylor, Associate Professor; M.S., SUNY at Binghamton, 1970. Automatic controls, microprocessor applications, robotics. (ctaylor@spectra.net)

Peter Wagner, Professor; Ph.D, Berkeley, 1956. Semiconductor circuit elements, microwave resonance, surface electricity, applied optics. (pwagner@bingsuns.cc.binghamton.edu)

N.Eva Wu, Associate Professor; Ph.D, Minnesota, 1987. Approximation, optimization, and stabilization of distributed parameter systems; robust control synthesis theory; control of robotic manipulators; signal processing. (evawu@bingsuns.cc.binghamton.edu)

ADJUNCT FACULTY

Stephen Czarnecki, Loral Corporation; Ph.D, Princeton, 1983. Communications.

Mohammed Islam, IBM Corporation (Retired); Ph.D., Northeastern, 1964. Electromagnetics, microwaves.

John Pivnichny, IBM Corporation; Ph.D, Michigan, 1971. Control systems.

Theresa Sadeghi, M.S., Rensselaer, 1978. Control systems.

Charles Standish, IBM Corporation (Retired); Ph.D, Cornell, 1954. Systems theory.

RESEARCH AREAS OF SPECIALIZATION

Computer Engineering (Bergman, Bourbakis, Delgado-Frias, Phatak, Taylor).

The unifying theme to the department's research in computer engineering is the study of computer architectures and digital systems. Novel computer concepts are first simulated to demonstrate potential capabilities and constructed for demonstration and verification of the special features of interest. Such machines developed in the department include a loosely coupled machine, RISC processors, multiprocessor vision system architectures, a synaptic connection machine, and a fast neural network architecture. There is also widespread activity in the applications of artificial intelligence concepts, including neural network applications, genetic algorithms, and the development of computer vision systems. Industrial applications of digital and microprocessor systems and microcontrollers are also supported by a general purpose development system.

Electrophysics (Blose, Chatterjee, Constable, Fang, Head, Hopkins, Morris, Wagner)

The group has a strong focus on research related to electronics packaging. This interest includes interconnect development and evaluation, including research on electrically conductive adhesives, metal-polymer systems, predictive testing for interconnect reliability, contact resistance of engineered surfaces, and noise analysis. Thin-film research is supported by a range of vacuum deposition techniques and focuses on the properties and applications of discontinuous (island) metal films and on noise and electromigration in thin-film VLSI interconnect lines. There are also noise studies of MESFETS and photovoltaics. Recent work in device modeling includes pulse thyristors and RTDs. Power electronics includes research on high-voltage and high-temperature modules, very high density multilayer power structures for telecommunications, power supplies, and motor drives.

The department is nationally known for its work in computational electromagnetics and in accurate and efficient modeling of VLSI and printed circuit board interconnections. Other recent work in electromagnetics includes cellular phone field strength modeling and near field radio propagation. Recent projects in optoelectronics have included fiber-optics, soliton theory, holographic optical interconnects, spatial multiplexing of 3D scenes using pixelated computer-generated holography, optical logic gates using acoustooptic feedback, and electromagnetic propagation in complex media.

Systems (Bourbakis, Chatterjee, Sackman, Skormin, Taylor, Wagner, Wu).

Most recent research in signal processing has been concentrated in acoustics and digital audio. There is also an ongoing project in image processing (see computer vision). Within the communications category, work is concentrated in fiber optics and radio propagation.

The controls group enjoys strong ties to local industry, including aerospace, flight simulation, power generation and reticulation, electronics assembly, electrical vehicle, and materials processing the industries, among others. The control systems research group members have special interests in the applications of simulation, robotics, and embedded control in support of these areas and in the development of new theoretical techniques.

STATE UNIVERSITY OF NEW YORK AT BUFFALO

DEPARTMENT OF COMPUTER SCIENCE

PROGRAMS OF STUDY

The Department of Computer Science at Buffalo offers programs of study leading to the degrees of Doctor of Philosophy and Master of Science. Courses cover a wide range of interests, with particular research emphasis on the areas of artificial intelligence, expert systems, parallel systems, pattern recognition, parallel computations, natural-language processing, computer vision, analysis of algorithms, theory of computation, VLSI algorithms, performance evaluation, and numerical analysis.

Doctoral students are required to pass a comprehensive qualifying examination in computer science and submit a dissertation that describes original independent research. The Ph.D. is awarded in recognition of high achievement in research, and the program is intended for persons interested in research careers.

For the M.S. degree, students must complete at least 30 credits of course work. These 30 credits must include either a thesis (usually 6 credits) or a project (usually 3 credits), or the student must pass the Ph.D. qualifying examination at the master's level.

RESEARCH FACILITIES

The department's research facilities include more than fifty Sun Workstations, several SPARCserver systems, and numerous X-window terminals. The department is connected to Internet for electronic mail, file transfer, and remote log-in. Macintoshes are readily available. CIT, the University computing service, has a network of many terminals or workstations, a cluster of SPARC-based timesharing equipment, and a DEC Alpha running VMS.

FINANCIAL AID

A variety of assistantships and fellowships, available for qualified graduate students, carry support levels of up to $13,150 plus tuition remission for the nine-month 1997–98 academic year. Teaching assistants are assigned part-time duties in the instructional program or in support of departmental laboratories. Research assistants are supported part-time on faculty-supervised research projects.

Opportunities exist for summer support in both research and teaching.

COST OF STUDY

For 1997–98, tuition for full-time study (12 or more credits) is $5112 per academic year for New York State residents and $8424 per academic year for out-of-state students. (For supported students, 9 credits is considered full-time.) Other University fees and required health insurance total approximately $500 in the first year.

LIVING AND HOUSING COSTS

Graduate students live off campus or in university housing. In 1997–98, rooms in the residence halls cost $3330 for a single and $2710 for a double per academic year, plus approximately $2100 per year for board.

STUDENT GROUP

There are 90 full-time graduate students in the department. Most students are recent graduates, but some acquired professional experience before returning to graduate school.

STUDENT OUTCOMES

Recent Ph.D. employment is evenly divided between academics and industry. Many hold tenure-track, teaching, or postdoctoral positions in American universities, and others are research scientists, software engineers, and senior programmer/analysts at companies that include Xerox, AT&T Bell Labs, Hewlett-Packard, and Disney.

LOCATION

The University is located in western New York State just outside Buffalo and near Niagara Falls. The area's recreational activities include swimming, boating, and fishing on the Great Lakes in summer and skiing and sledding in winter. Hiking and camping are available in nearby parks. Buffalo is home to the Buffalo Philharmonic Orchestra, the Albright-Knox Art Gallery, and an active theater district. Many professional sports teams are based in Buffalo, including the Bills (football), Sabres (hockey), and Bisons (baseball). Toronto is an easy drive north. The weather, tempered by Lake Erie to the west, is cool in summer and mild in winter.

THE UNIVERSITY

With a student enrollment of 23,600 the State University of New York at Buffalo is the largest of the four University Centers of the State University of New York. It offers comprehensive study in the arts and sciences and in the schools of engineering, management, law, medicine, dentistry, and health-related professions.

APPLYING

Applications for the fall semester should be submitted by December 31. For further information and application forms, prospective applicants should write to the address given below.

CORRESPONDENCE AND INFORMATION

Director of Graduate Studies
Department of Computer Science
226 Bell Hall
State University of New York at Buffalo
Buffalo, New York 14260-2000

Telephone: 716-645-3180 Ext. 4
Fax: 716-645-3464
E-mail: benzel@cs.buffalo.edu
World Wide Web: http://www.cs.buffalo.edu/

STATE UNIVERSITY OF NEW YORK AT BUFFALO

THE FACULTY AND THEIR RESEARCH

Jin-Yi Cai, Professor; Ph.D., Cornell. Complexity theory.

Sreejit Chakravarty, Associate Professor; Ph.D., SUNY at Albany. VLSI testing, VLSI algorithms, design automation.

Ashim Garg, Assistant Professor; Ph.D., Brown. Graph visualization.

Xin He, Associate Professor; Ph.D., Ohio State. Parallel algorithms, data structures, combinatorial complexity.

Bharadwaj Jayaraman, Associate Professor; Ph.D., Utah. Declarative programming languages, parallel processing.

Helene Kershner, Lecturer and Assistant Chairman; M.S.E., Pennsylvania. Computer science education, computer literacy.

Russ Miller, Professor; Ph.D., SUNY at Binghamton. Algorithms for parallel architecture.

Bina Ramamurthy, Teaching Assistant Professor; Ph.D., SUNY at Buffalo. Computer systems.

William Rapaport, Associate Professor; Ph.D., Indiana. Artificial intelligence, cognitive science, logic.

Kenneth W. Regan, Associate Professor; D.Phil., Oxford. Theoretical computer science, mathematical logic.

Alan L. Selman, Professor; Ph.D., Penn State. Complexity theory.

Stuart C. Shapiro, Professor and Chairman; Ph.D., Wisconsin–Madison. Artificial intelligence, computational linguistics, representation of knowledge, inference.

Wennie Wei Shu, Associate Professor; Ph.D., Illinois at Urbana-Champaign. Operating systems, compiler optimization, computer architecture.

Sargur N. Srihari, Distinguished Professor of Computer Science; Ph.D., Ohio State. Artificial intelligence, computer vision, pattern recognition.

Deborah K. W. Walters, Associate Professor; Ph.D., Birmingham (England). Computational vision, interactive image processing.

Min-You Wu, Assistant Professor; Ph.D., Santa Clara. Parallel systems.

Aidong Zhang, Assistant Professor; Ph.D., Purdue. Databases.

Adjunct Faculty

Raj Acharya, Associate Professor, Department of Electrical and Computer Engineering; Ph.D., Minnesota.

Patrick Dowd, Assistant Professor, Department of Electrical and Computer Engineering; Ph.D., Syracuse. Computer architecture, photonic networks.

Herbert Hauptman, Professor, Department of Biophysical Sciences; Ph.D., Maryland. X-ray crystallography.

Shambhu Upadhyaya, Associate Professor, Department of Electrical and Computer Engineering; Ph.D., Newcastle (Australia).

Research Faculty

Venugopal Govindaraju, Research Assistant Professor; Ph.D., SUNY at Buffalo. Pattern recognition.

Henry Hexmoor, Research Assistant Professor; Ph.D., SUNY at Buffalo. Artificial intelligence.

Jeannette Neal, Research Assistant Professor; Ph.D., SUNY at Buffalo. Natural language understanding.

Rohini Srihari, Research Assistant Professor; Ph.D., SUNY at Buffalo. Natural language understanding, on-line handwriting recognition, vision-language interfaces.

Zhongfei Zhang, Research Assistant Professor; Ph.D., Massachusetts. Pattern recognition.

STATE UNIVERSITY OF NEW YORK
AT BUFFALO

DEPARTMENT OF ELECTRICAL AND COMPUTER ENGINEERING

PROGRAMS OF STUDY

The department offers M.S., M.Eng., and Ph.D. programs. The M.S. requires 1–1½ years of full-time study. Students taking the M.S. thesis option must complete at least eight graduate courses. Core courses are required in systems. Students electing the all-course option must take a minimum of ten graduate courses and pass a comprehensive examination. The Ph.D. generally requires a minimum of two years of full-time study beyond the master's degree. Students must pass a qualifying examination and successfully complete dissertation research. Students in the M.Eng. program must take at least eight graduate courses, including suggested courses, and successfully complete a project.

Specialization and research programs are in computer engineering, communications, signal processing, systems, materials, high voltage, and electronics. Computer engineering areas of research include computer networks, parallel and distributed computing, computer architecture, software engineering, VLSI, operating systems, switching networks, ATM- and WDM-based network research, reconfigurable distributed architectures for high-performance clustering, FPGS and VLSI design, and real-time fault-tolerant operating systems. Areas of systems research include systems theory, control theory, communications theory, photonic networks, estimation and detection, digital signal processing, radar systems, adaptive filtering, and biomedical image processing. The areas of materials, high voltage, and electronics include power and plasma devices, solid-state electronics, circuit interruption, fault current limiting, pulsed-power and high-power switching, and power conversion; high-voltage electrical insulation and dielectric materials; space power systems; plasma processing and plasma-material interactions; laser physics, laser-material interactions, laser optics, and quantum electronics; computational photonics and fiber optics; electron devices; semiconductor electronics, electromagnetic compatibility, microelectronics, and VLSI; photovoltaics, thin-film deposition and device processing, and semiconductor material and device characterization; compound semiconductor growth by LPE and MOCVD; carrier dynamics in semiconductors; lattice-mismatched and strained heteroepitaxial layers; sensors and electronic instrumentation; optical confocal microscopy; high-T_c superconductors and applications; atmospheric environment, air pollution, and particulate-emission control; and theoretical studies in wave propagation and diffraction.

RESEARCH FACILITIES

The University and the department have an extensive computing infrastructure, including Sun, SGI, and DEC Alpha workstations and workstation clusters; multiprocessors; a VAX Calphal cluster; and an IBM mainframe. Equipment is available for work in modern control systems, switching logic, sensors, and electronic instrumentation. Optical confocal microscopes supply images of biological and electronic samples. High-power facilities are available for use in high-voltage DC interruption experiments and power device research and development activities. Laser facilities include UV lasers, picosecond and femtosecond lasers, tunable lasers, and a streak camera. The microwave laboratory is equipped with four HP8510 network analyzers. The Plasma Processing Laboratory is equipped with a low-pressure plasma spray system and RF and DC discharge reactors. The laboratory also has advanced diagnostics, including emission spectroscopy and laser-Doppler velocimetry, for characterizing thermal plasmas. Computer programs are also available for numerical modeling of thermal plasmas and calculation of plasma properties. Facilities exist for semiconductor growth, thin-film deposition, device fabrication, and characterization, including LPE, MOCVD, SEM, DLTS, double-crystal X-ray rocking curve, and low-temperature Hall effect equipment. Modern facilities for processing and characterization of high-T_c superconductors are also available in the New York State Institute on Superconductivity, which is located in the department.

FINANCIAL AID

A number of teaching assistantships are available, with a minimum stipend of $10,000 plus a tuition scholarship. Research assistantships are available through research grants. There are also a number of Presidential Fellowships in the amount of $3000, which are available from the State University of New York as supplements to the teaching and research assistantship stipends.

COST OF STUDY

For 1996–97, full-time tuition was $2871 per semester for New York State residents and $4529 per semester for nonresidents. Students receiving financial aid from the University or the department are normally granted a tuition scholarship.

LIVING AND HOUSING COSTS

Graduate students generally live off campus, and the Off-Campus Housing Office maintains a file of housing accommodations in various price ranges.

STUDENT GROUP

The University's student population numbers about 25,000 and includes more than 6,800 graduate students. There are approximately 260 graduate students in electrical and computer engineering.

STUDENT OUTCOMES

Graduates of the M.S. and Ph.D. programs obtain positions in engineering, research, and research and development with companies ranging from multinationals to entrepreneurials. The graduates' professional areas include materials, semiconductors, telecommunications systems design, biomedical imaging, and multidimensional confocal imaging. Many of the doctoral graduates enter positions in academia (both domestic and international) and conduct research in areas such as semiconductors, MOCVD growth, optical communication systems, and large network system development.

LOCATION

Buffalo, in western New York along the Niagara River and the shores of Lake Erie, has a metropolitan-area population of 1 million. Cultural and recreational interests include museums, art galleries, a concert hall, a botanical garden, a zoological park, a sports auditorium, major-league football, a symphony orchestra, and several academic institutions. Western New York offers opportunities for many outdoor activities, and nearby Canada has numerous resources for cultural events and sports.

THE UNIVERSITY AND THE DEPARTMENT

Formerly named the University of Buffalo, the institution was founded in 1846 as a medical school. About 1947, the state of New York formed a state university system and in 1962, it selected the University of Buffalo as one of its units. The University has two principal campuses: the Main Street Campus (178 acres, located in the northeast corner of Buffalo) and the Amherst Campus (more than 1,000 acres, 3 miles away). The Department of Electrical and Computer Engineering, established in 1945, is located on the Amherst Campus.

APPLYING

Applications for admission with financial aid must be completed by February 1 for September admission in order to ensure consideration for aid and assistantships. If no financial assistance is desired, two months should be allowed for the processing of an application before the start of any semester; international students should allow more time. All new applicants (except those for the M.Eng. program) are required to take the GRE General Test. International applicants must also supply TOEFL scores.

CORRESPONDENCE AND INFORMATION

Graduate Admissions
Department of Electrical and Computer Engineering
201 Bell Hall
State University of New York at Buffalo
Amherst, New York 14260

Telephone: 716-645-2422
Fax: 716-645-3656
World Wide Web: http://www.eng.buffalo.edu

STATE UNIVERSITY OF NEW YORK AT BUFFALO

THE FACULTY AND THEIR RESEARCH

Department Chairman: James J. Whalen.
Department Associate Chairmen: Donald D. Givone and Wayne A. Anderson.

Raj S. Acharya, Ph.D., Minnesota. Multimedia computing, visualization, image processing, fractals.

Wayne A. Anderson, Ph.D., SUNY at Buffalo. Semiconductors, thin-film techniques, photovoltaics, microelectronics, defects in semiconductors.

Stella N. Batalama, Ph.D., Virginia. Wireless communications, adaptive signal processing, detection and estimation theory and applications.

David M. Benenson, Ph.D., Caltech. Arc plasmas, plasma physics, circuit breakers, switching, plasma diagnostics, plasma processing, power, gasdynamics, acoustics.

Alexander N. Cartwright, Ph.D., Iowa. Ultrafast laser spectroscopy and imaging of semiconductor heterostructures and photonic devices.

Ping-chin Cheng, Ph.D., Illinois. Microscopy and lithography, biomedical imaging.

Victor Demjanenko, Ph.D., SUNY at Buffalo. Computer networks, operating systems, computer architecture.

Patrick W. Dowd, Ph.D., Syracuse. Parallel and distributed computer systems, performance analysis, computer communication.

Kasra Etemadi, Ph.D., Minnesota. Thermal plasma processing, plasma diagnostics.

Adly T. Fam, Ph.D., California, Irvine. Digital signal processing, parallel computing, systems theory and digital control.

A. Scott Gilmour Jr., Emeritus; Ph.D., Cornell. Power conditioning, power conversion, electromagnetic fields, electron devices.

Donald D. Givone, Ph.D., Cornell. Switching-circuit theory, automata theory, digital systems.

Raj K. Kaul, Ph.D., Columbia. Mathematical analysis, wave propagation and diffraction theory.

Alfred M. Kriman, Ph.D., Princeton. Theory of quantum electronic devices, semiconductor plasmas.

Javaid R. Laghari, Ph.D., SUNY at Buffalo. High voltage, pulsed power, dielectrics and insulation.

Pao-Lo Liu, Ph.D., Harvard. Photonic devices and computational photonics.

Nihar R. Mahapatra, Ph.D., Minnesota. Parallel and distributed processing, low power, VLSI and architecture, high-speed networking, mobile computing and fault tolerance.

Dennis P. Malone, Ph.D., Yale. Metal vapor plasmas, plasma diagnostics, quantum electronics, atomic and molecular physics.

Stephen G. Margolis, Emeritus; Ph.D., Pittsburgh. Systems and computer engineering.

Hinrich R. Martens, Ph.D., Michigan State. Digital control systems, modeling of dynamic systems, computer interfacing.

Dimitris A. Pados, Ph.D., Virginia. Communications, adaptive antenna and radar arrays, neural networks.

Chunming Qiao, Ph.D., Pittsburgh. Parallel and distributed processing, switching, network architectures, optic communications.

Mohammed Safiuddin, Ph.D., SUNY at Buffalo. Industrial automation and control, energy conservation, technology management.

Walter J. Sarjeant, Ph.D., Western Ontario. Pulsed power, high-voltage engineering.

Erich Schmitt, Emeritus; Ph.D., Karlsruhe (Germany). Digital systems, computer applications.

Peter D. Scott, Ph.D., Cornell. Machine vision, systems analysis.

David T. Shaw, Ph.D., Purdue. Ultrathin films, superconducting materials processing, particle formation and measurement, nanophase materials, holographic techniques, laser-ablation techniques.

Mehrdad Soumekh, Ph.D., Minnesota. Signal and image processing, inverse scattering.

Ramalingam Sridhar, Ph.D., Washington State. Digital systems, computer architecture, VLSI design.

Ozan K. Tonguz, Ph.D., Rutgers. Mobile and personal communication systems, fiber-optic communications, photonic networks, telecommunications.

Shambhu J. Upadhyaya, Ph.D., Newcastle (Australia). Fault-tolerant computing, reliability, VLSI testing, diagnostic reasoning.

James J. Whalen, Ph.D., Johns Hopkins. Semiconductor electronics, electromagnetic compatibility, microelectronics.

Chu Ryang Wie, Ph.D., Caltech. Semiconductor materials, surfaces and interfaces, heterostructures of III-V compounds.

Darold C. Wobschall, Ph.D., SUNY at Buffalo. Experimental instrumentation, atmospheric ions.

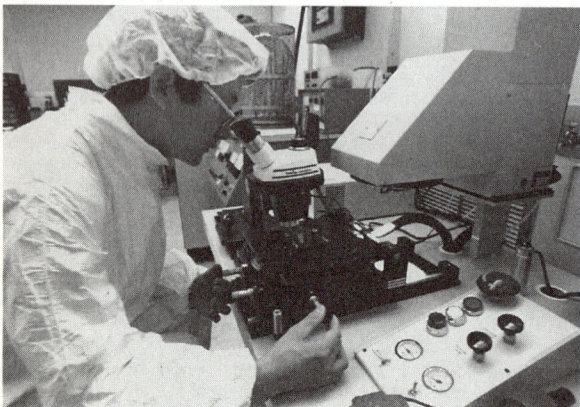

Clean Room. Making a pattern on a semiconductor wafer.

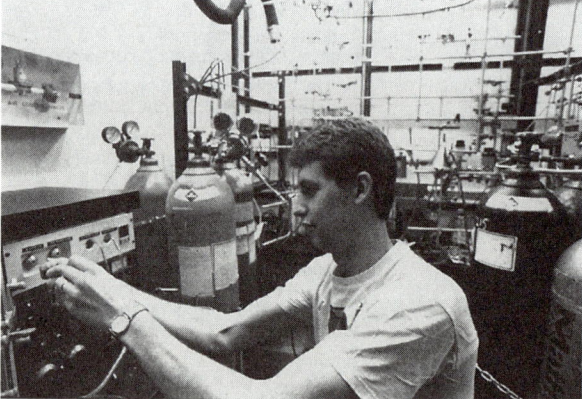

Setting up an experiment in a laboratory of the New York State Institute on Superconductivity.

STATE UNIVERSITY OF NEW YORK AT STONY BROOK

DEPARTMENT OF COMPUTER SCIENCE

PROGRAMS OF STUDY

The department offers graduate programs leading to the Ph.D. and M.S. degrees in computer science and the Certificate in Software Engineering. At present, active research areas include algorithms, automated deduction, computer architecture, computer networks, concurrency, database systems, distributed processing, graphics, knowledge representation, multimedia, operating systems, programming environments, programming languages, software engineering, theory of computation, transaction processing, and visualization. Specialized laboratories are listed below, as is the departmental World Wide Web site.

RESEARCH FACILITIES

The department has available some 190 machines, including forty-five Sun SLC/ELCs, twenty-two Sun IPX's, five SPARC10's, six SPARC5's, eight Sun IPCs, thirteen SPARC20's (4 CPU), a SPARC 1000, two Sun Ultras, twenty-three HP 9000's, three SGIs (4 CPU each), an SGI Power Challenge (16 CPU, 3 GB RAM), twelve 75-Mhz Pentiums, twenty 133-Mhz Pentiums, and eighteen Macs. The SPARC 20's, the SPARC 1000, and the Challenge are on a 155Mb/sec (OC3) ATM switch. The department network is a switched Ethernet with a 2.6 GB/sec backbone. Total disk storage space is more than 100 GB.

The engineering library adjunct for computer science, located within the Computer Science Building, provides a pleasant environment for serious study and houses a collection of more than 10,000 books, bound volumes of journals, conference proceedings, and technical reports.

Among the specialized laboratories supported by the department are ones dedicated to graphics, image processing, logic programming and database design, networking systems experimentation, transaction processing, visualization, and multimedia.

FINANCIAL AID

Teaching and research assistantships are available to qualified entering graduate students and carry support levels that can exceed $29,000. This includes summer supplements, fellowships, tuition remission, and health insurance benefits as described below.

Teaching assistantships are generally available only to first-year Ph.D. students and research assistantships to continuing Ph.D. students. The department also coordinates graduate assistantships (SPIR grants), which are funded by surrounding industry and available to M.S. students. A number of other support opportunities in the University and in nearby industry generally become available to CS graduate students each year.

Assistants are assigned part-time duties in the undergraduate instructional program or in faculty-supervised research projects, but are still able to carry a full academic program. For an assistant working 20 hours per week for the ten-month academic year, the 1997–98 New York State rate for stipends is expected to be $9922 plus tuition remission and health benefits. New York State pays 90 percent of the health insurance premium for single employees, or 75 percent of family coverage. The state estimates this benefit to be about 12 percent of salary for single employees.

The department also adds to the state stipends in the form of summer research supplements, generally in the range of $4000. A few summer fellowships are available at $6500, tenable for three years. This amount can be added to the stipend total.

COST OF STUDY

In 1997–98, full-time tuition (12 or more credits) is $2550 per semester ($4208 for out-of-state students). There are additional University fees that total approximately $350 in the first year.

LIVING AND HOUSING COSTS

University housing is available to graduate students. In 1997–98, rooms in the residence halls cost $2471 per academic year, plus $1994 per year for board. There is space in the residence halls for unmarried students, but University housing for married students is limited. Some off-campus housing is available, but students who live off campus must expect to furnish their own transportation.

STUDENT GROUP

The graduate student body of the department's program numbers about 140 full-time students. Most are recent college graduates, but some students have acquired some professional experience before returning to graduate school.

LOCATION

The 1,100-acre campus is located on the North Shore of Long Island, approximately 60 miles east of Manhattan. The community is primarily residential. The area combines the advantages of outdoor recreation in the summer months, such as swimming, boating, and fishing on Long Island Sound, with relative proximity to New York City and the cultural resources it offers. There are numerous opportunities on campus to participate in or attend programs of music, art, and drama or to go to the lectures given by visiting speakers in all fields of scholarship, as one might expect at a major university.

THE UNIVERSITY

The State University of New York at Stony Brook is one of four University Centers of the State University. It offers comprehensive study opportunities in its College of Arts and Sciences, College of Engineering and Applied Sciences, Center for Continuing Education, Health Sciences Center, and Marine Sciences Research Center. The student enrollment is approximately 17,700, and the campus is still being expanded. Graduate programs are offered by thirty-three of the thirty-six academic departments and by five of the six schools of the Health Sciences Center.

APPLYING

Applicants may download all application forms in postscript form from the department home page, listed below. Applications may also be made completely electronically; the status of the electronic application may be viewed at any time. To finalize the application, however, a signed copy of the main page must be returned. Those without access to the World Wide Web may obtain copies of the forms and instructions by contacting the address listed below.

CORRESPONDENCE AND INFORMATION

Graduate Program Administrator
Department of Computer Science
State University of New York at Stony Brook
Stony Brook, New York 11794-4400

Telephone: 516-632-8462
Fax: 516-632-8334
E-mail: pat@cs.sunysb.edu
World Wide Web: http://www.cs.sunysb.edu

STATE UNIVERSITY OF NEW YORK AT STONY BROOK

THE FACULTY AND THEIR RESEARCH

Esther Arkin, Associate Professor; Ph.D., Stanford, 1986. Combinatorial optimization, network flows, computational geometry.

Leo Bachmair, Associate Professor; Ph.D., Illinois at Urbana–Champaign, 1987. Computational logic, automated deduction, symbolic computation.

Hussein G. Badr, Associate Professor; Ph.D., Penn State, 1981. Computer communication networks and protocols, stochastic processes and queuing theory, simulation, performance evaluation, modeling and analysis.

Arthur J. Bernstein, Professor; Ph.D., Columbia, 1962. Distributed algorithms, design and correctness of operating systems, concurrent programming.

Tzi-cker Chiueh, Assistant Professor; Ph.D., Berkeley, 1992. VLSI computer architecture, parallel storage systems, virtual reality.

Peter B. Henderson, Professor; Ph.D., Princeton, 1975. Software engineering, programming environments, computer science education.

Arie Kaufman, Professor; Ph.D., Ben Gurion (Israel), 1977. Computer graphics, visualization, interactive systems, computer architecture, computer vision.

Michael Kifer, Associate Professor; Ph.D., Hebrew (Jerusalem), 1984. Database systems, logic programming, knowledge representation, artificial intelligence.

Ker-I Ko, Professor; Ph.D., Ohio State, 1979. Computational complexity, theory of computation, computational learning theory.

Philip M. Lewis, Leading Professor; Ph.D., MIT, 1956. Computational complexity, automata theory, compiler design, concurrent systems.

Prateek Mishra, Associate Professor; Ph.D., Utah, 1985. User-interface, software reliability and testing, programming languages.

Joseph Mitchell, Associate Professor; Ph.D., Stanford, 1986. Operations research, computational geometry, combinatorial optimization.

Theo Pavlidis, Leading Professor; Ph.D., Berkeley, 1964. Image analysis, document processing (including OCR), computer graphics.

I. V. Ramakrishnan, Professor; Ph.D., Texas at Austin, 1983. Functional and logic programming, parallel computation.

Steven Skiena, Associate Professor; Ph.D., Illinois at Urbana–Champaign, 1988. Computational geometry, combinatorial algorithms, discrete mathematics.

David R. Smith, Professor; Ph.D., Wisconsin–Madison, 1961. Hardware description languages and synthesis, VLSI design, tools and experimental chip architecture.

Scott A. Smolka, Professor; Ph.D., Brown, 1984. Semantics of concurrency, design of distributed languages and algorithms, visual environments for concurrent systems.

Eugene Stark, Associate Professor; Ph.D., MIT, 1984. Programming language semantics, theory of concurrency, formal specifications, verification, distributed algorithms.

Amitabh Varshney, Assistant Professor; Ph.D., North Carolina at Chapel Hill, 1994. Interactive 3-D graphics, scientific visualization, parallel graphics algorithms, geometric modeling, computational geometry.

David S. Warren, Professor and Chairman; Ph.D., Michigan, 1979. Logic programming, database systems, interactive systems, artificial intelligence, natural language and logic.

Anita Wasilewska, Associate Professor; Ph.D., Warsaw (Poland), 1975. Logic, knowledge representation, artificial intelligence, machine learning.

Larry D. Wittie, Professor; Ph.D., Wisconsin–Madison, 1973. Distributed shared-memory architectures, distributed operating systems, massively parallel algorithms, computer networks and interconnection topologies, computer architecture, neural networks.

STATE UNIVERSITY OF NEW YORK
AT STONY BROOK

DEPARTMENT OF ELECTRICAL ENGINEERING

PROGRAMS OF STUDY

The Department of Electrical Engineering offers programs of study leading to the degrees of Master of Science (M.S.) and Doctor of Philosophy (Ph.D.). Registration as a nondegree special student is also permitted. Active research areas include computer engineering, telecommunications, computer networks, digital image processing and machine vision, integrated circuit design, digital data compression and coding, signal processing, optical signal processing, fiber optics, physical electronics, solid-state electronic devices and circuits, systems and controls, and VLSI.

The M.S. program can be completed in one year, although many students elect to complete the program in three semesters (1½ years).

Graduate study is closely associated with research. Laboratories and associated faculty are listed on the reverse of this page.

RESEARCH FACILITIES

Students have access to extensive computing facilities that include the department's own Sun SPARCserver 330s with workstations, a network of Sun and HP workstations, and a VAX (VMS) cluster and IBM mainframe in the computer center. The computing system and laboratories are interconnected through Ethernet. The department has the following laboratories: Digital Signal Processing, Lasers, Computer Vision, Microelectronics/VLSI, Microprocessors System Design, Computer-aided Design, and Telecommunications.

FINANCIAL AID

The department makes an effort to support as many graduate students as possible. There are teaching and research assistantships and a limited number of fellowships. Assistantships normally pay up to $9572 per academic year; some also include tuition remission. Support levels ranged up to $14,300 for the calendar year, plus tuition remission, in 1996–97. There are also opportunities for summer research support that pay up to $3700 for three summer months.

COST OF STUDY

Tuition for full-time graduate study in 1996–97 was $2550 per semester for New York State residents and $4208 for nonresidents. Part-time students paid tuition of $213 per semester hour for residents and $351 for nonresidents.

LIVING AND HOUSING COSTS

A limited number of three- and four-bedroom units in University residence halls are available for unmarried graduate students at a cost of $223 to $331 per month. Housing for married students is available on the same basis as housing for single students. A limited amount of off-campus housing is available in the area. The University Housing Office maintains a file to assist both single and married students in finding suitable accommodations. Meals may be purchased at a reasonable cost in campus cafeterias.

STUDENT GROUP

There were 76 full-time and 26 part-time graduate students in the department in 1996–97. A total of 17,000 students are enrolled at the State University of New York at Stony Brook.

STUDENT OUTCOMES

The student body is international in character. Some graduates return to their native countries to pursue teaching or industrial jobs at such places as National Chaio-Tung University, Jordan Science and Technological University, and Microelectronics Tech. Taiwan. Graduates are now employed by AT&T Bell Labs, NYNEX, Jet Propulsion Lab., Panasonic Tech., and many other technological companies. Some are employed by nontechnological companies such as Lehman Brothers, Citicorp, and Mt. Sinai Hospital. Most graduates find employment within four months of graduation.

LOCATION

Stony Brook is located on the wooded North Shore of Long Island, about 60 miles east of Manhattan and at the geographical center of Long Island. There is a very substantial electronics industry nearby, and the department maintains excellent working relations with these firms. The location makes New York City's cultural life and Suffolk County's tranquil countryside and seashores conveniently accessible. Brookhaven National Laboratory and the Cold Spring Harbor (biological) Laboratory are close by.

THE UNIVERSITY

The State University of New York at Stony Brook was established as a comprehensive university center in 1960. Since that time, an internationally renowned faculty has been formed to offer courses in forty-five major areas and interdisciplinary programs. Externally funded research has steadily increased to reach the current level of more than $70 million. The campus now comprises more than 100 buildings located on approximately 1,100 acres.

APPLYING

Applications are due February 1 for the fall semester. The GRE General Test is required for all students. For international students the TOEFL, with a minimum score of 550 (600 for an assistantship), is also required.

CORRESPONDENCE AND INFORMATION

Professor Serge Luryi, Chair
Department of Electrical Engineering
State University of New York at Stony Brook
Stony Brook, New York 11794-2350
Telephone: 516-632-8420 or 8400
E-mail: grad@sbee.sunysb.edu
World Wide Web: http://www.ee.sunysb.edu:8080/

STATE UNIVERSITY OF NEW YORK AT STONY BROOK

THE FACULTY AND THEIR RESEARCH

Bradley S. Carlson, Assistant Professor; Ph.D., Syracuse. VLSI circuit design.

Sheldon S. L. Chang, Emeritus Professor; Ph.D., Purdue. Optimal control, computer architecture, robotics, artificial intelligence, signal processing, economic theory.

Chi-Tsong Chen, Professor; Ph.D., Berkeley. Systems and control theory, digital signal processing.

Harbans Singh Dhadwal, Associate Professor; Ph.D., London. Lasers and instrumentation.

Petar Djuric, Associate Professor; Ph.D., Rhode Island. Signal and systems analysis.

Mikhail Dorojevets, Assistant Professor; Ph.D., Computing Center, Novosibirsk (Russia). Computer architectures, systems design.

Gene Gindi, Associate Professor; Ph.D., Arizona. Neural network modeling, image processing. (Joint appointment with the Department of Radiology)

Vera Gorfinkel, Associate Professor; Ph.D., A.F. Ioffe Physical-Technical Institute, St. Petersburg (Russia). Semiconductor devices, including microwave and optoelectronics.

Ridha Kamoua, Assistant Professor; Ph.D., Michigan. Solid-state devices and circuits; microwave devices and integrated circuits.

Serge Luryi, Professor and Chair; Ph.D., Toronto. High-speed electronic and photonic devices, semiconductor physics and technology.

John H. Marburger III, Professor and President of the University; Ph.D., Stanford. Theoretical laser physics. (Joint appointment with the Department of Physics)

Velio A. Marsocci, Distinguished Service Professor; Eng.Sc.D., NYU. Solid-state electronics, integrated electronics, biomedical engineering. (Also Clinical Professor of Health Sciences)

John Murray, Associate Professor; Ph.D., Notre Dame. Systems, controls, signal processing, image processing and instrumentation.

Jayant Parekh, Professor; Ph.D., Polytechnic of Brooklyn. Microwave acoustics and magnetics, microwave electronics.

Theo Pavlidis, Professor; Ph.D., Berkeley. Machine vision, pattern recognition, computer graphics, robotics. (Joint appointment with the Department of Computer Science)

Nam Phamdo, Assistant Professor; Ph.D., Maryland. Digital communications, data compression and coding, speech processing.

Stephen S. Rappaport, Professor; Ph.D., NYU. Communications systems, telecommunications.

Thomas G. Robertazzi, Associate Professor; Ph.D., Princeton. Computer networks, local area networks.

Yacov Shamash, Professor and Dean; Ph.D., Imperial College (London). Control systems and robotics.

Kenneth L. Short, Professor; Ph.D., SUNY at Stony Brook. Digital system design, microprocessors, instrumentation.

David R. Smith, Professor; Ph.D., Wisconsin–Madison. Logic design, computer architecture. (Joint appointment with the Department of Computer Science)

Murali Subbarao, Associate Professor; Ph.D., Maryland. Machine vision, image processing, information processing.

Stephen Sussman-Fort, Associate Professor; Ph.D., UCLA. Electronic circuits, CAD, solid-state electronics, electromagnetics.

K. Wendy Tang, Assistant Professor; Ph.D., Rochester. Parallel and distributed processing, massively parallel systems, computer architecture.

Hang-Sheng Tuan, Professor; Ph.D., Harvard. Electromagnetic theory, integrated and fiber optics, microwave acoustics.

Armen H. Zemanian, Professor; Eng.Sc.D., NYU. Network theory, VLSI circuits.

Department Laboratories

Each of the following laboratories contains special research and teaching equipment.

Advanced IC Design and Simulation Laboratory: Professor Carlson.

Communications, Signal Processing, Speech and Vision Laboratory: Professors Rappaport, Djuric.

Computer Vision Laboratory: Professor Subbarao.

Digital Signal Processing: Professor Murray.

Embedded Systems Design Laboratory: Professor Short.

Fluorescent Detection Research Lab: Professors Luryi and Gorfinkel.

Microwave Electronics Laboratory: Professors Parekh, Sussman-Fort, Tuan.

Optical Signal Processing and Fiber Optics Sensors Laboratory: Professor Dhadwal.

Semiconductor Electronics and Optoelectronics Laboratory: Professor Luryi

TEXAS A&M UNIVERSITY

DEPARTMENT OF COMPUTER SCIENCE

PROGRAMS OF STUDY

The department offers graduate studies in computer science and computer engineering leading to the Master of Science, Master of Computer Science, Master of Engineering, and Doctor of Philosophy degrees. Computer engineering programs are offered jointly with the Department of Electrical Engineering. The fields of computer science and computer engineering are rapidly changing and expanding. This has generated a need for highly trained individuals. Graduate areas of specialization in computer science include architecture, artificial intelligence and cognitive modeling, computational mathematics, computer systems and networks, computer vision, data structures, distributed systems, fault-tolerant computing, graphics, hypertext/hypermedia, neural networks, real-time systems, robotics, simulation, software engineering, software systems, theoretical computer science, and VLSI design automation and simulation. The diverse research interests of the faculty provide opportunities for work in many areas, with curricula suited to individual interests.

RESEARCH FACILITIES

The Department of Computer Science has an installed base of more than $5 million in computing equipment. Research laboratories are equipped with state-of-the-art Sun, Silicon Graphics, Hewlett-Packard, and IBM workstations. The department manages two parallel systems: an NCUBE 6400 (sixty-four processors) and a MasPar (2,048 PEs). For general faculty and student use, the department has an instructional network of more than 400 workstations (UNIX, PC class, and Macintosh) coupled to several Sun servers. The real-time lab has six workstations controlling robot arms. Workstations, laser printers, and plotters are distributed throughout the department in fifteen power-conditioned laboratories.

The department was awarded a small-scale Infrastructure Grant by the National Science Foundation in 1992. This grant has provided a distributed systems lab, upgrades to the parallel machines, a department-wide FDDI network, and a new SGI Onyx.

Campus facilities include a CRAY Jedi and an SGI Power Challenge in the Supercomputing Center and several large mainframes with a wide assortment of supported software.

FINANCIAL AID

Graduate assistantships, research assistantships, and fellowships are available. In 1996–97, stipends varied from approximately $9000 to $10,800 for the nine-month academic year, depending upon the student's academic attainment and experience. Assistantships require 20 hours per week and permit the holder to carry a full academic program of graduate work. Students with financial support qualify for resident tuition fees.

COST OF STUDY

The tuition for the 1997–98 academic year is $7,598 for state residents, and $14,180 for nonresidents.

LIVING AND HOUSING COSTS

There is a waiting list for University-owned apartments; the current waiting time is three years. Town houses, patio homes, and apartments are available off campus. For information on University-owned apartments, students should contact: Student Apartments Office, Texas A&M University, College Station, Texas 77843. For off-campus housing information, students should contact: Off-Campus Center, Department of Student Affairs, Texas A&M University, College Station, Texas 77843-1257.

STUDENT GROUP

There are 250 graduate students in the computer science program. The department has student chapters of the ACM and IEEE Computer Society. It also has an active Upsilon Pi Epsilon and Graduate Student Association.

STUDENT OUTCOMES

Graduates of the programs in the Department of Computer Science can network with a large number of graduates across the country. University graduates are found in every area, with a significant activity in the computing profession. The majority of graduates stay within the state. The segments that are most common include telecommunications, software, systems, electronics, and applications to a wide array of industries.

LOCATION

Texas A&M University is located in the Bryan/College Station area (population approximately 114,000), 100 miles northwest of Houston and 170 miles south of Dallas. A growing industrial base, excellent housing, strong public school systems, and many recreational and entertainment activities characterize the area. The park systems include numerous parks, swimming pools, golf courses, and tennis courts. The area also has two lakes available for recreational activities.

THE UNIVERSITY

Texas A&M University, a land-grant university, was established in 1876 as Texas's first public institution of higher education. The spacious campus is within easy driving distance of the four largest cities in Texas. Texas A&M University is noted for its accomplishments in the areas of teaching, public service, and research. It is one of the few universities with space-grant, land-grant, and sea-grant titles. The high quality of Texas A&M's programs is based on the talented men and women who constitute the more than 2,400 members of the faculty. In fall 1995, the enrollment at Texas A&M University was 42,000. The Department of Computer Science is located in the College of Engineering, which has 9,300 students.

APPLYING

Inquiries regarding admission to the Graduate College should be addressed to the Office of Admissions and Records.

Admission to Texas A&M University and any of its sponsored programs is open to qualified individuals regardless of race, color, religion, sex, age, national origin, or educationally unrelated handicaps.

CORRESPONDENCE AND INFORMATION

Graduate Advisor
Department of Computer Science
Texas A&M University
College Station, Texas 77843-3112
Telephone: 409-845-8981
E-mail: csdept@cs.tamu.edu

TEXAS A&M UNIVERSITY
THE FACULTY AND THEIR RESEARCH

Richard A. Volz, Professor and Head; Ph.D., Northwestern. Real-time embedded in robotics and manufacturing, distributed program languages, task planning for robots, computer vision.

Bart Childs, Professor and Associate Department Head; Ph.D., Oklahoma State. Computational mathematics, automation of software, documentation.

Donald Friesen, Professor and Associate Department Head; Ph.D., Illinois at Urbana-Champaign. Algorithm analysis, computational complexity, artificial intelligence.

Professors

Laxmi Bhuyan, Ph.D., Wayne State. Parallel and distributed processing, distributed operating systems, interconnection networks, performance and reliability, evaluation.

William Lively, Ph.D., SMU. Software engineering, user-system interfaces, knowledge-based and intelligent systems.

Fabrizio Lombardi, Professor; Ph.D., London. Fault-tolerant computing, real-time systems, CAD VLSI/WSI.

Bruce McCormick, Ph.D., Harvard. Neural networks, scientific visualization and geometric modeling, artificial intelligence.

Paul Nelson, Ph.D., New Mexico. Mathematical software, numerical analysis, parallel numerical analysis.

Udo Pooch, Ph.D., Notre Dame. Operating systems, system architecture, computer networking, fault-tolerant systems, real-time systems.

Dhiraj K. Pradhan, Ph.D., Iowa. Electrical engineering, VLSI, fault-tolerant computing, parallel processing.

Sallie Sheppard, Associate Provost for Honors Programs and Undergraduate Studies; Ph.D., Pittsburgh. Simulation, software engineering, high-level languages.

Dick B. Simmons, Ph.D., Pennsylvania. Artificial intelligence, expert systems, software engineering, computer architecture.

Glen Williams, Ph.D., Texas A&M. Computational mathematics, computer graphics systems, scientific and engineering applications.

Associate Professors

Jianer Chen, Ph.D., NYU. Complexity theory, combinatorics and graph theory, algorithm analysis, computational number theory and cryptography.

Daniel Colunga, Ph.D., Texas at Austin. Management information systems, database design, data communications.

Richard Furuta, Ph.D., Washington (Seattle). Electronic publishing, hypertext.

John Leggett, Ph.D., Texas A&M. Hypertext/hypermedia, computer-human interaction, systems programming/operating systems.

Jyh-Charn (Steve) Liu, Ph.D., Michigan. High-performance computing, telecommunication switches, real-time distributed systems, computing systems, computer architecture, fault-tolerant computing.

Jeffrey Trinkle, Ph.D., Pennsylvania. Robotics, multibody mechanics, automated manufacturing.

Duncan Walker, Ph.D., Carnegie Mellon. VLSI, CAD.

Jennifer Welch, Ph.D., MIT. Distributed and parallel algorithms, distributed computing, fault tolerance.

John Yen, Ph.D., Berkeley. Artificial intelligence, software engineering, fuzzy logic, genetic algorithms.

Wei Zhao, Ph.D., Massachusetts. Real-time computing, distributed operating systems, computer networks.

Assistant Professors

Nancy Amato, Ph.D., Illinois at Urbana-Champaign. Parallel algorithms, computational geometry.

Riccardo Bettati, Ph.D., Illinois at Urbana-Champaign. Real-time systems.

Thomas Ioerger, Ph.D., Illinois at Urbana-Champaign. Artificial intelligence, computational biology.

Suely Oliveira, Ph.D., Colorado at Denver. Numerical analysis, multigrid methods.

Lawrence Rauchwerger, Ph.D., Illinois at Urbana-Champaign. Parallelizing compilers, runtime detection and exploitation of coarse-grained parallelism, architectures for parallel.

Nitin Vaidya, Ph.D., Massachusetts. Fault-tolerant computing, distributed systems, VLSI testing and applied coding, theory.

TEXAS A&M UNIVERSITY

COLLEGE OF ENGINEERING
DEPARTMENT OF ELECTRICAL ENGINEERING

PROGRAMS OF STUDY

The Department of Electrical Engineering offers programs of graduate study leading to the degrees of Master of Engineering, Master of Science, Doctor of Engineering, and Doctor of Philosophy.

The Master of Engineering is a professional, nonthesis degree that requires 36 hours of course work and includes an engineering report documenting an engineering/design project. The objective of the program is to give the student both advanced courses in electrical engineering concepts and experience in applying these concepts to actual engineering problems. The program can be completed in approximately one year.

The Doctor of Engineering degree requires 96 hours of graduate-level course work in engineering, management, and other areas related to the professional practice of engineering. A one-year internship in industry is also required. The program can be completed in three years.

The M.S. and Ph.D. are research degrees. The M.S. degree requires 32 hours of course work, including a thesis, and can be completed in one year. The Ph.D. requires approximately 96 hours of course work and research, including the dissertation, and requires at least three years to complete. There is no foreign language requirement.

Opportunities for graduate study and research exist in the areas of communications, computer-aided design of electronic circuits (including expert systems), computers and digital systems, control systems, digital signal processing, electric power systems and power electronics, electromagnetics, electronic materials, electrooptics, image processing, microelectronic circuits, microwaves, solid-state electronics, and VLSI. Interdisciplinary programs are also available.

RESEARCH FACILITIES

The Department of Electrical Engineering is housed in a modern building with extensive, well-equipped laboratory facilities. The department operates two SPARCserver 1000 computers as well as three high-performance laser printers for general graduate student use. In addition, there are more than forty-five SPARCstations in research laboratories and forty SPARCstations in student laboratories. There are more than twenty-five networked 486 class PCs available to students on a 24-hour basis. A power electronics laboratory including CAD, CAM, and MC development facilities, a power automation laboratory equipped with one Concurrent 5450 computer, and several PCs are available for research in power. Other University computing facilities available to electrical engineering students include a SPARCcenter 2000, a large VAXcluster, an IBM 3090, and an SGI Power Challenge XL shared memory parallel computer. The million-volume University library provides seating for more than 2,000 people and maintains substantial literature in all areas of electrical engineering. The department has access to IEEE publications on disc (IPO), which allows searching and full-text printing of almost all IEEE and IEE publications. Extensive solid-state and electrooptics facilities are available for device fabrication and testing.

FINANCIAL AID

Financial aid is available in the form of research or teaching assistantships, scholarships, and fellowships. Stipends for assistantships in 1996–97 varied between $800 and $1000 per month; they qualify out-of-state students for resident tuition. Assistantships require approximately 20 hours of work per week, and recipients must register for 9 to 12 hours of course work each semester. Research assistants work on one of the department's research projects; teaching assistants participate in undergraduate instruction. Various types of graduate fellowships are awarded to outstanding students; recipients are expected to register for 12 hours each semester.

COST OF STUDY

Tuition in 1996–97 for Texas residents was $64 per semester credit hour, with a minimum charge of $100 per semester. Other fees totaled approximately $200 per semester. Tuition for nonresident students was $278 per semester credit hour. (Costs are subject to change.)

LIVING AND HOUSING COSTS

For single students, fees for room and board on campus in 1996–97 ranged from $400 to $1000 per month. For married students, a limited number of University-owned apartments, both furnished and unfurnished, were available at $185 to $290 per month, plus electricity. A large number of privately owned apartments are available in the community.

STUDENT GROUP

The University is coeducational, and enrollment is more than 42,000, including about 7,000 graduate students. The enrollment in the College of Engineering is 7,000 undergraduates and 1,900 graduate students. There are 366 graduate students enrolled in electrical engineering—217 master's and 147 doctoral degree candidates and 2 nondegree students.

LOCATION

Texas A&M University is located about 100 miles northwest of Houston and 170 miles south of Dallas. The Bryan–College Station area is growing rapidly and has a population of about 113,000. Numerous athletic, cultural, and recreational activities take place in the area. There are two excellent public school systems and more than fifty churches of various denominations.

THE UNIVERSITY AND THE COLLEGE

Texas A&M was founded in 1876 as a land-grant college and is the state's oldest public institution of higher learning. Through its College of Engineering, Engineering Experiment Station, and Engineering Extension Service, it provides a wide range of high-quality programs of education, research, and public service. The campus and adjacent University facilities cover more than 5,200 acres of land and include a physical plant valued at $450 million. Texas A&M ranks higher than any other institution of higher learning in the South or Southwest in the total value of its sponsored research. Total expenditures for research during 1996–97 exceeded $100 million. Approximately one third of the University's research programs are in engineering.

APPLYING

To be admitted to the Department of Electrical Engineering, an applicant must hold a B.S. degree in engineering or physical science. The minimum grade point average for admission to the master's degree program is 3.0 (on a 4.0 scale); admission to the Ph.D. program requires a minimum grade point average of 3.6 (on a 4.0 scale). For both the M.S. and the Ph.D. programs, the applicant must have a minimum score of 525 on the verbal section and 700 on the quantitative section of the General Test of the Graduate Record Examinations. Prospective students whose native language is not English must submit a minimum score of 600 on the Test of English as a Foreign Language. Applications for U.S. citizens and permanent residents should be received no later than six weeks before the beginning of the semester in which admission is desired.

CORRESPONDENCE AND INFORMATION

Graduate Coordinator
Department of Electrical Engineering
College of Engineering
Texas A&M University
College Station, Texas 77843

TEXAS A&M UNIVERSITY
THE FACULTY AND THEIR RESEARCH

Communications and Signal Processing. Digital communications systems, information theory, coding, data compression, estimation and detection theory, digital signal processing, digital speech systems, image analysis, image processing, knowledge-based signal processing, architectures for signal processing, computer communication networks. Four MicroVAX 2000s and a VAX-11/750 are dedicated to research in communications and signal processing. Configured with the VAX-11/750 are analog-to-digital and digital-to-analog converters, two DEC graphics workstations, a Gould FD 5000 image processing system, and a Gould IP 8400 real-time video system. Also available are a GE vision system for research in computer vision, a Spatial Data image display system, and a spectrogram machine for speech analysis.

Faculty: P. E. Cantrell, Ph.D., Georgia Tech, 1981; E. Dougherty, Ph.D., Rutgers, 1974; C. Georghiades, D.Sc., Washington (St. Louis), 1985; J. D. Gibson, Ph.D., SMU, 1973; N. C. Griswold, D.Engr., Kansas, 1975; D. R. Halverson, Ph.D., Texas at Austin, 1979; N. Kehtarnavaz, Ph.D., Rice, 1986; J. Livingston, Ph.D., Virginia, 1989; J. H. Painter, Ph.D., SMU, 1972; V. Vaishampayan, Ph.D., Maryland, 1989.

Computers and Digital Systems Engineering. Computer engineering, digital system design and test, digital VLSI/WSI and ASIC design, minicomputers, microprocessors, digital signal processing, digital control, computer communications, fault-tolerant architectures, AI systems, real-time systems, parallel and distributed systems. Special laboratory facilities include CAD/CAE workstations, minicomputers, microprocessor system development facilities, and a well-equipped digital system design laboratory.

Faculty: P. E. Cantrell, Ph.D., Georgia Tech, 1981; G. S. Choi, Ph.D., Illinois, 1994; M. Lu, Ph.D., Rice, 1987; M. R. Mercer, Ph.D., Texas at Austin, 1980; J. H. Painter, Ph.D., SMU, 1972; A. L. N. Reddy, Ph.D., Illinois, 1990; K. Watson, Ph.D., Texas Tech, 1982.

Control Systems. Linear multivariable control systems, model following, distributed parameter systems, finite-element models, homomorphic digital filtering, nonlinear control systems, robust control and adaptive control.

Faculty: S. P. Bhattacharyya, Ph.D., Rice, 1971; A. Datta, Ph.D., USC, 1991; J. W. Howze, Ph.D., Rice, 1970; G. Huang, D.Sc., Washington (St. Louis), 1980; J. H. Painter, Ph.D., SMU, 1972.

Electric Power and Energy Systems. System planning, dynamic analysis, reliability evaluation, control, and protection applied to conventional as well as specialized terrestrial, airborne, and spaceborne power and energy systems; analysis and control of electrical machines and variable-speed drive systems; power electronics; energy storage and pulsed power systems; microcomputer control and monitoring of energy systems; applications of expert systems to power system problems. Research is supported by utility, aerospace, and other industrial companies as well as state, federal, and private research funding agencies.

Faculty: A. Abur, Ph.D., Ohio State, 1985; M. Ehsani, Ph.D., Wisconsin–Madison, 1981; P. Enjeti, Ph.D., Concordia (Montreal), 1987; G. Huang, D.Sc., Washington (St. Louis), 1980; M. Kezunovic, Ph.D., Kansas, 1980; A. D. Patton, Ph.D., Texas A&M, 1972; B. D. Russell, Ph.D., Oklahoma, 1975; C. Singh, Ph.D., Saskatchewan, 1972; H. Toliyat, Ph.D., Wisconsin–Madison, 1991.

Electromagnetic Fields. Antennas, electromagnetic wave propagation, electromagnetic theory, microwave systems, microwave solid-state circuits and devices, guided-wave structures, millimeter-wave circuits, microstrip and waveguide discontinuities, coupled-mode theory, numerical methods, microstrip antennas, antennas in stratified media. Special laboratories and facilities include a microwave anechoic chamber, a rooftop antenna range, an automatic microwave analyzer (HP8510), and Touchstone, Supercompact, and MW-Spice programs for microwave circuit design.

Faculty: A. K. Chan, Ph.D., Washington (Seattle), 1971; K. Chang, Ph.D., Michigan, 1976; K. A. Michalski, Ph.D., Kentucky, 1981; R. B. Nevels, Ph.D., Mississippi, 1979; C. Nguyen, Ph.D., Central Florida, 1990; S. M. Wright, Ph.D., Illinois at Urbana-Champaign, 1984.

Electronic Circuits. Integrated circuit design, very large scale integrated circuits, analog VLSI design, operational amplifier design and applications, switched-capacitor filters, low-noise front-end electronics, instrumentation, measurements, active and passive filter design, neural networks, data converters, expert systems for electronics applications.

Faculty: E. Sanchez-Sinencio, Ph.D., Illinois at Urbana-Champaign, 1973; M. A. Styblinski, Ph.D., 1974, D.Sc., 1981, Warsaw; K. Watson, Ph.D., Texas Tech, 1982.

Electrooptics. Optical waveguides, integrated optics, fiber optical devices, diode laser properties, optical materials; application of these technologies in communications, signal processing, sensing, and microwave systems. Extensive facilities are available for electrooptics research as well as optical waveguide device fabrication.

Faculty: J. Blake, Ph.D., Stanford, 1988; A. K. Chan, Ph.D., Washington (Seattle), 1971; O. Eknoyan, Ph.D., Columbia, 1975; R. K. Pandey, D.Sc., Cologne, 1967; C. B. Su, Ph.D., Brandeis, 1979; H. F. Taylor, Ph.D., Rice, 1967; M. H. Weichold, Ph.D., Texas A&M, 1983.

Microelectronics. Design of integrated circuits, including design methodology, analog and digital VLSI design, computer-aided design, simulation, systolic arrays, laser trimming of film resistors, application of AI methodologies to circuit analysis and design, biomedical applications, radiation-hardened IC circuit design, telecommunication applications, statistical circuit design, verification test and evaluation. Multiproject chips are fabricated by cooperating industries; department facilities include the VLSI CAD and AI Lab, with Apollo and Sun CAD/CAE color workstations, DEC VAX-11/750 and VAX-11/785 computer facilities, alphanumeric and color graphics terminals, digitizer and plotters, and the VLSI Diagnostic Lab, with probing, dicing, and bonding facilities and workstation-based semiautomated test systems for low-noise and high-frequency VLSI systems. The interdisciplinary Lab for Intelligent Design Systems has recently been initiated.

Faculty: S. Embabi, Ph.D., Waterloo, 1991; J. Pineda, Ph.D., University of Technology (Netherlands), 1991; E. Sanchez-Sinencio, Ph.D., Illinois at Urbana-Champaign, 1973; M. A. Styblinski, Ph.D., 1974, D.Sc., 1981, Warsaw; K. Watson, Ph.D., Texas Tech, 1982.

Solid-State Electronics. Solid-state materials, process-induced defects in silicon, X-ray topography, diffusion, ion implantation, solar cells, semiconductor memory devices, microwave devices, epitaxial growth of III-V compound semiconductor layers. Laboratories of the Institute for Solid State Electronics are fully equipped for research in solid-state materials, semiconductor devices, integrated circuits, single-crystal growth and characterization, and bulk and thin-film ferroelectric, magnetic, and semiconductor materials. The Molecular Beam Epitaxy Facility is equipped with two MBE machines (VG Instruments) for epitaxial growth of III-V heterojunction materials and silicon/silicon alloy superlattices. The silicon MBE has a special feature of two ion-implanters attached to the growth chamber. The Electron-Beam Lithography Facility is equipped for patterning semiconducting nanostructures.

Faculty: J. Blake, Ph.D., Stanford, 1988; O. Eknoyan, Ph.D., Columbia, 1975; R. K. Pandey, D.Sc., Cologne, 1967; D. L. Parker, Ph.D., Texas A&M, 1968; C. B. Su, Ph.D., Brandeis, 1979; H. F. Taylor, Ph.D., Rice, 1967; L. C. Wang, Ph.D., California, San Diego, 1991; M. H. Weichold, Ph.D., Texas A&M, 1983.

TEXAS A&M UNIVERSITY—CORPUS CHRISTI

DEPARTMENT OF COMPUTING AND MATHEMATICAL SCIENCES (CAMS)

PROGRAMS OF STUDY

The CAMS department offers master's degrees in both applied computer science and applied mathematics. Students in either degree program may apply course work from the other toward their individual program. Because the master's program in applied computer science is substantially larger with respect to the number of students, course offerings, and opportunities for assistantships, it is the only program described here.

The Master of Science with a major in computer science is designed to prepare graduate professionals to apply the necessary knowledge of computing to the information requirements of organizations in business, government, industry, and education. The program provides for the education of individuals who will develop, maintain, or manage complex computer-based information systems.

The Master of Science degree is offered under two options to meet the needs of two distinct groups of graduate students. The first option, software systems, is intended for students with a substantial background in computing (at least the equivalent of an undergraduate minor in computer science). The goal of this track is to prepare the student for a career in the development of complex computer software systems or for advanced study in academic computer science. The second option, information systems, is intended for students with a less extensive background in computing but with a substantial background in an area in which they wish to apply their gained knowledge of computing to develop area-specific software. The goal of this track is to prepare students to develop computer-based solutions to problems in their area of expertise. A typical candidate for this option would be a student with an undergraduate degree in business or a particular science who wishes to apply computing to the established area of the undergraduate major.

RESEARCH FACILITIES

The University and the department support a number of labs for general student use. These labs are equipped with more than 400 PCs, 100 Macintoshes, and twenty-six DEC Alpha workstations. A number of students and faculty members are employed by, or otherwise work on projects for, several on-campus research institutes using computing equipment ranging from workstations to real-time tide monitoring platforms stationed along the Texas coast.

FINANCIAL AID

The department makes available a number of graduate assistantships. Duties for these assistantships range from analysis and development for major research projects to user support for the campus community. Most assistantships are half-time positions, which require 20 hours per week for twelve months. The pay is $1000 per month, and graduate assistants qualify for benefits such as in-state tuition rates and health insurance.

COST OF STUDY

The total cost (tuition and fees) for a full load of 9 graduate hours is $757 per semester for resident students and $2683 per semester for nonresidents.

LIVING AND HOUSING COSTS

Furnished apartments that include all utilities, local phone service, and cable television are available on campus. The rate is $539 per month for a private one-bedroom efficiency apartment or $299 per month per person for a double-occupancy two-bedroom apartment.

STUDENT GROUP

In 1996–97, there were 80 graduate students enrolled in computer science. The student population varies widely from full-time students to part-time students who have full-time careers. The age and ethnic background of the student body is also widely varied. The Computer Science Club, which includes an ACM student chapter, sponsors local events and is actively involved in regional activities, such as programming contests.

LOCATION

Texas A&M University–Corpus Christi (TAMU–CC) is located on an island along Corpus Christi Bay, 10 miles from downtown Corpus Christi and 15 miles from the beaches of Padre Island on the Gulf of Mexico. The city of Corpus Christi, population 250,000, is 100 miles south of San Antonio and 200 miles southeast of Houston. Popular outdoor recreational activities in the area include sailing, windsurfing, golf, and saltwater fishing. The primary industries for the city are chemical manufacturing, oil refining, and the Port of Corpus Christi.

THE UNIVERSITY

Texas A&M University–Corpus Christi is a comprehensive urban university located on its own 240-acre island. The admission of freshman and sophomore students in 1994 signaled the transformation of the institution to a four-year university, with an enrollment of more than 5,500 students in 1995. TAMU-CC focuses on the higher education needs of South Texas and the entire state as well as on coastal and urban issues. Computer science is located in the Department of Computing and Mathematical Sciences in the College of Science and Technology.

APPLYING

Individuals seeking admission to the graduate program should write to the Office of Admissions, Texas A&M University–Corpus Christi, 6300 Ocean Drive, Corpus Christi, Texas 78412.

CORRESPONDENCE AND INFORMATION

Computing and Mathematical Sciences
Texas A&M University-Corpus Christi
6300 Ocean Drive
Corpus Christi, Texas 78412
Telephone: 512-994-2474
E-mail: compsci@tamucc.edu
World Wide Web: http://www.tamucc.edu

TEXAS A&M UNIVERSITY—CORPUS CHRISTI

THE FACULTY

Roy S. Ellzey, Professor and Department Chair; Ph.D., Texas.

Carol L. Binkerd, Associate Professor; M.S., Corpus Christi State.

Charlotte Busch, Associate Professor; M.S., Texas.

Nancy Cameron, Associate Professor; M.S., Texas A&M.

Stephen Dannelly, Assistant Professor; Ph.D., Auburn.

Steven Fant, Assistant Professor; M.S., Texas A&M.

Mario Guimaraes, Assistant Professor; Ph.D., Pontifical Catholic (Rio de Janeiro).

Herbert R. Haynes, Professor; Ph.D., Texas.

David Leasure, Associate Professor; Ph.D., Kansas.

Patrick Michaud, Associate Professor; Ph.D., Southwestern Louisiana.

Holly Patterson, Assistant Professor; Ph.D., Texas A&M.

Martina Schollmeyer, Assistant Professor; Ph.D., Missouri-Rolla.

David R. Thomas, Associate Professor; Ph.D., SUNY at Binghamton.

TEXAS TECH UNIVERSITY

COLLEGE OF ENGINEERING
DEPARTMENT OF ELECTRICAL ENGINEERING

PROGRAMS OF STUDY

The Department of Electrical Engineering offers programs leading to the Master of Science in Electrical Engineering and the Doctor of Philosophy degrees. Departmental research programs include pulsed-power techniques, optical and digital signal/image processing, optical computing, VLSI design, control systems, neural networks, plasma theory and applications, materials and optoelectronics, thin-film deposition, power semiconductor devices and electronics, electric propulsion, renewable energy systems, and systems theory.

The master's degree requires a minimum of 24 semester hours of graduate course work and 6 semester hours of thesis work; each student must complete a thesis on his or her research and undergo a final oral examination. The doctorate normally requires 60 semester hours of work beyond the bachelor's degree, exclusive of credit for the dissertation. Each doctoral student must pass a preliminary, a qualifying, and a final examination, the last consisting of the dissertation defense. The graduate program in electrical engineering is general in content (except for the thesis and dissertation), and both master's and doctoral students must become proficient in an extensive range of electrical engineering areas. Minor subjects are taken outside the department. Before being recommended for admission to a graduate program, a student may be required to enroll (without graduate credit) in specified undergraduate-level programs.

Under the direction of the Department of Electrical Engineering, the College of Engineering also offers a nonthesis Master of Engineering degree in systems engineering. This program is designed to accommodate working engineers who have an undergraduate degree in any engineering field. Students are required to take 36 semester hours of graduate engineering courses, 15 of which may be taken at another university. The program is structured so that a student can complete the on-campus work at Texas Tech during two summer sessions and all degree requirements within two years.

RESEARCH FACILITIES

The department is housed in a three-story building with a 40,000-square-foot two-story annex, and it contains specialized laboratories devoted to radio science, optical sciences, plasmas, pulsed power, and power semiconductors. These laboratories are equipped with all conventionally required and considerable state-of-the-art apparatus. The College of Engineering also has a variety of minicomputers and microcomputers. A fully equipped machine shop is maintained for research activities. Research faculty members also have close working relationships with industry and with many national laboratories.

FINANCIAL AID

Teaching and research assistantships are available to qualified students. Minimum nine-month stipends in electrical engineering in 1997–98 are $7200, and, in many cases, additional three-month stipends are available for the summer term. Minimum stipends for doctoral candidates are $9000 for nine months.

COST OF STUDY

In 1997–98, tuition for Texas residents is $64 per semester hour ($120 minimum total tuition); for nonresidents, tuition is $246 per semester hour. Teaching and research assistants employed at least half-time pay resident tuition during their employment. Fees are approximately $800 per term; these are optional for half-time graduate assistants.

LIVING AND HOUSING COSTS

The cost of living in Lubbock is relatively low. University facilities are available for single students, and moderately priced ($250 to $350 per month) apartments are available close to the University. Food and entertainment costs are also moderate.

STUDENT GROUP

The department has around 350 electrical engineering undergraduate majors and some 60 full-time graduate students. Most graduate students in electrical engineering have assistantships.

STUDENT OUTCOMES

Graduates have entered the professional field in industry, university, military, and national/government laboratories. In industry, positions range from scientist to president; in universities, positions range from assistant professor to dean; in the military, positions range from astronaut to director of highly technical projects; and in national/government labs, positions range from technical members to leaders.

LOCATION

Lubbock is the center of a metropolitan area of approximately 200,000. Dry, crisp air and sunny days throughout most of the year provide a healthy and invigorating climate. An excellent recreation center, an Olympic-size swimming pool, intramural sports fields, and tennis courts are available on the campus; local cultural activities include a symphony orchestra, a civic ballet, a civic chorale, and an arts festival.

THE UNIVERSITY

Texas Tech University, founded in 1923, is one of the state's four principal institutions of higher education, with seven colleges, graduate and law schools, and a health sciences center and teaching hospital; it has a total enrollment of around 25,000. The University also operates the Museum and Ranching Heritage Center. Texas Tech is located on 1,839 acres, and its buildings have a uniform Spanish architectural style. Its library, one of the finest in the Southwest, subscribes to more than 7,500 periodicals.

APPLYING

Prospective students should have a cumulative GPA of at least 3.0 for their final 60 hours of undergraduate work and a GRE General Test score (verbal and quantitative) of at least 1100, although some deviation from these numbers is possible. Students wishing to enter the program should also have an undergraduate degree in engineering, physics, or mathematics. Applications for admission and graduate assistantships for the fall term should be submitted no later than March 31, and for the spring term, no later than October 31. Applications from international students should be received at least one month earlier.

CORRESPONDENCE AND INFORMATION

Graduate Advisor
Department of Electrical Engineering
Box 43102
Texas Tech University
Lubbock, Texas 79409-3102
E-mail: michaelg@coe2.coe.ttu.edu

TEXAS TECH UNIVERSITY
THE FACULTY AND THEIR RESEARCH

Graduate Faculty

Jorge I. Auñón, Professor and Dean; Sc.D., George Washington. Brain-wave signal analysis, spectral estimation, biomedical signal processing.

Jon G. Bredeson, Professor and Chairman; Ph.D., Northwestern. Computer communications, local area networks, metropolitan area networks, digital signal processing, linear systems, computers and digital hardware.

Mary Baker, Associate Professor; Ph.D., Texas at Arlington. Pulsed power, electromagnetic mass driver, plasma vapor deposition of thin film.

Kwong S. Chao, Professor; Ph.D., Rice. Nonlinear and analog circuits.

John P. Craig, Professor Emeritus; Ph.D., Texas at Austin. Conventional, alternate, and pulsed power.

Michael G. Giesselmann, Associate Professor; Ph.D., Darmstadt (Germany). Pulsed power, power electronics, electric machines, and power systems.

Donald L. Gustafson, Professor; Ph.D., Minnesota. Microprocessors, control, digital signal processing.

Marion O. Hagler, Horn Professor; Ph.D., Texas at Austin. Optics, optical information processing, plasmas.

Osamu Ishihara, Professor; Ph.D., Tennessee. Plasma theory, plasma turbulence and instabilities.

Thomas F. Krile, Professor; Ph.D., Purdue. Optical signal processing, digital image processing, neural network theory and applications.

Magne Kristiansen, Thornton and Horn Professor; Ph.D., Texas at Austin. RF wave propagation, pulsed power, electrical space propulsion.

Hermann Krompholz, Professor; Ph.D., Darmstadt (Germany). Pulsed power, plasma physics and gas discharges, high speed diagnostics.

David Mehrl, Associate Professor; Ph.D., Iowa. Acoustooptics, optical signal/image processing, spatiotemporal image processing, holographic data storage.

Sunanda Mitra, Professor; Ph.D., Marburg (Germany). Digital image processing and analysis, pattern recognition, medical image processing.

Edgar O'Hair, Professor; Ph.D., Purdue. Solar thermal energy, electrical space propulsion.

Micheal Parten, Professor; Ph.D., Texas Tech. VLSI design and manufacture, instrumentation systems, control systems, neural networks, computer vision.

William M. Portnoy, Professor; Ph.D., Illinois at Urbana-Champaign. Power semiconductor devices, power electronics, semiconductor device reliability, deep levels in semiconductors.

Henryk Temkin, Maddox Chair Professor; Ph.D., Stevens. Materials and optoelectronics.

Thomas F. Trost, Professor; Ph.D., Case Western Reserve. Applied electromagnetics.

John F. Walkup, Horn Professor; Ph.D., Stanford. Optical information processing, digital image processing, statistical optics, communication theory.

Don C. Wunsch II, Assistant Professor; Ph.D., Washington (Seattle). Neural networks, artificial intelligence, industrial and business applications of computing, system theory, optical information processing.

Klaus Zieher, Associate Professor; Ph.D., Karlsruhe (Germany). Particle acceleration, particle-beam generation and diagnosis.

Adjunct Faculty

William Baker, Adjunct Professor; Ph.D., Pulsed power.

Arthur H. Guenther, Adjunct Professor; Ph.D., Penn State. Pulsed power.

Emanuel M. Honig, Adjunct Professor; Ph.D., Texas Tech. Pulsed power.

Ravinder Kachru, Adjunct Professor; Ph.D., Columbia. Optical data storage.

James A. Lacy, Adjunct Professor; M.S., SMU; PE. Systems engineering.

Arthur A. Petrosian, Adjunct Professor; Ph.D., Institute of Problems of Informatics & Automation (Armenia). Signal processing.

M. John Rowe III, Adjunct Professor; M.D., Michigan. Visual evoked potentials.

Yao-Yang Shieh, Adjunct Professor; Ph.D., Purdue. Optical imagery.

Harold V. Shurmer, Adjunct Professor; Sc.D., London. Sensors and transducers.

J. D. Van Wyk, Adjunct Professor; Sc.D., Eindhoven University of Technology (Netherlands). Power electronics, power semiconductor devices.

UNIVERSITY AT ALBANY,
STATE UNIVERSITY OF NEW YORK

DEPARTMENT OF COMPUTER SCIENCE

PROGRAMS OF STUDY

The Department of Computer Science at Albany offers programs of study leading to the degrees of Doctor of Philosophy and Master of Science. In addition, several members of the department participate in the University's interdisciplinary Ph.D. program in information science. Instruction covers a wide range of areas. The current areas of research include data structures and algorithms, automated reasoning and theorem proving, theory of computation, artificial intelligence, high-performance computing, operating systems and distributed systems, natural language processing and robotics, artificial neural networks, computational biology, knowledge representation, hardware and software specification and verification, computer algebra, VLSI circuit testing and analysis, fault-tolerant computing, database systems, information management, combinatorics, software engineering, and compiler design.

Doctoral students are required to pass examinations in several areas of computer science and an oral examination in their field of research interest and they must submit a dissertation that describes original research. The Ph.D. is awarded in recognition of high achievement in research. The doctoral program is intended for students with career interests in academia, industrial research and development, or government research agencies.

For the M.S. degree, students must complete at least 32 credits of approved course work, complete a programming project of significant scope, and pass a comprehensive exam in computer science. The programming project requirement may be waived for students with appropriate work experience.

RESEARCH FACILITIES

The Departmental Laboratory supports research in High-Performance Parallel Computation C and FORTRAN (HPF) compilers, operating systems, and networks with an ATM switch that joins two Sun SPARC20s, a multiprocessor SPARC1000E, and a Silicon Graphics Indigo2. It also includes an Ethernet subnetwork of other Sun, Silicon Graphics, and (Linux) PC-type workstations and a Pioneer I mobile robot. Central University Computing and Network Services provides networked UNIX workstation access to all computer science graduate students and a VAX cluster, IBM 3081, and other computing and information resources.

All of these systems are accessible from the University's high-speed (T3) Internet connection, modem pool, and dormitory/classroom network.

FINANCIAL AID

In 1997–98, teaching and research assistantships that provide tuition waivers and stipends of $8000 to $12,000 for the nine-month academic year are available. In some instances, summer appointments are also made. Applications for assistantships beginning in the fall session must be submitted by March 15, while applications for assistantships beginning in the spring session must be submitted by October 15.

Presidential fellowships with a stipend of $13,000 and an appropriate tuition waiver are open to students who have been admitted to the doctoral program. Applications for these awards must be submitted by February 15.

COST OF STUDY

Graduate tuition for New York State residents is $5100 per year for 12 or more credits and $213 per credit for fewer than 12 credits for 1997–98. Tuition for out-of-state residents is $8416 for 12 or more credits and $351 per credit for fewer than 12 credits. Other fees total approximately $555 for full-time students.

LIVING AND HOUSING COSTS

On-campus accommodations start at $5241 for room and board for the 1997–98 academic year. Off-campus apartments average $250–$300 per person per month. Total costs for a full year of study, including tuition, fees, books, room, board, and modest entertainment, are approximately $16,000. International students must have at least $19,300 available to meet all expenses for a calendar year.

STUDENT GROUP

The graduate student body of the department numbers 58 students, 26 of whom are Ph.D. students.

STUDENT OUTCOMES

Most M.S. graduates find employment as software professionals, including positions as analysts and developers. Recent doctoral graduates and some M.S. graduates have positions in government, industrial, or academic research. A concentration of class program, individual project, and research participation can lead to the career specialty in which the student is most interested. Graduates have located to large, as well as small, metropolitan areas.

LOCATION

Albany is the capital of New York State, and the Albany-Schenectady-Troy capital region metropolitan area has a population of more than 200,000. The Albany Medical Center, various professional schools, other colleges and universities, and technology parks, as well as museums, theaters, the Pepsi Arena, world-renowned classical and popular music, and nearby summer stock performing arts, all lend a cosmopolitan tone to the city.

THE UNIVERSITY

Albany, one of four university centers in the SUNY system, was founded in 1814 and has about 5,100 graduate and 12,400 undergraduate students.

APPLYING

Degree students may be admitted for the fall or spring terms, although the curriculum is oriented toward fall admission. Application deadlines are flexible, but financial aid applications for the fall semester are due March 15. Admission requirements for the M.S. and Ph.D. programs are a bachelor's degree, superior undergraduate achievement as indicated by transcripts and overall grade point average, three recommendations, and acceptable scores on the General Test of the Graduate Record Examinations. Ph.D. applicants are encouraged to take the GRE Subject Test in either mathematics, physics, computer science, or engineering.

CORRESPONDENCE AND INFORMATION

For application forms and admissions information:
Graduate Studies
AD-152
University at Albany–SUNY
Albany, New York 12222
Telephone: 518-442-3980
E-mail: graduate@cnsibm.albany.edu

For further information about graduate work:
Professor Daniel J. Rosenkrantz, Chair
Department of Computer Science, LI-67A
University at Albany–SUNY
Albany, New York 12222
Telephone: 518-442-4270
E-mail: info@cs.albany.edu
World Wide Web: http://www.cs.albany.edu

UNIVERSITY AT ALBANY, STATE UNIVERSITY OF NEW YORK

THE FACULTY AND THEIR RESEARCH

George Berg, Associate Professor; Ph.D., Northwestern. Artificial intelligence, artificial neural networks, natural-language processing, computational biology, architectures and training methods for networks to represent and process structurally sensitive language information (e.g., sentence structure and compositional semantics), connectionist models to predict the three-dimensional structure of proteins from their amino acid sequences (the "protein-folding" problem). Active research projects are in connectionist models of structured information.

Peter A. Bloniarz, Associate Professor and Research Director of the Center for Technology in Government; Ph.D., MIT. Software engineering, particularly data modeling and object-oriented databases; information management and the use of technology in the public and private sectors. Current research involves cost-benefit analysis of networked hypertext access to documents. The Center for Technology in Government is a research laboratory whose mission is to investigate and facilitate the use of technology in the public sector.

Seth Chaiken, Associate Professor; Ph.D., MIT. Combinatorics, electrical networks, analysis of algorithms, computer architecture. Current work involves mathematical foundations of electrical network theory, including graph and matroid theory and discrete models of the analog behavior of electronic circuits important in digital system design specification, analysis, and verification. Other research is in average system performance studies, environments for graph algorithm study, and window systems.

Mei-Hwa Chen, Assistant Professor; Ph.D., Purdue. Process modeling, software design, verification and validation, software reliability engineering and GUI. Current research focuses on object-oriented software testing and reliability estimation. Projects involve building a C++ testing and coverage analysis tool and developing white box reliability models for both traditional and object-oriented software.

Andrew Haas, Associate Professor; Ph.D., Rochester. Artificial intelligence, natural-language syntax and parsing, semantics, propositional attitudes, planning. Current research involves the construction of a simulated robot which carries out commands given in English. The robot can understand indexicals, demonstratives, and descriptions of objects that it has not yet seen. It plans not only to rearrange the physical world but also to acquire knowledge by perception.

Harry B. Hunt III, Professor; Ph.D., Cornell. Theory of computation, analysis of algorithms, combinatorial optimization, parallel and distributed computation, computation science. Current work involves the study of problems on various algebraic structures to obtain a precise characterization of the complexities of the decision, optimization, and counting versions of these problems. Applications in the areas of VLSI, database systems, recursive, hierarchical, or dynamic specifications have been demonstrated. Other topics under investigation include computational issues in distributed computing and model checking and high-performance parallel scientific computing.

Deepak Kapur, Professor; Ph.D., MIT. Formal methods, hardware and software specification and verification, hybrid systems, automated reasoning, rewriting, mechanization of proofs by induction, symbolic computation, Dixon resultants, geometry theorem proving. The theorem prover Rewrite Rule Laboratory (RRL) is being extended for specification ad verification analysis with a special focus on hardware and hybrid systems. In collaboration with Mundy's group at G.E.R&D, the use of geometric reasoning in image understanding is investigated.

Lenore M. R. Mullin, Associate Professor; Ph.D., Syracuse. Psi calculus, high-performance computing and communications, scientific computation and compilation, array processing: portable, scalable, deterministic performance. Current research involves the mechanization of the psi calculus into the psi compiler. One goal is to use the psi calculus to describe implicit partitioning and mapping strategies to one or many processors followed by its mechanization in the compiler. Another goal is to integrate the psi compiler in high-performance FORTRAN as a parallel tool for array optimizations. Research includes hardware address coprocessors to speed up compilation.

Neil V. Murray, Associate Professor; Ph.D., Syracuse. Automated deduction, knowledge representation. Current research is in the theoretical and experimental aspects of automated deduction. An automatic theorem prover based on inference techniques for negation normal form (NNF) formulas is under development. Other areas being pursued are inference techniques for multivalued logics and NNF-based techniques for generating prime implicants and prime implicates of formulas.

Paliath Narendran, Associate Professor; Ph.D., Rensselaer. Formal hardware specification and verification, automated reasoning, term rewriting systems, unification. Current interests include reasoning and specification methods suited for hardware, algebraic and computational aspects of term rewriting and unification, and applications of unification and pattern-matching in knowledge representation.

S. S. Ravi, Associate Professor; Ph.D., Pittsburgh. Design and analysis of algorithms, operations research, fault-tolerant computing, VLSI. Current research centers on the design and analysis of algorithms and/or heuristics for optimization problems that arise in areas such as network design, transportation, fault tolerant computing, and VLSI.

Daniel J. Rosenkrantz, Professor and Chair, ACM Fellow; Ph.D., Columbia. Database systems, algorithms, fault-tolerant computing, compiler design, software engineering, parallel computation. Current work includes transaction processing in distributed databases, algorithms for problems arising in the handling of hazardous materials, and automated fault-tolerant design.

Richard E. Stearns, Professor, ACM Fellow, and 1993 Turing Award Winner; Ph.D., Princeton. Automata theory and formal languages, compiler design, analysis of algorithms, game theory. Current work involves the development and application of an algebraic approach to problems that leads to a very general structure theory of problem instances. This work is now being extended to hierarchically specified problems and to approximation problems. Closely related is work involving the classification of NP-complete problems by precise characterizations of their complexities based on strong assumptions about the complexity of SAT.

Dan E. Willard, Professor; Ph.D., Harvard. Database systems, data structures, analysis of algorithms, computational geometry, and proof theory from mathematical logic. Most recent work has included the development of self-verifying axiom systems that can prove their own consistency and the study of faster than LogN methods for searching and faster than NlogN methods for sorting. Other work includes the design and analysis of algorithms for database retrieval, geometric search problems, range queries, and dynamic set manipulation.

Adjunct Faculty

Theodor J. Borys, Data Center Director, New York State Office of Mental Health; M.S., SUNY at Albany. Very large and complex databases, transaction processing, client-server models, local area networks.

Thomas Irvin, Chief of Computer Services, New York State Executive Chamber; M.S., SUNY at Albany. Database design, full text storage and retrieval.

Affiliated Faculty

Jacquelyn Fetrow, Associate Professor, Biological Sciences; Ph.D., Pennsylvania State University College of Medicine. Primary research interests include studying the protein-folding problem, predicting protein structure, and understanding protein structure and function relationships. Both computational and experimental techniques are developed and used to study these problems.

Joachim Frank, Professor, Biomedical Sciences; Ph.D., Technical University of Munich. Methods of three-dimensional reconstruction of biological macromolecules are being developed based on electron microscopic images of single particles. To this end, cross-correlation, multivariate statistical analysis, classification, weighted back-projection and SIRT (Simultaneous Iterative Reconstruction Technique) are utilized. These methods are being applied to ribosomes, hemocyanin, and calcium-release channels.

Pawel A. Penczek, Research Scientist, Wadsworth Center; Ph.D., Warsaw. Current research focuses on the three-dimensional (3D) reconstruction methods in application to electron microscopy. Several 3D reconstruction algorithms have been developed, most notably iterative techniques to deal with extremely noisy and inconsistent data. Research interests include signal processing and pattern recognition techniques. These techniques are employed in the studies of 3D structures of biological macromolecules. Some problems, such as transfer function correction, can be expressed as inverse problems and solved with the use of a priori information. Currently, work involves the improvement of the resolution of results. This can be achieved by collecting and processing very large amounts of data. To be able to process such a wealth of data in a reasonable time, attention is turned toward parallel algorithms and distributed processing.

Giri Kumar Tayi, Associate Professor, Department of Management Science and Information Systems; Ph.D., Carnegie Mellon. Current research is in the areas of data quality, information economics, mathematical models of manufacturing and service operations, design of algorithms and heuristics for problems in transportation, and environmental policy making and telecommunication networks.

UNIVERSITY AT ALBANY,
STATE UNIVERSITY OF NEW YORK

INFORMATION SCIENCE DOCTORAL PROGRAM

PROGRAM OF STUDY

The University at Albany offers an interdisciplinary program leading to the degree of Doctor of Philosophy in information science administered by the Nelson A. Rockefeller College of Public Affairs and Policy. It is a collaborative program of the School of Business; the Departments of Communication, Geography and Planning, and Computer Science of the College of Arts and Sciences; the School of Information Science and Policy; and the Department of Public Administration and Policy of the Graduate School of Public Affairs.

The program centers on advanced study and applied research in the nature of information as a phenomenon and in the character of the information transfer process. It prepares graduates both for academic and research careers in information science and for senior information management and policy positions in government or the private sector. The program requires a minimum of three years of full-time postbaccalaureate study or its part-time equivalent. A minimum of two terms of full-time resident study are required. The major components are four required interdisciplinary core proseminars, research tool and information technology competencies, course work in primary and secondary areas of specialization, and a doctoral dissertation. Areas of specialization are expert systems, geographic information systems, group decision support modeling, information decision systems, organization of knowledge records, and public information policy and a secondary specialization in organizational studies.

RESEARCH FACILITIES

The Center for Technology in Government seeks practical solutions to problems of information technology and management in government settings. Other research programs in which doctoral students are encouraged to participate are currently under way in research library and archival management and electronic records management.

The University libraries house more than 1.3 million volumes and maintain some 6,700 current periodical subscriptions. There are forty major libraries in the Albany area, including the New York State Library. Cooperative relationships with these and other research libraries provide access to collections nationwide.

The University provides access to mainframe computing, microcomputers, graphics equipment, laser printing, and regional and worldwide computer networks, as well as instruction in the use of these facilities. Public computer rooms are available at several campus locations.

FINANCIAL AID

Full-time students may apply for University fellowships and assistantships carrying annual stipends of up to $13,000 plus full or partial tuition scholarships in return for service in teaching, research, or administration. Similar teaching or research assistantships are available through the U.S. Department of Education's Library Career Training Program and the Center for Technology in Government. Information about other state and federal financial aid programs for which doctoral students may be eligible is available from the University's Office of Financial Aid. For 1996–97, all full-time students were supported through fellowships or assistantships.

COST OF STUDY

In 1997–98, estimated full-time graduate tuition is $5100 per year for residents of New York and $8416 per year for out-of-state students. Tuition for part-time students is $213 per credit hour for residents and $351 per credit hour for out-of-state students. Special fees, books, and supplies cost approximately $1000 per year.

LIVING AND HOUSING COSTS

University graduate student apartment rents are $1860 per term. Rents for off-campus studio and single-bedroom apartments begin at $350 and shared apartments at $300 per person per month. Total annual costs, including tuition, fees, books, room, board, and incidentals, are approximately $21,000–$27,000. International students must have at least $21,000 available to meet all expenses for each calendar year.

STUDENT GROUP

Enrollment for fall 1997 is 30 doctoral students, half of whom are full-time. Approximately half are women, and 10 percent are international students. Most are experienced information professionals holding master's degrees in information-related disciplines.

STUDENT OUTCOMES

Graduates hold university faculty positions in library and information science or computer information departments or senior information management positions in government.

LOCATION

Albany is headquarters for the state legislature and many major state agencies. The Empire State Plaza, with its Cultural Education Center, museum, and theater, lends a cosmopolitan tone to the city. Classic and popular music concerts are held during the winter season. The Saratoga Raceway, Saratoga Performing Arts Festival, Tanglewood (summer home of the Boston Symphony Orchestra), Jacob's Pillow, and Woodstock all come alive each summer with horse racing, theater, music, arts, and crafts.

THE UNIVERSITY AND THE PROGRAM

Founded in 1844, the University at Albany is one of four university centers in the sixty-four-member SUNY System. Albany currently enrolls about 16,000 students, 4,500 of whom are graduate students. The interdisciplinary doctoral program in information science enrolled its initial group of students in 1990–91. Information science is one of the University at Albany's eight major themes under the state's Graduate Education and Research Initiative.

APPLYING

New doctoral students are admitted only for the fall semester. Applications for admission and for financial aid for domestic students must be submitted to the Graduate Admissions Office, Nelson A. Rockefeller College of Public Affairs and Policy, Draper Hall, Room 112 by April 1. International applicants are expected to hold a degree from a U.S. university and must submit applications to the Office of Graduate Admissions, AD 112, State University of New York at Albany, New York, 12222. Candidates must have a substantial background of high-quality previous academic work, preferably at the graduate level, in a discipline concerned with perception, evaluation, and manipulation of information and should possess appropriate technical and analytical skills. Admission is highly selective, based on grade point average, scores on the General Test of the Graduate Record Examinations, and academic and professional references. Prospective students are strongly encouraged to arrange a personal interview.

CORRESPONDENCE AND INFORMATION

Dr. Thomas J. Galvin, Director
Information Science Doctoral Program
Draper Hall, Room 118
Nelson A. Rockefeller College of Public Affairs and Policy
University at Albany, State University of New York
Albany, New York 12222

Telephone: 518-442-3309
Fax: 518-442-5232
E-mail: tg504@cnsvax.albany.edu
World Wide Web: http://www.albany.edu/rcinf

UNIVERSITY AT ALBANY, STATE UNIVERSITY OF NEW YORK

THE FACULTY AND THEIR RESEARCH

Senior Program Faculty

David F. Andersen, Professor, Public Administration and Policy, Graduate School of Public Affairs; Ph.D., MIT, 1977. Public management, simulation and decision support systems in public policy, government information management. Coauthor *Government Information Management,* 1991.

Donald P. Ballou, Associate Professor, Management Science and Information Systems, School of Business; Ph.D., Michigan, 1969. Information systems, quantitative methods, impact of information quality on decision making, enhancing data quality.

Salvatore Belardo, Associate Professor, Management Science and Information Systems, School of Business; Ph.D., RPI, 1981. Information systems, management science, statistics, operations research, behavioral analysis.

Peter A. Bloniarz, Associate Professor, Computer Science, College of Arts and Sciences and Research Director, Center for Technology in Government; Ph.D., MIT, 1977. Software engineering, operating systems, computational complexity.

Anthony M. Cresswell, Associate Professor, Educational Administration and Policy Studies, School of Education; Ed.D., Columbia, 1970. Collective bargaining, public school finance, management and computer systems. International information systems development research projects for USAID in Haiti, Indonesia, Yemen.

Thomas J. Galvin, Professor, School of Information Science and Policy; Ph.D., Case Western Reserve, 1973. Director, Information Science Doctoral Program. Information and public policy, management of information services. Coeditor *Navigating the Networks,* 1995; author *Rights in Conflict: Issues in Information and Public Policy,* in preparation.

Jagdish S. Gangolly, Associate Professor, Accounting and Law, School of Business; Ph.D, Pittsburgh, 1977. Knowledge representation issues in the accounting domain. Author "Some Thoughts on the Engineering of Financial Accounting Standards," *Artificial Intelligence in Accounting and Auditing,* 1993.

Richard S. Halsey, Associate Professor, School of Information Science and Policy; Ph.D., Case Western Reserve, 1972. Information policy, management of information and library systems, organization of information. Author *Lobbying for Library and Information Services,* in preparation.

Floyd M. Henderson, Professor, Geography and Planning, College of Arts and Sciences; Ph.D., Kansas, 1973. Remote sensing, digital image analysis, geographic information systems applications. Symposium paper "An Analysis of Settlement Detectability in Central Europe Using SIR-B Radar Imagery," International Society of Photogrammetry and Remote Sensing, 1990.

William K. Holstein, Distinguished Professor, Management Science and Information Systems, School of Business; Ph.D., Purdue, 1964. Management of information systems, production management. Strategic issues in information systems development and implementation, information management in international settings.

Bruce Kingma, Associate Professor, Economics, College of Arts and Sciences and School of Information Science and Policy; Ph.D., Rochester, 1989. Information management and policy, nonprofit management and fund raising. Author *Economics of Information,* 1996; *Economics of Access Versus Ownership,* 1996.

Lakshmi Mohan, Associate Professor, Management Science and Information Systems, School of Business; Ph.D., Columbia, 1960. Decision support systems, executive information systems. Coauthor "Market Decision Support Systems in Transition," *The Information Revolution in Marketing.*

Jeryl L. Mumpower, Associate Professor, Public Administration and Policy, Graduate School of Public Affairs; Ph.D., Colorado, 1976. Director, Center for Policy Research. Social and quantitative psychology. Analysis of formal structure of negotiations, scientific disagreement about policy issues.

Neil V. Murray, Associate Professor, Computer Science, College of Arts and Sciences; Ph.D., Syracuse, 1979. Methods of logical deduction for formulas not necessarily in conjunctive or disjunctive normal form, multivalued logics. National Science Foundation research project "Implementation and Analysis of Proof Techniques Employing Negation Normal Form."

John S. Pipkin, Professor, Geography and Planning, College of Arts and Sciences; Associate Vice President; and Dean of Undergraduate Studies; Ph.D., Northwestern, 1974. Analytical and urban geography.

George P. Richardson, Associate Professor, Public Administration and Policy, Graduate School of Public Affairs; Ph.D., MIT, 1985. Policy-oriented research and computer simulation concerning significant dynamic problems. Author *Feedback Thought in Social Science and Systems Theory,* 1991.

John P. Seagle, Associate Professor, Management Science and Information Systems, School of Business; Ph.D., Stanford, 1967. Management science, information systems, statistics, operations research.

Roger W. Stump, Associate Professor, Geography and Planning, College of Arts and Sciences; Ph.D., Kansas, 1981. Spatial analysis, cultural geography, social applications of geographic information systems.

Affiliated Faculty

Sharon S. Dawes, Lecturer in Information Science and Executive Director, Center for Technology in Government; Ph.D., SUNY at Albany, 1991. Information management and policy in the public sector. Coauthor *Government Information Management,* 1991.

Edward J. DeFranco, Public Service Professor of Information Science and Assistant Director for Management Information and Analysis, New York State Division of Substance Abuse Services; Ph.D., NYU, 1967. Information systems. Quality, efficiency, and effectiveness of information infrastructure in the public sector. Research studies on public data systems.

Peter J. Duchessi, Associate Professor, Management Science and Information Systems, School of Business; Ph.D., Union (New York), 1982. Management science, information systems, knowledge-based systems. Coauthor "A Research Perspective: Artificial Intelligence, Management and Organizations," *International Journal of Intelligent Systems in Accounting, Finance and Management,* 1993.

Sue R. Faerman, Associate Professor, Public Administration and Policy, Graduate School of Public Affairs; D.P.A., SUNY at Albany. Research design, organizational behavior, managerial and leadership effectiveness. Coauthor "Productivity and the Personnel Process," *Handbook of Public Productivity,* 1991; *Electronic Information Access Technologies: A Faculty Needs Assessment,* 1993.

Richard Hall, Distinguished Service Professor, Sociology, College of Arts and Sciences, and Director, Organizational Studies Ph.D. Program; Ph.D., Ohio State, 1961. Organizational theory, sociology of organizations, sociology of information. Author *Sociology of Work,* 1994; *Organizations: Structures, Processes, and Outcomes,* 1993.

Hemalata Iyer, Associate Professor, School of Information Science and Policy; Ph.D., Mysore (India), 1984. Classification theory, information organization and retrieval, natural language representation. Author *Classificatory Structures 1995.*

Paul Miesing, Associate Professor, Management, School of Business; Ph.D., Colorado, 1977. Strategic management, organizational change, technology transfer. Coauthor "Size and Scope of Strategic Planning in State Agencies," *American Review of Public Administration,* 1991; "Market Forces or Technological Rate of Change," *Technology-Based Entrepreneurship,* in press.

James Mower, Associate Professor, Geography and Planning, College of Arts and Sciences; Ph.D., SUNY at Buffalo, 1989. Automated cartography, geographic information systems. Research in applications of parallel computing to automated projection of maps.

Giri Kumar Tayi, Associate Professor, Management Science and Information Systems, School of Business; Ph.D., Carnegie Mellon, 1982. Data communications and communication networks, information economics and policy, quantitative models for policy analysis. Coauthor "Heuristics and Special Case Algorithms for Dispersion Problems" and "Determining Priorities for Data Management," both in preparation.

M. Geraldene Walker, Assistant Professor, Information Science and Policy; Ph.D., Syracuse, 1987. Information retrieval systems and the user-system interface to on-line systems. Author *The Information Environment,* 1992.

UNIVERSITY OF ALABAMA

DEPARTMENT OF COMPUTER SCIENCE

PROGRAMS OF STUDY

Programs of study lead to the M.S. and Ph.D. degrees in computer science. Major areas of concentration include software engineering, artificial intelligence, databases, algorithms, systems, and human-computer interaction.

M.S. students are required to complete 30 hours, including a thesis or 36 hours with a research project.

Requirements for the Ph.D. include a minimum of 72 hours of courses, seminars, and research. Ph.D. students are strongly encouraged to become actively involved in research during the first year. Students must pass a written qualifying exam upon completion of their course work.

RESEARCH FACILITIES

Computer science graduate students have access to a wide range of computing equipment and other resources within the department, in the College of Engineering and the University, and externally through the Internet. The department's configuration is based on networked UNIX-based graphics workstations that are available for faculty and graduate student research. There are about 75 UNIX-based RISC workstations and approximately 130 PCs available for student use. Each UNIX-based workstation has a megapel color display, and all workstations share a common networked file system. The workstations are networked to all other computing resources on campus and are also connected to the Internet (via SURAnet). The PCs are 486-based machines with color monitors.

The campus network allows access to the University's IBM 3090/400E (complete with vector processor) as well as the library on-line card catalog computer and the Alabama Supercomputer Center which houses a CRAY X-MP/24 and an NCUBE 128-node machine. Dial-up access to the campus network is available.

FINANCIAL AID

Financial aid is available in the form of teaching and research assistantships and various University fellowships up to $10,000. The vast majority of the unconditionally admitted full-time students receive some form of assistance. Current stipend rates (nine-month appointment) are normally $8000 for master's-level students and $9000 for doctoral students. Half-time assistantships carry a full tuition waiver, and assistants are allowed to carry up to 10 hours of graduate courses. Graduate assistants on half-time appointments are expected to work 20 hours each week.

COST OF STUDY

Tuition and fees for Alabama residents who are full-time students are $1235 per semester, while nonresidents pay $3134 per semester for the 1997–98 academic year.

LIVING AND HOUSING COSTS

University housing includes dorm rooms at $940 per semester and more than 200 apartments ranging from unfurnished one-bedroom apartments at $290 to furnished three-bedroom apartments at $750 per month. The Off-Campus Housing Association assists students in selecting from a large number of off-campus apartments, many within walking distance of the campus. Meal plans are available on campus for all students. A single student sharing an apartment should budget at least $6500 for living expenses for an academic year.

STUDENT GROUP

The University has a total enrollment of 17,400 students, of whom 3,400 are graduate students. The Department of Computer Science has about 160 undergraduate students, 35 master's students, and 12 doctoral students. The College of Engineering ranks in the top five nationally with respect to enrollment of African-American students in non-historically black institutions.

STUDENT OUTCOMES

Ph.D. students can expect to find positions in academia and research. Most M.S. graduates find industrial jobs.

LOCATION

The University is located in Tuscaloosa, a city of about 100,000. The city is 50 miles southwest of Birmingham by interstate highway, not far from Atlanta and New Orleans. Several large lakes, as well as the Great Smoky Mountains and the Gulf of Mexico, offer recreational opportunities. Tuscaloosa is serviced by a local airport and Interstate I-59/I-20.

THE UNIVERSITY

Chartered in 1820, the University of Alabama, a comprehensive research institution, is one of the oldest state universities in the nation. As the "capstone" of the educational system within Alabama, the University of Alabama offers graduate degree programs in many areas, ranging from the sciences and engineering to business administration, education, and the fine arts. Library holdings are computerized with access through an on-line catalog system to more than 300 specialized databases. The University offers a wealth of cultural events, including music, theater, dance, and an impressive art collection.

APPLYING

Applications for admission are accepted from students with undergraduate degrees in computer science and, subject to remedial course work, from students with degrees in other areas. Applicants should have at least a 3.0 grade point average and present a GRE score of at least 1600 for the M.S. program and 1800 for the Ph.D. program. Students graduating from an accredited undergraduate program may omit the GRE, but the department still strongly recommends taking the exam. International students must score at least 550 on the TOEFL. A $25 application fee is required.

CORRESPONDENCE AND INFORMATION

Additional information may be obtained by sending e-mail to cs@cs.ua.edu or by accessing the World Wide Web (http://cs.ua.edu).

Graduate Admissions
Department of Computer Science
Box 870290
Tuscaloosa, Alabama 35487
Telephone: 205-348-6363
World Wide Web: http://cs.ua.edu

For an application package:

Office of the Graduate School
102 Rose Administration Building
Box 870118
University of Alabama
Tuscaloosa, Alabama 35487-0118

UNIVERSITY OF ALABAMA
THE FACULTY AND THEIR RESEARCH

David B. Brown, Professor and Head; Ph.D., Texas Tech, 1969. Information mining, large database systems, software testing, traffic safety applications.

Richard B. Borie, Associate Professor; Ph.D., Georgia Tech, 1988. Algorithm design and analysis, graph theory, parallel computation, computational complexity, data structures, combinatorial optimization, discrete mathematics, compilers.

Marcus E. Brown, Associate Professor; Ph.D., Texas A&M, 1988. Human-computer interface: hypertext, virtual reality, computer security, ethics.

Tracy K. Camp, Assistant Professor; Ph.D., William and Mary, 1993. Distributed computing systems, networks, performance analysis, simulation.

David W. Cordes, Associate Professor; Ph.D., LSU, 1988. Software engineering: systems modeling; object-based development and testing; requirements analysis, specification, and design.

Hui-Chuan Chen, Professor; Ph.D., SUNY at Buffalo, 1972. Artificial intelligence, expert systems, neural networks and fuzzy set theory.

Brandon Dixon, Assistant Professor; Ph.D., Princeton, 1993. Parallel and sequential algorithms, concurrent data structures, efficient implementations of parallel algorithms.

Allen S. Parrish, Associate Professor; Ph.D., Ohio State, 1990. Software engineering, software testing and verification, software reuse, programming languages.

Ron Sun, Assistant Professor; Ph.D., Brandeis, 1991. Artificial intelligence and cognitive science, especially every day reasoning, machine and human learning, and connectionist models/hybrid systems.

Susan V. Vrbsky, Assistant Professor; Ph.D., Illinois, 1993. Databases; object-oriented, temporal, and real-time systems; imprecise computation; database security.

RESEARCH AREAS

Software Engineering. Research is concentrated in two basic areas: (1) Testing of abstract data types independent of individual applications. Work on both specification-based and specification-independent techniques for testing of Ada packages and C++ classes is under way. This work includes the development of automated software tools to facilitate the testing process. (2) System modeling using object-based techniques. This includes both the elicitation of initial requirements information as well as the eventual transformation of these system models into a formal set of specifications for the system in question.

Artificial Intelligence. Research includes both theoretical and practical work. The practical work centers primarily on expert systems, including fuzzy expert systems. Expert system applications have included systems for mineral identification, oil and gas exploration, and interpretation of clastic sediments. The theoretical work is mainly concerned with connectionism and cognitive modeling with connectionist models. The theoretical foundation of neural networks is examined as an alternative paradigm for AI. The emphasis is on unified models of cognitive processes involving both neural and symbolic processing. Current research investigates the uses of connectionist networks for addressing hard problems in AI, such as common-sense reasoning, analogical reasoning, skill acquisition, and the issue of consciousness, which are important for both theoretical advances and practical applications.

Computer Networks and Distributed Computing Systems. Research focuses on communication issues. One way to classify asynchronous communication paradigms is by the delivery order restrictions placed upon messages. Allowing flexibility in the delivery order restrictions offers promise of providing ultra-high bandwidth interprocess communication, research activities consider this area. In addition, current research occurs in consideration of congestion techniques for ATM networks and various distributed algorithm implementations.

Database Research. This area includes theoretical and practical work. One research project focuses on approximate query processor that produces approximate results when real-time constraints will not allow completion of a query. This query processor works with a standard relational algebra framework and is currently being extended to include temporal data. Other projects center on information mining of large databases such as traffic accident records for several Southeastern states. In view of the obvious implications of this application, work is proceeding to automate this process using object-oriented technology and an inference engine.

Graph Algorithms. Research focuses on tree-decomposable graphs to provide algorithms more efficient than those for arbitrary graphs. This work with tree-decomposable graphs has led to research in parallel computation using a divide and conquer approach for the parts of the subtrees.

Human-Computer Interaction. This area concerns adapting the computer to better assist the human user. The research has several different aspects. Literate programming concentrates on programs written for programmer comprehension, often presented in a hypertext interface. Educational applications of hypermedia and virtual reality are also being explored. Another area of research in human-computer interaction has led to a user authentication technique based on typing characteristics alone, with application in computer system security.

UNIVERSITY OF ALABAMA AT BIRMINGHAM

DEPARTMENT OF COMPUTER AND INFORMATION SCIENCES

PROGRAMS OF STUDY

The department offers programs of study and research leading to the M.S. and Ph.D. degrees in computer and information sciences. Fields of specialization that are available include computer graphics, artificial intelligence, data mining and knowledge discovery, object-oriented technology, computer chess, and distributed systems. One of the features of the graduate program is the opportunity to participate in interdisciplinary research that includes researchers from the Academic Health Center, a world-class biomedical research center.

The M.S. program requires 36 semester hours of study and can be completed in six quarters by students entering with no undergraduate computer science background deficiencies. Both thesis and nonthesis options are available.

The Ph.D. program consists of three phases: preparation for the qualifying examination by taking a specified set of core courses, additional course work and development of a research proposal, and dissertation research and a final defense. There is no foreign language requirement.

RESEARCH FACILITIES

Graduate students have access to Sun and Silicon Graphics workstations and PC systems. All systems are networked within the department and to the campus network and the Internet through SURANet. The department has direct access to the Alabama Supercomputer Network Authority CRAY C90 supercomputer for research and instruction. Dial-up lines to the department networks are available for off-campus access.

The University of Alabama at Birmingham (UAB) library is an institutional member of the Association for Computing Machinery (ACM), the Institute of Electrical and Electronics Engineers (IEEE), and the Society for Industrial and Applied Mathematics (SIAM). These memberships provide complete and extensive collections of journals and other resources in the field of computer science.

FINANCIAL AID

Financial aid is available in the form of teaching and research assistantships. Laboratory assistant positions are also available. The number of research positions varies from year to year since many are related to faculty grant and contract activities. Most students are successful in obtaining assistantships or on-campus employment during their first year of study. Assistantship stipends vary from $9500 to $15,000 (twelve-month appointments), with half tuition for M.S. students and full tuition for Ph.D. students.

COST OF STUDY

Tuition is $83 per semester hour for Alabama residents and $166 per semester hour for nonresidents. Since UAB operates on a quarter calendar, which compresses a normal fifteen-week semester of work into a ten-week quarter timeframe, 6 semester hours per quarter is considered full-time. Other fees may be required, depending on the student's situation and courses involved, such as a student health fee and laboratory fees.

LIVING AND HOUSING COSTS

University housing includes furnished efficiency apartments, which range from $395 to $430 per month, and furnished one-bedroom apartments (shared occupancy), which rent for $228 to $252 per month per student. These rates include utilities, with the exception of telephone and cable. For families, unfurnished apartments that rent for $350 per month are available. Water is the only utility included in these rates. Off-campus housing information is available in the Student Housing and Residential Life Office.

STUDENT GROUP

Total UAB student enrollment exceeds 16,400, including more than 3,500 graduate students. The undergraduate computer science enrollment is about 150 students. There are about 40 M.S. and 25 Ph.D. students enrolled in the graduate programs. Graduate students are actively involved in the local student chapter of the Association for Computing Machinery (ACM) and the campus Graduate Student Association.

STUDENT OUTCOMES

Most recent graduates at both the M.S. and Ph.D. levels have accepted positions in the computer industry with such companies as Amdahl, American Airlines, AT&T Bell Labs, Bell Northern Research, BellSouth, Boeing, Borland, Cisco, DHL, GE Laboratories, IBM, Intel, Intergraph, Lockheed, LSI Logic, Mentor Graphics, Microsoft, NYNEX, Ricoh, Unisys, Xerox, and other national and regional corporations.

LOCATION

Birmingham is a dynamic, progressive urban center of great natural beauty. Almost a million people live in the metropolitan area, ranking it in the top fifty-eight nationwide. Birmingham is the cultural and entertainment center of the state and offers beautiful residential neighborhoods and parks, a thriving business climate, and a relatively low cost of living. Birmingham's high quality of life has been recognized nationally for many years, most recently by the U.S. Conference of Mayors, which awarded Birmingham its "Most Livable City" designation.

THE UNIVERSITY

UAB is a comprehensive urban institution in Alabama's major city and is a nationally and internationally respected center for educational, research, and service programs. The University is composed of twelve schools, as well as hospitals and clinics that house internationally renowned patient-care programs. The Department of Computer and Information Sciences is located in the School of Natural Sciences and Mathematics. UAB also includes the Schools of Arts and Humanities, Business, Dentistry, Education, Engineering, Health-Related Professions, Medicine, Natural Sciences and Mathematics, Nursing, Optometry, Public Health, and Social and Behavioral Sciences. The campus encompasses a seventy-block area on Birmingham's Southside, offering all of the advantages of a university within a city.

APPLYING

Application forms for admission can be obtained from the Graduate School. Scores on the Graduate Record Examinations General Test are required. Admission is competitive. 1100 and 1350 are typical GRE scores (verbal and quantitative) for admission to the M.S. and Ph.D. programs, respectively. Ph.D. applicants should include a personal statement of specific graduate study and research interests and objectives. International applicants are required to submit TOEFL scores of 600 or higher to be considered for admission.

Applicants who are interested in being considered for financial aid for fall 1998 should apply by March 15, 1998.

CORRESPONDENCE AND INFORMATION

Graduate Program Director
Department of Computer and Information Sciences
Room 114 Campbell Hall
University of Alabama at Birmingham
Birmingham, Alabama 35294-1170
Telephone: 205-934-2213
Fax: 205-934-5473
E-mail: gradinfo@cis.uab.edu
World Wide Web: http://www.cis.uab.edu

UNIVERSITY OF ALABAMA AT BIRMINGHAM

THE FACULTY AND THEIR RESEARCH

Anthony C. L. Barnard, Professor; Ph.D., Birmingham (England), 1957. Software and hardware architecture, microprocessor systems.

Barrett R. Bryant, Associate Professor; Ph.D., Northwestern, 1983. Programming languages, compiler design, object-oriented technology.

*Gary Grimes, Professor and Bunn Chair of Telecommunications; Ph.D., Colorado, 1973. Virtual reality, telecommunications systems.

Robert M. Hyatt, Associate Professor; Ph.D., Alabama at Birmingham, 1988. Parallel processing, parallel search, distributed processing using "Tuple Space."

*Merida L. Johns, Associate Professor of Health Information Systems; Ph.D., Ohio State, 1991. Health information systems, modeling, medical informatics.

John K. Johnstone, Associate Professor; Ph.D., Cornell, 1987. Computer graphics, geometric modeling, biomedical visualization medical informatics.

Warren T. Jones, Professor and Chair; Ph.D., Georgia Tech, 1973. Machine learning, data mining and knowledge discovery, information filtering, medical informatics.

*Charles R. Katholi, Associate Professor of Biostatistics and Biomathematics; Ph.D., Adelphi, 1970. Numerical analysis, parallel processing.

Kevin D. Reilly, Professor; Ph.D., Chicago, 1966. Simulation, artificial intelligence, software engineering.

Kenneth R. Sloan, Associate Professor; Ph.D., Pennsylvania, 1977. Computer graphics, vision, image processing, parallel search, medical informatics.

Alan P. Sprague, Associate Professor; Ph.D., Ohio State, 1988. Parallel algorithms, data mining and knowledge discovery, medical informatics.

*Ernest M. Stokely, Professor of Biomedical Engineering and Associate Dean of Engineering; Ph.D., Southern Methodist, 1972. Medical imaging.

*Tadao Takaoka, Adjunct Professor of Computer and Information Sciences and with Hitachi; Ph.D., Kyoto (Japan), 1971. Design and analysis of algorithms, compilers, formal semantics.

*Amy E. Zwarico, Adjunct Associate Professor and Manager with BellSouth Telecommunications; Ph.D., Pennsylvania, 1988. Programming languages, concurrency, object-oriented technologies.

*Faculty members whose primary appointment or position is outside the department.

RESEARCH AREAS

Computer Graphics and Geometric Modeling. Research directions include (1) reconstruction of three-dimensional surfaces, (2) geometric modeling of solids using rational Bezier representations of swept surfaces, and (3) visualization and modeling. This research involves collaboration with such biomedical research groups as Ophthalmology, Cardiac Rhythm Measurement Laboratory, Orthopaedics, and Biomedical Engineering.

Data Mining and Knowledge Discovery. This research involves data-driven extraction of information from large repositories of data. It is the process of automated presentation of patterns, rules, or functions to a knowledgeable user for review and examination. Various machine learning models are used. Research collaborators include the Department of Pathology and the Medical Informatics Section of the Department of Medicine.

Computer Chess. Research involves the development of a chess-playing program named Crafty, which is the successor of Cray Blitz, the program that was world computer champion from 1983 to 1989. This is a joint project with Lawrence Livermore National Laboratory and Cray Research. Strategies include (1) using parallel machines and search depth, (2) improving chess knowledge, and (3) selective search depth as a function of positions.

Distributed Systems. This research is involved with the study of various parallel machine architectures and how they can best be used to improve the speed of software applications. A recent result of this research is a distributed system called "Tuple Space," which simplifies the programming effort required to distribute an application over a heterogeneous network of machines.

Object-Oriented Technology. Ongoing research is concentrated in the areas of (1) automated generation of compilers for object-oriented programming languages from denotational semantics and (2) software reuse at the specification level. One recent result of this research is an object-oriented language called SmallC++, which generates parallel code in the form of Tuple Space primitives on a network of processors.

Artificial Intelligence. Current research activities include (1) combining artificial neural network and expert systems into mixed problem–solving systems, (2) use of combined discrete and continuous simulators with artificial neural network capabilities, (3) derivation strategies for artificial neural networks from fuzzy expert systems and vice versa, and (4) distributed artificial intelligence using Tcl-Dp, PVM, and Tuple Space and Java. Research collaborators are the Civitan International Research Center, the Department of Psychology, and the Cognitive Science Research Group.

Simulation Environments. A simulation environment includes elements that help in (1) building models, (2) executing (or exercising) them, (3) analyzing and interpreting modeling results, and (4) storing the knowledge representing all phases to include previous knowledge upon which building occurs, etc. Research involves defining SEs in general purpose frameworks and investigating key problems, e.g., the role of formal logic, automated tools in specifying systems, prototyping, model abstraction, distributing models, and animation.

UAH — THE UNIVERSITY OF ALABAMA IN HUNTSVILLE

DEPARTMENT OF ELECTRICAL AND COMPUTER ENGINEERING

PROGRAMS OF STUDY

The Department of Electrical and Computer Engineering (ECE) offers the Master of Science in Engineering (M.S.E.) in electrical engineering, computer engineering, and optics and photonics technology. Software engineering is offered as a concentration under the M.S.E. in computer engineering. The Ph.D. is awarded in electrical engineering and in computer engineering.

An interdisciplinary Ph.D. in optical science and engineering, offered jointly by the College of Science and the College of Engineering, enrolled its first students in 1993 and awarded its first degree in 1995. This flexible program prepares students with varied scientific backgrounds for research careers in such fields as classical optics, spectroscopy, optical processing and computing, optical inspection, optical materials, liquid crystal displays, and optoelectronics.

The ECE department encourages collaborative research and offers opportunities for students to work on broad programs of research extending across traditional disciplinary boundaries. Among such projects are 3-D displays, optical interconnect systems, and satellite communications. Faculty members from within and outside the department are actively involved with graduate student mentoring, ensuring that students develop the technical and communications skills necessary for successful careers.

RESEARCH FACILITIES

Students and faculty members have access to the Alabama Supercomputer Network's CRAY C94A and nCUBE2 as well as a variety of minicomputers and workstations through Ethernet connections in every office and laboratory. Personal computers are widely available throughout the Engineering Building. The department supports PC, Macintosh, Sun systems, and a Harris Nighthawk multiprocessor. Research laboratories include those for VLSI design, optical computing, nonlinear optics, optical communications, optical information processing, satellite communications, advanced display research, thin-film transistor development, nanofabrication, polymeric and liquid crystal photonics, real-time systems, and signal processing.

FINANCIAL AID

Teaching and research assistantships are available on a competitive basis. The assistantships carry a stipend and cover tuition. The optical science and engineering program offers NSF graduate traineeships for qualified U.S. permanent residents.

COST OF STUDY

Tuition for the 1996–97 academic year for a full-time Alabama resident enrolled for 9 semester hours averaged $1327 per semester. Rates for out-of-state students were double those of Alabama residents. The estimated average cost of books per semester for full-time students is $250.

LIVING AND HOUSING COSTS

UAH offers air-conditioned apartments. Each has its own entrance and is carpeted and equipped with a stove and a refrigerator. Interested students should apply at least two academic terms before anticipated enrollment. Costs range from $149 per month for a three-bedroom furnished dormitory suite (accommodates 2 students per bedroom) to $462 per month for a three-bedroom furnished apartments for student families. A new, private dormitory houses 4 students per suite. Numerous apartments are within walking distance of the campus.

STUDENT GROUP

The department is the largest on campus, enrolling 425 undergraduates and 174 graduate students, almost half of whom work in local industrial or government facilities. Many undergraduates take advantage of the Cooperative Program to alternate academic study with practical experience. Because of the large high-technology sector in Huntsville, almost all cooperative students live and work there, allowing them great flexibility in integrating their work and study.

STUDENT OUTCOMES

Most students remain in the Huntsville area, where many employment opportunities exist within the federal and private sectors in fields such as optoelectronics, communications, control systems, computer engineering, and signal processing.

LOCATION

Huntsville is the center of a diverse, dynamic metropolitan area of 250,000 that has developed around the high-technology focus of Redstone Arsenal (Army Missile Command, NASA Marshall Space Flight Center, Space and Strategic Defense Command) and the Cummings Research Park (ADTRAN, Nichols Research, Dynetics, BDM, SAIC, Rockwell, Lockheed-Martin, Teledyne Brown, Intergraph, and SCI, among others). The city is located on verdant rolling hills in the Tennessee Valley on the north bank of the Tennessee River in north-central Alabama.

THE UNIVERSITY AND THE DEPARTMENT

The department faculty members are research-active, with degrees from premier U.S. universities. With modern facilities for instruction and research, the department is the largest on campus, occupying 45,000 square feet of high-quality space.

APPLYING

Students may be admitted for any semester. Applicants attending on student visas must apply at least three months in advance on anticipated enrollment; all others should apply at least one month in advance. If assistantships are desired, applicants should apply early. All applicants must submit a completed application with a $20 application fee, official transcripts form each university previously attended, and the appropriate test scores.

CORRESPONDENCE AND INFORMATION

Director of Graduate Studies
Department of Electrical and Computer Engineering
The University of Alabama in Huntsville
Huntsville, Alabama 35899

Telephone: 205-890-6678 or 6316
Fax: 205-890-6803
E-mail: ece@ebs330.eb.uah.edu
World Wide Web: http://www.eb.uah.edu/ece

THE UNIVERSITY OF ALABAMA IN HUNTSVILLE

THE FACULTY AND THEIR RESEARCH

M. A. G. Abushagur. Optical signal processing, computing and metrology.
R. R. Adhami, Associate Chair. Digital signal processing, digital systems design.
N. F. Audeh. Electromagnetics.
P. P. Banerjee. Nonlinear wave phenomena, optical processing.
T. B. Boykin. Modeling compound and quantum semiconductor devices.
W. E. Cohen. Computer engineering, compilers.
K. B. Cook. Telecommunication systems.
R. L. Fork. Photonics, optical communications.
R. K. Gaede. Computer architecture, design for test, VHDL.
F. D. Ho. Microelectronic devices and integrated circuits, photovoltaic devices, electronic materials.
J. M. Jarem. Electromagnetics, antenna theory, microwave theory, optics.
C. D. Johnson. Control and dynamic systems.
C. Katsinis. Computer architecture.
S. T. Kowel, Chair. Optoelectronic materials, devices and systems.
J. H. Kulick. Computer design, computer-generated holography, medical image processing.
R. G. Lindquist. Electrooptics and nonlinear optics.
M. W. Maier. Radar signal processing, data compression, system architecture.
G. P. Nordin. Volume holographic optical memories, diffractive 3-D displays.
D. B. Pollock. Infrared optical systems.
W. A. Porter. Array architectures, pattern recognition, system theory and applications.
A. D. Poularikas. Statistical optics, signal processing.
V. R. Riasati. Optical pattern recognition.
D. Shen. Electronic materials and devices, thin-film deposition.
Y. Shtessel. Automatic control theory, sliding modes, multicriteria control.
N. Singh, Director of Graduate Studies. Electromagnetics, plasma, and space research.
J. Stensby. Communication systems and signal processing.
B. E. Wells. Computer architecture, parallel processing, digital design.

UNIVERSITY OF ALBERTA

DEPARTMENT OF COMPUTING SCIENCE

PROGRAMS OF STUDY

The department offers graduate programs leading to the M.Sc. and Ph.D. degrees. Instruction and opportunities for research exist in the areas of theoretical foundations, including analysis of algorithms, algebraic manipulation, and computational complexity; systems and architecture, including parallel and distributed computing, computer networks, and object-oriented programming; and applications, including software engineering and database systems, artificial intelligence, and graphics, vision, and robotics.

The M.Sc. requirements include a minimum of six graduate courses, a thesis, a seminar, and an oral examination. The Ph.D. requirements include a minimum of four graduate courses beyond those for the M.Sc. degree, the breadth requirement, a thesis, a seminar, and an oral examination.

RESEARCH FACILITIES

The department has its own research computing facility and maintains a central pool of resources—including programming, engineering, and operating staff—to support a wide diversity of computing science research by about 35 faculty members and 100 graduate students. Ethernet links this "backbone facility" to eight research labs containing specialized equipment. Besides using the equipment resident in the department, researchers have convenient access to the University's facilities, including a "farm" of thirty IBM RS6000s. In addition, facilities worldwide may be reached via the Internet direct connection.

The computer equipment consists of a network interconnecting a DEC AXP 3000/400, a four-processor Silicon Graphics 4D340S with 96 MB of memory, a sixty-four-processor Myrias SPS-2 parallel computer, and a variety of file servers supplying more than 40 gigabytes of storage. Workstations are generally accessible to graduate students; they are located in all faculty and staff offices, and many more are in the laboratories described below. There are four AppleTalk networks gatewayed to the backbone, with local printers and disk servers used by the many Macintoshes.

The AI laboratory contains six workstations, a scanner, a printer, and other equipment. Software includes LISP, PROLOG, LOOPS, ART-IM, and OPS83. The database systems laboratory is equipped with seven Sun SPARC and two IBM RS6000 workstations. Experiments are run using tools based on OStore, Smalltalk, PROLOG, and Exodus. The graphics laboratory supports virtual reality and animation with five SGI IRIS workstations, three DECStations, and four HP9000/7xx workstations. Attached to these are a TV camera, a 3-space digitizer, and a Data-Glove. Output devices include Eyephone stereo goggles, a single-frame VCR, and a color printer. The networking laboratory uses four SGI Indys to perform experiments in network performance and multimedia. The parallel systems laboratory has four Suns and an HP 9000/720. Many of their experiments are run on the CNS "farm" as well as other clusters of workstations using the NMP (Network Multiprocessor Package), PVM, and the Enterprise system under development. The software engineering laboratory uses four Sun SPARCstations and two IBM RS6000s to work with CASE tools such as Datrix, Concept Base, and Softbench. The theory laboratory contains six Sun SPARCstations supporting environments that include C, LISP, Mizar, Modula-2, Smalltalk-80, Cornell Program Synthesizer, and Maple. The vision and robotics laboratory has several robotic platforms, including a Puma 260 arm, a TRC mobile platform, a three-fingered hand, and a submarine. These are controlled by several real-time processors, including a DataCube MV-20 image analysis processor. Image understanding and compression for multimedia are supported with several cameras, digitizers, and workstations.

In addition to the extensive computing facilities available to departmental members, a satellite library housing more than 11,000 volumes and many journals exists within the department. This library is a part of the University Library system, which holds about 3.7 million volumes. The Department of Computing Science enjoys a close liaison with the Department of Electrical Engineering through the jointly administered Computer Engineering Program.

FINANCIAL AID

Normal stipends for a four-month term range from approximately $4300 to $5800 and require 12 hours of service per week. Summer support may be available.

COST OF STUDY

The full-time instruction fee for 1997–98 is about $2150, plus additional general fees of about $470. Student visitors (visa students) are assessed a differential fee of 100 percent of the graduate full-time instruction fee.

LIVING AND HOUSING COSTS

A single graduate student needs a total of approximately $9500 per year for living expenses in the Edmonton, Alberta, area.

STUDENT GROUP

The University of Alberta has an enrollment of about 29,000 students, of whom about 4,000 are pursuing graduate studies. Currently, the Department of Computing Science has 90 full-time graduate students in residence.

STUDENT OUTCOMES

Recent graduates of the Ph.D. program have found academic positions at Canadian and international universities, along with research and development positions in the computing industry.

The graduates of the M.Sc. program either find positions in industry or continue their studies at the Ph.D. level.

LOCATION

Edmonton, the capital of the province, is an attractive modern city of more than half a million people. The city is within a few hours' drive of Banff and Jasper national parks in the Canadian Rockies, which offer year-round recreational facilities. Edmonton not only is the home of the largest university of the province but also supports a variety of cultural activities, such as theater, opera, and symphony performances. Although predominantly English-speaking, the local community supports active French-, German-, Ukrainian-, and Chinese-speaking populations.

THE UNIVERSITY

In 1906, the Alberta legislature authorized the establishment of the University of Alberta. It experienced its greatest growth during the years 1945–69, during which time its enrollment increased from 5,000 to 17,000 students. It has continued to grow and now consists of sixteen faculties.

APPLYING

Canadian applicants may submit applications until June 1. Applications from international students and from all students requesting financial support must be received by March 1. Application forms are available from the department. Students from other countries should be aware that it takes three to six months to obtain a student visa.

CORRESPONDENCE AND INFORMATION

Graduate Program Coordinator
Department of Computing Science
University of Alberta
Edmonton, Alberta T6G 2H1
Canada
Telephone: 403-492-5198
Fax: 403-492-1071
E-mail: gradinfo@cs.ualberta.ca
World Wide Web: http://web.cs.ualberta.ca

UNIVERSITY OF ALBERTA
THE FACULTY AND THEIR RESEARCH

William W. Armstrong, Professor; Ph.D., British Columbia, 1966. Knowledge discovery in data, adaptive logic networks.

Anup Basu, Associate Professor; Ph.D., Maryland, 1990. Computer vision, robotics, image processing, teleconferencing/telepresence.

John W. Buchanan, Assistant Professor; Ph.D., British Columbia, 1994. Three dimensional textures, nonrealistic rendering, volume rendering, filtering of textures, vector field visualization.

Stanley Cabay, Professor; Ph.D., Toronto, 1971. Numerical analysis, symbolic and algebraic computation.

Joseph Culberson, Associate Professor; Ph.D., Waterloo, 1986. Data structures, algorithms and genetic algorithms.

Wayne A. Davis, Professor Emeritus; Ph.D., Ottawa, 1967. Interactive graphics, computer vision, spatial databases.

Renée Elio, Associate Professor; Ph.D., Carnegie Mellon, 1981. Knowledge-based and expert systems, machine learning, computer simulations of human cognitive processes, human reasoning.

Ehab S. Elmallah, Associate Professor; Ph.D., Waterloo, 1987. Combinatorial parallel and distributed algorithms, design and analysis of interconnection networks, fault tolerant computing.

Pawel Gburzynski, Professor; Ph.D., Warsaw, 1982. Local area networks, simulation, systems programming.

Randy G. Goebel, Professor and Associate Chair; Ph.D., British Columbia, 1985. Artificial intelligence, knowledge representation, logic programming.

Mark Green, Professor; Ph.D., Toronto, 1984. Computer graphics, human-computer interaction, virtual reality, computer animation.

Janelle J. Harms, Assistant Professor; Ph.D., Waterloo, 1992. Computer networks, performance evaluation, high-speed networks.

H. James Hoover, Associate Professor; Ph.D., Toronto, 1987. Theory of computation, complexity theory, circuit complexity, programming methodology.

Xiaobo Li, Professor; Ph.D., Michigan State, 1984. Pattern recognition, image processing, computer vision, computer architectures, parallel processing.

Ling Liu, Assistant Professor; Ph.D., Tilburg, 1993. Federated database systems, object-oriented database systems, software reuse and evolution.

T. Anthony Marsland, Professor; Ph.D., Washington (Seattle), 1967. Distributed systems studies, tree search algorithms, parallel processing methods.

Ursula M. Maydell, Associate Professor; M.Sc., Alberta, 1963. Analysis and design of communication networks; computer system and network performance (modeling, measurement, and evaluation); medical imaging on high-speed local area networks; high-speed circuit switched networks; integrated services.

Ioanis Nikolaidis, Assistant Professor; Ph.D., Georgia Tech, 1994. Computer networks, performance evaluation, parallel and distributed simulation.

M. Tamer Ozsu, Professor; Ph.D., Ohio State, 1983. Database systems, distributed databases, distributed parallel query processing, object-oriented databases, multimedia information systems.

Francis Jeffry Pelletier, Professor; Ph.D., UCLA, 1971. Computational linguistics, automated theorem proving, logic, artificial intelligence, philosophy of language, formal semantics, cognitive science. (Joint appointment with Philosophy)

Piotr Rudnicki, Associate Professor; Ph.D., Warsaw, 1979. Program correctness and verification, proof checkers, logic, programming languages.

Jonathan Schaeffer, Professor and Associate Chair; Ph.D., Waterloo, 1986. Distributed systems, parallel processing, search algorithms, heuristics, computer chess and checkers.

Keith W. Smillie, Professor Emeritus; Ph.D., Toronto, 1952. Programming languages, microcomputer software, history of computing.

Paul G. Sorenson, Professor and Chair; Ph.D., Toronto, 1974. Software engineering, software quality.

Lorna K. Stewart, Associate Professor; Ph.D., Toronto, 1985. Graph theory, design and analysis of algorithms.

Duane Szafron, Associate Professor; Ph.D., Waterloo, 1978. Object-oriented computing (programming languages, design and object bases), distributed computing, multimedia.

John Tartar, Professor Emeritus; Ph.D., Arizona State, 1967. Computer architectures, multiprocessor systems, graphics, local area networks.

Ron Unrau, Associate Professor; Ph.D., Toronto, 1993. Parallel compilers, operating systems.

Peter van Beek, Associate Professor; Ph.D., Waterloo, 1990. Artificial intelligence, temporal reasoning, knowledge representation and natural language question-answering systems.

Jia-Huai You, Professor; Ph.D., Utah, 1985. Logic programming, term rewriting systems, nonmonotonic reasoning.

Li Yan Yuan, Associate Professor; Ph.D., Case Western Reserve, 1986. Database management systems, logic programming and deductive databases, artificial intelligence.

Hong Zhang, Associate Professor; Ph.D., Purdue, 1986. Dextrous robot manipulation, tactile sensing, and collective robotics.

THE UNIVERSITY OF ARIZONA

DEPARTMENT OF COMPUTER SCIENCE

PROGRAMS OF STUDY

The Department of Computer Science at the University of Arizona offers programs leading to the Master of Science and Doctor of Philosophy degrees. Faculty research interests in both the experimental and theoretical aspects of computer science provide diversity and balance in preparing students for industrial or academic careers.

The Master of Science (M.S.) curriculum consists of 30 units of required course work followed by a comprehensive written examination. Students who are especially well prepared may elect a thesis option.

The department encourages qualified students to pursue the Doctor of Philosophy degree in computer science. Students with strong undergraduate records and training in computer science are admitted directly to the doctoral program, while students beginning graduate study at the University without extensive experience in computer science or a closely related field may first pursue the master's program. Because of the relationship between the two programs, taking the M.S. does not delay the completion of the Ph.D., and it gives students more opportunity to display their qualifications for doctoral work.

The Ph.D. curriculum in computer science consists of required course work and examinations, culminating in the dissertation and its defense. This program is supervised by the student's doctoral committee, made up of 3 faculty members from the Department of Computer Science and 2 from the minor department.

RESEARCH FACILITIES

Three multiprocessor systems—a Sun SPARCserver 1000, a Sun SPARCstation 20, and a Silicon Graphics 4D/340—provide mainframe shared computing support. Numerous Sun SPARC, DEC Alpha, and Intel Pentium workstations are used for research in distributed operating systems, programming environments, and other topics. Other research equipment includes a 16-processor Intel Paragon, an SGI Indigo2 graphics engine, and three different workstations clusters: an 8-node SPARC cluster, a 16-node Alpha cluster, and a 32-node PentiumPRO cluster. High-quality document preparation equipment such as a Linotype phototypesetter, Apple LaserWriters, a QMS color laser printer, film recorders, and document scanners are also available.

FINANCIAL AID

Several forms of financial assistance are available to graduate students through the University. These include scholarships, fellowships, work-study programs, and loan programs. In addition, a limited number of half-time assistantships are available directly through the Department of Computer Science.

COST OF STUDY

Legal residents of Arizona paid $1005 per semester in 1996–97, while the cost for nonresidents was $3149 (9 units). Nonresidents holding departmental assistantships pay resident tuition.

LIVING AND HOUSING COSTS

Private off-campus housing is readily available in a wide range of prices, much of it within a comfortable walking distance from campus. The University also has student family housing available ranging from $295 to $620 per month. For more information, students should write to Family Housing, 3401 North Columbus Boulevard, Tucson, Arizona 85712.

STUDENT GROUP

Total enrollment at the University is 33,504 students, including 7,090 graduate students. The department has 70 graduate students; 24 are in the Ph.D. program.

STUDENT OUTCOMES

Typically, the department's graduates find employment easily upon completion of their degrees. Students gain employment with corporations such as Microsoft, Hewlett-Packard, AT&T, Sun Microsystems, and Motorola, as well as with a variety of smaller companies. Ph.D. graduates have been recruited into such universities as Rice, Penn State, and the University of California, Davis.

LOCATION

Founded in 1775, and set in a valley surrounded by four mountain ranges, Tucson's population has grown to nearly 700,000 people. Nicknamed the "Old Pueblo," Tucson's identity has been shaped by the rich cultural heritage of the Old West. The influence of cowboys, pioneers, Mexicans, southwestern Native Americans, and Spaniards is evident throughout the area.

Tucson's mild winters and year-round sunshine attract many visitors and new residents. Although located in the Sonoran Desert upland, Tucson receives annual rainfall of 12 inches, comparable to that received by San Diego. Opportunities for recreation and sports are abundant all year, including skiing, spelunking, hiking, and golf. The beaches of Mexico are only a few hours south and provide scuba diving and deep-sea fishing.

For a city of moderate size, the variety and excellence of Tucson's arts community are remarkable. Attractions include the Tucson Symphony Orchestra, the Arizona Opera, the Arizona Theatre Company, the Arizona Dance Theater, and the Tucson Museum of Art, as well as a wide variety of University programs in the arts.

National observatories located on nearby Kitt Peak, Mt. Hopkins, and Mt. Lemmon make Tucson one of the world's major astronomical centers.

THE UNIVERSITY

The University of Arizona, located near the center of Tucson, was founded in 1885 as Arizona's land-grant university. Today it is one of the twenty-five largest universities in the nation, with advanced study and research taking place in 138 departments. The University is one of fifty-nine public universities classified as a Research Institute I by the Carnegie Commission on Higher Education, and it ranks fourteenth of all universities in external research funding and tenth among all public universities. The University's growing excellence attracts many recruiters from industry, government, education, and business representing the most prestigious companies and institutions.

APPLYING

Applicants to the master's program are expected to have a minimum undergraduate GPA of 3.2 out of 4.0 and scores above the 50th, 85th, and 75th percentiles, respectively, on the verbal, quantitative, and analytical portions of the GRE General Test. Applicants to the doctoral program should have a minimum undergraduate GPA of 3.5 (those with a master's degree in a related field are expected to have a graduate GPA of 3.7 or above) and GRE General Test scores above the 80th, 90th, and 85th percentiles. Doctoral applicants must also submit a GRE Subject Test score. Those with a degree in computer science must take the GRE Subject Test in computer science; non–computer science majors must take either the computer science Subject Test or the Subject Test in their major area. International applicants whose native language is not English must submit a TOEFL score of at least 600; the Test of Written English (TWE) is recommended; a score of at least 50 on the Test of Spoken English (TSE) is required to obtain a teaching assistantship.

CORRESPONDENCE AND INFORMATION

Department of Computer Science
The University of Arizona
Tucson, Arizona 85721-0077

Telephone: 520-621-6613
E-mail: gradadmissions@cs.arizona.edu
World Wide Web: http://www.cs.arizona.edu

THE UNIVERSITY OF ARIZONA

THE FACULTY AND THEIR RESEARCH

Gregory R. Andrews, Professor; Ph.D., Washington (Seattle), 1974. Design and implementation of concurrent programming languages, parallel and distributed computing, operating systems.

Saumya Debray, Associate Professor; Ph.D., SUNY at Stony Brook, 1986. Compilers, program analysis and optimization, programming language implementations, partial evaluation.

Peter J. Downey, Associate Professor; Ph.D., Harvard, 1974. Analysis of algorithms, stochastic analysis, performance modeling and evaluation, scheduling and sequencing problems.

Will Evans, Assistant Professor; Ph.D., Berkeley, 1994. Noisy computation, computational geometry, geographic information systems.

Ralph E. Griswold, Professor Emeritus; Ph.D., Stanford, 1962. Programming language design and implementation, graphics, human interface.

John Hartman, Assistant Professor; Ph.D., Berkeley, 1994. Network file systems, distributed systems, and operating systems.

Udi Manber, Professor; Ph.D., Washington (Seattle), 1982. Computer networks and the World Wide Web; software tools, especially search and resource discovery tools; design of algorithms; pattern matching.

Eugene W. Myers Jr., Professor; Ph.D., Colorado, 1981. Design and analysis of algorithms pertinent to applications in molecular biology, graphics, compilers, software tools.

Larry L. Peterson, Professor; Ph.D., Purdue, 1985. High-speed networks, operating systems, network appliances, mobile code.

Toni Pitassi, Assistant Professor; Ph.D., Toronto, 1992. Complexity theory, lower bounds, proof complexity, theorem proving, combinatorial algorithms.

Todd Proebsting, Assistant Professor; Ph.D., Wisconsin–Madison, 1992. Design and implementation of optimizing compilers, retargetable compilers, software tools.

Stuart Reges, Senior Lecturer; M.S., Stanford, 1983. Computer science education, object-oriented programming.

Richard D. Schlichting, Professor; Ph.D., Cornell, 1982. Fault-tolerant computing, distributed systems, heterogeneous computing, operating systems, networks, programming methodology.

Richard T. Snodgrass, Professor; Ph.D., Carnegie-Mellon, 1982. Temporal databases, data semantics, query languages, database management systems.

REPRESENTATIVE FACULTY PUBLICATIONS

Andrews, G. R., V. W. Freeh, and D. K. Lowenthal. Using fine-grain threads and run-time decision making in parallel computing. *J. Parallel Dist. Comput.* 37:41–54, 1996.

Andrews, G. R. *Concurrent Programming: Principles and Practice.* Redwood City, Calif.: Benjamin/Cummings Publishing Co., 1991.

Debray, S. K., and **T. A. Proebsting.** Interprocedural control flow analysis of first order programs with tail call optimization. *ACM Trans. Programming Lang. Syst.*, in press.

Debray, S. K. On the complexity of dataflow analysis of logic programs. *ACM Trans. Programming Lang. Syst.* 17(1), 1995.

Downey, P. J., J. Bruno, and E. G. Coffman. Scheduling independent tasks to minimize the makespan on identical machines. *Probability Eng. Information Sci.* 9:447–56, 1995.

Downey, P. J. Bounds and approximations for overheads in the time to join parallel forks. *ORSA J. Comput.* 7(2):176–86, 1995.

Evans, W., and N. Pippenger. Lower bounds for noisy Boolean decision trees. *28th Symposium on the Theory of Computation*, 1996. Submitted to *SIAM Journal of Computation.*

Evans, W., and L. Schulman. Signal propagation, with application to a lower bound on the depth of noisy formulas. *34th Symposium on Foundations of Computer Science*, 1993.

Griswold, R. E., and M. T. Griswold. *The Icon Programming Language*, 3rd edition. Peer-to-Peer Communications, 1996.

Griswold, R. E., C. L. Jeffery, and G. Townsend. Adding graphics capabilities to a high-level programming language. *Software Pract. Experience* 25(6), June 1995.

Hartman, J. H., and P. Sarkar. Efficient cooperative caching using hints. *Proceedings of the Second Symposium on Operating System Design and Implementation*, pp. 35–46, October 1996.

Hartman, J. H., and J. K. Ousterhout. The zebra striped network file system. *ACM Trans. Comput. Syst.* 13(3):279–310, 1995.

Manber, U. A simple scheme to make passwords based on one-way functions much harder to crack. *Comput. Secur.* 15(2):171–6, 1996.

Manber, U., et al. The Harvest Information Discovery and Access System. *Comput. Networks ISDN Syst.* 28:119–25, 1995.

Myers, E. W. Toward simplifying and accurately formulating fragment assembly. *J. Computational Biol.* 2(2):275–90, 1995.

Myers, E. W. A sublinear algorithm for approximate keyword matching. *Algorithmica* 12(4–5):345–74, 1994.

Peterson, L. L., and L. Brakmo. TCP Vegas: End-to-end congestion control in a global Internet. *IEEE J. Selected Areas Commun.* 13(8):1465–80, 1995.

Peterson, L. L., and P. Druschel. Fbufs: A high-bandwidth cross-domain transfer facility. In *Proceedings of the 14th Symposium on Operating Systems Principles*, pp. 202–15, December 1993.

Pitassi, T., et al. Lower bounds for Hilbert's nullstellensatz and propositional proofs. *Proc. London Math Soc.*, in press.

Pitassi, T., and A. Urquhart. The complexity of the Hajos calculus. *SIAM J. Discrete Mathematics* 8(3), 1995.

Proebsting, T., and C. N. Fischer. Demand-driven register allocation. *Trans. Prog. Languages Syst.*, in press.

Proebsting, T., S. M. Kurlander, and C. N. Fischer. Efficient instruction scheduling for delayed-load architectures. *Trans. Prog. Languages Syst.* 740–76, September 1995.

Reges, S. The effective use of undergraduates to staff large, introductory CS courses. *SIGCSE Bull.* February 1988.

Reges, S., and S. Fisher. *Pascal and Beyond: Data Abstraction and Data Structures using Turbo Pascal.* New York: John Wiley & Sons, 1992.

Schlichting, R. D., and D. Bakken. Supporting fault-tolerant parallel programming in Linda. *IEEE Trans. Parallel Distributed Syst.* 6(3):287–302, 1995.

Schlichting, R. D., and P. Homer. Using Schooner to support distribution and heterogeneity in the numerical propulsion system simulation project. *Concurrency, Software Pract. Experience* 6(4):271–87, 1994.

Snodgrass, R. T., and C. S. Jensen. Semantics of time-varying information. *Information Syst.* 21(4):311–52, 1996.

Snodgrass, R. T., ed. *The TSQL2 Temporal Query Language.* Dordrecht: Kluwer Academic Publishers, 1995.

THE UNIVERSITY OF ARIZONA

DEPARTMENT OF ELECTRICAL AND COMPUTER ENGINEERING

PROGRAMS OF STUDY

The department offers graduate programs leading to the M.S. and Ph.D. degrees with a major in electrical and computer engineering. A nonmajors program is available for qualified students who do not hold degrees in electrical or computer engineering.

The Master of Science degree requires a minimum of 30 units. There are thesis and nonthesis options. Candidates must pass a final oral examination.

The Ph.D. program must contain a minimum of 54 units of course work (including the Master of Science degree) and 18 units of dissertation study. To satisfy the residence requirement, the student must spend a minimum of two regular semesters of full-time study on campus. Students must pass a qualifying examination, which is usually taken during the first semester of residence beyond the master's degree, and are admitted to candidacy after passing a preliminary examination near the end of the study program. The final examination is a defense of the dissertation. There is no foreign language requirement.

RESEARCH FACILITIES

The department is active in research in the general areas of communications, controls, and signal processing; computer engineering; electromagnetics; and microelectronics. Specialized laboratories are available to support research efforts. Research programs are an integral part of the department's educational activities. All facilities are housed in a modern building that includes more than 50,000 square feet of laboratory space. Much of the research is supported by grants from federal agencies or by industrial contracts.

FINANCIAL AID

Fellowships, research and teaching assistantships, and tuition and academic scholarships are available for qualified students. In 1997–98, assistantships provide a stipend of $14,104 to $16,767 per academic year (ten months) plus a waiver of out-of-state tuition. Recipients devote 20 hours per week to research or teaching duties during the academic year and may significantly supplement their stipend by full-time research in the department during the summer. Supplemental scholarships are available for especially well qualified students.

COST OF STUDY

The registration fee for full-time Arizona residents was $2010 per academic year in 1996–97. Students who have not yet established Arizona residence paid an additional $6368 in out-of-state tuition; this is normally waived for students supported by an assistantship or fellowship.

LIVING AND HOUSING COSTS

The average cost of a room in the residence halls was $2200 per academic year in 1995–96. Comparably priced off-campus housing is available within easy walking distance.

STUDENT GROUP

There are about 225 full-time graduate students in the department. Research assistantships, teaching assistantships, scholarships, and fellowships are available to well-qualified applicants. The department has an active Graduate Student Association.

LOCATION

The University is located in Tucson, whose excellent climate, clean air, and mountain vistas have made it a magnet for visitors and new residents. The metropolitan area has a population of approximately 680,000. Tucson enjoys mild winters. In the Santa Catalina mountain range on the north edge of the city, ski slopes, ponderosa pines, canyons, and grassy meadows attract skiers, climbers, and hikers. Tucson has a symphony orchestra, an opera company, many art galleries, and the Arizona Sonora Desert Museum. The city is often visited by theater companies and musicians.

THE UNIVERSITY

Founded in 1885, the University of Arizona is ranked by the National Science Foundation as one of the top twenty research universities in the nation. The University has fourteen colleges and an enrollment of 35,000 students; of these, approximately 2,384 are enrolled in the fourteen departments of the College of Engineering and Mines. In the past decade, the University of Arizona Wildcat athletic teams, which compete in the Pacific-10 Conference, played in five postseason football bowl games, won six men's basketball conference titles, went to the men's NCAA Final Four in basketball three times, won four Collegiate World Series softball titles, and won national championships in both men's and women's golf. Most recently, the Cats won their first-ever NCAA championship in men's basketball in 1997.

APPLYING

Domestic applicants should submit applications for admission and all supporting material to the Graduate College as early as possible and no later than May 1 for the summer terms, June 1 for the fall term, and October 1 for the spring term. International applicants should submit applications for admission and all supporting material by February 1 for the summer and fall terms and August 1 for the spring term. Applicants for financial assistance must be accepted for admission and should submit supporting material by March 15 for the fall term and November 15 for the spring term. Applicants are required to submit GRE General Test scores, a statement of purpose, and three letters of recommendation directly to the department. All students whose native language is other than English must submit TOEFL scores directly to the Graduate College.

CORRESPONDENCE AND INFORMATION

Graduate Studies Office
Department of Electrical and Computer Engineering
ECE Building, Room 230
The University of Arizona
Tucson, Arizona 85721
Telephone: 520-621-6195

THE UNIVERSITY OF ARIZONA
THE FACULTY AND THEIR RESEARCH

John R. Brews, Professor; Ph.D., McGill, 1965. Semiconductor device physics, MOSFET design, electromagnetics of interconnections.

Andreas C. Cangellaris, Associate Professor; Ph.D., Berkeley, 1985. Numerical methods for electromagnetic wave scattering and propagation, analysis of microwave integrated circuits, electromagnetic characterization of high-speed interconnections for VLSI.

Jo Dale Carothers, Assistant Professor; Ph.D., Texas at Austin, 1989. VLSI design, physical design (partitioning, placement, and routing) for single and multichip modules, low-power design, engineering applications of graph theory.

Francois E. Cellier, Associate Professor; Ph.D., Swiss Federal Institute of Technology, 1979. Modeling, simulation, control, software engineering.

Thomas C. Cetas, Professor (also Professor in Radiation/Oncology); Ph.D., Iowa State, 1970. Thermal ionizing and non-ionizing radiation research for cancer and other medical therapies.

Donald G. Dudley, Professor Emeritus; Ph.D., UCLA, 1968. Target identification, transient scattering, coupling and penetration, microwave pulsed power, geophysical modeling.

Steven L. Dvorak, Associate Professor; Ph.D., Colorado at Boulder, 1989. Electromagnetic transients, wave propagation, analytical and computational electromagnetics, optics, applied mathematics, microwave measurements.

Jack D. Gaskill, Professor (also Professor in Optical Sciences); Ph.D., Stanford, 1968. Fourier optics, diffraction theory.

Glen C. Gerhard, Professor and Associate Department Head; Ph.D., Ohio State, 1963. Medical instrumentation and systems, technology and innovation in education.

Fredrick J. Hill, Professor; Ph.D., Utah, 1963. Digital systems, design languages, design automation, test generation.

W. Timothy Holman, Assistant Professor; Ph.D., Georgia Tech, 1994. Analog microelectronics.

Lawrence P. Huelsman, Professor Emeritus; Ph.D., Berkeley, 1960. Active and passive filters, computer-aided design.

Bobby R. Hunt, Professor; Ph.D., Arizona, 1967. Signal processing, digital image processing.

Raymond K. Kostuk, Associate Professor; Ph.D., Stanford, 1986. Optical interconnects, diffractive optical elements, fiber optics, optical data storage.

Marwan M. Krunz, Assistant Professor; Ph.D., Michigan State, 1995. Modeling and performance evaluation of high-speed computer networks, traffic characterization, video-on-demand architectures.

Ahmed Louri, Associate Professor; Ph.D., USC, 1988. Computer architecture, computer networks, parallel processing, parallel algorithms, optical computing.

Michael W. Marcellin, Associate Professor; Ph.D., Texas A&M, 1987. Data compression, digital communication and storage systems, digital signal processing.

Michael M. Marefat, Assistant Professor; Ph.D., Purdue, 1991. Machine intelligence, software engineering, robotics, computer vision, computer graphics, intelligent control, CAD/CAM.

Ralph Martinez, Associate Professor; Ph.D., Arizona, 1976. Computer systems application and design, distributed computing environments, computer networks, medical imaging and communications, telemedicine systems.

Pitu Mirchandani, Professor (also Professor in Systems and Industrial Engineering); D.Sc., MIT, 1975. Optimization, scheduling, integrated manufacturing, transportation.

Mark A. Neifeld, Associate Professor; Ph.D., Caltech, 1990. Optical memories and information processing, parallel coding and signal processing, pattern recognition, neural networks.

John F. O'Hanlon, Professor, Ph.D., Simon Fraser, 1967. Vacuum physics, microcontamination, semiconductor processing, physical electronics.

Olgierd A. Palusinski, Professor; Ph.D., Silesian Technical (Poland), 1966. Computer-aided design of integrated circuits, electronic packaging, circuit simulation.

Harold G. Parks, Associate Professor; Ph.D., RPI, 1980. Integrated circuit processing, defect studies, yield enhancement and modeling, semiconductor devices.

John L. Prince, Professor; Ph.D., North Carolina State, 1969. Microelectronics, electronic packaging.

John A. Reagan, Professor; Ph.D., Wisconsin–Madison, 1967. Electromagnetic remote sensing, atmospheric radiation and optics, optoelectronic instrumentation.

Jeffrey J. Rodriguez, Assistant Professor; Ph.D., Texas at Austin, 1990. Digital image processing, computer vision, digital signal processing, biomedical image processing.

Jerzy W. Rozenblit, Associate Professor; Ph.D., Wayne State, 1985. Modeling, simulation, artificial intelligence, knowledge-based design, intelligent systems, engineering of computer-based systems, codesign.

Larry C. Schooley, Professor; Ph.D., Kansas, 1968. Communications systems, digital communication networks, telemetry, telescience.

Robert A. Schowengerdt, Associate Professor; Ph.D., Arizona, 1975. Remote sensing systems and image processing, multispectral sensor and scene modeling, digital mapping techniques.

Robin N. Strickland, Associate Professor; Ph.D., Sheffield, 1979. Digital image processing, computer vision, signal processing.

Malur K. Sundareshan, Professor; Ph.D., Indian Institute of Science, 1973. Control systems, communication networks, statistical signal processing, neural network theory, applications to control system design.

Miklos N. Szilagyi, Professor; Ph.D., 1965, Leningrad Electrotechnical; D.Sc., Hungarian Academy of Sciences, 1979. Particle beams and optics, computer-aided synthesis of electron and ion optical systems, physical electronics.

Hal S. Tharp, Associate Professor; Ph.D., Illinois at Urbana-Champaign, 1986. Multivariable, multirate, robust, adaptive, and neural network control theory.

Kathleen L. Virga, Assistant Professor; Ph.D., UCLA, 1996. Antennas for wireless communications and radar systems, measurement-base characterization of high-density microwave and high-speed VLSI circuits.

Sarma Vrudhula, Associate Professor; Ph.D., USC, 1985. Design automation and testing of digital systems.

James R. Wait, Regents Professor Emeritus; Ph.D., Toronto, 1951. Electromagnetic theory, electrical geophysics.

Indra Widjaja, Assistant Professor; Ph.D., Toronto, 1992. High-speed packet switching, ATM traffic management, wireless networks.

Arthur F. Witulski, Associate Professor; Ph.D., Colorado at Boulder, 1988. Power electronics, resonant converters, distributed electronic power systems, low-voltage power converters.

James C. Wyant, Professor (also Professor in Optical Sciences); Ph.D., Rochester, 1968. Optical testing, interferometry, holography, computerized optical metrology.

Bernard P. Zeigler, Professor; Ph.D., Michigan, 1968. Modeling and simulation environments, high-performance discrete event simulation, distributed modeling and simulation.

Richard W. Ziolkowski, Professor; Ph.D., Illinois at Urbana-Champaign, 1980. Computational electromagnetics; transient linear and nonlinear electromagnetics, optics, and acoustic phenomena.

UNIVERSITY OF BRIDGEPORT

SCHOOL OF SCIENCE, ENGINEERING, AND TECHNOLOGY
PROGRAM IN COMPUTER SCIENCE

PROGRAM OF STUDY

The Computer Science and Engineering Department in the School of Science, Engineering, and Technology offers the M.S. in computer science, intended for individuals who wish to enhance their expertise, with an emphasis on professional applications. The core curriculum includes advanced C programming, advanced algorithms and data structures, operating systems, database design, and theory of computation. Among the electives offered are artificial intelligence, computer networking, robotics, parallel processing, computer music, computer animation, multimedia computing, computer vision, C++, and Java programming. Courses are available at both the main Bridgeport campus and the University's Stamford Center. The program may be pursued on a full-time, part-time, or weekend basis. Co-op and internship opportunities are frequently available, and graduates of the program are held in high demand by prospective employers.

The program in computer science requires the completion of 33 credit hours of study. At least one of the following is also required: a comprehensive examination, a thesis based on independent research, or the completion of an appropriate special project.

In addition, the department also offers the M.S. in the allied field of computer engineering. The program in computer engineering differs in its greater emphasis on computer hardware. Courses not found in the normal computer science curriculum include computer architecture, digital signal processing, digital system processing, VLSI design, logic synthesis with VHDL, and image processing.

RESEARCH FACILITIES

The computing facilities at the University of Bridgeport are among the best available. SPARC, digital design, digital signal processing, mixed-signal, image sequence, and microprocessor laboratories are among those available to students in the programs. Hardware platforms include Apple Power PCs, SPARC workstations from Sun Microsystems, and Pentium PCs. Software tools include those from Oracle, Macromedia, Microsoft, Altera, Xilinx, and Exemplar Logic. The University's Wahlstrom Library contains approximately 272,000 bound volumes, including bound journals and indexes and more than 1 million microforms, and subscribes to 1,600 periodicals and serials. On-line database searching is available on the Internet, Dialog, FirstSearch, and LEXIS/NEXIS. CD-ROM databases include ERIC, ABI/INFORM Global, Periodical Abstracts on disc, Dissertation Abstracts on disc, reQuest, Books in Print Plus (BIP Plus), and the National Trade Data Bank. All students have access to e-mail, Netscape, and word processing. Residence halls are wired for individual computer hookups.

FINANCIAL AID

Financial aid is available in the form of endowed scholarships, fellowships, Federal Stafford Student Loans, graduate assistantships, and internships. The University also hires graduate students as residence hall directors and assistant hall directors. Additional information can be obtained from the Financial Aid Office at 203-576-4568. The University also has a long-standing partnership with local corporations, which provide employees with excellent educational opportunities that lead to degrees and career advancement.

COST OF STUDY

In 1997–98, tuition is $340 per credit hour in the School of Science, Engineering, and Technology for students taking up to 12 credit hours per semester.

LIVING AND HOUSING COSTS

Graduate students may reside either in the University's on-campus residence halls or in private, off-campus apartments or rooms. The cost of off-campus living varies widely. Additional information related to on-campus residence may be obtained from the Office of Residential Life at 203-576-4395.

STUDENT GROUP

As of the fall 1996 semester, there were 67 students enrolled in the computer science program among approximately 1,200 graduate students enrolled at the University. Of the total University graduate population, approximately 52 percent are women, 18 percent are international, and 17 percent are members of minority groups.

LOCATION

The University of Bridgeport's 86-acre campus is situated on Long Island Sound. Both the Bridgeport and Stamford campuses are easily accessible from Westchester County, New York City, and northern New Jersey. Sixty-five percent of Connecticut's largest corporations are located in Fairfield County; these companies provide students with excellent opportunities for jobs both before and after graduation. University faculty members maintain close relationships with area corporations, school systems, and agencies.

THE UNIVERSITY

Founded in 1927, the University of Bridgeport is a private, nonsectarian, urban, comprehensive university. Professional accreditations include those from the ADA, ABA, ACBSP, NASAD, CCE, and ABET. The University's campus is composed of ninety-one buildings of diverse architectural styles. The Bernhard Arts and Humanities Center is a cultural hub, and the Wheeler Recreation Center is a complete recreation and physical fitness facility. The University's Stamford Center provides convenient access from southern Fairfield County and Westchester County, New York.

APPLYING

Students are encouraged to apply well in advance of the term they expect to enter but no later than thirty days before the beginning of the semester. Applications are accepted for fall, spring, and summer semesters.

CORRESPONDENCE AND INFORMATION

For general inquiries:
Office of Admissions
University of Bridgeport
126 Park Avenue
Bridgeport, Connecticut 06601
Telephone: 203-576-4552
        800-EXCEL-UB (toll-free)
Fax: 203-576-4941
E-mail: admit@cse.bridgeport.edu
World Wide Web: http://www.bridgeport.edu

For additional information:
Computer Science and Engineering Department
School of Science, Engineering, and Technology
Charles A. Dana Hall of Science
169 University Avenue
University of Bridgeport
Bridgeport, Connecticut 06601
Telephone: 203-576-4702
Fax: 203-576-4766
E-mail: deptcse@cse.bridgeport.edu

UNIVERSITY OF BRIDGEPORT
THE FACULTY AND THEIR RESEARCH

Julius Dichter, Visiting Assistant Professor of Computer Science and Engineering; M.S., New Haven. Neural networks, parallel processing.

Stephen Grodzinsky, Professor of Computer Science and Engineering (Chair); Ph.D., Illinois. Digital design, logic synthesis, VLSI design, microelectronics.

Gonhsin Liu, Associate Professor of Computer Science and Engineering; Ph.D., SUNY at Buffalo. Signal processing, image processing, computer vision, UNIX programming.

Douglas Lyon, Assistant Professor of Computer Science and Engineering; Ph.D., Rensselaer. Computer-generated music, diffraction rangefinding, image sequencing, signal processing.

Ausif Mahmood, Associate Professor of Computer Science and Engineering; Ph.D., Washington State. Algorithms, computer architecture, parallel VLSI simulation, compiler design, numerical methods.

Valluru Rao, Professor of Computer Science; D.Sc., Washington (St. Louis). Fuzzy logic, neural networks, programming languages.

Tarek Sobh, Associate Professor of Computer Science and Engineering; Ph.D., Pennsylvania. Control and simulation of electromechanical systems, parallel architecture, reverse engineering, robotics.

UNIVERSITY OF CALIFORNIA, DAVIS

GRADUATE GROUP IN COMPUTER SCIENCE

PROGRAMS OF STUDY

The Graduate Group in Computer Science (GGCS) is composed of the faculty members of the Department of Computer Science as well as faculty members from Electrical and Computer Engineering, Applied Science, and other campus departments. The GGCS offers programs of study leading to the M.S. and Ph.D. degrees. These programs offer students the opportunity to become involved in many areas of research specialization, including artificial intelligence, computer architecture, computer systems design, computer graphics, computer security, computational biology, database systems, distributed systems, computer networks, numerical analysis, operating systems, parallel algorithms and systems, programming languages, scientific computation, software engineering, program specification and verification, performance evaluation, robotics, computer science theory, and VLSI design. Since the group members from the Department of Applied Science are based at the Lawrence Livermore National Laboratory (LLNL), which supports a number of computer research projects and has substantial computer facilities, additional research opportunities exist in the laboratory for advanced students in the group.

The Ph.D. degree requires an approved program of course work, which includes a well-defined major area and one minor area, and a dissertation. In addition, a Ph.D. student must pass a written preliminary examination and an oral qualifying examination. Typically, it takes from four to six years to complete a Ph.D., depending on whether or not the program is entered with an M.S. degree.

The M.S. degree requires course work and either a thesis or a comprehensive examination. Typically, it takes from 1½ to 2 years to complete an M.S. degree.

RESEARCH FACILITIES

The major resources for graduate research in computer science are concentrated within the facilities and research laboratories of the Department of Computer Science. Several local area networks provide host-to-host services, connecting all of the systems available to students and faculty members of the graduate group. Gateways give these systems direct access to the Internet and to virtually all available research computer networks. Students have access to a wide variety of research resources, including numerous workstations, multiprocessors, and general purpose processors. Selected research facilities are also available through the research laboratories of interdisciplinary faculty members in the group, as well as through network links to several supercomputer centers, including the facilities at Lawrence Livermore National Laboratory. Every graduate student has direct access to a workstation.

FINANCIAL AID

Several forms of financial support are available, including fellowship stipends, nonresident tuition fee fellowships, research assistantships, and teaching assistantships. Fellowship applications are included in the general application packet. Those admitted to the program are automatically considered for teaching and/or research assistantships. Teaching assistants also receive partial in-state fee remission. Research assistants receive full in-state fee remission. Currently, more than 90 percent of full-time graduate students, and most incoming students, are awarded departmental support of some form. Around 85 percent of all incoming students receive full support.

COST OF STUDY

In 1996–97, California residents paid fees of $4419 per year; nonresidents paid fees of $12,813 per year. All fees are subject to change.

LIVING AND HOUSING COSTS

For 1996–97, accommodations in on-campus residence halls, with most meals included, were $6180 yearly (other meal options are available at reduced rates). Furnished and unfurnished one- and two-bedroom University-owned apartments are also available for both single and married students for rents ranging from $4524 to $6000 per year. Numerous privately owned apartments and houses are available in nearby areas.

STUDENT GROUP

Total campus enrollment is approximately 22,500 students, 5,200 of whom are graduate and professional students. Approximately 60 students are enrolled in the Graduate Group in Computer Science, divided evenly between the M.S. and Ph.D. programs. Recent graduates have been quite successful in seeking academic positions, with several having faculty offers prior to graduation. Recent graduates looking for industrial positions have had no difficulty in finding career positions prior to graduation.

LOCATION

The Davis campus lies 15 miles west of Sacramento. Approximately 50 miles of bicycle paths and 50,000 bicycles have given Davis a reputation for being one of the foremost cities in the country for bicycle transportation. An hour's drive away are the San Francisco Bay Area, the Napa Valley wine country, and the California Mother Lode. A 2- to 3-hour drive away are the Pacific coastal areas, from Mendocino in the north to Santa Cruz in the south, and the Sierra Nevada, with its excellent skiing and backpacking areas.

THE UNIVERSITY

UC Davis is one of nine campuses of the University of California System. Graduate, undergraduate, and professional programs are offered in a wide range of disciplines, giving UC Davis the most diversified teaching faculty and curriculum in the nine-campus system. The UC Davis faculty and graduate programs attract highly qualified students from diverse educational, social, ethnic, and cultural backgrounds. It is this global mix that contributes to the character of both the campus and the city of Davis. The campus has a tradition of close association between students and faculty members, and the style is one of informality and congeniality.

APPLYING

Students must begin graduate study in the fall quarter. Application materials may be requested from the Graduate Adviser at the address below. The application fee is $40 and subject to change without notice. Each applicant must take the GRE General Test. The Subject Test in computer science or mathematics is strongly recommended. To be considered for fellowships or scholarships, completed applications must be received by January 15. To receive consideration for all other forms of financial support, completed applications should be received by February 1. Later applications will continue to be considered for financial support as long as support is still available. Applications for admission without support must be submitted by April 1 for domestic students and by March 1 for international students.

CORRESPONDENCE AND INFORMATION

Graduate Adviser
Graduate Group in Computer Science
University of California, Davis
Davis, California 95616-8562

Telephone: 916-752-7004
E-mail: gradinfo@cs.ucdavis.edu
World Wide Web: http://www.cs.ucdavis.edu/graduate_info.html

UNIVERSITY OF CALIFORNIA, DAVIS

THE FACULTY AND THEIR RESEARCH

Computer Science

Matthew A. Bishop, Assistant Professor; Ph.D., Purdue. Computer and network security, vulnerability analysis, audit, formal models of access control, security of the UNIX operating system, cryptography, education, software engineering.

Frederic T. Chong, Assistant Professor; Ph.D., MIT. Architecture and applications for commodity multigrain parallel systems.

Matthew K. Farrens, Associate Professor; Ph.D., Wisconsin. Computer architecture, with a primary focus on the architecture and design of high-performance single-chip instruction level parallel processors and the optimal way to configure their memory hierarchies.

Dipak Ghosal, Assistant Professor; Ph.D., Southwestern Louisiana. Computer and telecommunication networks, parallel and distributed systems, performance evaluation.

Daniel M. Gusfield, Professor; Ph.D., Berkeley. Algorithm design and analysis, particularly algorithms for combinatorial optimization and graph theory; string and combinatorial problems that arise in computational biology, particularly from the Human Genome Project.

Bernd Hamann, Acting Associate Professor; Ph.D., Arizona State. Visualization, computer-aided geometric design, computer graphics, computer-aided design, unstructured mesh generation.

Kenneth I. Joy, Associate Professor; Ph.D., Colorado. Computer graphics, especially in the subfields of image synthesis and geometric modeling; free-form solid models and their integration into geometric modeling/computer graphics systems.

Alan J. Laub, Professor; Ph.D., Minnesota. Numerical analysis and algorithms, computer-aided control system design.

Karl N. Levitt, Professor; Ph.D., NYU. Techniques to improve security of large networks (such as the Internet) through intrusion detection, detection of malicious code (such as computer viruses), automated analysis of audit records, automated verification and testing of programs and hardware.

Charles U. Martel, Professor; Ph.D., Berkeley. Design and analysis of computer algorithms, with an emphasis on the effective use of parallel and distributed computer systems; design of efficient data structures; design of efficient parallel algorithms.

Norman S. Matloff, Professor; Ph.D., UCLA. Computer architecture, computer communication networks, data security, operating systems, Chinese-language computing.

Biswanath Mukherjee, Professor; Ph.D., Washington (Seattle). Computer-communication networks, lightwave networks, network security.

Ronald A. Olsson, Associate Professor; Ph.D., Arizona. Language design and implementation for programming concurrent systems, the SR concurrent programming language, debugging of sequential and concurrent programs.

Raju Pandey, Assistant Professor; Ph.D., Texas at Austin. Design and implementation of programming languages, parallel and distributed systems, object-oriented software construction.

Armand Prieditis, Assistant Professor; Ph.D., Rutgers. Artificial intelligence and program transformation, with an emphasis on machine learning and discovery and problem solving.

Phillip W. Rogaway, Assistant Professor; Ph.D., MIT. Cryptography, with an emphasis on provable security for problems of practical interest; protocol design and analysis; foundations of computer security; algorithms; complexity theory.

Manfred G. Ruschitzka, Professor; Ph.D., Berkeley. Experimental and theoretical studies of methods for improving the performance of computer systems and the accessibility of information in computer networks.

Richard F. Walters, Professor; Ph.D., Stanford. Computer technology used in support of distance learning; computer support of foreign languages and non-Latin character sets; medical informatics, especially computer support of medical records; databases (distributed, performance evaluation, interface between heterogeneous systems and designs).

Electrical and Computer Engineering

Tsu-Shuan Chang, Associate Professor; Ph.D., Harvard. Control systems, global and dynamic optimization, scheduling for manufacturing systems, neural networks.

Gary E. Ford, Professor; Ph.D., California, Davis. Signal and image processing, pattern recognition.

S. L. Hakimi, Professor; Ph.D., Illinois at Urbana-Champaign. Graph theory, analysis and design of communication and computer networks, fault identification in networks and computer systems, location theory, discrete optimization.

Vojin G. Oklobdzija, Associate Professor; Ph.D., UCLA. High-performance computer architecture, RISC and super-scalar architectures, massively parallel and supercomputer architectures.

G. Robert Redinbo, Professor; Ph.D., Purdue. Computer engineering, with emphasis on fault-tolerant computing.

Todd R. Reed, Associate Professor; Ph.D., Minnesota. Representation, processing, and encoding of images and image sequences; computer vision.

Michael A. Soderstrand, Professor; Ph.D., California, Davis. Digital filters and signal processing, system identification and deconvolution, active and passive networks.

Shih-Ho Wang, Professor; Ph.D., Berkeley. Control theory, robotics, computer-aided design of control systems and fuzzy logic.

Kent Wilken, Assistant Professor; Ph.D., Carnegie Mellon. Computer architecture, computer dependability, compilers.

Applied Science—Livermore

Meera M. Blattner, Professor; Ph.D., UCLA. Multimedia, user interfaces, virtual reality, audio output, human-computer interaction, assistive technology, distance education.

Nelson L. Max, Professor; Ph.D., Harvard. Computer graphics, with an emphasis on scientific visualization; application of visualization techniques to animations recorded on film or video or generated on real-time hardware.

Garry H. Rodrigue, Professor; Ph.D., USC. Scientific computing, parallel computing, numerical algorithms, high-performance computing, scientific computing environments.

Venkateswararao Vemuri, Professor; Ph.D., UCLA. Artificial neural networks; genetic algorithms and their application to signal processing, optimization, and modeling.

Other UCD Departments

Harry H. Cheng, Assistant Professor; Ph.D., Illinois at Chicago. Worldwide distributed computing; open-architecture enterprise-level system integration, including information of real-time machineries; programming environments and programming languages; evolution of C; robotics; mechatronics.

E. O. Milton, Professor; Ph.D., Duke. Databases.

Richard E. Plant, Professor; Ph.D., Cornell. Applied artificial intelligence; expert system development, with ongoing projects in the development of integrated decision support systems for crop and pest management; construction of qualitative simulation models for vegetation dynamics.

Donald M. Topkis, Professor; Ph.D., Stanford. Design and analysis of algorithms for the distributed control of communication networks, performance analysis of versions of flooding and other procedures for the concurrent broadcast of multiple messages from multiple nodes, combinatorial and qualitative properties of supermodular functions, mathematical economics.

David L. Woodruff, Assistant Professor; Ph.D., Northwestern. Production planning and heuristic search optimization.

UNIVERSITY OF CALIFORNIA, IRVINE

DEPARTMENT OF ELECTRICAL AND COMPUTER ENGINEERING

PROGRAMS OF STUDY

The Department of Electrical and Computer Engineering offers courses leading to the degrees of Master of Science and Doctor of Philosophy, with concentrations in electrical engineering and computer engineering. The electrical engineering concentration includes communication systems, control systems, digital systems, optoelectronic devices, semiconductor devices, electronics, electrooptics, machine vision, and signal processing. The computer engineering concentration covers VLSI design, computer architecture, parallel and distributed computer systems, fault-tolerant computing, real-time systems, and system software. The programs are designed for those who plan to enter the professional practice of engineering as it relates to design, research, teaching, and development—in industry, private practice, education, or public service. The fundamentals of engineering are emphasized so that graduates can continue professional development throughout their careers. Individual programs permit wide latitude in course work and research.

The M.S. degree may be attained by the successful completion of 36 approved units or by a combination of course work and a thesis.

The Ph.D. degree requires passing a preliminary examination, preparing research, advancing to candidacy, completing significant research investigation, and submitting and getting approval of a dissertation.

RESEARCH FACILITIES

Optical and solid-state research is performed in six laboratories, including facilities for integrated optics and microfabrication, quantum electronics, photonics, advanced semiconductor devices, optoelectronic devices, and optoelectronic materials research. These laboratories house cleanroom facilities; photolithography, thin-film deposition, and molecular beam epitaxy systems; solid-state, gas, dye, and semiconductor lasers; optical benches and microscopes; scanning acoustic and electron microscopes; computer-based data acquisition systems; cryogenic and high-current testing chambers; and a host of electronic testing equipment.

Computer engineering research laboratories include the VLSI design automation laboratory; the fault-tolerant multicomputer laboratory; the advanced computer architecture laboratory; the Distributed Real-time Ever Available Microcomputing (DREAM) Laboratory; the numerical processors and multiprocessors laboratory; the real-time systems laboratory; and the database systems laboratory. They are equipped with heterogeneous networks of state-of-the-art Sun, DEC, and Hewlett-Packard workstations; microprocessor development systems; an Intel hypercube; several high-performance file and compute servers; and a variety of advanced software packages such as VLSI CAD tools for layout, simulation, and synthesis and tools for performance evaluation and parallel programming.

Research in machine vision and image processing is carried out at several laboratories, including the image acquisition laboratory, the pattern recognition and image modeling laboratory, the visualization laboratory, and the imaging architectures laboratory. These laboratories are equipped with image acquisition equipment, digital video processing equipment, Sun Workstations, graphics displays, and graphics and image processing software packages. Within the department, there is access to high-performance parallel machines and tools for the development of custom chips.

The Power Electronics Laboratory is equipped with state-of-the-art instrumentation for design, simulation, layout, prototyping, and testing of switching/analog circuits.

FINANCIAL AID

Fellowships and teaching and research assistantships are available on a competitive basis. Except for students on visas, there are opportunities for part-time work in the engineering community of Orange County. With the same exception, financial aid may be obtained from UCI's Financial Aid Office.

COST OF STUDY

In 1997–98, student fees are $1666 per quarter for California residents and an additional $2995 per quarter for nonresidents. These fees are subject to change.

LIVING AND HOUSING COSTS

On-campus housing is available. In 1997–98, monthly apartment rents are from $250 to $465 for single students and from $460 to $620 for married students. Early application is advised for on-campus housing. Privately owned apartments are available close to the campus, and many types of housing can be found in the surrounding communities of Santa Ana, Newport Beach, Costa Mesa, Irvine, Tustin, and Laguna Beach.

STUDENT GROUP

Current campus enrollment is 17,888, including 1,161 undergraduate and 342 graduate students in the School of Engineering.

STUDENT OUTCOMES

M.S. graduates typically fill leading engineering positions in high-technology industries such as electronics, communications, computers, software, and aerospace. Ph.D. graduates most often obtain research and development positions with large industrial or governmental research laboratories or take academic positions that involve both teaching and research in their areas of specialization.

LOCATION

The 1,510-acre UCI campus is in Orange County, 40 miles south of Los Angeles. Irvine is one of the nation's fastest-growing residential, industrial, and business areas, yet within view of the campus is a wildlife sanctuary; Pacific Ocean beaches are nearby. Residential areas range from the beach communities of Newport Beach and Laguna Beach to the socially and economically diverse urban centers of Santa Ana, Tustin, and Costa Mesa.

THE UNIVERSITY

One of the nine campuses in the University of California system, UCI now enrolls 3,535 graduate and professional students. The University offers graduate degrees through the Schools of Biological Sciences, Engineering, Fine Arts, Humanities, Physical Sciences, Social Ecology, and Social Sciences; the Graduate School of Management; the College of Medicine; and the Department of Information and Computer Science.

APPLYING

Application forms may be obtained by writing to the department. The deadlines for applications are May 1 for the fall quarter, October 15 for the winter quarter, and January 15 for the spring quarter. Applicants who wish to be considered for fellowships or for teaching or research assistantships should apply by February 1. Applicants must submit official records covering all postsecondary academic work, three letters of recommendation, and official scores on the General Test of the Graduate Record Examinations. International students whose native language is not English must submit the results of the Test of English as a Foreign Language (TOEFL).

CORRESPONDENCE AND INFORMATION

For applications and information about the department:

Graduate Admissions
Department of Electrical and Computer Engineering
355 Engineering Tower
University of California
Irvine, California 92697-2625-10

Telephone: 714-824-5489
E-mail: ttle@uci.edu
World Wide Web: http://www.eng.uci.edu/ece/

UNIVERSITY OF CALIFORNIA, IRVINE

THE FACULTY AND THEIR RESEARCH

Nicolaos G. Alexopoulos, Professor; Ph.D., Michigan. Integrated microwave and millimeter-wave circuits and antennas, substrate materials and thin films, electromagnetic theory.

Nader Bagherzadeh, Associate Professor of Electrical and Computer Engineering and Information and Computer Science; Ph.D., Texas at Austin. Parallel processing, computer architecture, VLSI design.

Harut Barsamian, Adjunct Professor; M.S., USSR Academy of Sciences. Computer architectures, software engineering.

Neil J. Bershad, Professor Emeritus; Ph.D., RPI. Communication and information theory, signal processing.

Lubomir Bic, Professor of Information and Computer Science and Electrical and Computer Engineering; Ph.D., California, Irvine. Parallel processing, distributed systems, database machines.

Douglas M. Blough, Associate Professor of Electrical and Computer Engineering and Information and Computer Science; Ph.D., Johns Hopkins. Parallel processing, fault-tolerant computing, computer architecture.

Rui J. P. de Figueiredo, Professor; Ph.D., Harvard. Intelligent sensing and control, applied mathematics.

Nikil Dutt, Associate Professor of Information and Computer Science and Electrical and Computer Engineering; Ph.D., Illinois at Urbana–Champaign. Design modeling, languages and synthesis, CAD tools, computer architecture.

Daniel D. Gajski, Professor of Information and Computer Science and Electrical and Computer Engineering; Ph.D., Pennsylvania. Parallel algorithms and architectures, design methodology, design science, CAD algorithms and tools, software/hardware codesign.

Hideya Gamo, Professor Emeritus; D.Sc., Tokyo. Quantum electronics, electromagnetics, optics.

Michael Green, Associate Professor; Ph.D., Caltech. Analog integrated-circuit design, circuit simulation, nonlinear circuits.

Glenn E. Healey, Associate Professor; Ph.D., Stanford. Machine vision, computer engineering, image processing, computer graphics, intelligent machines.

Daniel Hirschberg, Professor of Information and Computer Science and Electrical and Computer Engineering; Ph.D., Princeton. Analysis of algorithms, data structures, models of computation.

K. H. (Kane) Kim, Professor of Electrical and Computer Engineering and Information and Computer Science; Ph.D., Berkeley. Ultrareliable distributed and parallel computing, real-time object-based system engineering.

Fadi J. Kurdahi, Associate Professor of Electrical and Computer Engineering and Information and Computer Science; Ph.D., USC. VLSI system design, design automation of digital systems.

Tomas Lang, Professor of Electrical and Computer Engineering and Information and Computer Science; Ph.D., Stanford. Numerical processors and multiprocessors, parallel computer systems.

Chin C. Lee, Professor; Ph.D., Carnegie Mellon. Electronic packaging, thermal management, integrated optics, photonics.

Henry P. Lee, Associate Professor; Ph.D., Berkeley. Optoelectronics, semiconductor materials and devices.

Guann-Pyng Li, Professor; Ph.D., UCLA. High-speed semiconductor technology, optoelectronic devices, integrated circuit fabrication and testing.

Kwei-Jay Lin, Professor of Electrical and Computer Engineering and Information and Computer Science; Ph.D., Maryland College Park. Real-time systems, distributed systems.

Orhan Nalcioglu, Professor of Radiological Sciences and Electrical and Computer Engineering; Ph.D., Oregon. Nuclear magnetic resonance imaging and spectroscopy, digital radiography.

Richard D. Nelson, Adjunct Professor; Ph.D., Michigan State. Sensors, microelectronics, photonics, medical imaging.

Alexandru Nicolau, Professor of Information and Computer Science and Electrical and Computer Engineering; Ph.D., Yale. Architecture, parallel computation, programming languages and compilers.

Robert M. Saunders, Professor Emeritus; Dr.Eng., Tokyo Institute of Technology; PE. Electromechanics, power systems.

Issac D. Scherson, Professor of Information and Computer Science and Electrical and Computer Engineering; Ph.D., Weizmann (Israel). Parallel computing architectures, massively parallel systems, parallel algorithms, interconnection networks, performance evaluation.

Roland Schinzinger, Professor Emeritus; Ph.D., Berkeley; PE. Electromagnetics, power systems, operations research.

Phillip C.-Y. Sheu, Professor of Electrical and Computer Engineering and Information and Computer Science; Ph.D., Berkeley. Robotics, database systems.

Jack Sklansky, Professor Emeritus of Electrical and Computer Engineering and Radiological Sciences; D.Sc., Columbia; PE. Pattern recognition, machine vision, medical imaging, neural learning, computer engineering.

Keyue M. Smedley, Assistant Professor; Ph.D., Caltech. Power electronics.

Gregory J. Sonek, Associate Professor; Ph.D., Cornell. Photonic devices, electrooptics and fiber optics, biomedical applications, optoelectronics.

Allen R. Stubberud, Professor and Chair of the Department; Ph.D., UCLA; PE. Control systems, digital signal processing, estimation and optimization.

Tatsuya Suda, Professor of Information and Computer Science and Electrical and Computer Engineering; Ph.D., Kyoto. Computer networks, distributed systems, performance evaluations.

Harry H. Tan, Associate Professor and Associate Dean of Undergraduate Student Affairs; Ph.D., UCLA. Communication systems, information theory, coding theory, stochastic processes.

Chen S. Tsai, Professor; Ph.D., Stanford. Integrated and fiber-optic devices and materials, acoustooptics, magnetooptics, acoustic microscopy.

Wei Kang (Kevin) Tsai, Associate Professor; Ph.D., MIT. Data communication networks, neural networks, parallel algorithms and architectures, CAD for VLSI systems engineering.

Rainer Zuleeg, Adjunct Professor; D.Eng., Tohoku. Semiconductor devices and technology.

UNIVERSITY OF CALIFORNIA, IRVINE

DEPARTMENT OF INFORMATION AND COMPUTER SCIENCE

PROGRAM OF STUDY

The graduate program leads to a Ph.D. degree in information and computer science with a concentration in one of the following six areas: artificial intelligence (constraint-based reasoning, neural modeling, machine learning); computer systems design (parallel processing, design science, computer architecture, high-speed multimedia net, distributed systems); computers, organizations, policy, and society (computer-supported cooperative work, human-computer interaction, social analysis of computing systems); software (software engineering, software environments, testing and validation); algorithms and data structures (design and analysis of algorithms, design and complexity analysis of theory); or computational biology.

Students are not admitted for graduate study leading only to the master's degree. The program is research oriented and encourages students to collaborate with faculty members to solve advanced problems in computer science. The program is full-time and normally takes six years to complete.

RESEARCH FACILITIES

Computing resources available on the campus include approximately 250 Sun Workstations and servers, 350 PCs and Macintoshes, 175 terminals, 90 printers, 250 Ethernet nodes, 2,500 MIPS, 50 GB disk storage capacity (not including PCs and Macintoshes), and 2 Sequents, 1 MasPar, 1 Hypercube computer, and 6 Lisp machines. In addition, the department hosts Irvine Research Units in both software and computer systems design.

FINANCIAL AID

University financial support for graduate students is available through three channels: teaching and research assistantships, fellowships, and GPOP fellowships for women and underrepresented minority students who are U.S. citizens. All prospective students are encouraged to apply for fellowship programs that are sponsored by federal agencies, the California Student Aid Commission, foundations, and other private organizations. More than half of the doctoral students receive financial assistance from the University.

COST OF STUDY

Graduate fees for the academic year 1997–98 are projected to be $4844.50 for California residents. Out-of-state and international students should expect to pay an additional $9000 per year. All graduate students are assessed $269 per quarter for health insurance. All fees are subject to change.

LIVING AND HOUSING COSTS

Approximately 50 percent of graduate and health sciences students currently live on campus. Three different types of housing options are available: Verano Place ($460–$640) or Palo Verde Apartments ($466–$1125); Quenya residence hall (approximately $6400 with meals); or a recreational vehicle park (space rental is $112 per month). Off-campus housing is also available.

STUDENT GROUP

Currently, 120 graduate students are enrolled full-time. Part-time study is not allowed. Of the current students, there are 27 women and 30 international students. Average GRE scores for fall 1997 accepted students are 635 (verbal), 777 (quantitative), and 732 (analytical). Faculty members are interested in students with experience in academic or industrial research and who share academic interests with faculty research interests.

STUDENT OUTCOMES

Recent Ph.D. graduates have found academic or research positions at Sonoma State University, Washington University, University of Pennsylvania, Cambridge University, and Stanford University. Others have found exciting opportunities working in such companies as IBM, Hewlett-Packard, Hughes, and Qualcom. A few entrepreneurs have opened their own companies in California.

LOCATION

Forty miles south of Los Angeles, 5 miles from the Pacific Ocean, and only a few hours away from deserts and mountains, University of California, Irvine (UCI) lies amid rapidly growing residential communities and a dynamic multinational business and industrial complex that affords many research and employment opportunities.

THE UNIVERSITY AND THE DEPARTMENT

Established in 1965, UCI is one of the nine campuses of the University of California. Graduate and undergraduate programs leading to the bachelor's, master's, M.D., and Ph.D. degrees are offered in a wide range of disciplines. The Department of Information and Computer Science is independent from any school within the UCI campus; as such, it allows a certain amount of flexibility for diversity among the faculty.

APPLYING

Completed applications should be submitted by January 15. Electronic applications are available on the World Wide Web (http://www.rgs.uci.edu/). Applicants are evaluated on the basis of their prior academic records and their potential for creative research and teaching in information and computer science. Applicants must take the GRE General Test and are strongly encouraged to take one advanced Subject Test. International applicants must also take the TOEFL test (minimum acceptable score is 550).

CORRESPONDENCE AND INFORMATION

Susan Moore
Graduate Counselor
Information and Computer Science
University of California, Irvine
Irvine, California 92697-3425
Telephone: 714-824-5597 or 2277
E-mail: gcounsel@ics.uci.edu
World Wide Web: http://www.ics.uci.edu

UNIVERSITY OF CALIFORNIA, IRVINE
THE FACULTY AND THEIR RESEARCH

Artificial Intelligence

Rina Dechter, Associate Professor; Ph.D., UCLA. Complexity of automated reasoning models: constraint-based reasoning, distributed connectionist models, causal models, probabilistic reasoning.

Richard H. Granger, Associate Professor; Ph.D., Yale. Computational and cognitive neuroscience.

Dennis F. Kibler, Professor; Ph.D., California, Irvine; Ph.D., Rochester. Learning control knowledge, planning and problem solving, parallel processing of logical problems, machine learning.

Richard H. Lathrop, Professor; Ph.D., MIT. Modeling structure and function, machine learning, intelligent systems and molecular biology, protein structure/function prediction.

Michael J. Pazzani, Associate Professor and Chair; Ph.D., UCLA. Human and machine learning, theory revision, learning with knowledge, cognitive science.

Padhraic Smyth, Assistant Professor; Ph.D., Caltech. Statistical pattern recognition, automated analysis of large data sets, applications of probability and statistics to problems in artificial intelligence.

Computer Systems Design

Lubomir Bic, Professor; Ph.D., California, Irvine. Parallel and distributed computing, biomedical simulation.

Nikil Dutt, Associate Professor; Ph.D., Illinois. Embedded systems design automation: specification, representation, and synthesis.

Daniel D. Gajski, Professor; Ph.D., Pennsylvania. Computer and information systems, software/hardware codesign, algorithms, system design and CAD tools.

Rajesh Gupta, Assistant Professor; Ph.D., Stanford. System-level design and CAD for embedded and portable systems, VLSI design, computer systems architecture and organization.

Alexandru Nicolau, Professor; Ph.D., Yale. Architecture, parallel computation, and programming languages and compilers.

Isaac Scherson, Professor; Ph.D., Weizmann (Israel). Parallel computing architectures, massively parallel systems, parallel algorithms, complexity, orthogonal multiprocessing systems.

Tatsuya Suda, Professor; Ph.D., Kyoto. Computer networks, distributed systems, performance evaluation.

Computing, Organizations, Policy and Society (CORPS)

Mark S. Ackerman, Assistant Professor; Ph.D., MIT. Computer-supported cooperative work, sociology of computing, human-computer interaction.

Jonathan T. Grudin, Associate Professor; Ph.D., California, San Diego. Computer-supported cooperative work, interactive systems development, human-computer interaction.

John L. King, Professor; Ph.D., California, Irvine. Economics of computing, policies for computer management and use in organizations, public policy and social impact aspects of computer use.

Software Engineering

Michael Franz, Assistant Professor; Dr.Sci., Swiss Federal Institute of Technology. Programming languages and their implementation, extensible systems: software architectures, component-ware and portable software that migrates across computer networks.

David F. Redmiles, Assistant Professor; Ph.D., Colorado at Boulder. Software engineering, knowledge representation, computer-supported cooperative work.

Debra J. Richardson, Associate Professor; Ph.D., Massachusetts at Amherst. Software engineering, program testing, life-cycle validation, software environments.

David S. Rosenblum, Assistant Professor; Ph.D., Stanford. Software specification, design, testing, and analysis; processes used to manage large software projects.

Richard W. Selby, Associate Professor; Ph.D., Maryland. Software engineering, software metrics, empirical evaluation of software methodologies.

Richard Taylor, Professor; Ph.D., Colorado. Software engineering, user interfaces, environments, team support systems.

Algorithms and Data Structures

Michael Dillencourt, Associate Professor; Ph.D., Maryland. Computational geometry, analysis of algorithms, data structures, computer vision.

David Eppstein, Associate Professor; Ph.D., Columbia. Analysis of algorithms, computational geometry, graph theory.

Daniel Hirschberg, Professor; Ph.D., Princeton. Analysis of algorithms, concrete complexity, data structures, models of computation.

Sandra S. Irani, Assistant Professor; Ph.D., Berkeley. Analysis of algorithms, on-line algorithms, graph theory and combinatorics.

George S. Lueker, Professor; Ph.D., Princeton. Computational complexity, probabilistic analysis of algorithms, data structures.

Thomas A. Standish, Professor; Ph.D., Carnegie Tech. Algorithms and data structures.

Emeritus Faculty

Alfred M. Bork, Professor; Ph.D., Brown. Computer-based learning, multimedia.

Julian Feldman, Professor; Ph.D., Carnegie Tech. Management of computing resources; the teaching of programming and development of techniques that will facilitate the learning of programming.

UNIVERSITY OF CALIFORNIA, LOS ANGELES

ELECTRICAL ENGINEERING DEPARTMENT

PROGRAMS OF STUDY

The department offers programs of study leading to the degrees of Master of Science and Doctor of Philosophy in electrical engineering in the areas listed under faculty research areas.

The M.S. program offers specializations in nine major fields; it requires a total of nine courses and either a thesis or a comprehensive examination. In the thesis plan, two of the nine courses relate to the research needed for writing the thesis. The program lasts from one to two years; some major fields offer the thesis plan only.

The program for the Ph.D. degree requires a course of study in one major field and two distinct but supporting minor fields, followed by research on a topic in the major field. Competence in the major field is determined by an 8-hour examination and in each of the two minor fields by passing the three prescribed courses with an adequate grade point average. The research topic is chosen following discussion with the student's adviser, who then guides the research as it progresses. The research is monitored by a doctoral committee, which administers two oral examinations and approves the dissertation describing the research. There is no foreign language requirement. The Ph.D. program is usually completed in four or five years after the award of the M.S. degree.

RESEARCH FACILITIES

Laboratories are available in the department for research in modern integrated semiconductor device processing, complete molecular beam epitaxy systems, analog and digital electronics, hybrid integrated circuits, microwaves and millimeter waves, fiber optics, speech and image processing, microelectromechanical systems, antennas, communications and networking, lasers and quantum electronics, and plasma electronics. The department is also associated with research centers for high-frequency and high-speed electronics and for plasma physics and fusion engineering, all located at UCLA.

Computer facilities for research and instruction range from the supercomputer to desktop workstations. The Electrical Engineering Department maintains a large network of UNIX platforms consisting of Sun, HP, and IBM workstations for the exclusive use of its graduate students and faculty members. A campuswide computing service offers access through remote terminals. All departments in the School of Engineering and Applied Science are linked by a common Ethernet (SEASNET), which provides access to the IBM 3090, the UNIX workstations, IBM PS/2, and Apple Macintosh classrooms.

The UCLA library, which ranks in the top three nationally, has more than 6 million volumes. One of its specialized branches, the Science & Engineering Library (SEL), contains more than 460,000 volumes and receives more than 7,000 serials and more than 1.9 million technical reports. SEL provides major access to library materials through Orion, the UCLA on-line information system, and Melvyl, the UC (nine campuses) on-line system.

FINANCIAL AID

Fellowships are available from a variety of sources for full-time students and are awarded on merit, mainly for the first year of study. For 1997–98, stipends range from $10,000 to $12,000. Many teaching and research assistantships are also offered, usually after the first year.

COST OF STUDY

For 1997–98, California residents pay $4494 for registration and incidental fees per academic year. Nonresidents pay an additional fee of $8984. The academic year consists of three quarters.

LIVING AND HOUSING COSTS

A typical budget for a California resident living in an off-campus apartment is approximately $17,290 a year and includes required books and supplies, board and room for the period classes are in session during the three quarters, and a minimum allowance for variable items. For students with families, the University has about 975 apartments, which rent for $586–$1027 per month in 1997–98. In addition, approximately 250 apartments are available for single students within walking distance of campus.

STUDENT GROUP

The department has approximately 350 graduate students, who come from all parts of the world. The great majority of them are in their mid-twenties and enter the department in the M.S. program. About 25 percent continue for the Ph.D. This is the preferred mode of entry to the Ph.D. program, but a few students are admitted directly after they receive an M.S. degree elsewhere. International students constitute about 32 percent of the total and women about 13 percent.

LOCATION

UCLA is located 5 miles from the Pacific Ocean on the north side of Los Angeles in the Westwood area, immediately adjacent to the Santa Monica Mountains. Los Angeles offers all the cultural and recreational amenities one expects in a major metropolitan area, such as theaters, cinemas, concert halls, museums, sports arenas, amusement parks, and facilities for swimming, sailing, skiing, and hiking.

THE UNIVERSITY AND THE DEPARTMENT

UCLA, one of the nine campuses that form the University of California, ranks among the leading universities in the United States. Student enrollment is about 35,000. Many undergraduates and a few graduate students commute from their homes; others live in apartments nearby or in the University dormitories on campus. Extensive programs for cultural events are presented on campus, and there are recreational facilities of all kinds available through the University.

The Electrical Engineering Department has been in existence as a separate entity since 1968, when the College of Engineering was divided into departments and became the School of Engineering and Applied Science. Since then it has risen rapidly in stature and now ranks among the top ten in the nation. It has a faculty of 39 full-time professors and a number of visiting and part-time professorial appointees.

APPLYING

Graduate students are admitted only in the fall quarter, and the application deadline is January 15. Applicants for financial aid are encouraged to apply earlier. Applications must include transcripts of all previous academic work, scores on the GRE General Test, three letters of recommendation, and a statement of study plans. The GRE should be taken no later than the previous October. Offers of fellowships are made by about March 15 and offers of admission by April 15. The UCLA Application for Graduate Admission is now available on the World Wide Web.

CORRESPONDENCE AND INFORMATION

Vice-Chairman for Graduate Affairs
Electrical Engineering Department
56-125B Engineering IV
Box 951594
University of California
Los Angeles, California 90095-1594

Telephone: 310-825-9383
World Wide Web: http://www.ee.ucla.edu

UNIVERSITY OF CALIFORNIA, LOS ANGELES

FACULTY RESEARCH AREAS

Communications and Telecommunications

Research is concerned with communications, telecommunications, networking, and information processing principles and their engineering applications. Communications research includes satellite, spread-spectrum, and digital communications systems. Fast estimation, detection, and optimization algorithms and processing techniques for communications, radar, and VLSI design are studied. Research is conducted in stochastic modeling of telecommunications engineering systems, switching, architectures, queuing systems, computer communications networks, local-area/metropolitan-area/long-haul communications networks, optical communications networks, packet-radio and cellular radio networks, and personal communications systems. Research in networking also includes studies of processor communications and synchronization for parallel and distributed processing in computer systems. Several aspects of communications networks and processing systems are thoroughly investigated, including system architectures, protocols, performance modeling and analysis, simulation studies, and analytical optimization. Investigations in information theory involve basic concepts and practices of channel and source coding. Significant multidisciplinary programs, including sensing and radio communication networks, exist.

Integrated Circuits and Systems

IC&S students and faculty members are engaged in research on communications and RF IC design; analog and digital signal processing microsystems; integrated microsensors, microelectromechanical systems, and the associated low-power microelectronics; reconfigurable computing systems; and multimedia and communications processors. Current projects include wireless transceiver ICs, including RF and baseband circuits; high-speed data communication ICs; A/D and D/A converters; networking electronics; distributed sensors with wireless networking; and digital processor design. M.S. and Ph.D. degrees require a thesis based on an ongoing IC&S project and full-time presence on campus. More information may be obtained via the World Wide Web (http://www.icsl.ucla.edu/general/profs.html).

Signal Processing

Signal processing encompasses the techniques, hardware, algorithms, and systems used to process one-dimensional and multidimensional sequences of data. Research being conducted in the Signal Processing Group reflects the broad, interdisciplinary nature of the field today. Areas of current interest include analysis, synthesis, and coding of speech signals; video signal processing; digital filter analysis and design; image compression; communications signal processing; synthetic aperture radar remote sensing; signal processing for hearing aids; auditory system modeling; automatic speech recognition; wireless communication; digital signal processor architectures; adaptive filtering; multirate signal processing; and the characterization and analysis of three-dimensional time-varying medical image data. M.S. and Ph.D. programs include a thesis project, and a full-time presence on campus is required.

Solid-State Electronics

Research involves studies of new and advanced devices with picosecond switching times and high-frequency capabilities up to submillimeter-wave ranges. Topics being investigated are hot-electron transistors, quantum devices, heterojunction bipolar transistors, HEMTs, and MESFETs, as well as more conventional scaled-down MOSFETs, SOI devices, bipolar devices, and photovoltaic devices. The studies of basic materials, submicron structures, and device principles range from Si, Si-Ge, Si-silicides, and III-V molecular beam epitaxy to the modeling of electron transport in high fields and short temporal and spatial scales. The research in progress also includes fabrication, testing, and reliability of new types of VLSI devices and circuits.

Control Systems

Research includes theoretical studies in optimal control, stabilization, identification, and estimation for finite and infinite dimensional systems, with applications to systems of current interest. Specific topics include identification, estimation, nonlinear filtering, feedback stabilization of distributed systems, and adaptive control of nonlinear systems. Application areas include control of smart structures, guidance and control of flight systems, intelligent control of vehicles, microrobotics, and control of micro-electromechanical systems.

Photonics and Optoelectronics

The area of photonics and optoelectronics includes the development and applications of new types of solid-state, gas, and semiconductor lasers. This research also extends into areas of nonlinear optics, ultrashort pulse generation and applications, very high speed detection, infrared detectors, optical logic, fiber optics, integrated optics, optoelectronics, and optical communications. The application of quantum electronics technology to the testing and control of solid-state devices is a fast-growing and particularly interesting project. Equipment used for research includes argon-ion lasers, mode-locked solid-state lasers, compressed femtosecond laser pulses, continuous-wave dye lasers, single-frequency tunable dye lasers, pulsed dye lasers, excimer lasers, and infrared TEA lasers, as well as the latest gigabit-rate electronics, fiber optics, and optical systems.

Electromagnetics

Research is being pursued on integrated microwave and millimeter-wave circuits and printed-circuit antennas, substrate material effects, and novel guiding structures; integrated optics and optical signal processing; antenna theory and design, mutual coupling effects, integrated antennas and antenna radar cross-section studies; scattering by complex bodies, radar cross-section reduction techniques, reflector antenna design and analysis, satellite and personal communication antennas, biological interactions, modern antenna measurement and diagnostic techniques, satellite/spacecraft antenna studies, atmospheric pollutant scattering, and multiple scattering; geometrical theory of diffraction and asymptotic techniques; advanced numerical techniques in electromagnetics; electromechanics; and nonlinear electrodynamics.

Operations Research

Research is being conducted in optimization theory (nonconvex programming, linear and nonlinear programming, and applications to networks with particular emphasis upon communications network problems and engineering design problems) and in stochastic processes (renewal and point processes, Markov processes, queuing theory, stochastic dynamic programming, and applications to communications and telecommunications engineering). The department offers a combined set of courses for those students interested in telecommunications engineering and operations research, and students of operations research are expected to have a strong interest in telecommunications networks and engineering. Students with backgrounds in engineering, physical science, or mathematics are encouraged to apply.

Plasma Electronics

Research is concerned with the electrodynamics of charged particles in electrified fluids. Originally developed for understanding the behavior of magnetically and inertially confined plasmas for controlled fusion energy, this field has moved to such active areas as the generation of high-power radiation sources, such as free-electron lasers, plasma-wave particle accelerators, far-infrared and submillimeter-wave plasma diagnostics, plasma processing, and alternative fusion concepts. Extensive laboratory facilities exist, including high-power laser systems, microwave and millimeter-wave sources and detectors, high- and low-density plasma sources for fundamental studies of nonlinear wave effects, and a variety of diagnostic instruments. The MARS CO_2 laser laboratory, a high-intensity subpicosecond laser facility, a plasma processing laboratory, a FEL laboratory, and a laser-plasma interaction laboratory are available for student training and research. In addition, experiments are conducted at several national laboratories and major fusion devices such as DIII-D Tokamak.

UNIVERSITY OF CALIFORNIA, RIVERSIDE

DEPARTMENT OF COMPUTER SCIENCE
PROGRAM IN COMPUTER SCIENCE

PROGRAM OF STUDY

The Department of Computer Science offers programs leading to the M.S. and Ph.D. degrees.

Instruction and opportunity for directed study exist in a variety of areas, including artificial intelligence, compiler design, complexity of computation, computer architecture, database systems, design and analysis of algorithms, modeling and simulation, operating systems, software engineering, VLSI design, and multimedia technologies and programming.

The master's degree program is usually completed within two years, although it is possible for a well-prepared student to earn a master's degree in one year. The student must pass qualifying examinations in theory of computation and computer systems or finish a thesis research.

RESEARCH FACILITIES

The campus library (a 3-minute walk from the Department of Computer Science) maintains extensive holdings of mathematics and computer science books and journals, including back issues. Publications not available locally may be obtained through interlibrary loan from all other campuses of the University of California.

The computer facilities for the department include a Sun 690 MP server, a Sun 1000 MP server, thirty-four SPARCstations, seventeen Pentium PCs, twelve 80486 PCs, a NeXT server, and thirty NeXT stations. All machines run UNIX and are connected to international computing through the Internet.

FINANCIAL AID

Fellowships are awarded by the Graduate Division on a competitive basis, with stipends ranging from $8500 to $15,000 for the nine-month academic year. These awards include payment of all assessed registration fees. The department offers teaching assistantships. A half-time appointment as a teaching assistant carries a stipend of $16,800 for the 1997–98 academic year.

COST OF STUDY

For 1997–98, California residents pay approximately $4866 a year in fees. Nonresidents are charged an additional tuition fee of $2798 per quarter. These amounts are subject to change.

LIVING AND HOUSING COSTS

Riverside offers graduate students one of the lowest costs of living of any city with a UC campus. Room and board in residence halls cost from $2565 to $5130 for the 1996–97 academic year. The University owns 268 houses that are available to married students and single students with children and rent from approximately $340 to $370 per month. Rents for the 150 apartments and 92 suites available for single students range from $295 to $688 per month. Off-campus housing is available within walking distance of the campus.

STUDENT GROUP

The department currently enrolls about 45 graduate students, who come from all sections of the United States and from abroad. Some are supported by teaching assistantships or fellowships. The campus has about 10,000 students, of whom more than 1,700 are graduate students.

LOCATION

The Riverside campus, consisting of more than 1,000 acres, is located 3 miles east of the center of Riverside in the shelter of the Box Springs Mountains. A community of more than 250,000 people, Riverside has excellent recreational facilities, a symphony orchestra, an opera association, a community theater, an art center, and several other colleges. Within a 60-mile radius are the mountains, the desert, the ocean, and Metropolitan Los Angeles. The average year-round maximum temperature is 79 degrees. The region is semiarid, with relatively low rainfall; consequently, students can spend much of their leisure time out of doors.

THE UNIVERSITY AND THE DEPARTMENT

The Riverside campus of the University of California began as a Citrus Experimental Station in 1907. In 1954 the College of Letters and Science opened for classes, and in 1959 Riverside became a general campus. The department began the graduate program in computer science in 1982.

APPLYING

Students may begin graduate study in the fall, spring, or winter quarters. Application materials may be obtained from the Student Affairs Office at the address below. Applicants are required to submit directly to the department scores from the GRE General Test, a statement outlining interests and professional goals, and a list of courses in progress or planned that do not appear on official transcripts. The Graduate School Application for Admission, the application fee, official transcripts, three letters of recommendation, and a TOEFL score (if applicable) should be submitted directly to the Graduate Admissions Office or to the Department of Computer Science.

To receive full consideration for financial support, applications, together with a $40 application fee, should be received by February 1. Later applications are considered if any support is still available.

CORRESPONDENCE AND INFORMATION

Student Affairs
Department of Computer Science
Bourns Hall A242
University of California, Riverside
Riverside, California 92521-0304
Telephone: 909-787-5639
Fax: 909-787-4643
E-mail: gradadmission@cs.ucr.edu

UNIVERSITY OF CALIFORNIA, RIVERSIDE

THE FACULTY AND THEIR RESEARCH

Marek Chrobak, Professor; Ph.D., Warsaw (Poland). Theory of computation, algorithms, data structures, combinatorics, graph theory.

Brett D. Fleisch, Assistant Professor; Ph.D., UCLA. Operating systems, distributed systems, parallel computer systems, shared memory.

Yang-Chang Hong, Associate Professor; Ph.D., Florida. Computer architecture, database systems.

Yu-Chin Hsu, Associate Professor; Ph.D., Illinois at Urbana-Champaign. VLSI, design automation, computer architecture.

Lawrence L. Larmore, Professor; Ph.D., California, Irvine. Algorithms, data structures.

Mart Molle, Professor; Ph.D., UCLA. Computer networking, performance evaluation, distributed algorithms.

Thomas H. Payne, Associate Professor; Ph.D., Notre Dame. Theory, computational logic, architecture.

Teodor C. Przymusinski, Professor; Ph.D., Polish Academy of Sciences. Computational logic, artificial intelligence, logic programming, deductive databases.

Frank Vahid, Assistant Professor; Ph.D., California, Irvine. System-level design, hardware/software codesign, high-level synthesis, functional partitioning, specification languages, design methodologies, embedded systems.

UNIVERSITY OF CALIFORNIA, SAN DIEGO

DEPARTMENT OF COMPUTER SCIENCE AND ENGINEERING

PROGRAMS OF STUDY

The Department of Computer Science and Engineering offers programs leading to the M.S. and Ph.D. degrees in computer science and computer engineering.

Graduate instruction takes place in a wide range of research areas, including algorithms and computation theory (computational complexity, algorithms, data structures, distributed algorithms, circuit complexity, operations research, probabilistic proof systems, approximation algorithms), cryptography and security (secure protocol design, provable security, electrical commerce), artificial intelligence (neural nets, automated reasoning, machine learning, cognitive modeling, genetic algorithms, vision, pattern recognition, expert systems, data mining, and natural language processing), computer architecture (computer architecture principles, high-performance processors, and parallel and concurrent machines), computer systems (operating distributed fault-tolerant systems, file systems, distributed high-performance communication and computing systems, highly dependable systems, real-time systems, performance evaluation, load balancing, and mass storage), communication networks (high-speed multimedia networks, ATM, wireless, Internet, protocols, performance analysis), multimedia systems (digital video and audio on-demand servers, media synchronization, and multimedia communication and collaboration), databases (relational database theory; complexity-tailored query language design; content-based retrieval; and deductive, object-oriented, temporal, multimedia, integration of heterogeneous data, semistructured data, and active databases), parallel computation (models of parallel algorithms and architectures, abstraction mechanism, compilers and programming languages, parallel programming environment and software tools, cluster and heterogeneous computing, and efficient large-scale computation), programming languages (language design and implementation, optimization for performance, and complexity and correctness of language), scientific computation (run-time support for concurrent execution, parallel algorithms, and efficient implementation techniques), software engineering (modular hierarchical system design techniques, programming tools, software maintenance, software specification and documentation, program testing and validation, functional program testing, and analysis of distributed and real-time protocols and systems), and VLSI/CAD (combinatorial and graph algorithms to solve circuit layout problems, high-level synthesis of VLSI circuits, hardware-software codesign, self-testable VLSI systems, on-line test, fault-resilient IC synthesis, and hardware-software issues of rapid system prototyping using field-programmable devices).

RESEARCH FACILITIES

The computer science and engineering department's computing facility provides research, instructional, and administrative resources. The computer hardware includes dozens of Macs, PCs, and X terminals; hundreds of workstations from a variety of vendors; and numerous fileservers as well as direct access to the vector and parallel supercomputers as well as a state-of-the-art scientific visualization laboratory at the San Diego Supercomputer Center (SDSC). There are more than a dozen separate networks in the department's computing facility with access to resources in all departments at UCSD, SDSC, Scripps Institution of Oceanography, and the UCSD Medical Center as well as to Internet and other networks.

FINANCIAL AID

Research assistantships are projected to provide $1212 per month during the 1997–98 academic year. Teaching assistantships are projected to pay $1452 per month for nine months. Various kinds of fellowships and scholarships for U.S. citizens are available and provide $9000–$15,000 for nine to twelve months, plus tuition and/or fees. A limited number of nonresident tuition or fee scholarships are sometimes available to Ph.D. students.

COST OF STUDY

Fees for the academic year 1997–98 are projected to be $4850.50 for California residents. Out-of-state tuition is projected to be $8982. California residents are exempted from paying tuition. United States citizens may become state residents after living in California for one year and fulfilling other requirements. Students supported by teaching or research assistantships usually also receive tuition and/or fees.

LIVING AND HOUSING COSTS

University Housing Services operates more than 1,300 apartments for couples, families, and single graduate students. They consist of studios and one-, two-, and three-bedroom apartments. Most of the two- and three-bedroom apartments are reserved for students with children. Studio apartments are offered only to single graduate students, and one-bedroom units are reserved for married couples without children. Rents range from $486 to $936 per month. The rent for some of the two- and three-bedroom apartments excludes utilities. Because University apartments cost much less than comparable private housing, there are long waiting lists for married couples without children and for single graduate students. For further information, students should contact the Residential Apartments Office, UC San Diego, 9224 B Regents Road, La Jolla, California 92093.

STUDENT GROUP

The total UCSD enrollment in the fall of 1996 was 19,099; approximately 50 percent of these students were women. There were 114 graduate students in the department; all full-time Ph.D. students received financial aid.

LOCATION

The University is in La Jolla, a suburban seaside resort north of San Diego. There are excellent beaches for swimming, sailing, surfing, and skin diving. La Jolla and San Diego offer a wide variety of cultural events.

THE UNIVERSITY

Established in 1964, UCSD is one of the nine campuses of the University of California System. Graduate and undergraduate programs leading to the bachelor's, master's, M.D., and Ph.D. degrees are offered in a wide range of disciplines. The campus structure is based on five undergraduate colleges, the Scripps Institution of Oceanography, the School of Medicine, the School of Engineering, the Graduate School of International Relations and Pacific Studies, and the School of Architecture, which accepted its first students in the fall of 1992.

APPLYING

A completed application should be submitted by January 15. Candidates must hold a bachelor's degree or its equivalent in computer science, mathematics, physics, electrical engineering, or a related area from an institution of acceptable standing. In special circumstances, alternative undergraduate preparation will be considered (e.g., a biology major may be appropriate for a student interested in the application of information and computer science to biological problems). Scores on the General Test of the Graduate Record Examinations should be sent to the department. It is recommended that applicants take the GRE Subject Test on a subject of their choice (not necessarily computer science). Students should apply for the fall quarter only. The University of California, San Diego, is an equal opportunity employer. The University encourages applications from men and women (including qualified handicapped students) of all racial, religious, and (within the limits imposed by University regulations) age groups.

CORRESPONDENCE AND INFORMATION

Julie Conner
Assistant to the Graduate Chair
Department of Computer Science and Engineering, 0123
University of California, San Diego
La Jolla, California 92093-0123
E-mail: grad_apps@cs.ucsd.edu
World Wide Web: http://www-cse.ucsd.edu

UNIVERSITY OF CALIFORNIA, SAN DIEGO
THE FACULTY AND THEIR RESEARCH

Donald W. Anderson, Professor of Computer Science; Ph.D. (mathematics), Berkeley. Computer graphics and applications of computers to education.

Scott B. Baden, Associate Professor of Computer Science; Ph.D. (computer science), Berkeley. Computational science, parallel processing, parallel programming abstractions, performance analysis of scientific applications, load balancing.

Michael J. Bailey, Associate Adjunct Professor of Computer Science and Senior Staff Scientist, San Diego Supercomputer Center; Ph.D. (engineering), Purdue. Computer graphics, scientific visualization, computational geometry, rapid prototyping.

Richard K. Belew, Associate Professor of Computer Science; Ph.D. (computer science), Michigan. Adaptive representations, including neural networks and genetic algorithms, computational biology and information retrieval (e.g., WWW) applications.

Mihir Bellare, Assistant Professor of Computer Science; Ph.D. (computer science), MIT. Cryptography and security, complexity theory, probabilistic proof systems, approximation algorithms.

Francine Berman, Professor of Computer Science; Ph.D. (mathematics), Washington (Seattle). Heterogeneous computing, parallel programming environments, mapping and scheduling of distributed high-performance systems.

Kenneth L. Bowles, Professor Emeritus; Ph.D., Cornell. Computer networks, intelligent terminals, computer-based instruction.

Walter A. Burkhard, Professor of Computer Science; Ph.D. (electrical engineering and computer science), Berkeley. Distributed systems, database systems, programming languages, data structures, storage subsystems.

Samuel R. Buss, Adjunct Professor of Computer Science; Ph.D. (mathematics), Princeton. Mathematical logic, complexity theory, proof theory.

Brad Calder, Assistant Professor of Computer Science and Engineering; Ph.D. (computer science), Colorado at Boulder. Computer architecture, compiler optimizations, instruction-level parallelism.

J. Lawrence Carter, Professor of Computer Science; Ph.D. (mathematics), Berkeley. Scientific computation, performance programming, parallel computation, machine and system architecture for high performance.

Chung-Kuan Cheng, Professor of Computer Science and Engineering; Ph.D. (electrical engineering and computer science), Berkeley. Computer-aided design, VLSI layout automation, circuit partitioning, network flow optimization, physical design of multichip modules for hybrid package.

Garrison W. Cottrell, Associate Professor of Computer Science; Ph.D. (computer science), Rochester. Connectionist models of cognitive processes, simple biological circuits, pattern recognition, dynamical systems, computational philosophy.

Flaviu Cristian, Professor of Computer Science; Ph.D. (computer science), Grenoble (France). Programming methodology, modular hierarchical software design techniques, distributed fault-tolerant systems, operating and communication systems, distributed algorithms, real-time systems.

Charles Elkan, Assistant Professor of Computer Science; Ph.D. (computer science), Cornell. Automated reasoning, machine learning, database systems, expert systems, computational biology, data mining.

Jeanne Ferrante, Professor and Chair of Computer Science; Ph.D. (mathematics), MIT. Compiling for high performance, automatic detection and exploitation of parallelism, optimizing data movement and resource usage.

Joseph A. Goguen, Professor of Computer Science and Director of Program in Advanced Manufacturing; Ph.D. (mathematics), Berkeley. Software engineering, requirements, algebraic semantics of computation, manufacturing, social issues in computing.

William G. Griswold, Assistant Professor of Computer Science; Ph. D. (computer science), Washington (Seattle). Software engineering, programming tools, software design, software maintenance, programming languages, parallel systems, and compilers.

William E. Howden, Professor of Computer Science; Ph.D. (computer science), California, Irvine. Software engineering, system design, software testing and validation, functional program testing, analysis of real-time systems.

T. C. Hu, Professor of Computer Science; Ph.D. (applied mathematics), Brown. Combinatorial algorithms, communications networks, computer-aided design, distributed computing, operations research.

Russell Impagliazzo, Associate Professor of Computer Science; Ph.D. (mathematics), Berkeley. Computational complexity, cryptography, circuit complexity, computational randomness.

Ramesh C. Jain, Professor of Computer Science and of Electrical Engineering; Ph.D. (computer and control engineering), Indian Institute of Technology. Multimedia databases, computer vision, artificial intelligence.

Sidney Karin, Adjunct Professor and Director of UCSD's Center for Advanced Computational Science and Engineering (CACSE); Ph.D. (nuclear engineering), Michigan. High-performance computing, computational science and engineering, distributed heterogeneous computing, scientific visualization, networking and communications, operating systems and data-intensive computing, integration of high-performance computing resources.

Walter H. Ku, Adjunct Professor of Computer Science, Professor of Electrical and Computer Engineering, and Director, NSF Center for Ultra-High Speed Integrated Circuits and Systems (ICAS); Ph.D. (electrical engineering and electrophysics), Polytechnic Institute of Brooklyn. Computer-aided design, VLSI chip design, VLSI algorithms and architectures.

Keith Marzullo, Associate Professor of Computer Science; Ph.D. (electrical engineering), Stanford. Fault-tolerance and high availability, distributed computing, group-based programming, responsive systems, application management.

Eric Mjolsness, Research Scientist; Ph.D. (physics and computer science), Caltech. Mathematical methods for neural networks; computer vision, pattern recognition, parallel optimization, biological modeling.

Alex Orailoglu, Associate Professor of Computer Science; Ph.D. (computer science), Illinois at Urbana-Champaign. Computer-aided design, synthesis of testable ICs, DSP test, high-level synthesis of fault-tolerant ASICs, microprocessor test, hardware/software codesign.

Yannis G. Papakonstantinou, Assistant Professor of Computer Science and Engineering; Ph.D. (computer science), Stanford. Databases, integration of heterogeneous sources, multimedia information systems.

Joseph Pasquale, Beyster Professor of Computer Science; Ph.D. (computer science), Berkeley. Operating systems, networks, multimedia, agent-based computing, mobile computing.

Ramamohan Paturi, Associate Professor of Computer Science; Ph.D. (computer science), Penn State. Complexity theory, circuit complexity, neural networks, learning theory, parallel computation, optical computing.

George Polyzos, Associate Professor of Computer Science; Ph.D. (computer science), Toronto. Communication networks and protocols, wireless mobile communications and computing, multiaccess channels, multimedia distributed systems, systems performance evaluation.

P. Venkat Rangan, Professor of Computer Science; Ph.D. (computer science), Berkeley. Multimedia (digital video and audio) systems, multimedia networking, visual asset management systems, multimedia content-based retrieval, database systems.

Jeffrey B. Remmel, Adjunct Professor of Computer Science and Professor of Mathematics; Ph.D. (mathematics), Cornell. Nonmonotonic logic, logic programming, knowledge representation, program verification, hybrid control.

J. Ben Rosen, Adjunct Professor of Computer Science; Ph.D. (applied mathematics), Columbia. Parallel numerical algorithms, large-scale optimization, global optimization with application to molecular structure, structure-preserving approximation algorithms.

Walter J. Savitch, Professor of Computer Science; Ph.D. (mathematics), Berkeley. Computational linguistics, formal language theory, complexity theory.

Terrence J. Sejnowski, Adjunct Professor of Computer Science; Ph.D. (physics), Princeton. Computational neuroscience, neural computation, massively parallel architectures.

Dean Tullsen, Assistant Professor of Computer Science and Engineering; Ph.D. (computer science), Washington (Seattle). Computer architecture, processor design, multithreading architectures, compiling for high-performance processors, cache design, multiprocessing.

Victor Vianu, Professor of Computer Science; Ph.D. (computer science), USC. Data and knowledge base systems.

S. Gill Williamson, Professor of Computer Science; Ph.D. (mathematics), California, Santa Barbara. Algorithms, combinatorial mathematics.

Richard Wolski, Research Scientist; Ph.D. (computer science), California, Davis. Distributed high-performance computing, parallel computing, scheduling and program mapping, distributed performance monitoring and forecasting.

Bennet S. Yee, Assistant Professor of Computer Science; Ph.D. (computer science), Carnegie Mellon. Computer security, electronic commerce, cryptography, distributed systems, operating systems.

UNIVERSITY OF CALIFORNIA, SAN DIEGO

DEPARTMENT OF ELECTRICAL AND COMPUTER ENGINEERING

PROGRAMS OF STUDY

The Department of Electrical and Computer Engineering (ECE) offers graduate programs leading to the M.S. and Ph.D. degrees in electrical engineering with specializations in each of the following areas: communication theory and systems, computer engineering, electronic circuits and systems, electronic devices and materials, intelligent systems, robotics and control, magnetic recording, photonics, radio and space science, and signal and image processing. In addition, there are interdepartmental curricula in advanced manufacturing, applied ocean sciences, and materials science. The M.S. program is intended to extend and broaden an undergraduate background and equip practicing engineers with fundamental knowledge in their particular fields. The degree may be terminal or obtained in the course of earning the Ph.D. Two plans of study are offered, both requiring successful completion of 48 quarter units of credit: Plan I is a combination of course work and research, culminating in the preparation of a thesis; Plan II involves course work only and culminates in a comprehensive examination. Course requirements for the M.S. and the Ph.D. programs are identical. The M.S. program is a terminal degree for students who wish to enter the workplace, while the Ph.D. program is designed to prepare students for a career in research or teaching.

RESEARCH FACILITIES

The department has state-of-the-art research facilities in a wide range of areas. Facilities for materials and device research include several molecular beam epitaxy and organometallic vapor phase epitaxy reactors, electron beam lithography, a complete microfabrication facility, and laboratories for microelectronic and photonic device research. In the area of optical systems and photonics, a wide variety of lasers, optical tables, light valves, modulators, characterization equipment, computing platforms, and CAD tools are in use. The circuits and systems laboratories include computational platforms, software tools, and equipment for evaluation of microwave devices and circuits. The radio and space science group operates its own workstation network and makes extensive use of the San Diego Supercomputer Center. A large 74-MHz phased array antenna for propagation research and radio astronomy is operated remotely from the campus. The Computer Vision and Resources Laboratories include optical systems for metric computer vision, a network of Sun and Silicon Graphics Workstations, two Puma Arms, and a mobile golf cart under computer control. Communications and networking research activities are supported by laboratories providing modern software tools for analysis and simulation using a variety of computational platforms. The department operates or participates in a variety of research centers, including the NSF Industrial/University Cooperative Research Center for Ultra-High Speed Integrated Circuits and Systems, the ARPA-sponsored Optoelectronics Technology Center, the Center for Magnetic Recording Research, the Center for Astronomy and Space Science, the California Space Institute, and the Institute for Nonlinear Science. The San Diego Supercomputer Center, one of four NSF national centers for supercomputing research, is located on the University of California, San Diego (UCSD) campus and is heavily used for electrical and computer engineering research. The Center for Wireless Communications supports graduate-level research in communications theory, communications networks, multimedia applications, circuit design, antenna design, and propagation measurements/modeling.

FINANCIAL AID

Financial aid is available in the form of fellowships, teaching assistantships, and research assistantships. The department attempts to support all full-time graduate students, especially at the Ph.D. level. Award of financial support is competitive, and stipends range from $9000 to $15,000 for the academic year, usually with tuition and fees. The most common form of support is a half-time research assistantship that provides approximately $16,770 during the calendar year plus tuition and fees.

COST OF STUDY

In 1997–98, full-time students who are California residents pay approximately $1625 per quarter in registration and incidental fees. Non-California residents pay approximately $4625 per quarter for registration, tuition, and incidental fees. There is a reduced-fee structure for students enrolled on a half-time basis. Costs are subject to change.

LIVING AND HOUSING COSTS

UCSD provides 802 residential apartments for graduate students. Current monthly rates range from $300 for a single student to $650 for a family. For off-campus housing, prevailing rates range from $270 per month for a room in a private home to $900 or more for a two-bedroom apartment. Further information may be obtained from the UCSD Residential Housing Office (telephone: 619-534-2952).

STUDENT GROUP

Current campus enrollment is about 18,200; of this number, 14,700 are undergraduates and 3,500 are graduate students. ECE has an undergraduate enrollment of about 550 and a graduate enrollment of about 230.

LOCATION

The 2,040-acre campus spreads from the coastline, where the Scripps Institution of Oceanography is located, across a large wooded portion to the Torrey Pines Mesa overlooking the Pacific Ocean. To the east and north lie mountains, with Mexico to the south. The climate in San Diego is generally mild and pleasant year-round.

THE UNIVERSITY

One of nine campuses in the University of California System, UCSD comprises the General Campus, the School of Medicine, and the Scripps Institution of Oceanography. Established in La Jolla in 1960, it is one of the newer campuses but in this short time has become one of the major research universities in the country. The UCSD campus and the School of Engineering are ranked in the top ten nationwide by the National Academy of Sciences.

APPLYING

Applicants are considered for admission for the fall quarter only. All applicants are required to take the GRE General Test. International applicants whose native language is not English are required to take the TOEFL and obtain a minimum score of 550. A minimum GPA of 3.0 (on a 4.0 scale) is required for admission. The deadline for filing applications is January 16, 1998.

CORRESPONDENCE AND INFORMATION

Department of Electrical and Computer Engineering
University of California, San Diego
9500 Gilman Drive
La Jolla, California 92093-0408
Telephone: 619-534-6606 or 4286
Fax: 619-534-2486
World Wide Web: http://www.ece.ucsd.edu

UNIVERSITY OF CALIFORNIA, SAN DIEGO

THE FACULTY AND THEIR RESEARCH

William S. C. Chang, Research Professor and Department Chair; Ph.D., Brown. Integrated optics, solid-state electronics.

Anthony Acampora, Professor; Ph.D., Polytechnic of Brooklyn. Wireless communications.

V. C. Anderson, Professor Emeritus; Ph.D., UCLA. Acoustics.

Peter M. Asbeck, Professor; Ph.D., MIT. Semiconductor device physics.

H. Neal Bertram, Professor; Ph.D., Harvard. Magnetic recording.

Paul M. Chau, Associate Professor; Ph.D., Cornell. VLSI systems, digital signal processing, computer engineering, CAD.

Teresa Cheeks, Assistant Professor; Ph.D., Cornell. Materials science, magnetic thin films.

William A. Coles, Professor; Ph.D., California, San Diego. Radio astronomy, space physics, antennas and electronic instrumentation.

Pamela C. Cosman, Assistant Professor; Ph.D., Stanford. Data compression, image processing.

Rene L. Cruz, Professor; Ph.D., Illinois. Communication networks.

Sadik C. Esener, Associate Professor; Ph.D., California, San Diego. Optoelectronic devices.

Shaya Fainman, Professor; Ph.D., Technion (Israel). Photonics, diffractive optics, information and image processing.

J. A. Fejer, Professor Emeritus; D.Sc., Witwatersrand (South Africa). Space physics.

Ian Galton, Associate Professor; Ph.D., Caltech. Signal processing and mixed-mode integrated circuits for communication systems.

Clark C. Guest, Associate Professor; Ph.D., Georgia Tech. Optical neural nets.

Robert Hecht-Nielsen, Adjunct Professor; Ph.D., Arizona State. Neural networks, neural computing.

Carl W. Helstrom, Professor Emeritus; Ph.D., Caltech. Communication theory, signal detection theory, optics.

John A. Hildebrand, Adjunct Professor; Ph.D., Stanford. Acoustics.

William S. Hodgkiss, Professor; Ph.D., Duke. Digital signal processing, underwater acoustics.

Ramesh Jain, Professor; Ph.D., Indian Institute of Technology. Computer engineering, robotics.

Karen L. Kavanagh, Professor; Ph.D., Cornell. Materials science.

Kenneth Kreutz-Delgado, Associate Professor; Ph.D., California, San Diego. Systems science, machine intelligence, robotics.

Walter H. Ku, Professor; Ph.D., Polytechnic of Brooklyn. VLSI, IC design for signal processing and communications.

S. S. Lau, Professor; Ph.D., Berkeley. Electronic materials science.

Sing H. Lee, Professor; Ph.D., Berkeley. Photonics, micro-optics, optoelectronic CAD and packaging.

James Lemke, Adjunct Professor; Ph.D., California, Santa Barbara. Magnetic recording.

Bill Lin, Assistant Professor; Ph.D., Berkeley. Computer engineering.

Ting-Ting Lin, Assistant Professor; Ph.D., Carnegie Mellon. Computer engineering.

Robert Lugannani, Professor; Ph.D., Princeton. Stochastic processes, communication theory.

Huey-Lin Luo, Professor Ph.D., Caltech. Solid-state physics, materials science, superconductivity.

Elias Masry, Professor; Ph.D., Princeton. Time series analysis, communication theory.

D. Asoka Mendis, Professor Emeritus; Ph.D., D.Sc., Manchester (England). Solar system physics, cometary physics.

Laurence B. Milstein, Professor; Ph.D., Polytechnic of Brooklyn. Digital communication systems, communication theory.

Farrokh Najmabadi, Associate Professor; Ph.D., Berkeley. Fusion.

Alon Orlitsky, Professor; Ph.D., Stanford. Information theory, learning theory, signal processing.

Kevin Quest, Professor; Ph.D., UCLA. Solar system physics.

Bhaskar Rao, Associate Professor; Ph.D., USC. Signal processing, estimation theory.

Ramesh R. Rao, Associate Professor; Ph.D., Maryland. Communication theory.

Barnaby J. Rickett, Professor; Ph.D., Manchester (England). Wave propagation in random media, radio, astronomy, solar wind.

Manuel Rotenberg, Professor Emeritus; Ph.D., MIT. Numerical methods, population dynamics.

M. Lea Rudee, Research Professor; Ph.D., Stanford. Materials science.

Anthony Sebald, Associate Professor; Ph.D., Illinois. Adaptive control systems, neural networks, fuzzy control.

Vitali Shapiro, Professor; Ph.D., Joint Institute for Nuclear Research (Russia). Space physics.

Paul H. Siegel, Professor; Ph.D., MIT. Communication and coding theory, magnetic recording, wireless communications.

David Sworder, Professor and Associate Dean, OGSR; Ph.D., UCLA. Systems control.

Mohan M. Trivedi, Professor; Ph.D., Utah State. Intelligent systems, machine vision, robotics.

Charles W. Tu, Professor; Ph.D., Yale. Molecular beam epitaxy, semiconductor materials and devices.

Harry H. Wieder, Professor Emeritus; D.Sc., Colorado State. Optical electronics, solid-state physics.

Jack K. Wolf, Professor; Ph.D., Princeton. Communication theory, magnetic recording.

Edward T. Yu, Assistant Professor; Ph.D., Caltech. Semiconductor materials and devices.

Paul K. L. Yu, Professor; Ph.D., Caltech. Optoelectronic devices.

Kenneth Y. Yun, Assistant Professor; Ph.D., Stanford. Asynchronous circuits, VLSI automation high-speed networks.

Kenneth Zeger, Associate Professor; Ph.D., California, Santa Barbara. Communications, data compression.

James Zeidler, Adjunct Professor; Ph.D., Nebraska. Solid-state devices, adaptive signal processing.

UNIVERSITY OF CALIFORNIA, SANTA BARBARA

DEPARTMENT OF COMPUTER SCIENCE

PROGRAMS OF STUDY

The Department of Computer Science offers graduate programs leading to M.S. and Ph.D. degrees. Course offerings reflect emphases in the following major areas of study: design and analysis of algorithms, theory of computation, computational complexity, parallel programming, databases, formal methods, VLSI/CAD, software engineering, operating systems, computer security, programming languages, compilers, networks and distributed systems, computer vision and image processing, and scientific computing.

The M.S. and Ph.D. programs offer advanced educational opportunities leading to a wide range of careers in research, teaching, and development; to positions in manufacturing organizations, business, and government; and to other positions of professional leadership.

Three quarters of residence are required in the M.S. program. Part-time students and those on assistantships may require additional quarters. Both thesis and nonthesis options are available, with a comprehensive examination required in the nonthesis option.

The Ph.D. requires an approved program, including course work that develops sufficient breadth in graduate-level computer science and a dissertation. In addition, a student must pass a screening examination early in the program and a qualifying examination approximately two to three years after admission. Six quarters of residence are required. There is no foreign language requirement.

RESEARCH FACILITIES

There are a number of research laboratories throughout the department, including the Computer Vision Lab, Distributed Systems Lab, Parallel Systems Lab, Reliable Software Lab, and Theory of Computation Lab. These labs are equipped with excellent computing facilities, including approximately 200 Sun and SGI workstations, file servers, Power Macintoshes, PCs, an ATM network of workstations, and an SGI-based workstation cluster. The College of Engineering computing facility houses workstations from Hewlett-Packard and Silicon Graphics.

The department operates a 64-node Meiko CS-2 MPP system, acquired through a major Computer and Information Science and Engineering (CISE) infrastructure grant from the National Science Foundation (NSF). The department is also a major participant in the Alexandria Digital Library Project—an integral part of the national Digital Library Initiative, funded jointly by the NSF, the Defense Advanced Research Projects Agency, and NASA—to design and implement a distributed test bed for searching, retrieving, and browsing images and maps.

FINANCIAL AID

Teaching and research assistantships and various fellowships are awarded on a competitive basis, mainly for the Ph.D. program. The application deadline for awards is January 15. Loans and work-study employment also are available.

COST OF STUDY

In 1997–98, all graduate students pay registration fees of $4066.80 per year ($1355.60 per quarter); nonresidents of California pay additional out-of-state tuition of $8984 ($2994.67 per quarter).

LIVING AND HOUSING COSTS

Accommodation in on-campus residence halls, with most meals included, costs $6131 yearly. One- and two-bedroom University-owned apartments are available for single and married students for rents of $5600 to $7440 per year. Privately owned apartments and houses are available in nearby areas at higher prices.

STUDENT GROUP

The total campus enrollment is about 20,000, with approximately 2,000 graduate students. The department has about 100 graduate students, who come from all parts of the United States and many other nations. Approximately 50 percent of the department's graduate students are international.

LOCATION

The University occupies a spacious 815-acre site on a promontory bordered on two sides by the Pacific Ocean and on another by Goleta Valley and the Santa Ynez mountains. The campus has a 7-mile system of bicycle paths that connect with those of surrounding communities. The Santa Barbara airport and Goleta Beach state park are immediately adjacent to the campus, which is 10 miles west of downtown Santa Barbara and 100 miles north of Los Angeles. In addition to providing an excellent academic environment, UCSB's location on the Southern California coast makes it one of the nicest places in the United States in which to live.

THE UNIVERSITY

UCSB is a major research institution. It is a member of the nine-campus University of California System, widely regarded as the most distinguished system of public higher education in the United States.

APPLYING

A bachelor's degree is required in some discipline of science, engineering, or mathematics. Applicants must have a grade point average of at least 3.0 in their last two years of undergraduate study. The GRE General Test is also required. International applicants whose native language is not English must submit a TOEFL score of at least 600. The TSE is strongly encouraged for international students applying for financial aid. All application materials must be received by May 1 for fall admission. An applicant is considered for fellowships and assistantships when all application materials are received by January 15.

CORRESPONDENCE AND INFORMATION

Graduate Advisor
Department of Computer Science
University of California
Santa Barbara, California 93106-5110
Telephone: 805-893-4323
Fax: 805-893-8553
E-mail: grad-advisor@cs.ucsb.edu
World Wide Web: http://www.cs.ucsb.edu

UNIVERSITY OF CALIFORNIA, SANTA BARBARA

THE FACULTY AND THEIR RESEARCH

Divyakant Agrawal, Associate Professor; Ph.D., SUNY at Stony Brook. Distributed systems, distributed databases.

John L. Bruno, Professor; Ph.D., CUNY, City College. Operating systems and distributed systems, scheduling theory, parallel computation.

Peter R. Cappello, Professor; Ph.D., Princeton. Concurrent computation, self-directed learning, globally distributed computing.

Laura Dillon, Associate Professor; Ph.D., Massachusetts. Testing and analysis of concurrent systems, semantics of programming languages, formal specification and verification, software systems.

Omer Egecioglu, Associate Professor; Ph.D., California, San Diego. Parallel algorithms, approximation algorithms, bijective and enumerative combinatorics, combinatorial algorithms.

Amr El Abbadi, Associate Professor; Ph.D., Cornell. Fault-tolerant distributed systems, distributed databases, digital libraries.

Teofilo Gonzalez, Professor; Ph.D., Minnesota. Computer-aided design, VLSI placement and routing algorithms, scheduling theory, design and analysis of algorithms.

Urs Hölzle, Assistant Professor; Ph.D., Stanford. Object-oriented programming languages, compilers, programming environments, computer architecture.

Oscar H. Ibarra, Professor; Ph.D., Berkeley. Theory of computation, design and analysis of algorithms, computational complexity, parallel computing.

Richard A. Kemmerer, Professor; Ph.D., UCLA. Specification and verification of systems, computer system security and reliability, programming and specification language design, software engineering.

Alan G. Konheim, Professor; Ph.D., Cornell. Computer communications, computer systems modeling and analysis, cryptography.

Marvin Marcus, Professor Emeritus; Ph.D., Berkeley. Linear and multilinear algebra, scientific computation, linear numerical analysis.

*Linda R. Petzold, Professor; Ph.D., Illinois at Urbana–Champaign. Numerical ordinary differential equations, differential algebraic equations and partial differential equations, numerical optimization, parameter estimation and optimal control for PDE systems, mathematical software, parallel computing, scientific computing.

Martin C. Rinard, Assistant Professor; Ph.D., Stanford. Parallelizing compilers, parallel and distributed computing.

Klaus E. Schauser, Assistant Professor; Ph.D., Berkeley. Parallel computing, parallel programming languages, compilers, computer architecture.

Ambuj K. Singh, Associate Professor; Ph.D., Texas at Austin. Parallel and distributed computing, formal specification and verification, databases.

Terence Smith, Professor; Ph.D., Johns Hopkins. Artificial intelligence, spatial databases.

Jianwen Su, Associate Professor; Ph.D., USC. Database theory, systems, and applications.

Yuan-Fang Wang, Associate Professor; Ph.D., Texas at Austin. Computer vision, computer graphics, artificial intelligence.

**Roger C. Wood, Professor Emeritus; Ph.D., UCLA. Computer system modeling, design and analysis, computer architecture.

Tao Yang, Assistant Professor; Ph.D., Rutgers. Algorithms and programming environments for parallel and distributed processing, program scheduling and compilation, parallel scientific computing, digital libraries.

——————

*Joint appointment with the Department of Mechanical and Environmental Engineering.
**Joint appointment with the Department of Electrical and Computer Engineering.

UNIVERSITY OF CALIFORNIA, SANTA BARBARA

DEPARTMENT OF ELECTRICAL AND COMPUTER ENGINEERING

PROGRAMS OF STUDY

Graduate studies leading to the M.S. and Ph.D. degrees in electrical and computer engineering are offered in the following areas of specialization: computer engineering; solid state; communications, control, and signal processing; and wave electronics and technology.

Three quarters of residence are required in the M.S. program, and it is possible to complete the program in that time. Part-time students and those on assistantships usually require additional quarters. Both thesis and nonthesis options are available; a comprehensive examination is required in the nonthesis option.

The Ph.D. degree requires an approved program, including course work in a well-defined major area, demonstrated competence in two minor areas, and a dissertation. In addition, a student must pass a screening examination early in the program and a qualifying examination approximately two to three years after admission. Six quarters of residence are required; typically, the Ph.D. program is completed in about three years after completion of the M.S. program. There is no foreign language requirement.

RESEARCH FACILITIES

The Department of Electrical and Computer Engineering maintains a wide range of facilities for research and is closely associated with interdisciplinary campus research units, including the Compound Semiconductor Research Center, the Center for Quantized Electronic Structures, the Center for Computational Sciences and Engineering, the Center for Control Engineering and Computation, the Optoelectronic Technology Center, and the Multidisciplinary Optical Switching Technology Center. Facilities are available for all processes of device and integrated-circuit technology, focused ion beam, scanning electron microscopy, and metalorganic and molecular beam epitaxy; an optics laboratory for compound semiconductor and materials research; a microwave and millimeter-wave laboratory; a high-speed optical communication laboratory; an acoustic imaging facility; facilities for image digitization and processing; and individual laboratories for research and graduate instruction in communications, control and scientific computation, signal processing, computer architecture, software engineering, artificial intelligence, systolic computation, and VLSI CAD and VLSI testing, each with a state-of-the-art computing environment.

FINANCIAL AID

Teaching and research assistantships and various fellowships are awarded on a competitive basis. The application deadline for awards is January 15. About 170 students received some form of financial aid in 1996–97.

COST OF STUDY

In 1997–98, all graduate students pay registration fees of approximately $4073 per year ($1358 per quarter); nonresidents of California pay additional out-of-state tuition of $8400 ($2800 per quarter).

LIVING AND HOUSING COSTS

One- and two-bedroom University-owned apartments are available for single and married students for rents of $424 to $932 per month. Privately owned apartments and houses are available in nearby areas. Most students share apartments or houses.

STUDENT GROUP

The total campus enrollment is about 18,500 (51 percent women), with approximately 2,250 graduate students. The department has about 200 graduate students who come from all parts of the United States and many other nations. Approximately 44 percent of the graduate students in the department are international students. Approximately 60 students are M.S. candidates and 170 are doctoral candidates; sixty M.S. and twenty-five Ph.D. degrees are awarded annually.

LOCATION

The University occupies a spacious site (815 acres) on a promontory bordered on two sides by the Pacific Ocean and on another by the Goleta Valley and Santa Ynez Mountains. The campus has a 7-mile system of bike paths that connect with those of surrounding communities. The Santa Barbara Airport and Goleta Beach State Park are immediately adjacent to the campus, which is 10 miles west of downtown Santa Barbara and 100 miles northwest of Los Angeles.

THE UNIVERSITY AND THE DEPARTMENT

UCSB is a research I institution offering undergraduate and graduate education in the arts, humanities, sciences and engineering, and social sciences. It is a member of the nine-campus University of California System, which is widely regarded to be the most distinguished system of public higher education in the United States. UCSB is now a member of the prestigious Association of American Universities (AAU), joining sixty leading institutions of higher learning in the U.S. and Canada that offer strong research and graduate education programs. The College of Engineering at UCSB ranks among the top four in the nation in terms of research funding per faculty member.

The Department of Electrical and Computer Engineering is a medium-size EE department with 35 faculty members, 190 undergraduate students, and 200 graduate students. There is a strong tradition of interdisciplinary education and research, with many multi-investigator research centers and programs, often involving faculty members and students from different areas in the department, other departments, and other universities. These projects also frequently include strong cooperation with industrial researchers.

APPLYING

Application deadlines for those who desire financial award consideration are January 15 for Ph.D. applicants and March 1 for M.S.- only or M.S./Ph.D. applicants. May 1 is the deadline for admission only. A bachelor's degree in electrical engineering, computer science, or some area of engineering or in mathematics, physics, or some related field of science is required. The GRE General Test is required of all applicants (the Subject Test is optional), and the TOEFL is required of international applicants.

CORRESPONDENCE AND INFORMATION

Graduate Assistant
Department of Electrical and Computer Engineering
University of California
Santa Barbara, California 93106-9560

Telephone: 805-893-3114
Fax: 805-893-3262
E-mail: admit@ece.ucsb.edu
World Wide Web: http://www.ece.ucsb.edu

UNIVERSITY OF CALIFORNIA, SANTA BARBARA

THE FACULTY AND THEIR RESEARCH

An asterisk (*) identifies faculty members who hold a joint appointment with the Department of Materials; a dagger (†) identifies those who hold a joint appointment with the Department of Computer Science; and a double dagger (††) identifies those who hold a joint appointment with the Department of Mathematics.

John E. Bowers, Professor; Ph.D., Stanford. High-speed photonic and electronic devices and integrated circuits, semiconductor laser physics and modelocking phenomena, compound semiconductor materials and processing.

Forrest D. Brewer, Associate Professor; Ph.D., Illinois. VLSI design automation, theory of design and design representations, symbolic techniques in high-level synthesis.

Steven E. Butner, Professor; Ph.D., Stanford. Computer architecture; reliability and computer-aided VLSI design of CMOS and gallium arsenate ICs, with emphasis on distributed organizations and fault-tolerant structures.

Shivkumar Chandrasekaran, Assistant Professor; Ph.D., Yale. Numerical analysis, numerical linear algebra, scientific computation.

Kwang-Ting (Tim) Cheng, Associate Professor; Ph.D., Berkeley. Design automation, VLSI testing, logic synthesis, design verification, algorithms.

*Larry A. Coldren, Professor; Ph.D., Stanford. Semiconductor integrated optoelectronics, widely tunable lasers, vertical-cavity lasers, optical fiber communication, growth and planar processing techniques.

Nadir Dagli, Associate Professor; Ph.D., MIT. Design, fabrication, and modeling of photonic integrated circuits, ultrafast eletrooptic modulators, solid-state microwave and millimeter-wave devices, experimental study of ballistic transport in quantum continued structures.

*Steven P. DenBaars, Associate Professor; Ph.D., USC. Metalorganic vapor phase epitaxy, optoelectronic materials, compound semiconductors, indium phosphide and gallium nitride, photonic devices.

Allen Gersho, Professor; Ph.D., Cornell. Speech, audio, image, and video compression; quantization and signal compression techniques and speech processing.

*Arthur Gossard, Professor; Ph.D., Berkeley. Epitaxial crystal growth, artificially structured materials, semiconductor structures for optical and electronic devices, quantum confinement structures.

Evelyn Hu, Professor; Ph.D., Columbia. High-resolution fabrication techniques for semiconductor device structures, process-related materials damage, contact/interface studies, superconductivity.

Ronald Iltis, Professor; Ph.D., California, San Diego. Digital spread spectrum communications, spectral estimation and adaptive filtering.

Atac Imamoglu, Assistant Professor; Ph.D., Stanford. Quantum optics, lasers without population inversion, quantum coherence in semiconductors, stochastic wave-function methods.

John P. J. Kelly, Associate Professor; Ph.D., UCLA. Dependable fault-tolerant software, software engineering, distributed computing, and database systems and machines.

Petar V. Kokotovic, Professor and Director, Center for Control Engineering and Computation; Ph.D., USSR Academy of Sciences. Control theory, singular perturbations, nonlinear systems, adaptive control, automotive and aerospace controls, sensitivity analysis, large-scale systems.

*Herbert Kroemer, Professor; Dr.rer.nat., Göttingen (Germany). General solid-state and device physics, heterostructures, molecular-beam epitaxy, compound semiconductor materials and devices, superconductivity.

Hua Lee, Professor; Director, Center for High-Speed Image Processing; Ph.D., California, Santa Barbara. High-performance image-formation algorithms, synthetic-aperture radar and sonar systems, acoustic microscopy, microwave nondestructive evaluation and dynamic vision systems, image system optimization.

Stephen I. Long, Professor; Ph.D., Cornell. Semiconductor devices and integrated circuits for high-speed digital and RF analog applications.

B. S. Manjunath, Assistant Professor; Ph.D., USC. Image processing, computer vision, pattern recognition, neural networks, content-based retrieval in multimedia databases and learning algorithms.

Malgorzata Marek-Sadowska, Professor; Ph.D., Warsaw Technical. Design automation, computer-aided design, integrated circuit layout, logic synthesis.

†P. Michael Melliar-Smith, Professor; Ph.D., Cambridge. Distributed systems, fault tolerance, formal specification and verification, communication networks and protocols, asynchronous systems.

Umesh K. Mishra, Professor; Ph.D., Cornell. High-speed transistors, semiconductor device physics, quantum electronics, design and fabrication of millimeter-wave devices, in situ processing and integration techniques, wide band gap materials and devices.

Sanjit K. Mitra, Professor; Ph.D., Berkeley. Digital signal processing, image processing, computer-aided design and optimization.

Louise E. Moser, Associate Professor; Ph.D., Wisconsin. Distributed systems, computer networks, software engineering, fault tolerance, formal specification, and verification; performance evaluation.

Venkatesh Narayanamurti, Professor; Ph.D., Cornell. Transport, ballistic electron emission microscopy, nanostructures, scanning tunneling microscopy, phonon physics, semiconductor heterostructures.

Behrooz Parhami, Professor; Ph.D., UCLA. Computer design, computer arithmetic, dependable (fault-tolerant) computing, parallel architectures and algorithms.

*Pierre M. Petroff, Professor; Director, Compound Semiconductor Research Center; Ph.D., Berkeley. Semiconductor device reliability, self-assembling nanostructures in semiconductors and ferromagnetic materials, spectroscopy of nanostructures, nanostructure devices.

Ian B. Rhodes, Professor; Ph.D., Stanford. Mathematical system theory and its applications, with emphasis on stochastic control, communication, and optimization problems, especially those involving decentralized information structures or parallel computational structures.

Mark J. W. Rodwell, Professor, Director, Compound Semiconductor Research Laboratories; Ph.D., Stanford. Heterojunction bipolar transistors, high-frequency integrated circuit design, electronics beyond 100 GHz.

Kenneth Rose, Associate Professor; Ph.D., Caltech. Information theory, source and channel coding, image coding, communications, pattern recognition.

John J. Shynk, Professor; Associate Director, Center for Information Processing Research; Ph.D., Stanford. Adaptive filtering, blind equalization, wireless communications, neural networks, array processing.

Roy S. Smith, Associate Professor; Ph.D., Caltech. Robust control with an emphasis on the modeling, identification, and control of uncertain systems, applications and experimental work, including process control, flexible structures, automotive systems, semiconductor manufacturing, levitated magnetic bearings, and dynamic aeromaneuvering of interplanetary spacecraft.

Emmanouel Varvarigos, Assistant Professor; Ph.D., MIT. Data networks, routing and communication aspects of parallel computations, communication systems, parallel processing architectures.

Pochi Yeh, Professor; Ph.D., Caltech. Optical computing, image processing, nonlinear optics, phase conjugation, dynamic holography, optical interconnection, neural networks.

Robert A. York, Associate Professor; Ph.D., Cornell. Electromagnetic theory, antennas, nonlinear circuits and dynamics, high-power/high-frequency devices and circuits, quasi-optics, microwave photonics.

UNIVERSITY OF CALIFORNIA, SANTA CRUZ

GRADUATE PROGRAM IN COMPUTER ENGINEERING

PROGRAMS OF STUDY

The Department of Computer Engineering (CE) offers M.S. and Ph.D. degree programs and conducts research in computer-aided design of digital systems, including placement and routing, timing analysis, logic synthesis, specification languages, fault modeling, test generation, and multichip module design; computer systems design and applications, including VLSI, special-purpose processors, high-speed arithmetic circuits, and real-time systems; data compression, image and video coding, signal processing, and image processing, retrieval, and transmission; computer architecture and parallel processing, including massively parallel architecture, parallel programming and visualization, and memory and IO systems; and performance evaluation, communication, and networks, including queuing theory, high-speed networks and switching, network measurement, and simulation. CE enjoys a close relationship with the Department of Computer and Sciences (CS), whose curriculum also covers the areas of machine learning, computer graphics and scientific visualization, operating systems, computational biology, distributed computing and debugging, theoretical computer science, and programming languages and environments. Faculty carry out joint research projects, supervise students, and teach courses for both departments. The department also has ties to nearby industry, employing computer professionals as visiting faculty and arranging for students to gain practical research experience through work in industrial labs. Students start the program with core courses in computer architecture and algorithms and then proceed to study thoroughly their area of specialization. The M.S. degree can be completed in one to two years. M.S. students may elect to complete a master's thesis. A Ph.D. degree is usually completed in five to six years. After completing the course requirements, students must pass an oral qualifying exam and write a dissertation. Part-time study is possible for students working in industry while going to school.

RESEARCH FACILITIES

The CS and CE departments operate the Computer Research Laboratory (CRL) of the Baskin Center for Computer Engineering and Information Sciences to support research and graduate instruction in computer science and computer engineering. The CRL provides a network of approximately 200 UNIX systems, with associated graphics devices, printers, and workstations, to facilitate research in computer engineering and information sciences. Network support includes full Ethernet connectivity at 10Mb/sec, as well as experimental fiber- and copper-based ATM connectivity at 155Mb/sec. In support of the computer needs of the graduate instruction and research in the above areas, the CRL provides a number of servers, including compute and file servers for the Sun SPARC, IBM RS6000, and DEC MIPS and Alpha architectures, as well as a 2-processor Silicon Graphics Challenge L central file server, a 4-processor Silicon Graphics Onyx Reality Engine 2 graphics engine, and a MasPar MP-2204 massively parallel compute server with 4096 processors. This server infrastructure supports in excess of 130 UNIX workstations from Sun, DEC, Silicon Graphics, IBM, and HP, as well as a number of X terminals and microcomputers. UCSC is a member of the San Diego Supercomputing Consortium, providing access to a CRAY C98/8128, a 400-node Intel Paragon, and other supercomputers. A weeklong Cray programming course is held annually.

FINANCIAL AID

A limited number of fellowships provide a stipend of $9999 plus payment of all University fees except nonresident tuition to first-year students. A number of nonresident tuition waivers are awarded to students who are not residents of California. Half-time teaching assistantships provide a salary of $5233 per quarter, half-time research assistantships provide a salary of $5188, and both allow time for taking two lecture courses per quarter.

COST OF STUDY

Fees for the 1997–98 academic year are approximately $5205. Students who are not California residents must pay the additional nonresident tuition fee of $8985 per year.

LIVING AND HOUSING COSTS

Housing for single students living on the University campus costs $4689. For married students and single parents, housing costs $5086. For students living off campus, the amount is about $6000, not including board.

STUDENT GROUP

Total enrollment at UC Santa Cruz is approximately 10,000 students; about 960 are graduate students. The number of graduate students currently in computer engineering is 90.

LOCATION

Santa Cruz is one of America's most beautiful campuses. Overlooking Monterey Bay, it occupies 2,000 acres in protected redwood forests and meadows above the city of Santa Cruz. Nearby Santa Clara Valley, one of the most important centers for the computer industry, is a significant resource.

THE UNIVERSITY

Founded 1965, Santa Cruz is a small collegiate university devoted to excellence in undergraduate education and enriched by a select group of graduate programs and the presence of major research units.

APPLYING

Students must begin the program in the fall quarter. Completed applications must be received by February 1, 1998. Files of applicants for 1998–99 are reviewed in late February 1998. Requests for applications should be directed to the Graduate Division, 399 Applied Sciences. The application fee is $40 and subject to increase without notification. Each applicant must take the GRE General Test and the Subject Test in either engineering or computer science and have the scores sent to the UCSC Graduate Division as part of the application file. The graduate brochure is available on-line (electronic mail: gradbrochure@cse.ucsc.edu).

CORRESPONDENCE AND INFORMATION

Graduate Representative, CE Department
University of California
Santa Cruz, California 95064

Telephone: 408-459-2576
E-mail: mullane@cse.ucsc.edu
World Wide Web: http://www.cse.ucsc.edu

UNIVERSITY OF CALIFORNIA, SANTA CRUZ
THE FACULTY AND THEIR RESEARCH

Computer Engineering

Alexandre Brandwajn, Professor; Ph.D. (computer science), Paris, 1975. Computer architecture, performance modeling, queuing network models of computer systems and operating systems.

Pak K. Chan, Associate Professor; Ph.D. (computer science), UCLA, 1987. Computer arithmetic, computer-aided design of VLSI circuits, circuit theory, systems prototyping.

Wayne Wei-ming Dai, Associate Professor; Ph.D. (electrical engineering), Berkeley, 1988. Computer-aided design of VLSI circuits, multichip modules, graph theory, computational geometry.

F. Joel Ferguson, Associate Professor; Ph.D. (computer engineering), Carnegie Mellon, 1987. Fault modeling, test generation and design-for-test of digital circuits and systems, fault-tolerant computing, VLSI design.

J. J. Garcia-Luna-Aceves, Associate Professor; Ph.D. (electrical engineering), Hawaii at Manoa, 1983. Computer networks and multimedia information systems.

Richard Hughey, Assistant Professor; Ph.D. (computer science), Brown, 1991. Computer architecture, parallel processing, parallel programming languages and environments, computer applications in biology, programmable systolic arrays.

Kevin Karplus, Associate Professor; Ph.D. (computer science), Stanford, 1983. Bioinformatic computational biology: applying information theory and stochastic modeling to biological sequence analysis, hidden Markov models, regularizers, mutual information, protein threading, multipurpose architecture for sequence analysis.

Harwood G. Kolsky, Adjunct Professor; Ph.D. (physics), Harvard, 1950. Scientific computing, compilers, image processing.

Glen G. Langdon Jr., Professor; Ph.D. (electrical engineering), Syracuse, 1968. Data compression, image and video coding, image segmentation.

Tracy Larrabee, Assistant Professor; Ph.D. (computer science), Stanford, 1990. Test pattern generation, design verification, logic synthesis.

Patrick E. Mantey, Professor; Ph.D. (electrical engineering), Stanford, 1965. Image storage and retrieval; electronic libraries and multimedia; educational applications of computer technology; image and signal processing; graphics and workstation hardware; system architecture, design, and performance; simulation and modeling of complex systems; real-time data acquisition and control systems; graphics and database applications, including geographic information systems; and user-machine interaction.

Martine D. F. Schlag, Associate Professor; Ph.D. (computer science), UCLA, 1986. VLSI design tools and algorithms; VLSI theory; formal specifications of VLSI circuits; Field-Programmable Gate Arrays.

Anujan Varma, Associate Professor; Ph.D. (computer engineering), USC, 1986. Computer networking, computer systems architecture, parallel processing.

Computer Information Systems

David Haussler, Professor; Ph.D. (computer science), Colorado, 1982. Machine learning, computational biology, neural networks, statistical decision theory, algorithms and complexity.

David Helmbold, Associate Professor; Ph.D. (computer science), Stanford, 1987. Machine learning, theoretical computer science, analysis of algorithms.

David A. Huffman, Professor Emeritus; Sc.D. (electrical engineering), MIT, 1953. Information theory and coding, scene analysis, graph theory, signal design and processing, discrete systems, sequential circuits.

Phokion Kolaitis, Professor; Ph.D. (mathematics), UCLA, 1978. Logic in computer science, database theory, logic programming, complexity theory.

Robert A. Levinson, Associate Professor; Ph.D. (computer science), Texas at Austin, 1985. Artificial intelligence, machine learning, heuristic search, hierarchical reinforcement learning, associate pattern retrieval, computer chess.

Suresh K. Lodha, Assistant Professor; Ph.D. (computer science), Rice, 1992. Computer graphics, scientific visualization, computer-aided geometric design, computer animation, image processing.

Darrell Long, Associate Professor; Ph.D. (computer science), California, San Diego, 1988. Distributed computing systems, operating systems, performance evaluation, data management.

Charles E. McDowell, Associate Professor; Ph.D. (computer science), California, San Diego, 1983. Computer architecture, parallel computing, microprogramming, compilers, operating systems.

Alex Pang, Assistant Professor; Ph.D. (computer science), UCLA, 1990. Visualization (scientific, environmental, and uncertainty), computer graphics, virtual reality interfaces, and collaborative software.

Ira Pohl, Professor; Ph.D. (computer science), Stanford, 1969. Artificial intelligence, programming languages, heuristic methods, educational and social issues, combinatorial algorithms.

R. Michael Tanner, Professor; Ph.D. (electrical engineering), Stanford, 1971. Information theory, error-correcting codes, complexity, VLSI systems, fault tolerance.

Allen Van Gelder, Associate Professor; Ph.D. (computer science), Stanford, 1986. Logic programming algorithms, parallel algorithms, complexity, programming languages, automated theorem proving, scientific visualization.

Manfred K. Warmuth, Professor; Ph.D. (computer science), Colorado, 1981. Machine learning, neural networks, parallel and distributed algorithms, on-line learning algorithms, complexity theory.

Jane P. Wilhelms, Associate Professor; Ph.D. (computer science), Berkeley, 1985. Computer graphics, computer animation, scientific visualization, modeling articulated bodies, physical simulation, behavioral animation.

UNIVERSITY OF CALIFORNIA, SANTA CRUZ
GRADUATE PROGRAM IN COMPUTER SCIENCE

PROGRAM OF STUDY

The Department of Computer Science (CS) offers M.S. and Ph.D. degrees and conducts research in theoretical computer science, including analysis of algorithms, parallel and distributed computation, and computational learning theory and logic; AI, including machine learning, pattern recognition and retrieval, heuristic search, computational biology and chemistry, nonmonotonic reasoning and theorem proving, and natural language understanding; programming languages and environments, including compilers, object-oriented programming, and parallel and logic programming; computer graphics and image processing, including scientific visualization, physical simulation, computer modeling, image synthesis and animation, signal processing, and image storage, retrieval, and transmission; computer architecture and operation systems, including parallel computers and distributed computing systems; and computer systems design and applications, including real-time systems, embedded systems, special-purpose processors, digital networks, data compression, design of high-speed adders, high-speed packet switching, and performance prediction, evaluation, and optimization. CS works closely with the Department of Computer Engineering, whose curriculum and research encompass some of those listed above as well as communications and networks and CAD of digital systems. Faculty members carry out joint research projects, supervise students, and teach courses for both departments. Students are provided with a general education in computer science and are then provided with the opportunity to begin research projects. M.S. degrees are usually completed in two years, although it is possible to complete the program in one year. A student must also write a master's thesis. Ph.D. degrees are usually completed in six years, although it is possible to complete in less time. After fulfilling the course requirements, a student must pass an oral qualifying exam in his or her research area and defend a dissertation.

RESEARCH FACILITIES

The CS and CE departments operate the Computer Research Laboratory (CRL) of the Baskin Center for Computer Engineering and Computer Science to support research and graduate instruction in computer science and computer engineering. The CRL provides a network of approximately 200 UNIX systems, with associated graphics devices, printers, and workstations, to facilitate research in computer engineering and computer science. Network support includes full Ethernet connectivity at 10Mb/sec, as well as experimental fiber- and copper-based ATM connectivity at 155Mb/sec. In support of the computing needs of graduate instruction and research in the above areas, the CRL provides a number of servers, including compute and file servers for the Sun SPARC, IBM RS6000, and DEC MIPS and Alpha architectures, as well as a 2-processor Silicon Graphics Challenge L central file server, a 4-processor Silicon Graphics Onyx Reality Engine 2 graphics engine, and a MasPar MP-2204 massively parallel compute server with 4096 processors. This server infrastructure supports in excess of 130 UNIX workstations from Sun, DEC, Silicon Graphics, IBM, and HP, as well as a number of X terminals and microcomputers. UCSC is a member of the San Diego Supercomputing Consortium, providing access to a CRAY C98/8128, a 400-node Intel Paragon, and other supercomputers. A weeklong Cray programming course is held annually.

FINANCIAL AID

A limited number of fellowships provide $9999 plus payment of all University fees except nonresident tuition to first-year students. A number of nonresident tuition waivers are awarded to students who are not residents of California. Half-time teaching assistantships provide a salary of $5233 per quarter, half-time research assistantships provide a salary of $6188 per quarter, and both allow time for taking two lecture courses per quarter.

COST OF STUDY

Fees for the 1997–98 academic year are approximately $5205. Students who are not California residents must pay the additional nonresident tuition fee of $8985 per year.

LIVING AND HOUSING COSTS

Housing for single students living on the University campus is $4689 for the academic year. For married students and single parents, housing costs $5080. For students living off campus, the amount is about $6000, not including board.

STUDENT GROUP

Total enrollment at UC Santa Cruz is approximately 10,000 students, of whom about 960 are graduate students. The number of graduate students currently in computer science is 70.

LOCATION

Santa Cruz is one of America's most beautiful campuses. Overlooking Monterey Bay, it occupies 2,000 acres in protected redwood forests and meadows above the city of Santa Cruz. Nearby Santa Clara Valley, one of the world's most important centers for the computer industry, is a significant resource.

THE UNIVERSITY

Founded in 1965, Santa Cruz is a small collegiate university devoted to excellence in undergraduate education and enriched by a select group of graduate programs and the presence of major research units.

APPLYING

Students must begin the program in the fall quarter. Completed applications must be received by February 1, 1998. Files of applicants for 1998–99 are reviewed in February 1998. Requests for applications should be directed to the Graduate Division, 399 Applied Sciences. The application fee is $40 and subject to increase without notification. Each applicant must take the GRE General Test and the Subject Test in either engineering or computer science and have the scores sent to the UCSC Graduate Division as part of the application file. The graduate brochure is available on-line (e-mail: gradbrochure@cse.ucsc.edu).

CORRESPONDENCE AND INFORMATION

Graduate Representative, CS Department
University of California
Santa Cruz, California 95064

Telephone: 408-459-2576
E-mail: mullane@cse.ucsc.edu
World Wide Web: http://www.cse.ucsc.edu

UNIVERSITY OF CALIFORNIA, SANTA CRUZ

THE FACULTY AND THEIR RESEARCH

Computer Engineering

Alexandre Brandwajn, Professor; Ph.D. (computer science), Paris, 1975. Computer architecture, performance modeling, queuing network models of computer systems and operating systems.

Pak K. Chan, Associate Professor; Ph.D. (computer science), UCLA, 1987. Computer arithmetic, computer-aided design of VLSI circuits, circuit theory, systems prototyping.

Wayne Wei-ming Dai, Associate Professor; Ph.D. (electrical engineering), Berkeley, 1988. Computer-aided design of VLSI circuits, multichip modules, graph theory, computational geometry.

Joel Ferguson, Associate Professor; Ph.D. (computer engineering), Carnegie Mellon, 1987. Fault modeling, test generation and design-for-test of digital circuits and systems, fault-tolerant computing, VLSI design.

J. J. Garcia-Luna-Aceves, Associate Professor; Ph.D. (electrical engineering), Hawaii at Manoa, 1983. Computer networks and multimedia information systems.

Richard Hughey, Assistant Professor; Ph.D. (computer science), Brown, 1991. Computer architecture, parallel processing, parallel programming languages and environments, computer applications in biology, programmable systolic arrays.

Kevin Karplus, Associate Professor; Ph.D. (computer science), Stanford, 1983. Bioinformatics (computational biology): applying information theory and stochastic modeling to biological sequence analysis, hidden Markov models, regularizers, mutual information, protein threading, multipurpose computer architecture for sequence analysis.

Harwood G. Kolsky, Adjunct Professor; Ph.D. (physics), Harvard, 1950. Scientific computing, compilers, image processing.

Glen G. Langdon Jr., Professor; Ph.D. (electrical engineering), Syracuse, 1968. Data compression, image and video coding, image segmentation.

Tracy Larrabee, Assistant Professor; Ph.D. (computer science), Stanford, 1990. Test pattern generation, design verification, logic synthesis.

Patrick E. Mantey, Professor; Ph.D. (electrical engineering), Stanford, 1965. Image storage and retrieval; electronic libraries and multimedia; educational applications of computer technology; image and signal processing; graphics and workstation hardware; system architecture, design, and performance; simulation and modeling of complex systems; real-time data acquisition and control systems; graphics and database applications, including geographic information systems; and user-machine interaction.

Martine D. F. Schlag, Associate Professor; Ph.D. (computer science), UCLA, 1986. VLSI design tools and algorithms; VLSI theory; formal specifications of VLSI circuits; Field-Programmable Gate Arrays.

Anujan Varma, Associate Professor; Ph.D. (computer engineering), USC, 1986. Computer networking, computer systems architecture, parallel processing.

Computer Science

David Haussler, Professor; Ph.D. (computer science), Colorado, 1982. Machine learning, computational biology, neural networks, statistical decision theory, algorithms and complexity.

David Helmbold, Associate Professor; Ph.D. (computer science), Stanford, 1987. Machine learning, theoretical computer science, analysis of algorithms.

David A. Huffman, Professor Emeritus; Sc.D. (electrical engineering), MIT, 1953. Information theory and coding, scene analysis, graph theory, signal design and processing, discrete systems, sequential circuits.

Phokion Kolaitis, Professor; Ph.D. (mathematics), UCLA, 1978. Logic in computer science, database theory, logic programming, complexity theory.

Robert A. Levinson, Associate Professor; Ph.D. (computer science), Texas at Austin, 1985. Artificial intelligence, machine learning, heuristic search, hierarchical reinforcement learning, associate pattern retrieval, computer chess.

Suresh K. Lodha, Assistant Professor; Ph.D. (computer science), Rice, 1992. Computer graphics, scientific visualization, computer-aided geometric design, computer animation, image processing.

Darrell Long, Associate Professor; Ph.D. (computer science), California, San Diego, 1988. Distributed computing systems, operating systems, performance evaluation, data management.

Charles E. McDowell, Associate Professor; Ph.D. (computer science), California, San Diego, 1983. Computer architecture, parallel computing, microprogramming, compilers, operating systems.

Alex Pang, Assistant Professor; Ph.D. (computer science), UCLA, 1990. Visualization (scientific, environmental, and uncertainty), computer graphics, virtual reality interfaces, collaborative software.

Ira Pohl, Professor; Ph.D. (computer science), Stanford, 1969. Artificial intelligence, programming languages, heuristic methods, educational and social issues, combinatorial algorithms.

R. Michael Tanner, Professor; Ph.D. (electrical engineering), Stanford, 1971. Information theory, error-correcting codes, complexity, VLSI systems, fault tolerance.

Allen Van Gelder, Associate Professor; Ph.D. (computer science), Stanford, 1986. Logic programming algorithms, parallel algorithms, complexity, programming languages, automated theorem proving, scientific visualization.

Manfred K. Warmuth, Professor; Ph.D. (computer science), Colorado, 1981. Machine learning, neural networks, parallel and distributed algorithms, on-line learning algorithms, complexity theory.

Jane P. Wilhelms, Associate Professor; Ph.D. (computer science), Berkeley, 1985. Computer graphics, computer animation, scientific visualization, modeling articulated bodies, physical simulation, behavioral animation.

UNIVERSITY OF CENTRAL FLORIDA

DEPARTMENT OF COMPUTER SCIENCE

PROGRAMS OF STUDY

The Department of Computer Science offers the Ph.D. and M.S. degrees. The Ph.D. program prepares students for academic and industrial careers. During the first two years of the Ph.D. program, students broaden their knowledge of programming systems and languages, computer architecture, algorithms, and computational methods. At the same time, they begin to specialize in a research area. A qualifying examination is taken in the first or second year. Ph.D. students must demonstrate a thorough knowledge of the fundamentals of computer science, depth in an area of specialization, and the creativity to make a new contribution to this area. Full-time Ph.D. students normally take four to five years to complete the program.

The M.S. degree requires a minimum of 30 semester hours of graduate credit; both thesis and nonthesis options are available.

Research interests of the faculty include parallel computation, computer architecture, VLSI systems, rapid prototyping, programming languages, object-oriented technology, operating systems, computer vision, artificial intelligence, computational linguistics, computer-assisted instruction, software engineering, database management systems, information storage/retrieval systems, multimedia systems, computer graphics, virtual environments, interactive simulation, computational biology, applied computational geometry, distributed processing/networking, algorithms, computational graph theory, and computational complexity.

RESEARCH FACILITIES

The department's infrastructure computing facilities are centered on several UNIX-based servers, including a Sun UltraSPARC Enterprise 3000 dual-processor server, an UltraSPARC Enterprise 2 Server, and an NT-based Dual Pentium server. These servers support a network of Sun SPARCstations, 486- and Pentium-based PCs, and Macintosh computers.

The specialized labs in the department are the Center for Parallel Computation, the VLSI Systems Architecture Laboratory, the Computer Vision Laboratory, the Artificial Intelligence Laboratory, the Distributed Computing and Networking Laboratory, the Database Systems Laboratory, and the Digital Media Laboratory. A Laboratory for Software Enabled Virtual Enterprises is also under development.

The resources available in these state-of-the-art laboratories include a DECmpp 12000 (MasPar MP-1) with 8,192 processors, an Intel Paragon XP/S-5, a Sun Ultra 2 Creator, several SPARCservers, an SGI High Impact, Symbolics 3653 LISP machines, specialized vision equipment, SGI Indys, Sun SPARCstations, IBM RS/6000s, and Macintosh and Pentium-based computers. Additional facilities are available through the Institute for Simulation and Training, including several Reality Engines and a variety of virtual reality equipment.

FINANCIAL AID

More than fifty teaching and research assistantships with partial tuition waivers are available. In 1997–98, assistantships with fellowships and tuition waivers pay between $10,000 and $15,000, depending on whether they are nine-month or twelve-month appointments and on residency status. These normally require 20 hours of service per week.

COST OF STUDY

For the 1997–98 academic year, students who are residents of Florida pay $128 per graduate credit hour; nonresidents pay $425 per graduate credit hour.

LIVING AND HOUSING COSTS

Apartments and private rooms are available both near the campus and throughout the city at a wide range of rents. The campus is easily accessible by major highways. The Orlando area has a relatively low cost of living; a graduate student can easily purchase housing, food, and the basic necessities for less than $1000 a month.

STUDENT GROUP

The University enrollment is approximately 28,000, including 2,000 graduate students. The Department of Computer Science has 200 regular graduate students, including M.S. and Ph.D. students. About one third of these are women. A substantial number of graduate students receive financial aid, and the rest hold employment outside the University.

STUDENT OUTCOMES

Of the Ph.D. graduates, about half take academic positions and half take industrial positions. Of the M.S. graduates, most take industrial positions, with the remaining students going on to further graduate studies.

LOCATION

Orlando is a growing metropolitan area and is served by many major airlines at one of the finest airports in the country. Central Florida is well known for Disney World and the Kennedy Space Center. The area is very attractive and has pleasant weather year-round.

THE UNIVERSITY

UCF, established in 1963, is a member of the State University System of Florida. The Department of Computer Science is one of the strongest academic units on campus and thrives on an exciting intellectual environment enhanced by renowned research units such as the Center for Research and Education in Optics and Lasers (CREOL) and the Institute for Simulation and Training (IST). The department also derives numerous benefits from its proximity to the Central Florida Research Park, a fast-growing center of high-tech industrial activity.

APPLYING

Applications are considered on a semester-by-semester basis. The *Graduate Catalog* should be consulted for specific deadlines. Admission requirements include a baccalaureate degree from an accredited college or university and an upper-division GPA of at least 3.0 or a minimum score of 1000 on the verbal plus quantitative sections of the GRE General Test. In recent years, most students obtaining department assistantships have scored in excess of 1200. Each student must also submit a score on the GRE Subject Test in computer science that is not more than two years old at the time of admission to regular graduate status. Students whose native language is not English and who do not possess a degree from a U.S. institution must obtain a minimum TOEFL score of 550.

An undergraduate degree in computer science is desirable but not required. Applicants without a strong undergraduate background in computer science are expected to obtain an undergraduate background in the core areas of computer science before being accepted as regular graduate students.

CORRESPONDENCE AND INFORMATION

Graduate Program Coordinator
Department of Computer Science
University of Central Florida
Orlando, Florida 32816-2362
Telephone: 407-823-2341
Fax: 407-823-5419
E-mail: gradprog@cs.ucf.edu
World Wide Web: http://www.cs.ucf.edu

UNIVERSITY OF CENTRAL FLORIDA
THE FACULTY AND THEIR RESEARCH

Mostafa A. Bassiouni, Professor of Computer Science; Ph.D. (computer science), Penn State, 1982. Distributed systems, operating systems, computer networks, databases.

Robert C. Brigham, Professor of Mathematics and Computer Science; Ph.D. (mathematics), NYU, 1970. Graph theory, combinatorics.

Larry K. Cottrell, Associate Professor of Computer Science; Ph.D. (science education), Purdue, 1976. Computer-based education systems, programming languages.

Niels da Vitoria Lobo, Assistant Professor of Computer Science; Ph.D. (computer science), Toronto, 1992. Computer vision, visual modeling for graphics.

Narsingh Deo, Charles N. Millican Endowed Chair Professor of Computer Science; Ph.D. (electrical engineering), Northwestern, 1965. Parallel computation, algorithms and data structures, graph theory, combinatorial optimization algorithms, complexity theory.

Ronald D. Dutton, Professor of Computer Science and Associate Chair; Ph.D. (computer science), Washington State, 1973. Computational complexity, design/analysis of algorithms, graph theory.

Terry J. Frederick, Distinguished Service Professor of Computer Science and Chair; Ph.D. (intelligent systems), Wisconsin–Madison, 1969. Mathematical modeling for intelligent systems, learning systems, computer science education.

Homer C. Gerber, Associate Professor of Computer Science; Ph.D. (mathematics education), Florida State, 1972. Distance learning, computer-assisted instruction, computer science education.

Fernando Gomez, Professor of Computer Science; Ph.D. (computer science), Ohio State, 1981. Artificial intelligence, natural-language processing, knowledge acquisition, knowledge representation.

Mark W. Goudreau, Assistant Professor of Computer Science; Ph.D. (electrical engineering), Princeton, 1993. Parallel computing, computer networks, artificial neural networks.

Ratan K. Guha, Professor of Computer Science; Ph.D. (computer science), Texas at Austin, 1970. Distributed simulation, networking and distributed computing, visualization.

Kien Hua, Associate Professor of Computer Science; Ph.D. (electrical engineering), Illinois, 1987. Database management systems, multimedia systems, parallel and distributed computing.

Charles E. Hughes, Professor of Computer Science; Ph.D. (computer science), Penn State, 1970. Distributed computing, interactive simulation, logic and computability.

Sheau-Dong Lang, Associate Professor of Computer Science; Ph.D. (mathematics), Penn State, 1979. Analysis of algorithms, databases, information retrieval.

John Leeson, Associate Professor of Computer Science; Ph.D. (mathematics), Miami (Florida), 1974. Programming environments, programming languages, object-oriented technology, distance learning.

Michael Moshell, Professor of Computer Science; Ph.D. (computer science), Ohio State, 1975. Simulation, graphics, cooperative work and learning environments.

Amar Mukherjee, Professor of Computer Science; Ph.D. (computer science), Calcutta, 1963. VLSI algorithms and design tools, computer architecture, computational geometry, design methodology for direct rapid prototyping, data compression and visualization.

Ali Orooji, Associate Professor of Computer Science; Ph.D. (computer science), Ohio State, 1984. Database systems, object-oriented systems.

Rebecca J. Parsons, Assistant Professor of Computer Science; Ph.D. (computer science), Rice, 1992. Computational biology, programming languages and semantics, semantics-based program optimization, distributed and parallel computation.

James Rogers, Assistant Professor of Computer Science; Ph.D. (computer and information science), Delaware, 1994. Computational linguistics, formal language theory, mathematical logic, artificial intelligence.

Mubarak A. Shah, Professor of Computer Science; Ph.D. (computer engineering), Wayne State, 1986. Computer vision, biomedical imaging, gesture recognition, lipreading, shape from shading, visual surveillance.

Udaya B. Vemulapati, Lecturer of Computer Science and Undergraduate Coordinator; Ph.D. (computer science), Penn State, 1990. Parallel and distributed computing, distributed simulation, high-performance computing, operating systems.

David A. Workman, Associate Professor of Computer Science; Ph.D. (computer science), Iowa, 1973. Visual programming languages, tools and environments, theory of parsing and translation, software engineering methodologies, tools and metrics.

UNIVERSITY OF CENTRAL FLORIDA

DEPARTMENT OF ELECTRICAL AND COMPUTER ENGINEERING

PROGRAMS OF STUDY

The Department of Electrical and Computer Engineering (ECE) offers programs leading to the Master of Science and Doctor of Philosophy degrees in electrical engineering, computer engineering, and optical sciences and engineering. Research areas include communication theory and systems, control and robotics, digital signal and image processing, digital systems and architecture, electrooptics, microelectronics and solid-state devices, microwaves and antennas, and software engineering and expert systems.

The master's degree with a thesis option requires a minimum of 30 semester hours, including 6 hours of thesis registration. All students completing a thesis on their research must undergo a final oral examination. A master's degree program without a thesis, requiring a minimum of 36 credit hours, is also available.

A maximum of 36 graduate semester hours taken in the master's degree can be accepted as credit toward the required minimum of 84 semester hours for the Ph.D. program. A minimum of 24 semester hours in basic sciences and engineering sciences is required with at least 9 hours taken outside the College of Engineering. A minimum of 36 hours within the field of specialization and a minimum of 24 dissertation hours must be earned to fulfill the requirements of 84 hours beyond the bachelor's degree.

RESEARCH FACILITIES

The department facilities include a Class 100 clean room, an RF/microwaves laboratory, a digital signal processing laboratory, and an image processing laboratory. Close interaction and research opportunities exist with the Center for Research and Education in Optics and Lasers (CREOL) and the Institute for Simulation and Training (IST). The laboratories in CREOL and IST have state-of-the-art equipment, including various lasers and associated data acquisition systems, and an ion-plating thin-film deposition system.

Computer support is provided by a college-wide computer network with a Sun-4/280 file server at its center. Distributed among the network are various IBM PC stations, Sun and IBM workstations, and an NCUBE (64001-E) 32-node supercomputer with a high-speed imaging display. The University library is well equipped with periodicals and books in electrical and computer engineering.

FINANCIAL AID

Financial aid is available in the form of a limited number of teaching and research assistantships. These require from one-quarter- to one-half-time work loads, with compensation in the range of $3400 to $6700 for nine months. Also, the nonresident and resident tuition fees can be waived in many cases. Fellowships with an annual stipend of $10,000, including tuition remission, as well as Graduate Enhancement Awards are available to outstanding entering graduate students through the UCF Division of Sponsored Research. Graduate assistantships are also available through CREOL for students in the electrooptics program.

COST OF STUDY

Tuition in 1996–97 was $110.11 per semester hour; out-of-state students paid $363.13 per hour. General fees paid by all students amounted to $143 per term. A 3 percent increase is expected for 1997–98.

LIVING AND HOUSING COSTS

Double-occupancy rooms on campus rented for $1320 per semester in 1996–97. Triple-occupancy rooms rented for $1005 per semester. Single rooms in apartments are available at a cost of $1535 per semester. Meal plans in 1996–97 ranged from $825 to $975 per semester. There are many apartments near UCF, some within walking distance.

STUDENT GROUP

The fall 1996 enrollment of the University was 26,325, the student body being almost equally divided between men and women. The enrollment of the department was 1,117, which included 364 graduate students. Most of the graduate courses are recorded on videotape and made available to five remote locations in the geographical area.

STUDENT OUTCOMES

M.S. and Ph.D. graduates in electrical engineering, computer engineering, and optical sciences and engineering are employed with companies, both in Florida and nationally, such as Lockheed Martin, Loral, Harris, Texas Instruments, Motorola, Vela Research, AT&T, Sawtek, Siemens, and Utilities.

LOCATION

UCF is located 15 miles from downtown Orlando. Central Florida has recently shown dramatic industrial growth, particularly in such high-technology industries as aerospace, communications, and electronics. The Kennedy Space Center, with its launch site for satellites and the space shuttle, is nearby. Central Florida has become a major tourist area since the 1971 opening of Walt Disney World, just southwest of Orlando. The Atlantic Ocean, the Gulf of Mexico, and numerous rivers and spring-fed lakes provide many opportunities for outdoor recreation.

THE UNIVERSITY AND THE DEPARTMENT

Established as a state university in 1963, UCF admitted its first students in 1968. Today, the modern campus covers 1,227 wooded acres. The University's central location makes it accessible from all parts of the state. In addition, campuses are located in Cocoa, Daytona Beach, and South Orlando.

The ECE department occupies the fourth floor of the engineering building as well as portions of other floors. It is the largest department in the College of Engineering and one of the largest in the University. CREOL and IST, where graduate students are often employed, are located in the nearby Central Florida Research Park.

APPLYING

Prospective students should apply to the Admissions Office at least five weeks before the start of classes for the term in which they plan to enroll. A $20 application fee, official transcripts from an accredited college, and GRE General Test scores are required. The minimum admissions requirements are based on an average of B or better of a baccalaureate program and a minimum combined score of 1000 on the verbal and quantitative portions of the GRE General Test. The deadline for financial aid applications is March 1.

CORRESPONDENCE AND INFORMATION

Requests for additional information should be directed to:
Graduate Committee Chair
ECE Department
University of Central Florida
P.O. Box 162450
Orlando, Florida 32816-2450
Telephone: 407-823-5339

Requests for research assistantships with CREOL should be directed to:
Graduate Affairs Committee
P.O. Box 162700
Orlando, Florida 32816-2700
Telephone: 407-823-6834

UNIVERSITY OF CENTRAL FLORIDA
THE FACULTY AND THEIR RESEARCH

Wasfy B. Mikhael, Chair; Ph.D., Concordia. Digital signal processing, circuits and systems.

Professors
Christian S. Bauer Jr., Ph.D., Florida. Real-time simulations, software engineering.
Avelino J. Gonzalez, Ph.D., Pittsburgh. Intelligent systems.
Donald C. Malocha, Ph.D., Illinois. Solid-state devices, microelectronics.
M. Gamal Moharam, Ph.D., British Columbia. Electrooptics, diffractive optics.
Ronald Phillips, Ph.D., Arizona State. Electrooptics, optical communications.
Marion J. Soileau, Ph.D., USC. Electrooptics, nonlinear optics.
C. Martin Stickley, Ph.D., Northeastern. Electrooptics.
Nicolaos S. Tzannes, Ph.D., Johns Hopkins. Communications, signal and image processing.

Associate Professors
Issa E. Batarseh, Ph.D., Illinois. Power electronics.
Madjid Belkerdid, Ph.D., Central Florida. Communications, spread spectrum systems.
Glenn Boreman, Ph.D., Arizona. Electrooptics, infrared sensors.
Christos Christodoulou, Ph.D., North Carolina State. Antennas and microwaves.
Peter Delfyett Jr., Ph.D., CUNY. Semiconductor lasers.
Michael Georgiopoulos, Ph.D., Connecticut. Communications systems and networks.
James E. Harvey, Ph.D., Arizona. Optical systems.
Takis Kasparis, Ph.D., CUNY, City College. Digital signal/image processing, electronics.
Harold I. Klee, Ph.D., Polytechnic. Systems and control, simulation.
Darrell C. Linton, Ph.D., Florida. Numerical methods, software engineering, simulation.
Jiun J. Liou, Ph.D., Florida. Microelectronics, semiconductors.
Richard Miller, Ph.D., SUNY at Buffalo. Electronics, circuits.
Amir Mortazawi, Ph.D., Texas at Austin. Microwave and millimeter-wave integrated circuits.
Harley R. Myler, Ph.D., New Mexico State. Control systems, image processing.
Brian Petrasko, E.Eng., Detroit. Computer engineering, computer architecture.
Zhihua Qu, Ph.D., Georgia Tech. Controls, robotics.
Samuel Richie, Ph.D., Central Florida. Surface acoustic wave devices, digital systems.
Nabeel Riza, Ph.D., Caltech. Optical information processing.
Kalpathy Sundaram, Ph.D., Indian Institute of Technology. Optoelectronic and semiconducting materials.
Parveen Wahid, Ph.D., Indian Institute of Science. Electromagnetics, antennas, microwaves.
Arthur R. Weeks Jr., Ph.D., Central Florida. Digital image processing.
Jiann S. Yuan, Ph.D., Florida. Microelectronics, device modeling and circuit simulation.
Janusz Zalewski, Ph.D., Warsaw (Poland).

Assistant Professors
Ronald DeMara, Ph.D., USC. Computer architecture, parallel processing.
Michael Haralambous, D.Sc., George Washington. Control systems.
Patrick Li Kam Wa, Ph.D., Sheffield (England). Ultrafast lasers, integrated optics, all-topical switching, MQW optoelectronics.
Jannick Rolland, Ph.D., Arizona. Optics design medical imaging.

Joint Appointees
Larry Andrews, Professor of Mathematics; Ph.D., Michigan State. Random processes, optical wave propagation.
Michael Bass, Ph.D., Michigan. Electrooptics, lasers, nonlinear optics.
Bruce H. T. Chai, Professor of Physics and Mechanical Engineering; Ph.D., Yale. Crystal growth.
David J. Hagan, Associate Professor of Physics; Ph.D., Heriot-Watt (Scotland). Electrooptics.
Robert Peale, Professor of Physics; Ph.D., Cornell. Physics.
Martin Richardson, Professor of Physics; Ph.D., London. X-ray sources, X-ray lithography.
William T. Silfvast, Ph.D., Utah. Electrooptics, lasers.
George Stegeman, Professor of Physics; Ph.D., Toronto. Optical wave guides, switching and integrated optics.
Eric Van Stryland, Professor of Physics; Ph.D., Arizona. Electrooptics, nonlinear optics.

UNIVERSITY OF CINCINNATI

COLLEGE OF ENGINEERING
DEPARTMENT OF ELECTRICAL & COMPUTER ENGINEERING AND COMPUTER SCIENCE

PROGRAMS OF STUDY

The Department of Electrical & Computer Engineering and Computer Science (ECECS) offers graduate degree programs leading to the following Master of Science (M.S.) degrees: computer engineering, computer science, and electrical engineering. It offers the Doctor of Philosophy (Ph.D.) degrees in electrical engineering or computer science and engineering. Students concentrate their work in one of the four graduate research areas within the ECECS department: computer engineering, computer science, electronic materials and devices, or systems engineering.

For each M.S. degree, a total of 45 quarter credits is required; 30 credits are for course work, and 15 credits are for thesis research performed under the supervision of a faculty member. The course work is usually completed in three quarters; the thesis is usually completed approximately one year thereafter. For the Ph.D. degree, a total minimum of 90 quarter credits is required beyond the master's degree. This includes 36 credits of graduate-level course work and 9 credits of graduate mathematics (but no foreign language requirement), and 45 credits of dissertation research performed under the direction of a faculty member. A Ph.D. dissertation must be written and successfully defended before the doctorate is conferred. For the direct route Ph.D., a total minimum of 135 quarter credit hours beyond the B.S. degree is required. This includes 75 quarter credits for graduate-level course work and 60 quarter credits for dissertation research. The Ph.D. qualifying examination is given in June and should be taken after the first year in the Ph.D. program.

Currently, there are 41 faculty members in the department, with more to be hired soon. The graduate programs involve more than 270 full-time and 70 part-time graduate students. The graduate research and education programs are well funded by internal and external research resources. The research environment, with a total expenditure of $4 million per year, provides excellent opportunities to work on exciting and challenging projects funded by national and state research agencies such as the National Science Foundation, National Institutes of Health, National Aeronautics and Space Administration, Defense Advanced Research Projects Agency, Army Research Office, Wright Patterson Air Force Base, Office of Naval Research, and Ohio Department of Transportation. The collaborative research projects are also well funded by international, national, and local industries such as IBM, Texas Instruments, Digital Equipment Corporation, Hewlett-Packard, General Electric, Motorola, MTL, Taitech, AT&T, TRW, and Industrial Technology Institute.

RESEARCH FACILITIES

The department has excellent research and teaching facilities, including research laboratories with state-of-the-art equipment in the areas of computer science, software systems, artificial intelligence, neural networks, image processing, electronic design automation, MEMS (MicroElectroMechanical Systems), microsensors, millimeter waves and photonics, nanoelectronics, and optoelectronics. The departmental computing resources consist of a large number of SUN Workstations. The local area network allows faculty members and students to obtain permanent accounts on University computers, as well as access to supercomputers via Internet II.

FINANCIAL AID

Fellowships, teaching and research assistantships, and tuition scholarships are available on a competitive basis to qualified full-time graduate students. Applicants are automatically considered for these awards during consideration for admission. Teaching assistantships include an average monthly stipend of $1000 and are accompanied by a tuition scholarship. Research assistantships are available with comparable stipends to incoming students who show exceptional promise and related research experience. Upper-level students are typically supported on externally sponsored research assistantships.

COST OF STUDY

For the 1997–98 academic year, full-time tuition for nonresidents of Ohio is $9876. The cost to Ohio residents for the same period is $4938. All students also pay a comprehensive fee, which amounts to $507 per academic year.

LIVING AND HOUSING COSTS

For the academic year 1997–98, the estimated expenses for room and board for a student living on campus are $8000. In addition, there are many apartments readily available within walking distance of the campus.

LOCATION

Cincinnati is the twenty-third–largest city in the United States, with a greater metropolitan area population of 1.7 million. The city offers many sites of architectural and historic interest as well as a full range of cultural attractions such as theaters, the symphony, and opera. The renowned College Conservatory of Music on campus offers frequent performances, many of them for free. The business and industrial base of the city is diverse, allowing qualified students to easily find part-time work. The largest companies in the city are Proctor & Gamble, General Electric, Merrell Dow, and Milacron. The city is served by the Greater Cincinnati International Airport, which is a major hub of Delta.

THE UNIVERSITY

The University of Cincinnati is a comprehensive state institution, with an average total enrollment of 35,000 students. Endowment funds, in excess of $390 million and $99 million in sponsored programs, places it in the top 2 percent of universities for funding. This allows it to provide the proper environment for innovative scholarship and research. A new Engineering Research Center (ERC) was dedicated in 1995. It has 110 laboratories, offices for 200 graduate students, and thirteen conference rooms, plus extensive computer facilities.

APPLYING

A Bachelor of Science degree with a minimum GPA of 3.0 (on a 4.0 scale) is the norm for admission into a Master of Science program or a direct route Ph.D. degree program. Students with an appropriate Master of Science degree may be admitted into a Ph.D. program. The Graduate Record Examinations (GRE) General Test is required for all students applying for admission. International students are also required to take Test of English as a Foreign Language (TOEFL), and they must achieve a minimum score of 550. In order to be considered for financial aid, the application deadline is February 1.

CORRESPONDENCE AND INFORMATION

Director of Graduate Studies
Department of Electrical & Computer Engineering
   and Computer Science
University of Cincinnati, ML 30
Cincinnati, Ohio 45221-0030
Telephone: 513-556-0635
E-mail: grad_dir@ececs.uc.edu
World Wide Web: http://www.ececs.uc.edu

UNIVERSITY OF CINCINNATI
THE FACULTY AND THEIR RESEARCH

Chong H. Ahn, Assistant Professor; Ph.D., Georgia Tech, 1993. Microelectromechanical systems (MEMS) bio/chemical microsensors, microfluidic systems, optoelectronic multichip modules.

W. Perry Alexander, Assistant Professor; Ph.D., Kansas, 1993. Formal methods, software engineering, formal synthesis, architectures, software reuse.

Fred S. Annexstein, Associate Professor; Ph.D., Massachusetts Amherst, 1991. Routing in networks, theory of parallel distributed processing, parallel algorithms.

Albert D. Baker, Assistant Professor; Ph.D., Rensselaer, 1991. Multiagent coordination and scheduling, autonomous agents, automatic factory control, industrial control description languages, discrete-event systems.

Kenneth A. Berman, Professor; Ph.D., Waterloo, 1979. Design and analysis of sequential and parallel algorithms, graph theory, combinatorics, numerical analysis, invariant theory.

Fred R. Beyette Jr., Assistant Professor; Ph.D., Colorado State, 1995. Optoelectronic device fabrication and testing, slotted plate optomechanic and optoelectronic systems development.

Dinesh K. Bhatia, Assistant Professor; Ph.D., Texas at Dallas, 1990. CAD and architecture of field-programmable gate arrays, VLSI system, CAD, reconfigurable and adaptive computing, hardware prototyping.

Raj Bhatnagar, Associate Professor; Ph.D., Maryland, 1989. Artificial intelligence models for reasoning and decision making, representation of uncertainty, reasoning under uncertainty, machine learning.

Punit Boolchand, Professor; Ph.D., Case Western Reserve, 1969. Molecular structure of noncrystalline materials-semiconducting glasses, optoelectronic materials, amorphous thin films.

Joseph T. Boyd, Professor; Ph.D., Ohio State, 1969. Integrated optoelectronics, optical characterization of materials, visible infrared detectors, optical processing of materials.

Marc M. Cahay, Associate Professor; Ph.D., Purdue, 1987. Carrier transport in semiconductors, quantum mechanical effects in superlattices and quantum wells, nanostructure devices, Josephson junction arrays, implementation of artificial neural networks.

Harold W. Carter, Professor; Ph.D., USC, 1980. VLSI architecture and design methodologics, mixed signal simulation, and parallel numerical analysis.

Yizong Cheng, Associate Professor; Ph.D., Purdue, 1986. Machine learning, uncertainty and similarity measures, cluster analysis, self-organization of memory and databases.

Karen C. Davis, Assistant Professor; Ph.D., Southwestern Louisiana, 1990. Object database systems, query languages and optimization, data modeling for engineering applications.

Howard Fan, Professor; Ph.D., Illinois, 1985. Digital signal processing, array processing, adaptive signal processing, signal processing for communication, system identification.

Altan M. Ferendeci, Associate Professor; Ph.D., Case Western Reserve, 1969. Microwave and millimeter-wave devices and circuits, high T superconductivity, electrooptics.

John V. Franco, Geier Professor of Computer Science and Associate Professor; Ph.D., Rutgers, 1981. Design and analysis of algorithms, probabilistic analysis of algorithms, graph theory, combinatorics, numerical analysis.

Patrick H. Garrett, Associate Professor; Ph.D., Ohio, 1970; PE. Computer I/O and real-time system design, control systems for process automation, intelligent sensors, and avionics engineering.

Chia-Yung Han, Associate Professor; Ph.D., Cincinnati, 1985. Knowledge engineering, computer vision, pattern recognition, CAD/CAM, computer graphics, multimedia systems.

Arthur J. Helmicki, Associate Professor; Ph.D., Rensselaer, 1989. Control-oriented modeling and identification of dynamical systems, robust multivariable control design, intelligent control system.

H. Thurman Henderson, Kartalia Professor; Ph.D., SMU, 1968. Microelectromechanical systems; microsensors for space, medical, and industrial applications; semiconductor device physics.

Peter B. Kosel, Professor; Ph.D., New South Wales (Australia), 1976. GaAs CCDs and CCD image scanners, GaAs integrated circuits, MBE and MOCVD processing modeling and simulation.

Ravi Kothari, Assistant Professor; Ph.D., West Virginia, 1991. Artificial neural network architectures and leaning paradigms, hybrid intelligent systems, machine vision.

Thomas D. Manteli, Professor; Ph.D., Stanford, 1967. High-density plasma-assisted etching of semiconductors, plasma-enhanced growth of diamond and silicon carbide.

Lawrence J. Mazlack, Associate Professor; Ph.D., Washington (Seattle), 1973. Expert and knowledge-based database systems, natural-language analysis, approximate reasoning, conceptualization.

Ali A. Minai, Assistant Professor; Ph.D., Virginia, 1991. Complex adaptive systems, neural models of cognition and memory, mathematical biology, nonlinear dynamics, fault-tolerant systems.

Joseph H. Nevin, Professor; Ph.D., Cincinnati, 1974; PE. Microelectromechanical systems, integrated sensors, analog systems, IC design, analog design automation.

Santosh Pande, Assistant Professor; Ph.D., North Carolina State, 1993. Compiler optimizations for parallel and distributed languages such as Java and for massively parallel multicomputers, and distributed mobile systems.

Jerome L. Paul, Professor; Ph.D., Case Western Reserve, 1965. Design and analysis of parallel and distributed algorithms, combinatorics, graph theory.

Marios M. Polycarpou, Assistant Professor; Ph.D., USC, 1992. Systems and control with emphasis on intelligent control, fault diagnosis, neural network learning, adaptive control, and nonlinear systems.

Carla C. Purdy, Associate Professor; Ph.D., Illinois, 1975; Ph.D., Texas A&M, 1986. VLSI algorithms, VLSI design, design and analysis of sequential and parallel algorithms.

George Purdy, Professor; Ph.D., Illinois, 1972. Cryptography and data security, algorithms for VLSI, discrete and computational geometry, computational number theory.

Anca L. Ralescu, Associate Professor; Ph.D., Indiana, 1983. Intelligent systems, soft computing, fuzzy information engineering, visual and auditory information processing and interpretation systems.

Panapakkam A. Ramamoorthy, Professor; Ph.D., Calgary, 1977. Digital signal processing and applications, neural networks and fuzzy expert systems, parallel processing, optical computing.

Kenneth P. Roenker, Professor; Ph.D., Iowa State, 1973. Compound semiconductor devices and fabrication, optoelectronic circuit applications, device physics, device reliability.

John Schlipf, Professor; Ph.D., Wisconsin, 1975. Logic programming, nonmonotonic inference and deductive databases, computability and complexity theory, model theory.

Dieter S. Schmidt, Professor; Ph.D., Minnesota, 1970. Symbolic computation, applications to problems in celestial mechanics, dynamical systems.

Andrew J. Steckl, Gieringer Professor and Ohio Eminent Scholar; Ph.D., Rochester, 1973. Semiconductor materials, devices and fabrication: focused ion beam implantation, thin-film growth (CVD, MBE), wide bandgap semiconductors (SiC, GaN).

Ranga R. Vemuri, Associate Professor; Ph.D., Case Western Reserve, 1989. Computer-aided design, VLSI design environments, formal verification, high-level synthesis, adaptive systems design, mixed signal synthesis, hardware/software cosynthesis.

William G. Wee, Professor; Ph.D., Purdue, 1967. Artificial intelligence; neural networks; computer vision, including 3-D modeling and applications; picture coding and compression.

Philip A. Wilsey, Assistant Professor; Ph.D., Southwestern Louisiana, 1987. Computer architecture, hardware description of languages, parallel simulation, formal methods for design and analysis.

RESEARCH AREAS

The department's graduate studies and research program are organized along the lines of faculty member interests and expertise. The faculty members are grouped together in interrelated but distinct research areas. This structure allows the critical mass necessary to facilitate innovative research efforts. Graduate programs, providing a balance between the formal classroom instruction and research, are tailored to the student's professional goals. At present, the four research areas within the department are: computer engineering, computer science, electronic materials and devices, and systems engineering.

UNIVERSITY OF COLORADO AT BOULDER

DEPARTMENT OF ELECTRICAL AND COMPUTER ENGINEERING

PROGRAMS OF STUDY

The Department of Electrical and Computer Engineering offers programs of graduate study leading to the degrees of M.S. in Electrical Engineering, Master of Engineering, and Ph.D. Major areas of study include atmospheric remote sensing; biomedical engineering; circuit and network theory; communications and digital signal processing; computer languages, digital system design, microprocessors, and computer architecture; CAD and VLSI; electromagnetic theory, microwave optics, antennas, and propagation; integrated-circuit computer-aided design and fabrication; millimeter and optical systems; power and power electronics and systems; solid-state devices, materials, and quantum electronics; and systems and control theory. The department also participates in an interdisciplinary master's program in telecommunications. The M.S. program requires at least one year of full-time study, which encompasses 30 semester hours of academic courses and may include a thesis. The courses are chosen by students in consultation with their adviser. At least two courses in a minor field are required. The Master of Engineering program requires a minimum of one year of full-time study and 30 semester hours of academic courses. It is broadly based and is designed primarily for practicing engineers who want to widen their vistas into areas other than those associated strictly with their major field. An example might be in technical administration, where course work in the business and management area would logically supplement advanced scientific study. Of the 30 semester hours required for graduation, 15 must be at the 5000 level or above in engineering courses, and the remainder may be in other areas. The Ph.D. program usually requires a minimum of two years of study beyond the master's degree. Excellent students are strongly urged to enter the Ph.D. program early. A master's degree is not a prerequisite for the Ph.D. degree. Each student is required to pass a preliminary examination upon entering the Ph.D. program and a comprehensive examination covering his or her course work before commencing thesis research.

RESEARCH FACILITIES

The department is housed in a portion of the Engineering Complex at the University and has approximately 60,000 square feet of laboratory space. Computers and microcomputers are available in various laboratories, including a CAD laboratory, microprocessor development laboratory, software development laboratory, and VLSI design systems laboratory. Also available are a silicon integrated-circuit laboratory for CAD and mask and circuit fabrication; facilities for reactive ion etching; state-of-the-art facilities for gallium arsenide and amorphous silicon devices and materials; crystal growth and thin-film deposition equipment; a microwave anechoic chamber and antenna range; microwave and millimeter-wave instrumentation; extensive optics laboratories for optical signal processing, optical computing, and holography; an optical metrology laboratory; a digital signal processing laboratory; a robotic manipulator and vision system; a multimedia signal processing laboratory and a power laboratory. These are augmented by standard and specialized test equipment and a well-equipped instrument shop. The University Computing Center is available for all research activities.

FINANCIAL AID

Financial aid is available from fellowships, scholarships, teaching assistantships, research assistantships, and student loans. Inquiries should be directed to the Graduate Office, Department of Electrical and Computer Engineering. In 1997–98, teaching assistantships pay approximately $10,500 per academic year on a half-time basis and provide full or partial tuition waivers; research assistantships pay approximately $10,500 or more per academic year on a half-time basis, plus tuition, with additional remuneration for summer activities.

COST OF STUDY

Tuition and fees for 1997–98 are $1225 for 6 hours for Colorado residents and $4796 for 6 hours for nonresidents. All students enrolled for 6 hours or more will be automatically assessed for health insurance, which is $550 per semester. Students who already have adequate coverage should complete a waiver to remove this charge from their bill.

LIVING AND HOUSING COSTS

Housing costs in residence halls (including meals) vary from $2250 to $2360 per semester. University apartments vary from $900 to $1150 per semester (without meals) and are available in units of buffet type to three bedrooms, both furnished and unfurnished. Married student housing ranges from $340 to $565 per month. Many privately owned accommodations near the campus are available at comparable rates.

STUDENT GROUP

There are approximately 250 graduate students in the electrical and computer engineering department on the Boulder campus, of whom about one half are working toward the Ph.D. The student population is widely varied and includes students from all parts of the world.

LOCATION

The University of Colorado is located in Boulder, a city of about 90,000 residents at the foot of the Rocky Mountains and only 20 miles from Denver. It is at the center of an unsurpassed recreational and cultural area and is surrounded by such technical centers as the Radio Propagation Laboratories of the National Institute of Standards and Technology, the National Center for Atmospheric Research, the U.S. Bureau of Reclamation, IBM, Ball Brothers Research Corporation, Exabyte, and Hewlett-Packard.

THE UNIVERSITY AND THE DEPARTMENT

The University of Colorado was established in 1876 and has grown to include four campuses with an enrollment of 42,000. The Boulder campus has about 24,440 students. The Department of Electrical and Computer Engineering was established in 1893 and now has a total undergraduate enrollment of 500. No evening courses are offered on the Boulder campus, although many of the graduate courses are available in the Denver campus evening program. Graduate courses are also available on the Colorado Springs campus, and it is possible to complete a program in Boulder, Denver, or Colorado Springs.

APPLYING

Completed applications, including transcripts, reference letters, and GRE General Test scores, must be in the departmental office at least two months prior to the beginning of the semester in which the applicant wishes to enroll. Application materials from students wishing to be considered for fellowships or scholarships for the following academic year must be received before January 15.

CORRESPONDENCE AND INFORMATION

Graduate Director
Department of Electrical and Computer Engineering
Campus Box 425
University of Colorado
Boulder, Colorado 80309

Telephone: 303-492-7671
E-mail: pam.wheeler@colorado.edu
World Wide Web: http://ece-www.colorado.edu/

UNIVERSITY OF COLORADO AT BOULDER
THE FACULTY AND THEIR RESEARCH

Research in the Department of Electrical and Computer Engineering covers a broad spectrum and can be categorized in the following general areas: atmospheric remote sensing; biomedical engineering; devices, materials, and quantum electronics; digital signal processing and communications; information systems; electromechanical energy conversion and power systems; systems, robotics, and control theory; circuits and electronics; fields and radio propagation; computer languages and logic circuits; optics and optoelectronics; microwave optics; and computer-aided design and VLSI.

A Ph.D. degree program in electrical engineering can be completed on the Boulder campus. The Colorado Springs campus has a separate Ph.D. program, but the degree is awarded from the University of Colorado at Boulder.

FACULTY

Boulder Campus

Lloyd J. Griffiths, Department Chairman. Adaptive antenna arrays and radar processing systems.
James P. Avery. Microprocessors, real-time computing.
Susan K. Avery. Radar and remote sensing.
Frank S. Barnes. Biomedical engineering, devices, and quantum electronics.
Richard C. Booton Jr. Numerical techniques and electromagnetics.
Elizabeth Bradley. Scientific computation and AI, nonlinear dynamics, network theory/circuit design.
Timothy Brown. Telecommunication systems, networking, neural networks, and novel computing.
W. Thomas Cathey. Imaging systems, optical information processing.
Roger S. Cheng. Multiuser communications and information theory.
Wayne V. Citrin. Visual programming, programming language design and implementation.
John M. Dunn. Fields and microwaves.
Robert W. Erickson. Power electronics.
Delores M. Etter. Digital signal processing, adaptive filtering, and speech processing.
Robert J. Feuerstein. Optical communications and computing.
Warren L. Flock. Radio propagation, remote sensing, satellite communications.
David C. Fritts. Experimental and theoretical atmospheric dynamics.
Ewald F. Fuchs. Energy conversion applied to traction, renewable and alternative energy, power quality.
K. C. Gupta. Fields and microwaves.
Gary D. Hachtel. Computer-aided design and VLSI.
John E. Hauser. Systems and control theory and applications.
Russell E. Hayes. Devices and quantum electronics.
Vincent P. Heuring. Programming language design and implementation, optical computer architectures.
H. Scott Hinton. Optical computing and photonic switching systems and architectures.
R. Brian Hooker. Optical system design and optoelectronic systems.
Kristina M. Johnson. Optoelectronic devices and computing.
Harry F. Jordan. Parallel processing, optical computing, and computer design.
Jerrold H. Krenz. Electronics, energy systems and policy.
Edward F. Kuester. Fields and radio propagation.
Michael Lightner. Computer-aided design and VLSI.
Arnoldo Majerfeld. Devices, materials, and quantum electronics.
Dragan Maksimovic. Power electronics.
Peter Mathys. Information theory and coding, communication networks.
William G. May. Integrated circuits.
David G. Meyer. Control theory and manufacturing.
Alan R. Mickelson. Fields and optical propagation.
Richard T. Mihran. Biomedical engineering and biotechnology.
Garret Moddel. Electronic materials and semiconductor devices.
Clifford T. Mullis. Communications and digital signal processing, VLSI.
John Neff. Optical interconnections in digital systems.
Jacques Pankove. Semiconductor materials and devices.
Lucy Pao. Control of flexible structures, multisensor data fusion and nonlinear filtering, robotics and haptic interfaces.
Melinda Piket-May. Computational electromagnetics.
Andrew Pleszkun. Computer architecture and VLSI design.
Zoya Popovic. Experimental microwave active devices.
Ruth H. Ravenel. Software engineering methodology.
Juan A. Rodriguez. Engineering project management.
Jon Sauer. Hardware and software for distributed high-performance computing, optical interconnect systems.
Louis A. Scharf. Statistical signal processing and communication.
Ernest K. Smith. Radio propagation, satellite communications, atmospheric physics.
Fabio Somenzi. Computer-aided design and VLSI.
Renjeng Su. Systems and control theory.
Bart J. Van Zeghbroeck. Optoelectronic devices and integrated circuits.
Mahesh K. Varanasi. Multiuser communications and statistical signal processing.
Howard Wachtel. Bioengineering.
Kelvin Wagner. Optical computing systems, nonlinear optics, neural networks, radar signal processing.
William M. Waite. Programming language design and implementation.
Min-Yen Wu. Systems and control theory.

Denver Campus

Marvin F. Anderson. Circuits and electronics.
Richard J. Auletta. Digital systems and electronic design automation.
Jan Bialasiewicz. Control systems.
Tamal Bose. Signal and image processing, communications.
Hamid Fardi. Electronics modeling and simulations.
Shelly Goggin. Image processing and neural networks.
Joseph L. Hibey. Stochastic systems.
Gary Leininger. Process control and management systems.
Miloje Radenkovic. Control systems, stochastic processes, signal processing.
William Roemish. Power systems.
Douglas Ross. Communications.
Pankaj K. Sen. Energy conversion and power systems.

UNIVERSITY OF CONNECTICUT

DEPARTMENT OF ELECTRICAL AND SYSTEMS ENGINEERING

PROGRAMS OF STUDY

The department offers programs of study leading to the M.S. and Ph.D. degrees in two major areas: control and communication systems and electromagnetics and physical electronics. The department also offers a general M.S. in electrical engineering and cooperates in an interdisciplinary program in biomedical engineering. The program in control and communication systems focuses on control theory, computational methods, digital signal processing, communications, estimation and detection theory, group decision making, manufacturing scheduling, power system scheduling, optical computing, and neural networks. The program in electromagnetics and physical electronics includes electromagnetic wave propagation, antenna theory, microwave and optical radars, lasers, optoelectronics, fiber optics, semiconductor devices and circuits, and dielectric materials.

The M.S. program offers two options. The thesis option requires at least 15 credit hours of graduate-level course work and completion of a thesis. The nonthesis option requires at least 24 credit hours of graduate-level course work. In either option, students must maintain at least a B average and pass a final M.S. exam.

Each Ph.D. program is unique. Students typically take 30 credit hours of graduate-level course work beyond the master's degree. A dissertation contributing to the body of knowledge in the chosen area of research must be presented. Students must maintain a minimum B average, pass a two-part general examination near the end of formal course work, and successfully defend the dissertation.

RESEARCH FACILITIES

Departmental facilities include many well-equipped laboratories: the Biomedical Instrumentation Laboratory; the Central Laboratory for Imaging Research; the Cyberlab, for decision and control research; the Electrical Insulation Research Laboratory; the Estimation and Signal Processing Laboratory; the Lasers and Electrooptics Laboratory; the Manufacturing Systems Laboratory; the Micro/Optoelectronics Laboratory; the Optical Fiber Communications Laboratory; the Optical Signal Processing/Computing Laboratory; the Sub-Micron Device Fabrication Laboratory; the Systems Optimization Laboratory; and the Photonics Research Center. Numerous dedicated computers are associated with these laboratories, including IBM RISC 6000, Apollo, and SUN Workstations (networked to mainframe) supporting a number of software packages for simulation of devices, circuits, and systems. The Booth Research Center, which houses laboratories and computer facilities to support interdisciplinary work in such areas as computer science, CAD/CAM, robotics, and manufacturing systems, contains Sun-4 server computers. The University Computer Center has a large IBM ES-9000/580 system that supports local, interactive and batch, and remote computing throughout all University components.

FINANCIAL AID

Financial aid is available in the form of fellowships and teaching and research assistantships, awarded individually or in combination. Students apply for financial aid through the graduate school. Stipends for fellowships are variable. Research and teaching assistantships require approximately 20 hours per week of work for the University during the academic year; stipends range from $13,466 to $15,750 in 1997–98, depending on the student's experience. A tuition waiver and health benefits are included with an assistantship. Financial support for summer research is also available.

COST OF STUDY

In 1997–98, tuition for residents of Connecticut enrolled as full-time students is $284 per credit hour up to a maximum of $2559 per semester. New England NEBHE Regional Student Program students (other than Connecticut residents) are charged $427 per credit hour up to a maximum of $3839 per semester; nonresidents are charged $739 per credit hour up to a maximum of $6649 per semester. Other mandatory fees for both residents and nonresidents are the general University fee ($109 up to a maximum of $327 per semester), the graduate activity fee of $10, the graduate matriculation fee of $42, and an infrastructure fee of $60. International students applying through and funded by governmental, quasi-governmental, public, and private organizations are charged $300 per semester. Fees are subject to change without notice.

LIVING AND HOUSING COSTS

On-campus housing costs are $1540 per semester for room and $1343 per semester for board, excluding summer sessions, tuition, and fees. The cost for room and board for the academic year per graduate student is about $4330. University housing is available for single and married graduate students but is not sufficient to meet the demand. Rooms and apartments may be secured in the surrounding area. The University maintains a housing office, which offers assistance in finding suitable housing on or off campus.

STUDENT GROUP

Approximately 6,000 students are pursuing graduate studies at the University of Connecticut. The Electrical and Systems Engineering Department has 105 graduate students. Of these students, 75 are full-time (27 master's, 48 Ph.D.) and 30 are part-time; approximately 19 M.S. and 14 Ph.D. degrees are awarded each year.

LOCATION

The University of Connecticut is situated in picturesque northeastern Connecticut. Centrally located between Boston (1½ hours away by car) and New York (2½ hours away), the area offers rural living with ready access to these and other nearby urban centers. Swimming, fishing, and boating are popular in neighboring lakes and state parks. Excellent skiing may be found within a 2–4-hours' drive. Connecticut and Rhode Island beaches are hardly more than an hour from Storrs. Located in historic New England, the University offers many cultural opportunities, including drama, music, art, dance, lectures, and tours.

THE UNIVERSITY

Founded in 1881, the University of Connecticut now includes the main campus at Storrs, five regional campuses, and many offices and centers throughout the state. More than 25,000 students are enrolled. Numerous centers, institutes, and laboratories support research and outreach activities.

APPLYING

Application materials may be obtained from the Graduate Admissions Office, Box U-6A, Storrs, Connecticut 06269-1006. Complete applications must be received prior to June 1 for admission in the fall semester or November 1 for admission in the spring semester. International applicants must apply by April 1 or October 1 for fall or spring admission, respectively. Applications for financial aid should be received prior to February 1 for the following academic year. To be admitted, applicants must hold a bachelor's degree or its equivalent. Applicants are required to submit all previous transcripts, three letters of recommendation, and a personal letter of application. The General Test of the GRE is strongly recommended. International students from non-English-speaking countries are required to submit acceptable TOEFL scores.

CORRESPONDENCE AND INFORMATION

Graduate Admissions Chairman, Electrical Engineering Program, U-157
Department of Electrical and Systems Engineering
University of Connecticut
260 Glenbrook Road
Storrs, Connecticut 06269-3157

Fax: 860-486-2447
E-mail: jenderle@eng2.uconn.edu
World Wide Web: http://www.eng2.uconn.edu/ese/

UNIVERSITY OF CONNECTICUT

THE FACULTY AND THEIR RESEARCH

The faculty consists of scientists and engineers who are actively engaged in both teaching and research and have received numerous honors. A number of members have gained extensive national and international reputations, have held editorial positions on the leading journals of their fields, and have chaired major national and international conferences.

A. F. M. Anwar, Associate Professor; Ph.D., Clarkson, 1988. Fabrication and modeling of quantum size effect devices.

J. E. Ayers, Associate Professor; Ph.D., RPI, 1990. Growth and characterization of semiconductors, GaAs and ZnSe materials.

R. Bansal, Professor; Ph.D., Harvard, 1981. Electromagnetic antennas and waves, dielectric materials, optical waveguides.

Y. Bar-Shalom, Professor; Ph.D., Princeton, 1970. Estimation, multitarget-multisensor tracking, stochastic control and optimization.

S. A. Boggs, Research Professor; Ph.D., Toronto, 1972. High-temperature superconducting transmission cable, gas-insulated substations.

J. Bronzino, Professor; Ph.D., Worcester Polytechnic, 1968. Quantification of bioelectric events and development of measures of brain maturation that can be utilized to evaluate the impact of various insults such as potential protein malnutrition and neonatal stress.

P. K. Cheo, Professor; Ph.D., Ohio State, 1964. Electrooptics, optoelectronics, and fiber optics.

S. Cheung, Research Assistant Professor; Ph.D., Connecticut, 1994. Fabrication and modeling of semiconductor devices.

A. De Maria, Research Professor; Ph.D., Connecticut, 1965. Lasers, electrooptics, fiber-optics devices and systems.

E. Donkor, Assistant Professor; Ph.D., Connecticut, 1988. Photonic switching, optical interconnects, semiconductor optics.

J. Enderle, Professor and Head of the Department; Ph.D., RPI, 1980. Modeling physiological systems, system identification, signal processing, control theory.

M. D. Fox, Professor; Ph.D., Duke, 1972; M.D., Miami (Florida), 1983. Biomedical imaging, Doppler ultrasound, ultrasound and X-ray imaging.

F. C. Jain, Professor; Ph.D., Connecticut, 1973. Fabrication and modeling of semiconductor devices for micro/optoelectronics, blue-green lasers.

B. Javidi, Professor; Ph.D., Penn State, 1986. Optical signal processing, information and pattern recognition, neural networks.

D. Jordan, Professor; Ph.D., Cornell, 1970. Classical and modern control theory and techniques; computational methods.

D. L. Kleinman, Professor; Sc.D., MIT, 1967. Man-machine systems, control systems, optimization algorithms.

P. B. Luh, Professor; Ph.D., Harvard, 1980. Planning, scheduling, and coordination of manufacturing and power systems.

L. Lynds, Research Professor; Ph.D., Caltech, 1970. Lasers, spectroscopy, electrooptic materials, superconducting.

M. Mashikian, Professor; D.Eng., Detroit, 1976. Power systems, high voltage, electrical insulation applications.

R. B. Northrop, Professor; Ph.D., Connecticut, 1964. Biomedical instrumentation, neurophysiology.

K. R. Pattipati, Professor; Ph.D., Connecticut, 1980. Queuing networks, fault-tolerant computer architecture performance and reliability.

C. Roychoudhuri, Research Professor; Ph.D., Rochester, 1973. Semiconductor lasers for sensing, spectroscopy and optical metrology.

G. Taylor, Professor; Ph.D., Toronto, 1971. Optoelectronics devices and integrated circuits; advanced materials.

L. Tong, Assistant Professor; Ph.D., Notre Dame, 1991. Wireless communication, statistical signal processing.

P. Willett, Associate Professor; Ph.D., Princeton, 1986. Representation and modeling of random processes, detection theory.

RESEARCH LABORATORIES AND CURRENT RESEARCH AREAS

Biomedical Instrumentation Laboratory, R. B. Northrop in charge. This laboratory contains the instrumentation used in electronic circuit development and physiology. Current research is focused on optical glucose sensors, closed-loop control of the self-administration of analgesic drugs, and modeling of the human immune system.

Central Laboratory for Imaging Research, M. D. Fox in charge. This laboratory focuses on the visualization of three-dimensional medical images and scientific and engineering data. The lab has various ultrasound imaging setups and Doppler ultrasound instrumentation. Research projects include optical glucose sensors, dual-energy radiography, drug delivery, early detection of breast cancer, and Lyme disease.

Cyberlab, D. L. Kleinman in charge. This lab is dedicated to man-machine and systems research. The heart of the extensive computational facilities within the laboratory is an Ethernet cluster of UNIX-based high-performance Sun SPARCstations. The primary application of the state-of-the-art computer complex lies in conducting real-time simulations for the empirical study of multihuman distributed decision making, distributed computation and networking, and team multitask sequencing and scheduling in addition to systems and control research.

Electrical Insulation Research Laboratory, M. Mashikian, Director. This laboratory operates in an interdisciplinary fashion with the Institute of Materials Science. It has high-voltage DC, AC, and impulse test equipment, a time domain spectrometer for the measurement of dielectric loss and complex permittivity, optical microscopes, infrared microspectrophotometers, a scanning electron microscope with EDX/WDX attachments, a computerized image analyzer, and an atomic absorption spectrometer.

Estimation and Signal Processing Laboratory, Y. Bar-Shalom in charge. The ESP laboratory deals with signal and information processing for remote sensing and data fusion for multiple moving targets (as in air traffic control) using heterogenous sensors (radar, sonar, and electrooptical).

Lasers and Electrooptics Laboratory, P. K. Cheo in charge. The lab is equipped with a variety of lasers, broadband electrooptic modulators, ultrafast detectors, and signal processors. It is augmented with optical, rf, submillimeter-wave, and microwave spectrum analyzers; frequency synthesizers; power amplifiers; stabilizers; lock-in amplifiers; and a vacuum FT-IR spectrometer. Current research focuses on tunable IR lasers for remote sensing of atmosphere and on high-resolution molecular spectroscopy.

Manufacturing Systems Laboratory, P. B. Luh in charge. This laboratory is dedicated to manufacturing systems research. Current research focuses on the development and implementation of high-performance planning, scheduling, and coordination systems. The facilities include an Ethernet cluster of seven Sun SPARC Workstations and extend to many industrial plants, including Pratt & Whitney, Cannondale, Toshiba, Delta, United Technologies, and Northeast Utilities.

Micro/Optoelectronics Research Laboratory, F. C. Jain in charge. This lab is equipped with CVD reactors for Ge and Si growth; MOCVD reactors for GaAs and ZnSe growth; a photolithographic clean room; reactive ion etcher and device processing setups; optoelectronic measurement instrumentation; and dedicated workstations for computer-aided design and simulation. Current research is focused on MQW optical modulators, blue-green lasers, flat panel EL displays, Quantum wire/dot optoelectronics devices, and single-mode MIS heterostructure lasers.

Optical Fiber Communications Laboratory, P. K. Cheo in charge. This lab offers continuously tunable fiber lasers with Bragg gratings and reflectors, Er-doped and Nd-doped fiber amplifiers, Ti-sapphire lasers and high-power diode lasers as pump sources, $LiNbO_3$ and GaAs waveguide modulators, fiber fusion splicer and spectrum analysis, and a high-speed photo detector. Current research is focused on all fiber-optic broadband communication networks.

Optical Signal Processing/Computing Laboratory, B. Javidi in charge. This laboratory is dedicated to research on optical signal processing, image processing, optoelectronic neural networks, and optical computing. The facilities include state-of-the-art spatial light modulators for real-time optical computing, high-power lasers, a stable table, optical benches with accessories, optoelectronic devices for real-time data acquisition, and workstations with extensive signal processing software packages.

Photonics Research Center, C. Roychoudhuri, Director. This center focuses on light-wave communications, remote sensing of the atmosphere, material processing, and laser manufacturing. It provides services and facilities to foster research and education in photonics. The facility contains equipment with state-of-the-art lasers, optical machine tools, an optical shop, and a Class 100 clean room for optoelectronic devices and circuits fabrication.

Signal Processing and Communication Laboratory, Lang Tong in charge. The focus of this laboratory is on theoretical and practical issues in modern signal processing and communication applications. In signal processing, research includes statistical methods in estimation and identification, array signal processing, and adaptive filtering. In communication, current activities include various equalization methods and multiuser communication theory. The lab is equipped with several SPARC Workstations, DSP modules (TMS320–C50 and TMS320–C30), and various simulation softwares.

Sub-Micron Device Fabrication Laboratory, G. Taylor in charge. This laboratory features a Class 100 clean room containing an MBE system for III–V material growth, reactive ion etching (RIE), refractory metal sputtering, metal and dielectric deposition, and rapid thermal annealing (RTA). Activities include device fabrication and characterization. Current research is dedicated to optoelectronic integrated devices for communications and optoelectronic computing.

System Optimization Laboratory, K. R. Pattipati in charge. This laboratory is dedicated to research on systems theory and optimization techniques to solve industrial problems. Current research is focused on automated testing, quality control, computer system performance optimization and scheduling, and multitarget tracking. The laboratory is equipped with seven Sun SPARC Workstations and enjoys a close relationship with local industries.

UNIVERSITY OF DELAWARE

DEPARTMENT OF COMPUTER AND INFORMATION SCIENCES

PROGRAMS OF STUDY

The Department of Computer and Information Sciences offers programs leading to the Master of Science and Doctor of Philosophy degrees. The M.S. program (normally completed in four semesters of full-time study) prepares students for doctoral studies or for professional employment. The doctoral program consists of additional course work and supervised research leading to a dissertation. There is no foreign language requirement.

Departmental research areas include algorithms: design and analysis, approximation algorithms, fully dynamic algorithms; artificial intelligence and human-computer interfaces: natural language generation and understanding, grammatical formalisms and parsing, multimodal interfaces, augmentative communication devices for people with disabilities, speech processing and synthesis, planning, rehabilitation robotics, neural networks, intelligent tutoring systems; computational theory: computational learning theory, recursive function theory; languages and compilers for parallel computing: optimizing and parallelizing compilers, compiler phase integration, language and compiler support for cluster computing, optimizing explicitly parallel programs, parallel compilers; networking: protocol specification and testing, network management, flow and congestion control, multiaccess protocols for packet radio and wireless environments, high-speed metropolitan area networks, internetworking virtual private networks, network security, distributed architectures, performance modeling and analysis; and symbolic mathematical computation: algebraic algorithms, analytic algorithms, parallelization.

Students normally enter as master's candidates and have had undergraduate preparation in mathematics and computer science. However, well-qualified students with varied backgrounds are encouraged to apply; minor deficiencies can be made up after matriculation.

The University of Delaware operates on a two-semester system, with additional summer sessions and a one-month winter session. No graduate courses are offered during the summer and winter sessions; however, graduate students often have an opportunity to teach and do research during these sessions.

RESEARCH FACILITIES

The department operates a joint research lab with the Department of Electrical Engineering that contains a Sequent Symmetry eight-processor system, several Sun file and print servers, and gateways to the NSFNET national network via SURAnet. A variety of single-user machines, including more than eighty Sun Workstations and four SGI Workstations, are available. All of the above machines are connected via Ethernet and an 80-megabit campus backbone network.

The University computing center operates a Cray Research J90, an IBM 3090-600E running MVS, several large Sun SPARCcenter time-sharing systems running SunOS 4.1, and an SGI Power Challenge computer. Numerous single-user machines are also available at more than twenty sites on campus, including Sun Workstations, IBM PCs, and Apple Macintoshes.

The recently expanded University library system contains more than 2.2 million bound volumes and is a government depository library, housing more than 400,000 government publications, including U.S. patents. The library subscribes to more than 20,000 periodicals, including a wide variety of computer science publications. Materials can be conveniently located using the DELCAT on-line computer catalog, which includes circulation status. DELCAT Plus provides access to a variety of on-line publication indices and summaries of journal contents.

FINANCIAL AID

Fellowships and teaching assistantships are available. For 1997–98, fellowship stipends range from $9940 upward, and teaching assistantships range from $9940 to $11,020; both include waiver of tuition. More than 50 percent of the full-time computer and information sciences graduate students receive fellowships or assistantships. Fellowships and traineeships are also available under a number of federal programs. Advanced students may be supported as research assistants. Some summer stipends are available.

COST OF STUDY

For 1997–98, course fees for full-time students are $3990 per academic year for residents of Delaware and $11,250 per academic year for nonresidents. Fees for the summer sessions and for part-time students are $222 per credit for Delaware residents and $625 per credit for nonresidents.

LIVING AND HOUSING COSTS

The University has a limited number of one- and two-bedroom apartments for married students and graduate students who are enrolled in full-time programs of study. Off-campus housing prices vary widely; typical monthly rents are $450 for an efficiency, $550 for one bedroom, and $650 for two bedrooms. The Off-Campus Housing Office maintains a listing of available accommodations near the University. For 1997–98, meals in the campus dining halls cost $1090 per semester for nineteen meals per week.

STUDENT GROUP

There are currently 74 graduate students in the department. Approximately 70 percent are full-time students, and most of these are supported by assistantships, fellowships, or external business organizations. The total campus enrollment is about 20,000, including 3,200 graduate students.

LOCATION

Newark (pronounced New Ark), Delaware, is a pleasant university community of 26,000 people. Located midway between Philadelphia and Baltimore, it offers the advantages of a small community but is still within easy traveling distance of New York and Washington, D.C. Newark is also close to the recreational areas along the Chesapeake Bay and Atlantic Ocean.

THE UNIVERSITY

The University of Delaware developed from a small private academy founded in 1743 and is today a state-assisted, privately controlled, coeducational land-grant and sea-grant university. The beautifully landscaped Newark campus consists of 1,100 acres with nearly 400 buildings in a predominantly Georgian architectural style.

APPLYING

The general application deadlines are July 1 and December 1 for the fall and spring semesters, respectively. Notification of the admissions decision is provided promptly upon receipt of credentials. In addition to the completed application form and the application fee of $40, applicants must forward official transcripts of their previous academic records, including at least three letters of recommendation, GRE General Test scores, and a TOEFL score if English is not their first language and they have not received a degree from a U.S. institution. Applications for fellowships and assistantships, including three letters of recommendation, are due by March 1 for the fall semester and November 1 for the spring semester; late applications are considered if positions exist. Interested students are invited to write to individual faculty members or the chairperson of the department, at the address below.

CORRESPONDENCE AND INFORMATION

Professor B. F. Caviness
Chair, Graduate Committee
Department of Computer and Information Sciences
University of Delaware
Newark, Delaware 19716
Telephone: 302-831-8234
Fax: 302-831-8458
E-mail: gradprgm@cis.udel.edu
World Wide Web: http://www.udel.edu (U. of Delaware home page)
    http://www.eecis.udel.edu/cis/index.html (CIS home page index)

UNIVERSITY OF DELAWARE
THE FACULTY AND THEIR RESEARCH

Gagan Agrawal, Assistant Professor; Ph.D., Maryland, 1996. Compiler optimizations, programming languages, parallel and distributed systems.

Paul D. Amer, Professor; Ph.D., Ohio State, 1979. Computer networks, performance measurement, formal description techniques for protocols (Estelle).

M. Sandra Carberry, Associate Professor; Ph.D., Delaware, 1985. Artificial intelligence, natural-language processing, planning systems.

John Case, Professor; Ph.D., Illinois, 1969. Computational learning theory, recursive function theory, algorithms and architecture design for massive parallelism.

B. F. Caviness, Professor; Ph.D., Carnegie Mellon, 1968. Computer algebra, analysis of algorithms.

Daniel L. Chester, Associate Professor; Ph.D., Berkeley, 1973. Artificial intelligence, natural-language processing, theorem proving, knowledge representation.

Keith S. Decker, Assistant Professor; Ph.D., Massachusetts, 1995. Distributed problem solving, multi-agent systems, real-time problem solving, computational organization design, concurrent engineering, parallel and distributed planning and scheduling, distributed information gathering.

Chandra Kambhamettu, Assistant Professor; Ph.D., South Florida, 1994. Computer vision, image processing, computer graphics and multimedia.

Errol L. Lloyd, Professor and Chair; Ph.D., MIT, 1980. Design and analysis of algorithms.

Kathleen F. McCoy, Associate Professor; Ph.D., Pennsylvania, 1985. Artificial intelligence, natural-language generation and understanding, knowledge representation.

Lori L. Pollock, Assistant Professor; Ph.D., Pittsburgh, 1986. Compiler construction, code optimization, incremental algorithms, parallel compilation, compilation for parallel machines, programming environments.

B. David Saunders, Associate Professor; Ph.D., Wisconsin, 1975. Computer algebra, analysis of algorithms, parallel computation.

Tuncay Saydam, Professor; Ph.D., Istanbul Technical, 1964. Performance evaluation, computer communication networks, discrete system simulation.

Adarshpal S. Sethi, Associate Professor; Ph.D., Indian Institute of Technology (Kanpur), 1978. Computer networks, performance modeling, distributed systems, computer architecture.

K. Vijayashanker, Associate Professor; Ph.D., Pennsylvania, 1987. Artificial intelligence, natural-language processing, unification-based grammatical systems, knowledge-representation languages.

Joint, Adjunct, and Research Faculty

Charles G. Boncelet, Professor (joint with Electrical Engineering); Ph.D., Princeton, 1984. Signal processing, algorithms, networking.

H. Timothy Bunnell, Research Associate Professor (A. I. DuPont Institute); Ph.D., Penn State, 1983. Speech perception, computer enhancement of speech.

George E. Collins, Professor; Ph.D., Cornell, 1955. Computer algebra.

Paul P. Eggermont, Associate Professor (joint with Mathematical Sciences); Ph.D., SUNY at Buffalo, 1981. Image reconstruction, numerical methods.

Richard A. Foulds, Research Professor (A. I. DuPont Institute); Ph.D., Tufts, 1985. Natural-language generation, robotics, augmentative communication.

Guang Gao, Associate Professor (joint with Electrical Engineering); Ph.D., MIT, 1996. Computer architecture and systems, parallel and distributed systems.

Robert P. Gilbert, Unidel Professor (joint with Mathematical Sciences); Ph.D., Carnegie Tech, 1958. Hybrid computation, mathematical modeling.

Ashfaq Khokhar, Assistant Professor (joint with Electrical Engineering); Ph.D., USC, 1993. Parallel computation and software systems, computational aspects of computer vision and multimedia.

Tariq Rahman, Research Assistant Professor; Ph.D., Drexel, 1990. Applied artificial intelligence, robotics.

Tom Ray, Associate Professor (joint with School of Life and Health Sciences); Ph.D., Harvard, 1981. Artificial life.

Renate Scheidler, Assistant Professor (joint with Mathematical Sciences); Ph.D., Manitoba (Canada), 1993. Computational number theory.

Richard L. Venezky, Unidel Professor (joint with Educational Studies); Ph.D., Stanford, 1965. Intelligent tutoring systems, natural-language processing, lexicography.

David Wood, Research Associate Professor; Ph.D., Rhode Island, 1972. Computer algebra, analysis of algorithms.

Professional Staff

Richard A. Albright, Associate to the Chair; Ph.D., Delaware, 1971. Numerical methods.

UNIVERSITY OF DETROIT MERCY

COLLEGE OF ENGINEERING AND SCIENCE
DEPARTMENT OF ELECTRICAL ENGINEERING

PROGRAMS OF STUDY

The Department of Electrical Engineering offers programs leading to the Master of Engineering and Doctor of Engineering. The areas of concentration include computer engineering (specifically computer architecture, parallel processing, and microprocessors) and signals and systems (specifically digital signal processing, electromagnetic compatibility, automotive electronics, and control systems). Students who are interested in management can pursue a Master of Engineering Management degree with an emphasis on electrical engineering. The Master of Engineering in electrical engineering may be completed by either a thesis or nonthesis plan. The thesis plan includes 24 credit hours of course work and 6 credit hours of thesis. The nonthesis plan consists of 30 credit hours of course work. The Doctor of Engineering in electrical engineering requires the following postbaccalaureate components: four core courses, 30 hours of course work in a specific discipline, 9 credit hours of approved technical electives, and 36 hours of dissertation. The doctoral candidate must pass qualifying examinations and a comprehensive examination. Upon entry into the graduate program, each student is assigned an academic adviser. This adviser works with the student to develop a course program that best corresponds to the student's career objectives.

RESEARCH FACILITIES

The program takes advantage of the rich automotive electronics environment of Detroit. State-of-the-art computing and faculty research facilities are also available for the graduate programs. In addition, the advanced computing laboratory, which consists of a network of workstations, provides simulation and analysis tools for research activities. All electrical engineering laboratories utilize computer-aided engineering technology via PC-based systems.

FINANCIAL AID

A variety of teaching and research fellowships/assistantships are available in the College of Engineering and Science. This financial aid is competitively awarded on a yearly basis. In addition, the Scholarship and Financial Aid Office accepts applications for grants, loans, and work-study assistance. Aid includes the Michigan Tuition Grant (for Michigan residents only), Federal Work-Study, and a variety of loans. The University also accepts third-party payments from employers and government agencies as well as offering payment plans of its own. For information regarding financial aid programs, students should call 313-993-3350.

COST OF STUDY

Tuition in 1997–98 is $490 per credit hour. Registration fees are $55 for full-time students.

LIVING AND HOUSING COSTS

Housing is available on campus. Double-occupancy rates range from $1260 to $2965. Single-occupancy rates range from $2185 to $2460. The University offers meal plans at costs ranging from $570 to $1180. All rates are for a sixteen-week term. For more information, students should call the Residence Life Office at 313-993-1230.

STUDENT GROUP

The graduate students in the electrical engineering department represent many groups: men, women, and minority and international students. Many students are pursuing their degree part-time in the evening while working full-time in industry. Approximately 7,500 students attend classes on four UDM campuses located in northwest and downtown Detroit.

LOCATION

Students enjoy a variety of activities offered on campus and throughout the metropolitan Detroit area, including sports, theater, concerts, and more.

THE UNIVERSITY

As Michigan's largest Catholic university, the University of Detroit Mercy has an outstanding tradition of academic excellence firmly rooted in a strong liberal arts curriculum. This tradition dates back to the formation of two Detroit institutions, the University of Detroit, founded in 1877 by the Society of Jesus (Jesuits), and Mercy College of Detroit, founded in 1944 by the Religious Sisters of Mercy. In 1990, these schools consolidated to become the University of Detroit Mercy. Today, UDM offers more than 120 majors and programs in nine different schools and colleges and is widely recognized for its programs in engineering, law, dentistry, nursing, and architecture. Faculty members are known for their excellence; more than 90 percent have a Ph.D. or comparable terminal degree. *Money* magazine recently named UDM as one of the top ten private commuter schools in the nation.

APPLYING

Applications for admission should be completed at least six weeks before the beginning of a term. Applications for financial aid should be submitted by April 1. International students are urged to complete their applications at least three months before classes begin. Admission requirements are a bachelor's degree from an accredited college; a B average in the total undergraduate program and in the proposed field of study; and, normally, an undergraduate major or the equivalent in the proposed field. Official transcripts are required from all colleges attended. Applicants with less than a B average who present other evidence of ability to perform graduate-level work may be admitted as probationary students upon the recommendation of the director of the program.

CORRESPONDENCE AND INFORMATION

Records Office
College of Engineering and Science
University of Detroit Mercy
4001 West McNichols
P.O. Box 19900
Detroit, Michigan 48219-0900
Telephone: 313-993-3335
Fax: 313-993-1187

Professor C. J. Lin, Chairman
Department of Electrical Engineering
University of Detroit Mercy
4001 West McNichols
P.O. Box 19900
Detroit, Michigan 48219-0900
Telephone: 313-993-3365
Fax: 313-993-1187
E-mail: lincj@udmercy.edu

UNIVERSITY OF DETROIT MERCY
THE FACULTY AND THEIR RESEARCH

Nizar Al-Holou, Assistant Professor; Ph.D., Dayton. Microprocessors, digital logic, parallel processing, computer architecture.

Armand Ashrafzadeh, Associate Professor; Ph.D., Oklahoma. Electrical engineering modeling and simulation (CAE), biomedical engineering, nonlinear filtering, sensor modeling.

Mohan Krishnan, Associate Professor; Ph.D., Windsor. Pattern recognition, speech processing, digital signal processing, communications.

Chun-Ju Lin, Professor; Ph.D., Michigan State. Electromagnetic compatibilities, circuits and systems, power distribution networks and machines.

Mark Paulik, Associate Professor; Ph.D., Oakland. Microprocessor design and implementation, microcontrollers, pattern recognition, digital signal processing.

Dipak Sengupta, Professor; Ph.D., Toronto. Microwave and radar, electromagnetic compatibility, communication.

Research Areas

The Department of Electrical Engineering has highly qualified faculty members with excellent academic and professional backgrounds. Some of the faculty members are internationally acclaimed for their research. Currently, faculty research interests are in the following areas: image processing and analysis, one- and two-dimensional sensor modeling and simulation, speech processing, parallel processing and distribution, electromagnetic interference, automotive electronics and antennas, and modeling and simulation (CAE).

UNIVERSITY OF DETROIT MERCY

COLLEGE OF ENGINEERING AND SCIENCE
DEPARTMENT OF MATHEMATICS AND COMPUTER SCIENCE

PROGRAM OF STUDY

The Master of Science in Computer Science degree is earned upon completion of a 33-credit-hour program of study. It is designed to prepare students for doctoral study or positions in industry or government service in computer-related areas. In recognition of various student interests, courses may be selected from areas related to computer science, primarily quantitative business decisions, software and hardware engineering, and mathematics appropriate for the theory of computers or computer applications. The strong blend of computer mastery with mathematics makes the program unique. This allows the faculty to lead students in both independent and team-based explorations. This paradigm of exploration and knowledge seeking leads to the development of a much stronger graduate. Most students complete the program within a two-year time frame. Some prerequisite courses are required if areas such as programming language or knowledge of calculus have not been previously completed. Students complete a research paper in their chosen area of computer science as a means of meeting one of the requisites in the program.

RESEARCH FACILITIES

Several computer labs are available on the campus. Each professor has a state-of-the-art computer available in his or her office to work with the students. Each computer has access to the Internet.

FINANCIAL AID

The University's Scholarship and Financial Aid Office accepts applications for grants, loans, and work-study assistance. Aid includes the Michigan Tuition Grant (for Michigan residents only), Federal Work-Study, and a variety of loans. The University also accepts third-party payments from employers and government agencies and offers payment plans of its own. For information regarding financial aid programs, students should call 313-993-3350.

COST OF STUDY

Tuition in 1997–98 is $468 per credit hour. Registration fees are $55 for full-time students.

LIVING AND HOUSING COSTS

Housing is available on campus. Double-occupancy rates range from $1260 to $2965. Single-occupancy rates range from $2185 to $2460. The University offers meal plans at costs ranging from $570 to $1180. All rates are for a sixteen-week term. For more information, students should call the Residence Life Office at 313-993-1230.

STUDENT GROUP

The average student population in the program is 30 students; currently, 60 percent are men, 40 percent are women. Both minority and international students are enrolled. Students in the program develop a great sense of camaraderie through working closely together on their projects. Approximately 7,300 students attend classes on four UDM campuses located in northwest and downtown Detroit.

LOCATION

Students enjoy a variety of activities offered on campus and throughout the metropolitan Detroit area, including sports, theater, concerts, and more.

THE UNIVERSITY AND THE DEPARTMENT

As Michigan's largest Catholic university, the University of Detroit Mercy has an outstanding tradition of academic excellence firmly rooted in a strong liberal arts curriculum. This tradition dates back to the formation of two Detroit institutions, the University of Detroit, founded in 1877 by the Society of Jesus (Jesuits), and Mercy College of Detroit, founded in 1944 by the Religious Sisters of Mercy. In 1990, these schools consolidated to become the University of Detroit Mercy. Today, UDM offers more than 120 majors and programs in nine different schools and colleges and is widely recognized for its programs in engineering, law, dentistry, nursing, and architecture. Faculty members are known for their excellence; more than 90 percent have a Ph.D. or comparable terminal degree. *Money* magazine recently named UDM as one of the top ten private commuter schools in the nation. Since its beginning 25 years ago, the department has served many students. These graduates have found rewarding employment in business and industry.

APPLYING

Applications for admission normally should be completed at least six weeks before the beginning of a term. Applications for financial aid should be submitted by April 1. International students are urged to complete their applications at least three months before classes begin. Admission requirements are a bachelor's degree from an accredited college; a B average in the total undergraduate program and in the proposed field of study; and, normally, an undergraduate major or the equivalent in the proposed field. Official transcripts are required from all colleges attended. Applicants with less than a B average who present other evidence of ability to perform graduate-level work may be admitted as probationary students upon the recommendation of the director of the program.

CORRESPONDENCE AND INFORMATION

Professor R. M. Canjar, Chairman
Department of Mathematics and Computer Science
University of Detroit Mercy
P.O. Box 19900
Detroit, Michigan 48219-0900
Telephone: 313-993-1209
E-mail: canjarrm@udmercy.edu

UNIVERSITY OF DETROIT MERCY

THE FACULTY AND THEIR RESEARCH

Elena Bankowski, Assistant Professor; Ph.D., Institute of Precise Mechanics and Optics (Russia). Fourier analysis, holography.

R. Michael Canjar, Professor and Chairman; Ph.D., Michigan. Object-oriented programming, mathematical logic.

John Dwyer, Associate Professor; Ph.D, Texas A&M. Statistics, computer science.

Robert Kane, Associate Professor; M.A., Detroit. Geometry and numerical analysis.

John O'Neill, S.J., Professor; Ph.D., Wayne State. Algebra, groups and rings.

Michael Skaff, Professor; Ph.D., UCLA. Model theory, operating systems.

Katherine Snyder, Instructor; M.S., Detroit. Artificial neural networks, evolutionary programming, cultural algorithms.

Raymond Travis, Associate Professor; M.A., Wayne State. Celestial mechanics and astrophysics.

James Van Ark, Assistant Professor; Ph.D., Iowa. Modeling of communicable diseases, differential equations.

Kathy Zhong, Assistant Professor; Ph.D., Wayne State. Complex analysis, wavelet theory.

UNIVERSITY OF FLORIDA

COMPUTER AND INFORMATION SCIENCE AND ENGINEERING DEPARTMENT

PROGRAMS OF STUDY

The Computer and Information Science and Engineering (CISE) Department offers the Master of Science degree through the Colleges of Engineering and Liberal Arts and Sciences. The Master of Engineering, Engineer and the Ph.D. degrees are offered through the College of Engineering only.

There are five broad areas of specialization in the department: computer systems and communications, which includes computer architecture, distributed systems, networks and communication, operating systems, simulation, and performance evaluation; database systems, which includes database management systems, database design, database theory and implementation, database machines, distributed databases, and information retrieval; high-performance computing, which includes parallel processing, parallel algorithms, and parallel software systems; intelligent systems, which includes computer vision and visualization, pattern recognition, image processing, computer graphics, robotics, expert systems, and machine learning and artificial intelligence; and software engineering, which includes large-scale software development and maintenance paradigms and processes for various computing systems (including parallel and distributed computing systems), software quality assurance, and programming environments and languages.

RESEARCH FACILITIES

The department has a variety of generalized and specialized computer systems, including a 64-processor NCUBE-2 parallel computer, a 1024-processor Maspar MP2, and numerous Sun, HP, Silicon Graphics, and IBM workstations and PCs. Along with the general campus computing facilities, a broad base of computing resources is provided. The departmental computers provide full connectivity to the Internet. The department is connected to the rest of the campus via a fiber-optic link, providing both video and digital data communications.

FINANCIAL AID

A number of research and teaching assistantships are available for CISE graduate students both within the department and within many other academic departments and research institutes on the campus. Based on one-half-time employment, assistantships paid $10,920–$18,500 for nine months in 1996–97. Appointments range from one-quarter time (requiring 10 hours of service per week) to one-half time (requiring 20 hours of service per week). Tuition payments may be granted for students holding assistantships.

COST OF STUDY

In 1996–97, Florida students paid $115.33 per graduate credit hour, and non-Florida students paid $386.07. A 10 percent rate increase is expected for 1997–98.

LIVING AND HOUSING COSTS

University and off-campus housing is available for single and married graduate students. Single students should allow $7150 to $12,150 per academic year for housing, food, and normal living expenses. International students must certify that they have a minimum of $19,005 available annually.

STUDENT GROUP

The total enrollment at the University is 40,000, including approximately 7,400 graduate students. The Department of Computer and Information Science and Engineering has approximately 165 graduate students, of whom 55 are enrolled in the Ph.D. program. Most of these are enrolled through the College of Engineering. The department has approximately 360 undergraduate students, and about one half of these are enrolled through the College of Engineering.

LOCATION

The University of Florida is located in Gainesville, a city with a metropolitan area population of approximately 220,000 and situated in north-central Florida, midway between the Atlantic Ocean and the Gulf of Mexico. The city has a strong research focus, with comprehensive University and medical research programs.

THE UNIVERSITY

The University of Florida is the senior institution in the State University System of Florida. A land-grant institution, it is one of the leading universities in the southeastern United States and is generally regarded as a major national university. There are thirteen upper-division colleges and four professional colleges. The University offers graduate programs in more than ninety-five fields at the master's level and in fifty-eight fields at the doctoral level.

APPLYING

Students are strongly encouraged to send all their application materials to the Admissions Office at least six months prior to the desired date of enrollment. The general admission requirements include a baccalaureate degree from an accredited college or university with an upper-division GPA of at least 3.0 and a combined score of not less than 1100 on the verbal and quantitative portions of the GRE General Test. International students are required to submit a TOEFL score greater than 550.

CORRESPONDENCE AND INFORMATION

The detailed description of the graduate program is available via the World Wide Web at http://www.cise.ufl.edu/. Students can also obtain this information by typing *ftp ftp.cise.ufl.edu* and using the login *anonymous*. Students should use their login ID as the password and then type *cd/cise/grad*. They should specify *binary* and use *get* or *ls* to view available files.

Information can also be obtained by contacting:

Graduate Secretary
Computer and Information Science and Engineering Department
P.O. Box 116120
301 Computer Science and Engineering Building
University of Florida
Gainesville, Florida 32611-6120
Telephone: 352-392-1090
Fax: 352-392-1220
E-mail: Internet gradsec@cise.ufl.edu

UNIVERSITY OF FLORIDA
THE FACULTY AND THEIR RESEARCH

Gerhard X. Ritter, Professor and Chairman; Ph.D., Wisconsin, 1971. Computer vision, pattern recognition. (E-mail: ritter@cise.ufl.edu)

Manuel E. Bermudez, Associate Professor; Ph.D., California, Santa Cruz, 1984. Programming languages, automata theory, compilers. (E-mail: manuel@cise.ufl.edu)

Sharma Chakravarthy, Associate Professor; Ph.D., Maryland, 1985. Query/rule optimization; active, heterogeneous, temporal, and deductive databases; logic programming. (E-mail: sharma@cise.ufl.edu)

Y. C. Chow, Professor; Ph.D., Massachusetts, 1977. Parallel processors, computer networks, performance evaluation. (E-mail: chow@cise.ufl.edu)

Douglas D. Dankel II, Assistant Professor; Ph.D., Illinois, 1979. Artificial intelligence, expert systems, software development environments. (E-mail: ddd@cise.ufl.edu)

Timothy A. Davis, Assistant Professor; Ph.D., Illinois, 1989. Parallel algorithms and architectures, parallel sparse matrix algorithms. (E-mail: davis@cise.ufl.edu)

Keith L. Doty, Professor; Ph.D., Berkeley, 1967. Microcomputers, robotics, concurrent processing. (E-mail: doty@milcise.ufl.edu)

Paul A. Fishwick, Associate Professor; Ph.D., Pennsylvania, 1986. Simulation, artificial intelligence, systems science, computer animation and visualization. (E-mail: fishwick@cise.ufl.edu)

Li-Min Fu, Associate Professor; Ph.D., Stanford, 1985. Artificial intelligence, expert systems, neural networks. (E-mail: fu@cise.ufl.edu)

Eric N. Hanson, Assistant Professor; Ph.D., Berkeley, 1987. Database management systems. (E-mail: hanson@cise.ufl.edu)

Theodore Johnson, Assistant Professor; Ph.D., NYU, 1990. Distributed and concurrent algorithms and systems, distributed and parallel database systems. (E-mail: ted@cise.ufl.edu)

Andrew F. Laine, Associate Professor; D.Sc., Washington (St. Louis), 1989. Computer vision, medical imaging, multidimensional signal processing, pattern recognition, wavelet analysis, nonlinear systems. (E-mail: laine@cise.ufl.edu)

Yann-Hang Lee, Associate Professor; Ph.D., Michigan, 1985. Distributed computing and parallel processing, database systems, performance evaluation. (E-mail: yhlee@cise.ufl.edu)

Panos E. Livadas, Assistant Professor; Ph.D., Florida, 1980. Computer graphics, data and file structures, software engineering. (E-mail: pel@cise.ufl.edu)

Richard Newman-Wolfe, Assistant Professor; Ph.D., Rochester, 1986. Distributed systems and networks, distributed conferencing and groupware, automata theory and complexity, parallel algorithms and architectures. (E-mail: nemo@cise.ufl.edu)

Jih-Kwon Peir, Associate Professor; Ph.D., Illinois, 1985. Parallel system architecture and algorithms. (E-mail: peir@cise.ufl.edu)

Hong Qin, Assistant Professor; Ph.D., Toronto, 1995. Physics-based modeling and simulation, computer graphics, and animation; computer-aided design, geometric modeling, human-computer interaction techniques and virtual reality. (E-mail: qin@cise.ufl.edu)

Sanjay Ranka, Associate Professor; Ph.D., Minnesota, 1988. Compilers and software environments for parallel machines, high-performance computing, design and analysis of parallel algorithms, models of parallel computation and neural networks. (E-mail: ranka@cise.ufl.edu)

Sartaj Sahni, Professor; Ph.D., Cornell, 1973. Design and analysis of algorithms, parallel computing, VLSI, CAD. (E-mail: sahni@cise.ufl.edu)

Rajasekaran Sanguthevar, Associate Professor; Ph.D., Harvard, 1988. Algorithms and parallel computation. (E-mail: raj@cise.ufl.edu)

Beverly Sanders, Associate Professor; Ph.D., Harvard, 1985. Parallel computation, formal method, software specification and verification, parallel and distributed systems. (E-mail: sanders@cise.ufl.edu)

Ralph G. Selfridge, Professor; Ph.D., Oregon, 1953. Language development and implementation, numerical analysis, computation theory, graphics. (E-mail: selfridg@cise.ufl.edu)

John Staudhammer, Professor; Ph.D., UCLA, 1963. Computer graphics, computer architecture. (E-mail: jstaudh@cise.ufl.edu)

Stanley Y. W. Su, Professor of Computer and Information Sciences and Electrical Engineering; Ph.D., Wisconsin, 1968. Database management, software systems, computer architecture for nonnumeric processing. (E-mail: su@cise.ufl.edu)

Fred Taylor, Professor of Computer and Information Sciences and Electrical Engineering; Ph.D., Colorado, 1969. Digital systems, signal processing. (E-mail: ft@gamma.ee@cise.ufl.edu)

Stephen M. Thebaut, Assistant Professor; Ph.D., Purdue, 1983. Software engineering, requirements elicitation, cost estimation. (E-mail: smt@cise.ufl.edu)

Baba C. Vemuri, Assistant Professor; Ph.D., Texas, 1987. Computer vision, image processing, geometric modeling, artificial intelligence. (E-mail: vemuri@cise.ufl.edu)

Joseph Wilson, Assistant Professor; Ph.D., Virginia, 1984. Programming languages, computer vision, image processing. (E-mail: jnw@cise.ufl.edu)

RESEARCH CENTERS

Center for Computer Vision and Visualization (Director: G. X. Ritter). This center is an interdisciplinary research center focusing on all aspects of computer vision technology. The center provides coordination, direction, and focus in the area of computer vision at the University of Florida as well as providing a structure for interaction between University faculty and graduate students and industrial and DoD laboratories.

Database Systems Research and Development Center (Director: S. Y. W. Su). This center deals with the following three categories of research and development activities: the database management aspects of information processing, the hardware aspects of information system design and development, and the behavioral aspects of information transfer.

Software Engineering and Research Center (Site Director: Stephen M. Thebaut). The Software Engineering and Research Center is a cooperative research program with Purdue University funded by the National Science Foundation and fifteen industrial sponsors. It is involved in developing software tools, environments, and metrics to assist the development and maintenance of reliable, efficient, reusable, and easily maintained software systems.

Space Communication Technology Center (Associate Director: R. E. Newman-Wolfe). The Space Communication Technology Center is a NASA-sponsored center for the commercial development of space (CCDS) with a primary focus on high-definition television (HDTV). Research is conducted in the area of digital signal handling and satellite networking, specifically in error control coding, signal modulation, terminal interconnect equipment, the Broadband Integrated Services Digital Network, protocols, and satellite network design, analysis, and management.

UNIVERSITY OF FLORIDA

DEPARTMENT OF ELECTRICAL AND COMPUTER ENGINEERING

PROGRAMS OF STUDY

The Department of Electrical and Computer Engineering offers programs of study leading to degrees of Master of Engineering, Master of Science, Engineer, and Doctor of Philosophy. The nine areas of major concentration are communications, computer engineering, device and physical electronics, digital signal processing, electric energy systems, electromagnetics, electronic circuits, photonics, and systems and controls. Course work and research opportunities are offered in many specializations, including control systems, digital communications, digital hardware and signal processing, electric energy and power electronics, electronic noise, image processing and computer graphics, integrated and fiber optics, laser electronics and fabrication, lightning, microprocessors, radar, reliability of semiconductor devices and circuits, robotics and machine intelligence, signal estimation, solid-state and semiconductor devices, space communications, spread spectrum systems, telecommunication systems, and VLSI circuit design, fabrication, and characterization.

The master's degree candidate may choose a thesis or nonthesis program. Although both programs require 33 semester hours of credit, the student who pursues the nonthesis option must pass a written examination that covers two of the above areas of concentration. The student who chooses the thesis option is expected to write a thesis and defend it during a final oral examination. The Master of Engineering degree is awarded to students with a baccalaureate in engineering, while the Master of Science degree is for those who have earned a bachelor's degree in engineering, math, or the sciences.

The Engineer degree requires a thesis and a minimum of 30 semester hours of course work beyond the master's degree. The Engineer degree is a terminal degree and should not be considered as a partial fulfillment of requirements for the Ph.D.

The doctoral candidate is required to pass a qualifying examination that is both written and oral. The student is also expected to complete a dissertation that reflects independent investigation and pass a related final examination. Ninety semester hours, which may include some or all of the master's degree course work, are required for the Ph.D. degree.

The Department of Electrical and Computer Engineering also offers an off-campus nonthesis master's degree program for employees of various Florida industries and government agencies through the statewide Florida Engineering Education Delivery System. Courses originating at the University of Florida are offered on site by videotape.

RESEARCH FACILITIES

The Department of Electrical and Computer Engineering occupies 85,000 square feet of space, much of which is devoted to funded research. The research facilities available include laboratories for IC processing in a Class 100 environment with 0.7 micron capability; VLSI circuit design and characterization; communications; computational neuroengineering; digital signal processing; electronic noise; lightning; optical measurement, photodetection, and optical waveguides; robotics; speech analysis and synthesis; and power system transient analysis and power electronics. All facilities contain up-to-date equipment either purchased via funded research or donated by supportive companies. The research computing facilities are excellent and include seventy minicomputers and workstations, hundreds of PCs, and extensive industrial software packages. The teaching facilities include an additional thirty UNIX workstations and forty Pentium-class PCs that run a wide variety of technical software. The computers are networked to provide access to other university computing resources and to the Internet.

FINANCIAL AID

Graduate teaching and research assistantships are available from the department and are awarded on the basis of academic performance, GRE scores, college transcripts, and letters of recommendation. Typical monthly stipends for one-third- and one-half-time assistantships were $500 and $750, respectively, in spring 1997. Fellowships are also available in limited number.

COST OF STUDY

In spring 1997, the registration fee for most graduate course work was $115.33 per credit hour for Florida residents and $386.07 per credit hour for out-of-state students. The tuition fee may be waived for students holding graduate assistantships and fellowships.

LIVING AND HOUSING COSTS

Rents for apartments provided by the University for single graduate and professional students begin at $226 per person per month. The University also operates five apartment villages for families, renting for $213 and up per month, excluding electricity. There are also many apartment complexes in the area, with rent for one-bedroom apartments starting at approximately $250 per month, not including utilities.

STUDENT GROUP

The total enrollment at the University of Florida is approximately 40,000. In the Department of Electrical and Computer Engineering, there are about 250 graduate students enrolled on campus.

LOCATION

The University of Florida is located in Gainesville, a city of approximately 95,000 inhabitants (190,500 in the metropolitan area) in north-central Florida. Gainesville is just over an hour's drive from both the Gulf of Mexico and the Atlantic Ocean, and there are facilities close by for sailing, canoeing, waterskiing, tennis, fishing, and golf. The city offers many cultural events, including professional theater, art exhibits, open-air festivals, and concerts.

THE UNIVERSITY

The University of Florida is one of the nation's ten largest universities and ranks among the top three in the number of academic programs offered. Undergraduate students can take classes in 140 departments, while graduate degrees are offered in more than 100 fields. There are sixteen upper-division colleges and schools and four professional colleges (Law, Dentistry, Medicine, and Veterinary Medicine).

APPLYING

Application forms may be obtained from the Graduate Studies Office of the Department of Electrical and Computer Engineering. Admission to the graduate program requires a baccalaureate degree from an accredited college and an upper-division grade point average of 3.0 or better on a 4.0 scale. Students must submit satisfactory scores on the General Test of the GRE and a score of 550 or better on the TOEFL (if applicable). Students may be admitted in any semester, but application forms, transcripts, and test scores should be submitted six months before the desired date of registration.

CORRESPONDENCE AND INFORMATION

Graduate Studies Office
Department of Electrical and Computer Engineering
P.O. Box 116200
225 Larsen Hall
University of Florida
Gainesville, Florida 32611

E-mail: gsbro@admin.ee.ufl.edu
World Wide Web: http://www.ece.ufl.edu

UNIVERSITY OF FLORIDA
THE FACULTY AND THEIR RESEARCH

Communications
Leon W. Couch II, Associate Chairman; Ph.D., Florida, 1968. Communication systems and applications.
Scott Miller, Ph.D., California, San Diego, 1988. Mobile communications and coding.
Peyton Z. Peebles Jr., Ph.D., Pennsylvania, 1967. Communication systems, radar system theory.

Computer Engineering
A. Antonio Arroyo, Ph.D., Florida, 1981. Artificial intelligence, microprocessing, digital design, computer graphics.
Keith L. Doty, Ph.D., Berkeley, 1967. Robotics, machine intelligence, microcomputers.
Alan D. George, Ph.D., Florida State, 1991. Parallel and distributed computing, high-performance computer networks, fault-tolerant computing.
Herman Lam, Ph.D., Florida, 1979. Computer engineering, database management, object-oriented computing.
Michel A. Lynch, Ph.D., Florida, 1972. Microprocessor applications and education.
John Staudhammer, Ph.D., UCLA, 1963. Computer graphics.
Stanley Y. W. Su, Ph.D., Wisconsin, 1968. Database management, database machines, software systems, parallel architecture and object-oriented knowledge base management.

Device and Physical Electronics
Gijs Bosman, Graduate Coordinator; Ph.D., Utrecht (Netherlands), 1981. Noise properties of solid-state devices, submicron electronic devices.
Jerry G. Fossum, Ph.D., Arizona, 1971. Semiconductor device theory and modeling, TCAD.
Sheng S. Li, Ph.D., Rice, 1968. Microelectronics, SOI materials and devices, photonic and quantum effect devices.
Fredrik A. Lindholm, Ph.D., Arizona, 1963. Semiconductor device physics.
Arnost Neugroschel, Ph.D., Technion (Israel), 1973. Semiconductor device physics and characterization.
Toshikazu Nishida, Ph.D., Illinois, 1988. VLSI reliability physics, submicron transistors, semiconductor device modeling.
Chih-Tang Sah, Graduate Research Professor and Eminent Scholar; Ph.D., Stanford, 1956. Semiconductor device physics, reliability physics.

Digital Signal Processing
John M. M. Anderson, Ph.D., Virginia, 1992. Statistical signal processing and application of higher-order statistics.
Donald G. Childers, Ph.D., USC, 1964. Algorithms, mind-machine interactions, intelligent systems, digital signal/speech/image processing.
William W. Edmonson, Ph.D., North Carolina State, 1990. Adaptive and multidimensional signal processing, neural networks.
John G. Harris, Ph.D., Caltech, 1991. Analog VLSI computer vision, neural networks.
Jian Li, Ph.D., Ohio State, 1991. Array processing, radar detection and estimation theory, image segmentation.
Jose C. Principe, Ph.D., Florida, 1979. Adaptive digital signal processing, neural networks, biomedical signal analysis.
Fred J. Taylor, Ph.D., Colorado, 1969. Digital system theory, architecture, and design; computer-aided design; VLSI design.

Electric Energy Systems
Dennis P. Carroll, Ph.D., Wisconsin, 1969. Electric energy systems, high-voltage transmission, power electronics, power system simulation.
Alexander Domijan Jr., Ph.D., Texas at Arlington, 1986. Electric energy systems, power quality, modeling and simulation, instrumentation.
Khai Ngo, Ph.D., Caltech, 1984. Power electronics, low-profile magnetics, power integrated circuits.
Vladimir A. Rakov, Ph.D., Tomsk (Russia), 1983. Lightning, atmospheric electricity, lightning protection.

Electromagnetics
Ewen M. Thomson, Ph.D., Queensland (Australia), 1985. Lightning.
Martin A. Uman, Chairman; Ph.D., Princeton, 1961. Lightning, atmospheric electricity, electromagnetics.
Henry Zmuda, Ph.D., Cornell, 1984. Microwave system design, photonics.

Electronic Circuits
William R. Eisenstadt, Ph.D., Stanford, 1984. Solid-state circuit electronics, VLSI design.
Robert M. Fox, Ph.D., Auburn, 1986. Analog and digital VLSI circuits.
Mark Law, Ph.D., Stanford, 1988. VLSI process and device simulation.
Kenneth K. O, Ph.D., MIT, 1989. Solid-state devices, circuits, processing technologies and materials.
Jack R. Smith, Ph.D., USC, 1964. Bioengineering, electronics, computers and signal detection.

Photonics
Chris S. Anderson, Ph.D., North Carolina State, 1991. Optics, optical signal processing, holography/interferometry, radar and communications.
Ramu V. Ramaswamy, Ph.D., Northwestern, 1969. Passive, active, linear, and nonlinear guided wave optical and optoelectronic devices.
Ramakant Srivastava, Ph.D., Indiana, 1973. Guided wave optics, lasers, nonlinear optics.
Peter S. Zory, Ph.D., Carnegie Tech, 1964. Lasers.

Systems and Control
Thomas E. Bullock, Ph.D., Stanford, 1966. Mathematical systems theory, filtering, digital control with microprocessors.
Jacob Hammer, D.Sc., Technion (Israel), 1980. Control systems.
Haniph A. Latchman, D.Phil., Oxford, 1986. Control systems and communications.

UNIVERSITY OF HOUSTON

DEPARTMENT OF COMPUTER SCIENCE
M.S. AND PH.D. DEGREE PROGRAMS

PROGRAMS OF STUDY

The Department of Computer Science at the University of Houston (UH) offers programs leading to the Master of Science (M.S.) and Doctor of Philosophy (Ph.D.) degrees in computer science. Fields of specialization include artificial intelligence (AI), databases, parallel and distributed computing, software engineering, virtual reality, and theory.

The M.S. degree requires 24 hours of course work and a thesis. Requirements for the Ph.D. degree include a dissertation and 48 hours of course work. Candidates must also meet specific requirements with respect to both breadth and depth in their academic background and may be assigned remedial work if these are not satisfied.

RESEARCH FACILITIES

The department maintains UNIX servers for Solaris, SunOS, and DEC Ultrix. Students have access to around 100 workstations and X-terminals in several open areas within the department. Remote access via dial-up, nongraphics connections is provided free by the University, utilizing more than 800 telephone lines. PPP graphics access is also available upon request, as are special University rates for Internet service providers. Access to University supercomputers such as a sixty-four-node IBM SP2, a sixteen-pipe SX-3, a thirty-two-node Cenju-3, and others is also provided. The University of Houston is on the Internet backbone and is part of the experimental Internet II.

FINANCIAL AID

Graduate students with teaching or research assistantships are provided a stipend of between $850 and $1200 per month, depending on the student's qualifications. Application for the assistantship should be made directly to the department. The deadlines are March 1 (for fall) and October 1 (for spring). Approximately 35 teaching assistants/fellows and 15 research assistants are currently employed by the department.

COST OF STUDY

Tuition and fees for Texas residents are approximately $1000 per semester in 1997–98; nonresidents, including international students, pay about $2800 per semester. Students receiving financial assistance qualify for resident status.

LIVING AND HOUSING COSTS

On-campus room and board cost approximately $2000 per semester. For students in off-campus housing, apartments begin at about $350 per month.

STUDENT GROUP

There are approximately 265 graduate students in the department, 100 of whom are Ph.D. students. These students come from all over the world, including Asia, Europe, the Middle East, and the Americas. The department maintains exchange student agreements with universities in Italy, France, and Mexico. Active student groups provide support.

STUDENT OUTCOMES

The Ph.D. graduates find employment in both academic institutions and industry, such as GTE labs, nationwide. The demand for graduates who earn a master's degree is great and most M.S. students find positions prior to graduation. Local employers include NASA/Johnson Space Center, Texas Medical Center, Shell Oil, and Compaq.

LOCATION

Houston is the fourth-largest city in the U.S. and maintains a high rate of economic growth. UH's 500-acre campus is within a short drive from downtown Houston and Texas Medical Center. Drawing upon the University's strong relationship with Houston business and research communities (e.g., Compaq, Exxon, Shell, NASA/JSC, Texas Medical Center), students may obtain numerous research and employment opportunities.

THE UNIVERSITY AND THE DEPARTMENT

The University of Houston is the only doctoral degree–granting component and the largest campus of the state-supported UH System and serves as a strong research and intellectual base for the city of Houston, the state of Texas, and the United States. Serving 32,000 students in fourteen colleges, UH ranks among the top eighty research universities in the country. Research grants and awards to UH exceeded $50 million in 1995.

The department, one of seven departments in the College of Natural Sciences and Mathematics, maintains strong ties with several research institutes on campus, including the High Performance Computer Center, the Virtual Environment Technology Laboratory, and the Texas Center for Advanced Molecular Design.

APPLYING

Applicants should have a bachelor's degree, a minimum GPA of 3.0 over the last 60 hours, a combined GRE (verbal and quantitative) score of 1150 or better, six or more hours of mathematics beyond Calculus II, and at least two programming courses. Students whose native language is not English must obtain a TOEFL score of 550 or above. For these students, a minimum GRE score of 1000 with at least 600 on the quantitative part is sufficient. Students with degrees in fields other than computer science may be admitted subject to additional course requirements.

CORRESPONDENCE AND INFORMATION

Dr. Ernst L. Leiss
Director of Graduate Studies
Department of Computer Science
University of Houston
Houston, Texas 77204-3475
Telephone: 713-743-3350
Fax: 713-743-3335
E-mail: gradinfo@cs.uh.edu
World Wide Web: http://www.cs.uh.edu

UNIVERSITY OF HOUSTON

THE FACULTY AND THEIR RESEARCH

Robert B. Anderson, Associate Professor and Director of Undergraduate Studies; Ph.D., Texas at Austin. Theory of computation, artificial intelligence.

Farokh Bastani, Professor; Ph.D., Berkeley. Software engineering, fault-tolerant computing, self-stabilizing systems, parallel and distributed systems, AI, multimedia computing.

Albert M. K. Cheng, Associate Professor and Director of Real-Time Systems Laboratory; Ph.D., Texas at Austin. Real-time systems, distributed systems, AI, software engineering, computer security, computer networks.

Kam-Hoi Cheng, Associate Professor; Ph.D., Minnesota. VLSI, parallel and distributed processing, networks, architecture, algorithm and complexity.

Jorge Cobb, Assistant Professor; Ph.D., Texas at Austin. Computer networks, mobile computing, concurrent and distributed computing.

Daniel B. Davison, Associate Professor of Biochemical and Biophysical Sciences and Computer Science; Ph.D., SUNY at Stony Brook. High-performance computing, parallel algorithm design, graph-theoretic techniques for sequence algorithms.

Christoph F. Eick, Associate Professor; Ph.D., Karlsruhe. Artificial intelligence, rule-based programming, expert systems, genetic algorithms, software reliability.

J. C. Huang, Professor; Ph.D., Pennsylvania. Software engineering, real-time computer systems, program analysis and testing.

S.-H. Stephen Huang, Associate Professor; Ph.D., Texas at Austin. Data structures, design and analysis of algorithms, parallel and distributed processing, data management.

Olin G. Johnson, Professor and Director of High Performance Computing Center; Ph.D., Berkeley. Numerical analysis, vector/array: processors, languages and algorithms.

S. Lennart Johnsson, Cullen Professor of Computer Science and Chairman; Ph.D., Chalmers Institute of Technology (Sweden). Parallel computing, scientific computation.

Willis K. King, Associate Professor; Ph.D., Pennsylvania. Computer architecture, distributed systems.

Ernst L. Leiss, Professor and Director of Graduate Studies; Dr. Techn., TU Wien (Vienna). Vector and parallel computing, data security, databases, formal and programming languages, geophysical data processing.

R. Bowen Loftin, Professor of Computer Science and Director of Virtual Environment Technology Laboratory; Ph.D., Rice. Computer graphics, data visualization, artificial intelligence, simulation.

Jehan-Francois Paris, Associate Professor; Ph.D., Berkeley. Distributed systems, file systems, fault-tolerant computing, performance evaluation.

B. Montgomery Pettitt, Cullen Professor of Chemistry, Computer Science, and Biochemical and Biophysical Sciences and Director of Institute for Molecular Design; Ph.D., Houston. High-performance computing, parallel processing, numerical analysis, visualization.

Nikos P. Pitsianis, Visiting Assistant Professor; Ph.D., Cornell. Parallel and high-performance scientific computing, numerical and symbolic algorithms, code transformations.

Marek Rusinkiewicz, Professor; Ph.D., Warsaw (Poland). Database management, distributed systems.

Ridgway Scott, Professor of Mathematics and Computer Science and Director of Texas Center for Advanced Molecular Design; Ph.D., MIT. Parallel languages and compilers, numerical algorithms for scientific computation, computer graphics and scientific visualization.

D. Sivakumar, Assistant Professor; Ph.D., SUNY at Buffalo. Computational complexity theory, randomized computation, probabilistic self-testing and self-correcting of programs.

Rakesh M. Verma, Associate Professor; Ph.D., SUNY at Stony Brook. Symbolic computation, declarative programming languages, automated deduction, parallel computing, temporal and spatial databases.

CURRENT RESEARCH PROJECTS

Input/output management in high-performance computing, including parallel I/O.
Data security in object-oriented and in multimedia systems.
Language equations.
Appropriateness evaluation of drug prescriptions.
Learning Bayesian rule-sets for classification tasks.
Knowledge discovery in databases.
Graph embedding algorithms with applications to parallel processing.
Distributed environment for interactive data and document review.
Smaran: an efficient congruence-closure-based system for equational systems.
Techniques for analyzing recursive algorithms.
Efficient sequential and parallel storage and access methods for temporal and spatial databases.
Virtual environments for training.
Assessing the potential of virtual reality in science education.
Data visualization science and engineering.
Rigorous reliability assessment of embedded safety-critical systems.
Program transformation for high-performance parallel computing.
Self-stabilizing safety-critical applications over wide area networks.
OMNIBASE: a multidatabase management system.
NARADA: interoperability in a heterogeneous computing environment.
High-performance robust parallel and distributed multi-agent systems.
Software reliability for payloads in space.
Parallel and distributed algorithms.
Fundamental properties of rule-based systems.

UNIVERSITY OF HOUSTON

DEPARTMENT OF ELECTRICAL AND COMPUTER ENGINEERING

PROGRAMS OF STUDY

The department offers the Master of Electrical Engineering (M.E.E.), Master of Science (M.S.), and Doctor of Philosophy (Ph.D.) degrees. Fields of specialization include antennas and applied electromagnetics, bioelectromagnetics, biomedical engineering, communications, computers, control systems, high-temperature superconductivity, microelectronics, nondestructive evaluation, optics, pattern recognition, power systems, seismic exploration, signal and image analysis, systems analysis, ultrasonics, and well logging. The department also administers interdisciplinary graduate programs in biomedical engineering and computer and systems engineering.

The M.S. degree requires 24 hours of course work and a research thesis. The M.E.E. degree is a nonthesis option and requires 36 course hours. Requirements for the Ph.D. degree include a dissertation and 24 course hours beyond the master's degree. Candidates must also meet specific requirements with respect to both breadth and depth in their professional knowledge and may be assigned remedial work if these are not satisfied.

In response to the rapid growth in the telecommunications industry, a nonthesis Master of Electrical Engineering in telecommunications is offered. The degree requirements are similar to those of the M.E.E. and additionally include a 6-credit-hour internship at one of many participating telecommunications companies. Scholarships are also available to outstanding individuals in this program.

RESEARCH FACILITIES

The department has extensive research facilities for work in antenna engineering; biomedical engineering; digital systems; electron beam and ion optics; high-temperature superconductivity; microwaves; power systems; seismic data analysis; semiconductor fabrication, including rapid thermal processing, advanced lithography, and defect characterization; well logging; and other areas. The University computing center maintains an AS/9000 mainframe and a cluster of VAX computers. A central campus facility maintains 140 workstations available 24 hours a day, 7 days a week. The Engineering Computing Center in the College of Engineering has more than 125 personal computers and workstations available for student use. In addition, personal computers and workstations are located throughout ECE department offices and laboratories.

FINANCIAL AID

Graduate students with teaching or research assistantships are provided a stipend of up to $1100 per month, depending on qualifications and level. At present, about 80 percent of full-time M.S. and Ph.D. students are supported by the department. Applications for assistantships should be made directly to the department well before the intended enrollment date.

COST OF STUDY

Tuition and fees vary, but typical payments for 12 semester credit hours are $1260 for Texas residents and $3564 for nonresidents.

LIVING AND HOUSING COSTS

On-campus room and board costs are in the range of $475 to $585 per month. Off-campus apartments (room only) begin at about $250 per month.

STUDENT GROUP

There are about 3,000 students enrolled in the Cullen College of Engineering and about 1,000 in the Department of Electrical and Computer Engineering.

LOCATION

The University's 390-acre campus is only a short drive from downtown Houston, the fourth-largest city in the nation. Also within a short distance is the internationally known Texas Medical Center, a 200-acre area in which are located the Baylor College of Medicine, the University of Texas College of Medicine, and the University of Texas Health Science Center at Houston, to name a few of its components. These institutions, together with the Johnson Space Center and other organizations, offer numerous interdisciplinary research opportunities. Texas Instruments and Compaq are among major high-technology companies with headquarters in Houston. The world-renowned Houston Symphony and Alley Theater present two of many exciting cultural opportunities. Houston is also home to many professional sports teams, including the Astros baseball team and the two-time World Champion Houston Rockets basketball team.

THE UNIVERSITY AND THE DEPARTMENT

A large majority of the University's 30,000 students commute. Although daytime enrollment now predominates, a tradition of providing night courses for part-time students at both the undergraduate and graduate levels is maintained. The wide scope of academic and research opportunities provided by the 44 doctoral and 106 master's-degree programs attracts a highly heterogeneous group of students and faculty. An international flavor results from a large enrollment of students from other nations.

Established in 1947, the Department of Electrical and Computer Engineering has experienced its greatest growth since 1963, when the previously private university became state supported. The electrical and computer engineering faculty members, most of whom have international reputations in their specialties, reflect an emphasis on excellence in research as well as teaching. As a consequence, the department enjoys a high level of research funding from outside agencies.

APPLYING

For unconditional admission to either master's degree program, a grade point average of at least 3.0 in the previous 60 hours of study, a satisfactory GRE score (verbal, math, and analytical), a bachelor's degree in electrical engineering (or a related discipline) from an accredited department, and three recommendations are required. Admission to the Ph.D. program requires a master's degree or 30 hours of graduate credit in electrical engineering (or a related field). GRE scores and a GPA appreciably above those specified for the master's level are expected.

Applications for admission, GRE scores, three recommendations, and two copies of all transcripts must be submitted directly to the Department of Electrical and Computer Engineering. International students and those seeking financial assistance are urged to apply several months in advance of their anticipated enrollment date. Results of the TOEFL (minimum score 550) are required of international applicants from non-English-speaking countries.

CORRESPONDENCE AND INFORMATION

Graduate Admissions Analyst
Department of Electrical and Computer Engineering
University of Houston
4800 Calhoun
Houston, Texas 77204-4793

Telephone: 713-743-4403
Fax: 713-743-4444
E-mail: mmm05866@jetson.uh.edu
World Wide Web: http://www.egr.uh.edu/Departments/ECE

UNIVERSITY OF HOUSTON
THE FACULTY AND THEIR RESEARCH

Wallace L. Anderson, Professor and Chairman; Sc.D., New Mexico; PE. Ultrasonics, nondestructive evaluation, signal analysis, statistical estimation, pattern recognition, Fourier optics.

Betty J. Barr, Assistant Professor; Ph.D., Houston. Applied mathematics.

Guanrong Chen, Associate Professor; Ph.D., Texas A&M. Nonlinear systems—dynamics and control, robotics, fuzzy systems control, chaotic systems control.

Ovidiu Crisan, Professor; D.Eng., Polytechnic Institute of Timisoara (Romania). Power systems operation, control and optimization, electric machine modeling, superconductivity in power systems.

John R. Glover Jr., Professor; Ph.D., Stanford. Adaptive systems, digital signal processing, biomedical signal processing, expert systems applications, educational software.

Thomas J. Hebert, Associate Professor; Ph.D., USC. Image and signal processing.

Martin C. Herbordt, Assistant Professor; Ph.D., Massachusetts. Computer architecture, high-performance systems, parallel processing, computer system simulation.

David R. Jackson, Associate Professor; Ph.D., UCLA. Electromagnetic theory, microstrip antennas, microwave and millimeter-wave antennas, bioelectromagnetics.

Ben H. Jansen, Professor; Ph.D., Free University (Amsterdam). Biomedical signal analysis, pattern recognition, artificial intelligence, biomedical engineering, complex dynamic systems modeling, nonlinear dynamics, self-organizing systems.

Nicolaos B. Karayiannis, Assistant Professor; Ph.D., Toronto. Artificial neural networks, supervised and unsupervised learning, fuzzy pattern recognition and vector quantization, image processing and analysis.

Tony L. King, Assistant Professor; Ph.D., Illinois. Control systems, electronic circuit design, instrumentation.

Periklis Y. Ktonas, Professor; Ph.D., Florida. Biomedical engineering, bioelectrical signal analysis, random data analysis.

Ce Liu, Assistant Professor; Ph.D., Jiaotong (China). Well logging, ground-penetrating radar, and EM tomography.

Stuart A. Long, Professor; Ph.D., Harvard; PE. Applied electromagnetics, printed-circuit and millimeter-wave antennas, high-temperature superconducting materials and devices.

Pauline Markenscoff, Associate Professor; Ph.D., Minnesota. Computer architecture, performance evaluation of computer systems, distributed processing.

Haluk Ogmen, Associate Professor; Ph.D., Laval. Neural networks, biological and computer vision, biological sensory-motor control and adaptive robotics.

Poen S. Ong, Associate Professor; D.Sc., Delft (Netherlands); PE. X-ray and electron optics, wavelength and energy-dispersive X-ray analysis, X-ray microscopy, scanning electron microscopy.

David M. Pai, Associate Professor; Ph.D., British Columbia. Seismic data modeling and inversion, well logging.

Gerhard F. Paskusz, Professor; Ph.D., UCLA; PE. Computer-aided circuit analysis and design.

Steven Pei, Professor; Ph.D., SUNY at Stony Brook. Heterostructure FETs and heterojunction bipolar transistors based on wide bandgap III-V compounds, optoelectronic ICs.

William P. Schneider, Professor; S.M., MIT; PE. Controls, electronic instrumentation, dynamic positioning systems, sonar drill-pipe control systems, marine systems, control of unstable systems.

David P. Shattuck, Associate Professor; Ph.D., Duke; PE. Acoustic imaging and well logging.

Liang C. Shen, Professor; Ph.D., Harvard; PE. Antennas and wave propagation, underground antennas, printed-circuit antennas, electromagnetic techniques in well logging, subsurface sensing.

Leang S. Shieh, Professor; Ph.D., Houston; PE. Control systems; model reduction, identification, and design; optimal control; adaptive control; digital control; multivariable control systems.

Leonard Trombetta, Associate Professor; Ph.D., Lehigh. Electronic materials, MOS oxide reliability, semiconductor defect studies, electron devices.

Jeffery T. Williams, Associate Professor; Ph.D., Arizona. Applied electromagnetics, wave propagation, numerical techniques, antenna measurements and design, high-frequency superconductor characterization and applications.

Donald R. Wilton, Professor; Ph.D., Illinois. Electromagnetic theory, mathematical methods, numerical techniques.

John C. Wolfe, Professor; Ph.D., Rochester. Materials research, electron and ion-beam devices, microfabrication.

Wanda Zagozdzon-Wosik, Associate Professor; Ph.D., Warsaw Technical. Semiconductor integrated circuit processing technology, electron devices.

THE UNIVERSITY OF ILLINOIS AT CHICAGO

DEPARTMENT OF ELECTRICAL ENGINEERING AND COMPUTER SCIENCE
PROGRAM IN COMPUTER SCIENCE AND ENGINEERING

PROGRAMS OF STUDY

The Department of Electrical Engineering and Computer Science offers a broad range of programs in computer science and engineering and electrical engineering leading to the M.S. and Ph.D. degrees. The M.S. degree requires 36 semester hours of study, including an optional thesis. The Ph.D. degree requires an additional 72 semester hours of credit. Ph.D. students are required to pass a written qualifying examination, an oral thesis proposal examination, and a final examination defending the thesis at the conclusion of the research.

While the department offers a comprehensive range of courses in computer science and engineering, it has special strengths in the areas of computer graphics, software engineering, database systems, parallel and distributed systems, human-computer interaction, theory, computer architecture, programming languages and environments, computer vision, and artificial intelligence.

RESEARCH FACILITIES

The department maintains a large, modern instructional computing facility, including ten UNIX file servers managing a total of more than forty GB of disk space, four UltraSPARC compute servers, and 105 student-accessible Sun Workstations for software development, database programming, VLSI design, HTML development, and numerical computing. There are also four Silicon Graphics workstations equipped with 24-bit graphics and thirty-four Macintosh computers used for assembly language programming and HTML development. All computers are networked via ten Megabit switched Ethernet.

In addition to the modern instructional computing facility, the department contains several specialized research laboratories, most of which are housed in the $30-million Engineering Research Facility. The Electronic Visualization Laboratory (EVL), the Interactive Computing Environments Laboratory, the Concurrent Software Systems Laboratory, the Intelligent Vehicle Highway Systems and Artificial Intelligence Laboratory, the Software Engineering Laboratory, the Knowledge and Database Systems Laboratory, the Distributed Real-Time Intelligent Systems Laboratory, the Parallel Systems Laboratory, the Laboratory for Advanced Computing, the Vision Interface and Systems Laboratory, and the Signal and Image Research Laboratory contain well over 100 additional workstations and servers as well as an extensive array of computer-based multimedia equipment. The Microfabrication Applications Laboratory, the Communications Laboratory, the Electromagnetics and Optics Laboratory, the Power Electronics Laboratory, the Visual/Motor Laboratory, and the Biomedical Functional Imaging and Computational Laboratory contain a wide array of specialized equipment for advanced research in electrical engineering.

The departmental computing facilities are networked to general University computing resources and national networks, permitting high-speed access to specialized computing facilities, such as Connection Machine, Power Challenge Array, and Convex supercomputers at the National Center for Supercomputing Applications (NCSA) at the University of Illinois at Urbana-Champaign and to the IBM SP-2 at Argonne National Laboratory.

FINANCIAL AID

Financial aid is available in the form of teaching and research assistantships as well as various University fellowships, and opportunities are excellent for research-oriented students with solid undergraduate backgrounds in computer science and engineering. Half-time assistantships for new graduate students require 19 hours per week and pay $10,000 for the academic year ($12,222 for the calendar year). In 1996–97, the electrical engineering and computer science department supported more than 120 graduate students, about a third of whom were teaching assistants. Approximately 75 graduate students were supported by external research grants totaling more than $4.8 million.

COST OF STUDY

For 1996–97, Illinois residents paid $2574 and nonresidents paid $5701 per semester if registered for 12 or more hours, with a sliding scale for registration of fewer than 12 hours. Tuition and fees are waived for recipients of teaching and research assistantships, tuition and fee awards, and some University fellowships. Fees are subject to change.

LIVING AND HOUSING COSTS

In addition to UIC residence halls, off-campus apartments and rooms are available. Meals may be taken in campus dining facilities or a variety of nearby commercial establishments. Food, housing, transportation, medical care, personal items, clothing, and incidentals are estimated to cost $11,000 per calendar year.

STUDENT GROUP

The department has an undergraduate student body of approximately 1,055 students and 450 graduate students. The graduate student body includes about 220 full-time (average of 12 or more hours) graduate students, of whom over 100 are pursuing the Ph.D. degree. Most graduate students are affiliated with one of the research laboratories listed above.

LOCATION

Chicago is a vibrant, friendly, beautiful city where there is never a dull moment. The city has countless restaurants, signature blues clubs, fantastic museums, and 12 miles of lakefront beach. The University, a 5-minute train ride from the center-city Loop, is situated on the original site of Jane Addam's Hull House, the first social settlement house in the United States. The University is bordered by Greektown to the north and Little Italy to the west. Chinatown is a 10-minute drive away.

THE UNIVERSITY

The University of Illinois at Chicago (UIC), with approximately 25,000 students, is the largest institution of higher learning in the Chicago area. UIC is listed among the Research-I universities in the United States in external research funding. The University offers master's degrees in eighty-seven fields and doctorates in fifty-four areas.

APPLYING

Application materials for admission and financial aid may be obtained by writing to the address below. Requests for applications for teaching assistantships and fellowships (including tuition and fee waivers) should also be directed to the address below. Each student seeking a research assistantship is advised to write directly to faculty members in his or her area of interest. Students are not required to take the Graduate Record Examinations for admission, but the GRE is recommended for applicants for financial aid. Applications for teaching and research assistantships should be received no later than March 1. To be considered for a fellowship, students should submit applications before the January 1 deadline. For fall 1998, the application for admission deadlines are March 20 for international students and June 1 for all other students. Applicants from non-English-speaking countries must take the TOEFL and score at least 570 to be considered for admission.

CORRESPONDENCE AND INFORMATION

Director of Graduate Admissions (M/C 154)
Department of Electrical Engineering and Computer Science
The University of Illinois at Chicago
851 South Morgan Street (1120 SEO)
Chicago, Illinois 60607-7053

Telephone: 312-996-2290
             312-413-2291
Fax: 312-413-0024
E-mail: grad-info@eecs.uic.edu
World Wide Web: http://www.eecs.uic.edu

THE UNIVERSITY OF ILLINOIS AT CHICAGO

THE FACULTY AND THEIR RESEARCH

Artificial Intelligence and Computer Vision

Simon Kasif, Associate Professor; Ph.D., Maryland, 1985. High-performance intelligent systems machine learning, data mining, computational biology, computational neuroscience, parallel computation.

Peter C. Nelson, Associate Professor; Ph.D., Northwestern, 1988. AI research in heuristic search and applied AI research in the areas of transportation, optimizing manufacturing scheduling problems (genetic algorithms and rule-based systems), and automated DNA restriction mapping.

Francis K. H. Quek, Assistant Professor; Ph.D., Michigan, 1990. Human-computer interaction, computer vision, robot navigation.

Boaz Super, Assistant Professor; Ph.D., Texas at Austin, 1992. Computer and biological vision, image processing, pattern recognition.

Communications and Control

Gyan C. Agarwal, Professor; Ph.D., Purdue, 1965. Automatic control, systems analysis, bioengineering, neuroscience, neural networks.

Charles A. Brooks, Assistant Professor; Ph.D., Berkeley, 1994. Stochastic modeling and communication networks, discrete event systems.

Roger C. Conant, Associate Professor; Ph.D., Illinois at Urbana-Champaign, 1968. General systems theory, artificial intelligence, cybernetics and information transfer in complex systems.

William D. O'Neill, Professor; Ph.D., Notre Dame, 1965. Information theory, communications, image processing, time-series modeling.

Chathilingath K. Sanathanan, Professor; Ph.D., Case Western Reserve, 1964. Industrial control system design, control of large-scale systems.

Computer Architecture and VLSI Systems

Wai-Kai Chen, Professor; Ph.D., Illinois at Urbana-Champaign, 1964. Broadband matching, applied graph theory, networks, systems, filters, VLSI placement, routing, and layout.

Krishna Shenai, Associate Professor; Ph.D., Stanford, 1986. Solid-state and microelectronics, power electronics, semiconductor manufacturing.

Jon A. Solworth, Associate Professor; Ph.D., NYU, 1987. Computer architecture, programming language design and compilation techniques for parallel processors, I/O, object stores and file systems.

Alexander Veidenbaum, Associate Professor; Ph.D., Illinois at Urbana-Champaign, 1985. High-performance and multiprocessor system architecture, system design and packaging, interconnection networks.

Database Systems

Jorge Lobo, Assistant Professor; Ph.D., Maryland, 1990. Knowledge representation, logic and databases, logic programming, nonmonotonic reasoning.

Ouri Wolfson, Associate Professor; Ph.D., NYU, 1984. Database systems, distributed systems, rule processing, mobile computing.

Clement T. Yu, Professor; Ph.D., Cornell, 1973. Database management, information retrieval and knowledge-base management, multimedia retrieval.

Electromagnetics and Power Electronics

Wolfgang-M. Boerner, Professor; Ph.D., Pennsylvania, 1967. Electromagnetics, inverse scattering, modern optics, geoelectromagnetism, electromagnetic imaging, remote sensing, wideband radar, optical polarimetry.

Rhonda F. Drayton, Assistant Professor; Ph.D., Michigan, 1996. Electromagnetics, microwave and millimeter wave circuit and system design.

Sharad R. Laxpati, Associate Professor; Ph.D., Illinois at Urbana-Champaign, 1965. Antennas, electromagnetic theory, computational electromagnetic scattering, microwaves, wave propagation and communication.

Chuo Q. Lee, Professor; Ph.D., IIT, 1966. Power electronics, electromagnetic field theory, ultrasound.

James C. Lin, Professor; Ph.D., Washington (Seattle), 1971. Electromagnetics in biology and medicine, biomedical instrumentation, telemedicine.

Korada R. Umashankar, Professor; Ph.D., Mississippi, 1974. Electromagnetic field theory and applications, microwave and millimeter waves, analytical and numerical techniques for electromagnetic scattering and interaction by complex materials, time-domain inverse-scattering methods.

Piergiorgio L. E. Uslenghi, Professor; Ph.D., Michigan, 1967. Electromagnetics, scattering theory, modern optics, solid-state, applied mathematics.

Hung-Yu Yang, Assistant Professor; Ph.D., UCLA, 1988. Applied electromagnetics in ferromagnetic integrated circuits and antennas, novel microstrip antennas and arrays, planar integrated transformers for power electronics, advanced computational techniques.

Graphics and Interactive Systems

Thomas A. DeFanti, Professor; Ph.D., Ohio State, 1973. Computer graphics and video animation, virtual reality, electronic art, educational technology, operating systems, scientific and volume visualization, networks, parallel computers, supercomputers.

Robert V. Kenyon, Associate Professor; Ph.D., Berkeley, 1978. Human visual and motor systems, human spatial orientation, computer graphics and display technology, virtual environments, flight simulation, spaceflight and human adaptation.

Thomas G. Moher, Associate Professor; Ph.D., Minnesota, 1983. Human-computer interaction, programming environments, cognitive models.

Signal and Image Processing

Rashid Ansari, Associate Professor; Ph.D., Princeton, 1981. Image/video processing, coding, transmission, layered video coding schemes for ATM networks, packet video transmissions, theoretical work on general framework for multirate processing of two-dimensional signals.

Jezekiel Ben-Arie, Associate Professor; Ph.D., Technion (Israel), 1986. Object and target recognition, image understanding and processing, shape and signal representation, wavelets and nonorthogonal expansions, neural networks, biomedical engineering.

Earl E. Gose, Professor; Ph.D., Berkeley, 1960. Pattern recognition and image processing with applications of medical images and industrial inspection techniques.

Daniel Graupe, Professor; Ph.D., Liverpool, 1963. Control systems, time-series analysis, signal processing, neural networks, wavelets and electrical stimulation.

Bin He, Assistant Professor; Ph.D., Tokyo Institute of Technology, 1988. Imaging systems, signal and image processing, bioelectric phenomena.

Arye Nehorai, Professor; Ph.D., Stanford, 1983. Signal and image processing, biomedicine and communications.

Roland Priemer, Associate Professor; Ph.D., IIT, 1969. Optimal and adaptive digital signal processing, digital filters, control systems, microprocessor-based system design.

Dan Schonfeld, Associate Professor; Ph.D., Johns Hopkins, 1990. Signal and image processing, pattern recognition, and computer vision.

Software Engineering

Ugo A. Buy, Associate Professor; Ph.D., Massachusetts, 1990. Software engineering, concurrency and real-time analysis.

Carl K. Chang, Associate Professor; Ph.D., Northwestern, 1982. Software engineering: specification, verification, and validation; testing: real-time systems, distributed computer systems, telecommunication software, and object-oriented methods.

Tadao Murata, Professor; Ph.D., Illinois at Urbana-Champaign, 1966. Petri net modeling and analysis of concurrent computer systems.

Sol M. Shatz, Associate Professor; Ph.D., Northwestern, 1983. Distributed computing systems, software engineering, operating systems.

Jeffrey J. P. Tsai, Associate Professor; Ph.D., Northwestern, 1986. Knowledge-based software systems, artificial intelligence, expert systems, requirements specification language, distributed real-time software testing, debugging, and software metrics.

Solid State and Microfabrication

Davorin Babic, Assistant Professor; Ph.D., Pennsylvania, 1988. Physical principles of nanoscale Si particles, their modeling and application to optical modulator, physics and chemistry of silicon interfaces and surfaces.

Alan D. Feinerman, Associate Professor; Ph.D., Northwestern, 1987. Miniaturization of the scanning electron microscope, linear accelerator/undulator and other analytical instruments, 3-D fabrication techniques.

Gary D. Friedman, Associate Professor; Ph.D., Maryland, 1989. Electromagnetics, magnetic and dielectric materials, microfabrication.

Peter J. Hesketh, Associate Professor; Ph.D., Pennsylvania, 1987. Solid-state sensors and actuators, biosensors and microfabrication.

G. Jordan Maclay, Associate Professor; Ph.D., Yale, 1972. Microsensors and microfabricated devices, quantum devices and micromachining.

David L. Naylor, Associate Professor; Ph.D., USC, 1988. Development and application of microfabricated photonic materials and devices, diffractive optics: design, fabrication, and systems applications.

Theory and Algorithms

Gianfranco Bilardi, Professor; Ph.D., Illinois at Urbana-Champaign, 1985. Parallel processing, VLSI architectures and systems, signal processing, physical limitations to computing systems.

A. Prasad Sistla, Associate Professor; Ph.D., Harvard, 1989. Distributed systems, semantics and verification of concurrent systems and database management systems.

Robert H. Sloan, Associate Professor; Ph.D., MIT, 1989. Design and analysis of algorithms, computational learning theory, machine learning, cryptography, software engineering, analysis of real-time programs, automatic program verification.

UIC   THE UNIVERSITY OF ILLINOIS AT CHICAGO

DEPARTMENT OF ELECTRICAL ENGINEERING AND COMPUTER SCIENCE
PROGRAM IN ELECTRICAL ENGINEERING

PROGRAMS OF STUDY

The Department of Electrical Engineering and Computer Science offers a broad range of programs in electrical engineering and computer science and engineering leading to the M.S. and Ph.D. degrees. The M.S. degree requires 36 semester hours of study, including an optional thesis. The Ph.D. degree requires an additional 72 semester hours of credit. Ph.D. students are required to pass a written qualifying examination, an oral thesis proposal examination, and a final examination defending the thesis at the conclusion of the research.

While a wide range of courses comprising many areas in electrical engineering is offered, the department has special strengths in the areas of microelectronics and microfabrication, electromagnetics and optics, power electronics, communications, controls, networks, biomedical applications, and signal processing.

RESEARCH FACILITIES

The department maintains a large, modern instructional computing facility, including ten UNIX file servers managing a total of more than forty GB of disk space, four UltraSPARC compute servers, and 105 student-accessible Sun Workstations for software development, database programming, VLSI design, HTML development, and numerical computing. There are also four Silicon Graphics workstations equipped with 24-bit graphics and thirty-four Macintosh computers used for assembly language programming and HTML development. All computers are networked via ten Megabit switched Ethernet.

In addition to the modern instructional computing facility, the department contains several specialized research laboratories, most of which are housed in the $30-million Engineering Research Facility. The Microfabrication Applications Laboratory, the Communications Laboratory, the Electromagnetics and Optics Laboratory, the Power Electronics Laboratory, the Visual/Motor Laboratory, and the Biomedical Functional Imaging and Computational Laboratory contain a wide array of specialized equipment for advanced research in electrical engineering. The Electronic Visualization Laboratory (EVL), the Interactive Computing Environments Laboratory, the Concurrent Software Systems Laboratory, the Intelligent Vehicle Highway Systems and Artificial Intelligence Laboratory, the Software Engineering Laboratory, the Knowledge and Database Systems Laboratory, the Distributed Real-Time Intelligent Systems Laboratory, the Parallel Systems Laboratory, the Laboratory for Advanced Computing, the Vision Interface and Systems Laboratory, and the Signal and Image Research Laboratory contain well over 100 additional workstations and servers as well as an extensive array of computer-based multimedia equipment for advanced research in computer science and engineering.

The departmental computing facilities are networked to general University computing resources and national networks, permitting high-speed access to specialized computing facilities, such as Connection Machine, Power Challenge Array, and Convex supercomputers at the National Center for Supercomputing Applications (NCSA) at the University of Illinois at Urbana-Champaign and to the IBM SP-2 at Argonne National Laboratory.

FINANCIAL AID

Financial aid is available in the form of teaching and research assistantships as well as various University fellowships, and opportunities are excellent for research-oriented students with solid undergraduate backgrounds in computer science and engineering. Half-time assistantships for new graduate students require 19 hours per week and pay $10,000 for the academic year ($12,222 for the calendar year). In 1996–97, the electrical engineering and computer science department supported more than 120 graduate students, about a third of whom were teaching assistants. Approximately 75 graduate students were supported by external research grants totaling more than $4.8 million.

COST OF STUDY

For 1996–97, Illinois residents paid $2574 and nonresidents paid $5701 per semester if registered for 12 or more hours, with a sliding scale for registration of fewer than 12 hours. Tuition and fees are waived for recipients of teaching and research assistantships, tuition and fee awards, and some University fellowships. Fees are subject to change.

LIVING AND HOUSING COSTS

In addition to UIC residence halls, off-campus apartments and rooms are available. Meals may be taken in campus dining facilities or a variety of nearby commercial establishments. Food, housing, transportation, medical care, personal items, clothing, and incidentals are estimated to cost $11,000 per calendar year.

STUDENT GROUP

The department has a student body of approximately 1,055 undergraduate students and 450 graduate students. The graduate student body includes about 220 full-time (average of 12 or more hours) students, of whom over 100 are pursuing the Ph.D. degree. Most graduate students are affiliated with one of the research laboratories listed above.

LOCATION

Chicago is a vibrant, friendly, beautiful city where there is never a dull moment. The city has countless restaurants, signature blues clubs, excellent museums, and 12 miles of lakefront beach. The University, a 5-minute train ride from the center-city Loop, is situated on the original site of Jane Addams' Hull House, the first social settlement house in the United States. The University is bordered by Greektown to the north and Little Italy to the west. Chinatown is a 10-minute drive away.

THE UNIVERSITY

The University of Illinois at Chicago (UIC), with approximately 25,000 students, is the largest institution of higher learning in the Chicago area. UIC is listed among the Research-I universities in the country in external research funding. The University offers master's degrees in eighty-seven fields and doctorates in fifty-four areas.

APPLYING

Application materials for admission and financial aid may be obtained by writing to the address below. Requests for applications for teaching assistantships and fellowships (including tuition and fee waivers) should also be directed to the address below. Students seeking research assistantships are advised to write directly to faculty members in their area of interest. Students are not required to take the Graduate Record Examinations for admission, but the GRE is recommended for applicants for financial aid. Applications for teaching and research assistantships should be received no later than March 1. To be considered for a fellowship, applications are due no later than January 1. For fall 1998, the application for admission deadlines are March 20 for international students and June 1 for all other students. Applicants from non-English-speaking countries must take the TOEFL and score at least 570 to be considered for admission.

CORRESPONDENCE AND INFORMATION

Director of Graduate Admissions (M/C 154)
Department of Electrical Engineering and Computer Science
The University of Illinois at Chicago
851 South Morgan Street (1120 SEO)
Chicago, Illinois 60607-7053

Telephone: 312-996-2290
           312-413-2291
Fax: 312-413-0024
E-mail: grad-info@eecs.uic.edu
World Wide Web: http://www.eecs.uic.edu

THE UNIVERSITY OF ILLINOIS AT CHICAGO

THE FACULTY AND THEIR RESEARCH

Artificial Intelligence and Computer Vision

Simon Kasif, Associate Professor; Ph.D., Maryland, 1985. High-performance intelligent systems machine learning, data mining, computational biology, computational neuroscience, parallel computation.

Peter C. Nelson, Associate Professor; Ph.D., Northwestern, 1988. AI research in heuristic search and applied AI research in the areas of transportation, optimizing manufacturing scheduling problems (genetic algorithms and rule-based systems), and automated DNA restriction mapping.

Francis K. H. Quek, Assistant Professor; Ph.D., Michigan, 1990. Human-computer interaction, computer vision, robot navigation.

Boaz Super, Assistant Professor; Ph.D., Texas at Austin, 1992. Computer and biological vision, image processing, pattern recognition.

Communications and Control

Gyan C. Agarwal, Professor; Ph.D., Purdue, 1965. Automatic control, systems analysis, bioengineering, neuroscience, neural networks.

Charles A. Brooks, Assistant Professor; Ph.D., Berkeley, 1994. Stochastic modeling and communication networks, discrete event systems.

Roger C. Conant, Associate Professor; Ph.D., Illinois at Urbana-Champaign, 1968. General systems theory, artificial intelligence, cybernetics and information transfer in complex systems.

William D. O'Neill, Professor; Ph.D., Notre Dame, 1965. Information theory, communications, image processing, time-series modeling.

Chathilingath K. Sanathanan, Professor; Ph.D., Case Western Reserve, 1964. Industrial control system design, control of large-scale systems.

Computer Architecture and VLSI Systems

Wai-Kai Chen, Professor; Ph.D., Illinois at Urbana-Champaign, 1964. Broadband matching, applied graph theory, networks, systems, filters, VLSI placement, routing, and layout.

Krishna Shenai, Associate Professor; Ph.D., Stanford, 1986. Solid-state and microelectronics, power electronics, semiconductor manufacturing.

Jon A. Solworth, Associate Professor; Ph.D., NYU, 1987. Computer architecture, programming language design and compilation techniques for parallel processors, I/O, object stores and file systems.

Alexander Veidenbaum, Associate Professor; Ph.D., Illinois at Urbana-Champaign, 1985. High-performance and multiprocessor system architecture, system design and packaging, interconnection networks.

Database Systems

Jorge Lobo, Assistant Professor; Ph.D., Maryland, 1990. Knowledge representation, logic and databases, logic programming, nonmonotonic reasoning.

Ouri Wolfson, Associate Professor; Ph.D., NYU, 1984. Database systems, distributed systems, rule processing, mobile computing.

Clement T. Yu, Professor; Ph.D., Cornell, 1973. Database management, information retrieval and knowledge-base management, multimedia retrieval.

Electromagnetics and Power Electronics

Wolfgang-M. Boerner, Professor; Ph.D., Pennsylvania, 1967. Electromagnetics, inverse scattering, modern optics, geoelectromagnetism, electromagnetic imaging, remote sensing, wideband radar, optical polarimetry.

Rhonda F. Drayton, Assistant Professor; Ph.D., Michigan, 1996. Electromagnetics, microwave and millimeter wave circuit and system design.

Sharad R. Laxpati, Associate Professor; Ph.D., Illinois at Urbana-Champaign, 1965. Antennas, electromagnetic theory, computational electromagnetic scattering, microwaves, wave propagation and communication.

Chuo Q. Lee, Professor; Ph.D., IIT, 1966. Power electronics, electromagnetic field theory, ultrasound.

James C. Lin, Professor; Ph.D., Washington (Seattle), 1971. Electromagnetics in biology and medicine, biomedical instrumentation, telemedicine.

Korada R. Umashankar, Professor; Ph.D., Mississippi, 1974. Electromagnetic field theory and applications, microwave and millimeter waves, analytical and numerical techniques for electromagnetic scattering and interaction by complex materials, time-domain inverse-scattering methods.

Piergiorgio L. E. Uslenghi, Professor; Ph.D., Michigan, 1967. Electromagnetics, scattering theory, modern optics, solid-state, applied mathematics.

Hung-Yu Yang, Assistant Professor; Ph.D., UCLA, 1988. Applied electromagnetics in ferromagnetic integrated circuits and antennas, novel microstrip antennas and arrays, planar integrated transformers for power electronics, advanced computational techniques.

Graphics and Interactive Systems

Thomas A. DeFanti, Professor; Ph.D., Ohio State, 1973. Computer graphics and video animation, virtual reality, electronic art, educational technology, operating systems, scientific and volume visualization, networks, parallel computers, supercomputers.

Robert V. Kenyon, Associate Professor; Ph.D., Berkeley, 1978. Human visual and motor systems, human spatial orientation, computer graphics and display technology, virtual environments, flight simulation, spaceflight and human adaptation.

Thomas G. Moher, Associate Professor; Ph.D., Minnesota, 1983. Human-computer interaction, programming environments, cognitive models.

Signal and Image Processing

Rashid Ansari, Associate Professor; Ph.D., Princeton, 1981. Image/video processing, coding, transmission, layered video coding schemes for ATM networks, packet video transmissions, theoretical work on general framework for multirate processing of two-dimensional signals.

Jezekiel Ben-Arie, Associate Professor; Ph.D., Technion (Israel), 1986. Object and target recognition, image understanding and processing, shape and signal representation, wavelets and nonorthogonal expansions, neural networks, biomedical engineering.

Earl E. Gose, Professor; Ph.D., Berkeley, 1960. Pattern recognition and image processing with applications of medical images and industrial inspection techniques.

Daniel Graupe, Professor; Ph.D., Liverpool, 1963. Control systems, time-series analysis, signal processing, neural networks, wavelets and electrical stimulation.

Bin He, Assistant Professor; Ph.D., Tokyo Institute of Technology, 1988. Imaging systems, signal and image processing, bioelectric phenomena.

Arye Nehorai, Professor; Ph.D., Stanford, 1983. Signal and image processing, biomedicine and communications.

Roland Priemer, Associate Professor; Ph.D., IIT, 1969. Optimal and adaptive digital signal processing, digital filters, control systems, microprocessor-based system design.

Dan Schonfeld, Associate Professor; Ph.D., Johns Hopkins, 1990. Signal and image processing, pattern recognition, and computer vision.

Software Engineering

Ugo A. Buy, Associate Professor; Ph.D., Massachusetts, 1990. Software engineering, concurrency and real-time analysis.

Carl K. Chang, Associate Professor; Ph.D., Northwestern, 1982. Software engineering: specification, verification, and validation; testing: real-time systems, distributed computer systems, telecommunication software, and object-oriented methods.

Tadao Murata, Professor; Ph.D., Illinois at Urbana-Champaign, 1966. Petri net modeling and analysis of concurrent computer systems.

Sol M. Shatz, Associate Professor; Ph.D., Northwestern, 1983. Distributed computing systems, software engineering, operating systems.

Jeffrey J. P. Tsai, Associate Professor; Ph.D., Northwestern, 1986. Knowledge-based software systems, artificial intelligence, expert systems, requirements specification language, distributed real-time software testing, debugging, and software metrics.

Solid State and Microfabrication

Davorin Babic, Assistant Professor; Ph.D., Pennsylvania, 1988. Physical principles of nanoscale Si particles, their modeling and application to optical modulator, physics and chemistry of silicon interfaces and surfaces.

Alan D. Feinerman, Associate Professor; Ph.D., Northwestern, 1987. Miniaturization of the scanning electron microscope, linear accelerator/undulator and other analytical instruments, 3-D fabrication techniques.

Gary D. Friedman, Associate Professor; Ph.D., Maryland, 1989. Electromagnetics, magnetic and dielectric materials, microfabrication.

Peter J. Hesketh, Associate Professor; Ph.D., Pennsylvania, 1987. Solid-state sensors and actuators, biosensors and microfabrication.

G. Jordan Maclay, Associate Professor; Ph.D., Yale, 1972. Microsensors and microfabricated devices, quantum devices and micromachining.

David L. Naylor, Associate Professor; Ph.D., USC, 1988. Development and application of microfabricated photonic materials and devices, diffractive optics: design, fabrication, and systems applications.

Theory and Algorithms

Gianfranco Bilardi, Professor; Ph.D., Illinois at Urbana-Champaign, 1985. Parallel processing, VLSI architectures and systems, signal processing, physical limitations to computing systems.

A. Prasad Sistla, Associate Professor; Ph.D., Harvard, 1989. Distributed systems, semantics and verification of concurrent systems and database management systems.

Robert H. Sloan, Associate Professor; Ph.D., MIT, 1989. Design and analysis of algorithms, computational learning theory, machine learning, cryptography, software engineering, analysis of real-time programs, automatic program verification.

UNIVERSITY OF ILLINOIS
AT URBANA—CHAMPAIGN

DEPARTMENT OF ELECTRICAL AND COMPUTER ENGINEERING

PROGRAMS OF STUDY

Graduate work in the Department of Electrical and Computer Engineering is offered in four general areas: circuits and systems, which includes control, power and communication systems, and networks; computers and information systems, which includes computer architecture, computational complexity, fault-tolerant computing, VLSI systems, digital signal and image processing, coding and information theory, and artificial intelligence; electromagnetic fields, including aeronomy, the upper atmosphere and ionosphere, antennas, holography, propagation, and radio and optical remote sensing; and physical and quantum electronics, which includes the areas of semiconductor devices, optical electronics, nanoelectronics, electrophysics, charged particles, and gaseous electronics and plasmas. In addition to conducting work in these areas, many faculty members and graduate students in electrical engineering participate in interdisciplinary programs in other departments and laboratories, including bioengineering, biophysics, computer systems, decision and control, nuclear engineering, radio astronomy, and electronic music. The M.S. and the Ph.D. are awarded; each requires an acceptable thesis.

Classes are generally small, with approximately 30 students in a class. The graduate students are more or less equally divided among the four general areas, with a smaller number of students in the interdisciplinary areas.

RESEARCH FACILITIES

The Department of Electrical and Computer Engineering has extensive state-of-the-art laboratories and facilities for research in the areas of acoustics, aeronomy, the upper atmosphere and ionosphere, antennas and electromagnetic theory, bioengineering, bioacoustics, computer-aided design of VLSI systems, control systems, electrophysics, fusion technology, laser physics and molecular spectroscopy, gaseous electronics and plasmas, optical electronics, power and energy systems, radio astronomy, radio-wave propagation, and semiconductors and solid-state devices, including molecular beam epitaxy, metalorganic chemical vapor deposition, and scanning tunneling microscopy–based nanofabrication. The department is also the home of multiple national research centers, which include the NSF Engineering Research Center for Compound Microelectronics (ERC), the NSF Center for Computational Electronics, the ARPA Center for Optoelectronic Science and Technology (COST), the Air Force Center for Computational Electromagnetics, and the Army Federated Laboratory for Human-Computer Interface.

FINANCIAL AID

Various forms of financial aid are available, including University and industrial fellowships. Fellowships range from $5000 to $15,000 per academic year. They are normally tax-free and include exemption from tuition and fees. Many provide dependency allowances.

Part-time teaching and research assistantships are available; for 1997–98, a half-time teaching assistantship pays a minimum of $11,080 for nine months, plus exemption from tuition and fees. Other assistantships with differing degrees of work responsibility are available.

COST OF STUDY

For students who have fellowships or staff appointments of 25 percent to 67 percent time, tuition and fees are waived and only the health and insurance fee of $532 per semester must be paid. Full-time students without appointments or tuition and fee waivers paid $2563 per semester in 1996–97 if they were Illinois residents, $5740 per semester if they were nonresidents. Summer session charges were $1618 for residents and $3604 for nonresidents. These amounts are subject to upward revision.

LIVING AND HOUSING COSTS

For single students, University graduate residence halls have double rooms for $2180 and $2600 per academic year. Board is an additional $3104 per academic year. Married student housing rents for $349 to $489 per month (gas and electricity are not included). These amounts are subject to upward revision. Privately owned rooms and apartments are available at similar and higher rents.

STUDENT GROUP

There are approximately 450 graduate students in the Department of Electrical and Computer Engineering. The 88 budgeted faculty members and the graduate students come from all over the United States and the world. There are approximately 2,000 students enrolled in the undergraduate and graduate programs.

LOCATION

The University is located 130 miles south of Chicago in the twin cities of Urbana and Champaign. Willard Airport, Amtrak, and three interstate highways provide rapid access to all points. Many cultural and recreational facilities are available that would normally be found only in a very large city. The cities have an excellent public school system, with thirty-four elementary and secondary schools.

THE UNIVERSITY AND THE DEPARTMENT

Each year the University Star Course series brings outstanding entertainers to the campus, many of whom perform in the $20-million Krannert Center for the Performing Arts, while others appear in the 16,000-seat Assembly Hall. Allerton Park, a 1,500-acre estate owned by the University, is one of a group of public parks and recreation areas. Many conferences and symposia are held in Allerton's lovely and graceful setting.

Because of the extended nature of the research programs in electrical and computer engineering, the department's activities are housed in a number of buildings on the Urbana campus, including the Everitt Laboratory, the Computer and Systems Research Laboratory, the Gaseous Electronics Laboratory, and the Microelectronics Laboratory. In addition, the department has research sites within 30 miles of the campus for research programs that require isolation from electromagnetic interference. A large proportion of the graduate students are engaged in work on the research projects of the department. Other graduate students assist in the undergraduate teaching program. The department cooperates closely with the Departments of Physics, Mathematics, Computer Science, Music, and Physiology and Biophysics and with the Beckman Institute for Advanced Science and Technology, the Coordinated Science Laboratory, the Materials Research Laboratory, the Atmospheric Research Laboratory, and the National Center for Supercomputing Applications, in order to complement the interdisciplinary programs. The University is an affirmative action, equal opportunity employer.

APPLYING

Information and application forms are available upon request. Applicants are required to take the General Test of the Graduate Record Examinations. Applications must be completed by January 15 for August admission. Awards are announced April 1. Applications for January admission are due by October 1, and awards are announced November 15. Women and members of minority groups are encouraged to apply.

CORRESPONDENCE AND INFORMATION

N. Narayana Rao, Associate Head
Department of Electrical and Computer Engineering
University of Illinois at Urbana-Champaign
1406 West Green Street
Urbana, Illinois 61801
Telephone: 217-333-2302 or 0207

UNIVERSITY OF ILLINOIS AT URBANA–CHAMPAIGN
THE FACULTY AND THEIR RESEARCH

Professors

I. Adesida: semiconductor electronics, microfabrication technology. N. Ahuja: computer vision, robotics, artificial intelligence. M. T. Basar: control systems, dynamic games, stochastic control and estimation. S. Bishop: semiconductor physics, optical spectroscopy. M. Blahut: signal processing, digital communications systems, statistical information processing. R. Campbell: software engineering, operating systems. K. Y. Cheng: molecular beam epitaxy, optoelectronic devices and integrated circuits, high-speed devices. W. C. Chew: electromagnetic scattering, geophysical probing, remote sensing, microwave integrated circuits. A. Y. Cho: semiconductors. S. L. Chuang: electromagnetics, integrated optics, quantum electronics. J. J. Coleman: semiconductor materials and devices. G. DeJong: artificial intelligence, natural-language processing, machine learning. T. A. DeTemple: quantum electronics. J. G. Eden: laser physics, quantum electronics, molecular spectroscopy, semiconductors. M. Feng: high-frequency and high-speed integrated circuits. S. J. Franke: wave propagation, remote sensing, microwaves. L. A. Frizzell: ultrasonic biophysics, bioengineering. C. S. Gardner: optical communications, laser radar, fiber optic systems. G. Gross: power and energy systems. B. E. Hajek: communication networks, stochastic process. I. N. Hajj: computer-aided design, VLSI circuits and systems. K. Hess: semiconductors. N. Holonyak Jr.: solid-state devices (semiconductors). T. S. Huang: computers and pattern recognition. W.-M. Hwu: computer architecture. R. K. Iyer: computers, reliability and fault tolerance, measurement and experimentation. W. K. Jenkins: circuits and signal analysis. S. M. Kang: reliable VLSI circuits, computer-aided design and layout of VLSI, device and circuit modeling of high-speed IC. K. Kim: fusion plasma engineering, lasers, charged-particle dynamics. W. J. Kubitz: computers. E. Kudeki: radar studies of the atmosphere and ionosphere, ionospheric plasmas. P. R. Kumar: systems and control theory, stochastic systems. M. Kushner: simulation in plasma physics. D. H. Lawrie: high-performance computer architecture and software. P. Lauterbur: medical information sciences. J. P. Leburton: theory of semiconductor devices. C. L. Liu: computer-aided design of integrated circuits. J. W. S. Liu: computer networks, distributed systems, databases, software engineering. M. C. Loui: parallel and distributed computation, computational complexity theory. J. W. Lyding: charge transport properties, reduced-dimensional materials and devices. R. L. Magin: bioengineering. J. V. Medanic: systems analysis, multivariable control systems. G. H. Miley: fusion, high-temperature plasmas, energy conversion. D. C. Munson Jr.: digital signal and image processing. S. Muroga: logic design of computers, computer-aided design. B. Oakley II: bioengineering. W. D. O'Brien Jr.: biological effects, bioengineering, biophysics, measurements and dosimetry of ultrasound. M. A. Pai: power and energy systems. J. H. Patel: computers. W. R. Perkins: control systems, systems theory and applications. D. Pines: condensed-matter theory, theoretical astrophysics. C. Polychronopoulos: computer systems. P. L. Ransom: holography, optical processing. N. N. Rao: ionosphere, radio-wave propagation. U. Ravaioli: simulation and plasma physics. S. R. Ray: computers. D. V. Sarwate: communication theory, error-control coding. P. W. Sauer: power and energy systems. P. D. Schomer: architectural acoustics, special measurements, noise control, environmental noise. B. S. Song: integrated circuits. M. W. Spong: control theory, robotics. G. E. Stillman: semiconductors, physics and device physics. G. Swenson: atmospheric remote sensing, atmospheric dynamics and chemistry, space environment measurements and modeling. T. N. Trick: integrated circuits, computer-aided analysis and design. J. R. Tucker: superconductive devices. R. J. Turnbull: energy conversion technology. P. Van Dooren: digital signal processing, image processing. B. W. Wah: computer architecture, parallel processing, computer networks, distributed databases, artificial intelligence, operating systems, VLSI systems. P. Yang: 2-D and 3-D device simulation, parallel processing, new algorithms for advanced circuit simulation.

Associate Professors

J. Bentsman: automatic control systems. D. Brady: optics, artificial neural networks, volume holographic information processing using photorefractive crystals. Y. Bresler: signal and image processing. D. J. Brown: VLSI design, analysis of algorithms. A. Chien: concurrent computer systems. K. Hsieh: characterization and development of optoelectronic materials growth. S. Hutchinson: robotics, computer vision. J. Jin: computational electromagnetics, MRI instrumentation. D. L. Jones: signal and image processing. L. Kale: design of parallel execution schemes and architectures for unpredictably structured computations. T. Kerkhoven: semiconductor simulation, mathematical analysis of algorithms for physical problems, nonlinear partial differential equations, scientific computation. P. T. Krein: power electronics. H. Merkelo: quantum electronics, optical electronics, lasers, luminescence. S. Meyn: communications, stochastic control theory. H. Morkoc: high-speed devices. F. Najm: circuits. T. Overbye: power and energy systems. G. Papen: optical information processing, quantum optics, application of nonlinear wave mixing. J. Ponce: computer vision, robotics. L. Rendell: artificial intelligence, probabilistic learning. W. H. Sanders: computers, performance/dependability evaluation, fault-tolerant computing, computer networks and protocols. J. Schutt-Aine: electromagnetic measurements, computer-controlled measurements. A. Vardy: coding theory, decoding algorithms, modulation codes for storage systems. B. C. Wheeler: bioengineering, sensor arrays, neural recording.

Assistant Professors

B. Bamieh: robust control, intelligent control. D. Beebe: microelectromechanical systems for biological applications, including tactile interfaces and microfluidic instruments. R. M. Fish: bioengineering, bioacoustics. Z.-P. Liang: MRI and spectroscopy techniques, image processing and neural networks. C. Liu: microfabrication, integrated sensors and actuators, microelectromechanical systems. U. Madhow: communication systems, communication networks, wireless channels. E. Michielssen: electromagnetic simulation, high-speed circuits. P. Moulin: signal processing. K. Ramchandran: image processing, video compression. E. Rosenbaum: reliability physics, IC reliability. N. Shanbag: VLSI design, algorithm development, signal processing. J. Torellas: computer architecture, memory hierarchies, parallel processing. B. Vaduvur: computer engineering. A. Webb: MRI, temperature measurement. Y. Zhao: signal processing, automatic speech recognition, human-computer interaction.

Lecturers

T. Basar: communication systems. R. B. Uribe: cybernetics and digital systems. P. E. Weston: computers. J. Zhang: electronic circuits.

UNIVERSITY OF IOWA

DEPARTMENT OF COMPUTER SCIENCE

PROGRAMS OF STUDY

Graduate programs leading to Doctor of Philosophy and Master of Science degrees are offered.

The Ph.D. program requires demonstrated excellence in research and superior comprehension of the discipline. Students complete a minimum of 72 semester hours of credit (including 18 semester hours of research) pursuing a program of course work that concentrates on a well-defined specialty area. In addition, they take a two-part comprehensive examination (the second part in the specialty area), and, most important, execute a significant research project that culminates in a dissertation. Ph.D. candidates need not take an M.S. degree but may acquire one as part of their Ph.D. program.

The separate M.S. program requires at least 30 semester hours of academic work, which may include 6 semester hours of thesis research or 12 semester hours for a subtrack in software engineering. Students not defending a thesis as a final examination must pass an exam that is a culmination of the student's work in the form of a written report and an oral presentation of an independently performed study on a student-selected topic.

Graduates from either degree program are well prepared for careers in education or industry.

RESEARCH FACILITIES

Departmental facilities include an 8-processor Silicon Graphics Onyx; ten SGI graphic workstations; eight IBM RS/6000 workstations; thirty 700 Series HP workstations plus many X-terminals, Macintoshes, and PCs; two PUMA 562 robots; high-speed image-processing hardware; and computer-controlled video equipment.

An extensive library is provided in the building.

FINANCIAL AID

The department offers financial aid in various forms, including research assistantships, teaching assistantships, and teaching-research fellowships. The criteria used in awarding aid are generally the same as for admission for new students. A total of approximately fifty half-time appointments are supported each year. Other departments seeking computer expertise support numerous other computer science students. Computer science stipends range from $11,500 to approximately $14,000 for a half-time appointment for the academic year. Students holding a graduate appointment pay tuition at the Iowa resident rate.

COST OF STUDY

For the academic year 1997–98, full-time graduate students (those taking 9 or more credits) who are residents of Iowa pay annual tuition of $3048; nonresident full-time annual tuition is $9820. Part-time tuition ranges from $680 (1–2 credits) to $2720 (8 credits) for Iowa residents and from $680 to $8736 for nonresidents.

LIVING AND HOUSING COSTS

The monthly rent for University-owned housing, available for married students and single parents, ranges between $187 and $353. A large number of privately owned apartments are available in the community. Students living off campus typically pay between $400 and $700 per month for food and rent. The University Housing Office can supply additional information.

STUDENT GROUP

The student body consists of approximately 28,000 students, including 6,700 enrolled in graduate programs. Nearly 70 percent come from Iowa, 17 percent from adjoining states, and 6 percent from the remaining states. International students from ninety-three countries make up 7 percent of the University's enrollment. The graduate enrollment in computer science is approximately 115 students.

LOCATION

The University is located on 900 acres of rolling land along the Iowa River. More than 100 major structures dot the campus, most within walking distance of each other and all fully accessible to those with physical disabilities. Iowa City offers numerous cultural and outdoor activities including restaurants, concerts, lakes, and athletic facilities.

The campus offers a wide variety of cultural and recreational activities. Several lakes and wooded recreational areas are immediately adjacent to Iowa City.

THE UNIVERSITY

The University of Iowa is a major research university and a world-class medical center. The University is a member of the Big Ten Athletic Conference, and its football and basketball programs are often nationally ranked; its program in women's sports is also a national leader. The University of Iowa was the first U. S. public university to admit men and women on an equal basis.

APPLYING

Application forms for admission and financial support, as well as additional information about the department and the M.S. and Ph.D. programs, can be obtained from the address given below. Applicants are judged on the basis of their academic record, specific computer science background, and GRE scores. The GRE Subject Test in computer science is required, and a good score on it can strengthen the application of a student whose academic performance or breadth of background might otherwise seem inadequate.

Prospective applicants are encouraged to consult informally with members of the graduate faculty and, if possible, visit the campus to meet with faculty and graduate students.

CORRESPONDENCE AND INFORMATION

Director of the Graduate Program
Department of Computer Science
14 MacLean Hall
University of Iowa
Iowa City, Iowa 52242
Telephone: 319-335-0713
E-mail: gradinfo@cs.uiowa.edu
World Wide Web: http://www.cs.uiowa.edu

UNIVERSITY OF IOWA
THE FACULTY AND THEIR RESEARCH

Donald A. Alton, Professor; Ph.D., Cornell, 1970. Database management systems, object-oriented databases, semantic data modeling.

Robert J. Baron, Professor; Ph.D., Cornell, 1968. Brain theory, perception, vision, movement control.

Maria-Paola Bonacina, Assistant Professor; Ph.D., SUNY at Stony Brook, 1992. Automated reasoning, problem solving in distributed systems, term rewriting systems, logic programming.

Steven C. Bruell, Professor and Chairman; Ph.D., Purdue, 1978. Queueing network and petri net models of computer systems, operating and computer system theory, distributed systems, simulation.

James Cremer, Associate Professor; Ph.D., Cornell, 1989. Physical system simulation, software systems and programming environments, symbolic computation.

William F. Decker, Adjunct Associate Professor; M.S., Iowa, 1968. Data communications, protocols and network architectures, software engineering methodology.

Donald L. Epley, Professor; Ph.D., Illinois, 1960. Real-time systems, network protocols, distributed control algorithms.

Arthur C. Fleck, Professor; Ph.D., Michigan State, 1964. Data abstraction, programming languages, formal languages, automata theory.

Margaret M. Fleck, Assistant Professor; Ph.D., MIT, 1988. Computer vision, robotics, mathematical models, computational linguistics, natural language processing.

Sukumar Ghosh, Professor; Ph.D., Calcutta, 1971. Distributed systems, synchronization, fault-tolerance, petri nets, computer architecture.

Ted Herman, Assistant Professor; Ph.D., Texas at Austin, 1991. Reliable software construction, distributed computing, verification, programming languages, information systems.

Douglas W. Jones, Associate Professor; Ph.D., Illinois, 1980. Discrete event simulation, resource protection in architecture, operating systems and system programming languages.

Joseph Kearney, Professor; Ph.D., Minnesota, 1983. Animation, graphics, virtual environments, computer vision, robotics.

Gregg Oden, Professor; Ph.D., California, San Diego, 1974. Models of cognition, psycholinguistics, artificial intelligence.

Florian Potra, Professor (joint appointment with Mathematics); Ph.D., Bucharest (Romania), 1980. Numerical optimization, numerical solution of differential equations, parallel algorithms.

Teodor Rus, Professor; Ph.D., Romanian Academy, 1965. Formal tools for language specification, technology for compiler design and implementation, operating system design and implementation, parallel programming.

Alberto Segre, Adjunct Associate Professor; Ph.D., Illinois, 1987. Artificial intelligence, machine learning, planning and scheduling, theorem proving.

Kenneth Slonneger, Assistant Professor; Ph.D., Illinois, 1971. Programming language semantics, functional programming, logic programming.

Hantao Zhang, Associate Professor; Ph.D., Rensselaer, 1988. Automatic theorem proving, rewriting systems, equational specifications, software and hardware design verification.

The scenic Iowa River intersects the campus.

Old Capitol, center of the University of Iowa campus.

MacLean Hall, home of the Department of Computer Science.

UNIVERSITY OF KANSAS

DEPARTMENT OF ELECTRICAL ENGINEERING AND COMPUTER SCIENCE
PROGRAMS IN ELECTRICAL ENGINEERING AND COMPUTER SCIENCE

PROGRAM OF STUDY

The Department of Electrical Engineering and Computer Science at the University of Kansas offers graduate programs of study and research leading to the degrees of M.S., Ph.D., and D.E. in electrical engineering and the M.S. and Ph.D. in computer science.

Specializations include algorithms, artificial intelligence, computer-aided design, computer systems, digital signal processing, distributed and parallel computing, electromagnetics, expert systems, graphics, high-speed networking, image processing, information retrieval, information systems, language processing, lightwave systems, performance modeling and analysis, programming languages, radar remote sensing, radar systems, semiconductor processing, telecommunications, theory of computing, and wireless communications.

The M.S. programs require 30 semester hours of graduate work with thesis and nonthesis options. The Ph.D. programs require 24 hours of course work beyond the M.S. and 18 hours of dissertation. The D.E. program requires 30 hours of course work beyond the M.S. and 12 to 18 hours of industrial internship.

RESEARCH FACILITIES

Almost all of the graduate research is conducted using facilities of four major laboratories: the Telecommunications and Information Sciences Laboratory (TISL), the Radar Systems and Remote Sensing Laboratory (RSL), The Center for Excellence in Computer-Aided Systems Engineering (CECASE), and the Design Technologies Laboratory (DesignLab).

All research is supported by an extensive network of workstations. Special facilities include a multigigabit experimental telecommunications network called "MAGIC," radar systems ranging from VHF through 140 GHz and lightwaves, wide-screen wall-panel graphics, and a new scalable multiprocessor computer for research in computer-aided design and graphics computing.

FINANCIAL AID

Fellowships, research assistantships, teaching assistantships, graduate assistantships, and scholarships are available to the best qualified applicants. Teaching assistants receive a tuition waiver, and research assistants receive resident tuition. The department offers a competitive package of financial support. More than 135 of the graduate students receive some support.

COST OF STUDY

During the 1997–98 academic year, tuition and fees are estimated at $94 per credit hour for residents and at $309 per credit hour for nonresidents. An equipment fee of $15 per credit hour is assessed on all School of Engineering students and is used solely for student-accessible laboratory equipment.

LIVING AND HOUSING COSTS

Housing is available both on and off campus. Lawrence is a relatively inexpensive place to live compared to the national average.

STUDENT GROUP

There are approximately 160 graduate students in the department, including 40 in doctoral programs. The student body is composed of both traditional and nontraditional students, who may also be engaged in industry or the military. The student population is diverse, coming from all parts of the world and from all parts of the United States.

LOCATION

Kansas is located in the heart of the United States. The city of Lawrence is in the eastern part of the state, and has a cosmopolitan population of 78,000 people.

THE UNIVERSITY AND THE DEPARTMENT

The University of Kansas is a major educational and research institution with nearly 29,000 students and 2,100 faculty members. The university includes the main campus in Lawrence and several satellite campuses throughout the state.

The Department of Electrical Engineering began in 1887. It has continued to grow and develop along with the state-of-the-art, incorporating programs in computer science, begun in 1967, and computer engineering, begun in 1987. The department has cutting-edge facilities and 31 faculty members who conduct research with funding exceeding $3 million per year.

APPLYING

To quality for admission, the applicant must hold a four-year baccalaureate degree or its equivalent from an accredited institution and meet other criteria demonstrating potential for success. Application forms, transcripts, GRE general test scores, three letters of recommendation, a statement of objectives, and an application fee of $30 are required. In addition, for persons whose native language is not English, a minimum TOEFL score of 600 is required. Deadlines and other details are explained in the application materials.

CORRESPONDENCE AND INFORMATION

Department of Electrical Engineering and Computer Science
Graduate Admissions
415 Snow Hall
University of Kansas
Lawrence, Kansas 66045

Telephone: 913-864-4487
Fax: 913-864-3226
E-mail: grad_admissions@eecs.ukans.edu

UNIVERSITY OF KANSAS
THE FACULTY AND THEIR RESEARCH

Christopher T. Allen, Assistant Professor; Ph.D., Kansas, 1984. Radar systems, high-speed digital circuits.

Allen L. Ambler, Associate Professor; Ph.D., Wisconsin, 1973. Programming paradigms and languages; program design principles, approaches, and tools; visual languages; end-user programming systems; scientific visualization; functionally distributed programming.

J. Michael Ashley, Assistant Professor; Ph.D., Indiana, 1995. Programming language design and implementation, static program analysis, program transformations.

Frank M. Brown, Associate Professor; Ph.D., Edinburgh, 1978. automatic deductions, artificial intelligence.

Swapan Chakrabarti, Associate Professor; Ph.D., Nebraska, 1986. Neural networks and fuzzy systems, pattern classification, signal processing.

Don G. Daugherty, Professor; Ph.D., Wisconsin, 1964. Electronic circuits for communications and control.

Raymond H. Dean, Professor; Ph.D., Princeton, 1968. Digital control, system modeling, simulation, alternative energy sources.

Kenneth R. Demarest, Associate Professor; Ph.D., Ohio State, 1980. Electromagnetic theory and computational techniques, antennas, electromagnetic interference and compatibility.

Harvey H. Doemland, Associate Professor Emeritus; Ph.D., Illinois, 1963. Electronic circuits, pulse circuits, biomedical engineering.

Joseph B. Evans, Associate Professor; Ph.D., Princeton, 1988. Networking, communications, signal processing, VLSI design.

Victor S. Frost, Professor; Ph.D., Kansas, 1982. Telecommunications, communications network control, modeling and analysis.

John M. Gauch, Assistant Professor, Ph.D., North Carolina, 1989. Image processing, computer vision, computer graphics.

Susan E. Gauch, Assistant Professor; Ph.D., North Carolina, 1990. Information retrieval, corpus linguistics, multimedia databases.

Siva Prasad Gogineni, Professor; Ph.D., Kansas, 1984. Radar systems, microwave engineering.

Jerzy W. Grzymala-Busse, Professor; Ph.D., Technical University of Poznan (Poland), 1969. Expert systems, reasoning under uncertainty, knowledge acquisition, machine learning, rough set theory.

Nancy G. Kinnersley, Associate Professor; Ph.D., Washington State, 1989. Design and analysis of algorithms, graph algorithms, discrete mathematics, tree automata, computational complexity.

Man C. Kong, Associate Professor; Ph.D., Nebraska, 1986. Design and analysis of algorithms, graph and network algorithms, parallel algorithms, combinatorial optimization, computational complexity, operations research.

James R. Miller, Associate Professor; Ph.D., Purdue, 1979. Geometric modeling and computer-aided design, computer graphics, scientific visualization, object-oriented programming.

Gary J. Minden, Associate Professor; Ph.D., Kansas, 1982. Digital systems, microprocessors, artificial intelligence.

Richard K. Moore, Distinguished Professor Emeritus; Ph.D., Cornell, 1951. Radar remote sensing, radio wave propagation, communications systems, antennas, radar imaging and backscatter systems.

Douglas Niehaus, Assistant Professor; Ph.D., Massachusetts, 1994. Operating systems, real-time and distributed systems, programming environments.

Karen J. Nordheden, Assistant Professor; Ph.D., Illinois, 1988. Plasma processing of semiconductors.

David W. Petr, Assistant Professor; Ph.D., Kansas, 1990. Communications, networking, digital signal processing.

Richard G. Plumb, Associate Professor; Ph.D., Syracuse, 1988. Electromagnetics, inverse scattering, ground-penetrating radars, antennas.

Glenn E. Prescott, Associate Professor; Ph.D., Georgia Tech, 1984. Communications theory, digital signal processing.

James A. Roberts Jr., Professor and Chair; Ph.D., Santa Clara, 1979. Telecommunications, information theory, wireless communications.

James R. Rowland, Professor; Ph.D., Purdue, 1966. Stochastic systems modeling and analysis, control systems, radar detection and estimation.

Dale I. Rummer, Professor Emeritus; Ph.D., Kansas, 1963. Design of digital systems, design of microprocessor-based systems, computer-aided design tools.

Earl J. Schweppe, Professor; Ph.D., Illinois, 1955. Computer architecture, computer organization, computer history, personal computers, computer communications, interactive systems, concurrent processes, computer science curriculum.

K. Sam Shanmugan, Southwestern Bell Distinguished Professor; Ph.D., Oklahoma State, 1970. Telecommunications, pattern recognition, general systems theory, statistical communications theory, image processing, digital signal processing techniques.

William P. Smith, Professor Emeritus; Ph.D., Texas, 1950. Electrical power systems and alternate energy sources.

James M. Stiles, Assistant Professor; Ph.D., Michigan, 1995. Radar remote-sensing, propagation and scattering in random media, electromagnetic theory.

Harry E. Talley, Professor Emeritus; Ph.D., Kansas, 1954. Semiconductor devices, solid-state physics and electronics.

Costas Tsatsoulis, Associate Professor; Ph.D., Purdue, 1987. Artificial intelligence, expert systems.

Hillel Unz, Professor Emeritus; Ph.D., Berkeley, 1957. Electromagnetic theory, antenna arrays, plasma propagation, acoustic waves, applied mathematics.

Victor L. Wallace, Professor; Ph.D., Michigan, 1969. Operating systems, computer graphics, user-machine interaction, computer networks, distributed systems, queuing theory, numerical analysis, performance evaluation.

UNIVERSITY OF KENTUCKY

DEPARTMENT OF COMPUTER SCIENCE

PROGRAMS OF STUDY

The Department of Computer Science offers the Master of Science and Doctor of Philosophy degrees. Two years of study are usually required for the M.S. degree and four or more years for the Ph.D.

Two master's options are available. Students may either complete 24 hours of course work and write a thesis, which often involves a major implementation of existing algorithms but can also contain original research, or they may complete 30 hours of course work and complete a project. The project often involves software development. Three credit hours of course work may be devoted to the project. Both options require a final examination directed by a committee chaired by the thesis or project director.

Ph.D. candidates must demonstrate reading proficiency in any natural language other than their native tongue. The Ph.D. program includes a qualifying examination with both written and oral parts, typically completed by the end of the third year of study. The written part includes two general examinations in approved areas and one that covers the major area in detail. The final step toward the degree is preparing and defending a dissertation that displays independent research.

All students must take the problem seminar course and must pass foundational examinations to demonstrate breadth of knowledge at the undergraduate level in the areas of theory and algorithms, numerical methods, and systems.

RESEARCH FACILITIES

The Department of Computer Science has an excellent research computing facility composed mostly of SPARCstations running UNIX (Solaris). These machines include SPARCstation 20 (thirty machines, 125MHz/64M), SPARCstation 5 (ten machines, 80MHz/32M), and SPARCclassics (two machines). The department also has DecStation 3000/400 (one), IBM RS 6000 (two), SGI Power Challenge (one with eight R10000 CPUs), SGI Indy (four), SGI Indigo (two), and PCs (eight, mostly Pentium); all run UNIX versions as well. The department regularly upgrades to the most recent stable versions of the operating systems except when older versions are needed for research. The University provides high-end computing on its 32-processor Convex Exemplar computer, but the department's research generally does not require this machine.

The CS department owns and operates the MultiLab instructional facility, composed of twenty-two PC clones (Pentium 1000/32M/1.6G). One acts as a file server and the others can be rebooted by students to run Windows NT, OS/2 Warp, or Linux. Students are allowed to modify test versions of the Linux kernel.

CS students have access to the SunLab, which has thirty SPARCstations. Graduate students often use the Engineering Computing Center, which has several Sun and HP machines running UNIX. Undergraduates usually get an account on the Student Access Computer, which is an HP K200 (2 CPUs, 768M/24G/UNIX).

The department has exceptional networking facilities. Fast Ethernet (100 Mbps) serves as the primary network connection for most machines. In addition, an ATM network consisting of seven FORE and CISCO ATM switches connects the machines in three labs. A CISCO 7000 router connects the research labs and the CS department and also ties directly into the campus backbone FDDI network. The research networks are also connected to a high-speed ATM network called the SEPSCoR network, which connects the flagship universities of six southeastern states. A recent NSF award will also connect the department's research networks to the NSF vBNS backbone via a DS3 connection.

FINANCIAL AID

Teaching assistantships and research assistantships are available through the department. In 1996–97 these have stipends of about $10,700–$11,100 for 20 hours of work per week. Graduate assistants are nominated for partial or full tuition scholarships offered by the Graduate School. Teaching assistants usually teach introductory courses, and research assistants lend support to research projects. Half assistantships, which provide half the stipend, are also granted. Competitive fellowships are available through the department, the Graduate School, and the University. Fellowships usually include payment of tuition. Part-time employment opportunities are abundant on campus.

COST OF STUDY

Full-time tuition, including all fees, is $2976 for in-state students and $8256 for out-of-state students for the 1997–98 academic year (two semesters).

LIVING AND HOUSING COSTS

There is extensive on-campus graduate housing, both for single students and for families. On-campus graduate student apartment housing ranges from $305 per month for a single/efficiency to $520 per month for a two-bedroom. Numerous apartments are also available within walking distance of campus.

STUDENT GROUP

The department has approximately 405 undergraduates, 47 master's degree students, and 23 Ph.D. students. About 15 percent of the graduate students are women; approximately 50 percent are American. The largest international groups are Indian (20 percent) and Chinese (25 percent). Twenty-four students have teaching assistantships, 15 have research assistantships, and 4 have competitive fellowships.

LOCATION

The University is in the heart of the beautiful Bluegrass region. The Appalachian mountains are several hours to the east, and many scenic parks are within an easy drive of the city. Lexington, with a population of about 230,000, is a thriving community whose major industries are the University and Lexmark. No heavy industry exists in the area, and the city is becoming more cosmopolitan yearly. There is fairly good theater, a ballet company, and an orchestra. Two tracks (harness and flat) and the Kentucky Horse Park (steeplechase and polo) provide equine attractions, but the major spectator sport is the University's nationally ranked basketball team. Both Louisville and Cincinnati are within a 2 hours' drive.

THE UNIVERSITY

The University of Kentucky, with a total enrollment of more than 23,000 students (of whom 20 percent are graduate students), is the flagship educational institution in Kentucky. It places a high priority on educational training at the postdoctoral, graduate, and undergraduate levels. The Carnegie Foundation classified it as a Research I University in 1987, placing it among the top forty-five public research institutions in the nation.

APPLYING

Application are processed throughout the year, and students may enter at the beginning of any semester. Applications for fall semester are due February 1 for international students and for those wishing to be considered for fellowships. Applications from students applying for assistantships are due by March 1. All application materials (two official transcripts, GRE scores, and various forms) must be on file by those dates. International applicants whose native language is not English must satisfactorily complete the TOEFL. Additional information can be received by sending e-mail to csgradpro@cs.engr.uky.edu with the subject line INFORMATION REQUEST.

CORRESPONDENCE AND INFORMATION

For application forms:

The Graduate School
351 Patterson Office Tower
University of Kentucky
Lexington, Kentucky 40506-0027
Telephone: 606-257-4613

For Computer Science information:

DGS, Department of Computer Science
773 Anderson Hall
University of Kentucky
Lexington, Kentucky 40506-0046
Telephone: 606-257-4997
E-mail: csgradpro@cs.engr.uky.edu (subject: Info Request)
World Wide Web: http://www.cs.engr.uky.edu

UNIVERSITY OF KENTUCKY
THE FACULTY AND THEIR RESEARCH

Anthony Q. Baxter, Associate Professor and Associate Chairman; Ph.D., Virginia, 1973. Programming and systems, performance monitoring and evaluation, database systems. (e-mail: tony@cs.engr.uky.edu)

Yuri Breitbart, Professor; Ph.D., Technion (Israel), 1973. Distributed database systems, query optimization in heterogeneous distributed database environments, databases and logic. (e-mail: yuri@cs.engr.uky.edu)

Fuhua Cheng, Associate Professor; Ph.D., Ohio State, 1982. Computer-aided geometric design, computer graphics, numerical analysis. (e-mail: cheng@cs.engr.uky.edu)

Duncan Clarke, Assistant Professor; Ph.D., Pennsylvania, 1996. Real-time systems, tools and techniques for applying formal methods, systems software. (e-mail: dclarke@cs.engr.uky.edu)

Raphael A. Finkel, Professor; Ph.D., Stanford, 1976. Operating systems, distributed algorithms, programming languages. (e-mail: raphael@cs.engr.uky.edu)

Judy Goldsmith, Assistant Professor; Ph.D., Wisconsin, 1988. Structural complexity. (e-mail: goldsmit@cs.engr.uky.edu)

James Griffioen, Assistant Professor; Ph.D., Purdue, 1991. Computer networks, operating systems. (e-mail: griff@cs.engr.uky.edu)

J. Robert Heath, Associate Professor; Ph.D., Auburn, 1973. Computer engineering, digital signal processing, software engineering. (Joint appointment with Electrical Engineering) (e-mail: ele185@ukcc.uky.edu)

Jerzy W. Jaromczyk, Associate Professor; Ph.D., Warsaw, 1984. Computational geometry, algorithms and applications. (e-mail: jurek@cs.engr.uky.edu)

Andrew Klapper, Assistant Professor; Ph.D., Brown, 1982. Cryptography. (e-mail: klapper@cs.engr.uky.edu)

Kenneth K. Kubota, Professor; Ph.D., Facultés des Sciences de Paris, 1969. Number theory, operating systems. (Joint appointment with Mathematics) (e-mail: ken@ms.uky.edu)

Forbes D. Lewis, Professor; Ph.D., Cornell, 1970. Computational complexity, CAD algorithms for VLSI systems. (e-mail: lewis@cs.engr.uky.edu)

Victor W. Marek, Professor; Ph.D., 1968, D.Sc., 1972, Warsaw. Logical foundations of AI, theory of databases, logic programming. (e-mail: marek@cs.engr.uky.edu)

A.C.R. Newbery, Professor; Ph.D., London 1962. Numerical analysis, interpolation. (e-mail: ode@cs.engr.uky.edu)

Brent Seales, Assistant Professor; Ph.D., Wisconsin, 1991. Image processing, graphics. (e-mail: seales@cs.engr.uky.edu)

Robert Tannenbaum, Adjunct Professor; Ed.D., Columbia, 1968. Graphics, fractals, CAI. (Joint appointment with Computing Center) (e-mail: rst@pop.uky.edu)

Mirek Truszczynski, Professor and Chairman; Ph.D., Warsaw Technical, 1980. Artificial intelligence, knowledge representation, logic programming. (e-mail: mirek@cs.engr.uky.edu)

Grzegorz W. Wasilkowski, Professor and Director of Graduate Studies; Ph.D., Warsaw, 1980. Computational complexity, numerical analysis. (e-mail: greg@cs.engr.uky.edu)

A research lab for distributed computing and ATM networking.

Anderson Hall, which houses the College of Engineering and the Department of Computer Science.

UNIVERSITY OF MARYLAND
GRADUATE SCHOOL, BALTIMORE

DEPARTMENT OF COMPUTER SCIENCE AND ELECTRICAL ENGINEERING

PROGRAMS OF STUDY

The Department of Computer Science (CS) and Electrical Engineering (EE) administers graduate programs leading to the M.S. and Ph.D. degrees and provides opportunities for studies in a broad selection of six research areas in computer science and electrical engineering. These research areas are algorithms, theory, and scientific computation; communications and signal processing; computer systems and networks; databases, information, and knowledge management; graphics, animation, and visualization; and photonics and microelectronics.

The M.S. program consists of 30 credit hours of course work with the option of either writing a scholarly paper (3 additional credit hours) and taking a comprehensive examination or writing a research thesis and taking an oral examination based on that thesis. The Ph.D. program consists of course work, comprehensive and preliminary examinations, a dissertation based on original research, and an oral examination on the dissertation.

RESEARCH FACILITIES

The department is housed in a new building devoted to engineering and computer science. The department maintains an extensive research computing facility that includes a large network of more than 50 UNIX workstations (SGI, Sun, and IBM), several large computer servers (SGI, Sun), and numerous other machines. The department is part of the University of Maryland Institute of Advanced Computer Science (UMIACS) and has access to its research facilities, including a Connection Machine CM-5. The University is a member of the San Diego Supercomputing Center Consortium through which it has access to a number of large supercomputers. The department has a number of well-equipped laboratories that support the research activities of the faculty. They include a CAIBE facility; the Advanced Information Technology Lab; a MOCVD lab; a nonlinear EM theory computations lab; the Computer Graphics, Animation, and Visualization Lab; the Crypto Lab; the Center For Telecommunications Research; the Communications and Signal Processing Lab; the DIODE Laser Lab; the Information Technology Lab; the Parallel Processing Lab; and the Remote Sensing, Signal, and Image Processing Lab.

The University's computing system for instructional and research use consists of UNIX-based and VAX/VMS multiuse systems. These include a new 20-processor SGI Challenge XL UNIX system augmented by two SGI Crimsons, seventy-three Indigo graphic workstations, and a new VAX 4000 model 500. The College of Engineering has also recently acquired a Cray System model YMP-EL. In addition, UMBC is a component of the larger University of Maryland Instructional and Research Computer Network, which provides access to computers at other University of Maryland campuses. From UMBC, users may communicate with other researchers on a national and international basis via BITNET and Internet.

UMBC's library ranks among the nation's leading university libraries in providing automated-enhanced systems. There is an integrated on-line catalog and circulation system that also provides access to the holdings at other University of Maryland libraries, the Uncover database of journal articles, and other databases. There are 550,000 monographs and bound periodicals as well as a current standing subscription order for 4,000 journals. Library patrons can request interlibrary loans from other Maryland campuses through the on-line catalog. The library staff also places requests for books and articles nationally, through the OCLC system.

FINANCIAL AID

Research and teaching assistantships are available for well-qualified applicants. In 1997–98, stipends range from $10,249 to $13,770, plus tuition, for ten months. Graduate School fellowships are offered, as well as fellowships and grants-in-aid for eligible students from minority groups.

COST OF STUDY

In 1997–98, tuition is $212 per credit hour for Maryland residents and $382 per credit hour for nonresidents. Fees of approximately $125 per semester are also levied.

LIVING AND HOUSING COSTS

UMBC housing and board in campus apartments for graduate students cost approximately $1390, plus utilities, per semester for the 1997–98 academic year. Off-campus housing is available at varying rates.

STUDENT GROUP

The department has 200 graduate students (120 CS and 80 EE), including 112 full-time students and 80 Ph.D. students. UMBC has a graduate enrollment of 1,600 students.

LOCATION

UMBC is located on a 488-acre site adjacent to the Baltimore Beltway at Catonsville, in suburban Baltimore County, south of Baltimore city. Exit 47 off Interstate 95 leads directly to the campus. UMBC is conveniently located near both Baltimore and Washington, D.C., and is able to benefit from the immense concentration of academic, government, cultural, and recreational facilities in these urban centers.

THE UNIVERSITY AND THE DEPARTMENT

UMBC is the newest campus in the University of Maryland system. It was founded in 1966 and was designed to offer the greater Baltimore area a major public research university. Currently, it has approximately 10,700 students enrolled in undergraduate and graduate programs. The department's full-time faculty of 24 has substantial industrial experience. A large number of research scientists and engineers from local industry and government laboratories serve as visiting and part-time faculty members. Several international scientists serve as visiting and research faculty members.

APPLYING

In addition to the completed application form and official college transcripts, applicants should have three letters of recommendation submitted on their behalf. A score on the Graduate Record Examinations General Test (school code 5835) is also required. Applicants whose native language is not English must take the TOEFL (Test of English as a Foreign Language). Application deadlines are specified by the Graduate School, but the review process begins by December 15 for admission in the fall semester and by June 15 for admission in the following spring. The application fee is $40. Potential candidates are encouraged to obtain more details via the World Wide Web and to fill out the free on-line preapplication.

CORRESPONDENCE AND INFORMATION

For information on programs or assistantships:
Director, Graduate Program
Department of Computer Science and
  Electrical Engineering
University of Maryland Baltimore County
1000 Hilltop Circle
Baltimore, Maryland 21250
Voice mail: 410-455-3500
Fax: 410-455-3969 or 1048
E-mail: cmscgrad@csee.umbc.edu
World Wide Web: http://www.cs.umbc.edu
        http://engr.umbc.edu/~itl/ee.html

For application forms and general information:
Vice President for Graduate Studies and Research
University of Maryland Graduate School, Baltimore
1000 Hilltop Circle
Baltimore, Maryland 21250
Voice mail: 410-455-2538
Fax: 410-455-1092

UNIVERSITY OF MARYLAND GRADUATE SCHOOL, BALTIMORE

THE FACULTY AND THEIR RESEARCH

Computer Science Faculty

Richard Chang, Assistant Professor; Ph.D., Cornell. Computational complexity theory, structural complexity, analysis of algorithms.

David Ebert, Assistant Professor; Ph.D., Ohio State. Realistic interactive volumetric visualization; procedural modeling; modeling gases, water, and fire; advanced rendering and animation techniques; and volumetric rendering.

Tim Finin, Professor; Ph.D., Illinois at Urbana-Champaign. Artificial intelligence, knowledge representation and reasoning, knowledge and database systems, natural language processing, intelligent agents.

Konstantinos Kalpakis, Assistant Professor; Ph.D., Maryland Baltimore County. Digital library, electronic commerce, databases, multimedia, parallel and distributed computing, combinatorial optimization.

Samuel Lomonaco, Professor; Ph.D., Princeton. Algebraic coding theory, cryptography, programming languages, supercomputing, parallel processing, heterogeneous computing.

James Mayfield, Associate Professor; Ph.D., Berkeley. Agent-based architectures, natural language processing, information extraction, and hypertext.

Ethan Miller, Assistant Professor; Ph.D., Berkeley. Massive storage systems, parallel file systems, multiterabyte storage hierarchies.

Howard E. Motteler, Associate Professor; Ph.D., Maryland College Park. Parallel and distributed processing and scientific computation.

Charles Nicholas, Associate Professor; Ph.D., Ohio State. Electronic document processing, software engineering, and intelligent information systems.

Yun Peng, Assistant Professor; Ph.D., Maryland College Park. Artificial intelligence, neural network computing, and machine learning.

Alan T. Sherman, Associate Professor; Ph.D., MIT. Discrete algorithms, cryptology, VLSI layout algorithms.

Deepinder Sidhu, Professor; Ph.D., SUNY at Stony Brook. Computer networks, distributed systems, distributed and heterogeneous databases, parallel and distributed algorithms, computer and communication security, distributed artificial intelligence, high-performance computing.

Brooke Stephens, Associate Professor; Ph.D., Maryland College Park. Numerical analysis, combinatorics, resource allocation, optimization.

Russell Turner, Assistant Professor; Ph.D., Swiss Federal. Interactive 3-D graphics, physically based modeling, object-oriented graphics, animation.

Yaacov Yesha, Professor; Ph.D., Weizmann (Israel). Parallel computing, computational complexity, algorithms, source coding, speech and image compression.

Yelena Yesha, Professor; Ph.D., Ohio State. Distributed systems, database systems, digital libraries, electronic commerce, performance modeling, design tools for optimizing availability in replicated database systems, efficient and highly fault tolerant mutual exclusion algorithms, and analytical performance models for distributed and parallel systems.

Electrical Engineering Faculty

Tulay Adali, Assistant Professor; Ph.D., North Carolina State. Communications and signal processing, detection and estimation, artificial neural networks, biomedical signal processing.

Gary M. Carter, Professor; Ph.D., MIT. Optoelectronics, diode lasers, nonlinear optics, coherent optical communications.

Chein-I Chang, Associate Professor; Ph.D., Maryland College Park. Information theory and coding, signal detection and estimation, image processing, medical imaging, remote sensing, neural networks.

Jyh-Chia Chen, Assistant Professor; Ph.D., SUNY at Buffalo. Optoelectronic materials/devices, thin-film technology.

Yung-Jui Chen, Professor; Ph.D., Pennsylvania. Integrated optics and optoelectronics, optical and electronic properties of materials, ultra-short optical pulse spectroscopy.

Fow-Sen Choa, Assistant Professor; Ph.D., SUNY at Buffalo. Semiconductor lasers, optoelectronic integrated circuits.

Curtis R. Menyuk, Professor; Ph.D., UCLA. Light propagation, optical fibers, nonlinear phenomena.

Joel M. Morris, Professor and Chair; Ph.D., Johns Hopkins. Communications and signal processing, signal detection and estimation, information theory, joint time-frequency/time-scale representations and analysis techniques.

Andrew Veronis, Professor (Visiting), Ph.D., Manchester. Computer architecture, microprocessors, digital and logic design, parallel processing, digital signal processing.

Li Yan, Assistant Professor; Ph.D., Maryland College Park. Quantum electronics, ultrashort pulse formation, ultrafast nonlinear optics, general aspects of laser physics.

The Engineering/Computer Science Building was dedicated in 1992.

UNIVERSITY OF MARYLAND
GRADUATE SCHOOL, BALTIMORE

DEPARTMENT OF INFORMATION SYSTEMS

PROGRAMS OF STUDY

The Department of Information Systems offers programs leading to the M.S. and Ph.D. degrees. The principal objective of the information systems graduate program is to provide professional, graduate-level training in computer-based information systems. The course work encompasses the theoretical foundations upon which information systems are constructed as well as the current range of information systems applications. Completion of the program provides career opportunities in every organization in the nation that uses computer-based information services. Information systems program instruction provides the competence needed to become systems analysts, database designers, software designers, decision support system administrators, documentation and technical manual designers, interfacers between engineering and management personnel, expert system designers, administrators of databases, and information systems scholars for higher education institutions.

The graduate program is an acknowledgment of the need for trained information specialists and scholars to continue the exploration of the synergism evolving among computers, information systems, and humans. The graduate program endeavors to meet these needs by providing trained professionals and contributing scholars. Areas of specialization include health sciences information, management information, operations research, public services information, and expert systems. The M.S. typically takes two to three years to complete, and the Ph.D. takes three to five.

RESEARCH FACILITIES

The department maintains extensive hardware and software facilities. These include UNIX-based workstations from Sun Microsystems and Silicon Graphics, high-end Macintosh computers, and numerous Pentium and 486 machines. The department has multiple network laser and ink-jet printers with graphics and color capabilities. The department has X-Windows software, high-end network laser printers, graphics capabilities, and more. The department has a graduate laboratory for personal applications and graphic terminal interfaces with machines capable of producing object-oriented simulations, multimedia demonstrations, and other graphic adventures. Housed on a Sun workstation is a CD-ROM based player for reading applications with a great amount of storage.

All equipment is networked via Ethernet, allowing access to all hardware resources from any one location and to additional computing resources, including a VAX/VMS multiuser server, various high-end Silicon Graphics/UNIX servers, and other departmental computers across the Internet that allow networking services such as SMTP e-mail, Usenet news, and the World Wide Web.

The department maintains three dedicated laboratories. One lab houses frame-creation machines and numerous Septre terminals. This facility is dedicated to studying videotext as a delivery mechanism for decision-support systems. Another lab supporting psychophysiological research focused on stress effects of VDT-based performance and countermeasures to those effects includes blood pressure, heart rate, and EMG monitoring equipment with on-line graphical displays. The department also maintains the Health Informatics Lab containing a variety of hardware platforms and software systems for studying the delivery of health care through advanced computing technology. The department maintains the latest in graphical interfaces and working environments and is one of a few that integrate PC, Macintosh, and UNIX computers into a fully operational working environment. The department houses many applications that facilitate everyday operations such as word processing, spreadsheet, and graphical presentation software; it also has many applications specific to its undergraduate and graduate courses.

FINANCIAL AID

The graduate program offers a limited number of research and teaching assistantships. These awards include full remission of tuition fees and an annual stipend. Assistantships are awarded for one year only, but they can be renewed from year to year. Inquiries about availability should be made to the department.

COST OF STUDY

Tuition for graduate study during 1997–98 is $253 per credit hour for residents and $455 per credit hour for nonresidents. Books and other supplies average $650 to $850 per academic year.

LIVING AND HOUSING COSTS

Single students should anticipate off-campus living costs of between $4000 and $8000 per year. The campus is surrounded by numerous apartment and town-house communities.

STUDENT GROUP

Current enrollment reflects 90 percent master's students and 10 percent doctoral students. Degree-seeking students have prior degrees in every field from arts and humanities to business, representing the broad range of computer-based information systems applications.

STUDENT OUTCOMES

To date, the department has produced 15 Ph.D.'s, of whom 12 have gone into academia and the rest into high-level research. Virtually all M.S. graduates have progressed and advanced in their professional careers.

LOCATION

The campus is located close to Baltimore and Washington, D.C., with convenient interstate highway access to both. The area abounds with opportunities for practical experience, research, and employment in business and government.

THE UNIVERSITY AND THE DEPARTMENT

The University of Maryland Graduate School, Baltimore campus, a public institution founded in 1968, is one of the four campuses of the University of Maryland System. It has grown to be identified with high-technology research and application programs, with an approximate day and evening enrollment of 10,000 students. The department has the largest undergraduate major on the campus, enrolling more than 1,300 students yearly. The IFSM graduate program includes faculty members whose expertise crosses all areas of computer-based information systems applications.

APPLYING

Students should review course prerequisites or their equivalents required for graduate admission. These prerequisites are never waived. Students who do not satisfy these prerequisites are not admitted. If they do not meet the prerequisites, applicants should apply for admission as a non–degree-seeking undergraduate special student. When prerequisites are satisfied, the student should apply for admission to the appropriate degree program. Students who wish to be considered for an assistantship should send a letter that describes any teaching, research, or other experiences directly to the department. Deadlines for assistantships are the same as admissions deadlines. International students should submit completed applications one year in advance of expected enrollment. Financial aid applications should be submitted to the Graduate School.

CORRESPONDENCE AND INFORMATION

Director of Graduate Programs
Department of Information Systems
University of Maryland Graduate School, Baltimore
1000 Hilltop Circle
Baltimore, Maryland 21250

Telephone: 410-455-3688
Fax: 410-455-1073
Internet: ifsm-gradinfo@umbc.edu

Administration Building
University of Maryland Graduate School, Baltimore
1000 Hilltop Circle
Baltimore, Maryland 21250

UNIVERSITY OF MARYLAND GRADUATE SCHOOL, BALTIMORE

THE FACULTY

Monica Adya, Assistant Professor; Ph.D. (information systems), Case Western Reserve, 1996.
Marion Ball, Affiliate Professor; Ph.D. (continuing medical education), Pennsylvania, 1978.
John C. Bertot, Assistant Professor; Ph.D. (information resources), Syracuse, 1995.
Gerald Canfield, Associate Professor; Ph.D. (medical informatics), Utah, 1990.
Henry H. Emurian, Associate Professor; Ph.D. (psychology), American, 1975.
Patricia Fletcher, Assistant Professor; Ph.D. (information studies), Syracuse, 1991.
Guisseppi A. Forgionne, Professor; Ph.D. (management science), California, Riverside, 1973.
Aryya Gangopadhyay, Assistant Professor; Ph.D. (information systems), Rutgers, 1993.
David Millis, Affiliate Assistant Professor; M.D., Howard, 1983.
Anthony F. Norcio, Professor; Ph.D. (psychology), Catholic University, 1978.
Jennifer J. Preece, Professor; Ph.D. (interpreting Cartesian graphs), Open (London), 1985.
James Smith, Adjunct Professor; Ph.D. (physics); Michigan, 1970.
James Sorace, Affiliate Professor; M.D. (pathology), Virginia, 1982.
Henry H. Walbesser, Professor Emeritus; Ph.D. (mathematics and education), Maryland.

UNIVERSITY OF MARYLAND, COLLEGE PARK

ELECTRICAL ENGINEERING DEPARTMENT

PROGRAMS OF STUDY

The department offers graduate study leading to the Master of Science and Doctor of Philosophy degrees. The department's research and educational activities can be broadly divided into two areas: information sciences and systems and electronic sciences and devices. Within information sciences and systems, concentration is possible in communications and signal processing (random processes, detection and estimation, coding and information theory, digital signal processing, image processing, signal compression, communication networks, wireless and cellular systems, and satellite communications), computer engineering (digital system design, design automation, parallel algorithms and architectures, VLSI architectures, fault-tolerant computing, neural networks, computer networking, operating systems, software engineering, and computer security), and controls (adaptive control, intelligent control, stochastic control, robust control, control of bifurcations and chaos, geometric control theory and robotics, control of discrete event systems, smart structure control, numerical optimization and optimization-based design, and control applications, including biomedical). Within electronic sciences and devices, concentration is possible in electrophysics (electromagnetic theory, plasmas, intense charged-particle beams and applications to accelerators, relativistic electronics and high-power microwave generation, high-power microwave components, nonlinear dynamics and chaos, quantum electronics, millimeter waves, optical engineering, lasers, nonlinear optics, ultrafast optoelectronics, femtosecond phenomena, RF photonics, optical-microwave interaction, optoelectronic devices, integration, assembly and packaging, photonic networks for computing and communication, optical communication, optical control of phased array antenna, and chemical physics and biophysics) and microelectronics (circuits, classical and quantum devices, VLSI, semiconductor modeling and computer-aided design, neural networks, microwave and integrated circuits, semiconductor materials and technology, and ion beam lithography). The M.S. program consists of course work plus either a scholarly paper with a final examination or a research thesis and an oral examination on the thesis. The Ph.D. program comprises course work, a qualifying examination, a dissertation based on original research, and an oral examination on the dissertation. Joint programs are maintained with other departments within the school of engineering and the mathematics, physics, and computer science departments as well as with the Institute for Plasma Research, the Institute for Systems Research, the Institute for Advanced Computer Studies, the Institute for Physical Science and Technology, the Engineering Research Center, the Center for Superconductivity Research, the laboratory for physical sciences, and the chemical physics and transportation programs. Opportunities also exist for programs of study in conjunction with many national and international laboratories and technical facilities.

RESEARCH FACILITIES

The department is equipped with an extensive computer facility consisting of state-of-the-art mainframes, workstations, and personal computers located in several open laboratories and in a large number of specialized research laboratories. Faculty and students affiliated with the Institute for Advanced Computer Studies have access to a Connection Machine that is housed in that institute. In addition, there are more than thirty specialized research laboratories supporting activities in speech and image processing, communication networks, robotics, control systems, VLSI design and testing, semiconductor materials and devices, photonics, fiber optics, microwave sources, ion beam lithography, and plasma science, among others. A complete engineering library is housed nearby.

FINANCIAL AID

A significant number of graduate fellowships and teaching and research assistantships are available for well-qualified applicants. In 1997–98, typical stipends for first-year students without an M.S. degree are $10,200 for an academic-year assistantship, $15,565 for a 12-month assistantship, and $20,565 for a 12-month "superfellowship." Government traineeships are awarded through the University to exceptionally well qualified students. Part-time support is available through many national laboratories and technical facilities located nearby. The University also has resident assistantships, summer dissertation fellowships, and various types of loans.

COST OF STUDY

In 1997–98, tuition and fees for full-time study (9 credit hours) are $2691 per semester for Maryland residents and $3843 for nonresidents.

LIVING AND HOUSING COSTS

Board and lodging are available in many private homes and apartments in College Park and the vicinity. Rooms in private homes range in cost from $250 to $350 a month, and one-bedroom apartments rent for an average of $600 per month. A list of accommodations, both University and private, is maintained by the University's housing bureau.

STUDENT GROUP

In fall 1996, there were 335 graduate students in electrical engineering; 218 were Ph.D. candidates. There were 206 full-time students and 129 part-time students.

STUDENT OUTCOMES

During the past few years, the department has placed its Ph.D. graduates on the faculties of such academic institutions as Harvard University, Princeton University, Penn State University, SUNY at Stony Brook, University of Wisconsin, and Queens University, Canada, as well as at corporate and national research labs such as AT&T Bell Laboratories, IBM Research Laboratories, General Electric, Texas Instruments, Hewlett-Packard, Philips Laboratory, Microsoft, Allied Signal, Advance Micro Devices, Micron Technologies, Bell Northern Research, Silicon Valley Research, Fore Systems, Comsearch, LCC, SAIC, Los Alamos National Laboratory, Oak Ridge National Laboratory, Laboratory for Physical Sciences, and Army Research Laboratory.

LOCATION

The central campus of the University of Maryland is located in College Park, Maryland, a suburban area roughly between and within easy commuting distance of Washington and Baltimore. The campus is 12 miles from the White House. The museums, galleries, theaters, federal and special libraries, universities, concert halls, and abundant cultural activities of both cities offer students unlimited opportunities to participate in the culture and social life of this thriving area. The immediate presence of many great national laboratories and technical facilities offers a particularly good opportunity to the graduate student in electrical engineering.

THE UNIVERSITY

The University is one of the oldest and largest state universities in the country. The College of Engineering is located on the central campus, which has a total student population of approximately 33,000. The University offers many cultural and entertainment activities and operates its own golf course and athletic facilities.

APPLYING

Applicants seeking admission should hold a B.S. degree with a B+ average or better from an accredited institution. Applications should be filed early; for best consideration, those seeking financial aid should apply by January 1 for fall admission and August 1 for spring admission (June 1 for international applicants). The submission of three recommendation letters and scores on the General Test of the Graduate Record Examinations is required.

CORRESPONDENCE AND INFORMATION

Office of Graduate Studies
Electrical Engineering Department
University of Maryland
College Park, Maryland 20742
Telephone: 301-405-3681

UNIVERSITY OF MARYLAND, COLLEGE PARK

THE FACULTY AND THEIR RESEARCH

Communications and Signal Processing

R. Chellappa, Ph.D., Purdue. Signal/image processing, computer vision, pattern recognition.

L. Davisson (Emeritus), Ph.D., UCLA. Communications theory, information theory, signal processing.

A. Ephremides, Ph.D., Princeton. Communication theory, communication systems and networks.

N. Farvardin, Ph.D., RPI. Communication systems, information theory, signal/image processing.

T. Fuja, Ph.D., Cornell. Digital communications, coding and information theory.

E. Geraniotis, Ph.D., Illinois at Urbana-Champaign. Communication networks, spread-spectrum systems, coding, robust signal processing.

R. Harger, Ph.D., Michigan. Signal/image processing.

K. J. Liu, Ph.D., UCLA. Signal/image processing, VLSI, communications.

A. Makowski, Ph.D., Kentucky. Stochastic control, queuing systems, applied stochastic processes.

P. Narayan, D.Sc., Washington (St. Louis). Information theory, multiuser communications, estimation and detection.

A. Papamarcou, Ph.D., Cornell. Statistical communications.

S. Shamma, Ph.D., Stanford. Microelectronics, integrated-circuit technology, neural networks, speech processing.

L. Tassiulas, Ph.D., Maryland. Wireless communication networks, communication theory systems.

S. Tretter, Ph.D., Princeton. Communication theory, coding, signal processing.

Computer Engineering

N. DeClaris, Sc.D., MIT. Computer and decision support systems, neural networks, knowledge engineering.

V. Gligor, Ph.D., Berkeley. Operating systems, computer security, distributed systems.

R. Greenberg, Ph.D., MIT. VLSI, parallel computation, algorithms.

J. JáJá, Ph.D., Harvard. Computers, VLSI signal processing, theory of computing, parallel computation.

P. Ligomenides (Emeritus), Ph.D., Stanford. Information processing systems, AI, cybernetic and cognitive systems.

K. Nakajima, Ph.D., Northwestern. VLSI layout, system diagnosis, combinatorial algorithms, graph theory.

A. Oruc, Ph.D., Syracuse. Computer architecture, interconnection network theory, multiprocessing systems.

J. Pugsley (Emeritus), Ph.D., Illinois at Urbana-Champaign. Computer systems, multiple-valued logic.

C. Silio, Ph.D., Notre Dame. Computer engineering, multivalued digital systems, computer networks.

D. Stewart, Ph.D., Carnegie Mellon. Software engineering, real-time systems, robotics and automated systems.

U. Vishkin, D.S., Technion (Israel). Parallel computation, design and analysis of algorithms, pattern matching, theory of computing.

Controls

E. Abed, Ph.D., Berkeley. Nonlinear systems, singular perturbations, power systems.

J. Baras, Ph.D., Harvard. Control systems, signal processing, queuing systems, symbolic computing.

G. Blankenship, Ph.D., MIT. Stochastic and nonlinear control, adaptive control, AI in engineering design.

W. Dayawansa, Sc.D., Washington (St. Louis). Control theory, geometric control theory, robotics, smart structures.

F. Emad, Ph.D., Northwestern. Power systems and control.

P. Krishnaprasad, Ph.D., Harvard. Control and system theory, robotics.

W. Levine, Ph.D., MIT. Control theory and its applications in neurophysiology, aerospace, and networks.

S. Marcus, Ph.D., MIT. Control and systems engineering, stochastic systems, discrete event systems.

M. Shayman, Ph.D., Harvard. Control theory, robotics.

A. Tits, Ph.D., Berkeley. Optimization-based design, nonlinear programming, robust linear system stability.

Electrophysics

T. Antonsen, Ph.D., Cornell. Plasma physics.

M. Dagenais, Ph.D., Rochester. Integrated photonics, optical communication, photonic integrated circuits, photonic switching.

C. Davis, Ph.D., Manchester (England). Quantum electronics, biophysics, laser sensors.

W. Destler, Ph.D., Cornell. Microwave and millimeter-wave sources, accelerator technology.

J. Goldhar, Ph.D., MIT. High-power lasers, nonlinear optics.

R. Gomez, Ph.D., Maryland. Information storage technology, experimental micromagnetics, physics of magnetism, scanned probe microscopy and experimental surface science.

V. Granatstein, Ph.D., Columbia. Free-electron lasers and gyrotrons, plasma physics.

P.-T. Ho, Sc.D., MIT. Quantum electronics.

U. Hochuli (Emeritus), Ph.D., Catholic University. Gas laser technology, cold cathodes.

W. Lawson, Ph.D., Maryland. High-power microwave source development, accelerator technology.

C. Lee, Ph.D., Harvard. Quantum electronics, nonlinear optics, picosecond optical electronics, millimeter waves.

I. Mayergoyz, Doktor Nauk, Ukrainian Academy of Sciences. Power, electromagnetic theory, semiconductor device modeling.

H. Milchberg, Ph.D., Princeton. Subpicosecond lasers and plasma interactions, atomic physics.

E. Ott, Ph.D., Polytechnic of Brooklyn. Chaotic dynamics, plasmas.

H. Rabin, Ph.D., Maryland. Nonlinear optics, space science.

M. Reiser, Ph.D., Mainz (Germany). Charged-particle dynamics, accelerators.

M. Rhee, Ph.D., Catholic University. Particle dynamics, plasma accelerators.

C. Striffler, Ph.D., Michigan. Plasma physics.

L. Taylor (Emeritus), Ph.D., New Mexico State. Biomedical engineering, electromagnetic theory, atmospheric optics.

T. Venkatesan, Ph.D., CUNY, Brooklyn. Superconducting electronics, epitaxial metal-oxide thin films and devices.

K. Zaki, Ph.D., Berkeley. Microwaves, millimeter waves and optical devices, computer-aided design.

Microelectronics

D. Barbe, Ph.D., Johns Hopkins. Solid-state devices, integrated circuits, electronic images, signal processing.

J. Frey, Ph.D., Berkeley. Semiconductor devices for digital and microwave applications.

N. Goldsman, Ph.D., Cornell. Device physics, electron transport in high-electric fields, microelectronic device reliability, device modeling.

A. Iliadis, Ph.D., Manchester (England). Molecular beam epitaxy (MBE), devices of III–V semiconductors.

H. Lin (Emeritus), D.E.E., Polytechnic of Brooklyn. Integrated circuits, semiconductor devices.

J. Melngailis, Ph.D., Carnegie Mellon. Microfabrication, ion lithography, focused ion beams.

L. Milor, Ph.D., Berkeley. Integrated circuit testing and failure mode prediction.

R. Newcomb, Ph.D., Berkeley. Microsystems, network theory, robotics, biomedical engineering.

J. Orloff, Ph.D., Oregon Graduate Center. High-brightness ion and electron sources, charged particle optics, micromachining with ion beams.

M. Peckerar, Ph.D., Maryland. Microelectronics, integrated circuits, microstructures.

C.-H. Yang, Ph.D., Princeton. Semiconductor physics and devices, quantum transport, silicon laser.

UNIVERSITY OF MASSACHUSETTS AMHERST

DEPARTMENT OF COMPUTER SCIENCE

PROGRAMS OF STUDY

The Department of Computer Science at the University of Massachusetts Amherst has a broad, flexible program that allows students to focus on those areas most relevant to their career objectives. The M.S. and Ph.D. programs provide a combination of practical training for students interested in a professional career in industry and advanced research training for students interested in research or teaching careers. The basic graduate program is a blend of courses in computer systems, theory of computation, robotics, and artificial intelligence.

Courses and research span a wide range of interests, including databases, distributed and real-time systems, networks, object-oriented systems, parallel processing, software development, cooperative distributed problem solving, computer architecture, planning, case-based reasoning, natural-language processing, information retrieval, computer vision, theory of computation, and parallel architectures. Graduate seminars expose students to advanced research results in an informal atmosphere that encourages frequent and close interactions between members of the faculty and students.

RESEARCH FACILITIES

The department operates an extensive network of more than 300 UNIX workstations plus PCs (most of which are Macintoshes), Lisp machines, servers, and special purpose computer systems. This network is connected to a campus-wide network and to regional, national, and international networks. There is a broad collection of special purpose equipment to support research in robotics, vision, graphics, and parallel and distributed processing. Graduate students participate in a variety of research programs that rely on the department's state-of-the-art computing environment. The department also runs an Educational Laboratory of more than fifty workstations to support course-related computing needs.

The University operates a sophisticated computer center with several PC labs distributed throughout the campus. Primary computer systems are VAX/VMS and UNIX mainframes. Students are also offered research opportunities in the department's collaborative research center, CRICCS. This center supplements the traditional university approach of conducting basic research by working on real problems that high-technology companies are facing. Collaborative research teams of industry and University scientists and students work on creating solutions to real problems.

FINANCIAL AID

Financial aid is available in the form of teaching and research assistantships as well as various University fellowships. Stipends vary with the type and amount of work involved but are normally $10,800 for the academic year or $14,750 for the calendar year for a 20-hour-per-week assignment. Fellowships and assistantships usually include a waiver of tuition and fees. An assistant is permitted to carry up to 15 semester hours of courses. Financial aid packets may be picked up in the Financial Aid Office in December for the forthcoming academic year. The deadline for financial aid applications is February 15 for the fall semester. For more information, students should write to the Financial Aid Office, 243 Whitmore Administration Building.

COST OF STUDY

For 1997–98, full-time tuition is expected to be $2640 for Massachusetts residents, $3960 for the New England Regional Student Program, and $8952 for out-of-state students. Additional fees of $2916 are charged to all full-time graduate students. Tuition and most fees are waived with most assistantships.

LIVING AND HOUSING COSTS

The minimum living cost (room, board, books, and incidentals) was estimated at $6000 per year in 1995–96. University housing is available for single and married graduate students but is not adequate to meet the demand. Rooms and apartments are available in the surrounding area. The University maintains a housing office, located in Berkshire House, which assists in finding suitable housing on or off campus.

STUDENT GROUP

In 1995–96, approximately 6,100 students were pursuing graduate degrees, and about 160 graduate students were studying in the Department of Computer Science.

LOCATION

The University of Massachusetts is situated in one of the most picturesque sections of New England. The University at its Amherst campus joins with its academic neighbors—Amherst, Hampshire, Smith, and Mount Holyoke colleges—in maintaining the rich tradition of education and cultural activity associated with the beautiful Connecticut Valley region. The area is rural in character but is within 4 hours' drive of any East Coast location from New York City to Portland, Maine. Local skiing is available, and the large ski areas of Vermont and New Hampshire are 2 to 4 hours away by car.

THE UNIVERSITY

One of today's leading centers of public higher education in the Northeast, the University of Massachusetts Amherst was established in 1863 under the Morrill Land Grant Act as an agricultural college. It became Massachusetts State College in 1931 and the University of Massachusetts in 1947. The University has grown to be the largest state university in New England.

The Amherst campus has more than 110 main buildings on 1,100 acres. Facilities are also maintained in Belchertown, East Wareham, Waltham, Nantucket, and South Deerfield. There were about 23,600 students enrolled at the University of Massachusetts Amherst in 1995–96. Within its ten schools, colleges, and faculties, the University offers bachelor's degrees in more than ninety areas, associate degrees in six, master's degrees in seventy, and the doctorate in forty-eight fields.

APPLYING

Applications for graduate study in computer science for the 1998–99 academic year should be submitted by January 15 for fall enrollment. International applicants should have all materials submitted before January 15 for fall enrollment. (There is no spring admission.) An undergraduate cumulative grade point average of 2.8 or higher is required for admission to degree candidacy. The Graduate School requires that all applicants take the GRE General Test. Students should exhibit a strong preparation in computer science and basic mathematics or should show other evidence of special aptitude for the graduate program. Admission to the program and award of assistantships are made on a competitive basis. The University follows a policy of equal educational opportunity without regard to race, sex, or religion.

CORRESPONDENCE AND INFORMATION

Graduate School
Goodell Building
University of Massachusetts
Amherst, Massachusetts 01003

Department of Computer Science
Room A243, Box 34610
Lederle Graduate Research Center
University of Massachusetts
Amherst, Massachusetts 01003-4610
Telephone: 413-545-2744
Fax: 413-545-1249
E-mail: csinfo@cs.umass.edu

UNIVERSITY OF MASSACHUSETTS AMHERST
THE FACULTY AND THEIR RESEARCH

W. Richards Adrion, Professor; Ph.D., Texas at Austin, 1971.
James Allan, Research Assistant Professor; Ph.D., Cornell, 1995.
David A. Barrington, Associate Professor; Ph.D., MIT, 1986.
Andrew G. Barto, Professor; Ph.D., Michigan, 1975.
James P. Callan, Research Assistant Professor; Ph.D., Massachusetts, 1993.
Lori A. Clarke, Professor; Ph.D., Colorado, 1976.
Paul R. Cohen, Professor; Ph.D., Stanford, 1983.
W. Bruce Croft, Professor; Ph.D., Cambridge, 1979.
Robert M. Graham, Professor Emeritus; M.A., Michigan, 1957.
Roderic A. Grupen, Associate Professor; Ph.D., Utah, 1988.
Allen R. Hanson, Professor; Ph.D., Cornell, 1969.
Neil Immerman, Professor; Ph.D., Cornell, 1980.
David Jensen, Research Assistant Professor; D.Sc., Washington (St. Louis), 1992.
James F. Kurose, Professor; Ph.D., Columbia, 1984.
Susan Landau, Research Associate Professor; Ph.D., MIT, 1983.
Wendy G. Lehnert, Professor; Ph.D., Yale, 1977.
Barbara S. Lerner, Research Assistant Professor; Ph.D., Carnegie Mellon, 1989.
Victor R. Lesser, Professor; Ph.D., Stanford, 1972.
Kathryn S. McKinley, Assistant Professor; Ph.D., Rice, 1992.
Robert N. Moll, Associate Professor; Ph.D., MIT, 1973.
J. Eliot Moss, Associate Professor; Ph.D., MIT, 1981.
Leon J. Osterweil, Professor; Ph.D., Maryland, 1971.
Robin J. Popplestone, Professor; B.Sc. (hons. mathematics), 1960; advanced studies, Manchester (England), 1960–64.
Krithivasan Ramamritham, Professor; Ph.D., Utah, 1981.
Edward M. Riseman, Professor; Ph.D., Cornell, 1969.
Edwina Rissland, Professor; Ph.D., MIT, 1977.
Arnold L. Rosenberg, Distinguished University Professor; Ph.D., Harvard, 1966.
Ramesh K. Sitaraman, Assistant Professor; Ph.D., Princeton, 1993.
D. N. Spinelli, Professor; M.D. (medicine and surgery), Milan (Italy), 1958.
David W. Stemple, Professor and Chair; Ph.D., Massachusetts, 1977.
Richard Sutton, Research Associate Professor; Ph.D., Massachusetts, 1984.
Donald F. Towsley, Professor; Ph.D., Texas at Austin, 1975.
Paul E. Utgoff, Associate Professor; Ph.D., Rutgers, 1984.
Charles C. Weems, Associate Professor; Ph.D., Massachusetts, 1984.
Richard S. Weiss, Research Assistant Professor; Ph.D., Harvard, 1976.
Jack C. Wileden, Professor; Ph.D., Michigan, 1978.
Conrad A. Wogrin, Professor Emeritus; D.Eng., Yale, 1955.
Beverly P. Woolf, Research Assistant Professor; Ph.D., Massachusetts, 1984.
Shlomo Zilberstein, Assistant Professor; Ph.D., Berkeley, 1993.

Adjunct and Affiliated Faculty
George S. Avrunin, Professor of Mathematics.
Lyn Frazier, Professor of Linguistics.
Rakesh Kumar, Adjunct Assistant Professor of Computer Science.
Ernest G. Manes, Professor of Mathematics.
Catherine McGeoch, Assistant Professor of Computer Science, Amherst College.
Lyle McGeoch, Assistant Professor of Computer Science, Amherst College.
John W. Moore, Professor of Psychology.
Hamid Nawab, Assistant Professor of Electrical Engineering and Computer Science, Boston University.
Barbara Partee, Professor of Linguistics and of Philosophy.
Howard A. Pellee, Professor of Education.
Alexander Pollatsek, Professor of Psychology.
Howard Schultz, Senior Research Fellow, Computer Science.
Klaus Schultz, Professor of Education.
Oliver G. Selfridge, GTE Laboratories.
William T. Verts, Assistant Professor.

RESEARCH ACTIVITIES
Algorithms and complexity (Barrington, Immerman, Landau, Rosenberg, Sitaraman).
Applied graph theory (Rosenberg, Sitaraman).
Computational neuroscience (Barto, Spinelli).
Computational strategies in learning and education (Rissland, K. Schultz, Selfridge, Woolf).
Computer vision and image understanding (Hanson, Riseman, H. Schultz, Spinelli, Weems, Weiss, Wogrin).
Connectionist learning (Barto, Lehnert).
Cooperative distributed problem solving (Lesser, Zilberstein).
Database systems and information retrieval (Callan, Croft, Immerman, Lehnert, Moss, Rissland, Stemple).
Distributed software systems (Graham, Kurose, McKinley, Ramamritham, Stemple, Towsley, Wileden).
Formal analysis of concurrency (Adrion, Clarke, Osterweil, Ramamritham, Wileden).
Intelligent user interfaces and office automation (Cohen, Croft, Lesser, Rissland, Woolf).
Knowledge-based systems (Cohen, Moll, Rissland, Utgoff).
Machine learning and knowledge acquisition (Barto, Callan, Cohen, Lehnert, Rissland, Utgoff, Woolf).
Natural-language processing (Lehnert).
Networking (Adrion, Kurose, Ramamritham, Towsley).
Operating systems (Kurose, Towsley).
Parallel computation (McKinley, Rosenberg, Sitaraman, Weems).
Programming languages and systems (McKinley, Moss, Popplestone).
Real-time computing (Ramamritham, Wileden).
Software development environments (Adrion, Clarke, Graham, Kurose, Lerner, Osterweil, Wileden).
Software testing and analysis (Adrion, Avrunin, Clarke, Osterweil, Wileden).
Theory of computation (Barrington, Immerman, Landau, C. McGeoch, L. McGeoch, Rosenberg, Sitaraman).
Visual and tactile control of robots (Grupen, Hanson, Popplestone, Riseman, Weiss).

UNIVERSITY OF MASSACHUSETTS DARTMOUTH

COLLEGE OF ENGINEERING
DEPARTMENT OF ELECTRICAL AND COMPUTER ENGINEERING

PROGRAMS OF STUDY

The Department of Electrical and Computer Engineering at the University of Massachusetts Dartmouth offers graduate programs leading to the Master of Science degree and the Doctor of Philosophy degree in electrical engineering. The programs offer opportunities for graduate studies in the broadly defined areas of communications; electrooptics; parallel computer architectures and supercomputing; database systems; intelligent systems and advanced automation; microwave and solid-state electronics; remote and in situ ocean-sensing systems; and signals, systems, control, and estimation theory. An emphasis in the marine applications of these broad areas is supported by specialized courses and dissertation research. The marine emphasis in electrical engineering graduate studies at the Dartmouth campus is unique within the UMass system.

The programs offer small classes, close contact with a diverse faculty, and easy access to well-supported research facilities to provide state-of-the-art learning and research experiences. Courses are scheduled to permit either full-time or part-time study and are offered at times that are convenient for students employed in industry and government.

RESEARCH FACILITIES

The Department of Electrical and Computer Engineering maintains and operates a wide variety of facilities for applications in engineering education and research. Some special facilities in the department are the Applied Signal Processing Laboratory, Speech Research Laboratory, Digital Signal Processing Laboratory, Marine Electronics Laboratory, Microcomputer Laboratory, Microwave Laboratory, Optics Research Laboratory, Robotics Laboratory, Scanning Electron Microscope Laboratory (operated jointly with the Department of Biology), VLSI Design Laboratory, and the Signal, Image Processing and Artificial Intelligence Laboratory. In addition to ten well-equipped undergraduate laboratories, the department maintains both DEC and Sun SPARC workstations. The department faculty members also have access to supercomputers at the Pittsburgh Supercomputing Center.

The Advanced Technology Center (ATC) for Business, Textiles and Manufacturing is a cooperative effort within the University to support local and regional industries in their efforts to lead the world in technology development, product quality, and competitiveness. The ATC acts as an interface with the resources of industry and those of the University to effect a combined effort in education and in economic development.

Located near campus is the Laboratory for Marine Science, Environment and Technology. The laboratory provides space for researchers and support staff and is a multidisciplinary facility shared by biologists, chemists, and electrical engineers. The University also maintains a 50-foot research vessel, the R/V *Lucky Lady*.

FINANCIAL AID

The department awards a number of teaching assistantships each year ($9000 for 20 hours per week). There are also research assistantship awards, subject to availability of faculty research funds. Information concerning loans and other forms of financial aid may be obtained through the University Financial Aid Office.

COST OF STUDY

For the 1997–98 academic year, the tuition (based on 9 graduate credits per semester) for Massachusetts residents is $2491 and for nonresidents, $5394. Graduate students are also assessed several fees totaling $3405, as well as an engineering equipment fee of $150 per semester. Those students not covered by an outside health insurance plan are assessed $430 for health insurance coverage. Teaching and research assistants receive remission of tuition but must pay all applicable fees.

LIVING AND HOUSING COSTS

The minimum cost of living (room, board, books, and incidentals) is approximately $6470 per year. University and off-campus housing is available for graduate students. The University housing office offers assistance for those seeking both on- and off-campus housing. Applicants are encouraged to contact this office early in the admission process.

STUDENT GROUP

The department has approximately 70 matriculated M.S. and Ph.D. degree students. About 20 students are pursuing their degree full-time.

STUDENT OUTCOMES

Department graduates are often employed by companies that are nationally recognized leaders in their respective areas. Department graduates are also employed by local firms, some of which have marine-related interests. In addition, department graduates have gone on to successful academic careers. Many M.S. program graduates have continued their education to pursue doctorates at the University and at premier graduate schools across the country.

LOCATION

The University is located approximately 60 miles south of Boston and 30 miles east of Providence, Rhode Island, between the cities of Fall River and New Bedford, Massachusetts, in the town of Dartmouth. The location is ideal for exploring the many cultural and educational activities of a large metropolitan area such as Boston, while still maintaining a residence in a more suburban setting. Cape Cod is less than an hour's drive, with most New England attractions and New York City less than a four-hour drive from campus.

THE UNIVERSITY

Southeastern Massachusetts University was renamed the University of Massachusetts Dartmouth in 1991 when it became part of the University of Massachusetts system. The history of the University dates back more than 100 years, to when the two institutions that were merged in 1962 to become the present institution of higher learning were chartered.

APPLYING

Applications for fall enrollment should be completed by February 1 for full consideration for financial aid in the form of teaching assistantships. Spring applications should be completed by November 1 for similar consideration. Scores from the GRE General Test are required, and the TOEFL is required of international students whose native language is not English. In addition, transcripts from all colleges and universities attended, three letters of recommendation, and a statement of career goals are required of all applicants. The application fee is $20 for Massachusetts residents; $40 for nonresidents.

CORRESPONDENCE AND INFORMATION

Graduate Admissions Office
Foster Administration Building
University of Massachusetts Dartmouth
North Dartmouth, Massachusetts 02747-2300
Telephone: 508-999-8026
Fax: 508-999-8901
E-mail: cnovo@umassd.edu
World Wide Web: http://www.ece.umassd.edu

UNIVERSITY OF MASSACHUSETTS DARTMOUTH

THE FACULTY AND THEIR RESEARCH

Ardsher Ahmed, Assistant Professor; Ph.D., SUNY at Binghamton, 1992. Parallel processing, computer architectures, supercomputing, parallel algorithm design.

David A. Brown, Assistant Professor; Ph.D., Naval Postgraduate School, 1991. Underwater acoustics, fiber-optic acoustic sensors and systems, acoustic transducer design, acoustic materials characterization.

John R. Buck, Assistant Professor; Ph.D., MIT/Woods Hole Oceanographic Institute, 1996. Underwater acoustics, signal processing, marine mammal bioacoustics.

Paul R. Caron, Professor; Ph.D., Brown, 1963. Computer architecture, microprocessors.

Robert H. Caverly, Professor; Ph.D., Johns Hopkins, 1983. Microwave and solid-state electronics, analog and digital VLSI design.

Chi-Hau Chen, Professor; Ph.D., Purdue, 1965. Pattern recognition, neural networks, image processing and machine vision, communications theory.

Lester W. Cory, Professor; M.S.E.E., Northeastern, 1970; D.Sc. (hon.), Rhode Island, 1996. Rehabilitation engineering, computer systems, HF/VHF communications.

Antonio H. Costa, Associate Professor; Ph.D., Rhode Island, 1994. Mixed time-frequency representations, spectral estimation, signal processing.

Thomas J. Curry, Professor and Dean; Ph.D., Rhode Island, 1975. Signal processing, underwater systems, engineering management.

Lee E. Estes, Professor; Ph.D., Worcester Polytechnic, 1969. Electrooptics, underwater acoustics, ocean optics, remote sensing of the ocean.

Gilbert Fain, Professor and ECE Chairperson; Ph.D., Rhode Island, 1968. Ocean systems, instrumentation and measurement systems, underwater acoustics, active circuits.

Paul Fortier, Associate Professor; D.Sc., Massachusetts Lowell, 1993. Database systems, real-time systems, operating systems, computer architecture, networks, computer performance evaluation.

John W. Gray, Professor; Ph.D., Ohio State, 1966. Operating systems, distributed systems, computer networks.

Robert W. Green, Professor; Ph.D., Michigan, 1972. Software engineering, programming languages, artificial neural networks.

Robert C. Helgeland, Professor; M.S.E.E., Northeastern, 1970; PE. Marine electronic systems.

Dayalan Kasilingam, Assistant Professor; Ph.D., Caltech, 1987. Remote sensing, electromagnetics, microwaves, signal processing.

Gerald Lemay, Professor; Ph.D., Rhode Island, 1988. Renewable energy.

Daniel J. Murphy, Chancellor Professor; Ph.D., Northeastern, 1969; PE. Ocean systems, signal processing, estimation and control.

Steven C. Nardone, Professor; Ph.D., Rhode Island, 1982. Systems theory, modern control and estimation theory, signal processing, fuzzy systems.

Karen L. Payton, Associate Professor; Ph.D., Johns Hopkins, 1986. Digital signal processing, speech processing, speech acoustics, auditory perception.

N. A. Pendergrass, Professor; Ph.D., Berkeley, 1975. Digital signal processing, adaptive signal processing, communications theory, estimation theory.

David Rancour, Associate Professor; Ph.D., Purdue, 1988. Semiconductor defects, solid-state devices and materials.

Roman Rutman, Professor; Ph.D., USSR Academy of Sciences, 1963. Control theory, systems analysis.

Dean Schmidlin, Associate Professor; Ph.D., NYU, 1972. Digital signal processing, linear discrete-time systems (both time-varying and time-invariant).

UNIVERSITY OF MICHIGAN

DEPARTMENT OF ELECTRICAL ENGINEERING AND COMPUTER SCIENCE

PROGRAMS OF STUDY

The Department of Electrical Engineering and Computer Science (EECS) offers graduate programs leading to the degrees of Master of Science, Master of Science in Engineering, and Doctor of Philosophy. Professional and Master of Engineering (M.Eng.) degrees are available in some programs. EECS comprises three divisions: Electrical Science and Engineering (ESE), System Science and Engineering (SSE), and Computer Science and Engineering (CSE). The ESE Division is organized into five broad areas: electromagnetics, optics, VLSI, circuits and electronics, and solid state. This program is intended for students wishing to major in topics such as circuits, electronics, electrodynamics, electromagnetics, electrooptics, microwave systems, remote sensing, solid-state materials, devices, and integrated circuits. The VLSI option bridges the areas of electrical and computer engineering. The SSE Division is organized into four broad areas: communications, control, signal processing, and bioelectrical sciences. SSE programs are intended for students wishing to major in topics such as bioelectrical sciences, communications, networks, control, manufacturing, signal processing, information theory, random processes, and systems theory. The graduate programs in the CSE Division are organized into four broad areas: hardware systems, intelligent systems, software and programming languages, and the theory of computation. This program is intended for students wishing to major in topics such as programming languages, software engineering, operating systems, computer architecture, databases, fault tolerance, reliable computing, computer-aided design, natural system modeling, artificial intelligence, robotics, computer vision, graphics, distributed systems, VLSI, and all aspects of theoretical computer science. This distinctive academic structure allows students to pursue diverse academic programs, enabling them to study and hone their research skills in more than one area.

RESEARCH FACILITIES

EECS departmental academic units, faculty members, and most of the research laboratories are housed in the modern EECS Building and in several nearby research buildings. EECS is home to more than a dozen state-of-the-art research laboratories, and it supports other interdepartmental research laboratories. The optics laboratories include the country's foremost center for research in ultrafast optical science. The Solid State Laboratory has one of the most advanced facilities for solid-state device research in the world. The Radiation Laboratory is home to the NASA/Center for Space Terahertz Technology. The area of systems and control is involved in theoretical and applied projects that run the gamut from aerospace vehicles and automotive systems, to manufacturing and highway systems, to computer and communications networks. Communications research spans a broad spectrum of interests, including digital modulation, channel coding, source coding, information theory, optical communications, detection and estimation, spread spectrum, and multiuser communications and techniques. The Biosystems Laboratory collaborates with faculty members in the Medical School of the University of Michigan to offer excellent research opportunities. Signal processing, which focuses on the representation, manipulation, and analysis of signals, particularly natural ones, overlaps with many research areas. Computer hardware systems research, including architecture and CAD, is centered in the Advanced Computer Architecture Laboratory. The Artificial Intelligence Laboratory houses a multidisciplinary group of researchers involved in theoretical, experimental, and applied aspects of intelligent systems. Areas of excellence in theoretical computer science research include logic and parallel algorithms. Software research draws on all areas of computer science from architecture, databases, and distributed systems to fault-tolerant and real-time systems and is housed in the Software Systems and Real-Time Computing laboratories. The EECS research environment is strengthened by a University-wide computer network infrastructure. The College of Engineering's CAEN network, one the largest campus networks, supports both instructional and research computing and has links to research facilities throughout Michigan, the nation, and the world.

FINANCIAL AID

A variety of fellowships, teaching assistantships, and research assistantships are available to students. Departmental aid is awarded on a merit basis. For recipients of NSF Fellowships, the University provides an additional stipend and the balance of tuition.

COST OF STUDY

For 1996–97, precandidate tuition and fees were $5452 per term for state residents and $10,265 per term for nonresidents. Candidacy rates were $3749, regardless of residency status. (Costs are subject to change each year.)

LIVING AND HOUSING COSTS

University-owned residence facilities provide a variety of single rooms and suites in dormitories, co-ops, and apartments. Many privately owned apartments are within walking distance of the North and Central campuses, and many others are serviced by the Ann Arbor Transit Authority's extensive bus system. A no-cost University bus system is available to provide service between the campuses and student housing. Food and living costs are equivalent with the national level.

STUDENT GROUP

Approximately 600 graduate students are enrolled in the EECS department. More than half of the enrolled students are pursuing a Ph.D. degree. The student population includes excellent scholars from throughout the United States and the world whose diverse backgrounds and interests add much to the educational environment.

LOCATION

The University of Michigan is located in the heart of Ann Arbor, a cosmopolitan community that has retained its small-town atmosphere and friendliness. It has an environment rich in opportunities to enjoy the fine arts, popular entertainment, sports, and widely varied recreational activities.

THE UNIVERSITY

The University of Michigan, founded in 1817, was the nation's first public university and has a long-standing tradition of excellence in engineering.

APPLYING

Applications and additional information may be obtained electronically or by writing to the EECS department.

CORRESPONDENCE AND INFORMATION

Department of Electrical Engineering and Computer Science
3314 EECS Building
University of Michigan
Ann Arbor, Michigan 48109-2122
E-mail: admit@eecs.umich.edu
World Wide Web: http://www.eecs.umich.edu

UNIVERSITY OF MICHIGAN
THE FACULTY AND THEIR RESEARCH

ELECTRICAL SCIENCE AND ENGINEERING DIVISION

Applied Electromagnetics. Professors Anthony England, Brian Gilchrist, Linda Katehi, Gabriel Rebeiz, Kamal Sarabandi, Thomas Senior, Fawwaz Ulaby, and John Volakis.

Recent theory research activities have concentrated on the numerical simulations of scattering by composite material structures. The research in circuit, antenna, and system technology covers a wide range of EM-related problems extending from pure EM theory to fabrications of submillimeter antenna arrays. Finding effective analytical or numerical solutions for problems of wave emission, propagation, and reception is an integral part of designing new microstrip transmission lines, filters, and antennas. The University of Michigan has an institutional commitment to global change research, and this is expressed through an aggressive program of environmental remote sensing research based on microwave and millimeter-wave technologies.

Optical Science. Professors Mohammed Islam, Henry Kapteyn, Emmett Leith, Gerard Mourou, Margaret Murnane, Theodore Norris, Stephen Rand, Duncan Steel, and Herbert Winful.

The rapidly expanding optics program encompasses four broad areas of interest: electrooptics, quantum optoelectronics, optical physics, and ultrafast optical science. The electrooptics area involves research in optical information processing, interferometry, and holography. Methods for making holographic lenses operating on diffractive rather than refractive principles have also been of concern. Other activities include optical tomography, holograms for white light, and viewing and imaging through homogeneous media. Research in quantum optoelectronics is concerned with optical studies of optical and electronic properties and semiconductor heterostructures as well as with studies of quantum-optical properties of radiations from these systems. This area includes the NSF-STC Center for Ultrafast Science.

Solid-State Electronics. Professors Pallab Bhattacharya, Richard Brown, Donald Calahan, Ward Getty, George Haddad, Jerzy Kanicki, Ronald Lomax, Carlos Mastrangelo, Leo McAfee, Khalil Najafi, Clark Nguyen, Stella Pang, Dimitris Pavlidis, Jasprit Singh, Fred Terry, and Kensall Wise.

Activities extend from the growth and characterization of advanced materials and devices to the development of microcomputer-based instrumentation. The primary focus is on the development of novel solid-state device structures for the acquisition and high-speed processing of information and the extension of microelectronics in areas such as telecommunications, radar, computing, health care, transportation, and automated manufacturing. Major research thrusts include material growth and characterization, including various types of narrow and wide bandgap semiconductor materials; monolithic integrated-circuit chips for analog and digital applications; optoelectronic devices and monolithic optoelectronic integrated circuits; integrated sensors; and automated semiconductor manufacturing. Within the Solid-State Electronics Laboratory (SSEL) there are several major research programs and four major centers: the Center for High-Frequency Microelectronics, the Center for Integrated Sensors and Circuits, the Center for Optoelectric Science & Technology, and the Center for Display Technology & Manufacturing.

VLSI. Faculty from both Solid-State Electronics and Computer Systems and Hardware.

Research in VLSI ranges from technology through CAD tool development to digital system applications.

Vehicular Engineering. Professors William Ribbens and Chelsea White III.

Efforts center on system identifications of various automotive subsystems for control and instrumentation applications, on development of new sensors for automotive applications, and on development of computer-aided failure diagnosis methods and algorithms for automotive systems. Exciting research is being done on "Intelligent Transportation Systems," which will integrate "smart" cars with "smart" highways.

COMPUTER SCIENCE AND ENGINEERING DIVISION

Artificial Intelligence. Professors William Birmingham, Lynn Conway, Edmund Durfee, Keki Irani, Stephen Kaplan, David Kieras, Daniel Koditschek, John Laird, Sang Wook Lee, William Rounds, Elliot Soloway, and Michael Wellman.

Many projects are now under way combining research in machine vision, natural-language understanding, distributed problem solving, machine learning, cognitive modeling, AI-aided design, collaboration technology, autonomous and teleautonomous robotic systems, automated knowledge acquisition, medical diagnosis and imaging, and AI-supported software development.

Systems and Hardware. Professors Daniel Atkins, William Birmingham, Peter Chen, Edward Davidson, John Hayes, Pinaki Mazumder, John Meyer, Trevor Mudge, Marios Papaefthymiou, Yale Patt, Steven Reinhardt, Karem Sakallah, and Gary Tyson.

Research on computer systems broadly covers the analysis and design of computers, computer-based systems, and their major components, with a focus on computer architecture and logic design. The computer systems hardware field has strong links with software (operating systems, programming languages), solid-state circuits (VLSI design), and several computer application areas (robotics, artificial intelligence, instrumentation, numerical methods). Research into VLSI design ranges from CAD tools such as logic simulation programs to the design of components for advanced computer systems.

Theoretical Computer Science. Professors Kevin Compton, Yuri Gurevich, William Rounds, and Quentin Stout.

This area uses formal descriptions to capture the essential features of problems, languages, algorithms, programs, machines, or systems and then uses these descriptions to prove properties of the objects described.

Software & Distributed Computing Systems. Professors Peter Chen, Larry Flanigan, Farnam Jahanian, Sugih Jamin, Atul Prakash, Steven Reinhardt, Elke Rudensteiner, Kang Shin, Nandit Soparkar, Toby Teorey, and Gary Tyson.

Research in software bridges the gap between sophisticated applications and the challenging raw power of machines. This is difficult because large software systems are among the most complex systems ever built. Their enormous complexity can be managed only through the development of new abstractions, techniques, structures, and languages. There is a major focus on distributed computing from the perspective of computer network design and analysis, distributed file and storage systems, database systems, and collaborative computing. Another focus area is the specification, design, analysis, and implementation of real-time computing systems and applications.

SYSTEMS SCIENCE AND ENGINEERING DIVISION

Biosystems. Professors David Anderson, Spencer BeMent, Charles Cain, Emad Ebbini, Jeffrey Fessler, Daniel Green, Janice Jenkins, Matthew O'Donnell, Clyde Owings, and Kimberly Wasserman.

Ongoing projects include computerized electrocardiography, medical images from several areas, therapeutic and diagnostic ultrasound, processing of complex sounds by the central auditory system, coding of images by the retina, pattern recognition and classification of visual evoked potentials, and evaluation of multichannel recordings from small neural circuits. This area includes the NIH Center for Neural Communications.

Communications and Signal Processing. Professors John Coffey, Alfred Hero III, David Neuhoff, Wayne Stark, Demosthenis Teneketzis, Gregory Wakefield, William Williams, Kim Winick, and Andrew Yagle.

Communications research focuses on system design, optimization, and performance analysis as well as on the development of theory to characterize the fundamental limits of communication system performance, including its mathematical foundations. Techniques include digital modulation, channel coding, source coding, information theory, optical communications, detection and estimation, spread spectrum, and multiuser communications and networks. Signal processing overlaps with many other research activities, particularly those of communication and bioengineering. Signal processing focuses on the representation, manipulation, and analysis of signals, particularly natural signals.

Systems and Control. Professors James Freudenberg, Jessy Grizzle, Pramod Khargonekar, Daniel Koditschek, Stéphane Lafortune, Semyon Meerkov, and Demosthenis Teneketzis.

This area is concerned with the investigation of fundamental properties of dynamic systems and the development of methods for their modification. It emphasizes the use of system-theoretical approaches to problems in robotics and automation, manufacturing, semiconductor processing, automotive systems, computer systems, and communications networks.

UNIVERSITY OF MINNESOTA

INSTITUTE OF TECHNOLOGY
GRADUATE PROGRAM IN COMPUTER ENGINEERING

PROGRAM OF STUDY

Computer engineering is an interdisciplinary graduate program offered jointly by the Department of Electrical Engineering and the Department of Computer Science. Students in this program develop a broad understanding of both hardware and software design issues. Two different degree options are available. The Master of Science (M.S.) in computer engineering degree is a traditional research-oriented graduate degree that prepares students to work in industry or to continue with their graduate studies in either electrical engineering or computer science. The Master of Computer Engineering (M.Comp.E.) degree is a course work-only professional engineering degree tailored to practicing computer scientists and engineers. Faculty members in the program work closely with graduate students conducting research in a wide variety of computer engineering topics, including computer architecture and system design, computer graphics, distributed systems, fault-tolerant computing, optimizing and parallelizing compilers, computer-aided design, databases, networks, operating systems, parallel computing, software engineering, and VLSI design and testing. Students begin their studies with a core program of courses in system software, computer architecture and networking, VLSI and digital design, and data structures and algorithms and then proceed to in-depth study in their area of specialization. M.S. students may elect to complete a master's thesis or an independent project. The comprehensive final exam for the M.S. degree is oral; no final exam is required for the M.Comp.E. degree. These degrees typically require one to two years of full-time study. Part-time study is encouraged for students who work in industry while attending classes.

RESEARCH FACILITIES

The Departments of Electrical Engineering and Computer Science provide access to numerous specialized and general-purpose computing facilities and laboratories. Current computing resources include several hundred workstations and personal computers from vendors such as Hewlett-Packard, Silicon Graphics, Sun, Apple, and IBM. Research programs have access to departmental computing resources, including a cluster of multiprocessor SGI Challenge computers connected via HIPPI and Fibre Channel, eight IBM RS6000/590 computers connected via ATM, and an IBM SP-2 parallel computing system. Workstation access is also provided by the Institute of Technology public labs, which have several hundred Sun and SGI computers. The Minnesota Supercomputer Institute supports research that is carried out using the supercomputers and other resources of the Minnesota Supercomputer Center, Inc. The systems available include a Cray C-90, a Cray T3D, and numerous graphics workstations. The Laboratory for Computational Science and Engineering provides access to extensive computing, storage, and graphics and visualization facilities. University library facilities are excellent and have on-line access to the catalog. Extensive networking and dial-in facilities are provided to access all of these systems.

FINANCIAL AID

Both fellowships and half-time teaching assistantships are available through the Departments of Electrical Engineering and Computer Science, and research assistantships are available through individual faculty members. Typically, a half-time teaching assistant is expected to teach laboratory sections for one of the introductory courses or to assist with grading and other duties. These appointments typically require up to 20 hours per week, including preparation, student consulting, and grading. Research assistants are normally expected to devote an equivalent amount of time to funded research work. Because of the concentration of computer and computer-based industries in the Twin Cities area, graduate students often can find a variety of interesting part-time and summer job opportunities. Students with fellowships or half-time assistantships are given tuition waivers and personal health insurance.

COST OF STUDY

For 1996–97, resident tuition for graduate students is $1560 per quarter (7–12 credits); nonresident tuition is $3130 per quarter (7–12 credits). While assistants and fellows obtain tuition waivers for up to 12 credits per quarter, all students must pay certain fees each quarter. Rates for tuition and fees are subject to increases by the Board of Regents.

LIVING AND HOUSING COSTS

For information about housing, students should contact University Housing Services, Comstock Hall-East, 210 Delaware Street SE, Minneapolis, Minnesota 55455 (telephone: 612-624-2994; fax: 612-624-6987; E-mail: housing @cafe.tc.umn.edu). Students who intend to live in a residence hall on campus or in nearby married-student housing should contact this office as soon as possible because housing is very limited.

STUDENT GROUP

The Twin Cities campus of the University is one the largest campuses in the country, with approximately 10,000 graduate students in diverse programs. In addition to students taking courses on campus, many students working in industry take courses via real-time interactive television. The program includes people from many states and countries.

STUDENT OUTCOMES

This is a new program and has not yet graduated any students. However, most students graduating in electrical engineering and computer science find positions in industry immediately upon completion of their degree programs.

LOCATION

The Twin Cities area offers diverse cultural and recreational opportunities, many within easy travel from campus. Two nationally known orchestras have full seasons, and there are many professional and community theaters in the cities, including the world-renowned Guthrie Theater. Minnesota has more than 10,000 lakes, including several within the metropolitan area, that offer both winter and summer fishing and summer boating. The Twin Cities are clean and attractive and have a low crime rate among metropolitan areas. The campus is within the city of Minneapolis and straddles the Mississippi River.

THE UNIVERSITY

The University of Minnesota was established in 1869 as Minnesota's land-grant university. It consists of four campuses, with the majority of students studying on the Twin Cities campus, where most of the engineering departments are located.

APPLYING

Graduate study in computer engineering is open to students with an undergraduate degree in computer engineering, electrical engineering, computer science, or a closely related field, such as mathematics or physics. In some instances, additional preparatory work may be required after admission. Applicants should contact the Director of Graduate Studies to request official application forms. The application deadline for students requesting financial aid is December 15 for admission for the following fall. All applicants requesting financial aid must submit scores from the GRE General Test, and all students from non-English-speaking countries must submit a recent TOEFL score.

CORRESPONDENCE AND INFORMATION

Director of Graduate Studies
Graduate Program in Computer Engineering
4-174 Electrical Engineering/Computer Science Building
University of Minnesota
200 Union Street S.E.
Minneapolis, Minnesota 55455

Telephone: 612-625-3300
Fax: 612-625-4583
E-mail: gradinfo@compengr.umn.edu
World Wide Web: http://www.compengr.umn.edu/

UNIVERSITY OF MINNESOTA
THE FACULTY AND THEIR RESEARCH

Vladimir Cherkassky, Associate Professor; Ph.D., Texas at Austin, 1985. Pattern recognition, neural networks, computer networks.

David H.-C. Du, Professor; Ph.D., Washington (Seattle), 1981. High-speed networking, multimedia applications, high-performance computing over clusters of workstations, database design, CAD for VLSI.

Larry Kinney, Professor; Ph.D., Iowa, 1968. Testing of digital systems, built-in-self-test, computer design, microprocessor-based systems, error-correcting codes.

Vipin Kumar, Professor; Ph.D., Maryland College Park, 1982. Parallel computing for sparse linear systems, scalability analysis.

Zhiyuan Li, Assistant Professor; Ph.D., Illinois at Urbana-Champaign, 1989. Parallelizing compilers, interprocedural analysis, hardware-software interactions, operating systems.

David J. Lilja, Associate Professor and Director of Graduate Studies; Ph.D., Illinois at Urbana-Champaign, 1991. Computer architecture, parallel and distributed computing, hardware-software interactions, performance analysis.

Lori Lucke, Assistant Professor; Ph.D., Minnesota, 1992. VLSI architectures and algorithms for signal processing and image processing, high-level synthesis, CAD algorithms.

Matthew T. O'Keefe, Associate Professor; Ph.D., Purdue, 1990. Computer architecture, compilers, parallel processing, applications, mass storage.

Shashi Shekhar, Associate Professor; Ph.D., Berkeley, 1989. Databases, geographic information systems, parallel computing, real-time computing.

Eugene B. Shragowitz, Professor; Ph.D., National Scientific Research Laboratory (Moscow), 1971. Computer-aided design of VLSI, fuzzy logic, nonlinear network theory, combinatorial optimization, learning algorithms.

Gerald E. Sobelman, Associate Professor; Ph.D., Harvard, 1979. VLSI design, digital signal processing, error-correcting codes.

Jaideep Srivastava, Associate Professor; Ph.D., Berkeley, 1988. Databases, distributed systems, multimedia computing.

Wei-tek Tsai, Professor; Ph.D., Berkeley, 1982. Software engineering.

Bapiraju Vinnakota, Assistant Professor; Ph.D., Princeton, 1991. VLSI design and test, CAD for testing, fault-tolerant computing.

Pen-Chung Yew, Professor; Ph.D., Illinois at Urbana-Champaign, 1981. Computer architecture, parallel machine organization, compilers, performance evaluation, parallel processing.

UNIVERSITY OF MINNESOTA

INSTITUTE OF TECHNOLOGY
DEPARTMENT OF COMPUTER SCIENCE

PROGRAM OF STUDY

The department offers a program of study leading to the M.S. and Ph.D. degrees in computer and information science. Applicants with related U.S. industrial experience can apply for a terminal M.S. course-work-only program. Students can select a program of study and research in all core areas of computer science, or they can structure a more interdisciplinary program to match their own special interests. The faculty conduct instruction and research in software engineering, parallel processing, numerical analysis, artificial intelligence, computer graphics, computer-aided design, theory of computation, computer networks, distributed systems, fault-tolerant computing, computer vision, robotics, neural networks, computer security, and computer architecture. Many faculty members actively participate in the graduate minors in scientific computation and in cognitive science. The objective of the graduate program is to prepare the student to carry out advanced research and development in the rapidly expanding areas of computer and information science. M.S. students may elect a course work or a thesis degree program. In addition to fulfilling course requirements for the M.S. degree, a candidate for the Ph.D. degree must pass a written preliminary examination. A typical Ph.D. program requires four years of graduate study, including the completion of an original Ph.D. dissertation with one of the department's faculty members. Lectures on significant current work in computer and information science are presented in a weekly colloquium series by visiting and local faculty members. In addition, seminars on special research topics are offered.

RESEARCH FACILITIES

The department has specialized laboratories in the areas of artificial intelligence, distributed computing, computer-aided design, robotics, vision, database, and music. Current computing resources include more than 250 workstations and personal computers from vendors such as Hewlett-Packard, SGI, Sun, Apple, and IBM in a mixture of research, instructional, and administrative roles. Research programs have access to departmental computing resources, such as four 4-processor SGI Challenge Computers connected via HIPPI and Fibre Channel, and eight IBM RS6000/590 and IBM SP2 computers connected via ATM. Workstation access is also provided by the Institute of Technology public labs, which have more than 300 Sun-, SGI-, and Macintosh- and Pentium-based computers. Dial-in SLIP service is provided up to 36.6 KBaud. The Minnesota Supercomputer Institute supports research carried out using the supercomputers and other resources of the Minnesota Supercomputer Center, Inc. The supercomputers available include a Cray 2 with four processors and 4 gigabytes of RAM, a Cray Y-MP with four processors and 512 megabytes of RAM, a Cray C-90 with nine processors and 4 gigabytes of RAM, and a Cray T3D with 128 Processing Elements (PE) and 64 megabytes of RAM/PE. Research access to supercomputers is also provided by the Army High Performance Computing Research Center, which has a Thinking Machines, Inc. CM5 with 896 PE and 32 megabytes of RAM and 4 vector units/PE. Library facilities are excellent and have on-line access to the catalog.

FINANCIAL AID

Fellowships and half-time assistantships are available. Fellowships may be awarded to outstanding graduate students in their first year of study. Teaching and research assistants receive a stipend and full or partial tuition waivers. Summer support is also available. Typically, a half-time teaching assistant is expected to teach laboratory sections for one of the introductory courses; this involves up to 20 hours per week including preparation, consulting, and grading. Research assistants are normally expected to devote an equivalent amount of time to funded research work. Because of the concentration of computer and computer-based industry in the Twin Cities area, graduate students often can find a variety of interesting part-time and summer job opportunities.

COST OF STUDY

Tuition is based on the number of credits, with a plateau from 7 to 14 credits. For 1997–98, resident tuition for graduate students is $1660 per quarter for 7 to 14 credits; tuition is $210 per credit above 14 credits. Nonresident tuition is $3260 per quarter for 7 to 14 credits; tuition is $420 per credit above 14 credits. Teaching assistants receive full or partial tuition waivers and health insurance but are responsible for certain fees each quarter.

LIVING AND HOUSING COSTS

Housing options include University residence halls, married student housing cooperatives, and rental properties throughout the Twin Cities. Detailed housing information can be obtained from Housing Services in Comstock Hall.

STUDENT GROUP

There are approximately 250 full- and part-time M.S. and Ph.D. students in the department. At least fifteen Ph.D. degrees have been awarded in each of the past five years. Many of the students who have received a Ph.D. from the department now hold faculty positions in other computer science departments offering doctoral study.

LOCATION

The Twin Cities area of Minneapolis and St. Paul justly deserves its reputation for providing a high quality of life. Recreational opportunities abound, ranging from sailing, canoeing, and camping in the summer to skiing and skating in the winter. The internationally known Tyrone Guthrie Theatre, the Walker Art Center, Orchestra Hall, Fitzgerald Theatre, and Ordway Music Center are but a few of the cultural attractions to be found. The Twin Cities area is also a center for computer research and design, and contacts are encouraged between the University and local industry.

THE UNIVERSITY AND THE DEPARTMENT

The computer science department is a part of the Institute of Technology, which also includes all of the engineering departments, mathematics, and the physical sciences. This broad spectrum of disciplines under a single administrative umbrella is an unusual arrangement and provides students with an excellent opportunity for study in a wide variety of related fields. The University is also well known for its medical and health sciences program, the Carlson School of Management, and the College of Biological Sciences. The computer science department maintains close ties with many of these other areas. In particular, various faculty members from electrical engineering, mathematics, health sciences, and the management information systems program are also part of the computer and information science graduate faculty. The structure of the University's Graduate School encourages multidisciplinary research.

APPLYING

To be admitted to the Graduate School, an applicant must have a bachelor's degree from a U.S. institution or a comparable degree from a recognized college or university outside the United States. Minimum preparation normally includes an undergraduate degree in computer science or in a related field with some computational experience. All applicants for the M.S. and Ph.D. must submit scores on the GRE General Test. GRE Subject Test scores are highly recommended, especially for those applicants seeking financial assistance. Application for admission should be made directly to the Graduate School. Admission applications received by January 2 for the following fall quarter will be considered for financial aid.

CORRESPONDENCE AND INFORMATION

Admission and Awards Committee
Department of Computer Science
University of Minnesota
200 Union Street, SE
Minneapolis, Minnesota 55455
Telephone: 612-625-4002

UNIVERSITY OF MINNESOTA
THE FACULTY AND THEIR RESEARCH

Professors

David Hung-Chuang Du, Ph.D., Washington (Seattle). Computer-aided design for VLSI, computer networking, database design, parallel and distributed architectures and processing.

Ding-Zhu Du, Ph.D., California, Santa Barbara. Complexity theory, theory of computation, combinatorial optimization.

David W. Fox, Ph.D., Maryland. Applied mathematics, eigenvalue problems.

Maria Gini, Doctor of Physics, Milan. Artificial intelligence, robotics.

Vipin Kumar, Ph.D., Maryland. Parallel processing, artificial intelligence.

Arthur Norberg, Ph.D., Wisconsin. History of science and technology.

Yousef Saad, Department Head; Doctorat, Grenoble (France). Sparse matrix computations, parallel computation, nonlinear equations, control theory, partial differential equations.

Eugene Shragowitz, Ph.D., Moscow. Combinatorial optimization, CAD of VLSI and computers, parallel and learning algorithms, learning automata, nonlinear networks.

James R. Slagle, Ph.D., MIT. Artificial intelligence.

Wei-Tek Tsai, Ph.D., Berkeley. Software engineering, parallel and distributed processing, computer security, artificial intelligence.

Pen-Chung Yew, Associate Head; Ph.D., Illinois at Urbana-Champaign. Computer architecture, optimizing compiler, parallel systems, performance evaluation.

Associate Professors

Daniel Boley, Ph.D., Stanford. Numerical analysis, linear algebra, control theory.

John Carlis, Ph.D., Minnesota. Database systems, management information systems, systems analysis and design.

Ravi Janardan, Ph.D., Purdue. Computational geometry, graph algorithms, data structures, distributed computation.

Haesun Park, Ph.D., Cornell. Numerical analysis, parallel computing, signal processing algorithms.

Nikolaos Papanikolopoulos, Ph.D., Carnegie Mellon. Computer vision, robotics, computer engineering, computer integrated manufacturing.

John Riedl, Ph.D., Purdue. Collaborative systems, database systems, fault tolerance, computer networks, object-oriented systems.

Shashi Shekhar, Ph.D., Berkeley. Neural networks, software engineering databases, geographic information systems, intelligent transportation systems.

Jaideep Srivastava, Director of Graduate Studies; Ph.D., Berkeley. Databases, distributed and parallel processing.

Shang-Hua Teng, Ph.D., Carnegie Mellon. Parallel processing, scientific computing, computational geometry, cryptography.

Anand Tripathi, Ph.D., Texas at Austin. Architecture, operating systems, distributed systems, parallel computing.

Assistant Professors

Mats Per Erik Heimdahl, Ph.D., California, Irvine. Software engineering, formal methods, requirements specification, embedded systems, safety-critical systems.

Joseph Konstan, Ph.D., Berkeley. Human-computer interaction, user interface tool kits and frameworks, multimedia systems.

Richard M. Voyles, Ph.D., Carnegie Mellon. Robotics, computer vision, mechatronics, MEMS, manufacturing methods, entrepreneurial engineering, computer engineering.

Zhi-Li Zhang, Ph.D., Massachusetts Amherst. Computer networks, real-time, distributed, multimedia systems.

UNIVERSITY OF MINNESOTA

DEPARTMENT OF ELECTRICAL AND COMPUTER ENGINEERING

PROGRAMS OF STUDY

Four master's degree plans and one doctoral degree plan are available. The Master of Science degree, the M.S.E.E., can be earned via Plan A, which includes a research thesis and 28 quarter credits in courses, with at least 20 credits from the major and at least 8 credits from other departments. The Plan B option for the M.S.E.E. requires 44 course credits plus a paper; at least 20 credits must come from the major and at least 8 from the minor. The Master of Engineering degree, the M.E.E., requires 44 course credits, with major and minor requirements similar to those of the M.S.E.E. degree. The Ph.D. program requires 60 total credits, with at least 21 course credits in the major and 18 credits in the minor; there are requirements for advanced courses within these credit guidelines. A written preliminary examination based on undergraduate material must be passed within the first or second year of study. An oral preliminary examination is taken when the course work is substantially complete. There is an oral paper presentation requirement, which is satisfied through a seminar offered within the department. A student with an assistantship can complete the master's program in two years and the Ph.D. program in five or six years after the B.S.

RESEARCH FACILITIES

The department's research utilizes both computational and experimental facilities. Experimental support includes access to a state-of-the-art microelectronic laboratory run by the Institute of Technology, which is vibration-isolated and has a class-10 clean room. Both silicon and III-V compound semiconductor devices and circuits, as well as optical devices, are routinely fabricated in the laboratory; micromechanical devices are also fabricated. The laboratory has epitaxial growth facilities and processing equipment for fabrication. The nanostructure lab houses state-of-the-art equipment for fabrication and characterization of nanodevices, including an ultrahigh-resolution e-beam lithography system, an atomic force microscope, femtosecond pulse lasers, and a terahertz electrooptical sampling system. The signal processing lab includes sensor arrays and data and image processing systems. The coherent optics laboratory includes lasers, optical tables, and computer facilities. The gaseous electronics laboratory has several ultrahigh-vacuum systems that can be modified to perform studies of plasma collisions and plasma-surface interactions. The magnetics laboratory includes sputtering and evaporation systems for thin-film fabrication and various diagnostic and test equipment. The microwave laboratory includes network and spectrum analyzers and a compact antenna test range. Diverse computing facilities are available to students in the program. There are workstations, personal computers, and central computing facilities.

FINANCIAL AID

Exceptional students may receive fellowship support. Most fellowships support either the first year of study or the final year of Ph.D. dissertation writing. Research assistantships are available from faculty members who have research grants; the number and sponsorship of these projects may vary. Research assistants may be able to use their research projects for their theses. During the 1996–97 academic year, there were approximately 105 research assistants and 30 teaching assistants in the program. Students with fellowships or 50 percent appointments as assistants are given full tuition waivers and personal health insurance.

COST OF STUDY

Tuition is based on the number of credits, with a plateau for 7–15 credits. For 1996–97, resident graduate tuition was $1560 per quarter for 7–15 credits. Nonresident tuition was $3130 per quarter. Assistants and fellows may obtain total or partial tuition waivers, but all students must pay certain fees each quarter. More detailed information may be obtained via the World Wide Web (http://www.umn.edu/tc/students/finances/tuition_and_fees.html). Rates for tuition and fees are subject to increases by the Regents.

LIVING AND HOUSING COSTS

Housing options include University residence halls, married student housing cooperatives, and rental properties throughout the Twin Cities. Detailed housing information can be obtained via the World Wide Web at http://www.umn.edu/tc/students/life/housing.html or from the Housing Bureau in Comstock Hall.

STUDENT GROUP

The Twin Cities campus of the University is one of the largest campuses in the country; there are approximately 10,000 graduate students in diverse programs on the campus. The electrical engineering program has about 160 graduate students on campus and another 90 taking courses in industry via real-time interactive television. The department's graduate group includes people from many states and countries.

STUDENT OUTCOMES

Recent graduates have been offered positions in industry and on university faculties. Some remain in the upper Midwest, but others have moved toward the coasts. Most graduates find positions immediately upon completion of their degree programs.

LOCATION

The Twin Cities area offers diverse cultural and recreational opportunities, many within easy travel from the campus. Two nationally known orchestras, the Minnesota Orchestra and the St. Paul Chamber Orchestra, have full seasons, and the Minnesota Orchestra holds a summer festival in downtown Minneapolis. There are many professional and community theaters in the cities, including the world-renowned Guthrie Theater. Minnesota has more than 10,000 lakes offering both winter and summer fishing and summer boating; there are more than 10 lakes within the Twin Cities area. The Twin Cities are clean and attractive and have a low crime rate among metropolitan areas. The campus is within the city of Minneapolis and straddles the Mississippi River.

THE UNIVERSITY

The University of Minnesota was established in 1869 and has four campuses. The majority of the students study on the Twin Cities campus, where most of the engineering departments are located.

APPLYING

Applicants should contact the Director of Graduate Studies by mail to request official application forms. Since many course sequences start in the fall, students are strongly encouraged to enter the program at that time. The application deadline for those desiring financial aid is December 15 for fall quarter admission. This date concerns the arrival of the completed forms; applicants are encouraged to send review material well in advance of December 15. Students who do not require aid may submit completed applications up to July 1. All students from non-English-speaking countries must submit a recent TOEFL score, which must exceed 550. All applicants desiring financial aid must submit scores on the GRE General Test. Applicants must have a bachelor's degree from an engineering or science program; people with engineering technology degrees are not accepted.

CORRESPONDENCE AND INFORMATION

Director of Graduate Studies
Department of Electrical and Computer Engineering
University of Minnesota, Twin Cities
200 Union Street
Minneapolis, Minnesota 55455

Telephone: 612-625-3564
E-mail: graduate_studies@ee.umn.edu
World Wide Web: http://www.ee.umn.edu

UNIVERSITY OF MINNESOTA
THE FACULTY AND THEIR RESEARCH

Fredric N. Bailey, Professor; Ph.D., Michigan, 1964. Control system theory and applications, control of mechanical motion.

Stephen A. Campbell, Associate Professor; Ph.D., Northwestern, 1981. Fabrication and characterization of high-speed devices, microelectronics.

Vladimir S. Cherkassky, Associate Professor; Ph.D., Texas at Austin, 1985. Pattern recognition, neural networks, computer networks.

Stephen Y. Chou, Professor; Ph.D., MIT, 1986. Nanofabrication and nanoscale electronic, optoelectronic, and magnetic devices.

Philip I. Cohen, Professor; Ph.D., Wisconsin, 1975. Molecular-beam epitaxy of artificially structured microelectronic materials.

Douglas W. Ernie, Associate Professor; Ph.D., Minnesota, 1980. Plasma physics and plasma chemistry, DC and radio-frequency plasma discharges.

Tryphon T. Georgiou, Professor; Ph.D., Florida, 1983. System theory and control engineering.

Anand Gopinath, Professor; Ph.D., 1965, D.Eng., 1978, Sheffield (England). Optoelectronic devices and circuits, including lasers, switches, modulators, guided wave structures, microwave devices, and circuits.

Ramesh Harjani, Associate Professor; Ph.D., Carnegie Mellon, 1989. Analog and mixed-signal design, CAD for analog and mixed-signal design.

Ted Higman, Associate Professor; Ph.D., Illinois, 1989. Atomic force microscopy, nanolithography.

James E. Holte, Associate Professor; Ph.D., Minnesota, 1960. Bioelectrical science with applications in medicine, aids for handicapped persons.

Jack H. Judy, Professor; Ph.D., Minnesota, 1965. Magnetic thin films, magnetic recording media and heads, micromagnetics, magnetic measurements, magnetic sensors, magnetic memories.

Richard Y. Kain, Professor; Sc.D., MIT, 1962. Computer system architecture, secure computer systems.

Mostafa Kaveh, Professor; Ph.D., Purdue, 1974. Communication theory, signal processing, parameter estimation, image processing.

John C. Kieffer, Professor; Ph.D., Illinois, 1970. Information theory, communication theory, techniques for reliable data transmission.

Larry L. Kinney, Professor; Ph.D., Iowa, 1968. Fault-tolerant computer design, test vector generation, fault simulation, concurrent error detection.

K. S. P. Kumar, Professor; Ph.D., Purdue, 1964. Control and systems.

E. Bruce Lee, Professor; Ph.D., Minnesota, 1960. Control and systems, mathematical models, synthesis techniques for control systems.

Thomas S. Lee, Associate Professor; Ph.D., Minnesota, 1961. Applied electrostatics, electrodynamics, and fluid-mechanical phenomena.

James Leger, Professor; Ph.D., California, San Diego, 1980. Electrooptics, Fourier optics and holography, microoptical devices, diffractive optics, semiconductor and solid state lasers.

David J. Lilja, Associate Professor; Ph.D., Illinois at Urbana-Champaign, 1991. High-performance computing, parallel and distributed computing, computer architecture, compilers.

Lori E. Lucke, Assistant Professor; Ph.D., Minnesota, 1992. Architectures for signal processing, high-level synthesis, CAD algorithms.

Ned Mohan, Professor; Ph.D., Wisconsin, 1973. Electric power systems, power electronics, motion control.

Jay Moon, Associate Professor; Ph.D., Carnegie Mellon, 1990. Communications, magnetic recording, signal processing.

Marshall I. Nathan, Professor; Ph.D., Harvard, 1958. Molecular-beam epitaxy and its use to fabricate layered semiconductors, semiconductor device physics, large gap semiconductors.

Matthew T. O'Keefe, Associate Professor; Ph.D., Purdue, 1990. Computer architecture, compilers, parallel processing, applications, mass storage.

Keshab K. Parhi, Professor; Ph.D., Berkeley, 1988. Signal processing systems on VLSI chips, computer-aided design, signal processing, computer arithmetic.

William T. Peria, Professor; Ph.D., British Columbia, 1957. Physical electronics, semiconductor epitaxy, IC fabrication.

Dennis L. Polla, Professor; Ph.D., Berkeley, 1985. Microelectromechanical systems, biomedical microinstruments, solid-state materials and devices, integrated circuits.

Mahmoud Riaz, Professor; Sc.D., MIT, 1955. Electric energy processing and control, computer-aided analysis of electromechanical and power systems.

William P. Robbins, Professor; Ph.D., Washington (Seattle), 1971. Acoustic sensing, ultrasonics, surface-wave devices, microactuators, power electronics.

P. Paul Ruden, Professor; Ph.D., Stuttgart, 1982. Semiconductor materials and physics of novel electronic devices.

Sachin Sapatnekar, Associate Professor; Ph.D., Illinois at Urbana-Champaign, 1992. CAD of VLSI systems, VLSI design.

Guillermo Sapiro, Assistant Professor; Ph.D., Technion (Israel), 1993. Computer vision, systems, image processing.

Gerald E. Sobelman, Associate Professor; Ph.D., Harvard, 1979. Digital VLSI design with applications in digital signal processing and digital communications.

Joseph Talghader, Assistant Professor; Ph.D., Berkeley, 1995. Optoelectronics, microelectronics.

Allen R. Tannenbaum, Professor; Ph.D., Harvard, 1976. Robust feedback control systems, mathematical analysis of control systems, computer vision, image processing.

Andrew R. Teel, Assistant Professor; Ph.D., Berkeley, 1992. Nonlinear systems analysis and control.

Ahmed H. Tewfik, Professor; Sc.D., MIT, 1987. Multimedia data coding and management, wavelets in signal processing, medical and radar imaging, solitons, stochastic resonance.

Bapiraju Vinnakota, Assistant Professor; Ph.D., Princeton, 1991. Fault-tolerant computing, digital system testing, CAD for testing.

Bruce Wollenberg, Professor; Ph.D., Pennsylvania, 1974. Electric power system analytical methods.

UNIVERSITY OF MISSOURI–COLUMBIA

DEPARTMENT OF COMPUTER ENGINEERING AND COMPUTER SCIENCE

PROGRAMS OF STUDY

The Department of Computer Engineering and Computer Science at the University of Missouri–Columbia offers graduate programs of study leading to Master of Science degrees in computer science and computer engineering and the Doctor of Philosophy in computer engineering and computer science. Faculty research areas include fuzzy set theory and fuzzy logic, neural networks, computer vision, parallel and distributed computing, computer networking, advanced computing and high-speed networking systems and applications, digital libraries, artificial intelligence, computer graphics and scientific visualization, multimedia systems, information systems and design, biomedical engineering, and database theory and design.

An M.S. candidate must complete a minimum of 30 semester credit hours and pass a final examination to demonstrate mastery of the work included in a thesis or substantial independent project. To achieve Ph.D. candidacy, a student must pass a qualifying examination. The Ph.D. program requires a minimum of 72 semester hours beyond the B.S. degree. The candidate must pass both a written and an oral examination, complete a doctoral dissertation on a topic approved by the candidate's advisory committee, and defend the dissertation in an oral final examination.

RESEARCH FACILITIES

A wide range of computing and networking resources are available to the students in the department, the college, and the campus. These resources provide ready access to state-of-the-art computing systems and networking facilities ranging from small desktop systems to large computational systems that are interconnected by traditional and advanced networking facilities. These connections also provide links to the Internet for global access to information, software, machines, and colleagues. All of these facilities provide a wealth of opportunity for students to use and study state-of-the-art computing.

FINANCIAL AID

Financial aid is available through departmental teaching and research assistantships as well as campus fellowship programs. All assistantships and fellowships carry a full tuition waiver. Stipends vary based on level of employment and level of achievement in the degree program.

COST OF STUDY

For the 1996–97 academic year, the graduate educational fee was $153.20 per credit hour for Missouri residents and $460.60 per credit hour for nonresidents. An activities fee of $103.25 per semester is charged to students enrolling in 12 or more credit hours. For part-time enrollment, the student activities fee is calculated per credit hour. An additional fee of $33.70 per credit hour is charged to students enrolled in courses offered by the College of Engineering.

LIVING AND HOUSING COSTS

Housing is available for graduate students both on and off campus. Columbia living conditions are pleasant and of moderate cost comparable to the regional (Big 12 institutions) average.

STUDENT GROUP

There are currently 130 graduate students in the Department of Computer Engineering and Computer Science; approximately 70 are enrolled in the M.S. in computer science program, 30 in the M.S. in computer engineering program, and 30 in the Ph.D. program. The average age is approximately 26, and approximately 12 percent of the students are women. Students come from all over the United States and from sixteen other countries.

STUDENT OUTCOMES

M.S. graduates typically find employment with a wide range of business, scientific, and research organizations as engineers, software designers, and application developers. Ph.D. graduates typically take research positions in industry or positions as faculty members in major universities across the country. International graduates often find employment in industry or academia in their home countries.

LOCATION

The University is located in Columbia, a city of approximately 75,000. It is located in the center of Missouri, near the Missouri River valley. It is approximately a 2-hour drive from either St. Louis or Kansas City on Interstate 70.

THE UNIVERSITY AND THE DEPARTMENT

The University of Missouri–Columbia is the flagship campus of the University of Missouri System and has more than 22,000 students and 1,800 faculty members. It is a member of the American Association of Universities (AAU) and a Carnegie Research I institution. In addition to engineering, the University offers degrees in agriculture, business, education, journalism, law, medicine, nursing, veterinary medicine, and the arts and sciences.

The department was created as an independent department in the College of Engineering in July 1995. The department was formed by combining the strengths in computational science from elements of the electrical and computer engineering department and the computer science department. Both electrical and computer engineering and computer science have long-standing histories at MU, and the new department was formed to capitalize upon the strengths of these two programs in a single unit.

APPLYING

Applicants should have earned a B.S. degree in computer engineering or computer science; if a B.S. in another field was obtained, accepted applicants will most likely have to complete preparatory courses in addition to their degree program requirements. To apply, an application form, GRE General Test scores, three confidential letters of recommendation, a personal statement describing the applicant's background and academic objectives, transcripts of all previous college work, and an application fee ($25 for U.S. residents or $50 for international applicants) must be submitted. Students whose native language is not English must also submit TOEFL scores.

CORRESPONDENCE AND INFORMATION

Director of Graduate Studies
Department of Computer Engineering and Computer Science
201 Engineering Building West
University of Missouri–Columbia
Columbia, Missouri 65211
Telephone: 573-882-3843
Fax: 573-882-8318
E-mail: cecsdgs@condor.cecs.missouri.edu
World Wide Web: http://www.cecs.missouri.edu

UNIVERSITY OF MISSOURI—COLUMBIA

THE FACULTY AND THEIR RESEARCH

Professors

Su-Shing Chen, Chair; Ph.D., Maryland, 1970. Digital libraries, intelligent agent architectures, digital information environments, content-based indexing for spatial (information) objects.

Harry Tyrer, Associate Chair; Ph.D., Duke, 1972. Computer architecture, object-oriented languages, software engineering, biomedical engineering, biophysics, instrumentation.

James Keller, Ph.D., Missouri—Columbia, 1978. Fuzzy set theory and fuzzy logic, computer vision, pattern recognition, neural networks.

Otho R. Plummer, Ph.D., Texas at Austin, 1966. Application systems, database systems, scientific programming, graphics applications and virtual reality.

Frederick N. Springsteel, Ph.D., Washington (Seattle), 1967. Database design, theory of parallel algorithms, foundations of computing.

Xinhua Zhuang, Ph.D., Peking, 1963. Computer vision, image processing, pattern recognition, neural net computing, speech recognition, artificial intelligence.

Associate Professors

Paul Gader, Ph.D., Florida, 1986. Character and handwriting recognition, image algebra and math, morphology, pattern recognition.

Raghu Krishnapuram, Ph.D., Carnegie Mellon, 1987. Fuzzy set theory, pattern recognition, image processing, computer vision.

Youran Lan, Ph.D., Michigan State, 1988. Parallel and distributed systems, parallel algorithm design, computer networking.

Kannappan Palaniappan, Ph.D., Illinois, 1991. Computer graphics, scientific visualization, remote sensing, stereo and nonrigid motion analysis, parallel algorithms for image analysis, sequence analysis.

Youssef G. Saab, Ph.D., Illinois, 1990. Combinatorial optimization, design automation, graph and geometric algorithms, stochastic algorithms.

Gordon K. Springer, Director of Graduate Studies; Ph.D., Penn State, 1970. Computer networking, advanced computing and high-speed networking systems and applications, distributed computing, software system design.

Assistant Professors

Anupam Joshi, Ph.D., Purdue, 1993. Networked and mobile computing, artificial and computational intelligence, computer and human vision, computer-mediated instruction.

Hongchi Shi, Ph.D., Florida, 1994. Parallel and distributed computing, image processing, computer vision.

UNIVERSITY OF MISSOURI–COLUMBIA

DEPARTMENT OF ELECTRICAL ENGINEERING

PROGRAMS OF STUDY

The Department of Electrical Engineering at the University of Missouri–Columbia offers graduate programs of study and research leading to the degrees of Master of Science and Doctor of Philosophy in electrical engineering. Faculty research areas include signal processing and wireless communication, computer communication, antenna design and remote sensing, solid-state device and optoelectronics, physical electronics, control, power electronics, digital power measurements, and biomedical engineering.

An M.S. candidate must complete a minimum of 30 total semester credit hours and pass a final examination to demonstrate mastery of the work included in a thesis or a substantial independent project. To achieve Ph.D. candidacy, a student must pass a qualifying exam. The Ph.D. program requires a minimum of 72 semester hours beyond the B.S., with research on the doctoral dissertation generally taking about one full year. The candidate must pass both a written and an oral comprehensive examination, complete a doctoral dissertation on a topic approved by his or her advisory committee, and defend the dissertation in an oral final examination.

RESEARCH FACILITIES

Research activities in electrical engineering are conducted in laboratories designed to support work in microcircuit design and processing, power electronics and power quality, electron beam radiation, molecular beam epitaxy, microcomputer development, and high-frequency measurements. Research is enhanced by an extensive network of computer facilities. The department, college, and University computing facilities are connected to one another and the Internet through both fiber-optic and wire cables.

FINANCIAL AID

Financial aid is available through departmental teaching and research assistantships as well as campus fellowship programs. All assistantships and fellowships carry a full tuition waiver. Stipends vary based on level of employment and level of achievement in degree program.

COST OF STUDY

For the 1996–97 academic year, the graduate educational fee was $153.20 per credit hour for Missouri residents and $460.60 per credit hour for nonresidents. An activities fee of $103.25 per semester was charged to students enrolling in 12 or more credit hours. For part-time enrollment, the student activities fee is calculated per credit hour. An additional fee of $33.70 per credit hour was charged to all students enrolled in courses offered by the College of Engineering.

LIVING AND HOUSING COSTS

Housing is available for graduate students both on and off campus. Columbia living conditions are pleasant and of moderate cost, comparable to the regional (Big 12 institutions) average.

STUDENT GROUP

There are currently 101 graduate students in the Department of Electrical Engineering: 55 are enrolled in the Ph.D. program, and the remaining students are seeking M.S. degrees. The average age is 30, and approximately 14 percent of the students are women. Students come from all over the United States and from nineteen countries.

STUDENT OUTCOMES

M.S. graduates typically find employment in companies such as McDonnell Douglas, Intel, Emerson Electric, Texas Instruments, and Motorola. Ph.D. graduates take research positions in organizations such as IBM and Bell Laboratories or as faculty members in major universities across the country. International graduates often find employment in industry or academia in their home countries.

LOCATION

The department's main location is in Columbia; it administers a coordinated engineering program in Kansas City. Columbia, a city of approximately 75,000, is located in the center of Missouri, near the Missouri River valley. It is approximately a 2-hour drive from either St. Louis or Kansas City and only 1 hour from the scenic Ozark recreational areas. Kansas City has a population of approximately 1 million.

THE UNIVERSITY AND THE DEPARTMENT

The University of Missouri–Columbia is the flagship campus of the University of Missouri System and has 22,483 students and more than 1,800 faculty members. It is a member of the American Association of Universities (AAU) and a Carnegie Research I institution. In addition to engineering, the University offers degrees in agriculture, business, education, journalism, law, medicine, nursing, veterinary medicine, and the arts and sciences.

One of the pioneering electrical engineering programs in the country, the department at UMC was founded in 1885 and was the first such program west of the Mississippi. The department consists of 23 faculty members, 6 of whom are located at the Kansas City campus.

APPLYING

Applicants should have earned a B.S. degree in electrical engineering; if a B.S. in a field other than electrical engineering was obtained, accepted applicants will most likely be required to complete preparatory courses in addition to their degree program requirements. To apply, an application form, GRE General Test scores, three confidential letters of recommendation, a personal statement describing the applicant's background and academic objectives, transcripts of all previous college work, and an application fee ($25 for U.S. resident applicants or $50 for international applicants) must be submitted. Students whose native language is not English must also submit TOEFL scores.

CORRESPONDENCE AND INFORMATION

Director of Graduate Studies
Department of Electrical Engineering
219 Engineering Building West
University of Missouri–Columbia
Columbia, Missouri 65211
Telephone: 573-882-3539
Fax: 573-882-0397
E-mail: unk@ece.missouri.edu

UNIVERSITY OF MISSOURI–COLUMBIA

THE FACULTY AND THEIR RESEARCH

Columbia Campus

Andrew J. Blanchard, Professor; Ph.D., Texas A&M, 1977. Microwave engineering, radar systems, remote sensing, long wavelength imaging, antennas.

Earl J. Charlson, Professor; Ph.D., Carnegie Mellon, 1964. Solid-state devices, thin-film technology, instrumentation.

Chang Wen Chen, Assistant Professor; Ph.D., Illinois at Urbana-Champaign, 1992. Image and signal processing, wireless communications.

Randy Curry, Assistant Professor; Ph.D., St. Andrews (Scotland), 1992. Physical electronics, pulse power applications, diagnostics.

Michael Devaney, Associate Professor; Ph.D., Missouri–Columbia, 1971. Digital systems, digital power measurement, power electronics, computer simulation.

T. Greg Engel, Assistant Professor; Ph.D., Texas Tech, 1990. Pulse power, high-power switching concepts, physical electronics.

Kevin Gillis, Assistant Professor; Ph.D., Washington (St. Louis), 1993. Biomedical problems.

Huber Graham, Associate Professor; Ph.D., MIT, 1969. Digital system design, circuit design.

Robert Leavene, Associate Professor; Ph.D., Missouri–Columbia, 1972. Digital system design, microprocessor applications, digital signal processing.

Kai-Fong Lee, Professor and Chair; Ph.D., Cornell, 1966. Antenna theory and design, applied electromagnetics.

Chun-Shin Lin, Associate Professor; Ph.D., Purdue, 1980. Robotics, computer vision.

Robert McLaren, Professor; Ph.D., Purdue, 1966. Artificial intelligence, robotics, image processing, computer process control.

Jon Meese, Professor; Ph.D., Purdue, 1970. Irradiations, optics, semiconductor theory, solid-state physics.

William Nunnally, Professor; Ph.D., Texas Tech, 1975. Physical electronics, pulsed power, antennas, applied electromagnetics.

Robert M. O'Connell, Associate Professor; Ph.D., Illinois at Urbana-Champaign, 1975. Semiconductor device modeling, laser effects in optical networks, power electronics.

Kayvan Sadra, Assistant Professor; Ph.D., Texas at Austin, 1993. Molecular beam epitaxy of semiconductor heterostructures, novel materials and devices, low-dimensional systems.

Wes B. Sherman, Professor; Ph.D., Missouri–Columbia, 1966. Electromagnetics, communications, instrumentation.

Charles Slivinsky, Professor; Ph.D., Arizona, 1969. Power systems, digital signal processing, multimedia.

Kenneth Unklesbay, Professor; Ph.D., Missouri–Columbia, 1972. Control system design, food processing engineering.

Coordinated Engineering Program In Kansas City

Ghulam M. Chaudhry, Assistant Professor; Ph.D., Wayne State, 1989. Computer networking, parallel processing.

Curt Davis, Assistant Professor; Ph.D., Kansas, 1992. Microwave engineering, radar systems, satellite remote sensing.

Suat M. Ertem, Associate Professor; Ph.D., Missouri–Columbia, 1985. Application of computer methods in power systems analysis, expert system application on power systems.

Yanpeng Guo, Assistant Professor; Ph.D., California, Davis, 1994. Wireless communication.

Jerome Knopp, Associate Professor; Ph.D., Texas at Austin, 1976. Optical systems, information processing, holography, high-energy laser systems, scalar diffraction theory, dimensional analysis, modeling.

David G. Skitek, Assistant Professor; Ph.D., Arizona State, 1973. Active network synthesis, simulations, digital signal processing.

UNIVERSITY OF MISSOURI–KANSAS CITY

COMPUTER SCIENCE TELECOMMUNICATIONS

PROGRAMS OF STUDY

Computer Science Telecommunications (CST) at the University of Missouri–Kansas City (UMKC) offers courses leading to M.S. degrees in computer networking, software engineering, and telecommunications networking and Ph.D. degrees in computer networking, software architecture, and telecommunications networking through the University's interdisciplinary Ph.D. program. Computer Science Telecommunications holds an exciting and unique niche position, blending the telecommunications aspects of engineering, the networking aspects of computer science, and the software architecture aspects of information technology. The program offers in-depth education in the new technologies and skills most in demand in these areas. Graduate students have the opportunity to get a concentrated, state-of-the-art education in the most dynamic, challenging, and professionally significant specialty areas. The M.S. degrees are designed to prepare graduates for professional careers as project leaders and managers, to do research, and to go on to advanced studies. The M.S. degree requires 30 credit hours of course work in addition to the thesis or 36 credit hours with the nonthesis option. The Ph.D. degrees are designed to prepare graduates for research, teaching, and high-level management in the specialty areas of computer networking, software architecture, and telecommunications networking. The Ph.D. program entails course work beyond the master's degree and a dissertation based on original, supervised research in the specialty area. All of the graduate degrees address the theory, design, and application levels of communications software, hardware, and networks.

RESEARCH FACILITIES

CST is fully equipped with three instructional laboratories for teaching and student use. Equipment includes Alpha-based UNIX machines, a Windows NT Pentium-based network, and fully networked Macintosh workstations. CST also houses state-of-the-art laboratories for graduate student and faculty research in each department. There is also a lab with graphic and character-based terminals. CST has a number of ATM switches and conducts research on a 38-gigahertz radio communications link. The location of UMKC in the telecommunications industry hub of Kansas City provides opportunities for students to do research and internships in cutting-edge industry laboratories by special arrangement. Library facilities include the UMKC Libraries, which maintain comprehensive journal subscriptions and offer a full range of reference services, and the private Linda Hall Library on campus, which is an internationally known science and technology resource.

FINANCIAL AID

The Computer Science Telecommunications program has approximately twenty-five graduate teaching and research assistantships each year for quarter-time or half-time support. Research assistantships are also available for advanced students from faculty members with research grants and contracts. The Chancellor's Non-Resident Award, which covers the nonresident portion of UMKC tuition and fees for the first semester of study, is awarded to students who are nominated to the University Scholarship Office by the graduate faculty. Other forms of financial support include grants and loans from state and national programs.

COST OF STUDY

In 1997–98, graduate tuition is $175.70 per credit hour for Missouri residents and $492.70 for nonresidents. For Computer Science Telecommunications courses, there is a fee of $16.50 per credit hour to support student-directed equipment purchases. Additional costs include application fees, books and course materials, and thesis processing.

LIVING AND HOUSING COSTS

The UMKC Office of Financial Aid suggests that the costs of housing, food, medical and dental insurance, and transportation average $10,200 per year for graduate students. On-campus housing is limited; however, off-campus housing is readily available.

STUDENT GROUP

In fall 1996, the Computer Science Telecommunications program had 290 undergraduates, 113 master's students, and 31 Ph.D. students. Of the graduate students, approximately half were full-time. Seventy-three percent were men and 27 percent were women, and 79 percent were international students. Approximately half of the full-time students received financial aid. The CST graduate faculty seeks student applicants with a solid technical preparation and a strong interest in high-level applications and theoretical training in its specialized fields.

STUDENT OUTCOMES

Computer Science Telecommunications graduates have gone on to technical, research, and managerial positions with industry leaders, including AT&T, Cisco Systems, Digital Equipment, GTE, Hewlett-Packard, IBM, LiTel Communications, MCI, Nortel, Sprint, and Sprint PCS. Graduates also manage information systems and communications networks across a wide range of industries. The demand for graduates is high, and most students have a wide range of employment opportunities upon graduation.

LOCATION

UMKC is located in the cultural heart of Kansas City, three blocks from the Nelson-Atkins Gallery of Art and the shopping and entertainment facilities of the Country Club Plaza. Major-league soccer, football, and baseball, in addition to numerous trendy shopping and historic sites, round out the recreational opportunities in this culturally rich, medium-sized (population 1.6 million) metropolitan area.

THE UNIVERSITY AND THE PROGRAM

UMKC is one of four campuses in the University of Missouri System. It was chartered in 1929 as the University of Kansas City, a private liberal arts college established by business and civic leaders, and in 1963 merged with the University of Missouri System to become UMKC. Computer Science Telecommunications was established in 1984 with support from the Sprint Corporation to meet the growing needs for research and highly trained employees in the telecommunications industry.

APPLYING

Application deadlines are March 1 for fall admission and financial aid consideration, April 15 for summer or fall, and August 15 for winter. Applicants should have a sound background in computer science and mathematics. A minimum GPA of 3.5 (for Ph.D.) or 3.0 (for M.S.) and a GRE quantitative score in at least the 85th (for Ph.D.) or 75th (for M.S.) percentile are required. International applicants also need a score of at least 550 on the TOEFL.

CORRESPONDENCE AND INFORMATION

For application and general information:
Computer Science Telecommunications
University of Missouri–Kansas City
5100 Rockhill Road, Room 207
Kansas City, Missouri 64110
Telephone: 816-235-1193
E-mail: info@cstp.umkc.edu
World Wide Web: http://www.umkc.edu

For specific questions about the program:
Dr. Richard G. Hetherington, Director and Professor
Computer Science Telecommunications
University of Missouri–Kansas City
5100 Rockhill Road, Room 207
Kansas City, Missouri 64110
Telephone: 816-235-1193
E-mail: hetherington@cstp.umkc.edu

UNIVERSITY OF MISSOURI–KANSAS CITY
THE FACULTY AND THEIR RESEARCH

Jagan Agrawal, Professor; Ph.D., North Carolina State, 1972. Computer communications, telecommunications, digital communications, digital signal processing.

Kenneth Blundell, Associate Professor; Ph.D., Nottingham (England), 1977. Software engineering, artificial intelligence, neural networks.

Lein Harn, Associate Professor; Ph.D., Minnesota, 1984. Digital signal processing, digital filter design, digital speech and image processing, cryptosystem design, data/video encryption.

Richard Hetherington, Professor and Director; Ph.D., Wisconsin–Madison, 1961. Computer networking, numerical analysis.

Mary Lou Hines, Assistant Professor; Ph.D., Kansas State, 1992. Object-oriented databases, software metrics, software engineering.

Vijay Kumar, Associate Professor; Ph.D., Southampton (England), 1983. Database management systems, distributed systems, main memory database management systems, concurrency control, database recovery, real-time systems.

Deep Medhi, Associate Professor; Ph.D., Wisconsin–Madison, 1987. Computer/communications network modeling, routing, and design; teletraffic science; large-scale optimization algorithms; network management.

Jonathan Oh, Associate Professor; Ph.D., Hawaii, 1971. Artificial intelligence, natural-language processing, ontological engineering, programming language theory.

E. K. Park, Professor; Ph.D., Northwestern, 1988. Software engineering, software architectures, object-oriented design/analysis, formal methods, programming methods, distributed systems, real-time processing.

Jerry Place, Associate Professor; Ph.D., Kansas, 1984. Distributed systems, parallel computer architecture, computer and network performance analysis, simulation and queuing theory, real-time systems.

Xiaojun Shen, Associate Professor; Ph.D., Illinois at Urbana-Champaign, 1989. Parallel processing, interconnection networks, algorithms.

Khosrow Sohraby, Professor; Ph.D., Toronto, 1985. Design and analysis of high-speed computer and communication networks, networking and design aspects of wireless and mobile communications, analysis of algorithms, parallel processing and large-scale computations.

Jerry Stach, Assistant Professor; Ph.D., Union (Ohio), 1995. Formalisms required for network software architecture, domain theory, concurrency algebras, computational models of network services.

Adrian Tang, Professor; Ph.D., Princeton, 1974. Computer networks, operating systems, programming languages and semantics, domain theory, protocol specifications.

Appie Van de Liefvoort, Associate Professor; Ph.D., Nebraska, 1982. Queuing theory and performance modeling, matrix-exponential distribution, performance modeling of computer and communication networks, algorithms and complexity.

UNIVERSITY OF NEBRASKA–LINCOLN

DEPARTMENT OF COMPUTER SCIENCE AND ENGINEERING

PROGRAMS OF STUDY

The Department of Computer Science and Engineering offers the degree of Doctor of Philosophy and both thesis and nonthesis options for the Master of Science (the nonthesis option requires a project). Master's students with a computer engineering background may enroll in the specialization area in computer engineering. Cooperative Doctor of Philosophy programs are also offered in conjunction with the Department of Mathematics and Statistics and under the unified engineering Ph.D. program.

RESEARCH FACILITIES

The Department of Computer Science and Engineering has extensive computing facilities for research. These include a Silicon Graphics Challenge L, fifty workstations, and a large number of PCs. All graduate offices are furnished with state-of-the-art computing facilities. Advanced laboratories in cryptology, graphics, human factors and multimedia, vision and image processing, and VLSI are available for specialized research. A high-speed distributed computing system interconnected by an ATM network is also available for research in networking and distributed computing. All the machines are connected by a campuswide high-performance network utilizing a fiber-optic backbone.

FINANCIAL AID

Financial support is available in the form of teaching assistantships, research assistantships, tuition waivers, and fellowships to highly qualified candidates. These carry academic-year stipends of $10,000 to $12,000 plus tuition remission. Graduate students may also apply for loans through the Office of Scholarships and Financial Aid, 16 Administration Building.

There are numerous part-time employment opportunities both on and off campus for experienced programmers, but these normally require application in person.

COST OF STUDY

Graduate tuition in 1997–98 is approximately $105 per credit hour for Nebraska residents and approximately $250 per credit hour for nonresidents. Fees for all full-time students are $205 per semester. Teaching and research assistants pay at the same rate as Nebraska residents, except that their first 9 credit hours each semester are free.

LIVING AND HOUSING COSTS

Room and board charges for students living on campus are approximately $3560–$4625 for the 1997–98 academic year.

STUDENT GROUP

The University of Nebraska–Lincoln has a total enrollment of 23,887 students. The Department of Computer Science and Engineering has 66 M.S. and 22 Ph.D. candidates and grants about 50 B.S. degrees per year. Students actively participate in student and state chapters of the Association for Computing Machinery (ACM) and the Institute of Electrical and Electronics Engineers (IEEE).

LOCATION

Lincoln, a city of 200,000, is an educational and state government center. It is situated in a gently rolling terrain and has attractive wide streets, fine parks, and excellent public transportation and bicycle routes. The city has a strong, progressive public school system. The average educational level of Lincoln's citizens is one of the highest in the country. The University, two other colleges, and the community together offer a wide variety of recreational and cultural activities.

THE UNIVERSITY

The University of Nebraska, founded in 1869, has an enrollment of 48,759 students on its four campuses. It was the first institution west of the Mississippi River to offer degree work beyond the baccalaureate level. The University is a member of the Association of American Universities. It is among the top twenty-five American universities in terms of the number of its graduates listed in *Who's Who*. The Carnegie Foundation for Advancement of Teaching has designated the University of Nebraska–Lincoln a Research One University.

APPLYING

An application form and official transcripts of all college work must be filed with the Graduate College. At the same time, three letters of reference, a statement of purpose, and a brief résumé should be filed with the department. For admission in the fall semester the application deadline is March 1, and for admission in the spring semester the application deadline is October 1. Admission to full graduate standing in the M.S. program requires the equivalent of the undergraduate major in computer science or computer engineering, as determined by the department. Students applying to the Ph.D. program must generally have an M.S. degree in computer science or the equivalent. Students seeking financial assistance should complete the application by January 15. Nebraska law requires tests of spoken English before non-native speakers are allowed to lecture. High scores on the General Test of the GRE and the Subject Test in computer science or in engineering may increase the student's chances of getting an assistantship, and it is advisable for applicants to submit these scores.

CORRESPONDENCE AND INFORMATION

Department of Computer Science and Engineering
Ferguson Hall
University of Nebraska
Lincoln, Nebraska 68588-0115

Telephone: 402-472-2401
E-mail: gradinfo@cse.unl.edu (information inquiries only)
World Wide Web: http://www.cse.unl.edu

UNIVERSITY OF NEBRASKA—LINCOLN
THE FACULTY AND THEIR RESEARCH

Prabir Bhattacharya, Professor; D.Phil., Oxford. Computer vision, parallel algorithms, discrete mathematics and combinatorics, applications of algebra. E-mail: prabir@cse.unl.edu

Jean-Camille Birget, Associate Professor; Ph.D., Berkeley. Algorithmic problems in algebra, complexity, automata theory. E-mail: birget@cse.unl.edu

Cecilia R. Daly, Assistant Professor Emeritia; M.S., Nebraska. Applications, education. E-mail: daly@cse.unl.edu

Jitender S. Deogun, Professor; Ph.D., Illinois at Urbana-Champaign. Design and analysis of algorithms, VLSI design automation, graph algorithms, information retrieval, combinatorics. E-mail: deogun@cse.unl.edu

Scott Henninger, Assistant Professor; Ph.D., Colorado at Boulder. Software engineering, multimedia design, human-computer interaction, cognitive science. E-mail: scotth@cse.unl.edu

Hong Jiang, Associate Professor; Ph.D., Texas A&M. Computer architecture, interconnection networks, parallel/distributed processing, supercomputing, performance evaluation. E-mail: jiang@cse.unl.edu

Roy F. Keller, Professor Emeritus; Ph.D., Missouri–Columbia. Language design and implementation, program verification, projection methods for solving systems of algebraic equations. E-mail: keller@cse.unl.edu

Roger Kieckhafer, Associate Professor; Ph.D., Cornell. Computer architecture, fault tolerance, real-time systems, reliability and performance modeling. E-mail: rogerk@cse.unl.edu

David A. Klarner, Professor Emeritus; Ph.D., Alberta. Combinatorics. E-mail: klarner@cse.unl.edu

Joseph Y.-T. Leung, Professor; Ph.D., Penn State. Scheduling theory, real-time systems, operating systems, algorithms and complexity, combinatorial optimization. E-mail: jyl@cse.unl.edu

Spyros Magliveras, Henson Professor; Ph.D., Birmingham (England). Data encryption, symbolic and algebraic computation, combinatorics, computational group theory. E-mail: spyros@cse.unl.edu

Stuart Margolis, Adjunct Professor; Ph.D., Berkeley. Automata and formal languages; relationships among algebra, automata, and logic; complexity theory; theory of computation. E-mail: margolis@cse.unl.edu

Sarit Mukherjee, Assistant Professor; Ph.D., Maryland. Computer network architecture and protocol, multimedia, distributed and real-time systems. E-mail: sarit@cse.unl.edu

Don J. Nelson, Professor; Ph.D., Stanford. Simulation and error analysis, especially power production in electrical utilities and communication networks, software engineering. E-mail: system2@engvms.unl.edu

Stephen E. Reichenbach, Associate Professor and Interim Chair; Ph.D., William and Mary. Digital image processing, computer vision, multimedia computing. E-mail: reich@cse.unl.edu

Peter Revesz, Assistant Professor; Ph.D., Brown. Database systems, logic programming, constraint programming, computer vision, sign language translation. E-mail: revesz@cse.unl.edu

Charles Riedesel, Assistant Professor; Ph.D., Nebraska. Algorithms, graph theory. E-mail: riedesel@cse.unl.edu

Ashok Samal, Associate Professor; Ph.D., Utah. Computer vision, document analysis, parallel and distributed computing. E-mail: samal@cse.unl.edu

Sharad C. Seth, Professor; Ph.D., Illinois at Urbana-Champaign. Digital testing and parallel algorithms for computer-aided design, document image analysis. E-mail: seth@cse.unl.edu

Sunil Shende, Associate Professor; Ph.D., Pennsylvania. Parallel and sequential algorithms, computational linguistics, theory of computation. E-mail: sunil@cse.unl.edu

Douglas Stinson, Professor; Ph.D., Waterloo. Cryptography, coding theory, algorithms and complexity, combinatorics. E-mail: stinson@cse.unl.edu

Alvin Surkan, Professor; Ph.D., Western Ontario. Machine intelligence by simulation and methods of soft computing, pattern learning by neural networks, genetic algorithms and fuzzy logic in database mining. E-mail: surkan@cse.unl.edu

Susan Wiedenbeck, Associate Professor; Ph.D., Pittsburgh. Cognition of programming, human-computer interaction, intelligent tutoring. E-mail: susan@cse.unl.edu

UNIVERSITY OF NEBRASKA–LINCOLN

COLLEGE OF ENGINEERING AND TECHNOLOGY
DEPARTMENT OF ELECTRICAL ENGINEERING

PROGRAMS OF STUDY

The Department of Electrical Engineering offers graduate degree programs leading to the Master of Science in Electrical Engineering (M.S.E.E.) and the Ph.D.

There are currently 27 faculty members, and two more may be added in fall 1997. The following are the seven designated programs of study: solid-state devices and materials, remote sensing and electromagnetics, communications, digital signal processing, controls engineering, power engineering, and electrooptics. These programs are funded by various federal, state, and private agencies with an annual research expenditure exceeding $2 million and growing rapidly. Faculty members on the Lincoln campus collaborate in their research with faculty members in the computer and electronics engineering department at the University of Nebraska's Omaha campus, located 50 miles to the east.

The M.S.E.E. degree is offered under three options. In the thesis option, a student is required to complete at least 24 hours of approved course work and a minimum of 6 hours of thesis research, followed by an oral thesis defense. In the nonthesis option, the student must complete at least 36 hours of course work and pass a written examination, with no thesis requirement. However, the student must declare a minor area and take a minimum of 9 hours out of the required 36 hours in that area. In the third option, a student continuing on to the Ph.D. can obtain an M.S.E.E. degree after completing 36 hours of course work (including research credits) if, in the opinion of the Graduate Committee, the student has demonstrated the ability to conduct research. Usually this requires that the student publish a refereed article, based on his or her work, in an internationally reputed journal. In all cases, the graduate committee can require a student to demonstrate proficiency by taking an oral examination if the student's performance is deemed unsatisfactory. The Ph.D. requires a minimum of 90 hours of graduate work beyond the bachelor's degree, out of which a maximum of 45 hours can be for the dissertation. Other requirements are stipulated in the University's *Graduate Bulletin*. Graduate work completed elsewhere can be transferred for credit subject to the approval of the department's Graduate Committee.

RESEARCH FACILITIES

The department has excellent and extensive research facilities in all seven of its program areas. Computing resources include many workstations, a UNIX OS two-processor Alpha Model A500MP, and a six-processor CRAY J916 supercomputer with 1 GB RAM and 37 GB disk space, maintained by the College of Engineering. The Solid State Laboratories have the full gamut of material processing and device fabrication facilities along with specialized equipment for measurement. The Center for Microelectronic and Optical Materials Research was established several years ago under the Nebraska Research Initiative and involves 5 faculty members. It has extensive facilities for thin film deposition and characterization, a large ellipsometry facility for in situ monitoring of growth processes, facilities for plasma etching and study of breakdown phenomena, a rare water/alcohol system for diamond film growth at low temperatures, and a triple spectrograph Raman system with macroprobes and microprobes. The Nanostructures Research Group is engaged in research on self-assembly of quantum dots and wires and study of their properties in cryogenic, noise-isolated environments. It maintains an electrochemical facility and magnetic fields. The Solar Cell Research Group is involved with the design and fabrication of amorphous silicon solar cells and maintains ultrahigh vacuum sputter deposition systems, e-beam deposition systems, an Auger spectrometer, and scanning electron microscopes. The solid state faculty members are also members of the University's Center for Materials Research and Analysis, which involves 56 faculty members from several disciplines and receives annual research funding of approximately $8 million. The center maintains the full gamut of characterization equipment, including X-ray, TEM and fine-line lithography, electron beam and X-ray direct-write facilities, and cryogenic measurements facilities and magneto-optical measurements equipment. The Center for Electro-optics was also established under the Nebraska Research Initiative and focuses on femtosecond laser techniques, sensor development, and creation of nanostructures. The Remote Sensing Group is a part of this center and conducts research on rough surface characterization, polarimetric scattering theory and experiment, remote sensing of soils and vegetation, atmospheric remote sensing, and passive microwave remote sensing. The center has its own computational and graphics facilities, a femtosecond high-power laser, optical diagnostics and spectroscopy, active microwave radar and mid-infrared laser remote sensing capability, ground-penetrating radar, coherent random noise radar, a van-mounted 10-meter telescoping boom, a passive remote sensing facility, a lower atmospheric profiler system with a radio acoustic sounding system, an optical polarimetric scatterometer, and an atomic force/scanning tunneling microscope facility. The communications group maintains an image capture and digitization facility. The Center for Laser Analytical Studies maintains an assortment of tunable diode laser spectrometers for analysis and diagnostics.

FINANCIAL AID

Fellowships and teaching and research assistantships are available on a competitive basis for qualified full-time graduate students. Assistantships carry a monthly stipend of $900 for M.S. students and $1050 for Ph.D. students. This amount will be raised by $50 every year, starting in fall 1998, for an unspecified period. All assistantships carry a tuition waiver. Stipends for U.S. citizens in the Ph.D. program currently can be augmented by $200 per month by virtue of a private endowment. About 62.5 percent of the students receive financial assistance in the form of fellowships or assistantships. Many of the remaining students find grading work in the department.

COST OF STUDY

For the 1997–98 academic year, the tuition for Nebraska residents is approximately $99.25 per credit hour; for nonresidents it is $245.25 per credit hour. Students are charged an additional $194 in fees per semester.

LIVING AND HOUSING COSTS

The estimated expenses for room and board are $3700 per academic year. There are many apartments available for rent within walking distance of the campus.

STUDENT GROUP

Approximately 55 percent of the graduate student body consists of international students. Seven percent of the students are women.

LOCATION

The Walter Scott Engineering Center, which houses the electrical engineering department and a few other engineering departments, is located on the University's downtown city campus. Lincoln, the capital of Nebraska, is a sprawling, fast-growing metropolis of 200,000 residents. It is replete with recreation, entertainment, arts, parks, museums, and old-world charm.

THE UNIVERSITY

Founded in 1869 as a land-grant university, the University of Nebraska–Lincoln is the flagship campus of the University of Nebraska system. It is a comprehensive state institution with an average enrollment of 25,000 students. It has been ranked by the Carnegie Foundation as a Research I institution, placing it in the top 3 percent of the nation's leading research universities.

APPLYING

The application deadline for admission and financial aid is March 31. A bachelor's degree with a GPA of 3.0 or above on a 4.0 scale is required. Students not possessing a bachelor's degree granted by an ABET-accredited electrical engineering program generally must take remedial courses as determined by the appropriate departmental committee. The GRE General Test is required; international students must also report TOEFL scores.

All international students are required to take a test administered by the University upon their arrival in order to qualify as a teaching assistant who is allowed to lecture.

CORRESPONDENCE AND INFORMATION

Director of Graduate Studies
Department of Electrical Engineering
University of Nebraska
Lincoln, Nebraska 68588-0511

UNIVERSITY OF NEBRASKA—LINCOLN

THE FACULTY AND THEIR RESEARCH

Dennis R. Alexander, Kingerey Professor; Ph.D., Kansas State, 1976. Femtosecond laser machining, sensor development, creation of nanostructures, aerosol analysis.

Marcelo C. Algrain, Associate Professor; Ph.D., IIT, 1992. Control system applications, active vibration control, guidance stabilization, pointing and tracking systems.

Sohrab Asgarpoor, Associate Professor; Ph.D., Texas A&M, 1989. Advanced computer applications, optimization techniques, fuzzy sets, Monte Carlo simulation related to power systems.

Ezekiel Bahar, George Holmes Distinguished Professor; Ph.D., Colorado, 1967. Scattering from inhomogeneous anisotropic media, polarimetric scatterometry theory and experiment.

Supriyo Bandyopadhyay, Professor; Ph.D., Purdue, 1985. Nanoelectronics, self-assembly of quantum dots and wires, physics of computation, transport theory, nonlinear optics.

David P. Billesbach, Research Assistant Professor; Ph.D., Nebraska, 1987. Global climate change and trace gas exchange.

A. John Boye, Associate Professor; Ph.D., Nebraska, 1984. Systems simulation and modeling, nonlinear systems and control, estimation filtering and prediction, optimization and optimal control.

Muh-Lin Chen, Research Assistant Professor; Ph.D. Nebraska, 1992. Object-oriented software engineering, network and database programming.

Rodney O. Dillon, Associate Professor; Ph.D., Maryland, 1974. Thin film deposition and characterization with focus on diamond, diamondlike carbon, wide-gap semiconductors, photochromic and piezoelectric films.

Michael W. Hoffman, Assistant Professor; Ph.D., Minnesota, 1992. Digital signal processing, sensor array processing, adaptive and real-time digital signal processing.

Natale J. Ianno, Professor; Ph.D., Illinois, 1981. Plasma processing of semiconductors and related materials, plasma and sputter deposition of hard coatings and optical materials.

Stanley R. Liberty, Professor; Ph.D., Notre Dame, 1971. Stochastic control and dynamic games.

Ram M. Narayanan, Associate Professor; Ph.D., Massachusetts, 1988. Scattering from surface and volume targets, radar and laser remote sensing, geophysical parameter estimation.

Don J. Nelson, Professor; Ph.D., Stanford, 1962. Computer simulations, communication networks, random processes, numerical analysis.

Robert D. Palmer, Assistant Professor; Ph.D., Oklahoma, 1989. Study of atmospheric phenomena using Doppler radar techniques.

Lance C. Perez, Assistant Professor; Ph.D., Notre Dame, 1995. Error-control coding, information theory, wireless and multiuser communications.

Khallid Sayood, Professor; Ph.D., Texas A&M, 1982. Data compression, joint source-channel coding, communication theory.

Paul G. Snyder, Associate Professor; Ph.D., USC, 1984. Optical characterization of thin films for microelectronics, real-time study of etching processes.

Rodney J. Soukup, Professor and Chair; Ph.D., Minnesota, 1969. Solid-state devices, amorphous silicon solar cells, plasma torch deposition of thin films, scanning electron microscopy.

Karen St. Germain, Assistant Professor; Ph.D., Massachusetts, 1993. Passive remote sensing of the environment, including ocean surface winds, polar sea ice properties, soil moisture, atmospheric water vapor, and precipitation.

Robert D. Throne, Associate Professor; Ph.D., Michigan, 1990. Inverse problems and optimization methods.

Hamid Vakilzadian, Associate Professor; Ph.D., Arizona, 1985. Hardware description languages, switching theory, fuzzy logic, interconnection networks, direct-executing simulation languages, computer architecture.

Jerald L. Varner, Associate Professor; Ph.D., Nebraska, 1972. Digital signal processing, processing of physiological signals.

P. Frazer Williams, Lott Professor; Ph.D., USC, 1973. Plasma processing of semiconductors, optical and infrared spectroscopy of plasmas, electrical breakdown of gases and semiconductor surfaces.

John A. Woollam, George Holmes Distinguished Professor; Ph.D., Michigan State, 1967. Thin films, vacuum deposition, plasma-surface interactions, optics, ellipsometry.

Walter H. Yao, Research Associate Professor; Ph.D., Kansas State, 1989. Optical characterization of semiconductor materials, radiation detectors, microelectronics.

UNLV UNIVERSITY OF NEVADA, LAS VEGAS

HOWARD R. HUGHES COLLEGE OF ENGINEERING
DEPARTMENT OF COMPUTER SCIENCE

PROGRAMS OF STUDY

Programs of study lead to the degrees of Master of Science (M.S.) in computer science and Doctor of Philosophy (Ph.D.) in computer science. The Master of Science degree requires 24 semester hours of course credits and a thesis or 27 credits and a project.

The Doctor of Philosophy degree requires 30 credits of course work, a written comprehensive exam, an oral qualifying exam, and a dissertation.

RESEARCH FACILITIES

The Department of Computer Science is housed in the Thomas E. Beam Engineering Complex. Department facilities include an open workstation laboratory shared with the other departments in engineering, a graphics laboratory, and a networks laboratory. The open laboratory is equipped with Sun, DEC, and NeXT workstations. The graphics laboratory is equipped with Silicon Graphics workstations, including an Onyx Reality Engine, Indigo Extremes, and Indies with multimedia capabilities. The networks laboratory is equipped with DEC workstations.

Associated with the department is the Information Sciences Research Institute (ISRI), which studies issues concerning document analysis, optical character recognition, and information retrieval.

FINANCIAL AID

Teaching and research assistantships are available from the department. The ISRI also offers research assistantships. M.S. student awards start at $8000 per academic year, while Ph.D. student awards start at $9000 per academic year. These awards also pay 85 percent of the credit-hour fee up to 10 credit hours and all of the out-of-state tuition if required. Assistantships are normally awarded for the nine-month academic year, but a few summer awards are available from ISRI.

COST OF STUDY

Tuition in 1996–97 was $90 per credit hour for Nevada residents, with additional fees for out-of-state students. These charges are waived for graduate assistants.

LIVING AND HOUSING COSTS

The Graduate College estimates that a single graduate student needs $16,000 per year for food, rent, books, and health-care insurance. This amount does not include out-of-state tuition or travel to and from Las Vegas. In general, housing and other living costs are quite reasonable in the Las Vegas area.

STUDENT GROUP

There are about 50 master's students in the department, and 4 doctoral students were enrolled in 1996–97.

LOCATION

The Las Vegas metropolitan area has a population of more than 1 million and is growing very rapidly. Not only is Las Vegas the entertainment capital of the world, but it has a substantial and growing industrial base. Off-campus part-time jobs are normally plentiful.

The University's campus of about 335 acres is located in the southeastern part of the city, near McCarran Airport. Although located in the desert, Las Vegas is less than an hour's drive from both water sports on Lake Mead and winter skiing on Mount Charleston. Los Angeles is 5 hours away by car.

THE UNIVERSITY

The University opened in 1957. Today, enrollment exceeds 19,000, and there are approximately 600 faculty members. Recently UNLV was designated a National Flagship University. The College of Engineering has approximately 60 faculty members, of whom 11 are in the Department of Computer Science.

APPLYING

Applicants to the Master of Science program should have earned a bachelor's degree in computer science with a minimum GPA of 2.75 and must take the GRE General Test. Applicants to the Doctor of Philosophy program should have earned a master's degree in computer science and must take the GRE General Test and the Subject Test in computer science.

A complete application consists of the application form, official transcripts of all previous University work, and two (three for the Ph.D. program) letters of recommendation. International students must file a financial statement and complete the TOEFL with a score of at least 550. The deadlines for application for admission are June 15 for the fall and November 15 for the spring. The deadlines for application for assistantships are April 1 for fall assistantships and November 1 for spring assistantships.

CORRESPONDENCE AND INFORMATION

For program information:
Graduate Secretary
Department of Computer Science
University of Nevada, Las Vegas
4505 Maryland Parkway
Box 454019
Las Vegas, Nevada 89154-4019
Telephone: 702-895-3681

For application forms and admission questions:
Graduate College
University of Nevada, Las Vegas
4505 Maryland Parkway
Box 451017
Las Vegas, Nevada 89154-1017
Telephone: 702-895-3346

UNIVERSITY OF NEVADA, LAS VEGAS

THE FACULTY AND THEIR RESEARCH

Lawrence L. Larmore, Professor and Chair; Ph.D. (mathematics), Northwestern; Ph.D. (computer science), California, Irvine. Theoretical computer science, data structures, on-line algorithms, parallel algorithms, dynamic programming, applications to computer-aided design.

Ajoy K. Datta, Associate Professor; Ph.D. (computer science), Jadavpur (India). Distributed computing, fault-tolerant computing, self-stabilization, networks, modeling and analysis of concurrent systems.

Laxmi Gewali, Associate Professor; Ph.D. (computer science), Texas at Dallas. Design and analysis of algorithms, computational geometry, pattern recognition, robot motion planning.

Junichi Kanai, Assistant Professor; Ph.D. (computer and systems engineering), Rensselaer. Pattern recognition, document understanding, image processing, computational geometry.

Kia Makki, Associate Professor; Ph.D. (computer science), California, Davis. Algorithm design and analysis, parallel and distributed systems and algorithms, approximation algorithms, VLSI computations, computer communication networks, parallel and distributed databases, temporal databases, digital libraries, distributed GIS, object-oriented environments.

John T. Minor, Associate Professor; Ph.D. (computer science), Texas at Austin. Artificial intelligence, logic representations, automated deduction techniques, rule-based expert systems, logic programming systems.

Thomas A. Nartker, Professor; Ph.D. (chemical engineering), Texas A&M. Formal requirements specification, metrics in image understanding, user interface development environments.

Roy H. Ogawa, Associate Professor; Ph.D. (mathematics), Berkeley. Programming languages, concurrent programming, computational linguistics, natural languages.

Kazem Taghva, Professor; Ph.D. (mathematics), Iowa. Database management systems, information retrieval, applications of formal logic in computer science.

Evangelos A. Yfantis, Professor; Ph.D. (statistics), Wyoming. Computer graphics, compiler construction, principles of programming languages, computer simulation.

UNIVERSITY OF NEW HAMPSHIRE

DEPARTMENT OF COMPUTER SCIENCE

PROGRAMS OF STUDY

The department offers Ph.D. and M.S. programs in computer science. A major emphasis in the Ph.D. program is the blending of theoretical and applied aspects of computer science. All students pursuing research in computer science theory are required to develop a strong background in systems and are encouraged whenever possible to identify potential or actual applications for theory. Similarly, all students pursuing research in the applied areas of computer science are required to base their work on strong theoretical foundations. Students are formally declared candidates for the Ph.D. once they have completed the qualifying examination, which consists of a written component that tests the breadth of a student's knowledge and a depth component that demonstrates the student's ability to do research in a given field. The qualifying examination should be completed by the end of a student's second year of residence. The completion of the dissertation typically requires 1½ to 2 additional years.

The M.S. program has a depth option, requiring a thesis, and a breadth option, requiring a comprehensive examination.

RESEARCH FACILITIES

Most research computing is done on the department's own computing facilities, which consist of a network of Sun, VAXstation, DECstation, and Linux workstations and a 32-node parallel computer.

University facilities include DEC Alpha machines, Linux workstations, and Macintosh and IBM-compatible microcomputer clusters.

UNIX is the primary software environment, with extensive programming done in C, C++, and LISP.

FINANCIAL AID

A number of teaching and research assistantships are available with stipends of $9800 for the 1997–98 academic year. Assistantships generally require the student to work approximately 20 hours per week during the academic year. Students receiving assistantships are also awarded a tuition waiver. Tuition-only scholarship awards are also available. Some summer support is available in the form of both research and teaching positions.

COST OF STUDY

Tuition for the 1996–97 academic year was $4641 for New Hampshire residents and $12,990 for out-of-state students. Mandatory fees amounted to about $620 per year.

LIVING AND HOUSING COSTS

A single room in the graduate residence hall costs $2978 for the 1997–98 academic year and $59.50 per week during the summer. A full meal plan is available for $1800 for the academic year. As of July 1997, a one-bedroom apartment in married student housing costs $400 per month, including all utilities.

STUDENT GROUP

The department currently has 22 full-time and 28 part-time graduate students.

STUDENT OUTCOMES

Most of the M.S. graduates have completed theses in applied areas such as networks, parallel computing, and graphics. Recent M.S. graduates have accepted positions at major companies, including Microsoft Research, BayNetworks, Open Software Foundation, SoftDesk, and Cabletron. The department graduated its first Ph.D. in 1995; he operates his own networking company. Current Ph.D. students are actively working on dissertations in constraint programming, network error diagnosis, and scientific data modeling and visualization.

LOCATION

The home of the University is Durham, one of the oldest towns in northern New England. The town is semirural and still retains traces of its Colonial past. Easy accessibility to Boston's cultural opportunities (65 miles to the south); the unsurpassed skiing, hiking, and scenery of the White Mountains (60 miles to the north); and the sandy beaches and rocky coast of New Hampshire and Maine (10 miles to the east) make it an excellent location.

THE UNIVERSITY

The University of New Hampshire was founded in 1866 as the New Hampshire College of Agriculture and the Mechanic Arts. The 200-acre campus contains seventy-four buildings for teaching, research, and service and thirty-six residence halls. The campus is surrounded by more than 3,000 acres of fields, farms, and woodlands owned by the University. The University has a full-time faculty of about 600 and offers ninety-four undergraduate and seventy-five graduate programs. The student body of about 10,500 includes about 1,200 graduate students.

APPLYING

Applicants should have a strong academic record and a bachelor's or master's degree in computer science or a closely related area with a strong concentration in computer science. Students with some computer science background who have demonstrated their academic potential in a related area (e.g., mathematics or physics) may be provisionally admitted to graduate study contingent upon the satisfactory completion of appropriate additional undergraduate course work. All applicants are required to take the GRE General Test and the GRE Subject Test in computer science. International applicants must also take the Test of English as a Foreign Language (TOEFL). Although there is no rigid deadline, students requesting financial assistance should have their applications completed prior to February 15 (for fall admission), and applications from international students should be completed by June 1 (for fall admission). Students can be admitted for the spring semester, but less financial assistance is available for students starting in the spring. Additional information about the programs can be accessed via the network: ftp: ftp.cs.unh.edu; www: www.cs.unh.edu; and gopher: gopher.cs.unh.edu.

CORRESPONDENCE AND INFORMATION

Graduate Program Secretary
Department of Computer Science
Kingsbury Hall
University of New Hampshire
Durham, New Hampshire 03824
Telephone: 603-862-3778
Fax: 603-862-3493
E-mail: gradinfo@cs.unh.edu

UNIVERSITY OF NEW HAMPSHIRE
THE FACULTY AND THEIR RESEARCH

Radim Bartos, Assistant Professor; Ph.D., Denver, 1997. High-speed computer networks and parallel and distributed systems.

R. Daniel Bergeron, Professor; Ph.D., Brown, 1973. Computer graphics, scientific visualization, parallel algorithms, user interfaces. (E-mail: rdb@cs.unh.edu)

Pilar de la Torre, Associate Professor; Ph.D., Maryland, 1987. Design and analysis of algorithms, data structures, computational complexity. (E-mail: dltrr@cs.unh.edu)

Eugene C. Freuder, Professor; Ph.D., MIT, 1975. Artificial intelligence, constraint-directed reasoning, machine learning. (E-mail: ecf@cs.unh.edu)

Raymond Greenlaw, Associate Professor; Ph.D., Washington (Seattle), 1988. Parallel computation, theory of computation. (E-mail: greenlaw@cs.unh.edu)

Philip J. Hatcher, Associate Professor; Ph.D., IIT, 1985. Programming language design and implementation. (E-mail: pjh@cs.unh.edu)

Robert D. Russell, Associate Professor; Ph.D., Stanford, 1972. Operating systems, computer networks. (E-mail: rdr@cs.unh.edu)

Sylvia Weber Russell, Adjunct Assistant Professor; Ph.D., Stanford, 1975. Natural-language understanding, computational linguistics. (E-mail: swr@cs.unh.edu)

Ted M. Sparr, Professor and Chairman; Ph.D., Texas A&M, 1972. Database and knowledge systems, scientific databases. (E-mail: tms@cs.unh.edu)

Elizabeth Varki, Assistant Professor; Ph.D., Vanderbilt, 1997. Modeling and performance evaluation of computer systems.

James L. Weiner, Associate Professor; Ph.D., UCLA, 1979. Computer-supported group work, logic programming, computational linguistics. (E-mail: jlw@cs.unh.edu)

RESEARCH AREAS

Parallel Computing

Research in parallel computing at UNH covers both theoretical studies of models of parallel computation and applied research related to parallel programming and algorithm development. The department's 64-processor hypercube multicomputer is the springboard for innovative research, integrating traditional computer science disciplines with the latest advances in parallel computing. Of particular interest is a major effort to develop effective paradigms for parallel algorithm specification along with compilers for generating efficient codes for a variety of parallel architectures.

Artificial Intelligence

Research in artificial intelligence is focused on three major areas: constraint-directed reasoning, natural-language understanding, and planning. There is also interest in logic programming, intelligent tutoring systems, and the interface between artificial intelligence and other major research areas of the department, such as computer graphics and parallel algorithms.

Computer Graphics

Current research in computer graphics is focused on the development of systems and methodology for multidimensional scientific visualization and the evaluation of parallel graphics and visualization algorithms. This research is supported by the facilities of the Parallel Computing Laboratory and several high-performance graphics workstations.

Programming Environments

The design and implementation of environments that support group work is being investigated. Such environments create and maintain group goals, responsibilities, and identity through conversation. The investigation builds on research from several disciplines—linguistics, sociology, cognitive science, and computer science.

Database Systems

Database research at UNH focuses on the needs of multidisciplinary teams of collaborating scientists. The goal is to create an integrated approach to the analysis, visualization, and management of scientific data. This research is related to work in scientific data visualization and cooperative environments.

Computer Networking

In cooperation with the University's InterOperability Laboratory, current research centers on simulation, testing, performance measurement, and evaluation and monitoring of the latest network technologies, including FDDI and ATM. The application of high-speed network technology to parallel computing is also being investigated.

UNIVERSITY OF NEW HAMPSHIRE

DEPARTMENT OF ELECTRICAL AND COMPUTER ENGINEERING

PROGRAMS OF STUDY

Featuring a master's degree program that is strongly coupled with interdisciplinary faculty research efforts, the department offers courses of study leading to the Master of Science (M.S.) degree in electrical engineering and the Ph.D. in engineering, with specialization in electrical engineering. Areas of departmental strength include computational and applied electromagnetics, reconfigurable and testable fault-tolerant computing structures, robotics and neural networks, biomedical engineering, signal and image processing hardware and techniques, wireless communications, space systems engineering, fiber optics, and ocean instrumentation engineering. Both master's and Ph.D. degree students work closely with faculty members on research, and they often lead multidisciplinary teams of undergraduate engineering students in the design and implementation of complex projects (e.g., a small satellite with multiple X-ray imaging instruments).

Two program options are offered for the Master of Science degree. The thesis option requires the completion of at least 24 credits of course work and 6 credits of thesis work. The nonthesis option requires the completion of at least 27 credits of course work and a one-semester, 3-credit project. Most students complete their degrees within 1½ to two years.

Ph.D. programs are planned on an individual basis, but they typically involve at least 24 credits of study beyond the master's degree. The Ph.D. student must successfully complete written and oral preliminary exams at the beginning of the program and prepare and present a dissertation prospectus near the end of Ph.D. course work. A written dissertation on the results of the student's original research must be defended in an oral final exam. At least three years of study beyond the baccalaureate level are necessary to obtain the Ph.D. degree.

RESEARCH FACILITIES

Within the department are special laboratories for research on design automation (including VHDL, digital and mixed-mode VLSI, and MCM design and testing), fiber optics, human factors and biomedical engineering, robotics, synthetic vision (including image processing and pattern analysis), and wireless communication. A unique meteor radar facility adjacent to the campus is used for remote sensing of upper-atmospheric wind dynamics. The extensive test facilities of the University of New Hampshire (UNH) Interoperability Laboratory enable students to study the most advanced computer network protocols. The Laboratory for Advanced Small Satellites of the UNH Institute for the Study of Earth, Oceans, and Space provides equipment for the design and prelaunch testing of satellite-borne space- and earth-observing instruments.

The department maintains its own cluster of networked engineering workstations with Internet access. The University operates multiple DEC Alpha™ computers for general use through the campus network. The Dimond Library houses 1.5 million volumes, 6,000 periodicals, and microfilm, audio, and video archives. Branch libraries contain special collections for mathematics, engineering, and computer sciences; physics; chemistry; and life sciences.

FINANCIAL AID

Teaching and research assistantships are awarded on a competitive basis and provide a full tuition waiver and living stipend for the academic year. For the 1997–98 academic year, stipends range from $9800 to $10,100, depending upon degree level. Additional support is available during the summer. The department's prestigious Walker and Industrial Associates Program fellowships are reserved for exceptional students and provide a full tuition waiver and stipend without the normal duties of an assistantship. A limited number of tuition scholarships for full- and part-time students are awarded by the Graduate School. Work-study and student loan programs are also available to qualified students.

COST OF STUDY

For the 1996–97 academic year, tuition for a student enrolled in full-time graduate study in the College of Engineering and Physical Sciences was $4495 for New Hampshire residents and $13,465 for nonresidents. Additional mandatory fees for health services, recreation, and support of the student Memorial Union totaled $763 per year.

LIVING AND HOUSING COSTS

Single rooms on campus for graduate students cost $2876 for the 1996–97 academic year. Studio and one- or two-bedroom apartments were available to students with families at monthly rates ranging from $332 to $441. Off-campus housing in Durham is somewhat more expensive, but numerous rentals of all types are available at a lower cost in nearby communities. A standard meal plan (nineteen meals per week) in the University dining halls costs $900 per semester.

STUDENT GROUP

Approximately 45 M.S. students and 7 Ph.D. students are presently enrolled in the department. More than 70 percent of the department's full-time graduate students are supported by assistantships, while most of the others work part-time in local engineering firms. About 30 percent are considered part-time students, and 20 percent are international students. Due to the extensive involvement of master's degree students in advanced research efforts, the Graduate Admissions Committee especially seeks academically strong applicants with prior independent project or research experience.

LOCATION

The University is located in Durham, a quintessential New England village. The 200-acre campus is surrounded by more than 2,400 acres of farms, gently rolling fields, and woodlands. It is ideally situated for access to year-round recreational and cultural opportunities. Portsmouth, an active seaport 10 miles to the east, is a regional center for the performing arts, while Boston's vast array of cultural diversions is just an hour's drive south. Spectacular skiing, hiking, and scenic vistas in the White Mountains, 60 miles north, and the sandy beaches and rocky coast of New Hampshire and Maine (10 miles east) beckon for enjoyment.

THE UNIVERSITY AND THE DEPARTMENT

The University of New Hampshire, founded in 1866, is a land-, sea-, and space-grant institution with a rich history of service to the state's people and its technological and agricultural business communities. Enrolling more than 12,000 students (including 1,500–2,000 graduate students) under the direction of about 630 full-time faculty members, the University offers seventy-five graduate degree programs in addition to its 100 undergraduate programs. Founded in 1908, the Department of Electrical and Computer Engineering prides itself upon the fact that its graduate degree recipients are highly respected by both industry and other academic institutions.

APPLYING

Although applications are reviewed throughout the year, maximum opportunity for financial assistance is ensured if one's complete portfolio is received by the Graduate School no later than February 15 for fall semester admission. The Test of English as a Foreign Language (TOEFL) is required of all international applicants. The General Test of the Graduate Record Examinations (GRE) is normally required of any applicant whose baccalaureate degree is from a non-U.S. institution and is recommended for all applicants.

CORRESPONDENCE AND INFORMATION

Graduate Program Coordinator
Department of Electrical and Computer Engineering
University of New Hampshire
33 College Road
Durham, New Hampshire 03824-3591
Telephone: 603-862-1357
Fax: 603-862-1832
E-mail: ece.gradstudy@unh.edu
World Wide Web: http://www.ece.unh.edu

UNIVERSITY OF NEW HAMPSHIRE

THE FACULTY AND THEIR RESEARCH

Jennifer T. Bernhard, Assistant Professor; Ph.D., Duke, 1994. Wireless communications, electromagnetics for industrial and medical applications, microwave antennas and circuits.

Michael J. Carter, Associate Professor; Ph.D., Michigan, 1984. Computational neuroscience, neural network models of brain disorders, artificial neural network architectures and learning algorithms, engineering for sustainable communities.

Kent A. Chamberlin, Professor; Ph.D., Ohio, 1982. Computer modeling of electromagnetic systems, particularly for applications involving communication and navigation systems.

Ronald R. Clark, Professor; Ph.D., Syracuse, 1963. Meteor radar techniques, upper-atmosphere winds, signal processing techniques, communications, RF circuit design, ionospheric measurement and propagation.

Allen D. Drake, Associate Professor; Ph.D., Tufts, 1978. Fiber optics, instrumentation, biomedical engineering, electrooptics, physiological acoustics.

Francis C. Hludik Jr., Instructor; M.S., New Hampshire, 1985. Design of microprocessor-based systems, applications of modern CAD techniques, full- and semi-custom VLSI technologies in digital systems, operating systems and software development.

L. Gordon Kraft III, Professor; Ph.D., Connecticut, 1977. Control systems, neural networks, estimation and filtering, system identification, robotics.

John R. LaCourse, Professor; Ph.D., Connecticut, 1981. Biomedical and physical instrumentation, modeling of biological systems, rehabilitation engineering, human factors engineering, electrosurgery.

Richard A. Messner, Associate Professor; Ph.D., Clarkson, 1985. Optical signal processing, image processing, smart visual sensors, associative memory, adaptive pattern recognition, machine vision.

W. Thomas Miller III, Professor; Ph.D., Penn State, 1977. Adaptive dynamic balance of legged walking robots, learning/adaptive digital control of robotic manipulators, neural network learning for control and signal processing.

Paul J. Nahin, Professor; Ph.D., California, Irvine, 1972. Physics and mathematics of time travel, history of technology and science, philosophy of science.

John L. Pokoski, Professor; Ph.D., Montana State, 1967. Distributed computing, computing architectures.

Andrzej Rucinski, Professor; Ph.D., Gdansk Technical, 1982. Artificial intelligence, collaborative engineering, computer-aided design, computer architectures, distributed computers, fault-tolerant computing, VHDL, VLSI.

Kondagunta U. Sivaprasad, Professor; Ph.D., Harvard, 1963. Applied electromagnetics, wave propagation in inhomogeneous media, underwater acoustics, remote sensing.

UNIVERSITY OF NEW MEXICO

DEPARTMENT OF ELECTRICAL AND COMPUTER ENGINEERING

PROGRAMS OF STUDY

Graduate work leading to the M.S. and Ph.D. degrees is offered by the department in the areas of physical electronics and photonics and signals, systems, and computers. Tracks within the signals, systems, and computers area are circuits and control systems, computer engineering, microelectronics design, and signal processing and communications. The M.S. degree is also offered in manufacturing engineering. The master's degree program requires 30 semester credit hours for a thesis option and 33 hours for a nonthesis option. The Ph.D. program requires that a minimum of 24 graduate credit hours beyond the master's degree be completed at the University of New Mexico. Additional course work and research leading to the dissertation are geared to the individual student's needs and interests. As a potential candidate for the Ph.D. program, each student must pass the Ph.D. qualifying examination to establish levels and areas of scholastic capabilities.

RESEARCH FACILITIES

The various laboratories (computer vision and image processing, laser/electrooptics, microprocessors, robotics, solid-state fabrication, and virtual reality) contain Sun, DEC, and SGI workstations. The department uses the computational resources of the Local Albuquerque Resource Center, which is part of the High Performance Computer Education and Research Center (HPCERC). These resources include RS6000 workstations, a 32-node DBM SP1 parallel processor, and others. The HPCERC operates the Maui High Performance Computing Center, which features the IBM SP2 parallel processor. Local national laboratories provide researchers access to various supercomputers, such as the CRAY Y-MP, Intel Paragon, and CM-5. The UNM computer center provides students access to both workstations and PC pods located throughout campus. Student offices are typically equipped with workstations and PCs.

FINANCIAL AID

A limited amount of financial support is available in the form of teaching assistantships and research assistantships. Graduate internship programs are conducted with local industries, such as Sandia National Laboratories. Annual stipends for full-time teaching assistantships require no more than 20 hours of service per week for the academic year. A tuition waiver for 12 credit hours per semester is also made. Research assistants are paid on a scale of $850 to $1500 per month (half-time).

COST OF STUDY

In 1997–98, tuition and other fees for students carrying 12 or more credit hours are $1174.40 for state residents and $4193 for nonresidents. All residents carrying 11 or fewer credit hours pay $99.20 per semester credit hour; nonresidents also pay $99.20 per semester credit hour for up to 6 credit hours. For more than 6 semester credit hours, nonresidents pay $350.75 per credit hour. Domestic students can meet the requirements for resident status by living continuously in New Mexico for not less than one year prior to registration for the following semester and by providing satisfactory evidence of their intent to retain residence in New Mexico.

LIVING AND HOUSING COSTS

Living costs in Albuquerque are somewhat lower than those in other cities of comparable size. In addition to tuition and fees, a single American student's expenses are estimated at $9955 per year; expenses for a single international student are approximately $16,750 per year, including tuition and fees, and proof of financial competence is required prior to admission.

STUDENT GROUP

Students are drawn from all parts of the United States, as well as from many other countries. The graduate enrollment in the department, including part-time students, is 221, of whom 88 are Ph.D. candidates. During the past two years, the department has awarded 82 master's degrees and 18 Ph.D. degrees.

STUDENT OUTCOMES

The current demand for graduate engineers is excellent, and the employment rate for electrical engineering and computer engineering graduates has been almost 100 percent. Graduates of the department have been employed in various positions, such as senior engineer; VP, manufacturing; electronics engineer; and systems engineer. Examples of companies that hire the department's graduates include Intel, Motorola, Array Communications, Honeywell, and Philips Semiconductors as well as small entrepreneurial companies.

LOCATION

Albuquerque, with a metropolitan population exceeding 500,000, is the largest city in New Mexico. With an unusual blend of three cultures—Native American (Indian), Spanish-American, and Western—it is able to offer a wide variety of cultural, artistic, and aesthetic events. Several of these take place on campus, others are in the city and neighboring pueblos. The All-Pueblo Indian Art Center, the Atomic Museum (Sandia), and the Maxwell Museum of Anthropology on campus offer facilities of particular interest. The city lies between the lowland of the Rio Grande and the towering, 11,000-foot Sandia mountains. In this "Land of Enchantment" environment, the sun shines every day, and warm days are followed by cool nights. Hunting, fishing, ballooning, mountain climbing, and skiing are only a few of the recreational activities available.

THE UNIVERSITY

The University of New Mexico is the largest university in the state, with more than 30,000 students. It was established in 1889 and is situated on 600 acres in the center of metropolitan Albuquerque. The School of Engineering has an enrollment of 1,402 undergraduate students and 575 graduate students. The resources of the University and its proximity to Sandia National Laboratories, Kirtland Air Force Base, and Los Alamos National Laboratories provide an excellent environment for advanced studies and research.

APPLYING

Prospective applicants should contact the Office of Graduate Studies as well as the Department of Electrical and Computer Engineering. The GRE General Test is required for admission to both the M.S. and Ph.D. programs. U.S. applications, fees, and transcripts should be on file with the Office of Graduate Studies by May 31 for the following fall semester, by October 31 for the following spring semester, and by March 31 for the summer session. International applicants' materials should arrive six months prior to the semester for which the applicant is applying. Financial aid applications are due by March 15.

CORRESPONDENCE AND INFORMATION

Coordinator of Graduate Studies
Department of Electrical and Computer Engineering
University of New Mexico
Albuquerque, New Mexico 87131-1356
Telephone: 505-277-2600
E-mail: gradinfo@eece.unm.edu
World Wide Web: http://www.eece.unm.edu/

UNIVERSITY OF NEW MEXICO
THE FACULTY AND THEIR RESEARCH

Kenneth C. Jungling, Professor and Chairman; Ph.D., Illinois at Urbana-Champaign. Lasers and thin films, microanalytical thin-film diagnostics, optical detection, high-power laser damage testing.

Ronald C. DeVries, Professor, Associate Chairman of Computer Engineering, and Graduate Coordinator; Ph.D., Arizona. Logic design, computer organization, fault detection, fault-tolerance computing, safety, parallel processing.

Donald A. Neamen, Professor and Associate Chairman of Electrical Engineering; Ph.D., New Mexico. Effects of nuclear radiation on solid-state devices.

Shlomo Karni, Professor and Director of Undergraduate Studies; Ph.D., Illinois at Urbana-Champaign. System and circuit theory, engineering education.

Chaouki T. Abdallah, Associate Professor; Ph.D., Georgia Tech. Control systems, adaptive control, nonlinear systems, robot control and coordination.

Nasir Ahmed, Professor and Associate Provost for Research; Ph.D., New Mexico. Digital signal and image processing, pattern recognition, computer applications.

Steven R. J. Brueck, Professor; Ph.D., MIT. Laser-material interactions, electrooptic devices, laser spectroscopy.

Thomas P. Caudell, Associate Professor; Ph.D., Arizona. Neural networks, virtual reality, machine vision, robotics, genetic algorithms.

Julian Cheng, Professor; Ph.D., Harvard. Electrooptics, theoretical physics.

Peter Dorato, Professor; D.E.E., Polytechnic of Brooklyn. Optimal control, robust design in feedback control systems.

Charles B. Fleddermann, Associate Professor; Ph.D., Illinois at Urbana-Champaign. Plasma processing, laser diagnostics, physical electronics, photovoltaics.

Paul A. Fleury, Professor and Dean of School of Engineering; Ph.D., MIT. Condensed-matter physics.

John Michel Gahl, Associate Professor; Ph.D., Texas Tech. Physical electronics.

Charles F. Hawkins, Professor; Ph.D., Michigan. VLSI design and testability, biomedical applications.

Gregory L. Heileman, Associate Professor; Ph.D., Central Florida. Parallel processing, neural networks, image processing, pattern recognition.

Stephen D. Hersee, Professor; Ph.D., Brighton Polytechnic (England). Semiconductor materials and optoelectronics devices.

Rhonda Hill, Associate Professor; M.S.E.E., Purdue. Circuit analysis, digital logic and systems, microprocessors.

Stanley Humphries, Professor; Ph.D., Berkeley. Plasma physics, accelerator technology.

Don Hush, Associate Professor; Ph.D., New Mexico. Neural networks, pattern recognition, computer vision.

Ravi Jain, Professor; Ph.D., Berkeley. Quantum electronics, optoelectronics, electrooptics, experimental solid-state physics.

Mohammad Jamshidi, Professor; Ph.D., Illinois at Urbana-Champaign. Large-scale system theory and applications, soft computing.

Ramiro Jordan, Associate Professor; Ph.D., Kansas State. Computer networks, signal processors and microprocessors.

Don L. Kendall, Professor; Ph.D., Stanford. Semiconductor diffusion, micromachining.

Luke F. Lester, Assistant Professor; Ph.D., Cornell. High-speed optical devices, integrated optoelectronics, device physics.

Neeraj Magotra, Associate Professor; Ph.D., New Mexico. Adaptive signal processing, hardware implementation of signal processors.

Gary K. Maki, Professor; Ph.D., Missouri–Rolla. Digital design, fault-tolerant digital design, error correction codes, VLSI design and architectures.

Kevin Malloy, Associate Professor; Ph.D., Purdue. Semiconductor physics, device physics.

John R. McNeil, Professor; Ph.D., Colorado State. Thin-film optics, electrooptics, physical electronics.

Marek Osinski, Associate Professor; Ph.D., Warsaw. Semiconductor lasers, optoelectronics, integrated and fiber optics, optical communication.

L. Howard Pollard, Assistant Professor; Ph.D., Illinois at Urbana-Champaign. Computer architecture, digital design, fault tolerance, microprocessors.

John R. Rasure, Research Associate Professor; Ph.D., Kansas State. VLSI for signal processing, robotic systems, computer vision, computer design, visual languages.

Edl Schamiloglu, Associate Professor; Ph.D., Cornell. Plasma physics, charged particle beam propagation, accelerator technology.

John Sobolewski, Associate Professor and Associate Vice President of Computer and Information Research and Technology. Ph.D., Washington State. Data communications, networking, computer architecture, system information and design, medical application of computers.

Robert Whitman, Assistant Professor; Ph.D., Colorado. Digital signal processing, speech signal processing.

Richard H. Williams, Professor; Sc.D., New Mexico; Instrumentation, signal processing, reliability.

RESEARCH CENTERS

Center for High Technology Materials

Creating a leading optoelectronics and laser research center is the primary goal of the Center for High Technology Materials (CHTM), an interdisciplinary organization that sponsors and encourages research efforts in the Departments of Electrical and Computer Engineering, Physics and Astronomy, Chemistry, and Chemical and Nuclear Engineering. CHTM's multilateral mission involves both research and education, dedicated to encouraging and strengthening interactions and the flow of technology among the University, government laboratories, and private industry while promoting economic development in the state.

Microelectronics Research Center

The goal of the Microelectronics Research Center (MRC) is to advance special-purpose very large scale integrated (VLSI) processors and VLSI electronics to benefit the electronics industry and the nation. Industrial needs are addressed through close interaction with major electronic companies, and national needs through involvement with national research laboratories in NASA, DOD, and DOE.

Center for Autonomous Control Engineering

The Center for Autonomous Control Engineering (ACE) is an interdisciplinary and committed program for research and education in autonomous control engineering and relevant areas. An outgrowth of a strong support and financial commitment from NASA and the Jet Propulsion Laboratory, ACE is a vital resource for cost-effective education and research in control technology related to NASA's mission and U.S. industrial needs. ACE provides an organizational structure for collaborative education and research among the faculty members, whose focus transcends the boundaries of the University's colleges and schools. Its scope spans the School of Engineering, College of Arts and Science, College of Pharmacy, and School of Medicine.

UNIVERSITY OF NORTH CAROLINA AT CHAPEL HILL

DEPARTMENT OF COMPUTER SCIENCE

PROGRAMS OF STUDY The department offers the Ph.D. and a professional M.S. degree. Study for the M.S. degree includes data representation, algorithms, programming languages, and hardware, as well as important areas of application. The doctoral program requirements subsume those of the M.S. program. Students delve into areas of their choice and are actively involved in research. The curricula emphasize the design and application of real computer systems and that portion of theory that guides and supports practice. The department's orientation is experimental, with clusters of research in compilation, computational geometry, computer architectures, computer graphics, image analysis and vision, computer-supported cooperative work, distributed systems, functional and logic programming, geometric and solid modeling, hardware systems and design, human-machine interaction, hypertext, Monte Carlo methods, multimedia systems, neural networks, object-oriented programming, parallel computing, real-time systems, software engineering and environments, and theorem proving and term rewriting. Students holding an assistantship can typically expect to earn the M.S. degree in two academic years and the Ph.D. in four or five years.

RESEARCH FACILITIES All of the department's computing facilities are housed in a four-story computer science building that features specialized research laboratories for graphics and image processing; computer building and design; and distributed, parallel, and collaborative systems. The labs, offices, conference areas, and classrooms are bound together by the department's fully integrated distributed computing environment, which includes more than 450 computers ranging in performance from 3 MIPS to more than 250 MIPS. These systems are integrated by high-speed networks and by software that is consistent at the user level over the many architectural platforms. Several of the department's research labs include specialized equipment and facilities. General computing systems include approximately 51 Sun, 100 DEC, 70 Hewlett-Packard, 4 IBM, and 13 SGI workstations; 150 Apple Macintosh systems; and 30 Intel-based personal computers. The parallel computing facilities comprise both the department's own designs, such as the two Pixel-Planes 5 graphics multicomputers, and commercial machines, including several parallel SGI Onyx and Power Onyx machines and several Sun multiprocessor systems.

The department also has access to computing facilities at the University's Department of Academic Technology and Networks, which operates a number of UNIX systems. The department has access to Cray supercomputers, parallel machines, and high-performance clustered workstations at the North Carolina Supercomputer Center. The nearby Brauer Library has extensive holdings in mathematics, physics, statistics, operations research, and computer science.

FINANCIAL AID During the academic year, most students are supported by assistantships and fellowships. The stipend for research and teaching assistantships for the nine-month academic year in 1997–98 is $12,500 (20 hours per week). Full-time summer employment on a research project is normally available to students wishing support. The current rate is $610 (40 hours per week) for ten to twelve weeks. This produces a combined annual financial package for graduate assistants of approximately $19,000. The assistantship qualifies a student for the North Carolina resident tuition rate, currently $1075 per semester for 9 or more credit hours. Students are also covered by a comprehensive major medical insurance program, underwritten by Blue Cross/Blue Shield of North Carolina. To apply for an assistantship, the applicant should check the appropriate item on the admission application form. Applicants for assistantships are automatically considered for all available fellowships. Students can expect continued support, contingent upon satisfactory work performance and academic progress. Opportunities also exist for part-time employment elsewhere in the University and in the Research Triangle area.

COST OF STUDY For the 1997–98 academic year, tuition and fees for those attending UNC at Chapel Hill are $2172 for state residents and $10,704 for nonresidents.

LIVING AND HOUSING COSTS Annual living costs for single graduate students in the Chapel Hill area are estimated by University staff to be $9000 or higher. On-campus housing is available for both married and single students attending the University.

STUDENT GROUP The Department of Computer Science enrolls 140 graduate students, most of whom attend full-time.

STUDENT OUTCOMES A majority of the department's master's graduates works in industry, in companies ranging from small start-up operations to government research labs and large research and development corporations. Ph.D. graduates work in both academia and industry. Academic employment ranges from positions in four-year colleges, where teaching is the primary focus, to positions at major research universities. Some graduates take postdoctoral positions at research laboratories prior to continuing in industry or joining academia.

LOCATION Chapel Hill (population 44,000) is a scenic college town located in the heart of North Carolina, where small-town charm mixes with a cosmopolitan atmosphere to provide students with a rich and varied living experience. The town and the surrounding area offer many cultural advantages, including excellent theater and music, museums, and a planetarium. There are also many opportunities to watch and to participate in sports. The Carolina beaches, Cape Hatteras, Great Smoky Mountains National Park, and the Blue Ridge Mountains are only a few hours' drive away.

The Research Triangle of North Carolina is formed by the University of North Carolina at Chapel Hill, Duke University in Durham, and North Carolina State University in Raleigh. The universities have a combined enrollment of approximately 60,000 students, have libraries with more than 8 million volumes with interconnected catalogs, and have national prominence in a variety of disciplines.

THE UNIVERSITY AND THE DEPARTMENT The 689-acre central campus of UNC at Chapel Hill is among the most beautiful in the country. Of the approximately 24,100 students enrolled, nearly 9,000 are graduate and professional students. The department's primary missions are graduate teaching and research, and it offers graduate degree programs only. The Computer Science Students' Association sponsors both professional and social events and represents the students in departmental matters. Its president is a voting member at faculty meetings. There is much interaction between students and faculty, and students contribute to nearly every aspect of the department's operation.

APPLYING Applications for fall admission, complete with a personal statement, all transcripts, and recommendations, should be received by the Graduate School no later than January 1. To ensure meeting that deadline, students should take the GRE no later than December. Early submission of applications is encouraged. A few assistantships are sometimes available for those who wish to begin in the spring semester. To be considered for these, students should submit completed applications by October 15 and take the GRE no later than June. International applicants should have their applications completed earlier to allow time for processing visa paperwork. Applicants whose native language is not English must submit TOEFL scores.

CORRESPONDENCE AND INFORMATION For written information about graduate study:

Admissions and Graduate Studies
Department of Computer Science
Campus Box 3175, 147 Sitterson Hall
University of North Carolina
Chapel Hill, North Carolina 27599-3175

Telephone: 919-962-1900
Fax: 919-962-1799
E-mail: admit@cs.unc.edu
World Wide Web: http://www.cs.unc.edu

For applications and admissions information

The Graduate School
Campus Box 4010, 200 Bynum Hall
University of North Carolina
Chapel Hill, North Carolina 27599-4010

Telephone: 919-966-2611

UNIVERSITY OF NORTH CAROLINA AT CHAPEL HILL

THE FACULTY AND THEIR RESEARCH

James Anderson, Associate Professor; Ph.D., Texas at Austin, 1990. Distributed and concurrent algorithms, real-time systems, fault-tolerant computing, formal methods.

Gary Bishop, Associate Professor; Ph.D., North Carolina at Chapel Hill, 1984. Hardware and software for man-machine interaction, 3-D interactive computer graphics.

Frederick P. Brooks Jr., Kenan Professor; Ph.D., Harvard, 1956. 3-D interactive computer graphics, human-computer interaction, virtual worlds, molecular graphics, computer architecture.

Christina A. Burbeck, Research Professor; Ph.D., California, Irvine, 1981. Visual perception, visual object representation, visual background representation, virtual worlds.

Peter Calingaert, Professor Emeritus; Ph.D., Harvard, 1955.

Siddhartha Chatterjee, Assistant Professor; Ph.D., Carnegie Mellon, 1991. High-level programming languages, compilation for highly parallel machines, object-oriented programming, parallel algorithms and architectures.

Vernon L. Chi, Lecturer and Director of the Microelectronic Systems Laboratory; B.S., Antioch (Ohio), 1964. Hardware solutions for information processing problems: novel architectural solutions, system design and integration, signal propagation and clock distribution; physical layer technology properties: electronic, optical, mechanical, acoustic, physical first-principles models of computation.

James M. Coggins, Associate Professor and Associate Chairman for Academic Affairs; Ph.D., Michigan State, 1983. Artificial visual systems, pattern recognition, computer graphics, human-computer interaction, object-oriented design and programming, distributed systems.

Prasun Dewan, Associate Professor; Ph.D., Wisconsin–Madison, 1986. User interfaces, distributed collaboration, software engineering environments, object-oriented databases.

Nick England, Research Professor; E.E., North Carolina State, 1974. Systems architectures for graphics and imaging, scientific visualization, volume rendering, interactive surface modeling.

John G. Eyles, Research Assistant Professor; Ph.D., North Carolina at Chapel Hill, 1982. Graphics architectures, rapid system prototyping, virtual environments, VLSI design.

Henry Fuchs, Federico Gil Professor; Ph.D., Utah, 1975. High-performance graphics hardware, 3-D medical imaging, head-mounted display and virtual environments.

John H. Halton, Professor; D.Phil., Oxford, 1960. Applications of combinatorial and probabilistic methods and of scientific and mathematical analysis to computational, scientific, and engineering problems.

Kye S. Hedlund, Associate Professor; Ph.D., Purdue, 1982. Computer-aided design, computer architecture, algorithm design and analysis, parallel processing.

Kevin Jeffay, Associate Professor; Ph.D., Washington (Seattle), 1989. Real-time systems, operating systems, distributed systems, multimedia networking, computer-supported cooperative work, performance evaluation.

Anselmo A. Lastra, Research Assistant Professor; Ph.D., Duke, 1988. Computer graphics, parallel computing.

Gyula A. Magó, Professor; Ph.D., Cambridge, 1970. Parallel computation, computer architecture, programming languages.

Dinesh Manocha, Assistant Professor; Ph.D., Berkeley, 1992. Geometric and solid modeling, physically-based modeling, computer graphics, simulation-based design, symbolic and scientific computation, computational geometry.

Steven E. Molnar, Research Assistant Professor; Ph.D., North Carolina at Chapel Hill, 1991. Architectures for real-time computer graphics, VLSI-based system design, parallel rendering algorithms.

Lars S. Nyland, Research Assistant Professor, Ph.D., Duke, 1991. High-performance computing, parallel algorithms, parallel computer architecture and hardware systems, programming languages, program transformation and optimization techniques, scientific computing.

Stephen M. Pizer, Kenan Professor; Ph.D., Harvard, 1967. Image analysis and display, human and computer vision, graphics, numerical computing, medical imaging.

David A. Plaisted, Professor; Ph.D., Stanford, 1976. Mechanical theorem proving, term rewriting systems, logic programming, algorithms.

John Poulton, Research Professor; Ph.D., North Carolina at Chapel Hill, 1980. Graphics architectures, VLSI-based system design, design tools, rapid system prototyping.

Jan F. Prins, Associate Professor and Director of Graduate Studies; Ph.D., Cornell, 1987. Parallel algorithms, languages and architectures, high-level programming languages, formal techniques in program development.

Timothy L. Quigg, Lecturer and Associate Chairman for Administration; M.P.A., North Carolina State, 1979. Human services' needs assessment and planning, resource allocation.

Raj K. Singh, Research Associate Professor; Ph.D., SUNY at Albany, 1986. High-performance systems design and integration, CAD tools, parallel architectures and algorithms, VLSI design and fabrication, networking, computational biology, scientific computing.

F. Donelson Smith, Research Professor; Ph.D., North Carolina at Chapel Hill, 1978. Distributed systems, computer-supported cooperative work, operating systems, computer networks.

John B. Smith, Professor; Ph.D., North Carolina at Chapel Hill, 1970. Computer-supported cooperative work, hypermedia systems, human-computer interaction, text and natural language processing.

Donald F. Stanat, Professor Emeritus; Ph.D., Michigan, 1966.

David Stotts, Associate Professor; Ph.D., Virginia, 1985. Computer-supported cooperative work, hypermedia, software engineering and formal methods, programming languages and concurrency, interoperable distributed systems.

Russell M. Taylor II, Research Assistant Professor; Ph.D., North Carolina at Chapel Hill, 1994. 3-D interactive computer graphics, virtual worlds, distributed computing, scientific visualization, human-computer interaction.

Jeannie M. Walsh, Lecturer; M.S., Oklahoma State, 1984. Computer education, information technology and social issues.

Stephen F. Weiss, Professor and Chairman; Ph.D., Cornell, 1970. Information storage and retrieval, natural language processing, communications and distributed systems, computer-supported cooperative work.

Gregory F. Welch, Research Assistant Professor; Ph.D., North Carolina at Chapel Hill, 1997. Human-machine interaction, 3-D interactive computer graphics, virtual/augmented environment tracking systems, shared virtual environments and telecollaboration.

Turner Whitted, Research Professor; Ph.D., North Carolina State, 1978. Computer graphics.

Mary C. Whitton, Research Assistant Professor and Project Manager for Virtual Environments Research; M.S., North Carolina State, 1984. Virtual and augmented reality systems for data visualization, computer graphics system architectures.

William V. Wright, Research Professor Emeritus; Ph.D., North Carolina at Chapel Hill, 1972. Interactive systems for supporting scientific research, molecular graphics, architecture and implementation of computing systems.

Adjunct Faculty

Hussein Abdel-Wahab, Adjunct Professor; Ph.D., Waterloo, 1976. Computer-supported cooperative work, multimedia systems and communications, distance learning, distributed systems, operating systems and networking.

Stephen R. Aylward, Adjunct Assistant Professor; Ph.D., North Carolina at Chapel Hill, 1997. Statistical pattern recognition, shape-based object representation, image processing, neural networks.

Ming C. Lin, Adjunct Assistant Professor; Ph.D., Berkeley, 1993. Physically-based and geometric modeling, applied computational geometry, robotics, distributed interactive simulation, virtual environments and algorithm analysis.

Julian Rosenman, Adjunct Professor; Ph.D., Texas at Austin, 1971; M.D., Texas Health Science Center at Dallas, 1977. Computer graphics for treatment of cancer patients, contrast enhancement of poor quality X rays.

UNIVERSITY OF NORTH TEXAS

DEPARTMENT OF COMPUTER SCIENCES

PROGRAMS OF STUDY

The Department of Computer Sciences offers programs leading to the M.S. and Ph.D. degrees. A wide range of courses and research areas are available to graduate students. These include algorithm analysis, artificial intelligence, database systems, distributed computing, image processing, neural networks, numerical analysis, operating systems, parallel computing, pattern recognition, programming languages, and simulation and modeling. Through its Center for Research in Parallel and Distributed Computing, the department offers special emphases in all areas of parallel and distributed computing.

RESEARCH FACILITIES

The Department of Computer Sciences provides students and faculty with a broad assortment of hardware and software. The facilities and equipment include a Sun Ultra Enterprise 4000; Sequent Symmetry; Intel's iPSC/2 hypercube; three IBM RS/6000s; and laboratories with X-window terminals, Macintoshes, and IBM PC compatibles, all connected via the departmental Ethernet. The department also has a 9-node INMOS transputer network. In addition to the graphics lab and several open-use labs, the University Computing Center's equipment includes an HDS 8083 mainframe, a dual processor VAX 6310, and a Solbourne.

FINANCIAL AID

Approximately thirty-five teaching assistantships and research fellowships with stipends beginning at $3500 per semester are available to qualified graduate students. Remission of out-of-state tuition is also included.

COST OF STUDY

In 1996–97, graduate tuition and fees were $300 per semester credit hour for out-of-state students and $90 per semester credit hour for in-state students.

LIVING AND HOUSING COSTS

The University housing system offers ample facilities for single graduate students and a limited number of residences for married students. Room and board at the residence halls cost about $4000 for the academic year. A wide variety of off-campus accommodations is available. The UNT Student Association's annual apartment survey lists apartments beginning at approximately $250 per month.

STUDENT GROUP

Nearly 25 percent of the University's more than 27,000 students are in the Graduate School. The department has approximately 30 doctoral students and 90 master's students. In the past four years, a total of ten Ph.D. degrees have been awarded; approximately twenty master's degrees are conferred yearly.

LOCATION

The University of North Texas is located in Denton, Texas. Denton, located 35 miles north of the Dallas–Fort Worth metroplex, combines a small-town atmosphere with the advantages of a major metropolitan area. With a population of more than 4 million, the metropolitan area is the largest in Texas and the seventh-largest in the United States. There is a wide range of employment, cultural, and recreational opportunities.

THE UNIVERSITY

Founded in 1890, the University of North Texas is a comprehensive state-supported institution that combines education and research with public service. The Governor's Select Committee recommended in 1986 that the University be designated as one of Texas's five major research and graduate institutions. UNT is the most comprehensive graduate and research university in the region and the fourth-largest in the state of Texas. There are 133 buildings on the 424-acre campus.

APPLYING

Students applying to the master's degree program must hold the equivalent of a bachelor's degree and submit GRE scores (a minimum of 650 on the quantitative portion of the GRE and 1050 on the combined quantitative and verbal portions) and transcripts (a minimum grade point average of 3.0 on a 4.0 scale). Students applying to the Ph.D. program must submit three letters of recommendation, GRE scores (700 quantitative, 1150 combined quantitative and verbal), and transcripts (3.5 minimum grade point average).

Applications for admission must be received by the School of Graduate Studies by June 1 for the fall semester and October 1 for the spring semester. Students requesting financial aid should send their completed application to the Department of Computer Sciences by March 1 for the fall semester and September 15 for the spring semester. Students whose native language is not English must submit minimum TOEFL scores 580.

Application forms and information may be obtained by writing the Office of Graduate Admissions or the department. The application fee is $25 for U.S. citizens, $50 for all others.

CORRESPONDENCE AND INFORMATION

Department of Computer Sciences
University of North Texas
Denton, Texas 76203-3886
Fax: 817-565-2799
E-mail: gradinfo@cs.unt.edu
World Wide Web: http://www.cs.unt.edu/

School of Graduate Studies
University of North Texas
Denton, Texas 76203-5446

UNIVERSITY OF NORTH TEXAS

THE FACULTY AND THEIR RESEARCH

Robert Brazile, Associate Professor; Ph.D., Texas at Dallas, 1985. Databases.

Sajal Das, Associate Professor; Ph.D., Central Florida, 1988. Parallel algorithms and data structures, multiprocessor interconnections networks, cellular mobile computing.

Paul Fisher, Professor; Ph.D., Arizona State, 1969. Pattern recognition.

Tom Irby, Assistant Professor; Ph.D., SMU, 1976. Data structures.

Tom Jacob, Associate Professor; Ph.D., Emory, 1974. Distributed computing.

Robert Kallman, Professor; Ph.D., MIT, 1968. Signal processing, image processing, engineering optimization.

Ian Parberry, Associate Professor; Ph.D., Warwick (England), 1984. Computational complexity, parallel computing, neural networks, computer games.

Robert Renka, Associate Professor; Ph.D., Texas at Austin, 1981. Numerical analysis, mathematical software, curve and surface fitting.

Don Retzlaff, Lecturer; M.S., North Texas State, 1979. Software engineering.

Farhad Shahrokhi, Associate Professor; Ph.D., Western Michigan, 1987. Design and analysis of algorithms, combinatorial optimization, graph theory, theory of VLSI.

Weiping Shi, Assistant Professor; Ph.D., Illinois, 1992. Defect and fault tolerance, computer-aided design, VLSI.

Kathleen Swigger, Professor; Ph.D., Iowa, 1977. Artificial intelligence, human factors.

Steve Tate, Assistant Professor; Ph.D., Duke, 1992. Algorithms, computational complexity, data compression.

Chao-Chih Yang, Professor; Ph.D., Northwestern, 1966. Artificial intelligence, databases.

Cui-Qing Yang, Associate Professor; Ph.D., Wisconsin, 1987. Operating systems, distributed systems, computer networks, graphical user interfaces.

UNIVERSITY OF NOTRE DAME

COLLEGE OF ENGINEERING
DEPARTMENT OF COMPUTER SCIENCE AND ENGINEERING

PROGRAMS OF STUDY

The department offers programs of study and research leading to the M.S. and Ph.D. degrees. Research emphases within the department are VLSI, parallel and distributed computing, new parallel computing architectures (especially those that map well into VLSI implementations), and parallel computing algorithms. Other research efforts are also under way in artificial intelligence and electronic design automation.

All new graduate students are admitted to the master's program unless they hold an equivalent degree. This program requires a minimum of 24 semester hours of course work credit beyond the bachelor's degree, plus a thesis. These requirements can be completed by a full-time student in three regular academic semesters plus the summer, although many students take four semesters. The student must, upon the acceptance of the thesis, successfully pass an oral thesis defense examination. Students who complete the master's program may apply for admission to the doctoral program during their final semester of master's work. Doctoral students are normally required to accumulate a minimum of 42 hours of satisfactory course credit beyond the bachelor's degree plus a dissertation. Additional requirements for the Ph.D. include three years in resident study and passing of qualifying and candidacy examinations and the final examination.

RESEARCH FACILITIES

Notre Dame's College of Engineering maintains a cluster of ninety-nine Sun UltraSPARC 140s and fifteen PowerMac 7200s, all for research and instruction. This workstation cluster also includes six Hewlett-Packard 4SI laser printers and a color printer.

The University's Computing Center provides more than 400 gigabytes of AFS file storage space for the campus community. The center also maintains a cluster of IBM RS/6000s, a sixteen-processor IBM SP-1, an eight-processor IBM SP-2, and two Silicon Graphics compute servers.

The computer science and engineering department maintains a dozen Sun UltraSPARC systems and five Sun SPARCstation 5s. These systems supplement an existing inventory of thirty Sun SPARCstation 2 and IBM RS/6000 workstations, a Sun 4/630 four-processor server, a dozen Pentium-Pro workstations, an IBM RS/6000 model 590, and twenty-one printer-plotters.

The department's Design Automation Laboratory is equipped with three SPARCstation 2 workstations and several PC graphics stations. A full suite of Mentor Graphics design automation tools is available on these and all departmental workstations. FPGA development tools are also installed on machines in this laboratory.

A specialized College of Engineering research library holds more than 50,000 volumes. The University's Theodore M. Hesburgh Library contains more than 1.8 million volumes and subscribes to 625 journals related to engineering.

FINANCIAL AID

Teaching assistantships provide stipends as well as remission of academic-year tuition. Research assistantships, with remuneration commensurate with an applicant's qualifications, are available in numbers that depend upon the scope of the research program in progress. Fellowships and traineeships supported by federal agencies, industry, and the University are also available.

COST OF STUDY

Tuition is $9900 per semester for full-time study in 1997–98. For part-time study, the cost is $1100 per credit hour.

LIVING AND HOUSING COSTS

A limited number of on-campus living accommodations are available for graduate students. Rooms in private homes adjacent to the campus in South Bend rent for $65–$75 per week. Apartment rentals are from $250 to $450 per month, depending on occupancy and size.

STUDENT GROUP

Forty-four graduate students are enrolled in the department's programs; 41 are full-time and 3 are part-time. There are 33 men and 11 women. Seventeen of the department's students are from the U.S. and 27 are international.

STUDENT OUTCOMES

Graduates of the department's programs find challenging employment as professors in universities, researchers in government/academic laboratories, research and development team leaders in software and hardware firms, and project managers working within technical consulting organizations.

LOCATION

The University is a cultural center of the northern Indiana–southwestern Michigan area and offers cultural, social, athletic, and political events throughout the year. Saint Mary's College, a liberal arts college for women, augments Notre Dame's offerings. The Morris Civic Auditorium hosts road shows of Broadway plays and is the home of a symphony orchestra. Notre Dame is 2 hours by automobile from Chicago.

THE UNIVERSITY AND THE COLLEGE

The University was founded in 1842 by the Reverend Edward Frederick Sorin and 6 brothers of the Congregation of Holy Cross. It was chartered as a university by a special act of the Indiana legislature in 1844, and engineering studies were begun in 1873. The University's 1,250-acre campus is situated immediately north of the city of South Bend, an industrial center of about 130,000 people, approximately 90 miles east of Chicago. Its twin lakes and many wooded areas provide a setting of natural beauty for more than seventy University buildings, many of which have been erected in the past thirty years.

APPLYING

Applicants should arrange for GRE General Test scores, two original transcripts showing previous academic credits and degrees earned, and letters of recommendation from 3 or 4 college teachers to be sent to the dean of the Graduate School at least six months prior to the beginning of the academic session in which enrollment is sought. The GRE should be taken no later than December preceding the academic year of enrollment.

CORRESPONDENCE AND INFORMATION

Director of Graduate Studies
Department of Computer Science and Engineering
University of Notre Dame
Notre Dame, Indiana 46556
Telephone: 219-631-8320
Fax: 219-631-9260
E-mail: cse@cse.nd.edu

UNIVERSITY OF NOTRE DAME
THE FACULTY AND THEIR RESEARCH

Steven C. Bass, Professor and Schubmehl-Prein Chair; Ph.D., Purdue, 1971. VLSI and parallel computing architectures.

Jay B. Brockman, Assistant Professor; Ph.D., Carnegie Mellon, 1992. VLSI, computer-aided design frameworks.

Ziyi D. Chen, Assistant Professor; Ph.D., Purdue, 1992. Parallel algorithms in computational geometry, theoretical computer science, robot motion and navigation.

Nikos P. Chrisochoides, Assistant Professor; Ph.D., Purdue, 1992. Parallel compilers and problem-solving environments for scientific computing.

David L. Cohn, Professor; Ph.D., MIT, 1970. Distributed computing, workstation operating systems, languages for parallel and distributed processing, reliable transaction systems.

Vincent W. Freeh, Assistant Professor; Ph.D., Arizona, 1996. Programming languages, compilers, and operating systems in distributed and parallel computing.

J. Curt Freeland, Assistant Professional Specialist; B.S.E., Purdue, 1985. System administration and network management.

Eugene W. Henry, Professor; Ph.D., Stanford, 1960. Electronic design automation, VLSI design, computer simulation.

Sharon Hu, Assistant Professor; Ph.D., Purdue, 1989. Algorithm design and analysis in VLSI, hardware-software codesign, real-time embedded systems.

Peter M. Kogge, McCourtney Chaired Professor; Ph.D., Stanford, 1972. High-performance computing, parallel computing, computer architectures.

Andrew Lumsdaine, Assistant Professor; Ph.D., MIT, 1992. Parallel processing, scientific computing, numerical analysis, VLSI circuit and semiconductor device simulation, mathematical software.

Edwin Sha, Assistant Professor; Ph.D., Princeton, 1992. VLSI processor arrays, parallel computer architectures, software for parallel systems.

John J. Uhran Jr., Professor and Associate Dean; Ph.D., Purdue, 1967. Electronic design automation, neural networks, robot motion, computer vision.

Adjunct and Visiting Appointment

Ramzi Bualuan, Lecturer; M.S., Notre Dame, 1986. Database techniques, knowledge engineering.

Professor Andrew Lumsdaine teaches in one of his research specialties, software engineering.

The Fitzpatrick/Cushing Hall of Engineering.

Sunrise at the University of Notre Dame as seen from the opposite shore of Lake St. Mary's.

UNIVERSITY OF NOTRE DAME

COLLEGE OF ENGINEERING
DEPARTMENT OF ELECTRICAL ENGINEERING

PROGRAMS OF STUDY

The department offers programs leading to the Ph.D. and the M.S. degrees in electrical engineering, with emphasis on the former. Research areas include electronic circuits and systems—communications systems, control systems, and signal and image processing and electronic materials and devices—solid-state nanoelectronic and optoelectronic materials and devices. A research M.S. degree requires 24 hours of course credits beyond the bachelor's degree and 6 hours for a thesis. The nonresearch M.S. degree requires 30 course credits. Both can normally be completed by a full-time student in about three semesters. All continuing students must pass the qualifying examination, which is administered at the end of the second semester. Students who show potential for doctoral-level work may apply for admission into the Ph.D. program after their second semester. Doctoral students are required to accumulate a minimum of 36 semester hours of satisfactory course credit beyond the bachelor's degree, pass the qualifying and candidacy examinations, spend at least two years in resident study, and write and defend a Ph.D. dissertation.

RESEARCH FACILITIES

Several major research laboratories for the study of electronic and photonic materials and devices and for the analysis and design of circuits and systems serve the department. The Microelectronics Lab houses extensive clean room facilities for IC and device fabrication, including 10-nm 50-kV electron-beam lithography; a photomask generator; mask aligners; a wafer stepper; sixteen furnace tubes; six evaporators; an ion implanter; a plasma etcher; PECVD; RIE; and RTA. Inspection includes a JEOL SEM and Hitachi S-4500 FESEM, a prism coupler, an ellipsometer, a surface profiler, and a 4-point probe. Advanced measurements utilize a 300-mK–11T cryostat, a 10-mK–11T dilution refrigerator, an HP 4145B SPA, a Tek 20-GHz TDR, an HP 18-GHz network analyzer, and DLTS, Hall effect, and Keithley I-V and C-V systems. The Device Simulation Laboratory has a cluster of high-end Sun Workstations and supercomputer access for large-scale computations and visualization. The Nanospectroscopy Lab includes a 15-W Ar$^+$ laser; a femtosecond mode-locked Ti:sapphire laser; a He-Cd laser; He cryostats with high spatial resolution and magnetic fields to 12T, and AFM and NSOM systems. The Optoelectronics Lab has a 10-W Ar$^+$ laser and a CW Ti:sapphire laser, spectrometers, and related optical characterization instrumentation. The Laboratory for Image and Signal Analysis features a dozen high-end Sun Workstations, equipment for the processing and real-time display of HDTV sequences, cameras, frame grabbers, a flat-bed scanner, and several high-definition 24-bit color monitors and specialized printers. The Controls Systems Research Laboratory consists of several Sun Workstations and additional facilities required for the design and prototyping of control systems. The Structural Dynamics and Control/Earthquake Engineering Laboratory, jointly operated with the Department of Civil Engineering and Geological Sciences, employs a 2-inch displacement, 35 in/s, +4g acceleration, 0-50 Hz slip table for 1,000 pound test loads. There are two Communications Laboratories: one with the latest workstations for performing simulations of communications systems and another with a full complement of RF measurement equipment, wide-band digitizers, and connections to roof antennas. The department has its own electronics shop run by a full-time technician. The Solid-State Laboratories are overseen by a full-time professional and a full-time technician; another full-time professional manages the department's computer facilities. The College supports a cluster of ninety-nine Sun UltraSPARC 1 and fifteen PowerMac Workstations for research and instruction. The University Computing Center supports IBM SP-1, SP-2, 9121 mainframe, and several RS/6000-590 systems. A College research library receives 850 engineering-related journals and provides easy access to numerous databases. Its 55,000 volumes augment the University's Theodore M. Hesburgh Library collection of more than 2 million volumes.

FINANCIAL AID

Several prestigious fellowships are available to highly qualified first-time applicants, women, and students from minority groups. Also available are about twenty teaching assistantships and several research assistantships that provide stipends of at least $1250 per month each. All appointments include full remission of academic-year tuition.

COST OF STUDY

Tuition for graduate students is $9905 per semester for full-time study in 1997–98 (waived for fellowship and assistantship recipients).

LIVING AND HOUSING COSTS

Two large modern apartment complexes are available on campus for single graduate students. Married student housing and apartments adjacent to the campus in South Bend are also available, renting for $250 to $400 per month. The cost of living is below the national average.

STUDENT GROUP

The department has about 75 undergraduates and 70 graduate students. It awards about fifteen M.S. degrees and ten Ph.D. degrees per year.

LOCATION

The University is the cultural center of the northern Indiana–southwestern Michigan area and offers cultural, social, and sports events throughout the year. Its 2,150-acre campus is just north of South Bend, a city of about 130,000 people, and approximately 90 miles east of Chicago (a 2-hour trip by car or train). South Bend's Morris Civic Auditorium hosts performances of Broadway plays and is the home of a first-rate symphony orchestra.

THE UNIVERSITY AND THE COLLEGE

The University was founded in 1842 by the Reverend Edward Frederick Sorin and 6 brothers of the Congregation of Holy Cross. It was chartered as a university in 1844, and engineering studies were begun in 1873. The campus's twin lakes and many wooded areas provide a setting of natural beauty for more than 102 University buildings. The engineering buildings, Cushing and Fitzpatrick Halls, were erected in 1931 and 1979, respectively.

APPLYING

GRE General Test scores, TOEFL scores for international students, two transcripts showing academic credits and degrees, and letters of recommendation from 3 or 4 college faculty members should be sent to the Graduate Admissions Office, University of Notre Dame, 312 Main Building, Notre Dame, Indiana 46556. The GRE should be taken no later than January preceding the academic year of enrollment, particularly if financial aid is desired. The application deadline is February 1 for fall admission and November 1 for spring. The application fee for fall admission is $25 for applications submitted by December 1 and $40 for applications submitted after this date.

CORRESPONDENCE AND INFORMATION

Graduate Admissions
Department of Electrical Engineering
University of Notre Dame
Notre Dame, Indiana 46556-5637
Telephone: 219-631-5480
E-mail: eegrad@nd.edu
World Wide Web: http://www.nd.edu/~ee/

UNIVERSITY OF NOTRE DAME
THE FACULTY AND THEIR RESEARCH

Panos J. Antsaklis, Professor and Director of Graduate Studies; Ph.D., Brown, 1977. Systems and control theory, intelligent control, control of hybrid systems, discrete event systems, neural networks.

Peter H. Bauer, Associate Professor; Ph.D., Miami (Florida), 1988. System theory, digital signal processing, stability theory, multidimensional systems.

Gary H. Bernstein, Associate Professor; Ph.D., Arizona State, 1987. Nanostructure fabrication, electron beam lithography.

William B. Berry, Professor and Associate Chair; Ph.D., Purdue, 1964. Solid-state energy conversion, thermoelectrics, photovoltaics.

David L. Cohn, Professor; Ph.D., MIT, 1970. Information and coding theory, communications, speech processing, microprocessors.

Oliver O. Collins, Associate Professor; Ph.D., Caltech, 1989. Information theory, coding, communications.

Daniel J. Costello Jr., Professor and Chair; Ph.D., Notre Dame, 1969. Information, coding, and communication theory.

Garabet J. Gabriel, Associate Professor; Ph.D., Northwestern, 1964. Statistical electrodynamics, optical and microwave radiation.

Douglas C. Hall, Assistant Professor; Ph.D., Illinois at Urbana-Champaign, 1991. Optoelectronics device characterization, fabrication, and materials studies.

Eugene W. Henry, Professor; Ph.D., Stanford, 1960. Computers, controls, simulation, computer-aided design.

Yih-Fang Huang, Professor; Ph.D., Princeton, 1982. Statistical signal processing and communications image-source coding.

Gerald J. Iafrate, Professor; Ph.D., Polytechnic of Brooklyn, 1970. Microelectronic and nanoelectronic devices and device physics.

Thomas H. Kosel, Associate Professor; Ph.D., Berkeley, 1975. Wear, erosion, electron microscopy.

Michael D. Lemmon, Associate Professor; Ph.D., Carnegie Mellon, 1990. Control systems, parameter estimation, pattern recognition, neural networks.

Craig S. Lent, Professor; Ph.D., Minnesota, 1983. Solid-state physics and devices.

Ruey-wen Liu, Freimann Professor; Ph.D., Illinois at Urbana-Champaign, 1960. Large-scale system theory, nonlinear circuits and systems, feedback control theory, stability theory, fault diagnosis.

James L. Merz, Freimann Professor; Ph.D., Harvard, 1967. Semiconductor physics, materials, and devices; optical properties of solids; defects; nanostructures.

Anthony N. Michel, Freimann Professor and McCloskey Dean; Ph.D., Marquette, 1968; D.Sc., Graz (Austria), 1973. Circuit and system theory, large-scale systems.

Wolfgang Porod, Professor; Ph.D., Graz (Austria), 1981. Solid-state devices, computational electronics, nanoelectronics.

Michael K. Sain, Freimann Professor; Ph.D., Illinois at Urbana-Champaign, 1965. Multivariable control systems, engine control, applied algebraic system theory.

Ken D. Sauer, Associate Professor; Ph.D., Princeton, 1989. Tomographic imaging, multivariate detection and estimation, image compression.

Gregory L. Snider, Assistant Professor; Ph.D., California, Santa Barbara, 1991. Design and fabrication of microelectromechanical devices and mesoscopic devices.

Robert L. Stevenson, Associate Professor; Ph.D., Purdue, 1990. Statistical and multidimensional signal and image processing, computer vision.

John J. Uhran Jr., Professor; Ph.D., Purdue, 1967. Communication theory, digital processing, large-scale simulation, computer applications for path planning and the disabled.

RESEARCH AREAS

Electronic Circuits and Systems. Approximately half of the faculty members have research interests in this area, which includes systems and control, signal and image processing, and communications. Projects are conducted in the following areas: bandwidth efficient coding and modulation—design of efficient coding and modulation schemes for reliable transmission over band-limited channels; radio architecture and codes for deep space and satellite communications; multimedia communication—combined source and channel coding and restoration techniques for robust transmission of video/audio; statistical signal processing—array signal processing (radar, sonar) and applications to wireless communications; identification and estimation—blind identification, set membership estimation, adaptive equalization, and spectral analysis; digital filtering—analysis and design of multidimensional filters, floating point realizations, robust stability of discrete-time systems, and nonlinear discrete-time systems; digital image processing—data compression for image sequences, video data processing, tomographic image reconstruction, and image restoration/enhancement; control systems—investigations of stability, robust control, restructurable control, zero dynamics, modeling, and nonlinear servomechanism design; autonomous control systems—theoretical developments for realization of control systems with enhanced operational capabilities; hybrid control; and large-scale dynamic systems—qualitative properties of large-scale dynamical systems addressing Lyapunov stability, input-output properties, and decomposition problems.

Electronic Materials and Devices. Approximately half of the faculty members have research interests in this area, which includes solid-state, nanoelectronic, and optoelectronic materials and devices. Current research projects include quantum device phenomena—optical properties, localization, universal conductance fluctuations, transport, interference, and resonant tunneling; nanoelectronic systems—novel circuits-and-systems architectures for the nanoelectronic regime; experimental nanoelectronics—nanofabrication of quantum dots, cryogenic characterization of single-electron effects, and ultra-small resonant tunneling diodes for ultra-high–speed digital ICs; nanospectroscopy—high-spatial, spectral, and temporal resolution investigations of quantum dots via atomic force microscopy and near-field scanning optical microscopy; device degradation—studies of the electromigration behavior of ultrasmall metal interconnects and hot carrier effects in MOS oxide breakdown phenomena; optoelectronic materials—studies of the optical and material properties of compound semiconductor native oxides; optoelectronic devices—fabrication and characterization of waveguides and optical components for integrated photonic ICs, semiconductor lasers, and optical amplifiers; and micromachining—fabrication of microelectromechanical devices utilizing Si processing, particularly reactive ion etching.

Golden dome atop historic Main Building, Basilica of the Sacred Heart, and other campus buildings.

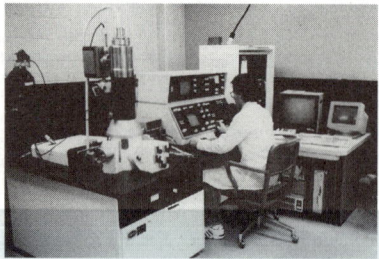

Electron-beam nanolithography system capable of writing 10-nm feature sizes.

Pergola and fountains outside of the Fitzpatrick Hall of Engineering.

UNIVERSITY OF OREGON

COLLEGE OF ARTS AND SCIENCES
DEPARTMENT OF COMPUTER AND INFORMATION SCIENCE

PROGRAMS OF STUDY

The Department of Computer and Information Science offers programs leading to the degrees of Master of Arts (M.A.), Master of Science (M.S.), and Doctor of Philosophy (Ph.D.). The primary research areas are artificial intelligence (natural language processing, expert systems, human interfaces, logic programming, vision); theoretical computer science (computational complexity, models of computation, algorithm design and analysis, graph theory); software engineering (transformation systems, systems analysis); architecture, operating systems, parallel processing, distributed systems, and performance evaluation; graphics; information processing and database systems; and programming languages and compilers. The University's interdisciplinary program in cognitive science provides for joint study between the department and the Departments of Psychology and Linguistics in the areas of human vision and natural language. Interdisciplinary research with the Department of Mathematics includes ongoing work in algebraic algorithms stressing both computational complexity and symbolic computation. Doctorates in numerical analysis and combinatorics are available through the Department of Mathematics.

The M.S. program usually consists of five quarters of full-time graduate course work. The degree requirements are 54 credits, with a minimum of 42 credit hours in computer science. Twelve credit hours may be taken in a related minor area. The M.S. program has a thesis option, which is recommended for those continuing to the Ph.D. program. Students in the Ph.D. program must take six courses in the core area of the master's program or show equivalencies. Courses, along with a directed research project, are completed in the first or second year. Students then choose their dissertation research area, survey current research, and learn problem-solving methods, while gradually assuming more of an independent role. Advancement to candidacy follows the passing of an oral comprehensive examination and a research proposal exam. A research dissertation is required. Students in both the M.S. and Ph.D. programs receive close guidance from faculty advisers.

RESEARCH FACILITIES

The department has a local area network of several workstations for instruction, research, and administration. The facilities include an instructional laboratory with Sun SPARCstations. A Real World Interfaces B12 mobile robot is used for student robotics projects. Research laboratories operate a variety of UNIX workstations, HPs, PCs, SPARCs, and Macintoshes. Workstations are supported by two 2-processor Sun SPARCcenter 1000s and laser printers. Individual laboratories use specialized research equipment: Two 8-processor SGI Power Challenges with Extreme graphics and one 6-processor SGI Power Onyx with Reality Engine and video cameras, recorders, and editors in the Knowledge Based Interface Laboratory; a digital convolver and frame grabber and an SGI Indigo Elan 4000 in the Computational Vision Laboratory; a MassPar Model 1101, SGI indys, IBM rs6000s, SGI Indigos, SGI Indigo 2s, SGI O2s, and UltraSPARCs in the Parallel Processing and Distributed Systems Laboratories; and in the Computer Graphics Laboratory, an HP Apollo 720 CTX-24Z, an HP Apollo 755 CRX-48Z, and an HP Apollo 433s Turbo VRX T2. The department's local network has a gateway to the campus fiber-optic network, giving access to machines in other departments. The University is connected to the Internet via a 1.544-Mbps link to NorthWestNet.

FINANCIAL AID

Teaching and research assistantships are available for qualified graduate students. In 1996–97, stipends ranged from $8665 to $10,037 for the nine-month academic year, with the amount of the award depending on the entry level of the student. The stipends also included a waiver of tuition. The department attempts to support all of its Ph.D. candidates through teaching and research assistantships. A few teaching fellowships are available from the summer school. Also, the Computing Center regularly employs students as programmers, consultants, and computer operators. Various scholarships and work-study opportunities are available through the University's Office of Student Financial Aid.

COST OF STUDY

Graduate tuition for 1996–97 was $1963 per term for Oregon residents; nonresident tuition was $3354 per term. Students with graduate assistantships paid only a fee of $192 per term.

LIVING AND HOUSING COSTS

The rate for single occupancy in University dormitories with a complete meal plan was $5428 for the academic year in 1996–97. Married student housing was available with rent between $250 and $550 per month. Off-campus one-bedroom apartments rented for approximately $500 per month excluding electricity.

STUDENT GROUP

The current student enrollment at the University is more than 17,000 students (more than 3,100 graduate students). The department has more than 60 graduate students.

LOCATION

The University is located in Eugene, a city of approximately 119,000 at the south end of the Willamette Valley. Parks with bike and running paths are built around the confluence of the city's two rivers, the Willamette and the McKenzie. Adjacent to the University are shops, restaurants, parks, and jogging and biking trails along the Willamette River. Within 60 miles of the campus are the Pacific coast to the west and the Cascade mountain range to the east. Thus there are extensive opportunities for camping, hiking, boating, white-water rafting, and cross-country and downhill skiing. Downtown Eugene is the site of a major center for the performing arts (home of the city's symphony orchestra, ballet, opera, and ensembles). The city itself is a compact convention center with major hotels, yet it is within a short distance of wilderness areas.

THE UNIVERSITY AND THE DEPARTMENT

The University of Oregon, which dates from 1876, has 750 full-time faculty members engaged in teaching and research. The University operates on the quarter system with a shortened summer session. The campus is richly landscaped with broad lawns and more than 400 varieties of trees and flowering plants. It includes extensive athletic facilities.

The Department of Computer and Information Science is housed in its own building. This three-story, 27,000-square-foot science facility has extensive laboratory space for research and instruction.

APPLYING

A $50 fee is required of all applicants. Applications for graduate admission should be submitted to the department. All applications should be received by February 1 for the following academic year. All graduate applicants must submit GRE General Test scores, and Ph.D. program applicants should submit scores on the computer science Subject Test of the GRE. International students must pass the TOEFL for admission to the University (the department requires a score of at least 610) and the TSE (Test of Spoken English) for teaching award consideration.

CORRESPONDENCE AND INFORMATION

Department of Computer and Information Science
1202 University of Oregon
Eugene, Oregon 97403-1202

Telephone: 541-346-4408
E-mail: info@cs.uoregon.edu
World Wide Web: http://www.cs.uoregon.edu/

UNIVERSITY OF OREGON
THE FACULTY AND THEIR RESEARCH

Zena M. Ariola, Assistant Professor; Ph.D., Harvard, 1992. Programming languages.

John S. Conery, Associate Professor; Ph.D., California, Irvine, 1983. Architecture, parallel processing.

Jan Cuny, Associate Professor; Ph.D., Michigan, 1981. Parallel processing, programming environments.

Sarah A. Douglas, Associate Professor; Ph.D., Stanford, 1983. User interfaces, artificial intelligence.

Arthur M. Farley, Professor; Ph.D., Carnegie-Mellon, 1974. Artificial intelligence, graph algorithms.

Stephen F. Fickas, Associate Professor; Ph.D., California, Irvine, 1982. Artificial intelligence, expert systems, software engineering.

Virginia M. Lo, Associate Professor; Ph.D., Illinois at Urbana-Champaign, 1984. Distributed systems, operating systems.

Eugene M. Luks, Professor; Ph.D., MIT, 1966. Computational complexity, algebraic algorithms.

Allen D. Malony, Associate Professor; Ph.D., Illinois at Urbana-Champaign, 1990. Performance evaluation of parallel and supercomputing systems.

Gary Meyer, Associate Professor; Ph.D., Cornell, 1986. Computer graphics, color synthesis and reproduction.

Andrzej Proskurowski, Professor; Ph.D., Royal Institute of Technology (Stockholm), 1974. Algorithmic graph theory, computational complexity.

Amr Sabry, Assistant Professor; Ph.D., Rice, 1994. Programming languages, semantics, compilers.

Zary Segall, Professor and Department Head; D.Sc., Technion (Israel), 1979. Performance efficient programming, system validation, wearable computers, binary translations.

Kent A. Stevens, Professor; Ph.D., MIT, 1979. Human and machine vision.

Christopher B. Wilson, Associate Professor; Ph.D., Toronto, 1984. Computational complexity, models of computation.

Computer and Information Science faculty.

Deschutes Hall.

UNIVERSITY OF PENNSYLVANIA

SCHOOL OF ENGINEERING AND APPLIED SCIENCE
DEPARTMENT OF COMPUTER AND INFORMATION SCIENCE

PROGRAMS OF STUDY

Research and teaching at the Department of Computer and Information Science covers a wide range of topics in theory and applications, including algorithms, architecture, programming languages, compilers, operating systems, logic and computation, software engineering, databases, parallel and distributed systems, real-time systems, high-speed networks, graphics, computational biology, natural-language processing, artificial intelligence, machine vision, and robotics. Much of this work involves multidisciplinary collaborations with other departments, including the Departments of Electrical Engineering, Systems Science and Engineering, Decision Sciences, Mechanical Engineering and Applied Mechanics, Chemical Engineering, Mathematics, Linguistics, Philosophy, Psychology, Bioengineering, and Neuroscience. The department also has a number of ongoing research collaborations with national and international organizations and laboratories. The main educational goal is to prepare students for research and teaching careers in either academic institutions or industry.

The Ph.D. program combines both course work and research in one of the major computer science areas. Students must pass a written qualifying examination testing breadth in computer science and an oral examination testing depth in the general area of research.

The department also offers a Master of Science in Engineering program that provides basic course work and research training for students who already have some experience in computer science.

RESEARCH FACILITIES

The primary educational equipment is a collection of Sun Workstations and servers, running Sun's version of UNIX. In addition to the vast array of utilities provided with manufacturer's UNIX, the department provides various software packages and languages, including C++, C, LISP, PROLOG, Standard ML, FORTRAN 77, most GNU utilities, the MIT/X Consortium release of the X-window system, LaTex, and elm. Each CIS computer is connected to an Ethernet network and supports the TCP/IP protocol. The Ethernet is gatewayed to the Penn Campus Network and to the Internet. All faculty members and graduate students have workstations or terminals in their offices capable of accessing any system in the department. The CIS Computing Facility has five groups of computers configured for specific applications.

The General Robotics and Active Sensory Perception (GRASP) Laboratory includes one Sun 4/280, several Sun SPARCstations, and numerous smaller Sun and MicroVAX machines, all running the manufacturer's version of UNIX. They are used mainly for research in robotics and manipulator control and vision. Users are CIS researchers in robotics and vision.

The Language Information and Computation (LINC) Laboratory includes a Sun 4/490, a Sun 4/280, two Sun 4/110s, and several HP 9000s, all running the manufacturer's version of UNIX, plus numerous Symbolics LISP Machines and X-terminals. The primary applications are for research in artificial intelligence. Users are researchers in artificial intelligence.

The Graphics Laboratory includes about twenty Silicon Graphics workstations running UNIX. The primary applications are for research in computer graphics and animation. The user community consists of CIS researchers in graphics and non-CIS researchers sponsored by CIS faculty members.

The Distributed Systems Laboratory (DSL) includes several Sun 3 Workstations, an IBM PC/RT running the manufacturer's version of UNIX, and numerous microcomputer systems. Some of the computer systems include special-purpose subsystems for distributed or parallel operations. The primary applications are for research in digital design and distributed systems. The user community for this lab includes graduate and undergraduate students in electrical engineering and computer science taking classes assigned to the lab and CIS researchers in distributed systems.

The General Research Computing Facilities of CIS include a SPARCserver 2, several desktop Sun Workstations, and numerous HP 9000s, all running the manufacturer's version of UNIX. In addition, numerous X-terminals are used to connect to server machines. The primary applications used are general programming and research and administrative support (text formatting, electronic mail, and others). The user community includes CIS faculty members, staff, graduate students, and non-CIS researchers as sponsored by CIS faculty members. The CIS department also has a Thinking Machines Corporation Connection Machine (CM2a) that is shared by several of the labs. The CM2a is used for research in massively parallel applications such as image and language processing.

FINANCIAL AID

A limited number of fellowships and scholarships are available for Ph.D. candidates; competition for this funding is very intense. No funding is available for part-time students, and funding for M.S.E. candidates is extremely limited; candidates may contact the University of Pennsylvania Center for Graduate and Professional Students, Franklin Building, Philadelphia, Pennsylvania 19104-6270, for information regarding loans.

COST OF STUDY

Tuition for full-time study for the academic year 1997–98 is $21,738, with a general fee of $1420 and a $420 technology fee. For part-time study, the cost is $2906 per course unit (one course), with a general fee of $164 and a $52 technology fee.

LIVING AND HOUSING COSTS

On-campus housing is available for both single and married students. In 1997–98, residences for single students cost approximately $7335 per nine-month term for one bedroom with a living room and kitchen and $4095 for a single room without kitchen. The cost for married student housing ranges from $7605 to $9450. There are also numerous apartments in the immediate area.

STUDENT GROUP

In 1996–97, the department had 140 full-time students and 57 part-time students, 82 master's candidates, and 115 Ph.D. candidates.

LOCATION

The University is located in west Philadelphia, just a few blocks from the heart of the city. Philadelphia is a twentieth-century city with seventeenth-century origins. Renowned museums, concert halls, theaters, and sports arenas provide cultural outlets for students. Fairmount Park extends through large sections of Philadelphia, occupying both banks of the Schuylkill River. The Jersey shore is not far to the east, Pennsylvania Dutch country to the west, and the Poconos to the north. Equidistant from New York City and Washington, D.C., the city of Philadelphia is a patchwork of distinctive neighborhoods that range from Colonial Society Hill to Chinatown.

THE SCHOOL

The School of Engineering and Applied Science has a distinguished reputation for the quality of its programs. Its alumni have achieved international distinction in research, management, industrial development, government service, and engineering education. Its faculty lead a research program that is at the forefront of modern technology and has made major contributions in a wide variety of fields. The School is in fact the birthplace of the modern computer, for it was at its Moore School of Electrical Engineering that ENIAC, the world's first electronic large-scale, general-purpose digital computer, was created.

APPLYING

Candidates who have obtained a bachelor's degree may apply for admission by submitting an application in writing to the Office of Graduate Education and Research, School of Engineering and Applied Science, University of Pennsylvania. Admission is based on the student's past record as well as on letters of recommendation. Scores on the GRE General Test (but not the Subject Test) are required. All students whose native language is not English must arrange to take the Test of English as a Foreign Language (TOEFL) prior to making application; the minimum score accepted is 600.

CORRESPONDENCE AND INFORMATION

Graduate Admissions
Department of Computer and Information Science
University of Pennsylvania
Philadelphia, Pennsylvania 19104-6389

Telephone: 215-898-8560
E-mail: cis-grad-admin@central.cis.upenn.edu

UNIVERSITY OF PENNSYLVANIA
THE FACULTY AND THEIR RESEARCH

Norman I. Badler, Cecilia Fitler Moore Professor; Ph.D., Toronto. Computer graphics, human movement simulation, three-dimensional modeling and interaction techniques.

Ruzena Bajcsy, Professor; Ph.D., Stanford. Computer vision, biomedical imaging, language and vision, robotics.

Peter Buneman, Professor; Ph.D., Warwick. Database/knowledge-base systems, programming languages, environments, semantics.

Susan Davidson, Associate Professor; Ph.D., Princeton. Distributed systems, database systems, real-time systems.

Magda El Zarki, Associate Professor of Computer and Information Science (secondary appointment) and of Electrical Engineering; Ph.D., Columbia. Network modeling and management.

David Farber, Professor of Computer and Information Science and of Electrical Engineering (secondary appointment); M.S., Stevens. High-speed networking, distributed computer systems, distributed collaboration and software productivity.

Peter Freyd, Professor of Computer and Information Science (secondary appointment) and of Mathematics; Ph.D., Princeton. Category theory, logic, type theory, semantics of programming languages.

Jean Gallier, Professor; Ph.D., UCLA. Logic programming, proof theory, automated deduction, theory of computation, programming languages, compilers.

Carl Gunter, Associate Professor; Ph.D., Wisconsin. Programming language theory; mathematical models for computational languages; logic, λ-calculus, category theory, and their applications in computer science, domain theory, and programming language semantics; type theory; models and proof systems for concurrency.

Aravind K. Joshi, Henry Salvatori Professor of Computer and Cognitive Science; Ph.D., Pennsylvania. Natural-language processing, natural-language interfaces, artificial intelligence, cognitive science.

Sampath Kannan, Assistant Professor; Ph.D., Berkeley. Program checking, probabilistic algorithms, learning theory, graph theory and combinatorics, computational biology, algorithms for code generation.

Insup Lee, Associate Professor; Ph.D., Wisconsin. Distributed systems, real-time computing, operating systems, software engineering methods and tools, formal specification and analysis of time-dependent systems.

Mark Liberman, Professor of Computer and Information Science (secondary appointment) and of Linguistics; Ph.D., MIT. Phonetics, prosody, natural-language processing, speech communication.

Mitchell Marcus, RCA Professor of Artificial Intelligence and Chair; Ph.D., MIT. Natural-language processing, computational theories of grammar, cognitive science, automatic acquisition of linguistic structure from text corpora.

Dimitri Metaxas, Assistant Professor; Ph.D., Toronto. Physics-based modeling and simulation, computer graphics and animation, computer vision, scientific visualization.

Dale Miller, Associate Professor; Ph.D., Carnegie Mellon. Logic and functional programming, computational logic, proof theory, automated reasoning.

Max Mintz, Associate Professor; Ph.D., Cornell. Decision making under uncertainty, stochastic modeling, multisensor fusion with applications to multiagent robotic systems.

Scott Nettles, Assistant Professor; Ph.D., Carnegie Mellon. Design, implementation, and evaluation of programming languages, operating systems, and database systems; memory management and garbage collection.

Richard Paul, Professor of Computer and Information Science and of Mechanical Engineering (secondary appointment); Ph.D., Stanford. Robotics, teleoperation, real-time numerical methods.

Ellen Prince, Professor of Computer and Information Science (secondary appointment) and of Linguistics; Ph.D., Pennsylvania. Pragmatics/discourse, language contact, Yiddish.

Noah S. Prywes, Professor; Ph.D., Harvard. Automatic software generation, programming languages, operating systems, visual programming.

Keith Ross, Associate Professor of Computer and Information Science (secondary appointment) and of Systems Engineering; Ph.D., Michigan. Performance modeling of telecommunications networks.

Andre Scedrov, Professor of Computer and Information Science (secondary appointment) and of Mathematics; Ph.D., SUNY at Buffalo. Logic, type theory, category theory, semantics of programming languages.

Jonathan Smith, Associate Professor; Ph.D., Columbia. Distributed systems, operating systems, multimedia communications systems, applications of randomness, computer security and cryptology.

Mark Steedman, Professor; Ph.D., Edinburgh. Natural-language processing, spoken-language systems, artificial intelligence, cognitive sciences.

Val Tannen, Associate Professor; Ph.D., MIT. Programming languages, databases, mathematical foundations, logic in computer science.

Lyle Ungar, Associate Professor of Computer and Information Science (secondary appointment) and of Chemical Engineering; Ph.D., MIT. Machine learning, knowledge-based systems, qualitative physics, real and artificial neural networks.

Tandy Warnow, Assistant Professor; Ph.D., Berkeley. Algorithms, graph theory, combinatorics, computational biology.

Bonnie Lynn Webber, Professor; Ph.D., Harvard. Natural-language processing (computational approaches to discourse, question-answering, animation from instructions), planning and reasoning about action, medical applications of artificial intelligence.

Scott Weinstein, Professor of Computer and Information Science (secondary appointment) and of Philosophy; Ph.D., Rockefeller. Computational learning theory, logic in computer science.

UNIVERSITY OF PENNSYLVANIA

SCHOOL OF ENGINEERING AND APPLIED SCIENCE
MOORE SCHOOL OF ELECTRICAL ENGINEERING
DEPARTMENT OF ELECTRICAL ENGINEERING

PROGRAM OF STUDY

The graduate program in electrical engineering encompasses the physical, device, and signal-processing aspects of electrical engineering. There are four areas of specialization in which the course work and research are coordinated: electromagnetic field phenomena, including diffraction scattering, propagation, remote sensing of the environment, microwave and long-wavelength holographic imaging, electrooptics, and integrated optics; signal processing and communication theory with emphasis on high-resolution microwave imaging, spectrum estimation and adaptive techniques, image processing, statistical techniques, digital signal processing, and neural networks; solid-state and chemical electronics, including integrated sensors, interface phenomena, integrated-circuit and other devices, and electronic properties of materials and their applications; and telecommunications, including packet and circuit switching, network design, performance modeling, communication architectures, and protocols. The department also offers a program in intelligent sensor technologies leading to the Master of Science in Engineering (M.S.E.) degree.

The minimum requirements for the M.S.E. are either 8 course units of formal course work and a 2-course-unit thesis describing the results of independent research or 10 course units of formal course work.

The Ph.D. requirements are 20 course units of studies, including the core areas of electrical engineering; a written qualifying examination; a departmental seminar; a dissertation, which includes a final oral presentation and defense of the work; and fulfillment of the equivalent of 2 course units as a teaching assistant for the department.

RESEARCH FACILITIES

The research program utilizes several modern laboratory facilities in the Moore School and other parts of the University. Major facilities include the Microfabrication Laboratory, the Center for Sensor Technologies, the Center for Telecommunications, the Electro-Optics/Microwave-Optics Holography Laboratory, the Optical Spectroscopy Laboratory, and the Valley Forge Research Center. Phased-array facilities are available at Valley Forge. There are excellent facilities for the study of synthetic metals, and the Laboratory for Research on the Structure of Matter is available for special measurements. Extensive optical measurement equipment covering the spectrum from 40 μm to less than 0.1 μm is available. Standard semiconductor processing facilities exist for support of the solid-state and chemical electronics program. Submicron device processing and studies utilize laser holography and electron-beam writing and an ion implanter. A microwave anechoic chamber and an automated network analyzer covering the 1–19 GHz range are available for antenna, radar cross-section, imaging, microwave component, and other electromagnetic studies. The Signal Processing Research Laboratory offers facilities for computational and simulation aspects of signal-processing research, including facilities for image processing on dedicated minicomputers and microcomputers.

FINANCIAL AID

Financial aid is available to qualified students in the Ph.D. program in the form of fellowships and research assistantships. In 1996–97, the awards covered tuition and fees plus a stipend of $15,000 for twelve months.

COST OF STUDY

Tuition and fees for the academic year 1997–98 for full-time study are approximately $29,600. For part-time study, the tuition and fees are approximately $2960 per course unit (one course).

LIVING AND HOUSING COSTS

On-campus housing is available for both single and married students and costs from approximately $370 to $775 per month, depending on the type of accommodation and the length of the lease. Detailed information is available from the Department of Residential Living at 3901 Locust. There are also numerous privately owned apartments in the immediate area.

STUDENT GROUP

Of the 22,952 students at the University, 11,332 are in graduate or professional schools. Of these, 610 are in graduate engineering programs, including 64 in electrical engineering.

LOCATION

The University is located in West Philadelphia, just a few blocks from the heart of the city. Philadelphia is a twentieth-century city with seventeenth-century origins. Renowned museums, concert halls, theaters, and sports arenas provide cultural outlets for students. Fairmount Park extends through large sections of Philadelphia, occupying both banks of the Schuylkill River. The New Jersey shore is not far to the east, Pennsylvania Dutch country to the west, and the Poconos to the north. Equidistant from New York City and Washington, D.C., the city of Philadelphia is a patchwork of distinctive neighborhoods ranging from Colonial Society Hill to Chinatown.

THE SCHOOL

The School of Engineering and Applied Science has a distinguished reputation for the quality of its programs. Its alumni have achieved international distinction in research, management, industrial development, government service, and engineering education. Its faculty leads a research program that is at the forefront of modern technology and has made major contributions in a wide variety of fields. The School is in fact the birthplace of the modern computer, for it was at its Moore School of Electrical Engineering that ENIAC, the world's first electronic large-scale, general-purpose digital computer was created.

APPLYING

Candidates who have obtained a bachelor's degree may apply for admission by submitting an application in writing to the Office of Graduate Education and Research, School of Engineering and Applied Science, Room 113 Towne Building, University of Pennsylvania. Admission is based on the student's past record as well as on letters of recommendation. Scores on the Graduate Record Examinations are not required. All international students whose native language is not English must arrange to take the Test of English as a Foreign Language (TOEFL) prior to applying; the minimum acceptable score is 600.

CORRESPONDENCE AND INFORMATION

Dr. Nader Engheta, Graduate Group Chair
Department of Electrical Engineering
University of Pennsylvania
200 South 33rd Street
Philadelphia, Pennsylvania 19104-6390
Telephone: 215-898-9241

UNIVERSITY OF PENNSYLVANIA
THE FACULTY AND THEIR RESEARCH

Joseph Bordogna, Ph.D., Pennsylvania, 1964. Electrooptics, optical recording materials, educational technology.

Takeshi Egami, Ph.D., Pennsylvania, 1971. Physics of solids: magnetism, amorphous metals, glasses, X-ray and neutron diffraction. (Primary appointment in Materials Science and Engineering)

Lawrence Eisenberg, D.Eng.Sc., NJIT, 1966. Large-scale electric power systems.

Magda El Zarki, Ph.D., Columbia, 1987. Telecommunication networks, performance analysis of adaptive protocols for integrated local area networks.

Nader Engheta, Ph.D., Caltech, 1982. Applied electromagnetics associated with antennas, wave polarization, and wave scattering.

David Farber, M.S., Stevens, 1962. Telecommunications and information systems, computer communications and local area networks (LANs). (Primary appointment in Computer and Information Science)

Nabil H. Farhat, Ph.D., Pennsylvania, 1963. Microwave and acoustic holography and imaging, inverse scattering, electrooptics, optical computing.

William R. Graham, D.Phil., Oxford, 1965. Surfaces and interfaces: atomic structure and adsorption on metal surfaces, thin-film surface alloys, metal semiconductor interfaces. (Primary appointment in Materials Science and Engineering)

Dwight L. Jaggard, Ph.D., Caltech, 1976. Optics and applied electromagnetic fields, imaging, inverse scattering, integrated optics, resonant sensors.

Saleem A. Kassam, Ph.D., Princeton, 1975. Signal processing and communication theory: nonlinear filters, sensor array processing, adaptive schemes, spectrum estimation, detection and estimation.

Frederick D. Ketterer, Ph.D., MIT, 1965. Organ preservation, microwave effects on tissues.

Haralambos N. Kritikos, Ph.D., Pennsylvania, 1961. Applied electromagnetic fields, remote sensing, electromagnetic radiation hazards.

Kenneth R. Laker, Ph.D., NYU, 1973. Analog and digital signal processing, sampled data systems, VLSI design.

Sohrab Rabii, Chair; Ph.D., MIT, 1966. Theory of electronic properties of solids, defects in solids, alloy theory, relativistic effects in molecules and solids.

Jorge J. Santiago, Ph.D., Penn State, 1971. Materials for electronics, thin-film physics.

Bernard D. Steinberg, Director, Valley Forge Research Center; Ph.D., Pennsylvania, 1971. Adaptive spatial signal processing, high-angular-resolution microwave imaging, development of the world's first radio camera.

Jan Van der Spiegel, Ph.D., Leuven (Belgium), 1979. Integrated sensors, signal conditioning, integrated-circuit technology, photosensitive devices such as CCD.

Santosh S. Venkatesh, Ph.D., Caltech, 1986. Pattern recognition, neural networks and cellular systems, distributed computing systems, digital signal processing, image processing, systems theory.

Jay N. Zemel, Director, Center for Sensor Technologies; Ph.D., Syracuse, 1956. Chemically sensitive semiconductor devices, semiconductor surface physics, integrated-circuit technology.

UNIVERSITY OF PITTSBURGH

DEPARTMENT OF ELECTRICAL ENGINEERING

PROGRAMS OF STUDY

The department offers programs leading to the degrees of Master of Science (M.S.) and Doctor of Philosophy (Ph.D.) in electrical engineering. Graduate studies and research are concentrated in seven major areas: bioengineering, computer engineering, control, electronics, image processing/computer vision, power, and signal processing/communications. The department has 33 faculty members.

The M.S. degree has both the thesis and nonthesis options. The thesis option provides the student with an opportunity to work on a specific research project (applied or basic in nature) under the close supervision of a faculty adviser. The minimum requirements for the thesis option are 24 credits of graduate course work and preparation and defense of a thesis on a topic in the student's primary area of interest. For the nonthesis option, the minimum requirements are 33 credits of graduate course work and passing a comprehensive exam. The M.S. degree program can usually be completed in 1 to 1½ years on a full-time basis.

Students who have an M.S. in electrical engineering and pass the Ph.D. Preliminary Exam are admitted to the Ph.D. program. After a student has been formally admitted, a faculty program committee is established for the purpose of advising and approving an appropriate plan of study for the student. A minimum of 48 credits of course work beyond the B.S. degree is required (54 credits are required for students who take the M.S. nonthesis option). The Ph.D. student is expected to pass a comprehensive exam and complete a dissertation embodying an independent and original investigation of a problem of significance in his or her major area of specialization. The validity and contributions of the dissertation work are then defended in a final oral examination.

Completion of the Ph.D. degree usually takes three years beyond the M.S. degree.

RESEARCH FACILITIES

The University of Pittsburgh has extensive computational facilities that include VMS and UNIX services. A very powerful computing capability is also available through the CRAY Y-MP C90 supercomputer, which is located in one of five National Science Foundation Supercomputer Centers in the United States. Access to the University's computers is provided by a fiber-optic network with ports located at numerous points around the campus, including the Benedum Hall of Engineering. All students have access to the central computing facility.

The Department of Electrical Engineering has numerous personal computers and Sun and Apollo workstations. The department has research and instructional laboratories in computer vision and pattern recognition, VLSI design and CAD, lasers and nonlinear optics, microprocessor systems, neural networks, optoelectronics, and signal processing. The optoelectronics laboratory contains a metal-organic chemical vapor deposition (MOCVD) system for epitaxial growth of GaAs, AlAs, and InAs for fabrication of quantum wells, superlattices, and electronic devices.

The University Library System maintains collections totaling more than 5.7 million volumes including microtext. The Bevier Engineering Library currently houses more than 60,000 volumes, 63,000 microforms, and 950 serials.

FINANCIAL AID

Teaching assistantships are available from the department and are awarded on the basis of scholastic record, GRE General Test scores, and letters of reference. Research assistantships are typically awarded to graduate students who have been in the department for at least one term and who have distinguished themselves by superior performance in course work or project work. A limited number of fellowships are also available. In 1996–97, typical stipends for teaching and research assistantships ranged from $1193 to $1300 per month, plus tuition and medical benefits.

COST OF STUDY

For the 1996–97 academic year, tuition was $8808 for state residents and $17,964 for out-of-state students.

LIVING AND HOUSING COSTS

Students can rent furnished and unfurnished rooms and apartments near campus. The Department of Property Management (412-624-4317) provides University housing, which is available to students.

STUDENT GROUP

The department has 114 graduate students, 56 of whom are Ph.D. students. Roughly one half of the graduate students are part-time, employed by industry in the Pittsburgh area.

Efforts are under way to double the number of full-time students in the Ph.D. program.

LOCATION

Pittsburgh, one of the most livable cities in the United States, is a cultural city and has been a major center for industrial activity and technological innovation for many decades. In recent years, the city has been undergoing a phase of corporate growth, emphasizing high technology. Pittsburgh is one of the nation's largest corporate headquarters cities. It offers many cultural and recreational resources, such as the Pittsburgh Symphony, the Pittsburgh Opera Company, the Pittsburgh Ballet Theatre, and major-league sports.

THE UNIVERSITY

The University of Pittsburgh is located in the Oakland section of the city, about 3 miles from downtown. The University began in 1787 and thus is one of the oldest in the country. Today, the University has approximately 28,500 students enrolled in sixteen professional schools and the arts and sciences, including the School of Medicine, which is a world leader in organ transplantation.

APPLYING

An outstanding scholastic record and GRE General Test scores are required of all applicants. International students, except those who attended U.S. schools, must submit TOEFL scores. Women, African Americans, and Hispanics are encouraged to apply. If financial support is requested, completed applications must be received by February 1 for the fall term. Application materials can be obtained by writing to the Graduate Program Coordinator.

CORRESPONDENCE AND INFORMATION

Graduate Program Coordinator
Department of Electrical Engineering
348 Benedum Hall
University of Pittsburgh
Pittsburgh, Pennsylvania 15261
Telephone: 412-624-8001
Fax: 412-624-8003
E-mail: eedept@ee.pitt.edu

UNIVERSITY OF PITTSBURGH
THE FACULTY AND THEIR RESEARCH

Individual electronic mail addresses are listed in parentheses after each faculty name.

Carolyn L. Beck, Assistant Professor; Ph.D., Caltech, 1995. Control systems theory with emphasis in model reduction methods and realization theory for multidimensional and uncertain systems.

J. Robert Boston, Associate Professor and Undergraduate Program Coordinator; Ph.D., Northwestern, 1971. Knowledge-based signal processing, control of artificial organs, modeling coordination of movement in people with chronic pain, representation of uncertainty using fuzzy logic and Dempster-Shafer theory. (boston@ee.pitt.edu)

David M. Brienza, Assistant Professor of Health and Rehabilitation Sciences and of Electrical Engineering; Ph.D., Virginia, 1991. Control theory, soft tissue biomechanics, assistive technology, rehabilitation science. (dab3@pitt.edu)

J. Thomas Cain, Associate Professor; Ph.D., Pittsburgh, 1970. Algorithm development, digital implementation of real-time systems. (cain@ee.pitt.edu)

Shi-Kuo Chang, Professor of Computer Science, Electrical Engineering, and Information Science and Intelligent Systems; Ph.D., Berkeley, 1969. Pictorial information systems, visual languages, knowledge-based systems. (chang@cs.pitt.edu)

Luis F. Chaparro, Associate Professor and Graduate Program Coordinator; Ph.D., Berkeley, 1980. Statistical signal processing, time frequency, multidimensional system theory, image processing. (chaparro@ee.pitt.edu)

Panos K. Chrysanthis, Associate Professor of Computer Science and Electrical Engineering; Ph.D., Massachusetts, 1991. Database systems, distributed systems, operating systems, real-time systems. (panos@cs.pitt.edu)

Henry Y. H. Chuang, Associate Professor of Computer Science and Electrical Engineering; Ph.D., North Carolina, 1966. Computer architecture, parallel processing, fault-tolerant computing. (chuang@cs.pitt.edu)

R. Gerald Colclaser, Professor; D.Sc., Pittsburgh, 1968. Electrical transients in power systems, pulse power components and systems. (rgc@ee.pitt.edu)

Amro A. El-Jaroudi, Associate Professor; Ph.D., Northeastern, 1988. Digital processing of speech signals, spectral estimation, neural networks. (amro@ee.pitt.edu)

Mahmoud El-Nokali, Associate Professor; Ph.D., McGill, 1980. Microelectronics, semiconductor device modeling, computer-aided design, analog circuit design. (elnokali@ee.pitt.edu)

Joel Falk, Professor; Ph.D., Stanford, 1971. Linear and nonlinear optical devices, solid-state lasers, high speed electrooptic modulators, electrooptic field sensors, phase conjugation. (falk@ee.pitt.edu)

Joseph M. Furman, Professor of Otolaryngology, Neurology, and Electrical Engineering; M.D., 1977, Ph.D., 1979, Pennsylvania. Balance disorders, vestibular function, eye movements. (furman@vms.cis.pitt.edu)

Ilan Gravé, Assistant Professor; Ph.D., Caltech, 1993. Optoelectronic integrated devices, low dimensional structures, resonant tunneling, quantum well infrared detectors, nonlinear optics, semiconductor lasers. (grave@ee.pitt.edu)

Richard W. Hall, Associate Professor; Ph.D., Northwestern, 1975. Computer vision, parallel algorithms and architectures for image processing, digital topology. (hall@ee.pitt.edu)

Ronald G. Hoelzeman, Associate Professor; Ph.D., Pittsburgh, 1970. Multiprocessor systems, parallel computer architectures, education innovation, computer-aided engineering. (hoelzema@ee.pitt.edu)

Steven P. Jacobs, Visiting Assistant Professor of Electrical Engineering; D.Sc., Washington (St. Louis), 1997. Model-based estimation, automated systems for joint tracking and recognition, high-resolution radar. (spj1+@pitt.edu)

Morton Kanefsky, Associate Professor; Ph.D., Princeton, 1964. Stochastic signal processing as applied to communications, image coding, and optical processing. (mk1@ee.pitt.edu)

Hong Koo Kim, Associate Professor; Ph.D., Carnegie Mellon, 1989. Semiconductor materials and devices, optoelectronic devices, integrated optics. (kim@ee.pitt.edu)

George L. Kusic, Associate Professor; Ph.D., Carnegie Mellon, 1967. Real-time computer control of power systems. (kusic@ee.pitt.edu)

Dietrich W. Langer, Professor; Dr.Ing., Berlin Technical, 1961. Devices for optoelectronic applications. (dwl@ee.pitt.edu)

Steven P. Levitan, Wellington C. Carl Faculty Fellow and Associate Professor; Ph.D., Massachusetts, 1984. Parallel computer architecture, optical computing, VLSI architectures, computer-aided design for VLSI. (steve@ee.pitt.edu)

Ching-Chung Li, Professor of Electrical Engineering and Computer Science; Ph.D., Northwestern, 1961. Computer vision, pattern recognition, biomedical image/signal processing, applications of wavelet transform. (ccl@ee.pitt.edu)

Patrick J. Loughlin, Fulton C. Noss Faculty Fellow and Assistant Professor, Ph.D., Washington (Seattle), 1992. Nonstationary signal processing, time-frequency distributions, biomedical signal analysis, machine fault monitoring. (pat@ee.pitt.edu)

Rami G. Melhem, Professor of Computer Science and Electrical Engineering; Ph.D., Pittsburgh, 1983. Design and verification of parallel fault-tolerant and optical systems. (melhem@cs.pitt.edu)

Marlin H. Mickle, Professor; Ph.D., Pittsburgh, 1967. Microprocessor systems, parallel architectures, homogenous and heterogeneous architectures, parallel performance modeling and analysis, computer and communication networks.

Douglas C. Noll, Assistant Professor of Radiology and Electrical Engineering; Ph.D., Stanford, 1991. Medical imaging, magnetic resonance imaging, image reconstruction and processing, functional neuroimaging. (doug@spiff.mrctr.upmc.edu)

Charles J. Robinson, Professor of Rehabilitation Science and Technology, Electrical Engineering, and Orthopaedic Surgery; D.Sc., Washington (St. Louis), 1979. Biomedical engineering, rehabilitation engineering, neurophysiology. (c.robinson@ieee.org)

Robert J. Sclabassi, Professor of Neurological Surgery, Electrical Engineering, Mechanical Engineering, and Behavioral Neuroscience; Ph.D., USC, 1971; M.D., Pittsburgh, 1981. Acquisition and analysis of electrical and magnetic data from the central nervous system. (bob@neuronet.pitt.edu)

Dorothy E. Setliff, Associate Professor; Ph.D., Carnegie Mellon, 1989. Real-time system software synthesis and design, VLSI CAD, computer engineering, computer architecture. (dottie@ee.pitt.edu)

Chris C. Shaw, Associate Professor of Radiology, Environmental and Occupational Health, and Electrical Engineering; Ph.D., Wisconsin–Madison, 1981. Physics and instrumentation of digital radiography, digital mammography, quantitative image processing and analysis, dual-energy subtraction imaging. (shaw@rad.arad.upmc.edu)

Marwan A. Simaan, Bell of PA/Bell Atlantic Professor and Chairman, Department of Electrical Engineering; Ph.D., Illinois at Urbana–Champaign, 1972. Signal processing, array signal processing, geophysical applications, knowledge-based signal processing and control, statistical process control. (simaan@ee.pitt.edu)

Richard Thompson, Professor and Co-Director of Telecommunications and Electrical Engineering; Ph.D., Connecticut, 1971. Communication switching: system architecture, photonic switching, switching network architectures and control algorithms, intelligent networks; communication terminals: integrated services, human-computer interaction, and multimedia services. (rat@icarus.lis.pitt.edu)

UNIVERSITY OF PITTSBURGH

DEPARTMENT OF INFORMATION SCIENCE AND TELECOMMUNICATIONS
GRADUATE PROGRAM IN INFORMATION SCIENCE

PROGRAMS OF STUDY

Programs of study lead to the Master of Science in Information Science (M.S.I.S.), the Ph.D. in information science, and a post-master's Certificate of Advanced Study. Graduate degrees in telecommunications are described in the telecommunications listing. The M.S.I.S. requires 36 credit hours of course work and can be completed in four terms of full-time study. Students may pursue such specialties as cognitive science (including artificial intelligence, neural networks, natural language processing, and human cognition), human-computer interface and visualization, information retrieval, networks and telecommunications, and systems analysis and design. The M.S.T. degree, designed for both beginning and experienced telecommunications professionals, is described in a separate listing. The Ph.D. programs provide research-oriented study and professional specialization in the sciences of information and telecommunications. Candidates must give evidence of superior scholarship, mastery of a specialized field of knowledge, and the ability to do significant and relevant research. The Ph.D. in information science requires 36 course or seminar credits beyond the master's degree, successful completion of the preliminary and comprehensive examinations, three terms of full-time academic study on campus, 6 credits of linguistics, at least 18 dissertation credits, and submission and defense of a dissertation.

RESEARCH FACILITIES

Departmental computing and networking labs are housed in a modern 5,000-square-foot area. A Sun ULTRAsparc compute server cluster with attached RAID-array is employed for various research activities, while a HYPERsparc upgraded Sun 670 serves as a general student access system. Workstations in the labs include Sun SPARC 5s, IPXs, and IPCs. Two labs are configured as classrooms, one with Pentium class systems running Windows95 and the other containing 486 systems. The internal labs network environment is being upgraded to employ a mixture of both ATM and fast Ethernet technology. Laser printing is provided throughout the labs. The telecommunications and network labs are built around a heterogeneous collection of UNIX workstations and microcomputer systems. Ethernet, token ring, and ATM test network environments are maintained for research as well as to supplement classroom instruction. These labs also house training, diagnostic, and testing equipment for AT&T phone systems, T1 and T3 connections, and M13, FT3C, and TASI transmission equipment. All workstations and PCs in the labs are linked via a local area network to general-purpose University UNIX and VMS systems as well as to the facilities of the Pittsburgh Supercomputing Center, which includes CRAY 90, CRAY T3E, and clustered workstations. Additional University computer facilities include an advanced technology and computer graphics lab and other labs located throughout the campus. All students have access to national and international electronic mail and assorted other network services.

FINANCIAL AID

In 1996–97, 42 percent of full-time graduate students received financial aid, mainly in the form of full or half graduate assistantships. Full graduate student assistants (GSAs) earned $4075 per term plus remission of tuition and assist a faculty member for 20 hours per week. Half GSAs earned half the stipend and remission of half the tuition for 10 hours of work per week. Financial aid awards are granted on the basis of academic achievement and financial need. Assistantships are normally awarded for the fall and spring terms. Budget permitting, they may also be offered for the summer term.

COST OF STUDY

The tuition per term (four months) in 1996–97 for full-time study (9–15 credits) was $7912. Because Pitt is state-related, the University receives funding from the state that enables it to reduce tuition for Pennsylvania residents to $3880 per term. Tuition for part-time students is $657 per credit for out-of-state students and $321 per credit for residents of Pennsylvania.

LIVING AND HOUSING COSTS

Pittsburgh, ranked by Rand McNally among the most livable cities in the United States, is noted for its low cost of living. Average monthly rent is $400 for a one-bedroom apartment and $575 for a two-bedroom apartment; it is estimated that students require at least $2200 per term to cover living expenses exclusive of tuition. Comfortable and affordable housing in attractive residential neighborhoods is readily available within walking distance of the University.

STUDENT GROUP

The current enrollment in information science and telecommunications graduate programs is 214 graduate students, of whom approximately 37 percent are full-time. Nineteen percent are international students and 42 percent are women. Members of minority groups represent approximately 6 percent of the U.S. enrollment.

LOCATION

The University is located in the heart of the city's educational center, with museums of art and natural history, music and lecture halls, Carnegie Mellon University and two smaller colleges, restaurants and shops, and a 450-acre park adjacent to the campus. The downtown corporate and cultural center is just a 10-minute bus ride away.

THE UNIVERSITY

The University of Pittsburgh, a privately organized state-related institution, enrolls approximately 32,000 students. The School of Information Sciences has an enrollment of 699 students in four programs (three graduate and one undergraduate).

APPLYING

Applicants for all programs must submit a recent score (within three years) from the GRE General Test. Requirements for admission to the M.S.I.S. degree program are a degree from an accredited college or university with a 3.0 GPA and a 3-credit course in a structured programming language (preferably C), math, statistics, and cognitive science. Ph.D. applicants must have a master's degree from an accredited program with a QPA of 3.3 or better, the same prerequisites as the M.S.I.S. degree program, and additional courses in mathematics. Provisional acceptance into any of the degree programs may be granted to students lacking some of the prerequisites, with the condition that deficiencies be made up during the first two terms. A $30 application fee is required ($40 for international applicants). Deadlines for receipt of application materials are July 1 for fall admission, November 1 for spring admission, and March 1 for summer admission. Applications for financial aid should be submitted by January 15 for fall term and October 1 for spring term. Candidates are usually notified of acceptance within six weeks of receipt of all application materials.

CORRESPONDENCE AND INFORMATION

Admissions Coordinator
505 SLIS Building
University of Pittsburgh
Pittsburgh, Pennsylvania 15260

Telephone: 412-624-5146
Fax: 412-624-2788
E-mail: isadmit@sis.pitt.edu
World Wide Web: http://www.sis.pitt.edu/~dist

UNIVERSITY OF PITTSBURGH
THE FACULTY AND THEIR RESEARCH

Toni Carbo, Professor and Dean, School of Information Sciences; Ph.D., Drexel. National and international information policies, measurement and use of scientific and technical information, role of information in the economy, education for the information professions.

Stephen C. Hirtle, Associate Professor and Chair; Ph.D., Michigan. Spatial information classification, mathematical psychology, cognitive science, geographic information systems, hypertext and multimedia systems, visualization, neural networks.

Sujata Banerjee, Assistant Professor; Ph.D., USC. Design and analysis of high-speed networking protocols, traffic modeling, network reliability, concurrency control, failure recovery of distributed database systems.

Marek Druzdzel, Assistant Professor; Ph.D., Carnegie Mellon. Decision support systems, strategic business planning, decision making under uncertainty, decision-theoretic methods in intelligent information systems.

Ida M. Flynn, Assistant Professor and Director of the Undergraduate Program; Ph.D., Pittsburgh. Information science, computer science, mathematics, education, information retrieval systems for young users, multimedia systems.

Roger R. Flynn, Associate Professor; Ph.D., Pittsburgh. Education in information science, knowledge representation and inference, database design, artificial intelligence, systems analysis and design, data structures, human-computer interaction, database management systems.

Charles P. Friedman, Professor and Director, Center for Biomedical Informatics; Ph.D., North Carolina at Chapel Hill. Biomedical informatics, clinical reasoning, program evaluation.

Wesley Jamison, Associate Professor (Greensburg Campus); Ph.D., Penn State. Human-computer interaction, computer-supported cooperative work, information technology, human factors, telecommunications.

Robert R. Korfhage, Professor; Ph.D., Michigan. Information storage and retrieval, visual languages and interfaces, abstract data structures and types, graph theory, integrated media systems, genetic algorithms.

Michael Lewis, Associate Professor; Ph.D., Georgia Tech. Operator modeling in human-machine systems, ecological models of visualization, virtual realities.

Dirk Mahling, Assistant Professor; Ph.D., Massachusetts. Visual languages, computer-supported collaborative learning, knowledge management, intelligent workflow, cooperation and coordination, CSCW and group work.

Douglas Metzler, Associate Professor; Ph.D., California, Davis. Artificial intelligence, cognitive science, knowledge representation, natural language processing, expert systems, information storage and retrieval, cognitive modeling, intelligent tutoring systems, education systems, research methods and statistics.

Paul Munro, Associate Professor; Ph.D., Brown. Connectionist systems, neural information processing, image processing, modeling and simulation, cognitive science, models of learning, visualization, genetic algorithms and artificial life.

Kai A. Olsen, Professor; Molde College (Norway); M.S., Norwegian Institute of Technology. Visualization, visual languages, information retrieval, programming languages, operating systems, computers in society.

Edie M. Rasmussen, Associate Professor and Chair, Department of Library and Information Science; Ph.D., Sheffield (England). Information storage and retrieval, applications of parallel processors to information retrieval, geographic information systems, indexing systems and software, microcomputer applications.

Kenneth M. Sochats, Assistant Professor; M.S.E.E., Pittsburgh. Information networks, simulation, databases, artificial intelligence, management information systems (MIS), systems analysis and design, software engineering, network design, microcomputer applications, graphics.

Michael B. Spring, Associate Professor; Ph.D., Pittsburgh. Collaborative authoring, document processing and office automation, client server systems, interactive system design, standards and standardization.

Daniel Suthers, Research Associate, Learning Research and Development Center; Ph.D., Massachusetts. Technology for knowledge communication and construction, including groupware for learning, network-based educational technology, coaching and tutoring systems, and discourse planning; related interests in cognitive and social aspects of learning and discourse processes.

Richard A. Thompson, Professor and Codirector, Telecommunications Program; Ph.D., Connecticut. Communications switching systems, especially photonic switching; intelligent networks; terminals, user services, and the human interface; fault tolerance and cellular automata; probabilistic formal languages.

David W. Tipper, Associate Professor; Ph.D., Arizona. Design and performance analysis of computer and telecommunication networks, control of communication networks, simulation methodology, queuing theory with emphasis on nonstationary/transient behavior, network survivability, application of control theory to communication networks and queuing systems.

Martin B. H. Weiss, Associate Professor and Codirector, Telecommunications Program; Ph.D., Carnegie Mellon. Telecommunications policy, technical standards, information system capacity management, network management and control.

James G. Williams, Professor; Ph.D., Pittsburgh. Information systems, networks, systems design, software engineering, simulation, system architecture, client server computing, database management.

Taieb Znati, Associate Professor; Ph.D., Michigan State. Real-time communication; networks and protocols to support multimedia environments, multimedia synchronization and presentation, design and analysis of medium access control protocols to support distributed real-time systems, network performance.

UNIVERSITY OF ROCHESTER

DEPARTMENT OF COMPUTER SCIENCE

PROGRAM OF STUDY

The Department of Computer Science at the University of Rochester offers an intensive research-oriented program leading to the degree of Doctor of Philosophy. Emphasis is currently being placed on the areas of artificial intelligence and machine perception, systems software for parallel and distributed computing, and the theory of computation. A number of joint faculty appointments and programs with other departments (including the Departments of Linguistics, Mathematics, Philosophy, Electrical Engineering, Psychology, Cognitive Science and Neuroscience) add breadth to the program. Additional enrichment is gained from an extensive program of seminar presentations and the participation of visiting professors.

Milestones in the doctoral program include a broad comprehensive exam at the end of the first year, a deeper area exam in the student's chosen subfield at the end of the second year (at which point the master's degree is generally awarded), and a thesis proposal at the end of the third year. Completion of a doctoral dissertation typically requires one to two more years, with formal feedback from the student's thesis committee twice a year.

The department is entering its twenty-fourth year of operation and has a young, energetic faculty, with a student-faculty ratio of 3.5:1. Students can receive individual attention in the shaping of their graduate programs and have an active role in the design of laboratory facilities and software.

RESEARCH FACILITIES

The department is well equipped. Its local area network connects sixty Sun SPARCstations, miscellaneous other workstations and file servers, a twelve-node Silicon Graphics Challenge multiprocessor, an 8-processor Sun SPARCcenter 2000, and a 32-processor, 233 MHz cluster connected by DEC's Memory Channel backbone. The Computer Vision and Robotics Laboratory is equipped with two Unimation Puma robot arms, a Utah/MIT four-fingered anthropomorphic hand, a custom-designed "robot head," and numerous DataCube real-time image processing boards. In the Virtual Reality Laboratory are eye trackers, a head-mounted stereo display, and a high-performance graphics workstation. The department's network has a high-speed connection to the University network, the NYSERNet regional network, and the Internet.

FINANCIAL AID

The department works to ensure that all doctoral students are fully supported by graduate assistantships or fellowships. In return, students are expected to participate in the department's research activities from the outset of their graduate career and to assist with teaching duties during two or three semesters over the course of the graduate program. The appointment in 1997–98 provides an assistantship stipend of $12,132 for nine months as well as full tuition remission. Many students accept summer research support from the department (a twelve-month total of $16,176); most others take summer jobs in industry.

COST OF STUDY

Full-time graduate tuition for the 1997–98 academic year is $20,544 for 32 credit hours but is waived for supported students. Mandatory health fees ($320 for 1997–98) are the responsibility of the student; required major medical insurance is available from the University for $672.

LIVING AND HOUSING COSTS

University-owned housing facilities include more than 800 apartments. Rents range from $358 per month for a single furnished sleeping room to $635 per month for a furnished two-bedroom apartment. The Housing Office maintains a listing of accommodations near the University. A comprehensive board plan is available.

STUDENT GROUP

The current full-time population at the University of Rochester is about 7,300 students, including more than 2,500 graduate students. There are 40 full-time graduate students in the Department of Computer Science, all of whom are supported by assistantships, fellowships, or tuition grants.

STUDENT OUTCOMES

Many of the department's graduates have gone on to academic appointments at top schools, including Carnegie Mellon, Stanford, Maryland, Illinois, Pennsylvania, North Carolina, Wisconsin, Northwestern, Rice, Boston, Virginia, Princeton, Chicago, and MIT. Those accepting nonacademic positions have gone to top research labs, including Bell Labs, IBM, Xerox, Olivetti Research Center, Philips Laboratories, Lockheed, Matsushita, the International Computer Science Institute, Microsoft, Martin Marietta, David Sarnoff Research Center, Siemens, and Digital Equipment Corporation.

LOCATION

Located on the south shore of Lake Ontario, a short drive from the Finger Lakes region, Rochester is a cultural center of upstate New York and has a metropolitan area population of just over a million. Opportunities for cultural activities are offered the year round by the Strasenburgh Planetarium, the University's Memorial Art Gallery, the International Museum of Photography, the Rochester Museum and Science Center, and the Eastman Theatre. Rochester and the surrounding area have many lovely parks, and in the winter there are many ski areas within an hour's drive. Known as the photographic and optical capital of the world, Rochester is the home of Eastman Kodak, the Xerox Corporation, Bausch & Lomb, and many other high-tech companies.

THE UNIVERSITY

The University of Rochester is an independent university that offers more than forty-five doctoral programs and some ninety master's degree programs in the following schools and colleges: the College that is made up of Arts and Sciences and the School of Engineering and Applied Sciences, the Eastman School of Music, the School of Medicine and Dentistry, the School of Nursing, the William E. Simon Graduate School of Business Administration, and the Margaret Warner Graduate School of Education and Human Development. The River Campus, where the Department of Computer Science is located, is situated on the east bank of the Genesee River, about 2 miles south of downtown Rochester.

APPLYING

Applicants are urged to apply electronically (see addresses below) or write directly to the department for application forms and additional information. For maximum consideration for the fall term, the application, transcripts, recommendations, and scores on the Graduate Record Examinations (GRE) must be submitted no later than February 1. A $25 application fee is waived if Part I is postmarked by December 15. The GRE should be taken no later than December. The General Test is required, and the Subject Test in computer science, math, or physics is highly recommended. International students should also submit their scores on the Test of English as a Foreign Language (TOEFL).

CORRESPONDENCE AND INFORMATION

Admissions Committee
Department of Computer Science
University of Rochester
Rochester, New York 14627-0226

Telephone: 716-275-5478
E-mail: admissions@cs.rochester.edu
World Wide Web: http://www.cs.rochester.edu/home.html

UNIVERSITY OF ROCHESTER
THE FACULTY AND THEIR RESEARCH

James F. Allen, John H. Dessauer Professor of Computer Science; Ph.D., Toronto, 1979. Artificial intelligence; natural language processing; dialog systems; planning; representation of plans, goals, time, and action.

Dana H. Ballard, Professor of Computer Science; Ph.D., California, Irvine, 1974. Computer vision, artificial intelligence, computational neuroscience.

Christopher M. Brown, Professor of Computer Science; Ph.D., Chicago, 1972. Artificial intelligence, computer vision, graphics, robotics.

Sandhya Dwarkadas, Assistant Professor of Computer Science; Ph.D., Rice, 1992. Parallel and distributed computing, compiler and run-time support for parallelism, computer architecture, networks, simulation methodology, performance evaluation, parallel applications research.

Lane A. Hemaspaandra, Associate Professor of Computer Science; Ph.D., Cornell, 1987. Computational complexity theory, algorithms from complexity, probabilistic and unambiguous computation, approximate computation, fault-tolerant computation, semi-feasible algorithms, cryptography, complexity-theoretic aspects of voting systems.

Henry Kyburg, Gideon Webster Burbank Professor of Moral and Intellectual Philosophy and Professor of Computer Science; Ph.D., Columbia, 1954. Uncertain inference, nonmonotonic logic, logical foundations of probability and statistical inference, measurement theory, cognitive science and artificial intelligence.

Thomas J. LeBlanc, Professor of Computer Science and College Dean of the Faculty of Arts, Sciences, and Engineering; Ph.D., Wisconsin, 1982. Parallel programming environments, multiprocessor systems, parallel program debugging and performance tuning.

Nathaniel G. Martin, Lecturer and Scientist of Computer Science; Ph.D., Rochester, 1993. Artificial intelligence, planning, representation of uncertain information.

Randal C. Nelson, Associate Professor of Computer Science; Ph.D., Maryland, 1988. Artificial intelligence, computer vision with an emphasis on the use of visual information for control of systems in real-world environments, robotics.

Mitsunori Ogihara, Assistant Professor of Computer Science; Ph.D., Tokyo Institute of Technology, 1993. Computational complexity theory, recursive function theory, number-theoretic algorithms.

Lenhart K. Schubert, Professor of Computer Science; Ph.D., Toronto, 1970. Knowledge representation and organization, general and specialized inference methods, natural language understanding, planning and acting.

Michael L. Scott, Associate Professor and Chair of Computer Science; Ph.D., Wisconsin, 1985. Parallel and distributed systems software, operating systems, programming languages, program development tools.

Joel I. Seiferas, Associate Professor of Computer Science; Ph.D., MIT, 1974. Computational, descriptive, and combinatorial complexity; lower bound techniques.

UNIVERSITY OF ROCHESTER

DEPARTMENT OF ELECTRICAL ENGINEERING

PROGRAMS OF STUDY

The department offers programs of study leading to the M.S. and Ph.D. degrees. Special features of graduate study in electrical engineering at the University of Rochester are flexible degree programs, opportunities for interdisciplinary study, close faculty-student cooperation, major sponsored projects, excellent computing resources, and leading research facilities. Research emphases include biomedical ultrasound and medical imaging, solid-state devices, optoelectronics, superconductivity, VLSI systems, computer architecture, manufacturing and robotics, and signal and image processing. The M.S. degree requires 30 credit hours of graduate study and may be earned in one year of full-time study. Both thesis (Plan A) and nonthesis (Plan B) options exist. The Ph.D. degree requires 90 credit hours of graduate study, or 60 credit hours beyond the master's degree. Each student must pass a qualifying examination, submit a satisfactory written thesis proposal in his or her third year of full-time graduate study, and serve as a teaching assistant. Teaching experience involves a maximum of 15 hours of total time per week for two semesters and includes lecturing in problem sessions and laboratories.

RESEARCH FACILITIES

The University of Rochester is ranked in the Research I category and maintains outstanding research facilities. In 1991, the University research impact in electronics was ranked second worldwide by Science Watch, which measured scientific citations to published research in electronics literature. The Faculty of Electrical Engineering are directors or key researchers in a number of specialized research centers, including the Center for Superconducting Digital Electronics, the Center for Biomedical Ultrasound, the Center for Electronic Imaging Systems, and the Laboratory for Laser Energetics.

The Center for Superconducting Digital Electronics, sponsored by the Department of Defense, is creating digital circuits and filters that are faster than any now in use. To measure the performance of these ultrafast devices, novel electrooptic sampling techniques have been developed.

The Center for Biomedical Ultrasound, funded by NIH and industry, brings together the largest group of academic clinicians, scientists, and engineers in the world to advance medical imaging and ultrasound instrumentation.

The Center for Electronic Imaging Systems, sponsored by NSF, NYS, and industry, has superb laboratories covering electronic imaging sensors, displays, image and video processing, and computer facilities for image encoding, transmission, and restoration techniques.

The Laboratory for Laser Energetics, a laser fusion lab, is supported by DOE and has developed some of the most advanced laser and optoelectronic devices in the world.

These outstanding, on-campus research centers provide students with access to leading experimental and computer facilities. In addition, other electrical engineering department laboratory clusters are in place with extensive workstations and specialized equipment. These include the high-performance VLSI/IC laboratory, the advanced computer architecture laboratory, the ultrasound laboratories, the solid-state device laboratories and clean room facility, and the 3-D image processing laboratory. The University Library system contains more than 2 million volumes. The Carlson Library maintains complete collections in the research areas of engineering and applied science.

FINANCIAL AID

Financial aid is available in the form of research or teaching assistantships and fellowships. Graduate assistants and fellows receive a stipend of up to $15,200 for twelve months and a tuition scholarship.

COST OF STUDY

Tuition for 1997–98 is $642 per credit hour; the maximum charge is $10,272 for a 16-credit-hour semester. The annual health fee of approximately $902 includes medical insurance.

LIVING AND HOUSING COSTS

University housing (furnished and unfurnished) for single and married graduate students is available near the River Campus. Rents for apartments range from $300 to $560 per month for single students and from $550 to $875 per month for married students. The Housing Office maintains a listing of students seeking shared accommodations. A board plan is available, and several dining areas offer meals on a cash basis.

STUDENT GROUP

The University's enrollment is 9,690, including 5,016 full-time undergraduates and 2,271 graduate students. Approximately 70 graduate students are in the Department of Electrical Engineering.

LOCATION

The city of Rochester, situated on the falls of the Genesee River about 10 miles south of Lake Ontario, is the heart of an urban-suburban community of more than 600,000. Noted for its high-tech industries, Rochester is the site of the Eastman Kodak Research Laboratories, the Xerox Webster Research Center, and many other R&D laboratories such as those of Bausch & Lomb, Taylor Instruments, and General Railway Signal. Many cultural and social activities are available in the community, with special emphasis on music in all forms.

THE UNIVERSITY

The University of Rochester is an independent, nonsectarian, coeducational institution of higher learning and research. Founded in 1850, it is one of the nation's most distinguished small universities. Academic and research programs are conducted by eight schools and colleges situated on three campuses. Programs ranging from the undergraduate to the postdoctoral level are offered in the humanities, the social sciences, the natural sciences, education, engineering, management, medicine, music, and nursing. The River Campus, which includes the School of Engineering and Applied Science, is situated on the Genesee River about 3 miles south of the city. The Medical Center is adjacent to the River Campus.

APPLYING

Applications are invited from students with a bachelor's degree in electrical engineering or in a related field, such as physics, mathematics, computer science, or another engineering discipline. Full-time study is normally started at the beginning of the fall semester. Part-time students may begin study in either semester. Applications should be submitted by February 1 for fall admission with financial aid. Students should submit a completed application form, a transcript, two letters of recommendation, and a $25 fee. The GRE tests are required, and international students must submit scores on the TOEFL. To arrange a visit to see the department and meet with the faculty, students should call 716-275-4054.

CORRESPONDENCE AND INFORMATION

Graduate Admissions Committee
Department of Electrical Engineering
204 Hopeman Building
University of Rochester
Rochester, New York 14627
E-mail: gradinfo@ee.rochester.edu
World Wide Web: http://www.ceas.rochester.edu:8080/ee/homepage.html

UNIVERSITY OF ROCHESTER
THE FACULTY AND THEIR RESEARCH

Professors

Alexander Albicki, Ph.D., Warsaw, 1973. Logic design, VLSI, low-power systems, asynchronous circuits, design for testability, data communications.

Edwin L. Carstensen (Professor Emeritus), Ph.D., Pennsylvania, 1955. Biomedical ultrasound, bioelectric phenomena, studies of the interaction of acoustic and electric fields with biological materials.

Phillipe M. Fauchet, Ph.D., Stanford, 1984. Optoelectronics and photonic materials and devices, semiconductor physics, light-emitting porous silicon, femtosecond lasers, optical diagnostics.

Thomas Y. Hsiang, Ph.D., Berkeley, 1977. Optoelectronics, ultrafast phenomena, superconductivity, electronic noise.

Thomas B. Jones, Ph.D., MIT, 1970. Electromechanics of particles, xerography, biological dielectrophoresis, electrostatic hazards.

Edwin Kinnen (Professor Emeritus), Ph.D., Purdue, 1958. VLSI systems, routing and placement, CAD tools.

Charles W. Merriam, Sc.D., MIT, 1958. Computer architecture, computer organization, programming languages.

Kevin J. Parker, Ph.D., MIT, 1981. Medical imaging, Doppler imaging techniques, digital halftoning.

A. Murat Tekalp, Ph.D., Rensselaer, 1984. Image processing, digital video processing, image restoration, image compression, pattern recognition.

Edward L. Titlebaum, Ph.D., Cornell, 1964. Multiple access communications, radar, sonar, signal design and coding psychoacoustics, echolocation, computer languages.

Robert C. Waag, Ph.D., Cornell, 1965. Bio-ultrasound, ultrasonic signal processing, tissue characterization, nondestructive testing.

Associate Professors

Mark F. Bocko, Ph.D., Rochester, 1984. Superconducting electronics, quantum noise, tunneling, electromechanical transducers, gravitational wave detection.

Eby G. Friedman, Ph.D., California, Irvine, 1989. VLSI circuits and systems, synchronization, clock distribution, pipelining, register allocation, speed/power/area tradeoffs, CMOS circuits, WSI.

Alan M. Kadin, Ph.D., Harvard, 1979. Superconducting thin films and devices, nonequilibrium effects, high-temperature superconductors, thin-film fabrication and processing, optoelectronic switching, magnetic thin films.

Jack G. Mottley, Ph.D., Washington (St. Louis), 1985. Quantitative ultrasonic tissue and materials characterization, biomedical ultrasound, anisotropy of ultrasonic parameters, contractile-state-dependence of ultrasonic parameters, ultrasonic contrast agents.

Vassillios D. Tourassis, Ph.D., Carnegie-Mellon, 1985. Robotics, manufacturing, intelligent control.

Assistant Professor

David Albonesi, Ph.D., Massachusetts, 1996. Computer architecture, microprocessor design, multiprocessor systems, computer systems performance analysis, experimental systems, high-speed reconfigurable architectures, digital systems design.

Research Professors

Diane Dalecki, Ph.D., Rochester, 1993. Biomedical ultrasound, nonlinear acoustics, lithotripsy, biological effect of ultrasound.

Marc J. Feldman, Ph.D., Berkeley, 1975. Superconducting digital electronics, millimeter-wave devices, noise.

Roman Sobolewski, Ph.D., Warsaw, 1983. Optoelectronics, solid-state technology, nonequilibrium and ultrafast phenomena in condensed matter, superconductivity, microwaves and millimeter waves.

Research Scientists

Xucai Chen, Ph.D., Yale, 1991. Acoustics, medical imaging, echocardiography, contrast agents.

A. Tanju Erdem, Ph.D., Rochester, 1990. Digital video processing, motion tracking, object-based video analysis and compositing, video data compression, image and video restoration and reconstruction.

Krzysztof Gaj, Ph.D., Warsaw, 1992. High-performance digital circuits, cryptography, computer network security, CAD of VLSI systems, superconductive electronics.

Research Associates

Roger Cramblitt, Ph.D., Purdue, 1994. Image processing, coherent imaging, ultrasound, compression, speckle, remote sensing, detectors.

Bilge Gunsel, Ph.D., Istanbul Technical, 1993. Digital video analysis, indexing, retrieval, sensor fusion, stochastic modeling, neural networks.

Petrus van Beek, Ph.D., Delft (Netherlands), 1995. Digital image processing, image (sequence) analysis, object-based video coding.

Adjuncts

David Blackstock, Ph.D., Harvard, 1960. Acoustics, shock waves, nonlinear acoustics.

Erich C. Everbach, Ph.D., Yale, 1989. Biomedical ultrasound, lithotripsy, echocardiography, transduction, nonlinear effects.

Andrzej Krasniewski, Ph.D., 1983, D.Sc., 1989, Warsaw. Self-testable VLSI circuits, adaptive control in telecommunications, networks.

Michael Kriss, Ph.D., UCLA, 1969. Digital imaging systems, image quality, image processing, imaging.

M. Ibrahim Sezan, Ph.D., RPI, 1984. Image restoration and reconstruction, image recovery, tomography.

Lecturer

Victor V. Derefinko, M.S., Virginia, 1967. Electronic design, including analog and digital processors and microprocessors.

Joint Appointments

Nicholas George, Ph.D., Caltech, 1959. Optoelectronic systems, electronic imaging, automatic pattern recognition, speckle, holography.

Stephen F. Levinson, Ph.D., Purdue, 1981; M.D., Indiana, 1983. Ultrasonic characterization of muscle and other soft tissues, exercise physiology and biomechanics of human motion.

Denham S. Ward, Ph.D., UCLA, 1975; M.D., Miami (Florida), 1977. Control systems in respiration and bioengineering.

RESEARCH SPECIALTIES

Electronics and computer systems. (Albicki, Albonesi, Friedman, Kinnen, Merriam)
Optoelectronics. (Fauchet, Hsiang, Sobolewski)
Signal processing and biomedical imaging. (Carstensen, Dalecki, Mottley, Parker, Tekalp, Titlebaum, Waag)
Superconductivity and solid-state devices. (Bocko, Feldman, Kadin)
Electromechanics and systems. (Jones, Tourassis)

UNIVERSITY OF SOUTH CAROLINA

COLLEGE OF SCIENCE AND MATHEMATICS
DEPARTMENT OF COMPUTER SCIENCE

PROGRAMS OF STUDY

The Department of Computer Science offers programs leading to Master of Science (M.S.) and Doctor of Philosophy (Ph.D.) degrees.

The requirements for the M.S. degree can be satisfied in two ways: with a project thesis and eleven courses or with a research thesis and nine courses. About one third of the M.S. program course work is in the core areas of algorithms, architecture, and compiler construction. This leaves two thirds of the course work as electives that can be focused as the student desires. This program generally requires two years, but frequently has been completed in less time.

Requirements for the Ph.D. degree include a written qualifying examination and a public defense of the dissertation. There are no required courses for the Ph.D., which allows students to focus their course work in support of their research. Strong research groups in computer networks, image compaction, object-oriented methodologies, information systems, and artificial intelligence welcome new students and provide substantial opportunities for research support.

RESEARCH FACILITIES

The department has newly renovated and equipped laboratories for research in image processing, mobile computing, image compaction, artificial intelligence, scientific modeling and visualization, database, and networks. The department has approximately 80 UNIX workstations, including a lab of DEC alpha machines with dual 160 MHz processors. These machines and several PC labs are connected to each other and the Internet via Ethernet and an FDDI ring. The department houses a 56-processor mesh machine and has remote access to the University's 1024 processor hypercube machine.

FINANCIAL AID

Financial aid is available to students in the form of research assistantships, teaching assistantships, and fellowships. The typical starting stipend for assistantships is $10,000 for nine months, with additional support available for the summer. In addition, many of the M.S. students find assistantships in other departments on campus. There are also many opportunities for internships in local industry, such as NCR.

COST OF STUDY

Tuition and fees per semester currently cost $735 for graduate assistants, $1840 for non-assistant residents of South Carolina, and $3709 for nonresident non-assistants.

LIVING AND HOUSING COSTS

For 1996–97, University housing provided single dorm rooms for $344 per month and two-bedroom apartments for $589 per month. These prices included all utilities, local phone, and cable service.

STUDENT GROUP

The department has 115 graduate students, 30 of whom are in the Ph.D. program. At the university level, more than 26,000 students are enrolled on the Columbia campus, of whom 10,000 are enrolled in graduate programs.

STUDENT OUTCOMES

Many of the recent M.S. graduates have worked on internships and co-op opportunities in local industry, which led to full-time employment at the completion of their degrees. Examples of such companies include AT&T, NCR, IBM, and Summus. Many graduates have found employment in the NC Research Triangle Park and Atlanta areas.

LOCATION

The University is located in Columbia, the capital of South Carolina. Columbia has many attractive features and combines the advantages of a metropolitan area with the pace of smaller cities. There are nearby lakes for recreation, a very nice zoological park, and numerous cultural activities. Columbia is only a short distance from the South Carolina beaches and the Blue Ridge Mountains.

THE UNIVERSITY

The University was founded in 1801 and has grown to an eight campus system with 38,000 students. The graduate school offers master's degrees in 167 areas, the Ph.D. in sixty-eight, and professional doctorates in law, medicine, pharmacy, and public health. About 1,800 master's and 250 Ph.D. degrees are awarded annually.

APPLYING

Applications for admission are considered throughout the year, but must be received by March 1 to receive full consideration for financial aid. Applicants are required to supply GRE General Test scores, official copies of transcripts of prior academic work, and two letters of recommendation. International applicants are also required to take the TOEFL and score at least 560.

CORRESPONDENCE

Director of Graduate Studies
Department of Computer Science
University of South Carolina
Columbia, South Carolina 29208

Telephone: 803-777-7849
E-mail: graduate@cs.sc.edu
World Wide Web: http://www.cs.sc.edu

UNIVERSITY OF SOUTH CAROLINA

THE FACULTY AND THEIR RESEARCH

Robert L. Cannon, Professor and Chair; Ph.D., North Carolina, 1973. Digital image processing, expert systems, text collation.

Carter Bays, Professor; Ph.D., Oklahoma, 1974. Algorithms, simulation, programming languages, functional programming, operating systems.

Karel Culik II, Professor; Ph.D., Czechoslovak Academy of Sciences, 1966; RNDr., Charles University, 1967. Formal languages and automata theory, theory of programming languages, systolic systems, cellular automata.

Caroline M. Eastman, Professor; Ph.D., North Carolina, 1977. Information retrieval, database management systems, file organizations, programming and natural languages.

Terrance L. Huntsberger, Associate Professor; Ph.D., South Carolina, 1978. Biomedical image processing, computer vision, computer graphics, artificial intelligence, parallel architectures.

Manton M. Matthews, Associate Professor; Ph.D., South Carolina, 1980. Artificial intelligence, parallel processing, user interfaces, graph theory.

Robert L. Oakman, Professor; Ph.D., Indiana University, 1971. Computer literacy, computational linguistics, natural language processing, humanities applications.

John R. Rose, Assistant Professor; Ph.D., SUNY at Stony Brook, 1991. Machine learning, knowledge discovery in databases, computational chemistry knowledge-based systems.

Abhijit Sengupta, Professor; Ph.D., Calcutta (India), 1976. Fault-tolerant computing, multiple-valued logic, parallel architectures.

Suresh Singh, Assistant Professor; Ph.D., Massachusetts, 1990. Distributed and parallel computing and operating systems.

M. A. Sridhar, Associate Professor; Ph.D., Wisconsin, 1986. Analysis of algorithms, automata theory, compiler design, complexity theory.

Marco Valtorta, Associate Professor; Ph.D., Duke, 1987. Artificial intelligence, expert systems.

UNIVERSITY OF SOUTHERN CALIFORNIA

COMPUTER SCIENCE DEPARTMENT

PROGRAMS OF STUDY

The department offers the degrees of Master of Science and Doctor of Philosophy. In addition, the department offers an M.S. degree with specialization in computer networks, an M.S. degree with specialization in software engineering, an M.S. degree with specialization in multimedia and creative technologies, and an M.S. degree with specialization in robotics and automation. The M.S. degree requires completion of 27 units of course work with a minimum grade point average of 3.0. No thesis is required for the M.S. degree. Full- or part-time study is possible, and one year is the expected time for completion of the M.S. program for full-time students with adequate backgrounds.

The doctoral program in computer science requires 60 units of course work, with a minimum grade point average of 3.5, and at least 4 units of dissertation research. All course work beyond the M.S. must be taken in residence at USC. Ph.D. students must pass through a screening process about a year into the program. Students must then pass the qualifying examination to be admitted to candidacy and later complete the dissertation to receive the Ph.D. A well-qualified full-time student should be able to finish the program within four to five years of entering graduate school.

The USC Interactive Instructional Television Network broadcasts regular University courses to companies in the Los Angeles area. Students employed at these companies may take some of their degree courses through this system without having to commute frequently to campus.

RESEARCH FACILITIES

The research facilities of the Computer Science Department are divided into the following laboratories: Programmable Automation, Robotics, Computer Vision, Molecular Robotics, Brain Simulation, Computational and Biological Vision, Molecular Science, Computer Networks and Distributed Systems, Database, Software Engineering, Computer Graphics and Creative Technologies, and Computer Animation. Each lab is run by 1 or more faculty members and each has a wide variety of equipment. Most laboratories have Sun-3 and Sun-4 Workstations, some have IBM RISC System 600 workstations and servers, and others have Symbolics Lisp Machines. In addition to the individual laboratory facilities, the department and graduate students have access to a Sun-4/490 with 64 MB of memory that is used for homework, word processing, and general departmental administration. The graduate students have a private laboratory that contains a variety of Sun-4, IBM, and DEC workstations plus personal computers, including Apple Macintosh and NeXT machines. Laser printers are available for output. All machines are connected to the local network and to the Internet, providing access to researchers all over the world.

FINANCIAL AID

Teaching and research assistantships are available for qualified Ph.D. students. These awards cover 12 units of tuition each semester and during the summer, in addition to providing a nine-month stipend of $1259 to $1395 per month in 1997–98. In addition, the Graduate School awards certain fellowships and scholarships. Interested individuals should contact the Graduate School directly. Information on other types of state and federal programs can be obtained from the Financial Aid Office.

COST OF STUDY

In 1997–98, tuition is $10,039 per semester for full-time students and $676 per unit for students taking fewer than 15 units. Student fees are $207, and the optional parking fee is $306.

LIVING AND HOUSING COSTS

For students living on campus, the cost of room and board ranges from $3000 to $3500 per semester in 1997–98. Comparable housing is available in the immediate vicinity of the campus for about 25 to 40 percent more. Housing can be found at all price ranges in the Greater Los Angeles area.

STUDENT GROUP

USC has a total enrollment of approximately 27,000 students, 36 percent of whom are women. The School of Engineering has about 3,500 students, of whom 54 percent are graduate students.

The Computer Science Department has a total of about 300 graduate students; roughly 175 are M.S. students, and the remaining 130 are Ph.D. students. The student body is very diverse, with students from all over the United States and many other countries.

LOCATION

Only 5 minutes by freeway from the center of Los Angeles, the University is secluded on an extensive, landscaped campus with a quiet academic atmosphere. Students may take advantage of the broad cultural offerings of a major metropolis. USC is situated midway between the mountains and the sea—less than an hour from each—offering students a choice of many outdoor diversions, such as surfing, boating, hiking, and skiing.

THE UNIVERSITY

The University of Southern California is private, nonsectarian, and coeducational. It is the oldest major university in the West. USC's diversity of programs has marked it as one of the most distinguished universities in the world. Its membership in the Association of American Universities attests to its educational excellence in general and graduate and research excellence in particular. Attracted by the variety and high quality of the University's offerings, faculty members and students come from every corner of the globe to engage in teaching, learning, and research. At USC, freedom and responsibility characterize the atmosphere—for the freshman as well as the postdoctoral student.

APPLYING

Admission to the Computer Science Department is highly competitive. Applicants are required to have a bachelor's degree from an accredited college or university and must have taken the GRE General Test. The GRE Subject Test in computer science, mathematics, or engineering is recommended. Three letters of recommendation from professors and an essay on specific research goals must be submitted to the department. International students whose native language is not English must take the Test of English as a Foreign Language and submit their scores to the department. Applicants with a background in computer science or programming are given particular consideration. The application fee is $55.

CORRESPONDENCE AND INFORMATION

Graduate Admissions
Computer Science Department
Room 300
Henry Salvatori Computer Science Center
University of Southern California
Los Angeles, California 90089-0781

Telephone: 213-740-4496
E-mail: csdept@pollux.usc.edu
World Wide Web: http://www.usc.edu/dept/cs

UNIVERSITY OF SOUTHERN CALIFORNIA
THE FACULTY AND THEIR RESEARCH

Leonard Adleman, Henry Salvatori Professor; Ph.D., Berkeley, 1976. Complexity theory, public key cryptosystems, number theory, computer viruses.

Cengiz Alaettinoglu, Research Assistant Professor; Ph.D., Maryland, 1994. Computer networks, operating systems, distributed algorithms, performance analysis.

Michael Arbib, Professor; Ph.D., MIT, 1963. Neural networks, visuomotor coordination, dextrous hands, artificial intelligence and cognition, schema theory.

Robert Balzer, Research Professor; Ph.D., Carnegie Mellon, 1966. Automatic programming, artificial intelligence, program specification.

George Bekey, Gordon Marshall Professor; Ph.D., UCLA, 1962. Robotics, artificial intelligence, biological systems.

Irving Biederman, William Keck Professor; Ph.D., Michigan, 1966. Computational, neural, and biological models of shape recognition.

Edward Blum, Professor; Ph.D., Columbia, 1952. Numerical analysis and computer programming theory, neural modeling.

Barry Boehm, TRW Professor; Ph.D., UCLA, 1964. Software engineering, software processes, metrics and architectures.

Melvin Breuer, Charles Lee Powell Professor; Ph.D., Berkeley, 1965. Testing, design-for-testability, computer-aided design of VLSI systems.

Steve Chien, Adjunct Assistant Professor; Ph.D., Illinois, 1991. AI: planning and scheduling, machine learning, intelligent scientific data systems.

Peter Danzig, Associate Professor; Ph.D., Berkeley, 1989. Performance analysis of operating systems, computer networks, distributed systems.

Alvin Despain, Charles Lee Powell Professor; Ph.D., Utah, 1966. AI: architecture, machine organization, and design automation.

Deborah Estrin, Associate Professor; Ph.D., MIT, 1985. Computer networks, security and organizational context of computing.

Robert Felderman, Adjunct Assistant Professor; Ph.D., UCLA, 1991. Parallel and distributed systems, high-speed LAN, distributed simulation.

Martin Frank, Research Assistant Professor; Ph.D., Georgia Tech, 1995. End-user programming, high-quality user interfaces, programming tools.

Shahram Ghandeharizadeh, Associate Professor; Ph.D., Wisconsin–Madison, 1990. Database management systems; parallel hypermedia and relational systems.

Yolanda Gil, Research Assistant Professor; Ph.D., Carnegie Mellon, 1992. AI: machine learning, planning, problem solving, robotics.

Seymour Ginsburg, Fletcher Jones Professor; Ph.D., Michigan, 1952. Databases theory, automata, formal languages.

Ramesh Govindan, Research Assistant Professor; Ph.D., Berkeley, 1992. Network operating systems, media software systems, next-generation Internet protocol.

Jonathan Gratch, Research Assistant Professor; Ph.D., Illinois, 1995; AI: machine learning, planning, uncertainty reasoning, decision theory.

Mary Hall, Research Assistant Professor; Ph.D., Rice, 1991. Compilers, program analysis, automatic parallelization.

Randall W. Hill Jr., Research Assistant Professor; Ph.D., USC, 1993. AI: perception, agent modeling, plan recognition, cognitive modeling.

Ellis Horowitz, Professor; Ph.D., Wisconsin–Madison, 1970. Software engineering, programming environments, computer-based instruction.

Eduard Hovy, Research Assistant Professor; Ph.D., Yale, 1987. AI: natural language processing, computational linguistics.

Ming-Deh Huang, Associate Professor; Ph.D., Princeton, 1984. Theory of parallel computation, computational complexity and number-theoretic algorithms, cryptography.

Kai Hwang, Professor; Ph.D., Berkeley, 1972. Computer architecture, parallel processing.

Douglas Ierardi, Adjunct Assistant Professor; Ph.D., Cornell, 1989. Algorithms in algebra and number theory, computational complexity.

Lewis Johnson, Research Assistant Professor; Ph.D., Yale, 1985. Software specification and design.

Kevin Knight, Research Assistant Professor; Ph.D., Carnegie Mellon, 1991. AI: natural language processing and machine translation.

Craig Knoblock, Research Assistant Professor; Ph.D., Carnegie Mellon, 1991. AI: planning, problem solving, machine learning and abstraction.

Sukhan Lee, Adjunct Associate Professor; Ph.D., Purdue, 1982. Robotics, AI: planning, problem solving, problem reformulation, and machine learning.

Stephen C. Y. Lu, David Packard Chair Professor; Ph.D., Carnegie Mellon, 1984. Development of information technologies to support engineering decision making as collaborative negotiation.

Raymond J. Madachy, Adjunct Assistant Professor; Ph.D., USC, 1994. Software engineering: software metrics, cost estimation, risk management, process modeling and improvement.

Larry Mathies, Adjunct Assistant Professor; Ph.D., Carnegie Mellon, 1989. Computer vision, including 3-D shape and motion estimation; mobile robotics.

Dennis McLeod, Professor; Ph.D., MIT, 1978. Database systems, knowledge management systems.

Gerard Medioni, Associate Professor; Ph.D., USC, 1983. Computer vision, artificial intelligence.

Robert Neches, Research Associate Professor; Ph.D., Carnegie Mellon, 1981. Intelligent interfaces, very large knowledge bases, computer supported cooperative work.

Clifford Neuman, Research Assistant Professor; Ph.D., Washington (Seattle), 1992. Parallel and distributed systems, operating systems, computer security and pervasive computing.

Ulrich Neumann, Assistant Professor; Ph.D., North Carolina, 1993. High-performance interactive computer graphics, virtual environments, parallel systems, volume visualization, medical imaging, multimedia.

Ramakant Nevatia, Professor; Ph.D., Stanford, 1975. Machine vision, robotics, artificial intelligence.

Katia Obraczka, Research Assistant Professor; Ph.D., USC, 1994. Computer networks, distributed systems, operating systems.

Pavel A. Pevzner, Professor; Ph.D., Moscow Institute of Physics and Technology, 1988. Computational molecular biology, combinatorical and theoretical computer science.

Keith Price, Research Associate Professor; Ph.D., Carnegie Mellon, 1977. Computer vision, artificial intelligence.

Irving Reed, Charles Lee Powell Professor; Ph.D., Caltech, 1949. Computer architecture, VLSI design, neural networks, coding theory.

Aristides Requicha, Professor; Ph.D., Rochester, 1970. Geometric modeling, AI in computer-aided design and manufacturing.

Jeff Rickel, Research Assistant Professor; Ph.D., Texas, 1995. Knowledge representation and reasoning, knowledge acquisition, machine learning, explanation generation, intelligent tutoring.

Paul Rosenbloom, Associate Professor; Ph.D., Carnegie Mellon, 1983. AI: machine learning, integrated intelligent architectures, cognitive science.

Rafael Saavedra, Assistant Professor; Ph.D., Berkeley, 1992. Parallel programming and architecture, performance analysis.

Herbert Schorr, Research Professor; Ph.D., Princeton, 1963. Expert systems, design automation, system architecture, artificial intelligence.

Mark Seidenberg, Professor; Ph.D., Columbia, 1980. Computational models of normal and distorted language.

Cyrus Shahabi, Research Assistant Professor; Ph.D., USC. Multimedia database management systems, parallel databases, continuous media services.

Wei Min Shen, Research Assistant Professor; Ph.D., Carnegie Mellon, 1989. Machine learning, autonomous agents and robots, data mining, models of the brain.

Scott Shenker, Adjunct Associate Professor; Ph.D., Chicago, 1983. Internet architecture.

Stuart Stubblebine, Adjunct Assistant Professor; Ph.D., Maryland, 1992. Distributed systems, networking, software engineering and security.

William Swartout, Research Associate Professor; Ph.D., MIT, 1981. AI: expert systems and knowledge acquisition.

Pedro Szekely, Research Assistant Professor; Ph.D., Carnegie Mellon, 1987. User interfaces.

Milind Tambe, Research Assistant Professor; Ph.D., Carnegie Mellon, 1991. Intelligent agents, agent modeling, multiagent systems, rule-based systems.

Joseph Touch, Research Assistant Professor; Ph.D., Pennsylvania, 1992. Protocols, networks, distributed systems.

Christoph von der Malsburg, Professor; Ph.D., Heidelberg (Germany), 1970. Brain theory, neural computer vision.

Michael Waterman, Professor; Ph.D., Michigan State, 1969. Computational biology.

Richard Weinberg, Research Assistant Professor; Ph.D., Minnesota, 1982. Computer graphics and animation.

David Wile, Research Professor; Ph.D., Carnegie Mellon, 1974. Programming languages and environment.

Wayne W. Zhang, Research Assistant Professor; Ph.D., UCLA, 1994. Heuristic search, combinatorial optimization problems, distributed multiagent systems, parallel and distributed algorithms, robotics.

UNIVERSITY OF SOUTHERN CALIFORNIA
DEPARTMENT OF ELECTRICAL ENGINEERING

PROGRAMS OF STUDY

The Department of Electrical Engineering consists of two separate areas, Systems and Electrophysics. The Systems area offers the M.S. degree in systems architecture engineering and the M.S. and Ph.D. degrees in computer engineering with concentrations in architecture, computer-aided design, computer networks, fault-tolerant computing, parallel processing, and VLSI systems. It also offers the M.S., Engineer, and Ph.D. degrees in electrical engineering in the following areas of concentration: biomedical engineering (M.S. only), communications, control theory, multimedia systems, signal and image processing, optics, and systems theory. The Electrophysics area offers the M.S., Engineer, and Ph.D. degrees in the following areas of concentration: electrical machines, electromagnetics and plasmas, integrated circuits, laser systems (M.S. and Engineer only), optics, photonics, power systems, quantum electronics, and solid-state electronics.

Almost all Systems and many Electrophysics graduate courses are broadcast over the Interactive Instructional Television Network, a one-way video, two-way audio broadcast system designed to enable part-time students working in companies in the area to take courses for credit without commuting frequently to campus.

RESEARCH FACILITIES

With approximately $12 million in funded research annually, the USC Department of Electrical Engineering ranks as one of the most prominent university research centers in the nation. Research institutes connected with the department are the Center for Laser Studies, the Center for Photonics Technology, the Southern California Center for Advanced Transportation Technologies, the Communication Sciences Institute, the Institute for Robotics and Intelligent Systems, the Integrated Media Systems Center, and the Signal and Image Processing Institute. The department is also affiliated with the Biomedical Engineering Center and the Information Sciences Institute at Marina Del Rey.

The Systems area has an extensive and diverse computing environment. The primary component is a large number of UNIX-based systems from a variety of vendors, such as Sun, Hewlett-Packard, and DEC. Most of these are desktop workstations, supported by a collection of file servers and time-sharing systems and located in individual offices or common rooms. All of these systems are connected by Ethernet to the main campus network and to the Internet, which provides access to resources on a worldwide basis. In addition to the UNIX systems, the department has a large installed base of Apple Macintosh and IBM PC–type systems. These are used extensively for both word processing and research activities. Most are connected in some manner to the campus network. A large number of output devices, such as laser printers, color plotters, and film recorders, are available. A variety of input devices, such as drum scanners, flatbed scanners, rangefinders, and video cameras, are used for both research and word processing applications.

FINANCIAL AID

Teaching and research assistantships, fellowships, and work-study programs are available. In 1996–97, assistantship stipends ranged from $5700 to $12,800 per academic year and carried tuition remission. U.S. citizens may apply for fellowships sponsored by the American Electronics Association and the U.S. Army Research Office. Fellowships available to all entering graduate students include the USC Predoctoral Merit Fellowship. Many local industries offer full- or part-time employee fellowships for graduate study at USC. Department fellowships are offered to outstanding U.S. citizens to supplement teaching and research awards.

COST OF STUDY

In 1997–98, tuition is $676 per semester unit and mandatory fees are $350 per semester. Graduates typically take 8–9 units per semester.

LIVING AND HOUSING COSTS

In 1997–98, the cost of on-campus room and board is approximately $7000 per year. Comparable housing off campus is available in the immediate vicinity.

STUDENT GROUP

The University enrolls 27,558 students, 46 percent of whom are women. In 1995–96, the department's enrollment was 1,600, including about 1,300 graduate students.

STUDENT OUTCOMES

Ph.D. graduates have taken university positions world-wide as well as positions in government and private research laboratories. M.S. and Ph.D. graduates compete successfully for jobs across the spectrum of electronic industries, including Silicon Valley computer firms, multimedia technology industries, telephonic network service providers, photonic and wireless communication system manufacturers, and Southern California aerospace companies.

LOCATION

USC is only 5 minutes by freeway from the center of Los Angeles and is secluded on an extensive, landscaped campus with a quiet academic atmosphere. Situated midway between the mountains and the sea—less than an hour from each—USC offers easy access to many outdoor diversions, such as surfing, boating, hiking, and skiing.

THE UNIVERSITY AND THE DEPARTMENT

The University of Southern California, the oldest major university in the West, is private, nonsectarian, and coeducational. It is a member of the Association of American Universities, which requires members to have educational excellence in general and graduate and research excellence in particular. The variety and quality of the University's programs and resources attract faculty and students from every corner of the globe.

The Department of Electrical Engineering has more than 60 full-time faculty members, many of whom have international reputations in their area of specialty. The faculty has been honored with numerous awards and distinctions: 8 are members of the National Academy of Engineering, and 28 have been elected Fellows of the IEEE.

APPLYING

To be admitted to full graduate standing, the student must have a bachelor's degree and acceptable scores on the General Test of the Graduate Record Examinations. Application forms for financial aid awards may be obtained from the department upon request and should be returned by January 1.

CORRESPONDENCE AND INFORMATION

Dr. Hans H. Kuehl, Co-Chairman
Department of Electrical Engineering—Electrophysics
University of Southern California
Los Angeles, California 90089-0271
Telephone: 213-740-4700

Dr. Robert A. Scholtz, Co-Chairman
Department of Electrical Engineering—Systems
University of Southern California
Los Angeles, California 90089-2560
Telephone: 213-740-4433
Fax: 213-740-4449
E-mail: eesystem@pollux.usc.edu
World Wide Web: http://www.usc.edu:80/dept/ee/

UNIVERSITY OF SOUTHERN CALIFORNIA
THE FACULTY AND THEIR RESEARCH

Electrophysics

Joe E. Baker, Instructor; Engineer, USC, 1970. Power electronics.
Milton Birnbaum, Research Professor; Ph.D., Maryland, 1953. Quantum electronics.
Tsen-Chung Cheng, Lloyd Hunt Professor; Sc.D., MIT, 1974. Power systems.
John Choma Jr., Professor; Ph.D., Pittsburgh, 1969. Integrated circuits.
Clarence Crowell, Professor; Ph.D., McGill, 1955. Solid state.
P. Daniel Dapkus, W. M. Keck Professor; Ph.D., Illinois at Urbana-Champaign, 1970. Quantum electronics.
Jack Feinberg, Professor; Ph.D., Berkeley, 1977. Nonlinear optics, lasers.
Martin Gundersen, Professor; Ph.D., USC, 1972. Quantum electronics.
Robert Hellwarth, George Pfleger Professor; D.Phil., Oxford, 1955. Quantum electronics, lasers.
Kirby Holte, Adjunct Professor; Ph.D., Washington State, 1971. Electromagnetic fields.
Thomas C. Katsouleas, Associate Professor; Ph.D., UCLA, 1984. Plasma physics, advanced acceleration, light sources.
Hans H. Kuehl, Professor and Co-Chairman; Ph.D., Caltech, 1959. Plasmas and electromagnetics.
Anthony F. J. Levi, Professor; Ph.D., Cambridge, 1983. Quantum electronics.
Virendra Mahajan, Adjunct Professor; Ph.D., Arizona, 1974. Optical sciences.
Lute Maleki, Adjunct Assistant Professor; Ph.D., LSU, 1975. Lasers.
Alan McCurdy, Associate Professor; Ph.D., Yale, 1987. Applied physics.
Ram C. Mukherji, Adjunct Associate Professor; M.S.E.E., USC, 1970. Economic operation of power systems.
Richard N. Nottenburg, Associate Professor; Ph.D., Swiss Federal Institute of Technology, 1984. Quantum electronics, photonics.
Aluizio Prata Jr., Assistant Professor; Ph.D., USC, 1990. Applied electromagnetics.
Hanna Reisler, Research Assistant Professor; Ph.D., Weizmann (Israel), 1972. Lasers, quantum electronics.
Steven B. Sample, Professor and President; Ph.D., Illinois, 1965. Electromagnetics and antennas.
Bing J. Sheu, Associate Professor; Ph.D., Berkeley, 1985. VLSI, signal and image processing.
Keith Soohoo, Adjunct Associate Professor; Ph.D., USC, 1964. Electromagnetics.
William H. Steier, Professor; Ph.D., Illinois, 1960. Lasers, optical devices.
Armand R. Tanguay, Associate Professor; Ph.D., Yale, 1976. Solid state, electronic devices.
William G. Wagner, Professor; Ph.D., Caltech, 1962. Quantum electronics.
Curt F. Wittig, Professor; Ph.D., Illinois at Urbana-Champaign, 1970. Quantum electronics.

Systems

Michael A. Arbib, Professor; Ph.D., MIT, 1963. Computer science.
George A. Bekey, Professor; Ph.D., UCLA, 1962. Control systems, signal processing.
Peter Beerel, Assistant Professor; Ph.D., Stanford, 1994. Computer engineering.
Melvin A. Breuer, Professor; Ph.D., Berkeley, 1965. Computer engineering.
Keith M. Chugg, Assistant Professor; Ph.D., USC, 1995. Digital communications.
Alvin M. Despain, Professor; Ph.D., Utah, 1966. Computer engineering.
Michel Dubois, Professor; Ph.D., Purdue, 1982. Computer engineering.
Robert Gagliardi, Professor; Ph.D., Yale, 1960. Communications.
Jean-Luc Gaudiot, Professor; Ph.D., UCLA, 1982. Computer engineering.
Seymour Ginsburg, Fletcher Jones Professor; Ph.D., Michigan, 1952. Computer science.
Solomon W. Golomb, Professor; Ph.D., Harvard, 1957. Communications.
Sandeep K. Gupta, Associate Professor; Ph.D., Massachusetts at Amherst, 1991. Computer engineering.
Ellis Horowitz, Professor; Ph.D., Wisconsin, 1970. Computer science.
Kai Hwang, Professor; Ph.D., Berkeley, 1972. Computer engineering.
Petros Ioannou, Professor; Ph.D., Illinois at Urbana-Champaign, 1982. Adaptive and feedback control systems.
Keith Jenkins, Associate Professor; Ph.D., USC, 1984. Signal and image processing.
Edmond Jonckheere, Professor; Ph.D., USC, 1978. Control theory.
Bart Kosko, Associate Professor; Ph.D., California, Irvine, 1987. Signal processing.
P. Vijay Kumar, Professor; Ph.D., USC, 1983. Communications.
Chung-Chieh (Jay) Kuo, Associate Professor; Ph.D., MIT, 1987. Signal processing.
Chris Kyriakakis, Assistant Professor; Ph.D., USC, 1993. Immersive audio.
Richard Leahy, Professor; Ph.D., Newcastle, 1984. Signal and image processing.
Victor O. K. Li, Professor; Ph.D., MIT, 1981. Communications.
William C. Lindsey, Professor; Ph.D., Purdue, 1962. Communications.
Toyone Mayeda, Adjunct Assistant Professor; M.S.E.E., USC, 1979. Computer engineering.
Gerard G. Medioni, Associate Professor; Ph.D., USC, 1983. Computer science.
Jerry M. Mendel, Professor; Ph.D., Polytechnic of Brooklyn, 1963. Signal processing.
Ramakant Nevatia, Professor; Ph.D., Stanford, 1975. Computer science.
Chrysostomos L. Nikias, Professor and Associate Dean; Ph.D., SUNY at Buffalo, 1982. Signal and image processing.
Antonio Ortega, Assistant Professor; Ph.D., Columbia, 1994. Signal and image processing.
George Papavassilopoulos, Professor; Ph.D., Illinois at Urbana-Champaign, 1979. Control systems.
Alice C. Parker, Professor and Vice Provost for Research and Graduate Studies; Ph.D., North Carolina State, 1975. Computer engineering.
Massoud Pedram, Associate Professor; Ph.D., Berkeley, 1991. Computer engineering.
Timothy Pinkston, Assistant Professor; Ph.D., Stanford, 1993. Computer engineering.
Andreas Polydoros, Professor; Ph.D., USC, 1982. Communication theory.
Viktor Prasanna, Professor; Ph.D., Penn State, 1983. Computer engineering.
Keith E. Price, Research Associate Professor; Ph.D., Carnegie Mellon, 1976. Computer science.
Gandhi Puvvada, Adjunct Assistant Professor; M.S.E.E., Houston, 1987. Computer engineering.
Eberhardt Rechtin, Emeritus Professor; Ph.D., Caltech, 1950. System architecting.
Irving S. Reed, Emeritus Professor; Ph.D., Caltech, 1949. Communications.
Aristides Requicha, Professor; Ph.D., Rochester, 1970. Computer science.
Michael G. Safonov, Professor; Ph.D., MIT, 1977. Control systems.
Alexander A. Sawchuk, Professor; Ph.D., Stanford, 1972. Signal processing.
Robert A. Scholtz, Professor and Co-Chairman; Ph.D., Stanford, 1964. Communications.
Leonard M. Silverman, Professor and Dean of the School of Engineering; Ph.D., Columbia, 1966. Control systems.
John A. Silvester, Professor and Interim Vice-Provost for Academic Computing; Ph.D., UCLA, 1979. Computer engineering.
Monte Ung, Adjunct Professor; Ph.D., USC, 1970. Computer engineering.
Charles L. Weber, Professor; Ph.D., UCLA, 1964. Communications.
Lloyd R. Welch, Professor; Ph.D., Caltech, 1958. Communications.
Alan Willner, Associate Professor; Ph.D., Columbia, 1988. Communications.
Zhen Zhang, Professor; Ph.D., Cornell, 1984. Communications.

UNIVERSITY OF SOUTH FLORIDA

DEPARTMENT OF COMPUTER SCIENCE AND ENGINEERING

PROGRAMS OF STUDY

The Department of Computer Science and Engineering offers the degrees of Master of Science in Computer Science and Computer Engineering and Doctor of Philosophy in Computer Science and Engineering. The major areas of research are image processing, computer vision, robotics, graphics, artificial intelligence, expert systems, coding theory, databases, computer networks, VLSI design, computer architecture, and fault-tolerant computing.

The master's degree program requires a total of 30 to 33 semester credit hours of work beyond the baccalaureate. Courses in four core areas are required; other courses are chosen to serve the individual student's interest.

The doctoral degree is attained by completing course work as advised by the doctoral committee and a minimum of 20 hours of dissertation beyond the master's degree. Other requirements include passing a written screening and a written preliminary examination, achieving candidacy by means of thesis proposal and oral examination, and presenting and defending thesis research.

RESEARCH FACILITIES

The Department of Computer Science and Engineering operates a research-oriented local area network consisting of several DEC/IBM machines, several SG workstations, more than sixty Sun SPARC workstations, image-processing workstations, and an Intel Hypercube of 16 nodes. The department's facilities also include a microprocessor laboratory, a hardware/architecture laboratory, and a PC-compatible laboratory for instructional purposes. College of Engineering facilities available to the department include a second network of Sun Workstations. In addition, the University operates a large IBM mainframe, which is available for the department's instructional and research purposes.

FINANCIAL AID

Teaching and research assistantships are available to qualified students, with estimated stipends of $7000–$12,000 for nine months for M.S. degree students and $7,000–$16,000 for Ph.D. students. A thesis is required on the subject covered by the research assistantship. Duties normally require 20 hours per week. Students holding assistantships are eligible for partial in-state and out-of-state tuition waivers. Fellowship appointments are available with stipends ranging upwards from $7000 through the graduate school.

COST OF STUDY

Fall semester 1997 in-state tuition was $120 per semester credit hour; out-of-state students paid $391 per semester credit hour.

LIVING AND HOUSING COSTS

The cost of living in the Tampa Bay area compares favorably with that of most other parts of the United States. Limited facilities for unmarried students are available on campus. A wide range of off-campus housing is available immediately adjacent to the University. Meal plans are available in the University's dining halls. Excluding tuition, books, and transportation, minimum living costs are estimated at $2000 per semester.

STUDENT GROUP

There are more than 36,000 students at the University of South Florida, with 6,200 enrolled in graduate programs. Students come from virtually all states of the Union and many other countries. The College of Engineering has an enrollment of about 3,000, including more than 500 graduate students. The department has more than 80 full-time graduate students with a total enrollment of 150.

LOCATION

The Tampa Bay area, with a population of more than 1.5 million, is rich in recreational, cultural, and athletic activities. The University is located approximately 10 miles from downtown Tampa, 35 miles from Clearwater and St. Petersburg. Symphonies, operas, professional theater, chamber music, and professional sports events are regularly available. Fine beaches and parks make the area an elite resort and vacation spot. Tampa Bay is undergoing rapid industrial growth and houses divisions of many internationally known high-technology industries.

THE UNIVERSITY

The University of South Florida opened its doors in 1960 and now has more than 35,000 students on five campuses. The Tampa campus is the largest, with more than 28,148 students. It comprises the Colleges of Engineering, Arts and Sciences, Business Administration, Education, Fine Arts, Medicine, Nursing, and Social and Behavioral Sciences and the School of Public Health. The campus is modern, airy, and attractive and provides a wide range of recreational facilities, including a golf course. More than $100 million in sponsored research is conducted annually.

The College of Engineering maintains close contact with local industry, where many of its students find part-time or full-time employment. Several of the department facility's research projects are funded by various federal and state agencies and local industries. The college is housed in two modern, 100,000-square-foot, four-story facilities.

APPLYING

Applicants for the master's program must have a bachelor's degree in computer science, computer engineering, or a closely related area. Students must have either a grade point average of 3.3 or higher during the last two years of their undergraduate work and a combined verbal and quantitative score of 1200 or better on the GRE General Test. Applicants for the doctoral program are expected to have an academic record that exceeds the foregoing minimum requirements. Applications for admissions should be received by the University's Office of Graduate Admissions at least three months prior to first expected enrollment.

CORRESPONDENCE AND INFORMATION

Graduate Program Coordinator
Department of Computer Science and Engineering
University of South Florida
Tampa, Florida 33620
Telephone: 813-974-3033
E-mail: msphd@csee.usf.edu
World Wide Web: http//www.csee.usf.edu

UNIVERSITY OF SOUTH FLORIDA
THE FACULTY AND THEIR RESEARCH

Sami Al-Arian, Associate Professor; Ph.D., North Carolina State, 1985. Digital systems and microcomputer-based design, fault-tolerant computing, VLSI/WSI system testing, architecture.

Kevin Bowyer, Professor; Ph.D., Duke, 1980. Image processing and computer vision, pattern recognition, computer science education.

Ken Christensen, Assistant Professor; Ph.D., North Carolina State, 1991. Computer networking, high-speed LANs, performance evaluation, simulation modeling, queueing systems.

Dmitry Goldgof, Associate Professor; Ph.D., Illinois, 1989. Computer vision, image processing, biomedical applications, pattern recognition, parallel algorithms for computer vision, visualization techniques.

Lawrence Hall, Professor; Ph.D., Florida State, 1986. Pattern recognition, intelligent systems development, fuzzy set theory, connectionist/symbolic learning.

Abraham Kandel, Professor and Chair; Ph.D., New Mexico, 1977. Intelligent autonomous systems, expert and hybrid systems, neural networks, fuzzy set theory, robotics.

Srinivas Katkoori, Assistant Professor; Ph.D., Cincinnati, 1996. VLSI design, CAD.

Sridhar Mahadevan, Assistant Professor; Ph.D., Rutgers, 1990. Machine learning, artificial intelligence, robotics, and aids for expert systems.

Peter Maurer, Associate Professor; Ph.D., Iowa State, 1982. Computer architecture, VLSI, VLSI logic simulation, VLSI layout verification, multiprocessors and parallel programming.

Rafael Perez, Professor; Ph.D., Pittsburgh, 1973. Genetic algorithms, neural networks and expert systems.

Les Piegl, Professor; Ph.D., Eotvos Lorand (Budapest), 1982. Geometric modeling, computer graphics, computer-aided geometric design, data structures, engineering and applied computing.

Dimitrios Plexousakis, Assistant Professor; Ph.D., Toronto, 1996. Databases, knowledge-based systems.

N. Ranganathan, Associate Professor; Ph.D., Central Florida, 1988. VLSI design, hardware algorithms, computer architecture, parallel algorithms and architecture, VLSI for vision, image processing and pattern recognition.

Dewey Rundus, Associate Professor; Ph.D., Stanford, 1971. User interface design, software engineering, computer graphics.

Sudeep Sarkar, Assistant Professor; Ph.D., Ohio State, 1993. Computer vision in the area of signals as opposed to symbols, perceptual organization, and image processing.

Michael D. Soo, Assistant Professor; Ph.D., Arizona, 1995. Temporal databases, data modeling, query optimization and evaluation, architectural issues.

Murali Varanasi, Professor; Ph.D., Maryland, 1973. Coding theory, computer arithmetic, implementation of communication and signal processing algorithms, fault-tolerant computing.

UNIVERSITY OF SOUTH FLORIDA

COLLEGE OF ENGINEERING
DEPARTMENT OF ELECTRICAL ENGINEERING

PROGRAMS OF STUDY

Ph.D. and master's (M.E., M.S.E., M.E.E., and M.S.E.E.) degrees in electrical engineering are granted by the department. Master's program options include circuit theory, control theory, communications and signal processing, electric power, microelectronics, and wireless systems. Ph.D. studies emphasize microelectronic design and test (VLSI, VHSIC, MMIC, and ASIC design; microwave and high-frequency analog and digital circuit modeling and testability; interconnection systems; and reliability and failure mode studies); communications and signal processing (digital communications, networks, packet switching, digital video and HDTV, ISDN, optical-fiber, and comm-software); systems and controls; solid-state material and device processing and characterization; electrooptics; electromagnetics, microwave, and millimeter-wave engineering (antennas, devices, and systems); CAD and microprocessors; and biomedical engineering. Special interdisciplinary study is available through the engineering science program.

Master's degree programs require a year's full-time study beyond the bachelor's degree. Master's degrees may be pursued with or without a thesis (30 semester hours minimum with a thesis, 33 semester hours minimum without a thesis). The thesis accounts for 6 semester hours. The doctoral degree program normally requires three years of full-time study and research beyond the bachelor's degree or two years beyond the master's degree. The program culminates in the submission of a dissertation that demonstrates the student's capacity for considerable original thought, talent for significant research and/or design, and ability to organize and present his or her findings.

Students must achieve and maintain a minimum grade point average of 3.0 (on a 4.0 scale) in all courses taken for graduate credit.

RESEARCH FACILITIES

The Department of Electrical Engineering is housed in the College of Engineering building, which provides excellent graduate research facilities and computing capabilities. Students have access to Ardents, Suns, and PC laboratories as well as to the Ethernet and ISN networks. Laboratories include compound semiconductor materials processing and microfabrication facilities with MOCVD reactors and CVD and plasma processing equipment; thin-film and hybrid circuit facilities; extensive semiconductor characterization equipment (DC through optical, including a semiconductor parameter tester, a network analyzer, a scanning electron microscope, a deep-level transient spectroscope, and electrochemical profilers and beam characterization tools); a noise research laboratory with cryogenics for superconductor studies; a communications and signal processing laboratory focusing on integrated-services (data/voice/video) telecommunications, information transport networks, VLSI and microprocessor-based algorithm implementations, speech and image processing, and digital communications; a coherent fiber optics laboratory with extensive instrumentation; a Restructurable VLSI lab; and CAD and modeling laboratories for analog, digital, and microwave monolithic circuits and devices, as well as antennas and scattering characteristics. The VLSI CAD facility includes extensive software and an automated system.

FINANCIAL AID

Teaching and research assistantships and fellowships are available to qualified students. In 1996–97, assistantships and fellowships carried estimated stipends of $5000–$12,000 for twelve months for master's students and $10,000–$16,000 for twelve months for Ph.D. students. (A thesis may be written on the subject covered by the research assistantship.) Duties normally require 20 hours per week. A major portion of the fees may be waived for employed students.

COST OF STUDY

For 1997–98, the in-state tuition fee is $116 per semester hour. Out-of-state students pay $383 per semester hour. Tuition and fee waivers may be available for graduate assistants.

LIVING AND HOUSING COSTS

The cost of living in the Tampa Bay area compares favorably with most other parts of the United States. There are limited facilities on campus for unmarried students. Off-campus housing is available immediately adjacent to the University. Meal plans are available in the University's dining halls. Excluding tuition, books, and transportation, minimum living costs for single students are about $1600 per semester.

STUDENT GROUP

There are more than 37,000 students at the University of South Florida. About 5,000 are enrolled in graduate programs. Students come from virtually all states of the Union and many other countries. The Department of Electrical Engineering has an enrollment of about 500 undergraduate and 200 graduate students.

STUDENT OUTCOMES

Students completing master's degrees have opted for employment in the growing microelectronics, wireless systems, and communications segments of industry. Recruitment by companies such as Texas Instruments, AT&T, Motorola, Honeywell, E-Systems, Intel, Harris, and Raytheon have resulted in challenging technical opportunities. Students completing Ph.D. degrees have also been in great demand, primarily by industrial organizations.

LOCATION

The Tampa Bay area is rich in recreational, cultural, and athletic activities. The University is located about 10 miles from downtown Tampa and 35 miles from Clearwater and St. Petersburg. Symphonies, operas, theaters, chamber music orchestras, and sports events are regularly available.

THE UNIVERSITY AND THE COLLEGE

The University opened its doors in 1960 and now has more than 36,000 students on its four campuses. The Tampa campus is the largest, with approximately 30,000 students. It comprises the Colleges of Engineering, Arts and Sciences, Business Administration, Education, Fine Arts, Medicine, Nursing, and Public Health. The campus is modern, airy, and attractive. The College of Engineering maintains close contact with local industry. Many engineering students find part-time or full-time employment with these companies.

APPLYING

Applicants for a master's program in engineering must have a bachelor's degree in an accredited engineering or related program. They must present a GPA of 3.0 or higher (for the last two years of undergraduate work) or a combined (verbal and quantitative) GRE General Test score of 1000 or better. All applicants must submit recent GRE General Test scores when applying. Applicants for the doctoral program should have an academic record that exceeds the foregoing minimum requirements. Applications for admission should be received by the Office of Graduate Admissions at least two months prior to expected enrollment. International applications need to be submitted at least four months prior to expected enrollment. For more information, students should see the World Wide Web site (http://www.eng.usf.edu/EE/ee.html). Applicants can download the USF Graduate School Application Form and can communicate directly via e-mail.

CORRESPONDENCE AND INFORMATION

Dr. Kenneth A. Buckle, Graduate Program Coordinator
Department of Electrical Engineering
University of South Florida
Tampa, Florida 33620-5350

Telephone: 813-974-2369
Fax: 813-974-5250
E-mail: eegrad@eng.usf.edu

UNIVERSITY OF SOUTH FLORIDA

THE FACULTY AND THEIR RESEARCH

Kenneth Buckle, Associate Professor; Ph.D., Wisconsin, 1984. Plasma processing, electromagnetics, microwave engineering in the deposition of thin films and their etching.

Charles T. M. Chen, Professor; Ph.D., Minnesota, 1964. Electrical and noise properties of hybrid microcircuits, reliability and noise properties of semiconductor devices and VLSI, analysis and design of low noise sensors and devices.

Yun-Leei Chiou, Professor; Ph.D., Purdue, 1969. Solid-state devices, hybrids, thin oxide films, breakdown mechanism, GaAs photonic devices, thick film, VLSI devices, silicon oxidation.

Lawrence P. Dunleavy, Assistant Professor; Ph.D., Michigan, 1988. Microwave and millimeter wave circuits, MMIC implementation, microwave CAD, measurements and modeling of passive and active microwave components, quasi-optic millimeter-wave grid array analysis.

Christos Ferekides, Assistant Professor; Ph.D., South Florida, 1991. Thin-film electronic materials and devices for optoelectronic applications, thin-film depositions and properties, device fabrication and characterization.

Paul Flikkema, Assistant Professor; Ph.D., Maryland, 1992. Communication theory and digital communications, spread spectrum theory and applications, wireless networking, signal detection and processing, satellite communications.

Samuel Garrett, Professor; Sc.D., Pittsburgh, 1963. Control theory, power electronics, computer-aided design, circuit theory.

Horace Gordon, Lecturer; M.S.E., South Florida, 1970. Low-frequency and microwave circuit theory and design, communication theory and system design, digital signal processing theory and hardware design.

Worth Henley, Assistant Professor; Ph.D., South Florida, 1993. Electronic materials processing and characterization, advanced VLSI MOSFET device design and fabrication.

Rudolf E. Henning, Professor; D.Eng.Sc., Columbia, 1954; PE. Microwave and millimeter-wave microelectronic design; application of microwave theory and electromagnetics to instrumentation, sensing, and detection; properties and applications of microwave and millimeter-wave propagation; microwave/optical interactions and subsystems.

Vijay K. Jain, Professor; Ph.D., Michigan State, 1964. Communication systems and networks (data/voice/video/multimedia); digital signal, image, and speech processing; VLSI and WSI implementations; parallel architectures; computer arithmetic and algorithms; pattern recognition by computers.

Lubek Jastrzebski, Professor; Ph.D., Polish Academy of Sciences, 1974. Silicon technology, material synthesis and characterization, material and devices modeling.

Firman Dean King, Assistant Professor; Ph.D., Florida, 1980. Control, estimation, and systems theory; random processes; robotics.

Keith Klontz, Assistant Professor; Ph.D., Wisconsin, 1995. Power systems and energy conversion, electric vehicles and related infrastructure, electric machines, power electronics.

Michael Kovac, Dean and Professor; Ph.D., Northwestern, 1970. Solid-state devices, reliability, VLSI, optical image sensors, novel transducers.

Gerard Lachs, Professor; Ph.D., Syracuse, 1964. Fiber-optic communication theory, digital communication, quantum electronics, laser applications, signal detection and processing in human sensory perception.

Jacek Lagowski, Professor; Ph.D., 1968, Habil.Dr.Sci., 1972, Polish Academy of Sciences. Semiconductor materials and devices: properties, growth, characterization, and defect engineering.

James Leffew, Assistant Professor; Ph.D., South Florida, 1985. Electromagnetics, microwave engineering, microwave CAD, network synthesis.

Don L. Morel, Professor; Ph.D., Tulane, 1971. Photovoltaic solar energy conversion, compound semiconductor and Group IV amorphous thin-film electronic materials and devices, large-area display and memory technology.

Harry Nienhaus, Associate Professor; M.S., Saint Louis, 1964. Computer-aided design, device modeling, speech processing, fault detection, power electronics, CMOS/VLSI design, DSP architecture, array processors, behavioral simulations.

Ravi Sankar, Associate Professor; Ph.D., Penn State, 1985. Communication/computer networking (high-speed local and wide area networks), speech processing and recognition, signal processing and its applications, telecommunications, applications of neural networks, simulation and modeling.

Arthur David Snider, Professor; Ph.D., NYU, 1971. Spectral analysis, optimization, math modeling in electromagnetics, communications, electronics, heat transfer.

Elias (Lee) Stefanakos, Professor and Chairman; Ph.D., Washington State, 1969; PE. Electric vehicles, clean energy, photovoltaics.

Thomas Wade, Professor; Ph.D., Florida, 1974. Solid-state microelectronics, VLSI multilevel interconnection systems, test structure development, solid-state material characterization (e.g., polyimides and refractory silicides).

Thomas M. Weller, Assistant Professor; Ph.D., Michigan, 1995. Numerical electromagnetics, applications of micromachining to microwave/millimeter-wave circuit/system design.

Paris Wiley, Associate Professor; Ph.D., Virginia Tech, 1973. Analog and digital electronics, biomedical instrumentation, theoretical electromagnetics, microwave communications.

UNIVERSITY OF SOUTHWESTERN LOUISIANA

CENTER FOR ADVANCED COMPUTER STUDIES

PROGRAMS OF STUDY

The primary mission of the Center for Advanced Computer Studies (CACS) is to conduct research and provide graduate-level education in computer engineering and computer science. The Center offers four graduate degrees: Ph.D. in computer engineering and in computer science, M.S.C.E., and M.S.C.S. Areas of specialization are artificial intelligence and cognitive science, fault-tolerant computing, parallel and distributed computing, VLSI, database systems, information retrieval, software systems and engineering, formal aspects of computing, robotics and automation, visual and image computing, neural networks, information technology, and multimedia systems architectures.

RESEARCH FACILITIES

The Computing Research Laboratory includes a network of eighty-six Sun Workstations connected to seven file servers with more than 10 gigabytes of on-line storage; two Cogent XTM-110 parallel computing systems, thirty-two processing nodes each; a comprehensive digital design laboratory (including VLSI design); and numerous peripherals (color laser printers and plotters). UNIX is the primary operating system. A wide variety of software is available for applications ranging from artificial intelligence to VLSI design. The following specialized laboratories are equipped with state-of-the-art computing facilities: automated reasoning, computer vision and pattern recognition, intelligent robotic systems, software research, VLSI research, and media technology.

FINANCIAL AID

A number of fellowships valued at up to $18,000 for up to four years are available for entering Ph.D. students with a superior academic record and exceptional GRE scores. Fellowships valued at up to $10,000 are available for entering M.S. students with superior academic records and strong GRE scores. All fellowship application materials must be received by February 15 for consideration. The Center has a large number of teaching and research assistantships and scholarships. The value of financial support ranges from about $6000 to more than $10,000 for the academic year. Figures quoted include tuition and most fees.

COST OF STUDY

Graduate resident fees for the 1997 fall semester for full-time students (minimum of 9 hours) are $942 for U.S. citizens and $1010 for international residents, $2742 for nonresident U.S. citizens, and $2810 for nonresident international students. Tuition and fee amounts are subject to change without notice.

LIVING AND HOUSING COSTS

The cost of room and board (fifteen meals per week) for single students living in residence halls in 1997–98 is $1470 per semester. A limited number of rooms in the University Conference Center cost $893 per semester. Married student apartments are available at $300 per month. All costs are subject to change. Fellowship students receive preferred housing. The community of Lafayette provides a wide selection of privately owned housing convenient to the campus.

STUDENT GROUP

Total University enrollment is 16,586 students. There are 189 students enrolled in the Center's graduate programs, including 84 pursuing the Ph.D. degree. USL is known to attract international graduate students in the fields of computer science and engineering at both the master's and Ph.D. levels. The master's degree program is currently serving 79 computer science majors and 26 computer engineering majors; the Ph.D. program is currently serving 60 computer science majors and 24 computer engineering majors.

STUDENT OUTCOMES

Among the universities employing some of the Center's recent graduates are Texas at Austin, Arkansas, South Carolina, Houston, Stevens Institute of Technology, South Alabama, Tulane, Louisiana Tech, Grambling State, Haceteppe (Turkey), National Institute of Saudi Arabia, and Chungbuk National University (Korea). Some Ph.D, graduates have accepted employment in industry with IBM (Durham, Boca Raton), MIT, Schlumberger (Austin), Intel (San Jose, Portland), LSI Logic (Milpitas, California), Centigram Communication (San Jose), and Stock Exchange of Thailand.

LOCATION

The University of Southwestern Louisiana is located in Lafayette, the central city of the geographic area known as Acadiana. The more than 500,000 inhabitants of this locale are mainly descendants of the exiled Acadians of Nova Scotia. Culturally, the region is characterized by a joie de vivre that has given it an international reputation. Lafayette is located approximately 52 miles from the state capital of Baton Rouge and 129 miles from New Orleans.

THE UNIVERSITY AND THE DEPARTMENT

The University has an impressive physical plant that is steadily being enlarged on all parts of the campus. It includes the administrative complex; Dupre Library; French House; academic buildings; athletic facilities; housing for men, women, and married students; art museum; and a Student Union Complex situated on Cypress Lake. Located on the agricultural extension of the campus are Blackham Coliseum, Cajun Field, and the Cajun Dome, which seats approximately 12,000. Since its inception in 1984, the Center for Advanced Computer Studies has demonstrated a strong contribution to both the quality of education and the quality of research in the fields of computer science and engineering. The University and CACS have created an environment unique in the nation. The Center is one of the first to merge the overlapping, yet disjoint, disciplines of computer science and computer engineering into a successful graduate program. CACS has 17 faculty and 7 support staff members.

APPLYING

Applications for admission for the fall semester must be submitted to the Graduate School thirty days before classes begin. Applications for graduate assistantships for the fall semester must be submitted to the Graduate School by March 1 and for the spring semester by November 1. Students will be notified by April 1 and December 1, respectively, of their acceptance. Requirements for admission include a baccalaureate degree from an accredited institution, an excellent GPA, GRE and TOEFL scores (if the degree is earned outside the United States), three letters of recommendation, and a fluent command of English. Application fees (nonrefundable) are $5 for U.S. citizens and $15 for students who are non-U.S. citizens. Applications, inquiries, letters of recommendation, transcripts, and GRE and TOEFL scores should be sent to the address below.

CORRESPONDENCE AND INFORMATION

The Graduate School
University of Southwestern Louisiana
P.O. Box 44610
Lafayette, Louisiana 70504-4610

Telephone: 318-482-6965
Fax: 318-482-6195

UNIVERSITY OF SOUTHWESTERN LOUISIANA
THE FACULTY AND THEIR RESEARCH

Professors

Magdy A. Bayoumi, Ph.D., Windsor, 1984. VLSI design, image and video signal processing, parallel processing, neural networks, wide-band, multimedia network architectures.

Subrata Dasgupta, Ph.D., Alberta, 1976. Theory of design, cognitive aspects of creativity in science and technology.

Vijay V. Raghavan, Ph.D., Alberta, 1978. Information storage and retrieval, rough sets and knowledge discovery in databases, content-based image retrieval.

T. R. N. Rao, Ph.D., Michigan, 1964. Fault-tolerant computers, information theory and coding, cryptology and data security.

Harold Szu, Ph.D., Rockefeller, 1971. Optics, neural networks, adaptive wavelet transforms, statistical and mathematical physics.

Kimon P. Valavanis, Ph.D., RPI, 1986. Control systems, robotics, intelligent systems and machines, automated manufacturing systems.

Associate Professors

Chee-Hung Henry Chu, Ph.D., Purdue, 1988. Computer vision, signal and image processing, data compression.

William R. Edwards Jr., Ph.D., Kansas, 1973. Theory of computation, software engineering, artificial intelligence.

Kemal Efe, Ph.D., Leeds (England), 1985. Parallel and distributed computer systems, data parallel algorithms.

Gui-Liang Feng, Ph.D., Lehigh, 1990. Fault-tolerant computing, error correcting code, fast algorithm design.

Jung Kim, Ph.D., Iowa, 1987. Neural networks and fault tolerance.

Arun Lakhotia, Ph.D., Case Western Reserve, 1989. Program understanding, software reengineering, programming flow analysis.

Rasiah Loganantharaj, Ph.D., Colorado State, 1985. Temporal reasoning, knowledge-based systems, KB-approaches for design of artifacts, artificial intelligence.

Niki Pissinou, Ph.D., USC, 1991. Databases, database system modeling, design and evolution, information sharing and integration.

Nian-Feng Tzeng, Ph.D., Illinois, 1986. Parallel and distributed processing, high-speed networking, fault-tolerant computing, high-performance computer systems.

Assistant Professors

Anthony S. Maida, Ph.D., SUNY at Buffalo, 1980. Artificial intelligence, cognitive science.

Gunasekaran Seetharaman, Ph.D., Miami (Florida), 1988. Computer vision, image and signal processing, algorithm analysis, data compression, 3-D displays.

Adjunct Faculty

Claude G. Cech, Ph.D., Illinois, 1981. Models of mental comparisons, discourse processes, categories and attention.

Sherri L. Condon, Ph.D., Texas at Austin, 1983. Discourse analysis, computational linguistics, Louisiana languages.

Joan Francioni, Ph.D., Florida State, 1981. Debugging tools for parallel programs, operating systems for parallel computers.

Steve Giambrone, Ph.D., Australian National, 1984. Logic language and automata communication.

Robert R. Henry, Ph.D., New Mexico State, 1976. Computer design and architecture, telecommunications.

Mohammad R. Madani, Ph.D., LSU, 1990. VLSI circuit processing and manufacturing, ion implantation, VLSI circuit characterization and testing.

Bill Manaris, Ph.D., Southwestern Louisiana, 1990. Artificial intelligence, natural-language processing, human-computer interaction, software engineering.

Renee McCauley, Ph.D., Southwestern Louisiana, 1992. Computer science education, software measurement, theory of computation.

Daniel J. Povinelli, Ph.D., Yale, 1991. Origin of self-recognition systems, attributions of intention and belief in young children, chimpanzees and other primates.

Jill Seaman, Ph.D., Penn State, 1993. Formal semantics of programming languages, static analysis, type systems.

THE UNIVERSITY OF TENNESSEE, KNOXVILLE

DEPARTMENT OF COMPUTER SCIENCE

PROGRAMS OF STUDY

The Department of Computer Science offers programs of study leading to the degrees of Doctor of Philosophy and Master of Science. The principal requirements for the Ph.D. are successful completion of certain comprehensive examinations and submission of a dissertation that describes original independent research. The degree of Doctor of Philosophy is awarded in recognition of high achievement in research. The M.S. degree may be earned by completing 30 semester hours of approved course work or course work plus a thesis. A comprehensive examination is required in lieu of a thesis.

RESEARCH FACILITIES

The department operates research laboratories with more than 200 UNIX-based machines, including Sun Workstations and servers, IBM RS/6000 workstations, HP series 700 workstations, and a 4096-processor MasPar MP-2. Faculty members collaborate with scientists at the Oak Ridge National Laboratory (ORNL) and have access to their facilities, including a 16-processor IBM SP2, a 64-processor Kendall Square Research KSR1-64, a 70-processor Intel Paragon XP/S 5, a 512-processor Intel Paragon XP/S 35, and a 1024-processor Intel Paragon XP/S 150. Local area networking technologies include 10Mbps Ethernet, 100Mbps Ethernet, and 155Mbps ATM. SLIP, PPP, and ISDN connections to the department from off campus are available. The Knoxville campus has three T1 connections to BBN Planet, providing connections from the campus to the Internet. A 155Mbps ATM link is used to route Internet traffic between the Knoxville campus and ORNL.

FINANCIAL AID

Financial aid is available in the form of graduate teaching assistantships and research assistantships. In 1997–98, assistantships pay a stipend of $8700–$9700 for nine months and offer a waiver of tuition and fees. Additional supplements are available under the state-funded Science Alliance and faculty research grants.

Graduate fellowships, awarded on the basis of scholastic record, are available through the Graduate School.

COST OF STUDY

Tuition for 1997–98 for full-time study is about $1500 per semester for Tennessee residents and $3500 per semester for out-of-state students, plus nominal activities and technology fees. All computer science students are encouraged to own a personal computer; to facilitate this, discount programs are available at the University bookstore.

LIVING AND HOUSING COSTS

Living accommodations of all types, ranging from residence halls to privately owned apartments, are available within walking distance of the campus. Single students may live in the residence halls for approximately $1875 per semester in 1997–98, including room and board.

STUDENT GROUP

The department has about 50 undergraduates and 140 graduate students majoring in computer science.

STUDENT OUTCOMES

Graduates of the department are highly sought by prospective employers such as AT&T, Cray Research, DuPont, Federal Express, Hewlett-Packard, IBM, and Oak Ridge National Laboratory, as well as a number of universities and colleges.

LOCATION

The University of Tennessee is located in Knoxville, which was previously listed in a national survey as one of the most livable cities in the nation. Knoxville provides a variety of athletic, cultural, and entertainment activities. The area has several lakes that offer excellent fishing, boating, and swimming. Knoxville is located 40 miles from the Great Smoky Mountains, where numerous outdoor activities, including skiing and white-water canoeing, are available. The Oak Ridge National Laboratory, 30 miles from the campus, is an important part of the intellectual community. The area has a relatively mild climate with a moderate range of temperatures.

THE UNIVERSITY

The University of Tennessee, with a statewide enrollment of about 43,000, has all the intellectual and social characteristics associated with a state university system. Students may specialize in a great number of professional and occupational fields. There is a distinguished group of faculty members, nationally recognized for their professional accomplishments. The Knoxville campus, with an enrollment of 26,000, is the main campus of the multicampus system and is the center for advanced graduate studies.

APPLYING

Admission applications are processed throughout the year, and students may enter at the beginning of any semester. Applications for assistantships beginning in August should be submitted to the department by March 1. Consideration may be given to applications received after that date. Fellowship applications must be received in the Office of Graduate Admissions and Records by February 15. The Graduate Admissions Office will supply specific deadlines for international applicants.

CORRESPONDENCE AND INFORMATION

Department of Computer Science
107 Ayres Hall
The University of Tennessee, Knoxville
Knoxville, Tennessee 37996-1301

Telephone: 423-974-5067
Fax: 423-974-4404
E-mail: straight@cs.utk.edu
World Wide Web: http://www.cs.utk.edu

For fellowship applications:

Assistant Director
Office of Graduate Admissions and Records
The University of Tennessee, Knoxville
Knoxville, Tennessee 37996-0220

THE UNIVERSITY OF TENNESSEE, KNOXVILLE
THE FACULTY AND THEIR RESEARCH

Micah Beck, Assistant Professor; Ph.D., Cornell. Parallel and distributed computing, automatic program parallelization, program development tools, distributed and fault-tolerant systems, networking, collaborative computing.

Michael W. Berry, Associate Professor; Ph.D., Illinois. Scientific computing, parallel numerical algorithms, information retrieval, computational science and performance evaluation.

Jack Dongarra, Distinguished Professor and Oak Ridge National Laboratory Distinguished Scientist; Ph.D., New Mexico. Scientific computing, numerical linear algebra, parallel processing, software tools, mathematical software and software repositories.

Jens Gregor, Assistant Professor; Ph.D., Aalborg (Denmark). Pattern and image analysis, computed imaging.

Mark Jones, Assistant Professor; Ph.D., Duke. Scientific computing: scalable parallel algorithms for numerical linear algebra, computational science, parallel discrete algorithms for unstructured computations (on leave).

Michael A. Langston, Professor; Ph.D., Texas A&M. Analysis of algorithms, graph theory, operations research, parallel computing, VLSI design.

Michael R. Leuze, Associate Professor and Director of the Joint Institute for Computational Science; Ph.D., Duke. Parallel linear algebra, sparse matrix computations, multiprocessor performance characterization and modeling.

Bruce J. MacLennan, Associate Professor; Ph.D., Purdue. Neural networks and connectionism, theory of knowledge, massively parallel analog computation, emergent computation.

J. Wallace Mayo, Instructor; M.S., Tennessee. Responsible for teaching and developing core courses, supervising graduate teaching assistants, and student advising.

James S. Plank, Assistant Professor; Ph.D., Princeton. Fault-tolerance and checkpointing, operating systems, parallel programming, architecture.

Jesse H. Poore, Professor; Ph.D., Georgia Tech. Economical production of high-quality software, federal software policy.

Padma Raghavan, Assistant Professor; Ph.D., Penn State. Parallel processing, graph algorithms, sparse matrices, linear algebra, scientific computing.

Thomas H. Rowan, Associate Professor and ORNL Collaborating Scientist; Ph.D., Texas. Mathematical software, numerical analysis, stability of numerical algorithms, optimization of noisy functions, software engineering.

Gordon R. Sherman, Professor Emeritus; Ph.D., Purdue. Probability and statistics, discrete optimization, high-performance computing resources, administration of computer services.

David W. Straight, Assistant Professor; Ph.D., Texas. LANS architecture, parallel processing.

Michael G. Thomason, Professor; Ph.D., Duke. Image and pattern analysis, stochastic processes, parallel algorithms.

Bradley T. VanderZanden, Associate Professor; Ph.D., Cornell. Graphical programming environments, programming languages, constraint solving.

Michael D. Vose, Associate Professor; Ph.D., Texas. Genetic algorithms.

Robert C. Ward, Professor and Department Head; Ph.D., Virginia. Numerical linear algebra, scientific computing.

Adjunct Faculty

Stephen G. Batsell, Assistant Professor and Network Research Group Leader, Oak Ridge National Laboratory; Ph.D., Texas Tech. Networks, network protocols, data security, optical computing.

Jean R. S. Blair, Associate Professor of Electrical Engineering and Computer Science, United States Military Academy; Ph.D., Pittsburgh. Design and analysis of algorithms, sparse matrix computations, VLSI theory, algorithmic game theory, graph algorithms.

Heather Booth, Assistant Professor; Ph.D., Princeton. Data structures, graph algorithms, computational geometry.

Shirley Browne, Assistant Professor and Research Associate, Computer Science Department; Ph.D., Purdue. Software reuse in high-performance computing, wide-area information retrieval, security aspects of safe execution environments.

Jeffrey Case, Associate Professor and President, SNMP Research Inc.; Ph.D., Illinois. Networking, network protocols, network management.

June M. Donato, Assistant Professor and Research Staff Member, Computer Science and Mathematics Division, Oak Ridge National Laboratory; Ph.D., UCLA. Information discovery, visualization, computational science, numerical methods, computational science and distributed computing.

Thomas H. Dunigan, Associate Professor and Staff Research Scientist at Oak Ridge National Laboratory; Ph.D., North Carolina at Chapel Hill. Operating systems, networks, parallel programming.

Sara R. Jordan, Associate Professor and Project Manager at Lockheed Martin Energy Systems, Inc.; Ph.D., Wisconsin. Advanced information technologies, information architectures.

Steven L. Lee, Assistant Professor and Staff Member, Mathematical Sciences Section, Oak Ridge National Laboratory; Ph.D., Illinois. Iterative linear equation solvers, differential-algebraic equations, preconditioning techniques, parallel computing.

Ronald P. Leinius, Professor and Director of Computing and Telecommunications Services at Lockheed Martin Energy Systems, Inc. (retired); Ph.D., Wisconsin. Operating systems, architecture, formal languages.

Reinhold C. Mann, Associate Professor and Section Head of Intelligent Systems Section at Oak Ridge National Laboratory; Dipl.Math., Dr.rer.nat., Mainz (Germany). Computer vision, pattern recognition, intelligent multisensor systems for mobile robots, nonlinear dynamical systems, parallel computing.

William McClain, Associate Professor and Staff Member, Technical Oversight Organization, Computing and Telecommunications Services at Lockheed Martin Energy Systems, Inc. (retired); Ph.D., Tennessee. Networks, data security, digital circuits, architecture, database management systems.

Noel Nachtigal, Assistant Professor and 1993 Householder Fellow at Oak Ridge National Laboratory; Ph.D., MIT. Numerical linear algebra, sparse matrix computations, iterative solution of linear systems.

Esmond Ng, Professor and Computer Scientist in the Mathematical Sciences Section at Oak Ridge National Laboratory; Ph.D., Waterloo. Sparse matrix computations, numerical linear algebra, parallel computing.

Nageswara S. V. Rao, Assistant Professor and Research Staff Member, Center for Engineering Systems Advanced Research, Oak Ridge National Laboratory; Ph.D., LSU. Massively parallel stochastic approximation algorithms, robot path planning algorithms, distributed sensor systems, fault diagnoses, parallel and distributed computing, application algorithms.

Charles H. Romine, Associate Professor and Research Staff Member at Oak Ridge National Laboratory; Ph.D., Virginia. Numerical linear algebra, parallel computing, analysis of parallel numerical algorithms, development of software environments for parallel computing.

Richard F. Sincovec, Professor and Division Director of Computer Science and Mathematics Division at Oak Ridge National Laboratory; Ph.D., Iowa State. Scientific computing, parallel algorithms and software, software engineering.

Carmen J. Trammell, Assistant Professor; Ph.D., Tennessee. Software engineering processes, methods, environments, and standards.

UNIVERSITY OF TEXAS AT ARLINGTON

COLLEGE OF ENGINEERING
DEPARTMENT OF COMPUTER SCIENCE AND ENGINEERING

PROGRAMS OF STUDY

The Department of Computer Science and Engineering offers graduate programs leading to Master of Science, Master of Computer Science, Master of Engineering, Master of Software Engineering (M.Sw.E.), and Doctor of Philosophy degrees. Studies may be pursued over a spectrum of areas covering computer architecture, database systems, fault-tolerant computing, image processing, intelligent systems, parallel processing, operating systems, real-time systems, and software engineering. The M.S. is a thesis degree that requires a minimum of 31 semester hours, of which at least 24 hours must be in approved course work and 6 hours in thesis. The M.Comp.Sci. and M.Engr. require at least 37 semester hours of approved course work, which may include a 6-semester-hour master's project. The M.Sw.E. is a practice-oriented program requiring a minimum of 37 semester hours of course work that includes an 18-hour core, 6 hours of design studio courses, and the remainder in approved electives. The Ph.D. is a research-oriented degree that has no specific course or credit-hour requirements and usually takes three years of full-time study after the master's degree.

RESEARCH FACILITIES

The University operates a wide spectrum of computing systems, which include IBM, Digital, and Convex mainframes; Sun and Digital workstations; and Macintosh and DOS personal computers. The department operates a multiuser VAX, a Sequent S27, a Sun-4/490 SPARCserver, a 128-processor nCube, and several clusters of UNIX workstations and personal computers. Most computers on campus are connected to a local area network and are accessible from both on and off campus. The department also operates laboratories supporting the design and development of microcomputer-based and/or special-purpose digital systems. The UTA Automation and Robotics Research Institute offers networks of workstations, robots, and other facilities for use by department students and faculty members with interests in robotics and automated manufacturing.

FINANCIAL AID

Teaching assistantships and research assistantships are available in limited numbers to qualified students. Unconditional admittance to the program is required for a student to be eligible for an assistantship. Stipends range from $4500 to $9000 for nine months. Assistant instructorships are sometimes available for qualified students in the final stages of a Ph.D. program. Part-time employment is often available for full-time students who are not receiving assistantships or other financial support from the University.

COST OF STUDY

For 1997–98, tuition and fees for a 12-semester-hour load are $1452 per semester for Texas residents and $4104 per semester for nonresidents. Half-time teaching or research assistants qualify for Texas resident rates. One-time fees include a general property deposit of $10, a diploma fee of $10, a library fee of $15, a thesis or dissertation binding fee of $22.50, and a thesis or dissertation microfilming fee of $40 or $50, respectively. Tuition and fees are subject to change by legislative or administrative action.

LIVING AND HOUSING COSTS

University apartments are available at rates ranging from $282 to $500 per month. Dormitory rooms range from $694 to $803 per semester. Numerous private apartments are available.

STUDENT GROUP

Enrollment at the University is 18,098, with students coming from forty-five states and sixty-five countries. College of Engineering enrollment is 2,485, including approximately 350 undergraduates and 350 graduate students in computer science and engineering. About 150 of the graduate students are full-time, with about 75 of them receiving financial support from the department. Most of the part-time students are practicing computer scientists or engineers pursuing advanced degrees.

STUDENT OUTCOMES

Alumni are employed in attractive academic positions and exciting jobs in leading companies throughout the state and the nation, including AT&T, E-Systems, Fujitsu, Lockheed-Martin, Motorola, NASA–Johnson Space Center, Nortel (Bell Northern Research), and Texas Instruments.

LOCATION

Arlington has a population of more than 280,000 and is within a few minutes' driving time of either Dallas or Fort Worth. The metropolitan area offers a variety of cultural and recreational opportunities.

THE UNIVERSITY AND THE DEPARTMENT

The University is located on a modern 347-acre campus in the center of the Dallas–Fort Worth metropolitan area. The University was founded in 1895 as Arlington College, a small private liberal arts school. The college changed with the times and its surroundings, undergoing a succession of names and affiliations until 1967, when it became the University of Texas at Arlington (UTA). Currently, UTA is the fifth-largest institution of higher learning in the state of Texas. The College of Engineering consists of six departments, including Computer Science and Engineering. The graduate degree programs in computer science and computer engineering were started in 1973 and were administered by the Department of Industrial Engineering until formation of the Department of Computer Science and Engineering in 1979.

APPLYING

Applications for admission to the program should be submitted to the Graduate School at least two months (U.S. students) or four months (international students) prior to the start of new student registration for the semester in which the student plans to enroll. Students seeking financial support should submit applications for admission and for support by March 1 for fall or by October 1 for spring enrollment. Applications for financial support should be submitted to the CSE department. General requirements for acceptance to the master's programs include a minimum combined quantitative and verbal GRE score of 1150 and a minimum GPA of 3.0 out of 4.0 for the last 60 hours of undergraduate course work. The Ph.D. program requires a minimum combined quantitative and verbal GRE score of 1250 and a GPA of 3.5 out of 4.0 for master's-level course work. All international students must submit a TOEFL score. International students who do not meet the above GRE combined score requirements may be accepted if their quantitative scores exceed 750 for the master's programs or 780 for the Ph.D. program. Students whose primary language is not English must have scored 250 or higher on the TSE-A or SPEAK in order to be eligible for a teaching assistantship.

CORRESPONDENCE AND INFORMATION

For catalogs and application forms:
Graduate School
University of Texas at Arlington
P.O. Box 19088, UTA Station
Arlington, Texas 76019
Telephone: 817-272-2688
E-mail: graduate.school@uta.edu

For departmental information:
Graduate Advisor
Department of Computer Science and Engineering
University of Texas at Arlington
P.O. Box 19015, UTA Station
Arlington, Texas 76019
Telephone: 817-272-3785
E-mail: csegrad@cse.uta.edu
World Wide Web: http://www-cse.uta.edu

UNIVERSITY OF TEXAS AT ARLINGTON

THE FACULTY AND THEIR RESEARCH

Carl T. Bruggeman, Assistant Professor; Ph.D., Indiana, 1995. Programming languages, compilers, computer architecture.

Eric J. Byrne, Assistant Professor; Ph.D., Kansas State, 1993. Software engineering, software maintenance, software reengineering, program comprehension, software processes.

Bill D. Carroll, Professor and Chairman; Ph.D., Texas at Austin, 1969. Fault-tolerant computing, computer architecture, distributed computing.

Diane J. Cook, Associate Professor; Ph.D., Illinois at Urbana–Champaign, 1990. Machine learning, planning, parallel algorithms.

Ramez A. Elmasri, Professor; Ph.D., Stanford, 1980. Databases, temporal databases, distributed and multidatabase systems.

Leonidas Fegaras, Assistant Professor; Ph.D., Massachusetts at Amherst, 1993. Databases, programming languages.

Piotr J. Gmytrasiewicz, Assistant Professor; Ph.D., Michigan, 1992. Artificial intelligence, multiagent coordination and communication, planning.

Karan A. Harbison, Associate Professor; Ph.D., Texas at Arlington, 1986. Real-time knowledge-based system, artificial intelligence.

Lawrence B. Holder, Associate Professor; Ph.D., Illinois at Urbana–Champaign, 1991. Artificial intelligence, machine learning, knowledge acquisition, parallel computing.

Pei Hsia, Professor; Ph.D., Texas at Austin, 1972. Software engineering, requirements engineering, scenario-based prototyping, incremental delivery, object-oriented software testing, formal languages.

Farhad A. Kamangar, Associate Professor; Ph.D., Texas at Arlington, 1980. Artificial intelligence, computer graphics, digital signal/image processing, neural networks, time series analysis.

David C. Kung, Professor; Ph.D., Norwegian Institute of Technology, 1984. Object-oriented software testing, object-oriented real-time systems, modeling and verification.

Lynn L. Peterson, Professor and Associate Dean; Ph.D., Texas Health Science Center at Dallas, 1978. Artificial intelligence, computer-based instructional systems, medical computer science.

Chien-Chung Shen, Assistant Professor; Ph.D., UCLA, 1992. Networks, operating systems, distributed systems.

Behrooz Shirazi, Professor and Associate Chairman; Ph.D., Oklahoma, 1985. Software development tools, computer architecture, parallel and distributed processing, task allocation and load balancing.

L. David Umbaugh, Senior Lecturer; Ph.D., Ohio State, 1983. Computer networks and data communications, systems programming.

Roger S. Walker, Professor; Ph.D., Texas at Austin, 1972. Digital signal processing, microcomputer applications.

Bob P. Weems, Associate Professor; Ph.D., Northwestern, 1984. Parallel algorithms, parallel processing, automated deduction, relational dependency theory.

Lonnie R. Welch, Associate Professor; Ph.D., Ohio State, 1990. Parallel and distributed computing, real-time systems, software and systems engineering, metrics and measurement, object-oriented methods, fault tolerance and compilers.

Hee Yong Youn, Associate Professor; Ph.D., Massachusetts at Amherst, 1988. Parallel and distributed computing, computer architecture, fault-tolerant computing, multimedia systems.

UNIVERSITY OF TEXAS AT ARLINGTON

DEPARTMENT OF ELECTRICAL ENGINEERING

PROGRAMS OF STUDY

The Department of Electrical Engineering offers graduate programs leading to the M.S. and Ph.D. degrees. Course work and research are offered in the following areas: applied physical electronics; control and robotics; digital signal and image processing; digital and microcomputer systems; electromagnetic fields and remote sensing; energy systems; manufacturing systems; microelectronics and semiconductors; microwave, millimeter-wave, and optoelectronic devices; optics and electrooptics; telecommunications; and VLSI design and implementation.

The master's degree is normally completed in two years and requires 24 hours of course work and 6 hours of thesis work. A nonthesis option may also be selected.

The Ph.D. program requires additional course work, the passing of a written diagnostic exam and a qualifying exam, and successful defense of the Ph.D. dissertation. The average time for completion is about three years beyond the Master of Science degree in engineering.

RESEARCH FACILITIES

Equipment for graduate student research in electrical engineering is spread over 67,000 square feet of space in four buildings, plus another 48,000 square feet in the Automation and Robotics Research Center. Specific equipment is listed on the reverse side of this page. Major research centers and faculty groups include the following: Center for Electronics, Materials, Devices, and Systems; Wave Scattering Research Center; Energy Systems Research Center; Human Performance Institute; Applied Physical Electronics Research Center; Electro-Optics Research Laboratory; Telecommunications and Signal and Image Processing Laboratories; Image Processing and Neural Networks Laboratory; and the Automation and Robotics Research Institute. In addition, several graduate projects involve work at local industries and at the University of Texas Southwestern Medical School at Dallas. Computing facilities are accessible over campuswide Ethernet and dial-up modems and include Sun and HP UNIX workstations, PC and Macintosh networks, a multiuser VAX, and a Convex mainframe.

FINANCIAL AID

Aid is available in the form of fellowships, research assistantships, and teaching assistantships. Stipends vary from $6300 to $24,000 for the calendar year, with recipients paying Texas resident tuition. Approximately ninety stipends are awarded each year.

COST OF STUDY

In 1997–98, tuition and fees for 12 credit hours are $1452 for Texas residents and $4104 for nonresident students each semester. Half-time teaching or research assistants and holders of competitive fellowships are entitled to Texas resident rates.

LIVING AND HOUSING COSTS

University apartments are available at rates ranging from $255 to $512 per month. Dormitory rooms range from $714 to $826 per semester. University food service plans are available. Numerous private apartments are available at a wide range of prices. Rates are subject to change.

STUDENT GROUP

There are approximately 300 M.S. and 100 Ph.D. students in electrical engineering and a total of 19,000 students at UT Arlington. Approximately half of the electrical engineering graduate students attend full-time, while many others are employed part-time in local industry.

STUDENT OUTCOMES

Students completing advanced degrees are actively recruited by the area's sizeable electronics, telecommunications, and aerospace industries. Recent graduates have been employed by Motorola, Nortel, Lucent Technologies, Ericsson Radio Systems, Hughes Training, Texas Instruments, E-Systems, and National Semiconductor.

LOCATION

The city of Arlington, 15 miles south of the Dallas–Fort Worth Airport, is located in the heart of the Dallas–Fort Worth metroplex, one of the fastest-growing areas in the nation. Dallas, 20 miles to the east, is a cosmopolitan city of tall buildings, distribution centers, fashion and technology-based industries, and the arts. Fort Worth, once a city of the Old West, 10–15 miles to the west of Arlington, now has art museums and many cultural activities as well as a variety of industries. Arlington is the home of the Texas Rangers and Six Flags over Texas. The area offers, in addition to campus activities, a full range of cultural and recreational opportunities, including museums, concerts, ballet, theater, amusement parks, and professional sports.

THE UNIVERSITY AND THE DEPARTMENT

The University of Texas at Arlington is located on a modern 300-acre campus a few blocks from downtown Arlington. Arlington State originated in 1895 as Arlington College, a private liberal arts institution; its founders located it "far from the temptations of city life." The school changed with the times and its surroundings. The final name change came in 1967 when the institution became the University of Texas at Arlington. The high-technology industries in telecommunications, electronics, and aerospace are helping to shape the College of Engineering into a premier high-tech research and education center. The department has 27 faculty members.

APPLYING

Students holding a B.S. degree in electrical engineering with a minimum upper-level grade point average of 3.0 (on a scale of 4.0) and a minimum combined GRE score of 1100 on the verbal and quantitative sections of the General Test are invited to apply for admission.

Applications for admission should be submitted by April 1 for the fall semester and November 1 for the spring semester. Admission materials can be obtained from the Graduate School office. Applicants for financial aid should submit a financial aid application directly to the department by March 1 to be considered for fall awards; applicants should also include copies of transcripts and GRE scores.

CORRESPONDENCE AND INFORMATION

For catalogs and application forms:
Graduate School
University of Texas at Arlington
Arlington, Texas 76019
Telephone: 817-272-2688

For department information:
Graduate Advisor
Department of Electrical Engineering
University of Texas at Arlington
Arlington, Texas 76019-0016
Telephone: 817-272-2671
Fax: 817-272-2253
World Wide Web: http://www-ee.uta.edu

UNIVERSITY OF TEXAS AT ARLINGTON
THE FACULTY AND THEIR RESEARCH

Kambiz Alavi, Professor; Ph.D., MIT, 1981. Molecular-beam epitaxy, heterojunction, quantum well and superlattice devices.

Jonathan W. Bredow, Associate Professor; Ph.D., Kansas, 1989. Radar systems design and remote sensing.

Ronald L. Carter, Professor; Ph.D., Michigan State, 1971. Semiconductor device physics, modeling and simulation, semiconductor electronics manufacturing.

Mo-Shing Chen, Professor; Ph.D., Texas, 1962. Power systems transmission, distribution, and generation.

Michal P. Chwialkowski, Associate Professor; Ph.D., Warsaw Technical, 1982. Digital instrumentation, magnetic resonance imaging.

W. Alan Davis, Associate Professor; Ph.D., Michigan, 1971. Microwave devices and circuits.

Venkat Devarajan, Associate Professor; Ph.D., Texas at Arlington, 1980. Image processing applications, including flight simulation, digital photogrammetry, virtual reality, and virtual prototyping.

Atam P. Dhawan, Professor; Ph.D., Manitoba, 1985. Medical imaging, intelligent biomedical image analysis, artificial neural networks, wavelet processing, pattern recognition.

William E. Dillon, Associate Professor; Ph.D., Texas at Arlington, 1972. Energy conversion, space power.

Jack Fitzer, Professor and Chairman; D.Sc., Washington (St. Louis), 1962. Controls and robotics, energy conversion.

Adrian K. Fung, Professor; Ph.D., Kansas, 1965. Wave scattering, radar image simulation and interpretation, remote sensing of air pollution.

Lloyd B. Gordon, Assistant Professor; Ph.D., Texas Tech, 1983. Space power, pulsed power, electrical insulation, electrical safety.

George V. Kondraske, Professor; Ph.D., Texas at Arlington and Texas Health Science Center at Dallas, 1982. Microprocessor-based instrumentation, software systems, human sensory and motor functions.

Wei-Jen Lee, Associate Professor; Ph.D., Texas at Arlington, 1985. Power system stability, power system protection, load flow analysis.

Frank L. Lewis, Professor; Ph.D., Georgia Tech, 1981. Systems and controls, robotics, adaptive systems, nonlinear systems, neural networks, manufacturing.

Menahem Lowy, Associate Professor; Ph.D., Berkeley, 1983. VLSI and ultralow power applications, digital signal processing.

Robert Magnusson, Professor; Ph.D., Georgia Tech, 1976. Diffractive optics, holography, electrooptics, integrated optics.

Theresa A. Maldonado, Associate Professor; Ph.D., Georgia Tech, 1990. Electrooptics, integrated optics, nonlinear optics.

Michael T. Manry, Professor; Ph.D., Texas at Austin, 1976. Digital signal and image processing, neural networks.

John H. McElroy, Professor; Ph.D., Catholic University, 1978. Communication satellites, earth observations.

Vasant K. Prabhu, Professor; Sc.D., MIT, 1966. Telecommunications, digital portable and cellular radio networks.

K. R. Rao, Professor; Ph.D., New Mexico, 1966. Digital signal and image processing, orthogonal transforms.

Raymond R. Shoults, Professor; Ph.D., Texas at Arlington, 1974. Electric power systems, computer methods.

Charles V. Smith Jr., Professor and Associate Chairman; Ph.D., MIT, 1968. Continuum electromagnetics, energy conversion.

Saibun Tjuatja, Assistant Professor; Ph.D., Texas at Arlington, 1992. Remote sensing of the environment, wave scattering and propagation, wireless communications, radar image processing and interpretation.

Kai-Shing Yeung, Professor; Dr.Ing., Karlsruhe (Germany), 1977. Nonlinear control, systems theory, robotics.

RESEARCH LABORATORIES AND FACILITIES

Applied Physical Electronics. Facilities include a space environment chamber; power modulator laboratory; optoelectronics laboratory with ns-Nd:YAG, ns-Nd:Glass, cw-argon ion, ps-Nd:YAG, and ns-Copper Vapor lasers; multichannel, multi-GHz transient digitizer; and time-resolved spectroscopic systems.

Controls, Robotics, and Manufacturing. UTA's Automation and Robotics Research Institute (ARRI) is a 48,000-square-foot off-campus extension housing robotics labs, intelligent material handling stations, and controls labs with industrial motion system test beds and real-time controllers capable of implementing advanced algorithms, including feedback linearization, adaptive control, neural net and fuzzy logic control. Supervisory controllers are capable of implementing discrete event rule-based control algorithms for dispatching shared resources and part routing with deadlock avoidance.

Electro-Optics. Facilities include many common laser systems (argon-ion, Nd:YAG [cw and pulsed], He-Ne, Ti:sapphire, He-Cd, CO_2); optics isolation tables; spectral analysis equipment; power and energy meters; wavemeters; and optical fabrication, testing, and control equipment.

High-Frequency Circuits and Devices. Facilities include a class 10/100 GaAs clean room with Karl Suss UV aligner, rapid thermal processor, reactive ion etch, scanning electron microscope, e-beam evaporator and sputter deposition; Varian GEN II modular molecular-beam epitaxy with e-beam evaporator and Auger analysis; automated microwave network analyzers, 45 MHz-60 GHz, 90-100 GHz; time domain reflectometry; cascade wafer probes; 250X step and repeat photomask facilities; DC measurement and analyzer facilities; and CAD design and simulation facilities: HP, Super Compact, Touchstone, Harmonica, etc.

Image Processing and Neural Networks. Facilities include a Panasonic FX-RS307U high-resolution image scanner, a Sony TV camera with Data Translation frame grabber, and extensive libraries of image processing and neural network simulation software that have been developed in the lab. The lab has access to a model 6400 nCUBE 2 parallel processing computer, a Convex, and Sun4 workstations.

Medical Imaging. Facilities are available through the Magnetic Resonance Imaging Center, UTSWMC Dallas, and include three clinical MR scanners (0.35, 0.5 Tesla, and a high-performance EPI-capable 1.5 Tesla instrument). In addition, an ultra-high-field 4.7 Tesla research-only instrument is available for animal studies. Computing facilities include Stardent and several SPARC and DEC-Alpha workstations as well as two LANs with a total of twenty-five high-end PCs.

Power Systems. Facilities include a unique physical scale model power system simulation laboratory complete with an Energy Management System (EMS), protective relaying, 1,050 miles of AC transmission lines, 700 miles of DC transmission lines, power plant models (M-G sets), actual load models, and digital computer-based load control; a state-of-the-art digital computer-based Black-Start Training Simulator; and numerous sophisticated computer analysis programs, including power flow analysis, transient stability analysis, and dynamic stability analysis.

Remote Sensing and Wave Scattering. There are a bistatic RCS measurement facility, 2–20 GHz, fully polarimetric imaging capability; a 75–110 GHz spectrometer; a bistatic laser scattering (663 nm) measurement system; an open-path Fourier transform infrared (FT-IR) spectrometer and a long-path ultraviolet spectrometer for environmental monitoring.

Robotics and Controls. There are digital control, vision, laser ranging, and force sensing systems; Puma and Adept robots; modular assembly components; abrasive water jet cutting; automated machining and reverse engineering; and CAD and simulation software: CADAM, CATIA, SILMA, custom human performance instrumentation, and DAP.

Signal Processing and Telecommunications. Facilities include extensive communication system simulation software on UNIX workstations, a TAAC-1 image and array processing module, high-resolution color displays, 560 Mb/s long-haul fiber-optic terminals, and an operational 150 Mb/s fiber-optic system including two duplex video channels with additional T1 Service over a 10-mile path.

Virtual Environment. An International Imaging Systems' M-75/S-600 suite and a Sun Workstation running a current version of Khoros and KBVISION provide the visual database tools. Two Hughes Micropoly-II image generation systems and Rend386 running on a 486DX-66 allow real-time rendering. A PowerGlove and stereo viewer are also available.

VLSI Design. A cluster of HP 700 family workstations is available with a complete set of Mentor Graphics tools that includes a Versatec plotter. Fabrication done by MOSIS or at industrial companies, if available.

UNIVERSITY OF TEXAS AT AUSTIN

DEPARTMENT OF COMPUTER SCIENCES

PROGRAMS OF STUDY

The Department of Computer Sciences offers programs leading to the M.S.C.S., M.A., and Ph.D. degrees. Programs provide students with a broad education in the various areas of computer sciences and allow specialization through a thesis. The master's program with thesis requires 30 semester hours of course work. The M.S.C.S. is a nonthesis option and requires 36 hours of course work. The Ph.D. requires 18 semester hours of general course work and about 15 more in the area of specialization. This is followed by an examination (based on the student's preliminary dissertation proposal) and by a dissertation.

RESEARCH FACILITIES

Many different computer systems are available for research use by faculty members and graduate students in the department. Machines available for parallel processing research include a four-processor SPARC 20, an eleven-processor IBM SP2 server, an Intel Paragon XP/E model 4, a four-processor IBM SP2 that was donated to the department by IBM in fall 1995 and upgraded in fall 1996, and 2 four-processor Sun Enterprise 5000 machines donated by Sun in spring 1997. The department has a Silicon Graphics Indigo 2, an SGI Indy, and six SGI O2s for graphics research. Five Pentium 90s with video conferencing and video compression and a Duo Pentium server, donated by Intel, are dedicated to multimedia research. Other research workstations include more than fifty Sun SPARC workstations, twenty-five Sun Ultra workstations, a DECstation 3000/600 Alpha/AXP, and six IBM RS6000s. In addition, there are fifty-three IBM Xstation 140s and seven PowerServer 25Ts donated by IBM in faculty member and graduate offices. There is also a network of more than seventy-five microcomputers, located in graduate offices, consisting of Macintosh Quadras, Dell 486s, and Pentium machines. In fall 1996, the department was awarded an NSF CISE grant with a total of $1.6 million to be devoted to the research infrastructure of the department. All departmental computers are networked together using Ethernet, with several server and research subnets of 100 Mbps. There is also an ATM research subnet. Network servers include a Sun Enterprise 4000 with more than 150 gigabytes of disk capacity that is used for home directory service, a Sun SPARC 1000e Web server, many file servers, laser print servers, and communications servers. The department continues to expand these existing departmental computing facilities, both through donations of equipment from manufacturers and also through funds provided by the University.

The equipment mentioned above is used for research; there is substantial additional equipment for educational computing.

FINANCIAL AID

The Doctoral Fellows program provides $1250 per month for twenty-four months for new Ph.D. students. Two semesters as a teaching assistant are required. The remaining fifteen months leave the student free for course work and preliminary research.

The department also employs students as research and teaching assistants at a minimum starting salary of $1109 per month. The computation center has opportunities for qualified students as systems programmers and consultants, and local industries such as MCC, IBM, TI, Schlumberger, and Motorola employ students on a part-time basis. Low-interest loans are also available.

COST OF STUDY

In 1996–97, tuition and fees for 9 credit hours were approximately $1229 per semester for Texas residents and $3155 per semester for nonresidents.

LIVING AND HOUSING COSTS

The cost of a dormitory room averages $4235 for nine months (including board). University housing for married students ranges in cost from $340 to $500 per month. Private housing is available in all price ranges.

STUDENT GROUP

There are 185 graduate students in computer sciences; more than half of them are Ph.D. candidates. The department confers thirty to thirty-five master's degrees and fifteen to twenty Ph.D. degrees annually.

LOCATION

Austin, a metropolitan area of approximately 485,000 people, is set in the scenic Hill Country of central Texas. The Colorado River, which flows through the city, has been dammed to form the chain of Highland Lakes, which provide opportunities for swimming, boating, and fishing. There are many fine parks and playgrounds. Austin also has five theater groups, several ballet troupes, an excellent symphony orchestra, and about fifty art galleries.

THE UNIVERSITY AND THE DEPARTMENT

The University of Texas, founded in 1883, is one of the largest universities in the country, with an enrollment of more than 48,000 on the Austin campus alone. There are other branches of the University in Houston, Galveston, San Antonio, and Dallas.

The graduate program in computer sciences was initiated in 1966. The undergraduate program was started in 1974 and has grown to include more than 1,600 computer sciences majors.

APPLYING

The department deadline for fall applications is January 2. Although the University deadline for graduate students' applications is February 1, all applicants are urged to submit materials by January 2. Financial aid applications should also be submitted by January 2. Applications are accepted for the spring semester, and the deadline for spring admission is September 1 for all applicants. The GRE General Test and Subject Test in computer science are required of all applicants. International applicants are strongly urged to take the TOEFL. Admission standards are high. Normally, a student admitted to the Ph.D. program has a bachelor's degree in computer science, at least a 3.5 GPA, a combined verbal and quantitative GRE score of at least 1400, and a minimum score of 85 percent on the computer science Subject Test.

In addition to obtaining information and application forms, all applicants should notify the graduate admissions secretary of the Department of Computer Sciences of their application and should ask the graduate admissions secretary to send them a *Graduate Information Bulletin* containing the most current information about applications and the department. (The graduate school catalog from the admissions office does not always have the most up-to-date information.)

When contacting the admissions office for an application, students should specify the type of application needed: U.S./permanent resident or international.

CORRESPONDENCE AND INFORMATION

For application forms and further information:

Graduate Admissions
Department of Computer Sciences
University of Texas at Austin
Austin, Texas 78712-1188

E-mail: csadmis@cs.utexas.edu
World Wide Web: http://www.cs.utexas.edu

UNIVERSITY OF TEXAS AT AUSTIN

THE FACULTY AND THEIR RESEARCH

The following list is limited to those faculty members whose primary appointment is in the Department of Computer Sciences.

Lorenzo Alvisi. Distributed computing and fault tolerance in distributed systems.

Don Batory. Software architectures, extensible and object-oriented databases, domain modeling, software system generators.

Robert Blumofe. Parallel computation, combinatorial approximation and optimization algorithms, communication networks, and operating systems.

Robert S. Boyer. Program verification, automatic theorem proving, artificial intelligence.

James C. Browne. Parallel computation, with the major focus on parallel programming, high-level specification languages, and integration of computer science with application areas.

Jeffrey A. Brumfield. Performance analysis, distributed systems, operating systems.

Alan K. Cline. Mathematical software and numerical analysis.

Michael D. Dahlin. Operating systems, distributed systems, networking.

Edsger Wybe Dijkstra. Program correctness, algorithms, systems.

Chris C. Edmondson-Yurkanan. Computer networks, computer science education, managing large software projects, mobile networking, database design.

E. Allen Emerson. Formal methods, logics and semantics of programs, concurrent and distributed computing.

Donald S. Fussell. Computer architecture, computer graphics, VLSI systems design, database concurrency control.

Suzy C. Gallagher. Computer science education, library and information processing.

Mohamed Gawdat Gouda. Distributed and concurrent computing, fault-tolerant computing, computer networks, network protocols.

Roy M. Jenevein Jr. Interconnection networks and parallel processing in computer architecture.

David R. Kincaid. Mathematical software, high-performance computers, numerical analysis.

Benjamin J. Kuipers. Artificial intelligence, robotics, qualitative reasoning.

Simon S. Lam. Network protocols, performance models, formal verification methods, security.

Vladimir Lifschitz. Mathematical logic, logic programming, knowledge representation.

Calvin Lin. Compilers and languages for parallel computing, parallel performance analysis, and scientific computing.

Risto Miikkulainen. Neural networks, natural language processing, cognitive modeling.

Daniel P. Miranker. Parallel computer architecture, active/expert database system, high-performance artificial intelligence systems.

Jayadev Misra. Parallel programming.

Aloysius K. Mok. Fault-tolerant hard-real-time systems, system architecture, computer-aided system design tools, software engineering.

Raymond J. Mooney. Artificial intelligence, machine learning, natural language understanding.

Gordon S. Novak Jr. Artificial intelligence, automatic programming, physics problem solving, expert systems, compilers.

C. Greg Plaxton. Parallel computation, analysis of algorithms, lower bounds, randomization.

Bruce W. Porter. Artificial intelligence, machine learning, knowledge-based systems.

Vijaya Ramachandran. Design and analysis of algorithms, parallel computation, computational complexity.

Hamilton Richards Jr. Functional programming, concurrent processing, object-oriented programming.

Robert A. van de Geijn. Numerical analysis, high-performance parallel computing.

Harrick M. Vin. Multimedia systems, high-speed networking, databases, mobile computing, distributed systems.

John S. Werth. Parallel programming, software engineering, compilers, computer science education.

Laurie Honour Werth. Software engineering, cognitive science.

Paul R. Wilson. Design and implementation of programming languages, operating systems, and debuggers; memory hierarchies.

Martin D. F. Wong. Computer-aided design of VLSI, design and analysis of algorithms.

David M. Young. Numerical analysis, partial differential equations, numerical linear algebra.

David I. Zuckerman. Role of randomness in computation, complexity theory, design and analysis of algorithms.

UNIVERSITY OF TEXAS AT AUSTIN

DEPARTMENT OF ELECTRICAL AND COMPUTER ENGINEERING

PROGRAMS OF STUDY

The Department of Electrical and Computer Engineering offers programs leading to the degrees of Master of Science in Engineering and Doctor of Philosophy. Advanced studies may be pursued in the following technical areas: biomedical engineering, computer engineering (including software engineering), electromagnetics and acoustics, energy systems, manufacturing systems engineering, plasma/quantum electronics/optics, solid-state electronics, and telecommunications and information systems engineering.

The master's degree program is normally completed in 1–1½ years with the completion of either 30 semester hours of course work, including a 6-semester-hour thesis, or 33 semester hours of course work, including a 3-semester-hour report. A no-thesis/no-report option is also available upon completion of 36 hours of course work.

The Ph.D. program requires the passing of an oral and/or written qualifying examination, the completion of an individualized program of course work as set by the Qualifying Examination Committee, and the completion and final oral defense of the Ph.D. dissertation. The average time for completion is about three years beyond the Master of Science in Engineering degree.

RESEARCH FACILITIES

Equipment with capabilities approaching the state of the art is available for research in the computer and information systems, power, quantum electronics and optics, electromagnetics-acoustics, biomedical, and solid-state electronics areas. Major research centers where ECE graduate students perform thesis- and dissertation-related work include the Electronics Research Center, the Center for Energy Studies, the Center for Electromechanics, the Center for Fusion Engineering, the Electrical Engineering Research Laboratory, the Computer and Vision Research Center, the Microelectronics Research Center, the Computer Engineering Research Center, and the Applied Research Laboratories. The annual rate of state, federal, and industrial funding for research in the department is in excess of $15 million.

FINANCIAL AID

Financial support is available in the form of fellowships, research assistantships, and teaching assistantships. The large number of highly qualified applicants makes fellowship awards extremely competitive. These awards are mainly for the fall semester, and recipients are eligible for Texas-resident tuition. Research and teaching assistantships normally require the recipient to work 20 hours per week and take a course load of 9 semester hours. These stipends vary from approximately $7500 to $15,000 per calendar year. Recipients of 20-hours-per-week appointments are eligible for Texas-resident tuition.

COST OF STUDY

In 1997–98, Texas residents pay $1231 per semester in tuition and required fees for 9 semester credit hours, while nonresidents pay $3157 for 9 semester credit hours. Students awarded competitive fellowships or holding a half-time teaching assistantship or research assistantship automatically qualify for resident tuition. These amounts do not include advising fees, lab fees, or incidental or supplemental fees; these may add several hundred dollars to the total.

LIVING AND HOUSING COSTS

Both University and privately owned housing accommodations are available. University dormitory rates range from $3900 to $4100 for the 1997–98 academic year (nine months), depending on the type of room and board selected. University family apartments for married students vary in cost from $365 per month for an unfurnished one-bedroom unit to $535 for a modern three-bedroom apartment. Privately owned housing may be found in all price ranges. The temperate climate allows for casual, inexpensive dress. Prices for food and other necessities are reasonable.

STUDENT GROUP

There are approximately 500 graduate students in electrical and computer engineering at the University of Texas at Austin, representing nearly every part of the United States and the world. Although the majority of these are full-time students, a sizable number are employed in the growing electronics industries in and around Austin.

LOCATION

Located on the edge of the Texas hill country—a region with abundant lakes, forests, wildlife, recreational opportunities, and a Sun Belt climate—Austin has recently been cited in a number of national publications as one of the nation's most desirable places in which to live. With a population around 568,000, Austin is large enough to provide widely varied leisure and entertainment opportunities without some of the congestion characteristic of larger cities. Culturally, the city is a fascinating mix of Western, Southern, and Spanish influences. In earlier years, the economic activity in Austin stemmed primarily from the state government and the University, but in recent years there has been a rapid expansion of industrial activities dominated by plants and laboratories of major corporations, primarily in the electronics area.

THE UNIVERSITY AND THE DEPARTMENT

The University, with an enrollment of about 45,500, has all the intellectual and social characteristics one would associate with the main campus of the state university system in a large, populous state. There is a wide diversity in student backgrounds, life-styles, and goals. Many of the University's graduate and professional programs, including those in the Department of Electrical and Computer Engineering, have a high national standing.

The department consists of 62 faculty members whose research interests and expertise encompass nearly every specialty area within electrical and computer engineering.

APPLYING

January 2 is the departmental deadline date for summer, fall, and spring (of the following year) admissions and for consideration for financial assistance. The admission application, transcripts, GRE General Test scores, and TOEFL scores (international students only) must be submitted directly to the Graduate and International Admissions Center by the above deadline date. Copies of these official documents, plus additional materials required by the department, should be sent directly to the department by the January 2 deadline.

CORRESPONDENCE AND INFORMATION

Graduate Advisor
Department of Electrical and Computer Engineering
University of Texas at Austin, MC C0803
Austin, Texas 78712-1084
Telephone: 512-471-8510 or 8511

UNIVERSITY OF TEXAS AT AUSTIN
THE FACULTY AND THEIR RESEARCH

Biomedical Engineering

L. E. Baker, Ph.D. Biomedical engineering, physiology.

J. A. Pearce, Ph.D. Biomedical engineering, tissue thermal damage, thermographic imaging, electrosurgery, electrophysiology.

R. Richards-Kortum, Ph.D. Biomedical engineering, laser spectroscopy, light propagation in scattering media.

H. G. Rylander III, M.D. Biomedical engineering, transducers, visual information processing, lasers in medicine.

J. W. Valvano, Ph.D. Biomedical instrumentation, heat transfer in biological systems, applications of microcomputers.

A. J. Welch, Ph.D. Biomedical engineering, lasers in medicine, optical-thermal laser-tissue interaction.

Computer Engineering

J. A. Abraham, Ph.D. Fault-tolerant computing, VLSI design and test, formal verification, software engineering.

J. K. Aggarwal, Ph.D. Computer vision, image processing, pattern recognition, multimedia systems.

A. P. Ambler, Ph.D. Computer engineering, CAD for test and design for test, economics of test, safety-critical systems.

A. Aziz, Ph.D. Design automation for VLSI systems: logic synthesis and formal verification.

K. S. Barber, Ph.D. Knowledge-intensive planning and control, software engineering, agent-based systems.

C. M. Chase, Ph.D. Parallel computer architecture, distributed computing environments.

H. G. Cragon, B.S. Digital computer architecture.

B. L. Evans, Ph.D. Embedded systems; CAD tools; signal, image, and video processing.

V. K. Garg, Ph.D. Distributed systems, software engineering, control of discrete event systems.

J. Ghosh, Ph.D. Artificial neural systems, parallel processing, artificial intelligence machines.

M. J. Gonzalez, Ph.D. Computer architecture, distributed systems.

M. F. Jacome, Ph.D. CAD frameworks, design theory, X H/S codesign, design reuse.

L. K. John, Ph.D. Computer architecture, high-performance processors and memory systems, compiler optimization, reconfigurable computing.

G. J. Lipovski, Ph.D. Digital systems architecture, microcomputers, nonnumeric processors, hardware description languages.

A. Ricciardi, Ph.D. Fault-tolerant distributed systems; high-performance, wide-area applications; formal methods.

C. H. Roth, Ph.D. Microcomputer systems and applications, theory and design of digital systems.

E. E. Swartzlander, Ph.D. Architecture for application-specific processors, computer arithmetic, computer architecture.

N. A. Touba, Ph.D. VLSI design and test, CAD, fault-tolerant computing.

T. J. Wagner, Ph.D. Information theory, computers.

Electromagnetics and Acoustics

F. X. Bostick, Ph.D. Electronic systems, electromagnetic theory, electrical geoscience.

J. H. Davis, Ph.D. Radio astronomy instrumentation, microwave systems engineering.

M. D. Driga, Ph.D. Electromagnetic field theory, advanced computational electromagnetics.

E. L. Hixson, Ph.D. Electroacoustics, acoustics, noise control.

H. Ling, Ph.D. Computational electromagnetics, synthetic aperture radar imaging, automatic target identification.

D. P. Neikirk, Ph.D. Electromagnetics in integrated circuits and solid-state devices.

H. W. Smith, Ph.D. Electrical geophysics, digital data processing.

Energy Systems

R. Baldick, Ph.D. Optimization of power system operations, transmission regulatory policy, algorithms for discrete optimization.

M. L. Baughman, Ph.D. Engineering economics, electrical power economics, transmission pricing and planning.

J. R. Cogdell, Ph.D. Electromechanical systems.

M. D. Driga, Ph.D. Electromechanical systems, pulsed power systems, electromagnetic macroparticle accelerators.

W. M. Grady, Ph.D. Power systems analysis, electromagnetics, power system harmonics.

W. F. Weldon, M.S. Design of electromechanical systems, pulsed power technology, electromechanical accelerators.

Manufacturing Systems Engineering

K. S. Barber, Ph.D. Knowledge-intensive planning and control, software engineering and agent-based systems.

M. D. Driga, Ph.D. Intelligent robotics, application of electromagnetism to manufacturing processes.

R. H. Flake, Ph.D. Computer vision systems applied to manufacturing, nondestructive circuit test and characterization.

Plasma/Quantum Electronics/Optics

M. F. Becker, Ph.D. Optical materials, electrooptics.

J. C. Campbell, Ph.D. Optoelectronic devices, photonic integrated-circuit lightwave systems.

R. T. Chen, Ph.D. Optical interconnects, photonic integrated circuits, optical signal processing, holographic optical elements.

G. A. Hallock, Ph.D. Thermonuclear fusion, plasma diagnostics, plasma turbulence and transport, plasma processing.

E. J. Powers, Ph.D. Applications of digital time-series analysis to nonlinear-wave and turbulence phenomena.

Solid-State Electronics

S. K. Banerjee, Ph.D. Solid-state devices and materials.

A. B. Buckman, Ph.D. Optical sensors/transducers, fiber and guided-wave optics, optical properties of materials, semiconductor devices.

D. Deppe, Ph.D. Optoelectronic semiconductor devices.

R. D. Dupuis, Ph.D. Compound semiconductor materials and devices, metalorganic chemical vapor deposition, epitaxial growth.

J. B. Goodenough, Ph.D. Physics and chemistry of transition-metal compounds and their application, fast ionic transport, fuel cells.

D.-L. Kwong, Ph.D. VLSI technology, semiconductor process and device modeling, solid-state materials and devices.

J. C. Lee, Ph.D. Semiconductor devices, materials, and technologies, including advanced submicron structures.

C. M. Maziar, Ph.D. Solid-state devices and materials, device modeling and simulation.

B. G. Streetman, Ph.D. Semiconductor materials and devices.

A. F. Tasch, Ph.D. Semiconductor processes and devices, VLSI/ULSI technology, device/process modeling.

R. M. Walser, Ph.D. Solid-state devices and materials research.

Telecommunications and Information Systems Engineering

A. Arapostathis, Ph.D. Systems, nonlinear dynamical systems, controlled Markov chains, stochastic hybrid systems.

A. C. Bovik, Ph.D. Image processing, digital video, computer vision.

G. de Veciana, Ph.D. Analysis and design of telecommunication systems, applied probability, information theory.

T. Konstantopoulos, Ph.D. Stochastic systems, communication networks, applied probability, queueing theory, operations research.

S.-Q. Li, Ph.D. Telecommunication network theory, queueing theory, and traffic modeling in integrated services digital networks.

E. J. Powers, Ph.D. Applications of higher-order statistical and wavelet-based processing.

A. Ricciardi, Ph.D. Wide-area networks, high-performance large-scale systems.

I. W. Sandberg, Ph.D. Nonlinear systems, network and system theory.

G. L. Wise, Ph.D. Statistical communication theory, random processes, signal processing, probability theory, real analysis.

B. F. Womack, Ph.D. Computer engineering, biomedical engineering, adaptive control and cybernetics.

G. Xu, Ph.D. Wireless communications, digital signal processing, fast algorithms, microwave and RF engineering.

UNIVERSITY OF TEXAS AT DALLAS

ENGINEERING AND COMPUTER SCIENCE SCHOOL
COMPUTER SCIENCE PROGRAM

PROGRAMS OF STUDY

The Computer Science Program offers a broad range of computer science– and engineering-related courses leading to the M.S. and Ph.D. degrees. There are three separate tracks leading to an M.S. degree: traditional computer science, networks/telecommunications, and software engineering.

A total of 36 credit hours is required for the M.S. Normally, a student takes one year of full-time work or two years of part-time work to complete the M.S. degree requirements. A total of 90 credit hours and a Ph.D. dissertation are required for the Ph.D. Typically, a student takes four years of full-time work to complete the Ph.D. degree requirements.

RESEARCH FACILITIES

The Academic Computer Center maintains an IBM 4381 with a wide range of peripherals. The Engineering and Computer Science School has a Convex C-2 supercomputer and a high-speed link to the University of Texas System's CRAY YMP/864 in Austin. An Ethernet connects various components of the system. The Computer Science Program has an NCUBE with sixty-four processors, and faculty and graduate student offices are equipped with Sun Workstations, PCs with 486 and Pentium processing terminals, and similar equipment for personal use. There are PC laboratories and terminal rooms available for general student access to computing facilities. The Computer Science Program is also connected to national and international networks such as the Internet and CSnet. The University library contains a complete collection of computer science journals and other publications.

FINANCIAL AID

Financial aid is available in the form of scholarships, research and teaching assistantships, and work-study arrangements with local industry. In 1996–97, stipends for research and teaching assistantships at level 1 (entry level) were $944.44 per month and at level 2 (after Ph.D. written qualifying exam) were $1100 per month. Additional compensation is generally available in the summertime, as a full schedule of classes is usually offered each summer. There are several additional government-, University-, and industry-backed sources for the support of graduate students. Interested prospective students may write for specific information to the graduate secretary of the department, EC 3.1, University of Texas at Dallas.

COST OF STUDY

In 1995–96, tuition and fees for Texas residents were $1466.50 for 15 semester hours; for nonresident and international students, tuition and fees were $4346.50 for 15 semester hours.

LIVING AND HOUSING COSTS

The cost of an apartment varies from $300 per month to more than $500 per month. The University has a limited amount of housing. Some students find housing in neighboring apartment complexes.

STUDENT GROUP

There are more than 4,000 graduate students and about 4,000 undergraduate students at UTD, representing most states in the United States and many other countries. Freshman and sophomore students were admitted for the first time in fall 1990. A large number of the undergraduate and part-time graduate students work in industry in the surrounding high-technology corridor.

LOCATION

UTD is located on the north side of Richardson, a suburb about 17 miles north of downtown Dallas. The campus is surrounded by University-owned land that is often used for soccer, jogging, bicycle riding, and other recreational activities. There are several lakes in the Dallas and surrounding north Texas area. Dallas has museums, concert halls, a zoo, and other facilities that offer a rich cultural life to students and their families. The area is the home of many computer, electronics, and communication companies that are large supporters of UTD engineering and computer science programs.

THE UNIVERSITY AND THE PROGRAM

The University of Texas at Dallas was created in 1969 by an act of the Texas legislature that enabled the transfer of the Southwest Center for Advanced Studies to the state of Texas. The University began as a graduate school. The enrollment of undergraduate juniors and seniors began in 1975. Electrical engineering programs were approved in 1985. The Computer Science Program was part of the general program in mathematical sciences until 1982, when it became an independent program in the School of Natural Sciences and Mathematics. In 1986, the program became part of the new Engineering and Computer Science School. In 1992, the Computer Science Program moved into the Engineering and Computer Science Building, which is equipped with offices, laboratories, and working areas.

APPLYING

M.S. students should have a bachelor's degree that includes a full calculus sequence and the following: (1) a GPA of at least 3.0, (2) a combined GRE General Test score of at least 1100 or a quantitative GRE score of at least 750 and a TOEFL score of at least 550, and (3) a GPA in computer science, math, engineering, and related courses of at least 3.3.

Students seeking direct admission to the Ph.D. program (and not entering the M.S. program first) must satisfy the requirements stated above for M.S. students, plus either (1) have an M.S. degree with a GPA of at least 3.5, or (2) have a GPA of at least 3.5 in upperclass undergraduate and graduate (if any) courses and either a combined GRE General Test score of at least 1300 or a quantitative GRE score of at least 750 and a TOEFL score of at least 550.

Applications for admission and all supporting documents should be submitted well in advance of the preferred semester of entry. Since department awards for teaching assistantships, research assistantships, and other scholarships are usually made in the spring for the next full academic year, applicants requesting financial aid should submit all required documents as early as possible to ensure consideration. U.S. citizens and permanent residents pay a $25 application fee and international students pay a $75 application fee.

CORRESPONDENCE AND INFORMATION

Dr. Ivor Page, Chairman
Computer Science Program
EC 31
University of Texas at Dallas
Richardson, Texas 75083-0688
Telephone: 972-883-6810
Fax: 972-883-2349

UNIVERSITY OF TEXAS AT DALLAS
THE FACULTY AND THEIR RESEARCH

Ivor Page, Program Chairman; Ph.D., Brunel (England). Operating systems, computer architecture, computer graphics.

Wolfgang Bein, Ph.D., Osnabrück (Germany). Transportation problems, parallel computation.

Biao Chen, Ph.D., Texas A&M. Communication network protocols (ATM, FDDI, etc.), network management, fault tolerance, real-time systems, wireless networks, distributed systems, multimedia.

Lawrence Chung, Ph.D., Toronto. Software development.

G. R. Dattatreya, Ph.D., Indian Institute of Science. Pattern recognition, digital and statistical signal processing and applications, artificial intelligence, applied probabilistic systems, estimation theory, adaptive learning.

Martha Dinwiddie, Senior Lecturer; M.S., Texas at Dallas.

Michael Durbin, Senior Lecturer; M.S., Texas at Dallas.

Donald Evans, Senior Lecturer; Ph.D., North Texas State.

Dung T. Huynh, Ph.D., Saarlandes (Germany). Automata-based complexity theory and analysis of algorithms, including classification of the intrinsic complexity of computational problems and computational algebra.

Rym Mili, Ph.D., Ottawa. Software engineering, software reuse and reusability measures, software maintenance and reengineering, software metrics, formal specifications.

Simeon Ntafos, Ph.D., Northwestern. Software reliability, computational geometry, design automation, parallel algorithms.

William J. Pervin, Ph.D., Pittsburgh. Program verification, programming languages, numerical analysis, computer organization and operation.

Balaji Raghavachari, Ph.D., Penn State. Design and analysis of sequential and parallel algorithms, graphs and networks, combinatorial optimization, approximation algorithms, string matching.

Haim Schweitzer, Ph.D., Hebrew (Jerusalem). Artificial intelligence, algorithms, vision, learning, and neural networks.

I. Hal Sudborough, Ph.D., Penn State. Parallel computation, interconnection networks, VLSI layout and design, algorithms and their complexity, language and compiler theory, various computer models (automata theory), theory of computation.

Violet Syrotiuk, Ph.D., Waterloo. Distributed system and distributed database systems, computer networks.

Ioannis Tollis, Ph.D., Illinois at Urbana-Champaign. Computer-aided design for VLSI, VLSI computation, layout algorithms, computational geometry, parallel computation.

Klaus Truemper, Ph.D., Case Western Reserve. Combinatorics and artificial intelligence, network optimization, graph analysis, decomposition of graphs and matroids, design of algorithms and computer systems to control and schedule large-scale automated systems and mobile robots.

Subbarayan Venkatesan, Ph.D., Pittsburgh, Distributed processing systems, fault tolerance, distributed debugging, computer networks, distributed database systems.

A friendly group of students at the University.

Erik Jonsson School of Engineering and Computer Science.

A typical graduation day.

UNIVERSITY OF TEXAS AT DALLAS

ENGINEERING AND COMPUTER SCIENCE SCHOOL
PROGRAMS IN ELECTRICAL ENGINEERING AND COMPUTER SCIENCE

PROGRAM OF STUDY

The principal concentration areas for the Master of Science in Electrical Engineering (M.S.E.E) program are communications and signal processing engineering; digital systems engineering; wireless communication systems engineering; digital microelectronic systems engineering; optical devices, materials, and systems engineering; and solid-state devices and circuits engineering. Besides core courses, a comprehensive set of electives is available in each area. The M.S.E.E. requires a minimum of 33 semester hours. All students must have an academic adviser and an approved degree plan. These are based upon the student's choice of concentration area. Courses that are taken without adviser approval will not count toward the 33-semester-hour requirements. Successful completion of the approved course of study leads to the M.S.E.E., M.S.E.E.-Telecommunications, or M.S.E.E.-Microelectronics degree. The M.S.E.E. program has both a thesis and a nonthesis option. All part-time M.S.E.E. students are assigned initially to the nonthesis option. Those wishing to elect the thesis option may do so by obtaining the approval of a faculty thesis supervisor. All full-time, supported students are required to participate in the thesis option. The thesis option requires 6 semester hours of research, a written thesis submitted to the graduate school, and a formal public defense of the thesis.

The Master of Science in Computer Science (M.S.C.S.) is also offered. The program of study in computer science is designed to offer students an opportunity to prepare for an industrial, business, or governmental career in a rapidly changing profession. The student may choose a thesis or nonthesis plan. The thesis plan requires 27 hours of courses plus completion of an approved thesis (6 thesis hours). The nonthesis plan requires 36 hours of courses.

RESEARCH FACILITIES

The Erik Jonsson School of Engineering and Computer Science has developed a state-of-the-art engineering computational facility consisting of a network of Sun servers and Sun Engineering Workstations. All systems are connected via an extensive fiber-optic Ethernet and have direct access to most major national and international networks. In addition, many microcomputers are available for student use. The Engineering and Computer Science Building provides extensive facilities for research in microelectronics engineering, telecommunications engineering, and computer science engineering. A Class 1000 microelectronics clean room facility, including optical lithography, sputter deposition, and evaporation, is available for student projects and research. An electron beam lithography pattern generator capable of submicron resolution is also available for microelectronics research. The Plasma Applications Laboratory has state-of-the-art facilities for mass spectrometry, microwave interferometry, optical spectroscopy, and optical detection. In addition, a Gaseous Electronics Conference Reference Reactor is available for plasma processing and particulate generation studies. The Optical Communications Laboratory includes attenuators, optical power meters, lasers, APD/p-i-n photodetectors, optical tables, couplers, etc., and is available to support system-level research in optical communications. The Electrical Materials Processing Laboratory has extensive facilities for fabricating and characterizing semiconductor and optical devices. The Laser Electronics Laboratory houses engineering graduate research projects centered around the characterization, development, and application of ultrafast dye and diode lasers. Engineering research in characterization, development, and application of devices is performed in the Nanoelectronics Laboratory. The Computer Systems Laboratory includes a network of workstations, personal computers, FPGA development systems, and a wide spectrum of state-of-the-art commercial and academic design tools to support graduate research in VLSI design and computer architecture. In the Digital Signal Processing Laboratory, several multi-CPU workstations are available in a network configuration for simulation experiments. Hardware development facilities for real-time experimental systems are available and include microphone arrays, active noise controllers, speech compressors, and echo cancellers. The engineering department also has an Image Processing Laboratory. In addition to the facilities on campus, cooperative arrangements have been established with many local industries to make their facilities available to UTD graduate engineering students.

FINANCIAL AID

Financial aid is available in the form of scholarships, research and teaching assistantships, and work-study arrangements with local industry. Additional compensation is generally available in the summer, as a full schedule of classes is usually offered. There are several additional government-, University-, and industry-backed sources for the support of graduate students. Interested prospective students may write for specific information to the graduate secretary of the engineering department, EC33, University of Texas at Dallas, or graduate secretary of the computer science department, EC31.

COST OF STUDY

In 1997–98, tuition and fees for Texas residents are $1646 for 15 semester hours; for nonresident and international students, tuition and fees are $4856 for 15 semester hours.

LIVING AND HOUSING COSTS

The cost of an apartment varies from $300 per month to more than $500 per month. The University has a limited amount of housing. Most students find housing in UTD apartment complexes.

STUDENT GROUP

There are more than 4,000 graduate students and about 4,000 undergraduate students at UTD, representing most states and many other countries. Freshman and sophomore students were admitted for the first time in fall 1990. A large number of undergraduate and part-time graduate students work in industry in the surrounding high-technology corridor.

LOCATION

UTD is located on the north side of Richardson, a suburb 17 miles north of downtown Dallas in the heart of the Telecom Corridor. The campus is surrounded by University-owned land that is used for soccer, jogging, bicycle riding, softball, and other recreational activities. There are several lakes in the Dallas and surrounding north Texas area. Dallas has museums, concert halls, a zoo, and other facilities that offer a rich cultural life to students and their families. The area is the home of many computer, electronics, and communication companies that are large supporters of UTD engineering and computer science programs.

THE UNIVERSITY AND THE PROGRAM

The University of Texas at Dallas was created in 1969 by an act of the Texas legislature that enabled the transfer of the Southwest Center for Advanced Studies to the state of Texas. The University began as a graduate school. The enrollment of undergraduate juniors and seniors began in 1975. Electrical engineering programs were approved in 1985. The Computer Science Program was part of the general program in mathematical sciences until 1982, when it became an independent program in the School of Natural Sciences and Mathematics. In 1986, the program became part of the new Engineering and Computer Science School. In the summer of 1992, the Computer Science Program moved into the new Engineering and Computer Science Building, which is equipped with entirely new offices, laboratories, and working areas.

APPLYING

The student entering the M.S.E.E. or M.S.C.S. program must meet the following guidelines: an undergraduate preparation equivalent to a baccalaureate in electrical engineering from an accredited engineering program, a grade point average in upper division quantitative course work of 3.0 or better on a 4.0 scale, a satisfactory score on the GRE, three letters of recommendation from individuals able to judge the candidate's probability of success in pursuing master's study, and an essay outlining the candidate's background and education and professional goals. Students from other engineering disciplines or from other science and math areas may be considered for admission to the program; however, some remedial course work may be necessary before starting the Master's program.

Applications for admission and all supporting documents should be submitted well in advance of the preferred semester of entry. Since department awards for teaching assistantships, research assistantships, and other scholarships are usually made in the spring for the next full academic year, applicants requesting financial aid should submit all required documents as early as possible to ensure consideration. A nonrefundable application fee of $25, payable by check, is required of all students applying for admission to the University of Texas at Dallas.

CORRESPONDENCE AND INFORMATION

Dr. William Frensley, Program Head
Electrical Engineering
P.O. Box 830688 MS-EC33
University of Texas at Dallas
Richardson, Texas 75083-0688
Telephone: 972-883-6755 or 2967

UNIVERSITY OF TEXAS AT DALLAS

THE FACULTY AND THEIR RESEARCH

ENGINEERING

PROFESSORS

Larry P. Ammann, Ph.D., Florida State. Robust multivariate methods, remote sensing.

Blake E. Cherrington, Ph.D., Illinois. Properties and applications of weakly ionized plasmas, fundamental mechanisms in gas discharges, plasma chemistry and applications of plasmas to materials processing.

C. D. Cantrell III, Director of the Center for Applied Optics; Ph.D., Princeton. Quantum and nonlinear optics; optical physics; propagation of laser beams in nonlinear optical waveguides and bulk media; optical bistability, chaos and switching, laser-semiconductor and laser-molecular interactions.

William R. Frensley, Electrical Engineering Program Head; Ph.D., Colorado. Semiconductor heterostructures and devices, device simulation and modeling, quantum transport theory, development of interactive software design.

Louis R. Hunt, Ph.D., Rice. Nonlinear systems and control theory, signal processing.

William P. Osborne, L. M. Ericsson Professor of Electrical Engineering and Dean; Ph.D., New Mexico State. Communication systems; detection, estimation, and coding theory; wireless networks.

Grover Wetsel, Ph.D., Rice. Nanoelectronics, scanned-probed characterization of materials, and nanoscale devices; applied optics.

Jan P. Van Der Ziel, Ph.D., Harvard. Evaluation of III-V materials, semiconductor lasers, and detectors; quantum well optical devices and processing.

ASSOCIATE PROFESSORS

Poras Balsara, Ph.D., Penn State. VLSI design, computer architecture; parallel computing; special-purpose hardware.

Dale M. Byrne, Ph.D., Arizona. Electromagnetic wave propagation, scattering and diffraction theory and applications, optical characterization of materials, infrared ellipsometry.

Ronald D. DeGroat, Ph.D., Colorado. Nonlinear modeling, signal processing algorithms, array processing, spectral estimations, fixed-point digital filters.

Eric Dowling, Ph.D., Florida. Statistical and subspace-based signal processing, adaptive signal processing and experimental systems.

John P. Fonseka, Ph.D., Arizona State. Digital modulation, continuous phase modulation, error control coding, combined modulation and coding techniques.

David T. Harper III, Ph.D., Rice. Parallel computer architectures, memory and I/O systems, interconnection networks.

Kamran Kiasaleh, Ph.D., USC. Digital communications, high-speed optical communication networks, network synchronization.

Darel Linebarger, Ph.D., Rice. Array processing, spectrum estimation, adaptive signal processing methods, nonlinear systems.

Duncan MacFarlane, Ph.D., Portland State. Electromagnetics, lasers and their applications.

Lawrence J. Overzet, Ph.D., Illinois. Deposition and etching of materials in glow discharges, negative ions in discharges, basic studies of particulate contamination in discharges.

Lakshman S. Tamil, Ph.D., Rhode Island. Fiber and integrated optics, nonlinear guided waves, optical computing, applied mathematics.

COMPUTER SCIENCE

PROFESSORS

Doug T. Huynh, Ph.D., Saarlandes (Germany), 1978. Computational complexity theory, automata and formal languages, concurrency theory, communications networks and protocols, parallel computation, software metrics.

Simeon Ntafos, Ph.D., Northwestern, 1979. Program testing, software reliability estimation, testing of distributed and concurrent software, computational geometry, robotics.

William J. Pervin, Ph.D., Pittsburgh, 1957. Software engineering, tools for program testing, program verification, processes in distributed and parallel systems, programming languages, applications to hearing disabilities and management.

Klaus Truemper, Ph.D., Case Western Reserve, 1973. Computational logic and intelligent computer systems; ongoing applications projects: natural language processing, handwriting interpretation, traffic control, and expert systems providing optimal decisions.

ASSOCIATE PROFESSORS

G. R. Dattatreya, Ph.D., Indian Institute of Science, 1981. Stochastic modeling, parameter estimation and performance; optimization in communication; signal and image processing; computer network systems.

Ivor Page, Program Head, Ph.D., Brunel (England), 1979. Distributed algorithms, including resource allocation problems; computer graphics.

Ioannis G. Tollis, Ph.D., Illinois at Urbana-Champaign, 1987. Graph drawing and visualization, computer-aided design, telecommunication networks, VLSI layout, graph layout, computational geometry, algorithms and applications.

S. Venkatesan, Ph.D., Pittsburgh, 1988. Distributed systems, fault tolerance, telecommunication networks, and mobile/nomadic computing.

ASSISTANT PROFESSORS

Biao Chen, Ph.D., Texas A&M, 1996. Communications networks, real-time computing systems, distributed systems, and fault-tolerant systems.

Lawrence Chung, Ph.D., Toronto, 1993. Software engineering, requirements engineering, nonfunctional requirements, information systems (Re-) engineering, software architectures, knowledge-based software engineering, computer-aided software engineering, software processes.

Rym Mili, Ph.D. Tunis (Tunisia), 1991; Ph.D., Ottawa, 1996. Software engineering, software reuse and reusability measures, software maintenance and reengineering, software metrics, formal specifications.

Balaji Raghavachari, Ph.D., Penn State, 1992. Design and analysis of algorithms, graphs, telecommunication networks, topological network design, combinatorial optimization, approximation algorithms, sequencing problems.

Haim Schweitzer, Ph.D., Hebrew (Jerusalem), 1986. Artificial intelligence, computer vision, machine learning, multimedia neural nets.

SENIOR LECTURERS

Wolfgang Bein, Ph.D., Osnabrueck (Germany), 1986. Algorithms, combinatorial optimization, software engineering, parallel computation, the Internet, computing in society.

Martha Dinwiddie, M.S., Texas at Dallas, 1982. Beginning and advanced Pascal programming, discrete mathematics, computer organization.

Michael Durbin, M.S., Texas at Dallas, 1983. Discrete mathematics, object-oriented technology, modern operating systems, programmer productivity.

Don Evans, D.M.A., North Texas State, 1994. 8086-based assembler, systems programming, Pascal programming, object-oriented programming, visual basic.

Violet Syrotiuk, Ph.D., Waterloo, 1992. Distributed algorithms (especially orientation problems), tiling problems, distributed systems.

FOUNDERS PROFESSOR

Hal Sudborough, Ph.D., Penn State, 1971. Telecommunication networks, parallel computation networks, efficient parallel (and sequential) algorithms, structure of complexity classes, picture processing, automata and formal languages, graph/network algorithms (especially embedding and layout problems), combinatorial problems (especially sorting by prefix reversals), computational biology.

UNIVERSITY OF TEXAS–PAN AMERICAN

COLLEGE OF SCIENCE AND ENGINEERING
DEPARTMENT OF COMPUTER SCIENCE

PROGRAM OF STUDY

The Master of Science in Computer Science program provides a broad range of courses in computer science as well as optional in-depth studies in the areas of distributed computing, artificial intelligence and cognitive science, multimedia and interactive systems, and object-oriented systems. The degree requires 36 semester credit hours of course work, including a core of 18 hours of computer science courses. Further courses are selected from the fourteen additional computer science courses and graduate courses in other departments. A 3- to 6-hour master's project is required instead of a thesis. The program is designed to prepare students to assume applied computing and computer management positions in government, industry, and education, enhance skills for practicing professionals, and supply a foundation for study at the doctoral level.

RESEARCH FACILITIES

Computer science education and research at the University of Texas–Pan American is supported by modern computing facilities, including a central computer (VAX cluster), about 500 personal computers, and a laboratory of Sun Workstations. Departmental research is supported with Sun workstations and Pentium PCs. All of these computers have direct access to the Internet.

The Department of Computer Science offices are in the new Engineering Building, and laboratories are housed in the adjacent Academic Services Building, a University-wide computing facility completed in 1993.

FINANCIAL AID

Teaching assistantships are awarded by the department on a competitive basis. Research assistantships are awarded on a project-by-project basis by the principal investigator on research and contract projects.

For more information concerning application materials for assistantships and fellowships, students may contact the Graduate Coordinator. Loans and work-study are available through the Financial Aid Office; the Free Application for Federal Student Aid (FAFSA) must be filed. Information regarding loans, work-study, and employment opportunities is available from the Financial Aid Office at 956-381-2501.

COST OF STUDY

In 1997–98, tuition for graduate students is expected to be $54 per semester credit hour for Texas residents and $248 for nonresidents. With mandatory fees, a full-time graduate student enrolled for nine semester credit hours pays $778.32 if a resident of Texas and $2524.32 if a nonresident. Tuition and fees are subject to change.

LIVING AND HOUSING COSTS

Housing on campus is available for single students in the Women's Residence Hall and in Troxel Hall for Men. Each residence hall houses almost 200 undergraduate and graduate students. The cost is expected to be $1311.25 per semester in 1997–98. All fees are subject to change. For students who prefer off-campus living, there are many apartments available near the University.

STUDENT GROUP

The Master of Science in Computer Science is a new program; the University was authorized to offer the degree in October 1996. The first group of students begin taking classes in fall 1997.

LOCATION

UT–Pan American is located in Edinburg, Texas, close to the Mexican border and the Gulf of Mexico. Popular South Padre Island is only 75 miles away. The Rio Grande Valley, one of the nation's fastest-growing areas, is semitropical and culturally diverse, with many people who speak both English and Spanish.

THE UNIVERSITY AND THE COLLEGE

UT–Pan American is a comprehensive, public, coeducational institution with more than 12,000 students. Established in 1927, it joined the University of Texas System in 1989 and is the tenth largest of the state's thirty-five senior institutions. About 85 percent of its students are Hispanic, which reflects the demographic characteristics of the area.

The computer science program was established in 1983, and in fall 1995 the Department of Computer Science was separated from the former Department of Mathematics and Computer Science. The Department of Computer Science is now part of the College of Science and Engineering, which also includes the Department of Biology, Department of Chemistry, Department of Engineering, Department of Mathematics, and Department of Physics and Geology.

APPLYING

Admission to the master's program in computer science requires admission to the graduate school, a GPA of 3.0 in the most recent 60 semester hours, letters of recommendation, and a bachelor's degree. For international applicants whose primary language is not English, the TOEFL is also required. For applicants who do not hold a bachelor's degree in computer science, a sequence of courses will be prescribed to prepare the student for graduate work. Application forms and further information can be obtained from the address below.

Separate applications are required for the UT–Pan American graduate school and the computer science graduate program. Application to the graduate school requires submission of Graduate Record Examination (GRE) scores and college transcripts. Graduate school admission criteria are based on the most recent 60 semester hours attempted. Tentative admission for one semester is granted by the graduate school to applicants who have not taken the GRE. To obtain an application packet, students may contact the Office of Admissions and Records at 956-381-2206.

CORRESPONDENCE AND INFORMATION

Graduate Coordinator
Department of Computer Science
University of Texas–Pan American
1201 W. University Drive
Edinburg, Texas 78539-2999
Telephone: 956-381-2320
Fax: 956-384-5099
E-mail: graduate-studies@cs.panam.edu
World Wide Web: http://www.cs.panam.edu

UNIVERSITY OF TEXAS–PAN AMERICAN
THE FACULTY AND THEIR RESEARCH

Ongoing faculty research projects are in the areas of artificial intelligence, interactive systems, information visualization, Internet-based systems, multimedia systems, distributed systems, robotics, and object-oriented systems.

John P. Abraham, Associate Professor; Ed.D., Houston, 1986. Computer networks.

Pearl W. Brazier, Assistant Professor and Department Chair; M.S., Virginia Tech, 1981. Programming languages, software engineering, operating systems.

Richard Fowler, Associate Professor; Ph.D., Houston, 1980. Interactive systems, artificial intelligence.

Richard Fox, Assistant Professor; Ph.D., Ohio State, 1992. Artificial intelligence, knowledge-based systems.

Wendy A. Lawrence-Fowler, Assistant Professor; Ph.D., Ohio State, 1983. Databases, information retrieval, multimedia systems.

Xiannong Meng, Assistant Professor; Ph.D., Worcester Polytechnic, 1990. Operation systems, computer networks, distributed systems, performance analysis.

Michael L. Nelson, Assistant Professor; Ph.D., Central Florida, 1988. Object-oriented systems, computer networks, distributed systems, performance analysis

UNIVERSITY OF UTAH

DEPARTMENT OF COMPUTER SCIENCE

PROGRAMS OF STUDY

The Department of Computer Science offers programs leading to the M.S. and Ph.D. degrees. The graduate programs are open to computer science majors and also to students whose preparation is outside of computer science. Most of a doctoral student's time is devoted to course work and research, including participation in the research and teaching environment of the department on a day-to-day basis. The Ph.D. normally requires five years of graduate study, assuming that students undertake some teaching obligations during that time. A full-time student working on an M.S. program normally completes the degree requirements, including thesis, within two calendar years. The Department of Computer Science has an active, highly visible faculty engaged in a variety of research areas: asynchronous digital systems, computer-aided geometric design, computer graphics, computer vision, constraint-based modeling, educational computing, formal VLSI design methods, high-speed GaAs circuits, information-based complexity, information retrieval, natural-language processing, numerical analysis, operating systems, parallel and distributed computing, programming languages, robotics, scientific computing, scientific visualization, VLSI design, and virtual reality and teleoperation. Some of the graduate courses offered by the department include computer architecture, computer vision, robotics, programming languages and data structures, compiler construction, natural-language processing, machine learning, logic design, program verification, switching circuit theory, digital systems, theoretical computer science, operating systems, LSI circuits design, computational complexity, software engineering, multisensor integration, VLSI tools, scientific computing, and scientific visualization.

RESEARCH FACILITIES

The major research computing facilities are composed of six laboratories: Computer-Aided Design and Graphics, Computer Systems Laboratory, Asynchronous Digital Systems and VLSI, Robotics and Vision, Scientific Computing and Imaging, and Information Retrieval and Natural Language Processing. The department is divided into two computing environments; one is dedicated to research computing, and the other is for general/instructional computing.

The Research Computing Facility is a heterogeneous network comprised of twenty file and application servers, with more than 600 Gb of disk storage. These servers utilize AFS and NFS and are connected by eighteen Ethernet, five fast Ethernet, and four FDDI rings to more than 200 workstations from DEC, Hewlett-Packard, Sun, IBM, and Silicon Graphics. General research equipment includes a six-processor Power Challenge with an Extreme Graphics console, a processor SGI Power Onyx with two RE2 Graphics consoles, and a two-processor SGI DM file server. Individual laboratories contain specialized equipment dedicated for research. The latter includes high-end graphics workstations; a 60-cpu Origin 2000 with eight infinite reality graphics engines; three FDDI and two fast Ethernet workstation clusters comprised of IBM RS 6000s, IBM Power PCs, HP 700s, and SGI Indigo2s; and a state-of-the-art multisource video-editing environment. Robot arms and a variety of specialized equipment for image analysis, plus specialized equipment for real-time signal processing, are also housed in departmental laboratories.

The General Computing Facility includes more than 100 UNIX workstations from HP, Sun, SGI, and DEC and thirty Hewlett-Packard Pentium/NT machines for instructional use, connected to ten file and application servers with a total of 75 Gb of disk storage using AFS and NFS file systems. The Department of Computer Science also has access to the College of Engineering Workstation Laboratory, which consists of five servers, 100 Sun Workstations, and twenty-five HP workstations. The machines are divided into two separate rooms and are used for undergraduate and graduate instruction.

FINANCIAL AID

Teaching and research assistantships are available to all full-time graduate students. Stipends are $9450 for M.S. students and $10,350 for Ph.D. students for the nine-month 1997–98 academic year. Research support is also available for the summer.

COST OF STUDY

In 1997–98, resident tuition is $591 per quarter ($1773 per academic year) for 9 credit hours. Nonresident tuition is $1721 per quarter ($5163 per academic year) for 9 credit hours. Tuition waivers are available for all supported teaching and research assistants.

LIVING AND HOUSING COSTS

In 1997–98, dormitory room and board costs are approximately $5382 for the academic year. Apartments in University apartment communities rent for $255 to $595 per month; utilities are included. Off-campus housing is moderately priced. The cost of living in the area is close to or slightly less than the national average.

STUDENT GROUP

The department has approximately 105 full-time graduate students.

LOCATION

Forty-five minutes from campus are some of the world's finest ski and recreational areas. Hiking, fishing, mountaineering, river-running, and desert solitude are only hours away, as are ten national parks, and numerous national monuments and wilderness areas. Cultural activities include the Utah Symphony, Ballet West, Repertory Dance Theatre, and Utah Opera Company. Utah is home to professional basketball, hockey, and baseball teams. Computer-related industries include Evans & Sutherland, Unisys, Signetics, Intersil, Hercules, National Semiconductor, Terratek, and Novell.

THE UNIVERSITY AND THE DEPARTMENT

The 1,500-acre University of Utah campus, located in the foothills of the Wasatch Mountains, is the oldest state university west of the Missouri River. The University operates on the quarter system with a shortened summer session. With more than 3,400 regular and auxiliary faculty members, who are among the nation's most prolific researchers, Utah ranks consistently among the top thirty-five American colleges and universities in funded research. The University offers its nearly 27,000 students excellent recreational facilities, including a nine-hole golf course, racquetball and squash courts, an indoor jogging track, indoor swimming pools, and comprehensive physical education facilities. The Department of Computer Science is located in the Merrill Engineering Building at the northern edge of the campus.

APPLYING

Forms for admission and financial aid, advice concerning application procedures and official deadlines, and copies of the department handbook and research brochure may be obtained from the address below. Applications for admission, official transcripts, letters of recommendation, GRE scores on the General Test and Subject Test in computer science, and a statement addressing specific research goals should be sent to the Department of Computer Science. TOEFL scores are required of all international students whose native language is not English and should be sent to the University of Utah Admissions Office. Admission decisions are made by the department's Graduate Admissions Committee after careful review of each complete application.

CORRESPONDENCE AND INFORMATION

Graduate Coordinator
Department of Computer Science
University of Utah
Salt Lake City, Utah 84112

Telephone: 801-581-8224
E-mail: grad-coordinator@cs.utah.edu
World Wide Web: http://www.cs.utah.edu/

UNIVERSITY OF UTAH
THE FACULTY AND THEIR RESEARCH

Erik L. Brunvand, Associate Professor; Ph.D., Carnegie Mellon, 1990. Computer architecture, VLSI, self-timed circuit design.

John B. Carter, Assistant Professor; Ph.D., Rice, 1993. Operating systems, computer architecture and networking.

Tony M. Carter, Research Associate Professor; Ph.D., Utah, 1983. VLSI and CAD applications.

Elaine Cohen, Professor; Ph.D., Syracuse, 1974. Computer-aided geometric design, computer graphics.

Alan L. Davis, Professor; Ph.D., Utah, 1972. Concurrent processing and programming languages, self-timed circuit design, parallel machine architecture.

Samuel H. Drake, Research Associate Professor; Sc.D., MIT, 1977. Mechanical design, industrial code.

Ganesh Gopalakrishnan, Associate Professor; Ph.D., SUNY at Stony Brook, 1986. VLSI design and methodology.

David Hanscom, Clinical Professor; Ph.D., Case Western Reserve, 1970. Undergraduate education.

Charles Hansen, Research Associate Professor; Utah, 1987. Scientific visualization, computer graphics, computer vision.

Thomas C. Henderson, Professor; Ph.D., Texas at Austin, 1979. Artificial intelligence, computer vision, robotics.

Lee A. Hollaar, Professor; Ph.D., Illinois at Urbana-Champaign, 1975. Computer architecture, logic design, information retrieval systems programming, data communications.

John M. Hollerbach, Professor; Ph.D., MIT, 1978. Robotics, teleoperation, virtual reality, human motor control.

Stephen C. Jacobsen, Research Professor; Ph.D., MIT, 1973. Robotics, artificial intelligence.

Chris Johnson, Associate Professor; Ph.D., Utah, 1989. Scientific computing, scientific visualization, numerical analysis.

Robert R. Johnson, Emeritus Professor; Ph.D., Caltech, 1956. Computer architecture, system design, graphical programming, information theory.

Robert Kessler, Associate Professor and Chairman; Ph.D., Utah, 1981. LISP, computer software, software engineering and visual languages.

Gary E. Lindstrom, Professor; Ph.D., Carnegie Mellon, 1971. Programming language design and implementation, data structures.

Chris Myers, Research Assistant Professor; Ph.D., Stanford, 1995. Digital VLSI systems, computer architectures.

Richard F. Riesenfeld, Professor; Ph.D., Syracuse, 1973. Computer-aided geometric design.

Ellen M. Riloff, Assistant Professor; Ph.D., Massachusetts Amherst, 1994. Natural-language processing, information retrieval, artificial intelligence.

Peter Shirley, Assistant Professor; Ph.D., Illinois, 1990. Virtual reality, computer graphics.

Kris Sikorski, Associate Professor; Ph.D., Utah, 1982. Computational complexity, information-based complexity, numerical analysis.

Kent F. Smith, Professor; Ph.D., Utah, 1982. Integrated-circuit design and the application of integrated circuits to computer systems.

Frank Stenger, Professor; Ph.D., Alberta, 1965. Numerical analysis, geometric modeling.

Mark Swanson, Research Assistant Professor; Ph.D., Utah, 1991. Computer architecture, computer simulation performance analysis.

William B. Thompson, Professor; Ph.D., USC, 1975. Artificial intelligence, computer vision.

Joseph Zachary, Clinical Associate Professor; Ph.D., MIT, 1987. Software engineering, programming and specification languages.

UNIVERSITY OF VIRGINIA

DEPARTMENT OF COMPUTER SCIENCE

PROGRAMS OF STUDY

The Department of Computer Science offers programs leading to the degrees of Master of Computer Science, Master of Science in computer science, and Ph.D. in computer science. Students at all levels have the opportunity to begin research in their first year on algorithm analysis, computation theory, computer networks, databases, graphics, human-computer interaction, parallel computers and systems, programming environments, programming languages/compilers, software engineering, and VLSI design. The department has a strong research orientation and believes in close interaction between faculty and students. It has an excellent student-faculty ratio, and the faculty encourage students to publish their research.

Students typically complete the master's degree programs in two years, writing a scholarly thesis on their research. The Ph.D. degree requires approximately four years, with qualifying examinations taken during the first or second year depending on the status of the student. The department requires that students complete a core curriculum of computer science courses to ensure breadth of knowledge in the field.

RESEARCH FACILITIES

The department owns and operates a diverse network of more than 100 workstations and personal computers and makes them available to all graduate students.

The University, through the Information and Telecommunications Center (ITC), provides access to several IBM RS/6000s and networks of Sun computers. There are also several labs with 486- and Pentium-based PCs and Apple Macintosh systems. ITC also provides access to various supercomputer centers when needed.

FINANCIAL AID

Financial aid is available through research assistantships, teaching assistantships, and fellowships. In-state students are eligible for tuition fellowships, and tuition waivers are available for out-of-state students. Assistants are normally supported through the summer.

COST OF STUDY

For 1997–98, in-state tuition for the academic year is approximately $5000; out-of-state tuition is approximately $14,000.

LIVING AND HOUSING COSTS

The cost of living for the 1997–98 year is estimated to be $10,000.

STUDENT GROUP

The department has approximately 100 graduate students, over one third of whom are in the Ph.D. program. Most students attend full-time and receive financial aid, including tuition and fees.

STUDENT OUTCOMES

Of the graduate students receiving master's degrees in 1996, 72 percent sought employment with an average starting salary of $43,000. Twenty-four percent continued on to Ph.D. programs. Ph.D. recipients were evenly divided between industry and academic employment.

LOCATION

Charlottesville, Virginia, was settled before the Revolutionary War. The Charlottesville metropolitan area is composed of approximately 100,000 residents and is located within 2 hours of several major metropolitan areas. The area around the town is still primarily agricultural, and the nearby Shenandoah National Park provides excellent recreational opportunities. The University is located on the edge of Charlottesville, with shopping and cultural events accessible through the town's public transportation system.

THE UNIVERSITY AND THE DEPARTMENT

The University was founded by Thomas Jefferson in 1819, and his spirit is still in evidence today. The original University buildings are considered an outstanding example of American architecture. To continue Jefferson's tradition of togetherness, the University has remained small compared to other major state institutions, with an enrollment of 17,500. The student-run honor system fosters an environment of community trust.

Computer science was instituted as part of the Department of Applied Mathematics and Computer Science in 1965. In 1984, computer science became a separate department. It is part of the School of Engineering and Applied Science, and its faculty encourage the cross-disciplinary nature of the subject.

APPLYING

Applications for both fall and spring semesters, with or without financial aid, will be considered. Admission to the graduate school requires a bachelor's degree (or the equivalent), scores on the GRE General and Subject Tests, relevant transcripts, three letters of recommendation, and TOEFL scores from applicants whose native language is not English. Applications for the fall semester must be received by February 1 for financial aid consideration.

CORRESPONDENCE AND INFORMATION

Department of Computer Science
Olsson Hall
University of Virginia
Charlottesville, Virginia 22903-2442
Telephone: 804-924-7605

UNIVERSITY OF VIRGINIA
THE FACULTY AND THEIR RESEARCH

Alan Batson, Professor; Ph.D., Birmingham, 1956. Computer systems, modeling and performance evaluation.

Stephen J. Chapin, Research Assistant Professor; Ph.D., Purdue, 1993. Operating and distributed systems.

James Cohoon, Associate Professor; Ph.D., Minnesota, 1982. Algorithms, design automation, parallel computing.

Jack Davidson, Associate Professor; Ph.D., Arizona, 1981. Compilers, computer architecture, systems software.

James French, Research Assistant Professor; Ph.D., Virginia, 1982. Parallel processing, database management, information retrieval.

Andrew Grimshaw, Associate Professor; Ph.D., Illinois, 1988. Parallel, distributed, and object-oriented systems.

Anita Jones, Professor; Ph.D., Carnegie Mellon, 1973. Software systems.

John C. Knight, Professor; Ph.D., Newcastle, 1973. Software reliability, software engineering, software testing, software verification.

Jorg Liebeherr, Assistant Professor; Ph.D., Georgia Tech, 1991. Computer networks, data communications, distributed systems.

Worthy Martin, Associate Professor; Ph.D., Texas at Austin, 1981. Artificial intelligence, computer vision, graphics.

James Ortega, Professor and Chair; Ph.D., Stanford, 1962. Numerical algorithms for parallel architectures.

Randy Pausch, Associate Professor; Ph.D., Carnegie Mellon, 1988. Graphics, human-computer interaction.

John Pfaltz, Professor; Ph.D., Maryland, 1968. Databases, parallel processes, graph theory.

Norman Ramsey, Research Assistant Professor; Ph.D., Princeton, 1993. Programming languages and environments.

Paul Reynolds, Associate Professor; Ph.D., Texas at Austin, 1979. Parallel and distributed systems.

Gabriel Robins, Associate Professor; Ph.D., UCLA, 1992. Combinatorial optimization, computational geometry, algorithms.

Sang Son, Associate Professor; Ph.D., Maryland, 1986. Databases, distributed systems, real-time systems.

John A. Stankovic, BP America Professor and Chair; Ph.D., Brown, 1979. Real-time systems.

Kevin Sullivan, Assistant Professor; Ph.D., Washington (Seattle), 1994. Software design and engineering.

Alfred Weaver, Professor; Ph.D., Illinois, 1976. Computer networks.

William Wulf, AT&T Professor of Engineering; Ph.D., Virginia, 1968. Architecture, compilers.

UNIVERSITY OF VIRGINIA

DEPARTMENT OF ELECTRICAL ENGINEERING

PROGRAMS OF STUDY

The Department of Electrical Engineering offers programs leading to the degrees of Master of Science, Master of Engineering, and Doctor of Philosophy. The M.S. degree requires a minimum of 24 semester hours of graduate courses and submission of a thesis. The M.E. degree requires a minimum of 30 semester hours. Either master's degree can be completed in a calendar year of full-time study, but most students spend three to four semesters in the program. For the Ph.D. degree, students are expected to complete a minimum of 24 semester hours beyond the master's degree, pass an oral qualifying examination, and submit and defend a dissertation. The normal full-time graduate course load is three or four courses, depending upon the research load. The principal areas of instruction in the department are communication theory, computer engineering, control systems, microwaves, optoelectronics, pattern recognition and image processing, signal processing, and solid-state devices and materials. Research is in progress in these fields, and the active involvement of every graduate student is encouraged.

A program in computer engineering is available at the master's level. The program includes courses offered by the computer science department and computer engineering courses offered by the electrical engineering department.

The department also offers a special program that encourages students with a bachelor's degree in a related area, such as physics or mathematics, to earn a master's degree in electrical engineering. The program is designed to be completed in fifteen to twenty-four months.

RESEARCH FACILITIES

The Department of Electrical Engineering is well endowed with modern electronic research equipment. The Semiconductor Device Laboratory (SDL) has a 2,000-square-foot clean-room facility capable of complete fabrication of submicron semiconductor and superconductor devices. Major processing capabilities include deep UV lithography, reactive ion etching, ion milling, RF and DC sputtering, e-beam deposition, CVD oxide grown, organometallic chemical vapor deposition (OMCVD) and molecular beam epitaxy (MBE) of GaAs and related compounds, and field emission scanning electron microscopy. The SDL also shares a Far-Infrared Receiver Laboratory with the Department of Physics. This facility houses laser local oscillator sources to 3 THz and a variety of submillimeter wavelength measurement and test equipment. The Laboratory for Optics and Quantum Electronics (LOQE) is fully equipped for optical spectroscopy and the optical characterization of semiconductor devices. Major equipment includes an MBE system for III-V compound semiconductors, a photoluminescence system, and a tunable Ti:sapphire laser system. The Millimeter-wave Research Laboratory (MRL) is equipped with a variety of test and fabrication equipment, including an HP-8510 vector network analyzer to 100 GHz and Apollo workstations. The Center for Semicustom Integrated Systems, a research center within the department, operates Sun and Hewlett-Packard computers that contain a number of VLSI design tools and software packages, including the Full Mentor Graphics Tool Suite. The center also operates a Calcomp 68436 electrostatic plotter, an HP 82000-100 IC test system, high-speed logic analyzers, and high-speed digital oscilloscopes. In addition, the center supports digital designs incorporating programmable parts (e.g., PLD, FPGA, EPROM, and custom integrated circuits). The Communication Control and Signal Processing Laboratory utilizes computing resources available on Sun and RS6000 workstations, MATLAB signal processing software, and Gould and Pixar image processing hardware for still picture and image sequence research. The University's computing center operates numerous IBM RS6000, Silicon Graphics, and Sun computers.

FINANCIAL AID

Financial aid is available in the form of University fellowships, national fellowships, and research and teaching assistantships. Fellowships in 1996–97 carried stipends of $9000 and up, plus tuition and fees, for the academic year. Research assistantships, supported by nonclassified sponsored research projects, provided stipends of $8000–$15,000 for the calendar year.

COST OF STUDY

In 1996–97, tuition and fees were $4658 per academic year for state residents and $14,444 per academic year for nonresidents.

LIVING AND HOUSING COSTS

Dormitory facilities were available for single students at $2100–$2400 per academic year for 1996–97. University-operated accommodations for student families ranged from one-bedroom apartments for $416 per month to three-bedroom apartments for $520 per month (apartments are furnished and include utilities).

STUDENT GROUP

There are 18,398 students at the University of Virginia, including 6,106 graduate students. The School of Engineering and Applied Science enrolls 2,235 students; 605 are graduate students. There are 104 full-time graduate students in the electrical engineering department.

LOCATION

Charlottesville and its environs, situated in the foothills of the Blue Ridge Mountains, constitute a community of approximately 100,000 people. The climate is relatively mild, and opportunities for outdoor recreation extend throughout most of the year. Shenandoah National Park is 20 miles away, and Washington, D.C., is 110 miles away. The area contains many places of historic interest.

THE UNIVERSITY

The University of Virginia, founded in 1819 by Thomas Jefferson, is a state-aided institution that recognizes the importance of having a student body drawn from many parts of the country. It is widely known for its outstanding programs in a variety of areas, including engineering and applied science.

Approximately 155 full-time faculty members are active in teaching, research, and public service in the School of Engineering and Applied Science.

APPLYING

Applications are considered at any time, but students seeking financial aid should apply by February 1 of the year in which they plan to enroll. All applicants are required to submit GRE scores, and international students must have a minimum TOEFL score of 600.

CORRESPONDENCE AND INFORMATION

Electrical Engineering Graduate Committee
Thornton Hall
University of Virginia
Charlottesville, Virginia 22903-2442

Telephone: 804-924-6077
E-mail: eegrad@virginia.edu
World Wide Web: http://www.ee.virginia.edu

UNIVERSITY OF VIRGINIA
THE FACULTY AND THEIR RESEARCH

J. H. Aylor, Ph.D., Professor and Chair of the Department. Design automation, digital systems, VLSI systems, test technology.

J. C. Bean, Ph.D., John Marshall Money Professor. Molecular beam epitaxy, novel electronic materials.

R. Bradley, Ph.D., Research Assistant Professor. Microwave and millimeter-wave semiconductor devices and integrated circuitry, radio astronomy instrumentation.

M. Brandt-Pearce, Ph.D., Assistant Professor. Communication theory, optical communications, multiuser networks.

T. W. Crowe, Ph.D., Research Professor. High-frequency solid-state devices, novel solid-state devices, terahertz sources and receivers.

J. B. Dugan, Ph.D., Professor. Dependability analysis of fault-tolerant systems, hardware and software reliability engineering.

G. B. Giannakis, Ph.D., Professor. Signal processing using higher-order statistics, nonstationary and nongaussian time-series analysis, wavelets, and system identification algorithms with applications to channel equalization, seismic, speech, array, and image data processing.

T. Globus, Ph.D., Associate Professor. Electrical and optical characterization of electron materials and devices.

B. W. Johnson, Ph.D., Professor. Fault-tolerant systems, VLSI testing, VLSI systems.

S. H. Jones, Ph.D., Associate Professor. Compound semiconductor materials and devices.

A. W. Lichtenberger, Ph.D., Research Assistant Professor. Superconducting materials and devices.

H. Liu, Ph.D., Assistant Professor. Wireless communication, array signal systems, array signal processing, system identification and parameter estimation.

P. P. Marshall, Ph.D., Associate Professor. Electric power and machinery, power electronics, energy policy, renewable energy.

M. L. Reed, Associate Professor. Medical and industrial application of microelectromechanical systems, microfabrication technology and piezoelectronically-tuned electrooptic devices.

N. Sidiropoulos, Ph.D., Assistant Professor. Statistical and nonlinear signal processing and mathematical imaging, optimal filtering, estimation and detection, regression coding, deconvolution and similarity testing.

M. Stan, Ph.D., Assistant Professor. Low power VLSI, FPGAs, mixed mode analog and digital VLSI, embedded systems and hardware/software codesign.

G. Tao, Ph.D., Assistant Professor. Adaptive control, nonlinear systems, control applications, multivariable control systems, robust adaptive systems, robotics.

E. Towe, Ph.D., Associate Professor. Optics, quantum electronics, solid-state devices.

R. Weikle, Ph.D., Assistant Professor. Microwave and millimeter-wave circuits and radiating structures.

R. D. Williams, Ph.D., Associate Professor. Computer design, real-time systems, VLSI design/VLSI testing, speech synthesis.

S. G. Wilson, Ph.D., Professor. Communications and information theory.

ACTIVE RESEARCH PROJECTS

Communications and Control
Adaptive control.
Communication network protocols and analysis.
Digital speech encoding and image encoding at low bit rates.
Distributed signal processing.
Error control coding.
Indoor wireless infrared systems.
Microelectronic system design, fabrication, and testing.
Multiuser communications.
Optical communications.
Robust signal processing.
Signal design for band- and power-limited satellite channels.
Statistical modeling and system identification.

Computer Engineering
A high-performance memory controller.
Automated design of digital systems.
Computer-aided design tools for circuit layout.
Concurrent error detection techniques.
Fault simulation using VHDL.
Fault-tolerant electronics for powered wheelchairs.
Integrated performance and reliability modeling of fault-tolerant systems.
Modeling and simulation using VHDL.
Reliable architectures for magnetic bearing systems.
Safety critical systems for automatic train control.
Test-pattern generation in a parallel environment.
Test-pattern generation using genetic algorithms.
Uninterpreted/interpreted modeling and simulation.

Millimeter-Wave Research
Integrated circuit antennas.
Microwave and millimeter-wave power combining.
Millimeter-wave diode characterization and applications.
Millimeter- and submillimeter-wave receivers and sources.
Planar transmission lines and active circuits.
Quasi-optical arrays and circuits.

Optics and Quantum Electronics
Integrated optics.
Intersubband transition quantum well detectors.
Optical modulators.
Optical neural networks.
Optical polymer materials.
Vertical cavity surface-emitting lasers.
Visible second-harmonic semiconductor lasers.

Solid-State Devices
Design and analysis of novel three-terminal devices based on GaAs and related compounds.
Epitaxial growth of GaAs and related compounds by OMCVD and MBE.
High-frequency semiconductor device physics.
Mixer and varactor diodes for submillimeter-wave applications.
Noise theory and microwave noise measurement.
Solid-state device fabrication and processing technology.
Superconductive electronics.
Superconductor-insulator-superconductor (SIS) structures for millimeter- and submillimeter-wave mixer applications.
Terahertz receiver systems.
Thin-film transistors.
Transferred electron oscillators.
Wide band gap semiconductor technology.

UNIVERSITY OF WASHINGTON

DEPARTMENT OF COMPUTER SCIENCE AND ENGINEERING

PROGRAMS OF STUDY

The Department of Computer Science and Engineering offers M.S. and Ph.D. degrees. The M.S. degree program typically takes two years. The Ph.D. degree program typically takes approximately five years and includes both a comprehensive evaluation and a depth exam in addition to the dissertation.

The department has significant strengths in most aspects of the field, with particular emphasis on VLSI, embedded systems, and CAD; architecture; operating systems, networks, and communication; programming systems; software engineering, safety, and human-computer interaction; computer graphics and computer vision; artificial intelligence; theory of computation; and computational biology. With a small undergraduate program, a moderate-sized graduate program, and an open, active faculty, the department feels that graduate student/faculty interaction, both within and across specialties, is one of the strengths of the programs.

RESEARCH FACILITIES

The department is well equipped to support advanced course work and research in computer science. General research equipment includes more than 300 UNIX and Windows-based workstations and servers, including Intel Pentium and Pentium-Pro PCs, DEC Alphas, IBM RS/6000, SGI Indy, and Sun SPARCstations. All graduate student desks are equipped with workstations or X-terminals. A wide variety of special-purpose equipment supports research in graphics, computer vision, VLSI, parallel computing, and other areas.

FINANCIAL AID

Most full-time graduate students receive some financial aid from the department, such as a teaching or research assistantship. For 1996–97, these paid $1046–$1330 per month, plus a waiver of most tuition and fees (including nonresident tuition).

COST OF STUDY

Tuition and fees for 1997–98 are approximately $1682 per quarter for Washington State residents and approximately $4159 per quarter for nonresidents. (U.S. citizens are often able to establish state residency after twelve months.)

LIVING AND HOUSING COSTS

The University provides some low-cost housing for both married and unmarried students. Otherwise, Seattle is moderately priced for a major metropolitan area.

STUDENT GROUP

There are approximately 150 graduate students in the program, with 30 new students entering each year. About 80 percent of the entering students are seeking a Ph.D. Most are full-time. Students come from all over the United States and from about twenty other countries. Graduates receive job offers from major universities and industrial labs throughout the world.

LOCATION

Seattle is a cosmopolitan city of approximately 500,000 people, situated between Puget Sound on the west and Lake Washington on the east. Consistently rated as one of the most livable cities in the United States, Seattle has lively regional theater, music, dance, and opera; a wide selection of movies; and other cultural activities. Opportunities for outdoor recreation abound, including boating, hiking, biking, camping, fishing, rock-climbing, mountain-climbing, and skiing, both downhill and cross-country. Thirty miles to the east, the Cascade Mountains offer alpine lakes, trails, blueberry picking in the fall, and skiing during the winter. Mount Rainier, height 14,408 feet, is visible from campus on a clear day and is about 2 hours away by car. Across Puget Sound by ferry is the Olympic Peninsula, with Olympic National Park, the rain forest, and isolated ocean beaches. Winters are mild, but it does rain—about 34 inches per year, much of it drizzle.

THE UNIVERSITY AND THE DEPARTMENT

The University of Washington was founded in 1861. It is the one of the major research institutions in the United States, averaging twelfth nationally over a variety of disciplines in a recent assessment, routinely ranking among the top five nationally in total federal awards for research and development, and among the top ten in industrial support of research and development. The enrollment is about 34,000, with approximately 8,000 in professional and graduate programs.

The Department of Computer Science and Engineering was formed in 1967 and has conferred 183 Ph.D. and 550 M.S. degrees. In the 1995 National Research Council study, the department was again ranked among the top ten in the nation both for excellence of faculty and for effectiveness of graduate program. Current faculty members have received fifteen prestigious Presidential/NSF Young Investigator awards from the National Science Foundation, two Guggenheim Fellowships, three ONR Young Investigator Awards, two Presidential Faculty Fellow Awards, one Sloan Research Fellowship, eight Fulbright Research Scholarships, nine ACM Fellowships, six IEEE Fellowships, the Turing Award, and the National Medal of Science, among other honors. The department has been continuously supported by the NSF CER/II program since its inception, and essentially all faculty members have research support from federal agencies, such as DARPA, NSF, and ONR. The faculty and students have presented papers at, and/or served on the program committees of, most major computer science conferences for the last decade.

APPLYING

Applicants must have a baccalaureate or equivalent degree. A solid background in computer science is the norm, but lack of formal training can be offset by strong evidence of potential. Transcripts, letters of recommendation, and GRE General Test scores are required; a GRE Subject Test score in computer science or another area is strongly recommended. Admission is very competitive. The department receives many more applications than it can accept. The typical undergraduate GPA of successful applicants is above 3.5, and typical GRE scores are above the 90th percentile. All application materials should reach the department by January 10.

CORRESPONDENCE AND INFORMATION

Graduate Admissions
Department of Computer Science and Engineering, Box 352350
University of Washington
Seattle, Washington 98195-2350
Telephone: 206-543-1695
E-mail: grad-admissions@cs.washington.edu
World Wide Web: http://www.cs.washington.edu/

UNIVERSITY OF WASHINGTON
THE FACULTY AND THEIR RESEARCH

Richard Anderson, Associate Professor; Ph.D., Stanford, 1985. Parallel algorithms. Recipient of NSF Presidential Young Investigator award, 1987.

Jean-Loup Baer, Professor; Diplome d'Ingenieur, 1960, Doctorat 3e cycle, 1963, Grenoble; Ph.D., UCLA, 1968. Parallel and distributed processing, computer architecture.

Paul Beame, Associate Professor; Ph.D., Toronto, 1987. Sequential and parallel computational complexity theory. Recipient of NSF Presidential Young Investigator award, 1988.

Brian Bershad, Associate Professor; Ph.D., Washington (Seattle), 1990. Operating systems, architecture, distributed systems, parallel systems. Recipient of NSF Presidential Young Investigator award, 1991.

Alan Borning, Professor; Ph.D., Stanford, 1979. Computer languages, constraint systems, object-oriented languages.

Gaetano Borriello, Associate Professor; Ph.D., Berkeley, 1988. CAD for VLSI design and system integration, user interfaces, expert systems applications in CAD, VLSI processor and controller architecture. Recipient of NSF Presidential Young Investigator award, 1988.

Craig Chambers, Assistant Professor; Ph.D., Stanford, 1992. Object-oriented language design and implementation.

Martin Dickey, Lecturer; Ph.D., Arizona State, 1992. Computational linguistics, computer science education.

Carl Ebeling, Associate Professor; Ph.D., Carnegie-Mellon, 1986. Special-purpose hardware, VLSI, computer-aided design of complex systems. Recipient of NSF Presidential Young Investigator award, 1987.

Susan Eggers, Associate Professor; Ph.D., Berkeley, 1989. Computer architecture, memory system design, trace-driven methodology. Recipient of NSF Presidential Young Investigator award, 1990.

Oren Etzioni, Associate Professor; Ph.D., Carnegie Mellon, 1990. Artificial intelligence: machine learning, integrated architectures, planning. Recipient of NSF Young Investigator award, 1993.

Steve Hanks, Associate Professor; Ph.D., Yale, 1990. Automated planning, temporal reasoning, logic as a tool for AI.

Alistair Holden, Professor (joint appointment with Electrical Engineering); Ph.D., Washington (Seattle), 1964. AI, vision, CAD.

Anna R. Karlin, Associate Professor; Ph.D., Stanford, 1987. On-line algorithms, probabilistic algorithms, and probabilistic analysis.

Richard M. Karp, Professor; Ph.D., Harvard, 1959. Combinatorial algorithms, computational complexity, parallel algorithms, computational biology.

Theodore H. Kehl, Professor (joint appointment with Physiology and Biophysics); Ph.D., Wisconsin, 1961. Hardware systems, real-time systems as applied to medical research, VLSI CAD, microprogramming.

Richard E. Ladner, Professor; Ph.D., Berkeley, 1971. Distributed computing theory, specification and analysis of distributed protocols, computational complexity theory, design/analysis of algorithms, learning theory, applications to aid deaf/deaf-blind people.

Edward D. Lazowska, Professor; Ph.D., Toronto, 1977. Distributed and parallel computer systems and system performance analysis, using queuing network models.

Nancy Leveson, Professor; Ph.D., UCLA, 1980. Software engineering, software and system safety, software reliability and fault tolerance.

Henry M. Levy, Professor; M.S., Washington (Seattle), 1981. Operating systems, architecture, distributed and parallel systems.

David Notkin, Professor; Ph.D., Carnegie-Mellon, 1984. Extendable software systems, heterogeneous computer systems, environments for parallel programming. Recipient of the NSF Presidential Young Investigator award, 1988.

Walter L. Ruzzo, Professor; Ph.D., Berkeley, 1978. Computational complexity and parallel computation.

David Salesin, Associate Professor; Ph.D., Stanford, 1991. Computer graphics, user interfaces, computational geometry. Recipient of NSF Young Investigator award, 1993.

Linda Shapiro, Professor (joint appointment with Electrical Engineering); Ph.D., Iowa, 1974. Computer vision, AI, robotics.

Alan Shaw, Professor; Ph.D., Stanford, 1968. Operating systems, real-time systems, software specification methods.

Lawrence Snyder, Professor; Ph.D., Carnegie-Mellon, 1973. Parallel computation and VLSI.

Arun Somani, Professor (joint appointment with Electrical Engineering); Ph.D., McGill, 1985. Fault tolerance.

Steven Tanimoto, Professor; Ph.D., Princeton, 1975. Computer analysis of images, computer graphics, artificial intelligence.

Martin Tompa, Professor; Ph.D., Toronto, 1978. Computational complexity. Recipient of NSF Presidential Young Investigator award, 1984.

Daniel Weld, Associate Professor; Ph.D., MIT, 1988. Qualitative reasoning, qualitative physics, artificial intelligence. Recipient of NSF Presidential Young Investigator award, 1989.

Paul Young, Professor; Ph.D., MIT, 1963. Computational complexity, general theory of algorithms, mathematical logic.

John Zahorjan, Professor; Ph.D., Toronto, 1980. Computer systems, analytic modeling. Recipient of NSF Presidential Young Investigator award, 1984.

Adjunct, Affiliate, and Emeritus Appointments

Loyce Adams, Associate Professor of Applied Mathematics. Parallel processing, numerical linear algebra.

Les Atlas, Associate Professor of Electrical Engineering. Neural networks, digital signal processing, speech processing.

Philip Bernstein, Affiliate Professor; Microsoft. Databases.

James Brinkley, Research Assistant Professor of Biological Structure. Systems, biomedical applications of computers.

Steve Burns, Affiliate Professor; Intel. VLSI.

David Callahan, Affiliate Assistant Professor and Corporate Scientist, Tera Computers, Seattle. Parallel programming, compilers.

David Cutler, Affiliate Professor of Computer Science; Microsoft. Implementation of extremely large hardware and software systems.

David B. Dekker, Associate Professor Emeritus of Mathematics and Computer Science. Differential geometry and numerical analysis.

Tony DeRose, Affiliate Professor; Pixar. Computer graphics.

Tom Duchamp, Professor of Mathematics. Differential geometry, applications to graphics.

Hellmut Golde, Professor Emeritus of Computer Science; Ph.D., Stanford, 1959. Computer networks, compilers.

Terence Gray, Affiliate Professor and Director of University Network and Distributed Computing. Operating systems, networks.

Philip Green, Associate Professor of Molecular Biotechnology. Genome analysis.

Robert M. Haralick, Professor of Electrical Engineering. Computer vision, artificial intelligence, image processing, pattern recognition.

Leroy Hood, Professor of Molecular Biotechnology. Molecular immunology and evolution, large-scale DNA mapping.

Earl Hunt, Professor of Psychology. Human and artificial intelligence, computer applications in teaching.

Ira J. Kalet, Associate Professor of Radiation Oncology. Medical applications of artificial intelligence, computer graphics, interface design, process control systems, distributed computing applications.

Gretchen Kalonji, Professor of Materials Science and Engineering. Computer simulation techniques in materials science.

Yongmin Kim, Professor of Electrical Engineering. Image processing and microprocessing.

Victor Klee, Professor of Mathematics. Convex sets, functional analysis, analysis of algorithms, linear programming, combinatorics.

Janusz Kowalik, Affiliate Professor of Computer Science and Manager of Technology Transfer, Boeing Computer Services. Parallel processing systems.

Paul Leach, Affiliate Professor; Microsoft. Distributed and object-oriented systems.

John Lewis, Associate Technical Fellow; Boeing Computer Services. Numerical mathematics and scientific computing.

Jerre D. Noe, Professor Emeritus of Computer Science. Distributed computer systems, operating systems, performance evaluation.

Maynard Olson, Professor of Molecular Biotechnology. DNA sequencing.

Eve Riskin, Assistant Professor of Electrical Engineering. Data compression, image processing, signal processing, information theory.

Burton Smith, Affiliate Professor and Chairman and Chief Scientist, Tera Computers, Seattle. Computer architecture.

Werner Stuetzle, Professor of Statistics. Computational and graphical methods in multivariate analysis, computer vision.

Gregory L. Zick, Professor of Electrical Engineering. Computer engineering, sorting, I/O subsystems, image databases.

UNIVERSITY OF WASHINGTON

DEPARTMENT OF ELECTRICAL ENGINEERING

PROGRAMS OF STUDY
The Department of Electrical Engineering offers graduate programs leading to the degrees of Master of Science (M.S.E.E.) and Doctor of Philosophy (Ph.D.). Graduate courses and research programs are offered in modern VLSI, sensors, and semiconductor technology; mechatronics and intelligent control; advanced digital systems and communication; applied signal and image processing; advanced power technology; and applied electromagnetics, optics, and remote sensing. Opportunities also exist for participation in research on medical instrumentation in the Bioengineering Program and in marine acoustics and instrumentation systems at the Applied Physics Laboratory.

For the M.S.E.E. degree, a minimum of 45 credits is required. Students writing a thesis must register for 9 to 12 credits. Students selecting the nonthesis option can either complete their degree by total course work or by a one-term project of 4 to 8 credits. Course work for any of the above-mentioned options must be selected with each student's supervisory committee approval to prepare the student in an area of specialization. If more flexibility is desired than the M.S.E.E. requirements allow, the interdisciplinary degree of Master of Science in Engineering is available.

The M.S.E.E. degree is also offered to part-time students, employed in local industries, through the Televised Instruction in Engineering (TIE) program. Regular graduate courses are offered over cable television or via videotape to enable working engineers to participate in the program without traveling to campus.

For the Ph.D. degree, the student must pass the departmental qualifying examination, pass an advanced general examination, pursue an original research problem, and report the results of the research in a dissertation that must be a contribution to knowledge. At least one year of course work beyond the M.S.E.E. degree is usually desirable. Exceptionally qualified students are encouraged to pursue the Ph.D. degree directly without first earning a master's degree.

RESEARCH FACILITIES
Facilities in the Electrical Engineering Building include laboratories for solid-state materials, microtechnology, microwaves and millimeter waves, computer technology, computer systems, machine vision, analog and digital electronics, energy systems, power electronics and electric drives, bioelectronics, control systems, statistical data analysis, neural networks, and signal processing and classification. Extensive computer facilities are available, and there is an integrated circuit and semiconductor sensor fabrication facility as well as an interactive facility for speech and sonar analyses.

FINANCIAL AID
Approximately 155 teaching and research assistantships, scholarships, and fellowships (optional graduate appointee health insurance included) are available for qualified graduate students in all areas of electrical engineering. Teaching assistantships pay $9414 per academic year in 1997–98 for an entering graduate student. Higher amounts are paid for research assistants and doctoral students. All graduate assistants must pay a modest resident operating fee.

COST OF STUDY
Tuition and fees are $1682 per quarter for state residents and $4159 for nonresidents in 1997–98; these costs are subject to change.

LIVING AND HOUSING COSTS
The cost of board and room in University residences is $4671 plus a $60 deposit for the 1997–98 academic year. Housing for married students is available for qualified applicants. Apartments and rooms are also available off campus at varying costs.

STUDENT GROUP
The department's on-campus graduate enrollment is 260 students, about 60 percent of whom are in the M.S.E.E. program and 40 percent of whom are in the Ph.D. program. An additional 50 students are enrolled in the off-campus televised M.S.E.E. program.

LOCATION
The University is located on the shores of Lake Washington in a residential area near downtown Seattle. The metropolitan region has 2.5 million people. Seattle is a cosmopolitan city with many cultural and scenic attractions. It enjoys a temperate marine climate and is located on Puget Sound between the Cascade and Olympic mountain ranges, which offer a rich assortment of recreational opportunities.

THE UNIVERSITY
The University's campus comprises 2.8 square kilometers of beautifully landscaped evergreens, flowering shrubs, and buildings. The University is the premier institution of higher learning in the Northwest and is a major graduate education and research center. It offers a full spectrum of academic disciplines and is a sea-grant institution.

APPLYING
Prospective students should request additional information and admission application forms from the graduate program coordinator. A separate application form is required for financial aid. The application deadline is February 1 for admission and financial aid awards. The General Test of the Graduate Record Examinations (GRE) is required of all students. Students are normally admitted in the fall quarter of the academic year. A $45 application fee must accompany the application.

CORRESPONDENCE AND INFORMATION
Graduate Program Coordinator
Department of Electrical Engineering, Box 352500
University of Washington
Seattle, Washington 98195
Telephone: 206-543-4924
E-mail: grad@ee.washington.edu
World Wide Web: http://www.ee.washington.edu

UNIVERSITY OF WASHINGTON
THE FACULTY AND THEIR RESEARCH

Communications
M. Azizoglu. Optical communication networks, high-speed network protocols, communication theory.

J. S. Meditch. Broadband communication networks, video and multimedia systems.

J. A. Ritcey. Communications, statistical signal processing for radar, underwater acoustics, biomedicine.

Controls and Robotics
R. W. Albrecht. Mobile robotics, nuclear systems.

F. J. Alexandro. Control systems.

B. Hannaford. Telerobotics, bioengineering, human-machine systems, neurological control systems and models.

D. R. Meldrum. Automated laboratory systems, robotics and control, applications in biotechnology and transportation systems.

R. B. Pinter. Cybernetics, nonlinear and adaptive control systems, biophysics.

F. A. Spelman (Adjunct, Department of Bioengineering). Biological systems and models, cochlear implants, tissue resistivity.

J. Vagners (Adjunct, Department of Aeronautics and Astronautics). Dynamics, control systems analysis and synthesis, and optimal control and estimation.

Digital Systems
B. Gordon. VLSI, low power, video and multimedia processing.

A. D. C. Holden. Speech recognition, computer-aided design, neural networks, artificial intelligence.

Y. Kim. Computer architecture, imaging systems, medical imaging, multimedia systems.

J. S. Meditch. Broadband communication networks, video and multimedia systems.

M. Soma. Integrated circuits: design, test, and reliability; bioelectronics.

A. K. Somani. Computer architecture, fault-tolerant computing, parallel computer systems, computer communication networks.

S. L. Tanimoto (Adjunct, Department of Computer Science and Engineering). Image analysis, artificial intelligence, computer graphics.

G. L. Zick. Image and multimedia databases, medical imaging.

Electromagnetics, Optics, and Acoustics
C. H. Chan. Computational electromagnetics, microwave integrated circuits, scattering and antennas, bioengineering.

L. A. Crum (Research). Physical acoustics, medical ultrasonics, underwater acoustics.

A. Ishimaru. Electromagnetics, optics, acoustics, applied mathematics, scattering theory.

D. R. Jackson (Research). Underwater acoustics.

Y. Kuga. Remote sensing, electromagnetics, optics.

R. P. Porter. Acoustics, electromagnetics, signal processing.

C. Ramon (Research Adjunct, Department of Bioengineering). Biomagnetic imaging, image reconstruction, inverse problems, bioelectromagnetics.

E. I. Thorsos (Research). Rough surface scattering, underwater acoustics, electromagnetic scattering.

L. Tsang. Electromagnetics, remote sensing, optics of semiconductors, wave scattering.

D. P. Winebrenner (Research). Microwave remote sensing, wave scattering, electromagnetics, polarimetry, scattering statistics.

Electronic Devices and Photonics
M. A. Afromowitz. Microfabrication, integrated and fiber-optic sensors, biomedical instrumentation.

W. R. Babbitt (Research). Optical memories, processors, interconnects, smart pixels.

R. B. Darling. Solid state, semiconductor devices, optoelectronics, microelectronics.

T. P. Pearsall. Technology and physics of semiconductor devices, materials growth and characterization.

S. S. Yee. Semiconductor devices, optical sensors and microsensors and integrated optics.

Electronics
J. Andersen. Circuits, systems, CAD.

W. J. Helms. Integrated circuits, analog and digital circuit design.

C. M. Sechen. Design and computer-aided design of analog and digital integrated circuits.

M. Soma. Integrated circuits: design, test, and reliability; bioelectronics.

A. T. Yang. VLSI, CAD, modeling and simulation of GaAs/Si devices, optoelectronics.

Energy Systems
R. D. Christie. Power system operations, real-time expert systems, software engineering.

M. J. Damborg. Control systems theory, power system dynamics, computer applications, expert systems and database applications.

M. A. El-Sharkawi. Intelligent system applications to power, dynamic analysis and control of power systems, electric drives and power electronics.

P. O. Lauritzen. Power electronics, modeling and simulation, semiconductor devices.

C. C. Liu. Power systems, expert systems, power electronics.

H. P. Yee (Research). Power semiconductor devices, intelligent power devices and integrated circuits.

Signal and Image Processing
L. E. Atlas. Digital signal processing and time-frequency representations, applications in speech processing and manufacturing.

D. J. Dailey (Research). Digital signal processing, time series analysis, networks, distributed computing.

R. M. Haralick. Computer vision, artificial intelligence, pattern recognition, image processing.

J.-N. Hwang. Digital signal/image processing, pattern recognition, artificial neural networks.

P. L. Katz (Research). Underwater acoustics, image processing, digital signal processing, automatic target recognition, classification.

T. K. Lewellen (Adjunct, Department of Radiology). Medical imaging, PET, detectors, reconstruction algorithms.

R. J. Marks. Artificial neural networks, fuzzy systems, signal analysis, statistical communication theory, optical processing.

R. Reed (Research). Neural networks.

E. A. Riskin. Data compression, image processing.

J. D. Sahr. Radar, signal processing, ionospheric physics.

L. G. Shapiro. Computer vision, robotics, artificial intelligence, database systems.

M. T. Sun. Video coding and systems, multimedia networking, VLSI.

E-mail for electrical engineering faculty members is lastname@maxwell.ee.washington.edu

UNIVERSITY OF WISCONSIN–MADISON

DEPARTMENT OF COMPUTER SCIENCES

PROGRAMS OF STUDY

The Department of Computer Sciences offers M.S. and Ph.D. degrees in computer science. Research areas include artificial intelligence, computer architecture, computer networks, computer vision, database systems, distributed systems, mathematical programming, modeling and analysis of computer systems, numerical analysis, operating systems, performance evaluation, programming languages, software development environments, and theory of computation. Ongoing collaborative research with other departments includes projects in computational biology, computational chemistry, robotics, space sciences, and medical diagnosis.

Requirements for the Ph.D. degree include course work and a preliminary examination based on initial and proposed thesis research. The M.S. degree usually takes two years to complete.

RESEARCH FACILITIES

There are over 500 departmental machines, mostly high-performance Intel, DEC, Sun, and HP workstations, and all supported graduate students have their own workstations. Parallel computing facilities include a Thinking Machines CM-5 parallel computer, an IBM SP2 parallel computer, seven Sun Ultra Enterprise multiprocessors, and an integrated cluster of workstations (COW).

FINANCIAL AID

Almost all full-time graduate students are supported by a departmental assistantship or fellowship. Several students are offered fellowships each year, and most of the other new students receive teaching assistantships, with a four-year guarantee of support. Most graduate students who have passed the Ph.D. preliminary examination are supported as research assistants.

COST OF STUDY

Tuition for 1996–97 was $2187.45 per semester for students with assistantships. For others, in-state tuition was $2187.45 per semester, and the nonresident tuition was $6647.95 per semester.

LIVING AND HOUSING COSTS

In addition to dormitories, University-operated one- and two-bedroom apartments are available for married students; these cost $356–$631 per month. Off-campus housing is abundant and relatively inexpensive.

STUDENT GROUP

The department has about 250 graduate students, with about 60 new students entering each year. Approximately fifteen Ph.D. degrees and sixty M.S. degrees are awarded each year.

STUDENT OUTCOMES

M.S. students are in high demand at a range of major computer companies. Half of Ph.D. students accept academic positions and half accept positions in industry. Many major corporations regularly visit the department to describe their work and to recruit graduating students.

LOCATION

Built on an isthmus between two large lakes, Madison—the state capital of Wisconsin—has a population of about 200,000 people. Madison offers a rich cultural life and is regularly rated as one of America's most livable cities. The area is a four-season display of beauty, encouraging recreational activities such as sailing, bicycling, hiking, and skiing. The campus extends 1½ miles along the shores of Lake Mendota, covering over 1,000 acres. The University has over 100 sailboats at its docks next to the student union.

THE UNIVERSITY AND THE DEPARTMENT

Founded in 1849 as a public, land-grant institution, the University of Wisconsin–Madison is one of America's top research universities; a recent National Academy of Sciences study ranked 16 UW–Madison research-doctorate programs in the top ten and 35 programs in the top twenty-five. The campus ranks second nationally in total research spending. There are 130 departments, making it one of the most comprehensive universities in the nation.

The Department of Computer Sciences, formed in 1963, is consistently ranked as one of the top ten computer science departments in the country. Research funding for 1996–97 exceeded $7.5 million, supporting about eighty grants and contracts.

APPLYING

Applications for admission and all supporting materials must be received by December 31. No distinction is made at admission time between M.S. and Ph.D. applicants. Applicants must take both the GRE General Test and a GRE Subject Test in any area. The TSE is strongly recommended for applicants whose native language is not English and whose primary medium of instruction is not English. Although applicants need not have pursued an undergraduate major in computer science, significant related course work is expected.

CORRESPONDENCE AND INFORMATION

Graduate Admissions
Department of Computer Sciences
1210 West Dayton Street
University of Wisconsin
Madison, Wisconsin 53706
Telephone: 608-262-1204
Fax: 608-262-9777
E-mail: admissions@cs.wisc.edu
World Wide Web: http://www.cs.wisc.edu/

UNIVERSITY OF WISCONSIN–MADISON
THE FACULTY AND THEIR RESEARCH

Eric Bach, Professor; Ph.D., Berkeley, 1984. Theoretical computer science, computational number theory, algebraic algorithms, complexity theory, cryptography, six-string automata.

Pei Cao, Assistant Professor; Ph.D., Princeton, 1995. Operating systems, storage management, parallel and distributed systems.

Anne Condon, Associate Professor; Ph.D., Washington (Seattle), 1987. Complexity theory, randomized complexity classes, theory of parallel computation, interactive proof systems.

Carl de Boor, Steenbock Professor of Mathematical Sciences; Ph.D., Michigan, 1966. Approximation theory, numerical analysis.

Edouard J. Desautels, Professor; Ph.D., Purdue, 1969. Systems programming, personal computer systems and applications.

David J. DeWitt, Professor and Romnes Fellow; Ph.D., Michigan, 1976. Object-oriented database systems, parallel database systems, database benchmarking, geographic information systems.

Charles R. Dyer, Professor; Ph.D., Maryland College Park, 1979. Computer vision, 3-D shape representation, appearance modeling, active vision.

Michael C. Ferris, Associate Professor of Computer Sciences and Industrial Engineering; Ph.D., Cambridge, 1989. Large-scale optimization: theory, algorithms, and applications.

Charles N. Fischer, Professor; Ph.D., Cornell, 1974. Compiler theory and design, interactive program development environments, automatic register allocation and code generation, optimization.

James R. Goodman, Professor of Computer Sciences and of Electrical and Computer Engineering; Ph.D., Berkeley, 1980. Computer architecture, large-scale computing, parallel computing, shared-memory multiprocessors.

Mark D. Hill, Associate Professor of Computer Sciences and of Electrical and Computer Engineering; Ph.D., Berkeley, 1987. Computer architecture, parallel computing, memory systems, performance evaluation.

Susan Horwitz, Professor; Ph.D., Cornell, 1985. Software development environments, language-based tools, static analysis of programs, program slicing.

Yannis E. Ioannidis, Associate Professor; Ph.D., Berkeley, 1986. Database management systems, complex query optimization, scientific databases, user interfaces.

Deborah A. Joseph, Associate Professor of Computer Sciences and Mathematics; Ph.D., Purdue, 1981. Structural and applied complexity theory, mathematical logic, computational biology.

Sheldon Klein, Professor of Computer Sciences and Linguistics; Ph.D., Berkeley, 1963. Archaeology of cognition, simulation of language transmission and language change, language understanding and generation in the context of knowledge structures.

Kenneth Kunen, Professor of Computer Sciences and Mathematics; Ph.D., Stanford, 1968. Mathematical logic, logic programming, automated deduction.

Lawrence H. Landweber, Professor; Ph.D., Purdue, 1967. Computer networks and protocols, high-speed networks, electronic mail.

James R. Larus, Associate Professor; Ph.D., Berkeley, 1989. Programming languages, parallel languages, compilers.

Miron Livny, Professor; Ph.D., Weizmann (Israel), 1984. Resource management algorithms, performance modeling and analysis, discrete-event simulation.

Olvi L. Mangasarian, John von Neumann Professor of Mathematics and Computer Sciences; Ph.D., Harvard, 1959. Mathematical programming, machine learning, parallel computing.

Robert R. Meyer, Professor of Computer Sciences and Industrial Engineering; Ph.D., Wisconsin, 1968. Linear and nonlinear network optimization, parallel algorithms for large-scale optimization.

Barton P. Miller, Professor; Ph.D., Berkeley, 1984. Parallel and distributed debugging, parallel program performance tools, network management and name services, user interface design, operating systems.

Jeffrey F. Naughton, Professor; Ph.D., Stanford, 1987. Parallel database systems, persistent object bases.

Seymour V. Parter, Professor of Computer Sciences and Mathematics; Ph.D., NYU, 1958. Numerical methods for partial differential equations.

Raghu Ramakrishnan, Professor; Ph.D., Texas, 1987. Declarative database programming languages, data models and query languages, sequence and image data management.

Thomas Reps, Professor; Ph.D., Cornell, 1982. Programming languages, language-based programming environments, program slicing, interprocedural dataflow analysis, incremental algorithms.

Stephen M. Robinson, Professor of Computer Sciences and Industrial Engineering; Ph.D., Wisconsin, 1971. Operations research, management science.

Amos Ron, Associate Professor; Ph.D., Tel Aviv, 1987. Approximation theory, spline theory, radial function approximation, wavelets, polynomial interpolation, windowed Fourier transform.

Jude W. Shavlik, Associate Professor; Ph.D., Illinois, 1988. Machine learning, neural networks, artificial intelligence, computational biology, cognitive science, software agents.

Gurindar S. Sohi, Professor of Computer Sciences and of Electrical and Computer Engineering; Ph.D., Illinois, 1985. Instruction-level parallel processing, compiling for parallel architectures, memory systems.

Marvin H. Solomon, Professor and Chair; Ph.D., Cornell, 1977. Object-oriented database systems, distributed operating systems, computer networks, program development systems, programming languages.

John C. Strikwerda, Professor; Ph.D., Stanford, 1976. Numerical analysis, scientific computing, applied mathematics.

Mary K. Vernon, Professor of Computer Sciences and Industrial Engineering; Ph.D., UCLA, 1983. Techniques and applications for computer systems performance analysis, performance of parallel systems, parallel architectures and operating systems.

David A. Wood, Associate Professor; Ph.D., Berkeley, 1990. Computer architecture, performance evaluation, parallel processing, VLSI design.

UNIVERSITY OF WYOMING

DEPARTMENT OF COMPUTER SCIENCE

PROGRAMS OF STUDY

The Department of Computer Science at the University of Wyoming offers M.S. and Ph.D. degrees. A Ph.D. in computer science and mathematics is offered jointly with the Department of Mathematics. The primary research areas in the department are artificial intelligence and parallel and distributed systems. Graduates are prepared for careers in both academics and industry.

The Ph.D. in computer science requires completion of 72 semester hours, 42 of which must be course work. A minimum of 12 hours of dissertation research must be included. A written qualifying examination is required, as well as preliminary and final examinations related to the dissertation research. The joint Ph.D. in computer science and mathematics has similar requirements, with two exceptions: the qualifying examination includes sections from both departments, and course work must include at least 15 hours in each department.

The M.S. in computer science can be achieved under one of two plans. The Plan A program (thesis option) requires a minimum of 29 hours of course work and 4 hours of thesis research. The Plan B program requires a minimum of 33 hours of course work; no thesis is required, but a research paper based on one or more courses must be completed and a written examination passed.

The department expects Ph.D. candidates to complete their program within six years of admission if they hold a bachelor's degree or 4 years if they hold a master's. The typical time for completion of the M.S. degree is two years of full-time study, although thesis preparation under the Plan A program may extend this by a semester or more.

RESEARCH FACILITIES

Six research laboratories within the department are directed by individual faculty members and focus on these specific areas: knowledge representation, applied artificial intelligence, distributed computing, parallel systems, dependable computing, and high-speed networking. The equipment available for research in these labs includes Silicon Graphics multiprocessor Challenges, SGI Indys and O2s, and Sun IPCs, as well as several Pentium PCs, Power Macintoshes, and X-terminals. The department runs its own local networks, including an ATM network for high-speed distributed and parallel computing research. A variety of other equipment is available for general graduate student use. The department networks are connected to the campus fiber-optic network, which in turn provides access to over 2,000 workstations and mainframes on campus as well as to the Internet.

The University's Science Library has an extensive collection of holdings in computer science and subscribes to most major journals, including all IEEE and ACM publications.

FINANCIAL AID

The department offers several graduate assistantships (GA's), which typically involve undergraduate teaching as well as duties such as those of a laboratory assistant or grader. Additional GA's are available through cooperative programs with other University divisions. The nine-month GA stipend is $8471, including a tuition and fees waiver.

Research assistantships (RA's) are funded by faculty grants. The RA stipend varies, but is typically at least equal to that of a department GA and includes a tuition and fees waiver. Additional money can be earned through hourly employment as a laboratory assistant or grader, but these positions do not carry a tuition waiver.

COST OF STUDY

Full-time (9–17 hours) graduate student tuition and fees for 1997–98 are $1406 per semester for Wyoming residents and $3950.75 for nonresidents. Part-time tuition is $142.25 per credit hour for residents and $425 for nonresidents. Graduate students taking more than 17 hours are charged the appropriate hourly tuition for the excess.

LIVING AND HOUSING COSTS

Residence hall semester room rates are $862 for a double room and $1294 for a single. Semester board rates in the residence halls range from $1037.50 (twelve meals weekly) to $1260 (unlimited access).

University apartments are available for $285–$385 monthly (plus utilities) for one bedroom and $350–$525 (utilities included) for two or three bedrooms. Off-campus housing at varying rates is available in rooms, apartments, and condominiums.

STUDENT GROUP

The University has approximately 12,000 students, including about 3,000 graduate students in sixty-eight master's and twenty-seven doctoral degree programs. The computer science department typically has 30–40 graduate students, roughly half of whom are international students. One quarter of all students are enrolled part-time.

Successful graduate students have a good preparation in computer science, with courses including computer architecture, languages, operating systems, and theoretical foundations. Mathematics or engineering backgrounds are also valuable.

STUDENT OUTCOMES

About half of recent Ph.D. graduates have taken faculty positions in other computer science departments, including positions with schools in South Dakota, Nebraska, and New York. The others, like most M.S. graduates, work in government or industry. Many graduates find jobs as software or hardware developers in the high-tech corridor of Colorado, but others work in Washington, New Jersey, Texas, Idaho, and California for employers such as Microsoft, AT&T, Hewlett-Packard, and IBM.

LOCATION

Laramie, founded in 1868 by a surveyor for the Union Pacific Railroad, has approximately 26,000 residents. It lies between two ranges of the Rocky Mountains at an elevation of 7,200 feet. Summers are cool and dry; winters are cold and crisp but generally free from major storms. Skiing, snowmobiling, camping, and hiking are popular activities in the nearby mountains.

THE UNIVERSITY AND THE DEPARTMENT

The University of Wyoming began in 1886 as one building on the prairie, but is now a major land-grant institution on a 78-acre campus. Numerous cultural activities are available, many free to students. The University sponsors twelve NCAA Division I athletic teams.

The Department of Computer Science was founded in 1966 by faculty members from mathematics and the Computer Center. Computer science master's degrees have been offered since 1971, joint doctorates with mathematics since 1983, and computer science doctorates since 1988.

APPLYING

Application deadlines for admission and financial aid are March 1 for fall and summer and October 1 for spring. A minimum combined verbal and quantitative GRE score of 900 for master's applicants and 1000 for doctoral applicants is required, including a high score on the quantitative test. Students whose native language is not English must complete the TOEFL with a score of at least 550, including a 58 in section 1. A nonrefundable $40 fee must accompany the application.

CORRESPONDENCE AND INFORMATION

Department of Computer Science
University of Wyoming
P.O. Box 3682
Laramie, Wyoming 82071-3682
Telephone: 307-766-5190
Fax: 307-766-4036
E-mail: cosc@uwyo.edu
World Wide Web: http://www.cs.uwyo.edu/

UNIVERSITY OF WYOMING
THE FACULTY AND THEIR RESEARCH

Thomas A. Bailey, Associate Professor; Ph.D., Michigan State. Analysis of algorithms, models of parallel computation.
Henry R. Bauer III, Professor; Ph.D., Stanford. Programming languages, compiler construction, compiling for parallel computation.
L. Karl Branting, Assistant Professor; Ph.D., Texas. Artificial intelligence, case-based reasoning, AI application to law and natural resources.
John R. Cowles, Professor; Ph.D., Penn State. Theory of computation, automated reasoning.
Rex E. Gantenbein, Professor; Ph.D., Iowa. Software engineering, distributed real-time control systems, fault-tolerant computing.
Matthew D. Haines, Assistant Professor; Ph.D., Colorado State. Distributed systems, database management, task and data parallelism.
Shivakant Mishra, Assistant Professor; Ph.D., Arizona. Distributed systems, fault-tolerant computing, communication protocols.
John H. Rowland, Professor; Ph.D., Penn State. Software engineering, software testing.
Jeffrey Van Baalen, Assistant Professor; Ph.D., MIT. Artificial intelligence, knowledge representation and reasoning.

VILLANOVA UNIVERSITY

COLLEGE OF ENGINEERING
DEPARTMENT OF ELECTRICAL AND COMPUTER ENGINEERING

PROGRAMS OF STUDY

The Department of Electrical and Computer Engineering offers programs of study leading to the degrees of Master of Science in Electrical Engineering and Master of Science in Computer Engineering. In electrical engineering, graduate study and research are concentrated in the following areas: systems and signal processing, electromagnetics, solid state devices and optics, and electronic systems. In computer engineering, graduate courses and research are offered in the following subjects: computer organization and design, advanced computer architectures, VLSI design, artificial intelligence, computer vision, and neural networks. The master's program requires 33 semester credit hours of study, including at least 24 course credits and up to 9 credits of research. Students may elect to write a thesis or choose a nonthesis option. The main objective of graduate programs is to provide a balance of theory and practical knowledge needed either to practice in the profession or to advance to a doctoral program.

RESEARCH FACILITIES

The laboratories of the Department of Electrical and Computer Engineering are constantly updated to reflect state-of-the-art instrumentation and equipment. Equipment includes Sun Workstations; DEC graphics terminals; microcomputer development systems; IBM, HP, and other personal computers; robot manipulators; an HP microwave analyzer; a digital music synthesizer; Motorola 68000 microprocessor systems; and HP CAE workstations. The department also has use of the College's excellent academic engineering computation facility.

FINANCIAL AID

Teaching assistantships are available that provide a stipend for the academic year, payable in ten installments, plus a waiver of tuition and fees. In the awarding of assistantships, consideration is given to performance on the Graduate Record Examinations and/or Test of English as a Foreign Language, the undergraduate academic record, and letters of reference indicating outstanding ability. Research and tuition scholarships may also be available. Eligibility for low-interest loans is determined by the University's Office of Financial Aid.

COST OF STUDY

Tuition for 1996–97 was $580 per credit. Books and supplies were about $200 per semester. Miscellaneous fees and parking amounted to approximately $60 per semester.

LIVING AND HOUSING COSTS

Normally, there is no on-campus housing available for graduate students unless they are counselors employed in undergraduate dormitories. Applications for counselorships should be directed to the Director of Resident Living in Tolentine Hall, not to the College of Engineering. Costs of off-campus housing vary greatly depending on the type of accommodation. Listings of rooms and apartments are maintained by the University's Off-Campus Housing Service.

STUDENT GROUP

The department has 30 full-time and 70 part-time graduate students.

LOCATION

The University's handsomely landscaped 240-acre campus is located on suburban Philadelphia's historic Main Line, 12 miles from the city. This beautiful residential area contains excellent restaurants and shopping centers and is near Valley Forge National Park. Philadelphia, with its many cultural, historic, and sports attractions, is directly accessible by rail and bus from the campus. The University is within driving distance of the New Jersey and Delaware beaches, New York City, and the Poconos' recreational area.

THE UNIVERSITY

Villanova University was founded in 1842 by the Fathers of the Order of Saint Augustine. The engineering college was established in 1905. The University is composed of the College of Arts and Sciences, the College of Nursing, the College of Engineering, the College of Commerce and Finance, and the School of Law.

APPLYING

A B.S. in electrical engineering is normally required for admission, but students with a B.S. in non–electrical engineering areas such as physics, mathematics, and applied sciences are considered for admission. Accepted students may be required to complete undergraduate prerequisites as determined by the department. The Graduate Record Examinations (GRE) are recommended for all applicants. For those applicants who hold a degree from a U.S. college or university, the school must be a regionally or nationally accredited institution of higher education. In the case of applicants who hold a degree from an institution outside the United States, the GRE is required. In addition, if the native language of the applicant is not English, a minimum score of 550 on the test of English as a Foreign Language (TOEFL) is required. Application materials may be obtained from the department.

CORRESPONDENCE AND INFORMATION

Dr. S. S. Rao
Professor and Chairperson
Department of Electrical and Computer Engineering
Villanova University
800 Lancaster Avenue
Villanova, Pennsylvania 19085-1681
Telephone: 610-519-4228 or 4970
Fax: 610-519-4436
E-mail: rao@ece.vill.edu or gradadm@ece.vill.edu
World Wide Web: http://www.ece.vill.edu

VILLANOVA UNIVERSITY
THE FACULTY AND THEIR RESEARCH

Moeness G. Amin, Professor; Ph.D., Colorado, 1984. Multidimensional signal processing, time-varying spectral analysis, adaptive filtering, signal detection and enhancement, noise canceling, system identification.

Julia V. Bukowski, Associate Professor; Ph.D., Pennsylvania, 1979. Large-scale systems; network theory; hardware, network, and software reliability.

Frank N. DiMeo, Associate Professor; Ph.D., Pennsylvania, 1969. Real-time control and automation, robotics, man-machine interfacing, image processing, FORTH language, neural networks.

Ahmad Hoorfar, Associate Professor; Ph.D., Colorado, 1984. Electromagnetic field theory, microwave and millimeter-wave antennas and circuits, transient electromagnetics, mathematical physics, numerical techniques.

Mark A. Jupina, Assistant Professor; Ph.D., Pennsylvania, 1990. Physical and electrical characterization of microelectronic materials and devices, modeling and analysis of microwave devices.

Stephen Konyk Jr., Assistant Professor; Ph.D., Drexel, 1985. Nonlinearly constrained adaptive filtering and estimation with applications to detective systems, e.g., radar, sonar, etc.; intelligent control and dynamics with applications to robotic design and automation.

Joseph L. Kozikowski, Associate Professor; Ph.D., Pennsylvania, 1969. Analog and digital integrated electronics; analysis and design of filters, oscillators, regulators, PLLs, interface circuits, and others; digital pulse transmission and crosstalk.

Edward Kresch, Associate Professor; Ph.D., Pennsylvania, 1968. Computers: programming, microprocessors and microcomputer design, combinational and sequential circuits, computer architecture; biomedical engineering: nerve conduction, gait analysis, cardiovascular dynamics.

William E. Mattis Jr., Associate Professor; Ph.D., Drexel, 1972. Digital systems, digital design, integrated circuit design, microprocessors, real-time processing and applications, computer communications, neural systems.

Frank J. Mercede, Assistant Professor; Ph.D., Drexel, 1989. Power electronics and systems.

Bijan Mobasseri, Associate Professor; Ph.D., Purdue, 1978. Computer vision and machine intelligence, intelligent robotics, hierarchical representations, parallel architectures for vision, pattern recognition, image processing.

Richard J. Perry, Associate Professor; Ph.D., Drexel, 1981. Computational algorithms and software, VLSI design, multivariable systems.

S. S. Rao, Professor and Chairperson; Ph.D., Kansas, 1966. Digital signal processing; estimation, detection, and identification algorithms; spectral analysis and estimation; nonlinear signal processing; digital filtering and implementation; statistical communication theory.

Pritpal Singh, Associate Professor; Ph.D., Delaware, 1984. Fabrication and characterization of electronic materials and devices, especially solar cells, infrared detectors, and bulk high T_c superconductors; modeling and analysis of semiconductor devices.

Anthony Zygmont, Professor; Ph.D., Pennsylvania, 1971. Applications of artificial intelligence, expert systems, numerical computation, and symbolic computation to the analysis and design of electrical engineering devices and systems.

Adjunct Faculty

Eric A. Alfonsi, M.S.E.E., Penn State, 1977. Digital systems and computers.

Edward L. Hepler, Ph.D., Drexel, 1979. Computer architecture and VLSI design.

Steven T. Kacenjar, Ph.D., Rochester, 1977. Electrooptics and fiber-optic communication systems.

James L. Marshall, M.S., MIT, 1949. Audio engineering.

Purusottam Mookerjee, Ph.D., Connecticut, 1986. Systems and control.

Kistareddy Pallegadda, M.S.E.E., Villanova, 1984. Computer communications.

Louis Pitale, Ph.D., Drexel, 1980. Electromagnetics and nonlinear wave propagation.

Louis P. Rubinfield, Ph.D., Washington (St. Louis), 1980. Digital systems and computer engineering.

Louis J. Ruggeri, M.S.E.E., Penn State, 1973. Computers and electronics.

Bradley Keith Taylor, Ph.D., Carnegie Mellon, 1988. Optical information processing.

Suzanne A. Liebowitz Taylor, Ph.D., Carnegie Mellon, 1989. Image processing.

Richard Teti, Ph.D., Pennsylvania, 1991. Electromagnetics, signal theory, communications, microwave remote sensing.

Luke J. Turgeon, Ph.D., Massachusetts, 1977. Analog and integrated circuits.

Sydney S. Weinstein, M.S., Massachusetts, 1978. Software engineering.

VIRGINIA POLYTECHNIC INSTITUTE AND STATE UNIVERSITY

COLLEGE OF ARTS AND SCIENCES
DEPARTMENT OF COMPUTER SCIENCE

PROGRAMS OF STUDY

The computer science faculty seeks talented graduate students to participate in study and research leading to the degrees of Master of Science and Doctor of Philosophy in computer science. These programs offer research opportunities in a wide range of areas, including algorithms, artificial intelligence, computer-aided education, digital libraries, human-computer interaction, information storage and retrieval, numerical analysis, parallel processing, real-time computation, simulation, and software engineering.

Master's degree candidates in computer science may choose to write a thesis or they may complete a course work–only degree. All students take a final examination: an oral exam for thesis students and either a written or oral exam for nonthesis students. Completion of the program takes 1½ to 2 years.

Each Ph.D. student must take 90 semester hours beyond the baccalaureate. The dissertation usually represents 45–60 of the 90 hours. Up to 30 hours may be transferred from another institution. Students working toward the Ph.D. degree must pass three examinations: qualifying (tests background knowledge), preliminary (tests the student's ability to undertake the dissertation research), and final (an oral defense of the dissertation).

At Virginia Tech's Graduate Center in northern Virginia, the department offers both the M.S. and Ph.D. in computer science as well as a Master of Information Systems. This interdisciplinary program requires a minimum of 33 credits, including courses in five specified areas and a student-selected area of specialization.

RESEARCH FACILITIES

The Department of Computer Science facilities house computers and related equipment for both instruction and research. The department shares a 119-node Intel Paragon parallel computer and a state-of-the-art digital video editing system for multimedia production and jointly operates a 2-terabyte digital library server with the University's Computing Center. The department's computational environment also includes more than 150 DEC RISC- and Alpha-based, Intel Pentium-based, Sun, SGI, Apple, and NeXT workstations, all of which are connected via a high-speed network. There are specially equipped laboratories offering opportunity for work in human-computer interaction, software engineering, reactive systems, CD-ROM/multimedia, and parallel computation.

FINANCIAL AID

A number of graduate teaching and research assistantships are available to qualified students each year. The stipend associated with assistantships is based on the student's academic level. In 1997–98, stipends range from $1260 to $1320 per month for nine months. Students on assistantships are exempt from tuition. A limited number of students receive offers of multiple-year assistantships as Computer Science Scholars; several multiple-year Graduate Research Traineeships are available for Ph.D. applicants in human-computer interaction.

COST OF STUDY

In 1997–98, tuition is $2061 per semester for full-time in-state students and $3276 per semester for full-time out-of-state students. All students also pay a comprehensive fee of $324 per semester.

LIVING AND HOUSING COSTS

Graduate student housing is available on campus, and there are many modestly priced private apartment complexes nearby. Information about housing may be obtained from the Office of Housing and Residence Life.

STUDENT GROUP

Students in the department's on-campus graduate programs come from a variety of academic backgrounds and geographic areas. Of the 85 students enrolled in 1996–97, approximately 60 percent were in the master's program and 40 percent were working on the Ph.D.

STUDENT OUTCOMES

Master's students readily find jobs in industry all over the United States, ranging from North Carolina, Virginia, and Maryland on the East Coast (e.g., Northern Telecom, TRW, Hughes Network Systems) to California, Oregon, and Washington on the West Coast (e.g., Qualcomm, Intel, Microsoft). Ph.D. graduates divide about equally between those going to research-oriented jobs in industry (e.g., Lucent Technologies, IBM, Mitre) and those going into teaching (e.g., Arizona State, James Madison, Iowa).

LOCATION

Blacksburg is a small university community of 35,000 people in the Appalachian Mountains. This area of southwest Virginia is noted for its scenic beauty and outdoor recreational opportunities. The Blue Ridge Parkway and the Appalachian Trail are within an hour's drive of the campus. Roanoke, Virginia, with a population of 100,000, is 45 miles northeast of Blacksburg.

THE UNIVERSITY AND THE DEPARTMENT

Virginia Tech, Virginia's land-grant university, is the largest university in the state. Of the 25,000 students enrolled, approximately 4,000 are graduate students. More than 1,250 faculty members participate in the University's seventy-six graduate degree programs.

APPLYING

The program accepts both students with undergraduate degrees in computer science and students with degrees in such technical areas as the mathematical sciences, the physical sciences, and engineering who have had at least one course or equivalent training in each of the following areas: discrete mathematics, calculus, calculus-based statistics, computer organization, data structures, and operating systems. Deficiencies can be made up by taking undergraduate courses. Applicants who have completed significant research work (e.g., a thesis, conference paper, or journal article) are invited to submit abstracts or copies of this work. The GRE General Test is required of all applicants. The deadline for applications both for admission and for support is February 1.

CORRESPONDENCE AND INFORMATION

Computer Science Department
660 McBryde Hall
Virginia Polytechnic Institute and State University
Blacksburg, Virginia 24061-0106
Telephone: 540-231-6932
E-mail: gradprog@cs.vt.edu
World Wide Web: http://www.cs.vt.edu

VIRGINIA POLYTECHNIC INSTITUTE AND STATE UNIVERSITY

THE FACULTY AND THEIR RESEARCH

Marc Abrams, Associate Professor; Ph.D., Maryland. Visualization and performance modeling of communication networks and parallel and distributed programs, parallel discrete event simulation.

Donald C. S. Allison, Professor; Ph.D., Queen's (Belfast). Computational geometry, analysis of algorithms, mathematical software, parallel computation.

James D. Arthur, Associate Professor; Ph.D., Purdue. Software engineering, verification and validation, parallel and distributed computation, user support environments, programming languages and translation.

Osman Balci, Associate Professor; Ph.D., Syracuse. Software engineering, simulation and modeling, World Wide Web.

N. Dwight Barnette, Instructor; M.S., Virginia Tech. Instructional computing, hypermedia/multimedia development.

**John M. Carroll, Professor and Head; Ph.D., Columbia. Human-computer interaction, scenario-based system development, education and design applications.

Csaba J. Egyhazy, Associate Professor; Ph.D., Case Western Reserve. Operations research; management information systems; data, text, and knowledge processing.

*Roger W. Ehrich, Professor; Ph.D., Northwestern. Digital picture processing, automatic visual inspection, human-computer interface design and evaluation.

Edward A. Fox, Professor; Ph.D., Cornell. Multimedia information storage and retrieval, digital libraries, hypertext/hypermedia, electronic publishing and text processing, educational technology, library automation, network/WWW information and modeling.

William B. Frakes, Associate Professor and Director, Northern Virginia Program; Ph.D., Syracuse. Software reusability, software engineering, experimental methods, information storage and retrieval.

Sanjay Gupta, Assistant Professor; Ph.D., Ohio State. Computational complexity theory, theoretical computer science, design and analysis of algorithms, neural networks.

H. Rex Hartson, Professor; Ph.D., Ohio State. Human-computer interaction, usability methods, human factors in computing, interactive system development, software engineering.

Lenwood S. Heath, Associate Professor; Ph.D., North Carolina. Algorithms, graph theory, computational biology, symbolic computation, computational geometry, theoretical computer science, combinatorics, topology, information retrieval.

Sallie M. Henry, Associate Professor; Ph.D., Iowa State. Software engineering, software metrics, operating systems, human factors, object-oriented paradigm.

Deborah Hix, Research Scientist; Ph.D., Virginia Tech. Human-computer interaction, development, and evaluation; interactive multimedia systems, virtual environments.

Dennis G. Kafura, Associate Professor; Ph.D., Purdue. Operating systems, software engineering, object-oriented systems.

John A. N. Lee, Professor; Ph.D., Nottingham (England). Programming languages, compiler design, industry standards, software engineering, history of computing, computer ethics.

Richard E. Nance, Professor; Ph.D., Purdue. Computer simulation, distributed systems, software engineering, performance evaluation.

†Calvin J. Ribbens, Associate Professor; Ph.D., Purdue. Numerical analysis, parallel computation, mathematical software, scientific problem-solving environments.

*John W. Roach, Associate Professor; Ph.D., Texas. Artificial intelligence, agents, logic programming, natural language, robot problem solving, scene analysis.

Mary Beth Rosson, Associate Professor; Ph.D., Texas. Human-computer interaction, psychology of programming, object-oriented paradigm, community networks.

Clifford A. Shaffer, Associate Professor; Ph.D., Maryland. Data structures and algorithms, computer-aided education, CSCW, data visualization, computer graphics.

†Layne T. Watson, Professor; Ph.D., Michigan. Numerical analysis, nonlinear programming, mathematical software, fluid mechanics, solid mechanics, image processing, parallel computation.

Courtesy Appointments in the Department of Computer Science

Christopher A. Beattie, Associate Professor; Ph.D., Johns Hopkins. Numerical analysis, computational linear algebra, spectral approximation of linear operators, scientific computing.

F. Gail Gray, Professor; Ph.D., Michigan. Fault-tolerant computing, switching and automata theory, computer architecture, algebraic coding theory, modeling and design with hardware description languages.

Charles E. Nunnally, Associate Professor; Ph.D., Virginia. Microprocessor/microcontroller systems, sensor-based real-time systems, embedded systems.

Joseph G. Tront, Professor; Ph.D., SUNY at Buffalo. VLSI design and testing, parallel processing, multimedia design, microprocessor systems, fault-tolerant computing.

Robert C. Williges, Professor; Ph.D., Ohio State. Human factors engineering, human-computer interface design, multimedia information presentation, computer-based training, usability testing, experimental design, human factors research methodology.

Courtesy appointment in the Department of Electrical Engineering.
†*Courtesy appointment in the Department of Mathematics.*
**Courtesy appointment in the Department of Psychology.*

VIRGINIA POLYTECHNIC INSTITUTE AND STATE UNIVERSITY

BRADLEY DEPARTMENT OF ELECTRICAL ENGINEERING

PROGRAMS OF STUDY

The Bradley Department of Electrical Engineering offers programs of graduate study leading to the degrees of Master of Science and Doctor of Philosophy.

The M.S. degree usually requires the equivalent of one year of full-time study, with a minimum of 30 semester credits of work acceptable for graduate credit. Although an M.S. degree may be earned with or without a thesis, research assistantships are awarded only to those who elect the thesis option. A final exit exam is required of all M.S. nonthesis candidates, while students electing the thesis option must take an oral examination on the thesis.

The Ph.D. program usually requires a minimum of three years of full-time work beyond the master's degree. Each student in the Ph.D. program must pass a written qualifying examination early in the program, a preliminary written and oral examination before dissertation work is begun, and a final oral examination on the dissertation and related topics.

RESEARCH FACILITIES

The University Computing Center has an IBM 3090 model 300E/3VF, an IBM 3084 model Q, a VAX 8800, a DEC System 5810, and several IBM RS/6000s. College resources include a multimedia and scientific visualization lab. The electrical engineering department has a computing facility that includes networked Sun and DEC workstations, personal computers, and software packages to support graduate work and research. Other computers, instrumentation, and specialized equipment are available to support specific research activities. Laboratories for research in acoustooptics; alternative energy; antenna design; computers; control systems; design automation; digital and image processing; digital signal processing; electric power; electronic materials and device fabrication; energy systems; fiber optics and electrooptics; high-frequency device modeling and testing; hybrid microelectronics; mobile and portable radio; motor drives; power electronics; radio frequency and microwave communication systems; robotics/AI lab, including a MERLIN 6540 industrial robot; satellite communications; and wideband time domain and microwave characterization and modeling are also available.

FINANCIAL AID

The department offers half-time teaching and research assistantships. For 1996–97, both types carried stipends of $1135 to $1800 per month for nine months, depending upon the student's academic record and previous experience. Research assistantships are available in acoustooptics, applied electromagnetics, computer engineering, control, electric power, fiber optics, image processing, microelectronics, mobile and portable radio, power electronics, robotics, satellite communications, and signal processing. All half-time assistantships also cover in-state tuition costs.

Bradley Fellowships of $16,000 and some additional fellowships are available. The department participates in a graduate co-op program with various companies and government agencies throughout the country.

COST OF STUDY

In 1996–97, full-time in-state graduate students paid an instructional fee of $2376.50 per semester ($3492.50 if out-of-state); in-state students who took fewer than 9 hours paid $229 per credit hour ($353 per credit hour if out-of-state). The above full-time fees include a $315.50 comprehensive fee, which is required of all students.

LIVING AND HOUSING COSTS

Only limited campus housing is available for graduate students, but there is an ample supply of suitable off-campus apartments costing from $170 to $350 per month, depending upon size and location. Meals are available in the student center dining areas at reasonable prices.

STUDENT GROUP

There are about 600 graduate students in electrical engineering, of whom about 350 are on the Blacksburg campus and the remainder are taking courses on a part-time basis at Falls Church, VCU, Dahlgren, and other locations within Virginia.

LOCATION

Virginia Tech is located 40 miles west of Roanoke in the town of Blacksburg, on a plateau (elevation 2,100 feet) between the Blue Ridge and Allegheny mountains. Interstate 81 provides easy access to Roanoke. Recreational facilities in the area include many opportunities for picnicking, swimming, fishing, hunting, and camping in state parks and national forests.

THE UNIVERSITY

Virginia Tech is a public land-grant university with particularly extensive offerings in the fields of engineering and agriculture. The University sponsors a film series and performances by visiting lecturers, musicians, and drama groups in addition to offering productions by the University orchestra, chorus, and drama department. Nearby Radford University also sponsors a series of concerts and plays, to which students may subscribe. The Singles Club and the Association of Married Students sponsor various social activities.

APPLYING

Applications can be submitted at any time. At least two months should be allowed for processing an application and obtaining references. Applications for financial assistance for the 1998–99 academic year should be submitted no later than January 15, 1998.

CORRESPONDENCE AND INFORMATION

For application forms and a catalog:
Dean Len Peters
Graduate School
Virginia Polytechnic Institute and State University
Blacksburg, Virginia 24061

For specific program information:
Loretta Estes, Graduate Counselor
Bradley Department of Electrical Engineering
Virginia Polytechnic Institute and State University
Blacksburg, Virginia 24061-0111
E-mail: esteslc@vt.edu

VIRGINIA POLYTECHNIC INSTITUTE AND STATE UNIVERSITY

THE FACULTY AND THEIR RESEARCH

A. L. Abbott, Associate Professor; Ph.D., Illinois at Urbana-Champaign. Computers.

J. R. Armstrong, Professor; Ph.D., Marquette. Computer engineering.

P. M. Athanas, Associate Professor; Ph.D., Brown. Computers.

W. T. Baumann, Associate Professor; Ph.D., Johns Hopkins. Systems and control.

J. S. Bay, Associate Professor; Ph.D., Ohio State. Robotics.

A. A. Beex, Professor; Ph.D., Colorado State. Signal processing.

I. M. Besieris, Professor; Ph.D., Case Tech. Theoretical and applied electromagnetics.

D. Borojevic, Associate Professor; Ph.D., Virginia Tech. Power electronics.

C. W. Bostian, Clayton Ayre Professor; Ph.D., North Carolina State. Microwave systems, antennas and propagation.

R. P. Broadwater, Professor; Ph.D., Virginia Tech. Power systems.

G. S. Brown, Professor; Ph.D., Illinois at Urbana-Champaign. Electromagnetics.

D. D. Chen, Professor; Ph.D., Duke. Power electronics.

R. O. Claus, Willis G. Worcester Professor; Ph.D., Johns Hopkins. Fiber optics.

R. W. Conners, Associate Professor; Ph.D., Missouri–Columbia. Image processing.

W. R. Cyre, Associate Professor; Ph.D., Florida. Computers.

N. J. Davis, Associate Professor; Ph.D., Purdue. Computer communications and architecture.

W. A. Davis, Professor; Ph.D., Illinois at Urbana-Champaign. Electromagnetic fields and communication systems.

J. De La Ree López, Associate Professor; Ph.D., Pittsburgh. Power systems.

S. B. Desu, Professor; Ph.D., Illinois at Urbana-Champaign. Electronic materials.

D. A. de Wolf, Professor; Ph.D., Eindhoven (Netherlands). Electromagnetics.

R. W. Ehrich, Professor; Ph.D., Northwestern. Computer science.

A. A. Elshabini-Riad, Professor; Ph.D., Colorado. Semiconductor electronics.

L. A. Ferrari, Professor and Department Head; Ph.D., California, Irvine. Image processing.

F. G. Gray, Professor; Ph.D., Michigan. Digital computers.

D. S. Ha, Associate Professor; Ph.D., Iowa. Fault-tolerant computing.

Q. Huang, Assistant Professor; Ph.D., Cambridge (England). Power electronics.

I. Jacobs, Professor; Ph.D., Purdue. Fiber optics and communications.

M. T. Jones, Assistant Professor; Ph.D., Duke. Computer engineering.

P. Kachroo, Assistant Professor; Ph.D., Berkeley. Transportation and controls.

F. C. Lee, Lewis A. Hester Chair; Ph.D., Duke. Power electronics, nonlinear systems.

D. K. Lindner, Associate Professor; Ph.D., Illinois at Urbana-Champaign. Control theory.

Y. Liu, Associate Professor; Ph.D., Ohio State. Power systems, computer simulations and animations.

G. Q. Lu, Assistant Professor; Ph.D., Harvard. Electronic materials.

S. F. Midkiff, Associate Professor; Ph.D., Duke. Computer architecture.

L. M. Mili, Associate Professor; Ph.D., Liège (Belgium). Power systems.

R. L. Moose, Associate Professor; Ph.D., Duke. Electronics and statistical communication theory.

K. A. Murphy, Associate Professor; Ph.D., Virginia Tech. Fiber optics.

C. E. Nunnally, Associate Professor and Assistant Department Head; Ph.D., Virginia. Digital computers and digital control.

A. G. Phadke, American Electric Power Professor; Ph.D., Wisconsin–Madison. Power systems.

T. C. Poon, Professor; Ph.D., Iowa. Electrooptics.

T. Pratt, Professor; Ph.D., Birmingham (England). Electromagnetics.

S. Rahman, Professor; Ph.D., Virginia Tech. Energy and environment.

K. Ramu, Professor; Ph.D., Concordia (Montreal). Motor drives.

T. S. Rappaport, James S. Tucker Professor; Ph.D., Purdue. Wave propagation and communications.

J. H. Reed, Associate Professor; Ph.D., California, Davis. Communications.

S. M. Riad, Professor; Ph.D., Toledo. Time domain techniques.

F. J. Ricci, Professor; Ph.D., Catholic University. Communications.

J. W. Roach, Associate Professor; Ph.D., Texas. Computer science.

A. Safaai-Jazi, Associate Professor; Ph.D., McGill. Optical fibers.

W. A. Scales, Assistant Professor; Ph.D., Cornell. Electromagnetics.

F. W. Stephenson, Professor and Dean, College of Engineering; Ph.D., Newcastle (England). Active networks, hybrid microelectronics.

W. L. Stutzman, Thomas L. Phillips Professor; Ph.D., Ohio State. Antennas and propagation.

K. S. Tam, Associate Professor; Ph.D., Wisconsin–Madison. Power systems.

W. H. Tranter, Harry Lynde Bradley Professor; Ph.D., Alabama at Tuscaloosa. Wireless communications.

J. G. Tront, Professor; Ph.D., SUNY at Buffalo. Digital computers.

H. F. VanLandingham, Professor; Ph.D., Cornell. Digital control and signal processing.

A. Wang, Associate Professor; Ph.D., Dalian (China). Fiber optics.

B. D. Woerner, Associate Professor; Ph.D., Michigan. Wireless communications.

WASHINGTON UNIVERSITY
DEPARTMENT OF COMPUTER SCIENCE

PROGRAMS OF STUDY

Both M.S. and D.Sc. degrees are offered. The doctorate requires written and oral qualifiers and a dissertation demonstrating independent research abilities of the highest standard. Students intending to obtain the doctorate may enter without a master's degree. Time to complete the doctorate is typically four to six years.

The master's program can be completed by course work alone or can include a thesis or project. Approximately ten courses are required (about three semesters). Many master's students are encouraged to remain for the doctoral program.

RESEARCH FACILITIES

Faculty and graduate student offices are housed in two modern research buildings. Most graduate students are in 2-person offices with individual workstations and have full access to the Internet. The department has extensive ATM network connections that reach across the campus and has dedicated laboratory facilities in networking and communications, visualization, and parallel and distributed computing. Strong systems staff support is provided for the computing and network infrastructure.

FINANCIAL AID

Graduate assistantships are currently $1320 per month plus tuition. Most doctoral degree students and some master's degree students are supported through research or teaching. It is expected that students making good progress will have their assistantships renewed.

COST OF STUDY

For students in the Department of Computer Science at Washington University, tuition is $875 per unit in 1997–98, and most courses are 3 units.

LIVING AND HOUSING COSTS

Compared to most large cities, St. Louis is very affordable. Students prefer to live off campus because of the variety of housing in attractive neighborhoods within walking or short driving distance. Two-bedroom apartments range from $450 to $700 a month.

STUDENT GROUP

Of approximately 90 graduate students, about two thirds are full-time, and half of those are pursuing doctorates. Mean GRE scores for incoming doctoral students are 790 (quantitative), 720 (analytical), 670 (verbal); for master's candidates, 720 (quantitative), 600 (analytical), and 510 (verbal).

STUDENT OUTCOMES

Doctoral graduates have gone on to a variety of positions in academia and industry. Some recent graduates have taken positions at Georgia Tech, AT&T Bell Labs, Columbia University, and MCNC.

LOCATION

No city is more American than St. Louis, which mixes Eastern, Southern, and Western culture and is often highly ranked among the best places to live. St. Louis is easily accessible from anywhere in the U.S. and is the national hub for Trans World Airlines. Winning national acclaim are the art museum and sculpture park, science center, botanical gardens, and various zoological and municipal parks, as well as the symphony, the opera, and dance and music companies; many buildings have been praised for their architectural design. There are a dozen Fortune 500 companies and three professional sports franchises.

THE UNIVERSITY AND THE DEPARTMENT

Washington University seeks excellence and prestige in everything that it does. It is an independent institution founded in 1853 and now has 11,500 students and nearly 2,000 full-time faculty members. Parts of the 1904 World's Fair and Olympics were held on the 169-acre campus, which is bordered on the east by St. Louis's famed Forest Park and on the north, west, and south by well-established suburbs. Twenty Nobel Prize winners have been associated with the University.

The department is an innovator in research relationships with industry. Research support is approximately $4.2 million per year (an average of $268,000 per full-time faculty person), and all faculty members are active in research. The adviser-student ratio for doctoral supervision averages 1:2; no adviser currently supervises more than five doctoral candidates. The department's small size and collegial atmosphere provide a supportive and friendly environment. The department has a history of strong ties to biomedical computing, and faculty members collaborate extensively with those from other departments. About 30 external speakers arrive each year, and visiting researchers come from all over the world.

APPLYING

Applicants should include GRE General Test scores as well as scores on an appropriate Subject Test. A strong computing background is recommended regardless of undergraduate major.

Applications for graduate assistantships must be received by January 15. Applicants whose native language is not English must submit a minimum score of 575 on the TOEFL and 4.5 on the TWE.

CORRESPONDENCE AND INFORMATION

Admissions
Department of Computer Science, Campus Box 1045
Washington University
St. Louis, Missouri 63130-4899

Telephone: 314-935-6160
Fax: 314-935-7302
E-mail: admissions@cs.wustl.edu
URL: http://www.cs.wustl.edu

WASHINGTON UNIVERSITY
THE FACULTY AND THEIR RESEARCH

Jerome R. Cox Jr., Harold B. and Adelaide G. Welge Professor; Sc.D., MIT, 1954. Computer visualization, digital communication, biomedical computing.

Ron K. Cytron, Associate Professor; Ph.D., Illinois, 1984. Program optimization and transformation, parallel computations.

Richard A. Dammkoehler, Professor; M.S.I.E., Washington (St. Louis), 1958. Computer programming theory and systems, information retrieval.

Mark A. Franklin, Professor; Ph.D., Carnegie Mellon, 1970. Computer architecture and systems analysis, parallel processing, VLSI design.

Will D. Gillett, Associate Professor; Ph.D., Illinois, 1977. Compiler theory and implementation, algorithm analysis and DNA mapping.

Kenneth J. Goldman, Associate Professor; Ph.D., MIT, 1990. Distributed systems, distributed applications, programming methodology.

Sally A. Goldman, Associate Professor; Ph.D., MIT, 1990. Computational learning theory, algorithms and computational geometry.

Philip M. Hubbard, Assistant Professor; Ph.D., Brown, 1994. Computer graphics, human-computer interaction, computational geometry, scientific visualization.

Takayuki Dan Kimura, Professor; Ph.D., Pennsylvania, 1971. Visual programming languages, user interfaces, neural networks.

Eileen T. Kraemer, Assistant Professor; Ph.D., Georgia Tech, 1995. Concurrent systems, visualization, parallel programming environments, computational biology.

Ronald P. Loui, Associate Professor; Ph.D., Rochester, 1988. Artificial intelligence.

Gurudatta M. Parulkar, Associate Professor; Ph.D., Delaware, 1987. High-speed protocols, multimedia communication, remote visualization.

Gruia-Catalin Roman, Professor; Ph.D., Pennsylvania, 1976. Concurrent systems design, software engineering, formal methods, programming languages, visualization.

Tuomas W. Sandholm, Assistant Professor; Ph.D., Massachusetts Amherst, 1996. Artificial intelligence, multiagent systems, machine learning, resource-bounded reasoning.

Douglas C. Schmidt, Assistant Professor; Ph.D., California, Irvine, 1994. Parallel and distributed systems, distributed object computing, object-oriented design patterns.

Subhash Suri, Associate Professor; Ph.D., Johns Hopkins, 1987. Computational geometry, algorithms and complexity network design, computer graphics.

Jonathan S. Turner, Chairman and Henry Edwin Sever Professor of Engineering; Ph.D., Northwestern, 1982. Networking and communications, algorithms and complexity, VLSI applications.

George Varghese, Associate Professor; Ph.D., MIT, 1993. Distributed algorithms, network protocols, fault tolerance.

Affiliate Faculty Grouped by Area

Biomedical applications: G. James Blaine (biomedical computing), A. Maynard Engebretson (speech and hearing applications), Mark Frisse (information retrieval).

Artificial Intelligence: Barry Kalman (neural networks), Stan C. Kwasny (natural language), L. Andrew Oldroyd (robotics), Robert Rouse (expert systems).

Systems: Keith Bennett (software engineering), Roger Chamberlain (parallel computation), Martin Dubetz (graphics, networks), Harold Mack (architecture, languages), Kenneth Wong (performance evaluation).

Other: I. Norman Katz (numerical analysis), Robert Benson (technology and information management).

Students enjoy a fall day on the Washington University campus.

WASHINGTON UNIVERSITY

DEPARTMENT OF ELECTRICAL ENGINEERING

PROGRAMS OF STUDY

The Department of Electrical Engineering offers courses of study leading to M.S.E.E. and D.Sc. degrees. Graduate students may pursue studies in the departmental faculty's areas of research. These include solid-state engineering (semiconductor and superconductor theory and devices, plasma processing and nonlinear plasma theory, optoelectronics, microwave and magnetic information devices and systems), computer engineering (architecture, parallel processing; special-purpose systems design and implementation, VLSI systems), communication theory and systems, information theory, and signal and image processing. There is also an interdepartmental program in biomedical engineering.

Candidates for the master's degree may elect a course option (30 hours of graduate course credit) or a thesis option (30 credit hours, including 6 hours of research). Candidates for the doctoral degree accumulate a minimum of 72 hours of graduate credit, with 48 credit hours in course work and 24 credit hours in research. Flexible course requirements permit the selection of a program of study designed for individual needs and career goals.

Washington University's academic year begins August 27 and ends May 7.

RESEARCH FACILITIES

The department operates several modern research laboratories. Research in the Computer and Communications Research Center is focused on high-speed wide-area communications systems, applications and performance analysis of parallel processing, and discrete-event analysis of digital systems. The Microelectronics Systems Laboratory performs research in the areas of electronics packaging, superconducting devices, plasma processing, and microfabrication technology. The Electronic Systems and Signals Research Laboratory has projects in medical imaging algorithms and technology, information theory applications, radar and sonar systems, ultrasonic imaging, astronomical imaging, and the design of digital hearing aids. The Center for Imaging Science, a federally funded research center in the department, is devoted to the development of mathematical and algorithmic foundations for the representation and understanding of complex multidimensional scenes. Other laboratories include the Optoelectronics Research Laboratory, the Microwave Laboratory, the Photonics Research Laboratory, and the Magnetic Information Systems Center.

The School of Engineering and Applied Science runs the Center for Engineering Computing, which has computer workstations dedicated to supporting course work. The laboratories have more than thirty Sun Workstations, two Silicon Graphics workstations, and numerous personal computers. The department has parallel processing capabilities, including AMT/DAP Models 510 and 610, SIMD machines with 1024 and 4096 processing elements, respectively, a DEC MPP machine, and a Sun SPARCcenter 2000 MIMD parallel processor. Modern facilities for VLSI chip design, simulation, and testing are also available.

Olin Library, a modern, fully equipped structure located in the center of the campus, contains more than 2 million volumes. These materials are augmented by the collections of several departmental libraries.

FINANCIAL AID

The Department of Electrical Engineering offers financial aid to full-time students enrolled in programs leading to the M.S.E.E. (thesis option) and D.Sc. degrees. Offers of financial aid are limited to available funds. For exceptionally qualified applicants, the department annually awards a number of doctoral fellowships that include tuition remission and a stipend for nine months each year. Women are eligible to apply for the prestigious Olin four-year fellowships. Financial aid in the form of research assistantships is also available through research grants and contracts administered by individual faculty members.

COST OF STUDY

Graduate tuition is $875 per credit hour in 1997–98.

LIVING AND HOUSING COSTS

The average cost of room and board for single graduate students in University residence facilities is $6032 per academic year. Nearby off-campus apartments also are available for students at reasonable costs.

STUDENT GROUP

The department's 1996–97 graduate enrollment of 88 full-time, 35 part-time, and 9 special students reflects the average composition of the graduate student body in recent years. Approximately 42 percent of the full-time graduate students currently enrolled in the department are working toward the doctoral degree.

STUDENT OUTCOMES

M.S.E.E. graduates have attended the top doctoral programs in the nation, including the program at Washington University, as well as other professional degree programs in medicine, law, and business. They are employed by industry leaders from all regions and by national laboratories. A number of D.Sc. graduates have been appointed to faculty positions in top research or teaching institutions and have been sought after by industrial, academic, and national laboratories.

LOCATION

Because of Washington University's location in metropolitan St. Louis, students are able to enjoy a stimulating, cosmopolitan environment. Among the city's many social and cultural assets are an excellent art museum, a science center, a history museum, an outstanding symphony, a planetarium, a highly regarded botanical garden, and the well-known zoo. For sports entertainment, there are professional teams in baseball, football, hockey, and soccer.

THE UNIVERSITY

Washington University is an independent, privately endowed and supported institution located on 169 acres in the center of the greater St. Louis area. It was founded in 1853.

Washington University has 8,499 full-time students, about half of whom are undergraduates. The evening division has 3,137 part-time students. The University has 2,089 full-time and 404 part-time faculty members and is composed of several major divisions: Arts and Sciences; the Graduate Schools of Arts and Sciences, Architecture, Business and Public Administration, Engineering and Applied Science, Fine Arts, Law, Medicine, and Social Work; the School of Continuing Education; and the Summer School. The University ranks among the top ten in the nation in the number of Nobel laureates associated with it.

APPLYING

Application materials may be obtained by writing to the address below. There is no deadline for applying for admission. The deadline for filing applications for financial aid is February 1 preceding the academic year for which assistance is sought. All applicants for financial aid must submit test scores on the General Test of the Graduate Record Examinations (GRE).

CORRESPONDENCE AND INFORMATION

Chairman
Department of Electrical Engineering
Box 1127
Washington University
St. Louis, Missouri 63130
E-mail: admissions@ee.wustl.edu
World Wide Web: http://ee.wustl.edu/ee

WASHINGTON UNIVERSITY
THE FACULTY AND THEIR RESEARCH

The faculty members of the department participate in both undergraduate and graduate education and in interdepartmental graduate programs, interschool programs, and industrial projects. Therefore, students receive a program of education that is designed to meet their interests and is guided by the experience of an active resident faculty involved in state-of-the-art research and development. Many faculty members have significant industrial experience, and many are registered professional engineers.

R. Martin Arthur, Professor; Ph.D., Pennsylvania, 1968. Ultrasonic imaging, electrocardiography.

Roger D. Chamberlain, Associate Professor; D.Sc., Washington (St. Louis), 1989. Computer engineering, parallel computation, computer architecture, multiprocessor systems.

Jerome R. Cox Jr., Harold B. and Adelaide G. Welge Professor; Sc.D., MIT, 1954. Computer visualization, digital communication, biomedical computing.

Mark A. Franklin, Hugo F. and Ina Champ Urbauer Professor; Ph.D., Carnegie Mellon, 1970. Digital computers, systems analysis and simulation.

Daniel R. Fuhrmann, Associate Professor; Ph.D., Princeton, 1984. Statistical signal processing, image compression, numerical linear algebra.

H. Richard Grodsky, Assistant Professor; D.Sc., Washington (St. Louis), 1971. Artificial intelligence, expert systems, intelligent tutoring systems, object-oriented modeling.

Ronald S. Indeck, Professor; Ph.D., Minnesota, 1987. Magnetics, microelectronic devices, thin-film technology.

Raymond M. Kline, Professor; Ph.D., Purdue, 1962. Computer engineering, computer-aided design, control systems.

Robert R. Krchnavek, Assistant Professor; Ph.D., Columbia, 1986. Laser/material interactions, materials processing for electronics, photonics.

Michael I. Miller, Newton R. and Sarah Louisa Glasgow Wilson Professor; Ph.D., Johns Hopkins, 1983. Auditory neuroscience, signal and image processing, speech recognition, shape recognition.

Paul S. Min, Associate Professor; Ph.D., Michigan, 1987. Routing and control of telecommunications networks, fault-tolerance and reliability, software systems, network management.

Robert E. Morley Jr., Associate Professor; D.Sc., Washington (St. Louis), 1977. Computer and communication systems, VLSI design, digital signal processing.

Marcel W. Muller, Research Professor and Professor Emeritus; Ph.D., Stanford, 1957. Solid-state physics, microwave electronics, magnetics.

Joseph A. O'Sullivan, Associate Professor; Ph.D., Notre Dame, 1986. Statistical signal processing, radar systems, information theory, nonlinear control theory.

William F. Pickard, Professor; Ph.D., Harvard, 1962. Biological transport, electrobiology, energy engineering.

William D. Richard, Associate Professor; Ph.D., Missouri, 1988. Computer engineering, machine vision, medical instrumentation.

Bixio E. Rimoldi, Associate Professor; Dr.Tech.Sc., Swiss Federal Institute of Technology, 1988. Information theory, communication theory, coding.

Daniel L. Rode, Professor; Director, Optoelectronics Research Laboratory; Ph.D., Case Western Reserve, 1968. Optoelectronics and fiber optics; semiconductor materials, processing, and devices.

Barbara A. Shrauner, Professor; Ph.D., Harvard (Radcliffe), 1962. Plasma processing, semiconductor transport, symmetries of nonlinear differential equations.

Donald L. Snyder, Samuel C. Sachs Professor; Ph.D., MIT, 1966. Communication theory, random process theory, signal processing, biomedical engineering, image processing, radar.

Barry E. Spielman, Professor and Chairman of the Department; Ph.D., Syracuse, 1971. High-frequency/high-speed devices, integrated circuits, superconducting electronics.

Charles M. Wolfe, Professor; Ph.D., Illinois, 1965. Semiconductor materials and devices, statistical physics, optimization.

Professors Emeriti

Lloyd R. Brown, D.Sc., Washington (St. Louis), 1960. Automatic control, electronic instrumentation.

Marvin J. Fisher, Ph.D., Illinois, 1957. Energy conversion, power electronics.

Robert O. Gregory, D.Sc., Washington (St. Louis), 1964. Electronic instrumentation, microwave theory, circuit design.

Harold W. Shipton, F.I.E.R.E., Shrewsbury Technical, 1949. Biomedical engineering, electronic instrumentation.

Affiliated Faculty

Frank R. Agovino, J.D., Cincinnati, 1973. Intellectual property of electronics.

G. James Blaine, D.Sc., Washington (St. Louis), 1974. Biomedical computing, digital communications and information systems.

Andreas Bovopoulos, Ph.D., Columbia, 1988. Design and performance evaluation of telecommunication networks.

John D. Corrigan, Ph.D., Missouri, 1973. Control systems theory.

Julius L. Goldstein, Ph.D., Rochester, 1965. Mathematical models of sensory communication, normal and impaired processing.

Russell E. Hermes, M.S., Washington (St. Louis), 1981. Computer systems.

Douglas J. Hunt, Ph.D., Duke, 1989. Image processing, signal detection and estimation theory.

Tom R. Miller, Ph.D., Stanford, 1971; M.D., Missouri, 1976. Medical imaging.

Stanley Misler, Ph.D./M.D., NYU, 1977. Patch clamp characterization of ion channel in stimulus-secretion coupling stimulus.

William J. Murphy, D.Sc., Washington (St. Louis), 1967. Control systems.

John W. Parks Jr., Ph.D., Missouri, 1980. Radar antenna analysis, electromagnetic counter measures and word systems.

Gurudatta M. Parulkar, Ph.D., Delaware, 1987. Computer communications, local area networks, distributed processing.

Frederick U. Rosenberger, Ph.D., Washington (St. Louis), 1969. Computer systems.

Prodeep K. Sood, Ph.D., Wisconsin, 1987. Electromechanical devices.

Jonathan S. Turner, Ph.D., Northwestern, 1982. Communications systems, algorithms and complexity, VLSI applications.

WAYNE STATE UNIVERSITY
DEPARTMENT OF COMPUTER SCIENCE

PROGRAMS OF STUDY

The department offers programs leading to the Master of Arts, Master of Science, and Doctor of Philosophy degrees. Courses offered in the department cover a broad range of interests, with particular emphasis on the areas of artificial intelligence, computational modeling of biological systems, computer graphics, computer vision, database systems, multimedia information systems, natural language processing, numerical analysis, parallel distributed systems, and software engineering.

Doctoral students are required to complete 90 credits beyond the bachelor's degree. This includes 30 credits of a Ph.D. dissertation that describes original, independent research. In addition, all doctoral students are required to pass a comprehensive proficiency examination in computer science.

For the M.A. degree, students must complete 31 credits of course work and a comprehensive exit exam. Those seeking the M.S. degree are required to complete 33 credits of course work, including a master's thesis of 8 credits.

RESEARCH FACILITIES

The departmental computing facilities are organized into ten laboratories, including the Artificial Intelligence Laboratory, the Computer Graphics and Animation Laboratory, the Information Management Laboratory, the Research Laboratory, the Software Environments Laboratory, the Undergraduate Laboratory, the Undergraduate Resource Center, and the Vision and Neural Networks Laboratory. All labs are interconnected by a 10 Mbps Ethernet and are accessible to the Internet. The labs are equipped with a total of approximately sixty Unix workstations (SPARCS and RS6000) and seventy-five Pentium PCs. The labs also contain two dual-processor SPARC-20s, an SGI Indigo Extreme, a MaxVideo 20 image processing system, and a MasPar 1024-node massively parallel computer. In addition to the department's facilities, the University's Computing Center operates an IBM 3081, an Amdahl 5890, and a Cray J916.

FINANCIAL AID

Twenty-five graduate teaching assistantships are offered by the department on a nine-month basis. Teaching assistants are assigned part-time duties in the instructional program. The department also employs a number of graduate assistants during the summer for instructional and laboratory development purposes. Furthermore, students support themselves through research assistantships with faculty members who are pursuing various projects funded by government and private agencies.

COST OF STUDY

For 1997–98, Michigan state resident graduate tuition is $225 for the first credit hour and $153 for subsequent hours per term. Nonresident graduate tuition is $401 for the first credit hour and $329 for subsequent hours per term. These fees include a $72 registration fee, which is required for both residents and nonresidents. (Tuition and fees are subject to change without notice by action of the Board of Governors.)

LIVING AND HOUSING COSTS

A single student needs approximately $18,000 per year for living expenses, including tuition, housing, and other costs.

STUDENT GROUP

The graduate student enrollment of the department consists of approximately 175 full-time students and 200 part-time students. The majority of the part-time students are working professionals whose special skills enrich the classroom experience.

LOCATION

Wayne State University is located in the cultural center of Detroit along with the world-renowned Detroit Institute of Arts, Detroit Public Library, Detroit Historical Museum, Detroit Science Center, and African-American Museum. The international headquarters of the General Motors and Unisys corporations are nearby.

THE UNIVERSITY

The main campus with its 185 acres of landscaped pedestrian malls is the meeting ground for over 30,000 students enrolled in its thirteen schools and colleges. More than 10,000 students are enrolled in Wayne's graduate and professional programs. There are 120 master's, specialist, and graduate certificate programs and 50 doctoral majors. Over 1,200 master's and 150 doctoral degrees are awarded each year. The University enjoys an excellent international reputation and enrolls more than 1,100 students from other countries. Wayne State is committed to a leadership role in research and creative activity. It offers students the opportunity to work closely with a variety of research centers and institutes. Examples in the physical sciences are the Center for Automotive Research, the Bioengineering Center, the Center for Molecular Biology, the Institute of Chemical Toxicology, and the Institute for Manufacturing Research.

APPLYING

Application forms for admission and financial aid may be obtained by writing to the address given below. Completed forms should be received in the department by February 15 for the fall semester and by October 15 for the winter semester. Admission and financial aid decisions are made after careful review of the applicant's research goals, undergraduate background in computer science, scores from a recent GRE General Test (verbal, quantitative, and analytical), and letters of recommendation. International students whose native language is not English must submit scores from the Test of English as a Foreign Language (TOEFL) or the Michigan English Language Assessment Battery (MELAB).

CORRESPONDENCE AND INFORMATION

Director of Graduate Studies
Department of Computer Science
431 State Hall
Wayne State University
5143 Cass Avenue
Detroit, Michigan 48202
Telephone: 313-577-2477
Fax: 313-577-6868
World Wide Web: http://www.cs.wayne.edu

WAYNE STATE UNIVERSITY
THE FACULTY AND THEIR RESEARCH

Anthony T. Chronopoulos, Associate Professor; Ph.D., Illinois at Urbana-Champaign, 1987. Computational science, distributed systems, numerical analysis, parallel computing.

Michael Conrad, Professor; Ph.D., Stanford, 1970. Biological information processing, computational modeling, molecular computing, brain models and intelligence, adaptability theory, evolutionary programming.

Farshad Fotouhi, Associate Professor; Ph.D., Michigan State, 1988. Multimedia/hypermedia information systems, object-oriented databases, data warehouses, user interface.

Narendra Goel, Professor; Ph.D., Maryland, 1965. Computer simulation, computer graphics and animation, modeling of physical engineering and biological systems, remote sensing.

William I. Grosky, Professor and Chairman; Ph.D., Yale, 1971. Multimedia information systems, databases, World Wide Web.

Lucja Iwanska, Assistant Professor; Ph.D., Illinois at Urbana-Champaign, 1992. Artificial intelligence: natural language processing (computational models of semantics, pragmatics and context, logical and nonlogical reasoning, discourse processing), knowledge representation systems based on natural language.

Vaclav Rajlich, Professor; Ph.D., Case Western Reserve, 1971. Software development methods, tools, and environments; software maintenance and program comprehension, Legacy software.

Robert G. Reynolds, Associate Professor; Ph.D., Michigan, 1979. Artificial intelligence, machine learning, genetic algorithms, cultural algorithms, knowledge-based software development environments, software reuse, software metrics, expert systems, evolutionary computation, evolutionary programming.

Ishwar Sethi, Professor; Ph.D., Indian Institute of Technology (Kharagpur), 1978. Computer vision, pattern recognition, neural nets, multimedia information retrieval.

Nai-Kuan Tsao, Associate Professor; Ph.D., Hawaii, 1970. Analysis and implementation of numerical algorithms in analysis and linear algebra.

Richard Weinand, Lecturer; M.S.C.S., Wayne State, 1985. Information processing and problem solving in the immune system, modeling and simulation of complex systems.

Seymour Wolfson, Associate Professor; Ph.D., Wayne State, 1965. Internet, numerical methods, computer systems.

WAYNE STATE UNIVERSITY

DEPARTMENT OF ELECTRICAL AND COMPUTER ENGINEERING

PROGRAMS OF STUDY

The Department of Electrical and Computer Engineering offers graduate programs leading to the Master of Science (M.S.) and Doctor of Philosophy (Ph.D.) degrees in electrical and computer engineering. Electrical engineering is organized into six areas: biomedical systems, communication and circuits, control systems, optical engineering, power systems, and solid-state electronics. Computer engineering is divided into four areas: general, computer architecture and digital design, parallel and distributed systems, and machine intelligence and applications. Thirty-two graduate credits are required for the master's degree; 90 are required for the Ph.D.

RESEARCH FACILITIES

The department has the following research laboratories: applied optics; computation and neural network; computer; enabling technologies; materials, device, and circuit simulations; microcomputer; microelectronic and photonic materials; optoelectronics; parallel and distributed computing; power electronics; and VLSI design.

Advanced computer facilities are available to students through the College of Engineering's computer center and the University Computing Center. The College maintains an Ethernet TCP/IP-based local area network, numerous UNIX-based servers and workstations, and more than 60 Windows-based PCs for student use. A wide variety of software is available on these systems, including Abaqus, Ansys, AutoCAD, Dads, Disspla, Exponent Graphics, Hypermesh, IMSL, Matlab, Mathematica, Mentor Graphics, Nastran, MatrixX, Patran, PDGS, PlotiT, and Polymath. The University Computing Center maintains supercomputers, including a Cray J916, accessible through the engineering network. The new Undergraduate Library, adjacent to the Engineering Building, has more than 700 PCs.

FINANCIAL AID

Many full-time students are supported through fellowships and graduate teaching and research assistantships. Fellowships, traineeships, and assistantships normally provide stipends of $7000 to $17,000 per academic year, tuition and full medical benefits, and, in some cases, a housing allowance.

COST OF STUDY

Fall 1997 tuition for a resident graduate student is $153 per credit hour; the nonresident rate is $329 per credit hour. (These rates are subject to change by action of the Board of Governors.)

LIVING AND HOUSING COSTS

The University offers housing for single and married graduate students. The Housing Office provides a list of approved off-campus accommodations. The Housing Office telephone number is 313-577-2116.

STUDENT GROUP

There are approximately 33,000 students enrolled at Wayne State University, about one half of whom attend part-time. Approximately 10,000 graduate students are enrolled in a variety of programs. The College of Engineering has nearly 1,600 undergraduates and more than 1,700 graduate students. The Department of Electrical and Computer Engineering has more than 450 graduate students.

LOCATION

Located in the nation's sixth-largest city, Wayne State University offers a personalized education in the heart of the city's cultural center. Wayne State University students are a short walk from the Detroit Institute of Arts, the Detroit Historical Museum, Orchestra Hall, the Detroit Public Library, the Detroit Science Center, and the nation's largest African-American history museum. In addition, five theater groups are active at the University.

THE UNIVERSITY

Founded as Detroit Medical College in 1868, Wayne State University has evolved into a large and respected national research university. Wayne State became a state university in 1956 and is one of only eighty-seven schools to have been designated as a Research I Institution by the Carnegie Commission. Wayne State University ranks thirty-sixth nationally in total enrollment. More than 1,900 master's and 200 doctoral degrees are awarded each year.

APPLYING

Applications for graduate admission and support are available from the department. The deadlines are July 1 for the fall term, November 1 for the winter term, and March 15 for the spring term. TOEFL scores are required for international students; a minimum score of 550 is necessary for consideration. Applicants seeking financial aid must submit GRE scores.

CORRESPONDENCE AND INFORMATION

Department of Electrical and Computer Engineering
Wayne State University
Detroit, Michigan 48202
World Wide Web: http://www.eng.wayne.edu

WAYNE STATE UNIVERSITY
THE FACULTY AND THEIR RESEARCH

Raymond Arrathoon, Professor. Optical engineering and optoelectronics, optical computing and fiber optics, with applications ranging from computer architecture to optoelectronic programmable logic arrays. (telephone: 313-577-3738; e-mail: rarratho@eng.wayne.edu)

Gregory Auner, Associate Professor. Wide bandgap semiconductors, graded pyroelectric materials, magnetic materials for sensors and device development, smart sensors. (telephone: 313-577-3904; e-mail: gauner@eng.wayne.edu)

Robert Barnard, Professor Emeritus. Application of functional analysis to tracking and state-estimation problems, specifically related to the feedback control of large-scale uncertain nonlinear systems. (telephone: 313-577-3788; e-mail: rbarnard@eng.wayne.edu)

Jatinder Bedi, Associate Professor. Real-time distributed processing of applications using microprocessors, design of controllers using Fuzzy-Neuro systems, optical and digital communications systems. (telephone: 313-577-3850; e-mail: jbedi@eng.wayne.edu)

Vipin Chaudhary, Assistant Professor. Parallelizing compilers and run-time support systems, parallel and distributed systems (algorithms, architectures, and applications), ATM, computer vision and image processing, graphics, biomedical engineering. (telephone: 313-577-0605; e-mail: vipin@eng.wayne.edu)

Robert Erlandson, Associate Professor and head of department's biomedical engineering effort. System methodologies suitable for analysis and evaluation of large complex systems, particularly physiological structures; development of decision-making methodologies utilizing multivalued logic and nonparametric techniques. (telephone: 313-577-3900; e-mail: rerlands@eng.wayne.edu)

Mohamad Hassoun, Professor. Artificial neural systems; associative memories; machine learning; pattern recognition; application of artificial neural networks to physiologic signal processing, optimization, and control. (telephone: 313-577-3966; e-mail: hassoun@brain.eng.wayne.edu)

Feng Lin, Associate Professor. Systems and control, hierarchical structure of discrete event systems, decision analysis for complex processes, control and optimization of flexible manufacturing systems. (telephone: 313-577-3428; e-mail: flin@eng.wayne.edu)

Syed M. Mahmud, Associate Professor. Microprocessor-based system design, digital system design, special purpose computer architectures, cache-based multiprocessor system design and performance analysis. (telephone: 313-577-3855; e-mail: smahmud@eng.wayne.edu)

Jerome Meisel, Professor. Electromechanical energy conversion, bulk power system planning and operation, power conditioning, power electronic circuitry, applied control theory. (telephone: 313-577-3530; e-mail: jmeisel@eng.wayne.edu)

Vladimir Mitin, Professor. Theoretical investigations and simulation of transport and noise phenomena in submicron and low-dimensional semiconductor structures, such as quantum wells and quantum wires; light emission and absorption; laser simulation; simulation of growth of semiconductor heterostructures. (telephone: 313-993-7651; e-mail: mitin@eng.wayne.edu)

Andrzej Olbrot, Professor. Control and dynamical systems theory, time delay systems, robust stability and stabilization, worst case design problems, observability and observers for linear and nonlinear systems, polynomial and ring-theoretic models, infinite-dimensional systems. (telephone: 313-577-3648; e-mail: aolbrot@eng.wayne.edu)

Melvin Shaw, Professor. Experimental and theoretical studies of microwave properties of semiconducting materials and devices; instabilities in semiconductors, particularly the behavior of thin amorphous chalcogenide and silicon films; phenomena in two-dimensional electron gases. (telephone: 313-577-0764; e-mail: mshaw@eng.wayne.edu)

Donald Silversmith, Professor. Microelectromechanical system design and fabrication technology, solid-state and microsystem device design, integrated circuit fabrication technology, VLSI design. (telephone: 313-577-0248; e-mail: silversm@ece.eng.wayne.edu)

Harpreet Singh, Professor. State-variables and system theoretic and Petri Net approach to computer hardware and software, vehicle guidance, software engineering, expert systems, VLSI design. (telephone: 313-577-3917; e-mail: hsingh@eng.wayne.edu)

Pepe Siy, Associate Professor. Pattern recognition, image processing, parallel discrete computational problems, analog and digital VLSI, smart sensor technology. (telephone: 313-577-3841; e-mail: psiy@eng.wayne.edu)

Loren Schwiebert, Assistant Professor. Parallel computer architecture, particularly for efficient communication and synchronization; interconnection network routing; computer graphics; ATM networking; parallel algorithms. (telephone: 313-577-3990; e-mail: loren@eng.wayne.edu)

Le Yi Wang, Associate Professor. H-infinity optimization, stabilization and optimization of slowly time-varying systems, frequency-domain systems identification, hybrid control systems, automotive control systems, nonlinear control. (telephone: 313-577-4715; e-mail: lywang@eng.wayne.edu)

Paul Watta, Assistant/Research Professor. Artificial neural networks, associative neural memory, Boolean and automata networks, application of artificial neural networks to optimization and control. (telephone: 313-577-3646; e-mail: watta@brain.eng.wayne.edu)

Franklin Westervelt, Professor and Chair. Computer systems, VLSI design, special purpose computer architectures for handling very large databases. (telephone: 313-577-3764; e-mail: fwesterv@eng.wayne.edu)

James Woodyard, Associate Professor. Ion beam analysis and modification of thin-film devices and device materials; hydrogenation, dehydrogenation, and radiation resistance of amorphous semiconductor materials; optical and electrical characterization of device materials and device fabrication. (telephone: 313-577-3758, e-mail: woodyard@eng.wayne.edu)

Cunkai Wu, Visiting Associate Professor. Laser systems without population inversion, nonlinear optics of photoretractive crystals and semiconductors, selective detection of rare molecules. (telephone: 313-577-3788; e-mail: cwu@eng.wayne.edu)

Chengzhong Xu, Assistant Professor. Parallel computing, particularly run-time and operating system support for irregularly structured applications; distributed shared memory systems; multiprocessor server technologies. (telephone: 313-577-3856; e-mail: czxu@eng.wayne.edu)

Yang Zhao, Associate Professor. Nonlinear optical devices for communications and computing, novel optical materials, remote sensing and imaging, lasers. (telephone: 313-577-3404; e-mail: yzhao@eng.wayne.edu)

WORCESTER POLYTECHNIC INSTITUTE

DEPARTMENT OF COMPUTER SCIENCE

PROGRAMS OF STUDY

The Department of Computer Science offers programs leading to the Master of Science (M.S.) and Doctor of Philosophy (Ph.D.) degrees. Graduate courses are scheduled in the late afternoon or evening to accommodate both full-time and part-time students.

In the M.S. program, students take courses in the core areas of computer science to provide a strong basis for further study. Additional courses are required to expose students to the major areas of computer science research. The master's program consists of eleven computer science courses or of eight courses and a thesis. Some students undertake thesis research in cooperation with local industry or are supported by research grants. Full-time students may complete their degree requirements in about two years, while part-time students typically take longer. A practice-oriented master's degree in computer and communications networks (CCN), consisting of nine courses plus an industrial internship, is also available.

The Ph.D. program consists of an additional nine courses in computer science, qualifying and comprehensive examinations, and completion of research leading to a dissertation.

Many applied and theoretical areas of computer science are available for course work and research. Research interests of the faculty include analysis of algorithms, artificial intelligence, computer graphics, computer vision, database systems, distributed systems, electronic publishing, expert systems, graph theory, networks, performance evaluation, programming languages and compilers, software engineering, user interfaces, and visualization.

RESEARCH FACILITIES

The department is housed in Fuller Laboratories, WPI's newest academic building, which was designed specifically for multimedia, high-tech education. A wide variety of computing equipment is available to graduate students in computer science. Offices are equipped with Xterms or PCs, with access to servers. Research labs provide workstations and specialized software. The College Computer Center has many general-access labs. These resources are interconnected by a campuswide voice/data communications network providing easy access from every classroom, lab, and office.

FINANCIAL AID

Financial aid is available to qualified students in the form of fellowships and assistantships. Robert H. Goddard Fellowships provide a stipend in the amount of $12,000 for twelve months plus remission of tuition. Assistantships are also available and generally require half-time teaching or research assistance. Stipends for assistantships start at $9828 for the academic year plus remission of tuition. Additional assistance may be available for the summer. Many part-time students receive tuition support from their employers.

COST OF STUDY

Graduate tuition for the 1997–98 academic year is $612 per credit hour. There are nominal extra charges for thesis, health insurance, and other fees.

LIVING AND HOUSING COSTS

Although graduate students do not generally live in dormitory rooms, they may use the Institute's dining facilities. Apartments and rooms in private homes are available near the campus at varying costs. Graduate students should plan on living expenses of around $9280 for the academic year, not including tuition.

STUDENT GROUP

The computer science department has about 50 full-time and 50 part-time graduate students. Approximately half of the full-time students receive financial aid from the Institute or from faculty research grants. Recent graduates are employed in a variety of jobs in industry and in academia.

LOCATION

The Institute is located in an attractive residential section of Worcester, which is a community of about 170,000 in central Massachusetts. Worcester is located near Massachusetts's high-technology corridor, creating many opportunities for industrial-academic cooperation.

The city, the second-largest in New England, has many colleges and a wide variety of cultural opportunities. The nationally famous Worcester Art Museum is located three blocks from campus. A civic center, the Worcester Centrum, is a regular venue of touring music groups and sports events. The cultural and academic activities of Boston are nearby, and there are recreational activities in Cape Cod to the east, the Berkshires to the west, and the ski areas to the north.

THE INSTITUTE

Worcester Polytechnic Institute, founded in 1865, is the third-oldest college of engineering and science in the United States. Graduate study has been part of the Institute's activity for more than ninety years. The computer science department was established in 1969 and began its graduate program in the same year. Classes are small and provide for close student-faculty relationships. In keeping with the Institute's dedication to project-based education, many graduate courses involve a significant component of individual or group projects. The Institute's modern facilities are located on a pleasant 80-acre campus within walking distance of the center of Worcester. Complete athletic and recreational facilities and a program of concerts, movies, and special events are available to graduate students.

APPLYING

Applications for admission and financial assistance should be submitted by February 15 but are considered at any time. An applicant must submit an application form, official transcripts from all colleges attended, and three letters of recommendation. The Graduate Record Examinations General Test is required of all applicants. International students who have not completed an undergraduate degree from an English-speaking country are required to take the Test of English as a Foreign Language (TOEFL). Applicants for the Ph.D. program should have a B.S. or an M.S. degree in computer science.

CORRESPONDENCE AND INFORMATION

For program information and application forms, interested students should contact:

Graduate Coordinator
Department of Computer Science
Worcester Polytechnic Institute
Worcester, Massachusetts 01609

Telephone: 508-831-5357
Fax: 508-831-5776
E-mail: graduate@cs.wpi.edu
World Wide Web: http://cs.wpi.edu/

WORCESTER POLYTECHNIC INSTITUTE

THE FACULTY AND THEIR RESEARCH

Lee A. Becker, Associate Professor; Ph.D., Illinois, 1978. Artificial intelligence, object-oriented analysis and design, visual communication. Professor Becker is interested in automated knowledge acquisition, machine learning, and cognitive modeling. He is also investigating knowledge reuse in object-oriented systems and a visual interlingua.

David C. Brown, Professor; Ph.D., Ohio State, 1984. Knowledge-based design systems, expert systems, artificial intelligence. Professor Brown's research is concerned with modeling the way humans design things, such as mechanical components, electronics, or buildings. He is also investigating the use of AI techniques for systems used in manufacturing. Applications include knowledge-based criticism, serviceability estimation, data interpretation, and intelligent interfaces.

David Finkel, Professor; Ph.D., Chicago, 1971. Computer system performance evaluation, distributed computing systems. Professor Finkel's current research is concerned with the performance of distributed and multiprocessor operating systems. He is also investigating computer networking systems, specifically networking systems for multimedia applications.

Michael A. Gennert, Associate Professor; Sc.D., MIT, 1987. Computer vision, spatio-temporal databases, theoretical computer science. Professor Gennert conducts research in computational vision, including stereo, motion, and fractal image modeling, with applications in biomedicine and automated inspection; image and multimedia databases, including temporal data modeling, with applications in global change analysis; category theory and abstraction theory, with applications in programming language design.

Nabil I. Hachem, Associate Professor; Ph.D., Syracuse, 1988. Management of very large data and knowledge bases, computer architecture and database machines. Professor Hachem is investigating modeling techniques for the integration of data management and analysis in very large distributed scientific databases.

George T. Heineman, Assistant Professor; Ph.D., Columbia, 1996. Software engineering, database systems, transaction processing. Professor Heineman is interested in advances in object-oriented technology and its impact on software engineering. He also investigates extended transaction models as applied to database and workflow management systems.

Robert E. Kinicki, Associate Professor and Head of the Department of Computer Science; Ph.D., Duke, 1978. Network management, computer system performance evaluation, computer networks. Professor Kinicki's current research involves network management and electronic commerce.

Karen A. Lemone, Associate Professor; Ph.D., Northeastern, 1979. Automatic document processing, language translation. Professor Lemone is interested in the problems involved in electronic publishing. In particular, she is interested in the creation of systems that allow a document to be described separately from its content for the efficient production of high-quality documents.

Elke A. Rundensteiner, Assistant Professor; Ph.D., California, Irvine, 1992. Database systems. Professor Rundensteiner is currently leading research projects in object-oriented databases, multimedia, Web-based database tools, and spatial and other advanced database technologies. In general, her research is concerned with building software systems or running experimental evaluation studies.

Carolina Ruiz, Assistant Professor; Ph.D., Maryland, 1996. Formal methods in artificial intelligence, deductive databases, logic programming, machine learning. Professor Ruiz's most recent work is in knowledge-based systems capable of combining various types of default reasoning. She is also working on applications of automated theorem proving techniques to inductive learning.

Gabor N. Sarkozy, Assistant Professor; Ph.D., Rutgers, 1994. Graph theory, combinatorics, algorithms. Professor Sarkozy's research is concerned with extremal graph theory, especially its relationship with other fields such as theoretical computer science and number theory. His current research includes the development of a new method for finding certain special subgraphs in dense graphs. He is also investigating algorithmic implementations of this method.

Stanley Selkow, Professor; Ph.D., Pennsylvania, 1970. Combinatorial algorithms, graph theory, analysis of algorithms. Professor Selkow is studying polynomial-time algorithms to solve problems in graph theory and other discrete combinatorial problems. He is also investigating the analysis of algorithms and data structures.

Matthew O. Ward, Associate Professor; Ph.D., Connecticut, 1981. Data and information visualization, computer graphics, and spatial data analysis and management. Professor Ward is investigating methods for the visual exploration of large multivariate data sets. He is also interested in the integration of management, analysis, and display of scientific data.

Craig E. Wills, Associate Professor; Ph.D., Purdue, 1988. Distributed systems, networking, user interfaces. Professor Wills is interested in issues concerning a user's access to a computer system, particularly when the system is a distributed network of machines. His current work involves the management, location, access, and visualization of information available for the user.

SELECTED RECENT PUBLICATIONS

Becker, L. A., and T. Guay. Case-based reasoning for knowledge acquisition suggestions. *Int. J. Artif. Tools,* vol. 3, no. 1, pp. 23–45, 1994.

Dunskus, B., D. L. Grecu. **D. C. Brown,** and I. Berker. Using single function agents to investigate conflicts. In *AI EDAM: AI in Engineering Design, Analysis and Manufacturing,* vol. 9, no. 4, pp. 299–312, ed. I. Smith. Cambridge University Press, September 1995.

Finkel, D., X. Meng, and S. Parikh. Load sharing that supports fault tolerance in a distributed computing system. *Comput. Syst. Sci. Eng.,* 1994.

Gennert, M. A., N. I. Hachem, and A. Bansal. Distributed retrieval, computation, and storage of GIS data. *Proc. 2nd ACM Workshop. Advances in Geographic Information Systems,* pp. 160–5, Gaithersburg, Md., December 1994.

Hachem, N. I. An approximate analysis of the performance of extendible hashing with elastic buckets. *Inf. Process. Lett.,* vol. 48, October 1993.

Hachem, N. I., M. A. Gennert, and **M. O. Ward.** An overview of the Gaea Project. *IEEE Database Eng. Bull.,* vol. 16, no. 1, March 1993.

Ben-Shaul, I. Z., and **G. T. Heineman.** A 3-level atomicity model for decentralized workflow management systems. *Distrib. Syst. Eng. J.,* 1997.

Lemone, K. A. *Design of Compilers: Techniques of Programming Language Translation.* CRC Press, 1992.

Zhou, L., **E. A. Rundensteiner,** and K. G. Shin. Schema evolution of an object-oriented real-time database system for manufacturing automation. *IEEE Transactions on Data and Knowledge Engineering,* 1997.

Ruiz, C., and J. Minker. Combining closed world assumptions with stable negation. *Fundamenta Informaticae,* 1997.

Sarkozy, G. N. Proof of a packing conjecture of Bollobas. *Probability, Combinatorics and Computing,* vol. 4, pp. 241–55, 1995.

Christian, C. A., G. Coray, and **S. M. Selkow.** A characterization of n-component graphs. *Discrete Mathematics,* vol. 149, pp. 279–81, 1996.

Ward, M. O., W. L. Power, and P. Ketelaar. A computational environment for the management, processing, and analysis of geological data. *Comput. Geosciences* 22(10):1123–31, 1996.

Wills, C. E. Process synchronization and IPC. *ACM Computing Surveys,* 50th anniversary issue. 28(1):209–11, 1996.

Wills, C. E., and **D. Finkel.** Experience with peer learning in an introductory computer science course. *Comput. Sci. Educ.,* vol. 5, no. 2, pp. 165–87, 1994.

WRIGHT STATE UNIVERSITY

COMPUTER ENGINEERING PROGRAM

PROGRAMS OF STUDY

The Department of Computer Science and Engineering offers graduate programs leading to the Master of Science in Computer Engineering (M.S.C.E.) and the Doctor of Philosophy in computer science and engineering. A Master of Science in Computer Science program is also available. Interested students should also see the Computer Science Program in this volume.

The M.S.C.E. program requires 48 graduate quarter credit hours in a department-approved program of study. Typically, students must complete ten courses and orally defend a thesis or complete twelve courses in the nonthesis option. The Ph.D. program requires 91 graduate quarter credit hours after completion of the M.S.C.E. or 136 hours after completion of a bachelor's degree. Students without a master's degree must complete the requirements for the M.S.C.E. as the first phase of their Ph.D. program.

Ph.D. students must complete 76 hours of formal course work (courses completed in the master's program may partially satisfy this requirement), pass the Ph.D. qualifying examinations and candidacy examination, and successfully complete and defend a dissertation.

RESEARCH FACILITIES

Modern laboratory facilities provide ample equipment for research in a number of areas. The College of Engineering and Computer Science provides access to DEC Alpha servers and workstations, a Silicon Graphics (SGI) Reality Engine 2, and SGI, DEC, and Sun workstations as well as numerous networked PCs and X-Windows terminals. In addition to these machines, dedicated research labs containing SGI, DEC, and Sun equipment are available. The University provides access to a Hitachi EX44 mainframe as well as DEC and Sun servers and workstations. Wright State is a member of OARnet, which provides access to the resources of the Ohio Supercomputer Center. Wright State's Center for Information Technology, a collaboration of academia, industry, and government, provides opportunities for research in all areas of modern information technology.

Laboratories specifically dedicated to student and faculty research support studies in artificial intelligence, networking, human-computer interaction, parallel and concurrent computing, control and robotics, digital communications, graphics, computer vision and imaging, computer-aided design, digital design, VLSI, software engineering, and optical computing. Research at Wright State is not limited to on-campus laboratory facilities. Several industrial laboratories, as well as Wright-Patterson Air Force Base laboratories, are involved in joint research efforts with the University and have excellent facilities available for faculty and graduate research that complement and extend those of the University.

FINANCIAL AID

Financial aid available to graduate students includes research assistantships, teaching assistantships, Federal Perkins Loans, Federal Stafford Student Loans, short-term loans, and academic tuition fellowships. Scholarships are also available through the Dayton Area Graduate Studies Institute. Competitive stipends for research and teaching assistantships are available.

COST OF STUDY

Tuition in 1997 for residents of Ohio is $143 per quarter hour for part-time study (1–10½ hours) and $1517 for full-time study (11–18 hours). Tuition for out-of-state students is $255 per quarter hour for part-time study and $2717 for full-time study.

LIVING AND HOUSING COSTS

Many students commute to classes; however, campus housing is available. Room and board cost about $1600 per quarter. There are a variety of apartments and houses for rent in the area. The cost of living in Dayton is low compared with that in most other metropolitan areas.

STUDENT GROUP

Approximately 3,800 graduate students are enrolled at Wright State University in forty graduate degree programs that lead to master's, Ed.S., Ph.D., M.D., and Psy.D. degrees.

STUDENT OUTCOMES

Graduates are employed in a variety of professional positions both in- and out-of-state. Typical positions include software engineer, computer engineer, systems analyst, and systems programmer.

LOCATION

Although Wright State has a suburban setting, it is closely tied to Dayton, the fourth-largest metropolitan area in Ohio. Dayton is a manufacturing center and is also the home of Wright-Patterson Air Force Base, the center of Air Force research and procurement. This combination of industrial and military development has produced an unusual concentration of scientific, technical, and research activity. Dayton has a considerable and varied cultural life. In the surrounding area there are at least fifteen other colleges and universities.

THE UNIVERSITY

Wright State University is an exciting and expanding university that continues in the scientific and engineering innovative spirit of aviation pioneers Orville and Wilbur Wright. The University has modern buildings that facilitate access for all, and the 557-acre main campus has accommodations for academics, support programs, sports, housing, and arts activities. Wright State's phenomenal growth as an institution—from one building, 92 employees, and 3,200 students in 1964 to forty-two modern buildings, nearly 2,000 employees, and more than 15,000 students in 1997—has necessarily stimulated a comparable growth in the areas that surround the University.

APPLYING

The basic requirement for admission to the master's degree program in computer engineering is a bachelor's degree in computer engineering or a related area with an overall undergraduate grade point average of at least 3.0 (on a 4.0 scale) or 2.7 with an average of 3.0 or better in the major field. A minimum grade point average of 3.3 is expected for admission to the Ph.D. program. Scores on the GRE General Test are required of all applicants. Specific prerequisites for admission include calculus, differential equations, linear algebra, physics, and circuit analysis. The student's background should include a knowledge of a higher-level language, data structures, concurrent programming, computer organization, operating systems, digital hardware design, and electronics. Minor background deficiencies may be made up after admission to the program by taking appropriate courses.

There is no deadline for admission applications since admission decisions are made on a rolling basis and programs may be started in any quarter; however, the deadline to apply for teaching assistantships is February 1.

CORRESPONDENCE AND INFORMATION

Oscar N. Garcia, Chair
Department of Computer Science and Engineering
Wright State University
Dayton, Ohio 45435
Telephone: 937-775-5131
Fax: 937-775-5133
E-mail: cse_dept@.cs.wright.edu
World Wide Web: http://www.cs.wright.edu/cse/general.html

WRIGHT STATE UNIVERSITY

THE FACULTY AND THEIR RESEARCH

A. A. S. Awwal, Associate Professor; Ph.D., Dayton, 1989. Digital optical computing, neural networks, computer arithmetic, digital systems, hardware systems and communications, pattern recognition.

Paul L. Bergstein, Assistant Professor; Ph.D., Northeastern, 1994. Database systems, intelligent interfaces, object-oriented software engineering, algorithms.

Chien-In Henry Chen, Associate Professor; Ph.D., Minnesota, 1989. CAD, simulation and test of VLSI circuits (design for testability, built-in test, automated synthesis of digital systems, and fault-tolerant multicomputer systems).

Chun-Lung Philip Chen, Associate Professor; Ph.D., Purdue, 1988. Robotics, CAD/CAM, intelligent systems and interfaces, neural networks and applications, knowledge-based systems.

Jer-Sen Chen, Assistant Professor; Ph.D., USC, 1989. Computer graphics and visualization, machine intelligence.

Soon M. Chung, Associate Professor; Ph.D., Syracuse, 1990. Database multimedia, parallel processing, computer architecture.

Oscar N. Garcia, Professor; Ph.D., Maryland, 1969. Speech recognition, K-B systems, computer architecture, human-computer interaction; intelligent interfaces; machine intelligence.

A. Ardeshir Goshtasby, Associate Professor; Ph.D., Michigan State, 1983. Intelligent interfaces, machine vision, computer graphics and visualization, geometric modeling, medical image analysis.

Jack S. N. Jean, Associate Professor; Ph.D., USC, 1988. Parallel algorithms and architecture, hardware systems and communications, intelligent interfaces, neural networks.

Prabhakar Mateti, Associate Professor; Ph.D., Illinois at Urbana-Champaign, 1976. Software systems.

S. Narayanan, Assistant Professor; Ph.D., Georgia Tech, 1994. Modeling, simulation, human-computer interaction, cognitive systems engineering.

Kuldip Rattan, Professor; Ph.D., Kentucky, 1975. Digital control systems, robotics, fuzzy control, prosthetic/orthotics and microprocessor applications.

Mateen M. Rizki, Associate Professor; Ph.D., Wayne State, 1985. Modeling, simulation, biological information processing, machine intelligence, pattern recognition, image processing.

Charles B. Ross, Associate Professor; Ph.D., Purdue, 1969. Hardware systems and communications, computer graphics and visualization.

Robert C. Shock, Associate Professor; Ph.D., North Carolina at Chapel Hill, 1969. Database systems, software engineering.

Raymond E. Siferd, Professor; Ph.D., Air Force Tech, 1977. VLSI design and parallel computing.

Thomas A. Sudkamp, Professor; Ph.D., Notre Dame, 1978. Approximate reasoning, machine intelligence.

Krishnaprasad Thirunarayan, Associate Professor; Ph.D., SUNY at Stony Brook, 1989. Knowledge-representation and reasoning, logic programming, hardware verification, programming languages.

Karen A. Tomko, Assistant Professor; Ph.D., Michigan, 1995. Parallel computing, application optimization, compilation.

WRIGHT STATE UNIVERSITY

COMPUTER SCIENCE PROGRAM

PROGRAMS OF STUDY

The Department of Computer Science and Engineering offers graduate programs leading to the Master of Science in Computer Science (M.S.C.S.) and the Doctor of Philosophy in computer science and engineering. A Master of Science in Computer Engineering program is also available. Interested students should also see the Computer Engineering Program in this volume.

The M.S.C.S. program requires 48 graduate quarter credit hours in a department-approved program of study. Typically, students must complete ten courses and orally defend a thesis or complete twelve courses in the nonthesis option. The Ph.D. program requires 91 graduate quarter credit hours after completion of the M.S.C.S. or 136 hours after completion of a bachelor's degree. Students without a master's degree must complete the requirements for the M.S.C.S. as the first phase of their Ph.D. program.

Ph.D. students must complete 76 hours of formal course work (courses completed in the master's program may partially satisfy this requirement), pass the Ph.D. qualifying examinations and candidacy examination, and successfully complete and defend a dissertation.

RESEARCH FACILITIES

Modern laboratory facilities provide ample equipment for research in a number of areas. The College of Engineering and Computer Science provides access to DEC Alpha servers and workstations, a Silicon Graphics (SGI) Reality Engine 2, and SGI, DEC, and Sun workstations as well as numerous networked PCs and X-Windows terminals. In addition to these machines, dedicated research labs containing SGI, DEC, and Sun equipment are available. The University provides access to a Hitachi EX44 mainframe as well as DEC and Sun servers and workstations. Wright State is a member of OARnet, which provides access to the resources of the Ohio Supercomputer Center. Wright State's Center for Information Technology, a collaboration of academia, industry, and government, provides opportunities for research in all areas of modern information technology.

Laboratories specifically dedicated to student and faculty research support studies in artificial intelligence, networking, human-computer interaction, parallel and concurrent computing, control and robotics, digital communications, graphics, computer vision and imaging, computer-aided design, digital design, VLSI, software engineering, and optical computing. Research at Wright State is not limited to on-campus laboratory facilities. Several industrial laboratories, as well as Wright-Patterson Air Force Base laboratories, are involved in joint research efforts with the University and have excellent facilities available for faculty and graduate research that complement and extend those of the University.

FINANCIAL AID

Financial aid available to graduate students includes research assistantships, teaching assistantships, Federal Perkins Loans, Federal Stafford Student Loans, short-term loans, and academic tuition fellowships. Scholarships are also available through the Dayton Area Graduate Studies Institute. Competitive stipends for research and teaching assistantships are available.

COST OF STUDY

Tuition in 1997 for residents of Ohio is $143 per quarter hour for part-time study (1–10½ hours) and $1517 for full-time study (11–18 hours). Tuition for out-of-state students is $255 per quarter hour for part-time study and $2717 for full-time study.

LIVING AND HOUSING COSTS

Many students commute to classes; however, campus housing is available. Room and board cost about $1600 per quarter. There are a variety of apartments and houses for rent in the area. The cost of living in Dayton is low compared with that in most other metropolitan areas.

STUDENT GROUP

Approximately 3,800 graduate students are enrolled at Wright State University in forty graduate degree programs that lead to master's, Ed.S., Ph.D., M.D., and Psy.D. degrees.

STUDENT OUTCOMES

Graduates are employed in a variety of professional positions both in and out of the state. Typical positions include software engineer, computer engineer, systems analyst, and systems programmer.

LOCATION

Although Wright State has a suburban setting, it is closely tied to Dayton, the fourth-largest metropolitan area in Ohio. Dayton is a manufacturing center and is also the home of Wright-Patterson Air Force Base, the center of Air Force research and procurement. This combination of industrial and military development has produced an unusual concentration of scientific, technical, and research activity. Dayton has a considerable and varied cultural life. In the surrounding area there are at least fifteen other colleges and universities.

THE UNIVERSITY

Wright State University is an exciting and expanding university that continues in the scientific and engineering innovative spirit of aviation pioneers Orville and Wilbur Wright. The University has modern buildings that facilitate access for all, and the 557-acre main campus has accommodations for academics, support programs, sports, housing, and arts activities. Wright State's phenomenal growth as an institution—from one building, 92 employees, and 3,200 students in 1964 to forty-two modern buildings, nearly 2,000 employees, and more than 15,000 students in 1996—has necessarily stimulated a comparable growth in the areas that surround the University.

APPLYING

The basic requirement for admission to the master's degree program in computer science is a bachelor's degree in computer science or a related area with an overall undergraduate grade point average of at least 3.0 (on a 4.0 scale) or 2.7 with an average of 3.0 or better in the major field. A minimum grade point average of 3.3 is expected for admission to the Ph.D. program. Scores on the GRE General Test are required of all applicants. Specific prerequisites for admission include calculus, linear algebra, discrete math for computing, and physics. The student's background should include knowledge of a higher-level language, data structures, concurrent programming, computer organization, operating systems, and digital hardware design. Minor background deficiencies may be made up after admission to the program by taking appropriate courses.

There is no deadline for admission applications, since admission decisions are made on a rolling basis, and programs may be started in any quarter. The deadline to apply for teaching assistantships, however, is February 1.

CORRESPONDENCE AND INFORMATION

Oscar N. Garcia, Chair
Department of Computer Science and Engineering
Wright State University
Dayton, Ohio 45435

Telephone: 937-775-5131
Fax: 937-775-5133
E-mail: cse_dept@.cs.wright.edu
World Wide Web: http://www.cs.wright.edu/cse/general.html

WRIGHT STATE UNIVERSITY

THE FACULTY AND THEIR RESEARCH

A. A. S. Awwal, Associate Professor; Ph.D., Dayton, 1989. Digital optical computing, neural networks, computer arithmetic, digital systems, hardware systems and communications, pattern recognition.

Paul L. Bergstein, Assistant Professor; Ph.D., Northeastern, 1994. Database systems, intelligent interfaces, object-oriented software engineering, algorithms.

Chien-In Henry Chen, Associate Professor; Ph.D., Minnesota, 1989. CAD, simulation and test of VLSI circuits (design for testability, built-in test, automated synthesis of digital systems, and fault-tolerant multicomputer systems).

Chun-Lung Philip Chen, Associate Professor; Ph.D., Purdue, 1988. Robotics, CAD/CAM, intelligent systems and interfaces, neural networks and applications, knowledge-based systems.

Jer-Sen Chen, Assistant Professor; Ph.D., USC, 1989. Computer graphics and visualization, machine intelligence.

Soon M. Chung, Associate Professor; Ph.D., Syracuse, 1990. Database multimedia, parallel processing, computer architecture.

Oscar N. Garcia, Professor; Ph.D., Maryland, 1969. Speech recognition, K-B systems, computer architecture, human-computer interaction, intelligent interfaces, machine intelligence.

A. Ardeshir Goshtasby, Associate Professor; Ph.D., Michigan State, 1983. Intelligent interfaces, machine vision, computer graphics and visualization, geometric modeling, medical image analysis.

Jack S. N. Jean, Associate Professor; Ph.D., USC, 1988. Parallel algorithms and architecture, hardware systems and communications, intelligent interfaces, neural networks.

Prabhakar Mateti, Associate Professor; Ph.D., Illinois at Urbana-Champaign, 1976. Software systems.

S. Narayanan, Assistant Professor; Ph.D., Georgia Tech, 1994. Modeling, simulation, human-computer interaction, cognitive systems engineering.

Kuldip Rattan, Professor; Ph.D., Kentucky, 1975. Digital control systems, robotics, fuzzy control, prosthetic/orthotics and microprocessor applications.

Mateen M. Rizki, Associate Professor; Ph.D., Wayne State, 1985. Modeling, simulation, biological information processing, machine intelligence, pattern recognition, image processing.

Charles B. Ross, Associate Professor; Ph.D., Purdue, 1969. Hardware systems and communications, computer graphics and visualization.

Robert C. Shock, Associate Professor; Ph.D., North Carolina at Chapel Hill, 1969. Database systems, software engineering.

Raymond E. Siferd, Professor; Ph.D., Air Force Tech, 1977. VLSI design and parallel computing.

Thomas A. Sudkamp, Professor; Ph.D., Notre Dame, 1978. Approximate reasoning, machine intelligence.

Krishnaprasad Thirunarayan, Associate Professor; Ph.D., SUNY at Stony Brook, 1989. Knowledge-representation and reasoning, logic programming, hardware verification, programming languages.

Karen A. Tomko, Assistant Professor; Ph.D., Michigan, 1995. Parallel computing, application optimization, compilation.

YALE UNIVERSITY

DEPARTMENT OF COMPUTER SCIENCE

PROGRAMS OF STUDY
The department features four areas of concentration: artificial intelligence, scientific computation (numerical analysis), systems and programming languages, and theory of computation, but research often crosses area boundaries.

The graduate degree program in computer science stresses original research by the student both as an individual and as a member of the community of scholars. To this end, course requirements are minimal, and students normally begin research by the fall term of their second year of graduate study.

RESEARCH FACILITIES
The department operates a high-bandwidth, local area computer network based mainly on distributed workstations and servers, with connections to worldwide networks. Workstations include Sun SPARCstations, IBM PowerPCs, and NeXTstations. A vision laboratory contains specialized equipment for vision and robotics research. Various printers, including color printers, as well as image scanners are also available. The primary educational facility consists of thirty-seven IBM PowerPC workstations supported by a large IBM server. This facility is used for courses and unsponsored research by computer science majors and first-year graduate students. Access to computing, via both the workstations and remote login facilities, is available to everyone in the department.

FINANCIAL AID
Most students receive financial aid in the form of a fellowship or research assistantship. For 1997–98, fellowship stipends are $12,000 for nine months; assistantship stipends are $12,000 for nine months and $16,000 for twelve months. Financial aid includes tuition in addition to the stipend. Students may supplement their income with teaching assistantships.

COST OF STUDY
Tuition for the two-semester academic year is $21,200 for 1997–98.

LIVING AND HOUSING COSTS
During the 1997–98 academic year, the cost of living is approximately $12,370 for a single student and $19,095 for a married student. A wide range of privately owned accommodations is available within easy commuting distance.

STUDENT GROUP
There are 34 students studying for the Ph.D. and 5 students studying for the master's degree.

LOCATION
A small Yankee town of 136,000 lies outside the Yale campus. New Haven dates back to 1638, and, in the midst of a busy urban center, several areas of the city retain the atmosphere of earlier days. The city has a rich cultural life, independent of that provided by the University. Furthermore, there is hourly train service to New York City, which is only 75 miles away.

THE UNIVERSITY AND THE DEPARTMENT
Yale was established in 1701 and today is one of the leading universities in the world. It draws students from every part of the United States and from many other countries.

Founded in 1969 as a small graduate program, the Yale computer science department is now a rapidly expanding academic community dedicated to education and research in computer science. The department numbers 15 faculty members, 6 research associates, 39 graduate students, and 94 undergraduate majors.

APPLYING
An applicant should have a strong preparation in mathematics, engineering, or science. He or she should be competent in programming but does not need to know computer science beyond that basic level. Application for admission in fall 1998 should begin in fall 1997.

CORRESPONDENCE AND INFORMATION
Graduate Admissions
Department of Computer Science
Yale University
P.O. Box 208236
New Haven, Connecticut 06520-8236
Telephone: 203-432-2770

YALE UNIVERSITY
THE FACULTY AND THEIR RESEARCH

James Aspnes, Assistant Professor; Ph.D., Carnegie Mellon, 1992. Randomized, distributed, on-line algorithms.

Stanley C. Eisenstat, Professor; Ph.D., Stanford, 1972. Numerical linear and nonlinear algebra, direct and iterative methods for solving sparse linear systems, eigenvalue problems, parallel computing.

Michael J. Fischer, Professor; Ph.D., Harvard, 1968. Cryptography and computer security, distributed systems and protocols, communication networks, analysis of algorithms and data structures, complexity theory.

David Gelernter, Associate Professor; Ph.D., SUNY at Stony Brook, 1982. Parallel programming, programming languages and applied AI.

Gregory Hager, Associate Professor; Ph.D., Pennsylvania, 1988. Real-time vision, robotic hand-eye coordination, robot navigation, reasoning under uncertainty.

Paul R. Hudak, Professor; Ph.D., Utah, 1982. Functional programming, formal methods, compilers and interpreters, computer music.

Bradley C. Kuszmaul, Assistant Professor; Ph.D., MIT, 1994. High-performance computer architecture, algorithmic parallel programming, computer systems.

László Lovász, Professor; Ph.D., Eötvös Loránd (Budapest), 1971. Combinatorial optimization, discrete mathematics, randomized algorithms, complexity theory.

Drew McDermott, Professor; Ph.D., MIT, 1976. Reasoning about space and time, planning, vision, robotics.

Willard Miranker, Adjunct Professor; Ph.D., NYU (Courant), 1956. Parallel computing, computational neuroscience, neural nets, models of computation.

Vladimir Rokhlin, Professor; Ph.D., Rice, 1983. Numerical scattering theory, elliptic partial differential equations, numerical solution of integral equations.

Martin H. Schultz, Arthur K. Watson Professor of Computer Science; Ph.D., Harvard, 1965. Numerical analysis, scientific computing, parallel computation.

Zhong Shao, Assistant Professor; Ph.D., Princeton, 1994. Efficient compilation of high-level languages, interaction of compilers and languages with modern architectures and operating systems, systems environments, programming languages, formal methods.

Lenore D. Zuck, Associate Professor; Ph.D., Weizmann (Israel), 1987. Logics of programs, distributed systems, and formal verification.

Steven Zucker, Professor of Computer Science and Electrical Engineering; Ph.D., Drexel, 1975. Computational vision, computational neuroscience, robotics, psychophysics.

PROGRAM INDEX

This index gives the page locations of various entries for all the colleges and universities in this book. The page numbers for the college profiles are printed in regular type, and those for in-depth descriptions are in boldface type.

Electrical Engineering

Information Science

SCHOOL INDEX

This index gives the page locations of various entries for all the colleges and universities in this book. The page numbers for the college profiles are printed in regular type, and those for in-depth descriptions are in boldface type.